SERIES

(ex•ploring)

1. Investigating in a systematic way: examining. 2. Searching into or ranging over for the purpose of discovery.

1. Investigating in a systematic way: examining. 2. Searching into or ranging over for the purpose of discovery.

Microsoft® Office 2010 Volume 1 Second Edition

Robert T. Grauer

Mary Anne Poatsy | Keith Mulbery | Michelle Hulett | Cynthia Krebs | Keith Mast

PEARSON

Boston Columbus Indianapolis New York San Francisco Upper Saddle River
Amsterdam Cape Town Dubai London Madrid Milan Munich Paris Montreal Toronto
Delhi Mexico City São Paulo Sydney Hong Kong Seoul Singapore Taipei Tokyo

Editor in Chief: Michael Payne
Acquisitions Editor: Samantha McAfee
Product Development Manager: Laura Burgess
Editorial Project Manager: Anne Garcia
Development Editor: Jennifer Campbell
Editorial Assistant: Laura Karahalis
Director of Digital Development: Zara Wanlass
Executive Editor, Digital Learning & Assessment: Paul Gentile
Director, Media Development: Cathi Profitko
Senior Editorial Media Project Manager: Alana Coles
Production Media Project Manager: John Cassar
Director of Marketing: Patrice Jones
Marketing Coordinator: Susan Osterlitz
Marketing Assistant: Darshika Vyas
Senior Managing Editor: Cynthia Zonneveld
Associate Managing Editor: Camille Trentacoste
Senior Operations Specialist: Nick Sklitsis
Operations Specialist: Maura Zaldivar
Senior Art Director: Jonathan Boylan
Manager of Rights & Permissions: Hessa Albader
Manager, Cover Visual Research & Permissions: Karen Sanatar
Cover Design: Jonathan Boylan
Cover Illustration/Photo: Courtesy of Shutterstock® Images
Composition: PreMediaGlobal
Full-Service Project Management: Andrea Stefanowicz, PreMediaGlobal
Typeface: Minion Pro 9/11

Photos in the PowerPoint chapters are reprinted courtesy of: Andy Sorensen Photography, Ryan Phillips at Xeric Landscape and Design, Jo Porter Photography, David and Ali Valeti, Brad and Jenalee Behle, Katherine Hulse Photography, Shanna Michelle Photography, Alan Jensen Photography, and Jaron and Jennifer Krebs.

YouTube screenshot on page 999 is reprinted by permission of Common Craft, LLC.

Images reprinted by permission of Shutterstock.com appear in the text on pages 819, 868, 878, 883, 886, 1066 (© Stephen Coburn), 1067 (© Stephen Coburn), and 1106 (slide 4, left: © Manuel Fernandes; slide 4, right: © Konstantin Sutyagin; slide 5: © Terence Mendoza; slide 6: © Simone van den Berg).

Screenshot on page 572 is courtesy of US Patriot, military and law enforcement gear. www.uspatriottactical.com

Selected content in the PowerPoint chapters is used with permission from: Cameron Martin, Ph.D., Utah Valley University; Quinn Foote, Dustin Miller, and Tyler Fox, Utah Valley University DGM Students; Bryan Stinson, Survival Solutions; and Jan Bentley, Kathleen Richards, and Diane Hartman, Utah Valley University.

Library of Congress Cataloging-in-Publication Data
Microsoft Office 2010 / Robert T. Grauer... [et al.].
v. cm. — (Exploring series)
"Volume 1, Second edition."
Rev. ed. of: Microsoft Office 2007 / Robert T. Grauer... [et al.].
ISBN-13: 978-0-13-287360-4
ISBN-10: 0-13-287360-5
1. Microsoft Office. 2. Business—Computer programs. I. Grauer, Robert T., 1945–
HF5548.4.M525M52496 2013
005.5—dc23

2011042939

10 9 8 7 6 5 4 3 2 1

ISBN-13: 978-0-13-287360-4
ISBN-10: 0-13-287360-5

DEDICATIONS

For my husband Ted, who unselfishly continues to take on more than his fair share to support me throughout this process; and for my children, Laura, Carolyn, and Teddy, whose encouragement and love have been inspiring.

Mary Anne Poatsy

I dedicate this book in loving memory to Grandma Ida Lu Etta (Billie) Hort, who was a positive role model for me through her patience, caring personality, and perseverance through challenging situations. I treasure her support and encouragement throughout my personal and professional endeavors, including years of textbook writing.

Keith Mulbery

I would like to dedicate this book to my wonderful husband John and my sweet baby girl Dakota. They have shown an amazing amount of patience and support as I put in hours and hours of work on this project. And to my amazing friends, family, and students who offer encouragement and motivate me to be the best I can be. God bless you all.

Michelle Hulett

To my precious children—your strength, and the love and support you share with one another amazes me. Your love sustains me. To my family (those who have been, those who are now, and those who will be)—we are one, and our love endures forever.

Cynthia Krebs

I would like to dedicate this book to my amazing Ellen. Thanks for being there for all these years.

Keith Mast

I wholeheartedly dedicate this book to my father in recognition of his support, guidance, and encouragement. His steady influence and unwavering confidence continue to be an inspiration in my life. He is truly my hero.

Lynn Hogan

ABOUT THE AUTHORS

Mary Anne Poatsy, Series Editor

Mary Anne is a senior faculty member at Montgomery County Community College, teaching various computer application and concepts courses in face-to-face and online environments. She holds a B.A. in psychology and education from Mount Holyoke College and an M.B.A. in finance from Northwestern University's Kellogg Graduate School of Management.

Mary Anne has more than 12 years of educational experience. She is currently adjunct faculty at Gwynedd-Mercy College and Montgomery County Community College. She has also taught at Bucks County Community College and Muhlenberg College, as well as conducted professional training. Before teaching, she was vice president at Shearson Lehman in the Municipal Bond Investment Banking Department.

Dr. Keith Mulbery, Consulting Series Editor and Excel Author

Dr. Keith Mulbery is the Department Chair and a Professor in the Information Systems and Technology Department at Utah Valley University (UVU), where he teaches computer applications, C# programming, systems analysis and design, global and ethical issues in information systems and technology, and MIS classes. Keith also served as Interim Associate Dean, School of Computing, in the College of Technology and Computing at UVU.

Keith received the Utah Valley State College Board of Trustees Award of Excellence in 2001, School of Technology and Computing Scholar Award in 2007, and School of Technology and Computing Teaching Award in 2008. He has authored more than 18 textbooks, served as Series Editor for the Exploring Office 2007 series, and served as developmental editor on two textbooks.

Keith received his B.S. and M.Ed. in Business Education from Southwestern Oklahoma State University and earned his Ph.D. in Education with an emphasis in Business Information Systems at Utah State University. His dissertation topic was computer-assisted instruction using Prentice Hall's Train and Assess IT program to supplement traditional instruction in basic computer proficiency courses.

Michelle Hulett, Word Author

Michelle Hulett received a B.S. degree in CIS from the University of Arkansas and an M.B.A. from Missouri State University. She has worked for various organizations as a programmer, network administrator, computer literacy coordinator, and educator. She currently serves as a Senior Instructor in the CIS department and Director of International Business Programs at Missouri State University.

When not teaching or writing, she enjoys flower gardening, traveling (Alaska and Hawaii are favorites), hiking, canoeing, and camping with her husband John, dog Dakota, and any friends or neighborhood kids who tag along.

Cynthia Krebs, PowerPoint Author

Cynthia Krebs is the Director of Business and Marketing Education and a professor in the Digital Media Department at Utah Valley University (UVU). In 2008, she received the UVU College of Technology and Computing Scholar Award. She has also received the School of Business Faculty Excellence Award twice during her tenure at UVU. Cynthia teaches the Methods of Teaching Digital Media class to future teachers, as well as classes in basic computer proficiency, business presentations, business graphics, and introduction to digital media.

Cynthia, who is a CME with Certiport, is active in Utah Business and Computer Education Association, Western Business Education Association, the National Business Education Association, and the Utah Association of Career and Technical Educators. In 2009/2010, she served on the Executive Board of UACTE, as President of UBCEA, and as Computer Workshop Chair for WBEA. She was awarded the WBEA Outstanding Educator at the University Level in 2009. Cynthia has written multiple texts on Microsoft Office software, consulted with government and business, and has presented extensively at the local, regional, and national levels to professional and business organizations.

Cynthia lives by a peaceful creek in Springville, Utah. When she isn't teaching or writing, she enjoys spending time with her children, spoiling her grandchildren, and traveling.

Keith Mast, Access Author

Keith A. Mast develops a wide range of Microsoft Access applications that solve challenging business problems and improve efficiency. His solutions help businesses and organizations in manufacturing, pharmaceutical, financial services, and agriculture, among other industries. Clients include Visible Filing Concepts, Inc.; Moyer's Chicks, Inc.; Marcho Farms, Inc.; LANsultants, Inc.; Spector, Roseman, Kodroff, & Willis, PC; Sunshine Therapy Club, Inc.; DuPont; and Sony Entertainment. He is an adjunct faculty member at Montgomery County Community College, Blue Bell, PA. He has also been a high school teacher, a business school instructor, and an Access seminar leader. Keith resides in Norristown, PA, a suburb of Philadelphia. In his free time, he enjoys biking, running, kayaking, ballroom dancing, and being in nature. For more information, visit him on Facebook or at www.keithmast.com.

Dr. Lynn Hogan, Office Fundamentals and File Management and Windows 7 Author

Lynn Hogan has taught in the Computer Information Systems area at Calhoun Community College for 29 years. She is the author of *Practical Computing* and has contributed chapters for several computer applications textbooks. Primarily teaching in the areas of computer literacy and computer applications, she was named Calhoun's outstanding instructor in 2006. She received an M.B.A. from the University of North Alabama and a Ph.D. from the University of Alabama. Lynn resides in Alabama with her husband and two daughters.

Dr. Robert T. Grauer, Creator of the Exploring Series

Bob Grauer is an Associate Professor in the Department of Computer Information Systems at the University of Miami, where he is a multiple winner of the Outstanding Teaching Award in the School of Business, most recently in 2009. He has written numerous COBOL texts and is the vision behind the Exploring Office series, with more than three million books in print. His work has been translated into three foreign languages and is used in all aspects of higher education at both national and international levels. Bob Grauer has consulted for several major corporations including IBM and American Express. He received his Ph.D. in operations research in 1972 from the Polytechnic Institute of Brooklyn.

BRIEF CONTENTS

WINDOWS 7

OFFICE FUNDAMENTALS AND FILE MANAGEMENT

WORD

EXCEL

ACCESS

POWERPOINT

CAPSTONE EXERCISES

CONTENTS

WINDOWS 7

CHAPTER ONE ➤ Getting Started with Windows 7 1

OFFICE FUNDAMENTALS AND FILE MANAGEMENT

CHAPTER ONE ➤ Office Fundamentals and File Management 53

MICROSOFT OFFICE WORD 2010

CHAPTER ONE ➤ Introduction to Word 123

CHAPTER TWO ➤ Document Presentation 171

CHAPTER THREE ➤ Collaboration and Research 225

CHAPTER FOUR ➤ Document Productivity 271

APPLICATION CAPSTONE EXERCISE ➤ Word 321

COLLABORATION EXERCISES ➤ Word 324

MICROSOFT OFFICE EXCEL 2010

CHAPTER ONE ➤ Introduction to Excel 327

CHAPTER TWO ➤ Formulas and Functions 393

CHAPTER THREE ➤ Charts 449

CHAPTER FOUR ➤ Datasets and Tables 505

CHAPTER THREE ➤ Customize, Analyze, and Summarize Query Data 687

CHAPTER FOUR ➤ Creating and Using Professional Forms and Reports 733

APPLICATION CAPSTONE EXERCISE ➤ Access 800

COLLABORATION EXERCISES ➤ Access 803

CHAPTER ONE ➤ Introduction to PowerPoint 807

CHAPTER TWO ➤ Presentation Development 861

CHAPTER THREE ➤ Presentation Design 903

CHAPTER FOUR ➤ PowerPoint Rich Media Tools 973

APPLICATION CAPSTONE EXERCISE ➤ PowerPoint 1036

COLLABORATION EXERCISES ➤ PowerPoint 1038

CAPSTONE EXERCISES

DISCIPLINE-SPECIFIC CAPSTONES ➤ Paralegal 1043

DISCIPLINE-SPECIFIC CAPSTONES ➤ Medical 1069

DISCIPLINE-SPECIFIC CAPSTONES ➤ Theater 1091

ACKNOWLEDGMENTS

The Exploring team would like to acknowledge and thank all the reviewers who helped us prepare for the Exploring Office 2010 revision by providing us with their invaluable comments, suggestions, and constructive criticism:

Allen Alexander
Delaware Technical & Community College

Andrea Marchese
Maritime College, State University of New York

Andrew Blitz
Broward College, Edison State College

Angela Clark
University of South Alabama

Astrid Todd
Guilford Technical Community College

Audrey Gillant
Maritime College, State University of New York

Barbara Stover
Marion Technical College

Barbara Tollinger
Sinclair Community College

Ben Brahim Taha
Auburn University

Beverly Amer
Northern Arizona University

Beverly Fite
Amarillo College

Bonnie Homan
San Francisco State University

Brad West
Sinclair Community College

Brian Powell
West Virginia University

Carol Buser
Owens Community College

Carol Roberts
University of Maine

Cathy Poyner
Truman State University

Charles Hodgson
Delgado Community College

Cheryl Hinds
Norfolk State University

Cindy Herbert
Metropolitan Community College–Longview

Dana Hooper
University of Alabama

Dana Johnson
North Dakota State University

Daniela Marghitu
Auburn University

David Noel
University of Central Oklahoma

David Pulis
Maritime College, State University of New York

David Thornton
Jacksonville State University

Dawn Medlin
Appalachian State University

Debby Keen
University of Kentucky

Debra Chapman
University of South Alabama

Derrick Huang
Florida Atlantic University

Diana Baran
Henry Ford Community College

Diane Cassidy
The University of North Carolina at Charlotte

Diane Smith
Henry Ford Community College

Don Danner
San Francisco State University

Don Hoggan
Solano College

Elaine Crable
Xavier University

Erhan Uskup
Houston Community College–Northwest

Erika Nadas
Wilbur Wright College

Floyd Winters
Manatee Community College

Frank Lucente
Westmoreland County Community College

G. Jan Wilms
Union University

Gail Cope
Sinclair Community College

Gary DeLorenzo
California University of Pennsylvania

Gary Garrison
Belmont University

Gerald Braun
Xavier University

Gladys Swindler
Fort Hays State University

Heith Hennel
Valencia Community College

Irene Joos
La Roche College

Iwona Rusin
Baker College; Davenport University

J. Roberto Guzman
San Diego Mesa College

Jan Wilms
Union University

Janet Bringhurst
Utah State University

Jim Chaffee
The University of Iowa Tippie College of Business

Joanne Lazirko
University of Wisconsin–Milwaukee

Jodi Milliner
Kansas State University

John Hollenbeck
Blue Ridge Community College

John Seydel
Arkansas State University

Judith A. Scheeren
Westmoreland County Community College

Judith Brown
The University of Memphis

Karen Priestly
Northern Virginia Community College

Karen Ravan
Spartanburg Community College

Kathleen Brenan
Ashland University

Ken Busbee
Houston Community College

Kent Foster
Winthrop University

Kevin Anderson
Solano Community College

Kim Wright
The University of Alabama

Kristen Hockman
University of Missouri–Columbia

Kristi Smith
Allegany College of Maryland

Laura McManamon
University of Dayton

Leanne Chun
Leeward Community College

Lee McClain
Western Washington University

Linda D. Collins
Mesa Community College

Linda Johnsonius
Murray State University

Linda Lau
Longwood University

Linda Theus
Jackson State Community College

Lisa Miller
University of Central Oklahoma

Lister Horn
Pensacola Junior College

Lixin Tao
Pace University

Loraine Miller
Cayuga Community College

Lori Kielty
Central Florida Community College

Lorna Wells
Salt Lake Community College

Lucy Parakhovnik (Parker)
California State University, Northridge

Marcia Welch
Highline Community College

Margaret McManus
Northwest Florida State College

Margaret Warrick
Allan Hancock College

Marilyn Hibbert
Salt Lake Community College

Mark Choman
Luzerne County Community College

Mary Duncan
University of Missouri–St. Louis

Melissa Nemeth
Indiana University Purdue University Indianapolis

Melody Alexander
Ball State University

Michael Douglas
University of Arkansas at Little Rock

Michael Dunklebarger
Alamance Community College

Michael G. Skaff
College of the Sequoias

Michele Budnovitch
Pennsylvania College of Technology

Mike Jochen
East Stroudsburg University

Mike Scroggins
Missouri State University

Nanette Lareau
University of Arkansas Community College– Morrilton

Pam Uhlenkamp
Iowa Central Community College

Patrick Smith
Marshall Community and Technical College

Paula Ruby
Arkansas State University

Peggy Burrus
Red Rocks Community College

Peter Ross
SUNY Albany

Philip H. Nielson
Salt Lake Community College

Ralph Hooper
University of Alabama

Ranette Halverson
Midwestern State University

Richard Cacace
Pensacola Junior College

Robert Dušek
Northern Virginia Community College

Robert Sindt
Johnson County Community College

Rocky Belcher
Sinclair Community College

Roger Pick
University of Missouri at Kansas City

Ronnie Creel
Troy University

Rosalie Westerberg
Clover Park Technical College

Ruth Neal
Navarro College

Sandra Thomas
Troy University

Sophie Lee
California State University, Long Beach

Steven Schwarz
Raritan Valley Community College

Sue McCrory
Missouri State University

Susan Fuschetto
Cerritos College

Susan Medlin
UNC Charlotte

Suzan Spitzberg
Oakton Community College

Sven Aelterman
Troy University

Terri Holly
Indian River State College

Thomas Rienzo
Western Michigan University

Tina Johnson
Midwestern State University

Tommy Lu
Delaware Technical and Community College

Troy S. Cash
NorthWest Arkansas Community College

Vicki Robertson
Southwest Tennessee Community College

Weifeng Chen
California University of Pennsylvania

Wes Anthony
Houston Community College

William Ayen
University of Colorado at Colorado Springs

Wilma Andrews
Virginia Commonwealth University

Yvonne Galusha
University of Iowa

We'd also like to acknowledge the reviewers of previous editions of Exploring:

Aaron Schorr
Fashion Institute of Technology

Alan Moltz
Naugatuck Valley Technical Community College

Alicia Stonesifer
La Salle University

Allen Alexander
Delaware Tech & Community College

Alok Charturvedi
Purdue University

Amy Williams
Abraham Baldwin Agriculture College

Andrea Compton
St. Charles Community College

Annette Duvall
Central New Mexico Community College

Annie Brown
Hawaii Community College

Antonio Vargas
El Paso Community College

Barbara Cierny
Harper College

Barbara Hearn
Community College of Philadelphia

Barbara Meguro
University of Hawaii at Hilo

Barbara Sherman
Buffalo State College

Barbara Stover
Marion Technical College

Bette Pitts
South Plains College

Beverly Fite
Amarillo College

Bill Daley
University of Oregon

Bill Morse
DeVry Institute of Technology

Bill Wagner
Villanova

Bob McCloud
Sacred Heart University

Bonnie Homan
San Francisco State University

Brandi N. Guidry
University of Louisiana at Lafayette

Brian Powell
West Virginia University–Morgantown Campus

Carl Farrell
Hawaii Pacific University

Carl M. Briggs
Indiana University School of Business

Carl Penzuil
Ithaca College

Carlotta Eaton
Radford University

Carole Bagley
University of St. Thomas

Carolyn DiLeo
Westchester Community College

Cassie Georgetti
Florida Technical College

Catherine Hain
Central New Mexico Community College

Charles Edwards
University of Texas of the Permian Basin

Cheryl Slavik
Computer Learning Services

Christine L. Moore
College of Charleston

Cody Copeland
Johnson County Community College

Connie Wells
Georgia State University

Dana Johnson
North Dakota State University

Dan Combellick
Scottsdale Community College

Daniela Marghitu
Auburn University

David B. Meinert
Southwest Missouri State University

David Barnes
Penn State Altoona

David Childress
Ashland Community College

David Douglas
University of Arkansas

David Langley
University of Oregon

David Law
Alfred State College

David Rinehard
Lansing Community College

David Weiner
University of San Francisco

Delores Pusins
Hillsborough Community College

Dennis Chalupa
Houston Baptist

Diane Stark
Phoenix College

Dianna Patterson
Texarkana College

Dianne Ross
University of Louisiana at Lafayette

Don Belle
Central Piedmont Community College

Douglas Cross
Clackamas Community College

Dr. Behrooz Saghafi
Chicago State University

Dr. Gladys Swindler
Fort Hays State University

Dr. Joe Teng
Barry University

Dr. Karen Nantz
Eastern Illinois University

Duane D. Lintner
Amarillo College

Elizabeth Edmiston
North Carolina Central University

Erhan Uskup
Houston Community College

Ernie Ivey
Polk Community College

Fred Hills
McClellan Community College

Freda Leonard
Delgado Community College

Gale E. Rand
College Misericordia

Gary R. Armstrong
Shippensburg University of Pennsylvania

Glenna Vanderhoof
Missouri State

Gregg Asher
Minnesota State University, Mankato

Hank Imus
San Diego Mesa College

Heidi Gentry-Kolen
Northwest Florida State College

Helen Stoloff
Hudson Valley Community College

Herach Safarian
College of the Canyons

Hong K. Sung
University of Central Oklahoma

Hyekyung Clark
Central New Mexico Community College

J. Patrick Fenton
West Valley College

Jack Zeller
Kirkwood Community College

James Franck
College of St. Scholastica

James Gips
Boston College

Jana Carver
Amarillo College

Jane Cheng
Bloomfield College

Jane King
Everett Community College

Janis Cox
Tri-County Technical College

Janos T. Fustos
Metropolitan State College of Denver

Jean Kotsiovos
Kaplan University

Jeffrey A. Hassett
University of Utah

Jennifer Pickle
Amarillo College

Jerry Chin
Southwest Missouri State University

Jerry Kolata
New England Institute of Technology

Jesse Day
South Plains College

Jill Chapnick
Florida International University

Jim Pepe
Bentley College

Jim Pruitt
Central Washington University

John Arehart
Longwood University

John Lee Reardon
University of Hawaii, Manoa

John Lesson
University of Central Florida

John Shepherd
Duquesne University

Joshua Mindel
San Francisco State University

Judith M. Fitspatrick
Gulf Coast Community College

Judith Rice
Santa Fe Community College

Judy Brown
The University of Memphis

Judy Dolan
Palomar College

Karen Tracey
Central Connecticut State University

Karen Wisniewski
County College of Morris

Karl Smart
Central Michigan University

Kathleen Brenan
Ashland University

Kathryn L. Hatch
University of Arizona

Kevin Pauli
University of Nebraska

Kim Montney
Kellogg Community College

Kimberly Chambers
Scottsdale Community College

Krista Lawrence
Delgado Community College

Krista Terry
Radford University

Lancie Anthony Affonso
College of Charleston

Larry S. Corman
Fort Lewis College

Laura McManamon
University of Dayton

Laura Reid
University of Western Ontario

Linda Johnsonius
Murray State University

Lisa Prince
Missouri State University

Lori Kelley
Madison Area Technical College

Lucy Parker
California State University, Northridge

Lynda Henrie
LDS Business College

Lynn Band
Middlesex Community College

Lynn Bowen
Valdosta Technical College

Malia Young
Utah State University

Margaret Thomas
Ohio University

Margie Martyn
Baldwin Wallace

Marguerite Nedreberg
Youngstown State University

Marianne Trudgeon
Fanshawe College

Marilyn Hibbert
Salt Lake Community College

Marilyn Salas
Scottsdale Community College

Marjean Lake
LDS Business College

Mark Olaveson
Brigham Young University

Martin Crossland
Southwest Missouri State University

Mary McKenry Percival
University of Miami

Meg McManus
Northwest Florida State College

Michael Hassett
Fort Hayes State University

Michael Stewardson
San Jacinto College–North

Midge Gerber
Southwestern Oklahoma State University

Mike Hearn
Community College of Philadelphia

Mike Kelly
Community College of Rhode Island

Mike Thomas
Indiana University School of Business

Mimi Duncan
University of Missouri–St. Louis

Minnie Proctor
Indian River Community College

Nancy Sardone
Seton Hall University

Pam Chapman
Waubonsee Community College

Patricia Joseph
Slippery Rock University

Patrick Hogan
Cape Fear Community College

Paul E. Daurelle
Western Piedmont Community College

Paula F. Bell
Lock Haven University of Pennsylvania

Paulette Comet
Community College of Baltimore County, Catonsville

Pratap Kotala
North Dakota State University

Ranette Halverson
Midwestern State University

Raymond Frost
Central Connecticut State University

Richard Albright
Goldey-Beacom College

Richard Blamer
John Carroll University

Richard Herschel
St. Joseph's University

Richard Hewer
Ferris State University

Robert Gordon
Hofstra University

Robert Marmelstein
East Stroudsburg University

Robert Spear
Prince George's Community College

Robert Stumbur
Northern Alberta Institute of Technology

Roberta I. Hollen
University of Central Oklahoma

Roland Moreira
South Plains College

Ron Murch
University of Calgary

Rory J. de Simone
University of Florida

Rose M. Laird
Northern Virginia Community College

Ruth Neal
Navarro College

Sally Visci
Lorain County Community College

Sandra M. Brown
Finger Lakes Community College

Sharon Mulroney
Mount Royal College

Shawna DePlonty
Sault College of Applied Arts and Technology

Stephen E. Lunce
Midwestern State University

Steve Schwarz
Raritan Valley Community College

Steven Choy
University of Calgary

Stuart P. Brian
Holy Family College

Susan Byrne
St. Clair College

Susan Fry
Boise State University

Suzan Spitzberg
Oakton Community College

Suzanne Tomlinson
Iowa State University

Thomas Setaro
Brookdale Community College

Todd McLeod
Fresno City College

Vernon Griffin
Austin Community College

Vickie Pickett
Midland College

Vipul Gupta
St. Joseph's University

Vivek Shah
Texas State University–San Marcos

Wei-Lun Chuang
Utah State University

William Dorin
Indiana University Northwest

Additionally, we'd like to thank our Instructor Resource authors:

Anci Shah
Houston Community College

Ann Rovetto
Horry-Georgetown Technical College

Arlene Eliason
Minnesota School of Business

Barbara Stover
Marion Technical College

Carol Roberts
University of Maine

David Csuha
Passaic County Community College

James Powers
University of Southern Indiana

Jayne Lowery
Jackson State Community College

Julie Boyles
Portland Community College

Kyle Stark
Macomb Community College

Linda Lau
Longwood University

Lisa Prince
Missouri State University

Lynn Bowen
Valdosta Technical College

Lynn Hogan
Calhoun Community College

Mary Lutz
Southwestern Illinois College

Meg McManus
Northwest Florida State College

Sally Baker
DeVry University

Sharon Behrens
Mid-State Technical College

Stephanie Jones
Texas Tech University

Steve Rubin
California State University, Monterey Bay

Suzan Spitzberg
Oakton Community College

Tom McKenzie
James Madison University

Finally, we'd like to extend our thanks to the Exploring 2010, second edition, technical editors:

Julie Boyles

Elizabeth Lockley

Joyce Nielsen

PREFACE

The Exploring Series and You

Exploring is Pearson's Office Application series which requires students like you to think "beyond the point and click." With Office 2010, Exploring has embraced today's student learning styles to support extended learning beyond the classroom.

The goal of Exploring is, as it has always been, to go further than teaching just the steps to accomplish a task—the series provides the theoretical foundation for you to understand when and why to apply a skill. As a result, you achieve a deeper understanding of each application and can apply this critical thinking beyond Office and the classroom.

You are plugged in constantly, and Exploring has evolved to meet you half-way to work within your changing learning styles. Pearson has paid attention to the habits of students today, how you get information, how you are motivated to do well in class, and what your future goals look like. We asked you and your peers for acceptance of new tools we designed to address these points, and you responded with a resounding "YES!"

Here Is What We Learned About You

You go to college now with a different set of skills than students did five years ago. The new edition of Exploring moves you beyond the basics of the software at a faster pace, without sacrificing coverage of the fundamental skills that you need to know. This ensures that you will be engaged from page 1 to the end of the book.

You and your peers have diverse learning styles. With this in mind, we broadened our definition of "student resources" to include Compass, an online skill database; movable Visual Reference cards; relevant Set-Up Videos filmed in a familiar, commercial style; and the most powerful online homework and assessment tool around, my**it**lab. Exploring will be accessible to all students, regardless of learning style.

You read, prepare, and study differently than students used to. You use textbooks like a tool—you want to easily identify what you need to know and learn it efficiently. We have added key features that make the content accessible to you and make the text easy to use.

You are goal-oriented. You want a good grade and you want to be successful in your future career. With this in mind, we used motivating case studies and Set-Up Videos to aid in the learning now and to show the relevance of the skills to your future careers.

Moving Beyond the Point and Click and Extending Your Learning Beyond the Classroom

In the second edition, we have added even more to help you learn this material inside and out and prepare for your future careers. Quick Concept Checks have been added in the chapter before every Hands-On Exercise to help you focus on the key concepts from the previous section of white pages. Collaboration Exercises have been added to help expose you to new technologies and get experience working in groups, as you will in the workforce. New "From Scratch" Exercises have been added to help test your understanding and critical thinking skills. Discipline Specific Capstones have been added at the end of the book to help you see how these Office skills apply to a variety of different fields. This tremendously talented team of Office Applications authors have devoted themselves to teaching you the ins and outs of Microsoft Word, Excel, Access, and PowerPoint. Led by series editor Mary Anne Poatsy, the whole team is dedicated to the Exploring mission of **moving you beyond the point and click, and extending your learning beyond the classroom**.

Key Features of Exploring Office 2010

- **White Pages/Yellow Pages** clearly distinguish the theory (white pages) from the skills covered in the Hands-On Exercises (yellow pages) so students always know what they are supposed to be doing.
- **Objective Mapping** enables students to skip the skills and concepts they know and quickly find those they do not know by scanning the chapter opener pages for the page numbers of the material they need.
- **Pull Quotes** entice students into the theory by highlighting the most interesting points.
- **Case Study** presents a scenario for the chapter, creating a story that ties the Hands-On Exercises together.

- **FYI Icon** indicates that an exercise step includes a skill that is common to more than one application. Students who require more information on that skill may utilize the Office Fundamentals and File Management chapter, the Visual Reference Cards, or Compass for assistance.

- **Set-Up Video** introduces the chapter's Case Study to generate student interest and attention and shows the relevance of the skills to students' future work.
- **Key Terms** are defined in the margins to ensure student comprehension.
- **End-of-Chapter Exercises** offer instructors several options for assessment. Each chapter has approximately 12–15 exercises ranging from multiple choice questions to open-ended projects.

CREATIVE CASE DISCOVER

- **Enhanced Mid-Level Exercises** include a **Creative Case**, which allows students some flexibility and creativity, not being bound by a definitive solution, as well as **Discover Steps**, which encourage students to use Help or to problem-solve to accomplish a task.

New to Exploring Office 2010 Volume 1 Second Edition

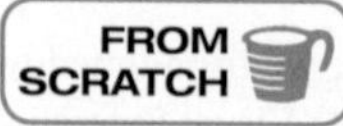

- **From Scratch Icon** indicates a project without a starting data file, which requires students to use critical thinking skills in developing the file from a blank document.
- **Quick Concept Check** helps students focus on the key concepts from the white page section preceding a Hands-On Exercise.
- **Full Application Capstones** bring all of the key skills and concepts of each application all together in a single, comprehensive project.
- **Collaboration Exercises** introduce students to new technologies to help them work collaboratively, one of the most essential skills in today's workforce.
- **Discipline-Specific Capstones** introduce students to using and integrating Office applications in different career fields, such as paralegal, theater, and medical fields.

Instructor Resources

The Instructor's Resource Center, available at www.pearsonhighered.com/exploring includes the following:

- **Annotated Solution Files with Scorecards** assist with grading the Hands-On Exercises and end-of-chapter exercises.
- **Data and Solution Files.**
- **Capstone Production Tests** allow instructors to assess all skills covered in a chapter with a single project.
- **Rubrics** for Mid-Level Creative Cases and Beyond the Classroom Cases in Microsoft® Word format enable instructors to customize the assignments for their classes.
- **PowerPoint® Presentations** with notes for each chapter are included for out-of-class study or review.
- **Audio PowerPoint Presentations** provide an alternate version of the PowerPoint presentations in which all the lecture notes have been prerecorded.
- **Lesson Plans** provide a detailed blueprint to achieve chapter learning objectives and outcomes.
- **Objectives List** maps chapter objectives to Hands-On Exercises and end-of-chapter exercises.
- **Multiple Choice Answer Key.**

- **Complete Test Bank**, also available in TestGen format.
- **Set-Up Video Exercises** provide companion exercises for the Set-Up Video for each chapter.
- **Syllabus templates** for 8-week, 12-week, and 16-week courses.
- **Grader projects** provide live-in-the-application assessment for each chapter's Capstone Exercise and additional capstone exercises.
- **Instructor Reference Cards**, available electronically and as printed cards, for each chapter, include:
  - **Concept Summary** outlines the KEY objectives to cover in class with tips on where students get stuck as well as how to get them unstuck.
  - **Scripted Lecture** provides instructors with a lecture outline that mirrors the Hands-On Exercises.

Online Course Cartridges

Flexible, robust, and customizable content is available for all major online course platforms that include everything instructors need in one place. Please contact your Sales Representative for information on accessing course cartridges for WebCT, Blackboard, or CourseCompass.

Student Resources

Online Student Resources

- Student Data Files
- Set-Up Videos introduce the chapter's Case Study to generate student interest and attention and show the relevance of the skills to students' future work.
- Compass access for PC and mobile phone

Visual Reference Cards

A two-sided reference card for each application provides students with a visual summary of information and tips specific to each application that provide answers to the most common student questions. The cards can be easily attached to and detached from the book's spiral binding to be used as a bookmark, and all cards are clearly color-coded by application.

Compass

Compass is a searchable database of Microsoft Office 2010 skills that is available for use online on a computer or on your mobile phone. Using a keyword look-up system on your computer, the database provides multimedia instructions via videos and at-a-glance frames to remind students how to perform a skill. For students on the go, you can use your mobile phone to search and access a brief description of a skill and the click-stream instructions for how to perform the skill. This is a resource for the tech savvy student, who wants help and answers right away. Students get access to Compass through my**it**lab and/or the Student CD.

Prentice Hall's Companion Website

www.pearsonhighered.com/exploring offers expanded IT resources and downloadable supplements. Students can find the following self-study tools for each chapter:

- Online Study Guide
- Chapter Objectives
- Glossary
- Chapter Objectives Review
- Web Resources
- Student Data Files

myitlab

my**it**lab for Office 2010 is a solution designed by professors for professors that allows easy delivery of Office courses with defensible assessment and outcomes-based training. The new *Exploring Office 2010* system will seamlessly integrate online assessment, training, and projects with my**it**lab for Microsoft Office 2010!

myitlab for Office 2010 Features....

- **Assessment and training built to match *Exploring Office 2010*** instructional content so that my**it**lab works with *Exploring* to move students beyond the point and click.
- **Both project-based and skill-based assessment and training** allow instructors to test and train students on complete exercises or individual Office application skills.
- **Full course management functionality** includes all instructor and student resources, a complete Gradebook, and the ability to run a variety of reports including detailed student clickstream data.
- **The most open, realistic, high-fidelity simulation** of Office 2010 so students feel like they are learning Office, not just a simulation.
- **Grader, a live-in-the-application project-grading tool,** enables instructors to assign projects taken from the end-of-chapter material and additional projects included in the instructor resources. These are graded automatically, with detailed feedback provided to both instructors and students.

WINDOWS 7

1 GETTING STARTED WITH WINDOWS 7

An Introduction to the Operating System

CASE STUDY | Cedar Cove Elementary School

A good friend recently graduated with a degree in Elementary Education and is excited to begin her first job as a fifth-grade teacher at Cedar Cove Elementary School. The school has a computer lab for all students as well as a computer system in each classroom. The computers were acquired through a state technology grant so they are new models running Windows 7. Your friend's lesson plans must include a unit on operating system basics and an introduction to application software. Because you have a degree in Computer Information Systems, she has called on you for assistance with the lesson plans. She also hopes you will occasionally visit her classroom to help present the material.

The elementary school is located in a low-income area of the city, so you cannot assume that all students have been exposed to computers at home, especially to those configured with Windows 7. Your material will need to include very basic instruction in Windows 7, along with a general overview of application software. You will probably focus on application software that is included with Windows 7, including WordPad, Paint, and Calculator. Your friend's lesson plans must be completed right away, so you are on a short timeline but are excited about helping students learn!

OBJECTIVES AFTER YOU READ THIS CHAPTER, YOU WILL BE ABLE TO:

Windows 7 Fundamentals

Computer activities that you enjoy might include e-mail, games, social networking, and digital photo management. If you have a computer at work, you probably use such software as spreadsheet, database, word processing, and other job-specific applications. Those applications are necessary for your enjoyment or career, but they would not be possible without an ***operating system***. The operating system is software that directs such computer activities as checking all components, managing system resources, and communicating with application software.

Windows 7 is a Microsoft operating system produced in 2009 and available on most new microcomputer systems.

An **operating system** is software that directs computer activities such as recognizing keyboard input, sending output to a display, and keeping track of files and folders.

Windows 7 is a Microsoft operating system produced in 2009 and available on most new microcomputer systems. Because you are likely to encounter Windows 7 on computers at school, work, and home, it is well worth your time to explore it and learn to appreciate its computer management and security features. In this section, you will explore the desktop and its components, including the Start menu and taskbar. You will also learn to customize the desktop with a background and color scheme of your choice.

Understanding the Desktop

The **desktop** is the screen that displays when you turn on a computer. It contains icons and a taskbar.

A **window** is an onscreen rectangular area representing a program or system resource, or data.

An **icon** is a small picture on the desktop representing a program, file, folder, or other item.

The ***desktop*** is the display that you see after you turn on a computer and respond to any username and password prompts. The Windows 7 desktop includes components that enable you to access system resources, work with software, and manage files and folders. It is called a *desktop* because it serves the purpose of a desk, on which you can manage tasks and complete paperwork. Just as you can work with multiple projects on a desk, you can work with several software applications, each occupying a ***window***, or area of space, on the desktop.

Identify Desktop Components

One of the first things that you will notice about the desktop is the presence of a few small pictures, each with a description underneath. Those pictures, or ***icons***, represent programs, files, folders, or other items related to your computer. The desktop that you see on your home computer might differ from the one that you use at school or work because each computer has a unique configuration of installed programs and files. Invariably, most desktops contain one or more icons such as the one shown in Figure 1.1. You can easily add and remove icons

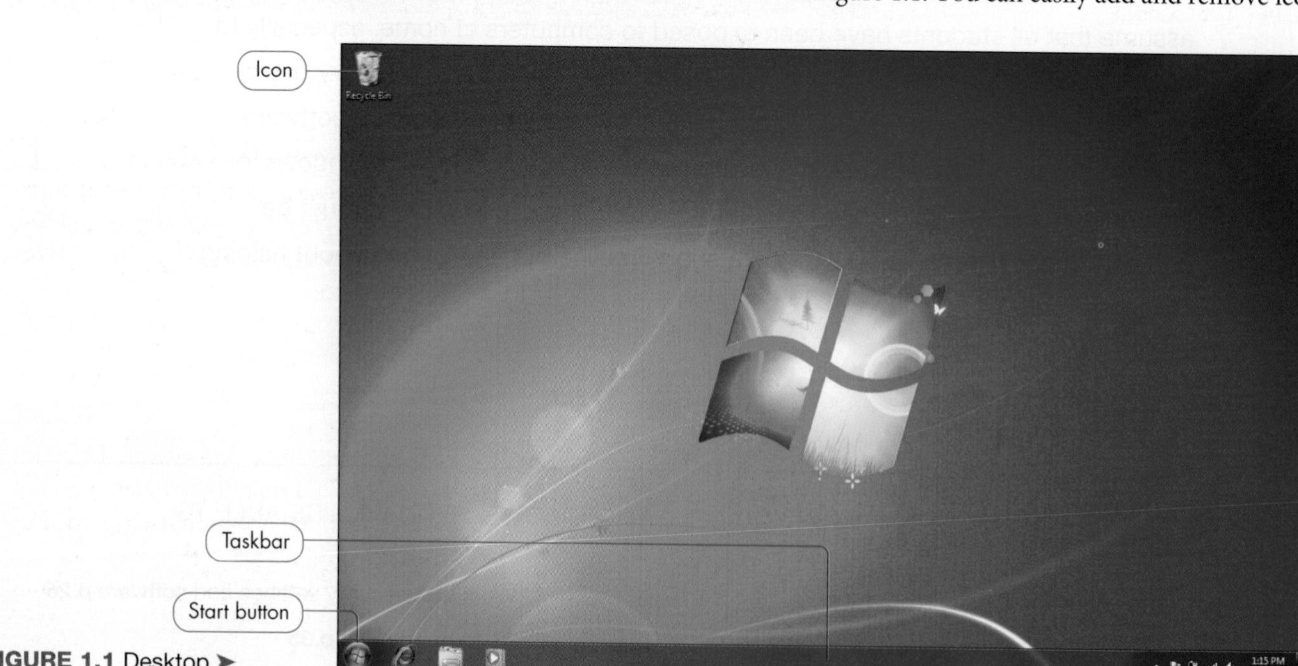

FIGURE 1.1 Desktop ➤

so that the desktop includes only those items that are important to you or that you access often. You can even include desktop folders in which you can organize files and programs.

A **shortcut** is a pointer, or link, to a program or computer resource.

As you work with a computer, you will find that you access some programs, or software, more often than others. Instead of searching for the program on a program list, you will find it convenient to add a program icon to the desktop. The icon is not actually the program, but a link to the program, called a ***shortcut***. Such shortcut icons are identified by a small arrow in the bottom-left corner of the icon. Figure 1.2 shows a shortcut icon. A computer provides a large amount of storage space, some of which you might use to house files, such as documents, worksheets, and digital photos related to particular projects or work-related activities. Because the desktop is so convenient to access, you could create a folder, identified by a folder icon, on the desktop to organize such files. See the folder icon in Figure 1.2. If you save files to the desktop, you should organize them in desktop folders. That way, the desktop will not become too cluttered and you can easily find related files later. Keep in mind that just as you strive to keep a desk relatively clear, you will also want to maintain order on the Windows desktop.

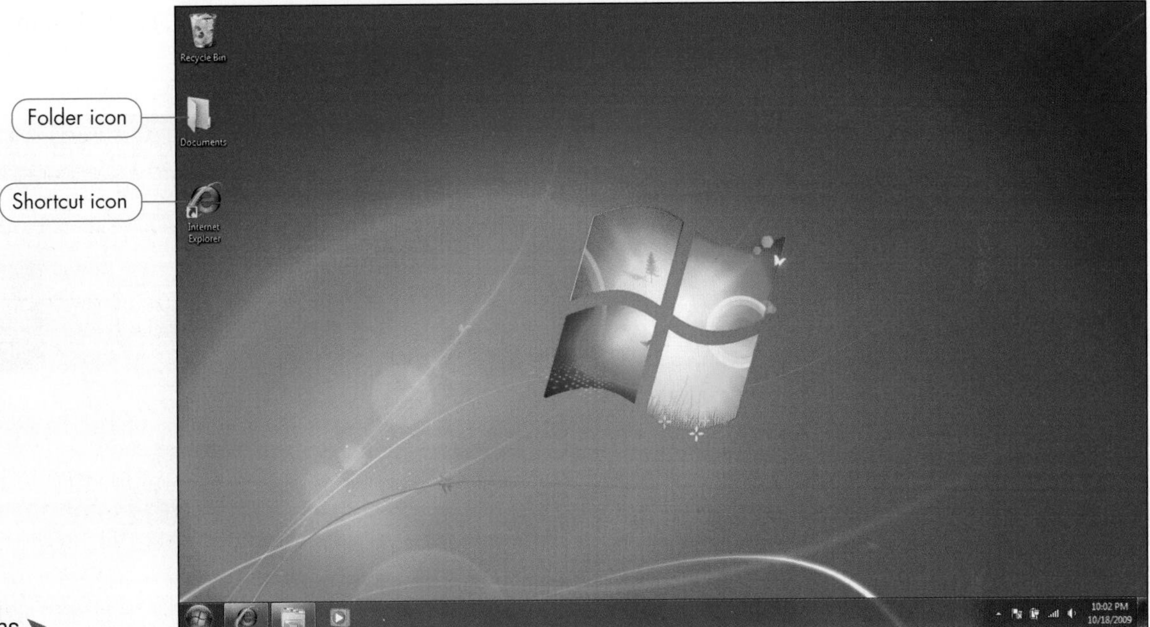

FIGURE 1.2 Icons ➤

You can easily add icons to the desktop, but the way in which you add an icon depends on the icon's purpose.

- **To add a program shortcut to the desktop**, you must first locate the program. Most often, you can simply click the Start button (located in the bottom-left corner of the desktop). Point to All Programs. Navigate the menu to display the program, but do not open it. Instead, right-click and drag the program name to the desktop. Release the mouse button. Click Create shortcuts here.
- **To add a folder to the desktop**, right-click an empty area of the desktop. Point to New and click Folder. Type a folder name and press Enter.

You can also delete and rename icons, as described below.

- **To delete an icon**, right-click the icon and click Delete. Respond affirmatively if asked whether to place the icon in the Recycle Bin. Remember that deleting a program shortcut icon does not remove, or uninstall, the program itself. You simply remove the desktop pointer (shortcut) to the program.
- **To rename an icon**, right-click the icon and click Rename. Type the new name and press Enter.

TIP Auto Arrange Icons

A desktop can easily become cluttered and disorganized. To avoid clutter, make sure that you maintain only desktop icons that are accessed often or that are important to keep handy. To neatly organize the desktop, you can auto arrange the icons. Right-click an empty area of the desktop, point to View, and click Auto arrange icons (unless Auto arrange icons already has a checkmark). Icons are maintained in straight columns and cannot be moved out of line.

A **gadget** is a desktop item that represents such items as games or puzzles, or constantly changing data, such as a clock or a calendar. Gadgets can be selected or downloaded and opened on the desktop.

Another item that can be placed on the desktop is a desktop ***gadget***. A gadget represents data that is constantly changing, or an item such as a game or puzzle. Although some gadgets are available when you install Windows 7, you can add additional gadgets from the Microsoft Windows Web site. To view the gadgets that are available within Windows, right-click an empty area of the desktop and click Gadgets. The gallery shown in Figure 1.3 displays. Double-click a gadget to place it on the desktop. Click Get more gadgets online to download others. To remove a gadget from the desktop, right-click the gadget and click Close gadget.

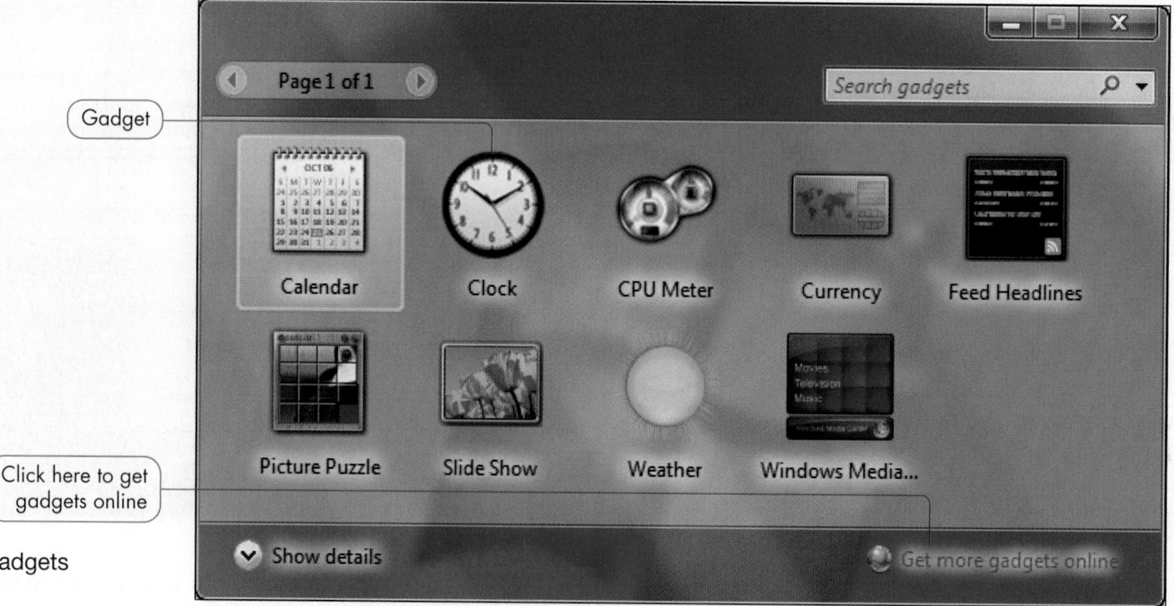

FIGURE 1.3 Gadgets Gallery ➤

By default, gadgets are grouped together on the right side of the desktop. By changing a few settings, you can resize gadgets, cause them to always appear on top of any open windows, adjust the opacity level, and move them. All of these options are available when you right-click a gadget on the desktop.

Explore the Taskbar

You can have several projects, papers, and other items on a desk. In fact, you can have so many things on a desk that it becomes difficult to sort through them all. Similarly, you can have several windows, or applications, open on a computer desktop at one time. Unlike a desk, however, the Windows desktop provides a tool for keeping

The Windows desktop provides a tool for keeping track of open computer projects—the taskbar.

The **taskbar** is the horizontal bar at the bottom of the desktop that enables you to move among open windows and provides access to system resources.

The **Start button**, located on the left side of the taskbar, is the place to begin when you want to open programs, get help, adjust computer settings, access system resources, or even shut down a computer.

The **Notification area**, on the right side of the taskbar, displays icons for background programs and system resources. It also provides status information in pop-up windows.

track of open computer projects—the ***taskbar***. The taskbar is a long horizontal bar located at the bottom of the desktop. The taskbar is the location of the ***Start button***, toolbars, open window buttons, and the ***Notification area***.

When you open a program or work with a file, the item will display in a window on the desktop. It is not unusual to have several windows open at one time. When that happens, the windows sometimes overlap, making it difficult to see what is underneath or to remember what you have open. The taskbar simplifies the task of keeping track of the desktop. Every open window has a corresponding icon on the taskbar. Icons often represent programs, such as Excel and Word. To move from one window to another, simply click the taskbar icon representing the window. It works much like shifting paper on a desk but is easier. Figure 1.4 shows two windows open on the desktop, with corresponding taskbar program icons. Although several windows can be open at one time, only one is active (in front of other windows).

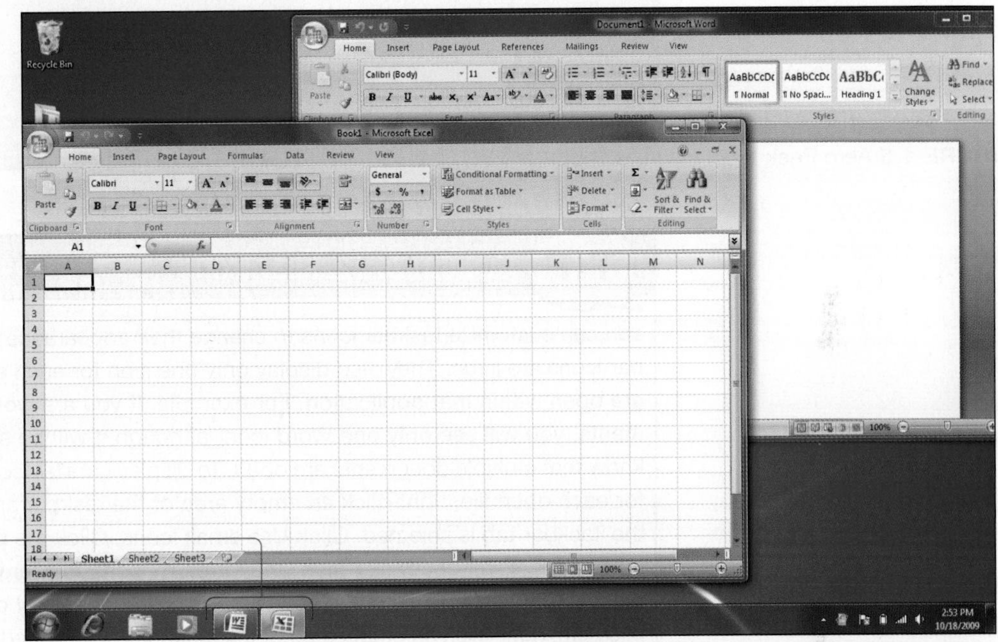

FIGURE 1.4 Program Icons on the Taskbar ➤

Aero Peek provides a preview of an open window without requiring you to click away from the window that you are currently working on. Place the mouse pointer over any icon that represents an open window to view its contents.

Windows 7 taskbar icons are large and unlabeled, unlike icons found in earlier Windows versions. The size and simplicity gives a clean uncluttered feel to the taskbar. Even if you have multiple files open for one icon, such as when you have several word processing documents open, you will see only one program icon. If several programs are open, you will see a taskbar icon for each open window. To get a sneak preview of any open window, even if it is obscured by another, place the mouse pointer over the program's icon on the taskbar. The resulting preview is called ***Aero Peek***. Place the mouse pointer over the thumbnail (previewed window), without clicking, to temporarily view the window in full size. When you move the mouse pointer away, the active window reappears. If you click the thumbnail (window preview) you will switch to the previewed window. See Figure 1.5 for an example of Aero Peek.

FIGURE 1.5 Aero Peek ➤

TIP Customize Taskbar Icons

You can customize taskbar icons to change their appearance and behavior. By default, taskbar icons are large. They also display only one icon for each application, even if several files are open within that application. For example, if you are working with several Word documents, you will see only one Word icon, although it will be slightly overlapped, letting you know that multiple documents are open. To display smaller icons and to show separate icons for each open file, right-click an empty area of the taskbar and click Properties. Make sure the Taskbar tab is selected. Click Use small icons. Click the button beside the Taskbar buttons. Click Never combine. Click OK. To return icons to a larger size, reverse the process of making them smaller. To combine taskbar icons so that only one icon is shown for each application, right-click an empty area of the taskbar, click Properties, click the button beside the Taskbar buttons, and click Always combine, hide labels. Click OK.

The **Start menu** is a list of programs, folders, and utilities that displays when you click the Start button.

When you click the Start button, you will see the ***Start menu***, as shown in Figure 1.6. As its name implies, the Start menu is the place to begin when you want to open programs, get help, adjust computer settings, access system resources, or even shut down your computer. The Start menu is comprised of three areas. The *left pane* displays a short list of commonly accessed programs on your computer. When you point to All Programs, you will see a more complete list of programs. The *right pane* provides access to system folders, such as Documents, Pictures, and Music. It also enables you to adjust system settings, log off a user account, shut down the computer, and get help. The Search box, located at the bottom of the left side of the Start menu (see Figure 1.6), is where you can type keywords of an item you are looking for, such as a file or folder. You will explore the topic of searching later in this chapter.

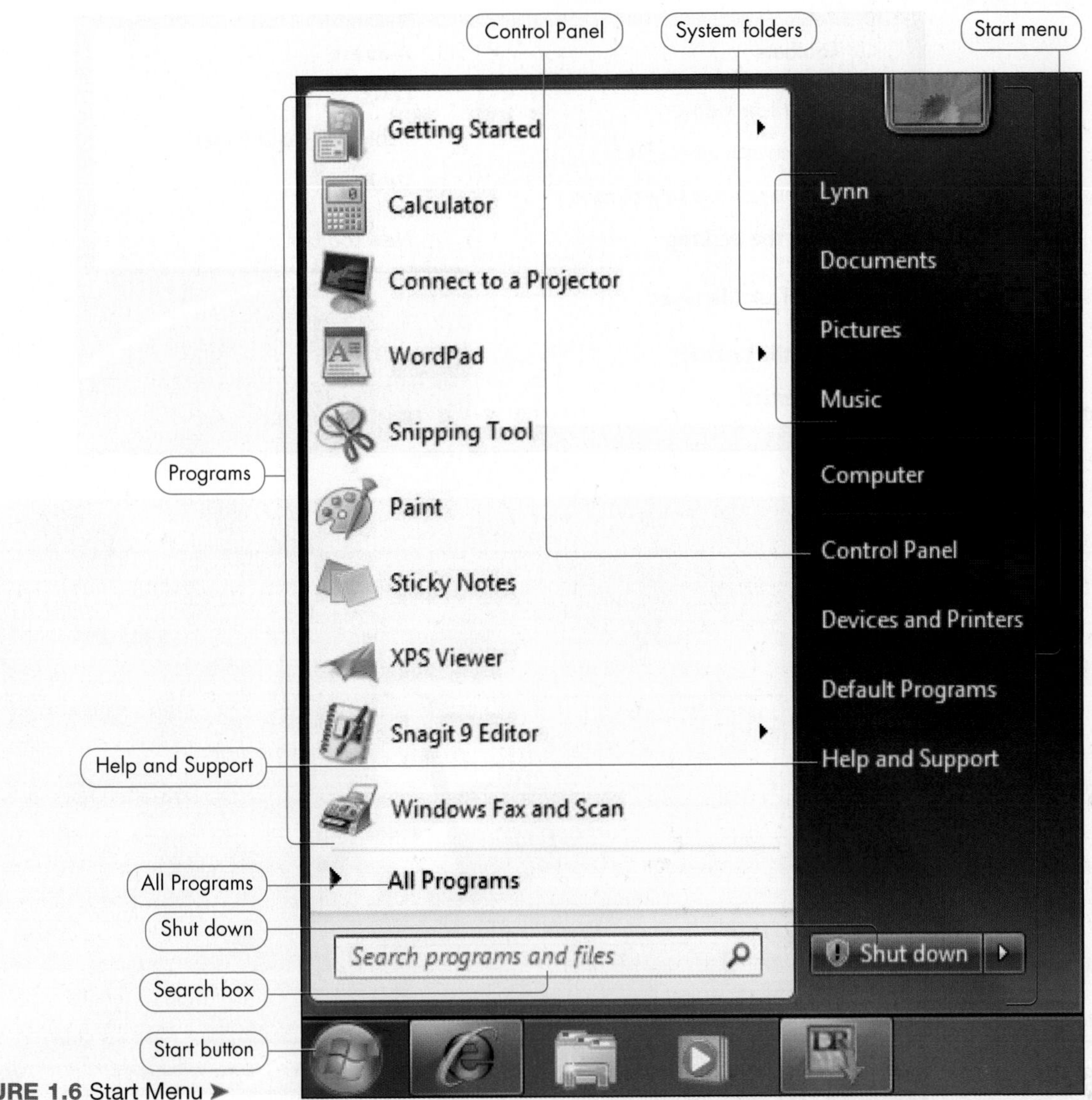

FIGURE 1.6 Start Menu ➤

TIP Hide the Taskbar

Although it is very helpful, the taskbar can occupy space on your work area that you need. To temporarily hide the taskbar, right-click an empty area of the taskbar. Click Properties. In the Taskbar appearance area of the Taskbar and Start Menu Properties window, click to select Auto-hide the taskbar, and then click OK. The taskbar immediately disappears. When you move the mouse pointer to the previous location of the taskbar, it will appear, but only until you move the mouse pointer away. To return the taskbar to view, reverse the process described above, clicking to deselect Auto-hide the taskbar.

A **toolbar** is an area of items that you can select, usually displayed on the taskbar or within an application.

The taskbar is a convenient place to display ***toolbars***, which provide shortcuts to Web resources and enable you to quickly move to a specified address. Specifically the Links and Address toolbars are handy additions to the taskbar but are not automatically displayed. To see a list of available toolbars, right-click an empty part of the taskbar and point to Toolbars. See Figure 1.7 for an example of a toolbar list. Click any item in the list to add or remove it. If you see a checkmark beside a toolbar, the toolbar is already open on the taskbar. Figure 1.8 shows a taskbar that includes an Address toolbar.

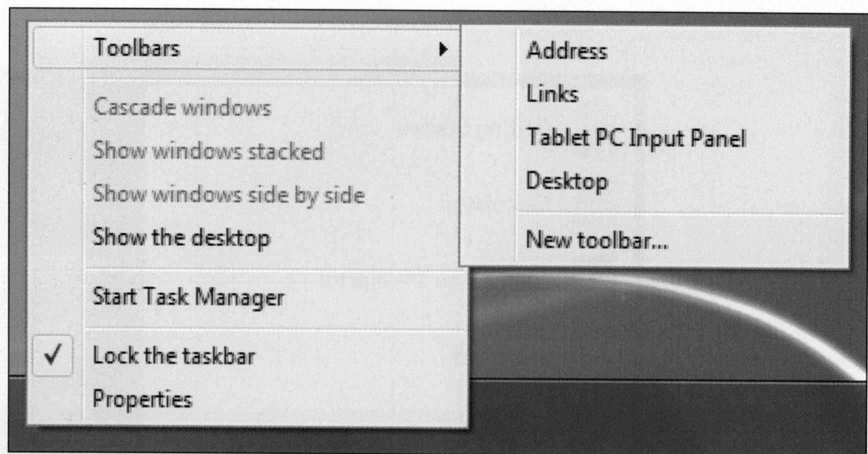

FIGURE 1.7 Taskbar Toolbars List ➤

FIGURE 1.8 Toolbar Example ➤

When you **pin** an item, it becomes a permanent part of the taskbar, accessible with a single click.

A **Jump List** is a list of actions or resources associated with an open window button or pinned item on the taskbar.

You can place, or ***pin***, icons of frequently used programs on the taskbar for quick access later. When you pin a program, the program icon becomes a permanent part of the taskbar, as shown in Figure 1.9. You can then open the program by single-clicking its icon. If the program that you want to pin is not already open, click Start, browse to the program name, right-click the name, and click Pin to Taskbar. If the program that you want to pin is already open, right-click the program icon on the taskbar to open its ***Jump List*** (see Figure 1.9). Click Pin this program to taskbar. A Jump List is a list of shortcuts to pinned items, most often simply the program name, an option to pin or unpin an item, and a close option.

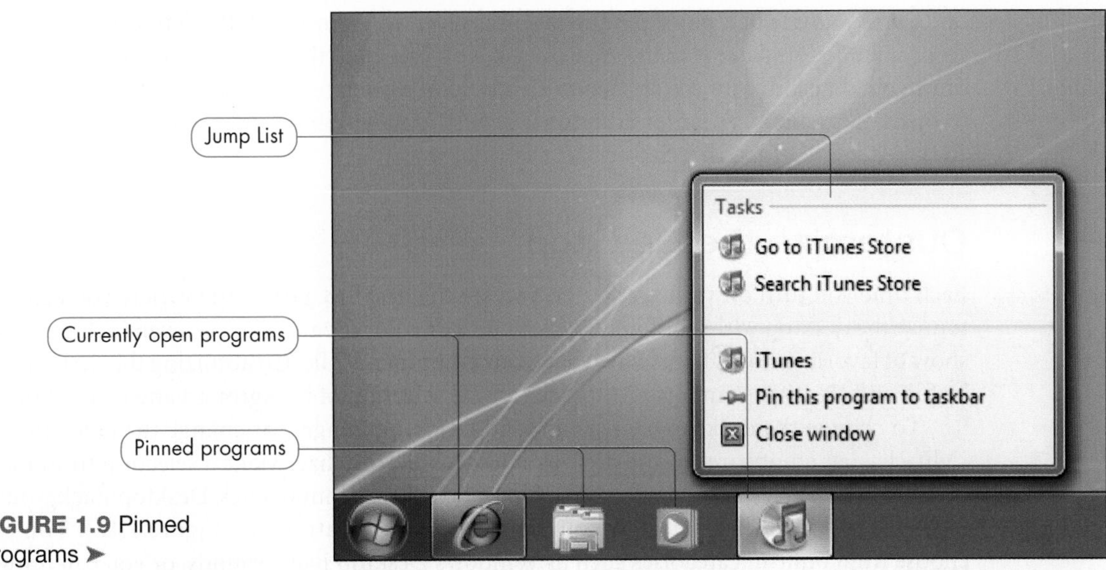

FIGURE 1.9 Pinned Programs ➤

TIP Pin Items to the Start Menu

Just as you can pin programs to the taskbar, you can pin items to the Start menu. When you pin a program to the Start menu, it becomes a permanent selection on the left side of the Start menu. A pinned program always shows on the Start menu so that you can find the program easily and open it with a single click. To pin a program, locate its name on the Start menu, right-click it, and click Pin to Start Menu. You can pin a program from the Start menu to both the Start menu and the taskbar, but you cannot pin a program from the taskbar to the Start menu.

A major purpose of the Notification area is providing important status information that appears in a pop-up window when you click the Action Center icon.

You will find the Notification area (see Figure 1.10) on the right side of the taskbar. It displays icons for programs running in the background, such as a virus scanner, and provides access to such system activities as managing wireless networks and adjusting volume. A major purpose of the Notification area is to provide important status information that appears in a pop-up window when you click the Action Center icon. Status information could include the detection of new devices, the availability of software updates, or recommended maintenance and security

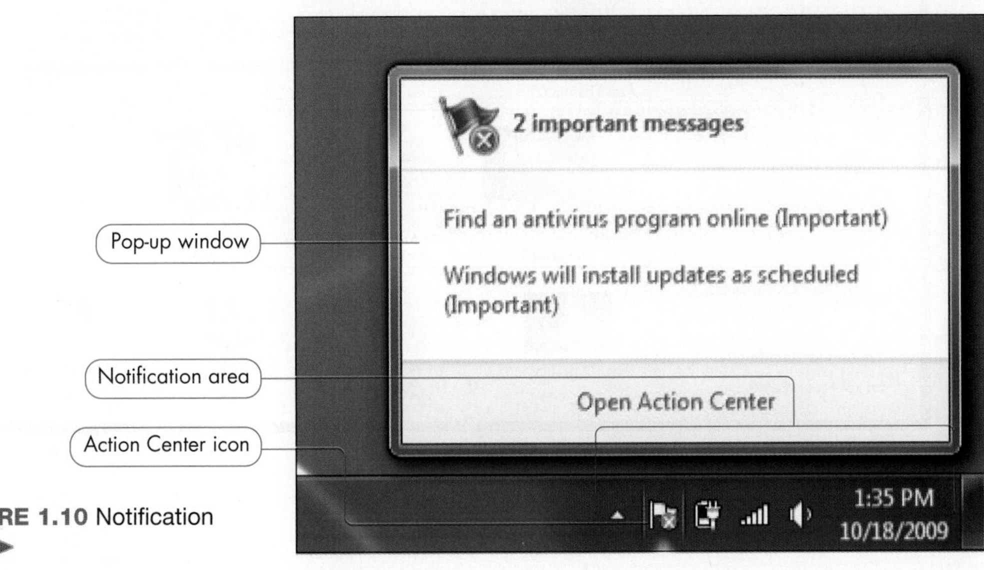

FIGURE 1.10 Notification Area ➤

tasks. An example of a pop-up notification is given in Figure 1.10. If the notification is of a recommended update or maintenance task, you can click the message to perform the recommended task. If you see an ***Action Center*** icon associated with the notification, click it to open the Action Center for additional details. You will find more information about the Action Center later in this chapter.

The **Action Center** monitors maintenance and security settings, providing alerts when necessary.

Customize the Desktop

Each time you turn on your computer, you see the desktop. For a little variety you can customize the desktop with a different background or color theme. You can even include a slide show of favorite photos to display when your computer is idle. Customizing the desktop can be fun and creative. Windows 7 provides a wide selection of background and color choices.

To change the desktop background, add moving images, or change the color theme, right-click an empty area of the desktop and click Personalize. Make a selection from those shown in Figure 1.11. If you choose to change the background, click Desktop Background (see Figure 1.11). Then select or confirm the picture location (see Figure 1.12). You can choose from built-in categories such as Windows Desktop Backgrounds, or you can browse for a folder containing your personal pictures. If you select Windows Desktop Backgrounds, you can select from several categories (nature, architecture, etc.). Click Window Color (see Figure 1.11) to change the color of window borders, the Start menu, and the taskbar. You can also select a ***screen saver*** (see Figure 1.11). A screen saver is a moving series of pictures or images that appears when your computer has been idle for a specified period of time. You might use a screen saver for privacy, so that when you are away from your desk, the display is obscured by the moving images. Figure 1.13 shows the Screen Saver Settings dialog box from which you can select a screen saver and adjust settings. Settings include how long the computer must be idle before a screen saver is displayed, as well as the option to require a log on before the screen saver disappears. Click Save Changes (see Figure 1.12) after making any of the above selections or Cancel to ignore changes. Close any open windows.

A **screen saver** is a series of moving images that appears on the desktop when a computer has been idle for a specified period of time.

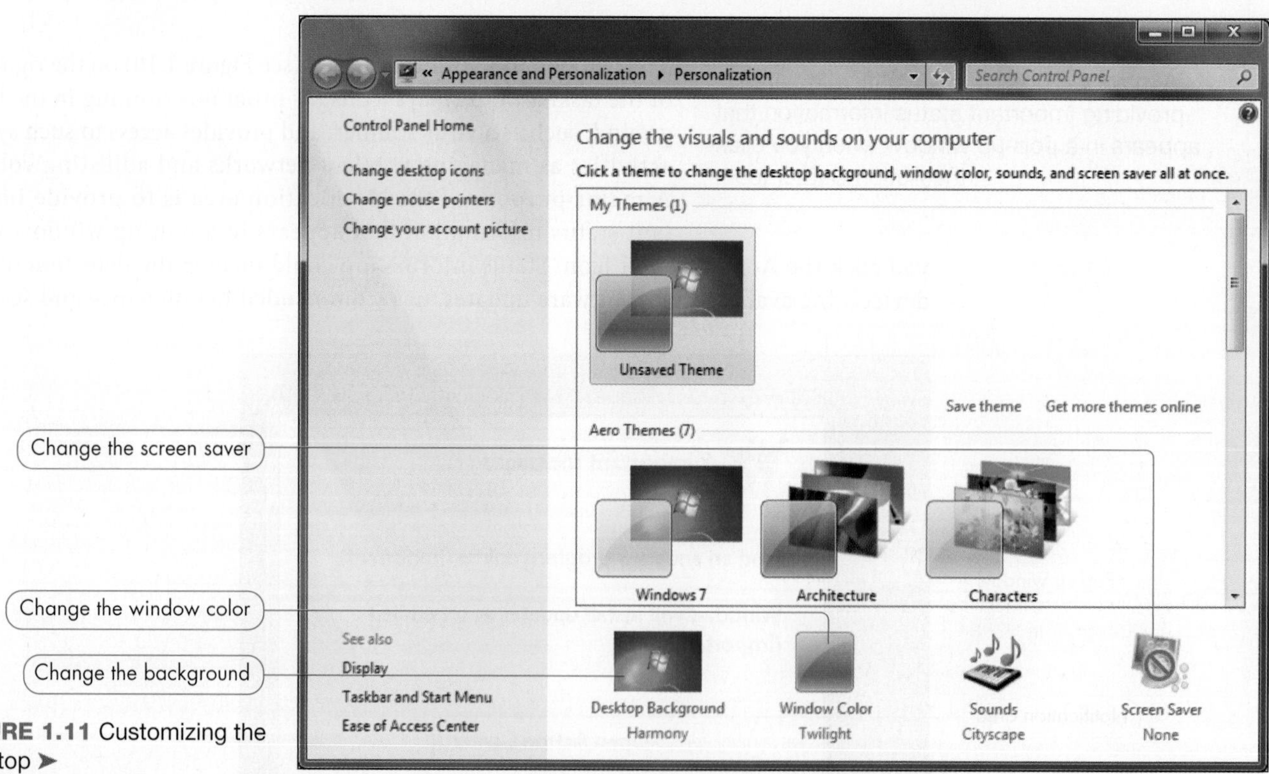

FIGURE 1.11 Customizing the Desktop ➤

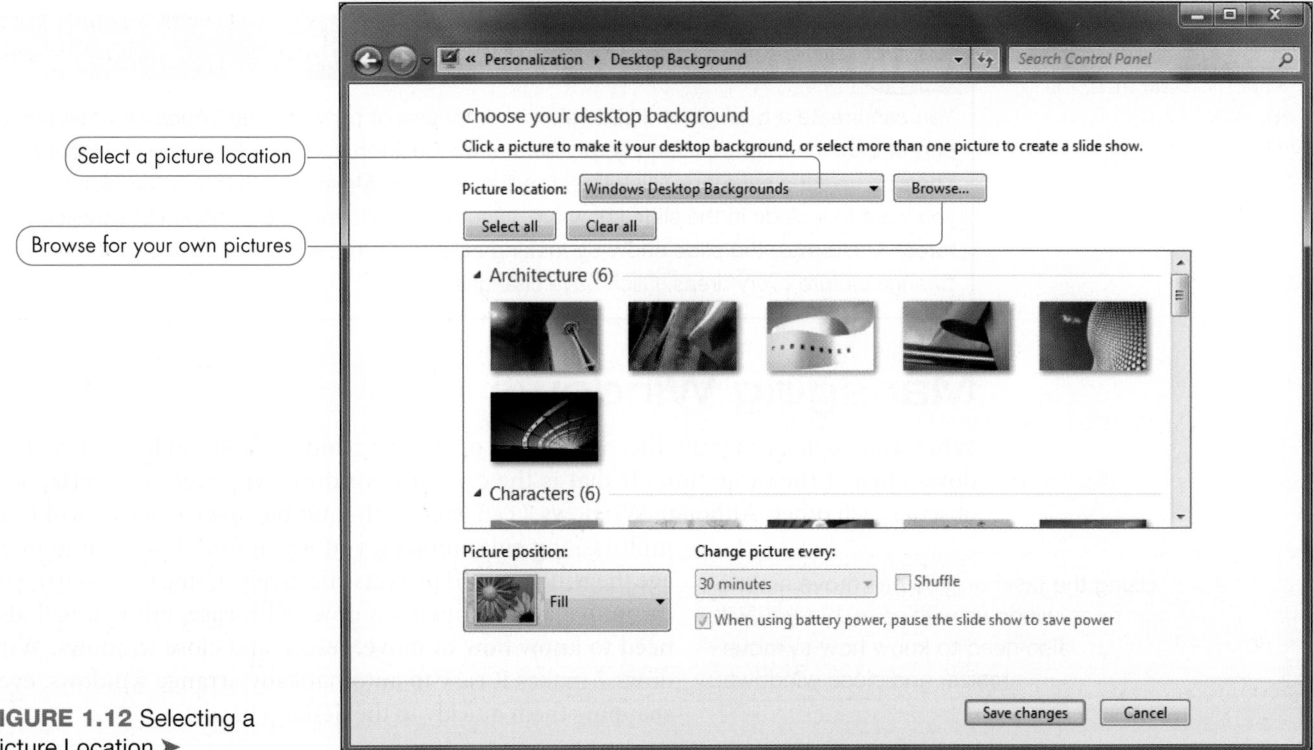

FIGURE 1.12 Selecting a Picture Location ➤

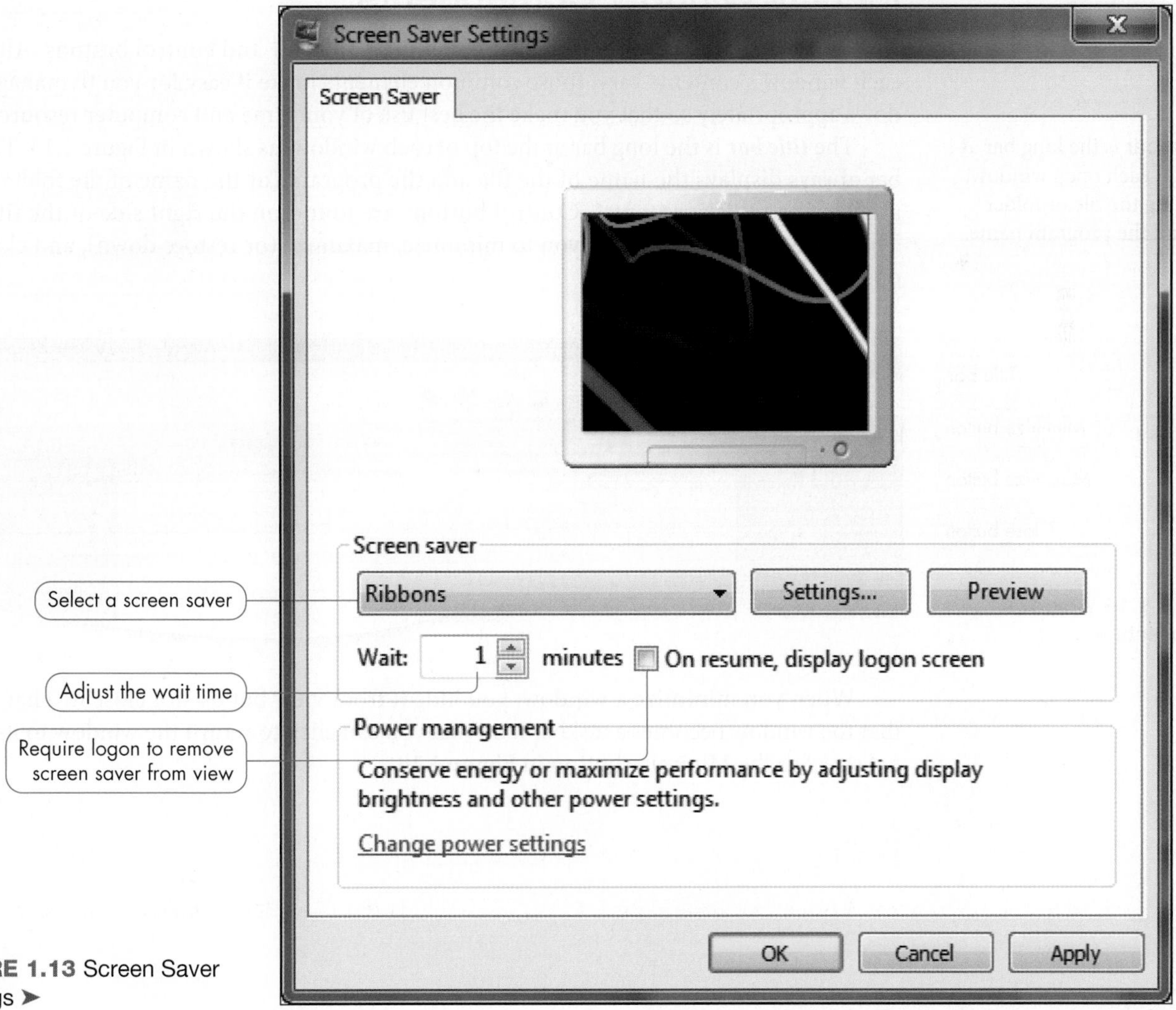

Screen Saver Settings

Screen Saver

Screen saver

Ribbons | Settings... | Preview

Wait: 1 minutes On resume, display logon screen

Power management

Conserve energy or maximize performance by adjusting display brightness and other power settings.

Change power settings

OK | Cancel | Apply

Select a screen saver

Adjust the wait time

Require logon to remove screen saver from view

FIGURE 1.13 Screen Saver Settings ➤

> **TIP** Create a Desktop Background Slide Show
>
> You can create a background slide show comprised of pictures that Windows provides as part of a theme. Right-click an empty area of the desktop and click Personalize. Under Aero Themes, select a category. Click Desktop Background. Make sure that only the pictures that you want to include in the slide show are selected (as evidenced by checkmarks beside pictures). Customize the slide show by making selections in the *Picture position*, *Shuffle*, and *Change picture every* areas. Click Save changes.

Managing Windows

When you open a program, file, or folder, it opens in a window. You can have many windows open at the same time. If that is the case, the windows will begin to overlap and obscure each other. Although Windows 7 can work with multiple open windows within its multitasking environment, you might find it difficult to manage the windows and projects effectively. Using the taskbar, you can move among open windows with ease, but you will also need to know how to move, resize, and close windows. Windows 7 makes it easy to automatically arrange windows, even snapping them quickly to the desktop borders.

> Using the taskbar, you can move among open windows with ease, but you will also need to know how to move, resize, and close windows.

Identify Window Components

All windows share common elements including a title bar and control buttons. Although each window's contents vary, those common elements make it easy for you to manage windows appropriately so that you make the best use of your time and computer resources.

The **title bar** is the long bar at the top of each open window, containing the file or folder name and the program name.

The ***title bar*** is the long bar at the top of each window, as shown in Figure 1.14. The title bar always displays the name of the file and the program (or the name of the folder if you are viewing folder contents). Control buttons are found on the right side of the title bar. Those control buttons enable you to minimize, maximize (or restore down), and close any open window.

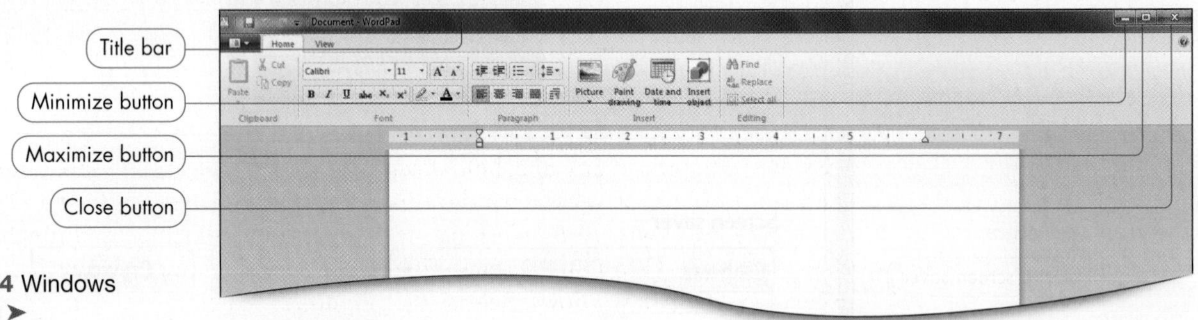

FIGURE 1.14 Windows Components ➤

When you minimize a window, you hide it from view but do not close it. That means that the window becomes a taskbar icon that you can click to return the window to its original size. See the Minimize button in Figure 1.14.

The middle control button shares two functions depending on the current size of the window. One is to maximize a window and one is to restore down to a smaller size. If a window is less than full size, click the middle button to maximize the window so that it occupies the entire desktop. The Maximize button looks like a small box. The Restore Down button appears as two overlapped boxes. The middle button in Figure 1.14 is the Maximize button. You can also maximize or restore down a window by double-clicking the title bar of the open window.

TIP Maximize a Window and Expand a Window Vertically

You can quickly maximize a window by dragging the title bar to the top of the desktop. The window immediately becomes full sized. To expand a window vertically without changing the window's width, drag a top or bottom border to the corresponding top or bottom edge of the desktop. When you place the mouse pointer on a border of a window, the pointer assumes the shape of a double-headed arrow. Only then should you drag the window to the top or bottom edge of the desktop. Release the mouse button to expand the window vertically.

The button on the far right side of the title bar is used to close a window. It is always displayed as an X. When you close a window, you remove the file or program from memory. If you have not saved a file that you are closing, Windows 7 will prompt you to save it before closing.

Work with Windows

It is sometimes necessary to move or resize a window. If multiple windows are open, you will need to know how to switch between windows and how to rearrange them. Windows 7 provides easy ways to select among windows, including the Aero Flip 3D experience.

If a window is obscuring something that you need to see, you can move or resize the window to reveal what is behind.

If a window is obscuring something that you need to see, you can move or resize the window to reveal what is behind. You can only move or resize a window that is not maximized. To move a window, drag the title bar. To resize a window, place the mouse pointer on a border of the window. The pointer will become a double-headed arrow. Drag to make the window larger or smaller. If the pointer is on a corner of the window, forming a diagonal double-headed arrow, you can resize two adjacent sides of the window at once by dragging.

Aero Flip 3D is a feature that shows windows in a rotating 3D stack so that you can select a window.

You can also use the keyboard to switch to another window. To cycle through all open windows, stopping at any one, hold down Alt on the keyboard and repeatedly press Tab. Release Alt when you see the window that you want to display. ***Aero Flip 3D*** arranges all open windows in a three-dimensional stack that you can quickly flip through. Figure 1.15 shows a sample Aero Flip 3D stack. Hold down the Windows logo key and press Tab to cycle through open windows. Release the Windows logo key to stop on any window. You can also click any window in the stack to display it.

Given what you know about resizing and moving windows, you can rearrange windows to suit your purposes. You can minimize or close those that are not necessary, returning to them later. Even so, you might prefer to let Windows 7 arrange your windows automatically. Windows 7 can arrange windows in a cascading fashion, vertically stacked, or side by side. If multiple windows are open on the desktop, right-click an empty part of the taskbar. Click Cascade windows, Show windows stacked, or Show windows side by side.

Snap arranges windows automatically along the left and right sides of the desktop.

Snap is a Windows 7 feature that will automatically place a window on the side of the desktop, resulting in a well-ordered arrangement of windows. Simply drag the title bar of a window to the left or right side of the desktop until an outline of the window appears. Release the mouse button. Do the same with another window.

Earlier in this section, you learned about Aero Peek. Another function of Aero Peek is to provide a quick way to show the desktop without actually removing or minimizing windows. Simply

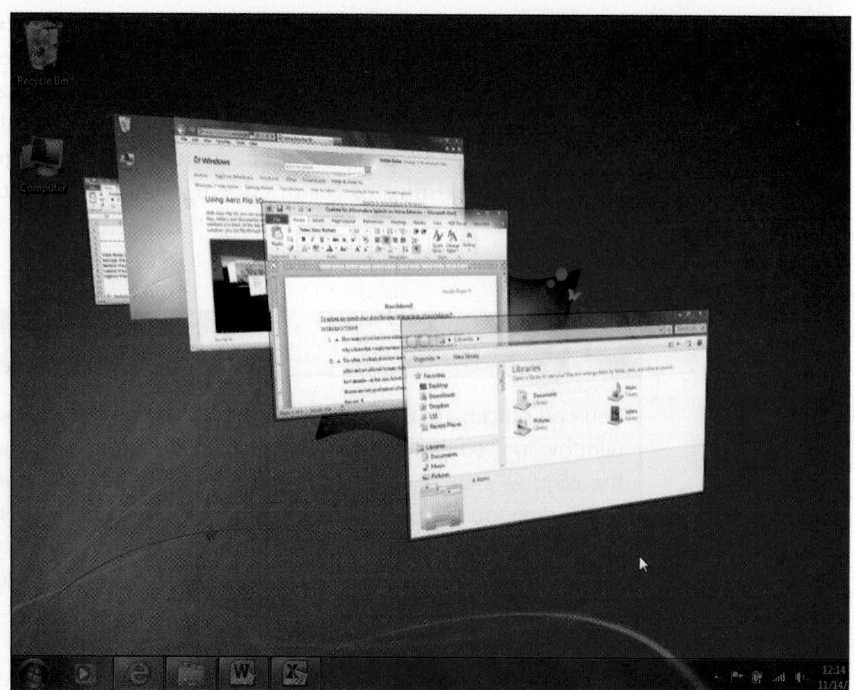

FIGURE 1.15 Aero Flip 3D Stack ➤

point to the Show desktop button, shown in Figure 1.16. To see the desktop temporarily, do point to the Show desktop button to display the desktop. Move the insertion point off of the button to make windows reappear. To minimize all open windows, click the Show desktop button. Click the button again to return the windows to view (or click the corresponding icons on the taskbar).

A **dialog box** is a special window that opens when you are accomplishing a specific task and when your confirmation or interaction is required.

The preceding discussion of windows focused on those windows that represent programs, files, or folders. Those could be considered standard windows. A ***dialog box*** is a special window that displays when an operation requires confirmation or additional information. A dialog box asks for interaction with you before completing a procedure. By responding to areas of the dialog box, you can indicate how you want an operation to occur and how the program should behave. You cannot minimize or maximize a dialog box, but you can move it. You can close it or make selections, get help by clicking the ? button (if present), and click OK (or Cancel if you want to ignore any selections you have made). The Print dialog box is shown in Figure 1.17 and summarized below.

- *Option buttons* indicate mutually exclusive choices, one of which *must* be chosen, such as the page range. In this example, you can print all pages, the selection (if it is available), the current page, or a specific set of pages (such as pages 1–4), but you

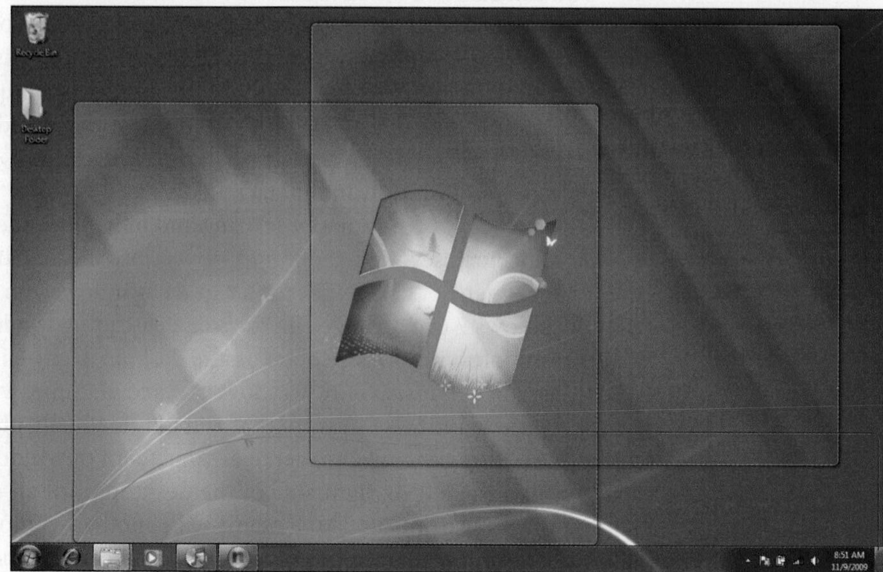

FIGURE 1.16 Showing the Desktop ➤

must choose *one and only one* option. When you select an option, any previously selected option is deselected.

- A *text box*, such as the one shown beside the *Pages* option in Figure 1.17, enables you to enter information. In this case, you would type the pages you want to print.
- A *spin arrow* is provides a quick method of increasing or decreasing a setting. For example, clicking the spin arrow (or spinner) beside *Number of copies* enables you to increase or decrease the number of copies of the document to print.
- *Check boxes* are used instead of option buttons if the choices are not mutually exclusive. Clicking a check box toggles the setting on and off. In Figure 1.17, you can select either or both options of printing to a file or using manual duplex. Unlike an option button, check boxes enable you to make several selections.
- A *list box* displays some or all of the available choices, any of which can be selected by clicking the list item. For example, you can choose from several print options, including printing all pages, or only odd or even pages.
- All dialog boxes also contain one or more *command buttons* that provide options to either accept or cancel your selections. OK, for example, initiates the printing process shown in Figure 1.17. Cancel does just the opposite and ignores (cancels) any changes made to the settings, closing the dialog box.

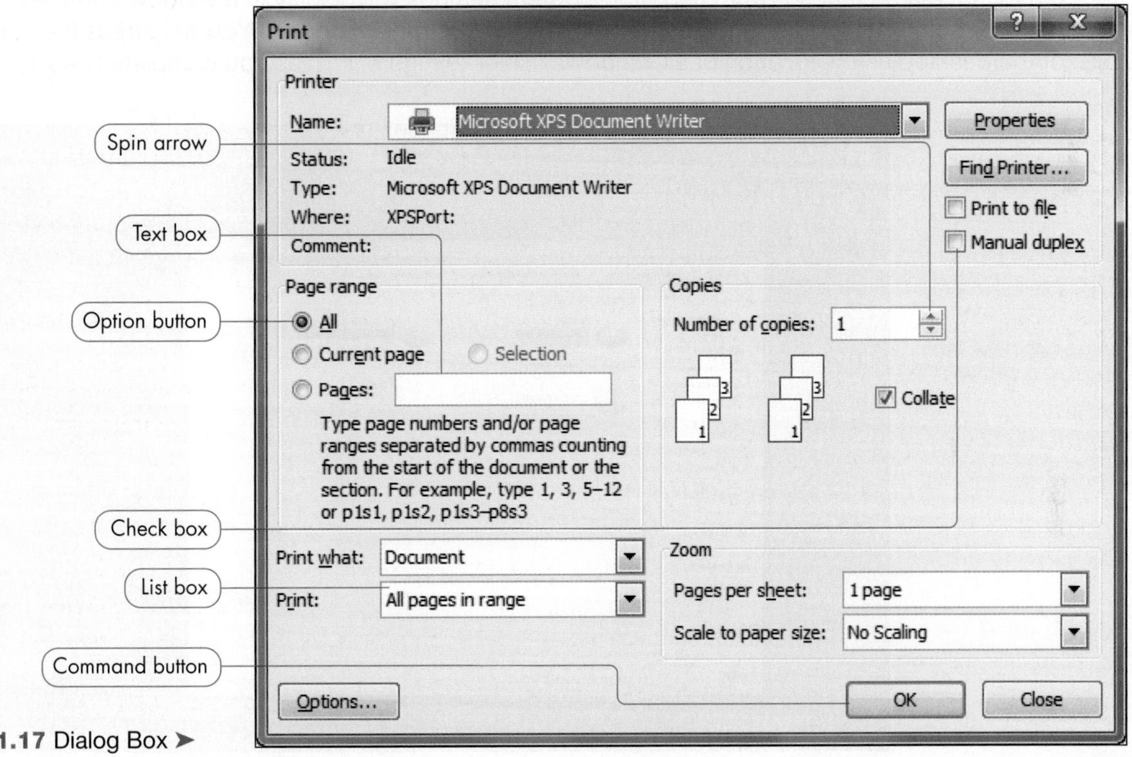

FIGURE 1.17 Dialog Box ➤

Quick Concepts Check

1. The taskbar serves several purposes in the Windows 7 operating system. Name and describe two of the reasons a taskbar is helpful.
2. The Start menu is comprised of three areas. Name and describe those areas.
3. Although pinning a program and creating a shortcut are different activities, they do share similarities. How are the two activities similar and how are they different?
4. In what ways can you customize the desktop when you right-click an empty area of the desktop and then click Personalize?
5. Windows enables you to work with several applications at one time, with each application represented in a window. Windows on the desktop can easily overlap and obscure one another. Describe at least two ways that you can organize open windows or cycle through them so that they are visible and easily accessible.

NDS-ON EXERCISES

1 Windows 7 Fundamentals

Tomorrow, you will meet with the Cedar Cove class to present an introduction to Windows 7. Only one computer is present in the classroom, and it is connected to a projector. You plan to demonstrate a few basics of working with the operating system including managing windows, adding gadgets, and working with the taskbar and Start menu. Above all, you want to keep it simple so that you encourage class enthusiasm. You have prepared a script that you plan to follow and you will practice it in the steps that follow.

Skills covered: Open, Resize, Move, and Close a window • Manage Multiple Windows, Arrange Windows Automatically, Arrange Windows Using *Snap* • Add and Remove Gadgets, Add Shortcuts to the Desktop, Identify Icons • Explore the Start Menu, Pin Items to the Start Menu, Customize the Taskbar, Pin Items to the Taskbar • Change the Desktop Background and Screen Saver

STEP 1 OPEN, RESIZE, MOVE, AND CLOSE A WINDOW

Before the students can work with software, they must learn to work with windows. Specifically, they must understand that software and other system settings will display in a window and they must become comfortable opening, closing, resizing, and moving windows. You will stress the importance of the desktop as the location of all windows. Refer to Figure 1.18 as you complete Step 1.

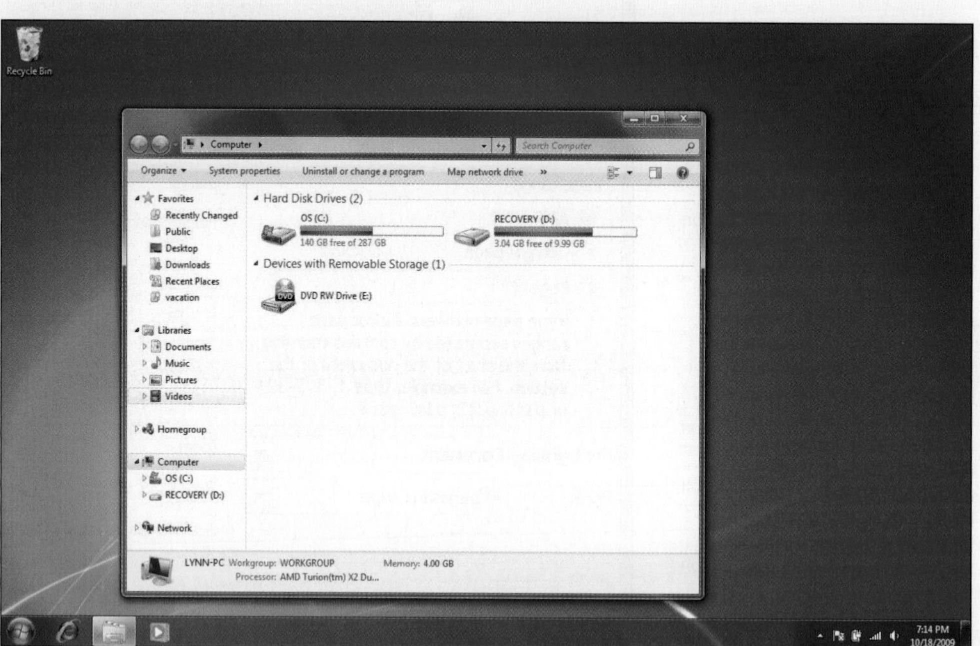

FIGURE 1.18 Computer Window ➤

a. Click the **Start button**. Click **Computer** in the right pane.

   You have opened the Computer window, giving a summary of your computer's disk configuration. The window contents are not important at this time; you are interested in it only as an example of a window that you can use to demonstrate Windows basics.

b. Compare the window to that shown in Figure 1.18. If the window already fills the desktop, click the **Restore Down button** (the middle button) to restore the window to a smaller size. If it is less than full size, leave it as is.

c. Place the mouse pointer on a corner of the window. The pointer should appear as a double-headed arrow. Drag to make the window slightly smaller.

d. Place the mouse pointer on the title bar of the window. Drag to move it to another location on the desktop.

e. Place the mouse pointer on the top border of the window. Drag to make the window slightly larger.

f. Click the **Close button** (shown as an X) in the top-right corner of the window to close it.

STEP 2 MANAGE MULTIPLE WINDOWS, ARRANGE WINDOWS AUTOMATICALLY, ARRANGE WINDOWS USING *SNAP*

Because there will be occasions when several windows are open simultaneously, students must learn to arrange them. You will show them various ways that Windows 7 can help arrange open windows. Refer to Figure 1.19 as you complete Step 2.

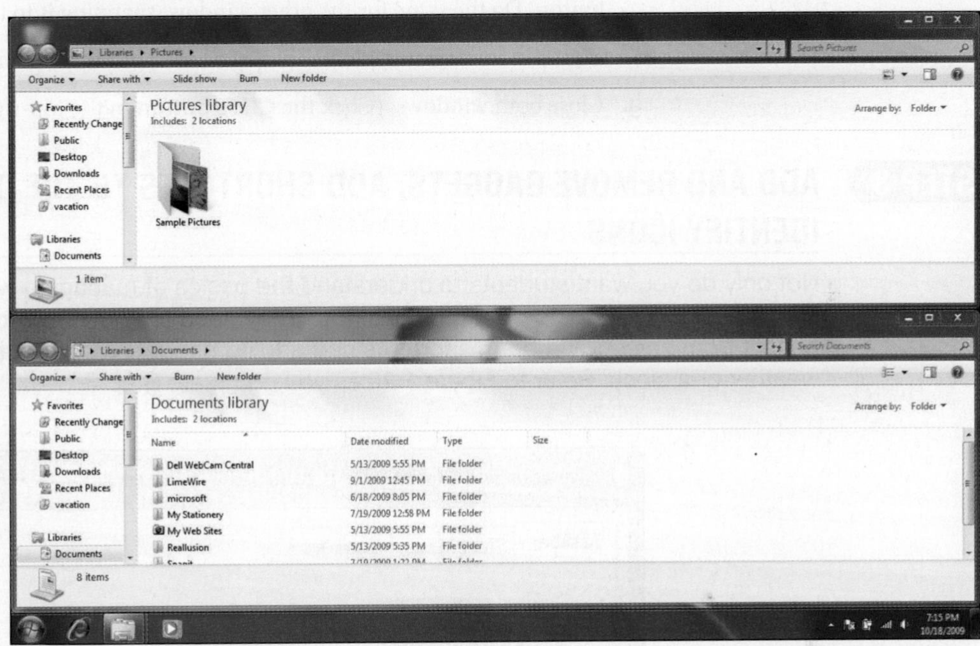

FIGURE 1.19 Working with Two Windows ➤

a. Click the **Start button**. Click **Documents** in the right pane. Click the **Start button**. Click **Pictures** in the right pane.

> **TROUBLESHOOTING:** If the two windows open so that one is directly on top of the other, obscuring the lower window, drag the title bar of the topmost window to move the window so that you can see both.

You have opened two windows—Pictures and Documents. You are going to show students various ways to arrange the open windows. The two open windows are most likely overlapped, but if yours are not, that's OK. Just make sure both windows are open.

b. Right-click an empty part of the taskbar. Click **Show windows stacked**. Compare your desktop with Figure 1.19.

The contents of the windows will vary, but the arrangement should be similar.

> **TROUBLESHOOTING:** If your desktop displays more than two stacked windows, you have more than two windows open. You should make sure that only the Pictures and Documents windows are open. Close any others by right-clicking the corresponding taskbar icon and clicking Close window.

c. Right-click an empty part of the taskbar. Click **Show windows side by side**.

The two windows should line up vertically.

d. Click the **Close button** in both windows to close them.

e. Click the **Start button**. Click **Computer**. Click the **Start button**. Click **Control Panel**.

> **TROUBLESHOOTING:** If either window opens at full size (maximized), click the Restore Down button (middle button) at the top-right side of the title bar to make the window smaller.

You have opened two windows—Computer and Control Panel. You will use the Windows Snap feature to position each window on a side of the desktop.

f. Drag the title bar of one of the windows to one side of the desktop. Keep dragging the window, even beyond the desktop edge, until a window outline appears. Release the mouse button. Do the same for the other window, snapping it to the opposite side of the desktop.

Both windows should be evenly spaced, each occupying half of the desktop.

g. Close both windows. (Click the **Close button** in the top-right corner of each.)

STEP 3 ADD AND REMOVE GADGETS, ADD SHORTCUTS TO THE DESKTOP, IDENTIFY ICONS

Not only do you want students to understand the basics of managing windows, but you know that they will also enjoy customizing the desktop. They need to know how to identify icons. They will also benefit from creating program shortcuts and adding gadgets for constantly changing items like the weather or a clock. Refer to Figure 1.20 as you complete Step 3.

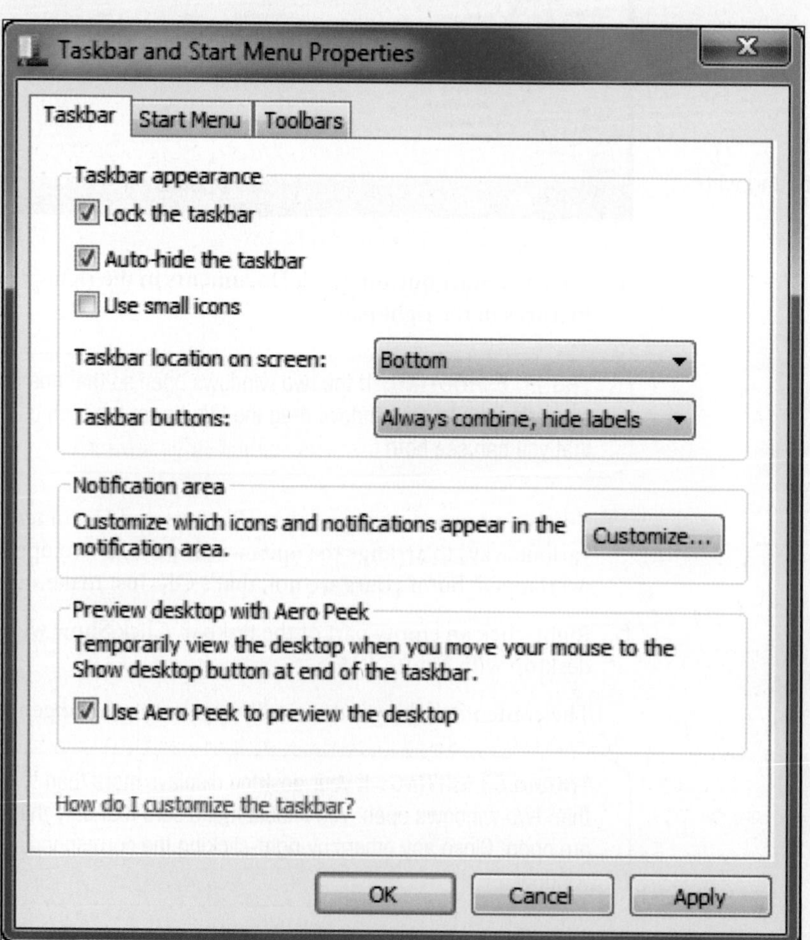

FIGURE 1.20 Taskbar and Start Menu Properties ➤

a. Note any icons on the desktop that have an arrow in the bottom-left corner. They represent programs or system resources. Double-click an icon to open the item window. Close the window by clicking the **Close button** in the top-right corner.

b. Right-click an empty area of the taskbar. Click **Properties**. Click the **Auto-hide the taskbar check box** (unless a checkmark already appears), as shown in Figure 1.20. Click **OK**.

   The taskbar will only show if you place the mouse pointer near where it should show. When you move the mouse pointer away, the taskbar disappears. You will explain to students that they can use the Taskbar and Start Menu Properties dialog box to customize the appearance and behavior of the taskbar.

c. Move the mouse pointer to the location of the taskbar. Right-click an empty area of the taskbar. Click **Properties**. Click to deselect the **Auto-hide the taskbar check box**. Click **OK**.

d. Click the **Start button**. Point to **All Programs**. Click **Accessories**. Right-click and drag Paint to the desktop. Release the mouse button. Click **Create shortcuts here**.

   TROUBLESHOOTING: To create a shortcut on the desktop, you must be able to see the desktop. Therefore, all windows should be closed before you drag the program from the Start menu. Also, be sure to use the right mouse button to drag, not the left.

   You have placed a program shortcut on the desktop so that you can easily find it later. The arrow in the lower-left corner of the Paint icon indicates that it is a shortcut.

e. Right-click the **Paint shortcut icon** on the desktop. Click **Delete**. Click **Yes** to confirm the deletion.

   Because you want to leave the classroom's computer just as you found it, you will delete the Paint shortcut from the desktop.

f. Right-click an empty area of the desktop. Click **Gadgets**. Double-click **Clock**. The Clock gadget appears on the right side of the desktop. Double-click **Weather** to add a Weather gadget.

   TROUBLESHOOTING: You must be connected to the Internet for the Weather gadget to display. If you are not connected, you will see a note to that effect where the gadget would have been placed.

g. Right-click the **Clock gadget**, and then click **Close gadget**. Do the same for the Weather gadget.

   Because you want to leave the classroom's computer as you found it, you will close the Clock and Weather gadgets.

h. Click the **Close button** to close the Gadgets window.

STEP 4 EXPLORE THE START MENU, PIN ITEMS TO THE START MENU, CUSTOMIZE THE TASKBAR, PIN ITEMS TO THE TASKBAR

Upon completing the fifth grade, the students with whom you are working will advance to middle school. There, they will be expected to be comfortable with Windows 7. You will be with them for only a couple of class sessions, so you want to use your time to make sure they are introduced to the Start menu, understand the purpose of icons, and are confident with customizing the taskbar. With just a little practice, they will be well-prepared for middle school computer work. Refer to Figure 1.21 as you complete Step 4.

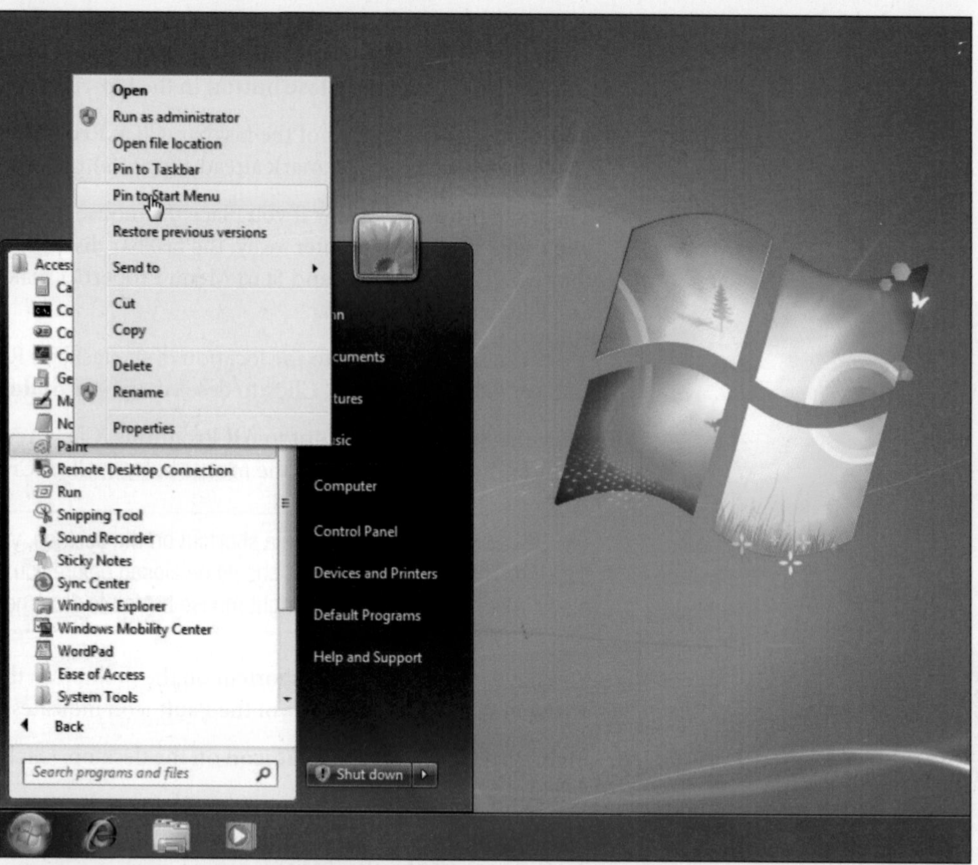

FIGURE 1.21 Pin a Program to Start Menu ➤

a. Click the **Start button**. Note the programs that display on the left side of the menu. Take a look at the right side of the menu. Click **Pictures**. Close the window that represents the Pictures folder.

   You will explain to students that the left side of the Start menu contains commonly accessed programs or those that have been pinned to the Start menu. The right side includes system folders, such as Pictures, Documents, and Music; the Control Panel; and Help and Support. The Search box, located at the bottom-left side of the Start menu, enables searches based on keywords.

b. Click the **Start button**. Point to **All Programs**. Click **Accessories**. Scroll, if necessary, to show Paint. Right-click **Paint**. Click **Pin to Start Menu**, as shown in Figure 1.21. Click outside the Start menu to remove it from view.

   The example you will give students is that in some classes they will have a recurring need to open the Paint program. You want them to practice pinning the program to the Start menu.

c. Click the **Start button**. Check to make sure Paint appears on the left side of the menu. Click **Paint** to open it. Click the **Close button** to close the program.

   TROUBLESHOOTING: If you have recently opened Paint files, you might find it necessary to click Paint twice to open the program.

d. Click the **Start button**. Note that because Paint is a pinned program, it appears above the line on the left side of the Start menu. Right-click **Paint**. Click **Unpin from Start Menu**. Click outside the Start menu to remove it from view.

   Because you want to leave the classroom's computer as you found it, you will unpin the Paint program from the Start menu.

e. Click the **Start button**. Point to **All Programs**. Click **Accessories**. Point to **WordPad** and right-click. Click **Pin to Taskbar**. Click outside the Start menu to remove the menu from view.

Students will need to know that if they open a program often, it is easy to pin it to the taskbar for quick access. That way, they won't have to find it on the Start menu or double-click an icon on the desktop. Instead, they can single-click the icon on the taskbar.

f. Click the **WordPad icon** on the taskbar. If you are not sure which icon is WordPad, place the mouse pointer over any icon and see the program name. Then locate WordPad. After WordPad opens, close it. Right-click the **WordPad icon** on the taskbar, and then click **Unpin this program from taskbar**.

After demonstrating the use of a pinned icon (by opening the associated program), you remove the pinned icon from the taskbar.

STEP 5 CHANGE THE DESKTOP BACKGROUND AND SCREEN SAVER

To end the class session on a creative note, you want the students to have fun changing the desktop background and experimenting with screen savers. Refer to Figures 1.22 and 1.23 as you complete Step 5.

TROUBLESHOOTING: If you are working in a campus lab, you might not be able to change the desktop background or screen saver. In that case, you cannot complete this step of the Hands-On Exercise.

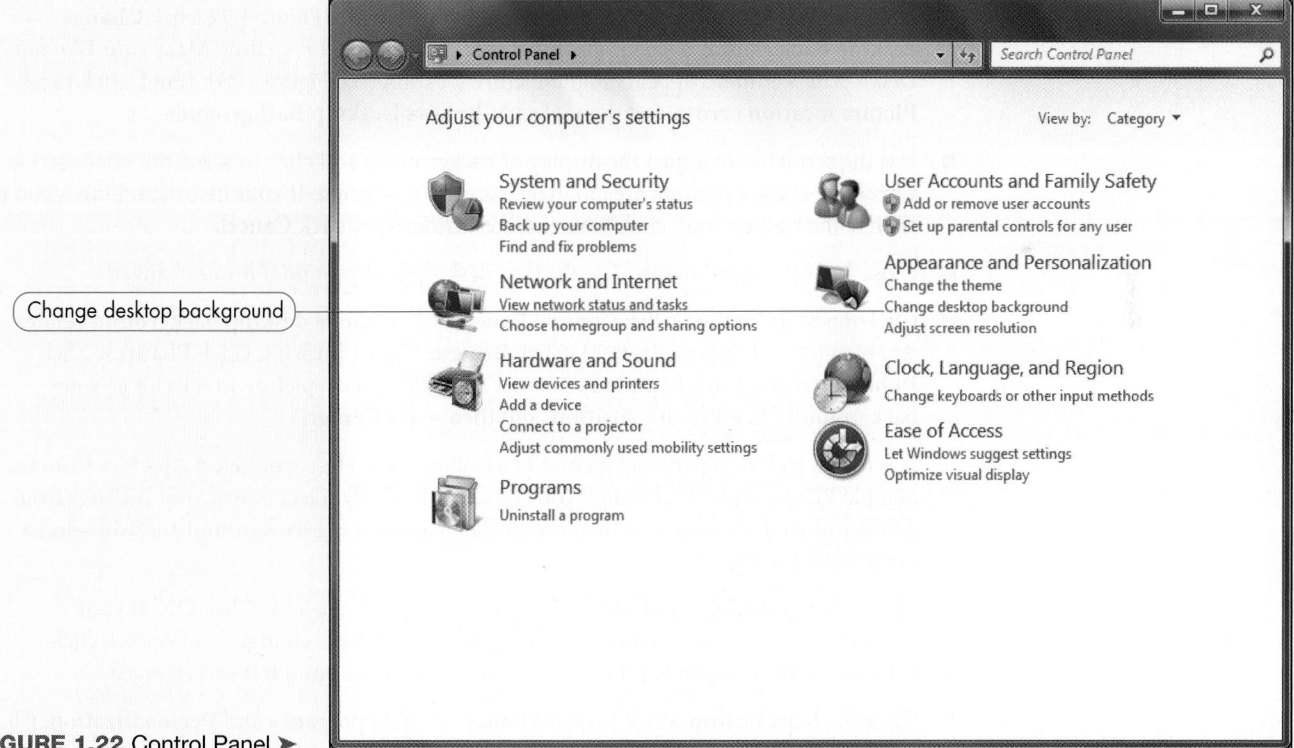

FIGURE 1.22 Control Panel ➤

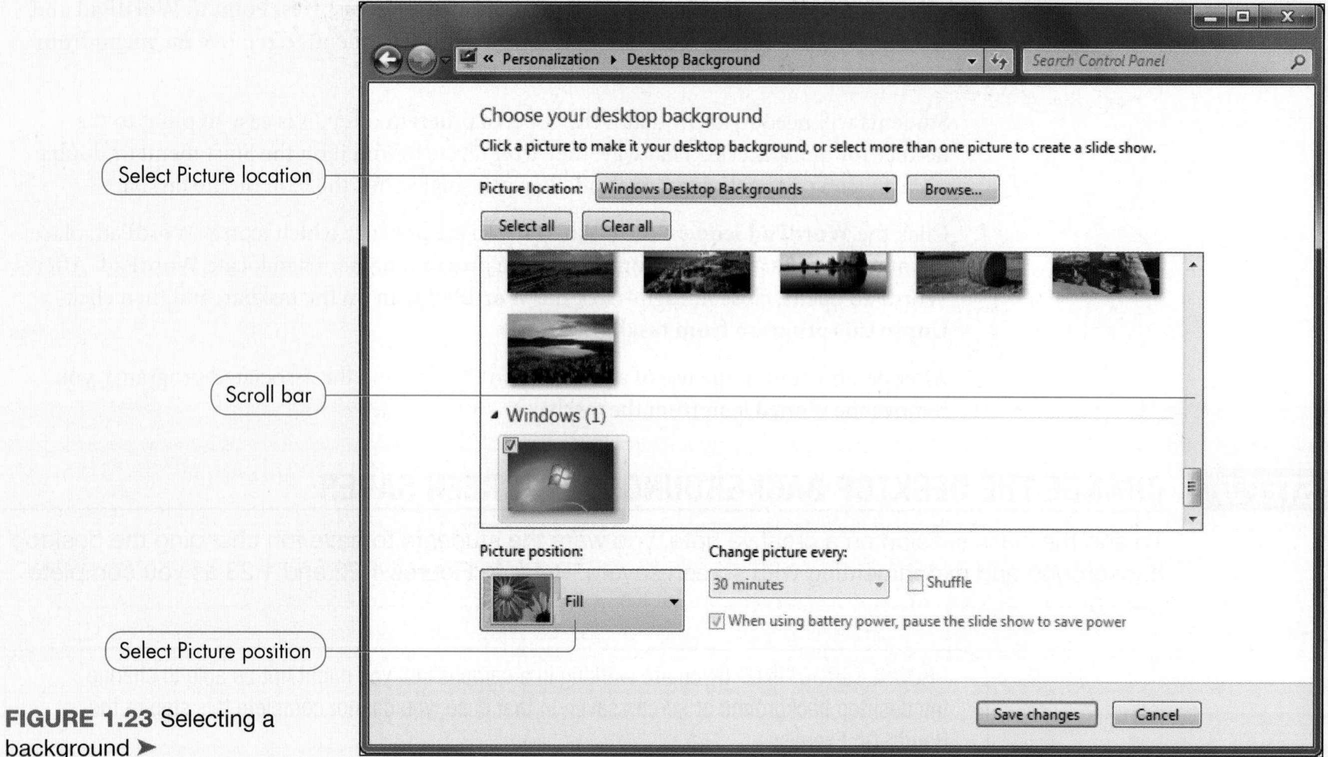

FIGURE 1.23 Selecting a background ➤

a. Click the **Start button**. Click **Control Panel**. As shown in Figure 1.22, click **Change desktop background** in the *Appearance and Personalization* section. Make sure *Windows Desktop Backgrounds* appears in the Picture location (see Figure 1.23). If not, click the **Picture location arrow**, and then select **Windows Desktop Backgrounds**.

b. Use the scroll bar to adjust the display of backgrounds and click to select one that you like. Check the *Picture position* area to make sure *Fill* is selected. If your instructor allows you to change the background, click **Save changes**. Otherwise, click **Cancel**.

c. Close any open windows to view the new desktop background if it was changed.

d. Click the **Start button**. Click **Control Panel**. Click **Change desktop background** (under *Appearance and Personalization*). Click **Browse**. Click **Libraries**. Click **Pictures**. Click **Public Pictures**. Click **Sample Pictures**. Click **OK**. Click a picture to select it as your background. Click **Picture position**, and then select **Center**.

   It is fun to include a personal picture as a background. Here, you select a picture from the Sample Pictures folder (although you could just as easily select one of your pictures from a folder of your choice). You then center the picture on the background and will select a border color in the next step.

e. Click **Change background color**. Select a color from the palette. Click **OK**. If your instructor allows you to change the background, click **Save changes**. Otherwise, click **Cancel**. Close any open windows to view the new background if it was changed.

f. Click the **Start button**. Click **Control Panel**. Click **Appearance and Personalization**. Click **Change screen saver** (under *Personalization*). Click the **Screen saver arrow**. Select a screen saver. Click **Preview**. Press **Esc** to remove the screen saver from view. Note that you can also change the Wait time to specify the number of minutes the computer must remain idle before the screen saver appears. Click **Cancel** to avoid making the change permanent, or click **OK** if you are allowed to change the screen saver. Close any open windows.

   Unless you saved the screen saver change and unless you wait the required wait time for the screen saver to appear, you will see no changes.

Windows Programs and Security Features

Windows 7 is a full-featured operating system, including built-in programs for such tasks as word processing, creating graphics, and system security. With only a little effort, you can learn to use those programs. Regardless of how many programs you install on your computer system, you can take comfort in knowing that you will always have access to software supporting basic tasks and that your computer is protected against spyware and hacking. In this section, you will learn to work with Windows 7 accessory and security programs.

You can take comfort in knowing that you will always have access to software supporting basic tasks and that your computer is protected against spyware and hacking.

Identifying Windows Accessories

You use a computer for many purposes, but a primary reason to enjoy a computer is to run programs. A program is software that accomplishes a specific task. You use a word processing program to prepare documents, an e-mail program to compose and send e-mail, and a database program to maintain records. You can customize a computer by installing programs of your choice. Windows 7 provides a few programs for basic tasks, as well. Those programs include WordPad, Notepad, Paint, Snipping Tool, and Calculator.

Use Notepad and WordPad

Notepad is a text editing program built in to Windows 7.

WordPad is a basic word processing program built in to Windows 7.

Notepad and ***WordPad*** are programs that enable you to create and print documents. Notepad is a basic text editing program used primarily to edit text files, files that are identified with a .txt extension. Programmers sometimes use Notepad to prepare basic program statements. Notepad is not at all concerned with style and does not include the features of typical word processing software such as document formatting and character design.

WordPad, on the other hand, is a basic word processing program, and includes the capability of formatting text and inserting graphics. Not as full-featured as Microsoft Word, WordPad is still a handy alternative when you do not have access to Word or when you want to quickly create a simple document. WordPad saves documents in a Microsoft Word format, so you can open WordPad files in Word.

Figure 1.24 shows both WordPad and Notepad windows. Note the bare-bones appearance of Notepad when compared with WordPad. Access either program by clicking the Start button. Point to All Programs. Click Accessories. Make a program selection.

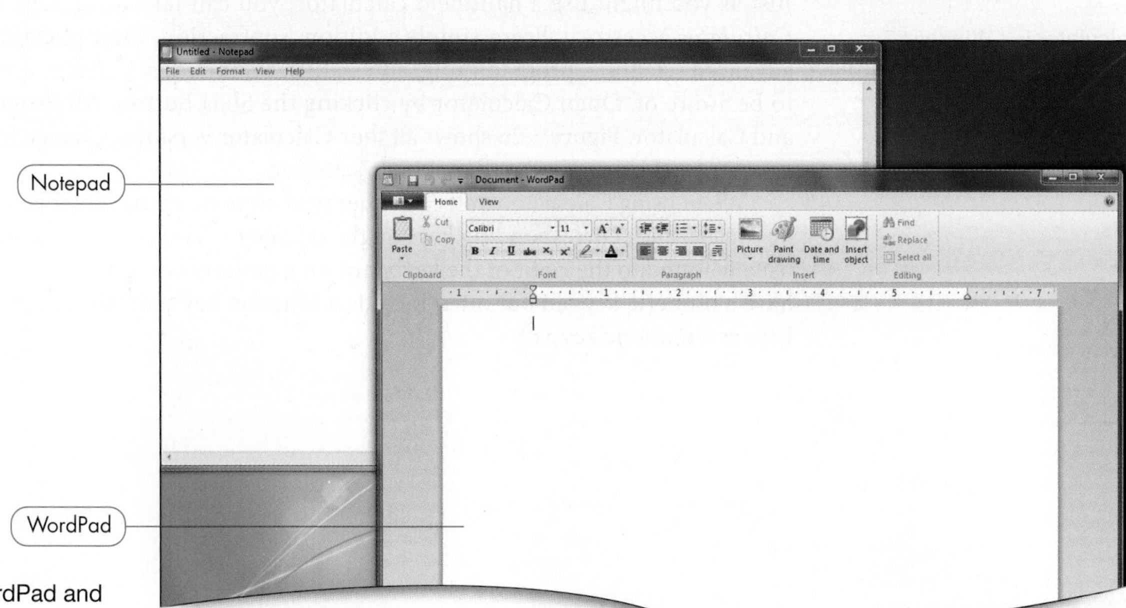

FIGURE 1.24 WordPad and Notepad ➤

Use Paint

Paint is a Windows 7 accessory that enables you to create graphics by drawing and adding text.

Paint is a Windows 7 program that enables you to create drawings and to open digital pictures. You will recall that you opened Paint in Hands-On Exercise 1. Figure 1.25 shows the Paint interface. Note the Ribbon at the top of the Paint window that includes such items as the Pencil tool, Brushes, Colors, and Shapes. Open Paint by clicking the Start button, All Programs, Accessories, and Paint. The palette in the center of the Paint window acts as an easel on which you can draw.

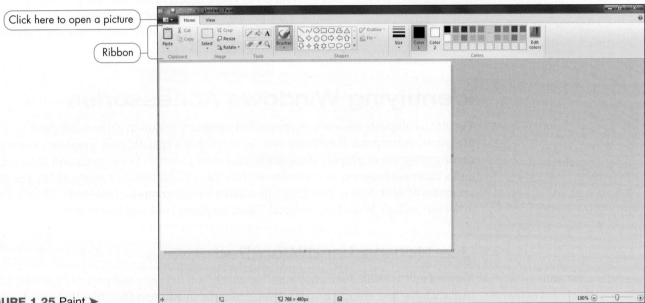

FIGURE 1.25 Paint ➤

When you open Paint, you can create and save a colorful drawing, including text, shapes, and background color. You can also open a digital photo and add comments, shapes, or drawings. If you want to work with an existing picture, open the photo by clicking the button in the top-left corner of the Paint window (see Figure 1.25). Click Open, browse to the location of the picture, and double-click the picture. Then use Paint tools to add to the picture, saving it when done.

Use the Calculator

Calculator is a Windows 7 accessory that acts as a handheld calculator with different views—standard, scientific, programming, and statistical.

Just as you might use a handheld calculator, you can take advantage of the Windows 7 ***Calculator*** accessory. From simple addition, subtraction, multiplication, and division to advanced scientific, programming, and statistical functions, Calculator is a very handy tool to be aware of. Open Calculator by clicking the Start button, All Programs, Accessories, and Calculator. Figure 1.26 shows all four Calculator versions. Change from one version to another by clicking View and making a selection.

When using Calculator, you can either type numeric entries and operators (+, –, *, and /) or you can click corresponding keys on the calculator. You can also use the numeric keypad, usually found to the right of the keyboard on a desktop computer. Laptops do not typically have a numeric keypad but often include a function key that you can press to use alternate keys as a numeric keypad.

FIGURE 1.26 Calculator Views ➤

> **TIP** Use Sticky Notes
>
> Sticky Notes is a fun and useful Windows 7 accessory. Open Sticky Notes by clicking the Start button, All Programs, Accessories, and Sticky Notes. Use the program as you would a paper sticky note, recording to-do lists, phone numbers, or anything else. Your notes appear as stick-up notes on the desktop. Click New Note to add another note, click Delete Note to delete a note, and right-click a note to change the color.

Use the Snipping Tool

The **Snipping Tool** is a Windows 7 accessory that enables you to capture and save a screen display.

A **snip** is a screen display that you have captured with the Snipping Tool.

The ***Snipping Tool*** is a Windows 7 accessory program that enables you to capture, or ***snip***, a screen display so that you can save, annotate, or share it. On occasion, you might need to capture an image of the screen for use in a report or to document an error for later troubleshooting. Using the Snipping Tool (see Figure 1.27), you can capture screen elements in a rectangular, free-form, window, or full-screen fashion. Then you can draw on or annotate the screen captures, save them, or send them to others.

FIGURE 1.27 Snipping Tool ➤

Open the Snipping Tool by clicking the Start button, All Programs, Accessories, and Snipping Tool. Click the New arrow and select a snip type (rectangular, free-form, etc.). If you select a window snip type, you will click the window to capture. If you select rectangular or free-form, you must drag to identify the area to capture. Of course, it is not necessary to specify an area when you select full-screen capture.

After you capture a snip, it is displayed in the mark-up window, where you can write or draw on it. The screen capture is also copied to the Clipboard, which is a temporary holding area in your computer's memory. You can then paste the screen capture in a word processing document when the document is displayed by clicking Paste on the word processor's toolbar. The Clipboard is temporary storage only. Because the Clipboard's contents are lost when your computer is powered down, you should immediately paste a copied screen image if it is your intention to include the screen capture in a document or other application. Otherwise, you can save a screen capture by clicking Save Snip and indicating a location and file name for the snip.

Working with Security Settings and Software

So that you can enjoy your computer for a long time, you will want to protect it from security threats such as viruses, spyware, and hacking. Windows 7 monitors your security status, providing recommendations for security settings and software updates as needed. Although Windows 7 provides a firewall and antispyware software, you should make sure your computer is also protected against viruses. Such protection requires that you install antivirus software that is not included with Windows 7. Although you are not protected against viruses automatically, Windows 7 does have security features. ***Windows Defender*** is antispyware software included with Windows 7. It identifies and removes ***spyware***, which is software that is usually downloaded without your awareness, collecting personal information from your computer. Windows 7 also includes a ***firewall*** to protect against unauthorized access (hacking).

Windows 7 monitors your security status, providing recommendations for security settings and software updates as needed.

Windows Defender is a program that identifies and removes spyware.

Spyware is software that gathers information through a user's Internet connection, usually for advertising purposes. Spyware is most often installed without a user's permission.

A **firewall** is software or hardware that protects a computer or network from unauthorized access.

Understand the Action Center

Windows 7 monitors your system for various maintenance and security settings, recommending action through the Action Center when necessary. Open the Action Center by clicking the Start button, Control Panel, System and Security, and then Action Center. In

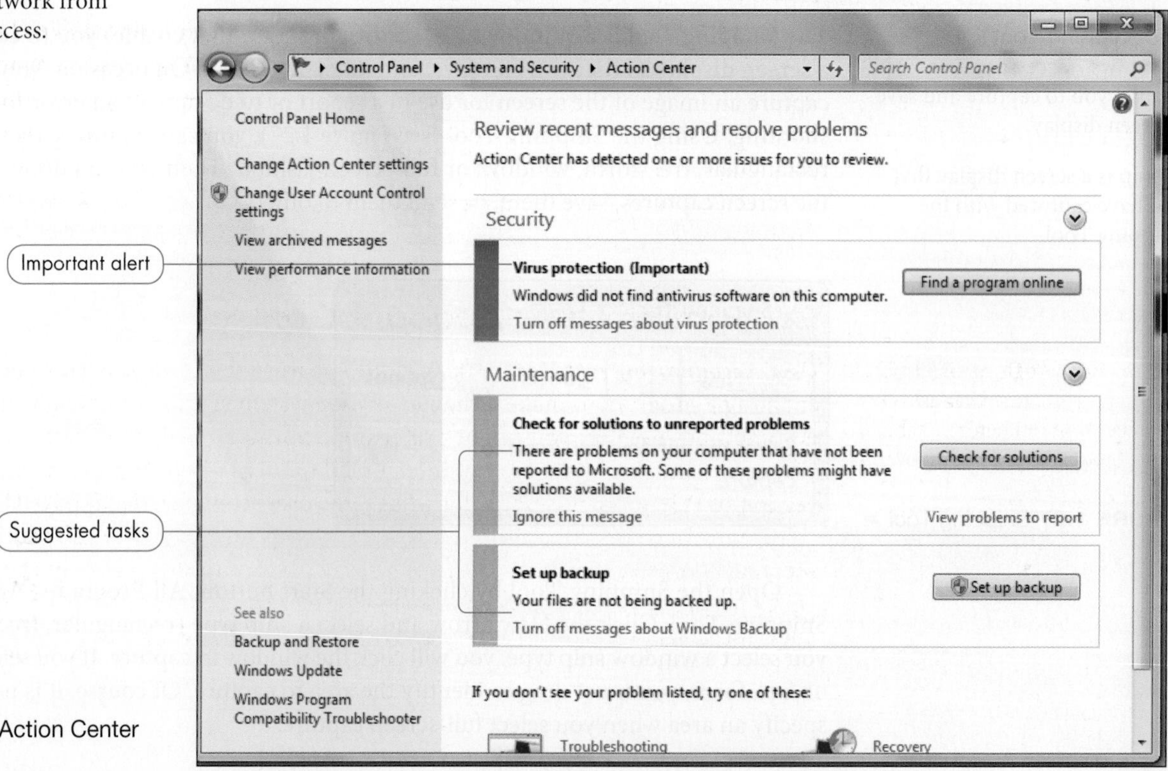

FIGURE 1.28 Action Center Alerts ➤

Figure 1.28, the Action Center gives several messages in order of severity. Red flags are for potentially serious or important alerts that should be addressed soon. Yellow items are suggested tasks, usually maintenance such as backing up files. For a quick summary of Action Center items, you can click the Action Center icon in the Notification area. Click a link on the summary list to explore a recommended action. When the status of a monitored item changes, perhaps when antivirus software becomes out of date, Action Center will display a message in a balloon (pop-up) on the Notification area (see Figure 1.29).

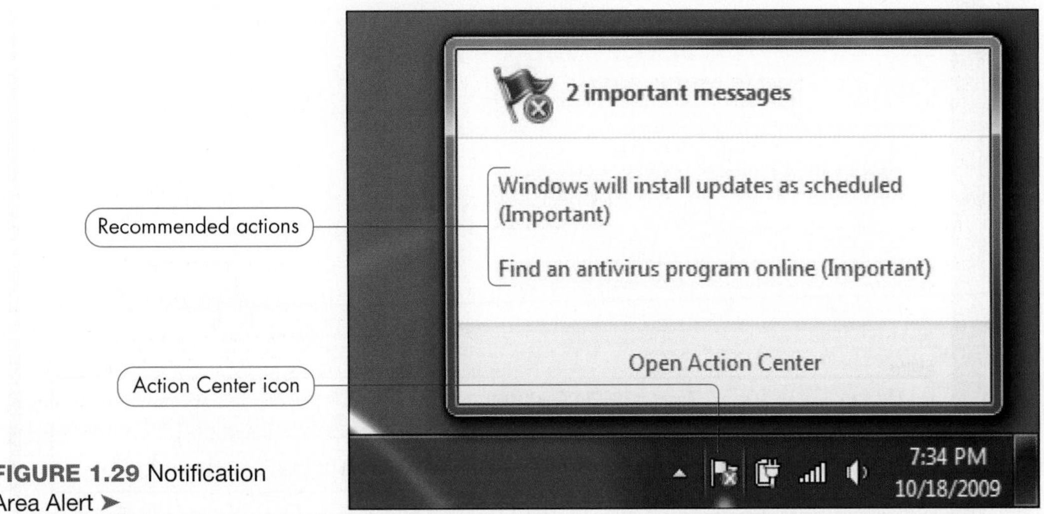

FIGURE 1.29 Notification Area Alert ➤

Use Windows Defender

You probably enjoy accessing Web sites and downloading programs. Although such activity is a great way to have fun, it carries a serious risk—downloading spyware along with the program. Actually, spyware can be installed on your computer whenever you connect to the Internet, regardless of whether you download anything. Spyware is usually installed without your knowledge. It can do anything from keeping track of Web sites you visit (for marketing purposes) to changing browser settings to recording keystrokes. Obviously, spyware is unwelcome and a potential security risk.

Windows Defender is antispyware software that is included with Windows 7. Windows Defender can be set to run in real time, which means that it is always on guard against spyware, alerting you when spyware attempts to install itself or change your computer settings. You can also schedule routine scans so that Windows Defender checks your system for malicious software. Open Windows Defender by clicking the Start button, typing Windows Defender in the Search box, and pressing Enter (or clicking the corresponding link in the Results list). Figure 1.30 shows the Windows Defender program window.

Customize User Account Control

User Account Control (UAC) is a Windows feature that asks for your permission before enabling any changes to your computer settings.

User Account Control (UAC) is a Windows feature that asks for your permission before enabling a program to make a change to your system settings. Although such information is sometimes helpful, you might prefer to be notified only when substantial changes are attempted; that way, you are not interrupted quite as often. Windows Vista, the previous version of Windows, was noted for what some users considered excessive UAC prompts.

If you have only one user account on your computer, it is an administrator-level account. Most likely, you are the administrator, which means that only you can respond to UAC messages. Other user accounts are considered standard accounts, with varying levels of permissions that you can choose to grant.

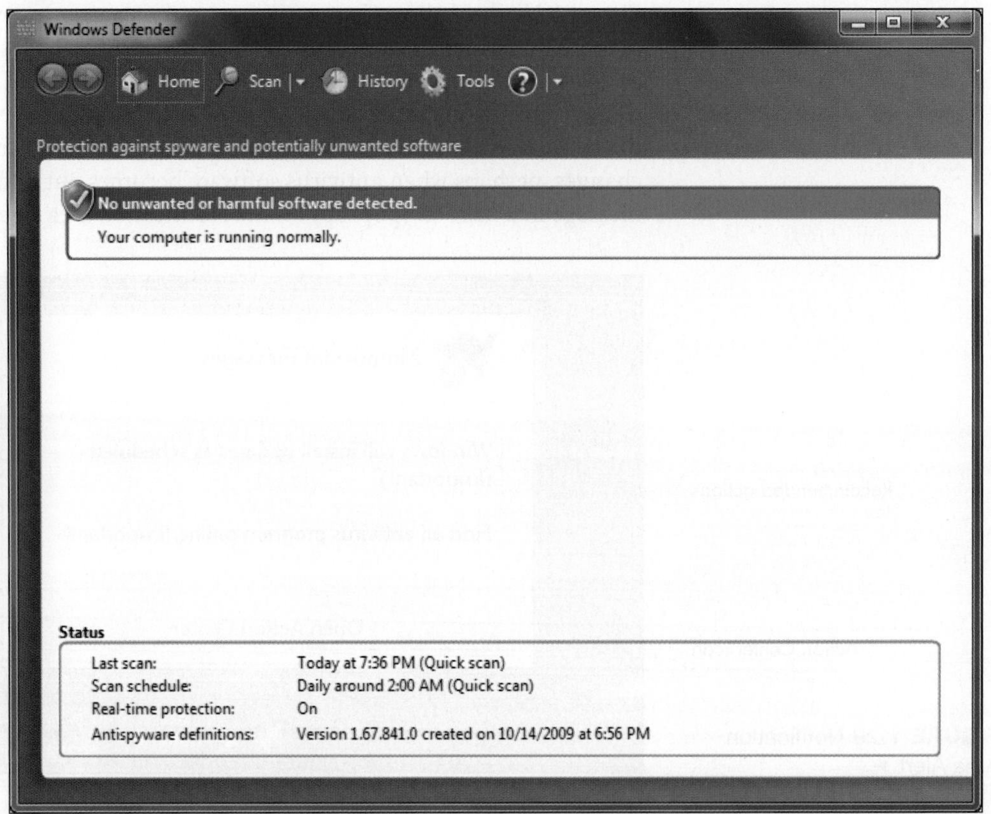

FIGURE 1.30 Windows Defender ➤

You might want to be informed of any changes that occur, even those that you initiate, that change your Windows settings. Or perhaps you prefer to know of only those changes attempted by programs. In either case, you can modify the level of UAC through the Action Center. Click the Start button, Control Panel, System and Security, and then Action Center. Click Change User Account Control settings. Adjust the bar in the dialog box shown in Figure 1.31.

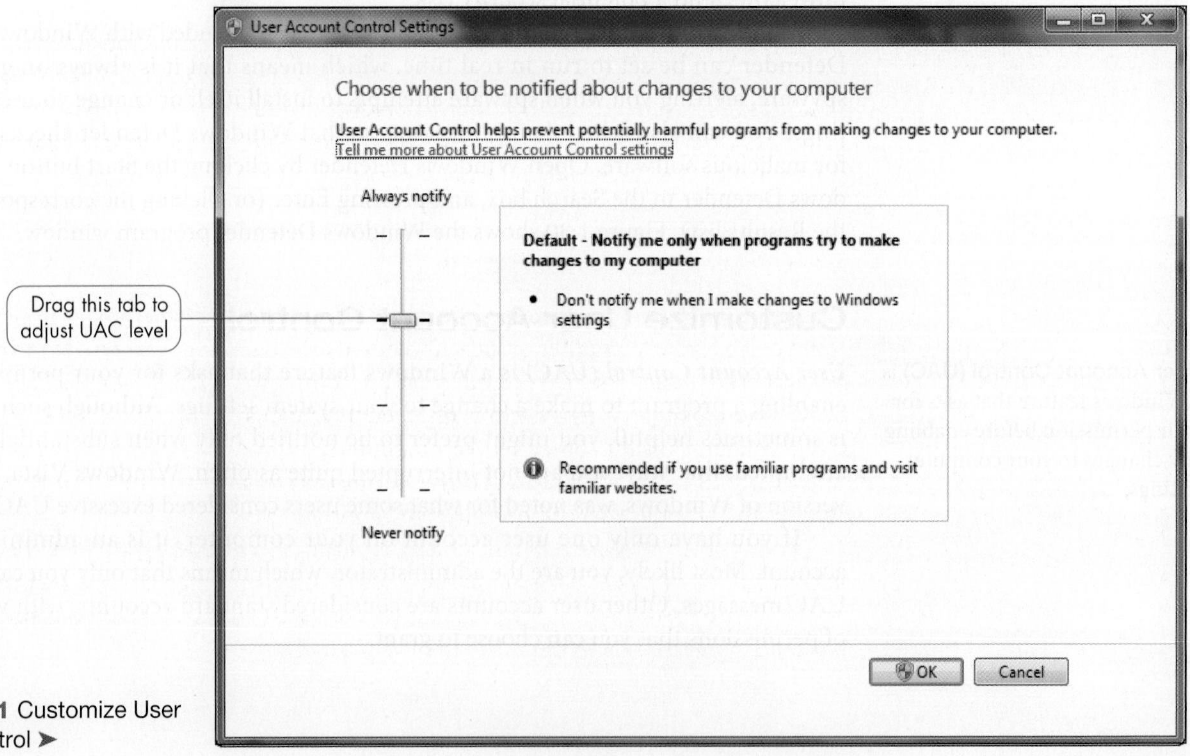

FIGURE 1.31 Customize User Account Control ➤

Access Windows Update

A **Windows Update** is an addition to the operating system that prevents or corrects problems, including security concerns.

When Microsoft makes changes to Windows 7 to enhance its security or fix problems that occur you can make sure that your computer is set to automatically download any updates (fixes). Such modifications to the operating system are called ***Windows Updates***.

Microsoft strongly recommends that you configure your computer to automatically download and install any updates. To schedule automatic updates, click the Start button, All Programs, and then Windows Update. Click Change settings. As shown in Figure 1.32, you can click to select the level of updates. You can have Windows both download and install updates automatically, only download but let you install them, or never check for updates. You can also schedule a time for updates to occur.

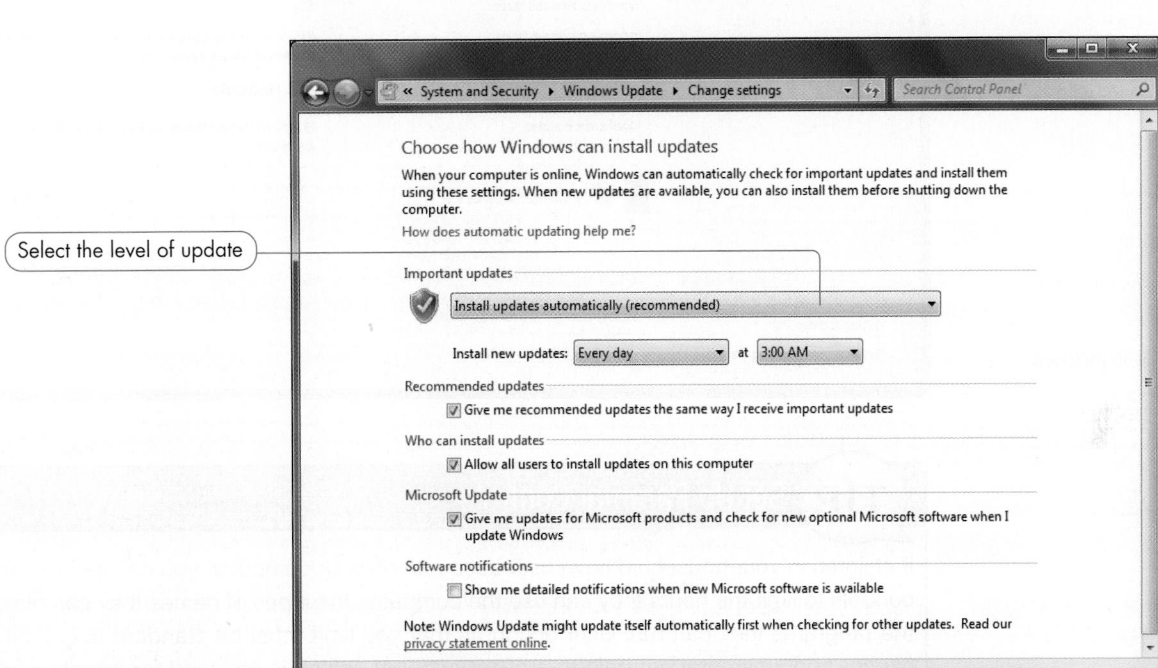

FIGURE 1.32 Windows Update ➤

Even between scheduled downloads, you can have your computer check for updates. Click the Start button, All Programs, Windows Update, and then Check for updates. If you want to check for updates for other Microsoft products, such as Microsoft Office, open Windows Update, and click Change settings. Select Give me updates for Microsoft products and check for new optional Microsoft software when I update Windows.

Use Windows Firewall

When you work with the Internet, the possibility that a self-replicating virus or another user could disable your computer or view its contents always exists. To keep that from occurring, it is imperative that you use firewall software. Windows 7 includes firewall software that is active when the operating system is installed. It remains on guard whenever your computer is on, which means that other people, computers, or programs are not allowed to communicate with your computer unless you give permission. Also, programs on your system are not allowed to communicate online unless you approve them.

To make sure your firewall has not been turned off accidentally. Click the Start button, select the Control Panel, select System and Security, and then click Check firewall status (under Windows Firewall). From the dialog box (see Figure 1.33), you can turn the firewall on or off. You can also adjust other firewall settings.

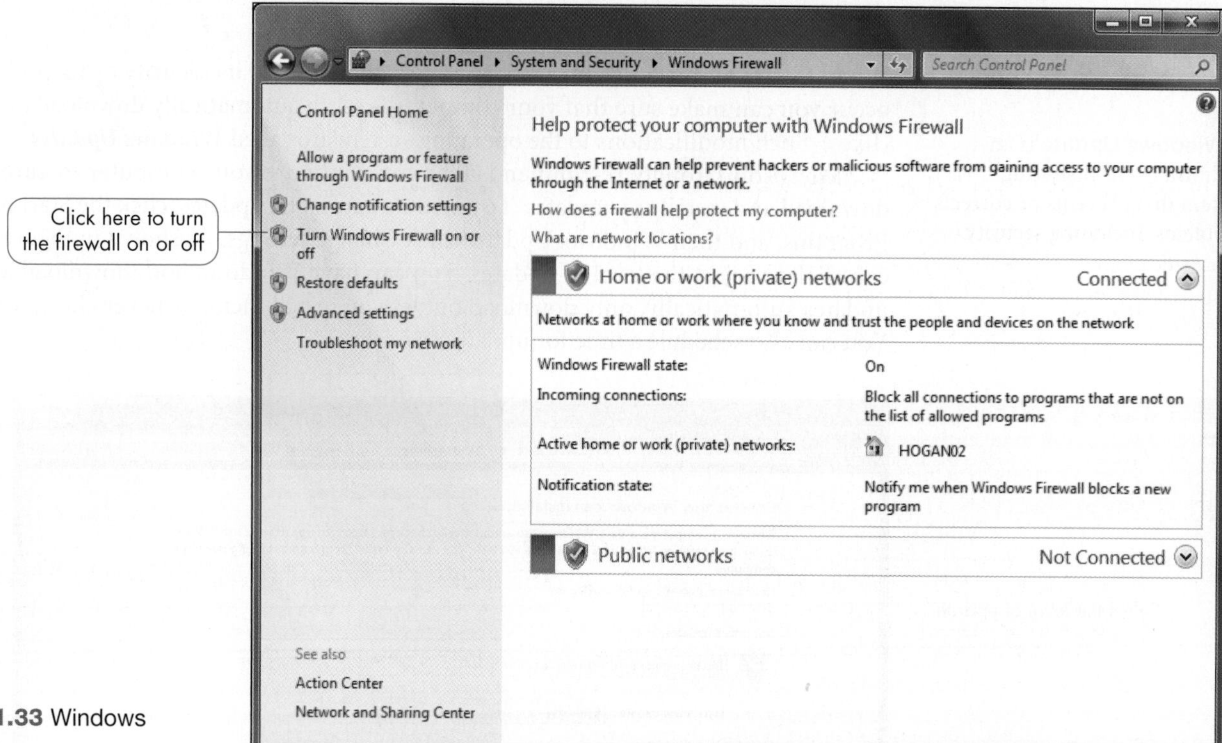

FIGURE 1.33 Windows Firewall ➤

TIP Set Up Parental Controls

If children in your household have user accounts on your computer, you can set up parental controls to limit the hours they can use the computer, the types of games they can play, and the programs they can run. User accounts that you limit must be standard accounts. You cannot apply parental controls to a guest account, which is reserved for people who use your computer on a temporary basis. If you plan to use parental controls, turn off the guest account (open the Control Panel, click Add or remove user accounts, click Guest, click Turn off the guest account). Open the Control Panel to create user accounts and assign standard privileges. To assign parental controls, open the Control Panel and click Set up parental controls for any user (under User Accounts and Family Safety). After selecting the user account to limit, apply any parental controls.

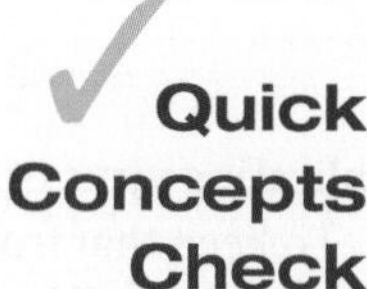

Quick Concepts Check

1. Notepad and WordPad are Windows 7 accessories that share commonalities. However, they are also unique in purpose. Compare and contrast the two programs, explaining how they are similar and how they are different.
2. The Action Center monitors a computer system for various maintenance and security concerns, displaying color-coded alerts. How can you open the Action Center? How is color used to indicate the severity of the alert? Where on the taskbar is the Action Center icon located and what happens when you access it?
3. Why is it important that you configure your system to automatically check for Windows Updates? Explain the process you would follow to schedule automatic updates. What steps would you follow to make sure the Windows firewall is active?
4. Why is it necessary to protect a computer with a firewall? Windows 7 provides a bidirectional firewall. What does the term "bidirectional" mean?

HANDS-ON EXERCISES

2 Windows Programs and Security Features

Windows is a gateway to using application software. You know that the fifth-grade students are most interested in the "fun" things that can be done with software. You want to excite them about having fun with a computer but you also want them to understand that along with the fun comes some concern about security and privacy. In this section of your demonstration, you will encourage them to explore software and to understand how Windows can help address security concerns.

Skills covered: Create a Wordpad Document, Use Calculator • Use the Action Center to Check Security and Privacy Settings • Use the Snipping Tool

STEP 1 CREATE A WORDPAD DOCUMENT, USE CALCULATOR

Because all computers are configured with different software, your demonstration to the class will focus on only those programs (software) that are built in to Windows (those that students are most likely to find on any computer). Specifically, you will use WordPad and Calculator for your brief discussion. Refer to Figure 1.34 as you complete Step 1.

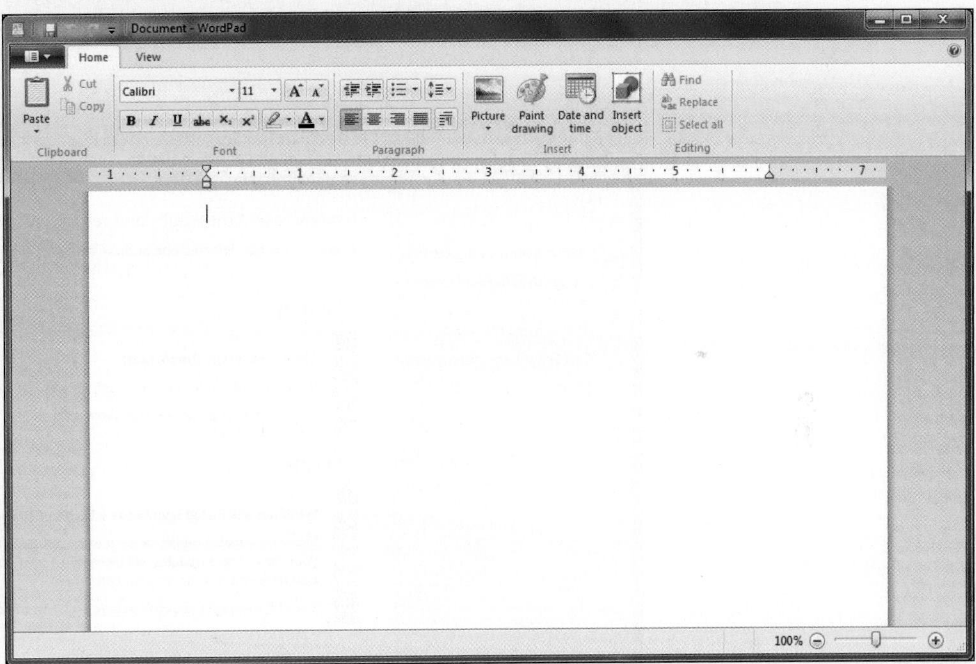

FIGURE 1.34 WordPad ➤

a. Click the **Start button**. Point to **All Programs**. Click **Accessories**. Click **WordPad**. The WordPad window opens, as shown in Figure 1.34.

   WordPad is a word processing program that is installed along with Windows 7 (and earlier Windows versions).

b. Be sure the insertion point is located in the WordPad window. Type your first and last names. Press **Enter**. Type your street address. Press **Enter**. Type your city, state, and zip.

> **TROUBLESHOOTING:** Before typing your name, you should see a blinking black bar (insertion point) in the white WordPad document area. If you do not, click in the document area to position the insertion point.

c. Close the WordPad document. Click **Don't Save** when prompted to save your changes.

   Having demonstrated the use of a word processor, you will close the document without saving it.

d. Click the **Start button**. Point to **All Programs**. Click **Accessories**. Click **Calculator**. Click **View**. If you do not see a bullet beside *Standard*, click **Standard**. If you do see a bullet beside *Standard*, press **Esc** (on the keyboard).

e. Click the corresponding keys on the calculator to complete the following formula: **87+98+100/3**. Click the = sign when you have typed the formula.

   You use the calculator to show how a student might determine his average, assuming he has taken three exams (weighted equally) with scores of 87, 98, and 100. The result should be 95.

f. Close the Calculator.

STEP 2 USE THE ACTION CENTER TO CHECK SECURITY AND PRIVACY SETTINGS

The Action Center will occasionally display messages regarding security and privacy settings. You want the Cedar Cove students to be aware of how important those messages are, so you will show them how to use the Action Center. Refer to Figure 1.35 as you complete Step 2.

TROUBLESHOOTING: If you are working in a campus lab, you might not have access to the Action Center or Windows Update. In that case, you should proceed to Step 3 of this Hands-On Exercise.

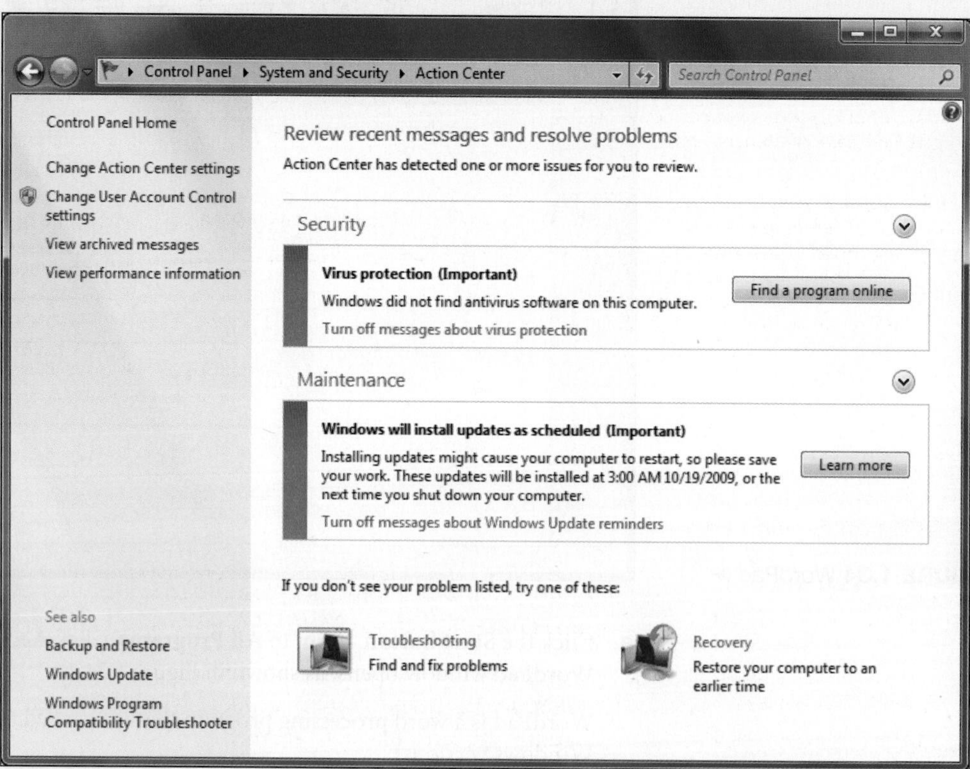

FIGURE 1.35 Action Center ➤

a. Click the **Start button**. Click **Control Panel**. Click **System and Security**. Click **Action Center**.

   Although any alerts displayed on your computer may vary from those shown in Figure 1.35, the general appearance should be similar.

b. Click **Change Action Center settings**. Take a look at the items monitored by the Action Center. Note that you can select or deselect any of them. Click **Cancel**. Close the Action Center.

c. Click the **Start button**. Point to **All Programs**. Scroll through the list of programs if necessary and click **Windows Update**. Click **Change settings**. Is your system scheduled for a routine check for or installation of updates? Click **Back** (arrow pointing left at the top-left corner of the window).

d. Click **View update history**. You should see a summary of recent updates and their level of importance. Click **OK**. Close any open windows.

STEP 3 USE THE SNIPPING TOOL

As students progress and are required to use a computer in many facets of their education, they might find occasion to include screen captures in reports or presentations. Windows 7 includes a Snipping Tool that enables you to select any part of the screen and save it as a picture file. You plan to present the Snipping Tool to the Cedar Cove class. Refer to Figures 1.36 and 1.37 as you complete Step 3.

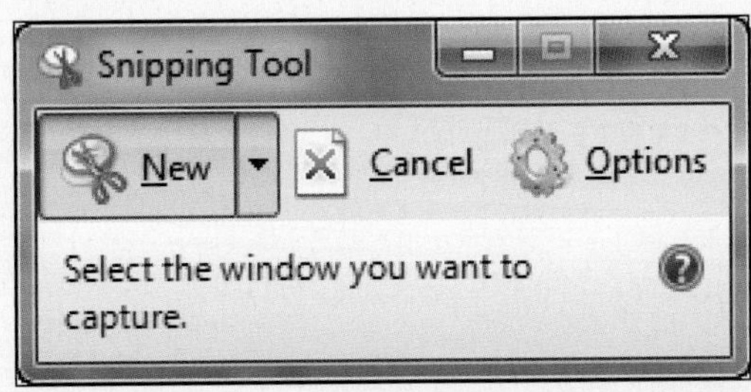

FIGURE 1.36 Snipping Tool ➤

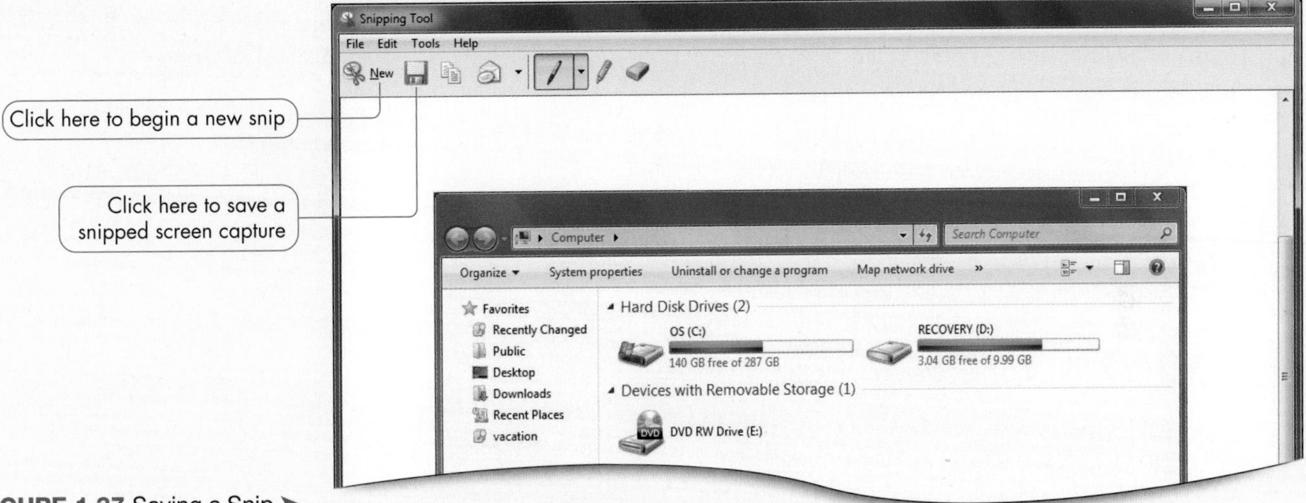

FIGURE 1.37 Saving a Snip ➤

a. Click the **Start button**. Click **Computer**. If the Computer window opens in full size (maximized), click the **Restore Down button** to reduce the window size.

   Assume that as part of a report, students are to insert a picture of the Computer window. After opening the Computer window, you will illustrate the use of the Snipping Tool to capture the screen in a picture file.

b. Click the **Start button**. Point to **All Programs**. Click **Accessories**. Click **Snipping Tool**. The Snipping Tool displays as shown in Figure 1.36. Click the **New arrow**. Click **Window Snip**. Click in the Computer window to select it.

   You have selected a window as a screen capture.

c. Click the **Save Snip icon** in the Snipping Tool window (see Figure 1.37). Scroll up in the left pane of the Save As dialog box, if necessary, and then click **Favorites**. Click **Desktop** (in the left pane, not the right). Click in the **File name box** (where you most likely see the word *Capture*). Drag to select the word *Capture* (if it is not already selected). Type **Computer window** (to change the file name). Click **Save**.

You have saved the picture of the Computer window to the desktop.

d. Close any open windows. You should see the *Computer window* file on the desktop. Double-click to open it. Close the file.

e. Right-click **Computer window** on the desktop. Click **Delete**. Confirm the deletion.

You will remove the file from the desktop.

Windows Search and Help

No matter how well prepared you are or how much you know about your computer, you will occasionally have questions about a process or tool. And no matter how careful you are to save files in locations that will be easily located later, you will sometimes lose track of a file or folder. In those cases, Windows 7 can help! You can take advantage of an extensive Help and Support library to get some questions answered and you can search for items, using anything that you know—part of the file name, the file type, or even a bit of the contents. In this section, you will learn to search for items such as files, folders, and programs. You will also explore the Help and Support feature.

You can take advantage of an extensive Help and Support library to get some questions answered and you can search for items, using anything that you know.

Performing a Search

If you know anything about an item you are looking for, you are likely to find it if it is on your computer. Windows 7 provides several ways to search. You can use the Search box found on the Start menu or you can use the Search box located at the top-right corner of some open windows. You can customize a search to look at specific folders, libraries, or storage media, and you can narrow the search by filters (file type, date modified, etc.). After conducting a search, you can save it so that you can access it later without recreating search criteria.

Conduct a Search

A **tag** is a custom file property that you create to further identify a file. A tag could be a rating that you apply to a file. You can set tags and view file properties in the details pane of a window.

You will find a Search box on the Start menu and at the top-right corner of most open windows (see Figure 1.38). You will probably find the Search box on the Start menu the most convenient place to begin a search. You can find files, folders, programs, and e-mail messages saved on your computer by entering one or more keywords in the Search box. As you type, items that match your search will appear in the list above the Search box. Click any item to be directed to that location or file. The search will occur based on text in the file, text in the file name, ***tags***, and other ***file properties***.

You can find files, folders, programs, and e-mail messages saved on your computer by entering one or more keywords in the Search box.

If you are certain a program is installed on your computer, but you cannot find the program on the Start menu or elsewhere, or perhaps you just don't know where to find the program, you can type some or all of the program name in the Search box on the Start menu. Immediately, you will see any matching program names in the list above. Simply click the name in the list to open the program.

A **file property** is an identifier of a file, such as author or date created. You can find file properties in the details pane of a window.

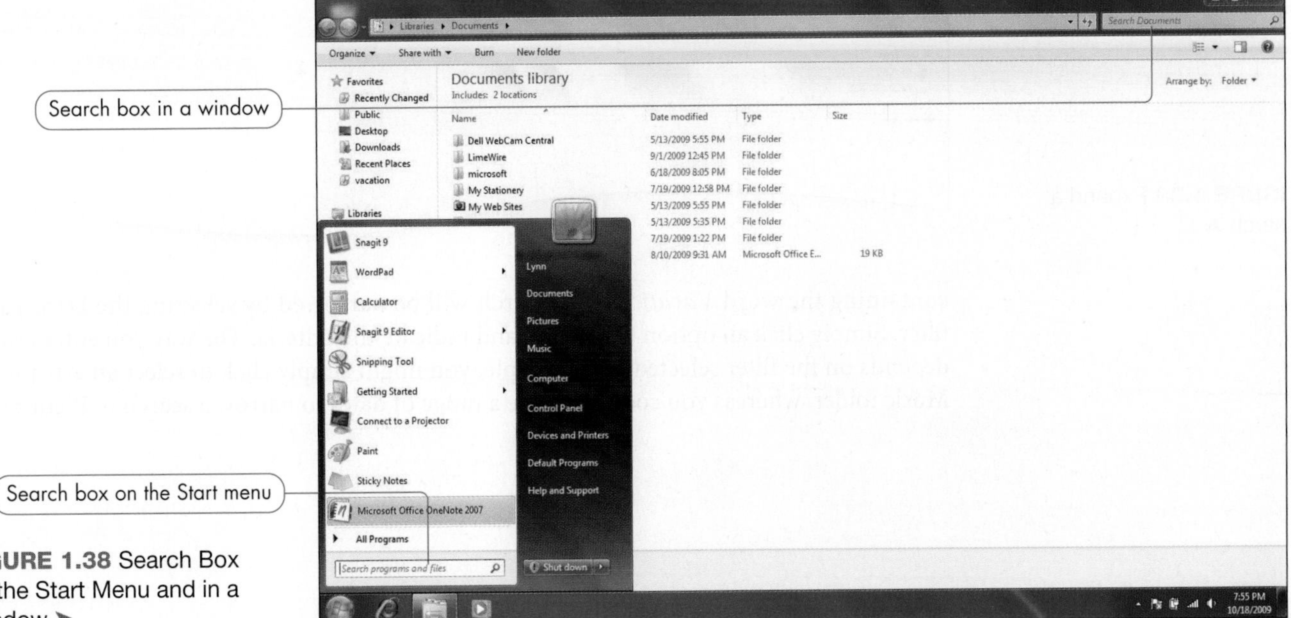

FIGURE 1.38 Search Box on the Start Menu and in a Window ➤

When you perform a search, Windows 7 searches quickly through indexed locations. All folders in Libraries are automatically included in an index. If you search in locations that are not indexed, the search can be much slower than it would be otherwise. To get a list of indexed locations and to add additional folders or disk drives to the index, click the Start button and type Indexing Options in the Search box. Click Indexing Options from the list that displays above. If you want to add locations, click Modify.

Suppose you cannot find a document that you feel sure you saved in the Documents folder. Open the Documents folder (click the Start button and click Documents). Click in the Search box at the top-right corner of the Documents window. Type any identifier (part or all of the file name, some file contents, or a file tag or property). As you type, any matching file in the Documents folder is displayed.

When you conduct a search through a window (not the Start menu), only the contents of the current folder are searched. You can expand the search to include other folders or libraries and other storage media. You can also narrow the search to seek only specific file types or for properties specific to the folder. For example, if you are searching for music in the Music folder, you might want to narrow the search to a particular artist.

Expand or Narrow a Search

To expand the search, begin typing a search term in the Search box of a window and then scroll to the bottom of the list of search results. Point to a selection in the Search again in area (see Figure 1.39) and select another area to search. Selecting Computer searches the entire computer system, even those areas that are not indexed, as well as Libraries (including Documents, Music, Pictures, and Videos). Use Custom to search a specific location, or Internet to search online.

To narrow a search, click in the Search box of a window and click the appropriate search filter below the search area. Depending on the folder or file type you are searching for, specific filters will vary. Figure 1.40 shows a search of the Pictures folder for any files

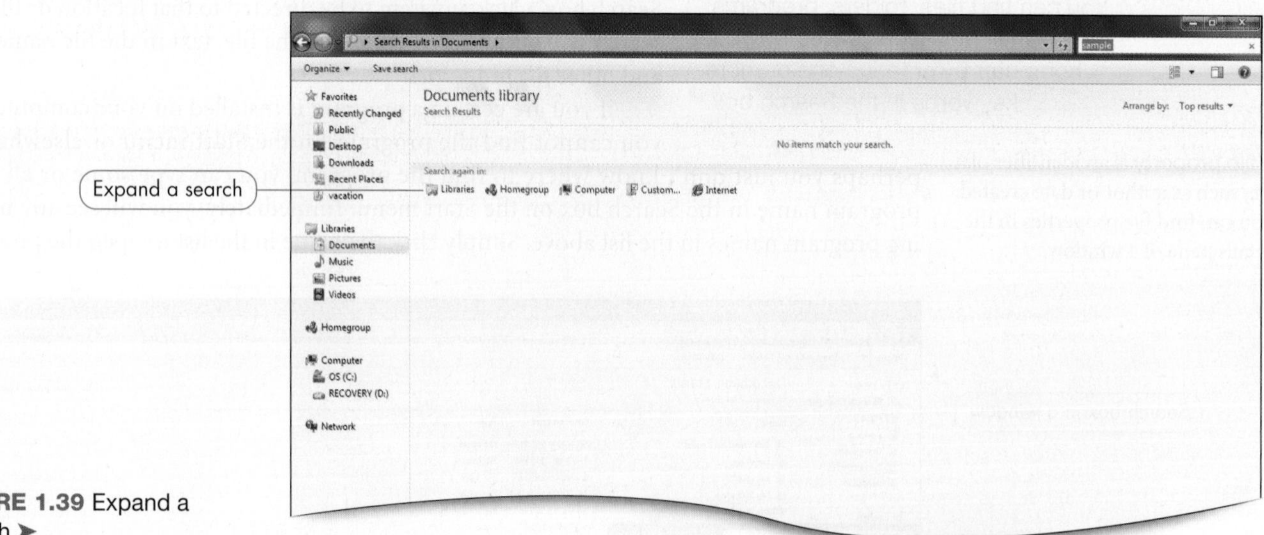

FIGURE 1.39 Expand a Search ➤

containing the word *Vacation*. The search will be narrowed by selecting the Date Taken filter. Simply click an option to filter by and indicate the criteria. The way you enter criteria depends on the filter selected. For example, you might simply click to select an artist in the Music folder, whereas you could indicate a range of dates to narrow a search of Pictures.

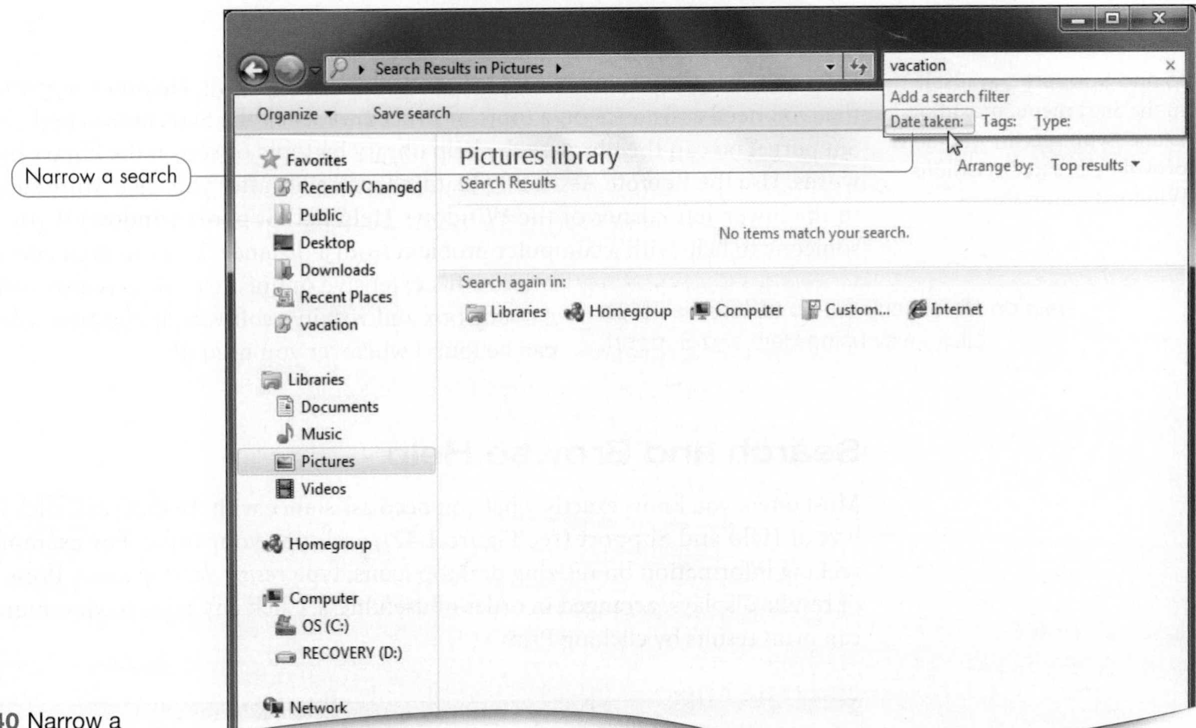

FIGURE 1.40 Narrow a Search ➤

Save a Search

If you know that you will conduct the same search often, you might find it helpful to save the search so that you do not have to continually enter the same search criteria. Perform the search once. On the toolbar, click Save search. Type a name for the search and click Save. The next time you want to conduct the search, open the Computer window. The saved search name is displayed in the Favorites section, as shown in Figure 1.41. Simply click the link to get new results.

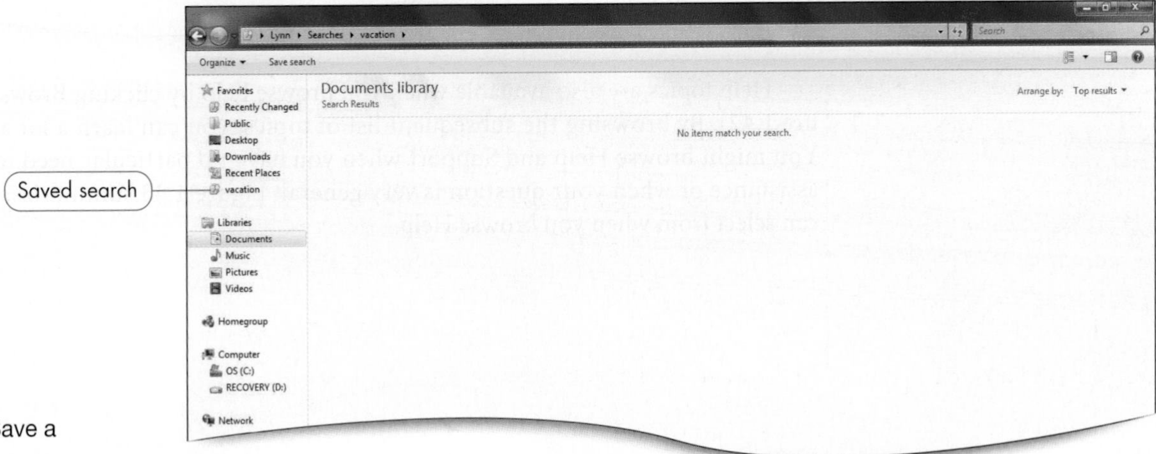

FIGURE 1.41 Save a Search ➤

Getting Help

Help and Support is available from the Start menu, providing assistance with specific questions or providing broad discussions of Windows features.

Help on almost any Windows topic is only a click away using ***Help and Support***. As you find that you need assistance on a topic or procedure, click the Start button and click Help and Support. You can then browse the help library by topic or search the library by typing keywords. Use the Remote Assistance feature (accessible after you click More support options in the lower-left corner of the Windows Help and Support window) if you want to ask someone to help with a computer problem from a distance. You can even take advantage of Microsoft's extensive online help. Help is also available within a dialog box and within a software application. Obviously, help can be found wherever you need it!

Help on almost any Windows topic is only a click away using Help and Support.

Search and Browse Help

Most often, you know exactly what you need assistance with. In that case, click in the Search box of Help and Support (see Figure 1.42), and type your topic. For example, if you are seeking information on resizing desktop icons, type *resize desktop icons.* Press Enter. A list of results displays, arranged in order of usefulness. Click any topic to view more detail. You can print results by clicking Print.

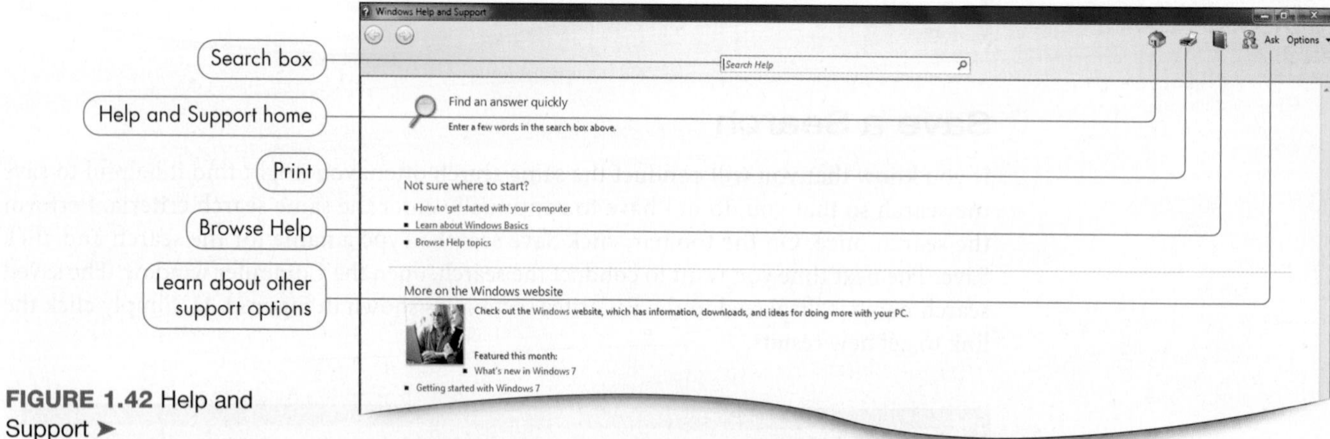

FIGURE 1.42 Help and Support ➤

Help topics are also available when you browse help by clicking Browse Help (see Figure 1.42). By browsing the subsequent list of topics, you can learn a lot about Windows. You might browse Help and Support when you have no particular need for topic-specific assistance or when your question is very general. Figure 1.43 summarizes topics that you can select from when you browse Help.

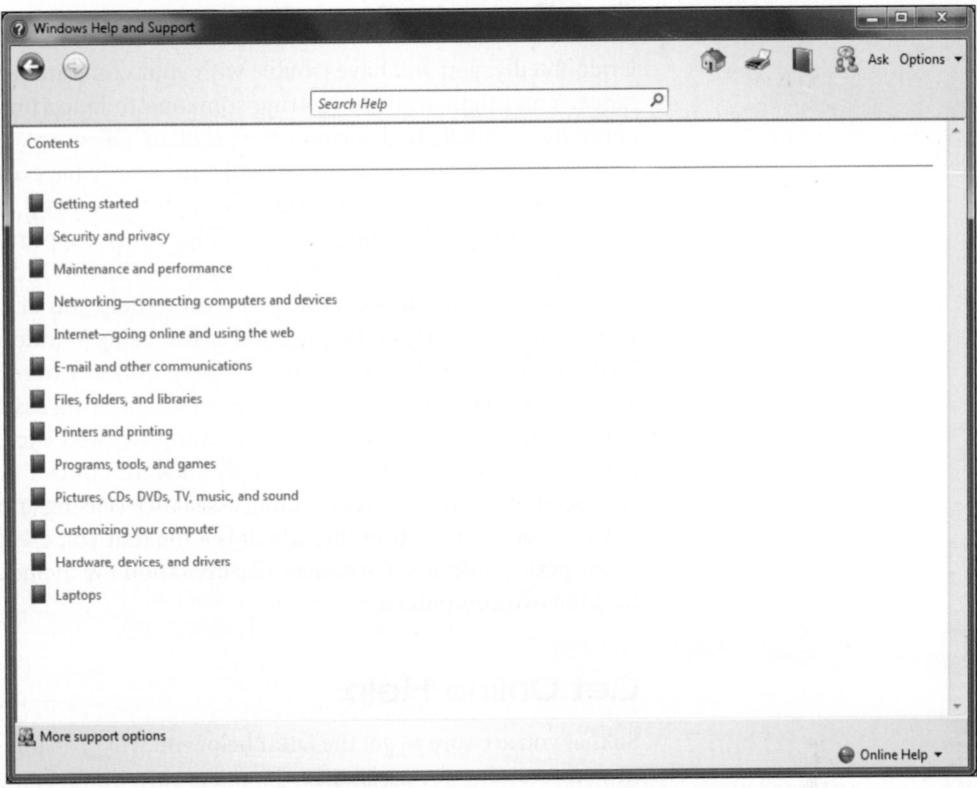

FIGURE 1.43 Browse Topics ➤

Windows Help and Support is an excellent tool when you need assistance on general topics related to the operating system, but you might also need help with a specific application, as well. For example, you will be working with a software application, such as a word processing program, and find that you have a question. Invariably, you can locate a Help button that enables you to type search terms or browse application-specific help topics. When you are working with a task in an application, you will often be responding to a dialog box. If you have a question at that time, click the ? button, usually located in the top-right corner of a window, for help related to the specific task. Some dialog boxes, but not all, include a Help button. Figure 1.44 shows a dialog box with a Help button.

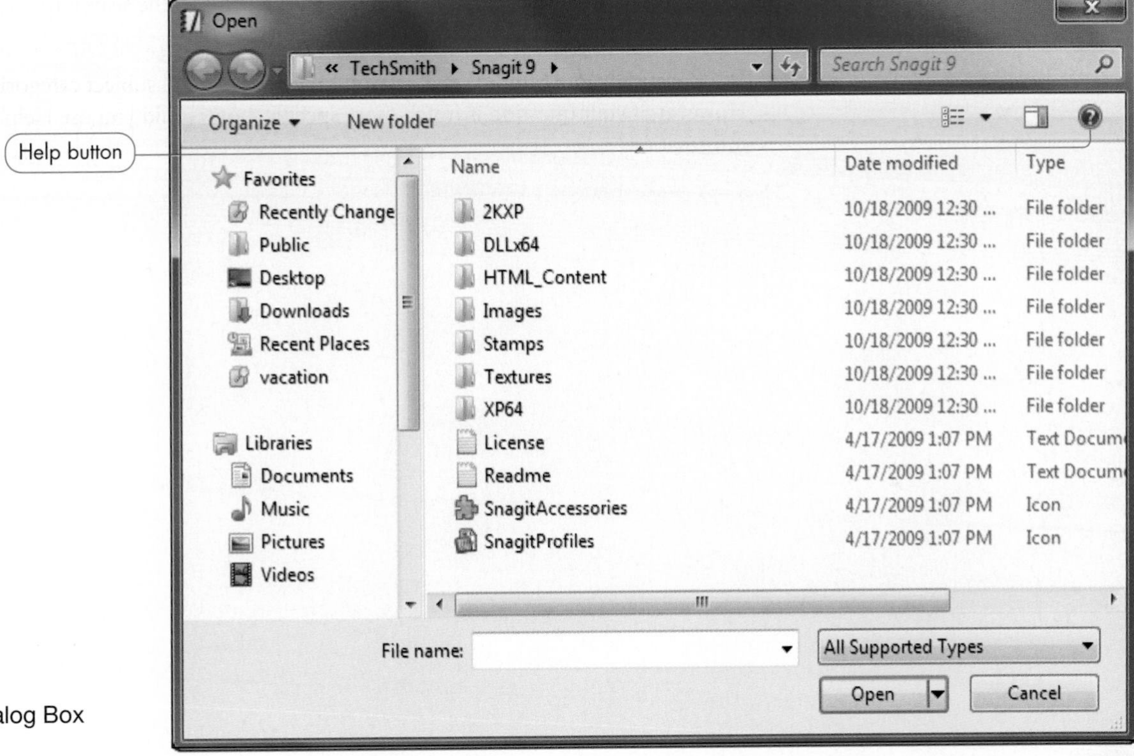

FIGURE 1.44 Dialog Box Help ➤

Get Remote Assistance

Undoubtedly, you will have trouble with your computer at some time and need some assistance. You might consider getting someone to help you by letting them connect to your computer remotely to determine the problem. Of course, you will only want to ask someone that you trust because that person will temporarily have access to your files.

Remote Assistance is available through Windows 7 Help and Support. Click the Start button, and then Help and Support. Click More support options, in the lower-left corner of the Windows Help and Support window. Click Windows Remote Assistance. Click an option to either invite someone you trust to help you or to help someone who has invited you. If the person who is helping you is also using Windows 7, you can use a method called Easy Connect. The first time you use Easy Connect to request assistance, you will receive a password that you then give to the person offering assistance. Using that password, the helper can remotely connect to your computer and exchange information. Thereafter, a password is not necessary—you simply click the contact information for the helper to initiate a session. If the person providing assistance is using another Windows operating system, you can use an invitation file, which is a file that you create that is sent (usually by e-mail) to the person offering assistance. The invitation file includes a password that is used to connect the two computers.

Get Online Help

So that you are sure to get the latest help, you will probably want to include online Help files in your searches for assistance. To make sure that is happening, open Help and Support, click Options, and then click Settings. Click to select Improve my search results by using online Help (recommended). Click OK. Of course, you must be connected to the Internet before accessing online Help.

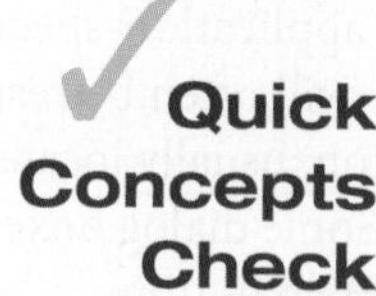

Quick Concepts Check

1. In which two places is a Windows Search box located in Windows 7? Which Search box would you use if you are looking for a particular program that you think is installed on your system?
2. You have just conducted a search of the Documents folder (in Windows Explorer) for all files with a particular extension. You now want to expand the search to include the entire Computer. Explain how you would do that.
3. Windows Help and Support enables you to browse general subject categories for assistance. However, if your question is much more specific, how would you use Help and Support to get information?

3 Windows Search and Help

As you close your presentation to the Cedar Cove class, you want the students to be confident in their ability but well aware that help is available. You plan to demonstrate several ways they can get assistance. You also want them to know how to conduct searches for files and folders. Although they might not give it much thought, you know that there will be many times when they will forget where they saved a very important file. Therefore, it is imperative that you include the topic of searching in your presentation.

Skills covered: Explore Windows Help, Search Using Keywords • Use the Search Box to Conduct a Search, Expand a Search • Get Help in an Application, Get Help in a Dialog Box.

STEP 1 EXPLORE WINDOWS HELP, SEARCH USING KEYWORDS

As students in your class progress to middle and high school, they may have opportunities to use laptops for class work. They also are likely to find themselves in locations where they can connect to the Internet wirelessly. Using that example, you will help the class understand how to use Windows Help and Support to learn how to find and safely connect to an available wireless network. Refer to Figure 1.45 as you complete Step 1.

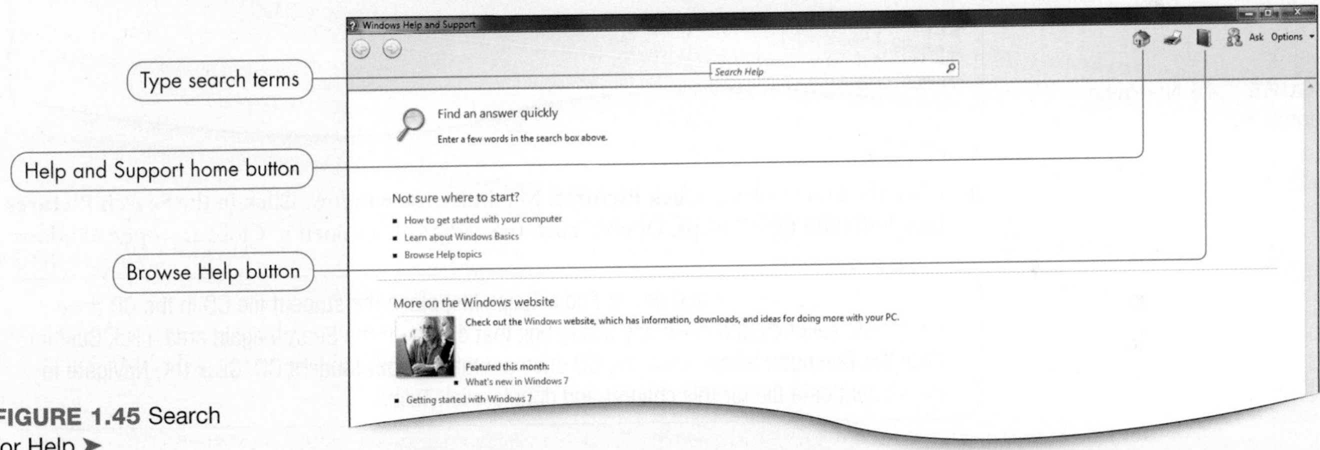

FIGURE 1.45 Search for Help ➤

a. Click the **Start button**. Click **Help and Support** in the right pane. Maximize the Windows Help and Support window.

> **TROUBLESHOOTING:** Your computer should be connected to the Internet before completing this exercise. That way, you can include online help resources.

b. Click the **Browse Help button**. Click **Networking—connecting computers and devices**. Click **Connecting to a network**. Click **View and connect to available wireless networks**. Read through the topic. Pay close attention to any warning about safely connecting to a wireless network.

   You will show students how to use Help and Support browsing to locate help on a topic—in this case, connecting to a wireless network.

c. Click the **Help and Support home button**. Click in the **Search Help box**, and then type **Connect to a wireless network**. Press **Enter**. Click **View and connect to available wireless**

networks. Note that you arrived at the same topic as in the previous step, but took a different route. Close the Windows Help and Support window.

d. Use any method of getting Help and Support to answer the question "How can I make sure a wireless connection is secure?" What did you find?

STEP 2 USE THE SEARCH BOX TO CONDUCT A SEARCH, EXPAND A SEARCH

You want to show students how to search for files, but you are not familiar enough with the classroom computer to know what files to search for. You know, however, that Windows-based computers will include some picture files so you feel certain you can use the example of searching for files with a .jpg (picture) type. You will also illustrate expanding and narrowing a search. Refer to Figure 1.46 as you complete Step 2.

FIGURE 1.46 Narrow a Search ➤

a. Click the **Start button**. Click **Pictures**. Maximize the window. Click in the **Search Pictures box**, and then type **Tulips**. Double-click the *Tulips* file to open it. Close any open windows.

> **TROUBLESHOOTING:** If you do not find a Tulips file, place the student file CD in the CD drive. Wait a few seconds and close any dialog box that opens. In the Search again area, click Custom. Click the Computer arrow. Click the CD drive containing your student CD. Click OK. Navigate to the student data file for this chapter and double-click Tulips.

You search for a file by name—Tulips. Because one of the desktop backgrounds provided by Windows 7 is a file named Tulips, you should be able to find it on the classroom computer in the Pictures folder.

b. Click the **Start button**. Click **Pictures**. Maximize the window, if necessary. Click in the **Search Pictures box**. Look beneath the *Search* box to find the *Add a search filter* area. Click **Type**, as shown in Figure 1.46. Click **.jpg**. All files of that type should display to the left. Double-click any file to open it. Close the picture.

You want to find a few picture files that are saved in the Pictures folder. Because you know that many picture files are of the .jpg file type, you can limit the search to that file type.

c. Click **Documents** in the left pane. Click in the **Search Documents box**, and then type **Sample**. Regardless of whether any results are found, expand the search to include Libraries. Click **Libraries** in the *Search again in* area. Double-click the **Sample Music folder** to view the folder contents. Close all open windows.

d. Click the **Start button**. Click in the **Search box** on the Start menu, and then type **Getting Started**. If more than one Getting Started link appears, place the mouse pointer over each link. Click the one with a ScreenTip that reads *Learn about Windows features and start* *using them.* Click **Go online to learn more**. You will be directed to a Microsoft Web page that provides information on Windows 7. Take a look, click any links that look interesting, and then close any open windows.

TROUBLESHOOTING: After clicking Go online to learn more, you will view a Web page only if your computer is currently connected to the Internet.

Windows 7 provides a Getting Started tip box, but since you are not sure where that information resides, you will use the Search box on the Start menu to find it.

STEP 3 GET HELP IN AN APPLICATION, GET HELP IN A DIALOG BOX

As you complete the session with the fifth-graders, you want them to understand that they will never be without assistance. If they need help with general computer and operating system questions, they can access Help and Support from the Start menu. If they are working with an application, such as a word processor, they will most likely find a Help link that will enable them to search for help related to keywords. Within an application, if they have a dialog box open, they can sometimes get help related to the dialog box's activities. You will demonstrate application help and dialog box help. Refer to Figure 1.47 as you complete Step 3.

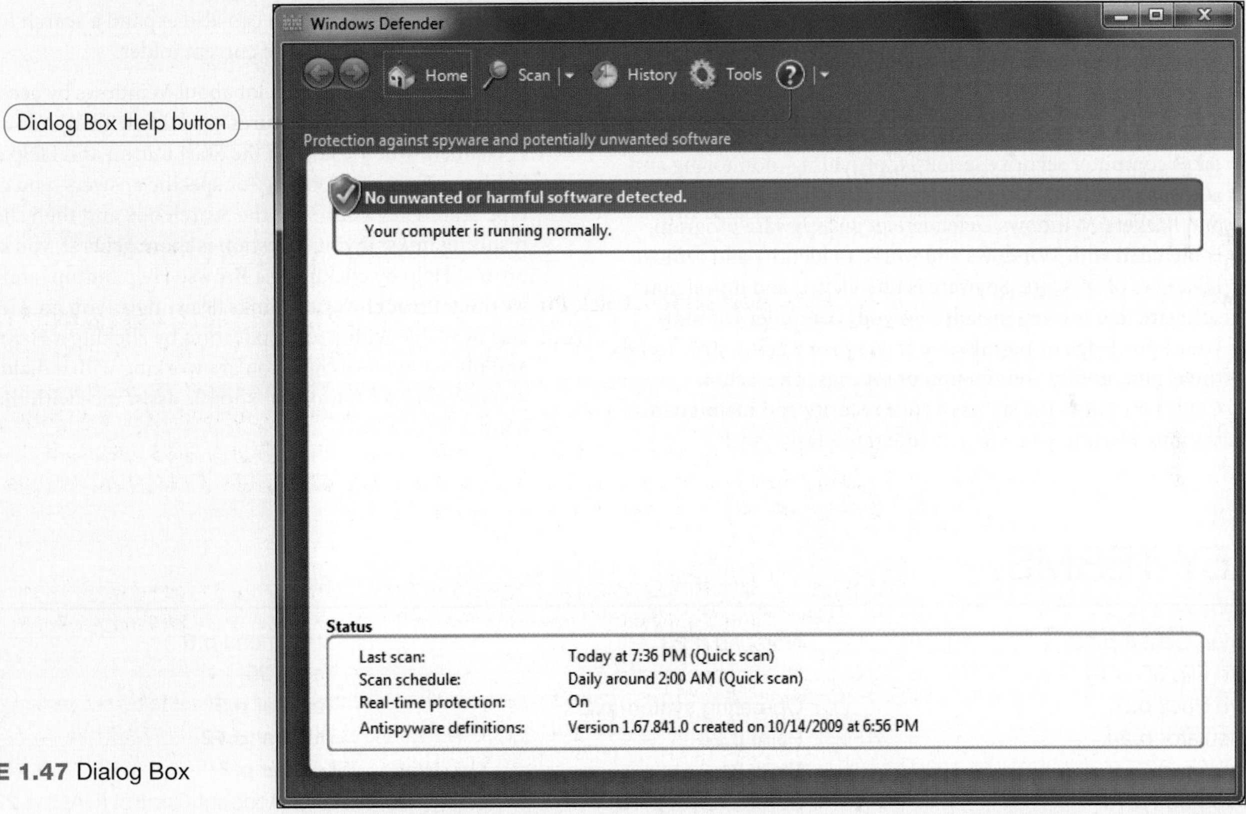

FIGURE 1.47 Dialog Box Help ➤

a. Click the **Start button**. Click in the **Search box** on the Start menu. Type **Windows Defender**. Click the **Windows Defender link** that appears in the results list.

b. Click the question mark (**?**) shown in Figure 1.47 on the right side of the Windows Defender toolbar. Maximize the Windows Help and Support window. Click **Scan for spyware and other potentially unwanted software**. Read about how to conduct a Windows Defender scan. Close all open windows.

c. Click the **Start button**. Click **Control Panel**. Click **Appearance and Personalization**. Click **Change the theme** in the *Personalization* section. Click the **?** in the top-right corner of the dialog box to open dialog box Help. Read about themes. Close any open windows.

CHAPTER OBJECTIVES REVIEW

After reading this chapter, you have accomplished the following objectives:

1. **Understand the desktop.** The desktop is the display that appears when you turn on a computer. It contains icons (small pictures) that represent programs, files, folders, and system resources. The taskbar is the horizontal bar along the bottom of the desktop. It includes a Start button, pinned icons, icons of open windows, and the Notification area. You can customize the desktop to include a background and a screen saver.
2. **Manage windows.** Programs, folders, and other computer projects open in individual windows on the desktop, much like papers on a desk. You can manage windows by moving, resizing, stacking, or snapping them into position so that multiple windows are easier to work with and identify.
3. **Identify Windows accessories.** Windows 7 provides several accessory programs, including a word processor (WordPad), text editor (Notepad), calculator (Calculator), and screen capture tool (Snipping Tool). You will find accessory programs when you click the Start button, All Programs, and Accessories.
4. **Work with security settings and software.** Windows 7 takes computer security seriously, providing monitoring and software that helps keep your computer safe from spyware and hackers. Windows Defender, an antispyware program, is included with Windows and works to identify and remove instances of spyware. Spyware is unsolicited and unwelcome software that is often installed on your computer without your knowledge or permission. It can then track your Internet travel and modify your computer settings. The Action Center monitors the status of your security and maintenance settings, alerting you when maintenance tasks (such as backing up your system) are overlooked or when your security is at risk (when antivirus software is out of date, for example). A Windows firewall protects against unauthorized access to your computer from outside entities and prohibits Internet travel by programs from your computer without your permission.
5. **Perform a search.** As you work with a computer, it is inevitable that you will forget where you saved a file or that you misplace a file or folder. Windows 7 provides ample support for finding such items, providing a Search box on the Start menu and in every open window. As you type search keywords in either of those areas, Windows immediately begins a search, showing results. From an open window, you can begin a search and then narrow it by file type or other criteria unique to the searched folder. You might, for example, narrow a search by Date Taken if you are searching in the Pictures folder. You can also expand a search to include more search areas than the current folder.
6. **Get Help.** You can learn a lot about Windows by accessing the Help and Support features available with Windows 7. Get help when you click the Start button and Help and Support. If you are looking for specific answers, you can type search keyword(s) in the Search box and then click any resulting links. If your question is more general, you can browse Help by clicking the Browse Help button, and then working through various links, learning as you go. Help is also available within an application by clicking a Help button and phrasing a search. If you are working with a dialog box, you can click a ? button for specific assistance with the task at hand.

KEY TERMS

Action Center ***p.10***
Aero Flip 3D ***p.13***
Aero Peek ***p.5***
Calculator ***p.24***
Desktop ***p.2***
Dialog box ***p.14***
File property ***p.35***
Firewall ***p.26***
Gadget ***p.4***
Help and Support ***p.38***
Icon ***p.2***
Jump List ***p.8***
Notepad ***p.23***
Notification area ***p.5***
Operating system ***p.2***
Paint ***p.24***
Pin ***p.8***
Screen saver ***p.10***
Shortcut ***p.3***
Snap ***p.13***
Snip ***p.25***
Snipping Tool ***p.25***
Spyware ***p.26***
Start button ***p.5***
Start menu ***p.6***
Tag ***p.35***
Taskbar ***p.5***
Title bar ***p.12***
Toolbar ***p.7***
User Account Control (UAC) ***p.27***
Window ***p.2***
Windows Defender ***p.26***
Windows Update ***p.29***
WordPad ***p.23***

MULTIPLE CHOICE

1. The Windows 7 feature that alerts you to any maintenance or security concerns is the:
   (a) Action Center.
   (b) Security Center.
   (c) Windows Defender.
   (d) Control Pane.

2. Snapping windows means that you:
   (a) Minimize all open windows simultaneously so that the desktop displays.
   (b) Auto arrange all open windows so that they are of uniform size.
   (c) Manually reposition all open windows so that you can see the content of each.
   (d) Move any open windows to an opposing side of the desktop until they snap into place.

3. Which of the following accessory programs is primarily a text editor?
   (a) Notepad
   (b) Snipping Tool
   (c) Journal
   (d) Calculator

4. A calendar, which is an example of a constantly changing desktop item, is a(n):
   (a) Icon.
   (b) Thumbnail.
   (c) Gadget.
   (d) Action.

5. Open windows are displayed as icons, or buttons, on the:
   (a) Desktop.
   (b) Taskbar.
   (c) Notification area.
   (d) Start menu.

6. A shortcut icon on the desktop is identified by:
   (a) An arrow at the lower-left corner of the icon.
   (b) The word *shortcut* included as part of the icon name.
   (c) A checkmark at the lower-left corner of the icon.
   (d) Its placement on the right side of the desktop.

7. Help and Support is available from which of the following?
   (a) Start menu
   (b) Desktop icon
   (c) Notification area
   (d) Taskbar

8. Which of the following is NOT a method of switching between open windows?
   (a) Alt+Tab
   (b) Shift+Tab
   (c) Click an open window icon on the taskbar.
   (d) Windows logo+Tab

9. When you maximize a window, you:
   (a) Fill the screen with the window.
   (b) Prioritize the window so that it is always placed on top of all other open windows.
   (c) Expand the window's height but leave its width unchanged.
   (d) Expand the window's width but leave its height unchanged.

10. When you enter search keywords in the Search box of a folder window (such as the Documents window):
    (a) The search is not limited to the selected folder.
    (b) The search cannot be further narrowed.
    (c) The search is automatically expanded to include every folder on the hard drive.
    (d) The search is limited to the selected folder, but can be expanded if you like.

PRACTICE EXERCISES

1 Senior Academy

As a requirement for completing graduate school, you must submit a thesis, which is a detailed research report. Your degree is in Education with a minor in Information Technology. Your thesis will center on generational learning styles, comparing the way students learn across the generations. Although you have not yet conducted your research, you suspect that students aged 55 and older have a very different way of learning than do younger students. You expect the use of technology in learning to be much more intimidating to older students who have not been exposed to such learning at a high level. As a researcher, however, you know that such suppositions must be supported or proven incorrect by research. As part of your thesis preparation, you are surveying a group of senior adults and a group of college students who are less than 25 years old. The local senior center will distribute your survey to seniors who are currently enrolled in a non-credit computer literacy course sponsored by the senior center. The same survey will be given to students enrolled in a computer literacy college course. The survey covers Windows 7 basics and includes the following steps. You should go over the steps before finalizing the survey instrument. This project follows the same set of skills as used in Hands-On Exercises 1, 2, and 3 in the chapter. Refer to Figure 1.48 as you complete this exercise.

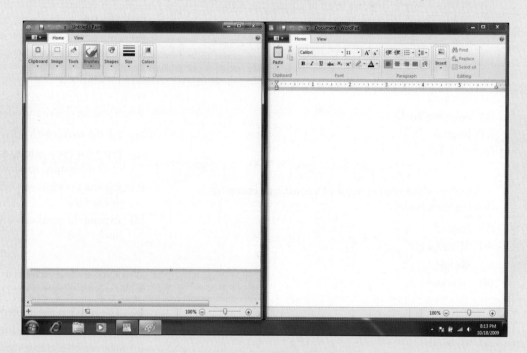

FIGURE 1.48 Paint and WordPad windows ➤

a. Click the **Start button**. Click **Control Panel**. Click **Change desktop background**. Make sure Picture location shows Windows Desktop Backgrounds. Scroll through the picture choices and select one. Click **Save Changes** if you are allowed to make a change to the desktop, or **Cancel** if you are not. Close all open windows.

b. Click the **Start button**. Point to **All Programs**. Click **Accessories**. Right-click **WordPad**, and then click **Pin to Taskbar**. Click outside the Start menu to remove it from view.

c. Click the **Start button**. Point to **All Programs**. Click **Accessories**. Right-click **Paint**. Click **Pin to Start Menu**. Click outside the Start menu to remove it from view.

d. Click the **Start button**. Point to **All Programs**. Click **Accessories**. Right-click and drag **Notepad** to the desktop. Release the mouse button. Click **Create shortcuts here**.

e. Click the **WordPad icon** on the taskbar. With WordPad still open, click the **Start button**. Click **Paint**. If you have recently opened Paint files, you may have to click Paint twice to open it.

f. Right-click an empty area of the taskbar. Click **Show windows side by side**. Compare your screen to Figure 1.48.

g. Click the **Close button** at the top-right corner of the Paint window to close the program.
h. Click the **Maximize button** (middle control button) on the right side of the WordPad window to maximize the window.
i. Click the **Start button**. Click **Help and Support**. Click **Browse Help**. Click **Security and privacy**. Scroll down the list if necessary and click **Helping to protect your computer from viruses**. Click **How can I tell if my computer has a virus?**. Identify some symptoms of a virus.
j. Right-click an empty area of the taskbar. Click **Show windows stacked**. Click in the WordPad window and in your own words, list at least three virus symptoms.
k. Click the **Start button**. Point to **All Programs**. Click **Accessories**. Click **Snipping Tool**. Click the **New arrow**. Click **Full-screen Snip**. Click **Save Snip**. Scroll down the left side of the **Save As dialog box**, and then click to select the disk drive where you will save your student files. Click in the **File name box**, and then type **win01p1survey_LastnameFirstname**. Click **Save**.
l. Close all open windows without saving.
m. Right-click the **WordPad icon** on the taskbar. Click **Unpin this program from taskbar**. Click the **Start button**. Right-click **Paint**. Click **Unpin from Start Menu**. Click outside the Start menu to remove it from view.
n. Right-click the **Notepad icon** on the desktop. Click **Delete**. Confirm the deletion.

2 Silent Auction

As part of your responsibility as vice president of the National Youth Assembly of College Athletes, you are soliciting donated items for a silent auction at the national conference. You accept items and tag them with an estimated value and a beginning bid requirement. You will use a computer to keep a record of the donor, value, and minimum bid requirement. Because you will not always be in the office when an item is donated, you will configure the desktop and taskbar of the computer to simplify the job of data entry for anyone who happens to be at the desk. This project follows the same set of skills as used in Hands-On Exercises 1, 2, and 3 in the chapter. Refer to Figure 1.49 as you complete this exercise.

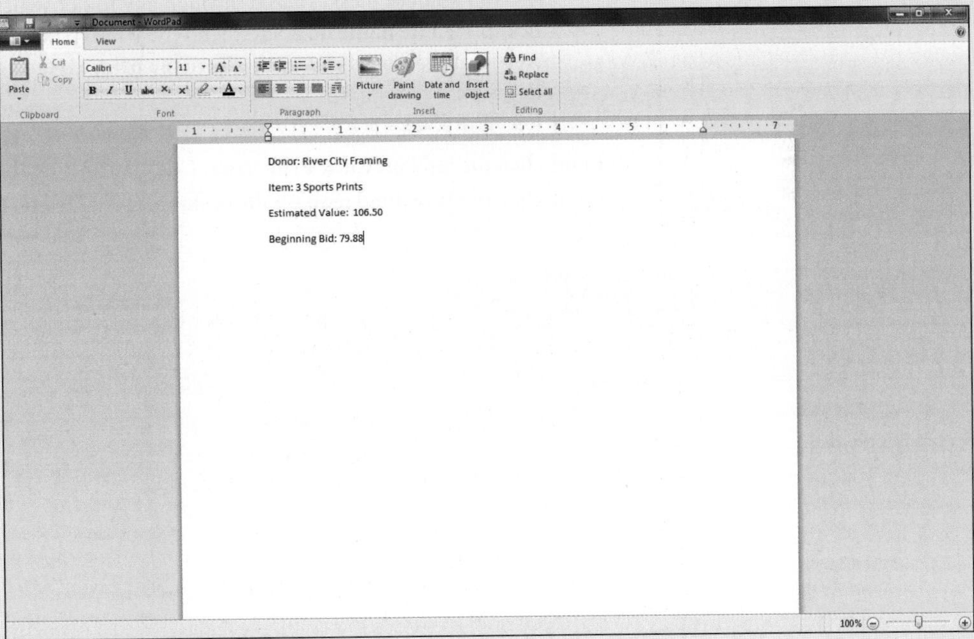

FIGURE 1.49 Silent Auction Items ➤

a. Click the **Start button**. Point to **All Programs**. Click **Accessories**. Right-click and drag **WordPad** to the desktop. Click **Create shortcuts here**.
b. Right-click an empty area of the taskbar. Click **Properties**. Click the **Auto-hide the taskbar check box** (if no check mark appears). Click **OK**.

c. Double-click the **WordPad icon** on the desktop. WordPad will open.
   - Click the **Maximize button**. If no insertion point (blinking bar) appears in the upper-left corner of the white space, click to position it there.
   - Type **Donor: River City Framing**. Press **Enter**.
   - Type **Item: 3 Sports Prints**. Press **Enter**.
   - Type **Estimated Value:**. Press **Spacebar**.

d. Click the **Start button**. Point to **All Programs**. Click **Accessories**. Click **Calculator**.

   The estimated value of each print is $35.50, but the frames will be sold as a unit. Therefore, you need to determine the total value ($35.50 multiplied by 3). Because you are in the middle of typing a WordPad document, you do not want to close it. Instead, you will open the Calculator program and compute the value.

e. Use the mouse to click **35.50*3** and click =. The total value should show on the calculator. Minimize the Calculator.

f. Type the total in the WordPad document. Press **Enter**. Type **Beginning Bid:**. Press the spacebar.

g. Click the **Calculator icon** on the taskbar. The amount from step (e) should still be displayed on the Calculator. Click the **multiplication key** (*) and **.75**. Click =. Jot down the value shown on the Calculator and close the Calculator.

   The beginning bid will be 75% of the estimated value. So the calculation should be Estimated Value multiplied by .75.

h. Click after the word *Bid:* in the WordPad window, if necessary. Type the value that you recorded in step (g), rounded up to the nearest hundredth. Press **Enter**. Compare your screen to Figure 1.49.

i. Click the **Start button**. Click **Help and Support**. Maximize the Windows Help and Support window. Click in the **Search box**, and then type **WordPad**. Press **Enter**. Click **Using WordPad**. Click **Create, open, and save documents** on the right side. If necessary, click **Create, open, and save documents** to expand the detail. Look at the displayed table to determine how to save a document. Close Windows Help and Support.

j. Click **WordPad** (just to the left of the Home tab) as you were directed in the Help and Support tip.
   - Click **Save**.
   - Scroll down the left side of the dialog box to Computer and click the disk drive where you save your student files. Proceed through any folder structure, as directed by your instructor.
   - Click in the **File name box**, and then type **win01p2auction_LastnameFirstname**. You might first need to remove the current file name before typing the new one.
   - Click **Save**.
   - Close WordPad.

k. Right-click the taskbar. Click **Properties**. Click **Auto-hide the taskbar**. Click **OK**.

l. Right-click the **WordPad icon** on the desktop. Click **Delete**. Confirm the deletion.

MID-LEVEL EXERCISES

1 Junk Business

You and a college friend have signed on as a franchise for JUNKit, a company that purchases unwanted items and disposes of or recycles them. A recent pickup included a desktop computer that appeared to be reusable. Because you had a few spare parts and some hardware expertise, you rebuilt the computer and installed Windows 7. Now you will check the system to verify that it is workable and configured correctly.

a. Open WordPad and type as directed when you complete the following items.

b. Open the Action Center. Are there any alerts? Make note of them and close the Action Center. In the WordPad document, type **Step b:** and then list any alerts or indicate that there are none. Press **Enter**.

c. Open Windows Defender and check to see when the last scan occurred. Click the WordPad icon on the taskbar, click in the document on the line following your response for Step b, type **Step c:** and then record when the last scan occurred. Press **Enter**. Right-click the **Windows Defender** icon on the taskbar, and then click **Close window**.

d. Check the firewall status. Is the firewall on? Close the System and Security window. If necessary, click in the WordPad document on the line following your response for Step c. Type **Step d:** and then record whether the firewall is on or off. (Note that the firewall may not be on for the lab computer because the campus lab is likely to be behind another campus-wide firewall. Your computer at home is more likely to have the firewall turned on.) Press **Enter**.

e. Check Windows Update. When did the last update occur? Click the **WordPad icon** on the taskbar. If necessary, click in the WordPad document on the line following your response for Step d. Type **Step e:** and then record the date of the last update. Press **Enter**. Right-click the **Windows Update icon** on the taskbar, and then click **Close window**.

f. Check for available desktop backgrounds. Identify one that you plan to use, but click **Cancel** without selecting it. Close any open windows other than WordPad. If necessary, click in the WordPad document on the line following your response for Step e. Type **Step f:** and then list the name of the background that you would have selected in the WordPad document. Press **Enter**.

DISCOVER

g. Open Help and Support. Find information on the Aero desktop. Specifically, identify a definition of the Aero desktop and requirements for its use (computer specifications and Windows 7 versions that support Aero). Going a little further, find out what Aero Shake is and how it could be beneficial in managing a desktop. Click the **WordPad icon** on the taskbar, type **Step g:** and then summarize your findings in the WordPad document. Press **Enter**.

h. Click the **Restore Down button** to reduce the size of the WordPad window. Snap the Windows Help and Support window to one side of the desktop and the WordPad document to the other.

i. Close the Windows Help and Support window. Save the WordPad document by clicking **Save** (second from left on the topmost row of the WordPad window). Scroll down in the left pane of the dialog box and click **Computer**. Double-click the disk drive where you save your student files (as directed by your instructor). Click in the **File name box**, and then type **win01m1junk_LastnameFirstname**. Click **Save**. Close WordPad.

2 Technical Writing

You are employed as a software specialist with Wang Design, a firm that provides commercial and residential landscape design and greenscape services. The landscape designers use a wide array of software that assists with producing detailed plans and lawn layouts. The firm has just purchased several new computers, configured with Windows 7. Because the operating system is new to all employees, you have been assigned the task of producing a small easy-to-follow manual summarizing basic Windows 7 tasks. Use WordPad or Microsoft Word to produce a report, no more than 10 pages, based on the following topic outline. Where appropriate, use the Snipping Tool to include screen captures that illustrate a topic or process. Use this chapter and Windows Help and Support to find information for your report. Save your report as **win01m2writing_LastnameFirstname**.

1. Desktop Components
2. Customizing the Desktop
3. Windows Accessories
4. Windows Search

CAPSTONE EXERCISE

You are enrolled in a Directed Studies class as one of the final courses required for your degree. The class is projects-based, which means that the instructor assigns open-ended cases for students to manage and report on. You will prepare teaching materials for a Windows 7 community education class. The class is a new effort for the college, and given early enrollment figures, it appears that most students are over the age of 45 with very little computer background. Most students indicate that they have recently purchased a computer with Windows 7 and want to learn to work with the operating system at a minimal level. The class is short, only a couple of Saturday mornings, and it is fast approaching. In this exercise, you will prepare and test class material introducing students to the desktop, managing windows, working with accessory programs and security settings, getting help, and finding files. Your instructor wants screen shots of your progress, so you will use the Snipping Tool to prepare those.

Explore the Desktop and Manage Windows

The instructor will spend the first hour of class introducing students to the Windows 7 desktop and to the concept of windows. He will assume that students are complete novices, so he wants an outline that begins with the basics. You have prepared the series of steps given below. You will go through those steps, preparing a screen shot to accompany your submission.

a. Auto arrange icons on the desktop (if they are not already set to auto arrange).
b. Create a desktop shortcut for the Notepad program.
c. Pin the WordPad program to the taskbar.
d. Open the Notepad shortcut. If necessary, restore down the window so that it is not maximized.
e. Open WordPad from the taskbar. If necessary, restore down the window so that it is not maximized.
f. Snap each window to opposing sides of the desktop.
g. Show the windows stacked.
h. Use the Snipping Tool to capture a copy of the screen. Save it as **win01c1desktop_LastnameFirstname**.
i. Close all open windows.

Work with Accessory Programs and Security Settings

The instructor wants to make sure students understand that some software is included with a Windows 7 installation. Because using any type of software most often involves Internet access, you know that the class must include instruction on security risks and solutions. You have prepared some notes and will test them in the steps that follow.

a. Open WordPad. Maximize the window, if necessary. Students in class will be instructed to type a paragraph on Windows 7 security features. Use Windows 7 Help and Support if necessary to identify Windows 7 security features, and then compose a paragraph in the WordPad document. Minimize WordPad but do not close it.
b. Open Paint. Maximize the window, if necessary. Click the top half of **Brushes**. Click and drag to write your name in the *Paint* area. Click the top half of **Select**. Click and drag in a rectangle around your name. Click **Copy**. Close Paint without saving.
c. Click the **WordPad icon** on the taskbar. Click the top half of **Paste** to add your "signature" to the paragraph.
d. Save the WordPad document as **win01c1paragraph_LastnameFirstname**.
e. Close WordPad.

Get Help and Find Files

You know from personal experience that things usually work well when an instructor is available to help. You also know that as students leave the Windows 7 class, they will have questions and must know how to find help themselves. They will also undoubtedly misplace files. The steps that follow should help them understand how to get help and how to find files, programs, and folders.

a. Browse Help and Support to find information on the Start menu.
b. Search Help and Support to find a description of remote assistance.
c. Minimize the Windows Help and Support window.
d. Click the **Start button**, click in the **Start menu Search box**, and then type **Word**. You will search for any program with the word *word* in the program name. At the very least, you should see *WordPad* in the results list. Click the program name to open it. If WordPad is maximized, restore it down to less than full size.
e. Click the **Help and Support icon** on the taskbar to open the window.
f. Show the windows stacked.
g. Use the Snipping Tool to capture the screen, saving it as **win01c1help_LastnameFirstname**. Close all open windows.
h. Unpin the **WordPad icon** from the taskbar.
i. Delete the **NotePad icon** from the desktop.

BEYOND THE CLASSROOM

Speech Class

GENERAL CASE 

You are taking a Speech class and must develop a demonstration speech, complete with a sheet of notes. A demonstration speech is one in which you teach or direct the class on how to do something. Because Windows 7 is a relatively new operating system, you decide to demonstrate some of its features. You will use WordPad to record a few notes that will help you make your presentation. After completing your notes, save the document as **win01b1speech_LastnameFirstname** in a location as directed by your instructor. In a 1, 2, 3 fashion (listing your points in numerical order), provide directions to the class on how to:

- Customize the desktop with a background and screen saver.
- Pin programs to the taskbar and the Start menu.
- Use the Start menu Search box to find and open a program that you think is installed on your computer system.
- Get Help on an item related to Windows 7.
- Make sure your computer is protected against spyware and hacking.

Campus Chatter

RESEARCH CASE 

As a reporter for the college newspaper *Campus Chatter,* you are responsible for the education section. Each month, you contribute a short article on an educational topic. This month, you will summarize a feature of Windows 7. You are having writer's block, however, and need a nudge, so you will use the Internet for an idea. Click Start, All Programs, Accessories, Getting Started. Click Go online to learn more. You will be directed to the Windows 7 Web site. Peruse some links, locate a topic of interest, and use WordPad to write a minimum one-page typed report on a topic related to Windows 7. Save the report as **win01b2chatter_LastnameFirstname** in a location as directed by your instructor.

Laptop Logic

DISASTER RECOVERY 

Your job in sales with an educational software company requires a great deal of travel. You depend on a laptop computer for most of what you do, from keeping sales records to connecting with an overhead projector when you make presentations to groups. In short, you would be lost without your computer. A recent scare, when you temporarily misplaced the laptop, has led you to consider precautions you can take to make sure your computer and its data are protected. Since you have a little free time before leaving for your next trip, you will use Windows 7 Help and Support to explore some suggestions on protecting your laptop. Open Help and Support and search for information on *protecting a laptop*. Create a one- to two-page typed report covering two topics. First, describe how you would protect data (including passwords and financial information) on your laptop. Second, provide some suggestions on steps you can take to make sure you do not lose your laptop or have it stolen. Use WordPad to record the report, saving the report as **win01b3laptop_LastnameFirstname** in a location as directed by your instructor.

1 OFFICE FUNDAMENTALS AND FILE MANAGEMENT

Taking the First Step

CASE STUDY | Rails and Trails

You are an administrative assistant for a local historical preservation project. The project involves creating a series of trails designed for hikers, bikers, and horseback riders. The trails generally follow the route of a historic railroad line that traversed the northwestern corner of Kentucky from the early 1900s until it was discontinued in 1991. The 78 miles of trails follow the original rail route, which passed through natural hardwood forests and open meadows. Considered a major impetus of the Kentucky Historical Preservation Society, the project has received both public and private funding through legislative appropriations and private and federal grants.

As the administrative assistant, you are responsible for overseeing the production of documents, spreadsheets, newspaper articles, and presentations that will be used to increase public awareness of the Rails and Trails project. Other clerical assistants who are familiar with Microsoft Office will prepare the promotional materials, and you will proofread, make necessary corrections, adjust page layouts, save and print documents, and identify appropriate templates to simplify tasks. Your experience with Microsoft Office 2010 is limited, but you know that certain fundamental tasks that are common to Word, Excel, and PowerPoint will help you accomplish your oversight task. You are excited to get started on the project!

OBJECTIVES AFTER YOU READ THIS CHAPTER, YOU WILL BE ABLE TO:

Files and Folders

If you stop to consider why you use a computer, you will most likely conclude that you want to produce some type of output. That output could be games, music, or the display of digital photographs. Perhaps you use a computer at work to produce reports, financial worksheets, or schedules. All of those items are considered computer ***files***. Files include electronic data such as documents, databases, slide shows, and worksheets. Even digital photographs, music, videos, and Web pages are saved as files.

Windows 7 provides tools that enable you to create folders and to save files in ways that make locating them simple.

A **file** is a document or item of information that you create with software and to which you give a name.

A **folder** is a named storage location where you can save files.

You use software to create and save files. For example, when you type a document on a computer, you first open a word processor such as Microsoft Word. Similarly, you could use a type of Web-authoring software to create a Web page. In order to access files later, you must save them to a computer storage medium such as a hard drive or flash drive. And just as you would probably organize a filing cabinet into a system of folders, you can organize storage media by ***folders*** that you name and into which you place data files. That way, you can easily retrieve the files later. Windows 7 provides tools that enable you to create folders and to save files in ways that make locating them simple. In this section, you will learn to use Windows Explorer to manage folders and files.

Using Windows Explorer

Windows Explorer is a Windows component that can be used to create and manage folders.

A **subfolder** is a folder that is housed within another folder.

Windows Explorer is a component that can be used to create and manage folders. The sole purpose of a computer folder is to provide a labeled storage location for related files so that you can easily organize and retrieve items. A folder structure can occur across several levels, so you can create folders within other folders (called ***subfolders***), arranged according to purpose. Windows 7 introduces the concept of libraries, which are folders that gather files from different locations and display the files as if they were all saved in a single folder, regardless of where they are physically stored. Using Windows Explorer, you can manage folders, work with libraries, and view favorites (areas or folders that are frequently accessed).

Understand and Customize the Interface

To open Windows Explorer, click Windows Explorer on the taskbar as shown in Figure 1.1. You can also right-click the Start button and click Open Windows Explorer. Figure 1.2 shows the Windows Explorer interface containing several areas. Some of those areas are described in Table 1.1.

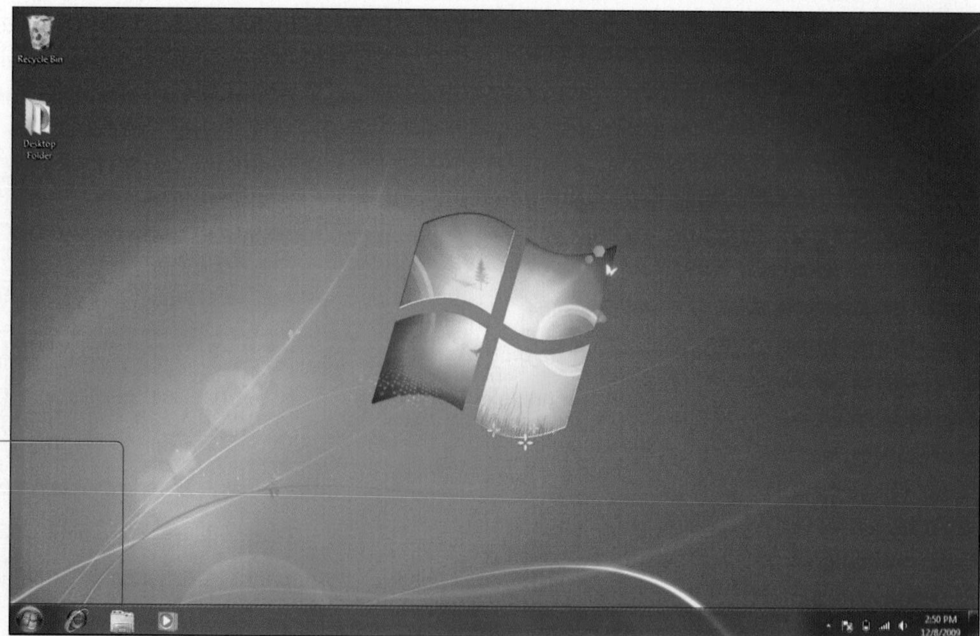

FIGURE 1.1 Windows Explorer Button ➤

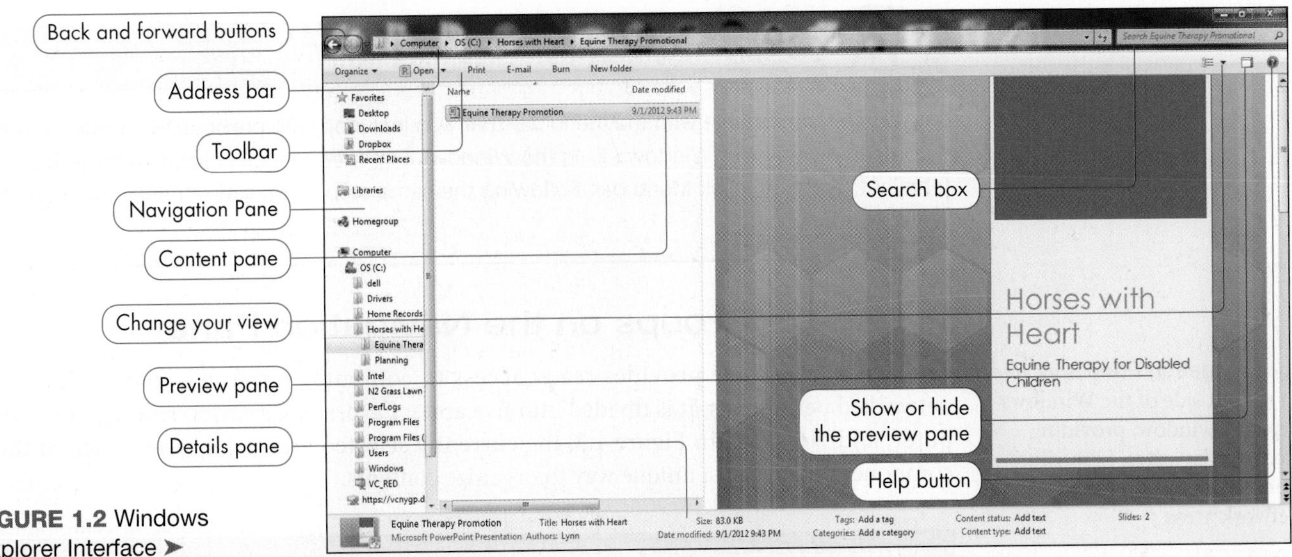

FIGURE 1.2 Windows Explorer Interface ➤

TABLE 1.1 Windows Explorer Interface	
Navigation Pane	The Navigation Pane contains five areas: Favorites, Libraries, Homegroup, Computer, and Network. Click an item in the Navigation Pane to display contents and to manage files that are housed within a selected folder.
Back and Forward Buttons	Use these buttons to visit previously opened folders or libraries.
Toolbar	The Toolbar includes buttons that are relevant to the currently selected item. If you are working with a music file, the toolbar buttons might include one for burning to a CD, whereas if you have selected a document, the toolbar would enable you to open or share the file.
Address Bar	The Address bar enables you to navigate to other folders or libraries.
Content Pane	The Content pane shows the contents of the currently selected folder or library.
Search Box	Find files and folders by typing descriptive text in the Search box. Windows immediately begins a search after you type the first character, further narrowing results as you type.
Details Pane	The Details pane shows properties that are associated with a selected file. Common properties include information such as the author name and the date the file was last modified.
Preview Pane	The Preview pane provides a snapshot of a selected file's contents. You can see file contents before actually opening the file. The Preview pane does not show the contents of a selected folder.

As you work with Windows Explorer, you might find that the view is not how you would like it. The file and folder icons might be too small for ease of identification, or you might want additional details about displayed files and folders. Modifying the view is easy. To make icons larger or to provide additional detail, click the Change your view arrow (see Figure 1.2), and select from the views provided. If you want additional detail, such as file type and size, click Details. You can also change the size of icons by selecting Small, Medium, Large, or Extra Large icons. The List view shows the file names without added detail, whereas Tiles and Content views are useful to show file thumbnails (small pictures describing file contents) and varying levels of detail regarding file locations. To show or hide Windows Explorer panes, click Organize (on the Toolbar), point to Layout, and then select the pane to hide or show. You can widen or narrow panes by dragging a border when the mouse changes to a double-headed arrow. When you click Show or hide the Preview pane, you toggle—or change between—views. If the Preview pane is not shown, clicking the button shows the pane. Conversely, if the pane is already open, clicking the button will hide it.

TIP Displaying the Windows Explorer Menu Bar

If you are comfortable with the menu bar that was included with previous Windows versions, you can display it in Windows 7. In the Windows Explorer window, click Organize. Point to Layout, and then click Menu bar. Following the same steps, you can remove a menu that is displayed.

Work with Groups on the Navigation Pane

The **Navigation Pane** is located on the left side of the Windows Explorer window, providing access to Favorites, Libraries, Homegroup, Computer, and Network areas.

The ***Navigation Pane*** provides ready access to computer resources, folders, files, and networked peripherals. It is divided into five areas: Favorites, Libraries, Homegroup, Computer, and Network. In Figure 1.3, the currently selected area is Libraries. Each of those components provides a unique way to organize contents.

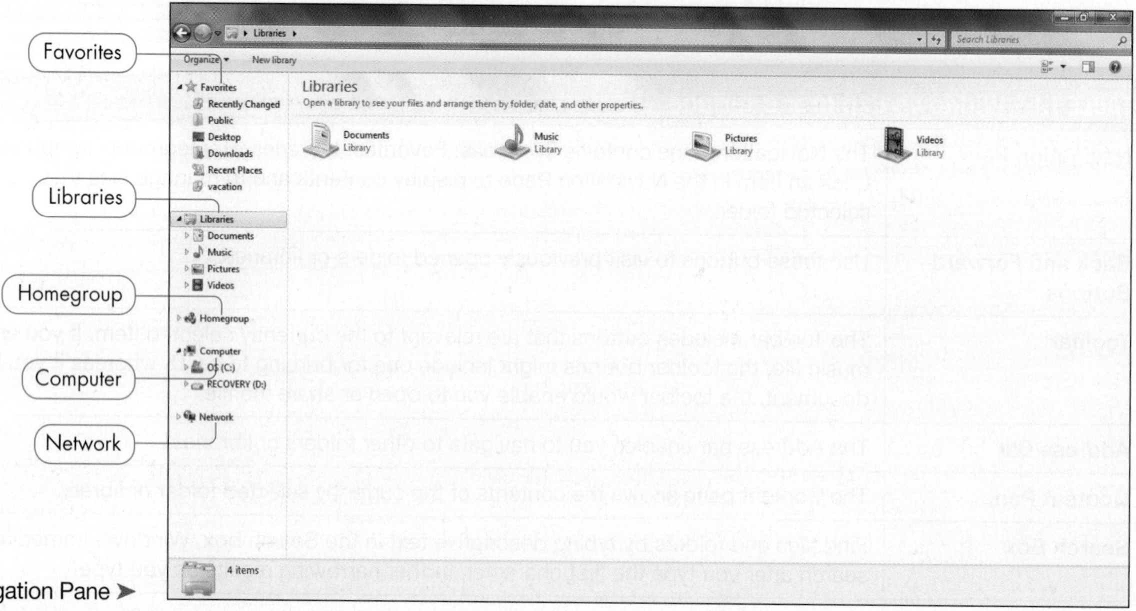

FIGURE 1.3 Navigation Pane ➤

A **library** is an organization method that collects files from different locations and displays them as one unit.

Earlier, we used the analogy of computer folders to folders in a filing cabinet. Just as you would title folders in a filing cabinet according to their contents, computer folders are also titled according to content. Folders are physically located on storage media such as a hard drive or flash drive. You can also organize folders into ***libraries***, which are collections of files from different locations that are displayed as single units. For example, the Pictures library includes files from the Pictures folder and from the Public Pictures folder, both of which are physically housed on the hard drive. Although the library content comes from two separate folders, contents are displayed as a unit.

Windows 7 includes several libraries that include default folders or devices. For example, the Documents library includes the My Documents and Public Documents folders, but you can add other folders if you wish so that they are also housed within the Documents library. To add a folder to a library, right-click the folder, and then point to Include in library. Then select a library, or select Create new library and create a new one. To remove a folder from a library, open Windows Explorer, and then click the library from which you want to remove the folder. In the Library pane shown at the right side of the Windows Explorer window, click the locations link (next to the word *Includes*). The link will indicate the number of physical locations in which the folders are housed. For example, if folders in the Pictures library are drawn from two locations, the link will read *2 locations*. Click the folder that you want to remove, click Remove, and then click OK.

The Computer area provides access to specific storage locations, such as a hard drive, CD/DVD, and removable media (including a flash drive). Files and folders housed on those storage media are accessible when you click Computer. For example, click drive C, shown under Computer in the Navigation Pane, to view its contents in the Content pane on the right. If you simply want to see the subfolders of the hard drive, click the arrow to the left of drive C to expand the view, showing all subfolders. Click the arrow again to collapse the view, removing subfolder detail. It is important to understand that clicking the arrow (as opposed to clicking the folder or area name) does not actually select an area or folder. It merely displays additional levels contained within the area. Clicking the folder or area, however, does select the item. Figure 1.4 illustrates the difference between clicking the area in the Navigation Pane and clicking the arrow to the left.

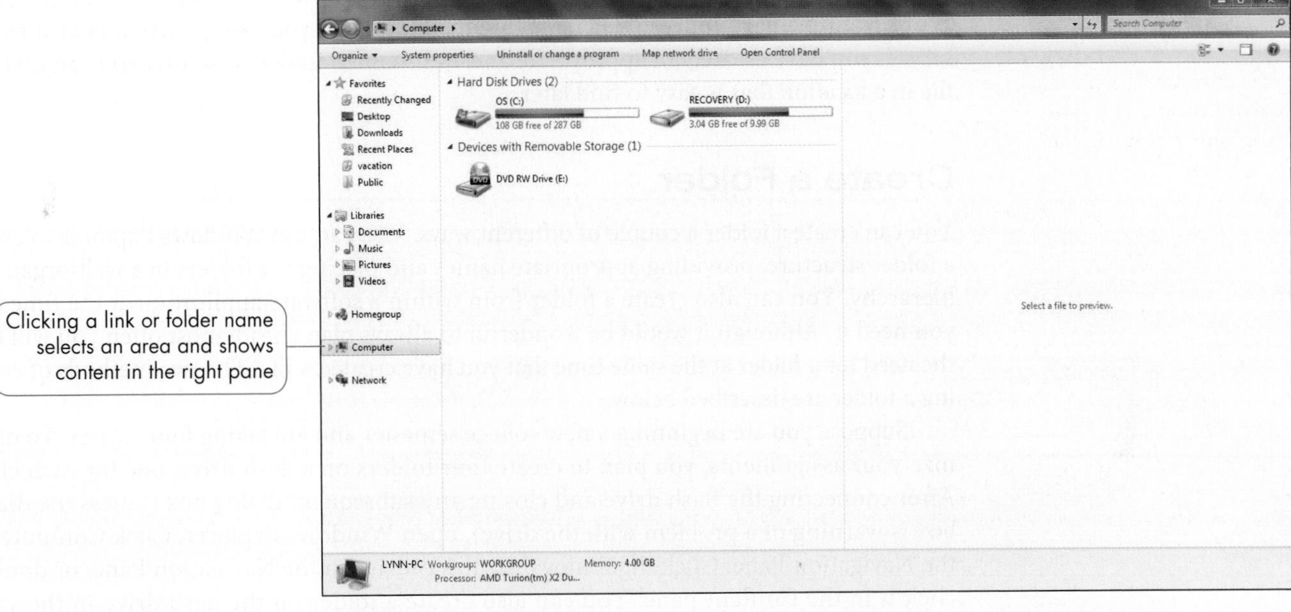

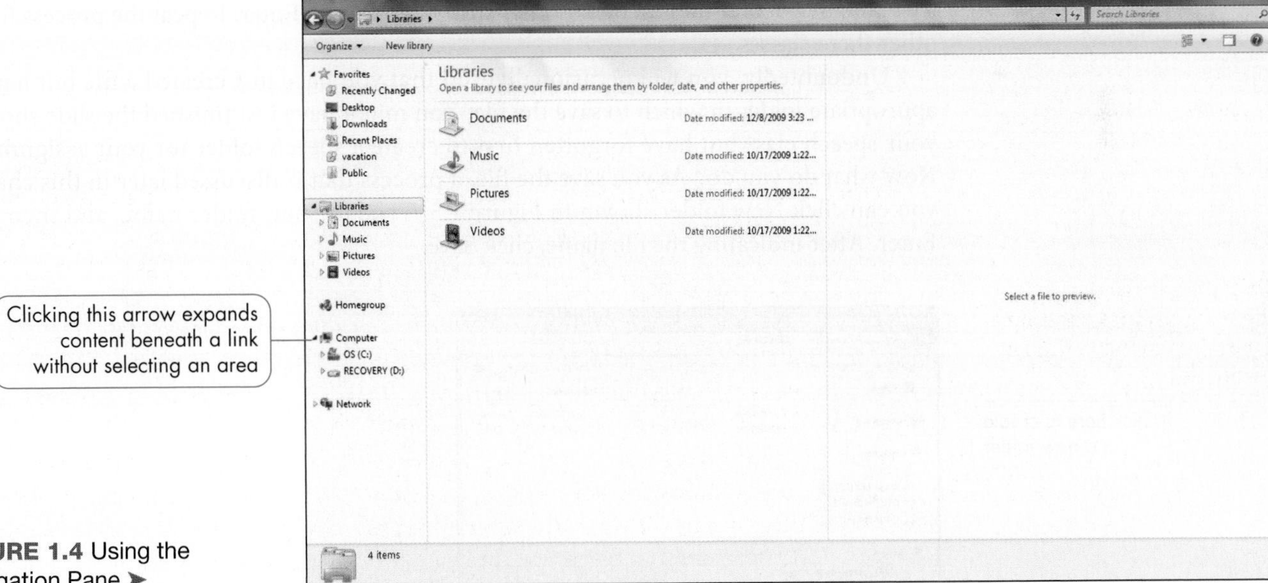

FIGURE 1.4 Using the Navigation Pane ➤

Click the drive in the Navigation Pane (or double-click the drive in the Content pane). Continue navigating through the folder structure until you find the folder that you seek. Double-click the folder (in the Content pane) or single-click the folder (in the Navigation Pane) to view its contents.

The Favorites area contains frequently accessed folders and recent searches. You can drag a folder, a saved search, a library, or a disk drive to the Favorites area. To remove a favorite, simply right-click the favorite, and then click Remove. You cannot add files or Web sites as favorites.

Homegroup is a Windows 7 feature that enables you to share resources on a home network. You can easily share music, pictures, videos, and libraries with other people in your home through a homegroup. It is password protected, so you do not have to worry about privacy.

Windows 7 makes creating a home network easy, sharing access to the Internet and peripheral devices such as printers and scanners. The Network area provides quick access to those devices, enabling you to see the contents of network computers.

Working with Folders and Files

As you work with software to create a file, such as when you type a report using Microsoft Word, your primary concern will be saving the file so that you can retrieve it later if necessary. If you have created an appropriate and well-named folder structure, you can save the file in a location that is easy to find later.

Create a Folder

You can create a folder a couple of different ways. You can use Windows Explorer to create a folder structure, providing appropriate names and placing the folders in a well-organized hierarchy. You can also create a folder from within a software application at the time that you need it. Although it would be wonderful to always plan ahead, most often you will find the need for a folder at the same time that you have created a file. The two methods of creating a folder are described below.

Suppose you are beginning a new college semester and are taking four classes. To organize your assignments, you plan to create four folders on a flash drive, one for each class. After connecting the flash drive and closing any subsequent dialog box (unless the dialog box is warning of a problem with the drive), open Windows Explorer. Click Computer in the Navigation Pane. Click the removable (flash) drive in the Navigation Pane, or double-click it in the Content pane. You can also create a folder on the hard drive in the same manner, clicking drive C instead of the removable drive. Click New folder on the Toolbar. Type the new folder name, such as English 101, and press Enter. Repeat the process for the other three classes.

Undoubtedly, you will occasionally find that you have just created a file but have no appropriate folder in which to save the file. You might have just finished the slide show for your speech class but have forgotten first to create a speech folder for your assignments. Now what do you do? As you save the file, a process that is discussed later in this chapter, you can click New folder shown in Figure 1.5. Type the new folder name, and then press Enter. After indicating the file name, click Save.

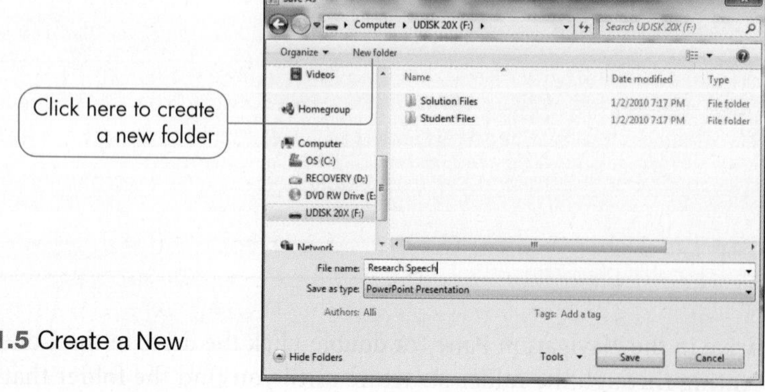

FIGURE 1.5 Create a New Folder ➤

TIP Working with the Address Bar

As you manage folders and work with files in Windows Explorer, keep a close eye on the Address bar (shown in Figure 1.2). It will always inform you of the current drive or folder, which is a very important detail. For example, if you have created a folder titled Summer Semester, and you want to create a subfolder for each class that you plan to take during the semester, you will want to be sure the Summer Semester folder is selected before creating the subfolders. If the Address bar does not show the correct folder, you should select the correct folder in the Navigation Pane before proceeding.

Open, Rename, and Delete Folders and Files

You have learned that folders can be created in Windows Explorer but that files must be created in other ways, such as within a software package. Although Windows Explorer cannot create files, you can use it to open, rename, and delete files just as you use it for folders.

Using the Navigation Pane, you can locate and select a folder containing a file that you want to open. For example, you will want to open the speech slide show so that you can practice before giving the presentation to the class. Open Windows Explorer, and navigate to the speech folder on your removable drive (flash drive). The file will display in the right pane. Double-click the file. The program that is associated with the file will open the file. For example, if you used PowerPoint to create the slide show, then PowerPoint will open the file. To open a folder and display the contents, just single-click the folder in the Navigation Pane or double-click it in the Content pane.

At times, you may find a more suitable name for a file or folder than the one that you originally gave it. Or perhaps you made a typographical mistake when you entered the name. In these situations, you should rename the file or folder. In Windows Explorer, move through the folder structure to find the folder or file. Right-click the name, and then click Rename. Type the new name, and then press Enter. You can also rename an item when you click the name twice, but much more slowly than a double-click. Type the new name, and then press Enter. Finally, you can click a file or folder once to select it, click Organize, click Rename, type the new name, and then press Enter.

TIP Renaming Several Files at Once

Suppose you are collecting digital photos that you took during a recent trip to Las Vegas. The camera gives the photo files very cryptic names, so you want to give them names that will identify them as Las Vegas photos. You can rename all the files at once. In Windows Explorer, select all of the files. To do so, click the first file, hold down Shift, and then click the last file in the list. Right-click any selected file, click Rename, and then type a new name—perhaps *Las Vegas*. Press Enter. All files will be saved with the new name and a different sequential number. Your photos will be named *Las Vegas (1)*, *Las Vegas (2)*, and so forth.

It is much easier to delete a folder or file than it is to recover it if you remove it by mistake. Therefore, be very careful when deleting items so that you are sure of your intentions before proceeding. When you delete a folder, all subfolders and all files within the folder are also removed. If you are certain you want to remove a folder or file, the process is simple. Right-click the item, click Delete, and then click Yes if asked to confirm removal to the Recycle Bin. Items are only placed in the Recycle Bin if you are deleting them from a hard drive. Files and folders deleted from a removable storage medium, such as a flash drive, are permanently deleted, with no easy method of retrieval. You can also delete an item (file or folder) when you click to select the item, click Organize, and then click Delete.

Save a File

As you create or modify a project such as a document, presentation, or worksheet, your work is placed in RAM, which is the computer's temporary memory. When you shut down the computer or inadvertently lose electrical power, the contents of RAM are erased. Even with a loss of electrical power, however, RAM on a laptop will not be erased until the battery runs down. Because you will most likely want to continue the project at another time or keep it for later reference, you need to save it to a storage medium such as a hard drive, CD, or flash drive. When you save a file, you will be working within a software package. Therefore, you must follow the procedure dictated by that software to save the file. Thankfully, most software requires that you save files in a similar fashion, so you can usually find your way through the process fairly quickly.

The first time that you save a file, you must indicate where the file should be saved, and you must assign a file name. Of course, you will want to save the file in an appropriately named folder so that you can find it easily later. Thereafter, you can quickly save the file with the same settings, or you can change one or more of those settings, perhaps saving the file to a different storage device as a backup copy. Figure 1.6 shows a typical Save As dialog box that enables you to confirm or change settings before finally saving the file.

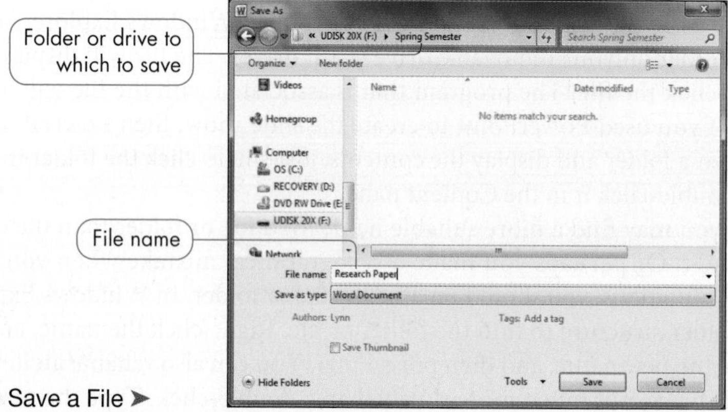

FIGURE 1.6 Save a File ➤

Selecting, Copying, and Moving Multiple Files and Folders

You will want to select folders and files when you need to rename, delete, copy, or paste them, or open files and folders so that you can view the contents. Single-click a file or folder to *select* it; double-click a file or folder (in the Content pane) to *open* it. To apply an operation to several files at once, such as deleting or moving them, you will want to select all of them.

Select Multiple Files and Folders

You can select several files and folders, regardless of whether they are adjacent to each other in the file list. Suppose that your digital pictures are contained in the Pictures folder. You might want to delete some of the pictures because you want to clear up some hard drive space. To select pictures in the Pictures folder, open Windows Explorer, and then click the Pictures library. Locate the desired pictures in the Content pane. To select the adjacent pictures, select the first picture, press and hold Shift, and then click the last picture. All pictures will be highlighted, indicating that they are selected. At that point, you can delete, copy, move, or rename the selected pictures.

If the files or folders to be selected are not adjacent, click the first item. Press and hold Ctrl while you click all files or folders, releasing Ctrl only when you have finished.

To select all items in a folder or disk, use Windows Explorer to navigate to the desired folder. Open the folder, press and hold Ctrl, and press A on the keyboard. You can also click Organize, and then Select All to select all items.

TIP Using a Check Box to Select Items

In Windows 7, it is easy to make multiple selections, even if the items are not adjacent. Open Windows Explorer, and then change the view to Details. Click Organize, and then select Folder and search options. The Folder Options dialog box opens. Click the View tab, scroll down in the Advanced settings box, click Use check boxes to select items (see Figure 1.7), and then click OK. As you move the mouse pointer along the left side of files and folders, a check box appears. Click in the check box to select the file. If you want to quickly select all items in the folder, click the check box that appears in the Name column.

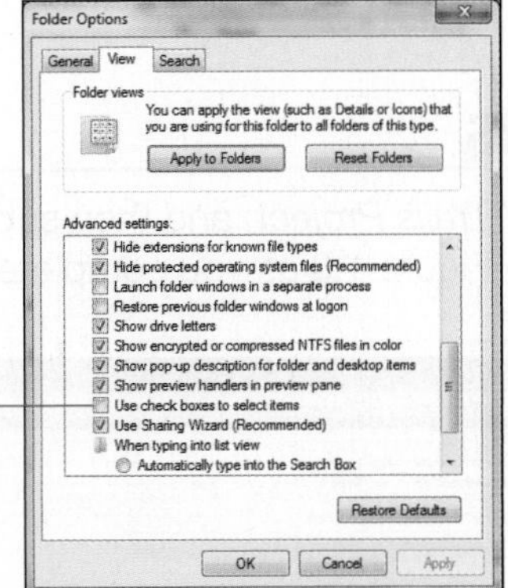

FIGURE 1.7 Use Check Boxes to Select Items ➤

Copy and Move Files and Folders

A **backup** is a copy of a file, usually on another storage medium.

When you copy or move a folder, you move both the folder and any files that it contains. You can move or copy a folder or file to another location on the same drive or to another drive. If your purpose is to make a ***backup*** copy of an important file or folder, you will probably want to copy it to another drive.

To move or copy an item in Windows Explorer, select the item. If you want to copy or move multiple items, follow the directions in the previous section to select them all at once. Right-click the item(s), and select either Cut or Copy on the shortcut menu. In the Navigation Pane, locate the destination drive or folder, right-click the destination drive or folder, and then click Paste.

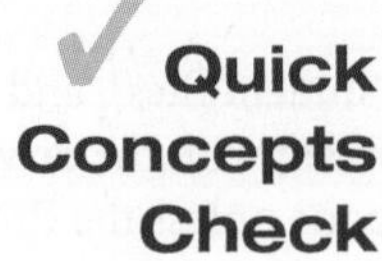

Quick Concepts Check

1. The Navigation Pane in Windows Explorer contains five major areas. Name and briefly describe each area.
2. If the Preview pane is open, it shows the contents of a selected file. When might it be helpful to see a file preview and when might it not be beneficial?
3. A library is not actually a folder, although it does help organize files. How does a library differ from a folder?
4. After creating a file, such as a Word document, you will most likely want to save it. However, as you begin to save the file, you realize that you have not yet created a folder in which to place the file. Is it possible to create a folder as you are saving the file? If so, how?
5. You want to delete several files, but the files are not consecutively listed in Windows Explorer. How would you select and delete them? What should you consider when deleting files or folders from a removable storage medium such as a flash drive?

HANDS-ON EXERCISES

1 Files and Folders

You will soon begin to collect files from volunteers who are preparing promotional and record-keeping material for the Rails and Trails project. It is important that you save the files in appropriately named folders so that you can easily access them later. Therefore, you plan to create folders. You can create folders on a flash drive or a hard drive. You will select the drive on which you plan to save your student files. As you create a short document, you will save it in one of the folders. You will then make a backup copy of the folder structure, including all files, so that you do not run the risk of losing the material if the drive is damaged or misplaced.

Skills covered: Create Folders and Subfolders • Create and Save a File • Rename and Delete a Folder • Open and Copy a File

STEP 1 CREATE FOLDERS AND SUBFOLDERS

You decide to create a folder titled *Rails and Trails Project*, and then subdivide it into subfolders that will help categorize the project files. Refer to Figure 1.8 as you complete Step 1.

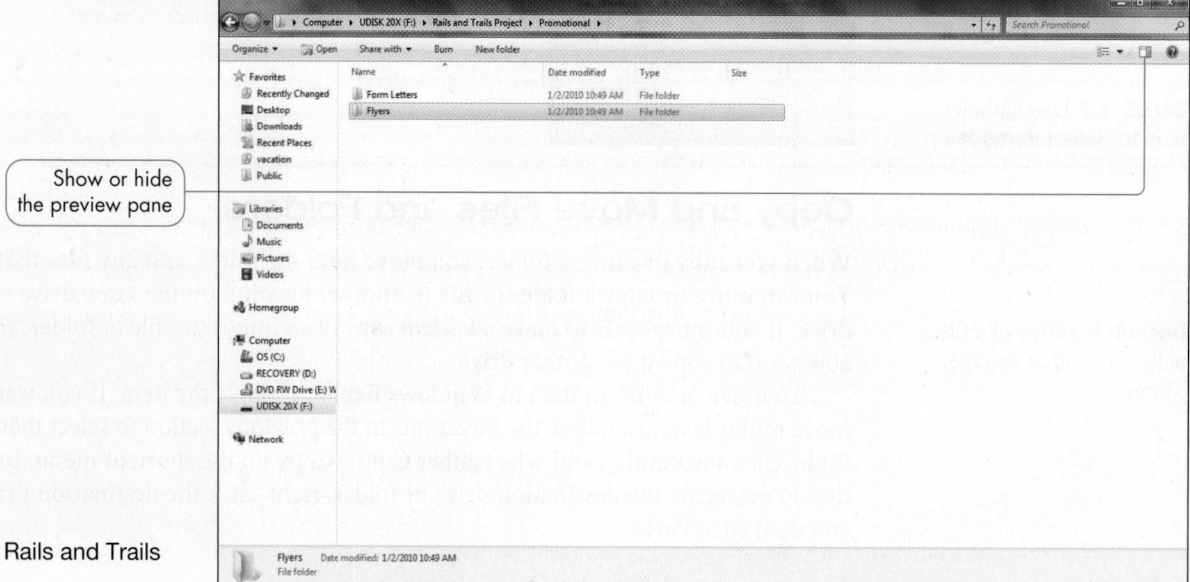

FIGURE 1.8 Rails and Trails Folders ➤

a. Insert your flash drive (if you are using a flash drive for your student files), and close any dialog box that opens (unless it is informing you of a problem with the drive). Click **Windows Explorer** on the taskbar. Click **Show the preview pane** unless the Preview pane is already displayed.

   The removable drive shown in Figure 1.8 is titled UDISK 20X (F:), describing the drive manufacturer and the drive letter. Your removable drive will be designated in a different manner, perhaps also identified by manufacturer. The drive letter identifying your flash drive is likely to be different because the configuration of disk drives on your computer is unique.

   TROUBLESHOOTING: If you do not have a flash drive, you can use the hard drive. In the next step, simply click drive C in the Navigation Pane instead of the removable drive.

b. Click the removable drive in the Navigation Pane (or click **drive C** if you are using the hard drive). Click **New folder** on the Toolbar, type **Rails and Trails Project**, and then press **Enter**.

   You create a folder where you can organize subfolders and files for the Rails and Trails project.

TROUBLESHOOTING: If the folder you create is called *New folder* instead of *Rails and Trails Project*, you probably clicked away from the folder before typing the name, so that it received the default name. To rename it, right-click the folder, click Rename, type the correct name, and then press Enter.

c. Double-click **Rails and Trails Project** in the Content pane (middle pane). The Address bar should show that it is the currently selected folder. Click **New folder**, type **Promotional**, and then press **Enter**.

You decide to create subfolders of the Rails and Trails Project folder to contain promotional material, presentations, and office records. You create three subfolders, appropriately named.

d. Check the Address bar to make sure *Rails and Trails Project* is still the current folder. Click **New folder**, type **Presentations**, and then press **Enter**.

e. Click **New folder**, type **Office Records**, and then press **Enter**.

f. Double-click **Promotional** in the middle pane. Click **New folder**, type **Form Letters**, and then press **Enter**. Click **New folder**, type **Flyers**, and then press **Enter**.

To subdivide the promotional material further, you create two subfolders, one to hold form letters and one to contain flyers. Your screen should appear as in Figure 1.8.

g. Close Windows Explorer.

STEP 2 CREATE AND SAVE A FILE

As the project gears up, you assign volunteers to take care of certain tasks. After creating an Excel worksheet listing those responsibilities, you will save it in the Office Records folder. Refer to Figure 1.9 as you complete Step 2.

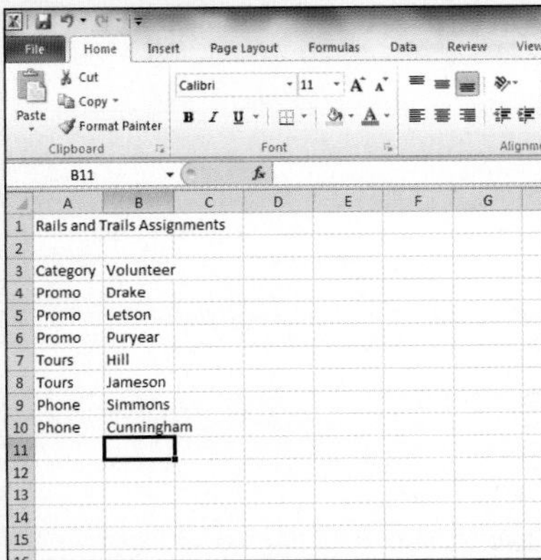

FIGURE 1.9 Volunteers Worksheet ➤

a. Click the **Start button**, and then point to **All Programs**. Scroll down the program list, if necessary, and then click **Microsoft Office**. Click **Microsoft Excel 2010**.

You use Microsoft Excel to create the volunteers worksheet.

b. Type **Rails and Trails Assignments** in **cell A1**. Press **Enter** twice.

Your cursor will be in cell A3.

c. Type **Category**. Press **Tab** to move the cursor one cell to the right, and then type **Volunteer**. Press **Enter**. Complete the remaining cells of the worksheet as shown in Figure 1.9.

TROUBLESHOOTING: If you make a mistake, click in the cell and retype the entry.

d. Click the **File tab** (in the top-left corner of the Excel window). Click **Save**.

The Save As dialog box displays. The Save As dialog box is where you determine the location, file name, and file type of any document. You can also create a new folder in the Save As dialog box.

e. Scroll down if necessary, and then click **Computer** in the left pane. In the Content pane, double-click the drive where you will save the file. Double-click **Rails and Trails Project** in the Content pane. Double-click **Office Records**. Click in the **File name box**. Type **f01h1volunteers_LastnameFirstname** in the **file name box**, replacing *LastnameFirstname* with your own last name and first name. Click **Save**.

The file is now saved as *f01h1volunteers_LastnameFirstname*. You can check the title bar of the workbook to confirm the file has been saved with the correct name.

f. Click the **Close button** in the top-right corner of the Excel window to close Excel.

> **TROUBLESHOOTING:** If you click the lower X instead of the one in the top-right corner, the current Excel worksheet will close, but Excel will remain open. In that case, click the remaining X to close Excel.

The Volunteers workbook is saved in the Office Records subfolder of the Rails and Trails Project folder.

STEP 3 RENAME AND DELETE A FOLDER

As often happens, you find that the folder structure is not exactly what you need. You will remove the Flyers folder and the Form Letters folder and will rename the Promotional folder to better describe the contents. Refer to Figure 1.10 as you complete Step 3.

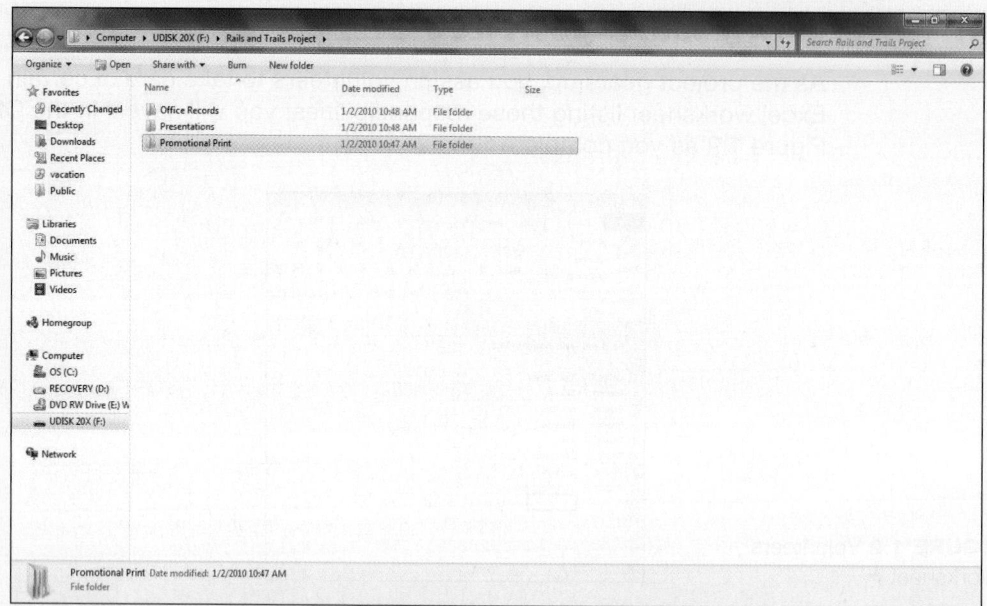

FIGURE 1.10 Rails and Trails Project Folder Structure ➤

a. Right-click the **Start button**. Click **Open Windows Explorer**. Click the disk drive where you save your files (under Computer in the Navigation Pane). Double-click **Rails and Trails Project** in the Content pane.

b. Click the **Promotional folder** to select it.

> **TROUBLESHOOTING:** If you double-click the folder instead of using a single-click, the folder will open and you will see its title in the Address bar. To return to the correct view, click Rails and Trails Project in the Address bar.

c. Click **Organize**, click **Rename**, type **Promotional Print**, and then press **Enter**.

Since the folder will be used to organize all of the printed promotional material, you decide to rename the folder to better reflect the contents.

d. Double-click **Promotional Print**. Click **Flyers**. Hold down **Shift**, and then click **Form Letters**. Both folders should be selected (highlighted). Right-click either folder, and then click **Delete**. If asked to confirm the deletion, click **Yes**. Click **Rails and Trails Project** in the **Address bar**. Your screen should appear as shown in Figure 1.10. Leave Windows Explorer open for the next step.

You decide that dividing the promotional material into flyers and form letters is not necessary, so you delete both folders.

STEP 4 OPEN AND COPY A FILE

You hope to recruit more volunteers to work with the Rails and Trails project. The Volunteers worksheet will be a handy way to keep up with people and assignments, and as the list grows, knowing exactly where the file is saved will be important for easy access. You will modify the Volunteers worksheet and then make a backup copy of the folder hierarchy. Refer to Figure 1.11 as you complete Step 4.

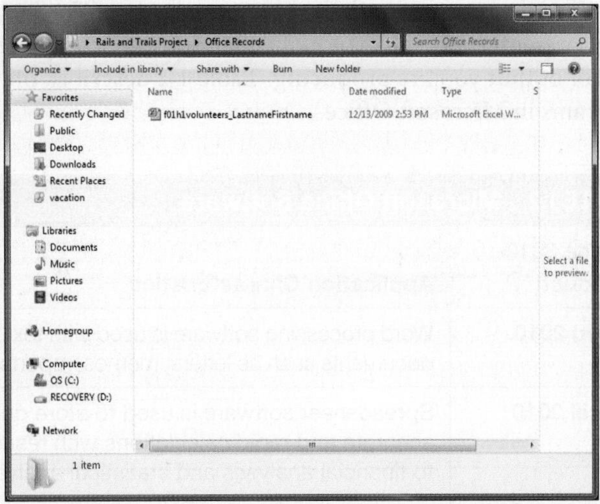

FIGURE 1.11 Rails and Trails Folder Structure ➤

a. Double-click the **Office Records folder**. Double-click *f01h1volunteers_LastnameFirstname.*

Because the file was created with Excel, that program opens, and the volunteers worksheet is displayed.

b. Click **cell A11**, and then type **Office**. Press **Tab**, type **Adams**, and then press **Enter**. Click the **File tab** in the top-left corner of the Excel window, and then click **Save**. The file is automatically saved in the same location with the same file name as before. Close Excel.

A neighbor, Samantha Adams, has volunteered to help in the office. You record that information on the worksheet and save the updated file in the Office Records folder.

c. Click the location where you save files in the Navigation Pane in Windows Explorer. Right-click **Rails and Trails Project** in the right pane. Click **Copy**.

d. Right-click **Desktop** in the Favorites group on the Navigation Pane, and then click **Paste**. Close Windows Explorer. If any other windows are open, close them also.

You make a copy of the Rails and Trails Project folder on the desktop.

e. Double-click **Rails and Trails Project** on the desktop. Double-click **Office Records**. Is the volunteers worksheet in the folder? Your screen should appear as shown in Figure 1.11. Close Windows Explorer.

f. Right-click the **Rails and Trails Project folder** on the desktop, click **Delete**, and then click **Yes** when asked to confirm the deletion.

You delete the Rails and Trails Project folder from the desktop of the computer because you may be working in a computer lab and want to leave the computer as you found it.

Microsoft Office Software

Organizations around the world rely heavily on ***Microsoft Office*** software to produce documents, spreadsheets, presentations, and databases. Microsoft Office is a productivity software suite including four primary software components, each one specializing in a particular type of output. You can use ***Word*** to produce all sorts of documents, including memos, newsletters, forms, tables, and brochures. ***Excel*** makes it easy to organize records, financial transactions, and business information in the form of worksheets. With ***PowerPoint***, you can create dynamic presentations to inform groups and persuade audiences. ***Access*** is relational database software that enables you to record and link data, query databases, and create forms and reports. You will sometimes find that you need to use two or more Office applications to produce your intended output. You might, for example, find that a Word document you are preparing for your investment club should also include a summary of stock performance. You can use Excel to prepare the summary and then incorporate the worksheet in the Word document. Similarly, you can integrate Word tables and Excel charts in a PowerPoint presentation. The choice of which software component to use really depends on what type of output you are producing. Table 1.2 describes the major tasks of the four primary programs in Microsoft Office.

Microsoft Office is a productivity software suite including four primary software components, each one specializing in a particular type of output.

Microsoft Office is a productivity software suite that includes word processing, spreadsheet, presentation, and database software components.

Word is a word processing program included in Microsoft Office.

Excel is software that specializes in organizing data in worksheet form. It is included in Microsoft Office.

PowerPoint is a Microsoft Office software component that enables you to prepare slideshow presentations for audiences.

Access is a database program included in Microsoft Office.

TABLE 1.2 Microsoft Office Software

Office 2010 Product	Application Characteristics
Word 2010	Word processing software is used with text to create, edit, and format documents such as letters, memos, reports, brochures, resumes, and flyers.
Excel 2010	Spreadsheet software is used to store quantitative data and to perform accurate and rapid calculations with results ranging from simple budgets to financial analyses and statistical analyses.
PowerPoint 2010	Presentation graphics software is used to create slide shows for presentation by a speaker, to be published as part of a Web site, or to run as a stand-alone application on a computer kiosk.
Access 2010	Relational database software is used to store data and convert it into information. Database software is used primarily for decision-making by businesses that compile data from multiple records stored in tables to produce informative reports.

As you become familiar with Microsoft Office, you will find that although each software component produces a specific type of output, all components share common features. Such commonality gives a similar feel to each software application so that learning and working with primary Microsoft Office software products is easy. In this section, you will identify features common to Microsoft Office software, including such interface components as the Ribbon, Backstage view, and the Quick Access Toolbar. You will also learn how to get help with an application.

Identifying Common Interface Components

A **user interface** is a collection of onscreen components that facilitates communication between the software and the user.

As you work with Microsoft Office, you will find that each application shares a similar ***user interface***. The user interface is the screen display through which you communicate with the software. Word, Excel, PowerPoint, and Access share common interface elements, as shown in Figure 1.12. As you can imagine, becoming familiar with one application's interface makes it that much easier to work with other Office software.

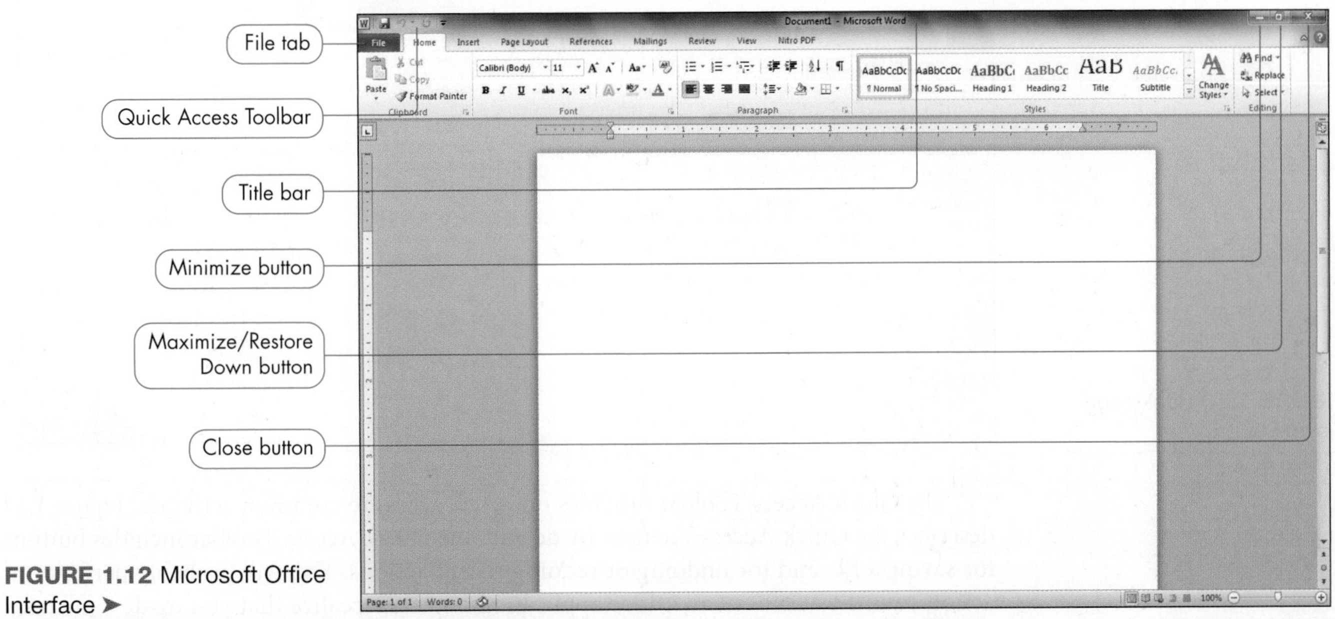

FIGURE 1.12 Microsoft Office Interface ➤

Use the Backstage View and the Quick Access Toolbar

The ***Backstage view*** is a new component of Office 2010 that provides a concise collection of commands related to an open file. Using the Backstage view, you can print, save, open, close, and share a file. In addition, you can view properties and other information related to the file. A file's properties include the author, file size, permissions, and date modified. You can access the Backstage view by clicking the File tab. The ***Quick Access Toolbar***, located at the top-left corner of the Office window, provides handy access to commonly executed tasks such as saving a file and undoing recent actions. The ***title bar*** identifies the current file name and the application in which you are working. It also includes control buttons that enable you to minimize, maximize, restore down, or close the application window. Refer to Figure 1.12 for the location of those items on the title bar.

Using the Backstage view, you can print, save, open, close, and share a file.

The **Backstage view** displays when you click the File tab. It includes commands related to common file activities and provides information on an open file.

The **Quick Access Toolbar** provides one-click access to commonly used commands.

The **title bar** contains the current file name, Office application, and control buttons.

When you click the File tab, you will see the Backstage view, as shown in Figure 1.13. Primarily focusing on file activities such as opening, closing, saving, printing, and beginning new files, the Backstage view also includes options for customizing program settings, getting help, and exiting the program. It displays a file's properties, providing important information on file permission and sharing options. When you click the File tab, the Backstage view will occupy the entire application window, hiding the file with which you might be working. For example, suppose that as you are typing a report you need to check the document's properties. Click the File tab to display a Backstage view similar to that shown in Figure 1.13. You can return to the application—in this case, Word—in a couple of ways. Simply click the File tab again (or any other tab on the Ribbon). Alternatively, you can press Esc on the keyboard. The Ribbon is described in the next section.

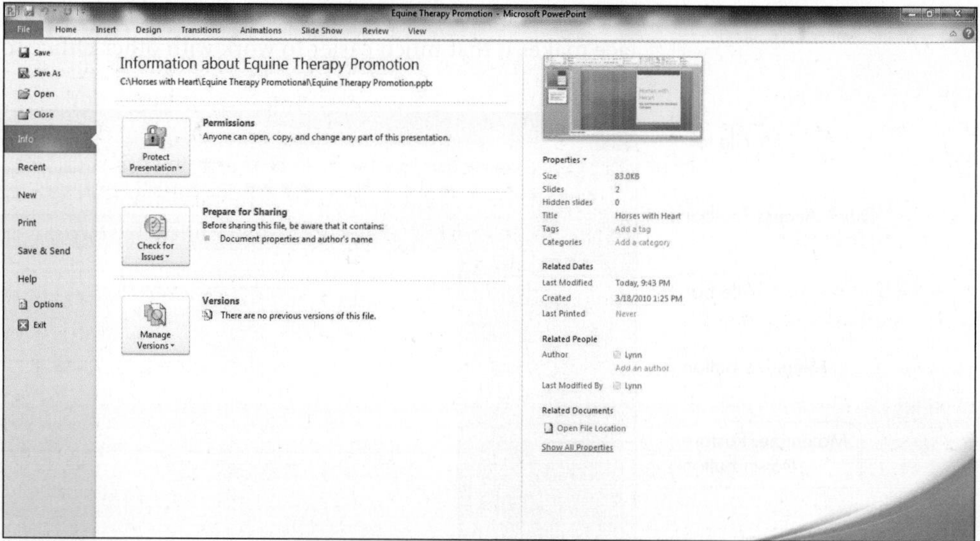

FIGURE 1.13 Backstage View ➤

The Quick Access Toolbar provides one-click access to common activities. Figure 1.14 describes the Quick Access Toolbar. By default, the Quick Access Toolbar includes buttons for saving a file and for undoing or redoing recent actions. You will probably perform an action countless times in an Office application and then realize that you made a mistake. You can recover from the mistake by clicking Undo on the Quick Access Toolbar. If you click the arrow beside Undo, you can select from a list of previous actions in order of occurrence. The Undo list is not maintained when you close a file or exit the application, so you can only erase an action that took place during the current Office session. Similar to Undo, you can also Redo (or Replace) an action that you have just undone. You can customize the Quick Access Toolbar to include buttons for frequently used commands such as printing or opening files. Because the Quick Access Toolbar is onscreen at all times, the most commonly accessed tasks are just a click away.

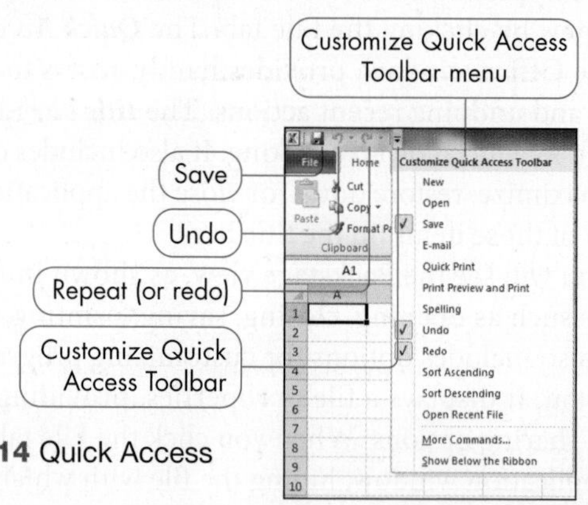

FIGURE 1.14 Quick Access Toolbar ➤

TIP Customizing the Quick Access Toolbar

To customize the Quick Access Toolbar, click Customize Quick Access Toolbar, as shown in Figure 1.14, and select from a list of commands. If a command that you want to include on the toolbar is not on the list, you can simply right-click the command on the Ribbon, and then click Add to Quick Access Toolbar. Similarly, remove a command from the Quick Access Toolbar by right-clicking the icon on the Quick Access Toolbar, and then clicking Remove from Quick Access Toolbar. If you want to display the Quick Access Toolbar beneath the Ribbon, click Customize Quick Access Toolbar (Figure 1.14), and then click Show Below the Ribbon.

Familiarize Yourself with the Ribbon

The **Ribbon** is the long bar of tabs, groups, and commands located just beneath the Title bar.

Each **tab** on the Ribbon contains groups of related tasks.

A **group** is a subset of a tab that organizes similar tasks together.

A **command** is a button or area within a group that you click to perform tasks.

The ***Ribbon*** is the command center of Office applications. It is the long bar located just beneath the Title bar, containing tabs, groups, and commands. Each ***tab*** is designed to appear much like a tab on a file folder, with the active tab highlighted. The File tab is always a darker shade than the other tabs, and a different color depending on the application. Remember that clicking the File tab opens the Backstage view. Other tabs on the Ribbon enable you to create and modify a file. The active tab in Figure 1.15 is the Home tab.

When you click a tab, the Ribbon displays several task-oriented ***groups***, with each group containing related ***commands***. Microsoft Office is designed to provide the most functionality possible with the fewest clicks. For that reason, the Home tab, displayed when you first open an Office software application, contains groups and commands that are commonly used. For example, because you will often want to change the way text is displayed, the Home tab in each Office application includes a Font group with activities related to modifying text. Similarly, other tabs contain groups of related actions, or commands, many of which are unique to the particular Office application.

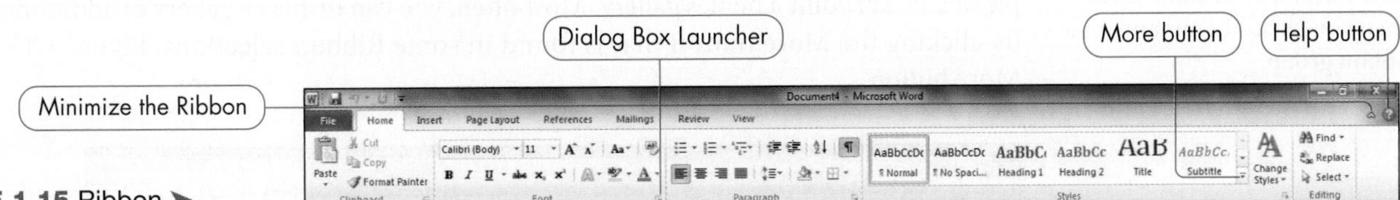

FIGURE 1.15 Ribbon ➤

Because Word, PowerPoint, Excel, and Access all share a similar Ribbon structure, you will be able to move at ease among those applications. Although the specific tabs, groups, and commands vary among the Office programs, the way in which you use the Ribbon and the descriptive nature of tab titles is the same regardless of which program you are working with. For example, if you want to insert a chart in Excel, a header in Word, or a shape in PowerPoint, you will click the Insert tab in any of those programs. The first thing that you should do as you begin to work with an Office application is to study the Ribbon. Take a look at all tabs and their contents. That way, you will have a good idea of where to find specific commands and how the Ribbon with which you are currently working differs from one that you might have used previously in another application.

Because Word, PowerPoint, Excel, and Access all share a similar Ribbon structure, you will be able to move at ease among those applications.

TIP Hiding the Ribbon

The Ribbon occupies a good bit of space at the top of the Office interface. If you are working with a large project, you might want to maximize your workspace by temporarily hiding the Ribbon. You can hide the Ribbon in several ways. Double-click the active tab to hide the Ribbon, and then double-click any tab to redisplay it. Alternatively, you can press Ctrl+F1 to hide the Ribbon, with the same shortcut key combination redisplaying it. Finally, you can click Minimize the Ribbon (see Figure 1.15), located at the right side of the Ribbon, clicking it a second time to redisplay the Ribbon.

A **dialog box** is a window that enables you to make selections or indicate settings beyond those provided on the Ribbon.

A **Dialog Box Launcher** is an icon in Ribbon groups that you can click to open a related dialog box. It is not found in all groups.

The Ribbon provides quick access to common activities such as changing number or text formats or aligning data or text. Some actions, however, are not so common but are related to commands displayed on the Ribbon. For example, you might want to change the background of a PowerPoint slide to include a picture. In that case, you will need to work with a ***dialog box*** that provides access to more precise, but less frequently used, commands. Figure 1.16 shows a dialog box. Some commands display a dialog box when they are clicked. Other Ribbon groups include a ***Dialog Box Launcher*** that, when clicked, opens a corresponding dialog box. Figure 1.15 shows a Dialog Box Launcher.

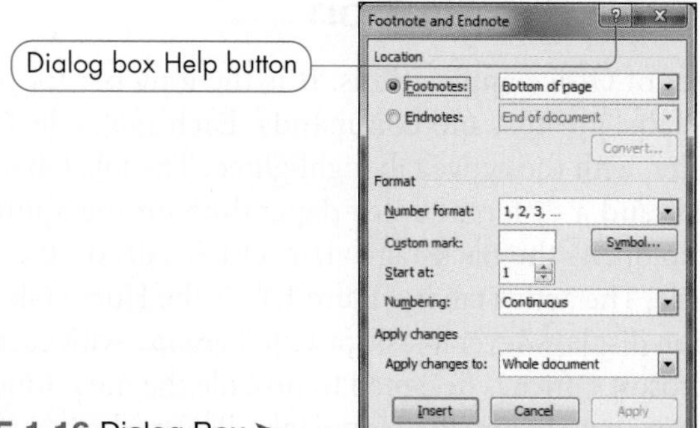

FIGURE 1.16 Dialog Box ➤

A **gallery** is a set of selections that appears when you click a More button, or in some cases when you click a command, in a Ribbon group.

The Ribbon contains many selections and commands, but some selections are too numerous to include in the Ribbon's limited space. For example, Word provides far more text styles than it can easily display at once, so additional styles are available in a ***gallery***. A gallery also provides a choice of Excel chart styles and PowerPoint transitions. Figure 1.17 gives an example of a PowerPoint Themes gallery. Most often, you can display a gallery of additional choices by clicking the More button that is found in some Ribbon selections. Figure 1.15 shows a More button.

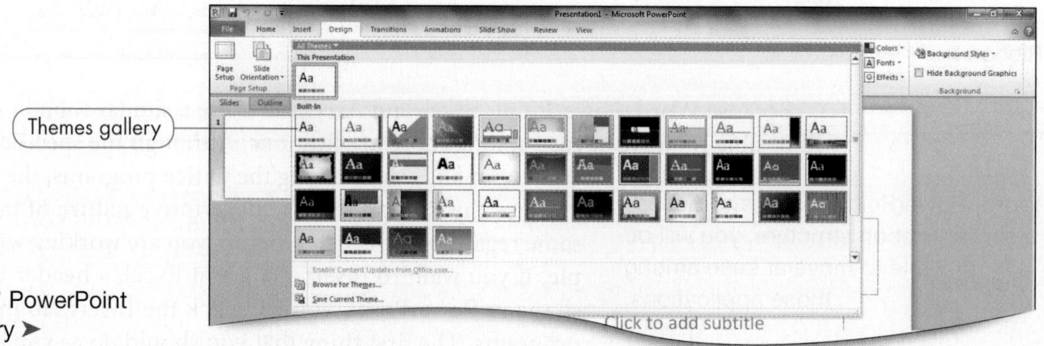

FIGURE 1.17 PowerPoint Themes Gallery ➤

When editing a document, worksheet, or presentation, it is helpful to see the results of formatting changes before you make final selections. You might be considering changing the font color of a selection in a document or worksheet. As you place the mouse pointer over a color selection in a Ribbon gallery or group, the selected text will temporarily display the color to which you are pointing. Similarly, you can get a preview of how color designs would appear on PowerPoint slides by pointing to specific themes in the PowerPoint Themes group and noting the effect on a displayed slide. When you click the item, such as the font color, the selection is applied. The feature enabling a preview of the results of a selection is called ***Live Preview***. It is available in various Ribbon selections among the Office applications.

Live Preview is an Office feature that provides a preview of the results of a selection when you point to an option in a list. Using Live Preview, you can experiment with settings before making a final choice.

Office applications make it easy for you to work with objects such as pictures, clip art, shapes, charts, and tables. When you include such objects in a project, they are considered separate components that you can manage independently. To work with an object, you must click to select it. When you select an object, the Ribbon is modified to include one or more ***contextual tabs*** containing groups of commands related to the selected object. Figure 1.18 shows a contextual tab related to a selected object in a Word document. When you click outside the selected object, the contextual tab disappears.

A **contextual tab** is a Ribbon tab that displays when an object, such as a picture or clip art, is selected. A contextual tab contains groups and commands specific to the selected object.

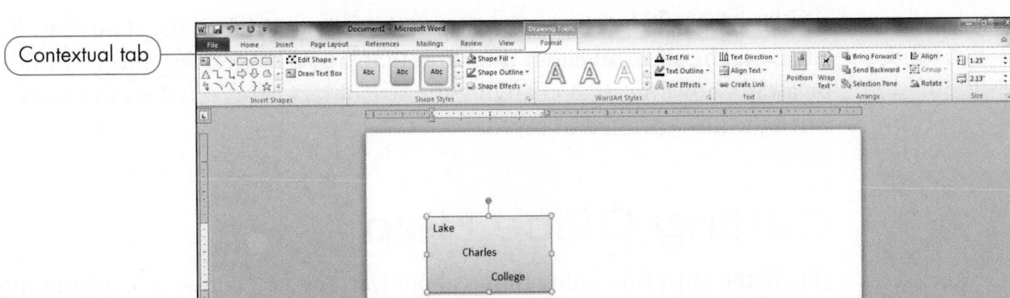

FIGURE 1.18 Contextual Tab ➤

TIP Using Keyboard Shortcuts

You might find that you prefer to use keyboard shortcuts, which are keyboard equivalents for software commands, when they are available. Keyboard shortcuts make it possible for you to keep your hands on the keyboard instead of reaching for the mouse to make Ribbon selections. Press Alt to display keyboard shortcuts, called ***Key Tips***, for items on the Ribbon and Quick Access Toolbar. You can press the letter or number corresponding to Ribbon items to invoke the action from the keyboard. Press Alt again to remove the Key Tips. You can also use universal keyboard shortcuts that have been available in past Office versions and in other Windows software, such as Ctrl+C (copy), Ctrl+X (cut), Ctrl+V (paste), and Ctrl+Z (undo). You will want to remember two very important keyboard shortcuts—Ctrl+Home and Ctrl+End. To move to the beginning of a Word document, to cell A1 in Excel, or to the first PowerPoint slide, press Ctrl+Home. To move to the end of those items, press Ctrl+End.

A **Key Tip** is the letter or number that displays over features on the Ribbon and Quick Access Toolbar. Typing the letter or number is the equivalent of clicking the corresponding item.

Use the Status Bar

The **status bar** is the horizontal bar located at the bottom of an Office application containing information relative to the open file.

The ***status bar*** is found at the bottom of the program window and contains information relative to the open file. It also includes tools for changing the view of the file and for changing the size of onscreen file contents. Contents of the status bar are unique to each specific application. When you work with Word, the status bar informs you of the number of pages and words in an open document. Excel's status bar displays summary information, such as average and sum, of selected cells. The PowerPoint status bar shows the slide number, total slides in the presentation, and the applied theme.

Changing the **view** of a file changes the way it appears onscreen.

Regardless of the application in which you are working, the status bar includes view buttons and a Zoom slider. You can also use the View tab on the Ribbon to change the current view or zoom level of an open file. The status bar's view buttons, shown in Figure 1.19, enable you to change the ***view*** of the open file. You might, for example, view a PowerPoint slide presentation with multiple slides displayed (Slide Sorter view) or with only one slide in large size (Normal view). In Word, you could view a document in Print Layout view (showing margins, headers, and footers), Full Screen Reading view, Web Layout view, or Draft view (with the greatest amount of typing space possible). As you learn more about Office applications in the following chapters, you will become aware of the views that are specific to each application.

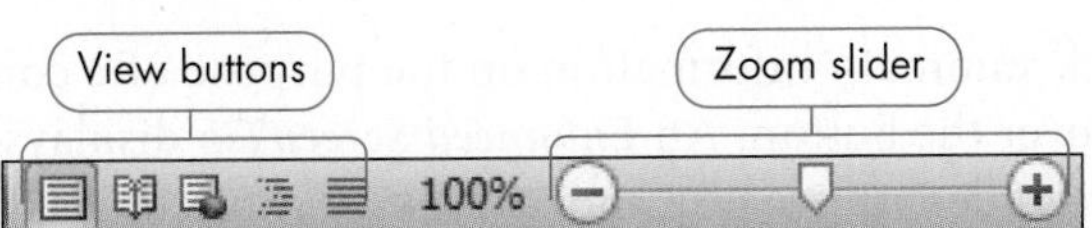

FIGURE 1.19 Word Status Bar ➤

The **Zoom slider** enables you to increase or decrease the size of file contents onscreen.

The ***Zoom slider*** always displays at the far right side of the status bar. You can drag the tab along the slider in either direction to increase or decrease the magnification of the file. Be aware, however, that changing the size of text onscreen does not increase the font size when the file is printed or saved.

Getting Office Help

One of the most frustrating things about learning new software is determining how to complete a task. Thankfully, Microsoft includes comprehensive help in Office so that you are less likely to feel such frustration. As you work with any Office application, you can access help online as well as within the current software installation. Help is also available through a short description that displays when you rest the mouse pointer on a command. Additionally, you can get help related to a currently open dialog box by clicking a question mark in the top-right corner of the dialog box or when you click the Help button in the Backstage view.

Use Office Help

To access the comprehensive library of Office Help, click the Help button, displayed as a question mark, on the far right side of the Ribbon (see Figure 1.15). You can get the same help by pressing F1 on the keyboard. The Backstage view also includes a Help feature, providing assistance with the current application as well as a direct link to online resources and technical support. Figure 1.20 shows the Help window that will display when you press F1, when you click the Help button, or when you click File, Help, Microsoft Office Help. For general information on broad topics, click a link in the window. However, if you are having difficulty with a specific task, it might be easier to simply type the request in the Search box. Suppose you are seeking help with using the Goal Seek feature in Excel. Simply type *Goal Seek* or a phrase such as *find specific result by changing variables* in the Search box, and press Enter (or click the magnifying glass on the right). Then select from displayed results for more information on the topic.

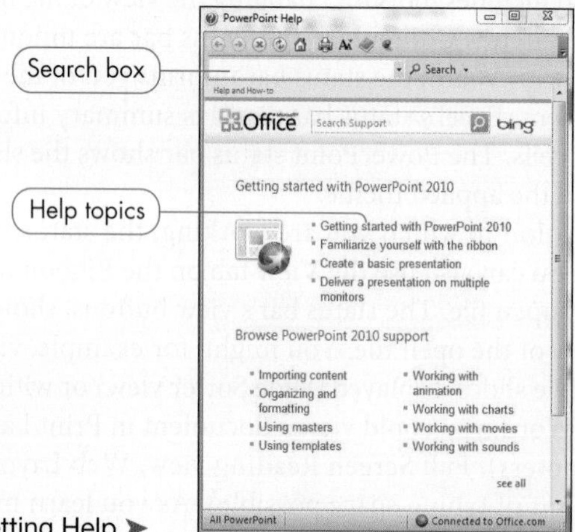

FIGURE 1.20 Getting Help ➤

Use Enhanced ScreenTips

An **Enhanced ScreenTip** provides a brief summary of a command when you place the mouse pointer over the command button.

For quick summary information on the purpose of a command button, place the mouse pointer over the button. An ***Enhanced ScreenTip*** displays, giving the purpose of the command, short descriptive text, and a keyboard shortcut if applicable. Some ScreenTips include a suggestion for pressing F1 for additional help. The Enhanced ScreenTip in Figure 1.21 provides context-sensitive assistance.

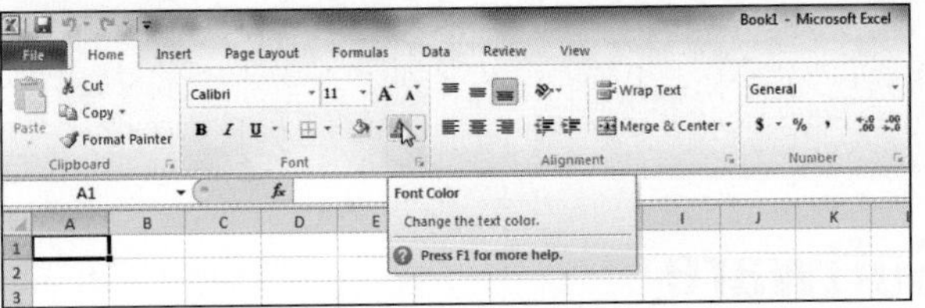

FIGURE 1.21 Enhanced ScreenTip ➤

Get Help with Dialog Boxes

Getting help while you are working with a dialog box is easy. Simply click the Help button that appears as a question mark in the top-right corner of the dialog box (see Figure 1.16). The subsequent Help window will offer suggestions relevant to your task.

Quick Concepts Check

1. What is the purpose of the Quick Access Toolbar? Suppose that you often engage in an activity—for example, printing—and want to include that command on the Quick Access Toolbar. What steps would you take to do that?
2. Suppose that you want to increase the font size of selected text. As you point to various font sizes in the Font Size list, the selected text temporarily displays each font size. What feature is demonstrated in that process? How can it be helpful as you develop a document?
3. Occasionally, the Ribbon is modified to include a contextual tab. Define a contextual tab and give an example of when a contextual tab is displayed.
4. After using Word to develop a research paper, you learn that the margins you used are incorrect. You plan to use Word's built-in Help feature to obtain information on how to change margins. Explain the process of obtaining help on that topic. Be specific.

HANDS-ON EXERCISES

2 Microsoft Office Software

As the administrative assistant for the Rails and Trails project, you need to get the staff started on a proposed fund-management worksheet. Although you do not have access to information on current donations, you want to provide a suggested format for a worksheet to keep up with donations as they come in. You will use Excel to begin design of the worksheet.

Skills covered: Open an Office Application, Get Enhanced ScreenTip Help, and Use the Zoom Slider • Get Help, Use the Backstage View • Change the View and Use Live Preview • Use the Quick Access Toolbar and Explore PowerPoint Views

STEP 1 OPEN AN OFFICE APPLICATION, GET ENHANCED SCREENTIP HELP, AND USE THE ZOOM SLIDER

Because you will use Excel to create the fund-raising worksheet, you will open the application. You will familiarize yourself with items on the Ribbon by getting Enhanced ScreenTip Help. For a better view of worksheet data, you will use the Zoom slider to magnify cell contents. Refer to Figure 1.22 as you complete Step 1.

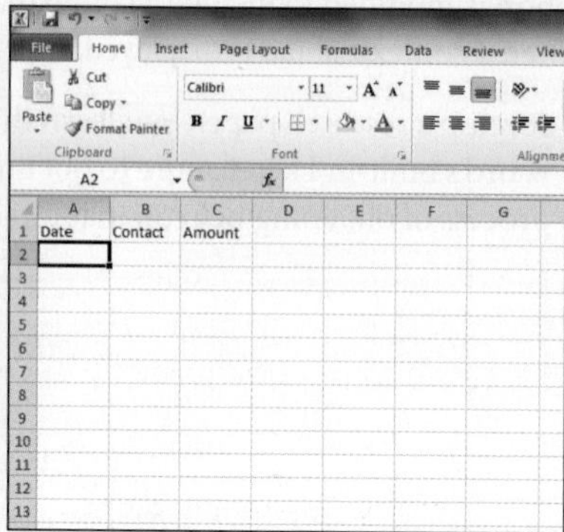

FIGURE 1.22 Fund-Raising Worksheet ➤

a. Click the **Start button** to display the Start Menu. Point to **All Programs**. Scroll down the list, if necessary, and click **Microsoft Office**. Click **Microsoft Excel 2010**.

   You have opened Microsoft Excel because it is the program in which the fund-raising worksheet will be created.

b. Type **Date**. As you type, the text appears in the current worksheet cell, **cell A1**. Press **Tab**, and then type **Contact**. Press **Tab**, and then type **Amount**. Press **Enter**. Your worksheet should look like the one in Figure 1.22.

   The worksheet that you create is only a beginning. Your staff will later suggest additional columns of data that can better summarize the hoped-for donations.

c. Hover the mouse pointer over any command on the Ribbon and note the Enhanced ScreenTip that displays, informing you of the purpose of the command. Explore other commands and identify their purpose.

d. Click the **Page Layout tab**, click **Orientation** in the Page Setup group, and then click ***Landscape***.

   The Page Layout tab is also found in Word, enabling you to change margins, orientation, and other page settings. Although you will not see much difference in the Excel screen display after you change the orientation to landscape, the worksheet will be oriented so that it is wider than it is tall when printed.

e. Drag the tab on the **Zoom slider**, located at the far right side of the status bar, to the right to temporarily magnify the text. Click the **View tab**, and then click **100%** in the Zoom group to return the text to its original size. Keep the workbook open for the next step in this exercise.

When you change the zoom, you do not change the text size that will be printed or saved. The change merely magnifies or decreases the view while you work with the file.

STEP 2 GET HELP, USE THE BACKSTAGE VIEW

Because you are not an Excel expert, you occasionally rely on the Help feature to provide information on tasks. You need assistance with saving a worksheet, previewing it before printing, and printing the worksheet. From what you learn, you will find that the Backstage view enables you to accomplish all of those tasks. Refer to Figure 1.23 as you complete Step 2.

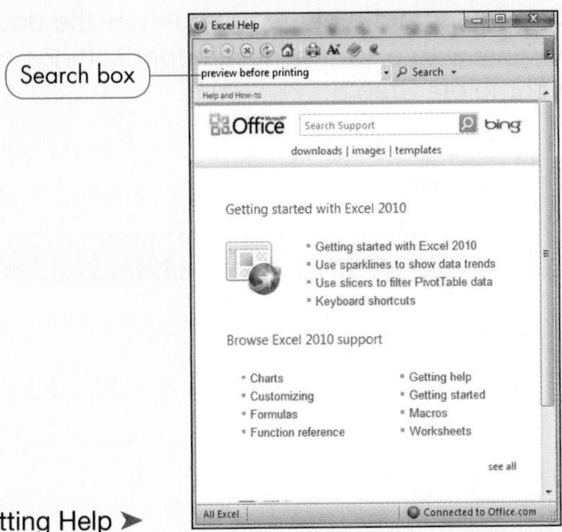

FIGURE 1.23 Getting Help ➤

a. Click the **Help button**, which is the question mark in the top-right corner of the Ribbon. The Help dialog box displays.

b. Click in the white text box to the left of the word *Search* in the Help dialog box, as shown in Figure 1.23. Type **preview before printing** and click **Search**. In the Help window, click **Preview worksheet pages before printing**. Read about how to preview a worksheet before printing. From what you read, can you identify a keyboard shortcut for previewing worksheets? Click the **Close button**.

Before you print the worksheet, you would like to see how it will look when printed. You can use Help to find information on previewing before printing.

> **TROUBLESHOOTING:** You must be connected to the Internet to get context-sensitive help.

c. Click the **File tab**, and then click **Print**.

Having used Office Help to learn how to preview before printing, you follow the directions to view the document as it will look when printed. The preview of the worksheet displays on the right. To print the worksheet, you would click Print. However, you can first select any print options, such as the number of copies, from the Backstage view.

d. Click the **Help button.** Excel Help presents several links related to the worksheet. Explore any that look interesting. Return to previous Help windows by clicking **Back** at the top-left side of the Help window. Close the Help dialog box.

e. Click the **Home tab**. Point to **Bold** in the Font group.

You will find that, along with Excel, Word and PowerPoint also include formatting features in the Font group, such as Bold and Italic. When the Enhanced ScreenTip appears, identify the shortcut key combination that could be used to bold a selected text item. It is indicated as Ctrl plus a letter. What is the shortcut?

f. Click the **Close button** in the red box in the top-right corner of the Excel window to close both the workbook and the Excel program. When asked whether you want to save changes, click **Don't Save**.

You decide not to print or save the worksheet right now. Instead, you will get assistance with its design and try it again later.

> **TROUBLESHOOTING:** If you clicked the Close button on the second row from the top, you closed the workbook but not Excel. Click the remaining Close button to close the program.

STEP 3 CHANGE THE VIEW AND USE LIVE PREVIEW

It is important that the documents you prepare or approve are error-free and as attractive as possible. Before printing, you will change the view to get a better idea of how the document will look when printed. In addition, you will use Live Preview to experiment with font settings before actually applying them. Refer to Figure 1.24 as you complete Step 3.

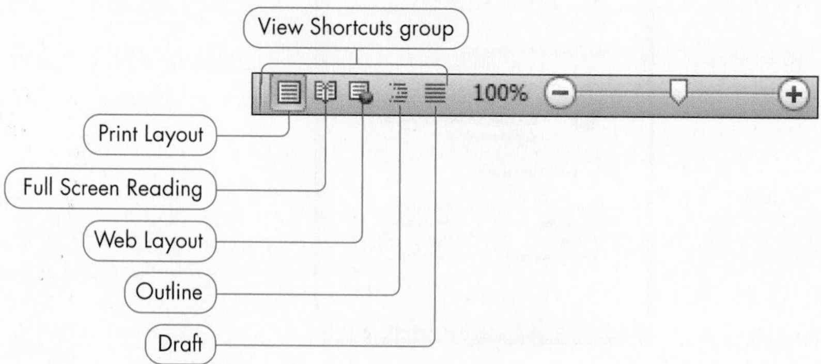

FIGURE 1.24 Word Views ➤

a. Click the **Start button**, and then point to **All Programs**. Scroll down, if necessary, and click **Microsoft Office**. Click **Microsoft Word 2010**.

You have opened a blank Word document. You plan to familiarize yourself with the program for later reference.

b. Type your full name, and then press **Enter**. Drag to select your name (or position the mouse pointer immediately to the left of your name so that the pointer looks like a white arrow, and then click). Your name should be shaded, indicating that it is selected.

You have selected your name because you want to experiment with using Word to change the way text looks.

c. Click the **Font Size arrow** in the Font group on the Home tab. If you need help locating Font Size, check for an Enhanced ScreenTip. Place the mouse pointer over any number in the subsequent list, but do not click. As you move to another number, notice the size of your name change. The feature you are using is called Live Preview. Click any number in the list to change the text size of your name.

d. Click **Draft** in the View Shortcuts group on the status bar to change the view (see Figure 1.24).

When creating a document, you might find it helpful to change the view. Word's Print Layout view is useful when you want to see both the document text and such features as margins and page breaks. Draft view provides a full screen of typing space without displaying margins or other print features, such as headers or footers. PowerPoint, Excel, and Access also provide view options, although they are unique to the application. The most common view options are accessible from View Shortcuts on the status bar of each application.

e. Click the **Close button** in the top-right corner of the Word window to close both the current document and the Word program. When asked whether you want to save the file, click **Don't Save**.

STEP 4 USE THE QUICK ACCESS TOOLBAR AND EXPLORE POWERPOINT VIEWS

During the course of the Rails and Trails project, you will be asked to review documents, presentations, and worksheets. It is important that you explore each application to familiarize yourself with operations and commonalities. Specifically, you know that the Quick Access Toolbar is common to all applications and that you can place commonly used commands there to streamline processes. Also, learning to change views will enable you to see the project in different ways for various purposes. Refer to Figure 1.25 as you complete Step 4.

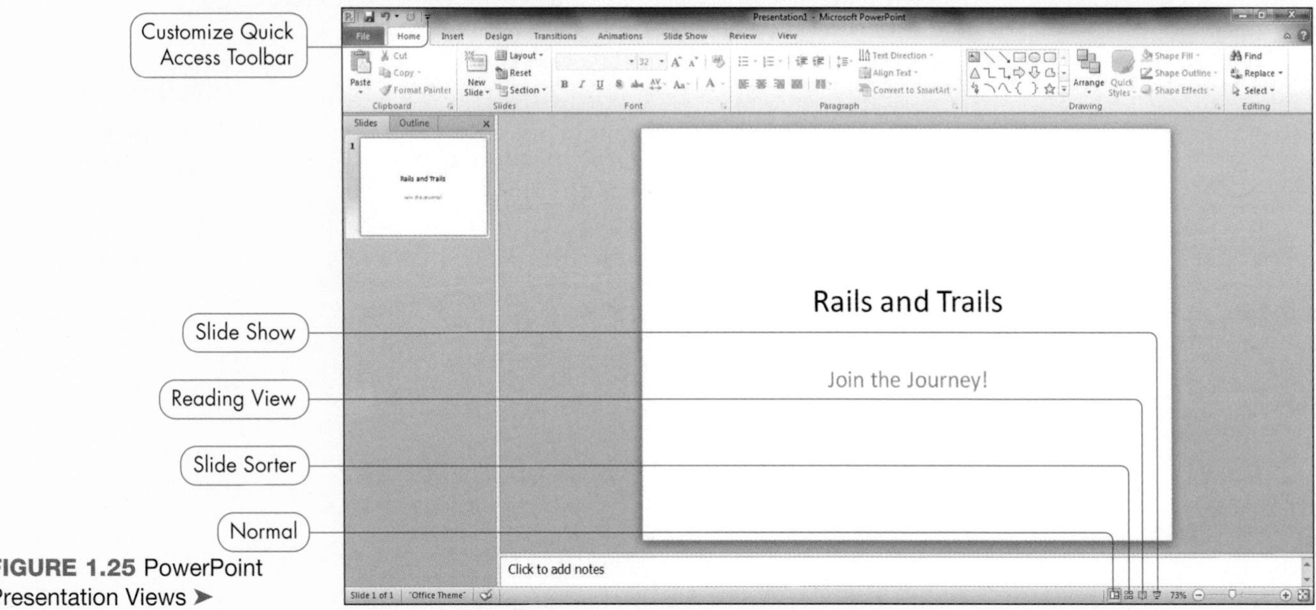

FIGURE 1.25 PowerPoint Presentation Views ➤

a. Click the **Start button**, and then point to **All Programs**. Scroll down, if necessary, and click **Microsoft Office**. Click **Microsoft PowerPoint 2010**.

   You have opened PowerPoint. You see a blank presentation.

b. Click **Click to add title**, and then type **Rails and Trails**. Click in the bottom, subtitle box, and then type **Join the Journey!** Click the bottom-right corner of the slide to deselect the subtitle. Your PowerPoint presentation should look like that shown in Figure 1.25.

c. Click **Undo** on the Quick Access Toolbar.

   The subtitle on the current slide is removed because it is the most recent action.

d. Click **Slide Sorter** in the View Shortcuts group on the status bar.

   The Slide Sorter view shows thumbnails of all slides in a presentation. Because this presentation has only one slide, you see a small version of one slide.

e. Move the mouse pointer to any button on the Quick Access Toolbar and hold it steady. See the tip giving the button name and the shortcut key combination, if any. Move to another button and see the description.

   The Quick Access Toolbar has at least three buttons, Save, Undo, and Redo (or Repeat). In addition, a small arrow is included at the far-right side. If you hold the mouse pointer steady on the arrow, you will see the ScreenTip Customize Quick Access Toolbar.

f. Click **Customize Quick Access Toolbar**. From the menu, click **New**. The New button enables you to quickly create a new presentation (also called a document).

g. Click **Customize Quick Access Toolbar**, and then click **New**. The button is removed from the Quick Access Toolbar.

   You can customize the Quick Access Toolbar by adding and removing items.

h. Click **Normal** in the View Shortcuts group on the status bar.

The presentation returns to the original view in which the slide displays in full size.

i. Click **Slide Show** in the View Shortcuts group on the status bar.

The presentation is shown in Slide Show view, which is the way it will be presented to audiences.

j. Press **Esc** to end the presentation.

k. Close the presentation without saving it. Exit PowerPoint.

Backstage View Tasks

When you work with Microsoft Office files, you will often want to open previously saved files, create new ones, print items, and save and close files. You will also find it necessary to indicate options, or preferences, of settings. For example, you might want a spelling check to occur automatically, or you might prefer to initiate a spelling check only occasionally. Getting Help is also a common selection that you want to find easily. Because those tasks are applicable to each software application within the Office 2010 suite, they are accomplished through a common area in the Office interface—the Backstage view. Open the Backstage view by clicking the File tab. Figure 1.26 shows the area that displays when you click the File tab. The Backstage view also enables you to exit the application and to identify file information, such as the author or date created. In this section, you will explore the Backstage view, learning to create, open, close, and print files.

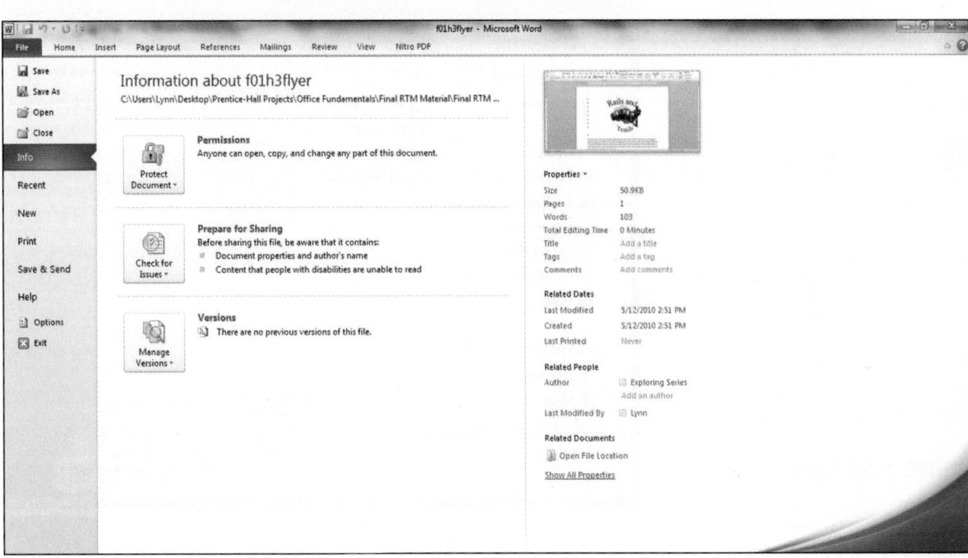

FIGURE 1.26 Backstage View ➤

Opening a File

When working with an Office application, you can begin by opening an existing file that has already been saved to a storage medium, or you can begin work on a new file. Both actions are available when you click the File tab. When you first open Word, Excel, or PowerPoint, you will be presented with a new blank work area that you can begin using immediately. When you first open Access, you will need to save the file before you can begin working with it. You can also open a project that you previously saved to a disk.

Create a New File

After opening an Office application, such as Word, Excel, or PowerPoint, you will be presented with a blank document area. The word *document* is sometimes used generically to refer to any Office file, including a Word document, an Excel worksheet, or a PowerPoint presentation. Perhaps you are already working with a document in an Office application but want to create a new file. Simply click the File tab, and then click New. Double-click Blank document (or Blank presentation or Blank workbook, depending on the specific application). You can also single-click Blank document, and then click Create.

Open a File Using the Open Dialog Box

If you choose to open a previously saved file, as you will need to do when you work with the data files for this book, you will work with the Open dialog box as shown in Figure 1.27. That dialog box appears after you select Open from the File tab. Using the Navigation Pane, you will make your way to the file to be opened. Double-click the file or click the file name once, and then click Open. Most likely, the file will be located within a folder that is appropriately named to make it easy to find related files. Obviously, if you are not well aware of the file's location and file name, the process of opening a file could become quite cumbersome. However, if you have created a well-designed system of folders, as you learned to do in the *Files and Folders* section of this chapter, you will know exactly where to find the file.

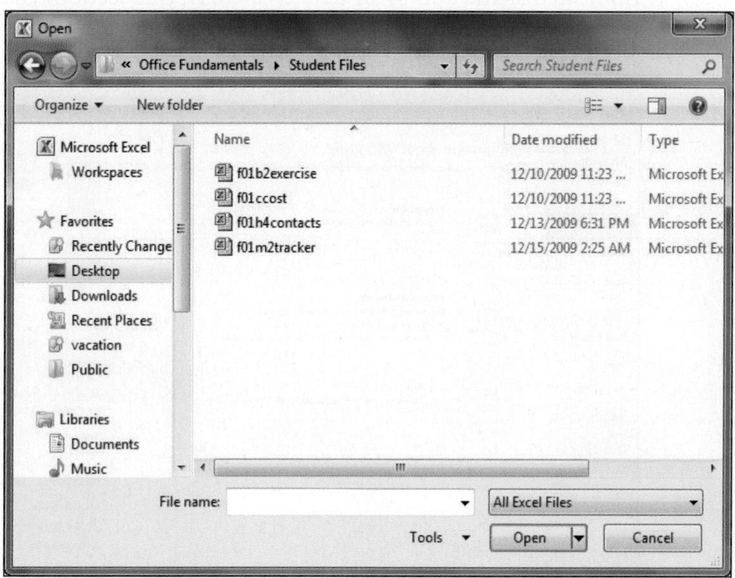

FIGURE 1.27 Open Dialog Box ➤

Open a File Using the Recent Documents List

You will often work with a file, save it, and then continue the project at a later time. Office simplifies the task of reopening the file by providing a Recent Documents list with links to your most recently opened files. See Figure 1.28 for an example of a Recent Documents list. To access the list, click the File tab, and then click Recent. Select from any files listed in the right pane. The list constantly changes to reflect only the most recently opened files, so if it has been quite some time since you worked with a particular file, you might have to work with the Open dialog box instead of the Recent Documents list.

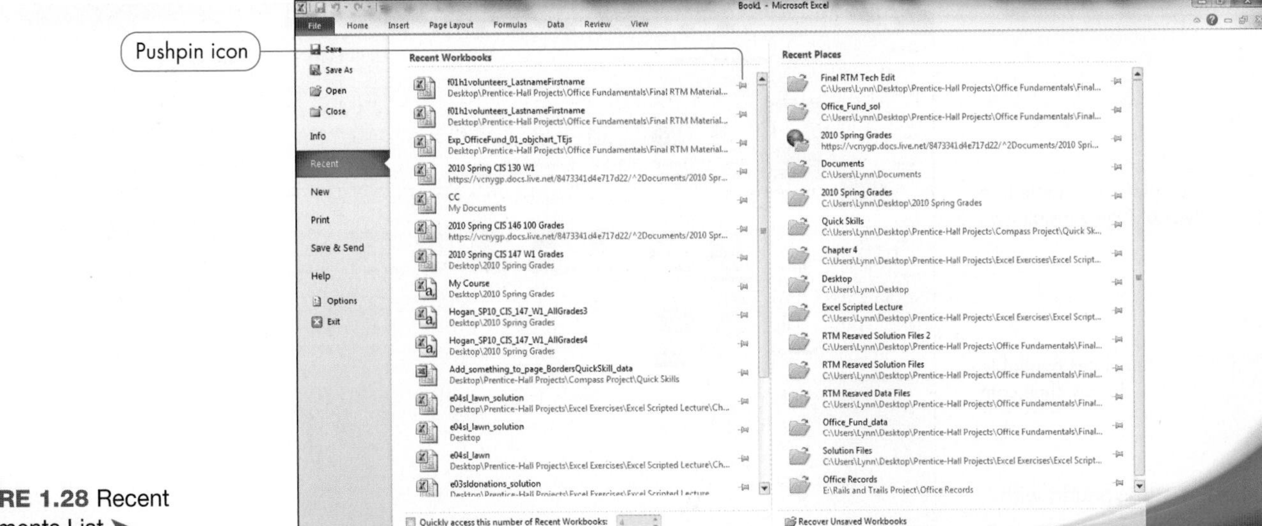

FIGURE 1.28 Recent Documents List ➤

TIP Keeping Files on the Recent Documents List

The Recent Documents list displays a limited list of only the most recently opened files. You might, however, want to keep a particular file in the list regardless of how recently it was opened. In Figure 1.28, note the pushpin icon that appears to the right of each file. Click the icon to cause the file to remain in the list. At that point, you will always have access to the file by clicking the File tab and selecting the file from the Recent Documents list. The pushpin of the "permanent" file will change direction so that it appears to be inserted, indicating that it is a pinned item. If later you want to remove the file from the list, simply click the inserted pushpin, changing its direction and allowing the file to be bumped off the list when other, more recently opened, files take its place.

Open a File from the Templates List

A **template** is a predesigned file that you can modify to suit your needs.

You do not need to create a new file if you can access a predesigned file that meets your needs or one that you can modify fairly quickly to complete your project. Office provides such files, called ***templates***, making them available when you click the File tab and then New. Refer to Figure 1.29 for an example of a Templates list. The top area is comprised of template groups available within the current Office installation on your computer. The lower category includes template groups that are available from Office.com. When you click to select a group, you are sometimes presented with additional choices to narrow your selection to a particular file. For example, you might want to prepare a home budget. After opening Excel, click the File tab, and then click New. From the template categories, you could click Budgets from the Office.com Templates area, click Monthly Family Budget, and then click Download to display the associated worksheet (or simply double-click Monthly Family Budget). If a Help window displays along with the worksheet template, click to close it, or explore Help to learn more about the template. If you know only a little bit about Excel, you could then make a few changes so that the worksheet would accurately represent your family's financial situation. The budget would be prepared much more quickly than if you began the project with a blank workbook, designing it yourself.

You do not need to create a new file if you can access a predesigned file that meets your needs or one that you can modify fairly quickly to complete your project. Office provides such files, called templates.

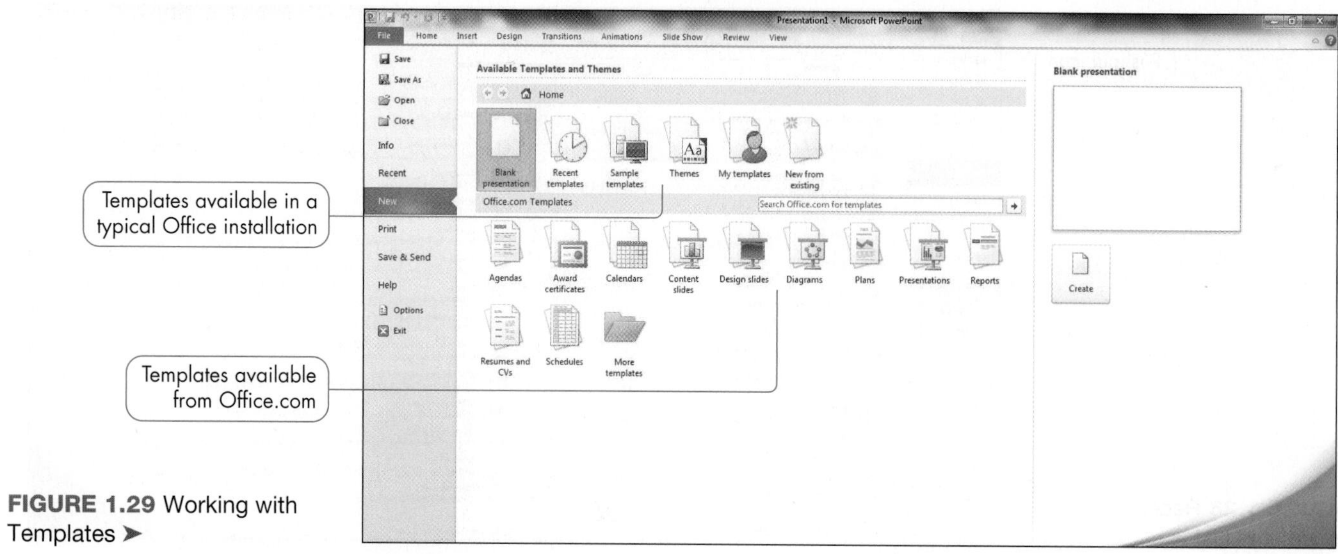

FIGURE 1.29 Working with Templates ➤

Printing a File

There will be occasions when you will want to print an Office project. Before printing, you should preview the file to get an idea of how it will look when printed. That way, if there are obvious problems with the page setup, you can correct them before wasting paper on something that is not correct. When you are ready to print, you can select from various print options, including the number of copies and the specific pages to print. If you know that the page setup is correct and that there are no unique print settings to select, you can simply print the project without adjusting any print settings.

It is a good idea to take a look at how your document will appear before you print it. The Print Preview feature of Office enables you to do just that.

It is a good idea to take a look at how your document will appear before you print it. The Print Preview feature of Office enables you to do just that. In Print Preview, you will see all items, including any headers, footers, graphics, and special formatting. To view a project before printing, click the File tab, and then click Print. The subsequent Backstage view shows the file preview on the right, with print settings located in the center of the Backstage screen. Figure 1.30 shows a typical Backstage print view.

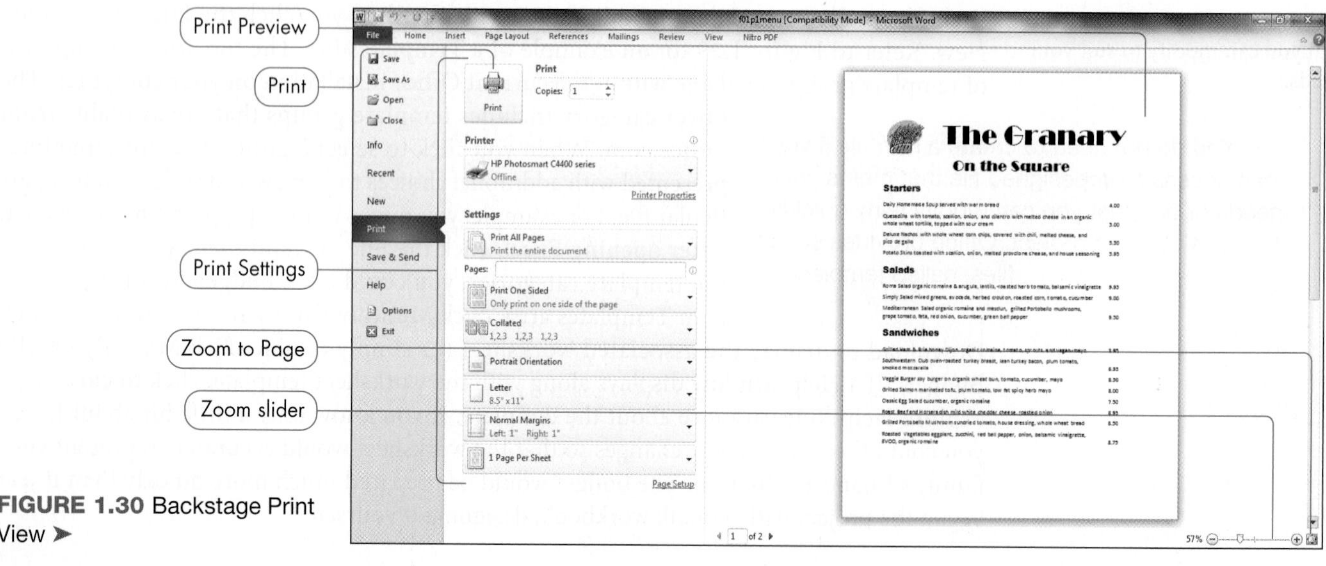

FIGURE 1.30 Backstage Print View ➤

To increase the size of the file preview, drag the Zoom slider to the right. The Zoom slider is found on the right side of the status bar, beneath the preview. Remember that increasing the font size by adjusting the zoom only applies to the current display. It does not actually increase the font size when the document is printed or saved. To return the preview to its original size, click Zoom to Page found at the right of the Zoom slider. See Figure 1.30 for the location of the Zoom slider and Zoom to Page.

Other options in the Backstage Print view vary, depending on the application in which you are working. Regardless of the Office application, you will be able to access Print Setup options from the Backstage view, including page orientation (landscape or portrait), margins, and page size. You will find a more detailed explanation of those settings in the *Page Layout Tab Tasks* section later in this chapter. To print a file, click Print (shown in Figure 1.30).

The Backstage Print view shown in Figure 1.30 is very similar across all Office applications. However, you will find slight variations specific to each application. For example, PowerPoint's Backstage Print view includes options for printing slides and handouts in various configurations and colors, whereas Excel's focuses on worksheet selections and Word's includes document options. Regardless of software, the manner of working with Backstage's print options remains consistent.

Closing a File and Application

Although you can have several documents open at one time, limiting the number of open files is a good idea. Office applications have no problem keeping up with multiple open files, but you can easily become overwhelmed with them. When you are done with an open project, you will need to close it along with the application itself.

You can easily close any files that you no longer need. With the desired file on the screen, click the File tab, and then click the Close button. Respond to any prompt that might appear suggesting that you save the file. The application remains open, but the selected file is closed. To close the application, click the File tab, and then click Exit.

TIP Closing a File and Application

When you close an application, all open files within the application are also closed. You will be prompted to save any files before they are closed. A quick way to close an application is to click the X in the top-right corner of the application window.

Quick Concepts Check

1. As part of your job search, you plan to develop a letter of application. However, you find it difficult to determine the right words to begin your letter, and wish you could begin with a predesigned document that you could modify. Is that possible with Word? If so, what steps would you take to locate a predesigned letter of application?
2. Closing a file is not the same as closing an application, such as Excel. What is the difference?
3. You want to continue to work with a PowerPoint presentation that you worked with yesterday, but cannot remember where you saved the presentation on your hard drive. How can you open a file that you recently worked with?

HANDS-ON EXERCISES

3 Backstage View Tasks

Projects related to the Rails and Trails project have begun to come in for your review and approval. You have received an informational flyer to be distributed to civic and professional groups around the city. It contains a new logo along with descriptive text. Another task on your agenda is to keep the project moving according to schedule. You will identify a calendar template to print and distribute. You will explore printing options, and you will save the flyer and the calendar to a disk as directed by your instructor.

Skills covered: Open and Save a File • Preview and Print a File • Open a File from the Recent Documents List and Open a Template

STEP 1 OPEN AND SAVE A FILE

You have asked your staff to develop a logo that can be used to promote the Rails and Trails project. You will open a Word document that includes a proposed logo and you will save the document to a disk drive. Refer to Figure 1.31 as you complete Step 1.

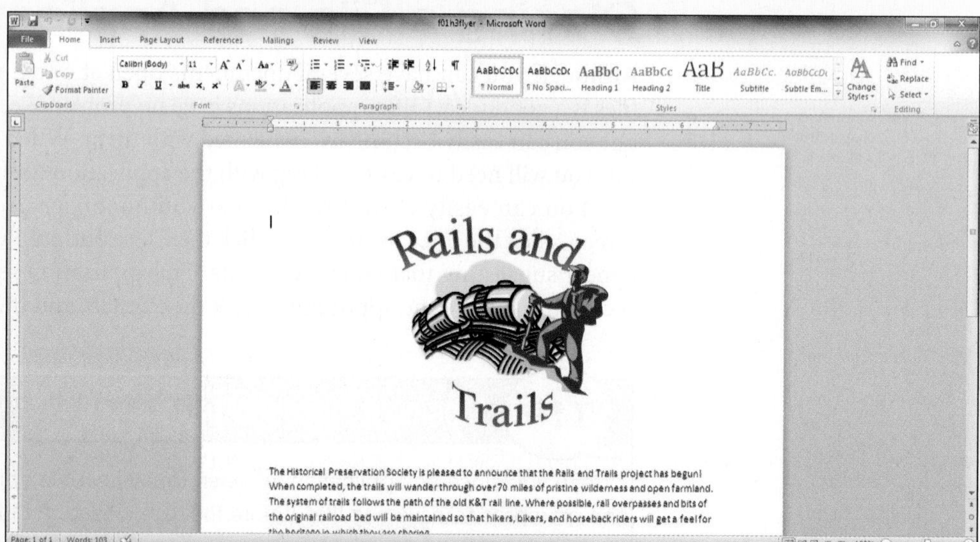

FIGURE 1.31 Promotional Flyer (Word Document) ➤

a. Click the **Start button** to display the Start Menu, and then click **All Programs**. Scroll down the list, if necessary, and then click **Microsoft Office**. Click **Microsoft Word 2010**.

   You have opened Microsoft Word because it is the program in which the promotional flyer is saved.

b. Click the **File tab**, and then click **Open**. Navigate to the location of your student files. Because you are working with Microsoft Word, the only files listed are those that were created with Microsoft Word. Double-click *f01h3flyer* to open the file shown in Figure 1.31. Familiarize yourself with the document.

   The logo and the flyer are submitted for your approval. A paragraph underneath the logo will serve as the launching point for an information blitz and the beginning of the fund-raising drive.

c. Click the **File tab**, and then click **Save As**.

   You choose the Save As command because you know that it enables you to indicate the location to which the file should be saved, as well as the file name.

d. Click the drive where you save your files, and then double-click **Rails and Trails Project**. Double-click **Office Records**, click in the **File name box**, type **f01h3flyer_LastnameFirstname**, and then click **Save**. Keep the file open for the next step in this exercise.

STEP 2 PREVIEW AND PRINT A FILE

You approve of the logo, so you will print the document for future reference. You will first preview the document as it will appear when printed. Then you will print the document. Refer to Figure 1.32 as you complete Step 2.

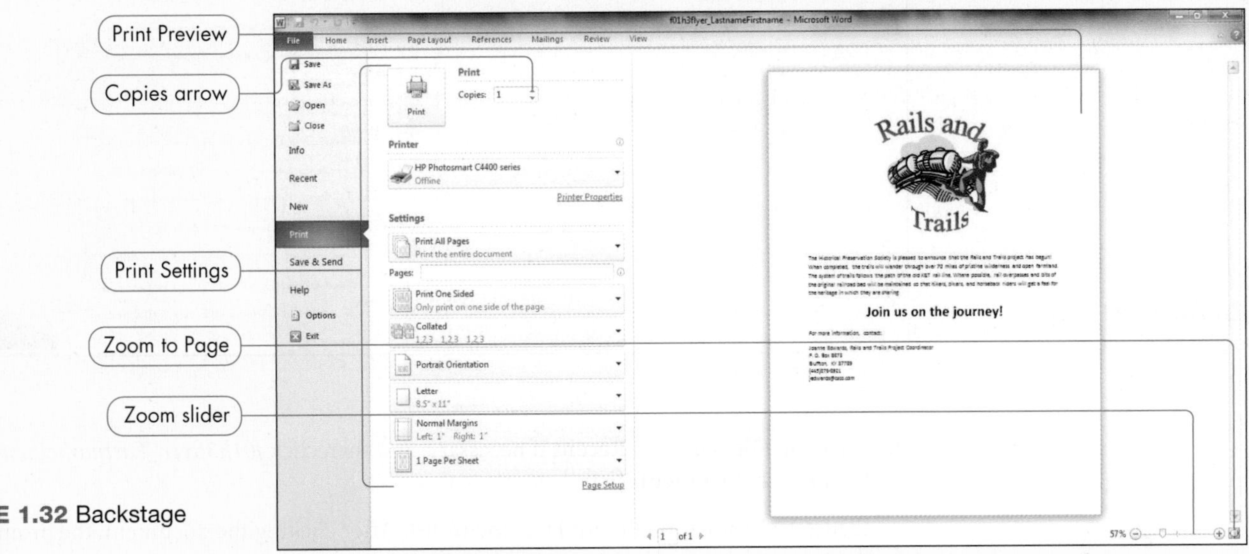

FIGURE 1.32 Backstage Print ➤

a. Click the **File tab**, and then click **Print**.

Figure 1.32 shows the flyer preview. It is always a good idea to check the way a file will look when printed before actually printing it.

b. Drag the **Zoom slider** to increase the document view. Click **Zoom to Page** to return to the original size.

c. Click **Portrait Orientation** in the Print settings area in the center of the screen. Click **Landscape Orientation** to show the flyer in a wider and shorter view.

d. Click **Landscape Orientation**, and click **Portrait Orientation** to return to the original view.

You decide that the flyer is more attractive in portrait orientation, so you return to that setting.

e. Click the **Copies arrow** repeatedly to increase the copies to **5**.

You will need to print five copies of the flyer to distribute to the office assistants for their review.

f. Press **Esc** to leave the Backstage view.

You choose not to print the flyer at this time.

g. Click the **File tab**, and then click the **Close button**. When asked, click **Don't Save** so that changes to the file are not saved. Leave Word open for the next step in this exercise.

STEP 3 OPEN A FILE FROM THE RECENT DOCUMENTS LIST AND OPEN A TEMPLATE

A large part of your responsibility is proofreading Rails and Trails material. You will correct a typo in a phone number in the promotional flyer. You must also keep the staff on task, so you will identify a calendar template on which to list tasks and deadlines. Refer to Figure 1.33 as you complete Step 3.

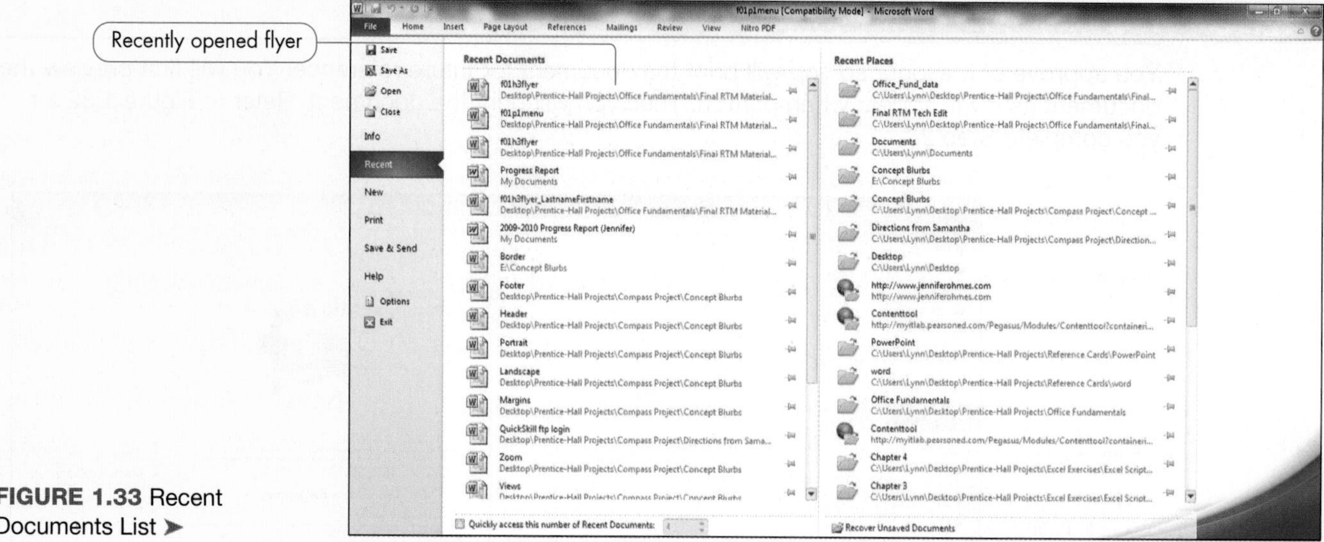

FIGURE 1.33 Recent Documents List ➤

a. Click the **File tab**, click **Recent** if necessary, and then click *f01h3flyer_LastnameFirstname* in the **Recent Documents list.**

   Figure 1.33 shows the Recent Documents list. After clicking the document, the promotional flyer opens.

b. Scroll down, and then click after the number 1 in the telephone number in the contact information. Press **Backspace** on the keyboard, and then type **2**.

   You find that the phone number is incorrect, so you make a correction.

c. Click **Save** on the Quick Access Toolbar, click the **File tab**, and then click the **Close button**.

   When you click Save on the Quick Access Toolbar, the document is saved in the same location with the same file name as was indicated in the previous save.

d. Click the **File tab**, and then click **New**. From the list of template categories available from Office.com, click **Calendars**, and then click the current year's calendar link.

   Office.com provides a wide range of calendar choices. You will select one that is appealing and that will help you keep projects on track.

e. Click a calendar of your choice from the gallery, and then click **Download**. Close any Help window that may open.

   The calendar that you selected opens in Word.

TROUBLESHOOTING: It is possible to select a template that is not certified by Microsoft. In that case, you might have to confirm your acceptance of settings before you click Download.

f. Click **Save** on the Quick Access Toolbar. If necessary, navigate to **Office Records** (a subfolder of Rails and Trails Project) on the drive where you save your student files. Save the document as **f01h3calendar_LastnameFirstname**. Click **OK**, if necessary. Close the document, and then exit Word.

   Because this is the first time to save the calendar file, the Save button on the Quick Access Toolbar opens a dialog box in which you must indicate the location of the file and the file name.

Home Tab Tasks

You will find that you will repeat some tasks often, whether in Word, Excel, or PowerPoint. You will frequently want to change the format of numbers or words, selecting a different font or changing font size or color. You might also need to change the alignment of text or worksheet cells. Undoubtedly, you will find a reason to copy or cut items and paste them elsewhere in the document, presentation, or worksheet. And you might want to modify file contents by finding and replacing text. All of those tasks, and more, are found on the Home tab of the Ribbon in Word, Excel, and PowerPoint. The Access interface is unique, sharing little with other Office applications, so this section will not address Access. In this section, you will explore the Home tab, learning to format text, copy and paste items, and find and replace words or phrases. Figure 1.34 shows Home tab groups and tasks in the various applications. Note the differences and similarities between the groups.

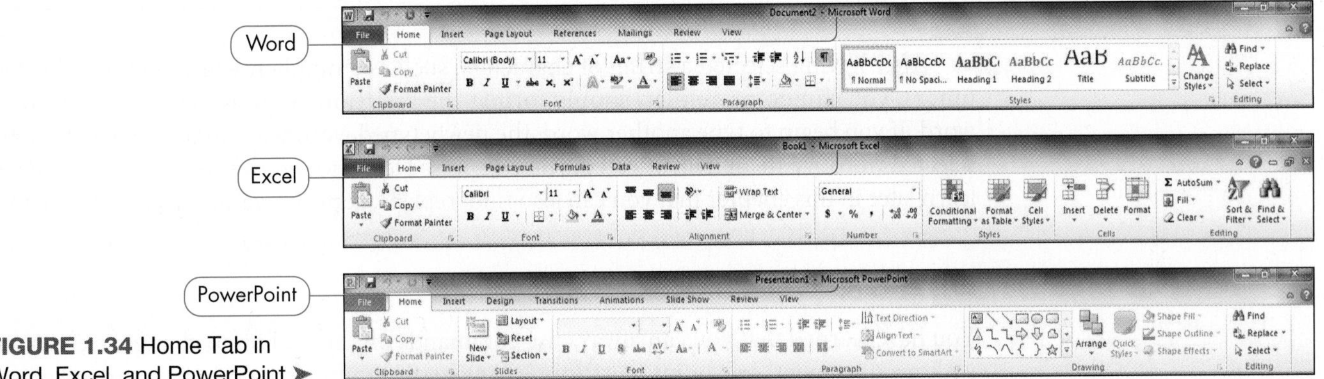

FIGURE 1.34 Home Tab in Word, Excel, and PowerPoint ➤

Selecting and Editing Text

After creating a document, worksheet, or presentation, you will probably want to make some changes. You might prefer to center a title, or maybe you think that certain worksheet totals should be formatted as currency. You can change the font so that typed characters are larger or in a different style. You might even want to underline text to add emphasis. In all Office applications, the Home tab provides tools for selecting and editing text. You can also use the Mini toolbar for quick changes to selected text.

Select Text to Edit

Before making any changes to existing text or numbers, you must first select the characters. A general rule that you should commit to memory is "Select, then do." A foolproof way to select text or numbers is to place the mouse pointer before the first character of the text you want to select, and then drag to highlight the intended selection. Before you drag, be sure that the mouse pointer takes on the shape of the letter *I*, called the I-bar. Although other methods for selecting exist, if you remember only one way, it should be the click-and-drag method. If your attempted selection falls short of highlighting the intended area, or perhaps highlights too much, simply click outside the selection and try again.

Before making any changes to existing text or numbers, you must first select the characters. A general rule that you should commit to memory is "Select, then do."

Sometimes it can be difficult to precisely select a small amount of text, such as a single character or a single word. Other times, the task can be overwhelming, such as when selecting an entire 550-page document. Shortcut methods for making selections in Word and PowerPoint are shown in Table 1.3. When working with Excel, you will more often need to select multiple cells. Simply drag the intended selection, usually when the mouse pointer appears as a large white plus sign. The shortcuts shown in Table 1.3 are primarily applicable to Word and PowerPoint.

TABLE 1.3 Shortcut Selection in Word and PowerPoint

Item Selected	Action
One Word	Double-click the word.
One Line of Text	Place the mouse pointer at the left of the line, in the margin area. When the mouse changes to a right-pointing arrow, click to select the line.
One Sentence	Press and hold Ctrl while you click in the sentence to select.
One Paragraph	Triple-click in the paragraph.
One Character to the Left of the Insertion Point	Press and hold Shift while you press l.
One Character to the Right of the Insertion Point	Press and hold Shift while you press r.
Entire Document	Press and hold Ctrl while you press the letter A on the keyboard.

After having selected a string of characters, such as a number, word, sentence, or document, you can do more than simply format the selection. Suppose you have selected a word. If you begin to type another word, the newly typed word will immediately replace the selected word. With an item selected, you can press Delete to remove the selection. You will learn later in this chapter that you can also find, replace, copy, move, and paste selected text.

Use the Mini Toolbar

The **Mini toolbar** is an Office feature that provides access to common formatting commands. It is displayed when text is selected.

You have learned that you can always use commands on the Ribbon to change selected text within a document, cell, or presentation. All it takes is locating the desired command on the Home tab and clicking to select it. Although using Home tab commands is simple enough, an item called the ***Mini toolbar*** provides an even shorter way to accomplish some of the same formatting changes. When you select any amount of text within a worksheet, document, or presentation, you can move the mouse pointer only slightly within the selection to display the Mini toolbar, as shown in Figure 1.35. The Mini toolbar provides access to the most common formatting selections, such as boldfacing, italicizing, or changing font type or color. Unlike the Quick Access Toolbar, the Mini toolbar is not customizable, which means that you cannot add or remove options from the toolbar. The Mini toolbar will only appear when text is selected. The closer the mouse pointer is to the Mini toolbar, the darker the toolbar. As you move the mouse pointer away from the Mini toolbar, it becomes almost transparent. Make any selections from the Mini toolbar by clicking the corresponding button.

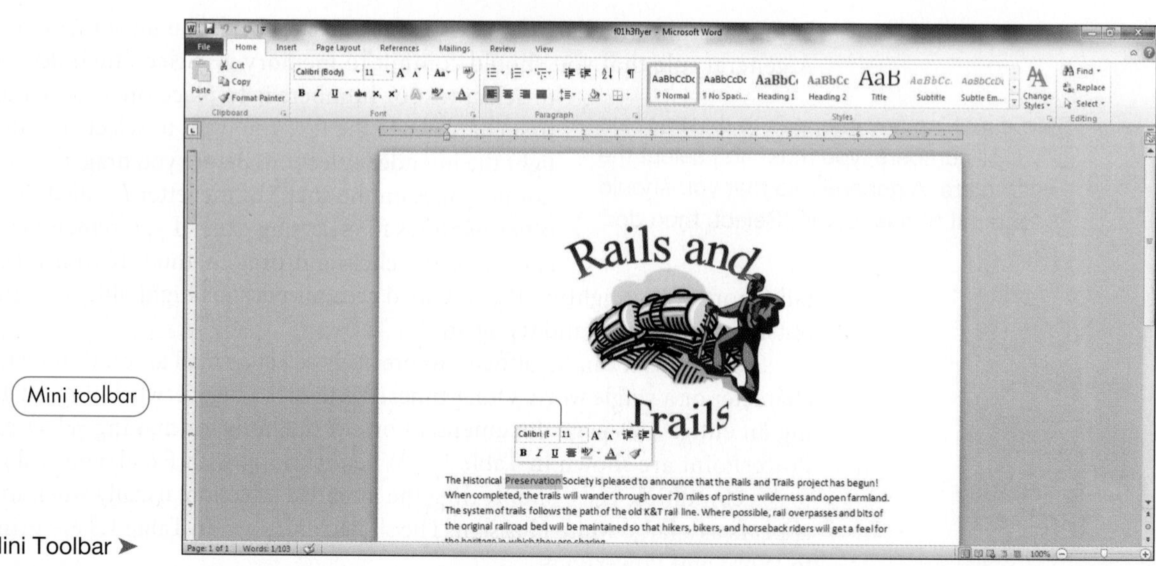

FIGURE 1.35 Mini Toolbar ➤

To temporarily remove the Mini toolbar from view, press Esc. If you want to permanently disable the Mini toolbar so that it does not appear in any open file when text is selected, click the File tab and click Options. As shown in Figure 1.36, click General, if necessary. Deselect the Show Mini Toolbar on selection setting by clicking the check box to the left of the setting and clicking OK.

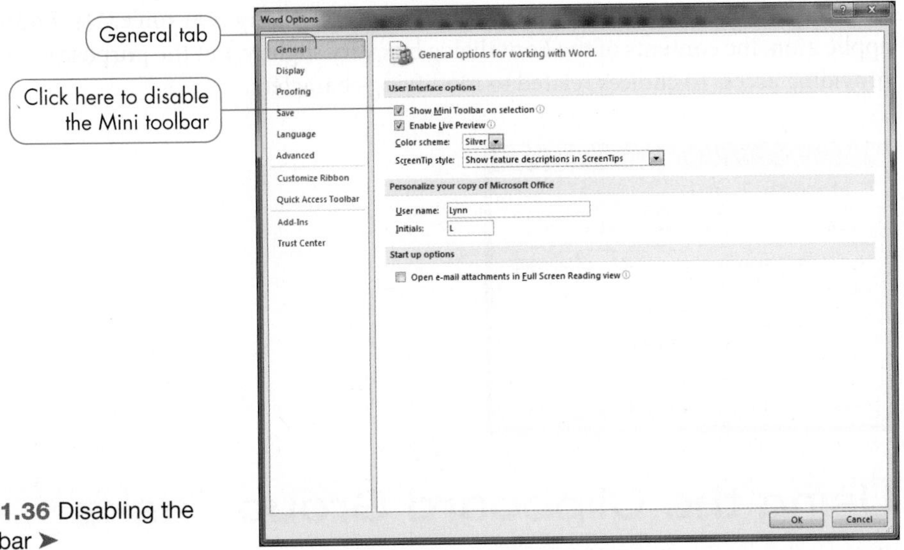

FIGURE 1.36 Disabling the Mini Toolbar ➤

Apply Font Attributes

A **font** is a character design that includes size, spacing, and shape.

To **toggle** is to switch from one setting to another. Several Home tab tasks, such as Bold and Italic, are actually toggle commands.

A ***font*** is a character design. More simply stated, it is the way characters appear onscreen, including qualities such as size, spacing, and shape. Each Office application has a default font, which is the font that will be in effect unless you change it. Other font attributes include boldfacing, italicizing, and font color, all of which can be applied to selected text. Some formatting changes, such as Bold and Italic, are called ***toggle*** commands. They act somewhat like light switches that you can turn on and off. For example, after having selected a word that you want to boldface, click Bold in the Font group of the Home tab to turn the setting "on." If at a later time you want to remove boldface from the word, select it again, and then click Bold. This time, the button turns "off" the bold formatting.

Change the Font

All applications within the Office suite provide a set of fonts from which you can choose. If you prefer a font other than the default, or if you want to apply a different font to a section of your project, you can easily make the change by selecting a font from within the Font group on the Home tab. You can also change the font by selecting from the Mini toolbar, although that only works if you have first selected text.

Change the Font Size, Color, and Attributes

At times, you want to make the font size larger or smaller, change the font color, underline selected text, or apply other font attributes. Because such changes are commonplace, Office places those formatting commands in many convenient places within each Office application.

You can find the most common formatting commands in the Font group on the Home tab. As shown in Figure 1.34, Word, Excel, and PowerPoint all share very similar Font groups that provide access to tasks related to changing the character font. Remember that you can place the mouse pointer over any command icon to view a summary of the icon's purpose, so although the icons might at first appear cryptic, you can use the mouse pointer to quickly determine the purpose and applicability to your desired text change. You can also find a subset of those commands plus a few additional choices on the Mini toolbar, which becomes available when you make a text selection.

If the font change that you plan to make is not included as a choice on either the Home tab or the Mini toolbar, you can probably find what you are looking for in the Font dialog box. Click the Dialog Box Launcher in the bottom-right corner of the Font group. Figure 1.37 shows a sample Font dialog box. Since the Font dialog box provides many formatting choices in one window, you can make several changes at once. Depending on the application, the contents of the Font dialog box vary slightly, but the purpose is consistent—providing access to choices related to modifying characters.

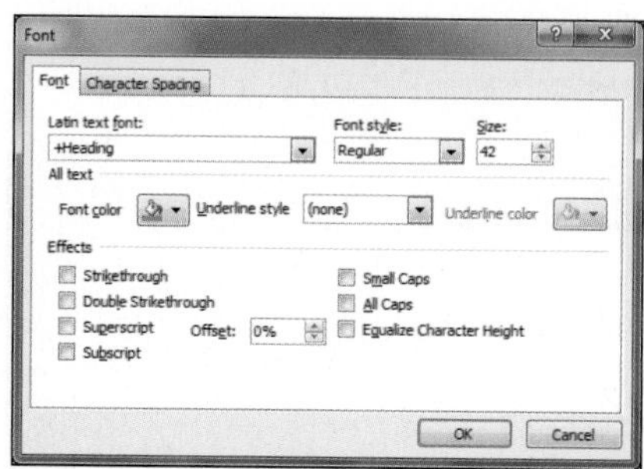

FIGURE 1.37 Font Dialog Box ➤

Using the Clipboard Group Tasks

The **Clipboard** is an Office feature that temporarily holds selections that have been cut or copied. It also enables you to paste those selections in other locations within the current or another Office application.

When you **cut** a selection, you remove it from the original location and place it in the Office Clipboard.

When you **copy** a selection, you duplicate it from the original location and place the copy in the Office Clipboard.

On occasion, you will want to move or copy a selection from one area to another. Suppose that you have included text on a PowerPoint slide that you believe would be more appropriate on a previous slide. Or perhaps an Excel formula should be copied from one cell to another because both cells should be totaled in the same manner. You can easily move the slide text and copy the Excel formula by using options found in the Clipboard group on the Home tab. The ***Clipboard*** is an area of memory reserved to temporarily hold selections that have been ***cut*** or ***copied***. Although the Clipboard can hold up to 24 items at one time, the usual procedure is to ***paste*** the cut or copied selection to its final destination fairly quickly. When the computer is shut down or loses power, the contents of the Clipboard are erased, so it is important to finalize the paste procedure during the current session.

The Clipboard group enables you not only to copy and cut items, but also to copy formatting. Perhaps you have applied a font style to a major heading of a report and you realize that the same formatting should be applied to other headings. Especially if the heading includes multiple formatting features, you will save a great deal of time by copying the entire package of formatting to the other headings. In so doing, you will ensure the consistency of formatting for all headings because they will appear exactly alike. Using the Clipboard group's ***Format Painter***, you can quickly and easily copy all formatting from one area to another in Word, PowerPoint, and Excel.

The Clipboard group enables you not only to copy and cut text, but also to copy formatting.

When you **paste** a selection, you place a cut or copied item in another location.

The **Format Painter** is a Clipboard group command that copies the formatting of text from one location to another.

A **shortcut menu** provides choices related to the selection or area at which you right-click.

TIP Using a Shortcut Menu

In Office, you can usually accomplish the same task in several ways. Although the Ribbon provides ample access to formatting and Clipboard commands (such as Format Painter, cut, copy, and paste), you might find it convenient to access the same commands on a ***shortcut menu***. Right-click a selected item or text to open a shortcut menu such as the one shown in Figure 1.38. A shortcut menu is also sometimes called a *context menu* because the contents of the menu vary depending on the location at which you right-clicked.

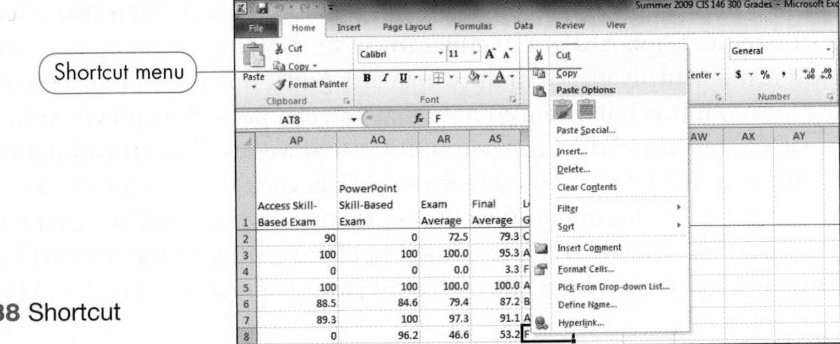

FIGURE 1.38 Shortcut Menu ➤

Copy Formats with the Format Painter

As described earlier, the Format Painter makes it easy to copy formatting features from one selection to another. You will find the Format Painter command conveniently located in the Clipboard group of the Home tab. Figure 1.39 shows Clipboard group tasks. To copy a format, you must first select the text containing the desired format. If you want to copy the format to only one other selection, *single-click* Format Painter. If, however, you plan to copy the same format to multiple areas, *double-click* Format Painter. As you move the mouse pointer, you will find that it has the appearance of a paintbrush with an attached I-bar. Select the area to which the copied format should be applied. If you single-clicked Format Painter to copy the format to one other selection, Format Painter turns off once the formatting has been applied. If you double-clicked Format Painter to copy the format to multiple locations, continue selecting text in various locations to apply the format. Then, to turn off Format Painter, click Format Painter again, or press Esc.

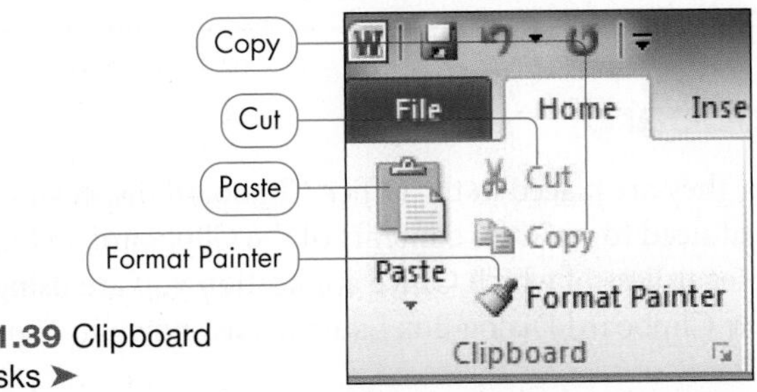

FIGURE 1.39 Clipboard Group Tasks ➤

Move and Copy Text

Undoubtedly, there will be times when you want to revise a project by moving or copying items such as Word text, PowerPoint slides, or Excel cell contents, either within the current application or among others. For example, a section of a Word document might be appropriate as PowerPoint slide content. To keep from retyping the Word text in the PowerPoint slide, you can copy the text and paste it in a blank PowerPoint slide. At other times, it might be necessary to move a paragraph within a Word document or to copy selected cells from one Excel worksheet to another. The Clipboard group contains a Cut command with which you can select text to move. You can also use the Copy command to duplicate items and the Paste command to place moved or copied items in a final location. See those command icons in Figure 1.39.

TIP Using Ribbon Commands with Arrows

Some commands, such as Paste in the Clipboard group, contain two parts: the main command and an arrow. The arrow may be below or to the right of the command, depending on the command, window size, or screen resolution. Instructions in the Exploring series use the command name to instruct you to click the main command to perform the default action (e.g., Click Paste). Instructions include the word *arrow* when you need to select an additional option (e.g., Click the Paste arrow).

The first step in moving or copying text is to select the text. After that, click the appropriate icon in the Clipboard group either to cut or copy the selection. Remember that cut or copied text is actually placed in the Clipboard, remaining there even after you paste it to another location. It is important to note that you can paste the same item multiple times because it will remain in the Clipboard until you power down your computer or until the Clipboard exceeds 24 items. To paste the selection, click the location where you want the text to be placed. The location can be in the current file or in another open file within any Office application. Then click Paste in the Clipboard group. In addition to using the Clipboard group icons, you can also cut, copy, and paste in any of the ways listed in Table 1.4.

TABLE 1.4 Cut, Copy, and Paste Options

Result	Actions
Cut	• Click Cut in Clipboard group. • Right-click selection, and then click Cut. • Press Ctrl+X
Copy	• Click Copy in Clipboard group. • Right-click selection, and then click Copy. • Press Ctrl+C.
Paste	• Click in destination location, and then click Paste in Clipboard group. • Right-click in destination location, and then click Paste. • Click in destination location, and then press Ctrl+V. • Click the Clipboard Dialog Box Launcher to open the Clipboard task pane. Click in destination location. With the Clipboard task pane open, click the arrow beside the intended selection, and then click Paste.

Use the Office Clipboard

When you cut or copy selections, they are placed in the Office Clipboard. Especially if you cut or copy multiple items, you might need to view the contents of the Clipboard so that you can select the correct item to paste. Regardless of which Office application you are using, you can view the Clipboard by clicking the Clipboard Dialog Box Launcher as shown in Figure 1.40.

FIGURE 1.40 Clipboard Task Pane ➤

Unless you specify otherwise when beginning a paste operation, the most recently added Clipboard item is pasted. You can, however, select an item from the Clipboard task pane to paste. Similarly, you can delete items from the Clipboard by making a selection in the Clipboard task pane. You can remove all items from the Clipboard by clicking Clear All. The Options button in the Clipboard task pane enables you to control when and where the Clipboard is displayed. Close the Clipboard task pane by clicking the Close button in the top-right corner of the task pane or by clicking the arrow in the title bar of the Clipboard task pane and selecting Close.

Using the Editing Group Tasks

The process of finding and replacing text is easily accomplished through options in the Editing group of the Home tab. You will at times find it necessary to locate each occurrence of a text item so that you can replace it with another or so that you can delete, move, or copy it. If you have consistently misspelled a person's name throughout a document, you can find the misspelling and replace it with the correct spelling in a matter of a few seconds, no matter how many times the misspelling occurs in the document. The Editing group also enables you to select all contents of a project document, all text with similar formatting, or specific objects, such as pictures, clip art, or charts. The Editing group is found at the far-right side of the Home tab in all Office applications except Access.

The Excel Editing group is unique in that it also includes provisions for sorting, filtering, and clearing cell contents; filling cells; and summarizing numeric data. Because those commands are relevant only to Excel, this chapter will not address them specifically. Figure 1.41 shows the Editing group of Excel, Word, and PowerPoint. Note the differences.

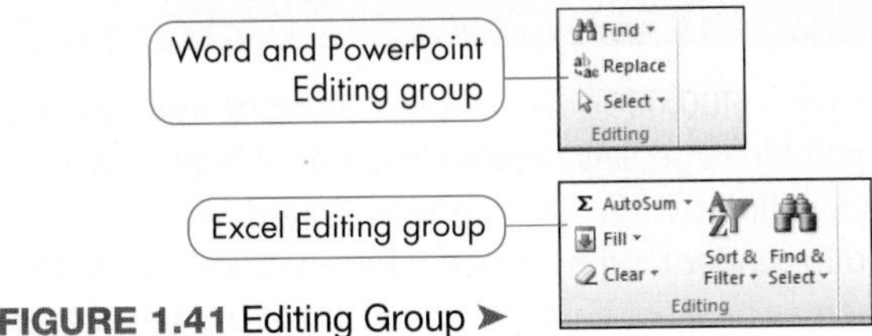

FIGURE 1.41 Editing Group ➤

Find and Replace Text

Find locates a word or phrase that you indicate in a document.

Replace finds text and replaces it with a word or phrase that you indicate.

Especially if you are working with a lengthy project, manually seeking a specific word or phrase can be time-consuming. Office enables you not only to ***find*** each occurrence of a series of characters, but also to ***replace*** what it finds with another series.

To begin the process of finding a specific item, click Replace in the Editing group on the Home tab of Word or PowerPoint. To begin a find and replace procedure in Excel, you must click Find & Select, and then click Replace. The subsequent dialog box enables you to indicate a word or phrase to find and replace. See Figure 1.42 for the Find and Replace dialog box in each Office application.

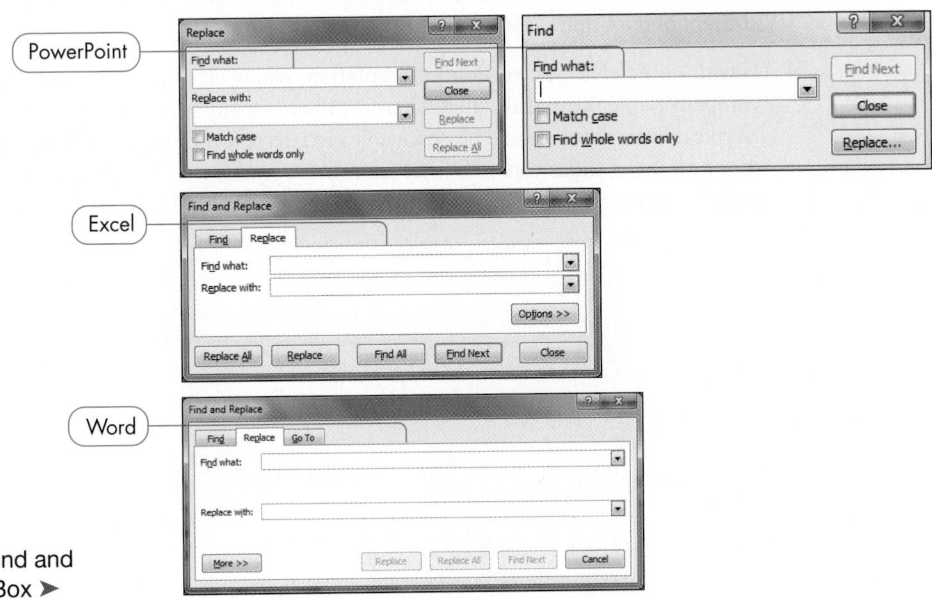

FIGURE 1.42 Find and Replace Dialog Box ➤

TIP Using a Shortcut to Finding Items

Ctrl+F is a shortcut to finding items in a Word, Excel, or PowerPoint file. When you press Ctrl+F, the Find and Replace dialog box shown in Figure 1.42 displays in Excel and PowerPoint. Pressing Ctrl+F in Word displays a feature—the Navigation task pane—at the left side of a Word document. When you type a search term in the Search Document area, Word finds and highlights all occurrences of the search term. The Navigation task pane also makes it easy to move to sections of a document based on levels of headings. The Navigation task pane is only found in Word 2010.

To find and replace selected text, type the text to locate in the *Find what* box and the replacement text in the *Replace with* box. You can narrow the search to require matching case or find whole words only. If you want to replace all occurrences of the text, click Replace All. If you want to replace only some occurrences, click Find Next repeatedly until you reach the occurrence that you want to replace. At that point, click Replace. Click the Close button (or Cancel).

TIP Go to a Location in a File

An Excel worksheet can include more than 1,000,000 rows of data. A Word document's length is unlimited. Moving to a specific point in large files created in either of those applications can be a challenge. That task is simplified by the Go To option, found in the Editing group as an option of the Find command (or under Find & Select in Excel). Click Go To and enter the page number (or other item, such as section, comment, bookmark, or footnote) or the specific Excel cell. Click Go To (in Word) or OK in Excel.

Quick Concepts Check

1. After selecting text in a presentation or document, you see a small transparent bar with formatting options displayed just above the selection. What is the bar called and what is its purpose? If the bar becomes distracting, how would you temporarily remove it from view?
2. You can use Format Painter to copy formatting from one selection to other areas of a document. When would you want to single-click Format Painter and when would you want to double-click the command?
3. What is the first step in cutting or copying text? How are cutting and copying related to the concept of the Clipboard?
4. Having completed a PowerPoint presentation, you realize that you consistently misused a company name. You realize that wherever the company name occurs in the presentation, Krypton Enterprises should be changed to Ace Krypton Enterprises. Without going through the entire set of slides yourself, what feature can you use to very quickly locate and replace the name? Provide an example of when you might want to find text but not replace it.

HANDS-ON EXERCISES

4 Home Tab Tasks

You have created a list of potential contributors to the Rails and Trails project. You have used Excel to record that list in worksheet format. Now you will review the worksheet and format its appearance to make it more attractive. You will also modify the promotional flyer that you reviewed in the last Hands-On Exercise. In working with those projects, you will put into practice the formatting, copying, moving, and editing information from the preceding section.

Skills covered: Move, Copy, and Paste Text • Select Text, Apply Font Attributes, and Use the Mini Toolbar • Use Format Painter and Work with a Shortcut Menu • Use the Font Dialog Box and Find and Replace Text

STEP 1 MOVE, COPY, AND PASTE TEXT

Each contributor to the Rails and Trails project is assigned a contact person from the project. You manage the worksheet that keeps track of those assignments, but the assignments sometimes change. You will copy and paste some worksheet selections to keep from having to retype data. You will also reposition a clip art image to improve the worksheet's appearance. Refer to Figure 1.43 as you complete Step 1.

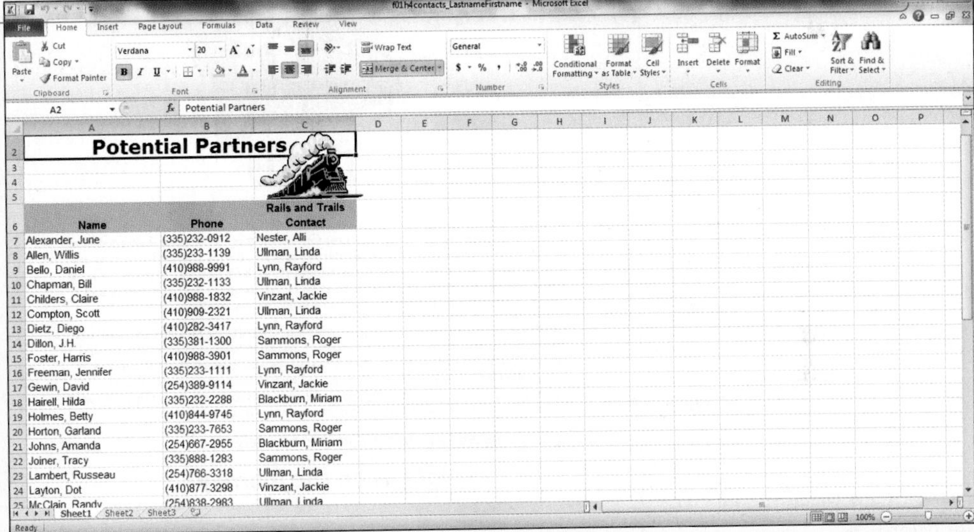

FIGURE 1.43 Contributor List (Excel) ➤

a. Click the **Start button** to display the Start menu, point to **All Programs**, scroll down the list if necessary, and then click **Microsoft Office**. Click **Microsoft Excel 2010**.

   The potential contributors list is saved as an Excel worksheet. You will first open Excel.

b. Open the student data file *f01h4contacts*. Save the file as **f01h4contacts_LastnameFirstname** in the Office Records folder on the drive where you save your files.

   The potential contributors list shown in Figure 1.43 is displayed.

c. Click **cell C7** to select the cell that contains *Alli Nester*, and then click **Copy** in the Clipboard group on the Home tab. Click **cell C15** to select the cell that contains *Roger Sammons*, click **Paste** in the Clipboard group, and then press **Esc** to remove the selection from *Alli Nester*.

   Alli Nester has been assigned as the Rails and Trails contact for Harris Foster, replacing Roger Sammons. You make that replacement on the worksheet by copying and pasting Alli Nester's name in the appropriate worksheet cell.

d. Click the picture of the train. A box displays around the image, indicating that it is selected. Click **Cut** in the Clipboard group, click **cell A2**, click **Paste**, and then click anywhere outside the train picture to deselect it.

> **TROUBLESHOOTING:** A Paste Options icon might appear in the worksheet after you have moved the train picture. It offers additional options related to the paste procedure. You do not need to change any options, so ignore the button.

You decide that the picture of the train will look better if it is placed on the left side of the worksheet instead of the right. You move the picture by cutting and pasting the object.

e. Click **Save** on the Quick Access Toolbar. Click the **Minimize button** to minimize the worksheet without closing it.

STEP 2 SELECT TEXT, APPLY FONT ATTRIBUTES, AND USE THE MINI TOOLBAR

As the opening of Rails and Trails draws near, you are active in preparing promotional materials. You are currently working on an informational flyer that is almost set to go. You will make a few improvements before approving the flyer for release. Refer to Figure 1.44 as you complete Step 2.

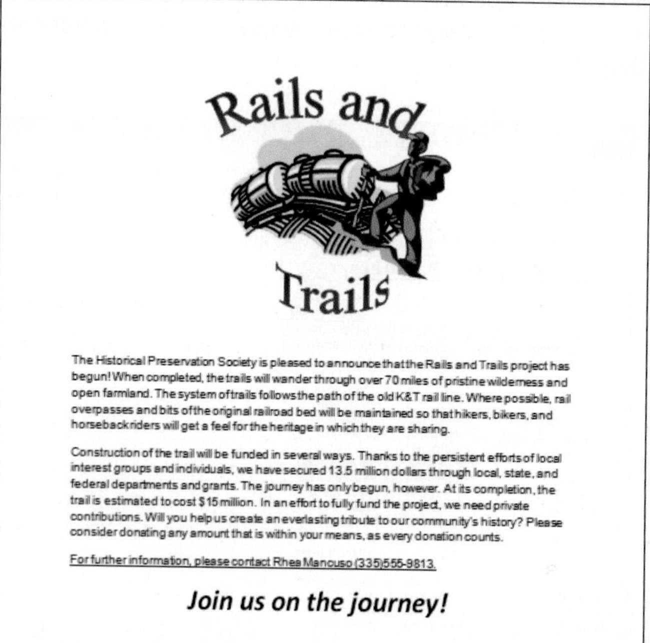

Rails and Trails

The Historical Preservation Society is pleased to announce that the Rails and Trails project has begun! When completed, the trails will wander through over 70 miles of pristine wilderness and open farmland. The system of trails follows the path of the old K&T rail line. Where possible, rail overpasses and bits of the original railroad bed will be maintained so that hikers, bikers, and horsebackriders will get a feel for the heritage in which they are sharing.

Construction of the trail will be funded in several ways. Thanks to the persistent efforts of local interest groups and individuals, we have secured 13.5 million dollars through local, state, and federal departments and grants. The journey has only begun, however. At its completion, the trail is estimated to cost $15 million. In an effort to fully fund the project, we need private contributions. Will you help us create an everlasting tribute to our community's history? Please consider donating any amount that is within your means, as every donation counts.

For further information, please contact Rhea Mancuso (335)555-9813.

Join us on the journey!

FIGURE 1.44 Promotional Flyer (Word) ➤

a. Click the **Start button** to display the Start menu. Click **All Programs**, scroll down if necessary, and then click **Microsoft Office**. Click **Microsoft Word 2010**. Open *f01h4flyer* and save the document as **f01h4flyer_LastnameFirstname** in the Promotional Print folder (a subfolder of Rails and Trails project) on the drive where you save your files.

You plan to modify the promotional flyer slightly to include additional information about the Rails and Trails project.

> **TROUBLESHOOTING:** If you make any major mistakes in this exercise, you can close the file without saving it, open *f01h4flyer* again, and start this exercise over.

b. Click after the period after the word *sharing* at the end of the first paragraph. Press **Enter**, and then type the text below. As you type, do not press Enter at the end of each line. Word will automatically wrap the lines of text.

Construction of the trail will be funded in several ways. Thanks to the persistent efforts of local interest groups and individuals, we have secured $13.5 million through local, state, and federal departments and grants. The journey has only begun, however. At its completion, the trail is estimated to cost $15 million. In an effort to fully fund the project, we need private

contributions. Will you help us create an everlasting tribute to our community's history? Please consider donating any amount that is within your means, as every donation counts. For further information, please contact Rhea Mancuso at (335)555-9813.

> **TROUBLESHOOTING:** If you make any mistakes while typing, press Backspace and correct them.

c. Scroll down and select all of the text at the end of the document, beginning with **For more information, contact:**. Press **Delete**.

   When you press Delete, selected text (or characters to the right of the cursor) are removed. Deleted text is not placed in the Clipboard.

d. Select the words *Join us on the journey!* Click **Italic** in the Font group, and then click anywhere outside the selection to see the result.

e. Select both paragraphs but not the final italicized line. While still within the selection, move the mouse pointer slightly to display the Mini toolbar, click the **font arrow** on the Mini toolbar, and then select **Arial**.

> **TROUBLESHOOTING:** If you do not see the Mini toolbar, you might have moved too far away from the selection. In that case, click outside the selection, and then drag to select it once more. Without leaving the selection, move the mouse pointer slightly to display the Mini toolbar.

   You have changed the font of the two paragraphs.

f. Click after the period following the word *counts* before the last sentence in the second paragraph. Press **Enter**, and then press **Delete** to remove the extra space before the first letter, if necessary. Move the mouse pointer to the margin area at the immediate left of the new line. The mouse pointer should appear as a white arrow. Click once to select the line, click **Underline** in the Font group, and then click anywhere outside the selected area. Your document should appear as shown in Figure 1.44.

   You have underlined the contact information to draw attention to the text.

g. Save the document and keep it open for the next step in this exercise.

STEP 3 USE FORMAT PAINTER AND WORK WITH A SHORTCUT MENU

You are on a short timeline for finalizing the promotional flyer, so you will use a few shortcuts to avoid retyping and reformatting more than is necessary. You know that you can easily copy formatting from one area to another using Format Painter. Shortcut menus can also help make changes quickly. Refer to Figure 1.45 as you complete Step 3.

The Historical Preservation Society is pleased to announce that the **Rails and Trails** project has begun! When completed, the trails will wander through over 70 miles of pristine wilderness and open farmland. The system of trails follows the path of the old K&T rail line. Where possible, rail overpasses and bits of the original railroad bed will be maintained so that hikers, bikers, and horseback riders will get a feel for the heritage in which they are sharing.

Construction of the trail will be funded in several ways. Thanks to the persistent efforts of local interest groups and individuals, we have secured $13.5 million through local, state, and federal departments and grants. The journey has only begun, however. At its completion, the trail is estimated to cost $15 million. In an effort to fully fund the project, we need private contributions. Will you help us create an everlasting tribute to our community's history? Please consider donating any amount that is within your means, as every donation counts.

For further information, please contact Rhea Mancuso at (335)232-9813.

Join us on the journey!

FIGURE 1.45 Promotional Flyer (Word) ➤

a. Select the words **Rails and Trails** in the first paragraph, and then click **Bold** in the Font group.

b. Click **Format Painter** in the Clipboard group, and then select the second to last line of the document, containing the contact information. Click anywhere outside the selection to deselect the line.

   The format of the area that you first selected (Rails and Trails) is applied to the line containing the contact information.

c. Select the text *Join us on the journey!* Right-click in the selected area, click **Font** on the shortcut menu, click **22** in the **Size box** to reduce the font size slightly, and then click **OK**. Click outside the selected area.

   Figure 1.45 shows the final document as it should now appear.

d. Save the document and close Word.

   The flyer will be saved with the same file name and in the same location as it was when you last saved the document in Step 2. As you close Word, the open document will also be closed.

STEP 4 USE THE FONT DIALOG BOX AND FIND AND REPLACE TEXT

The contributors worksheet is almost complete. However, you first want to make a few more formatting changes to improve the worksheet's appearance. You will also quickly change an incorrect area code by using Excel's Find and Replace feature. Refer to Figures 1.46 and 1.47 as you complete Step 4.

FIGURE 1.46 Excel Dialog Box Launcher ➤

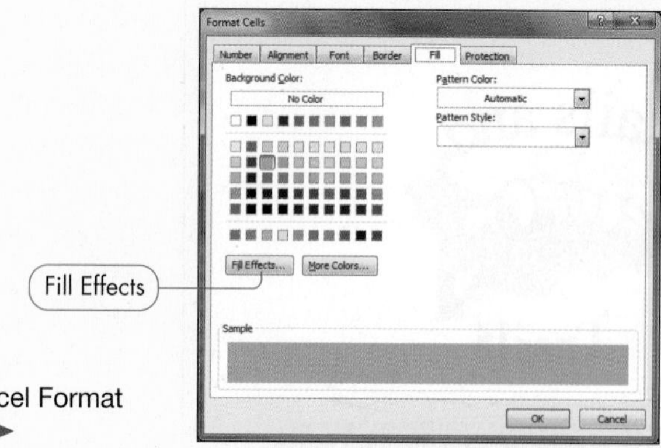

FIGURE 1.47 Excel Format Cells Dialog Box ➤

a. Click the **Excel icon** on the taskbar to redisplay the contributors worksheet that you minimized in Step 1.

   The Excel potential contributors list displays.

b. Drag to select **cells A6 through C6**.

TROUBLESHOOTING: Make sure the mouse pointer looks like a large white plus sign before dragging. It is normal for the first cell in the selected area to be a different shade. If you click and drag when the mouse pointer does not resemble a white plus sign, text may have been moved or duplicated. In that case, click Undo on the Quick Access Toolbar.

c. Click the **Dialog Box Launcher** in the Font group as shown in Figure 1.46. Click the **Fill tab**, and then click **Fill Effects** as shown in Figure 1.47. Click any style in the Variants group, click **OK**, and then click **OK** once more to close the Format Cells dialog box. Click outside the selected area to see the final result.

The headings of the worksheet are shaded more attractively.

d. Click **Find & Select** in the Editing group, click **Replace**, and then type **410** in the **Find what box**. Type **411** in the **Replace with box**, click **Replace All**, and then click **OK** when notified that Excel has made 10 replacements. Click **Close**.

You discover that you consistently typed an incorrect area code. You use Find and Replace to make a correction quickly.

e. Save the *f01h4contacts_LastnameFirstname* workbook. Close the workbook and exit Excel.

The workbook will be saved with the same file name and in the same location as it was when you last saved the document in Step 1. As you exit Excel, the open workbook will also be closed.

Insert Tab Tasks

As its title implies, the Insert tab enables you to insert, or add, items into a file. Much of the Insert tab is specific to the particular application, with little commonality to other Office applications. Word's Insert tab includes text-related commands, whereas Excel's is more focused on inserting such items as charts and tables. PowerPoint's Insert tab includes multimedia items and links. Despite their obvious differences in focus, all Office applications share a common group on the Insert tab—the Illustrations group. In addition, all Office applications enable you to insert headers, footers, text boxes, and symbols. Those options are also found on the Insert tab in various groups, depending on the particular application. In this section, you will work with common activities on the Insert tab, including inserting pictures and clip art.

Despite their obvious differences in focus, all Office applications share a common group on the Insert tab—the Illustrations group.

Inserting Objects

With few exceptions, all Office applications share common options in the Illustrations group of the Insert tab. PowerPoint places some of those common features in the Images group. You can insert pictures, clip art, shapes, screenshots, and SmartArt. Those items are considered objects, retaining their separate nature when they are inserted in files. That means that you can select them and manage them independently of the underlying document, worksheet, or presentation.

After an object has been inserted, you can click the object to select it or click anywhere outside the object to deselect it. When an object is selected, a border of small dots, or "handles," surrounds it, appearing at each corner and in the middle of each side. Figure 1.48 shows a selected object, surrounded by handles. Unless an object is selected, you cannot change or modify it. When an object is selected, the Ribbon expands to include one or more contextual tabs. Items on the contextual tabs relate to the selected object, enabling you to modify and manage it.

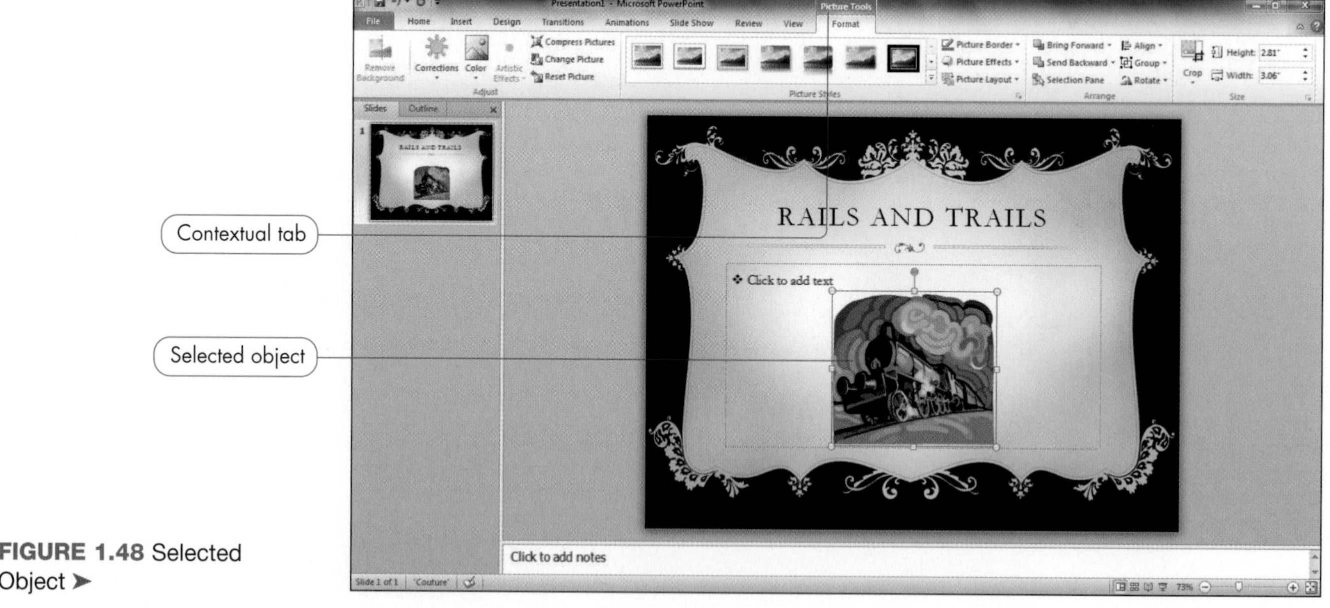

FIGURE 1.48 Selected Object ➤

> **TIP** Resizing and Moving a Selected Object
>
> You can resize and move a selected object. Place the mouse pointer on any handle, and then drag (when the mouse pointer looks like a two-headed arrow) to resize the object. Be careful! If you drag a side handle, the object is likely to be skewed, possibly resulting in a poor image. Instead, drag a corner handle to proportionally resize the image. To move an object, drag the object when the mouse pointer looks like a four-headed arrow.

Insert Pictures

A **picture** is a graphic file that is retrieved from storage media and placed in an Office project.

Documents, worksheets, and presentations can include much more than just words and numbers. You can easily add energy and description to the project by including pictures and other graphic elements. Although a ***picture*** is usually just that—a digital photo—it is actually defined as a graphic element retrieved from storage media such as a hard drive or a CD. A picture could actually be a clip art item that you saved from the Internet onto your hard drive.

The process of inserting a picture is simple. First, click in the project where you want the picture to be placed. Make sure you know where the picture that you plan to use is stored. Click the Insert tab. Then, in the Illustrations group (or Images group in PowerPoint), click Picture. The Insert Picture dialog box shown in Figure 1.49 displays. Select a picture and click Insert (or simply double-click the picture). In addition, on some slide layouts, PowerPoint displays an Insert Picture from File button (Figure 1.50) that you can click to select and position a picture on the slide.

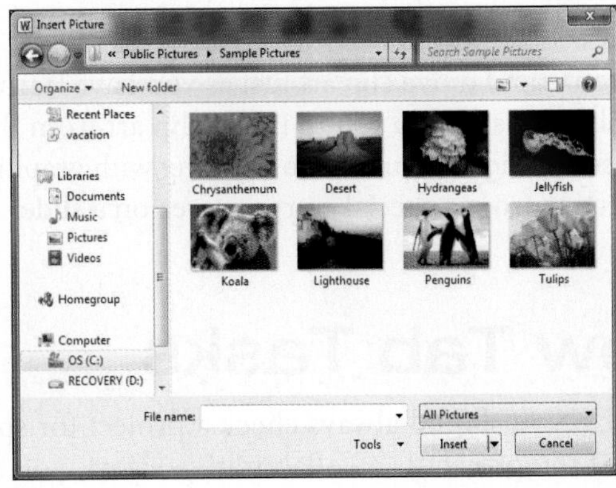

FIGURE 1.49 Insert Picture Dialog Box ➤

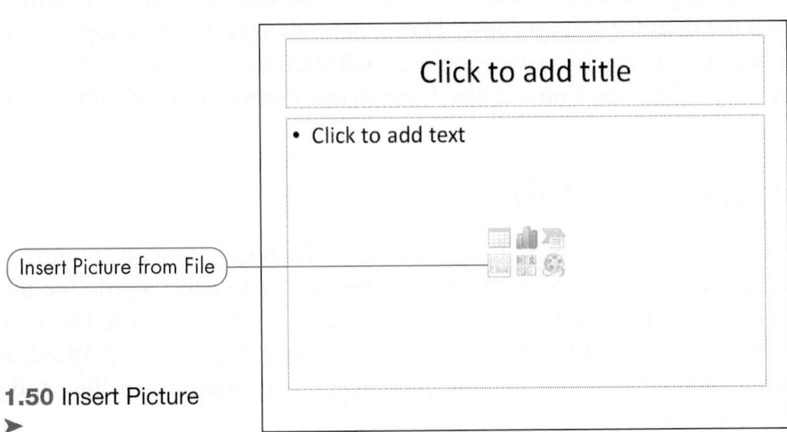

FIGURE 1.50 Insert Picture from File ➤

Insert Clip Art

Clip art is an electronic illustration that can be inserted into an Office project.

A large library of ***clip art*** is included with each Office installation. Office.com, an online resource providing additional clip art and Office support, is also available from within each Office application. To explore available clip art, click the Insert tab within an Office program, and then click Clip Art in the Illustrations group (or the Images group in PowerPoint). Figure 1.51 shows the Clip Art task pane that displays. Suppose that you are looking for some clip art to support a fund-raising project. Having opened the Clip Art task pane, you could click in the *Search for* box and type a search term, such as *money*. To limit the results to a particular media type, click the arrow beside the *Results should be* box, and make a selection. Click Go to initiate the search.

FIGURE 1.51 Clip Art Task Pane ➤

You can resize and move clip art just as you have learned to similarly manage pictures. All Office applications enable you to insert clip art from the Illustrations group. However, PowerPoint uses a unique approach to working with graphics, including the ability to insert clip art by selecting from a special-purpose area on a slide.

Review Tab Tasks

As a final touch, you should always check a project for spelling, grammatical, and word-usage errors. If the project is a collaborative effort, you and your colleagues might add comments and suggest changes. You can even use a thesaurus to find synonyms for words that are not quite right for your purpose. The Review tab in each Office application provides all these options and more. In this section, you will learn to review a file, checking for spelling and grammatical errors. You will also learn to use a thesaurus to identify synonyms.

Reviewing a File

As you create or edit a file, you will want to make sure no spelling or grammatical errors exist. You will also be concerned with wording, being sure to select words and phrases that best represent the purpose of the document, worksheet, or presentation. On occasion, you might even find yourself at a loss for an appropriate word. Not to worry. Word, Excel, and PowerPoint all provide standard tools for proofreading, including a spelling and grammar checker and a thesaurus.

Check Spelling and Grammar

In general, all Office applications check your spelling and grammar as you type. If a word is unrecognized, it is flagged as misspelled or grammatically incorrect. Misspellings are identified with a red wavy underline, grammatical problems are underlined in green, and word usage errors (such as using *bear* instead of *bare*) have a blue underline. If the word or phrase is truly in error—that is, it is not a person's name or an unusual term that is not in the application's dictionary—you can correct it manually or you can let the software correct it for you. If you right-click a word or phrase that is identified as a mistake, you will see a shortcut menu similar to that shown in Figure 1.52. If the application's dictionary can make a suggestion as to the correct spelling, you can click to accept the suggestion and make the change. If a grammatical rule is violated, you will have an opportunity to select a correction. However, if the text is actually correct, you can click Ignore (to bypass that single occurrence) or Ignore All (to bypass all occurrences of the flagged error in the current document). Click Add to Dictionary if you want the word to be considered correct whenever it appears in all documents. Similar selections on a shortcut menu enable you to ignore grammatical mistakes if they are not errors.

In general, all Office applications check your spelling and grammar as you type.

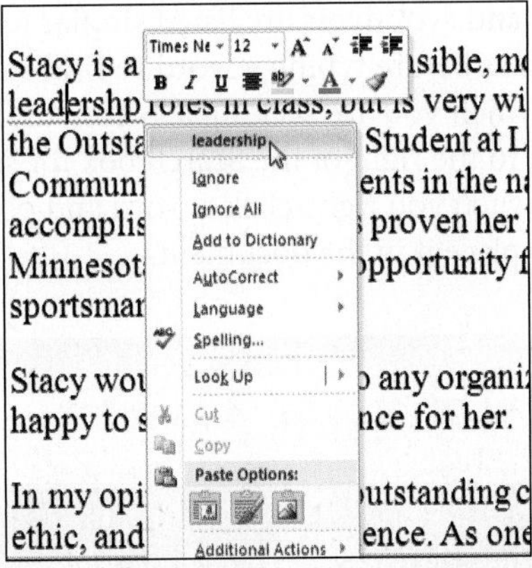

FIGURE 1.52 Correcting Misspelling ➤

You might prefer the convenience of addressing possible misspellings and grammatical errors without having to examine each underlined word or phrase. To do so, click Spelling & Grammar in the Proofing group of the Review tab. Beginning at the top of the document, each identified error is highlighted in a dialog box similar to Figure 1.53. You can then choose how to address the problem by making a selection in the dialog box.

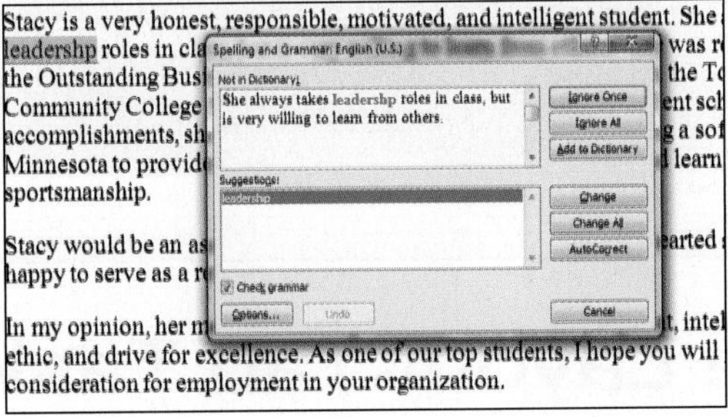

FIGURE 1.53 Checking for Spelling and Grammatical Errors ➤

TIP Understanding Software Options

A **default** setting is one that is in place unless you specify otherwise.

Many Office settings are considered ***default*** options. Thus, unless you specify otherwise, the default options are in effect. One such default option is the automatic spelling and grammar checker. If you prefer to enable and disable certain options or change default settings in an Office application, you can click the File tab and click Options. From that point, you can work through a series of categories, selecting or deselecting options at will. For example, if you want to change how the application corrects and formats text, you can select or deselect settings in the Proofing group.

Use the Thesaurus

As you write, there will be times when you are at a loss for an appropriate word. Perhaps you feel that you are overusing a word and want to find a suitable substitute. The Thesaurus is the Office tool to use in such a situation. Located in the Proofing group of the Review tab, Thesaurus enables you to search for synonyms, or words with similar meanings. Select a word, then click Thesaurus, in the Proofing group on the Review tab. A task pane displays on the right side of the screen, and synonyms are listed similar to those shown in Figure 1.54. You can also use the Thesaurus before typing a word to find substitutes. Simply click Thesaurus and type the word for which you are seeking a synonym in the Search for box. Press Enter or click the green arrow to the right of the Search box for some suggestions. Finally, you can also identify synonyms when you right-click a word and point to Synonyms (if any are available). Click any word to place it in the document.

FIGURE 1.54 Thesaurus Task Pane ➤

Page Layout Tab Tasks

When you prepare a document or worksheet, you are concerned with the way the project appears onscreen and possibly in print. Unlike Word and Excel, a PowerPoint presentation is usually designed as a slide show, so it is not nearly as critical to concern yourself with page layout settings. The Page Layout tab in Word and Excel provides access to a full range of options such as margin settings and page orientation. In this section, you will identify page layout settings that are common to Office applications. These settings include margins and page orientation.

The Page Layout tab in Word and Excel provides access to a full range of options such as margin settings and page orientation.

Changing Page Settings

Because a document is most often designed to be printed, you will want to make sure it looks its best in printed form. That means that you will need to know how to adjust margins and how to change the page orientation. Perhaps the document or spreadsheet should be centered on the page vertically or the text should be aligned in columns. By adjusting page settings, you can do all these things and more. You will find the most common page settings, such as margins and page orientation, in the Page Setup group of the Page Layout tab. For less common settings, such as determining whether headers should print on odd or even pages, you can use the Page Setup dialog box.

Change Margins

A **margin** is the blank space around the sides, top, and bottom of a document or worksheet.

A ***margin*** is the area of blank space that appears to the left, right, top, and bottom of a document or worksheet. Margins are only evident if you are in Print Layout or Page Layout view or if you are in the Backstage view, previewing a document to print. To change or set margins, click the Page Layout tab. As shown in Figure 1.55, the Page Setup group enables you to change such items as margins and orientation. To change margins, click Margins. If the margins that you intend to use are included in any of the preset margin options, click a selection. Otherwise, click Custom Margins to display the Page Setup dialog box in which you can create custom margin settings. Click OK to accept the settings, and close the dialog box. You can also change margins when you click Print on the File tab.

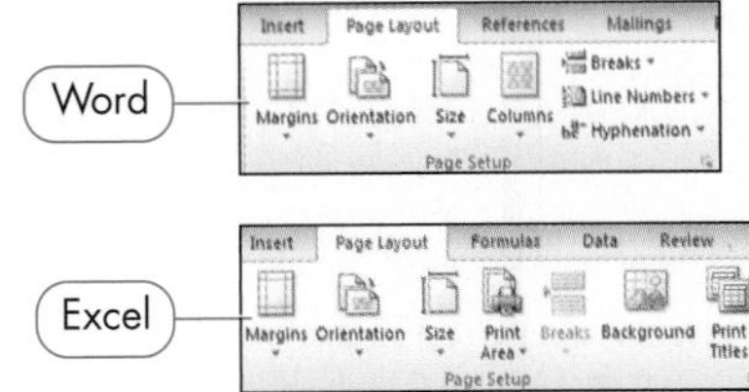

FIGURE 1.55 Page Setup Group ➤

Change Page Orientation

A page or worksheet displayed in **portrait** orientation is taller than it is wide.

A page or worksheet displayed in **landscape** orientation is wider than it is tall.

Documents and worksheets can be displayed in ***portrait*** orientation or in ***landscape***. A page displayed or printed in portrait orientation is taller than it is wide. A page in landscape orientation is wider than it is tall. Word documents are usually more attractive displayed in portrait orientation, whereas Excel worksheets are often more suitable in landscape. To select page orientation, click Orientation in the Page Setup group on the Page Layout tab. See Figure 1.55 for the location of the Orientation command. Orientation is also an option in the Print area of the Backstage view.

Use the Page Setup Dialog Box

The Page Setup group contains the most commonly used page options in the particular Office application. Some are unique to Excel, and others are more applicable to Word. Other less common settings are only available in the Page Setup dialog box, displayed when you click the Page Setup Dialog Box Launcher. The subsequent dialog box includes options for customizing margins, selecting page orientation, centering vertically, printing gridlines, and creating headers and footers, although some of those options are only available when working with Word, and others are unique to Excel. Figure 1.56 gives a glimpse of both the Excel and Word Page Setup dialog boxes.

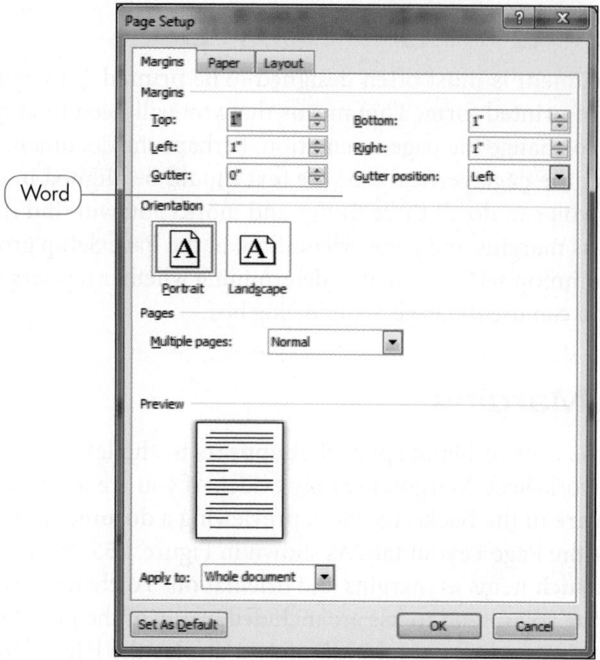

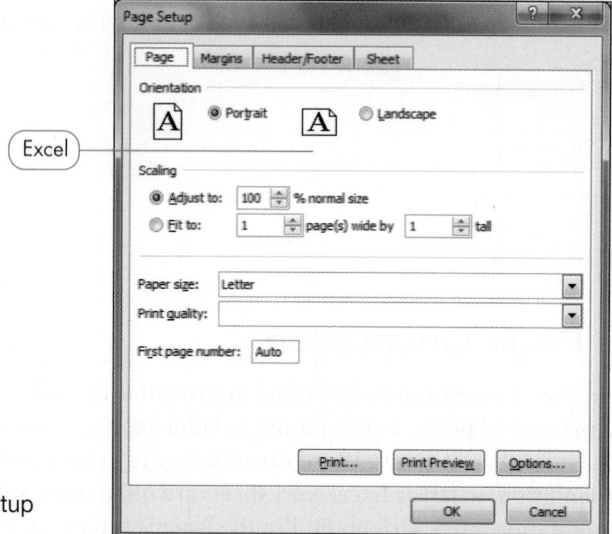

FIGURE 1.56 Page Setup Dialog Boxes ➤

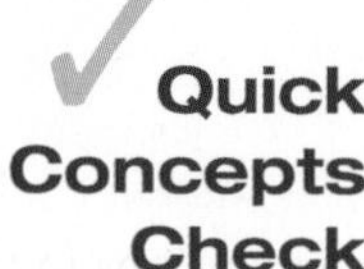

Quick Concepts Check

1. Give two ways to resize an object, such as clip art, that has been inserted in a document and selected.
2. Often, an Office application will identify a word as misspelled that is not actually misspelled. How can that happen? If a word is flagged as misspelled, how can you correct it (or ignore it if it is not actually an error)?
3. Give two ways to change a document from portrait orientation to landscape. Identify at least one document type that you think would be better suited for landscape orientation rather than portrait.
4. What dialog box includes options for selecting margins, centering vertically, and changing page orientation?

5 Tasks on the Insert Tab, Page Layout Tab, and Review Tab

The Rails and Trails project is nearing kickoff. You are helping plan a ceremony to commemorate the occasion. To encourage interest and participation, you will edit a PowerPoint presentation that is to be shown to civic groups, the local retiree association, and to city and county leaders. You know that pictures and clip art add energy to a presentation when used appropriately, so you will check for those elements, adding whatever is necessary. A major concern is making sure the presentation is error free and that it is available in print so that meeting participants can review it later. As a reminder, you also plan to have available a handout giving the time and date of the dedication ceremony. You will use the Insert tab to work with illustrations and the Review tab to check for errors, and you will use Word to generate an attractive handout as a reminder of the date.

Skills covered: Check Spelling and Use the Thesaurus • Insert Clip Art and Pictures • Select Margins and Page Orientation

STEP 1 CHECK SPELLING AND USE THE THESAURUS

As you check the PowerPoint presentation that will be shown to local groups, you make sure no misspellings or grammatical mistakes exist. You also use the Thesaurus to find a suitable substitution for a word you feel should be replaced. Refer to Figure 1.57 as you complete Step 1.

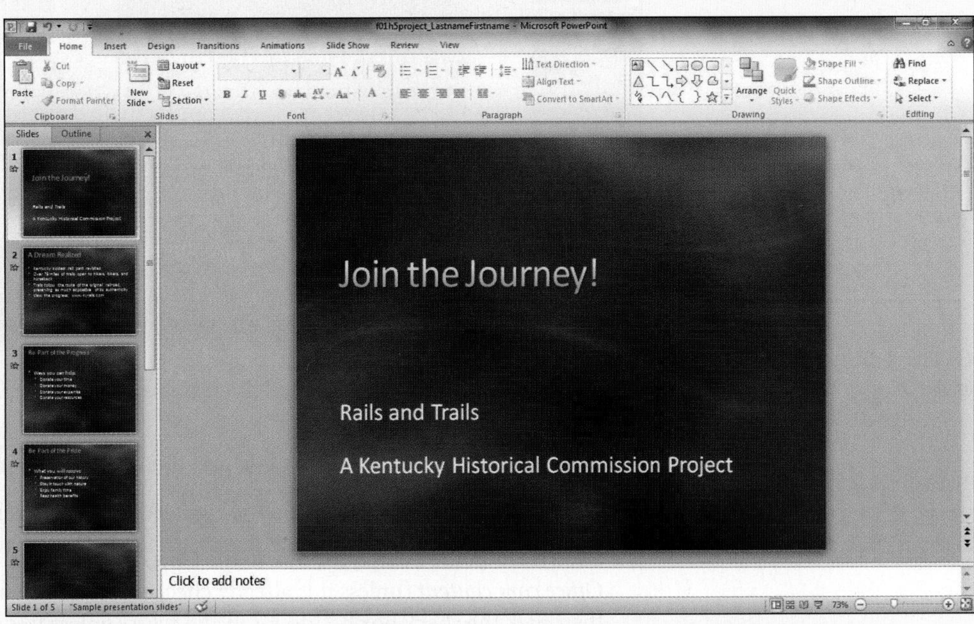

FIGURE 1.57 Project Presentation ➤

a. Click the **Start button** to display the Start menu, and then point to **All Programs**. Click **Microsoft Office**, and then click **Microsoft PowerPoint 2010**. Open *f01h5project* and save it as **f01h5project_LastnameFirstname** in the Presentations folder (a subfolder of Rails and Trails Projects) on the drive where you save your files. The presentation displays as shown in Figure 1.57.

   The PowerPoint presentation opens, with Slide 1 shown in Normal view.

b. Click **Slide Show** and the **Slide Show tab**, and then click **From Beginning** in the Start Slide Show group to view the presentation. Click to advance from one slide to another. After the last slide, click to return to Normal view.

c. Click the **Review tab**, and then click **Spelling** in the Proofing group. The first misspelling is not actually misspelled. It is the name of a city. Click **Ignore** to leave it as is. The next flagged misspelling is truly misspelled. With the correct spelling selected, click **Change** to correct the mistake. Correct any other words that are misspelled. Click **OK** when the spell check is complete.

d. Click **Slide 2** in the Slides pane on the left. Double-click the word *route*, click **Thesaurus** in the Proofing group, point to **path** in the Research pane, click the arrow to the right of the word path, and then click **Insert**. Press the **Spacebar**.

   The word *route* is replaced with the word *path*.

e. Click the **Close button** in the top-right corner of the Research pane.

f. Save the presentation and keep it open for the next step.

STEP 2 INSERT CLIP ART AND PICTURES

Although the presentation provides the necessary information and encourages viewers to become active participants in the project, you believe that pictures and clip art might make it a little more exciting. Where appropriate, you will include clip art and a picture. Refer to Figures 1.58 and 1.59 as you complete Step 2.

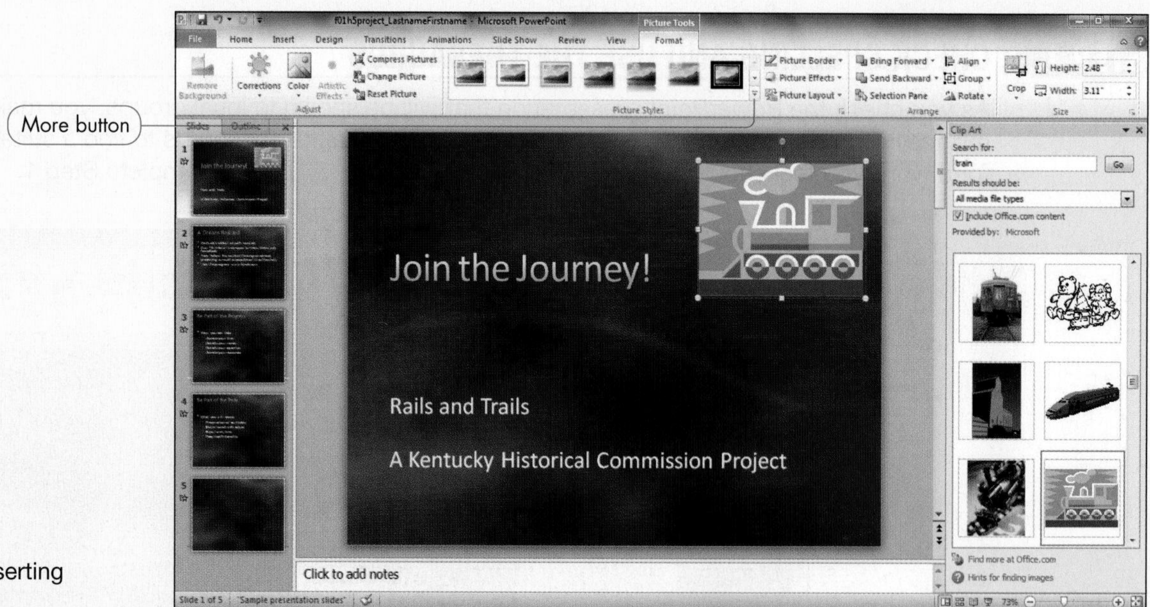

FIGURE 1.58 Inserting Clip Art ➤

a. Display Slide 1, click the **Insert tab**, and then click **Clip Art**.

   The Clip Art task pane opens on the right side of the screen.

b. Type **train** in the **Search for box** in the Clip Art task pane. Click the check box beside *Include Office.com content* (unless it is already checked), click the arrow beside *Results should be*, and then click the check box beside *All media types* (unless it is already checked). Narrow results to illustrations by clicking the check box beside *Illustrations*, and then click **Go**.

   You will identify clip art to be displayed on Slide 1.

c. Click to select any clip art image of a train.

TROUBLESHOOTING: Be sure to click the clip art image, not the arrow to the right. If you click the arrow, you will then need to click Insert to place the clip art image on the slide.

TROUBLESHOOTING: It is very easy to make the mistake of inserting duplicate clip art images on a slide, perhaps because you clicked the image more than once in the Clip Art task pane. If that should happen, you can remove any unwanted clip art by clicking to select it on the slide and pressing Delete.

The clip art image probably will not be placed as you would like, but you will move and resize it in the next substep. Also, the clip art is selected, as indicated by the box and handles surrounding it.

d. Click a corner handle (small circle) on the border of the clip art. Make sure the mouse pointer appears as a double-headed arrow. Drag to resize the image so that it appears similar to that shown in Figure 1.58. Click in the center of the clip art. The mouse pointer should appear as a four-headed arrow. Drag the clip art to the top-right corner of the slide. Make sure the clip art is still selected (it should be surrounded by a box and handles). If it is not selected, click to select it.

e. Click the **More button** of the Picture Styles group (see Figure 1.58) to reveal a gallery of styles. Position the mouse pointer over any style to see a preview of the style applied to the clip art. Click to apply a style of your choice. Close the Clip Art task pane.

f. On Slide 5, type **The Journey Begins** in the **Title box**. Click **Insert Picture from File** in the Content Placeholder (see Figure 1.50), navigate to the student data files, and then double-click *f01h5rails*.

A picture is placed on the final slide.

g. Click to select the picture, if necessary. Drag a corner handle to resize the picture. Click the center of the picture and drag the picture to reposition it in the center of the slide as shown in Figure 1.59.

> **TROUBLESHOOTING:** You can only move the picture when the mouse pointer looks like a four-headed arrow. If instead, you drag a handle, the picture will be resized instead of moved. Click Undo on the Quick Access Toolbar and try it again.

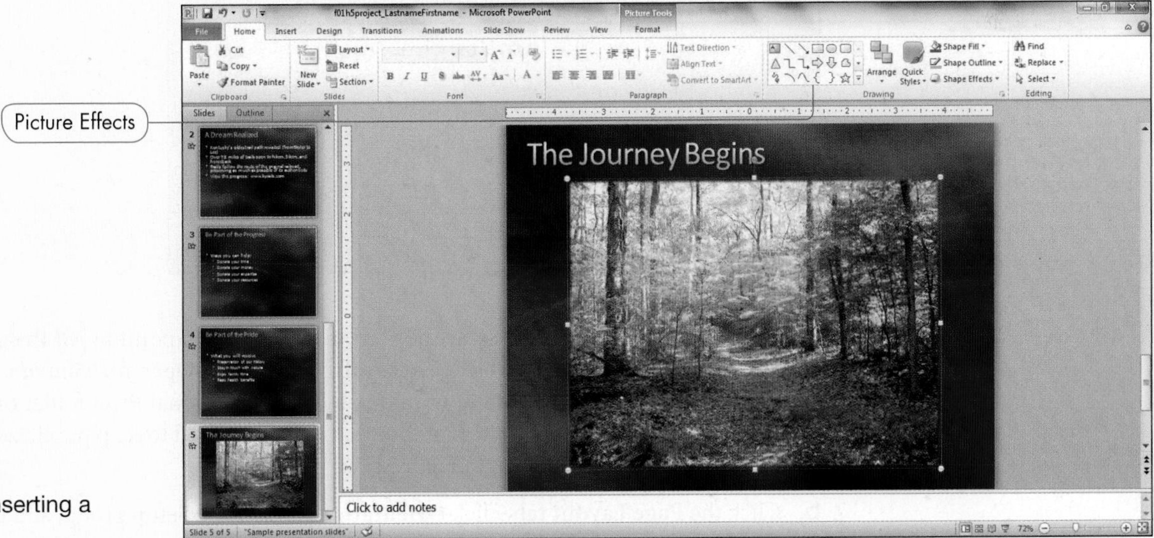

FIGURE 1.59 Inserting a Picture ➤

h. Click **Picture Effects** in the Picture Styles group on the Format tab, point to **Soft Edges**, and then click **5 Point**.

i. Click the **Slide Show tab**, and then click **From Beginning** in the Start Slide Show group. Click to advance from one slide to another. After the last slide, click to return to Normal view.

j. Save the presentation and exit PowerPoint.

STEP 3 SELECT MARGINS AND PAGE ORIENTATION

You are ready to finalize the flyer, but before printing it you want to see how it will look. You wonder if it would be better in landscape or portrait orientation, so you will try both. After adjusting the margins, you are ready to save the flyer for later printing and distribution. Refer to Figure 1.60 as you complete Step 3.

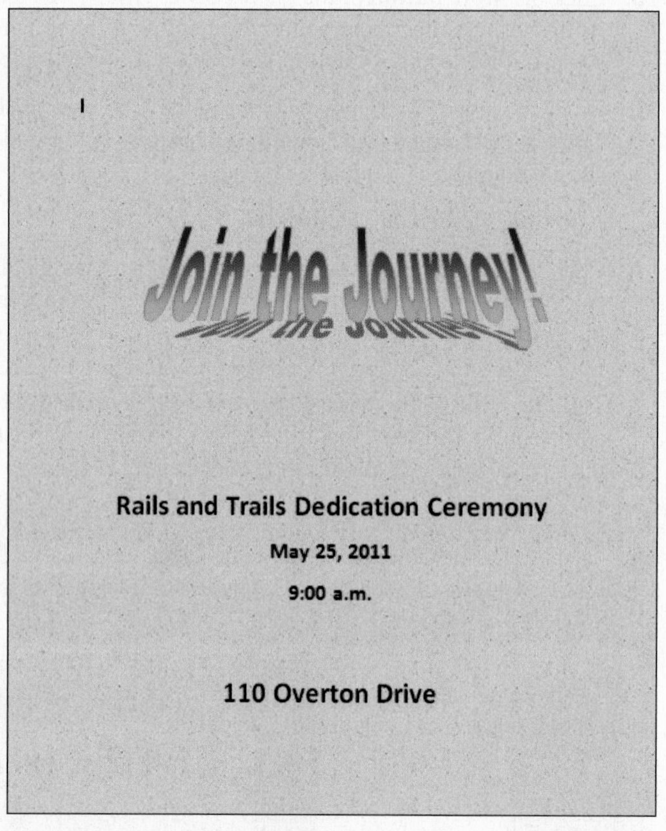

Join the Journey!
Rails and Trails Dedication Ceremony
May 25, 2011
9:00 a.m.
110 Overton Drive

FIGURE 1.60 Word Handout ➤

a. Click the **Start button** to display the Start menu, and then point to **All Programs**. Click **Microsoft Office**, and then click **Microsoft Word 2010**. Open *f01h5handout* and save it as **f01h5handout_LastnameFirstname** in the Promotional Print folder on the drive where you save your files. The handout that you developed to help publicize the dedication ceremony displays as shown in Figure 1.60.

b. Click the **Page Layout tab**, click **Orientation** in the Page Setup group, and then click **Landscape** to view the flyer in landscape orientation.

   You want to see how the handout will look in landscape orientation.

c. Click the **File tab**, click **Print**, and then click **Next Page** (right-directed arrow at the bottom center of the preview page).

   The second page of the handout shows only the address. You can see that the two-page layout is not an attractive option.

d. Click the **Home tab**. Click **Undo** on the Quick Access Toolbar. Click the **File tab**, and then click **Print**.

   The document fits on one page. Portrait orientation is a much better choice for the handout.

e. Click the **Page Layout tab**, click **Margins**, and then select **Custom Margins**. Click the **spin arrow** beside the Left margin box to increase the margin to **1.5**. Similarly, change the right margin to **1.5**. Click **OK**.

f. Save the document and exit Word.

CHAPTER OBJECTIVES REVIEW

After reading this chapter, you have accomplished the following objectives:

1. **Use Windows Explorer.** You can use Windows Explorer to manage files and folders and to view contents of storage media. In addition to viewing the contents of physical folders, you can also manage libraries, which are collections of related data from various physical locations. Windows Explorer provides information on networked resources and shared disk drives, as well. Using the Favorites area of Windows Explorer, you can locate areas of frequent access.
2. **Work with folders and files.** Using Windows Explorer, you can create folders and rename, delete, move, and copy files and folders. You can also open files through Windows Explorer.
3. **Select, copy, and move multiple files and folders.** Backing up, or copying, files and folders is necessary to ensure that you do not lose important data and documents. You can quickly move or copy multiple items by selecting them all at one time.
4. **Identify common interface components.** You can communicate with Office software through the Microsoft Office user interface. Common interface components, found in all Microsoft Office applications, include the Ribbon, Quick Access Toolbar, title bar, status bar, and the Backstage view. The Ribbon is organized by commands within groups within tabs on the Ribbon. The Quick Access Toolbar provides one-click access to such activities as Save, Undo, and Repeat (Redo). The Backstage view is an Office feature that enables such common activities as opening, closing, saving, and printing files. It also provides information on an open file. The status bar contains information relative to the open file. The title bar identifies the open file's name and contains control buttons (minimize, maximize/restore down, and close).
5. **Get Office Help.** You can get help while you are using Microsoft Office by clicking the Help button, which appears as a question mark in the top-right corner of the Ribbon. You can also click the File tab to open the Backstage view, and then click the Help button. Assistance is available from within a dialog box by clicking the Help button in the top-right corner of the dialog box. When you rest the mouse pointer over any command on the Ribbon, you will see an Enhanced ScreenTip that provides a brief summary of the command.
6. **Open a file.** After a file has been saved, you can open it by clicking the File tab and selecting Open. If you recently worked with a file, you can reopen it from the Recent Documents list, which is displayed when you click Recent in the Backstage view. Finally, you can open a file from a template. Templates are predesigned files supplied by Microsoft from within the current Office installation or from Office.com.
7. **Print a file.** Often, you will want to print a file (a document, worksheet, or presentation). The Backstage view makes it easy to preview the file, change print settings, and print the file.
8. **Close a file and application.** When you close a file, it is removed from memory. If you plan to work with the file later, you will need to save the file before closing it. The Office application will prompt you to save the file before closing if you have made any changes since the last time the file was saved. When you close an application, all open files within the application are also closed.
9. **Select and edit text.** The Home tab includes options to change the appearance of text. You can change the size, color, and type of font, as well as other font attributes. The font is the typeface, or the way characters appear and are sized. Before changing existing text, you must select what you want to change. Although shortcuts to text selection exist, you can always select text by dragging to highlight it. Any formatting changes that you identify apply only to selected text or to text typed after the changes are invoked.
10. **Use the Clipboard group tasks.** The Clipboard is a holding area for selections that you have cut or copied. Although you can view the Clipboard by clicking the Dialog Box Launcher in the Clipboard group, doing so is not necessary before pasting a cut or copied item to a receiving location. Another option in the Clipboard group is Format Painter, which enables you to copy formatting from one area to another within a file.
11. **Use the Editing group tasks.** You can easily find selected words or phrases and replace them, if necessary, with substitutions. There may be occasions when you simply want to find an occurrence of selected text without replacing it, whereas at other times you want to make replacements immediately. The Find option enables you to locate text, whereas Replace enables you to find all occurrences of an item quickly and replace it with another.
12. **Insert objects.** Pictures, clip art, shapes, screenshots, headers and footers, and text boxes are objects that you can insert in Office projects. After you have inserted an object, you can click to select it and manage it independently of the underlying worksheet, document, or presentation. When you select an object, a contextual tab appears on the Ribbon to provide formatting options specific to the selected object.
13. **Review a file.** You can check spelling, grammar, and word usage using any Office application. In fact, applications are usually set to check for such errors as you type, underlining possible misspellings in red, grammatical mistakes in green, and incorrect word usage in blue. Errors are not always correctly identified, as the Office application might indicate a misspelling when it is simply a word that is not in its dictionary. You can also check spelling and grammar by selecting Spelling & Grammar in the Proofing group on the Review tab.
14. **Change page settings.** You can change margins and page orientation through commands in the Page Setup group of the Page Layout tab. The Page Setup dialog box, accessible when you click the Dialog Box Launcher in the Page Setup group, provides even more choices of page settings.

KEY TERMS

Access ***p.66***
Backstage view ***p.67***
Backup ***p.61***
Clip art ***p.102***
Clipboard ***p.90***
Command ***p.69***
Contextual tab ***p.70***
Copy ***p.90***
Cut ***p.90***
Default ***p.104***
Dialog box ***p.69***
Dialog Box Launcher ***p.69***
Enhanced ScreenTip ***p.72***
Excel ***p.66***
File ***p.54***
Find ***p.93***
Folder ***p.54***
Font ***p.89***
Format Painter ***p.90***
Gallery ***p.70***
Group ***p.69***
Key Tip ***p.71***
Landscape ***p.105***
Library ***p.56***
Live Preview ***p.70***
Margin ***p.105***
Microsoft Office ***p.66***
Mini toolbar ***p.88***
Navigation Pane ***p.56***
Paste ***p.90***
Picture ***p.101***
Portrait ***p.105***
PowerPoint ***p.66***
Quick Access Toolbar ***p.67***
Replace ***p.93***
Ribbon ***p.69***
Shortcut menu ***p.90***
Status bar ***p.71***
Subfolder ***p.54***
Tab ***p.69***
Template ***p.81***
Title bar ***p.67***
Toggle ***p.89***
User interface ***p.66***
View ***p.71***
Windows Explorer ***p.54***
Word ***p.66***
Zoom slider ***p.72***

MULTIPLE CHOICE

1. The Recent Documents list:
   (a) Shows documents that have been previously printed.
   (b) Shows documents that have been previously opened.
   (c) Shows documents that have been previously saved in an earlier software version.
   (d) Shows documents that have been previously deleted.

2. Which of the following Windows Explorer features collects related data from folders and gives them a single name?
   (a) Network
   (b) Favorites
   (c) Libraries
   (d) Computer

3. When you want to copy the format of a selection, but not the content:
   (a) Double-click Copy in the Clipboard group.
   (b) Right-click the selection, and then click Copy.
   (c) Click Copy Format in the Clipboard group.
   (d) Click Format Painter in the Clipboard group.

4. Which of the following is not an object that can be inserted in an Office document?
   (a) Picture
   (b) Clip art
   (c) Paragraph box
   (d) Text box

5. What does a red wavy underline in a document, spreadsheet, or presentation mean?
   (a) A word is misspelled or not recognized by the Office dictionary.
   (b) A grammatical mistake exists.
   (c) An apparent word-usage mistake exists.
   (d) A word has been replaced with a synonym.

6. When you close a file:
   (a) You are prompted to save the file (unless you have made no changes since last saving it).
   (b) The application (Word, Excel, or PowerPoint) is also closed.
   (c) You must first save the file.
   (d) You must change the file name.

7. Live Preview:
   (a) Opens a predesigned document or spreadsheet that is relevant to your task.
   (b) Provides a preview of the results of a choice you are considering before you make a final selection.
   (c) Provides a preview of an upcoming Office version.
   (d) Enlarges the font onscreen.

8. You can get help when working with an Office application in which one of the following areas?
   (a) Help tab
   (b) Status bar
   (c) The Backstage view
   (d) Quick Access Toolbar

9. The Find and Replace feature enables you to do which of the following?
   (a) Find all instances of misspelling and automatically correct (or replace) them.
   (b) Find any grammatical errors and automatically correct (or replace) them.
   (c) Find any specified font settings and replace them with another selection.
   (d) Find any character string and replace it with another.

10. A document or worksheet printed in portrait orientation is:
    (a) Taller than it is wide.
    (b) Wider than it is tall.
    (c) A document with 2" left and right margins.
    (d) A document with 2" top and bottom margins.

1 Editing a Menu

You have gone into partnership with a friend to open a health food restaurant in a golf and tennis community. With the renewed emphasis on healthy living and the large number of high-income renters and condominium owners in the community, the specialty restaurant should do well. In preparation for the opening, your partner has begun a menu that you will review and edit. This exercise follows the same set of skills as used in Hands-On Exercises 1, 2, 3, 4, and 5 in the chapter. Refer to Figure 1.61 as you complete this exercise.

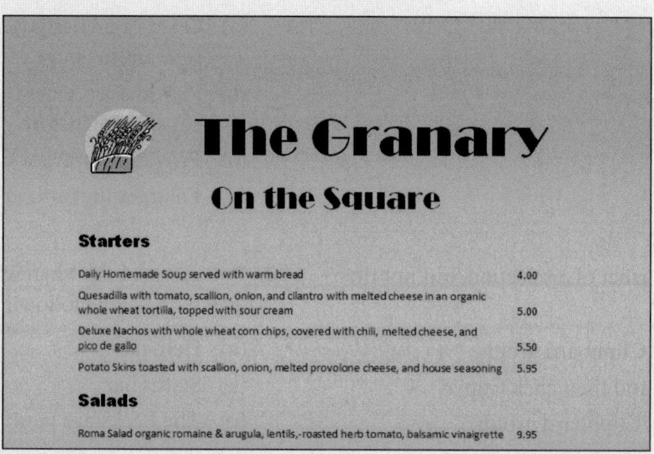

The Granary

On the Square

Starters

Daily Homemade Soup served with warm bread 4.00

Quesadilla with tomato, scallion, onion, and cilantro with melted cheese in an organic whole wheat tortilla, topped with sour cream 5.00

Deluxe Nachos with whole wheat corn chips, covered with chili, melted cheese, and pico de gallo 5.50

Potato Skins toasted with scallion, onion, melted provolone cheese, and house seasoning 5.95

Salads

Roma Salad organic romaine & arugula, lentils,-roasted herb tomato, balsamic vinaigrette 9.95

FIGURE 1.61 Restaurant Menu ➤

a. Click **Windows Explorer** on the taskbar, and then select the location where you save your files. Click **New folder**, type **The Granary**, and then press **Enter**. Close Windows Explorer.
b. Start Word. Open *f01p1menu* and save it as **f01p1menu_LastnameFirstname** in the The Granary folder.
c. Click the **Review tab**, and then click **Spelling & Grammar** in the Proofing group. The words *pico*, *gallo*, and *mesclun* are not misspelled, so you should ignore them when they are flagged. Other identified misspellings should be changed.
d. Click after the word *bread* in the first item under *Starters*. Press the **Spacebar**, and then type **or cornbread**.
e. Double-click **Desserts** on page 2 to select the word, and then type **Sweets**.
f. Drag to select the **Sandwiches section**, beginning with the word *Sandwiches* and ending after *8.75*. Click the **Home tab**, click **Cut** in the Clipboard group, click to place the insertion point before the word *Salads*, and then click **Paste** in the Clipboard group. The *Sandwiches* section should be placed before the *Salads* section.
g. Click **Undo** twice on the Quick Access Toolbar to return the *Sandwiches* section to its original location.
h. Change the price of Daily Homemade Soup to **4.95**.
i. Press **Ctrl+End** to place the insertion point at the end of the document, and then type your name.
j. Click the **Page Layout tab**, click **Orientation**, and then click **Landscape**. Click the **File tab**, and then click **Print** to see a preview of the document. Click the **Home tab**. Because the new look does not improve the menu's appearance, click **Undo** to return to the original orientation.
k. Press **Ctrl+Home** to move to the top of the document. Compare your results to Figure 1.61.
l. Drag the **Zoom slider** on the status bar slightly to the right to magnify text. Click the **View tab**, and then click **100%** in the Zoom group to return to the original size.
m. Save and close the file, and submit based on your instructor's directions.

2 Web Design Business

You have always been interested in Web design and have worked in the field for several years. You now have an opportunity to devote yourself full-time to your career as the CEO of a company dedicated to designing and supporting Web sites. One of the first steps in getting the business off the ground is developing a business plan so that you can request financial support. You will use PowerPoint to present your business plan. This exercise follows the same set of skills as used in Hands-On Exercises 2, 3, and 4 in the chapter. Refer to Figure 1.62 as you complete this exercise.

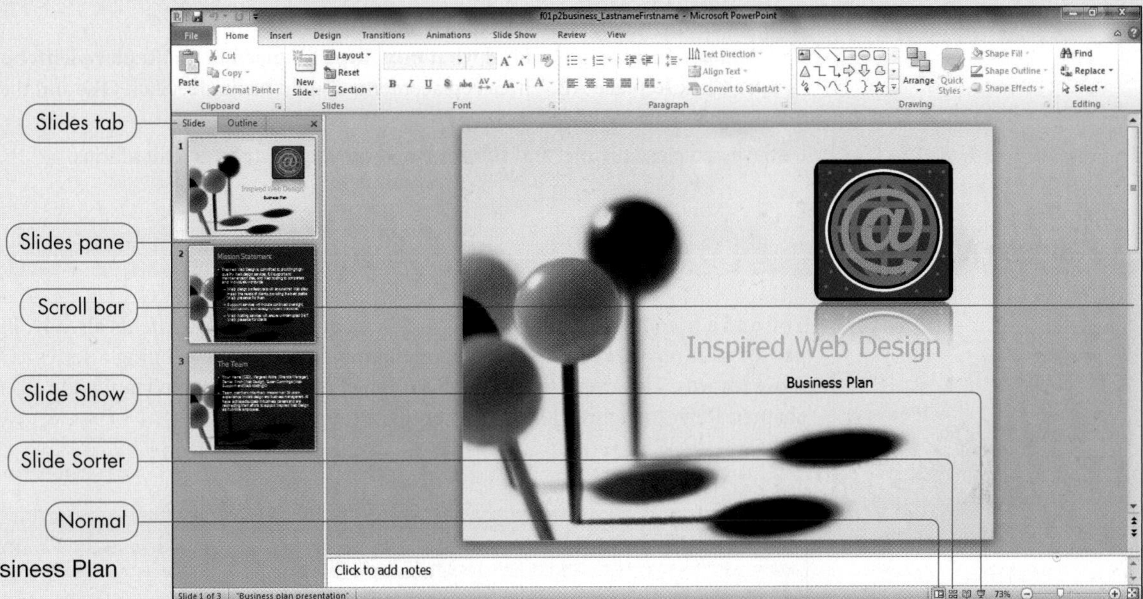

FIGURE 1.62 Business Plan Presentation ➤

a. Start PowerPoint. Open *f01p2business* and save it as **f01p2business_ LastnameFirstname.**

b. Click the **Slides tab** in the Slides pane (on the left), if necessary. Slide 1 should be displayed. If not, click the first slide in the left pane.

c. Position the mouse pointer to the immediate left of the word *Company*. Drag to select the words *Company Name*, and then type **Inspire Web Design**.

d. Click the **Insert tab**, and then click **Clip Art** in the Images group.
   - Click in the **Search for box** in the Clip Art task pane, remove any text that might be in the box, and then type **World Wide Web**. Make sure *Include Office.com content* is checked, and then click **Go**.
   - Select any image (or the one shown in Figure 1.62). Resize and position the clip art as shown. *Hint: To reposition clip art, drag when the mouse pointer is a four-headed arrow.*
   - Click the **Format tab**, click the **More button** in the Picture Styles group, and then click the **Reflected Rounded Rectangle picture style** (fifth from the left on the top row).
   - Click outside the clip art and compare your slide to Figure 1.62. Close the Clip Art task pane.

e. On Slide 2, click after the period on the bulleted point ending with *them*, and then press **Enter**. Type **Support services will include continued oversight, modification, and redesign of client Web sites.**

f. Press **Enter**, and then type **Web hosting services will ensure uninterrupted 24/7 Web presence for clients.**

g. On Slide 3, complete the following steps:
   - Position the mouse pointer over the first bullet so that the pointer appears as a four-headed arrow, and then click the bullet. All of the text in the bullet item is selected. As you type text, it will replace the selected text.
   - Type **your name (CEO)** [replacing *your name* with your first and last names]**, Margaret Atkins (Financial Manager), Daniel Finch (Web Design), Susan Cummings (Web Support and Web Hosting).**

h. Click the second bullet, and then type **Team members collectively possess over 28 years' experience in Web design and business management. All have achieved success in business careers and are redirecting their efforts to support Inspire Web Design as full-time employees.**
i. Click to select the **third bullet**, and then press **Delete**, removing the bullet and text.
j. On Slide 1, click **Slide Show** on the status bar. After viewing a slide, click the mouse button to proceed to the next slide. Continue to click until the slide show ends.
k. Click **Slide Sorter** on the status bar. You and your partners have decided to rename the company. The new name is **Inspired Web Design**.
   - Click the **Home tab**, and then click **Replace** in the Editing group. Be careful to click the button, not the arrow to the right.
   - Type **Inspire** in the **Find what box**. Type **Inspired** in the **Replace with box**.
   - Click **Replace All**. Three replacements should be made. Click **OK**, and then click **Close** in the Replace dialog box.
l. Save and close the file, and submit based on your instructor's directions.

3 Planning Ahead

You and a friend are starting a lawn care service and have a few clients already. Billing will be a large part of your record keeping, so you are planning ahead by developing a series of folders to maintain those records. This exercise follows the same set of skills as used in Hands-On Exercises 1 and 4 in the chapter. Refer to Figure 1.63 as you complete this exercise.

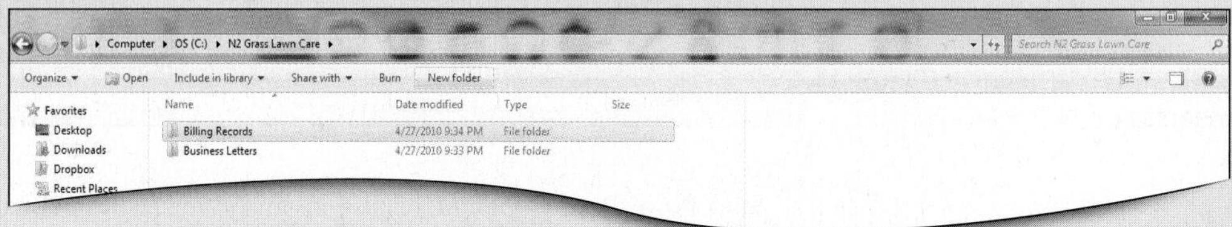

FIGURE 1.63 N2 Grass Folder Structure ➤

a. Click **Windows Explorer** on the taskbar, and then select the location where you save your files. Click **New folder**, type **N2 Grass Lawn Care**, and then press **Enter**.
b. Double-click **N2 Grass Lawn Care** in the Content pane.
   - Click **New folder**, type **Business Letters**, and then press **Enter**.
   - Click **New folder**, type **Billing Records**, and then press **Enter**. Compare your results to Figure 1.63. Close Windows Explorer.
c. Start Word. Open *f01p3lawn*. Use Find and Replace to replace the text *Your Name* with your name.
d. Click the **File tab**, and then click **Save As**.
   - Click **Computer** in the left pane.
   - Click the drive (in the Navigation Pane) where you save your student files. Double-click **N2 Grass Lawn Care**, and then double-click **Business Letters**.
   - Save the file as **f01p3lawn_LastnameFirstname**. Click **OK**, if necessary. Close the document and exit Word.
e. Open Windows Explorer.
   - Click **Computer** in the Navigation Pane.
   - In the Content pane, double-click the drive where you earlier placed the N2 Grass Lawn Care folder. Double-click **N2 Grass Lawn Care**.
   - Right-click **Billing Records**, click **Rename**, type **Accounting Records,** and then press **Enter**.
f. Click the **Start button**, click **All Programs**, click **Accessories**, and then click **Snipping Tool**. You will use the Snipping Tool to capture the screen display for submission to your instructor.
   - Click the **New arrow**, and then click **Full-screen Snip**.
   - Click **File**, and then click **Save As**.
g. Save the file as **f01p3snip_LastnameFirstname**. Close the file and submit based on your instructor's directions.

4 Theater Press Release

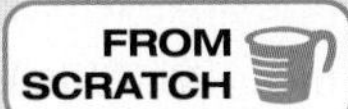

You are a member of a local theater league, Zodiac Players. Your group is preparing for a production of *Our Town*, a play by Thornton Wilder. You have agreed to develop a short press release for the local newspaper to promote the performance. You will use Word 2010 to develop the document. This exercise follows the same set of skills as used in Hands-On Exercises 1–5. Refer to Figure 1.64 as you complete this exercise.

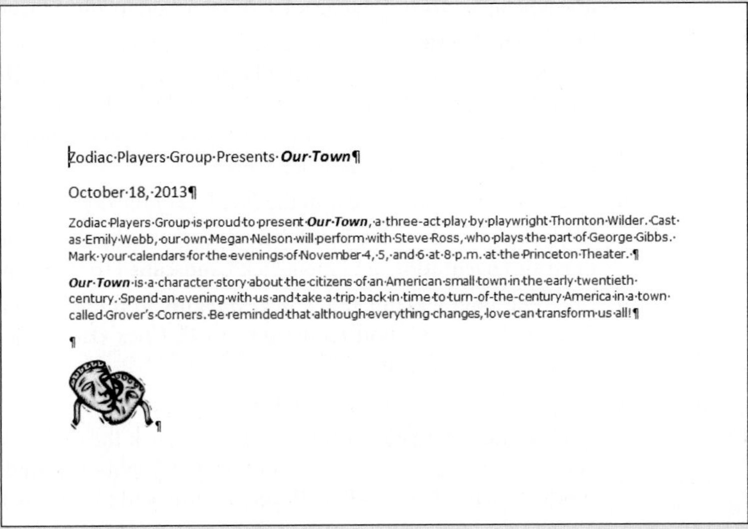

FIGURE 1.64 ➤

a. Click **Windows Explorer** on the taskbar or using the Start menu, and then select the location where you save your files. Click **New folder**, type **Zodiac**, and then press **Enter**. Close Windows Explorer.

b. Start Word. Save the blank document in the Zodiac folder as **f01p3zodiac_LastnameFirstname**.

c. Click the **Home tab** if necessary. If nonprinting characters are not displayed, click **Show/Hide** in the Paragraph group. Type **Zodiac Players Present Our Town**, and then press **Enter**.

d. Type **October 18, 2013**, and then press **Enter**. Type the following paragraph, but do not press Enter at the end of each line. After typing the entire paragraph, press **Enter**.

   Zodiac Players is proud to present Our Town, a three-act play by playwright Thornton Wilder. Mark your calendars for the evenings of November 4, 5, and 6 at 8 p.m. at the Princeton Theater. Cast as Emily Webb, our own Megan Nelson will perform with Steve Ross, who plays the part of George Gibbs. Our Town is a character story about the citizens of an American small town in the early twentieth century. Spend an evening with us and take a trip back in time to turn-of-the-century America in a town called Grover's Corners. Be reminded that although everything changes, love can transform us all!

e. Press **Ctrl+Home** to place the insertion point at the beginning of the document. Drag to select the words *Our Town* in the first line. Click **Bold** in the Font group, and then click **Italic** in the Font group. Place the pointer at the left of the first line in the document so that the pointer resembles a right-directed arrow. Click to select the first line. Click the **Font Size arrow** on the Mini toolbar, and then click **18**. Do not deselect the line.

f. With the first line still selected, click **Format Painter** in the Clipboard group. Point to the left of the second line in the document, and then click to select the line and copy the formatting from the first line.

g. Review the document to find any occurrence of the words *Our Town*. Bold and italicize the words.

h. Press **Ctrl+Home**. Click the **Review tab**, and then click **Spelling & Grammar** in the Proofing group. Correct any spelling or grammatical errors.

i. Triple-click the last text paragraph in the document to select the paragraph. Click the **Home tab**. Click the **Font arrow**, scroll through the font choices, and then click **Verdana**. Click the **Font Size arrow**, and then click **12**.

j. Click to place the insertion point before the words *Our Town* in the third sentence from the end of the last text paragraph. Press **Enter**.

k. Select the last sentence in the paragraph beginning with *Zodiac Players is proud to present*, but do not select the paragraph mark. Click **Cut** in the Clipboard group. Click to place the insertion point before the word *Mark* in the same paragraph. Click **Paste**.

l. Press **Ctrl+End**, and then press **Enter**. Click the **Insert tab**, and then click **Clip Art**. Click in the **Search for box**, remove any existing text, and then type **Theater**. Make sure **Include Office.com content** is selected. Click the **Results should be arrow**, and then deselect all categories except *Illustrations*. Click **Go**. Click any illustration that you like. Close the Clip Art pane.

m. With the clip art selected, make sure the **Format tab** is selected. Click the **Shape Height spin down or up arrow** to change the clip art height to 1 inch. Click outside the clip art to deselect it.

n. Press **Ctrl+Home** to place the insertion point at the beginning of the document. Zodiac Players has changed its name to Zodiac Players Group. Click the **Home tab** if necessary, and then click **Replace** in the Editing group. Click in the **Find what box**, and then type **Zodiac Players**. Click in the **Replace with box**, and then type **Zodiac Players Group.** Click **Replace All**. Two replacements should be made. Click **OK**. Click **Close**.

o. Click after the word *Present* in the first line of the document. Type **s**.

p. Click the **File tab**. Click **Print**. The document should be shown as a preview on the right. Click **Portrait Orientation**, and then click **Landscape Orientation**.

q. Click the **Page Layout tab**. Click **Margins** in the Page Setup group. Click **Custom Margins**. Change the top and bottom margins to **2"**. Click **OK**. Click the **File tab**, and then click **Print** to preview the document.

r. Save the document and close Word.

s. Click **Windows Explorer** on the taskbar. Click the drive on which your student files are saved. Locate the Zodiac folder, but do not open it. Right-click **Zodiac**, and then click **Rename** from the shortcut menu. Type **Zodiac Players Group**, and then press **Enter**. Close Windows Explorer.

t. Submit *f01p3zodiac_LastnameFirstname* according to your instructor's directions.

MID-LEVEL EXERCISES

1 Reference Letter

You are an instructor at a local community college. A student has asked you to provide her with a letter of reference for a job application. You have used Word to prepare the letter, but now you need to make a few changes before it is finalized.

a. Open Windows Explorer. Create a new folder on the drive where you save your student files, naming it **Letters of Reference**. Close Windows Explorer.
b. Start Word. Open *f01m1letter* and save it in the Letters of Reference folder as **f01m1letter_LastnameFirstname**.
c. Type your name, address, and the current date in the address area, replacing the generic text. The letter is to go to **Ms. Samantha Blake, CEO**, **Ridgeline Industries**, **410 Wellington Parkway**, **Huntsville AL 35611**. The salutation should read **Dear Ms. Blake:**.
d. Bold the student's first and last names in the first sentence.
e. Find each occurrence of the word *Stacy* and replace it with **Stacey**.
f. Find and insert a synonym for the word *intelligent* in the second paragraph.
g. Move the last paragraph (beginning with *In my opinion*) to position it before the third paragraph (beginning with *Stacey*).
h. Press **Ctrl+Home** to move the insertion point to the beginning of the document. Check spelling, selecting a correction for each misspelled word and ignoring spelling or grammatical mistakes that are not actually incorrect.
i. Type your name and title in the area beneath the word *Sincerely*.
j. Preview the document as it will appear when printed.
k. Save and close the file, and submit based on your instructor's directions.

2 Medical Monitoring

You are enrolled in a Health Informatics program of study in which you learn to manage databases related to health fields. For a class project, your instructor requires that you monitor your blood pressure, recording your findings in an Excel worksheet. You have recorded the week's data and will now make a few changes before printing the worksheet for submission.

a. Start Excel. Open *f01m2tracker* and save it as **f01m2tracker_LastnameFirstname**.
b. Preview the worksheet as it will appear when printed.
c. Change the orientation of the worksheet to **Landscape**. Preview the worksheet again. Click the **Home tab**.
d. Click in the cell beside *Name*, and then type your first and last names. Press **Enter**.
e. Change the font of the text in **cell C1** to **Verdana** and the font size to **20**.
f. Copy the function in **cell E22** to **cells F22 and G22**. *Hint: After selecting cell E22 and clicking Copy, drag cells F22 and G22. Before you drag, be sure the mouse pointer has the appearance of a large white plus sign. Then click Paste to copy the formula to those two cells.* Press **Esc** to remove the selection from around **cell E22**.

DISCOVER 

g. Get Help on showing decimal places. You want to increase the decimal places for the values in **cells E22, F22, and G22**, so that each value shows two places to the right of the decimal. Use Excel Help to learn how to do that. You might use *Increase Decimals* as a Search term. When you find the answer, select the three cells and increase the decimal places to **2**.
h. Click **cell A1**, and insert a **clip art image** of your choice related to blood pressure. Be sure the images include content from Office.com. If necessary, resize and position the clip art attractively. *Hint: To resize clip art, drag a corner handle (small circle). To reposition, drag the clip art when the mouse pointer is a four-headed arrow.*
i. Open the Backstage view, and adjust print settings to print two copies. You will not actually print two copies unless directed by your instructor.
j. Save and close the file, and submit based on your instructor's directions.

CAPSTONE EXERCISE

You are a member of the Student Government Association (SGA) at your college. As a community project, the SGA is sponsoring a "Stop Smoking" drive designed to provide information on the health risks posed by smoking cigarettes and to offer solutions to those who want to quit. The SGA has partnered with the local branch of the American Cancer Society as well as the outreach program of the local hospital to sponsor free educational awareness seminars. As the SGA Secretary, you will help prepare a PowerPoint presentation that will be displayed on plasma screens around campus and used in student seminars. You will use Microsoft Office to help with those tasks.

Manage Files and Folders

You will open, review, and save an Excel worksheet providing data on the personal monetary cost of smoking cigarettes over a period of years.

a. Create a folder called **SGA Drive** on the drive where you save your files.

b. Start Excel. Open *f01ccost* from the student data files and save it in the SGA Drive folder as **f01ccost_LastnameFirstname**.

c. Click **cell A10**, and then type your first and last names. Press **Enter**.

Modify Font

To highlight some key figures on the worksheet, you will format those cells with additional font attributes.

a. Draw attention to the high cost of smoking for 10, 20, and 30 years by changing the font color in **cells G3 through I4** to **Red**.

b. Italicize the Annual Cost cells (**F3 and F4**).

c. Click **Undo** on the Quick Access Toolbar to remove the italics. Click **Redo** to return the text to italics.

Insert Clip Art

You will add a clip art image to the worksheet and then resize it and position it.

a. Click **cell G7**, and then insert clip art appropriate for the topic of smoking.

b. Resize the clip art and reposition it near cell B7, if necessary.

c. Click outside the clipart to deselect it. Close the Clip Art task pane.

Preview Print, Change Page Layout, and Print

To get an idea of how the worksheet will look when printed, you will preview the worksheet. Then you will change the orientation and margins before printing it.

a. Preview the document as it will appear when printed.

b. Change the page orientation to **Landscape**. Click the **Page Layout tab**, and then change the margins to **Narrow**.

c. Preview the document as it will appear when printed.

d. Adjust the print settings to print two copies. You will not actually print two copies unless directed by your instructor.

e. Save the workbook and exit Excel.

Find and Replace

You have developed a PowerPoint presentation that you will use to present to student groups and for display on plasma screens across campus. The presentation is designed to increase awareness of the health problems associated with smoking. The PowerPoint presentation has come back from the reviewers with only one comment: A reviewer suggested that you spell out Centers for Disease Control and Prevention, instead of abbreviating it. You do not remember exactly which slide or slides the abbreviation might have been on, so you use Find and Replace to make the change quickly.

a. Start PowerPoint. Open *f01c1quit* and save it in the SGA Drive folder as **f01c1quit_LastnameFirstname**.

b. Replace all occurrences of *CDC* with **Centers for Disease Control and Prevention**.

Cut and Paste and Insert a Text Box

The Mark Twain quote on Slide 1 might be more effective on the last slide in the presentation, so you will cut and paste it there in a text box.

a. On Slide 1, select the entire Mark Twain quote, including the author name, and then cut it.

b. On Slide 22, paste the quote, reposition it more attractively, and then format it in a larger font size.

Check Spelling and Change View

Before you call the presentation complete, you will spell check it and view it as a slide show.

a. Check spelling. The word *hairlike* is not misspelled, so it should not be corrected.

b. View the slide show, and then take the smoking quiz. Click after the last slide to return to the presentation.

c. Save and close the presentation. Exit PowerPoint. Submit both files included in this project as directed by your instructor.

Employment Résumé

GENERAL CASE 

You have recently graduated from a university and are actively seeking employment. You know how important it is to have a comprehensive résumé to include with job applications, so you will use Word to prepare one. Instead of beginning a new document, you will modify a résumé template that is installed with Word. You can locate an appropriate résumé template by clicking the File tab and then clicking New. Select a résumé template from the Office.com area. Save the résumé as **f01b1resume_LastnameFirstname** in an appropriately named folder where you save your student files. Modify the résumé in any way you like, but make sure to complete the following activities:

- Include your name on the résumé. All other information, including address, education, employment history, and job objective, can be fictional.
- Format some text differently. The choice of text is up to you, but you should change font size and type and apply appropriate character attributes to improve the document's appearance.
- Find and replace all occurrences of the word *education* with **academic preparation**.
- Check the document for spelling errors, correcting or ignoring any that you find.
- Change the margins to **1.5"** right and left. Preview the document as it will appear when printed. Save and close the document. Keep Word open.
- Open a new blank document. Create a cover letter that will accompany the résumé. You can use a template for the cover letter if you find an appropriate one. The letter should serve as your introduction, highlighting anything that you think makes you an ideal employee.
- Save the cover letter as **f01b1cover_LastnameFirstname** and exit Word. Submit the file as directed by your instructor.

Fitness Planner

RESEARCH CASE 

Microsoft Excel is an excellent organizational tool. You will use it to maintain a fitness planner. Start Excel. Open *f01b2exercise*, and then save it as **f01b2exercise_LastnameFirstname**. The fitness planner is basically a template, which means that all exercise categories are listed, but without actual data. To personalize the planner to improve its appearance, complete the following activities:

- Change the orientation to **Landscape**. Preview the worksheet as it will appear when printed.
- Move the contents of **cell A2** (*Exercise Planner*) to **cell A1**.
- Click **cell A8**, and then use **Format Painter** to copy the format of that selection to **cells A5 and A6**. Increase the font size of **cell A1** to **26**.
- Use Excel Help to learn how to insert a header. Then insert a header on the worksheet with your first and last names.
- Insert a fitness-related clip art item in **cell A21**, positioning and sizing it so that it is attractive. Click outside the clip art to deselect it.
- Begin the fitness planner, entering at least one activity in each category (warm-up, aerobics, strength, and cool-down). Use **Find and Select** to replace all occurrences of *Exercises* with **Activities**. Save and close the file, and submit as directed by your instructor.

Household Records

DISASTER RECOVERY 

You recently received a newsletter from the insurance company with which you have homeowners insurance. An article in the newsletter suggested that you maintain detailed records of your household appliances and other items of value that are in your home. In case of burglary or disaster, an insurance claim is expedited if you are able to itemize what was lost along with identifying information such as serial numbers. You will use Excel to prepare such a list. You will then make a copy of the record on another storage device for safekeeping outside your home (in case your home is destroyed by a fire or weather-related catastrophe).

- Connect a flash drive to your computer, and then close any dialog box that may appear (unless it is informing you of a problem with the drive). Use Windows Explorer to create a folder on the hard drive titled **Home Records**.
- Start Excel. Design a worksheet listing at least five fictional appliances and electronic equipment along with the serial number of each. Design the worksheet in any way you like. Save the workbook as **f01b3household_LastnameFirstname** in the Home Records folder of the hard drive. Close the workbook and exit Excel.

- Use Windows Explorer to copy the Home Records folder from the hard drive to your flash drive. Click the **flash drive** in the Navigation Pane of Windows Explorer. Double-click the **Home Records folder** in the Content pane.
- Click the **Start button**, click **All Programs**, click **Accessories**, and then click **Snipping Tool**. Click the **New arrow**, and then click **Full-screen Snip**. Click **File**, and then click **Save As**. Save the screen display as **f01b3disaster_LastnameFirstname**.
- Close all open windows and submit the files as directed by your instructor.

WORD

1 INTRODUCTION TO WORD

Organizing a Document

Watch the
Set-up Video
for this Case Study!

CASE STUDY | First River Outfitter

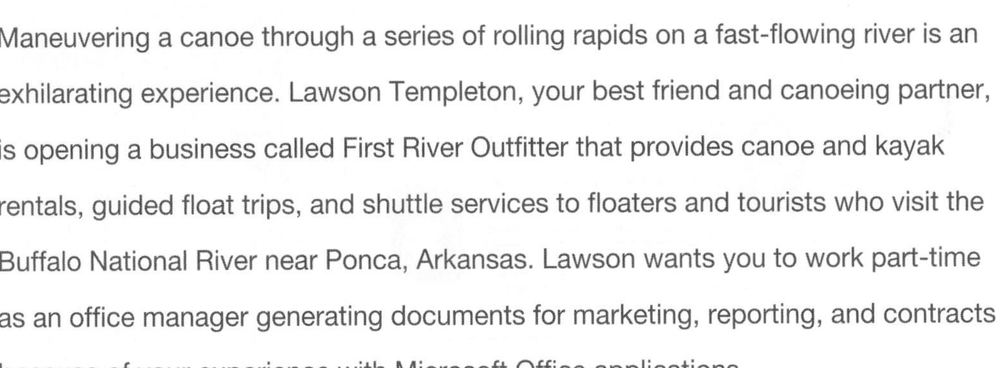

Maneuvering a canoe through a series of rolling rapids on a fast-flowing river is an exhilarating experience. Lawson Templeton, your best friend and canoeing partner, is opening a business called First River Outfitter that provides canoe and kayak rentals, guided float trips, and shuttle services to floaters and tourists who visit the Buffalo National River near Ponca, Arkansas. Lawson wants you to work part-time as an office manager generating documents for marketing, reporting, and contracts because of your experience with Microsoft Office applications.

Preparation for the new business includes acquiring real estate and equipment, but it also demands the development of marketing materials that generate new business. Your first project is to transform the rough draft of a document about river distances, safety precautions, and rental fees into a professional-looking article. This article will not only be posted on the First River Outfitter's Web site, but also printed and mailed to customers after they book a trip or reserve a rental. Your training in Microsoft Office Word 2010 enables you to modify the document easily and efficiently. After you complete the modifications, you both can go float the river!

OBJECTIVES AFTER YOU READ THIS CHAPTER, YOU WILL BE ABLE TO:

1. Understand how word processors work ***p.125***
2. Customize Word ***p.130***
3. Use features that improve readability ***p.137***
4. Check spelling and grammar ***p.141***
5. Display a document in different views ***p.142***
6. Prepare a document for distribution ***p.150***
7. Modify document properties ***p.155***

Introduction to Word Processing

Word processing software is the most commonly used type of software. You can create letters, reports, research papers, newsletters, brochures, and other documents with Word. You can even create and send e-mail, produce Web pages, and update blogs with Word.

Word processing software, often called a word processor, is the most commonly used type of software. People around the world—students, office assistants, managers, and professionals in all areas—use word processing programs such as Word for a variety of tasks. You can create letters, reports, research papers, newsletters, brochures, and other documents with Word. You can even create and send e-mail, produce Web pages, and update blogs with Word. Figure 1.1 shows examples of documents created in Word.

Word processing software enables you to produce documents such as letters, reports, and research papers.

2012 Annual Summary

SIMSERV-PITKA ENTERPRISES
JANUARY 2013

Corporate Overview

The consumer products industry has seen dramatic change in the last decade, due to increasing costs in manufacturing, need for innovative products, and decrease in brand loyalty. These changes have created the need to modify previous tactics to continue operating in this competitive industry.

Acquisition of Pitka Industries

In November, Simserv completed the process for acquiring Pitka Industries to form Simserv-Pitka Enterprises. The combined resources provide a stronger, more versatile organization to create innovative products and compete during the next decade. Here is a breakdown of the combined organization's divisions, their locations, and number of employees:

Simserv Headquarters	Cleveland	1,355
Pitka Division	Seattle	1,235
Product Development	Cincinnati	350
West Coast Distribution	Fresno	123

2012 Management Changes

On January 1, 2012, ***Dewey A. Larson*** was named Chairman of the Board and Chief Executive Officer by the Company's Board of Directors, replacing Jeff K. Andrews, who retired this year after 25 years of service. Mr. Larson first joined Simserv in January 1992 and over a period of nineteen years, has held a variety of senior executive positions.

In March 2012, ***Jerri Reed*** joined Simserv as its Chief Financial Officer. Ms. Reed has an impressive record in the industry over the past 20 years, which includes a position as CFO in a British company worth £50,000,000. She adds strength to our management team, particularly as the Company faces the important challenge of improving the financial and operating performance. Ms. Reed has stated:

> In 2013, we take the bull by the horns. Everyone at Simserv-Pitka must pull together and work toward our mutual success. I'm counting on every employee to focus on our common goals to

Page | 1

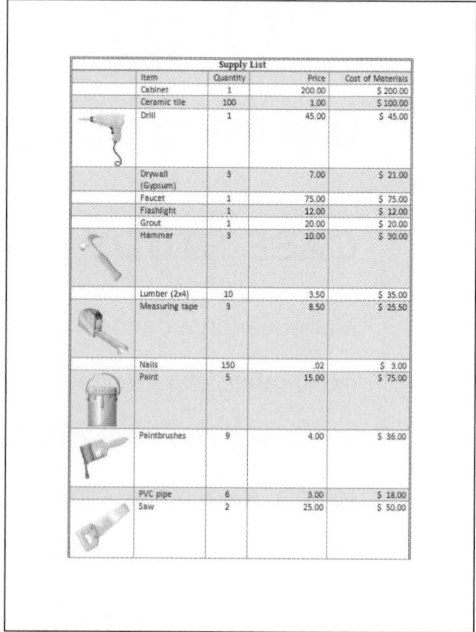

Supply List				
	Item	Quantity	Price	Cost of Materials
	Cabinet	1	200.00	$ 200.00
	Ceramic tile	100	1.00	$ 100.00
	Drill	1	45.00	$ 45.00
	Drywall (Gypsum)	3	7.00	$ 21.00
	Faucet	1	75.00	$ 75.00
	Flashlight	1	12.00	$ 12.00
	Grout	1	20.00	$ 20.00
	Hammer	3	10.00	$ 30.00
	Lumber (2x4)	10	3.50	$ 35.00
	Measuring tape	3	8.50	$ 25.50
	Nails	150	.02	$ 3.00
	Paint	5	15.00	$ 75.00
	Paintbrushes	9	4.00	$ 36.00
	PVC pipe	6	3.00	$ 18.00
	Saw	2	25.00	$ 50.00

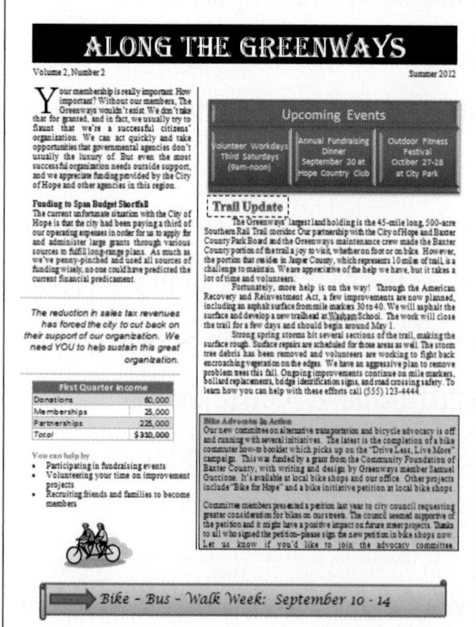

ALONG THE GREENWAYS

Volume 2, Number 2 — Summer 2012

Your membership is really important. How important? Without our members, The Greenways wouldn't exist. We don't take that for granted, and in fact, we usually try to flaunt that we're a successful citizens' organization. We can act quickly and take opportunities that governmental agencies don't usually the luxury of. But even the most successful organization needs outside support, and we appreciate funding provided by the City of Hope and other agencies in this region.

Funding to Span Budget Shortfall

The current unfortunate situation with the City of Hope is that the city had been paying a third of our operating expenses in order for us to apply for and administer large grants through various sources to fulfill long-range plans. As much as we've penny-pinched and used all sources of funding wisely, no one could have predicted the current financial predicament.

The reduction in sales tax revenues has forced the city to cut back on their support of our organization. We need YOU to help sustain this great organization.

First Quarter Income	
Donations	60,000
Memberships	25,000
Partnerships	225,000
Total	$310,000

You can help by

- Participating in fundraising events
- Volunteering your time on improvement projects
- Recruiting friends and families to become members

Upcoming Events

Volunteer Workdays Third Saturdays (9am-noon)	Annual Fundraising Dinner September 20 at Hope Country Club	Outdoor Fitness Festival October 27-28 at City Park

Trail Update

The Greenways' largest land holding is the 45-mile long, 500-acre Southern Rail Trail corridor. Our partnership with the City of Hope and Baxter County Park Board and the Greenways maintenance crew made the Baxter County portion of the trail a joy to visit, whether on foot or on bike. However, the portion that resides in Jasper County, which represents 10 miles of trail, is a challenge to maintain. We are appreciative of the help we have, but it takes a lot of time and volunteers.

Fortunately, more help is on the way! Through the American Recovery and Reinvestment Act, a few improvements are now planned, including an asphalt surface from mile markers 30 to 40. We will asphalt the surface and develop a new trailhead at Washam School. The work will close the trail for a few days and should begin around May 1.

Strong spring storms hit several sections of the trail, making the surface rough. Surface repairs are scheduled for those areas as well. The storm tree debris has been removed and volunteers are working to fight back encroaching vegetation on the edges. We have an aggressive plan to remove problem trees this fall. Ongoing improvements continue on mile markers, bollard replacements, bridge identification signs, and road crossing safety. To learn how you can help with these efforts call (555) 123-4444.

Bike Advocates In Action

Our new committee on alternative transportation and bicycle advocacy is off and running with several initiatives. The latest is the completion of a bike commuter how-to booklet which picks up on the "Drive Less, Live More" campaign. This was funded by a grant from the Community Foundation of Baxter County, with writing and design by Greenways member Samuel Guccione. It's available at local bike shops and our office. Other projects include "Bike for Hope" and a bike initiative petition at local bike shops.

Committee members presented a petition last year to city council requesting greater consideration for bikes on our streets. The council seemed supportive of the petition and it might have a positive impact on future street projects. Thanks to all who signed the petition–please sign the new petition in bike shops now. Let us know if you'd like to join the advocacy committee

Bike - Bus - Walk Week: September 10 - 14

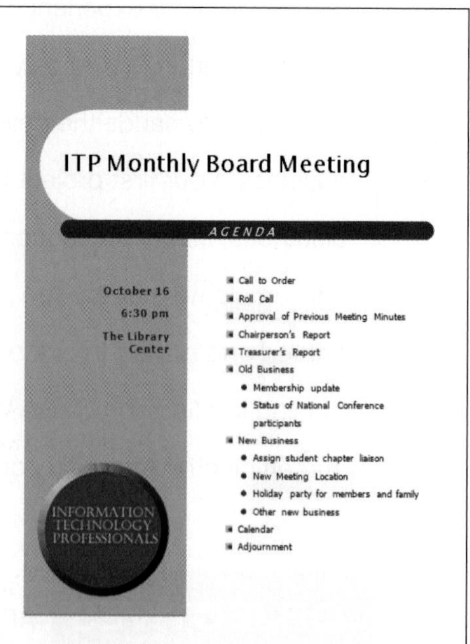

ITP Monthly Board Meeting

AGENDA

October 16
6:30 pm
The Library Center

- Call to Order
- Roll Call
- Approval of Previous Meeting Minutes
- Chairperson's Report
- Treasurer's Report
- Old Business
  - Membership update
  - Status of National Conference participants
- New Business
  - Assign student chapter liaison
  - New Meeting Location
  - Holiday party for members and family
  - Other new business
- Calendar
- Adjournment

INFORMATION TECHNOLOGY PROFESSIONALS

FIGURE 1.1 Versatility of Microsoft Office Word 2010 ➤

Word provides several features that enable you to enhance documents with only a few clicks of the mouse. You can change colors, add interesting styles of text, insert graphics, use a table to present data, track changes made to a document, view comments made about document content, combine several documents into one, and quickly create reference pages such as a table of contents, an index, or a bibliography.

This chapter provides a broad-based introduction to word processing and Word in general. All word processors adhere to certain basic concepts that must be understood to use the program effectively.

In this section, you will learn about the Word interface and word wrap. You will also learn how to move around quickly in a document and how to turn features on and off quickly by toggling. Finally, you will learn about breaks in a document, how to add page numbers, how to insert cover pages quickly, and how to customize Word.

Understanding How Word Processors Work

The Exploring series authors used Word to write this book. You will use Word to complete the exercises in this chapter. When you start Word, your screen might look different than the screen shown in Figure 1.2. This is because the commands are customizable, and elements that display will be affected. However, you should recognize the basic elements emphasized in Figure 1.2.

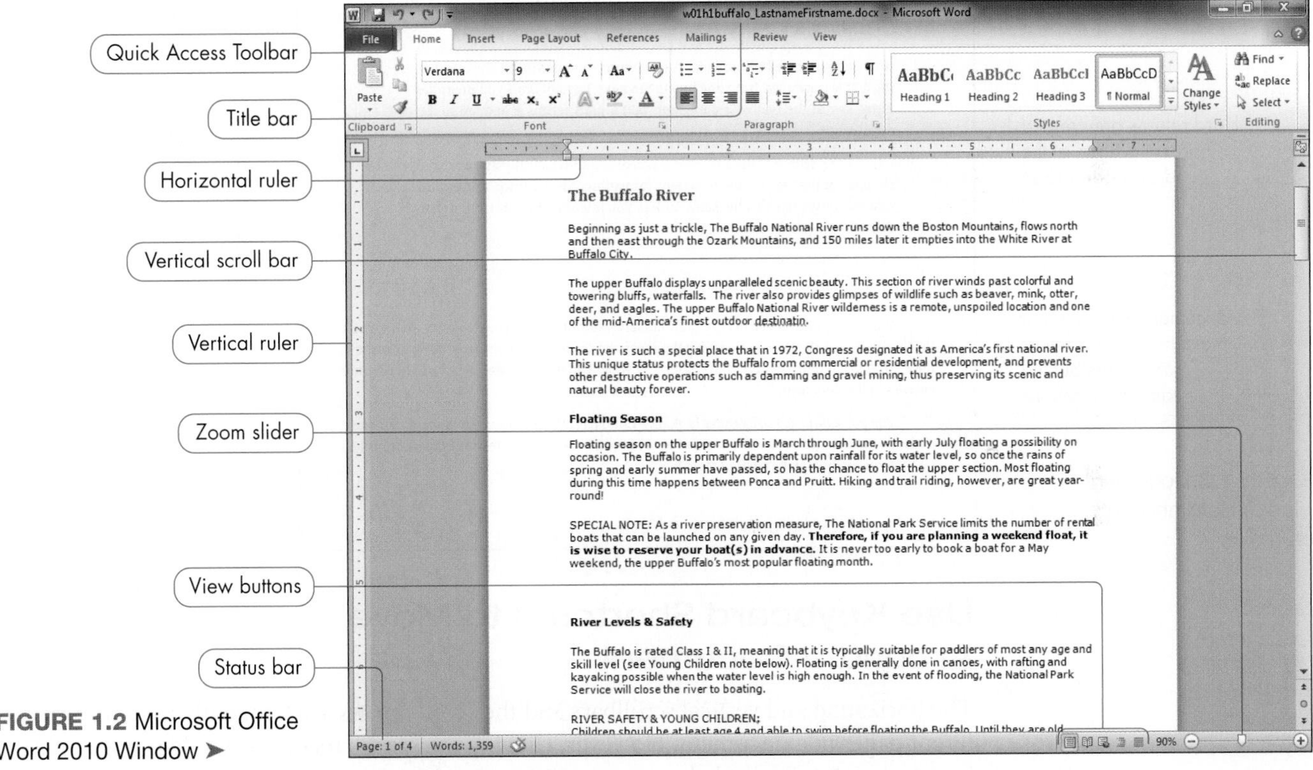

FIGURE 1.2 Microsoft Office Word 2010 Window ➤

When Word opens, several basic features are available. These features include the Ribbon, the Quick Access Toolbar, vertical and horizontal scroll bars, and the status bar, which you learned about in the Office Fundamentals chapter. The status bar at the bottom of the window displays information about the open Word document such as the page number where the insertion point is currently positioned, the total number of pages in the document, and the total number of words in the document.

Learn About Word Wrap

Whether you are new to using a word processor or have been using one for a period of time, you will notice that certain functions seem to happen automatically. As you type, you probably do not think about how much text can fit on one line or where the sentences roll from

Word wrap moves words to the next line if they do not fit on the current line.

A **hard return** is created when you press Enter to move the insertion point to a new line.

A **soft return** is created by the word processor as it wraps text to a new line.

one line to the other. Fortunately, Word takes care of that for you. This feature is called ***word wrap*** and enables you to type continuously without pressing Enter at the end of a line within a paragraph. The only time you press Enter is when you want the insertion point to move to the next line.

Word wrap is closely associated with another concept: the hard and soft return. A ***hard return*** is created when you press Enter at the end of a line or paragraph. A ***soft return*** is created by the word processor as it wraps text from one line to the next. The locations of the soft returns change automatically as text is inserted or deleted. Only the user, who must intentionally insert or delete each hard return, can change the location of such returns.

The paragraphs at the top of Figure 1.3 show two hard returns, one at the end of each paragraph. Figure 1.3 also includes four soft returns in the first paragraph (one at the end of every line except the last) and three soft returns in the second paragraph. Now, assume the margins in the document are made smaller (that is, the line is made longer), as shown in the bottom paragraphs of Figure 1.3. The number of soft returns decreases as more text fits on a line and fewer lines are needed. The revised document still contains the two original hard returns—one at the end of each paragraph.

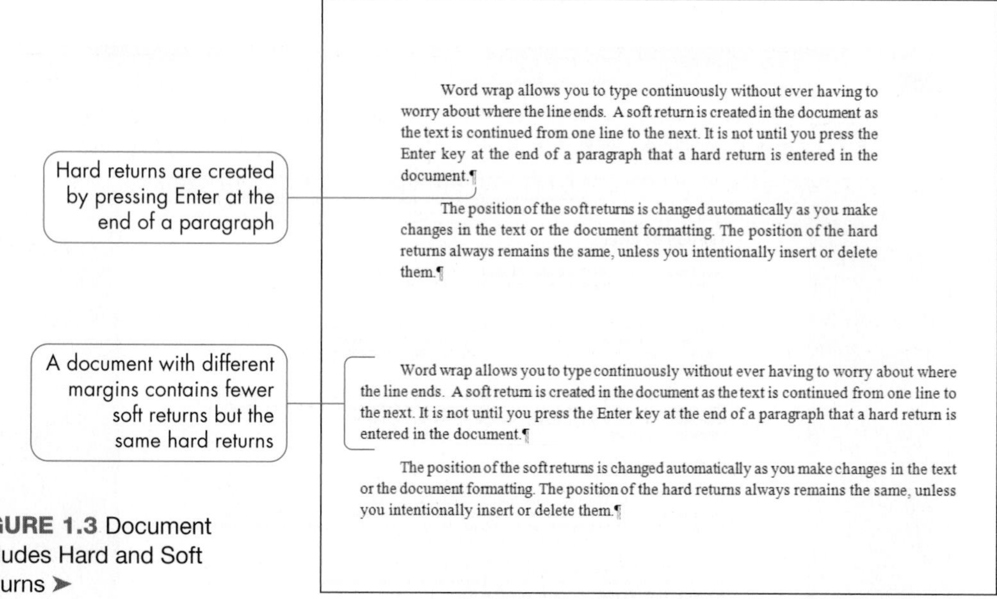
Hard returns are created by pressing Enter at the end of a paragraph
A document with different margins contains fewer soft returns but the same hard returns

Word wrap allows you to type continuously without ever having to worry about where the line ends. A soft return is created in the document as the text is continued from one line to the next. It is not until you press the Enter key at the end of a paragraph that a hard return is entered in the document.¶

The position of the soft returns is changed automatically as you make changes in the text or the document formatting. The position of the hard returns always remains the same, unless you intentionally insert or delete them.¶

Word wrap allows you to type continuously without ever having to worry about where the line ends. A soft return is created in the document as the text is continued from one line to the next. It is not until you press the Enter key at the end of a paragraph that a hard return is entered in the document.¶

The position of the soft returns is changed automatically as you make changes in the text or the document formatting. The position of the hard returns always remains the same, unless you intentionally insert or delete them.¶

FIGURE 1.3 Document Includes Hard and Soft Returns ➤

Use Keyboard Shortcuts to Move Around a Document

The horizontal and vertical scrollbars and the scroll arrows are frequently used to view different pages in a document. However, clicking the scrollbars or arrows does not move the insertion point; it merely lets you see different parts of the document and leaves the insertion point where it was last positioned. To move the insertion point in a document you use the mouse or the keyboard. Table 1.1 shows useful keyboard shortcuts for navigating a document and relocating the insertion point.

TABLE 1.1 Keyboard Navigation Controls

Keys	Moves the Insertion Point	Keys	Moves the Insertion Point
←	One character to the left	**Ctrl+Home**	To the beginning of the document
→	One character to the right	**Ctrl+End**	To the end of the document
↑	Up one line	**Ctrl+←**	One word to the left
↓	Down one line	**Ctrl+→**	One word to the right
Home	To the beginning of the line	**Ctrl+↑**	Up one paragraph
End	To the end of the line	**Ctrl+↓**	Down one paragraph
Page Up	Up to the previous page	**Ctrl+Page Up**	To the top of the previous page
Page Down	Down to the next page	**Ctrl+Page Down**	To the top of the next page

Discover Toggle Switches

To **toggle** is to switch from one setting to another.

A ***toggle***, when pressed or clicked, causes the computer to switch from one setting to another. Caps Lock is an example of a toggle button. Each time you press it, newly typed text will change from uppercase to lowercase, or vice versa. In the Office Fundamentals chapter you read about other toggle buttons. Sometimes you can invoke a toggle by pressing keys on the keyboard, such as Caps Lock. You invoke many toggle features, such as the Bold, Italic, and Underline commands, by clicking a combination of keys or a ribbon command to turn the feature on and off.

The **Show/Hide feature** reveals where formatting marks, such as spaces, tabs, and returns, are used in the document.

A toggle that enables you to reveal formatting applied to a document is the ***Show/Hide feature***. Click Show/Hide (¶) in the Paragraph group on the Home tab to reveal where formatting marks, such as spaces, tabs, and hard returns, are in the document. Figure 1.4 displays formatting marks when the Show/Hide (¶) feature is on.

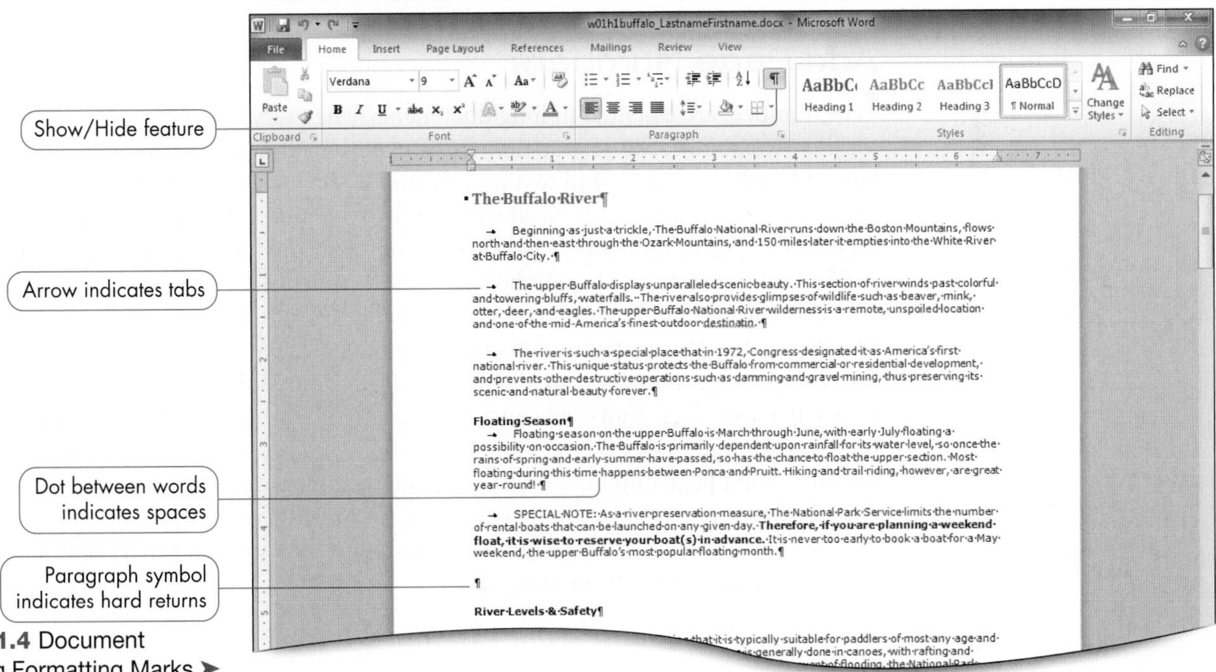

FIGURE 1.4 Document Displaying Formatting Marks ➤

Insert Page Breaks

A **soft page break** is inserted when text fills an entire page, then continues onto the next page.

When you type more text than can fit on a page, Word continues the text on another page using soft and hard page breaks. The ***soft page break*** is a hidden marker that automatically continues text on the top of a new page when text no longer fits on the current page. These breaks adjust automatically when you add and delete text. For the most part, you rely on soft page breaks to prepare multiple-page documents. However, at times you need to start a new page before Word inserts a soft page break.

A **hard page break** forces the next part of a document to begin on a new page.

When this occurs, you can insert a ***hard page break***, a hidden marker, to force text to begin on a new page. You can insert a hard page break into a document using the Breaks command in the Page Setup group on the Page Layout tab or using Page Break in the Pages group on the Insert tab. To view the page break markers in Print Layout view you must click Show/Hide (¶) on the Home tab to toggle on the formatting marks, as shown in Figure 1.5. You can view the page break markers without Show/Hide toggled on when you switch to Draft view.

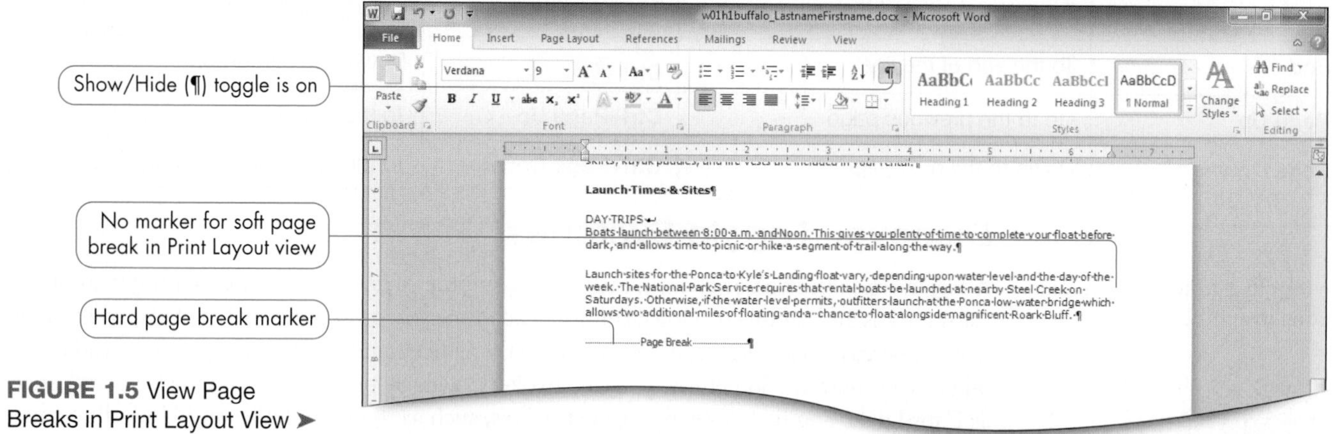

FIGURE 1.5 View Page Breaks in Print Layout View ➤

> **TIP** Hard Page Break Shortcut
>
> You can use the keyboard shortcut Ctrl+Enter to insert a hard page break.

Add Page Numbers

Page numbers are essential in long documents. They serve as convenient reference points for the writer and reader. If you do not include page numbers in a long document, you will have difficulty trying to find text on a particular page or trying to tell someone where to locate a particular passage in the document. Have you ever tried to reassemble a long document without page numbers that was out of order? It can be very frustrating, and it makes a good case for inserting page numbers in your documents.

The Page Number command in the Header & Footer group on the Insert tab is the easiest way to place page numbers in a document. When you use this feature, Word not only inserts page numbers, but also automatically adjusts the page numbers when you add or delete pages. Page numbers can appear at the top or bottom of a page in the header or footer areas, and can be left, center, or right aligned. Word 2010 provides several options for formatting page numbers. Your decision on where to place page numbers might stem from personal preference, the writing specifications for your paper, or other information you must include with the page number. Figure 1.6 displays a few gallery options for placing a page number at the bottom of a page.

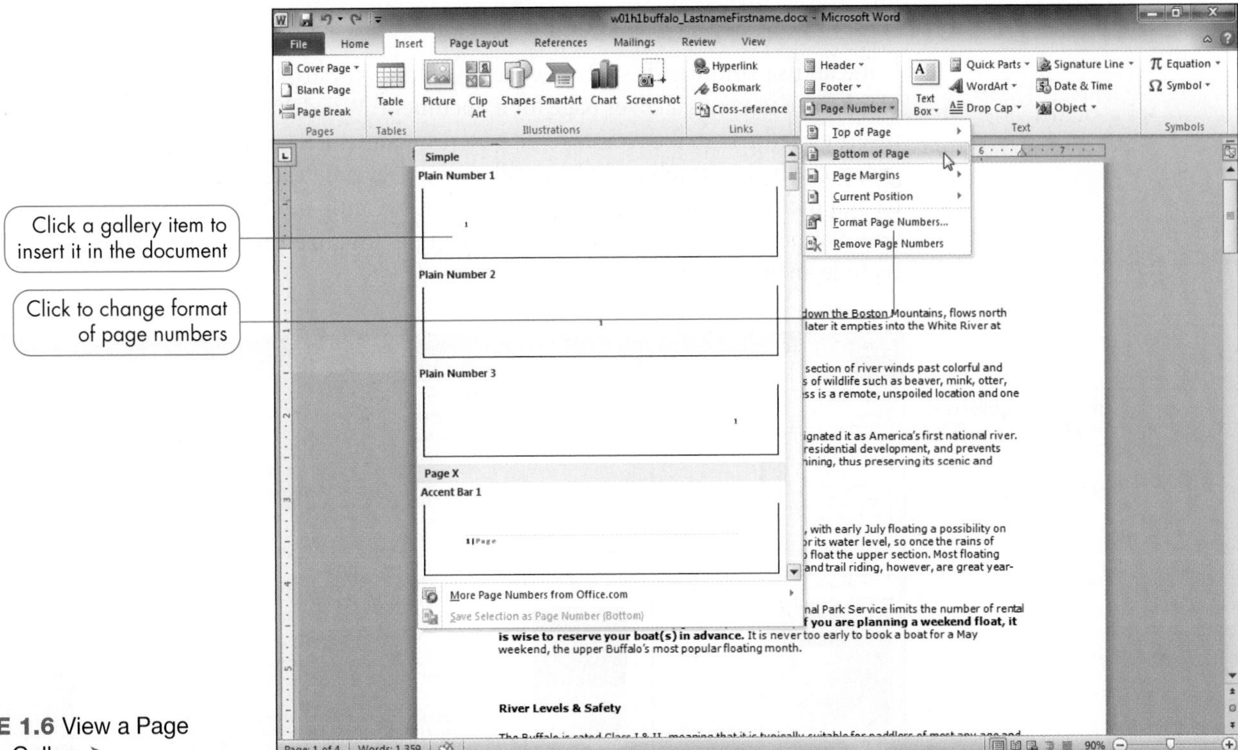
Click a gallery item to insert it in the document
Click to change format of page numbers

FIGURE 1.6 View a Page Number Gallery ➤

Word enables you to customize the format of page numbers. For example, at the beginning of a document you can use Roman numerals instead of Arabic numerals for preface pages. You also can adjust the page numbering so that it starts numbering on a page other than the first. This is useful when you have a report with a cover page; you typically do not consider the cover as page one and therefore begin numbering the page that follows it. You use the Format Page Number feature to display the Page Number Format dialog box (see Figure 1.7). If you are not satisfied with the page numbering in a document, use the Remove Page Numbers command to remove them.

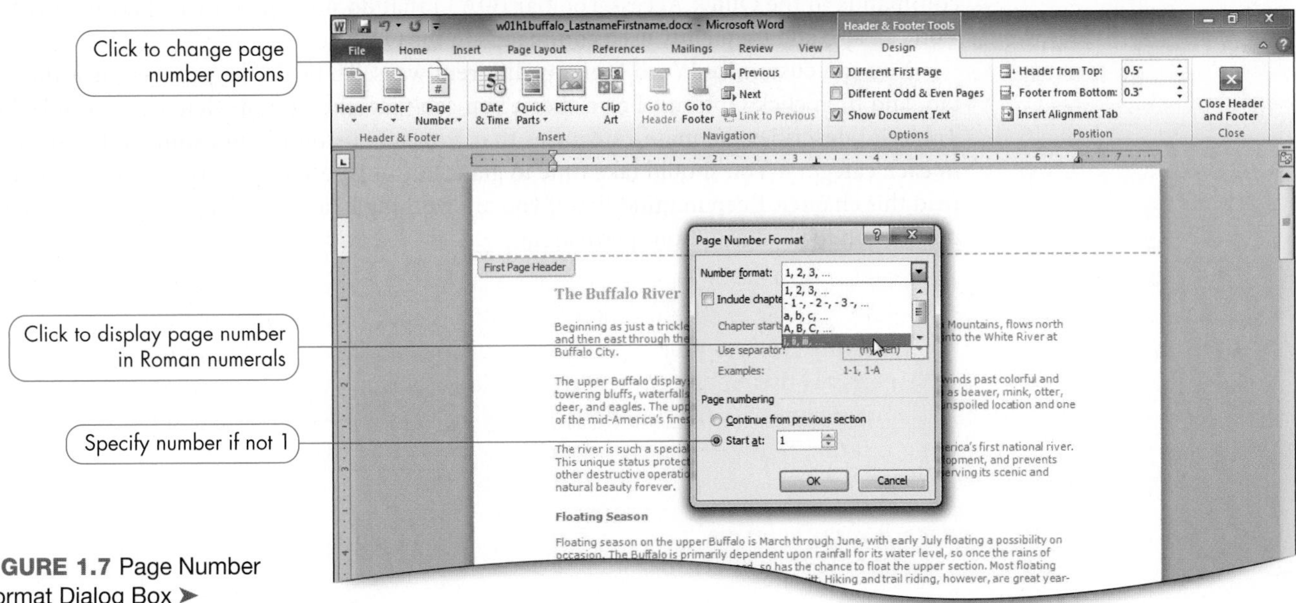
Click to change page number options
Click to display page number in Roman numerals
Specify number if not 1

FIGURE 1.7 Page Number Format Dialog Box ➤

Insert a Cover Page

You can use commands such as page break and keystrokes such as Ctrl+Enter to insert a blank page to use as a cover page for a document. Word 2010 also offers a feature to quickly insert a preformatted cover page into your document. The Cover Page feature in the Pages group on the Insert tab includes a gallery with several designs, as shown in Figure 1.8. Each design includes fields such as Document Title, Company Name, Date, and Author, which you can personalize or remove. After you personalize this feature, your document will include an attractive cover page.

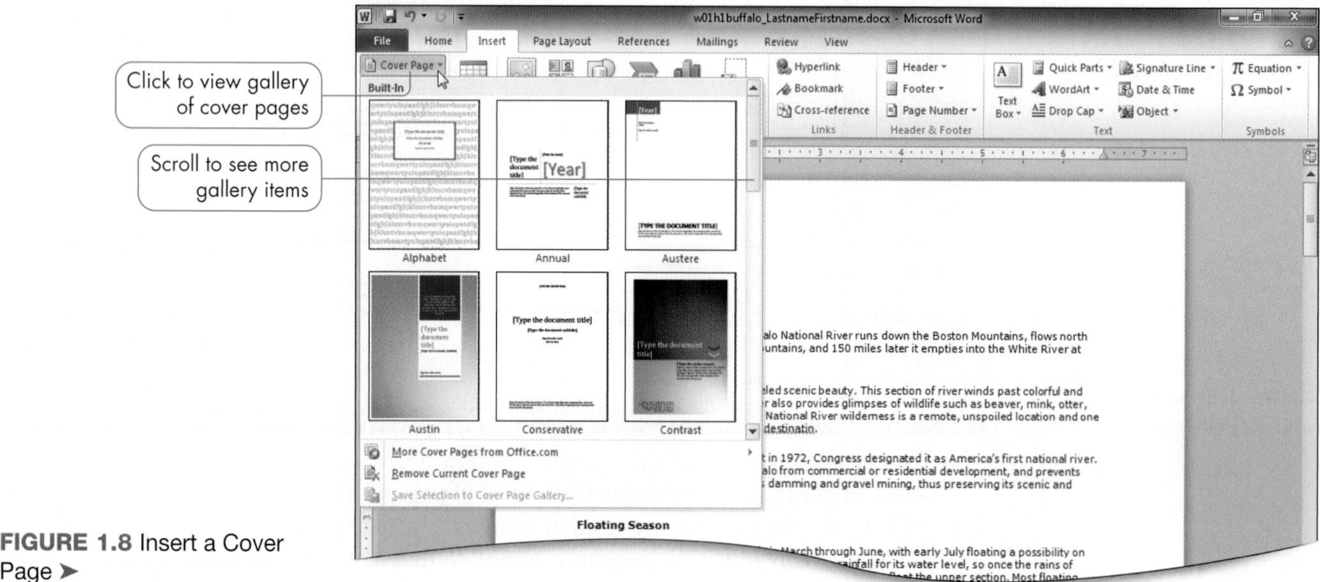

FIGURE 1.8 Insert a Cover Page ➤

Customizing Word

As installed, Word is immediately useful. However, you might find options that you would prefer to customize, add, or remove from the document window. For example, you can add commands to the Quick Access Toolbar (QAT) that do not currently display on any tab. You can also add frequently used commands to the QAT.

You can customize Word in many different ways. To begin the process, click the File tab, and then click Options. From there, you can view the options that are customizable. Table 1.2 describes the main categories that you can customize and some of the features in each category. You should take time to glance through each category as you continue to read this chapter. Keep in mind that if you are working in a school lab, you might not have permission to change options permanently.

Document Organization

Throughout your college and professional career, you will create a variety of documents. As you compose and edit you want to set the documents up so that some parts display differently than others when you view or print them. Word has settings that enable you to segment a document just for this purpose.

In this section, you will learn how to make changes to a Word document, such as inserting section breaks, adding headers and footers, and displaying watermarks. You will also learn about features that help you monitor spelling and grammar, and you will learn about different view modes.

Using Features That Improve Readability

When you create a document you consider the content you will insert, but you also should consider how you want the document to look when you print or display it. Many of the settings you use for this purpose are on the Page Layout tab. For example, when you create a short business letter, you want to increase the margins to a width such as 1.5" on all sides, so the letter contents are balanced on the printed page. If you print a formal or research paper, you want to use a 1.5" left margin and a 1" right margin to provide extra room on the left for binding.

When you create a document, you consider the content you will insert, but you also should consider how you want the document to look when you print or display it.

Another setting to consider for a document is orientation. Most documents, such as letters and research papers, use portrait orientation. However, a brochure, large graphic, chart, or table might display better on a page with landscape orientation.

If you need to print a document on special paper, such as legal size (81/2" × 14") paper or an envelope, you should select the paper size before you create the document text. The Size command in the Page Setup group on the Page Layout tab contains several different document sizes that you can use. If you have special paper requirements, you can select More Paper Sizes to enter your own custom size. If you do not select the special size before you print, you will waste paper and find yourself with a very strange-looking printout.

Insert Headers and Footers

A **header** is information that displays at the top of each document page.

A **footer** is information that displays at the bottom of each document page.

Headers and footers give a professional appearance to a document. A ***header*** consists of one or more lines at the top of each page. A ***footer*** displays at the bottom of each page. The advantage of using a header or footer is to specify the content only once, after which it appears automatically on all pages. Although you can type the text yourself at the top or bottom of every page, it is time-consuming, and the possibility of making a mistake is great. You also can insert a field, such as a page number or file name, and Word will automatically insert the correct information. A document may display headers but not footers, footers but not headers, both headers and footers, or neither. A page number is a simple header or footer and can be created by clicking Page Number, selecting the location where it will display, and selecting the style you prefer. Footers might also contain the date the document was created or the file name. Headers might contain the name of an organization, the author, or the title of the document. Take a moment to notice the type of information you see in the headers and footers of the books or magazines you are reading.

Headers and footers are added from the Insert tab and are formatted like any other paragraph. They can be center, left, or right aligned. You can format headers and footers in any typeface or point size and can include special fields to insert automatically information such as author, date, or time a document is saved. The content of the headers and footers is adjusted for changes in page breaks caused by modifications to the body of the document. This happens most often for page numbers because the addition or deletion of information in a document can alter the page numbering.

Word 2010 offers many built-in formatting options that enable you to add a professional look quickly. It also enables you to control how headers and footers display throughout a document. These options display on the Header & Footer Tools Design tab (see Figure 1.13). For instance, you can specify a different header or footer for the first page; this is advisable when you have a cover page and do not want the header (or footer) to display on that page. You can also have different headers and footers for odd and even pages. This feature is useful when you plan to print a document that will be bound as a book. Notice the different information this book prints on the footer of odd versus even pages and how the page numbers display in the corners of each page. If you want to change the header (or footer) midway through a document, you need to insert a section break at the point where the new header (or footer) is to begin. These breaks are discussed in the next section.

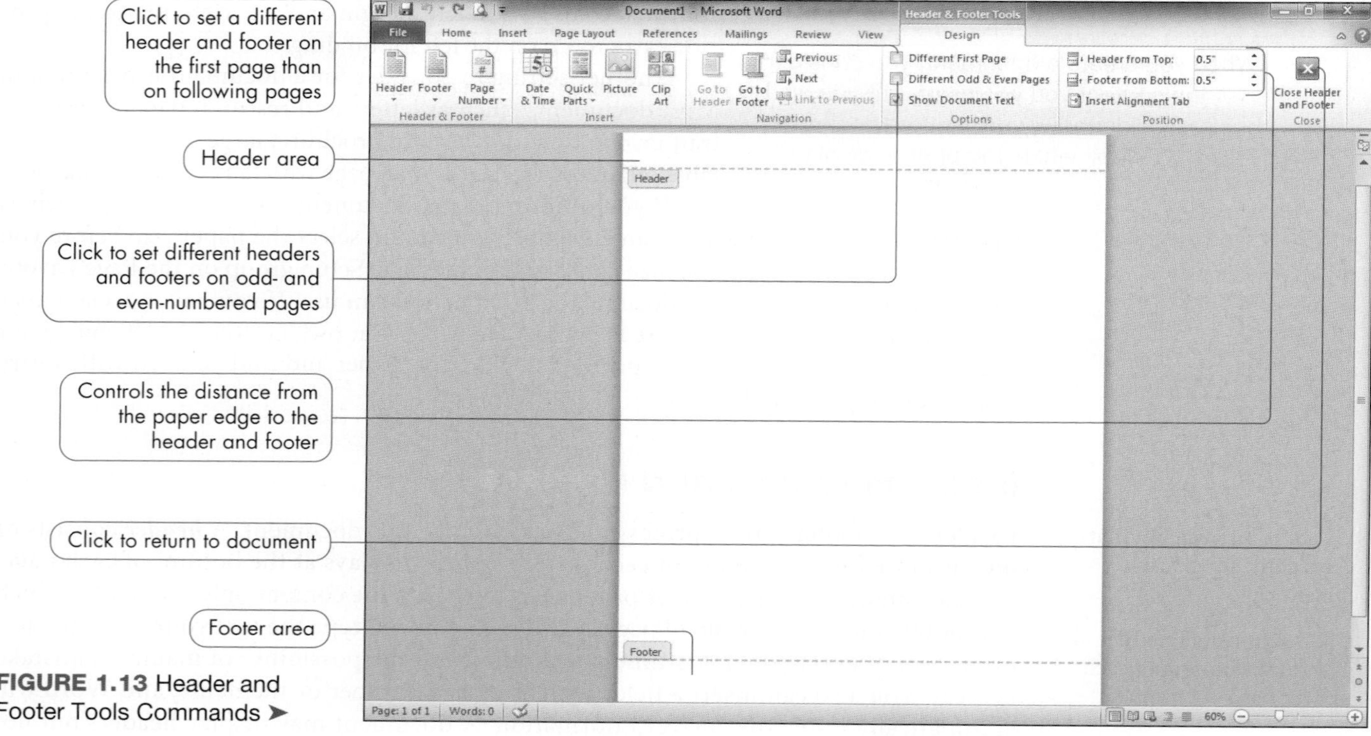

FIGURE 1.13 Header and Footer Tools Commands ➤

Create Sections

Formatting in Word occurs on three levels: character, paragraph, and section. Formatting at the section level controls headers and footers, page numbering, page size and orientation, margins, and columns. Most documents you work with, unless intentionally changed, probably consist of a single section, and thus any formatting is applied to the entire document. You can, however, divide a document into sections and format each section independently.

A **section break** is a marker that divides a document into sections, thereby enabling different formatting in each section.

You determine where one section ends and another begins by clicking Breaks in the Page Setup group on the Page Layout tab. A ***section break*** is a marker that divides a document into sections. It enables you to control where text is placed and how it will be formatted on the printed page; that is, you can specify that text in the new section displays on the same page or on a new page. Formatting at the section level gives you the ability to create more sophisticated documents. Word stores the formatting characteristics of each section within the section break at the end of a section. Thus, deleting a section break also deletes the section formatting, causing the text above the break to assume the formatting characteristics of the next section.

Word has four types of section breaks, as shown in Table 1.3.

TABLE 1.3 Section Breaks

Type	Description	Example
Next Page	When inserted, text that follows must begin at the top of the next page.	Use to force a chapter to start at the top of a page.
Continuous	When inserted, text that follows can continue on the same page.	Use to format text in the middle of the page into columns.
Even Page	When inserted, text that follows must begin at the top of the next even-numbered page.	Use to force a chapter to begin at the top of an even-numbered page.
Odd Page	When inserted, text that follows must begin at the top of the next odd-numbered page.	Use to force a chapter to begin at the top of an odd-numbered page.

When you use section breaks, you can do the following:

- Change the margins within a multipage letter, where the section containing only the first page (the letterhead) requires a larger top margin than the other pages in the letter.
- Change the orientation in one section from portrait to landscape to accommodate a wide table or graphic in the middle or end of the document.
- Change the page numbering in one section to use Roman numerals for a table of contents and Arabic numerals thereafter on pages in remaining sections.
- Change the number of columns in a newsletter, which may contain a section with a single column at the top of a page for the masthead and another section with two or three columns in the body of the newsletter.

Figure 1.14 displays the last page of the Buffalo River document. The document has been divided into two sections, and the insertion point is currently on the last page of the document, which is also the first page of the second section. Note the difference in page number on the footer and in the status bar.

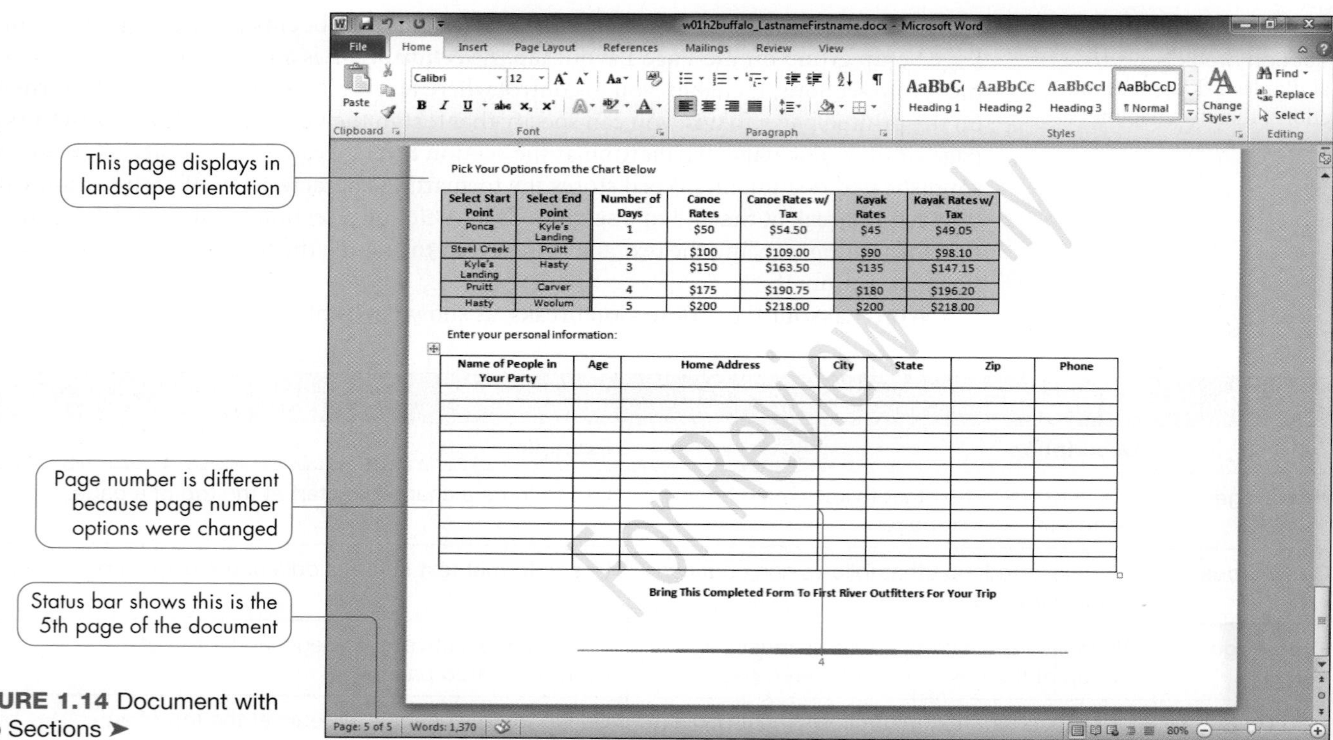

FIGURE 1.14 Document with Two Sections ➤

When a document has multiple sections, the Link to Previous feature in the Header & Footer Tools tab is important to consider. If you want page numbering to continue sequentially so the numbering is not interrupted from section to section, activate the Link to Previous toggle. It displays with an orange color when active. If you want to restart page numbering when a section changes, turn off the Link to Previous toggle. Additionally, you can move from the header or footer of one section to another section by clicking Next or Previous in the Navigation group on the Design tab, as shown in Figure 1.15.

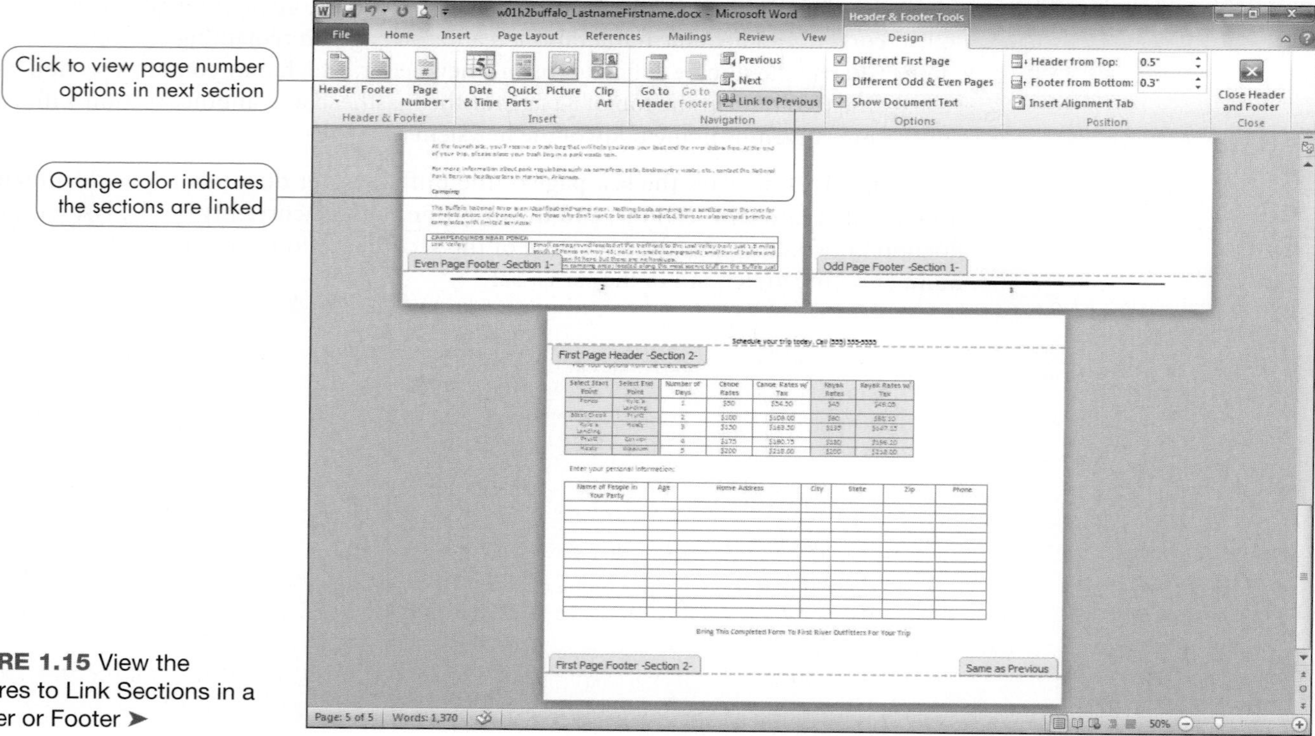

FIGURE 1.15 View the Features to Link Sections in a Header or Footer ➤

TIP Viewing Section Breaks

The best way to view the location of a section break in a document is to change to Draft view. The best way to determine which section each page is in is to double-click on the header or footer of a page. If a document has multiple sections, the section number is indicated with the header and footer.

Insert a Watermark

A **watermark** is text or a graphic that displays behind text.

A ***watermark*** is text or a graphic that displays behind text. Watermarks are often used to display a very light, washed-out logo for a company. They are also frequently used to indicate the status of a document, such as *FOR REVIEW ONLY*, as shown in Figure 1.16. Watermarks do not display on a document that is saved as a Web page, nor will they display in Web Layout view.

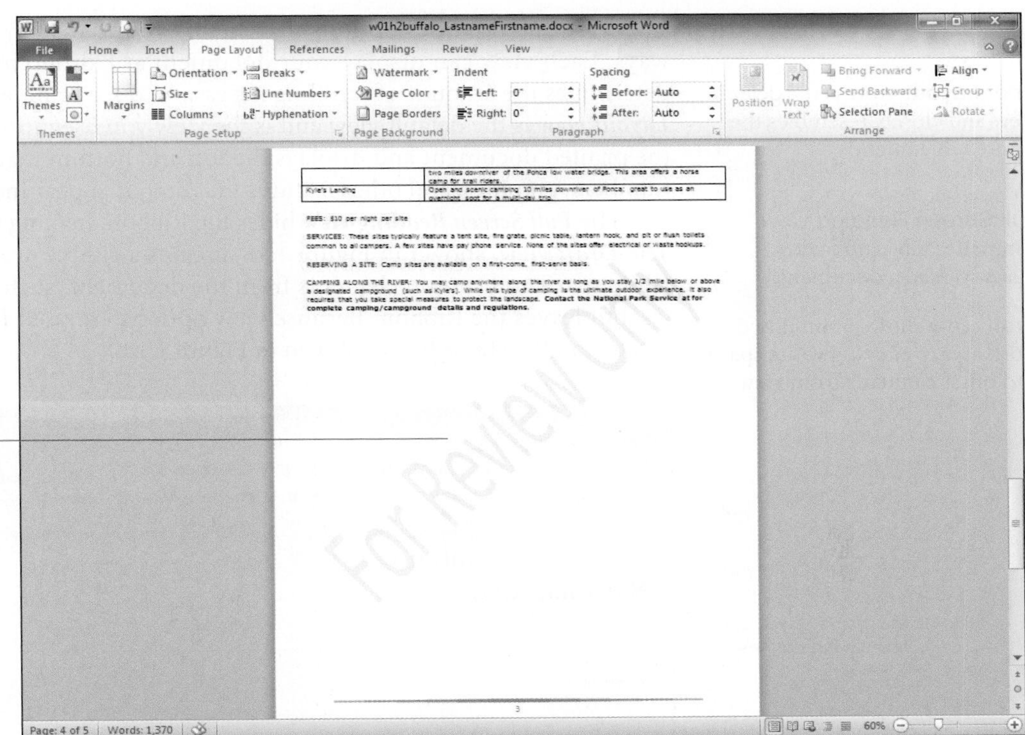

For Review Only displays as a watermark behind text on the page

FIGURE 1.16 Document That Includes a Watermark ➤

Checking Spelling and Grammar

It is important to create a document that is free of typographical and grammatical errors. With the automated spelling and grammar checker tools in Word, it is relatively easy to do so. However, you should always proofread a document because the spelling and grammar checker will not always find every possible error.

In addition to spelling and grammar checking, Word provides many features that correct a variety of grammatical mistakes. Word has a contextual spelling feature that attempts to locate a word that is spelled correctly but used incorrectly. For example, many people confuse the usage of words such as *their* and *there*, *two* and *too*, and *which* and *witch*. The visual indication that a contextual spelling error exists is a blue wavy line under the word, as shown in Figure 1.17.

When you invoke the spelling and grammar checking feature, contextual spelling mistakes will also display, and you can change them during this process.

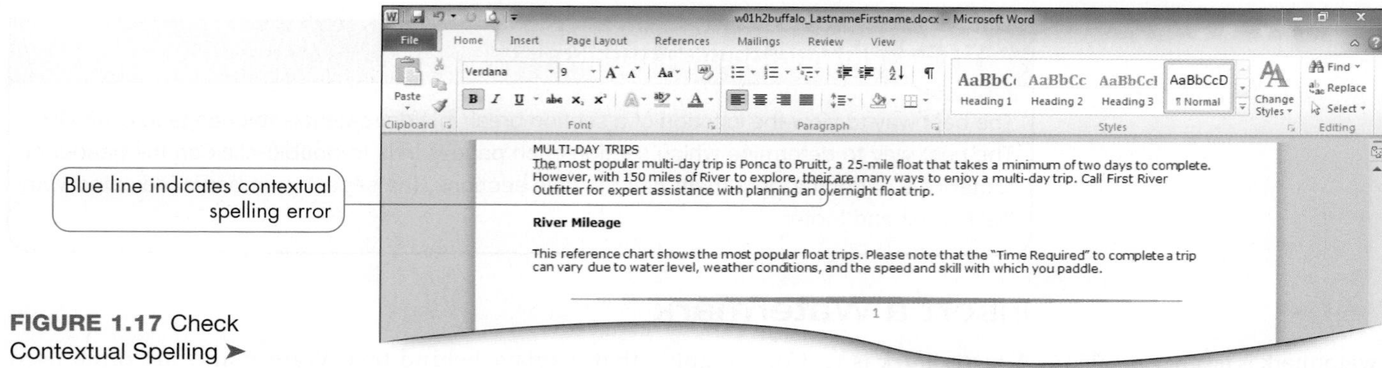

FIGURE 1.17 Check Contextual Spelling ➤

Displaying a Document in Different Views

Print Layout view is the default view and closely resembles the printed document.

Full Screen Reading view eliminates tabs and makes it easier to read a document.

Draft view shows a simplified work area, removing white space and other elements from view.

The View tab provides options that enable you to display a document in many different ways. Each view can display your document at a different magnification, which in turn determines the amount of scrolling necessary to see remote parts of a document. The ***Print Layout view*** is the default view and is the view you use most frequently. It closely resembles the printed document and displays the top and bottom margins, headers and footers, page numbers, graphics, and other features that do not appear in other views.

The ***Full Screen Reading view*** hides the Ribbon, making it easier to read your document. The ***Draft view***, shown in Figure 1.18, creates a simple area in which to work; it removes white space and certain elements from the document, such as headers, footers, and graphics, but leaves the Ribbon. Because view options are used frequently, buttons for each are located on the status bar, as shown in Figure 1.18.

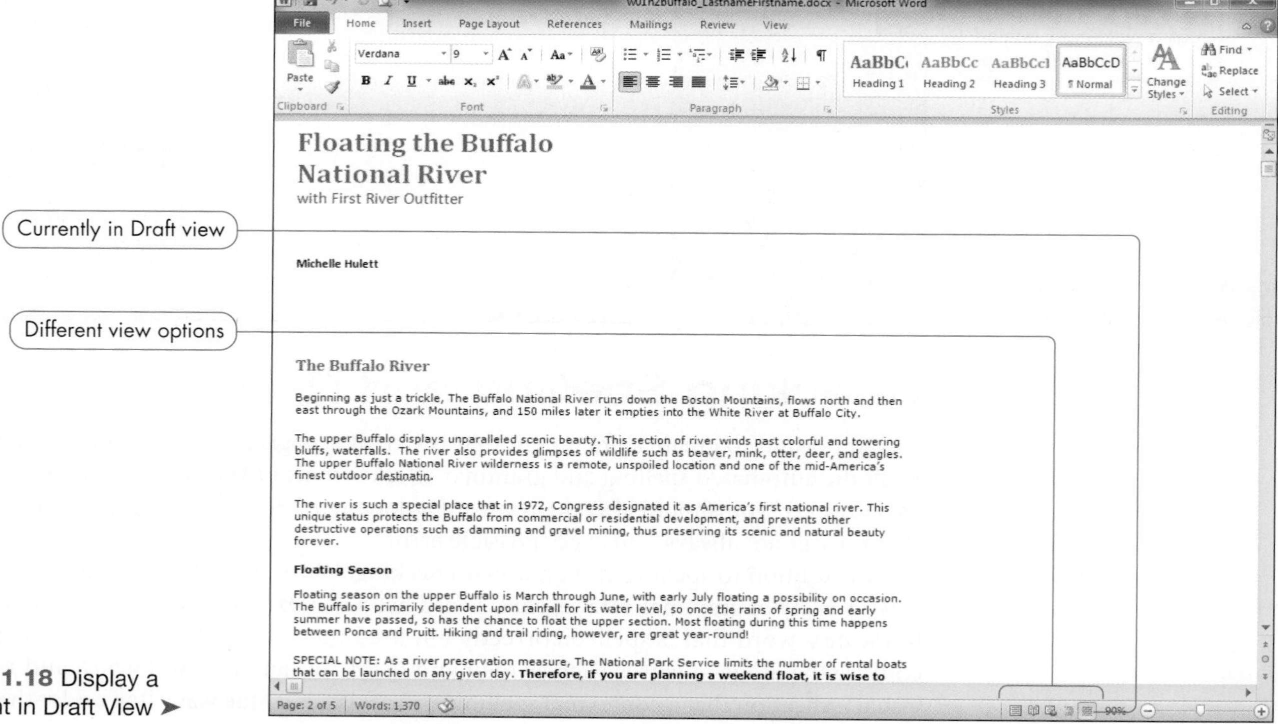

FIGURE 1.18 Display a Document in Draft View ➤

When you click Zoom in the Zoom group on the View tab, the Zoom dialog box displays with several options (see Figure 1.19). You can use the Zoom controls to display the document onscreen at different magnifications—for example, 75%, 100%, or 200%. This command does not affect the size of the text on the printed page. It is helpful to be able to zoom in to view details or to zoom out and see the effects of your work on a full page.

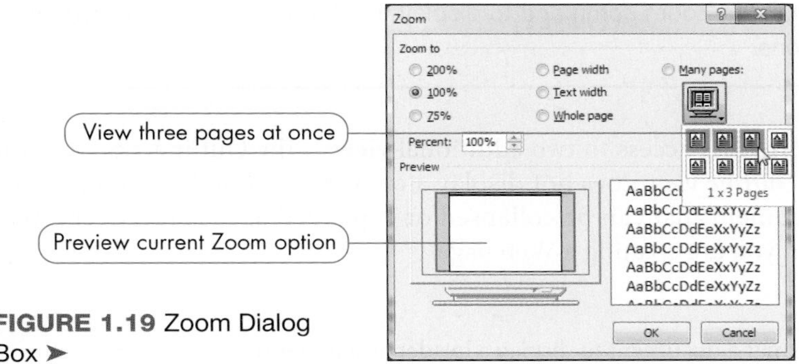

FIGURE 1.19 Zoom Dialog Box ➤

Word will automatically determine the magnification if you select one of the Zoom options—Page width, Text width, Whole page, or Many pages (Whole page and Many pages are available only in the Print Layout view). Figure 1.20, for example, displays the Buffalo River document in Print Layout view. The 27% magnification is determined automatically after you specify the number of pages, in this case 2 × 2. If you use a wide screen, the magnification size might differ slightly.

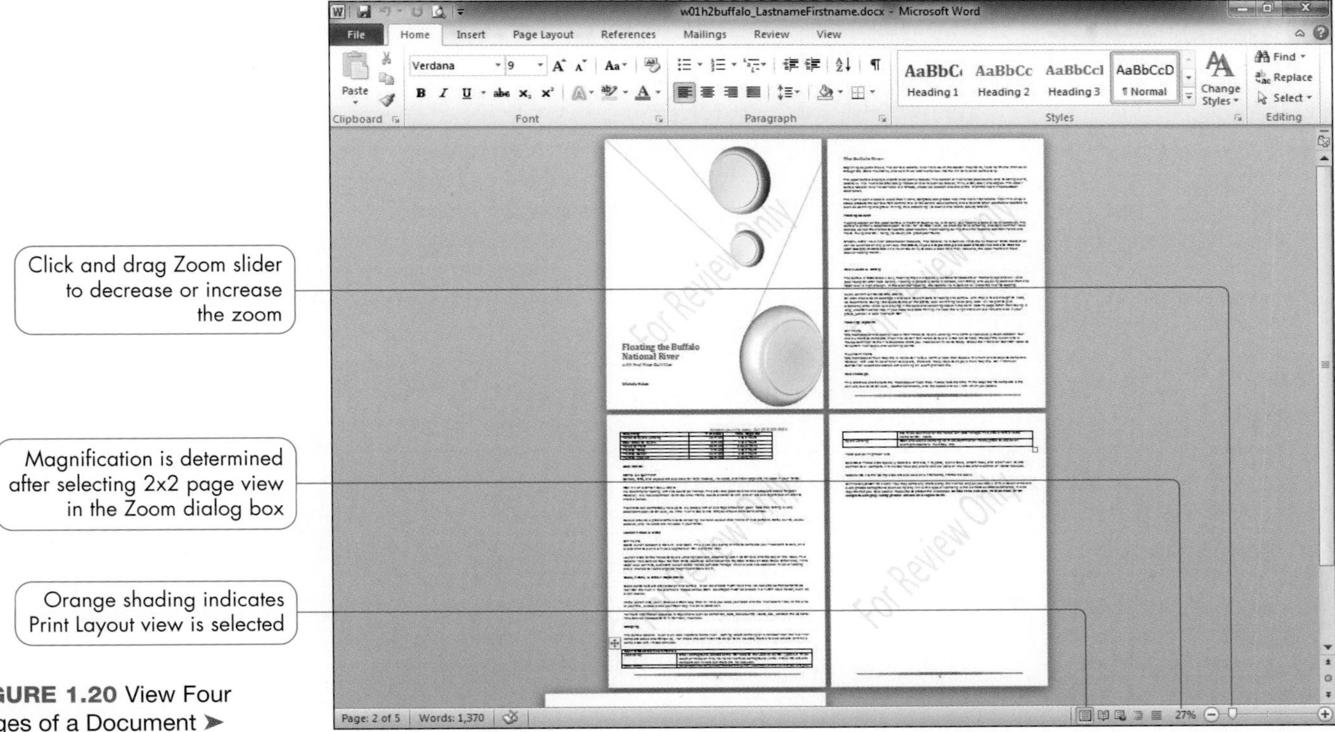

FIGURE 1.20 View Four Pages of a Document ➤

TIP Use the Status Bar to Change View Options

The status bar repeats commands from the View tab in a handy location for quick access. You can switch to Print Layout, Full Screen Reading, Web Layout, Outline, or Draft view from the buttons on the status bar. You also can use the Zoom slider to change the zoom of the current document or click the Zoom command to display the Zoom dialog box, which contains more viewing options.

The **Outline view** displays a structural view of the document that can be collapsed or expanded.

The **Web Layout view** is used when creating a Web page.

The View tab also provides access to two additional views—the Outline view and the Web Layout view. The ***Outline view*** does not display a conventional outline, but rather a structural view of a document that can be collapsed or expanded as necessary. The ***Web Layout view*** is used when you are creating a Web page.

Quick Concepts Check

1. Describe how you format a document to display a header and footer on all pages except the first page.
2. Name three different types of breaks and a situation in which each one is most appropriate to use.
3. Name three types of mistakes that might display when you invoke the spelling and grammar checking feature.
4. Describe the different document views that display by clicking on a view button on the status bar.

HANDS-ON EXERCISES

2 Document Organization

You have made some introductory edits to the document that will be used in marketing the First River Outfitter, but you plan to make more changes that will improve organization and readability. These improvements require a section break at the end that will enable you to format the last page differently from the others. You also remember to check spelling and grammar.

Skills covered: Change Page Margins and Insert a Page Break • Insert Headers in Sections • Add a Watermark • Check Spelling and Grammar

STEP 1 CHANGE PAGE MARGINS AND INSERT A PAGE BREAK

One step in conserving the amount of paper used in marketing materials is to reduce the margins on the pages that will print. In this step you change margins and insert a page break to create a new section at the end of the document. Then you change orientation on the last page to make it easier to view a lengthy table. Refer to Figure 1.21 as you complete Step 1.

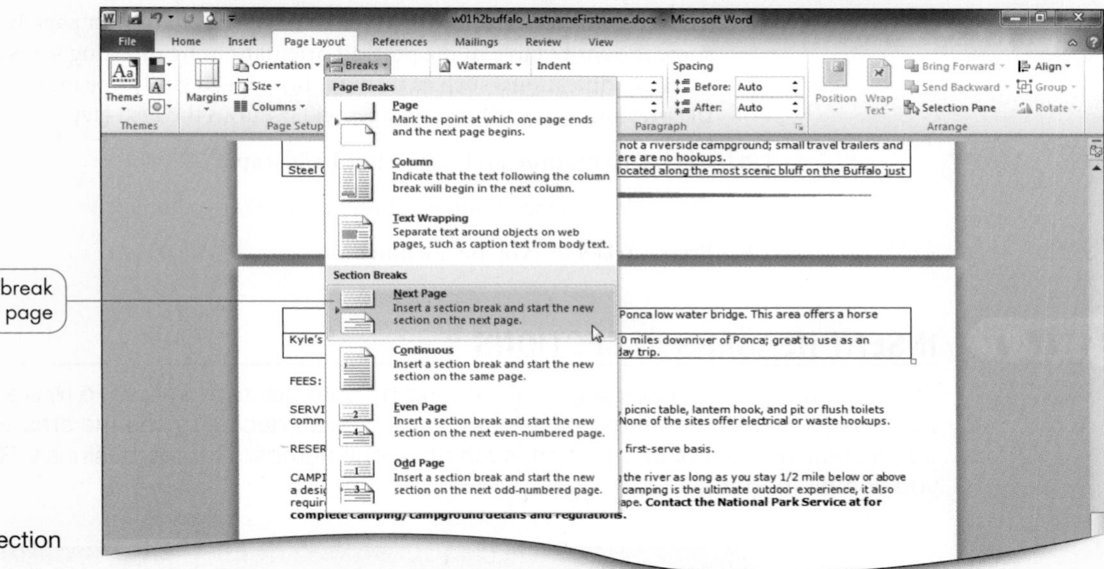

FIGURE 1.21 Insert a Section Break ➤

a. Open *w01h1buffalo_LastnameFirstname* if you closed it at the end of Hands-On Exercise 1. Save the document with the new name **w01h2buffalo_LastnameFirstname**, changing *h1* to *h2*.

b. Click the **Page Layout tab**, and then click **Margins** in the Page Setup group. Click **Custom Margins**.

   The Page Setup dialog box displays.

c. Click the **Margins tab**, if necessary. Type **.5** in the **Top margin box**. Press **Tab** to move the insertion point to the Bottom margin box. Type **.5** and press **Tab** to move to the Left margin box.

   0.5" is the equivalent of 1/2 of one inch.

d. Click the **Left margin arrow** to set the left margin at **0.6**, and then repeat the procedure to set the right margin to **0.6**.

The top and bottom margins are now set at 0.5", and the left and right margins are set at 0.6".

e. Check that these settings apply to the **Whole document**, located in the lower portion of the dialog box. Click **OK** to close the dialog box.

You can see the change in layout as a result of changing the margins. The content now displays with less white space around the text. And the page break at the beginning of the *Glass, Trash, & Other Regulations* section that you inserted earlier is no longer needed.

f. Scroll down and position the insertion point on the left side of the *Glass, Trash, & Other Regulations* title. Press **Backspace**.

TROUBLESHOOTING: If the page break does not disappear immediately, you might have to press Backspace a second time.

g. Scroll down and place the insertion point on the left side of the heading *Plan Your Trip Now!* Click **Breaks** in the Page Setup group, and then click **Next Page** under *Section Breaks*, as shown in Figure 1.21.

The table for personal information that displays on the last page is very wide and does not show the entire table in the portrait orientation. By inserting this section break you can now make modifications, such as turning this page to landscape orientation, without changing the previous pages. Those changes will occur in the next steps.

h. Click **Orientation**, and then select **Landscape**.

The table of personal information now displays completely.

i. Press **Ctrl+S** to save the document.

STEP 2 INSERT HEADERS IN SECTIONS

The document you are preparing will be read by potential customers. To make sure you maximize all areas of the document to market the company, you decide to use the area at the top of a page to add a small amount of information, such as phone numbers for the business. Refer to Figure 1.22 as you complete Step 2.

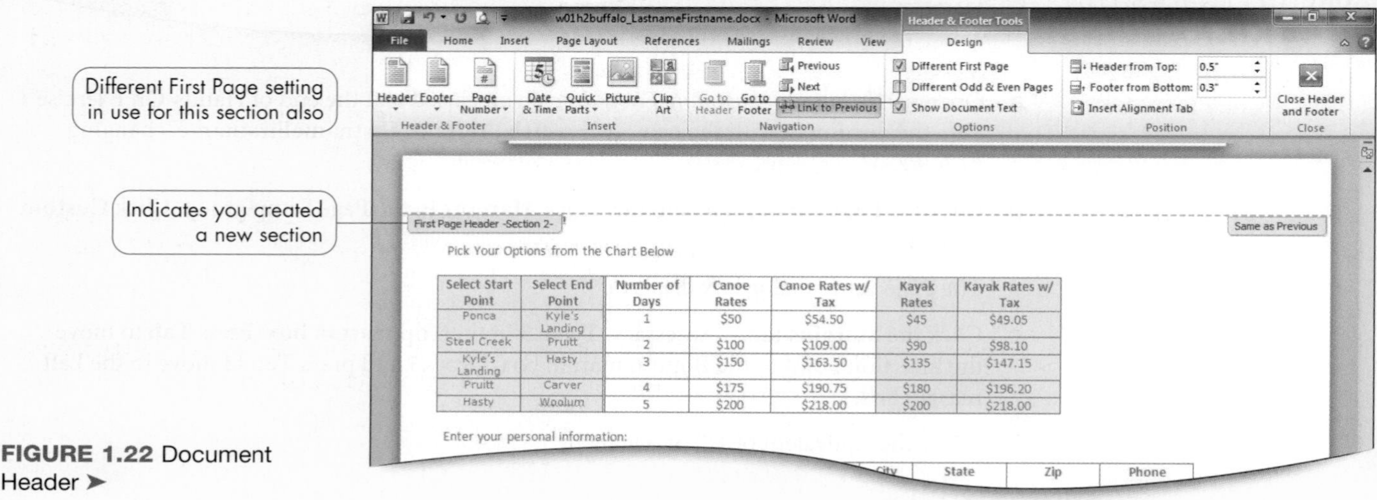

Select Start Point	Select End Point	Number of Days	Canoe Rates	Canoe Rates w/ Tax	Kayak Rates	Kayak Rates w/ Tax
Ponca	Kyle's Landing	1	$50	$54.50	$45	$49.05
Steel Creek	Pruitt	2	$100	$109.00	$90	$98.10
Kyle's Landing	Hasty	3	$150	$163.50	$135	$147.15
Pruitt	Carver	4	$175	$190.75	$180	$196.20
Hasty	Woolum	5	$200	$218.00	$200	$218.00

FIGURE 1.22 Document Header ➤

a. Click the **Insert tab**, click **Header** in the Header & Footer group, and then click **Edit Header**.

The Insertion point displays in the header of the last page, and the Header & Footer Tools Design tab displays in the Ribbon. Notice also that the Header tab for this page indicates this is Section 2, as seen in Figure 1.22.

b. Scroll up and click in a header or footer in Section 1. Click **Different Odd & Even Pages** in the Options group to turn on this feature.

c. Scroll and click to position the insertion point in a header identified as *Even Page Header -Section 1-*, if necessary.

Any information you insert in this header will only show up on even-numbered pages. It looks more professional to omit headers from the first page of text and add them on following pages. This enables you to place information on only even-numbered pages throughout the document. The setting can be used in addition to the Different First Page feature, which is already being used to prevent any header or footer from displaying on the cover page.

d. Press **Tab** two times to move the insertion point to the right side of the header. Type **Schedule your trip today. Call (555) 555-5555.**

The text and phone number display in the header. Scroll down and notice the header displays on this page only.

e. Scroll down and position the insertion point in the header for Section 2. Click **Link to Previous** in the Navigation group to turn that setting off.

The creation of the new section automatically invokes the Link to Previous command. When turned on, it enables the same header or footer to display on the first page in each section. To prevent this contact information from displaying on the cover page you disable that setting in Section 2.

f. Press **Tab** two times, and then type **Schedule your trip today. Call (555) 555-5555**.

Because you insert a separate section for the last page, the headers and footers in the previous section do not automatically display there. To continue the trend of placing the contact information at the top of every even-numbered page, you must insert it again in the new section.

g. Scroll up to the previous page, select the entire odd page footer from Section 1, and then click **Ctrl+C**.

Another consequence of invoking the Different Odd & Even Pages setting is that the footers for the even pages in Section 1 were removed. The next steps copy the footer from the odd pages and insert it into the even pages.

h. Scroll up to the *Even Page Footer -Section 1-*, and then place the insertion point in the footer. Press **Ctrl+V** to insert the page number and heavy line.

TROUBLESHOOTING: If you insert an extra line return and the cursor displays on the line below the page number at the end of the paste operation, press Backspace to remove the extra line return so it does not needlessly extend the space for the footer.

i. Scroll through the document and notice the sequential page numbering only on the middle pages, not the cover sheet or last page. Click **Close Header and Footer**.

j. Save the document.

STEP 3 ADD A WATERMARK

You plan to send a copy of your current work to Lawson for review. You want to make sure this document is marked so anyone who views it will know it is not complete or ready to distribute to customers. You insert a watermark that will display faintly on each page. Later, when the document is complete, you will remove the watermark. Refer to Figure 1.23 as you complete Step 3.

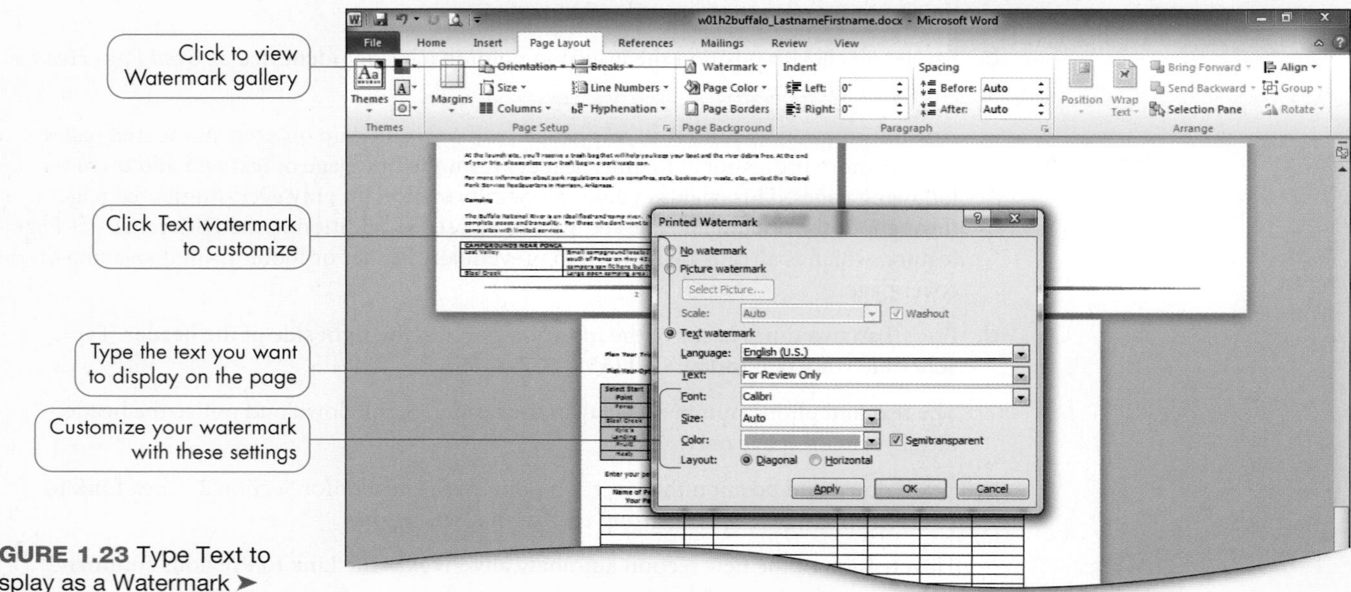

FIGURE 1.23 Type Text to Display as a Watermark ➤

a. Click the **Page Layout tab**. Click **Watermark** in the Page Background group, and then click **Custom Watermark.**

   The Watermark dialog box displays with several options available. You decide to enter your own words to communicate the message that displays as a watermark on this page.

b. Click **Text watermark.**

c. Select the text *ASAP* that displays beside *Text*, and then type **For Review Only** to replace *ASAP*, as shown in Figure 1.23. Click **OK**. Scroll to page 4, which displays *3* as the page number in the footer, to get a better view of the watermark.

   The watermark is in place and displays on each page in each section. It is easier to see it on page 4 because this page has less text.

> **TIP** Frequently Used Watermarks
>
> When you click Watermark in the Page Background group, several of the most commonly used watermark statements display, such as *DRAFT* or *CONFIDENTIAL*. You can also select the option to view more Watermarks from Office.com.

d. Click **Print Preview** in the Quick Access Toolbar, and notice the watermark in the preview of the document.

e. Click the **File tab** to close Print Preview. Press **Ctrl+S** to save the document.

STEP 4 CHECK SPELLING AND GRAMMAR

You are always careful to check spelling and grammar before distributing a document for others to read. After several edits, you decide it is time to run the spelling and grammar check feature in Word and make changes to remove any mistakes. Refer to Figure 1.24 as you complete Step 4.

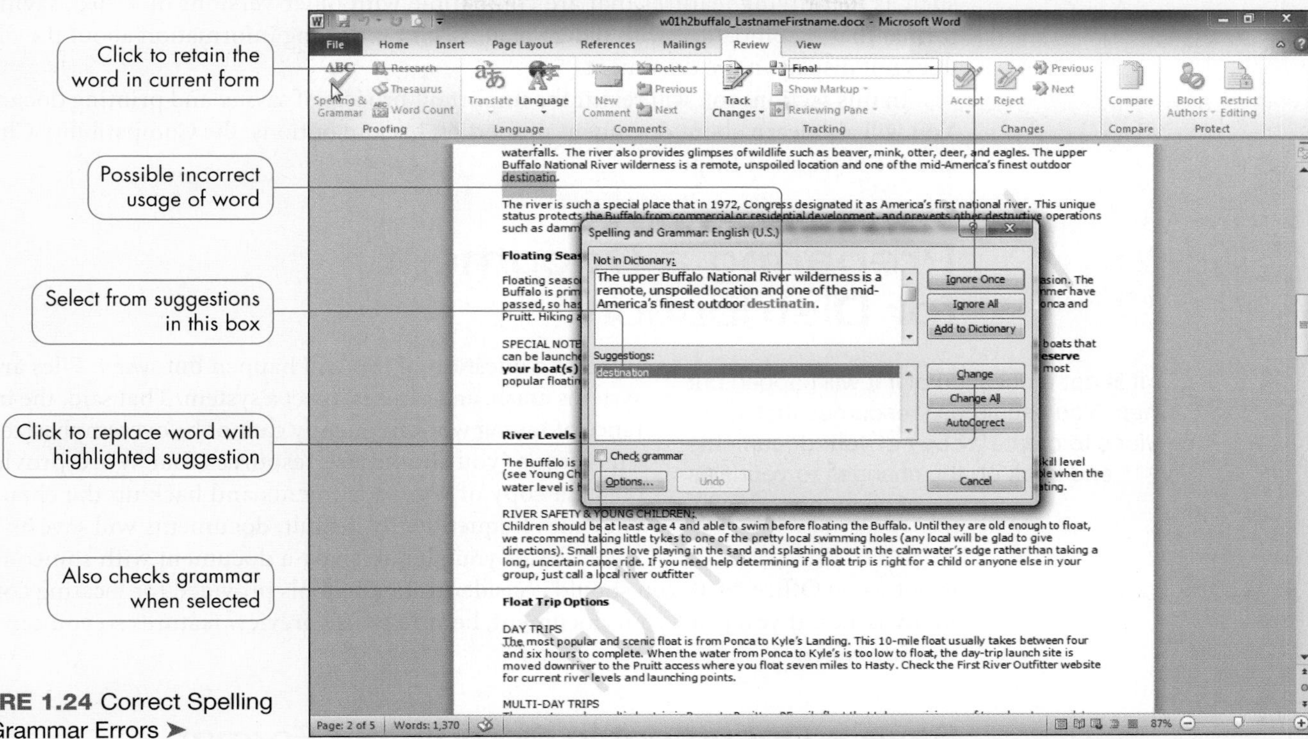

FIGURE 1.24 Correct Spelling and Grammar Errors ➤

a. Place the cursor at the top of page 2, on the left side of the text *The Buffalo River*. Click the **Review tab**, and then click **Spelling & Grammar** in the Proofing group.

The Spelling and Grammar dialog box displays with the first error indicated in red text, as shown in Figure 1.24.

b. Remove the check from the *Check grammar* option. If necessary, click **Yes** in the dialog box that asks if you want to continue checking the document.

Many of the headings in the document will be flagged for incorrect grammar, so this will let you bypass all of them and check the spelling only.

TROUBLESHOOTING: If additional text is flagged, such as *you've*, click Ignore All. This indicates that Word is checking grammar and style. To do a simple spelling and grammar check, click the File tab, click Options, click Proofing, click the Writing Style arrow, choose Grammar Only, and then click OK.

c. Click **Change All** to replace all misspellings of the word *destinatin* with the correct *destination*, and then view the next error.

d. Click **Change** to replace the contextual spelling error *their are* with *there are* near the bottom of the first page.

e. Click **Ignore once** to the remaining spelling errors in the document. These words are spelled correctly, but are not included in the spelling checker dictionary, and therefore, are flagged as spelling errors. Click **OK** in the box that informs you the spelling and grammar check is complete.

f. Save the document and keep it onscreen if you plan to continue with the next Hands-On Exercise. If not, close the document and exit Word.

Finalize a Document

After you organize your document and make all the formatting changes you desire, you need to save the document in its final form and prepare it for use by others. You can take advantage of features in Word that enable you to manipulate the file in a variety of ways, such as identifying features that are compatible with older versions of Word, saving in a format that is compatible with older versions, and including information about the file that does not display in the document.

In this section, you will revisit the important process of saving and printing documents. You will also learn about document properties, backup options, the Compatibility Checker, and the Document Inspector.

Preparing a Document for Distribution

It is not a question of *if* it will happen but *when*. You should use resources that Word provides to create a copy of your documents and back up the changes to your files at every opportunity.

It is not a question of *if* it will happen but *when*. Files are lost, systems crash, and viruses infect a system. That said, the importance of saving work frequently cannot be overemphasized. For this reason, you should use resources that Word provides to create a copy of your documents and back up the changes to your files frequently. By default, documents will save as Word 2010 files. If you plan to share a document with someone who is not using Office 2010, you should consider using the tools provided for locating compatibility issues. If you print your document, be sure to use preview features so you can avoid wasting paper.

Save a Document in Compatible Format

Because some people may have a different version of Word, you should know how to save a document in a format that they can use. People cannot open a Word 2010 document in the 97-2003 versions of Word unless they install the Compatibility Pack that contains a converter. If you are sure they have not installed the Compatibility Pack, you should save the document in Word 97-2003 format.

After reading the Office Fundamentals chapter, you know the Save and Save As commands are used to copy your documents to disk and should be used frequently to avoid loss of work and data. To save a document so that someone with a 97-2003 version of Office can open it, do the following:

1. Click the File tab.
2. Click Save As.
3. Select the Save as type arrow, and then select Word 97-2003 (see Figure 1.25).
4. Enter a name for your file in the Save As dialog box. The saved file will have the .doc extension instead of the Word 2010 extension, .docx.

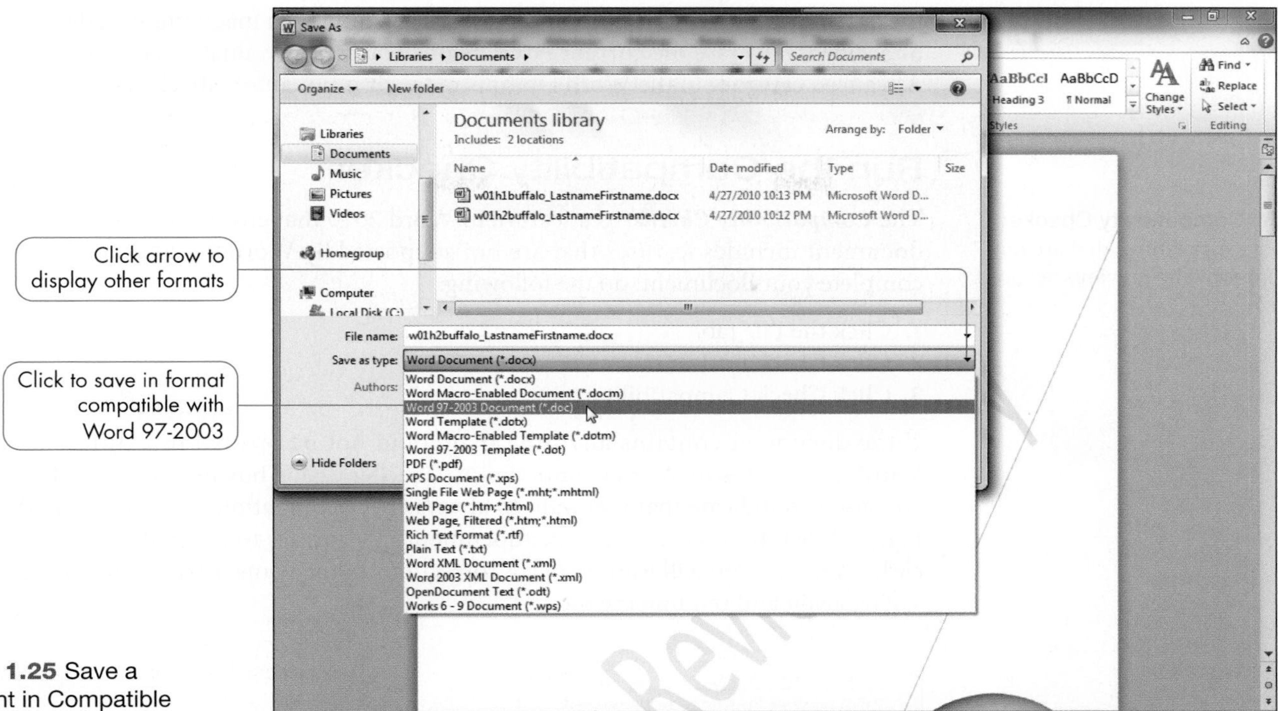

FIGURE 1.25 Save a Document in Compatible Format ➤

If you open a Word document created in an earlier version, such as Word 2003, the title bar will include *(Compatibility Mode)* at the top. You can still work with the document and even save it back in the same format for Word 97-2003 users. However, some features introduced in Word 2007 and used in Word 2010, such as SmartArt and graphic enhancement options used in the cover page, are not viewable or available for use in compatibility mode.

To remove the file from compatibility mode, click the File tab, and then click Convert. It will convert the file and remove the *(Compatibility Mode)* designator, but the .doc extension will still display. The next time you click Save, the extension will change to .docx, indicating that the file is converted into a Word 2010 file; you will then be able to use all of the Word 2010 features.

Understand Backup Options

AutoRecover enables Word to recover a previous version of a document.

Word enables you to back up files in different ways. One option is to use a feature called ***AutoRecover***. If Word crashes when AutoRecover is enabled, the program will be able to recover a previous version of your document when you restart the program. The only work you will lose is anything you did between the time of the last AutoRecover operation and the time of the crash, unless you happen to save the document in the meantime. The default *Save AutoRecover information every 10 minutes* ensures that you will never lose more than 10 minutes of work. AutoRecover is enabled from the Save category in the Word Options menu.

You can also set Word to create a backup copy with every save. Assume that you have created the simple document with the phrase *The fox jumped over the fence*, and have saved it under the name *Fox*. Assume further that you edit the document to read *The quick brown fox jumped over the fence*, and that you save it a second time. The second Save command changes the name of the original document from *Fox* to *Backup of Fox*, then saves the current contents of memory as *Fox*. In other words, the disk now contains two versions of the document: the current version *Fox* and the most recent previous version *Backup of Fox*.

The cycle goes on indefinitely, with *Fox* always containing the current version and *Backup of Fox* the most recent previous version. So, if you revise and save the document a third time, the original (first) version of the document disappears entirely because only two versions are kept. The contents of *Fox* and *Backup of Fox* are different, but the existence of the latter enables you to retrieve the previous version if you inadvertently edit beyond repair or accidentally erase the current *Fox* version. You set this valuable backup option from the Advanced category in the Word Options menu; it is not automatically enabled.

Run the Compatibility Checker

The **Compatibility Checker** looks for features that are not supported by previous versions of Word.

The ***Compatibility Checker*** is a feature in Word 2010 that enables you to determine if your document includes features that are not supported by Word 97-2003 versions. After you complete your document, do the following:

1. Click the File tab.
2. Click Check for Issues.
3. Click Check Compatibility.

If the document contains anything that could not be opened in a different version of Word, the Microsoft Word Compatibility Checker dialog box lists it. From this dialog box you also can indicate that you want to always check compatibility when saving this file (see Figure 1.26). If you are saving the document in a format to be used by someone with an earlier version, you will want to make corrections to the items listed in the dialog box before saving again and sending the file.

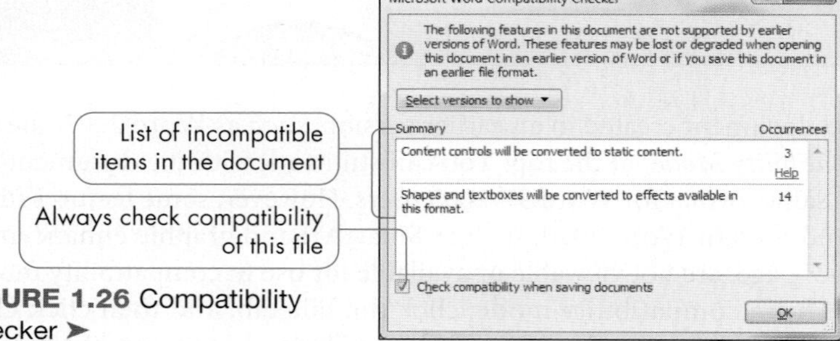

FIGURE 1.26 Compatibility Checker ➤

Run the Document Inspector

The **Document Inspector** checks for and removes different kinds of hidden and personal information from a document.

Before you send or give a document to another person, you should run the ***Document Inspector*** to reveal any hidden or personal data in the file. For privacy or security reasons, you might want to remove certain items contained in the document such as author name, comments made by one or more persons who have access to the document, or document server locations. Some inspectors are specific to individual Office applications, such as Excel and PowerPoint. Word provides inspectors that you can invoke to reveal different types of information, including the following:

- Comments, Revisions, Versions, and Annotations
- Document Properties and Personal Information
- Custom XML Data
- Headers, Footers, and Watermarks
- Invisible Content
- Hidden Text

The inspectors can also locate information in documents created in older versions of Word. Because some information that the Document Inspector might remove cannot be recovered with the Undo command, you should save a copy of your original document, using a different name, just before you run any of the inspectors. After you save the copy, do the following:

1. Click the File tab.
2. Click Check for Issues.
3. Click Inspect Document.

The Document Inspector dialog box displays first, enabling you to select the types of content you want it to check (see Figure 1.27). When the check is complete, Word lists the results and enables you to choose whether to remove the content from the document. If you forget to save a backup copy of the document, you can use the Save As command to save a copy of the document with a new name after you run the inspector.

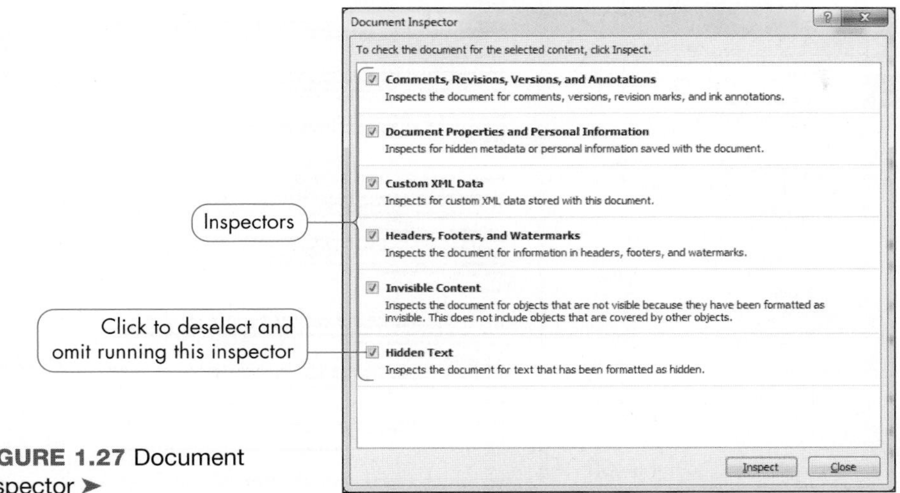

FIGURE 1.27 Document Inspector ➤

Select Printing Options

People often print an entire document when they want to view only a few pages. All computer users should be mindful of the environment, and limiting printer use is a perfect place to start. Millions of sheets of paper have been wasted because someone did not take a moment to preview his or her work and then had to reprint due to a minor error that is easily noticed in a preview window.

Click the File tab, and click Print to view the Backstage view settings and options for printing. Fortunately, the print preview displays automatically, so you know how your document will print in its current form. You see one page at a time, but you can use the Previous Page and Next Page arrows to navigate to other pages. You can also use the zoom slider or Zoom to Page setting at the bottom of the Preview pane to magnify the page or preview several pages at once.

After evaluating the preview carefully, you can select from many print options in the Backstage view, as shown in Figure 1.28. At the top of the screen you can scroll to select the number of copies. To select a different printer, if you have access to more than one, click the Printer arrow. Word has other print settings; Table 1.4 lists a sampling of options available for each setting. Settings might vary from one computer to another because of the difference in printers.

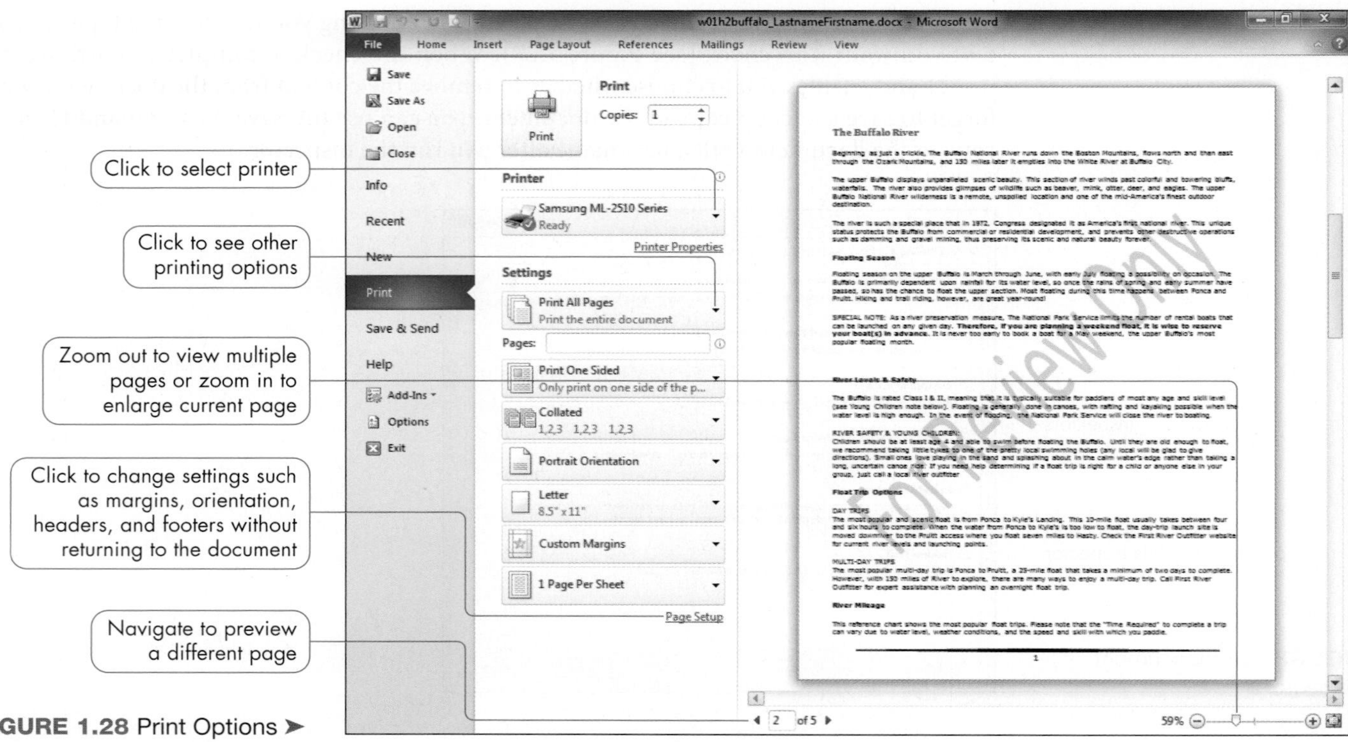

FIGURE 1.28 Print Options ➤

TABLE 1.4 Print Settings	
Setting	**Options**
Print All Pages	Print Selection Print Current Page Print Custom Range Document Properties Only Print Odd Pages Only Print Even Pages
Print One Sided	Print Both Sides (only listed if your printer is capable of duplex printing) Manually Print on Both Sides
Collated	Collated (1,2,3; 1,2,3; 1,2,3) Uncollated (1,1,1; 2,2,2; 3,3,3)
Portrait Orientation	Portrait Orientation Landscape Orientation
Letter	Legal (8.5"× 14") A4 (8.27" × 11.69") More Paper Sizes
Normal Margins	Normal Narrow Custom Margins
1 Page Per Sheet	2 Pages Per Sheet 4 Pages Per Sheet 16 Pages Per Sheet Scale to Paper Size

Modifying Document Properties

Sometimes, you want to record detailed information about a document but do not want to display the information directly in the document window. You use the Document Panel to store descriptive information such as a title, subject, author, keywords, and summary.

Sometimes, you want to record detailed information about a document but do not want to display the information directly in the document window. For example, you might want to record some notes to yourself about a document, such as the document's author, purpose, or intended audience. You use the ***Document Panel*** to store descriptive information such as a title, subject, author, keywords, and summary.

The **Document Panel** enables you to enter descriptive information about a document.

When you click the File tab and display the Backstage view, you see a thumbnail version of the current page. Below that thumbnail you see information about the document such as the size, number of pages, word count, title, date modified, and author. You can modify some document information in this view, but you can also display the full Document Panel to view and edit other properties. To display the Document Panel, as shown in Figure 1.29, do the following:

1. Click the File tab.
2. Click the Properties arrow.
3. Click Show Document Panel.

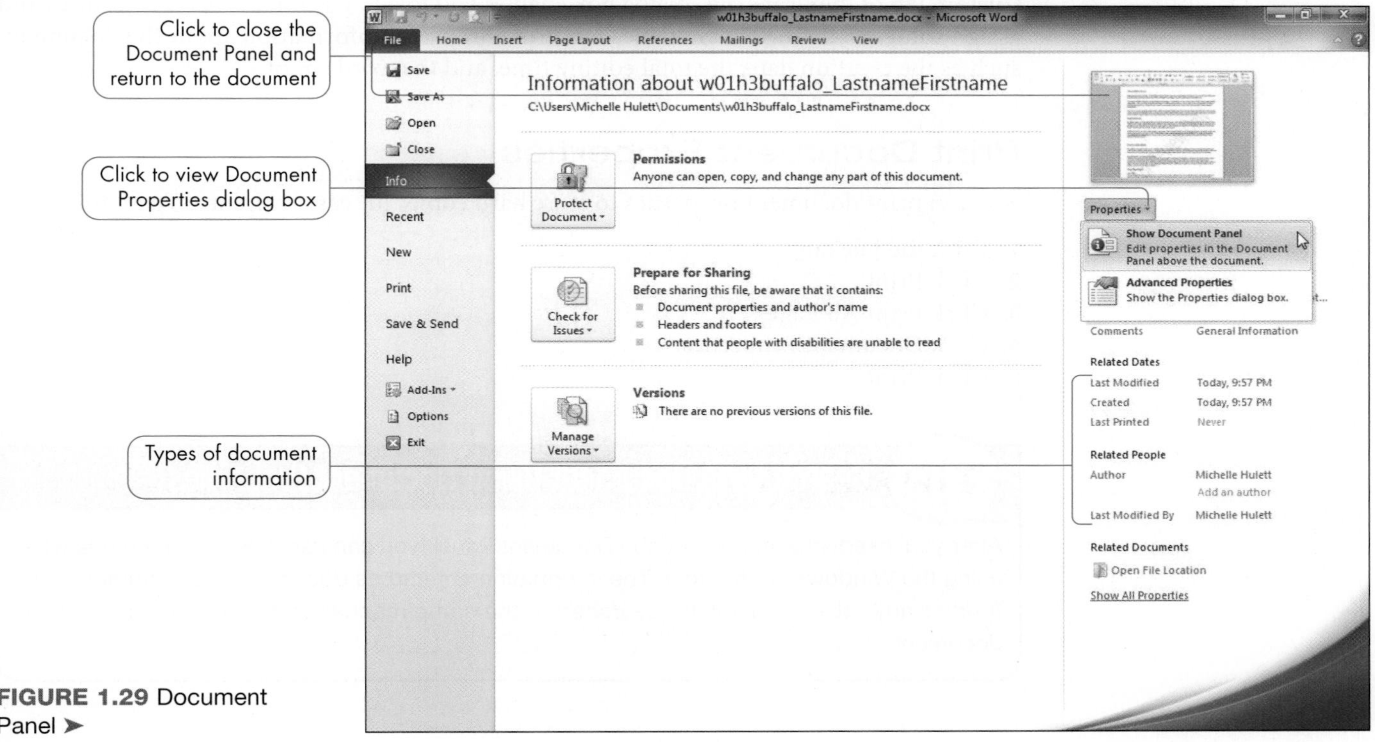

FIGURE 1.29 Document Panel ➤

When you save the document, Word saves this information with the document. You can update the descriptive information at any time by opening the Document Panel for the respective document.

> **TIP** **Exiting the Backstage View**
>
> You can return to a document from the Backstage view in three ways:
>
> - Click the File tab.
> - Click the document thumbnail.
> - Click ESC on the keyboard.

Customize Document Properties

In addition to creating, modifying, and viewing a document summary, you may want to customize the document properties in the Document Panel. For example, you might want to add a *Date completed* property and specify an exact date for reference. This date would reflect the completion date, not the date the file was last saved—in case someone opens a file and saves it without making changes. You also might create a field to track company information such as warehouse location or product numbers.

When you click Document Properties and then click Advanced Properties, the Properties dialog box displays. Most commonly used properties display in the General tab. The Custom tab of the Properties dialog box enables you to add custom property categories and assign values to them. The Statistics tab provides useful information about the document, such as the creation date, the total editing time, and the word count.

Print Document Properties

You can print document properties to store hard copies for easy reference. To do this,

1. Click the File tab.
2. Click Print.
3. Click Print All Pages.
4. Click Document Properties.
5. Click Print.

> **TIP** **Search for a Document Using Document Properties**
>
> After you insert information into the Document Panel, you can use it as search criteria when using the Windows search tool. The information entered as document title, comments, author, or any other field will be searched in the same manner as text that displays in the document.

Quick Concepts Check

1. List the steps to save a document so it can be opened by an associate who uses a different version of Microsoft Word.
2. Describe the differences in how the AutoRecover and backup features work in Microsoft Word.
3. Before you send a document to an associate, what features might you run to make sure the associate can open and view the entire contents of your file?
4. Name three Print options you will consider using on a regular basis to prevent unnecessary waste of paper?
5. What feature can you use to add information to your document, but which does not display in the document? What type of information can you add?

3 Finalize a Document

As office manager for First River Outfitter, you are responsible for the security, management, and backup of all documents the business uses. Your formatting changes to the marketing document make it look more professional; now you must perform last-minute checks before sending it to Lawson for a final check. You also change document properties so it will be easy to locate and identify from your system storage device.

Skills covered: Modify Document Properties • Run the Document Inspector and a Compatibility Check • Save in a Compatible Format • Use Print Preview Features

STEP 1 MODIFY DOCUMENT PROPERTIES

You want to add data to your document so you can identify information such as the author, title, purpose, and date that it was completed—not just the last revision date, which is assigned by the computer. Since you don't want this information to show up in your document, you include it in the Document Properties. Refer to Figure 1.30 as you complete Step 1.

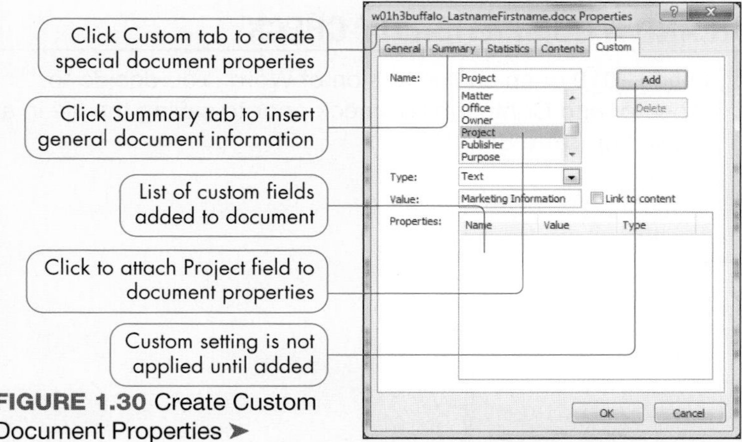

FIGURE 1.30 Create Custom Document Properties ➤

a. Open *w01h2buffalo_LastnameFirstname* if you closed it at the end of Hands-On Exercise 2. Save the document with the new name **w01h3buffalo_LastnameFirstname**, changing *h2* to *h3*.

b. Click the **File tab**, click **Properties**, and then click **Show Document Panel**.

   The Document Panel displays above your document. The document title and author name you entered on the cover page display in their respective boxes here. The subtitle you entered on the cover page displays in the Subject box.

> **TROUBLESHOOTING:** If the Document Panel disappears, repeat step b above to display it again.

c. Click one time in the **Comments box**, and then type **General Information**.

d. Click the **Document Properties arrow** in the top-left of the Document Properties panel, and then select **Advanced Properties** to display the w01h3buffalo_LastnameFirstname.docx Properties dialog box.

e. Create a custom property by completing the following steps:

- Click the **Custom tab**, and then select **Project** in the **Name list**.
- Type **Marketing Information** in the **Value box**, as shown in Figure 1.30, and then click **Add**.
- Click **OK** to close the dialog box.

  You want to catalog the documents you create for First River Outfitter, and one way to do that is to assign a project scope using the custom properties that are stored with each document. Because you set up a custom field in the Document Properties, you can later perform searches and find all documents in that Project category.

f. Click **Close the Document Information Panel** in the top-right corner of Document Properties. Save the document.

TIP Document Properties and Windows Explorer

When you hover your mouse over a document in Windows Explorer, information stored as Document Properties will display.

STEP 2 RUN THE DOCUMENT INSPECTOR AND A COMPATIBILITY CHECK

You cannot remember if Lawson is using Office 2010 or an earlier version of Word. You decide to take precautions and run the Document Inspector and Compatibility check prior to saving the file in a compatible version. Refer to Figure 1.31 as you complete Step 2.

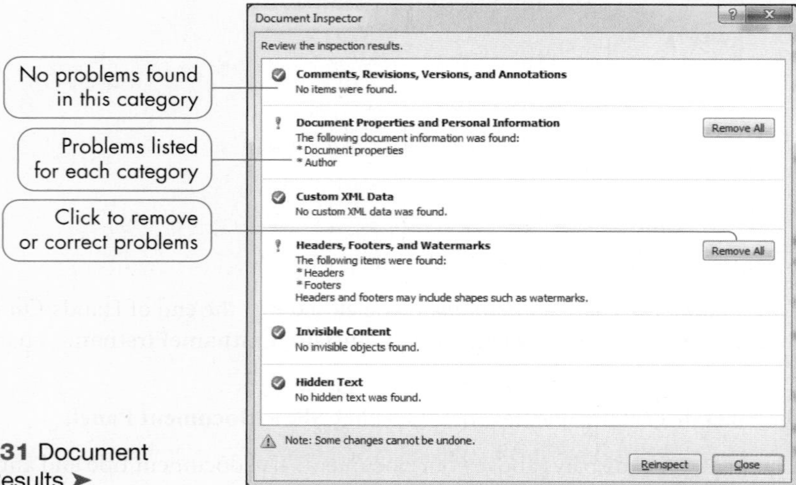

FIGURE 1.31 Document Inspector Results ➤

a. Click the **File tab**, click **Check for Issues** in the center part of the window, and then select **Check Compatibility**.

   Any noncompatible items in the document will display in the Microsoft Office Word Compatibility Checker dialog box. For this document, 17 occurrences of a feature are not compatible with earlier versions of Word.

b. Click **OK** after you view the incompatible listings.

c. Click the **File tab**, and then click **Save As**. Save the document as **w01h3buffalo2_LastnameFirstname**, adding the number *2* at the end of *buffalo*.

   Before you run the Document Inspector, you save the document with a different name in order to have a backup. You should always create a backup of the document because the Document Inspector might make changes that you cannot undo.

d. Click the **File tab**, click **Check for Issues**, and then select **Inspect Document**.

> **TROUBLESHOOTING:** An informational window might display with instructions to save the document before you run the Document Inspector. You should always create a backup of the document because the Document Inspector might make changes that you cannot undo.

e. Click to select any inspector check box that is not already checked. Click **Inspect**.

   The Document Inspector results display and enable you to use Remove All buttons to eliminate the items found in each category.

f. Click the **Close button**; do not remove any items at this time.

g. Save the document as **w01h3buffalo_LastnameFirstname**, deleting the *2* at the end of *buffalo* and reverting back to the previous name. Click **OK** to replace the existing file with the same name.

STEP 3 SAVE IN A COMPATIBLE FORMAT

You know Lawson is anxious to review a copy of this document. You have learned that Lawson is running Word 2000 in his office, so you decide to convert the file so he will be able to open and view it easily. After you save it in compatible mode, you convert it again so Lawson can view your work using the current version. Refer to Figure 1.32 as you complete Step 3.

FIGURE 1.32 File Saved in Word 97-2003 Format ➤

a. Click the **File tab**, click **Save As**, click the **Save as type arrow**, and then select **Word 97-2003 Document**.

b. Confirm the Save as type box displays *Word 97-2003 Document (*.doc)*, and then click **Save**.

   The Microsoft Word Compatibility Checker dialog box displays to confirm the compatibility issues you have already seen.

c. Click **Continue** to accept the alteration.

   The title bar displays *(Compatibility Mode)* following the file name *w01h3buffalo_LastnameFirstname.doc*. If you set the option to display file extensions on your computer, the document extension .doc displays in the title bar, as shown in Figure 1.32.

d. Click the **File tab**, and then click **Convert**.

   The Compatibility Mode designation is removed from the title bar. If a dialog box displays stating the document will be converted to the newest file format, click OK. You can check the option that prevents the dialog box from displaying each time this situation occurs.

e. Click **Save** on the Quick Access Toolbar. Click **Save** in the Save As dialog box, and then click **OK** if the authorization to replace the current file displays.

   The document extension has been restored to .docx.

STEP 4 USE PRINT PREVIEW FEATURES

Since you believe you have made the final changes to the document for now, you preview it onscreen. When you preview it this way, you are not wasting paper on unnecessary printouts. Refer to Figure 1.33 as you complete Step 4.

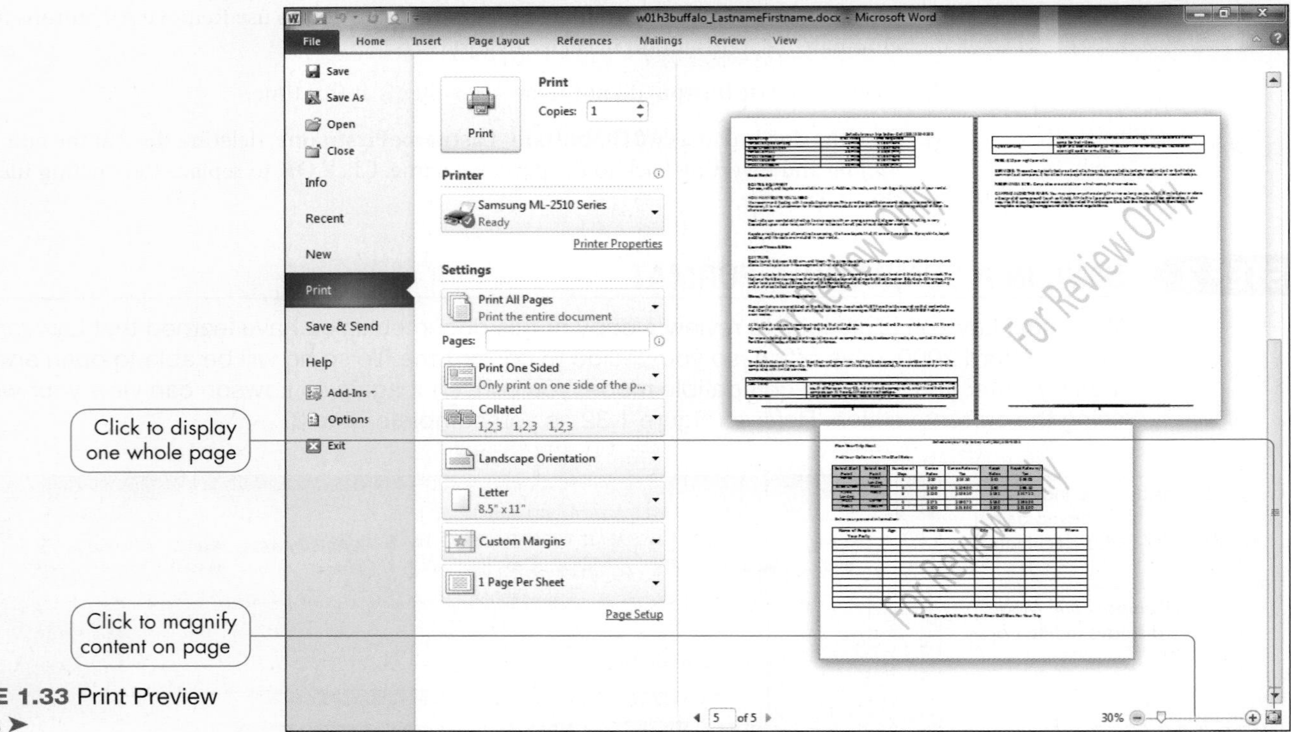

FIGURE 1.33 Print Preview Options ➤

a. Click **Ctrl+Home**, if necessary, to move to the beginning of the document. Click the **File tab**, and then click **Print**.

   The Print Preview window displays the first page.

b. Click **Zoom out** on the Zoom slider until the first four pages display.

   The display can vary depending on your settings, but you should see four pages of the document.

c. Click the **Next Page** navigation arrow four times until the last page of the document displays.

   You can see how the last page is formatted differently due to the section break inserted previously.

d. Click the **File tab** again to return to the application.

e. Close *w01h3buffalo_LastnameFirstname* and submit based on your instructor's directions.

CHAPTER OBJECTIVES REVIEW

After reading this chapter, you have accomplished the following objectives:

1. **Understand how word processors work.** Word provides a multitude of features that enable you to enhance documents easily while typing or with only a few clicks of the mouse. As you type, the word wrap feature automatically positions text for you using soft returns; however, you can insert a hard return to force text to the next page or to increase spacing between paragraphs. Keyboard shortcuts are useful for navigating a document, and toggle switches are often used to alternate between two states while you work. Page numbers are easy to add, and they serve as a convenient reference point to assist in reading through a document. Word also offers a feature to quickly insert a preformatted cover page in your document. The Cover Page feature includes a gallery with several designs.
2. **Customize Word.** Word is useful immediately. However, many options can be customized. The Word Options dialog box contains ten categories of options that you can change, including General, Proofing, and Add-Ins.
3. **Use features that improve readability.** When you create a document, you should consider how it will look when you print or display it. Margins determine the amount of white space from the text to the edge of the page, and you can set pages to display in portrait or landscape orientation. Headers and footers give a professional appearance to a document and are the best location to store page numbers. A section break is a marker that divides a document into sections, thereby enabling different formatting in each section. By using section breaks, you can change the margins within a multipage letter, where the first page (the letterhead) requires a larger top margin than the other pages in the letter. You can also change the page numbering within a document.
4. **Check spelling and grammar.** In conjunction with the spelling and grammar check feature, the contextual spelling feature attempts to locate a word that is spelled correctly but used incorrectly. For example, it looks for the correct usage of the words *there* and *their*. A contextual spelling error is underlined with a blue wavy line.
5. **Display a document in different views.** The View tab provides options that enable you to display a document in many different ways. Views include Print Layout, Full Screen Reading, Web Layout, Outline, and Draft. To change the view quickly, click a button on the status bar in the lower-right corner of the window. The Zoom dialog box includes options to change to whole page or multipage view.
6. **Prepare a document for distribution.** To prevent loss of data you should save and back up your work frequently. You should also be familiar with commands that enable you to save your documents in a format compatible with older versions of Word. Several backup options can be set, including an AutoRecover setting you can customize. You can also require Word to create a backup copy in conjunction with every save operation. Word 2010 includes a compatibility checker to look for features that are not supported by previous versions of Word, and it also offers a Document Inspector that checks for and removes different kinds of hidden or personal information from a document. The Backstage view print area contains many useful options including options to print only the current page, a specific range of pages, or a specific number of copies.
7. **Modify document properties.** You can create a document summary that provides descriptive information about a document, such as a title, subject, author, keywords, and comments. When you create a document summary, Word saves the document summary with the saved document. You also can print document properties.

KEY TERMS

AutoRecover ***p.151***
Compatibility Checker ***p.152***
Document Inspector ***p.152***
Document Panel ***p.155***
Draft view ***p.142***
Footer ***p.137***
Full Screen Reading view ***p.142***
Hard page break ***p.128***
Hard return ***p.126***
Header ***p.137***
Outline view ***p.144***
Print Layout view ***p.142***
Section break ***p.139***
Show/Hide feature ***p.127***
Soft page break ***p.127***
Soft return ***p.126***
Toggle ***p.127***
Watermark ***p.141***
Web Layout view ***p.144***
Word processing software ***p.124***
Word wrap ***p.126***

MULTIPLE CHOICE

1. How do you display the Backstage view Print options?
   (a) Click Print on the Quick Access Toolbar.
   (b) Click the File tab, and then click Print.
   (c) Click the Print Preview command.
   (d) Click the Home tab.

2. Which view removes white space, headers, and footers from the screen?
   (a) Full Screen Reading
   (b) Print Layout
   (c) Draft
   (d) Print Preview

3. You are the only person in your office to upgrade to Word 2010. Before you share documents with coworkers you should do which of the following?
   (a) Print out a backup copy.
   (b) Run the Compatibility Checker.
   (c) Burn all documents to CD.
   (d) Have no concerns that coworkers can open your documents.

4. A document has been entered into Word using the default margins. What can you say about the number of hard and soft returns if the margins are increased by 0.5" on each side?
   (a) The number of hard returns is the same, but the number and/or position of the soft returns increases.
   (b) The number of hard returns is the same, but the number and/or position of the soft returns decreases.
   (c) The number and position of both hard and soft returns is unchanged.
   (d) The number and position of both hard and soft returns decreases.

5. Which of the following is detected by the contextual spelling checker?
   (a) Duplicate words
   (b) Use of the word *their* when you should use *there*
   (c) Irregular capitalization
   (d) Improper use of commas

6. If your cursor is near the bottom of a page and you want to display the next paragraph you type at the top of a new page, you should use which of the following?
   (a) Enter
   (b) Ctrl+Page Down
   (c) Ctrl+Enter
   (d) Page Layout, Breaks, Line Numbers

7. You need to insert a large table in the middle of a report that contains page numbers in the footer. The table is too wide to fit on a standard page. Which of the following is the best option to use in this case?
   (a) Put the table in a separate document, and do not worry about page numbering.
   (b) Insert a section break, and change the format of the page containing the table to landscape orientation.
   (c) Change the whole document to use landscape orientation.
   (d) Change margins to 0" on the right and left.

8. What feature adds organization to your documents?
   (a) Print Preview
   (b) Orientation
   (c) Page Numbers
   (d) Find and Replace

9. If you cannot determine why a block of text starts at the top of the next page, which toggle switch should you invoke to view the formatting marks in use?
   (a) Word wrap
   (b) Show/Hide
   (c) Bold font
   (d) Caps Lock

10. What visual clue tells you that a document is not in Word 2010 format?
    (a) The status bar includes the text *(Compatibility Mode)*.
    (b) The file extension is .docx.
    (c) The title bar is a different color.
    (d) The title bar includes *(Compatibility Mode)* after the file name.

PRACTICE EXERCISES

1 Study Abroad Reference Forms

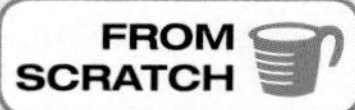

You are the Executive Assistant in the Study Abroad Office of a local university and are creating a new reference form that students must deliver to anyone from whom they plan to get a recommendation for their planned study abroad activities. You will begin creating the document by including basic requirements of the reference form. Your supervisor has an older version of Microsoft Office, so you will save it in a format he can read before you send it to him to review. This exercise follows the same set of skills as used in Hands-On Exercises 1–3 in the chapter. Refer to Figure 1.34 as you complete this exercise.

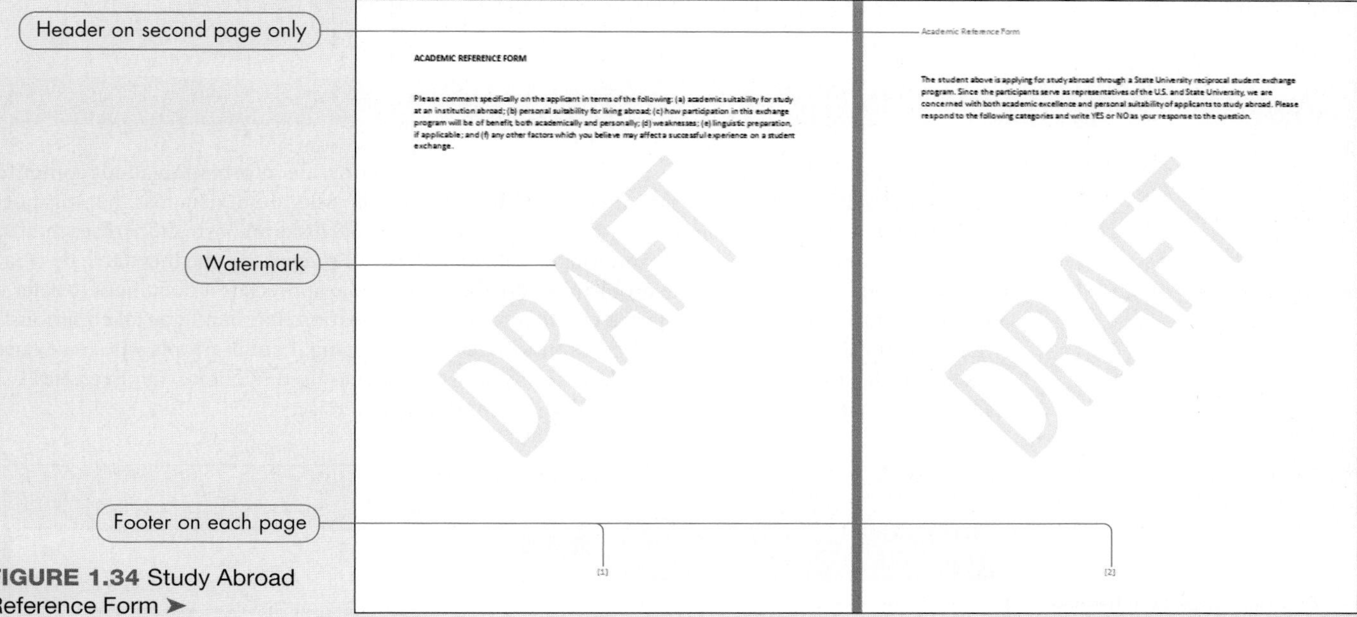

FIGURE 1.34 Study Abroad Reference Form ➤

a. Click the **File tab**, click **New**, and then double-click **Blank document**. Click the **File tab**, click **Save As**, click the **Save As type arrow**, and then select **Word 97-2003 Document (*.doc)**. Name the file ***w01p1reference_LastnameFirstname***, and then click **Save**.

b. Type **Please comment specifically on the applicant in terms of the following: (a) academic suitability for study at an institution abroad; (b) personal suitability for living abroad; (c) how participation in this exchange program will be of benefit, both academically and personally; (d) weaknesses; (e) linguistic preparation, if applicable; and (f) any other factors which you believe may affect a successful experience on a student exchange.**

c. Press **Ctrl+Home** to move the insertion point to the top of the document. Press **Ctrl+B**, type **ACADEMIC REFERENCE FORM**, and then press **Enter** twice. Press **Ctrl+End** to move the cursor to the end of the document.

d. Press **Ctrl+Enter** to insert a hard page break. Click **Show/Hide (¶)** in the Paragraph group to display formatting marks. Click **Draft** on the status bar to display the document in Draft view.

e. Type **The student above is applying for study abroad through a State University reciprocal student exchange program. Since the participants serve as representatives of the U.S. and State University, we are concerned with both academic excellence and personal suitability of applicants to study abroad. Please respond to the following categories and write YES or NO as your response to the question.**

f. Click the **Page Layout tab**, click **Watermark** in the Page Background group, and then click **Custom Watermark**. Click **Text watermark**, click the **Text arrow**, and then click **DRAFT**. Click **OK**.

g. Click the **Insert tab**, click **Page Number** in the Header & Footer group, point to **Bottom of Page**, and then click **Brackets 1** from the gallery.

h. Click **Different First Page** in the Options group to select it. Click **Header** in the Header & Footer group, and then select **Edit Header**. Confirm you are in the Page 2 header, and then type **Academic Reference Form**.

   After you select the option for Different First Page, the headers and footers on the first page are removed. This enables you to insert information on the first page which will not display in the header or footer of the remaining pages.

i. Move the insertion point to the first page footer. Click **Page Number** in the Header & Footer group, point to **Bottom of Page**, and then click **Brackets 1** from the gallery. Click **Close Header and Footer** in the Close group.

j. Click the **Zoom level** in the status bar, click the **Many pages icon**, and then drag to select **1 x 2 Pages**. Click **OK** to close the Zoom dialog box. Click **Show/Hide (¶)** in the Paragraph group on the Home tab to toggle off the formatting marks. Compare your document to Figure 1.34.

k. Click the **File tab**, click **Print**, click the **Pages per sheet arrow**, and then click **2 Pages Per Sheet**. Click the **File tab** to return to the document.

l. Save and close the file, and submit based on your instructor's directions.

2 Aztec Computers

As the owner of Aztec Computers, you are frequently asked to provide information about computer viruses and backup procedures. You are quick to tell anyone who asks about data loss that it is not a question of if it will happen, but when—hard drives die, removable disks are lost, and viruses may infect systems. You advise customers and friends alike that they can prepare for the inevitable by creating an adequate backup before the problem occurs. Because people appreciate a document to refer to about this information, you have started one that contains information that should be taken seriously. After a few finishing touches, you will feel comfortable about passing it out to people who have questions about this topic. This exercise follows the same set of skills as used in Hands-On Exercises 1, 2, and 3 in the chapter. Refer to Figure 1.35 as you complete this exercise.

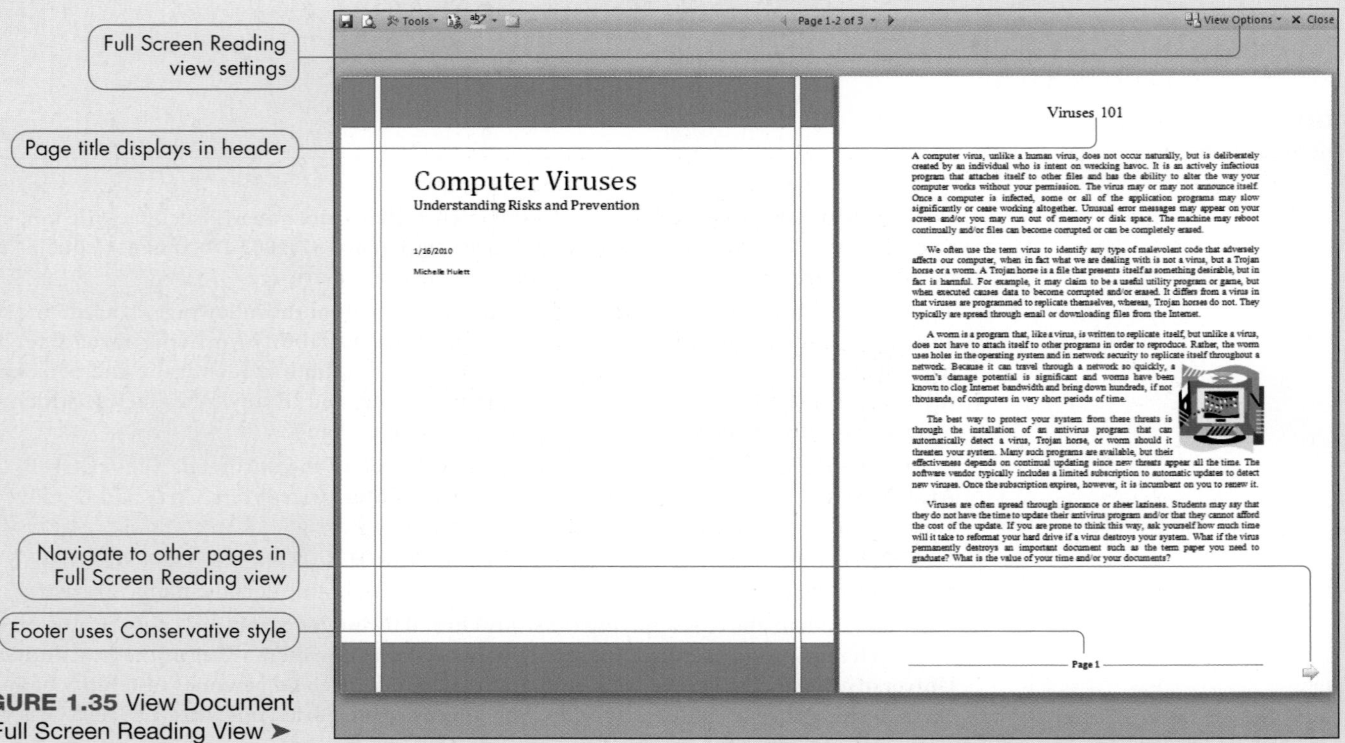

FIGURE 1.35 View Document in Full Screen Reading View ➤

a. Open *w01p2virus* and save it as **w01p2virus_LastnameFirstname**.

b. Create a cover page by completing the following steps:

   - Click the **Insert tab**, click **Cover Page** in the Pages group, and then click **Pinstripes**.
   - Click **Type the document subtitle**, and then type the text **Understanding Risks and Prevention**.
   - Click **Pick the Date**, click the arrow, and then select **Today**.
   - Right-click **Type the company name**, and then select **Cut**.
   - Click **Type the author name**, and then type your name.

c. Scroll to the bottom of the first page of the report, and then place the insertion point on the left side of the title *The Essence of Backup*. Click the **Page Layout tab**, click **Breaks**, and then click **Next Page**.

d. Set up headers and footers by completing the following steps:

   - Click the **Insert tab**, click **Footer**, and then click **Conservative**. A page number footer is added to *First Page Footer -Section 2-*.
   - Select the page number footer in *First Page Footer -Section 2-*, and then press **Ctrl+C** to copy the page number footer to the clipboard.
   - Click **Previous** in the Navigation group to place the insertion point in the Section 1 footer, and then press **Ctrl+V** to paste the page number and graphic into this footer. Since this document has two sections, you must duplicate the steps when you want to display the same footer (or header) in both.
   - Place the insertion point in *First Page Header -Section 2-*. Click **Page Number** in the Header & Footer group, click **Format Page Numbers**, and then click **Continue from Previous Section**. Click **OK**.
   - Click **Previous** in the Navigation group to place the insertion point in *Header -Section 1-*. Type **Viruses 101** and press **Ctrl+E** to center it. Use the Mini toolbar to increase the font to **20 pt**.
   - Place the insertion point in *First Page Header -Section 2-*. Click **Link to Previous** in the Navigation group to turn the setting off and enable you to create a unique header for this section instead of displaying the header from the previous section.
   - Type **The Essence of Backup**, press **Ctrl+E** to center it, and then use the Mini toolbar to increase the font to **20 pt**.
   - Click **Close Header and Footer**.

e. Delete the lines that contain the text *Viruses 101* and *The Essence of Backup* from the two pages of the report because these titles now display in the header.

f. Click the **Review tab**, and click **Spelling & Grammar**. Click **Change** to correct the contextual spelling error reported on backup, and then click **OK** when complete.

g. Complete the following steps to display the document in different views:

   - Click **Draft** in the status bar, and then scroll to view the location of the section break.
   - Click **Full Screen Reading** on the status bar.
   - Click **View Options** in the top-right corner, and then click **Show Two Pages**, if necessary.
   - Click **View Options** again, and then click **Show Printed Page**.
   - Click the arrows in the bottom corners to view each page, and then return to the first page. Compare your document to Figure 1.35.
   - Click the **Close button** to return to Print Layout view.

h. Click the **File tab**, click **Properties**, and then select **Show Document Panel**. Click in the **Comments box**, and then type **General information for understanding computer viruses**. Click **Close the Document Information Panel**.

i. Save the document. Click the **File tab**, click **Check for Issues**, and then click **Check Compatibility**. Click **OK** to close the Microsoft Word Compatibility Checker dialog box after you review the results.

j. Click the **File tab**, click **Check for Issues**, select **Inspect Document**, and then click **Inspect**. Click **Close** after you review the results.

k. Save and close the file, and submit based on your instructor's directions.

MID-LEVEL EXERCISES

1 Heart Disease Prevention

Millions of people suffer from heart disease and other cardiac-related illnesses. Of those people, several million will suffer a heart attack this year. Your mother volunteers for the American Heart Association and has brought you a document that explains what causes a heart attack, the signs of an attack, and what you can do to reduce your risk of having one. The information in the document is very valuable, but she needs you to put the finishing touches on this document before she circulates it in the community.

a. Open *w01m1heart* and save it as **w01m1heart_LastnameFirstname**.
b. Convert *w01m1heart_LastnameFirstname* so it does not save in Compatibility Mode.
c. Create a cover page for the report. Use Stacks in the cover page gallery. Add text where necessary to display the report title **Heart Attacks:** and the subtitle **What You Should Know**. Insert your name as author, replacing *Exploring Series*.
d. Change the document margins to **0.75"** on all sides.
e. Create a section break between the cover page and the first page of the report.

DISCOVER 

f. Create a footer in Section 2 by typing the text **Page**, leave a space, and then insert a page number field. The page number should only display at the bottom of the pages in Section 2. The first page of Section 2, not the cover page, should display page number 1.
g. Create a header that displays the report title and subtitle. It should not display on the cover or first page of the report. Confirm that the headers and footers in the second section are not linked to the first section.
h. Insert hard page breaks where necessary to prevent a paragraph or list from breaking across pages. View the document in Full Screen Reading view to confirm it is formatted as instructed and ready for printing.
i. Check spelling in the document. Change the document properties to include a custom field for Date completed.
j. Check Word Options and verify that AutoRecover backups occur every five minutes or less.
k. Print the document properties if approved by your instructor.
l. Save and close the file, and submit based on your instructor's directions.

2 Diabetes

You are taking a Personal Fitness class this semester, and your instructor wants you to write a paper about preventing and controlling diabetes. Perform a search on the Internet and view the Web site for non-profit organizations such as www.diabetesatwork.org/index.cfm, where all the materials and information are copyright-free. Follow the instructions below, review the Web site materials, and proceed to write a paper that is at least one page. You may copy and paste some of the materials from the Web site but you need to rewrite the content using your own words.

a. Open Microsoft Word. Open a blank document and save it as **w01m2diabetes_LastnameFirstname**.
b. Set margins to **.75"** on the top, bottom, left, and right.
c. Insert a footer using the **Alphabet style**. Type the source of your Web site on the left.
d. Insert a Blank header that starts on page 1 and displays the title of the paper on the left and your name on the right.
e. Insert a watermark that displays **Draft**.
f. Add the **Conservative** cover page from the gallery. Type the title, subtitle, your name, and the date onto the cover page. Delete the Company and Abstract placeholders.

g. Use the Spelling & Grammar tool to check the document.
h. Insert Page Breaks where necessary to display the document in a manner that prevents paragraphs from breaking across a page.
i. Run the Compatibility Checker and Document Inspector, and then save the document in Word 97-2003 format.
j. Save and close the file, and submit based on your instructor's directions.

CAPSTONE EXERCISE

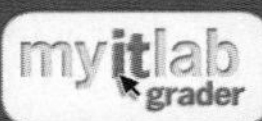

Ethical conflicts occur all the time and result when one person or group benefits at the expense of another. Your Philosophy 101 instructor assigned a class project whereby students must consider the question of ethics and society. The result of your research includes a collection of questions every person should ask him- or herself. Your paper is nearly complete but needs a few modifications before you submit it.

Spelling, Margins, and Watermarks

You notice Word displays spelling and grammar errors with the colored lines, so you must correct those as soon as possible. Additionally, you want to adjust the margins and then insert a watermark that displays when you print so that you will remember that this is not the final version.

a. Open *w01c1ethics* and save it as **w01c1ethics_LastnameFirstname**.

b. Display the Word Options dialog box, and then engage the Contextual Spelling feature if it is not already in use.

c. Run the Spelling & Grammar tool to correct all misspelled words and contextual errors.

d. Change the margins to use a setting of **0.75"** on all sides.

e. Insert a watermark that displays **Version 1** when printed.

Cover Page, Headers, and Footers

You want to add a cover page that will attractively introduce your paper. Then you will set up page numbering, but it must not display on the cover page. Because you are going to customize headers and footers very precisely, you must use several of the custom settings available for Headers and Footers.

a. Insert a Cover Page that uses the Puzzle style. Select **Today** in the two Date fields. Type the title of the paper in the appropriate field, and then add your name as author, but remove all other fields from the cover page.

b. Insert a page number at the bottom of the first page of the report (the page that follows the cover page) using **Accent Bar 2 style**. There should be no header on this page.

c. Display the page number in the header of the remaining page of the report using the **Accent Bar 2 style**. (Hint: Use the Different Odd & Even Pages Header & Footer option.) In the footer of this page, display the report title on the left and your name on the right.

Set Properties and Finalize Document

After improving the readability of the document, you remember that you have not yet saved it. Your professor still uses an older version of Word, so you save the document in a compatible format that will display easily. You also remove the watermark just before saving the final copy.

a. Save the document.

b. Run the Compatibility Checker and Document Inspector, but do not take any suggested actions at this time.

c. Add **Ethics**, **Responsibility**, and **Morals** to the Keywords: field in the document properties.

d. Remove the watermark.

e. Save the document again, in Word 97-2003 format, as **w01c1ethics_LastnameFirstname**.

f. Use the Print Preview and Print feature to view the document before printing. If allowed by your instructor, print one copy of the document using the 2 Pages per sheet setting.

More Career Choices

GENERAL CASE

FROM SCRATCH

Have you taken time to think about the career you wish to pursue when you complete your education? You will author a paper about a career field that interests you. After you write your documentary using Word, use the skills from this chapter to format it with a professional look, and then name the document **w01b1job_LastnameFirstname**. Save and close the file, and submit based on your instructor's directions.

Endangered Species

RESEARCH CASE

FROM SCRATCH

There are many varieties of plants and animals that are endangered. Do you know if any are native to your home state? Use a search engine and find reliable Web sites that describe the species that are currently on the endangered list. Start from a blank document and save it as **w01b2endangered_LastnameFirstname**. Describe at least five different species of endangered plants or animals, and write a paragraph about each one. Do not copy information directly from a Web site; make sure the information is phrased in your own words. At the end of each paragraph type the URL of the Web site where you find information about each species. Use your knowledge of formatting techniques, such as hard returns, page numbers, and margin settings, to create an attractive document. Create a cover page for the document, and add headers and/or footers to improve readability. Check the spelling, and then preview the document before submitting this assignment to your instructor. Save and close the file, and submit based on your instructor's directions.

Logo Policy

DISASTER RECOVERY

Open *w01b3policy.doc*, convert it, and then save it as **w01b3policy_LastnameFirstname.docx**. (*Note*: you must save it as a different document type as well as rename the file). The document was started by an office assistant, but she quickly gave up on it after she realized it needs significant formatting changes to display the contents in a more professional manner. Use your knowledge of page layout options, section and page breaks, page numbering, and other Word features to revise this policy statement so that it can be distributed to members of the organization. Save and close the file, and submit based on your instructor's directions.

WORD

2 DOCUMENT PRESENTATION

Editing and Formatting

CASE STUDY | Simserv-Pitka Enterprises

Watch the
Set-up
Video
for this
Case Study!

Simserv Enterprises, a consumer products manufacturing company, has recently acquired a competitor in an effort to become a stronger company poised to meet the demands of the market. Each year, Simserv generates a corporate annual summary and distributes it to all employees and stockholders. You are the executive assistant to the president of Simserv, and your responsibilities include preparing and distributing the corporate annual summary. This year, the report emphasizes the importance of acquiring Pitka Industries to form Simserv-Pitka Enterprises.

The annual report always provides a synopsis of recent changes to upper management, and this year, it will introduce a new Chairman of the Board and Chief Executive Officer, as well as a new Chief Financial Officer. Information about these newly appointed executives and other financial data has been gathered, but the report needs to be formatted to display the information clearly and professionally before it can be distributed to employees and stockholders.

OBJECTIVES AFTER READING THIS CHAPTER, YOU WILL BE ABLE TO:

1. Apply font attributes through the Font dialog box *p.172*
2. Control word wrap *p.176*
3. Set off paragraphs with tabs, borders, lists, and columns *p.180*
4. Apply paragraph formats *p.186*
5. Understand styles *p.195*
6. Create and modify styles *p.195*
7. Format a graphical object *p.205*
8. Insert symbols into a document *p.209*

Text Formatting Features

Typography is the appearance of printed matter.

The arrangement and appearance of printed matter is called ***typography***. You may also define it as the process of selecting typefaces, type styles, and type sizes. The importance of these decisions is obvious, for the ultimate success of any document depends greatly on its appearance. Typeface should reinforce the message without calling attention to itself and should be consistent with the information you want to convey. For example, a paper prepared for a professional purpose, such as a résumé, should have a standard typeface instead of one that looks funny or cute. Additionally, you want to minimize the variety of typefaces in a document to maintain a professional look.

The ultimate success of any document depends greatly on its appearance. Typeface should reinforce the message without calling attention to itself and should be consistent with the information you want to convey.

A **typeface** or **font** is a complete set of characters.

A **serif typeface** contains a thin line at the top and bottom of characters.

A **sans serif typeface** does not contain thin lines on characters.

A ***typeface*** or ***font*** is a complete set of characters—upper- and lowercase letters, numbers, punctuation marks, and special symbols. A definitive characteristic of any typeface is the presence or absence of thin lines that end the main strokes of each letter. A ***serif typeface*** contains a thin line or extension at the top and bottom of the primary strokes on characters. A ***sans serif typeface*** (*sans* from the French meaning *without*) does not contain the thin lines on characters. Times New Roman is an example of a serif typeface. Arial is a sans serif typeface.

Serifs help the eye to connect one letter with the next and generally are used with large amounts of text. The paragraphs in this book, for example, are set in a serif typeface. A sans serif typeface is more effective with smaller amounts of text such as titles, headlines, corporate logos, and Web pages. For example, the blue heading Text Formatting Features and the quote by the first paragraph on this page are set in a sans serif font.

A **monospaced typeface** uses the same amount of horizontal space for every character.

A **proportional typeface** allocates horizontal space to each character.

Type style is the characteristic applied to a font, such as bold.

A second characteristic of a typeface is whether it is monospaced or proportional. A ***monospaced typeface*** (such as `Courier New`) uses the same amount of horizontal space for every character regardless of its width. A ***proportional typeface*** (such as Times New Roman or Arial) allocates space according to the width of the character. For example, the lowercase *m* is wider than the lowercase *i*. Monospaced fonts are used in tables and financial projections where text must be precisely lined up, one character underneath the other. Proportional typefaces create a more professional appearance and are appropriate for most documents, such as research papers, status reports, and letters. You can set any typeface in different ***type styles*** such as regular, bold, *italic*, or ***bold italic***.

In this section, you will apply font attributes through the Font dialog box, change case, and highlight text so that it stands out. You will also control word wrap by inserting nonbreaking hyphens and nonbreaking spaces between words.

Applying Font Attributes Through the Font Dialog Box

In the Office Fundamentals chapter, you learn how to use the Font group on the Home tab to apply font attributes. In addition to applying commands from the Font group, you can display the Font dialog box when you click the Font Dialog Box Launcher. Making selections in the Font dialog box before entering text sets the format of the text as you type (see Figure 2.1).

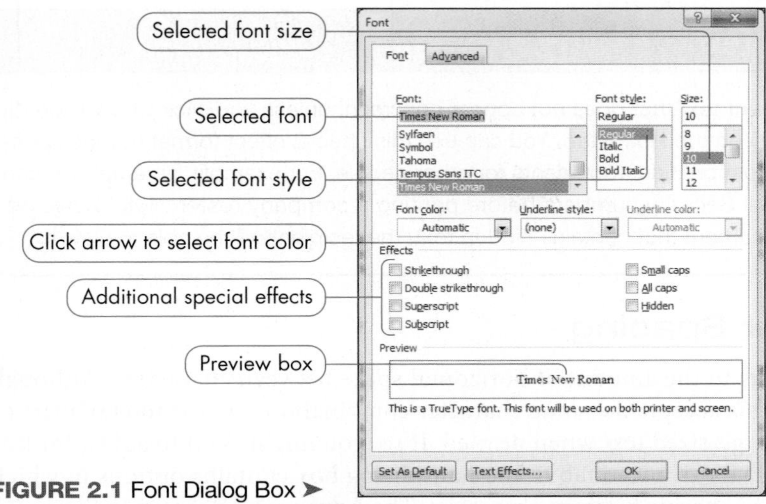

FIGURE 2.1 Font Dialog Box ➤

Select Font Options

In addition to changing the font, font style, and size, you can apply other font attributes to text. Although the Font group on the Home tab contains special effects commands such as strikethrough, subscript, and superscript, the Effects section in the Font tab in the Font dialog box contains other options for applying color and effects, such as small caps and double strikethrough. From this dialog box you can change the underline options and indicate if spaces are to be underlined or just words. You can even change the color of the text and the color of the underline.

New to Office 2010 is the Text Effects feature in the Font group. When you click Text Effects you can choose from a variety of colors and styles to immediately apply to text. The feature enables you to customize the effects by selecting colors, line widths, and amount of transparency. In addition to the Home tab, you can access Text Effects from the Font dialog box. When you use that path, another dialog box opens, showing custom options for each effect. Table 2.1 gives a general description of these special effects.

TABLE 2.1 Font Effects

Effect	Description and Options	Sample of Options to Change	Sample of Effect
Text Fill	Select a color to apply to the font.	No fill Solid fill Gradient fill	Sample
Text Outline	Select a color and line type to outline the font.	No line Solid line Gradient line	Sample
Outline Style	Select line width, type (solid, dashed), and cap on the font.	Width Dash type Arrow settings	Sample
Shadow	Select amount of shadow to apply to the font.	Color Transparency Angle	Sample
Reflection	Select a reflection style to apply to the font.	Presets Size Blur	Sample
Glow and Soft Edges	Select a glow or soft edge that displays around the font.	Color Size Presets	Sample
3-D Format	Select features that present the font in 3-D form.	Bevel Depth Surface	Sample

Hidden text does not appear onscreen.

> **TIP Hidden Text**
>
> ***Hidden text*** is document text that does not appear onscreen, unless you click Show/Hide (¶) in the Paragraph group on the Home tab. You can use this special effect format to hide confidential information before printing documents for other people. For example, an employer can hide employees' Social Security numbers before printing a company roster. Note, however, that if you e-mail a document that contains hidden text, the recipient will be able to view it.

Set Character Spacing

Character spacing is the horizontal space between characters.

Character spacing refers to the amount of horizontal space between characters. Although most character spacing is acceptable, some character combinations appear too far apart or too close together in large-sized text when printed. If so, you might want to adjust for this spacing discrepancy. The Advanced tab in the Font dialog box contains options in which you manually control the spacing between characters. The Advanced tab shown in Figure 2.2 displays four options for adjusting character spacing: Scale, Spacing, Position, and Kerning.

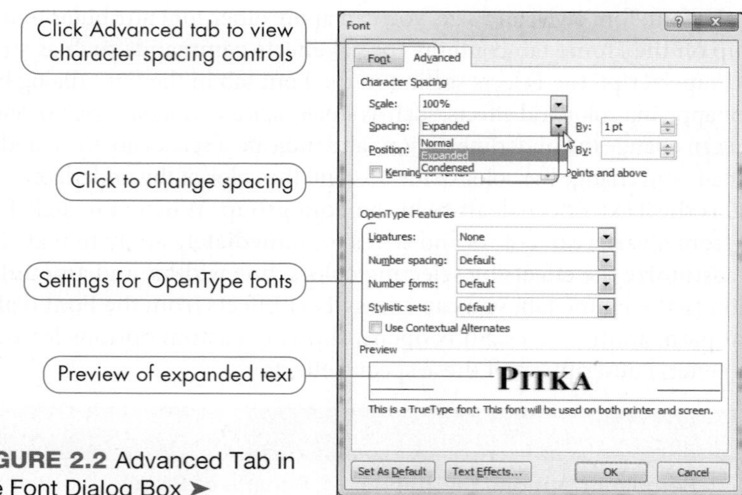

FIGURE 2.2 Advanced Tab in the Font Dialog Box ➤

Scale or scaling is the adjustment of height or width by a percentage of the image's original size.

Scale or ***scaling*** adjusts height and width by a percentage of the original size. For text, adjustments to scale will increase or decrease the text horizontally as a percentage of its size; it does not change the vertical height of text. You may use the scale feature on justified text, which does not produce the best-looking results—adjust the scale by a low percentage (90%–95%) to improve text flow without a noticeable difference to the reader. You may select the Expanded option to stretch a word or sentence so it fills more space; for example, use it on a title you want to span across the top of a page. The Condensed option is useful to squeeze text closer together, such as when you want to prevent one word from wrapping to another line.

Position raises or lowers text from the baseline.

Kerning enables more even spacing between characters.

Position raises or lowers text from the baseline without creating superscript or subscript size. Use this feature when you want text to stand out from other text on the same line, or use it to create a fun title by raising and/or lowering every few letters. ***Kerning*** automatically adjusts spacing between characters to achieve a more evenly spaced appearance. Kerning primarily enables letters to fit closer together, especially when a capital letter can use space unoccupied by a lowercase letter beside it. For example, you can kern the letters *Va* so the top of the *V* extends into the empty space above the *a* instead of leaving an awkward gap between them.

OpenType is a form of font designed for use on all platforms.

Word 2010 introduces support for OpenType fonts. ***OpenType*** is an advanced form of font that is designed for all platforms, including Windows and Macintosh. OpenType font technology has advantages over the commonly used TrueType Font because it can hold more characters in a set and is more compact, enabling smaller file sizes. If you install OpenType fonts on your PC, you can use the OpenType font settings in the Advanced tab of the Font dialog box.

Change Text Case (Capitalization)

Use **Change Case** to change capitalization of text.

To change the capitalization of text in a document quickly, use ***Change Case*** in the Font group on the Home tab. When you click Change Case, the following list of options display:

- **Sentence case** (capitalizes only the first word of the sentence or phrase).
- **lowercase** (changes the text to all lowercase).
- **UPPERCASE** (changes the text to all capital letters).
- **Capitalize Each Word** (capitalizes the first letter of each word; effective for formatting titles, but remember to lowercase first letters of short prepositions, such as *of*).
- **tOGGLE cASE** (changes lowercase to uppercase and uppercase to lowercase).

This feature is useful when generating a list and you want to use the same case formatting for each item. If you do not select text first, the casing format will take effect on the text where the insertion point is located. You can toggle among uppercase, lowercase, and sentence case formats by pressing Shift+F3.

Apply Text Highlighting

Use the **Highlighter** to mark text that you want to locate easily.

People often use a highlighting marker to highlight important parts of textbooks, magazine articles, and other documents. In Word, you use the ***Highlighter*** to mark text that you want to stand out or locate easily. Highlighted text draws the reader's attention to important information within the documents you create, as illustrated in Figure 2.3. The Text Highlight Color command is located in the Font group on the Home tab and on the Mini toolbar. You can click Text Highlight Color before or after selecting text. When you click Text Highlight Color before selecting text, the mouse pointer resembles a pen that you can click and drag across text to highlight it. The feature stays on so you can highlight additional text. When you finish highlighting text, click Text Highlight Color again, or press Esc to turn it off. If you select text first, click Text Highlight Color to apply the color. To remove highlights, select the highlighted text, click the Text Highlight Color arrow, and choose No Color.

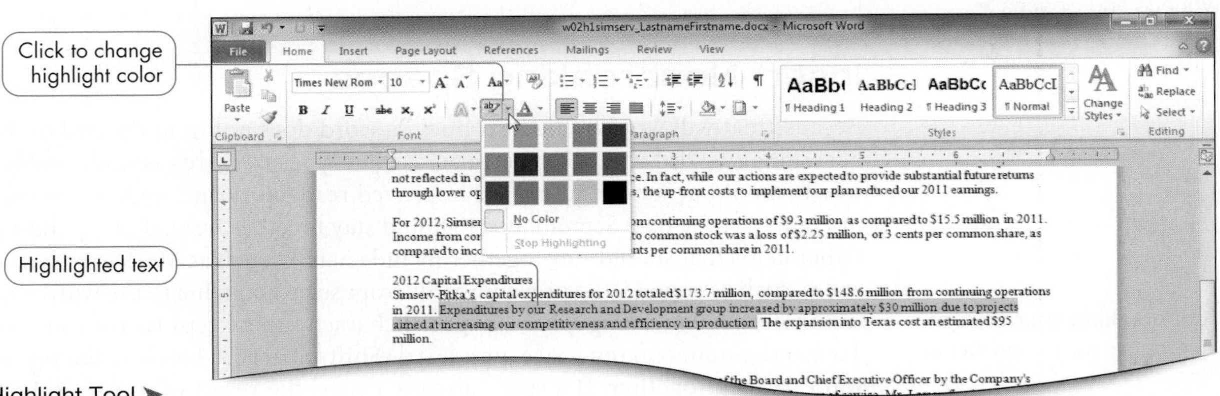

FIGURE 2.3 Highlight Tool ➤

If you use a color printer, you see the highlight colors on your printout. If you use a monochrome printer, the highlight appears in shades of gray. Use Print Preview prior to printing to be sure that you can easily read the text with the gray highlight. If not, select a lighter highlight color, and preview your document again. You can create a unique highlighting effect by choosing a dark highlight color, such as Dark Blue, and applying a light font color, such as White.

Controlling Word Wrap

In Word, text wraps to the next line when the current line of text is full. Most of the time, the way words wrap is acceptable. Occasionally, however, text may wrap in an undesirable location. To improve the readability of text, you need to proofread word-wrapping locations and insert special characters. Two general areas of concern are hyphenated words and spacing within proper nouns.

Insert Nonbreaking Hyphens

A **nonbreaking hyphen** prevents a word from becoming separated at the hyphen.

If a hyphenated word falls at the end of a line, the first word and the hyphen may appear on the first line, and the second word may wrap to the next line. However, certain hyphenated text, such as phone numbers, should stay together to improve the readability of the text. To keep hyphenated words together, replace the regular hyphen with a nonbreaking hyphen. A ***nonbreaking hyphen*** keeps text on both sides of the hyphen together, thus preventing the hyphenated word from becoming separated at the hyphen, as shown in Figure 2.4. To insert a nonbreaking hyphen, press Ctrl+Shift+Hyphen. When you click Show/Hide in the Paragraph group on the Home tab to display formatting symbols, a regular hyphen looks like a hyphen, and a nonbreaking hyphen appears as a wider hyphen. However, the nonbreaking hyphen looks like a regular hyphen when printed.

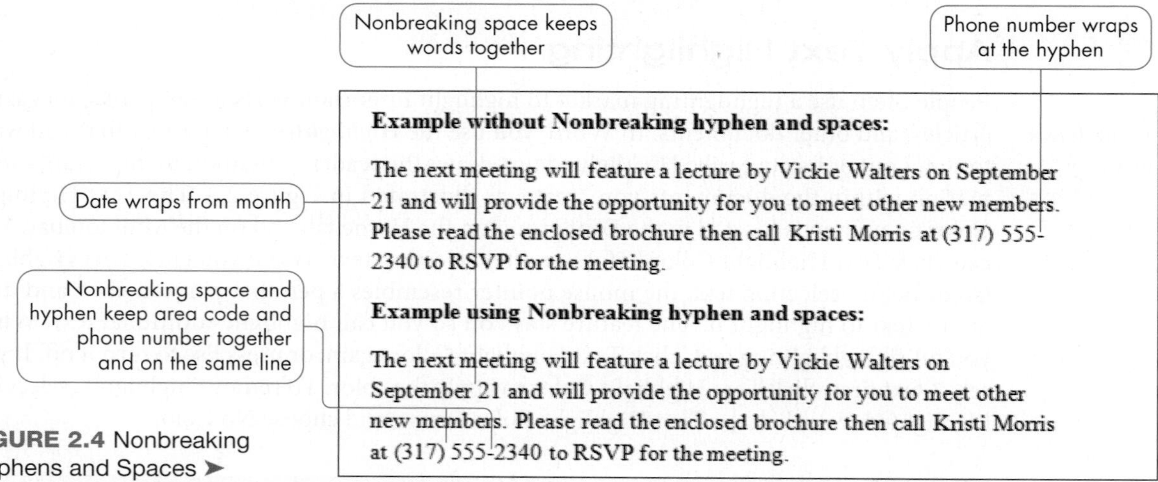

Nonbreaking space keeps words together
Phone number wraps at the hyphen
Date wraps from month
Nonbreaking space and hyphen keep area code and phone number together and on the same line
Example without Nonbreaking hyphen and spaces:
The next meeting will feature a lecture by Vickie Walters on September
21 and will provide the opportunity for you to meet other new members.
Please read the enclosed brochure then call Kristi Morris at (317) 555-
2340 to RSVP for the meeting.
Example using Nonbreaking hyphen and spaces:
The next meeting will feature a lecture by Vickie Walters on
September 21 and will provide the opportunity for you to meet other
new members. Please read the enclosed brochure then call Kristi Morris
at (317) 555-2340 to RSVP for the meeting.

FIGURE 2.4 Nonbreaking Hyphens and Spaces ➤

Insert Nonbreaking Spaces

A **nonbreaking space** keeps two or more words together on a line.

Because text will wrap to the next line if a word does not fit at the end of the current line, occasionally word wrapping between certain types of words is undesirable; that is, some words should be kept together for improved readability and understanding. For example, in Figure 2.4 the date September 21 should stay together instead of separating on two lines. Other items that should stay together include names, such as Ms. Stevenson, and page references, such as page 15. To prevent words from separating due to the word wrap feature, you can insert a ***nonbreaking space***—a special character that keeps two or more words together. To insert a nonbreaking space, press Ctrl+Shift+Spacebar between the two words that you want to keep together. If a space already exists, the result of pressing the Spacebar, you should delete it before you insert the nonbreaking space.

Quick Concepts Check

1. Describe both a serif and a sans serif typeface and give an example of each.
2. Describe three new special effects you can apply to a font using Office 2010.
3. Give an example of why you would change character spacing and which options you apply to create the new effect.
4. Give two examples describing the benefit of using nonbreaking hyphens and nonbreaking spaces.

HANDS-ON EXERCISES

1 Text Formatting Features

As the executive assistant to the president at Simserv-Pitka Enterprises, you are responsible for preparing and distributing the Annual Summary. A report of this importance should be easy to read, attractive, and professional. You have the basic information to include in the report, and your first step is to change the formatting of some text so that it displays nicely in print, to include highlighting where appropriate, and to look for places where you might need to insert nonbreaking hyphens or spaces.

Skills covered: Change Text Appearance • Insert Nonbreaking Spaces and Nonbreaking Hyphens • Highlight Text

STEP 1 CHANGE TEXT APPEARANCE

As you begin to prepare the report for the Board and stockholders, you know the first thing that requires your attention is changing the font of the whole document so that it is easier to read. Additionally, you will change the font properties of the heading and subheading so they stand out from the rest of the text. Refer to Figure 2.5 as you complete Step 1.

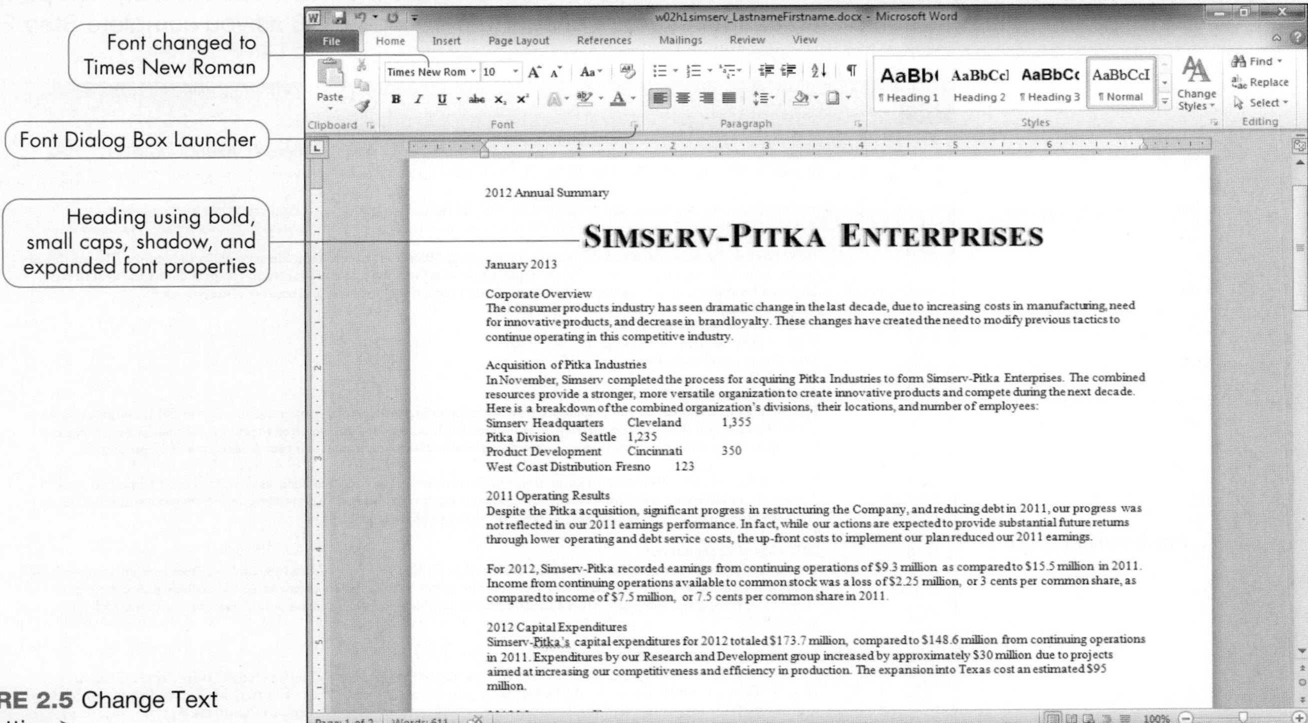

FIGURE 2.5 Change Text Formatting ➤

a. Open *w02h1simserv* and save it as **w02h1simserv_LastnameFirstname**.

> **TROUBLESHOOTING:** If you make any major mistakes in this exercise, you can close the file, open *w02h1simserv* again, and then start this exercise over.

b. Click **Ctrl+A** to select all of the text in the document. Click the **Font arrow** in the Font group on the Home tab, and then select **Times New Roman**.

   You use a serif font on the whole document because it is easier to read in print.

c. Select the second line of the document, *Simserv-Pitka Enterprises*. Click **Center** on the Mini toolbar.

d. Click the **Font Dialog Box Launcher** in the Font group.

   The Font dialog box displays with the Font tab options.

e. Click the **Font tab**, if necessary, and then click **Bold** in the Font style box. Select **26** in the Size box. Click to select the **Small caps Effect**.

f. Click **Text Effects**. Click **Shadow**, click **Presets**, and then click **Offset Left** (third row, third column). Click the **Close button** to return to the Font dialog box.

g. Click the **Advanced tab**, and then click the **Spacing arrow**. Select **Expanded**, and then notice how the text changes in the preview box. Click **OK.**

   Word expands the spacing between letters in the subtitle as shown in Figure 2.5. You will apply this formatting to the third line in a later exercise.

h. Save the document.

STEP 2 INSERT NONBREAKING SPACES AND NONBREAKING HYPHENS

Since the company's new name, Simserv-Pitka, is hyphenated, you want to keep the name together and not split it if it appears at the end of a text line. Therefore, you will replace existing hyphens in Simserv-Pitka, as well as in other areas of the document, with nonbreaking hyphens. You will also replace existing spaces with nonbreaking spaces to make sure the information displays properly when the report is completed and ready for printing. Refer to Figure 2.6 as you complete Step 2.`

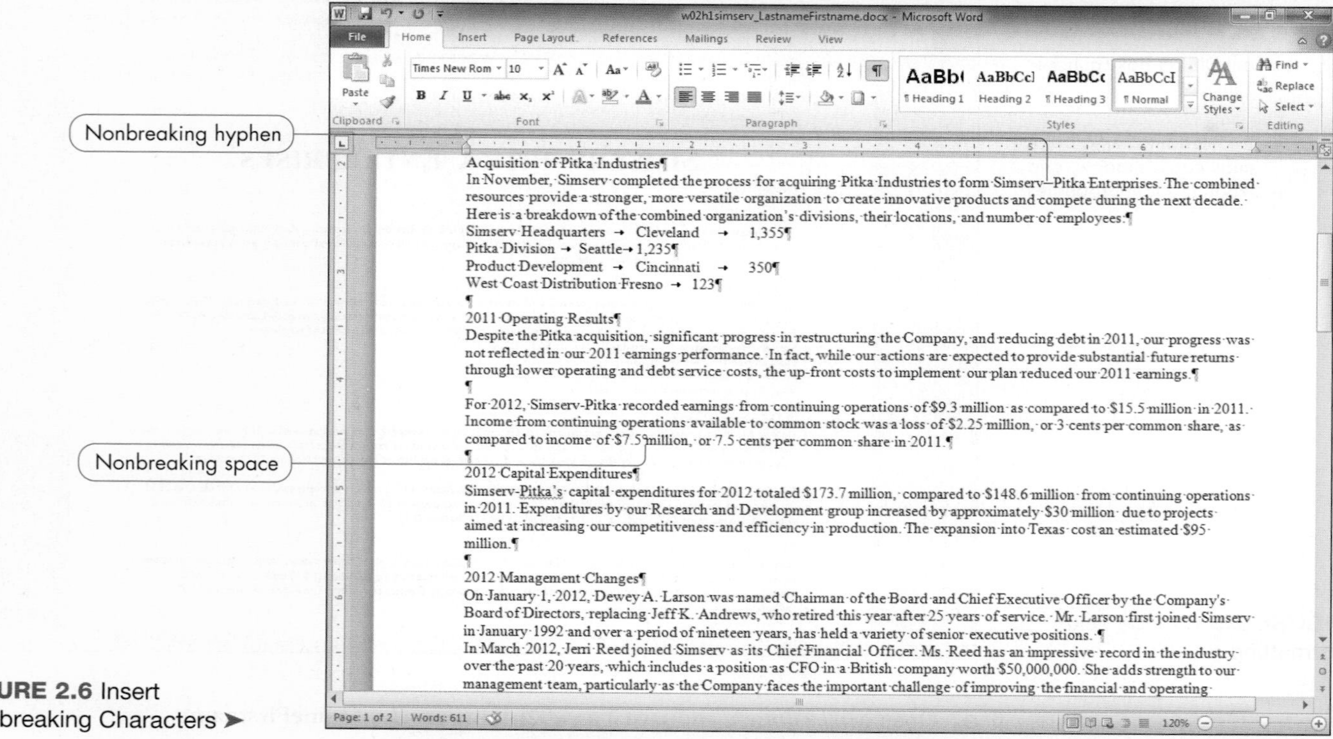

FIGURE 2.6 Insert Nonbreaking Characters ➤

a. Select the hyphen between the text *Simserv-Pitka* in the first sentence of the *Acquisition of Pitka Industries* paragraph. Press **Delete**, and then press **Ctrl+Shift+Hyphen** to insert a nonbreaking hyphen.

> **TROUBLESHOOTING:** If text continues word wrapping between two words after you insert a nonbreaking space or nonbreaking hyphen, click Show/Hide (¶) in the Paragraph group on the Home tab to display symbols, and then identify and delete regular spaces or hyphens that still exist between words.

b. Place the insertion point between *$7.5* and *million* in the last sentence of the second paragraph under the *2011 Operating Results* heading.

   Before inserting a nonbreaking space, you must position the insertion point between the two words you want to keep together.

c. Delete the existing space, and then press **Ctrl+Shift+Spacebar** to insert a nonbreaking space.

d. Click **Show/Hide** (¶) in the Paragraph group, and then notice the different format for the nonbreaking hyphen and space, as seen in Figure 2.6.

   If text is enlarged, the nonbreaking space keeps *$7.5 million* together, preventing word wrapping between the two words.

e. Click **Show/Hide** (¶) again to remove the formatting marks. Save the document.

TIP Another Way to Insert Nonbreaking Spaces and Hyphens

An alternative to using keyboard shortcuts to insert nonbreaking spaces and hyphens is to use the Symbols gallery on the Insert tab. From the Insert tab, click the Symbol arrow and click More Symbols to display the Symbol dialog box. Click the Special Characters tab, select the Nonbreaking Hyphen or the Nonbreaking Space character option, and click Insert to insert a nonbreaking hyphen or a nonbreaking space, respectively. Close the Symbol dialog box after inserting the nonbreaking hyphen or nonbreaking space.

STEP 3 HIGHLIGHT TEXT

Some information in a document is so important that you want to be sure to draw attention to it. The Highlighting tool is useful for this purpose and you use it in the next step to make sure the reader knows about the great investment in Research and Development at Simserv-Pitka Enterprises. Refer to Figure 2.7 as you complete Step 3.

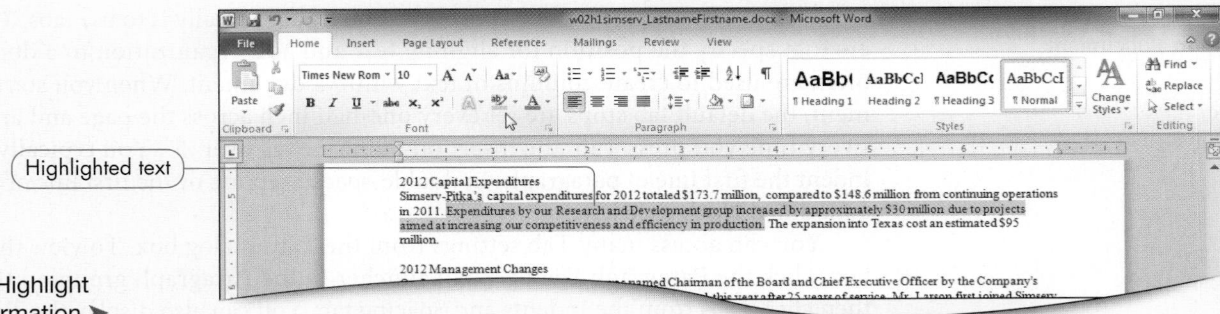

FIGURE 2.7 Highlight Important Information ➤

a. Select the second sentence in the *2012 Capital Expenditures* paragraph that starts with *Expenditures by our Research and Development group*.

b. Click **Text Highlight Color** in the Font group.

   Word highlighted the selected sentence in the default highlight color, yellow, as seen in Figure 2.7.

TROUBLESHOOTING: If Word applies a color other than yellow to the selected text, that means another highlight color was selected after starting Word. If this happens, select the text again, click the Text Highlight Color arrow, and select Yellow.

c. Save the document and keep it onscreen if you plan to continue with the next Hands-On Exercise. If not, close the document and exit Word.

Paragraph Formatting Features

A change in typography is only one way to alter the appearance of a document. You also can change the alignment, indentation, tab stops, or line spacing for any paragraph(s) within the document. You can control the pagination and prevent the occurrence of awkward page breaks by specifying that an entire paragraph must appear on the same page, or that a heading should appear on the same page as the next paragraph. You can include borders or shading for added emphasis around selected paragraphs.

A change in typography is only one way to alter the appearance of a document. You also can change the alignment, indentation, tab stops, or line spacing for any paragraph(s) within the document.

Word implements all of these paragraph formats for all selected paragraphs. If no paragraphs are selected, Word applies the formats to the current paragraph (the paragraph containing the insertion point), regardless of the position of the insertion point within the paragraph when you apply the paragraph formats.

In this section, you will set tabs, apply borders, create lists, and format text into columns to help offset text for better readability. You will also change text alignment, indent paragraphs, set line and paragraph spacing, and control pagination breaks.

Setting Off Paragraphs with Tabs, Borders, Lists, and Columns

Many people agree that their eyes tire and minds wander when they read page after page of plain black text on white paper. To break up long blocks of text or draw attention to an area of a page, you can format text with tabs, borders, lists, or columns. These formatting features enable you to modify positioning, frame a section, itemize for easy reading, order steps in a sequence, or create pillars of text for visual appeal and easy reading. For example, look through the pages of this book and notice the use of bulleted lists, tables for reference points, and borders around TIP boxes to draw your attention and enhance the pages.

Set Tabs

A **tab** is a marker for aligning text in a document.

One way to enhance the presentation of text on a page visually is to use tabs. ***Tabs*** are markers that specify the position for aligning text and add organization to a document. They often are used to create columns of text within a document. When you start a new document, the default tab stops are set every one-half inch across the page and are left aligned. Every time you press Tab, the insertion point moves over .5". You typically press Tab to indent the first line of paragraphs in double-spaced reports or the first line of paragraphs in a modified block style letter.

You can access many Tab settings from the Tabs dialog box. To view the Tabs dialog box, click the Paragraph Dialog Box Launcher in the Paragraph group on the Home tab, then click Tabs from the Indents and Spacing tab. You can also display the Tabs dialog box by double-clicking a tab setting on the ruler. Table 2.2 describes the different types of tabs.

A **left tab** marks the position to align text on the left.

A **center tab** marks where text centers as you type.

A **right tab** marks the position to align text on the right.

A **decimal tab** marks where numbers align on a decimal point as you type.

A **bar tab** marks the location of a vertical line between columns.

TABLE 2.2 Tab Markers

Tab Icon on Ruler	Type of Tab	Function
⌊	***left tab***	Sets the start position on the left so as you type, text moves to the right of the tab setting.
⊥	***center tab***	Sets the middle point of the text you type; whatever you type will be centered on that tab setting.
⌋	***right tab***	Sets the start position on the right so as you type, text moves to the left of that tab setting and aligns on the right.
⊥.	***decimal tab***	Aligns numbers on a decimal point. Regardless of how long the number, each number lines up with the decimal in the same position.
|	***bar tab***	This tab does not position text or decimals, but inserts a vertical bar at the tab setting. This bar is useful as a separator for text printed on the same line.

An alternative to using the Tabs dialog box is to set tabs directly on the ruler. Click the Tabs selector on the left side of the ruler (refer to Figure 2.8) until it displays the tab alignment you want. Then click the ruler in the location where you want to set the type of tab you selected. To delete a tab, click the tab marker on the ruler, and then drag it down and off the ruler.

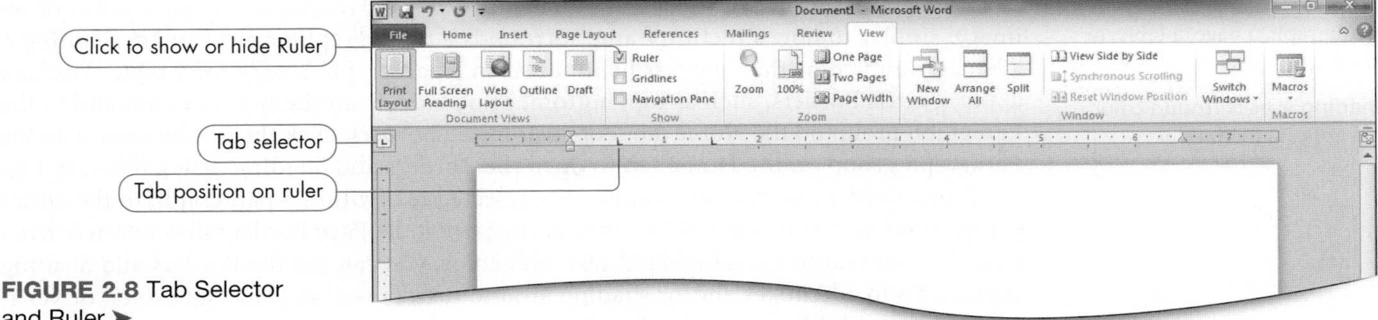

FIGURE 2.8 Tab Selector and Ruler ➤

TIP Deleting Tabs

When you set a new tab by clicking on the ruler, Word deletes all tab settings to the left of the tab you set. If you need to delete a single tab setting, for example the tab at 1.5", click the 1.5" tab marker on the ruler and drag it off of the ruler. When you release the mouse, you delete only that tab setting. If a marker does not display on the ruler for a tab, use the Tabs dialog box to adjust tab settings.

A **leader character** is dots or hyphens that connect two items of information.

In the Tabs dialog box, you also can specify a ***leader character***, typically dots or hyphens, which display on the left side of the tab and serve to draw or lead the reader's eye across the page to connect two items of information. For example, in Figure 2.9, it is easier to read the location and number of employees for each division because tab leader characters connect each piece of information. When dot characters connect items, they are often called *dot leaders* or just *leaders*. Notice also in the Tab dialog box in Figure 2.9, the default tab settings have been cleared and new tab settings are in place at .5" and 2.5"; additionally, a right tab is set at 4".

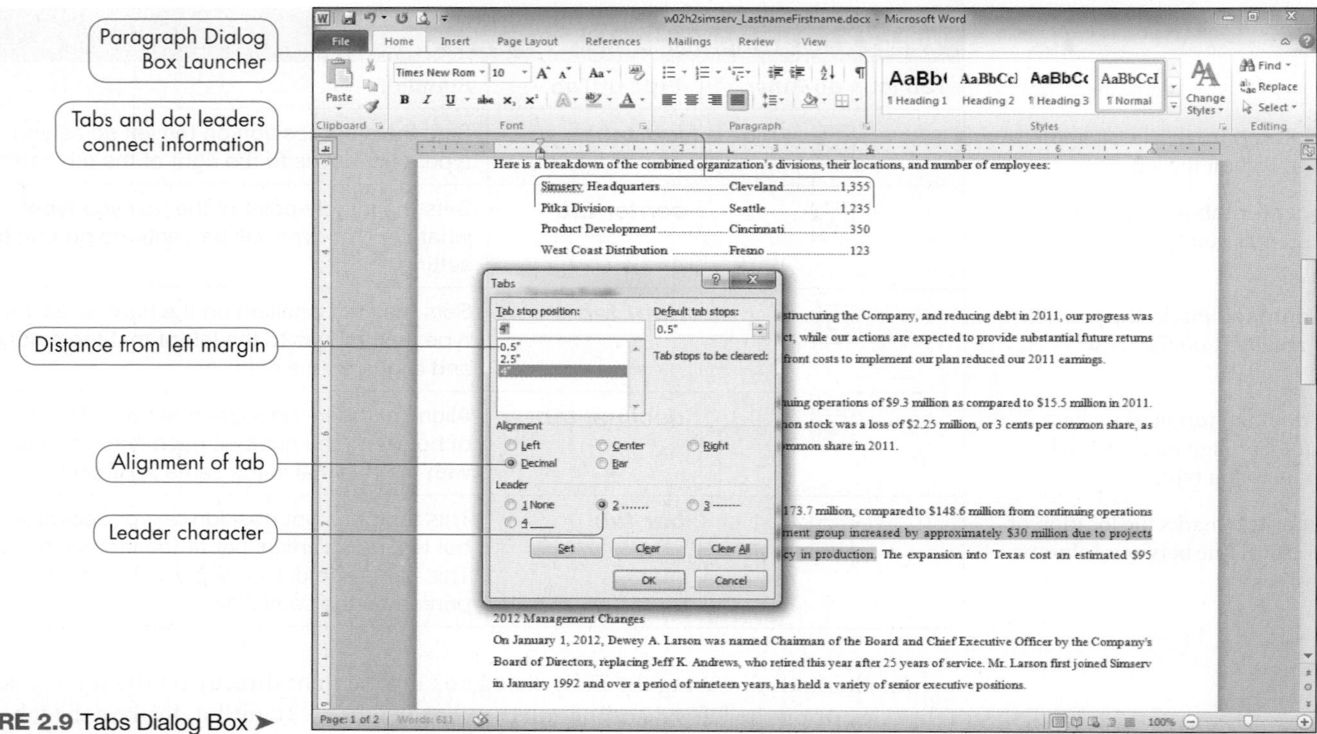

FIGURE 2.9 Tabs Dialog Box ➤

Apply Borders and Shading

A **border** is a line that surrounds a paragraph, a page, a table, or an image.

Shading is background color that appears behind text.

You can draw attention to a document or an area of a document by using the Borders and Shading command. A ***border*** is a line that surrounds a paragraph, a page, a table, or an image, similar to how a picture frame surrounds a photograph or piece of art. ***Shading*** is a background color that appears behind text in a paragraph, a page, or a table. You can apply specific borders, such as top, bottom, or outside, from the Border command in the Paragraph group on the Home tab. For customized borders, click the Borders arrow in the Paragraph group on the Home tab to open the Borders and Shading dialog box (see Figure 2.10). Borders or shading is applied to selected text within a paragraph, to the entire paragraph if no text is selected, or to the entire page if the Page Border tab is selected. Even though other features can highlight text with color, you can use the Borders and Shading commands to add boxes and/or shading around text, as well as place horizontal or vertical lines around different quantities of text. A good example of this practice is used in the Exploring series: The TIP boxes are surrounded by a border with dark shading and use a white font color for the headings to attract your attention.

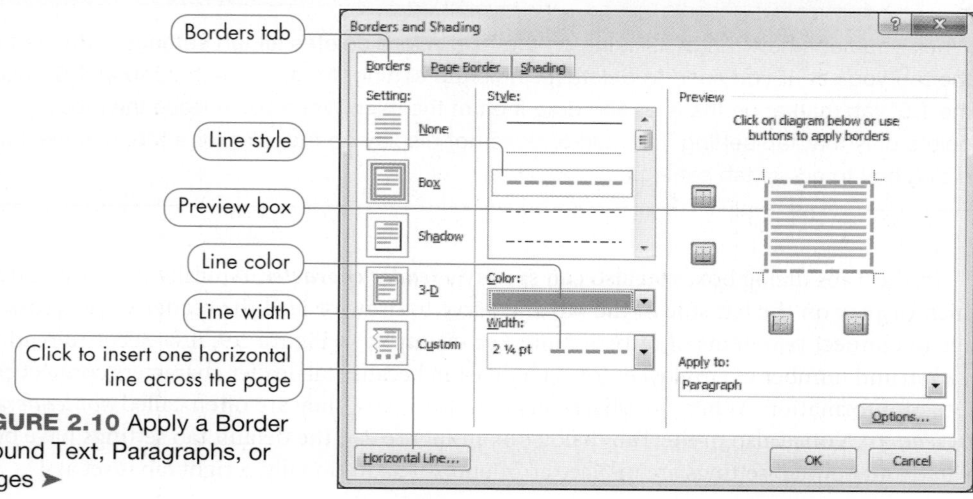

FIGURE 2.10 Apply a Border Around Text, Paragraphs, or Pages ➤

You can choose from several different line styles in any color, but remember you must use a color printer to display the line colors on the printed page. Colored lines appear in gray on a monochrome printer. Using the Box setting, you can place a uniform border around a paragraph, or you can choose a shadow effect with thicker lines at the right and bottom. You also can apply lines to selected sides of a paragraph by selecting a line style, and then clicking the desired sides as appropriate.

The horizontal line button at the bottom of the Borders and Shading dialog box provides access to a variety of attractive horizontal line designs. This is useful for displaying a horizontal line across a page to separate two elements. It also makes a nice border in a header or footer.

The Page Border tab enables you to place a decorative border around one or more selected pages. As with a paragraph border, you can place the border around the entire page, or you can select one or more sides. The page border also provides an additional option to use preselected clip art as a border instead of ordinary lines. Note that it is appropriate to use page borders on documents such as fliers, newsletters, and invitations, but not on formal documents such as research papers and professional reports.

Use page borders on ... fliers, newsletters, and invitations, but not on formal documents such as research papers and professional reports.

Shading is applied independently of the border and is accessed from the Borders and Shading dialog box or from Shading in the Paragraph group on the Home tab. Clear (no shading) is the default. Solid (100%) shading fills in a box around the text, and in some instances, the text is turned white so you can read it. Shading of 10% or 20% generally is most effective to add emphasis to the selected paragraph (see Figure 2.11). The Borders and Shading command is implemented on the paragraph level and affects the entire paragraph unless text has been selected within the paragraph.

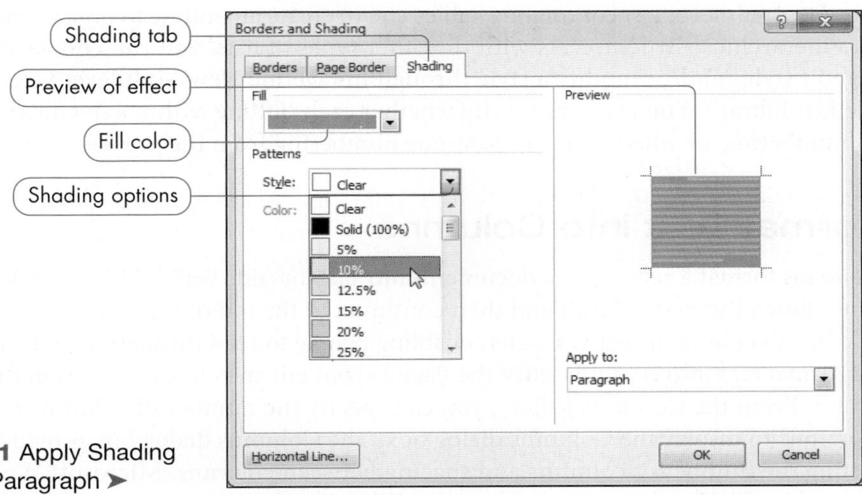

FIGURE 2.11 Apply Shading to Text or a Paragraph ➤

Create Bulleted and Numbered Lists

A **bulleted list** itemizes and separates paragraph text to increase readability.

A **numbered list** sequences and prioritizes items.

A **multilevel list** extends a numbered list to several levels.

A list helps you organize information by highlighting important topics. A ***bulleted list*** itemizes and separates paragraphs to increase readability. A ***numbered list*** sequences and prioritizes the items and is automatically updated to accommodate additions or deletions. A ***multilevel list*** extends a numbered list to several levels, and it too is updated automatically when topics are added or deleted. You create each of these lists from the Paragraph group on the Home tab.

To apply bullet formatting to a list, click the Bullets arrow and choose one of several predefined symbols in the Bullet library (see Figure 2.12). Position your mouse over one of the bullet styles in the Bullet Library and a preview of that bullet style will display in your document. To use that style, simply click the bullet. If you want to use a different bullet symbol, click the Define New Bullet option below the Bullet Library to choose a different symbol or picture for the bullet.

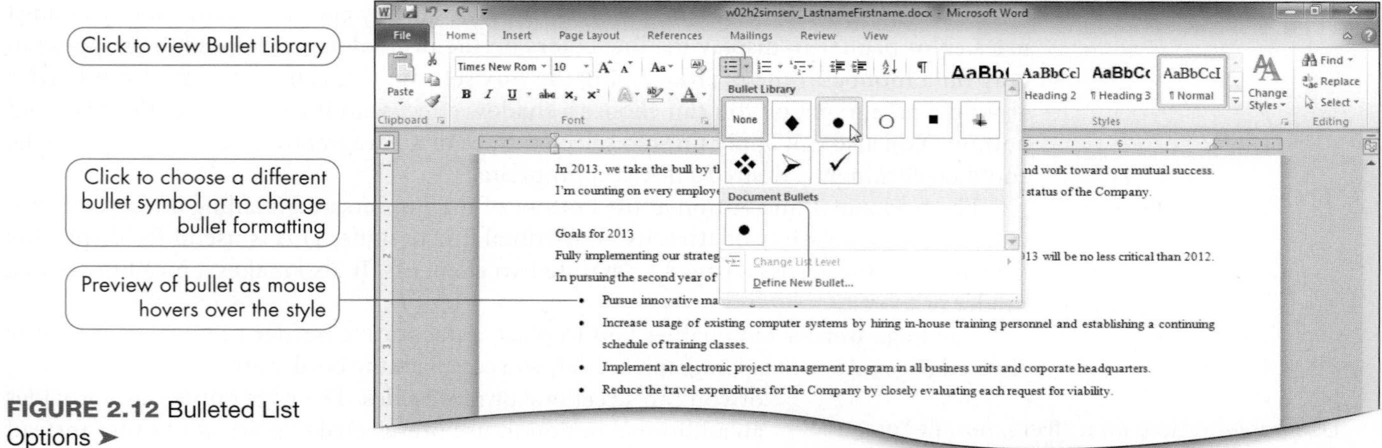
Click to view Bullet Library
Click to choose a different bullet symbol or to change bullet formatting
Preview of bullet as mouse hovers over the style

FIGURE 2.12 Bulleted List Options ➤

After you select text, you can click the Numbering arrow in the Paragraph group to apply Arabic or Roman numerals, or upper- or lowercase letters, for a numbered list. When you position the mouse pointer over a style in the Numbering Library, you see a preview of that numbering style in your document. As with a bulleted list, you can define a new style by selecting the Define New Number Format option below the Numbering Library. Note, too, the options to restart or continue numbering found by selecting the Set Numbering Value option. These become important if a list appears in multiple places within a document. In other words, each occurrence of a list can start numbering anew, or it can continue from where the previous list left off.

The Multilevel List command enables you to create an outline to organize your thoughts in a hierarchical structure. As with the other types of lists, you can choose one of several default styles and/or modify a style through the Define New Multilevel List option below the List Library. You also can specify whether each outline within a document is to restart its numbering, or whether it is to continue numbering from the previous outline.

Format Text into Columns

A **column** formats a section of a document into side-by-side vertical blocks.

Columns format a section of a document into side-by-side vertical blocks in which the text flows down the first column and then continues at the top of the next column. The length of a line of columnar text is shorter, enabling people to read through each document faster. To format text into columns, click the Page Layout tab and click Columns in the Page Setup group. From the Columns gallery, you can specify the number of columns or select More Columns to display the Columns dialog box. The Columns dialog box provides options for setting the number of columns and spacing between columns. Microsoft Word calculates the width of each column according to the left and right document margins on the page and the specified (default) space between columns.

The dialog box in Figure 2.13 implements a design of two equal columns. The width of each column is computed based on current left and right document margins and the spacing between columns. The width of each column is determined by subtracting the sum of the margins and the space between the columns from the page width of 8.5". The result of the subtraction results in column widths of 3.25".

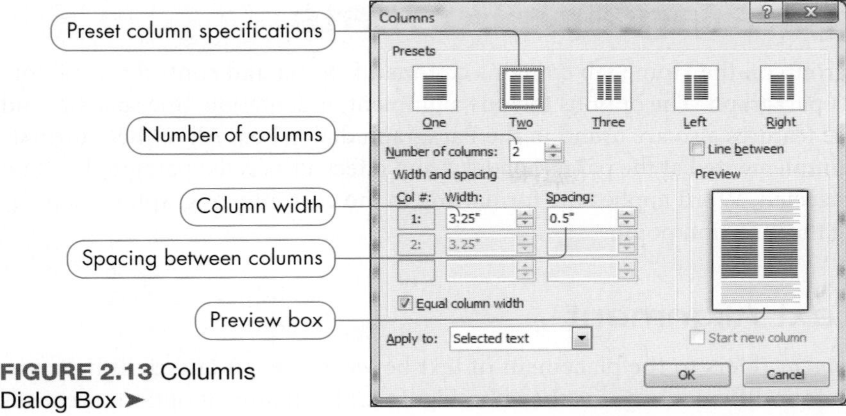

FIGURE 2.13 Columns Dialog Box ➤

One subtlety associated with column formatting is the use of sections, which control elements such as the orientation of a page (landscape or portrait), margins, page numbers, and the number of columns. Most of the documents you work with consist of a single section, so section formatting is not an issue. It becomes important only when you want to vary formatting in different parts, or sections, of the document. For example, you could use section formatting to create a document that has one column on its title page and two columns on the remaining pages. Creating this type of formatting requires you to divide the document into two sections by inserting a section break. You then format each section independently and specify the number of columns in each section.

Display Nonprinting Formatting Marks

As you type text, Word inserts nonprinting marks or symbols. While these symbols do not display on printouts, they do affect the appearance. For example, Word inserts a code every time you press Spacebar, Tab, and Enter. When you press Enter, it leaves a paragraph mark, no matter whether it is at the end of a single word, a single line, or a complete group of sentences. Word interprets the Paragraph mark as the completion of a paragraph, and so the paragraph mark (¶) at the end of a paragraph does more than just indicate the presence of a hard return. It also stores all of the formatting in effect for the paragraph. To preserve the formatting when you move or copy a paragraph, you must include the paragraph mark in the selected text. Click Show/Hide (¶) in the Paragraph group on the Home tab to display the paragraph mark and make sure it has been selected. Table 2.3 lists several common formatting marks. Both the hyphen and nonbreaking hyphen look like a regular hyphen when printed.

Word interprets the Paragraph mark as the completion of a paragraph.... It also stores all of the formatting in effect for the paragraph.

TABLE 2.3 Nonprinting Symbols

Symbol	Description	Create by
•	Regular space	Pressing Spacebar
°	Nonbreaking space	Pressing Ctrl+Shift+Spacebar
-	Regular hyphen	Pressing Hyphen
—	Nonbreaking hyphen	Pressing Ctrl+Shift+Hyphen
→	Tab	Pressing Tab
¶	End of paragraph	Pressing Enter
... **(shows under text)**	Hidden text	Selecting Hidden check box in Font dialog box
↵	Line break	Pressing Shift+Enter

Applying Paragraph Formats

The Paragraph group on the Home tab contains commands to set and control several format options for a paragraph. The options include alignment, indentation, line spacing, and pagination. These features also are found in the Paragraph dialog box. All of these formatting features are implemented at the paragraph level and affect all selected paragraphs. If no paragraphs are selected, Word applies the formatting to the current paragraph—the paragraph containing the insertion point.

Change Text Alignment

Horizontal alignment refers to the placement of text between the left and right margins.

Horizontal alignment refers to the placement of text between the left and right margins. Text is aligned in four different ways, as shown in Figure 2.14. Alignment options are justified (flush left/flush right), left aligned (flush left with a ragged right margin), right aligned (flush right with a ragged left margin), or centered within the margins (ragged left and right). The default alignment is left aligned.

We, the people of the United States, in order to form a more perfect Union, establish justice, insure domestic tranquility, provide for the common defense, promote the general welfare, and secure the blessings of liberty to ourselves and our posterity, do ordain and establish this Constitution for the United States of America.

Justified (flush left/flush right)

We, the people of the United States, in order to form a more perfect Union, establish justice, insure domestic tranquility, provide for the common defense, promote the general welfare, and secure the blessings of liberty to ourselves and our posterity, do ordain and establish this Constitution for the United States of America.

Left Aligned (flush left/ragged right)

We, the people of the United States, in order to form a more perfect Union, establish justice, insure domestic tranquility, provide for the common defense, promote the general welfare, and secure the blessings of liberty to ourselves and our posterity, do ordain and establish this Constitution for the United States of America.

Right Aligned (ragged left/flush right)

We, the people of the United States, in order to form a more perfect Union, establish justice, insure domestic tranquility, provide for the common defense, promote the general welfare, and secure the blessings of liberty to ourselves and our posterity, do ordain and establish this Constitution for the United States of America.

Centered (ragged left/ragged right)

FIGURE 2.14 Horizontal Alignment ➤

Left-aligned text is perhaps the easiest to read. The first letters of each line align with each other, helping the eye to find the beginning of each line. The lines themselves are of irregular length. Uniform spacing exists between words, and the ragged margin on the right adds white space to the text, giving it a lighter and more informal look.

Justified text, sometimes called fully justified, produces lines of equal length, with the spacing between words adjusted to align at the margins. Look closely and you will see many books, magazines, and newspapers fully justify text to add formality and "neatness" to the text. Some find this style more difficult to read because of the uneven (sometimes excessive) word spacing and/or the greater number of hyphenated words needed to justify the lines. However, it also can enable you to pack more information onto a page when space is constrained.

Text that is centered or right aligned is usually restricted to limited amounts of text where the effect is more important than the ease of reading. Centered text, for example, appears frequently on wedding invitations, poems, or formal announcements. In research papers, first-level titles often are centered as well. Right-aligned text is used with figure captions, in short headlines, and in document headers and footers.

The Paragraph group on the Home tab contains the four alignment options: Align Text Left, Center, Align Text Right, and Justify. To apply the alignment, select text, then click the alignment option on the Home tab. You can also set alignment from the Paragraph dialog box; the Indents and Spacing tab contains an Alignment arrow in the General section from which you can choose one of the four options.

TIP Alignment Keyboard Shortcuts

You can quickly apply alignment by using keyboard shortcuts. After you select the text, click Ctrl+L to align left, click Ctrl+E to align center, click Ctrl+R to align right, or click Ctrl+J to justify.

Indent Paragraphs

You can indent individual paragraphs so they appear to have different margins from the rest of a document. Indentation is established at the paragraph level; thus, it is possible to apply different indentation properties to different paragraphs. You can indent one paragraph from the left margin only, another from the right margin only, and a third from both the left and right margins. For example, the sixth edition of the *Publication Manual of the American Psychological Association,* which establishes the APA editorial style of writing, specifies that quotations consisting of 40 or more words should be contained in a separate paragraph that is indented .5" from the left margin. Additionally, you can indent the first line of any paragraph differently from the rest of the paragraph. Finally, a paragraph may have no indentation at all, so that it aligns on the left and right margins.

Three settings determine the indentation of a paragraph: the left indent, the right indent, and a special indent (see Figure 2.15). The left and right indents are set to 0 by default, as is the special indent, and produce a paragraph with no indentation at all. Positive values for the left and right indents offset the paragraph from both margins.

A **first line indent** marks the location to indent only the first line in a paragraph.

A **hanging indent** marks how far to indent each line of a paragraph except the first.

The two types of special indentation are first line and hanging. The ***first line indent*** affects only the first line in the paragraph, and you apply it by pressing the Tab key at the beginning of the paragraph or by setting a specific measurement in the Paragraph dialog box. Remaining lines in the paragraph align at the left margin. A ***hanging indent*** aligns the first line of a paragraph at the left margin and indents the remaining lines. Hanging indents are often used with bulleted or numbered lists and to format citations on a bibliography page.

When you view the ruler, characters display to identify any special indents that are in use. A grey triangle pointing down identifies the indention for a First Line Indent, a grey arrow pointing up identifies the indention for a Hanging Indent, and a grey square identifies the Left Indent. You can slide the characters along the ruler to modify the location of the indents.

TIP Decrease Indent and Increase Indent

You can click Decrease Indent in the Paragraph group on the Home tab to decrease (bring text to the left) indented text by .5". Click Increase Indent to move text to the right for an additional 1/2".

Set Line and Paragraph Spacing

Line spacing is the space between the lines in a paragraph.

Line spacing determines the space between the lines in a paragraph and between paragraphs. Word provides complete flexibility and enables you to select any multiple of line spacing (single, double, line and a half, and so on). You also can specify line spacing in terms of points (1" vertical contains 72 pt). Click Line and Paragraph Spacing in the Paragraph group on the Home tab to establish line spacing for the current paragraph. You can also set line spacing in the *Spacing* section on the Indents and Spacing tab in the Paragraph dialog box.

Paragraph spacing is the amount of space before or after a paragraph.

Paragraph spacing is the amount of space before or after a paragraph, as indicated by the paragraph mark when you press Enter between paragraphs. Unlike line spacing that controls *all* spacing within and between paragraphs, paragraph spacing controls only the spacing between paragraphs.

Sometimes you need to single-space text within a paragraph but want to have a blank line between paragraphs. Instead of pressing Enter twice between paragraphs, you can set the paragraph spacing to control the amount of space before or after the paragraph. You can set paragraph spacing in the *Spacing* section on the Indents and Spacing tab in the Paragraph dialog box. Setting a 12-pt After spacing creates the appearance of a double-space after the paragraph even though the user presses Enter only once between paragraphs.

The Paragraph dialog box is illustrated in Figure 2.15. The Indents and Spacing tab specifies a hanging indent, 1.5 line spacing, and justified alignment. The Preview area within the Paragraph dialog box enables you to see how the paragraph will appear within the document.

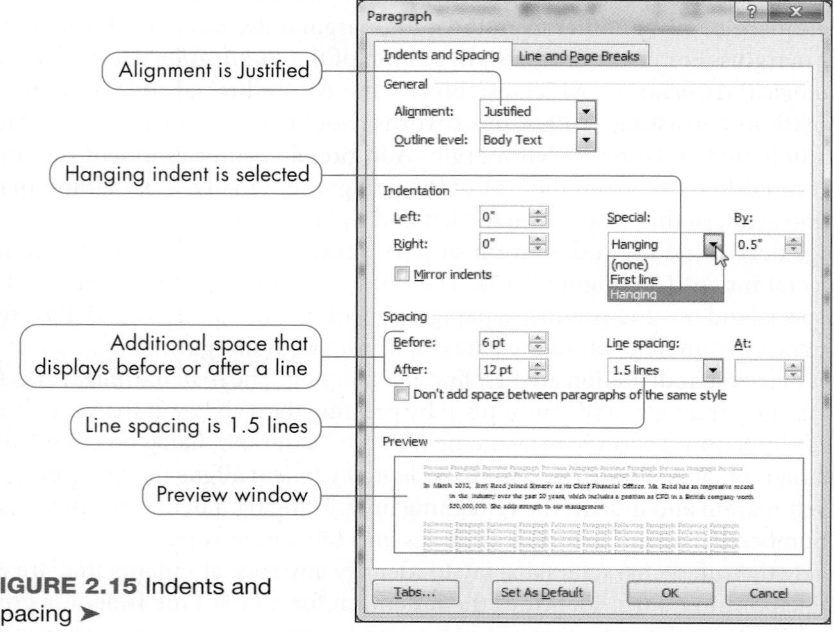

FIGURE 2.15 Indents and Spacing ➤

> **TIP** Indents and Paragraph Spacing
>
> To avoid opening the Paragraph dialog box, you can quickly change Indent or Paragraph Spacing from the Paragraph group on the Page Layout tab.

Control Widows and Orphans

A **widow** is the last line of a paragraph appearing by itself at the top of a page.

An **orphan** is the first line of a paragraph appearing by itself at the bottom of a page.

Some lines become isolated from the remainder of a paragraph and seem out of place at the beginning or end of a multipage document. A ***widow*** refers to the last line of a paragraph appearing by itself at the top of a page. An ***orphan*** is the first line of a paragraph appearing by itself at the bottom of a page. You can prevent these from occurring by checking the Widow/Orphan control in the *Pagination* section of the Line and Page Breaks tab of the Paragraph dialog box.

To prevent a page break from occurring within a paragraph and ensure that the entire paragraph appears on the same page use the *Keep lines together* option in the *Pagination* section of the Line and Page Breaks tab of the Paragraph dialog box. The paragraph is moved to the top of the next page if it does not fit on the bottom of the current page. Use the *Keep with next* option in the *Pagination* section to prevent a soft page break between the two paragraphs. This option is typically used to keep a heading (a one-line paragraph) with its associated text in the next paragraph. Figure 2.16 displays the Paragraph dialog box settings to control soft page breaks that detract from the appearance of a document.

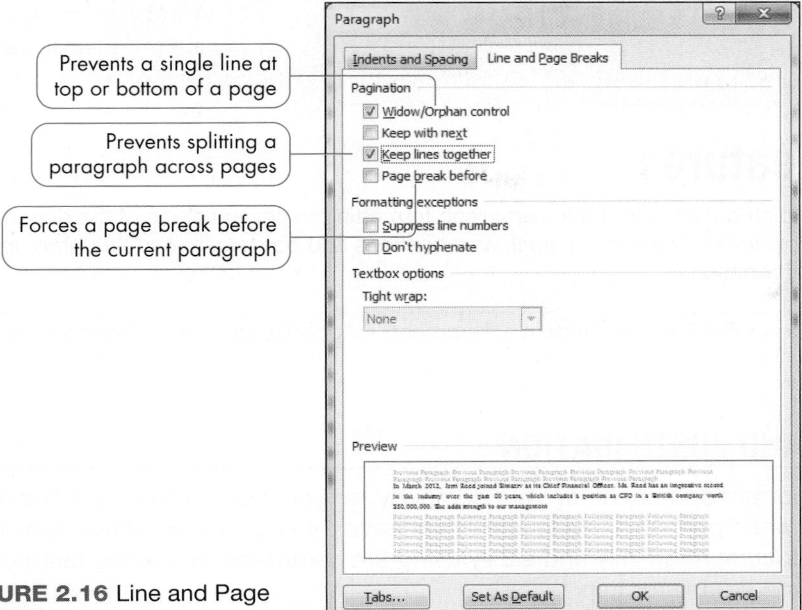

FIGURE 2.16 Line and Page Breaks ➤

The Section Versus the Paragraph

Line spacing, alignment, tabs, and indents are implemented at the paragraph level. Change any of these parameters anywhere within the current (or selected) paragraph(s) and you change *only* those paragraph(s). Margins, page numbering, orientation, and columns are implemented at the section level. Change these parameters anywhere within a section and you change the characteristics of every page within that section.

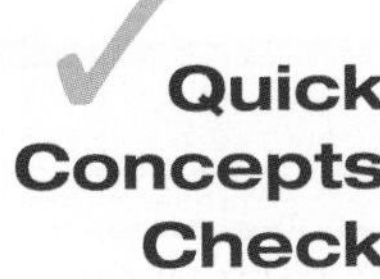

Quick Concepts Check

1. Describe the five types of tab markers you can use in a document.
2. Describe three different features you can use to draw attention to your text.
3. List three non-printing symbols and tell how they affect the appearance of text in your document.
4. Describe the different methods of aligning text in a document.
5. What is the difference between a widow and an orphan in word processing?

HANDS-ON EXERCISES

2 Paragraph Formatting Features

The next step in preparing the Annual Summary for distribution is to apply paragraph formatting to several areas of the document that will make it easier to read. You also want to apply special formatting, such as indentions and borders, to certain paragraphs for emphasis and to draw the readers' eye to that information.

Skills covered: Specify Line Spacing and Justification • Set Tabs and Indent a Paragraph • Apply Borders and Shading • Create a Bulleted and Numbered List • Create Columns

STEP 1 SPECIFY LINE SPACING AND JUSTIFICATION

The Annual Summary is an important document for your company, so you want to be sure it is easy to read and looks professional when printed. To help in that endeavor, you increase the line spacing and adjust justification of this document quickly and easily using the paragraph formatting features in Word. Refer to Figure 2.17 as you complete Step 1.

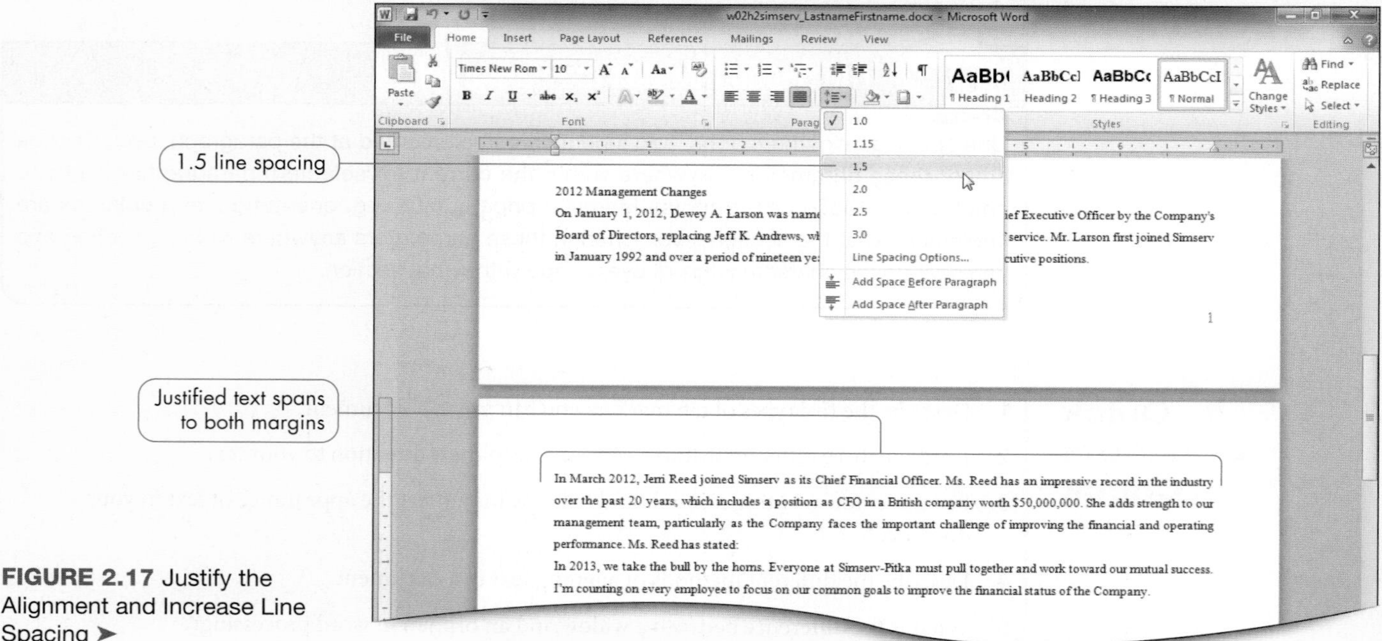

FIGURE 2.17 Justify the Alignment and Increase Line Spacing ➤

a. Open the *w02h1simserv_LastnameFirstname* document if you closed it at the end of Hands-On Exercise 1, and save it as **w02h2simserv_LastnameFirstname**, changing *h1* to *h2*.

b. Drag to select all of the text in the document, starting with the first sentence, *The consumer products industry has seen dramatic change …*, and then click **Justify** in the Paragraph group.

c. Click **Line and Paragraph Spacing** in the Paragraph group, and then select **1.5**, as seen in Figure 2.17.

   These settings align the text on the right and left margins and add spacing before and after lines of text, making it easier to read.

d. Save the document.

STEP 2 SET TABS AND INDENT A PARAGRAPH

You want to display the information about divisions that were acquired so that it is easy to read across the page and not jumbled together as you see it now. You decide to insert two tabs to line up the division and cities. A third tab is needed for the number of employees, and since you are aligning a number, you wisely insert a decimal tab. You also decide to indent a quotation by the new CFO so it does not blend in with the rest of the paragraph. Refer to Figure 2.18 as you complete Step 2.

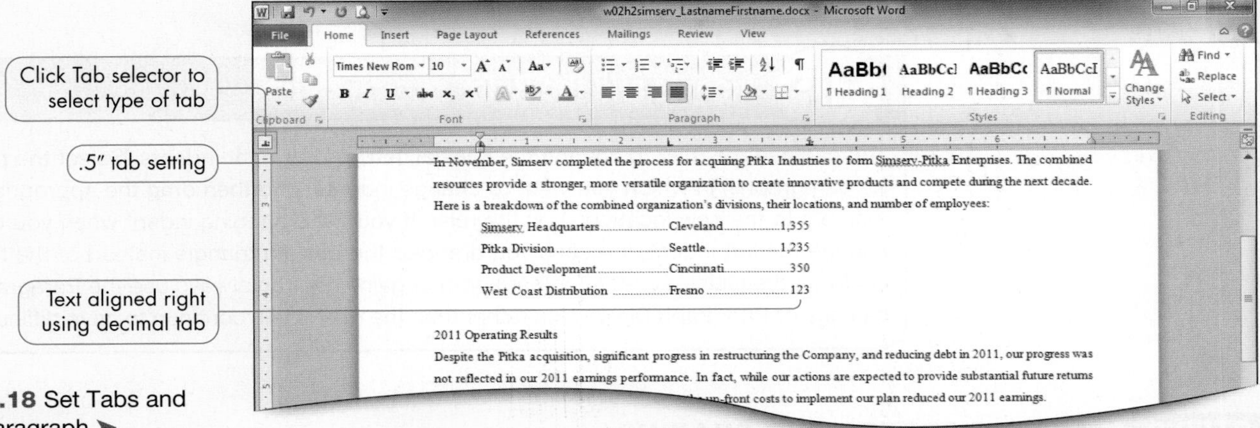

FIGURE 2.18 Set Tabs and Indent a Paragraph ➤

a. Select the last four lines of the *Acquisition of Pitka Industries* paragraph.

   These lines describe facility locations and number of employees at each.

b. Click the **Paragraph Dialog Box Launcher** in the Paragraph group. Click **Tabs** in the bottom left to display the Tabs dialog box.

c. Type **.5** in the **Tab stop position box**, confirm *Left* is selected in the Alignment area, and then click **Set**.

d. Type **2.5** in the **Tab stop position box**, confirm it is a Left-aligned tab, click **2…** in the Leader area, and then click **Set** again. Click **OK** to close the Tabs dialog box.

   You set two tab stops for the Division and locations.

e. Click the **View tab**, and then click **Ruler**, if necessary, to view the Ruler at the top of the window. Select the last four lines again, if necessary, and then click the **Tab selector** at the left end of the ruler until the Decimal tab displays.

TROUBLESHOOTING: If you miss the Decimal tab selector, keep clicking. All tab selections will cycle through the selector area and then repeat as you click.

f. Click the **4"** mark on the ruler to apply the Decimal tab.

   When you set the decimal tab, the numbers line up along the right edge. It is always best to display numbers aligning on the right.

g. Right-click the selected text, click **Paragraph**, and then click **Tabs**. Click the **4" tab**, click **2…** in the Leader area, and then click **OK**.

   When you add the dot leaders, it is easier to follow the information across the page for each location.

h. Click the **Home tab**, and then click **Increase Indent** in the Paragraph group to indent the list to the first tab stop.

i. Place your cursor on the left side of *Fresno* on the last line, and press **Tab** to align the data at the new tab stops, as shown in Figure 2.18.

j. Select the quote by Jerri Reed at the end of the second paragraph following the *2012 Management Changes* heading. The quote starts *In 2013, we take the bull by the horns.*

k. Click the **Page Layout tab**. Click the **Indent Left arrow** until *0.5*" displays.

l. Click the **Indent Right arrow** until *0.5*" displays.

   The paragraph is equally indented from the right and left margins and now displays with additional white space on the right and left sides.

m. Save the document.

TIP Indents and the Ruler

You can use the ruler to change the special, left, and/or right indents. Select the paragraph (or paragraphs) in which you want to change indents, and then drag the appropriate indent markers to the new location(s) on the ruler. If you get a hanging indent when you wanted to change the left indent, it means you dragged the bottom triangle instead of the box. Click Undo on the Quick Access Toolbar and try again. You can always use the Paragraph group settings or Paragraph Dialog Box rather than the ruler if you continue to have difficulty.

STEP 3 APPLY BORDERS AND SHADING

To make sure your company's financial position is recognized, you decide to place a border around that paragraph and shade it with color to make it really stand out. You know that this is another way to draw the reader's attention to important data—by highlighting with color and borders. Refer to Figure 2.19 as you complete Step 3.

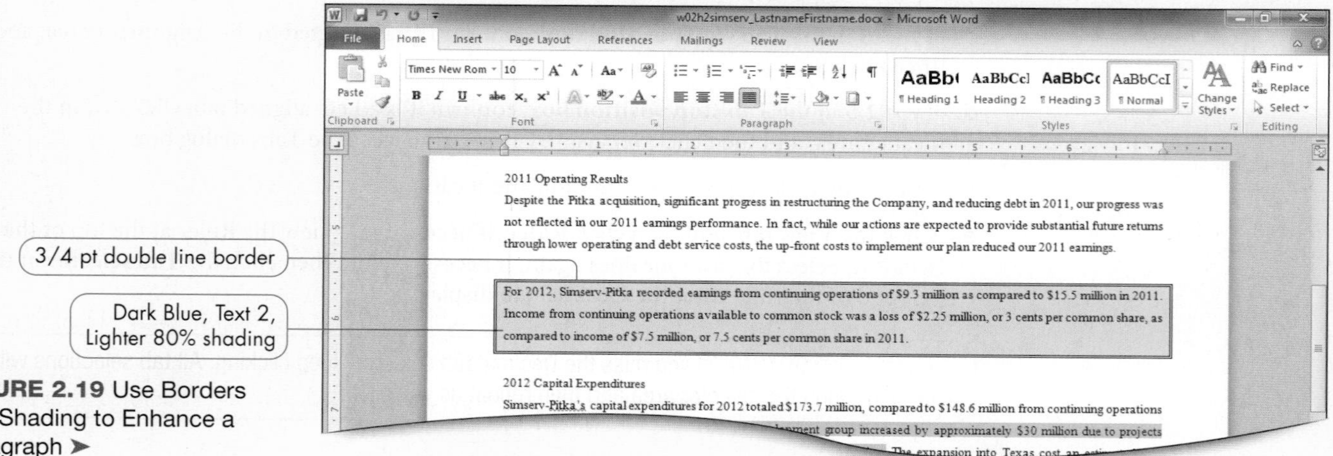

FIGURE 2.19 Use Borders and Shading to Enhance a Paragraph ➤

a. Select the second paragraph following the *2011 Operating Results* heading, which starts *For 2012, Simserv-Pitka recorded earnings.*

b. Click the **Home tab**, click the **Borders arrow**, and then click **Borders and Shading** to display the Borders and Shading dialog box.

c. Click the **Borders tab**, if necessary, and then select the **double line style** in the **Style list**. Click the **Width arrow**, select **3/4 pt**, and then click **Box** in the *Setting* section.

   A preview of these settings will display on the right side of the window in the Preview area.

d. Click the **Shading tab**, click the **Fill arrow**, and then select **Dark Blue, Text 2, Lighter 80%** from the palette (second row, fourth column). Click **OK** to accept the settings for both Borders and Shading.

The paragraph is surrounded by a 3/4-pt double-line border, and light blue shading appears behind the text.

e. Click outside the paragraph to deselect it, and then compare your work to Figure 2.19.

f. Save the document.

STEP 4 CREATE A BULLETED AND NUMBERED LIST

The Annual Summary includes paragraphs that describe the goals for 2012. To display the key goals so each one is easily distinguishable, you decide to format them into a bulleted list. The goals described in the final paragraph should be formatted similarly, but since they are described as steps, which assume an order, you format them using a numbered list instead of simple bullets. Refer to Figure 2.20 as you complete Step 4.

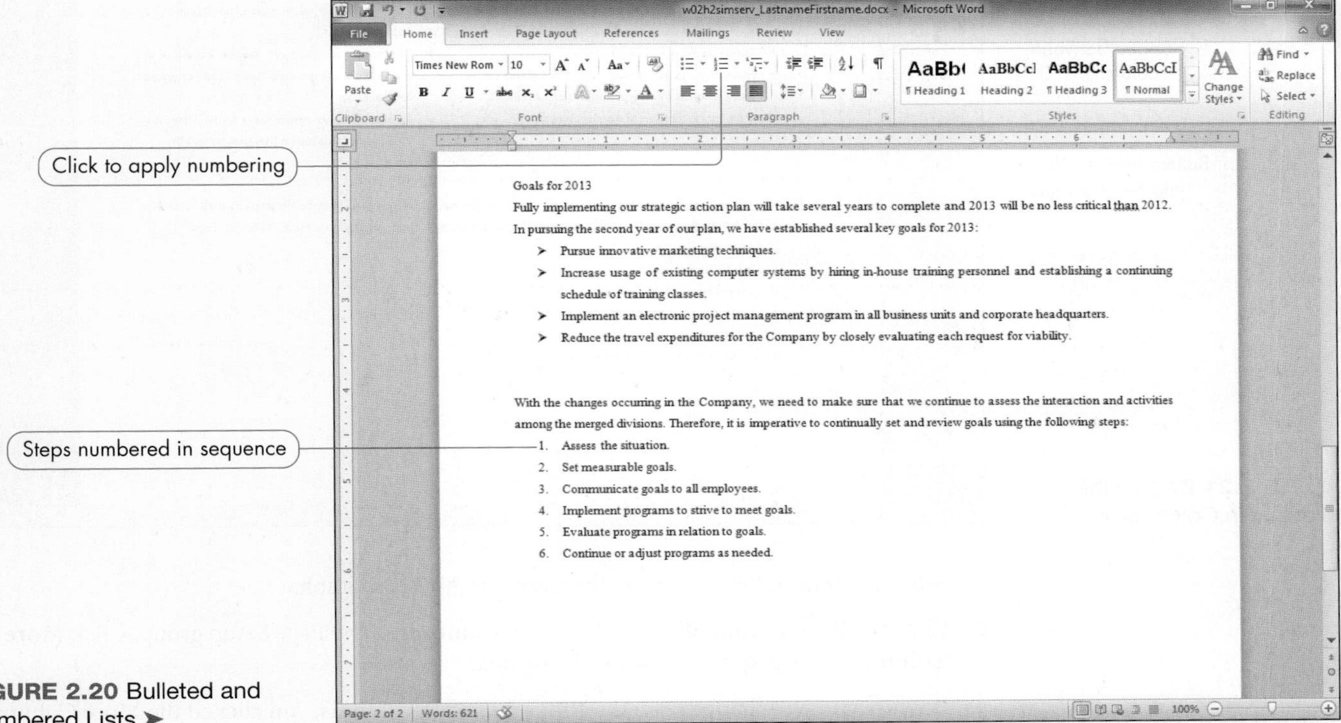

FIGURE 2.20 Bulleted and Numbered Lists ➤

a. Select the five lines of text in the first paragraph that follows the *Goals for 2013* heading, starting with *Pursue innovative marketing techniques.*

b. Click the **Home tab**, if necessary, and then click the **Bullets arrow** to display the Bullet Library.

   Here you select from a variety of bullet styles. The most recently used bullets display at the top.

c. Click a bullet that is in the shape of an arrow or arrowhead. If that style does not display, click the bullet of your choice.

d. Select the last six lines of text in the last paragraph that follows the *Goals for 2013* heading.

e. Click **Numbering** in the paragraph group.

   The steps are numbered in sequence from 1 to 6 as shown in Figure 2.20. Because it is important to perform these steps in this order, you use a numbered list instead of bullets.

f. Save the document.

STEP 5 CREATE COLUMNS

The goals you formatted with bullets in the last step look fine, but you realize the bullets are somewhat short and would look good if displayed in columns on the page. Columns would also add an element of variety to the way the information displays on the page. Refer to Figure 2.21 as you complete Step 5.

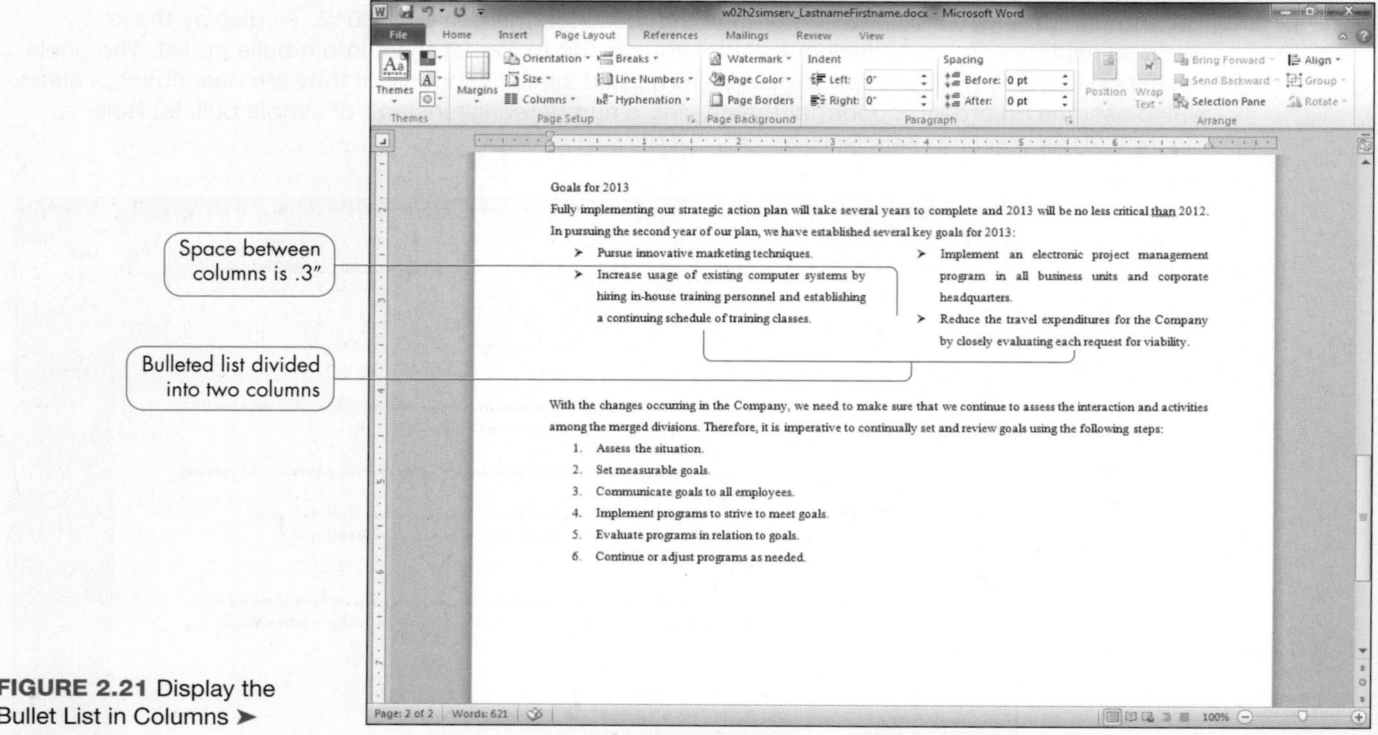

FIGURE 2.21 Display the Bullet List in Columns ➤

a. Select the four bulleted items in the *Goals for 2013* paragraph.

b. Click the **Page Layout tab**, and then click **Columns** in the Page Setup group. Click **More Columns** to display the Columns dialog box.

   Because you will change several settings related to columns, you clicked the More Columns option instead of clicking the gallery option to create columns.

c. Click **Two** in the *Presets* section of the dialog box. The default spacing between columns is 0.5", which leads to a column width of 3.25". Change the Spacing to **.3**", which automatically changes the column Width to *3.35*".

d. Click **OK** to close the Columns dialog box, and compare your document to Figure 2.21.

   The bulleted list is now formatted in two columns and makes efficient use of space on the page.

e. Click the **View tab**, and then click **Ruler** to turn off the ruler.

f. Save the document and keep it onscreen if you plan to continue with the next Hands-On Exercise. If not, close the document and exit Word.

Styles

As you complete reports, assignments, and projects for other classes or in your job, you probably apply the same text, paragraph, table, and list formatting for similar documents. Instead of formatting each document individually, you can create your own custom style to save time in setting particular formats for titles, headings, and paragraphs. Styles and other features in Word then can be used to automatically generate reference pages such as a table of contents and indexes. In this section, you will create and modify styles.

Understanding Styles

Styles automate the formatting process and provide a consistent appearance to a document... Change the style and you automatically change all text defined by that style.

One characteristic of a professional document is the uniform formatting that is applied to similar elements throughout the document. Different elements have different formatting. For headings you can use one font, color, style, and size, and then use a completely different format design on text below those headings. The headings may be left aligned, whereas the text is fully justified. You can format lists and footnotes in entirely different styles.

A **style** is a set of formatting options you apply to characters or paragraphs.

One way to achieve uniformity throughout the document is to use the Format Painter to copy the formatting from one occurrence of each element to the next. If you change your mind after copying the formatting throughout a document, you have to repeat the entire process all over again. A much easier way to achieve uniformity is to store all the formatting information together, which is what we refer to as a ***style***. Styles automate the formatting process and provide a consistent appearance to a document. It is possible to store any type of character or paragraph formatting within a style, and once a style is defined, you can apply it to any element within a document to produce identical formatting. Change the style and you automatically change all text defined by that style.

Creating and Modifying Styles

A **character style** stores character formatting and affects only selected text.

A **paragraph style** stores formats used on text in an entire paragraph.

Styles are created on the character or paragraph level. A ***character style*** stores character formatting (font, size, and style) and affects only the selected text. A ***paragraph style*** stores paragraph formatting such as alignment, line spacing, indents, tabs, text flow, and borders and shading, as well as the font, size, and style of the text in the paragraph. A paragraph style affects the current paragraph or, if selected, multiple paragraphs. You cannot apply a paragraph style to only part of a paragraph. You create and apply styles from the Styles group on the Home tab, as shown in Figure 2.22.

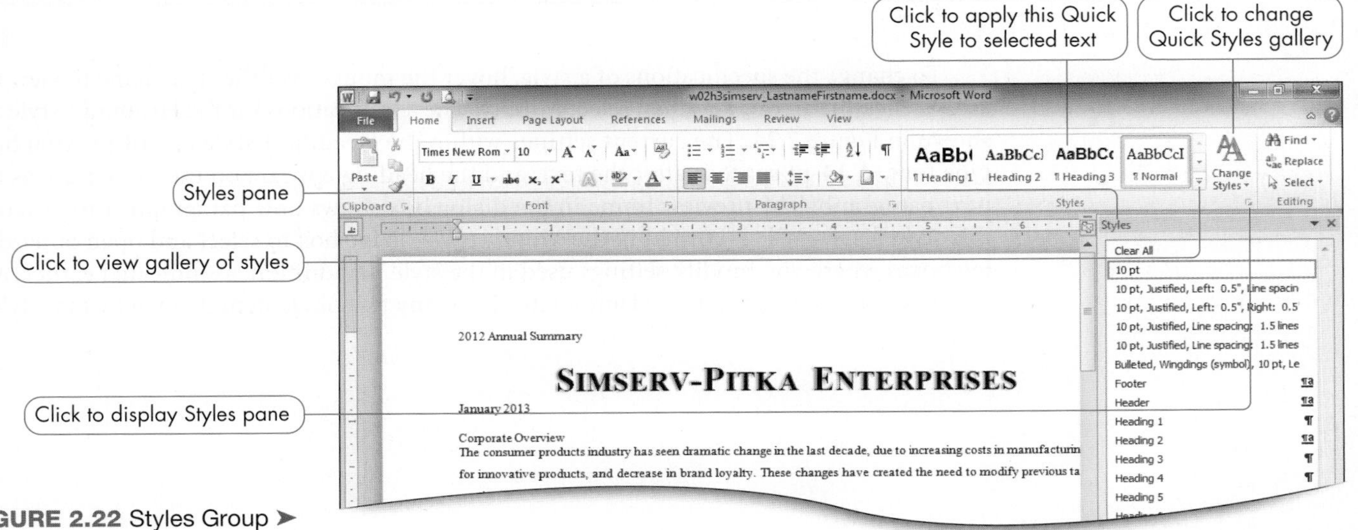

FIGURE 2.22 Styles Group ➤

The Normal template contains more than 100 styles. Unless you specify a style, Word uses the Normal style. The Normal style contains these settings: 11-pt Calibri, 1.15 line spacing, 10-pt spacing after, left horizontal alignment, and Widow/Orphan control. To apply a different style to an existing paragraph, place the insertion point anywhere within the paragraph, click the Styles Dialog Box Launcher on the Home tab to display the Styles pane, and then click the name of the style you want to use. You can create your own styles to use in a document, modify or delete an existing style, and even add your new style to the Normal template for use in other documents. The Clear All style removes all formatting from selected text.

In Figure 2.23, the task pane displays all of the styles available for use in the Simserv-Pitka Enterprises Annual Summary. The Normal style contains the default paragraph settings (left aligned, 1.15 line spacing, 10-pt spacing after, and 11-pt Calibri font) and is assigned automatically to every paragraph unless a different style is specified. It is the Heading 1 and Heading 3 styles, however, that are of interest to us, as these styles have been applied throughout the document to titles and paragraph headings. To view the style names with their styles applied, click the Show Preview check box near the bottom of the Styles pane.

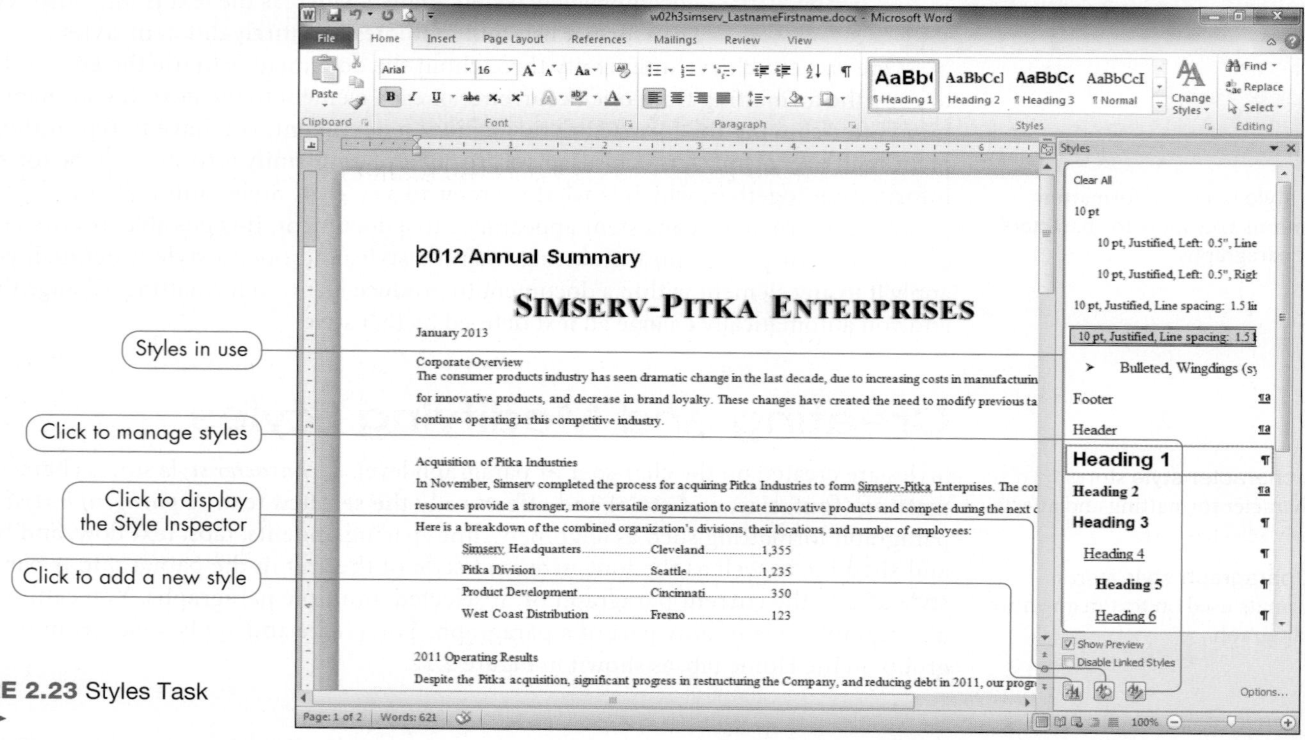

FIGURE 2.23 Styles Task Pane ➤

To change the specifications of a style, hover the mouse over the style name to view the arrow, click the arrow, and then select Modify. The specifications for the Heading 1 style are shown in Figure 2.24. The current settings within the Heading 1 style use 18-pt Arial bold type font. A 14-pt space is after the text, and the heading appears on the same page as the next paragraph. The preview frame in the dialog box shows how paragraphs formatted in this style display. Click Format in the Modify Style dialog box to select and open other dialog boxes where you modify settings used in the style. In addition, as indicated earlier, any changes to the style are reflected automatically in any text or element defined by that style.

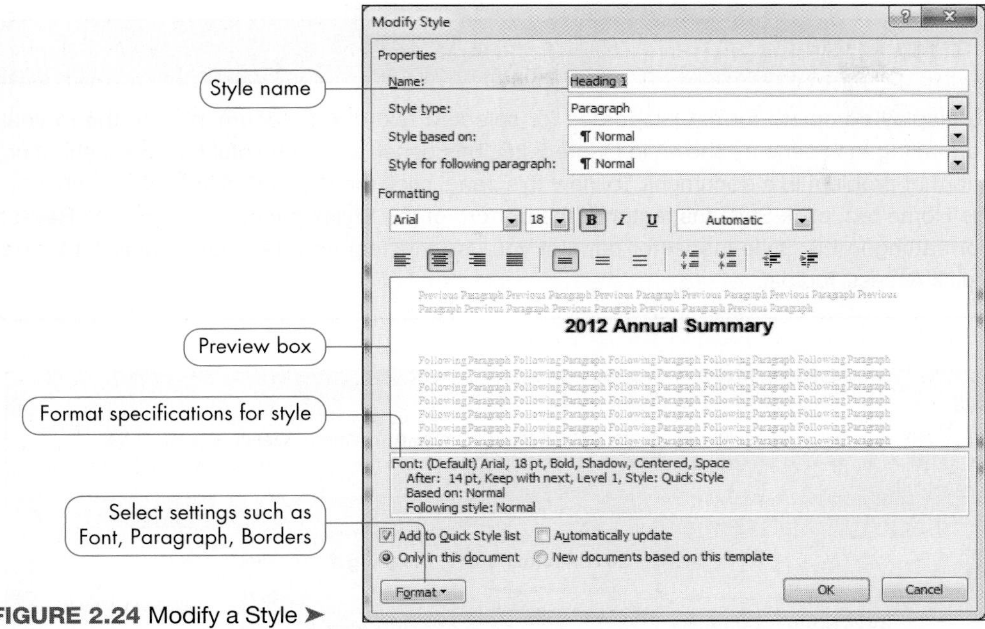

FIGURE 2.24 Modify a Style ➤

Use the Styles Pane Options

The Styles pane can display in several locations. Initially it might display as a floating window, but you can drag the title bar to move it. Drag to the far left or right side, and it will dock on that side of the window. When you display the Styles pane in your document, it might contain only the styles used in the document, as in Figure 2.23, or it might list every style in the Word document template. If the Styles pane only displays styles used in the document, you are unable to view or apply other styles.

You can change the styles that display in the Styles pane by using the Styles Pane Options dialog box, which displays when you click Options in the bottom-right corner of the Styles pane. In the *Select styles to show* box, you select from several options including Recommended, In use, In current document, and All styles, as shown in Figure 2.25. Select *In use* to view only styles used in this document; select *All styles* to view all styles created for the document template as well as any custom styles you create. Other options are available in this dialog box, including how to sort the styles when displayed, and whether to show Paragraph or Font or both types of styles.

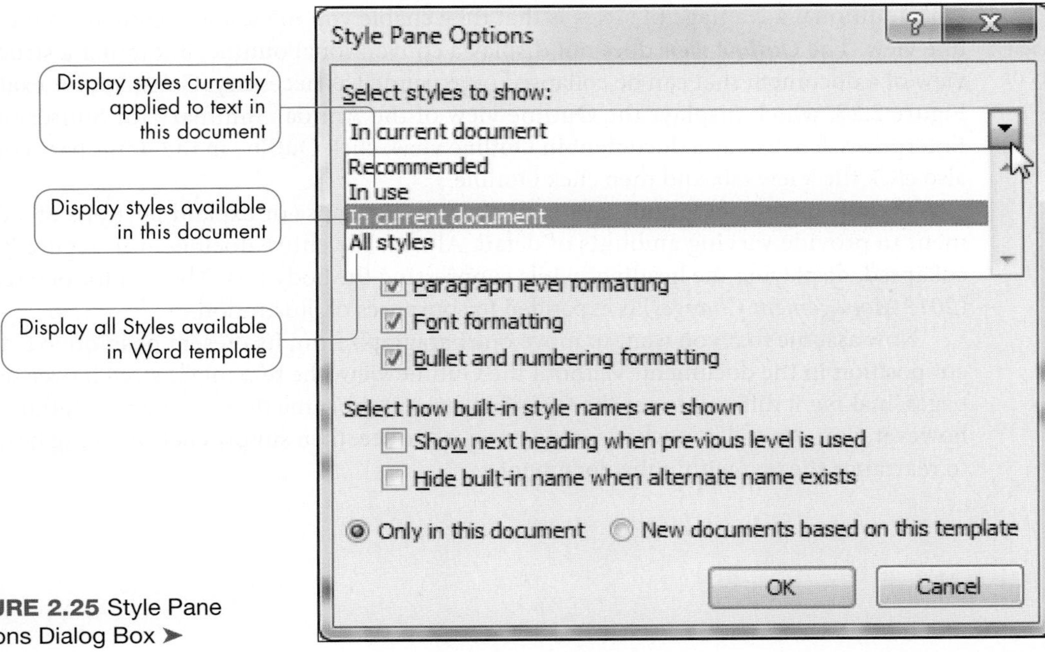

FIGURE 2.25 Style Pane Options Dialog Box ➤

TIP Reveal Formatting

To display complete format properties for selected text in the document, use the Reveal Formatting task pane as shown in Figure 2.26. This panel is often helpful for troubleshooting a format problem in a document. To view this pane, click the Styles Dialog Box Launcher on the Home tab, click Style Inspector at the bottom of the Styles pane, and then click Reveal Formatting in the Style Inspector pane. If you use this feature often, you can add it to the Quick Access Toolbar.

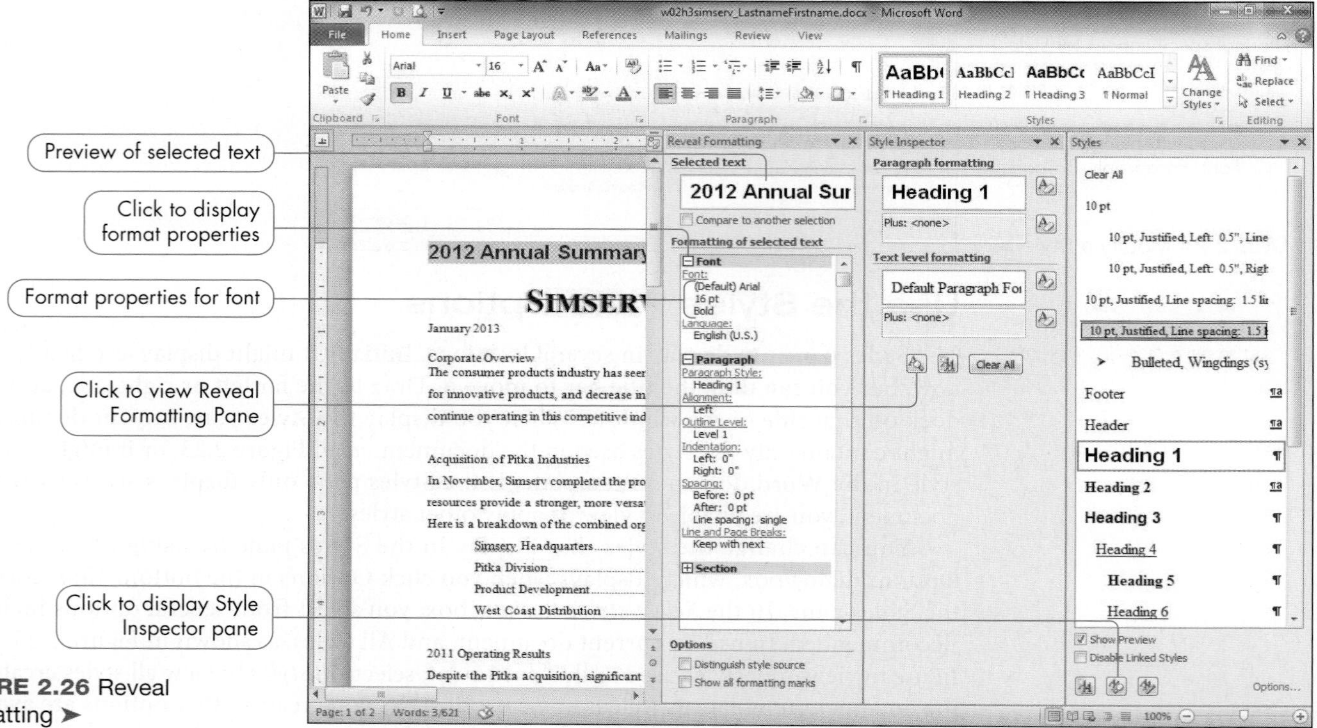

FIGURE 2.26 Reveal Formatting ➤

Use the Outline View

Outline view is a structural view that displays varying amounts of detail.

One additional advantage of styles is that they enable you to view a document in the Outline view. The ***Outline view*** does not display a conventional outline, but rather a structural view of a document that can be collapsed or expanded as necessary. Consider, for example, Figure 2.27, which displays the Outline view of the Annual Summary for Simserv-Pitka Enterprises. To display a document in Outline view, click Outline in the status bar. You can also click the View tab, and then click Outline.

The advantage of Outline view is that you can collapse or expand portions of a document to provide varying amounts of detail. Almost the entire document in Figure 2.27 is collapsed, displaying the headings while suppressing the body text. The text for one section (*2012 Management Changes)* is expanded for purposes of illustration.

Now assume that you want to move one paragraph from its present position to a different position in the document. Without the Outline view, the text might stretch over several pages, making it difficult to see the text of all areas at the same time. Using the Outline view, however, you can collapse what you do not need to see, then simply click and drag headings to rearrange the text within the document.

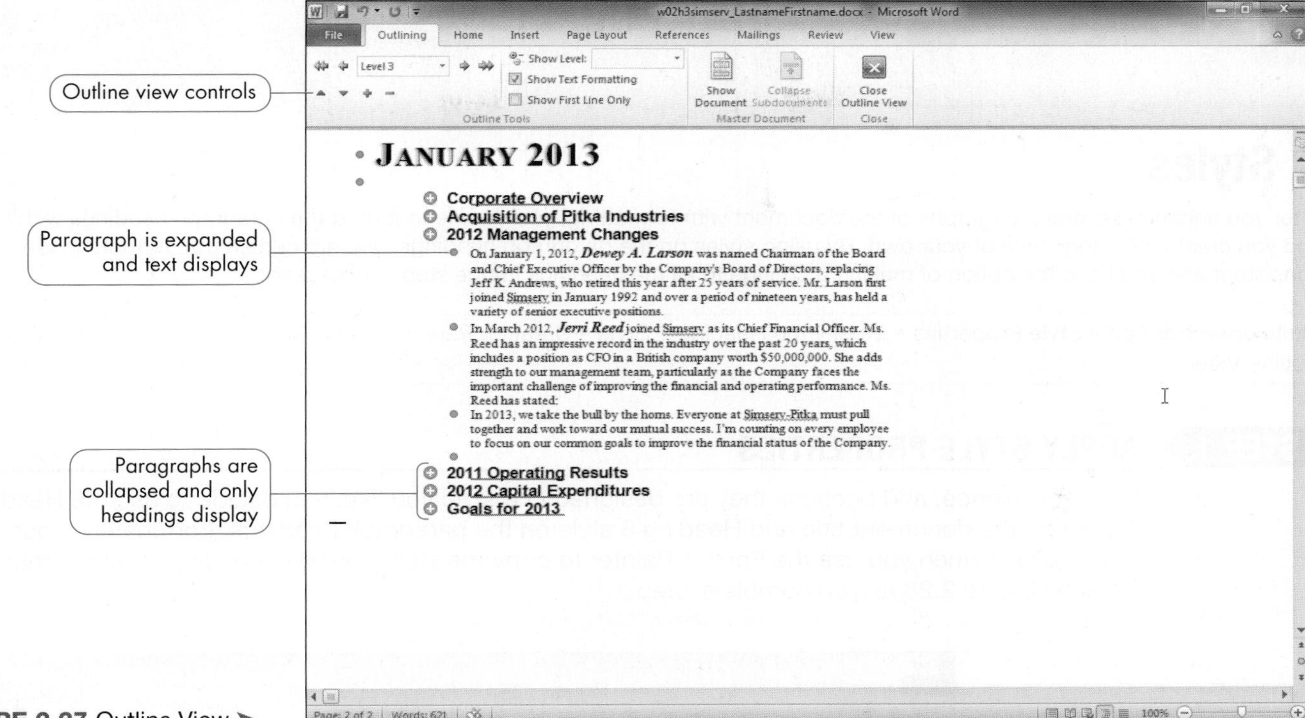

FIGURE 2.27 Outline View ➤

TIP The Outline Versus the Outline View

A conventional outline is created as a multilevel list using the Multilevel List command in the Paragraph group on the Home tab. Text for the outline is entered in the Print Layout view, *not* the Outline view. The latter provides a condensed view of a document that is used in conjunction with styles.

Quick Concepts Check

1. Describe the benefit of using styles in a document.
2. Explain the differences between a character style and a paragraph style.
3. Explain what happens to text in a document when you modify a style applied to that text.
4. Describe the different ways to display styles in the Styles pane.
5. What is the relationship between styles and the Outline view?

HANDS-ON EXERCISES

3 Styles

After you enhance several paragraphs of the document with formatting, you decide to format the paragraph headings with styles, and you create a custom style of your own. By using styles on the paragraph headings, you are certain that formatting is consistent and you have the option of making a change to all the headings in one step, if necessary.

Skills covered: Apply Style Properties • Modify the Heading 1 Style • Create a Paragraph and Character Style • Select the Outline View

STEP 1 APPLY STYLE PROPERTIES

For convenience, and because they are designed in a style you like, you decide to use the Heading 1 style on the document title and Heading 3 style on the paragraph headings. Fortunately, your work goes quickly when you use the Format Painter to copy the style from one heading to all the rest. Refer to Figure 2.28 as you complete Step 1.

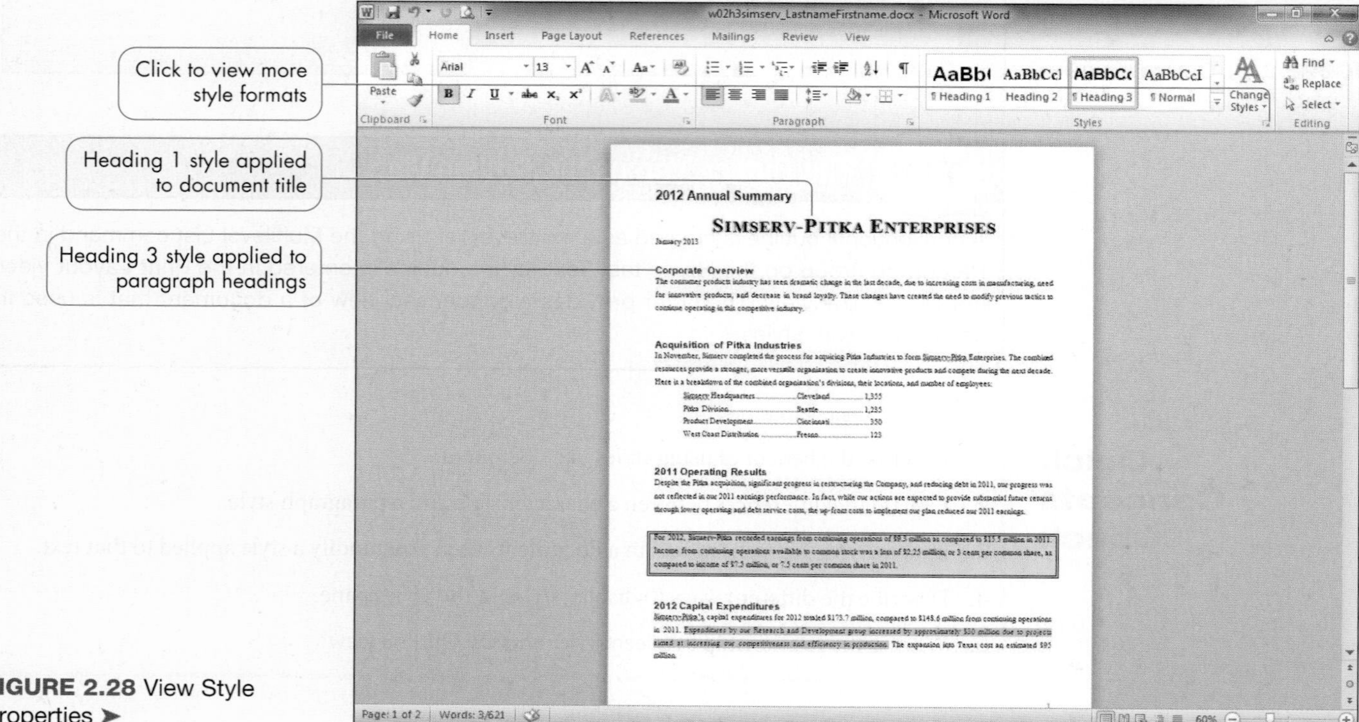

FIGURE 2.28 View Style Properties ➤

a. Open *w02h2simserv_LastnameFirstname* if you closed it at the end of Hands-On Exercise 2, and save it as **w02h3simserv_LastnameFirstname**, changing *h2* to *h3*.

b. Press **Ctrl+Home** to move to the beginning of the document.

c. Select the first line of the document, *2012 Annual Summary*, click the **Home tab**, if necessary, and then click **Heading 1** from the Quick Style gallery in the Styles group.

   When you hover your mouse over the different styles in the gallery, the Live Preview feature displays the style on your selected text but will not apply it until you click the style.

d. Select the paragraph heading *Corporate Overview*. Click the **More buttom** on the right side of the Quick Style gallery to display more styles, and then click the **Heading 3 style**.

e. Double-click the **Format Painter** in the Clipboard group, and then select the five remaining paragraph headings in the document to apply the **Heading 3 style**. Press **Esc** to turn off the Format Painter.

All paragraph headings in this document are formatted as shown in Figure 2.28.

f. Save the document.

STEP 2 MODIFY THE HEADING 1 STYLE

After you look at the document title, you decide it should be centered on the page and formatted to match the subtitle. Because you anticipate using that style frequently, you decide to modify the style to add center alignment and to include the font attributes used on the subtitle. Refer to Figure 2.29 as you complete Step 2.

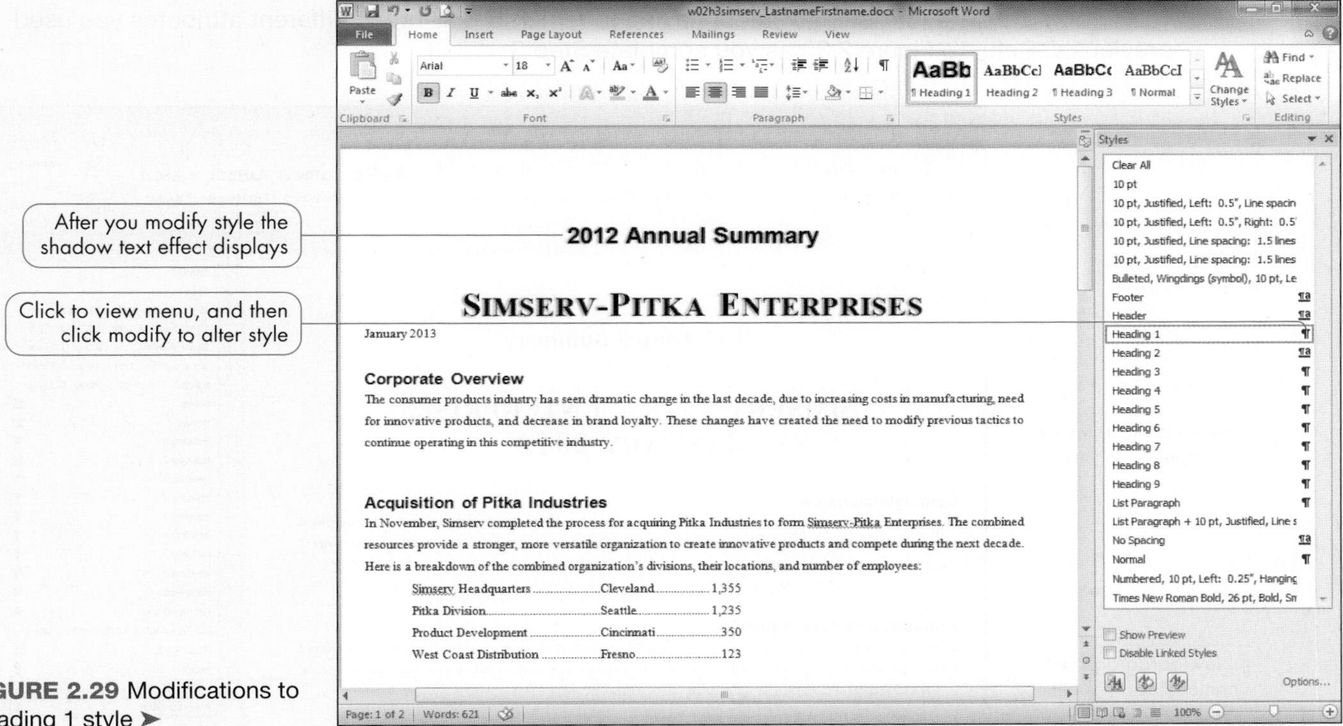

FIGURE 2.29 Modifications to Heading 1 style ➤

a. Click the **Styles Dialog Box Launcher** in the Styles group. Double-click the title bar of the Styles pane to dock it, if necessary, so it does not float on the screen.

b. Click **Ctrl+Home** to move to the beginning of the document. Notice the Heading 1 style is selected in the Styles pane. Hover your mouse over the style description in the Styles pane to display the arrow, click the arrow, and then select **Modify** to display the Modify Style dialog box.

TROUBLESHOOTING: If you click the style name instead of the arrow, you will apply the style to the selected text instead of modifying it. Click Undo on the Quick Access Toolbar to cancel the command. Click the arrow next to the style name to display the associated menu, and select the Modify command to display the Modify Style dialog box.

c. Click **Center** in the *Formatting* section to change the alignment of this title. Click **Format** in the bottom-left corner of the window, and then click **Font** to display the Font dialog box. If necessary, click the **Font tab**. Change Font size to **18**, and then click **OK** to close the Font dialog box and return to the Modify Style dialog box.

d. Click **Format**, and then select **Text Effects**. Click **Shadow**, click **Presets,** and then click **Offset Left** (second row, third column). Click the **Close button**.

e. Click **Format**, and then select **Paragraph**. If necessary, click the **Indents and Spacing tab**. In the *Spacing* section, type **14** in the **After box**.

   Since 14 is not one of the predefined options you see when scrolling in the Spacing After box, you must type it in.

f. Click **OK** to close the Paragraph dialog box, and then click **OK** to close the Modify Style dialog box. Compare your results to Figure 2.29.

g. Save the document.

STEP 3 CREATE A PARAGRAPH AND CHARACTER STYLE

You decide the format used on the subtitle should also be saved as a style so you can apply it to other text. You also decide to create a character style that you use on specific text to make it stand out from other text in the paragraph. Creating the paragraph and character styles enables you to duplicate the formatting without having to remember all of the different attributes you used previously. Refer to Figure 2.30 as you complete Step 3.

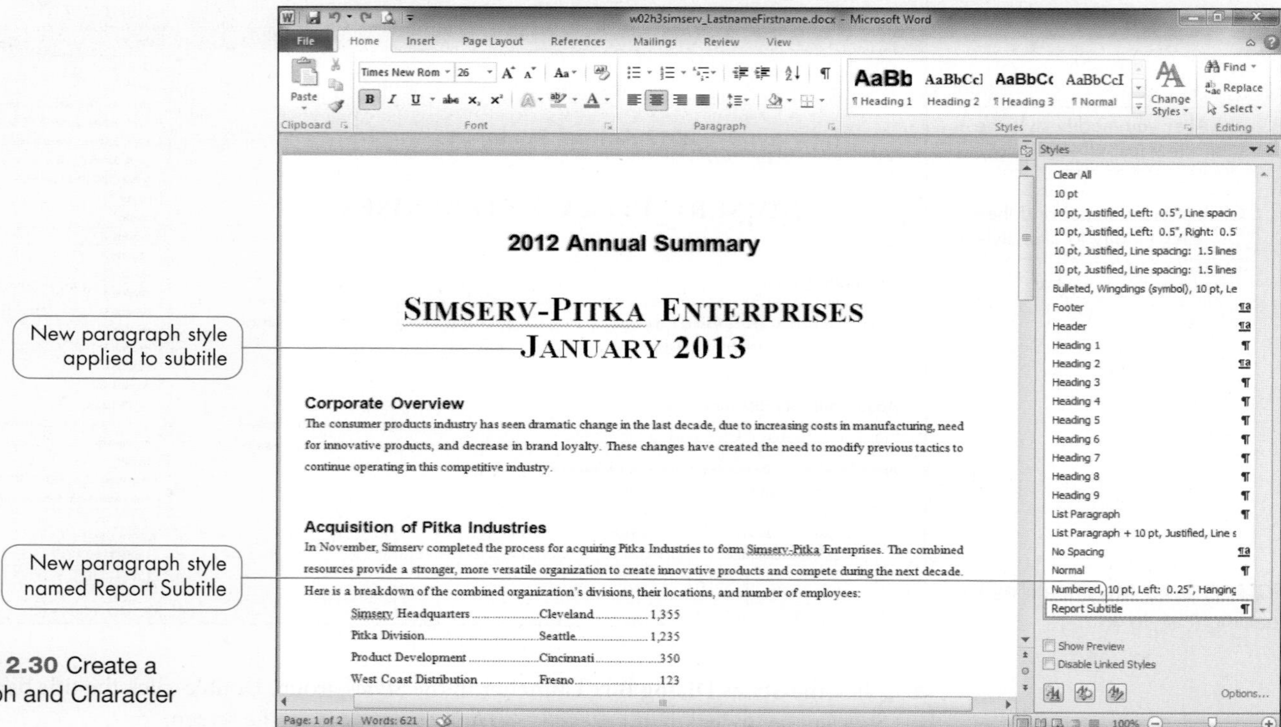

FIGURE 2.30 Create a Paragraph and Character Style ➤

a. Move the insertion point to the left side of the subtitle *Simserv-Pitka Enterprises* that displays just below the main title. Point to the description for this subtitle on the Styles Pane (you may only be able to see the first or last few format effects listed), hover your mouse over the description to display the arrow, click the arrow, and then select **Modify Style** to display the Modify Style dialog box.

   The Styles task pane displays the specifications for this style. You have created a new style by changing the font options earlier, but the style is not yet named.

b. Click in the **Name box** in the Properties area, and then type **Report Subtitle** as the name of the new style. Click **OK**.

c. Select the third line of the document, *January 2013*, and then click **Report Subtitle** in the Styles pane to apply the new style to this line of text.

The two lines of text that make up the subtitle of the document share the same formatting, as shown in Figure 2.30. However, the shadow special effect does not save. You will modify the style to add it back and it will then display on all text that uses the Report Subtitle style.

d. Hover your mouse over the *Report Subtitle* style until the arrow displays, and then click **Modify**. Click **Format**, and then click **Text Effects**. Click **Shadow**, click **Presets**, and then click **Offset Left** (third row, third column). Click the **Close button**. Click **OK** to close the dialog box.

Notice the shadow effect displays on both lines of text that use the Report Subtitle style. Once you apply a style, any modifications to that style will automatically show on all text that uses the style; you do not have to change text individually.

e. Select the name *Dewey A. Larson* that appears within the *2012 Management Changes* paragraph. Click **Bold** and **Italic** in the Font group. Click **Grow Font** in the Font group two times to increase the size to **12**.

f. Click **New Style** on the bottom of the Styles pane, and then type **Emphasize** as the name of the style.

g. Click the **Style type arrow**, and then select **Character**. Click **OK** to close the dialog box.

The style named *Emphasize* is listed in the Style pane and can be used throughout your document. You create and use this character style because you only want to use it on certain words, not entire paragraphs.

h. Select the name *Jerri Reed*, also in the *2012 Management Changes* paragraph. Click **Emphasize** in the Quick Style gallery to apply the newly created Emphasize character style to the selected text.

You can also select this character style from the Styles pane.

i. Close the Styles task pane and save the document.

STEP 4 SELECT THE OUTLINE VIEW

You want to view the structure of the document quickly by looking only at titles and paragraph headings, so you invoke the Outline view in Word. By viewing the outline, you determine you should move one paragraph up, and you quickly make it so by using the Outline tools on the Ribbon. Refer to Figure 2.31 as you complete Step 4.

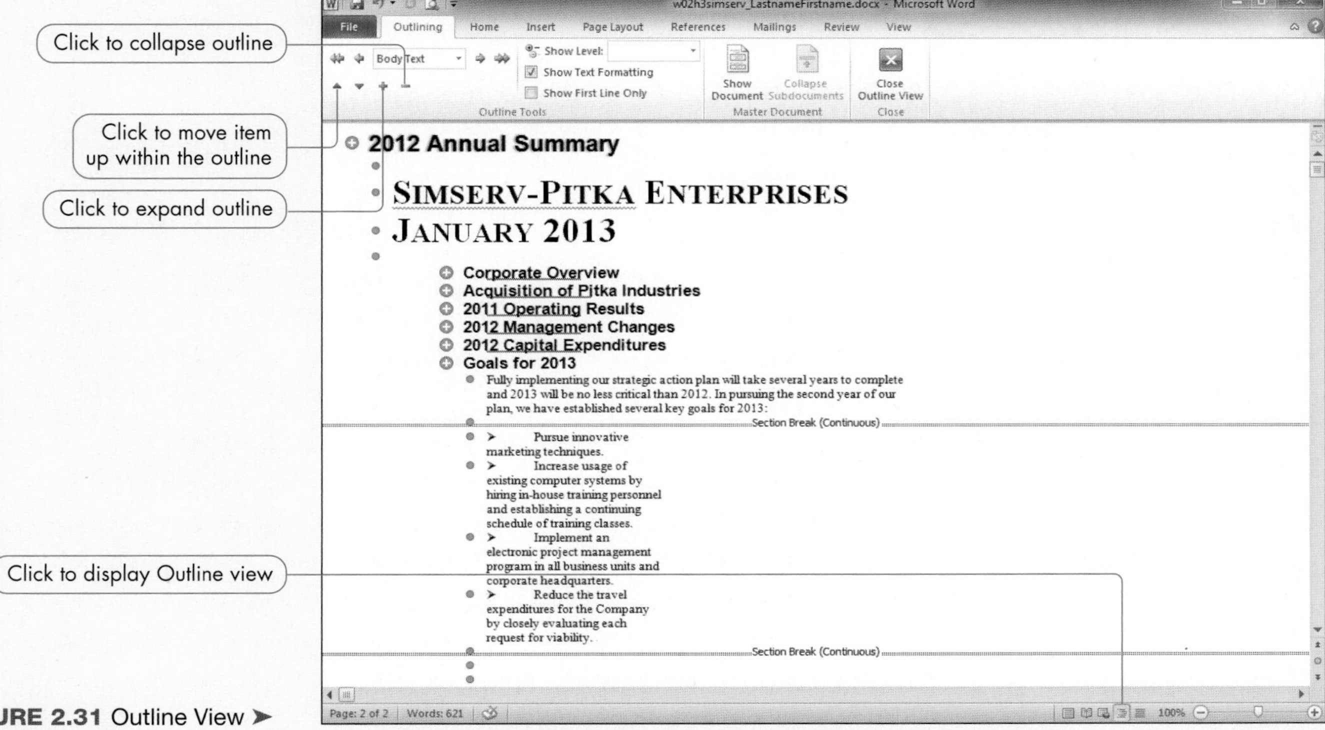

FIGURE 2.31 Outline View ➤

a. Click the **View tab**, then click **Outline** to display the document in Outline view.

b. Place the insertion point to the left of the first paragraph heading, *Corporate Overview*, and then select the rest of the document. Click the **Outlining tab**, if necessary, and then click **Collapse** in the Outline Tools group.

   The entire document collapses so that only the headings display.

c. Click in the heading titled *Goals for 2013*, and then click **Expand** in the Outline Tools group to expand the subordinate paragraphs under this heading.

d. Select the paragraph heading *2012 Management Changes*, and then click **Move Up** in the Outline Tools group one time.

   You moved the paragraph above the paragraph that precedes it in the outline. It now displays just below the *2011 Operating Results* paragraph, as shown in Figure 2.31. Note that you also can drag and drop a selected paragraph.

e. Click **Print Layout** in the status bar so you can view the entire document.

f. Save the document and keep it onscreen if you plan to continue with the next Hands-On Exercise. If not, close the document and exit Word.

Graphical Objects

One of the most exciting features of Word is its graphic capabilities. You can use clip art, images, drawings, scanned photographs, and symbols to visually enhance brochures, newsletters, announcements, and reports. After inserting a graphical object, you can adjust size, choose placement, and perform other formatting options.

One of the most exciting features of Word is its graphic capabilities. You can use clip art, images, drawings, and scanned photographs to visually enhance brochures, newsletters, announcements, and reports.

In this section, you will format the image by changing the height and width, applying a text-wrapping style, applying a quick style, and adjusting graphic properties. Finally, you will insert symbols in a document.

Formatting a Graphical Object

In addition to the collection of clip art and pictures that you can access from Word, you also can insert your own pictures into a document. If you have a scanner or digital camera attached to your computer, you can scan or download a picture for use in Word. After you insert the picture, many commands are available that you can use to format the picture or any other graphical element you use in the document. Remember that graphical elements should enhance a document, not overpower it.

Adjust the Height and Width of an Image

When you insert an image in a document, it comes in a predefined size. For example, the graphic image in Figure 2.32 was very large and took up much space on the page before it was resized. Most times, you need to adjust an image's size so it fits within the document and does not greatly increase the document file size.

Word provides different tools you can use to adjust the height or width of an image, depending on how exact you want the measurements. The Picture Tools Format tab contains Height and Width commands that enable you to specify exact measurements. You can use ***sizing handles***, the small circles and squares that appear around a selected object, to size an object by clicking and dragging any one of the handles. When you use the circular sizing handles in the corner of a graphic to adjust the height (or width), Word also adjusts the width (or height) simultaneously. If needed, hold down Shift while dragging the corner-sizing handle to maintain the correct proportion of the image. If you use square sizing handles on the right, left, top, or bottom, you adjust that measurement without regard to any other sides.

Sizing handles are the small circles and squares that appear around a selected object and enable you to adjust the height and width of an object.

For more precise measurements use the scale or scaling feature. Similar to the effects on text mentioned earlier in the chapter, you can adjust the height or width of an image by a percentage of its original size. The scale adjustment is located in the Size dialog box, which you display by clicking the Size Dialog Box Launcher on the Format tab.

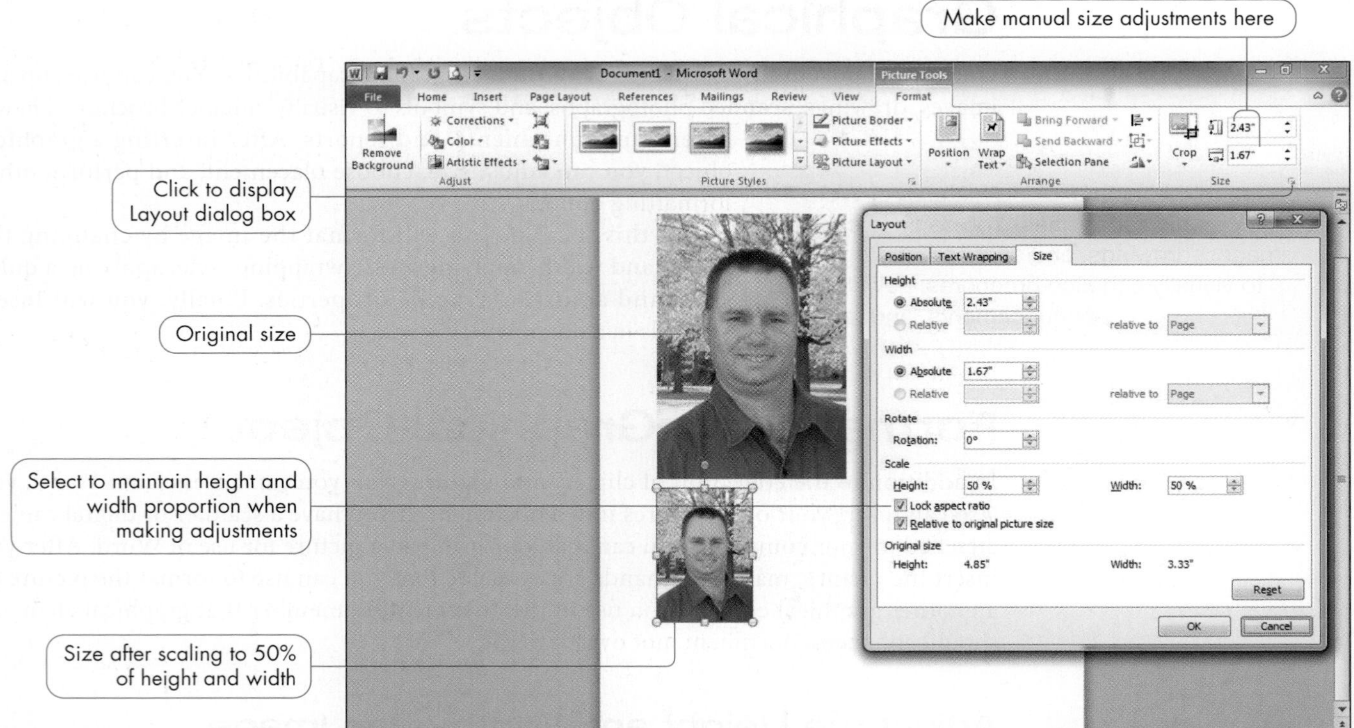
Make manual size adjustments here
Click to display Layout dialog box
Original size
Select to maintain height and width proportion when making adjustments
Size after scaling to 50% of height and width

FIGURE 2.32 Adjusting the Size of a Graphic Object ➤

Adjust Text Wrapping

Text wrapping style refers to the way text wraps around an image.

When you first insert an image, Word treats it as a character in the line of text, which leaves a lot of empty space on the left or right side of the image. You may want it to align differently, perhaps enabling text to display very tightly around the object or even placing it behind the text. ***Text wrapping style*** refers to the way text wraps around an image. Table 2.4 describes the different options, which may also display as Wrap Text options.

TABLE 2.4 Text Wrapping Styles

Wrap Text Style	Description
In Line with Text	Graphic displays on the line where inserted so that as you add or delete text, causing the line of text to move, the image moves with it.
Square	Enables text to wrap around the graphic frame that surrounds the image.
Tight	Enables text to wrap tightly around the outer edges of the image itself instead of the frame.
Through	Select this option to wrap text around the perimeter and inside any open portions of the object.
Top and Bottom	Text wraps to the top and bottom of the image frame, but no text appears on the sides.
Behind Text	Enables the image to display behind the text in such a way that the image appears to float directly behind the text and does not move if text is inserted or deleted.
In Front of Text	Enables the image to display on top of the text in such a way that the image appears to float directly on top of the text and does not move if text is inserted or deleted.

Apply Picture Quick Styles

The **Picture Styles** gallery contains preformatted options that can be applied to a graphical object.

Word includes a ***Picture Styles*** gallery that contains many preformatted picture formats. The gallery of styles you can apply to a picture or clip art is extensive, and you can modify the style after you apply it. The quick styles provide a valuable resource if you want to improve the appearance of a graphic but are not familiar with graphic design and format tools. For example, after you insert a graphic, with one click you can choose a style from the Quick Styles gallery that adds a border and displays a reflection of the picture. You might want to select a style that changes the shape of your graphic to an octagon, or select a style that applies a 3-D effect to the image. To apply a quick style, select the graphical object, then choose a quick style from the Picture Styles group on the Picture Tools Format tab. Other style formatting options, such as Soft Edges or 3-D Rotation, are listed in Picture Effects on the Picture Styles group as shown in Figure 2.33.

FIGURE 2.33 Quick Changes Using the Picture Styles Gallery ➤

Adjust Graphic Properties

Cropping (or to **crop**) is the process of trimming the edges of an image or other graphical object.

After you insert a graphic or an image, you might find that you need to edit it before using a picture style. One of the most common changes is to ***crop*** (also called ***cropping***), which is the process of trimming edges or other portions of an image or other graphical object that you do not wish to display. Cropping enables you to call attention to a specific area of a graphical element while omitting any unnecessary detail, as shown in Figure 2.34. When you add images to enhance a document, you may find clip art that has more objects than you desire, or you may find an image that has damaged edges that you do not wish to appear in your document. You can solve the problems with these graphics by cropping. The cropping tool is located in the Size group on the Format tab.

FIGURE 2.34 Cropping a graphic ➤

Even though cropping enables you to adjust the amount of a picture that displays, it does not actually delete the portions that are cropped out. Nor does cropping reduce the size of the graphic and the Word document in which it displays. Therefore, if you want to reduce the size of an image so it does not greatly increase the size of the file, you should not use only the crop tool.

Contrast is the difference between light and dark areas of an image.

Brightness is the ratio between lightness and darkness of an image.

Other common adjustments to a graphical object include contrast and/or brightness. Adjusting the ***contrast*** increases or decreases the difference in dark and light areas of the image. Adjusting the ***brightness*** lightens or darkens the overall image. These adjustments often are made on a picture taken with a digital camera in poor lighting or if a clip art image is too bright or dull to match other objects in your document. Adjusting contrast or brightness can improve the visibility of subjects in a picture. You may want to increase contrast for a dramatic effect or lower contrast to soften an image. The Brightness and Contrast adjustment is combined in the Adjust group on the Format tab, as shown in Figure 2.35.

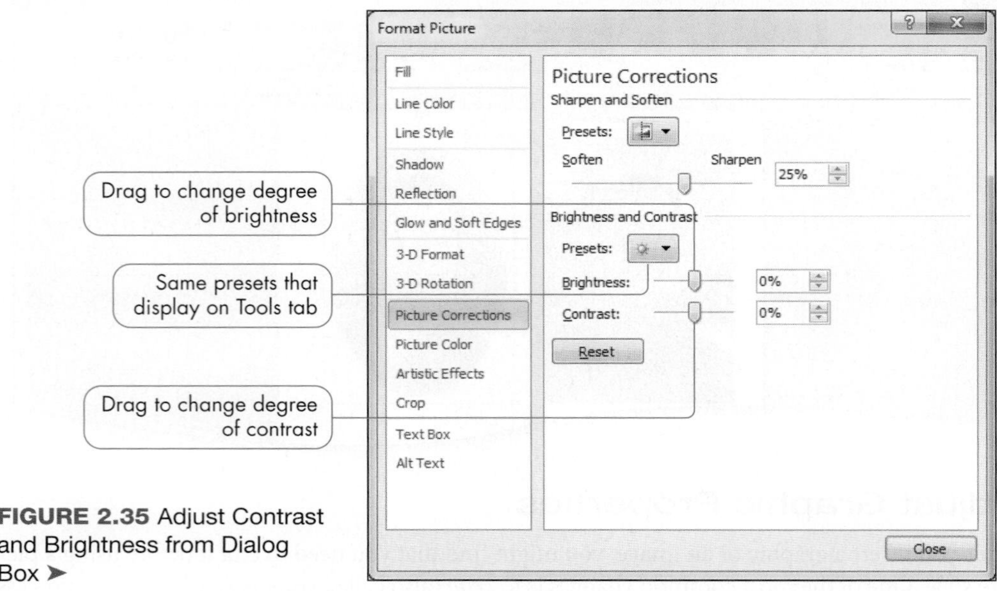

FIGURE 2.35 Adjust Contrast and Brightness from Dialog Box ➤

Even though graphical objects add a great deal of visual enhancement to a document, they also can increase the file size of the document. If you add several graphics to a document, you should view the file size before you copy or save it to a portable storage device, and then confirm the device has enough empty space to hold the large file. Additional consideration should be given to files you send as e-mail attachments. Many people have space limitations in their mailboxes, and a document that contains several graphics can fill their space or take a long time to download. To decrease the size of a graphic, you can use the ***Compress*** feature, which reduces the size of an object. After you select a graphical object, click the Compress Pictures command in the Adjust group on the Picture Tools Format tab to display the Compress Pictures dialog box. Here, you can select from options that enable you to reduce the size of the graphical elements, thus reducing the size of the file when you save. You can also select the option to compress all pictures in the document.

Compress reduces the file size of an object.

New to Office 2010 is the ability to remove the background or other portions of a picture you do not want to keep. When you select a picture and click the Remove Background tool in the Adjust group on the Format tab, Word creates automatic marquee selection area in the picture that determines the ***background***, or area to be removed, and the ***foreground***, or area to be kept. Word identifies the background selection with magenta coloring. You can then adjust Word's automatic selection by marking areas you want to keep, marking areas you want to remove, and deleting any markings you do not want. You can discard any changes you have made or keep your changes.

The **background** of a picture is the portion of a picture to be removed.

The **foreground** of a picture is the portion of the picture to be kept.

The Picture Tools Format tab offers many graphic editing features, some of which are described in Table 2.5.

TABLE 2.5 Graphic Editing Features		
Feature	**Button**	**Description**
Height	1.5"	Height of an object in inches.
Width	1.37"	Width of an object in inches.
Crop		Remove unwanted portions of the object from top, bottom, left, or right to adjust size.
Align		Adjust edges of object to line up on right or left margin or center between margins.
Group		Process of selecting multiple objects so you can move and format them together.
Rotate		Ability to change the position of an object by rotating it around its own center.
Wrap Text		Refers to the way text wraps around an object.
Position		Specify location on page where object will reside.
Picture Border		The outline surrounding an object; it can be formatted using color, shapes, or width, or can be set as invisible.
Picture Effects		Enhance an object by adding effects such as shadow, bevel, or reflection.
Compress Pictures		Reduce the file size of an object.
Corrections		Increase or decrease brightness of an object. Increase or decrease difference between black and white colors of an object (contrast).
Color		Apply color alterations for effect, such as grayscale, sepia, or match document content colors.
Artistic Effects		Apply effects that make a picture appear as a painting or sketch.
Remove Background		Remove unwanted background in a picture. Enables customization to define unwanted areas.

Inserting Symbols into a Document

The Symbol command enables you to enter typographic symbols and/or foreign language characters into a document in place of ordinary typing—for example, ® rather than (R), © rather than (c), ½ and ¼ rather than 1/2 and 1/4, and the accented letter é in résumé. These special characters give a document a very professional look.

The installation of Microsoft Office adds a variety of fonts onto your computer, each of which contains various symbols that can be inserted into a document. Selecting "normal text," however, as was done in Figure 2.36, provides access to the accented characters as well as other common symbols. Other fonts—especially the Wingdings, Webdings, and Symbol fonts—contain special symbols, including the Windows logo. Each font contains a variety of symbols that are actually pictures. You can insert any of these symbols into a document as text, or custom bullets, or you can even select the character and enlarge the point size, change the color, then copy the modified character to create a truly original document.

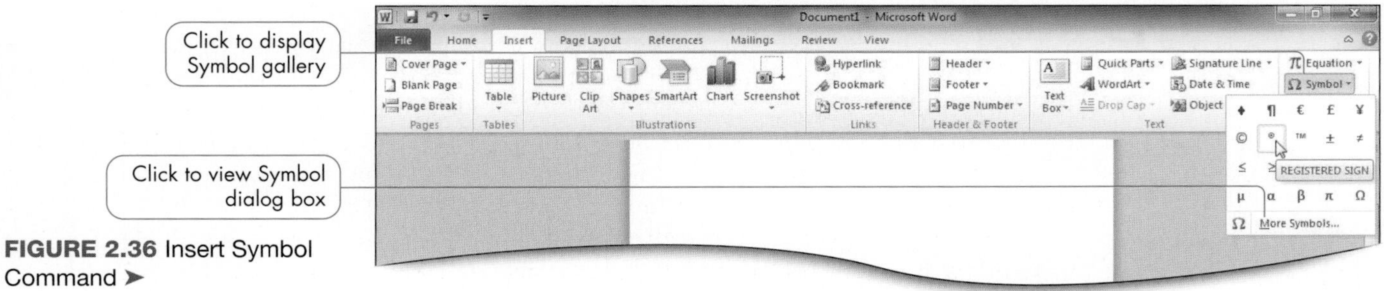

FIGURE 2.36 Insert Symbol Command ➤

Quick Concepts Check

1. Describe two methods to modify the height and width of an image.
2. List and describe at least five different text wrapping styles that might be applied to a graphical object.
3. What feature enables you to change the appearance of a graphical object with one click and where do you find it on the Ribbon?
4. Describe three formatting effects which you can apply to a graphical image to change its appearance.
5. Describe the steps you take to insert a symbol into a document from the Symbol dialog box.

4 Graphical Objects

To finalize the Annual Summary for Simserv-Pitka Industries, you decide to include pictures of the two new executives. As is the case with most pictures inserted into a document, they need to be resized and formatted so they will display next to the paragraphs where you insert them. You also insert a euro symbol into the document, and finish by inserting a page number in the footer.

Skills covered: Insert Picture Objects • Change Picture Formatting • Insert a Symbol

STEP 1 INSERT PICTURE OBJECTS

The new executives hired to lead Simserv-Pitka are important assets to the company, so you want to honor them by placing their pictures in the Annual Summary. You display the picture of each person beside the paragraph that describes his or her position and credentials. Refer to Figure 2.37 as you complete Step 1.

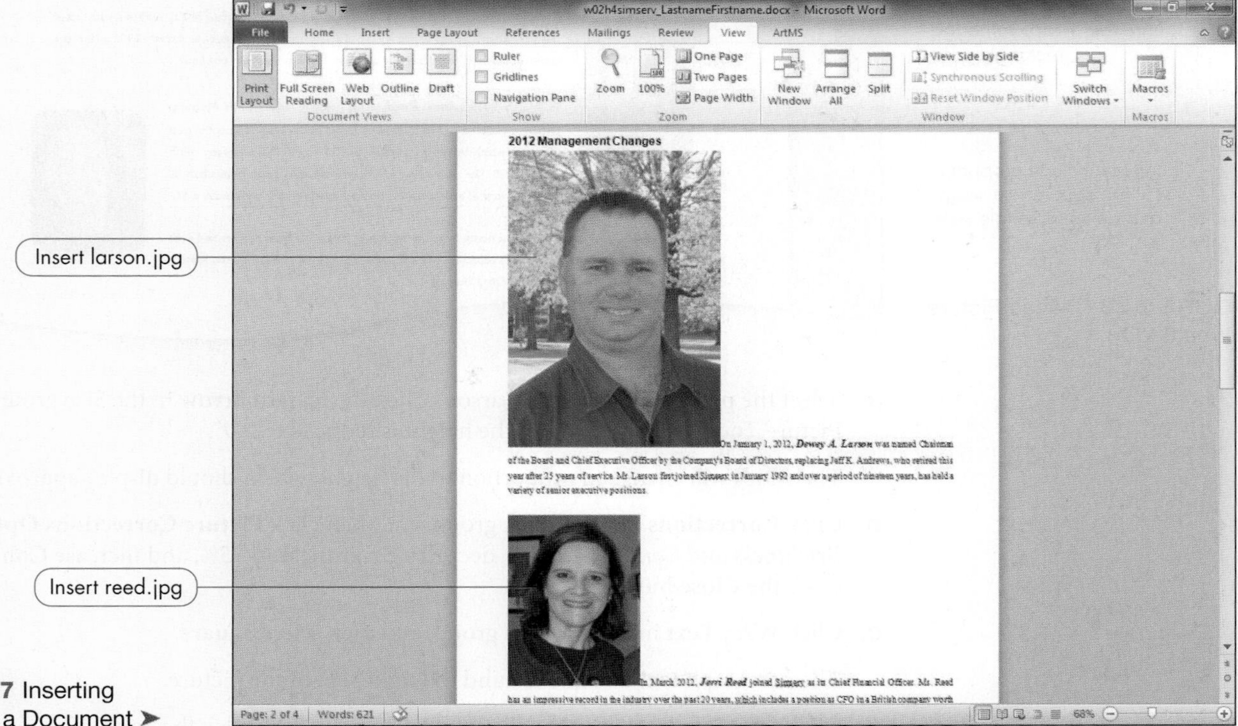

FIGURE 2.37 Inserting Pictures into a Document ➤

a. Open *w02h3simserv_LastnameFirstname* if you closed it at the end of Hands-On Exercise 3, and save it as **w02h4simserv_LastnameFirstname**, changing *h3* to *h4*.

b. Click to the left of the *2012 Management Changes* paragraph heading. Press **Ctrl+Enter** to insert a page break. Click the **Insert tab**, and then click **Picture** in the Illustrations group. Navigate to the location where files for this book are stored, and then double-click **larson.jpg** to insert the picture of Dewey A. Larson into your document.

> **TROUBLESHOOTING:** If the graphic files for these photos do not display, click the File type arrow, and then select All Files **(*.*)** so all file types display rather than just Word documents. Also, be certain you are clicking Insert Picture, not File, Open, to insert the graphic files.

c. Click to the left of the text *In March 2012* in the *2012 Management Changes* section. Press **Enter** to insert a blank line. Click the **Insert tab**, if necessary, and then click **Picture**. This time, double-click **reed.jpg** to insert the picture of Jerri Reed into your document. Compare your results to Figure 2.37.

d. Save the document.

STEP 2 CHANGE PICTURE FORMATTING

After you insert the pictures, you must adjust them, by changing size or cropping, so they are not disproportionate in size to the rest of the text in the document. You also want to adjust the wrapping style of each picture so you have the control you need to position them with the paragraphs they support. You correct colors as needed, and finally, for effect, you decide to add a border around the pictures. Refer to Figure 2.38 as you complete Step 2.

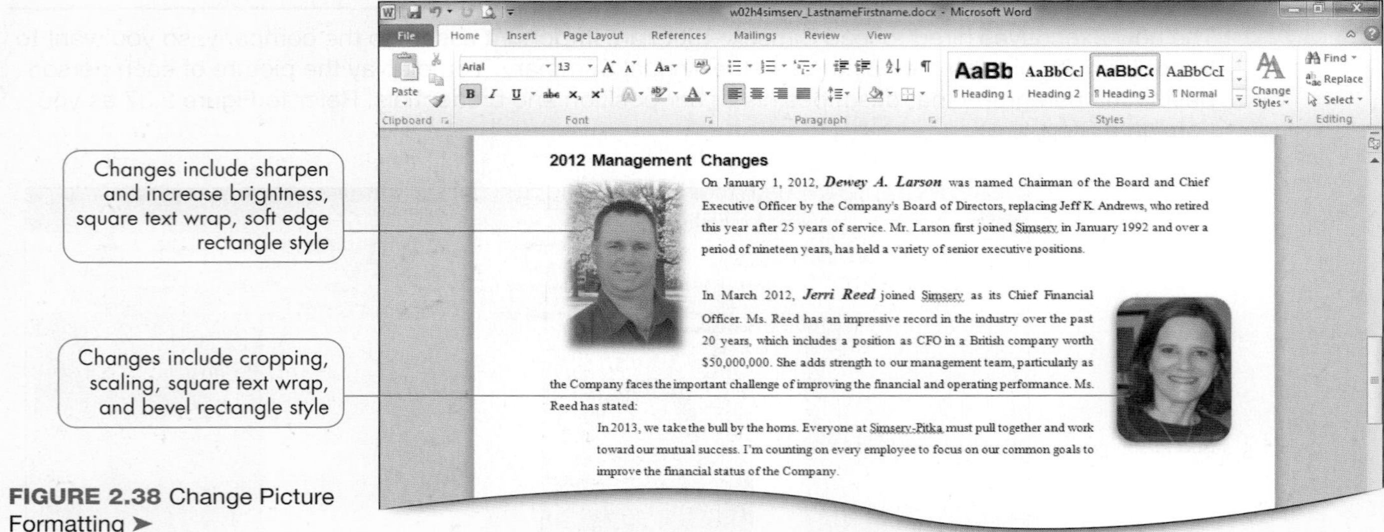

FIGURE 2.38 Change Picture Formatting ➤

a. Select the picture of Dewey A. Larson. Click the **Height arrow** in the Size group on the Picture Tools Format tab until the height is reduced to *2.0"*.

The width will change in proportion to the height, which should display approximately 1.38".

b. Click **Corrections** in the Adjust group, and then click **Picture Corrections Options**. In the *Brightness and Contrast* section, decrease **Brightness** to *–5%*, and increase **Contrast** to *5%*. Click the **Close button**.

c. Click **WrapText** in the Arrange group, and then select **Square**.

The paragraph text displays around the right side of the picture.

d. Click the **More button** in the Picture Styles group to display the entire Picture quick style gallery. Click **Soft Edge Rectangle** (second row, first column).

e. Use your mouse to drag the picture down slightly so the paragraph heading displays on the left margin and the picture displays on the left of the paragraph text only.

Nudging a Picture

You can use the arrow keys on your keyboard to move a graphical image around a document in very small increments.

f. Click **Compress Pictures** in the Adjust group. Click **Apply only to this picture** to deselect the option, and then click **OK**.

Most digital picture files are quite large and can increase the size of the document substantially when you insert them. The Compression feature is vital to use in that situation. This picture of Dewey A. Larson is not extremely large, but you decide to compress the picture and make sure the size of the document stays small. By deselecting the option in this step, all graphics in the document will compress as well.

g. Select the picture of Jerri Reed. Click the **Size Dialog Box Launcher**. In the *Scale* section, click **Lock aspect ratio**, if necessary. Click the **height arrow** until *70%* displays. Click **OK**.

Because you locked the aspect ratio, which preserves proportions as the picture is resized, the Width percentage changed automatically when you reduced the height.

h. Click **Crop**, and then drag the crop lines inward from right, left, and bottom until she displays from the shoulders up. When complete, press **Crop** again to remove the crop lines.

The size of the picture should be approximately 1.6" by 1.25". You crop out the bill of a cap worn by a person who was standing beside her and also remove excess space on the left and bottom of the picture.

> **TROUBLESHOOTING:** If you want to revise the crop, click the picture, and then click Crop. The crop lines and original picture size display, and you can move the lines to a new position. Click Crop again to remove all crop lines.

i. Click **Wrap Text** in the Arrange group, and then click **Square**. Drag the picture of Jerri Reed to the right side of the paragraph that introduces her.

j. Click the **More button** in the Picture Styles group to display the entire Picture quick style gallery. Click **Bevel Rectangle** (fifth row, first column). Compare your work to Figure 2.38.

k. Save the document.

STEP 3 INSERT A SYMBOL

The financial manager at Simserv-Pitka reminds you that it is appropriate to use the correct currency symbols when referring to monetary assets in a document such as this, especially when the currency is not U.S. dollars. To conform to that rule, you change the symbol used to reference the value of a European company to the euro instead of using the dollar symbol. To complete the document, you insert a page number in the footer of the document. Even though it is short, page numbering helps the reader follow the order of the document. Refer to Figure 2.39 as you complete Step 3.

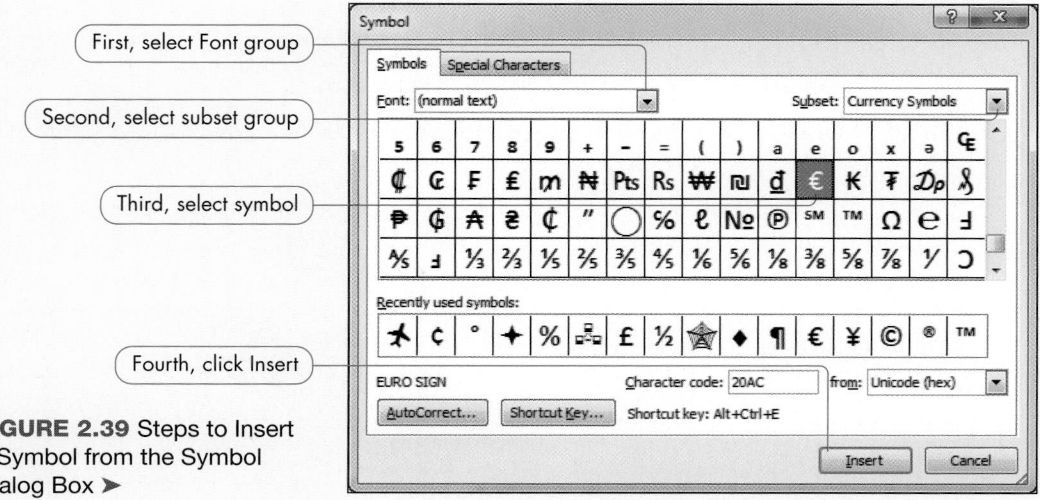

FIGURE 2.39 Steps to Insert a Symbol from the Symbol Dialog Box ➤

a. Select $ in the second sentence in the paragraph that describes the new CFO, Jerri Reed. Press **Delete** to remove the dollar sign.

b. Click the **Insert tab**, and then click **Symbol** in the Symbols group. Click **More Symbols** to view the Symbol dialog box, as seen in Figure 2.39.

c. Change the Font group to **(normal text)**, if necessary, and then change the Subset to **Currency Symbols**. Click the **Euro sign (€)**, click **Insert**, and then click the **Close button**.

When you click Insert, the symbol appears in your document at the location of your cursor. While the Symbol dialog box is open, you can return to your document, move your cursor, then return to the symbol dialog box and insert other symbols before you close.

d. Click **Page Number** in the Header and Footer group, hover the mouse over *Bottom of Page*, and then scroll down and select **Accent Bar 4**. Click **Close Header and Footer**.

e. Save and close *w02h4simserve_LastnameFirstname*, and submit based on your instructor's directions.

CHAPTER OBJECTIVES REVIEW

After reading this chapter, you have accomplished the following objectives:

1. **Apply font attributes through the Font dialog box.** Formatting occurs at the character, paragraph, or section level. The Font dialog box enables you to change the spacing of the characters and you can change attributes including font size, font color, underline color, and effects. Use the character spacing options to control horizontal spacing between letters and also adjust the scale, position, and kerning of characters. You can quickly modify the capitalization and text highlight color from the Home tab.
2. **Control word wrap.** Occasionally, text wraps in an undesirable location in your document, or you just want to keep words together for better readability. To keep hyphenated words together on one line, use a nonbreaking hyphen to replace the regular hyphen. You also can keep words together on one line by inserting a nonbreaking space instead of using the spacebar.
3. **Set off paragraphs with tabs, borders, lists, and columns.** You can change appearance and add interest to documents by using paragraph formatting options. Tabs enable you to set markers in the document to use for aligning text. Borders and shading enable you to use boxes and/or shading to highlight an area of your document. A bulleted or numbered list helps to organize information by emphasizing or ordering important topics. Columns add interest by formatting text into side-by-side vertical blocks of text.
4. **Apply paragraph formats.** The Paragraph dialog box contains many formatting options, such as alignment. Another option to adjust the distance from margins is indention. Line spacing determines the space between lines in a document, such as single or double, and can be customized. You also can specify an amount of space to insert before or after a paragraph, which is more efficient than pressing Enter. Widow/Orphan control prevents a single line from displaying at the top or bottom of a page, separate from the rest of a paragraph.
5. **Understand styles.** A style is a set of formatting instructions that has been saved under a distinct name. Styles are created at the character or paragraph level and provide a consistent appearance to similar elements throughout a document. Styles provide the foundation to use other tools such as outlines and the table of contents.
6. **Create and modify styles.** You can modify any existing style to change the formatting of all text defined by that style. You can even create a new style for use in the current or any other document.
7. **Format a graphical object.** Graphics are often added to enhance a document. After you insert one, a variety of tools can make it fit and display where you want—such as changing height and width, scaling, or cropping unwanted portions. You can position the graphic more exactly by wrapping text, and you can use the Picture Styles gallery to add borders or reflections. You can refine imperfections or add creative touches to pictures using features to sharpen, change brightness, and adjust contrast. You can compress a graphic to reduce its size as well as the size of the document.
8. **Insert symbols into a document.** Insert Symbol makes it easy to place typographic characters in a document. The symbols can be taken from any font and can be displayed in any point size.

KEY TERMS

Background ***p.208***
Bar tab ***p.181***
Border ***p.182***
Brightness ***p.208***
Bulleted list ***p.183***
Center tab ***p.181***
Change Case ***p.175***
Character spacing ***p.174***
Character style ***p.195***
Column ***p.184***
Compress ***p.208***
Contrast ***p.208***
Cropping or crop ***p.207***
Decimal tab ***p.181***
First line indent ***p.187***
Font ***p.172***
Foreground ***p.208***
Hanging indent ***p.187***
Hidden text ***p.174***
Highlighter ***p.175***
Horizontal alignment ***p.186***
Kerning ***p.174***
Leader character ***p.181***
Left tab ***p.181***
Line spacing ***p.187***
Monospaced typeface ***p.172***
Multilevel list ***p.183***
Nonbreaking hyphen ***p.176***
Nonbreaking space ***p.176***
Numbered list ***p.183***
OpenType ***p.174***
Orphan ***p.188***
Outline view ***p.198***
Paragraph spacing ***p.187***
Paragraph style ***p.195***
Picture Styles ***p.207***
Position ***p.174***
Proportional typeface ***p.172***
Right tab ***p.181***
Sans serif typeface ***p.172***
Scale or scaling ***p.174***
Serif typeface ***p.172***
Shading ***p.182***
Sizing handles ***p.205***
Style ***p.195***
Tab ***p.180***
Text wrapping style ***p.206***
Type style ***p.172***
Typeface ***p.172***
Typography ***p.172***
Widow ***p.188***

MULTIPLE CHOICE

1. Which of the following is not true about typeface?
   - (a) A serif typeface helps the eye connect one letter with the next.
   - (b) A monospaced typeface allocates space according to the width of the character.
   - (c) A san serif typeface is more effective with titles and headlines.
   - (d) A typeface is a complete set of characters.

2. What is the easiest way to change the alignment of five paragraphs scattered throughout a document, each of which is formatted with the same style?
   - (a) Select the paragraphs individually, then click the appropriate alignment button.
   - (b) Use CTRL to select all of the paragraphs, then click the appropriate alignment button on the Home tab.
   - (c) Change the format of the existing style, which changes the paragraphs.
   - (d) Retype the paragraphs according to the new specifications.

3. If you want to be sure the date June 21, 2012, does not word wrap what should you do?
   - (a) Use a nonbreaking hyphen in place of the comma.
   - (b) Use expanded spacing on the whole number.
   - (c) Use nonbreaking spaces between the month, date, and year.
   - (d) Press Ctrl+Enter before you type the date.

4. Which wrap style enables text to wrap around the graphic frame that surrounds the image?
   - (a) Square
   - (b) Tight
   - (c) Behind Text
   - (d) Right and Left

5. A(n) _________ occurs when the first line of a paragraph is isolated at the bottom of a page and the rest of the paragraph continues on the next page.
   - (a) widow
   - (b) section break
   - (c) footer
   - (d) orphan

6. Which of the following is a false statement about the Outline view?
   - (a) It can be collapsed to display only headings.
   - (b) It can be expanded to show the entire document.
   - (c) It requires the application of styles.
   - (d) It is used to create a multilevel list.

7. What happens if you modify the Body Text style in a Word document?
   - (a) Only the paragraph where the insertion point is located is changed.
   - (b) All paragraphs in the document will be changed.
   - (c) Only those paragraphs formatted with the Body Text style will be changed.
   - (d) It is not possible to change a Word default style such as Body Text.

8. If you want to display text in side-by-side sections, what feature should you use to format the text?
   - (a) Styles
   - (b) Borders
   - (c) Multilevel lists
   - (d) Columns

9. Which of the following is a true statement regarding indents?
   - (a) Indents are measured from the edge of the page.
   - (b) The left, right, and first line indents must be set to the same value.
   - (c) The insertion point can be anywhere in the paragraph when indents are set.
   - (d) Indents must be set within the Paragraph dialog box.

10. The spacing in an existing multipage document is changed from single spacing to double spacing throughout the document. What can you say about the number of hard and soft page breaks before and after the formatting change?
    - (a) The number of soft page breaks is the same, but the number and/or position of the hard page breaks are different.
    - (b) The number of hard page breaks is the same, but the number and/or position of the soft page breaks are different.
    - (c) The number and position of both hard and soft page breaks are the same.
    - (d) The number and position of both hard and soft page breaks are different.

PRACTICE EXERCISES

1 Engler, Guccione, & Partners

You are the Marketing Director for the Architect firm Engler, Guccione, & Partners. Lately, the firm has less work due to a reduction in construction spending. In order to bring in new business, you design a marketing plan to pursue new customers by advertising your ability to consult in legal cases. The plan is typed and in a raw form, so you use formatting features to enhance the document and impress the partners with your own skills. This exercise follows the same set of skills as used in Hands-On Exercises 1, 2, 3, and 4 in the chapter. Refer to Figure 2.40 as you complete this exercise.

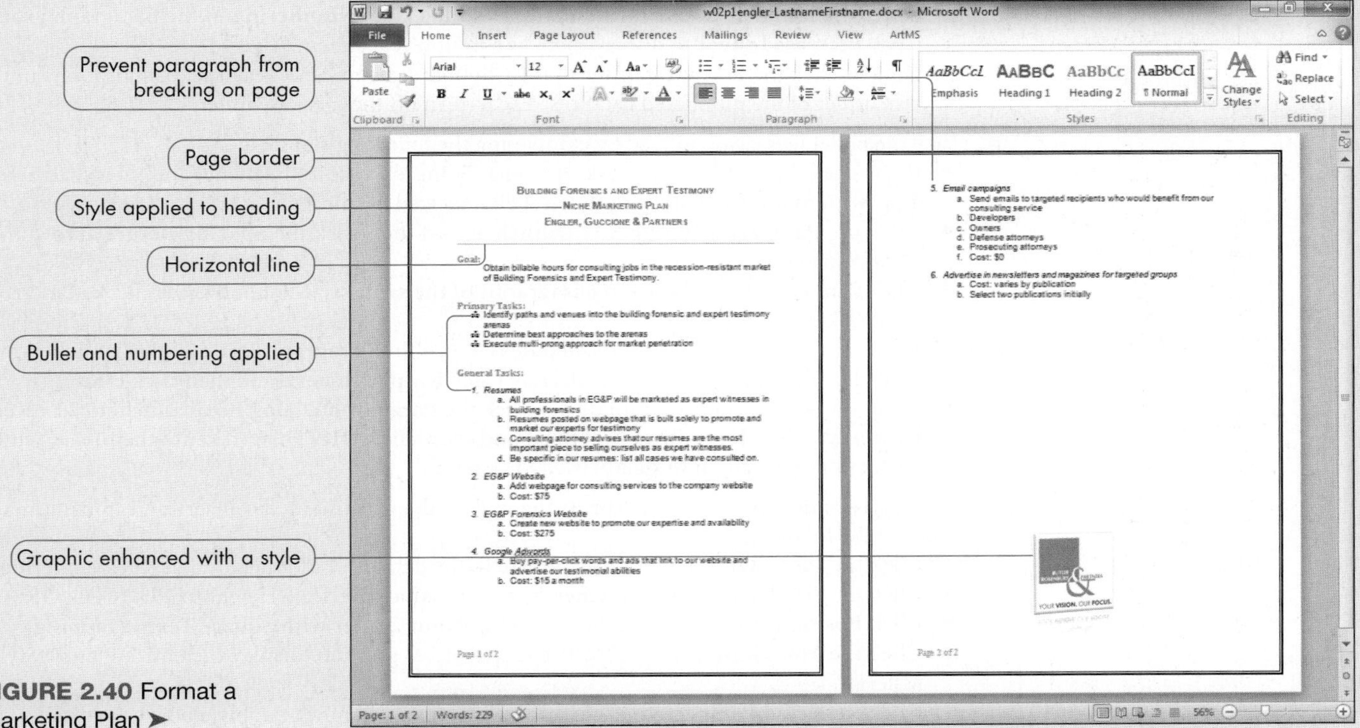

FIGURE 2.40 Format a Marketing Plan ➤

a. Open *w02p1engler* and save the document as **w02p1engler_LastnameFirstname**.

b. Add a page border around the text by completing the following steps:
   - Click the **Home tab**, and then click the **Borders arrow** in the Paragraph group.
   - Select **Borders and Shading** to open the dialog box.
   - Click the **Page Border tab**, and then click **Box** in the *Setting* section.
   - Scroll down and select the **ninth** style—a double line border with a thick line outside and a thin line inside.
   - Click **OK** to close the Borders and Shading dialog box.

c. Click **Ctrl+A** to select the whole document. Click the **Font arrow** in the Font group on the Home tab, and then select **Arial**.

d. Select the first three lines, which make up the document title, and complete the following steps:
   - Click **Heading 1** in the Quick Styles gallery.
   - Right-click the **Heading 1 entry** in the Quick styles pane, and then select **Modify**.
   - Change the alignment to **Center**.
   - Change the font to **Arial**.
   - Click **Format, Font**, and then click **Small caps**. Click **OK** to close the Font dialog box.
   - Click **Format, Paragraph**, and then click the **Indents and Spacing tab**, if necessary.
   - Reduce the **Spacing Before** to **0 pt**.
   - Increase **Spacing After** to **6 pt**.

- Click **OK** to close the Paragraph dialog box.
- Click **OK** to close the Modify Style dialog box.

e. Place the insertion point on the blank line that follows the third line of the title. Click the **Borders and Shading arrow**, and then click **Horizontal Line**.

f. Select the three lines under the *Primary Tasks:* paragraph heading, and then click the **Bullets arrow** in the Paragraph group. Click **Define New Bullet**, click **Symbol** to open the Symbol dialog box, and then select **Webdings** from the **Font list**. Select the symbol that resembles a computer network (character code 194) located in the third row, third column, and then click **OK**. Click **OK** to create the bullet list, and then close the Define New Bullet dialog box.

g. Create a numbered list for the General Tasks by completing the following steps:
   - Right-click the italicized word *Resumes* directly under *General Tasks*, point to *Styles* in the menu, and then click **Select Text with Similar Formatting** to select all italicized headings.
   - Click the **Numbering arrow**, and then select the format that displays lowercase alphabet numbering (*a.*, *b.*, *c.*).
   - Select the four sub-points for *Resumes*, and then click **Numbering** in the paragraph group. Click **Increase Indent** to display them as a multilevel list item.
   - Double-click the **Format Painter** in the Clipboard group. Select each set of sub-points in the remainder of the numbered list. Press **Esc** to turn off the format painter.

h. Make the bullet lists easier to read by completing the following steps:
   - Right-click the first General Task, *Resumes*. Point to *Styles* in the menu, and then click **Select Text with Similar Formatting** to select all italicized headings.
   - Click the **Paragraph Dialog Box Launcher**, and then click the **Spacing Before arrow** until *12 pt* displays.
   - Click **Don't add space between paragraphs of the same style** to remove the check mark from the check box. Click **OK**.
   - Select item number five, *Email campaigns*. Click the **Paragraph Dialog Box Launcher**, and then click the **Line and Page Breaks tab**. Click **Keep with next**, and then click **OK**.
   - Select the six sub-points for item five. Click the **Paragraph Dialog Box Launcher**, click **Keep with next**, click **Keep lines together**, and then click **OK**. This prevents the break, which enables one paragraph to split between two pages.

i. Press **Ctrl+End** to move the cursor to the end of the document. To insert a graphical image complete the following steps:
   - Click the **Insert tab**, click **Picture**, browse to the data files, and then double-click **englerlogo**.
   - Click the **Size Dialog Box Launcher**, and then reduce the Scale Height to **25%**. Click **OK**.
   - Click **Position**, and then click **Position in Bottom Center with Square Text Wrapping**.
   - Click the **More button** in the Picture Quick Styles group to display the entire Picture Styles gallery.
   - Click **Reflected Perspective Right** (fifth row, third column) to apply a border and reflective effects around the graphic.
   - Click **Compress Pictures** in the Adjust group, and then click **OK**.

j. Click the **Insert tab**, click **Page Number**, point to *Bottom of Page*, and select **Bold Numbers 1**. Click **Close Header and Footer**.

k. Press **Ctrl+Home**. Click the **Styles Dialog Box Launcher**. Click **Options**, and then click the **Select styles to show arrow**. Click **All styles**, and then click **OK**. Right-click the **Emphasis style** in the Styles gallery, and then select **Select All 3 Instance(s)**. Scroll down the Styles pane, and then select **Heading 2** to change all headings to a new style. Close the Style pane.

l. Place the insertion point on the left side of the paragraph under the *Goal:* heading. Press **Tab**. Press **Ctrl+T** to indent the whole paragraph the same distance as the tab setting.

m. Compare your work to Figure 2.40. Save and close the file, and submit based on your instructor's directions.

2 International Student Shopping List

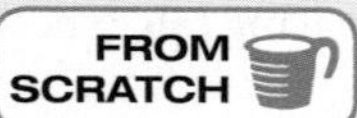

You are the Program Director for an Executive MBA program at the local university and are responsible for making sure the incoming international students receive assistance in settling into their new apartments. One of your graduate assistants recommends that you generate a list of essential items that each student should consider purchasing as soon as they arrive, so you create a document to hand to each student. Your assistant provided you with a list of items, so you only need to add a welcome paragraph and contact information, insert the list, and add some formatting for a refined look. This exercise follows the same set of skills as used in Hands-On Exercises 1–2 in the chapter. Refer to Figure 2.41 as you complete this exercise.

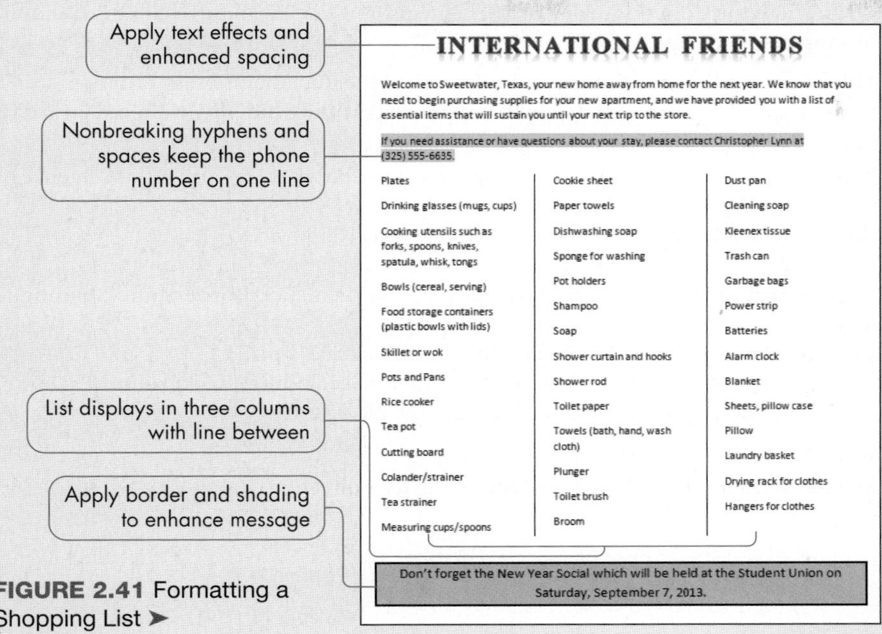

FIGURE 2.41 Formatting a Shopping List ➤

a. Click the **File tab**, click **New**, and then double-click **Blank document**. Save the document as **w02p2shopping_LastnameFirstname**.

b. Type **International Friends**, and then press **Enter**. Select the words you just typed, and then format them by completing the following steps:
   - Click **Center** in the Paragraph group on the Home tab, click **Change Case** in the Font group, and then select **UPPERCASE**. Click the **Font arrow**, and then select **Times New Roman**.
   - Click the **Font Size arrow**, and then select **24**. Click the **Text Effects arrow**, and then click **Gradient Fill – Purple, Accent 4, Reflection** (fourth row, fifth column).
   - Click the **Font Dialog Box Launcher**, and then click the **Advanced tab**. Click the **Spacing arrow**, and then select **Expanded**. Click the increase arrow in the By box until **2 pt** displays. Click **OK** to close the Font dialog box.

c. Place the insertion point at the beginning of the blank line that follows the heading you just formatted, and then type the following paragraph: **Welcome to Sweetwater, Texas, your new home away from home for the next year. We know that you need to begin purchasing supplies for your new apartment, and we have provided you with a list of essential items that will sustain you until your next trip to the store. If you need assistance or have questions about your stay, please contact Christopher Lynn at (325) 555-6635.**

d. Place the insertion point at the beginning of the last sentence, which begins with *If you need*, and then press **Enter** to move the sentence to a new line.

e. Click **Show/Hide** (¶) in the Paragraph group to display formatting marks. Make format changes to the phone number in the last sentence by completing these steps:
   - Select the blank space between the area code and phone number, and then press **Shift+Ctrl+Space** to insert a nonbreaking space.
   - Select the hyphen in the middle of the phone number, and then press **Shift+Ctrl+Hyphen** to insert a nonbreaking hyphen.
   - Select the entire sentence, including the period at the end, and then click the **Text Highlight Color arrow,** and then click **Yellow**.

f. Open the file *w02p2list*, and then press **Ctrl+A** to select the entire document. Press **Ctrl+C** to copy the list to the Clipboard. Close the file without saving.

g. Press **Ctrl+End** to move to the end of the first document, press **Enter**, and then press **Ctrl+V** to insert the shopping list.

h. Display the list of items in three columns, so you can print the list on one sheet of paper instead of two, by completing these steps:
   - Select every item on the list, but do not select the paragraph markers above or below.
   - Click the **Page Layout tab**, click **Columns**, and then select **More Columns**.
   - Click **Three** in the *Presets* section in the Columns dialog box, and then select the **Line between check box**.
   - Click **OK** to close the Columns dialog box. The items now display in three columns, and the entire document fits on one page.

i. Press **Ctrl+End** to move the insertion point to the end of the document. Press **Enter**, and then type **Don't forget the New Year Social, which will be held at the Student Union on Saturday, September 7, 2013.**

j. Select the entire sentence you just typed, including the paragraph marker. Format this sentence by completing these steps:
   - Click the **Home tab**. Click **Grow Font** in the Paragraph group twice.
   - Click **Center** in the Paragraph group.
   - Click the **Borders arrow** in the Paragraph group, and then click **Borders and Shading** to open the Borders and Shading dialog box.
   - Click the **Box setting**, click the **Width arrow**, and then click **2¼ pt**.
   - Click the **Shading tab**, click the **Fill arrow**, and then select **White, Background 1, Darker 25%** (fourth row, first column). Click **OK** to close the dialog box.

k. Click **Show/Hide (¶)** to turn off formatting marks.

l. Save and close the file, and submit based on your instructor's directions.

MID-LEVEL EXERCISES

1 Technology Training Conference

You created a status report to inform committee members about an upcoming conference of which you are in charge. You want the report to look attractive and professional, so you decide to create and apply your own styles rather than use those already available in Word. You create a paragraph style named Side Heading to format the headings, and then you create a character style named Session to format the names of the conference sessions and apply these formats to document text. You then copy these two styles to the Normal template.

a. Open *w02m1conference* and save it as **w02m1conference_LastnameFirstname**.
b. Create a new paragraph style named **Side Heading** using the following properties: Style based on is **Normal**, style for following paragraph is **Normal**. Font properties are **Arial**, **14 pt**, **Bold**; and font color is **Red, Accent 2, Darker 50%.**
c. Set the following paragraph formats for this style: **12 pt Before** paragraph spacing, **6 pt After** paragraph spacing.
d. Apply the **Side Heading style** to the two-line report title, and then **Center** both lines. Apply the **Side Heading style** to the three headings *The Committee*, *Training Sessions*, and *Training Goal.*
e. Create a new character style named **Session** using the following specifications: **Bold** and **Red, Accent 2, Darker 50%** font color. Apply the **Session style** to the following words in the highlighted area: *Word*, *Web Page Development*, *Multimedia*, and *Presentation Graphics*.
f. Use the highlighted text to create a bulleted list. Remove the highlighting, and then indent the bullet list **.8"** from the right side.
g. Modify the Side Heading style to use the **Small caps font effect** and expand spacing by **1.5 pt**.
h. Save *w02m1conference_LastnameFirstname*.

DISCOVER 

i. Open the Manage Styles dialog box, and then export the **Side Heading** and **Session styles** from *w02m1conference_ LastnameFirstname.docx* to *Normal.dotm*.
j. Open a new document. Display the Styles pane, if necessary, and then verify that the Session and Side Heading styles display. After confirming they are imported, delete the two styles from the *Normal.dotm* list. If working in a computer lab, this resets the Normal template for the next user. Close the blank document without saving it.
k. Insert a nonbreaking hyphen and a nonbreaking space in the phone number that displays at the end of the report.
l. Save and close *w02m1conference_LastnameFirstname*, and submit based on your instructor's directions.

2 Dental Information Meeting

You are the office manager for a pediatric dentist who periodically conducts informational sessions for young children. You have written a letter to children in the neighborhood reminding them about the upcoming monthly session, but you want to make the letter more professional looking. You decide to use paragraph formatting such as alignment, paragraph spacing, paragraph borders, and shading, as well as a customized bulleted list that describes some of the fun activities for the day. You also want to add the dentist's e-mail address and clip art to the letter.

a. Open the document *w02m2dentist* and save it as **w02m2dentist_LastnameFirstname**.
b. Change the capitalization of the recipient *Ms. Catherine Ellis* and her address so that each word is capitalized and the state abbreviation displays in uppercase. Change Dr. Block's name to your full name in the signature block. Type your e-mail address on the next line below your name.

c. Apply **Justified alignment** to each paragraph in the document. Delete the asterisk (*), and then create a customized bulleted list, selecting a picture bullet of your choice. Type the following items in the bulleted list:

Participating in the dental crossword puzzle challenge.
Writing a convincing letter to the tooth fairy.
Digging through the dental treasure chest.
Finding hidden toothbrushes in the dental office.

d. Select text from the salutation *Dear Catherine:* through the last paragraph that ends with *seeing you on July 14.* Set **12 pt spacing After paragraph**.

e. Use the **Small caps font effect** on *Dr. Block Pediatric Dental Center* in the first paragraph.

f. Replace the question mark, which displays at the end of the title of the presentation described in the second full paragraph, with the inverted question mark symbol found in the (normal text) Latin-1 Supplement subset.

g. Select the italicized lines of text that give the date, time, and location of the meeting. Remove the italics, and then complete the following:
   - Increase left and right indents to **1.25"**, and then set **0 pt spacing After paragraph**.
   - Apply a double-line border using the color **Purple, Accent 4, Darker 50%, ¾ pt border width**, and **Purple, Accent 4, Lighter 40% shading color**.

h. Click the line containing the text *Richmond, VA 23060*, and then set **12 pt spacing After paragraph**.

i. Select the entire document, and then change the font to **12 pt Bookman Old Style**. Delete the extra tab formatting marks to the left of the lines containing *July 14, 2012, 4:00 p.m.* and *Dr. Block Pediatric Dental* to prevent them from word wrapping.

j. Use nonbreaking hyphens and nonbreaking spaces to display the date on one line.

k. Display the Clip Art task pane, and then search for *tooth*. Insert any clip of a tooth, and then display it in the top-right corner of the document. Resize the graphic so it does not display larger than 1.1" × 1.1". Apply the **Bevel Perspective Left, White picture style** (fifth row, fourth column) to the graphic. Increase the Brightness setting by **20%**.

l. Adjust all margins to **1"**, and then delete any extra lines so that all content fit on one page.

m. Save and close the file, and submit based on your instructor's directions.

CAPSTONE EXERCISE

In this project, you work with a document prepared for managers involved in the hiring process. This report analyzes the validity of the interview process and suggests that selection does not depend only on quality information, but on the quality of the interpretation of information. The document requires formatting to enhance readability and important information; you will use skills from this chapter to format multiple levels of headings and figures. To make it easy for readers to locate topics in your document, create and use various supplemental document components such as a table of contents and index.

Applying Styles

This document is ready for enhancements, and the styles feature is a good tool that enables you to add them quickly and easily.

a. Open *w02c1interview* and save it as **w02c1interview_LastnameFirstname**.

b. Create a paragraph style named **Title_Page_1** with these formats: **22-pt font size**, **Shadow font effect Offset Diagonal Top Right**, **character spacing expanded by 2 pt**, **horizontally centered**, using Font color **Dark Blue, Text 2, Darker 50%**. Apply this style to the first line of the document, *Understanding the Personal Interview*.

c. Create a paragraph style named **Title_Page_2** based on the first style you created, with these additional formats: **20-pt font size**, **custom color 66, 4, 66**. Apply this style to the subtitle, *A Study for Managers Involved in the Hiring Process*.

d. Replace the * in the middle of the first page with your name. Change the capitalization for your name to uppercase.

e. Select the remainder of the text in the document that follows your name, starting with *Understanding the Personal Interview*. **Justify** the alignment of all paragraphs and change line spacing to **1.15**. Place your cursor on the left side of the title *Understanding the Personal Interview*, and then insert a page break so the document starts at the top of the page.

f. Apply the **Heading 1 style** to the main headings throughout the document and the **Heading 2 style** to the paragraph headings, such as *Introduction* and *Pre-interview Impressions*.

g. Modify the Heading 2 style to use **Dark Red font color**.

Formatting the Paragraphs

Next, you will apply paragraph formatting to the document. These format options will further increase the readability and attractiveness of your document.

a. Apply a bulleted list format for the five-item list in the *Introduction*. Use the symbol of a four-sided star from the Wingdings group (symbol 170) for the bullet.

b. Select the second paragraph in the *Introduction* section that begins with *Personal interviewing continues*, and then apply these formats: **0.6" left and right indent**, **6 pt spacing after the paragraph**, **boxed 11/2 pt border using the color Blue, Accent 1, Darker 25%**, and the shading color **Blue, Accent 1, Lighter 80%**.

c. Apply the first numbered-list format (1., 2., 3.) for the three phases in the *Pre-Interview Impressions* section.

d. Select the second and third paragraphs in *The Unfavorable Information Effect* section, and then display them in two columns with a line between the columns.

Inserting Graphics and Page Numbers

To put the finishing touches on your document, you will add graphics that enhance the explanations given in some paragraphs. Captions are already in place for the graphics, but final formatting must occur to display them properly. Additionally, you will create a footer to display page numbers in this long document.

a. Insert the picture file **perceptions.jpg** at the beginning of the line that contains the caption *Figure 1: Perception in the Interview* and that displays at the bottom of page 2. Center the graphic horizontally, change text wrapping, and then insert any line breaks necessary so the graphic displays on a line by itself just above the caption. Use scaling to reduce the size to 75% of the original size. Apply the **Rounded Diagonal Corner**, **White picture style**.

b. Insert the picture file **phases.jpg** at the beginning of the line that contains the caption *Figure 2: Diboye's Interview phases*. Change text wrapping, and then insert any line breaks necessary so the graphic displays on a line by itself just above the caption. Apply **Offset Center shadow effect** to the graphic.

c. Display a page number in the footer of each page using the **Accent Bar 4 format**. Prevent the footer from displaying on the title page, and then start numbering on the page that follows the title page.

d. Review the entire document, and if necessary, use **Keep Lines Together controls** to prevent headings and paragraphs from being separated across pages. Invoke the **Widow/Orphan control** also.

e. Insert nonbreaking spaces and nonbreaking hyphens where appropriate.

f. Display the document in Outline view. Collapse all paragraphs so only the headings display.

g. Save and close the file, and submit based on your instructor's directions.

Review the Skills

GENERAL CASE 

You learned many skills and features of Word 2010 in this chapter. Take a few minutes to refresh yourself on these and other features by creating an outline of this chapter. Use the Multilevel list feature to type out each heading and subheading, and write a short paragraph to summarize the skills. Adjust tabs as necessary so the second and third level headings are indented at least .5 beyond the first. Use styles for each type of heading so they appear different (as they do in the chapter). Save your work as **w02b1outline_Lastname Firstname** and submit based on your instructor's directions.

Money Management Brochure

RESEARCH CASE 

You are very concerned that many young people do not know how to manage their personal finances. Create a 3-column, 2-sided brochure on money management to be distributed to high school students. Search the Internet to gather enough information to write the brochure. Provide your e-mail address as contact information and several non-profit financial Web sites as resources. Start each paragraph with a drop cap, insert clip art and/or images, adjust the margins, and format your content so that you have one or two full pages of helpful materials. Do not forget to include a list of the Web sites you consulted. Save your work as **w02b2brochure_LastnameFirstname** and submit based on your instructor's directions.

Food Drive Flyer

DISASTER RECOVERY 

To fulfill a community project requirement for your Citizenship class, you are organizing a food drive for a local food bank. You want to create a one-page flyer soliciting food items and post it around campus. You created a draft yesterday and saved it as *w02b3flyer*, but it was neither formatted nor organized. Today, you want to open the document and create a more professionally looking document by using features such as columns, tables, tabs, bullets, page borders, and any additional pictures or clip art as desired. Save your work as **w02b3flyer_LastnameFirstname** and submit based on your instructor's directions.

WORD

3 COLLABORATION AND RESEARCH

Communicating Easily and Producing Professional Papers

CASE STUDY | Marketing Plan for Take Note Paperie

Watch the
Set-up Video
for this Case Study!

Your marketing professor assigned you to work with Rachel Starkey and your team project is to create a marketing plan for a new small business. You and Rachel have chosen a custom printing service named Take Note Paperie as the company for which you will develop a plan.

The research is complete, and the document is typed. Rachel last updated the document and has sent it to you to view and modify as you see fit. You check the comments Rachel made and perform modifications based on her notes. You also notice it is lacking vital features of a research paper that all professors require, such as the table of contents, bibliography, and table of figures, so you plan to add those. However, you also want to provide Rachel the opportunity to view your changes to the document and to provide feedback before you submit it for grading, so you leave a note for her as well. You hope this is the last round of changes before you turn it in and earn an A!

OBJECTIVES AFTER YOU READ THIS CHAPTER, YOU WILL BE ABLE TO:

Document Revisions

This chapter introduces several Word features that you can use for research papers while in school. These same skills will also be useful as you work with others on collaborative projects. One of the first things you need to do when working on a collaborative project is workgroup editing, where suggested revisions from one or more individuals can be stored electronically within a document. This feature enables the original author to review each suggestion individually before it is incorporated into the final version of the document, and further, enables multiple people to work on the same document in collaboration with one another. Another feature that is useful in workgroup settings enables you to insert comments in a document for other editors to view and respond to.

In this section, you will insert comments to provide feedback or to pose questions to the document author. Then you will track editing changes you make so that others can see your suggested edits.

Inserting Comments in a Document

In today's organizational environment, teams of people with diverse backgrounds, skills, and knowledge prepare documentation.... When you work with a team, you can use collaboration tools in Word such as the Comments feature.

In today's organizational environment, teams of people with diverse backgrounds, skills, and knowledge prepare documentation. Team members work together while planning, developing, writing, and editing important documents. If you have not participated in a team project yet, most likely you will. When you work with a team, you can use collaboration tools in Word such as the Comments feature. A ***comment*** is a note or annotation that appears in the document to ask a question or provide a suggestion about the content of a document. Frequently, the comment appears in a balloon on the side of the document.

A **comment** is a note or annotation about the content of a document.

Before you use the comments and other collaboration features, you should click File, click Options, and then view the General section of the Word Options dialog box to confirm that your name and initials display as the user. Word uses this information to identify the person who uses collaboration tools, such as Comments. If you are in a lab environment, you might not have permission to modify settings or change the User name; however, you should be able to change these settings on a home computer.

Add a Comment

You add comments to a document to remind a reviewer, or yourself, of action that needs to be taken. To insert a comment, select a word or phrase where you want it to appear, display the Review tab, click New Comment in the Comments group to open the markup balloon (see Figure 3.1), and then type the text of the comment. If you do not select anything prior to clicking New Comment, Word assigns the comment to the word or object closest to the insertion point. When you click outside the comment area, the comment is recorded in the document. Most comments display in ***markup balloons***, which are colored circles in the margin with a line drawn to the object of the comment. After you complete the comment, the text and markup balloon are highlighted in the color assigned to the reviewer.

A **markup balloon** is a colored circle that contains comments and displays in the margin.

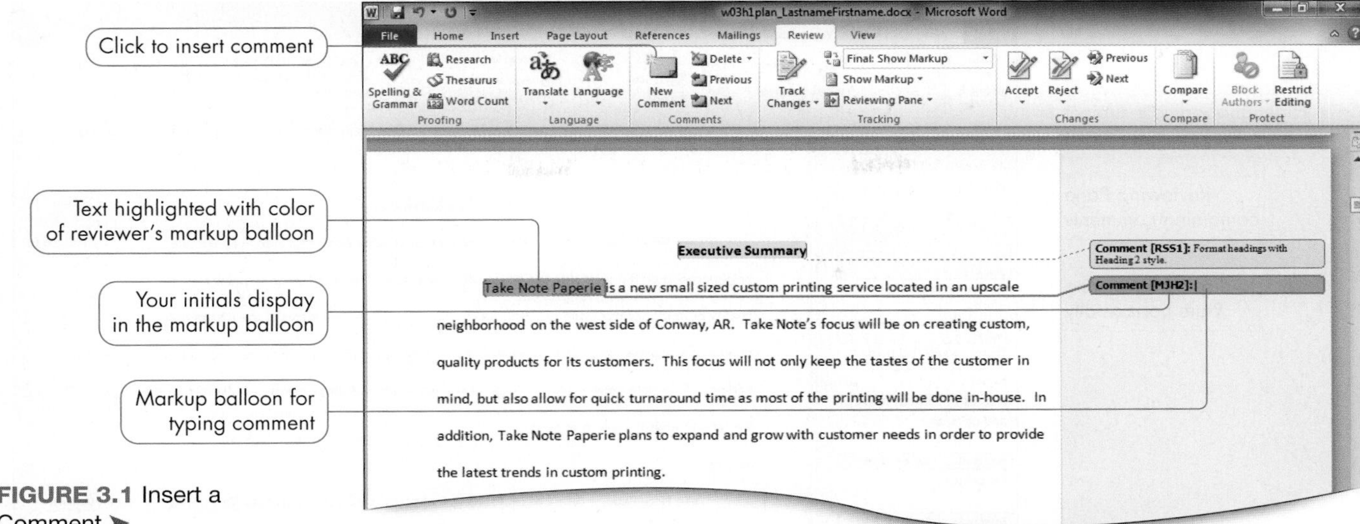

FIGURE 3.1 Insert a Comment ➤

TIP Response Comments

You can build a dialog through comments. If you select or put the insertion point in a comment markup balloon, and then click New Comment, a new markup balloon displays adjoining the first balloon, and *R1* will follow the reviewer's initials that display inside. The *R* stands for response, so the reader knows it is a response to the original comment.

View, Modify, and Delete Comments

The **Reviewing Pane** displays comments and changes made to a document.

Comments appear in markup balloons in Print Layout, Full Screen Reading, and Web Layout views. In Draft view, comments appear as tags embedded in the document; when you hover the cursor over the tag, it displays the comment. In any view, you can display the ***Reviewing Pane***, which displays all comments and editorial changes made to the main document. To display the Reviewing Pane vertically on the left side of the document, as shown in Figure 3.2, click Reviewing Pane on the Review tab. To hide the Reviewing Pane click Reviewing Pane again—it is a toggle. You can display the Reviewing Pane horizontally at the bottom when you click the Reviewing Pane arrow. The Reviewing Pane is useful when the comments are too long to display completely in a markup balloon.

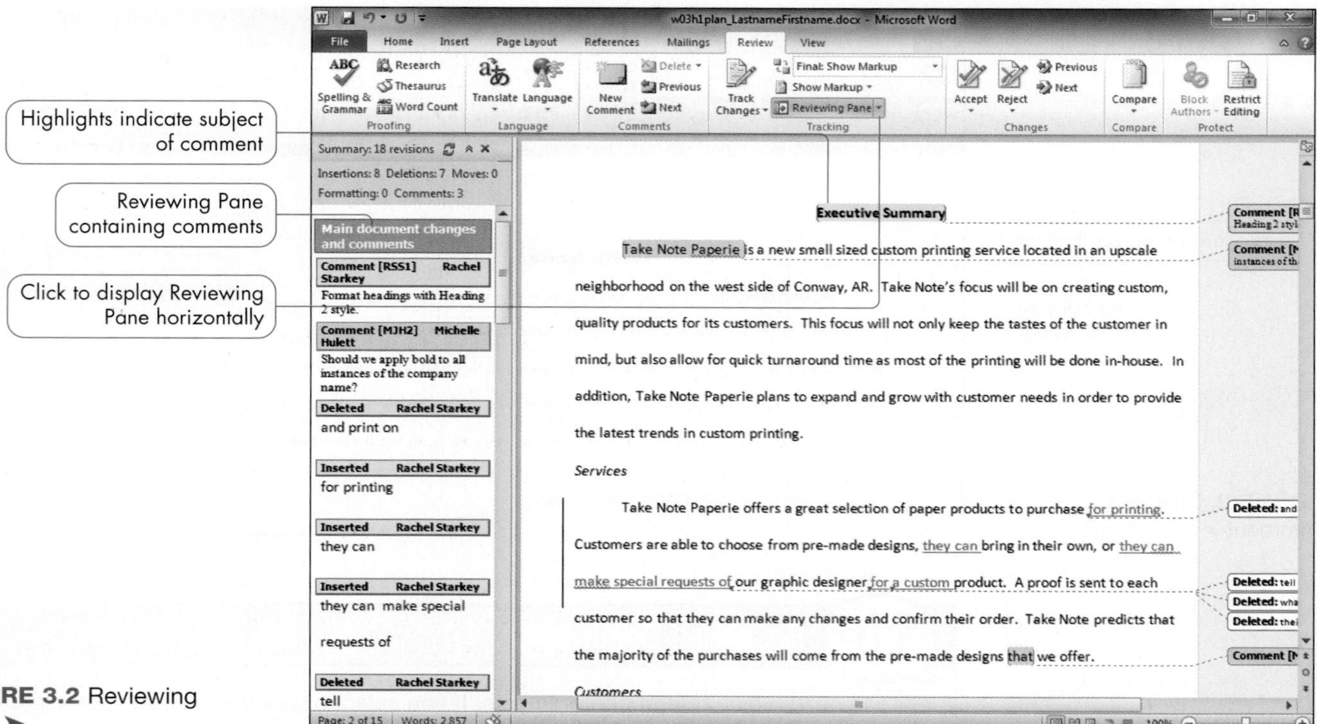
Highlights indicate subject of comment
Reviewing Pane containing comments
Click to display Reviewing Pane horizontally

FIGURE 3.2 Reviewing Pane ➤

Show Markup enables you to view document revisions by reviewers.

If you do not see comments initially, click Show Markup on the Review tab and confirm that Comments is toggled on. The ***Show Markup*** feature enables you to view document revisions by reviewers. It also enables you to choose which type of revisions you want to view such as Comments, Ink annotations (made on a tablet PC), insertions and deletions, or formatting changes. Each can be toggled on or off, and you can view several at the same time, as shown in Figure 3.3. Show Markup also color-codes each revision or comment by using a different color for each reviewer. If you want to view only changes by a particular reviewer, click Show Markup, click Reviewers, and deselect all reviewers except the one you prefer.

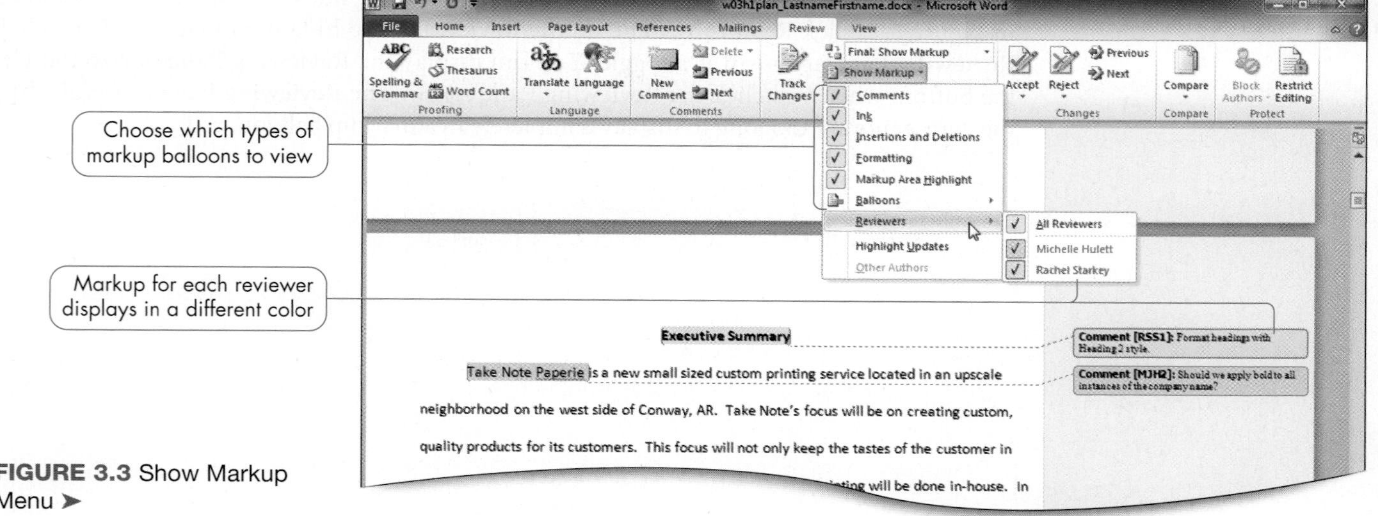
Choose which types of markup balloons to view
Markup for each reviewer displays in a different color

FIGURE 3.3 Show Markup Menu ➤

You can modify comments easily. When you click inside a markup balloon, the insertion point will relocate in the balloon, and you can use word processing formatting features, such as bold, italic, underline, and color, in the comment. If a document contains many comments, or the document is lengthy, you can click Previous and Next in the Comments group on the Review tab to navigate from comment to comment. This is a quick way to move between comments without scrolling through the entire document, and it places the insertion point in the comment automatically. You can edit comments when viewing them in the Reviewing Pane also.

After reading or acting on comments, you can delete them from the document or the Reviewing Pane by clicking Delete in the Comments group on the Review tab. When you click the Delete arrow, your options include deleting the current comment, all comments shown, or deleting all comments in the document at one time. You also can right-click a comment markup balloon and select Delete Comment from the shortcut menu. If you print a document that has comments, the comments also print. To omit the comments from the printout, click File, click Print, click the first Settings arrow (which shows Print All Pages by default), and then click Show Markup to remove the checkmark.

Tracking Changes in a Document

Use **Track Changes** to insert revision marks and markup balloons for additions, deletions, and formatting changes.

Whether you work individually or with a group, you can monitor any revisions you make to a document. The ***Track Changes*** feature monitors all additions, deletions, and formatting changes you make. It is useful in situations where a document must be reviewed by several people—each of whom can offer suggestions or changes—and then returned to one person who will finalize the document.

A **revision mark** indicates where text is added, deleted, or formatted while the Track Changes feature is active.

A **changed line** is a vertical bar in the margin to pinpoint the area where changes are made.

When Track Changes is not active, any change you make to a document is untraceable and no one will know what you change unless he or she compares your revised document with the previous version. When Track Changes is active, it applies ***revision marks***, which indicate where a person added, deleted, or formatted text. Like Comments, the revision marks will be colored differently for each reviewer. Revision marks can vary depending on your preference in viewing them, but include strikeout lines for deleted text, underlines for inserted text, markup balloons, and changed lines. ***Changed lines*** are vertical bars that display in the right or left margins to specify the line that contains revision marks. You can position the mouse pointer over revision marks or markup balloons to see who made the change and on what date and time, as shown in Figure 3.4.

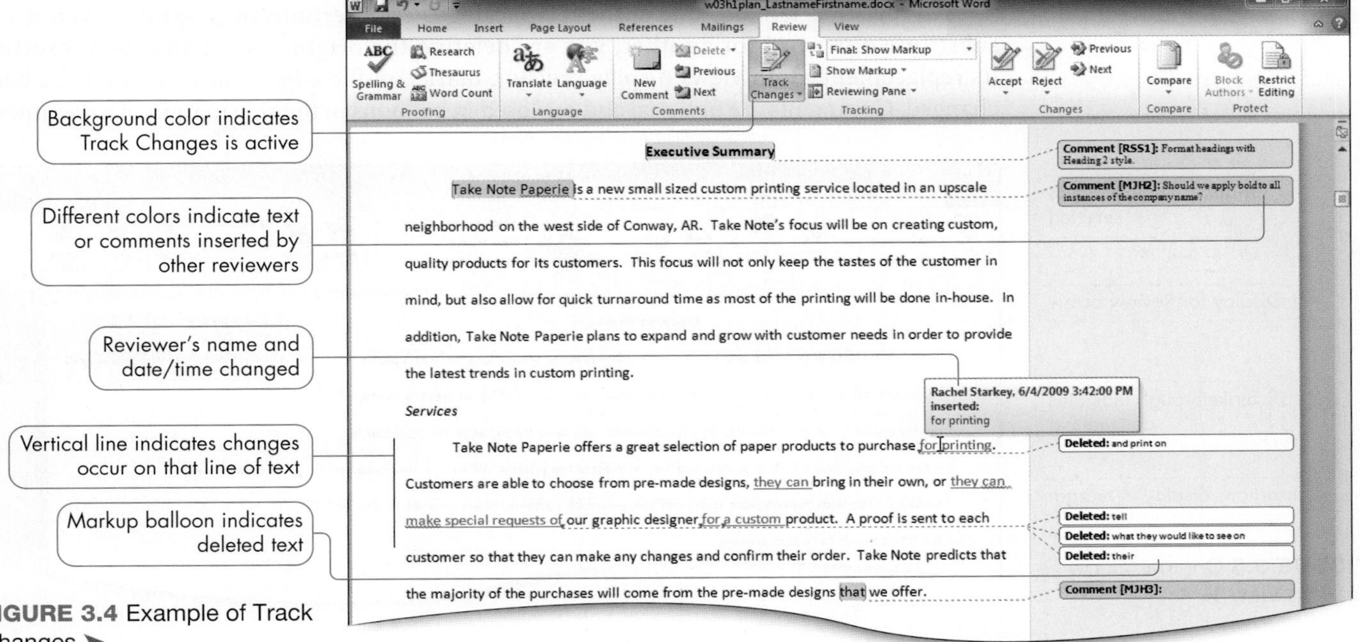

FIGURE 3.4 Example of Track Changes ➤

Word also includes markup tools, which enable you to accept or reject changes indicated by revision marks. The Changes group on the Review tab includes Accept, to accept a suggested change, and Reject, to remove a suggested change. When you accept or reject a change, the revision marks, markup balloon, and changed lines disappear. The Changes group also includes Previous and Next. When you click Previous, the insertion point moves to the beginning of any comment or change that occurs just prior to the current position. Similarly, clicking Next will move the insertion point to the beginning of the next comment or change.

If the review process takes place using paper copies of a document, it is difficult to visualize all the suggested changes at one time, and then the last person must manually change the original document. While writing the Exploring series, the authors, editors, and reviewers each inserted comments and tracked changes to the manuscript for each chapter using Word. Each person's comments or changes displayed in different colored balloons, and because all edits were performed in the same document, the Series Editor could accept and reject changes before sending the manuscript to the production department.

TIP Accepting or Rejecting All Changes

To accept all changes in a document at once, click the Accept arrow on the Review tab and select Accept All Changes in Document. To delete all changes in a document at once, click the Reject arrow on the Review tab and select Reject All Changes in Document.

Select Markup Views

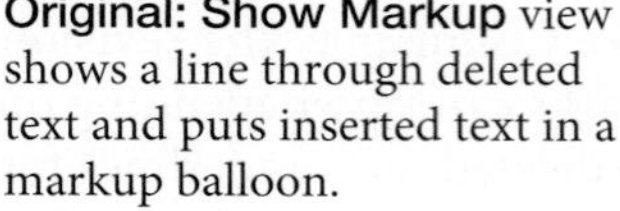

Original: Show Markup view shows a line through deleted text and puts inserted text in a markup balloon.

Final: Show Markup view shows inserted text in the body and puts deleted text in a markup balloon.

The suggested revisions from the various reviewers display in one of two ways, as the Original Showing Markup or as the Final Showing Markup. The ***Original: Show Markup*** view shows the deleted text within the body of the document (with a line through the deleted text) and displays the inserted text in a balloon to the right of the actual document, as shown in Figure 3.5. The ***Final: Show Markup*** view is the opposite; that is, it displays the inserted text in the body of the document and shows the deleted text in a balloon. The difference is subtle and depends on personal preference with respect to displaying the insertions and deletions in a document. You can change the way markups display by clicking Show Markup, Balloons, and selecting from three choices: Show Revisions in Balloons, Show All Revisions Inline, or Show Only Comments and Formatting in Balloons.

All revisions fall into one of these two categories: insertions or deletions. Even if you substitute one word for another, you are deleting the original word and then inserting its replacement. Both views display revision marks on the edge of any line that has been changed. Comments are optional and enclosed in balloons in the side margin of a document.

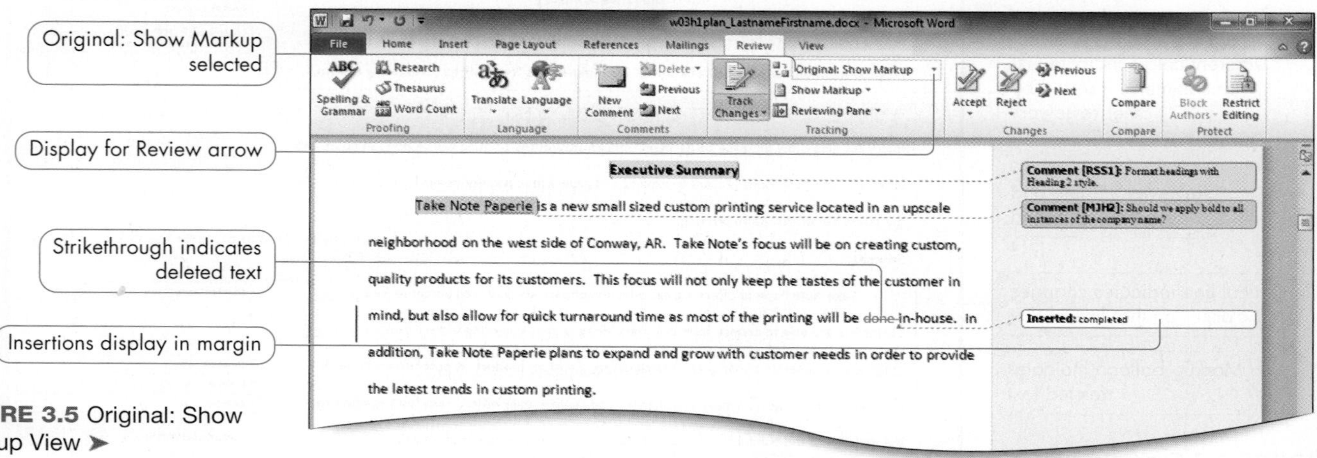

FIGURE 3.5 Original: Show Markup View ➤

To select one of the markup views you click the Display for Review arrow in the Tracking group on the Review tab (see Figure 3.5). When you click the Display for Review arrow, two additional view options are listed—Final and Original. Final shows how the document looks if you accept and incorporate all tracked changes. Original shows the document prior to using the Track Changes feature.

Customize Track Changes Options

The Track Changes feature has many options for viewing and displaying changes, which you can customize. When you click Change Tracking Options from the Track Changes arrow, the Track Changes Options dialog box displays with many features you can change. For example, you can choose the type of underline to display under inserted text (single line or double line). You can choose the type of strikethrough line to display on deleted text (strikethrough or double strikethrough). You can choose the location where the balloons display (right or left margins), and you can even choose the size of the balloons.

The beginning of this chapter mentioned that you should check the Word Options, making changes if necessary, so your name and initials are associated with any tracked changes you make in the document. You also can access those settings from the Review tab when you click the Track Changes arrow and select Change User Name, as shown in Figure 3.6. This step takes you to the General category of the Word Options dialog box, where you have the opportunity to enter your name and initials in the *Personalize your copy of Microsoft Office* section.

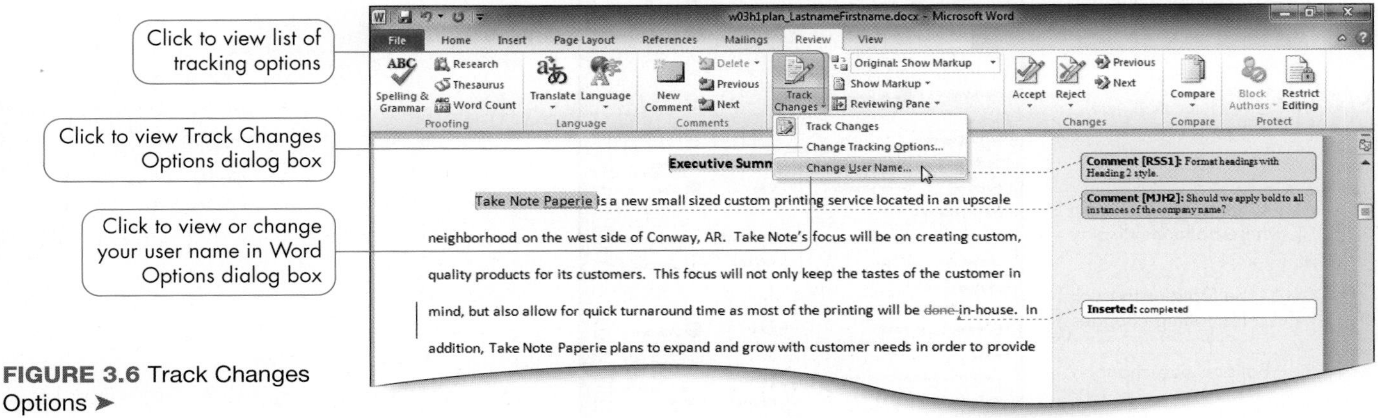

FIGURE 3.6 Track Changes Options ➤

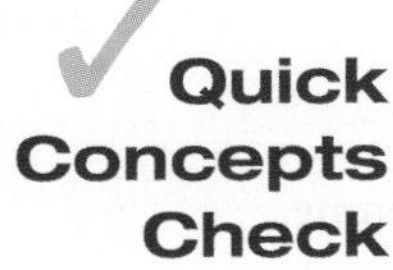

Quick Concepts Check

1. How can you change the name of a Word user so they are identified when a comment is inserted?
2. How does Word assign a comment to the text in the document?
3. List three types of revisions you can view using the Show Markup feature.
4. When using the Track Changes feature, name at least three visual cues that Word can display to show the changes made in the document.
5. Name and describe two different ways to view a document that was edited using the Track Changes feature.

HANDS-ON EXERCISES

1 Document Revisions

You open the document that Rachel Starkey prepared and find the comments she left for you. You also see her recent edits because she tracked her changes. Your task is to address any questions or requests in the comment balloons and also accept or reject the changes she made when revising the document.

Skills covered: Set User Name and Customize the Track Changes Options • Track Document Changes • View, Add, and Delete Comments • Accept and Reject Changes

STEP 1 SET USER NAME AND CUSTOMIZE THE TRACK CHANGES OPTIONS

You want to make sure the Word Options are customized so your name displays when comments are added or changes are tracked in a document. Then you decide to modify some of the track changes options to use settings that are distinguishable from those other editors might use. Refer to Figure 3.7 as you complete Step 1.

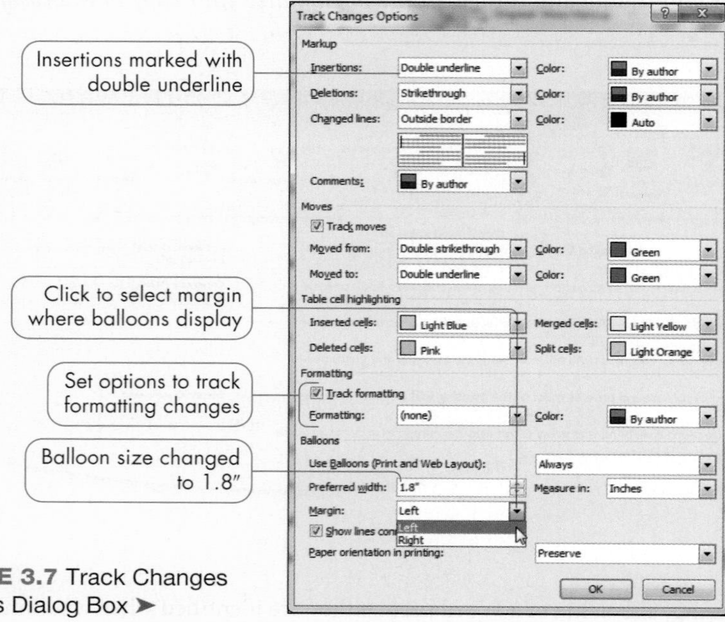

FIGURE 3.7 Track Changes Options Dialog Box ➤

a. Open *w03h1plan* and save it as **w03h1plan_LastnameFirstname**.

> **TROUBLESHOOTING:** If you make any major mistakes in this exercise, you can close the file, open *w03h1plan* again, and then start this exercise over.

b. Delete the text *YourName* in the subtitle and insert your first and last names. Click the **Review tab**, and then click **Track Changes** in the Tracking group.

> **TROUBLESHOOTING:** Track Changes in the Tracking group, like some other commands in Word, contain two parts: the main command icon and an arrow. Click the main command icon when instructed to click Track Changes and turn on the feature. Click the arrow when instructed to click the Track Changes arrow for additional command options.

The command displays with an orange background color, indicating the feature is turned on. When you click Track Changes, you toggle the feature on or off.

c. Click the **Track Changes arrow**, and then click **Change User Name**. In the *Personalize your copy of Microsoft Office* section, type your name in the **User name box**, and then type your initials in the **Initials box**, if necessary. Click **OK** to close the Word Options dialog box.

   You want to be sure your name and initials are correct before you add any comments or initiate any changes in the document. After you update the user information, your initials display with all comments or changes you make.

TROUBLESHOOTING: Personalizing your copy of Microsoft Office might not be possible in a lab environment. If you cannot make the change, just continue with the exercise.

d. Click the **Track Changes arrow**, and then click **Change Tracking Options** to open the dialog box. In the *Markup* section, click the **Insertions arrow**, and then click **Double underline**. In the *Formatting* section, click the **Track formatting check box**, if necessary, to turn on this feature.

   Your revisions to the Track Changes options enable you to view any additions to the document quickly because they will be identified in balloons and your insertions will display with a double underline. Markups on formatting may not display automatically, but you confirm that option is on so you will see marks next to formatting changes that you make.

e. Click the **Use Balloons (Print and Web Layout) arrow** in the *Balloons* section, and then click **Always**, if necessary. Click the **Preferred width arrow** until **1.8"** displays. Click the **Margin arrow**, and then select **Left**, as shown in Figure 3.7. Click **OK** to close the Track Changes Options dialog box.

   You altered the location of all comment and editing balloons to display on the left side of your document instead of on the right, which is the default. You also decreased the width of the markup balloons so they will take up less space in the margins.

f. Save the document.

STEP 2 TRACK DOCUMENT CHANGES

Now that the settings are set to your preference, you make a few changes so you can see how your editing is tracked separately from Rachel's. You first change the views so you can see the tracked changes made by both of you while you work, and then you later change the view so you see how the document looks as a final version. Refer to Figure 3.8 as you complete Step 2.

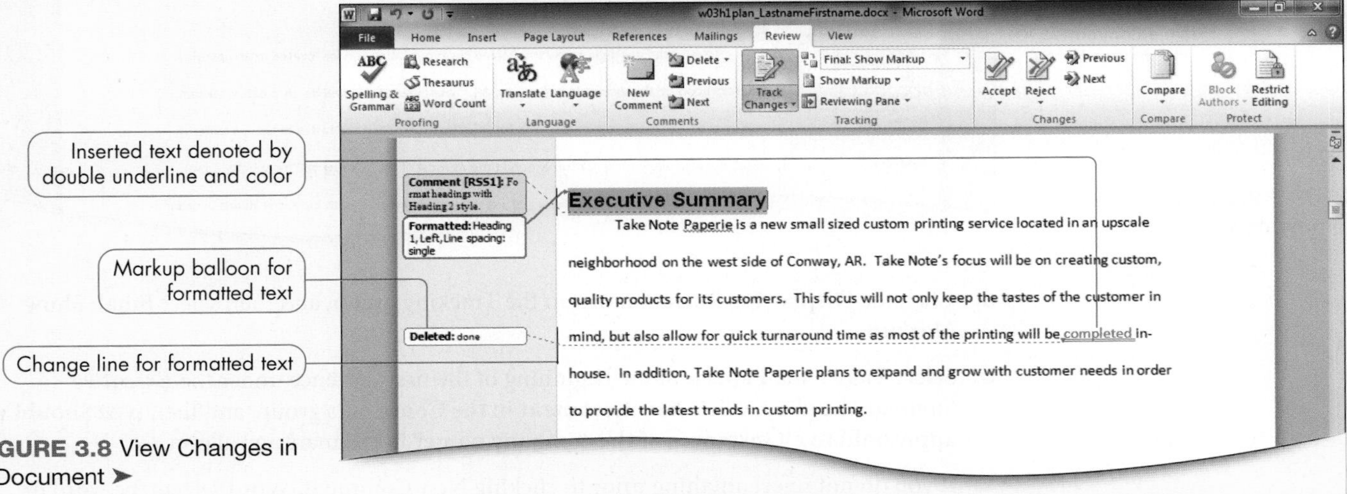

FIGURE 3.8 View Changes in a Document ➤

a. Click the **Display for Review arrow** in the Tracking group on the Review tab, and then select **Final: Show Markup**, if necessary. Scroll down the document until you see the heading *Executive Summary* on the second page of the document.

One comment displays in a balloon and several changes are marked in color. Because of the changes you made in Step 1, any future changes you make in the document also display in balloons in the margin of the document.

b. Replace the word *done* with **completed** in the third sentence of the first paragraph that follows the *Executive Summary* heading.

The text you inserted is colored and has a double underline beneath it.

> **TROUBLESHOOTING:** If a balloon does not display, indicating the word replacement, make sure Track Changes is on. When on, Track Changes is highlighted in an orange color on the Review tab. If necessary, click Undo, click Track Changes again to turn it on, and then repeat Step 2b.

c. Select the **Executive Summary heading**, click the **Home tab**, and then apply the **Heading 1 style** from the Styles gallery.

The heading is now left justified, and a changed line appears on the left side. A markup balloon describes the formatting change, as seen in Figure 3.8.

d. Click the **Review tab**, click the **Display for Review arrow** in the Tracking group, and then select **Final**.

The formatting change indicators do not display, and the *Executive Summary* heading displays in the new style.

e. Save the document.

STEP 3 VIEW, ADD, AND DELETE COMMENTS

As you work through the document, you think of a question you would like to ask Rachel before the plan is finalized, so you insert a comment of your own. You also remove one of her comments about an issue that is resolved. Refer to Figure 3.9 as you complete Step 3.

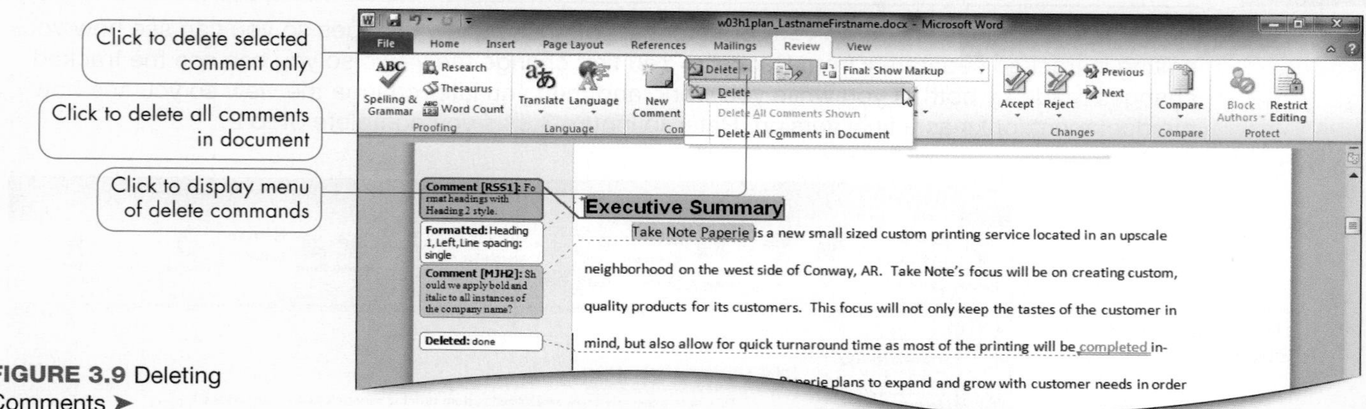

FIGURE 3.9 Deleting Comments ➤

a. Click the **Display for Review arrow** in the Tracking group, and then select **Final: Show Markup**.

b. Select **Take Note Paperie** at the beginning of the first sentence under the *Executive Summary* heading. Click **New Comment** in the Comments group, and then type **Should we apply bold to all instances of the company name?** in the markup balloon.

If you do not select anything prior to clicking New Comment, Word selects the word or object nearest the insertion point for the comment reference.

c. Click inside the markup balloon you created. Place your cursor to the left of the word *to*, edit the comment by typing **and italic**, and then press **Spacebar**. Click outside of the balloon to deselect it.

Your comment now displays *Should we apply bold and italic to all instances of the company name?*

d. Position the mouse pointer over the comment balloon attached to the *Executive Summary* heading.

When you position the mouse pointer over a markup balloon, Word displays a ScreenTip that tells you who created the comment and when.

e. Click Rachel Starkey's comment one time to select it, and then click **Delete** in the Comments group.

You removed the selected comment and the markup balloon. If you click the arrow on the right side of Delete in the Comments group, you can select from several options, including Delete all Comments in Document (see Figure 3.9). You can also right-click a comment and select Delete Comment.

f. Save the document.

STEP 4 ACCEPT AND REJECT CHANGES

Now you are ready to consider the changes that Rachel made and tracked. Some are good and will improve the readability of the paper; some will not. You remember how quick and easy it is to accept and reject changes by using features on the Review tab and that makes you smile. Refer to Figure 3.10 as you complete Step 4.

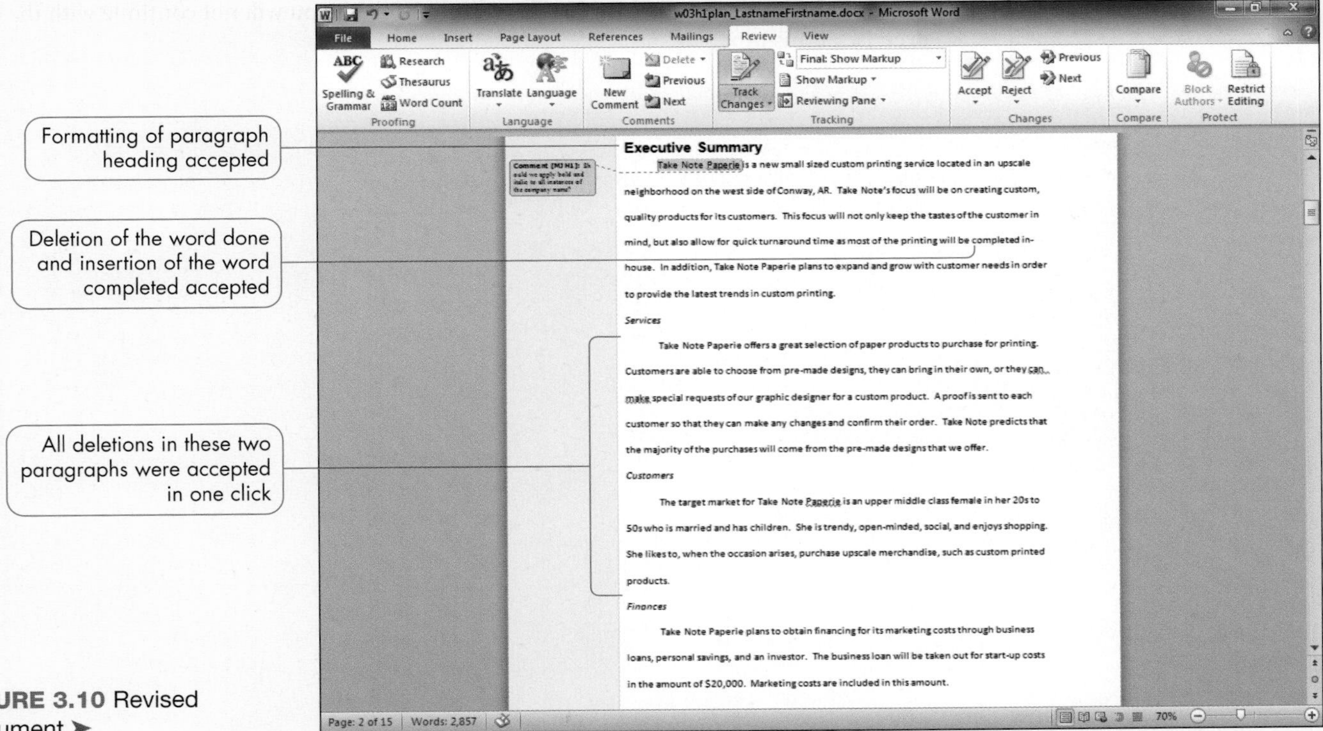

FIGURE 3.10 Revised Document ➤

a. Press **Ctrl+Home** to place the insertion point at the beginning of the document.

b. Click **Next** in the Changes group to highlight the first change, and then position the mouse pointer over the tracked change.

The formatting change to the *Executive Summary* heading is highlighted. When you position the mouse pointer on the revision, a ScreenTip appears that tells you who made the change and the date and time the change was made.

TROUBLESHOOTING: If you click Next in the Comments group instead of Next in the Changes group, click Previous in the Comments group to return the cursor to the beginning of the document, and then click Next in the Changes group.

c. Click **Accept** in the Changes group.

The formatting change is accepted. When the suggested change is accepted, the markup balloons and other Track Changes markups disappear. Additionally, the markup balloon for the next change or comment is highlighted. As with other commands, you can click Accept to accept this change only, or you can click the Accept arrow to view options for accepting changes.

d. Click **Next** in the Changes group to pass the comment and view the next markup balloon. Click **Accept** two times to accept the replacement of *done* to *completed.*

The first time you accept the change it applies to the deletion of the word *done*. The second time you accept the change it applies to the insertion of *completed.*

e. Select the entire second and third paragraphs in the *Executive Summary* section. Click **Accept** to retain all revisions in the paragraphs. Click **Reject** to remove the empty comment that displays in this paragraph.

All the changes in those paragraphs are accepted, the blank comment is removed, and the next change, a deletion of a complete section of the report, is highlighted. Figure 3.10 shows the first page after accepting changes.

f. Click **Reject** in the Changes group to retain the *Goals* heading and following paragraphs.

g. Save *w03h1plan_LastnameFirstname* and keep it onscreen if you plan to continue with the next Hands-On Exercise. Close the file and exit Word if you will not continue with the next exercise at this time.

Research Paper Basics

Well-prepared documents often include notes that provide supplemental information or citations for sources quoted in the document. Some documents also contain other valuable supplemental components, such as a list of figures or legal references. Word includes many features that can help you create these supplemental references, as well as many others described in the following paragraphs.

In this section, you will use Word to create citations used for reference pages, create a bibliography page that displays works cited in the document, and select from a list of writing styles that are commonly used to dictate the format of reference pages. You will also create and modify footnote and endnote citations, which display at the bottom of a page or the end of the document.

Acknowledging a Source

Plagiarism is the act of using and documenting the works of another as one's own.

It is common practice to use a variety of sources to supplement your own thoughts when writing a paper, report, legal brief, or many other types of document. Failure to acknowledge the source of information you use in a document is a form of plagiarism. *Webster's New Collegiate Dictionary* defines ***plagiarism*** as the act of using and documenting the ideas or writings of another as one's own. It may also apply to spoken words, multimedia works, or graphics. Plagiarism has serious moral and ethical implications and is taken seriously in the academic community; it is often classified as academic dishonesty.

Failure to acknowledge the source of information you use in a document is a form of plagiarism.... Word includes a robust feature for tracking sources and producing the supplemental resources to display them.

To assist in your efforts to avoid plagiarism, which is frequently a thoughtless oversight rather than a malicious act, Word includes a robust feature for tracking sources and producing the supplemental resources to display them.

Create a Source

A **citation** is a note recognizing a source of information or a quoted passage.

Word provides the citation feature to track, compile, and display your research sources for inclusion in several types of supplemental references. To use this feature you use the Insert Citation command in the Citations & Bibliography group on the References tab to add data about each source, as shown in Figure 3.11. A ***citation*** is a note recognizing the source of information or a quoted passage. The Create Source dialog box includes fields to catalog information, such as author, date, publication name, page number, or Web site address, from the following types of sources:

- Book
- Book Section
- Journal Article
- Article in a Periodical
- Conference Proceedings
- Report
- Web site
- Document from Web site
- Electronic Source
- Art
- Sound Recording
- Performance
- Film
- Interview
- Patent
- Case
- Miscellaneous

After you create the citation sources, you can insert them into a document using the Insert Citation command. When you click the command, a list of your sources displays; click a source from the list, and the proper citation format is inserted in your document.

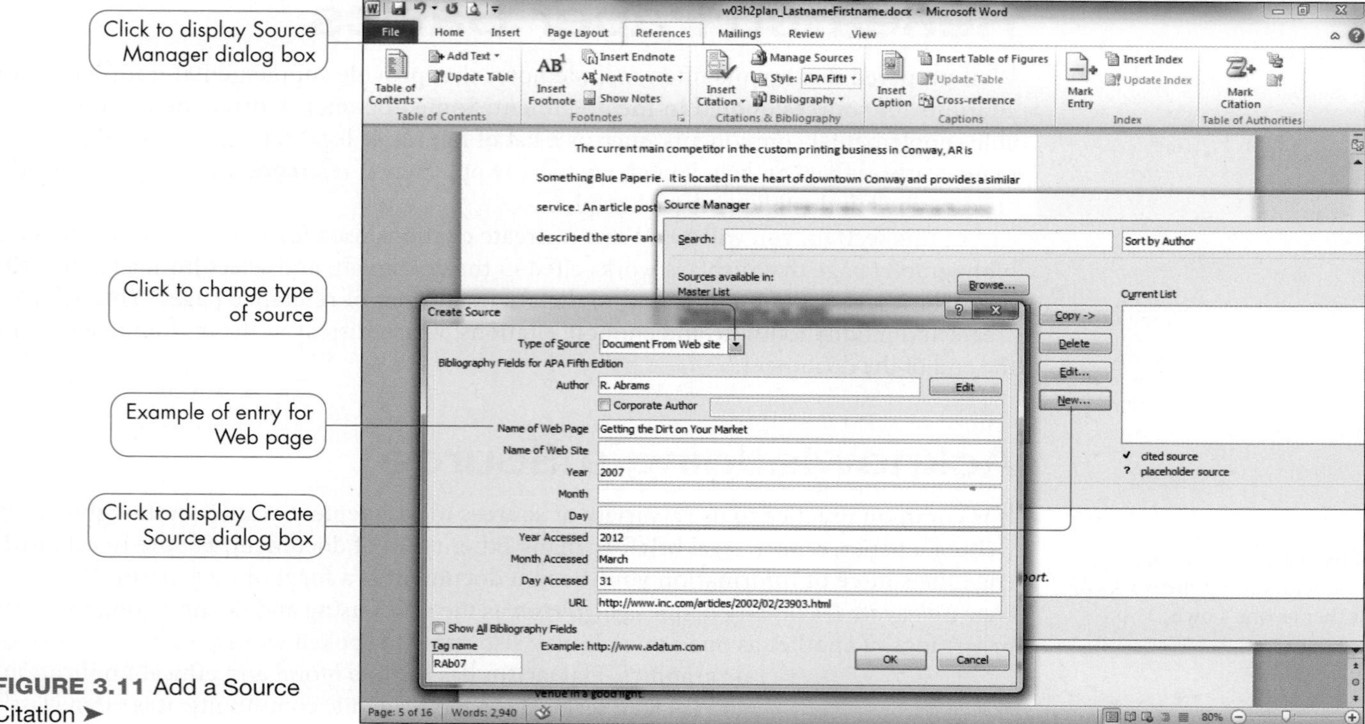

FIGURE 3.11 Add a Source Citation ➤

The **Master List** is a database of all citation sources created in Word.

The **Current List** includes all citation sources you use in the current document.

Share and Search for a Source

After you add sources, they are saved in a Master List. The ***Master List*** is a database of all citation sources created in Word on a particular computer. The source also is stored in the ***Current List***, which contains all sources you use in the current document. Sources saved in the Master List can be used in any Word document. This feature is helpful to those who use the same sources on multiple occasions. Master Lists are stored in XML format, so you can share the Master List file with coworkers or other authors, eliminating the need to retype the information and ensuring accuracy. The Master List file is stored in \AppData\Roaming\Microsoft\Bibliography, which is a subfolder of the user account folder stored under C:\Users. For example, a path to the Master File might be C:\Users\MichelleHulett\AppData\Roaming\Microsoft\Bibliography\Sources.xml.

The Source Manager dialog box (see Figure 3.12) displays the Master List you created, and you also can browse to find other XML files that contain source information. After you open a Master List, you can copy sources to your Current List. You can also copy, delete, or edit sources in either the Master or Current List from the Source Manager.

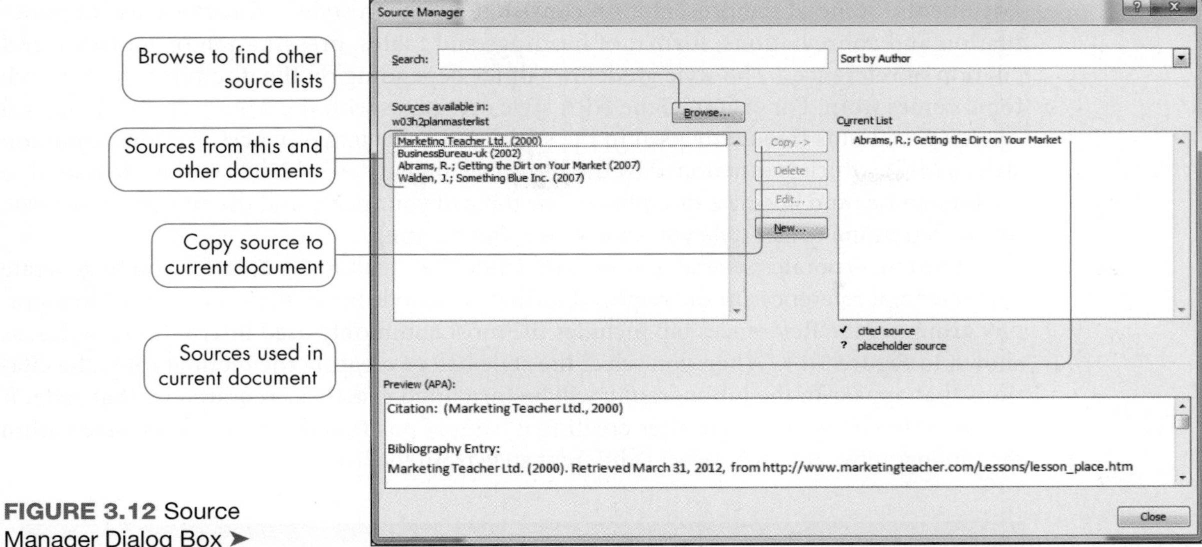

FIGURE 3.12 Source Manager Dialog Box ➤

Creating a Bibliography

A **bibliography** is a list of works cited or consulted by an author in a document.

A ***bibliography*** is a list of works cited or consulted by an author and should be included with the document when published. Some reference manuals use the terms Works Cited or References instead of Bibliography. A bibliography is just one form of reference that gives credit to the sources you consulted or quoted in the preparation of your paper. The addition of a bibliography to your completed work demonstrates respect for the material consulted. In addition to the bibliography, you should cite your source within a document, near any quotations or excerpts, to avoid plagiarizing. It also gives the reader an opportunity to validate your references for accuracy.

Word includes a bibliography feature that makes the addition of this reference page very easy. After you add the sources using the Insert Citation feature, you click Bibliography in the Citations & Bibliography group on the References tab, and then click Insert Bibliography. Any sources used in the current document will display in the appropriate format as a bibliography, as shown in Figure 3.13.

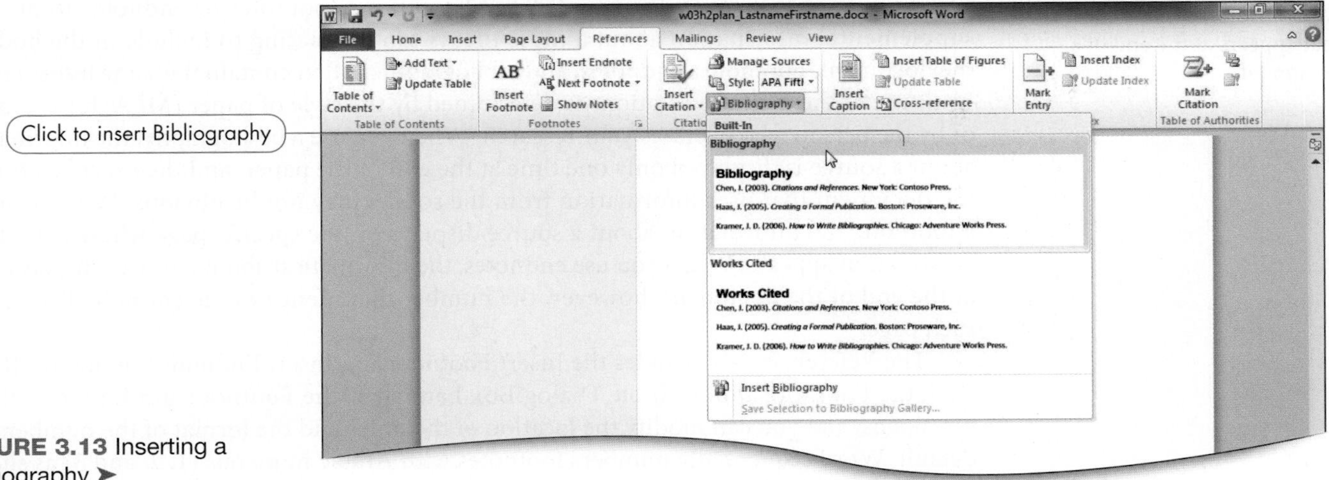

FIGURE 3.13 Inserting a Bibliography ➤

Selecting the Writing Style

When research papers are prepared the author often must conform to a particular writing style. The writing style, also called an editorial style, consists of rules and guidelines set forth by a publisher of a research journal to ensure consistency in presentation of research documents. Some of the presentation consistencies that a style enforces are use of punctuation and abbreviations, format of headings and tables, presentation of statistics, and citation of references. The style guidelines differ depending on the discipline the research topic comes from. For example, the APA style originates with the American Psychological Association, but is frequently used in the social and behavioral sciences. Another common style is MLA, which is sanctioned by the Modern Language Association and is often used in the humanities and business disciplines. The topic of your paper and the audience you write to will determine which style you should use while writing.

Word incorporates several writing style guidelines, making it easier for you to generate supplemental references in the required format. The Style list in the Citations & Bibliography group on the References tab includes the most commonly used international styles, as shown in Figure 3.14. When you select the style before creating the bibliography, the citations that appear in the bibliography will be formatted exactly as required by that style. If you want to change the style after creating it, simply position the cursor anywhere within the bibliography, and then select a different style from the list.

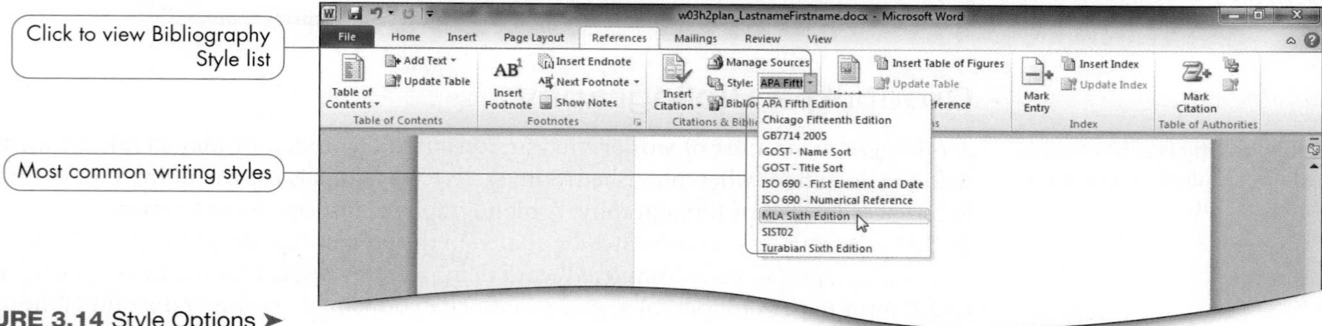

FIGURE 3.14 Style Options ➤

Creating and Modifying Footnotes and Endnotes

A **footnote** is a citation that appears at the bottom of a page.

An **endnote** is a citation that appears at the end of a document.

A ***footnote*** is a citation that appears at the bottom of a page, and an ***endnote*** is a citation that appears at the end of a document. You use footnotes or endnotes to credit the sources you quote or cite in your document. You also can use footnotes or endnotes to provide supplemental information about a topic that is too distracting to include in the body of the document. Footnotes, endnotes, and bibliographies often contain the same information. Your use of these citation options is determined by the style of paper (MLA, for example) or by the person who oversees your research. When you use a bibliography, the information about a source is displayed only one time at the end of the paper, and the exact location in the document that uses information from the source may not be obvious. When you use a footnote, the information about a source displays on the specific page where a quote or information appears. When you use endnotes, the information about a source displays only at the end of the document; however, the number that identifies the endnote displays on each page.

The References tab includes the Insert Footnote and Insert Endnote commands. If you click the Footnote and Endnote Dialog Box Launcher, the Footnote and Endnote dialog box opens, and you can modify the location of the notes and the format of the numbers. By default, Word sequentially numbers footnotes with Arabic numerals (1, 2, and 3) as shown in Figure 3.15. Endnotes are numbered with lowercase Roman numerals (i, ii, and iii) based on the location of the note within the document. If you add or delete notes, Word renumbers the remaining notes automatically.

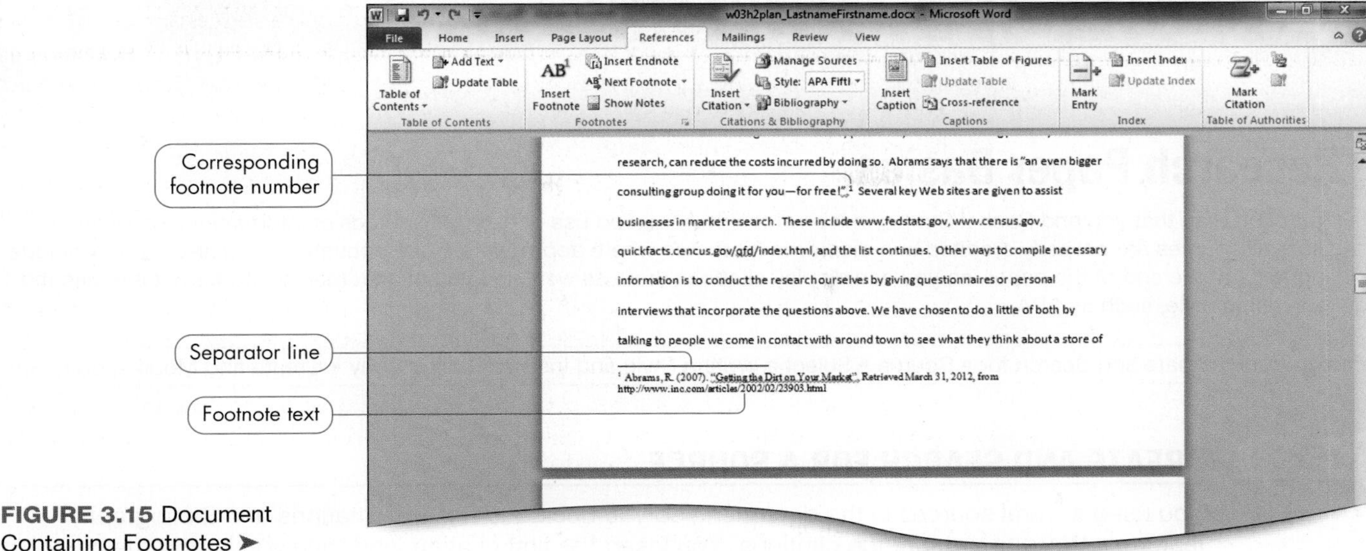

FIGURE 3.15 Document Containing Footnotes ➤

You can easily make modifications to footnotes and endnotes. In Print Layout view, scroll to the bottom of the page (or for endnotes, to the end of the document or section), click inside the note, and then edit it. In Draft view, double-click the footnote or endnote reference mark to display the Footnotes or Endnotes pane, and then you can edit the note.

TIP Relocating a Footnote or Endnote

If you created a note in the wrong location, select the note reference mark within the text, cut it from its current location, and then paste it in the correct location within the document text. You also can use the drag-and-drop method to move a selected note reference mark to a different location.

1. Define a citation and explain why citations should be used in a research paper.
2. Describe the difference between a Master List and a Current List, both of which you find in the Source Manager dialog box.
3. Name three features on the References tab to assist with creating a bibliography and how each contributes to the end product.
4. What is the difference between a footnote and an endnote, and how do you know when to use each one?

HANDS-ON EXERCISES

2 Research Paper Basics

The Marketing Plan that you and Rachel Starkey have written makes good use of external sources of information. You want to make sure all sources are properly credited and display in footnotes where appropriate in the document. You also plan to include a bibliography at the end of the paper, so you can display citations there as well, and you must remember to format it to use the required writing style, such as APA.

Skills covered: Create and Search for a Source • Select a Writing Style and Insert a Bibliography • Create and Modify Footnotes

STEP 1 CREATE AND SEARCH FOR A SOURCE

You used several sources in the document, so you decide to use the Citations and Bibliography feature in Word to prepare the citations. You insert the first citation, and then you import the other citations from a document that Rachel sent you, thus eliminating duplication of efforts. Refer to Figure 3.16 as you complete Step 1.

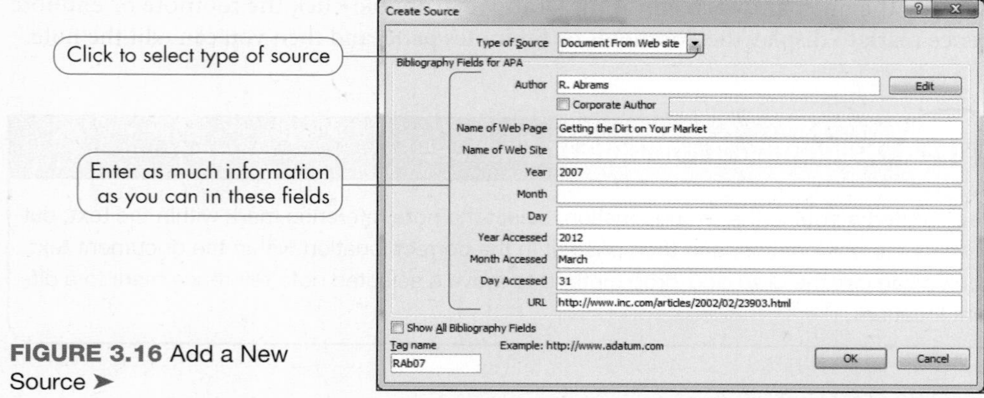

FIGURE 3.16 Add a New Source ➤

a. Open the *w03h1plan_LastnameFirstname* document if you closed it after the last Hands-On Exercise, and save it as **w03h2plan_LastnameFirstname**, changing *h1* to *h2*.

b. Click the **Display for Review arrow** in the Tracking group on the Review tab, and then select **Final**.

You are still tracking changes in the document, but the information that displays can distract your attention, so you change the view to display it as if all your changes are accepted.

c. Click the **References tab**, click **Manage Sources** in the Citations & Bibliography group, and then click **New** in the middle of the dialog box.

The Source Manager dialog box displays, as shown in Figure 3.16. Because you want to create a citation source without inserting the citation directly into the document, you use the Source Manager instead of clicking Insert Citation, Add New Source. After you click New in the Source Manager, the Create Source dialog box displays.

d. Click the **Type of Source arrow**, and then select **Document From Web site**. Type the source information as noted in the following table and as seen in Figure 3.16. After you enter each entry, click **OK** to add the source to your document and return to the Source Manager dialog box.

Author	R. Abrams
Name of Web Page	Getting the Dirt on Your Market
Year	2007
Year Accessed	2012
Month Accessed	March
Day Accessed	31
URL	http://www.inc.com/articles/2002/02/23903.html

To cite a source properly, you need as much information as you can provide, but you do not have to fill out all of the boxes in the Create Source dialog box. In some sources, such as the one above, the URL is more descriptive than the Web site name, and therefore more informative to anyone who wants to check your source.

e. Click **Browse** in the Source Manager dialog box to display the Open Source List dialog box. Click the drive and folder in the Folders list on the left side of the Open Source List dialog box where the student data files that accompany this book are located. Select *w03ho2planmasterlist*, and then click **OK**.

You return to the Source Manager dialog box, and three sources that Rachel Starkey had created in a separate document display in the *Sources available in* box along with the source you just created.

f. Click the first source entry, if necessary, to select it. Then press and hold **Ctrl** and select the other two new entries. Click **Copy** to insert the sources into the current document.

The three sources you copied and the one source you created display in the Current List box as well as in the Master List.

g. Click **Close** to return to the document. Save the document.

STEP 2 SELECT A WRITING STYLE AND INSERT A BIBLIOGRAPHY

Now that sources are cited and stored in the document, you can quickly insert the bibliography at the end. You also select the writing style, which affects the way each source displays in the bibliography listing. Luckily, you can select the style before or after inserting the bibliography and Word changes it accordingly. Refer to Figure 3.17 as you complete Step 2.

FIGURE 3.17 Bibliography in MLA Style ➤

a. Click the **Style arrow** in the Citations and Bibliography group, and then select **MLA Sixth Edition**.

b. Press **Ctrl+End** to position the insertion point at the end of the document, press **Ctrl+Enter** to add a blank page, and then type **Bibliography** at the top of the new page. Click the **Home tab**, and then apply the **Heading 1 style** from the Styles gallery. Press **End**, and then press **Enter** two times.

c. Click the **References tab**, click **Bibliography** in Citations & Bibliography, and then click **Insert Bibliography**.

The sources cited in the document display in the MLA format for bibliographies, as shown in Figure 3.17.

d. Click the **Style arrow** again, and then select **APA Fifth Edition**.

The format of the bibliography changes to reflect the standards of the APA style.

e. Save the document.

STEP 3 CREATE AND MODIFY FOOTNOTES

Rachel inserted some footnotes, but you realize she forgot one, so you add it. You also notice one footnote needs revising so that it accurately reflects the source information. Refer to Figure 3.18 as you complete Step 3.

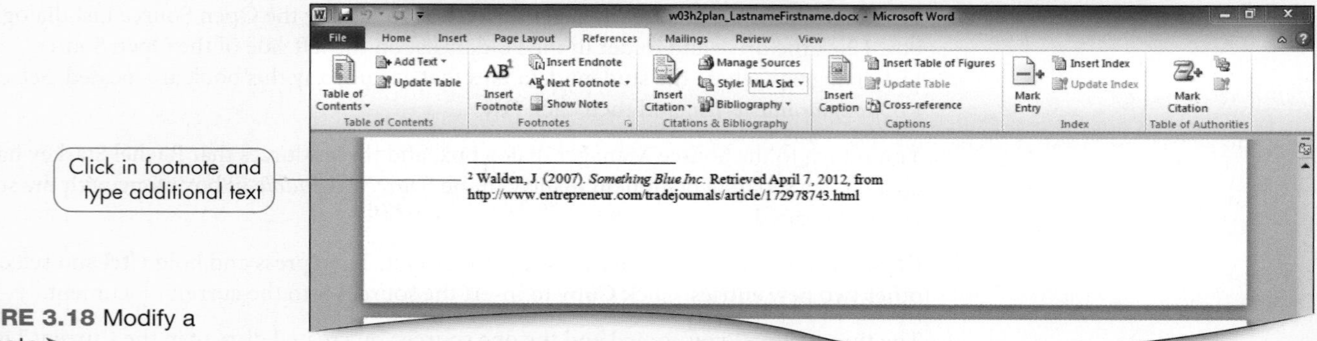

FIGURE 3.18 Modify a Footnote ➤

a. Scroll to the middle of page 4. Click one time at the end of the sentence that ends with *doing it for you—for free!* to relocate the insertion point. Click **Insert Footnote** in the Footnotes group.

The insertion point displays at the bottom of the page, below a horizontal line. This is where your footnote displays in the document.

b. Type **Abrams, R. (2007). "Getting the Dirt on Your Market". Retrieved March 31, 2012,** from **http://www.inc.com/articles/2002/02/23903.html**. Format the footnote as displayed with periods and commas, but do not bold the citation.

c. Scroll to the bottom of page 6. Click one time at the end of the footnote, a reference to an article written by J. Walden in 2007. Replace the date of retrieval with the date **April 7, 2012**.

You edited the footnote as shown in Figure 3.18.

d. Save *w03h2plan_LastnameFirstname* and keep it onscreen if you plan to continue with the next Hands-On Exercise. Close the file and exit Word if you will not continue with the next exercise at this time.

Research Paper Enhancements

The previous section mentioned several types of reference features that should be used when a document refers to outside information or sources. Some reference features are used less frequently, yet are valuable for creating professional quality documents. These supplements include a list of captions used on figures, a list of figures presented in a document, references to other locations in a document, and a list of legal sources referenced. You also can attach information that refers to the contents and origin of a document.

In this section, you will generate a table of contents at the beginning of a document. You will then learn how to designate text to include in an index and then generate the index at the end of a document. You will add captions to visual elements and create a list of the visuals used in a document, and you will create a list of references from a legal document. Finally, you will create a cross-reference, or note that refers the reader to another location in the document.

Inserting a Table of Contents and Index

Well-prepared long documents include special features to help readers locate information easily. For example, people often refer to the table of contents or the index in a long document—such as a book, reference manual, or company policy—to locate particular topics within that document. You can use Word to help you create these supplemental document components with minimal effort.

Well-prepared long documents include special features to help readers locate information easily.... You can use Word to help you create these supplemental document components with minimal effort.

Create a Table of Contents

A **table of contents** lists headings and the page numbers where they appear in a document.

A ***table of contents*** lists headings in the order they appear in a document and the page numbers where the entries begin. Word can create the table of contents automatically, if you apply a style to each heading in the document. You can use built-in styles, Heading 1 through Heading 9, or identify your own custom styles to use when generating the table of contents. Word also will update the table to accommodate the addition or deletion of headings or changes in page numbers brought about through changes in the document.

The table of contents feature is located on the References tab. After you apply a heading style to selected text in the document, you click the References tab and click Table of Contents to insert a predefined table of the styled text and page numbers. If you want more control over the way the table of contents displays in your document, you can click the Insert Table of Contents command to select from other styles such as Classic and Formal, as well as determine how many levels to display in the table; the latter correspond to the heading styles used within the document using the custom feature. You can determine whether to right-align the page numbers, and you also can choose to include a leader character to draw the reader's eyes across the page from a heading to a page number. Table 3.1 shows the variety of styles you can choose for your table of contents.

TABLE 3.1 Table of Contents Styles

Fancy Format

Table of Contents

Formal Format

Table of Contents

Modern Format

Table of Contents

Simple Format

Table of Contents

Create an Index

An **index** is a listing of topics and the page numbers where the topics are discussed.

An index puts the finishing touch on a long document. The ***index*** provides an alphabetical listing of topics covered in a document, along with the page numbers where the topic is discussed. Typically, the index appears at the end of a book or document. Word will create an index automatically, provided that the entries for the index have been previously marked. This requires you to go through a document, select the terms to be included in the index, and mark them accordingly. You can select a single occurrence of an entry and select an option to mark all occurrences of that entry for the index. You also can refer the reader to a different location in the document when you create an index entry, such as "see also Internet."

To mark an Index entry you follow these steps:

1. Select the word or phrase in your document that you want to display in the Index.
2. Click the References tab, and then click Mark Entry in the Index group. You can also use the shortcut Alt+Shift+X.
3. If necessary, revise the Main Entry text that displays in the Mark Index Entry dialog box. For example, if you mark a word that is not capitalized in the document, you want to revise the Main Entry so it is capitalized in the Index. The text that displays in the Main Entry box will display in the Index.
4. Click Mark for this selected word or phrase or click Mark All to include all occurrences of this word or phrase in the Index.
5. In a long document, it is helpful to use the Find feature to locate the next word or phrase to mark.
6. When all words or phrases are marked, close the Mark Entry dialog box.

After you specify the entries, create the index by choosing Insert Index in the Index group on the References tab. You can choose a variety of styles for the index, just as you can for the table of contents, as shown in Table 3.2. Word arranges the index entries in alphabetical order and enters the appropriate page references. You also can create additional index entries or move text within a document, then update the index with the click of a mouse.

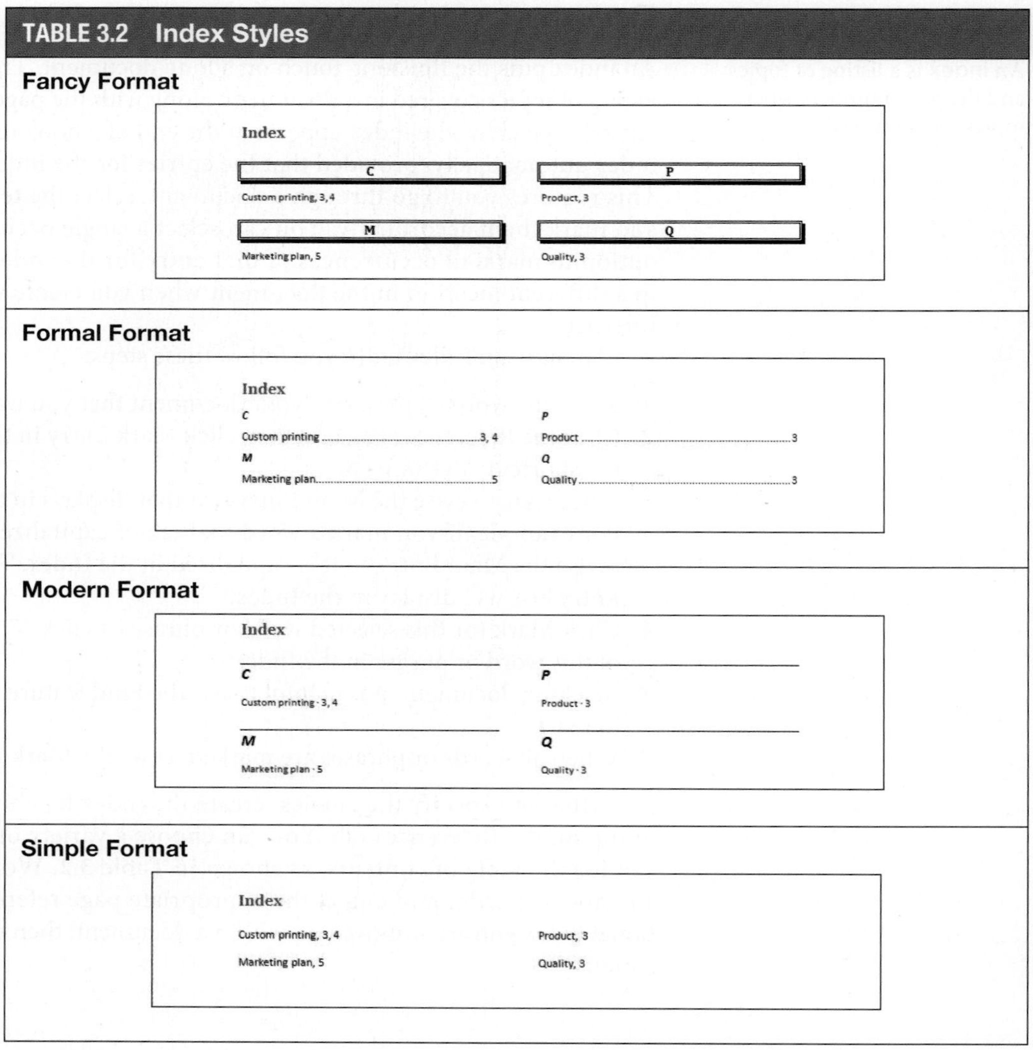

TABLE 3.2 Index Styles

Format	Example
Fancy Format	Index C Custom printing, 3, 4 M Marketing plan, 5 P Product, 3 Q Quality, 3
Formal Format	Index C Custom printing .... 3, 4 M Marketing plan .... 5 P Product .... 3 Q Quality 3
Modern Format	Index C Custom printing · 3, 4 M Marketing plan · 5 P Product · 3 Q Quality · 3
Simple Format	Index Custom printing, 3, 4 Marketing plan, 5 Product, 3 Quality, 3

To modify an Index entry, you must display the index fields by clicking Show/Hide (¶) in the Paragraph group on the Home tab. Locate the entry that you wish to modify and edit the text inside the quotation marks. Do not change the entry in the finished Index, or the next time you update the index, your changes will be lost. To delete an entry, select the entire entry field, including the braces {}, and then press Delete. After you modify or delete a marked entry, click Update Index in the Index group on the References tab to display the changes in the table.

TIP AutoMark Index Entries

When you have a lengthy list of words to mark for index entries, you can use a separate Word document as a source to help you automatically mark all occurrences of each word. When you select the AutoMark command from the Index dialog box it prompts you to open the Word document that contains a list of terms you want to mark for an index. It then marks the entries automatically. The advantage is that it is fast. The disadvantage is that every occurrence of an entry is marked and displays in the index so that a commonly used term may have too many page references. You can, however, delete superfluous entries by manually deleting the field codes. Click Show/Hide (¶) in the Paragraph group of the Home tab if you do not see the entries in the document.

Adding Other Reference Tables

You will likely use the Table of Contents and Index features most often in your research and other long documents. However, you can include additional reference tables to highlight other important information in your document. Some documents might contain so many tables or pictures that listing each one in a format similar to a table of contents can be helpful. Legal documents also often include a listing of the documents they use as a reference. Word includes features to enable you to include reference tables correctly for these situations.

Assign Figure Captions

A **caption** is a descriptive title for an equation, a figure, or a table.

Documents and books often contain several images, charts, or tables. For example, this textbook contains several screenshots in each chapter. To help readers refer to the correct image or table, you can add a caption. A ***caption*** is a descriptive title for an image, a figure, or a table. To add a caption click Insert Caption in the Captions group on the References tab. By default, Word assigns a number to the equation, figure, or table at the beginning of the caption. When you click Insert Caption, the Caption dialog box appears, as shown in Figure 3.19, and you can edit the default caption by adding descriptive text.

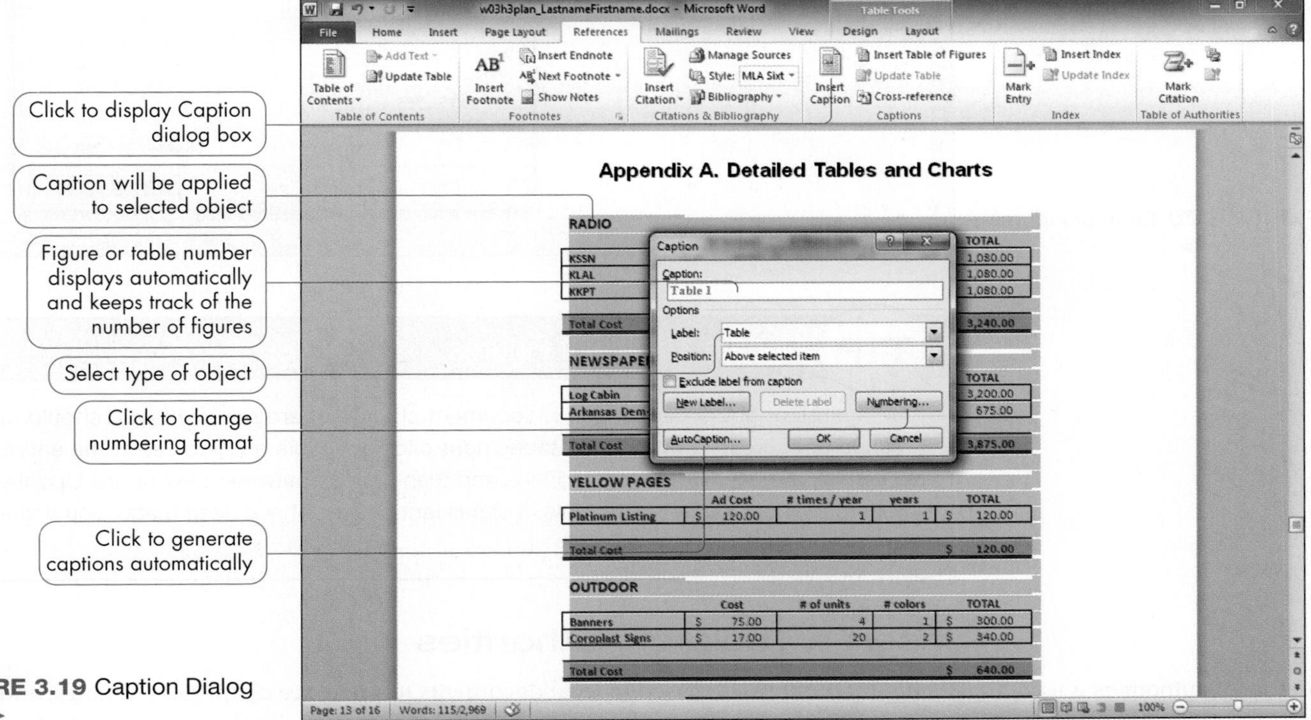
Click to display Caption dialog box
Caption will be applied to selected object
Figure or table number displays automatically and keeps track of the number of figures
Select type of object
Click to change numbering format
Click to generate captions automatically
Appendix A. Detailed Tables and Charts
Caption
Table 1
Above selected item
AutoCaption...
OK
Cancel

FIGURE 3.19 Caption Dialog Box ➤

To automatically generate captions, click AutoCaption in the Caption dialog box. In the *Add caption when inserting* list, in the AutoCaption dialog box, click the check box next to the element type for which you want to create AutoCaptions. Specify the default caption text in the *Use label* box, and specify the location of the caption by clicking the Position arrow. If your document will contain several captions, this feature helps to ensure each caption is named and numbered sequentially.

Insert a Table of Figures

A **table of figures** is a list of the captions in a document.

If your document includes pictures, charts and graphs, slides, or other illustrations along with a caption, you can include a ***table of figures***, or list of the captions, as a reference. To build a table of figures, Word searches a document for captions, sorts the captions by number, and displays the table of figures in the document. A table of figures is placed after the table of contents for a document. The Insert Table of Figures command is in the Captions group on the References tab. The Table of Figures dialog box, shown in Figure 3.20, enables you to select page number, format, and caption label options.

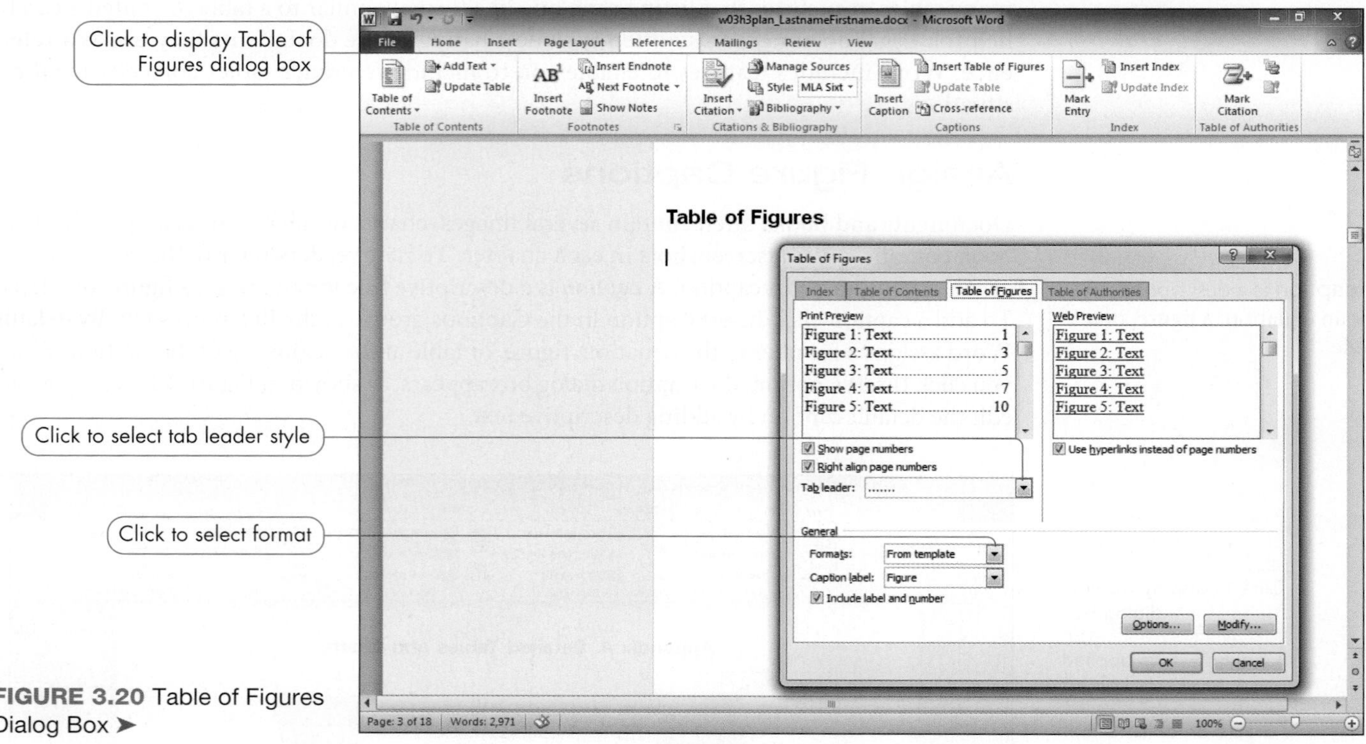

FIGURE 3.20 Table of Figures Dialog Box ➤

> **TIP** Update a Table of Figures
>
> If the figures or figure captions in a document change or are removed, you should update the table of figures. To update the table, right-click any table entry to select the entire table and display a menu. Click Update Field, and then choose between the options Update Page Numbers only or Update entire table. If significant changes have been made, you should update the entire table.

Insert a Table of Authorities

A **table of authorities** is used in legal documents to reference cases and other documents referred to in a legal brief.

A ***table of authorities*** is used in legal documents to reference cases, rules, treaties, and other documents referred to in a legal brief. You typically compile the table of authorities on a separate page at the beginning of a legal document. Word's Table of Authorities feature enables you to track, compile, and display citations, or references to specific legal cases and other legal documents, to be included in the table of authorities. Before you generate the table of authorities, you must indicate which citations you want to include using the Mark Citation command in the Table of Authorities group on the References tab. To mark citations, select text, and then click Mark Citation. The Mark Citation dialog box displays, as shown in Figure 3.21, and you can choose to mark this one case or mark all references to this case in the document. After you mark the citations in your document, click Insert Table of Authorities in the Table of Authorities group to generate the table at the location of your insertion point.

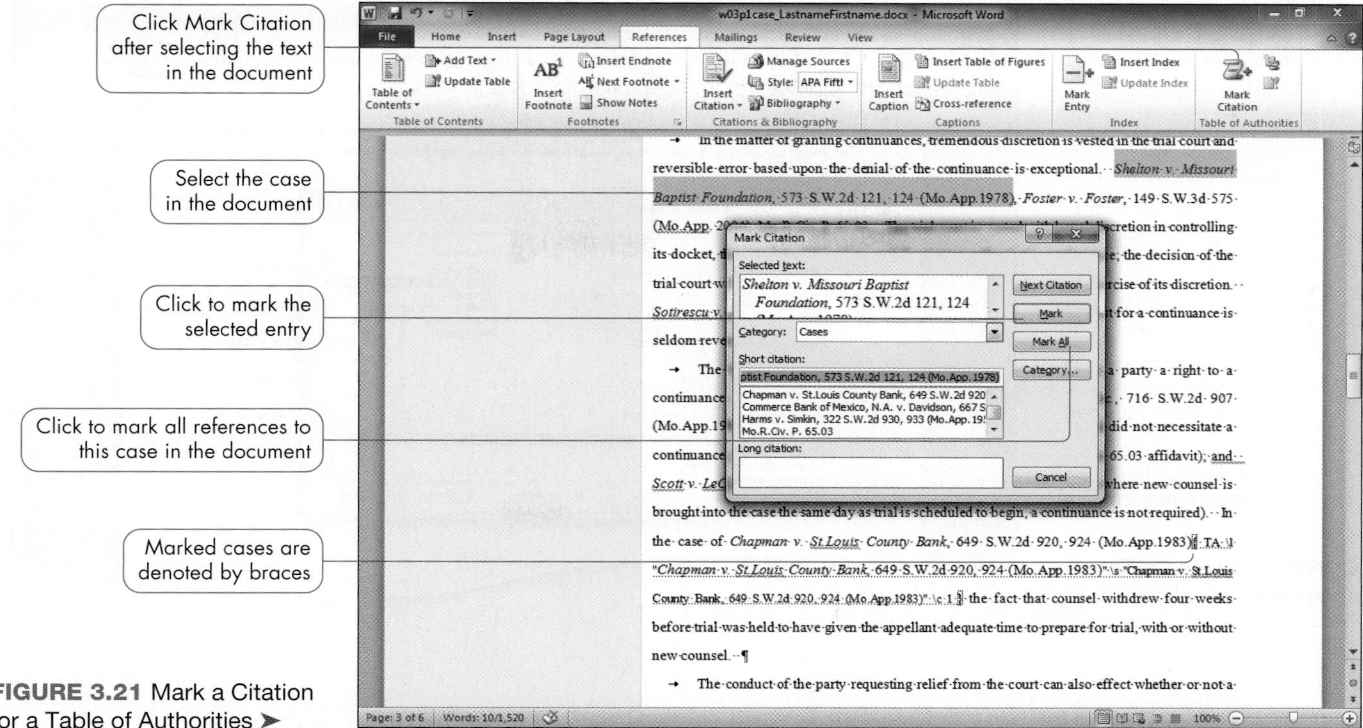
Click Mark Citation after selecting the text in the document
Select the case in the document
Click to mark the selected entry
Click to mark all references to this case in the document
Marked cases are denoted by braces

FIGURE 3.21 Mark a Citation for a Table of Authorities ➤

To modify an entry in the table of authorities, you must display the table of authorities fields by clicking Show/Hide (¶) in the Paragraph group on the Home tab. Locate the entry that you wish to modify and edit the text inside the quotation marks. Do not change the entry in the finished table of authorities, or the next time you update the table of authorities, your changes will be lost.

To delete a table of authorities entry, select the entire entry field, including the braces {}, and press Delete. After you modify or delete a marked entry, click Update Table in the Table of Authorities group on the References tab to display the changes in the table.

Creating Cross-References

A **cross-reference** is a note that refers the reader to another location for more information about a topic.

A ***cross-reference*** is a note that refers the reader to another location for more information about a topic. You can create automated cross-references to headings, bookmarks, footnotes, endnotes, captions, and tables. A typical cross-reference looks like this: *See page 4 for more information about local recreation facilities.* When using the automated cross-reference feature, Word tracks the location of the reference and inserts the correct page number in the place you designate in the document. For files you make available via e-mail or on an intranet, this creates an electronic cross-reference that enables the reader to hyperlink to that location.

To create a cross-reference, position the insertion point in the location where the reference occurs. On the References tab click Cross-reference in the Captions group. When the Cross-reference dialog box displays, as shown in Figure 3.22, you choose the type of reference (such as Heading, Bookmark, Figure, or Footnote) and then the reference element to display (such as page number or paragraph text). You can specify whether it displays as a hyperlink in the document, causing a ScreenTip to appear when the mouse pointer is over the cross-reference and moving you to that location when clicked, or as a static entry that simply displays a page number.

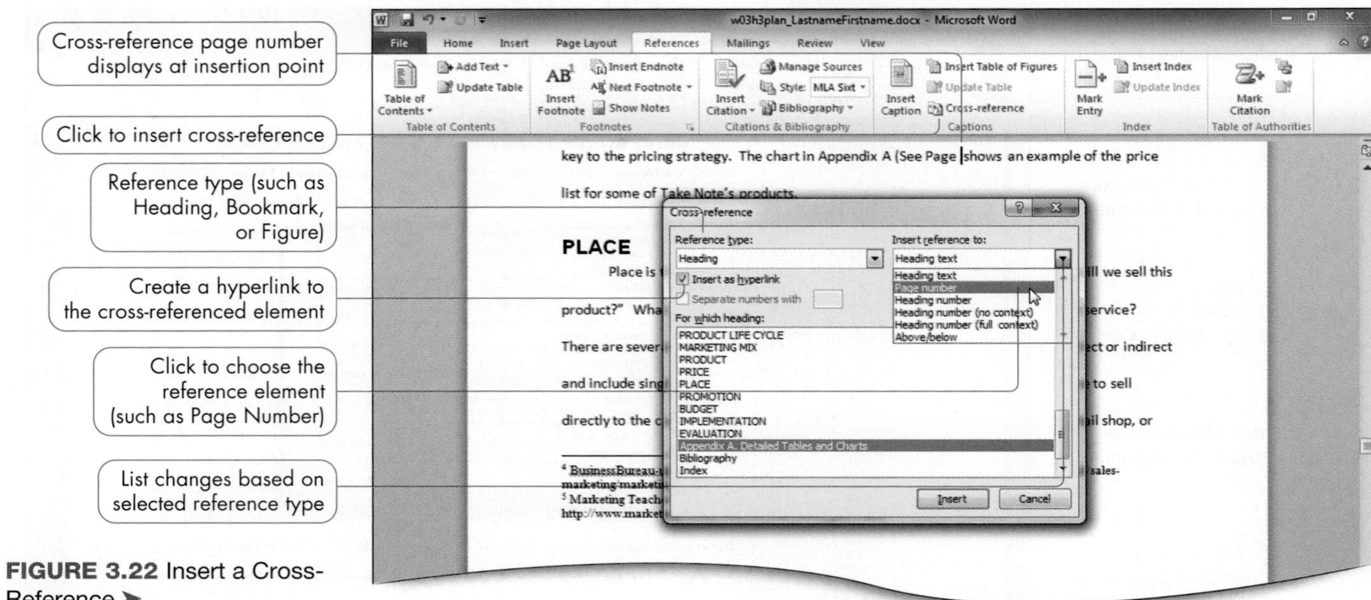

Cross-reference page number displays at insertion point
Click to insert cross-reference
Reference type (such as Heading, Bookmark, or Figure)
Create a hyperlink to the cross-referenced element
Click to choose the reference element (such as Page Number)
List changes based on selected reference type

FIGURE 3.22 Insert a Cross-Reference ➤

Quick Concepts Check

1. What feature in Word must you use in order to insert a table of contents?
2. What are the steps you must follow to mark text which you will include in an index?
3. List three ways you can modify a caption using the Caption dialog box.
4. What information do you use to generate a table of figures in a document, and where should you insert the table of figures?
5. Why would you insert a cross-reference in your document?

HANDS-ON EXERCISES

3 Research Paper Enhancements

This version of the marketing plan is nearly done. Only a few more enhancements will make it complete, so you decide to add a table of contents to the beginning of the document. Because of the number of graphic elements, you also decide to include a table of figures. An index will help the reader find information in this lengthy document, and you insert a cross-reference as well.

Skills covered: Apply Styles and Insert a Table of Contents • Define an Index Entry • Create the Index and Add Page Numbers • Add Captions and Create a Table of Figures • Create a Cross-Reference • Update the Table of Contents and View the Completed Document

STEP 1 APPLY STYLES AND INSERT A TABLE OF CONTENTS

Adding a table of contents (ToC) will enhance the professionalism of the marketing plan you and Rachel have developed for your class. You know that a table of contents is easy to insert if you apply styles to text first, so you take care of that and then insert the ToC. Refer to Figure 3.23 as you complete Step 1.

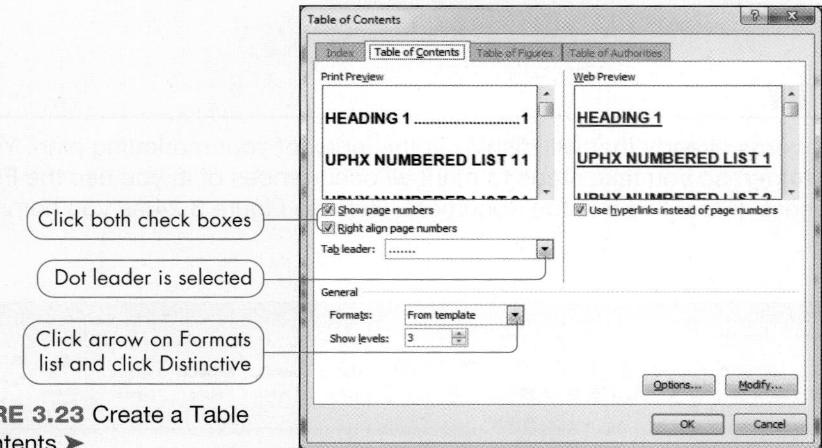

FIGURE 3.23 Create a Table of Contents ➤

a. Open the *w03h2plan_LastnameFirstname* document if you closed it after the last Hands-On Exercise. Save the document as **w03h3plan_LastnameFirstname**, changing *h2* to *h3*.

b. Click to the left of the *Executive Summary* title on the second page. Type **Table of Contents** and press **Enter** two times. Press **Ctrl+Enter** to insert a page break.

   The ToC displays on a page between the title page and the body of the document using the Heading 1 style you applied in the previous exercise.

TROUBLESHOOTING: If the Heading 1 style does not display, apply Heading 1 from the Quick Style gallery on the Home Tab to the *Table of Contents* heading.

c. Select the entire **Table of Contents heading**. Click the **Home tab**, and then apply the **Strong style**. **Center** the heading.

   If you continue to use the Heading 1 style, the *Table of Contents* heading will display in the ToC itself.

d. Apply the **Heading 1 style** to the paragraph heading *Organizational Overview* on the fourth page. Continue to apply the **Heading 1 style** to the paragraph headings on the next three pages using the Format Painter.

e. Scroll up and place the insertion point on the line following the *Table of Contents* title.

f. Click the **References tab**, and then click **Table of Contents** in the Table of Contents group. Select **Insert Table of Contents.**

   The Table of Contents dialog box displays (see Figure 3.23). You will see several preformatted styles provided when you click Table of Contents, but you are not using them because you want to customize the table. To customize you will select features in the Table of Contents dialog box, which you do in the next steps.

g. Click the **Show page numbers check box** and the **Right align page numbers check box**, if necessary.

h. Click the **Formats arrow** in the *General* section, and then select **Distinctive**. Click the **Tab leader arrow** in the *Print Preview* section, and then choose a dot leader. Click **OK**.

   Word takes a moment to create the table of contents and then displays all paragraph headings and their associated page numbers in the location of your insertion point.

> **TROUBLESHOOTING:** If your Table of Contents includes text from the paragraphs instead of just paragraph headings, check the style applied to the text. Remove the Heading 1 or 2 styles, if they are in use, and apply a different one to avoid inclusion in the ToC. Press F9 to update your table to reflect the change.

i. Save the document.

STEP 2 DEFINE AN INDEX ENTRY

Rachel has marked several words already that will display in the index of your marketing plan. You decide to add the word *customer*, so you take steps to mark all occurrences of it; you use the Find feature to speed up the process of locating it in the document. Refer to Figure 3.24 as you complete Step 2.

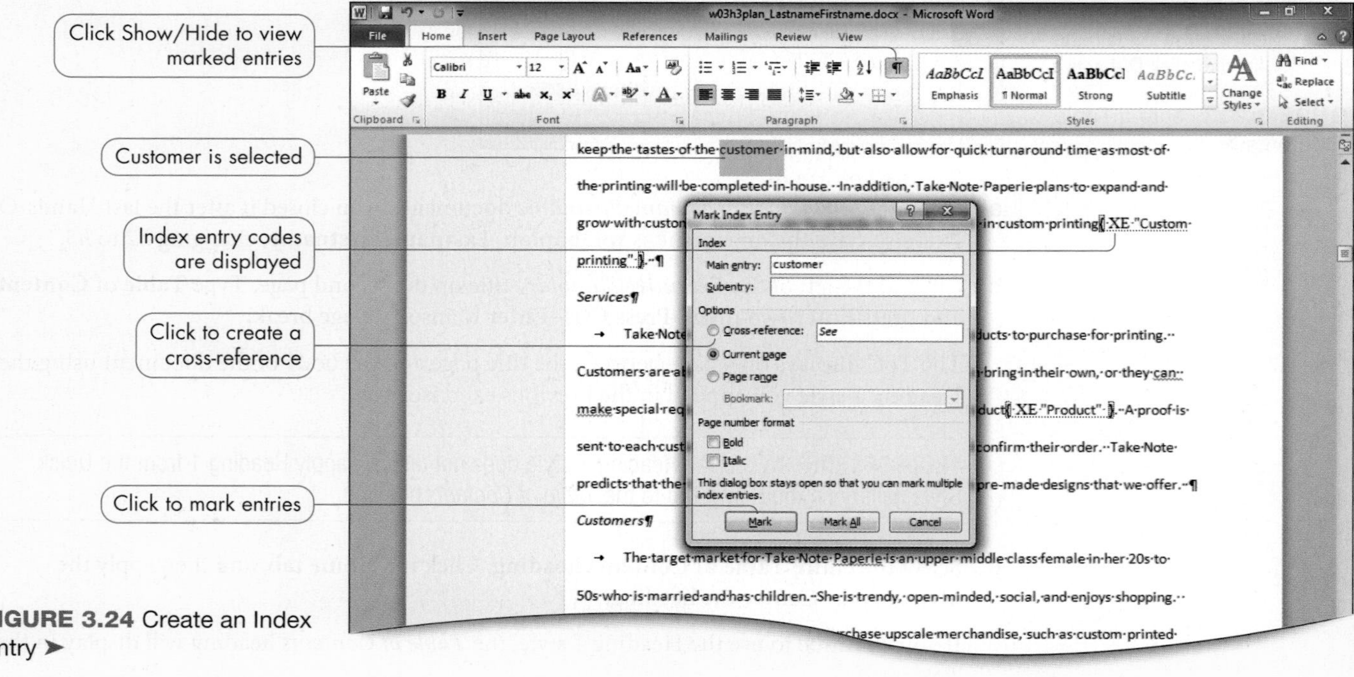

FIGURE 3.24 Create an Index Entry ➤

a. Press **Ctrl+Home** to move to the beginning of the document. Click **Ctrl+F** to display the Navigation Pane, and type **Customer** in the **text box**. Click the second entry in the results list.

   You click the second occurrence because it is in singular form. The first occurrence is in plural form, but that is not what you want to mark for the index.

b. Click the **Home tab**, if necessary, and then click **Show/Hide** (¶) in the Paragraph group so you can see the nonprinting characters in the document.

   The index entries already created by Rachel appear in curly brackets and begin with the letters *XE*.

c. Confirm that the entry for *customer* you just found is selected within the document. Click the **References tab**, and then click **Mark Entry** to display the Mark Index Entry dialog box, as shown in Figure 3.24.

d. Replace the lowercase *c* in the **Main Entry box** with a capital **C** so the word *Customer* displays capitalized.

   The word that displays in the dialog box, and later as a hidden mark in the document text, will display in the index, so you want it to be capitalized. Capitalizing it in the index entry does not affect the way it displays in the document.

e. Click **Mark** to create the index entry.

   After you create the index entry, you see the field code *{XE "Customer"}* to indicate that the index entry is created. The Mark Index Entry dialog box stays open so that you can create additional entries by selecting additional text.

f. Type **customer** in the **text box** in the Navigation Pane, if necessary, and then click the fourth entry, which is the next occurrence of the word *customer* in the document. Close the Navigation Pane.

g. Click anywhere on the Mark Index Entry dialog box, change capitalization to display *Customer* in the **Main Entry box**, and then click **Mark All** to create the index entry on all instances of the word in the remainder of the document.

   You know this word occurs many times in the document and each should be referenced in the Index; this is the most efficient way to mark all occurrences simultaneously.

h. Click **Close** to close the Mark Index Entry dialog box. Click the **Home tab**, and then click **Show/Hide** (¶) to hide the formatting marks.

i. Save the document.

STEP 3 CREATE THE INDEX AND ADD PAGE NUMBERS

You have just marked all the words you want to include in the Index, so it is time to add it. You remember to insert the index on a blank page at the end of the document, after the bibliography, You also decide it is time to add page numbers, which are appropriate to display in a multi-page document. Refer to Figure 3.25 as you complete Step 3.

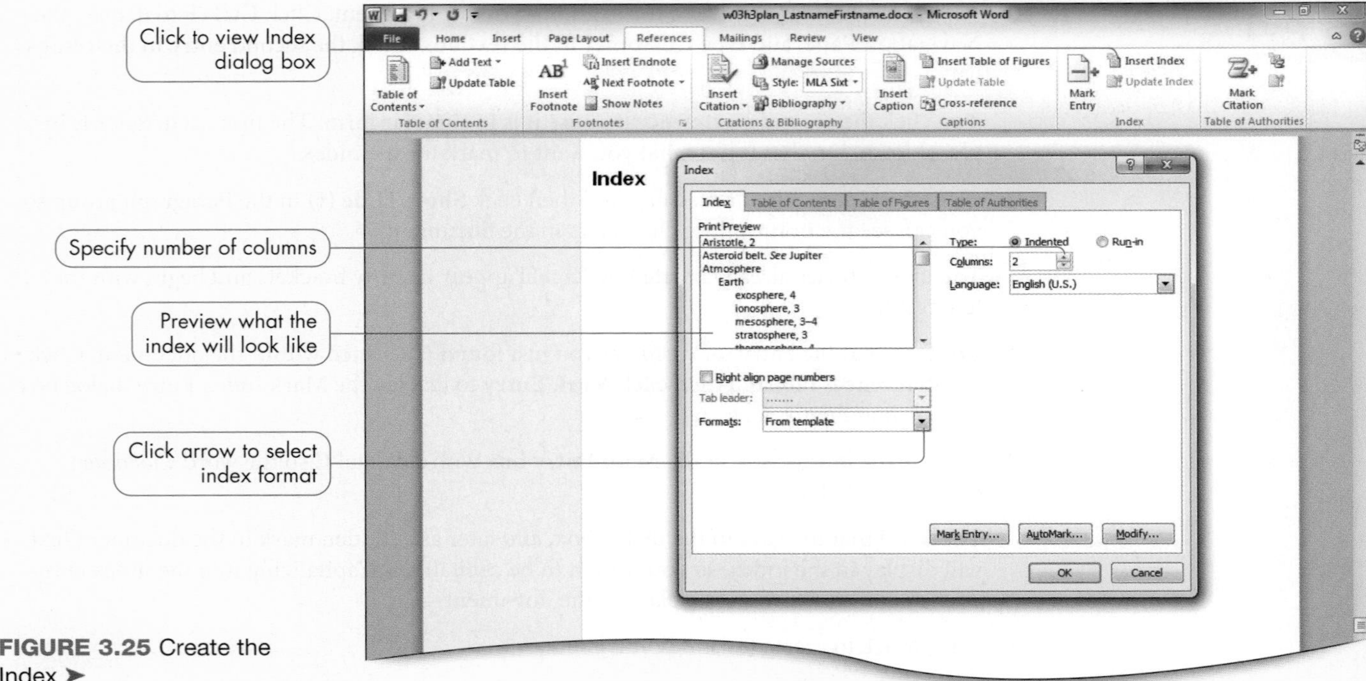
Click to view Index dialog box
Specify number of columns
Preview what the index will look like
Click arrow to select index format

FIGURE 3.25 Create the Index ➤

a. Press **Ctrl+End** to move to the end of the document, and then press **Ctrl+Enter** to add a new blank page.

   This is where you will insert the index.

b. Type **Index** and press **Enter** one time. Select **Index**, and then click **Heading 1** in the Styles gallery. Position your cursor on the line that follows the *Index* heading.

c. Click the **References tab**, and then click **Insert Index** in the Index group.

   The Index dialog box displays as shown in Figure 3.25.

d. Click the **Formats arrow**, and then select **Classic**. If necessary, click the **Columns arrow** until **2** displays. Click **OK** to create the index.

TROUBLESHOOTING: Click Undo on the Quick Access Toolbar if the index does not display at the end of the document, reposition the cursor, and then repeat Steps 3c and 3d.

TIP Check the Index Entries

Every entry in the index should begin with an uppercase letter. If this is not the case, it is because the original entry within the body of the document was marked improperly. Click Show/Hide (¶) in the Paragraph group on the Home tab to display the indexed entries within the document, which appear within brackets, e.g., {XE "Customer"}. Change each entry to begin with an uppercase letter as needed.

e. Click the **Insert tab**, click **Page Number** in the Header & Footer group, point to **Bottom of Page**, and then click **Plain Number 3**. Click **Close Header and Footer**.

f. Save the document.

STEP 4 ADD CAPTIONS AND CREATE A TABLE OF FIGURES

Because the marketing plan contains multiple tables and a graphic, you take steps to insert a table of figures. Similar to other reference items you insert, before you create this table you must do some preliminary work by adding captions to the tables and graphic first, which are then used in the table. Refer to Figure 3.26 as you complete Step 4.

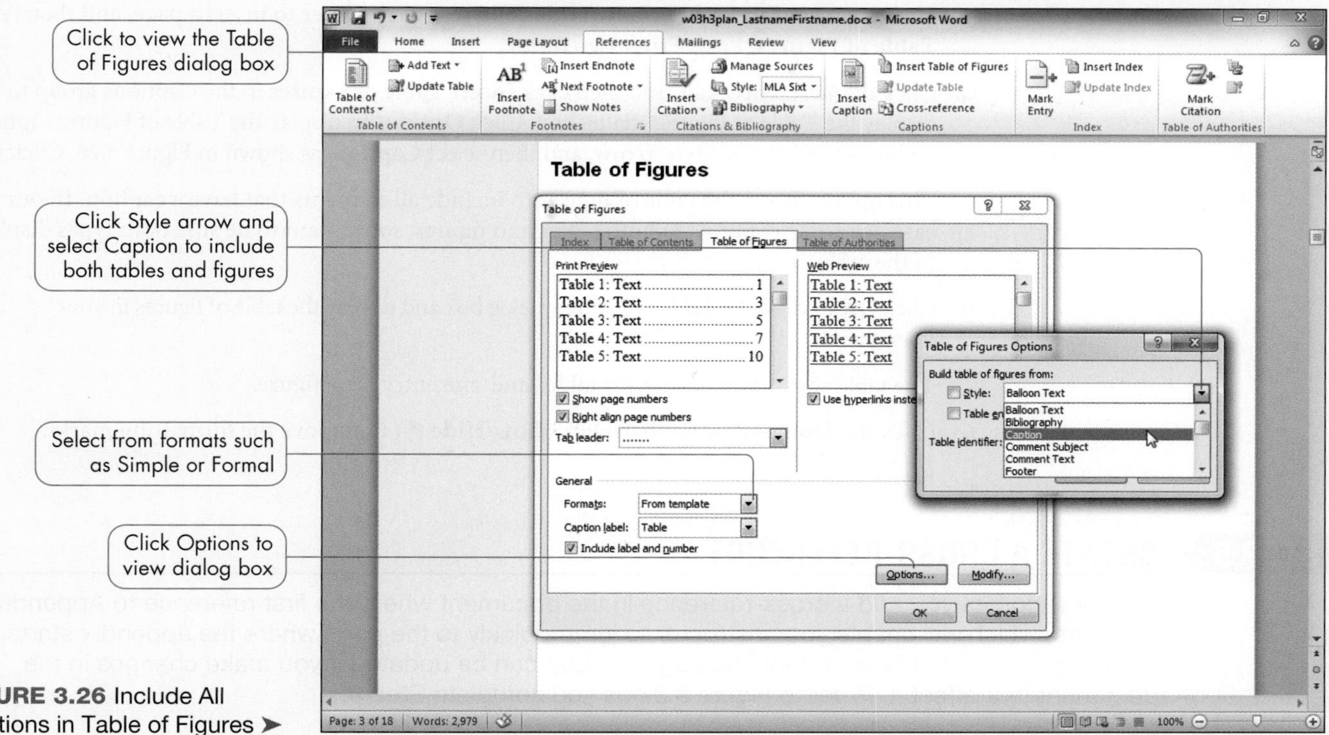

Click to view the Table of Figures dialog box
Click Style arrow and select Caption to include both tables and figures
Select from formats such as Simple or Formal
Click Options to view dialog box
w03h3plan_LastnameFirstname.docx - Microsoft Word
Table of Figures
Table of Figures Options

FIGURE 3.26 Include All Captions in Table of Figures ➤

FYI

a. Go to page 14 where Appendix A begins. Hold your mouse over the top-left corner of the table until the cursor turns into a crosshair with arrows on each end. Click once to select the entire table. Click the **References tab**, and then click **Insert Caption** in the Captions group.

> **TROUBLESHOOTING:** Your page numbers may vary slightly. If so, find the page where *Appendix A* displays.

The Caption dialog box displays, and the insertion point is positioned at the end of the caption text that displays automatically.

b. Press the **Colon key (:)**, and then press **Spacebar** two times. Type **Initial Advertising Plan Budget** in the **Caption box**. Click the **Position arrow**, and then select **Above selected item**, if necessary. Click **OK**.

The caption *Table 1: Initial Advertising Plan Budget* displays above the chart. By default, captions for tables are placed above the table, and captions for images are placed below the image. However, you can relocate them by making a change in the Caption dialog box.

c. Scroll to the top of the next page, and then select the organization chart. Click **Insert Caption** in the Captions group to open the Caption dialog box.

d. Click the **Label arrow**, and then select **Figure**. Click to place the cursor after *Figure 1* in the **Caption box**, press the **Colon key (:)**, press **Spacebar** two times, and then type **Marketing Organization**. Click the **Position arrow**, and then click **Above selected item**. Click **OK** to close the dialog box.

The caption for this figure now displays *Figure 1: Marketing Organization.*

e. Scroll to the top of the next page, and then select the chart. Click **Insert Caption**, press the **Colon key (:)**, press **Spacebar** one time, and then type **Take Note Paperie—Price List** in the **Caption box**. Click the **Label arrow**, and then select **Table**. Click the **Position arrow**, and then select **Above selected item**, if necessary. Click **OK** to close the dialog box.

   You have now created three captions in this paper—two for tables and one for a figure.

f. Move your insertion point to the bottom of page 2, which contains the ToC. Click the **Home tab**, and then click **Show/Hide (¶)**. Press **Ctrl+Enter** to insert a page, and then type **Table of Figures**. Press **Enter** two times.

g. Click the **References tab**, and then click **Insert Table of Figures** in the Captions group to display the Table of Figures dialog box. Click **Options** to display the Table of Figures Options dialog box. Click the **Style arrow**, and then select **Caption**, as shown in Figure 3.26. Click **OK**.

   This option forces the table of figures to include all elements that have a caption. In our case, we apply captions to both tables and figures, so we want to be sure both types display in the table.

h. Click **OK** to close the Table of Figures dialog box and display the table of figures in your document.

   The table shows two entries for tables and one entry for a figure.

i. Click the **Home tab**, and then click **Show/Hide (¶)** to remove the formatting marks.

j. Save the document.

STEP 5 ➤ CREATE A CROSS-REFERENCE

Rachel suggests you add a cross-reference in the document where the first reference to Appendix A occurs, which will enable your instructor to jump quickly to the page where the appendix starts. By using the cross-reference tool, the page number can be updated if you make changes in the document that affect it. Refer to Figure 3.27 as you complete Step 5.

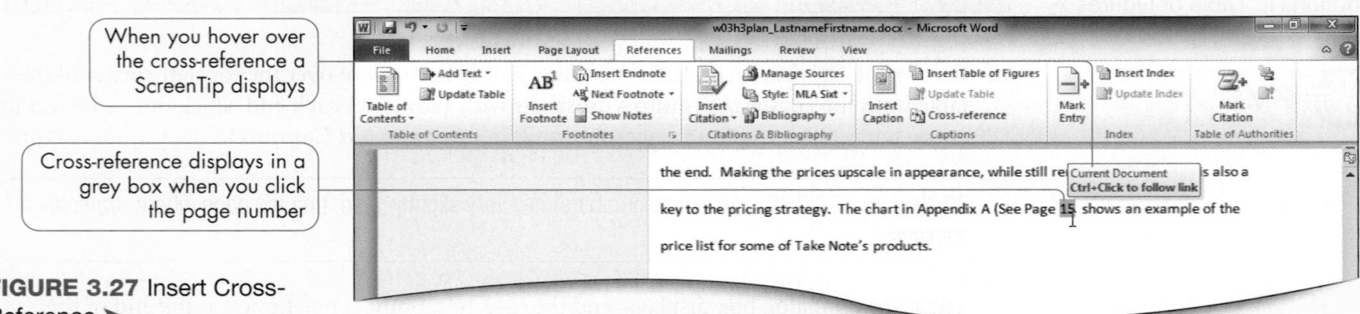

FIGURE 3.27 Insert Cross-Reference ➤

a. Scroll to page 11, and then place the insertion point on the right side of the text *Appendix A* in the last sentence of the *Price* section.

b. Press **Spacebar**, and then type **(See page** . Click the **References tab**, if necessary, and then click **Cross-reference** in the Captions group. Click the **Reference type arrow**, and then select **Heading**. Click **Appendix A. Detailed Tables and Charts** in the **For which heading list**. Click the **Insert reference to arrow**, select **Page number**, and then click **Insert**. Click **Close** to close the Cross-reference dialog box.

   The cross-reference displays the number *15*, which is the page where the chart displays.

c. Type) to close the parenthesis around the cross-reference. Click one time on the number *15* in the cross-reference, and then notice it is shaded with a dark grey box. Hold your mouse over the cross-reference page number, and then view the ScreenTip, as shown in Figure 3.27.

   The ScreenTip instructs you to press *Ctrl+Click to follow link* while you click the number *15*; if you do, Word will move the insertion point to the location of the chart on page 15.

d. Save the document.

STEP 6 UPDATE THE TABLE OF CONTENTS AND VIEW THE COMPLETED DOCUMENT

Before you finish you want to make sure the additions of the table of figures, bibliography, and index display in your table of contents, so you take steps to update it and all page numbers. Then you view the marketing plan as a final copy without markup. Then you save it so Rachel can look at it before you submit it to your professor. Refer to Figure 3.28 as you complete Step 6.

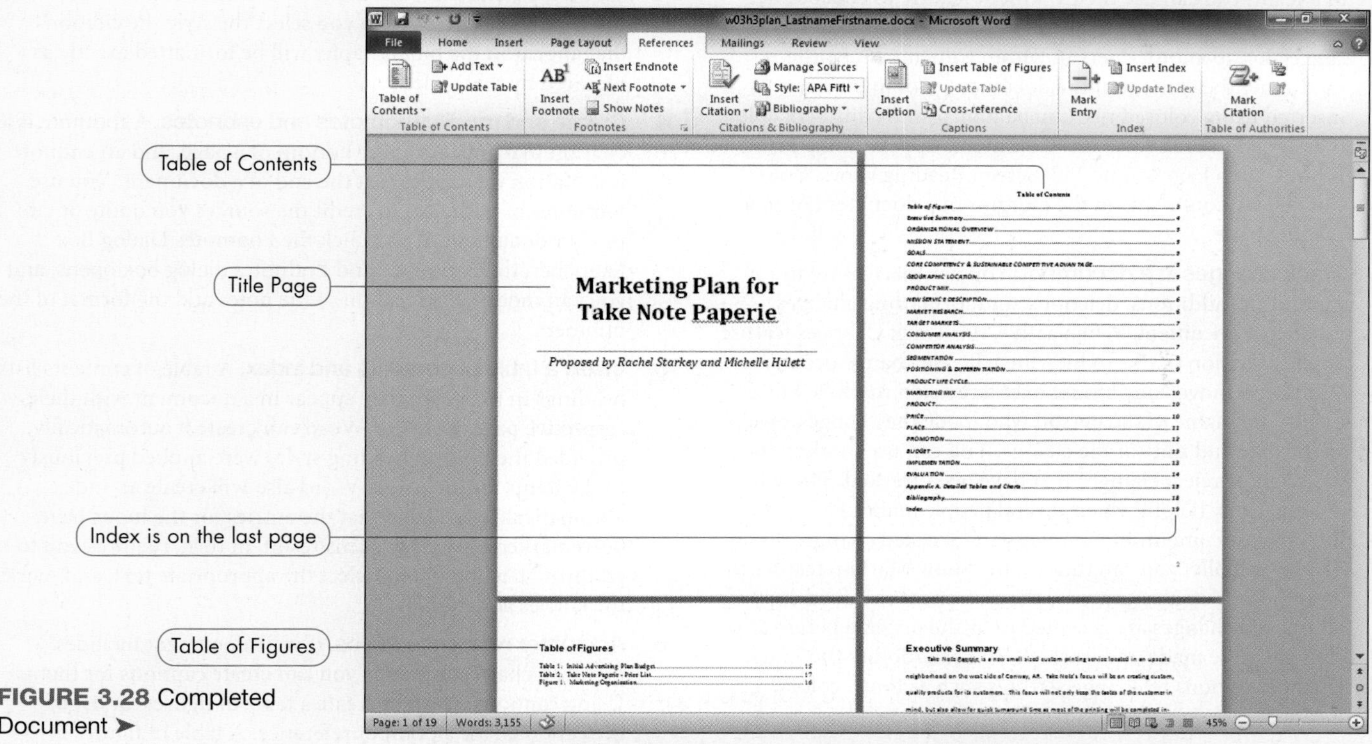

FIGURE 3.28 Completed Document ➤

a. Scroll to view the page that contains the *Table of Contents*. Right-click anywhere in the ToC, click **Update Field**, click **Update Entire Table**, and then click **OK**.

The entries for *Table of Figures*, *Bibliography*, and *Index* display, and page numbers adjust throughout the ToC to reflect these additions.

> **TROUBLESHOOTING:** If one or more of these tables do not display in the ToC, reapply the Heading 1 style to them, and update the ToC again. Also, remove any extra page breaks that might occur when you refresh the table—you do not want blank pages in between reference pages.

b. Click **Zoom level** on the status bar. Click the **Many pages icon** and drag to display **2 × 2 Pages**. Click **OK**.

You view several pages of the document, as seen in Figure 3.28.

c. Save and close the *w03h3plan_LastnameFirstname* file, and submit based on your instructor's directions.

CHAPTER OBJECTIVES REVIEW

After reading this chapter, you have accomplished the following objectives:

1. **Insert comments in a document.** When you work as part of a team, you can use the Comment feature to collaborate. Comments enable you to ask a question or provide a suggestion to another person within a document, without modifying the content of the document. Comments are inserted using colored markup balloons, and a different color is assigned to each reviewer. Comments appear in the Print Layout, Web Layout, and Full Screen Reading views. You can display comments in the margins of a document or in a reading pane.
2. **Track changes in a document.** You use this feature to monitor all additions, deletions, and formatting changes made to a document. When active, the Track Changes feature applies revision marks to indicate where a change occurs. When you move your mouse over a revision mark, it will display the name of the person who made the change as well as the date and time of the change. You can use markup tools to accept or reject changes that have been tracked. These tools are especially helpful when several people make changes to the same document. If comments and tracked changes do not display initially, you can turn on the Show Markup feature to view them. You also can view the document as a final copy if all tracked changes are accepted or as the original before any changes were made and tracked. You can modify the Track Changes options to change settings such as fonts, colors, location, and size of markup balloons.
3. **Acknowledge a source.** It is common practice to use a variety of sources to supplement your own thoughts when authoring a paper, report, legal brief, or many other types of document. Failure to acknowledge the source of information you use in a document is a form of plagiarism. Word provides the citation feature to track, compile, and display your research sources for inclusion in several types of supplemental references such as a bibliography. A bibliography is a list of works cited or consulted by an author and should be included with the document when published. Any sources added with the citation feature and used in the current document will display in the appropriate format as a bibliography. When research papers are prepared, the author often must conform to a particular writing style. The Style list on the References tab includes the most commonly used international styles. When you select the style the citations that appear in the bibliography will be formatted exactly as required by that style.
4. **Create and modify footnotes and endnotes.** A footnote is a citation that appears at the bottom of a page, and an endnote is a citation that appears at the end of a document. You use footnotes or endnotes to credit the sources you quote or cite in your document. If you click the Footnotes Dialog Box Launcher, the Footnotes and Endnotes dialog box opens, and you can modify the location of the notes and the format of the numbers.
5. **Insert a table of contents and index.** A table of contents lists headings in the order they appear in a document with their respective page numbers. Word can create it automatically, provided the built-in heading styles were applied previously to the items for inclusion. Word also will create an index automatically, provided that the entries for the index have been marked previously. This result, in turn, requires you to go through a document, select the appropriate text, and mark the entries accordingly.
6. **Add other reference tables.** If your document includes pictures, charts, or graphs you can create captions for them. Using captions, you can create a table of figures, or list of the captions, for a point of reference. A table of figures is commonly placed after the table of contents for a document. A table of authorities is used in legal documents to reference cases, rules, treaties, and other documents referred to in a legal brief. Word's Table of Authorities feature enables you to mark, track, compile, and display citations, or references to specific legal cases and other legal documents, to be included in the table of authorities.
7. **Create cross-references.** A cross-reference is a note that refers the reader to another location in the document for more information about a topic. You can create cross-references to headings, bookmarks, footnotes, endnotes, captions, and tables.

KEY TERMS

Bibliography ***p.239***
Caption ***p.249***
Changed line ***p.229***
Citation ***p.237***
Comment ***p.226***
Cross-reference ***p.251***
Current List ***p.238***
Endnote ***p.240***
Final: Show Markup ***p.230***
Footnote ***p.240***
Index ***p.247***
Markup balloon ***p.226***
Master List ***p.238***
Original: Show Markup ***p.230***
Plagiarism ***p.237***
Reviewing Pane ***p.227***
Revision mark ***p.229***
Show Markup ***p.228***
Table of authorities ***p.250***
Table of contents ***p.245***
Table of figures ***p.249***
Track Changes ***p.229***

MULTIPLE CHOICE

1. Which of the following statements about comments is true?
   (a) You cannot edit a comment that was created by another person.
   (b) Comment balloons appear on the right side in Print Layout view by default.
   (c) You cannot ever print comments with the rest of the document.
   (d) You can use the Show Markup feature on the Review tab to filter markup balloons so comments display both inline and also in balloons.

2. What option enables you to preview how a document will look if you accept all tracked changes?
   (a) Final: Show Markup
   (b) Final
   (c) Original: Show Markup
   (d) Original

3. How do you view and edit footnote text?
   (a) Position the mouse pointer over the footnote reference mark and click inside the ScreenTip that appears.
   (b) Open the Footnote and Endnote dialog box.
   (c) Double-click the footnote reference mark and type in the footnote.
   (d) Click Citation on the References tab.

4. Which option is not true about plagiarism?
   (a) It is the act of using another person's work and claiming it as your own.
   (b) It is considered academic dishonesty in academic communities.
   (c) It only applies to written works; ideas, spoken words, or graphics are not included.
   (d) It has serious moral and ethical implications.

5. What document item directs a reader to another location in a document by mentioning its location?
   (a) Cross-reference
   (b) Bookmark
   (c) Endnote
   (d) Thumbnail

6. A table of figures is generated from what type of entries?
   (a) Index
   (b) Bookmarks
   (c) Comments
   (d) Captions

7. What does a table of authorities display?
   (a) A list of pictures, tables, and figures in a document
   (b) A list of cases, rules, treaties, and other documents cited in a legal document
   (c) A list of key words and phrases in the document
   (d) A sequential list of section headings and their page numbers

8. Select the sequence of events to include a bibliography in your document.
   (a) Select writing style, insert bibliography, and then insert citations.
   (b) Type footnotes into document, insert bibliography, and then select writing style.
   (c) Select writing style, mark legal references, and then insert bibliography.
   (d) Insert a citation, select writing style, and then insert bibliography.

9. After you create and insert a table of contents into a document:
   (a) Any subsequent page changes arising from the insertion or deletion of text to existing paragraphs must be entered manually.
   (b) Any additions to the entries in the table arising due to the insertion of new paragraphs defined by a heading style must be entered manually.
   (c) An index cannot be added to the document.
   (d) You can right-click, then select Update Field to update the table of contents.

10. You are participating in a group project in which each member makes changes to the same document. Which feature in Word should you suggest the members use so each can see the edits made by fellow group members?
    (a) Mark index entries.
    (b) Track changes.
    (c) Mark citations.
    (d) Create cross-references.

PRACTICE EXERCISES

1 Odom Law Firm

You work as a clerk in the Odom Law Firm and are responsible for preparing documentation used in all phases of the judicial process. A senior partner in the firm asks you to work on a document by inserting a table of authorities based on the cases cited in the document. As you work you notice it also needs another footnote and a caption on a graphic. So that the partner can double-check your work, you track the changes you make to the document. This exercise follows the same set of skills as used in Hands-On Exercises 1, 2, and 3 in the chapter. Refer to Figure 3.29 as you complete this exercise.

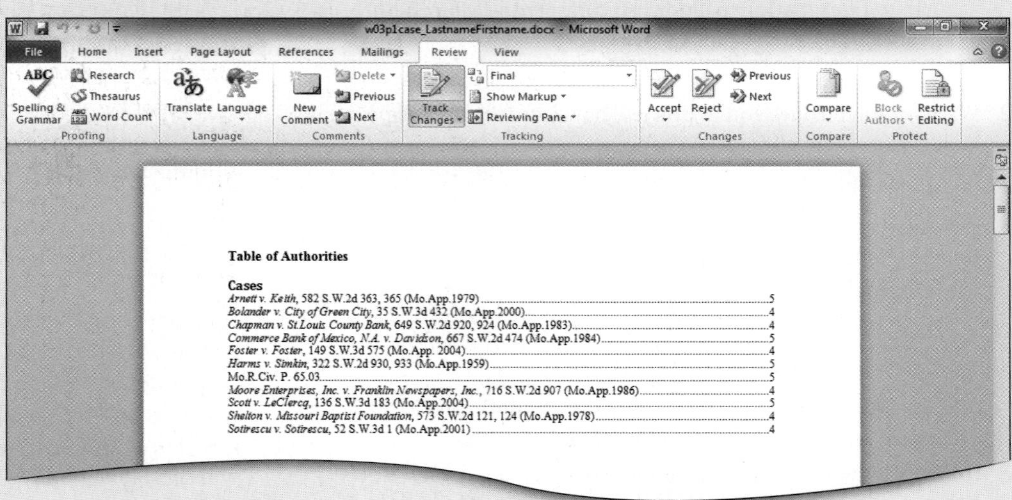

FIGURE 3.29 Table of Authorities ➤

a. Open *w03p1case* and save it as **w03p1case_LastnameFirstname**.

b. Press **Ctrl+Home** to move the insertion point to the beginning of the document.

c. Click the **Review tab**, click the **Track Changes arrow** in the Tracking group, and click **Change User Name**. Verify that your name displays as the *User Name* on this PC, and that your initials display in the Initials box; if necessary, type your name and initials in the appropriate text box, and then click **OK** to close the Word Options dialog box.

d. Click **Track Changes** in the Tracking group so the feature displays in orange and your edits are marked as you work.

e. Click **New Comment** in the Comments group, and then type **Second edit by *your name* on *date*.**

f. Click **Next** in the Comments group two times to select the balloon containing the comment about a change you need to make to the footer. Read the comment.

g. Place the insertion point at the end of the footer on the bottom of the first page. Replace the year *2008* with **2012**.

h. Click **Previous** in the Comments group to select the comment balloon you previously read. Move the insertion point to the end of the comment inside the balloon, and then type the sentence **Completed by *your name*** after the existing text. Remember to use your name.

i. Scroll to the bottom of page 2. Position your cursor at the end of the last sentence in the first paragraph under the heading *Attorney Blanchard's withdrawal.* When your cursor is on the right side of the period after the words *anything on the case*, click the **References tab**, and then click **Insert Footnote** in the Footnotes group. Type **See Exhibit 9, attached** in the **footnote area** where your cursor is blinking at the bottom of the page.

j. Press **Ctrl+End** to move to the end of the document. Select the picture of the bicycle, and then click **Insert Caption** in the Captions group. If necessary, click the **Label arrow**, and then select **Figure** so that *Figure 1* displays as the caption. Place the insertion point at the end of the caption, press **colon** (:), press **Spacebar** one time, and then type **Assembled Bicycle**. Click **OK** to close the Caption dialog box.

k. Go to page 3 in the document. Locate the *Shelton v. Missouri Baptist Foundation* case, and then select the case information from *Shelton* through and including the date *(1978)*. Select the closing parenthesis but not the comma after it. Click **Mark Citation** in the Table of Authorities group. Click **Mark All**, and then click **Close**.

l. Scan the remainder of that page, and then mark all citations for the following cases: *Foster*, *Sotirescu*, *Moore Enterprises*, *Scott*, *Chapman*, *Bolander*, and *Arnett*. After you mark the final citation on that page, click **Cancel** to close the dialog box. Click the **Home tab**, and then click **Show/Hide (¶)** in the Paragraph group to turn off display of formatting marks.

m. Press **Ctrl+Home** to position the insertion point at the beginning of the document, and then press **Ctrl+Enter** to add a blank page. Press **Ctrl+Home** to place the insertion point at the top of the new page, type **Table of Authorities**, and then press **Enter** one time. Click the **References tab**, and then click **Insert Table of Authorities** in the Table of Authorities group. Click **OK**.

n. Right-click the comment by William Kincaid on page 2 that says *Please add the Table of Authorities to this document*, and then click **Delete Comment**.

o. Press **Ctrl+F**, and then type **bike** in the **text box**. Place the insertion point after the first occurrence of the word *bike* that displays in the first sentence of the *Background* paragraph. Press **Spacebar** one time, and then type (**See picture on page** . Be sure to add a blank space after you type the word *page*. Click the **References Tab**, and then click **Cross-reference** in the Captions group.

p. Click the **Reference type arrow**, and then select **Figure**. Click **Figure 1 Assembled Bicycle** in the **For which caption list**, click the **Insert reference to arrow**, select **Page Number**, and then click **Insert** to complete the cross-reference. Click **Close** to close the Cross-reference dialog box. Type) to complete the parentheses that hold the cross-reference.

q. Click the **Review tab**, click the **Display for Review arrow**, and then click **Final** to display the document without markup. Press **Ctrl+Home** to view the table of authorities, and then compare to Figure 3.29.

r. Save and close the file, and submit based on your instructor's directions.

2 Social Networking Web Sites

In your business communications class, you have to write a three-page research paper about social communications. You decide to discuss the impacts of popular social networking Web sites on our society. Besides enhancing your description of each site with the company's trademark logo, you want to impress your instructor with your word processing skills by using features such as citations, endnotes, a table of contents, and a table of figures. This exercise follows the same set of skills as used in Hands-On Exercises 1–3 in the chapter. Refer to Figure 3.30 as you complete this exercise.

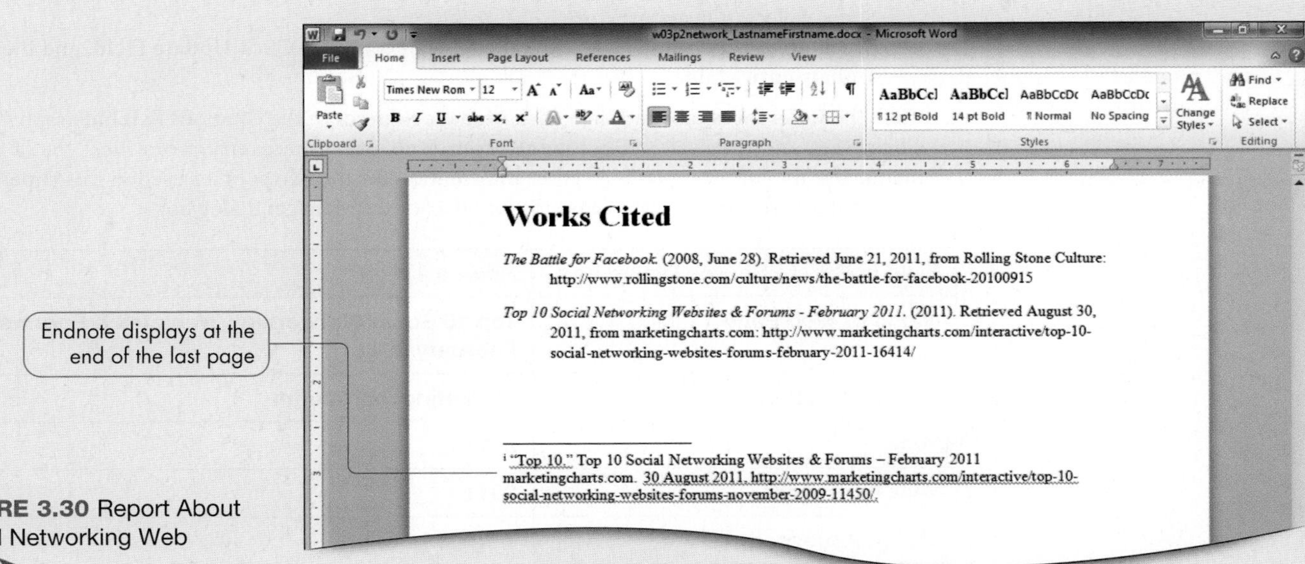

FIGURE 3.30 Report About Social Networking Web Sites ➤

a. Open *w03p2network* and save it as **w03p2network_LastnameFirstname**.

b. Click the **Insert tab**, and then click **Cover Page** in the Pages group. Update the cover page by completing the following steps:

- Choose the **Conservative style**, click the **company name placeholder**, and then press **Delete**.

- Click the **document title placeholder**, and then type **Social Networking Web Sites:** as the document title.
- Click the **document subtitle placeholder**, and then type **Impacts on Our Society**.
- Select the text in the **author placeholder** that displays *Exploring Series*, and type your name.
- Click **Pick the date**, click the **date arrow**, and then select **Today**.
- Click the **Abstract placeholder**, and then type **This research paper will introduce several popular social networking Web sites and will also briefly discuss the positive and negative impacts of these Web sites on our society.**

c. Press **Ctrl+Home** to move the insertion point to the beginning of the document. Click the **Review tab**, and then click **Next** in the Changes group. Click the **Accept arrow**, and then click **Accept All Changes in Document**. Click **Track Changes** in the Tracking group to turn off track changes.

d. Place the insertion point on the left side of the heading *Introduction* at the top of page 2. Press **Ctrl+Enter** to create a page break. Select the **Introduction heading** at the top of page 3, click the **Home tab**, and then apply the **Heading 1 style** from the Styles gallery. Apply the **Heading 1 style** to the remaining boldfaced paragraph headings in the document using the Format Painter.

e. Scroll to the top of page 2, and place the insertion point on the first line. Click the **References tab**, click **Table of Contents**, and then click **Automatic Table 2**.

f. Scroll down to the third page, and then select the graphic. Click **Insert Caption** in the Captions group. Press **Spacebar** twice, and then type **Top 10 Social Networking Web Sites**. Click the **Position arrow**, and then click **Below selected item**, if necessary. Click **OK** to close the Caption dialog box.

g. Use the instructions from step f to apply the following captions to the remaining pictures in the document:
   - **Facebook Logo**
   - **YouTube Logo**
   - **Myspace Logo**
   - **Twitter Logo**

h. Insert a table of figures and update the table of contents by completing the following steps:
   - Place the insertion point at the end of the table of contents on page 2. Press **Ctrl+Enter** to insert a page break.
   - With the insertion point on the first line, type **Table of Figures**, and then press **Enter** two times.
   - Click **Insert Table of Figures** in the Captions group, and then click **OK**.
   - Select the **Table of Figures heading**, click the **Home tab**, and then click **Heading 1** from the Styles gallery, if necessary.
   - Scroll up to page 2 and right-click the table of contents. Click **Update Field**, and then click **Update entire table**.

i. Click the **References tab**, and then click **Manage Sources** in the Citations & Bibliography group. Click **New**, and then select **Document From Web site**, if necessary, from the Type of Source menu. Use the following table to enter information for the two sources used in this paper. After both sources are created, click **Close** to close the Source Manager dialog box.

Field in Create Source Dialog box	Source # 1
Name of Web Page	Top 10 Social Networking Websites & Forums – February 2011
Name of Web Site	Marketingcharts.com
Year	2011
Year Accessed	2011
Month Accessed	August
Day Accessed	30
URL	http://www.marketingcharts.com/interactive/top-10-social-networking-websites-forums-february-2011-16414/

Field in Create Source Dialog box	Source # 2
Name of Web Page	The Battle for Facebook
Name of Web Site	Rolling Stone Culture
Year	2008
Month	June
Day	28
Year Accessed	2011
Month Accessed	June
Day Accessed	21
URL	http://www.rollingstone.com/culture/news/the-battle-for-facebook-20100915

j. Press **Ctrl+End** to move the insertion point to the end of the document, and then press **Ctrl+Enter** to insert a hard page break. Click the **Style arrow** in the Citations & Bibliography group, and then click **APA Fifth Edition**, if necessary. Click **Bibliography**, and then click **Works Cited**. Use the mini toolbar to change the font type and size of the references to **Times New Roman, 12 point**.

k. Place the insertion point after the period at the end of the first sentence on page 4 in the first paragraph under the *Social Networking Sites* paragraph heading, which starts with *Figure 1 shows*. Click **Insert Endnote** in the Footnotes group on the Home tab. Type the following: **"Top 10." Top 10 Social Networking Websites & Forums–February 2011 Marketingcharts.com. 30 August 2011, http://www.marketingcharts.com/interactive/top-10-social-networking-websites-forums-november-2009-11450/**. Change the font type and size of the endnote to **Times New Roman, 12 point**. Compare your work to Figure 3.30.

l. Scroll to the page that contains the table of contents. Click one time anywhere in the table of contents, and then press **F9**. Click **Update entire table**, and then click **OK**.

m. Save and close the file, and submit based on your instructor's directions.

MID-LEVEL EXERCISES

1 WWW Web Services Agency

You work as a Web designer at WWW Web Services Agency and have been asked to provide some basic information to be used in a senior citizens workshop. You want to provide the basic elements of good Web design and format the document professionally. Use the basic information you have already, in a Word document, and revise it to include elements appropriate for a research-oriented paper.

a. Open *w03m1web* and save it as **w03m1web_LastnameFirstname**.
b. Insert your name at the bottom of the cover page.
c. Place the insertion point at the end of the *Proximity and Balance* paragraph on the second page of the document. Insert the following text into an endnote: **Max Rebaza, Effective Web Sites, Chicago: Windy City Publishing, Inc. (2004): 44.**

DISCOVER 

d. Change all endnotes into footnotes.
e. Insert a table of contents after the cover page. Use a style of your choice.
f. In preparation for adding a bibliography to your document, create a citation source using the source from step c. (Hint: It is a book section.) Use the **Source Manager** to create the source and prevent the citation from displaying in the document. Also create citation sources for the two additional sources identified in the document footnotes.
g. Insert a bibliography at the end of the document using the Chicago style. Use the default format and settings for the bibliography. Apply **Heading 2 style** to the *Bibliography* heading.
h. Add captions to each graphic that displays in the paper. Use the default caption for each; you do not have to create a description. Display the caption below the graphic. Add a caption to the table on page 6 and display the caption below the table.
i. Create a table of figures at the beginning of the document on a separate page after the table of contents. The table should provide a list of figures only. Give the page an appropriate heading and format the heading using the **Heading 2 style**.
j. Insert a cross-reference at the end of the *Font Size and Attributes* paragraph on the seventh page. Type **See also** and insert a cross-reference that uses the **Heading reference type** and the *Contrast and Focus* heading. End the sentence with a period.
k. Update the entire table of contents and the table of figures. Remove any unnecessary blank pages in the document.
l. Save and close the file, and submit based on your instructor's directions.

2 New York City Trip

CREATIVE CASE 

Your family is planning a seven-day trip to New York City next summer. Your responsibility is to research the city and develop a list of activities that your family will enjoy. You used the Internet to complete your research. Now you want to format the Word document to impress your family with your word processing skills by incorporating different styles and formats, and including a cover page, table of contents, and index.

a. Open *w03m2nyc* and save it as **w03m2nyc_LastnameFirstname**.
b. Scroll through the document to view the formatting changes that are currently marked in the document, and then accept each change. Turn on **Track Changes** so any further changes will also be flagged. Change the Track Changes Options to display all formatting changes in color only.
c. Apply the **Heading 1 style** to section headings that display in all capital letters, **Heading 2 style** to section headings that display in title case (the first letter of each word is capitalized), and **Body Text style** to all the paragraphs throughout the document. It has been completed on the first and last sections already. The first Heading 1, the first Heading 2, and the first paragraph are already formatted.

d. Insert a blank page at the beginning of the document to create a title page for the document consisting of the title, **Trip to New York City**, and the subtitle, **Prepared by *your name***. Replace *your name* with your name. Center the title and your name.
e. Create a footer for the document consisting of the title, **Trip to New York City**, and a page number—use the page number style of your choice. The footer should not appear on the title page; that is, page 1 is actually the second page of the document.
f. Create a page specifically for the table of contents, and then generate a table of contents using Heading 1 and Heading 2 styles. Use a dashed leader to connect the headings to the page numbers in the table.
g. Mark all occurrences of the following text for inclusion in the index: *Central Park*, *Rockefeller*, *Staten Island*, *Statue of Liberty*, *Museum*. At the end of your document, create the index and take necessary steps so the index heading displays in the table of contents. Format the indexes as **Times New Roman**, **12 point**. Update the table of contents.
h. Change the Display for Review setting to show the document as a final copy.

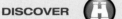

i. Print only a **List of markup**, if allowed by your instructor.
j. Save and close the file, and submit based on your instructor's directions.

3 Table of Authorities

As the junior partner in a growing law firm, you must proofread and update all legal briefs before they are submitted to the courts. You are in the final stage of completing a medical malpractice case, but the brief cannot be filed without a table of authorities.

a. Open *w03m3legal* and save it as **w03m3legal_LastnameFirstname**.
b. Mark all references to legal cases throughout the document.
c. Insert a table of authorities at the beginning of the document. Insert an appropriate heading at the top of the page, and format it using **Heading 1 style**.
d. Insert a comment at the beginning of the document, and then type **Ready to include in court records**.
e. Save and close the file, and submit based on your instructor's directions.

CAPSTONE EXERCISE

You are a member of the Horticulture Society and have been asked to assist in the development of information packets about a variety of flowers and plants. A report about tulips has been started, and you are responsible for completing the document so that it is ready for the fall meeting. You know of many features in Word that you can use to finish and present an easy-to-follow report.

Track Revisions

The document you receive has a few comments and shows the last few changes by the author. You will accept or reject the changes, and then make a few of your own. You will turn on track changes to differentiate between your changes and the author's.

a. Open *w03c1tulip* and save it as **w03c1tulip_Lastname Firstname**.

b. Scroll through the document and review the comment. Return to the third page and reject the insertion of a sentence about squirrels.

c. Accept all other tracked changes in the document. Keep all comments.

d. Change all headings that use Heading 3 style so they use **Heading 1 style**, as per the comment left by the author

e. Click inside the author's comment, and then insert a new comment. In the new comment, type a message indicating you have made the style replacement. This new comment will display *R1* after your name in the balloon to indicate it is a response to the previous comment.

Credit Sources

You are now ready to add the citations for resources that the author used when assembling this report. The author sent some source citations as an external file, and she typed some of the source information at the end of the document. She did not format it appropriately for use as a citation, nor did she insert citations in the appropriate places in the document as a footnote or endnote.

a. Use the **Source Manager tool** to open the file *tulips.xml*, and then copy the citations into the current list for this document.

b. Scroll to the end of the document to view a list of sources. Use the **Source Manager tool** to create new citations for each source. After you create the citations, delete the *Sources* paragraph heading and each source below it.

c. Modify the source from the Gardenersnet Web site to indicate the information was retrieved on June 7, 2012. Modify the source only in your current list.

d. Create a bibliography using MLA style on a separate page at the end of the document.

e. Insert an endnote on page 3, at the end of the third paragraph in the *Planting* section, which ends with *made by the planter*. Type the following for the endnote: **Swezey, Lauren Bonar, A Westerner's Guide to Tulips (Sunset, October 1999).** Change the number format for endnotes to **1, 2, 3** in the Footnotes dialog box launcher.

Figure References

The graphics in the document are quite informative, and you want to add descriptive captions to them and to list them on a reference page.

a. Select the tulip picture on the left side of the first row, and then assign the following caption below the photo: **Figure 1. Angelique**.

b. Assign captions to the remaining tulip photos on that page using information in the comments fields. Delete the comments after you create the captions.

c. Assign the caption **Planting Depth Guide** to the graphic titled *Planting Guide at a Glance*.

d. Create a blank page following the cover page, and then insert a table of figures, using the **Distinctive format**. Type **Table of Figures** at the top, and then format with the **Heading 1 style**.

Finish with Table of Contents and Index

To put the finishing touches on your document, you add a table of contents and an index. The document is short, but you decide to include both because they demonstrate a higher level of professionalism in your work.

a. Automatically generate a table of contents and display it on a page between the cover page and the table of figures.

b. Mark the following words as index entries: *Holland*, *perennials*, *deadheading*, *soil*, *store*. Create an index cross-reference entry using the word *storage* in the index to indicate where the word *store* is used in the document.

c. Add an index to the end of the document. Use the **Classic index format**. Format the Index title using the **Heading 1 style**.

d. Find the sentence *See the depth chart in Figure 6*, which displays in the third paragraph in the *Planting* section. Before the period and following the number 6, add the following text: **on page** . Then insert a cross reference to Figure 6. If correct, it informs the reader that the graphic is found on page 5.

e. Display a page number in the footer of the document using **Accent Bar 4 format**. Start numbering on the page that contains the Table of Contents. Also, in the left side of the footer, display the text **Compiled by *your name***, but use your first and last name.

f. Update all tables to reflect any changes made throughout this project.

g. Save and close the file, and submit based on your instructor's directions.

Group Collaboration

GENERAL CASE

This is a research paper written by a group of three students about American presidents. The first student will open a blank document, turn on Track Changes, save it as **w03b1group_LastnameFirstname**, and then start the draft by creating headings such as **Introduction**, **History**, **The American Government**, and **Our Favorite Presidents**. In the last section, the first student will write a short paragraph about one of his or her favorite presidents and also include a photo of the chosen president. After typing his or her full name in the footer, the student will save and send the document to the next group member. The second group member will continue writing with the Track Changes feature on and add a paragraph and a photo describing his or her favorite president. This student will also narrate a brief history of this country. After adding his or her full name in the footer, this student will save and send the document to the next member. In addition to including a description of another president, the third member will write a short paragraph explaining how the American government works. Each student is allowed to make modifications to the content without accepting or rejecting any changes at this time. Each student can also customize the track changes options. After the last student has made his or her entry, he or she will print two copies of the document: one will show markup and the other will show final without markup. Once all students have made their edits, save and close the file, and submit the final copy based on your instructor's directions.

An Ethics Paper on Cheating

RESEARCH CASE

FROM SCRATCH

Cheating and the violation of schools' honor codes has become a major problem in many school systems. We often hear stories of how high school and college students can easily cheat on their tests or written papers without being caught. You will use the Internet to research the topic of plagiarism, the honor code, and the honor and judicial program at your university and several other universities in your state. You should use more than five sources, with at least one each from the Internet, a book, and a journal. After your research is complete, you will write a three-page, double-spaced report, describing your findings. Include the definition of plagiarism, the penalty for violating the honor code at your school, and the statistics for cheating in high schools and colleges. Cite all the sources in your paper, insert at least one footnote, and develop a bibliography for your paper based on the APA Fifth Edition writing style. Save the report as **w03b2cheating_LastnameFirstname**. Save and close the file, and submit based on your instructor's directions.

Repairing Tables

DISASTER RECOVERY

You work in the city's Planning and Zoning department as an analyst. You begin to prepare the *Guide to Planned Developments* document for posting on the city's intranet. The administrative clerk who typed the document attempted to insert a table of contents and a table of figures, but he was not successful in displaying either table accurately. Open his file, *w03b3table*, and save your revised document as **w03b3table_LastnameFirstname**. He also attempted to insert cross-references, but they do not work correctly either. Before this document can be posted, you must repair both tables at the beginning of the document and the erroneous cross-references. The cross-references are highlighted in the document so you can locate them easily; the highlights should be removed when you have corrected the references. When you have corrected the problems, save and close the file, and submit based on your instructor's directions.

WORD

4 DOCUMENT PRODUCTIVITY

Working with Tables and Mail Merge

CASE STUDY | Community Disaster Relief Center

Watch the
Set-up
Video
for this
Case Study!

Wacey Rivale is the Director of Fundraising at the local Community Disaster Relief Center (CDRC). She spends many hours giving speeches to local companies, organizations, and civic groups so they will be familiar with the efforts and activities of the Relief Center. Because the CDRC is a nonprofit organization, Wacey and other CDRC staffers must demonstrate the need, the benefits, and the success of the service they provide.

Wacey always sends a letter of appreciation to the people who donate and support the CDRC, but her latest marketing efforts have increased the response of the community. Typically, she sends one or two per week, but now she is in a position where she needs to send several dozen letters. She asks you, her co-worker, to start a list of donors, their addresses, and their contribution amounts so no donor is overlooked when it comes time to send the letters. You decide to document donor information in a table in Word. Then it will be part of a mail merge to create thank-you letters quickly and efficiently.

OBJECTIVES AFTER YOU READ THIS CHAPTER, YOU WILL BE ABLE TO:

1. Insert a table ***p.272***
2. Format a table ***p.274***
3. Sort and apply formulas to table data ***p.283***
4. Convert text to a table ***p.285***
5. Select a main document ***p.292***
6. Select or create recipients ***p.293***
7. Insert merge fields ***p.297***
8. Merge a main document and a data source ***p.298***

Tables

A **table** is a series of columns and rows that organize data.

A **cell** is the intersection of a column and row in a table.

A ***table*** is a series of columns and rows that organizes data effectively. The columns and rows in a table intersect to form ***cells***. The table feature is one of the most powerful in Word and is an easy way to organize a series of data in a columnar list format. For example, you can create tables to organize data such as employee lists with phone numbers and e-mail addresses. The donor registry in Figure 4.1, for example, is actually an 8 × 13 table (8 columns and 13 rows). The completed table looks impressive, but it is very easy to create once you understand how a table works. In addition to the organizational benefits, tables make an excellent alignment tool. Although you can align text with tabs, you have more format control when you create a table. (See the Practice Exercises at the end of the chapter for other examples.)

The table feature is one of the most powerful in Word and is an easy way to organize a series of data.... In addition to the organizational benefits, tables make an excellent alignment tool.

Table Move handle

Column 2

Cell that intersects at row 7 and column 2

Row 7

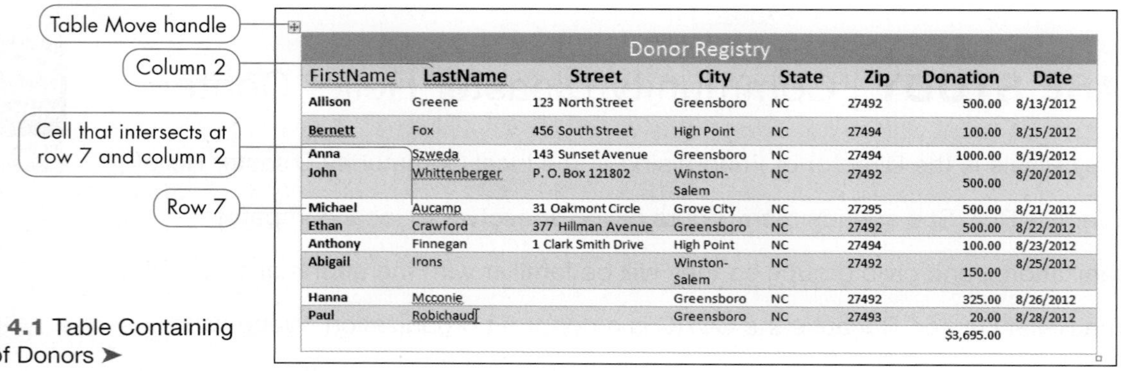

Donor Registry							
FirstName	LastName	Street	City	State	Zip	Donation	Date
Allison	Greene	123 North Street	Greensboro	NC	27492	500.00	8/13/2012
Bernett	Fox	456 South Street	High Point	NC	27494	100.00	8/15/2012
Anna	Szweda	143 Sunset Avenue	Greensboro	NC	27494	1000.00	8/19/2012
John	Whittenberger	P. O. Box 121802	Winston-Salem	NC	27492	500.00	8/20/2012
Michael	Aucamp	31 Oakmont Circle	Grove City	NC	27295	500.00	8/21/2012
Ethan	Crawford	377 Hillman Avenue	Greensboro	NC	27492	500.00	8/22/2012
Anthony	Finnegan	1 Clark Smith Drive	High Point	NC	27494	100.00	8/23/2012
Abigail	Irons		Winston-Salem	NC	27492	150.00	8/25/2012
Hanna	Mcconie		Greensboro	NC	27492	325.00	8/26/2012
Paul	Robichaud		Greensboro	NC	27493	20.00	8/28/2012
						$3,695.00	

FIGURE 4.1 Table Containing Names of Donors ➤

After you create a basic table, you want to enhance the appearance to create interest for the reader and improve readability. Word includes many tools to assist with these efforts, and you will use several of them to complete the table used for the Donor Registry. In this section, you will insert a table in a document. After inserting the table, you can insert or delete columns and rows if you need to change the structure. Furthermore, you will learn how to merge and split cells within the table and how to change the row height and column width to accommodate data in the table. You also will learn how to format a table using borders, shading, and the styles provided by Word. Finally, you will modify table alignment and position.

Inserting a Table

You create a table from the Insert tab. Click Table in the Tables group on the Insert tab to see a gallery of cells on which you drag to select the number of columns and rows you require in the table, or you can choose the Insert Table command below the gallery to display the Insert Table dialog box and enter the table composition you prefer. When you select the table dimension from the gallery or from the Insert Table dialog box, Word creates a table structure with the number of columns and rows you specify. After you create a table, you can enter text, numbers, or graphics in individual cells. The text wraps as it is entered within a cell, so that you can add or delete text without affecting the entries in other cells.

You format the contents of an individual cell the same way you format an ordinary paragraph; that is, you change the font, apply boldface or italic, change the text alignment, or apply any other formatting commands. You can select multiple cells, rows, or columns and apply formatting to the selection all at once, or you can format a cell independently of every other cell.

After you insert a table in your document, use commands in the Table Tools Design and Layout tabs to modify and enhance it. Place the insertion point anywhere in the table, and then click either the Design or Layout tab to view the commands. In either tab just point to a command and a ScreenTip describes its function. When you hover the mouse over any cell of a table the ***Table Move handle*** displays (see Figure 4.1). You can click this handle once to select the whole table at one time, which is useful when working with design and layout features.

Click the **Table Move handle** to select a whole table at one time.

TIP Using Tabs to Move Within Tables

The Tab key on your keyboard functions differently in a table than in a regular document. Press Tab to move to the next cell in the current row, or to the first cell in the next row if you are at the end of a row. Press Tab when you are in the last cell of a table to add a new blank row to the bottom of the table. Press Shift+Tab to move to the previous cell in the current row (or to the last cell in the previous row). You must press Ctrl+Tab to insert a regular tab character within a cell.

Insert and Delete Rows and Columns

You can change the structure of a table after it has been created. If you need more rows or columns to accommodate additional data in your table, it is easy to add or insert them using the Rows & Columns group on the Table Tools Layout tab. The Insert and Delete commands enable you to add new or delete existing rows or columns. When you add a column, you can specify if you want to insert it to the right or left of the current column. Likewise, you can specify where to place a new row—either above or below the currently selected row.

You can delete complete rows and columns using the commands mentioned previously, or you can delete only the data in those rows and columns using the Delete key on your keyboard. Keep in mind that when you insert or delete a complete row or a column, the remaining rows and columns will adjust to the positioning. For example, if you delete the third row of a 5 × 5 table, the data in the fourth and fifth rows move up and become the third and fourth rows. If you delete only the data in the third row, the cells would be blank and the fourth and fifth rows would not change at all.

TIP Inserting Multiple Rows (or Columns) Simultaneously

If you need to insert more than one row (or column) at a time, simply select multiple rows (or columns), right-click, and select the Insert command, and the same number of blank rows (or columns) you selected will display. For example, if you select three rows before you click the Insert row command, three blank rows will appear.

Merge and Split Cells

You can use the Merge Cells command in the Merge group on the Table Tools Layout tab to join individual cells together (merge) to form a larger cell, as was done in the first row of Figure 4.1. People often merge cells to enter a main title at the top of a table. Conversely, you can use the Split Cells command in the Merge group to split a single cell into multiple cells if you require more cells to hold data.

Change Row Height and Column Width

Row height is the vertical space from the top to the bottom of a row.

Column width is the horizontal space or length of a column.

When you create a table, Word builds evenly spaced columns. Frequently you need to change the row height or column width to fit your data. ***Row height*** is the vertical distance from the top to the bottom of a row. ***Column width*** is the horizontal space or width of a column. You might increase the column width to display a wide string of text, such as first and last name, to prevent it from wrapping in the cell. You might increase row height to better fit a header that has been enlarged for emphasis.

The Table command is easy to master, and as you might have guessed, you will benefit from reviewing the available commands listed in the Design and Layout tabs. Features in the Layout tab are described in Table 4.1. You will use many of these commands as you create a table in the Hands-On Exercises.

TABLE 4.1 Table Tools Layout Tab

Group	Commands	Enables You to
Table	Select ▾ View Gridlines Properties Table	• Select particular parts of a table (cell, column, row, or entire table). • Show or hide the gridlines around the table. • Display the Table Properties dialog box to format the table.
Rows & Columns	Delete Insert Above Insert Below Insert Left Insert Right Rows & Columns	• Delete cells, columns, rows, or the entire table. • Insert rows and columns. • Display the Insert Cells dialog box.
Merge	Merge Cells Split Cells Split Table Merge	• Merge (join) selected cells together. • Split cells into separate cells. • Split the table into two tables.
Cell Size	6.65" 0.25" AutoFit ▾ Cell Size	• Adjust the row height and column width. • Adjust the column width automatically based on the data in the column. • Display the Table Properties dialog box.
Alignment	Text Direction Cell Margins Alignment	• Specify the combined horizontal and vertical alignment of text within a cell. • Change the text direction. • Set margins within a cell.
Data	Sort Repeat Header Rows Convert to Text Formula Data	• Sort data within a table. • Repeat header rows when tables span multiple pages. • Convert tabulated text to table format. • Insert a formula in a table.

Formatting a Table

Shading affects the background color within a cell.

Border refers to the line style around each cell.

You can use basic formatting options to enhance the appearance of your table. The Borders and Shading commands, for example, offer a wide variety of choices for formatting the table structure. ***Shading*** affects the background color within a cell or group of cells. Table shading is similar to the Highlight feature that places a color behind the contents in a cell. You often apply shading to the header row of a table to make it stand out from the data. ***Border*** refers to the line style around each cell in the table. The default is a single line, but you can choose from many styles to outline a table such as a double, triple, or a wavy line. You can even choose invisible borders if you want only data to display in your document without the outline of a table. Borders and Shading commands are located on both the Home tab and the Table Tools Design tab, but you will probably find it more convenient to access the command from the Table Tools Design tab while you work with tables. The Design tab features are described in Table 4.2.

TIP Right-Click for Table Formatting Options

As an alternative to using the Layout tab, you can find many table options in the context-sensitive menu that displays when you right-click the mouse. The insertion point can be anywhere in the table, and after you right-click you see several table options including Insert, Delete Cells, and Split Cells. You also can change format and alignment of table cells using the Borders and Shading, Cell Alignment, and Text Direction commands in this menu. The Table Properties option is available in the menu if you need to access features such as table alignment and cell spacing.

TABLE 4.2 Table Tools Design Tab

Group	Commands	Enables You to
Table Style Options	Header Row, First Column, Total Row, Last Column, Banded Rows, Banded Columns (Table Style Options)	• Turn Header Row on or off. • Turn Total Row on or off. • Display banded rows; formats even- and odd-numbered rows differently. • Display special formatting for first column. • Display special formatting for last column. • Display banded columns; formats even- and odd-numbered columns differently.
Table Styles	Shading, Borders (Table Styles)	• Select predefined style from gallery. • Apply color behind the selected cell(s) or table. • Customize borders of selected cell(s) or table.
Draw Borders	½ pt, Pen Color, Draw Table, Eraser (Draw Borders)	• Alter style of line used around border of cell or table. • Alter size of line used for borders. • Change Pen Color feature; use with Draw Table feature. • Manually draw borders of cell(s) or table. • Erase borders of cell(s) or table. • Display the Borders and Shading dialog box.

Apply Table Styles

A **table style** contains borders, shading, and other attributes to enhance a table.

Word provides many predefined ***table styles*** that contain borders, shading, font sizes, and other attributes that enhance the readability of a table. The Table Styles feature is helpful in situations where you want to apply a professional-looking format to a table; when you are coordinating the design of a table with other features in Word, Excel, or PowerPoint; or when you do not have time to apply custom borders and shading. The styles are available in the Table Styles group on the Design tab. To use a predefined table style, click anywhere in your table, and then click a style from the Table Styles gallery. A few styles from the gallery display, but you can select from many others by clicking the More button on the right side of the gallery, as shown in Figure 4.2. The Live Preview of a style displays on your table when you hover your mouse over it in the gallery. To apply a style, click it one time.

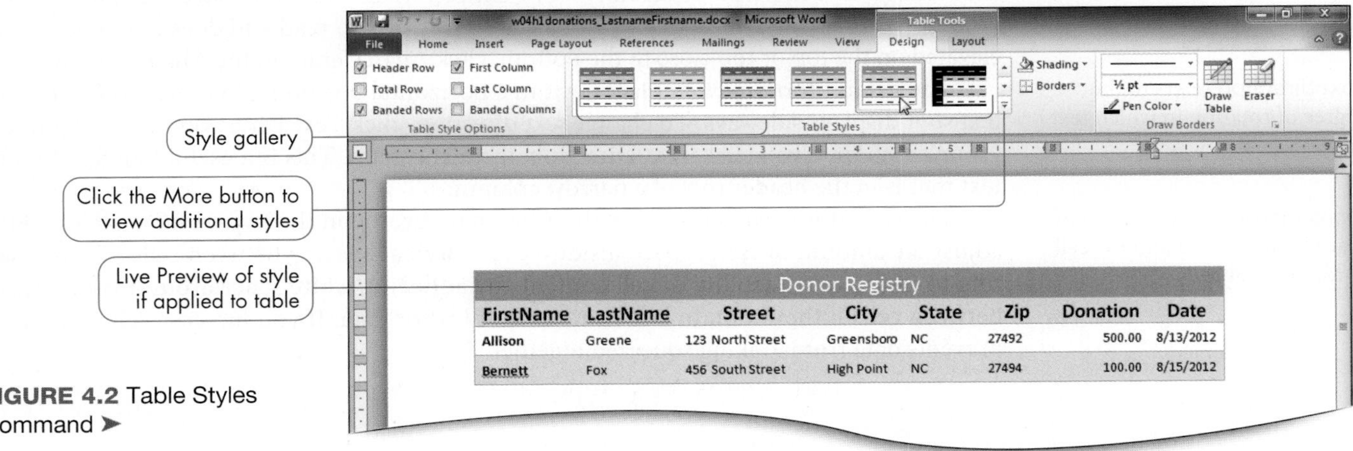

FIGURE 4.2 Table Styles Command ➤

You can modify a predefined style if you wish to make changes to features such as color or alignment. You also can create your own table style and save it for use in the current document, or add it to a document template for use in other Word documents. Click the More button in the Table Styles group to access the Modify Table Style and New Table Style commands.

Select the Table Position and Alignment

Table alignment is the position of a table between the left and right margins.

Table alignment refers to the position of a table between the left and right document margins. When you insert a table, Word aligns it at the left margin by default. However, you can click Properties in the Table group on the Layout tab to display the Table Properties dialog box. The *Alignment* section of the dialog box offers four choices for table alignment—Left, Center, Right, or a custom setting in which you specify an amount that the table is indented from the left margin, as seen in Figure 4.3. For example, you might want to use the custom setting to indent the table exactly two inches from the left margin so it aligns with other indented text.

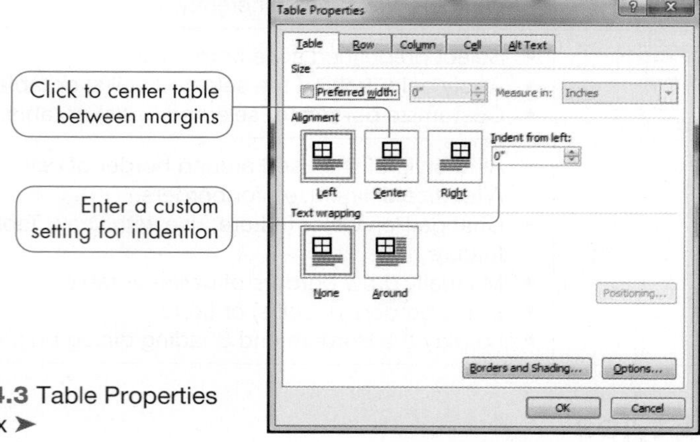

FIGURE 4.3 Table Properties Dialog Box ➤

You can also choose from two text wrapping options in the Table Properties dialog box. The option to wrap text Around will enable you to display text on the side of the table. This is useful if you have a small table so you will not waste a great deal of space on the page by displaying the table and text close together. The option for None prevents text from displaying beside the table, and will force text to display above or below it. If your table is small, this will enable a large amount of white space to display beside it.

You also can change alignment of the data in a table separately from the table itself using commands on the Layout tab. The Alignment group contains many options to quickly format table data. Table data can be formatted to align in many different horizontal and vertical combinations. We often apply horizontal settings, such as Center, to our data, but using vertical settings also increases readability. For example, when you want your data to be centered both horizontally and vertically within a cell so it is easy to read and does not appear to be elevated on the top or too close to the bottom, click Align Center in the Alignment group.

Text direction refers to the degree of rotation in which text displays.

The default ***text direction*** places text in a horizontal position. However, you can rotate text so it displays sideways. To change text direction, click Text Direction in the Alignment group. Each time you click Text Direction, the text rotates. This is a useful tool for aligning text that is in the header row of a narrow column.

A **cell margin** is the amount of space between data and the cell border in a table.

The ***Cell Margins*** command in the Alignment group on the Layout tab enables you to adjust the amount of white space inside a cell as well as spacing between cells. Use this setting to improve readability of cell contents by adjusting white space around your data or between cells if they contain large amounts of text or data. If you increase cell margins, it prevents data from looking squeezed together.

1. Using the correct terminology, explain how data is organized in a table.
2. Explain six different ways you can modify the structure of an existing table.
3. Describe three different formatting options you can apply to change the appearance of a table.
4. Describe the different ways to align a table within the text in a document.

HANDS-ON EXERCISES

1 Tables

Since you will be tracking information about the donors and donations that Wacey Rivale receives for the Community Disaster Relief Center (CDRC), you quickly determine that a table is the logical choice for a professional and easy-to-read document. It also gives you flexibility in adding more information because you expect the donations to keep pouring in.

Skills covered: Create a Table • Insert Data, Rows, and Columns • Change Row Height and Column Width • Merge Cells to Create a Title Row • Apply a Table Style and Align Data

STEP 1 CREATE A TABLE

After a discussion with Wacey, you now know the donor information that should be documented. You determine the size of the table you will use is based on the fact that it must display the donor's name, address, date, and amount of donation. Refer to Figure 4.4 as you complete Step 1.

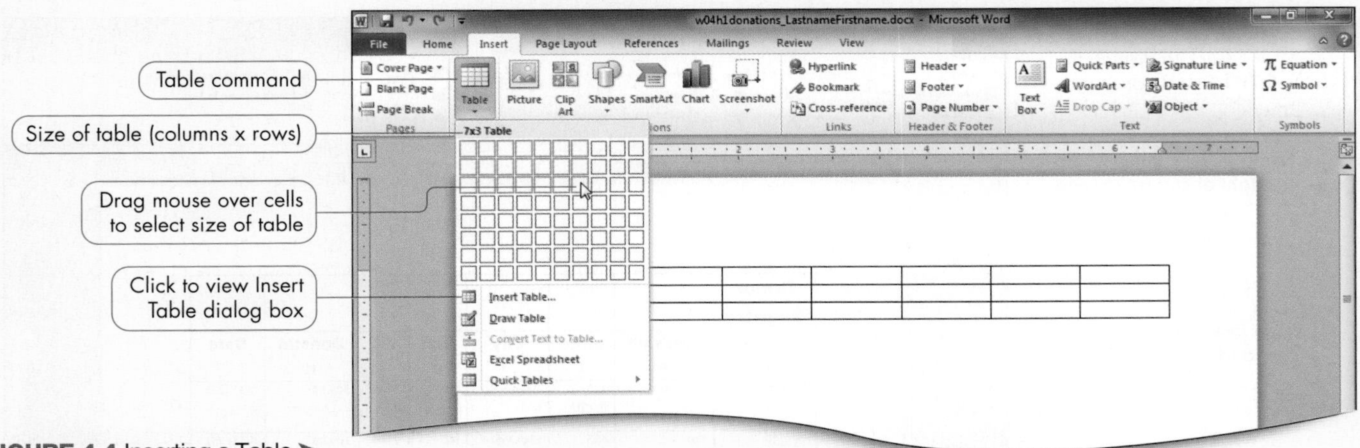

FIGURE 4.4 Inserting a Table ➤

a. Open a new blank document and save it as **w04h1donations_LastnameFirstname**.

b. Press **Enter** twice in the blank document, and then click the **Insert tab**.

   You will find it easier to work with a table if it does not begin on the very first line of the document. The Insert tab contains the Table command.

c. Click **Table** in the Tables group, and then drag your mouse over the cells until you select seven columns and three rows; you will see the table size, 7 × 3, displayed above the cells, as shown in Figure 4.4. Click the bottom-right cell (where the seventh column and the third row intersect) to insert the table into your document.

   Word creates an empty table that contains seven columns and three rows. The default columns have identical widths, and the table spans from the left to the right margin.

d. Practice selecting various elements from the table, something that you will have to do in subsequent steps:

   - Select a single cell by pointing inside the left grid line. The pointer changes to a black slanted arrow when you are in the proper position, and then you can click to select the cell.

- Select a row by clicking in the left margin of the first cell in that row (the pointer changes to a right slanting white arrow).
- Select a column by pointing just above the top of the column (the pointer changes to a small black downward pointing arrow) and click.
- Select adjacent cells by clicking a cell and dragging the mouse over the adjacent cells.
- Select the entire table by dragging the mouse over the table or by clicking the Table Move handle that appears at the top-left corner of the table.

e. Save the document.

STEP 2 INSERT DATA, ROWS, AND COLUMNS

With the table in place, you can now begin entering the headings for each column, and then you can add the donor information later. When you realize you need one more column, you relax because Word makes it easy to add one just where you need it. Refer to Figure 4.5 as you complete Step 2.

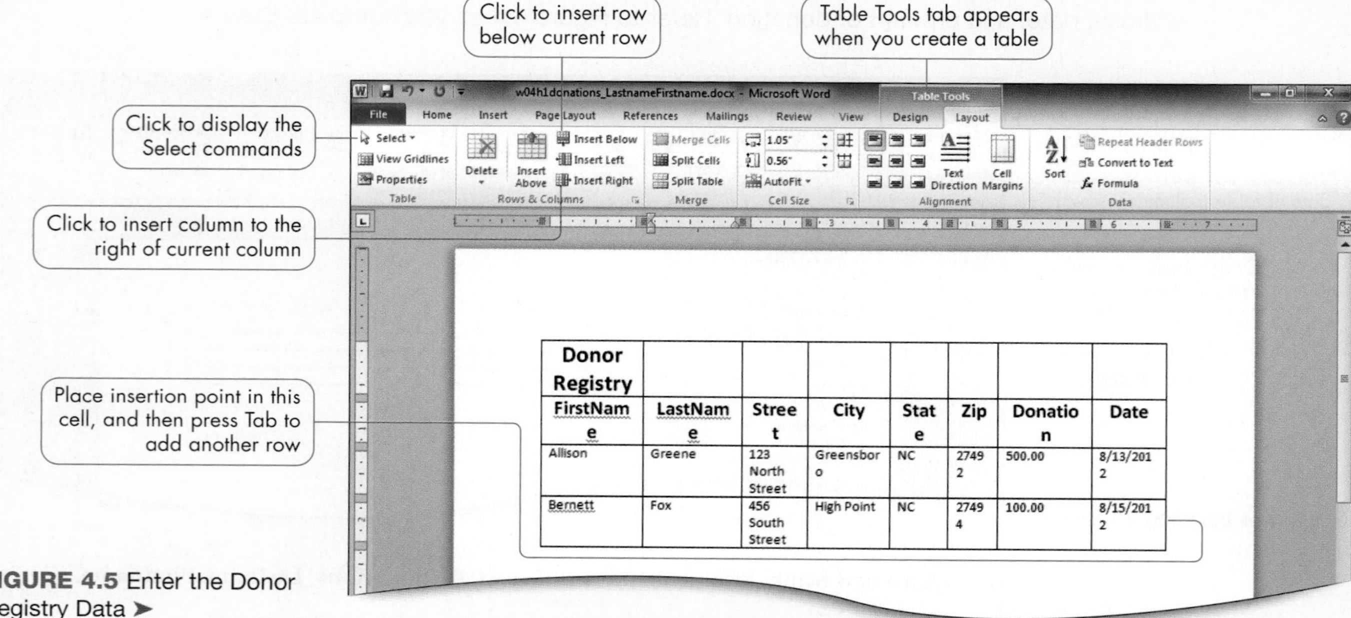

FIGURE 4.5 Enter the Donor Registry Data ➤

a. Enter data into the table by completing the following steps:

- Click in the first cell of the first row, and then type **Donor Registry**.
- Press ↓ to move to the first cell in the second row, and then type **FirstName** (this displays directly below *Donor Registry*).

  You do not insert spaces in the First Name column heading because this format is used in documents we later use to associate with this information.
- Press **Tab** (or →) to move to the next cell, and then type **LastName**.
- Press **Tab** to move to the next cell, and then type **Street**.
- Enter the following labels in the next four cells: **City**, **State**, **Zip**, and **Donation**.

You realize you need one more column for the date of the donation.

b. Add another column by completing the following steps:

- Click anywhere in the last column of your table, and then click the **Layout tab**, if necessary. Click **Insert Right** in the Rows & Columns group to add a new column to your table.
- Click in the second row of the new column, and then type **Date**.

  You added a new column on the right side of the table. Notice that the column widths decrease to make room for the new column you just added.

TROUBLESHOOTING: If the column you insert is not in the correct location within the table, click Undo on the Quick Access Toolbar, confirm your insertion point is in the last column, and then click the appropriate Insert command.

c. Select the text *Donor Registry* in the first row. On the Mini toolbar, click the **Font Size arrow**, select **18**, click **Bold**, and then click **Center** to center the heading within the cell.

The table title stands out with the larger font size, bold, and center horizontal alignment.

d. Click in the left margin to select the entire second row. On the Mini toolbar, click the **Font Size arrow**, select **16**, and then click **Bold** and **Center**.

Now the labels in the second row stand out as well. They are not quite as large as the first row because they should not overpower the title.

e. Insert the donor information into your new table using data in the table below. When you get to the last column and find you need another row to hold the next row of data, press **Tab** to add a row to the end of your table, and then enter the next item and amounts. Compare your results to Figure 4.5.

FirstName	LastName	Street	City	State	Zip	Donation	Date
Allison	Greene	123 North Street	Greensboro	NC	27492	500.00	8/13/2012
Bernett	Fox	456 South Street	High Point	NC	27494	100.00	8/15/2012

f. Save the document.

Other Ways to Select a Table

You can click Select in the Table group on the Layout tab to display commands for selecting a cell, a column, a row, or the entire table. Figure 4.5 shows the location of the Select command.

STEP 3 CHANGE ROW HEIGHT AND COLUMN WIDTH

Now that you have donor information in the table, you decide to adjust the way it displays so it is easier to read. Adjusting the orientation of the page enables you to increase column widths so text does not need to wrap as much. This is especially useful for addresses, which are easier to read if they do not wrap. Refer to Figure 4.6 as you complete Step 3.

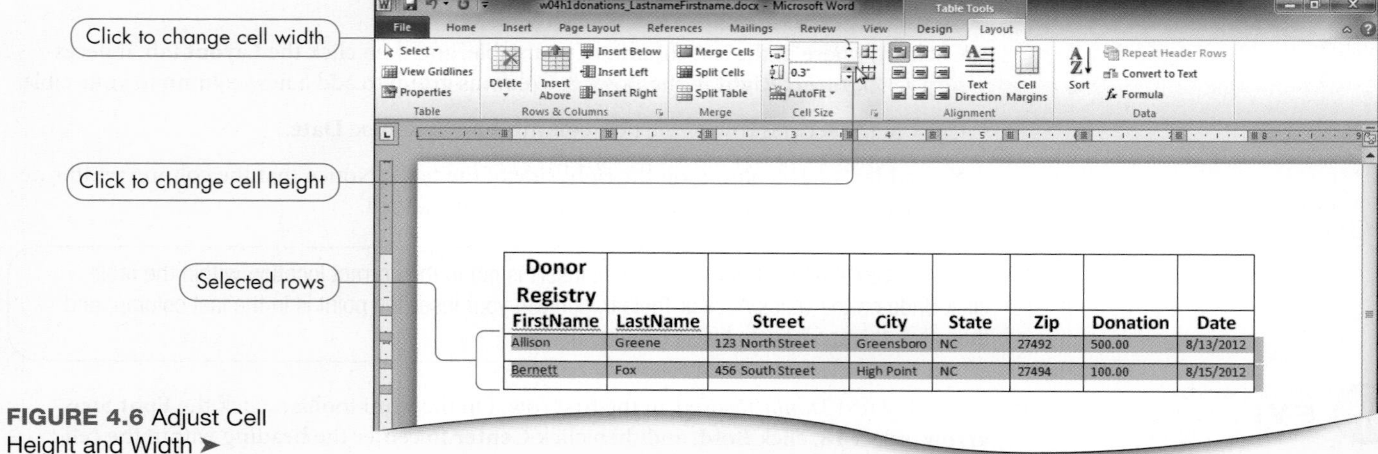
Click to change cell width
Click to change cell height
Selected rows

FIGURE 4.6 Adjust Cell Height and Width ➤

a. Click the **Page Layout tab**, click **Orientation**, and then click **Landscape**.

   You have more room to display the donor information without wrapping the text if your page orientation is in landscape mode.

b. Hold your mouse above the top cell in the third column of data until the small black arrow appears, and then click to select the column that displays the street address.

c. Click the **Layout tab**, and then click the **Width arrow** in the Cell Size group until **1.5"** displays.

   You changed the width of the column so that the whole address displays without wrapping. Other column widths did not change, even though the table stretches to the right of the page.

d. Change the height of the row by completing the following steps:

   - Place the insertion point anywhere in the cell that contains the text *Allison*, and then click **Select** in the Table group.
   - Click **Select Row**, and then hold down **Shift** and press ↓ on your keyboard to select the remaining row in the table.
   - Click the **Height arrow** in the Cell Size group until **.3"** displays, as shown in Figure 4.6.

     You changed the height of the last two rows in the table to 0.3" tall, which makes the data easier to read.

e. Save the document.

> **TIP Adjusting Column Width and Row Height**
>
> If you are not certain of the exact measurements needed for row height or column width, you can use the mouse to increase or decrease the size. Position the mouse pointer on the gridline that separates the rows (or columns) until the pointer changes to a two-headed arrow. The two-headed arrow indicates you can adjust the height (or width) by dragging the gridline up or down (right or left) to resize the cell.

STEP 4 MERGE CELLS TO CREATE A TITLE ROW

Any table that displays important information should have a title to explain the contents, and it should be easy to read and look professional. You recognize this table fits that description, so you merge the cells in the first row and center the text. Refer to Figure 4.7 as you complete Step 4.

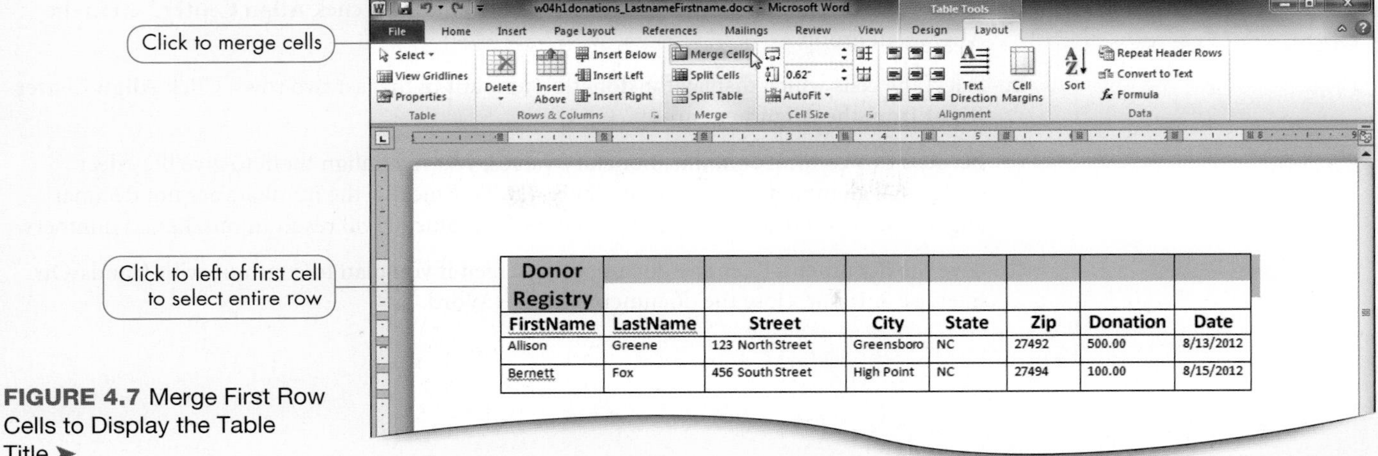
Click to merge cells
Click to left of first cell to select entire row

FIGURE 4.7 Merge First Row Cells to Display the Table Title ➤

a. Click outside the table to the left of the first cell in the first row to select the entire first row.

b. Click **Merge Cells** in the Merge group, as shown in Figure 4.7.

   You merged the selected cells. The first row now contains a single cell.

c. Right-click the row to display the Mini toolbar, and then click **Center**.

d. Save the document.

STEP 5 APPLY A TABLE STYLE AND ALIGN DATA

The table is sufficient for holding information, but you want to format it using Table Styles in Word so that the information is easy to read when it displays. Using alternating colors across the rows prevents the data from being blurred together or mixed up when you read it. It is also a good practice to apply proper alignment to the columns that contain monetary values. Refer to Figure 4.8 as you complete Step 5.

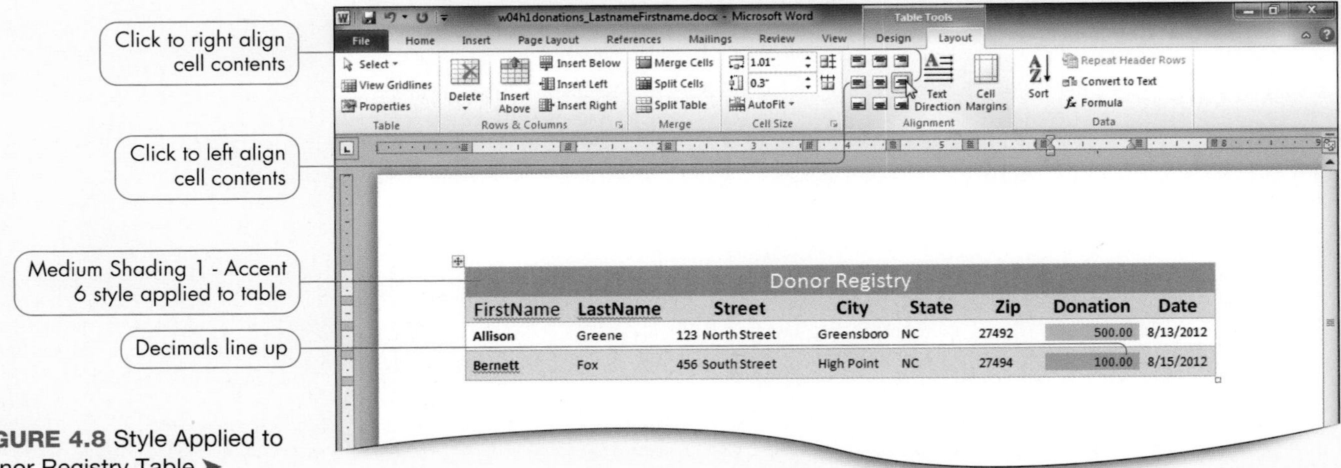
Click to right align cell contents
Click to left align cell contents
Medium Shading 1 - Accent 6 style applied to table
Decimals line up

FIGURE 4.8 Style Applied to Donor Registry Table ➤

a. Apply a style to your table by completing the following steps:

   - Click the **Design tab**, and then click the **More button** in the Table Styles group.
   - Hover your mouse over several styles and notice how the table changes to preview that style.
   - Click **Medium Shading 1 - Accent 6** (last column, fourth row) to apply it to your table.

   Previous formatting such as alignment and cell shading, if it exists, may be replaced by the formatting attributes for a style when applied to a table.

b. Select rows three and four. Click the **Layout tab**, and then click **Align Center Left** in the Alignment group.

c. Select the cells which display the donation amount in the last two rows. Click **Align Center Right** from the Alignment group.

Because this column contains monetary values, you right align them to give the effect of decimal alignment, as shown in Figure 4.8. Technically, the numbers are not decimal aligned, so if you display an additional digit in a value, it will result in misaligned numbers.

d. Save the document. Keep the document onscreen if you plan to continue with Hands-On Exercise 2. If not, close the document and exit Word.

Advanced Table Features

You now have a good understanding of table features and realize there are many uses for them in your Word documents. But did you know you can use tables to perform simple tasks that are typically performed in a spreadsheet? Word includes features that enable the user to sort and perform simple mathematical calculations to data in a table. You can also convert plain text into a table.

Word includes features that enable the user to sort and perform simple mathematical calculations to data in a table.

In this section, you will learn how to sort data within a table and insert formulas to perform calculations. Finally, you convert text to a table format.

Sorting and Applying Formulas to Table Data

Sorting is the process of arranging data in a specific order.

Because tables provide an easy way to arrange numbers within a document, it is important to know how to use table calculations. This feature gives a Word document the power of a simple spreadsheet. Additional organization of table data is possible by ***sorting***, or rearranging, data based on certain criteria. Figure 4.9 displays the donor list you created previously, but this table illustrates two additional capabilities of the table feature—sorting and calculating.

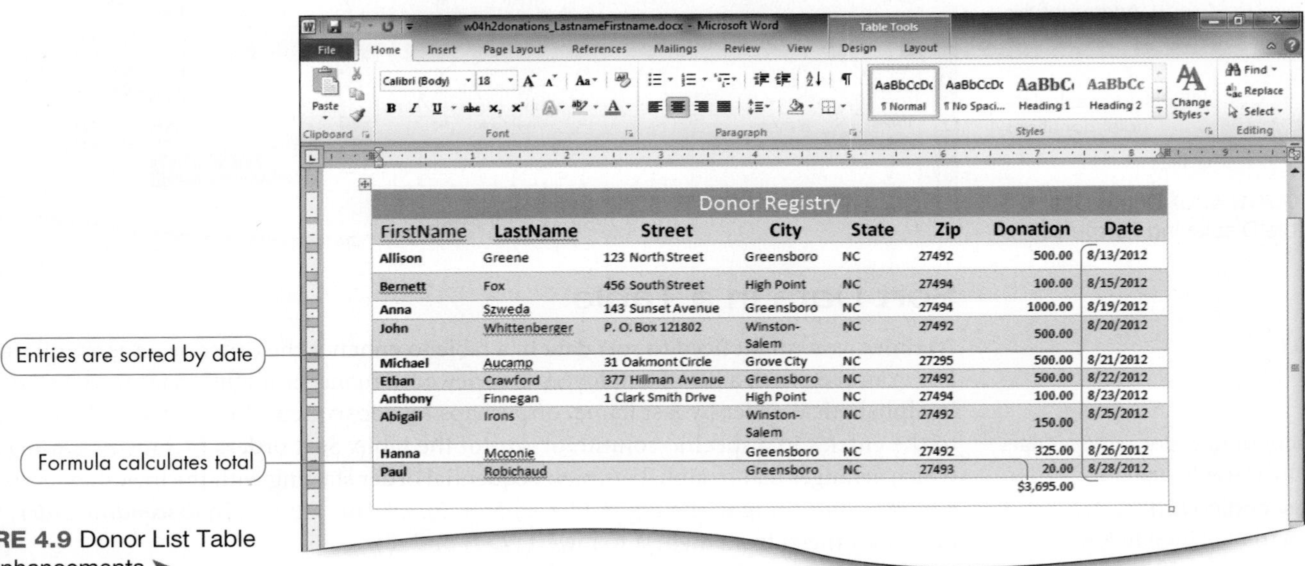

Donor Registry							
FirstName	LastName	Street	City	State	Zip	Donation	Date
Allison	Greene	123 North Street	Greensboro	NC	27492	500.00	8/13/2012
Bernett	Fox	456 South Street	High Point	NC	27494	100.00	8/15/2012
Anna	Szweda	143 Sunset Avenue	Greensboro	NC	27494	1000.00	8/19/2012
John	Whittenberger	P. O. Box 121802	Winston-Salem	NC	27492	500.00	8/20/2012
Michael	Aucamp	31 Oakmont Circle	Grove City	NC	27295	500.00	8/21/2012
Ethan	Crawford	377 Hillman Avenue	Greensboro	NC	27492	500.00	8/22/2012
Anthony	Finnegan	1 Clark Smith Drive	High Point	NC	27494	100.00	8/23/2012
Abigail	Irons		Winston-Salem	NC	27492	150.00	8/25/2012
Hanna	Mcconie		Greensboro	NC	27492	325.00	8/26/2012
Paul	Robichaud		Greensboro	NC	27493	20.00	8/28/2012
						$3,695.00	

FIGURE 4.9 Donor List Table with Enhancements ➤

Calculate Using Table Formulas

You know that the intersection of a row and column forms a cell, and the rows and columns are identified by numbers and letters, respectively. Word uses the column letter and row number of that intersection to identify the cell and to give it an address. Thus, the rows in the Donor Registry table are numbered top to bottom from 1 to 13 while the columns are labeled left to right from A to H. The row and column labels do not appear in the table, but are used in the formula for reference. The last entry in the Donation column in the table in Figure 4.9 is actually a formula entered into the table to perform a calculation. The entry is similar to that in a spreadsheet because it is adding the values in all the cells above it.

Syntax refers to the rules for constructing an equation.

The formula is not entered (typed) into the cell explicitly, but is created using the Formula command in the Data group on the Layout tab. You often do not need to know the formula ***syntax***, or rules for constructing the formula, because Word provides a dialog box that supplies basic formulas such as sum and average. But sometimes you construct a unique formula from your table entries. Once you use the table formula feature to create a formula, you will find it easy to understand because it uses field codes to identify the data and formats you use in the formula. You could, of course, use a calculator and type in the total in the cell. However, it is better to use the Formula command to calculate totals than to type the result because if you add data or change data already in the table, you can use formula tools to recalculate the total for you.

Figure 4.10 is a slight variation of Figure 4.9 in which the field codes have been toggled on to display formulas, as opposed to the calculated values. The cells are shaded to emphasize that these cells contain formulas (also called *fields*), as opposed to numerical values. The field codes are toggled on and off by selecting the formula and pressing Shift+F9 or by right-clicking the entry and selecting the Toggle Field Codes command.

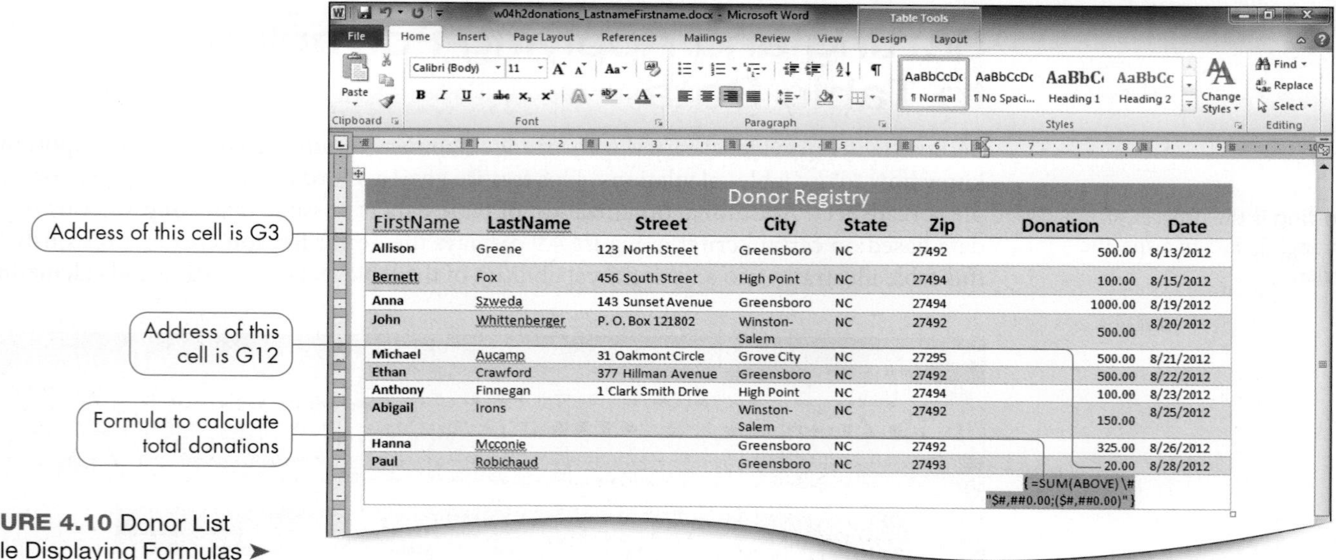

FIGURE 4.10 Donor List Table Displaying Formulas ➤

Sort Data in a Table

Ascending order arranges data from lowest to highest.

Descending order arranges data from highest to lowest.

At times, you might need to sort data in a table to enhance the order or understand the data. For example, when a list of employees is reviewed, a manager might prefer to view the names in alphabetical order by last name, or perhaps by department. You can sort data according to the entries in a specific column or row of the table. Sort orders include ***ascending order***, which arranges text in alphabetical or sequential order starting with the lowest letter or number and continuing to the highest (A–Z or 0–9). Or you can sort in ***descending order***, where data is arranged from highest to lowest (Z–A or 9–0).

You can sort the rows in a table to display data in different sequences, as shown in Figure 4.11, where the donor list items are sorted by date. You also could sort the data in descending (high to low) sequence according to the donation amount or alphabetically by last name. In descending order the largest amount displays at the top of the list, and the smallest amount appears last. The first row of the table contains the title and the second row contains the field names for each column, so they are not included in the sort. The next 11 rows contain the sorted data; the last row is not included in the sort because it displays the total amount donated.

To perform a sort of data in a table you select the rows that are to be sorted, rows 2 through 12 in this example, and then you click Sort in the Data group on the Layout tab. The Sort dialog box displays, as shown in Figure 4.12, which enables you to select the direction and sort criteria. In this case, you include the second row, which contains field names, and then select the option on the Sort dialog box that indicates your data includes a Header row. When you include the header row and then identify it to the sort program, it displays the header row names in the Sort by list so you can identify your sort criteria easily. Identifying the header row also removes it from the sort.

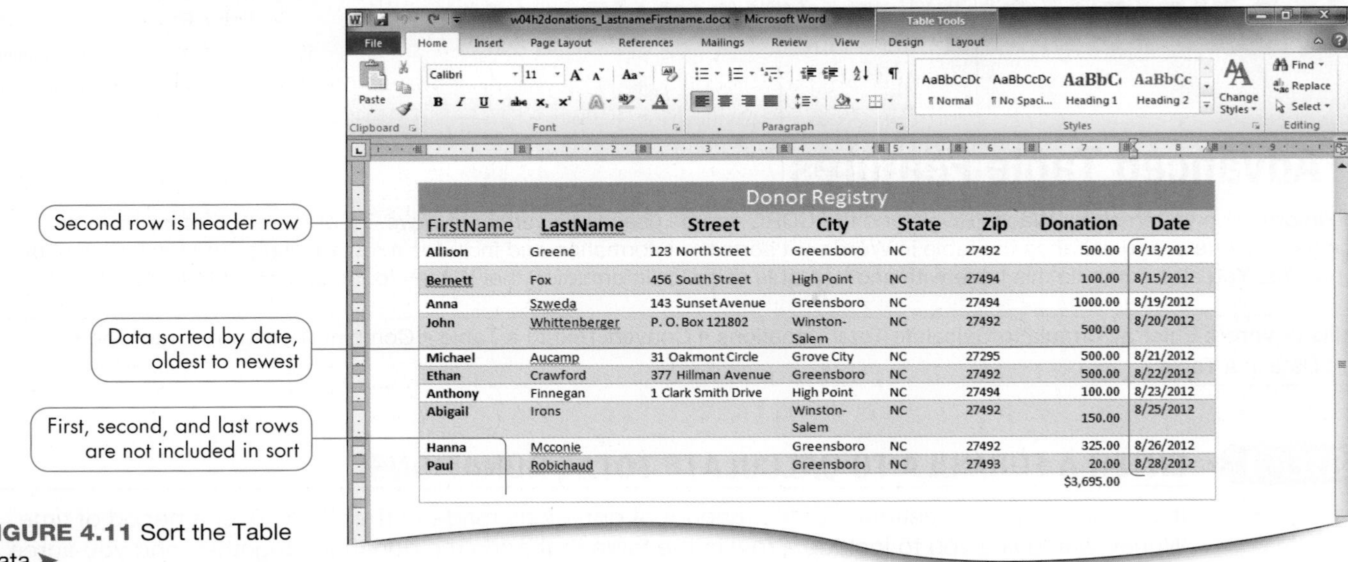

Second row is header row
Data sorted by date, oldest to newest
First, second, and last rows are not included in sort

Donor Registry							
FirstName	LastName	Street	City	State	Zip	Donation	Date
Allison	Greene	123 North Street	Greensboro	NC	27492	500.00	8/13/2012
Bernett	Fox	456 South Street	High Point	NC	27494	100.00	8/15/2012
Anna	Szweda	143 Sunset Avenue	Greensboro	NC	27494	1000.00	8/19/2012
John	Whittenberger	P. O. Box 121802	Winston-Salem	NC	27492	500.00	8/20/2012
Michael	Aucamp	31 Oakmont Circle	Grove City	NC	27295	500.00	8/21/2012
Ethan	Crawford	377 Hillman Avenue	Greensboro	NC	27492	500.00	8/22/2012
Anthony	Finnegan	1 Clark Smith Drive	High Point	NC	27494	100.00	8/23/2012
Abigail	Irons		Winston-Salem	NC	27492	150.00	8/25/2012
Hanna	Mcconie		Greensboro	NC	27492	325.00	8/26/2012
Paul	Robichaud		Greensboro	NC	27493	20.00	8/28/2012
						$3,695.00	

FIGURE 4.11 Sort the Table Data ➤

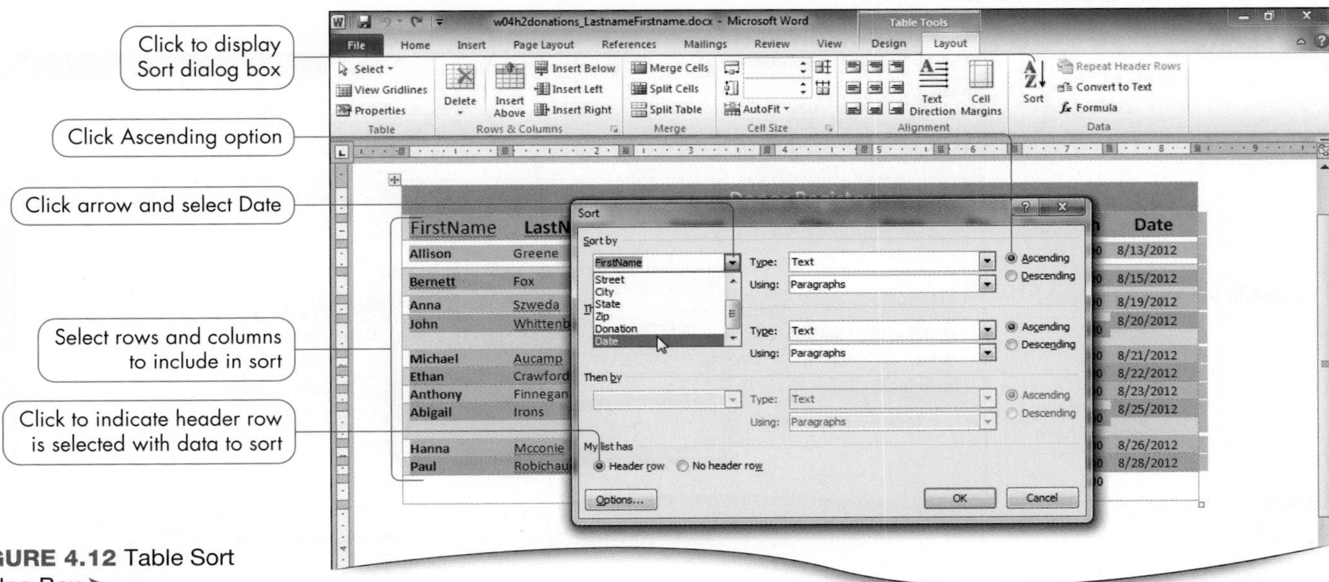

Click to display Sort dialog box
Click Ascending option
Click arrow and select Date
Select rows and columns to include in sort
Click to indicate header row is selected with data to sort

FIGURE 4.12 Table Sort Dialog Box ➤

Converting Text to a Table

The table feature is outstanding, but what if you are given a lengthy list of items that should have been formatted as a table but is currently just text? For example, you have a document containing a list of two items per line separated by a tab, and the list needs to be sorted. The Table command on the Insert tab includes the Convert Text to Table command, and it can aid you in this transformation. After you select the text and choose this command, the Convert Text to Table dialog box displays and offers several options to assist in a quick conversion of text into a table. The command also works in reverse; you can convert a table to text. You will perform a table conversion in the next Hands-On Exercise.

Quick Concepts Check

1. Explain how a table formula uses table data to perform mathematical calculations.
2. Describe the two primary ways to order or sort data in a table.
3. What steps should you take to convert a list of names and addresses into a table?

2 Advanced Table Features

The information you track for Wacey Rivale and the CDRC can be useful in a variety of ways. To prepare the information for reports and letters, you enhance the table in Word so it sorts the information and includes a row to display the total amount of donations. You also combine this table with another table of donor information that Wacey found on her flash drive.

Skills covered: Enter a Formula to Calculate Total Donations • Convert Text to a Table • Combine Two Tables into One • Sort Data in a Table

STEP 1 ENTER A FORMULA TO CALCULATE TOTAL DONATIONS

It is good to have an estimate of the amount of donations made to the CDRC over a period of time. Wacey would like you to include a row in the table that adds the donations together, and you agree that it can be done quickly and easily using the formula tool for tables. Refer to Figure 4.13 as you complete Step 1.

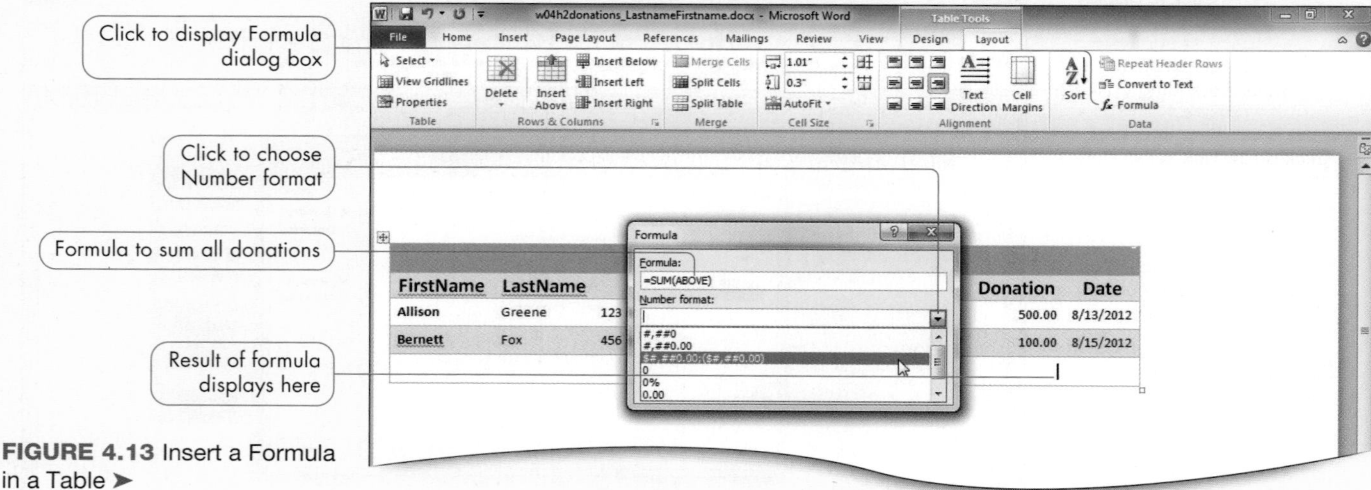

FIGURE 4.13 Insert a Formula in a Table ➤

a. Open the *w04h1donations_LastnameFirstname* document if you closed it after the last Hands-On Exercise, and save it as **w04h2donations_Lastname Firstname**, changing *h1* to *h2*.

TROUBLESHOOTING: If you make any major mistakes in this exercise, you can close the file, open *w04h1donations_LastnameFirstname* again, and then start this exercise over.

b. Click in the last row of the table. Click the **Layout tab**, if necessary, and then click **Insert Below** in the Rows & Columns group.

   You add a new row where you can sum the total amount of donations.

c. Click in **cell G5**, the cell in the seventh column and fifth row. Click **Formula** in the Data group to display the formula box.

   Notice the formula *=SUM(ABOVE)* is entered by default. We can use the default formula because it will add the contents of cells directly above this one. The formula is not case sensitive; you can type formula references in lowercase or capital letters.

d. Click the **Number format arrow**, select **$#,##0.00;($#,##0.00)**, as shown in Figure 4.13, and then click **OK**.

The result of *$600.00* displays in a number format with a dollar sign and two decimal places because these numbers represent a monetary value.

e. Save the document and leave it open.

> **TIP Updating Formula Results**
>
> If you add or remove cells that affect the results of a formula in a table, the formula result will not change automatically. Right-click the formula, and then select Update Field to display the new results.

STEP 2 CONVERT TEXT TO A TABLE

Wacey remembered that she previously saved some raw data about donations received and asks you to put it in a table like the other information. You agree, knowing Word includes a feature for conversions of text to a table. Refer to Figure 4.14 as you complete Step 2.

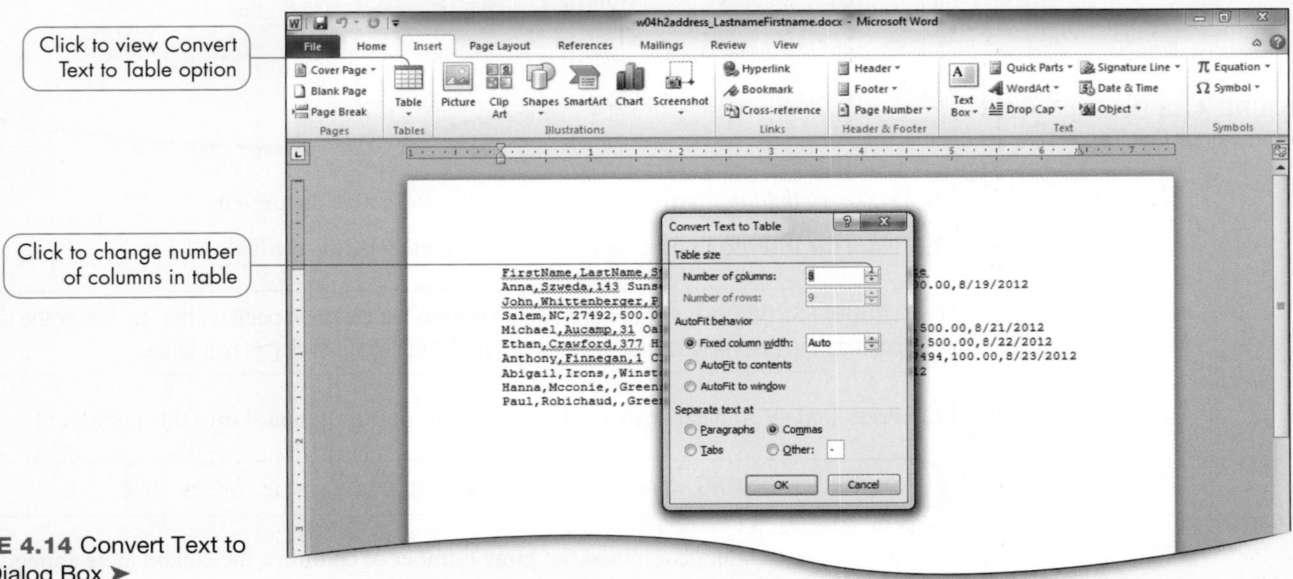

FIGURE 4.14 Convert Text to Table Dialog Box ➤

a. Open *w04h2address* and save it as **w04h2address_LastnameFirstname**.

b. Press **Ctrl+A** to select all text in this document, and then click the **Insert tab**.

c. Click **Table** in the Tables group, and then click **Convert Text to Table**. View the options in the Convert Text to Table dialog box, as shown in Figure 4.14, but do not make any changes at this time. Click **OK**.

The listing of donors and their related information now displays in a table and the commas that separated the data are removed.

d. Press **Ctrl+C** to copy the table to the clipboard.

> **TROUBLESHOOTING:** If you deselect the table after step C, click the Table Move handle to select the entire table, and then perform step D.

e. Save the document.

STEP 3 COMBINE TWO TABLES INTO ONE

Now that you have converted the additional data into a table, you want to combine it with the first table so you can manipulate all the data together. It is not always possible to combine two tables easily, but in this case, you can use Copy and Paste to merge the two tables that contain similar information into one. Refer to Figure 4.15 as you complete Step 3.

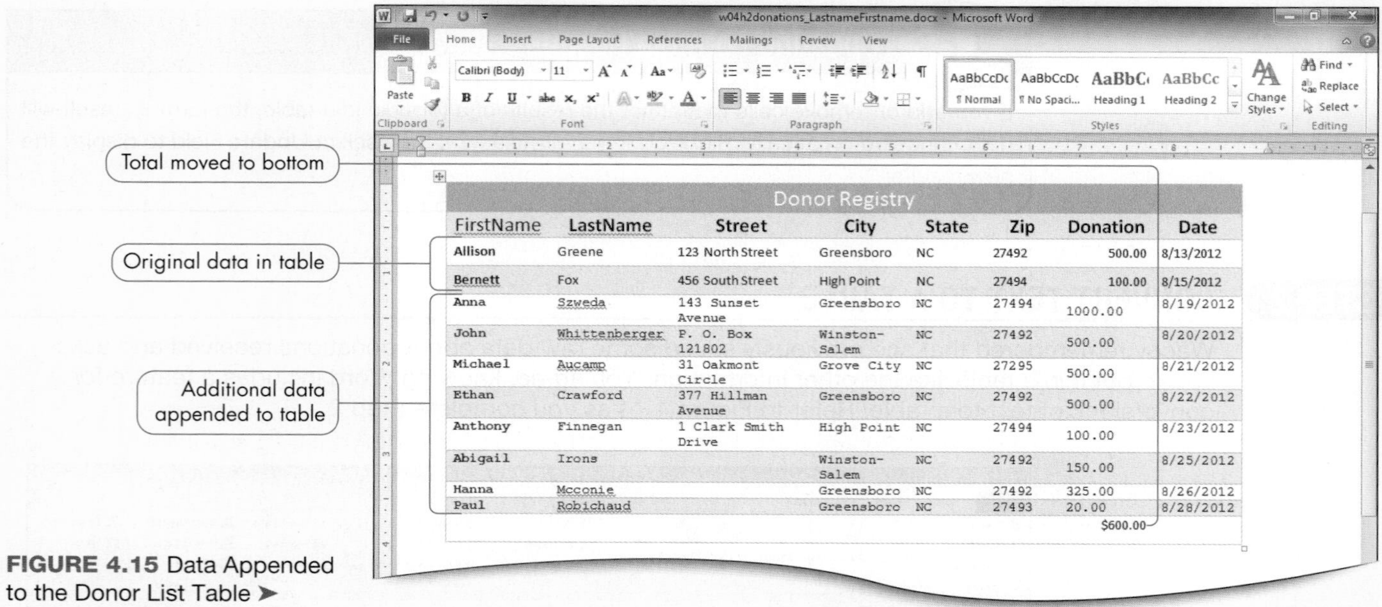

FIGURE 4.15 Data Appended to the Donor List Table ➤

a. Make *w04h2donations_LastnameFirstname* the active document.

b. Place the insertion point on the line immediately below the table.

> **TROUBLESHOOTING:** If you have trouble placing the insertion point on the line below the table, position the insertion point in the last cell of the table and click → two times.

c. Press **Ctrl+V** to paste the rows from the table in the clipboard into this document.

> **TROUBLESHOOTING:** If necessary, click Paste Options and select Merge Table.

Because both tables contained the same number of columns, the copied table appends directly to the existing table, displaying a table with many more rows of donor information. Unfortunately, there is an extra header row which needs to be removed, and the row containing the total line is no longer at the bottom, so you must move it.

d. Select the entire sixth row, which is a repeat of the column headings. Right-click and select **Delete Rows**.

e. Select the entire fifth row, which displays the formula to total the donations. Press **Ctrl+X** to cut the row. Place the insertion point on the line directly below the last row of the table, and then press **Ctrl+V**.

The row now displays at the bottom of the table, but the formula results are the same (as seen in Figure 4.15). Next, you update the formula to reflect the additional donations that now display in the table.

f. Right-click the formula that displays on the last row of the table, and then select **Update Field**.

The new total of *$3,695.00* now displays.

g. Save the document but leave it open for the next step. Close *w04h2address_LastnameFirstname.*

STEP 4 SORT DATA IN A TABLE

The data are combined and you are almost ready to turn the document over to Wacey for review. You know that it will be helpful to display the information sorted by date so she can try to remember the people she visited with on certain occasions. You complete the sort and then make a few last adjustments so the information displays nicely on paper. Refer to Figure 4.16 as you complete Step 4.

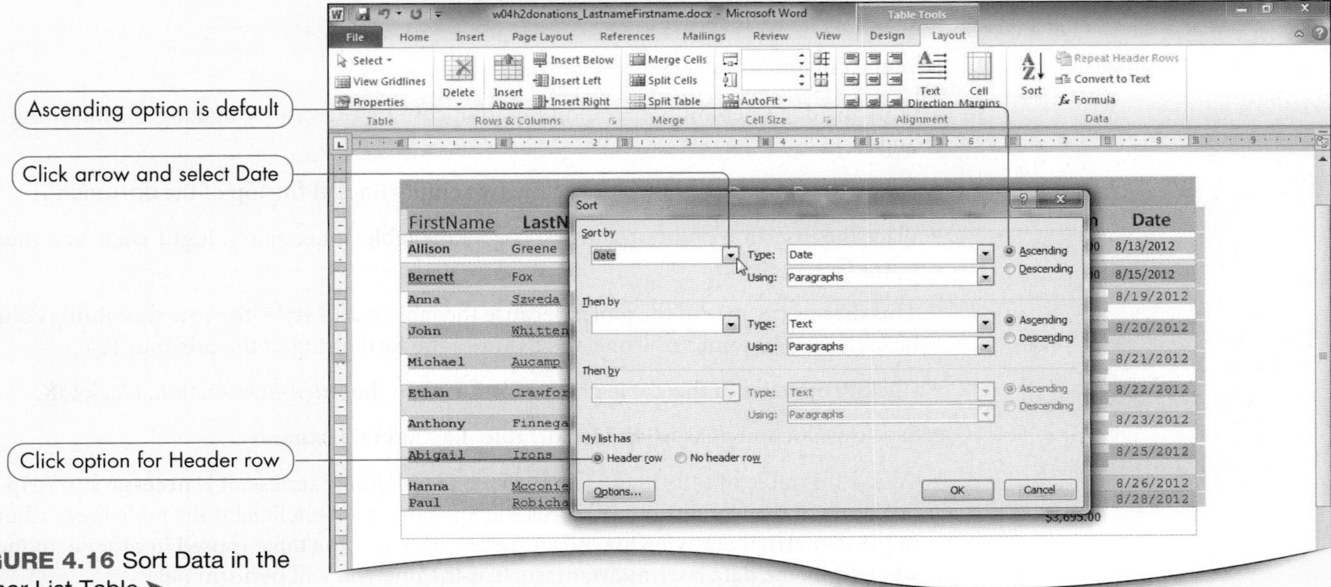

FIGURE 4.16 Sort Data in the Donor List Table ➤

a. Drag to select rows 2 through 12 in the table. That is, select all table rows *except* the first and last row. Click the **Layout tab**, and then click **Sort** in the Data group.

b. Click **Header row** in the *My list has* section, at the bottom of the dialog box.

c. Click the **Sort by arrow**, and then select **Date** (the column heading for the last column). Click **Ascending**, if necessary, and compare your settings to Figure 4.16. Click **OK**.

The entries in the table are rearranged chronologically from the oldest to most recent date of donation.

> **TROUBLESHOOTING:** If you do not first click Header row, the headings for each column will not display in the Sort by list; instead you will see the column numbers listed. You can sort by column number (1, 2, 3, or 4), but it is important to click the Header row option before you leave this dialog box so the header row is not included in the sort.

d. Select **cells G5 through G12** (the donation data from the added table), and then click **Align Center Right** in the Alignment group.

Now the donation amounts for the data appended to this table are aligned with the other amounts that you typed in earlier.

e. Change the font of the newly inserted donors to match the first two donors by completing the following steps:

- Select the rows that contain the data appended to the table, and then right-click to display the Mini toolbar.
- Click the **Font arrow** on the Mini toolbar, and then click **Calibri**.
- Right-click the selected rows again to display the Mini toolbar, if necessary, click the **Font Size arrow**, and then click **11**.

f. Click **Properties** in the Table group.

g. Click the **Table tab**, if necessary, and then click **Center** in the *Alignment* section. Click **OK**. Click anywhere to deselect the table.

Your table is now centered between the left and right margins. This alignment alters the location of the table, but not the data inside the table. It also creates an attractively styled and easy-to-read document.

h. Save the document.

i. Modify the document in preparation for an upcoming exercise by making the following changes:

- Press **Ctrl+Home**, and then delete the two empty lines at the top of the document.
- Place the insertion point on the first row of the table, if necessary. Right-click, and then select **Delete Rows**.

  This deletes the title of the table. Because the table uses a style, the row containing column headers now becomes row one and assumes the formatting of the previous title.
- Click **Properties** in the Table group. Click **Left** in the *Alignment* section. Click **OK**.
- Save this document as **w04h2donortable_LastnameFirstname**.

  To use this table of information in the next Hands-On Exericse, it is necessary to strip out some of the formatting. Whereas the formatting is beneficial if the table is distributed in print or strictly for viewing, it is unnecessary when the table is used in other activities where only the data are important, such as the one you will perform next.

j. Close the document.

Mail Merge

At some point in your personal or professional life, you will need to send the same message to a number of different people. For example, you will send a graduation announcement to all your family and friends, you might send a cover letter with a résumé to several organizations, or you might need to send a letter to a group of customers informing them of an upcoming sale. In each case, you will need to personalize either the letter or the recipient's address on the letter or an envelope. You can use Word's Mail Merge feature to generate these types of documents easily and efficiently. ***Mail merge*** is a process that combines content from a main document and a data source, with the option of creating a new document.

Mail merge is a process that combines content from a main document and a data source.

A **form letter** is a letter you will print or e-mail many times, personalizing each one for the recipient.

Mail merge is used most frequently to create a set of ***form letters***, which are letters you might print or e-mail many times, personalizing or modifying each one for the recipient. When you apply for a job after graduation, you might send the same cover letter to many different companies. You could spend hours personalizing and resaving individual letters, but when you use mail merge, you can update several letters simultaneously and quickly. An example of a mail merge is illustrated in Figures 4.17, 4.18, and 4.19, in which Wacey Rivale has written a letter of appreciation to each person who donated to the CDRC, then merges that letter with her log that contains addresses, donation amount, and dates. When complete, she produces letters addressed to each donor individually.

... you might send the same cover letter to many different companies. You could spend hours personalizing and resaving individual letters, but when you use mail merge, you can update several letters simultaneously and quickly.

In this section, you will learn about the mail merge process by creating a main document and selecting a recipient list. You then will create form letters by combining the information from both sources.

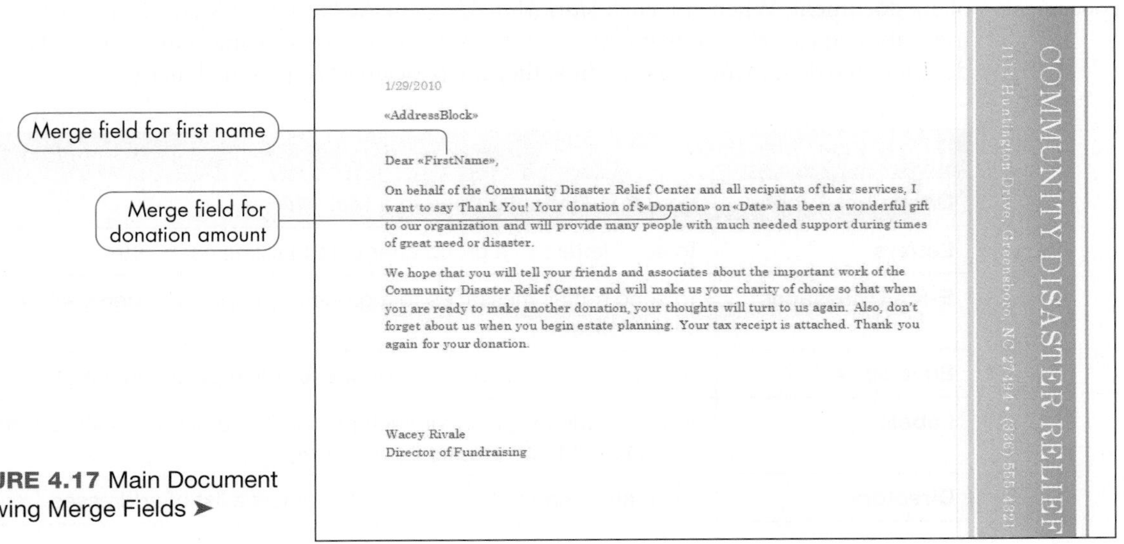

1/29/2010

«AddressBlock»

Dear «FirstName»,

On behalf of the Community Disaster Relief Center and all recipients of their services, I want to say Thank You! Your donation of $«Donation» on «Date» has been a wonderful gift to our organization and will provide many people with much needed support during times of great need or disaster.

We hope that you will tell your friends and associates about the important work of the Community Disaster Relief Center and will make us your charity of choice so that when you are ready to make another donation, your thoughts will turn to us again. Also, don't forget about us when you begin estate planning. Your tax receipt is attached. Thank you again for your donation.

Wacey Rivale
Director of Fundraising

FIGURE 4.17 Main Document Showing Merge Fields ➤

FirstName	LastName	Street	City	State	Zip	Donation	Date
John	Whittenberger	P. O. Box 121802	Winston-Salem	NC	27492	500.00	8/20/2012
Anna	Szweda	143 Sunset Avenue	Greensboro	NC	27494	1000.00	8/19/2012
Paul	Robichaud		Greensboro	NC	27493	20.00	8/28/2012
Hanna	Mcconie		Greensboro	NC	27492	325.00	8/26/2012
Abigail	Irons		Winston-Salem	NC	27492	150.00	8/25/2012
Allison	Greene	123 North Street	Greensboro	NC	27492	500.00	8/13/2012
Bernett	Fox	456 South Street	High Point	NC	27494	100.00	8/15/2012
Anthony	Finnegan	1 Clark Smith Drive	High Point	NC	27494	100.00	8/23/2012
Ethan	Crawford	377 Hillman Avenue	Greensboro	NC	27492	500.00	8/22/2012
Michael	Aucamp	31 Oakmont Circle	Grove City	NC	27295	500.00	8/21/2012

FIGURE 4.18 List of Names, Addresses, and Donations ➤

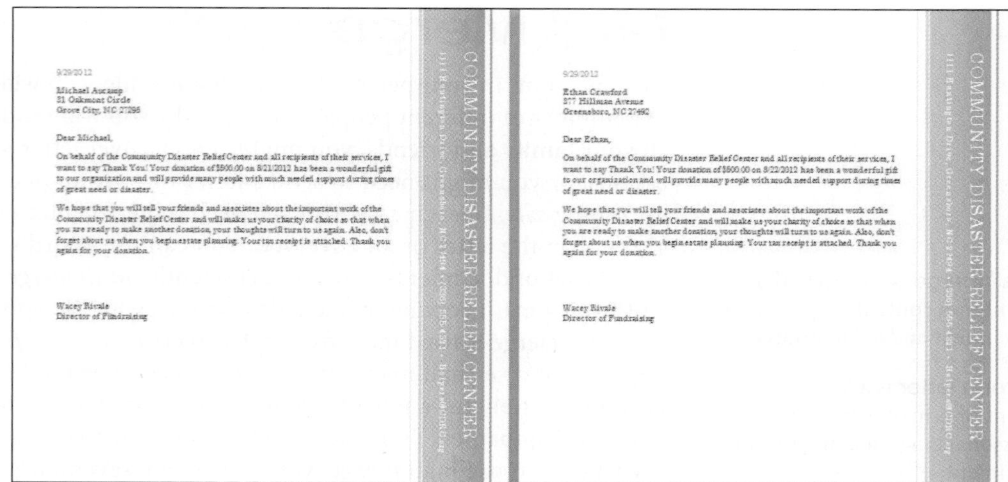

9/29/2012

Michael Aucamp
31 Oakmont Circle
Grove City, NC 27296

Dear Michael,

On behalf of the Community Disaster Relief Center and all recipients of their services, I want to say Thank You! Your donation of $500.00 on 8/21/2012 has been a wonderful gift to our organization and will provide many people with much needed support during times of great need or disaster.

We hope that you will tell your friends and associates about the important work of the Community Disaster Relief Center and will make us your charity of choice so that when you are ready to make another donation, your thoughts will turn to us again. Also, don't forget about us when you begin estate planning. Your tax receipt is attached. Thank you again for your donation.

Wacey Rivale
Director of Fundraising

COMMUNITY DISASTER RELIEF CENTER

9/29/2012

Ethan Crawford
377 Hillman Avenue
Greensboro, NC 27492

Dear Ethan,

On behalf of the Community Disaster Relief Center and all recipients of their services, I want to say Thank You! Your donation of $500.00 on 8/22/2012 has been a wonderful gift to our organization and will provide many people with much needed support during times of great need or disaster.

We hope that you will tell your friends and associates about the important work of the Community Disaster Relief Center and will make us your charity of choice so that when you are ready to make another donation, your thoughts will turn to us again. Also, don't forget about us when you begin estate planning. Your tax receipt is attached. Thank you again for your donation.

Wacey Rivale
Director of Fundraising

COMMUNITY DISASTER RELIEF CENTER

FIGURE 4.19 Merged Form Letters ➤

Selecting a Main Document

The **main document** contains the information that stays the same for all recipients.

A **merge field** serves as a placeholder for data that will be inserted into the main document during the mail merge.

The mail merge process uses two files as input, a main document and a data source; by merging these two files you can create a set of individualized letters, envelopes, e-mails, or other documents. The ***main document***, also known as a source or starting document, contains the information that stays the same for all recipients. The main document also includes one or more ***merge fields*** that serve as placeholders for the variable data that will be inserted into the individual letters, as shown in Figure 4.17.

You can use an existing document as a main document, or you can create one from a blank document. When you click *Start Mail Merge* in the Start Mail Merge group of the Mailings tab, you can choose from several categories to use as your main document. Table 4.3 describes the document types and how they are typically used in a mail merge.

TABLE 4.3 Main Document Types

Document Type	How It Is Typically Used in a Mail Merge
Letters	To send letters to a group after personalizing each letter.
E-Mail Messages	To send e-mail messages to a group of people after personalizing each message.
Envelopes	To print an address on an envelope for each person in the group.
Labels	To print address labels for each person in the group, which can then be attached to an envelope for mailing.
Directory	To create a single document that contains a list of addresses.

A **wizard** makes a process easier by asking a series of questions, then creating a document structure based on your answers.

The last option displayed when you click *Start Mail Merge* is the Step by Step Mail Merge Wizard. A ***wizard*** makes a process easier by asking a series of questions, then creating a customized document structure based on your answers. In this case, the wizard simplifies the process of creating form letters and other types of merge documents through step-by-step directions that appear automatically on the Mail Merge pane. The options for the current step appear in the top portion of the pane and are self-explanatory. Click the link to the next step at the bottom of the pane to move forward in the process, or click the link to the previous step to correct any mistakes you might have made. This is a very easy-to-follow process and helps you work through the mail merge procedure without knowing exactly what you need to click in the Mailings tab.

> **TIP: Printing Mailing Labels or Envelopes**
>
> If you want to create mailing labels or envelopes, the Create group on the Mailings tab includes commands that help you select the correct settings. You can use these options to print items that would not necessarily be included in a mail merge, such as a single envelope or a sheet of return address labels.

Selecting or Creating Recipients

A **data source** is a listing of information.

A **field** is a single piece of data used in a source document, such as last name.

A **record** is a group of related fields.

After you choose the type of document you will use in a merge, the next step is to create or select a list of recipients. Typically, this is the information you need to insert in an address block, or specific information, such as a company name. A recipient list, sometimes called a ***data source***, contains individual pieces of data and each is known as a ***field***. Common fields in a data source include first name, last name, address, city, state, ZIP code, phone number, and e-mail address. A group of fields for a particular person or thing is called a ***record***. Figure 4.18 demonstrates a sample data source. Your data source might come from:

- A Word document that contains information stored in a table
- An Access database
- An Excel worksheet
- Your Outlook Contacts

The **header row** is the first row in a data source.

The first row in the data source is called the ***header row*** and identifies the fields in the remaining rows. Each additional row contains a record, and every record contains the same fields in the same order—for example, Title, FirstName, LastName, and so on.

> **TIP: Using a Word Table as a Data Source**
>
> When your source data are stored in a table in Word, you can ensure the mail merge will work correctly if you save the table by itself in a separate file with no blank lines above the table. The first row of the table must contain field names. To use your table as a recipient list, click Use Existing List after you click Select Recipients in the Start Mail Merge group on the Mailings tab. Navigate to the location where the document is saved, select the file, and click Open.

If you do not have a preexisting list to use as a data source, you can create one in Word. Click Select Recipients in the Start Mail Merge group of the Mailings tab, and then click Type New List. A New Address List dialog box displays with the most commonly used fields for a mail merge, as shown in Figure 4.20. You can enter data immediately or click Customize Columns to add, delete, or rename the fields to meet your particular needs. When you save, the list is saved as a database file with the .mdb extension.

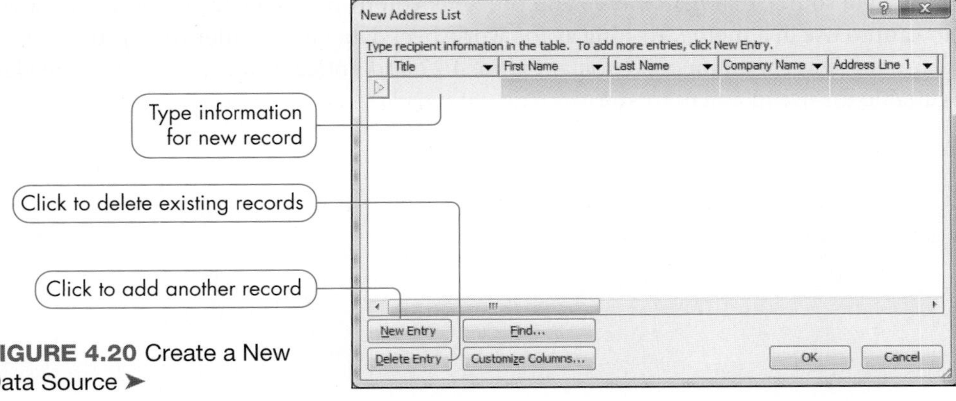

FIGURE 4.20 Create a New Data Source ➤

If you want to add new records to a source file you created in Word, you can click Edit Recipient List in the Start Mail Merge group of the Mailings tab. Note that you can only edit the list after it has been selected as a recipient list for the mail merge. When the Mail Merge Recipients dialog box displays, click the name of the data source, and then click Edit. The Edit Data Source dialog box displays. Click Add New and a blank form displays as the last record, and you can immediately populate the fields with your data (see Figure 4.21).

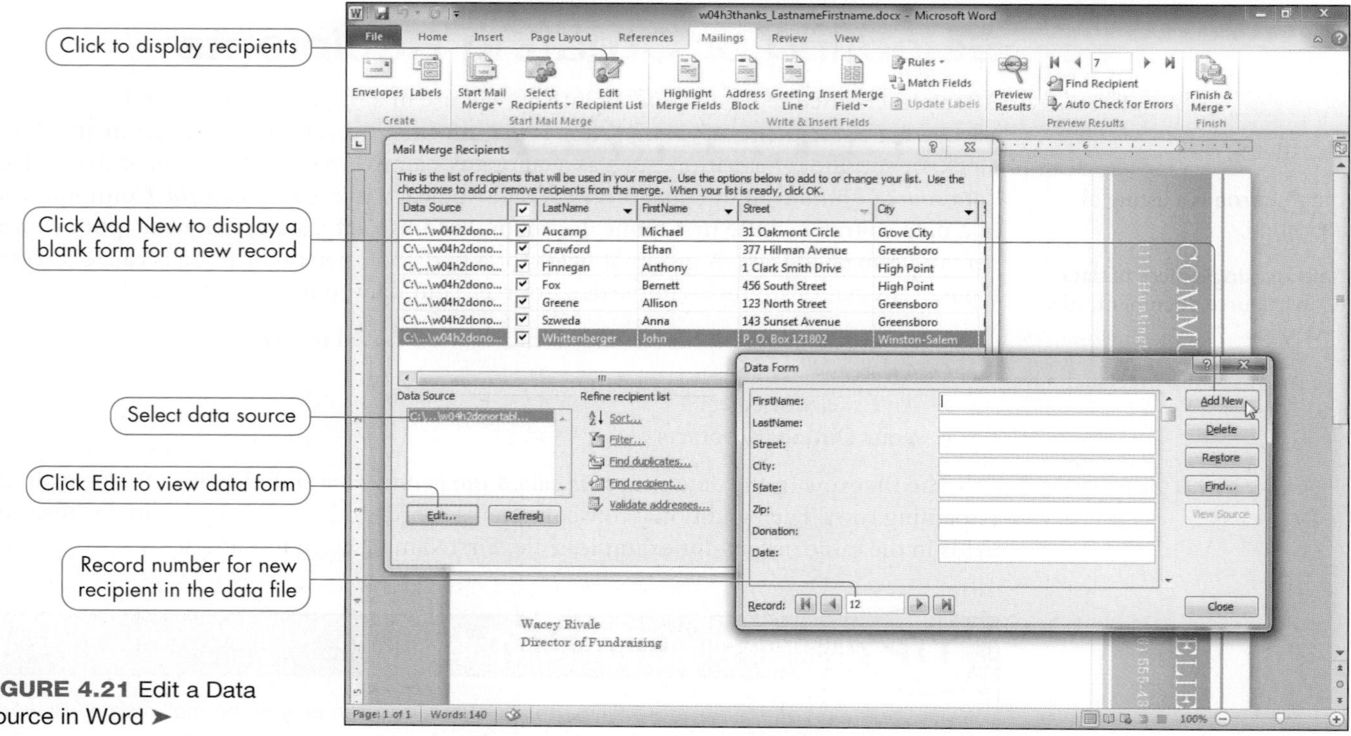

FIGURE 4.21 Edit a Data Source in Word ➤

Using Excel Worksheets as a Data Source

Even though you can create and use data sources in Word, there is a very good probability you will also need to perform a mail merge with a data source that was created and saved in a different Office application such as Access or Excel. The database and spreadsheet applications are designed to organize large amounts of information, so they are perfect candidates to hold the source data you want to use in a mail merge.

The database and spreadsheet applications are designed to organize large amounts of information, so they are perfect candidates to hold the source data you want to use in a mail merge.

An Excel worksheet is comparable to a giant table in Word; it can contain hundreds of rows and columns of data. A manager who must keep track of large amounts of information probably stores it in a spreadsheet, which makes a good candidate for a data source in a mail merge and prevents you from having to retype any data you might want to use in a merge. As long as the worksheet data has a header row, you can use it as a data source in a mail merge. Look at Figure 4.22 and notice how the worksheet displays data suitable for use in a mail merge.

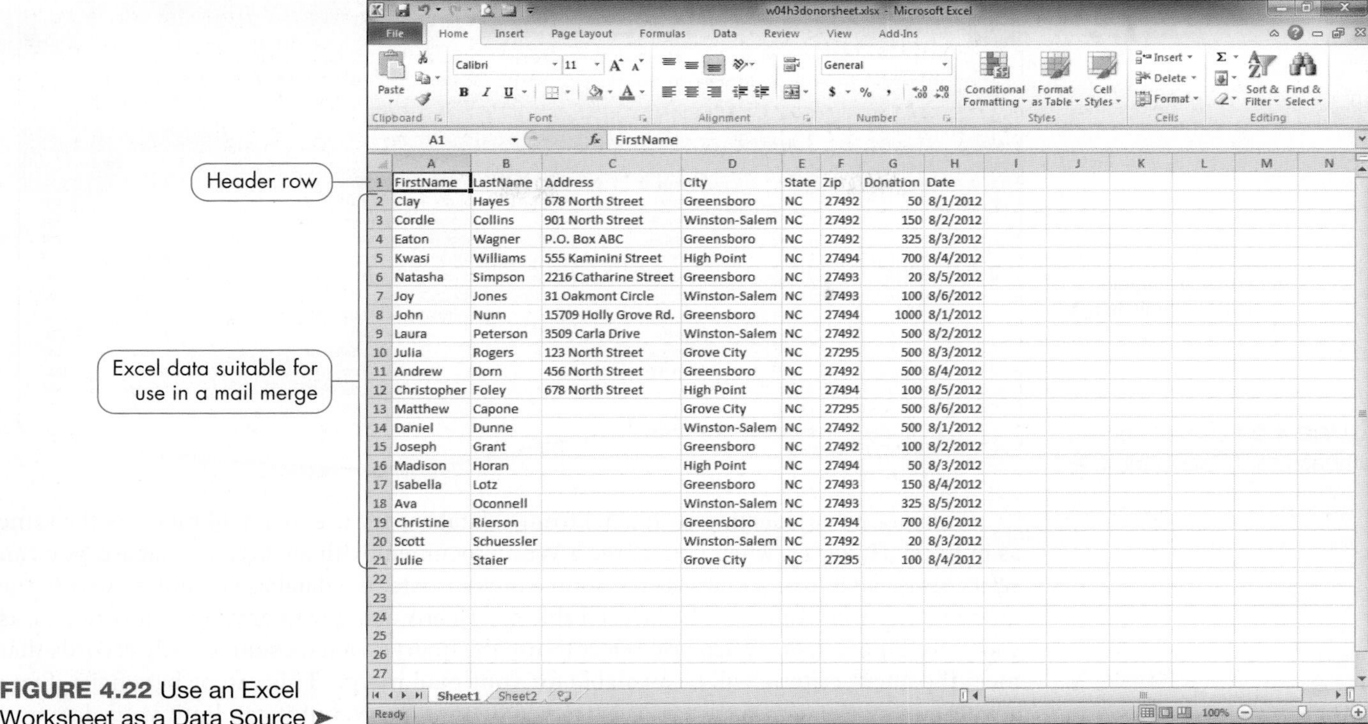

FirstName	LastName	Address	City	State	Zip	Donation	Date
Clay	Hayes	678 North Street	Greensboro	NC	27492	50	8/1/2012
Cordle	Collins	901 North Street	Winston-Salem	NC	27492	150	8/2/2012
Eaton	Wagner	P.O. Box ABC	Greensboro	NC	27492	325	8/3/2012
Kwasi	Williams	555 Kaminini Street	High Point	NC	27494	700	8/4/2012
Natasha	Simpson	2216 Catharine Street	Greensboro	NC	27493	20	8/5/2012
Joy	Jones	31 Oakmont Circle	Winston-Salem	NC	27493	100	8/6/2012
John	Nunn	15709 Holly Grove Rd.	Greensboro	NC	27494	1000	8/1/2012
Laura	Peterson	3509 Carla Drive	Winston-Salem	NC	27492	500	8/2/2012
Julia	Rogers	123 North Street	Grove City	NC	27295	500	8/3/2012
Andrew	Dorn	456 North Street	Greensboro	NC	27492	500	8/4/2012
Christopher	Foley	678 North Street	High Point	NC	27494	100	8/5/2012
Matthew	Capone		Grove City	NC	27295	500	8/6/2012
Daniel	Dunne		Winston-Salem	NC	27492	500	8/1/2012
Joseph	Grant		Greensboro	NC	27492	100	8/2/2012
Madison	Horan		High Point	NC	27494	50	8/3/2012
Isabella	Lotz		Greensboro	NC	27493	150	8/4/2012
Ava	Oconnell		Winston-Salem	NC	27493	325	8/5/2012
Christine	Rierson		Greensboro	NC	27494	700	8/6/2012
Scott	Schuessler		Winston-Salem	NC	27492	20	8/3/2012
Julie	Staier		Grove City	NC	27295	100	8/4/2012

FIGURE 4.22 Use an Excel Worksheet as a Data Source ➤

To merge a Word document with data stored in Excel, click Select Recipients in the Start Mail Merge group on the Mailings tab, and then click Use Existing List. When the Select Data Source dialog box opens, browse to the location where the Excel worksheet is stored, click the file name, and then click Open. Excel worksheets have the extension .xlsx (or .xls if an older version), so you might need to change the type of file in the *Files of type* box at the bottom of the window.

Using Access Databases as a Data Source

A **database table** is a collection of related records that contain fields to organize data.

Access is a database program, and databases are designed to store large amounts of data. Information in a database is stored in tables. A ***database table*** is a collection of related records that contain fields to organize data. Access also includes features that enable you to query the database tables so you can extract and view only data that meet your search criteria. Figure 4.23 provides a look at a database file. Because database files can contain so much data, it is advisable to use the query feature to narrow down the data to only that which will be needed in the mail merge. Filtering the data from the database is much more efficient and easier than sorting and deleting unwanted pages in a Word document after a mail merge.

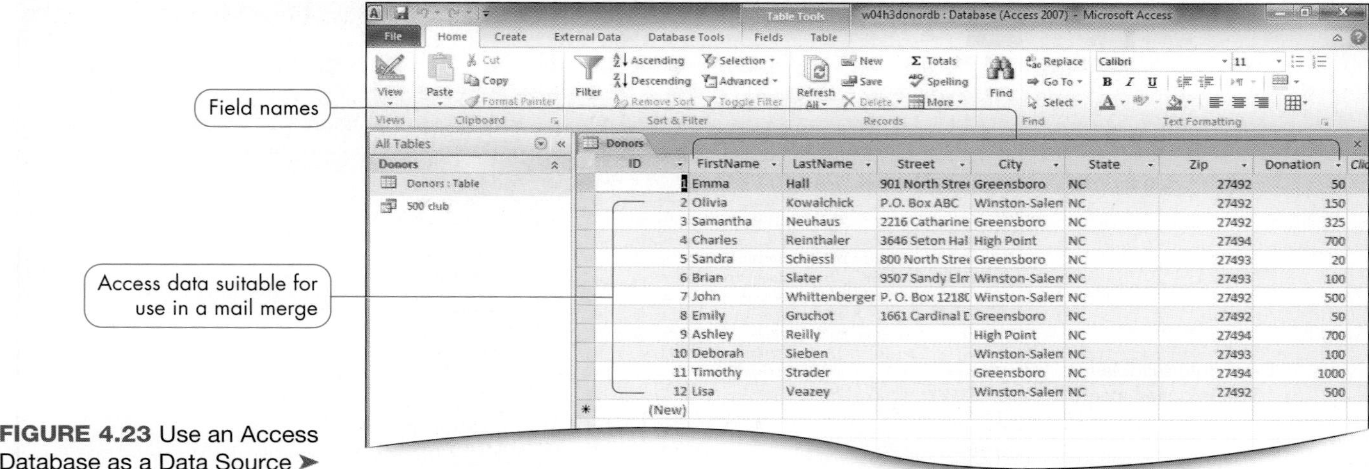

FIGURE 4.23 Use an Access Database as a Data Source ➤

The process of selecting recipients from a database for use in a mail merge is the same as in Excel. However, when you merge a Word document with an Access database, you can select to use a table or a query as the source of your data. If a database includes queries, the query names will display in the Select Table dialog box along with any tables it contains, as shown in Figure 4.24. When you select to use the query as a data source, only records that meet the query criteria will be available for your mail merge. This can be beneficial if you are certain all the data you need is extracted by that query, but it can limit your data and omit necessary records if the query is too restrictive.

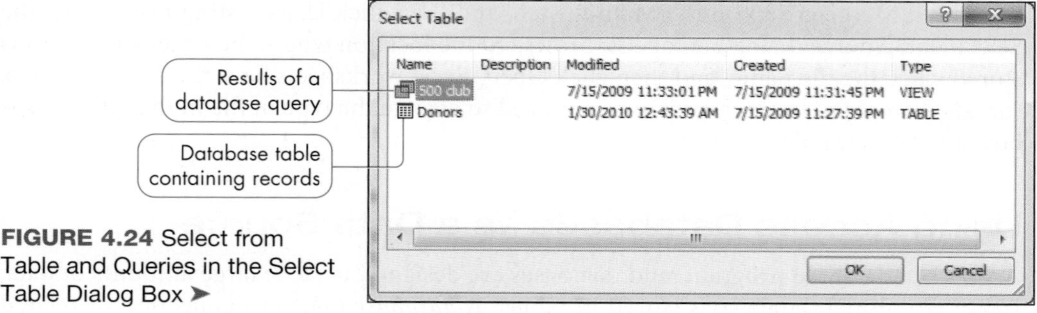

FIGURE 4.24 Select from Table and Queries in the Select Table Dialog Box ➤

Access database files have the extension .accdb (or .mdb if an older version). A database uses field names to classify the data it contains, which makes it very compatible for a mail merge. However, the Access file you use as a data source might not use the same field names as Word expects; for example, a database may use LNAME as a field name instead of Last-Name. In this situation, you can use the Match Fields command to create a link between the Word document fields and the Access database fields. After you select the recipient list for your mail merge, click Match Fields to display a list of fields that Word often uses and a list of the fields found in the data source. You can then select a database field that matches the required fields in Word.

Sorting and Filtering Records in a Data Source

Before merging the data source with the main document, you might want to rearrange the records in the data source. For example, you might want to sort the data source in alphabetical order by last name, or in descending order by sales, if included. If you have a large number of form letters to send, you can receive a discount at the post office if you follow certain procedures. One procedure is to sort the letters by ZIP code. You can save a lot of work hours if you sort the data source before merging instead of after merging and printing. When you click Edit Recipient List in the Start Mail Merge group on the Mailings tab to display the Mail Merge Recipients dialog box, several options offer a variety of methods to sort the source data, as shown in Figure 4.25.

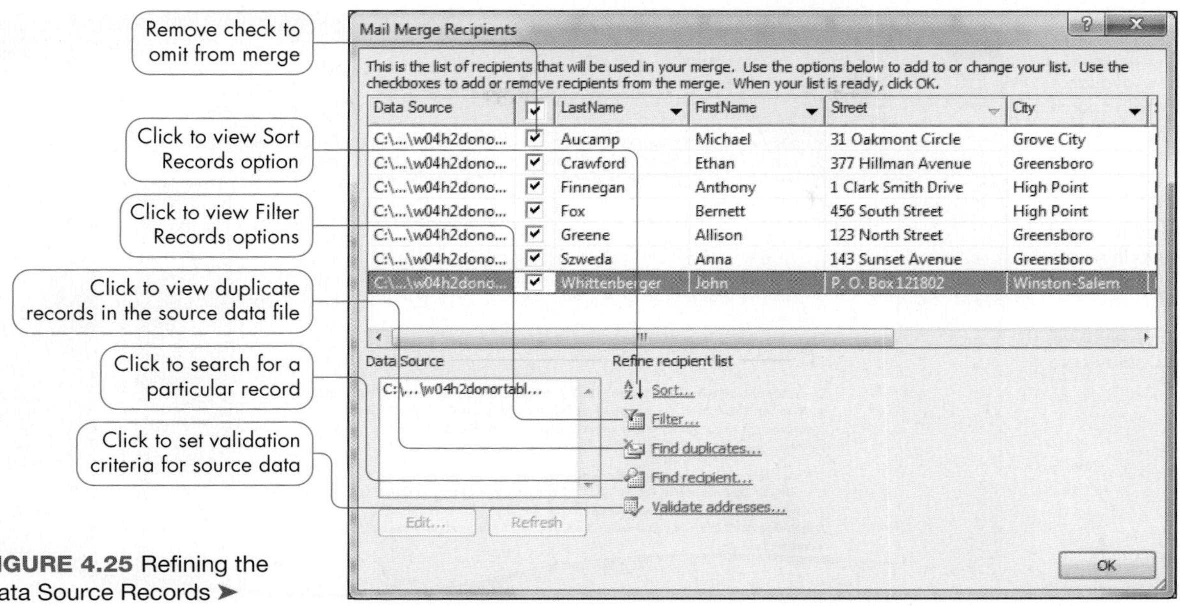

FIGURE 4.25 Refining the Data Source Records ➤

A **filter** specifies criteria for including records that meet certain conditions.

When you click Sort or Filter, the Filter and Sort dialog box displays and enables you to perform more complex sorts. The Filter Records tab enables you to ***filter***, or specify criteria for including records that meet certain conditions during the merge process. For example, you may want to filter the source data by state so only companies in the state of California are included in the mail merge.

The Sort Records tab enables you to specify up to three levels for sorting records. For example, you can first sort by state, further sort by city within state, and finally sort by last name within city (see Figure 4.26).

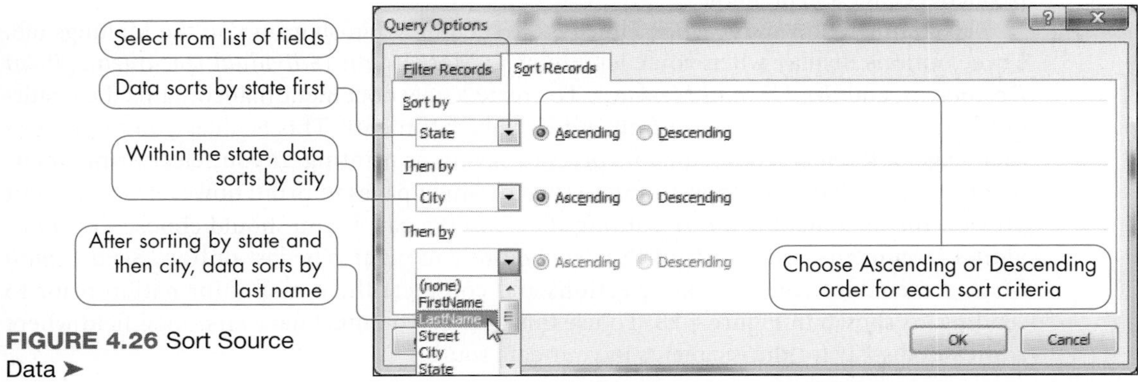

FIGURE 4.26 Sort Source Data ➤

Inserting Merge Fields

When you write a letter or set up your e-mail in preparation for a mail merge, you insert a merge field in the main document. The merge field is a placeholder that specifies where information from the data source will display in the main document. Because it corresponds with a field in the data source, matching the two fields guarantees that the right data will be inserted into the main document when you complete the merge. View Figure 4.17 again to view the merge fields that correspond to the fields in the source document in Figure 4.18.

The merge fields display in the main document within angle brackets, for example «AddressBlock», «FirstName», or «Donation». These entries are not typed explicitly but are entered automatically when you select one of the source data fields that display when you click Insert Merge Field from the Write & Insert Fields group of the Mailings tab. (See Figure 4.27.)

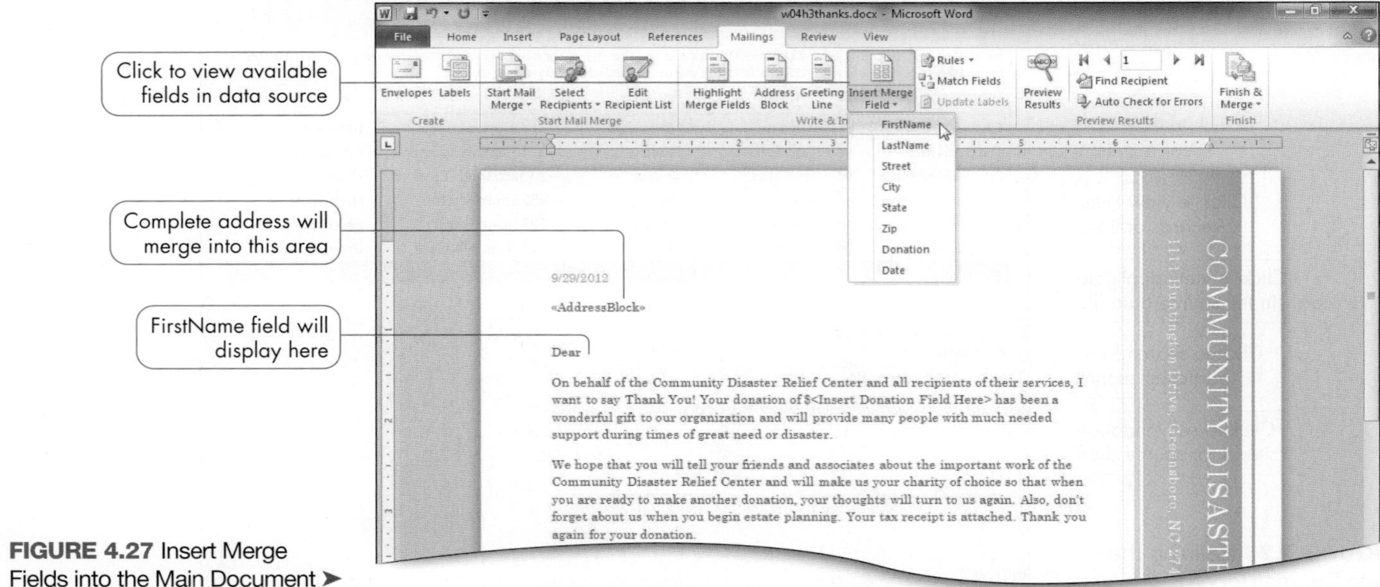

FIGURE 4.27 Insert Merge Fields into the Main Document ➤

Merging a Main Document and a Data Source

After you create the main document and identify the source data, you are ready to begin the merge process. The merge process examines each record in the data source, and when a match is found, it replaces the merge field in the main document with the information from the data source. A copy of the main document is created for each record in the data source, thus creating individual form letters, for example. Figure 4.19 displays two of the personalized letters after a mail merge.

To complete the merge, click Finish & Merge in the Finish group on the Mailings tab. Three options display when you click Finish & Merge: *Edit Individual Documents*, *Print Documents*, and *Send E-mail Messages*. To create a new document that contains the results of the merge, you should select Edit Individual Documents. This enables you to preview each page of the merged documents prior to saving or printing. If you select Print Documents, you will have the opportunity to specify which pages to print; however, you cannot preview the document prior to printing. To conserve paper, you should choose *Edit Individual Documents* and use Print Preview before you print. The last option, *Send E-mail Messages*, enables you to make selections and complete the e-mail information prior to sending, as shown in Figure 4.28. To use this option, you must have an e-mail field where addresses display for the recipients in your data source.

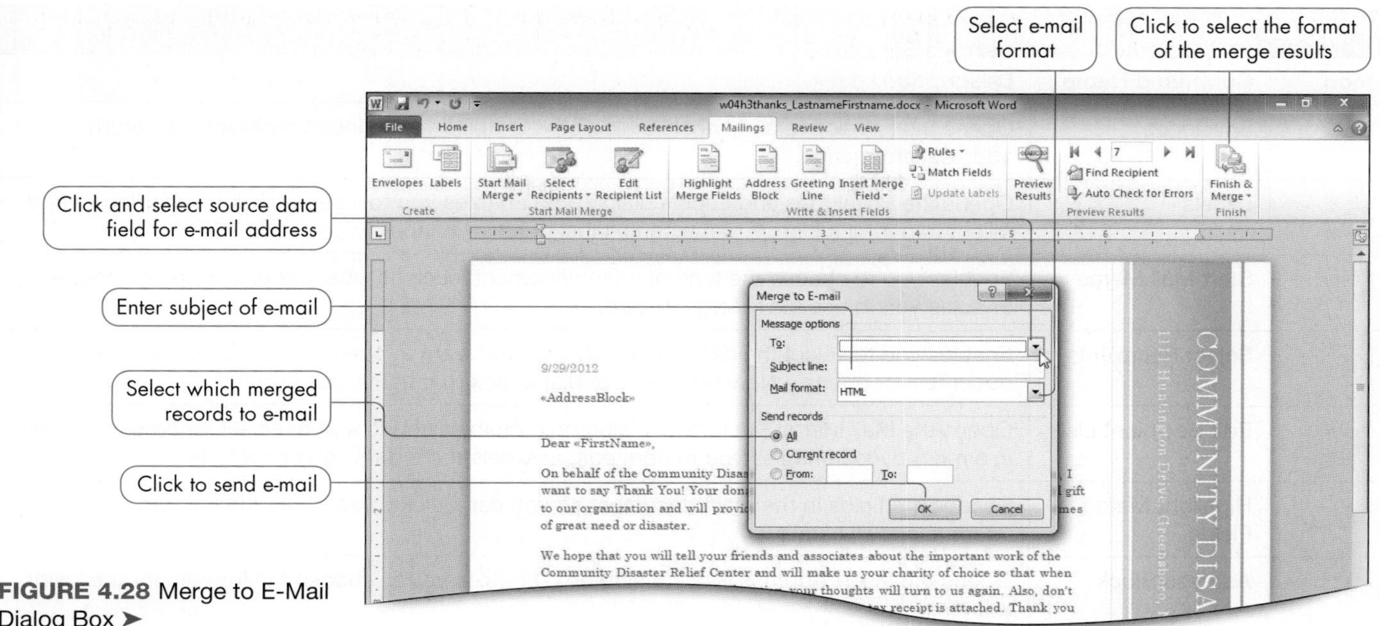
Select e-mail format
Click to select the format of the merge results
Click and select source data field for e-mail address
Enter subject of e-mail
Select which merged records to e-mail
Click to send e-mail
Merge to E-mail
Message options
To:
Subject line:
Mail format:
HTML
Send records
All
Current record
From:
To:
OK
Cancel

FIGURE 4.28 Merge to E-Mail Dialog Box ➤

The same data source can be used to create multiple sets of form documents. You could, for example, create a marketing campaign in which you send an initial letter to the entire list, and then send follow-up letters at periodic intervals to the same mailing list. Alternatively, you could filter the original mailing list to include only a subset of names, such as the individuals who responded to the initial letter. You could also create a different set of documents, such as envelopes or e-mail messages.

If you want to generate a list from the source data, you can use a Directory mail merge. Select Directory as your source document type and Word will merge all the source data onto the same page instead of merging each record onto a separate page.

The Mail Merge feature is exciting, yet a bit complex. Use Table 4.4 to acquaint yourself with the commands on the Mailings tab. Once you successfully complete a mail merge, you will enjoy finding ways to use it over and over!

TABLE 4.4 Mail Merge Commands		
Icon	**Command Name**	**Description**
	Envelopes	Opens the Envelopes and Labels dialog box. Enables you to insert recipient and return address information.
	Labels	Opens the Envelopes and Labels dialog box. Enables you to insert an address for labels and select to print a full page of the same label or a single label.
	Start Mail Merge	Enables you to choose the type of main document, such as letters or envelopes, to create. Enables you to use Mail Merge Wizard.
	Select Recipients	Enables you to select the data source file that you want to open and use with the main document or opens a New Address List dialog box to create a data source.
	Edit Recipient List	Opens the Mail Merge Recipients dialog box. Enables you to sort or select records to include in a merge. Also enables you to add, edit, and delete the data source records.
	Highlight Merge Fields	Shades the fields in the main document so you can quickly see where the merged information will display.
	Address Block	Opens the Insert Address Block dialog box. Enables you to choose the formats for the inside address.
	Greeting Line	Opens the Greeting Line dialog box. Enables you to choose the level of formality for the salutation.
	Insert Merge Field	Opens the Insert Merge Field dialog box. Enables you to select and insert fields in the main document.
	Rules	Displays decision-making criteria to increase your options for filtering records.
	Match Fields	Opens the Match Fields dialog box. Enables you to select fields from another data source, such as an Access database table, to match with required fields in Word.
	Update Labels	Copies the merge fields from the first label to the other labels.
	Preview Results	Displays the data from the data source in the respective fields in the main document so that you can verify correct placement.
	First Record	Displays the first merged record. Works with Preview Results.
	Previous Record	Displays the previous merged record. Works with Preview Results.
1	Go to Record	Enables you to enter the number of a specific record to go to.
	Next Record	Displays the next merged record. Works with Preview Results.
	Last Record	Displays the last merged record. Works with Preview Results.
	Find Recipient	Opens the Find Entry dialog box. Enables you to find data in a specific field or in all fields.
	Auto Check for Errors	Enables you to check for errors and report those errors during the merge process.
	Finish & Merge	Enables you to choose how to display or process the results of the mail merge.

Quick Concepts Check

1. Explain the benefit of using the Mail Merge feature to generate letters in Word.
2. Describe how a merge field is used in a main document.
3. List three types of data sources that can be used in a mail merge.
4. What forms of output can you create as a product of your mail merge?

3 Mail Merge

Wacey Rivale always sends a letter of gratitude to the people who have donated to the CDRC. You will use an existing letter as the main document and use the table you recently created as a recipient list in a mail merge process, which makes sending letters quick and easy. Wacey later finds more donor information, created in Excel and Access, which you also use to generate letters. Lastly, you create mailing labels for the letters.

Skills covered: Start the Mail Merge Process and Select a Recipient List • Complete the Main Document • Complete the Mail Merge and View Results • Use an Excel Spreadsheet Recipient List • Use an Access Database Recipient List • Use Mail Merge Wizard to Create Mailing Labels

STEP 1 START THE MAIL MERGE PROCESS AND SELECT A RECIPIENT LIST

You open the letter of gratitude to use as a source document in the mail merge process. Then you must select recipient information, which includes address and amount received from each donor. The document that contains the table of donor information you created recently will work perfectly in this process. Refer to Figure 4.29 as you complete Step 1.

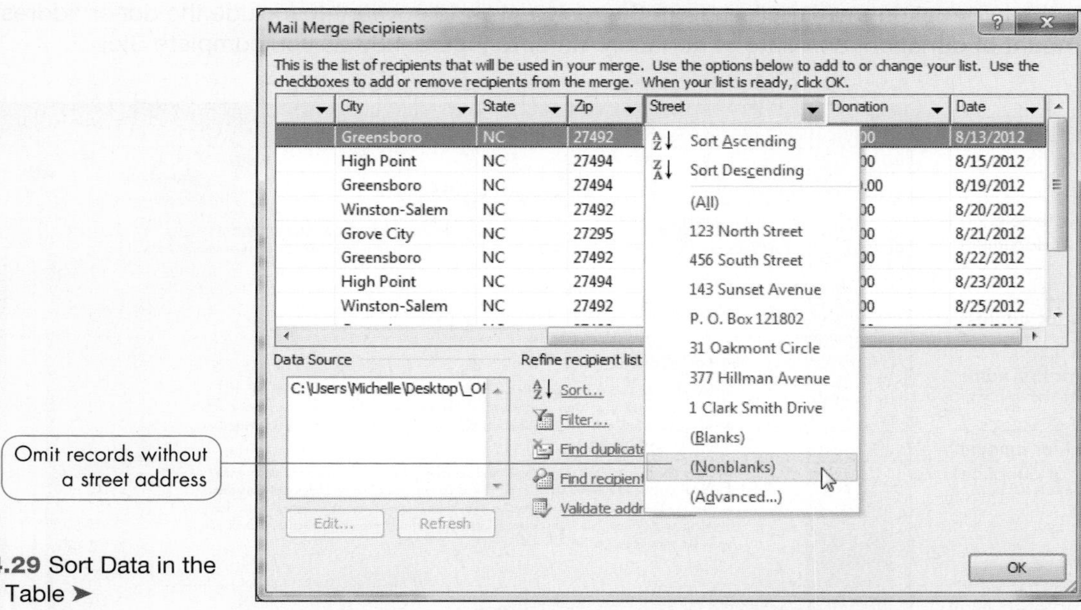

FIGURE 4.29 Sort Data in the Donor List Table ➤

a. Open *w04h3thanks*, and then save it as **w04h3thanks_LastnameFirstname**.

   The document contains a letter that you will mail to the people who have donated to the CDRC.

b. Click the **Mailings tab**, click **Start Mail Merge** in the Start Mail Merge group, and then click **Letters**.

   You are telling Word that this document onscreen is the main document you are using for the mail merge operation.

c. Click **Select Recipients** in the Start Mail Merge group, and then click **Use Existing List**. Navigate to the location where you store your documents, and then select *w04h2donortable_LastnameFirstname.*

   This is the last document you created in Hands-On Exercise 2, which contains the donor information in a table with no title row.

d. Click **Edit Recipient List** in the Start Mail Merge group.

The Mail Merge Recipients dialog box opens and displays information about donors. It also provides features you use later, such as sort and filter.

e. Filter and sort the data used in the mail merge by completing the following steps:

- Scroll to the right to view more columns.
- Click the **Street arrow**, and then click **(Nonblanks)**, as shown in Figure 4.29.
- Click **Sort**.
- Click the **Sort by arrow**, and then select **LastName**. Click **OK** to close the Query Options dialog box.
- Click **OK** to close the Mail Merge Recipients dialog box.

When the process is complete, letters will only be generated to people for whom Wacey has an address. When printed, the letters will be sorted by the donor's last name. This simplifies the process of matching letters with tax receipts before mailing.

f. Save the document.

STEP 2 COMPLETE THE MAIN DOCUMENT

Now you need to update the source of your mail merge, the letter of gratitude, to include placeholders for the information that it pulls in from the recipient list. You want to include the donor address, name, amount of donation, and date of donation. Refer to Figure 4.30 as you complete Step 2.

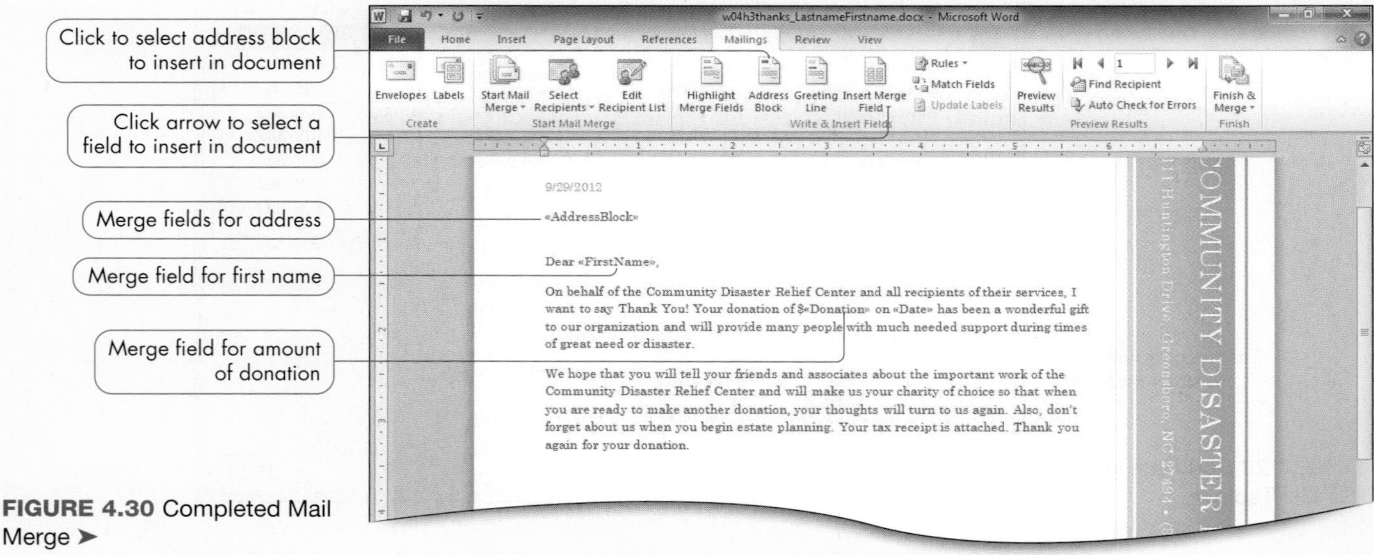

FIGURE 4.30 Completed Mail Merge ➤

a. Click **Pick the Date**, click the arrow, and then click **Today**.

b. Insert the address by completing the following steps:

- Place the insertion point on the left side of the text *Insert Name and.*
- Click **Address Block** in the Write & Insert Fields group. Look at the address in the Preview panel.

Notice the first and last name display on the first line and the city, state, and ZIP display on the second line. The street address does not display, which is not correct. This is a problem with matching the names of the fields in the main letter and the source document which holds the recipient information.

- Click **Match Fields** in the bottom-right corner of the Insert Address Block dialog box.
- Locate *Address 1* in the column that displays fields in the Required for Address Block column.
- Click the **Address 1 arrow**, and then click **Street**.
- Click **OK** to close the Match Fields dialog box.

  In the Preview window, the address displays for the first recipient, *Michael Aucamp*.
- Click **Next** (an arrow pointing right) in the *Preview* section of the Insert Address Block dialog box.

  The entry for *Ethan Crawford* displays in the *Preview* section of the dialog box.
- Click **OK** to close the Address Block dialog box.

  The AddressBlock field displays in the document.

c. Select and delete the three lines that display *Insert Name and, Street and, City, ST, ZIP fields Here.*

d. Insert a salutation by completing the following steps:

- Click one time to position the cursor on the left side of *Insert Greeting Line here.* Type **Dear** and press the **spacebar**.
- Click the **Insert Merge Field arrow** in the Write & Insert group.
- Click **FirstName**. Press **,** to display a comma after the name.
- Delete the text *Insert Greeting Line here* from that line.

  The merge fields show the recipient's first name in the salutation line.

e. Insert the donation date and amount in the letter for each person by completing the following steps:

- Select the text *<Insert Donation Field Here>* in the second line of the first paragraph.

TROUBLESHOOTING: If you find it difficult to drag to select the exact text and symbols to remove from this paragraph, position the insertion point at the left edge of the text, hold down Shift, and then press and hold → until all text is selected.

- Click **Insert Merge Field**.
- Click **Donation**, click **Insert**, and then click **Close**.
- Press **Spacebar**, type **on**, and then press **Spacebar**.
- Click the **Insert Merge Field arrow**.
- Click **Date.**

  The placeholder for donation and date displays in the paragraph, as shown in Figure 4.30. You now know two different ways to insert the individual fields into the main document.

f. Save the document.

STEP 3 COMPLETE THE MAIL MERGE AND VIEW RESULTS

You preview the final product before completing the mail merge, just to be sure you inserted the information correctly and included spaces where needed so words do not run together. Then you complete the merge and display the letters in a new document in which you can make individual edits if needed. Refer to Figure 4.31 as you complete Step 3.

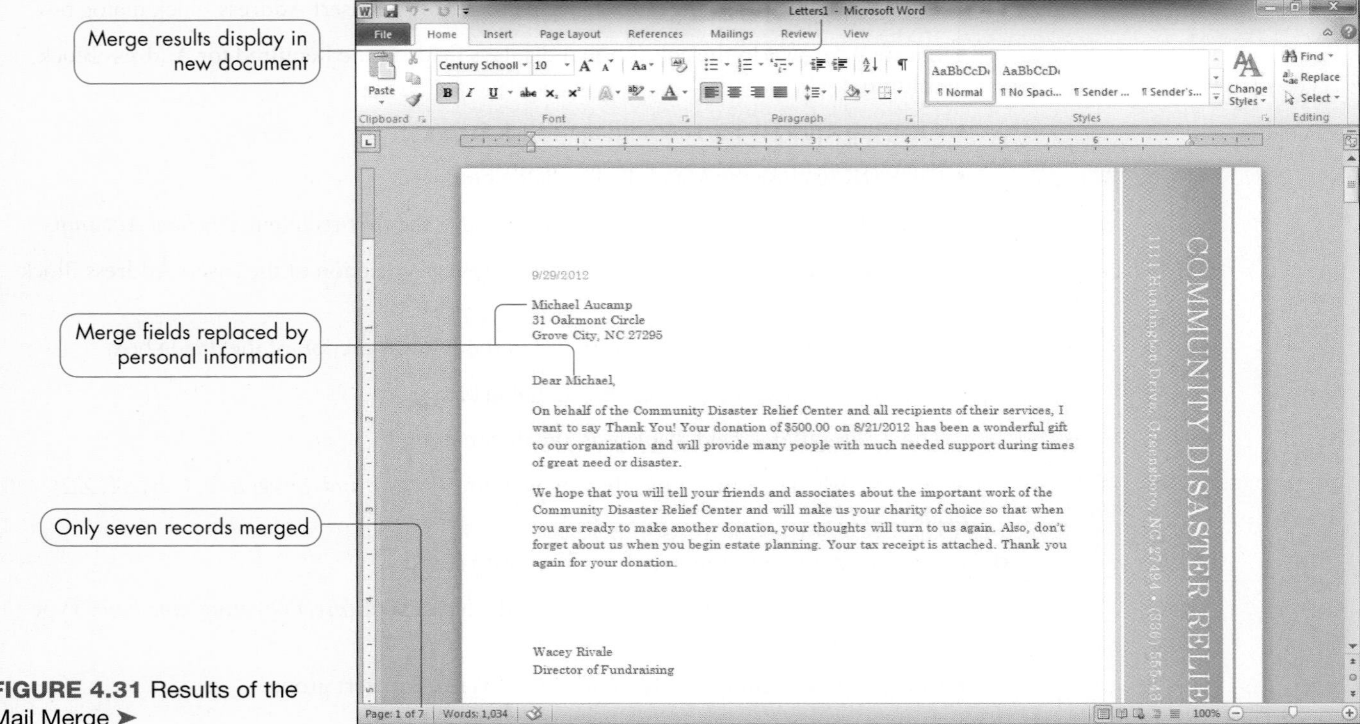

FIGURE 4.31 Results of the Mail Merge ➤

a. Click **Preview Results** in the Preview Results group. Click **Last Record** to preview the letter addressed to *John Whittenberger*.

   You can navigate from record to record or specify a record to preview using the First Record, Previous Record, Go To Record, Next Record, and Last Record navigational commands in the Preview Results group on the Mailings tab.

b. Click **Preview Results** to return to the letter and view the mail merge fields.

   The Preview Results command is a toggle that alternates between the original source document and a preview of the final documents.

c. Click **Finish & Merge** in the Finish group, and then click **Edit Individual Documents**. Click **OK** to merge all records with the letter.

   The letter merges with the recipients and displays in a completely new document, as shown in Figure 4.31. Scroll through the new document and view the seven pages, one for each letter.

d. Press **Ctrl+S** to display the Save As dialog box, and then save the merged letters as **w04h3letters_LastnameFirstname**.

e. Save and close all documents.

STEP 4 ➤ USE AN EXCEL SPREADSHEET RECIPIENT LIST

Wacey has found another list of donor information which was stored in an Excel spreadsheet. You tell her you can print another set of letters with this information because the letter you use in the mail merge can be modified to use information from a different source or recipient list, such as a spreadsheet, just as easily as a Word table. Refer to Figure 4.32 as you complete Step 4.

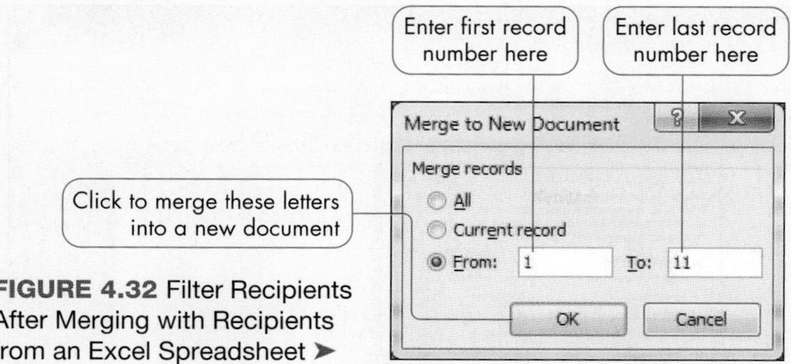
Enter first record number here
Enter last record number here
Merge to New Document
Merge records
All
Current record
From: 1
To: 11
OK
Cancel
Click to merge these letters into a new document

FIGURE 4.32 Filter Recipients After Merging with Recipients from an Excel Spreadsheet ➤

a. Open *w04h3thanks_LastnameFirstname*, and then click **Yes** if a screen displays the message *Opening this document will run the following SQL command.*

b. Click the **Mailings tab**, click **Select Recipients**, and then click **Use Existing List**.

   The Select Data Source dialog box displays.

c. Navigate to the location of your data files, select *w04h3donorsheet.xlsx*, and then click **Open**. When the Select Table dialog box displays, click **OK**.

d. Click **Preview Results** to view the first merged letter. Click **Last Record** to view the last letter.

   The last letter is number 20. Notice that there is no street address for that record. You do not want to print letters to people for whom addresses are unknown. You can do a manual filter when you complete the final merge step.

e. Click **Previous Record** again until you determine which letter has the last complete address.

   You find that the 11th letter has a complete address displaying.

f. Click **Finish & Merge**, and then click **Edit Individual Documents**. Click **From**, type **1** in the first box, and then type **11** in the second box, as shown in Figure 4.32. Click **OK**.

   You create a new document that contains letters for only the first 11 individuals in the recipient list.

g. Save the new file as **w04h3exletters_LastnameFirstname** and close the document. Leave *w04h3thanks_LastnameFirstname* open for the next step.

STEP 5 USE AN ACCESS DATABASE RECIPIENT LIST

Just as you finish the second mail merge, Wacey runs in to tell you she found another file that contains donor information. However, this list is in an Access database. You assure her that Word accepts Access tables and queries as source data too, so with one more round of mail merge, more letters will be ready today. Refer to Figure 4.33 as you complete Step 5.

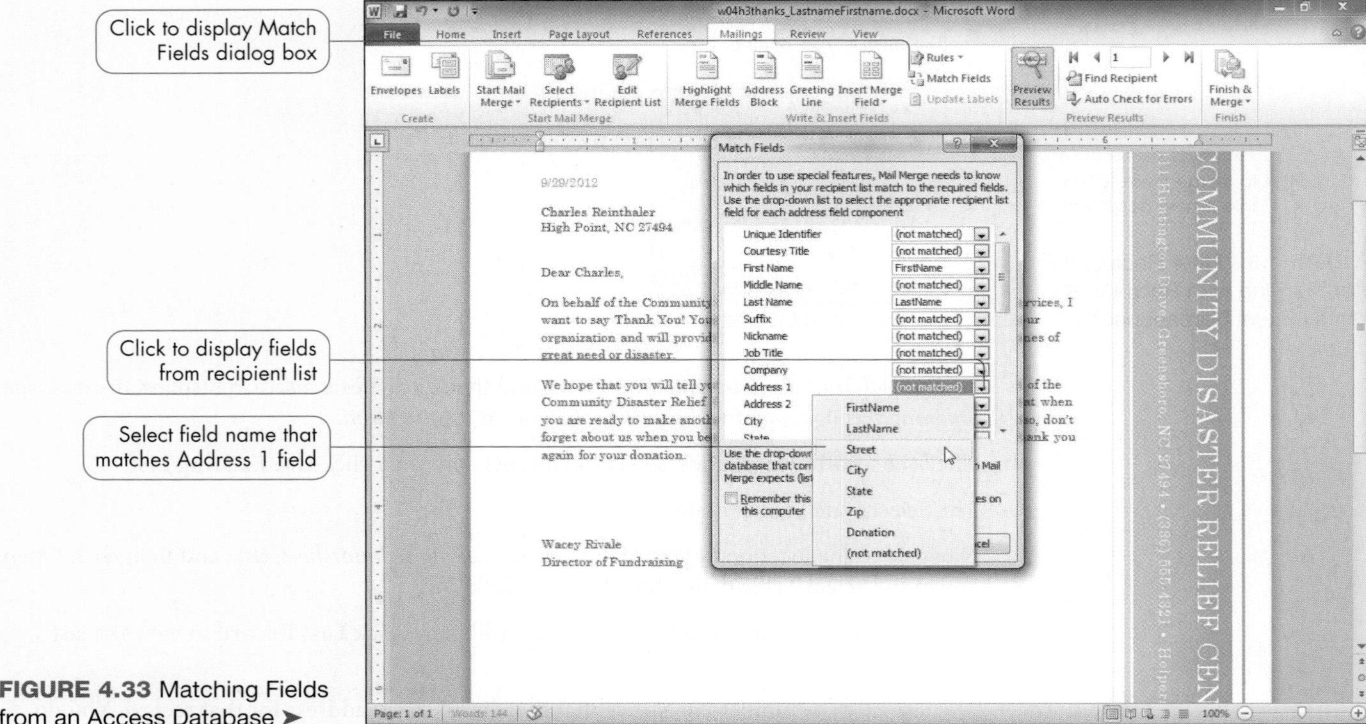

FIGURE 4.33 Matching Fields from an Access Database ➤

a. Click **Select Recipients** in the Start Mail Merge group, and then click **Use Existing List**.

b. Navigate to the location of your data files, select *w04h3donordb.accdb*, and then click **Open**. When the Select Table dialog box displays, click **OK** to select the data in a query named *500 club*.

   The Access database file contains a table of data, but it also includes a query created to extract specific information from the table. In this case, the query displays only patrons who donated more than $500.

> **TROUBLESHOOTING:** If you click the Donors table in the Select Table dialog box by mistake, you can repeat steps a and b to select the 500 Club query. You can use the Donors table for the merge, but you will have more fields to select from than you have in the 500 Club query.

c. Click **Remove Field** in the Invalid Merge Field dialog box.

   An Invalid Merge Field dialog box displays because your letter includes a merge field for date (of donation) and the data in the query does not have a match for the field. Since that information is not available, you will remove the merge field in the source document (the letter).

d. Click **Preview Results**, if necessary, to view the first merged letter.

   Notice you are viewing the letter to Charles Reinthaler but the address block does not include a street address. Next, you check for unmatched fields between the query and the letter.

e. Click **Match Fields** in the Write & Insert Fields group. Click the **Address 1 arrow**, select **Street** (shown in Figure 4.33), and then click **OK**.

f. Click **Next Record**, and then click **Previous Record** in the Preview Results group.

   Now the complete address for Charles Reinthaler displays.

g. Delete the word *on* and the space that follows it from the second sentence in the first paragraph.

   Since you are no longer displaying the date of the donation, the sentence must be corrected.

h. Ensure the letter is only mailed to people for whom we have a complete mailing address by completing the following steps:

- Click **Edit Recipient List** in the Start Mail Merge group.
- Click **Filter** to display the Filter and Sort dialog box.
- Click the **Filter Records tab**, if necessary.
- Click the **Field arrow**, and then select **Street**.
- Click the **Comparison arrow**, and then select **Not equal to**.
- Click **OK** to close the dialog box. Click **OK** to close the Mail Merge Recipients dialog box.

You have set a filter so any record containing blanks in the address field will not be used in the mail merge. Only two records meet all criteria.

i. Click **Finish & Merge** in the Finish group, click **Edit Individual Documents**, click **All**, and then click **OK**.

In a new document, two letters display.

j. Save the new document as **w04h3acletter_LastnameFirstname**, and then close it. Close *w04h3thanks_LastnameFirstname* without saving, but do not exit Word.

TIP Saving Merged Letters

Typically, you only save the original documents and recipient lists used in a mail merge. The document that contains the individual letters as a result of the mail merge is usually printed and mailed. You save the merged documents in this exercise so you can submit them to your instructor, if necessary.

STEP 6 USE MAIL MERGE WIZARD TO CREATE MAILING LABELS

Wacey is hoping you can help with one last request—she needs to send out the first set of letters today. If you can create mailing labels to put on the envelopes, it will prevent another assistant from having to address envelopes manually. You agree to do it because creating labels is as easy as generating a letter. Refer to Figure 4.34 as you complete Step 6.

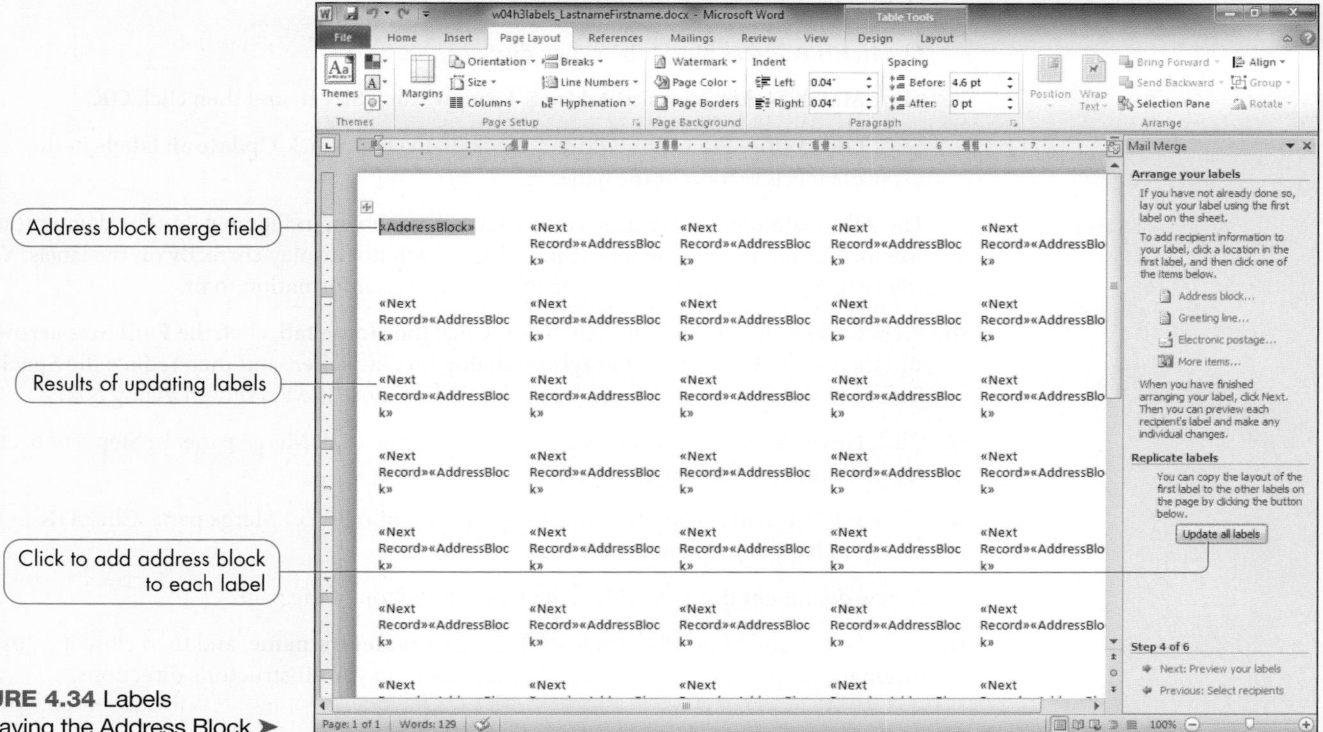

FIGURE 4.34 Labels Displaying the Address Block ➤

a. Press **Ctrl+N** to display a new document. Save the document as **w04h3labels_LastnameFirstname**.

b. Click the **Mailings tab**, click **Start Mail Merge**, and then click **Step by Step Mail Merge Wizard**.

   The Mail Merge pane displays.

c. Click **Labels** in the *Select document type* section of the Mail Merge pane, and then click **Next: Starting document** at the bottom of the pane.

d. Click **Label options** in the *Change document layout* section of the pane.

   The Label Options dialog box displays.

e. Click the **Label vendors arrow**, and then click **Avery A4/A5**. Click **C2651** from the Product number list. Click **OK**. Click **Next: Select recipients** at the bottom of the pane.

> **TROUBLESHOOTING:** If you do not have the Avery A4/A5 label, consult with your instructor for an alternative product.

   Most packages of labels will display a product number on the package that will also display in this list. This product number helps Word to set up a template that matches the layout of the labels, which then ensures the labels print correctly.

f. Click **Browse** in the *Use an existing list* section of the pane, and then navigate to the location where you saved the recipient list, *w04h2donortable_LastnameFirstname*. Select the file, and then click **Open**.

   The Mail Merge Recipients dialog box displays.

g. Click the **Last Name arrow**. Click **Sort Ascending**.

h. Click the **Street arrow**, and then click **(Nonblanks)**.

i. Click **OK** to select the remaining recipients, and then close the dialog box.

   The document displays the Next Record code throughout the document to indicate the labels are ready.

j. Click **Next: Arrange your labels** in the bottom of the Mail Merge pane. Click **Address block** in the *Arrange your labels* section of the pane.

   The Insert Address Block dialog box displays.

k. Click **Match Fields**, click the **Address 1 arrow**, click **Street**, and then click **OK**.

l. Click **OK** to close the Insert Address Block dialog box. Click **Update all labels** in the *Replicate labels* section of the pane.

   The Address Block field displays on each label, as shown in Figure 4.34. The default font size for the document is so large the addresses will not display correctly on the labels. You will reduce the size of the font to enable the address information to fit.

m. Press **Ctrl+A** to select all the label fields. Click the **Home tab**, click the **Font Size arrow**, and then select **9**. Click the **Paragraph dialog box launcher**, and then reduce the **Spacing Before** in the *Spacing* section to **0 pt**. Click **OK** to close the Paragraph dialog box.

n. Click **Next: Preview your labels** in Step 4 of 6 of the Mail Merge pane. In Step 5 of 6, click **Next: Complete the merge**.

o. Click **Edit individual labels** in the *Merge* section of the Mail Merge pane. Click **OK** in the Merge to New Document dialog box.

   A new document displays with seven labels at the top of the page.

p. Save the document as **w04h3mergelabels_LastnameFirstname**, and then close it. Close the original document without saving. Submit based on your instructor's directions.

CHAPTER OBJECTIVES REVIEW

After reading this chapter, you have accomplished the following objectives:

1. **Insert a table.** Tables represent a very powerful capability within Word and are used to organize a variety of data in documents. Tables are made up of rows and columns; the intersection of a row and column is called a *cell*. You can insert additional rows and columns if you need to add more data to a table, or you can delete a row or column if you no longer need data in the respective row or column. Individual cells can be merged to create a larger cell. Conversely, you can split a single cell into multiple cells. The rows in a table can be different heights and/or each column can be a different width.
2. **Format a table.** Each cell in a table is formatted independently and may contain text, numbers, and/or graphics. To enhance readability of table data, you can apply a predefined style, which Word provides, or use Borders and Shading tools to add color and enhance it. Furthermore, you can align table data—at the left margin, at the right margin, or centered between the margins. You also can change the text direction within a cell.
3. **Sort and apply formulas to table data.** You can sort the rows in a table to display the data in ascending or descending sequence, according to the values in one or more columns in the table. Sorting is accomplished by selecting the rows within the table that are to be sorted, and then executing the Sort command on the Layout tab. Calculations can be performed within a table using the Formula command in the same tab.
4. **Convert text to a table.** If you have a list of tabulated items that would be easier to manipulate in a table, you can use the Convert Text to Table command. The command also works in reverse, enabling you to remove data from a table and format it as tabulated text.
5. **Select a main document.** The mail merge process uses two files as input, a main document and a data source; by merging these two files, you can create a set of individualized letters, envelopes, e-mails, or other documents. The main document, also known as a *source* or *starting document*, contains the information that stays the same for all recipients. A wizard makes a process easier by asking a series of questions, and then creating a template based on your answers. If you want to create individual envelopes or a sheet of mailing labels, which are not part of a mail merge process, the Create group on the Mailings tab includes commands that you use to select the correct settings.
6. **Select or create recipients.** A recipient list, sometimes called a *data source*, contains individual pieces of data known as *fields*. Common fields in a data source include first name, last name, street, city, state, ZIP code, phone number, and e-mail address. You can sort or filter the recipient list to specify criteria for including records that meet certain conditions during the merge process. The Sort Records tab enables you to specify up to three levels for sorting records. You can also use Excel spreadsheets or Access databases or queries as source data for a mail merge.
7. **Insert merge fields.** When you write your letter or set up your e-mail in preparation for a mail merge, you insert a merge field in the main document. The merge field is a placeholder that specifies where information from the data source will display in the main document. The merge fields display in the main document within angle brackets. Because it corresponds with a field in the data source, matching the two fields guarantees that the right data will be inserted into the main document when you complete the merge.
8. **Merge a main document and a data source.** The merge process examines each record in the data source, and when a match is found, it replaces the merge field in the main document with the information from the data source. A copy of the main document is created for each record in the data source, thus creating individual form letters.

KEY TERMS

Ascending order ***p.284***
Border ***p.274***
Cell ***p.272***
Cell margin ***p.276***
Column width ***p.273***
Data source ***p.293***
Database table ***p.295***
Descending order ***p.284***
Field ***p.293***
Filter ***p.297***
Form letter ***p.291***
Header row ***p.293***
Mail merge ***p.291***
Main document ***p.292***
Merge field ***p.292***
Record ***p.293***
Row height ***p.273***
Shading ***p.274***
Sorting ***p.283***
Syntax ***p.283***
Table ***p.272***
Table alignment ***p.276***
Table Move handle ***p.273***
Table style ***p.275***
Text direction ***p.276***
Wizard ***p.292***

MULTIPLE CHOICE

1. You have created a table containing numerical values and have entered the SUM(ABOVE) function at the bottom of a column. You then delete one of the rows included in the sum. Which of the following is true?
   (a) The row cannot be deleted because it contains a cell that is included in the sum function.
   (b) The sum is updated automatically.
   (c) The sum cannot be updated.
   (d) The sum will be updated after you right-click the cell and click the Update Field command.

2. What happens when you press Tab from within the last cell of a table?
   (a) A Tab character is inserted just as it would be for ordinary text.
   (b) Word inserts a new row below the current row.
   (c) Word inserts a new column to the right of the current column.
   (d) The insertion point appears in the paragraph below the table.

3. What happens when you type more than one line of text into a cell?
   (a) The cell gets wider to accommodate the extra text.
   (b) The row gets taller as word wrapping occurs to display the additional text.
   (c) The first line is hidden by default.
   (d) A new column is inserted automatically.

4. Assume you created a table with the names of the months in the first column. Each row lists data for that particular month. The insertion point is in the first cell on the third row, which lists goals for April. You realize that you left out the goals for March. What should you do?
   (a) Display the Insert tab, and then click the Table command.
   (b) Display the Table Tools Design tab, and then click the Insert Cell command.
   (c) Display the Table Tools Layout tab, and then click the Insert Left command.
   (d) Display the Table Tools Layout tab, and then click the Insert Above command.

5. You have a Word document that contains a list of people who were sent an invitation to a wedding. You are responsible for monitoring their responses to the invitation, whether they will attend or not, and to determine the grand total of those attending. Using skills learned in the chapter, what would be a good way to track this information?
   (a) Copy the names into an Excel spreadsheet, and then use mail merge to populate a table in Word.
   (b) Convert the list of names to a table; add columns that enable you to mark their response, including the number who will attend, and use a formula to add up the numbers when all responses are received.
   (c) Type the list of names into a Word table; add columns to mark a response, and a formula to add up responses.
   (d) Insert a two-column table beside the names and mark the responses as declined or attending.

6. When you generate a new data source during the mail merge process, what type of file do you create when it saves?
   (a) Document (.docx)
   (b) Worksheet (.xlsx)
   (c) Database (.mdb))
   (d) Rich text (.rtf)

7. During a mail merge process, what operation can you perform on a data source so only data that meet specific criteria, such as a particular city, are included in the merge?
   (a) Sort
   (b) Propagate
   (c) Delete
   (d) Filter

8. When you click Edit Individual Documents on the Mail Merge pane, and then click OK, the merged document ______.
   (a) appears in a new document window
   (b) is automatically printed
   (c) is saved to a new document file
   (d) overwrites the main document

9. When you use mail merge to create address labels, what option do you click to copy the address field from the first label to the rest of the labels before performing the merge?
   (a) Copy and paste
   (b) Update all labels
   (c) Edit recipient list
   (d) Sort and filter

10. Which of the following is not a good use for mail merge?
    (a) To print mailing labels for Christmas cards from a list of addresses in an Excel spreadsheet
    (b) To send the same personalized letter to all your business clients
    (c) To create return address labels that display your home address
    (d) To e-mail a meeting announcement to every member of your professional organization

PRACTICE EXERCISES

1 Letter and Check Payment to Suppliers

You are the manager of a local steak and seafood restaurant. At the end of each month, you balance the books and process the accounts payable. You then write a letter to all your suppliers, thank them for the prompt delivery services, and enclose a check for the monthly balance. Since you already have the suppliers' information stored in a spreadsheet, you decide to create a mail merge document that you can use to quickly create letters to send to each supplier. There is no need to send payments to suppliers with a zero balance, so you use a filter to remove their names from the merge process. This exercise follows the same set of skills as used in Hands-On Exercise 3 in the chapter. Refer to Figure 4.35 as you complete this exercise.

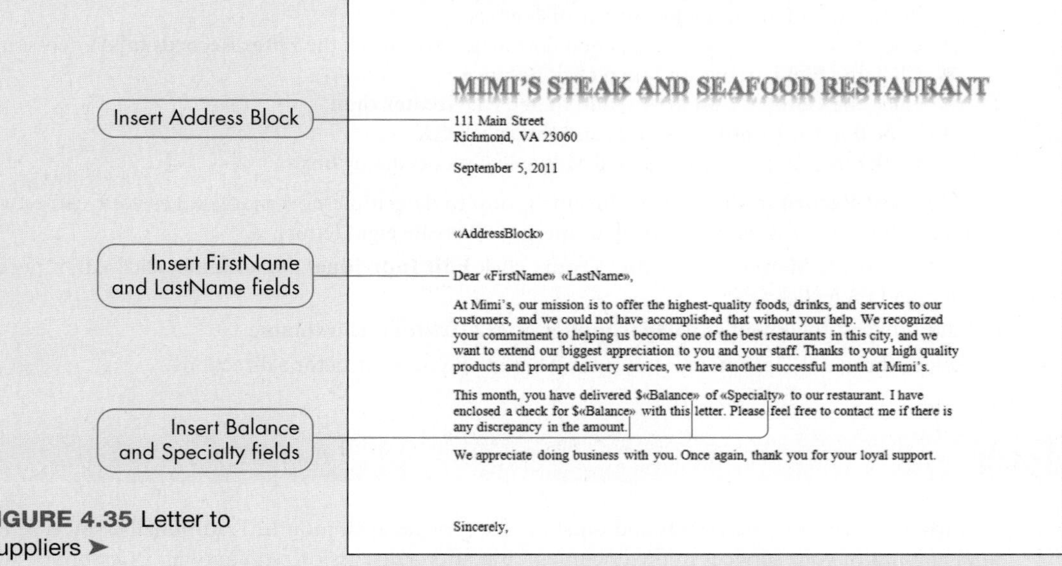

MIMI'S STEAK AND SEAFOOD RESTAURANT

111 Main Street
Richmond, VA 23060

September 5, 2011

«AddressBlock»

Dear «FirstName» «LastName»,

At Mimi's, our mission is to offer the highest-quality foods, drinks, and services to our customers, and we could not have accomplished that without your help. We recognized your commitment to helping us become one of the best restaurants in this city, and we want to extend our biggest appreciation to you and your staff. Thanks to your high quality products and prompt delivery services, we have another successful month at Mimi's.

This month, you have delivered $«Balance» of «Specialty» to our restaurant. I have enclosed a check for $«Balance» with this letter. Please feel free to contact me if there is any discrepancy in the amount.

We appreciate doing business with you. Once again, thank you for your loyal support.

Sincerely,

FIGURE 4.35 Letter to Suppliers ➤

a. Open *w04p1letter* and save it as **w04p1letter_LastnameFirstname**.

b. Click the **Mailings tab**, click **Start Mail Merge** in the Start Mail Merge group, and then click **Letters**.

c. Select a recipient by completing the following steps:
   - Click **Select Recipients**, and then click **Use Existing List**.
   - Navigate to the location where data files are stored, click **w04p1suppliers.xlsx**, and then click **Open**.
   - Make sure *Sheet1$* is selected, and then click **OK** when the Select Table dialog box displays.

d. Insert merge fields by completing the following steps:
   - Move the insertion point two lines below the date. Click **Address Block** in the Write & Insert Fields group, and then click **OK** to insert the default format of the supplier's address at the top of the letter.
   - Move the insertion point to the left side of the comma in the salutation line *Dear*, if necessary, and then click **Insert Merge Field** in the Write & Insert Fields group. Click **FirstName**, click **Insert**, and then click **Close**. Move the insertion point to the right of *FirstName*, press **Spacebar**, click **Insert Merge Field**, make sure *LastName* is selected and click **LastName**, click **Insert**, and then click **Close**.
   - Place the insertion point on the right side of the dollar sign in the first sentence of the second body paragraph. Click the **Insert Merge Field arrow**, and then click **Balance**. Repeat the insertion of *Balance* after the dollar sign in the second sentence of the same paragraph.
   - Place the insertion point on the right side of the word *of* in the first sentence of the second paragraph. Press **Spacebar**, click the **Insert Merge Field arrow**, and then click **Specialty**. Compare your letter to Figure 4.35.

TROUBLESHOOTING: If you find it difficult to determine where to place the cursor, click the Show/Hide (¶) button on the Home tab to display formatting marks such as spaces.

e. Click **Preview Results** in the Preview Results group. To correct the extra lines around the address block, complete these steps:
   - Select the four lines that make up the address block.
   - Click the **Page Layout tab**.
   - Click the **Spacing After arrow** in the Paragraph group until **0 pt** displays.

f. Finish the merge by completing these steps:
   - Click the **Mailings tab**, click **Finish & Merge** in the Finish group, and then click **Edit Individual Documents**.
   - Click **All**, if necessary, and then click **OK**. There should be 10 records (pages).
   - Save the new document as **w04p1supplierletter1_LastnameFirstname**. Close the file.

g. Save *w04p1letter_LastnameFirstname* as **w04p1letter2_LastnameFirstname**.

h. Filter the recipient list in preparation for creating letters to only suppliers with a positive balance by completing the following steps:
   - Click the **Mailings tab**, and then click **Edit Recipient List** in the Start Mail Merge group to display the Mail Merge Recipients dialog box.
   - Click **Filter** to display the Filter and Sort dialog box. Click the **Filter Records tab**, if necessary.
   - Click the **Field arrow**, and then click **Balance**.
   - Click the **Comparison arrow**, and then click **Greater than**.
   - Type **0** in the **Compare to box**, and then click **OK**.
   - Click **OK** again to close the Mail Merge Recipients dialog box.

i. Click **Last Record** in the Preview Results group to determine how many pages your merge will create. If the filter is set correctly, your merge will create eight letters.

j. Click **Finish & Merge** in the Finish group, click **Edit Individual Documents**, click **All**, if necessary, and then click **OK**.

k. Save the new document as **w04p1supplierletter2_LastnameFirstname**.

l. Save and close all documents, and submit based on your instructor's directions.

2 Marti Appraisal Company

You work as a real estate assessor and must bill for services each month. Traditionally, you type the total amount of your services in the document, but after a discussion with another assessor you discover how to use table formulas and begin to use them to calculate your total fees on the invoice. In this exercise, you develop a professional-looking invoice and use formulas to calculate totals within the table. This exercise follows the same set of skills as used in Hands-On Exercises 1 and 2 in the chapter. Refer to Figure 4.36 as you complete this exercise.

Marti Appraisal Company, LLC

Invoice Number: 300	Invoice Date: 8/20/2012
Bill to: Heartcountry Bank 33252 S. Campbell Ave. Springfield, MO 65807	Submit Payment to: Marti Appraisal Company, LLC 2048 S. Glenn Ave. Springfield, MO 65807

File #	Appraisal Date	Property Address	Appraisal Fee Due
75	8/1/2012	335 Valley Vista Dr., Springfield	800.00
70	8/2/2012	105 Amanda Ln., Nixa	300.00
65	8/4/2012	2402 E. Lee St., Republic	300.00
77	8/4/2012	3324 N. Hickory Hills Ct., Nixa	100.00
		Total	$1,500.00
Thank You for your business!			

FIGURE 4.36 Completed Invoice ➤

a. Open a blank document and save it as **w04p2invoice_LastnameFirstname**.
b. Click the **Insert tab**, and then click **Table**. Drag to select one column and three rows (1 × 3 table).
c. Add information in the first row by completing the following steps:
   - Type **Marti Appraisal Company, LLC**.
   - Right-click to display the Mini toolbar, and then click **Center**.
   - Select the text, click the **Font size arrow** on the Mini toolbar, and then select **28**.
   - Click the **Page Layout tab**, and then click the **Spacing After arrow** until **12 pt** displays.
   - Press → to move the insertion point to the right side of the text.
   - Click the **Insert tab**. Click **Clip Art**.
   - Search for **House** and insert a graphic in the first row next to the Company name. Close the Clip Art pane.
   - Click the **Format tab**, if necessary, click **Position** in the Arrange group, and then click **Position in Middle Right with Square Text Wrapping**.
   - Reduce the height of the Clip Art so it is no more than 1" high; the width can adjust proportionally to the height.
d. Select the second and third rows. Click the **Layout tab**, click **Split Cells** in the Merge group, and then click **OK** to accept the new size of 2 columns by 2 rows.
e. Fill in the last two rows of the table with the following information:

Invoice Number: 300	**Invoice Date: 8/20/2012**
Bill to: Heartcountry Bank 33252 S. Campbell Ave. Springfield, MO 65807	Submit Payment to: Marti Appraisal Company, LLC 2048 S. Glenn Ave. Springfield, MO 65807

f. Select the text you just typed and use the Mini toolbar to increase the font size to **14**. Press **Ctrl+L** to left justify, if necessary.
g. Select the second row of the table, click the **Page Layout tab**, and increase both **Spacing before** and **Spacing after** to **6 pt**.
h. Format the table borders by completing the following steps:
   - Click the **Table Move handle** to select the whole table.
   - Click the **Design tab,** click the **Borders arrow** in the Table Styles group, and then click **Borders and Shading**.
   - Click the **Borders tab** in the Borders and Shading dialog box, if necessary.
   - Click **Box** in the Setting area on the left side. Click **OK**.
   - Select the second row of the table.
   - Click the **Borders arrow** in the Table Styles group, and then click **Bottom Border**.
   - Select the first row of the table.
   - Click the **Borders arrow**, click **Borders and Shading**, and then click the **Shading tab**.
   - Click the **Fill arrow**, select **Red, Accent 2, Darker 25%**, and then click **OK**.
i. Add a second table for invoice details by completing the following steps:
   - Press **Ctrl+End** to move your cursor to the end of the document.
   - Press **Enter** two times.
   - Click the **Insert tab**.
   - Click **Table**.
   - Drag to select a four column by five row table (4 × 5).
j. Type the following column headings in the first row:

File #	**Appraisal Date**	**Property Address**	**Appraisal Fee Due**

k. Modify the size of the columns in this table by completing the following steps:
   - Click the **Table Move handle** to select the whole table.
   - Click the **Layout tab**, if necessary.
   - Click the **Width arrow** until **1"** displays.
   - Place the insertion point in the third column.
   - Click the **Width arrow** until **2.5"** displays.

l. Type the following appraisal information in rows 2 through 4.

65	8/4/2012	2402 E. Lee St., Republic	300.00
70	8/2/2012	105 Amanda Ln., Nixa	300.00
75	8/1/2012	335 Valley Vista Dr., Springfield	800.00

m. Add the total amount due in row five by completing the following steps:
- Drag to select the first three cells in row five. Click **Merge Cells** in the Merge group on the Layout tab.
- Type **Total** in this new larger cell, and then press **Ctrl+R**.
- Place the insertion point in the last column of this row (**cell D5**), and then click **Formula** in the Data group.
- Make sure *=SUM(ABOVE)* displays in the Formula box. Click the **Number format arrow**, select **$#,##0.00;($#,##0.00)**, and then click **OK**.

n. Press **Tab** to add one more row to the table. In that row, complete the following steps:
- Drag your mouse across each cell in the last row to select the whole row.
- Click **Merge Cells** in the Merge group.
- Type **Thank you for your business!**
- Press **Ctrl +E** to center the sentence in the row.

o. Place the insertion point in the first cell of the fourth row, and then click **Insert Below** in the Rows & Columns group. In the new blank row, type the following:

77	8/4/2012	3324 N. Hickory Hills Ct., Nixa	100.00

p. Sort the information in the table by date by completing the following steps:
- Select rows one through five.
- Click **Sort** in the Data group.
- Click **Header row** under *My list has.*
- Click the **Sort by arrow**, and then select **Appraisal Date**.
- Click **OK**.

q. Click in **cell D6**, which holds the formula. Right-click, and then select **Update Field**.

r. Format the table for readability by completing the following steps:
- Click the **Design tab**.
- Click anywhere in the second table, and then click the **More button** in the Table Styles group.
- Select **Medium Shading 1 - Accent 2** (third column, fourth row) from the gallery.
- Select **cells D1 through D6** (the first six rows of the last column), and then press **Ctrl+R** to right align.
- Click the **Layout tab**, click **AutoFit**, and then click **AutoFit Window** to expand the size of the table to the right margin.
- Select the total amount due in **cell D6**, and then click **Bold** on the Mini toolbar.
- Click the **Table Move handle** to select the whole table, and then increase the font size to **12 pt** using the Mini toolbar.
- Select the *Thank you* sentence in the last row, and then select **Bold** from the Mini toolbar, if necessary. Compare your results to Figure 4.36.

s. Save and close the document, and then submit based on your instructor's directions.

MID-LEVEL EXERCISES

1 Regional Science Fair

The Regional Science Fair will occur on the campus of Missouri State University in the spring, and students from schools across the southwest portion of the state compete in areas such as physics, chemistry, environment, meteorology, and astronomy. As the volunteer coordinator, you must maintain a list of people who will donate their time to the event. You decide to send a reminder to each volunteer so they will be sure to arrive at their designated time.

a. Open *w04m1reminder* and save it as **w04m1reminder_LastnameFirstname**.
b. Use the reminder as the main document in a mail merge.
c. Use *w04m1times.xlsx* as your data source. Insert fields for first and last name, time in (start time), and time out (end time) in the appropriate locations in the reminder document. Center the start and end time fields in the table.
d. Preview the merge results, and then edit the recipient list. Sort the source data so that it sorts the Time In field in ascending order.
e. Filter the source data so that any record containing a Time Out of *9:00:00 PM* will not be included in the merge.
f. Merge the documents, and then display the results in a new file. Save the merged reminders as **w04m1mergedreminder_LastnameFirstname**.
g. Save and close all documents, and then submit based on your instructor's directions.

2 Building Materials

You are the executive assistant to a general contractor, and your duties include listing the materials that will be used on a home remodeling project. Due to the large number of people who work on the project, from plumbers to electricians to carpenters, it is necessary to keep detailed records of the materials and supplies to use during the remodel. After the first job, you decide to provide the crew with a table of materials that includes pictures. This also might be helpful for any crew member who does not speak English. Refer to Figure 4.37 as you complete this exercise.

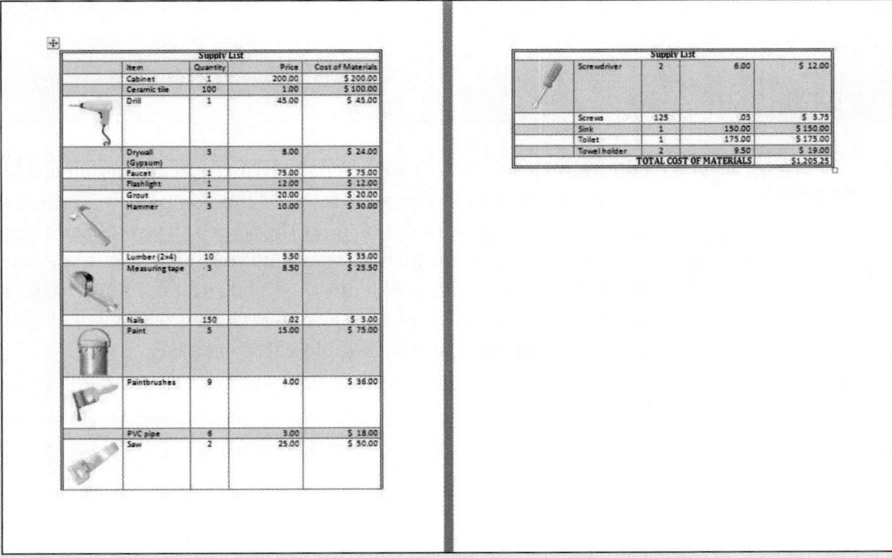

Supply List				
	Item	Quantity	Price	Cost of Materials
	Cabinet	1	200.00	$ 200.00
	Ceramic tile	100	1.00	$ 100.00
	Drill	1	45.00	$ 45.00
	Drywall (Gypsum)	3	8.00	$ 24.00
	Faucet	1	75.00	$ 75.00
	Flashlight	1	12.00	$ 12.00
	Grout	1	20.00	$ 20.00
	Hammer	3	10.00	$ 30.00
	Lumber (2x4)	10	3.50	$ 35.00
	Measuring tape	3	8.50	$ 25.50
	Nails	150	.02	$ 3.00
	Paint	5	15.00	$ 75.00
	Paintbrushes	9	4.00	$ 36.00
	PVC pipe	6	3.00	$ 18.00
	Saw	2	25.00	$ 50.00

Supply List				
	Screwdriver	2	6.00	$ 12.00
	Screws	125	.03	$ 3.75
	Sink	1	150.00	$ 150.00
	Toilet	1	175.00	$ 175.00
	Towel holder	2	9.50	$ 19.00
			TOTAL COST OF MATERIALS	$1,205.25

FIGURE 4.37 Supply List ➤

a. Open *w04m2construction* and save it as **w04m2construction_LastnameFirstname**.
b. Convert this list to a three-column table so you can organize the list of materials and add more data.
c. Insert two rows at the top to use for a heading and item descriptions.
   - Create a title row on the table by merging cells in the first row.
   - Insert the text **Supply List** as the title.
   - Use the second row as a header for the columns.
   - Enter the following labels for each column: **Item**, **Quantity**, **Price**.
d. Align the prices of each item in the third column. The prices should appear to align on the decimal point.
e. Center the data in the second column, which displays the quantity of each item you will use in the project.
f. Sort the data in ascending order by Item.
g. Use the **Split cell option** to split the third column in two. The label for the fourth column is **Total Cost**.
h. Insert a column to the left of the first column. Insert a picture of the supplies in the first column.
   - Use symbols, clip art, or pictures to visually describe the following materials in your table: drill, hammer, paint, paintbrushes, saw, and screwdriver. You might not be able to locate a graphic for each item, but you should be able to find at least five to use in the table.
   - Include Office.com content in your search, if needed.
   - Resize the graphics as necessary so they do not exceed 1" in height or width.
   - Align each graphic in the center of the cell.

DISCOVER 

i. Use a formula to calculate the total cost of each item and display it in the fifth column. To calculate the cost of materials, multiply the cell that contains the quantity by the cell that contains the price. For example, the formula for the cabinet is =C3*D3. You might also explore the Product function to calculate the cost of items. If you use a function, you can copy the formula from cell to cell, but must update each one to reflect the different data they calculate.
j. Add a row at the bottom of the table. Merge the first four columns of this row into one cell, and then type **TOTAL COST OF MATERIALS**. Insert a formula in the last column to calculate the total cost of materials used in this project.
k. Apply the **Light Grid - Accent 1** (sixth column, nineth row) style to the table. Use the Borders (and Shading) feature on the Design tab to add a double-line outside border to the table. (Hint: Use the Custom setting.) Center the table horizontally on the page.

DISCOVER 

l. Use Help if needed to indicate the first row will repeat as a header row at the top of each page if your table spans more than one page. Merge cells in the first row to enlarge the cell containing the title.
m. Save and close the document, and then submit based on your instructor's directions.

3 Looking for a Roommate

CREATIVE CASE 

You found a very nice 2-bedroom apartment in an upscale neighborhood, but you need a responsible roommate to share the rent with you. After asking your friends to spread the word, you also decide to create a flyer to post in the neighborhood grocery stores and shops. Figure 4.38 displays a flyer that is intended to provide information about your apartment and tags with your contact information that interested parties can pull from the flyer and take home. Use a table as the basis of this document. You can use your own picture and description while working this exercise, or use the one provided. Refer to Figure 4.38 as you complete this exercise.

FIGURE 4.38 Looking for a Roommate ➤

a. Open a new document and save it as **w04m3roommate_LastnameFirstname**.

b. Create a table with five columns and four rows (5 × 4 table).

c. Merge all the cells in the first row, and type the text **Looking for a Roommate**. Select the text, and then change the font size to **26 pt**. The row height will increase automatically to accommodate the larger text. Center the text in the cell.

d. Merge the cells in row 2. Use shading to place a black background in the cell. Locate pictures of your apartment; we have provided a picture of a living room, *livingroom.jpg*, in the folder containing files for Exploring Word Chapter 4. When you locate the file, insert the picture in the second table row. The row height will expand automatically to accommodate the picture. Center the picture in the cell. You should use the Size features in Word to reduce the size of the photo if it displays too large for the page.

e. Merge cells in the third row, and then enter text to describe your new apartment. Feel free to duplicate the information provided in Figure 4.38. Change the font size to **14 pt**, and then center the text in the cell.

DISCOVER 

f. Use the Draw Table tool to double the number of columns in the last row from 5 to 10. Use Help if needed to learn about this tool.

g. Type your name and phone number in the first cell of the fourth row. Use the Text Direction feature to rotate the text, as shown in Figure 4.38. Center and align the text at the top of the cell and increase the height of the cell, if necessary, to display the contents on two lines.

h. Use Copy and Paste to populate the remaining cells with your information. Rotate, center, and align the text again, if necessary.

i. Change the formatting of the fourth row to display a dashed line around each of the cells.

j. Save and close the document, and submit based on your instructor's directions.

CAPSTONE EXERCISE

You work as the business manager for the local Sports Medicine Clinic and are responsible for many forms of correspondence. This week, you want to send a letter of welcome to three physical therapists recently hired at the clinic. Additionally, you need to send your weekly reminders to patients who are scheduled for upcoming treatment or consultations. In the past, the letters were generated manually and names were typed in each letter separately. However, because you now use Word 2010, you decide to create and use source data documents and implement a mail merge so you can produce the letters quickly and accurately.

Create a Table Containing Therapist Information

You will create a new document that includes a table of information about the new physical therapists. Then you personalize the welcome letter created for the therapists and use information from the table to create a personal letter for each person.

a. Open a new, blank document and save it as **w04c1therapists_LastnameFirstname.**

b. Create a table with the following information:

Name	Credentials	Street	Days working	Salary
Mike Salat	M.S., ATC	2342 W. Cardinal Street	Monday–Thursday	$60,000
Justin Ebert	M.S., ATC	34234 S. Callie Place	Monday–Friday	$65,000
Karen Rakowski	ATC, PT	98234 E. Shepherd Lane	Monday–Friday	$65,000

c. Separate the name into two columns because it will be easier to use in form letters using mail merge features. Make necessary changes to the table to display the therapists' first and last names in two separate columns. (Hint: Uncheck the option *Merge cells before split* in the Split Cells dialog box.)

d. Create three new columns for the City, State, and ZIP Code information, and then populate each one with **Conway, AR 72032.**

e. Create a new row, and then use a formula to total the Salary column. This amount is referenced in the letter, although you do not use it in the mail merge. Use Currency formatting, which will cause total salary amount to display with two decimal places, unlike the salary entries in the cells above.

f. Sort the data in the table by Last Name.

g. Save the document.

Merge Therapist Information into a Welcome Letter

Now that you have documented information about the new Physical Therapists, you can use it as a source for the welcome letter.

a. Open *w04c1welcome* and save it as **w04c1welcome_LastnameFirstname.**

b. Start a mail merge using the welcome letter as the source document. The recipient information will come from *w04c1therapists_LastnameFirstname.*

c. Replace the starred placeholders in the letter with the fields from the recipient table. Insert today's date in the appropriate place.

d. Preview the results before merging. Filter the recipients so the fourth record does not generate a letter.

e. Complete the mail merge, displaying the results in a new document. Save the merged letters as **w04c1ptwelcome_LastnameFirstname.** Close all files.

Produce a Reminder Letter for Patients

Your second project for the day is the generation of a letter to remind patients of their appointment with the therapists. For this project, you use an Access database as the source because that is how your office stores patient information.

a. Open a new document and save it as **w04c1reminder_LastnameFirstname.** Start a mail merge letter and pull your recipients from *w04c1patients.accdb.* When you select the database file, use the Patients table.

b. Press **Enter** two times in your new blank document, and then insert today's date aligned on the left margin of the letter. Press **Enter** three times, and then insert an address block in the return address area of the letter. Press **Enter** twice, and then insert an appropriate salutation of greeting to the patient.

c. Press **Enter** twice, and then type the following for the body of the reminder letter: **Please remember that you have an appointment at the Sports Medicine Clinic of Conway on **date**, at **time**. If you have paperwork to fill out, please arrive at our office 15 minutes prior to your appointment time stated above. Thank you!**

d. Press **Enter** two times, and then finish the letter by typing the closing salutation:

Sincerely,
The Sports Medicine Clinic of Conway
(501) 555-5555

e. Insert the fields for date and time in the first sentence and remove the markers.

f. Change the formatting of the document so the letter is single spaced with no additional spacing before or after any paragraph.

g. Edit the recipient list and add your name, address, and a date for an appointment. If file or network security does not enable you to modify the source data file, copy the file to your own disk and redirect the mail merge to use the file from the new location. If you cannot copy the file, omit this step.

h. Sort the recipient list by appointment date, and then appointment time. Do not print letters for people who do not have a scheduled appointment.

i. Merge the documents into a new document, and then save it as **w04c1appointments_LastnameFirstname**. If a Mail Merge dialog box displays indicating Word found locked fields during the update, click **OK** to clear the dialog box.

j. Save and close all documents, and submit based on your instructor's directions.

Thank You Letter

GENERAL CASE

FROM SCRATCH

Recently, you attended a Career Fair at your university and have collected more than ten business cards from companies who participated in the job fair. You want to send a thank you letter to all your new contacts and hope to establish a communication rapport with them. You use Word to create a directory for your contacts, write a thank you letter, and then use Mail Merge to generate the letters. Open a new document, insert a table, and then enter the contact information from the fictional business cards onto the table. Save the document as **w04b1contacts_LastnameFirstname**, and then close the file. Open another new document, write your thank you letter, which includes address blocks and fields you can use in a mail merge, and then save the document as **w04b1careerfairletter_LastnameFirstname**. Using Mail Merge and *w04b1contacts_LastnameFirstname* as your data source, create and save the result of your mail merge as **w04b1thankyouletter_LastnameFirstname**. Use the Microsoft Help feature, if necessary. Close all documents and submit based on your instructor's directions.

Personal Budget Report

RESEARCH CASE

FROM SCRATCH

You are taking a Personal Finance class this semester and one of the assignments is to provide a report about your income, expenses, and spending habits for a 12-month period. Open a new document and type two paragraphs that describe your spending habits. In the first paragraph, include your primary sources of income and how you allocate your income to different sources such as savings accounts and expenses. In the second paragraph, describe your major expenses. Create a table in Word that details your budget under various major categories such as **Income**, **Expenses**, and **Savings**, and subcategories such as **Fixed Expenses** and **Variable Expenses**. Examples of fixed expenses include tuition, rent, auto insurance, cable, and cell phone subscriptions, while examples of variable expenses include food, books, school supplies, and utilities. Create multiple columns that enable you to break down your income and costs by category and by month, and then add formulas to show subtotals for each month and the grand total for the 12-month period. Use the Internet to help you find ways to reduce your monthly expenses, and then describe some of these cost-saving strategies in the last paragraph. Save your work as **w04b2budget_LastnameFirstname**. Close the document and submit based on your instructor's directions.

Wedding Invitations

DISASTER RECOVERY

Your friend is experiencing high levels of anxiety because she cannot complete a mail merge operation to create labels for her wedding invitations. She has used the Mail Merge feature previously; however, when you open the labels, a dialog box appears and indicates there is no link from that main document to the data source (address list). You decide to troubleshoot the operation by first opening the file *w04b3labels*, to see how it was set up to use the addresses in *w04b3labeladdresses.accdb*, and then determine if you can find the reason why it does not work. If you can solve the problem, create mailing labels for the wedding and save the new file as **w04b3weddinglabels_LastnameFirstname**. Rename and save the original file you fix as **w04b3labels_LastnameFirstname**. Close all documents and submit based on your instructor's directions.

WORD APPLICATION CAPSTONE EXERCISE

You are a manager at an IT consulting firm and are often asked to provide general information about technology to local schools and organizations. You recently received a request to write a short report about the history of personal computers. You spent a few minutes to gather a few facts about various systems and now you are ready to format the document so that it is easy to read and understand. Upon completion, you will print and mail copies of the report to three teachers who recently requested a report on this topic.

Add a Graphic and Update Properties

As the first of many changes to improve the readability and professionalism of this document, you add a graphic for visual effects. You also change the document properties for easier searching, and you change the margins. You enlarge the document title on the first page because this is important in explaining the content and purpose of the report.

a. Start Word. Open *waccap.docx* and save it as **waccap_LastnameFirstname.docx**.
b. Insert the graphic file **wacboard.jpg** under the *Altair 8800* heading, immediately to the left of the sentence that begins *The Altair 8800 is generally*. Change the height of the picture to **1.75"**. Change the wrapping style of the picture to **Tight**.
c. Enter the caption **Figure 1-Circuit Board** below the image.
d. Modify the document properties, and then enter **A Brief History of the Personal Computer** in the **Title field**. Close the Document Properties panel.
e. Set the margins of the document to **Normal**.
f. Select the first line of text in the document, *A Brief History of the Personal Computer*. Format the text as bold, italic, 24 pt, and centered.
g. Format the same text with a 2¼ pt box border using the default line style. Set the fill color to **Blue, Accent 1, Lighter 80%**.

Add Footers and Heading Styles

Any multi-page document should include page numbers, so you add a footer that will automatically number the pages for you. You also decide to format a grouping of information into a bulleted list that spans two columns, which will be easier to read and take up less space on the page. And you also format all paragraph headings with a built-in style to improve readability.

a. Insert a page number at the bottom of the page using the Accent Bar 1 style.
b. Type your last name in the header, aligned with the left margin.
c. Format the nine paragraph headings with the Heading 1 style, beginning with the *Altair 8800* heading and ending with the *Index* heading on page 3.
d. Select the list under the *Windows* heading on page 2 that begins with *Windows 1.0* and ends with *Windows 7*. Format as a bulleted list using solid round bullets (character code: 183 in the Symbol font).
e. Change the layout of the bulleted list you just created to two columns.

Add a Table and Footnote

You want to include a short amount of information on page 2, and you decide to display that text in a table. You will modify the table so longer lines of information display completely in one cell, and then apply a style to the table. You also add a footnote to explain where you found the information.

a. Insert a one-row by two-column table on page 2 in the blank line immediately above the *Timeline* heading. Type **Descended from DOS** in the first cell. Type **Windows 1.0-Windows ME** in the second cell.

b. Add a new row below the existing row. Merge the cells of the second row. Type ***Internet Explorer debuted in 1995 with Windows 95*** in the merged cell. Center align all the text in the table.
c. Format the table with the style **Light Shading - Accent 1**.
d. Click after the text **Internet Explorer debuted in 1995 with Windows 95** in the merged cell. Insert the following footnote: **Source: http://www.microsoft.com/windows/WinHistoryIE.mspx**.

Set Tabs and Add an Index

You wisely decide to use tabs to separate some information in the report so that it will be easier to read. You also decide to add an index at the end of the document. In order to use the feature that creates the index automatically, you first mark text in the document that you want to include in the index.

a. Select the seven lines of text under the *Timeline* heading, beginning with *1975* and ending with *Windows*. Set left-aligned tab stops at **2.5"** and **4"**. Add a dotted leader to the 4" tab stop.
b. Select each paragraph title that was previously formatted with the Heading 1 style, except the *Index* heading, and then mark them as index entries.
c. Mark each occurrence of *personal computer* as an index entry, and then revise the entry to display *Personal Computer* so each word is capitalized in the index.
d. Press **Ctrl+End** to move the last line of the document. Insert an index using the default settings.

Add a Comment, a Table of Contents, and a Cover Page

You use the comment feature to leave yourself a reminder of something to change later. Additionally, you insert a cover page and table of contents, which will both display at the beginning of the report.

a. Turn on Track Changes. Display the beginning of the document, and then change the title of the document to **A Brief History of the Personal Computer—Altair to Windows**. Do not include a period at the end of the title. Observe the tracked change in the document, and then accept it.
b. Turn off Track Changes.
c. Select the newly added text *Altair to Windows*, and then insert a comment that reads **Need to update document properties with new title.** Include a period at the end of the sentence in the comment.
d. At the beginning of the document, insert a page break immediately to the left of the title, *A Brief History of the Personal Computer—Altair to Windows*. Insert a table of contents at the top of the new page using the Automatic Table 2 built-in style.
e. Insert a cover page at the beginning of the document that uses the Cubicles style.
f. Replace the company name with your own name. Remove the placeholders *Type the document subtitle* and *Date*.

Perform a Mail Merge

You will be sending this report to three colleagues, so you decide to create mailing labels using the mail merge feature and a document that contains addresses. After you create the labels, you decide to copy the mailing label table into this document so you can remember to whom you sent the report.

a. Insert a page break at the end of the document. Save, but do not close, the *waccap_LastnameFirstname* document.
b. Open a new blank Word document. In the new blank Word document, start the Step by Step Mail Merge Wizard.
c. Set the document type to **Labels**, and then proceed to step 2. Select **Label options**, and then select **Avery US Letter labels, product number 5160**. Accept the settings, and then proceed to step 3 of the wizard.
d. Browse for the downloaded file *wacaddresses.docx* as the recipients list. Accept the settings, and then proceed to step 4.

e. Insert an address block using the default settings at the insertion point. Update all of the labels to match the first label, and then proceed to step 5.
f. After previewing the labels, proceed to step 6. Merge all the records into a new document.
g. View the merged labels document. Select and copy the entire table containing the mailing labels.
h. Return to the *waccap_LastnameFirstname.docx* file, and then paste the copied mailing labels at the top of the seventh page (which displays *Page 6* in the footer).
i. Update the index and table of contents.
j. Save and close *waccap_LastnameFirstname*. Close any other open documents without saving, and then exit Word. Submit the saved file based on your instructor's directions.

WORD COLLABORATION EXERCISES

1 The Career Connection Annual Report

Group collaboration is the normal method of operation in many successful companies. It is important that you learn to use several forms of communication and collaboration as you transition from college to the business environment. Some companies provide the technology that you will use in group project collaborations, but many tools are available for free on the Internet. Some applications you use on a regular basis, such as Facebook, can also serve as a collaboration tool. In this exercise, you will have an online discussion with members of your group to determine who will be responsible for each of the six steps that are necessary to update and finalize an annual report for The Career Connection.

a. Use an online collaboration tool such as Google Groups or Skype to message with or conduct a live chat with your group members.

b. Discuss who will be the group leader during the chat session, and then choose a name for the group. Then decide which team members will be responsible for steps d through i below. The group leader should use the Snipping Tool to capture the chat session at several stages and save it to a document that will be submitted to your instructor. This document will demonstrate each member's contribution to the discussion.

c. The group leader will open *w01t1ccreport* and save it as **w01t1ccreport_GroupName**. The team leader will then post the document to a central location, such as SkyDrive or Dropbox.com, where each team member can share and open it as a Microsoft Word document.

d. Insert document properties that display each group member's name in the Author area.

e. Set custom margins at **0.5"** on the top and bottom, and **0.55"** on the right and left. Insert a comment in the Comments area of the document properties panel which displays your name and explain how you completed this step. Save the document.

f. Add breaks where appropriate so paragraphs do not break across pages. Display the document in different views to determine where page breaks should be added or removed. Insert a comment in the Comments area of the document properties panel which displays your name and explain how you completed this step. Save the document.

g. Add a section break between the last paragraph and the first graphic to display the graphics on a separate page, and then change the last page to display the contents in Landscape orientation. Insert a comment in the Comments area of the document properties panel which displays your name and explain how you completed this step. Save the document.

h. Add a footer that displays the document name and page number on every page except the first page. Insert a comment in the Comments area of the document properties panel which displays your name and explain how you completed this step. Save the document.

i. Check the spelling and grammar in the document and make any necessary corrections. Insert a comment in the Comments area of the document properties panel which displays your name and explain how you completed this step. Save the document.

j. Save the document in both Word 2010 and Word 97-2003 formats, and then close all documents.

k. Post the final versions of each document as well as the document that displays the screenshots of the chat session to the central storage location. Inform your instructor that the documents are ready for grading, and also give directions on where they are located.

2 Recipe Favorites Book

Have you ever attended an event such as a reception or graduation party and wish you could walk away with recipes for all the wonderful dishes that were served and consumed at the event? In this exercise, you will collaborate with a group of your peers to develop a recipe booklet. You will each share a recipe and use font and paragraph tools in Word that enable you to format the recipes in a way that is easy to read and understand.

a. Determine which group member will create a new Word document, name it **w02t2recipes_Groupname**, and then that group member will type their favorite recipe.

b. The first member will store the document in a shared folder that other members and your instructor can access by using a storage tool such as Dropbox.com.
c. Begin each recipe on a new page of the document. Each member should type the name of the person who is contributing the recipe as well as the recipe itself.
d. Use formatting tools in Word such as bulleted or numbered lists, columns, tabs, borders, shading, and styles to create a consistent format in which each recipe displays. The first person to add their recipe can select the styles that each member should use.
e. Use a cell phone or digital camera to take pictures of dishes, if possible, and add the pictures to the document. Or, you can search for copyright-free images on the Internet using a site such as Morguefile.com (*Note:* Even though an image is copyright free, you still need to give credit for the image.) Display the pictures near the respective recipe.
f. Provide pictures of any hard-to-find ingredients, and then insert them into the document near the respective recipe.
g. Save the document. Inform your instructor that the document is ready for grading, and also give directions on where it is located.

3 Advantages of Cloud Computing

As you learn to use Word, you will notice that the application has many features that work well with online resources. So many resources are available online that it is hard to determine which one is the best fit for your needs. But with the help of your fellow students, you will develop a research paper that attempts to identify and evaluate several online resources, which are also referred to as cloud computing.

a. Use an online chat tool to discuss the division of duties within your group to determine who will be the group leader, and who will be responsible for completing steps d through h below.
b. Create a shared storage location for the document using your group name that will be modified by each team member and available for access by your instructor. Save the document as **w03t3cloud_GroupName**.
c. Turn on Track Changes, and then track the changes made by each member of the group. Use comments within the document to communicate to other group members.
d. Develop a research paper that answers these questions:
    - What is cloud computing?
    - What online resources are available for use as a word processor or spreadsheet application? Which resource is most popular for this purpose and why?
    - What online resources are available for use in saving and sharing information such as documents or pictures? Which resource is most popular for this purpose and why?
    - What online resources are available for use in collaborating with others? How are they used and why are they popular?
    - Are social media websites considered a cloud computing resource? Why or why not?
    - What are the advantages and disadvantages of using cloud computing resources for an individual, a small business, or a large business?
e. Use the Source Manager to store information from each resource you use or acknowledge in your paper. Create a bibliography from the sources.
f. Use headings throughout the paper to identify a topic. Use the style feature on the headings, and then create an automated table of contents.
g. Use footnotes or endnotes when appropriate.
h. Use other formatting features such as cover sheets, page numbering, and formatting tools to create a professional-looking research paper.
i. Save the document and inform your instructor that the document is ready for grading. Also give your instructor directions on where he or she can locate it.

4 Summer Study Abroad Programs

You and several of your friends would like to take classes abroad during the summer. You collectively decide that each person will research one program, and display the various program information in a table that shows information about each program. After the table is created, the group will collaborate and decide into which program the group members will enroll. After you each add your research to the table, the group will meet together and decide in which one you will all enroll. The group will choose one person to start the document; that person will save it on their SkyDrive and allow each of the remaining members to view and edit it from that location.

a. Open a new blank document and save it as **w04t4summer_GroupName**.
b. Save the document to your SkyDrive in a folder named Public. Give permission for your group members and instructor to view this folder, if necessary. Each person will modify this file and save it back to this location.
c. Insert a table in the document with the following column headings:

Location	Program	Overview	Dates	Deadlines	Credits	Cost

d. Insert a row above the first row in the table and merge it across so that it is only one column wide. Type **Summer Study Tours** in that new cell.
e. E-mail your group members to let them know the document is available and should be updated by each one as soon as possible. Group members will add a row to the table and insert the information about a different summer study away program.
f. Format the table using a built-in table style after all information is complete. Add other formatting as necessary to create an easy-to-read table.
g. Save the document and inform your instructor that the document is ready for grading from your SkyDrive.

EXCEL

1 INTRODUCTION TO EXCEL

What Is a Spreadsheet?

Watch the
Set-up Video
for this Case Study!

CASE STUDY | OK Office Systems

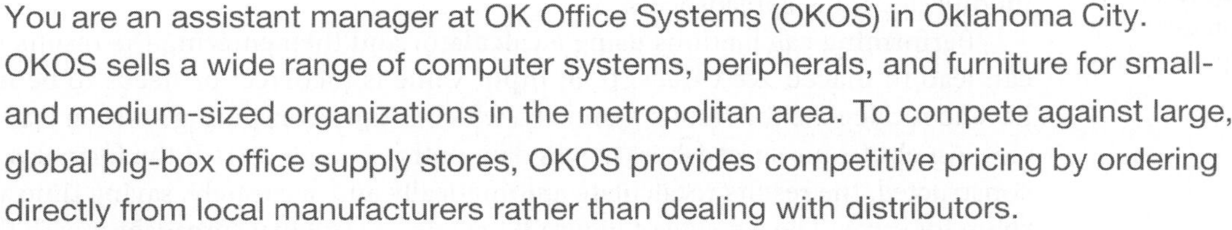

You are an assistant manager at OK Office Systems (OKOS) in Oklahoma City. OKOS sells a wide range of computer systems, peripherals, and furniture for small- and medium-sized organizations in the metropolitan area. To compete against large, global big-box office supply stores, OKOS provides competitive pricing by ordering directly from local manufacturers rather than dealing with distributors.

The manager asked you to help prepare a markup, discount, and profit analysis for selected items on sale. The manager has been keeping these data in a ledger, but you will develop a spreadsheet to perform the necessary calculations. After you create the initial pricing spreadsheet, you will be able to change values and see that the formulas update the results automatically. In addition, you will be able to insert data for additional sale items or delete an item based on the manager's decision.

Although your experience with Microsoft Office Excel 2010 may be limited, you are excited to apply your knowledge and skills to your newly assigned responsibility. When you get to the Hands-On Exercises, you will create and format the analytical spreadsheet to practice the skills you learn in this chapter.

OBJECTIVES AFTER YOU READ THIS CHAPTER, YOU WILL BE ABLE TO:

1. Plan for effective workbook and worksheet design ***p.328***
2. Explore the Excel window ***p.329***
3. Enter and edit cell data ***p.332***
4. Use symbols and the order of precedence ***p.337***
5. Use Auto Fill ***p.339***
6. Display cell formulas ***p.340***
7. Manage worksheets ***p.346***
8. Manage columns and rows ***p.349***
9. Select, move, copy, and paste ***p.353***
10. Apply alignment and font options ***p.363***
11. Apply number formats ***p.365***
12. Select page setup options ***p.371***
13. Print a worksheet ***p.375***

Introduction to Spreadsheets

The ability to organize, calculate, and evaluate quantitative data is one of the most important skills needed today for personal, as well as managerial, decision making. In your personal life, you track expenses for your household budget, maintain a savings plan, and determine what amount you can afford for a house or car payment. Retail managers create and analyze their organizations' annual budgets, sales projections, and inventory records. Charitable organizations track the donations they receive, the distribution of those donations, and overhead expenditures. Scientists track the results of their experiments and perform statistical analysis to draw conclusions and recommendations.

The ability to organize, calculate, and evaluate quantitative data is one of the most important skills needed today.

A **spreadsheet** is an electronic file that contains a grid of columns and rows containing related data.

A **spreadsheet program** is a computer application used to create and modify spreadsheets.

Regardless of what type of quantitative analysis you need to do, you can use a spreadsheet to help you maintain data and perform calculations. A ***spreadsheet*** is an electronic file that contains a grid of columns and rows used to organize related data and to display results of calculations, enabling interpretation of quantitative data for decision making. A ***spreadsheet program*** is a computer application, such as Microsoft Excel, that you use to create and modify electronic spreadsheets.

Performing calculations using a calculator and then entering the results into a ledger can lead to inaccurate values. If an input value is incorrect or needs to be updated, you have to recalculate the results manually, which is time-consuming and can lead to inaccuracies. An electronic spreadsheet makes data-entry changes easy. If the formulas are correctly constructed, the results recalculate automatically and accurately, saving time and reducing room for error. The left side of Figure 1.1 shows the original spreadsheet with the $450 cost, 75% markup rate, and calculated retail price. The right side shows the updated spreadsheet with a $500 cost, 65.5% markup, and automatically updated retail price.

Changed values

Automatically updated retail price

Original calculated retail price

Original values

Original Spreadsheet Values and Results

Product	Cost	Markup Rate	Retail Price
Electronics:			
Computer System	$ 400.00	50.00%	$ 600.00
28" Monitor	$ 195.00	83.50%	$ 357.83
Color Laser Printer	$ 450.00	75.00%	$ 787.50

Modified Spreadsheet Values and Results

Product	Cost	Markup Rate	Retail Price
Electronics:			
Computer System	$400.00	50.00%	$ 600.00
28" Monitor	$195.00	83.50%	$ 357.83
Color Laser Printer	$500.00	65.50%	$ 827.50

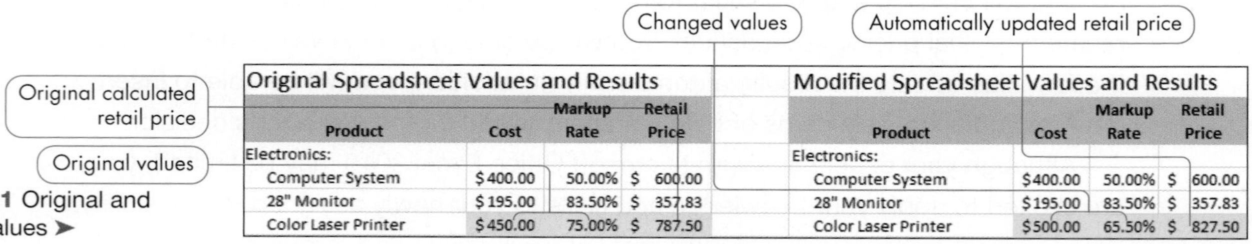

FIGURE 1.1 Original and Modified Values ➤

In this section, you will learn how to design workbooks and worksheets. In addition, you will explore the Excel window and learn the name of each window element. Then, you will enter text, values, dates, and formulas in a worksheet.

Planning for Effective Workbook and Worksheet Design

A **worksheet** is a spreadsheet that contains formulas, functions, values, text, and visual aids.

A **workbook** is a file containing related worksheets.

Microsoft Excel is the most popular spreadsheet program used today. In Excel, a ***worksheet*** is a single spreadsheet that typically contains descriptive labels, numeric values, formulas, functions, and graphical representations of data. A ***workbook*** is a collection of one or more related worksheets contained within a single file. By default, new workbooks contain three worksheets. Storing multiple worksheets within one workbook helps organize related data together in one file and enables you to perform calculations among the worksheets within the workbook. For example, you can create a budget workbook of 13 worksheets, one for each month to store your personal income and expenses and a final worksheet to calculate totals across the entire year.

You should plan the structure before you start entering data into a worksheet. Using the OKOS case study as an example, the steps to design the workbook and a worksheet include the following:

1. **State the purpose of the worksheet.** The purpose of the OKOS worksheet is to provide data, including a profit margin, on selected products on sale.

An **input area** is a range of cells containing values for variables used in formulas.

An **output area** is a range of cells containing results based on manipulating the variables.

2. **Decide what input values are needed.** Create an ***input area***, a range of cells to enter values for your variables or assumptions. Clearly label an input area so that users know where to change values. For the OKOS worksheet, list the product names, the costs OKOS pays the manufacturers, the markup rates, and the proposed discount rates for the sale. Enter these data in individual cells to enable changes if needed.
3. **Decide what outputs are needed to achieve the purpose of the worksheet.** Create an ***output area***, a range of cells that contains the results of manipulating values in the input area. As the OKOS assistant manager, you need to calculate the retail price (i.e., the selling price to your customers), the sale price, and the profit margin. As you plan your formulas, avoid constants (raw numbers); instead, use references to cells containing numbers.
4. **Assign the worksheet inputs and results into columns and rows, and consider labeling.** Typically, descriptive labels appear in the first column to represent each row of data. For the OKOS worksheet, enter the product names in the first column. Labels at the top of each column represent individual columns of data, such as cost, markup rate, and selling price.
5. **Enter the labels, values, and formulas in Excel.** Change the input values to test that your formulas produce correct results. If necessary, correct any errors in the formulas to produce correct results regardless of the input values. For the OKOS worksheet, change some of the original costs and markup rates to ensure the calculated retail price, selling price, and profit margin percentage results update correctly.
6. **Format the numerical values in the worksheet.** Align decimal points in columns of numbers. In the OKOS worksheet, use Accounting Number Format and the Percent Style to format the numerical data. Adjust the number of decimal places as needed.
7. **Format the descriptive titles and labels attractively but so as not to distract your audience from the purpose of the worksheet.** Include a descriptive title and label for each column. Add bold to headings, increase the font size for readability, and use color to draw attention to important values or trends. In the OKOS worksheet, you will center the main title over all the columns and apply a larger font size to it.
8. **Document the worksheet as thoroughly as possible.** Include the current date, your name as the author of the worksheet, assumptions, and purpose of the worksheet.
9. **Save the completed workbook.** Preview and prepare printouts for distribution in meetings, or send an electronic copy of the workbook to those who need it.

Figure 1.2 shows the completed worksheet in Excel.

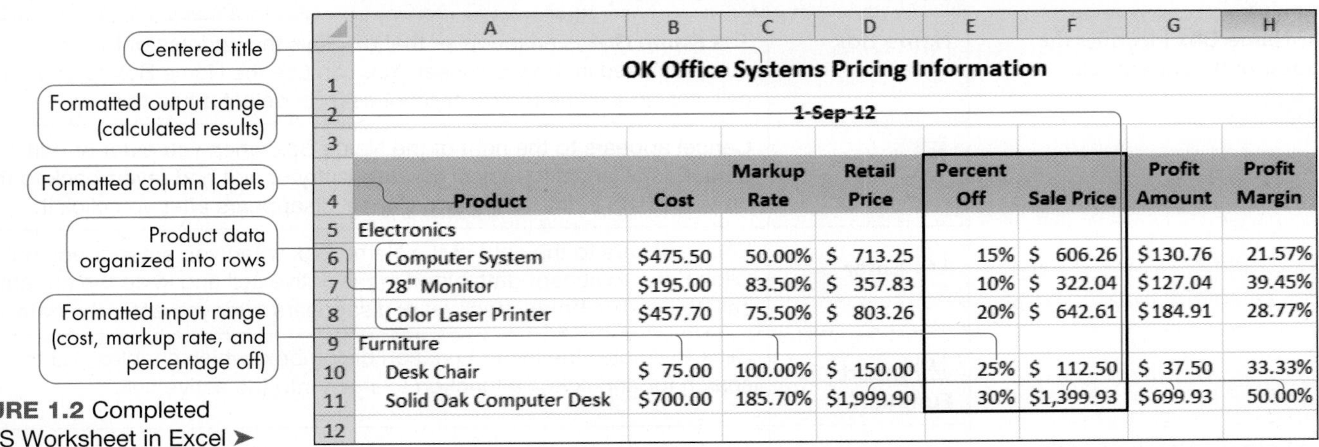

	A	B	C	D	E	F	G	H
1	OK Office Systems Pricing Information							
2	1-Sep-12							
3								
4	Product	Cost	Markup Rate	Retail Price	Percent Off	Sale Price	Profit Amount	Profit Margin
5	Electronics							
6	Computer System	$475.50	50.00%	$ 713.25	15%	$ 606.26	$130.76	21.57%
7	28" Monitor	$195.00	83.50%	$ 357.83	10%	$ 322.04	$127.04	39.45%
8	Color Laser Printer	$457.70	75.50%	$ 803.26	20%	$ 642.61	$184.91	28.77%
9	Furniture							
10	Desk Chair	$ 75.00	100.00%	$ 150.00	25%	$ 112.50	$ 37.50	33.33%
11	Solid Oak Computer Desk	$700.00	185.70%	$1,999.90	30%	$1,399.93	$699.93	50.00%
12								

FIGURE 1.2 Completed OKOS Worksheet in Excel ➤

Exploring the Excel Window

By now, you should be familiar with the standard interface of Microsoft Office applications: the Quick Access Toolbar, title bar, control buttons, Ribbon, Home tab, the Backstage view, and scroll bars. The Excel window includes screen elements that are similar to other Office applications and items that are unique to Excel. Figure 1.3 identifies elements specific to the Excel window, and Table 1.1 lists and describes the Excel window elements.

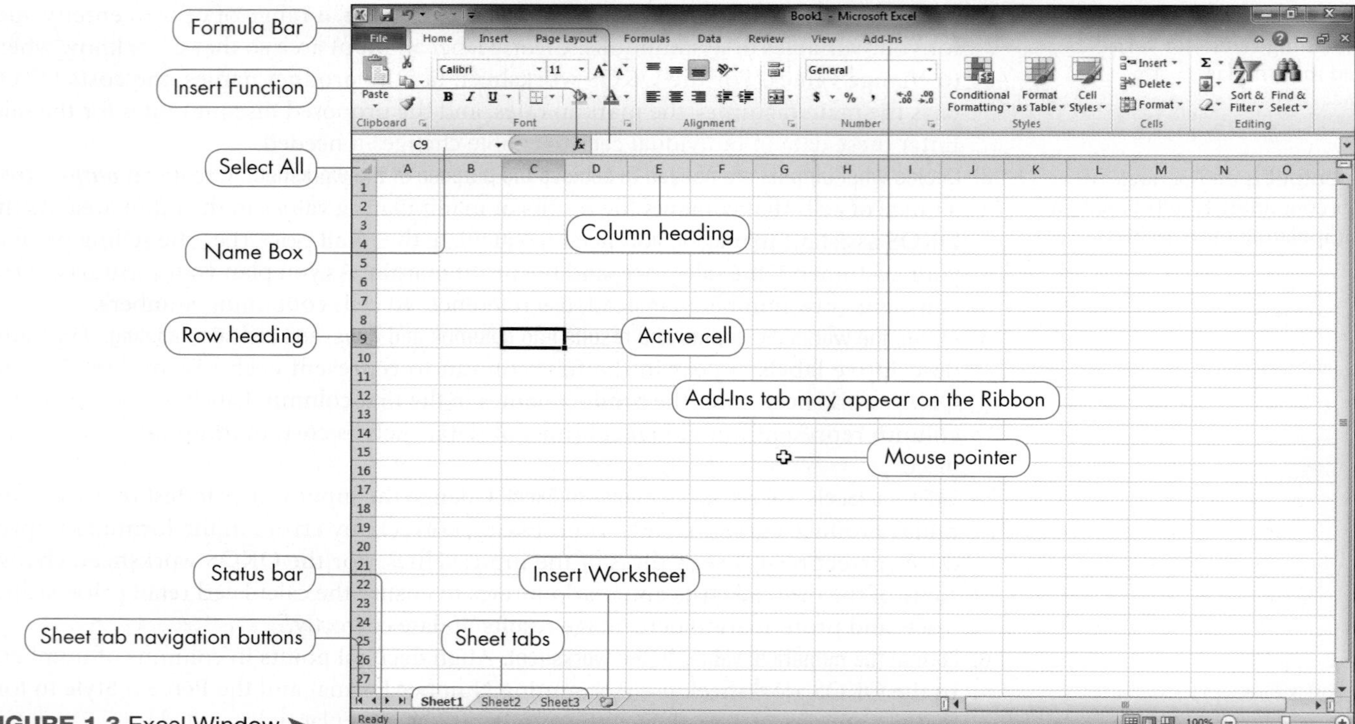

FIGURE 1.3 Excel Window ➤

TIP Add-Ins Tab

You may see an Add-Ins tab on the Ribbon. This tab indicates that additional functionality, such as an updated Office feature or an Office-compatible program, has been added to your system. Add-Ins are designed to increase your productivity.

The **Name Box** identifies the address of the current cell.

The **Formula Bar** displays the content (text, value, date, or formula) in the active cell.

TABLE 1.1 Excel Elements

Element	Description
Name Box	The ***Name Box*** is an identifier that displays the address of the cell currently used in the worksheet. You can use the Name Box to go to a cell, assign a name to one or more cells, or select a function.
Cancel	Cancel appears to the right of the Name Box when you enter or edit data. Click Cancel to cancel the data entry or edit and revert back to the previous data in the cell, if any. Cancel disappears after you click it.
Enter	Enter appears to the right of the Name Box when you enter or edit data. Click Enter to accept data typed in the active cell and keep the current cell active. The Enter check mark disappears after you enter the data.
Insert Function	Click to display the Insert Function dialog box, which enables you to search for and select a function to insert into the active cell.
Formula Bar	The ***Formula Bar***, the area that appears below the Ribbon and to the right of Insert Function, shows the contents of the active cell. You can enter or edit cell contents here or directly in the active cell. Drag the bottom border of the Formula Bar down to increase the space of the Formula Bar to display large amounts of data or a long formula contained in the active cell.
Select All	The square at the intersection of the row and column headings in the top-left corner of the worksheet. Click it to select everything contained in the active worksheet.

TABLE 1.1 (*Continued*)	
Element	**Description**
Column headings	The letters above the columns, such as A, B, C, and so on.
Row headings	The numbers to the left of the rows are row headings, such as 1, 2, 3, and so on.
Sheet tabs	***Sheet tabs***, located at the bottom-left corner of the Excel window, show the names of the worksheets contained in the workbook. Three sheet tabs, initially named Sheet1, Sheet2, and Sheet3, are included when you start a new Excel workbook. You can rename sheets with more meaningful names. To display the contents of a particular worksheet, click its sheet tab.
Sheet Tab Navigation buttons	If your workbook contains several worksheets, Excel may not show all the sheet tabs at the same time. Use the buttons to display the first, previous, next, or last worksheet.
Status bar	Located at the bottom of the Excel window, below the sheet tabs and above the Windows taskbar, the status bar displays information about a selected command or operation in progress. For example, it displays *Select destination and press ENTER or choose Paste* after you use the Copy command.

A **sheet tab** displays the name of a worksheet within a workbook.

Identify Columns, Rows, and Cells

A **cell** is the intersection of a column and row.

A **cell address** identifies a cell by a column letter and a row number.

A worksheet contains columns and rows, with each column and row assigned a heading. Columns are assigned alphabetic headings from columns A to Z, continuing from AA to AZ, and then from BA to BZ until XFD, which is the last of the possible 16,384 columns. Rows have numeric headings ranging from 1 to 1,048,576 (the maximum number of rows available).

The intersection of a column and row is a ***cell***; a total of over 17 billion cells are available in a worksheet. Each cell has a unique ***cell address***, identified by first its column letter and then its row number. For example, the cell at the intersection of column A and row 9 is cell A9. Cell references are useful when referencing data in formulas, or in navigation.

Navigate In and Among Worksheets

The **active cell** is the current cell, indicated by a dark border.

The ***active cell*** is the current cell. Excel displays a dark border around the active cell in the worksheet window, and the cell address of the active cell appears in the Name Box. The contents of the active cell, or the formula used to calculate the results of the active cell, appear in the Formula Bar. You can change the active cell by using the mouse to click in a different cell. If you work in a large worksheet, you may not be able to see the entire contents in one screen; use the vertical and horizontal scroll bars to display another area of the worksheet, and then click in the desired cell to make it the active cell.

To navigate to a new cell, click it, or use the arrow keys on the keyboard. When you press Enter, the next cell down in the same column becomes the active cell. Table 1.2 lists the keyboard methods for navigating within a worksheet. The Go To command is helpful for navigating to a cell that is not visible onscreen.

TABLE 1.2 Keystrokes and Actions	
Keystroke	**Used to**
↑	Move up one cell in the same column.
↓	Move down one cell in the same column.
←	Move left one cell in the same row.
→	Move right one cell in the same row.
Tab	Move right one cell in the same row.

(*Continued*)

TABLE 1.2 *(Continued)*	
Keystroke	**Used to**
Page Up	Move the active cell up one screen.
Page Down	Move the active cell down one screen.
Home	Move the active cell to column A of current row.
Ctrl+Home	Make cell A1 the active cell.
Ctrl+End	Make the rightmost, lowermost active corner of the worksheet—the intersection of the last column and row that contains data—the active cell. Does not move to cell XFD1048576 unless that cell contains data.
F5 or Ctrl+G	Display the Go To dialog box to enter any cell address.

To display the contents of another worksheet within the workbook, click the sheet tab at the bottom of the workbook window. The active sheet tab has a white background color. After you click a sheet tab, you can then navigate within that worksheet.

Entering and Editing Cell Data

Figure 1.4 shows examples of text, values, dates, and formula results.

AutoComplete

	A	B	C	D	E
1	Text	Date	Value	Value	Formula Result
2	Computer	10/1/2013	400	0.5	600
3	Computer				

FIGURE 1.4 Data Entered in Cells ➤

Enter Text

Text includes letters, numbers, symbols, and spaces.

Text is any combination of letters, numbers, symbols, and spaces not used in calculations. Excel treats phone numbers, such as 555-1234, and social security numbers, such as 123-45-6789, as text entries. You enter text for a worksheet title to describe the contents of the worksheet, as row and column labels to describe data, and as cell data. Text aligns at the left cell margin by default. To enter text in a cell, do the following:

1. Make sure the cell is active where you want to enter text.
2. Enter the text.
3. Press Enter, press an arrow key on the keyboard, or click Enter—the check mark between the Name Box and the Formula Bar. If you want to enter data without making another cell the active cell, click Enter instead of pressing Enter.

As soon as you begin typing a label into a cell, the AutoComplete feature searches for and automatically displays any other label in that column that matches the letters you typed (see Figure 1.4). Press Enter to accept the repeated label, or continue typing to enter a different label.

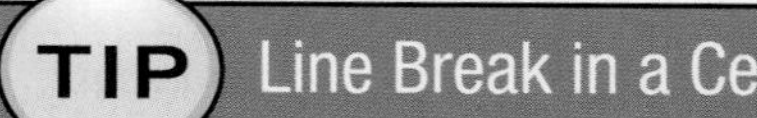

TIP Line Break in a Cell

If you have a long text label that does not fit well in a cell, you can insert a line break to display the text label on multiple lines within the cell. To insert a line break while you are typing a label, press Alt+Enter where you want to start the next line of text within the cell.

Enter Values

A **value** is a number that represents a quantity or an amount.

Values are numbers that represent a quantity or a measurable amount. Excel usually distinguishes between text and value data based on what you enter. The primary difference between text and value entries is that value entries can be the basis of calculations, whereas text cannot. Values align at the right cell margin by default. After entering values, you can align decimal places and add identifying characters, such as $ or %.

Enter Dates

You can enter dates and times in a variety of formats in cells, such as 9/15/2012; 9/15/12; September 15, 2012; or 15-Sep-12. You can also enter times, such as 1:30 PM or 13:30. You should enter a static date to document when you create or modify a workbook or to document the specific point in time when the data were accurate, such as on a balance sheet or income statement. Dates are values, so they align at the right cell margin.

Excel displays dates differently from the way it stores dates. For example, the displayed date 9/15/2012 represents the fifteenth day in September in the year 2012. Excel stores dates as serial numbers starting at 1 with January 1, 1900, so 9/15/2012 is stored as 41167 so that you can create formulas to calculate how many days exist between two dates.

Static Dates and Times

Press Ctrl+semicolon to insert the current date, such as 3/28/2012, or press Ctrl+Shift+semicolon to insert the current time, such as 4:35 PM.

Enter Formulas

A **formula** is a combination of cell references, operators, values, and/or functions used to perform a calculation.

Formulas combine cell references, arithmetic operations, values, and/or functions used in a calculation. You must start the formula with an equal sign (=). In Figure 1.4, cell E2 contains the formula =C2*D2+C2. The result of the formula (600) displays in the cell.

Edit and Clear Cell Contents

You can edit a cell's contents by doing one of the following:

- Click the cell, click in the Formula Bar, make the changes, and then click Enter on the left side of the Formula Bar.
- Double-click the cell, make changes in the cell, and then press Enter.
- Click the cell, press F2, make changes in the cell, and then press Enter.

You can clear a cell's contents by doing one of the following:

- Click the cell, and then press Delete.
- Click the cell, click Clear in the Editing group on the Home tab, and then select Clear Contents.

Quick Concepts Check

1. What are two major advantages of using an electronic spreadsheet instead of a paper-based ledger?
2. What are four planning steps you should follow before entering labels, values, and formulas into a worksheet?
3. What visual indicators let you know which cell is the active cell?
4. What are four major things you can enter into a cell? Give an example (different from those in the book) for each type.

HANDS-ON EXERCISES

HOE1 Training

1 Introduction to Spreadsheets

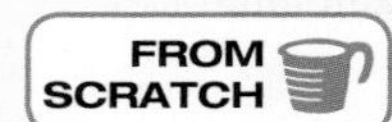

As the assistant manager of OKOS, you need to create a worksheet that shows the cost (the amount OKOS pays its suppliers), the markup percentage (the amount by which the cost is increased), and the retail selling price. In addition, you need to list the discount percentage (such as 25% off) for each product, the sale price, and the profit margin percentage. Most of the cells in the worksheet will contain formulas. You have already planned the design as indicated in the steps listed earlier in this chapter.

Skills covered: Enter Text • Enter Unformatted Values • Enter a Date and Clear Cell Contents

STEP 1 ENTER TEXT

Now that you have planned your worksheet, you are ready to enter labels for the title, row labels, and column labels. Refer to Figure 1.5 as you complete Step 1.

	A	B	C	D	E	F	G	H
1	OK Office Systems Pricing Information							
2	1-Sep-12							
3								
4	Product	Cost	Markup Ra	Retail Pric	Percent O	Sale Price	Profit Margin	
5	Computer System							
6	Color Laser Printer							
7	Filing Cabinet							
8	Desk Chair							
9	Solid Oak Computer Desk							
10	28" Monitor							
11								
12								

FIGURE 1.5 Text Entries ➤

a. Start Excel. Save the new workbook as **e01h1markup_LastnameFirstname**.

When you save files, use your last and first names. For example, as the Excel author, I would save my workbook as e01h1markup_MulberyKeith.

b. Type **OK Office Systems Pricing Information** in **cell A1**, and then press **Enter**.

When you press Enter, the next cell down—cell A2 in this case—becomes the active cell. The text does not completely fit in cell A1, and some of the text appears in cells B1, C1, and D1. If you make cell B1, C1, or D1 the active cell, the Formula Bar is empty, indicating that nothing is stored in those cells. If you were to type data in cell B1, that text would appear in cell B1, and although the contents of cell A1 would appear cut off, cell A1 still would contain the entire text.

c. Click **cell A4**, type **Product**, and then press **Enter**.

d. Continue typing the rest of the text in **cells A5** through **A10** as shown in Figure 1.5. Note that text appears to flow into column B.

When you start typing *Co* in cell A6, AutoComplete displays a ScreenTip suggesting a previous text entry starting with *Co—Computer System*—but keep typing to enter *Color Laser Printer* instead. You just entered the product labels to describe the data on each row.

e. Click **cell B4** to make it the active cell. Type **Cost** and press **Tab**.

Instead of pressing Enter to move down column B, you pressed Tab to make the cell to the right the active cell.

f. Type the following text in the respective cells, pressing **Tab** after typing each column heading:

- **Markup Rate** in **cell C4**
- **Retail Price** in **cell D4**
- **Percent Off** in **cell E4**
- **Sale Price** in **cell F4**
- **Profit Margin** in **cell G4**

Notice that the text looks cut off when you enter data in the cell to the right. Do not worry about this now. You will adjust column widths and formatting later in this chapter.

TROUBLESHOOTING: If you notice a typographical error, click in the cell containing the error, and then retype the label. Or press F2 to edit the cell contents, move the insertion point using the arrow keys, press Backspace or Delete to delete the incorrect characters, type the correct characters, and then press Enter. If you type a label in an incorrect cell, click the cell, and then press Delete.

g. Save the changes you made to the workbook.

You should develop a habit of saving periodically. That way if your system unexpectedly shuts down, you won't lose everything you worked on.

STEP 2 ENTER UNFORMATTED VALUES

Now that you have entered the descriptive labels, you need to enter the cost, markup rate, and percent off for each product. Refer to Figure 1.6 as you complete Step 2.

	A	B	C	D	E	F	G	H
1	OK Office Systems Pricing Information							
2	1-Sep-12							
3								
4	Product	Cost	Markup Ra	Retail Pric	Percent O	Sale Price	Profit Margin	
5	Computer	400	0.5		0.15			
6	Color Lase	457.7	0.75		0.2			
7	Filing Cab	68.75	0.905		0.1			
8	Desk Chai	75	1		0.25			
9	Solid Oak	700	1.857		0.3			
10	28" Monit	195	0.835		0.1			
11								
12								

FIGURE 1.6 Unformatted Values ➤

a. Click **cell B5** to make it the active cell.

You are ready to enter the amount each product cost your company.

b. Type **400** and press **Enter**.

c. Type the remaining costs in **cells B6** through **B10** as shown in Figure 1.6.

TIP Numeric Keypad

To improve your productivity, you should use the numeric keypad on the right side of your keyboard if your keyboard contains a numeric keypad. If you use a laptop, you can purchase a separate numeric keypad device to use. It is much faster to type values and use Enter on the number keypad rather than using the numbers on the keyboard. Make sure Num Lock is active before using the keypad to enter values.

d. Click **cell C5**, type **0.5**, and then press **Enter**.

You entered the markup rate as a decimal instead of a percentage. You will apply Percent Style later, but now you can concentrate on data entry. When you enter decimal values less than zero, you can type the period and value without typing the zero first, such as *.5*. Excel will automatically add the zero. You can also enter percentages as 50%, but the approach this textbook takes is to enter raw data without typing formatting such as % and then to use number formatting options through Excel to display formatting symbols.

e. Type the remaining markup rates in **cells C6** through **C10** as shown in Figure 1.6.

f. Click **cell E5**, type **0.15**, and then press **Enter**.

You entered the markdown or percent off sale value as a decimal.

g. Type the remaining markdown rates in **cells E6** through **E10** as shown in Figure 1.6, and then save the changes to the workbook.

STEP 3 ENTER A DATE AND CLEAR CELL CONTENTS

As you review the worksheet, you realize you need to provide a date to indicate when the sale starts. Refer to Figure 1.7 as you complete Step 3.

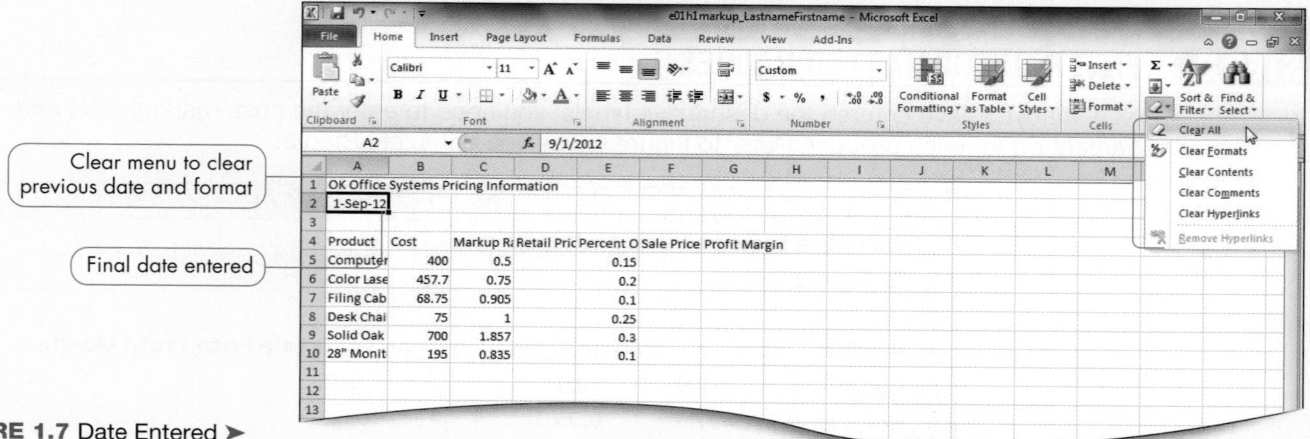

FIGURE 1.7 Date Entered ➤

a. Click **cell A2**, type **9/1/12**, and then press **Enter**.

The date aligns on the right cell margin by default. Note that Excel displays *9/1/2012* instead of *9/1/12* as you entered.

b. Click **cell A2**. Click **Clear** in the Editing group on the Home tab, and then select **Clear All**.

The Clear All command clears both cell contents and formatting in the selected cell(s).

c. Type **September 1, 2012** in **cell A2**, and then press **Enter**.

When you enter a date in the format *September 1, 2012*, Excel displays the date in the customer number format: *1-Sep-12*. However, you can select a date number format in the Format Cells dialog box.

d. Save the workbook. Keep the workbook onscreen if you plan to continue with Hands-On Exercise 2. If not, close the workbook and exit Excel.

Mathematics and Formulas

Formulas transform otherwise static numbers into meaningful results that can update as values change. For example, a payroll manager can build formulas to calculate the gross pay, deductions, and net pay for an organization's employees, or a doctoral student can create formulas to perform various statistical calculations to interpret his or her research data.

Formulas transform otherwise static numbers into meaningful results.

You can use formulas to help you analyze how results will change as the input data change. You can change the value of your assumptions or inputs and explore the results quickly and accurately. For example, if the interest rate changes from 4% to 5%, how would that affect your monthly payment? Analyzing different input values in Excel is easy after you build formulas. Simply change an input value and observe the change in the formula results.

In this section, you will learn how to use mathematical operations in Excel formulas. You will refresh your memory of mathematical order of precedence and how to construct formulas using cell addresses so that when a value of an input cell changes, the result of the formula changes without you having to modify the formula.

Using Symbols and the Order of Precedence

The four mathematical operations—addition, subtraction, multiplication, and division—are the basis of mathematical calculations. Table 1.3 lists the common arithmetic operators and their symbols.

TABLE 1.3 Arithmetic Operators and Symbols

Operation	Common Symbol	Symbol in Excel
Addition	+	+
Subtraction	–	–
Multiplication	×	*
Division	÷	/
Exponentiation	^	^

Enter Cell References in Formulas

Start a formula by typing the equal sign (=), followed by the arithmetic expression. Do not include a space before or after the arithmetic operator. To add the contents of cells A2 and A3, enter =A2+A3 or =A3+A2. Excel uses the value stored in cell A2 (10) and adds it to the value stored in cell A3 (2). The result—12—appears in the cell instead of the formula itself. You can see the formula of the active cell by looking at the Formula Bar. Figure 1.8 shows a worksheet containing data and results of formulas. The figure also displays the actual formulas used to generate the calculated results.

	A	B	C	D
1	Contents		Description	Results
2	10		First input value	10
3	2		Second input value	2
4	=A2+A3		Sum of 10 and 2	12
5	=A2-A3		Difference between 10 and 2	8
6	=A2*A3		Product of 10 and 2	20
7	=A2/A3		Results of dividing 10 by 2	5
8	=A2^A3		Results of 10 to the 2nd power	100

Input values

Output (formula results)

FIGURE 1.8 Formula Results ➤

If you type A2+A3 without the equal sign, Excel does not recognize that you entered a formula and stores the data as text.

You should use cell addresses instead of values as references in formulas where possible. You may include values in an input area—such as dates, salary, or costs—that you will need to reference in formulas. Referencing these cells in your formulas, instead of typing the value of the cell to which you are referring, keeps your formulas accurate if the values change. If you change the value of cell A2 to 5, the result of =A2+A3 displays 7 in cell A4. If you had typed actual values in the formula, =10+2, you would have to edit the formula each time a value changes. Always design worksheets in such a way as to be able to change input values without having to modify your formulas if an input value changes later.

TIP Constants in Formulas

Use cell references instead of actual values in formulas, unless the value is a constant. For example, to calculate the reciprocal of a percentage stored in cell B4, type =1-B4. The constant, 1, represents 100%, a value that never changes, although the percentage in cell B4 might change.

Control the Results with the Order of Precedence

Recall the basic rules of performing calculations from a high school or college math class. What is calculated first in the expression =A1+A2*A3? Remember that multiplication is performed before addition, so the value in cell A2 is multiplied by the value in cell A3. Excel then adds the product to the value in cell A1.

The **order of precedence** controls the sequence in which Excel performs arithmetic operations.

The ***order of precedence*** (also called order of operations) is a rule that controls the sequence in which arithmetic operations are performed, which affects the results of the calculation. Excel performs mathematical calculations left to right in this order: **P**arentheses, **E**xponentiation, **M**ultiplication or **D**ivision, and finally **A**ddition or **S**ubtraction. Some people remember the order of precedence with the phrase **P**lease **E**xcuse **M**y **D**ear **A**unt **S**ally. Therefore, if you want to add the values in A1 and A2 and *then* multiply the sum by the value in cell A3, you need to enclose the addition operation in parentheses =(A1+A2)*A3 since anything in parentheses is calculated first. Without parentheses, multiplication has a higher order of precedence than addition and will be calculated first. Figure 1.9 shows formulas, formula explanations, and formula results based on the order of precedence. The result in cell A12 displays only five digits to the right of the decimal point.

	A	B	C	D
1	10			
2	5			
3	2			
4	4			
5				
6	**Result**		**Formula**	**Explanation**
7	20		=A1+A2*A3	5 x 2 = 10. The product 10 is then added to 10 stored in cell A1.
8	30		=(A1+A2)*A3	10 + 5 = 15. The sum of 15 is then multiplied by 2 stored in cell A3.
9	24		=A1+A2*A3+A4	5 x 2 = 10. 10 + 10 + 4 = 24.
10	90		=(A1+A2)*(A3+A4)	10 + 5 = 15; 2+4 = 6. 15 x 6 = 90.
11	10		=A1/A2+A3*A4	10 / 5 = 2; 2 x 4 = 8; 2 + 8 = 10.
12	5.71429		=A1/(A2+A3)*A4	5 + 2 = 7. 10 / 7 = 1.428571429. 1.42857149 * 4 = 5.714285714

FIGURE 1.9 Formula Results Based on Order of Precedence ➤

Using Auto Fill

Auto Fill enables you to copy the contents of a cell or cell range or to continue a sequence by dragging the fill handle over an adjacent cell or range of cells.

The **fill handle** is a small black square at the bottom-right corner of a cell.

Auto Fill enables you to copy the contents of a cell or a range of cells by dragging the ***fill handle*** (a small black square appearing in the bottom-right corner of a cell) over an adjacent cell or range of cells. To use Auto Fill, do the following:

1. Click the cell with the content you want to copy to make it the active cell.
2. Position the pointer over the bottom-right corner of the cell until it changes to the fill pointer (a thin black plus sign).
3. Drag the fill handle to repeat the content in other cells.

Copying Formulas with Auto Fill. After you enter a formula in a cell, you can duplicate the formula down a column or across a row without retyping it by using Auto Fill. Excel adapts each copied formula based on the type of cell references in the original formula.

Completing Sequences with Auto Fill. You can also use Auto Fill to complete a sequence. For example, if you enter *January* in a cell, you can use Auto Fill to enter the rest of the months in adjacent cells. Other sequences you can complete are quarters (Qtr 1, etc.), weekdays, and weekday abbreviations, by typing the first item and using Auto Fill to complete the other entries. For numeric values, however, you must specify the first two values in sequence. For example, if you want to fill in 5, 10, 15, and so on, you must enter the first two values in two cells, select the two cells, and then use Auto Fill so that Excel knows to increment by 5. Figure 1.10 shows the results of filling in months, abbreviated months, quarters, weekdays, abbreviated weekdays, and increments of 5.

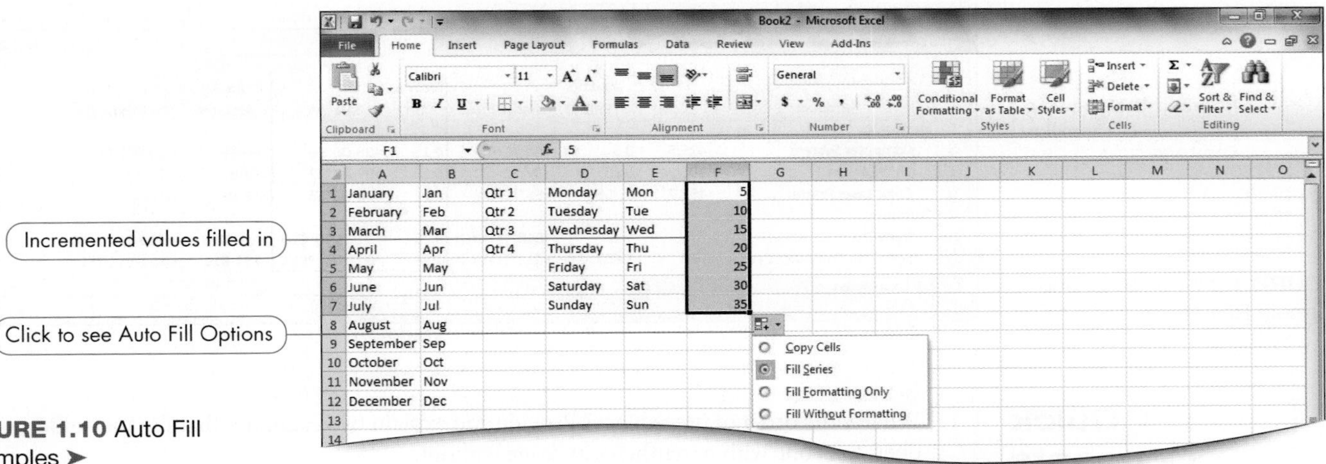

FIGURE 1.10 Auto Fill Examples ➤

Immediately after you use Auto Fill, Excel displays the Auto Fill Options button in the bottom-right corner of the filled data (see Figure 1.10). Click the button to display four options: Copy Cells, Fill Series, Fill Formatting Only, or Fill Without Formatting.

TIP Fill Handle

To copy a formula down a column, double-click the fill handle. Excel will copy the formula in the active cell for each row of data to calculate in your worksheet. Cell addresses change automatically during the Auto Fill process. For example, if the original formula is =A1+B1 and you copy the formula down one cell, the copied formula is =A2+B2.

Displaying Cell Formulas

When you enter a formula, Excel shows the result of the formula in the cell (see the top half of Figure 1.11); however, you might want to display the formulas instead of the calculated results in the cells (see the bottom half of Figure 1.11). The quickest way to display cell formulas is to press Ctrl and the grave accent (`) key, sometimes referred to as the tilde key, in the top-left corner of the keyboard, below Esc. You can also click Show Formulas in the Formula Auditing group on the Formulas tab to show and hide formulas. This is a toggle feature; do the same step to redisplay formula results.

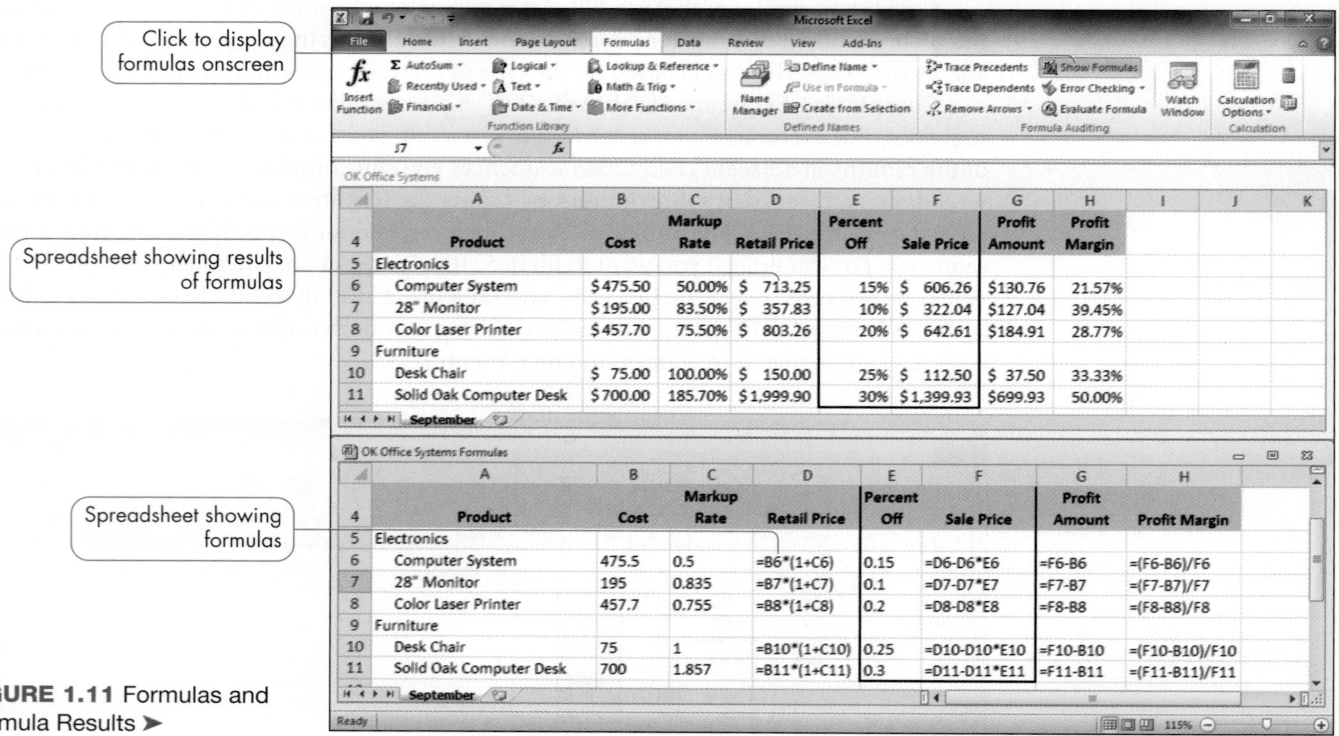

FIGURE 1.11 Formulas and Formula Results ➤

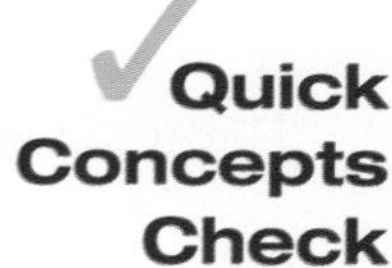

Quick Concepts Check

1. What is the order of precedence? Provide and explain two examples that use four different operators: one with parentheses and one without.
2. What is the purpose of Auto Fill? Provide at least three examples of data you can complete using Auto Fill.
3. Why would it be useful to display formulas instead of formula results in a worksheet?

HANDS-ON EXERCISES

2 Mathematics and Formulas

In Hands-On Exercise 1, you created the basic worksheet for OKOS by entering text, values, and a date for items on sale this week. Now you need to insert formulas to calculate the missing results—specifically, the retail (before sale) value, sale price, and profit margin. You will use cell addresses in your formulas, so when you change a referenced value, the formula results will update automatically.

Skills covered: Enter the Retail Price Formula • Enter the Sale Price Formula • Enter the Profit Margin Formula • Copy Formulas with Auto Fill • Change Values and Display Formulas

STEP 1 ENTER THE RETAIL PRICE FORMULA

The first formula you need to create is one to calculate the retail price. The retail price is the price you originally charge. It is based on a percentage of the original cost so that you earn a profit. Refer to Figure 1.12 as you complete Step 1.

Formula displayed in Formula Bar

Blue border and blue cell reference

Green border and green cell reference

SUM =B5*(1+C5)

	A	B	C	D	E	F	G	H
1	OK Office Systems Pricing Information							
2	1-Sep-12							
3								
4	Product	Cost	Markup Ra	Retail Pric	Percent O	Sale Price	Profit Margin	
5	Computer	400	0.5	=B5*(1+C5)				
6	Color Lase	457.7	0.75		0.2			
7	Filing Cab	68.75	0.905		0.1			
8	Desk Chai	75	1		0.25			
9	Solid Oak	700	1.857		0.3			
10	28" Monit	195	0.835		0.1			
11								
12								

FIGURE 1.12 Retail Formula ➤

a. Open the *e01h1markup_LastnameFirstname* workbook if you closed it after the last Hands-On Exercise, and then save it as **e01h2markup_LastnameFirstname**, changing *h1* to *h2*.

TROUBLESHOOTING: If you make any major mistakes in this exercise, you can close the file, open *e01h1markup_LastnameFirstname* again, and then start this exercise over.

b. Click **cell D5**, the cell where you will enter the formula to calculate the retail selling price of the first item.

c. Type **=B5*(1+C5)** and view the formula and the colored cell borders on the screen.

As you type or edit a formula, each cell address in the formula displays in a specific color, and while you type or edit the formula, the cells referenced in the formula have a temporarily colored border. For example, in the formula =B5*(1+C5), B5 appears in blue, and C5 appears in green. Cell B5 has a temporarily blue border and cell C5 has a temporarily green border to help you identify cells as you construct your formulas (see Figure 1.12).

d. Click **Enter** to the left of the Formula Bar and view the formula.

The result of the formula, 600, appears in cell D5, and the formula displays in the Formula Bar. This formula first adds 1 (the decimal equivalent of 100%) to 0.5 (the value stored in cell C5). Excel multiplies that sum of 1.5 by 400 (the value stored in cell B5). The theory behind this formula is that the retail price is 150% of the original cost.

TIP Alternative Formula

An alternative formula also calculates the correct retail price: =B5*C5+B5 or =B5+B5*C5. In this formula, 400 (cell B5) is multiplied by 0.5 (cell C5); that result (200) represents the dollar value of the markup. Excel adds the value 200 to the original cost of 400 to obtain 600, the retail price. You were instructed to enter =B5*(1+C5) to demonstrate the order of precedence.

TROUBLESHOOTING: If the result is not correct, click the cell and look at the formula in the Formula Bar. Click in the Formula Bar, edit the formula to match the formula shown in step 1c, and then click Enter. Make sure you start the formula with an equal sign.

e. Save the workbook with the new formula.

STEP 2 ENTER THE SALE PRICE FORMULA

Now that you calculated the retail price, you want to calculate a sale price. This week, the computer is on sale for 15% off the retail price. Refer to Figure 1.13 as you complete Step 2.

F5 fx =D5-D5*E5

	A	B	C	D	E	F	G	H
1	OK Office Systems Pricing Information							
2	1-Sep-12							
3								
4	Product	Cost	Markup Ra	Retail Pric	Percent O	Sale Price	Profit Margin	
5	Computer	400	0.5	600	0.15	510		
6	Color Lase	457.7	0.75		0.2			
7	Filing Cab	68.75	0.905		0.1			
8	Desk Chai	75	1		0.25			
9	Solid Oak	700	1.857		0.3			
10	28" Monit	195	0.835		0.1			
11								
12								

FIGURE 1.13 Sale Price Formula ➤

a. Click **cell F5**, the cell where you will enter the formula to calculate the sale price.

b. Type **=D5-D5*E5** and notice the color-coding in the cell addresses. Press **Ctrl+Enter** to keep the current cell the active cell.

The result is 510. Looking at the formula, you might think D5-D5 equals zero; remember that because of the order of precedence rules, multiplication is calculated before subtraction. The product of 600 (cell D5) and 0.15 (cell E5) equals 90, which is then subtracted from 600 (cell D5), so the sale price is 510. If it helps to understand the formula better, add parentheses: =D5-(D5*E5).

TIP Spot-Check Your Work

You can check the result for logic. Use a calculator to spot-check the accuracy of formulas. If you mark down merchandise by 15% of its regular price, you are charging 85% of the regular price. You can spot-check your formula to ensure that 85% of 600 is 510 by multiplying 600 by 0.85.

c. View the Formula Bar, and then save the workbook with the new formula.

The Formula Bar displays the formula you entered.

STEP 3 ENTER THE PROFIT MARGIN FORMULA

After calculating the sale price, you want to know the profit margin you earn. You paid $400 for the computer and will sell it for $510. The profit is $110, which gives you a profit margin of 21.57%. Refer to Figure 1.14 as you complete Step 3.

G5 =(F5-B5)/F5

	A	B	C	D	E	F	G	H
1	OK Office Systems Pricing Information							
2	1-Sep-12							
3								
4	Product	Cost	Markup Ra	Retail Pric	Percent O	Sale Price	Profit Margin	
5	Computer	400	0.5	600	0.15	510	0.215686	
6	Color Lase	457.7	0.75		0.2			
7	Filing Cab	68.75	0.905		0.1			
8	Desk Chai	75	1		0.25			
9	Solid Oak	700	1.857		0.3			
10	28" Monit	195	0.835		0.1			
11								
12								

FIGURE 1.14 Profit Margin Formula ➤

a. Click **cell G5**, the cell where you will enter the formula to calculate the profit margin.

The profit margin is the profit (difference in sales price and cost) percentage of the sale price. This amount represents the amount to cover operating expenses and tax, which are not covered in this analysis.

b. Type **=(F5-B5)/F5** and notice the color-coding in the cell addresses. Press **Ctrl+Enter**.

The formula must first calculate the profit, which is the difference between the sale price (510) and the original cost (400). The difference (110) is then divided by the sale price (510) to determine the profit margin of 0.215686 or 21.6%.

TROUBLESHOOTING: If you type a backslash (\) instead of a forward slash (/), Excel will display an error message box. Make sure you type / as the division operator.

c. Look at the Formula Bar, and then save the workbook with the new formula.

The Formula Bar displays the formula you entered.

STEP 4 COPY FORMULAS WITH AUTO FILL

After double-checking the accuracy of your calculations for the first product, you are ready to copy the formulas down the columns to calculate the retail price, sale price, and profit margin for the other products. Refer to Figure 1.15 as you complete Step 4.

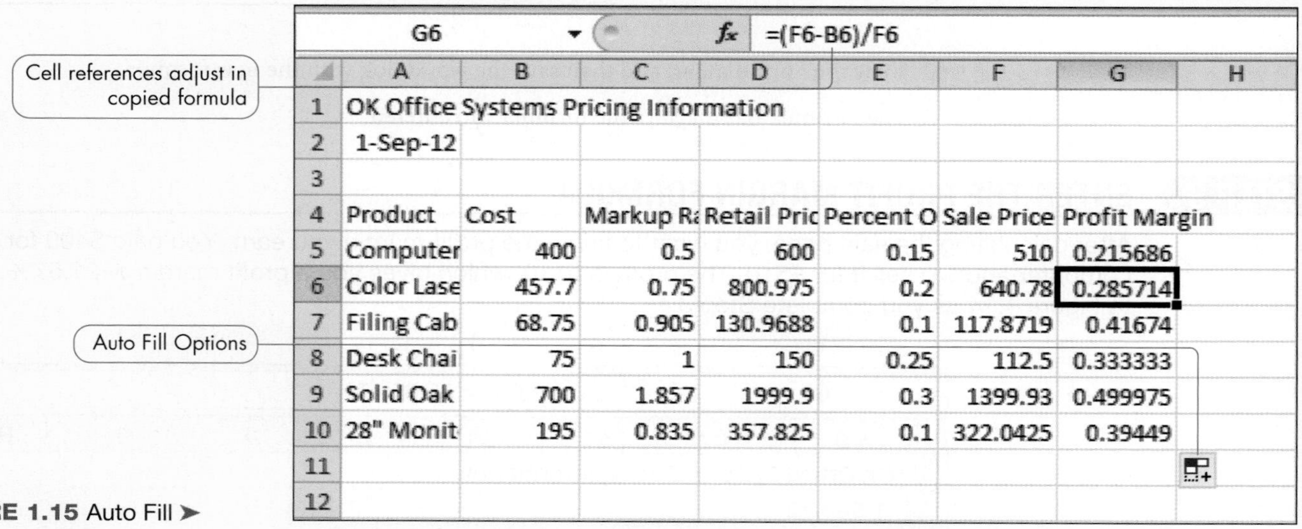

	A	B	C	D	E	F	G	H
1	OK Office Systems Pricing Information							
2	1-Sep-12							
3								
4	Product	Cost	Markup Ra	Retail Pric	Percent O	Sale Price	Profit Margin	
5	Computer	400	0.5	600	0.15	510	0.215686	
6	Color Lase	457.7	0.75	800.975	0.2	640.78	0.285714	
7	Filing Cab	68.75	0.905	130.9688	0.1	117.8719	0.41674	
8	Desk Chai	75	1	150	0.25	112.5	0.333333	
9	Solid Oak	700	1.857	1999.9	0.3	1399.93	0.499975	
10	28" Monit	195	0.835	357.825	0.1	322.0425	0.39449	
11								
12								

FIGURE 1.15 Auto Fill ➤

a. Click **cell D5**, the cell containing the formula to calculate the retail price for the first item.

b. Position the mouse pointer on the fill handle in the bottom-right corner of **cell D5**. When the pointer changes from a white plus sign to a thin black plus sign, double-click the **fill handle**.

Excel's Auto Fill feature copies the retail price formula for the remaining products in your worksheet. Excel detects when to stop copying the formula when it encounters a blank row, such as in row 11.

c. Click **cell D6**, the cell containing the first copied retail price formula, and look at the Formula Bar.

The original formula was =B5*(1+C5). The copied formula in cell D6 is =B6*(1+C6). Excel adjusts the cell addresses in the formula as it copies the formula down a column so that the results are based on each row's data rather than using the original formula's cell addresses for other products.

d. Select the **range F5:G5**. Double-click the **fill handle** in the bottom-right corner of **cell G5**.

Auto Fill copies the selected formulas down their respective columns. Notice Auto Fill Options down and to the right of the cell G10 fill handle, indicating you could select different fill options if you want.

e. Click **cell F6**, the cell containing the first copied sale price formula, and view the Formula Bar.

The original formula was =D5-D5*E5. The copied formula in cell F6 is =D6-D6*E6.

f. Click **cell G6**, the cell containing the first copied profit margin formula, and look at the Formula Bar. Save the changes to your workbook.

The original formula was =(F5-B5)/F5. The copied formula in cell G6 is =(F6-B6)/F6.

STEP 5 CHANGE VALUES AND DISPLAY FORMULAS

You want to see how the prices and profit margins are affected when you change some of the original values. For example, the supplier might notify you that the cost to you will increase. In addition, you want to see the formulas displayed in the cells temporarily. Refer to Figures 1.16 and 1.17 as you complete Step 5.

E8 | f_x 0.25

	A	B	C	D	E	F	G	H
1	OK Office Systems Pricing Information							
2	1-Sep-12							
3								
4	Product	Cost	Markup Ra	Retail Pric	Percent O	Sale Price	Profit Margin	
5	Computer	475.5	0.5	713.25	0.15	606.2625	0.215686	
6	Color Lase	457.7	0.755	803.2635	0.2	642.6108	0.287749	
7	Filing Cab	68.75	0.905	130.9688	0.05	124.4203	0.447437	
8	Desk Chai	75	1	150	0.25	112.5	0.333333	
9	Solid Oak	700	1.857	1999.9	0.3	1399.93	0.499975	
10	28" Monit	195	0.835	357.825	0.1	322.0425	0.39449	
11								
12								

Updated formula results

Changed values

FIGURE 1.16 Results of Changed Values ➤

a. Click **cell B5**, type **475.5**, and then press **Enter**.

The results of the retail price, sale price, and profit margin formulas change based on the new cost.

b. Click **cell C6**, type **0.755**, and then press **Enter**.

The results of the retail price, sale price, and profit margin formulas change based on the new markup rate.

c. Click **cell E7**, type **0.05**, and then press **Enter**.

The results of the sale price and profit margin formulas change based on the new markdown rate. Note that the retail price did not change since that formula is not based on the markdown rate.

d. Press **Ctrl+`** (the grave accent mark).

The workbook now displays the formulas rather than the formula results (see Figure 1.17). This is helpful when you want to review several formulas at one time.

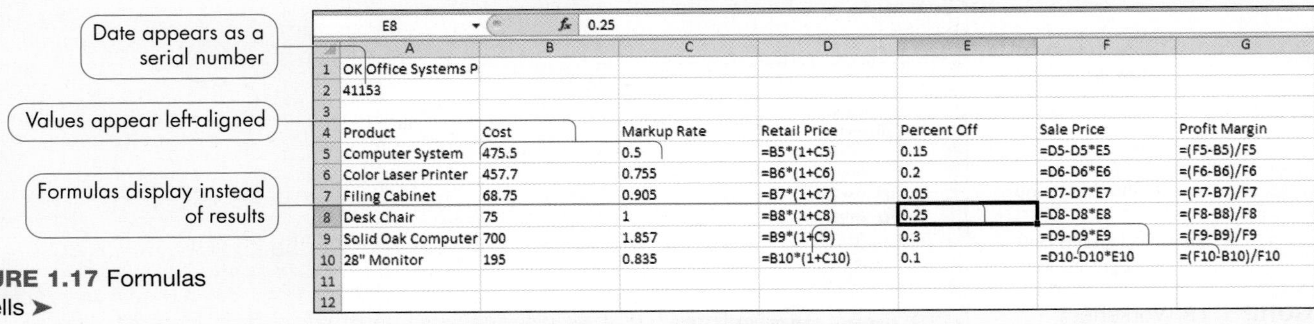

	A	B	C	D	E	F	G
1	OK Office Systems P						
2	41153						
3							
4	Product	Cost	Markup Rate	Retail Price	Percent Off	Sale Price	Profit Margin
5	Computer System	475.5	0.5	=B5*(1+C5)	0.15	=D5-D5*E5	=(F5-B5)/F5
6	Color Laser Printer	457.7	0.755	=B6*(1+C6)	0.2	=D6-D6*E6	=(F6-B6)/F6
7	Filing Cabinet	68.75	0.905	=B7*(1+C7)	0.05	=D7-D7*E7	=(F7-B7)/F7
8	Desk Chair	75	1	=B8*(1+C8)	0.25	=D8-D8*E8	=(F8-B8)/F8
9	Solid Oak Computer	700	1.857	=B9*(1+C9)	0.3	=D9-D9*E9	=(F9-B9)/F9
10	28" Monitor	195	0.835	=B10*(1+C10)	0.1	=D10-D10*E10	=(F10-B10)/F10
11							
12							

FIGURE 1.17 Formulas in Cells ➤

e. Press **Ctrl+`** (the grave accent mark).

The workbook now displays the formula results in the cells again.

f. Save the workbook. Keep the workbook onscreen if you plan to continue with Hands-On Exercise 3. If not, close the workbook and exit Excel.

Workbook and Worksheet Management

When you start a new blank workbook in Excel, the workbook contains three worksheets named Sheet1, Sheet2, and Sheet3. The text, values, dates, and formulas you enter into the individual sheets are saved under the one workbook file name. Having multiple worksheets in one workbook is helpful to keep related items together. For example, you might want one worksheet for each month to track your monthly income and expenses for one year. When tax time rolls around, you have all your data stored in one workbook file.

Although you should plan the worksheet and workbook before you start entering data, you might need to add, delete, or rename worksheets. Furthermore, within a worksheet you may want to insert a new row to accommodate new data, delete a column that you no longer need, adjust the size of columns and rows, or move or copy data to other locations.

In this section, you will learn how to manage workbooks by renaming, inserting, and deleting worksheets. You will also learn how to make changes to worksheet columns and rows, such as inserting, deleting, and adjusting sizes. Finally, you will learn how to move and copy data within a worksheet.

Managing Worksheets

Creating a multiple-worksheet workbook takes some planning and maintenance. Worksheet tab names should reflect the contents of the respective worksheets. In addition, you can insert, copy, move, and delete worksheets within the workbook. You can even apply background color to the worksheet tabs so that they stand out onscreen. Figure 1.18 shows a workbook in which the sheet tabs have been renamed, colors have been applied to worksheet tabs, and a worksheet tab has been right-clicked so that the shortcut menu appears.

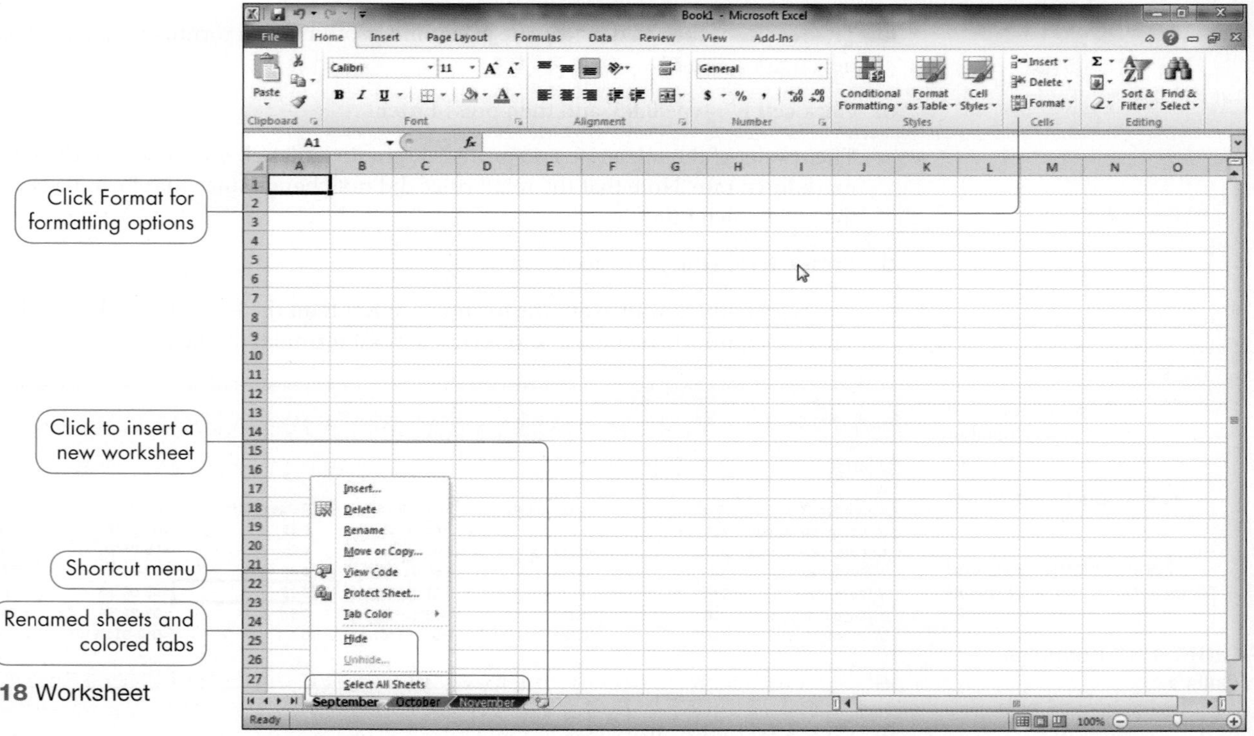

FIGURE 1.18 Worksheet Tabs ➤

Rename Worksheets

The default worksheet names—Sheet1, Sheet2, and Sheet3—are vague; they do not describe the contents of each worksheet. You should rename the worksheet tabs to reflect the sheet contents so that you, and anyone with whom you share your workbook, will be able to find data. For example, if your budget workbook contains monthly worksheets, name the worksheets *September*, *October*, etc. A teacher who uses a workbook to store a grade book for several classes should name each worksheet by class name or number, such as *MIS 1000* and *MIS 3430*. Although you can have spaces in worksheet names, you should keep worksheet names relatively short. The longer the worksheet names, the fewer sheet tabs you will see at the bottom of the workbook window without scrolling.

To rename a worksheet, do one of the following:

- Double-click a sheet tab, type the new name, and then press Enter.
- Click Format in the Cells group on the Home tab (see Figure 1.18), select Rename Sheet (see Figure 1.19), type the new sheet name, and then press Enter.
- Right-click the sheet tab, select Rename from the shortcut menu (see Figure 1.18), type the new sheet name, and then press Enter.

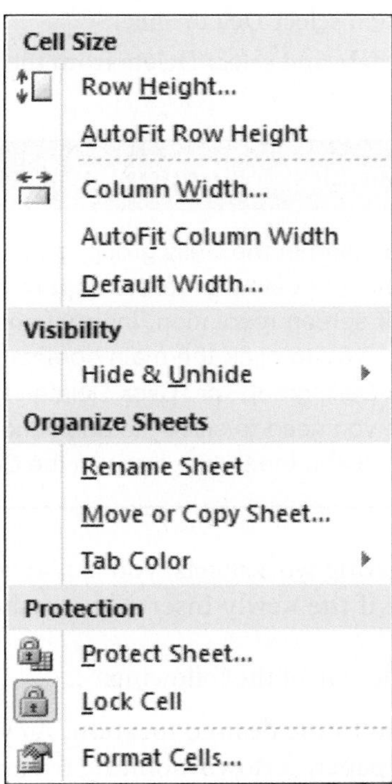

FIGURE 1.19 Format Menu ➤

Change Worksheet Tab Color

The active worksheet tab is white, whereas the default color of the tabs depends on the Windows color scheme. When you use multiple worksheets, you might want to apply a different color to each worksheet tab to make the tab stand out or to emphasize the difference between sheets. For example, you might apply red to the September tab, green to the October tab, and dark blue to the November tab.

To change the color of a worksheet tab, do one of the following:

- Click Format in the Cells group on the Home tab (see Figure 1.18), point to Tab Color (see Figure 1.19), and then click a color on the Tab Color palette.
- Right-click the sheet tab, point to Tab Color on the shortcut menu (see Figure 1.18), and then click a color on the Tab Color palette.

Insert, Delete, Move, and Copy Worksheets

Sometimes you need more worksheets in the workbook than the three default sheets. For example, you might create a workbook that contains 12 worksheets—a worksheet for each month of the year. Each new worksheet you insert starts with a default name, such as Sheet4, numbered consecutively after the last Sheet#. After inserting worksheets, you can rename them to be more descriptive. You can delete extra worksheets from your workbook to keep it streamlined.

To insert a new worksheet, do one of the following:

- Click Insert Worksheet to the right of the last worksheet tab.
- Click the Insert arrow—either to the right or below Insert—in the Cells group on the Home tab, and then select Insert Sheet.
- Right-click any sheet tab, select Insert from the shortcut menu (see Figure 1.18), click Worksheet in the Insert dialog box, and then click OK.
- Press Shift+F11.

To delete a worksheet in a workbook, do one of the following:

- Click the Delete arrow—either to the right or below Delete—in the Cells group on the Home tab, and then select Delete Sheet.
- Right-click any sheet tab, and select Delete from the shortcut menu (see Figure 1.18).

TIP Ribbon Commands with Arrows

Some commands, such as Insert in the Cells group, contain two parts: the main command and an arrow. The arrow may be below or to the right of the command, depending on the command, window size, or screen resolution. Instructions in the Exploring Series use the command name to instruct you to click the main command to perform the default action, such as "Click Insert in the Cells group" or "Click Delete in the Cells group." Instructions include the word *arrow* when you need to select an additional option, such as "Click the Insert arrow in the Cells group" or "Click the Delete arrow in the Cells group."

After inserting and deleting worksheets, you can arrange the worksheet tabs in a different sequence, especially if the newly inserted worksheets do not fall within a logical sequence.

To move a worksheet, do one of the following:

- Drag a worksheet tab to the desired location. As you drag a sheet tab, the pointer resembles a piece of paper. A down-pointing triangle appears between sheet tabs to indicate where the sheet will be moved when you release the mouse button.
- Click Format in the Cells group on the Home tab (see Figure 1.18) or right-click the sheet tab you want to move, and select Move or Copy to see the Move or Copy dialog box (see Figure 1.20). Select the workbook if you want to move the sheet to another workbook. In the *Before sheet* list, select the worksheet on whose left side you want the moved worksheet to be located, and then click OK. For example, assume the October worksheet was selected before displaying the dialog box. You then select November so that the October sheet moves before (or to the left) of November.

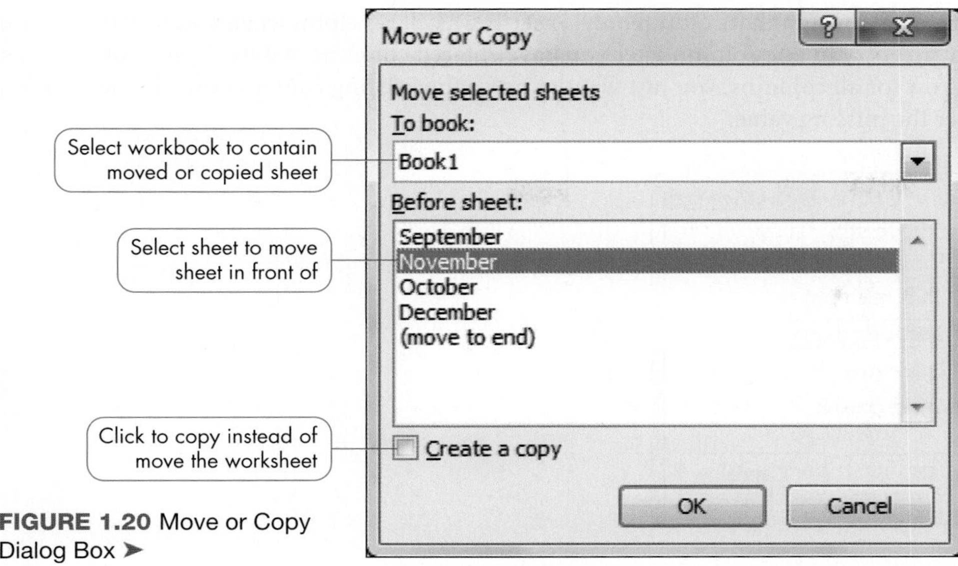

FIGURE 1.20 Move or Copy Dialog Box ➤

The process for copying a worksheet is similar to moving a sheet. To copy a worksheet, press and hold Ctrl as you drag the worksheet tab. Alternatively, display the Move or Copy dialog box, select the options (see Figure 1.20), click the *Create a copy* check box, and then click OK.

Managing Columns and Rows

As you enter and edit worksheet data, you can adjust the row and column structure. You can add rows and columns to accommodate new data, or you can delete data you no longer need. Adjusting the height and width of columns and rows can present the data better.

Insert Cells, Columns, and Rows

After you construct a worksheet, you might need to insert cells, columns, or rows to accommodate new data. For example, you might need to insert a new column to perform calculations or a new row to list a new product. When you insert cells, rows, and columns, cell addresses in formulas adjust automatically.

To insert a new column or row, do one of the following:

- Click in the column or row for which you want to insert a new column to the left or a new row above, respectively. Click the Insert arrow in the Cells group on the Home tab, and then select Insert Sheet Columns or Insert Sheet Rows.
- Right-click the column letter or row number for which you want to insert a new column to the left or a new row above, respectively, and select Insert from the shortcut menu.

Excel inserts new columns to the *left* of the current column and new rows *above* the current row. If the current column is column C and you insert a new column, the new column becomes column C, and the original column C data are now in column D. Likewise, if the current row is 5 and you insert a new row, the new row is row 5, and the original row 5 data are now in row 6.

You can insert a single cell in a particular row or column. To insert a cell, click in the cell where you want the new cell, click the Insert arrow in the Cells group on the Home tab, and then select Insert Cells. Select an option from the Insert dialog box (see Figure 1.21) to position the new cell, and then click OK. Alternatively, click Insert in the Cells group. The default action of clicking Insert is to insert a cell at the current location, which moves existing data down in that column only. Inserting a cell is helpful when you realize that you left out an entry in one column after you have entered columns of data. Instead of inserting a new row for all columns, you just want to move the existing content down in one column to enter the missing value.

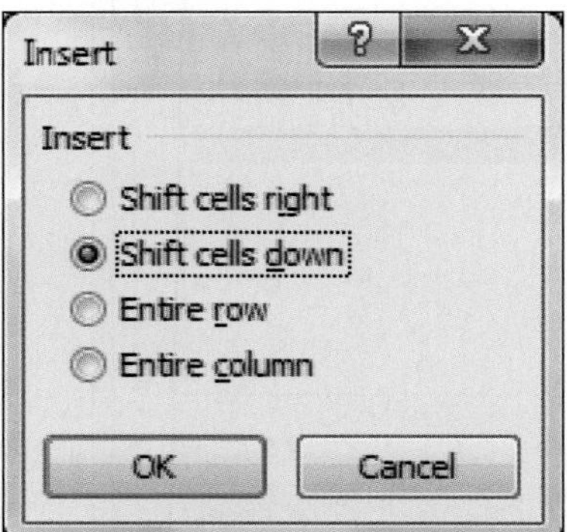

FIGURE 1.21 Insert Dialog Box ➤

Delete Cells, Columns, and Rows

If you no longer need a cell, column, or row, you can delete it. In these situations, you are deleting the entire cell, column, or row, not just the contents of the cell to leave empty cells. As with inserting new cells, any affected formulas adjust the cell references automatically. To delete a column or row, do one of the following:

- Click the column or row heading for the column or row you want to delete. Click Delete in the Cells group on the Home tab.
- Click in any cell within the column or row you want to delete. Click the Delete arrow in the Cells group on the Home tab, and then select Delete Sheet Columns or Delete Sheet Rows, respectively.
- Right-click the column letter or row number for the column or row you want to delete, and then select Delete from the shortcut menu.

To delete a cell or cells, select the cell(s), click the Delete arrow in the Cells group, and then select Delete Cells to display the Delete dialog box (see Figure 1.22). Click the appropriate option to shift cells left or up, and then click OK. Alternatively, click Delete in the Cells group. The default action of clicking Delete is to delete the active cell, which moves existing data up in that column only.

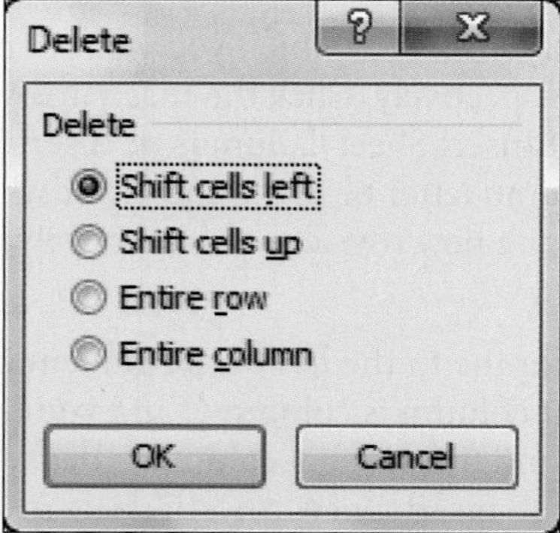

FIGURE 1.22 Delete Dialog Box ➤

Adjust Column Width

Column width is the horizontal measurement of a column.

After you enter data in a column, you often need to adjust the ***column width***—the number of characters that can fit horizontally using the default font or the number of horizontal pixels—to show the contents of cells. For example, in the worksheet you created in Hands-On Exercises 1 and 2, the labels in column A displayed into column B when those adjacent cells were empty. However, after you typed values in column B, the labels in column A appeared truncated, or cut off. You will need to widen column A to show the full name of all of your products. Numbers appear as a series of pound signs (######) when the cell is too narrow to display the complete value, and text appears to be truncated.

To widen a column to accommodate the longest label or value in a column, do one of the following:

- Position the pointer on the vertical border between the current column heading and the next column heading. When the pointer displays as a two-headed arrow, double-click the border. For example, if column B is too narrow to display the content in that column, double-click the border between the column B and C headings.
- Click Format in the Cells group on the Home tab (see Figure 1.18), and then select AutoFit Column Width (see Figure 1.19).

You can drag the vertical border to the left to decrease the column width or to the right to increase the column width. As you drag the vertical border, Excel displays a ScreenTip specifying the width (see Figure 1.23). Excel column widths range from 0 to 255 characters. The final way to change column width is to click Format in the Cells group on the Home tab (see Figure 1.18), select Column Width (see Figure 1.19), type a value in the Column width box in the Column Width dialog box, and then click OK.

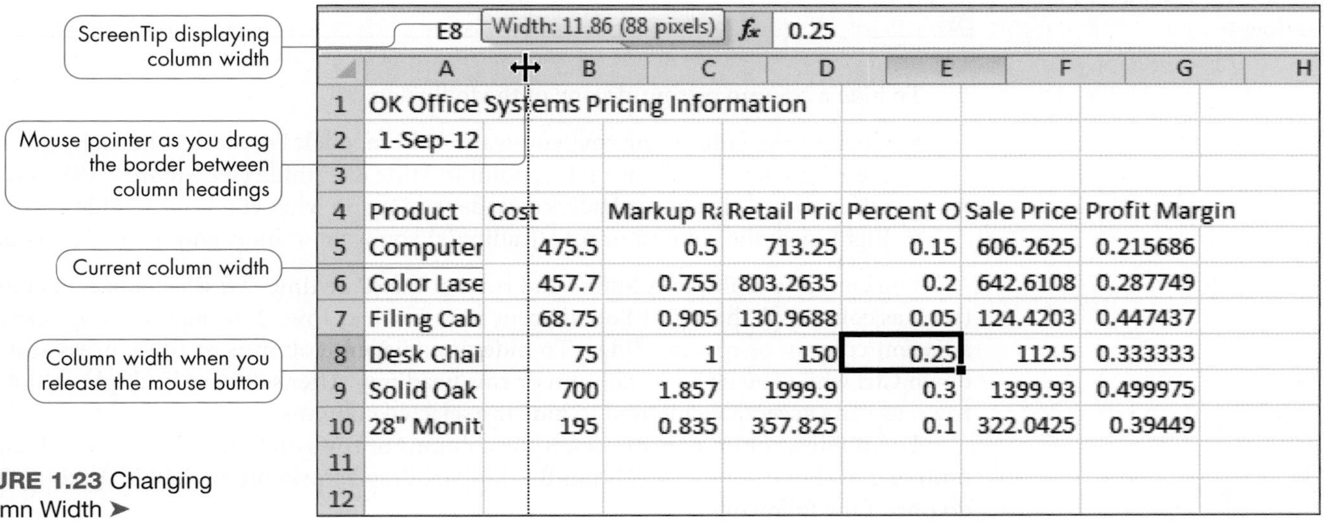

ScreenTip displaying column width

Mouse pointer as you drag the border between column headings

Current column width

Column width when you release the mouse button

E8 Width: 11.86 (88 pixels) fx 0.25

	A	B	C	D	E	F	G	H
1	OK Office Systems Pricing Information							
2	1-Sep-12							
3								
4	Product	Cost	Markup Ra	Retail Pric	Percent O	Sale Price	Profit Margin	
5	Computer	475.5	0.5	713.25	0.15	606.2625	0.215686	
6	Color Lase	457.7	0.755	803.2635	0.2	642.6108	0.287749	
7	Filing Cab	68.75	0.905	130.9688	0.05	124.4203	0.447437	
8	Desk Chai	75	1	150	0.25	112.5	0.333333	
9	Solid Oak	700	1.857	1999.9	0.3	1399.93	0.499975	
10	28" Monit	195	0.835	357.825	0.1	322.0425	0.39449	
11								
12								

FIGURE 1.23 Changing Column Width ➤

Adjust Row Height

Row height is the vertical measurement of a row.

When you increase the font size of cell contents, Excel automatically increases the ***row height***—the vertical measurement of the row. However, if you insert a line break to create multiple lines of text in a cell, Excel might not increase the row height. You can adjust the row height in a way similar to how you change column width by double-clicking the border between row numbers or by selecting Row Height or AutoFit Row Height from the Format menu (see Figure 1.19). In Excel, row height is a value between 0 and 409 based on point size (abbreviated as *pt*). Whether you are measuring font sizes or row heights, one point size is equal to 1/72 of an inch. Your row height should be taller than your font size. For example, with an 11 pt font size, the default row height is 15.

TIP Multiple Column Widths and Row Heights

You can set the size for more than one column or row at a time to make the selected columns or rows the same size. Drag across the column or row headings for the area you want to format, and then set the size using any method.

Hide and Unhide Columns and Rows

If your worksheet contains confidential information, such as social security numbers or salary information, you might need to hide some columns and/or rows before you print a copy for public distribution. When you hide a column or a row, Excel prevents that column or row from displaying or printing. However, the column or row is not deleted. If you hide column B, you will see columns A and C side by side. If you hide row 9, you will see rows 8 and 10 together. Figure 1.24 shows that column B and row 9 are hidden. Excel displays a thicker border between column headings (such as between A and C), indicating one or more columns are hidden, and between row headings (such as between 8 and 10), indicating one or more rows are hidden.

Column B hidden (thicker border)

Row 9 hidden (thicker border)

	A	C	D	E	F	G	H	I	J	K	L
1	OK Office Systems Pricing Information										
2	1-Sep-12										
3											
4	Product	Markup Ra	Retail Pric	Percent O	Sale Price	Profit Margin					
5	Computer System	0.5	713.25	0.15	606.263	0.21569					
6	Color Laser Printer	0.755	803.264	0.2	642.611	0.28775					
7	Filing Cabinet	0.905	130.969	0.05	124.42	0.44744					
8	Desk Chair	1	150	0.25	112.5	0.33333					
10	28" Monitor	0.835	357.825	0.1	322.043	0.39449					
11											
12											

FIGURE 1.24 Hidden Column and Row ➤

To hide a column or row, do one of the following:

- Click in the column or row you want to hide, click Format in the Cells group on the Home tab (see Figure 1.18), point to Hide & Unhide (see Figure 1.19), and then select Hide Columns or Hide Rows, depending on what you want to hide.
- Right-click the column or row heading(s) you want to hide, and then select Hide.

You can hide multiple columns and rows at the same time. To select adjacent columns (such as columns B through E) or adjacent rows (such as rows 2 through 4), drag across the adjacent column or row headings. To hide nonadjacent columns or rows, press and hold down Ctrl while you click the column or row headings. After selecting multiple columns or rows, use any acceptable method to hide the selected columns or rows.

To unhide a column or row, select the columns or rows on both sides of the hidden column or row. For example, if column B is hidden, drag across column letters A and C. Then do one of the following:

- Click Format in the Cells group on the Home tab (see Figure 1.18), point to Hide & Unhide (see Figure 1.19), and then select Unhide Columns or Unhide Rows, depending on what you want to display again.
- Right-click the column(s) or row(s) you want to hide, and then select Unhide.

TIP Unhiding Column A, Row 1, and All Hidden Rows/Columns

Unhiding column A or row 1 is different because you cannot select the row or column on either side. To unhide column A or row 1, type A1 in the Name Box, and then press Enter. Click Format in the Cells group on the Home tab, point to Hide & Unhide, and then select Unhide Columns or Unhide Rows to display column A or row 1, respectively. If you want to unhide all columns and rows, click Select All, and then use the Hide & Unhide submenu.

Selecting, Moving, Copying, and Pasting

In the Office Fundamentals chapter, you learned the basics of selecting, cutting, copying, and pasting data. These tasks are somewhat different when working in Excel.

Select a Range

A **range** is a rectangular group of cells.

A **nonadjacent range** contains multiple ranges of cells.

A ***range*** refers to a group of adjacent or contiguous cells. A range may be as small as a single cell or as large as the entire worksheet. It may consist of a row or part of a row, a column or part of a column, or multiple rows or columns, but will always be a rectangular shape, as you must select the same number of cells in each row or column for the entire range. A range is specified by indicating the top-left and bottom-right cells in the selection. For example, in Figure 1.25, the date is a single-cell range in cell A2, the Color Laser Printer data are stored in the range A6:G6, the cost values are stored in the range B5:B10, and the sales prices and profit margins are stored in range F5:G10. A ***nonadjacent range*** contains multiple ranges, such as C5:C10 and E5:E10. At times, you need to select nonadjacent ranges so that you can apply the same formatting at the same time, such as formatting the nonadjacent range C5:C10 and E5:E10 with Percent Style.

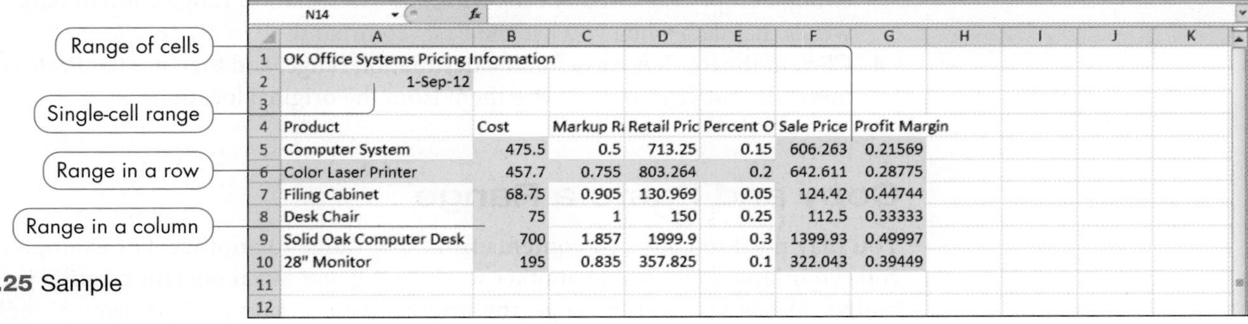

FIGURE 1.25 Sample Ranges ➤

Table 1.4 lists methods you can use to select ranges, including nonadjacent ranges.

TABLE 1.4 Selecting Ranges

To Select:	Do This:
A Range	Click the first cell and drag until you select the entire range. Alternatively, click the first cell in the range, press and hold down Shift, and then click the last cell in the range.
An Entire Column	Click the column heading.
An Entire Row	Click the row heading.
Current Range Containing Data	Click in the range of data and then press Ctrl+A.
All Cells in a Worksheet	Click Select All, or press Ctrl+A twice.
Nonadjacent Range	Select the first range, press and hold down Ctrl, and then select additional range(s).

A border appears around a selected range. Any command you execute will affect the entire range. The range remains selected until you select another range or click in any cell in the worksheet.

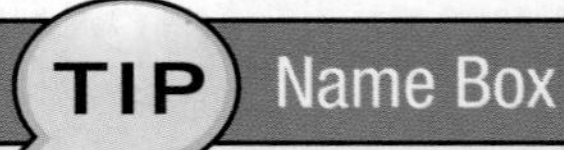

You can use the Name Box to select a range by clicking in the Name Box, typing a range address such as B15:D25, and then pressing Enter.

Move a Range to Another Location

You can move cell contents from one range to another. For example, you might need to move an input area from the right side of the worksheet to above the output range. When you move a range containing text and values, the text and values do not change. However, any formulas that refer to cells in that range will update to reflect the new cell addresses. To move a range, do the following:

1. Select the range.
2. Use the Cut command to copy the range to the Clipboard. Excel outlines the range you cut with a moving dashed border. Unlike cutting data in other Office applications, the data you cut in Excel remain in their locations until you paste them elsewhere. After you use Cut, the status bar displays *Select destination and press ENTER or choose Paste.*
3. Make sure the destination range—the range where you want to move the data—has enough empty cells. If any cells within the destination range contain data, Excel overwrites that data when you use the Paste command.
4. Click in the top-left corner of the destination range, and then use the Paste command to insert the cut cells and remove them from the original location.

Copy and Paste a Range

You may need to copy cell contents from one range to another. For example, you might copy your January budget to another worksheet to use as a model for creating your February budget. When you copy a range, the original data remain in their original locations. Cell references in copied formulas adjust based on their relative locations to the original data. To copy a range, do the following:

1. Select the range.
2. Use the Copy command to copy the contents of the selected range to the Clipboard. Excel outlines the range you copied with a moving dashed border. After you use Copy, the status bar displays *Select destination and press ENTER or choose Paste.*
3. Make sure the destination range—the range where you want to copy the data—has enough empty cells. If any cells within the destination range contain data, Excel overwrites that data when you use the Paste command.
4. Click in the top-left corner of the destination range where you want the duplicate data, and then use the Paste command. The original selected range remains selected with a moving dashed border around it.
5. Press Esc to deselect the range. Figure 1.26 shows a selected range and a copy of the range.

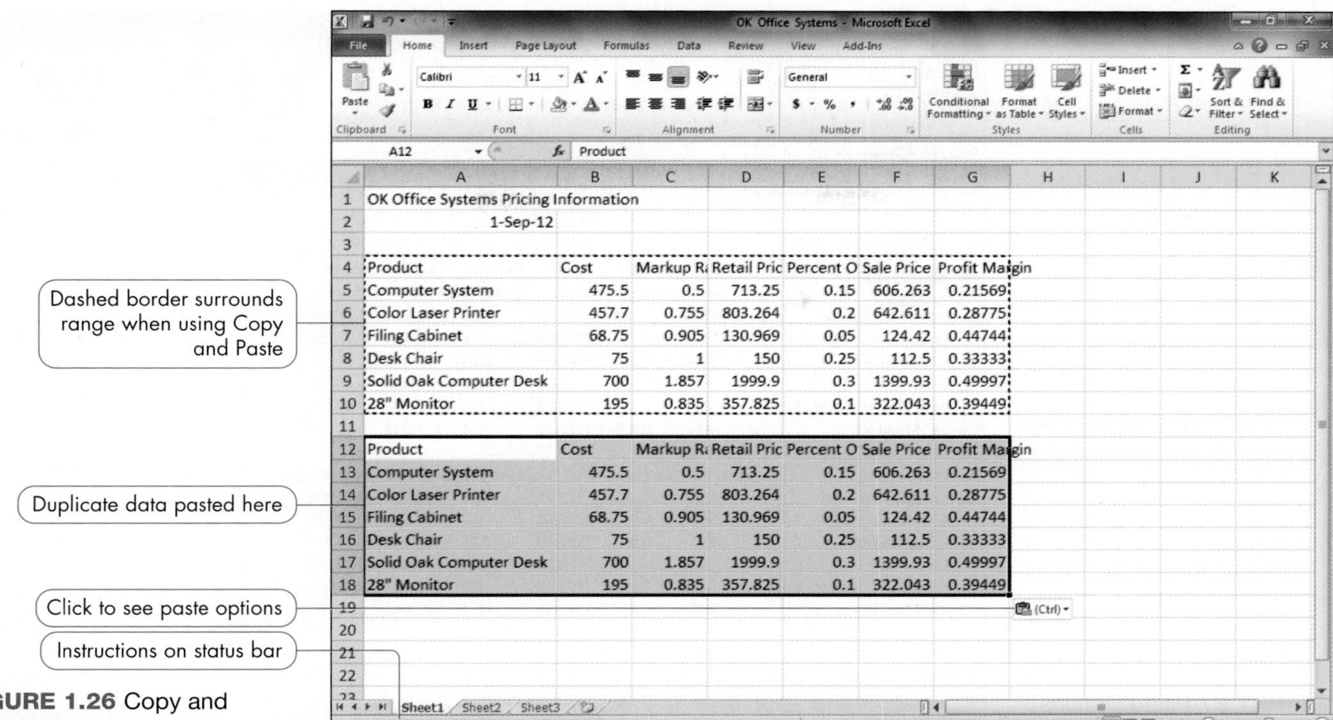

FIGURE 1.26 Copy and Pasted Range ➤

> **TIP** Copy as Picture
>
> Instead of clicking Copy, if you click the Copy arrow in the Clipboard group, you can select Copy (the default option) or Copy as Picture. When you select Copy as Picture, you copy an *image* of the selected data. You can then paste the image elsewhere in the workbook or in a Word document or PowerPoint presentation. However, when you copy the data as an image, you cannot edit individual cell data when you paste the image.

> **TIP** Paste Options Button
>
> When you copy or paste data, Excel displays Paste Options in the bottom-right corner of the pasted data (see Figure 1.26). Click Paste Options to see different results for the pasted data.

Use Paste Special

Sometimes you might want to paste data in a different format than they are in in the Clipboard. For example, you might want to copy a range containing formulas and cell references, and paste the range as values in another workbook that does not have the referenced cells. If you want to copy data from Excel and paste them into a Word document, you can paste the Excel data as a worksheet object, as unformatted text, or in another format. To paste data from the Clipboard into a different format, click the Paste arrow in the Clipboard group, and hover over a command to see a ScreenTip and a preview of how the pasted data will look. In Figure 1.27, the preview shows that a particular paste option will maintain formulas and number formatting; however, it will not maintain the text formatting, such as font color and centered text. After previewing different paste options, click the one you want in order to apply it.

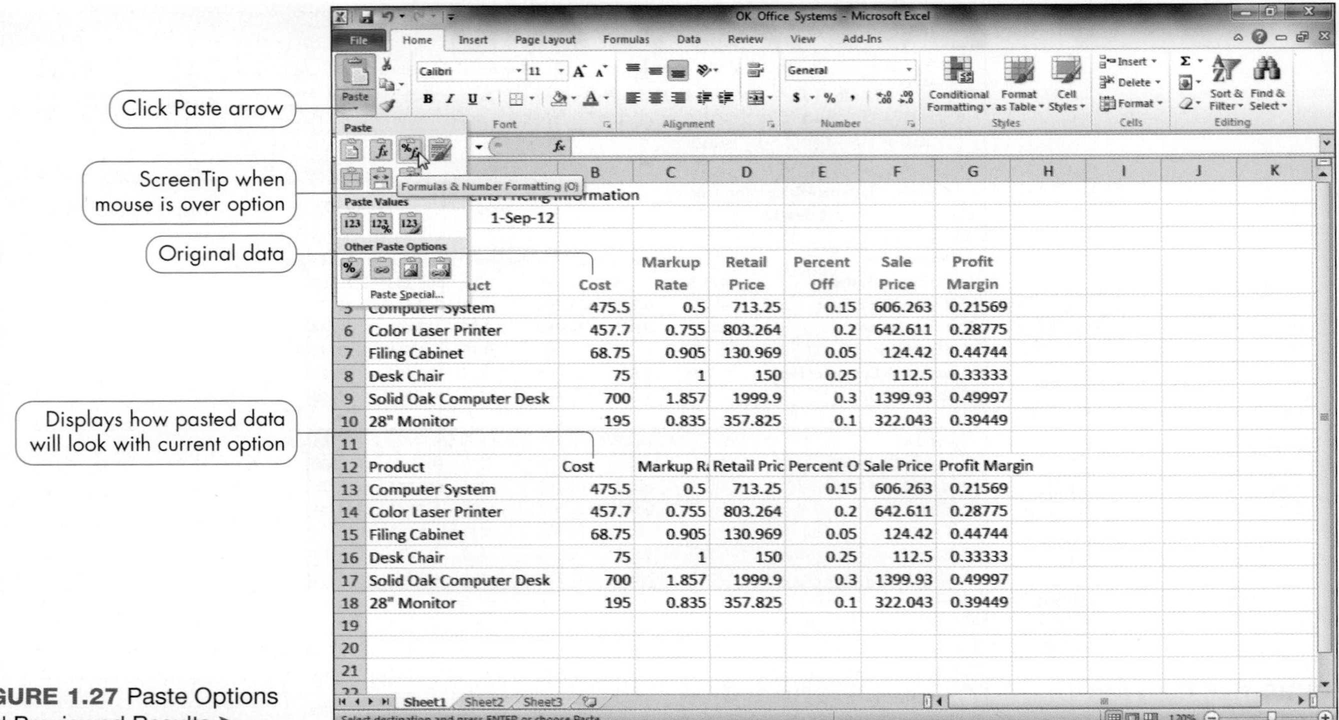

FIGURE 1.27 Paste Options and Previewed Results ➤

For more specific paste options, click the Paste arrow, and then select Paste Special to display the Paste Special dialog box (see Figure 1.28). This dialog box contains more options than the Paste menu. Click the desired option, and then click OK.

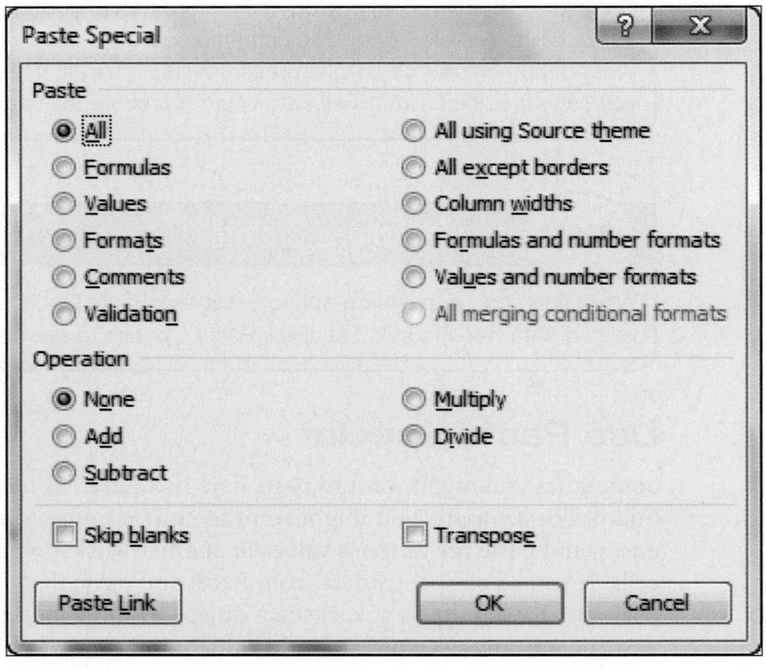

FIGURE 1.28 Paste Special Dialog Box ➤

TIP Transposing Columns and Rows

After entering data into a worksheet, you might want to transpose the columns and rows so that the data in the first column appear as column labels across the first row, or the column labels in the first row appear in the first column. To transpose worksheet data, select and copy the original range, click the top-left corner of the destination range, click the Paste arrow, and then click Transpose.

Copy Excel Data to Other Programs

You can copy Excel data and use it in other applications, such as in a Word document or in a PowerPoint slide show. Because Excel is designed for organizing data in columns and rows and enables you to create complex formulas, you should design spreadsheet data in Excel, and then copy it into other applications. For example, you might perform statistical analyses in Excel, and then copy the data into a research paper in Word or create a budget in Excel, and then copy the data into a PowerPoint slide show for a meeting.

After selecting and copying a range in Excel, you must decide how you want the data to appear in the destination application. Click the Paste arrow in the destination application to see a gallery of options or to select the Paste Special option. Table 1.5 describes some of the Paste options in Word you can use to paste Excel data. The PowerPoint Paste options are similar.

TABLE 1.5 Some Paste Options

Option Name	Result
Paste	Default paste inserts a copy of the Excel data as a Word table. Use the Table Tools Design and Layout tabs in Word to edit and format the copied data.
Link & Keep Source Formatting	Provides a link to the original Excel workbook so that changes in the workbook also update the pasted data. Maintains the original worksheet formatting.
Link & Use Destination Styles	Provides a link to the original Excel workbook so that changes in the workbook also update the pasted data. Applies the current document styles to the pasted data.
Picture	Inserts an image of the Excel data so that you can use the Picture Tools Format tab to apply a picture style, specify its position and wrapping, and adjust the height and width; however, you cannot edit the worksheet data displayed in the picture.
Keep Text Only	Pastes the data as regular text with tabs between columns.
Microsoft Excel Worksheet Object (in Paste Special dialog box)	Pastes the Excel data into the document so that you can edit it directly in the document. When you double-click the object, the Excel Ribbon displays within the Word window, giving you Excel functionality to make changes to the pasted data.

1. When you move or copy a worksheet, what are some of the decisions you must make?
2. What are two ways to insert a new row in a worksheet?
3. How can you delete cell B5 without deleting the entire row or column?
4. How can you select nonadjacent ranges, such as B5:B10 and F5:F10? Why would you select nonadjacent ranges?
5. Why would you use the Paste Special options in Excel?

HANDS-ON EXERCISES

3 Workbook and Worksheet Management

After reviewing the OKOS worksheet, you decide to rename the worksheet that contains the data and delete the other sheets. In addition, you decide to move the 28" Monitor data to display below the Computer System row and insert a column to calculate the amount of markup. You also need to adjust column widths to display data.

Skills covered: Manage Worksheets • Delete a Row • Insert a Column and Three Rows • Move a Row • Adjust Column Width and Row Height • Hide and Unhide Columns

STEP 1 MANAGE WORKSHEETS

You want to rename Sheet1 to describe the worksheet contents and add a color to the sheet tab. In addition, you want to delete the blank worksheets. Refer to Figure 1.29 as you complete Step 1.

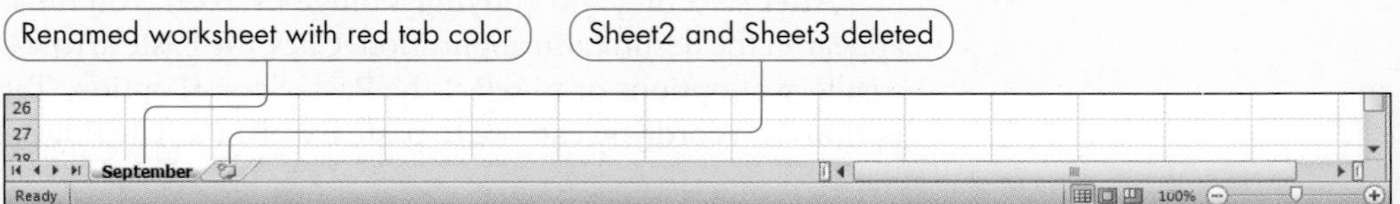

FIGURE 1.29 Worksheets Managed ➤

a. Open the *e01h2markup_LastnameFirstname* workbook if you closed it after the last Hands-On Exercise, and save it as **e01h3markup_LastnameFirstname**, changing *h2* to *h3*.

b. Double-click the **Sheet1 sheet tab**, type **September**, and then press **Enter**.

   You just renamed Sheet1 as September.

c. Right-click the **September sheet tab**, point to **Tab Color**, and then click **Red** in the Standard Colors section.

   The worksheet tab color is red.

d. Click the **Sheet2 sheet tab**, click the **Delete arrow** in the Cells group on the Home tab, and then select **Delete Sheet**.

   You deleted the Sheet2 worksheet from the workbook.

> **TROUBLESHOOTING:** Delete in the Cells group, like some other commands in Excel, contains two parts: the main command icon and an arrow. Click the main command icon when instructed to click Delete to perform the default action. Click the arrow when instructed to click the Delete arrow for additional command options.

> **TROUBLESHOOTING:** Notice that Undo is unavailable on the Quick Access Toolbar. You can't undo deleting a worksheet. It is deleted!

e. Right-click the **Sheet3 sheet tab**, and then select **Delete** to delete the sheet. Save the workbook.

STEP 2 DELETE A ROW

You just realized that you do not have enough filing cabinets in stock to offer on sale, so you need to delete the Filing Cabinet row. Refer to Figure 1.30 as you complete Step 2.

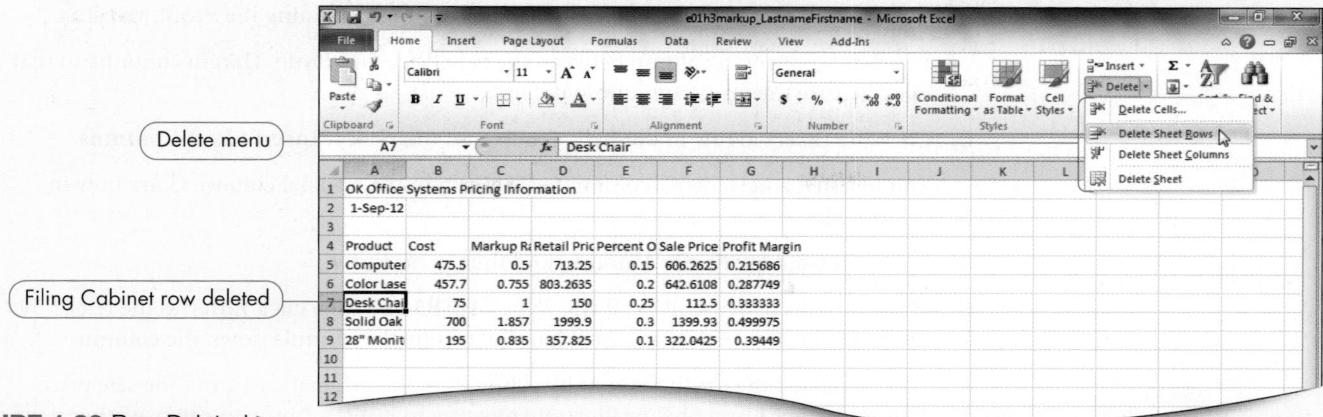

FIGURE 1.30 Row Deleted ➤

a. Click **cell A7** (or any cell on row 7), the row that contains data for the Filing Cabinet.

b. Click the **Delete arrow** in the Cells group.

c. Select **Delete Sheet Rows**, and then save the workbook.

The Filing Cabinet row is deleted, and the remaining rows move up one row.

> **TROUBLESHOOTING:** If you accidentally delete the wrong row or accidentally select Delete Sheet Columns instead of Delete Sheet Rows, click Undo on the Quick Access Toolbar to restore the deleted row or column.

STEP 3 INSERT A COLUMN AND THREE ROWS

You decide that you need a column to display the amount of profit. Because profit is a dollar amount, you want to keep the profit column close to another column of dollar amounts. Therefore, you will insert the profit column before the profit margin (percentage) column. You also want to insert new rows for product information and category names. Refer to Figure 1.31 as you complete Step 3.

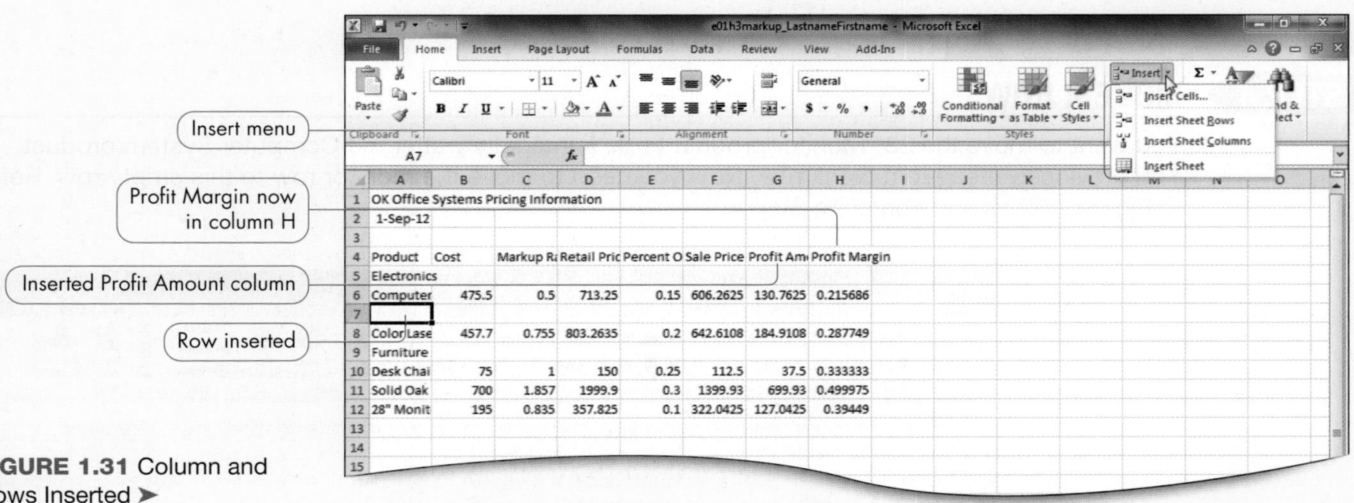

FIGURE 1.31 Column and Rows Inserted ➤

a. Click **cell G5** (or any cell in column G), the column containing the Profit Margin.

You want to insert a column between the Sale Price and Profit Margin columns so that you can calculate the profit amount in dollars.

b. Click the **Insert arrow** in the Cells group, and then select **Insert Sheet Columns**.

You inserted a new, blank column G. The data in the original column G are now in column H.

c. Click **cell G4**, type **Profit Amount**, and then press **Enter**.

d. Make sure the active cell is **cell G5**. Type **=F5-B5** and then click **Enter** to the left of the Formula Bar. Double-click the **fill handle** to copy the formula down the column.

You calculated the profit amount by subtracting the original cost from the sale price. Although steps e and f below illustrate one way to insert a row, you can use other methods presented in this chapter.

e. Right-click the **row 5 heading**, the row containing the Computer System data.

Excel displays a shortcut menu consisting of commands you can perform.

f. Select **Insert** from the shortcut menu.

You inserted a new blank row 5, which is selected. The original rows of data move down a row each.

g. Click **cell A5**. Type **Electronics** and then press **Enter**.

You entered the category name Electronics above the list of electronic products.

h. Right-click the **row 8 heading**, the row containing the Desk Chair data, and then select **Insert** from the shortcut menu.

i. Click **cell A8**. Type **Furniture** and then press **Enter**.

You entered the category name Furniture above the list of furniture products. Now you want to insert a blank row after the Computer System row so that you can move the 28" Monitor data to the new row.

j. Insert a row between Computer System and Color Laser Printer. Click **cell A7**, and then save the workbook.

STEP 4 MOVE A ROW

You want to move the 28" Monitor product to be immediately after the Computer System product. You previously inserted a blank row. Now you need to move the monitor row to this empty row. Refer to Figure 1.32 as you complete Step 4.

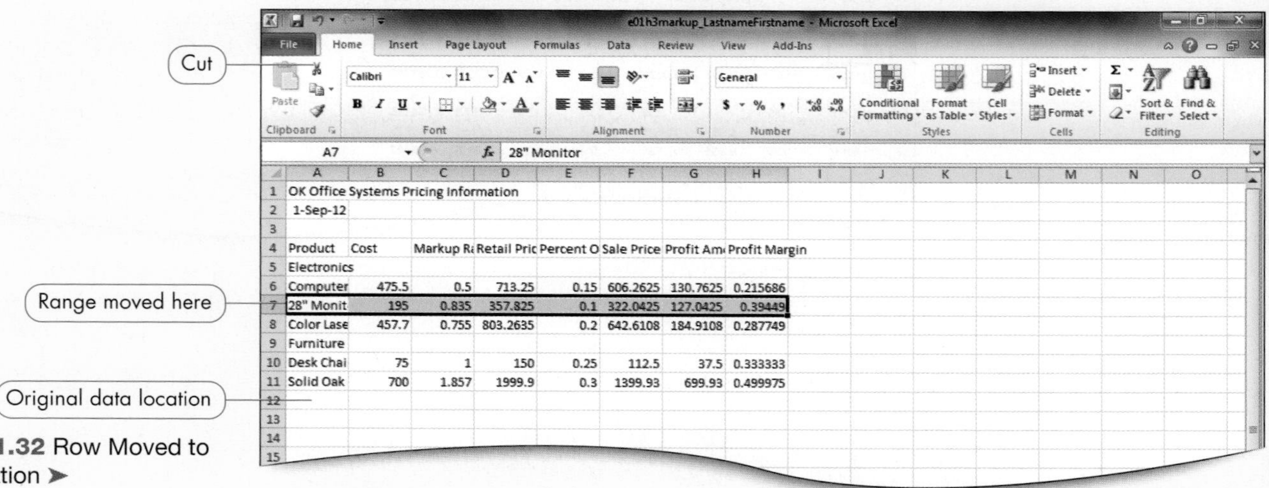

FIGURE 1.32 Row Moved to New Location ➤

FYI

a. Click **cell A12**, and then drag to select the **range A12:H12**.

You selected the range of cells containing the 28" Monitor data.

b. Cut the selected range.

A moving dashed border outlines the selected range. The status bar displays the message *Select destination and press ENTER or choose Paste.*

c. Click **cell A7**, the new blank row you inserted in step 3j.

This is the first cell in the destination range.

FYI

d. Paste the data that you cut, and then save the workbook.

The 28" Monitor data are now located on row 7.

> **TROUBLESHOOTING:** If you cut and paste a row without inserting a new row first, Excel will overwrite the original row of data, which is why you inserted a new row in step 3.

STEP 5 ADJUST COLUMN WIDTH AND ROW HEIGHT

As you review your worksheet, you notice that the labels in column A appear cut off. You need to increase the width of that column to display the entire product names. In addition, you want to make row 1 taller. Refer to Figure 1.33 as you complete Step 5.

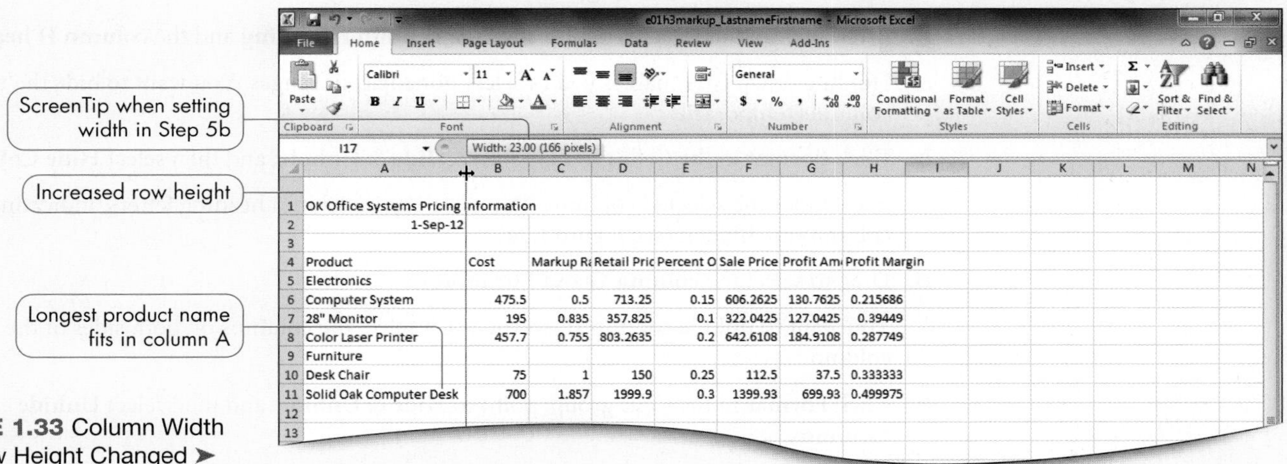

FIGURE 1.33 Column Width and Row Height Changed ➤

a. Position the pointer between the column A and B headings. When the pointer looks like a double-headed arrow, double-click the **border**.

When you double-click the border between two columns, Excel adjusts the width of the column on the left side of the border to fit the contents of that column. In this case, Excel increased the width of column A. However, it is based on the title in cell A1, which will eventually span over all columns. Therefore, you want to decrease the column to avoid so much empty space in column A.

b. Position the pointer between the column A and B headings again. Drag the border to the left until the ScreenTip displays **Width: 23.00 (166 pixels)**. Release the mouse button.

You decreased the column width to 23 for column A. The longest product name is visible. You won't adjust the other column widths until after you apply formats to the column headings in Hands-On Exercise 4.

c. Click **cell A1**. Click **Format** in the Cells group, and then select **Row Height** to display the Row Height dialog box.

d. Type **30** in the **Row height box**, and then click **OK**. Save the workbook.

You doubled the height of the first row.

STEP 6 HIDE AND UNHIDE COLUMNS

To focus on the dollar amounts, you decide to hide the markup rate, discount rate, and profit margin columns. Refer to Figure 1.34 as you complete Step 6.

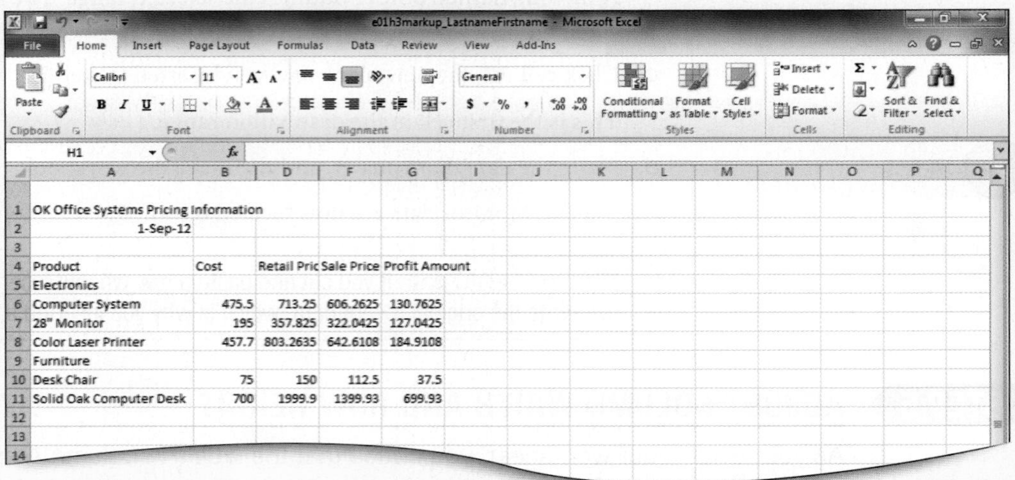

FIGURE 1.34 Hidden Columns ➤

a. Click the **column C heading**, the column containing the Markup Rate values.

b. Press and hold down **Ctrl** as you click the **column E heading** and the **column H heading**.

   Holding down Ctrl enables you to select nonadjacent ranges. You want to hide the rate columns temporarily.

c. Click **Format** in the Cells group, point to **Hide & Unhide**, and then select **Hide Columns**.

   Excel hides the selected columns. You see a gap in column heading letters, indicating columns are hidden (see Figure 1.34).

d. Drag to select the **column G and I headings**.

   You want to unhide column H, so you must select the columns on both sides of the hidden column.

e. Click **Format** in the Cells group, point to **Hide & Unhide**, and then select **Unhide Columns**.

   Column H, which contains the Profit Margin values, is no longer hidden. You will keep the other columns hidden to save the workbook as evidence that you know how to hide columns. You will unhide the remaining columns in the next Hands-On Exercise.

f. Save the workbook. Keep the workbook onscreen if you plan to continue with Hands-On Exercise 4. If not, close the workbook, and exit Excel.

Formatting

After entering data and formulas, you should format the worksheet. A professionally formatted worksheet—through adding appropriate symbols, aligning decimals, and using fonts and colors to make data stand out—makes finding and analyzing data easy. You apply different formats to accentuate meaningful details or to draw attention to specific ranges in a worksheet.

Different formats accentuate meaningful details or draw attention to specific ranges.

In this section, you will learn to apply different alignment options, including horizontal and vertical alignment, text wrapping, and indent options. In addition, you will learn how to format different types of values.

Applying Alignment and Font Options

Alignment refers to how data are positioned in cells. By now, you know that text aligns at the left cell margin, and dates and values align at the right cell margin. You can change the alignment of cell contents to improve the appearance of data within the cells. The Alignment group (see Figure 1.35) on the Home tab contains several features to help you align and format data.

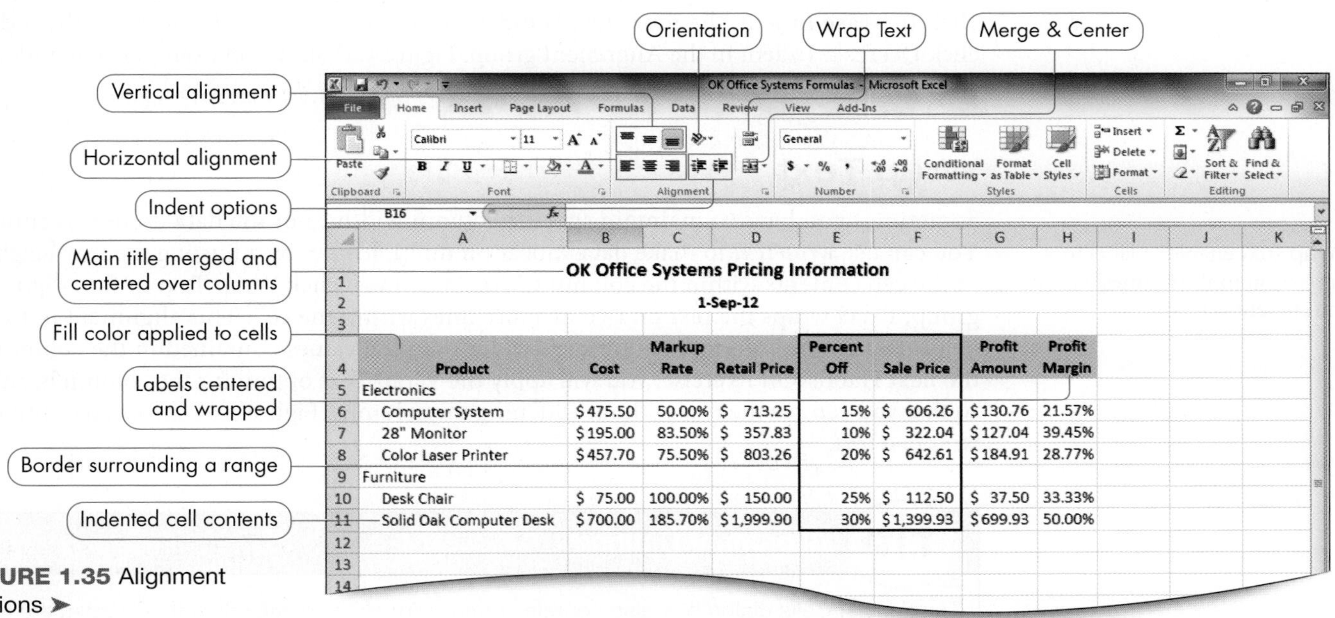

FIGURE 1.35 Alignment Options ➤

Change Horizontal and Vertical Cell Alignment

Horizontal alignment positions data between the left and right cell margins.

Vertical alignment positions data between the top and bottom cell margins.

Horizontal alignment specifies the position of data between the left and right cell margins, and ***vertical alignment*** specifies the position of data between the top and bottom cell margins. Bottom Align is the default vertical alignment, as indicated by the orange background of Bottom Align on the Ribbon. After adjusting row height, you might need to change the vertical alignment to position data better in conjunction with data in adjacent cells. To change alignments, click the desired alignment setting(s) in the Alignment group on the Home tab.

People sometimes rotate headings in cells. You can rotate data in a cell by clicking Orientation in the Alignment group, and then selecting an option, such as Angle Clockwise.

Merge and Center Labels

You may want to place a title at the top of a worksheet and center it over the columns of data in the worksheet. You can center main titles over all columns in the worksheet, and you can center category titles over groups of related columns. To create a title, enter the text in the far left cell of the range. Select the range of cells across which you want to center the title, and then click Merge & Center in the Alignment group on the Home tab. Any data in the merge area are lost, except what is in the far left cell in the range. Excel merges the selected cells together into one cell, and the merged cell address is that of the original cell on the left. The data are centered between the left and right sides of the merged cell. In Figure 1.35, the title *OK Office Systems Pricing Information* is merged and centered over the data columns.

If you merge too many cells and want to split the merged cell back into its original multiple cells, click the merged cell, and then click Merge & Center. Unmerging places the data in the top-left cell.

Increase and Decrease Indent

To offset labels, you can indent text within a cell. Accountants often indent the word Totals in financial statements so that it stands out from a list of items above the total row. Indenting helps others see the hierarchical structure of your spreadsheet data. To indent the contents of a cell, click Increase Indent in the Alignment group on the Home tab. The more you click Increase Indent, the more text is indented in the active cell. To decrease the indent, click Decrease Indent in the Alignment group. Figure 1.35 shows an example of an indented label.

Wrap Text

Wrap text enables a label to appear on multiple lines within the current cell.

Sometimes you have to maintain specific column widths, but the data do not fit entirely. You can use ***wrap text*** to make data appear on multiple lines by adjusting the row height to fit the cell contents within the column width. When you click Wrap Text in the Alignment group, Excel wraps the text on two or more lines within the cell. This alignment option is helpful when the column headings are wider than the values contained in the column. In the next Hands-On Exercise, you will apply the Wrap Text option for the column headings so that you can see the text without widening the columns. Figure 1.35 shows an example of wrapped text.

TIP Alignment Options

The Format Cells dialog box also contains options for aligning cell contents. To open the Format Cells dialog box, click the Alignment Dialog Box Launcher in the Alignment group on the Home tab. The Alignment tab in the dialog box contains the options for aligning data.

Apply Borders and Fill Color

A **border** is a line that surrounds a cell or a range.

You can apply a border or fill color to accentuate data in a worksheet. A ***border*** is a line that surrounds a cell or a range of cells. You can use borders to offset particular data from the rest of the data on the worksheet. To apply a border, select the cell or range that you want to have a border, click the Borders arrow in the Font group, and then select the desired border type. To remove a border, select No Border from the Borders menu.

Fill color is the background color appearing behind data in a cell.

To add some color to your worksheet to add emphasis to data or headers, you can apply a fill color. ***Fill color*** is a background color that displays behind the data. You should choose a fill color that contrasts with the font color. For example, if the font color is Black, you might want to choose Yellow fill color. If the font color is White, you might want to apply Blue or Dark Blue fill color. To apply a fill color, select the cell or range that you want to have a fill color, click the Fill Color arrow on the Home tab, and then select the color choice from the Fill Color palette. If you want to remove a fill color, select No Fill from the bottom of the palette.

For additional border and fill color options, display the Format Cells dialog box. Click the Border tab to select border options, including the border line style and color. Click the Fill tab to set the background color, fill effects, and patterns. Figure 1.35 shows examples of cells containing a border and fill color.

Applying Number Formats

Values appear in General format (i.e., no special formatting) when you enter data. You should apply number formats based on the type of values in a cell, such as applying either the Accounting or Currency number format to monetary values. Changing the number format changes the way the number displays in a cell, but the format does not change the number's value. If, for example, you entered 123.456 into a cell and format the cell with Currency number type, the value shows as $123.46 onscreen, but the actual value 123.456 is used for calculations. When you apply a number format, you can specify the number of decimal places to display onscreen.

Select an Appropriate Number Format

The default number format is General, which displays values as you originally enter them. General does not align decimal points in a column or include symbols, such as dollar signs, percent signs, or commas. Table 1.6 lists and describes the primary number formats in Excel.

TABLE 1.6 Number Formats

Format Style	Display
General	A number as it was originally entered. Numbers are shown as integers (e.g., 12345), decimal fractions (e.g., 1234.5), or in scientific notation (e.g., 1.23E+10) if the number exceeds 11 digits.
Number	A number with or without the 1000 separator (e.g., a comma) and with any number of decimal places. Negative numbers can be displayed with parentheses and/or red.
Currency	A number with the 1,000 separator and an optional dollar sign (which is placed immediately to the left of the number). Negative values are preceded by a minus sign or are displayed with parentheses or in red. Two decimal places display by default.
Accounting	A number with the 1,000 separator, an optional dollar sign (at the left border of the cell, vertically aligned within a column), negative values in parentheses, and zero values as hyphens. Two decimal places display by default.
Date	The date in different ways, such as March 14, 2012; 3/14/12; or 14-Mar-12.
Time	The time in different formats, such as 10:50 PM or 22:50 (24-hour time).
Percentage	The value as it would be multiplied by 100 (for display purpose), with the percent sign. The default number of decimal places is zero if you click Percent Style in the Number group or two decimal places if you use the Format Cells dialog box. However, you should typically increase the number of decimal points to show greater accuracy.
Fraction	A number as a fraction; use when no exact decimal equivalent exists. A fraction is entered into a cell as a formula such as =1/3. If the cell is not formatted as a fraction, the formula results display.
Scientific	A number as a decimal fraction followed by a whole number exponent of 10; for example, the number 12345 would appear as 1.23E+04. The exponent, +04 in the example, is the number of places the decimal point is moved to the left (or right if the exponent is negative). Very small numbers have negative exponents.

(Continued)

TABLE 1.6 (*Continued*)	
Format Style	**Display**
Text	The data left-aligned; is useful for numerical values that have leading zeros and should be treated as text, such as ZIP codes or phone numbers. Apply Text format before typing a leading zero so that the zero displays in the cell.
Special	A number with editing characters, such as hyphens in a Social Security number.
Custom	Predefined customized number formats or special symbols to create your own customized number format.

The Number group on the Home tab contains commands for applying Accounting Number Format, Percent Style, and Comma Style numbering formats. You can click the Accounting Number Format arrow and select other denominations, such as English pounds or euros. For other number formats, click the Number Format arrow and select the numbering format want to use. For more specific numbering formats than those provided, select More Number Formats from the Number Format menu or click the Number Dialog Box Launcher to open the Format Cells dialog box with the Number tab options readily available. Figure 1.36 shows different number formats applied to values. The first six values are displayed with two decimal places.

	A	B	C
1	General	1234.56	
2	Number	1234.56	
3	Currency	$1,234.56	
4	Accounting	$ 1,234.56	
5	Comma	1,234.56	
6	Percent	12.34%	
7	Short Date	3/1/2012	
8	Long Date	Thursday, March 01, 2012	

FIGURE 1.36 Number Formats ➤

Increase and Decrease Decimal Places

After applying a number format, you may need to adjust the number of decimal places that display. For example, if you have an entire column of monetary values formatted in Accounting Number Format, Excel displays two decimal places by default. If the entire column of values contains whole dollar values and no cents, displaying .00 down the column looks cluttered. You can decrease the number of decimal places to show whole numbers only.

To change the number of decimal places displayed, click Increase Decimal in the Number group on the Home tab to display more decimal places for greater precision or Decrease Decimal to display fewer or no decimal places.

Quick Concepts Check

1. What is the importance of formatting a worksheet?
2. Describe five alignment and font formatting techniques used to format labels that are discussed in this section.
3. What are the main differences between Accounting Number Format and Currency format? Which format has its own command on the Ribbon?

HANDS-ON EXERCISES

4 Formatting

In the first three Hands-On Exercises, you entered data about products on sale, created formulas to calculate markup and profit, and inserted new rows and columns to accommodate additional data. You are ready to format the worksheet. Specifically, you need to center the title, align text, format values, and apply other formatting to enhance the readability of the worksheet.

Skills covered: Merge and Center the Title • Wrap and Align Text • Apply Number Formats and Decimal Places • Apply Borders and Fill Color • Indent Cell Contents

STEP 1 MERGE AND CENTER THE TITLE

To make the title stand out, you want to center it over all the data columns. You will use the Merge & Center command to merge cells together and center the title at the same time. Refer to Figure 1.37 as you complete Step 1.

	A	B	C	D	E	F	G	H	I
1	OK Office Systems Pricing Information								
2	1-Sep-12								
3									
4	Product	Cost	Markup Ra	Retail Pric	Percent O	Sale Price	Profit Am	Profit Margin	
5	Electronics								
6	Computer System	475.5	0.5	713.25	0.15	606.2625	130.7625	0.215686	
7	28" Monitor	195	0.835	357.825	0.1	322.0425	127.0425	0.39449	
8	Color Laser Printer	457.7	0.755	803.2635	0.2	642.6108	184.9108	0.287749	
9	Furniture								
10	Desk Chair	75	1	150	0.25	112.5	37.5	0.333333	
11	Solid Oak Computer Desk	700	1.857	1999.9	0.3	1399.93	699.93	0.499975	
12									
13									

FIGURE 1.37 Formatted Title ➤

a. Open the *e01h3markup_LastnameFirstname* workbook if you closed it after the last Hands-On Exercise, and save it as **e01h4markup_LastnameFirstname**, changing *h3* to *h4*.

b. Select the **column B, D, and F headings**. Unhide columns C and E as you learned in Hands-On Exercise 3.

c. Select the **range A1:H1**.

   You want to center the title over all columns of data.

d. Click **Merge & Center** in the Alignment group.

   Excel merges cells in the range A1:H1 into one cell and centers the title horizontally within the merged cell, which is cell A1.

> **TROUBLESHOOTING:** If you merge too many or not enough cells, you can unmerge the cells and start again. To unmerge cells, click in the merged cell. The Merge & Center command has an orange border when the active cell is merged. Click Merge & Center to unmerge the cell. Then select the correct range to merge and use Merge & Center again.

e. Bold the title, and then select **14 pt** size.

f. Select the **range A2:H2**. Merge and center the date, and then bold it.

g. Save the workbook.

STEP 2 WRAP AND ALIGN TEXT

You will wrap the text in the column headings to avoid columns that are too wide for the data, but which will display the entire text of the column headings. In addition, you will horizontally center column headings between the left and right cell margins. Refer to Figure 1.38 as you complete Step 2.

Middle Align applied

Text wrapped, centered, and bold

	A	B	C	D	E	F	G	H	I
1	OK Office Systems Pricing Information								
2	1-Sep-12								
3									
4	Product	Cost	Markup Rate	Retail Price	Percent Off	Sale Price	Profit Amount	Profit Margin	
5	Electronics								
6	Computer System	475.5	0.5	713.25	0.15	606.2625	130.7625	0.215686	
7	28" Monitor	195	0.835	357.825	0.1	322.0425	127.0425	0.39449	
8	Color Laser Printer	457.7	0.755	803.2635	0.2	642.6108	184.9108	0.287749	
9	Furniture								
10	Desk Chair	75	1	150	0.25	112.5	37.5	0.333333	
11	Solid Oak Computer Desk	700	1.857	1999.9	0.3	1399.93	699.93	0.499975	
12									

FIGURE 1.38 Formatted Column Headings ➤

a. Select the **range A4:H4**.

You selected the multiple-word column headings.

b. Click **Wrap Text** in the Alignment group.

The column headings are now visible on two lines within each cell.

c. Click **Center** in the Alignment group. Bold the selected column headings.

The column headings are centered horizontally between the left and right edges of each cell.

d. Click **cell A1**, which contains the title.

e. Click **Middle Align** in the Alignment group. Save the workbook.

Middle Align vertically centers data between the top and bottom edges of the cell.

STEP 3 APPLY NUMBER FORMATS AND DECIMAL PLACES

You need to format the values to increase readability and look more professional. You will apply number formats and adjust the number of decimal points displayed. Refer to Figure 1.39 as you complete Step 3.

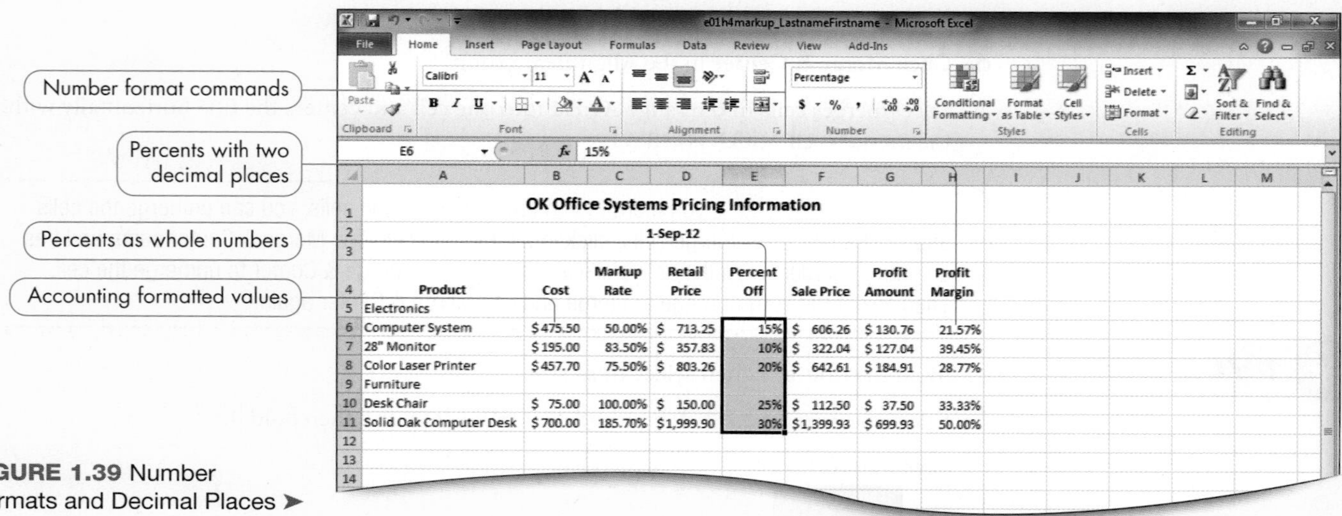

	A	B	C	D	E	F	G	H
1	OK Office Systems Pricing Information							
2	1-Sep-12							
3								
4	Product	Cost	Markup Rate	Retail Price	Percent Off	Sale Price	Profit Amount	Profit Margin
5	Electronics							
6	Computer System	$ 475.50	50.00%	$ 713.25	15%	$ 606.26	$ 130.76	21.57%
7	28" Monitor	$ 195.00	83.50%	$ 357.83	10%	$ 322.04	$ 127.04	39.45%
8	Color Laser Printer	$ 457.70	75.50%	$ 803.26	20%	$ 642.61	$ 184.91	28.77%
9	Furniture							
10	Desk Chair	$ 75.00	100.00%	$ 150.00	25%	$ 112.50	$ 37.50	33.33%
11	Solid Oak Computer Desk	$ 700.00	185.70%	$1,999.90	30%	$1,399.93	$ 699.93	50.00%

FIGURE 1.39 Number Formats and Decimal Places ➤

a. Select the **range B6:B11**, and then click **Accounting Number Format** in the Number group.

You formatted the selected range with Accounting Number Format. The dollar signs align on the left cell margins and the decimals align.

b. Select the **range D6:D11**. Press and hold down **Ctrl** as you select the **range F6:G11**.

Since you want to format nonadjacent ranges with the same formats, you hold down Ctrl.

c. Click **Accounting Number Format** in the Number group.

You formatted the selected nonadjacent ranges with the Accounting Number Format.

d. Select the **range C6:C11**, and then click **Percent Style** in the Number group.

You formatted the values in the selected ranges with Percent Style, showing whole numbers only.

e. Click **Increase Decimal** in the Number group twice.

You increased the decimal places to avoid misleading your readers by displaying the values as whole percentages.

f. Use Format Painter to copy the formats of the selected range to values in columns E and H.

g. Select the **range E6:E11**, and then click **Decrease Decimal** twice in the Number group. Save the workbook.

Since this range contained whole percentages, you do not need to show the decimal places.

STEP 4 APPLY BORDERS AND FILL COLOR

You want to apply a light purple fill color to highlight the column headings. In addition, you want to emphasize the percent off and sale prices. You will do this by applying a border around that range. Refer to Figure 1.40 as you complete Step 4.

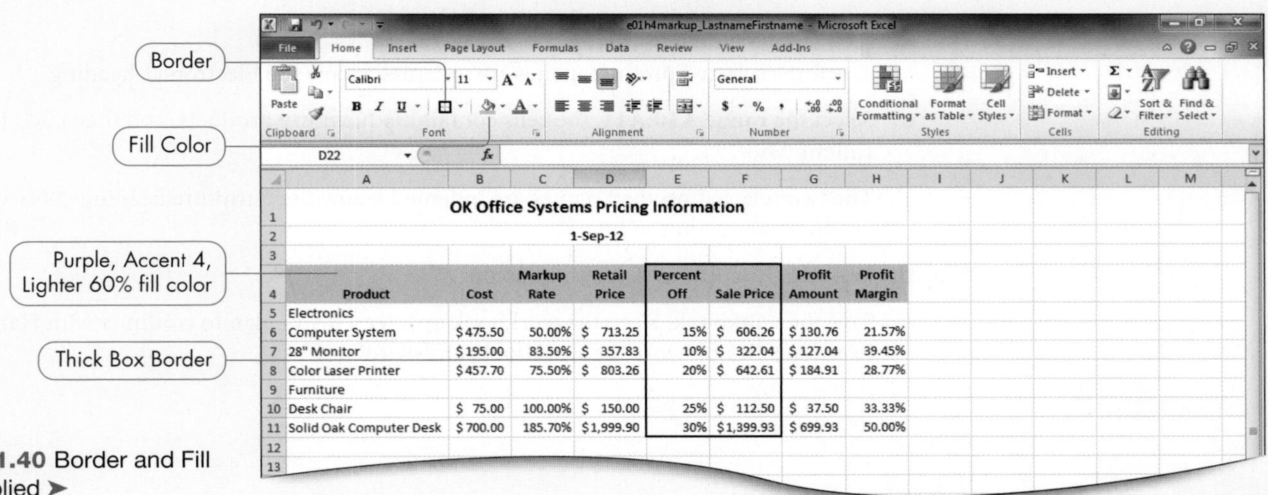

FIGURE 1.40 Border and Fill Color Applied ➤

a. Select the **range A4:H4**.

b. Click the **Fill Color arrow** in the Font group.

c. Click **Purple, Accent 4, Lighter 60%** in the *Theme Colors* section. It is the third color down in the third column from the right.

You applied a fill color to the selected cells to draw attention to these cells.

d. Select the **range E4:F11**.

e. Click the **Border arrow** in the Font group, and then select **Thick Box Border**.

You applied a border around the selected cells.

f. Click in an empty cell below the columns of data to deselect the cells. Save the workbook.

STEP 5 INDENT CELL CONTENTS

As you review the first column, you notice that the category names, Electronics and Furniture, don't stand out. You decide to indent the labels within each category to show which products are in each category. Refer to Figure 1.41 as you complete Step 5.

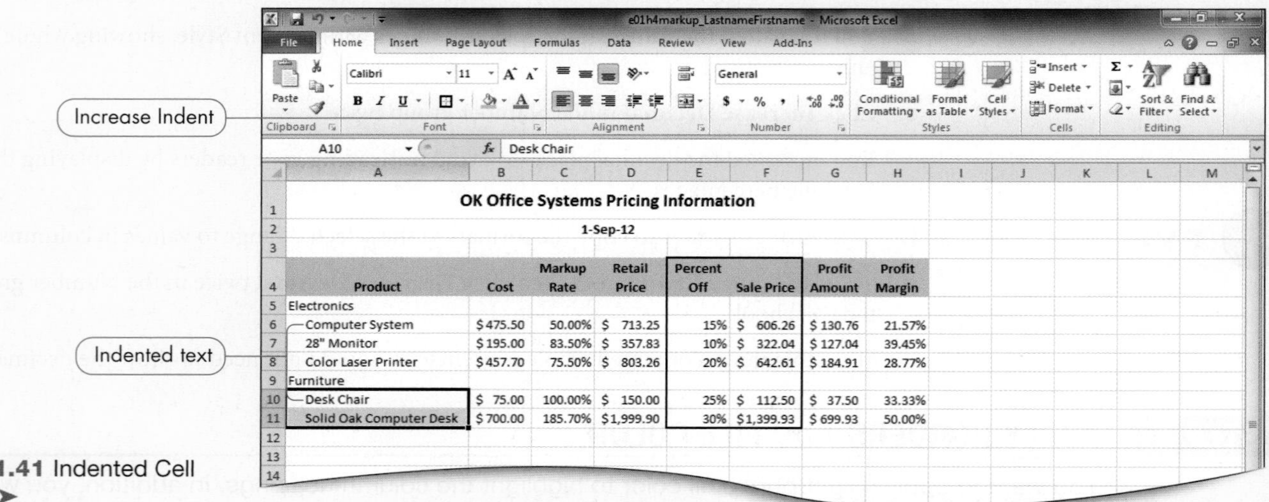

FIGURE 1.41 Indented Cell Contents ➤

a. Select the **range A6:A8**, the cells containing electronic products.

b. Click **Increase Indent** in the Alignment group twice.

The three selected product names are indented below the Electronics heading.

c. Select the **range A10:A11**, the cells containing furniture products, and then click **Increase Indent** twice.

The two selected product names are indented below the Furniture heading. Notice that the product names appear cut off.

d. Increase the **column A** width to **26.00**.

e. Save the workbook. Keep the workbook onscreen if you plan to continue with Hands-On Exercise 5. If not, close the workbook, and exit Excel.

Page Setup and Printing

Although you might distribute workbooks electronically as e-mail attachments or you might upload workbooks to a corporation server, you should prepare the worksheets in the workbook for printing. You should prepare worksheets in case you need to print them or in case others who receive an electronic copy of your workbook need to print the worksheets. The Page Layout tab provides options for controlling the printed worksheet (see Figure 1.42).

Page Setup Dialog Box Launcher

FIGURE 1.42 Page Layout Tab ➤

In this section, you will select options on the Page Layout tab. Specifically, you will use the Page Setup, Scale to Fit, and Sheet Options groups. After selecting page setup options, you are ready to print your worksheet.

Selecting Page Setup Options

The Page Setup group on the Page Layout tab contains options to set the margins, select orientation, specify page size, select the print area, and apply other options. The Scale to Fit group contains options for adjusting the scaling of the spreadsheet on the printed page. When possible, use the commands in these groups to apply page settings. Table 1.7 lists and describes the commands in the Page Setup group.

TABLE 1.7 Page Setup Commands

Command	Description
Margins	Displays a menu to select predefined margin settings. The default margins are 0.75" top and bottom and 0.7" left and right. You will often change these margin settings to balance the worksheet data better on the printed page. If you need different margins, select Custom Margins.
Orientation	Displays orientation options. The default page orientation is portrait, which is appropriate for worksheets that contain more rows than columns. Select landscape orientation when worksheets contain more columns than can fit in portrait orientation. For example, the OKOS worksheet might appear better balanced in landscape orientation because it has eight columns.
Size	Displays a list of standard paper sizes. The default size is 8.5" by 11". If you have a different paper size, such as legal paper, select it from the list.
Print Area	Displays a list to set or clear the print area. When you have very large worksheets, you might want to print only a portion of that worksheet. To do so, select the range you want to print, click Print Area in the Page Setup group, and select Set Print Area. When you use the Print commands, only the range you specified will be printed. To clear the print area, click Print Area, and select Clear Print Area.
Breaks	Displays a list to insert or remove page breaks.
Background	Enables you to select an image to appear as the background behind the worksheet data when viewed onscreen (backgrounds do not appear when the worksheet is printed).
Print Titles	Enables you to select column headings and row labels to repeat on multiple-page printouts.

Specify Page Options

To apply several page setup options at once or to access options not found on the Ribbon, click the Page Setup Dialog Box Launcher. The Page Setup dialog box organizes options into four tabs: Page, Margins, Header/Footer, and Sheet. All tabs contain Print and Print Preview buttons. Figure 1.43 shows the Page tab.

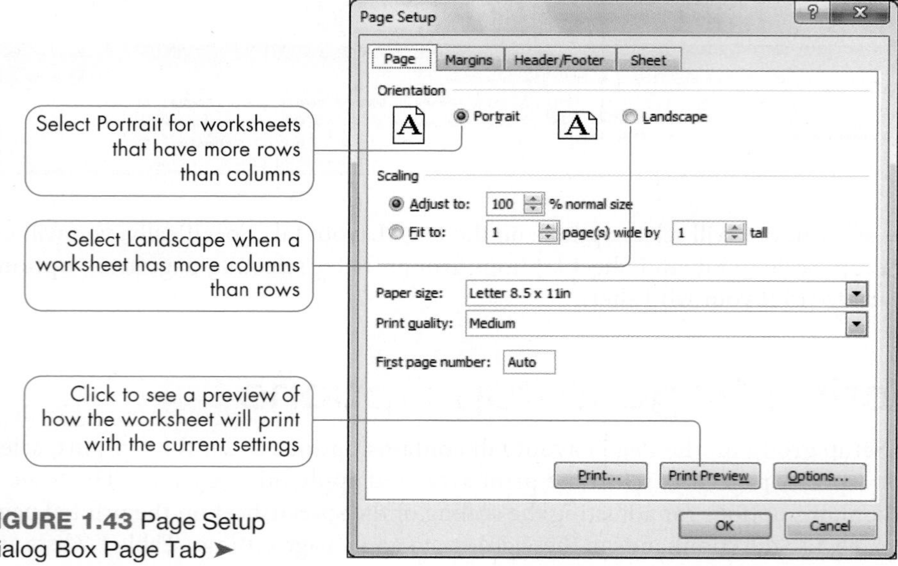

FIGURE 1.43 Page Setup Dialog Box Page Tab ➤

The Page tab contains options to select the orientation and paper size. In addition, it contains scaling options that are similar to the options in the Scale to Fit group on the Page Layout tab. You use scaling options to increase or decrease the size of characters on a printed page, similar to using a zoom setting on a photocopy machine. You can also use the Fit to option to force the data to print on a specified number of pages.

Specify Margins Options

The Margins tab (see Figure 1.44) contains options for setting the specific margins. In addition, it contains options to center the worksheet data horizontally or vertically on the page. To balance worksheet data equally between the left and right margins, Excel users often center the page horizontally.

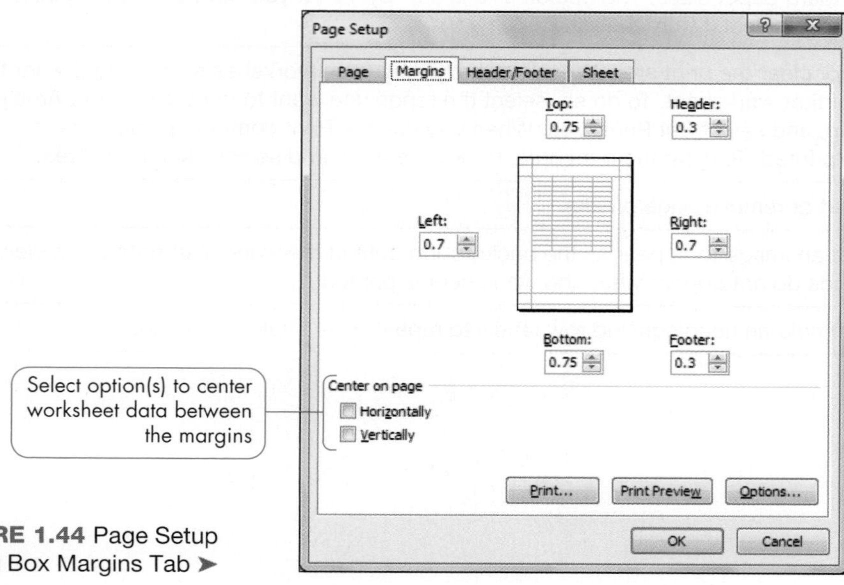

FIGURE 1.44 Page Setup Dialog Box Margins Tab ➤

Create Headers and Footers

The Header/Footer tab (see Figure 1.45) lets you create a header and/or footer that appear at the top and/or bottom of every printed page. Click the arrows to choose from several preformatted entries, or alternatively, you can click Custom Header or Custom Footer, insert text and other objects, and then click the appropriate formatting button to customize your headers and footers. You can use headers and footers to provide additional information about the worksheet. You can include your name, the date the worksheet was prepared, and page numbers, for example.

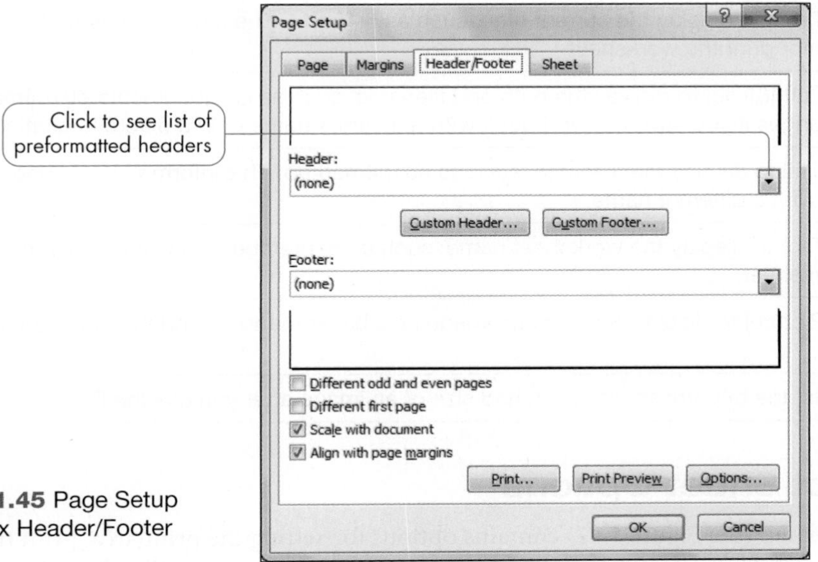

FIGURE 1.45 Page Setup Dialog Box Header/Footer Tab ➤

Instead of creating headers and footers using the Page Setup dialog box, you can click the Insert tab and click Header & Footer in the Text group. Excel displays the worksheet in Page Layout view with the insertion point in the center area of the header. If you click the View tab and then click Page Layout, you see an area that displays *Click to add header* at the top of the worksheet. You can click inside the left, center, or right section of a header or footer. When you do, Excel displays the Header & Footer Tools Design contextual tab (see Figure 1.46). You can enter text or insert data from the Header & Footer Elements group on the tab. Table 1.8 lists and describes the options in the Header & Footer Elements group. To get back to Normal view, click any cell in the worksheet, and then click Normal in the Workbook Views group on the View tab.

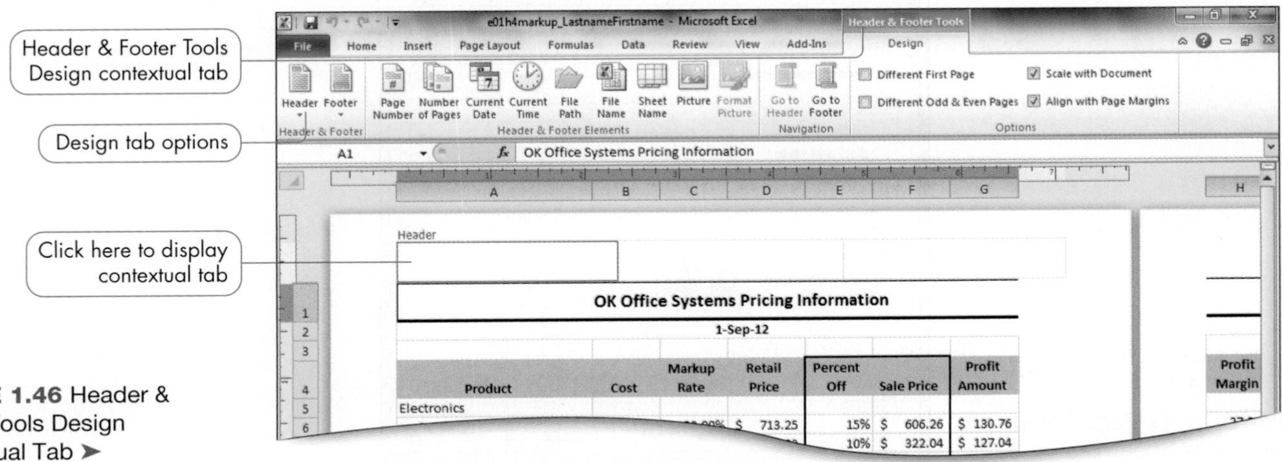

FIGURE 1.46 Header & Footer Tools Design Contextual Tab ➤

TABLE 1.8 Header & Footer Elements Options

Option Name	Result
Page Number	Inserts the code &[Page] to display the current page number.
Number of Pages	Inserts the code &[Pages] to display the total number of pages that will print.
Current Date	Inserts the code &[Date] to display the current date, such as 5/19/2013. The date updates to the current date when you open or print the worksheet.
Current Time	Inserts the code &[Time] to display the current time, such as 5:15 PM. The time updates to the current time when you open or print the worksheet.
File Path	Inserts the code &[Path]&[File] to display the path and filename, such as C:\Documents\e01h4markup. This information changes if you save the workbook with a different name or in a different location.
File Name	Inserts the code &[File] to display the filename, such as e01h4markup. This information changes if you save the workbook with a different name.
Sheet Name	Inserts the code &[Tab] to display the worksheet name, such as September. This information changes if you rename the worksheet.
Picture	Inserts the code &[Picture] to display and print an image as a background behind the data, not just the worksheet.
Format Picture	Enables you to adjust the brightness, contrast, and size of an image after you use the Picture option.

Select Sheet Options

The Sheet tab (see Figure 1.47) contains options for setting the print area, print titles, print options, and page order. Some of these options are also located in the Sheet Options group on the Page Layout tab on the Ribbon. By default, Excel displays gridlines onscreen to show you each cell's margins, but the gridlines do not print unless you specifically select the Gridlines check box in the Page Setup dialog box or the Print Gridlines check box in the Sheet Options group on the Page Layout tab. In addition, Excel displays row (1, 2, 3, etc.) and column (A, B, C, etc.) headings onscreen. However, these headings do not print unless you click the Row and column headings check box in the Page Setup dialog box or click the Print Headings check box in the Sheet Options group on the Page Layout tab.

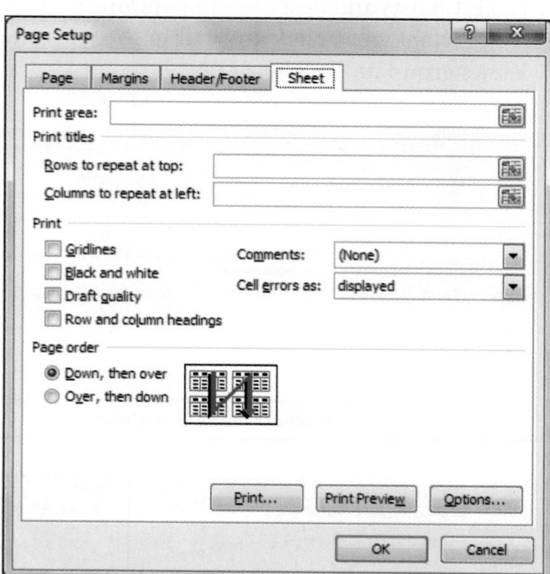

FIGURE 1.47 Page Setup Dialog Box Sheet Tab ➤

TIP Printing Gridlines and Headings

For most worksheets, you do not need to print gridlines and row/column headings. However, when you want to display and print cell formulas instead of formula results, you might want to print the gridlines and row/column headings. Doing so will help you analyze your formulas. The gridlines help you see the cell boundaries, and the headings help you know what data are in each cell. At times, you might want to display gridlines to separate data on a regular printout to increase readability.

Printing a Worksheet

Before printing a worksheet, you should click the File tab and then select Print. The Backstage view displays print options and displays the worksheet in print preview mode. This mode helps you see in advance if the data are balanced on the page or if data will print on multiple pages.

The Backstage view helps you see in advance if the data are balanced on the page.

You can specify the number of copies to print and which printer to use to print the worksheet. The first option in the Settings area enables you to specify what to print. The default option is Print Active Sheets. You can choose other options, such as Print Entire Workbook or Print Selection. You can also specify which pages to print. If you are connected to a printer that duplexes, you can print on only one side or print on both sides. You can also collate, change the orientation, specify the paper size, adjust the margins, and adjust the scaling.

The bottom of the Backstage view indicates how many total pages will print. If the settings are correct, you can specify the print options. If you do not like how the worksheet will print, click the Page Layout tab so that you can adjust margins, scaling, column widths, and so on until the worksheet data appear the way you want them to print.

Quick Concepts Check

1. What helps you determine whether to use Portrait or Landscape orientation for a worksheet?
2. Why would you select a *Center on page* option if you have already set the margins?
3. List at least five elements you can insert in a header or footer.
4. Why would you want to print gridlines and row and column headings?

HANDS-ON EXERCISES

5 Page Setup and Printing

You are ready to complete the OKOS worksheet. Before printing the worksheet for your supervisor, you want to make sure the data will appear professional when printed. You will adjust some page setup options to put the finishing touches on the worksheet.

Skills covered: Set Page Orientation • Set Margin Options • Create a Header • Print Preview and Print • Adjust Scaling and Set Sheet Options

STEP 1 SET PAGE ORIENTATION

Because the worksheet has several columns, you decide to print it in landscape orientation.

a. Open the *e01h4markup_LastnameFirstname* workbook if you closed it after the last Hands-On Exercise, and save it as **e01h5markup_LastnameFirstname**, changing *h4* to *h5*.

b. Click the **Page Layout tab**.

c. Click **Orientation** in the Page Setup group.

d. Select **Landscape** from the list. Save the workbook.

   If you print the worksheet, the data will print in landscape orientation.

STEP 2 SET MARGIN OPTIONS

You want to set a 1" top margin and center the data between the left and right margins.

a. Click **Margins** in the Page Setup group on the Page Layout tab.

   As you review the list of options, you notice the list does not contain an option to center the worksheet data horizontally.

b. Select **Custom Margins**.

   The Page Setup dialog box opens with the Margins tab options displayed.

c. Click the **Top spin box** to display *1*.

   You set a 1" top margin. You don't need to change the left and right margins since you will center the worksheet data horizontally between the original margins.

d. Click the **Horizontally check box** in the *Center on page* section, and then click **OK**. Save the workbook.

   The worksheet data will be centered between the left and right margins.

STEP 3 CREATE A HEADER

To document the worksheet, you want to include your name, the current date, and the worksheet tab name in a header. Refer to Figure 1.48 as you complete Step 3.

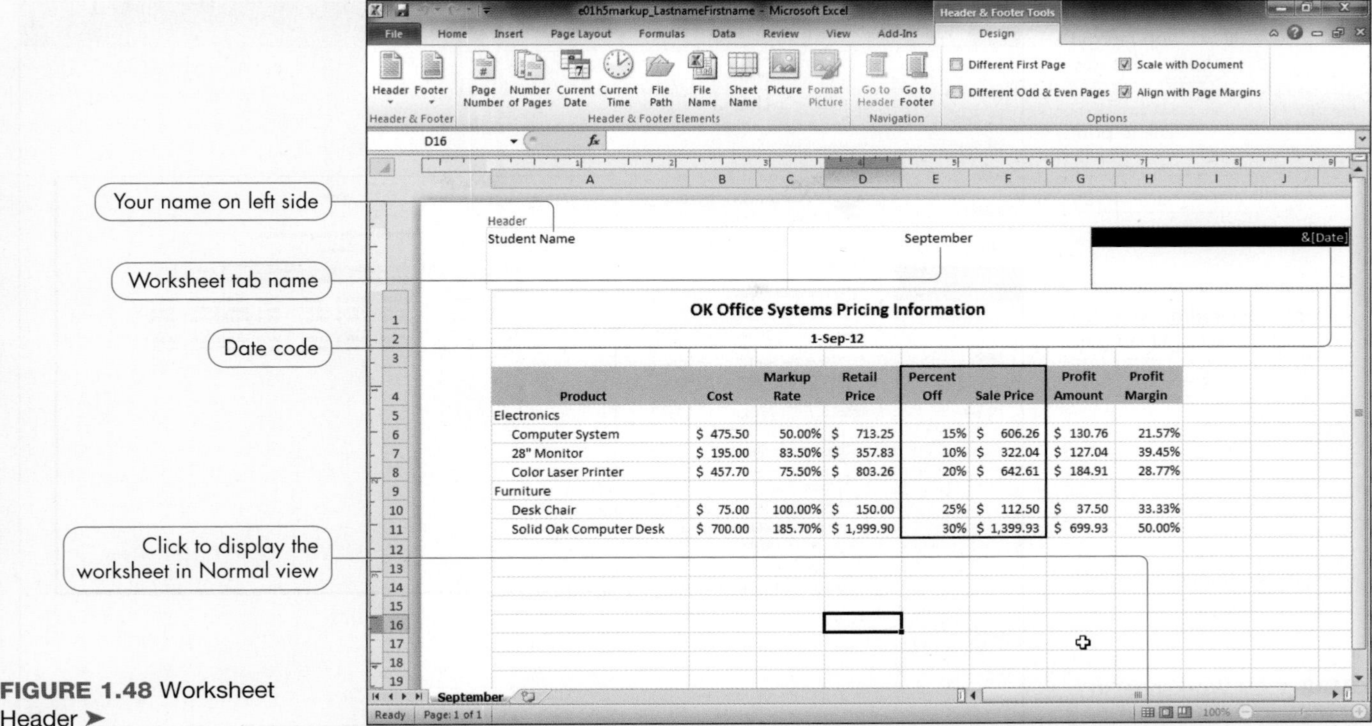

FIGURE 1.48 Worksheet Header ➤

a. Click the **Insert tab**, and then click **Header & Footer** in the Text group.

   Excel displays the Header & Footer Tools Design tab, and the worksheet displays in Page Layout view. The insertion point blinks inside the center section of the Header.

b. Click in the left section of the header, and then type your name.

c. Click in the center section of the header, and then click **Sheet Name** in the Header & Footer Elements group on the Design tab.

   Excel inserts the code &[Tab]. This code displays the name of the worksheet. If you change the worksheet tab name, the header will reflect the new sheet name.

d. Click in the right section of the header, and then click **Current Date** in the Header & Footer Elements group on the Design tab.

   Excel inserts the code &[Date]. This code displays the current date based on the computer clock when you print the worksheet. If you want a specific date to appear regardless of the date you open or print the worksheet, you would have to type that date manually. When you click in a different header section, the codes, such as &[Tab], display the actual tab name instead of the code.

e. Click in any cell in the worksheet, click **Normal** on the status bar, and then save the workbook.

STEP 4 PRINT PREVIEW AND PRINT

Before printing the worksheet, you should print preview it. Doing so helps you detect margin problems and other issues, such as a single row or column of data flowing onto a new page. Refer to Figure 1.49 as you complete Step 4.

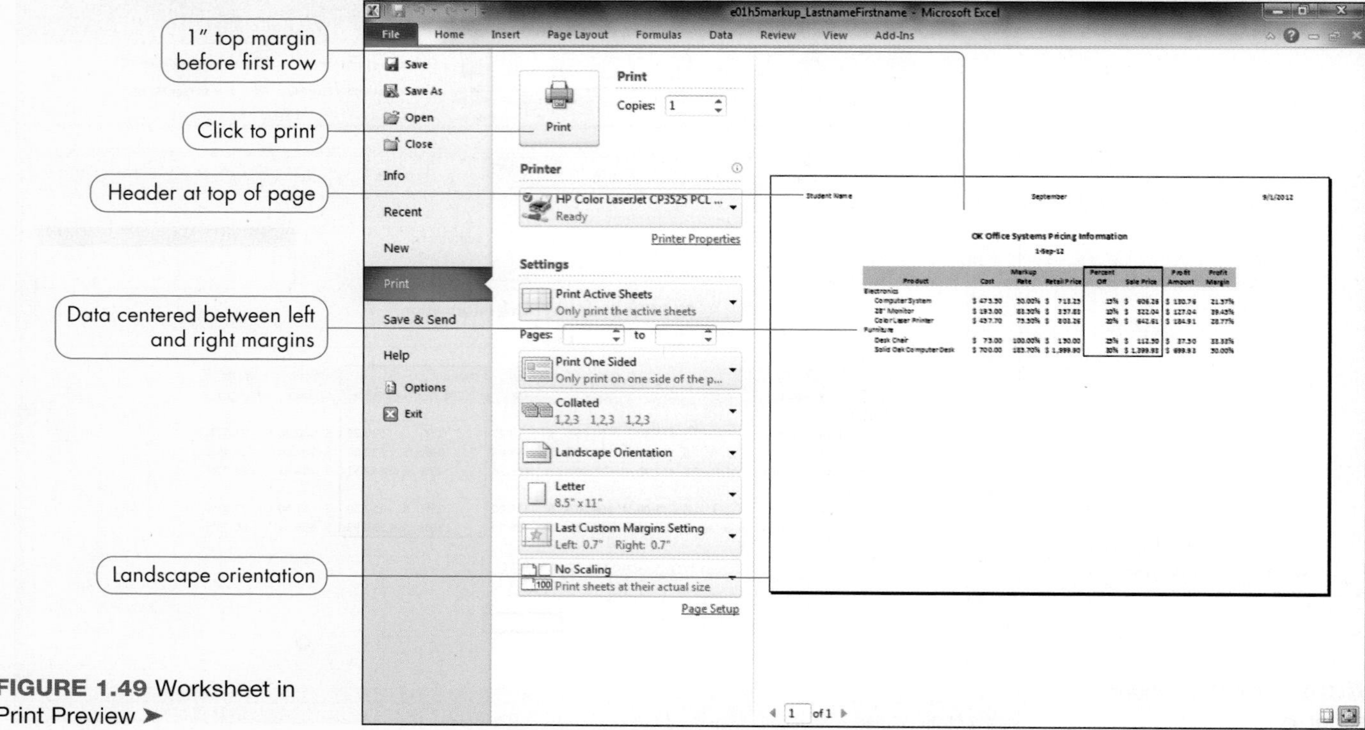

FIGURE 1.49 Worksheet in Print Preview ➤

a. Click the **File tab**, and then click **Print**.

The Backstage view displays print options and a preview of the worksheet.

b. Verify the Printer name displays the printer that you want to use to print your worksheet.

c. Click **Print** to print the worksheet, and then save the workbook.

Check your printed worksheet to make sure the data are formatted correctly. After you click Print, the Home tab is displayed. If you decide not to print at this time, you need to click the Home tab yourself.

STEP 5 ADJUST SCALING AND SET SHEET OPTIONS

You want to print a copy of the worksheet formulas to check the logic of the formulas. You need to display the formulas, select options to print gridlines and headings, and then decrease the scaling so that the data print on one page. Refer to Figure 1.50 as you complete Step 5.

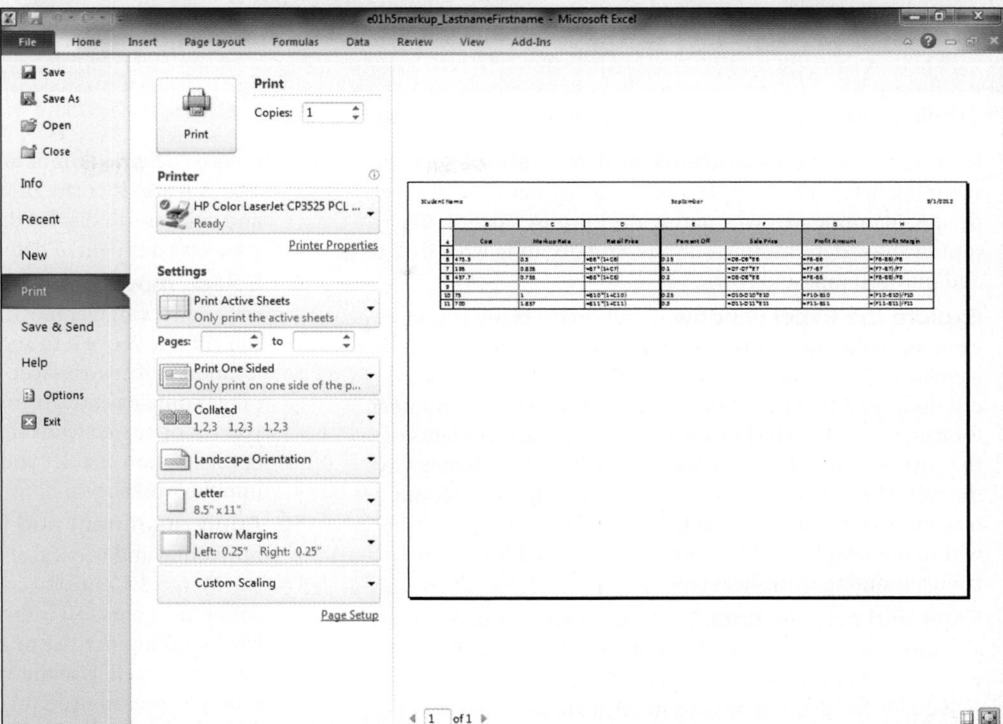

FIGURE 1.50 Worksheet in Print Preview ➤

a. Press **Ctrl+`** to display cell formulas.

b. Click the **Page Layout tab**. Click the **Print Gridlines check box**, and then click the **Print Headings check box** in the Sheet Options group.

   Since you want to print cell formulas, it is helpful to display the gridlines and row and column headings on that printout.

c. Click the **File tab**, and then click **Print**.

   The bottom of the Backstage view displays 1 of 2, indicating the worksheet no longer prints on one page.

d. Click **Next Page** (the right triangle at the bottom of the Backstage view), and then click the **Page Layout tab**.

e. Click **Margins** in the Page Setup group, and then select **Narrow**.

f. Select the **range B4:H11**, click **Print Area** in the Page Setup group, and then select **Set Print Area**.

g. Click the **Scale spin box** in the Scale to Fit group on the Page Layout tab until it displays **90%**.

   The dotted line indicating the page break now appears on the right side of the last column, indicating that the worksheet data will print on one page. If you want to verify that the worksheet will print on one page, display it in print preview.

h. Print the worksheet. Save and close the *e01h5markup_LastnameFirstname* workbook and submit the worksheet based on your instructor's directions.

   Check your printed worksheet to make sure the data are formatted correctly.

CHAPTER OBJECTIVES REVIEW

After reading this chapter, you have accomplished the following objectives:

1. **Plan for effective workbook and worksheet design.** Planning before entering data helps ensure better worksheet design. Planning involves stating the purpose, identifying input values, determining outputs, and deciding what data to add into columns and rows.
2. **Explore the Excel window.** Excel shares many common elements with other Office programs, but also includes unique elements. The Name Box identifies the location of the active cell, indicated first by column letter and then by row number, for example, A10. The Formula Bar displays the contents of the current cell. Select All enables users to select all items in the worksheet. Column and row headings identify column letters and row numbers. Sheet tabs provide different worksheets within the workbook. Navigation buttons enable users to navigate among worksheet tabs.
3. **Enter and edit cell data.** You can enter text, values, dates, and formulas in cells. Text aligns on the left cell margin, and values and dates align on the right cell margin. Values represent quantities that can be used in calculations. Dates may be entered in a variety of formats. You can edit or clear the contents of cells.
4. **Use symbols and order of precedence.** The basic arithmetic symbols are +, –, *, /, and ^ in Excel. The order of operations is the sequence in which mathematical operations is performed: parentheses, exponents, multiplication, division, addition, and subtraction. Formulas start with an equal sign, should include cell references containing values, and should not contain raw values except constants.
5. **Use Auto Fill.** To copy a formula down a column or across a row, double-click or drag the fill handle. You can use Auto Fill to copy formulas, number patterns, names of months, weekdays, etc.
6. **Display cell formulas.** By default, the results of formulas appear in cells instead of the actual formulas. You can display formulas within the cells to help troubleshoot formulas by pressing Ctrl+`.
7. **Manage worksheets.** The default worksheet tab names are Sheet1, Sheet2, and Sheet3. You can rename the worksheet tabs to be more meaningful, delete extra worksheets, insert new worksheets, and apply colors to worksheet tabs. In addition, you can move worksheets or copy worksheets.
8. **Manage columns and rows.** Although you should plan a worksheet before creating it, you can insert new columns and rows or delete columns and rows that you no longer need. You can also increase or decrease the height or width of rows and columns to display data better. Hiding rows and columns protects confidential data from being displayed or printed.
9. **Select, move, copy, and paste.** A range may be a single cell or a rectangular block of cells. After selecting a range, you can cut it to move it to another range or copy it to another location in the worksheet. You should ensure the designation range contains enough empty cells to accommodate the data you cut or copied to avoid overwriting existing data. The Paste Special option enables you to specify how the data are pasted into the worksheet.
10. **Apply alignment and font options.** You can apply horizontal and vertical alignment to format data in cells or use Merge & Center to combine cells and center titles over columns of data. To indicate hierarchy of data or to offset a label you can increase or decrease how much the data are indented in a cell. Use the Wrap Text option to present text on multiple lines in order to avoid having extra-wide columns. You can further improve readability of worksheets by adding appropriate borders around important ranges or applying fill colors to cells.
11. **Apply number formats.** The default number format is General, which does not apply any particular format to values. Apply appropriate formats to values to present the data with the correct symbols and decimal alignment. For example, Accounting is a common number format for monetary values. Other popular number formats include Percentage and Date. After applying a number format, you can increase or decrease the number of decimal points displayed.
12. **Select page setup options.** The Page Layout tab on the Ribbon contains options for setting margins, selecting orientation, specifying page size, selecting the print area, and applying other settings. In addition, you can display the Page Setup dialog box to specify these and other settings to control how data will print. You can insert a header or footer to display documentation, such as your name, date, time, and worksheet tab name.
13. **Print a worksheet.** Before printing a worksheet, you should display a preview in the Backstage view to ensure the data will print correctly. The Backstage view helps you see if margins are correct or if isolated rows or columns will print on separate pages. After making appropriate adjustments, you can print the worksheet.

KEY TERMS

Active cell **p.331**
Auto Fill **p.339**
Border **p.364**
Cell **p.331**
Cell address **p.331**
Column width **p.350**
Fill color **p.365**
Fill handle **p.339**
Formula **p.333**
Formula Bar **p.330**
Horizontal alignment **p.363**
Input area **p.329**
Name Box **p.330**
Nonadjacent range **p.353**
Order of precedence **p.338**
Output area **p.329**
Range **p.353**
Row height **p.351**
Sheet tab **p.331**
Spreadsheet **p.328**
Spreadsheet program **p.328**
Text **p.332**
Value **p.333**
Vertical alignment **p.363**
Workbook **p.328**
Worksheet **p.328**
Wrap text **p.364**

MULTIPLE CHOICE

1. What is the first step in planning an effective worksheet?
   (a) Enter labels, values, and formulas.
   (b) State the purpose of the worksheet.
   (c) Identify the input and output areas.
   (d) Decide how to format the worksheet data.

2. What Excel interface item is not displayed until you start typing or editing data in a cell?
   (a) Insert Function
   (b) Name Box
   (c) Formula Bar
   (d) Enter

3. Given the formula =B1*B2+B3/B4^2 where B1 contains 3, B2 contains 4, B3 contains 32, and B4 contains 4, what is the result?
   (a) 14
   (b) 121
   (c) 76
   (d) 9216

4. Why would you press Ctrl+` in Excel?
   (a) To display the print options
   (b) To undo a mistake you made
   (c) To display cell formulas
   (d) To enable the AutoComplete feature

5. Which of the following is a nonadjacent range?
   (a) C15:D30
   (b) L15:L65
   (c) A1:Z99
   (d) A1:A10, D1:D10

6. If you want to balance a title over several columns, what do you do?
   (a) Enter the data in the cell that is about midway across the spreadsheet.
   (b) Merge and center the data over all columns.
   (c) Use the Increase Indent command until the title looks balanced.
   (d) Click Center to center the title horizontally over several columns.

7. Which of the following characteristics is not applicable to the Accounting Number Format?
   (a) Dollar sign immediately on the left side of the value
   (b) Commas to separate thousands
   (c) Two decimal places
   (d) Zero values displayed as hyphens

8. If you want to see a preview of how a worksheet will appear on a hard copy, what do you do?
   (a) Change the Zoom to 100%.
   (b) Click the Page Layout tab, and then click the Print check box in the Sheet Options group.
   (c) Click the File tab, and then click Print.
   (d) Click the Page Setup Dialog Box Launcher.

9. Assume that the data on a worksheet consume a whole printed page and a couple of columns on a second page. You can do all of the following except what to force the data to print all on one page?
   (a) Decrease the Scale value.
   (b) Increase the left and right margins.
   (c) Decrease column widths if possible.
   (d) Select a smaller range as the print area.

10. What should you do if you see a column of pound signs (###) instead of values or results of formulas?
    (a) Increase the zoom percentage.
    (b) Delete the column.
    (c) Adjust the row height.
    (d) Increase the column width.

PRACTICE EXERCISES

1 Mathematics Review

After a nice summer break, you want to brush up on your math skills. Since you are learning Excel, you decide to test your logic by creating formulas in Excel. Your first step is to plan the spreadsheet design. After having read Chapter 1, you realize that you should avoid values in formulas most of the time. Therefore, you will create an input area that contains values you will use in your formulas. To test your knowledge of formulas, you need to create an output area that will contain a variety of formulas using cell references from the input area. You need to include a formatted title, the date prepared, and your name. After creating and verifying formula results, you plan to change the input values and observe changes in the formula results. After verifying the results, you will copy the data to Sheet2, display cell formulas, and apply page layout options. This exercise follows the same set of skills as used in Hands-On Exercises 1, 2, 3, and 5 in the chapter. Refer to Figure 1.51 as you complete this exercise.

	A	B	C	D	E
1	**Excel Formulas and Order of Precedence**				
2	Date Created:	9/1/2012		Student Name	
3					
4	**Input Area:**			**Output Area:**	
5	First Value	1		Sum of 1st and 2nd values	3
6	Second Value	2		Difference between 4th and 1st values	3
7	Third Value	3		Product of 2nd and 3rd values	6
8	Fourth Value	4		Quotient of 3rd and 1st values	3
9				2nd value to the power of 3rd value	8
10				1st value added to product of 2nd and 4th values and difference between sum and 3rd value	6
11				Product of sum of 1st and 2nd and difference between 4th and 3rd values	3
12				Product of 1st and 2nd added to product of 3rd and 4th values	14
13					

FIGURE 1.51 Formula Practice ➤

a. Start Excel. If Excel is already open, click the **File tab**, select **New**, and then click **Create** to display a blank workbook. Save the workbook as **e01p1math_LastnameFirstname**.

b. Type **Excel Formulas and Order of Precedence** in **cell A1**, and then press **Enter**.

c. Type the labels in **cells A2** through **A8** as shown in Figure 1.51, type the current date in **cell B2** in the format shown, and then type the values shown in **cells B5:B8**. Column A labels will appear cut off after you enter values in column B, and the column B values will be right-aligned at this point.

d. Type your name in **cell D2**, and then type the labels in **cells D4:D12** as shown in Figure 1.51. Column D labels will overlap into columns E through L at this point.

e. Adjust the column widths by doing the following:
   - Click in any cell in column A, and then click **Format** in the Cells group.
   - Select **Column Width**, type **12.5** in the **Column width box**, and then click **OK**.
   - Use the instructions in the first two bullets above to set a **35.5** width for **column D**.
   - Use the instructions in the first two bullets above to set a **11.43** width for **column B**.

f. Format the title:
   - Select the **range A1:E1**.
   - Click **Merge & Center** in the Alignment group.
   - Bold the title and apply **14 pt** size.

g. Apply the following font and alignment formats:
   - Bold **cells A4** and **D4**.
   - Select the **range B5:B8**, and then click **Center** in the Alignment group.
   - Select the **range D10:D12**, and then click **Wrap Text** in the Alignment group.

h. Enter the following formulas in **column E**:
   - Click **cell E5**. Type **=B5+B6** and press **Enter**. Excel adds the value stored in cell B5 (1) to the value stored in cell B6 (2). The result (3) appears in cell E5, as described in cell D5. You can check your results with the results shown in Figure 1.51.
   - Enter appropriate formulas in **cells E6:E8**, pressing **Enter** after entering each formula. Subtract to calculate a difference, multiply to calculate a product, and divide to calculate a quotient.
   - Type **=B6^B7** in **cell E9**, and then press **Enter**. Estimate the answer: 2*2*2 = 8.
   - Enter **=B5+B6*B8-B7** in **cell E10**, and then press **Enter**. Estimate the answer: 2*4=8; 1+8 = 9; 9-3 = 6. Multiplication occurs first, followed by addition, and finally subtraction.
   - Enter **=(B5+B6)*(B8-B7)** in **cell E11**, and then press **Enter**. Estimate the answer: 1+2 = 3; 4-3 = 1; 3*1 = 3. Notice that this formula is almost identical to the previous formula; however, the parentheses affect the order of operations. Calculations in parentheses occur before the multiplication.
   - Enter **=B5*B6+B7*B8** in **cell E12**, and then press **Enter**. Estimate the answer: 1*2 = 2; 3*4 = 12; 2+12 = 14.

i. Edit a formula and the input values:
   - Click **cell E12**, and then click in the **Formula Bar** to edit the formula. Add parentheses as shown: **=(B5*B6)+(B7*B8)**, and then click **Enter** to the left side of the Formula Bar. The answer is still 14. The parentheses do not affect order of precedence since multiplication occurred before the addition. The parentheses help improve the readability of the formula.
   - Click **cell B5**, type **2**, and then press **Enter**. Type **4**, press **Enter**, type **6**, press **Enter**, type **8**, and then press **Enter**.
   - Double-check the results of the formulas using a calculator or your head. The new results in cells E5:E12 should be 6, 6, 24, 3, 4096, 28, 12, and 56, respectively.

j. Double-click the **Sheet1 tab**, type **Results**, and then press **Enter**. Right-click the **Results tab**, select **Move or Copy**, click **(move to end)** in the *Before sheet* section, click the **Create a copy check box**, and then click **OK**. Double-click the **Results (2) tab**, type **Formulas**, and then press **Enter**. Right-click the **Sheet2 tab**, and then select **Delete**. Delete the Sheet3 tab.

k. Make sure the Formulas worksheet tab is active, click the **Page Layout tab**, and then do the following:
   - Click **Orientation** in the Page Setup group, and then select **Landscape**.
   - Click the **Print Gridlines check box**, and then click the **Print Headings check box** in the Sheet Options group.

l. Click the **Formulas tab**, and then click **Show Formulas** in the Formula Auditing group. Double-click between the column A and column B headings to adjust the column A width. Double-click between the column B and column C headings to adjust the column B width. Set **24.0** width for **column D**.

m. Click the **File tab**, and then click **Print**. Verify that the worksheet will print on one page. Click the **File tab** again to close the Backstage view.

n. Save and close the workbook, and submit the worksheet based on your instructor's directions.

2 Calendar Formatting

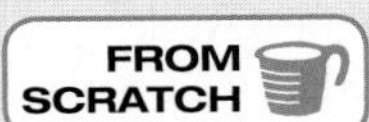

You want to create a calendar for October. The calendar will enable you to practice alignment settings, including center, merge and center, and indents. In addition, you will need to adjust column widths and increase row height to create cells large enough to enter important information, such as birthdays, in your calendar. You will use Auto Fill to complete the days of the week and the days within each week. To improve the appearance of the calendar, you will add fill colors, font colors, borders, and clip art. This exercise follows the same set of skills as used in Hands-On Exercises 1–5 in the chapter. Refer to Figure 1.52 as you complete this exercise.

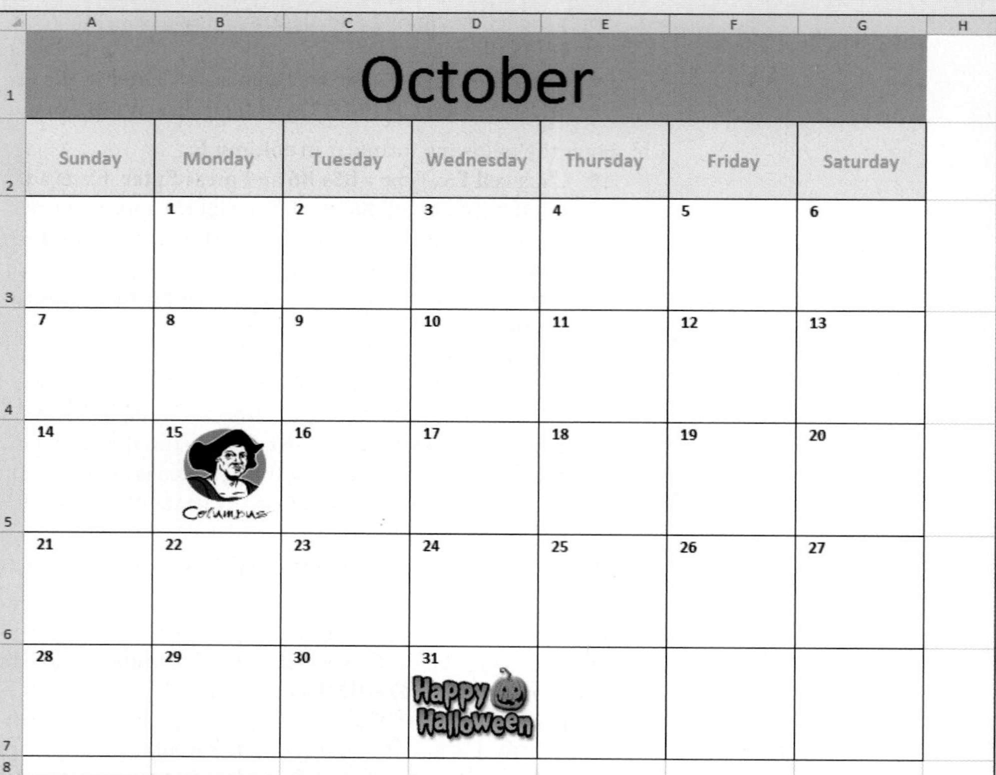

FIGURE 1.52 October Calendar Page ➤

a. Click the **File tab**, select **New**, and then click **Create** to display a blank workbook. Save the workbook as **e01p2october_LastnameFirstname**.

b. Type **October** in **cell A1**, and then click **Enter** on the left side of the Formula Bar.

c. Format the title:
   - Select the **range A1:G1**, and then click **Merge & Center** in the Alignment group.
   - Apply **48 pt** size.
   - Click the **Fill Color arrow**, and then click **Orange, Accent 6** on the top row of the *Theme Colors* section of the color palette.

d. Complete the days of the week:
   - Type **Sunday** in **cell A2**, and then click **Enter** on the left side of the Formula Bar.
   - Drag the fill handle in **cell A2** across the row through **cell G2** to use Auto Fill to complete the rest of the weekdays.
   - Click the **Fill Color arrow**, and then select **Orange, Accent 6, Lighter 80%**. Click the **Font Color arrow**, and then click **Orange, Accent 6**. Apply bold and **14 pt** size. Click **Middle Align**, and then click **Center** in the Alignment group.

e. Complete the days of the month:
   - Type **1** in **cell B3**, press **Tab**, type **2** in **cell C3**, and then click **Enter** on the left side of the Formula Bar.
   - Select the **range B3:C3**. Drag the fill handle in **cell C3** across the row through **cell G3** to use Auto Fill to complete the rest of the days for the first week.
   - Type **7** in **cell A4**, press **Tab**, type **8** in **cell B4**, and then click **Enter** on the left side of the Formula Bar. Use the fill handle to complete the days for the second week.
   - Type **14** in **cell A5**, press **Tab**, type **15** in **cell B5**, and then click **Enter** on the left side of the Formula Bar. Use the fill handle to complete the days for the third week.
   - Use the fill handle to complete the days of the month (up to 31).

f. Format the columns and rows:
   - Select **columns A:G**. Click **Format** in the Cells group, select **Column Width**, type **16** in the **Column width box**, and then click **OK**.
   - Select **row 2**. Click **Format** in the Cells group, select **Row Height**, type **54**, and then click **OK**.
   - Select **rows 3:7**. Set an **80** row height.

- Select the **range A2:G7**. Click the **Borders arrow** in the Font group, and then select **All Borders**.
- Select the **range A3:G7**. Click **Top Align** and **Align Text Left** in the Alignment group. Click **Increase Indent**. Bold the numbers and apply **12 pt** size.

FYI

g. Insert and size images:
   - Display the Clip Art task pane. Search for and insert the Halloween image in the **October 31 cell**. Size the image to fit within the cell.
   - Search for and insert an image of Columbus in the **October 15 cell**. Size the image to fit within the cell.

h. Double-click the **Sheet1 tab**, type **October**, and then press **Enter**. Right-click **Sheet2**, and then select **Delete**. Delete Sheet3.

i. Click the **Page Layout tab**. Click **Orientation** in the Page Setup group, and then select **Landscape**.

j. Click the **Insert tab**, and then click **Header & Footer** in the Text group. Click in the left side of the header, and then type your name. Click in the center of the header, and then click **Sheet Name** in the Header & Footer Elements group on the Design tab. Click in the right side of the header, and then click **File Name** in the Header & Footer Elements group on the Design tab. Click in any cell in the workbook, and then click **Normal** on the status bar.

k. Save and close the workbook, and submit based on your instructor's directions.

3 Bricktown Theatre

You are the assistant manager at Bricktown Theatre where touring Broadway plays and musicals are performed. You want to design a spreadsheet that helps you analyze ticket sales by seating chart for each performance. The spreadsheet you create will identify the seating sections, total seats in each section, and the number of seats sold for a performance. You will then be able to calculate the percentage of seats sold and unsold. This exercise follows the same set of skills as used in Hands-On Exercises 1–5 in the chapter. Refer to Figure 1.53 as you complete this exercise.

	A	B	C	D	E	F	G
1	**Downtown Theatre**						
2	Ticket Sales						
3	3/8/2013						
4							
5	**Section**	**Available Seats**	**Seats Sold**	**Percentage Sold**	**Percentage Unsold**		
6	Box Seats	16	12	75.0%	25.0%		
7	Front Floor	120	114	95.0%	5.0%		
8	Back Floor	132	108	81.8%	18.2%		
9	Tier 1	40	40	100.0%	0.0%		
10	Mezzanine	144	138	95.8%	4.2%		
11	Balcony	106	84	79.2%	20.8%		
12							

13	**Downtown Theatre**				
14	Ticket Sales				
15	41341				
16					
17					
18	Section	Available Seats	Seats Sold	Percentage Sold	Percentage Unsold
19	Box Seats	16	12	=C6/B6	=(B6-C6)/B6
20	Front Floor	120	114	=C7/B7	=(B7-C7)/B7
21	Back Floor	132	108	=C8/B8	=(B8-C8)/B8
22	Tier 1	40	40	=C9/B9	=(B9-C9)/B9
23	Mezzanine	144	138	=C10/B10	=(B10-C10)/B10
24	Balcony	106	84	=C11/B11	=(B11-C11)/B11
25					
26					

Seating

FIGURE 1.53 Theatre Seating Data ➤

a. Click the **File tab**, click **New**, make sure **Blank workbook** is selected, and then click **Create**. Save the workbook as **e01p3ticketsales_LastnameFirstname**.

b. Double-click the **Sheet1 tab**, type **Seating**, and then press **Enter**. Right-click **Sheet2**, and then select **Delete**. Delete Sheet3 as well.

c. Enter initial data in the worksheet by doing the following:
   - Type **Downtown Theatre** in **cell A1**, and then press **Enter**. Type **Ticket Sales by Seating Section** in **cell A2**, and then press **Enter**. Type **3/8/2013** in **cell A3**, and then press **Enter**.
   - Click **cell A5**, and then type the following data in the **range A5:A10**: **Section**, **Balcony**, **Box Seats**, **Floor**, **Tier 1**, and **Mezzanine**.
   - Click **cell B5**, and then type the following data in the **range B5:B10**: **Available Seats**, **106**, **16**, **120**, **40**, and **144**.
   - Click **cell C5**, and then type the following data in the **range C5:C10**: **Seats Sold**, **84**, **12**, **114**, **40**, and **138**.
   - Type **Percentage Sold** in **cell D5**, and then type **Percentage Unsold** in **cell E5**. The label in cell D5 will appear cut off after you type the label in cell E5. You will format the labels in steps d and i.

d. Adjust alignments and font attributes by doing the following from the Alignment and Font groups on the Home tab:
   - Select the **range A1:E1**, click **Merge & Center**, click **Bold**, click the **Font Size arrow**, and then select **16**.
   - Use the Merge & Center command to merge the **range A2:E2** and center the subtitle.
   - Use the Merge & Center command to merge the **range A3:E3** and center the date.
   - Select the **range A5:E5**, click **Wrap Text**, click **Center**, and then click **Bold** to format the column labels.

e. Right-click the **row 9 heading**, and then select **Insert** from the shortcut menu to insert a new row. Type the following data in the new row: **Back Floor**, **132**, **108**.

f. Double-click **cell A8**, press **Home** to position the insertion point on the left side of the existing text, type **Front**, making sure a space separates *Front* and *Floor*, and then press **Enter**.

FYI

g. Press **Ctrl+Home** to make **cell A1** the active cell. Spell check the worksheet and make any necessary changes.

h. Move the Balcony row to be the last row by doing the following:
   - Click the **row 6 heading**, and then click **Cut** in the Clipboard group on the Home tab.
   - Right-click the **row 12 heading**, and then select **Insert Cut Cells** from the menu.

i. Adjust column widths by doing the following:
   - Double-click between the column A and column B heading.
   - Select **columns B and C headings** to select the columns, click **Format** in the Cells group, select **Column Width**, type **9** in the **Column width box** in the Column Width dialog box, and then click **OK**. Because columns B and C contain similar data, you set the same width for these columns.
   - Set the width of columns D and E to **12**.

j. Select the **range B6:C11**, click **Align Text Right** in the Alignment group on the Home tab, and then click **Increase Indent** twice in the Alignment group.

k. Calculate and format the percentage of sold and unsold seats by doing the following:
   - Click **cell D6**. Type **=C6/B6** and then press **Tab** to enter the formula and make **cell E6** the active cell. This formula divides the number of seats sold by the total number of Box Seats.
   - Type **=(B6-C6)/B6** and then click **Enter** on the left side of the Formula Bar to enter the formula and keep **cell E6** the active cell. This formula must first subtract the number of sold seats from the available seats to calculate the number of unsold seats. The difference is divided by the total number of available seats to determine the percentage of unsold seats.
   - Select the **range D6:E6**, click **Percent Style** in the Number group on the Home tab, and then click **Increase Decimal** in the Number group. Keep the range selected.
   - Double-click the fill handle in the bottom-right corner of **cell E6** to copy the selected formulas down their respective columns. Keep the range selected.
   - Click **Align Text Right** in the Alignment group, and then click **Increase Indent** twice in the Alignment group. These actions will help center the data below the column labels. Do not click Center; doing so will center each value and cause the decimal points not to align.

l. Display and preserve a screenshot of the formulas by doing the following:
   - Select the **range A13:G25**, click the **Fill Color arrow** in the Font group, and then click **White, Background 1**. Applying this fill color will prevent the cell gridlines from bleeding through the screenshot you are about to embed.
   - Click the **Formulas tab**, and then click **Show Formulas** in the Formula Auditing group to display cell formulas.
   - Click **cell A1**, drag down to **cell E11** to select the range of data, click the **Home tab**, and click **Copy** in the Clipboard group.
   - Click **cell A13**, click the **Paste arrow**, and then click **Picture (U)** in the *Other Paste Options* section.
   - Click the **Formulas tab**, and then click **Show Formulas** in the Formula Auditing group to hide cell formulas. Notice that the picture image is a little distorted now.
   - Drag the middle-right sizing handle to the right side of column G to reduce the image distortion.

m. Click **cell A1** to deselect the image. Click the **Page Layout tab**, click **Margins** in the Page Setup group, and then select **Custom Margins**. Click the **Horizontally check box**, and then click **Print Preview**. Excel centers the data horizontally based on the widest item, which is the image. If the worksheet contains the data only, it would have been centered horizontally instead. Press **Esc** to get out of the Print Preview mode.

n. Click the **Insert tab**, and then click **Header & Footer** in the Text group. Click in the left side of the header, and then type your name. Press **Tab**, and then click **File Name** in the Header & Footer Elements group. Press **Tab**, and then click **Current Date** in the Header & Footer Elements group. Click **cell A1**, and then click **Normal** on the status bar.

o. Save and close the workbook, and submit based on your instructor's directions.

MID-LEVEL EXERCISES

1 Fuel Efficiency

Your summer vacation involved traveling through several states to visit relatives and to view the scenic attractions. While traveling, you kept a travel log of mileage and gasoline purchases. Now that the vacation is over, you want to determine the fuel efficiency of your automobile. The partially completed worksheet includes the beginning mileage for the vacation trips and the amount of fuel purchased.

a. Open the *e01m1fuel* workbook and save the workbook as **e01m1fuel_LastnameFirstname** so that you can return to the original workbook if necessary.
b. Insert a new column between columns B and C, and then type **Miles Driven** as the column heading.
c. Select the range of beginning miles in **cells A5:A12**. Copy the selected range to duplicate the values in **cells B4:B11** to ensure that the ending mileage for one trip is identical to the beginning mileage for the next trip.
d. Create the formula to calculate the miles driven for the first trip. Copy the formula down the **Miles Driven column**.
e. Create the formula to calculate the miles per gallon for the first trip. Copy the formula down the **Miles Per Gallon column**.
f. Merge and center the title over the data columns. Apply bold, **16 pt** size, and **Blue, Accent 1** font color.
g. Format the column headings: bold, centered, wrap text, and **Blue, Accent 1, Lighter 80% fill color**.
h. Apply **Comma Style** to the values in the Beginning and Ending columns, and then display these values as whole numbers. Display the values in the Miles Per Gallon column with two decimal places.
i. Delete Sheet2 and Sheet3. Rename *Sheet1* as **Mileage**.
j. Set these page settings: **2"** top margin, centered horizontally, **125%** scaling.
k. Insert a header with your name on the left side, the sheet name code in the center, and the file name code on the right side.
l. Save and close the workbook, and submit based on your instructor's directions.

2 Restaurant Receipt

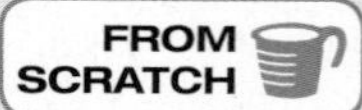

Matt, the owner of Matt's Sports Grill in Toledo, Ohio, asked you to help him create a receipt spreadsheet that he can use until his new system arrives. He wants an input area for the total food and beverage purchases, the sales tax rate, and the tip rate. The formatted receipt should include the subtotal, tax, tip, and total amount for a customer. Refer to Figure 1.54 as you complete this exercise..

	A	B	C	D	E
1	**Input Area**			**Matt's Sports Grill**	
2	Food & Beverages	$ 9.39		Toledo, Ohio	
3	Sales Tax Rate	6.5%			
4	Tip Rate	18.0%		Food & Beverages	$ 9.39
5				Sales Tax Amount	0.61
6				Subtotal	$ 10.00
7				Tip Amount	1.80
8				**Total Bill**	**$ 11.80**
9					
10				*Thank you for dining with us.*	

FIGURE 1.54 Matt's Sports Grill Receipt ➤

a. Open a new Excel workbook, save it as **e01m2receipt_LastnameFirstname**, rename *Sheet1* as **Receipt**, and delete the other sheets.

b. Enter the four labels in the **range A1:A4** in the Input Area as shown in Figure 1.54. Type **9.39**, **0.065**, and **.18** in the **range B2:B4**. Apply these formats to the Input Area:
   - Merge and center the Inputs Area title over both columns. Apply bold and **Tan, Background 2, Darker 25% fill color** to the title. Adjust the width of the first column.
   - Apply the **Accounting Number Format** and **Percent Style** formats with the respective decimal places as shown in the **range B2:B4**.

FYI

c. Enter the labels in the receipt area as shown in column D. Use Format Painter to copy the formats of the title in **cell A1** to **cell D1**. Format Painter will merge and center, bold, and apply the fill color to **cell D1**. Merge and center the city and state in the **range D2:E2**. Change the width of column D to **17**. Indent the *Subtotal* and *Tip Amount* labels twice each. Apply bold to *Total Bill*, and then italicize *Thank you for dining with us*.

d. Enter the following formulas for the receipt:
   - Food & Beverages: Enter a formula that reads the value in the Input Area; do not retype the value in cell E4.
   - Sales Tax Amount: Calculate the product of the food & beverages and the sales tax rate.
   - Subtotal: Determine the formula needed.
   - Tip Amount: Calculate the product of the subtotal and tip rate.
   - Total Bill: Determine the formula needed.

e. Apply **Accounting Number Format** to the Food & Beverages, Subtotal, and Total Bill values, if necessary. Apply **Comma Style** to and underline to the Sales Tax Amount and Tip Amount values. Apply the **Double Underline style** to the Total Bill value.

f. Set **1.5"** top margin, and then center the data horizontally on the page.

g. Insert a header with your name on the left side, the sheet name code in the center, and the file name code on the right side.

h. Create a copy of the Receipt worksheet, move the new sheet to the end, and then rename the copied sheet as **Formulas**. Display cell formulas on the Formulas worksheet, select **landscape orientation**, and then select the options to print gridlines and headings. Adjust column widths so that the data will fit on one page.

i. Save and close the workbook, and submit based on your instructor's directions.

3 Real Estate Sales Report

You own a small real estate company in Enid, Oklahoma. You want to analyze sales for selected properties. Your assistant prepared a spreadsheet with some of the data from the files. You need to calculate the number of days that the houses were on the market and their sales percentage of the list price. In one situation, the house was involved in a bidding war between two families that really wanted the house. Therefore, the sale price exceeded the list price.

a. Open the *e01m3sales* workbook and save the workbook as **e01m3sales_LastnameFirstname** so that you can return to the original workbook if necessary.

b. Delete the row that has incomplete sales data. The owners took their house off the market.

c. Calculate the number of days each house was on the market. Copy the formula down that column.

d. Calculate the sale price percentage of the list price. The second house was listed for $500,250, but it sold for only $400,125. Therefore, the sale percentage of the list price is 79.99%. Format the percentages with two decimal places.

e. Format prices with **Accounting Number Format** with zero decimal places.

f. Wrap the headings on row 4.

g. Insert a new column between the Date Sold and List Price columns. Move the Days on Market column to the new location. Then delete the empty column B.

h. Edit the list date of the 41 Chestnut Circle house to be **4/20/2012**. Edit the list price of the house on Amsterdam Drive to be **$355,000**.

i. Select the **property rows**, and then set a **20** row height. Adjust column widths as necessary.

j. Select **landscape orientation**, and then set the scaling to **130%**. Center the data horizontally and vertically on the page.
k. Insert a header with your name, the current date code, and the current time code.
l. Save and close the workbook, and submit based on your instructor's directions.

4 Guest House Rental Rates

You manage a beach guest house in Ft. Lauderdale. The guest house contains three types of rental units. You set prices based on peak and off-peak times of the year. You want to calculate the maximum daily revenue for each rental type, assuming all units of each type are rented. In addition, you want to calculate the discount rate for off-peak rental times. After calculating the revenue and discount rate, you want to improve the appearance of the worksheet by applying font, alignment, and number formats.

a. Open the *e01m4rentals* workbook and save the workbook as **e01m4rentals_LastnameFirstname** so that you can return to the original workbook if necessary.
b. Create and copy the following formulas:
   - Calculate the Peak Rentals Maximum Revenue based on the number of units and the rental price per day.
   - Calculate the Off-Peak Rentals Maximum Revenue based on the number of units and the rental price per day.

   - Calculate the discount rate for the Off-Peak rental price per day. For example, using the peak and off-peak per day values, the studio apartment rents for 75% of its peak rental rate. However, you need to calculate and display the off-peak discount rate, which is 25%.

c. Format the monetary values with **Accounting Number Format**. Format the discount rate in **Percent Style** with one decimal place.
d. Format the headings on row 4 as follows:
   - Merge and center *Peak Rentals* over the two columns of peak rental data. Apply bold, **Dark Red fill color**, and **White, Background 1 font color.**
   - Merge and center *Off-Peak Rentals* over the three columns of off-peak rental data. Apply bold, **Blue fill color**, and **White, Background 1 font color.**
e. Center, bold, and wrap the headings on row 5.
f. Apply **Red, Accent 2, Lighter 80% fill color** to the **range C5:D8**. Apply **Blue, Accent 1, Lighter 80% fill color** to the **range E5:G8**.
g. Set **1"** top, bottom, left, and right margins. Center the data horizontally on the page.
h. Insert a header with your name on the left side, the sheet name code in the center, and the file name code on the right side.
i. Insert a new worksheet, and then name it **Formulas**. Copy the data from the Rental Rates worksheet to the Formulas worksheet. On the Formulas worksheet, select **landscape orientation** and the options to print gridlines and headings. Display cell formulas and adjust column widths so that the data will fit on one page. Insert a header with the same specifications that you did for the Rental Rates worksheet.
j. Save and close the workbook, and submit based on your instructor's directions.

CAPSTONE EXERCISE

You manage a publishing company that publishes and sells books to bookstores in Austin. Your assistant prepared a standard six-month royalty statement for one author. You need to insert formulas, format the worksheets, and then prepare royalty statements for other authors.

Enter Data into the Worksheet

You need to enter and format a title, enter the date indicating the end of the statement period, and then delete a blank column. You also need to insert a row for the standard discount rate row, a percentage that you discount the books from the retail price to sell to the bookstores.

a. Open the *e01c1royal* workbook and save it as **e01c1royal_LastnameFirstname**.

b. Type **Royalty Statement** in **cell A1**. Merge and center the title over the four data columns. Select **16 pt** size, and apply **Purple font color**.

c. Type **6/30/2012** in **cell B3**, and then left-align the date.

d. Delete the blank column between the Hardback and Paperback columns.

e. Insert a new row between *Retail Price* and *Price to Bookstore*. Enter **Standard Discount Rate**, **0.55**, and **0.5**. Format the two values as **Percent Style**.

Calculate Values

You need to insert formulas to perform necessary calculations.

a. Enter the **Percent Returned formula** in the Hardback column. The percent returned indicates the percentage of books sold but returned to the publisher.

b. Enter the **Price to Bookstore formula**. This is the price at which you sell the books to the bookstore and is based on the retail price and the standard discount. For example, if a book has a $10 retail price and a 55% discount, you sell the book for $4.50.

c. Enter the **Net Retail Sales formula**. The net retail sales is the revenue from the net units sold at the retail price. Gross units sold minus the returned units equals net units sold.

d. Enter the **Royalty to Author formula**. Royalties are based on net retail sales and the applicable royalty rate.

e. Enter the **Royalty per Book formula**. This amount is the author's earnings on every book sold but not returned.

f. Copy the formulas to the Paperback column.

Format the Values

You are ready to format the values to improve the readability.

a. Apply **Comma Style** with zero decimal places to the quantities in the *Units Sold* section.

b. Apply **Percent Style** with one decimal place to the Units Sold values, **Percent Style** with zero decimal places to the Pricing values, and **Percent Style** with two decimal places to the Royalty Information values.

c. Apply **Accounting Number Format** to all monetary values.

Format the Worksheet

You want to improve the appearance of the rest of the worksheet.

a. Select the **Hardback** and **Paperback labels**. Apply bold, right-alignment, and **Purple font color**.

b. Select the **Units Sold section heading**. Apply bold and **Purple, Accent 4, Lighter 40% fill color**.

c. Use **Format Painter** to apply the formats from the Units Sold label to the Pricing and Royalty Information labels.

d. Select the individual labels within each section (e.g., *Gross Units Sold*) and indent the labels twice. Widen column A as needed.

e. Select the **range A7:C10** (the *Units Sold* section), and then apply the **Outside Borders border style**. Apply the same border style to the *Pricing* and *Royalty Information* sections.

Manage the Workbook

You want to duplicate the royalty statement worksheet to use as a model to prepare a royalty statement for another author. You will apply page setup options and insert a header on both worksheets.

a. Insert a new worksheet on the right side of the Jacobs worksheet. Rename the worksheet as **Lopez**.

b. Change the Jacobs sheet tab to **Red**. Change the Lopez sheet tab to **Dark Blue**.

c. Copy Jacobs' data to the Lopez worksheet.

d. Make these changes on the Lopez worksheet: **Lopez** (author), **5000** (hardback gross units), **15000** (paperback gross units), **400** (hardback returns), **175** (paperback returns), **19.95** (hardback retail price), and **7.95** (paperback retail price).

e. Click the **Jacobs sheet tab**, and then press and hold down **Ctrl** as you click the **Lopez sheet tab** to select both worksheets. Select the margin setting to center the data horizontally on the page. Insert a header with your name on the left side, the sheet name code in the center, and the file name code on the right side.

f. Change back to Normal view. Right-click the **Jacobs sheet name**, and then select **Ungroup Sheets**.

Display Formulas and Print the Workbook

You want to print the formatted Jacobs worksheet to display the calculated results. To provide evidence of the formulas, you want to display and print cell formulas in the Lopez worksheet.

a. Display the cell formulas for the Lopez worksheet.

b. Select options to print the gridlines and headings.

c. Adjust the column widths so that the formula printout will print on one page.

d. Submit either a hard copy of both worksheets or an electronic copy of the workbook to your professor as instructed. Close the workbook.

Tip Distribution from Access Table

GENERAL CASE

FROM SCRATCH

You are a server at a restaurant in Portland. You must tip the bartender 15% of the drink amount and the server assistant 10% of the total tip amount left. You entered data in an Access database table for one shift. Open *e01b1server* in Access, open the table, select the records including the field names, copy the data, start a new workbook in Excel, and then paste the data starting in **cell A6**. Save the workbook as **e01b1server_LastnameFirstname**. Close the Access database.

Insert a column labeled **Subtotal** between the Drinks and Tip Left columns. Calculate the food and drinks subtotal. In column F, enter a formula to calculate the tip percentage of the subtotal. Format the percentage with one decimal place. Type **15%** in **cell G7**, and then type **10%** in **cell H7**. Copy these percentage values down these two columns. In columns I and J, calculate the bartender's tip amount and the assistant's tip amount. Finally, in column K, calculate your net tip after giving the bartender and server their share of the tips. Insert appropriate column labels on row 6. Add three labels on row 5 to provide category labels over groups of columns: **Customer Subtotal and Tip** merged and centered in the **range B5:E5**, **Tip Rates** merged and centered in the **range F5:H5**, and **Tip Amounts** merged and centered in the **range I5:K5**. Apply borders, fill colors, and wrap text appropriately.

Include a notes section that explains the tipping rates for the bartender and server assistant. On the first three rows, add and format a descriptive title, date, and time of shift. Select appropriate options on the Page Layout tab that are appropriate for printing the worksheet. Rename the worksheet and delete the other worksheets. Include a header with appropriate information. Copy the original worksheet, and then place the copied worksheet on the right side of the original worksheet. On the copied worksheet, display cell formulas, print gridlines, print headings, adjust the column widths, and decrease the scaling. Add worksheet tab colors to both sheets. Save and close the workbook, and submit based on your instructor's directions.

Credit Card Rebate

RESEARCH CASE

FROM SCRATCH

You recently found out the Costco TrueEarnings® American Express credit card earns annual rebates on all purchases. You want to see how much rebate you would have received had you used this credit card for purchases in the past year. Use the Internet to research the percentage rebates for different categories. Plan the design of the spreadsheet. Enter the categories, rebate percentages, amount of money you spent in each category, and a formula to calculate the amount of rebate. Use the Excel Help feature to learn how to add several cells using a function instead of adding cells individually and how to apply a Double Accounting underline. Insert the appropriate function to total your categorical purchases and rebate amounts. Apply appropriate formatting and page setup options for readability. Underline the last monetary values for the last data row, and apply the Double Accounting underline style to the totals. Insert a header with imperative documentation. Save the workbook as **e01b2rebate_LastnameFirstname**. Save and close the workbook, and submit based on your instructor's directions.

Net Proceeds from House Sale

DISASTER RECOVERY

Garrett Frazier is a real estate agent. He wants his clients to have a realistic expectation of how much money they will receive when they sell their houses. Sellers know they have to pay a commission to the agent and pay off their existing mortgages; however, many sellers forget to consider they might have to pay some of the buyer's closing costs, title insurance, and prorated property taxes. The realtor commission and estimated closing costs are based on the selling price and the respective rates. The estimated property taxes are prorated based on the annual property taxes and percentage of the year. For example, if a house sells three months into the year, the seller pays 25% of the property taxes. Garrett created a worksheet to enter values in an input area to calculate the estimated deductions at closing and calculate the estimated net proceeds the seller will receive. However, the worksheet contains errors. Open *e01b3proceeds* and save it as **e01b3proceeds_LastnameFirstname**.

Use Help to learn how to insert comments into cells. As you identify the errors, insert comments in the respective cells to explain the errors. Correct the errors, including formatting errors. Apply landscape orientation, 115% scaling, 1.5" top margin, and centered horizontally. Insert your name on the left side of the header, the sheet name code in the center, and the file name code on the right side. Save and close the workbook, and submit based on your instructor's direction.

EXCEL

2 FORMULAS AND FUNCTIONS

Performing Quantitative Analysis

Watch the
Set-up Video
for this Case Study!

CASE STUDY | Denver Mortgage Company

You are an assistant to Erica Matheson, a mortgage broker at the Denver Mortgage Company. Erica spends her days reviewing mortgage rates and trends, meeting with potential clients, and preparing paperwork. She relies on your expertise in using Excel to help you analyze mortgage data.

Today, Erica provided you with a spreadsheet containing data for five mortgages. She asked you to perform some basic calculations so that she can check the output provided by her system. She needs you to calculate the amount financed, the periodic interest rate, the total number of payment periods, monthly payments, and other details for each mortgage. In addition, you will perform some basic statistics, such as totals and averages. After you complete these tasks, Erica wants you to create a separate worksheet with additional input data to automate calculations for future loans.

OBJECTIVES AFTER YOU READ THIS CHAPTER, YOU WILL BE ABLE TO:

1. Use semi-selection to create a formula ***p.394***
2. Use relative, absolute, and mixed cell references in formulas ***p.394***
3. Avoid circular references ***p.397***
4. Insert a function ***p.403***
5. Total values with the SUM function ***p.405***
6. Insert basic statistical functions ***p.406***
7. Use date functions ***p.409***
8. Determine results with the IF function ***p.417***
9. Use lookup functions ***p.420***
10. Calculate payments with the PMT function ***p.422***
11. Create and maintain range names ***p.428***
12. Use range names in formulas ***p.430***

Formula Basics

By increasing your understanding of formulas, you can build robust spreadsheets that perform a variety of calculations for quantitative analysis. Your ability to build sophisticated spreadsheets and to interpret the results increases your value to any organization. By now, you should be able to build simple formulas using cell references and mathematical operators and using the order of precedence to control the sequence of calculations in formulas.

Your ability to build sophisticated spreadsheets and to interpret the results increases your value to any organization.

In this section, you will use the semi-selection method to create formulas. In addition, you will create formulas in which cell addresses change or remain fixed when you copy them. Finally, you will learn how to identify and prevent circular references in formulas.

Using Semi-Selection to Create a Formula

You have learned how to create formulas by typing the cell references (for example, =A1+A2) to create a formula. To decrease typing time and ensure accuracy, you can use ***semi-selection***, a process of selecting a cell or range of cells for entering cell references as you create formulas. Semi-selection is often called ***pointing*** because you use the mouse pointer to select cells as you build the formula. To use the semi-selection technique to create a formula, do the following:

Semi-selection (or **pointing**) is the process of using the mouse pointer to select cells while building a formula.

1. Click the cell where you want to create the formula.
2. Type an equal sign (=) to start a formula.
3. Click the cell or drag to select the cell range that contains the value(s) to use in the formula. A moving marquee appears around the cell or range you select, and Excel displays the cell or range reference in the formula.
4. Type a mathematical operator.
5. Continue clicking cells, selecting ranges, and typing operators to finish the formula. Use the scroll bars if the cell is in a remote location in the worksheet, or click a worksheet tab to see a cell in another worksheet.
6. Press Enter to complete the formula.

Using Relative, Absolute, and Mixed Cell References in Formulas

When you copy a formula, Excel either adjusts or preserves the cell references in the copied formulas based on how the cell references appear in the original formula. Excel uses three different ways to reference a cell in a formula: relative, absolute, and mixed. When you create an original formula that you will copy to other cells, ask yourself the following: Do the cell references need to adjust for the copied formulas, or should the cell references always refer to the same cell location, regardless where the copied formula is located?

Use a Relative Cell Reference

A ***relative cell reference*** indicates a cell's relative location, such as two rows up and one column to the left, from the cell containing the formula. When you copy a formula containing a relative cell reference, the cell references in the copied formula change relative to the position of the copied formula. Regardless of where you copy the formula, the cell references in the copied formula maintain the same relative distance from the copied formula cell, as the cell references relative location to the original formula cell.

A **relative cell reference** indicates a cell's relative location from the cell containing the formula; the cell reference changes when the formula is copied.

In Figure 2.1, the formulas in column F contain relative cell references. When you copy the original formula =D2-E2 from cell F2 down to cell F3, the copied formula changes to =D3-E3. Because you copy the formula *down* the column to cell F4, the column letters in the formula stay the same, but the row numbers change, *down* one row number at a time. Using relative cell addresses to calculate the amount financed ensures that each borrower's down payment is subtracted from his or her respective house cost.

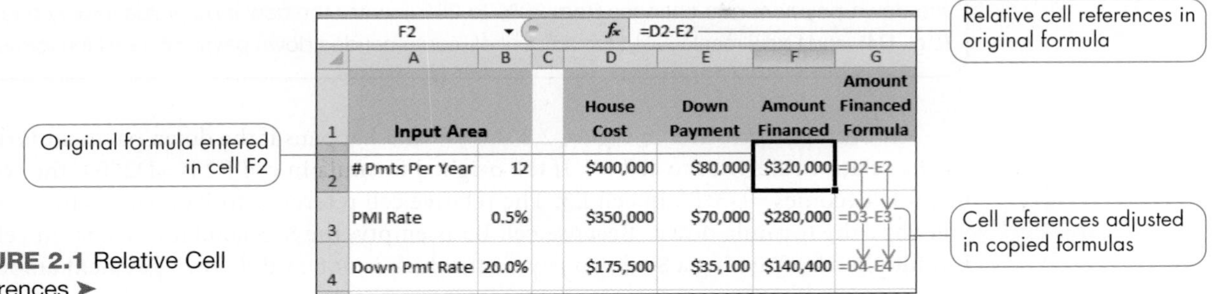

FIGURE 2.1 Relative Cell References ➤

Use an Absolute Cell Reference

An **absolute cell reference** indicates a cell's specific location; the cell reference does not change when you copy the formula.

An ***absolute cell reference*** provides a permanent reference to a specific cell. When you copy a formula containing an absolute cell reference, the cell reference in the copied formula does not change, regardless of where you copy the formula. An absolute cell reference appears with a dollar sign before both the column letter and row number, such as $B$4.

In Figure 2.2, each down payment is calculated by multiplying the respective house cost by the down payment rate (20%). In the top worksheet, cell E2 contains =D2*$B$4 to calculate the first borrower's down payment. When you copy the formula down the column, the copied formula in cell E3 is =D3*$B$4 whereby the relative cell reference D2 changes to D3 and the absolute cell reference $B$4 remains the same. This formula ensures that the cell reference to the house cost changes for each row but that the house cost is always multiplied by the rate in cell B4.

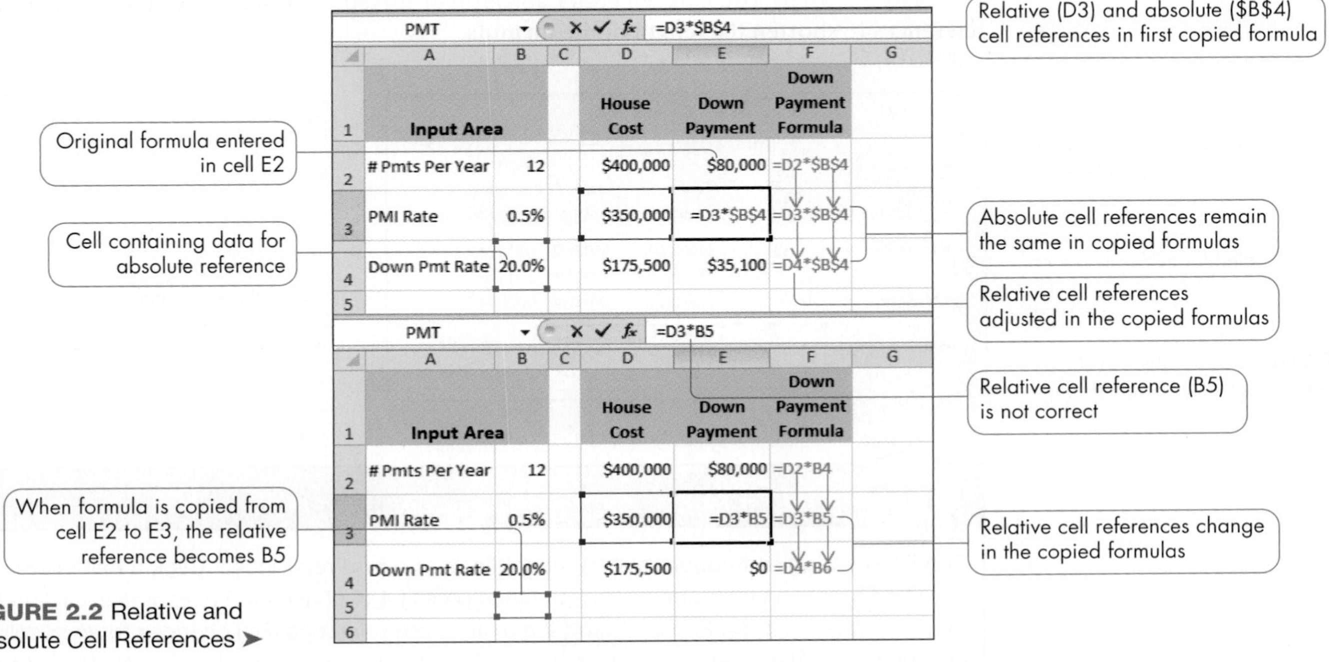

FIGURE 2.2 Relative and Absolute Cell References ➤

TIP Input Area and Absolute Cell References

The top worksheet in Figure 2.2 illustrates an effective use of an input area, a range in a worksheet that contains values that you can change. You build formulas using absolute references to the cells in the input area. By using cell references from an input area, you can change the value in the input area and the formulas that refer to those cells update automatically. If an input value changes (e.g., the down payment rate changes from 20% to 25%), enter the new input value in only one cell (e.g., B4), and Excel recalculates the amount of recommended down payment for all the formulas.

The bottom worksheet in Figure 2.2 shows what happens if the down payment formula used a relative reference to cell B4. If the original formula in cell E2 is =D2*B4, the copied formula becomes =D3*B5 in cell E3. The relative cell reference to B4 changes to B5 when you copy the formula down. Because cell B5 is empty, the $350,000 house cost in cell D3 is multiplied by 0, giving a $0 down payment, which is not a valid down payment amount.

Use a Mixed Cell Reference

A **mixed cell reference** contains both an absolute and a relative cell reference in a formula; the absolute part does not change but the relative part does when you copy the formula.

A ***mixed cell reference*** combines an absolute cell reference with a relative cell reference. When you copy a formula containing a mixed cell reference, either the column letter or the row number that has the absolute reference remains fixed while the other part of the cell reference that is relative changes in the copied formula. $B4 and B$4 are examples of mixed cell references. In the reference $B4, the column B is absolute, and the row number is relative; when you copy the formula, the column letter, B, does not change, but the row number will change. In the reference B$4, the column letter, B, changes, but the row number, 4, does not change. To create a mixed reference, type the dollar sign to the left of the part of the cell reference you want to be absolute.

In the down payment formula, you can change the formula in cell E2 to be =D2*B$4. Because you are copying down the same column, only the row reference 4 must be absolute; the column letter stays the same. Figure 2.3 shows the copied formula =D3*B$4 in cell E3. In situations where you can use either absolute or mixed references, consider using mixed references to shorten the length of the formula.

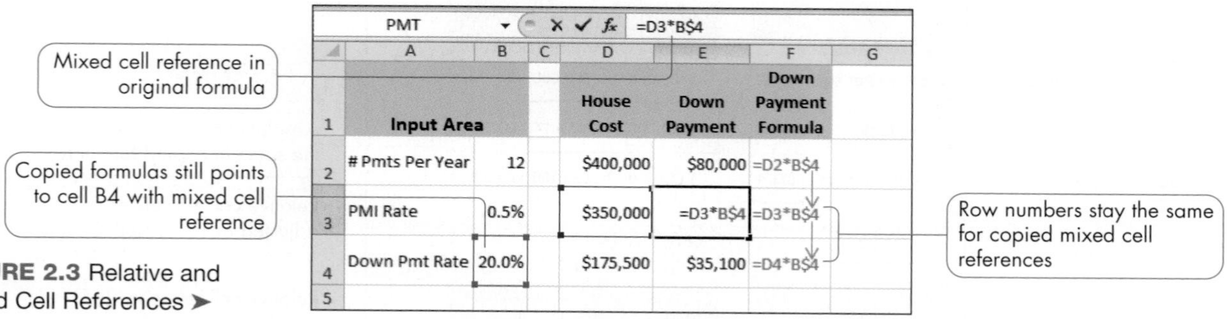

PMT =D3*B$4

	A	B	C	D	E	F	G
1	Input Area			House Cost	Down Payment	Down Payment Formula	
2	# Pmts Per Year	12		$400,000	$80,000	=D2*B$4	
3	PMI Rate	0.5%		$350,000	=D3*B$4	=D3*B$4	
4	Down Pmt Rate	20.0%		$175,500	$35,100	=D4*B$4	
5							

Mixed cell reference in original formula

Copied formulas still points to cell B4 with mixed cell reference

Row numbers stay the same for copied mixed cell references

FIGURE 2.3 Relative and Mixed Cell References ➤

TIP The F4 Key

The F4 key toggles through relative, absolute, and mixed references. Click a cell reference within a formula on the Formula Bar, and then press F4 to change it. For example, click in B4 in the formula =D2*B4. Press F4, and the relative cell reference (B4) changes to an absolute cell reference ($B$4). Press F4 again, and $B$4 becomes a mixed reference (B$4); press F4 again, and it becomes another mixed reference ($B4). Press F4 a fourth time, and the cell reference returns to the original relative reference (B4).

Avoiding Circular References

A **circular reference** occurs when a formula directly or indirectly refers to itself.

If a formula contains a direct or an indirect reference to the cell containing the formula, a ***circular reference*** exists. For example, assume you enter the formula =A8-C8 in cell C8. Because the formula is in cell C8, using the cell address C8 within the formula creates a circular reference. Circular references usually cause inaccurate results, and Excel displays a warning message when you enter a formula containing a circular reference or when you open an Excel workbook that contains an existing circular reference (see Figure 2.4). Click Help to display the *Remove or allow a circular reference* Help topic, or click OK to accept the circular reference. The status bar indicates the location of a circular reference until it has been resolved.

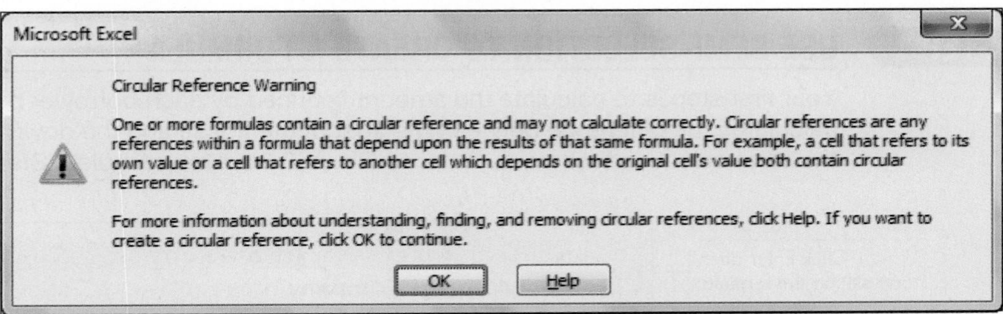

Microsoft Excel
Circular Reference Warning
One or more formulas contain a circular reference and may not calculate correctly. Circular references are any references within a formula that depend upon the results of that same formula. For example, a cell that refers to its own value or a cell that refers to another cell which depends on the original cell's value both contain circular references.
For more information about understanding, finding, and removing circular references, click Help. If you want to create a circular reference, click OK to continue.
OK
Help

FIGURE 2.4 Circular Reference Warning ➤

If the circular reference warning appears when creating a formula, use Help to activate formula auditing tools to help you identify what is causing the circular reference.

TIP Green Triangles

Excel displays a green triangle in the top-left corner of a cell if it detects a potential error in a formula. Click the cell to see the Trace Error button (yellow diamond with exclamation mark). When you click Trace Error, Excel displays information about the potential error and how to correct it. In some cases, Excel may anticipate an inconsistent formula or the omission of adjacent cells in a formula. For example, if a column contains values for the year 2012, the error message indicates that you did not include the year itself. However, the year is merely a label and should not be included; therefore, you would ignore that error message.

Quick Concepts Check

1. What are the advantages of using semi-selection when creating formulas?
2. What happens when you copy a formula containing a relative cell reference one column to the right?
3. Why would you use an absolute reference in a formula?
4. What is a circular reference? Provide an example.

HANDS-ON EXERCISES

1 Formula Basics

Erica prepared a workbook containing data for five mortgages financed with the Denver Mortgage Company. The data include house cost, down payment, mortgage rate, number of years to pay off the mortgage, and the financing date for each mortgage.

Skills covered: Use Semi-Selection to Create a Formula • Copy a Formula with a Relative Cell Reference • Enter a Formula with an Absolute Cell Reference • Enter a Formula with a Mixed Cell Reference • Create and Correct a Circular Reference

STEP 1 USE SEMI-SELECTION TO CREATE A FORMULA

Your first step is to calculate the amount financed by each borrower by creating a formula that calculates the difference between the cost of the house and the down payment. You decide to use the semi-selection technique. Refer to Figure 2.5 as you complete Step 1.

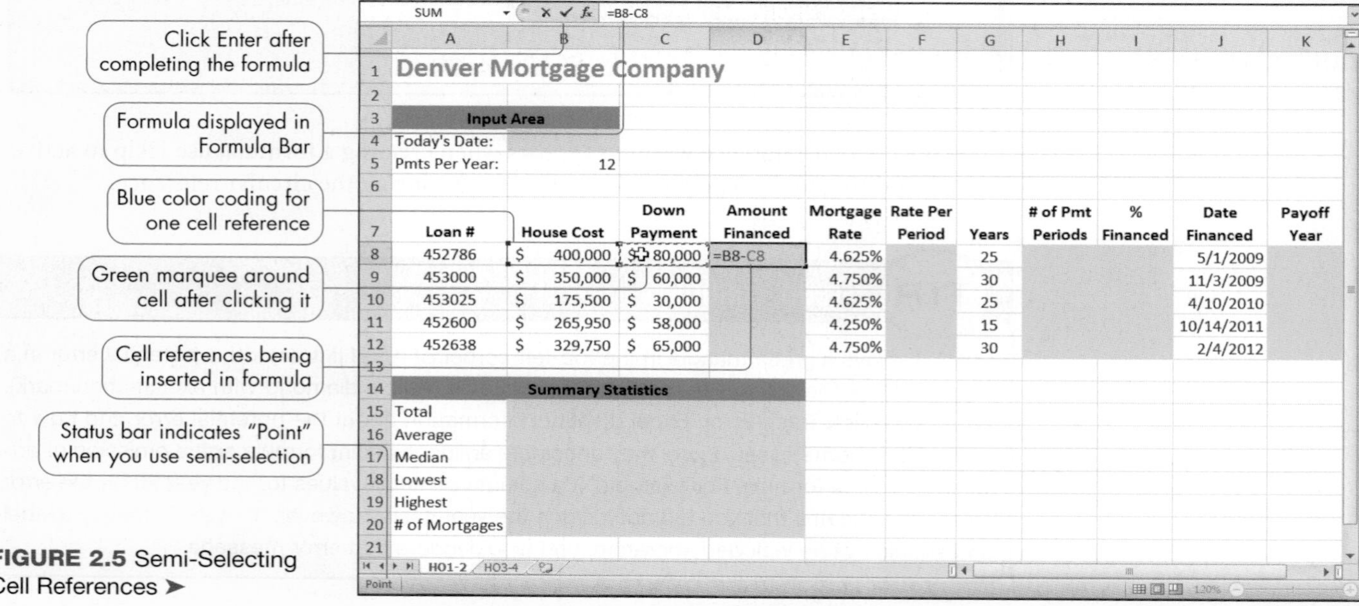

FIGURE 2.5 Semi-Selecting Cell References ➤

a. Open *e02h1loans* and save it as **e02h1loans_LastnameFirstname**.

> **TROUBLESHOOTING:** If you make any major mistakes in this exercise, you can close the file, open *e02h1loans* again, and then start this exercise over.

The workbook contains two worksheets: HO1-2 (for Hands-On Exercises 1 and 2) and HO3-4 (for Hands-On Exercises 3 and 4). You will enter formulas in the shaded cells.

b. Click the **HO1-2 worksheet tab**, and then click **cell D8**.

This is where you will create a formula to calculate the first borrower's amount financed.

c. Type = and click **cell B8**, the cell containing the first borrower's house cost.

You type an equal sign to start the formula, and then you click the first cell containing a value you want to use in the formula. A blue marquee appears around cell B8, and the B8 cell reference appears to the right of the equal sign in the formula.

d. Type - and click **cell C8**, the cell containing the down payment by the first borrower.

A green marquee appears around cell C8, and the C8 cell reference appears to the right of the subtraction sign in the formula (see Figure 2.5).

> **TROUBLESHOOTING:** If you click the wrong cell, click the correct cell to change the cell reference in the formula. If you realize the mistake after typing an arithmetic operator or after entering the formula, you must edit the formula to change the cell reference.

e. Click **Enter** to the left of the Formula Bar to complete the formula. Save the workbook.

The first borrower financed (i.e., borrowed) $320,000, the difference between the cost ($400,000) and the down payment ($80,000).

STEP 2 COPY A FORMULA WITH A RELATIVE CELL REFERENCE

After verifying the results of the amount financed by the first borrower, you are ready to copy the formula. Before copying the formula, determine if the cell references should be relative or absolute. For this formula, you want cell references to change for each row. For each borrower, you want to base the amount financed on his or her own data, so you decide to keep the relative cell references in the formula. Refer to Figure 2.6 as you complete Step 2.

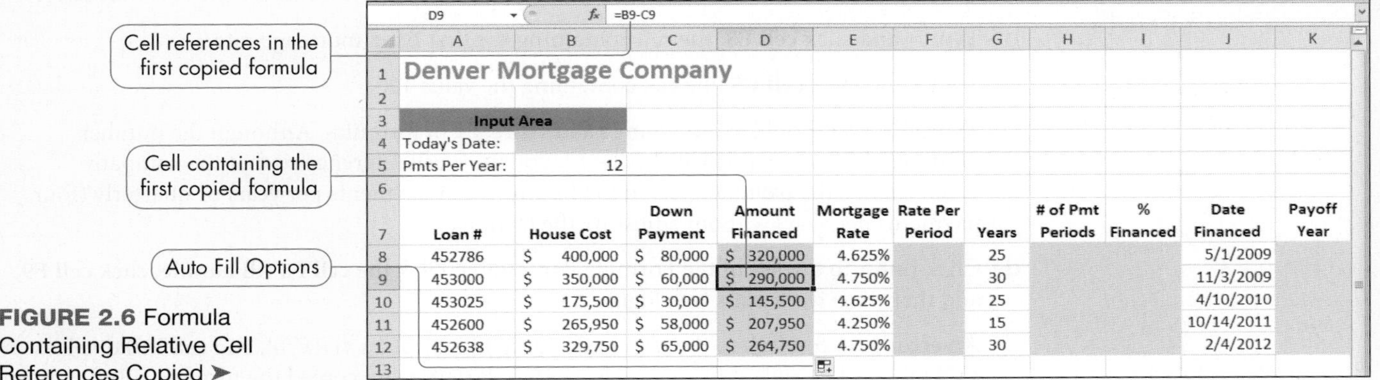

Denver Mortgage Company

Input Area	
Today's Date:	
Pmts Per Year:	12

Loan #	House Cost	Down Payment	Amount Financed	Mortgage Rate	Rate Per Period	Years	# of Pmt Periods	% Financed	Date Financed	Payoff Year
452786	$ 400,000	$ 80,000	$ 320,000	4.625%		25			5/1/2009	
453000	$ 350,000	$ 60,000	$ 290,000	4.750%		30			11/3/2009	
453025	$ 175,500	$ 30,000	$ 145,500	4.625%		25			4/10/2010	
452600	$ 265,950	$ 58,000	$ 207,950	4.250%		15			10/14/2011	
452638	$ 329,750	$ 65,000	$ 264,750	4.750%		30			2/4/2012	

FIGURE 2.6 Formula Containing Relative Cell References Copied ➤

a. Make sure that **cell D8** is the active cell but does not have a blinking insertion point.

b. Double-click the **cell D8 fill handle**.

You copied the formula down the Amount Financed column for each mortgage row.

> **TIP Auto Fill Options**
>
> The Auto Fill Options button appears in the bottom-right corner of the copied formulas. If you click it, you can see that the default is Copy Cells. If you want to copy only formatting, click Fill Formatting Only. If you want to copy data only, click Fill Without Formatting.

c. Click **cell D9**, and then view the formula in the Formula Bar.

The formula in cell D8 is =B8-C8. The formula pasted in cell D9 is =B9-C9. Because the original formula contained relative cell references, when you copy the formula down a column, the row numbers for the cell references change. Each result represents the amount financed for that particular borrower.

d. Press ↓ and look at the cell references in the Formula Bar to see how the references change for each formula you copied. Save the workbook with the new formula you created.

STEP 3 ENTER A FORMULA WITH AN ABSOLUTE CELL REFERENCE

Column E contains the annual percentage rate (APR) for each mortgage. Because the borrowers will make monthly payments, you need to calculate the monthly interest rate by dividing the APR by 12 (the number of payments in one year) for each borrower. Refer to Figure 2.7 as you complete Step 3.

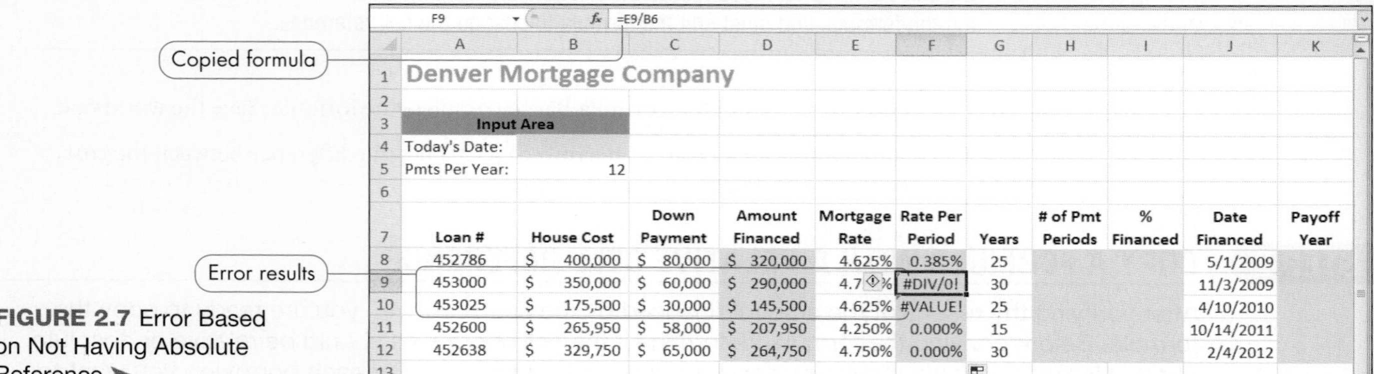

	A	B	C	D	E	F	G	H	I	J	K
1	Denver Mortgage Company										
2											
3	Input Area										
4	Today's Date:										
5	Pmts Per Year:	12									
6											
7	Loan #	House Cost	Down Payment	Amount Financed	Mortgage Rate	Rate Per Period	Years	# of Pmt Periods	% Financed	Date Financed	Payoff Year
8	452786	$ 400,000	$ 80,000	$ 320,000	4.625%	0.385%	25			5/1/2009	
9	453000	$ 350,000	$ 60,000	$ 290,000	4.7%	#DIV/0!	30			11/3/2009	
10	453025	$ 175,500	$ 30,000	$ 145,500	4.625%	#VALUE!	25			4/10/2010	
11	452600	$ 265,950	$ 58,000	$ 207,950	4.250%	0.000%	15			10/14/2011	
12	452638	$ 329,750	$ 65,000	$ 264,750	4.750%	0.000%	30			2/4/2012	
13											

FIGURE 2.7 Error Based on Not Having Absolute Reference ➤

a. Click **cell F8**.

You need to create a formula to calculate the monthly interest rate for the first borrower.

b. Type = and click **cell E8**, the cell containing the first fixed mortgage rate.

c. Type / and click **cell B5**, the cell containing the value 12.

Typically, you should avoid typing values directly in formulas. Although the number of months in one year will always be 12, you use a cell reference so that the company could change the payment period to bimonthly (24 payments per year) or quarterly (four payments per year) without adjusting the formula.

d. Click **Enter** to the left of the Formula Bar, double-click the **cell F8 fill handle**, click **cell F9**, and then view the results (see Figure 2.7).

An error icon displays to the left of cell F9, cell F9 displays #DIV/0!, and cell F10 displays #VALUE!. The original formula was =E8/B5. Because you copied the formula =E8/B5 down the column, the first copied formula is =E9/B6, and the second copied formula is =E10/B7. Although you want the mortgage rate cell reference (E8) to change (E9, E10, etc.) from row to row, you do not want the divisor to change. You need all formulas to divide by the value stored in cell B5, so you will edit the formula to make B5 an absolute reference.

TIP Error Icons

You can position the mouse pointer over the error icon to see a tip indicating what is wrong, such as *The formula or function used is dividing by zero or empty cells*. You can click the icon to see a menu of options to learn more about the error and how to correct it.

FYI

e. Undo the Auto Fill process. Click within or to the right of **B5** in the Formula Bar.

f. Press **F4**, and then click **Enter** to the left of the Formula Bar.

Excel changes the cell reference from B5 to $B$5, making it absolute.

g. Copy the formula down the Rate Per Period column. Click **cell F9**, and then view the formula in the Formula Bar. Save the workbook with the new formula you created.

The formula in cell F9 is =E9/$B$5. The reference to E9 is relative and B5 is absolute.

STEP 4 ENTER A FORMULA WITH A MIXED CELL REFERENCE

The next formula you need to enter will calculate the total number of payment periods for each loan. Refer to Figure 2.8 as you complete Step 4.

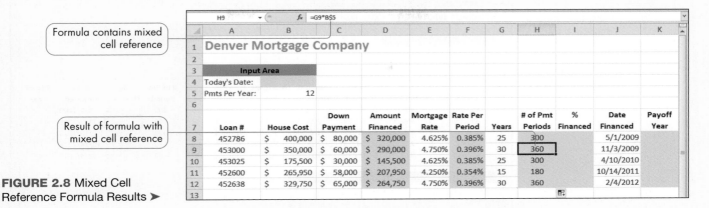

Formula contains mixed cell reference

Result of formula with mixed cell reference

H9 =G9*B$5

	A	B	C	D	E	F	G	H	I	J	K
1	Denver Mortgage Company										
2											
3	Input Area										
4	Today's Date:										
5	Pmts Per Year:	12									
6											
7	Loan #	House Cost	Down Payment	Amount Financed	Mortgage Rate	Rate Per Period	Years	# of Pmt Periods	% Financed	Date Financed	Payoff Year
8	452786	$ 400,000	$ 80,000	$ 320,000	4.625%	0.385%	25	300		5/1/2009	
9	453000	$ 350,000	$ 60,000	$ 290,000	4.750%	0.396%	30	360		11/3/2009	
10	453025	$ 175,500	$ 30,000	$ 145,500	4.625%	0.385%	25	300		4/10/2010	
11	452600	$ 265,950	$ 58,000	$ 207,950	4.250%	0.354%	15	180		10/14/2011	
12	452638	$ 329,750	$ 65,000	$ 264,750	4.750%	0.396%	30	360		2/4/2012	
13											

FIGURE 2.8 Mixed Cell Reference Formula Results ➤

a. Click **cell H8**.

b. Type = and click **cell G8**, the cell containing *25*, the number of years to pay off the loan for the first borrower.

   You need to multiply the number of years (25) by the number of payment periods in one year (12) using cell references.

c. Type * and click **cell B5**.

   You want B5 to be absolute so that the cell reference remains B5 when you copy the formula.

d. Press **F4** to make the cell reference absolute, and then click **Enter** to the left of the Formula Bar.

   The product of 25 years and 12 months is 300.

e. Copy the formula down the # of Pmt Periods column.

   The first copied formula is =G9*$B$5, and the result is 360. You want to see what happens if you change the absolute reference to a mixed reference and then copy the formula again. Because you are copying down a column, the column letter B can be relative since it will not change either way, but the row number 5 must be absolute.

f. Undo the copied formulas. Click **cell H8**, and then click within the **$B$5 cell reference** in the Formula Bar. Press **F4** to change the cell reference to a mixed cell reference, B$5. Press **Ctrl+Enter**, and then copy the formula down the # of Pmt Periods column. Click **cell H9**. Save the workbook with the new formula you created.

   The first copied formula is =G9*B$5, and the result is still 360. In this situation, using either an absolute reference or a mixed reference provides the same results.

STEP 5 CREATE AND CORRECT A CIRCULAR REFERENCE

Erica wants to know what percentage of the house cost each borrower will finance. As you create the formula, you enter a circular reference. After studying the results, you correct the circular error and plan future formulas that avoid this problem. Refer to Figure 2.9 as you complete Step 5.

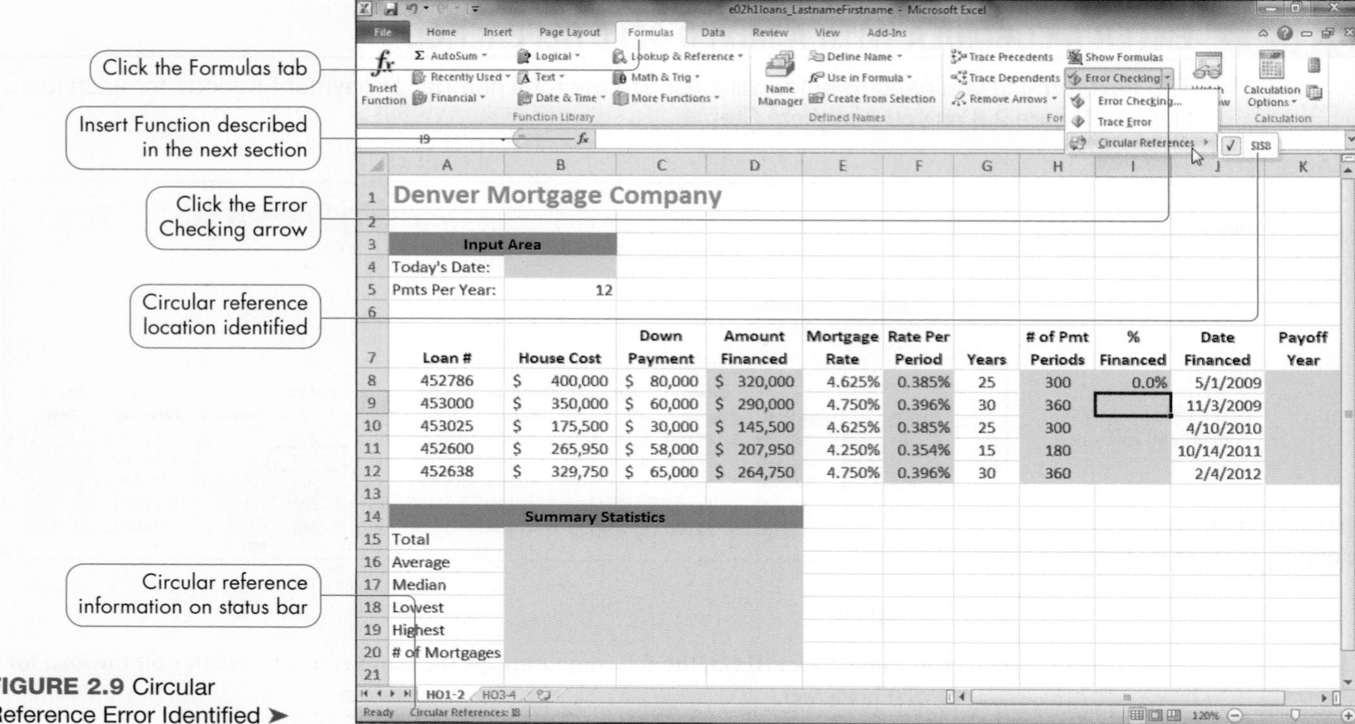

FIGURE 2.9 Circular Reference Error Identified ➤

a. Click **cell I8**, type **=I8/B8**, and then press **Enter**.

   The Circular Reference Warning message box appears.

b. Read the description of the error, and then click **Help**.

   A Help window opens, displaying information about circular references.

c. Read the Help topic information, and then close the Help window.

   Notice that the left side of the status bar displays *Circular References: I8*. You will follow the advice given in the Help window to fix it.

d. Click the **Formulas tab**, click the **Error Checking arrow** in the Formula Auditing group, and then point to **Circular References**.

   The Circular References menu displays a list of cells containing circular references.

e. Select **$I$8** from the list to make it the active cell.

   Because the formula is stored in cell I8, the formula cannot refer to the cell itself. You need to divide the value in the Amount Financed column by the value in the House Cost column.

f. Edit the formula to be **=D8/B8**. Copy the formula down the % Financed column.

   The first borrower financed 80% of the cost of the house: $320,000 financed divided by $400,000 cost.

g. Save the workbook. Keep the workbook onscreen if you plan to continue with Hands-On Exercise 2. If not, close the workbook and exit Excel.

Function Basics

A **function** is a predefined formula that performs a calculation.

An Excel ***function*** is a predefined computation that simplifies creating a formula that performs a complex calculation. Excel contains more than 325 functions, which are organized into categories. Table 2.1 lists and describes function categories.

TABLE 2.1 Function Categories and Descriptions

Category	Description
Compatibility	Contains functions compatible with Excel 2007 and earlier.
Cube	Returns values based on data in a cube, such as validating membership in a club, returning a member's ranking, and displaying aggregated values from the club data set.
Database	Analyzes records stored in a database format in Excel and returns key values, such as the number of records, average value in a particular field, or the sum of values in a field.
Date & Time	Provides methods for manipulating date and time values.
Engineering	Calculates values commonly used by engineers, such as value conversions.
Financial	Performs financial calculations, such as payments, rates, present value, and future value.
Information	Provides information about the contents of a cell, typically displaying TRUE if the cell contains a particular data type such as a value.
Logical	Performs logical tests and returns the value of the tests. Includes logical operators for combined tests, such as AND, OR, and NOT.
Lookup & Reference	Looks up values, creates links to cells, or provides references to cells in a worksheet.
Math & Trig	Performs standard math and trigonometry calculations.
Statistical	Performs common statistical calculations, such as averages and standard deviations.
Text	Manipulates text strings, such as combining text or converting text to lowercase.

Syntax is a set of rules that govern the structure and components for properly entering a function.

An **argument** is an input, such as a cell reference or value, needed to complete a function.

When using functions, you must adhere to correct ***syntax***, the rules that dictate the structure and components required to perform the necessary calculations. The basic syntax of a function requires a function to start with an equal sign, to contain the function name, and to specify its arguments. The function name describes the purpose of the function. For example, the function name SUM indicates that the function sums or adds values.

A function's ***arguments*** specify the inputs—such as cells, values, or arithmetic expressions—that are required to complete the operation. Arguments are enclosed in parentheses, with the opening parenthesis immediately following the function name. Some functions, such as TODAY, do not require arguments; however, you must include the parentheses with nothing inside them. In some cases, a function requires multiple arguments separated by commas.

In this section, you will learn how to insert common functions using the keyboard and the Insert Function and Function Arguments dialog boxes.

Inserting a Function

Formula AutoComplete displays a list of functions and defined names as you enter a function.

To insert a function by typing, first type an equal sign, and then begin typing the function name. ***Formula AutoComplete*** displays a list of functions and defined names that match letters as you type a formula. For example, if you type =SU, Formula AutoComplete displays a list of functions and names that start with *SU* (see Figure 2.10). You can double-click the function name from the list or continue typing the function name. You can even scroll through the list to see the ScreenTip describing the function.

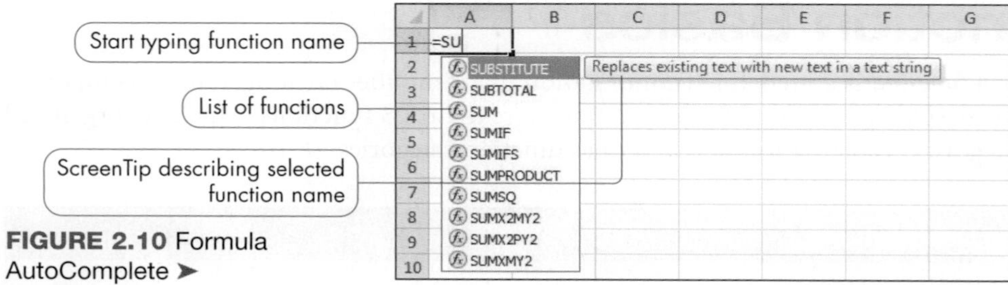

FIGURE 2.10 Formula AutoComplete ➤

A **function ScreenTip** is a small pop-up description that displays the arguments for a function as you enter it.

After you type the function name and opening parenthesis, Excel displays the ***function ScreenTip***, a small pop-up description that displays the function's arguments. The argument you are currently entering is bold in the function ScreenTip (see Figure 2.11). Square brackets indicate optional arguments. For example, the SUM function requires the number1 argument, but the number2 argument is optional. Click the argument name in the function ScreenTip to select the actual argument in the cell.

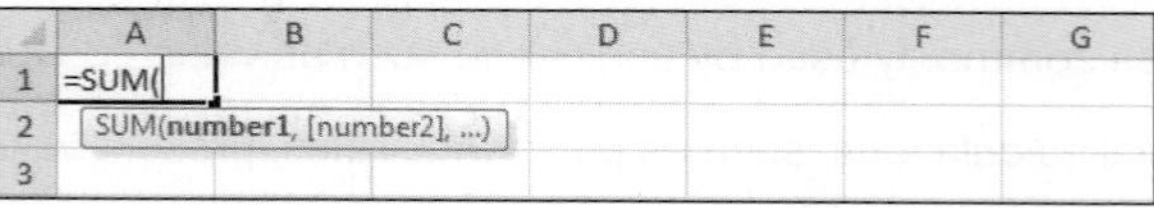

FIGURE 2.11 Function ScreenTip ➤

You can also use the Insert Function dialog box to search for a function, select a function category, and select a function from the list (see Figure 2.12). The dialog box is helpful if you want to browse a list of functions, especially if you are not sure of the function you need and want to see descriptions.

To display the Insert Function dialog box, click Insert Function, which looks like *fx*, between the Name Box and the Formula Bar, or click Insert Function in the Function Library group on the Formulas tab. From within the dialog box, select a function category, such as Most Recently Used, and then select a function to display the syntax and a brief description of that function. Click *Help on this function* to display details about the selected function.

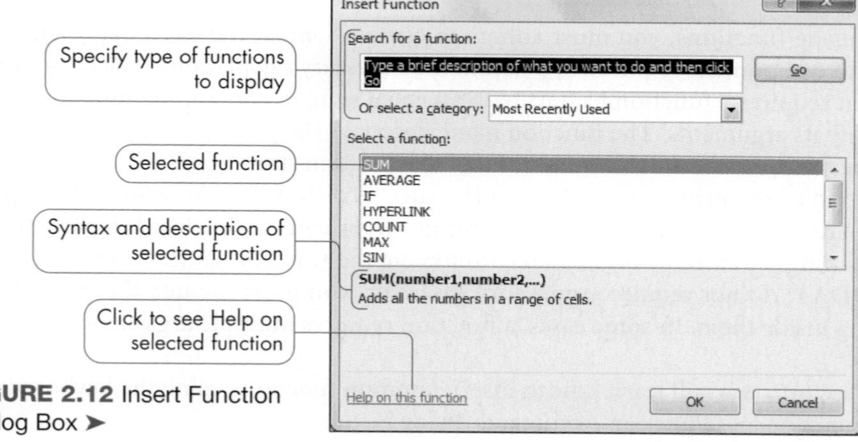

FIGURE 2.12 Insert Function Dialog Box ➤

When you find the function you want, click OK. The Function Arguments dialog box opens so that you can enter the arguments for that specific function (see Figure 2.13). Bold arguments are required; argument names that are not bold are optional. The function can operate without the optional argument, which is used when you need additional specifications to calculate a result. Type the cell references in the argument boxes, or click a collapse button to the right side of an argument box to select the cell or range of cells in the worksheet to designate as that argument. The value or results of a formula contained in the argument cell displays on the right side of the argument box. If the argument is not valid, Excel displays an error description on the right side of the argument box.

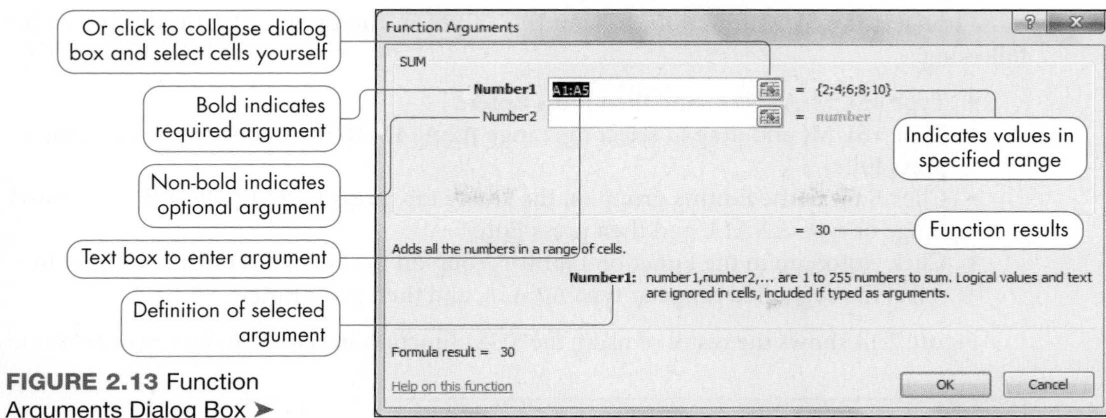

FIGURE 2.13 Function Arguments Dialog Box ➤

The bottom of the Function Arguments dialog box displays a description of the function and a description of the argument containing the insertion point. As you enter arguments, the dialog box also displays the results of the function.

TIP #Name?

If you enter a function, and #NAME? appears in the cell, you might have mistyped the function name. To avoid this problem, select the function name from the Formula AutoComplete list as you type the function name, or use the Insert Function dialog box. You can type a function name in lowercase letters. If you type the name correctly, Excel converts the name to all capital letters when you press Enter, indicating that you spelled the function name correctly.

Totaling Values with the SUM Function

The **SUM function** calculates the total of values contained in two or more cells.

One of the most commonly used functions is the ***SUM function***, which totals values in two or more cells and then displays the result in the cell containing the function. This function is more efficient to create when you need to add the values contained in three or more cells. For example, to add the contents of cells A2 through A14, you could enter =A2+A3+A4+A5+A6+A7+A8+A9+A10+A11+A12+A13+A14, which is time-consuming and increases the probability of entering an inaccurate cell reference, such as entering a cell reference twice or accidentally leaving out a cell reference. Instead, you could use the SUM function, =SUM(A2:A14).

=SUM(number 1, [number 2],…)

TIP Function Syntax

In this book, the function syntax lines are highlighted. Arguments enclosed by brackets [ ] are optional. However, you do not actually type the brackets in the functions.

The SUM function contains one required argument—number1—that represents a range of cells to add. The range, such as A2:A14, specifies the first and last cells containing values to SUM. Excel will sum all cells within that range. The number2 optional argument is used when you want to sum values stored in cells in nonadjacent cells or ranges, such as =SUM(A2:A14,F2:F14).

To insert the SUM function, to sum the values in the range A2:A14, do one of the following:

- Type =SUM(A2:A14) and then press Enter.
- Type =SUM(and drag to select the range A2:A14 with the mouse. Type) and then press Enter.
- Click Sum in the Editing group on the Home tab, press Enter to select the suggested range or type A2:A14, and then press Enter.
- Click AutoSum in the Function Library group on the Formulas tab, press Enter to select the suggested range or type A2:A14, and then press Enter.

Figure 2.14 shows the result of using the SUM function in cell D2 to total scores (898).

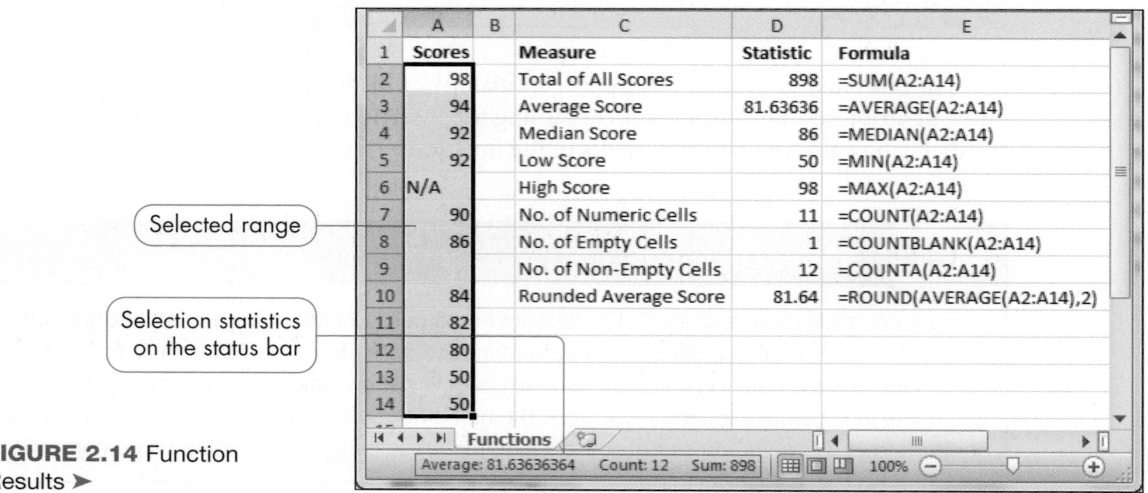

	A	B	C	D	E
1	Scores		Measure	Statistic	Formula
2	98		Total of All Scores	898	=SUM(A2:A14)
3	94		Average Score	81.63636	=AVERAGE(A2:A14)
4	92		Median Score	86	=MEDIAN(A2:A14)
5	92		Low Score	50	=MIN(A2:A14)
6	N/A		High Score	98	=MAX(A2:A14)
7	90		No. of Numeric Cells	11	=COUNT(A2:A14)
8	86		No. of Empty Cells	1	=COUNTBLANK(A2:A14)
9			No. of Non-Empty Cells	12	=COUNTA(A2:A14)
10	84		Rounded Average Score	81.64	=ROUND(AVERAGE(A2:A14),2)
11	82				
12	80				
13	50				
14	50				

FIGURE 2.14 Function Results ➤

TIP Avoiding Functions for Basic Formulas

Do not use a function for a basic mathematical expression. For example, although =SUM(B4/C4) produces the same result as =B4/C4, the SUM function is not needed to perform the basic arithmetic division. Use the most appropriate, clear-cut formula, =B4/C4.

Inserting Basic Statistical Functions

Excel includes commonly used statistical functions that you can use to calculate how much you spend on average per month on music downloads from iTunes®, what your highest electric bill is to control spending, and what your lowest test score is so you know what score you need to earn on your final exam to achieve the grade you desire. You can also use statistical functions to create or monitor your budget.

If you click AutoSum, Excel inserts the SUM function. However, if you click the AutoSum arrow in the Editing group on the Home tab, Excel displays a list of basic functions to select: Sum, Average, Count Numbers, Max, and Min. If you want to insert another function, select More Functions from the list.

Find Central Tendency with the AVERAGE and MEDIAN Functions

The **AVERAGE function** calculates the arithmetic mean, or average, of values in a range.

People often describe data based on central tendency, which means that values tend to cluster around a central value. Excel provides two functions to calculate central tendency: AVERAGE and MEDIAN. The ***AVERAGE function*** calculates the arithmetic mean, or average, for the values in a range of cells. You can use this function to calculate the class average on a biology test, or the average number of points scored per game by a basketball player. In Figure 2.14, =AVERAGE(A2:A14) in cell D3 returns 81.63636 as the average test score.

=AVERAGE(number 1,[number2],...)

The **MEDIAN function** identifies the midpoint value in a set of values.

The ***MEDIAN function*** finds the midpoint value, which is the value that one half of the population is above or below. The median is particularly useful because extreme values often influence arithmetic mean calculated by the AVERAGE function. In Figure 2.14, the two extreme test scores of 50 distort the average. The rest of the test scores range from 80 to 98. Cell D4 contains =MEDIAN(A2:A14). The median for test scores is 86, which indicates that half the test scores are above 86 and half the test scores are below 86. This statistic is more reflective of the data set than the average is.

=MEDIAN(number 1,[number 2],...)

Identify Low and High Values with MIN and MAX

The **MIN function** displays the lowest value in a range.

The ***MIN function*** analyzes an argument list to determine the lowest value, such as the lowest score on a test. Manually inspecting a range of values to identify the lowest value is inefficient, especially in large spreadsheets. If you change values in the range, the MIN function will identify the new lowest value and display it in the cell containing the MIN function. In Figure 2.14, =MIN(A2:A14) in cell D5 identifies that 50 is the lowest test score.

=MIN(number 1,[number 2],...)

The **MAX function** identifies the highest value in a range.

The ***MAX function*** analyzes an argument list to determine the highest value, such as the highest score on a test. Like the MIN function, when the values in the range change, the MAX function will display the new highest value within the range of cells. In Figure 2.14, =MAX(A2:A14) in cell D6 identifies 98 as the highest test score.

=MAX(number 1,[number 2],...)

TIP Nonadjacent Ranges

You can use multiple ranges as arguments, such as finding the largest number within two nonadjacent (nonconsecutive) ranges. For example, you can find the highest test score where some scores are stored in cells A2:A14, and others are stored in cells K2:K14. Separate each range with a comma in the argument list, so that the formula is =MAX(A2:A14,K2:K14).

Identify the Total Number with COUNT Functions

The **COUNT function** tallies the number of cells in a range that contain values.

Excel provides three basic count functions: COUNT, COUNTBLANK and COUNTA to count the cells in a range that meet a particular criterion. The ***COUNT function*** tallies the number of cells in a range that contain values you can use in calculations, such as numerical and date data, but excludes blank cells or text entries from the tally. In Figure 2.14, the selected range spans 13 cells; however, =COUNT(A2:A14) in cell D7 returns 11, the number of cells that contain numerical data. It does not count the cell containing the text *N/A* or the blank cell.

The **COUNTBLANK function** tallies the number of blank cells in a range.

The **COUNTA function** tallies the number of cells in a range that are not empty.

The ***COUNTBLANK function*** tallies the number of cells in a range that are blank. In Figure 2.14, =COUNTBLANK(A2:A14) in cell D8 identifies that one cell in the range A2:A14 is blank. The ***COUNTA function*** tallies the number of cells in a range that are not blank, that is, cells that contain data whether a value, text, or a formula. In Figure 2.14, =COUNTA(A2:A14) in cell D9 returns 12, indicating the range A2:A14 contains 12 cells that contain some form of data. It does not count the blank cell.

=COUNT(number 1,[number 2],...)

=COUNTBLANK(number 1,[number 2],...)

=COUNTA(number 1,[number 2],...)

Average, Count, and Sum

When you select a range of cells containing values, by default Excel displays the average, count, and sum of those values on the status bar (see Figure 2.14). You can customize the status bar to show other selection statistics, such as the minimum and maximum values for a selected range. To display or hide particular selection statistics, right-click the status bar, and then select the statistic.

Use Other Math and Statistical Functions

In addition to the functions you have learned in this chapter, Excel provides over 100 other math and statistical functions. Table 2.2 lists and describes some of these functions that you might find helpful in your business, education, and general statistics courses.

TABLE 2.2 Math and Statistical Functions

Function Syntax	Description
=ABS(number)	Displays the absolute (i.e., positive) value of a number.
=FREQUENCY(data_array,bins_array)	Counts how often values appear in a given range.
=INT(number)	Rounds a value number down to the nearest whole number.
=MODE.SNGL(number1,[number2],...)	Displays the most frequently occurring value in a list.
=PI()	Returns the value of *pi* that is accurate up to 15 digits.
=PRODUCT(number1,[number2],...)	Multiplies all values within the argument list.
=RANDBETWEEN(bottom,top)	Generates a random number between two numbers you specify.
=RANK.AVG(number,ref,[order])	Identifies a value's rank within a list of values; returns an average rank for identical values.
=RANK.EQ(number,ref,[order])	Identifies a value's rank within a list of values; the top rank is identified for all identical values.
=ROUND(number,num_digits)	Rounds a value to a specific number of digits. Rounds numbers of 5 and greater up and those less than 5 down.
=SUMPRODUCT(array1,[array2],[array3],...)	Finds the result of multiplying values in one range by the related values in another column and then adding those products.
=TRIMMEAN(array,percent)	Returns the arithmetic average of the internal values in a range by excluding a specified percentage of values at the upper and lower values in the data set. This function helps reduce the effect outliers (i.e., extreme values) have on the arithmetic mean.
=TRUNC(number,[num_digits])	Returns the integer equivalent of a number by truncating or removing the decimal or fractional part of the number. For example, =TRUNC(45.5) returns 45.

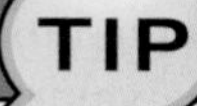

Round vs. Decrease Decimal Points

When you click Decrease Decimal in the Number group to display fewer or no digits after a decimal point, Excel still stores the original value's decimal places so that those digits can be used in calculations. The ROUND function changes the stored value to its rounded state.

Nest Functions as Arguments

A **nested function** is a function that contains another function embedded (i.e., nested) inside one or more of its arguments.

A ***nested function*** occurs when one function is embedded as an argument within another function. Each function has its own set of arguments that must be included. For example, cell D10 in Figure 2.14 contains =ROUND(AVERAGE(A2:A14),2). The ROUND function requires two arguments: number and num_digits. The AVERAGE function is nested in the *number* argument of the ROUND function. AVERAGE(A2:A14) returns 81.63636. That value is then rounded to two decimal places, indicated by 2 in the *num_digits* argument. The result is 81.64. If you change the second argument from 2 to 0, such as =ROUND(AVERAGE(A2:A14),0), the result would be 82.

Using Date Functions

Because Excel treats dates as serial numbers, you can perform calculations using dates. For example, assume today is January 1, 2013, and you graduate on May 10, 2013. To determine how many days until graduation, subtract today's date from the graduation date. Excel uses the serial numbers for these dates (41275 and 41404) to calculate the difference of 129 days.

Insert the TODAY Function

The **TODAY function** displays the current date.

The ***TODAY function*** displays the current date, such as 6/14/2013, in a cell. Excel updates the function results when you open or print the workbook. The function is expressed as =TODAY(). The TODAY() function does not require arguments, but you must include the parentheses for the function to work. If you omit the parentheses, Excel displays #NAME? in the cell with a green triangle in the top-left corner of the cell. When you click the cell, an error icon appears that you can click for more information.

Insert the NOW Function

The **NOW function** displays the current date and time.

The ***NOW function*** uses the computer's clock to display the current date and military time, such as 6/14/2013 15:30, you last opened the workbook. Military time expresses time on a 24-hour period where 1:00 is 1 a.m. and 13:00 is 1 p.m. The date and time will change every time the workbook is opened. Like the TODAY function, the NOW function does not require arguments, but you must include the parentheses. Omitting the parentheses creates a #NAME? error.

TIP Update the Date and Time

Both the TODAY and NOW functions display the date/time the workbook was last opened or last calculated. These functions do not continuously update the date and time while the workbook is open. To update the date and time, press F9 or click the Formulas tab, and then click Calculate now in the Calculation group.

Use Other Date Functions

Excel contains a variety of other date functions. You can use these functions to calculate when employees are eligible for certain benefits, what is the date 6 months from now, or what day of the week a particular date falls on. Table 2.3 describes and Figure 2.15 shows examples of some date functions.

TABLE 2.3 Date Functions	
Function Syntax	**Description**
=DATE(year,month,day)	Returns the serial number for a date.
=DAY(serial_number)	Displays the day (1–31) within a given month for a date or its serial number.
=EDATE(start_date,months)	Displays the serial number using the General format of a date a specified number of months in the future (using a positive value) or past (using a negative value). Displays the actual future or past date in Short Date format.
=EOMONTH(start_date,months)	Identifies the serial number of the last day of a month using General format or the exact last day of a month using Short Date format for a specified number of months from a date's serial number.
=MONTH(serial_number)	Returns the month (1–12) for a serial number, where 1 is January and 12 is December.
=WEEKDAY(serial_number,[return_type])	Identifies the weekday (1–7) for a serial number, where 1 is Sunday and 7 is Saturday (the default with no second argument); can specify a second argument for different numbers assigned to weekdays (see Help).
=YEAR(serial_number)	Identifies the year for a serial number.
=YEARFRAC(start_date,end_date,[basis])	Calculates the fraction of a year between two dates based on the number of whole days.

	A	B	C	D	E	F
1	**Inputs:**	**7**	**11**	**2013**	**10/11/2013**	
2						
3	**Description**			**Format**	**Result**	**Formula**
4	Today's Date			Short Date	6/14/2013	=TODAY()
5	Today's Date			Other Date	June 14, 2013	=TODAY()
6	Today's Date and Military Time			Date/Time	6/14/2013 19:38	=NOW()
7	Serial # of Date			General	41466	=DATE(D1,B1,C1)
8	Serial # of Date			Short Date	7/11/2013	=DATE(D1,B1,C1)
9	Day within the Month			General	14	=DAY(E4) or =DAY(TODAY())
10	Serial # of Date 3 Months in Future			General	41531	=EDATE(E4,3)
11	Date 3 Months in Future			Short Date	9/14/2013	=EDATE(E4,3)
12	Date 3 Years in Future			Short Date	6/14/2016	=EDATE(E4,3*12)
13	Date 2 Months Ago			Short Date	4/14/2013	=EDATE(E4,-2)
14	Serial # of Date 6 Months in Future			General	41650	=EDATE(DATE(D1,B1,C1),6)
15	Serial # of Last Day in 6 Months			General	41639	=EOMONTH(E4,6) or =EOMONTH(TODAY())
16	Last Day of 6 Months in Future			Short Date	12/31/2013	=EOMONTH(E4,6) or =EOMONTH(TODAY())
17	Month Number (where 6=June)			General	6	=MONTH(E5) or =MONTH(TODAY())
18	Week day (1=Sunday; 7=Saturday)			General	6	=WEEKDAY(E4)
19	Week day (1=Monday; 7=Sunday)			General	5	=WEEKDAY(E4,2)
20	Year for a Serial Date			General	2013	=YEAR(E4) or =YEAR(TODAY())
21	Fraction of Year 7/11/2013-10/11/2013			General	0.25	=YEARFRAC(DATE(D1,B1,C1),E1)

FIGURE 2.15 Date Function Examples ➤

You can nest a date function inside another date function, such as =DAY(TODAY()). This nested function TODAY() first identifies today's date and from that date, the DAY function identifies the day of the month. In Figure 2.15, cell E21 contains =YEARFRAC(DATE(D1,B1,C1),E1). The DATE function is nested to combine values in three cells (D1, B1, and C1) to build a date (7/11/2013). Excel finds the number of days between that date and 10/11/2013, the date stored in cell E1. From there, the YEARFRAC function calculates the fraction of a year (25%) between those two dates. Had 7/11/2013 been stored as a date in a single cell, the formula would simplify to something like =YEARFRAC(D1,E1).

You can combine date functions with arithmetic operations. For example, you sign a lease on June 14, 2013, for three years. The starting date is stored in cell E4. What date does your lease expire? Enter =EDATE(E4,3*12)-1 to calculate the expiration date. The first argument E4 is the cell containing the start date, and the second argument 3*12 equals three years containing 12 months each, or 36 months. (In an actual worksheet, you should store the value 36 in a cell instead of typing numbers in the argument.) That result is June 14, 2016, but the lease actually expires the day before. So you must then subtract 1 from the function result to calculate the June 13, 2016, date.

Quick Concepts Check

1. What visual features help guide you through typing a function directly in a cell?
2. What type of data do you enter in a Function Arguments dialog box, and what are five things the dialog box tells you?
3. What is the difference between the AVERAGE and MEDIAN functions?
4. What is a nested function and why would you create one?
5. Provide three examples of using date functions to determine something specific.

2 Function Basics

The Denver Mortgage Company's worksheet contains an area in which you must enter summary statistics. In addition, you need to include today's date and identify what year each mortgage will be paid off.

Skills covered: Use the SUM Function • Use the AVERAGE Function • Use the MEDIAN Function • Use the MIN, MAX, and COUNT Functions • Use the TODAY and YEAR Functions

STEP 1 USE THE SUM FUNCTION

The first summary statistic you need to calculate is the total value of the houses bought by the borrowers. You will use the SUM function. Refer to Figure 2.16 as you complete Step 1.

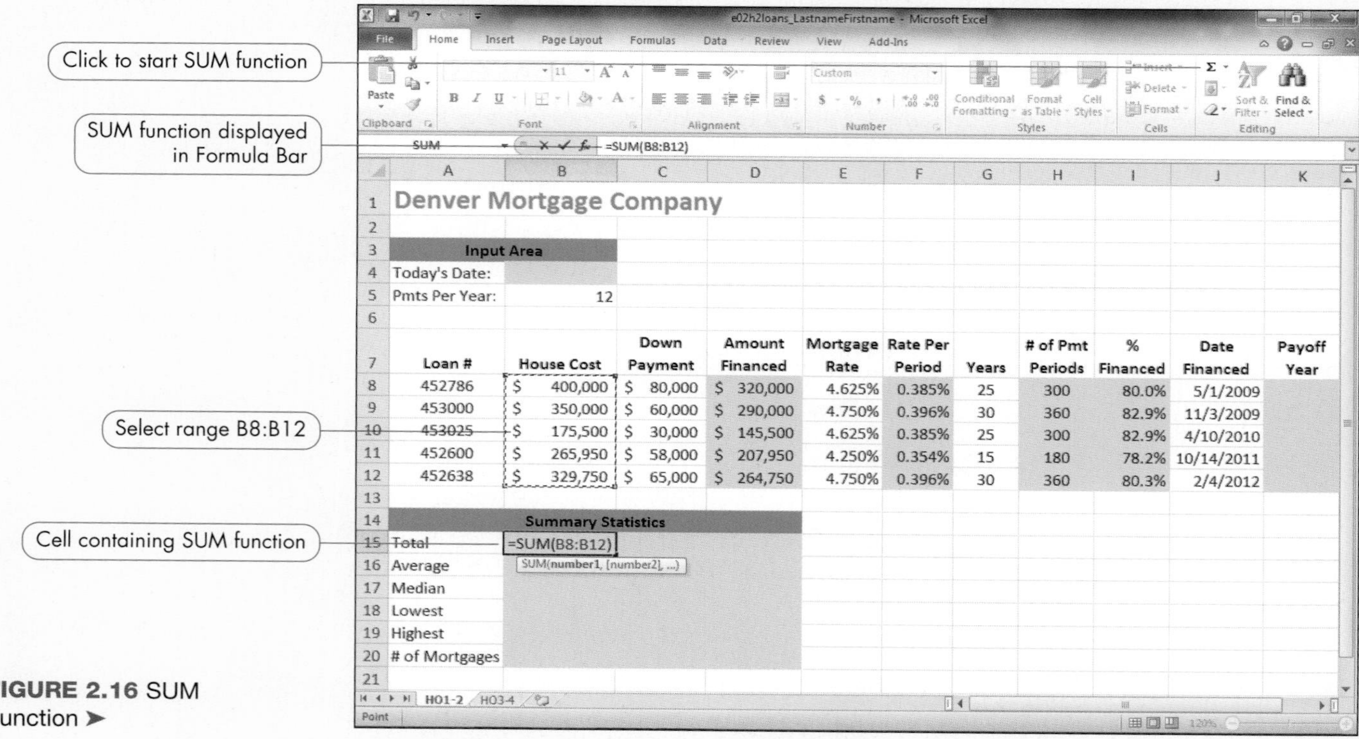

FIGURE 2.16 SUM Function ➤

a. Open *e02h1loans_LastnameFirstname* if you closed it at the end of Hands-On Exercise 1. Save the workbook with the new name **e02h2loans_LastnameFirstname**, changing *h1* to *h2*.

b. Click the **Home tab**, if needed, and then click **cell B15**, the cell where you will enter a formula for the total house cost.

c. Click **AutoSum** in the Editing group.

> **TROUBLESHOOTING:** Click the main part of the AutoSum command. If you click the AutoSum arrow, then select Sum.

Excel anticipates the range of cells containing values you want to sum based on where you enter the formula—in this case, A8:D14. This is not the correct range, so you must enter the correct range.

d. Select the **range B8:B12**, the cells containing house costs.

As you use the semi-selection process, Excel enters the range in the SUM function.

> **TROUBLESHOOTING:** If you accidentally entered the function without changing the arguments, you can repeat steps b–d, or you can edit the arguments in the Formula Bar by deleting the default range, typing B8:B12 between the parentheses, and then pressing Enter.

e. Click **Enter** to the left of the Formula Bar, and then save the workbook.

Cell B15 contains the function = SUM(B8:B12), and the result is $1,521,200.

STEP 2 USE THE AVERAGE FUNCTION

Before copying the functions to calculate the total down payments and amounts financed, you want to calculate the average value of houses bought by the borrowers. Refer to Figure 2.17 as you complete Step 2.

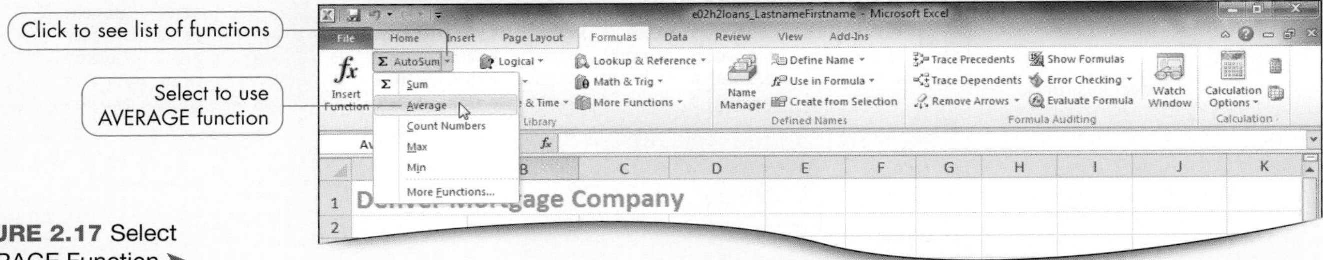

FIGURE 2.17 Select AVERAGE Function ➤

a. Click the **Formulas tab**, and then click **cell B16**, the cell where you will display the average cost of the houses.

b. Click the **AutoSum arrow** in the Function Library group, and then select **Average**.

Excel anticipates cell B15, which is the total cost of the houses. You need to change the range.

> **TROUBLESHOOTING:** AutoSum, like some other commands in Excel, contains two parts: the main command icon and an arrow. Click the main command icon when instructed to click AutoSum to perform the default action. Click the arrow when instructed to click AutoSum arrow for additional options. If you accidentally clicked AutoSum instead of the arrow, press Esc to cancel the SUM function from being completed, and then try step b again.

c. Select the **range B8:B12**, the cells containing the house costs.

The function is =AVERAGE(B8:B12).

d. Press **Enter** to complete the function and make **cell B17** the active cell, and then save the workbook.

The average house cost is $304,240.

STEP 3 USE THE MEDIAN FUNCTION

You realize that extreme values may distort the average. Therefore, you decide to identify the median value of houses bought to compare it to the average. Refer to Figure 2.18 as you complete Step 3.

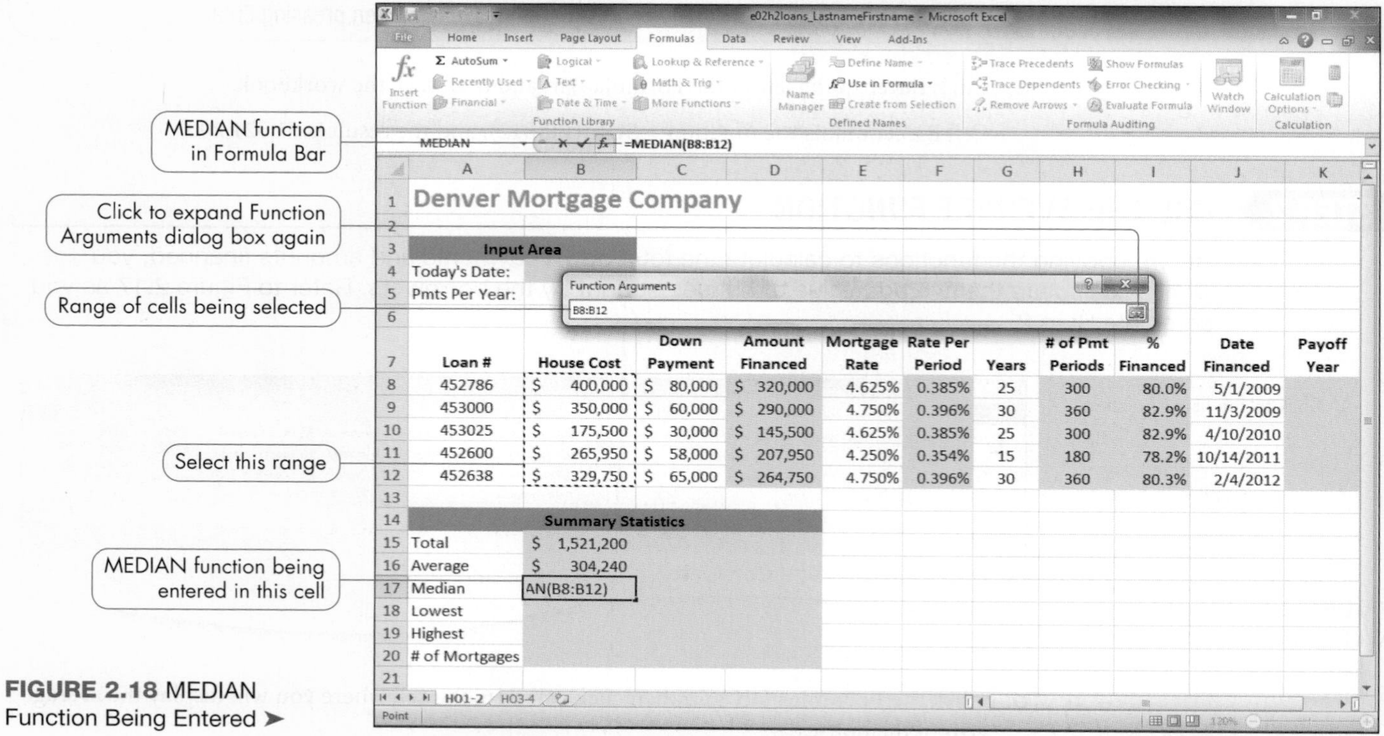

FIGURE 2.18 MEDIAN Function Being Entered ➤

a. Make sure **cell B17** is the active cell. Click **Insert Function** to the left of the Formula Bar or in the Function Library group.

   The Insert Function dialog box opens. Use this dialog box to select the MEDIAN function since it is not available on the Ribbon.

b. Type **median** in the **Search for a function box**, and then click **Go**.

   Excel displays a list of possible functions in the *Select a function* list. The MEDIAN function is selected at the top of the list; the bottom of the dialog box displays the syntax and the description.

c. Read the MEDIAN function's description, and then click **OK**.

   The Function Arguments dialog box opens. It contains one required argument, Number1, representing a range of cells containing values. It has an optional argument, Number2, which you can use if you have nonadjacent ranges that contain values.

d. Click the **collapse button** to the right of the Number1 box.

   You collapsed the Function Arguments dialog box so that you can select the range.

e. Select the **range B8:B12**, and then click the **expand button** in the Function Arguments dialog box.

   The Function Arguments dialog box expands again.

f. Click **OK** to accept the function arguments and close the dialog box. Save the workbook.

   Half of the houses purchased cost over the median, $329,750, and half of the houses cost less than this value. Notice the difference between the median and the average: The average is lower because it is affected by the lowest-costing house, $175,500.

STEP 4 USE THE MIN, MAX, AND COUNT FUNCTIONS

Erica wants to know the least and most expensive houses so that she can analyze typical customers of the Denver Mortgage Company. You will use the MIN and MAX functions to obtain these statistics. In addition, you will use the COUNT function to tally the number of mortgages in the sample. Refer to Figure 2.19 as you complete Step 4.

			Down	Amount	Mortgage	Rate Per		# of Pmt	%	Date	Payoff
7	Loan #	House Cost	Payment	Financed	Rate	Period	Years	Periods	Financed	Financed	Year
8	452786	$ 400,000	$ 80,000	$ 320,000	4.625%	0.385%	25	300	80.0%	5/1/2009	
9	453000	$ 425,000	$ 60,000	$ 365,000	4.750%	0.396%	30	360	85.9%	11/3/2009	
10	453025	$ 175,500	$ 30,000	$ 145,500	4.625%	0.385%	25	300	82.9%	4/10/2010	
11	452600	$ 265,950	$ 58,000	$ 207,950	4.250%	0.354%	15	180	78.2%	10/14/2011	
12	452638	$ 329,750	$ 65,000	$ 264,750	4.750%	0.396%	30	360	80.3%	2/4/2012	
13											
14	Summary Statistics										
15	Total	$ 1,596,200	$ 293,000	$1,303,200							
16	Average	$ 319,240	$ 58,600	$ 260,640							
17	Median	$ 329,750	$ 60,000	$ 264,750							
18	Lowest	$ 175,500	$ 30,000	$ 145,500							
19	Highest	$ 425,000	$ 80,000	$ 365,000							
20	# of Mortgages	5	5	5							
21											

H01-2 H03-4

Ready 120%

FIGURE 2.19 MIN, MAX, and COUNT Function Results ➤

a. Click **cell B18**, the cell to display the cost of the lowest-costing house.

b. Click the **AutoSum arrow** in the Function Library group, select **Min**, select the **range B8:B12**, and then press **Enter**.

   The MIN function identifies that the lowest-costing house is $175,500.

c. Click **cell B19**, if needed. Click the **AutoSum arrow** in the Function Library group, select **Max**, select the **range B8:B12**, and then press **Enter**.

   The MAX function identifies that the highest-costing house is $400,000.

d. Click **cell B20**, if needed. Type **=COUNT(B8:B12)** and press **Enter**.

   As you type the letter *C*, Formula AutoComplete suggests functions starting with *C*. As you continue typing, the list of functions narrows. After you type the beginning parenthesis, Excel displays the function ScreenTip, indicating the arguments for the function. The range B8:B12 contains five cells.

e. Select the **range B15:B20**.

   You want to select the range of original statistics to copy the cells all at one time to the next two columns.

f. Drag the fill handle to the right by two columns to copy the functions. Click **cell D20**.

   Because you used relative cell references in the functions, the range changes from =COUNT(B8:B12) to =COUNT(D8:D12).

g. Change the value in **cell B9** to **425000**. Save the workbook.

   The results of several formulas and functions change, including the total, average, and max house costs.

STEP 5 USE THE TODAY AND YEAR FUNCTIONS

You have two date functions to enter to complete the first worksheet. Refer to Figure 2.20 as you complete Step 5.

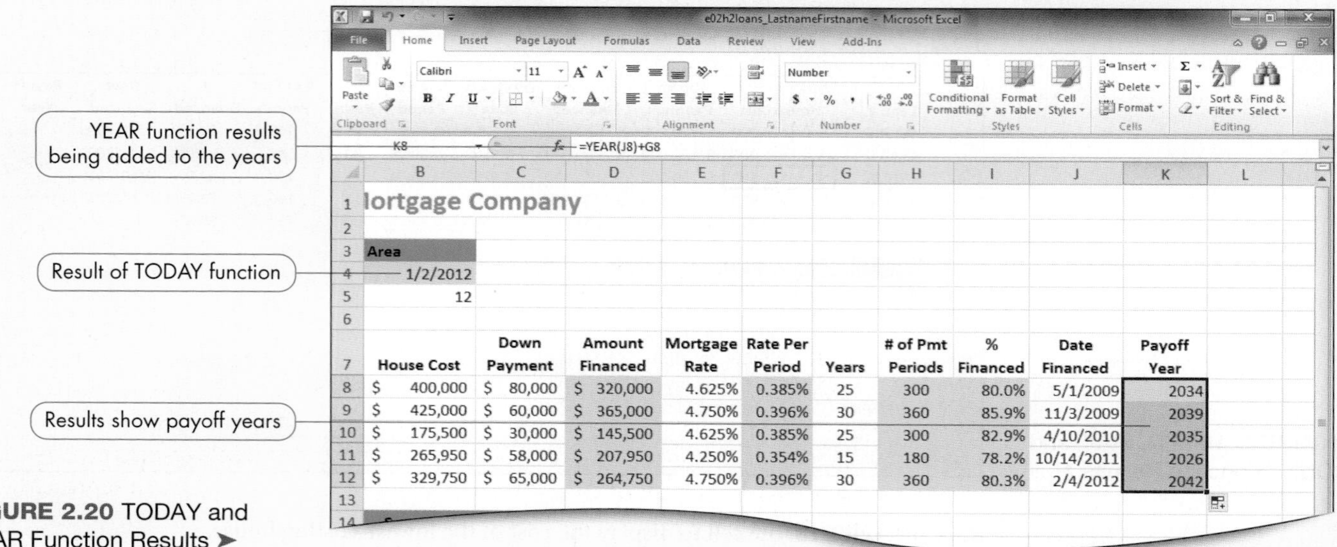

House Cost	Down Payment	Amount Financed	Mortgage Rate	Rate Per Period	Years	# of Pmt Periods	% Financed	Date Financed	Payoff Year
$ 400,000	$ 80,000	$ 320,000	4.625%	0.385%	25	300	80.0%	5/1/2009	2034
$ 425,000	$ 60,000	$ 365,000	4.750%	0.396%	30	360	85.9%	11/3/2009	2039
$ 175,500	$ 30,000	$ 145,500	4.625%	0.385%	25	300	82.9%	4/10/2010	2035
$ 265,950	$ 58,000	$ 207,950	4.250%	0.354%	15	180	78.2%	10/14/2011	2026
$ 329,750	$ 65,000	$ 264,750	4.750%	0.396%	30	360	80.3%	2/4/2012	2042

FIGURE 2.20 TODAY and YEAR Function Results ➤

a. Click **cell B4**, the cell to contain the current date.

b. Click **Date & Time** in the Function Library group, select **TODAY** to display the Function Arguments dialog box, and then click **OK** to close the dialog box.

   Excel inserts the current date in Short Date format, such as 1/2/2012, based on the computer system's date. The Function Arguments dialog box opens, although no arguments are necessary for this function.

c. Click **cell K8**, click **Date & Time** in the Function Library group, scroll through the list, and then select **YEAR**.

   The Function Arguments dialog box opens so that you can enter the argument, a serial number for a date.

d. Click **cell J8** to enter it in the **Serial_number box**. Click **OK**.

   The function returns 2009, the year the first mortgage was taken out. However, you want the year the mortgage will be paid off. The YEAR function returns the year from a date. You need to add the years to the result of the function to calculate the year that the borrower will pay off the mortgage.

e. Press **F2** to edit the formula stored in cell K8. With the insertion point on the right side of the closing parenthesis, type **+G8**, and then press **Ctrl+Enter**.

   Pressing Ctrl+Enter is the alternative to clicking Enter by the Formula Bar. It keeps the current cell as the active cell. The results show a date: 7/26/1905. You need to apply the Number format to display the year.

f. Click the **Home tab**, click the **Number Format arrow** in the Number group, and then select **Number**. Decrease the number of decimal points to show the value as a whole number.

   You applied the Number format instead of the Comma format because although the Comma format is correct for quantities, such as 2,034 units, it is not appropriate for the year 2034.

g. Copy the formula down the column.

h. Save the workbook. Keep the workbook onscreen if you plan to continue with Hands-On Exercise 3. If not, close the workbook and exit Excel.

Logical, Lookup, and Financial Functions

As you prepare complex spreadsheets using functions, you will frequently use three function categories: logical, lookup and reference, and finance. Logical functions test the logic of a situation and return a particular result. Lookup and reference functions are useful when you need to look up a value in a list to identify the applicable value. Financial functions are useful to anyone who plans to take out a loan or invest money.

Financial functions are useful to anyone who plans to take out a loan or invest money.

In this section, you will learn how to use the logical, lookup, and financial functions.

Determining Results with the IF Function

The **IF function** evaluates a condition and returns one value if the condition is true and a different value if the condition is false.

The most common logical function is the ***IF function***, which returns one value when a condition is met or is true and returns another value when the condition is not met or is false. For example, a company gives a $500 bonus to employees who sold *over* $10,000 in merchandise this week, but no bonus to employees who did not sell over $10,000 in merchandise. Figure 2.21 shows a worksheet containing the sales data for three representatives and their bonuses, if any.

F2 | fx =IF(E2>B$2,B$3,0)

	A	B	C	D	E	F	G
1	Input Area			Sales Rep	Sales	Bonus	
2	Sales Goal	$ 10,000		Anita	$ 11,000	$ 500	
3	Bonus	$ 500		Jacob	$ 10,000	$ -	
4				Tyson	$ 9,000	$ -	

FIGURE 2.21 IF Function to Calculate Bonus ➤

The IF function has three arguments: (1) a condition that is tested to determine if it is either true or false, (2) the resulting value if the condition is true, and (3) the resulting value if the condition is false.

```
=IF(logical_test,value_if_true,value_if_false)
```

You might find it helpful to create two flowcharts to illustrate an IF function. First, construct a flowchart that uses words and numbers to illustrate the condition and results. For example, the left flowchart in Figure 2.22 illustrates the condition to see if sales are greater than $10,000, the $500 bonus if the condition is true or $0 if the condition is false. Then, create a second flowchart similar to the one of the right side of Figure 2.22 that replaces the words and values with actual cell references. Creating these flowcharts can help you construct the IF function that is used in cell F2 in Figure 2.21.

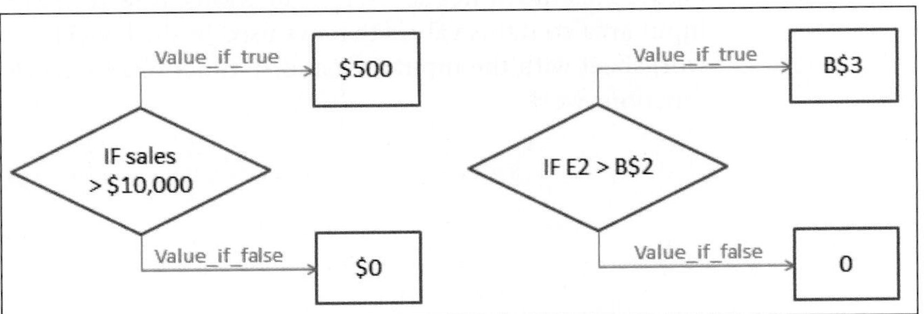

FIGURE 2.22 Flowcharts Illustrating IF Function ➤

Design the Logical Test

The **logical test** is an expression that evaluates to true or false.

The first argument for the IF function is the logical test. The ***logical test*** is a formula that contains either a value or an expression that evaluates to true or false. The logical expression is typically a binary expression, meaning that it requires a comparison between at least two variables, such as the values stored in cells E2 and B2. Table 2.4 lists and describes the logical operators to make the comparison in the logical test.

In Figure 2.21, cell F2 contains an IF function where the logical test is E2>B$2 to determine if Anita's sales in cell E2 are greater than the sales goal in cell B2. The reference to cell B2 can be mixed B$2 or absolute $B$2. Either way, copying the function down the column will correctly compare each sales representative's sales with the $10,000 value in cell B2.

TABLE 2.4 Logical Operators

Operator	Description
=	Equal to
<>	Not equal to
<	Less than
>	Greater than
<=	Less than or equal to
>=	Greater than or equal to

Design the Value_If_True and Value_If_False Arguments

The second and third arguments of an IF function are value_if_true and value_if_false. When Excel evaluates the logical test, the result is either true or false. If the logical test evaluates to true, the value_if_true argument executes. If the logical test evaluates to false, the value_if_false argument executes. Only one of the last two arguments is executed; both arguments cannot be executed, since the logical test is either true or false but not both.

The value_if_true and value_if_false arguments can contain text, cell references, formulas, or constants (not recommended unless –1, 1, or 0). In Figure 2.21, cell F2 contains an IF function in which the value_if_true argument is B$3 and the value_if_false argument is 0. Since the logical test (E2>B$2) is true, that is, Anita's sales of $11,000 are greater than the goal of $10,000, the value_if_true argument is executed, and the result displays the same value that is stored in cell B3, which is $500. Jacob's sales of $10,000 are not *greater than* $10,000. Therefore, the value_if_false argument is executed and returns no bonus in cell F3.

Create Other IF Functions

Figure 2.23 illustrates several IF functions, how they are evaluated, and their results. The input area contains values that are used in the logical tests and results. You can create this worksheet with the input area and IF functions to develop your understanding of how IF functions work.

	A	B	C
1	Input Values		
2	$1,000		
3	$2,000		
4	10%		
5	5%		
6	$250		
7			
8	IF Function	Evaluation	Result
9	=IF(A2=A3,A4,A5)	1000 is equal to 2000: FALSE	5%
10	=IF(A2<A3,A4,A5)	1000 is less than 2000: TRUE	10%
11	=IF(A2<>A3,"Not Equal","Equal")	1000 and 2000 are not equal: TRUE	Not Equal
12	=IF(A2>A3,(A2*A4),(A2*A5))	1000 is greater than 2000: FALSE	$50
13	=IF(A2>A3,A2*A4,MAX(A2*A5,A6))	1000 is greater than 2000: FALSE	$250

FIGURE 2.23 Sample IF Functions ➤

- **Cell A9.** The logical test A2=A3 compares the values in cells A2 and A3 to see if they are equal. Because $1,000 is not equal to $2,000, the logical test is false. The value_if_false argument is executed, which displays the value stored in cell A5, which is 5%.
- **Cell A10.** The logical test A2<A3 determines if the value in cell A2 is less than the value in A3. Because $1,000 is less than $2,000, the logical test is true. The value_if_true argument is executed, which displays the value stored in cell A4, which is 10%.
- **Cell A11.** The logical test A2<>A3 determines if the values in cells A2 and A3 are not equal. Because $1,000 and $2,000 are not equal, the logical test is true. The value_if_true argument is executed, which displays the text *Not Equal.*
- **Cell A12.** The logical test A2>A3 is false. The value_if_false argument is executed, which multiplies the value in cell A2 ($1,000) by the value in cell A5 (5%) and displays $50. The parentheses in the value_if_true (A2*A4) and value_if_false (A2*A5) arguments are optional. They are not required but may help you read the function arguments better.
- **Cell A13.** The logical test A2>A3 is false. The value_if_false argument, which contains a nested MAX function, is executed. The MAX function, MAX(A2*A5,A6), multiplies the values in cells A2 ($1,000) and A5 (5%), and then returns the higher of the product ($50) with the value stored in cell A6 ($250).

TIP Using Text in Formulas

You can use text within a formula. For example, you can build a logical test comparing the contents of cell A1 to specific text, such as A1="Input Values". The IF function in cell A11 in Figure 2.23 uses "Not Equal" and "Equal" in the value_if_true and value_if_false arguments. When you use text in a formula or function, you must enclose the text in quotation marks. However, remember not to use quotation marks around formulas, cell references, or values.

TIP Nest Functions in IF Functions

You can nest functions in the logical test, value_if_true, and value_if_false arguments of the IF function. When you nest functions as arguments, make sure the nested function contains the required arguments for it to work and that you nest the function in the correct argument to calculate accurate results. For example, cell C13 in Figure 2.23 contains a nested MAX function in the value_if_false argument.

Using Lookup Functions

You can use lookup and reference functions to look up values to perform calculations or display results. For example, when you order merchandise on a Web site, the Web server looks up the shipping costs based on weight and distance, or at the end of a semester, your professor uses your numerical average, such as 88%, to look up the letter grade to assign, such as B+.

Create the Lookup Table

A **lookup table** is a range that contains data for the basis of the lookup and data to be retrieved.

Before you insert lookup functions, you need to create a lookup table. A ***lookup table*** is a range containing a table of values or text that can be retrieved. The table should contain at least two rows and two columns, not including headings. For example, think of a telephone book. Figure 2.24 illustrates how telephone book entries are structured into three "columns." The first column contains people's names. You look up a person's name in the first column to see his or her address (second "column") and phone number (third "column").

Grauer, Robert 123 S Main 405-555-1234
Hulett, Michelle 68 Redwood 405-555-6789
Krebs, Cynthia 24 Pine Drive 405-555-3342
Mast, Keith 932 Oak Park 405-555-9320
Mulbery, Keith 117 Cedar Hills 405-555-8080
Poatsy, Mary 84 Manilla Drive 405-555-7254

FIGURE 2.24 Phone Book Lookup Table Analogy ➤

It is important to plan the table so that it conforms to the way in which Excel can utilize the data in it. Excel cannot interpret the structure of Table 2.5. To look up a value in a range (such as the range 80–89), you must arrange data from the lowest to the highest value and include only the lowest value in the range (such as 80) instead of the complete range. If the values you look up are *exact* values, you can arrange the first column in any logical order. The lowest value for a category or in a series is the ***breakpoint***. The first column contains the breakpoints—such as 60, 70, 80, and 90—or the lowest values to achieve a particular grade. The lookup table contains one or more additional columns of related data to retrieve. Table 2.6 shows how to construct the lookup table in Excel.

The **breakpoint** is the lowest value for a specific category or series in a lookup table.

TABLE 2.5 Grading Scale

Range	Grade
90–100	A
80–89	B
70–79	C
60–69	D
Below 60	F

TABLE 2.6 Grades Lookup Table

Range	Grade
0	F
60	D
70	C
80	B
90	A

Understand the VLOOKUP Function Syntax

The **VLOOKUP function** looks up a value in a vertical lookup table and returns a related result from the lookup table.

The ***VLOOKUP function*** accepts a value, looks the value up in a vertical lookup table, and returns a result. Use VLOOKUP to search for exact matches or for the nearest value that is less than or equal to the search value, such as assigning a B grade for an 87% class average. The VLOOKUP function has the following three required arguments and one optional argument: (1) lookup_value, (2) table_array, (3) col_index_number, and (4) range_lookup.

```
=VLOOKUP(lookup_value,table_array,col_index_number,[range_lookup])
```

Figure 2.25 shows a partial grade book that contains a vertical lookup table, as well as the final scores and letter grades. The function in cell F3 is =VLOOKUP(E3,$A$3:$B$7,2).

	A	B	C	D	E	F	G
1	Grading Scale			Partial Gradebook			
2	Breakpoint	Grade		Names	Final Score	Letter Grade	
3	0	F		Abbott	85	B	
4	60	D		Carter	69	D	
5	70	C		Hon	90	A	
6	80	B		Jackson	74	C	
7	90	A		Miller	80	B	
8				Nelsen	78	C	

FIGURE 2.25 VLOOKUP Function for Grade Book ➤

The **lookup value** is a reference to a cell containing a value to look up.

The **table array** is a range containing a lookup table.

The **column index number** is the argument in a VLOOKUP function that identifies which lookup table column from which to return a value.

The ***lookup value*** is the cell reference of the cell that contains the value to look up. The lookup value for the first student is cell E3, which contains 85. The ***table array*** is the range that contains the lookup table: $A$3:$B$7. The table array range must be absolute and cannot include column labels for the lookup table. The ***column index number*** is the column number in the lookup table that contains the return values. In this example, the column index number is 2.

TIP Using Values in Formulas

You know to avoid values in formulas because values might change. However, notice that the value 2 is the col_index_number argument of the VLOOKUP function. The value 2 refers to a particular column within the lookup table and is an acceptable use of a number within a formula.

Understand How Excel Processes the Lookup

The VLOOKUP function identifies the value stored in the lookup value argument and then searches the first column of the lookup table until it finds an exact match (if possible). If Excel finds an exact match, it returns the value stored in the column designated by the column index number on that same row. If the table contains breakpoints for ranges rather than exact matches, Excel identifies the correct range based on comparing the lookup value to the breakpoints in the first column. If the lookup value is larger than the breakpoint, it looks to the next breakpoint to see if the lookup value is larger than that breakpoint also. When Excel detects that the lookup value is not greater than the next breakpoint, it stays on that row. It then uses the column index number to identify the column containing the value to return for the lookup value. Because Excel goes sequentially through the breakpoints, it is mandatory that the breakpoints are arranged from the lowest value to the highest value for ranges.

For example, the VLOOKUP function to assign letter grades works like this: Excel identifies the lookup value (85 stored in cell E3) and compares it to the values in the first column of the lookup table (stored in cells A3:B7). It tries to find an exact match for the value 85; however, the table contains breakpoints rather than every conceivable numeric average. Because the lookup table is arranged from the lowest to the highest breakpoints, Excel detects that 85 is greater than the 80 breakpoint but is not greater than the 90 breakpoint. Therefore, it stays on the 80 row. Excel then looks at the column index number of 2 and returns the letter grade of B, which is located in the second column of the lookup table. The returned grade of B is then stored in cell F3, which contains the VLOOKUP function.

Use the Range_Lookup Argument

Instead of looking up values in a range, you can look up a value for an exact match using the optional range_lookup argument in the VLOOKUP function. By default, the range_lookup is set implicitly to TRUE, which is appropriate to look up values in a range. Omitting the optional argument or typing TRUE in it enables the VLOOKUP function to find the closest match in the table to the lookup value.

However, to look up an exact match, you must specify FALSE in the range_lookup argument. For example, if you are looking up product numbers, you must find an exact match to display the price. The function would look like this: =VLOOKUP(D15,$A$1:$B$50,2,FALSE). The VLOOKUP function returns a value for the first lookup value that matches the first column of the lookup table. If no exact match is found, the function returns #N/A.

Nest Functions inside the VLOOKUP Function

You can nest functions as arguments inside the VLOOKUP function. Figure 2.26 illustrates shipping amounts that are based on weight and location (Boston or Chicago). In the VLOOKUP function in cell C3, the lookup_value argument looks up the weight of a package in cell A3. That weight (14 pounds) is looked up in the table_array argument, which is $E$2:$G$5. To determine which column of the lookup table to use, an IF function is nested as the column_index_number argument. The nested IF function compares the city stored in cell B3 to the text *Boston*. If cell B3 contains *Boston*, it returns 2 to use as the column_index_number to identify the shipping value for a package that is going to Boston. If cell B3 does not contain *Boston* (i.e., the only other city in this example is *Chicago*), the column_index_number is 3.

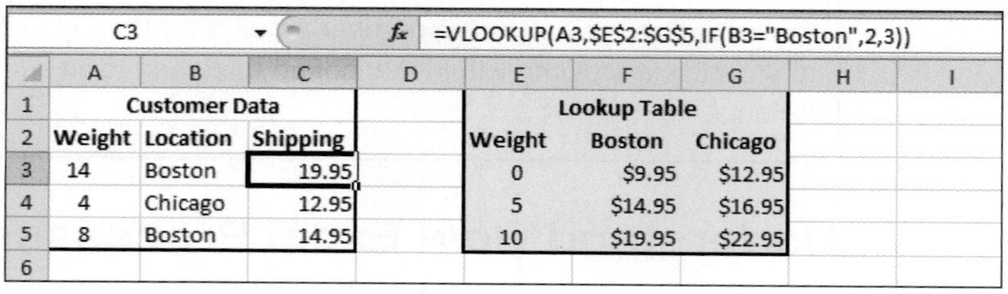

C3 fx =VLOOKUP(A3,$E$2:$G$5,IF(B3="Boston",2,3))

	A	B	C	D	E	F	G	H	I
1		Customer Data				Lookup Table			
2	Weight	Location	Shipping		Weight	Boston	Chicago		
3	14	Boston	19.95		0	$9.95	$12.95		
4	4	Chicago	12.95		5	$14.95	$16.95		
5	8	Boston	14.95		10	$19.95	$22.95		
6									

FIGURE 2.26 IF Function Nested in VLOOKUP Function ➤

Use the HLOOKUP Function

The **HLOOKUP function** looks up a value in a horizontal lookup table where the first row contains the values to compare with the lookup value.

You can design your lookup table horizontally, so that the first row contains the values for the basis of the lookup or the breakpoints, and additional rows contain data to be retrieved. With a horizontal lookup table, you must use the ***HLOOKUP function***. Table 2.7 shows how the grading scale would look as a horizontal lookup table.

TABLE 2.7 Horizontal Lookup Table

0	60	70	80	90
F	D	C	B	A

The syntax is almost the same as the syntax for the VLOOKUP function, except the third argument is row_index_number instead of col_index_number.

```
=HLOOKUP(lookup_value,table_array,row_index_number,[range_lookup])
```

Calculating Payments with the PMT Function

Excel contains several financial functions to help you perform calculations with monetary values. If you take out a loan to purchase a car, you need to know the monthly payment, which depends on the price of the car, the down payment, and the terms of the loan, in order to determine if you can afford the car. The decision is made easier by developing the worksheet in Figure 2.27 and then by changing the various input values as indicated.

B9 | f_x =PMT(B6,B8,-B3)

	A	B	C	D
1	Purchase Price	$25,999.00		
2	Down Payment	$ 5,000.00		
3	Amount to Finance	$20,999.00		
4	Payments per Year	12		
5	Interest Rate (APR)	5.250%		
6	Periodic Rate (Monthly)	0.438%		
7	Term (Years)	5		
8	No. of Payment Periods	60		
9	Monthly Payment	$ 398.69		
10				

FIGURE 2.27 Car Loan Worksheet ➤

Creating a loan model helps you evaluate your options. You realize that the purchase of a $25,999 car is prohibitive because the monthly payment is almost $398.69. Purchasing a less expensive car, coming up with a substantial down payment, taking out a longer term loan, or finding a better interest rate can decrease your monthly payments.

The **PMT function** calculates the periodic payment for a loan with a fixed interest rate and fixed term.

The ***PMT function*** calculates payments for a loan with a fixed amount at a fixed periodic rate for a fixed time period. The PMT function uses up to five arguments, three of which are required and two of which are optional: (1) rate, (2) nper, (3) pv, (4) fv, and (5) type.

=PMT(rate,nper,pv,[fv],[type])

The **rate** is the periodic interest rate, such as a monthly interest rate.

The ***rate*** is the periodic interest rate, the interest rate per payment period. If the annual percentage rate (APR) is 12% and you make monthly payments, the periodic rate is 1% (12%/12 months). With the same APR and quarterly payments, the periodic rate is 3% (12%/4 quarters). Divide the APR by the number of payment periods in one year. However, instead of dividing the APR by 12 within the PMT function, calculate the periodic interest rate in cell B6 in Figure 2.27 and use that calculated rate in the PMT function.

The **nper** is the number of total payment periods.

The ***nper*** is the total number of payment periods. The term of a loan is usually stated in years; however, you make several payments per year. For monthly payments, you make 12 payments per year. To calculate the nper, multiply the number of years by the number of payments in one year. Instead of calculating the number of payment periods in the PMT function, calculate the number of payment periods in cell B8 and use that calculated value in the PMT function.

The **pv** is the present value of the loan.

The ***pv*** is the present value of the loan. The result of the PMT function is a negative value because it represents your debt. However, you can display the result as a positive value by typing a minus sign in front of the present value cell reference in the PMT function.

Quick Concepts Check

1. Describe the three arguments for an IF function.
2. How should you structure a vertical lookup table if you need to look up values in a range?
3. What are the first three arguments of a PMT function? Why would you have to divide by or multiply an argument by 12?

HANDS-ON EXERCISES

3 Logical, Lookup, and Financial Functions

Erica wants you to complete a similar model that she might use for future mortgage data analysis. As you study the model, you realize you need to incorporate logical, lookup, and financial functions.

Skills covered: Use the VLOOKUP Function • Use the PMT Function • Use the IF Function

STEP 1 USE THE VLOOKUP FUNCTION

Rates vary based on the number of years to pay off the loan. Erica created a lookup table for three common mortgage years, and she entered the current APR. The lookup table will provide efficiency later when the rates change. You will use the VLOOKUP function to display the correct rate for each customer based on the number of years of the respective loans. Refer to Figure 2.28 as you complete Step 1.

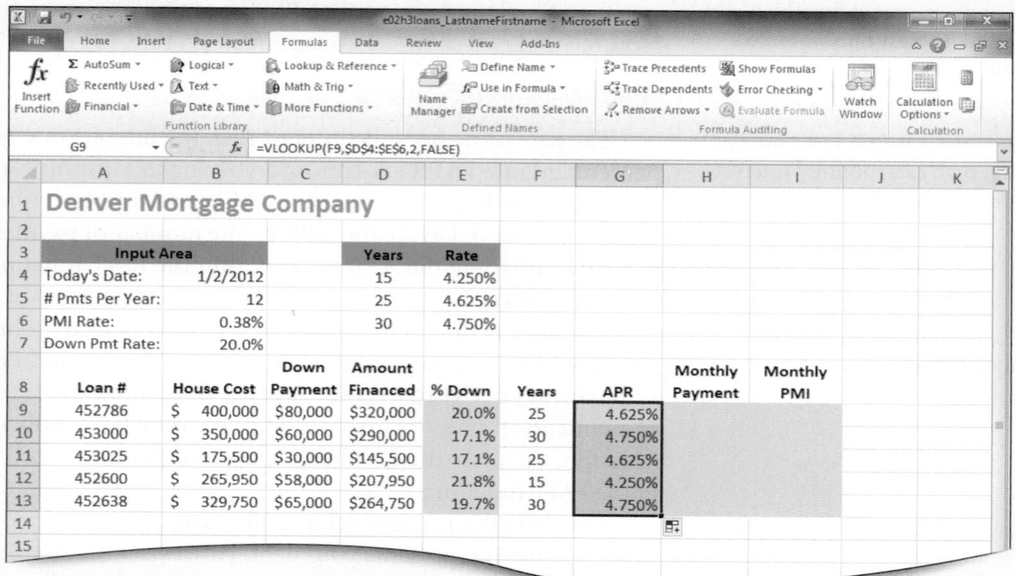

FIGURE 2.28 VLOOKUP Function ➤

a. Open *e02h2loans_LastnameFirstname* if you closed it at the end of Hands-On Exercise 2. Save the workbook with the new name **e02h3loans_LastnameFirstname**, changing *h2* to *h3*.

b. Click the **HO3-4 worksheet tab** to display the worksheet containing the data to complete. Click **cell G9**, the cell that will store the APR for the first customer.

c. Click the **Formulas tab**, click **Lookup & Reference** in the Function Library group, and then select **VLOOKUP**.

   The Function Arguments dialog box opens. You need to enter the three required and one optional argument.

d. Click **F9** to enter F9 in the **Lookup_value box**.

   Cell F9 contains the value you need to look up from the table: 25 years.

> **TROUBLESHOOTING:** If you cannot see the cell you need to use in an argument, click the Function Arguments dialog box title bar, and drag the dialog box on the screen until you can see and click the cell you need for the argument.

e. Press **Tab**, and then select the **range D4:E6** in the **Table_array box**.

This is the range that contains that data for the lookup table. The Years values in the table are arranged in ascending order (from lowest to highest). Do not select the column headings for the range. Anticipate what will happen if you copy the formula down the column. What do you need to do to ensure that the cell references always point to the exact location of the table? If your answer is to make the table array cell references absolute, then you answered correctly.

f. Press **F4** to make the range references absolute.

The Table_array box now contains $D$4:$E$6.

g. Press **Tab**, and then type **2** in the **Col_index_num box**.

The second column of the lookup table contains the APRs that you want to return and display in the cells containing the formulas.

h. Press **Tab**, and then type **False** in the **Range_lookup box**.

You want the formula to display an error if an incorrect number of years has been entered. To ensure an exact match to look up in the table, you enter *False* in the optional argument.

i. Click **OK**.

The VLOOKUP function looks up the first person's years (25), finds an exact match in the first column of the lookup table, and then returns the corresponding APR, which is 4.625%.

j. Copy the formula down the column, and then save the workbook.

Spot check the results to make sure the function returned the correct APR based on the number of years.

STEP 2 USE THE PMT FUNCTION

The worksheet now has all the necessary data for you to calculate the monthly payment for each loan: the APR, the number of years for the loan, the number of payment periods in one year, and the initial loan amount. You will use the PMT function to calculate the monthly payment, which includes paying back the principal amount with interest. This calculation does not include escrow amounts, such as property taxes or insurance. Refer to Figure 2.29 as you complete Step 2.

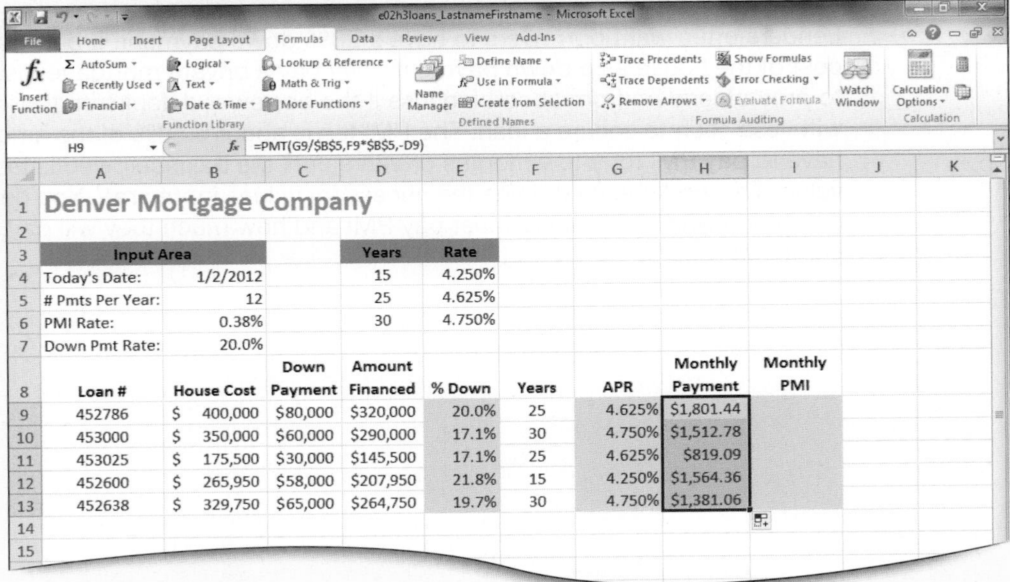

FIGURE 2.29 PMT Function ➤

a. Click **cell H9**, the cell that will store the payment for the first customer.

b. Click **Financial** in the Function Library group, scroll through the list, and then select **PMT**.

> **TROUBLESHOOTING:** Make sure you select PMT, not PPMT. The PPMT function calculates the principal portion of a particular monthly payment, not the total monthly payment itself.

The Function Arguments dialog box opens. You need to enter the three required arguments.

c. Type **G9/B5** in the **Rate box**.

Before going on to the next argument, think about what will happen if you copy the formula. The argument will be G10/B6 for the next customer. Are those cell references correct? G10 does contain the APR for the next customer, but B6 does not contain the correct number of payments in one year. Therefore, you need to make B5 an absolute cell reference because the number of payments per year does not vary.

d. Press **F4** to make the reference absolute.

e. Press **Tab**, and then type **F9*$B$5** in the **Nper box**.

You calculate the nper by multiplying the number of years by the number of payments in one year. Again, you must make B5 an absolute cell reference so that it does not change when you copy the formula down the column.

f. Press **Tab**, and then type **-D9** in the **Pv box**.

The bottom of the dialog box indicates that the monthly payment is 1801.444075 or $1,801.44.

> **TROUBLESHOOTING:** If the payment displays as a negative value, you probably forgot to type the minus sign in front of the D9 reference in the Pv box. Edit the function, and type the minus sign in the correct place.

g. Click **OK**. Copy the formula down the column, and then save the workbook.

STEP 3 USE THE IF FUNCTION

Lenders often want borrowers to have a 20% down payment. If borrowers do not put in 20% of the cost of the house as a down payment, they pay a private mortgage insurance (PMI) fee. PMI serves to protect lenders from absorbing loss if the borrower defaults on the loan, and it enables borrowers with less cash to secure a loan. The PMI fee is about 0.38% of the amount financed. Some borrowers have to pay PMI for a few months or years until the balance owed is less than 80% of the appraised value. The worksheet contains the necessary values input area. You need to use the IF function to determine which borrowers must pay PMI and how much they will pay. Refer to Figure 2.30 as you complete Step 3.

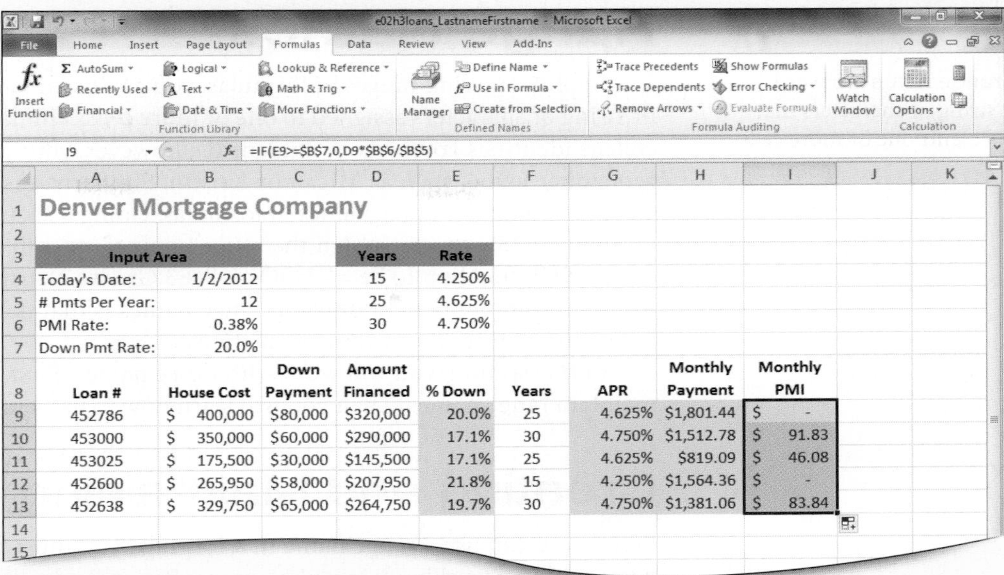

FIGURE 2.30 IF Function ➤

a. Click **cell I9**, the cell that will store the PMI, if any, for the first customer.

b. Click **Logical** in the Function Library group, and then select **IF**.

   The Function Arguments dialog box opens. You need to enter the three arguments.

c. Type **E9>=$B$7** in the **Logical_test box**.

   The logical test compares the down payment percentage to see if the customer's down payment is at least 20%, the threshold stored in B7, of the amount financed. The customer's percentage cell reference needs to be relative so that it will change when you copy it down the column; however, cell B7 must be absolute because it contains the threshold value.

d. Press **Tab**, and then type **0** in the **Value_if_true box**.

   If the customer makes a down payment that is at least 20% of the purchase price, the customer does not pay PMI. The first customer paid 20% of the purchase price, so he or she does not have to pay PMI.

e. Press **Tab**, and then type **D9*$B$6/$B$5** in the **Value_if_false box**.

   If the logical test is false, the customer must pay PMI, which is calculated by dividing the yearly PMI (0.38%) by 12 and multiplying the result by the amount financed.

f. Click **OK**, and then copy the formula down the column.

   The second, third, and fifth customers must pay PMI because their respective down payments were less than 20% of the purchase price.

TROUBLESHOOTING: If the results are not as you expected, check the logical operators. People often mistype < and > or forget to type = for >= situations. Correct any errors in the original formula, and then copy the formula again.

g. Save the workbook. Keep the workbook onscreen if you plan to continue with Hands-On Exercise 4. If not, close the workbook and exit Excel.

Range Names

A **range name** is a word or string of characters that represents one or more cells.

To simplify entering ranges in formulas, you can use range names. A ***range name*** is a word or string of characters assigned to one or more cells. Think of range names in this way: Your college identifies you by your student ID; however, your professors call you by an easy-to-remember name, such as Micah or Kristin. Similarly, instead of using cell addresses, you can use descriptive range names in formulas. Going back to the VLOOKUP example shown in Figure 2.25, you can assign the range name *Grades* to cells A3:B7 and then modify the VLOOKUP function to be =VLOOKUP(E3,Grades,2), using the range name *Grades* in the formula. Another benefit of using range names is that they are absolute references, which helps ensure accuracy in your calculations.

In this section, you will work with range names. First, you will learn how to create and maintain range names. Then you will learn how to use a range name in a formula.

Creating and Maintaining Range Names

Before you can use a range name in a formula, you must first create the name. Each range name within a workbook must be unique. For example, you can't assign the name *COST* to ranges on several worksheets or on the same sheet.

After you create a range name, you might need to change its name or change the range of cells. If you no longer need a range name, you can delete it. You can also insert a list of range names and their respective cell ranges for reference.

Create a Range Name

A range name can contain up to 255 characters, but it must begin with a letter or an underscore. You can use a combination of upper- or lowercase letters, numbers, periods, and underscores throughout the range name. A range name cannot include spaces or special characters. You should create range names that describe the range of cells being named, but names cannot be identical to the cell contents. Keep the range names relatively short to make them easier to use in formulas. Table 2.8 lists acceptable and unacceptable range names.

TABLE 2.8 Range Names

Name	Description
Grades	Acceptable range name
COL	Acceptable abbreviation for cost-of-living
Tax_Rate	Acceptable name with underscore
Commission Rate	Unacceptable name; can't use spaces in names
Discount Rate %	Unacceptable name; can't use special symbols and spaces
2009_Rate	Unacceptable name; can't start with a number
Rate_2012	Acceptable name with underscore and numbers

To create a range name, select the range of cells you want to name, and do one of the following:

- Click in the Name Box, type the range name, and then press Enter.
- Click the Formulas tab, click Define Name in the Defined Names group to open the New Name dialog box (see Figure 2.31), type the range name in the Name box, and then click OK.
- Click the Formulas tab, click Name Manager in the Defined Names group to open the Name Manager dialog box, click New, type the range name in the Name box, click OK, and then click Close.

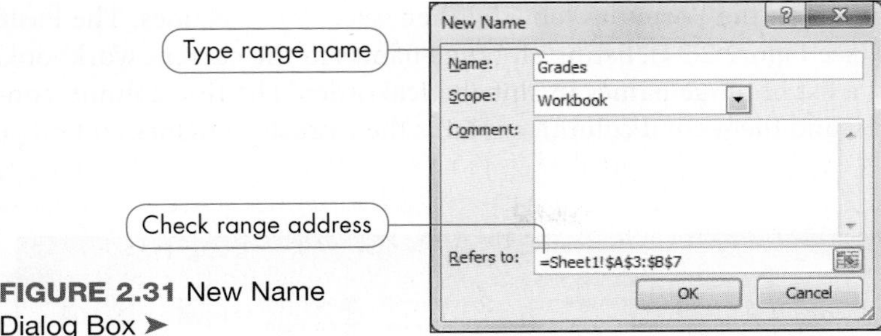

FIGURE 2.31 New Name Dialog Box ➤

You can create several range names at the same time if your worksheet already includes ranges with values and descriptive labels. To do this, select the range of cells containing the labels that you want to become names and the cells that contain the values to name, click Create from Selection in the Defined Named group on the Formulas tab, and then select an option in the Create Names from Selection dialog box (see Figure 2.32).

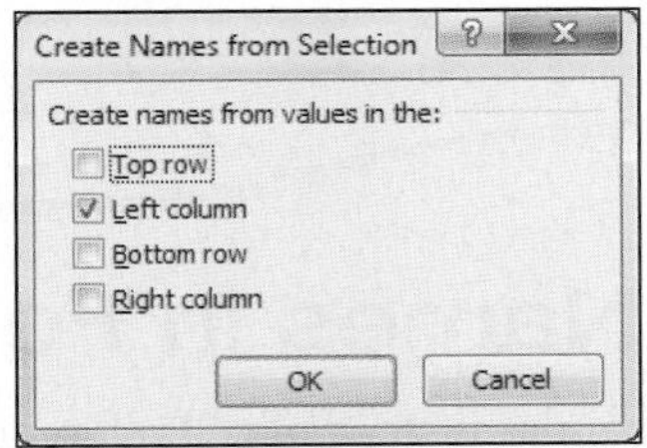

FIGURE 2.32 Create Names from Selection Dialog Box ➤

Edit or Delete a Range Name

Use the Name Manager dialog box to edit, delete, and create range names. To open the Name Manager dialog box shown in Figure 2.33, click Name Manager in the Defined Names group on the Formulas tab. To edit a range or range name, click the range name in the list, and then click Edit. In the Edit Name dialog box, make your edits, and then click OK.

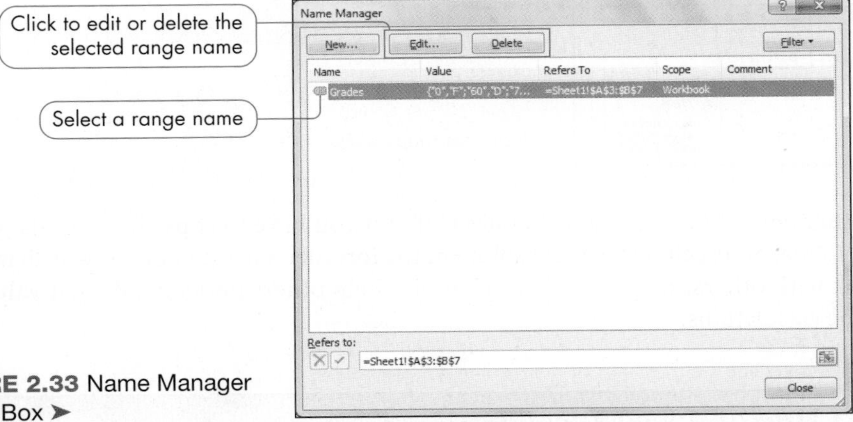

FIGURE 2.33 Name Manager Dialog Box ➤

To delete a range name, open the Name Manager dialog box, select the name you want to delete, click Delete, and then click OK in the confirmation message box.

If you change a range name, any formulas that use the range name reflect the new name automatically. For example, if a formula contains =cost*rate and you change the name rate to tax_rate, Excel updates the formula to be =cost*tax_rate. If you delete a range name and a formula depends on that range name, Excel displays #NAME?—indicating an Invalid Name Error.

Insert a Table of Range Names

Documentation is an important part of good spreadsheet design. People often document workbooks with date or time stamps that indicate the last date of revision, notes describing how to use a workbook, and so on. One way to document a workbook is to insert a list of range names in a worksheet. To insert a list of range names, click *Use in Formula* in the Defined Names group on the Formulas tab, and then select Paste Names. The Paste Name dialog box opens (see Figure 2.34), listing all range names in the current workbook. Click Paste List to insert a list of range names in alphabetical order. The first column contains a list of range names, and the second column contains the worksheet names and range locations.

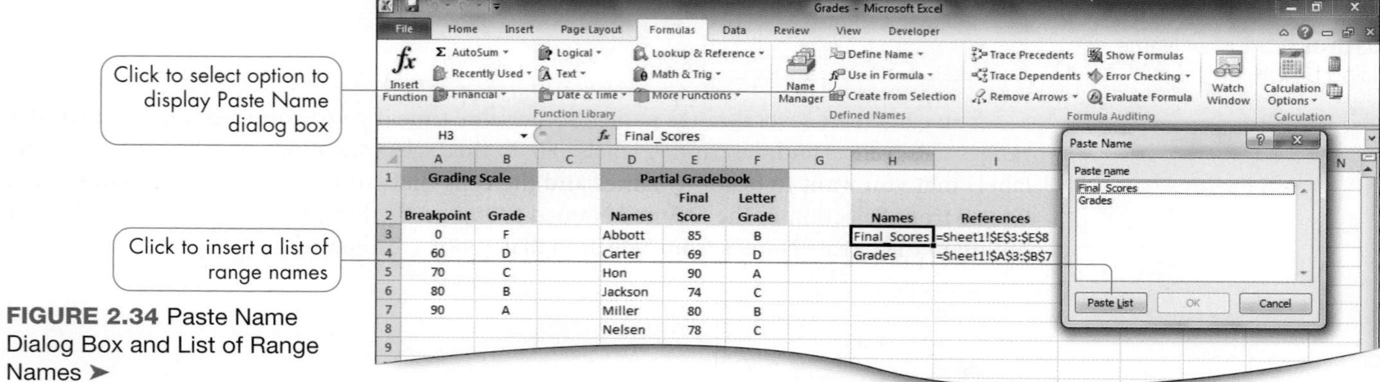

FIGURE 2.34 Paste Name Dialog Box and List of Range Names ➤

Using Range Names in Formulas

You can use range names in formulas instead of cell references. For example, if cell C15 contains a purchase amount, and cell C5 contains the sales tax rate, instead of typing =C15*C5, you can type the range names in the formula, such as =purchase*tax_rate. When you type a formula, Formula AutoComplete displays a list of range names, as well as functions, that start with the letters as you type (see Figure 2.35). Double-click the range name to insert it in the formula.

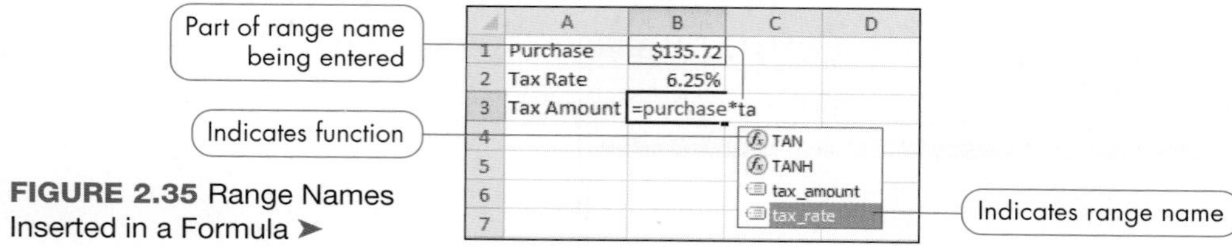

FIGURE 2.35 Range Names Inserted in a Formula ➤

Another benefit of using range names is that if you have to copy the formula, you do not have to make the cell reference absolute in the formula. Furthermore, if you share your workbook with others, range names in formulas help others understand what values are used in the calculations.

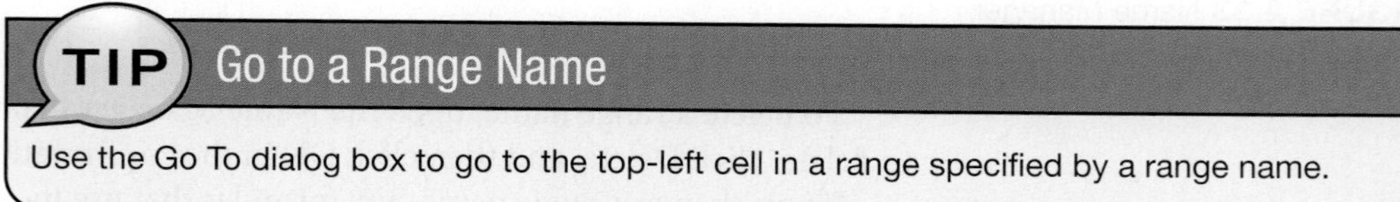

TIP Go to a Range Name

Use the Go To dialog box to go to the top-left cell in a range specified by a range name.

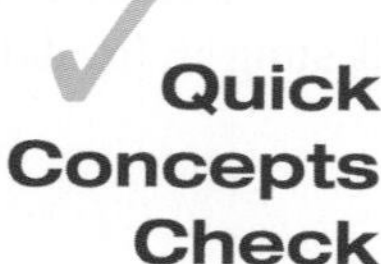

Quick Concepts Check

1. What is a range name?
2. List at least five guidelines and rules for naming a range.
3. What is the purpose of inserting a list of range names in a worksheet? What is contained in the list, and how is it arranged?

4 Range Names

You decide to simplify the VLOOKUP function by using a range name for the lookup table instead of the actual cell references. After creating a range name, you will modify some range names Erica created, and then create a list of range names.

Skills covered: Create a Range Name • Edit and Delete Range Names • Use a Range Name in a Formula • Insert a List of Range Names

STEP 1 CREATE A RANGE NAME

You want to assign a range name to the lookup table of years and APRs. Refer to Figure 2.36 as you complete Step 1.

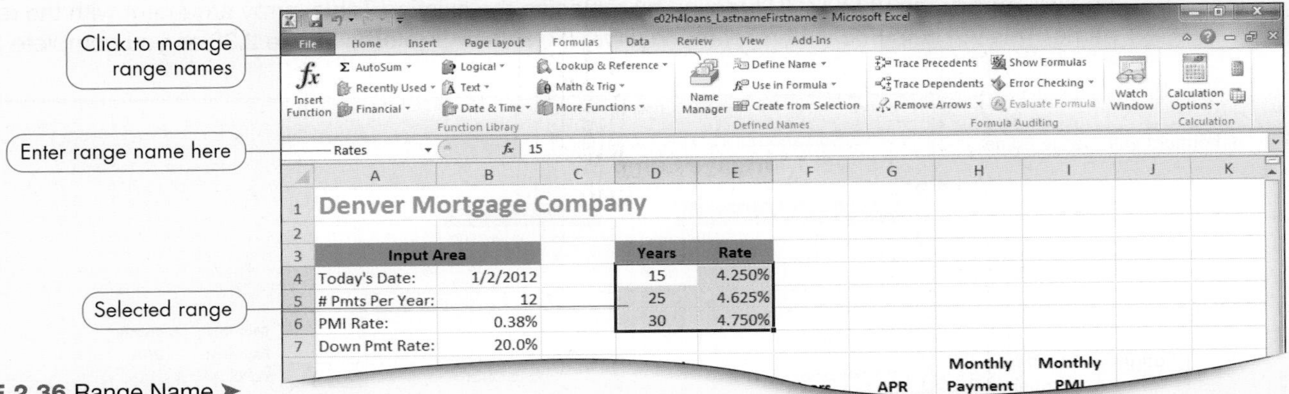

FIGURE 2.36 Range Name ➤

a. Open *e02h3loans_LastnameFirstname* if you closed it at the end of Hands-On Exercise 3. Save the workbook with the new name **e02h4loans_LastnameFirstname**, changing *h3* to *h4*.

b. Make sure the **HO3-4 worksheet tab** is active. Select **range D4:E6** (the lookup table).

c. Type **Rates** in the **Name Box**, and then press **Enter**. Save the workbook.

STEP 2 EDIT AND DELETE RANGE NAMES

You noticed that Erica added some range names. You will open the Name Manager dialog box to view and make changes to the range names. Refer to Figure 2.37 as you complete Step 2.

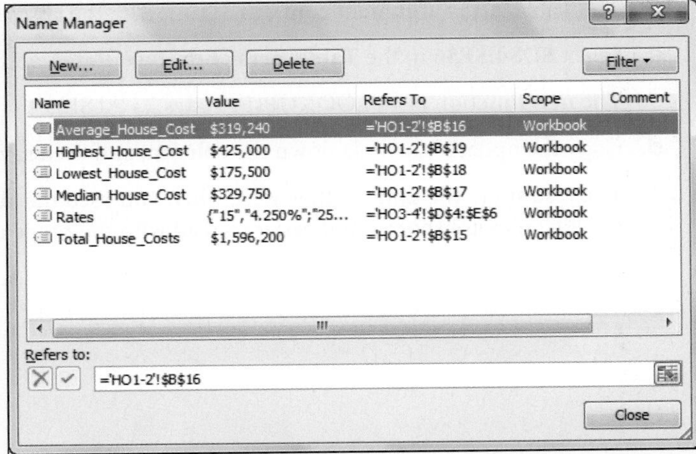

FIGURE 2.37 Updated Range Names ➤

a. Click **Name Manager** in the Defined Names group.

The Name Manager dialog box opens. The first name is *Avg_Cost*. You want to rename it to have a naming structure consistent with the other Cost names, such as Total_House_Costs.

b. Select **Avg_Cost**, and then click **Edit** to open the Edit Name dialog box.

c. Type **Average_House_Cost** in the **Name box**, and then click **OK**.

d. Select **Title** in the Name Manager dialog box.

This range name applies to a cell containing text, which does not need a name as it cannot be used in calculations. You decide to delete the range name.

e. Click **Delete**, read the warning message box, and then click **OK** to confirm the deletion of the Title range name.

f. Click **Close**, and then save the workbook.

STEP 3 USE A RANGE NAME IN A FORMULA

You will modify the VLOOKUP function by replacing the existing Table_array argument with the range name. This will help Erica interpret the VLOOKUP function. Refer to Figure 2.38 as you complete Step 3.

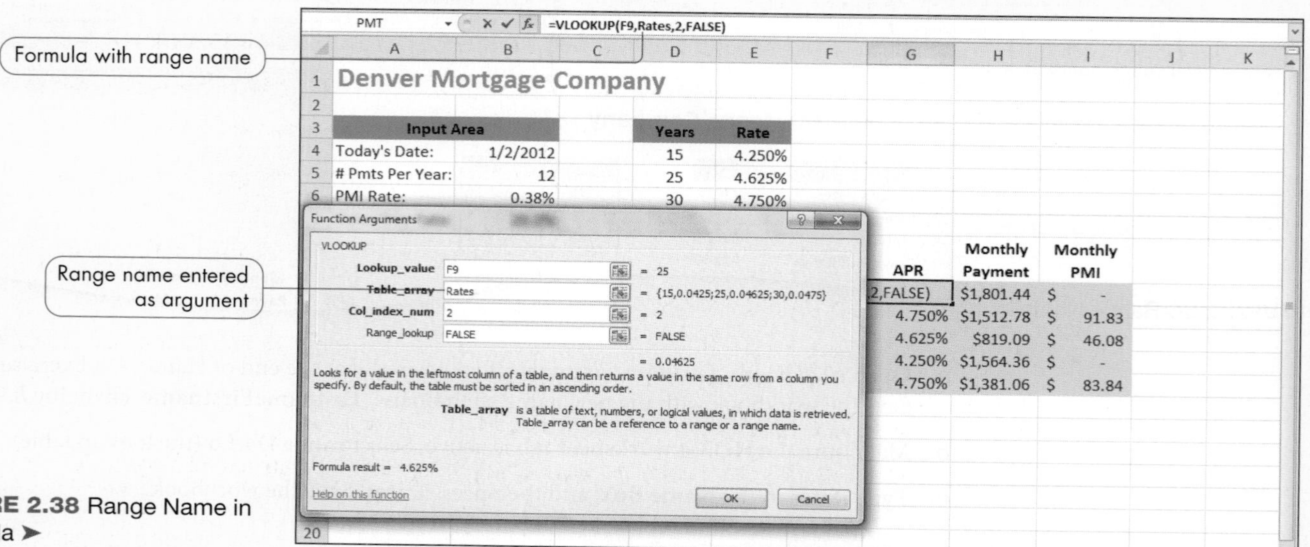

FIGURE 2.38 Range Name in Formula ➤

a. Click **cell G9**, the cell containing the VLOOKUP function.

b. Click **Insert Function** between the Name Box and the Formula Bar to open the Function Arguments dialog box.

The Table_array argument contains $D$4:$E$6, the absolute reference to the lookup table.

c. Select **$D$4:$E$6** in the **Table_array box**, type **Rates**, and then click **OK**.

The new function is =VLOOKUP(F9,Rates,2,FALSE).

d. Copy the updated formula down the column, and then save the workbook.

The results are the same as they were when you used the absolute cell references. However, the formulas are shorter and easier to read with the range names.

STEP 4 INSERT A LIST OF RANGE NAMES

Before submitting the completed workbook to Erica, you want to create a documentation worksheet that lists all of the range names in the workbook. Refer to Figure 2.39 as you complete Step 4.

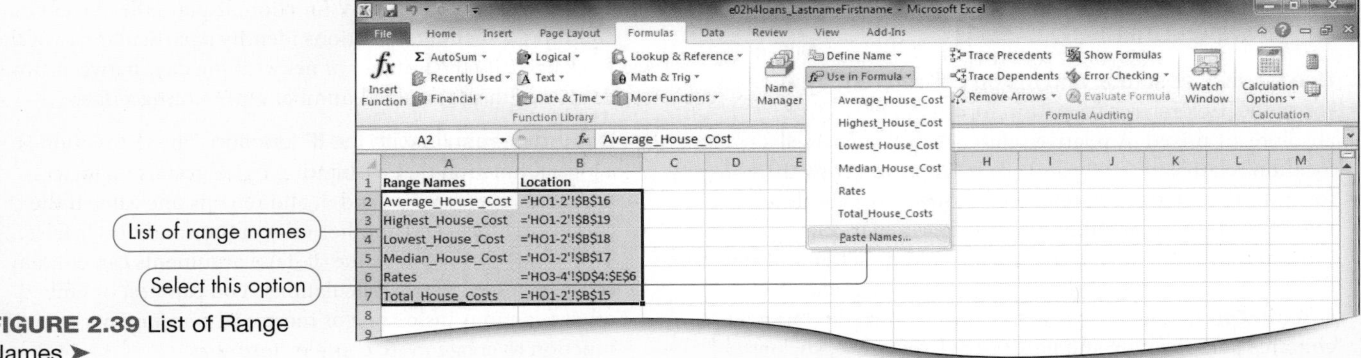

FIGURE 2.39 List of Range Names ➤

a. Click **Insert Worksheet** to the right of the worksheet tabs, and then double-click the default sheet name, **Sheet1**. Type **Range Names** and press **Enter**.

You inserted and renamed the new worksheet to reflect the data you will add to it.

b. Type **Range Names** in **cell A1**, and then type **Location** in **cell B1**. Bold these headings.

These column headings will appear above the list of range names.

c. Click **cell A2**, click **Use in Formula** in the Defined Names group on the Formulas tab, and then select **Paste Names**.

The Paste Name dialog box opens, displaying all of the range names in the workbook.

d. Click **Paste List**.

Excel pastes an alphabetical list of range names starting in cell A2. The second column displays the locations of the range names.

e. Increase the widths of columns A and B to fit the data.

f. Save and close the workbook, and submit based on your instructor's directions.

TIP List of Range Names

When you paste range names, the list will overwrite any existing data in a worksheet, so consider pasting the list in a separate worksheet. If you add, edit, or delete range names, the list does not update automatically. To keep the list current, you would need to paste the list again.

CHAPTER OBJECTIVES REVIEW

After reading this chapter, you have accomplished the following objectives:

1. **Use semi-selection to create a formula.** Semi-selection is a pointing process where you click or drag to select cells to add cell references to a formula.

2. **Use relative, absolute, and mixed cell references in formulas.** Cell references within formulas are relative, absolute, or mixed. A relative reference indicates a cell's location relative to the formula cell. When you copy the formula, the relative cell reference changes. An absolute reference is a permanent pointer to a particular cell, indicated with dollar signs before the column letter and row number, such as $B$5. When you copy the formula, the absolute cell reference does not change. A mixed reference contains part absolute and part relative reference, such as $B5 or B$5. Depending on the type of relative reference, either the column or row reference changes while the other remains constant when you copy the formula.

3. **Avoid circular references.** A circular reference occurs when a formula refers to the cell containing the formula. The status bar indicates the location of a circular reference. You should correct circular references to prevent inaccurate results.

4. **Insert a function.** A function is a predefined formula that performs a calculation. It contains the function name and arguments. Formula AutoComplete, function ScreenTips, and the Insert Function dialog box help you select and create functions. The Function Arguments dialog box guides you through entering requirements for each argument.

5. **Total values with the SUM function.** The SUM function calculates the total of a range of values. The syntax is =SUM(number1,[number2],...) where the arguments are cell references to one or more ranges.

6. **Insert basic statistical functions.** The AVERAGE function calculates the arithmetic mean of values in a range. The MEDIAN function identifies the midpoint value in a set of values. The MIN function identifies the lowest value in a range, whereas the MAX function identifies the highest value in a range. The COUNT function tallies the number of cells in a range, whereas the COUNTBLANK function tallies the number of blank cells in a range. Excel contains other math and statistical functions, such as FREQUENCY and MODE.

7. **Use date functions.** The TODAY function displays the current date, and the NOW function displays the current date and time. Other date functions identify a particular day of the week, identify the number of net working days between two dates, and display a serial number representing a date.

8. **Determine results with the IF function.** The IF function is a logical function that evaluates a logical test using logical operators, such as <, >, and =, and returns one value if the condition is true and another value if the condition is false. The value_if_true and value_if_false arguments can contain cell references, text, or calculations. You can nest or embed other functions inside one or more of the arguments of an IF function to create more complex formulas.

9. **Use lookup functions.** The VLOOKUP function looks up a value for a particular record, compares it to a lookup table, and returns a result in another column of the lookup table. Design the lookup table using exact values or the breakpoints for ranges. If an exact match is required, the optional fourth argument should be FALSE; otherwise, the fourth argument can remain empty. The HLOOKUP function looks up values by row (horizontally) rather than by column (vertically).

10. **Calculate payments with the PMT function.** The PMT function calculates periodic payments for a loan with a fixed interest rate and a fixed term. The PMT function requires the periodic interest rate, the total number of payment periods, and the original value of the loan. You can use the PMT function to calculate monthly car or mortgage payments.

11. **Create and maintain range names.** A range name is a descriptive name that corresponds with one or more cells. A range name may contain letters, numbers, and underscores, but must start with either a letter or an underscore. The quick way to create a range name is to select the range, type the name in the Name Box, and then press Enter. Use the Name Manager dialog box to edit, create, or delete range names. You can insert a list of range names on a worksheet.

12. **Use range names in formulas.** You can use range names in formulas instead of cell references. Range names are absolute and can make your formula easier to interpret by using a descriptive name for the value(s) contained in a cell or range.

KEY TERMS

MULTIPLE CHOICE

1. If cell D15 contains the formula =$C$5*D15, what is the D15 in the formula?
   (a) Mixed reference
   (b) Absolute reference
   (c) Circular reference
   (d) Range name

2. What function would most appropriately accomplish the same thing as =(B5+C5+D5+E5+F5)/5?
   (a) =SUM(B5:F5)/5
   (b) =AVERAGE(B5:F5)
   (c) =MEDIAN(B5:F5)
   (d) =COUNT(B5:F5)

3. When you type a function, what appears after you type the opening parenthesis?
   (a) Function ScreenTip
   (b) Formula AutoComplete
   (c) Insert Function dialog box
   (d) Function Arguments dialog box

4. A formula containing the entry =$B3 is copied to a cell one column to the right and two rows down. How will the entry appear in its new location?
   (a) =$B3
   (b) =B3
   (c) =$C5
   (d) =$B5

5. Cell B10 contains a date, such as 1/1/2012. Which formula will determine how many days are between that date and the current date, given that the cell containing the formula is formatted with Number Format?
   (a) =TODAY()
   (b) =CURRENT()-B10
   (c) =TODAY()-B10
   (d) =TODAY()+NOW()

6. Given that cells A1, A2, and A3 contain values 2, 3, and 10, respectively, and B6, C6, and D6 contain values 10, 20, and 30, respectively, what value will be returned by the function =IF(B6>A3,C6*A1,D6*A2)?
   (a) 10
   (b) 40
   (c) 60
   (d) 90

7. Given the function =VLOOKUP(C6,D12:F18,3), the entries in:
   (a) Range D12:D18 are in ascending order.
   (b) Range D12:D18 are in descending order.
   (c) The third column of the lookup table must be text only.
   (d) Range D12:D18 contain multiple values in each cell.

8. The function =PMT(C5,C7,-C3) is stored in cell C15. What must be stored in cell C7?
   (a) APR
   (b) Periodic interest rate
   (c) Loan amount
   (d) Number of payment periods

9. Which of the following is not an appropriate use of the SUM function?
   (a) =SUM(D15-C15)
   (b) =SUM(F1:G10)
   (c) =SUM(A8:A15,D8:D15)
   (d) =SUM(B3:B45)

10. Which of the following is not an acceptable range name?
    (a) FICA
    (b) Test_Weight
    (c) Goal for 2012
    (d) Target_2012

PRACTICE EXERCISES

1 Blue Skies Airlines

You are an analyst for Blue Skies Airlines, a regional airline headquartered in Kansas City. Blue Skies has up to 10 departures a day from the Kansas City Airport. Your assistant developed a template for you to store daily flight data about the number of passengers per flight. Each regional aircraft can hold up to 70 passengers. You need to calculate the occupancy rate, which is the percent of each flight that is occupied. In addition, you need daily statistics, such as total number of passengers, averages, least full flights, and so forth, so that decisions can be made for future flight departures out of Kansas City. You also want to calculate weekly statistics per flight number. This exercise follows the same set of skills as used in Hands-On Exercises 1 and 2 in the chapter. Refer to Figure 2.40 as you complete this exercise.

Blue Skies Airlines

Aircraft Capacity: 70

Daily Flight Information

Flight Info		Sunday		Monday		Tuesday		Wednesday		Thursday		Friday		Saturday	
Flight #	Destination	# Pass	% Full	# Pass	% Full	# Pass	% Full	# Pass	% Full	# Pass	% Full	# Pass	% Full	# Pass	% Full
4520	DEN	60	85.7%	65	92.9%	55	78.6%	65	92.9%	62	88.6%	50	71.4%		
3240	TUL	35	50.0%	57	81.4%			60	85.7%			55	78.6%		
425	DFW	50	71.4%	70	100.0%	48	68.6%	66	94.3%	68	97.1%			55	78.6%
345	ORD	69	98.6%	70	100.0%	61	87.1%	66	94.3%	70	100.0%	68	97.1%	67	95.7%
3340	TUL	45	64.3%	61	87.1%	64	91.4%	45	64.3%	48	68.6%	66	94.3%		
418	SLC	65	92.9%	67	95.7%	58	82.9%	66	94.3%	55	78.6%	69	98.6%	66	94.3%
4526	DFW	68	97.1%	70	100.0%	58	82.9%			63	90.0%	70	100.0%	68	97.1%
300	ORD	70	100.0%	70	100.0%			61	87.1%	70	100.0%	59	84.3%		
322	DEN	70	100.0%	60	85.7%	48	68.6%			65	92.9%	68	97.1%	69	98.6%
349	ORD	70	100.0%	64	91.4%	67	95.7%			66	94.3%	70	100.0%	55	78.6%

Daily Statistics

	Sunday		Monday		Tuesday		Wednesday		Thursday		Friday		Saturday	
Total # of Passengers	602		654		459		429		567		575		380	
Averages	60.2	86%	65.4	93%	57.375	82%	61.2857	88%	63	90%	63.8889	91%	63.3333	90%
Medians	66.5	95%	66	94%	58	83%	65	93%	65	93%	68	97%	66.5	95%
Least Full Flights	35	50%	57	81%	48	69%	45	64%	48	69%	50	71%	55	79%
Most Full Flights	70	100%	70	100%	67	96%	66	94%	70	100%	70	100%	69	99%
# of Flights per Day	10		10		8		7		9		9		6	

Stats

FIGURE 2.40 Blue Skies Airlines ➤

a. Open *e02p1flights* and save it as **e02p1flights_LastnameFirstname**.

b. Click **cell D6**, the cell to display the occupancy percent for Flight 4520 on Sunday, and do the following:
   - Type = and click **cell C6**. Type / and click **cell C2**.
   - Press **F4** to make cell C2 absolute.
   - Click **Enter** to the left of the Formula Bar. The completed formula is =C6/$C$2. The occupancy rate of Flight 4520 is 85.7%.
   - Double-click the **cell D6 fill handle** to copy the formula down the column.

c. Click **cell D7** and notice that the bottom border disappears from cell D15. When you copy a formula, Excel also copies the original cell's format. The cell containing the original formula did not have a bottom border, so when you copied the formula down the column, Excel formatted it to match the original cell with no border. To reapply the border, click **cell D15**, click the **Border arrow** in the Font group on the Home tab, and then select **Bottom Border**.

d. Select the **range D6:D15**, copy it to the Clipboard, and paste it starting in **cell F6**. Notice the formula in cell F6 changes to = E6/$C$2. The first cell reference changes from C6 to E6, maintaining its relative location from the pasted formula. $C$2 remains absolute so that the number of passengers per flight is always divided by the value stored in cell C2. The copied range is still in the Clipboard. Paste the formula into the remaining % Full columns (columns H, J, L, N, and P). Press **Esc** to turn off the marquee around the original copied range.

e. Clean up the data by deleting *0.0%* in cells, such as H7. The 0.0% is misleading as it implies the flight was empty; however, some flights do not operate on all days. Check your worksheet against the *Daily Flight Information* section in Figure 2.40.

f. Calculate the total number of passengers per day by doing the following:
    - Click **cell C18**.
    - Click **AutoSum** in the Editing group.
    - Select the **range C6:C15**, and then press **Enter**.
g. Calculate the average number of passengers per day by doing the following:
    - Click **cell C19**.
    - Click the **AutoSum arrow** in the Editing group, and then select **Average**.
    - Select the **range C6:C15**, and then click **Enter** to the left of the Formula Bar.
h. Calculate the median number of passengers per day by doing the following:
    - Click **cell C20**.
    - Click **Insert Function** to the left of the Formula Bar, type **median** in the **Search for a function box**, and then click **Go**.
    - Click **MEDIAN** in the **Select a function box**, and then click **OK**.
    - Select the **range C6:C15** to enter it in the **Number1 box**, and then click **OK**.
i. Calculate the least number of passengers on a daily flight by doing the following:
    - Click **cell C21**.
    - Click the **AutoSum arrow** in the Editing group, and then select **Min**.
    - Select the **range C6:C15**, and then press **Enter**.
j. Calculate the most passengers on a daily flight by doing the following:
    - Click **cell C22**.
    - Click the **AutoSum arrow** in the Editing group, and then select **Max**.
    - Select the **range C6:C15**, and then press **Enter**.
k. Calculate the number of flights for Sunday by doing the following:
    - Click **cell C23**.
    - Click the **AutoSum arrow** in the Editing group, and then select **Count Numbers**.
    - Select the **range C6:C15**, and then press **Enter**.
l. Calculate the average, median, least, and full percentages in **cells D19:D22**. Format the values with Percent Style with zero decimal places. Do not copy the formulas from column C to column D, as that will change the borders. You won't insert a SUM function in cell D18 because it does not make sense to total the occupancy rate percentage column. Select **cells C18:D23**, copy the range, and then paste in these cells: **E18**, **G18**, **I18**, **K18**, **M18**, and **O18**. Press **Esc** after pasting.
m. Create a footer with your name on the left side, the date code in the center, and the file name code on the right side.
n. Save and close the workbook, and submit based on your instructor's directions.

2 Central Nevada College Salaries

You work in the Human Resources Department at Central Nevada College. You are preparing a spreadsheet model to calculate bonuses based on performance ratings, where ratings between 1 and 1.9 do not receive bonuses, ratings between 2 and 2.9 earn $100 bonuses, ratings between 3 and 3.9 earn $250 bonuses, ratings between 4 and 4.9 earn $500 bonuses, and ratings of 5 or higher earn $1,000 bonuses. In addition, you need to calculate annual raises based on years employed. Employees who have worked five or more years earn a 3.25% raise; employees who have not worked at least five years earn a 2% raise. The partially completed worksheet does not yet contain range names. This exercise follows the same set of skills as used in Hands-On Exercises 1, 2, 3, and 4 in the chapter. Refer to Figure 2.41 as you complete this exercise.

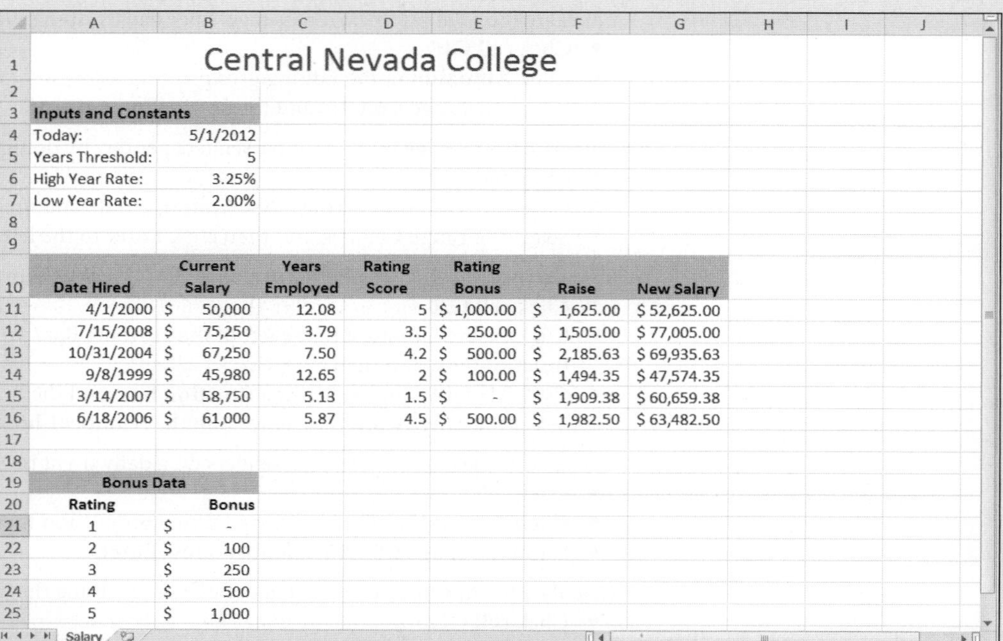

Central Nevada College

Inputs and Constants	
Today:	5/1/2012
Years Threshold:	5
High Year Rate:	3.25%
Low Year Rate:	2.00%

Date Hired	Current Salary	Years Employed	Rating Score	Rating Bonus	Raise	New Salary
4/1/2000	$ 50,000	12.08	5	$ 1,000.00	$ 1,625.00	$ 52,625.00
7/15/2008	$ 75,250	3.79	3.5	$ 250.00	$ 1,505.00	$ 77,005.00
10/31/2004	$ 67,250	7.50	4.2	$ 500.00	$ 2,185.63	$ 69,935.63
9/8/1999	$ 45,980	12.65	2	$ 100.00	$ 1,494.35	$ 47,574.35
3/14/2007	$ 58,750	5.13	1.5	$ -	$ 1,909.38	$ 60,659.38
6/18/2006	$ 61,000	5.87	4.5	$ 500.00	$ 1,982.50	$ 63,482.50

Bonus Data	
Rating	Bonus
1	$ -
2	$ 100
3	$ 250
4	$ 500
5	$ 1,000

Salary

FIGURE 2.41 Central Nevada College Salaries ➤

a. Open *e02p2salary* and save it as **e02p2salary_LastnameFirstname**.

b. Click **cell B4**, click the **Formulas tab**, click **Date & Time** in the Function Library, select **TODAY**, and then click **OK** to enter today's date in the cell.

c. Enter a formula to calculate the number of years employed by doing the following:
- Click **cell C11**.
- Click **Date & Time** in the Function Library group, scroll through the list, and then select **YEARFRAC**.
- Click **cell A11** to enter the cell reference in the **Start_date box**.
- Press **Tab**, and then click **cell B4** to enter the cell reference in the **End_date box**.
- Ask yourself if the cell references should be relative or absolute. You should answer *relative* for **cell A11** so that it will change as you copy it for the other employees. You should answer *absolute* or *mixed* for **cell B4** so that it always refers to the cell containing the TODAY function as you copy the formula.
- Press **F4** to make **cell B4** absolute, and then click **OK**. (Although you could have used the formula =($B$4-A11)/365 to calculate the number of years, the YEARFRAC function provides better accuracy since it accounts for leap years and the divisor 365 does not. The completed function is =YEARFRAC(A11,$B$4).
- Double-click the **cell C11 fill handle** to copy the YEARFRAC function down the Years Employed column. Your results will differ based on the date contained in cell B4.

d. Enter the breakpoint and bonus data for the lookup table by doing the following:
- Click **cell A21**, type **1**, and then press **Ctrl+Enter**.
- Click the **Home tab**, click **Fill** in the Editing group, and then select **Series**. Click **Columns** in the *Series in* section, leave the Step value at **1**, type **5** in the **Stop value box**, and then click **OK**.
- Click **cell B21**. Enter **0**, **100**, **250**, **500**, and **1000** down the column. The cells have been previously formatted with Accounting Number Format with zero decimal places.
- Select **range A21:B25**, click in the **Name Box**, type **Bonus**, and then press **Enter** to name the range.

e. Enter the bonus based on rating by doing the following:
- Click **cell E11**, and then click the **Formulas tab**.
- Click **Lookup & Reference** in the Function Library group, and then select **VLOOKUP**.
- Click **cell D11** to enter the cell reference in the **Lookup_value box**.
- Press **Tab**, and then type **Bonus** to enter the range name for the lookup table in the **Table_array box**.
- Press **Tab**, type **2** to represent the second column in the lookup table, and then click **OK**. The completed function is =VLOOKUP(D11,Bonus,2).
- Double-click the **cell E11 fill handle** to copy the formula down the Rating Bonus column.

f. Enter the raise based on years employed by doing the following:
   - Click **cell F11**.
   - Click **Logical** in the Function Library group, and then select **IF**.
   - Click **cell C11**, type >= and then click **cell B5**. Press **F4** to enter C11>=$B$5 to compare the years employed to the absolute reference of the five-year threshold in the **Logical_test box**.
   - Press **Tab**, click **cell B11**, type * and then click **cell B6**. Press **F4** to enter B11*$B$6 to calculate a 3.25% raise for employees who worked five years or more in the **Value_if_true box**.
   - Press **Tab**, click **cell B11**, type * and then click **cell B7**. Press **F4** to enter B11*$B$7 to calculate a 2% raise for employees who worked less than five years in the **Value_if_false box**. Click **OK**. The completed function is =IF(C11>=$B$5,B11*$B$6,B11*$B$7).
   - Double-click the **cell F11 fill handle** to copy the formula down the Raise column.

g. Click **cell G11**. Type **=B11+E11+F11** to add the current salary, the bonus, and the raise to calculate the new salary. Press **Ctrl+Enter** to keep **cell G11** the active cell, and then double-click the **cell G11 fill handle** to copy the formula down the column.

h. Create a footer with your name on the left side, the date code in the center, and the file name code on the right side.

i. Save and close the workbook, and submit based on your instructor's directions.

3 New Car Loan

After obtaining a promotion at work, you are ready to upgrade to a luxury car, such as a Lexus or Infinity. Before finalizing the purchase with the dealer, you want to create a worksheet to estimate the monthly payment based on the purchase price (including accessories, taxes, and license plate), APR, down payment, and years. You will assign range names and use range names in the formulas to make them easier to analyze. This exercise follows the same set of skills as used in Hands-On Exercises 1–4 in the chapter. Refer to Figure 2.42 as you complete this exercise.

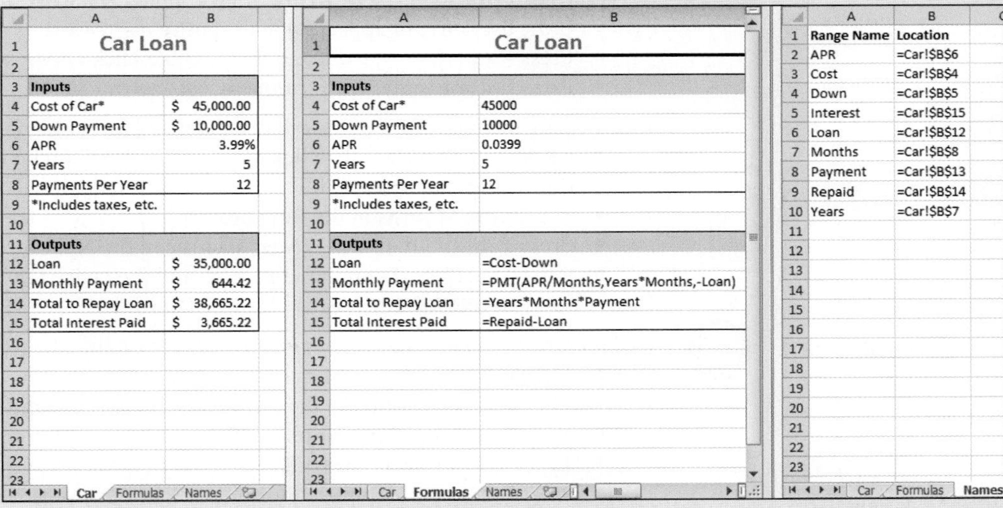

Car Loan
Inputs
Cost of Car* $ 45,000.00
Down Payment $ 10,000.00
APR 3.99%
Years 5
Payments Per Year 12
*Includes taxes, etc.
Outputs
Loan $ 35,000.00
Monthly Payment $ 644.42
Total to Repay Loan $ 38,665.22
Total Interest Paid $ 3,665.22
Car Formulas Names
Car Loan
Inputs
Cost of Car* 45000
Down Payment 10000
APR 0.0399
Years 5
Payments Per Year 12
*Includes taxes, etc.
Outputs
Loan =Cost-Down
Monthly Payment =PMT(APR/Months,Years*Months,-Loan)
Total to Repay Loan =Years*Months*Payment
Total Interest Paid =Repaid-Loan
Range Name Location
APR =Car!$B$6
Cost =Car!$B$4
Down =Car!$B$5
Interest =Car!$B$15
Loan =Car!$B$12
Months =Car!$B$8
Payment =Car!$B$13
Repaid =Car!$B$14
Years =Car!$B$7

FIGURE 2.42 Luxury Car Loan ➤

a. Start a new Excel workbook, save it as **e02p3carloan_LastnameFirstname**, rename Sheet1 as **Car**, and then delete Sheet2 and Sheet3.

b. Enter and format the title of the worksheet by doing the following:
   - Type **Car Loan** in **cell A1**, and then press **Ctrl+Enter**.
   - Select the **range A1:B1**, and then click **Merge & Center** in the Alignment group.
   - Apply bold, **18 pt font size**, and **Olive Green, Accent 3, Darker 25% font color**.

c. Click **cell A3**, and then type the labels for both the Inputs and the Outputs in column A as shown in the left screen of Figure 2.42. Double-click between column heading A and B to widen column A. Widen column B as needed.

d. Enter and format the Input values in column B by doing the following:
   - Click **cell B4**, type **45000**, and then press **Enter**.
   - Type **10000** in **cell B5**, and then press **Enter**.

- Type **0.0399** in **cell B6**, and then press **Enter**.
- Type **5** in **cell B7**, and then press **Enter**.
- Type **12** in cell **B8**, and then press **Enter**.
- Select the **range B4:B5**, and then click **Accounting Number Format** in the Number group.
- Click **cell B6**, click **Percent Style** in the Number group, and then click **Increase Decimal** twice.
- Select the **range B7:B8**, click **Comma Style** in the Number group, and then click **Decrease Decimal** twice.

DISCOVER 

e. Name the input values by doing the following:
   - Select the **range A4:B8**.
   - Click the **Formulas tab**, and then click **Create from Selection** in the Defined Names group.
   - Make sure *Left column* is selected, and then click **OK**.
   - Click each input value cell in the **range B4:B8** and look at the newly created names in the Name Box.

f. Edit the range names by doing the following:
   - Click **Name Manager** in the Defined Names group.
   - Click **Cost_of_Car**, click **Edit**, type **Cost**, and then click **OK**.
   - Change *Down_Payment* to **Down**.
   - Change *Payments_Per_Year* to **Months**.
   - Click **Close** to close the Name Manager.

g. Name the output values in the **range A12:B15** using the *Create from Selection* method you used in step e to assign names to the empty cells in the range B12:B15. However, you will use the range names as you build formulas in the next few steps. Edit the range names using the same approach you used in step f.
   - Change *Monthly_Payment* to **Payment.**
   - Change *Total_Interest_Paid* to **Interest**.
   - Change *Total_to_Repay_Loan* to **Repaid**.
   - Click **Close** to close the Name Manager.

h. Enter the formula to calculate the amount of the loan by doing the following:
   - Click **cell B12**. Type **=Cos** and then double-click **Cost** from the Function AutoComplete list. If the list does not appear, type the entire name **Cost**.
   - Press – and then type **do**, and then double-click **Down** from the Function AutoComplete list.
   - Press **Enter** to enter the formula =Cost-Down.

i. Calculate the monthly payment of principal and interest by doing the following:
   - Click the **Formulas tab**. Click **cell B13**. Click **Financial** in the Function Library group, scroll down, and then select **PMT**.
   - Type **APR/Months** in the **Rate box**.
   - Press **Tab**, and then type **Years*Months** in the **Nper box**.
   - Press **Tab**, type **–Loan** in the **Pv box**, and then click **OK**. The completed function is =PMT(APR/Months,Years*Months,-Loan).

DISCOVER 

j. Enter the total amount to repay loan formula by doing the following:
   - Click **cell B14**. Type = to start the formula.
   - Click **Use in Formula** in the Defined Names group, and then select **Years**.
   - Type *, click **Use in Formula** in the Defined Names group, and then select **Months**.
   - Type *, click **Use in Formula** in the Defined Names group, and then select **Payment**.
   - Press **Enter**. The completed formula is =Years*Months*Payment.

k. Use the skills from step j to enter the formula **=Repaid-Loan** in **cell B15**.

l. Select the **range B12:B15**, click the **Home tab**, and then click **Accounting Number Format** in the Number group.

m. Apply **Olive Green, Accent 3, Lighter 60% fill color** and bold to the **ranges A3:B3** and **A11:B11**. Apply the **Outside Borders style** to the **ranges A3:B8** and **A11:B15** as shown in Figure 2.42.

n. Select the option to center the worksheet data between the left and right margins in the Page Setup dialog box.

o. Create a footer with your name on the left side, the sheet name code in the center, and the file name code on the right side.

p. Right-click the **Car sheet tab**, select **Move or Copy** from the menu, click **(move to end)** in the *Before sheet* section, click the **Create a copy check box**, and then click **OK**. Rename the Car (2) sheet as **Formulas**.

q. Make sure the Formulas sheet is active. Click the **Formulas tab**, and then click **Show Formulas** in the Formula Auditing group. Widen column B to display entire formulas.

r. Click the **Page Layout tab**, and then click the **Gridlines Print check box** and the **Headings Print check box** in the Sheet Options group to select these two options.

s. Insert a new sheet, name it **Names**, type **Range Name** in **cell A1**, and then type **Location** in **cell B1**. Apply bold to these column labels. Click **cell A2**, click the **Formulas tab**, click **Use in Formula**, select **Paste Names**, and then click **Paste List** to paste an alphabetical list of range names in the worksheet. Adjust the column widths. Apply the same Page Setup settings and footer to the Formulas and Cars worksheets.

t. Save and close the workbook, and submit based on your instructor's directions.

MID-LEVEL EXERCISES

1 Sunrise Credit Union Weekly Payroll

As manager of the Sunrise Credit Union, you are responsible for managing the weekly payroll. Your assistant developed a partial worksheet, but you need to enter the formulas to calculate the regular pay, overtime pay, gross pay, taxable pay, withholding tax, FICA, and net pay. In addition, you want to total pay columns and calculate some basic statistics. As you construct formulas, make sure you use absolute and relative cell references correctly in formulas and avoid circular references.

a. Open the *e02m1payroll* workbook and save it as **e02m1payroll_LastnameFirstname**.

b. Study the worksheet structure, and then read the business rules in the Notes section.

c. Use IF functions to calculate the regular pay and overtime pay based on a regular 40-hour work-week in **cells E5** and **F5**. Pay overtime only for overtime hours. Calculate the gross pay based on the regular and overtime pay. Abram's regular pay is $398. With eight overtime hours, Abram's overtime pay is $119.40.

d. Create a formula in **cell H5** to calculate the taxable pay. Multiply the number of dependents by the deduction per dependent, and then subtract that from the gross pay. With two dependents, Abram's taxable pay is $417.40.

e. Use a VLOOKUP function in **cell I5** to identify and calculate the federal withholding tax. With a taxable pay of $417.40, Abram's tax rate is 25%, and the withholding tax is $104.35. The VLOOKUP function returns the applicable tax rate, which you must then multiply by the taxable pay.

f. Calculate FICA in **cell J5** based on gross pay and the FICA rate, and then calculate the net pay in **Cell K5**.

g. Calculate the total regular pay, overtime pay, gross pay, taxable pay, withholding tax, FICA, and net pay on row 17.

h. Copy all formulas down their respective columns.

i. Apply **Accounting Number Format** to the **range C5:C16**. Apply **Accounting Number Format** to the first row of monetary data and to the total row. Apply **Comma Style** to the monetary values for the other employees. Underline the last employee's monetary values, and then use the Format Cells dialog box to apply **Double Accounting Underline** for the totals.

j. Insert appropriate functions to calculate the average, highest, and lowest values in the Summary Statistics area **(range I21:K23)** of the worksheet.

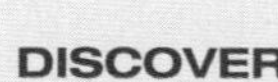

k. At your instructor's discretion, use Help to learn about the FREQUENCY function. The Help feature contains sample data for you to copy and practice in a new worksheet to learn about this function. You can close the practice worksheet containing the Help data without saving it. You want to determine the number (frequency) of employees who worked less than 20 hours, between 20 and 29 hours, between 30 and 40 hours, and over 40 hours. **Cells J28:J31** list the ranges. You need to translate this range into correct values for the Bin column in **cells I28:I30** and then enter the FREQUENCY function in **cells K28:K31**. The function should identify one employee who worked between 0 and 19 hours and six employees who worked more than 40 hours.

l. Apply other page setup formats as needed.

m. Insert a footer with your name on the left side, the date code in the center, and the file name code on the right side.

n. Save and close the workbook, and submit based on your instructor's directions.

2 House Loan

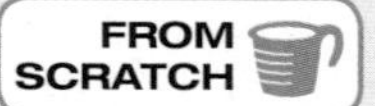

As a financial consultant, you work with people who are planning to buy a new house. You want to create a worksheet containing variable data (the price of the house, down payment, date of the first payment, and borrower's credit rating) and constants (property tax rate, years, and number of payments in one year). Borrowers pay 0.5% private mortgage insurance (PMI) of the loan amount if they do not make at least a 20% down payment. A borrower's credit rating determines the required down payment percentage and APR. For example, a person with an excellent credit rating may make only a 5% down payment with a 4.25% APR loan. A person with a fair credit rating will make a 15% down payment and have a higher APR at 5%. Your worksheet needs to perform various calculations. Refer to Figure 2.43 as you complete this exercise. The filled cells in column F indicate cells containing formulas, not values.

	A	B	C	D	E	F
1			**Mortgage Calculator**			
2						
3	**Inputs**				**Intermediate Calculations**	
4	Negotiated Cost of House		$ 350,000.00		APR Based on Credit Rating	4.25%
5	Additional Down Payment		$ 3,500.00		Min Down Payment Required	$ 17,500.00
6	Date of First Payment		5/1/2013		Annual Property Tax	$ 2,625.00
7	Credit Rating		Excellent		Annual PMI	$ 1,645.00
8						
9	**Constants**				**Outputs**	
10	Property Tax Rate		0.75%		Total Down Payment	$ 21,000.00
11	Down Payment to Avoid PM		20.00%		Amount of the Loan	$329,000.00
12	PMI Rate		0.50%		Monthly Payment (P&I)	$1,618.48
13	Term of Loan in Years		30		Monthly Property Tax	218.75
14	# of Payments Per Year		12		Monthly PMI	137.08
15					**Total Monthly Payment**	$ 1,974.32
16	**Credit**	**Down Payment**	**APR**		**Date of Last Payment**	**4/1/2043**
17	Excellent	5%	4.25%			
18	Good	10%	4.50%			
19	Fair	15%	5.00%			
20	Poor	20%	5.25%			
21						

FIGURE 2.43 House Loan Data ➤

a. Start a new Excel workbook, save it as **e02m2loan_LastnameFirstname**, rename Sheet1 as **Payment**, rename Sheet2 as **Range Names**, and then delete Sheet3.

b. Select the **Payment sheet**, type **Mortgage Calculator** in **cell A1**, and then merge and center the title on the first row in the **range A1:F1**. Apply bold, **18 pt size**, and **Aqua, Accent 5, Darker 25% font color**.

c. Create and format the Inputs and Constants areas by doing the following:
   - Type the labels in the **range A3:A20**. For each label, such as *Negotiated Cost of House*, merge the cells, such as the **range A4:B4**, and then apply **Align Text Left**. You will have to merge cells for nine labels.
   - Enter and format the *Inputs* and *Constants* values in column C.

d. Create the lookup table in the **range A16:C20** to use the credit ratings to identify the appropriate required percentage down payment and the respective APR by doing the following:
   - Type **Credit**, **Down Payment**, and **APR** in the **range A16:C16**.
   - Type the four credit ratings in the first column, the required down payment percentages in the second column, and the respective APRs in the third column.
   - Format the percentages, apply **Align Text Right**, and then indent the percentages in the cells as needed.

e. Assign range names to cells containing individual values in the Inputs and Constants sections. Do *not* use the *Create from Selection* feature since the labels are stored in merged cells. Assign a range name to the lookup table.

f. Type labels in the *Intermediate Calculations* and *Outputs* sections in column E, and then assign a range name to each cell in the **ranges F4:F7** and **F10:F12**. Widen column E as needed.

g. Enter formulas in the *Intermediate Calculations* and *Outputs* sections using range names to calculate the following:

   - **APR** based on the borrower's credit rating by using a lookup function. Include the range_lookup argument to ensure an *exact match*. For example, a borrower who has an Excellent rating gets a 4.25% APR.

   - **Minimum down payment required** amount by using a lookup function and calculation. Include the range_lookup argument to ensure an *exact match*. For example, a borrower who has an Excellent rating is required to pay a minimum of 5% down payment of the negotiated purchase price. Multiply the function results by the negotiated cost of the house. Hint: The calculation comes after the closing parenthesis.
   - **Annual property tax** based on the negotiated cost of the house and the annual property tax rate.
   - **Annual PMI**. If the borrower's total down payment (required and additional) is 20% or higher of the negotiated purchase price (multiply the cost by the PMI avoidance percentage),

PMI is zero. If the total down payment is less than 20%, the borrower has to pay PMI based on multiplying the amount of the loan by the PMI rate.

- **Total down payment**, which is sum of the required minimum down payment (calculated previously) and any additional down payment entered in the Inputs section.
- **Amount of the loan**, which is the difference between the negotiated cost of the house and the total down payment.
- **Monthly payment** of principal and interest using the PMT function.
- **Monthly property tax**, the **monthly PMI**, and the **total monthly payment**.
- **Last payment date** using the EDATE function. The function's second argument must calculate the correct number of months based on the total length of the loan. For example, if the first payment is 5/1/2013, the final payment is 4/1/2043 for a 30-year loan. The last argument of the function must subtract 1 to ensure the last payment date is correct. If the last payment date calculated to 5/1/2043, you would be making an extra payment.

h. Format each section with fill color, bold, underline, number formats, borders, and column widths as shown in the figure.

i. Paste a list of range names in the Range Names worksheet. Insert a row above the list, and then type and format column labels above the two columns in the list of range names.

j. Center the worksheet data horizontally between the left and right margins.

k. Insert a footer with your name on the left side, the sheet name code in the center, and the file name code on the right side of both sheets.

l. Save and close the workbook, and submit based on your instructor's directions.

3 Professor's Grade Book

You are a teaching assistant for Dr. Denise Gerber, who teaches an introductory C# programming class at your college. One of your routine tasks is to enter assignment and test grades into the grade book. Now that the semester is almost over, you need to create formulas to calculate category averages, the overall weighted average, and the letter grade for each student. In addition, Dr. Gerber wants to see general statistics, such as average, median, low, and high for each graded assignment and test, as well as category averages and total averages. Furthermore, you need to create the grading scale on the documentation worksheet and use it to display the appropriate letter grade for each student.

a. Open the *e02m3grades* workbook and save it as **e02m3grades_LastnameFirstname**.

b. Use breakpoints to enter the grading scale in the correct structure on the Documentation worksheet, and then name the grading scale range **Grades**. The grading scale is as follows:

95+	A
90–94.9	A–
87–89.9	B+
83–86.9	B
80–82.9	B–
77–79.9	C+

73–76.9	C
70–72.9	C–
67–69.9	D+
63–66.9	D
60–62.9	D–
0–59.9	F

c. Calculate the total lab points earned for the first student in **cell T8** in the Grades worksheet. The first student earned 93 lab points.

d. Calculate the average of the two midterm tests for the first student in **cell W8**. The student's midterm test average is 87.

e. Calculate the assignment average for the first student in cell I8. The formula should drop the lowest score before calculating the average. Hint: You need to use a combination of three functions: SUM, MIN, and COUNT. The argument for each function for the first student is B8:H8. Find the total points, and then subtract the lowest score. Then divide the remaining points by the number of assignments minus 1. The first student's assignment average is 94.2 after dropping the lowest assignment score.

f. Calculate the weighted total points based on the four category points (assignment average, lab points, midterm average, and final exam) and their respective weights (stored in the range B40:B43) in cell Y8. Use relative and absolute cell references as needed in the formula. The first student's total weighted score is 90.

g. Use a VLOOKUP function to calculate the letter grade equivalent in **cell Z8**. Use the range name in the function. The first student's letter grade is A–.

h. Copy the formulas down their respective columns for the other students.

i. Name the passing score threshold in **cell B5** with the range name **Passing**. Use an IF function to display a message in the last grade book column based on the student's semester performance. If a student earned a final score of 70 or higher, display *Enroll in CS 202*. Otherwise, display *RETAKE CS 101*. Remember to use quotation marks around the text arguments.

j. Calculate the average, median, low, and high scores for each assignment, lab, test, category average, and total score. Display individual averages with no decimal places; display category and final score averages with one decimal place. Display other statistics with no decimal places.

k. Insert a list of range names in the designated area in the Documentation worksheet. Complete the documentation by inserting your name, today's date, and a purpose statement in the designated areas.

DISCOVER 

l. At your instructor's discretion, add a column to display each student's rank in the class. Use Help to learn how to insert the RANK function.

m. Select page setup options as needed to print the Grades worksheet on one page.

n. Insert a footer with your name on the left side, the sheet name code in the center, and the file name code on the right side of each worksheet.

o. Save and close the workbook, and submit based on your instructor's directions.

CAPSTONE EXERCISE

You are a sales representative at the local fitness center, Buff and Tuff Gym. Your manager expects each representative to track weekly new membership data, so you created a spreadsheet to store data. Membership costs are based on membership type. Clients can rent a locker for an additional annual fee. You are required to collect a down payment based on membership type, determine the balance, and then calculate the monthly payment based on a standard interest rate. In addition, you need to calculate general statistics to summarize for your manager. Spot-check results to make sure you created formulas and functions correctly.

Perform Preliminary Work

You need to open the starting workbook you created, acknowledge the existing circular reference error, and assign a range name to the membership lookup table. You will correct the circular reference error later.

a. Open the *e02c1gym* workbook, click **Help**, read about circular references, close the Help window that appears, and save the workbook as **e02c1gym_LastnameFirstname**.

b. Assign the name **Membership** to the **range A18:C20**.

c. Insert a function to display the current date in **cell B2**.

Calculate Cost, Annual Total, and Total Due

You are ready to calculate the basic annual membership cost and the total annual cost. The basic annual membership is determined based on each client's membership type, using the lookup table.

a. Insert a lookup function in **cell C5** to display the basic annual membership cost for the first client.

b. Use an IF function in **cell E5** to calculate the annual total amount, which is the sum of the basic cost and locker fees for those who rent a locker. For people who do not rent a locker, the annual cost is only the cost shown in column C. The Locker column displays *Yes* for clients who rent a locker and *No* for those who don't.

c. Calculate the total amount due in **cell G5** for the first client based on the annual total and the number of years in the contract.

d. Copy the three formulas down their respective columns.

Determine the Down Payment and Balance

You need to collect a down payment based on the type of membership for each new client. Then you must determine how much each client owes.

a. Insert a lookup function in **cell H5** to display the amount of down payment for the first client based on the membership type.

b. Find and correct the circular reference for the balance. The balance is the difference between the total due and the down payment.

c. Copy the two formulas for the rest of the clients.

Calculate the Monthly Payment

Clients pay the remainder by making monthly payments. Monthly payments are based on the number of years specified in the client's contract and a standard interest rate.

a. Insert the function in **cell J5** to calculate the first client's monthly payment, using appropriate relative and absolute cell references.

b. Copy the formula down the column.

c. Edit the formula by changing the appropriate cell reference to a mixed cell reference. Copy the formula down.

Finalize the Workbook

You need to perform some basic statistical calculations and finalize the workbook with formatting and page setup options.

a. Calculate totals on row 14.

b. Insert the appropriate functions in the *Summary Statistics* section of the worksheet: **cells H18:H22**. Format the payments with **Accounting Number Format**, and format the number of new members appropriately.

c. Format the other column headings on rows 4 and 17 to match the fill color in the **range E17:H17**. Wrap text for the column headings.

d. Format the monetary values for Andrews and the total row with **Accounting Number Format**. Use zero decimal places for whole amounts, and display two decimal places for the monthly payment. Apply **Comma Style** to the internal monetary values. Underline the values before the totals, and then apply **Double Accounting Underline** (found in the Format Cells dialog box) for the totals.

e. Set **0.3"** left and right margins, and then ensure the page prints on only one page.

f. Insert a footer with your name on the left side, the date code in the center, and the file name code on the right side.

g. Save and close the workbook, and submit based on your instructor's directions.

Airline Ticket Prices

GENERAL CASE 

You work in the IT Department for a regional airline that provides flights to seven airports. A colleague started a workbook with sample ticketing data to ensure the business rules for ticket prices are correct. Open *e02b1tickets* and save it as **e02b1tickets_LastnameFirstname**. Ticket prices are based on several factors: destination, first class or coach seating, number of days purchased before travel date, and checked bags. First-class tickets cost almost double the price of a coach ticket. Purchasing a ticket 21 days in advance is less expensive than 7 days in advance. A surcharge is added to the base price based on the number of days the ticket is booked before departure. The airline charges $20 if the passenger checks a bag.

In the Lookup Tables worksheet, complete the Weekday Lookup table for days, where 1= Sunday and 7= Saturday. Complete the Ticket Booked X Days Before Travel lookup table: 21 or more days, $0; 14–20 days, $25; 7–13 days, $75; and less than 7 days, $100. Assign range names to each of the three lookup tables. Use range names when applicable in formulas. In the Tickets worksheet, use the WEEKDAY function nested in the VLOOKUP function to identify the departure day number. For example, 5/15/2013 is on a Wednesday. Use a lookup function to calculate the Base Ticket price by looking up the arrival airport code, using the second lookup table, and then nesting an IF function as the third argument to determine whether to use the first-class or coach price. This is an exact lookup, so use the optional range_lookup argument. Use a lookup function to calculate the surcharge by calculating the number of days between booking a ticket and the departure date (subtraction between two cells for the lookup_value argument). Use an IF function to determine if a checked baggage charge applies. Use a function to calculate the total cost per ticket. Apply Currency format with zero decimal places, Align Text Right, and indent for the values in the last four columns. Apply landscape orientation, and then insert a footer with your name on the left side, the sheet name code in the center, and the file name code on the right side of both worksheets. Save and close the workbook, and submit based on your instructor's directions.

College Sports Scores

RESEARCH CASE 

FROM SCRATCH

You want to create a spreadsheet to display data for your favorite college sports team. Conduct an Internet search to identify the game dates, your team's scores, the opponent, and the opponent's score for each game for the last complete season. Enter the data into a new workbook, and save the workbook as **e02b2sports_LastnameFirstname**. Games are usually scheduled 7 days apart. Enter this value on a second sheet, assign a range name, and then use the range name in a formula to calculate the game dates based on the original game date. In some instances, you may have to enter a date if more or fewer days exist between two game dates. In the fifth column, use an IF function to determine if your team won or lost each game; display either *Win* or *Lose*. In the sixth column, use an IF function to calculate how many points your team won each game or display an empty string by entering "" in the value_if_false argument if your team lost.

Create a statistics area to calculate the average, median, low, and high scores for your team. Below the won-by points column, use two different count functions to count the number of games won and lost. Use Help to learn about the COUNTIF function, and then use this function to count the number of games won based on the number of *Win* entries. Use mixed references in the function's first argument, copy the function, and then edit the second argument of the copied COUNTIF function to calculate the number of games lost. The summary area should have four count functions. Add titles and column labels, format data within the columns, and then include the URL of where you got the data. Include a footer with your name on the left side, the date code in the center, and the file name code on the right side. Save and close the workbook, and submit based on your instructor's directions.

Park City Condo Rental

DISASTER RECOVERY 

You and some friends are planning a Labor Day vacation to Park City, Utah. You have secured a four-day condominium that costs $1,200. Some people will stay all four days; others will stay part of the weekend. One of your friends constructed a worksheet to help calculate each person's cost of the rental. The people who stay Thursday night will split the nightly cost evenly. To keep the costs down, everyone agreed to pay $30 per night per person for Friday, Saturday, and/or Sunday nights. Depending on the number of people who stay each night, the group may owe more money. Kyle, Ian, Isaac, and Daryl agreed to split the difference in the total rental cost and the amount the group members paid. Open *e02b3parkcity*, address the circular reference error message that appears, and save the workbook as **e02b3parkcity_LastnameFirstname**. Review the worksheet structure, including the assumptions and calculation notes at the bottom of the worksheet. Check the formulas and functions, making necessary corrections. With the existing data, the number of people staying each night is 5, 7, 10, and 10, respectively. The total paid given the above assumptions is $1,110, giving a difference of $90 to be divided evenly among the first four people. Kyle's share should be $172.50. In the cells containing errors, insert comments to describe the error, and then fix the formulas. Verify the accuracy of formulas by entering an IF function in cell I1 to ensure the totals match. Nick, James, and Body inform you they can't stay Sunday night, and Rob wants to stay Friday night. Change the input accordingly. The updated total paid is now $1,200, and the difference is $150. Include a footer with your name on the left side, the date code in the center, and the file name code on the right side. Save and close the workbook, and submit based on your instructor's directions.

EXCEL

3 CHARTS

Depicting Data Visually

Watch the
Set-up
Video
for this
Case Study!

CASE STUDY | Hort University Majors

You are an assistant in the Institutional Research Department for Hort University, a prestigious university on the East Coast. You help conduct research using the university's information systems to provide statistics on the student population, alumni, and more. Your department stores an abundance of data to provide needed results upon request.

Dr. Alisha Musto, your boss, asked that you analyze the number of majors by the six colleges: Arts, Business, Education, Humanities & Social Science, Science & Health, and Technology & Computing. In addition, Dr. Musto wants you to include the undeclared majors in your analysis. You created an Excel worksheet with the data, but you want to create a series of charts that will help Dr. Musto analyze the enrollment data.

OBJECTIVES AFTER YOU READ THIS CHAPTER, YOU WILL BE ABLE TO:

Chart Basics

The expression "a picture is worth a thousand words" means that a visual can be a more effective way to communicate or interpret data than words or numbers. Storing, organizing, and performing calculations on quantitative data, such as in the spreadsheets you have created, are important, but you must also be able to analyze the data to determine what they mean. A ***chart*** is a visual representation of numerical data that compares data and helps reveal trends or patterns to help people make informed decisions. An effective chart depicts data in a clear, easy-to-interpret manner and contains enough data to be useful but not too much that the data overwhelm people.

An effective chart depicts data in a clear, easy-to-interpret manner....

A **chart** is a visual representation of numerical data.

In this section, you will learn chart terminology and how to choose the best chart type, such as pie or line, to fit your needs. You will select the range of cells containing the numerical values and labels from which to create the chart, choose the chart type, insert the chart, and designate the chart's location.

Deciding Which Chart Type to Create

Before creating a chart, study the data you want to represent visually. Look at the structure of the worksheet—the column labels, the row labels, the quantitative data, and the calculated values. Decide what you want to convey to your audience: Does the worksheet hold a single set of data, such as average snowfall at one ski resort, or multiple sets of data, such as average snowfall at several ski resorts? Do you want to depict data for one specific time period or over several time periods, such as several years or decades? Based on the data on which you want to focus, you decide which type of chart best represents that data. With Excel, you can create a variety of types of charts. The four most common chart types are column, bar, line, and pie.

You should organize the worksheet data before creating a chart by ensuring that the values in columns and rows are on the same value system (such as dollars or units) in order to make comparisons, that labels are descriptive, and that no blank rows or columns exist in the primary dataset. Figure 3.1 shows a worksheet containing the number of students who have declared a major within each college at Hort University. These data will be used to illustrate several chart types. Each cell containing a value is a ***data point***. For example, the value 1,330 is a data point for the Arts data in the 2012 column. A group of related data points that appear in row(s) or column(s) in the worksheet create a ***data series***. For example, the values 950, 1,000, 1,325, and 1,330 comprise the Arts data series. Textual information, such as column and row labels (college names, months, years, product names, etc.), is used to create ***category labels*** in charts.

A **data point** is a numeric value that describes a single value on a chart.

A **data series** is a group of related data points.

A **category label** is text that describes a collection of data points in a chart.

	A	B	C	D	E	F
1	Hort University					
2	Number of Majors by College					
3						
4		2009	2010	2011	2012	Average
5	Arts	950	1,000	1,325	1,330	1,151
6	Business	3,975	3,650	3,775	4,000	3,850
7	Education	1,500	1,425	1,435	1,400	1,440
8	Humanities & Social Science	2,300	2,250	2,500	3,500	2,638
9	Science & Health	1,895	1,650	1,700	1,800	1,761
10	Technology & Computing	4,500	4,325	4,400	4,800	4,506
11	Undeclared	5,200	5,500	5,000	4,700	5,100
12	Totals by Year	20,320	19,800	20,135	21,530	20,446
13						

FIGURE 3.1 Sample Dataset ➤

Create a Column Chart

A **column chart** displays data comparisons vertically in columns.

The **chart area** contains the entire chart and all of its elements.

The **plot area** contains a graphical representation of values in a data series.

The **X-axis** is a horizontal line that borders the plot area to provide a frame of reference for measurement.

The **Y-axis** is a vertical line that borders the plot area to provide a frame of reference for measurement.

The **category axis** provides descriptive group names for subdividing the data series.

The **value axis** displays incremental values to identify the values of the data series.

A ***column chart*** displays data vertically in columns. You use column charts to compare values across different categories, such as comparing revenue among different cities or comparing quarterly revenue in one year. Column charts are most effective when they are limited to small numbers of categories—generally seven or fewer. If more categories exist, the columns appear too close together, making it difficult to read the labels.

Before you create a chart, you need to know the names of the different chart elements. The ***chart area*** contains the entire chart and all of its elements, including the plot area, titles, legend, and labels. The ***plot area*** is the region containing the graphical representation of the values in the data series. Two axes form a border around the plot area. The ***X-axis*** is a horizontal border that provides a frame of reference for measuring data horizontally. The ***Y-axis*** is a vertical border that provides a frame of reference for measuring data vertically. Excel refers to the axes as the category axis and value axis. The ***category axis*** displays descriptive group names or labels, such as college names or cities, to identify data. The ***value axis*** displays incremental numbers to identify approximate values, such as dollars or units, of data points in the chart. In a column chart, the category axis is the X-axis, and the value axis is the Y-axis.

The column chart in Figure 3.2 compares the number of majors by college for only one year using the data from the worksheet in Figure 3.1. In Figure 3.2, the college labels stored in the first column—the range A5:A11—form the horizontal category axis, and the data points representing the number of majors in 2012 in the range E5:E11 form the vertical value axis. The height of each column represents the value of the individual data points: The larger the value, the taller the column. For example, Business has a taller column than the Arts and Education columns, indicating that more students major in Business than Arts or Education.

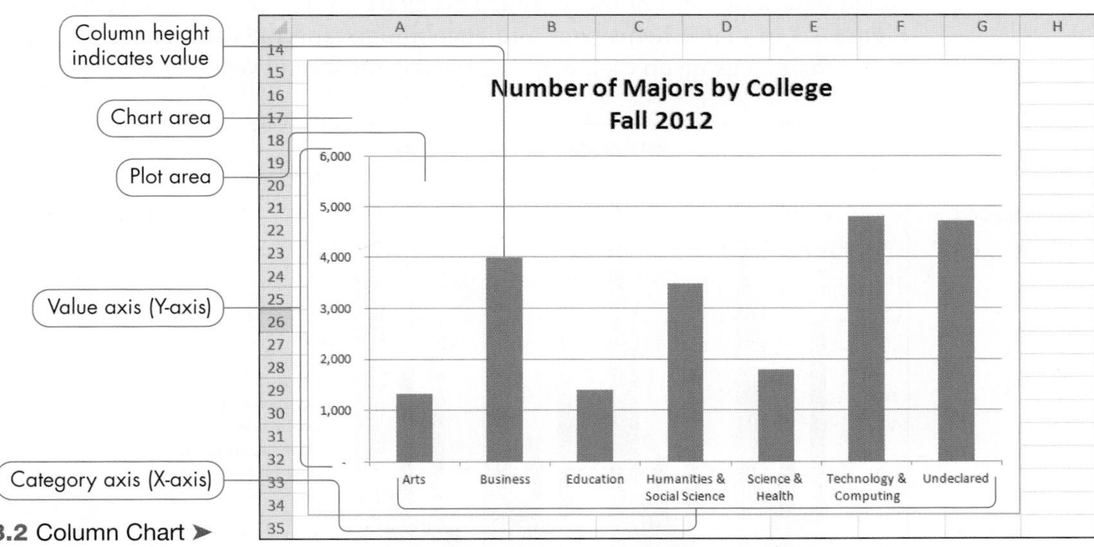

FIGURE 3.2 Column Chart ➤

A **single data series** compares values for one set of data.

A **multiple data series** compares two or more sets of data in one chart.

A **clustered column chart** groups or clusters similar data in columns to compare values across categories.

Figure 3.2 shows a column chart representing a ***single data series***—data for only Fall 2012. However, you might want to create a column chart that contains multiple data series. A ***multiple data series*** chart compares two or more sets of data, such as the number of majors by college for four years. After you select the chart category, such as Column or Line, select a chart subtype. Within each chart category, Excel provides many variations or subtypes, such as clustered, stacked, and 100% stacked.

A ***clustered column chart*** compares groups or clusters of columns set side-by-side for easy comparison. The clustered column chart facilitates quick comparisons across data series, and it is effective for comparing several data points among categories. Figure 3.3 shows a clustered column chart created from the data in Figure 3.1. By default, the row titles appear on the category axis, and the yearly data series appear as columns with the value axis

A **legend** is a key that identifies the color, gradient, picture, texture, or pattern fill assigned to each data series in a chart.

showing incremental numbers. Excel assigns a different color to each yearly data series and includes a legend. A ***legend*** is a key that identifies the color, gradient, picture, texture, or pattern assigned to each data series in a chart. For example, the 2012 data appear in purple. This chart clusters yearly data series for each college, enabling you to compare yearly trends for each major.

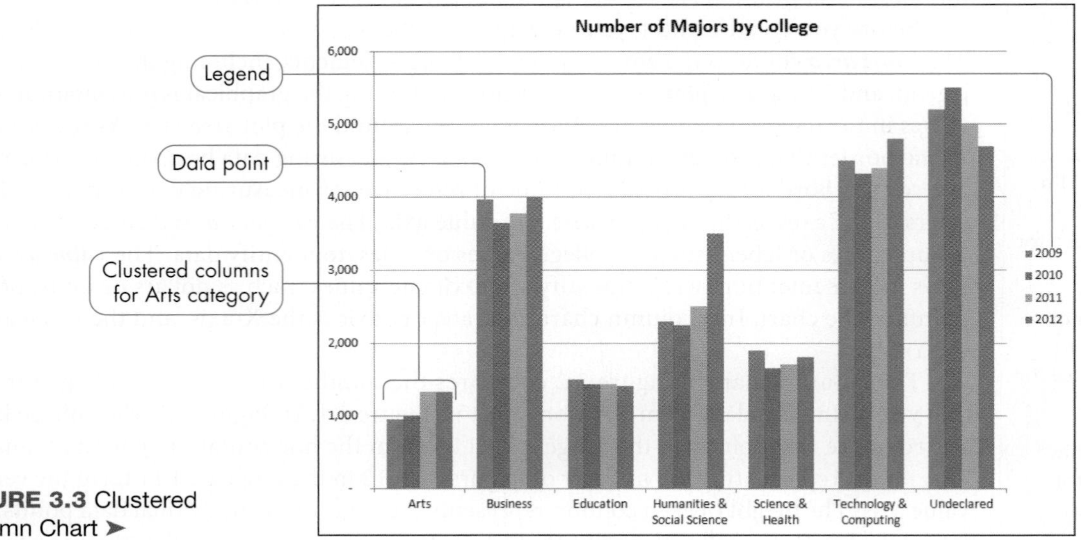

FIGURE 3.3 Clustered Column Chart ➤

Figure 3.4 shows another clustered column chart in which the categories and data series are reversed. The years appear on the category axis, and the colleges appear as color-coded data series and in the legend. This chart gives a different perspective from that in Figure 3.3 in that it helps your audience understand the differences in majors per year rather than focusing on each major separately for several years.

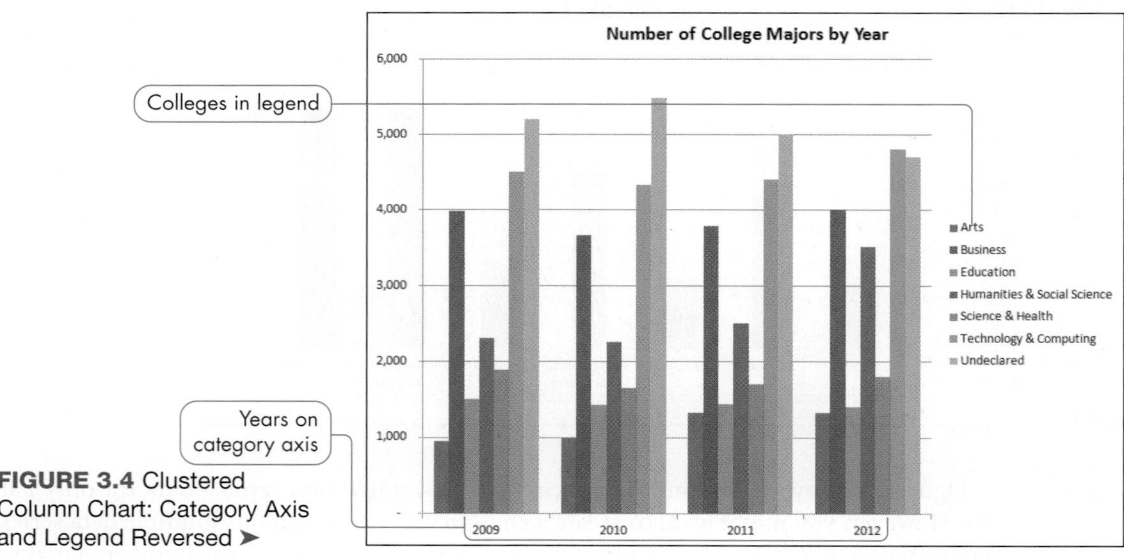

FIGURE 3.4 Clustered Column Chart: Category Axis and Legend Reversed ➤

A **stacked column chart** places stacks of data in segments on top of each other in one column, with each category in the data series represented by a different color.

A ***stacked column chart*** shows the relationship of individual data points to the whole category. Unlike a clustered column chart that displays several columns (one for each data series) for a category (such as Arts), a stacked column chart displays only one column for each category. Each category within the stacked column is color-coded for one data series. Use the stacked column chart when you want to compare total values across categories, as well as to display the individual category values. Figure 3.5 shows a stacked column chart in which a single column represents each categorical year, and each column stacks color-coded data-point segments representing the different colleges. The stacked column chart enables you to determine the total number of majors for each year. The height of each color-coded data point enables you to identify the relative contribution of each college to the total number of yearly majors. A disadvantage of the stacked column chart is that the segments within each column do not start at the same point, making it more difficult to compare individual segment values across categories.

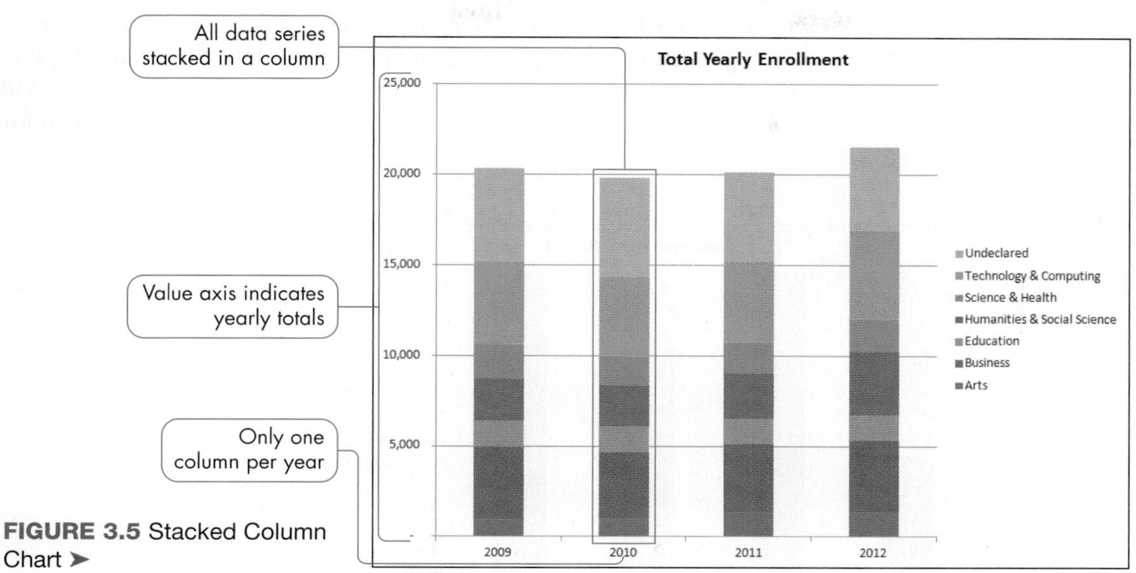

FIGURE 3.5 Stacked Column Chart ➤

When you create a stacked column chart, you must ensure data are *additive*, meaning that each column represents a sum of the data for each segment. Figure 3.5 correctly uses years as the category axis and the colleges as data series. Within each year, Excel adds the number of majors by college, and the columns display the sum of the majors. For example, the total number of majors in 2012 is over 20,000. Figure 3.6 shows an incorrectly constructed stacked column chart because the yearly number of majors by college is *not* additive. It is incorrect to state that the university has 15,000 total business majors for four years. Be careful when constructing stacked column charts to ensure that they lead to logical interpretation of data.

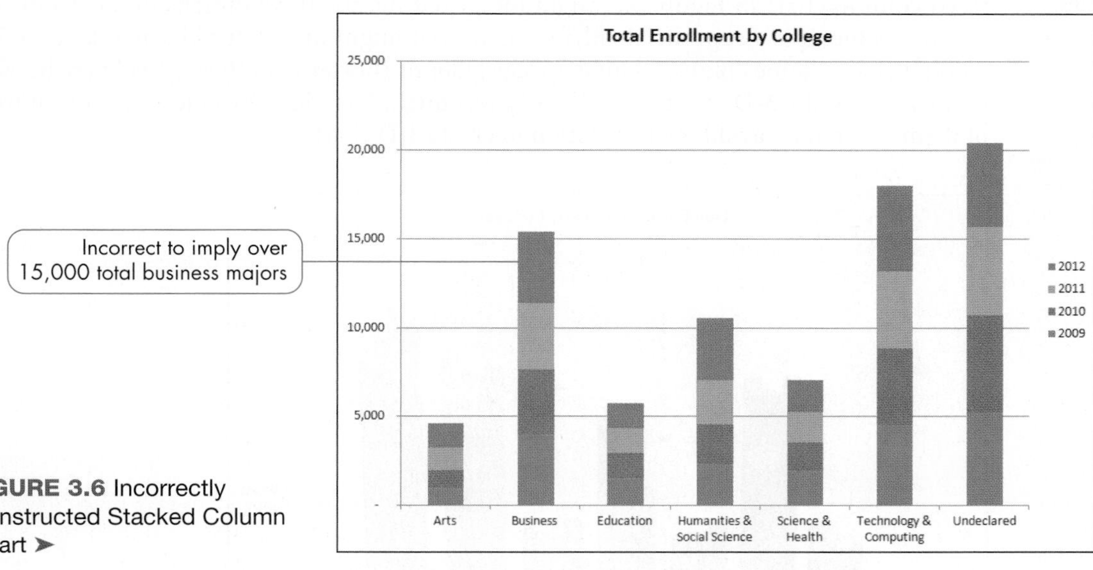

FIGURE 3.6 Incorrectly Constructed Stacked Column Chart ➤

A **100% stacked column chart** places (stacks) data in one column per category, with each column having the same height of 100%.

A ***100% stacked column chart*** compares the percentage each data point contributes to the total for each category. Similar to the stacked column chart, the 100% stacked column chart displays only one column per category. The value axis displays percentages rather than values, and all columns are the same height: 100%. Excel converts each data point value into a percentage of the total for each category. Use this type of chart when you are more interested in comparing relative percentage contributions across categories rather than actual values across categories. For example, a regional manager for a department store realizes that not every store is the same size and that the different stores have different sales volumes. Instead of comparing sales by department for each store, you might want to display percentage of sales by department to facilitate comparisons of percentage contributions for each department within its own store's sales.

Figure 3.7 shows a 100% stacked column chart. Excel computes the total 2012 enrollment (21,530 in our example), calculates the enrollment percentage by college, and displays each column segment in proportion to its computed percentage. The Arts College had 1,330 majors, which accounts for 6% of the total number of majors, where the total enrollment for any given year is 100%.

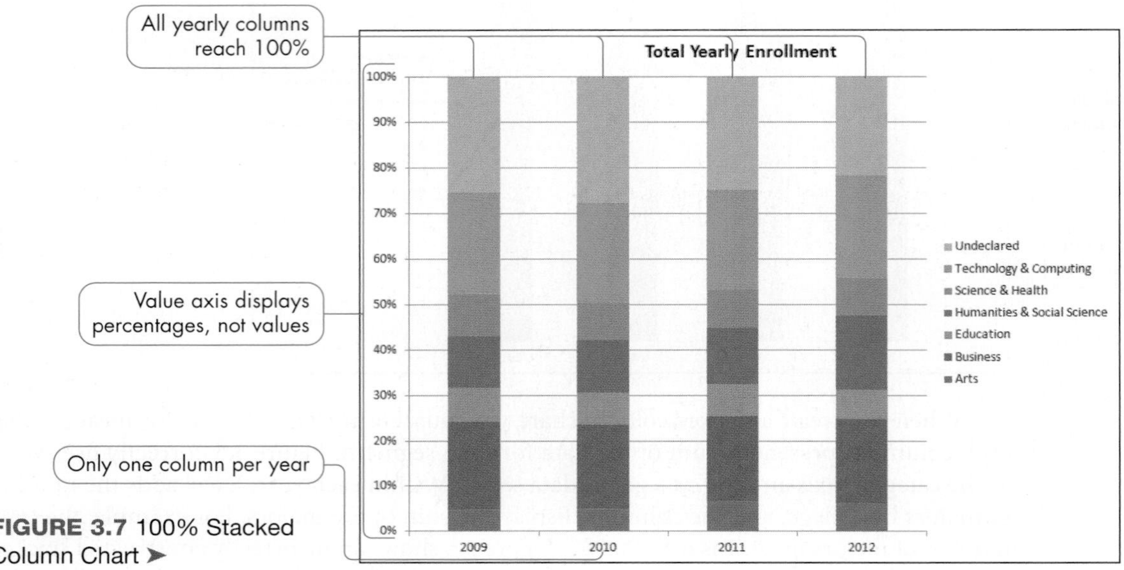

FIGURE 3.7 100% Stacked Column Chart ➤

A **3-D chart** adds a third dimension to each data series, creating a distorted perspective of the data.

Excel enables you to create special-effects charts, such as 3-D, cylinder, pyramid, or cone charts. A ***3-D chart*** adds a third dimension to each data series. Although the 3-D clustered column chart in Figure 3.8 might look exciting, the third dimension does not plot another value. It is a superficial enhancement that might distort the charted data. In 3-D column charts, some columns might appear taller or shorter than they actually are because of the angle of the 3-D effect, or some columns might be hidden by taller columns in front of them. Therefore, avoid the temptation to create 3-D charts.

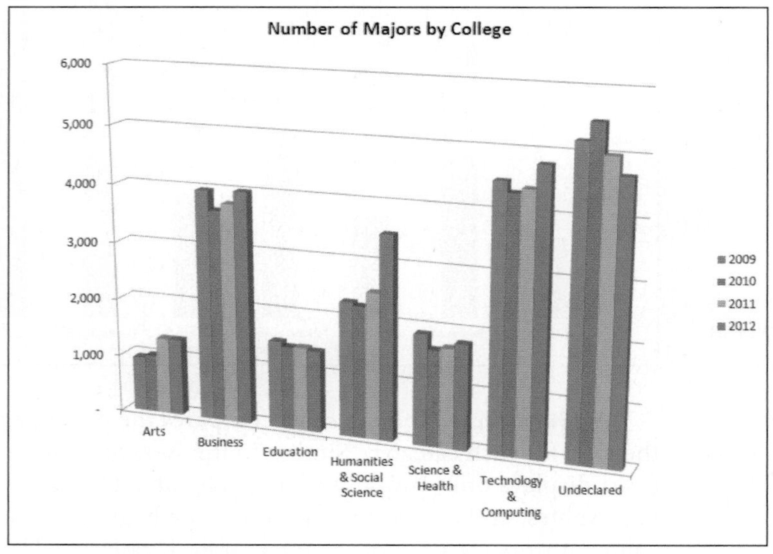

FIGURE 3.8 3-D Clustered Column Chart ➤

Create a Bar Chart

A **bar chart** compares values across categories using horizontal bars.

A ***bar chart*** compares values across categories using horizontal bars. In a bar chart, the horizontal axis displays values, and the vertical axis displays categories (see Figure 3.9). A bar chart conveys the same type of information as a column chart; however, a bar chart is preferable when category names are long, such as *Humanities & Social Science.* A bar chart enables category names to appear in an easy-to-read format, whereas a column chart might display category names at an awkward angle or smaller font size. Like column charts, bar charts have several subtypes, such as clustered, stacked, 100% stacked, 3-D, cylinder, cone, or pyramid subtypes.

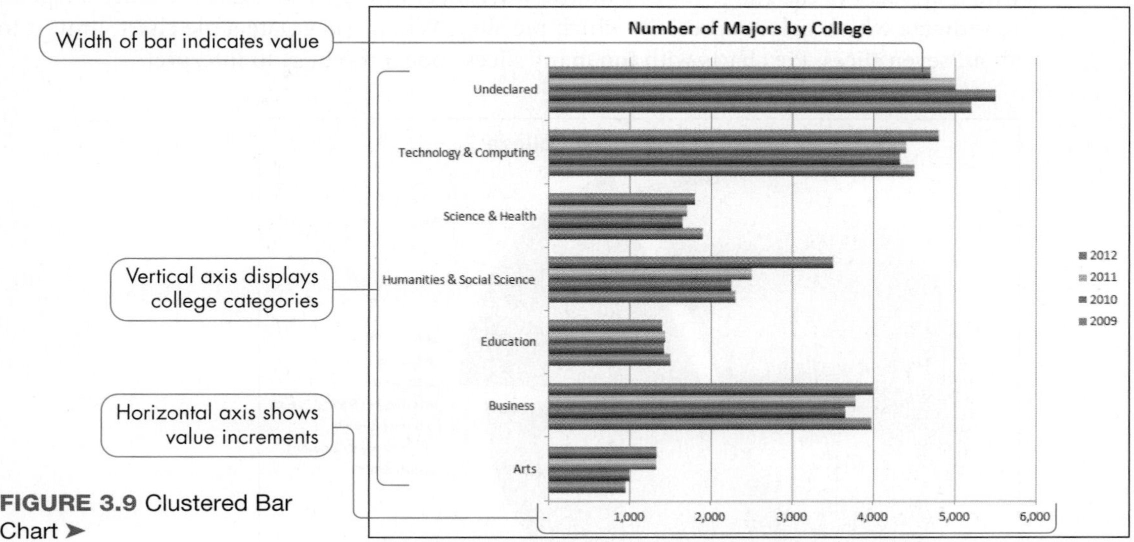

FIGURE 3.9 Clustered Bar Chart ➤

Create a Line Chart

A **line chart** uses a line to connect data points in order to show trends over a period of time.

A ***line chart*** displays lines connecting data points to show trends over equal time periods, such as months, quarters, years, or decades. With multiple data series, Excel displays each data series with a different line color. The category axis (X-axis) represents time, such as ten-year increments, whereas the value axis (Y-axis) represents the value, such as a monetary value or quantity. A line chart enables a user to easily spot trends in the data since the line continues to the next data point. The line, stacked, and 100% stacked line charts do not have specific indicators for each data point. To show each data point, select Line with Markers, Stacked Line with Markers, or 100% Stacked Line with Markers. Figure 3.10 shows a line chart indicating the number of majors by college over time, making it easy to see the enrollment trends. For example, the Arts enrollment spiked in 2010 while enrollments in other colleges decreased that year.

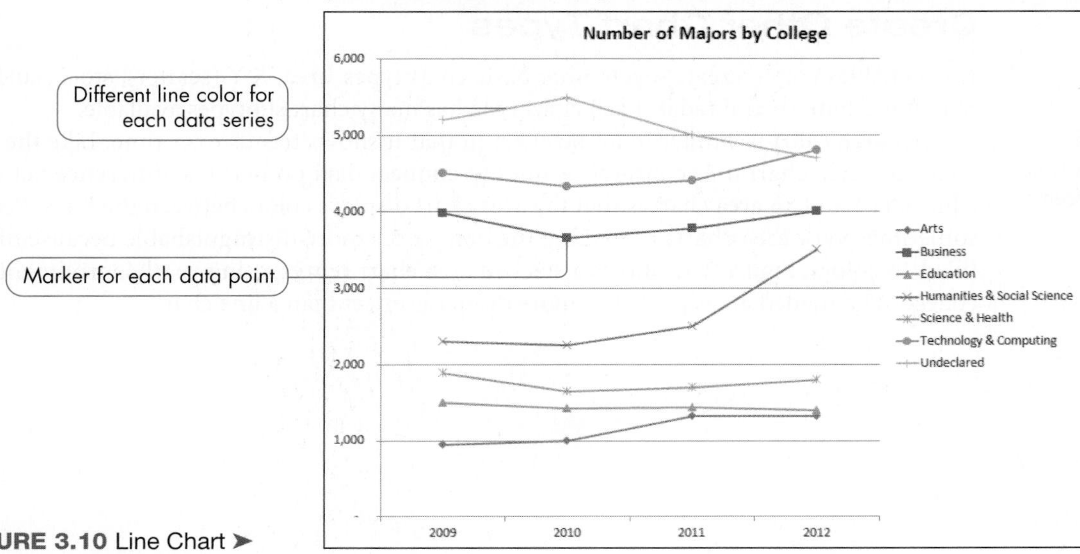

FIGURE 3.10 Line Chart ➤

Create a Pie Chart

A **pie chart** shows each data point in proportion to the whole data series as a slice in a circular pie.

A ***pie chart*** shows each data point as a proportion to the whole data series. The pie chart displays as a circle or "pie," where the entire pie represents the total value of the data series. Each slice represents a single data point. The larger the slice, the larger percentage that data point contributes to the whole. Use a pie chart when you want to convey percentage or market share. Unlike column, bar, and line charts, pie charts represent a single data series only.

The pie chart in Figure 3.11 divides the pie representing total Fall 2012 enrollment into seven slices, one for each college. The size of each slice is proportional to the percentage of total enrollment for that year. The chart depicts a single data series (Fall 2012 enrollment), which appears in the range E5:E11 on the worksheet in Figure 3.1. Excel creates a legend to indicate which color represents which pie slice. When you create a pie chart, limit it to about seven slices. Pie charts with too many slices appear too busy to interpret.

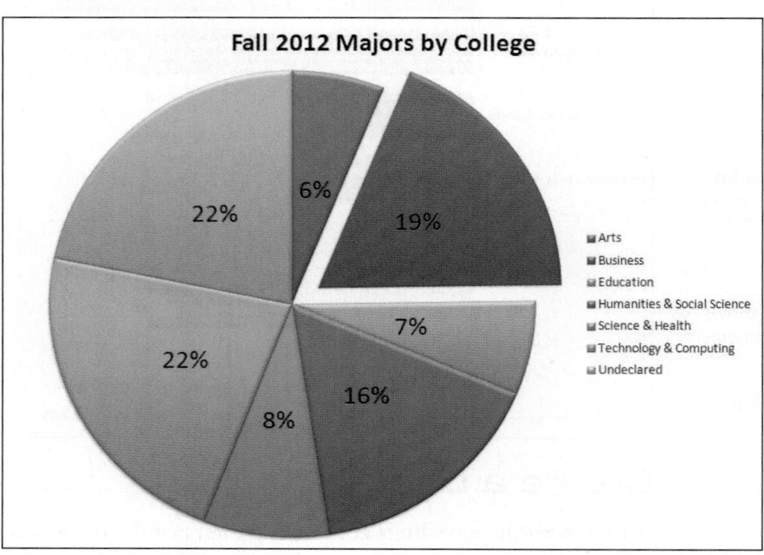

FIGURE 3.11 Pie Chart ➤

Similar to the way it creates a 100% stacked column chart, Excel creates a pie chart by computing the total 2012 enrollment (21,530 in our example), calculating the enrollment percentage by college and drawing each slice of the pie in proportion to its computed percentage. The Business College had 4,000 majors, which accounts for 19% of the total number of majors. You can focus a person's attention on a particular slice by separating one or more slices from the rest of the chart in an ***exploded pie chart***, as shown in Figure 3.11. Additional pie subtypes include pie of pie, bar of pie, and 3-D pie charts.

An **exploded pie chart** separates one or more pie slices from the rest of the pie chart.

Create Other Chart Types

Excel enables you to create seven other basic chart types: area, X Y (scatter), stock, surface, doughnut, bubble, and radar. Each chart type has many chart subtypes available.

An **area chart** emphasizes magnitude of changes over time by filling in the space between lines with a color.

An ***area chart*** is similar to a line chart in that it shows trends over time. Like the line chart, the area chart uses continuous lines to connect data points. The difference between a line chart and an area chart is that the area chart displays colors between the lines. People sometimes view area charts as making the data series more distinguishable because of the filled-in colors. Figure 3.12 shows a stacked area chart representing yearly enrollments by college. The shaded areas provide a more dramatic effect than a line chart.

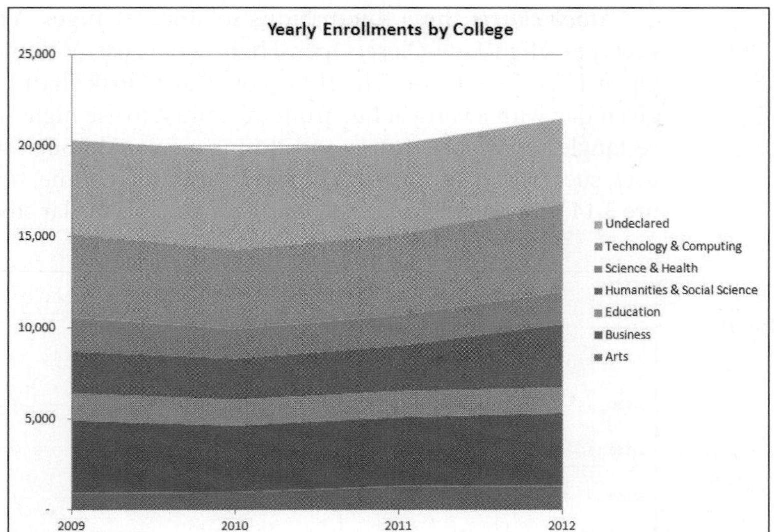

FIGURE 3.12 Stacked Area Chart ➤

> **TIP** Hidden Data
>
> When creating an area chart, be careful which subtype you select. For some subtypes such as a 3-D area chart, the chart might hide smaller data values behind data series with larger values. If this happens, you can change subtypes or apply a transparency fill to see any hidden data values.

An **X Y (scatter) chart** shows a relationship between two variables.

An ***X Y (scatter) chart*** shows a relationship between two variables using their X and Y coordinates. Excel plots one variable on the horizontal X-axis and the other variable on the vertical Y-axis. Scatter charts are often used to represent data in educational, scientific, and medical experiments. A scatter chart is essentially the plotted values without any connecting line. A scatter chart helps you determine if a relationship exists between two different sets of numerical data. For example, you can plot the number of minutes students view a computer-based training (CBT) module and their test scores to see if a relationship exists between the two variables (see Figure 3.13).

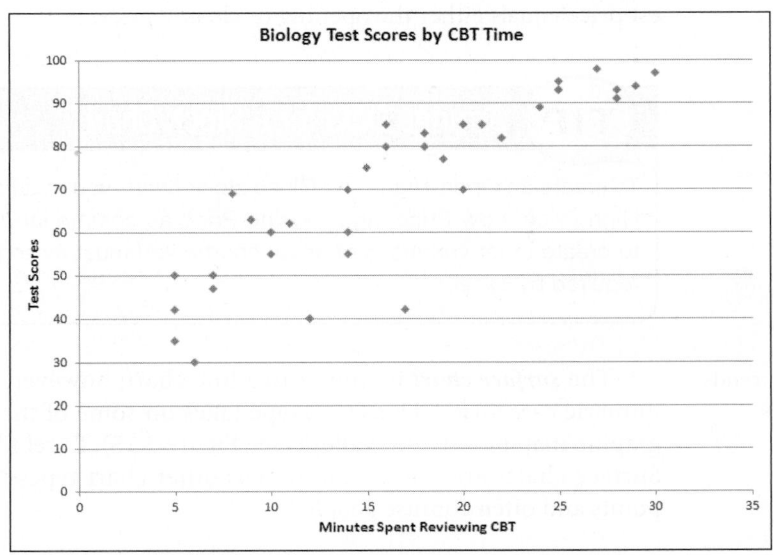

FIGURE 3.13 Scatter (X Y) Chart ➤

A **stock chart** shows the high, low, and close prices for individual stocks over time.

Stock charts show fluctuations in stock changes. You can select one of four stock subtypes: High-Low-Close, Open-High-Low-Close, Volume-High-Low-Close, and Volume-Open-High-Low-Close. The High-Low-Close stock chart marks a stock's trading range on a given day with a vertical line from the lowest to the highest stock prices. Horizontal bars or rectangles mark the opening and closing prices. Although stock charts may have some other uses, such as showing a range of temperatures over time, they usually show stock prices. Figure 3.14 shows three days of stock prices for a particular stock.

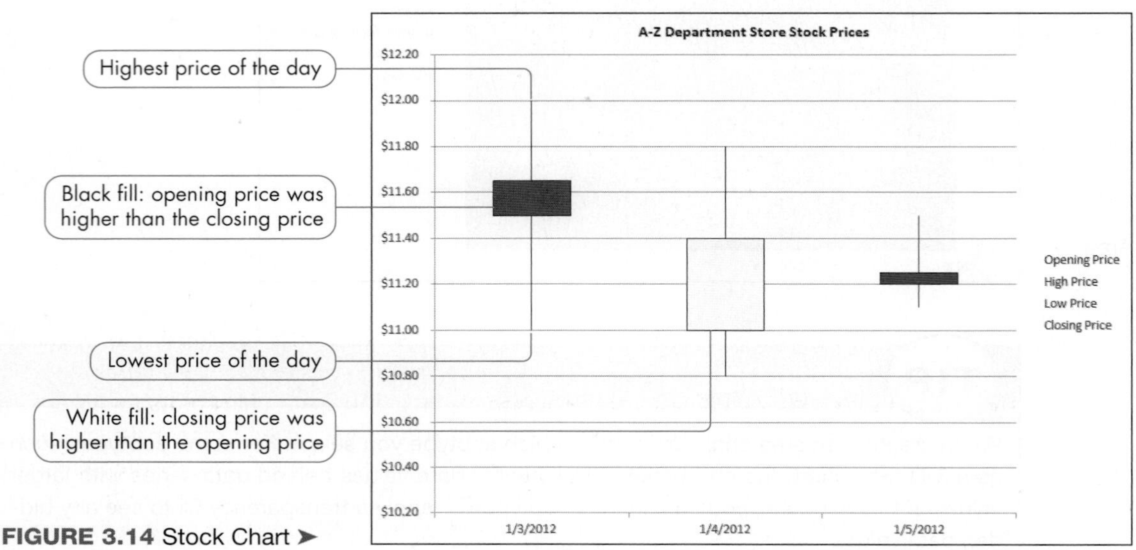

FIGURE 3.14 Stock Chart ➤

The stock chart legend may not explain the chart clearly. However, you can still identify prices. The rectangle represents the difference in the opening and closing prices. If the rectangle has a white fill, the closing price is higher than the opening price. If the rectangle has a black fill, the opening price is higher than the closing price. In Figure 3.14, the opening price was $11.65, and the closing price was $11.50 on January 3. A line below the rectangle indicates that the lowest trading price is lower than the opening and closing prices. In Figure 3.14, the lowest price was $11.00 on January 3. A line above the rectangle indicates the highest trading price is higher than the opening and closing prices. In Figure 3.14, the highest price was $12.00 on January 3. If no line exists below the rectangle, the lowest price equals either the opening or closing price, and if no line exists above the rectangle, the highest price equals either the opening or closing price.

TIP Arrange Data for a Stock Chart

To create an Open-High-Low-Close stock chart, you must arrange data with Opening Price, High Price, Low Price, and Closing Price as column labels in that sequence. If you want to create other variations of stock charts, you must arrange data in a structured sequence required by Excel.

A **surface chart** displays trends using two dimensions on a continuous curve.

The ***surface chart*** is similar to a line chart; however, it represents numeric data and numeric categories. This chart type takes on some of the same characteristics as a topographic map of hills and valleys (see Figure 3.15). Excel fills in all data points with colors. Surface charts are not as common as other chart types because they require more data points and often confuse people.

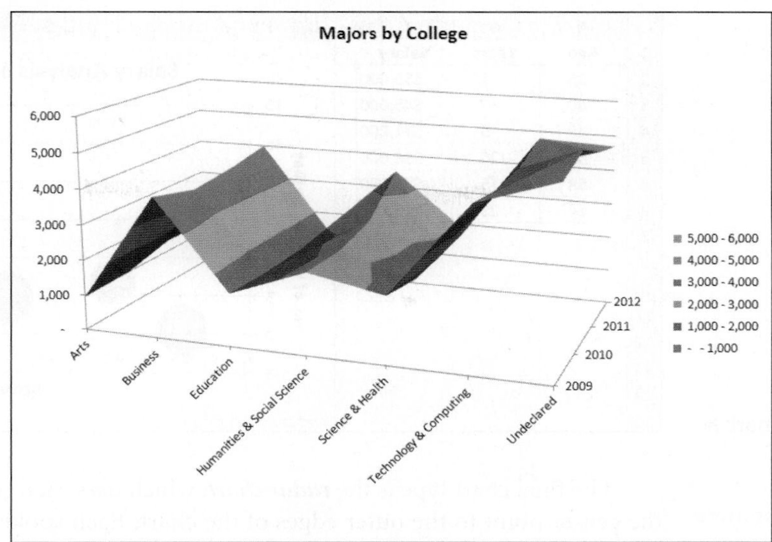

FIGURE 3.15 Surface Chart ➤

A **doughnut chart** displays values as percentages of the whole but may contain more than one data series.

The ***doughnut chart*** is similar to a pie chart in that it shows the relationship of parts to a whole, but the doughnut chart can display more than one series of data, and it has a hole in the middle. Like a clustered or stacked column chart, a doughnut chart plots multiple data series. Each ring represents a data series, with the outer ring receiving the most emphasis. Although the doughnut chart is able to display multiple data series, people often have difficulty interpreting it. Figure 3.16 illustrates the 2011 and 2012 data series, with the 2012 data series on the outer ring. The chart shows each college as a segment of each ring of the doughnut. The larger the segment, the larger the value.

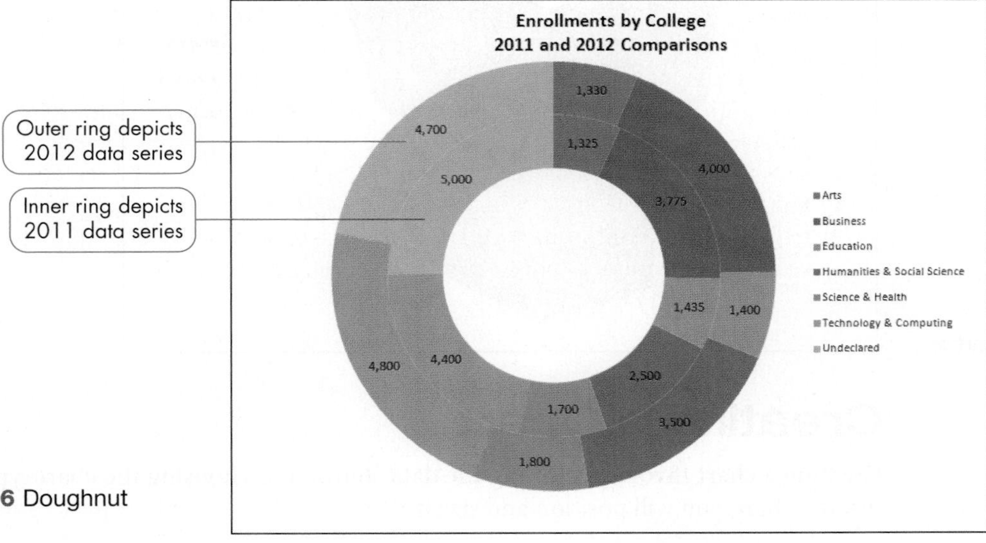

FIGURE 3.16 Doughnut Chart ➤

A **bubble chart** shows relationships among three values by using bubbles.

The ***bubble chart*** is similar to a scatter chart, but it uses round bubbles instead of data points to represent a third dimension. Similar to the scatter chart, the bubble chart does not contain a category axis. The horizontal and vertical axes are both value axes. The third value determines the size of the bubble where the larger the value, the larger the bubble. People often use bubble charts to depict financial data. In Figure 3.17, age, years at the company, and salaries are compared. When creating a bubble chart, do not select the column headings, as they might distort the data.

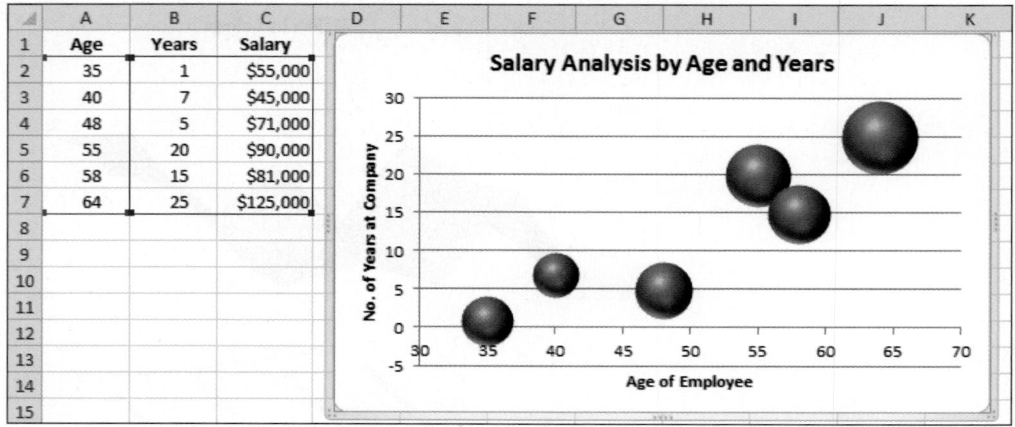

Age	Years	Salary
35	1	$55,000
40	7	$45,000
48	5	$71,000
55	20	$90,000
58	15	$81,000
64	25	$125,000

FIGURE 3.17 Bubble Chart ➤

A **radar chart** compares aggregate values of three or more variables represented on axes starting from the same point.

The final chart type is the ***radar chart***, which uses each category as a spoke radiating from the center point to the outer edges of the chart. Each spoke represents each data series, and lines connect the data points between spokes, similar to a spider web. You can create a radar chart to compare aggregate values for several data series. Figure 3.18 shows a radar chart comparing monthly house sales by house type (rambler, split level, 2 story). The house type categories appear in different colors, while the months appear on the outer edges of the chart.

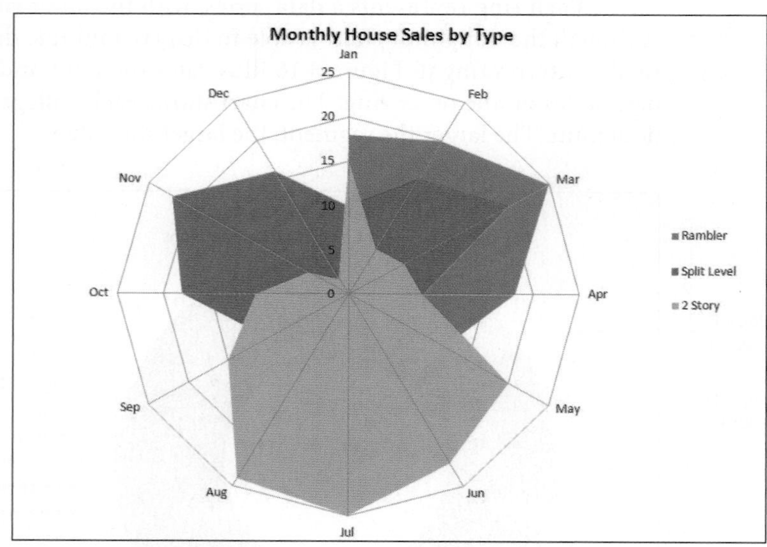

FIGURE 3.18 Radar Chart ➤

Creating a Chart

Creating a chart involves selecting the data source and choosing the chart type. After you insert a chart, you will position and size it.

Select the Data Source

Identify the chart data range by selecting the data series, any descriptive labels you need to construct the category labels, and the series labels you need to create the legend. Edit the row and column labels if they are not clear and concise. Table 3.1 describes what you should select for various charts. If the labels and data series are not stored in adjacent cells, press and hold Ctrl while selecting the nonadjacent ranges. Using Figure 3.1 as a guide, you would select the range A4:E11 to create a clustered column chart with multiple data series. To create the pie chart in Figure 3.11, select the range A5:A11, and then press and hold Ctrl while you select the range E5:E11. If your worksheet has titles and subtitles, you should not select them. Doing so would add unnecessary text to the legend.

TABLE 3.1 Data Selection for Charts		
Chart Type	**What to Select**	**Figure 3.1 Example**
Column, Bar, Line, Area, Doughnut	Row labels (such as colleges), column labels (such as years), and one or more data series	A4:E11
Pie	Row labels (such as colleges) and only one data series (such as 2012), but not column headings	A5:A11,E5:E11
Bubble	Three different data series (such as age, years, and salary)	A21:C26 (in Figure 3.17)
X Y (Scatter)	Two related numeric datasets (such as minutes studying and test scores)	*

*Figure 3.1 does not contain data conducive to an X Y (scatter) chart.

TIP Total Rows and Columns

Make sure that each data series uses the same scale. For example, don't include aggregates, such as totals or averages, along with individual data points. Doing so would distort the plotted data. Compare the clustered column chart in Figure 3.3 to Figure 3.19. In Figure 3.19, the chart's design is incorrect because it mixes individual data points with the totals and yearly averages.

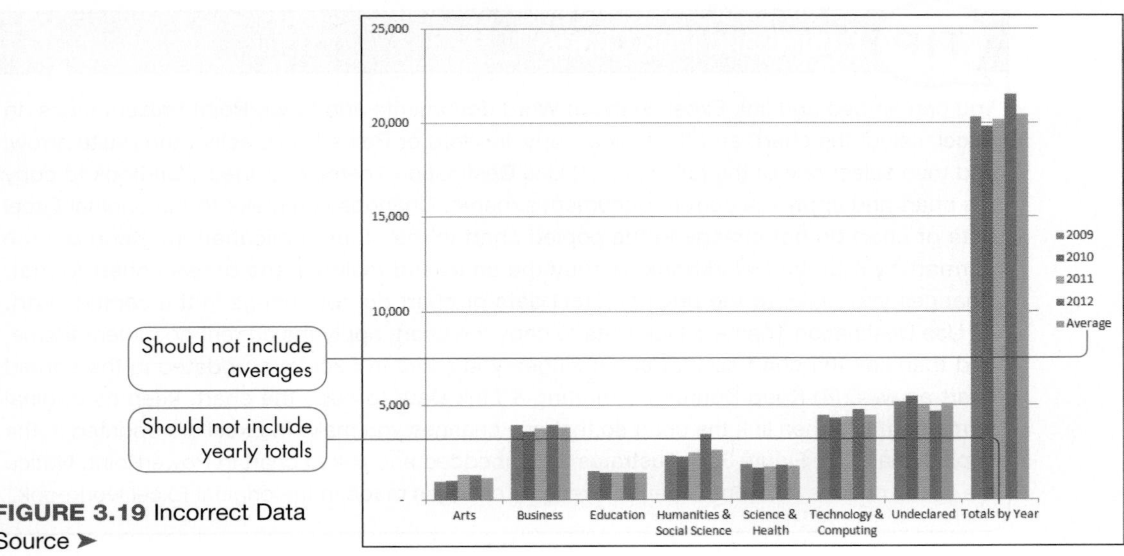

FIGURE 3.19 Incorrect Data Source ➤

Select the Chart Type

After you select the range of cells that you want to be the source for the chart, you need to select the chart type. To insert a chart for the selected range, click the Insert tab, and then do one of the following:

- Click the chart type (such as Column) in the Charts group, and then click a chart subtype (such as Clustered Column) from the chart gallery.
- Click the Charts Dialog Box Launcher to display the Insert Chart dialog box (see Figure 3.20), select a chart type on the left side, select a chart subtype, and then click OK.

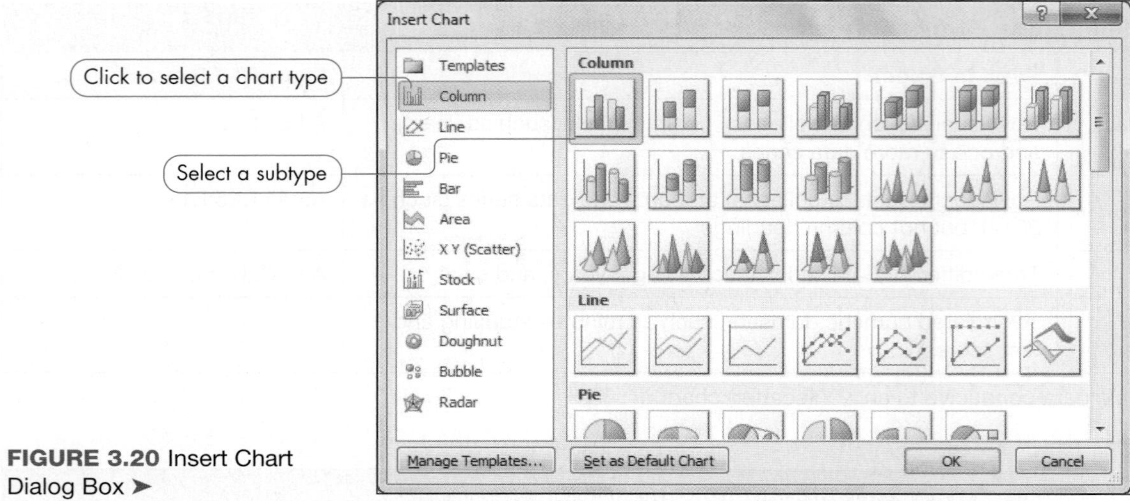

FIGURE 3.20 Insert Chart Dialog Box ➤

A **chart sheet** contains a single chart and no spreadsheet data.

Excel inserts the chart as an embedded object on the current worksheet. You can leave the chart on the same worksheet as the worksheet data used to create the chart, or you can place the chart in a separate worksheet, called a ***chart sheet***. A chart sheet contains a single chart only; you cannot enter data and formulas on a chart sheet. If you leave the chart in the same worksheet (see Figure 3.17), you can print the data and chart on the same page. If you want to print or view a full-sized chart, you can move the chart to its own chart sheet.

TIP Embed and Link Charts

You can embed and link Excel charts in Word documents and PowerPoint presentations. In Excel, select the chart, and then click Copy. In Word or PowerPoint, select the Paste arrow, and then select one of the following: (1) Use Destination Theme & Embed Workbook to copy the chart and apply the current document's theme. Changes you make to the original Excel data or chart do not change in the copied chart in the other application. (2) Keep Source Formatting & Embed Workbook to copy the chart and maintain the original chart format. Changes you make to the original Excel data or chart do not change in the copied chart. (3) Use Destination Theme & Link Data to copy the chart, apply the current document theme, and then link the chart so that any changes you make in Excel are updated in the copied chart as well. (4) Keep Source Formatting & Link Data to copy the chart, keep its original formatting, and then link the chart so that any changes you make in Excel are updated in the copied chart too. Figure 3.21 illustrates an embedded and linked chart in PowerPoint. Notice the linked chart is different because it reflects changes made in the original Excel workbook.

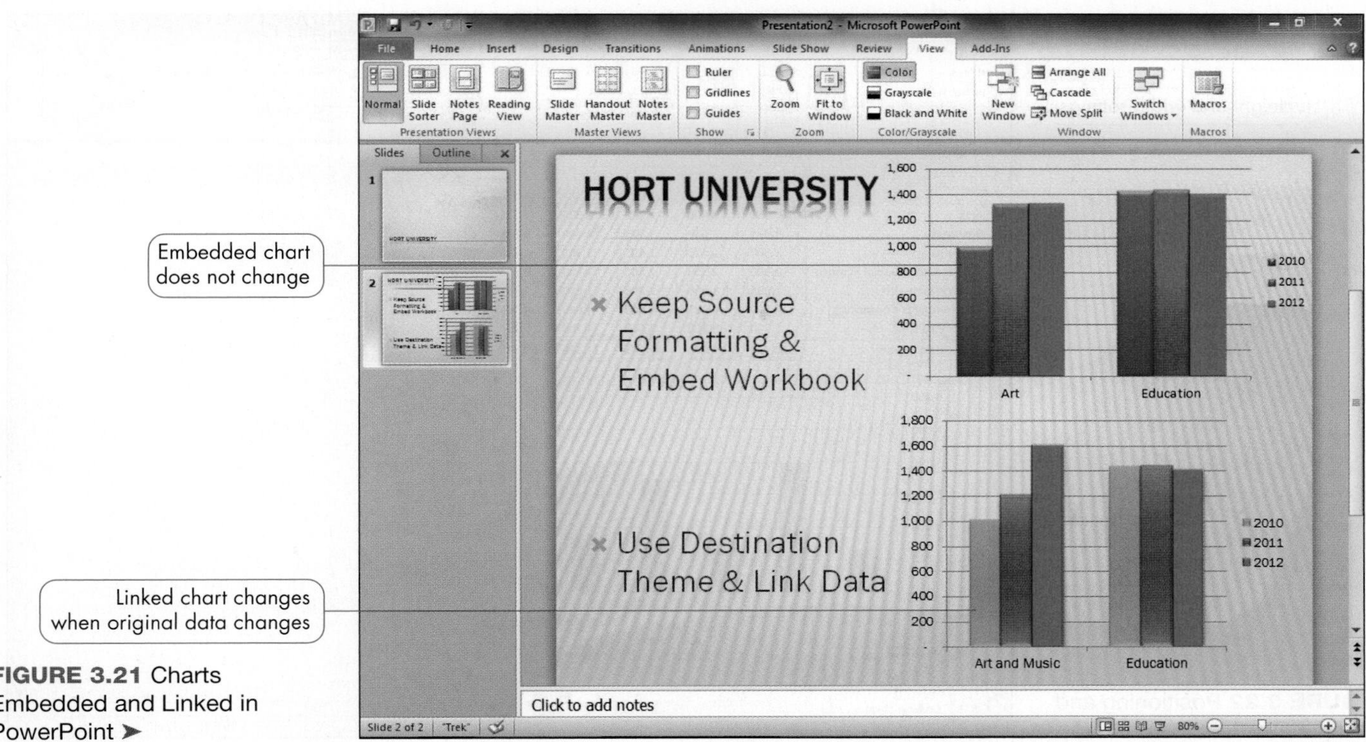

FIGURE 3.21 Charts Embedded and Linked in PowerPoint ➤

Position and Size the Chart

When you first create a chart, Excel inserts the chart in the worksheet, often to the right side of, but sometimes on top of and covering up, the data area. To move the chart to a new location, position the mouse pointer over the chart area. When you see the Chart Area ScreenTip and the mouse pointer includes the white arrowhead and a four-headed arrow (see Figure 3.22), drag the chart to the desired location.

A **sizing handle**, indicated by faint dots on the outside border of a selected chart, enables you to adjust the size of the chart.

To change the size of a chart, select the chart if necessary. Position the mouse pointer on the outer edge of the chart where you see three or four faint dots. These dots are called ***sizing handles***. When the mouse pointer changes to a two-headed arrow, drag the border to adjust the chart's height or width. Drag a corner sizing handle to increase or decrease the height and width of the chart at the same time. Press and hold down Shift as you drag a corner sizing handle to change the height and width proportionately. You can also change the chart size by clicking the Format tab and changing the height and width values in the Size group (see Figure 3.22).

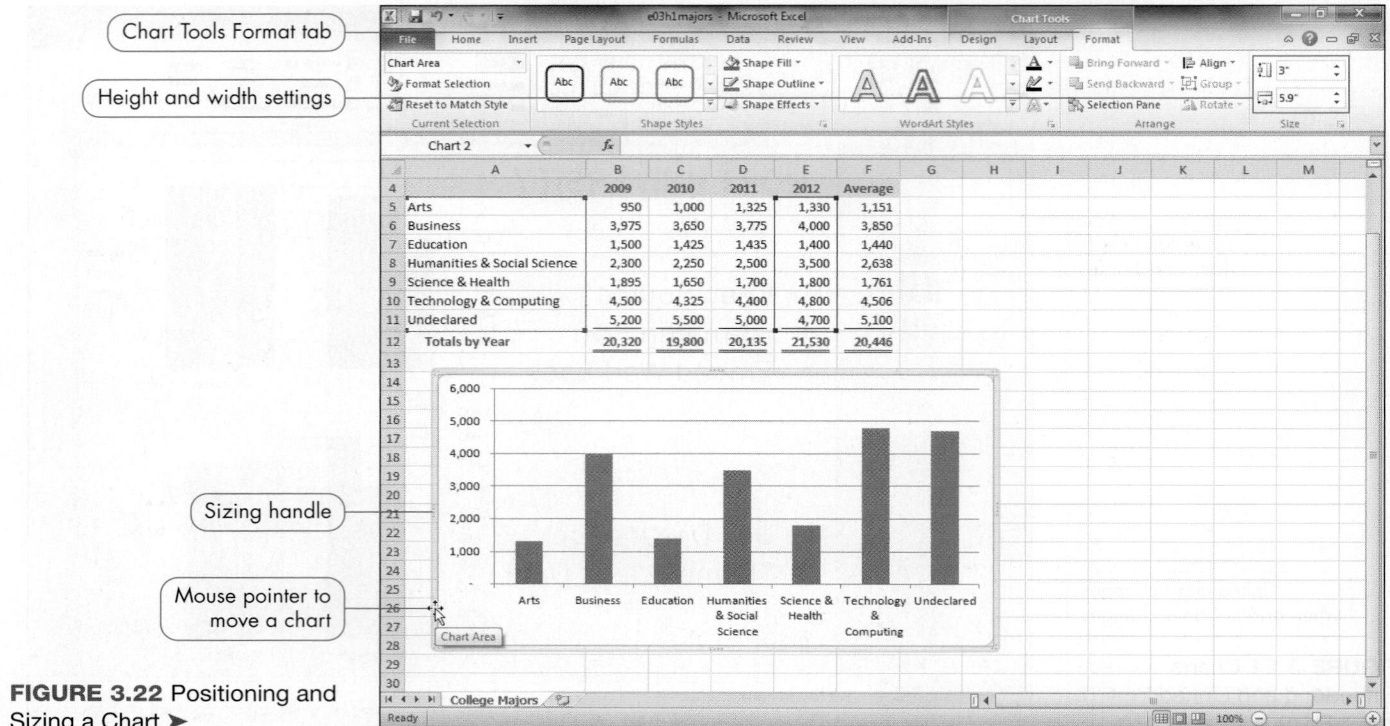

FIGURE 3.22 Positioning and Sizing a Chart ➤

Quick Concepts Check

1. What is the purpose of each of these chart types: (a) column, (b) bar, (c) line, and (d) pie?
2. What is the difference between a data point and a data series?
3. What is wrong with including aggregates, such as totals or averages, along with individual data in a chart?
4. What are the three major steps to creating a chart?

HANDS-ON EXERCISES

1 Chart Basics

Yesterday, you gathered the enrollment data for Hort University and organized it into a structured worksheet that contains the number of majors for the last four years, organized by college. You included yearly totals and the average number of majors. Now you are ready to transform the data into visually appealing charts.

Skills covered: Create a Clustered Column Chart • Change the Chart Position and Size • Create a Pie Chart • Explode a Pie Slice • Change Worksheet Data

STEP 1 CREATE A CLUSTERED COLUMN CHART

Dr. Musto wants to compare large amounts of data. You know that the clustered column chart is effective at depicting multiple data series for different categories, so you will create one first. Refer to Figure 3.23 as you complete Step 1.

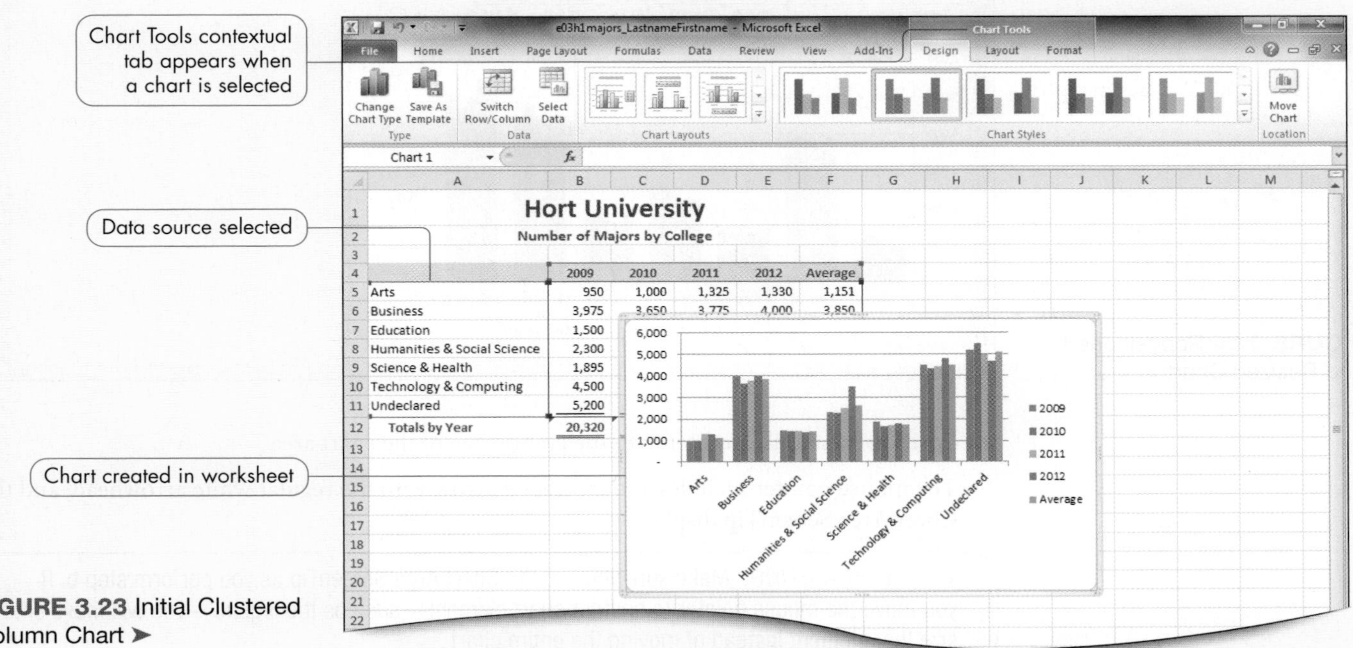

FIGURE 3.23 Initial Clustered Column Chart ➤

a. Open *e03h1majors* and save it as **e03h1majors_LastnameFirstname**.

> **TROUBLESHOOTING:** If you make any major mistakes in this exercise, you can close the file, open *e03h1majors* again, and then start this exercise over.

b. Select the **range A4:F11**.

You included the average column in your selection. Although you should not mix individual values and aggregates such as averages in the same chart, we will do this now and later show you how you can modify the data source after you create the chart.

c. Click the **Insert tab**, and then click **Column** in the Charts group.

The Column gallery opens, displaying the different column subtypes you can create.

d. Click **Clustered Column** in the *2-D Column* section of the gallery. Save the workbook.

Excel inserts the clustered column chart in the worksheet.

Chart Tools Contextual Tab

When you select a chart, Excel displays the Chart Tools contextual tab, containing the Design, Layout, and Format tabs. You can use the commands on these tabs to modify the chart.

STEP 2 CHANGE THE CHART POSITION AND SIZE

Excel inserts the chart next to the worksheet data. You want to reposition the chart and then adjust the size so that the college category labels do not display at an angle to make the chart readable for Dr. Musto. Refer to Figure 3.24 as you complete Step 2.

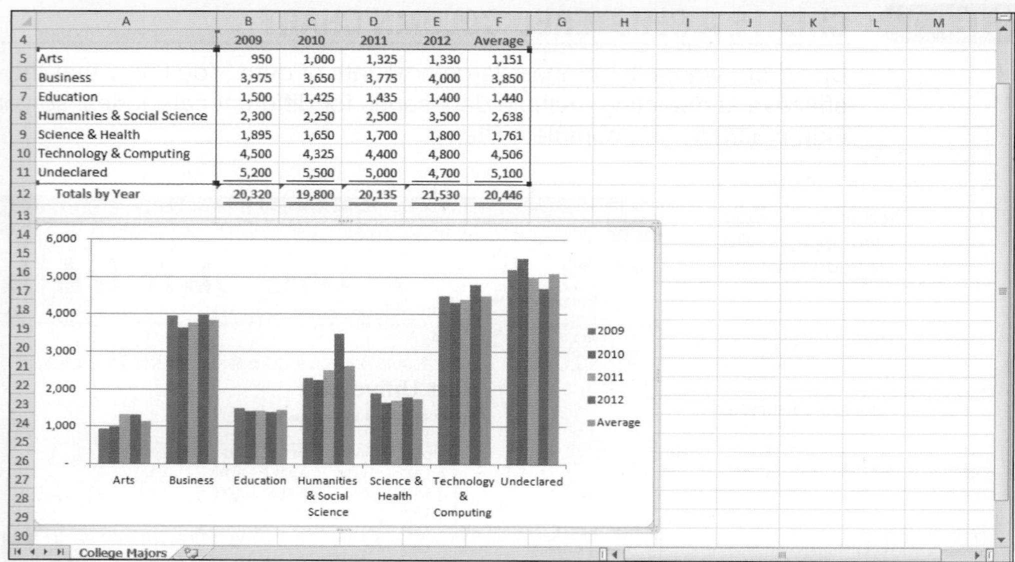

	2009	2010	2011	2012	Average
Arts	950	1,000	1,325	1,330	1,151
Business	3,975	3,650	3,775	4,000	3,850
Education	1,500	1,425	1,435	1,400	1,440
Humanities & Social Science	2,300	2,250	2,500	3,500	2,638
Science & Health	1,895	1,650	1,700	1,800	1,761
Technology & Computing	4,500	4,325	4,400	4,800	4,506
Undeclared	5,200	5,500	5,000	4,700	5,100
Totals by Year	20,320	19,800	20,135	21,530	20,446

FIGURE 3.24 Repositioned and Resized Chart ➤

a. Position the mouse pointer over the empty area of the chart area.

   The mouse pointer includes a four-headed arrow with the regular white arrowhead, and the Chart Area ScreenTip displays.

TROUBLESHOOTING: Make sure you see the Chart Area ScreenTip as you perform step b. If you move the mouse pointer to another chart element—such as the legend—you will move or size that element instead of moving the entire chart.

b. Drag the chart so that the top-left corner of the chart appears in **cell A14**.

   You positioned the chart below the worksheet data.

c. Drag the bottom-right sizing handle down and to the right to **cell H29**. Save the workbook.

   You increased both the height and the width at the same time. The college labels on the category axis no longer appear at an angle. You will leave the clustered column chart in its current state for the moment while you create another chart.

The F11 Key

Pressing F11 is a fast way to create a column chart in a new chart sheet. Select the worksheet data source, and then press F11 to create the chart.

STEP 3 CREATE A PIE CHART

Dr. Musto has also asked you to create a chart showing the percentage of majors for the current year. You know that pie charts are excellent for illustrating percentages and proportions. Refer to Figure 3.25 as you complete Step 3.

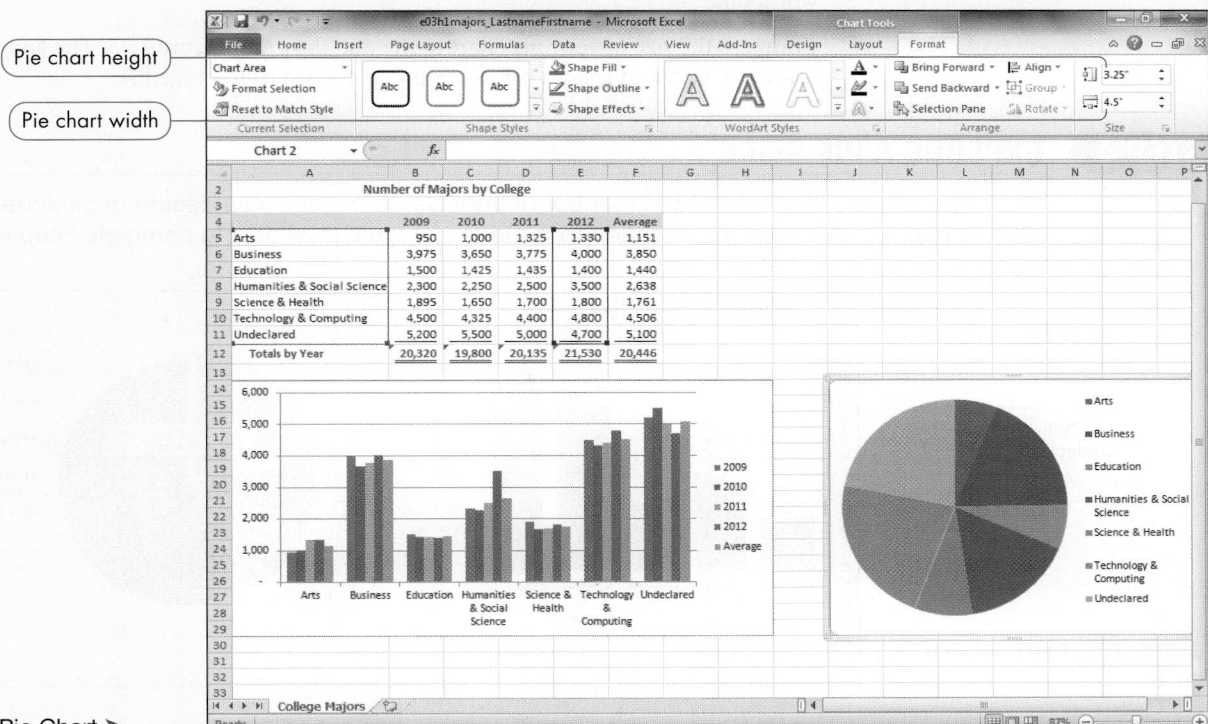

Number of Majors by College

	2009	2010	2011	2012	Average
Arts	950	1,000	1,325	1,330	1,151
Business	3,975	3,650	3,775	4,000	3,850
Education	1,500	1,425	1,435	1,400	1,440
Humanities & Social Science	2,300	2,250	2,500	3,500	2,638
Science & Health	1,895	1,650	1,700	1,800	1,761
Technology & Computing	4,500	4,325	4,400	4,800	4,506
Undeclared	5,200	5,500	5,000	4,700	5,100
Totals by Year	20,320	19,800	20,135	21,530	20,446

FIGURE 3.25 Pie Chart ➤

a. Select the **range A5:A11**, which contains the college category labels.

b. Press and hold **Ctrl** as you select the **range E5:E11**, which contains the 2012 values.

Remember that you have to press and hold Ctrl to select nonadjacent ranges.

> **TIP** Parallel Ranges
>
> Nonadjacent ranges should be parallel so that the legend will correctly reflect the data series. This means that each range should contain the same number of related cells. For example, A5:A11 and E5:E11 are parallel ranges in which E5:E11 contains values that relate to range A5:A11.

c. Click the **Insert tab**, click **Pie** in the Charts group, and then select **Pie** in the 2-D Pie group on the gallery.

Excel inserts a pie chart in the worksheet. The pie chart may overlap part of the worksheet data and the clustered column chart.

d. Drag the chart so that the top-left corner appears in **cell J14**.

> **TROUBLESHOOTING:** Make sure that you see the Chart Area ScreenTip before you start dragging. Otherwise, you might accidentally drag a chart element, such as the legend or plot area. If you accidentally move the legend or plot area, press Ctrl+Z to undo the move.

e. Click the **Format tab**.

f. Type **3.25** in the **Shape Height box** in the Size group, and then press **Enter**.

You increased the chart height to 3.25".

g. Type **4.5** in the **Shape Width box** in the Size group, and then press **Enter**. Save the workbook.

Compare the size of your pie chart to the one shown in Figure 3.25. The zoom in the figure was decreased to display a broader view of the two charts together.

STEP 4 EXPLODE A PIE SLICE

Dr. Musto is concerned about the number of undeclared majors. You decide to explode the Undeclared pie slice to draw attention to it. Refer to Figure 3.26 as you complete Step 4.

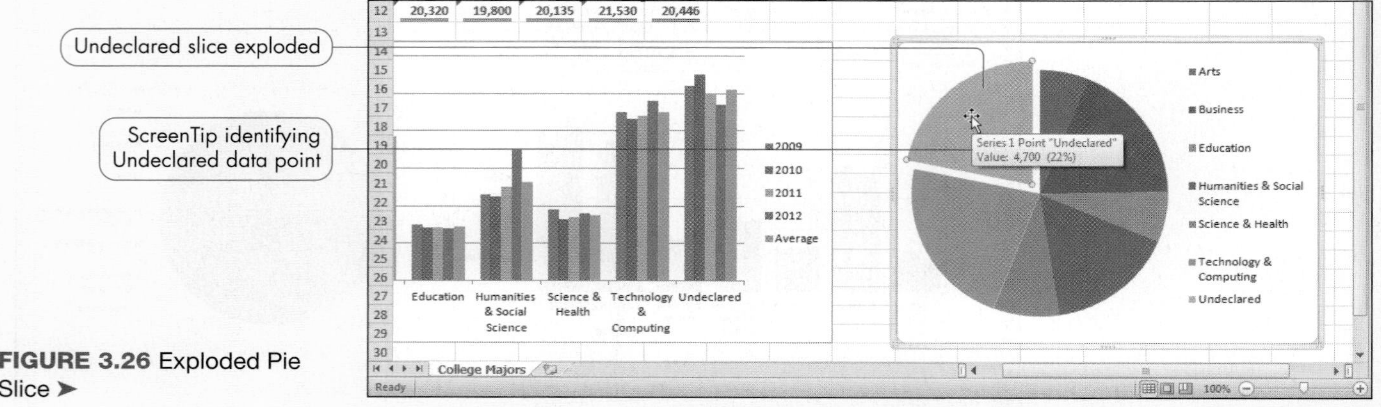

FIGURE 3.26 Exploded Pie Slice ➤

a. Make sure the pie chart is still selected.

b. Click any slice of the chart.

Excel selects all pie slices, as indicated by circular selection handles at the corner of each slice and in the center of the pie.

c. Click the **Undeclared slice**, the light blue slice in the top-left corner of the chart.

The Undeclared slice is the only selected slice.

TROUBLESHOOTING: If you double-click the chart instead of clicking a single data point, the Format Data Point dialog box appears. If this happens, click Close in the dialog box, and then click the individual pie slice to select that slice only.

d. Drag the **Undeclared slice** away from the pie a little bit. Save the workbook.

You exploded the pie slice by separating it from the rest of the pie.

STEP 5 CHANGE WORKSHEET DATA

While you have been preparing two charts, some updated data came into the Institutional Research Department office. You need to update the worksheet data to update the charts. Refer to Figure 3.27 as you complete Step 5.

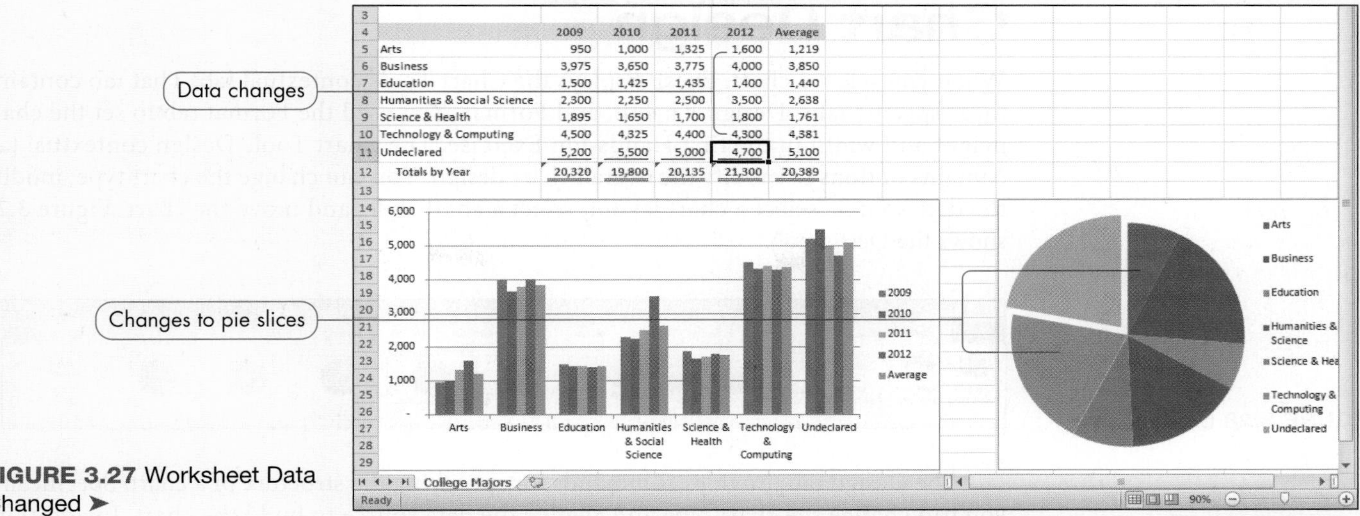

	2009	2010	2011	2012	Average
Arts	950	1,000	1,325	1,600	1,219
Business	3,975	3,650	3,775	4,000	3,850
Education	1,500	1,425	1,435	1,400	1,440
Humanities & Social Science	2,300	2,250	2,500	3,500	2,638
Science & Health	1,895	1,650	1,700	1,800	1,761
Technology & Computing	4,500	4,325	4,400	4,300	4,381
Undeclared	5,200	5,500	5,000	4,700	5,100
Totals by Year	20,320	19,800	20,135	21,300	20,389

FIGURE 3.27 Worksheet Data Changed ➤

a. Click **cell E5**, the cell containing *1,330*—the number of students majoring in the College of Arts in 2012.

b. Type **1600** and press **Enter**.

Notice that the total changes in cell E12, the average yearly number of Arts majors changes in cell F5, the total average students changes in cell F12, and the two charts are adjusted to reflect the new value.

c. Click **cell E10**, the cell containing *4,800*—the number of students majoring in the College of Technology and Computing.

d. Type **4300** and press **Enter**.

Compare the updated charts to those shown in Figures 3.26 and 3.27. Notice the changes in the worksheet and the chart. With a smaller value, the Technology & Computing slice is smaller, while the other slices represent proportionally higher percentages of the total majors for 2012.

e. Save the workbook. Keep the workbook onscreen if you plan to continue with Hands-On Exercise 2. If not, close the workbook and exit Excel.

Chart Design

When you select a chart, Excel displays the Chart Tools contextual tab. That tab contains three specific tabs: Design, Layout, and Format. You used the Format tab to set the chart height and width in the first Hands-On Exercise. The Chart Tools Design contextual tab contains options to modify the overall chart design. You can change the chart type, modify the data source, select a chart layout, select a chart style, and move the chart. Figure 3.28 shows the Design tab.

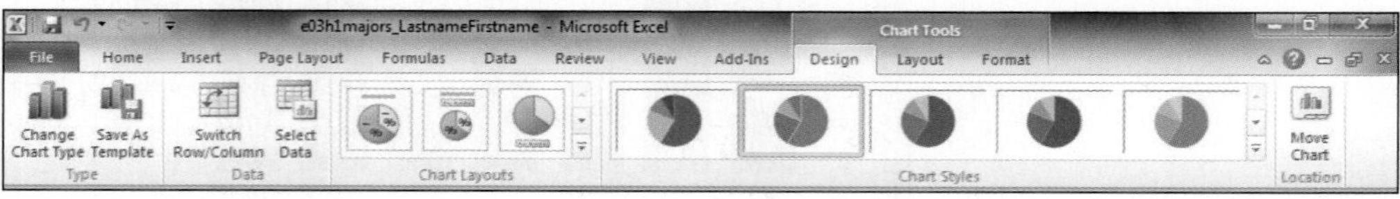

FIGURE 3.28 Design Tab ➤

The Design tab provides commands for specifying the structure of a chart. Specifically, you can change the chart type and change the data source to build the chart. In addition, you can specify a chart layout that controls which chart elements display and where, select a chart style, and move the chart to a different location.

In this section, you will learn about the Design tab options and how to make changes to a chart's design. In addition, you will learn how to insert and format sparkline charts.

Changing the Chart Type

After you create a chart, you might want to change how the data are depicted by using other chart types. For example, you might want to change a line chart to a surface chart to see the dramatic effect of the fill colors or change a stacked column chart to a 100% stacked column chart to compare the segment percentages within their respective categories. To change the chart type, do the following:

1. Select the chart.
2. Click the Design tab.
3. Click Change Chart Type in the Type group to open the Change Chart Type dialog box.
4. Select the desired chart type, and then click OK.

TIP Saving a Chart as a Template

Companies often require a similar look for charts used in presentations. After you spend time customizing a chart to your company's specifications, you can save it as a template to create additional charts. To save a chart as a template, select the chart, click the Design tab, and then click Save as Template in the Type group. The Save Chart Template dialog box opens, in which you can select the template location and type a template name. Click Save in the dialog box to save the template. To use a chart template that you have created, click Templates in the Insert Chart dialog box, select the desired chart template, and then click OK.

Changing the Data Source and Structure

By default, Excel displays the row labels in the first column (such as the college names in Figure 3.1) on the category axis and the column labels (such as years) as the data series and in the legend. You can reverse how the chart presents the data—for example, place the column labels (e.g., years) on the category axis and the row labels (e.g., colleges) as data series and in the legend. To reverse the data series, click Switch Row/Column in the Data group. Figure 3.29 shows two chart versions of the same data. The chart on the left shows the row labels (months) on the category axis and the housing types as data series and in the legend. The chart on the right reverses the category axis and data series. The first chart compares house types for each month, and the second chart compares the number of sales of each house type throughout the year.

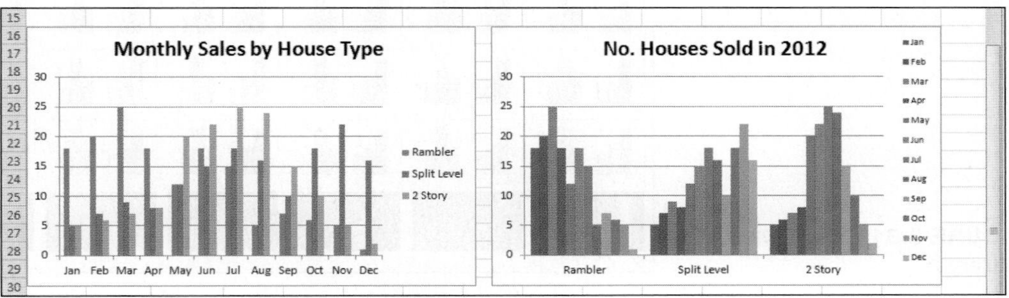

FIGURE 3.29 Original Chart and Reversed Row/Column Chart ➤

After creating a chart, you might notice extraneous data caused by selecting too many cells for the data source, or you might want to add to or delete data from the chart by clicking Select Data in the Data group to open the Select Data Source dialog box (see Figure 3.30). Select the desired range in the worksheet to modify the data source, or adjust the legend and horizontal axis within the dialog box.

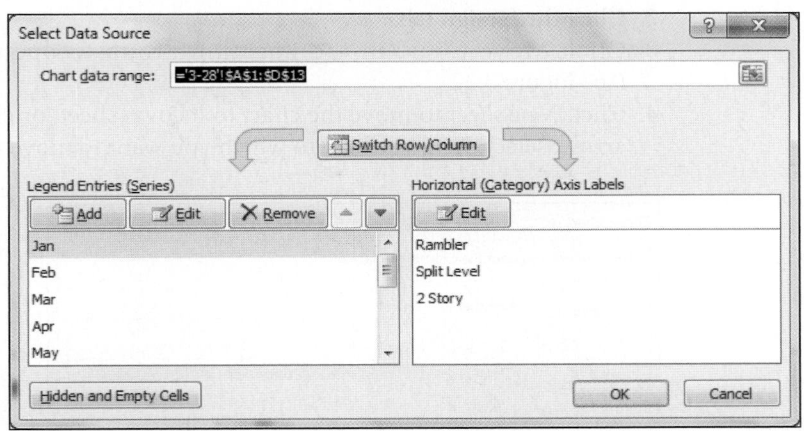

FIGURE 3.30 Select Data Source Dialog Box ➤

Applying a Chart Layout and a Chart Style

The Chart Layouts group enables you to apply predefined layouts to a chart. A chart layout determines which chart elements appear in the chart area and how they are positioned within the chart area. Chart layouts are useful when you are first learning about charts and chart elements or to create consistently laid out charts. As you learn more about charting, you may want to customize your charts by using the commands on the Layout tab.

The Chart Styles group contains predefined styles that control the color of the chart area, plot area, and data series. Styles also affect the look of the data series, such as flat, 3-D, or beveled. Figure 3.31 shows the Chart Styles gallery. When choosing a chart style, make sure the style complements the chart data and is easy to read. Also, consider whether you will display the chart onscreen in a presentation or print the chart. If you will display the chart in a presentation, select a style with a black background. If you plan to print the chart, select a chart style with a white background to avoid wasting toner printing a background. If you print with a black and white printer, use the first column of black and gray styles.

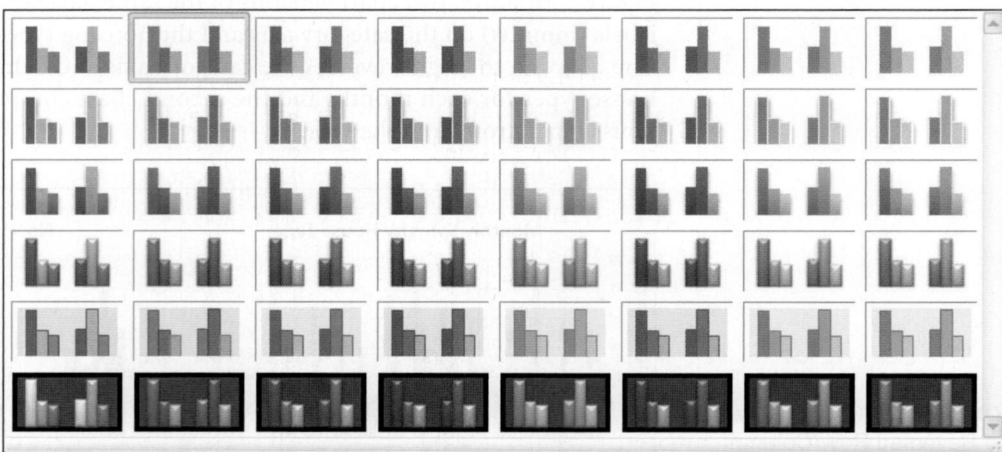

FIGURE 3.31 Chart Styles Gallery ➤

Moving a Chart

By default, Excel creates charts on the same worksheet as the original dataset, but you can move the chart to its own chart sheet in the workbook. To move a chart to another sheet or a new sheet, do the following:

1. Select the chart to display the Chart Tools contextual tab.
2. Click the Design tab.
3. Click Move Chart in the Location group to open the Move Chart dialog box (see Figure 3.32).
4. Click *New sheet* to move the chart to its own sheet, or click *Object in*, click the *Object in* arrow, select the worksheet to which you want to move the chart, and then click OK.

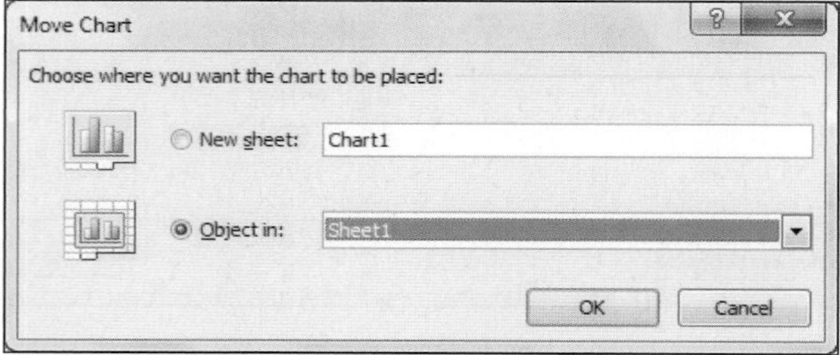

FIGURE 3.32 Move Chart Dialog Box ➤

TIP Chart Sheet Name

The default chart sheet name is Chart1, Chart2, etc. You can rename the sheet before you click OK in the Move Chart dialog box or by double-clicking the chart sheet tab, typing a new name, and then pressing Enter.

Printing Charts

Just like for printing any worksheet data, preview the chart in the Backstage view before you print to check margins, spacing, and page breaks to ensure a balanced printout.

Print an Embedded Chart

If you embedded a chart on the same sheet as the data source, you need to decide if you want to print the data only, the data *and* the chart, or the chart only. To print the data only, select the data, click the File tab, click Print, click the first arrow in the Settings section and select Print Selection, and then click Print. To print only the chart, select the chart, and then display the Backstage view. The default setting is Print Selected Chart, and clicking Print will print the chart as a full-page chart. If the data and chart are on the same worksheet, print the worksheet contents to print both, but do not select either the chart or the data before displaying the Backstage view. The preview shows you what will print. Make sure it displays what you want to print before clicking Print.

Print a Chart Sheet

If you moved the chart to a chart sheet, the chart is the only item on that worksheet. When you display the print options, the default is Print Active Sheets, and the chart will print as a full-page chart. You can change the setting to Print Entire Workbook.

Inserting and Customizing a Sparkline

A **sparkline** is a miniature chart contained in a single cell.

Excel 2010 enables you to create miniature charts called sparklines. A ***sparkline*** is a small line, column, or win/loss chart contained in a single cell. The purpose of a sparkline is to present a condensed, simple, succinct visual illustration of data. Unlike a regular chart, a sparkline does not include a chart title or axes labels. Inserting sparklines next to data helps your audience understand data quickly without having to look at a full-scale chart.

A sparkline presents a condensed, simple, succinct visual illustration of data.

Create a Sparkline

Before creating a sparkline, identify what data you want to depict and where you want to place it. To create a sparkline, do the following:

1. Click the Insert tab.
2. Click Line, Column, or Win/Loss in the Sparklines group. The Create Sparklines dialog box opens (see Figure 3.33).
3. Type the cell references in the Data Range box, or click the collapse button (if necessary), select the range, and then click the expand button.
4. Enter or select the range where you want the sparkline to appear in the Location Range box, and then click OK. The default cell location is the active cell unless you change it.

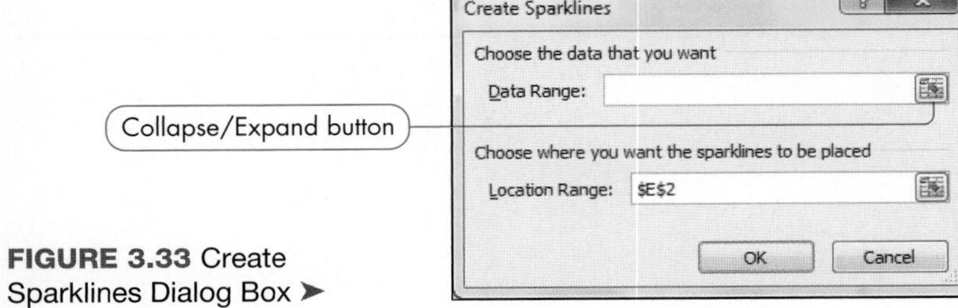

FIGURE 3.33 Create Sparklines Dialog Box ➤

Apply Design Characteristics to a Sparkline

After you insert a sparkline, the Sparkline Tools Design contextual tab displays, with options to customize the sparkline. Click Edit Data in the Sparkline group to change the data source or sparkline location and indicate how empty cells appear, such as gaps or zeros.

- The Type group enables you to select the sparkline type: Line, Column, or Win/Loss.
- The Show group enables you to display points within the sparkline. For example, click the Markers check box to display markers for all data points on the sparkline, or click High Point to display a marker for the high point, such as for the highest sales or highest price per gallon of gasoline for a time period.
- The Style group enables you to change the sparkline style, similar to how you can apply different chart styles to charts. Click Sparkline Color to change the color of the sparkline. Click Marker Color, point to a marker type—such as High Point—and then click the color for that marker. Make sure the marker color contrasts with the sparkline color.
- The Group you to specify the horizontal and vertical axis settings, group objects together, and ungroup objects.

Figure 3.34 shows a blue sparkline to indicate trends for the yearly students. The High Point marker is red.

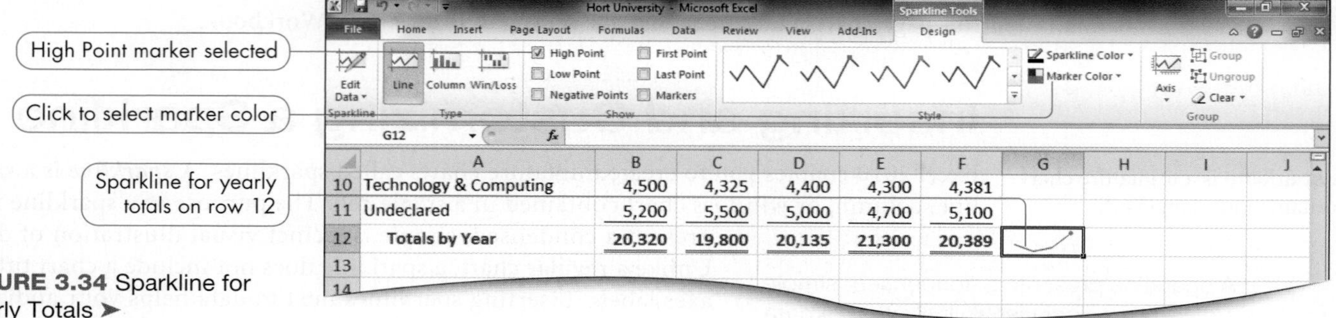

FIGURE 3.34 Sparkline for Yearly Totals ➤

> **TIP** Clear Sparklines
>
> To clear the sparklines, select the cells containing sparklines, click the Clear arrow in the Group group on the Sparkline Tools Design tab, and then select either Clear Selected Sparklines or Clear Selected Sparkline Groups.

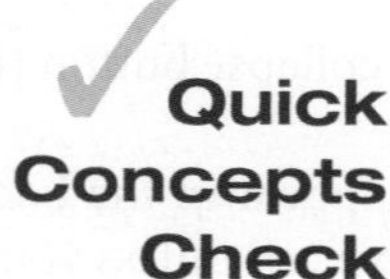

Quick Concepts Check

1. What are the steps to change a column chart to a line chart?
2. How can you change a chart so that the data in the legend is on the X-axis and the data on the X-axis is in the legend?
3. What is a sparkline and why would you create one?

HANDS-ON EXERCISES

2 Chart Design

You have studied the Design tab and decide to change some design elements on your two charts. You will move the pie chart to a chart sheet so that Dr. Musto can focus on the chart. You will use other options on the Design tab to modify the charts.

Skills covered: Move a Chart • Apply a Chart Style and Chart Layout • Change the Data • Change the Chart Type • Insert a Sparkline • Print a Chart

STEP 1 MOVE A CHART

Your first task is to move the pie chart to its own sheet so that the worksheet data and the clustered column chart do not distract Dr. Musto. Refer to Figure 3.35 as you complete Step 1.

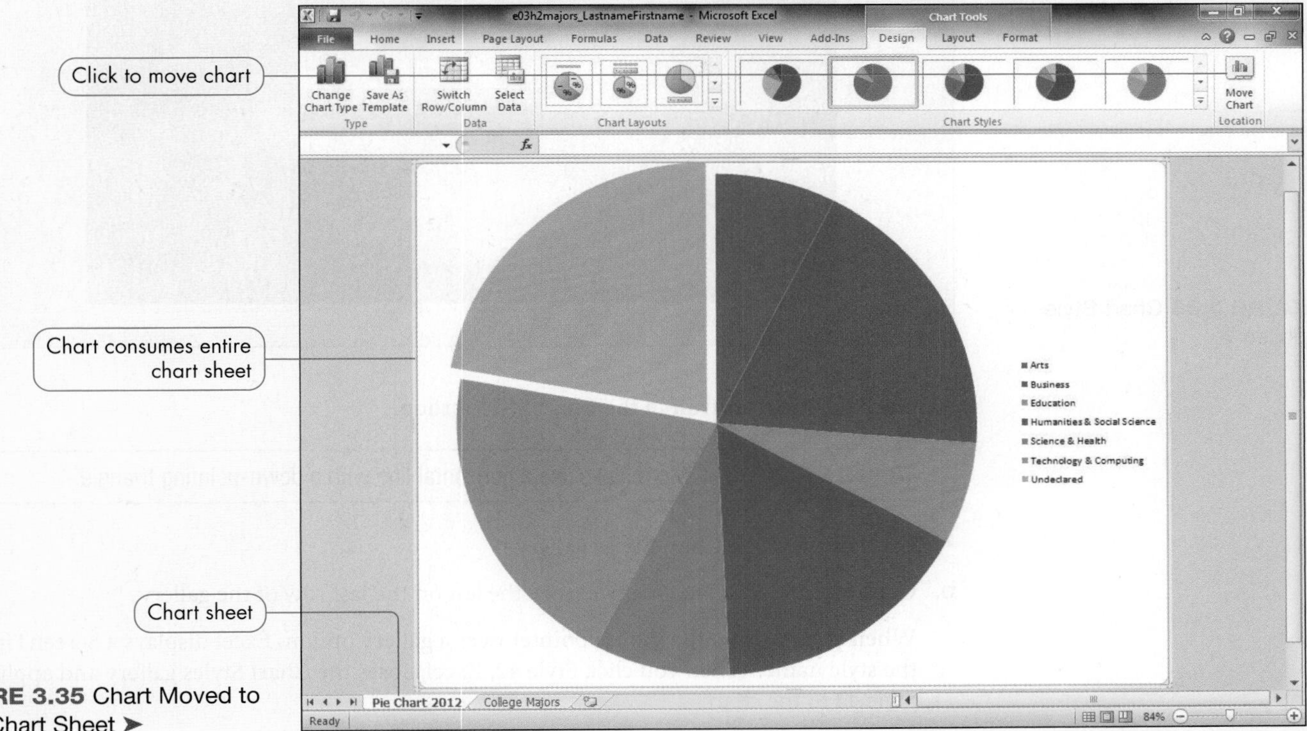

FIGURE 3.35 Chart Moved to New Chart Sheet ➤

a. Open *e03h1majors_LastnameFirstname* if you closed it at the end of Hands-On Exercise 1. Save the workbook with the new name **e03h2majors_LastnameFirstname**, changing *h1* to *h2*.

b. Click the outside border of the pie chart to select it.

c. Click the **Design tab**, and then click **Move Chart** in the Location group.

   The Move Chart dialog box opens so that you can specify a new or existing sheet to which to move the chart.

d. Click **New sheet**, type **Pie Chart 2012**, and then click **OK**. Save the workbook.

   Excel moves the pie chart out of the original worksheet, creates a new sheet named Pie Chart 2012, and inserts the chart on that sheet.

STEP 2 APPLY A CHART STYLE AND CHART LAYOUT

The pie chart looks a little flat, but you know that changing it to a 3-D pie chart could distort the data. A better solution is to apply an interesting chart style. In addition, you apply a layout to change the location of chart elements. Refer to Figure 3.36 as you complete Step 2.

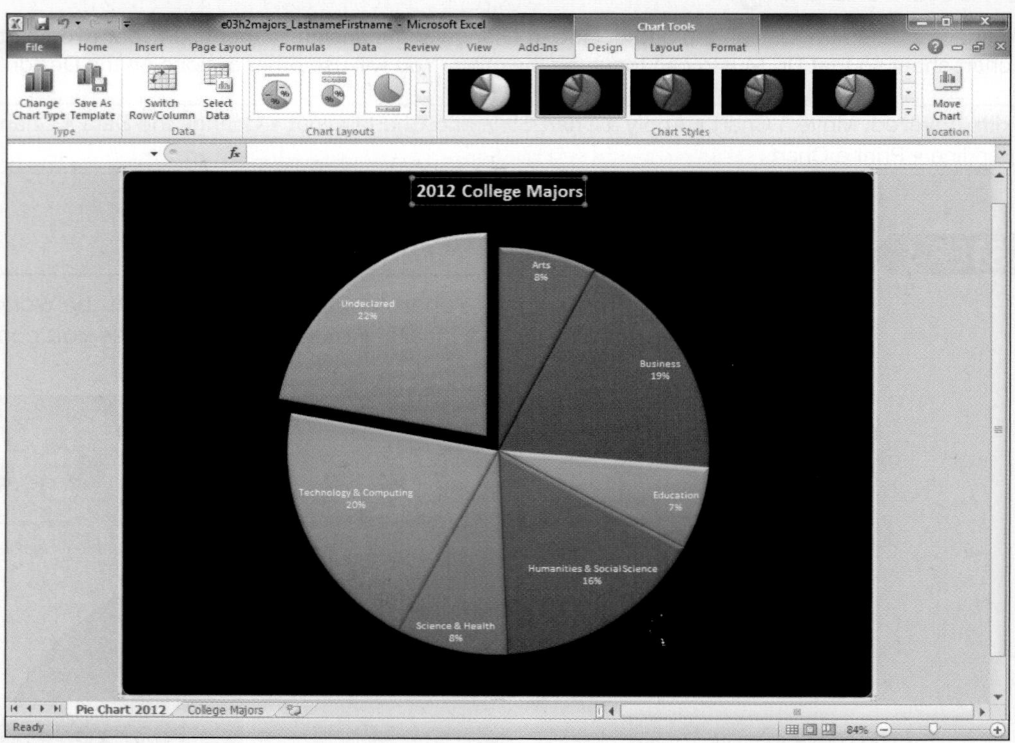

FIGURE 3.36 Chart Style Applied ➤

a. Click the **More button** in the Chart Styles group.

> **TROUBLESHOOTING:** More looks like a horizontal line with a down-pointing triangle.

Excel displays the Chart Styles gallery.

b. Click **Style 42**, the second style from the left on the last row of the gallery.

When you position the mouse pointer over a gallery option, Excel displays a ScreenTip with the style name. When you click Style 42, Excel closes the Chart Styles gallery and applies Style 42 to the chart.

c. Click **Layout 1** in the Chart Layouts group. Save the workbook.

Excel adds a Chart Title placeholder, removes the legend, and inserts the category labels and the respective percentages within the pie slices.

TIP Pie Chart Labels

The Layout 1 chart layout displays the category names and related percentages on the respective pie slices and removes the legend. This layout is helpful when a pie chart has more than four slices so that you do not have to match pie slice colors with the legend.

d. Click the **Chart Title placeholder**, type **2012 College Majors**, and then press **Enter**. Save the workbook.

> **TROUBLESHOOTING:** If you click inside the Chart Title placeholder instead of just the outer boundary of the placeholder, you may have to delete the placeholder text before typing the new title. Also, the text you type appears only in the Formula Bar until you press Enter. Then it appears in the chart title.

STEP 3 CHANGE THE DATA

You realize that the clustered column chart contains aggregated data (averages) along with the other data series. You need to remove the extra data before showing the chart to Dr. Musto. In addition, you notice that Excel placed the years in the legend and the colleges on the X-axis. Dr. Musto wants to be able to compare all majors for each year (that is, all majors for 2009, then all majors for 2010, and so on) instead of the change in Arts majors throughout the years. Refer to Figure 3.37 as you complete Step 3.

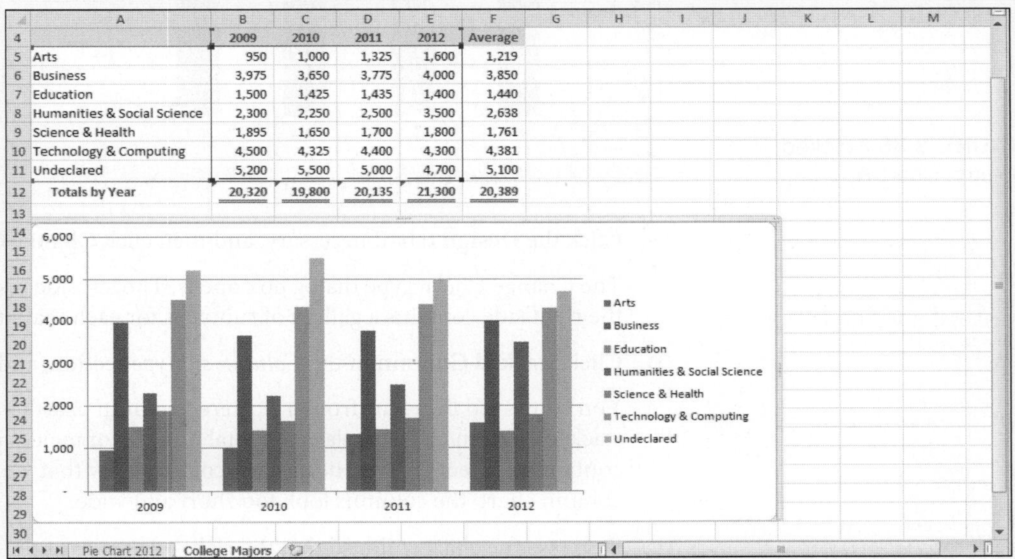

	2009	2010	2011	2012	Average
Arts	950	1,000	1,325	1,600	1,219
Business	3,975	3,650	3,775	4,000	3,850
Education	1,500	1,425	1,435	1,400	1,440
Humanities & Social Science	2,300	2,250	2,500	3,500	2,638
Science & Health	1,895	1,650	1,700	1,800	1,761
Technology & Computing	4,500	4,325	4,400	4,300	4,381
Undeclared	5,200	5,500	5,000	4,700	5,100
Totals by Year	20,320	19,800	20,135	21,300	20,389

FIGURE 3.37 Adjusted Data for Chart ➤

a. Click the **College Majors worksheet tab** to display the worksheet data and clustered column chart.

b. Click the clustered column chart to select it, and then click the **Design tab**, if necessary.

c. Click **Select Data** in the Data group.

The Select Data Source dialog box opens, and Excel selects the original data source in the worksheet.

d. Click **Average** in the **Legend Entries (Series) list.**

You need to remove the aggregated data.

e. Click **Remove**, and then click **OK**.

f. Click **Switch Row/Column** in the Data group.

Excel reverses the data series and category labels so that the years are category labels and the college data are data series and in the legend.

g. Drag the middle-right sizing handle to the right to the end of column J to widen the chart area. Save the workbook.

After reversing the rows and columns, the columns look tall and thin. You widened the chart area to make the columns appear better proportioned.

STEP 4 CHANGE THE CHART TYPE

Dr. Musto likes what you have done so far, but she would like the column chart to indicate total number of majors per year. You will change the chart to a stacked column chart. Refer to Figure 3.38 as you complete Step 4.

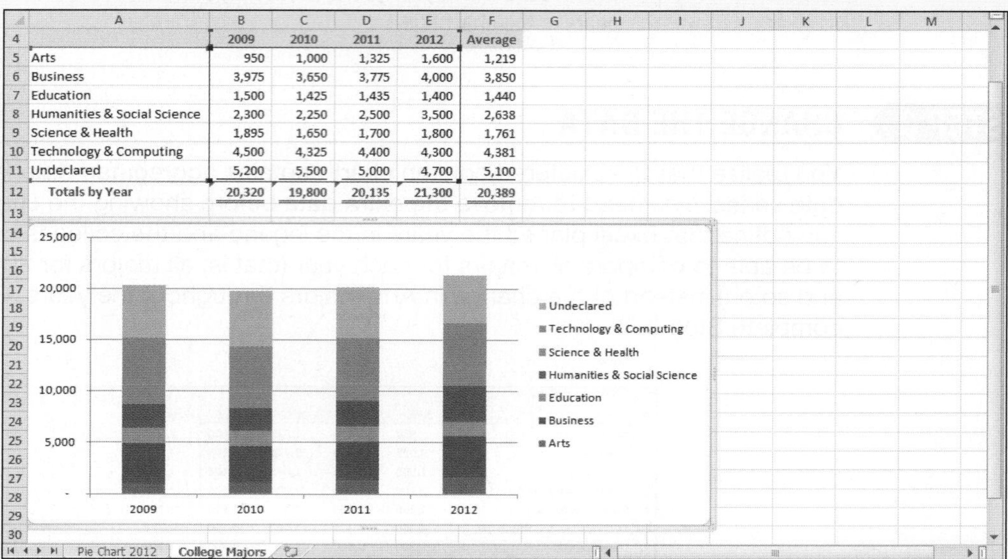

FIGURE 3.38 Stacked Column Chart ➤

a. Click the **Design tab**, if necessary, and then click **Change Chart Type** in the Type group.

   The Change Chart Type dialog box opens. The left side displays the main chart types, and the right side contains a gallery of subtypes for each main type.

b. Click **Stacked Column** in the *Column subtype* section, and then click **OK**.

   You converted the chart from a clustered column chart to a stacked column chart. The stacked column chart displays the total number of majors per year. Each yearly column contains segments representing each college. Now that you changed the chart to a stacked column chart, the columns look too short and wide.

c. Decrease the chart width so that the right edge ends at the end of column I. Save the workbook.

STEP 5 INSERT A SPARKLINE

You want to insert sparklines to show the enrollment trends for majors in each college at Hort University. After inserting the sparklines, you will display high points to stand out for Dr. Musto and other administrators who want a quick visual of the trends. Refer to Figure 3.39 as you complete Step 5.

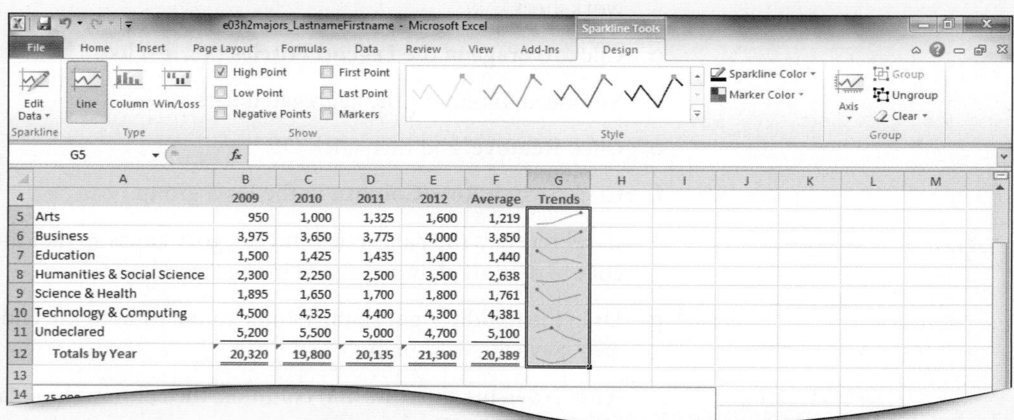

FIGURE 3.39 Sparklines Inserted to Show Trends ➤

a. Type **Trends** in **cell G4**, use **Format Painter** to apply the styles from **cell F4** to **cell G4**, and then click **cell G5**.

You entered a heading in the column above where you will insert the sparklines.

b. Click the **Insert tab**, and then click **Line** in the Sparklines group.

c. Select the **range B5:E12** to enter it in the **Data Range box**.

d. Press **Tab**, select the **range G5:G12** to enter it in the **Location Range box**, and then click **OK**.

Excel inserts sparklines in range G5:G12. Each sparkline depicts data for its row. The sparklines are still selected, and the Sparkline Tools Design contextual tab displays.

e. Click the **More button** in the Style group, and then click **Sparkline Style Colorful #4**, the fourth style on the last row of the gallery.

f. Click **High Point** in the Show group.

A marker appears for the high point of each data series for each Trendline. You want to change the marker color to stand out.

g. Click **Marker Color** in the Style group, point to **High Point**, and then click **Red** in the *Standard Colors* section. Save the workbook.

STEP 6 PRINT A CHART

Dr. Musto wants you to print the stacked column chart and the worksheet data for her as a reference for a meeting this afternoon. You want to preview the pie chart to see how it would look when printed as a full page.

a. Click **cell A4** to deselect the sparklines.

To print both the chart and the worksheet data, you must deselect the chart.

b. Click the **File tab**, and then click **Print**.

The Backstage view shows a preview that the worksheet data and the chart will print on one page.

c. Click **Print** if you or your instructor wants a printout.

d. Click the **Pie Chart 2012 worksheet tab**, click the **File tab**, click **Print** to preview the printout to ensure it would print on one page, and then click the **Home tab** to go back to the chart window.

e. Save the workbook. Keep the workbook onscreen if you plan to continue with Hands-On Exercise 3. If not, close the workbook and exit Excel.

Chart Layout

The Chart Tools Layout tab (see Figure 3.40) enables you to enhance your charts by selecting specific chart elements, inserting objects, displaying or removing chart elements, customizing the axes, formatting the background, and including analysis. When adding visual elements to a chart, make sure these elements enhance the effectiveness of the chart instead of overpowering it.

When adding visual elements to a chart, make sure these elements enhance the effectiveness of the chart instead of overpowering it.

Chart Elements command shows currently selected chart element, such as Chart Area

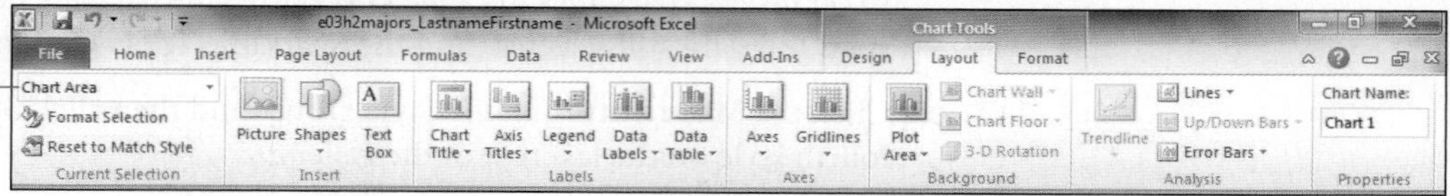

FIGURE 3.40 Chart Tools Layout Tab ➤

In this section, you will learn how to modify a chart by adjusting individual chart elements, such as the chart title and data labels. In addition, you will learn how to format chart elements, including applying fill colors to a data series.

Selecting and Formatting Chart Elements

A chart includes several elements—the chart area, the plot area, data series, the horizontal axis, the vertical axis, and the legend—each of which you can customize. When you position the mouse pointer over the chart, Excel displays a ScreenTip with the name of that chart element. To select a chart element, click it when you see the ScreenTip, or click the Chart Elements arrow in the Current Selection group, and then select the element from the list.

After you select a chart element, you can format it and change its settings. You can apply font settings, such as increasing the font size, from the Font group on the Home tab. You can format the values by applying a number style or by changing the number of decimal places on the value axis using the options in the Number group on the Home tab.

You can apply multiple settings at once using a Format dialog box, such as Format Data Series. To format the selected chart element, click Format Selection in the Current Selection group, or right-click the chart element, and then select Format *element* to display the appropriate dialog box (see Figure 3.41).

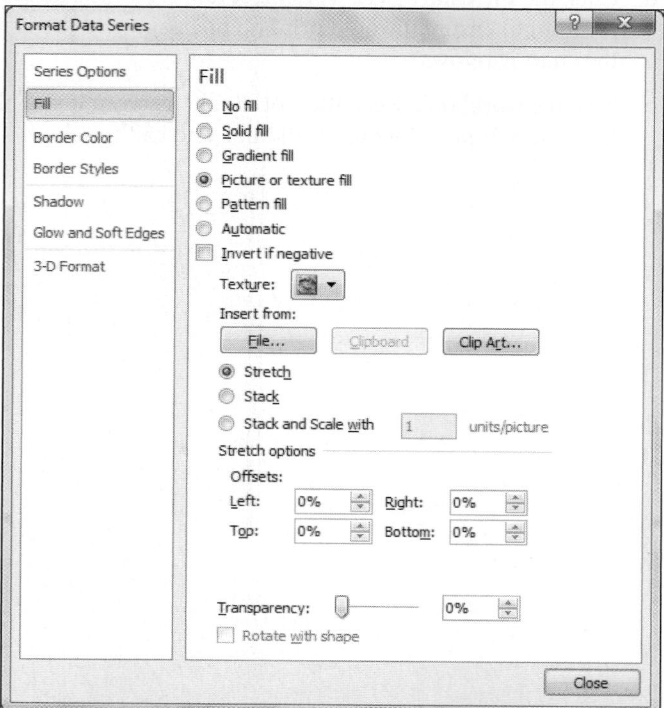

FIGURE 3.41 Format Data Series Dialog Box ➤

The left side of the dialog box lists major categories, such as Fill and Border Color. When you click a category, the right side of the dialog box displays specific options to customize the chart element. For example, when you select the Fill category, the right side displays fill options. When you click a specific option in the right side, such as *Picture or texture fill*, the dialog box displays additional fill options. You can use the Fill options to change the fill color of one or more data series. Avoid making a chart look busy with too many different colors. If you are changing the fill color of a chart area or plot area, make sure the color you select provides enough contrast with the other chart elements.

To format the plot area, click Plot Area in the Background group. Select None to remove any current plot area colors, select Show Plot Area to display the plot area, or select More Plot Area Options to open the Format Plot Area dialog box so that you can apply a fill color to the plot area, similar to selecting fill colors in the Format Data Series dialog box shown in Figure 3.41.

TIP Use Images or Textures

For less formal presentations, you might want to use images or a texture to fill the data series, chart area, or plot area instead of a solid fill color. To use an image or a texture, click *Picture or texture fill* in the Format Data Series dialog box. Click File or Clip Art in the *Insert from* section, and then insert an image file or search the Microsoft Web site to insert an image. Use the Stack option to avoid distorting the image. To add a texture, click Texture, and then select a textured background. Figure 3.42 shows a stacked image as the first data series fill, a texture fill for the second data series, and a gradient fill for the plot area. Generally, do not mix images and textures; in addition to illustrating different fill options, this figure also shows how adding too many features creates a distracting chart.

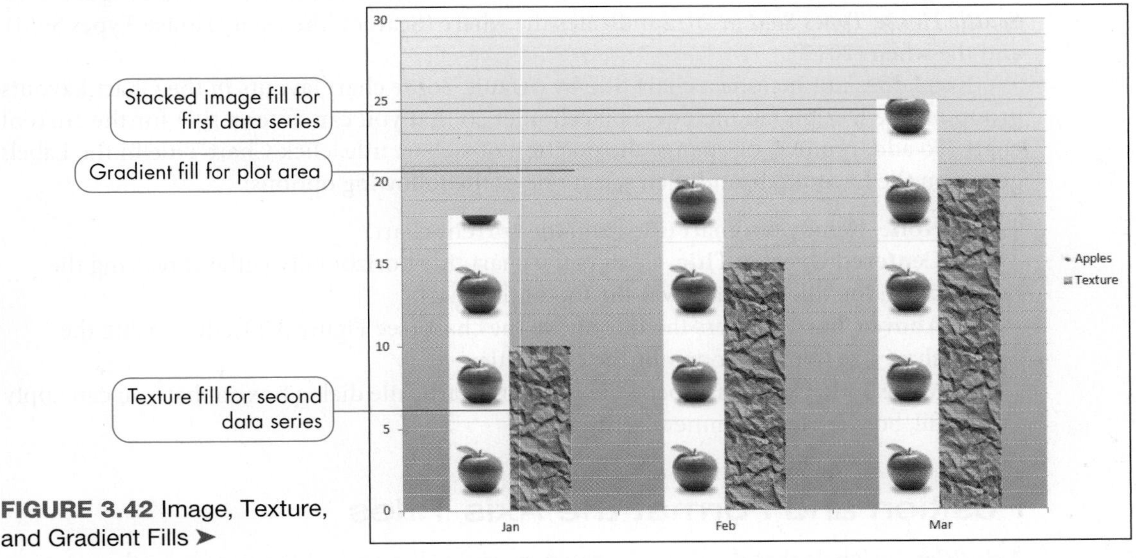

FIGURE 3.42 Image, Texture, and Gradient Fills ➤

Customizing Chart Labels

You should include appropriate labels to describe chart elements. The Chart Elements command in the Current Selection group on the Layout tab displays the name of the currently selected element, such as Chart Title, Vertical (Value Axis), Legend, etc. Figure 3.43 identifies basic chart labels.

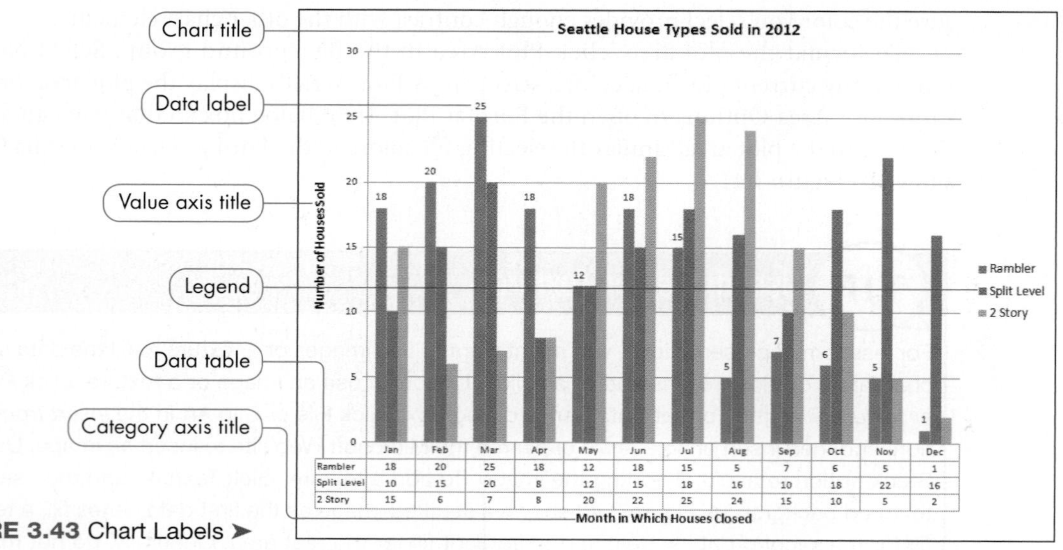

FIGURE 3.43 Chart Labels ➤

Insert and Format the Chart Title

A **chart title** is a label that describes the chart.

A ***chart title*** is the label that describes the entire chart. Chart titles should reflect the purpose of the chart. For example, *Houses Sold* would be too generic for the chart in Figure 3.43. *Seattle House Types Sold in 2012* indicates the where (Seattle), the what (House Types Sold), and the when (2012).

Excel does not include a chart title by default. Some chart layouts in the Chart Layouts group on the Design tab include a placeholder so that you can enter a title for the current chart. To add, remove, or change the position of a chart title, click Chart Title in the Labels group on the Layout tab, and then select one of the following options:

- **None.** Removes a chart title from the current chart.
- **Centered Overlay Title**. Centers the chart title horizontally without resizing the chart; the title appears over the top of the chart.
- **Above Chart.** Centers the title above the chart (see Figure 3.43), decreasing the chart size to make room for the chart title.
- **More Title Options.** Opens the Format Chart Title dialog box so that you can apply fill, border, and alignment settings.

Position and Format the Axis Titles

An **axis title** is a label that describes either the category axis or the value axis.

Axis titles are labels that describe the category and value axes. If the names on the category axis are not self-explanatory, you can add a label to describe it. The value axis often needs further explanation, such as *In Millions of Dollars* to describe the unit of measurement. To display category axis title options, click Axis Titles in the Labels group, point to Primary Horizontal Axis Title, and then select one of the following:

- **None**. Removes the horizontal axis title from the current chart.
- **Title Below Axis.** Displays the horizontal axis title below the category axis.
- **More Primary Horizontal Axis Title Options**. Opens the Format Axis Title dialog box so that you can apply fill, border, and alignment settings.

To display the value axis title options, click Axis Titles in the Labels group, point to Primary Vertical Axis Title, and then select one of the following:

- **None.** Removes the value axis title from the current chart.
- **Rotated Title.** Displays the value axis title on the left side of the value axis, rotated vertically. The chart in Figure 3.43 uses the Rotated Title setting.
- **Vertical Title.** Displays the vertical axis title on the left side of the value axis, with the letters in the title appearing vertically down the left edge.
- **Horizontal Title.** Displays the vertical axis title on the left side of the value axis; the title consumes more horizontal space.
- **More Primary Vertical Axis Title Options.** Opens the Format Axis Title dialog box so that you can apply fill, border, and alignment settings.

Customize the Legend

When you create a multiple series chart, the legend appears on the right side of the plot area (see Figure 3.43). Click Legend in the Labels group on the Layout tab to change the location of the legend or overlay the legend on either the left or right side of the plot area. Select More Legend Options from the Legend menu to open the Format Legend dialog box so that you can apply a background fill color, display a border around the legend, select a border color or line style, and apply a shadow effect. Remove the legend if it duplicates data found elsewhere in the chart.

Insert and Format Data Labels

A **data label** is the value or name of a data point.

Data labels are descriptive labels that show the exact value of the data points on the value axis. The chart in Figure 3.43 displays data labels for the Rambler data series. Only add data labels when they are necessary for a specific data series; adding data labels for every data point will clutter the chart.

When you select a data label, Excel selects all data labels in that data series. To format the labels, click Format Selection in the Current Selection group, or right-click and select Format Data Labels to open the Format Data Labels dialog box (see Figure 3.44).

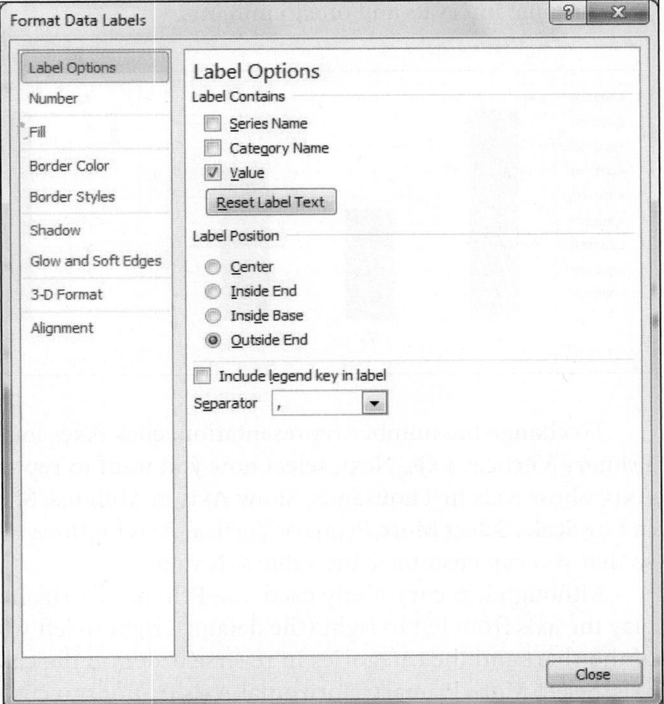

FIGURE 3.44 Format Data Labels Dialog Box ➤

The Format Data Labels dialog box enables you to specify what to display as the label. The default Label Contains setting displays values, but you can display additional data such as the category name. Displaying additional data can clutter the chart. You can also specify the position of the label, such as Center or Outside End. If the numeric data labels are not formatted, click Number on the left side of the dialog box, and then apply number formats.

TIP Pie Chart Data Labels

When you first create a pie chart, Excel generates a legend to identify the category labels for the different slice colors, but it does not display data labels. You can display values, percentages, and even category labels on or next to each slice. Pie charts often include percentage data labels. If you also include category labels, hide the legend to avoid duplicating elements.

Include and Format a Data Table

A data table is a grid that contains the data source values and labels. If you embed a chart on the same worksheet as the data source, you do not need to include a data table. Only add a data table with a chart to a chart sheet if you need the audience to know the exact values.

To display a data table, click Data Table in the Labels group, and then select Show Data Table. Figure 3.43 shows a data table at the bottom of the chart area. To see the color-coding along with the category labels, select Show Data Table with Legend Keys, which enables you to omit the legend.

Formatting the Axes and Gridlines

Based on the data source values and structure, Excel determines the starting, incremental, and stopping values that display on the value axis when you create the chart. You might want to adjust the value axis. For example, when working with large values such as 4,567,890, the value axis displays increments, such as 4,000,000 and 5,000,000. You can simplify the value axis by displaying values in millions, so that the values on the axis are 4 and 5 with the word *Millions* placed by the value axis to indicate the units. Figure 3.45 shows two charts—one with original intervals and one in millions.

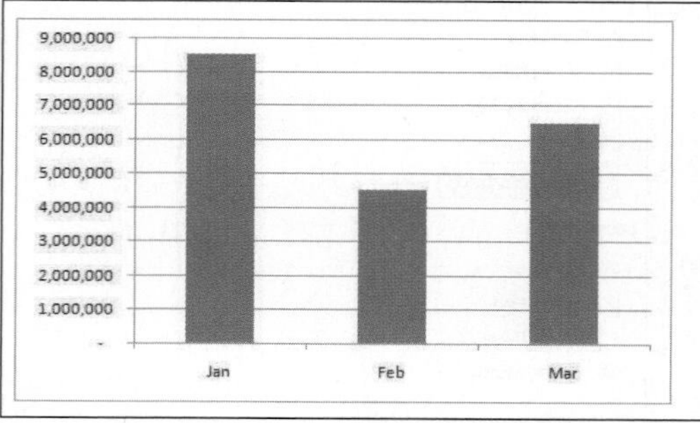

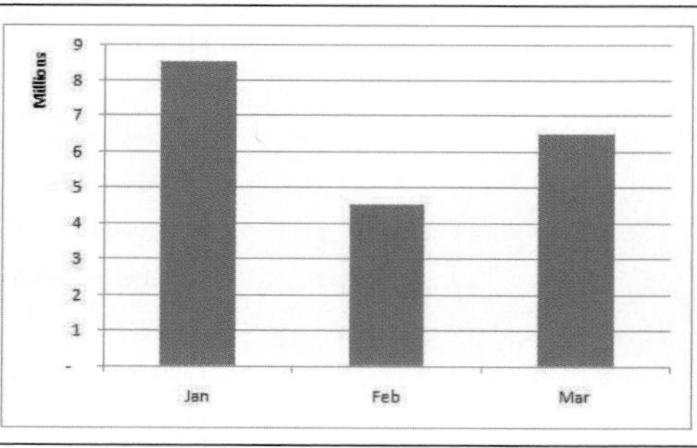

FIGURE 3.45 Value Axis Scaling ➤

To change the number representation, click Axes in the Axes group, and then point to Primary Vertical Axis. Next, select how you want to represent the value axis: Show Default Axis, Show Axis in Thousands, Show Axis in Millions, Show Axis in Billions, or Show Axis in Log Scale. Select More Primary Vertical Axis Options to open the Format Axis dialog box so that you can customize the value axis values.

Although less commonly used, the Primary Horizontal Axis menu enables you to display the axis from left to right (the default), right to left with the value axis on the right side of the chart and the categories in reverse order on the category axis, or without a category axis. Select More Primary Horizontal Axis Options to customize the horizontal axis.

A **gridline** is a horizontal or vertical line that extends from the horizontal or vertical axis through the plot area.

Gridlines are horizontal or vertical lines that span across the chart to help people identify the values plotted by the visual elements, such as a column. Excel displays horizontal gridlines for column, line, scatter, stock, surface, and bubble charts and vertical gridlines for bar charts. If you do not want to display gridlines in a chart, click Gridlines in the Axes group, point to either Primary Horizontal Gridlines or Primary Vertical Gridlines, and then select None. To add more gridlines, select Minor Gridlines or Major & Minor Gridlines.

Adding a Trendline

A **trendline** is a line used to depict trends and forecast future data.

Charts help reveal trends, patterns, and other tendencies that are difficult to identify by looking at values in a worksheet. A ***trendline*** is a line that depicts trends or helps forecast future data. Trendlines are commonly used in prediction, such as to determine the future trends of sales, or the success rate of a new prescription drug. You can use trendlines in unstacked column, bar, line, stock, scatter, and bubble charts. To add a trendline, click Trendline in the Analysis group, and then select the type you want: Linear Trendline, Exponential Trendline, Linear Forecast Trendline, or Two Period Moving Average. Figure 3.46 shows two linear forecast trendlines, one applied to the Business data series and one applied to the Undeclared data series. Notice that this trendline provides a forecast (prediction) for two additional time periods—2013 and 2014—although the years are not depicted on the X-axis. Excel analyzes the plotted data to forecast values for the next two time periods when you select the Linear Forecast Trendline. If you apply Linear Trendline only, Excel displays the trendline for the data but does not forecast data points for the future.

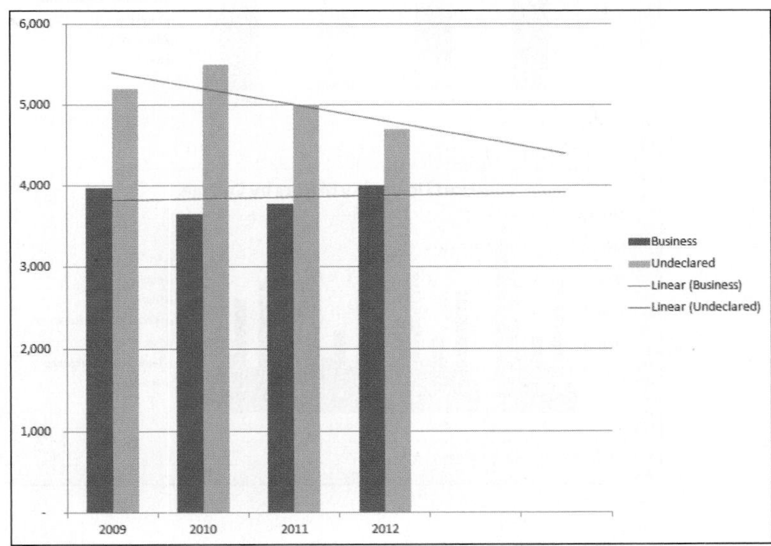

FIGURE 3.46 Trendlines ➤

Quick Concepts Check

1. What can you do if you do not like the default fill color of a data series in a column chart?
2. List at least four types of appropriate labels that describe chart elements. What types of things can you do to customize these labels?
3. What is a trendline?

HANDS-ON EXERCISES

3 Chart Layout

You want to enhance the column chart by using some options on the Layout tab to add the final touches needed before you give the charts to Dr. Musto to review.

Skills covered: Add a Chart Title • Add and Format Axis Titles • Add Data Labels • Apply Fill Colors • Insert a Trendline

STEP 1 ADD A CHART TITLE

When you applied a chart layout to the pie chart, Excel displayed a placeholder for the chart title. However, you need to add a chart title for the column chart. You also want to copy the chart and modify it so that you can provide two different perspectives for Dr. Musto. Refer to Figure 3.47 as you complete Step 1.

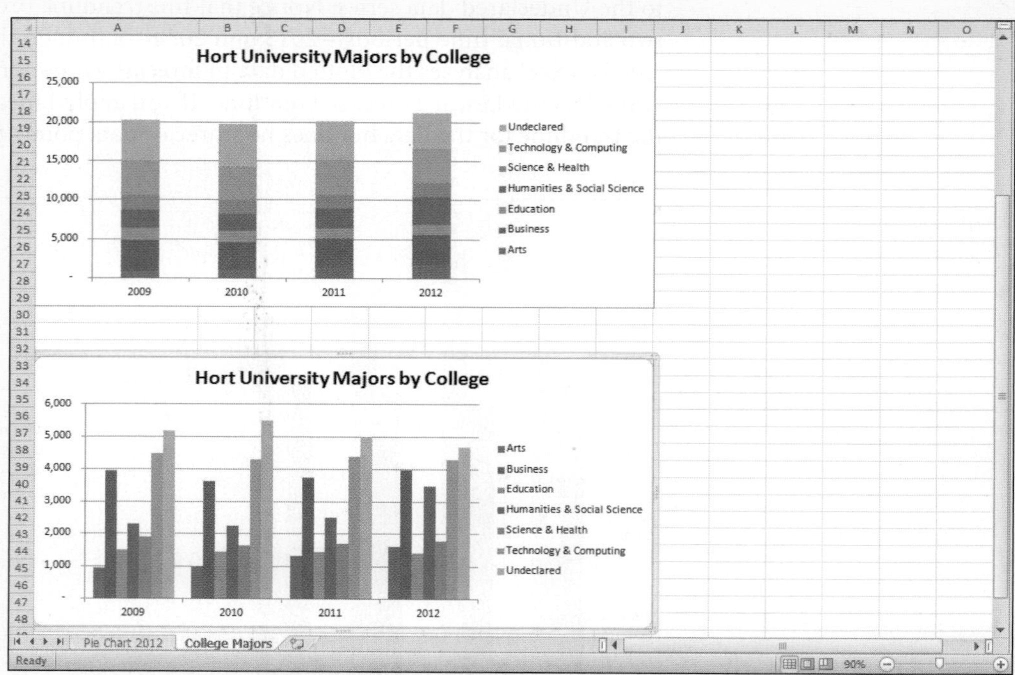

FIGURE 3.47 Charts with Titles ➤

a. Open *e03h2majors_LastnameFirstname* if you closed it at the end of Hands-On Exercise 2. Save the workbook with the new name **e03h3majors_LastnameFirstname**, changing *h2* to *h3*.

b. Click the stacked column chart to select it.

c. Click the **Layout tab**, click **Chart Title** in the Labels group, and then select **Above Chart**.

   Excel displays the Chart Title placeholder, and the plot area decreases to make room for the chart title.

d. Type **Hort University Majors by College** and press **Enter**.

e. Click the **Chart Elements arrow** in the Current Selection group (which currently displays *Chart Title*), and then select **Chart Area**.

   You selected the entire chart area so that you can copy it.

f. Press **Ctrl+C**, click **cell A33**, and then press **Ctrl+V** to paste the top-left corner of the chart here. Change the second chart to a **Clustered Column chart**. Save the workbook.

STEP 2 ADD AND FORMAT AXIS TITLES

You decide to add an axis title to the value axis to clarify the values in the clustered column chart. For the stacked column chart, you want to change the value axis increments. Refer to Figure 3.48 as you complete Step 2.

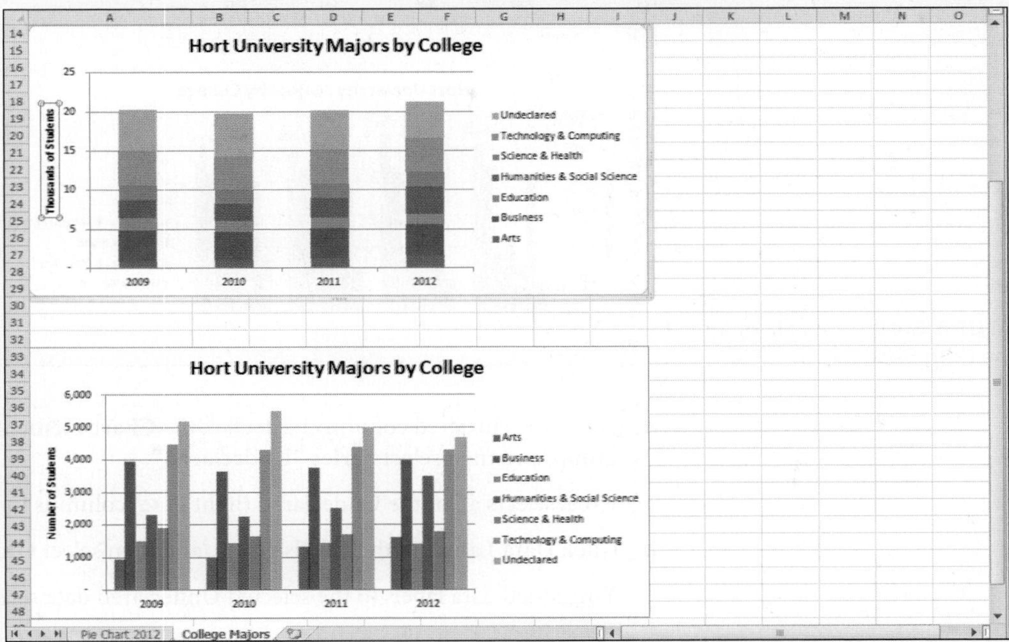

FIGURE 3.48 Axis Titles and Values Changed ➤

a. Make sure the clustered column chart is selected, and then use the scroll bars if necessary to view the entire chart.

b. Click the **Layout tab**, click **Axis Titles** in the Labels group, point to **Primary Vertical Axis Title**, and then select **Rotated Title**.

Excel inserts the Axis Title placeholder on the left side of the value axis.

c. Type **Number of Students** and press **Enter**.

The text you typed replaces the placeholder text after you press Enter.

d. Select the stacked column chart, click the **Layout tab** (if necessary), click **Axes** in the Axes group, point to **Primary Vertical Axis**, and then select **Show Axis in Thousands**.

Excel changes the value axis values to thousands and includes the label *Thousands* to the left side of the value axis.

e. Click **Thousands** to select it, type **Thousands of Students**, and then press **Enter**.

f. Drag the **Thousands of Students label** down to appear vertically centered with the value axis increments. Save the workbook.

STEP 3 ADD DATA LABELS

Dr. Musto wants you to emphasize the Undeclared majors data series by adding data labels for that data series. You will have to be careful to add data labels for only the Undeclared data series, as adding data labels for all data series would clutter the chart. Refer to Figure 3.49 as you complete Step 3.

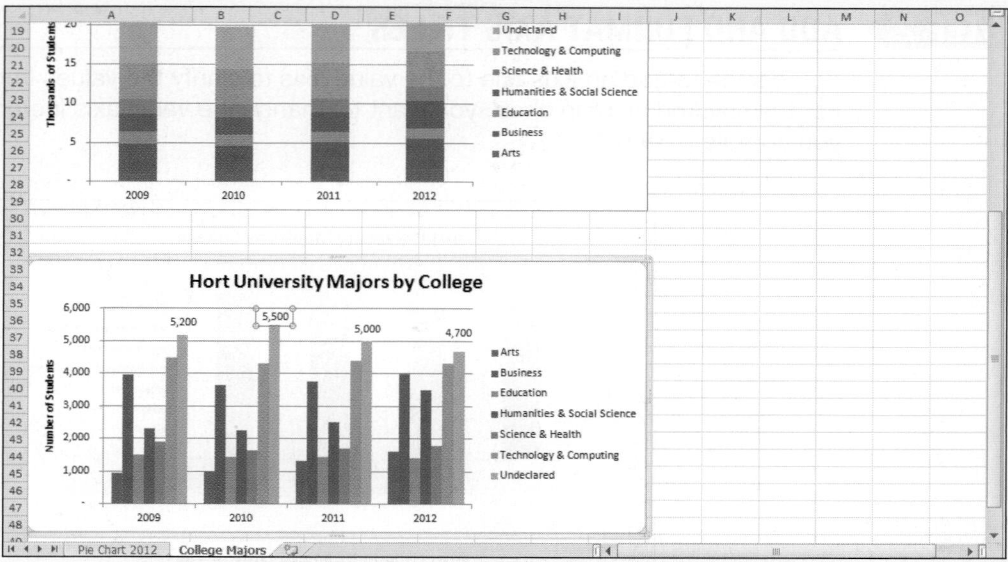

FIGURE 3.49 Data Labels for One Data Series ➤

a. Select the clustered column chart, click the **Chart Elements arrow** in the Current Selection group, and then select **Series "Undeclared"**.

   Excel selects all of the Undeclared (light blue) columns in the chart.

b. Click **Data Labels** in the Labels group, and then select **Outside End**.

   You added data labels to the selected Undeclared data series.

> **TROUBLESHOOTING:** If data labels appear for all columns, use the Undo feature. Make sure you select only the Undeclared data series columns, and then add data labels again.

c. Look at the data labels to see if they are on gridlines.

   The 4,700 and 5,500 data labels are on gridlines.

d. Click the **4,700 data label** twice, pausing between clicks.

   Only the 4,700 data label should be selected.

> **TROUBLESHOOTING:** If you double-click a data label instead of pausing between individual clicks, the Format Data Labels dialog box appears. If this happens, click Close in the dialog box, and then repeat step d, pausing longer between clicks.

e. Click the outer edge of the **4,700 data label border**, and then drag the label up a little so that it is off the gridline.

f. Select the **5,500 data label**, and then drag it below the top gridline. Save the workbook.

STEP 4 APPLY FILL COLORS

Dr. Musto wants the Business data series color to stand out, so you will apply a brighter red fill to that series. In addition, you want to apply a gradient color to the plot area so that the chart stands out from the rest of the page. Refer to Figure 3.50 as you complete Step 4.

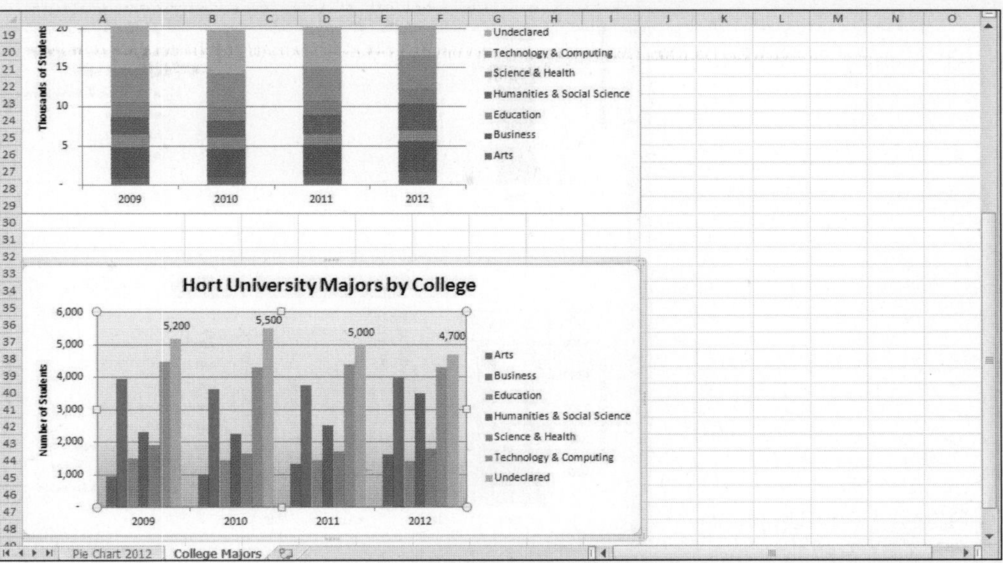

FIGURE 3.50 Chart with Different Fill Colors ➤

a. Make sure the clustered column chart is still selected, click the **Chart Elements arrow** in the Current Selection group, and then select **Series "Business"** or click one of the **Business columns**.

   The Business data series columns are selected.

b. Click **Format Selection** in the Current Selection group.

   The Format Data Series dialog box opens so that you can format the Business data series.

c. Click **Fill** on the left side of the dialog box, and then click **Solid fill**.

   The dialog box displays additional fill options.

d. Click **Color**, click **Red** in the *Standard Colors* section of the gallery, and then click **Close**.

   The Business data series appears in red.

e. Click **Plot Area** in the Background group, and then select **More Plot Area Options**.

   The Format Plot Area dialog box opens.

f. Click **Gradient fill**, click **Preset colors**, click **Parchment** (using the ScreenTips to help you find the correct preset color), and then click **Close**.

   Be careful when selecting plot area colors to ensure that the data series columns, bars, or lines still stand out. Print a sample on a color printer to help make the decision.

STEP 5 ➤ INSERT A TRENDLINE

Identifying trends is important when planning college budgets. Colleges with growing enrollments need additional funding to support more students. It looks like the numbers of humanities and social science majors are increasing, but you want to add a trendline to verify your analysis. Refer to Figure 3.51 as you complete Step 5.

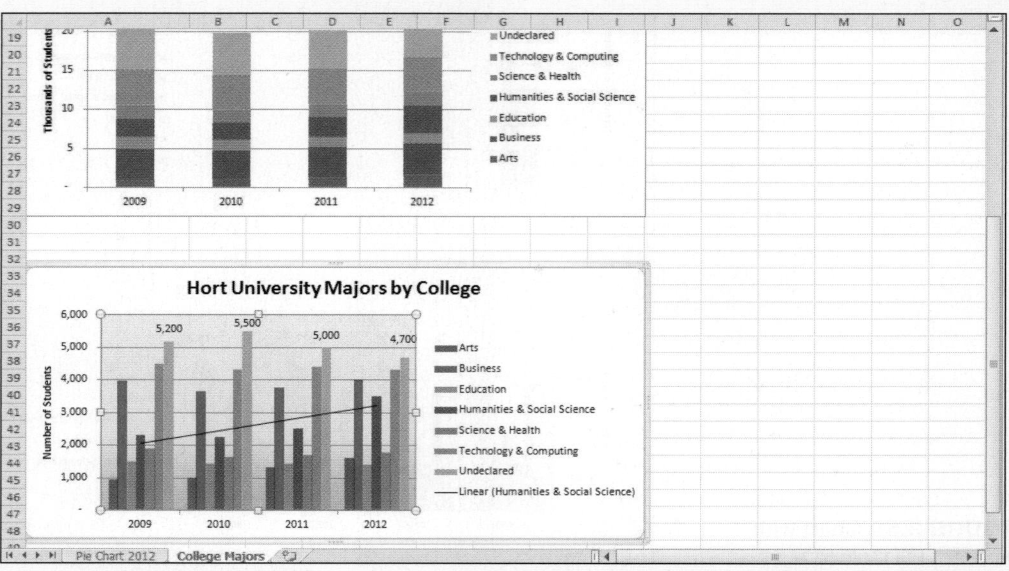

FIGURE 3.51 Trendline ➤

a. Make sure the clustered column chart is still selected.

b. Click **Trendline** in the Analysis group, and then select **Linear Trendline**.

The Add Trendline dialog box opens so that you can select which data series you want to use for the trendline.

c. Click **Humanities & Social Science**, and then click **OK**.

Excel adds a trendline based on the data series you specified. The trend is a steady increase in the number of majors in this discipline.

d. Save and close the workbook, and submit based on your instructor's directions.

CHAPTER OBJECTIVES REVIEW

After reading this chapter, you have accomplished the following objectives:

1. **Decide which chart type to create.** Choose a chart type that will present the data in a way that communicates the message effectively to your audience. Column charts compare categorical data, bar charts compare categorical data horizontally, line charts illustrate trends over time, and pie charts show proportions to the whole. Variations of each major chart type are called *subtypes*.
2. **Create a chart.** The first step in creating a chart is to identify and select the range of cells that will be used as the data source. Be careful to select similar data series to avoid distorting the chart. After selecting the data source, click the desired chart type on the Insert tab. Excel inserts charts on the same worksheet as the data. You can move the chart and adjust the size of the chart area. When you create a chart or select an existing chart, Excel displays the Chart Tools contextual tab with three tabs: Design, Layout, and Format.
3. **Change the chart type.** You can change a chart to a different chart type if you believe a different chart type will represent the data better.
4. **Change the data source and structure.** You can add or remove data from the data source to change the data in the chart. The Select Data Source dialog box enables you to modify the ranges used for the data series. Excel usually places the first column of data as the category axis and the first row of data as the legend, but you can switch the row and column layout. The Design tab contains options for changing the data source and structure.
5. **Apply a chart layout and a chart style.** You can apply a chart layout to control what chart elements are included and where they are positioned within the chart area. You can apply a chart style, which determines formatting, such as the background color and the data series color. The Design tab contains options for selecting the chart layout and chart style.
6. **Move a chart.** You can position a chart on the same worksheet as the data source, or you can move the chart to its own sheet. The Move Chart dialog box enables you to select a new sheet and name the new chart sheet at the same time. The chart sheet will then contain a full-sized chart and no data. You can also move a chart to an existing worksheet. When you do this, the chart is an embedded object on that sheet, and the sheet may contain other data.
7. **Print charts.** You can print a chart with or without its corresponding data source. To print a chart with its data series, the chart needs to be on the same worksheet as the data source. To ensure both the data and the chart print, make sure the chart is not selected. If the chart is on its own sheet or if you select the chart on a worksheet containing other data, the chart will print as a full-sized chart.
8. **Insert and customize a sparkline.** A sparkline is a miniature chart in one cell representing a single data series. It gives a quick visual of the data to aid in comprehension. You can customize sparklines by changing the data source, location, and style. In addition, you can display markers, such as High Point, and change the line or marker color.
9. **Select and format chart elements.** Because each chart element is an individual object in the chart area, you can select and format each element separately. The Format dialog boxes enable you to apply fill colors, select border colors, and apply other settings. For the value axis, you can format values and specify the number of decimal places to display. For basic formatting, such as font color, use the options in the Font group on the Home tab.
10. **Customize chart labels.** The Labels group on the Layout tab enables you to add or remove chart elements: chart title, axis titles, legend, data labels, and a data table. The chart title should clearly describe the data and purpose of the chart. Include axis titles when you need to clarify the values on the value axis or the categories on the category axis. Customize the legend when you want to change its position within the chart area or hide the legend. Display data labels to provide exact values for data points in one or more data series; however, be careful the data labels do not overlap. If a chart is contained on a chart sheet, you might want to show the data table that contains the values used from the data source.
11. **Format the axes and gridlines.** The Axes group on the Layout tab enables you to control the horizontal and vertical axes. You can select the minimum, maximum, and increments on the value axis, and you can display both major and minor gridlines to help your audience read across the plot area.
12. **Add a trendline.** A trendline is a line that depicts trends. Trendlines are used to help make predictions or forecasts based on the current dataset. Excel enables you to select different types of trendlines based on the type of statistical analysis you want to perform.

KEY TERMS

100% stacked column chart ***p.453***
3-D chart ***p.454***
Area chart ***p.456***
Axis title ***p.482***
Bar chart ***p.455***
Bubble chart ***p.459***
Category axis ***p.451***
Category label ***p.450***
Chart ***p.450***
Chart area ***p.451***
Chart sheet ***p.462***
Chart title ***p.482***
Clustered column chart ***p.451***
Column chart ***p.451***
Data label ***p.483***
Data point ***p.450***
Data series ***p.450***
Doughnut chart ***p.459***
Exploded pie chart ***p.456***
Gridline ***p.485***
Legend ***p.452***
Line chart ***p.455***
Multiple data series ***p.451***
Pie chart ***p.456***
Plot area ***p.451***
Radar chart ***p.460***
Single data series ***p.451***
Sizing handle ***p.463***
Sparkline ***p.473***
Stacked column chart ***p.452***
Stock chart ***p.458***
Surface chart ***p.458***
Trendline ***p.485***
Value axis ***p.451***
X Y (scatter) chart ***p.457***
X-axis ***p.451***
Y-axis ***p.451***

MULTIPLE CHOICE

1. Which type of chart is the **least** appropriate for depicting yearly rainfall totals for five cities for four years?
   (a) Pie chart
   (b) Line chart
   (c) Column chart
   (d) Bar chart

2. What is the typical sequence for creating a chart?
   (a) Select the chart type, select the data source, and then size and position the chart.
   (b) Select the data source, size the chart, select the chart type, and then position the chart.
   (c) Select the data source, select the chart type, and then size and position the chart.
   (d) Click the cell to contain the chart, select the chart type, and then select the data source.

3. Which of the following applies to a sparkline?
   (a) Chart title
   (b) Single-cell chart
   (c) Legend
   (d) Multiple data series

4. If you want to show exact values for a data series in a bar chart, what chart element should you display?
   (a) Chart title
   (b) Legend
   (c) Value axis title
   (d) Data labels

5. The value axis currently shows increments such as 50,000 and 100,000. What do you select to display increments of 50 and 100?
   (a) More Primary Vertical Axis Title Options
   (b) Show Axis in Thousands
   (c) Show Axis in Millions
   (d) Show Right to Left Axis

6. You want to create a single chart that shows each of five divisions' proportion of yearly sales for each year for five years. Which type of chart can accommodate your needs?
   (a) Pie chart
   (b) Surface chart
   (c) Clustered bar chart
   (d) 100% stacked column chart

7. Currently, a column chart shows values on the value axis, years on the category axis, and state names in the legend. What should you do if you want to organize data with the states on the category axis and the years shown in the legend?
   (a) Change the chart type to a clustered column chart.
   (b) Click Switch Row/Column in the Data group on the Design tab.
   (c) Click Layout 2 in the Chart Layouts group on the Design tab, and then apply a different chart style.
   (d) Click Legend in the Labels group on the Layout tab, and then select Show Legend at Bottom.

8. Which tab contains commands to apply a predefined chart layout that controls what elements are included, where, and their color scheme?
   (a) Design
   (b) Layout
   (c) Format
   (d) Page Layout

9. A chart and its related data source are located on the same worksheet. What is the default Print option if the chart is selected prior to displaying the Backstage view?
   (a) Print Entire Workbook
   (b) Print Selection
   (c) Print Selected Chart
   (d) Print Active Sheets

10. Which of the following is *not* a way to display the Format Data Series dialog box for the Arts data series in a column chart?
   (a) Press and hold Shift as you click each Arts column.
   (b) Click an Arts column, and then click Format Selection in the Current Selection group on the Layout tab.
   (c) Right-click an Arts column, and then select Format Data Series.
   (d) Click the Chart Elements arrow in the Current Selection group, select the Arts data series, and then click Format Selection in the Current Selection group on the Layout tab.

PRACTICE EXERCISES

1 Family Utility Expenses

Your cousin, Rita Dansie, wants to analyze her family's utility expenses for 2012. She wants to save money during months when utility expenses are lower so that her family will have money budgeted for months when the total utility expenses are higher. She gave you her files for the electric, gas, and water bills for the year 2012. You created a worksheet that lists the individual expenses per month, along with yearly totals per utility type and monthly totals. You will create some charts to depict the data. This exercise follows the same set of skills as used in Hands-On Exercises 1 and 2 in the chapter. Refer to Figure 3.52 as you complete this exercise.

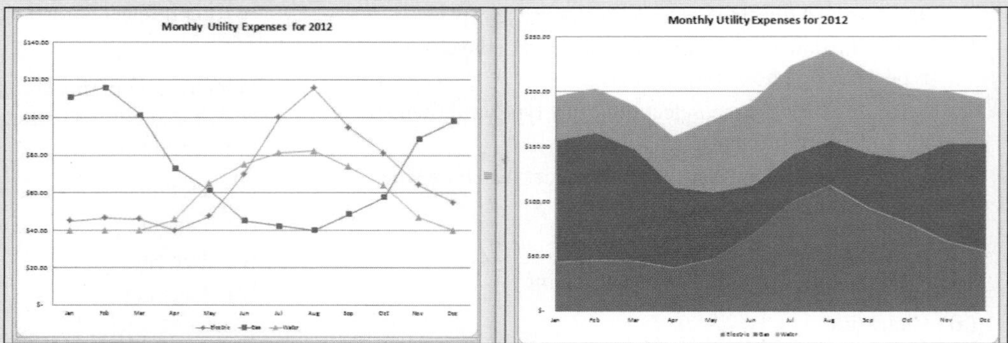

FIGURE 3.52 Dansie Family Utility Expenses ➤

a. Open *e03p1utilities* and save it as **e03p1utilities_LastnameFirstname**.
b. Select the **range A4:E17**, and then click the **Insert tab**.
c. Click **Column** in the Charts group, and then select **Clustered Column**. After creating the chart, you realize you need to adjust the data source because you included the monthly and yearly totals.
d. Click the **Design tab**, if necessary. Click **Select Data** in the Data group to open the Select Data Source dialog box, and then do the following:
   - Click **Monthly Totals** in the **Legend Entries (Series) list**, and then click **Remove**.
   - Click in the **Chart data range box**, and then change *17* to **16** at the end of the range.
   - Click **OK** to finalize removing the monthly and yearly totals from the chart.
e. Position the mouse pointer over the chart area. When you see the Chart Area ScreenTip, drag the chart so that the top-left edge of the chart is in **cell A19**.
f. Click the **Format tab**. Click in the **Shape Width box** in the Size group, type **6**, and then press **Enter**.
g. Click the **Design tab**, and then click **Layout 3** in the Chart Layouts group.
h. Click the **Chart Title placeholder**, type **Monthly Utility Expenses for 2012**, and then press **Enter**.
i. Click the **More button** in the Chart Styles group, and then click **Style 26** (second style, fourth row).
j. Click the clustered column chart, use the **Copy command**, and then paste a copy of the chart in **cell A36**. With the second chart selected, do the following:
   - Click the **Design tab**, click **Change Chart Type** in the Type group, select **Line with Markers** in the *Line* section, and then click **OK**.
   - Click the **More button** in the Chart Styles group, and then click **Style 2** (second style, first row).
   - Copy the selected chart, and then paste it in **cell A52**.
k. Make sure the third chart is selected, and then do the following:
   - Click the **Design tab**, if necessary, click **Change Chart Type** in the Type group, select **Area** on the left side, click **Stacked Area**, and then click **OK**.
   - Click **Move Chart** in the Location group, click **New sheet**, type **Area Chart**, and then click **OK**.
l. Click the **Expenses worksheet tab**, scroll up to see the line chart, and then select the line chart. Click the **Design tab**, if necessary, click **Move Chart** in the Location group, click **New sheet**, type **Line Chart**, and then click **OK**.

m. Create a footer with your name on the left side, the sheet name code in the center, and the file name code on the right side on the worksheet and on the two chart sheets.

n. Click the **File tab**, and then click **Print**. Look at the preview window for each worksheet. Print all three worksheets for your reference, based on your instructor's directions.

o. Save and close the workbook, and submit based on your instructor's directions.

2 Florida Population by Age and Sex

As a consultant for major corporations in Florida, you provide demographic data to managers to help them determine how to market their products to the population. Marketing professionals often look at demographics, such as age distributions and the male-to-female ratio, when developing marketing campaigns. For example, if a state's population is predominately females from 45–64 years old, a company would market products differently from a state that is predominately males from 25–44 years old. This exercise follows the same set of skills as used in Hands-On Exercises 1–3 in the chapter. Refer to Figure 3.53 as you complete this exercise.

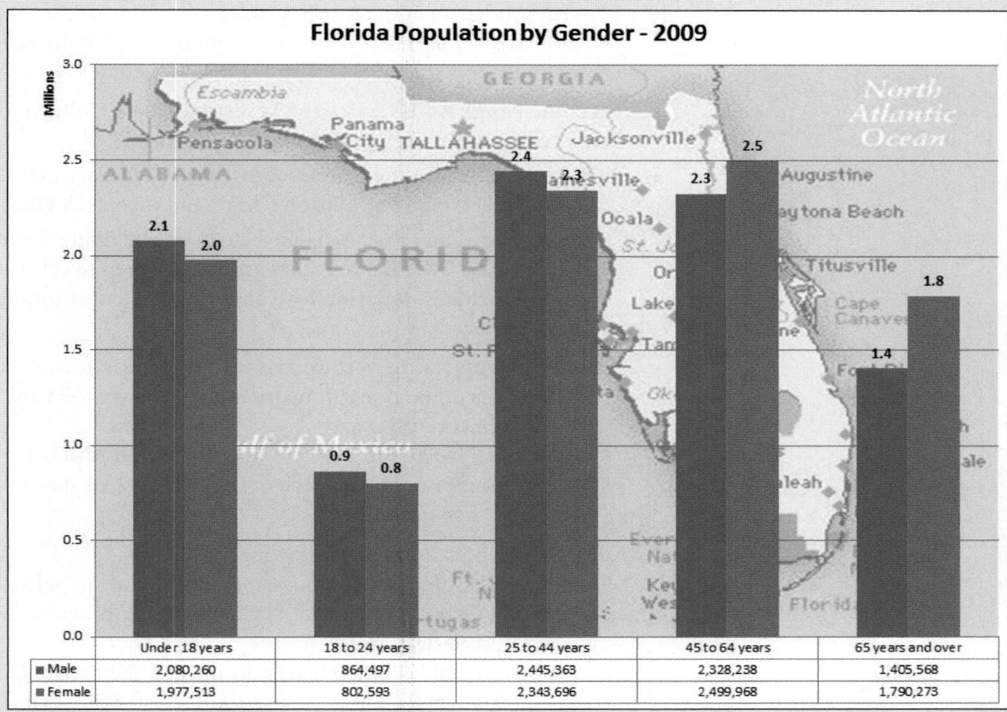

	Under 18 years	18 to 24 years	25 to 44 years	45 to 64 years	65 years and over
■ Male	2,080,260	864,497	2,445,363	2,328,238	1,405,568
■ Female	1,977,513	802,593	2,343,696	2,499,968	1,790,273

FIGURE 3.53 Florida Data ➤

a. Open a Web browser and go to **www.census.gov/popest/states/**. Click the **State estimates by demographic characteristics link**, click the **Median Age and Age by Sex link**, click the **Excel link** for Florida, and then click **Open** or **OK** to open the dataset in Excel. Click **Enable Editing.**

> **TROUBLESHOOTING:** If your data differs, the ranges you need to select may be in different rows. Use the labels as a guide to selecting the correct ranges and adapt the exercise as necessary.

b. Copy age group labels and data for the latest year posted from the downloaded dataset to a new workbook by doing the following:
   - Scroll through the dataset to find the *MALE* section. Select the **range A60:B60**, the label **Under 18 years**, and the population data for the latest year. Click **Copy**. Start a new workbook, click **cell A5**, and then click **Paste**. Type **Male** in **cell B4**. Save the workbook as **e03p2florida_LastnameFirstname**.
   - Make the downloaded dataset active, select the **range A65:B68**, which includes labels and data for age groups 18 years and older, click **Copy**, switch to the e03p2florida workbook, click **cell A6**, and then click **Paste**.

- Switch to the downloaded dataset, scroll through the dataset to find the *FEMALE* section, click **cell B95**, the data only for females under 18 years, click **Copy**, switch to the e03p2florida workbook, click **cell C5**, and then click **Paste**. Copy the **range B100:B103** (data only for the remaining female age groups) from the downloaded dataset, and then paste it starting in **cell C6** in the e03p2florida workbook. Type **Female** in **cell C4**. Close the downloaded data without saving it.

c. Complete the worksheet by doing the following:
   - Select the **range A4:A9**, click **Clear** in the Editing group on the Home tab, and then select **Clear Formats**.
   - Double-click between **column headings A** and **B** to widen column A.
   - Click **Find & Select** in the Editing group, select **Replace**, type **.** (a period) in the **Find what box**, leave the *Replace with* box empty, and then click **Replace All** to delete the period at the beginning of each label. Click **OK** when the replacement confirmation message displays. Click **Close** to close the Find and Replace dialog box.
   - Type **Florida Population** in **cell A1**, merge and center the title across the **range A1:C1**, apply bold, and then change the font size to **14 pt**.
   - Type **'July 2009** (substituting the latest year in the downloaded dataset) in **cell A2**. If you do not type the leading apostrophe, Excel will convert the date to a different format. Merge and center the date in the **range A2:C2**.
   - Bold and center horizontally the column labels in the **range B4:C4**.
   - Change the name of Sheet1 to **Data**, and then delete the other worksheets.

d. Select the **range A4:C9**, click the **Insert tab**, click **Column** in the Charts group, and then select **Clustered Column** in the *2-D Column* section.

e. Click **Move Chart** in the Location group on the Design tab to open the Move Chart dialog box. Click **New sheet**, type **Population Chart**, and then click **OK**.

f. Click the **Layout tab**, and then add a chart title by doing the following:
   - Click **Chart Title** in the Labels group, and then select **Above Chart**.
   - Type **Florida Population by Gender - 2009** (substituting the appropriate year), and then press **Enter**.

g. Change the units for the vertical axis by doing the following:
   - Click **Axes** in the Axes group, point to **Primary Vertical Axis**, and then select **More Primary Vertical Axis Options**.
   - Click the **Display units arrow**, and then select **Millions**.
   - Click **Number** on the left side of the Format Axis dialog box, type **1** in the **Decimal places box**, and then click **Close**.

h. Add data labels by doing the following:
   - Identify the Charts Elements arrow in the Current Selection group. It currently displays *Vertical (Value) Axis*. Click the **Chart Elements arrow** in the Current Selection group, and then select **Series "Male"**.
   - Click **Data Labels** in the Labels group, and then select **Outside End**.
   - Click **Data Labels** in the Labels group, select **More Data Label Options**, click **Number** on the left side of the Format Data Labels dialog box, select **Number** in the *Category* section, type **1** in the **Decimal places box**, and then click **Close**.
   - Click the **data labels** to select them if necessary, apply **bold**, and then apply **11-pt font size**.
   - Adapt these steps for the Female data series.

i. Click the **Layout tab**, if necessary, click **Data Table** in the Labels group, and then select **Show Data Table with Legend Keys**.

j. Click **Legend** in the Labels group, and then select **None**.

k. Click **Plot Area** in the Background group, and then select **More Plot Area Options**. Do the following in the Format Plot Area dialog box:
   - Click **Picture or texture fill**.
   - Click **Clip Art**, then in the Select Picture dialog box, search for and insert a map of Florida.
   - Select the image that matches the image in Figure 3.53, and then click **OK**.
   - Drag the **Transparency slider** to **60%**, and then click **Close**.

l. Click the **Data worksheet tab**, click **cell B10**, and then create sparklines by doing the following:
   - Click the **Insert tab**, and then click **Column** in the Sparklines group.
   - Select the **range B5:B9** to enter the range in the **Data Range box**.
   - Ensure *$B$10* appears in the **Location Range box**, and then click **OK**.
   - Increase the row height of row 10 to **34.50**.

m. Adapt step l to create a sparkline in **cell C10** for the female data. Click **Sparkline Color** in the Style group, and then select **Red, Accent 2**.

n. Create a footer with your name on the left side, the sheet name code in the center, and the file name code on the right side of both worksheets. For the Data worksheet, use the Page Layout tab to change the scaling to **125%** in the Scale to Fit group, and then select the **Horizontally check box** in the Margins tab of the Page Setup dialog box.

o. Save and close the workbook, and submit based on your instructor's directions. Close the Web browser window if necessary.

3 Gas Prices in Boston

You are interested in moving to Boston, but you want to know about the city's gasoline prices. You downloaded data from a government site, but it is overwhelming to detect trends when you have over 200 weekly data points. You create a chart to help you interpret the data. This exercise follows the same set of skills as used in Hands-On Exercises 1, 2, and 3 in the chapter. Refer to Figure 3.54 as you complete this exercise.

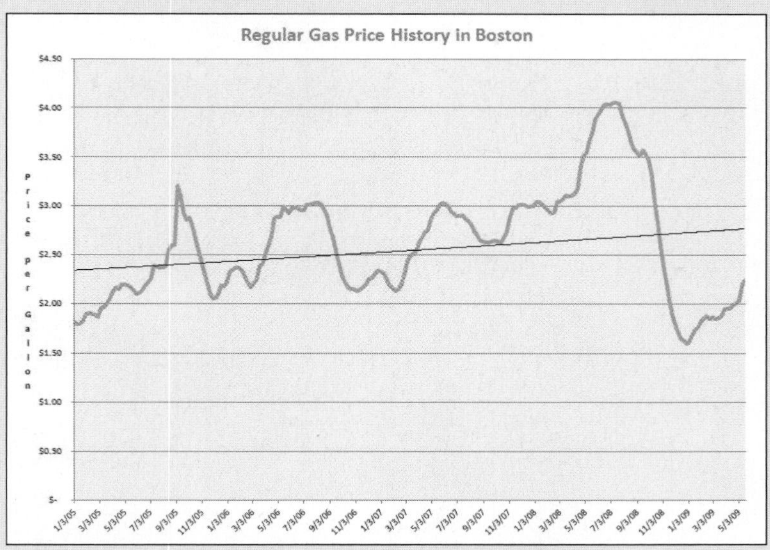

FIGURE 3.54 Boston Gas Prices ➤

a. Open *e03p3boston* and save it as **e03p3boston_LastnameFirstname**.

b. Select **cells A6:B235**, click the **Insert tab**, click **Line** in the Charts group, and then click **Line** in the *2-D Line* section. Excel creates the chart and displays the Chart Tools Design tab.

c. Click **Move Chart** in the Location group, click **New sheet**, type **Line Chart**, and then click **OK**.

d. Click the **Layout tab**, click **Legend** in the Labels group, and then select **None** to remove the legend.

e. Click the chart title to select it, type **Regular Gas Price History in Boston**, and then press **Enter**.

f. Click **Axis Titles** in the Labels group, point to **Primary Vertical Axis Title**, select **Vertical Title**, type **Price per Gallon**, and then press **Enter**.

g. Click **Axes** in the Axes group, point to **Primary Vertical Axis**, and then select **More Primary Vertical Axis Options**. Do the following in the Format Axis dialog box:
   - Make sure that **Axis Options** is selected on the left side of the Format Axis dialog box, click the **Display units arrow**, and then select **Hundreds**.
   - Click **Number** on the left side of the dialog box, click **Accounting** in the **Category list**, and then click **Close**.

h. Click the **Hundreds label**, and then press **Delete**. You converted the cents per gallon to dollars and cents per gallon.

i. Click **Axes** in the Axes group, point to **Primary Horizontal Axis**, and then select **More Primary Horizontal Axis Options**. Click **Number** on the left side of the Format Axis dialog box, click **Date** in the **Category list** if necessary, select **3/14/01** in the **Type list**, and then click **Close**.

j. Use the Home tab to change the category axis, value axis, and value axis labels to **9-pt** size. Apply the **Orange, Accent 6, Darker 25% font color** to the chart title.
k. Click the **Design tab**, click the **More button** in the Chart styles group, and then click **Style 40** (first style on the right side of the fifth row).
l. Click the **Layout tab**, click **Trendline**, and then select **Exponential Trendline**.
m. Create a footer with your name on the left side, the sheet name code in the center, and the file name code on the right side.
n. Click the **File tab**, click **Print**, and then look at the preview. Print the chart sheet if instructed.
o. Save and close the workbook, and submit based on your instructor's directions.

1 Employee Evaluations

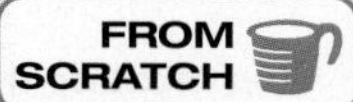

As the manager of a product development team, you are responsible for the annual employee evaluations. Employees are evaluated on five criteria with a score of 1 to 5. You need to create a worksheet that lists each employee's name and score for each category. After calculating categorical and employee averages, you want to create charts to depict the data visually. Refer to Figures 3.55 and 3.56 as you complete this exercise.

	A	B	C	D	E	F
1	2013 Employee Evaluations					
2						
3	Employee	Productivity	Work Quality	Initiative	Working Relations	Writing Skills
4	Adam	4.50	5.00	4.00	3.50	4.00
5	Belinda	5.00	4.50	5.00	4.00	5.00
6	Denise	3.00	3.00	2.00	4.00	3.50
7	Eli	4.00	4.50	4.00	3.50	3.00
8	Grant	3.50	2.50	3.00	4.00	3.50

FIGURE 3.55 Employee Evaluations ➤

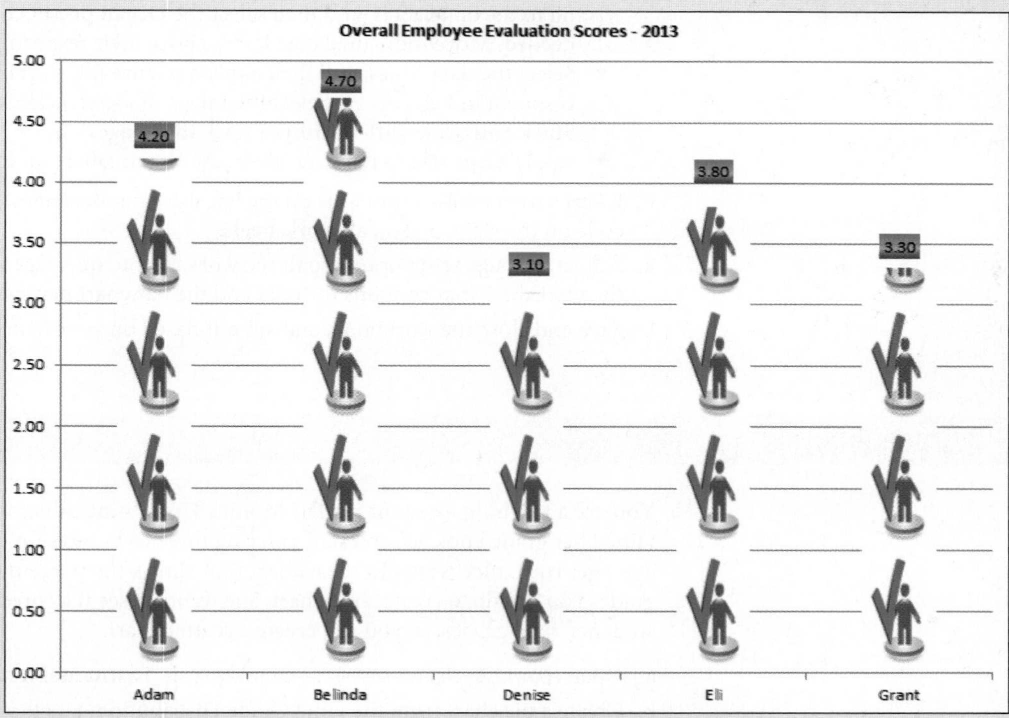

FIGURE 3.56 Employee Evaluations Chart ➤

a. Start a new Excel workbook, save it as **e03m1evals_LastnameFirstname**, rename Sheet1 as **Data and Chart**, and then delete the other sheets.

b. Enter and format the title and data shown in Figure 3.55 by doing the following:
   - Type the title in **cell A1**, merge and center the title over the **range A1:H1**, and then apply **18 pt size**, **bold**, and **Aqua, Accent 5, Darker 25% font color**.
   - Type the column labels on row 3, center, and wrap text, and then apply bold and the same font color as the title. Adjust column widths as needed.
   - Type the data for each employee, increase the decimal points as shown, and then center the data horizontally in the cells.

c. Calculate category averages in row 9, and then type a row label. Calculate employee averages in column G, type a column label, and then apply consistent formatting as the other column labels, if necessary. Apply the **Aqua, Accent 5, Lighter 60% fill color** to the row and column average values, and then center the averages.

d. Select the employee ratings in the **range B4:F8**, and then create column sparklines in column H. Show the high point, and then select the **Sparkline Style Accent 5, Darker 25% style**. Type an appropriate column label and apply consistent formatting as necessary. Change the row height to **24.75** for rows containing sparklines.

e. Select the **range A3:G8**, and then create a clustered column chart. After creating the chart, change it to a clustered bar chart, remove the Employee Average data series, and then position the chart in the **range A12:G40**.

f. Make the following design changes:
- Select **Layout 1** as the chart layout style.
- Change the chart title to **2013 Employee Evaluation Scores by Category**.
- Apply the **Style 26 chart style**.

DISCOVER 

g. Change the highest value on the horizontal axis to **5**.

h. Create a chart on a new chart sheet by doing the following:
- Select the nonadjacent **ranges A3:A8** and **G3:G8**.
- Create a clustered column chart, and then move it to its own chart sheet named **Overall Evaluations**.

i. Make the following changes to the column chart (see Figure 3.56):
- Remove the legend.
- Change the title to **Overall Employee Evaluation Scores - 2013**. Apply **13.2 pt font size** to the chart title.
- Add data labels in the **Outside End** position, and then bold the data labels. Apply a gradient fill to the data labels, and then select the **Ocean preset color**. Adjust the transparency as needed. Move individual data labels above their respective columns as needed.
- Select the data series, and then apply a picture fill, searching for clip art of a check mark that is shown in Figure 3.56. Select the image of a green check mark with a blue person. Select the **Stack and Scale with option** to stack the images.
- Apply **12 pt size** to the data labels, the Y-axis labels, and the X-axis labels.

j. Insert a footer with your name on the left side, the sheet name code in the center, and the file name code on the right side on all worksheets.

k. Adjust the page setup option to fit the worksheet to one page with 0.5" left and right margins. Print the worksheet that contains the data and the bar chart per your instructor's directions.

l. Save and close the workbook, and submit based on your instructor's directions.

2 Grade Analysis

You are a teaching assistant for Dr. Monica Unice's introductory psychology class. You have maintained her grade book all semester, entering three test scores for each student and calculating the final average. Dr. Unice wants to see a chart that shows the percentage of students who earn each letter grade. You decide to create a pie chart. She wants to see if a correlation exists between attendance and students' final grades, so you will create a scatter chart.

a. Open *e03m2psych* and save it as **e03m2psych_LastnameFirstname**.

b. Create a pie chart from the Final Grade Distribution data located below the student data, and then move the pie chart to its own sheet named **Grades Pie**.

c. Customize the pie chart with these specifications:
- **Layout 1 chart layout** with the title **PSY 2030 Final Grade Distribution - Fall 2012**
- F grade slice exploded
- **20-pt** size for the data labels, with a center label position, and gradient fill
- Border: no line

d. Apply these standard fill colors to the respective data points:
   - A (Blue)
   - B (Green)
   - C (Orange)
   - D (Purple)
   - F (Red)

DISCOVER 

e. Create a Scatter with only Markers chart using the attendance record and final averages from the Grades worksheet. Move the scatter chart to its own sheet named **Attend Grades**.
f. Apply these label settings to the scatter chart:
   - Legend: none
   - Chart title above chart: **Attendance - Final Average Relationship**
   - X-axis title: **Percentage of Attendance**
   - Y-axis rotated title: **Student Final Averages**
g. Use Help to learn how to apply the following axis settings:
   - Y-axis: 40 starting point, 100 maximum score, 10 point increments, and a number format with zero decimal places
   - X-axis: 40 starting point, automatic increments, automatic maximum
h. Add the **Parchment gradient fill** to the plot area, and then insert a linear trendline.
i. Center the worksheet horizontally between the left and right margins on the Grades worksheet.
j. Insert a footer with your name on the left side, the sheet name code in the center, and the file name code on the right side for all three worksheets.
k. Save and close the workbook, and submit based on your instructor's directions.

CAPSTONE EXERCISE

You are an assistant manager at Premiere Movie Source, an online company that enables customers to download movies for a fee. You are required to track movie download sales by genre. You gathered the data for September 2012 and organized it in an Excel workbook. You are ready to create charts to help represent the data so that you can make a presentation to your manager later this week.

Change Data Source, Position, and Size

You already created a clustered column chart, but you selected too many cells for the data source. You need to open the workbook and adjust the data source for the chart. In addition, you want to position and size the chart.

a. Open the *e03c1movies* workbook and save it as **e03c1movies_LastnameFirstname**.

b. Remove the Category Totals from the legend, and then adjust the data range to exclude the weekly totals.

c. Position and size the chart to fill the **range A18:L37**.

d. Change the row and column orientation so that the weeks appear in the category axis and the genres appear in the legend.

Add Chart Labels

You want to add a chart title and a value axis title and change the legend's position.

a. Add a chart title above the chart.

b. Enter the text **September 2012 Downloads by Genre**.

c. Add a rotated value axis title.

d. Enter the text **Number of Downloads**.

e. Move the legend to the top of the chart, and then drag the bottom of the chart area down to cover row 40.

Format Chart Elements

You are ready to apply the finishing touches to the clustered column chart. You will adjust the font size of the category axis and display additional gridlines to make it easier to identify values for the data series. You will add and adjust data labels to the Drama data series. Finally, you will add a linear trendline to the chart to visualize trends.

a. Format the category axis with **12-pt size**.

b. Display major and minor horizontal gridlines.

c. Select the **Drama data series**, and then add data labels in the Outside End position.

d. Add a **Yellow fill color** to the data labels.

e. Add a linear trendline to the Drama data series.

Insert and Format Sparklines

You want to show weekly trends for each genre by inserting sparklines in the column to the right of Category Totals.

a. Insert a **Line sparkline** for the weekly (but not category totals) data for Action & Adventure in **cell G5**.

b. Copy the sparkline down the column.

c. Format the sparklines by applying **Sparkline Style Dark #6**, display the high point, and format the high point marker in **Red**.

Create Another Chart

You want to create a chart that will show the monthly volume of downloads by genre. You decide to create a bar chart with genre labels along the left side of the chart.

a. Select the genres and weekly totals. Create a clustered bar chart.

b. Move the chart to its own sheet, and then name the sheet **Bar Chart**.

c. Change the chart type to a stacked bar chart.

d. Add a chart title above the chart, and then enter **Sept 2012 Total Monthly Downloads by Genre**.

Format the Bar Chart

You want to enhance the appearance of the chart by applying a chart style and adjusting the axis values.

a. Apply the **Style 31 chart style** to the bar chart.

b. Display the value axis in units of thousands.

c. Display the category axis names in reverse order using the Format Axis dialog box.

d. Apply the **Layout 3 layout style** to the chart.

Printing the Charts

You want to print the bar chart on its own page, but you want to print the clustered column chart with the original data. To ensure the worksheet data and chart print on the same page, you need to adjust the page setup options.

a. Create a footer on each worksheet with your name, the sheet name code, and the file name code.

b. Apply landscape orientation for the original worksheet.

c. Set 0.2" left, right, top, and bottom margins for the original worksheet.

d. Select the option that makes the worksheet print on only one page.

e. Print both worksheets.

f. Save and close the workbook, and submit based on your instructor's directions.

Top 5 Airport Statistics

GENERAL CASE 

You created a workbook that lists the top five U.S. airports based on passenger counts for three years. In addition to passenger counts, you created worksheets to depict the percentage of on-time arrivals and the percentage of on-time departures for those airports. Now you want to create charts to illustrate the data. Open *e03b1airports* and save it as **e03b1airports_LastnameFirstname**. Use the Passenger worksheet to create a bar chart of your choice in the **range A14:F34** depicting the passenger count for all three years. Apply **Layout 1 chart layout**, and then type an appropriate title. Change the display units to millions for the horizontal axis, and then edit the axis title to display **Millions of Passengers**. Select each data series individually, and then select a brighter replacement fill color. Format the chart area by adding a picture (clip art) of an airport, and then changing its transparency to **70%**. Format the plot area with no fill so that the chart area's picture will display.

On the Arrivals worksheet, create a line chart in the **range A14:H28**. Apply the **Layout 1 chart layout**, type an appropriate title, and then delete the axis title. Format the vertical axis with zero decimal places, and start the minimum value at **0.65**. Switch the data so that the years appear on the horizontal axis and the airport codes appear in the legend. Format the plot area with an image of a plane landing at sunset, and then change the transparency to **60%**.

On the Departures worksheet, create a line chart similar to the Arrivals chart, except start the minimum value at **0.75**, format the plot area with an image of a plane taking off, and then change the transparency to **70%**. Create a footer with your name on the left side, the sheet name code in the center, and the file name code on the right side of all three sheets. Fit each sheet to print on one page, and set the horizontal center page alignment.

Start PowerPoint. Click the **File tab**, and then click **New**. Type **airplane** in the **Search Office.com for templates box**, and then click **Start searching**. Select an appropriate airplane template to start a new slide show. Add a title and subtitle on the title slide, and then delete all other slides. Add three new slides, and then embed each Excel chart on a separate slide using the source formatting. Adjust the size of each chart in PowerPoint, add main titles to the actual slides, and then delete the chart titles from the charts. Remove the images from the plot and chart areas in the three charts. On the line charts, increase the font size of the vertical axis, horizontal axis, and legend. Select each line data series, click the **Format tab**, click **Shape Outline**, and then adjust the weight to **6 pt**. Change the ATL data series shape outline color to yellow. Add your name and the slide number to all slides except the title slide. Save the PowerPoint slide show as **e03b1airports_LastnameFirstname**, which will have the pptx file name extension. Save and close the workbook and slide show, and submit based on your instructor's directions.

Historical Stock Prices

RESEARCH CASE 

You are interested in investing in the stock market. But before you do, you want to research the historical prices for a particular stock. Launch a Web browser, go to **money.msn.com/investing/**, type a company name, such as Apple, and then select the desired company name from a list of suggested companies. Click the **HISTORICAL PRICES link**. Copy the stock data (date, high, low, open, close, volume) for a six-month period, and then paste it in a new workbook, adjusting the column widths to fit the data. Save the workbook as **e03b2stockdata_LastnameFirstname**. Keep only data for the first date listed for each month; hide rows containing data for other dates. Sort the list from the oldest date to the newest date. Use Help if needed to learn how to sort data and how to create a Volume-Open-High-Low-Close chart. After conducting the Help research, rearrange the columns of data in the correct sequence. Format the data and column labels. Insert a row to enter the company name, and then insert another row to list the company's stock symbol, such as AAPL. Copy the URL from the Web browser, and then paste it as a source below the list of data and the date you obtained the data. Merge the cells containing the company name and stock symbol through the last column of data, and then word-wrap the URL.

Create a Volume-Open-High-Low-Close chart on a new chart sheet named **Stock Chart**. Select a chart layout that includes a title, and then type an appropriate chart title. Set the primary vertical axis (left side) unit measurement to millions, and then include an axis title **Volume in Millions**. Include a secondary vertical axis (right side) title **Stock Prices**. Apply **Currency** number style with 0 decimal places for the secondary axis values. Use Help to research how to insert text boxes. Insert a text box that describes the stock chart: white fill rectangles indicate the closing price was higher than the opening price; black fill rectangles indicate the closing price was lower than the opening price; etc. Delete the extra worksheets, and then name the sheet containing the data. Create a footer with your name, the sheet name code, and the file name code on both worksheets. Print a copy of the chart for your records. Save and close the workbook, and submit based on your instructor's directions.

Harper County Houses Sold

DISASTER RECOVERY

You want to analyze the number of houses sold by type (e.g., rambler, two-story, etc.) in each quarter during 2012. Your intern created an initial chart, but it contains a lot of problems. Open *e03b3houses* and save it as **e03b3houses_LastnameFirstname**. Identify the errors and poor design. List the errors and your corrections in a two-column format below the chart. Then correct problems in the chart. Create a footer with your name, the sheet name code, and the file name code. Adjust the margins and scaling to print the worksheet data, including the error list, and chart on one page. Save and close the workbook, and submit based on your instructor's directions.

EXCEL

4 DATASETS AND TABLES

Managing Large Volumes of Data

Watch the
Set-up Video
for this Case Study!

CASE STUDY | The Spa Experts

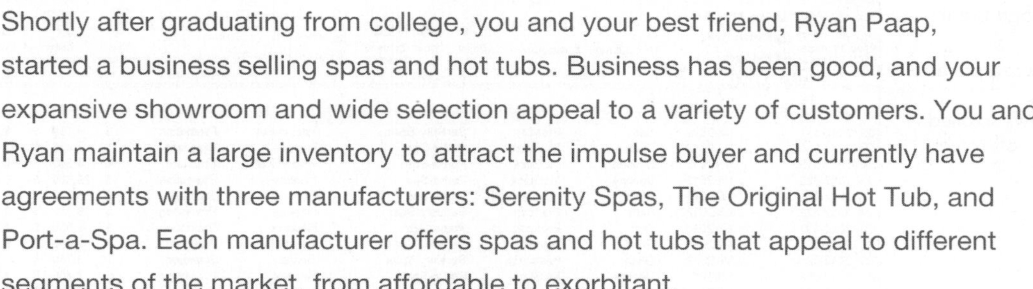

Shortly after graduating from college, you and your best friend, Ryan Paap, started a business selling spas and hot tubs. Business has been good, and your expansive showroom and wide selection appeal to a variety of customers. You and Ryan maintain a large inventory to attract the impulse buyer and currently have agreements with three manufacturers: Serenity Spas, The Original Hot Tub, and Port-a-Spa. Each manufacturer offers spas and hot tubs that appeal to different segments of the market, from affordable to exorbitant.

The business has grown rapidly, and you need to analyze the sales data in order to increase future profits. For example, which vendor generates the most sales? Who is the leading salesperson? Do most customers purchase or finance? Are sales promotions necessary to promote business, or will customers pay the full price?

You created a worksheet that has sales data for the current month. Each transaction appears on a separate row and contains the transaction number, date, sales representatives' first and last names, the spa manufacturer, payment type (financed or paid in full), transaction (standard or promotion), and the amount of the sale. You are ready to start analyzing the data in Excel.

OBJECTIVES AFTER YOU READ THIS CHAPTER, YOU WILL BE ABLE TO:

Large Datasets

So far you have worked with worksheets that contain small datasets, a collection of structured, related data in columns and rows. In reality, you will probably work with large datasets consisting of hundreds or thousands of rows and columns of data. When you work with small datasets, you can usually view most or all of the data without scrolling. When you work with large datasets, column and row labels scroll offscreen when you scroll through the worksheet. Large, widescreen monitors set at high resolutions display more data onscreen; however, you may not be able to view the entire dataset. You might want to keep some data always in view, even as you scroll throughout the dataset. Figure 4.1 shows the Spa Experts' January sales transactions. Because it contains a lot of transactions, the entire dataset is not visible. You could decrease the zoom level; however, doing so decreases the text size onscreen, making it hard to read the data.

> Working with large datasets is challenging because column and row labels scroll offscreen....

Click to see page breaks

Click to freeze panes

First 21 rows scrolled off screen

Page Break Preview on status bar

	A	B	C	D	E	F	G	H	I	J
22	2012-017	1/4/2012	Seth	Prescott	Serenity Spas	Paid in Full	Promotion	$ 6,780	$ 6,780	$ -
23	2012-018	1/5/2012	Deanne	McGuire	Port-a-Spa	Finance	Standard	$ 7,450	$ 1,863	$ 5,588
24	2012-019	1/5/2012	Deanne	McGuire	Port-a-Spa	Paid in Full	Standard	$ 8,560	$ 8,560	$ -
25	2012-020	1/6/2012	Deanne	McGuire	Port-a-Spa	Finance	Promotion	$ 26,500	$ 6,625	$ 19,875
26	2012-021	1/6/2012	Oleta	Fairbanks	Port-a-Spa	Finance	Standard	$ 5,000	$ 1,250	$ 3,750
27	2012-022	1/6/2012	Seth	Prescott	Serenity Spas	Finance	Promotion	$ 8,560	$ 2,140	$ 6,420
28	2012-023	1/7/2012	Seth	Prescott	Port-a-Spa	Finance	Promotion	$ 5,000	$ 1,250	$ 3,750
29	2012-024	1/7/2012	Grant	Ingersoll	Serenity Spas	Paid in Full	Standard	$ 5,400	$ 5,400	$ -
30	2012-025	1/8/2012	Oleta	Fairbanks	Serenity Spas	Finance	Standard	$ 3,240	$ 810	$ 2,430
31	2012-026	1/9/2012	Deanne	McGuire	Port-a-Spa	Finance	Promotion	$ 7,400	$ 1,850	$ 5,550
32	2012-027	1/9/2012	Grant	Ingersoll	Port-a-Spa	Finance	Promotion	$ 22,000	$ 5,500	$ 16,500
33	2012-028	1/9/2012	Grant	Ingersoll	The Original Hot Tub	Paid in Full	Promotion	$ 3,240	$ 3,240	$ -
34	2012-029	1/10/2012	Seth	Prescott	The Original Hot Tub	Paid in Full	Standard	$ 7,690	$ 7,690	$ -
35	2012-030	1/10/2012	Deanne	McGuire	Serenity Spas	Finance	Promotion	$ 6,000	$ 1,500	$ 4,500
36	2012-031	1/11/2012	Deanne	McGuire	The Original Hot Tub	Finance	Promotion	$ 7,500	$ 1,875	$ 5,625
37	2012-032	1/11/2012	Oleta	Fairbanks	Port-a-Spa	Paid in Full	Promotion	$ 7,500	$ 7,500	$ -
38	2012-033	1/11/2012	Seth	Prescott	Serenity Spas	Paid in Full	Promotion	$ 4,650	$ 4,650	$ -
39	2012-034	1/12/2012	Deanne	McGuire	Serenity Spas	Finance	Standard	$ 6,700	$ 1,675	$ 5,025
40	2012-035	1/13/2012	Grant	Ingersoll	The Original Hot Tub	Finance	Promotion	$ 6,540	$ 1,635	$ 4,905
41	2012-036	1/14/2012	Grant	Ingersoll	Serenity Spas	Paid in Full	Promotion	$ 4,800	$ 4,800	$ -
42	2012-037	1/15/2012	Deanne	McGuire	Port-a-Spa	Paid in Full	Standard	$ 7,200	$ 7,200	$ -
43	2012-038	1/16/2012	Oleta	Fairbanks	Serenity Spas	Paid in Full	Standard	$ 32,000	$ 32,000	$ -
44	2012-039	1/17/2012	Seth	Prescott	Port-a-Spa	Finance	Standard	$ 12,000	$ 3,000	$ 9,000
45	2012-040	1/18/2012	Deanne	McGuire	Port-a-Spa	Finance	Standard	$ 3,200	$ 800	$ 2,400
46	2012-041	1/18/2012	Seth	Prescott	The Original Hot Tub	Finance	Standard	$ 12,350	$ 3,088	$ 9,263
47	2012-042	1/18/2012	Deanne	McGuire	Port-a-Spa	Paid in Full	Promotion	$ 18,000	$ 18,000	$ -
48	2012-043	1/19/2012	Deanne	McGuire	Port-a-Spa	Paid in Full	Standard	$ 4,500	$ 4,500	$ -
49	2012-044	1/19/2012	Grant	Ingersoll	Port-a-Spa	Paid in Full	Standard	$ 12,500	$ 12,500	$ -
50	2012-045	1/20/2012	Oleta	Fairbanks	Serenity Spas	Finance	Promotion	$ 7,500	$ 1,875	$ 5,625
51	2012-046	1/21/2012	Grant	Ingersoll	The Original Hot Tub	Finance	Standard	$ 3,450	$ 863	$ 2,588
52	2012-047	1/21/2012	Oleta	Fairbanks	Port-a-Spa	Finance	Promotion	$ 8,000	$ 2,000	$ 6,000
53	2012-048	1/21/2012	Oleta	Fairbanks	The Original Hot Tub	Finance	Standard	$ 17,500	$ 4,375	$ 13,125

FIGURE 4.1 Large Dataset ➤

In order to view other columns, use the horizontal scroll bar to view one or more columns to the right. When the active cell is in the last visible column (cell J1, for example), pressing → displays one or two more columns on the right. Clicking the down arrow in the vertical scroll bar or pressing ↓ when the active cell is in the bottom visible row moves the screen down one row. As you scroll down and to the right, the rows and columns that were originally visible are no longer visible.

In this section, you will learn how to freeze panes and print large worksheets. In particular, you will learn how to keep labels onscreen as you scroll and how to adjust settings that control how large worksheets print.

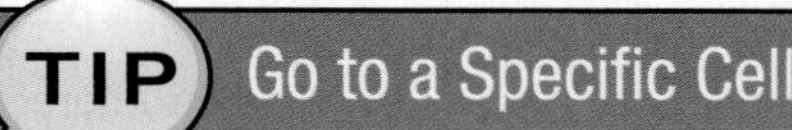

TIP Go to a Specific Cell

You can navigate through a large worksheet by using the Go To command. Click Find & Select in the Editing group on the Home tab and select Go To (or press F5 or Ctrl+G) to display the Go To dialog box, enter the cell address in the Reference box, and then press Enter to go to the cell. You can also click in the Name Box, type the cell reference, and then press Enter.

Freezing Rows and Columns

Freezing keeps rows and/or columns visible as you scroll through a worksheet.

When you scroll to parts of a dataset not initially visible, some rows and columns disappear from view. When the row and column labels scroll off the screen, you may not remember what each column represents. You can keep labels onscreen by freezing them. ***Freezing*** is the process of keeping rows and/or columns visible onscreen at all times even when you scroll through a large dataset. To freeze labels from scrolling offscreen, click the View tab, click Freeze Panes in the Window group, and then select a freeze option. Table 4.1 describes the three freeze options.

TABLE 4.1 Freeze Options

Option	Description
Freeze Panes	Keeps both rows and columns above and to the left of the active cell visible as you scroll through a worksheet.
Freeze Top Row	Keeps only the top row visible as you scroll through a worksheet.
Freeze First Column	Keeps only the first column visible as you scroll through a worksheet.

To freeze one or more rows and columns, use the Freeze Panes option. Before selecting this option, make the active cell one row below and one column to the right of the rows and columns you want to freeze. For example, to freeze the first five rows and the first two columns, make cell C6 the active cell before clicking a Freeze Panes option. As Figure 4.2 shows, Excel displays a horizontal line below the last frozen row (row 5) and a vertical line to the right of the last frozen column (column B). As you scroll down, the unfrozen rows, such as rows 6–14, disappear. As you scroll to the right, the unfrozen columns, such as columns C and D, disappear.

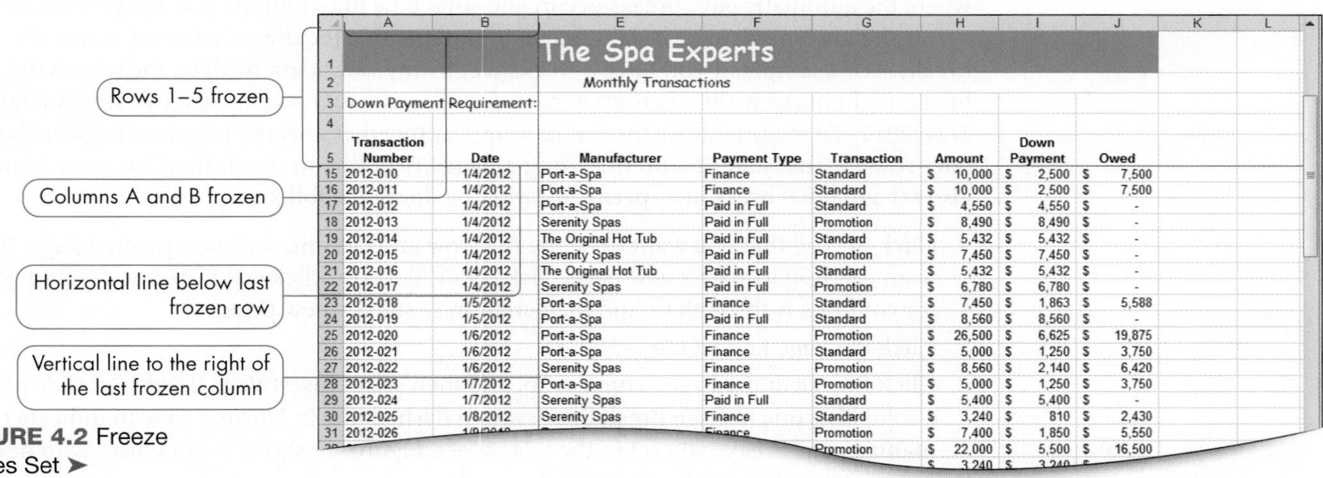

	A	B	E	F	G	H	I	J
5	Transaction Number	Date	Manufacturer	Payment Type	Transaction	Amount	Down Payment	Owed
15	2012-010	1/4/2012	Port-a-Spa	Finance	Standard	$ 10,000	$ 2,500	$ 7,500
16	2012-011	1/4/2012	Port-a-Spa	Finance	Standard	$ 10,000	$ 2,500	$ 7,500
17	2012-012	1/4/2012	Port-a-Spa	Paid in Full	Standard	$ 4,550	$ 4,550	$ -
18	2012-013	1/4/2012	Serenity Spas	Paid in Full	Promotion	$ 8,490	$ 8,490	$ -
19	2012-014	1/4/2012	The Original Hot Tub	Paid in Full	Standard	$ 5,432	$ 5,432	$ -
20	2012-015	1/4/2012	Serenity Spas	Paid in Full	Promotion	$ 7,450	$ 7,450	$ -
21	2012-016	1/4/2012	The Original Hot Tub	Paid in Full	Standard	$ 5,432	$ 5,432	$ -
22	2012-017	1/4/2012	Serenity Spas	Paid in Full	Promotion	$ 6,780	$ 6,780	$ -
23	2012-018	1/5/2012	Port-a-Spa	Finance	Standard	$ 7,450	$ 1,863	$ 5,588
24	2012-019	1/5/2012	Port-a-Spa	Paid in Full	Standard	$ 8,560	$ 8,560	$ -
25	2012-020	1/6/2012	Port-a-Spa	Finance	Promotion	$ 26,500	$ 6,625	$ 19,875
26	2012-021	1/6/2012	Port-a-Spa	Finance	Standard	$ 5,000	$ 1,250	$ 3,750
27	2012-022	1/6/2012	Serenity Spas	Finance	Promotion	$ 8,560	$ 2,140	$ 6,420
28	2012-023	1/7/2012	Port-a-Spa	Finance	Promotion	$ 5,000	$ 1,250	$ 3,750
29	2012-024	1/7/2012	Serenity Spas	Paid in Full	Standard	$ 5,400	$ 5,400	$ -
30	2012-025	1/8/2012	Serenity Spas	Finance	Standard	$ 3,240	$ 810	$ 2,430
31	2012-026			Finance	Promotion	$ 7,400	$ 1,850	$ 5,550
					Promotion	$ 22,000	$ 5,500	$ 16,500

FIGURE 4.2 Freeze Panes Set ➤

To unlock the rows and columns from remaining onscreen as you scroll, click Freeze Panes in the Window group, and then select Unfreeze Panes, which only appears on the menu when you have frozen rows and/or columns. After you unfreeze the panes, the Unfreeze Panes option disappears, and the Freeze Panes option appears on the menu again.

TIP Edit Data in Frozen Range

When you freeze panes and press Ctrl+Home, the first unfrozen cell is the active cell instead of cell A1. For example, with columns A and B and rows 1–5 frozen in Figure 4.2, pressing Ctrl+Home makes cell C6 the active cell. If you need to edit a cell in the frozen area, click the particular cell to make it active, and then edit the data.

Printing Large Datasets

Printing all or parts of a large dataset presents special challenges. For a large dataset, some columns and rows may print on several pages. Analyzing the data for individual printed pages is difficult when each page does not contain column and row labels. To prevent wasting paper, always preview large datasets in the Backstage view before printing data. Doing so enables you to adjust page settings until you are satisfied with how the data will print.

The Page Layout tab (see Figure 4.3) contains many options to help you prepare large datasets to print. Previously, you changed the page orientation, set different margins, and adjusted the scaling. In addition, you can manage page breaks, set the print area, and print titles.

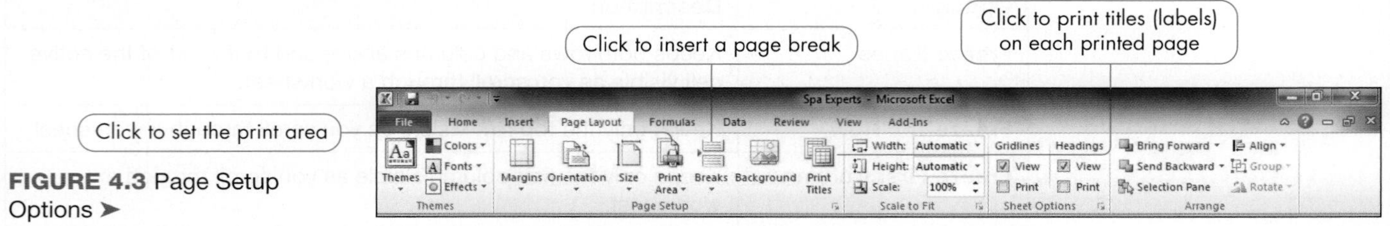

FIGURE 4.3 Page Setup Options ➤

Manage Page Breaks

A **page break** indicates where data starts on a new printed page.

Based on the paper size, orientation, margins, and other settings, Excel identifies how much data can print on a page. Then it displays a ***page break***, indicating where data will start on another printed page. To identify where these automatic page breaks will occur, click Page Break Preview on the status bar or in the Workbook Views group on the Views tab. If the Welcome to Page Break Preview message box appears, click OK. Excel displays watermarks, such as *Page 1*, indicating the area that will print on a specific page. Blue dashed lines indicate where the automatic page breaks occur, and solid blue lines indicate manual page breaks.

If the automatic page breaks occur in undesirable locations, you can adjust the page breaks. For example, if you have a worksheet listing sales data by date, the automatic page break might occur within a group of rows for one date, such as between two rows of data for 1/21/2012. To make all rows for that date appear together, insert a page break above the first data row for that date. To do this, drag a page break line to the desired location. You can also set a manual break at a specific location by doing the following:

1. Click the cell that you want to be the first row and column on a new printed page. If you want cell A50 to start a new page, click cell A50. If you click cell D50, you create a page for columns A through C, and then column D starts a new page.
2. Click the Page Layout tab.
3. Click Breaks in the Page Setup group, and then select Insert Page Break. Excel displays a solid blue line in Page Break Preview or a dashed line in Normal view to indicate the manual page breaks you set in the worksheet. Figure 4.4 shows a worksheet with both automatic and manual page breaks.

To remove a manual page break, click the cell below a horizontal page break or the cell to the right of a vertical page break, click Breaks in the Page Setup group, and then select Remove Page Break. To reset all page breaks back to the automatic page breaks, click Breaks in the Page Setup group, and then select Reset All Page Breaks.

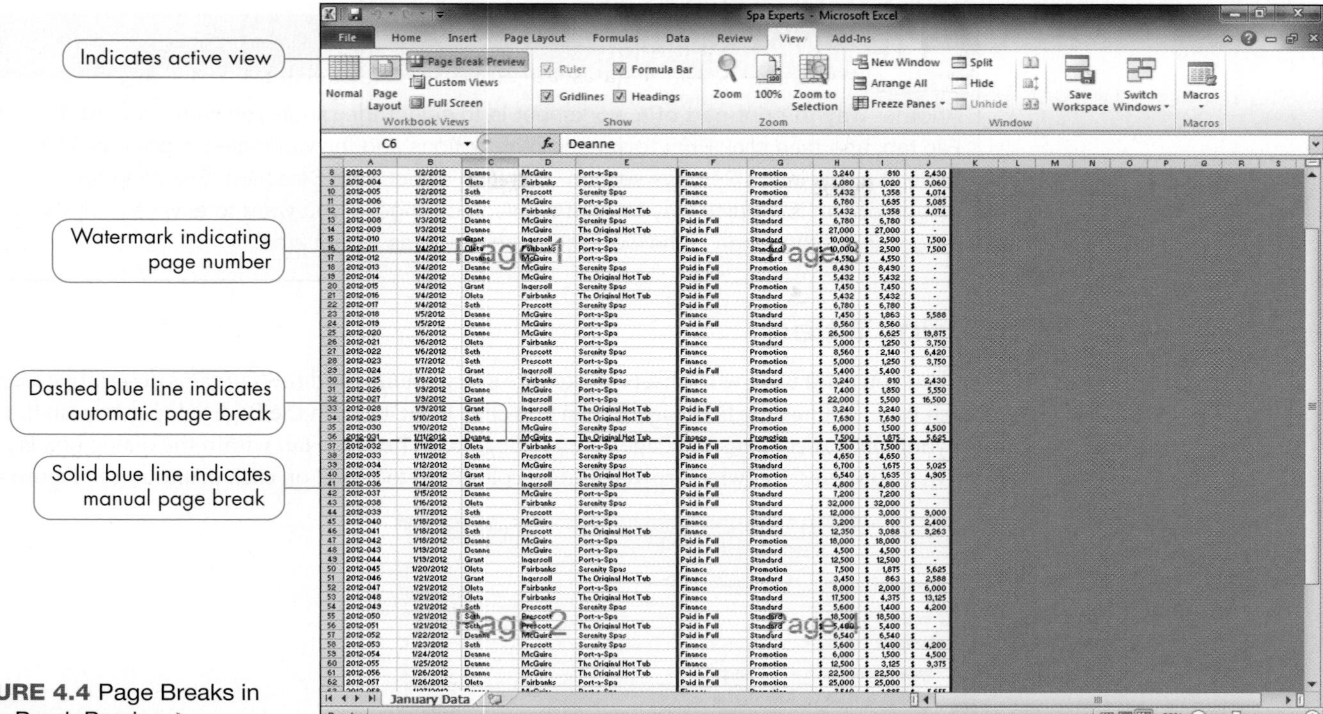

FIGURE 4.4 Page Breaks in Page Break Preview ➤

Set and Clear a Print Area

A **print area** defines the range of data to print.

The default settings send an entire dataset on the active worksheet to the printer. However, you might want to print only part of the worksheet data. For example, you might want to print an input area only or transactions that occurred on a particular date. You can set the ***print area***, which is the range of cells that will print. To print part of a worksheet, do the following:

1. Select the range you want to print.
2. Click the Page Layout tab, and then click Print Area in the Page Setup group.
3. Select Set Print Area. Excel displays solid blue lines in Page Break Preview or thin black dashed lines around the print area in Normal view or Page Layout view (see Figure 4.5).

FIGURE 4.5 Print Area ➤

When you use the Print command, only the print area will print. In Page Break Preview, the print area has a white background and solid blue border; the rest of the worksheet has a gray background. To add print areas, select the range you want to print, click Print Area, and then select Add to Print Area. Each print area will print on a separate page. To clear the print area, click Print Area in the Page Setup group, and then select Clear Print Area.

Print a Selection

Another way to print part of a worksheet is to select the range you want to print. Click the File tab, and then click Print to see the print options and the worksheet in print preview. Click the first arrow in the *Settings* section, and then select Print Selection. Selecting the Print Selection option is a quick way to print a selected range. If you want to always print the same range, select the range in the worksheet, and set it as a print area.

Print Titles

When you print large worksheets, make sure every column and row contains descriptive labels on each page, not just the first page. When you click Print Titles in the Page Setup group on the Page Layout tab, Excel opens the Page Setup dialog box. The Sheet tab within the dialog box is active so that you can select which row(s) and/or column(s) to repeat on each printout (see Figure 4.6).

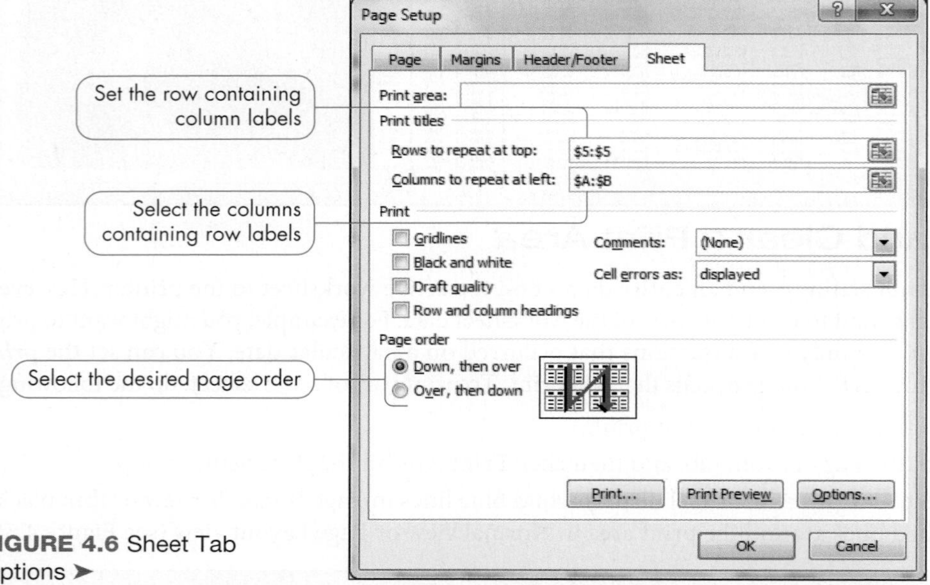

FIGURE 4.6 Sheet Tab Options ➤

In the Spa Experts dataset, not all of the rows will print on the same page as the column labels. To print the column labels at the top of each printout, select the range in the *Rows to repeat at top* box. For example, row 5 contains column labels, such as Manufacturer. If your worksheet has more columns that can print on a page, you might want to display the row labels. To print the row headings on the left side of each printout, select the range in the *Columns to repeat at left* box. For example, columns A and B contain the transaction numbers and dates.

Control Print Page Order

Print order is the sequence in which pages print.

Print order is the sequence in which the pages are printed. By default, the pages print in this order: top-left section, bottom-left section, top-right section, and bottom-right section. However, you might want to print the entire top portion of the worksheet before printing the bottom portion.

To change the print order, click the Page Setup Dialog Box Launcher in the Page Setup group, click the Sheet tab, and then click either *Down, then over* or *Over, then down* (see Figure 4.6).

Quick Concepts Check

1. What is the purpose of freezing panes in a worksheet?
2. Why would you want to insert page breaks instead of using the automatic page breaks?
3. What steps should you take to ensure that column labels display on each printed page of a large dataset?

HANDS-ON EXERCISES

1 Large Datasets

You want to review the large dataset you created that shows the January transactions for your business, Spa Experts. You want to view the data and adjust some page setup options so that you can print necessary headings on each printed page.

Skills covered: Freeze and Unfreeze Panes • Display and Change Page Breaks • Set and Clear a Print Area • Print Worksheet Titles • Change the Page Order

STEP 1 FREEZE AND UNFREEZE PANES

Before setting up the dataset to print, you want to view the data onscreen. The dataset contains more rows than will display onscreen at the same time. You decide to freeze the headings to stay onscreen as you scroll through the transactions. Refer to Figure 4.7 as you complete Step 1.

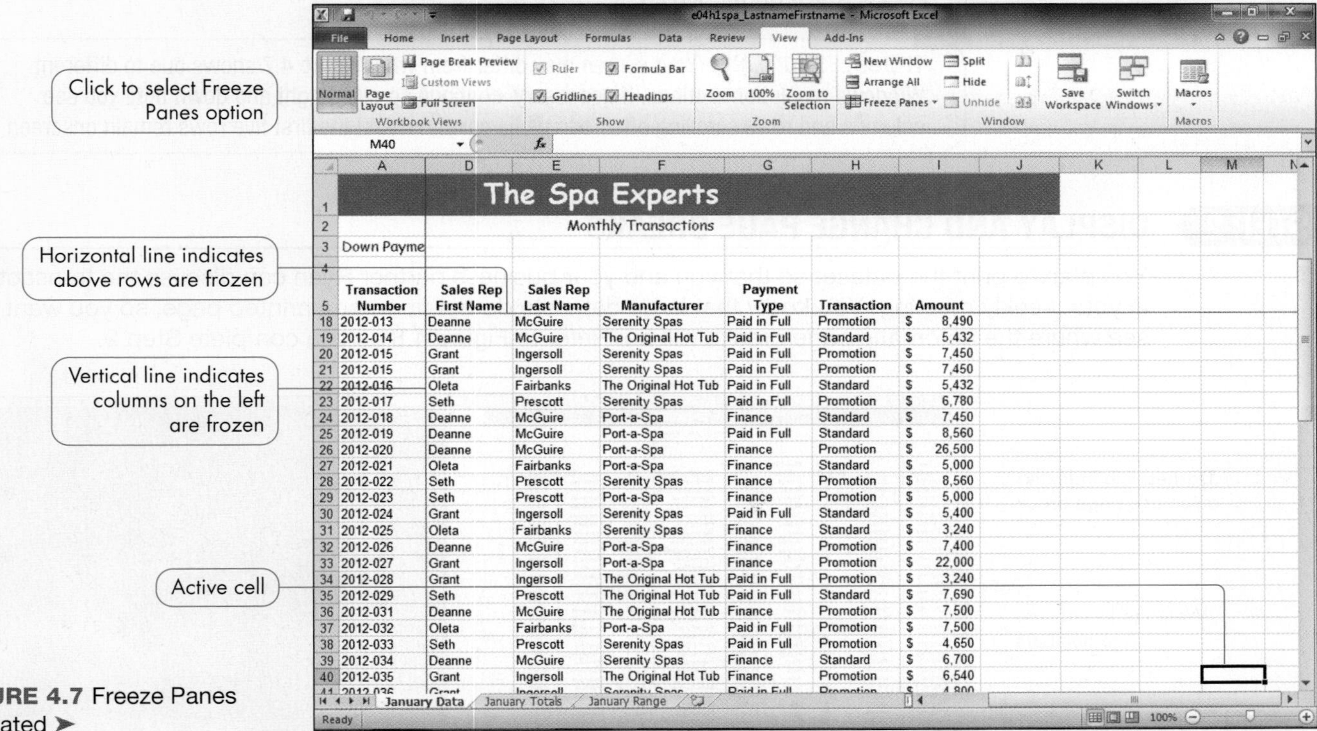

FIGURE 4.7 Freeze Panes Activated ➤

a. Open *e04h1spa* and save it as **e04h1spa_LastnameFirstname**.

> **TROUBLESHOOTING:** If you make any major mistakes in this exercise, you can close the file, open *e04h1spa* again, and then start this exercise over.

The workbook contains three worksheets: January Data (to complete tasks in Hands-On Exercises 1, 2, and 3), January Totals (to complete tasks in Hands-On Exercise 3), and January Range (to complete tasks in Hands-On Exercise 4).

b. Click the **View tab**, click **Freeze Panes** in the Window group, and then select **Freeze Top Row**.

A black horizontal line appears between rows 1 and 2.

c. Press **Page Down** to scroll down through the worksheet.

As rows scroll off the top of the Excel window, the first row remains frozen onscreen. The title by itself is not helpful; you need to freeze the column headings as well.

d. Click **Freeze Panes** in the Window group.

Notice that the first option is now Unfreeze Panes.

e. Select **Unfreeze Panes**.

The top row is no longer frozen.

f. Click **cell B6**, the cell below the row and one column to the right of what you want to freeze. Click **Freeze Panes** in the Window group, and then select **Freeze Panes**.

Excel displays a vertical line between columns A and B, indicating that column A is frozen, and a horizontal line between rows 5 and 6, indicating the first five rows are frozen.

g. Press **Ctrl+G**, type **M40** in the **Reference box** of the Go To dialog box, and then click **OK** to make **cell M40** the active cell. Save the workbook.

Notice that rows 6 through 17 are not visible, and columns B and C are not visible since they scrolled off the screen.

> **TROUBLESHOOTING:** Your screen may differ from what Figure 4.7 shows due to different Windows resolution settings. If necessary, continue scrolling right and down until you see columns and rows scrolling offscreen while column A and the first five rows remain onscreen.

STEP 2 DISPLAY AND CHANGE PAGE BREAKS

You plan to print the dataset so that you and your business partner Ryan can discuss the transactions in your weekly meeting. You know that large datasets do not fit on one printed page, so you want to see where the automatic page breaks will be. Refer to Figure 4.8 as you complete Step 2.

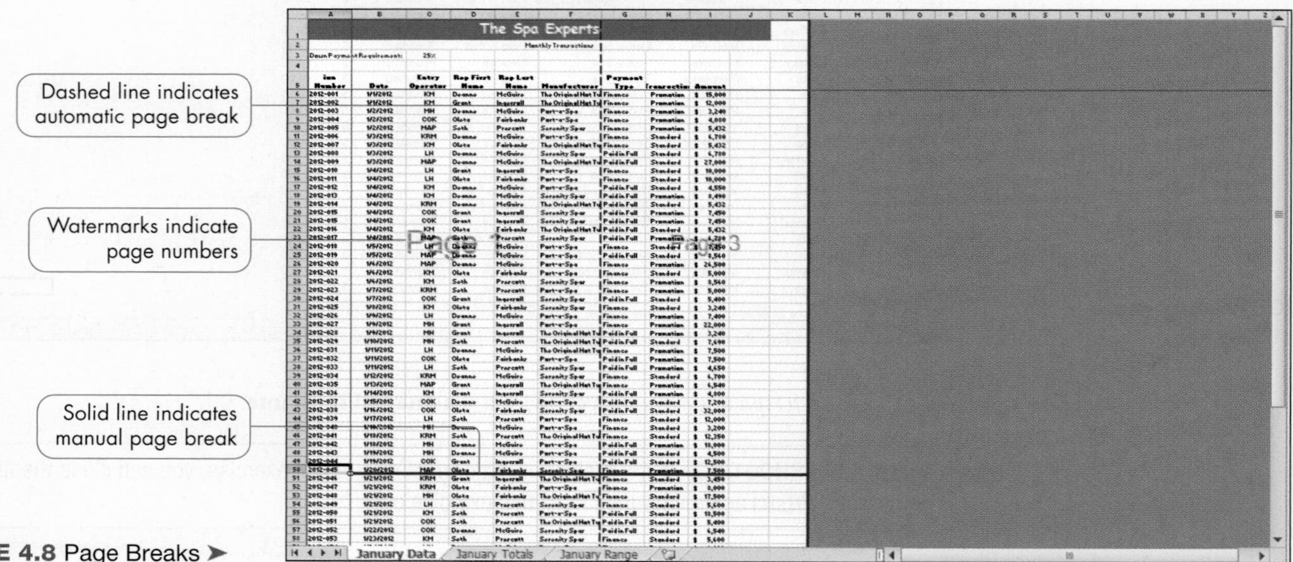

FIGURE 4.8 Page Breaks ➤

a. Press **Ctrl+Home** to jump to **cell B6**, the first cell in the unfrozen area. Click the **View tab** if necessary, and then click **Page Break Preview** in the Workbook Views group or on the status bar.

> **TROUBLESHOOTING:** If the Welcome to Page Break Preview message box opens instructing you how to adjust page breaks, click OK.

b. Drag the **Zoom slider** to the left until the zoom is **50%**.

Excel displays blue dashed lines to indicate the page breaks. The horizontal page break is between rows 51 and 52. You want to make sure all transactions for a particular day do not span between printed pages, so you need to move the page break up to keep all 1/21/2012 transactions together.

c. Click **cell A51**, the cell to start the top of the second page.

d. Click the **Page Layout tab**, click **Breaks** in the Page Setup group, and then select **Insert Page Break**. Save the workbook.

You inserted a page break between rows 50 and 51 so that the 1/21/2012 transactions will be on one page.

> **TROUBLESHOOTING:** If Excel displays a solid line between columns and removes the automatic vertical page break, you selected the wrong cell before inserting a page break. Excel inserts page breaks above and to the left of the active cell. If the page breaks are in the wrong place, click Undo on the Quick Access Toolbar and complete steps c and d again.

> **TIP** Using the Pointer to Move Page Breaks
>
> Instead of clicking Breaks in the Page Setup group, you can use the mouse pointer to adjust a page break. Position the pointer on the page break line to see the two-headed arrow. Drag the page break line to move it where you want the page break to occur.

STEP 3 SET AND CLEAR A PRINT AREA

You want to focus on the first five days of transactions. To avoid printing more data than you need, you can set the print area to only that data. Refer to Figure 4.9 as you complete Step 3.

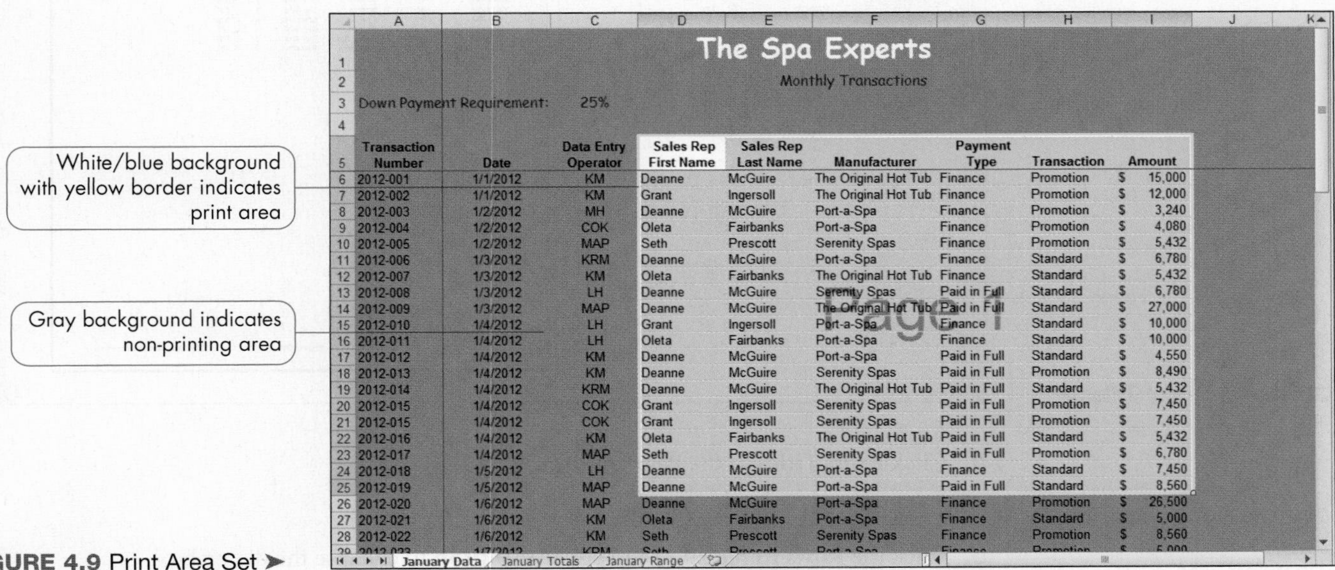

FIGURE 4.9 Print Area Set ➤

a. Change the zoom back to **100%**. Scroll up to see the first row of January data. Select the **range D5:I25**, the range of data for the first five days of the month.

b. Click the **Page Layout tab**, if necessary, click **Print Area** in the Page Setup group, and then select **Set Print Area**.

   Excel displays the print area with a solid yellow border. The rest of the worksheet displays with a gray background, as shown in Figure 4.9.

c. Click the **Page Setup Dialog Box Launcher** in the Page Setup group. Use the dialog box to create a footer with your name on the left side, the sheet name code in the center, and the file name code on the right side.

d. Click the **File tab**, and then click **Print** to verify that only the print area will print. Click the **File tab** to close the Backstage view.

e. Click **Print Area** in the Page Setup group, and then select **Clear Print Area**. Save the workbook.

STEP 4 PRINT WORKSHEET TITLES

When you looked at the entire dataset in Page Break Preview, you noticed it would print on four pages. Only the first page will print both row and column headings. Page 2 will print the remaining row headings, Page 3 will print the remaining column headings, and Page 4 will not print either heading. You want to make sure the column and row headings print on all pages. To do this, you will print titles. Refer to Figure 4.10 as you complete Step 4.

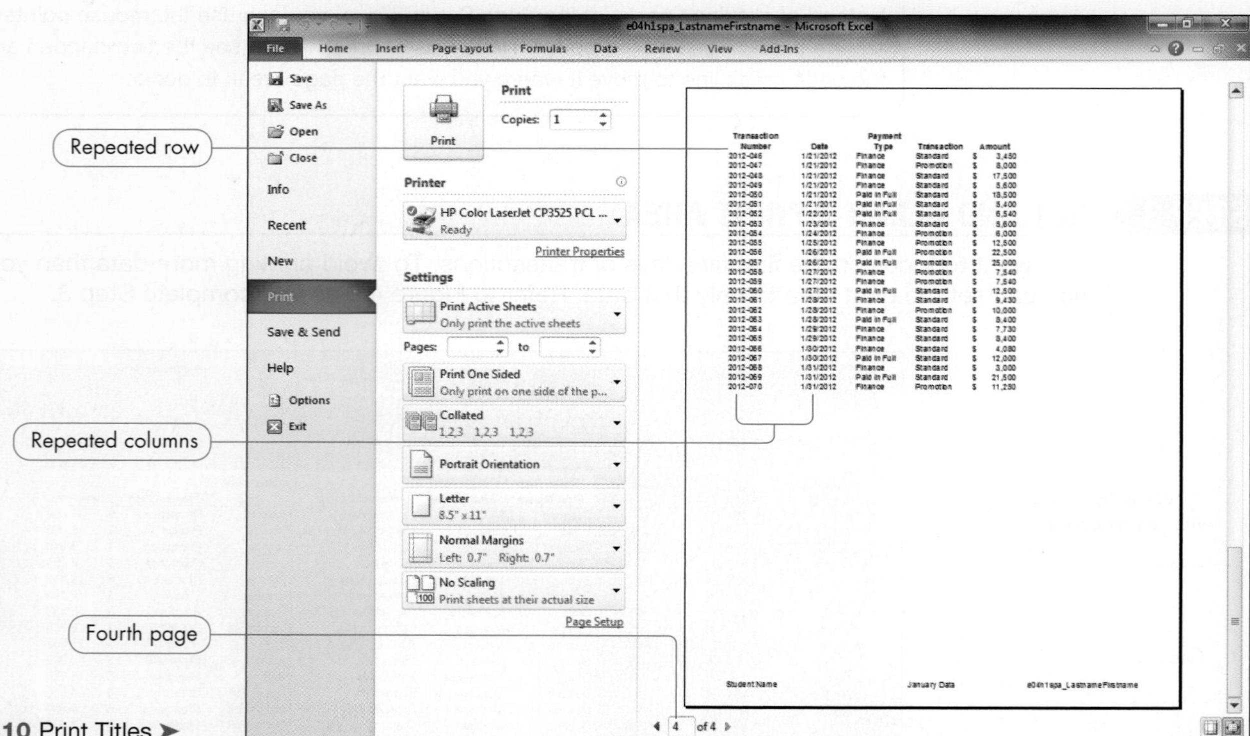

FIGURE 4.10 Print Titles ➤

a. Click **Print Titles** in the Page Setup group.

   The Page Setup dialog box opens, displaying the Sheet tab.

b. Click the **Rows to repeat at top collapse button** to collapse the dialog box.

c. Click the **row 5 heading**, and then click the **expand button** to expand the Page Setup dialog box again.

   You selected the fifth row, which contains the headings that identify content in the columns.

d. Click in the **Columns to repeat at left box**, type **A:B**, and then click **Print Preview**.

   You should verify the page breaks and titles in Print Preview.

e. Click **Next Page** at the bottom of the Backstage view. Look at the second page to see the column headings for the last 11 days of transactions. Click **Next Page** twice to see the third and fourth pages.

   Figure 4.10 shows a preview of the fourth page. The fifth row—the descriptive column headings—appears at the top of the page, and the first two columns of row headings (Transaction Number and Date) appear on all pages now.

f. Click the **Page Layout tab** to close the Backstage view. Save the workbook.

STEP 5 CHANGE THE PAGE ORDER

Although all four pages will print with titles, you want to print all columns for the first half of the monthly transactions rather than printing the first few columns of all transactions and then printing the last columns for all transactions. Refer to Figure 4.11 as you complete Step 5.

The Spa Experts

Monthly Transactions

Down Payment Requirement: 25%

	Transaction Number	Date	Data Entry Operator	Sales Rep First Name	Sales Rep Last Name	Manufacturer	Payment Type	Transaction	Amount
6	2012-001	1/1/2012	KM	Deanne	McGuire	The Original Hot Tub	Finance	Promotion	$ 15,000
7	2012-002	1/1/2012	KM	Grant	Ingersoll	The Original Hot Tub	Finance	Promotion	$ 12,000
8	2012-003	1/2/2012	MH	Deanne	McGuire	Port-a-Spa	Finance	Promotion	$ 3,240
9	2012-004	1/2/2012	COK	Oleta	Fairbanks	Port-a-Spa	Finance	Promotion	$ 4,080
10	2012-005	1/2/2012	MAP	Seth	Prescott	Serenity Spas	Finance	Promotion	$ 5,432
11	2012-006	1/3/2012	KRM	Deanne	McGuire	Port-a-Spa	Finance	Standard	$ 6,780
12	2012-007	1/3/2012	KM	Oleta	Fairbanks	The Original Hot Tub	Finance	Standard	$ 5,432
13	2012-008	1/3/2012	LH	Deanne	McGuire	Serenity Spas	Paid in Full	Standard	$ 6,780
14	2012-009	1/3/2012	MAP	Deanne	McGuire	The Original Hot Tub	Paid in Full	Standard	$ 27,000
15	2012-010	1/4/2012	LH	Grant	Ingersoll	Port-a-Spa	Finance	Standard	$ 10,000
16	2012-011	1/4/2012	LH	Oleta	Fairbanks	Port-a-Spa	Finance	Standard	$ 10,000
17	2012-012	1/4/2012	KM	Deanne	McGuire	Port-a-Spa	Paid in Full	Standard	$ 4,550
18	2012-013	1/4/2012	KM	Deanne	McGuire	Serenity Spas	Paid in Full	Promotion	$ 8,490
19	2012-014	1/4/2012	KRM	Deanne	McGuire	The Original Hot Tub	Paid in Full	Standard	$ 5,432
20	2012-015	1/4/2012	COK	Grant	Ingersoll	Serenity Spas	Paid in Full	Promotion	$ 7,450
21	2012-015	1/4/2012	COK	Grant	Ingersoll	Serenity Spas	Paid in Full	Promotion	$ 7,450
22	2012-016	1/4/2012	KM	Oleta	Fairbanks	The Original Hot Tub	Paid in Full	Standard	$ 5,432
23	2012-017	1/4/2012	MAP	Seth	Prescott	Serenity Spas	Paid in Full	Promotion	$ 6,780
24	2012-018	1/5/2012	LH	Deanne	McGuire	Port-a-Spa	Finance	Standard	$ 7,450
25	2012-019	1/5/2012	MAP	Deanne	McGuire	Port-a-Spa	Paid in Full	Standard	$ 8,560
26	2012-020	1/6/2012	MAP	Deanne	McGuire	Port-a-Spa	Finance	Promotion	$ 26,500
27	2012-021	1/6/2012	KM	Oleta	Fairbanks	Port-a-Spa	Finance	Standard	$ 5,000
28	2012-022	1/6/2012	KM	Seth	Prescott	Serenity Spas	Finance	Promotion	$ 8,560
29	2012-023	1/7/2012	KRM	Seth	Prescott	Port-a-Spa	Finance	Promotion	$ 5,000

Page 1 Page 2

January Data | January Totals | January Range

Page 2 instead of page 3 now

FIGURE 4.11 Different Page Order ➤

a. Click the **Page Layout tab**, if necessary, and then click the **Page Setup Dialog Box Launcher** in the Page Setup group.

b. Click the **Sheet tab** in the Page Setup dialog box.

c. Click **Over, then down.**

   The preview shows that the pages print left to right and then back down left to right, in a Z manner.

d. Click **OK.**

   Notice the Page 2 watermark appears on the right side of Page 1 rather than below it.

e. Save the workbook. Keep the workbook onscreen if you plan to continue with Hands-On Exercise 2. If not, close the workbook and exit Excel.

Excel Tables

All organizations maintain lists of data. Businesses maintain inventory lists, educational institutions maintain lists of students and faculty, and governmental entities maintain lists of contracts. Although more complicated related data should be stored in a database management program, such as Access, you can maintain structured lists in Excel tables. A ***table*** is a structured range that contains related data organized in such a way as to facilitate data management and analysis. Although you can manage and analyze a range of data, a table provides many advantages over a range of data:

All organizations maintain lists of data.

A **table** is an area in the worksheet that contains rows and columns of related data formatted to enable data management and analysis.

- Column headings that remain onscreen during scrolling without having to use Freeze Panes
- Filter lists for efficient sorting and filtering
- Predefined table styles to format table rows and columns with complementary fill colors
- Ability to create and edit calculated columns where the formulas copy down the columns automatically
- Calculated total row enabling the user to choose from a variety of functions
- Use of structured references instead of cell references in formulas
- Ability to export the table data to a SharePoint list

In this section, you will learn table terminology and rules for structuring data. You will create a table from existing data, manage records and fields, and remove duplicates. Then, you will apply a table style to format the table.

Understanding Table Design

A **field** is an individual piece of data, such as a last name.

An Excel table is like a database table: it provides a structured organization of data in columns and rows. Each column represents a ***field***, which is an individual piece of data, such as last names or quantities sold. You should create fields with the least amount of data. For example, instead of a Name field, separate data into First Name and Last Name fields. Instead of one large address field, separate addresses into Street Address, City, State, and ZIP Code fields. Storing data into the smallest units possible enables you to manipulate the data in a variety of ways for output.

A **record** is a complete set of data for an entity.

Each row in an Excel table represents a ***record***, which is a collection of data about one entity, such as data for one person. For example, your record in your professor's grade book contains specific data about you, such as your name, ID, test scores, etc. The professor maintains a record of similar data for each student in the class. In an Excel table, each cell represents one piece of data (in the respective field columns) for a particular record.

Often, people create tables from existing worksheet data. For example, a data-entry operator for the Spa Experts might enter data in a worksheet instead of creating a table first. Just as you spend time planning a worksheet, you should plan the structure for a table. Think about who will use the table, what types of reports you need to produce, and what types of searches might be done. The more thorough your planning process, the fewer changes you will have to make to the table after you create it. To help plan your table, follow these guidelines:

- Enter field names on the top row.
- Keep field names relatively short, descriptive, and unique. No two field names should be identical.
- Format the field names so that they stand out from the data.
- Enter data for each record on a row below the field names.
- Do not leave blank rows between records or between the field names and the first record.
- Delete any blank columns between fields in the dataset.

- Make sure each record has something unique about it, such as a transaction number or ID.
- Insert at least one blank row and one blank column between the table and other data, such as the main titles, input area, or other tables. When possible, place separate tables on separate worksheets.

Creating a Table

When your worksheet data are structured correctly, you can easily create a table. To create a table from existing data, do the following:

1. Click within the existing range of data.
2. Click the Insert tab, and then click Table in the Tables group. As Figure 4.12 shows, the Create Table dialog box opens, prompting you to enter the range of data. If Excel does not correctly predict the range, select the range for the *Where is the data for your table?* box. If the existing range contains column headings, select the *My table has headers* check box.
3. Click OK to create the table.

FIGURE 4.12 Create Table Dialog Box ➤

The Table Tools Design tab appears. Excel applies the default Table Style Medium 9 banded rows to your table, and each cell in the header row has filter arrows (see Figure 4.13). Excel assigns a name to each table, such as Table 1. You can change the table name by clicking in the Table Name box in the Properties group, typing a new name using the same rules you applied when assigning range names, and then pressing Enter.

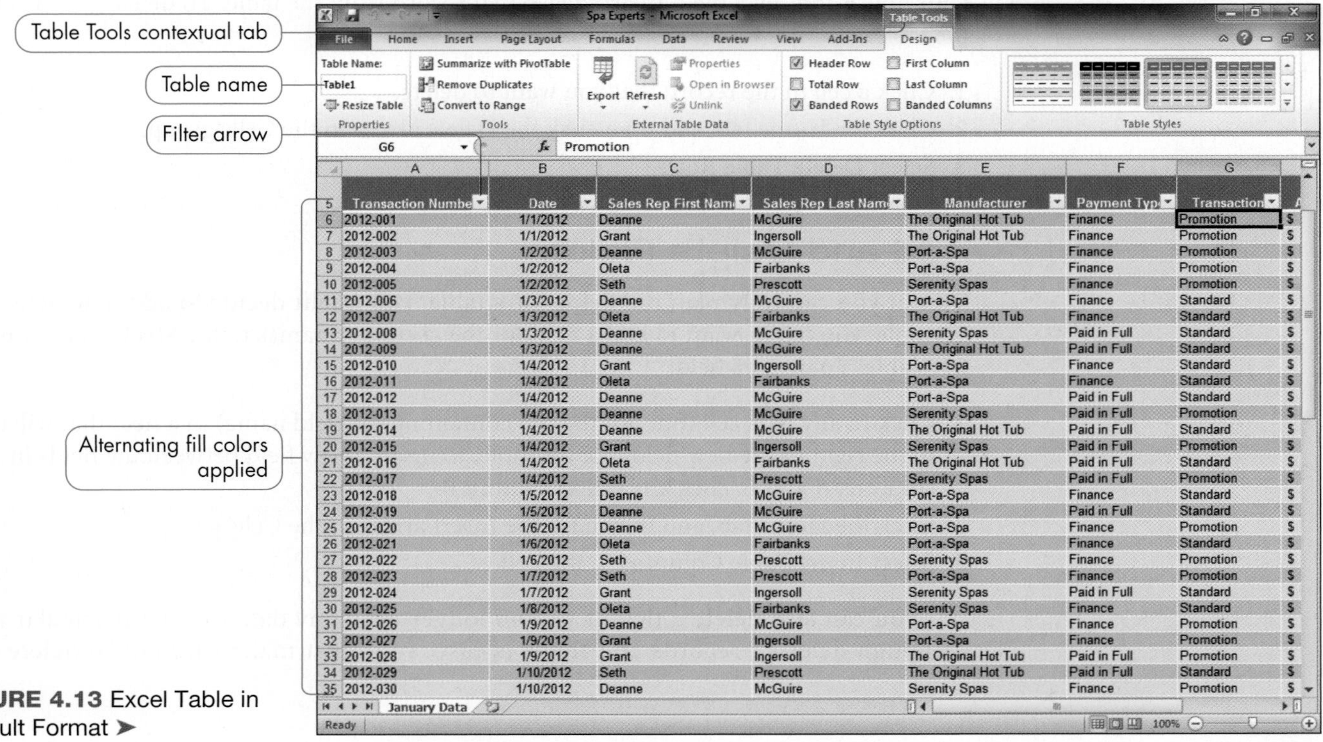

FIGURE 4.13 Excel Table in Default Format ➤

If you do not have existing data, you can create a table structure, and then add data to it later. Select an empty range, and then follow the above steps to create the range for the table. The default table style is Table Style Medium 2, and the default column headings are Column1, Column2, and so on. Click the column heading and type a descriptive label to replace the temporary heading. Excel applies table formatting to the empty rows. You are then ready to add data for each row in the empty table.

TIP Converting a Table to a Range

Tables provide an abundance of advantages to regular ranges. You might want to convert a table back to a range of data to accomplish other tasks. To convert a table back to a range, click within the table range, click the Table Tools Design tab, click Convert to Range in the Tools group, and then click Yes in the message box asking, *Do you want to convert the table to a normal range?*

Add, Edit, and Delete Records

After you create a table, you will need to maintain it, such as by adding new records. For example, you might need to add a new client or employee record, or add a new item to an inventory table or transaction table. To add a record to your table, do the following:

1. Click a cell in the record below where you want the new record inserted. If you want to add a new record below the last record, click the row containing the last record.
2. Click the Home tab, and then click the Insert arrow in the Cells group.
3. Select Insert Table Rows Above to insert a row above the current row, or select Insert Table Row Below if the current row is the last one and you want a row below it.

Sometimes, you need to change data for a record. For example, when a client moves, you need to change the client's address and phone number. You edit data in a table the same way you edit data in a regular worksheet cell.

Finally, you can delete records. For example, if you maintain an inventory of artwork in your house and sell a piece of art, delete that record from the table. To delete a record from the table:

1. Click a cell in the record that you want to delete.
2. Click the Home tab, and then click the Delete arrow in the Cells group.
3. Select Delete Table Rows.

Add and Delete Fields

Even if you carefully plan the fields for a table, you might decide to add new fields. For example, you might want to add a field for the customer names to the Spa Experts transaction table. To insert a field:

1. Click in any data cell (but not the cell containing the field name) in a field that will be to the right of the new field. For example, to insert a new field between the fields in columns A and B, click any cell in column B.
2. Click the Home tab, and then click the Insert arrow in the Cells group.
3. Select Insert Table Columns to the Left.

You can also delete a field if you no longer need any data for that particular field. Although deleting records and fields is easy, you must make sure not to delete data erroneously. If you accidentally delete data, click Undo immediately. To delete a field, do the following:

1. Click a cell in the field that you want to delete.
2. Click the Delete arrow in the Cells group on the Home tab.
3. Select Delete Table Columns.

Remove Duplicate Rows

You might accidentally enter duplicate records in a table, which can give false results when totaling or performing other calculations on the dataset. For a small table, you might be able to detect duplicate records by scanning the data. For large tables, it is more difficult to identify duplicate records by simply scanning the table with the eye. To remove duplicate records, do the following:

1. Click within the table, and then click the Design tab.
2. Click Remove Duplicates in the Tools group to display the Remove Duplicates dialog box (see Figure 4.14).
3. Click Select All to set the criteria to find a duplicate for every field in the record, and then click OK. If you select individual columns, Excel looks for duplicates in that one column only, and deletes all but one record that contains that data. For example, if you delete duplicate records where the manufacturer is Serenity Spas, only one transaction would remain. The other customers' transactions that contain Serenity Spas would be deleted. Excel will display a message box informing you how many duplicate rows it removed.

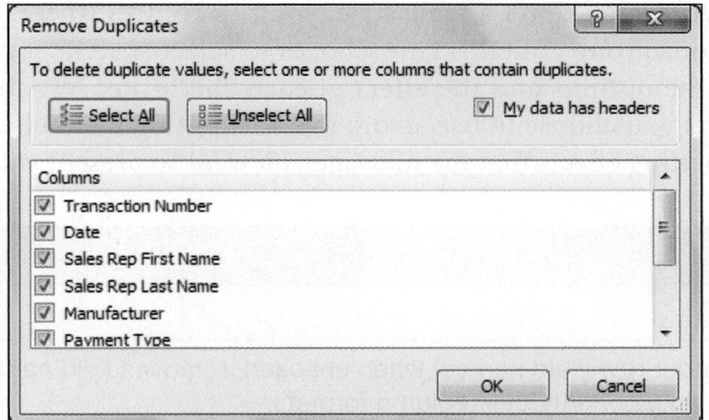

FIGURE 4.14 Remove Duplicates Dialog Box ➤

Applying a Table Style

A **table style** controls the fill color of the header row, columns, and records in a table.

Formatting tables can make them more attractive and easier to read, and can emphasize data. The Design tab provides a variety of formatting options for tables. Excel applies a table style when you create a table. ***Table styles*** control the fill color of the header row (the row containing field names) and rows of records. In addition, table styles specify bold and border lines. You can change the table style to a color scheme that complements your organization's color scheme or to emphasize data in the table. Click the More button to see the Table Styles gallery (see Figure 4.15). To see how a table style will format your table using Live Preview, position the pointer over a style in the Table Styles gallery. After you identify a style you want, click it to apply it to the table.

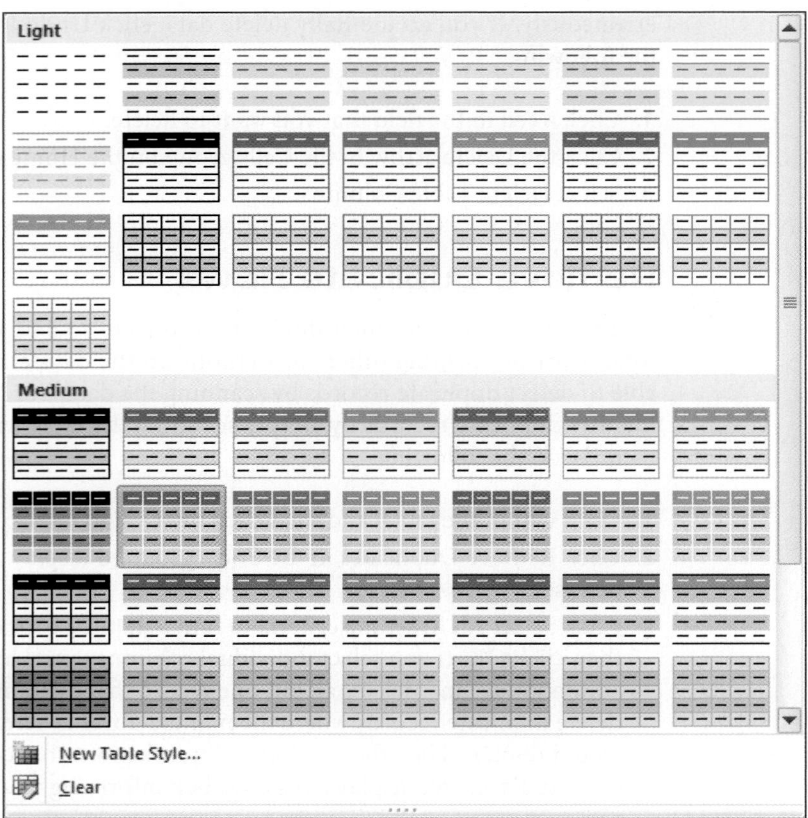

FIGURE 4.15 Table Styles Gallery ➤

After you select a table style, you can control what the style formats. The Table Style Options group contains check boxes to select specific format actions in a table. Table 4.2 lists the options and the effect of each check box. Whatever formatting and formatting effects you choose to use, avoid overformatting the table. It is not good to apply so many formatting effects that the message you want to present with the data is obscured or lost.

TABLE 4.2 Table Style Options

Check Box	Action
Header Row	Displays the header row (field names) when checked; removes field names when not checked. Header Row formatting takes priority over column formats.
Total Row	Displays a total row when selected. Total Row formatting takes priority over column formats.
First Column	Applies a different format to the first column so that the row headings stand out. First Column formatting takes priority over Banded Rows formatting.
Last Column	Applies a different format to the last column so that the last column of data stands out; effective for aggregated data, such as grand totals, per row. Last Column formatting takes priority over Banded Rows formatting.
Banded Rows	Displays alternate fill colors for even and odd rows to help distinguish records.
Banded Columns	Displays alternate fill colors for even and odd columns to help distinguish fields.

Quick Concepts Check

1. List at least four guidelines for planning a table in Excel.
2. How can you convert a range of data into an Excel table?
3. What are six options you can control after selecting a table style?

HANDS-ON EXERCISES

2 Excel Tables

Now that you understand Excel tables, you need to convert the January transactions data from basic worksheet data to a table. As you review the table, you will adjust its structure by deleting an unnecessary field and adding two missing fields. Then, you will focus on the transaction records by adding a missing record and removing a duplicate record. Finally, you will enhance the table appearance by selecting a table style.

Skills covered: Create a Table • Delete and Add Fields • Add a Record • Remove Duplicate Rows • Apply a Table Style

STEP 1 ➤ CREATE A TABLE

Although the Spa Experts' January transaction data are organized in an Excel worksheet, you know that you will have additional functionality if you convert the range to a table. Refer to Figure 4.16 as you complete Step 1.

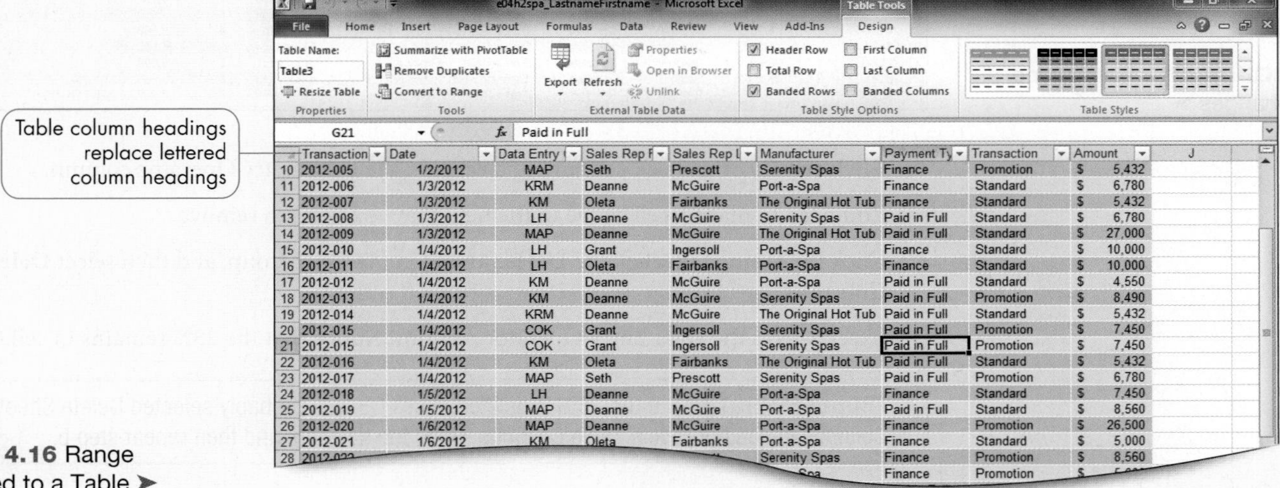

FIGURE 4.16 Range Converted to a Table ➤

a. Open *e04h1spa_LastnameFirstname* if you closed it at the end of Hands-On Exercise 1, and then save it as **e04h2spa_LastnameFirstname**, changing *h1* to *h2*.

b. Click **Normal** on the status bar, and then click the **Insert tab**.

c. Click in any cell within the transactional data. Click **Table** in the Tables group.

   The Create Table dialog box opens. The Where is the data for your table? box displays =$A$5:$I$75. You need to keep the *My table has headers* check box selected so that the headings on the fifth row become the field names for the table.

d. Click **OK**, and then click **cell A5**.

   Excel creates a table from the specified range and displays the Table Tools Design tab, filter arrows, and alternating fill colors for every other record. The columns widen to fit the field names, although the wrap text option is still applied to those cells.

e. Set **12.00 column widths** to these fields: Transaction Number, Data Entry Operator, Sales Rep First Name, Sales Rep Last Name, and Payment Type.

f. Unfreeze the panes, and then scroll through the table. Save the workbook.

   With a regular range of data, column headings scroll off the top of the screen if you don't freeze panes. When you scroll within a table, the table column headings remain onscreen by moving up to where the Excel column (letter) headings usually display (see Figure 4.16).

STEP 2 DELETE AND ADD FIELDS

The original range included the Data Entry Operator's initials. You decide that you no longer need this column, so you will delete it. In addition, you want to add a field to display down payment amounts in the future. Refer to Figure 4.17 as you complete Step 2.

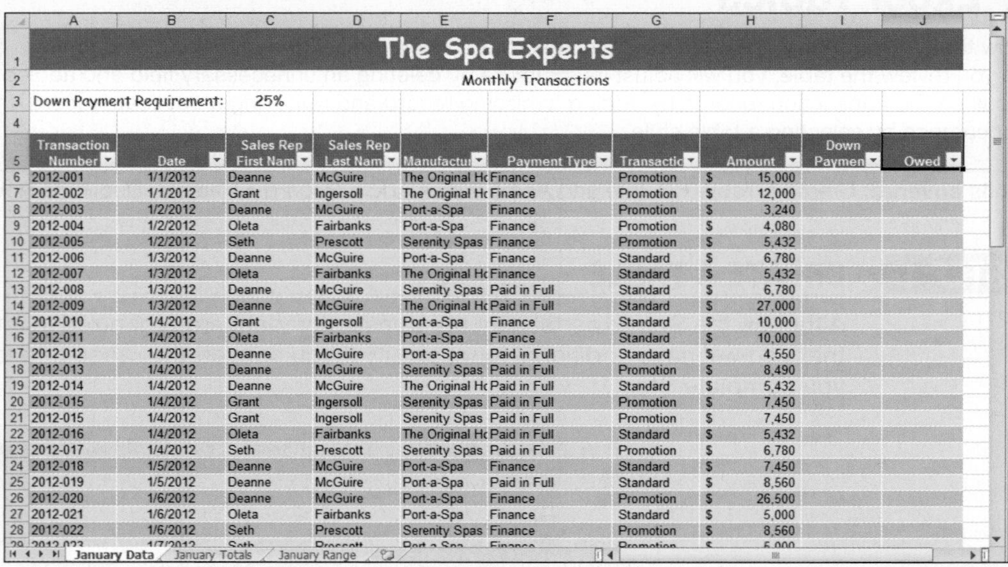

The Spa Experts

Monthly Transactions

Down Payment Requirement: 25%

Transaction Number	Date	Sales Rep First Nam	Sales Rep Last Nam	Manufactu	Payment Type	Transactio	Amount	Down Paymen	Owed
2012-001	1/1/2012	Deanne	McGuire	The Original Hc	Finance	Promotion	$ 15,000		
2012-002	1/1/2012	Grant	Ingersoll	The Original Hc	Finance	Promotion	$ 12,000		
2012-003	1/2/2012	Deanne	McGuire	Port-a-Spa	Finance	Promotion	$ 3,240		
2012-004	1/2/2012	Oleta	Fairbanks	Port-a-Spa	Finance	Promotion	$ 4,080		
2012-005	1/2/2012	Seth	Prescott	Serenity Spas	Finance	Promotion	$ 5,432		
2012-006	1/3/2012	Deanne	McGuire	Port-a-Spa	Finance	Standard	$ 6,780		
2012-007	1/3/2012	Oleta	Fairbanks	The Original Hc	Finance	Standard	$ 5,432		
2012-008	1/3/2012	Deanne	McGuire	Serenity Spas	Paid in Full	Standard	$ 6,780		
2012-009	1/3/2012	Deanne	McGuire	The Original Hc	Paid in Full	Standard	$ 27,000		
2012-010	1/4/2012	Grant	Ingersoll	Port-a-Spa	Finance	Standard	$ 10,000		
2012-011	1/4/2012	Oleta	Fairbanks	Port-a-Spa	Finance	Standard	$ 10,000		
2012-012	1/4/2012	Deanne	McGuire	Port-a-Spa	Paid in Full	Standard	$ 4,550		
2012-013	1/4/2012	Deanne	McGuire	Serenity Spas	Paid in Full	Promotion	$ 8,490		
2012-014	1/4/2012	Deanne	McGuire	The Original Hc	Paid in Full	Standard	$ 5,432		
2012-015	1/4/2012	Grant	Ingersoll	Serenity Spas	Paid in Full	Promotion	$ 7,450		
2012-015	1/4/2012	Grant	Ingersoll	Serenity Spas	Paid in Full	Promotion	$ 7,450		
2012-016	1/4/2012	Oleta	Fairbanks	The Original Hc	Paid in Full	Standard	$ 5,432		
2012-017	1/4/2012	Seth	Prescott	Serenity Spas	Paid in Full	Promotion	$ 6,780		
2012-018	1/5/2012	Deanne	McGuire	Port-a-Spa	Finance	Standard	$ 7,450		
2012-019	1/5/2012	Deanne	McGuire	Port-a-Spa	Paid in Full	Standard	$ 8,560		
2012-020	1/6/2012	Deanne	McGuire	Port-a-Spa	Finance	Promotion	$ 26,500		
2012-021	1/6/2012	Oleta	Fairbanks	Port-a-Spa	Finance	Standard	$ 5,000		
2012-022	1/6/2012	Seth	Prescott	Serenity Spas	Finance	Promotion	$ 8,560		

FIGURE 4.17 Field Name Changes ➤

a. Click **cell C6** or any cell containing a value in the Data Entry Operator column.

You need to make a cell active in the field that you want to remove.

b. Click the **Home tab**, click the **Delete arrow** in the Cells group, and then select **Delete Table Columns**.

Excel deletes the Data Entry Operator column. Notice that the 25% remains in cell C3.

> **TROUBLESHOOTING:** If the 25% is deleted in cell C3, you probably selected Delete Sheet Columns instead of Delete Table Columns. Undo the deletion, and then repeat step b.

c. Click **cell I5**, the first blank cell on the right side of the field names.

d. Type **Down Payment** and press **Ctrl+Enter**.

Excel extends the table formatting to column I automatically. A filter arrow appears for the newly created field name, and alternating fill colors appear in the rows below the field name.

e. Click **Wrap Text** in the Alignment group.

f. Click **cell J5**, type **Owed**, and then press **Ctrl+Enter** to keep cell J5 active. Click **Center** in the Alignment group. Save the workbook.

STEP 3 ADD A RECORD

As you review the January transaction table, you notice that transaction 2012-030 is missing. After finding the paper invoice, you are ready to add a record with the missing transaction data. Refer to Figure 4.18 as you complete Step 3.

	Transaction	Date	Sales Rep F	Sales Rep L	Manufacture	Payment Type	Transaction	Amount	Down Payi	Owed
7	2012-002	1/1/2012	Grant	Ingersoll	The Original Hc	Finance	Promotion	$ 12,000		
8	2012-003	1/2/2012	Deanne	McGuire	Port-a-Spa	Finance	Promotion	$ 3,240		
9	2012-004	1/2/2012	Oleta	Fairbanks	Port-a-Spa	Finance	Promotion	$ 4,080		
10	2012-005	1/2/2012	Seth	Prescott	Serenity Spas	Finance	Promotion	$ 5,432		
11	2012-006	1/3/2012	Deanne	McGuire	Port-a-Spa	Finance	Standard	$ 6,780		
12	2012-007	1/3/2012	Oleta	Fairbanks	The Original Hc	Finance	Standard	$ 5,432		
13	2012-008	1/3/2012	Deanne	McGuire	Serenity Spas	Paid in Full	Standard	$ 6,780		
14	2012-009	1/3/2012	Deanne	McGuire	The Original Hc	Paid in Full	Standard	$ 27,000		
15	2012-010	1/4/2012	Grant	Ingersoll	Port-a-Spa	Finance	Standard	$ 10,000		
16	2012-011	1/4/2012	Oleta	Fairbanks	Port-a-Spa	Finance	Standard	$ 10,000		
17	2012-012	1/4/2012	Deanne	McGuire	Port-a-Spa	Paid in Full	Standard	$ 4,550		
18	2012-013	1/4/2012	Deanne	McGuire	Serenity Spas	Paid in Full	Promotion	$ 8,490		
19	2012-014	1/4/2012	Deanne	McGuire	The Original Hc	Paid in Full	Standard	$ 5,432		
20	2012-015	1/4/2012	Grant	Ingersoll	Serenity Spas	Paid in Full	Promotion	$ 7,450		
21	2012-015	1/4/2012	Grant	Ingersoll	Serenity Spas	Paid in Full	Promotion	$ 7,450		
22	2012-016	1/4/2012	Oleta	Fairbanks	The Original Hc	Paid in Full	Standard	$ 5,432		
23	2012-017	1/4/2012	Seth	Prescott	Serenity Spas	Paid in Full	Promotion	$ 6,780		
24	2012-018	1/5/2012	Deanne	McGuire	Port-a-Spa	Finance	Standard	$ 7,450		
25	2012-019	1/5/2012	Deanne	McGuire	Port-a-Spa	Paid in Full	Standard	$ 8,560		
26	2012-020	1/6/2012	Deanne	McGuire	Port-a-Spa	Finance	Promotion	$ 26,500		
27	2012-021	1/6/2012	Oleta	Fairbanks	Port-a-Spa	Finance	Standard	$ 5,000		
28	2012-022	1/6/2012	Seth	Prescott	Serenity Spas	Finance	Promotion	$ 8,560		
29	2012-023	1/7/2012	Seth	Prescott	Port-a-Spa	Finance	Promotion	$ 5,000		
30	2012-024	1/7/2012	Grant	Ingersoll	Serenity Spas	Paid in Full	Standard	$ 5,400		
31	2012-025	1/8/2012	Oleta	Fairbanks	Serenity Spas	Finance	Standard	$ 3,240		
32	2012-026	1/9/2012	Deanne	McGuire	Port-a-Spa	Finance	Promotion	$ 7,400		
33	2012-027	1/9/2012	Grant	Ingersoll	Port-a-Spa	Finance	Promotion	$ 22,000		
34	2012-028	1/9/2012	Grant	Ingersoll	The Original Hc	Paid in Full	Promotion	$ 3,240		
35	2012-029	1/10/2012	Seth	Prescott	The Original Hc	Paid in Full	Standard	$ 7,690		
36	2012-030	1/10/2012	Deanne	McGuire	Serenity Spas	Finance	Promotion	$ 6,000		
37	2012-031	1/11/2012	Deanne	McGuire	The Original Hc	Finance	Promotion	$ 7,500		
38	2012-032	1/11/2012	Oleta	Fairbanks	Port-a-Spa	Paid in Full	Promotion	$ 7,500		

FIGURE 4.18 Missing Record Added ➤

a. Click **cell A36** or any cell within the table range on row 36.

   You need to make a cell active on the row in which you want to insert the new table row.

b. Click the **Home tab**, click the **Insert arrow** in the Cells group, and then select **Insert Table Rows Above**.

   Excel inserts a new table row on row 36. The rest of the records move down by one row.

c. Enter the following data in the respective fields on the newly created row. AutoComplete will help you enter the names, manufacturer, payment type, and transaction text. Then save the workbook.

   - Transaction Number: **2012-030**
   - Date: **1/10/2012**
   - Sales Rep First Name: **Deanne**
   - Sales Rep Last Name: **McGuire**
   - Manufacturer: **Serenity Spas**
   - Payment Type: **Finance**
   - Transaction: **Promotion**
   - Amount: **6000**

STEP 4 REMOVE DUPLICATE ROWS

As you continue checking the transaction records, you think the table contains some duplicate records. To avoid having to look at the entire table row-by-row, you want to have Excel find and remove the duplicate rows for you. Refer to Figure 4.19 as you complete Step 4.

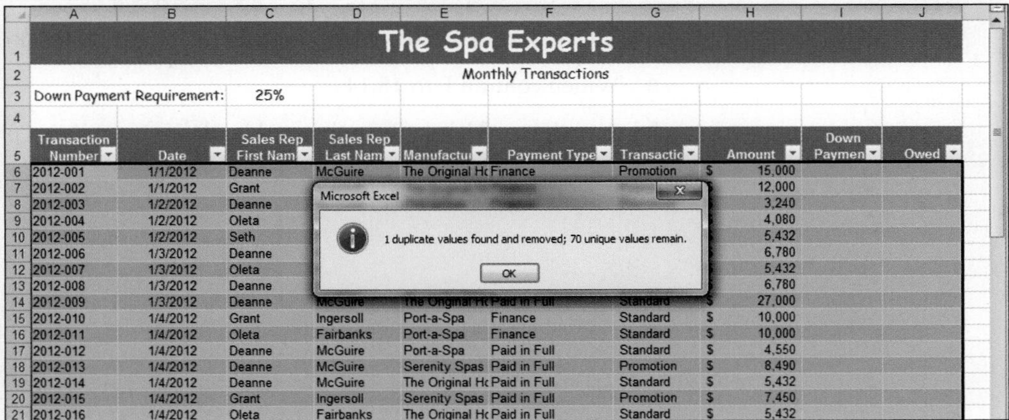

The Spa Experts

Monthly Transactions

Down Payment Requirement: 25%

	Transaction Number	Date	Sales Rep First Nam	Sales Rep Last Nam	Manufactu	Payment Type	Transactio	Amount	Down Paymen	Owed
6	2012-001	1/1/2012	Deanne	McGuire	The Original Hc	Finance	Promotion	$ 15,000		
7	2012-002	1/1/2012	Grant					12,000		
8	2012-003	1/2/2012	Deanne					3,240		
9	2012-004	1/2/2012	Oleta					4,080		
10	2012-005	1/2/2012	Seth					5,432		
11	2012-006	1/3/2012	Deanne					6,780		
12	2012-007	1/3/2012	Oleta					5,432		
13	2012-008	1/3/2012	Deanne					6,780		
14	2012-009	1/3/2012	Deanne	McGuire	The Original Hc	Paid in Full	Standard	$ 27,000		
15	2012-010	1/4/2012	Grant	Ingersoll	Port-a-Spa	Finance	Standard	$ 10,000		
16	2012-011	1/4/2012	Oleta	Fairbanks	Port-a-Spa	Finance	Standard	$ 10,000		
17	2012-012	1/4/2012	Deanne	McGuire	Port-a-Spa	Paid in Full	Standard	$ 4,550		
18	2012-013	1/4/2012	Deanne	McGuire	Serenity Spas	Paid in Full	Promotion	$ 8,490		
19	2012-014	1/4/2012	Deanne	McGuire	The Original Hc	Paid in Full	Standard	$ 5,432		
20	2012-015	1/4/2012	Grant	Ingersoll	Serenity Spas	Paid in Full	Promotion	$ 7,450		
21	2012-016	1/4/2012	Oleta	Fairbanks	The Original Hc	Paid in Full	Standard	$ 5,432		

FIGURE 4.19 Duplicate Record Removed ➤

a. Scroll to see rows 20 and 21. Click the **Design tab**.

The records on rows 20 and 21 are identical. You need to remove one row.

b. Click **Remove Duplicates** in the Tools group.

The Remove Duplicates dialog box opens.

c. Click **Select All**, if necessary, to select all table columns.

d. Click the **My data has headers check box**, if necessary, and then click **OK**.

Excel displays a message box indicating the number of duplicate records found and removed. The message box also specifies how many unique records remain.

e. Click **OK** in the message box. Save the workbook.

STEP 5 APPLY A TABLE STYLE

Now that you have modified fields and records, you want to apply a table style to format the table. Refer to Figure 4.20 as you complete Step 5.

The Spa Experts

Monthly Transactions

Down Payment Requirement: 25%

Transaction Number	Date	Sales Rep First Nam	Sales Rep Last Nam	Manufacturer	Payment Type	Transactio	Amount	Down Paymen	Owed
2012-001	1/1/2012	Deanne	McGuire	The Original Hot Tub	Finance	Promotion	$ 15,000		
2012-002	1/1/2012	Grant	Ingersoll	The Original Hot Tub	Finance	Promotion	$ 12,000		
2012-003	1/2/2012	Deanne	McGuire	Port-a-Spa	Finance	Promotion	$ 3,240		
2012-004	1/2/2012	Oleta	Fairbanks	Port-a-Spa	Finance	Promotion	$ 4,080		
2012-005	1/2/2012	Seth	Prescott	Serenity Spas	Finance	Promotion	$ 5,432		
2012-006	1/3/2012	Deanne	McGuire	Port-a-Spa	Finance	Standard	$ 6,780		
2012-007	1/3/2012	Oleta	Fairbanks	The Original Hot Tub	Finance	Standard	$ 5,432		
2012-008	1/3/2012	Deanne	McGuire	Serenity Spas	Paid in Full	Standard	$ 6,780		
2012-009	1/3/2012	Deanne	McGuire	The Original Hot Tub	Paid in Full	Standard	$ 27,000		
2012-010	1/4/2012	Grant	Ingersoll	Port-a-Spa	Finance	Standard	$ 10,000		
2012-011	1/4/2012	Oleta	Fairbanks	Port-a-Spa	Finance	Standard	$ 10,000		
2012-012	1/4/2012	Deanne	McGuire	Port-a-Spa	Paid in Full	Standard	$ 4,550		
2012-013	1/4/2012	Deanne	McGuire	Serenity Spas	Paid in Full	Promotion	$ 8,490		
2012-014	1/4/2012	Deanne	McGuire	The Original Hot Tub	Paid in Full	Standard	$ 5,432		
2012-015	1/4/2012	Grant	Ingersoll	Serenity Spas	Paid in Full	Promotion	$ 7,450		
2012-016	1/4/2012	Oleta	Fairbanks	The Original Hot Tub	Paid in Full	Standard	$ 5,432		

FIGURE 4.20 Table Style Applied ➤

a. Click the **More button** in the Table Styles group to display the Table Styles gallery.

b. Position the mouse pointer over the fourth style on the second row in the *Light* section.

Live Preview shows the table with the Table Style Light 10 style but does not apply it.

c. Click **Table Style Medium 6**, the sixth style on the first row in the *Medium* section.

Excel formats the table with the Table Style Medium 6 format.

d. Click in the **Name Box**, type **A1**, and press **Enter** to go to **cell A1**, the title. Click the **Home tab**, click the **Fill Color arrow** in the Font group, and then click **Aqua, Accent 5**.

You applied a fill color for the title to match the fill color of the field names.

e. Widen column E to **18.14**.

f. Save the workbook. Keep the workbook onscreen if you plan to continue with Hands-On Exercise 3. If not, close the workbook and exit Excel.

Table Manipulation and Aggregation

When you convert data to a table, you have a variety of options to manipulate that data, in addition to managing fields and records and applying predefined table styles. You can arrange data in different sequences, display only particular records instead of the entire dataset, and aggregate data. Although Excel provides many advantages for using tables over a range, you might need to convert a table back to a range to perform a few tasks that are not available for tables.

You can add more meaning to tables by aggregating data.

In this section, you will learn how to sort records by text, numbers, and dates in a table. In addition, you will learn how to filter data based on conditions you set. You will create structured formulas to perform calculations, and add a total row.

Sorting Data

Table data are easier to understand and work with if you organize the data. In Figure 4.1, the data are arranged by transaction number. You might want to organize the table by showing sales by sales associate, or to display all financed spas together, followed by all paid-in-full spas. ***Sorting*** arranges records by the value of one or more fields within a table.

Sorting arranges records in a table by the value in field(s) within a table.

Sort One Column

You can sort data by one or more columns. To sort by only one column, you can use any of the following methods for either a range of data or a table:

- Click Sort & Filter in the Editing group on the Home tab.
- Click Sort A to Z, Sort Z to A, or Sort in the Sort & Filter group on the Data tab.
- Right-click the field to sort, point to Sort from the shortcut menu, and select the type of sort you want.

When you format data as a table, the field names appear in a header row, which contains sort and filter arrows. Click the arrow for the column you want to sort and select the type of sort you want. Table 4.3 lists sort options by data type.

TABLE 4.3 Sort Options

Data Type	Options	Explanation
Text	Sort A to Z	Arranges data in alphabetical order.
	Sort Z to A	Arranges data in reverse alphabetical order.
Dates	Sort Oldest to Newest	Displays data in chronological order, from oldest to newest.
	Sort Newest to Oldest	Displays data in reverse chronological order, from newest to oldest.
Values	Sort Smallest to Largest	Arranges values from the smallest value to the largest value.
	Sort Largest to Smallest	Arranges values from the largest value to the smallest value.

Use the Sort Dialog Box to Sort Multiple Columns

At times sorting by only one field yields several records that have the same information—for example the same last name or the same manufacturer. Sales representative names and manufacturer names appear several times. A single sort field does not uniquely identify a record. You might need both last name and first name to identify an individual. Using multiple level sorts allows differentiation among records with the same data in the first (primary) sort level.

For example, you might want to sort by sales rep names, manufacturer, and then by price. Excel enables you to sort data on 64 different levels. To perform a multiple level sort:

1. Click in any cell in the table.
2. Click Sort in the Sort & Filter group on the Data tab to display the Sort dialog box.
3. Select the primary sort level by clicking the *Sort by* arrow and selecting the column to sort by, and then clicking the Order arrow and selecting the sort order from the list.
4. Click Add Level, select the second sort level by clicking the *Then by* arrow and selecting the column to sort by, clicking the Order arrow, and then selecting the sort order from the list.
5. Continue to click Add Level and add sort levels until you have entered all sort levels. See Figure 4.21. Click OK.

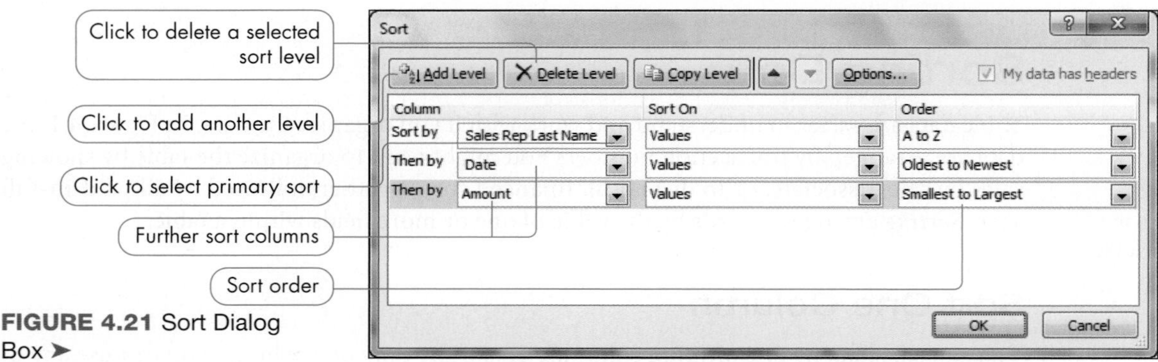

FIGURE 4.21 Sort Dialog Box ➤

Create a Custom Sort

Excel arranges data in defined sequences, such as alphabetical order. For example, weekdays are sorted alphabetically: Friday, Monday, Saturday, Sunday, Thursday, Tuesday, and Wednesday. However, you might want to create a custom sort sequence. For example, you can create a custom sort to arrange weekdays in order from Sunday to Saturday.

To create a custom sort sequence, click Sort in the Sort & Filter group on the Data tab. Click the Order arrow, and then select Custom List to display the Custom Lists dialog box (see Figure 4.22). Select an existing sort sequence in the *Custom lists* box, or select NEW LIST, click Add, and then type the entries in the desired sort sequence in the *List entries* box, pressing Enter between entries. Click Add, and then click OK.

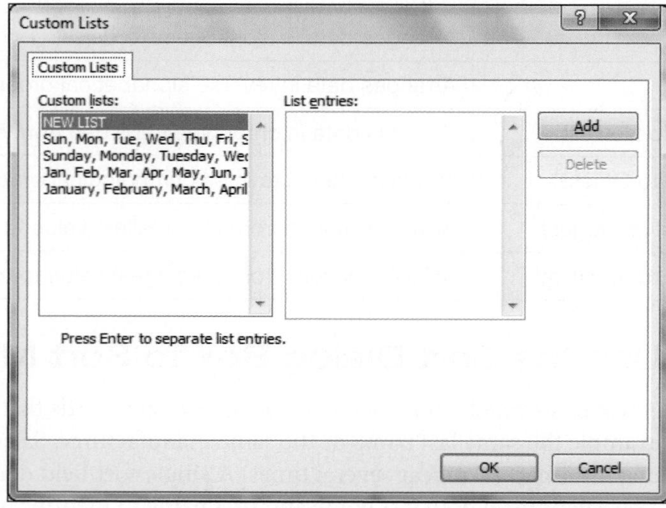

FIGURE 4.22 Custom Lists Dialog Box ➤

Filtering is the process of displaying only records that meet specific conditions.

Filtering Data

You might want to show only particular records. ***Filtering*** is the process of specifying conditions to display only those records that meet certain conditions. For example, you might want to filter the data to show transactions for only Oleta Fairbanks. To filter records by a particular field, click the column's filter arrow. The list displays each unique label, value, or date contained in the column. Deselect the (Select All) check box, and then click the check box for each value you want to include in the filtered results.

Often you will need to apply more than one filter to display the needed records. You can filter more than one column. Each additional filter is based on the current filtered data and further reduces a data subset. To apply multiple filters, click each column's filter arrow, and select the values to include in the filtered data results.

TIP Copying Before Filtering Data

Often, you need to show different filters applied to the same dataset. You can copy the data to another worksheet, and then filter the copied data to preserve the original dataset.

Apply Text Filters

When you apply a filter to a text column, the filter menu displays each unique text item. You can select one or more text items from the list. For example, select Fairbanks to show only records for this salesperson. To display records for both Fairbanks and Prescott, deselect the (Select All) check mark, and then click the Fairbanks and Prescott check boxes. You can also select Text Filters to see a submenu of additional options, such as *Begins With*, to select all records where the name begins with the letter G, for example.

Figure 4.23 shows the Last Name filter menu with two names selected. Excel displays records for these two reps only. The records for the other sales reps are hidden but not deleted. The filter arrow displays a filter icon, indicating which column is filtered. Excel displays the row numbers in blue, indicating that you applied a filter. The missing row numbers indicate hidden rows of data. When you remove the filter, all the records display again.

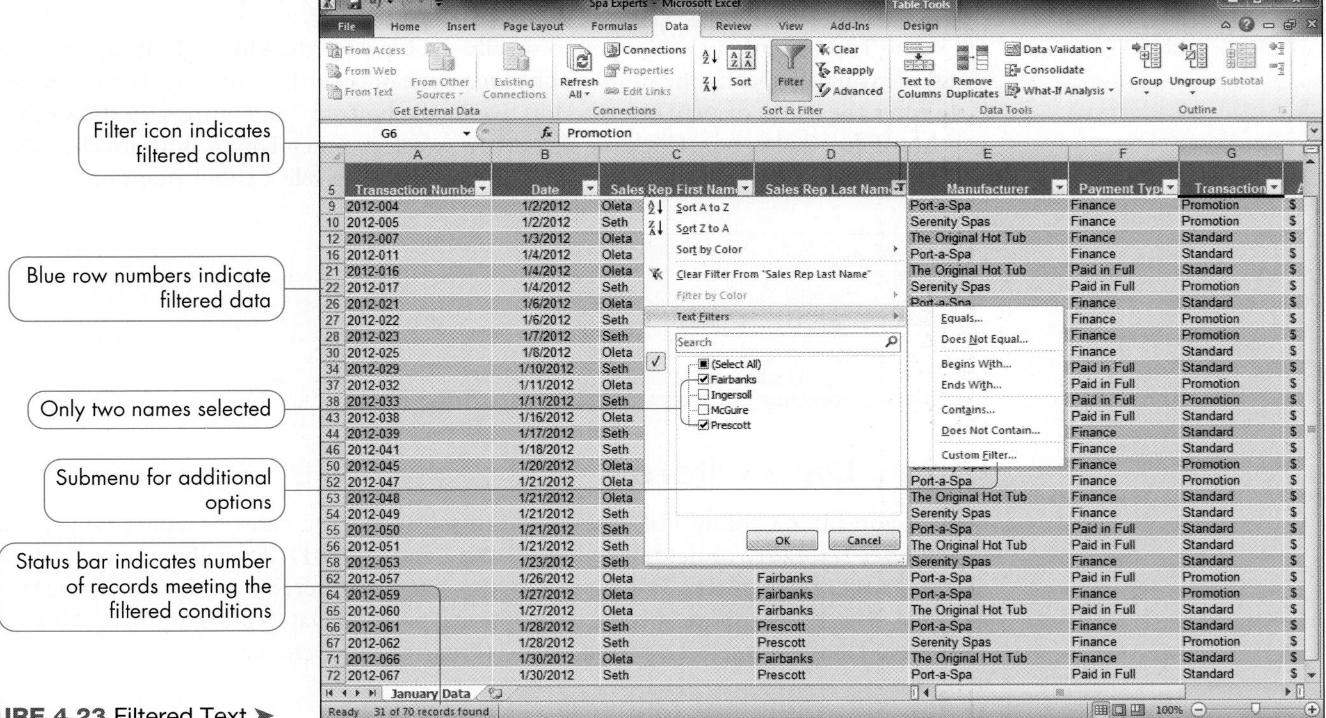

FIGURE 4.23 Filtered Text ➤

Filter Arrows

Before you filter a table, the Filter command in the Sort & Filter group on the Data tab is orange, indicating the filter arrows are displayed. Click Filter to toggle the filter arrows on and off. To filter a range of data instead of a table, activate the filter arrows by clicking Filter.

Apply Number Filters

When you filter a column of numbers, you can select specific numbers. You might want to filter numbers by a range, such as numbers greater than $5,000 or numbers between $4,000 and $5,000. The submenu enables you to set a variety of number filters. In Figure 4.24, the amounts are filtered to show only those that are above the average amount. In this situation, Excel calculates the average amount as $9,577. Only records above that amount display.

If the field contains a large number of unique entries, you can click in the Search box, and then type a value, text label, or date. Doing so narrows the visible list so that you do not have to scroll through the entire list. For example, if you enter $7, the list will display only values that start with $7.

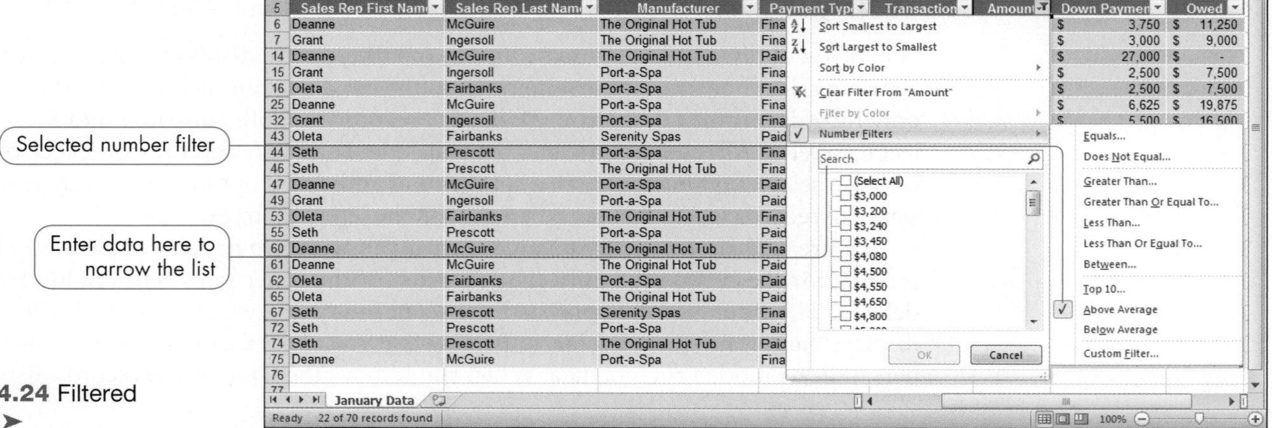

FIGURE 4.24 Filtered Numbers ➤

The Top 10 option enables you to specify the top records. Although the option name is Top 10, you can specify the number or percentage of records to display. For example, you can filter the list to display only the top five or the bottom 7%. Figure 4.25 shows the Top 10 AutoFilter dialog box. Click the first arrow to select either Top or Bottom, click the spin arrows to indicate a value, and then click the last arrow to select either Items or Percent.

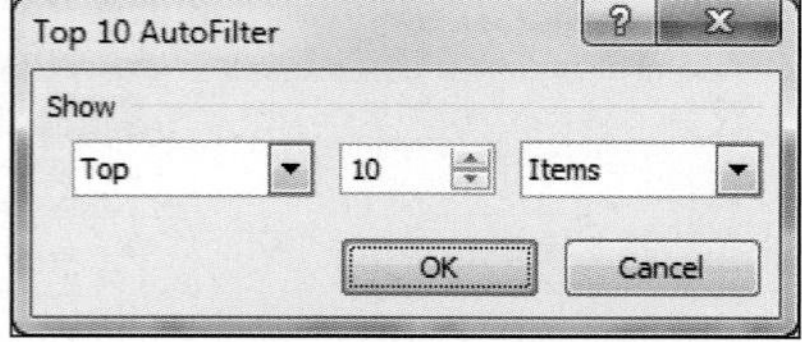

FIGURE 4.25 Top 10 AutoFilter Dialog Box ➤

Apply Date Filters

When you filter a column of dates, you can select specific dates or a date range, such as dates after 1/15/2012 or dates between 1/1/2012 and 1/7/2012. The submenu enables you to set a variety of date filters. In Figure 4.26, the dates are filtered to show only those that are after 1/15/2012. For more specific date options, point to Date Filters, point to All Dates in the Period, and then select a period, such as Quarter 2 or October.

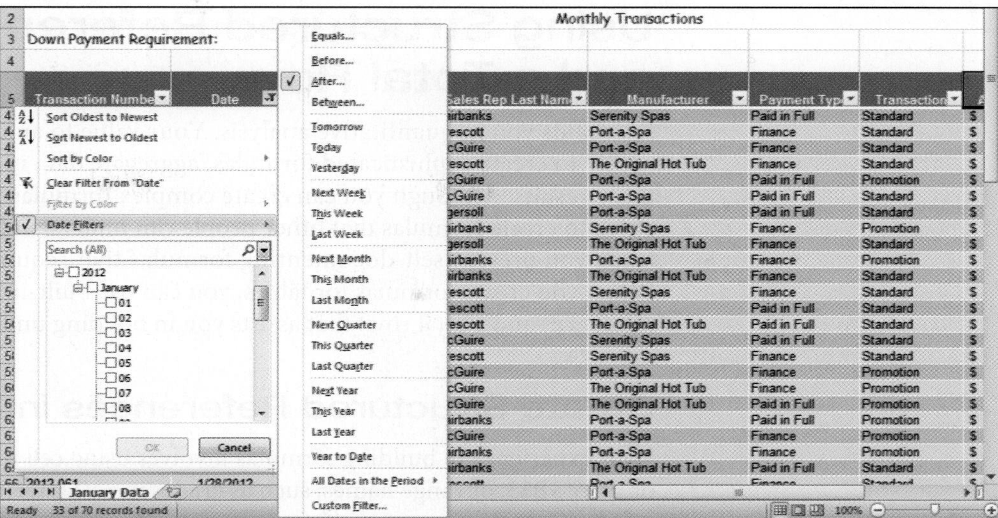

FIGURE 4.26 Filtered Dates ➤

Apply a Custom Filter

If you select options such as *Greater Than* or *Before*, Excel displays the Custom AutoFilter dialog box (see Figure 4.27). You can also select Custom Filter from the menu to display this dialog box, which is designed for more complex filtering requirements.

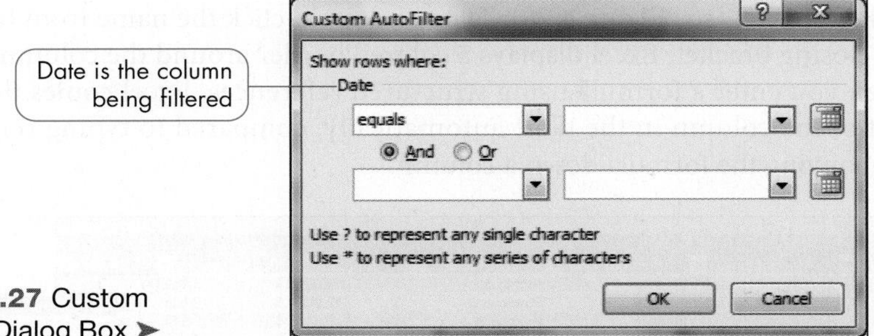

FIGURE 4.27 Custom AutoFilter Dialog Box ➤

The dialog box indicates the column being filtered, such as Date. To set the filters, click the arrows to select the comparison type, such as equals or contains. Click the arrow on the right to select a specific text, value, or date entry, or type the data yourself. For ranges of dates or values, click And, and then specify the comparison operator and value or date for the next condition row. For text, click Or. For example, if you want both Kansas and Kentucky, you must select Or because one data entry contains either Kansas or Kentucky but not both at the same time.

You can use wildcards to represent characters. For example, to select all states starting with New, type New * in the second box. The asterisk (*) represents any number of characters. If you want a wildcard for only a single character, type the question mark (?).

Clear Filters

After reviewing the filtered data, you can remove the filters to see the entire dataset again. To remove only one filter and keep the other filters, click the filter arrow for the column from which you wish to clear the filter, and then select Clear Filter From. Excel then removes that column's filter and displays records previously hidden by that filter. To remove all filters, click Filter in the Sort & Filter group on the Data tab, or click Sort & Filter in the Editing group on the Home tab and select Filter. Excel clears all filters and displays all records in the dataset.

Using Structured References and a Total Row

Excel aids you in quantitative analysis. Your value to an organization increases with your ability to create sophisticated formulas, aggregate data in a meaningful way, and interpret those results. Although you can create complex formulas that you understand, you should strive to create formulas that other people can understand. Creating easy-to-read formulas helps you present self-documenting formulas that require less explanation on your part. When you create formulas for tables, you can use built-in functionality (such as structured references and a total row) that assists you in building understandable formulas.

Create Structured References in Formulas

A **structured reference** is a tag or use of a table element as a reference in a formula.

Your experience in building formulas involves using cell references, such as =SUM(B1:B15) or =H6*$B$3, or range names, such as grades in =VLOOKUP(E5,grades,2). You can use cell references and range names in formulas to perform calculations in a table, as well as another type of reference for formulas in tables: structured references. A ***structured reference*** is a tag or use of a table element, such as a column heading, as a reference in a formula. Structured references in formulas clearly indicate what type of data is used in the calculations.

A structured reference requires brackets around column headings or field names, such as =[Amount]-[Down Payment]. The use of column headings without row references in a structured formula is called an *unqualified reference*. While creating a formula by typing, Formula AutoComplete displays a list of column headings after you type the equal sign and the opening bracket (see Figure 4.28). Type or double-click the name from the list, and then type the closing bracket. Excel displays a colored border around the column being referenced. When you enter a formula using structured references, Excel copies the formula down the rest of the column in the table automatically, compared to typing references in formulas and copying the formula down a column.

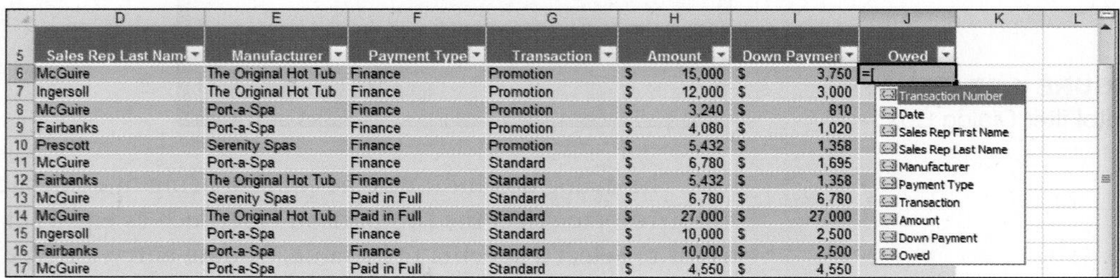

FIGURE 4.28 Structured Reference Creation ➤

You can still use the semi-selection process to create a formula. If you use the pointing process to enter a formula in a table, Excel builds a formula like this: =[@Amount]-[@Down Payment], where the @ indicates the current row. If you use the semi-selection process to create a formula outside the table, the formula includes the table name and row as well, such as =Table1[@Amount]-Table1[@Down Payment]. Table1 is the name of the table, and Amount and Down Payment are column headings. This structured formula that includes references, such as table numbers, is called a *fully qualified reference*. When you build formulas *within* a table, you can use either unqualified or fully qualified structured references. If you need to use table data in a formula *outside* the table boundaries, you must use fully qualified structured references.

TIP Complex Structured References

You can create structured reference tags to other elements, such as headers and totals. The more you know how to incorporate structured references, the more powerful your tables are to you. Look up *structured references* in Help for detailed explanations and examples of more complex use of structured references.

Create a Total Row

A **total row** appears as the last row of a table to display summary statistics, such as a sum.

Aggregating data provides more meaningful quantitative interpretation than individual values at times. For regular ranges of data, you use basic statistical functions, such as SUM, AVERAGE, MIN, and MAX, to provide meaning for a dataset. An Excel table provides the advantage of being able to display a total row automatically without creating the aggregate function yourself. A ***total row*** appears below the last row of records in an Excel table and enables you to display summary statistics, such as a sum of values displayed in a column. To display and use the total row:

1. Click the Design tab.
2. Click Total Row in the Table Style Options group. Excel displays the total row below the last record in the table. Excel displays *Total* in the first column of the total row. Excel either sums or counts data for the last column, depending on the type of data stored in that column. If the last column consists of values, Excel sums the values. If the last column is text, Excel counts the number of records.
3. Click a cell in the total row, and then click that cell's total row arrow and select the function results, such as Average, that you desire. To add a total to another column, click in the empty cell for that column in the total row, and then click the arrow to select the desired function. Select None to remove the function.

Figure 4.29 shows the active total row with totals applied to the Amount and Down Payment columns. A list of functions displays to change the function for the last column.

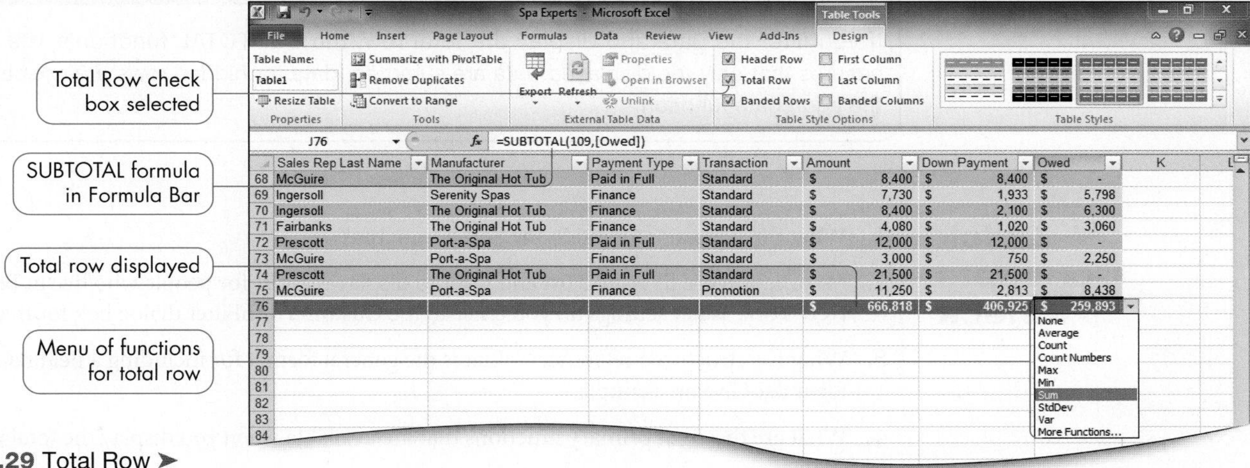

FIGURE 4.29 Total Row ➤

=SUBTOTAL(function_num,ref1,...

The **SUBTOTAL function** calculates an aggregate for values in a range or database.

The SUBTOTAL function calculates results on the total row. The ***SUBTOTAL function*** calculates an aggregate value, such as totals, for values in a range or database. The function for the total row looks like this: =SUBTOTAL(109,[Owed]). The function_num argument is a number that represents a function (see Table 4.4). The number 109 represents the SUM function. The ref1 argument indicates the range of values to calculate. In this case, [Owed] represents the Owed field. A benefit of the SUBTOTAL function is that it subtotals data for filtered records, so you have an accurate total for the visible records.

TABLE 4.4 SUBTOTAL Function Numbers		
Function	**Database Number**	**Table Number**
AVERAGE	1	101
COUNT	2	102
COUNTA	3	103
MAX	4	104
MIN	5	105
PRODUCT	6	106
STDEV	7	107
STDEVP	8	108
SUM	9	109
VAR	10	110
VARP	11	111

TIP Filtering Data and Subtotals

If you filter the data and display the total row, the SUBTOTAL function's 109 argument ensures that only the displayed data are summed; data for hidden rows are not calculated in the aggregate function.

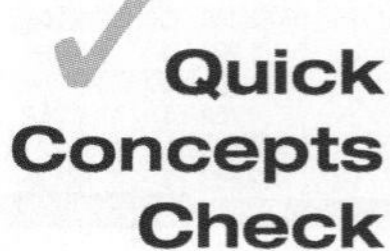

Quick Concepts Check

1. What three locations contain the Sort command?
2. Assume you are filtering a list and want to display records for people who live in Boston or New York. What settings do you enter in the Custom AutoFilter dialog box for that field?
3. What is a structured reference? What is the general format for including a field name in a formula? Give an example.
4. What are the eight primary functions that are available when you display the total row for a table?

HANDS-ON EXERCISES

3 Table Manipulation and Aggregation

You want to start analyzing the January transactions for Spa Experts by sorting and filtering data in a variety of ways to help you understand the transactions better. In addition, you need to calculate the required down payment amount and how much customers owe for their spas. Finally, you will convert the table back to a range.

Skills covered: Sort Individual Columns • Use the Sort Dialog Box • Apply Text Filters • Apply a Number Filter • Apply a Date Filter • Create Structured References • Add a Total Row • Convert a Table to a Range

STEP 1 SORT INDIVIDUAL COLUMNS

First, you want to compare the number of transactions by sales rep, so you will sort the data by the Last Name field. After reviewing the transactions by sales reps, you want to see what manufacturer's spas are sold most often. Refer to Figure 4.30 as you complete Step 1.

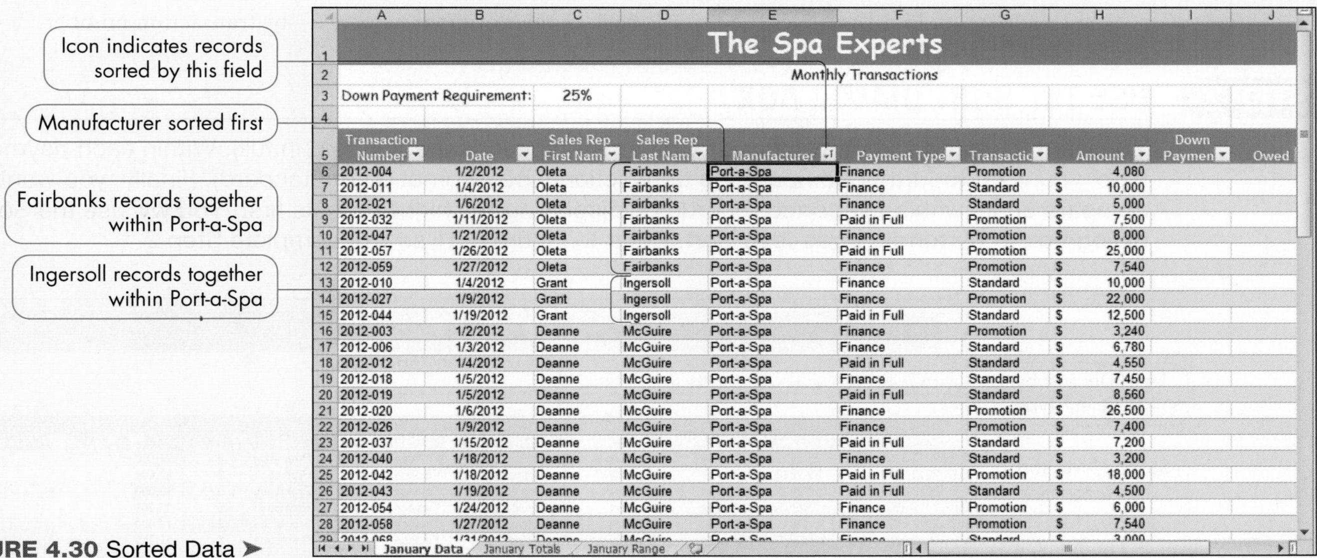

Transaction Number	Date	Sales Rep First Name	Sales Rep Last Name	Manufacturer	Payment Type	Transaction	Amount	Down Payment	Owed
2012-004	1/2/2012	Oleta	Fairbanks	Port-a-Spa	Finance	Promotion	$ 4,080		
2012-011	1/4/2012	Oleta	Fairbanks	Port-a-Spa	Finance	Standard	$ 10,000		
2012-021	1/6/2012	Oleta	Fairbanks	Port-a-Spa	Finance	Standard	$ 5,000		
2012-032	1/11/2012	Oleta	Fairbanks	Port-a-Spa	Paid in Full	Promotion	$ 7,500		
2012-047	1/21/2012	Oleta	Fairbanks	Port-a-Spa	Finance	Promotion	$ 8,000		
2012-057	1/26/2012	Oleta	Fairbanks	Port-a-Spa	Paid in Full	Promotion	$ 25,000		
2012-059	1/27/2012	Oleta	Fairbanks	Port-a-Spa	Finance	Promotion	$ 7,540		
2012-010	1/4/2012	Grant	Ingersoll	Port-a-Spa	Finance	Standard	$ 10,000		
2012-027	1/9/2012	Grant	Ingersoll	Port-a-Spa	Finance	Promotion	$ 22,000		
2012-044	1/19/2012	Grant	Ingersoll	Port-a-Spa	Paid in Full	Standard	$ 12,500		
2012-003	1/2/2012	Deanne	McGuire	Port-a-Spa	Finance	Promotion	$ 3,240		
2012-006	1/3/2012	Deanne	McGuire	Port-a-Spa	Finance	Standard	$ 6,780		
2012-012	1/4/2012	Deanne	McGuire	Port-a-Spa	Paid in Full	Standard	$ 4,550		
2012-018	1/5/2012	Deanne	McGuire	Port-a-Spa	Finance	Standard	$ 7,450		
2012-019	1/5/2012	Deanne	McGuire	Port-a-Spa	Paid in Full	Standard	$ 8,560		
2012-020	1/6/2012	Deanne	McGuire	Port-a-Spa	Finance	Promotion	$ 26,500		
2012-026	1/9/2012	Deanne	McGuire	Port-a-Spa	Finance	Promotion	$ 7,400		
2012-037	1/15/2012	Deanne	McGuire	Port-a-Spa	Paid in Full	Standard	$ 7,200		
2012-040	1/18/2012	Deanne	McGuire	Port-a-Spa	Finance	Standard	$ 3,200		
2012-042	1/18/2012	Deanne	McGuire	Port-a-Spa	Paid in Full	Promotion	$ 18,000		
2012-043	1/19/2012	Deanne	McGuire	Port-a-Spa	Paid in Full	Standard	$ 4,500		
2012-054	1/24/2012	Deanne	McGuire	Port-a-Spa	Finance	Promotion	$ 6,000		
2012-058	1/27/2012	Deanne	McGuire	Port-a-Spa	Finance	Promotion	$ 7,540		

FIGURE 4.30 Sorted Data ➤

a. Open *e04h2spa_LastnameFirstname* if you closed it at the end of Hands-On Exercise 2. Save the workbook with the new name **e04h3spa_LastnameFirstname**, changing *h2* to *h3*.

b. Click the **Sales Rep Last Name filter arrow**, and then select **Sort A to Z**.

Excel arranges the records in alphabetical order by last name. All transactions completed by Fairbanks display first. Within each sales rep, records appear in their original sequence by transaction number. Without actually counting the records, which sales rep appears to have the most sales? According to the sorted list, McGuire sold the most spas in January. The up arrow icon on the Last Name filter arrow indicates records are sorted in alphabetical order by that column.

Name Sorts

Always check the table to determine how many levels of sorting you need to apply. If your table contains several people with the same last name but different first names, you would first sort by the Last Name field, and then sort by First Name field individually. All the people with the last name Fairbanks would be grouped together and then further sorted by first name, such as Amanda and then Bradley. To ensure that Excel sorts in the sequence you desire, use the Sort dialog box instead of sorting columns individually.

c. Click the **Manufacturer filter arrow**, and then select **Sort A to Z**.

   Excel arranges the records in alphabetical order by manufacturer. Port-a-Spa displays first. Within the Port-a-Spa group, the records are further sorted by the previous sort: last name. Fairbanks appears before Ingersoll. The up arrow icon within the Manufacturer filter arrow indicates that records are sorted in alphabetical order by this column (see Figure 4.30).

d. Click the **Transaction Number filter arrow**, and then select **Sort A to Z**. Save the workbook.

   Excel arranges the records back in their original sequence—by transaction number.

STEP 2 USE THE SORT DIALOG BOX

You want to review the transactions by payment type (financed or paid in full). Within each payment type, you want to further compare the transaction type (promotion or standard). Finally, you want to compare costs within the sorted records by displaying the highest costs first. You will use the Sort dialog box to perform a three-level sort. Refer to Figure 4.31 as you complete Step 2.

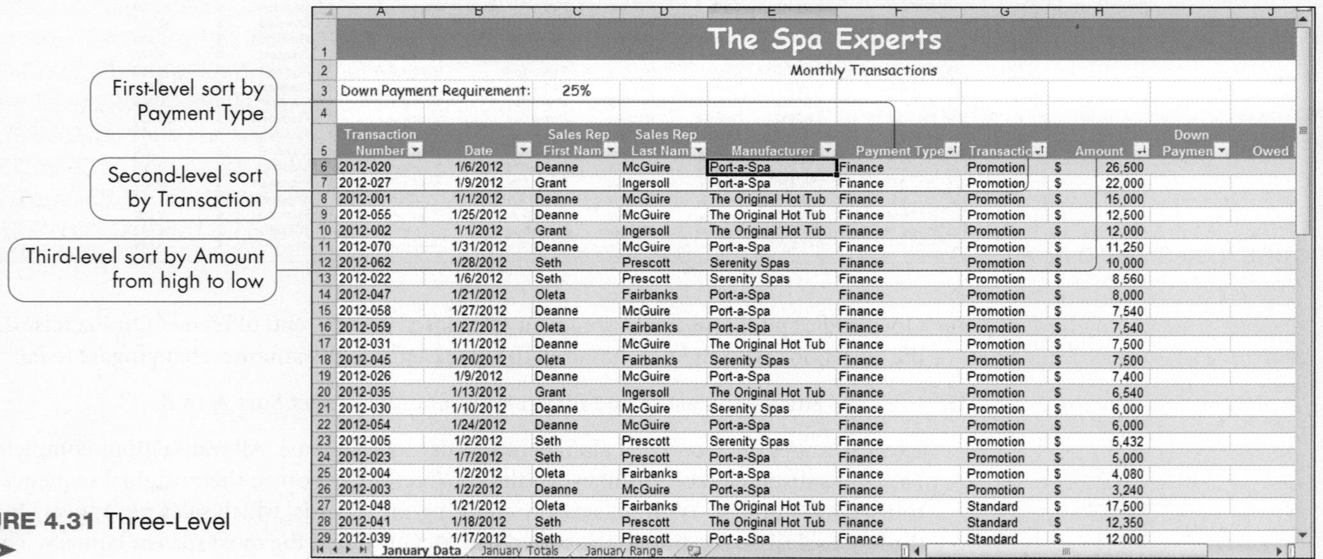

The Spa Experts

Monthly Transactions

Down Payment Requirement: 25%

Transaction Number	Date	Sales Rep First Nam	Sales Rep Last Nam	Manufacturer	Payment Type	Transactic	Amount	Down Paymen	Owed
2012-020	1/6/2012	Deanne	McGuire	Port-a-Spa	Finance	Promotion	$ 26,500		
2012-027	1/9/2012	Grant	Ingersoll	Port-a-Spa	Finance	Promotion	$ 22,000		
2012-001	1/1/2012	Deanne	McGuire	The Original Hot Tub	Finance	Promotion	$ 15,000		
2012-055	1/25/2012	Deanne	McGuire	The Original Hot Tub	Finance	Promotion	$ 12,500		
2012-002	1/1/2012	Grant	Ingersoll	The Original Hot Tub	Finance	Promotion	$ 12,000		
2012-070	1/31/2012	Deanne	McGuire	Port-a-Spa	Finance	Promotion	$ 11,250		
2012-062	1/28/2012	Seth	Prescott	Serenity Spas	Finance	Promotion	$ 10,000		
2012-022	1/6/2012	Seth	Prescott	Serenity Spas	Finance	Promotion	$ 8,560		
2012-047	1/21/2012	Oleta	Fairbanks	Port-a-Spa	Finance	Promotion	$ 8,000		
2012-058	1/27/2012	Deanne	McGuire	Port-a-Spa	Finance	Promotion	$ 7,540		
2012-059	1/27/2012	Oleta	Fairbanks	Port-a-Spa	Finance	Promotion	$ 7,540		
2012-031	1/11/2012	Deanne	McGuire	The Original Hot Tub	Finance	Promotion	$ 7,500		
2012-045	1/20/2012	Oleta	Fairbanks	Serenity Spas	Finance	Promotion	$ 7,500		
2012-026	1/9/2012	Deanne	McGuire	Port-a-Spa	Finance	Promotion	$ 7,400		
2012-035	1/13/2012	Grant	Ingersoll	The Original Hot Tub	Finance	Promotion	$ 6,540		
2012-030	1/10/2012	Deanne	McGuire	Serenity Spas	Finance	Promotion	$ 6,000		
2012-054	1/24/2012	Deanne	McGuire	Port-a-Spa	Finance	Promotion	$ 6,000		
2012-005	1/2/2012	Seth	Prescott	Serenity Spas	Finance	Promotion	$ 5,432		
2012-023	1/7/2012	Seth	Prescott	Port-a-Spa	Finance	Promotion	$ 5,000		
2012-004	1/2/2012	Oleta	Fairbanks	Port-a-Spa	Finance	Promotion	$ 4,080		
2012-003	1/2/2012	Deanne	McGuire	Port-a-Spa	Finance	Promotion	$ 3,240		
2012-048	1/21/2012	Oleta	Fairbanks	The Original Hot Tub	Finance	Standard	$ 17,500		
2012-041	1/18/2012	Seth	Prescott	The Original Hot Tub	Finance	Standard	$ 12,350		
2012-039	1/17/2012	Seth	Prescott	Port-a-Spa	Finance	Standard	$ 12,000		

January Data | January Totals | January Range

FIGURE 4.31 Three-Level Sort ➤

a. Click inside the table. Click the **Data tab**.

   Both the Data and Home tabs contain commands to open the Sort dialog box.

b. Click **Sort** in the Sort & Filter group.

   The Sort dialog box opens. You start by specifying the column for the primary sort. In this case, you want to sort the records first by the Payment Type column.

c. Click the **Sort by arrow**, and then select **Payment Type**.

   The default Sort On is Values, and the default Order is A to Z.

d. Click **Add Level**.

The Sort dialog box adds the *Then by* row, which adds a secondary sort.

e. Click the **Then by arrow**, and then select **Transaction**.

Excel will first sort the records by the Payment Type. Within each Payment Type, Excel will further sort records by Transaction.

f. Click **Add Level** to add another *Then by* row. Click the second **Then by arrow**, and then select **Amount**.

g. Click the **Order arrow** for the Amount sort, and then select **Largest to Smallest**.

Within the Payment Type and Transaction sorts, this will arrange the records with the largest amount first in descending order to the smallest amount.

h. Click **OK** and scroll through the records. Save the workbook.

Figure 4.31 shows the sorted records. Most customers finance their spas instead of paying for their spas in full. For the financed spas, about half were promotional sales and half were standard sales. For those spas paid in full, a majority of the transactions were standard sales, indicating that people with money don't necessarily wait for a promotional sale to buy their spas.

STEP 3 APPLY TEXT FILTERS

Now that you know McGuire had the most transactions, you want to focus on her sales for January. In particular, you want to filter the table to show only her records. You notice that she sells more Port-a-Spas and The Original Hot Tub than the Serenity Spas, so you will filter out the Serenity Spa sales. Refer to Figure 4.32 as you complete Step 3.

5	Transaction Number	Date	Sales Rep First Nam	Sales Rep Last Nam	Manufacturer	Payment Type	Transactio		Amount	Down Paymen	Owed
6	2012-020	1/6/2012	Deanne	McGuire	Port-a-Spa	Finance	Promotion	$	26,500		
8	2012-001	1/1/2012	Deanne	McGuire	The Original Hot Tub	Finance	Promotion	$	15,000		
9	2012-055	1/25/2012	Deanne	McGuire	The Original Hot Tub	Finance	Promotion	$	12,500		
11	2012-070	1/31/2012	Deanne	McGuire	Port-a-Spa	Finance	Promotion	$	11,250		
15	2012-058	1/27/2012	Deanne	McGuire	Port-a-Spa	Finance	Promotion	$	7,540		
17	2012-031	1/11/2012	Deanne	McGuire	The Original Hot Tub	Finance	Promotion	$	7,500		
19	2012-026	1/9/2012	Deanne	McGuire	Port-a-Spa	Finance	Promotion	$	7,400		
22	2012-054	1/24/2012	Deanne	McGuire	Port-a-Spa	Finance	Promotion	$	6,000		
26	2012-003	1/2/2012	Deanne	McGuire	Port-a-Spa	Finance	Promotion	$	3,240		
35	2012-018	1/5/2012	Deanne	McGuire	Port-a-Spa	Finance	Standard	$	7,450		
36	2012-006	1/3/2012	Deanne	McGuire	Port-a-Spa	Finance	Standard	$	6,780		
45	2012-040	1/18/2012	Deanne	McGuire	Port-a-Spa	Finance	Standard	$	3,200		
46	2012-068	1/31/2012	Deanne	McGuire	Port-a-Spa	Finance	Standard	$	3,000		
48	2012-056	1/26/2012	Deanne	McGuire	The Original Hot Tub	Paid in Full	Promotion	$	22,500		
49	2012-042	1/18/2012	Deanne	McGuire	Port-a-Spa	Paid in Full	Promotion	$	18,000		
58	2012-009	1/3/2012	Deanne	McGuire	The Original Hot Tub	Paid in Full	Standard	$	27,000		
64	2012-019	1/5/2012	Deanne	McGuire	Port-a-Spa	Paid in Full	Standard	$	8,560		
65	2012-063	1/28/2012	Deanne	McGuire	The Original Hot Tub	Paid in Full	Standard	$	8,400		
67	2012-037	1/15/2012	Deanne	McGuire	Port-a-Spa	Paid in Full	Standard	$	7,200		
70	2012-014	1/4/2012	Deanne	McGuire	The Original Hot Tub	Paid in Full	Standard	$	5,432		
74	2012-012	1/4/2012	Deanne	McGuire	Port-a-Spa	Paid in Full	Standard	$	4,550		
75	2012-043	1/19/2012	Deanne	McGuire	Port-a-Spa	Paid in Full	Standard	$	4,500		
76											
77											

January Data / January Totals / January Range

Ready 22 of 70 records found 100%

FIGURE 4.32 McGuire Sales for Two Manufacturers ➤

a. Click the **Sales Rep Last Name filter arrow**.

The (Select All) check box is selected.

b. Click the **(Select All) check box** to deselect all last names.

c. Click the **McGuire check box**, and then click **OK**.

The status bar indicates that 27 out of 70 records meet the filtering condition. The Last Name filter arrow includes a funnel icon, indicating that this column is filtered.

d. Click the **Manufacturer filter arrow**.

e. Click the **Serenity Spas check box** to deselect this manufacturer, and then click **OK**. Save the workbook.

You filtered out the Serenity Spas brand that McGuire sold. The remaining 22 records show McGuire's sales for the Port-a-Spas and The Original Hot Tub brands sold. The Manufacturer filter arrow includes a funnel icon, indicating that this column is also filtered.

STEP 4 APPLY A NUMBER FILTER

You now want to focus on the amount of sales for McGuire. In particular, you are interested in how much gross revenue she generated for spas that cost at least $10,000 or more. Refer to Figure 4.33 as you complete Step 4.

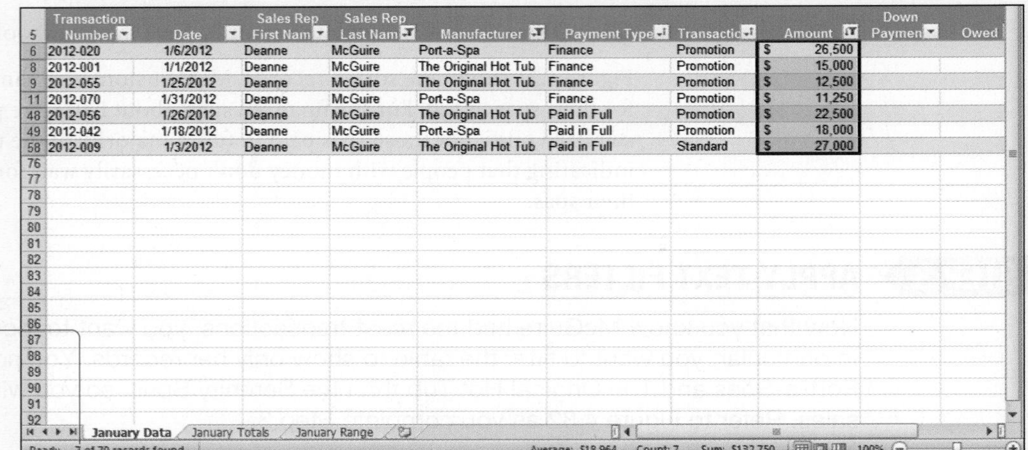

FIGURE 4.33 Filtered to Amounts Greater Than or Equal To $10,000 ➤

a. Select the **range H6:H75** of the filtered list, and then view the status bar.

The average transaction amount is $10,159 with 22 transactions (i.e., 22 filtered records). McGuire's total January sales are $223,502. You will use this total to see how much of the $223,502 sales generated are for higher-priced models she sold.

b. Click the **Amount filter arrow**.

c. Point to **Number Filters**, and then select **Greater Than Or Equal To**.

The Custom AutoFilter dialog box opens. The default comparison is *is greater than or equal to*, although you could change it if needed.

d. Type **10000** in the box to the right of *is greater than or equal to*, and then click **OK**. Save the workbook.

When typing numbers, you can type raw numbers such as 10000 or formatted numbers such as $10,000. Out of the original 27 spas McGuire sold, she sold only 7 of the Port-a-Spas and The Original Hot Tub brands that cost $10,000 or more. Out of the $223,502 total sales for those two brands, McGuire sold $132,750 in the higher-priced models costing $10,000 or more.

TROUBLESHOOTING: If no records display or if too many records display, you might have entered 100000 or 1000. Repeat steps b–d.

STEP 5 APPLY A DATE FILTER

Finally, you want to study McGuire's sales records for the week of January 22. You will add a date filter to identify those sales records. Refer to Figure 4.34 as you complete Step 5.

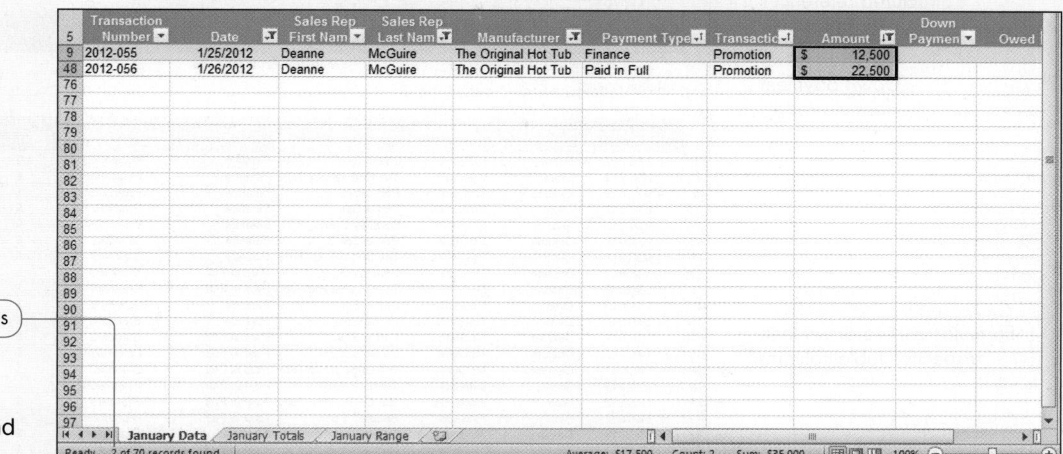

FIGURE 4.34 Filtered by Dates Between 1/22/2012 and 1/28/2012 ➤

a. Click the **Date filter arrow**.

b. Point to **Date Filters**, and then select **Between**.

   The Custom AutoFilter dialog box opens. The default comparisons are *is after or equal to* and *is before or equal to*, ready for you to enter the date specifications.

c. Type **1/22/2012** in the box on the right side of *is after or equal to*.

   You specified the starting date of the range of dates to include. You will keep the *And* option selected.

d. Type **1/28/2012** in the box on the right side of *is before or equal to*. Click **OK**. Save the workbook.

   McGuire had only two sales during that week, totaling $35,000.

STEP 6 CREATE STRUCTURED REFERENCES

To continue reviewing the January transactions, you need to calculate the required down payment for customers who financed their spas. The required down payment is located above the table data so that you can change that value if needed later. In addition, you need to calculate how much customers owe on their spas if they did not pay in full. You will use structured formulas to perform these calculations. Refer to Figure 4.35 as you complete Step 6.

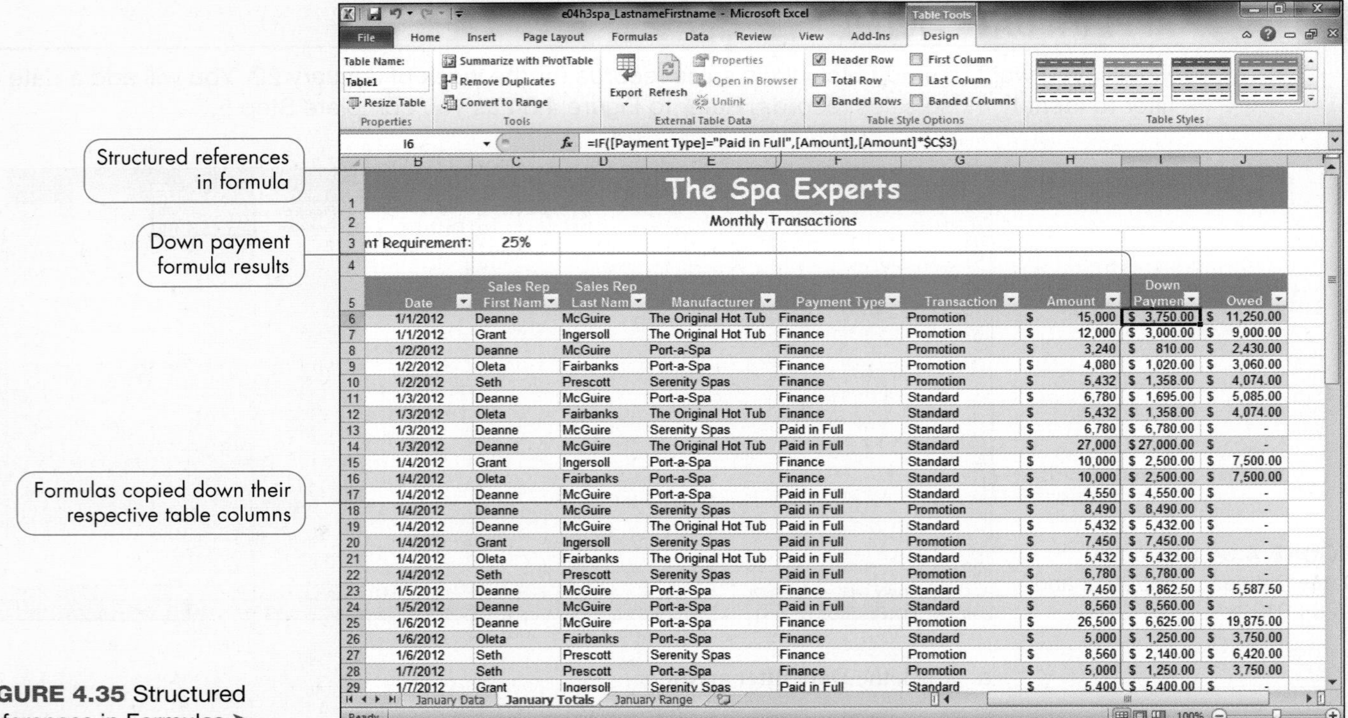

FIGURE 4.35 Structured References in Formulas ➤

a. Click the **January Totals worksheet tab.**

To preserve the integrity of the sorting and filtering in case your instructor wants to verify your work, you will continue with an identical table on another worksheet.

b. Click in the **Name Box**, type **I6**, and then press **Enter** to go to **cell I6**. Click **Insert Function** on the Formula Bar to open the Insert Function dialog box, select **IF** in the **Select a function list**, and then click **OK**.

c. Type **[Payment Type]="Paid in Full"** in the **Logical_test box.**

The logical test evaluates whether a customer paid in full, indicated in the Payment Type column. Remember to type the brackets around the column heading.

d. Type **[Amount]** in the **Value_if_true box.**

If a customer pays in full, their down payment is the full amount.

e. Type **[Amount]*$C$3** in the **Value_if_false box.**

If a customer does not pay in full, they must pay a required down payment. You use [Amount] to refer to the Amount column in the table. You must enclose the column heading in brackets. The amount of the spa is multiplied by the absolute reference to C3, the cell containing the required down payment percentage. You make this cell reference absolute so that it does not change when Excel copies the formula down the Down Payment column. Figure 4.35 shows the formula in the formula bar.

f. Click **OK** to enter the formula (see Figure 4.35).

Because you are entering formulas in a table, Excel copies the formula down the column automatically. The first customer must finance $3,750 (25% of $15,000). The columns in the current worksheet have been formatted as Accounting Number Format for you.

TROUBLESHOOTING: If the results seem incorrect, check your function. Errors will result if you do not enclose the field names in brackets, if you have misspelled a field name, if you omit the quotation marks around *Paid in Full*, and so on. Correct any errors.

g. Click **cell J6**. Type the formula **=[Amount]-[Down Payment]** and press **Enter**. Save the workbook.

The formula calculates how much customers owe if they finance their hot tubs. Excel copies the formula down the column.

STEP 7 ADD A TOTAL ROW

The table is almost complete, but you want to see the monthly totals for the Amount, Down Payment, and Owed columns. Instead of entering SUM functions yourself, you will add a total row. Refer to Figure 4.36 as you complete Step 7.

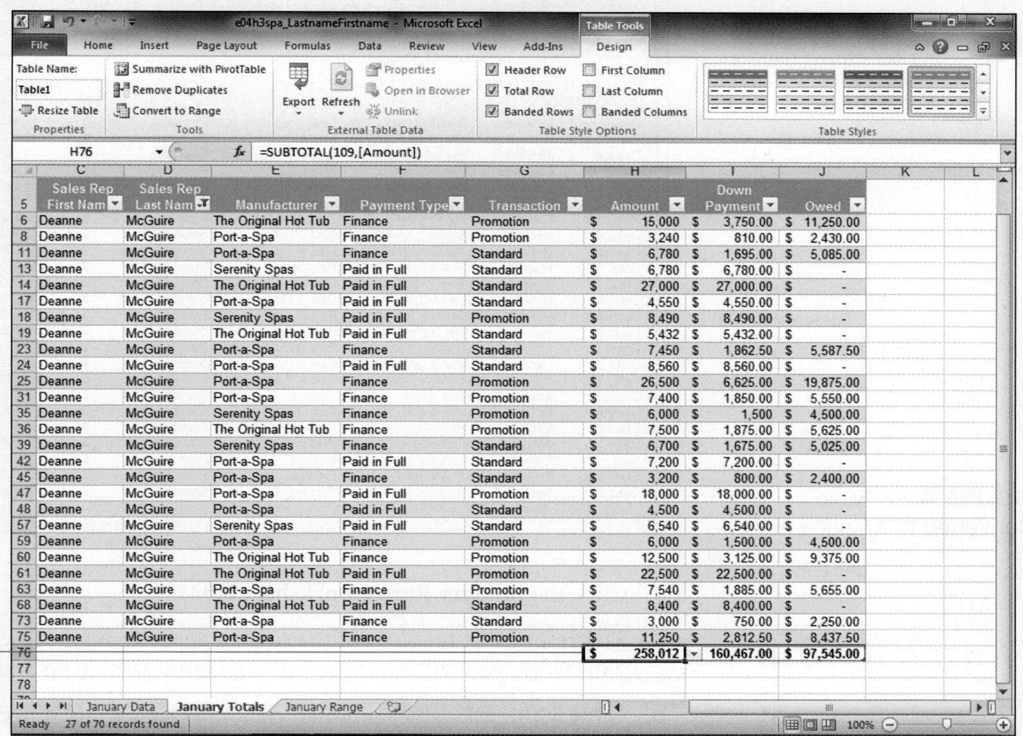

FIGURE 4.36 Totals for Filtered Table ➤

a. Click the **Design tab**, and then click **Total Row** in the Table Style Options group.

Excel displays the total row after the last record. It sums the last column of values automatically. The total amount customers owe is $259,893.00.

b. Click the **Down Payment cell** in row 76, click the **total arrow**, and then select **Sum**. Increase the Down Payment column width as needed.

You added a total to the Down Payment column. The total amount of down payment collected is $406,925.00. The formula appears as =SUBTOTAL(109,[Down Payment]) in the Formula Bar.

c. Click the **Amount cell** in row 76, click the **total arrow**, and then select **Sum**.

You added a total to the Amount column. The total amount of spa sales is $666,818. The formula appears as =SUBTOTAL(109,[Amount]) in the Formula Bar.

d. Filter by McGuire again. Save the workbook.

Notice that the total row values change to display the totals for only the filtered records.

STEP 8 CONVERT A TABLE TO A RANGE

Your last task for now is to convert a copy of the table to a range again so that you can apply other formats. Refer to Figure 4.37 as you complete Step 8.

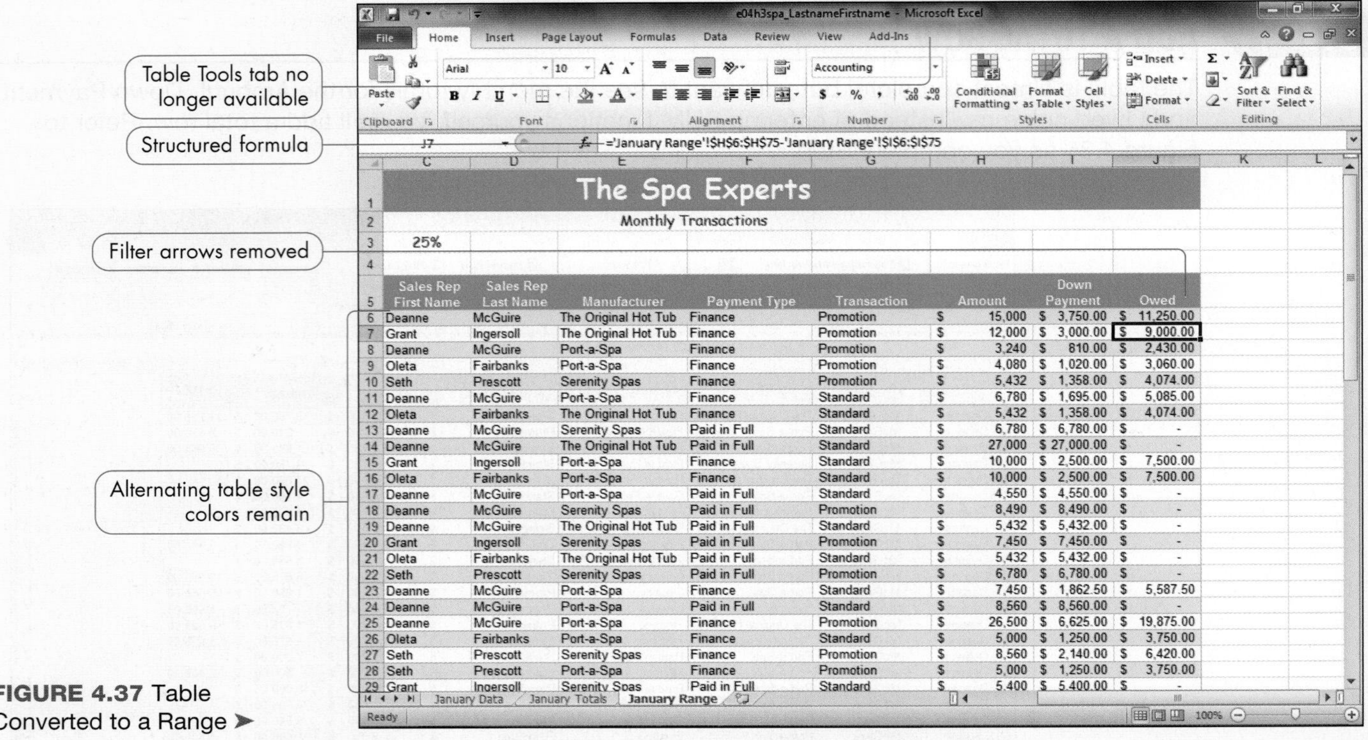

FIGURE 4.37 Table Converted to a Range ➤

a. Click the **January Range worksheet tab**.

   To preserve the integrity of the sorting and filtering in case your instructor wants to verify your work, you will continue with an identical table on another worksheet.

b. Click within the table, and then click the **Design tab**, if necessary.

c. Click **Convert to Range** in the Tools group.

   Excel displays a message box asking if you want to convert the table to a range.

d. Click **Yes**.

   Excel converts the table to a range. The filter arrows disappear, and the Table Tools no longer display. The range is still formatted using the table style you applied. The structured formula =[Amount]-[Down Payment] changes (see Figure 4.37).

e. Double-click the border between the column I and J headers to increase the width of column I so that the down payment total displays on the last row.

f. Save the workbook. Keep the workbook onscreen if you plan to continue with Hands-On Exercise 4. If not, close the workbook and exit Excel.

Conditional Formatting

You use table styles, or a variety of font, alignment, and number formats on the Home tab, to format a worksheet. You can also apply special formatting to cells that contain particular values or text using conditional formatting. ***Conditional formatting*** applies special formatting to highlight or emphasize cells that meet specific conditions. For example, a sales manager might want to highlight cells containing the top 10 sales amounts, or a professor might want to highlight test scores that fall below the average. You can also apply conditional formatting to point out data for a specific date or duplicate values in a range.

Conditional formatting highlights or emphasizes cells that meet certain conditions.

In this section, you will learn about the five conditional formatting categories and how to apply conditional formatting to a range of values based on a condition you set.

Applying Conditional Formatting

Conditional formatting helps you and your audience understand a dataset better because it adds a visual element to the cells. The term is called *conditional* because the formatting occurs when a condition is met. This is similar logic to the IF function you have used. Remember with an IF function, you create a logical test that is evaluated. If the logical or conditional test is true, the function produces one result. If the logical or conditional test is false, the function produces another result. With conditional formatting, if the condition is true, Excel formats the cell automatically based on that condition. If the condition is false, Excel does not format the cell. If you change a value in a conditionally formatted cell, Excel examines the new value to see if it should apply the conditional format. Table 4.5 lists and describes a number of different conditional formats that you can apply.

Conditional formatting helps you and your audience understand a dataset better because it adds a visual element to the cells.

TABLE 4.5 Conditional Formatting Options

Conditional Formatting	Description
Highlight Cells Rules	Highlights cells with a fill color, font color, or border (such as Light Red Fill with Dark Red Text) if values are greater than, less than, between two values, equal to a value, or duplicate values; text that contains particular characters; or dates when a date meets a particular condition, such as *In the last 7 days*.
Top/Bottom Rules	Formats cells with values in the top 10 items, top 10%, bottom 10 items, bottom 10%, values, above average, or below average. You can change the exact values to format the top or bottom items or percentages, such as top 5 or bottom 15%.
Data Bars	Applies a gradient or solid fill bar in which the width of the bar represents the current cell's value compared to other cells' values.
Color Scales	Formats different cells with different colors, assigning one color to the lowest group of values and another color to the highest group of values, with gradient colors to other values.
Icon Sets	Inserts an icon from an icon palette in each cell to indicate values compared to each other.

To apply a conditional format, select the cells for which you want to apply a conditional format, click the Home tab, click Conditional Formatting in the Styles group, and select the conditional formatting category you want to apply.

Apply the Highlight Cells Rules

The Highlight Cells Rules category enables you to apply a highlight to cells that meet a condition, such as a value greater than a particular value. This option contains predefined combinations of fill colors, font colors, and/or borders. This category is useful because it helps you identify and format automatically values of interest. For example, a weather tracker who developed a worksheet containing the temperatures for each day of a month might want to apply a conditional format to cells that contain temperatures between 70 and 75 degrees. To apply this conditional formatting, she would select Highlight Cells Rules, and then select Between. In the Between dialog box (see Figure 4.38), the weather tracker would type 70 in the *Format cells that are BETWEEN* box and 75 in the *and* box, select the type of conditional formatting, such as *Light Red Fill with Dark Red Text*, and then click OK to apply the formats.

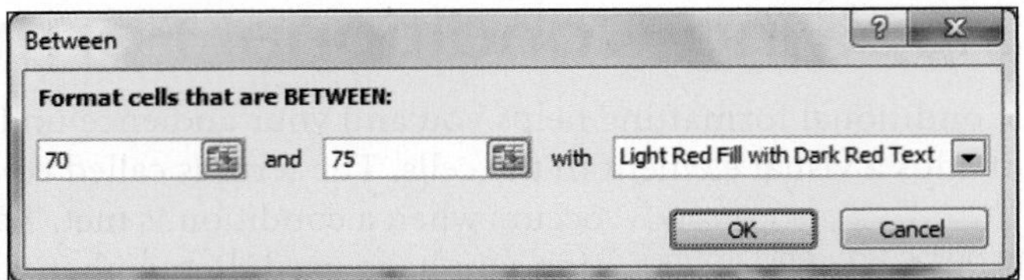

FIGURE 4.38 Between Dialog Box ➤

Figure 4.39 shows two columns of data that contain conditional formats. The Manufacturer column contains a conditional format to highlight text with a Light Red Fill with Dark Red Text for cells that contain *Serenity Spas*, and the Amount column contains a conditional format to highlight with Red Border values between $10,000 and $20,000.

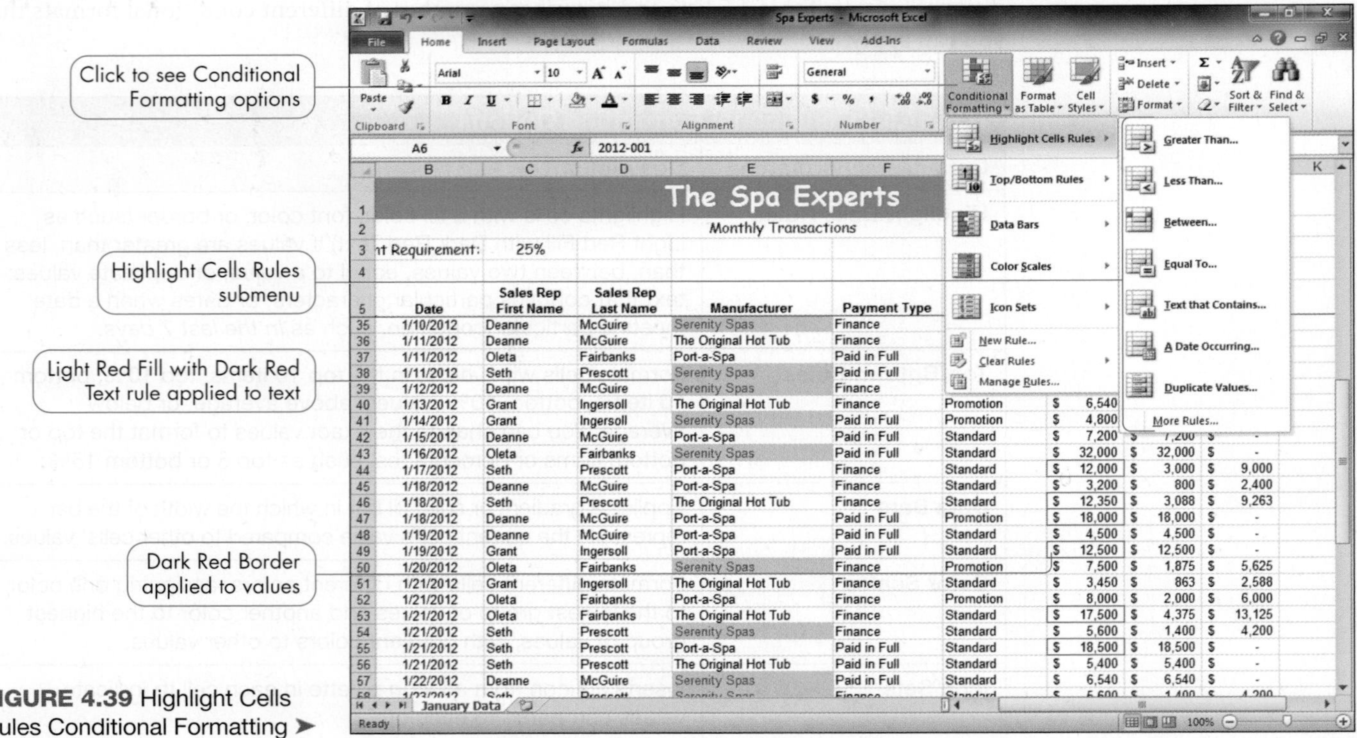

FIGURE 4.39 Highlight Cells Rules Conditional Formatting ➤

Specify Top/Bottom Rules

You may not know the exact values to format conditionally. You might be interested in identifying the top five sales to reward the sales associates, or want to identify the bottom 15% of automobile dealers so that you can close underperforming locations. The Top/Bottom Rules category enables you to specify the top or bottom number or percentage in a selected range. In addition, the Top/Bottom Rules category enables you to identify values that are above or below the average value in that range. In Figure 4.40, the selected range is conditionally formatted to highlight the top three amounts. Although the menu option is Top 10 Items, you can specify the exact number of items to highlight.

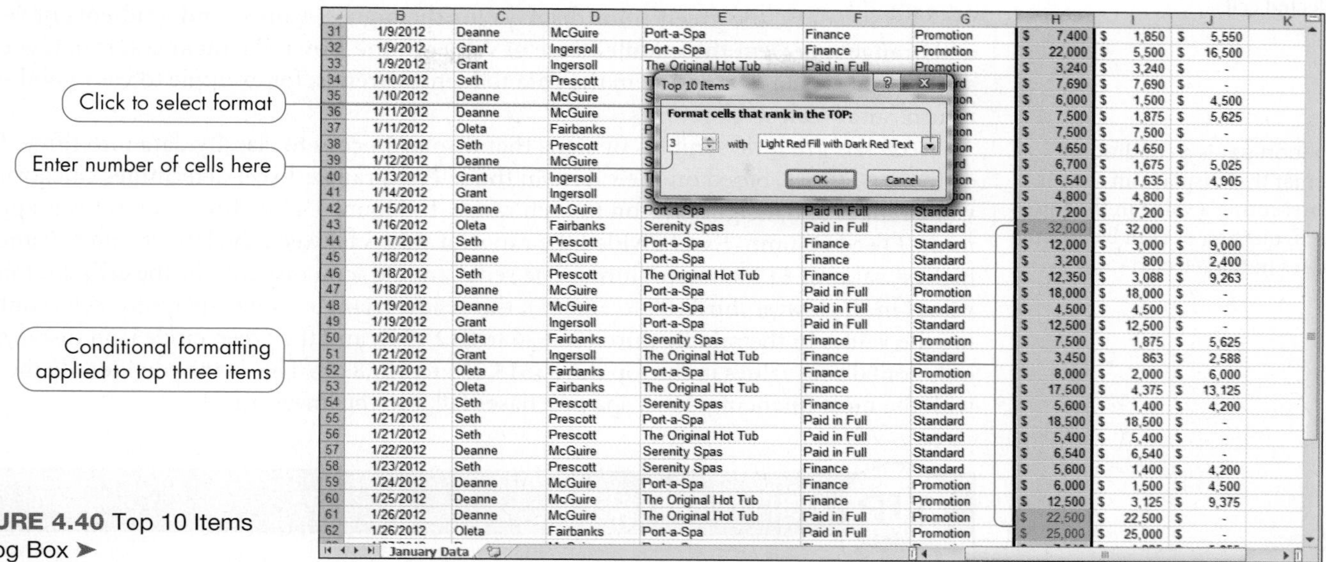

	B	C	D	E	F	G	H	I	J
31	1/9/2012	Deanne	McGuire	Port-a-Spa	Finance	Promotion	$ 7,400	$ 1,850	$ 5,550
32	1/9/2012	Grant	Ingersoll	Port-a-Spa	Finance	Promotion	$ 22,000	$ 5,500	$ 16,500
33	1/9/2012	Grant	Ingersoll	The Original Hot Tub	Paid in Full	Promotion	$ 3,240	$ 3,240	$ -
34	1/10/2012	Seth	Prescott	T		rd	$ 7,690	$ 7,690	$ -
35	1/10/2012	Deanne	McGuire	S		ion	$ 6,000	$ 1,500	$ 4,500
36	1/11/2012	Deanne	McGuire	T		ion	$ 7,500	$ 1,875	$ 5,625
37	1/11/2012	Oleta	Fairbanks	P		ion	$ 7,500	$ 7,500	$ -
38	1/11/2012	Seth	Prescott	S		ion	$ 4,650	$ 4,650	$ -
39	1/12/2012	Deanne	McGuire	S		rd	$ 6,700	$ 1,675	$ 5,025
40	1/13/2012	Grant	Ingersoll	T		ion	$ 6,540	$ 1,635	$ 4,905
41	1/14/2012	Grant	Ingersoll	S		ion	$ 4,800	$ 4,800	$ -
42	1/15/2012	Deanne	McGuire	Port-a-Spa	Paid in Full	Standard	$ 7,200	$ 7,200	$ -
43	1/16/2012	Oleta	Fairbanks	Serenity Spas	Paid in Full	Standard	$ 32,000	$ 32,000	$ -
44	1/17/2012	Seth	Prescott	Port-a-Spa	Finance	Standard	$ 12,000	$ 3,000	$ 9,000
45	1/18/2012	Deanne	McGuire	Port-a-Spa	Finance	Standard	$ 3,200	$ 800	$ 2,400
46	1/18/2012	Seth	Prescott	The Original Hot Tub	Finance	Standard	$ 12,350	$ 3,088	$ 9,263
47	1/18/2012	Deanne	McGuire	Port-a-Spa	Paid in Full	Promotion	$ 18,000	$ 18,000	$ -
48	1/19/2012	Deanne	McGuire	Port-a-Spa	Paid in Full	Standard	$ 4,500	$ 4,500	$ -
49	1/19/2012	Grant	Ingersoll	Port-a-Spa	Paid in Full	Standard	$ 12,500	$ 12,500	$ -
50	1/20/2012	Oleta	Fairbanks	Serenity Spas	Finance	Promotion	$ 7,500	$ 1,875	$ 5,625
51	1/21/2012	Grant	Ingersoll	The Original Hot Tub	Finance	Standard	$ 3,450	$ 863	$ 2,588
52	1/21/2012	Oleta	Fairbanks	Port-a-Spa	Finance	Promotion	$ 8,000	$ 2,000	$ 6,000
53	1/21/2012	Oleta	Fairbanks	The Original Hot Tub	Finance	Standard	$ 17,500	$ 4,375	$ 13,125
54	1/21/2012	Seth	Prescott	Serenity Spas	Finance	Standard	$ 5,600	$ 1,400	$ 4,200
55	1/21/2012	Seth	Prescott	Port-a-Spa	Paid in Full	Standard	$ 18,500	$ 18,500	$ -
56	1/21/2012	Seth	Prescott	The Original Hot Tub	Paid in Full	Standard	$ 5,400	$ 5,400	$ -
57	1/22/2012	Deanne	McGuire	Serenity Spas	Paid in Full	Standard	$ 6,540	$ 6,540	$ -
58	1/23/2012	Seth	Prescott	Serenity Spas	Finance	Standard	$ 5,600	$ 1,400	$ 4,200
59	1/24/2012	Deanne	McGuire	Port-a-Spa	Finance	Promotion	$ 6,000	$ 1,500	$ 4,500
60	1/25/2012	Deanne	McGuire	The Original Hot Tub	Finance	Promotion	$ 12,500	$ 3,125	$ 9,375
61	1/26/2012	Deanne	McGuire	The Original Hot Tub	Paid in Full	Promotion	$ 22,500	$ 22,500	$ -
62	1/26/2012	Oleta	Fairbanks	Port-a-Spa	Paid in Full	Promotion	$ 25,000	$ 25,000	$ -

FIGURE 4.40 Top 10 Items Dialog Box ➤

Display Data Bars, Color Scales, and Icon Sets

A **data bar** is a horizontal gradient or solid fill indicating the cell's relative value compared to other selected cells.

Data bars help you visualize the value of a cell relative to other cells, as shown in Figure 4.41. The width of the gradient or solid data bar represents the value in a cell, with a wider bar representing a higher value and a shorter bar a lower value. Use data bar conditional formatting when identifying high and low values. Excel locates the largest value and displays the widest data bar in that cell. Excel then finds the smallest value and displays the smallest data bar in that cell. Excel sizes the data bars for the remaining cells based on their relative values. If you change the values in your worksheet, Excel automatically updates the widths of the data bars. Data bars are more effective with wider columns than narrow columns. Figure 4.41 shows data bar conditional formatting applied to the Amount column. The widest data bar displays in the cell containing the largest amount of $27,000, and the smallest data bar appears in the cells containing the smallest value of $3,240. The data bar widths of other cells help you see the value differences. Excel uses the same color for each data bar, but each bar differs in size based on the value in the respective cells.

Data bars applied to Amount column

Icon set applied to Owed column

Color scales applied to Down Payment column

	B	C	D	E	F	G	H	I	J
5	Date	Sales Rep First Name	Sales Rep Last Name	Manufacturer	Payment Type	Transaction	Amount	Down Payment	Owed
6	1/1/2012	Deanne	McGuire	The Original Hot Tub	Finance	Promotion	$ 15,000	$ 3,750	$ 11,250
7	1/1/2012	Grant	Ingersoll	The Original Hot Tub	Finance	Promotion	$ 12,000	$ 3,000	$ 9,000
8	1/2/2012	Deanne	McGuire	Port-a-Spa	Finance	Promotion	$ 3,240	$ 810	$ 2,430
9	1/2/2012	Oleta	Fairbanks	Port-a-Spa	Finance	Promotion	$ 4,080	$ 1,020	$ 3,060
10	1/2/2012	Seth	Prescott	Serenity Spas	Finance	Promotion	$ 5,432	$ 1,358	$ 4,074
11	1/3/2012	Deanne	McGuire	Port-a-Spa	Finance	Standard	$ 6,780	$ 1,695	$ 5,085
12	1/3/2012	Oleta	Fairbanks	The Original Hot Tub	Finance	Standard	$ 5,432	$ 1,358	$ 4,074
13	1/3/2012	Deanne	McGuire	Serenity Spas	Paid in Full	Standard	$ 6,780	$ 6,780	$ -
14	1/3/2012	Deanne	McGuire	The Original Hot Tub	Paid in Full	Standard	$ 27,000	$ 27,000	$ -
15	1/4/2012	Grant	Ingersoll	Port-a-Spa	Finance	Standard	$ 10,000	$ 2,500	$ 7,500
16	1/4/2012	Oleta	Fairbanks	Port-a-Spa	Finance	Standard	$ 10,000	$ 2,500	$ 7,500
17	1/4/2012	Deanne	McGuire	Port-a-Spa	Paid in Full	Standard	$ 4,550	$ 4,550	$ -
18	1/4/2012	Deanne	McGuire	Serenity Spas	Paid in Full	Promotion	$ 8,490	$ 8,490	$ -
19	1/4/2012	Deanne	McGuire	The Original Hot Tub	Paid in Full	Standard	$ 5,432	$ 5,432	$ -
20	1/4/2012	Grant	Ingersoll	Serenity Spas	Paid in Full	Promotion	$ 7,450	$ 7,450	$ -
21	1/4/2012	Oleta	Fairbanks	The Original Hot Tub	Paid in Full	Standard	$ 5,432	$ 5,432	$ -
22	1/4/2012	Seth	Prescott	Serenity Spas	Paid in Full	Promotion	$ 6,780	$ 6,780	$ -
23	1/5/2012	Deanne	McGuire	Port-a-Spa	Finance	Standard	$ 7,450	$ 1,863	$ 5,588
24	1/5/2012	Deanne	McGuire	Port-a-Spa	Paid in Full	Standard	$ 8,560	$ 8,560	$ -
25	1/6/2012	Deanne	McGuire	Port-a-Spa	Finance	Promotion	$ 26,500	$ 6,625	$ 19,875
26	1/6/2012	Oleta	Fairbanks	Port-a-Spa	Finance	Standard	$ 5,000	$ 1,250	$ 3,750
27	1/6/2012	Seth	Prescott	Serenity Spas	Finance	Promotion	$ 8,560	$ 2,140	$ 6,420
28	1/7/2012	Seth	Prescott	Port-a-Spa	Finance	Promotion	$ 5,000	$ 1,250	$ 3,750
29	1/7/2012	Grant	Ingersoll	Serenity Spas	Paid in Full	Standard	$ 5,400	$ 5,400	$ -
30	1/8/2012	Oleta	Fairbanks	Serenity Spas	Finance	Standard	$ 3,240	$ 810	$ 2,430
31	1/9/2012	Deanne	McGuire	Port-a-Spa	Finance	Promotion	$ 7,400	$ 1,850	$ 5,550
32	1/9/2012	Grant	Ingersoll	Port-a-Spa	Finance	Promotion	$ 22,000	$ 5,500	$ 16,500
33	1/9/2012	Grant	Ingersoll	The Original Hot Tub	Paid in Full	Promotion	$ 3,240	$ 3,240	$ -
34	1/10/2012	Seth	Prescott	The Original Hot Tub	Paid in Full	Standard	$ 7,690	$ 7,690	$ -
35	1/10/2012	Deanne	McGuire	Serenity Spas	Finance	Promotion	$ 6,000	$ 1,500	$ 4,500

January Data

FIGURE 4.41 Data Bars, Color Scales, and Icon Sets ➤

A **color scale** is a conditional format that displays a particular color based on the relative value of the cell contents to other selected cells.

Color scales format cells with different colors based on the relative value of a cell compared to other selected cells. You can apply a two- or three-color scale. This scale assists in comparing a range of cells using gradations of those colors. The shade of the color represents higher or lower values. In Figure 4.41, for example, the red color scales display for the lowest values, the green color displays for the highest values, and gradients of yellow and orange represent the middle range of values in the Down Payment column. Use color scales to understand variation in the data to identify trends, for example to view good stock returns and weak stock returns.

An **icon set** is a conditional format that displays an icon representing a value in the top third, quarter, or fifth based on values in the selected range.

Icon sets are little symbols or signs that display in cells to classify data into three, four, or five categories, based on the values in the selected range. Excel determines categories of value ranges and assigns an icon to each range. In Figure 4.41, a three-icon set was applied to the Owed column. Excel divided the range of values between the lowest value $0 and the highest value of $19,875 into thirds. The red diamond icon displays for the cells containing values in the lowest third ($0 to $6,625), the yellow triangle icon displays for cells containing the values in the middle third ($6,626 to $12,150), and the green circle icon displays for cells containing values in the top third ($13,251 to $19,875). This helps you identify the spas with the most financing. Most spa purchases fall into the lowest third.

TIP Don't Overdo It!

Although conditional formatting helps identify trends, you should use this feature wisely. Apply conditional formatting when you want to emphasize important data. When you decide to apply conditional formatting, think about which category is best to highlight the data. Sometimes simple highlighting will suffice when you want to point out data meeting a particular condition; other times, you might want to apply data bars to point out relative differences among values. Finally, don't apply conditional formatting to too many columns.

Clear Rules

To clear conditional formatting from the entire worksheet, click Conditional Formatting in the Styles group on the Home tab, point to Clear Rules, and select Clear Rules from Entire Sheet. To remove conditional formatting from a range of cells, select cells. Then click Conditional Formatting, point to Clear Rules, and then select Clear Rules from Selected Cells.

Creating a New Rule

The default conditional formatting categories provide a variety of options. Excel also enables you to create your own rules to specify different fill colors, borders, or other formatting if you don't want the default settings. Excel provides three ways to create a new rule:

- Click Conditional Formatting in the Cell Styles group, and then select New Rule.
- Click Conditional Formatting in the Cell Styles group, select Manage Rules to open the Conditional Formatting Rules Manager dialog box, and then click New Rule.
- Click Conditional Formatting in the Cell Styles group, select a rule category such as Highlight Cells Rules, and then select More Rules.

The New Formatting Rule dialog box opens (see Figure 4.42) so that you can define your new conditional formatting rule. First, select a rule type, such as *Format all cells based on their values*. The *Edit the Rule Description* section changes, based on the rule type you select. With the default rule type selected, you can specify the format style (2-Color Scale, 3-Color Scale, Data Bar, or Icon Sets). You can then specify the minimum and maximum values, the fill colors for color sets or data bars or the icons for icon sets. After you edit the rule description, click OK to save your new conditional format.

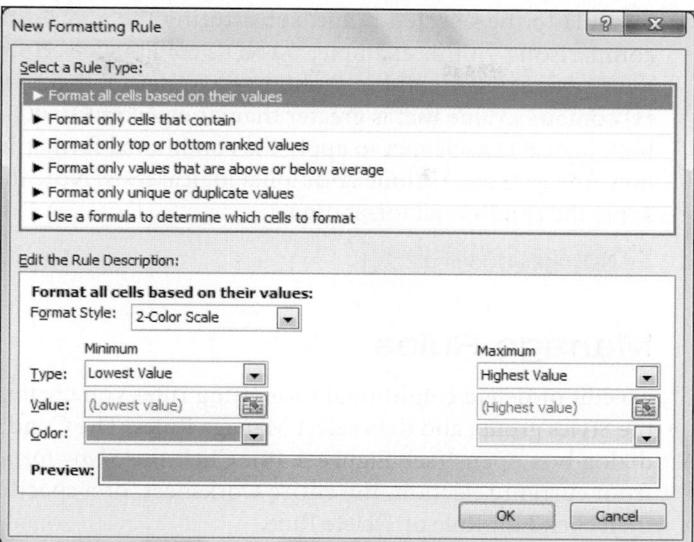

FIGURE 4.42 New Formatting Rule Dialog Box ➤

If you select any rule type except the *Format all cells based on their values* rule, the dialog box contains a Format button. When you click Format, the Format Cells dialog box opens so that you can specify number, font, border, and fill formats to apply to your rule.

> **TIP** Format Only Cells That Contain
>
> This option provides a wide array of things you can format: values, text, dates, blanks, no blanks, errors, or no errors. Formatting blanks is helpful to see where you are missing data, and formatting cells containing errors helps you find those errors quickly.

Use Formulas in Conditional Formatting

If you need to create a complex conditional formatting rule, you can select a rule that uses a formula to format cells. For example, you might want to format amounts of financed spas *and* amounts that are $10,000 or more. Figure 4.43 shows the Edit Formatting Rule dialog box and the corresponding conditional formatting applied to cells.

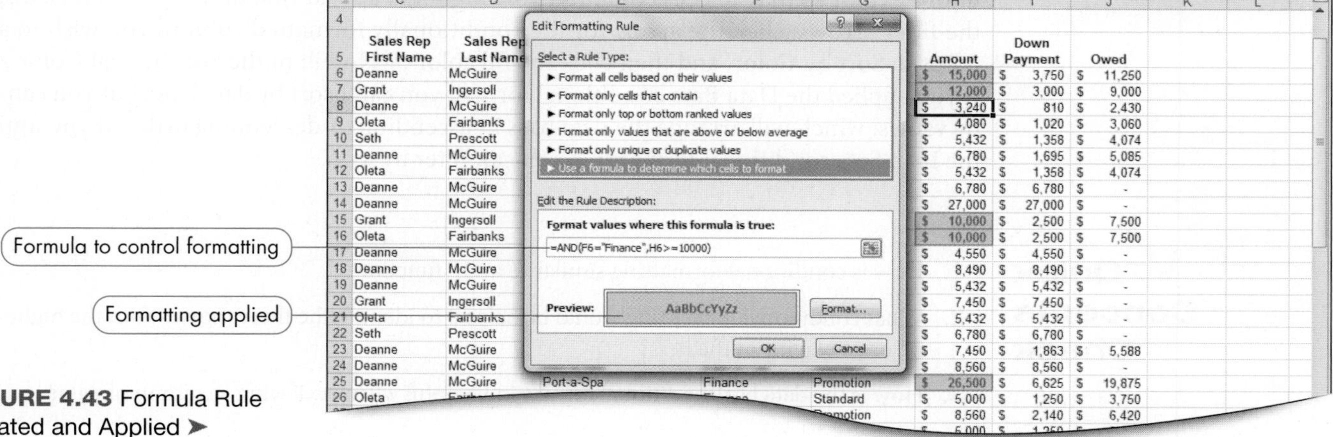

FIGURE 4.43 Formula Rule Created and Applied ➤

To create a formula-based conditional formatting rule, select the data and create a new rule. In the New Formatting Rule dialog box, select *Use a formula to determine which cells to format*, and then type the formula in the *Format values where this formula is true* box. You write the formula for the first data row, such as F6 and H6. Excel applies the general formula to the selected range, substituting the appropriate cell reference as it makes the comparisons. In this example, =AND(F6="Finance",H6>=10000) requires that the text in the Payment Type column (column F) contain Finance and the Amount column (column H) contain a value that is greater than or equal to $10,000. The AND function requires that both logical tests be met to apply the conditional formatting. Two logical tests are required; however, you can include additional logical tests. Note that *all* logical tests must be true to apply the conditional formatting.

= AND(logical1,logical2,...)

Manage Rules

To edit or delete conditional formatting rules you create, click Conditional Formatting in the Styles group, and then select Manage Rules. The Conditional Formatting Rules Manager dialog box opens (see Figure 4.44). Click the *Show formatting rules for* arrow and select from current selection, the entire worksheet, or a specific table. Then select the rule, and then click Edit Rule or Delete Rule.

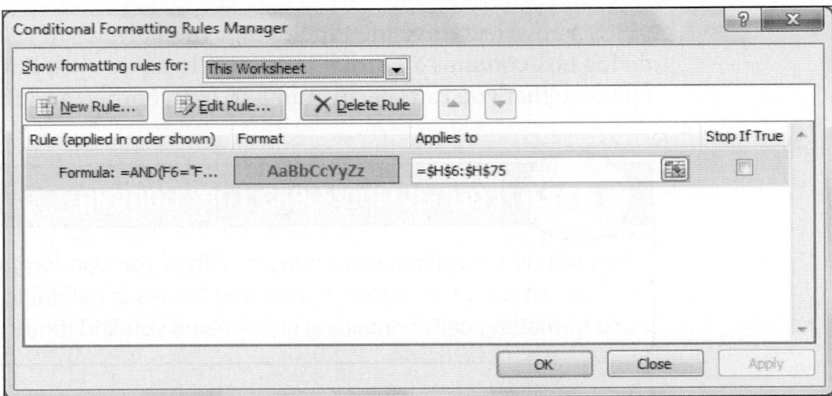

FIGURE 4.44 Conditional Formatting Rules Manager Dialog Box ➤

Sorting and Filtering Using Conditional Formatting

You can sort and filter by conditional formatting. For example, if you applied the Highlight Cells Rules, Top/Bottom Rules, or Color Scales conditional formatting, you can sort the column by color so that all cells containing the highlight appear first or last. To do this, display the filter arrows, click the arrow for the conditionally formatted column you wish to sort, point to Sort by Color, and then click the fill color or No Fill in the Sort by Cell Color area. If you applied the Data Bars conditional format, you can't sort by data bars, but you can sort by values, which will arrange the data bars in ascending or descending order. If you applied the Icon Sets conditional formatting, you can filter by icon.

Quick Concepts Check

1. How is conditional formatting similar to an IF function?
2. What conditional formatting would be helpful to identify the three movies with the highest revenue playing at theaters?
3. How is the data bar conditional formatting helpful when reviewing a column of data?

4 Conditional Formatting

Your business partner, Ryan, wants to review the transactions with you. He is interested in Fairbanks' sales record and the five highest spa amounts. In addition, he wants to compare the down payment amounts visually. Finally, he wants to analyze the amounts owed for sales completed by Prescott.

Skills covered: Highlight Cells Rules • Specify Top/Bottom Rules • Display Data Bars • Create a New Rule • Filter by Rule

STEP 1 HIGHLIGHT CELLS RULES

You want to identify Fairbanks' spa sales for January without filtering the data. You will apply a conditional format to apply a fill and font color so that cells containing her last name stand out. Refer to Figure 4.45 as you complete Step 1.

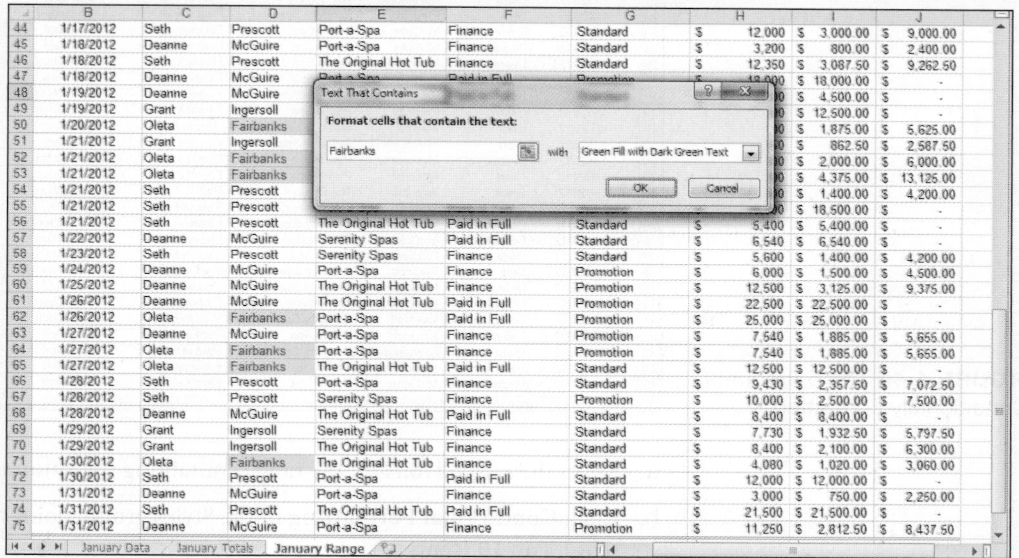

FIGURE 4.45 Text Formatted with Highlight Text Rules ➤

a. Open *e04h3spa_LastnameFirstname* if you closed it at the end of Hands-On Exercise 3. Save the workbook with the new name **e04h4spa_LastnameFirstname**, changing *h3* to *h4*.

b. Select **row headings 6 through 75** in the January Range worksheet. Click the **Home tab**, if necessary, click the **Fill Color arrow**, and then select **No Fill**.

   You removed the previous table style with banded rows. This will avoid having too many fill colors when you apply conditional formatting rules.

c. Select the **range D6:D75**, which is the column containing the sales representatives' last names.

d. Click **Conditional Formatting** in the Styles group, point to **Highlight Cells Rules**, and then select **Text that Contains**.

   The Text That Contains dialog box opens.

e. Type **Fairbanks** in the box, click the **with arrow**, and then select **Green Fill with Dark Green Text**. Click **OK**. Deselect the range, and then save the workbook.

   Excel formats only cells that contain Fairbanks with the fill and font color.

Apply Multiple Formats to One Column

While the range is selected, you can apply another conditional format, such as Light Yellow with Dark Yellow text for another last name.

STEP 2 SPECIFY TOP/BOTTOM RULES

Ryan is now interested in identifying the highest five spa sales in January. Instead of sorting the records, you will use the Top/Bottom Rules conditional formatting. Refer to Figure 4.46 as you complete Step 2.

	B	C	D	E	F	G	H		I		J
14	1/3/2012	Deanne	McGuire	The Original Hot Tub	Paid in Full	Standard	$	27,000	$ 27,000.00	$	-
15	1/4/2012	Grant	Ingersoll	Port-a-Spa	Finance	Standard	$	10,000	$ 2,500.00	$	7,500.00
16	1/4/2012	Oleta	Fairbanks	Port-a-Spa	Finance	Standard	$	10,000	$ 2,500.00	$	7,500.00
17	1/4/2012	Deanne	McGuire	Port-a-Spa	Paid in Full	Standard	$	4,550	$ 4,550.00	$	-
18	1/4/2012	Deanne	McGuire	Serenity Spas	Paid in Full	Promotion	$	8,490	$ 8,490.00	$	-
19	1/4/2012	Deanne	McGuire	The Original Hot Tub	Paid in Full	Standard	$	5,432	$ 5,432.00	$	-
20	1/4/2012	Grant	Ingersoll	Serenity Spas	Paid in Full	Promotion	$	7,450	$ 7,450.00	$	-
21	1/4/2012	Oleta	Fairbanks	The Original Hot Tub	Paid in Full	Standard	$	5,432	$ 5,432.00	$	-
22	1/4/2012	Seth	Prescott	Serenity Spas	Paid in Full	Promotion	$	6,780	$ 6,780.00	$	-
23	1/5/2012	Deanne	McGuire	Port-a-Spa	Finance	Standard	$	7,450	$ 1,862.50	$	5,587.50
24	1/5/2012	Deanne	McGuire	Port-a-Spa	Paid in Full	Standard	$	8,560	$ 8,560.00	$	-
25	1/6/2012	Deanne	McGuire	Port-a-Spa	Finance	Promotion	$	26,500	$ 6,625.00	$	19,875.00
26	1/6/2012	Oleta	Fairbanks	Port-a-Spa	Finance	Standard	$	5,000	$ 1,250.00	$	3,750.00
27	1/6/2012	Seth	Prescott	Serenity Spas	Finance	Promotion	$	8,560	$ 2,140.00	$	6,420.00
28	1/7/2012	Seth	Prescott	Port-a-Spa	Finance	Promotion	$	5,000	$ 1,250.00	$	3,750.00
29	1/7/2012	Grant	Ingersoll	Serenity Spas	Paid in Full	Standard	$	5,400	$ 5,400.00	$	-
30	1/8/2012	Oleta	Fairbanks	Serenity Spas	Finance	Standard	$	3,240	$ 810.00	$	2,430.00
31	1/9/2012	Deanne	McGuire	Port-a-Spa	Finance	Promotion	$	7,400	$ 1,850.00	$	5,550.00
32	1/9/2012	Grant	Ingersoll	Port-a-Spa	Finance	Promotion	$	22,000	$ 5,500.00	$	16,500.00
33	1/9/2012	Grant	Ingersoll	The Original Hot Tub	Paid in Full	Promotion	$	3,240	$ 3,240.00	$	-
34	1/10/2012	Seth	Prescott	The Original Hot Tub	Paid in Full	Standard	$	7,690	$ 7,690.00	$	-
35	1/10/2012	Deanne	McGuire	Serenity Spas	Finance	Promotion	$	6,000	$ 1,500.00	$	4,500.00
36	1/11/2012	Deanne	McGuire	The Original Hot Tub	Finance	Promotion	$	7,500	$ 1,875.00	$	5,625.00
37	1/11/2012	Oleta	Fairbanks	Port-a-Spa	Paid in Full	Promotion	$	7,500	$ 7,500.00	$	-
38	1/11/2012	Seth	Prescott	Serenity Spas	Paid in Full	Promotion	$	4,650	$ 4,650.00	$	-
39	1/12/2012	Deanne	McGuire	Serenity Spas	Finance	Standard	$	6,700	$ 1,675.00	$	5,025.00
40	1/13/2012	Grant	Ingersoll	The Original Hot Tub	Finance	Promotion	$	6,540	$ 1,635.00	$	4,905.00
41	1/14/2012	Grant	Ingersoll	Serenity Spas	Paid in Full	Promotion	$	4,800	$ 4,800.00	$	-
42	1/15/2012	Deanne	McGuire	Port-a-Spa	Paid in Full	Standard	$	7,200	$ 7,200.00	$	-
43	1/16/2012	Oleta	Fairbanks	Serenity Spas	Paid in Full	Standard	$	32,000	$ 32,000.00	$	-
44	1/17/2012	Seth	Prescott	Port-a-Spa	Finance	Standard	$	12,000	$ 3,000.00	$	9,000.00
45	1/18/2012	Deanne	McGuire	Port-a-Spa	Finance	Standard	$	3,200	$ 800.00	$	2,400.00

January Data | January Totals | January Range

FIGURE 4.46 Top 5 Amounts Conditionally Formatted ➤

a. Select the **range H6:H75**, the range containing the amounts.

b. Click **Conditional Formatting** in the Styles group, point to **Top/Bottom Rules**, and then select **Top 10 Items**.

The Top 10 Items dialog box opens.

c. Click the **spin arrow** to display *5*, click the **with arrow**, and then select **Light Red Fill**. Click **OK**.

d. Scroll through the worksheet to see the top five amounts (three of which are shown in Figure 4.46). Save the workbook.

STEP 3 DISPLAY DATA BARS

Now Ryan wants to compare all of the down payments. Data bars would add a nice visual element as Ryan compares down payment amounts. Refer to Figure 4.47 as you complete Step 3.

	B	C	D	E	F	G	H	I	J
44	1/17/2012	Seth	Prescott	Port-a-Spa	Finance	Standard	$ 12,000	$ 3,000.00	$ 9,000.00
45	1/18/2012	Deanne	McGuire	Port-a-Spa	Finance	Standard	$ 3,200	$ 800.00	$ 2,400.00
46	1/18/2012	Seth	Prescott	The Original Hot Tub	Finance	Standard	$ 12,350	$ 3,087.50	$ 9,262.50
47	1/18/2012	Deanne	McGuire	Port-a-Spa	Paid in Full	Promotion	$ 18,000	$ 18,000.00	$ -
48	1/19/2012	Deanne	McGuire	Port-a-Spa	Paid in Full	Standard	$ 4,500	$ 4,500.00	$ -
49	1/19/2012	Grant	Ingersoll	Port-a-Spa	Paid in Full	Standard	$ 12,500	$ 12,500.00	$ -
50	1/20/2012	Oleta	Fairbanks	Serenity Spas	Finance	Promotion	$ 7,500	$ 1,875.00	$ 5,625.00
51	1/21/2012	Grant	Ingersoll	The Original Hot Tub	Finance	Standard	$ 3,450	$ 862.50	$ 2,587.50
52	1/21/2012	Oleta	Fairbanks	Port-a-Spa	Finance	Promotion	$ 8,000	$ 2,000.00	$ 6,000.00
53	1/21/2012	Oleta	Fairbanks	The Original Hot Tub	Finance	Standard	$ 17,500	$ 4,375.00	$ 13,125.00
54	1/21/2012	Seth	Prescott	Serenity Spas	Finance	Standard	$ 5,600	$ 1,400.00	$ 4,200.00
55	1/21/2012	Seth	Prescott	Port-a-Spa	Paid in Full	Standard	$ 18,500	$ 18,500.00	$ -
56	1/21/2012	Seth	Prescott	The Original Hot Tub	Paid in Full	Standard	$ 5,400	$ 5,400.00	$ -
57	1/22/2012	Deanne	McGuire	Serenity Spas	Paid in Full	Standard	$ 6,540	$ 6,540.00	$ -
58	1/23/2012	Seth	Prescott	Serenity Spas	Finance	Standard	$ 5,600	$ 1,400.00	$ 4,200.00
59	1/24/2012	Deanne	McGuire	Port-a-Spa	Finance	Promotion	$ 6,000	$ 1,500.00	$ 4,500.00
60	1/25/2012	Deanne	McGuire	The Original Hot Tub	Finance	Promotion	$ 12,500	$ 3,125.00	$ 9,375.00
61	1/26/2012	Deanne	McGuire	The Original Hot Tub	Paid in Full	Promotion	$ 22,500	$ 22,500.00	$ -
62	1/26/2012	Oleta	Fairbanks	Port-a-Spa	Paid in Full	Promotion	$ 25,000	$ 25,000.00	$ -
63	1/27/2012	Deanne	McGuire	Port-a-Spa	Finance	Promotion	$ 7,540	$ 1,885.00	$ 5,655.00
64	1/27/2012	Oleta	Fairbanks	Port-a-Spa	Finance	Promotion	$ 7,540	$ 1,885.00	$ 5,655.00
65	1/27/2012	Oleta	Fairbanks	The Original Hot Tub	Paid in Full	Standard	$ 12,500	$ 12,500.00	$ -
66	1/28/2012	Seth	Prescott	Port-a-Spa	Finance	Standard	$ 9,430	$ 2,357.50	$ 7,072.50
67	1/28/2012	Seth	Prescott	Serenity Spas	Finance	Promotion	$ 10,000	$ 2,500.00	$ 7,500.00
68	1/28/2012	Deanne	McGuire	The Original Hot Tub	Paid in Full	Standard	$ 8,400	$ 8,400.00	$ -
69	1/29/2012	Grant	Ingersoll	Serenity Spas	Finance	Standard	$ 7,730	$ 1,932.50	$ 5,797.50
70	1/29/2012	Grant	Ingersoll	The Original Hot Tub	Finance	Standard	$ 8,400	$ 2,100.00	$ 6,300.00
71	1/30/2012	Oleta	Fairbanks	The Original Hot Tub	Finance	Standard	$ 4,080	$ 1,020.00	$ 3,060.00
72	1/30/2012	Seth	Prescott	Port-a-Spa	Paid in Full	Standard	$ 12,000	$ 12,000.00	$ -
73	1/31/2012	Deanne	McGuire	Port-a-Spa	Finance	Standard	$ 3,000	$ 750.00	$ 2,250.00
74	1/31/2012	Seth	Prescott	The Original Hot Tub	Paid in Full	Standard	$ 21,500	$ 21,500.00	$ -
75	1/31/2012	Deanne	McGuire	Port-a-Spa	Finance	Promotion	$ 11,250	$ 2,812.50	$ 8,437.50

January Data | January Totals | **January Range**

FIGURE 4.47 Data Bars Conditional Formatting ➤

a. Select the **range I6:I75**, which contains the down payment amounts.

b. Click **Conditional Formatting** in the Styles group, point to **Data Bars**, and then select **Purple Data Bar** in the *Gradient Fill* section. Scroll through the list, and then save the workbook.

   Excel displays data bars in each cell. The larger bar widths help Ryan identify quickly the largest down payments. However, the largest down payments are identical to the original amounts when the customers pay in full. This result illustrates that you should not accept the results at face value. Doing so would provide you with an inaccurate analysis.

STEP 4 CREATE A NEW RULE

Ryan's next request is to analyze the amounts owed by Prescott's customers. In particular, he wants to know how many customers owe more than $5,000. To do this, you realize you need to create a custom rule that evaluates both the Sales Rep Last Name column and the Owed column. Refer to Figure 4.48 as you complete Step 4.

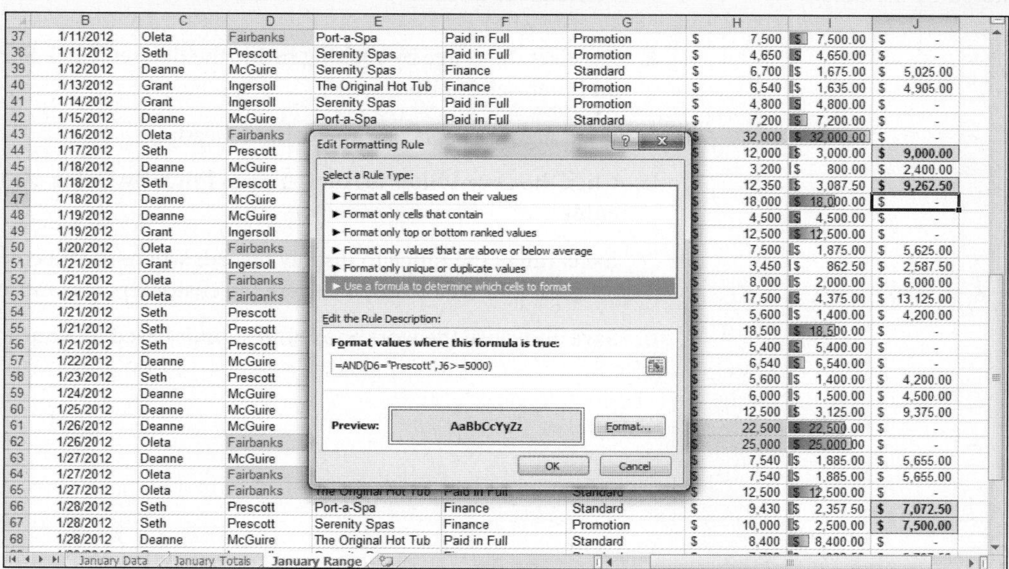

	B	C	D	E	F	G	H	I	J
37	1/11/2012	Oleta	Fairbanks	Port-a-Spa	Paid in Full	Promotion	$ 7,500	$ 7,500.00	$ -
38	1/11/2012	Seth	Prescott	Serenity Spas	Paid in Full	Promotion	$ 4,650	$ 4,650.00	$ -
39	1/12/2012	Deanne	McGuire	Serenity Spas	Finance	Standard	$ 6,700	$ 1,675.00	$ 5,025.00
40	1/13/2012	Grant	Ingersoll	The Original Hot Tub	Finance	Promotion	$ 6,540	$ 1,635.00	$ 4,905.00
41	1/14/2012	Grant	Ingersoll	Serenity Spas	Paid in Full	Promotion	$ 4,800	$ 4,800.00	$ -
42	1/15/2012	Deanne	McGuire	Port-a-Spa	Paid in Full	Standard	$ 7,200	$ 7,200.00	$ -
43	1/16/2012	Oleta	Fairbanks				$ 32,000	$ 32,000.00	$ -
44	1/17/2012	Seth	Prescott				$ 12,000	$ 3,000.00	$ 9,000.00
45	1/18/2012	Deanne	McGuire				$ 3,200	$ 800.00	$ 2,400.00
46	1/18/2012	Seth	Prescott				$ 12,350	$ 3,087.50	$ 9,262.50
47	1/18/2012	Deanne	McGuire				$ 18,000	$ 18,000.00	$ -
48	1/19/2012	Deanne	McGuire				$ 4,500	$ 4,500.00	$ -
49	1/19/2012	Grant	Ingersoll				$ 12,500	$ 12,500.00	$ -
50	1/20/2012	Oleta	Fairbanks				$ 7,500	$ 1,875.00	$ 5,625.00
51	1/21/2012	Grant	Ingersoll				$ 3,450	$ 862.50	$ 2,587.50
52	1/21/2012	Oleta	Fairbanks				$ 8,000	$ 2,000.00	$ 6,000.00
53	1/21/2012	Oleta	Fairbanks				$ 17,500	$ 4,375.00	$ 13,125.00
54	1/21/2012	Seth	Prescott				$ 5,600	$ 1,400.00	$ 4,200.00
55	1/21/2012	Seth	Prescott				$ 18,500	$ 18,500.00	$ -
56	1/21/2012	Seth	Prescott				$ 5,400	$ 5,400.00	$ -
57	1/22/2012	Deanne	McGuire				$ 6,540	$ 6,540.00	$ -
58	1/23/2012	Seth	Prescott				$ 5,600	$ 1,400.00	$ 4,200.00
59	1/24/2012	Deanne	McGuire				$ 6,000	$ 1,500.00	$ 4,500.00
60	1/25/2012	Deanne	McGuire				$ 12,500	$ 3,125.00	$ 9,375.00
61	1/26/2012	Deanne	McGuire				$ 22,500	$ 22,500.00	$ -
62	1/26/2012	Oleta	Fairbanks				$ 25,000	$ 25,000.00	$ -
63	1/27/2012	Deanne	McGuire				$ 7,540	$ 1,885.00	$ 5,655.00
64	1/27/2012	Oleta	Fairbanks				$ 7,540	$ 1,885.00	$ 5,655.00
65	1/27/2012	Oleta	Fairbanks				$ 12,500	$ 12,500.00	$ -
66	1/28/2012	Seth	Prescott	Port-a-Spa	Finance	Standard	$ 9,430	$ 2,357.50	$ 7,072.50
67	1/28/2012	Seth	Prescott	Serenity Spas	Finance	Promotion	$ 10,000	$ 2,500.00	$ 7,500.00
68	1/28/2012	Deanne	McGuire	The Original Hot Tub	Paid in Full	Standard	$ 8,400	$ 8,400.00	$ -

FIGURE 4.48 Custom Rule Created ➤

a. Select the **range J6:J75**, which contains the amounts owed.

b. Click **Conditional Formatting** in the Styles group, and then select **New Rule**.

   The New Formatting Rule dialog box opens.

c. Select **Use a formula to determine which cells to format.**

d. Type **=AND(D6="Prescott",J6>=5000)** in the **Format values where this formula is true box**.

   Because you are comparing the contents of cell D6 to text, you must enclose the text within quotation marks.

e. Click **Format** to open the Format Cells dialog box.

f. Click the **Font tab**, if necessary, and then click **Bold** in the **Font style list**. Click the **Border tab**, click the **Color arrow**, select **Purple**, and then click **Outline**. Click the **Fill tab**, click the **lightest purple background color** (the eighth color on the first row below the first horizontal line), and then click **OK**. Look at Figure 4.48 to compare your new rule.

   The figure shows the Edit Formatting Rule dialog box, but the options are similar to the New Formatting Rule dialog box.

g. Click **OK** in New Formatting Rule dialog box, and then scroll through the list to see which amounts owed are greater than $5,000 for Prescott only. Save the workbook.

STEP 5 FILTER BY RULE

Ryan commented that it is difficult to see which of Prescott's transactions were greater than $5,000 without scrolling. To help Ryan review the Owed column where you applied a formula-based conditional format, you will filter that column by the fill color. Refer to Figure 4.49 as you complete Step 5.

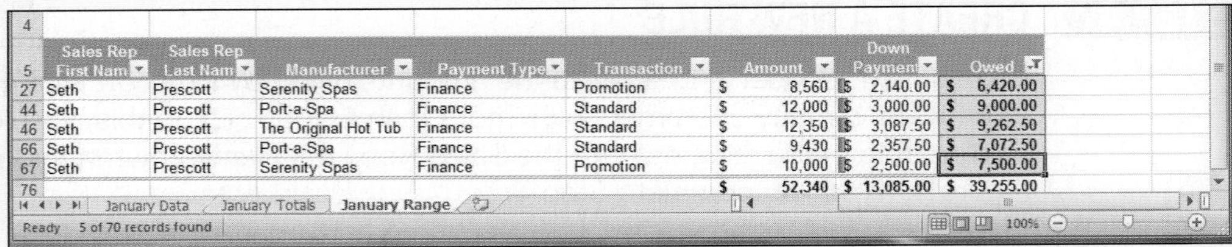

	Sales Rep First Nam	Sales Rep Last Nam	Manufacturer	Payment Type	Transaction	Amount	Down Payment	Owed
27	Seth	Prescott	Serenity Spas	Finance	Promotion	$ 8,560	$ 2,140.00	$ 6,420.00
44	Seth	Prescott	Port-a-Spa	Finance	Standard	$ 12,000	$ 3,000.00	$ 9,000.00
46	Seth	Prescott	The Original Hot Tub	Finance	Standard	$ 12,350	$ 3,087.50	$ 9,262.50
66	Seth	Prescott	Port-a-Spa	Finance	Standard	$ 9,430	$ 2,357.50	$ 7,072.50
67	Seth	Prescott	Serenity Spas	Finance	Promotion	$ 10,000	$ 2,500.00	$ 7,500.00
76						$ 52,340	$ 13,085.00	$ 39,255.00

FIGURE 4.49 Owed Column Filtered by Fill Color ➤

a. Deselect the range by clicking inside the dataset. Click **Sort & Filter** in the Editing group, and then select **Filter**.

   Filter arrows display for the column headings.

b. Click the **Owed filter arrow**, point to **Filter by Color**, and then select the **light purple fill color**.

   Excel filters the range to display records where the fill color is lavender. Now it is easy to see that Prescott sold five spas where the customers owe more than $5,000.

c. Save and close the workbook, and submit based on your instructor's directions.

CHAPTER OBJECTIVES REVIEW

After reading this chapter, you have accomplished the following objectives:

1. **Freeze rows and columns.** To prevent labels from scrolling offscreen, freeze rows or columns. The Freeze Panes setting freezes the row(s) above and the column(s) to the left of the active cell. When you scroll, those rows and columns remain onscreen so that you know what type of data is in each row or column. You can use Unfreeze Panes to clear the frozen rows and columns.
2. **Print large datasets.** Display the data in Page Break Preview to see the automatic page breaks. Dashed blue lines indicate automatic page breaks. You can insert manual page breaks, indicated by solid blue lines. If you do not want to print an entire worksheet, select a range and set a print area. Dotted lines surround the print area onscreen. When a dataset will print on several pages, you can control the sequence in which the pages will print.
3. **Understand table design.** A table is a structured range that contains related data. Tables have several benefits over regular ranges, such as keeping headings onscreen as you scroll. Each table column is a field. The column headings, called *field names*, appear on the first row of a table. Each row is a complete set of data for one record. You should plan a table. For example, create unique field names on the first row of the table, and enter data immediately below the field names, avoiding blank rows.
4. **Create a table.** You can create a table from existing structured data. Excel applies the Table Style Medium 9 format and assigns a default name, such as Table1, to the table. When the active cell is within a table, the Table Tools display with the Design tab. You can insert and delete table rows and columns and remove duplicate records in your table.
5. **Apply a table style.** Table styles control the fill color of the header row and records within the table. To further customize the formatting, click options, such as First Column or Total Row in the Table Style Options group.
6. **Sort data.** The data in a table are often easier to understand and work with if they are in some meaningful order. Sorting arranges records in a table by the value of one or more fields within the table. You can sort text in alphabetical or reverse alphabetical order, values from smallest to largest or largest to smallest, and dates from oldest to newest or newest to oldest. To sort a single field, click the filter arrow and select the sort method from the list. To sort multiple fields, open the Sort dialog box and add column levels and sort orders. You can create a custom sort for unique data.
7. **Filter data.** Filtering is the process of specifying conditions for displaying records in a table. Only records that meet those conditions display; the other records are hidden until you clear the filters. You can apply text, value, and date filters based on the data in a particular field.
8. **Use structured references and a total row.** A structured reference uses field names instead of cell references, such as =[Amount]-[Down Payment]. Field names must appear in brackets within the formula. When you press Enter, Excel copies the formula down the column. You can display a total row after the last record. Excel sums the values in the last column automatically or counts the number of text entries. You can add totals to other columns, and you can select a different function, such as Average.
9. **Apply conditional formatting.** Conditional formatting applies special formatting to cells that contain values that meet set conditions. The five major conditional formatting categories are Highlight Cells Rules, Top/Bottom Rules, Data Bars, Color Scales, and Icon Sets. Data bars display horizontal bars that compare values within the selected range. The larger the value, the wider the horizontal bar. Color scales indicate values that occur within particular ranges. Icon sets display icons representing a number's relative value compared to other numbers in the range. When you no longer need conditional formatting, you can clear it for the selected range or entire worksheet.
10. **Create a new rule.** You can create conditional format rules. The New Formatting Rule dialog box enables you to select a rule type. Based on the type you select, the *Edit the Rule Description* section changes to provide specific options for defining your rule. You can create rules based on formulas to set conditions based on content in multiple columns. Use the Conditional Formatting Rules Manager dialog box to edit and delete rules.
11. **Sort and filter using conditional formatting.** After you apply conditional formatting, you can sort or filter a column based on its formats. Use Sort by Color to select a sort sequence, or select Filter by Color to filter out records that do not meet the color condition you specify.

KEY TERMS

Color scale ***p.544***
Conditional formatting ***p.541***
Data bar ***p.543***
Field ***p.516***
Filtering ***p.527***
Freezing ***p.507***
Icon set ***p.544***
Page break ***p.508***
Print area ***p.509***
Print order ***p.510***
Record ***p.516***
Sorting ***p.525***
Structured reference ***p.530***
SUBTOTAL function ***p.531***
Table ***p.516***
Table style ***p.519***
Total row ***p.531***

MULTIPLE CHOICE

1. You have a large dataset that will print on several pages. You want to ensure that related records print on the same page with column and row labels visible and that confidential information is not printed. You should apply all of the following page setup options except which one to accomplish this?
   (a) Set a print area.
   (b) Print titles.
   (c) Adjust page breaks.
   (d) Change the print page order.

2. You are working with a large worksheet. Your row headings are in column A. Which command(s) should be used to see the row headings and the distant information in columns X, Y, and Z?
   (a) Freeze Panes command
   (b) Hide Rows command
   (c) New Window command and cascade the windows
   (d) Split Rows command

3. Which statement is not a recommended guideline for planning a table in Excel?
   (a) Avoid naming two fields with the same name.
   (b) Ensure no blank columns separate data columns within the table.
   (c) Leave one blank row between records in the table.
   (d) Include field names on the first row of the table.

4. You have a list of all the employees in your organization. The list contains employee name, office, title, and salary. You want to list all employees in each office branch. The branches should be listed alphabetically, with the employee earning the highest salary listed first in each office. Which is true of your sort order?
   (a) Branch office is the primary sort and should be in A to Z order.
   (b) Salary is the primary sort and should be from highest to lowest.
   (c) Salary is the primary sort and should be from lowest to highest.
   (d) Branch office is the primary sort and should be in Z to A order.

5. You suspect a table has several identical records. What should you do?
   (a) Do nothing; a logical reason probably exists to keep identical records.
   (b) Use the Remove Duplicates command.
   (c) Look at each row yourself, and manually delete duplicate records.
   (d) Find the duplicate records and change some of the data to be different.

6. Which check box in the Table Style Options group enables you to apply different formatting to the records in a table?
   (a) Header Row
   (b) Banded Rows
   (c) Banded Columns
   (d) Total Row

7. Which date filter option enables you to specify criteria for selecting a range of dates, such as between 3/15/2012 and 7/15/2012?
   (a) Equals
   (b) Before
   (c) All Dates in the Period
   (d) Between

8. You want to display a total row that identifies the oldest date in a field in your table. What function do you select from the list?
   (a) Max
   (b) Sum
   (c) Min
   (d) Count

9. What type of conditional formatting displays horizontal colors in which the width of the bar indicates relative size compared to other values in the selected range?
   (a) Color Scales
   (b) Icon Sets
   (c) Data Bars
   (d) Sparklines

10. When you select the ______ rule type, the New Formatting Rule dialog box does not show the Format button.
   (a) Format all cells based on their values
   (b) Format only cells that contain
   (c) Use a formula to determine which cells to format
   (d) Format only unique or duplicate values

PRACTICE EXERCISES

1 Fiesta® Items and Replacement Values

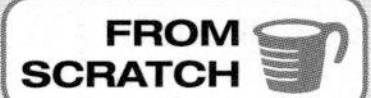

Marie Maier has collected Fiesta dinnerware, manufactured by the Homer Laughlin China Company, since it was reintroduced in 1986. Between 1986 and 2011, the company produced 29 colors, each with a unique name. Marie created a table in Word that lists the name, number, year introduced, and year retired (if applicable) for each color. She created another table in Word that lists the item number, item, replacement value, and source of information for each item in her Fiesta collection. Her main sources for replacement values are the Homer Laughlin's Web site (www.fiestafactorydirect.com); Replacements, Ltd. (www.replacements.com), eBay auctions (www.ebay.com), Mega China (www.megachina.com), and a local antique store. She needs your help to convert the data to Excel tables, apply table formatting, delete duplicate records, insert functions, and sort and filter the data based on how she wants to view the data. This exercise follows the same set of skills as used in Hands-On Exercises 1–3 in the chapter. Refer to Figure 4.50 as you complete this exercise.

	A	B	C	D	E	F	G	H	I
1	Color Numbe	Year Introduce	Year Retire	Status	Color	Item Numbe	Item	Replacement Value	Source
2	104	1986	1998	Retired	Apricot	495	Covered Casserole	70.95	Ebay Auction
3	104	1986	1998	Retired	Apricot	830	5 Piece Place Setting	69.95	Local Antique Store
4	104	1986	1998	Retired	Apricot	448	Carafe	64.95	Replacements, Ltd.
5	104	1986	1998	Retired	Apricot	484	Pitcher Large Disc	42.99	Ebay Auction
6	104	1986	1998	Retired	Apricot	821	Sugar/Cream Tray Set	38.00	Ebay Auction
7	104	1986	1998	Retired	Apricot	497	Salt and Pepper Set	27.99	Replacements, Ltd.
8	104	1986	1998	Retired	Apricot	453	Mug	24.99	Ebay Auction
9	104	1986	1998	Retired	Apricot	471	Bowl Large 1 qt	19.99	Ebay Auction
10	104	1986	1998	Retired	Apricot	492	Individual Creamer	19.99	Replacements, Ltd.
11	104	1986	1998	Retired	Apricot	465	Luncheon Plate	7.99	Ebay Auction
28	117	1997	1999	Retired	Chartreuse	495	Covered Casserole	84.95	Replacements, Ltd.
29	117	1997	1999	Retired	Chartreuse	467	Chop Plate	79.95	Replacements, Ltd.
30	117	1997	1999	Retired	Chartreuse	448	Carafe	75.95	Replacements, Ltd.
31	117	1997	1999	Retired	Chartreuse	830	5 Piece Place Setting	75.00	Ebay Auction
32	117	1997	1999	Retired	Chartreuse	821	Sugar/Cream Tray Set	59.99	Replacements, Ltd.
33	117	1997	1999	Retired	Chartreuse	484	Pitcher Large Disc	50.00	Ebay Auction
34	117	1997	1999	Retired	Chartreuse	489	Pyramid Candleholders	42.99	Ebay Auction
35	117	1997	1999	Retired	Chartreuse	486	Sauceboat	35.95	Ebay Auction
36	117	1997	1999	Retired	Chartreuse	471	Bowl Large 1 qt	30.99	Ebay Auction
37	117	1997	1999	Retired	Chartreuse	497	Salt and Pepper Set	29.99	Replacements, Ltd.
38	117	1997	1999	Retired	Chartreuse	478	AD Cup and Saucer	27.99	Replacements, Ltd.
39	117	1997	1999	Retired	Chartreuse	451	Rim Soup	24.99	Ebay Auction
40	117	1997	1999	Retired	Chartreuse	492	Individual Creamer	20.99	Ebay Auction
41	117	1997	1999	Retired	Chartreuse	453	Mug	19.95	Ebay Auction
42	117	1997	1999	Retired	Chartreuse	465	Luncheon Plate	15.00	Ebay Auction
43	117	1997	1999	Retired	Chartreuse	446	Tumbler	11.99	Replacements, Ltd.
56	102	2000	2010	Retired	Cinnabar	830	5 Piece Place Setting	35.99	Replacements, Ltd.
57	102	2000	2010	Retired	Cinnabar	484	Pitcher Large Disc	34.99	Megachina.com
58	102	2000	2010	Retired	Cinnabar	467	Chop Plate	19.99	Megachina.com
59	102	2000	2010	Retired	Cinnabar	497	Salt and Pepper Set	19.99	Megachina.com

Color List | Items | Retired

FIGURE 4.50 Fiesta® Collection ➤

a. Open *e04p1colors* in Word. Do the following to copy the Word table data into Excel and prepare the data to be used as a lookup table:
    - Click the **table icon** in the top-left corner of the table to select the table content, and then click **Copy** in the Clipboard group.
    - Start a new Excel workbook, click the **Paste arrow** in the Clipboard group in Excel, and then select **Match Destination Formatting (M)**.
    - Bold and horizontally center the labels on the first row. Center the data in the first, third, and fourth columns. Widen the second and third columns to fit the data.
    - Select the **range A2:D30**, click in the **Name Box**, type **colors**, and then press **Enter** to assign a name to the selected range.
    - Click **cell A2**, click **Sort & Filter** in the Editing group, and then select **Sort Smallest to Largest**. Remember that you must sort the first column in ascending order to use the table for an exact match for a VLOOKUP function.
    - Rename the *Sheet1* tab as **Color List**.
    - Save the Excel workbook as **e04p1collection_LastnameFirstname**. Close the Word document.

b. Open *e04p1items* in Word. Select and copy the table, display the Excel workbook, click the **Sheet2 tab**, make sure **cell A1** is the active cell, and then paste the table in the same way you did in step a. Rename *Sheet2* as **Items**. Close the Word document.

c. Click **cell A2** in the Items sheet, click the **View tab**, click **Freeze Panes** in the Window group, and then select **Freeze Top Row**.

d. Press **Ctrl+End** to go to the last data cell. Note that the first row is frozen so that the column labels remain onscreen. Press **Ctrl+Home** to go back to **cell A2**.

e. Click the **Insert tab**, click **Table** in the Tables group, and then click **OK** in the Create Table dialog box.

f. Click the **Design tab** if necessary, click the **More button** in the Table Styles group, and then click **Table Style Medium 5**.

g. Click the **Data tab**, click **Remove Duplicates** in the Data Tools group, click **Select All** to ensure all columns are selected, and then click **OK** in the Remove Duplicates dialog box. Click **OK** in the message box that informs you that *12 duplicate values were found and removed; 343 unique values remain*.

h. Click **cell B2**, click the **Home tab**, click the **Insert arrow** in the Cells group, and then select **Insert Table Columns to the Left**. Then, insert two more columns to the left. Do the following to insert functions and customize the results in the three new table columns:
   - Type **Year Introduced** in **cell B1**, **Year Retired** in **cell C1**, and **Color** in **cell D1**.
   - Click **cell B2**, type **=VLOOKUP([Color Number],colors,3,False)** and then press **Enter**. Excel copies the function down the Year Introduced column. This function looks up each item's color number using the structured reference [Color Number], looks up that value in the colors table, and then returns the year that color was introduced, which is in the third column of that table.
   - Click **cell B2**, click **Copy**, click **cell C2**, and then click **Paste**. Change the *3* to **4** in the col_index_num argument of the pasted function. Excel copies the function down the Year Retired column. This function looks up each item's color number using the structured reference [Color Number], looks up that value in the colors table, and then returns the year that color was retired if applicable, which is in the fourth column of that table. The function returns 0 if the retired cell in the lookup table is blank.

   - Click the **File tab**, click **Options**, click **Advanced**, scroll down to the *Display options for this worksheet* section, click the **Show a zero in cells that have zero value check box** to deselect it, and then click **OK**. The zeros disappear. (Note that this option hides zeros anywhere in the active worksheet. In some cases, this is not desirable if you need to show legitimate zeros. However, this particular worksheet is designed to avoid that issue.)
   - Click **cell C2**, click **Copy**, click **cell D2**, and then click **Paste**. Change the *4* to **2** in the col_index_num argument of the pasted function. Excel copies the function down the Color column. This function looks up each item's color number using the structured reference [Color Number], to look up that value in the colors table, and then returns the color name, which is in the second column of that table.

i. Apply wrap text, horizontal centering, and **30.75 row height** to the column labels row. Adjust column widths. Center data horizontally in the Color Number, Year Introduced, Year Retired, and Item Number columns. Apply **Comma Style** to the Replacement Values. Deselect the data.

j. Click **Sort & Filter** in the Editing group, and then select **Custom Sort** to display the Sort dialog box. Do the following in the Sort dialog box:
   - Click the **Sort by arrow**, and then select **Color**.
   - Click **Add Level**, click the **Then by arrow**, and then select **Replacement Value**.
   - Click the **Order arrow**, and then select **Largest to Smallest**. Click **OK**.

k. Right-click the **Items sheet tab**, select **Move or Copy**, click **(move to end)**, click the **Create a copy check box**, and then click **OK**. Rename the copied sheet as **Retired**. Delete Sheet3.

l. Make sure the active sheet is Retired. Insert a table column between the Year Retired and Color columns.
   - Type **Status** in **cell D1** as the column label.
   - Click **cell D2**, type **=IF([Year Retired]=0,"Current","Retired")**, and then press **Enter**. This function determines that if the cell contains a 0 (which is hidden), it will display the word *Current*. Otherwise, it will display *Retired*.

m. Click the **Status filter arrow**, deselect the **Current check box**, and then click **OK** to filter out the current colors and display only retired colors.

n. Click the **Design tab**, and then click **Total Row** in the Table Style Options group. Press **Ctrl+End** to go to the total row, click the **Source total cell** (which contains a count of visible items), click the **Source total arrow**, and then select **None**. Click **cell H345**, the Replacement Value total cell, click the **Replacement Value total arrow**, and then select **Sum**.

o. Prepare the Retired worksheet for printing by doing the following:
   - Set **0.2"** left and right page margins.
   - Select the **range E1:I345**, click the **Page Layout tab**, click **Print Area** in the Page Setup group, and then select **Set Print Area**.
   - Click **Print Titles** in the Page Setup group, click the **Rows to repeat at top collapse button**, click the **row 1 header**, and then click the **expand button**. Click **OK**.
   - Click the **View tab**, and then click **Page Break Preview** in the Worksbook Views group. If the message box appears, click **OK**.

p. Create a footer with your name on the left side, the sheet name code in the center, and the file name code on the right side of each worksheet.

q. Save and close the workbook, and submit based on your instructor's directions.

2 Salary Data

As the Human Resources Manager, you maintain employee salary data. You exported data from the corporate database into an Excel workbook. You want to convert the data to a table. You will use structured references to calculate raises and new salaries. Finally, you want to display a total row to show the total salaries. This exercise follows the same set of skills as used in Hands-On Exercises 1, 2, and 3 in the chapter. Refer to Figure 4.51 as you complete this exercise.

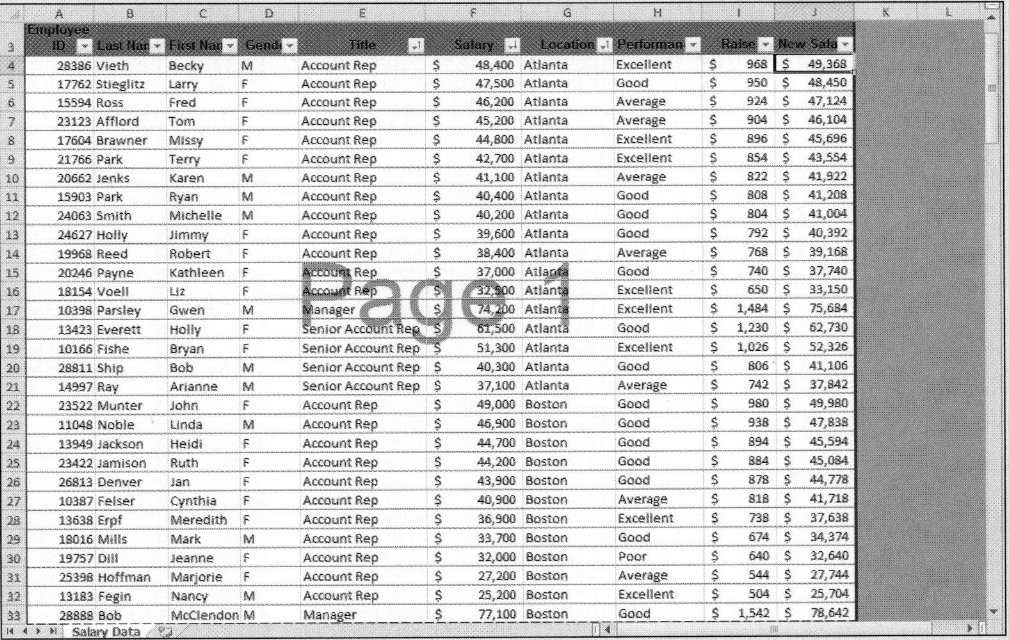

	A	B	C	D	E	F	G	H	I	J
3	Employee ID	Last Nar	First Nar	Gend	Title	Salary	Location	Performan	Raise	New Sala
4	28386	Vieth	Becky	M	Account Rep	$ 48,400	Atlanta	Excellent	$ 968	$ 49,368
5	17762	Stieglitz	Larry	F	Account Rep	$ 47,500	Atlanta	Good	$ 950	$ 48,450
6	15594	Ross	Fred	F	Account Rep	$ 46,200	Atlanta	Average	$ 924	$ 47,124
7	23123	Afflord	Tom	F	Account Rep	$ 45,200	Atlanta	Average	$ 904	$ 46,104
8	17604	Brawner	Missy	F	Account Rep	$ 44,800	Atlanta	Excellent	$ 896	$ 45,696
9	21766	Park	Terry	F	Account Rep	$ 42,700	Atlanta	Excellent	$ 854	$ 43,554
10	20662	Jenks	Karen	M	Account Rep	$ 41,100	Atlanta	Average	$ 822	$ 41,922
11	15903	Park	Ryan	M	Account Rep	$ 40,400	Atlanta	Good	$ 808	$ 41,208
12	24063	Smith	Michelle	M	Account Rep	$ 40,200	Atlanta	Good	$ 804	$ 41,004
13	24627	Holly	Jimmy	F	Account Rep	$ 39,600	Atlanta	Good	$ 792	$ 40,392
14	19968	Reed	Robert	F	Account Rep	$ 38,400	Atlanta	Average	$ 768	$ 39,168
15	20246	Payne	Kathleen	F	Account Rep	$ 37,000	Atlanta	Good	$ 740	$ 37,740
16	18154	Voell	Liz	F	Account Rep	$ 32,500	Atlanta	Excellent	$ 650	$ 33,150
17	10398	Parsley	Gwen	M	Manager	$ 74,200	Atlanta	Excellent	$ 1,484	$ 75,684
18	13423	Everett	Holly	F	Senior Account Rep	$ 61,500	Atlanta	Good	$ 1,230	$ 62,730
19	10166	Fishe	Bryan	F	Senior Account Rep	$ 51,300	Atlanta	Excellent	$ 1,026	$ 52,326
20	28811	Ship	Bob	M	Senior Account Rep	$ 40,300	Atlanta	Good	$ 806	$ 41,106
21	14997	Ray	Arianne	M	Senior Account Rep	$ 37,100	Atlanta	Average	$ 742	$ 37,842
22	23522	Munter	John	F	Account Rep	$ 49,000	Boston	Good	$ 980	$ 49,980
23	11048	Noble	Linda	M	Account Rep	$ 46,900	Boston	Good	$ 938	$ 47,838
24	13949	Jackson	Heidi	F	Account Rep	$ 44,700	Boston	Good	$ 894	$ 45,594
25	23422	Jamison	Ruth	F	Account Rep	$ 44,200	Boston	Good	$ 884	$ 45,084
26	26813	Denver	Jan	F	Account Rep	$ 43,900	Boston	Good	$ 878	$ 44,778
27	10387	Felser	Cynthia	F	Account Rep	$ 40,900	Boston	Average	$ 818	$ 41,718
28	13638	Erpf	Meredith	F	Account Rep	$ 36,900	Boston	Excellent	$ 738	$ 37,638
29	18016	Mills	Mark	M	Account Rep	$ 33,700	Boston	Good	$ 674	$ 34,374
30	19757	Dill	Jeanne	F	Account Rep	$ 32,000	Boston	Poor	$ 640	$ 32,640
31	25398	Hoffman	Marjorie	F	Account Rep	$ 27,200	Boston	Average	$ 544	$ 27,744
32	13183	Fegin	Nancy	M	Account Rep	$ 25,200	Boston	Excellent	$ 504	$ 25,704
33	28888	Bob	McClendon	M	Manager	$ 77,100	Boston	Good	$ 1,542	$ 78,642

FIGURE 4.51 Salary Data ➤

a. Open *e04p2salary* and save it as **e04p2salary_LastnameFirstname**.

b. Click in the dataset. Click the **Insert tab**, click **Table** in the Tables group, and then click **OK**.

c. Click the **More button** in the Table Styles group, and then click **Table Style Light 10**.

d. Click the **Data tab**, click **Sort** in the Sort & Filter group, and then do the following in the Sort dialog box:
   - Click the **Sort by arrow**, and then select **Location**.
   - Click **Add Level**, click the **Then by arrow**, and then select **Title**.
   - Click **Add Level**, click the **Then by arrow**, select **Salary**, click the **Order arrow**, and then select **Largest to Smallest**. Then click **OK**.

e. Click **cell I3**, type **Raise**, and then press **Tab**. Type **New Salary** in **cell J3**, and then press **Enter**.

f. Click **cell I4**, type =[and then double-click **Salary** from the list. Type]***$I$1** and press **Enter**.
g. Click **cell J4**, type =**[Salary]**+**[Raise]**, and then press **Enter**.
h. Format the last two columns with **Accounting Number Format** with no decimal places.
i. Click the **Design tab**, and then click **Total Row** in the Table Style Options group. Scroll to the bottom of the table, click the **Raise total cell** on row 159, click the **Raise total row arrow**, and then select **Sum**. Click the **Salary total cell** on row 159, click the **Salary total row arrow**, and then select **Sum**.
j. Prepare the worksheet to be printed by doing the following:
   - Click the **Page Layout tab**, and then set **landscape orientation**. Adjust column widths so that the data fits on one page, wrap text, and center align field names.
   - Click **Print Titles**, click the **Rows to repeat at top collapse button**, click **row 3**, click the **expand button**, and then click **OK**.
   - Click the **View tab**, and then click **Page Break Preview**. If a message box appears, click **OK**.
k. Drag the second page break to be between rows 58 and 59. Move the third page break to be between rows 81 and 82. Move the fourth page break to be between rows 110 and 111. Move the last page break to be between rows 139 and 140.
l. Create a footer with your name on the left side, the date code in the center, and the file name code on the right side.
m. Save and close the workbook, and submit based on your instructor's directions.

3 Dentist Association Donation List

The Midwest Regional Dentist Association is planning its annual meeting in Lincoln, Nebraska, this spring. Several members donated items for door prizes at the closing general session. You need to organize the list of donations and format it to highlight particular data for your supervisor, who is on the conference board of directors. This exercise follows the same set of skills as used in Hands-On Exercises 2, 3, and 4 in the chapter. Refer to Figure 4.52 as you complete this exercise.

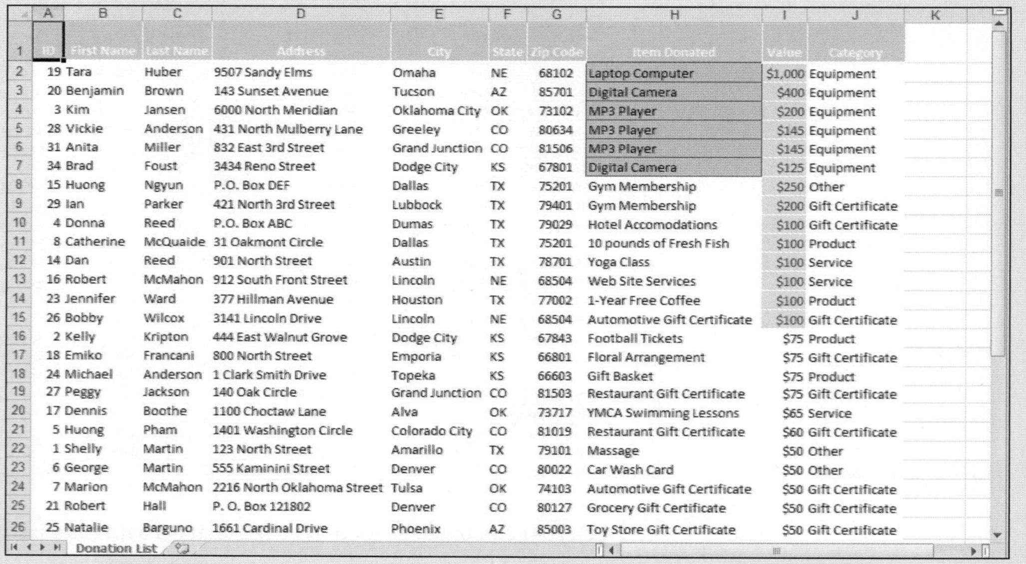

	A	B	C	D	E	F	G	H	I	J
1	ID	First Name	Last Name	Address	City	State	Zip Code	Item Donated	Value	Category
2	19	Tara	Huber	9507 Sandy Elms	Omaha	NE	68102	Laptop Computer	$1,000	Equipment
3	20	Benjamin	Brown	143 Sunset Avenue	Tucson	AZ	85701	Digital Camera	$400	Equipment
4	3	Kim	Jansen	6000 North Meridian	Oklahoma City	OK	73102	MP3 Player	$200	Equipment
5	28	Vickie	Anderson	431 North Mulberry Lane	Greeley	CO	80634	MP3 Player	$145	Equipment
6	31	Anita	Miller	832 East 3rd Street	Grand Junction	CO	81506	MP3 Player	$145	Equipment
7	34	Brad	Foust	3434 Reno Street	Dodge City	KS	67801	Digital Camera	$125	Equipment
8	15	Huong	Ngyun	P.O. Box DEF	Dallas	TX	75201	Gym Membership	$250	Other
9	29	Ian	Parker	421 North 3rd Street	Lubbock	TX	79401	Gym Membership	$200	Gift Certificate
10	4	Donna	Reed	P.O. Box ABC	Dumas	TX	79029	Hotel Accomodations	$100	Gift Certificate
11	8	Catherine	McQuaide	31 Oakmont Circle	Dallas	TX	75201	10 pounds of Fresh Fish	$100	Product
12	14	Dan	Reed	901 North Street	Austin	TX	78701	Yoga Class	$100	Service
13	16	Robert	McMahon	912 South Front Street	Lincoln	NE	68504	Web Site Services	$100	Service
14	23	Jennifer	Ward	377 Hillman Avenue	Houston	TX	77002	1-Year Free Coffee	$100	Product
15	26	Bobby	Wilcox	3141 Lincoln Drive	Lincoln	NE	68504	Automotive Gift Certificate	$100	Gift Certificate
16	2	Kelly	Kripton	444 East Walnut Grove	Dodge City	KS	67843	Football Tickets	$75	Product
17	18	Emiko	Francani	800 North Street	Emporia	KS	66801	Floral Arrangement	$75	Gift Certificate
18	24	Michael	Anderson	1 Clark Smith Drive	Topeka	KS	66603	Gift Basket	$75	Product
19	27	Peggy	Jackson	140 Oak Circle	Grand Junction	CO	81503	Restaurant Gift Certificate	$75	Gift Certificate
20	17	Dennis	Boothe	1100 Choctaw Lane	Alva	OK	73717	YMCA Swimming Lessons	$65	Service
21	5	Huong	Pham	1401 Washington Circle	Colorado City	CO	81019	Restaurant Gift Certificate	$60	Gift Certificate
22	1	Shelly	Martin	123 North Street	Amarillo	TX	79101	Massage	$50	Other
23	6	George	Martin	555 Kaminini Street	Denver	CO	80022	Car Wash Card	$50	Other
24	7	Marion	McMahon	2216 North Oklahoma Street	Tulsa	OK	74103	Automotive Gift Certificate	$50	Gift Certificate
25	21	Robert	Hall	P. O. Box 121802	Denver	CO	80127	Grocery Gift Certificate	$50	Gift Certificate
26	25	Natalie	Barguno	1661 Cardinal Drive	Phoenix	AZ	85003	Toy Store Gift Certificate	$50	Gift Certificate

Donation List

FIGURE 4.52 Donation List ➤

a. Open *e04p3donate* and save it as **e04p3donate_LastnameFirstname**.
b. Click the **Design tab**, click **Remove Duplicates** in the Tools group, and then click **OK**. Click **OK** in the message box that tells you that Excel removed three duplicate records.
c. Click **Convert to Range** in the Tools group, and then click **Yes** in the message box.
d. Select the **range A2:J35**, click the **Home tab**, click the **Fill Color arrow** in the Font group, and then select **No Fill** to remove the table fill colors.

e. Select the **range I2:I35**. Click **Conditional Formatting** in the Styles group, point to **Highlight Cells Rules**, and then select **Greater Than**. Type **99** in the **Format cells that are GREATER THAN box**, and then click **OK**.

f. Select **cells H2:H35**. Create a custom conditional format by doing the following:
   - Click **Conditional Formatting** in the Styles group, and then select **New Rule**.
   - Click **Use a formula to determine which cells to format**.
   - Type =(J2="Equipment") in the **Format values where this formula is true box**. The basic condition is testing to see if the contents of cell J2 equal the word *Equipment*. You type *Equipment* in quotation marks since you are comparing text instead of a value.
   - Click **Format**, click the **Fill tab** if necessary, and then click **Red, Accent 2, Lighter 60%** (sixth background color on the second row below the first horizontal line).
   - Click the **Border tab**, click the **Color arrow**, click **Dark Red**, and then click **Outline**.
   - Click **OK** in each dialog box.

g. Click anywhere in the table to deselect the range. Click **Sort & Filter** in the Editing group, and then select **Custom Sort**. The dialog box may contain existing sort conditions for the State and City fields, which you will replace. Set the following sort conditions:
   - Click the **Sort by arrow**, and then select **Item Donated.** Click the **Sort On arrow**, and then select **Cell Color**. Click the **Order arrow**, and then select the **RGB(242, 220, 219)** or **RGB(230, 184, 183) fill color**. The fill color displays for the Order.
   - Click the **Then by arrow**, and then select **Value**. Click the **Order arrow**, and then select **Largest to Smallest**.
   - Click **OK**.

h. Select **landscape orientation**, set appropriate margins, and adjust column widths so that all the data will print on one page. Do not decrease the scaling.

i. Create a footer with your name on the left side, the sheet name code in the center, and the file name code on the right side.

j. Save and close the workbook, and submit based on your instructor's directions.

MID-LEVEL EXERCISES

1 Biology Department Teaching Schedule

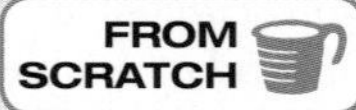

As the department head of the Biology Department at a state university, you must prepare and finalize the faculty teaching schedule. Scheduling preparation takes time because you must ensure that you do not book faculty for different courses at the same time or double-book a classroom with two different classes. You downloaded the Spring 2012 schedule as a starting point and edited it to prepare a draft for the Spring 2013 schedule, and now you need to sort and filter the schedule to review it from several perspectives.

a. Open *e04m1classes* and save it as **e04m1classes_LastnameFirstname**.

b. Freeze the panes so that the column labels do not scroll offscreen.

c. Convert the data to a table, and then name the table **Spring2013**.

d. Apply **Table Style Light 14** to the table.

DISCOVER 

e. Sort the table by Instructor, then Days, and then Start Time. Create a custom sort order for Days so that it appears in this sequence: MTWR, MWF, MW, M, W, F, TR, T, R. (The day abbreviations are as follows: M=Monday, T=Tuesday, W=Wednesday, R=Thursday, F=Friday.)

f. Remove duplicate records from the table. Excel should find and remove three duplicate records.

g. Copy the Faculty sheet, place the copied worksheet to the right of the Faculty sheet, and then rename the duplicate worksheet **Rooms**. Sort the data in the Rooms sheet by Room in ascending order, then by Days using the custom sort order you created in step e, and finally by Start Time from earliest to latest time.

h. Copy the Rooms sheet, place the copied worksheet to the right of the Rooms sheet, and then rename the duplicate worksheet **Prime Time**.

i. Filter the table in the Prime Time sheet to show only classes scheduled on any combination of Monday, Wednesday, and Friday. Include classes that meet four days a week (MTWR). Do not include any other combination of Tuesday or Thursday classes though. Also filter the table by classes that start between 9:00 AM and 12:00 PM. The status bar indicates 20 of 75 records found.

j. Insert a new worksheet named **Room Capacity**. Create the following lookup table, and then assign the range name **capacity** to the data except for the column labels. Bold and horizontally center the column labels in the lookup table.

Room	Capacity
ED 301	30
SCI 115	50
SCI 117	42
SCI 119	28
SCI 210	32
SCI 214	28
SCI 215	24
SCI 216	24

k. Insert a column on the right side of the Credits column in the Faculty sheet. Type the column label **Capacity**. Insert a lookup function that looks up the room number, compares it to the lookup table you created in step j, and returns the room capacity. Make sure the function copies down the entire column.

l. Select the first three sheet tabs, set **0.2"** left and right margins, **Landscape orientation**, and **95% scaling**. Repeat the column labels on all pages. On the Faculty sheet, decrease some column widths so that the Capacity column will print on the same page as the other columns.

m. Display the Faculty sheet in Page Break Preview. Adjust any page breaks so that classes for a particular instructor do not split between pages.

n. Display the Rooms sheet in Page Break Preview. Adjust any page breaks so that classes for a particular room do not split between pages, if necessary.

o. Insert a footer with your name on the left side, the sheet name code in the center, and the file name code on the right side of all four sheets.

p. Save and close the workbook, and submit based on your instructor's directions.

2 Credit Card Expenses

You started recording every credit card transaction so that you can analyze your monthly expenses. You used an Excel worksheet to track dates, places, categories, and amounts. Because you are a consultant who travels periodically, you also have business expenses. You included a column to indicate the business-related transactions. You are now ready to analyze the data. Refer to Figure 4.53 as you complete this exercise.

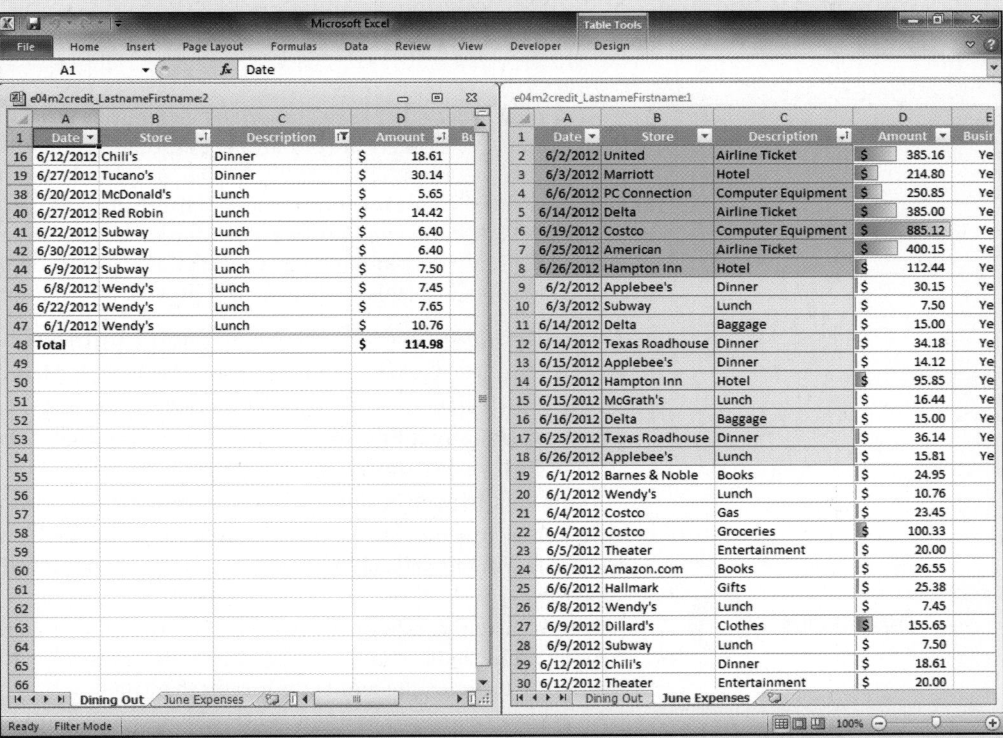

FIGURE 4.53 Credit Card Analysis ➤

a. Open *e04m2credit* and save it as **e04m2credit_LastnameFirstname**.

b. Make sure the Dining Out worksheet is active. Convert the data to a table, and then apply **Table Style Light 11**.

c. Sort the table by the description in alphabetical order, sort the store in alphabetical order, and then sort by amount from smallest to largest in that sequence.

d. Filter the records to show personal (i.e., non-business) lunches and dinner expenses. Add a total row to sum the amounts but do not include other totals.

e. Click the **June Expenses worksheet tab**, and then apply the **Green Data Bar** in the *Gradient Fill* section setting to the Amount column.

f. Create a conditional formatting rule with these specifications:
- Applies to the **range A2:C47**.
- Uses a formula to determine which cells to format based on amounts of $100 or more *and* that are classified as business expenses. Because this conditional formatting applies to several columns (A, B, and C), you must use mixed cell references in the formula.
- Formats data with a **Medium Green fill color** and a **Green line border** using the **Outline preset border style**.

g. Create a conditional formatting rule with these specifications:
   - Applies to the **range A2:C47**.
   - Uses a formula to determine which cells to format based on amounts less than $100 *and* that are classified as business expenses. Because this conditional formatting applies to several columns (A, B, and C), you must use mixed cell references in the formula.
   - Formats data with a **Light Green fill color** and a **Green line border** using the **Outline preset border style**.

DISCOVER 

DISCOVER 

h. Create a custom color sort for the Description column with these specifications:
   - Sorts on cell color.
   - Displays the **Medium Green fill color** on Top as the primary sort.
   - Displays the **Light Green fill color** on Top as the secondary sort.

i. Create a footer with your name on the left side, the sheet name code in the center, and the file name code on the right side on each worksheet.

j. Save and close the workbook, and submit based on your instructor's directions.

3 Artwork

You work for a gallery that is an authorized Greenwich Workshop fine art dealer (www.greenwich-workshop.com). Customers in your area are especially fond of James C. Christensen's art. Although customers can visit the Web site to see images and details about his work, they have requested a list of all his artwork. Your assistant prepared a list of artwork: art, type, edition size, release date, and issue price. In addition, you included a column to identify what pieces are sold out at the publisher, indicating the rare, hard-to-obtain artwork that is available on the secondary market. You now want to convert the data to a table so that you can provide information to your customers.

a. Open *e04m3fineart* and save it as **e04m3fineart_LastnameFirstname**.

b. Convert the data to a table, and then apply **Table Style Medium 5**.

c. Add a row (below the The Yellow Rose record) for this missing piece of art: **The Yellow Rose, Masterwork Canvas Edition, 50** edition size, **May 2009** release date, **$895** issue price. Enter **Yes** to indicate the piece is sold out.

d. Sort the table by type in alphabetical order and then by release date from newest to oldest.

e. Add a total row that shows the largest edition size and the most expensive issue price. Delete the Total label in **cell A173**. Add a descriptive label in **cell C173** to reflect the content on the total row.

DISCOVER 

f. Create a custom conditional format for the Issue Price column with these specifications:
   - 4 Traffic Lights icon set (Black, Red, Yellow, Green)
   - Red icon when the number is greater than 1000
   - Yellow icon when the number is less than or equal to 1000 and greater than 500
   - Green icon when the number is less than or equal to 500 and greater than 250
   - Black icon when the number is less than or equal to 250.

g. Filter the table by the Green Traffic Light conditional formatting icon.

h. Set the print area to print the **range C1:H173**, select the **first row to repeat at the top of each printout**, set **1"** top and bottom margins, set **0.3"** left and right margins, and then select **landscape orientation**.

i. Wrap text and horizontally center column labels, and then adjust column widths and row heights as needed.

j. Adjust the page break so that at least five Limited Edition Canvas records print on the second page.

k. Create a footer with your name on the left side, the sheet name code in the center, and the file name code on the right side.

l. Save and close the workbook, and submit based on your instructor's directions.

CAPSTONE EXERCISE

You just got an internship at Mountain View Realty, a real estate firm that focuses on the North Utah County area. The previous intern developed a spreadsheet listing houses listed and sold during the past several months. She included addresses, location, list price, selling price, listing date, and date sold. You need to convert the data to a table and manipulate the table. You will manage the large worksheet, prepare the worksheet for printing, sort and filter the table, include calculations, and format the table.

Prepare the Large Worksheet as a Table

You need to freeze the panes so that labels remain onscreen. You also want to convert the data to a table so that you can apply table options.

a. Open the *e04c1houses* workbook and save it as **e04c1houses_LastnameFirstname**.

b. Freeze the first row on the Sales Data worksheet.

c. Convert the data to a table, and then apply the **Table Style Medium 17**.

d. Remove duplicate records.

Add Calculated Fields and a Total Row

The office manager asked you to insert a column to display the percent of list price. The formula finds the sale price percentage of the list price. For example, if a house was listed at $100,000 and sells for $75,000, the percentage of list price is 75%. In some cases, the percentage is more than 100%. This happens when a bidding war occurs, and buyers increase their offers, which results in the seller getting more than the list price.

a. Insert a new field to the right of the Selling Price field. Name the new field **Percent of List Price**.

b. Create a formula with structured references to calculate the percent of the list price.

c. Format the column with **Percent Style** with one decimal place.

d. Insert a new field to the right of the Sale Date field. Name the new field **Days on Market**.

e. Create a formula with structured references to calculate the number of days on the market. If the result displays in a date format, apply the **General number format** to the average.

f. Add a total row to display the average percent of list price and average number of days on market. Format the average number of days on market as a whole number. Use an appropriate label for the total row.

Sort and Print the Table

To help the office manager compare house sales by city, you will sort the data. Then, you will prepare the large table to print.

a. Sort the table by city in alphabetical order, and add a second level to sort by days on market with the houses on the market the longest at the top within each city.

b. Adjust column widths so that the data is one page across (three pages total), and then wrap the column headings as needed.

c. Repeat the column headings on all pages.

d. Display the table in Page Break Preview.

e. Change page breaks so that city data does not span between pages, and then change back to Normal view.

f. Add a footer with your name on the left side, the sheet name code in the center, and the file name code on the right side.

Copy and Filter the Data

The office manager needs to focus on houses that took longer than 30 days to sell within 3 cities. To keep the original data intact for the agents, you will copy the table data to a new sheet and use that sheet to display the filtered data.

a. Copy the Sales Data worksheet, and then place the duplicate worksheet to the right of the original worksheet tab. Convert the table to a range of data, and delete the average row.

b. Rename the duplicate worksheet **Filtered Data**.

c. Display the filter arrows for the data.

d. Filter the data to display the cities of *Alpine*, *Cedar Hills*, and *Eagle Mountain*.

e. Filter the data to display records for houses that were on the market 30 days or more.

Apply Conditional Formatting

To highlight housing sales to illustrate trends, you will apply conditional formatting. Since data are sorted by city, you will use an icon set to color-code the number of days on market. You will also apply a data bar conditional formatting to the sale prices to help the office manager visualize the difference among the sales.

a. Apply the **3 Arrows (Colored) icon set** to the days on market values.

b. Apply the **Light Blue Data Bar conditional formatting** in the *Gradient Fill* section to the selling prices.

c. Create a new conditional format that applies **Yellow fill** and **bold font** to values that contain 95% or higher for the Percent of List Price column.

d. Edit the conditional format you created so that it formats values 98% or higher.

Finalize the Workbook

You are ready to finalize the workbook by adding a footer to the new worksheet and saving the final workbook.

a. Add a footer with your name on the left side, the sheet name code in the center, and the file name code on the right side.

b. Remove all page breaks in the Filtered Data worksheet.

c. Select **landscape orientation**, and then set appropriate margins so that the data will print on one page.

d. Save and close the workbook, and submit based on your instructor's directions.

House Sales Data

GENERAL CASE 

You are a real estate agent for Mountain View Realty in Utah. You created a workbook that lists houses sold in several cities in your area. Open *e04b1houses* and save it as **e04b1houses_LastnameFirstname**. Freeze the panes to keep the column labels from scrolling offscreen. Convert the data to a table, and then apply an appropriate table style. Add a calculated column to find the number of days on market between the listing and sales dates. If the formula result displays a date, select **General** as the number format for the last column. Increase the width of the calculated column so that the column label displays fully. Filter the table to show only those houses in Alpine and Cedar Hills that had asking prices less than $750,000. Sort the table by city, and then by asking price from high to low. Add a total row to find the average asking price, average selling price, and the average number of days on the market. Set a print area to print all columns except the Number column, and then select **Landscape orientation**. Select the option to center the worksheet data between the left and right margins. Insert a footer with your name on the left side, the sheet name code in the center, and the file name code on the right side of the worksheet. Save and close the workbook, and submit based on your instructor's directions.

Flight Arrival Status

RESEARCH CASE 

FROM SCRATCH

As an analyst for an airport, you want to study the flight arrivals for a particular day. Select an airport and find its list of flight arrival data. Some airport Web sites do not list complete details, so search for an airport that does, such as Will Rogers World Airport or San Diego International Airport. Copy the column labels and arrival data (airline, flight number, city, gate, scheduled time, status, etc.) for one day, and then paste it in a new workbook. The columns may be in a different sequence from what is listed here. However, you should format the data as needed. Leave two blank rows below the last row of data, and then enter the URL of the Web page where you got the data, the date, and the time. Save the workbook as **e04b2flights_LastnameFirstname**. Convert the list to a table, and then apply a table style.

Sort the table by scheduled time and then by gate number. Apply a conditional formatting to the Status column to highlight cells that contain the text *Delayed* (or similar text). Add a total row to calculate the MODE for the gate number and arrival time. You must select **More Functions** from the list of functions in the total row, and then search for and select **MODE**. Change the label in the first column from *Total* to **Most Frequent**. Use Help to refresh your memory on how to nest an IF function inside another IF function. Add a calculated column on the right side of the table using a nested IF function and structured references to display *Late* if the actual time was later than the scheduled time, *On Time or Early* if the actual time was earlier or equal to the scheduled time, or *Incomplete* if the flight has not landed yet.

Name the worksheet **Arrival Time**. Copy the worksheet, and then name the copied worksheet as **Delayed**. Filter the list by delayed flights. Include a footer with your name on the left side, the sheet name code in the center, and the file name code on the right side of both worksheets. Adjust the margins on both worksheets as necessary. Save and close the workbook, and submit based on your instructor's directions.

U.S. Population

DISASTER RECOVERY 

A colleague at an advertising firm downloaded U.S. population information from the government Web site. In the process of creating tables, he made some errors and needs your help. Open *e04b3populate* and save it as **e04b3populate_LastnameFirstname**. As you find the errors, document them on the Errors worksheet and make the corrections. Your documentation should include these columns: Error Number, Location, Problem, and Solution. Both tables in the U.S. Population worksheet should show grand total populations per year. The state table should be sorted by region and then by state. Your colleague wants to emphasize the top 15% state populations for the most recent year in the state table. The last column should show percentage changes from year to year, such as 0.6%. Your colleague wants to print only the state data. Select the sorted data population for one region at a time to compare to the regional totals in the first table to cross-check the totals. For example, when you select the July 1, 2008, Midwest values in the second table, the status bar should display the same value as shown for the Midwest July 1, 2008, values in the first table. Create a footer with your name, the sheet name code, and the file name code. Save and close the workbook, and submit based on your instructor's directions.

EXCEL APPLICATION CAPSTONE EXERCISE

You work for a travel company that specializes in arranging travel accommodations for student tours and vacations in exciting destinations such as Canada, Rome, and the Czech Republic. You created a workbook to store agent names, student IDs, and tour codes. The workbook also contains a worksheet to store lookup tables. You need to complete the workbook for your manager's approval. You will insert formulas and a variety of functions, convert data to a table, sort and filter the table, and prepare a chart.

Lookup Tables

The Lookup Tables worksheet contains two lookup tables: one to look up the base price to find the commission rate and the other table to look up the tour package code to find the tour description, departure date, and base cost. You need to assign a range name to each lookup table.

a. Start Excel. Open *e00a1trips*, and then save the workbook as **e00a1trips_LastnameFirstname**. Make sure the Lookup Tables sheet is active.
b. Assign the range name **rates** to the base price and commission range.
c. Assign the range name **tours** to the data for the package, tour description, departure, and base cost.

Insert Functions and Formulas

You need to insert lookup functions that look up the tour code, compare it to the lookup table, and then return the trip description, departure date, and base cost of the trip. Then you need to insert a formula to calculate the cost with taxes and fees, the monthly payment, and the agents' commissions.

a. Click **cell D13** on the Data sheet, and then insert a VLOOKUP function that looks up the tour code, compares it to the tours table, and returns the description.
b. Click **cell E13**, and then insert a lookup function that looks up the tour code, compares it to the tours table, and returns the departure date.
c. Click **cell F13**, and then insert a lookup function that looks up the tour code, compares it to the tours table, and returns the base cost of the trip.
d. Click **cell G13**, and then insert a formula that adds taxes and fees to the base cost of the trip (in cell F5) by using the percentage value in the Input area. Use a mixed reference to the cell containing 20% in the input area below the data.
e. Click **cell H13**, and then insert the PMT function to calculate the payments for students who want to pay for their trips in three installments. Use the interest rate and months in the input area below the data. Use appropriate relative, mixed, and/or absolute cell references in the formula. Make sure the result is a positive value.
f. Click **cell I13**, and then calculate the commission using the base cost of the trip and a VLOOKUP function that returns the commission rate based on the base cost of the trip using the rates lookup table. The function should then calculate the monetary value of the commission.
g. Copy the formulas and functions down their respective columns.

Format Data

You need to format the titles and numeric data in the Data sheet. In addition, you want to freeze the column labels so that they do not scroll offscreen. You also want to apply conditional formatting to emphasize values above the average value.

a. Merge and center the main title on the first row over all data columns on the Data sheet. Apply bold and **18 pt font size**.
b. Merge and center the subtitle on the second row over the data columns.
c. Apply **Currency number format** to the monetary values in columns F, G, H, and I.
d. Hide the Tour Code column.

e. Wrap text in the **range F4:I4**. Set the column widths for these columns to 11, if necessary. Adjust the row height, if necessary.
f. Freeze the panes so that the row of column labels do not scroll offscreen.
g. Apply the **Light Red Fill with Dark Red Text** conditional formatting to values in the Total Cost with Taxes column when the values are above average.

Add Summary Statistics

The Data worksheet contains a section for Summary Statistics. You need to insert functions to perform these calculations. Use the total cost including taxes and fees for the range in the functions.

a. Insert a function to calculate the total for all trips in **cell G46**, the average trip cost in **cell G47**, and the median trip cost in **cell G48**.
b. Insert a function to calculate the lowest trip cost in **cell G49** and the highest trip cost in **cell G50**.
c. Click **cell G51**, and then enter a function to display today's date.

Sort and Filter the Data

To preserve the integrity of the original data, you need to copy the worksheet. You will then convert the data in the copied worksheet to a table, apply a table style, sort and filter the data, and then display totals.

a. Copy the Data sheet, and then place the copied sheet before the Summary sheet. Remove the conditional formatting rule on the Data (2) sheet.
b. Convert the data range in the Data (2) sheet to a table.
c. Apply the **Table Style Medium 21 style** to the table.
d. Sort the table by departure date from oldest to newest and then alphabetically by trip description.
e. Apply a filter to display trips arranged by agents Avery and Ross only.
f. Display a total row. Add totals for all monetary columns.

Create Sparklines and Insert a Chart

The Summary sheet provides a six-month summary of sales. You want to insert sparklines to display trends for each agent, and then provide a $500 bonus if the sales were greater than the average combined sales. Finally, you want to create a chart.

a. Create Line sparklines in column H in the Summary sheet to display six-month trends for each agent. Show the high point in each sparkline.
b. Insert an IF function in column I that displays a $500 bonus if an agent's average sales are greater than the average of all sales for the six months. Use two nested AVERAGE functions in the logical _test argument of the IF function to make the comparison.
c. Create a column chart of the agents and their six month sales.
d. Move the chart to a chart sheet named **Sales Chart**.
e. Apply the **Layout 1 chart layout**.
f. Type **January-June 2012 Sales by Agent** for the chart title.
g. Apply the **Style 34 chart style**.
h. Select the **Overlay Legend at Right legend** location, and then move the legend up so that it does not overlay actual columns. If necessary, reduce the size of the legend chart element. Apply a solid white fill color to the legend.
i. Create a footer with your name on the left side, the sheet tab code in the center, and the file name code on the right side of each sheet.
j. Apply **0.2"** left and right margins and scale to one page for the Data and Data (2) sheets. Select **Landscape orientation** for the Data (2) sheet.
k. Save the workbook. Close the workbook, and then exit Excel. Submit the workbook as directed by your instructor.

EXCEL COLLABORATION EXERCISES

1 OK Office Systems Pricing Information

People who have a Windows Live account can access SkyDrive and Microsoft Office Web Apps, a virtual version of Microsoft Office. You can access Microsoft Office Web Apps using your Web browser, and then perform basic Excel tasks without having Microsoft Office installed on your computer. You can save Excel workbooks on your SkyDrive and then provide permission so that others can access your files and collaborate with you on team projects. Pair up with another classmate for this exercise and make sure both students have created a Windows Live account. You will complete the Chapter 1 Hands-On Exercises in teams, and then document the differences in the virtual Excel capabilities compared to the installed version of Excel.

Student 1:

a. Log in to your SkyDrive account using your Windows Live ID. Do the following to create a shared folder with your team member and instructor:
   - Click **Create folder** to the right of *Create*, and then type **Exploring Excel Group** ***X***, substituting the number assigned to your group, in the **Name box**.
   - Click **Change** in the *Share with* section, type the e-mail address of your student team member's e-mail address in the **Enter a name or an email address box**, and then press **Enter**. That person's e-mail address appears below the text box. Click the arrow to the right of the person's e-mail address, and then change the default from *Can view files* to **Can add, edit details, and delete files**.
   - Type your instructor's e-mail address in the **Enter a name or an email address box**, and then press **Enter**. That person's e-mail address appears below the text box. Click the arrow to the right of your instructor's e-mail address, and then change the default from *Can view files* to **Can add, edit details, and delete files**.
   - Click **Next**, and then click **Continue** to complete the shared folder process and return to SkyDrive.

b. Click **Excel workbook** to the right of *Create* in SkyDrive. A Web browser window opens, prompting you to name the workbook. Type **e01t1pricing_Group X**, and then click **Save** to save it in the new shared folder, Exploring Excel Group *X*. (The folder you just created is the default folder.) The Microsoft Excel Web App browser window opens.

c. Start a new Word document using the installed version of Word. Save the document as **e01t1pricing_Group*X*** where you normally save files. Type the heading **Microsoft Excel Web App**, click **Title** in the Styles group on the Home tab, and then press **Enter**. Click the **Insert tab**, click **Screenshot** in the Illustrations group, and then click the thumbnail representing the virtual Excel window. Adjust the size of the screenshot image, if necessary.

d. Type your name below the screenshot image, and then type a short paragraph describing your initial observations of the virtual Excel version compared to the installed version of Excel in the Word document. Press **Enter** twice, type **Hands-On Exercise 1 Observations by** ***your name***, and then press **Enter**.

e. Complete Hands-On Exercise 1 in Chapter 1 using Microsoft Excel Web App. Start with step 1b and continue through step 3. Then document any observations, differences, or challenges in the Word document below the first paragraph you typed. Indicate each step number in which the textbook instruction cannot be completed exactly. Press **Enter** twice, type **Hands-On Exercise 2 Observations by**, type your name, and then press **Enter**.

f. Complete Hands-On Exercise 2 in Chapter 1 using Microsoft Excel Web App. Start with step 1b and continue through step 5. Then document any observations, differences, or challenges in the Word document. Indicate each step number in which the textbook instruction cannot be completed exactly.

g. Close the Excel Web Apps workbook, but keep SkyDrive open. In Microsoft Excel Web App, workbooks save automatically to SkyDrive.

h. Save the Word document. Click the **File tab**, click **Save & Send**, click **Save to Web**, click **Sign In**, and then enter your username and password if necessary. After signing into Windows Live, double-click the **Exploring Excel Group*X* folder,** and then click **Save** in the Save As dialog box. Close Word, log out of Windows Live, and then contact the other student on your team that the files are uploaded to the shared folder.

Student 2:

i. Log in to your Windows Live account, and then display the contents of the shared Exploring Excel folder.

j. Hover the mouse pointer over the *e01t1pricing_Group1.docx* file name. Click the **Show information icon** on the right side of the file name details, and then click **Open in Word** on the right side of the window. Click **OK** when a warning message appears that the file could harm your computer (in this case, you should be safe). Leave the document open. At the end of the document, type **Hands-On Exercise 3 Observations by *your name***, and then press **Enter**.

k. Display the contents of the shared folder on SkyDrive. Open the *e01t1pricing_Group1* workbook in Microsoft Excel Web App.

l. Complete Hands-On Exercise 3 in Chapter 1 using Microsoft Excel Web App. Start with step 1b. Then document any observations, differences, or challenges in the Word document. Indicate each step number in which the textbook instruction cannot be completed exactly. Press **Enter** twice, type **Hands-On Exercise 4 Observations by *your name***, and then press **Enter**.

m. Complete Hands-On Exercise 4 in Chapter 1 using Microsoft Excel Web App. Start with step 1b. Then document any observations, differences, or challenges in the Word document. Indicate each step number in which the textbook instruction cannot be completed exactly.

n. Compose a paragraph to discuss the limitations of Excel Web App to complete Hands-On Exercise 5.

o. Save the Word document, and then upload it back to the shared Exploring Excel SkyDrive folder. Refer to step h above to save it back in the shared folder, if necessary. Close the Word document.

p. Save the Excel workbook, and then upload it back to the shared Exploring Excel SkyDrive folder.

q. Inform your instructor that the files are uploaded. Log out of Windows Live.

2 Facebook Collaboration

Social media extends past friendships to organizational and product "fan" pages. Organizations such as Lexus, Pepsi Co, Inc., and universities create pages to provide information about their organizations. Some organizations even provide product details, such as the Lexus ES350. Facebook includes a wealth of information about Microsoft Office products. People share information, pose questions, and reply with their experiences to share information in the community.

a. Log in to your Facebook account. If you do not have a Facebook account, sign up for one and add at least two classmates as friends. Search for Microsoft Excel, and then click **Like**.

b. Review postings on the Microsoft Excel wall. Notice that some people post what they like most about Excel or how much it has improved their productivity. Post a note about one of your favorite features about Excel that you have learned so far or how you have used Excel in other classes or on the job. Start Word, and then, using the Snipping Tool, insert a screenshot of your posting. Save the document as **e02t1_LastnameFirstname**.

c. Click the **Discussions link** on the Microsoft Excel Facebook page, and then find topics that relate to IF or VLOOKUP functions. Post a response to one of the discussions. Take a screenshot of your posting, and then insert it into your Word document.

d. Create a team of three students. Create one discussion that asks people to describe their favorite use of any of the nested functions used in Chapter 2. Each team member should respond to the posting. Monitor the discussion and, when you have a few responses, capture a screenshot of the dialogue and insert it into your Word document.

e. Save and close the document. Exit Word. Submit the document based on your instructor's directions.

f. Go to www.youtube.com and do a search for one of these Excel topics: absolute references, mixed references, semi-selection, IF function, VLOOKUP function, circular references, statistical functions shown in Table 2.2, data functions shown in Table 2.3, or range names.

g. Watch several video clips and find one of particular interest to you.

h. Post the URL on your Facebook wall. Specify the topic, and then describe why you like this particular video.

i. Watch videos from the links posted by other students on their Facebook walls. Comment on at least two submissions. Point out what you like about the video or any suggestions you have for improvement.

3 Box Office Movies

You and two of your friends like to follow the popularity of new movies at the theater. You will research current movies that have been showing for four weeks and decide which movies to report on. Work in teams of three for this activity. After obtaining the data, your team will create applicable charts to illustrate the revenue data. Team members will critique each other's charts.

a. Have all three team members log in to a chat client, like MSN Messenger, and engage in a dialogue about what movies are currently playing. Each member should research a different theater to see what is playing at that theater. Decide on six movies that have been in theaters for at least four weeks to research. Save a copy of your instant message dialogue and submit based on your instructor's directions.

b. Divide the six movies among the three team members. Each member should research the weekly revenue reported for two movies for the past four weeks. Make sure your team members use the same source to find the data.

Student 1:

c. Create a new Excel workbook, and then enter appropriate column labels and data for each week for all six movies. Name Sheet1 **Data**.

d. Format the data appropriately. Save the workbook as **e03t1movies_Group**. E-mail the workbook as an attachment to the next student.

Student 2:

e. Create a line chart to show the trends in revenue for the movies for the four-week period.

f. Add a chart title, format the axes appropriately, select a chart style, and then apply other formatting.

g. Move the chart to its own sheet named **Trends**. Save the workbook, and then e-mail it as an attachment to the next student.

Student 3:

h. Add a column to the right of the four-week data, and then total each movie's four-week revenue.

i. Create a pie chart depicting each movie's percentage of the total revenue for your selected movies.

j. Add a chart title, explode one pie slice, add data labels showing percentages and movie names, and then apply other formatting.

k. Move the chart to its own sheet named **Revenue Chart**. Save the workbook, and then e-mail it as an attachment to the first student.

Student 1:

l. Critique the charts. Insert a new worksheet named **Chart Critique** that provides an organized critique of each chart. Type notes that list each team member's name and specify what each student's role was in completing this exercise.

m. Save the workbook, and then e-mail it to the second student.

Student 2:

n. Read the critique of the line chart and make any appropriate changes for the line chart. On the critique worksheet, provide a response to each critique and why you made or did not make the suggested change.

o. Save the workbook, and then e-mail it to the third student.

Student 3:

p. Read the critique of the pie chart and make any appropriate changes for the pie chart. On the critique worksheet, provide a response to each critique and why you made or did not make the suggested change.

q. Save and close the workbook. Exit Excel. Submit the workbook based on your instructor's directions.

4 Party Music

You are planning a weekend party and want to create a mix of music so that most people will appreciate some of the music you will play at the party. To help you decide what music to play, you have asked five classmates to help you create a song list. The entire class should decide on the general format, capitalization style, and sequence: song, musician, genre, year released, and approximate song length.

a. Conduct online research to collect data for your favorite 25 songs.
b. Enter the data into a new workbook in the format, capitalization style, and sequence that was decided by the class.
c. Save the workbook as **e04t1playlist_LastnameFirstname**.
d. Upload the file to a shared folder on SkyDrive or Dropbox that everyone in the class has access to.
e. Download four workbooks from friends, and then copy and paste data from their workbooks into yours.
f. Convert the data to a table, and then apply a table style of your choice.
g. Detect and delete duplicate records. Make a note of the number of duplicate records found and deleted.
h. Sort the data by genre in alphabetical order, then by artist in alphabetical order, and then by release date with the newest year first.
i. Set a filter to hide songs that were released before 2000.
j. Display the total row, and then select the function to count the number of songs displayed.
k. Insert comments in the workbook to indicate which student's workbooks you used, the number of duplicate records deleted, and number of filtered records.
l. Save and close the workbook. Exit Excel. Submit the workbook based on your instructor's directions.

ACCESS

1 INTRODUCTION TO ACCESS

Finding Your Way Through a Database

CASE STUDY | Managing a Business in the Global Economy

Watch the
Set-up
Video
for this
Case Study!

Northwind Traders* is an international gourmet food distributor that imports and exports specialty foods from around the world. Northwind's products include meats, seafood, dairy products, beverages, and produce. Keeping track of customers, vendors, orders, and inventory is no small task. The owners of Northwind have just purchased an order-processing database created with Microsoft Office Access 2010 to help manage their customers, suppliers, products, and orders.

Because the owners do not have time to operate the new database, you have been hired to learn, use, and manage the database. The Northwind owners are willing to provide training about their business and on Access. They expect the learning process to take about three months. After three months, your job will be to support the order-processing team as well as to provide detail and summary reports to the sales force as needed. Your new job at Northwind Traders will be a challenge! It is also an opportunity to make a great contribution to a global company. Are you up to the task?

*Northwind Traders was created by the Microsoft Access Team and is shipped with Access as a sample database you can use to learn about Access. The names of companies, products, people, characters, and/or data are fictitious. The practice database you will use is a modified version of Northwind Traders.

OBJECTIVES AFTER YOU READ THIS CHAPTER, YOU WILL BE ABLE TO:

1. Navigate among the objects in an Access database ***p.573***
2. Understand the difference between working in storage and memory ***p.580***
3. Practice good database file management ***p.581***
4. Back up, compact, and repair Access files ***p.581***
5. Create filters ***p.589***
6. Sort table data on one or more fields ***p.592***
7. Know when to use Access or Excel to manage data ***p.593***
8. Use the Relationships window ***p.600***
9. Understand relational power ***p.601***

Databases Are Everywhere!

If you use the Internet, you use databases often. When you shop online or check your bank statement, you are connecting to a database. Even when you type a search phrase into Google and click Search, you are using Google's massive database with all of its stored Web page references and keywords. Look for something on eBay, and you are searching eBay's database to find a product on which you might want to bid. Need a new pair of boots? Log on to the U.S. Patriot Web site (see Figure 1.1), and find the right pair in your style, your size, and your price range. All this information is stored in its products database.

If you use the Internet, you use databases often.

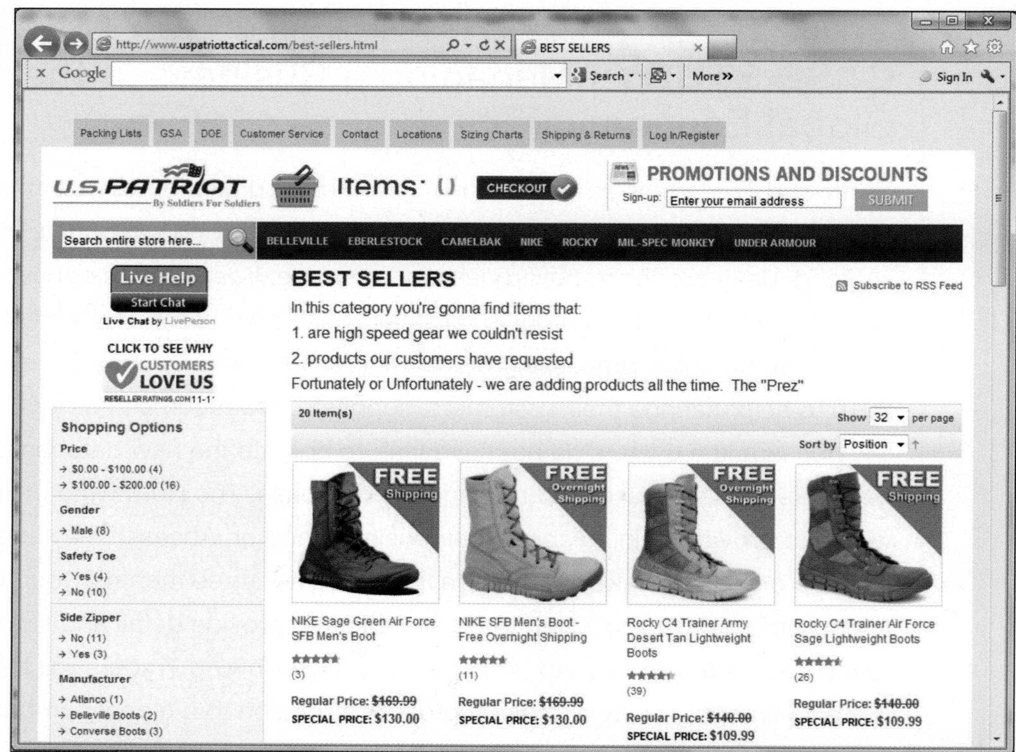

FIGURE 1.1 U.S. Patriot Web Site ➤

You are exposed to other databases on a regular basis outside of Internet shopping. For example, your community college or university uses a database to store the registration data. When you registered for this course, your data was entered into a database. The database probably told you the number of available seats but not the names of the other students who enrolled in the class. In addition, social networking Web sites such as Facebook and LinkedIn are storing data on large database servers.

Organizations rely on data to conduct daily operations, regardless of whether the organization exists as a profit or not-for-profit environment. Organizations maintain data about their customers, employees, orders, volunteers, activities, and facilities. Every keystroke and mouse click creates data about the organization that needs to be stored, organized, and available for analysis. Access is a valuable decision-making tool that many organizations are using or want to use.

In this section, you will explore Access database objects and work with table views. You will also learn the difference between working in storage and working in memory, and you will learn how changes to database objects are saved. Finally, you will practice good database maintenance techniques by backing up, compacting, and repairing databases.

Navigating Among the Objects in an Access Database

An **object** in an Access database is a main component that is created and used to make the database function.

A **field** is the smallest data element contained in a table. Examples of fields are first name, last name, address, and phone number.

A **record** is a complete set of all of the data elements (fields) about one person, place, event, or concept.

A **table**, the foundation of every database, is a collection of related records.

A **database** consists of one or more tables to store data, one or more forms to enter data into the tables, and one or more reports to output the table data as organized information.

The ***objects*** in an Access database are the main components that are created and used to make the database function. The four main object types are tables, queries, forms, and reports. Two other object types, macros and modules, are used less frequently. Throughout this chapter, you will learn how to use each type of object.

To understand how an Access database works and how to use Access effectively, you should first learn the terms of the key object—the table. A ***field*** is the smallest data element contained in a table. Fields define the type of data that is collected, for example, text, numeric, or date. Examples of fields are first name, last name, address, and phone number. A field may be required or optional. For example, a person's last name may be required, but a fax number may be optional. A ***record*** is a complete set of all of the data elements (fields) about one person, place, event, or concept. For example, your first name, last name, student ID, phone number, and e-mail address constitute your record in your instructor's class roster. A ***table***, the foundation of every database, is a collection of related records. For example, all the students in your class would be entered into the Class Roster table during registration.

A ***database*** consists of one or more tables to store data, one or more forms to enter data into the tables, and one or more reports to output the table data as organized information. The main functions of a database are to collect data, to store data logically, to manipulate data to make it more useful, and to output the data to the screen and printed reports. Databases also export data to files so the files can be imported by other databases or other information-processing systems.

TIP Data Versus Information

Data and *information* are two terms that are often used interchangeably. However, when it comes to databases, the two terms mean different things. *Data* is what is entered into the tables of the database. *Information* is the finished product that is produced by the database in a query or in a printed report. Data is converted to information by selecting, calculating, sorting, or summarizing records. Decisions in an organization are usually based on information produced by a database, rather than raw data.

Examine the Access Interface

Figure 1.2 shows the Access Interface for the Northwind Traders database, which was introduced in the Case Study at the beginning of this chapter. The top section, known as the Ribbon, remains the same no matter which database is open. Below the Ribbon, you find all the objects that are needed to make the current database function; these objects are stored in the Navigation Pane (on the left). To the right of the Navigation Pane, the currently open objects are displayed and are delimited with tabs. The title bar at the top of the window contains the name of the application (Microsoft Access), the name of the currently loaded database (Northwind), and the file format (Access 2007) of the loaded database. Because Access 2010 does not have a new file format, you will see Access 2007 in the title bar throughout this textbook. The Minimize, Maximize (or Restore), and Close icons can be found on the right of the title bar. The tab below the Ribbon shows that the Employees table is currently open. When more than one object is open at a time, one tab will be shown for each open object. Click on a tab to view or modify that object independently of the other objects.

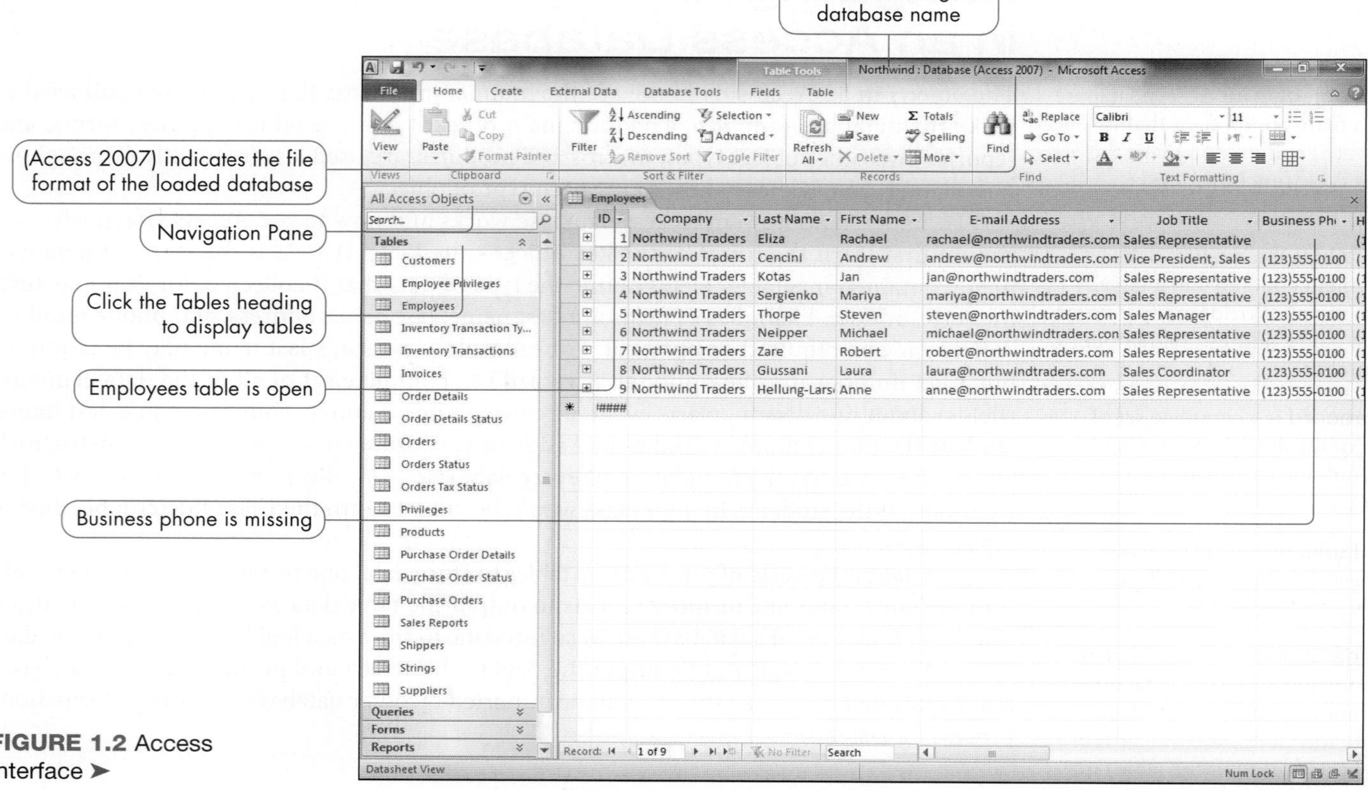
Title bar showing the database name
(Access 2007) indicates the file format of the loaded database
Navigation Pane
Click the Tables heading to display tables
Employees table is open
Business phone is missing

FIGURE 1.2 Access Interface ➤

Figure 1.2 shows that the Northwind database contains 20 tables: Customers, Employee Privileges, Employees, etc. Each table contains multiple records. The Employees table is currently open and shows nine records for the nine employees who work for the company. The Employees table contains 18 fields (or attributes) about each employee, including the employee's Last Name, First Name, E-Mail Address, Job Title, and so on. Occasionally, a field does not contain a value for a particular record. One of the employees, Rachael Eliza, did not provide a business phone. The value of that field is missing. Access shows a blank cell when data is missing.

The Suppliers table holds a record for each vendor from whom the firm purchases products; the Orders table holds one record for each order. The real power of Access is derived from a database with multiple tables and the relationships that connect the tables.

The **Navigation Pane** organizes and lists the database objects in an Access database.

The ***Navigation Pane*** organizes and lists the database objects in an Access database. As stated earlier, six types of objects—tables, queries, forms, reports, macros, and modules—can exist in a database. Most databases contain multiple tables, queries, forms, and reports. Tables store the data, forms enable users to enter information into the tables, reports enable users to display data in an organized format, and queries enable users to ask questions about the data. In Figure 1.2, the Tables group shows all the table objects; the other objects are hidden until you click a group heading to expand the group and display the objects. Click a visible group name to hide the group. To change the way objects are displayed within a group, right-click the group, and select from a list of options. For example, you can right-click the Queries category, point to View By, and then click Details to see when each query was created.

The Access Ribbon contains the icons that help you perform the database functions to maintain a database. These commands are described in detail on the following Reference page. You do not need to memorize every icon, group, and tab; however, it will be helpful to refer to this page as you are learning Access.

REFERENCE ACCESS RIBBON

Tab and Groups	Description
File	The File tab leads to the Backstage view, which gives you access to a variety of database tools such as Compact and Repair, Back Up Database, and Print.
Home Views Clipboard Sort & Filter Records Find Text Formatting	The default Access tab. Contains basic editing functions, such as cut and paste, filtering, find and replace, and most formatting actions.
Create Templates Tables Queries Forms Reports Macros & Code	This tab contains all the create tools, such as create Tables, create Forms, create Reports, and create Queries.
External Data Import & Link Export Collect Data Web Linked Lists	This tab contains all of the operations to facilitate data import and export.
Database Tools Tools Macro Relationships Analyze Move Data Add-Ins	This tab enables you to use the more advanced features of Access. Set relationships between tables, analyze a table or query, and migrate your data to SQL Server or SharePoint.

Work with Table Views

The **Datasheet view** is where you add, edit, and delete the records of a table.

The **Design view** is where you create tables, add and delete fields, and modify field properties.

Access provides two different ways to view a table: the Datasheet view and the Design view. The ***Datasheet view*** is a grid containing columns (fields) and rows (records), similar to an Excel spreadsheet. You can view, add, edit, and delete records in the Datasheet view. The ***Design view*** is used to create and modify a table's design by specifying the fields it will contain, the fields' data types, and their associated properties. Data types define the type of data that will be stored in a field, such as currency, numeric, text, etc. For example, if you need to store the pay rate of an employee, you would enter the field name Pay Rate and select the data type currency. The field properties define the characteristics of the fields in more detail. For example, for the field Pay Rate, you could set a field property that requires Pay Rate to be less than $25 (a higher rate would trigger a manager's approval). To accomplish this, you would set the validation rule to <25 to prevent users from entering a pay rate higher than $25.

Figure 1.3 shows the Design view for the Customers table. In the top portion, each row contains the field names, the data type, and an optional description for each field in the table. In the bottom portion, the Field Properties pane contains the properties (details) for each field. Click on a field, and the field properties will be displayed in the bottom portion of the Design view window.

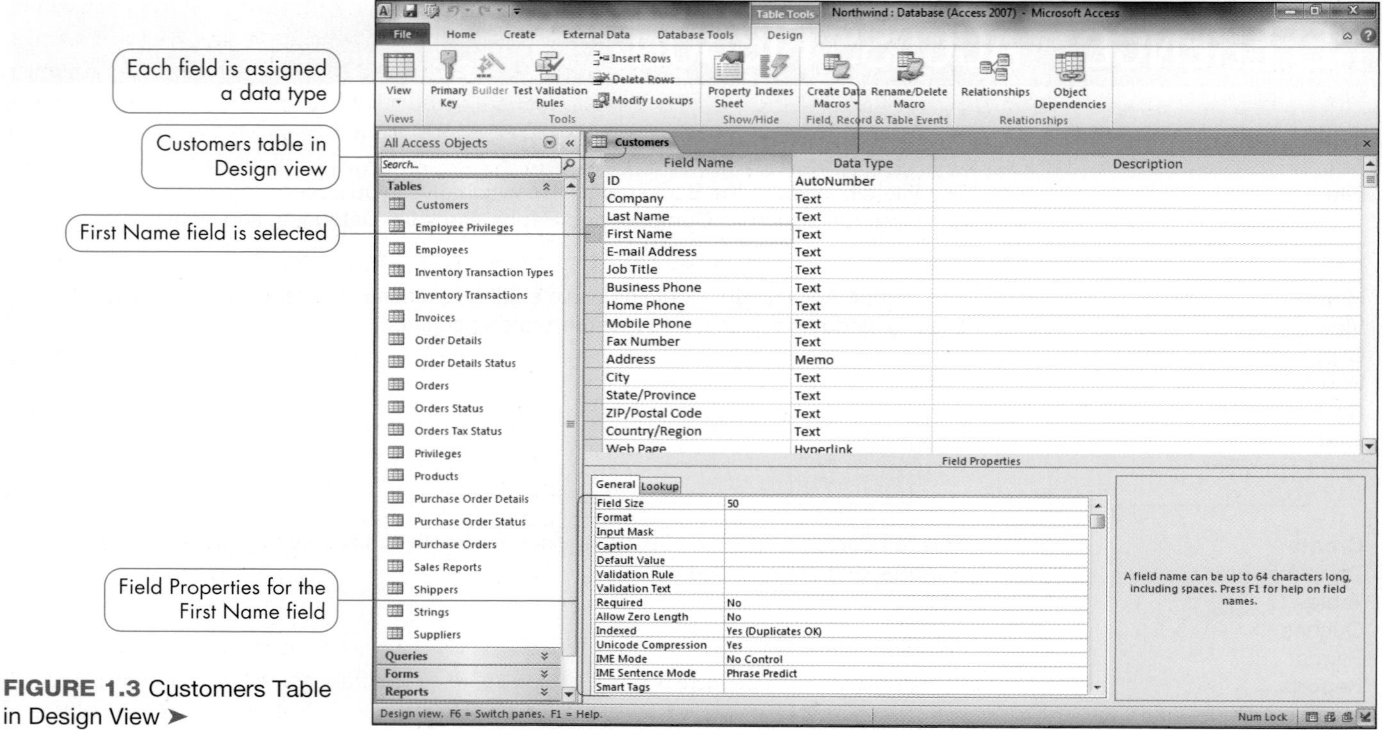
Each field is assigned a data type
Customers table in Design view
First Name field is selected
Field Properties for the First Name field

FIGURE 1.3 Customers Table in Design View ➤

Figure 1.4 shows the Datasheet view for the Customers table. The top row in the table contains the field names. Each additional row contains a record (the data for a specific customer). Each column represents a field (one attribute about a customer). Every record in the table represents a different customer; all records contain the same fields.

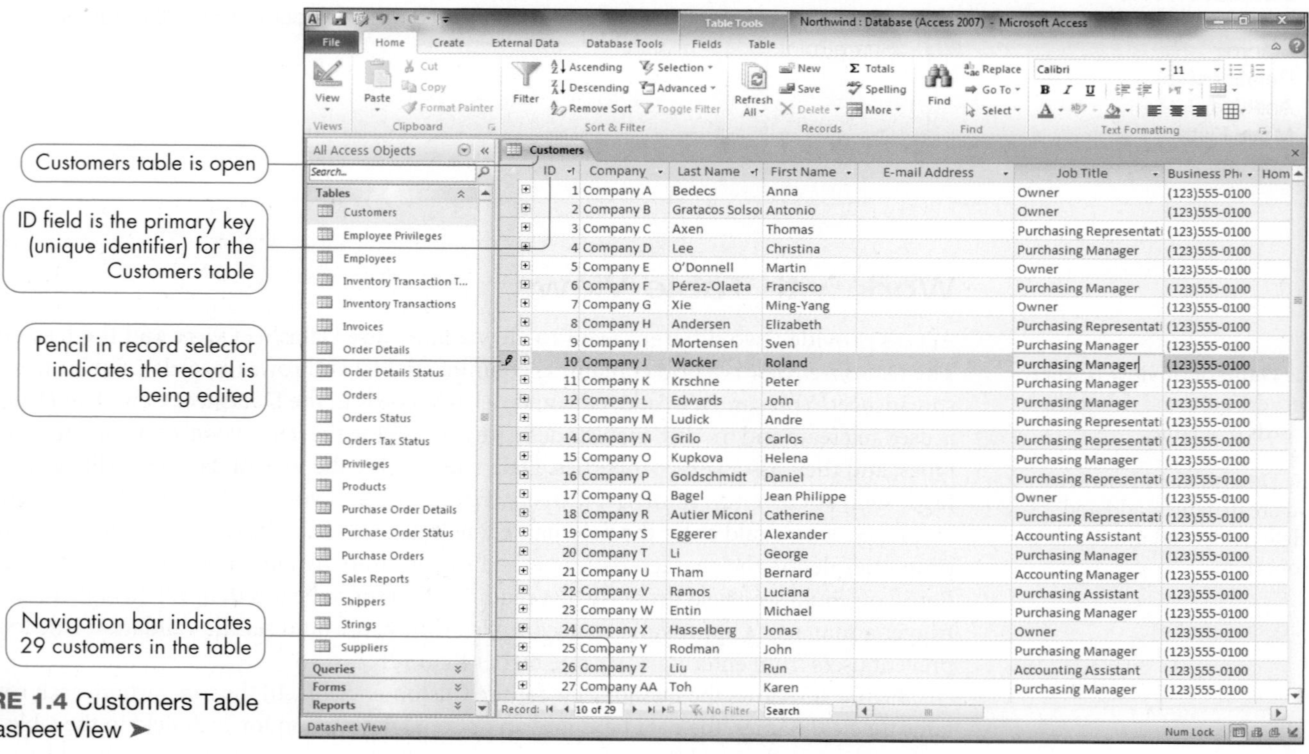
Customers table is open
ID field is the primary key (unique identifier) for the Customers table
Pencil in record selector indicates the record is being edited
Navigation bar indicates 29 customers in the table

FIGURE 1.4 Customers Table in Datasheet View ➤

The **primary key** is the field (or combination of fields) that uniquely identifies each record in a table.

The ***primary key*** is the field (or combination of fields) that uniquely identifies each record in a table. The ID field is the primary key in the Customers table; it ensures that each record in the table can be distinguished from every other record. It also helps prevent the occurrence of duplicate records. Primary key fields may be numbers, letters, or a combination of both. In this case, the primary key is an autonumber (a number that is generated by Access and is incremented each time a record is added). Another example of a primary key is Social Security Number, which is often used in an employee table.

The navigation bar at the bottom of Figure 1.4 shows that the Customers table has 29 records and that record number 10 is the current record. The vertical scroll bar on the right side of the window only appears when the table contains more records than can appear in the window at one time. Similarly, the horizontal scroll bar at the bottom of the window only appears when the table contains more fields than can appear in the window at one time.

The pencil symbol to the left of Record 10 indicates that the data in that record is being edited and that changes have not yet been saved. The pencil symbol disappears when you move to another record. It is important to understand that Access saves data automatically as soon as you move from one record to another. This may seem counter-intuitive at first, since Word and Excel do not save changes and additions automatically. With Word and Excel, you must click the Save icon in order to save your work (or set auto-save to save automatically in the background).

Figure 1.5 shows the navigation buttons that you use to move through the records in a table, query, or form. The buttons enable you to go to the first record, the previous record, the next record, or the last record. The button with the asterisk is used to add a new (blank) record. You can also type a number directly into the current record cell, and Access will take you to that record. Finally, the navigation bar enables you to locate a record based on a single word. Type a word in the search cell box, and Access will locate the first record that contains the word.

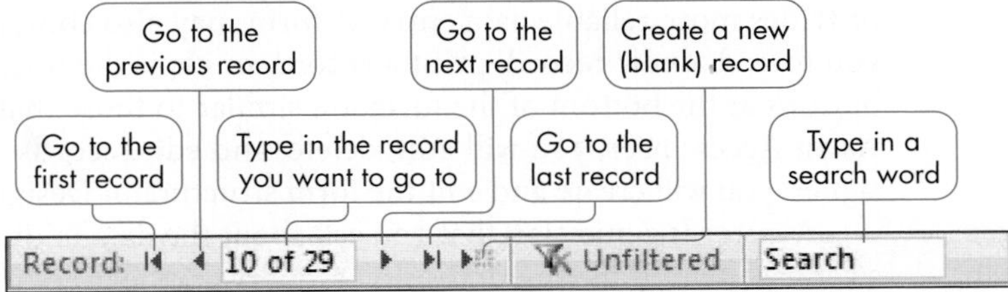

FIGURE 1.5 Navigation Buttons ➤

No system, no matter how sophisticated, can produce valid output from invalid input. Access database systems are built to anticipate data entry errors. These systems contain table validation rules created to prevent invalid data entry. Two types of validation rules exist: those built into Access and those a developer creates specifically for a database. For example, Access will automatically prevent you from adding a new record with the same primary key as an existing record. Access does not allow you to enter text or numeric data into a date field. A database developer can add validation rules, such as requiring a person's last name or requiring an employee's social security number. A developer can also limit the length of data, such as only enabling five digits for a zip code or two characters for a state abbreviation.

Use Forms, Queries, and Reports

As previously indicated, an Access database is made up of different types of objects together with the tables and the data they contain. The tables are the heart of any database because they contain the *actual* data. The other objects in a database—such as forms, queries, and reports—are based on one or more underlying tables. Figure 1.6 displays a form based on the Customers table shown earlier.

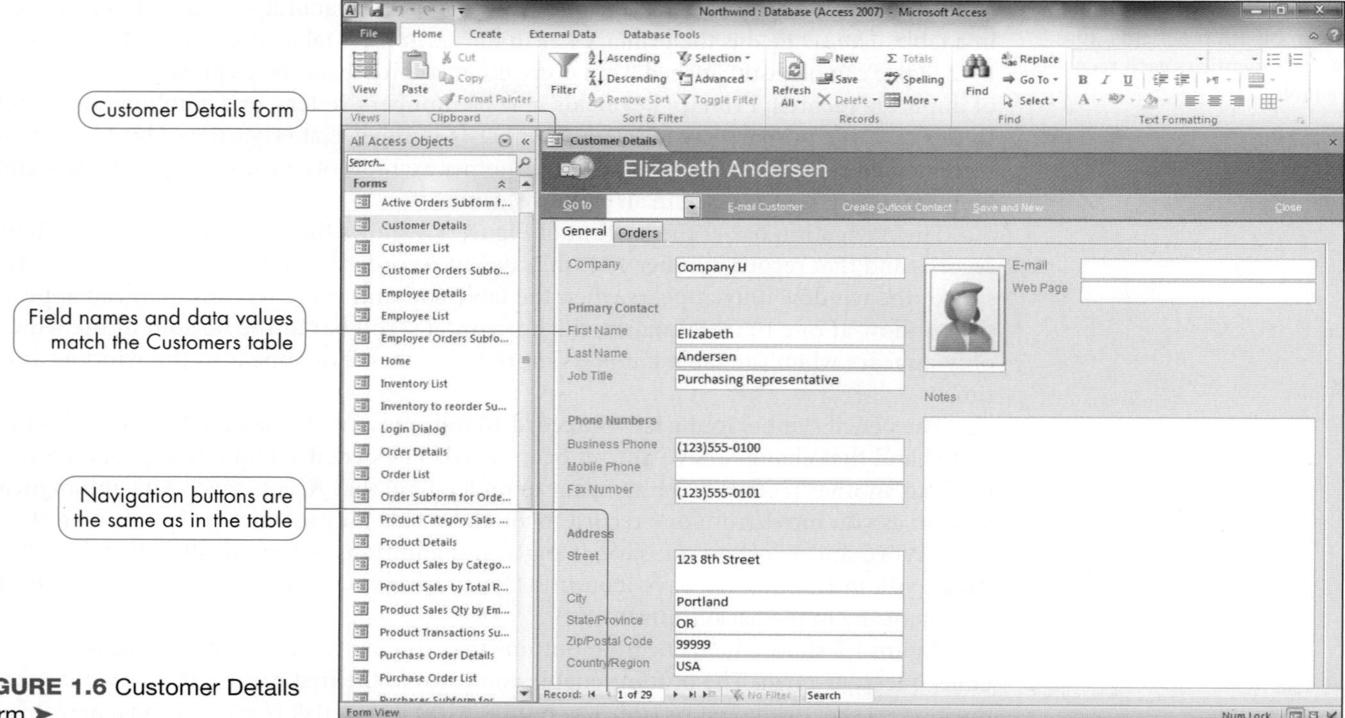

FIGURE 1.6 Customer Details Form ➤

A **form** is an object that enables you to enter, modify, or delete table data.

A ***form*** is an object that enables you to enter, modify, or delete table data. A form enables you to manipulate data in the same manner that you would in a table's Datasheet view. The difference is that you can create a form that will limit the user to viewing only one record at a time. This helps the user to focus on the data being entered or modified and also provides more reliable data entry. A form may also contain command buttons that enable you to add a new record, print a record, or close the form. The status bar and navigation buttons at the bottom of the form are similar to those that appear at the bottom of a table. As an Access user, you will add, delete, and edit records in Form view. As the Access designer, you will create and edit the form structure in Design view.

A **query** is a question that you ask about the data in the tables of your database.

A ***query*** is a question that you ask about the data in the tables of your database. The answer is shown in the query results. A query can be used to display only records that meet a certain criterion and only the fields that are required. Figure 1.7 shows the query design for the question "Which products does Northwind purchase from Supplier A?" The Products table contains records for many vendors, but the records shown in Figure 1.8 are only the products that were supplied by Supplier A. If you want to know the details about a specific supplier (such as Supplier A), you set the criterion in the query to specify which supplier you need to know about.

A **criterion** (**criteria**, pl) is a number, a text phrase, or an expression used to filter the records in a table.

A ***criterion*** (***criteria***, pl) is a number, a text phrase, or an expression used to filter the records in a table. If you need the names of all the suppliers in New York, you can set the supplier's state criterion to *New York*. The results would yield only those suppliers from New York. Query results are in Datasheet view and are similar in appearance to the underlying table, except that the query contains selected records and/or selected fields for those records. The query also may list the records in a different sequence from that of the table.

You also can use a query to add new records and modify existing records. If you open a query and notice an error in an address field, you can edit the record directly in the query results. When you edit a value in a query, you are also updating the data in the underlying table. Editing in a query is efficient but should be used with caution to avoid inadvertently updating the tables. Queries may be opened in Datasheet view or Design view. You use the Datasheet view to examine the query output; you use the Design view to specify which fields to display and what criteria you want.

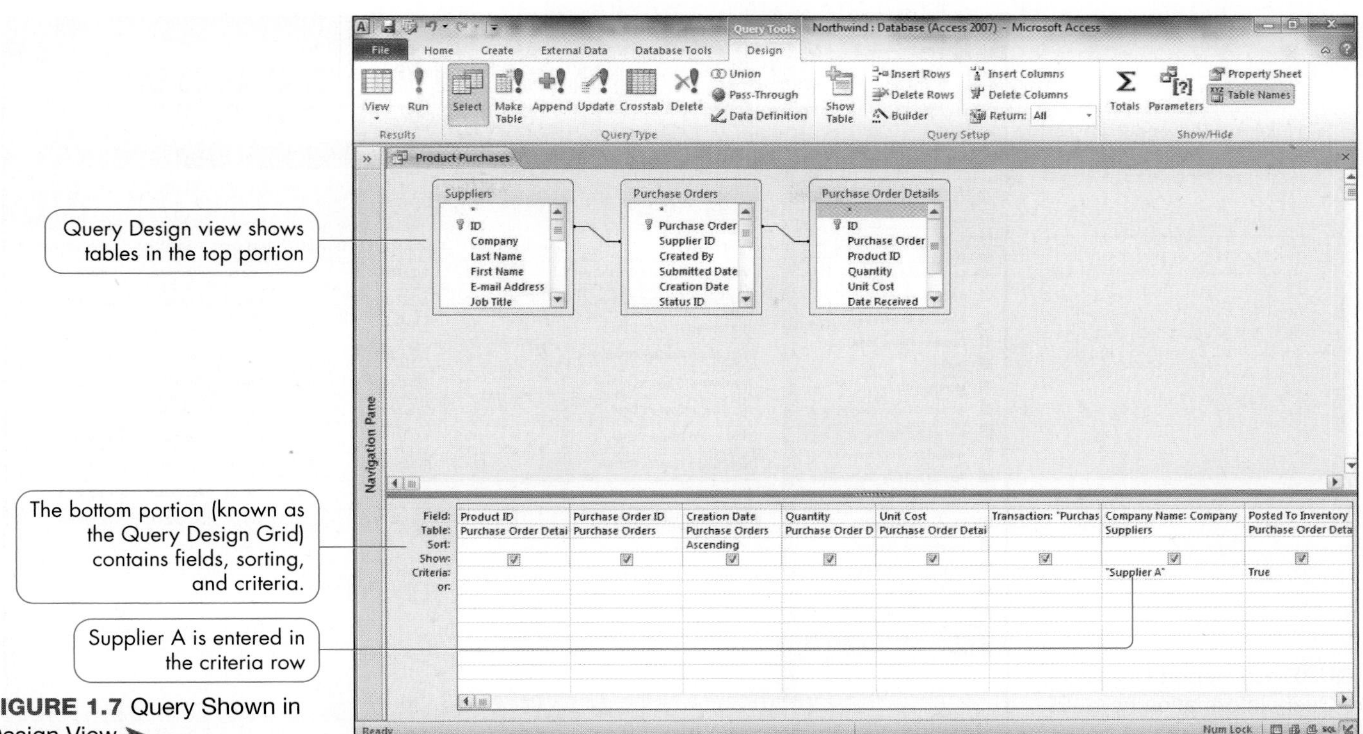
Query Design view shows tables in the top portion
The bottom portion (known as the Query Design Grid) contains fields, sorting, and criteria.
Supplier A is entered in the criteria row

FIGURE 1.7 Query Shown in Design View ➤

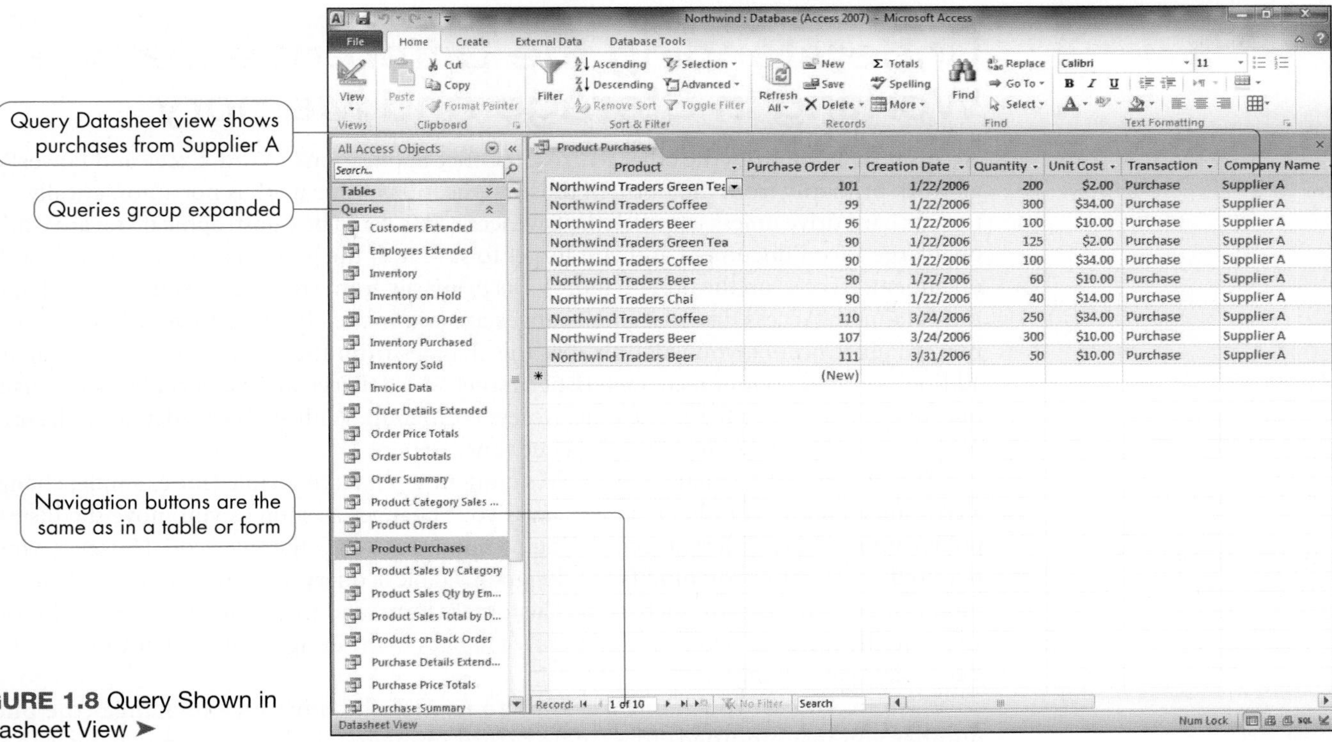
Query Datasheet view shows purchases from Supplier A
Queries group expanded
Navigation buttons are the same as in a table or form

FIGURE 1.8 Query Shown in Datasheet View ➤

A **report** contains professional-looking formatted information from underlying tables or queries.

A ***report*** contains professional-looking formatted information from underlying tables or queries. Figure 1.9 displays a report that contains the same information as the query in Figure 1.8. Because the report information contains a more professional look than a query or table, you normally present database information using a report. Access provides different views for designing, modifying, and running reports. Most Access users use only the Print Preview, Layout, and Report views of a report.

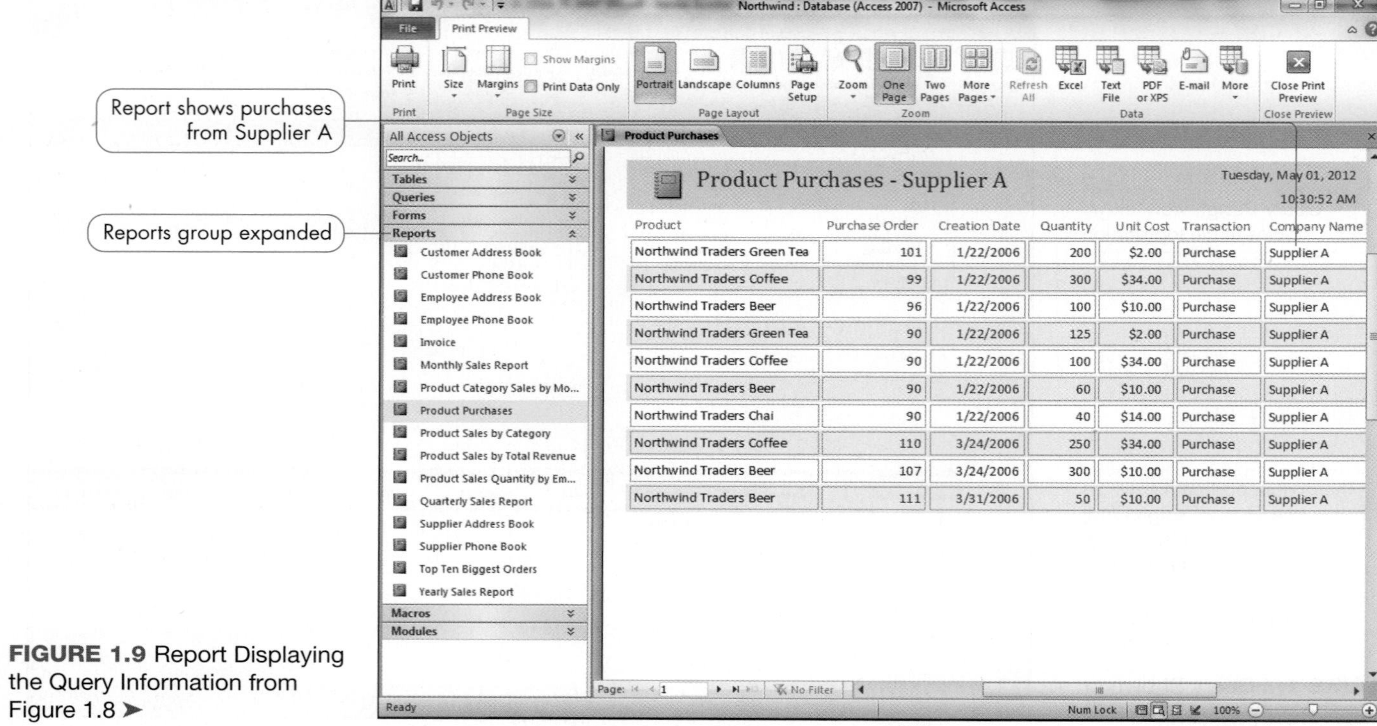

FIGURE 1.9 Report Displaying the Query Information from Figure 1.8 ➤

Understanding the Difference Between Working in Storage and Memory

Access is different from the other Microsoft Office applications. Word, Excel, and PowerPoint all work primarily from memory. In those applications, your work is not automatically saved to your hard drive unless you click the Save icon. This could be catastrophic if you are working on a large Word document and you forget to save it. If the power is lost, you may lose your document. Access, on the other hand, works primarily from storage. As you enter and update the data in an Access database, the changes are automatically saved to your hard drive. If a power failure occurs, you will only lose the changes from the record that you are currently editing. Another common characteristic among Word, Excel, and PowerPoint is that usually only one person uses a file at one time. Access is different. With an Access database file, several users can work in the same file at the same time.

When you make a change to a field's content in an Access table (for example, changing a customer's phone number), Access saves your changes as soon as you move the insertion point (or focus) to a different record. You do not need to click the Save icon. However, you are required to Save after you modify the design of a table, a query, a form, or a report. When you modify an object's design, such as the Customers form, and then close it, Access will prompt you with the message "Do you want to save changes to the design of form 'Customers'?" Click Yes to save your changes.

Also in Access, you can click Undo to reverse the most recent change (the phone number you just modified) to a single record immediately after making changes to that record. However, unlike other Office programs that enable multiple Undo steps, you cannot use Undo to reverse multiple edits in Access.

Multiple users, from different computers, can work on an Access database simultaneously. As long as two users do not attempt to change the same record at the same time, Access will enable two or more users to work on the same database file at the same time. One person can be adding records to the Customers table while another can be creating a query based on the Products table. Two users can even work on the same table as long as they are not working on the same record.

> **TIP: Save Edits While Keeping a Record Active**
>
> When you want to save changes to a record you are editing while remaining on the same record, press Shift+Enter. The pencil symbol disappears, indicating that the change is saved. Save is optional since Access saves changes automatically when you move to a different record.

Practicing Good Database File Management

Database files are similar to other files (spreadsheets, documents, and images) on your computer. They must be filed in an organized manner using folders and subfolders, they must be named appropriately, and they must be backed up in case of a computer failure. Access files require additional understanding and maintenance to avoid data loss.

Every time you open a student file, you will be directed to copy the file and to rename the copied file. As you are learning about Access databases, you will probably make mistakes. Since you'll be working from the copy, you can easily recover from one of these mistakes by reverting back to the original and starting over.

Access speed measures the time it takes for the storage device to make the file content available for use.

Access runs best from a local disk drive or network disk drive because those drives have sufficient access speed to support the software. ***Access speed*** measures the time it takes for the storage device to make the file content available for use. If your school provides you with storage space on the school's network, store your student files there. The advantage to using the network is that the network administration staff back up files regularly. If you have no storage on the school network, your next best storage option is a thumb drive, also known as a USB jump drive, a flash drive, a pen drive, or a stick drive.

Backing Up, Compacting, and Repairing Access Files

Compact and Repair reduces the size of the database.

Backup creates a duplicate copy of the database.

Data is the lifeblood of any organization. Access provides two utilities to help protect the data within a database: ***Compact and Repair*** and ***backup***. These two functions both help protect your data, but they each serve a different purpose. Compact and Repair reduces the size of the database. Backup creates a duplicate copy of the database.

Compact and Repair a Database

All Access databases have a tendency to expand with everyday use. Entering data, creating queries, running reports, deleting objects, and adding indexes will all cause a database file to expand. This growth may increase storage requirements and may also impact database performance. In addition, databases that are compacted regularly are less likely to become corrupt—resulting in loss of data. Access provides a utility—Compact and Repair Database—in the Backstage view that addresses this issue. When you run the Compact and Repair utility, it creates a new database file behind the scenes and copies all the objects from the original database into the new one. As it copies the objects into the new file, Access will remove temporary objects and unclaimed space due to deleted objects, resulting in a smaller database file. Compact and Repair will also defragment a fragmented database file if needed. When the utility is finished copying the data, it deletes the original file and renames the new one with the same name as the original. This utility can also be used to repair a corrupt database. In most cases, only a small amount of data—the last record modified—will be lost during the repair process. You should compact your database every day.

Back Up a Database

Imagine what would happen to a firm that loses the orders placed but not shipped, a charity that loses the list of donor contributions, or a hospital that loses the digital records of its patients. Fortunately, Access recognizes how critical backup procedures are to organizations and makes backing up the database files easy. You back up an Access file (and all of the objects inside) with just a few mouse clicks. To back up files, click the File tab, and then click Save & Publish from the list of options. From the list of Save & Publish options, double-click Back Up Database, and the Save As dialog box opens. You can designate the folder location and the file name for the backup copy of the database. Access provides a default file name that is the original file name followed by the current date. The default database type is accdb.

In the next Hands-On Exercise, you will work with the Northwind Traders database you read about in the Case Study at the beginning of the chapter. Northwind purchases food items from suppliers around the world and sells them to restaurants and specialty food shops. Northwind depends on the data stored in its Access database to process orders and make daily decisions.

1. Name the six objects in an Access database and briefly describe the purpose of each one.
2. What is the difference between Datasheet view and Design view in a table?
3. What is meant by the statement "Access works from storage"?
4. What is the purpose of the Compact and Repair utility in Access?

HANDS-ON EXERCISES

1 Databases Are Everywhere!

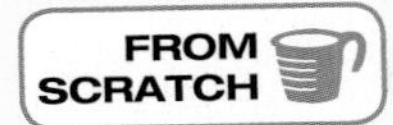

In your new position with Northwind Traders, you need to spend time getting familiar with its Access database. You will open its database and add, edit, and delete records using both tables and forms. Finally, you will perform management duties by compacting and backing up the database file.

Skills covered: Open an Access File, Save the File with a New Name, and Work with the New File • Edit a Record • Navigate an Access Form and Add Records • Recognize the Connection Between Table and Form, Delete a Record • Compact, Repair, and Back Up the Database

STEP 1 OPEN AN ACCESS FILE, SAVE THE FILE WITH A NEW NAME, AND WORK WITH THE NEW FILE

This exercise introduces you to the Northwind Traders database. You will use this database to practice working with database files. Refer to Figure 1.10 as you complete Step 1.

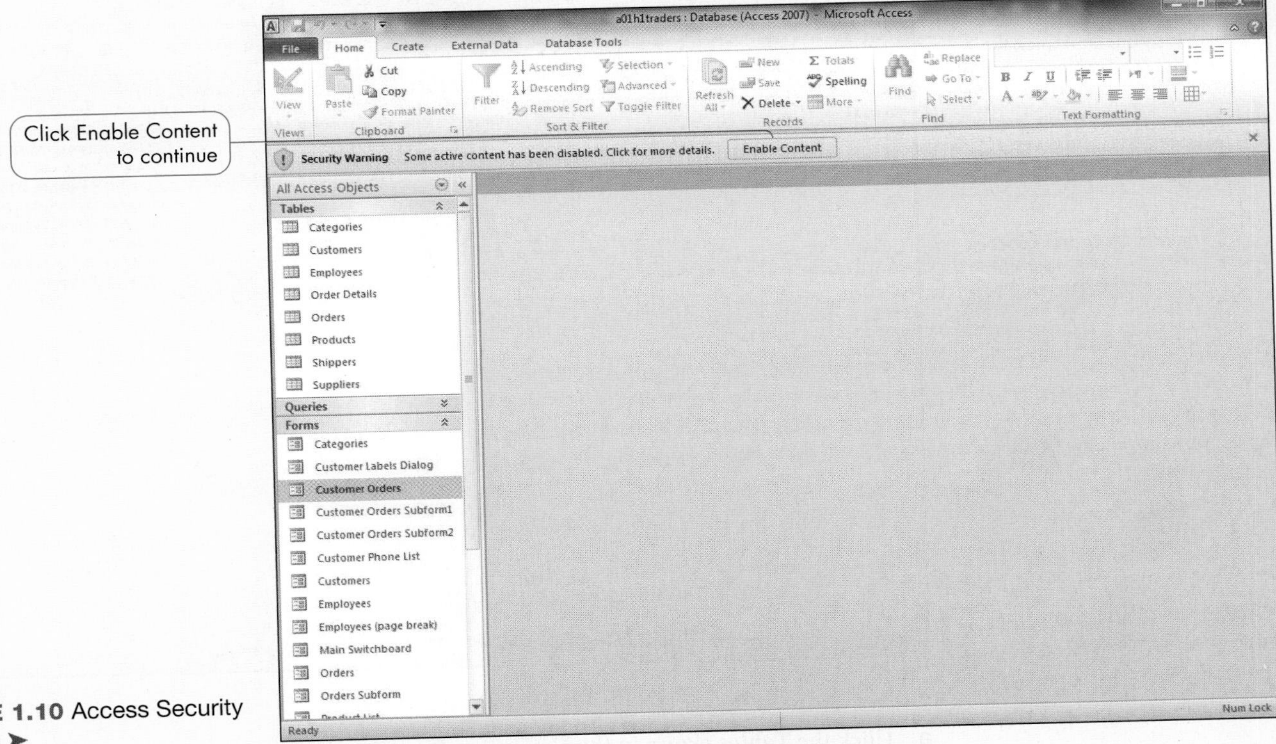

FIGURE 1.10 Access Security Warning ➤

a. Open the database named *a01h1traders* in the folder location designated by your instructor.

b. Click the **File tab**, click **Save Database As**, and then locate the folder location designated by your instructor.

When you name solution files, use your last and first names. For example, as the Access author, I would name my database a01h1traders_MastKeith.

TROUBLESHOOTING: If you make any major mistakes in this exercise, you can close the file, make another copy of *a01h1traders*, and then start this exercise over.

c. Type **a01h1traders_LastnameFirstname** as the new file name, and then click **Save** to create the new database.

This step creates the new Access database file. The Security Warning message bar may appear below the Ribbon, indicating that some database content is disabled.

d. Click **Enable Content** on the Security Warning message bar.

When you open an Access file from this book, you will need to enable the content. Several viruses and worms may be transmitted via Access files. You may be confident of the trustworthiness of the files in this book. However, if an Access file arrives as an attachment from an unsolicited e-mail message, you should not open it. Microsoft warns all users of Access that a potential threat exists every time a file is opened. Keep the database open for the rest of the exercise.

STEP 2 EDIT A RECORD

You need to modify the data in the Northwind database since customers will change their address, phone numbers, and order data from time to time. Refer to Figure 1.11 as you complete Step 2.

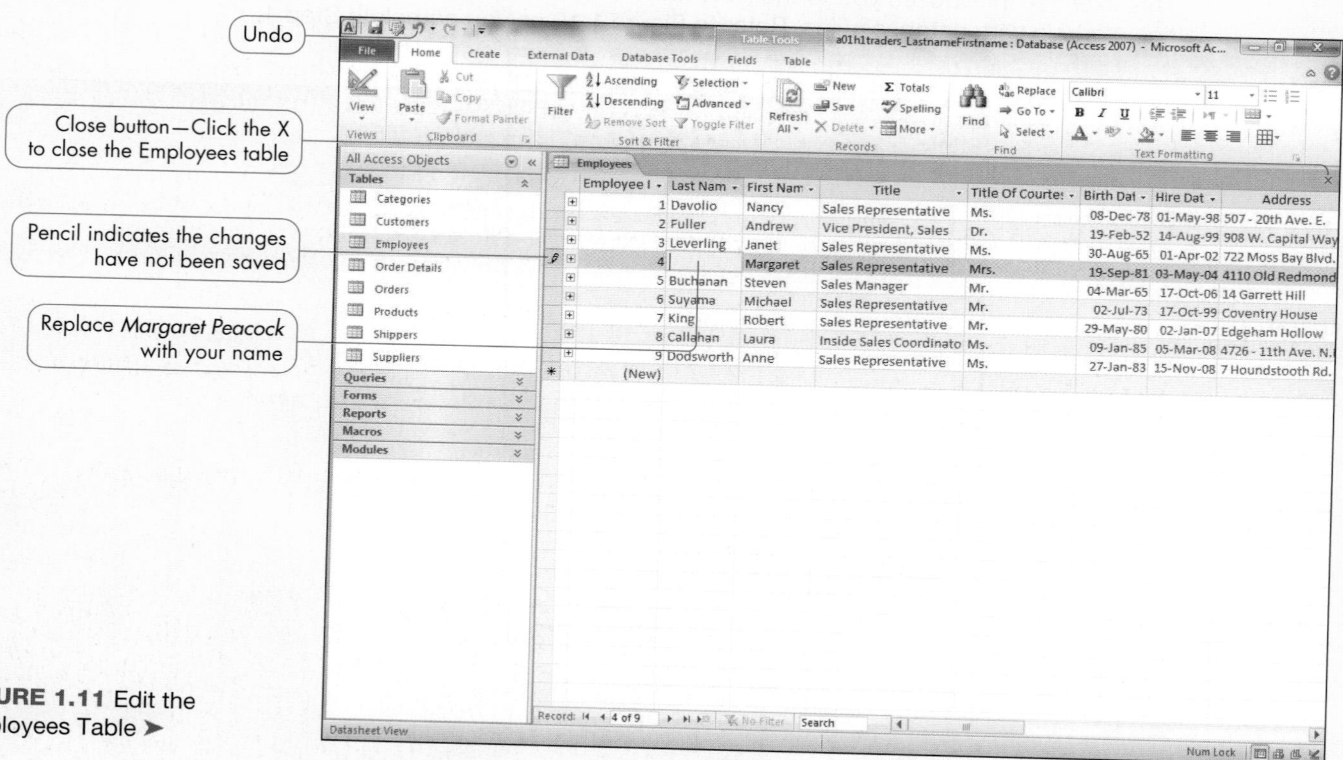

FIGURE 1.11 Edit the Employees Table ➤

a. Click the **Tables group** in the Navigation Pane (if necessary) to expand the list of available tables.

The list of tables contained in the database file opens.

b. Double-click the **Employees table** to open it (see Figure 1.11).

c. Click on the **Last Name field** in the fourth row. Double-click **Peacock**; the entire name highlights. Type your last name to replace *Peacock*.

d. Press **Tab** to move to the next field in the fourth row. Replace *Margaret* with your first name, and then press **Tab**.

You have made changes to two fields in the same record (row); note the pencil symbol on the left side in the row selector box.

e. Click **Undo** in the Quick Access Toolbar.

Your first and last names reverts back to *Margaret Peacock* because you have not yet left the record.

f. Type your first and last names again to replace *Margaret Peacock*. Press **Tab**.

You should now be in the Title field and your title, *Sales Representative*, is selected. The pencil symbol still displays in the row selector.

g. Click anywhere in the third row where Janet Leverling's data is stored.

The pencil symbol disappears, indicating your changes have been saved.

h. Click the **Address field** in the first record, the one for Nancy Davolio. Select the entire address, and then type **4004 East Morningside Dr**. Click anywhere on Andrew Fuller's record.

i. Click **Undo**.

Nancy's address reverts back to *507 - 20th Ave. E.* However, the Undo command is now faded. You can no longer undo the change that you made replacing Margaret Peacock's name with your own.

j. Click the **Close button** (the X at the top of the table) to close the Employees table.

The Employees table closes. You are not prompted about saving your changes; they have already been saved for you because Access works in storage, not memory. If you reopen the Employees table, you will see your name in place of Margaret Peacock's name.

> **TROUBLESHOOTING:** If you click the Close (X) button on the title bar at the top right of the window and accidentally close the database, locate the file, and then double-click it to start again.

STEP 3 NAVIGATE AN ACCESS FORM AND ADD RECORDS

You need to add new products to the Northwind database since the company will be adding a new line of products to the database. Refer to Figure 1.12 as you complete Step 3.

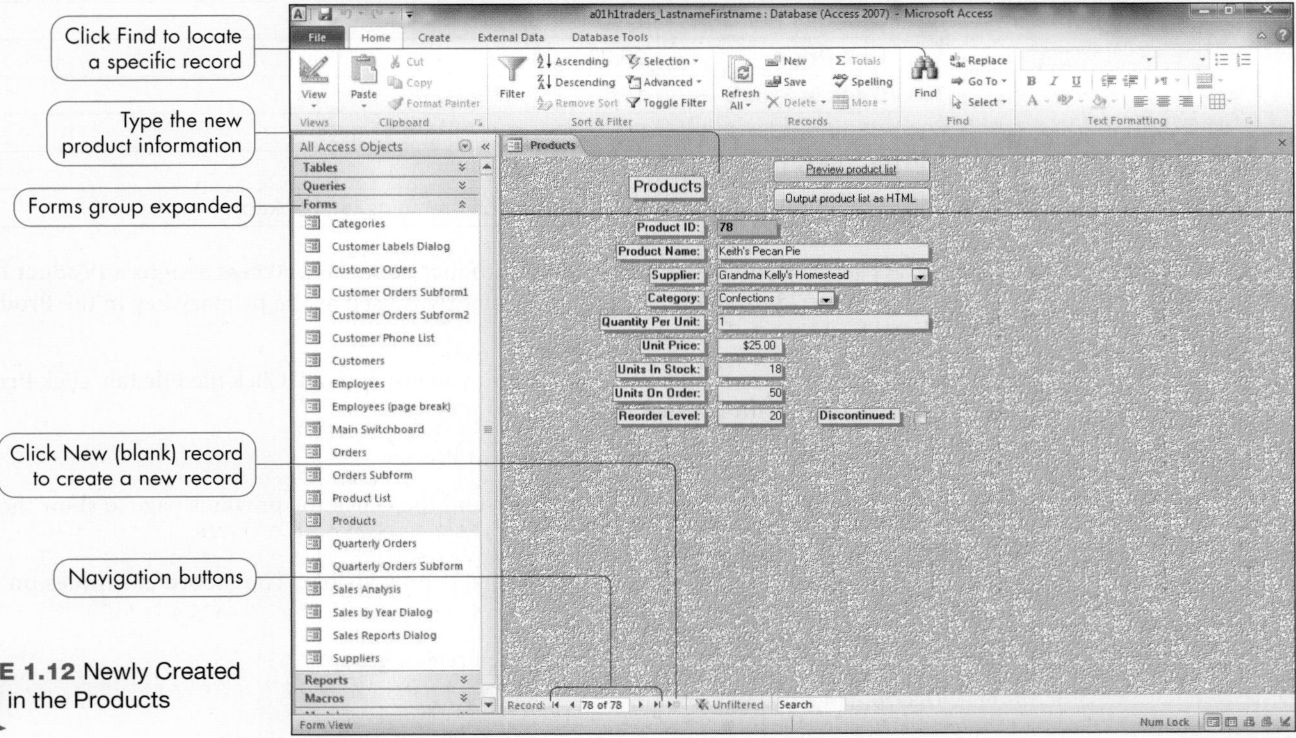

FIGURE 1.12 Newly Created Record in the Products Form ➤

a. Click the **Tables group** in the Navigation Pane to collapse it.

   The list of available tables collapses.

b. Click the **Forms group** in the Navigation Pane (if necessary) to expand the list of available forms.

c. Double-click the **Products form** to open it.

d. Use Figure 1.12 to locate the navigation buttons (arrows) at the bottom of the Access window. Practice moving from one record to the next. Click **Next record**, and then click **Last record**; click **Previous record**, and then **First record**.

e. Click **Find** in the Find group on the Home tab.

   The Find command is an ideal way to search for specific records within a table, form, or query. You can search a single field or the entire record, match all or part of the selected field(s), move forward or back in a table, or specify a case-sensitive search. The Replace command can be used to substitute one value for another. Be careful when using the Replace All option for global replacement because unintended replacements are possible.

f. Type **Grandma** in the **Find What box**, click the **Match arrow**, and select **Any Part of Field**. Click **Find Next**.

   You should see information about Grandma's Boysenberry Spread. Selecting the *any part of the field* option will return a match even if it is contained in the middle of a word.

g. Close the Find dialog box.

h. Click **New (blank) record** on the navigation bar.

i. Enter the following information for a new product. Press **Tab** to navigate through the form.

Field Name	Value to Type
Product Name	*your name* Pecan Pie
Supplier	**Grandma Kelly's Homestead** (Note: click the arrow to select from the list of Suppliers)
Category	**Confections** (Click the arrow to select from the list of Categories)
Quantity Per Unit	1
Unit Price	25.00
Units in Stock	18
Units on Order	50
Reorder Level	20
Discontinued	**No** (the checkbox remains unchecked)

   As soon as you begin typing in the product name box, Access assigns a Product ID, in this case 78, to the record. The Product ID is used as the primary key in the Products table.

j. Click anywhere on the Pecan Pie record you just entered. Click the **File tab**, click **Print**, and then click **Print Preview**.

   The first four records appear in the Print Preview.

k. Click **Last Page** in the navigation bar, and then click the previous page to show the new record you entered.

   The beginning of the Pecan Pie record is now visible. The record continues on the next page.

l. Click **Close Print Preview** in the Close Preview group.

m. Close the Products form.

STEP 4 RECOGNIZE THE CONNECTION BETWEEN TABLE AND FORM, DELETE A RECORD

You need to understand how Access stores data. After you add the new products using a form, you verify that the products are also in the table. You also attempt to delete a record. Refer to Figure 1.13 as you complete Step 4.

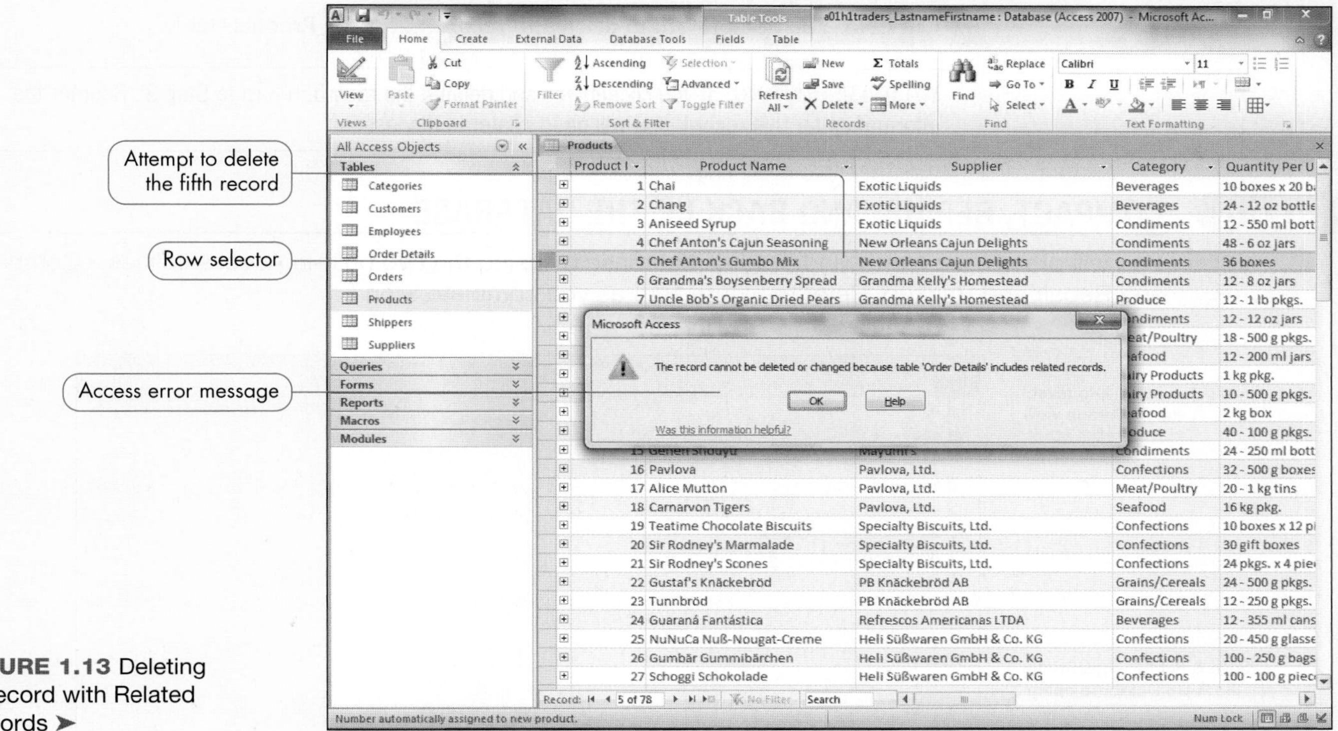

FIGURE 1.13 Deleting a Record with Related Records ➤

a. Click the **Forms group** in the Navigation Pane to collapse it.

   The list of available forms collapses.

b. Click the **Tables group** in the Navigation Pane to expand it.

   The list of available tables is shown. You need to prove that the change you made to the Products form will appear in the Products table.

c. Double-click the **Products table** to open it.

d. Click **Last record** in the navigation bar.

   The Pecan Pie record you entered in the Products form is listed as the last record in the Products table. The Products form was created from the Products table. Your newly created record, Pecan Pie, is stored in the Products table even though you added it in the form.

e. Navigate to the fifth record in the table, *Chef Anton's Gumbo Mix*.

f. Use the horizontal scroll bar to scroll right until you see the Discontinued field.

   The check mark in the Discontinued check box tells you that this product has been discontinued.

g. Click the **row selector box** to the left of the fifth record.

   The row highlights with a gold-colored border.

h. Click **Delete** in the Records group. Read the error message.

   An error message appears. It tells you that you cannot delete this record because the table Order Details has related records. (Customers ordered this product in the past.) Even though the product is now discontinued and none of it is in stock, it cannot be deleted from the Products table because related records exist in the Order Details table.

i. Click **OK**.

j. Navigate to the last record. Click the **row selector box** to highlight the entire row.

k. Click **Delete** in the Records group. Read the warning.

A warning box appears. It tells you that this action cannot be undone. Although this product can be deleted because it was just entered and no orders were created for it, you do not want to delete the record.

l. Click **No**. You do not want to delete this record. Close the Products table.

> **TROUBLESHOOTING:** If you clicked Yes and deleted the record, return to Step 3i. Reenter the information for this record. You will need it later in the lesson.

STEP 5 COMPACT, REPAIR, AND BACK UP THE DATABASE

You will protect the Northwind Traders database by using the two built-in Access utilities—Compact and Repair and Backup. Refer to Figure 1.14 as you complete Step 5.

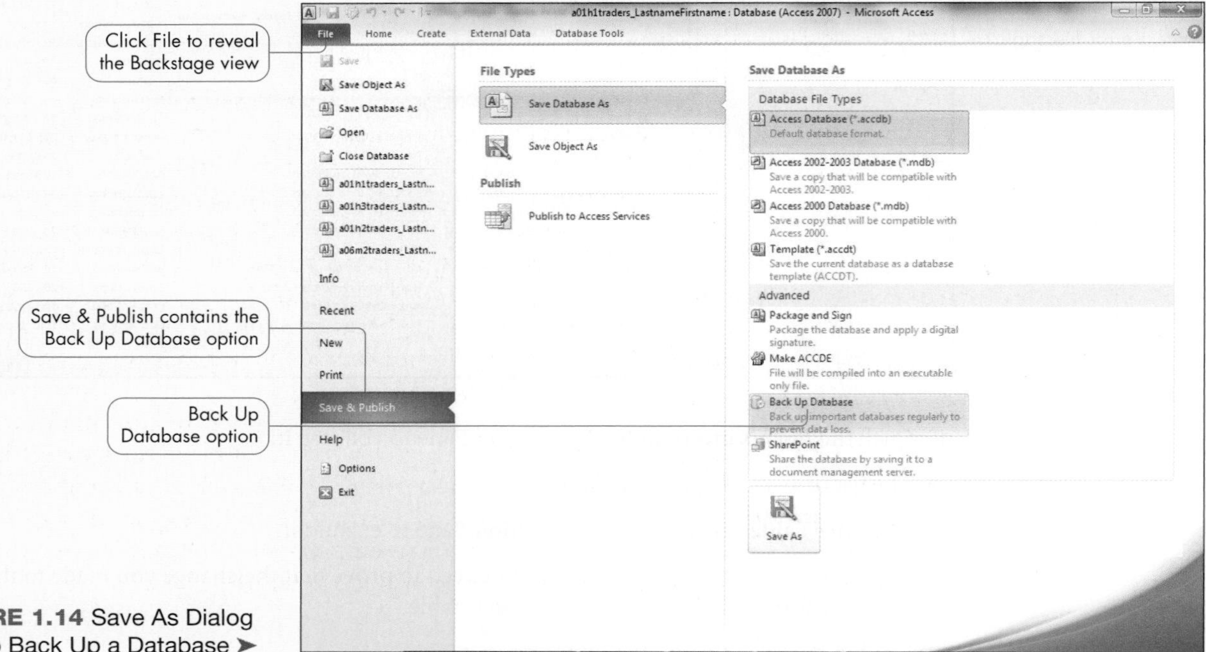

FIGURE 1.14 Save As Dialog Box to Back Up a Database ➤

a. Click the **File tab**.

The File tab reveals the Backstage view, which gives you access to a variety of database tools: Compact and Repair, Back Up Database, and Print, to name a few.

b. Click **Compact & Repair Database**.

Databases tend to get larger as you use them. This feature acts as a defragmenter and eliminates wasted space. Before running this feature, close any open objects in the database.

c. Click the **File tab**, click **Save & Publish**, and then double-click **Back Up Database**.

The Save As dialog box opens. Verify the Save in folder is correct before saving. The backup utility assigns a default name by adding a date to your file name.

d. Click **Save** to accept the default backup file name with today's date.

You just created a backup of the database after completing Hands-On Exercise 1. The original database *a01h1traders_LastnameFirstname* remains onscreen.

e. Keep the database onscreen if you plan to continue with Hands-On Exercise 2. If not, close the database and exit Access.

Filters, Sorts, and Access Versus Excel

Access provides you with many tools that you can use to identify and extract only the data needed at the moment. For example, you might need to know which suppliers are located in New Orleans or which customers have outstanding orders that were placed in the last seven days. You might use that information to identify possible disruptions to product deliveries or customers who may need a telephone call to let them know the status of their orders. Both Access and Excel contain powerful tools that enable you to extract the information you need and arrange it in a way that makes it easy to analyze. An important part of becoming a proficient Office user is learning how to use these tools to accomplish a task.

Access provides you with many tools that you can use to identify and extract only the data needed at the moment.

In this section, you will learn how to isolate records in a table based on certain criteria. You will also examine the strengths of Access and Excel in more detail so you can better determine when to use which application to complete a given task.

Creating Filters

In the first Hands-On Exercise, you added Pecan Pie to the Products table with a category of *Confections*, but you also saw many other products. Suppose you wanted a list of all of the products in the Confections category. To do this, you could open the Products table in Datasheet view and create a filter. A ***filter*** displays a subset of records based on specified criteria. A filter works with either a table's datasheet or a query's datasheet. You can use filters to analyze data quickly. Applying a filter does not delete any records; filters only *hide* records that do not match the criteria. Two types of filters are discussed in this section: Filter by Selection and Filter by Form. Filter by Selection selects only the records that match preselected single criteria, whereas Filter by Form offers a more versatile way to select a subset of records, including the use of comparison operators.

A **filter** displays a subset of records based on specified criteria.

Figure 1.15 displays the Customers table with 29 records. The records in the table are displayed in sequence according to the CustomerID, which is also the primary key (the field or combination of fields that uniquely identifies a record). The navigation bar at the bottom indicates that the active record is the first row in the table. Many times you will only want to see a subset of the customer records—you can accomplish this using a filter. For example, suppose you want a list of all customers whose Job Title is *Owner*.

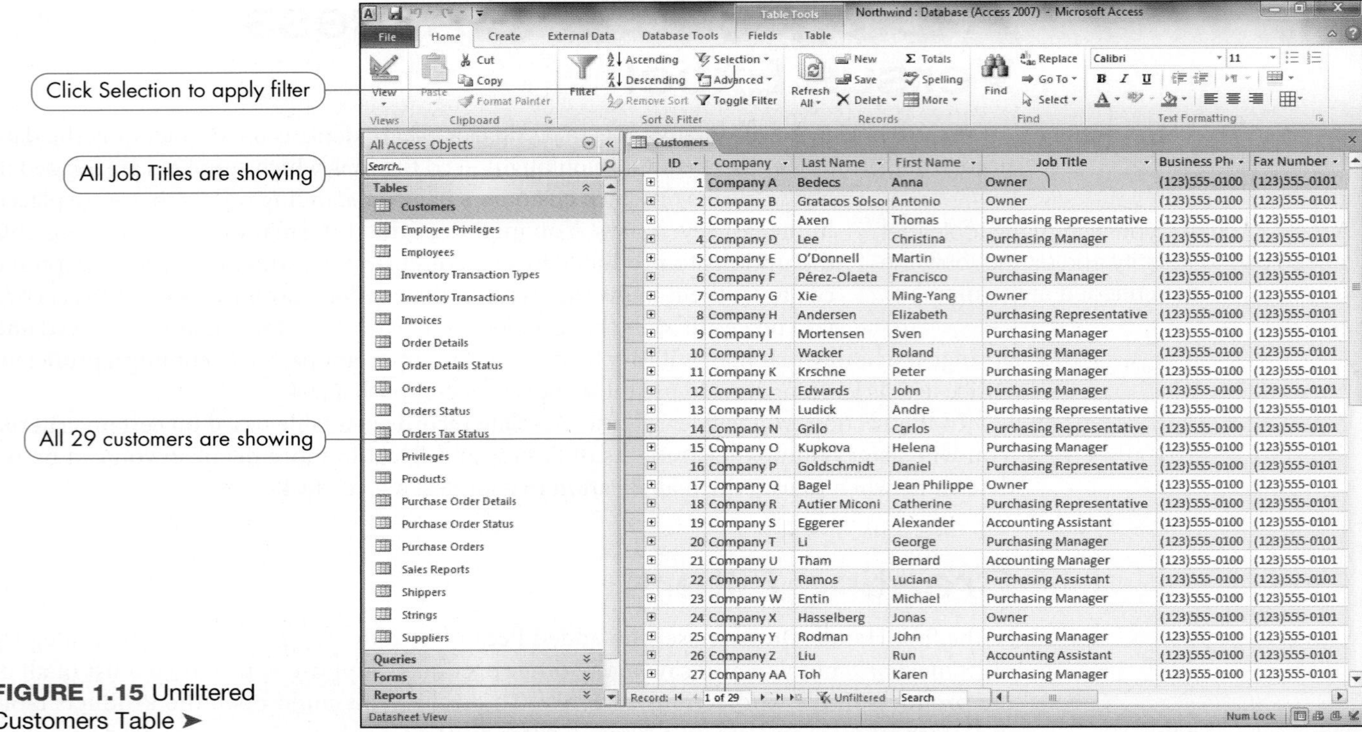
Click Selection to apply filter
All Job Titles are showing
All 29 customers are showing

FIGURE 1.15 Unfiltered Customers Table ➤

Figure 1.16 displays a filtered view of the Customers table, showing records with Job Title of *Owner*. The navigation bar shows that this is a filtered list containing 6 records matching the criteria. (The Customers table still contains the original 29 records, but only 6 records are visible with the filter applied.)

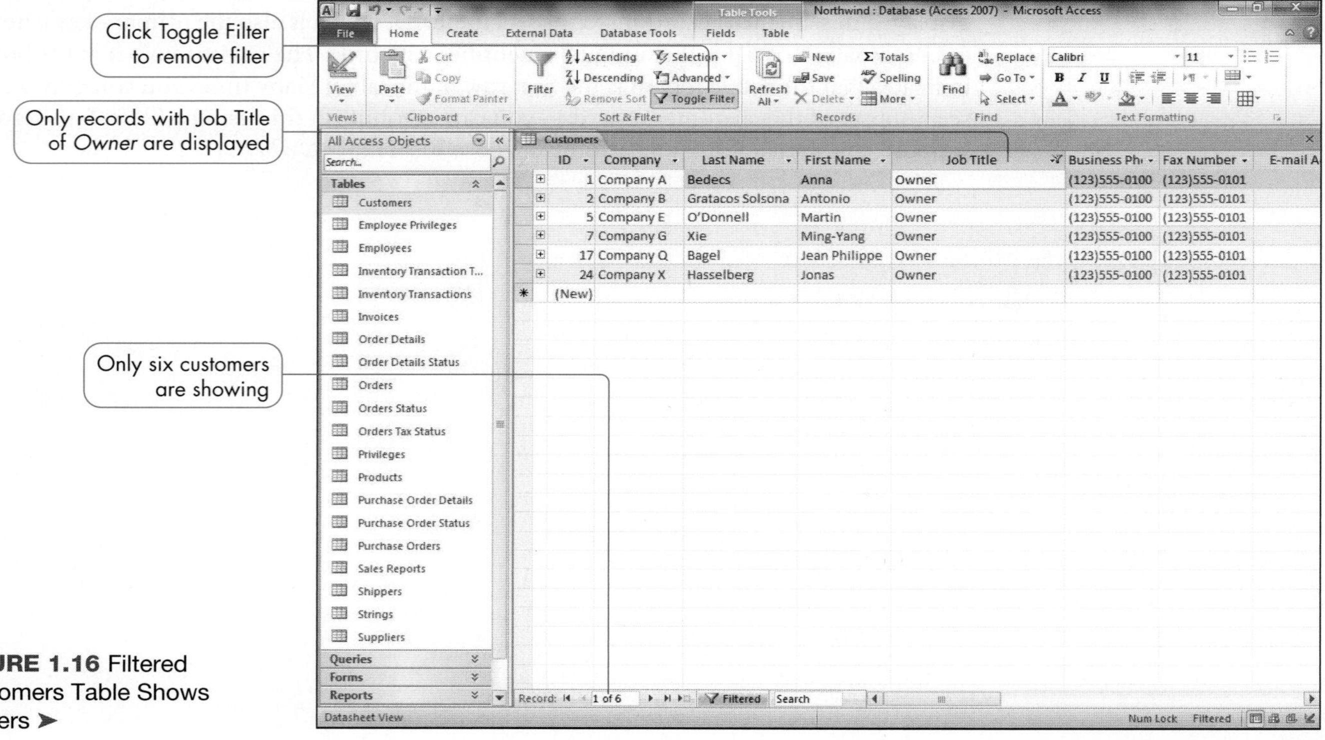
Click Toggle Filter to remove filter
Only records with Job Title of *Owner* are displayed
Only six customers are showing

FIGURE 1.16 Filtered Customers Table Shows Owners ➤

TIP Use Quick Keyboard Shortcuts

Look for underlined letters in Access menus. They indicate the letters to use for the keyboard shortcuts. For example, when you click the Selection arrow in the Sort & Filter group, you can click the Equals "xyz criterion" menu selection or simply type the letter *E*, because the letter *E* in *Equals* is underlined, indicating a shortcut key.

Filter by Selection displays only the records that match the selected criteria.

Filter by Selection displays only the records that match the selected criteria. The easiest way to implement a Filter by Selection is as follows:

1. Click in any field that contains the criterion on which you want to filter.
2. Click Filter by Selection in the Sort & Filter group.
3. Select Equals "criterion" from the list of options.

Only the records that match the selected criterion will be displayed.

Filter by Form displays table records based on multiple criteria. Filter by Form enables the user to apply the logical operators AND and OR.

A **comparison operator** is used to evaluate the relationship between two quantities to determine if they are equal or not equal; and, if they are not equal, a comparison operator determines which one is greater than the other.

Figure 1.17 illustrates another, more versatile, way to apply a filter, using Filter by Form. ***Filter by Form*** displays table records based on multiple criteria. Filter by Form enables the user to apply the logical operators AND and OR. For the AND operator, a record is included in the results if all the criteria are true; for the OR operator, a record is included if at least one criterion is true. Another advantage of the Filter by Form function is that you can use a comparison operator. A ***comparison operator*** is used to evaluate the relationship between two quantities to determine if they are equal or not equal; and, if they are not equal, a comparison operator determines which one is greater than the other. Comparison operator symbols include: equal (=), not equal (<>), greater than (>), less than (<), greater than or equal to (>=), and less than or equal to (<=). For example, you can use a comparison operator to select products with an inventory level greater than 30 (>30). Filter by Selection, on the other hand, requires you to specify criteria equal to an existing value. Figure 1.17 shows a Filter by Form designed to select Products with a reorder level of more than 10 units.

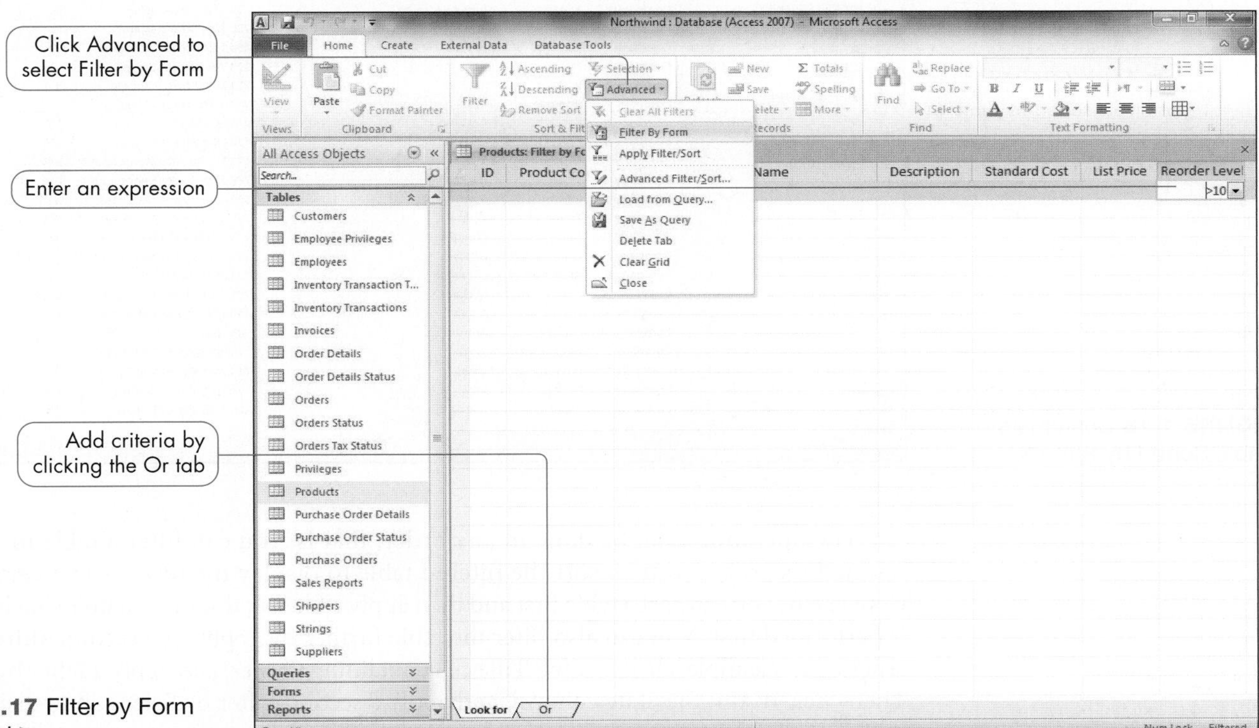

FIGURE 1.17 Filter by Form Design Grid ➤

To apply an OR comparison operator to a Filter by Form, click the Or tab at the bottom of the window. For example, you could add the criterion *Baked Goods & Mixes* to the category field, which would show all the Products with a reorder level of more than 10 units and all Products in the Baked Goods & Mixes category. (This OR example is not shown in Figure 1.17.) Filters enable you to obtain information from a database quickly without creating a query or a report.

Sorting Table Data on One or More Fields

A **sort** lists records in a specific sequence, such as ascending by last name or by ascending EmployeeID.

Ascending sorts a list of text data in alphabetical order or a numeric list in lowest to highest order.

Descending sorts a list of text data in reverse alphabetical order or a numeric list in highest to lowest order.

You can also change the order of the information by sorting by one or more fields. A ***sort*** lists records in a specific sequence, such as alphabetically by last name or by ascending EmployeeID.

To sort a table, do the following:

1. Click in the field that you want to use to sort the records.
2. Click Ascending or Descending in the Sort & Filter group.

Ascending sorts a list of text data in alphabetical order or a numeric list in lowest to highest order. ***Descending*** sorts a list of text data in reverse alphabetical order or a numeric list in highest to lowest order. Figure 1.18 shows the Customers table sorted in ascending order by state. You may apply both filters and sorts to tables or query results.

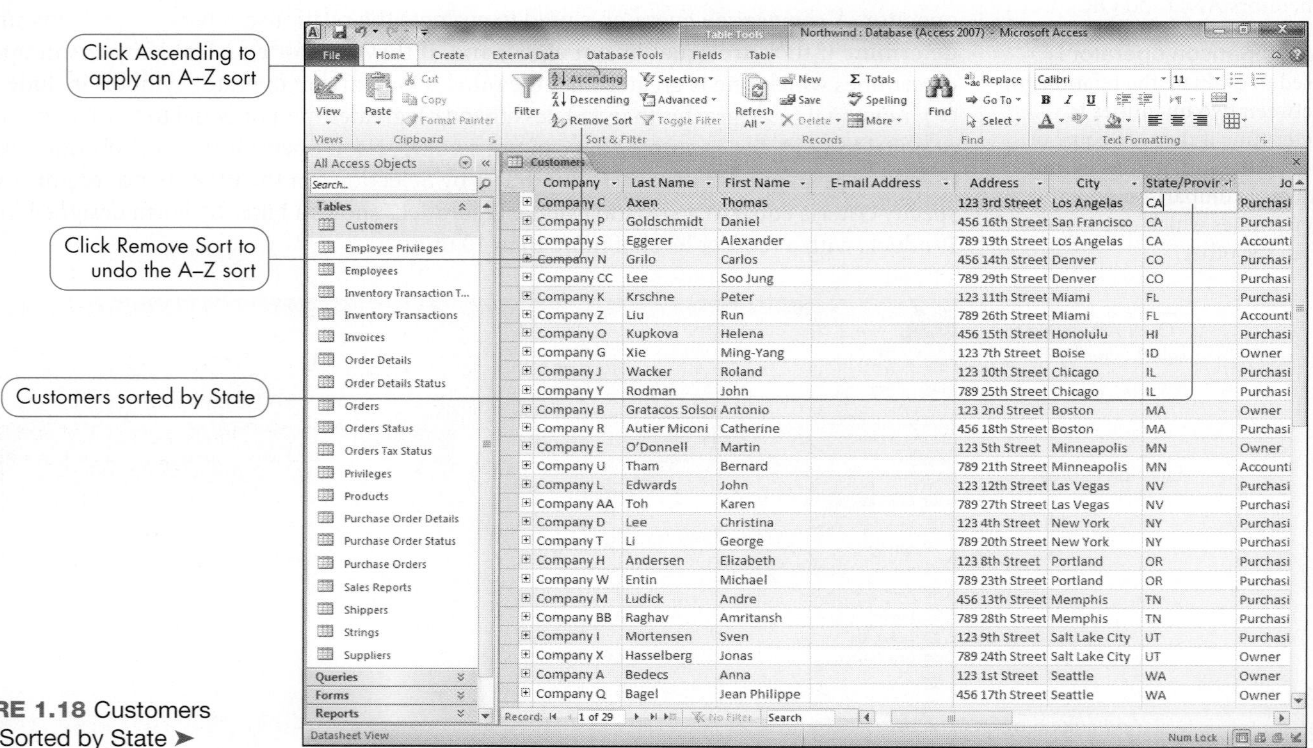
Click Ascending to apply an A–Z sort
Click Remove Sort to undo the A–Z sort
Customers sorted by State

FIGURE 1.18 Customers Table Sorted by State ➤

The operations can be done in any order; that is, you can filter a table to show only selected records, and then sort the filtered table to display the records in a certain order. Conversely, you can sort a table first and then apply a filter. It does not matter which operation is performed first. You can also filter the table further by applying a second, third, or more criteria; for example, click in a Job Title cell containing *Owner*, and apply a Filter by Selection. Then click *WA* in the State column, and apply a second Filter by Selection to display all the customers from WA. You can also click Toggle Filter at any time to remove all filters and display all of the records in the table. Filters are a temporary method for examining table data. If you close the filtered table and then reopen it, the filter will be removed, and all of the records will be restored.

Use Undo After Applying a Filter by Selection

You can apply one Filter by Selection to a table, and then a second, and then a third to display certain records based on three criteria. If you click Toggle Filter, all three filters will be removed. What if you only want the last filter removed? Click Undo to remove only the last filter. Click Undo again and remove the second-to-last filter. This feature will help you apply *and remove* multiple filters.

Knowing When to Use Access or Excel to Manage Data

You are probably familiar with working in an Excel spreadsheet. You type the column headings, then enter the data, perhaps add a formula or two, then add totals to the bottom. Once the data has been entered, you can apply a filter, or sort the data, or start all over—similar to what we learned to do in Access with filters. It is true that you can accomplish many of the same tasks using either Excel or Access. In this section, you will learn how to decide whether to use Access or Excel. Although the two programs have much in common, they each have distinct advantages. How do you choose whether to use Access or Excel? The choice you make may ultimately depend on how well you know Access. Users who only know Excel are more likely to use a spreadsheet even if a database would be better. When database features are used in Excel, they are generally used on data that is in one table. When the data is better suited to be on two or more tables, then using Access is preferable. Learning how to use Access will be beneficial to you since it will enable you to work more efficiently with large groups of data. Ideally, the type of data and the type of functionality you require should determine which program will work best.

Select the Software to Use

A contact list (e.g., name, address, phone number) created in Excel may serve your needs just fine at first. Each time you meet a new contact, you can add another row to the bottom of your worksheet, as shown in Figure 1.19. You can sort the list by last name for easier look-up of names. In Excel, you can easily move an entire column, insert a new column, or copy and paste data from one cell to another. This is the "ease of use" characteristic of Excel.

If you needed to expand the information in Excel, to keep track of each time you contacted someone on your contact list, for example, you may need an additional worksheet. This additional sheet would only list the contacts who you contacted and some information about the nature of the contact. Which contact was it? When was the contact made? Was it a phone contact or a face-to-face meeting? As you track these entries, your worksheet will contain a reference to the first worksheet using the Contact Name. As the quantity and complexity of the data increase, the need to organize your data logically also increases.

A **relationship** is a connection between two tables using a common field.

Access provides built-in tools to help organize data better than Excel. One tool that helps Access organize data is the ability to create relationships between tables. A ***relationship*** is a connection between two tables using a common field. The benefit of a relationship is to efficiently combine data from related tables for the purpose of creating queries, forms, and reports. Relationships are the reason why Access is referred to as a relational database. For example, assume you want to create a Contact Management Database. You would first create two tables to hold contact names and contact notes. You would then create a relationship between the Contact Name table and the Contact Notes table using ContactID as the common field. To create a Contacts Form or Query, you would take advantage of the two related tables.

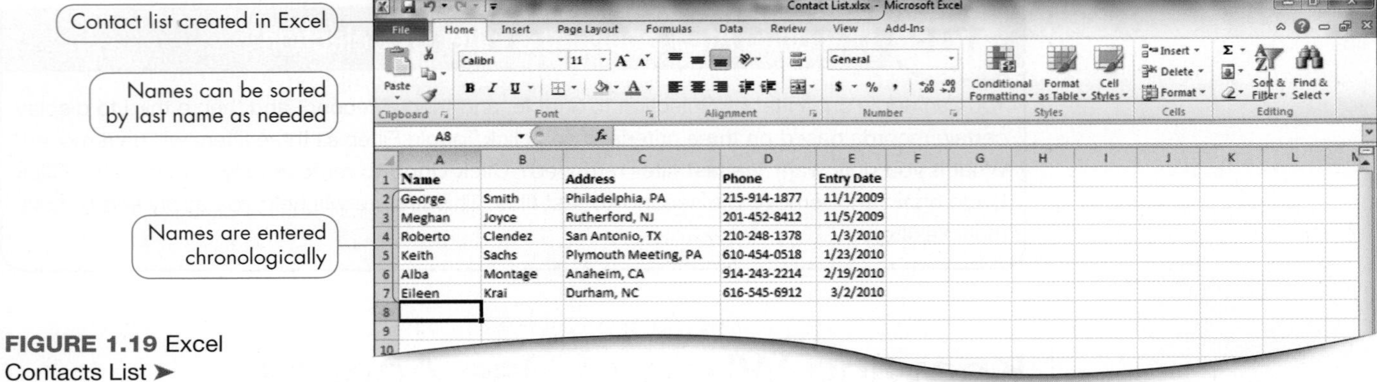

FIGURE 1.19 Excel Contacts List ➤

Use Access

You should use Access to manage data when you:

- Require multiple related tables to store your data.
- Have a large amount of data.
- Need to connect to and retrieve data from external databases, such as Microsoft SQL Server.
- Need to group, sort, and total data based on various parameters.
- Have an application that requires multiple users to connect to one data source at the same time.

Use Excel

You should use Excel to manage data when you:

- Only need one worksheet to handle all of your data (i.e., you do not need multiple worksheets).
- Have mostly numeric data—for example, you need to maintain an expense statement.
- Require subtotals and totals in your worksheet.
- Want to primarily run a series of "what if" scenarios on your data.
- Need to create complex charts and/or graphs.

In the next Hands-On Exercise, you will create and apply filters, create comparison operator expressions using Filter by Form, and sort records in the Datasheet view of the Customers table.

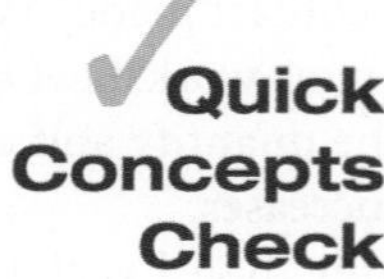

1. What is the purpose of creating a filter?
2. How are Filter by Form and Filter by Selection similar? How are they different?
3. What are the benefits of sorting the records in a table?
4. How can you determine when to use Access or Excel to manage data?

2 Filters, Sorts, and Access Versus Excel

The sales managers at Northwind Traders need quick answers to their questions about customer orders. You use the Access database to filter tables to answer most of these questions. Before printing your results, make sure you sort the records based on the managers' needs.

Skills covered: Use Filter by Selection with an Equal Condition • Use Filter by Selection with a Contains Condition • Use Filter by Form with a Comparison Operator • Sort a Table

STEP 1 USE FILTER BY SELECTION WITH AN EQUAL CONDITION

As you continue to learn about the Northwind Traders database, you are expected to provide answers to questions about the customers and products. In this exercise, you use filters to find customers who live in London. Refer to Figure 1.20 as you complete Step 1.

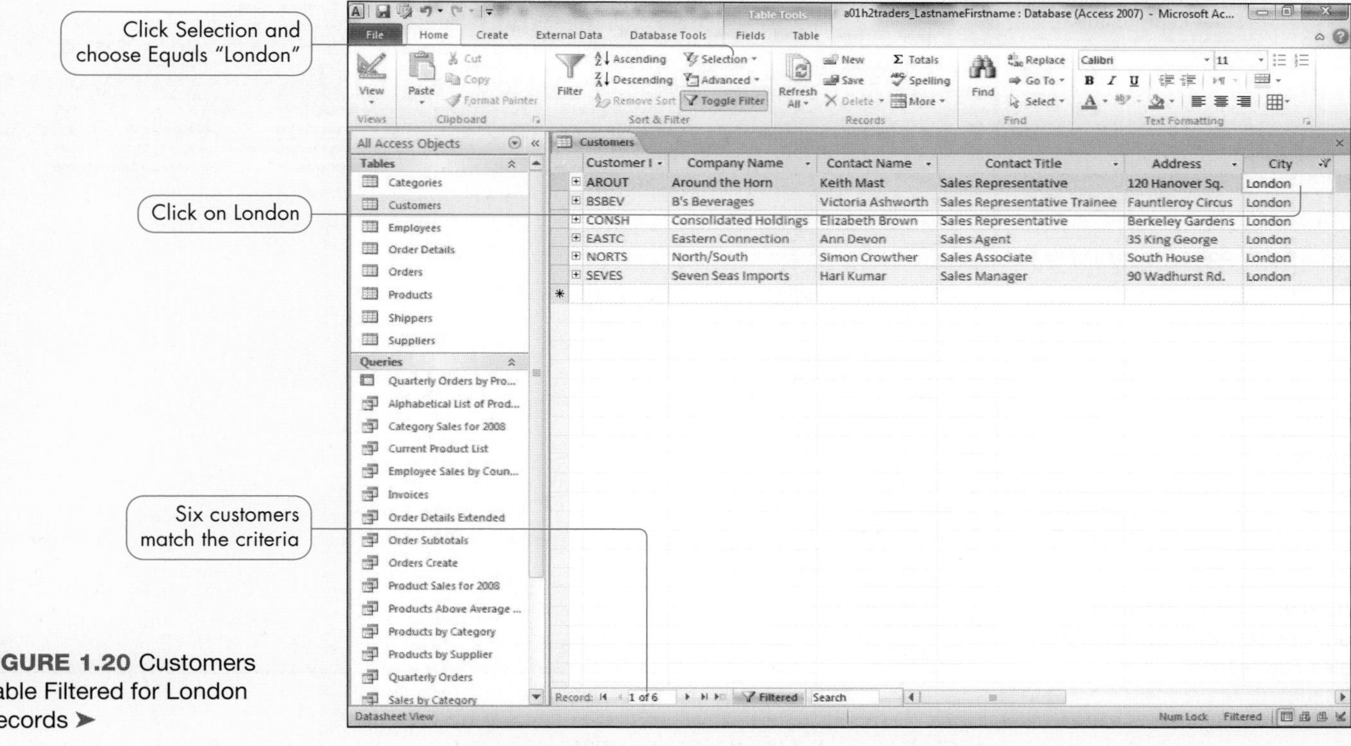

FIGURE 1.20 Customers Table Filtered for London Records ➤

a. Open *a01h1traders_LastnameFirstname* if you closed it at the end of Hands-On Exercise 1. Click the **File tab**, click **Save Database As**, and then type **a01h2traders_LastnameFirstname**, changing *h1* to *h2*. Click **Save**.

> **TROUBLESHOOTING:** If you make any major mistakes in this exercise, you can delete the *a01h2traders_LastnameFirstname* file, repeat step a above, and then start the exercise over.

b. Open the Customers table, navigate to record four, and then replace *Thomas Hardy* with your name in the Contact Name field.

c. Scroll right until the City field is visible. The fourth record has a value of *London* in the City field. Click on the field to select it.

   The word *London* has a gold-colored border around it to let you know that it is active.

d. Click **Selection** in the Sort & Filter group.

e. Choose **Equals "London"** from the menu.

   Six records should be displayed.

f. Click **Toggle Filter** in the Sort & Filter group to remove the filter.

g. Click **Toggle Filter** again to reset the filter. Leave the Customers table open for the next step.

STEP 2 USE FILTER BY SELECTION WITH A CONTAINS CONDITION

At times, you need to print information for the Northwind managers. In this exercise, you print your results. Refer to Figure 1.21 as you complete Step 2.

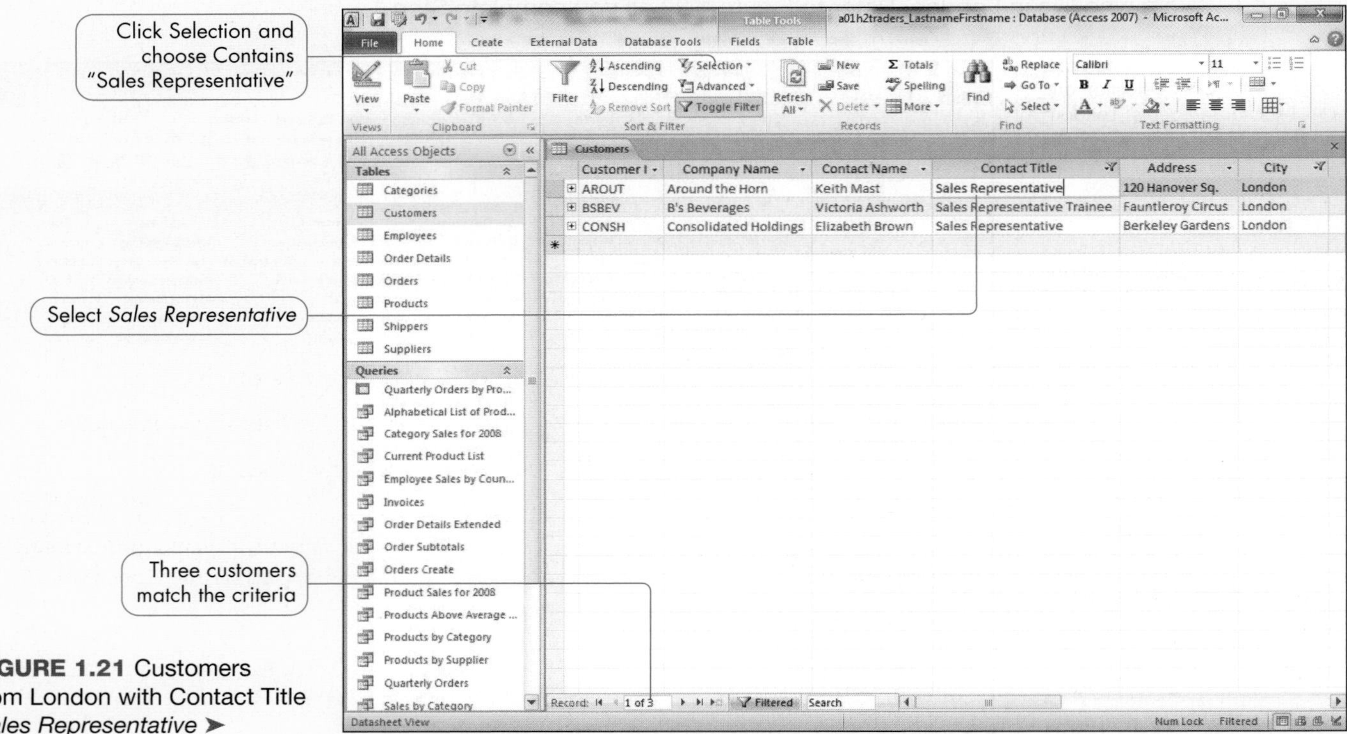

FIGURE 1.21 Customers from London with Contact Title *Sales Representative* ➤

a. Click in any field in the Contact Title column that contains the value *Sales Representative*.

   Sales Representative has a gold-colored border around it to let you know that it is activated.

b. Click **Selection** on the Sort & Filter group.

c. Click **Contains "Sales Representative"**.

   You have applied a second layer of filtering to the customers in London. The second layer further restricts the display to only those customers who have the words *Sales Representative* contained in their titles.

d. Scroll left until you see your name. Compare your results to those shown in Figure 1.21.

e. Click **Toggle Filter** in the Sort & Filter group to remove the filters.

f. Close the Customers table. Click **No** if a dialog box asks if you want to save the design changes to the Customers table.

STEP 3 USE FILTER BY FORM WITH A COMPARISON OPERATOR

At Northwind Traders, you are asked to provide a list of records that do not match just one set of criteria. Use a Filter by Form to provide the information when two or more criteria are needed. Refer to Figure 1.22 as you complete Step 3.

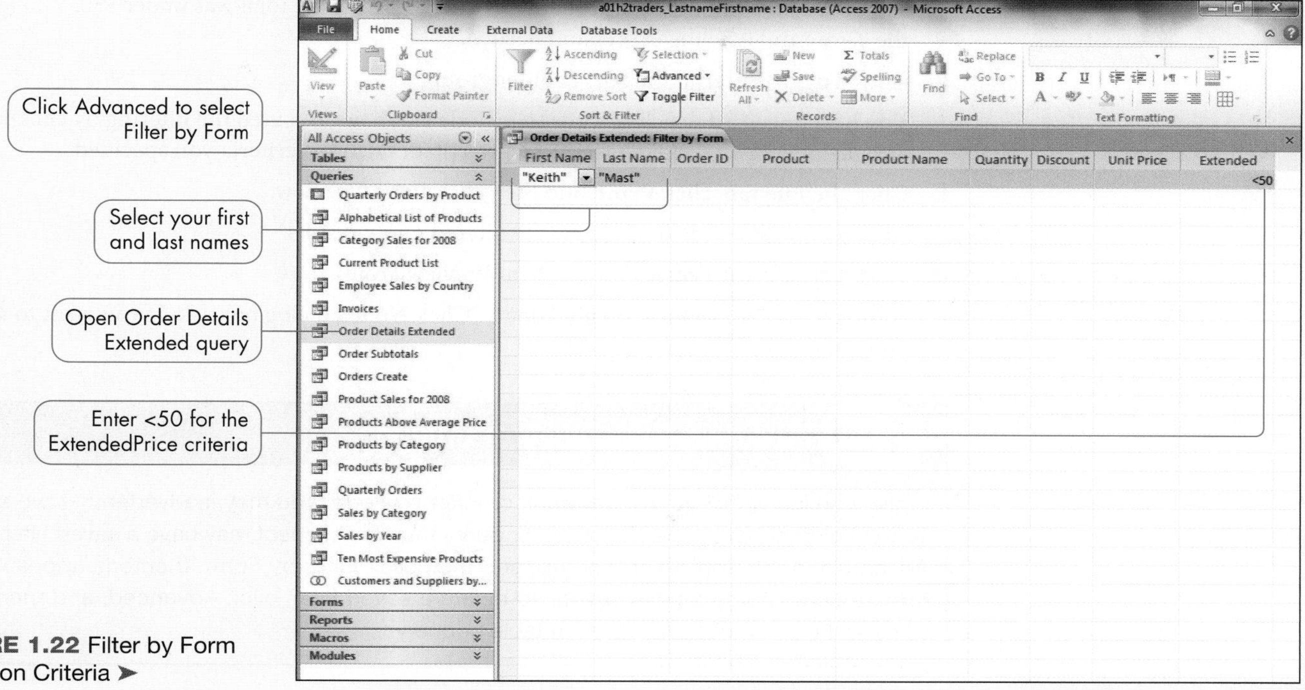

FIGURE 1.22 Filter by Form Selection Criteria ➤

a. Click the **Tables group** in the Navigation Pane to collapse the listed tables.

b. Click the **Queries group** in the Navigation Pane to expand the lists of available queries.

c. Locate and double-click the **Order Details Extended query** to open it.

This query contains information about orders. It has fields containing information about the salesperson, the Order ID, the product name, the unit price, quantity ordered, the discount given, and an extended price. The extended price is a field used to total order information.

d. Click **Advanced** in the Sort & Filter group.

While you are applying a Filter by Form to a query, you can use the same process to apply a Filter by Form to a table.

e. Select **Filter by Form** from the list.

All of the records are now hidden, and you only see field names with an arrow in the first field. Click on the other fields, and an arrow appears.

f. Click in the first row under the First Name field.

An arrow appears at the right of the box.

g. Click the **First Name arrow**.

A list of all available first names appears. Your name should be on the list. Figure 1.22 shows Keith Mast, which replaced Margaret Peacock in Hands-On Exercise 1.

> **TROUBLESHOOTING:** If you do not see your name and you do see Margaret on the list, you probably skipped Steps 3c and 3d in Hands-On Exercise 1. Close the query without saving changes, turn back to the first Hands-On Exercise, and rework it, making sure not to omit any steps. Then you can return to this spot and work the remainder of this Hands-On Exercise.

h. Select your first name from the list.

i. Click in the first row under the Last Name field to reveal the arrow. Locate and select your last name by clicking it.

j. Scroll right until you see the Extended Price field. Click in the first row under the Extended Price field, and then type **<50**.

This will select all of the items that you ordered where the total was under $50. You ignore the arrow and type the expression needed.

k. Click **Toggle Filter** in the Sort & Filter group.

You have specified which records to include and have executed the filtering by clicking Toggle Filter. You should have 31 records that match the criteria you specified.

l. Click the **File tab**, click **Print**, and then click **Print Preview**.

You instructed Access to preview the filtered query results.

m. Click **Close Print Preview** in the Print Preview group.

n. Close the Order Details Extended query. Click **No** if a dialog box asks if you want to save your changes.

> **TIP** Deleting Filter by Form Criterion
>
> While working with Filter by Selection or Filter by Form, you may inadvertently save a filter. To view a saved filter, open the table or query that you suspect may have a saved filter. Click Advanced in the Sort & Filter group, and then click Filter by Form. If criteria appear in the form, then a filter has been saved. To delete a saved filter, click Advanced, and then click Clear All Filters. Close and save the table or query.

STEP 4 SORT A TABLE

Your boss at Northwind is happy with your work; however, he would like some of the information to appear in a different order. Sort the records in the Customers table using the boss's new criteria. Refer to Figure 1.23 as you complete Step 4.

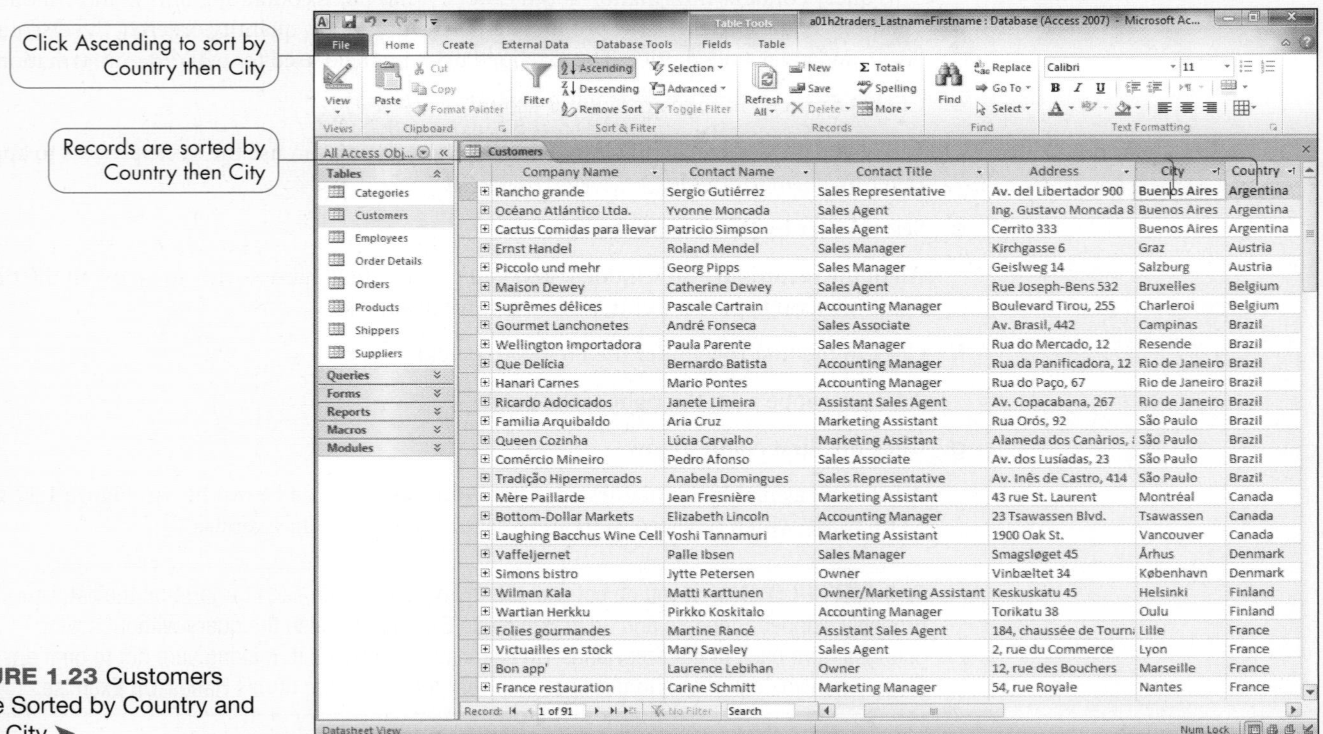

FIGURE 1.23 Customers Table Sorted by Country and Then City ➤

a. Click the **Queries group** in the Navigation Pane to collapse the listed queries.

b. Click the **Tables group** in the Navigation Pane to expand the lists of available tables.

c. Locate and double-click the **Customers table** to open it.

   This table contains information about customers. It is sorted in ascending order by the Customer ID field. Because this field contains text, the table is sorted in alphabetical order.

d. Click any value in the Customer ID field. Click **Descending** in the Sort & Filter group on the Home tab.

   Sorting in descending order on a character field produces a reverse alphabetical order.

e. Scroll right until you can see both the Country and City fields.

   If you close the Navigation Pane, locating the fields on the far right will be easier.

f. Click the **Country column heading**.

   The entire column is selected.

g. Click the **Country column heading** again, and hold down the **left mouse button**.

   A thick dark blue line displays on the left edge of the Country field column.

h. Check to make sure that you see the thick blue line. Drag the **Country field** to the left until the thick black line moves between the City and Region fields. Release the mouse and the Country field position moves to the right of the City field.

   You moved the Country field next to the City field so you can easily sort the table based on both fields.

i. Click any city name in the City field, and then click **Ascending** in the Sort & Filter group.

j. Click any country name in the Country field, and then click **Ascending**.

   The countries are sorted in alphabetical order. The cities within each country also are sorted alphabetically. For example, the customer in Graz, Austria, is listed before the customer in Salzburg, Austria.

k. Close the Customers table. Do not save the changes.

l. Click the **File tab**, and then click **Compact & Repair Database**.

m. Click the **File tab**, click **Save & Publish**, and then double-click **Back Up Database**. Accept *a01h2traders_LastnameFirstname_date* as the file name, and then click **Save**.

   You just created a backup of the database after completing Hands-On Exercise 2. The *a01h2traders_LastnameFirstname* database remains onscreen.

n. Keep the database onscreen if you plan to continue with Hands-On Exercise 3. If not, close the database and exit Access.

Relational Database

Access is known as a relational database management system (RDBMS).

Access is known as a **relational database management system** (RDBMS); using an RDBMS, you can manage groups of data (tables) and then set rules (relationships) between tables.

In the previous section, we compared Excel worksheets to Access relational databases. Access has the ability to create relationships between two tables, whereas Excel does not. Access is known as a ***relational database management system*** (RDBMS); using an RDBMS, you can manage groups of data (tables) and then set rules (relationships) between tables. When relational databases are designed properly, users can easily combine data from multiple tables to create queries, forms, and reports.

Good database design begins with grouping data into the correct tables. This practice, known as normalization, will take time to learn, but over time you will begin to understand the fundamentals. The design of a relational database management system is illustrated in Figure 1.24, which shows the table design of the Northwind Traders database. The tables have been created, the field names have been added, and the data types have been set. The diagram also shows the relationships that were created between tables using join lines. ***Join lines*** enable you to create a relationship between two tables using a common field. When relationships are established, three options are available to further dictate how Access will manage the relationship: Enforce referential integrity, Cascade update related fields, and Cascade delete related records. Later in this section, you will learn more about enforcing referential integrity. The other two options will be covered in another chapter. Using the enforce referential integrity option will help keep invalid data out of your database. Examples of invalid data include (1) entering an order for a customer that does not exist, (2) tagging a new product with a nonexistent category, and (3) entering a person's address with an invalid state abbreviation.

Join lines enable you to create a relationship between two tables using a common field.

Figure 1.24 shows the join lines between related tables as a series of lines connecting the common fields. For example, the Suppliers table is joined to the Products table using the common field SupplierID.

When the database is set up properly, the users of the data can be confident that searching through the Customers table will produce accurate results about their order history or their outstanding invoices.

In this section, you will explore relationships between tables and learn about the power of relational data.

Using the Relationships Window

The relationships in a database are represented by the lines between the tables, as shown in Figure 1.24. Relationships are set in the Relationships window by the database developer after the tables have been created but before any sample data is entered. The most common method of connecting two tables is to connect the primary key from one table to the foreign key of another. A ***foreign key*** is a field in one table that is also the primary key of another table. For example, the SupplierID (primary key) in the Suppliers table is joined to the SupplierID (foreign key) in the Products table. As you learned before, the primary key is a field that uniquely identifies each record in a table.

A **foreign key** is a field in one table that is also the primary key of another table.

To create a relationship between two tables, follow these guidelines:

1. Click Relationships in the Relationships group on the Database Tools tab.
2. Add the two tables that you want to join together to the Relationships window.
3. Drag the common field (e.g., SupplierID) from the primary table (e.g., Suppliers) onto the common field (e.g., SupplierID) of the related table (e.g., Products).
4. The data types of the common fields must be the same.
5. Check the Enforce Referential Integrity check box.
6. Close the Relationships window.

Enforce Referential Integrity

Enforce referential integrity ensures that data cannot be entered into a related table unless it first exists in the primary table.

Enforce referential integrity is one of the three options you can select when setting a table relationship. When ***enforce referential integrity*** is checked, Access ensures that data cannot be entered into a related table unless it first exists in the primary table. For example, in Figure 1.24, you cannot enter an order into the Order table for a Customer with CustomerID 9308 if Customer 9308 has not been entered in the Customer table. This rule ensures the integrity of the data in the database and improves overall data accuracy. Referential integrity also prohibits users from deleting a record in one table if it has records in related tables (i.e., you cannot delete Customer 8819 if Customer 8819 has any orders).

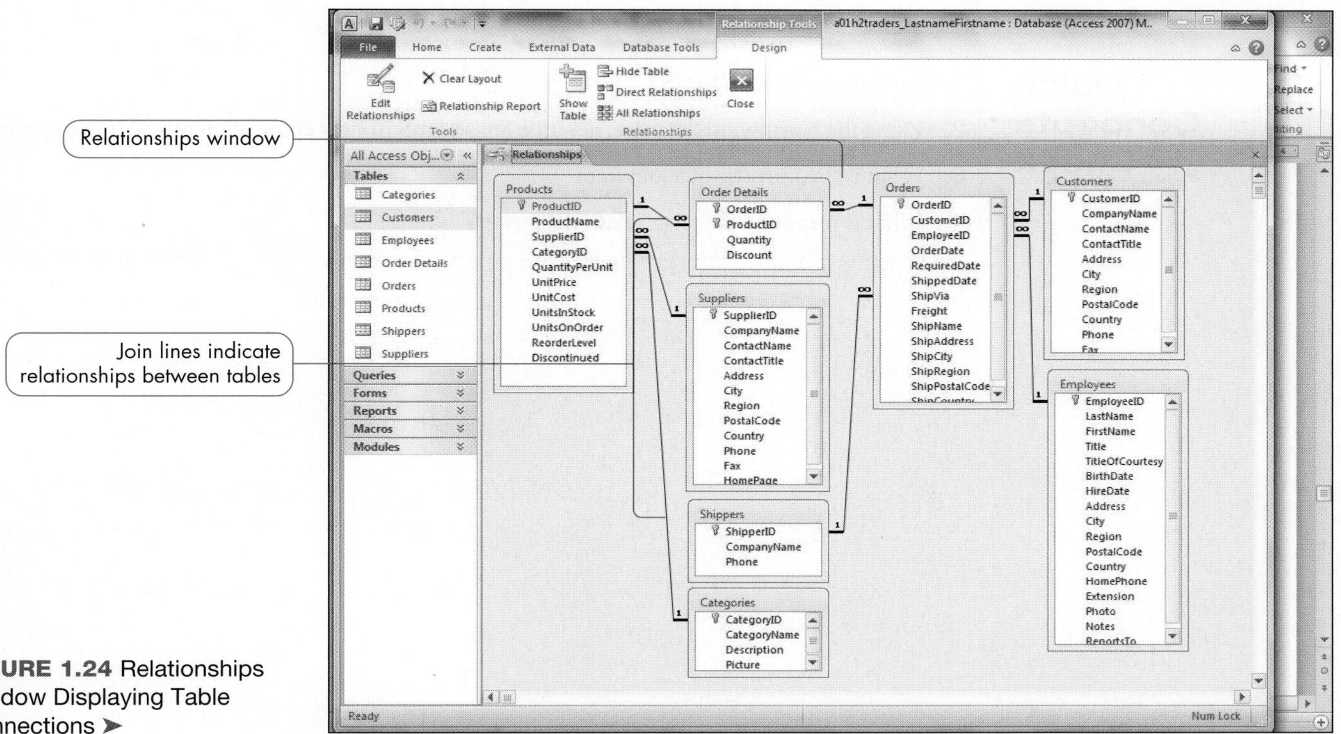

FIGURE 1.24 Relationships Window Displaying Table Connections ➤

Create Sample Data

When learning database skills, starting with a smaller set of sample data prior to entering all company records can be helpful. The same design principles apply regardless of the number of records. A small amount of data gives you the ability to check the tables and quickly see if your results are correct. Even though the data amounts are small, as you test the database tables and relationships, the results will prove useful as you work with larger data sets.

When learning database skills, starting with a smaller set of sample data prior to entering all company records can be helpful.

Understanding Relational Power

In the previous section, you learned that you should use Access when you have relational data. Access derives power from multiple tables and the relationships between those tables. This type of database is illustrated in Figure 1.24. This diagram describes the database structure of the Northwind Traders company. If you examine some of the connections, you will see that the EmployeeID is a foreign key in the Orders table. That means you can produce a report displaying all orders for a customer and the employee name (from the Employees table) that entered the order. The Orders table is joined to the Order Details table where the

OrderID is the common field. The Products table is joined to the Order Details table where ProductID is the common field. These table connections enable you to query (ask) the database for information stored in multiple tables. This feature gives the manager the ability to ask questions like "How many different beverages were shipped last week?" and "What was the total revenue generated from seafood orders last year?"

Suppose a customer called to complain that his orders were arriving late. Because the ShipperID is a foreign key field in the Orders table, you could query the database to find out which shipper delivered that customer's merchandise. Are the other orders also late? Does the firm need to reconsider its shipping options? The design of a relational database enables us to extract information from multiple tables in a single query or report.

In the next Hands-On Exercise, you will examine the Relationships window, create a filter in a query and a report, and remove a filter.

1. Explain the term RDBMS?
2. Using the Northwind database, describe an example of how enforce referential integrity works.
3. What is the purpose of a join line?
4. What is meant by the term relational power?

HANDS-ON EXERCISES

3 Relational Database

You continue to use the Access database to filter tables and provide answers to the Northwind employees' questions. When the same question is repeated by several employees, you look for a way to save your filter by form specifications.

Skills covered: Use the Relationships Window • Filter a Query • Use Filter by Form with a Comparison Operator and Reapply a Saved Filter • Filter a Report • Remove a Filter

STEP 1 USE THE RELATIONSHIPS WINDOW

In this exercise, you examine the relationships established in the Northwind Traders database to learn more about the overall design of the database. Refer to Figure 1.25 as you complete Step 1.

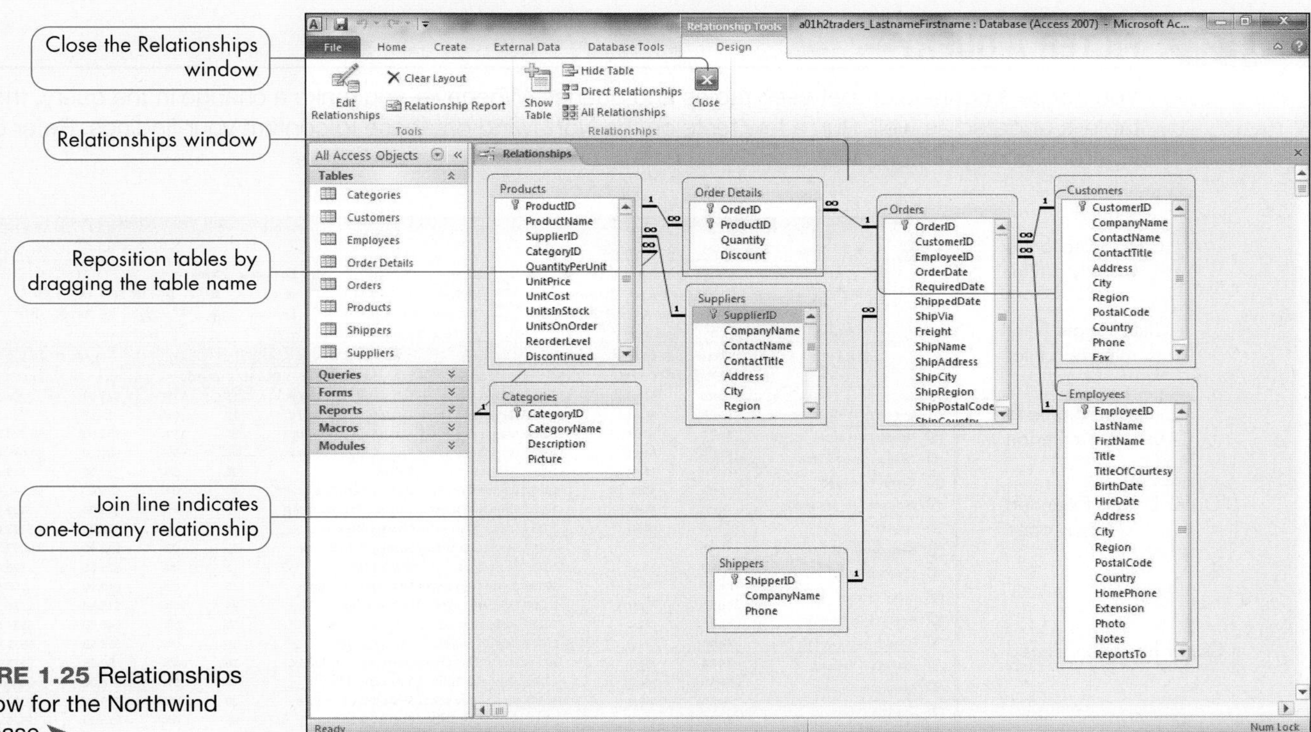

FIGURE 1.25 Relationships Window for the Northwind Database ➤

a. Open *a01h2traders_LastnameFirstname* if you closed it at the end of Hands-On Exercise 2. Click the **File tab**, click **Save Database As**, and then type **a01h3traders_LastnameFirstname**, changing *h2* to *h3*. Click **Save**.

> **TROUBLESHOOTING:** If you make any major mistakes in this exercise, you can delete the *a01h3traders_LastnameFirstname* file, repeat step a above, and then start the exercise over.

b. Click the **Database Tools tab**, and then click **Relationships** in the Relationships group.

Examine the relationships that connect the various tables. For example, the Products table is connected to the Suppliers, Categories, and Order Details tables.

c. Click **Show Table** in the Relationships group on the Relationship Tools Design tab.

The Show Table dialog box opens. It tells you that eight tables are available in the database. If you look in the Relationships window, you will see that all eight tables are in the relationships diagram.

d. Click the **Queries tab** in the Show Table dialog box.

You could add all of the queries to the Relationships window. Things might become cluttered, but you could tell at a glance where the queries get their information.

e. Close the Show Table dialog box.

f. Click **All Access Objects** on the Navigation Pane.

g. Select **Tables and Related Views**.

You now see each table and all the queries, forms, and reports that are based on each table. If a query is created using more than one table, it appears multiple times in the Navigation Pane.

h. Close the Relationships window. Click **All Tables** on the Navigation Pane, and then select **Object Type**.

STEP 2 FILTER A QUERY

You notice a connection between tables and queries. Whenever you make a change in the query, the table is updated as well. Run a few tests on the Northwind database to confirm your findings. Refer to Figure 1.26 as you complete Step 2.

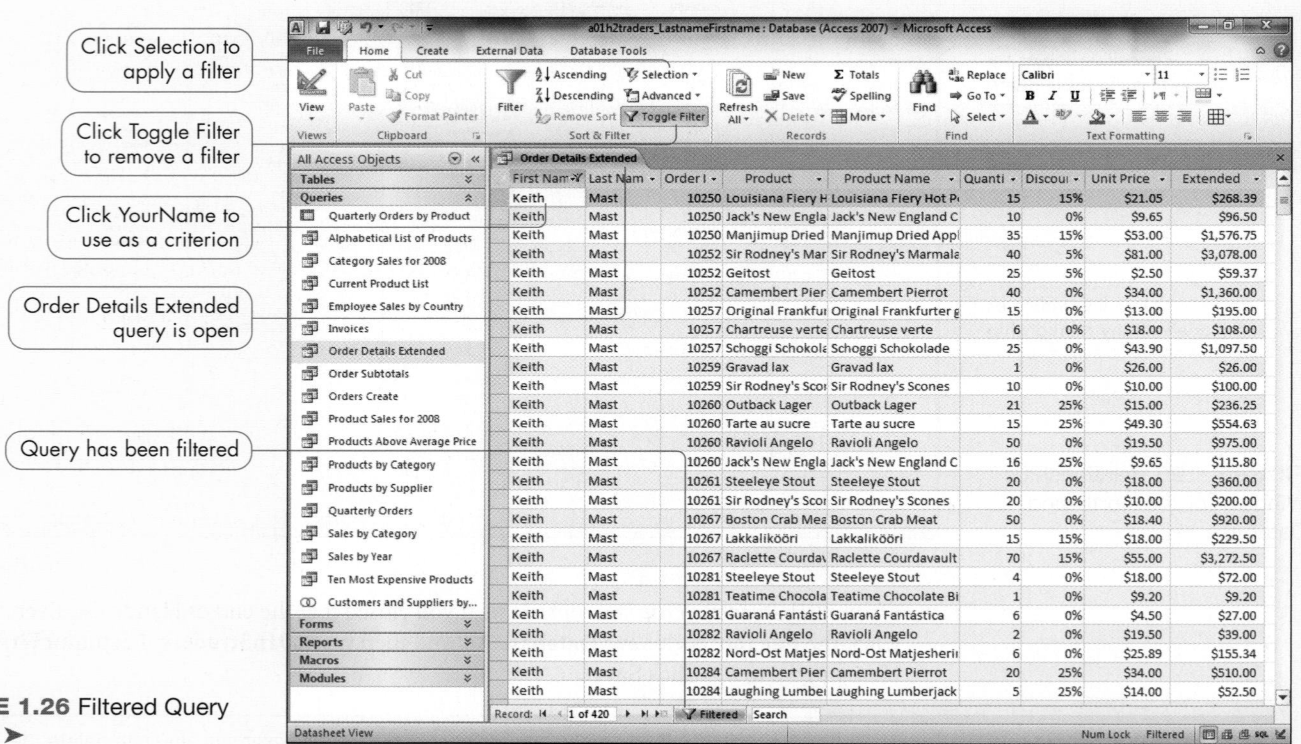

FIGURE 1.26 Filtered Query Results ➤

a. Collapse the Tables group, and expand the Queries group, and then locate and double-click the **Order Details Extended query**.

b. Find an occurrence of your last name, and then click it to select it.

c. Click **Selection** in the Sort & Filter group. Select **Equals "YourName"** from the selection menu.

The query results are reduced to 420 records.

d. Click **Toggle Filter** in the Sort & Filter group to remove the filter.

STEP 3 USE FILTER BY FORM WITH A COMPARISON OPERATOR AND REAPPLY A SAVED FILTER

Use Filter by Form to solve more complex questions about the Northwind data. After you retrieve the records, you save the Filter by Form specifications so you can reapply the filter later. Refer to Figure 1.27 as you complete Step 3.

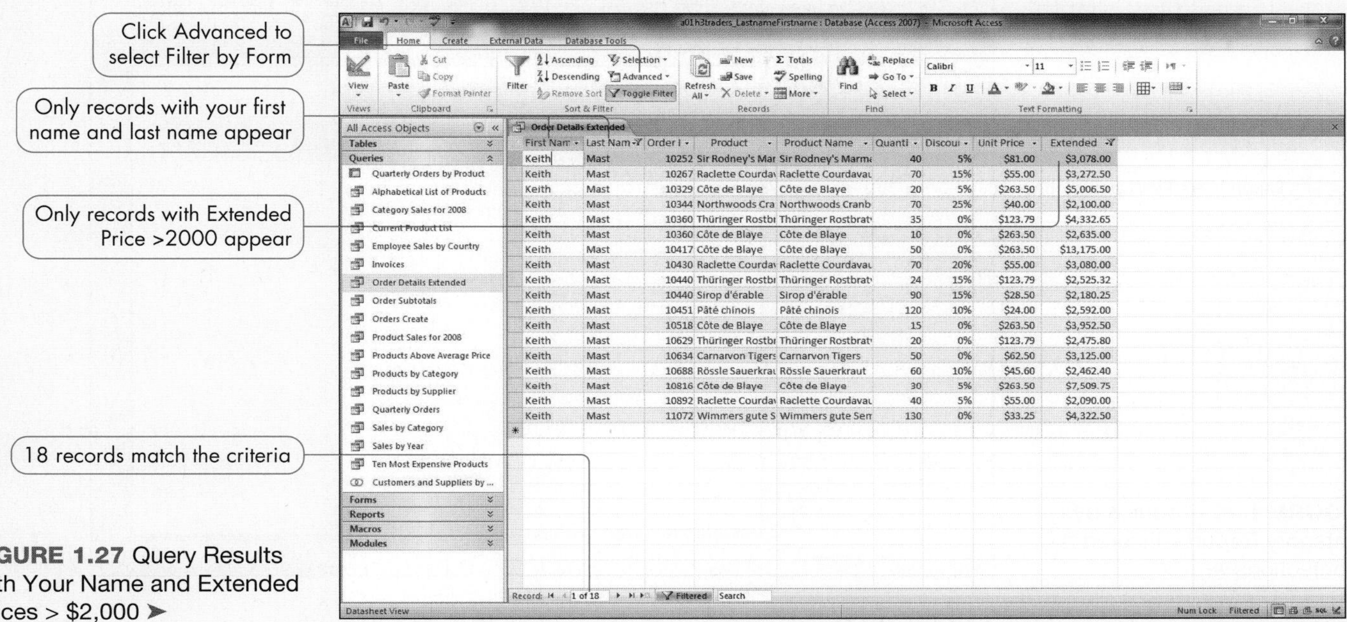
Click Advanced to select Filter by Form
Only records with your first name and last name appear
Only records with Extended Price >2000 appear
18 records match the criteria

FIGURE 1.27 Query Results with Your Name and Extended Prices > $2,000 ➤

a. Click **Advanced** in the Sort & Filter group.

b. Select **Filter By Form** from the list.

   Because Access will save the last filter you created, the Filter by Form design sheet opens with one criterion already filled in. Your name displays in the selection box under the Last Name field.

c. Scroll right (or press **Tab**) until the Extended Price field is visible. Click the first row in the Extended Price field.

d. Type >**2000**.

   The Extended Price field shows the purchased amount for each item ordered. If an item sold for $15 and a customer ordered 10, the Extended Price would display $150.

e. Click **Toggle Filter** in the Sort & Filter group. Examine the filtered results.

   Your comparison operator instruction, >2000, identified 18 items ordered where the extended price exceeded $2,000.

f. Close the Order Details Extended query by clicking the **Close button**. Answer **Yes** when asked *Do you want to save changes?*.

g. Open the Order Details Extended query again.

   The filter disengages when you close and reopen the object. However, the filter has been stored with the query. You may reapply the filter at any time by clicking the Toggle Filter command (until the next filter replaces the current one).

h. Click **Toggle Filter** in the Sort & Filter group.

i. Compare your results to Figure 1.27. If your results are correct, close and save the query.

STEP 4 FILTER A REPORT

You wonder if one report can serve several purposes. You discover that a report can be customized using the Filter by Selection feature. Refer to Figure 1.28 as you complete Step 4.

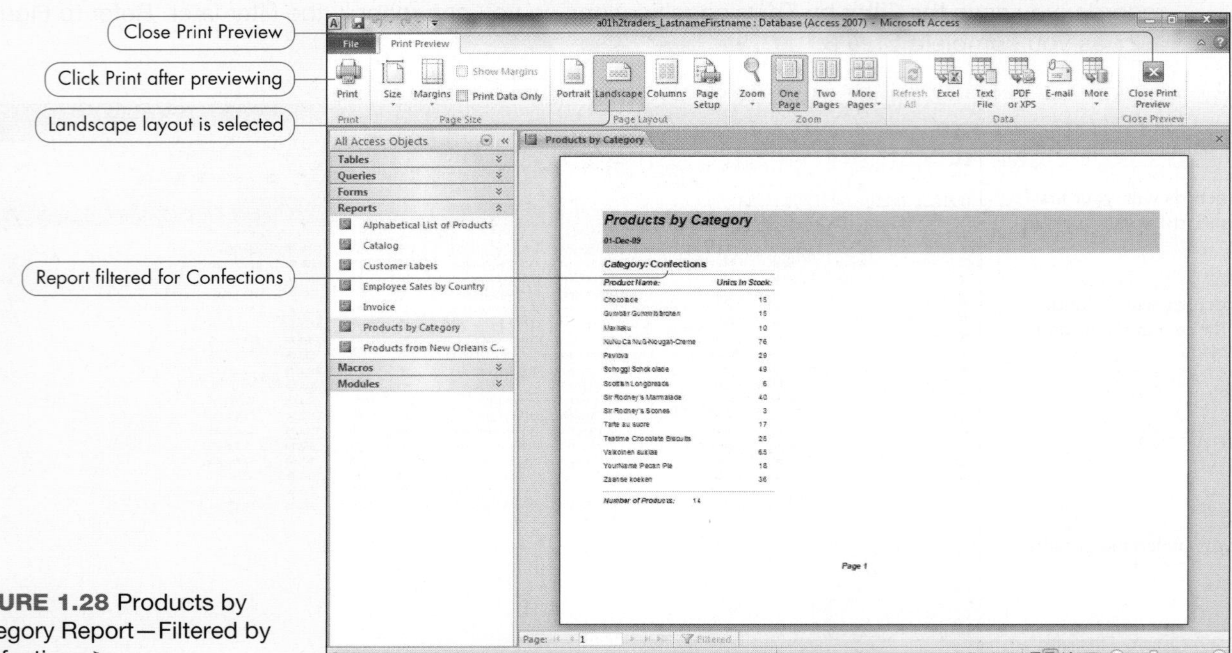

Close Print Preview
Click Print after previewing
Landscape layout is selected
Report filtered for Confections

FIGURE 1.28 Products by Category Report—Filtered by Confections ➤

a. Click the **Queries group** in the Navigation Pane to collapse the listed queries, and then click the **Reports group** in the Navigation Pane to expand the list of available reports.

b. Open the Products by Category report located in the Reports group on the Navigation Pane. You may need to scroll down to locate it.

   The report should open in Print Preview with a gray title background highlighting the report title. The Print Preview displays the report exactly as it will print. This report was formatted to display in three columns.

> **TROUBLESHOOTING:** If you do not see the gray title background and three columns, you probably opened the wrong object. The database also contains a Product by Category query. It is the source for the Products by Category report. Make sure you open the report (shown with the green report icon) and not the query. Close the query and open the report.

c. Examine the Confections category products. You should see *Your Name Pecan Pie.*

   You created this product by entering data in a form in Hands-On Exercise 1. You later discovered that changes made to a form affect the related table. Now you see that other related objects also change when the source data changes.

d. Right-click the **Products by Category tab**, and then select **Report View** from the shortcut menu.

   The Report view displays the information a little differently. It no longer shows three columns. If you clicked the Print command while in Report view, the columns would print even though you do not see them. The Report view permits limited data interaction (for example, filtering).

e. Scroll down in the report until you see the title *Category: Confections.* Right-click the word *Confections* in the title. Select **Equals "Confections"** from the shortcut menu.

   The report now displays only *Confections.*

f. Right-click the **Products by Category tab**, and then select **Print Preview** from the shortcut menu.

   If you need to print a report, always view the report in Print Preview prior to printing.

g. Click **Close Print Preview** in the Close Preview group.

h. Save and close the report.

   The next time the report opens in Report view, it will not be filtered. However, since the filter was saved, the filter can be reapplied by clicking Toggle Filter in the Sort & Filter group.

STEP 5 REMOVE A FILTER

You notice that Access keeps asking you to save your changes when you close a table or query. You say "Yes" each time since you do not want to lose your data. Now you need to remove the filters that you saved. Refer to Figure 1.29 as you complete Step 5.

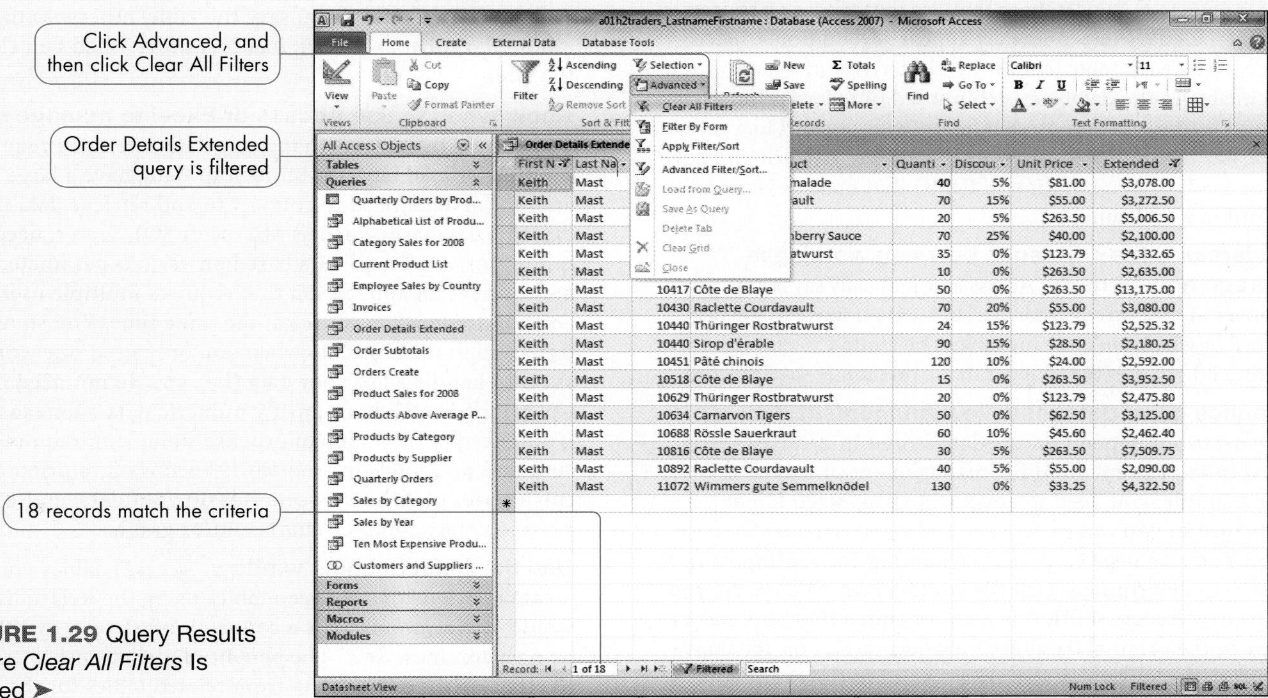

Click Advanced, and then click Clear All Filters
Order Details Extended query is filtered
18 records match the criteria

FIGURE 1.29 Query Results Before *Clear All Filters* Is Clicked ➤

a. Click the **Queries group** in the Navigation Pane to expand the list of available reports, then open the Order Details Extended query.

   All 2,155 records should display in the query. You have unfiltered the data. However, the filter from the previous step still exists.

b. Click **Toggle Filter** in the Sort & Filter group.

   You will see the same 18 filtered records that you created in Step 3.

c. Click **Advanced** in the Sort & Filter group, and then click **Clear All Filters.**

   All 2,155 records are shown again.

d. Close the query. A dialog box opens asking if you want to save changes. Click **Yes.**

e. Open the Order Details Extended query.

f. Click **Advanced** in the Sort & Filter group.

g. Check to ensure the Clear All Filters option is dim, indicating there are no saved filters. Save and close the query.

h. Click the **File tab**, and then click **Compact & Repair Database.**

i. Click the **File tab**, and then click **Exit** (to exit Access).

j. Submit based on your instructor's directions.

CHAPTER OBJECTIVES REVIEW

After reading this chapter, you have accomplished the following objectives:

1. **Navigate among the objects in an Access database.** An Access database has six types of objects: tables, forms, queries, reports, macros, and modules. The Navigation pane displays these objects and enables you to open an existing object or create new objects. You may arrange these by Object Type or by Tables and Related Views. The Tables and Related Views provides a listing of each table and all other objects in the database that use that table as a source. Thus, one query or report may appear several times, listed once under each table from which it derives information. Each table in the database is composed of records, and each record is in turn composed of fields. Every record in a given table has the same fields in the same order. The primary key is the field (or combination of fields) that makes every record in a table unique.
2. **Understand the difference between working in storage and memory.** Access automatically saves any changes in the current record as soon as you move to the next record or when you close the table. The Undo Current Record command reverses the changes to the previously saved record.
3. **Practice good database file management.** Because organizations depend on the data stored in databases, you need to implement good file management practices. For example, you need to develop an organized folder structure so you can easily save and retrieve your database files. You also need to develop a naming convention so it is easy to determine which file contains which data. As you learn new Access skills, it is recommended that you make a copy of the original database file and practice on the copy. This practice provides a recovery point in the event you make a fatal error.
4. **Back up, compact, and repair Access files.** Because using a database tends to increase the size of the file, you should always close any database objects and compact and repair the database prior to closing the file. Compact & Repair will reduce the size of the database by removing temporary objects and unclaimed space due to deleted objects. Adequate backup is essential when working with an Access database (or any other Office application). For increased security, a duplicate copy of the database can be created at the end of every session and stored externally (on a flash drive or an external hard drive).
5. **Create filters.** A filter is a set of criteria that is applied to a table to display a subset of the records in that table. Access lets you Filter by Selection or Filter by Form. The application of a filter does not remove the records from the table, but simply hides them temporarily from view.
6. **Sort table data on one or more fields.** The records in a table can be displayed in ascending or descending order by first selecting the appropriate column and clicking Ascending or Descending on the Home tab. The sort order will hold only if you save the table; otherwise the table will return to the original sort order when you close the table.
7. **Know when to use Access or Excel to manage data.** You should use Access to manage data when you require multiple related tables to store your data; have a large amount of data; need to connect to and retrieve data from external databases, such as Microsoft SQL Server; need to group, sort, and total data based on various parameters; and/or have an application that requires multiple users to connect to one data source at the same time. You should use Excel to manage data when you only need one worksheet to handle all of your data (i.e., you do not need multiple worksheets); have mostly numeric data—for example, if you need to maintain an expense statement; require subtotals and totals in your worksheet; want to primarily run a series of "what if" scenarios on your data; and/or need to create complex charts and/or graphs.
8. **Use the Relationships window.** Access enables you to create relationships between tables using the Relationships window. A *relationship* is a connection between two tables using a common field. The benefit of a relationship is to efficiently combine data from related tables for the purpose of creating queries, forms, and reports. Relationships are the reason why Access is referred to as a relational database.
9. **Understand relational power.** A relational database contains multiple tables and enables you to extract information from those tables in a single query. The related tables must be consistent with one another, a concept known as referential integrity. Once referential integrity is set, Access enforces data validation to protect the integrity of a database. No system, no matter how sophisticated, can produce valid output from invalid input. Changes made in one object can affect other related objects. Relationships are based on joining the primary key from one table to the foreign key of another table.

KEY TERMS

Access speed ***p.581***
Backup ***p.581***
Compact and Repair ***p.581***
Comparison operator ***p.591***
Criterion ***p.578***
Database ***p.573***
Datasheet view ***p.575***
Design view ***p.575***
Enforce referential integrity ***p.601***
Field ***p.573***
Filter ***p.589***
Filter by Form ***p.591***
Filter by Selection ***p.591***
Foreign key ***p.600***
Form ***p.578***
Join lines ***p.600***
Navigation Pane ***p.574***
Object ***p.573***
Primary key ***p.577***
Query ***p.578***
Record ***p.573***
Relational database management system ***p.600***
Relationship ***p.593***
Report ***p.579***
Sort ***p.592***
Sort Ascending ***p.592***
Sort Descending ***p.592***
Table ***p.573***

MULTIPLE CHOICE

1. Which sequence represents the hierarchy of terms, from smallest to largest?
   (a) Database, table, record, field
   (b) Field, record, table, database
   (c) Record, field, table, database
   (d) Field, record, database, table

2. You perform several edits in a table within an Access database. When should you execute the Save command?
   (a) Immediately after you add, edit, or delete a record
   (b) Each time you close a table or a query
   (c) Once at the end of a session
   (d) Records are saved automatically; the save command is not required.

3. You have opened an Access file. The left pane displays a table with forms, queries, and reports listed below a table name. Then another table and its objects display. You notice some of the object names are repeated under different tables. Why?
   (a) The Navigation Pane has been set to Object Type. The object names repeat because a query or report is frequently based on multiple tables.
   (b) The Navigation Pane has been set to Tables and Related Views. The object names repeat because a query or report is frequently based on multiple tables.
   (c) The Navigation Pane has been set to Most Recently Used View. The object names repeat because an object has been used frequently.
   (d) The database objects have been alphabetized.

4. Which of the following is not true of an Access database?
   (a) Every record in a table has the same fields as every other record.
   (b) Every table in a database contains the same number of records as every other table.
   (c) Text, Number, Autonumber, and Currency are valid data types.
   (d) Each table should contain a primary key; however, a primary key is not required.

5. Which of the following is true regarding the record selector box?
   (a) A pencil symbol indicates that the current record already has been saved.
   (b) An empty square indicates that the current record has not changed.
   (c) An asterisk indicates the first record in the table.
   (d) A gold border surrounds the active record.

6. You have finished an Access assignment and wish to turn it in to your instructor for evaluation. As you prepare to transfer the file, you discover that it has grown in size. It is now more than double the original size. You should:
   (a) Zip the database file prior to transmitting it to the instructor.
   (b) Turn it in; the size does not matter.
   (c) Compact and repair the database file prior to transmitting it to the instructor.
   (d) Delete extra tables or reports or fields to make the file smaller.

7. Which of the following will be accepted as valid during data entry?
   (a) Adding a record with a duplicate primary key
   (b) Entering text into a numeric field
   (c) Entering numbers into a text field
   (d) Omitting an entry in a required field

8. Which of the following conditions is available through Filter by Selection?
   (a) The AND condition
   (b) The OR condition
   (c) An Equals condition
   (d) A delete condition

9. You open an Access form and use it to update an address for customer Lee Fong. After closing the form, you later open a report that generates mailing labels. What will the address label for Lee Fong show?
   (a) The new address
   (b) The old address
   (c) The new address if you remembered to save the changes made to the form
   (d) The old address until you remember to update it in the report

10. You are looking at an Employees table in Datasheet view. You want the names sorted alphabetically by last name and then by first name—for example, Smith, Andrea is listed before Smith, William. To accomplish this, you must:
    (a) First sort ascending on first name and then on last name.
    (b) First sort descending on first name and then on last name.
    (c) First sort ascending on last name and then on first name.
    (d) First sort descending on last name and then on first name.

PRACTICE EXERCISES

1 Hotel Rewards

The Prestige Hotel chain caters to upscale business travelers and provides state-of-the-art conference, meeting, and reception facilities. It prides itself on its international, four-star cuisine. The hotel is launching a rewards club to help the marketing department track the purchasing patterns of its most loyal customers. All of the hotel transactions will be stored in an Access database. Your task is to create a member table and enter sample customers. You will practice filtering on the table data. This exercise follows the same set of skills as used in Hands-On Exercise 1 in the chapter. Refer to Figure 1.30 as you complete this exercise.

Members

ID	LastName	FirstName	Address	City	State	Zip	Phone	DateOfMembership
1	Gray	Mary	100 BIRDIE COURT	RALEIGH	NC	27612	555-787-7688	9/1/2011
2	Phillips	Harold	1511 OAKDALE RD	CHARLOTTE	NC	28218		5/4/2012
3	Hauser	Bob	10008 WHITESTONE RD	RALEIGH	NC	27613	555-783-8286	3/1/2011
4	Gregory	Anne	1001 QUEENS RD	RALEIGH	NC	27615	555-847-9431	12/18/2010
5	Johnson	Alicia	101 CORBEL PLACE	CHARLOTTE	NC	28217		9/19/2012
6	Kowalski	Karen	199 SAINT MARKS CT	CHARLOTTE	NC	28218		10/15/2011
7	McBride	Diane	2519 TIMBER LANE	CHARLOTTE	NC	28270	555-485-8914	5/16/2011
8	Hallsey	Betty	105 PINE CONE DR	CHARLOTTE	NC	28217		4/30/2012
9	Hanck	Bill	1066 CENTRAL DRIVE	CHARLOTTE	NC	28217		1/1/2013
10	Payne	Roger	3904 HUNT CHASE CT	WILMINGTON	NC	28412	555-791-5154	1/22/2012

FIGURE 1.30 Enter Data into the Members Table ➤

a. Open Access, and then type **a01p1hotel_LastnameFirstname** in the **File Name box.** Click **Browse** (to the right of the file name). Locate your Student Data Files folder in the File New Database dialog box, click **OK** to close the dialog box, and then click **Create** to create the new database.

b. Click **View** in the Views group on the Table Tools Fields tab to switch to Design view. Type **Members** in the **Save As dialog box**, and then click **OK**.

c. Type **LastName** under the ID field, and then press **Tab**. Accept **Text** as the Data Type. Type **FirstName** in the third row, and then press **Tab**. Accept **Text** as the Data Type.

d. Type the next five fields into the Field Name column: **Address**, **City**, **State**, **Zip** and **Phone**. Accept **Text** as the Data Type for each of these fields. Type **DateOfMembership** as the last Field Name, and select **Date/Time** as the Data Type.

e. Click **View** in the Views group to switch to Datasheet view. Click **Yes** to save the table. Type the data as shown in Figure 1.30. Increase the column widths to fit the data as necessary. Press **Tab** to move to the next field.

f. Find a record that displays *Charlotte* as the value in the City field. Click **Charlotte** to select that data value.

g. Click **Selection** in the Sort & Filter group on the Home tab. Select **Equals "Charlotte"**.

h. Find a record that displays *28217* as the value in the Zip field. Click **28217** to select that data value.

i. Click **Selection** in the Sort & Filter group on the Home tab. Select **Equals "28217"**.

j. Click any value in the FirstName field. Click **Ascending** in the Sort & Filter group on the Home tab. Click any value in the LastName field. Click **Ascending** in the Sort & Filter group on the Home tab.

k. Click the **File tab**, click **Print**, and then click **Print Preview** to preview the sorted and filtered table.

l. Click **Close Print Preview** in the Close Preview group. Close the table without saving changes.

m. Click the **File tab**, and then click **Compact & Repair Database**.

n. Click the **File tab**, click **Save & Publish**, and then double-click **Back Up Database**.

o. Click **Save** to accept the default backup file name with today's date.

p. Click the **File tab**, and then click **Exit** (to exit Access).

q. Submit the database based on your instructor's directions.

2 Custom Coffee

The Custom Coffee Company provides coffee, tea, and snacks to offices in Miami. Custom Coffee also provides and maintains the equipment for brewing the beverages. The firm has a reputation for providing outstanding customer service. To improve customer service even further, the owner recently purchased an Access database to keep track of customers, orders, and products. This database will replace the Excel spreadsheets currently maintained by the office manager. The Excel spreadsheets are out of date and they do not allow for data validation while data is being entered. The company hired a temp to verify and enter all the Excel data into the Access database. This exercise follows the same set of skills as used in Hands-On Exercises 2 and 3 in the chapter. Refer to Figure 1.31 as you complete this exercise.

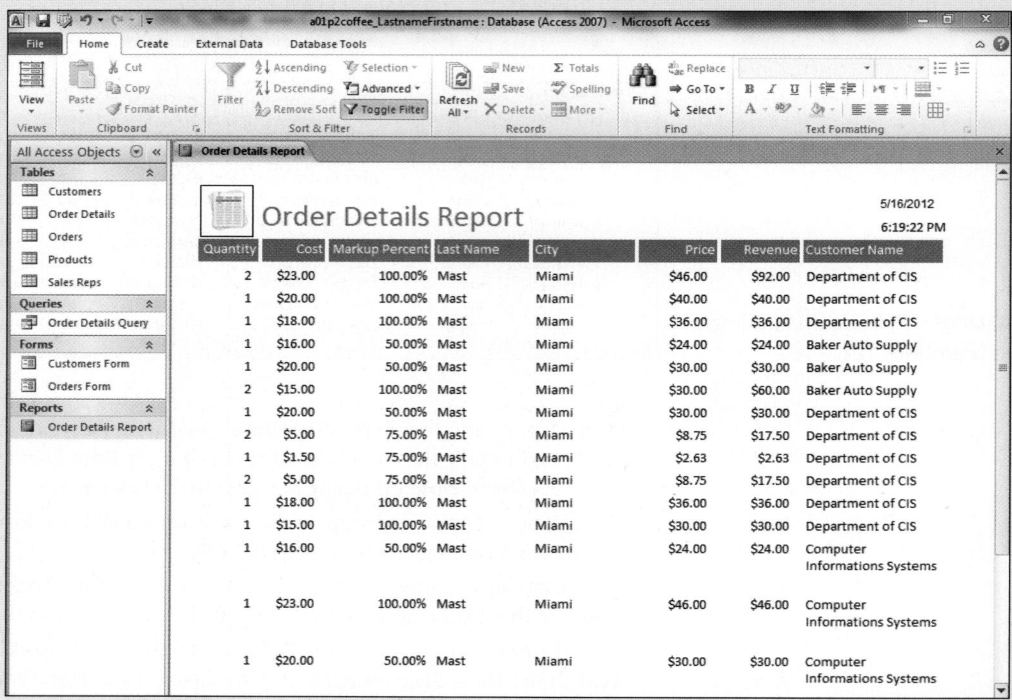

FIGURE 1.31 Order Details Report Filtered for *YourName* ➤

a. Open the *a01p2coffee* file, and then save the database as **a01p2coffee_LastnameFirstname.**

b. Click the **Database Tools tab**, and then click **Relationships** in the Relationships group. Review the table relationships. Take note of the join line between the Customers and Orders Tables.

c. Click **Close** in the Relationships group.

d. Double-click the **Sales Reps table** in the Navigation Pane to open it. Replace *YourName* with your name in both the LastName and FirstName fields. Close the table by clicking the **Close (X) button** on the right side of the Sales Reps window.

e. Double-click the Customers Form form to open it. Click New (blank) record in the navigation bar at the bottom of the window. Add a new record by typing the following information; press Tab after each field.

Customer Name:	***your name*** **Company**
Contact:	***your name***
Email:	***your name*****@yahoo.com**
Address1:	**123 Main St**
Address2:	**Skip**
City:	**Miami**
State:	**FL**
Zip Code:	**33133**
Phone:	**(305) 555-1234**
Fax:	**Skip**
Service Start Date:	**1/17/2012**
Credit Rating:	**A**
Sales Rep ID:	**2**

Notice the pencil in the top-left margin of the form window. This symbol indicates the new record has not been saved to storage. Press Tab. The pencil symbol disappears, and the new customer is automatically saved to the table.

f. Close the Customers Form form.

g. Double-click the **Orders Form form** to open it. Click **New (blank) record** in the navigation bar at the bottom of the window. Add a new record by typing the following information:

Customer ID:	**15** (Access will convert it to *C0015*)
Payment Type:	**Cash** (select using the arrow)
Comments:	**Ship this order in 2 days**
Product ID:	**4** (Access will convert it to *P0004*)
Quantity:	**2**

h. Add a second product using the following information:

Product ID:	**6** (Access will convert it to *P0006*)
Quantity:	**1**

i. Close the form (save changes if asked.)

j. Double-click the **Order Details Report** to open it in Report view. Right-click your name in the Last Name field, and then select **Equals "Your Name"** from the shortcut menu. Right-click **Miami** in the City field, and then select **Equals "Miami"** from the shortcut menu.

k. Click the **File tab**, click **Print**, and then click **Print Preview**.

l. Click **Close Print Preview** in the Close Preview group. Close the report.

m. Click the **File tab**, click **Info**, and then click **Compact and Repair Database**.

n. Click the **File tab**, click **Save & Publish**, and then double-click **Back Up Database**. Use the default backup file name.

o. Click the **File tab**, and then click **Exit** (to exit Access).

p. Submit based on your instructor's directions.

MID-LEVEL EXERCISES

1 Home Sales

You are the senior partner in a large, independent real estate firm that specializes in home sales. Most of your time is spent supervising the agents who work for your firm. The firm needs to create a database to hold all of the information on the properties it has listed. You will use the database to help find properties that match the goals of your customers. You will create the database, create two tables, add data to both tables, and create a relationship. Refer to Figure 1.32 as you complete this exercise.

FIGURE 1.32 Sample Properties ➤

Properties

ID	DateListed	DateSold	ListPrice	SalePrice	SqFeet	Beds	Baths	Address	SubDi	Agent	Style	Constructior	Garage	YearBuilt
1	5/28/2012		$146,000.00		928	2	2	1166 Avondale	3	1	Ranch	Brick	1 Car Attached	2000
2	7/22/2012		$163,600.00		896	2	2	1684 Riverdale	3	2	2 Story	Frame	1 Car Detached	1979
3	6/7/2012		$170,000.00		1023	2	2	1166 Silverdale	3	4	Split Level	Stone	2 Car Attached	1977
4	6/7/2012		$198,000.00		672	1	1	4520 Oakdale	3	3	Ranch	Brick	1 Car Attached	1987
5	6/22/2012		$212,000.00		1056	2	2	1838 Hillendale	3	4	Split Level	Frame	2 Car Detached	1993
6	7/24/2012		$239,600.00		1456	3	2	1255 Copperdale	3	5	Ranch	Stone	1 Car Detached	1998
7	6/22/2012		$239,600.00		1539	3	2	1842 Gardendale	3	3	2 Story	Brick	Carport	1963
8	8/12/2012		$239,600.00		1032	2	0	1605 Lakedale	3	2	Split Foyer	Frame	3 Car Attached	1992
9	6/22/2012		$279,600.00		1540	3	2	1775 Jerrydale	3	1	Ranch	Stone	1 Car Detached	2000
10	6/23/2012	9/14/2012	$72,500.00	$68,000.00	1030	3	1	214 Merrydale	3	3	Ranch	Brick	2 Car Detached	2000

a. Open Access, and then type **a01m1homes_LastnameFirstname** in the **File Name box**. Click **Browse** (to the right of the file name). Locate your Student Data Files folder in the File New Database dialog box, click **OK** to close the dialog box, and then click Create to create the new database.

b. Click View in the Views group to switch to Design view. Type **Properties** in the **Save As dialog box**, and then click **OK**.

c. Type **DateListed** under the ID field, and then press **Tab**. Select **Date/Time** as the Data Type. Type **DateSold** in the third row, and then press **Tab**. Select **Date/Time** as the Data Type.

d. Type the remainder of the fields and the Data Types as shown:

Field Name	Data Type
ListPrice	Currency
SalePrice	Currency
SqFeet	Number
Beds	Number
Baths	Number
Address	Text
SubDivision	Number
Agent	Number
Style	Text
Construction	Text
Garage	Text
YearBuilt	Number

e. Click **View** in the Views group to switch to Datasheet view. Click **Yes** to save the table. Type the first ten records as shown in Figure 1.32. Press **Tab** to move to the next field.

f. Open the *a01m1properties_import* workbook file in Excel. Click **row 2**, press and hold the left mouse button, and then drag through row 70 so that all of the data rows are selected. Click **Copy** in the Clipboard group.

g. Return to Access, and then click on the **asterisk (*)** on the first new row of the Properties table. Click **Paste** n the Clipboard group to paste all 69 rows into the Properties table. Save and close the table.

h. Click the **Create tab**, and then click **Table Design** in the Tables group. Type **ID** in the **Field Name column** of the first row, and then select **AutoNumber** as the Data Type.

i. Type **FirstName** in the **Field Name column** of the second row, and then accept Text as the Data Type. Type **LastName** in the **Field Name column** of the third row, and then accept **Text** as the Data Type. Type **Title** as the **Field Name column** of the fourth row, and then accept **Text** as the Data Type.

j. Click the **ID Field name**, and then click **Primary Key** in the Tools group. Click **View** in the Views group to switch to Datasheet view. Click **Yes** to save the table. Type **Agents** in the **Save As dialog box**, and then click **OK**.

k. Type **Juan** in the second column, and then press **Tab**. Type **Rosario** in the third column, and then press **Tab**. Type **President** in the fourth column, and then press **Tab**. Type the names and titles for the remaining agents as shown below. Note that the ID field is an AutoNumber field, so you will not need to type the ID.

ID	FirstName	LastName	Title
2	Kia	Hart	Broker
3	Keith	Martin	Agent
4	Kim	Yang	Agent
5	Steven	Dougherty	Agent in Training
6	Angela	Scott	Agent in Training

l. Close the table.

m. Click the **Database Tools tab**, and then click **Relationships** in the Relationships group. Add both tables to the Relationships window, and then close the Show Table dialog box.

n. Increase the height of the Properties table to display all fields. Drag the **ID field** from the Agents table and drop it onto the **Agent field** in the Properties table. Click the **Enforce Referential Integrity check box** in the Edit Relationships dialog box to turn it on. Click **Create**, and then close the Relationships window. Click **Yes** to save your changes.

o. Open the Properties table. Click **Advanced** in the Sort & Filter group, and then click **Filter By Form**. Set the criteria to identify properties with a list price less than $300,000 and with two bedrooms. (You will use the expression *<300000* for the criteria of list price.) Display the results, and then sort the results by ascending list price.

p. Save and close the table. Exit Access.

q. Submit the database based on your instructor's directions.

2 National Conference

The Association of Higher Education will host its National Conference on your campus next year. To facilitate the conference, the information technology department has replaced last year's Excel spreadsheets with an Access database containing information on the rooms, speakers, and sessions. Your assignment is to create a room itinerary that will list all of the sessions, dates, and times for each room. The list will be posted on the door of each room for the duration of the conference. Refer to Figure 1.33 as you complete this exercise.

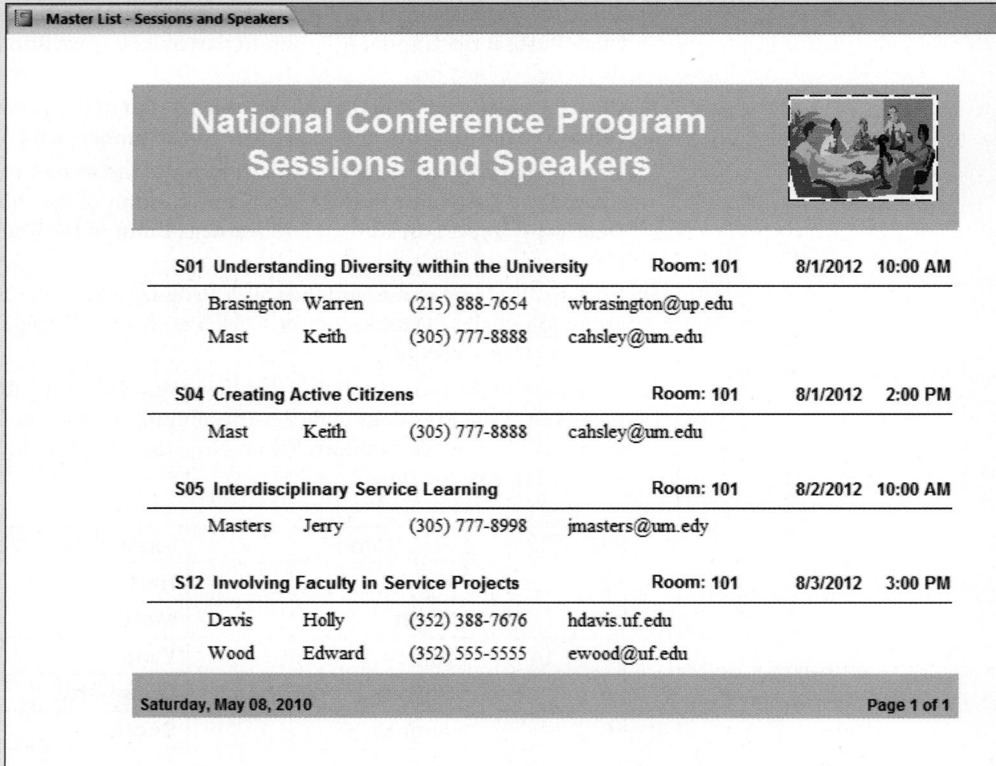

Master List - Sessions and Speakers
National Conference Program
Sessions and Speakers
S01 Understanding Diversity within the University Room: 101 8/1/2012 10:00 AM
Brasington Warren (215) 888-7654 wbrasington@up.edu
Mast Keith (305) 777-8888 cahsley@um.edu
S04 Creating Active Citizens Room: 101 8/1/2012 2:00 PM
Mast Keith (305) 777-8888 cahsley@um.edu
S05 Interdisciplinary Service Learning Room: 101 8/2/2012 10:00 AM
Masters Jerry (305) 777-8998 jmasters@um.edy
S12 Involving Faculty in Service Projects Room: 101 8/3/2012 3:00 PM
Davis Holly (352) 388-7676 hdavis.uf.edu
Wood Edward (352) 555-5555 ewood@uf.edu
Saturday, May 08, 2010
Page 1 of 1

FIGURE 1.33 Sessions and Speakers Report—Room 101 ➤

a. Open the *a01m2natconf* file, and then save the database as **a01m2natconf_LastnameFirstname**.
b. Open the Relationships window.
c. Review the objects in the database to see if any of the existing objects will provide the room itinerary information described above.

d. Open the SessionSpeaker table. Scroll to the first blank record at the bottom of the table, and then enter a new record using SpeakerID: **99** and SessionID: **09**. (Note: speaker 99 does not exist.) How does Access respond? Press **Esc**. Close the SessionSpeaker table. In the Relationships window, right-click on the join line between the Speakers table and SessionSpeaker table, and then click **Delete**. Click **Yes**, and then close the Relationships window. Open the SessionSpeaker table, and then enter the same record again. How does Access respond this time? Close the SessionSpeaker table. Open the Speakers table. Find and replace *YourName* with your name. Close the Speakers table.
e. Open the Speaker – Session Query query, and then apply a filter to identify the sessions where you or Holly Davis are the speakers. Use **Filter by Form** and the **Or tab**.
f. Sort the filtered results in ascending order by the RoomID field.
g. Save and close the query.
h. Open the Master List – Sessions and Speakers report in Report view.
i. Apply a filter that limits the report to sessions in Room 101 only.
j. Click the **File tab**, click **Print**, and then click **Print Preview**.
k. Click **Close Print Preview** in the Close Preview group.
l. Close the report.
m. Compact and repair the database.
n. Back up the database. Use the default backup file name.
o. Exit Access (and save the relationships layout when asked).
p. Submit based on your instructor's directions.

CAPSTONE EXERCISE

Your boss expressed a concern about the accuracy of the inventory reports in the bookstore. He needs you to open the inventory database, make modifications to some records, and determine if the changes you make carry through to the other objects in the database. You will make changes to a form and then verify those changes in a table, a query, and a report. When you have verified that the changes update automatically, you will compact and repair the database and make a backup of it.

Database File Setup

You will open an original database file, and then save the database with a new name. Use the new database to replace an existing employee's name with your name, examine the table relationships, and then complete the remainder of this exercise.

a. Open the *a01c1books* file, and then save the database as **a01c1books_LastnameFirstname**.

b. Open the Maintain Authors form.

c. Navigate to Record 7, and then replace *YourName* with your name.

d. Add a new Title: **Technology in Action**. The ISBN is **0-13-148905-4**, the PubID is **PH**, the PublDate is **2006**, the Price is **$89.95** (just type 89.95, no $), and StockAmt is **95** units.

e. Move to any other record to save the new record. The pencil that appeared in the record selector box on the left while you were typing has now disappeared. Close the form.

f. Open the Maintain Authors form again, and then navigate to Record 7. The changes are there because Access works from storage, not memory. Close the form.

Sort a Query and Apply a Filter by Selection

You need to reorder a detail query so that the results are sorted alphabetically by the publisher name.

a. Open the Publishers, Books, and Authors query.

b. Click in any record in the PubName column, and then sort the field in ascending order.

c. Check to make sure that three books list you as the author.

d. Click your name in the Author's Last Name field, and then filter the records to show only your books.

e. Close the query and save the changes.

View a Report

You need to examine the *Publishers, Books, and Authors* report to determine if the changes you made in the Maintain Authors form appear in the report.

a. Open the Publishers, Books, and Authors report.

b. Check to make sure that the report shows three books listing you as the author.

c. Check the layout of the report in Print Preview.

d. Close the report.

Filter a Table

You need to examine the Books table to determine if the changes you made in the Maintain Authors form carried through to the related table. You also will filter the table to display books published after 2006 with fewer than 100 copies in inventory.

a. Open the Books table.

b. Create a filter that will identify all books published after 2006 with fewer than 100 items in stock.

c. Apply the filter.

d. Preview the filtered table.

e. Close the table and save the changes.

Compact and Repair a Database, Back Up a Database

Now that you are satisfied that any changes made to a form or query carry through to the table, you are ready to compact, repair, and back up your file.

a. Compact and repair your database.

b. Create a backup copy of your database, accept the default file name, and save it.

c. Exit Access.

d. Submit based on your instructor's directions.

BEYOND THE CLASSROOM

Creating a New Database

GENERAL CASE 

Create a new database, name the file **a01b1students_LastnameFirstname**, and then save the database in your Student Data Files folder. Create a new Students table in Design view that will hold the information about all the students in your class. Add an ID field with data type AutoNumber, and then add the typical contact fields such as FirstName, LastName, Street, City, Major etc. All fields (except ID) should have the Text data type. Save the table, and then switch to Datasheet view. Enter the information about at least ten students using the real first and last names; enter real or fictitious data for the rest of the information. Create a filter to display students with a certain major. Compact, repair, and back up your database, and then exit Access. Submit the database based on your instructor's directions.

Filtering a Report

RESEARCH CASE 

Open the *a01b2nwind* file, and then save the database as a01b2nwind_LastnameFirstname. Open the Employees table and replace *YourName* with your first and last names. Before you can filter the Revenue report, you need to update the criterion in the underlying query to match the dates in the database. Right-click the Revenue query in the Navigation Pane, and then click Design View in the shortcut list. Scroll to the right until you see *Between #1/1/2007# And #3/31/2007#* in the OrderDate criteria row. Change the criterion to Between #1/1/2012# And #3/31/2012#. Save and close the query. Open the Revenue report. Use the tools that you have learned in this chapter to filter the report for only your sales of Confections. Close the report. Compact, repair, and back up your database, and then exit Access.

Error Setting Relationship

DISASTER RECOVERY 

You are having trouble with an Access 2010 database. One of the employees accidentally changed the CustomerID of Lugo Computer Sales. This change caused a problem in one of the relationships. Open the *a01b3recover* file, and then save the database as **a01b3recover_LastnameFirstname**. Open the Customers and Orders tables, and examine the data. Change the Lugo Computer Sales CustomerID in the Customers table back to the original number. Reset the relationship between the Customers table and the Orders table. Compact, repair, and back up your database, and then exit Access. Submit the database based on your instructor's directions.

ACCESS

2 RELATIONAL DATABASES AND QUERIES

Designing Databases and Extracting Data

CASE STUDY | Bank Auditor Uncovers Mishandled Funds

Watch the
Set-up Video
for this Case Study!

During a year-end review, a bank auditor uncovers mishandled funds at Commonwealth Federal Bank, in Wilmington, Delaware. In order to analyze the data in more detail, the auditor asks you to create an Access database so he can enter the compromised accounts, the associated customers, and the involved employees. Once the new database is created and all the data is entered, you will help the auditor answer questions by creating and running queries.

As you begin, you realize that some of the data is contained in Excel spreadsheets. After discussing this with the auditor, you decide importing this data directly into the new database would be best. Importing from Excel into Access is commonplace and should work well. Importing will also help avoid errors that are associated with data entry. Once the Excel data has been imported, you will use queries to determine which data does not belong in the database. Unaffected records will be deleted.

This chapter introduces the Bank database case study to present the basic principles of table and query design. You will use tables and forms to input data, and you will create queries and reports to extract information from the database in a useful and organized way. The value of that information depends entirely on the quality of the underlying data—the tables.

OBJECTIVES AFTER YOU READ THIS CHAPTER, YOU WILL BE ABLE TO:

1. Design data ***p.620***
2. Create tables ***p.624***
3. Understand table relationships ***p.636***
4. Share data with Excel ***p.638***
5. Establish table relationships ***p.642***
6. Create a single-table query ***p.653***
7. Specify criteria for different data types ***p.656***
8. Copy and run a query ***p.659***
9. Use the Query Wizard ***p.659***
10. Create a multi-table query ***p.665***
11. Modify a multi-table query ***p.666***

Table Design, Properties, Views, and Wizards

Good database design begins with the tables. Tables provide the framework for all of the activities you perform in a database. If the framework is poorly designed, the rest of the database will be poorly designed as well. Whether you are experienced in designing tables or just learning how, the process should not be done haphazardly. You should follow a systematic approach when creating tables for a database. This process will take practice; however, over time you will begin to see the patterns and eventually see the similarities among all databases.

In this section, you will learn the principles of table design and the other essential guidelines used when creating tables. After developing and testing the table design on paper, you will implement that design in Access. The first step is to list all the tables you need for the database and then list all the fields in each table. When you create the tables in Access, you will refine them further by changing the properties of various fields. You will also be introduced to the concept of data validation. You want to make sure the data entered into the database is valid for the field and valid for the organization. Allowing invalid data into the tables will only cause problems later.

Designing Data

Most likely you have a bank account and you know that your bank or credit union maintains data about you. Your bank has your name, address, phone number, and Social Security number. It also knows what accounts you have (checking, savings, money market), if you have a credit card with that bank, and what its balance is. Additionally, your bank keeps information about its branches. If you think about the data your bank maintains, you could make a list of the categories of data needed to store that information. These categories for the bank—customers, accounts, branches—become the tables in the bank's database. Previously, we defined a table as a collection of records. In this chapter, we expand on the definition—a ***table*** is a storage location in a database that holds related information. A table consists of records, and each record is made up of a number of fields. A bank's customer list is an example of a table: It contains a record for each bank customer, and each customer's details are contained in fields such as first and last name, street, city, state, and zip code. Figure 2.1 shows a customer table and two other tables found in a sample bank database.

A **table** is a storage location in a database that holds related information. A table consists of records, and each record is made up of a number of fields.

During the design process, it will help if you consider the output required for the database. Looking at the output will help determine the tables and fields needed to produce that output. Think of the specific fields you need in each table; list the fields under the correct table and assign each field a data type (such as text, number, or date) as well as its size (length) or format. The order of the fields within the table and the specific field names are not significant. What is important is that the tables contain all necessary fields so that the system can produce the required information.

Customers Table
o CustomerID
o FirstName
o LastName
o Street
o City
o State
o Zip
o Phone

Accounts Table
o AccountID
o CustomerID
o BranchID
o OpenDate

Branch Table
o BranchID
o Manager
o Location
o StartDate

FIGURE 2.1 Tables and Fields in a Sample Bank Database ➤

Figure 2.1 shows the tables and fields needed in a sample bank database. After the tables have been identified, add the necessary fields using these six guidelines:

1. Include the necessary data.
2. Design for now and the future.
3. Store data in its smallest parts.
4. Add calculated fields to a table.
5. Design to accommodate date arithmetic.
6. Link tables using common fields.

Include the Necessary Data

...ask yourself what information will be expected from the database, and then determine the data required to produce that information.

A good way to determine what data is necessary in the tables is to create a rough draft of the reports you will need and then to design tables that contain the fields necessary to create those reports. In other words, ask yourself what information will be expected from the system, and then determine the data required to produce that information. Consider, for example, the tables and fields in Figure 2.1. Is there required information that could not be generated from those tables?

- You can determine which branch a customer uses.
- You cannot, however, generate the monthly bank statement. In order to generate a customer bank statement (showing all deposits and withdrawals for the month), you would need to add an additional table—the Account Activity table.
- You can determine who manages a particular branch and which accounts are located there.
- You can determine how long a customer has banked with the branch because the date he or she opened the account is stored in the Accounts table.

If you discover a missing field, you can insert a row anywhere in the appropriate table and add the missing field. The databases found in a real bank are more complex, with more tables and more fields; however, the concepts illustrated here apply to both our sample bank database and to real bank databases.

Design for Now and the Future

As the data requirements of an organization evolve over time, the information systems that hold the data must change as well. When designing a database, try to anticipate the future needs of the system, and then build in the flexibility to satisfy those demands. For example, when you add a text field, make sure that the number of characters allocated is sufficient to accommodate future expansion. On the other hand, if you include all the possible fields that anyone might ever need, you could drive up the cost of the database. Each additional field can increase the cost of the database, since it will require additional employee time to enter and maintain the data. The additional fields will also require more storage space, which you will need to calculate, especially when working with larger databases. Good database design must balance the data collection needs of the company with the cost associated with collection and storage.

Good database design must balance the data collection needs of the company with the cost associated with collection and storage.

Suppose you are designing a database for a college. You would need to store each student's name, address, and phone number. You will need to store multiple phone numbers for most students—a cell phone number, a work number, and an emergency number. As a database designer, you will need to design the tables to accommodate multiple entries for similar data.

Store Data in Its Smallest Parts

The table design in Figure 2.1 divides a customer's name into two fields (Firstname and Lastname) to reference each field individually. You might think it easier to use a single field consisting of both the first and last name, but that approach is too limiting. Consider a list of customers stored as a single field:

- Sue Grater
- Rick Grater
- Nancy Gallagher
- Harry Weigner
- Barb Shank
- Pete Shank

The first problem in this approach is the lack of flexibility: You could not easily create a salutation for a letter of the form *Dear Sue* or *Dear Ms. Gallagher* because the first and last names are not accessible individually.

A second difficulty is that the list of customers cannot be easily displayed in alphabetical order by last name because the last name begins in the middle of the field. The names could easily be alphabetized by first name because the first name is at the beginning of the field. However, the most common way to sort names is by the last name, which can be done more efficiently if the last name is stored as a separate field.

Think of how an address might be used. The city, state, and postal code should always be stored as separate fields. Any type of mass mailing requires you to sort on postal codes to take advantage of bulk mail. Other applications may require you to select records from a particular state or postal code, which can be done more efficiently if you store the data as separate fields. Often database users enter the postal code, and the database automatically retrieves the city and state information. You may need to direct a mailing only to a neighborhood or to a single street. The guideline is simple: Store data in its smallest parts.

Add Calculated Fields to a Table

A **calculated field** produces a value from an expression or function that references one or more existing fields.

A ***calculated field*** produces a value from an expression or function that references one or more existing fields. Access 2010 enables you to store calculated fields in a table using the calculated data type. An example of a calculated field can be found in the bank database. Suppose the bank pays its customers 1.0% interest on the principal each month. A calculated field, such as Monthly Interest, could store the expression Principal × .01. The interest amount would then appear on the customer's monthly bank statement.

Previous versions of Access did not have the option of adding a calculated field to a table. Calculated fields were not available because they do not adhere to conventional database design principles. Database design principles avoid storing data that can be derived from other data. The Monthly Interest field mentioned above can be derived from the product of Principal × .01; therefore, you would not need to store the Monthly Interest value.

The new calculated field* can be very useful in certain circumstances, like a Monthly Interest field. Storing calculated data in a table enables you to add the data easily to queries, forms, and reports without the trouble of an additional calculation. Storing calculated data in a table may increase the size of the database slightly, but the benefits may outweigh this drawback. In the chapters ahead, you will examine calculations and calculated fields in greater detail. You will learn when to add calculated fields to a table and when to avoid them.

Design to Accommodate Date Arithmetic

Calculated fields are frequently created with numeric data, as the Monthly Interest field example above illustrates. You can also create calculated fields using date/time data. If you want to store the length of time a customer has been a customer, you would first create a field to hold the start date for each customer. Next, you would create a calculated field that contains an expression that subtracts the start date from today's date. The resulting calculation would store the number of days each customer has been a customer. Divide the results by 365 to convert days to years.

This same concept applies to bank accounts; a bank is likely to store the Open Date for each account in the Accounts table, as shown in Figure 2.1. Using this date, you can subtract the open date from today's date and calculate the number of days the account has been open. (Again, divide the results by 365 to convert to years.) If you open the Accounts table at least one day later, the results of the calculated field will be different.

A person's age is another example of a calculated field using date arithmetic—date of birth is subtracted from today's date and the results are divided by 365. It might seem easier to store a person's age rather than the birth date to avoid the calculation. But that would be a mistake because age changes over time and would need to be updated each time age changes. Storing the date of birth is much better since the data remains ***constant***. You can use ***date arithmetic*** to subtract one date from another to find out the number of days, months, or years that have lapsed between them. You can also add or subtract a constant from a date.

A **constant** is an unchanging value, like a birth date.

Date arithmetic is the process of subtracting one date from another, or adding or subtracting a constant from a date.

Link Tables Using Common Fields

As you create the tables and fields for the database, keep in mind that the tables will be joined in relationships using common fields. Draw a line between common fields to indicate the joins, as shown in Figure 2.2. These join lines will be created in Access when you learn to create table relationships later in the chapter. For now, you should name the common fields the same and make sure they have the same data type. For example, CustomerID in the Customers table will join to the CustomerID field in the Accounts table. CustomerID must have the same data type (in this case number/long integer) in both tables; otherwise, the join line will not be allowed.

Data redundancy is the unnecessary storing of duplicate data in two or more tables.

Avoid ***data redundancy***, which is the unnecessary storing of duplicate data in two or more tables. You should avoid duplicate information in multiple tables in a database, because errors may result. Suppose the customer address data was stored in both the

*If you add a calculated field to a table in Access 2010, you will not be able to open the table using Access 2007.

Customers and Accounts tables. If a customer moved to a new address, a possible outcome would be that the address would be updated in only one of the two tables. The result would be unreliable data. Depending on which table served as the source for the output, either the new or the old address might be given to the person requesting the information. Storing the address in only one table is more reliable.

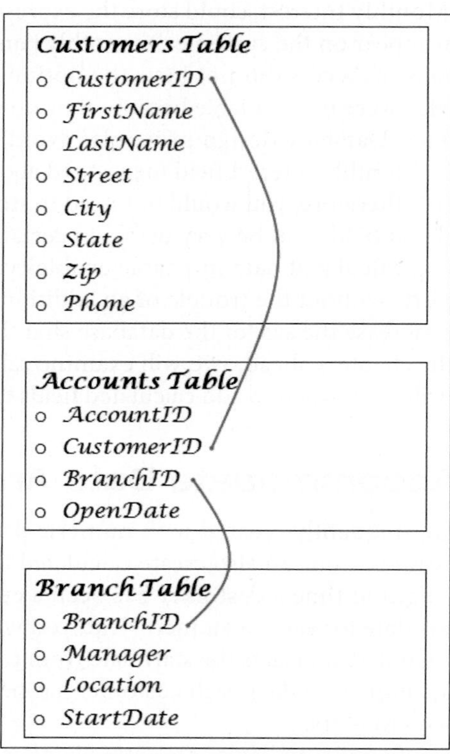

FIGURE 2.2 Create Relationships Using Common Fields ➤

Creating Tables

Before you can begin creating your tables, you must first create a new blank database and save it to a specific storage location. If you are creating tables in an existing database, you open the existing database and then create new tables or modify existing ones.

Access provides several ways to create a table. You can create a table by creating the fields in Design view (as shown in Figure 2.3) or by entering table data into a new row in Datasheet view, or you can import data from another database or application such as Excel. Regardless of how a table is first created, you can always modify it later to include a new field or to change an existing field.

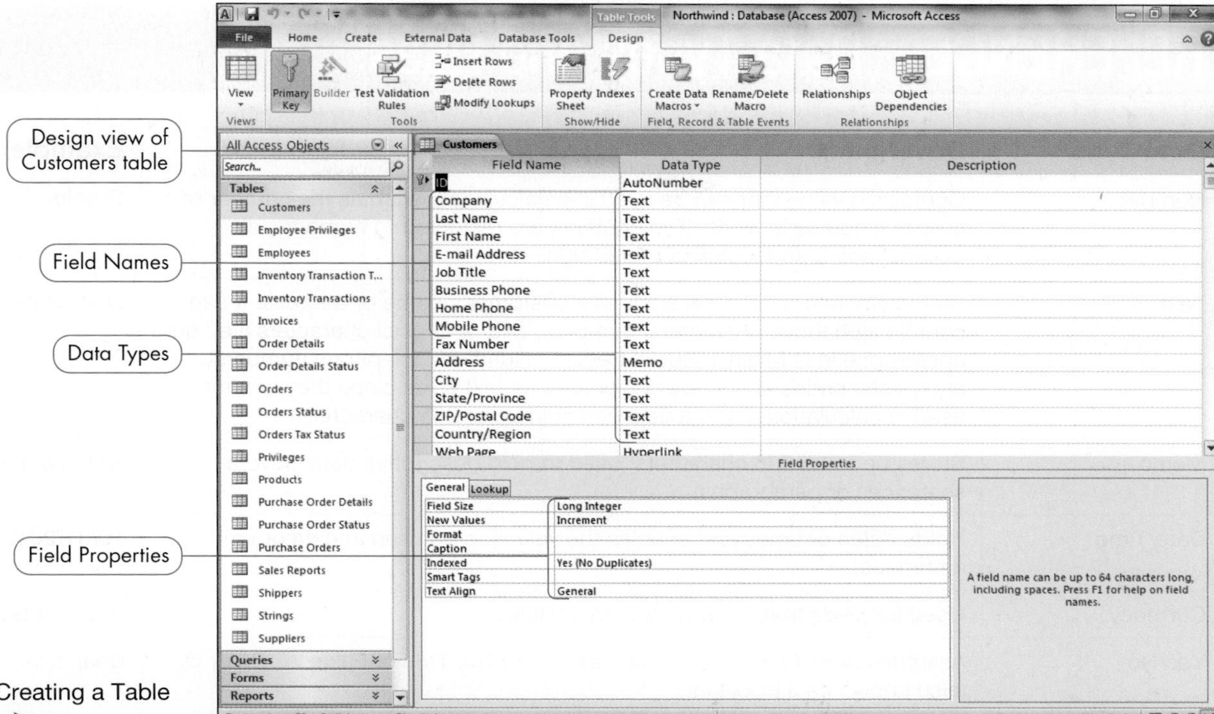

FIGURE 2.3 Creating a Table in Design View ➤

CamelCase notation uses no spaces in multi-word field names, but uses uppercase letters to distinguish the first letter of each new word.

The **data type** determines the type of data that can be entered and the operations that can be performed on that data.

Each field in a table has a field name to identify the data that it holds. The field name should be descriptive of the data and can be up to 64 characters in length, including letters, numbers, and spaces. Database developers use ***CamelCase notation*** for field names, object names, and filenames. Instead of spaces in multi-word field names, use uppercase letters to distinguish the first letter of each new word, for example, ProductCost or LastName. It is best to avoid spaces in field names, since spaces can cause problems when creating the other objects based on tables—such as queries, forms, and reports.

Every field also has a ***data type*** that determines the type of data that can be entered and the operations that can be performed on that data. Access recognizes 10 data types.

Establish a Primary Key

As you learned earlier, the primary key is the field (or combination of fields) that uniquely identifies each record in a table. Access does not require that each table have a primary key. However, good database design usually includes a primary key in each table. You should select unique and infrequently changing data for the primary key. For example, a complete address (street, city, state, and postal code) may be unique but would not make a good primary key because it is subject to change when someone moves.

The **AutoNumber** data type is a number that automatically increments each time a record is added.

You probably would not use a person's name as the primary key, because several people could have the same name. A customer's account number, on the other hand, is unique and is a frequent choice for the primary key, as in the Customers table in this chapter. The primary key can be easily identified in many tables; for example, a PartNumber in a parts table, the ISBN in the book database of a bookstore, or a Student ID that uniquely identifies a student. When no primary key occurs naturally, you can create a primary key field with the AutoNumber data type. The ***AutoNumber*** data type is a number that automatically increments each time a record is added.

REFERENCE Data Types and Uses

Data Type	Description	Example
Number	Contains a value that can be used in a calculation, such as the number of credits a course is worth. The contents are restricted to numbers, a decimal point, and a plus or minus sign.	Credits
Text	Stores alphanumeric data, such as a customer's name or address. It can contain alphabetic characters, numbers, and/or special characters (i.e., an apostrophe in O'Malley). Social Security Numbers, telephone numbers, and postal codes should be designated as text fields since they are not used in calculations. A text field can hold up to 255 characters.	Last name
Memo	Stores up to 65,536 characters; used to hold descriptive data (several sentences or paragraphs).	Notes or comments
Date/Time	Holds dates or times and enables the values to be used in date or time arithmetic.	10/31/2012
Currency	Used for fields that contain monetary values.	Account balance
Yes/No	Assumes one of two values, such as Yes or No, True or False, or On or Off (also known as a Boolean).	Dean's list
OLE	Contains an object created by another application. OLE objects include spreadsheets, pictures, sounds, or graphics.	One photo
AutoNumber	A special data type used to assign the next consecutive number each time you add a record. The value of an AutoNumber field is unique for each record in the file.	Customer ID
Hyperlink	Stores a Web address (URL) or the path to a folder or file. Hyperlink fields can be clicked to retrieve a Web page or to launch a file stored locally.	http://www.keithmast.com
Attachment	Used to store multiple images, spreadsheet files, Word documents, and other types of supported files.	An Excel workbook; a photo
Calculated	The results of an expression that references one or more existing fields.	[IntRate] + 0.25

In Figure 2.4, the book's ISBN is the natural primary key for the book table because no two book titles can have the same ISBN. This field uniquely identifies the records in the table. Figure 2.5 depicts the Speakers table, where no unique field can be identified from the data. When this happens, you can add the SpeakerID field with an AutoNumber data type. Access will automatically number each speaker record sequentially with a unique ID as each record is added.

ISBN provides a unique identifier

AuthorCode	Title	ISBN	PubID	PublDate	Price	StockAmt
15	Chasing the Dime	0-316-15391-5	LBC	2002	$51.75	400
13	Blackhills Farm	0-275-41199-7	KN	2002	$18.87	528
13	Blood and Gold	0-679-45449-7	KN	2001	$18.87	640
11	Reaching for Glory	0-684-80408-5	SS	2001	$24.00	480
14	From a Buick 8	0-743-21137-5	SS	2002	$16.80	368
15	City of Bones	0-316-15405-9	LBC	2002	$20.76	394
16	Follow the Stars Home	0-553-58102-3	BB	2000	$6.99	496
14	Hearts in Atlantis	0-684-85351-5	SS	1999	$28.00	528
12	Personality Injuries	0-742095692-X	FSG	1999	$27.00	403
15	Darkness More than Midnight	0-316-15407-5	LBC	2001	$20.76	432
13	Interview with the Vampire	0-394-49821-6	KN	1976	$19.57	371
16	True Blue	0-553-38398-0	BB	2002	$7.50	492

FIGURE 2.4 Books Table with a Natural Primary Key ➤

SpeakerID (AutoNumber data type) is the primary key

Next record will be assigned SpeakerID 17

Speakers

SpeakerID	First Name	Last Name	Address	City	Sta	Zip Co	Phone Number	Email
1	YourName	YourName	10000 SW 59 Court	Miami	FL	33146	(305) 777-8888	cahsley@um.edu
2	Warren	Brasington	9470 SW 25 Street	Philadelphia	PA	19104	(215) 888-7654	wbrasington@up.edu
3	James	Shindell	14088 Malaga Avenue	Miami	FL	33146	(305) 773-4343	jshindell@um.edu
4	Edward	Wood	400 Roderigo Avenue	Gainesville	FL	32611	(352) 555-5555	ewood@uf.edu
5	Kristine	Park	9290 NW 59 Steet	Athens	GA	30602	(706) 777-1111	kpark@ug.edu
6	William	Williamson	108 Los Pinos Place	Tuscaloosa	AL	35487	(205) 888-4554	wwilliamson@ua.edu
7	Holly	Davis	8009 Riviera Drive	Gainesville	FL	32611	(352) 388-7676	hdavis.uf.edu
8	David	Tannen	50 Main Street	Philadelphia	PA	19104	(215) 777-2211	dtannen@up.edu
9	Jeffrey	Jacobsen	490 Bell Drive	Athens	GA	30602	(706) 388-9999	jjacobsen@ug.edu
10	Jerry	Masters	2000 Main Highway	Miami	FL	33146	(305) 777-8998	jmasters@um.edy
11	Kevin	Kline	2980 SW 89 Street	Gainesville	FL	32611	(352) 877-8900	kkline@uf.edu
12	Jessica	Withers	110 Center Highway	Athens	GA	30602	(706) 893-8872	jwithers@ug.edu
13	Betsy	Allman	2987 SW 14 Avenue	Philadelphia	PA	19104	(215) 558-7748	ballman@up.edu
14	Mary	Miller	1008 West Marine Road	Miami	FL	33146	(305) 877-4993	mmiller@um.edu
15	Nancy	Vance	1878 W. 6 Street	Gainesville	FL	32611	(352) 885-4330	nvance@uf.edu
16	George	Jensen	42-15 81 Street	Elmhurst	NY	11373	(718) 555-6666	gjensen@school.edu
(New)								

FIGURE 2.5 Speakers Table with an AutoNumber Primary Key ➤

Explore Foreign Key

A foreign key, as defined earlier, is a field in one table that is also the primary key of another table. The CustomerID is the primary key in the Customers table. It serves to uniquely identify each customer. It also appears as a foreign key in a related table. For example, the Accounts table contains the CustomerID field to establish which customer owns the account. A CustomerID can appear only once in the Customers table, but it may appear multiple times in the Accounts table (when viewed in Datasheet view) since one customer may own multiple accounts (checking, money market, home equity).

If you were asked to create an Access database for the speakers at a national conference, you would create a database with the tables Speakers and SessionSpeaker. You would add a primary key field to the Speakers table (SpeakerID) along with the speaker's First Name and Last Name; you would add two fields to the SessionSpeaker table (SpeakerID and SessionID). The SpeakerID in the SessionSpeaker table enables you to join the two tables in a relationship. The SpeakerID field in the SessionSpeaker table is an example of a foreign key. Figure 2.6 shows portions of the Speakers and SessionSpeaker tables.

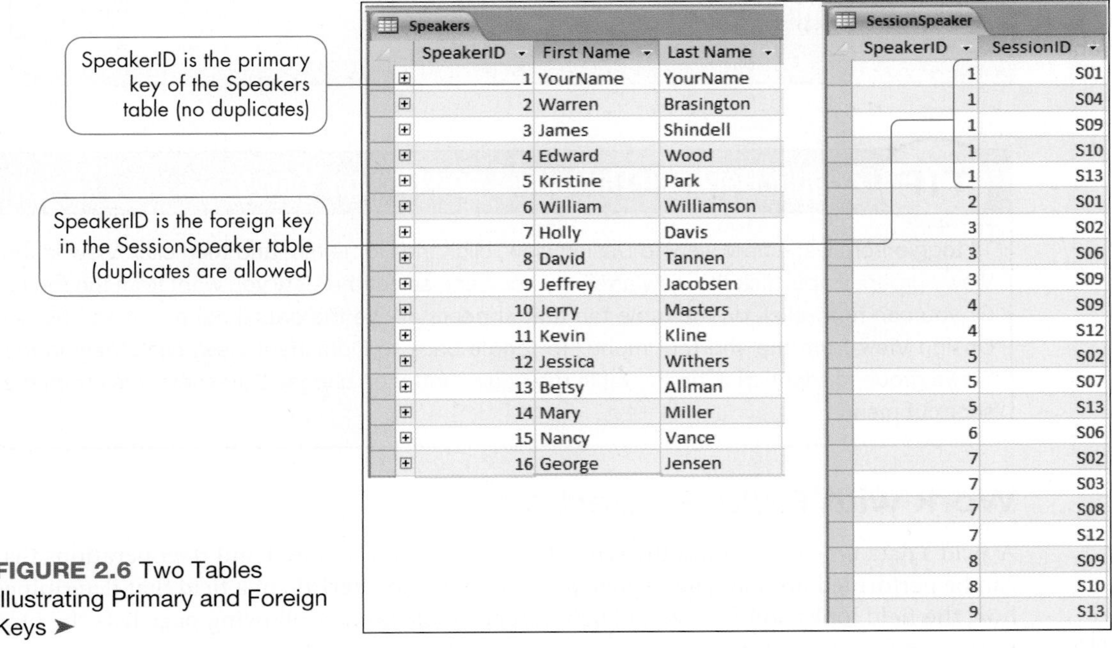
SpeakerID is the primary key of the Speakers table (no duplicates)
SpeakerID is the foreign key in the SessionSpeaker table (duplicates are allowed)

Speakers

SpeakerID	First Name	Last Name
1	YourName	YourName
2	Warren	Brasington
3	James	Shindell
4	Edward	Wood
5	Kristine	Park
6	William	Williamson
7	Holly	Davis
8	David	Tannen
9	Jeffrey	Jacobsen
10	Jerry	Masters
11	Kevin	Kline
12	Jessica	Withers
13	Betsy	Allman
14	Mary	Miller
15	Nancy	Vance
16	George	Jensen

SessionSpeaker

SpeakerID	SessionID
1	S01
1	S04
1	S09
1	S10
1	S13
2	S01
3	S02
3	S06
3	S09
4	S09
4	S12
5	S02
5	S07
5	S13
6	S06
7	S02
7	S03
7	S08
7	S12
8	S09
8	S10
9	S13

FIGURE 2.6 Two Tables Illustrating Primary and Foreign Keys ➤

Use Table Views

As defined earlier, users can work in Datasheet view to add, edit, and delete records. The Datasheet view of an Access table resembles an Excel spreadsheet and displays data in a grid format—rows represent records, and columns represent fields. Datasheet view indicates the current record using a gold border; you can select a record by clicking the record selector on the left side of each record, as shown in Figure 2.7. Use the new blank record (marked with an asterisk) at the end of the table to add a new record. Design view is used to create and modify the table structure by adding and editing fields and by setting the field properties. PivotTable view and PivotChart view will be covered in a later chapter.

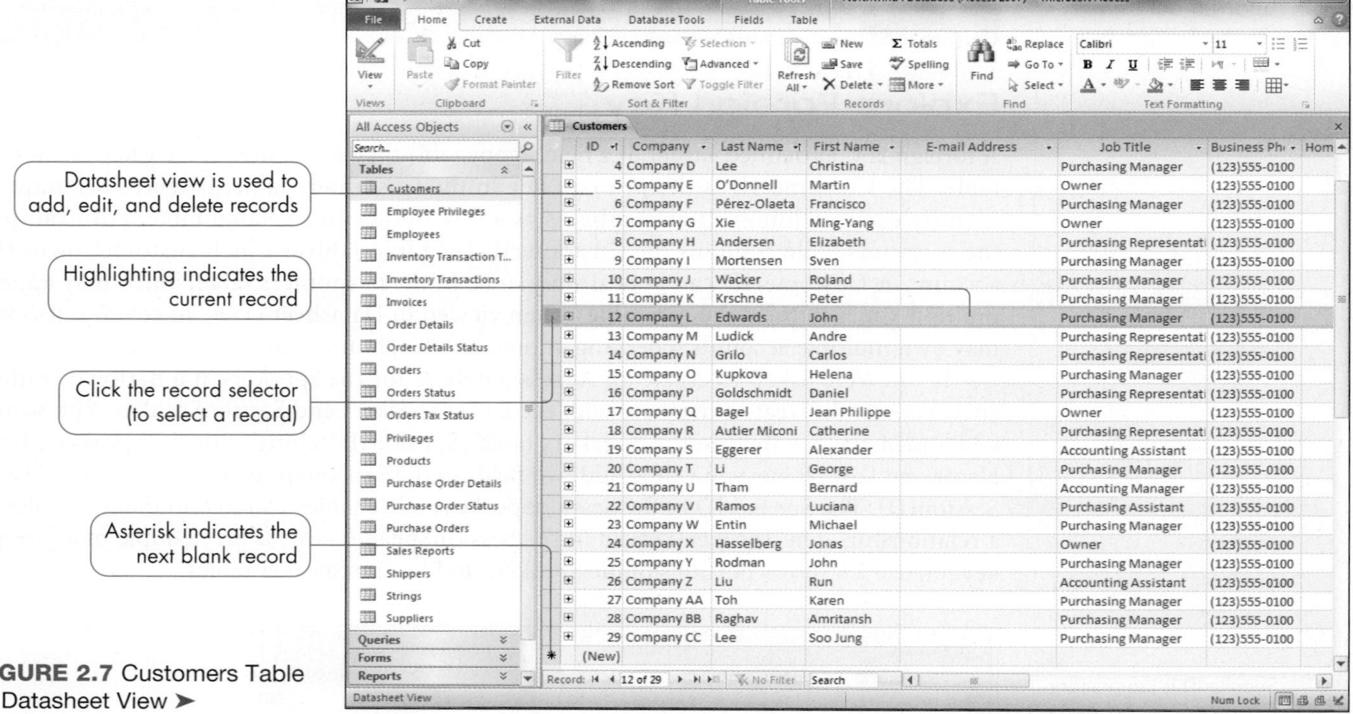

Datasheet view is used to add, edit, and delete records
Highlighting indicates the current record
Click the record selector (to select a record)
Asterisk indicates the next blank record

FIGURE 2.7 Customers Table in Datasheet View ➤

> **TIP** Toggle Between Datasheet and Design Views
>
> To toggle from Datasheet view to Design view, click the Home tab, and then click View in the Views group. If you click the view arrow by accident, select the view you want from the menu. Or you can right-click on the table tab that appears above the datasheet and then choose Design View from the shortcut menu. To toggle back to Datasheet view, click View in the Views group, or right-click on the table tab again, and then choose Datasheet View from the shortcut menu.

Work with Field Properties

A **field property** is a characteristic of a field that determines how the field looks and behaves.

A **text data type** can store either text or numerical characters.

A field's data type determines the type of data that can be entered and the operations that can be performed on that data. A ***field property*** is a characteristic of a field that determines how the field looks and behaves. (The reference table on the following page lists the field properties for a typical field.)

A field with a ***text data type*** can store either text or numerical characters. A text field can hold up to 255 characters; however, you can limit the characters by reducing the field size property. For example, you would limit the State field to only two characters since all

A **number data type** can store only numerical data.

A **caption property** is used to create a more readable label that appears in the top row in Datasheet view and in forms and reports.

A **validation rule** prevents invalid data from being entered into the field.

state abbreviations are two letters. A field with a ***number data type*** can store only numerical data. Set the Format field property to Integer to display the field contents as integers from –32768 to 32768. Set the Format field property to Long Integer for larger values.

You can use the ***caption property*** to create a more readable label that appears in the top row in Datasheet view and in forms and reports. For example, a field named ProductCostPerUnit could have the caption *Per Unit Product Cost*. The caption displays at the top of a table or query column in Datasheet view and when the field is used in a report or form. You must use the actual field name, ProductCostPerUnit, in any calculation.

Set the validation rule property to restrict data entry in a field to ensure the correct type of data is entered or that the data does not violate other enforced properties. The ***validation rule*** checks the data entered when the user exits the field. If the data entered violates the validation rule, an error message appears and prevents the invalid data from being entered into the field.

The field properties are set to default values according to the data type, but you can modify them if necessary. The property types are defined in the following Reference table.

In Hands-On Exercise 1, you will create a new database and enter data into a table. Then you will switch to the table's Design view to add additional fields and modify selected field properties of various fields within the table.

REFERENCE Access Table Property Types and Descriptions

Property Type	Description
Field Size	Determines the maximum characters of a text field or the format of a number field.
Format	Changes the way a field is displayed or printed, but does not affect the stored value.
Input Mask	Simplifies data entry by providing literal characters that are typed for every entry, such as hyphens in a Social Security Number or slashes in a date. It also imposes data validation by ensuring that data entered conforms to the mask.
Caption	This enables an alternate name to be displayed other than the field name; alternate names appear in datasheets, forms, and reports.
Default Value	This option automatically enters a predetermined value for a field each time a new record is added to the table. For example, if most of your customers live in Los Angeles, you might consider setting the default value for the City to Los Angeles to save data entry time.
Validation Rule	Requires the data entered to conform to the specified rule.
Validation Text	Specifies the error message that is displayed when the validation rule is violated.
Required	Indicates that a value for this field must be entered.
Allow Zero Length	Enables text or memo strings of zero length.
Indexed	Increases the efficiency of a search on the designated field.
Expression	Used for calculated fields only. Enter the expression you want Access to evaluate and store.
Result Type	Used for calculated fields only. Enter the format for the calculated field results.

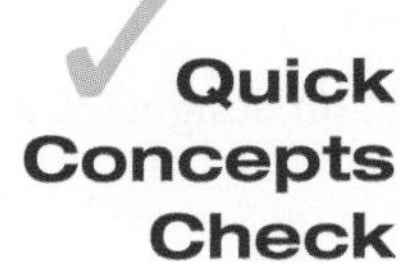

Quick Concepts Check

1. What is meant by "Design for now and the future" when designing database fields?
2. What is the difference between a primary key and a foreign key?
3. Describe the two table views and when to use each of them.
4. Field properties allow you to define how the data will look and behave. Explain.

HANDS-ON EXERCISES

1 Table Design, Properties, Views, and Wizards

Assisting the bank auditor at Commonwealth Federal Bank as he investigates the mishandled funds will be a great opportunity for you to showcase your Access skills. Be sure to check your work each step of the way since your work will come under substantial scrutiny. Do a good job with this Access project and more opportunities might come your way, along with a promotion.

Skills covered: Create a New Database • Create a Table by Entering Data • Change the Primary Key, Modify Field Properties, and Delete a Field • Modify Table Fields in Design View • Create a New Field in Design View • Switch Between the Table Design and the Table Datasheet Views

STEP 1 CREATE A NEW DATABASE

To start a new Access database project, you first need to create a new database. Use the Access interface to create a new file for the mishandled funds database. Refer to Figure 2.8 as you complete Step 1.

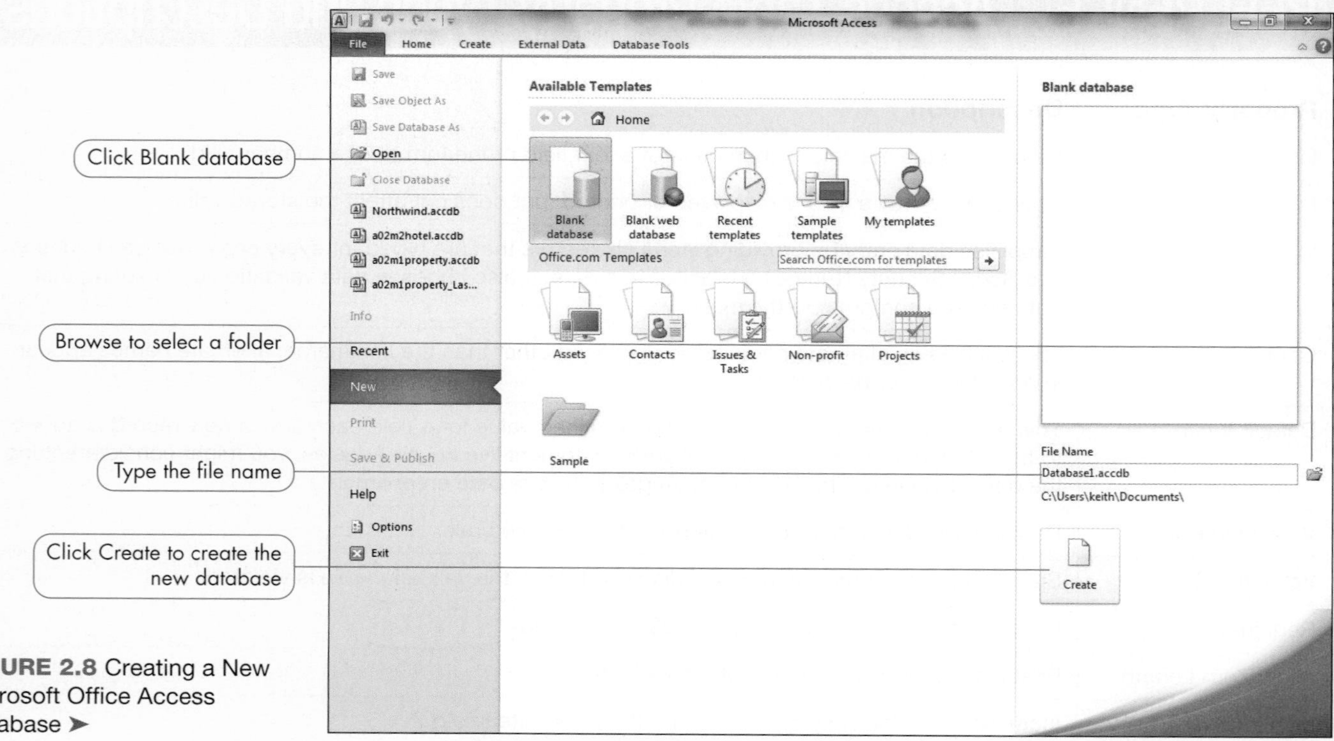

FIGURE 2.8 Creating a New Microsoft Office Access Database ➤

a. Start Microsoft Access.

   You will see the Backstage view with New selected by default.

b. Click **Blank database** in the Available Templates section of the Backstage view.

c. Type **a02h1bank_LastnameFirstname** into the **File Name box**.

d. Click **Browse**—the yellow folder icon—to find the folder location designated by your instructor, and then click **OK**.

e. Click **Create** to create the new database.

   Access will create the new database named *a02h1bank_LastnameFirstname*, and a new table will automatically appear in Datasheet view.

TROUBLESHOOTING: If you have a problem finding your file, use the Windows search tool to locate the file.

STEP 2 CREATE A TABLE BY ENTERING DATA

Create a new Branch table and enter the branch data as instructed. Only branches with suspicious data will be added. Refer to Figure 2.9 as you complete Step 2.

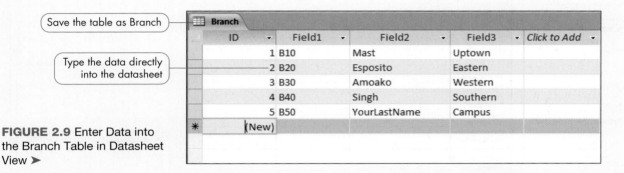

Save the table as Branch

Type the data directly into the datasheet

Branch

ID	Field1	Field2	Field3	Click to Add
1	B10	Mast	Uptown	
2	B20	Esposito	Eastern	
3	B30	Amoako	Western	
4	B40	Singh	Southern	
5	B50	YourLastName	Campus	
* (New)				

FIGURE 2.9 Enter Data into the Branch Table in Datasheet View ➤

a. Type **B10** in the second column, and then click **Click to Add**.

The column heading becomes Field1 and Click to Add now appears as the third column.

b. Type **Mast** in the third column, press **Tab**, and then type **Uptown** in the fourth column.

You can advance to the next field by pressing Tab or move to the previous field by pressing Shift+Tab.

c. Press **Tab** three times. Type **B20**, press **Tab**, type **Esposito**, press **Tab**, and then type **Eastern**.

d. Enter the additional data for the new table as shown in Figure 2.9. Replace *YourLastName* with your last name.

e. Click **Save** on the Quick Access Toolbar. Type **Branch** in the **Save As dialog box**, and then click **OK**.

Entering data provides an easy way to create the table initially. You can now modify the table in Design view as described in the next several steps.

STEP 3 CHANGE THE PRIMARY KEY, MODIFY FIELD PROPERTIES, AND DELETE A FIELD

It is common to modify tables even after data has been entered; however, pay attention to the messages from Access after you make a design change. In this example, you will be modifying the Branch table field names to match the auditor's requirements. Refer to Figure 2.10 as you complete Step 3.

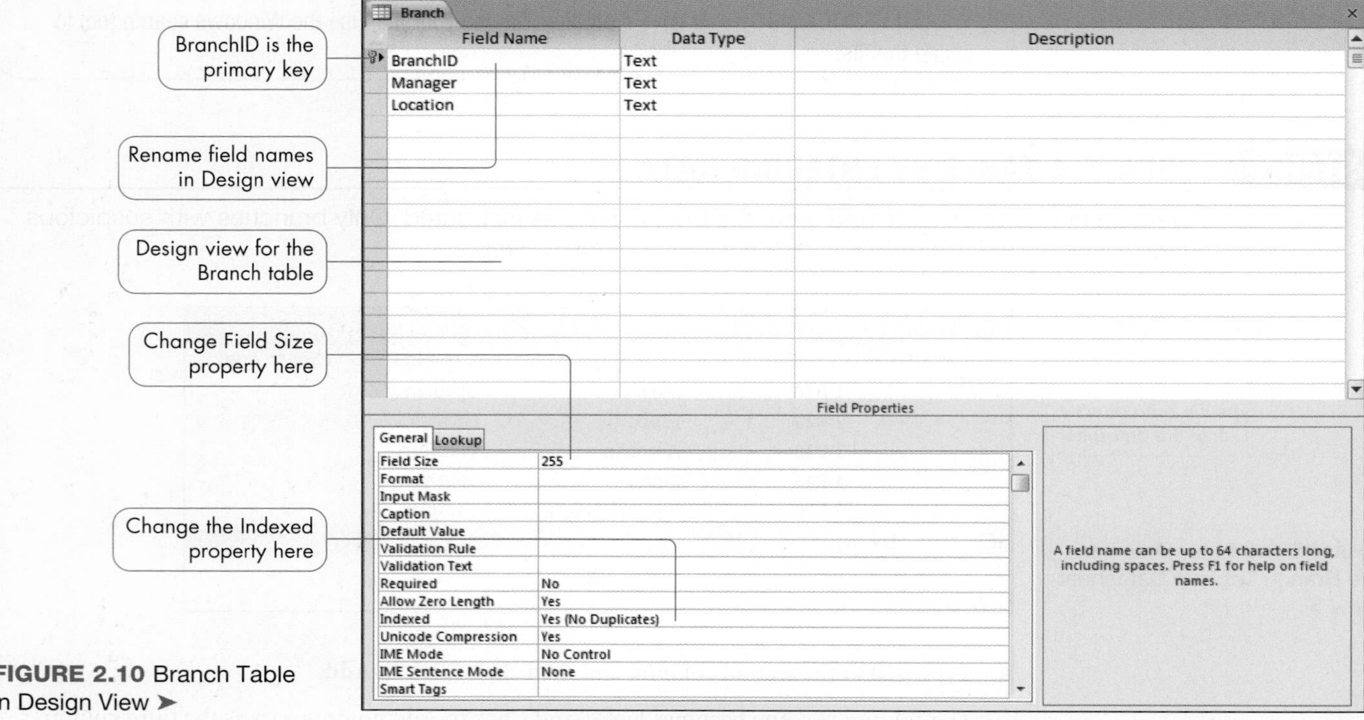

FIGURE 2.10 Branch Table in Design View ➤

a. Click **View** in the Views group to switch to the Design view of the Branch table.

   The fields are named ID, Field1, Field2, and Field3, because they are the default names given to the fields when you create the table in Datasheet view. These field names are not descriptive of the data, so you need to change Field1, Field2, and Field3 to BranchID, Manager, and Location, respectively. You will also delete the ID field.

b. Click the **ID field** to select it. Click **Delete Rows** in the Tools group. Click **Yes** to both warning messages.

   Access responds with a warning that you are about to permanently delete a field and a second warning that the field is the primary key. You delete the field since you will set a different field as the primary key.

c. Double-click the **Field1 field name** to select it, if necessary, and then type **BranchID**. Replace *Field2* with **Manager** and *Field3* with **Location**.

d. Click the **BranchID field.**

   The cell field name now has an orange border as shown in Figure 2.10.

e. Click **Primary Key** in the Tools group.

   You set BranchID as the primary key. The Indexed property in the *Field Properties* section at the bottom of the design window displays *Yes (No Duplicates).*

f. Click **Save** to save the table.

Shortcut Menu

You can right-click a row selector to display a shortcut menu to copy a field, set the primary key, and insert or delete rows. Use the shortcut menu to make these specific changes to the design of a table.

STEP 4 MODIFY TABLE FIELDS IN DESIGN VIEW

You need to modify the table design further to comply with the bank auditor's specifications. Be aware of messages from Access that indicate you may lose data. Refer to Figure 2.11 as you complete Step 4.

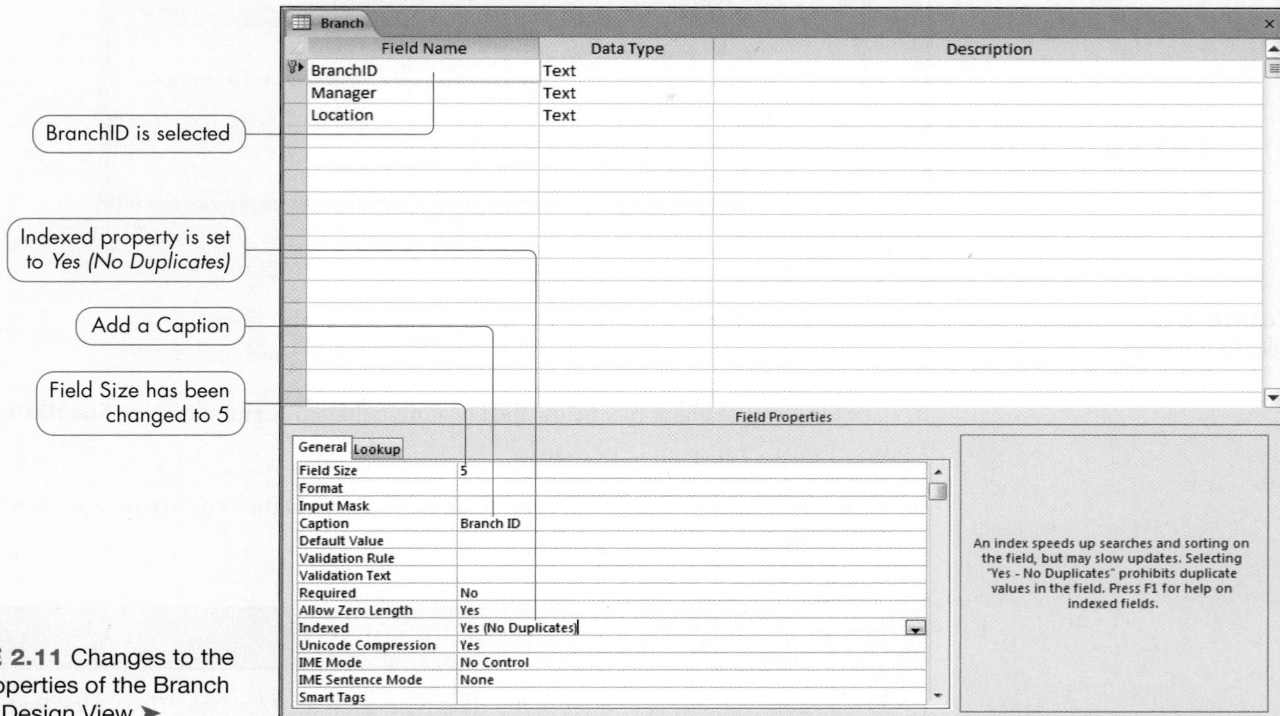

FIGURE 2.11 Changes to the Field Properties of the Branch Table in Design View ➤

a. Click the **BranchID field name** in the top section of the design window; modify the BranchID field properties in the bottom of the design window:

- Click in the **Field Size property**, and then change *255* to **5**.
- Click in the **Caption property**, and then type **Branch ID**. Make sure *Branch* and *ID* have a space between them.

  A caption provides a more descriptive field name. It will appear as the column heading in Datasheet view.
- Check the Indexed property; confirm it is *Yes (No Duplicates).*

b. Click the **Manager field name** at the top of the window; modify the following field properties:

- Change the **Field Size property** from *255* to **30**.
- Click in the **Caption property**, and then type **Manager's Name**.

c. Click the **Location field name**, and then modify the following field properties:

- Change the **Field Size property** from *255* to **30**.
- Click in the **Caption property**, and then type **Branch Location**.

STEP 5 CREATE A NEW FIELD IN DESIGN VIEW

You notify the auditor that a date field is missing in your new table. Modify the table and add the new field. The data can be entered at a later time. Refer to Figure 2.12 as you complete Step 5.

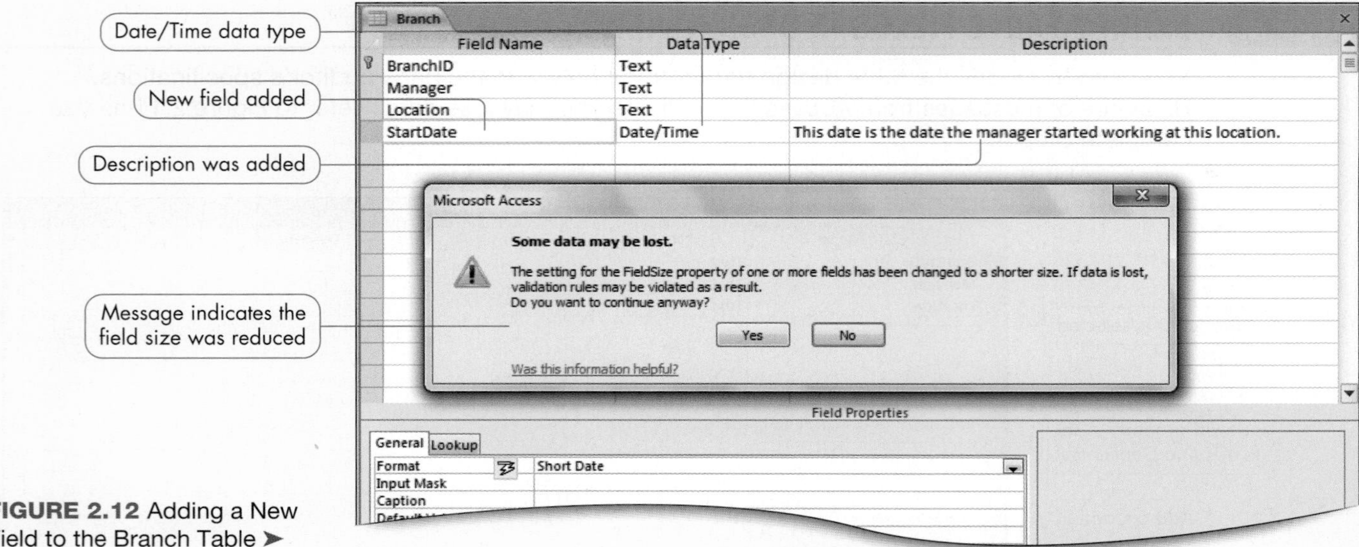

FIGURE 2.12 Adding a New Field to the Branch Table ➤

a. Click in the first blank row below the Location field name, and then type **StartDate**.

   You added a new field to the table.

b. Press **Tab** to move to the Data Type column. Click the **Data Type arrow**, and then select **Date/Time**.

> **TIP** Keyboard Shortcut for Data Types
>
> You also can type the first letter of the data type such as *d* for Date/Time, *t* for Text, or *n* for number. To use the keyboard shortcut, click on the field name, and then press Tab to advance to the Data Type column. Next, type the first letter of the data type.

c. Press **Tab** to move to the Description column, and then type **This is the date the manager started working at this location.**

d. Click in the **Format property**, click the arrow, and then select **Short Date** from the list of date formats.

e. Click in the **Caption property**, and then type **Manager's Start Date**.

f. Click **Save** on the Quick Access Toolbar to save the changes you made to the *a02h1bank_LastnameFirstname* database.

   A warning dialog box opens to indicate that "Some data may be lost" since the size of the BranchID, Manager, and Location field properties were shortened. It asks if you want to continue anyway. Always read the Access warnings! In this case, you can click Yes to continue. You changed the size of the BranchID field from 255 to 5 in Step 4a.

g. Click **Yes** in the warning box.

STEP 6 SWITCH BETWEEN THE TABLE DESIGN AND THE TABLE DATASHEET VIEWS

As you work with the auditor, you will need to modify tables in the bank database from time to time. To modify the table, you will need to switch between Design view and Datasheet view. Refer to Figure 2.13 as you complete Step 6.

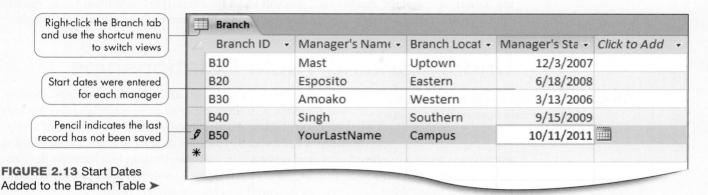

Right-click the Branch tab and use the shortcut menu to switch views

Start dates were entered for each manager

Pencil indicates the last record has not been saved

Branch

Branch ID	Manager's Name	Branch Locat	Manager's Sta	Click to Add
B10	Mast	Uptown	12/3/2007	
B20	Esposito	Eastern	6/18/2008	
B30	Amoako	Western	3/13/2006	
B40	Singh	Southern	9/15/2009	
B50	YourLastName	Campus	10/11/2011	
*				

FIGURE 2.13 Start Dates Added to the Branch Table ➤

a. Right-click the **Branch tab** shown in Figure 2.13, and then select **Datasheet View** from the shortcut menu. (To return to the Design view, right-click the tab again, and then select Design View.)

b. Click inside the **Manager's Start Date** in the first record, and then click the **Calendar**. Use the navigation arrows to find and select **December 3, 2007** from the calendar.

   You can also enter the dates by typing them directly into the StartDate field.

c. Type directly in each field the Start Date for the rest of the managers as shown in Figure 2.13.

d. Click the **Close button** at the top-right corner of the datasheet, below the Ribbon.

TROUBLESHOOTING: If you accidentally click the Close button on top of the Ribbon, you will exit out of Access completely. To start again, launch Access, click the File tab, click Recent, and then select the first database from the recent documents list.

e. Double-click the **Branch table** in the Navigation Pane to open the table. Check the start dates.

   The start dates are still there even though you did not save your work in the previous step. Access saves the data to the hard drive as soon as you move off the current record (or close an object).

f. Click the **File tab**, click **Print**, and then click **Print Preview**.

   Occasionally, users will print an Access table. However, database developers usually create reports to print table data.

g. Click **Close Print Preview**. Close the Branch table.

h. Click the **File tab**, and then click **Compact & Repair Database** (the top button).

i. Click the **File tab**, click **Save & Publish**, and then double-click **Back Up Database** in the right column. Accept *a02h1bank_LastnameFirstname_date* as the file name, and then click **Save**.

   You created a backup of the database. The original database, *a02h1bank_LastnameFirstname*, remains open.

j. Keep the database onscreen if you plan to continue with Hands-On Exercise 2. If not, close the database and exit Access.

Multiple Table Databases

In Figure 2.1, the sample bank database contains three tables—Customers, Accounts, and Branch. You already created one table, the Branch table, in the previous section using the Datasheet view. The two remaining tables will be created using a different method—importing data from Excel. In this section, you will learn how to import data from Excel, modify tables, create indexes, create relationships between tables, and enforce referential integrity.

Understanding Table Relationships

> The benefit of a relationship is to efficiently combine data from related tables.

Relationships between tables are set in the Relationships window. In this window, join lines are created to establish relationships between two tables. As discussed earlier, the benefit of a relationship is to efficiently combine data from related tables for the purpose of creating queries, forms, and reports. For example, the join line between the CustomerID in the Accounts table and the CustomerID in the Customers table (see Figure 2.14) enables you to combine data from the Accounts and the Customers tables.

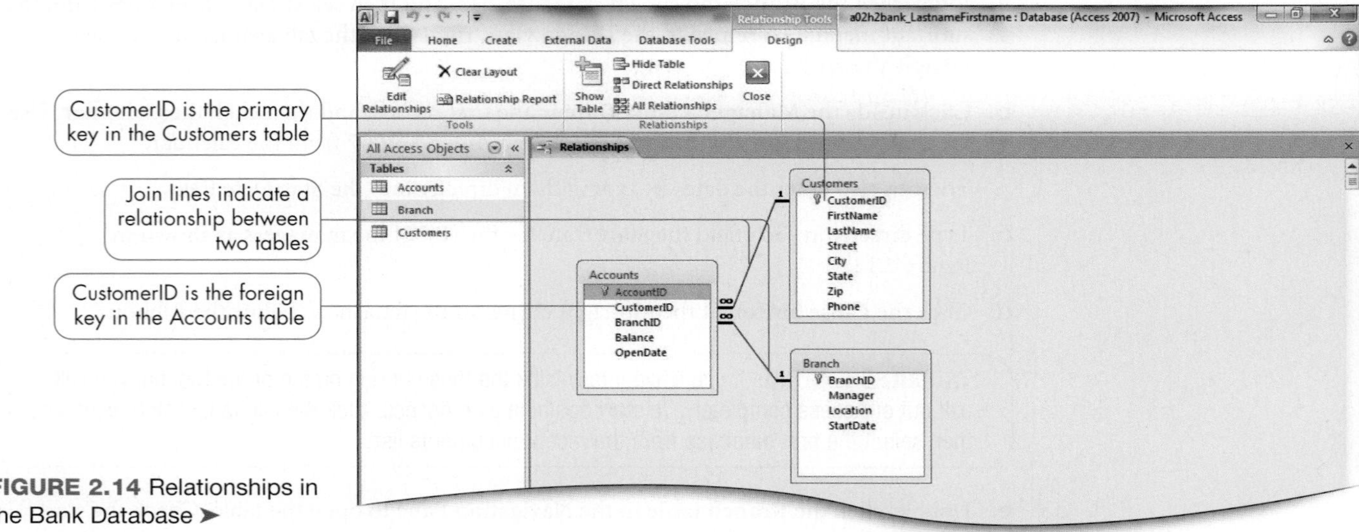

FIGURE 2.14 Relationships in the Bank Database ➤

The primary key of a table plays a significant role when setting relationships. You cannot join two tables unless a primary key has been set in the primary table. In our Bank database, the CustomerID has been set as the primary key in the Customers table. Therefore, a relationship can be set between the Customers table and the Accounts table. Similarly, the Branch table can be joined to the Accounts table since BranchID has been set as the primary key in the Branch table.

> Relationships between tables will almost always be set using primary and foreign keys.

The other side of the relationship join line is most often the foreign key of the related table. A foreign key is a field in one table that is also the primary key of another table. In the previous example, CustomerID in the Accounts table is a foreign key; BranchID in the Accounts table is a foreign key. Relationships between tables will almost always be set using primary and foreign keys.

Establish Referential Integrity

When **referential integrity** is enforced, you cannot enter a foreign key value in a related table unless the primary key value exists in the primary table.

When you create a relationship in Access, the Edit Relationships dialog box appears, as shown in Figure 2.15. The first check box, Enforce Referential Integrity, should be checked in most cases. When ***referential integrity*** is enforced, you cannot enter a foreign key value in a related table unless the primary key value exists in the primary table. In the case of the Bank database, a customer's account information (which includes CustomerID) cannot be entered into the Accounts table unless the customer information is first entered into the Customers table. If you attempt to enter an account prior to entering the customer information, an error will appear, as shown in Figure 2.16. When referential integrity is enforced, you cannot delete a record in one table if it has related records in other tables.

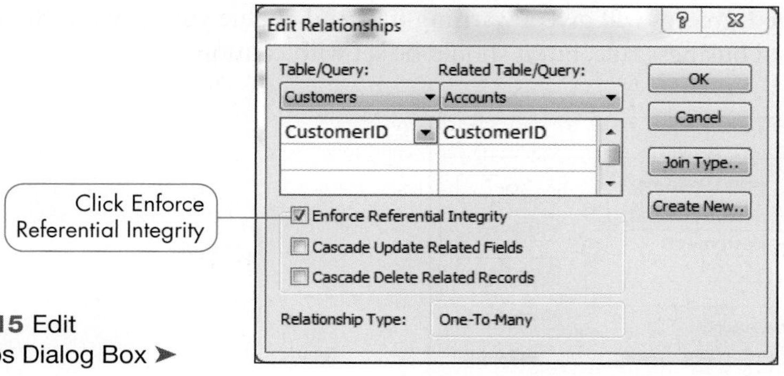

FIGURE 2.15 Edit Relationships Dialog Box ➤

Accounts

Account ID	Customer ID	Branch ID	Balance	OpenDate	Click to Add
1001	30010	B50	$5,600.00	4/28/2007	
1002	30001	B10	$1,200.00	4/13/2005	
1003	30004	B20	$15,490.00	5/28/2004	
1004	30003	B30	$630.00	9/21/2003	
1005	30009	B50	$1,300.00	7/22/2005	
1006	30003	B10	$550.00	7/3/2003	
1007	30007	B20	$1,620.00	6/7/2006	
1008	30004	B40	$2,100.00	9/30/2007	
1016	30001	B30	$18,700.00	3/13/2003	
1017	30010	B30	$980.00	9/5/2004	
1018	30005	B40	$7,800.00	5/6/2003	
1019	30004	B30	$14,250.00	1/4/2012	
1020	30001	B50	$12,000.00	4/13/2005	
1021	30011	B50	$21,004.00	7/2/2009	
1022	30003	B50	$4,000.00	4/13/2011	
1023	30011	B50	$1,000.00	1/1/1012	
1024	99999				

Microsoft Access

You cannot add or change a record because a related record is required in table 'Customers'.

OK Help

Was this information helpful?

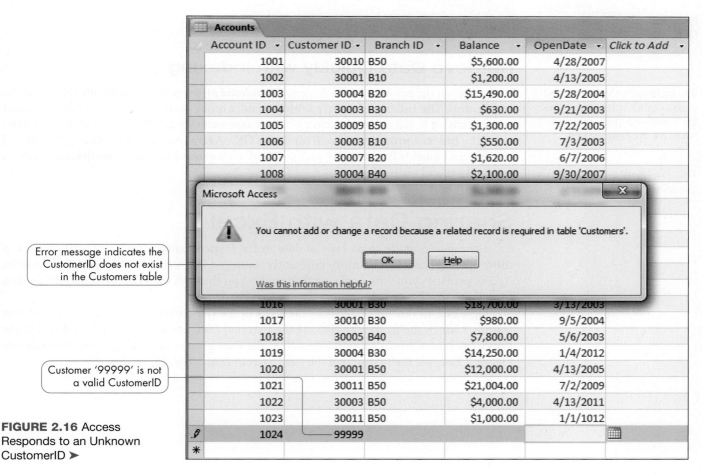

Error message indicates the CustomerID does not exist in the Customers table

Customer '99999' is not a valid CustomerID

FIGURE 2.16 Access Responds to an Unknown CustomerID ➤

Set Cascade Options

Cascade Update Related Fields is an option that directs Access to automatically update all foreign key values in a related table when the primary key value is modified in a primary table.

Cascade Delete Related Records is an option that directs Access to automatically delete all records in related tables that match the primary key that is deleted from a primary table.

When you create a relationship in Access and click the Enforce Referential Integrity checkbox, Access gives you two additional options—Cascade Update Related Fields and Cascade Delete Related Records. Check the ***Cascade Update Related Fields*** option so that when the primary key is modified in a primary table, Access will automatically update all foreign key values in a related table (see Figure 2.17). If a CustomerID is updated for some reason, all the CustomerID references in the Accounts table will automatically be updated.

Check the ***Cascade Delete Related Records*** option so that when the primary key is deleted in a primary table, Access will automatically delete all records in related tables that reference the primary key (see Figure 2.17). If one branch of a bank closes and its record is deleted from the Branch table, any account that was not transferred to a different branch would be deleted. Access will give a warning first and enable you to avoid the action. This may be a desired business rule, but it should be set with caution.

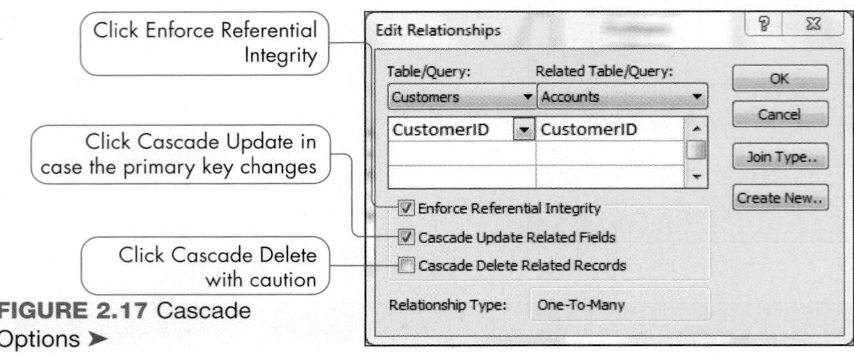

FIGURE 2.17 Cascade Options ➤

Retrieve Data Quickly with Indexing

The **indexed property** setting enables quick sorting in primary key order and quick retrieval based on the primary key.

When you set the primary key in Access, the ***indexed property*** is automatically set to *Yes (No Duplicates)*. The Indexed property setting enables quick sorting in primary key order and quick retrieval based on the primary key. For non-primary key fields, it may be beneficial to set the Indexed property to *Yes (Duplicates OK)*. Again, Access uses indexing to sort and retrieve data quickly based on the indexed field. As a general rule, indexed fields are usually foreign keys and are numeric.

Sharing Data with Excel

Most companies store some type of data in Excel spreadsheets. Often the data stored in those spreadsheets can be more efficiently managed in an Access database. Fortunately, Access provides you with a wizard that guides you through the process of importing data from Excel. Access can also export data to Excel easily.

Figures 2.18 through 2.24 show the steps of the *Get External Data - Excel Spreadsheet* feature. Launch the feature by clicking the External Data tab and then clicking Excel in the Import & Link Group. Table 2.1 describes the four groups on the External Data tab. See Figure 2.18 to see the first step of the *Get External Data - Excel Spreadsheet* feature.

TABLE 2.1 Options on the External Data Tab	
Group	**When Used**
Import & Link	To bring data into an Access database. The data sources include Excel, Access (other Access files), ODBC Database, Text File, XML File, and More.
Export	To send a portion of a database to other applications. You might use this to create a Mail Merge letter and envelopes in Word. You could create an Excel file for a coworker who is not using Access, or you could share your data over the Internet via a SharePoint List.
Collect Data	You could create an e-mail mail merge to send e-mails to your clients and then use Access to manage the clients' responses.
Web Linked Lists	Use these commands to interact with SharePoint lists on the Internet. If an Internet connection is unavailable, you can work offline and synchronize with SharePoint later.

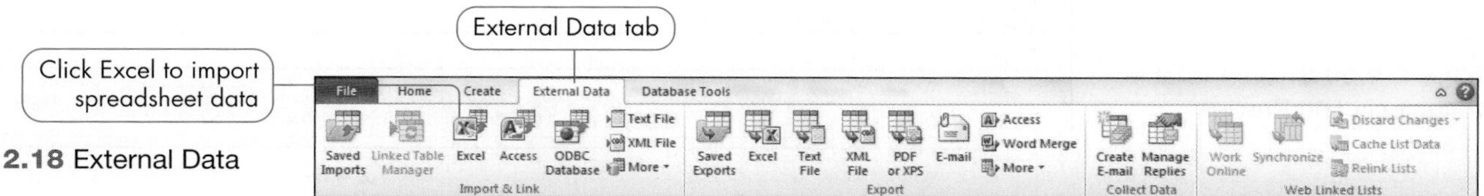

FIGURE 2.18 External Data Tab ➤

Figure 2.19 shows the *Get External Data - Excel Spreadsheet* dialog box. This step enables you to locate the Excel file you want to import by clicking Browse. It asks you to choose among three options for the incoming data: Place it in a new table, append the data to an existing table, or create a link to the Excel source.

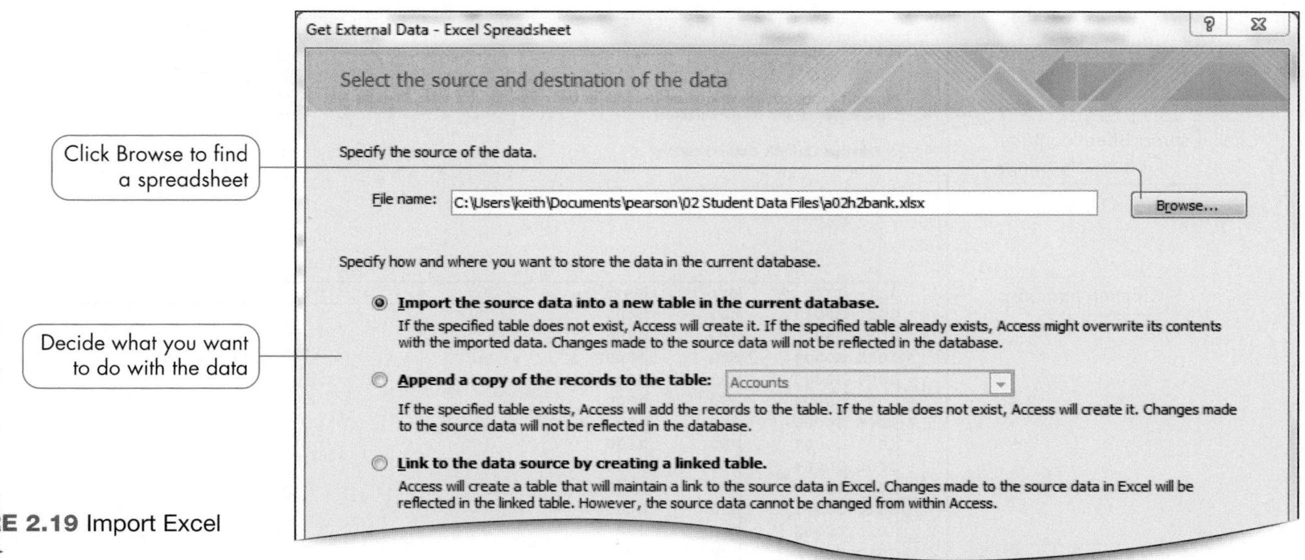

FIGURE 2.19 Import Excel Data ➤

After you select an Excel workbook and accept the default option, import the source data into a new table in the current database, and then click OK. The Import Spreadsheet Wizard dialog box launches and displays a list of the worksheets in the specified workbook. The Customers worksheet is selected; click the Accounts worksheet, which will be imported first (see Figure 2.20). The bottom of the Import Spreadsheet Wizard dialog box displays a preview of the data stored in the specified worksheet.

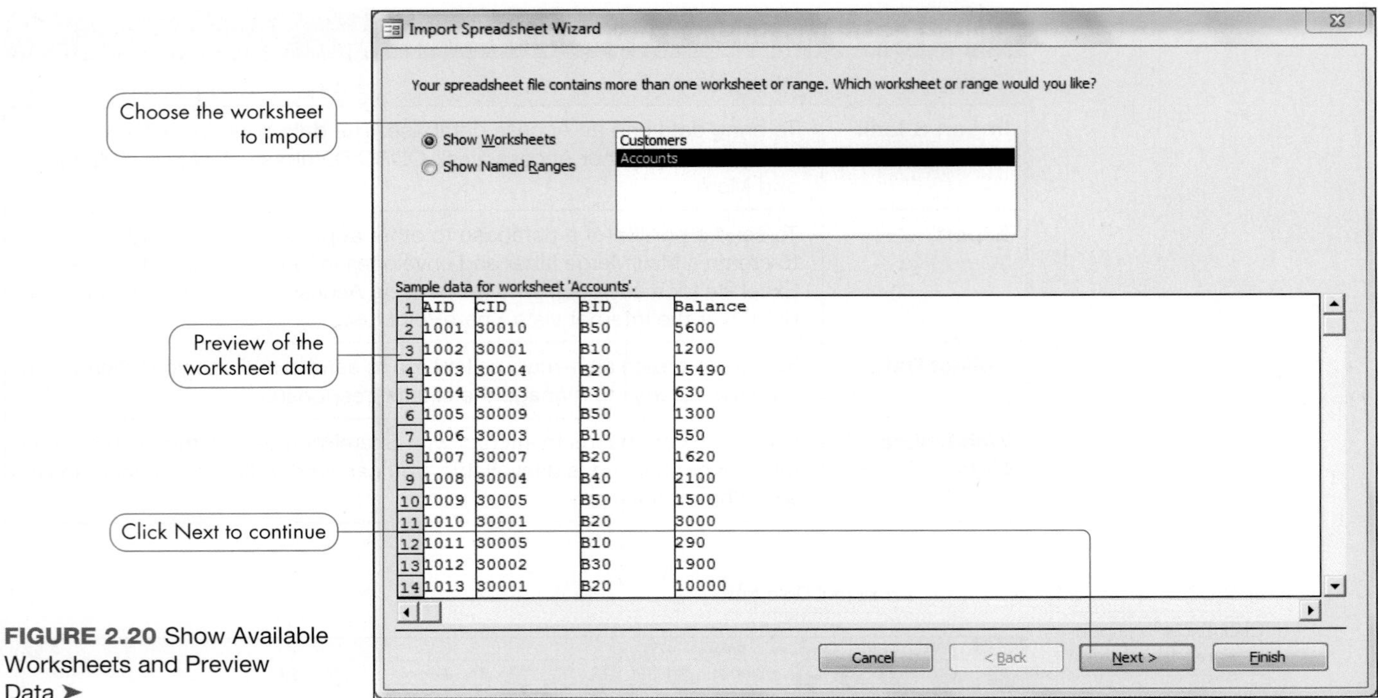

FIGURE 2.20 Show Available Worksheets and Preview Data ➤

Although a well-designed spreadsheet may include descriptive column headings, not all spreadsheets are ready to import. You may have to revise the spreadsheet before importing it. The second window of the Import Spreadsheet Wizard dialog box contains a check box that enables you to convert the first row of column headings to field names in Access (see Figure 2.21). If a column heading row exists in the spreadsheet, check the box. If no column headings exist, leave the check box unchecked, and the data will import using Field1, Field2, Field3, etc.

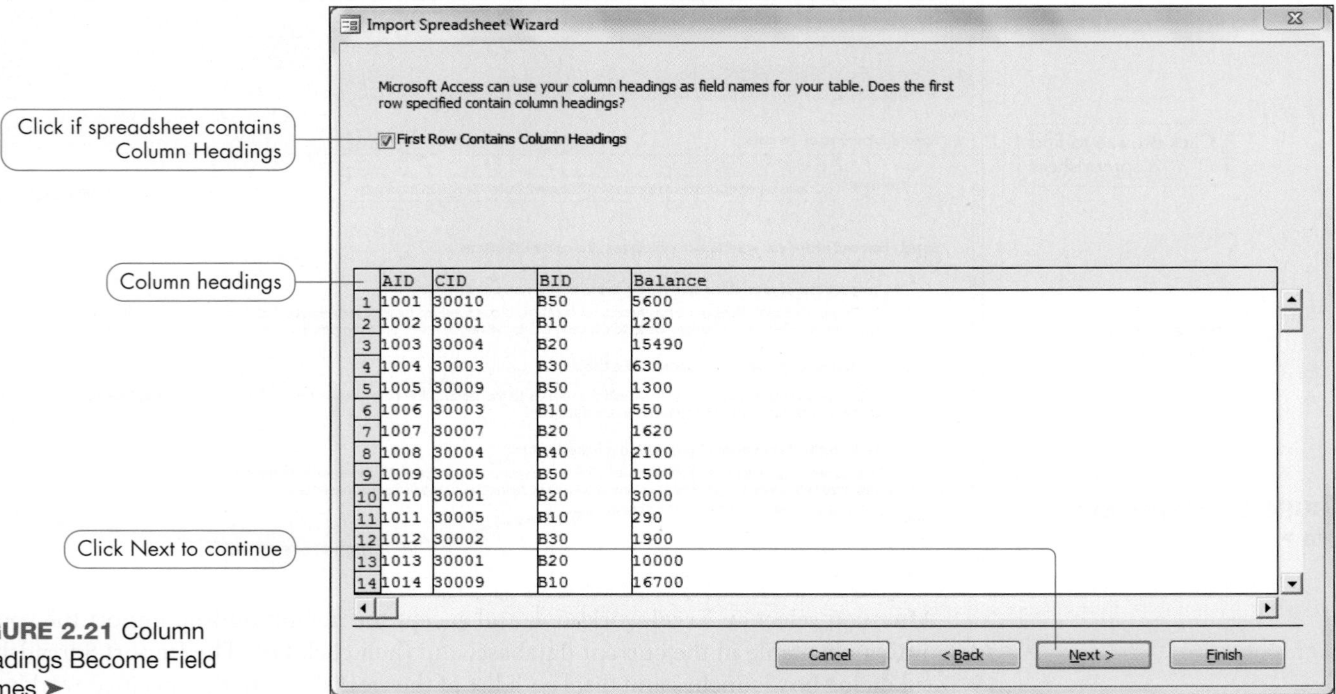

FIGURE 2.21 Column Headings Become Field Names ➤

The third window of the Import Spreadsheet Wizard dialog box enables you to specify field options (see Figure 2.22). The AID field is shown in this figure. Because it will become this table's primary key, you need to set the Indexed Property to *Yes (No Duplicates)*.

To modify the field options of the other fields, click the Field Name column heading, and then make the changes. Not all Access table properties are supported by the wizard. You will need to open the table in Design view after importing it to make additional field property changes.

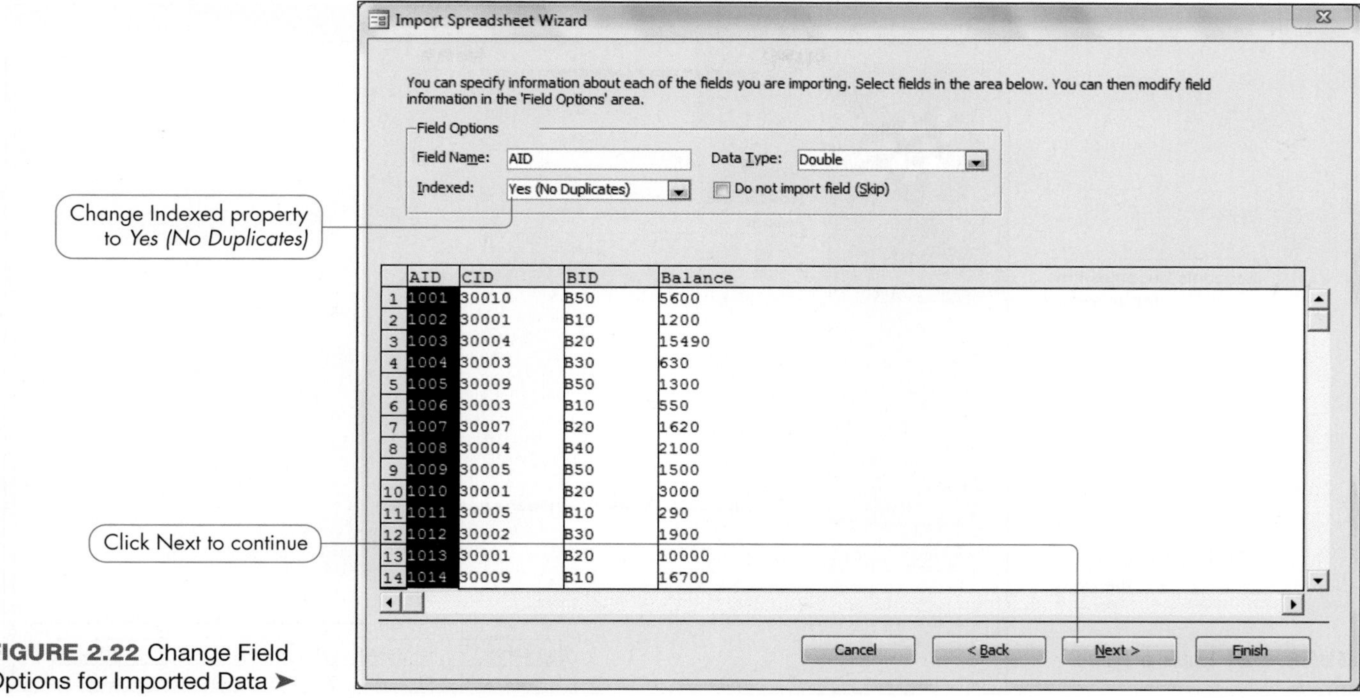

	AID	CID	BID	Balance
1	1001	30010	B50	5600
2	1002	30001	B10	1200
3	1003	30004	B20	15490
4	1004	30003	B30	630
5	1005	30009	B50	1300
6	1006	30003	B10	550
7	1007	30007	B20	1620
8	1008	30004	B40	2100
9	1009	30005	B50	1500
10	1010	30001	B20	3000
11	1011	30005	B10	290
12	1012	30002	B30	1900
13	1013	30001	B20	10000
14	1014	30009	B10	16700

FIGURE 2.22 Change Field Options for Imported Data ➤

The fourth window of the Import Spreadsheet Wizard dialog box enables you to choose a primary key before the import takes place (see Figure 2.23). If the option *Let Access add primary key* is selected, Access will generate an AutoNumber field and designate it as the primary key. Otherwise, you can designate a field to be the primary key. In the import described in the figure, the Excel data has a unique identifier (AID) that will become the table's primary key.

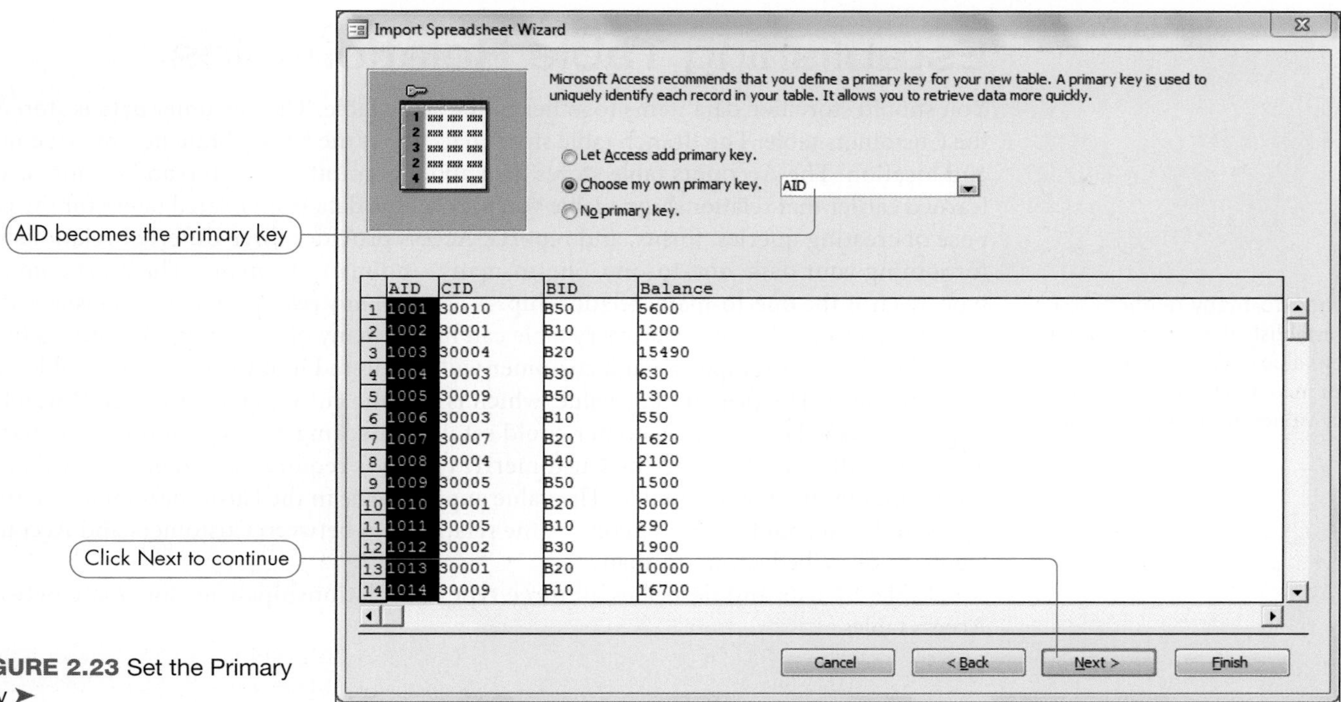

	AID	CID	BID	Balance
1	1001	30010	B50	5600
2	1002	30001	B10	1200
3	1003	30004	B20	15490
4	1004	30003	B30	630
5	1005	30009	B50	1300
6	1006	30003	B10	550
7	1007	30007	B20	1620
8	1008	30004	B40	2100
9	1009	30005	B50	1500
10	1010	30001	B20	3000
11	1011	30005	B10	290
12	1012	30002	B30	1900
13	1013	30001	B20	10000
14	1014	30009	B10	16700

FIGURE 2.23 Set the Primary Key ➤

Use the final window of the Import Spreadsheet Wizard to name the Access table. If the worksheet in the Excel workbook was named, Access uses the worksheet name as the table name (see Figure 2.24).

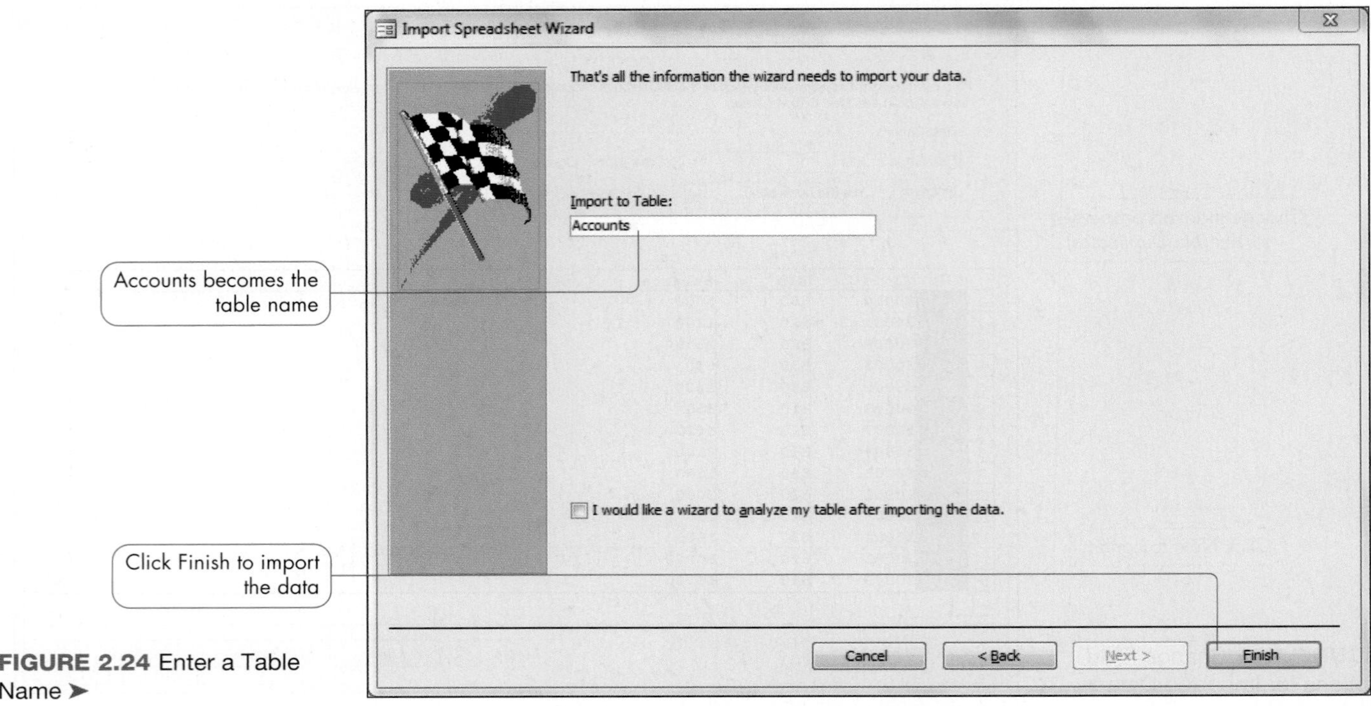

FIGURE 2.24 Enter a Table Name ➤

Finally, the Wizard will ask if you wish to save the import steps. If the same worksheet is imported from Excel to Access on a recurring basis, you could save the parameters and use them again. To save the import steps such as the indexing option and any new field names, click Saved Imports in the Import group. Saving the import steps will help you import the data the next time it is needed.

Establishing Table Relationships

A **one-to-many relationship** is established when the primary key value in the primary table can match many of the foreign key values in the related table.

You should store like data items together in the same table. The customer data is stored in the Customers table. The Branch table stores data about the bank's branches, management, and location. The Accounts table stores data about account ownership and balances. You learned earlier that relationships enable you to combine data from related tables for the purpose of creating queries, forms, and reports. Access provides three different relationships for joining your data: one-to-one, one-to-many, and many-to-many. The most common type by far is the one-to-many relationship. A ***one-to-many relationship*** is established when the primary key value in the primary table can match many of the foreign key values in the related table. For example, a bank customer will be entered into the Customers table once and only once. The primary key value, which is also the customer's CustomerID number, might be 1585. That same customer could set up a checking, savings, and money market account. With each account, the CustomerID (1585) is required and therefore will occur three times in the Accounts table. The value appears once in the Customers table and three times in the Accounts table. Therefore, the relationship between Customers and Accounts would be described as one-to-many.

Table 2.2 lists and describes all three types of relationships you can create between Access tables.

TABLE 2.2 Relationship Types	
Relationship Name	**Definition**
One-to-Many	This relationship is between a primary key in the first table and a foreign key in the second table. The first table must have only one occurrence of each value. For example, each customer must have a unique identification number in the Customers table, or each employee must have a unique EmployeeID in the Employee table. The foreign key field in the second table may have repeating values. For example, one customer may have many different account numbers, or one employee can perform many services.
One-to-One	Two different tables use the same primary key. Exactly one record exists in the second table for each record in the first table. Sometimes security reasons require a table to be split into two related tables. For example, anyone in the company can look in the Employee table and find the employee's office number, department assignment, or telephone extension. However, only a few people need to have access to the employee's salary, Social Security Number, performance review, or marital status. Both tables use the same unique identifier to identify each employee.
Many-to-Many	This is an artificially constructed relationship giving many matching records in each direction between tables. It requires construction of a third table called a junction table. For example, a database might have a table for employees and one for projects. Several employees might be assigned to one project, but one employee might also be assigned to many different projects. When Access connects to databases using Oracle or other software, you find this relationship type.

Establish a One-to-Many Relationship

Click the Database Tools tab, and then click Relationships in the Relationships group; the Relationships window opens (as shown in Figure 2.25). If this were an established database, this window would already contain tables and join lines indicating the relationships that were established in the database.

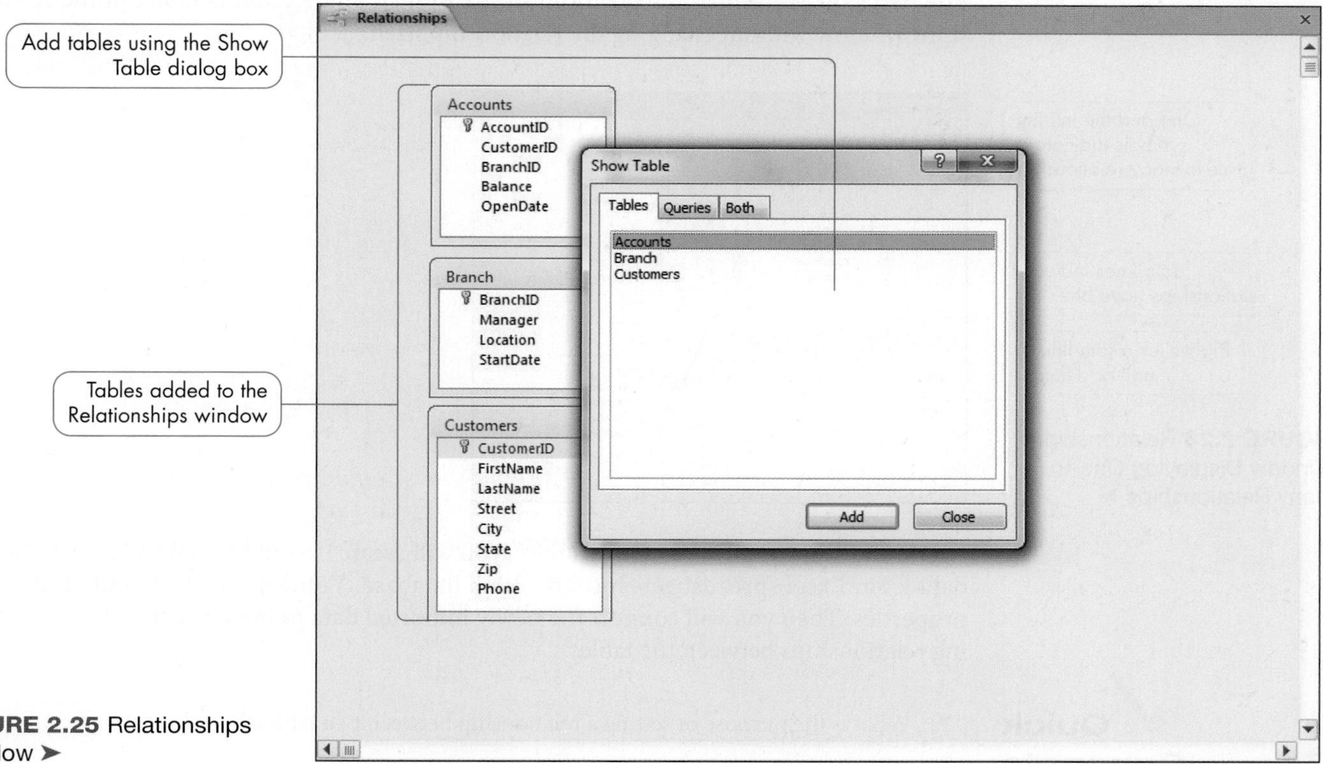

FIGURE 2.25 Relationships Window ➤

The first time you open the Relationships window, you will not see any established relationships; you must first use the Show Table dialog box to add the required tables to the Relationships window. Select the tables you want to use to set relationships, and then add them to the Relationships window by clicking Add (as shown in Figure 2.25).

TIP Navigating Between the Relationships Window and a Table's Design

When you right-click on a table's title bar in the Relationships window, the shortcut menu offers you a chance to open the table in Design view. This is a convenient feature because if you want to link **one** table to another table, the joined fields must have the same data type, and a table may contain a field with the wrong data type. This shortcut enables you to check the fields and revise them if necessary.

Where necessary, expand the table windows to display the complete list of field names shown in the table.

Establish the relationships by dragging the common field name from the primary table onto the common field name in the related table. (The common field name does not have to be an exact match, but the data type and field size must be the same.) When you release the mouse, the Edit Relationships dialog box opens (look back at Figure 2.15). Click Enforce Referential Integrity, and then click Create; Access checks the table data to ensure that the rules you are attempting to establish can be met. For example, in the bank database, if you attempt to enforce referential integrity between the Branch table and the Accounts table, Access will verify that one BranchID value exists in the Branch table for each BranchID value in the Accounts table. If one BranchID value (e.g., B80) in the Accounts table does not exist in the Branch table, Access cannot establish the relationship with referential integrity enforced. The data must be corrected prior to checking enforce referential integrity.

Figure 2.26 shows the Relationships window for the Bank database and all the relationships created using referential integrity. The join line between the CustomerID field in the Customers table and the CustomerID field in the Accounts table indicates that a one-to-many relationship has been set. You can rearrange the tables by dragging the tables by the title bar. You can switch the positions of the Branch and Accounts tables in the Relationships window without changing the relationship itself.

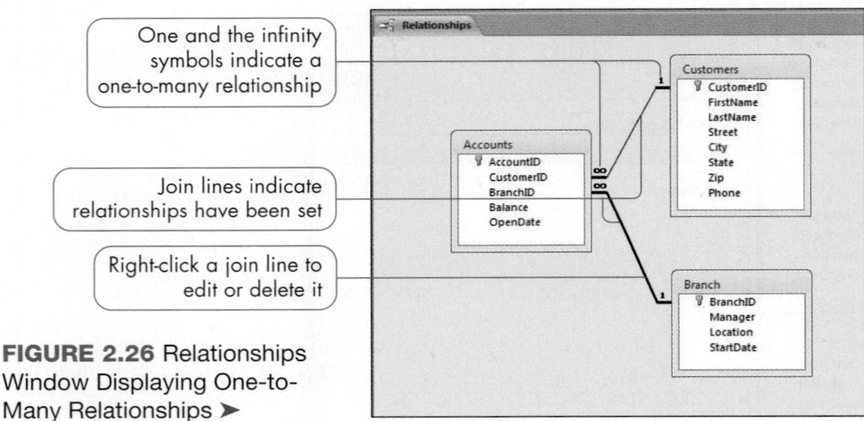

FIGURE 2.26 Relationships Window Displaying One-to-Many Relationships ➤

In the following Hands-On Exercise, you will create two additional tables by importing data from Excel spreadsheets into the Bank database. You will establish and modify field properties. Then you will connect the newly imported data to the Branch table by establishing relationships between the tables.

Quick Concepts Check

1. What is the purpose of setting a relationship between two tables?
2. Describe referential integrity when setting a relationship.
3. Describe a scenario that may require you to import Excel data into Access.
4. Give an example of two database tables that would contain a one-to-many relationship. Describe the relationship.

2 Multiple Table Databases

You created a new Bank database, and you created a new Branch table. Now you are ready to import Commonwealth Federal's customer and account data from Excel spreadsheets. Even though you believe the Excel data is formatted correctly, you decided to open the Excel spreadsheets before you import them into Access. Once you are satisfied the data is structured properly, you can begin the import process.

Skills covered: Import Excel Data into an Access Table • Import Additional Excel Data • Modify an Imported Table's Design • Add Data to an Imported Table • Establish Table Relationships • Test Referential Integrity

STEP 1 IMPORT EXCEL DATA INTO AN ACCESS TABLE

You and the auditor have discovered several of Commonwealth's Excel spreadsheets that contain customer data. These files need to be analyzed, so you decide to import the Excel data into Access. Refer to Figure 2.27 as well as Figures 2.19 through 2.24 as you complete Step 1.

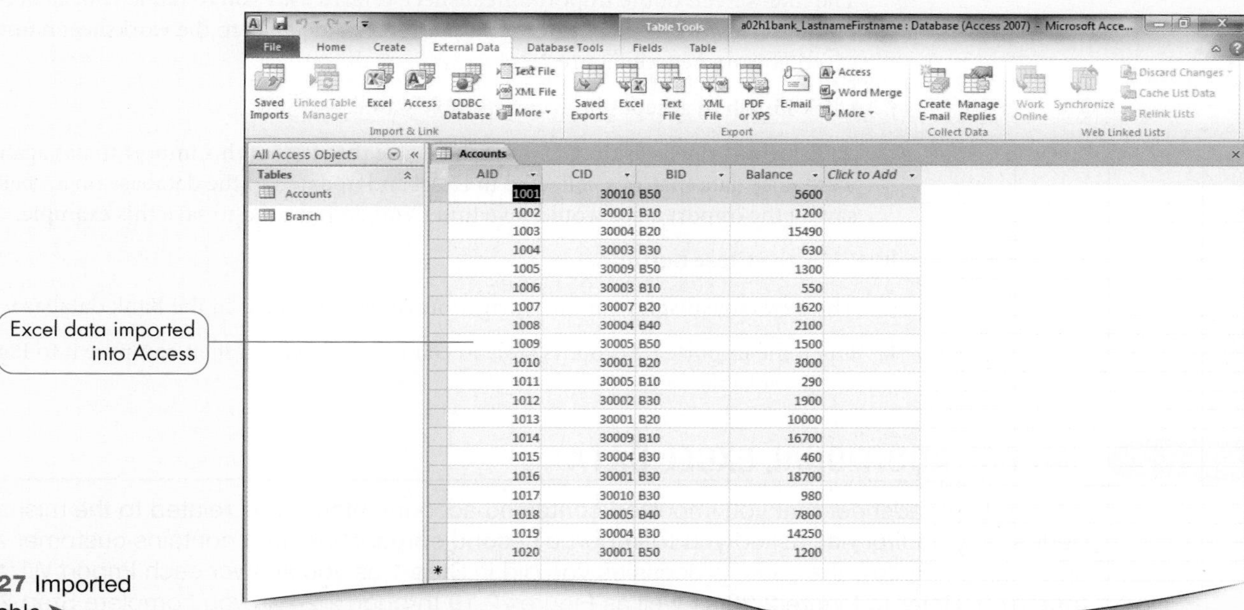

AID	CID	BID	Balance
1001	30010	B50	5600
1002	30001	B10	1200
1003	30004	B20	15490
1004	30003	B30	630
1005	30009	B50	1300
1006	30003	B10	550
1007	30007	B20	1620
1008	30004	B40	2100
1009	30005	B50	1500
1010	30001	B20	3000
1011	30005	B10	290
1012	30002	B30	1900
1013	30001	B20	10000
1014	30009	B10	16700
1015	30004	B30	460
1016	30001	B30	18700
1017	30010	B30	980
1018	30005	B40	7800
1019	30004	B30	14250
1020	30001	B50	1200

FIGURE 2.27 Imported Accounts Table ➤

a. Open *a02h1bank_LastnameFirstname* if you closed it at the end of Hands-On Exercise 1. Click the **File tab**, click **Save Database As**, and then type **a02h2bank_LastnameFirstname**, changing *h1* to *h2*. Click **Save**.

b. Click the Enable Content button below the Ribbon to indicate you trust the contents of the database.

TROUBLESHOOTING: Throughout the remainder of this chapter and textbook, click the Enable Content button whenever you are working with student files.

c. Click the **External Data tab**, and click **Excel** in the Import & Link group to launch the *Get External Data - Excel Spreadsheet* feature. Select the **Import the source data into a new table in the current database option**, if necessary, as shown in Figure 2.19.

d. Click **Browse**, and then go to the student data folder. Select the *a02h2bank* workbook. Click **Open**, and then click **OK** to open the Import Spreadsheet Wizard.

The top of the first window shows all of the worksheets in the workbook. This particular workbook contains only two worksheets: Customers and Accounts. The Customers worksheet is active, and a list of the data contained in the Customers worksheet displays in the Wizard.

e. Click **Accounts** (see Figure 2.20), and then click **Next**.

f. Ensure that the *First Row Contains Column Headings* check box is checked to tell Access that column headings exist in the Excel file (see Figure 2.21).

   The field names, AID, CID, BID, and Balance, will import from Excel along with the data stored in the rows in the worksheet. The field names will be modified later in Access.

g. Click **Next**.

   The AID (AccountID) will become the primary key in this table. It needs to be a unique identifier, so we must change the properties to no duplicates.

h. Ensure that *AID* is displayed in the Field Name box in Field Options. Then click the **Indexed arrow**, and then select **Yes (No Duplicates)**, as shown in Figure 2.22. Click **Next**.

i. Click the **Choose my own primary key option** (see Figure 2.23). Make sure that the *AID* field is selected. Click **Next**.

   The final screen of the Import Spreadsheet Wizard asks you to name your table. The name of the Excel worksheet was Accounts, and Access defaults to the worksheet name. It is an acceptable name (see Figure 2.24).

j. Click **Finish** to accept the Accounts table name.

   A dialog box opens asking if you wish to save the steps of this import to use again. If this were sales data that was collected in Excel and updated to the database on a weekly basis, saving the import steps would save time. You do not need to save this example.

k. Click the **Close button**.

   The new table displays in the Navigation Pane and resides in the Bank database.

l. Open the imported Accounts table in Datasheet view, and then compare it to Figure 2.27. Close the table.

STEP 2 IMPORT ADDITIONAL EXCEL DATA

The first spreadsheet that you imported contained account information related to the mishandled funds. The auditor has asked you to import a second spreadsheet that contains customer account information. Follow the same process as you did in Step 1 as you answer each Import Wizard question. Refer to Figure 2.28 as well as Figures 2.19 through 2.24 as you complete Step 2.

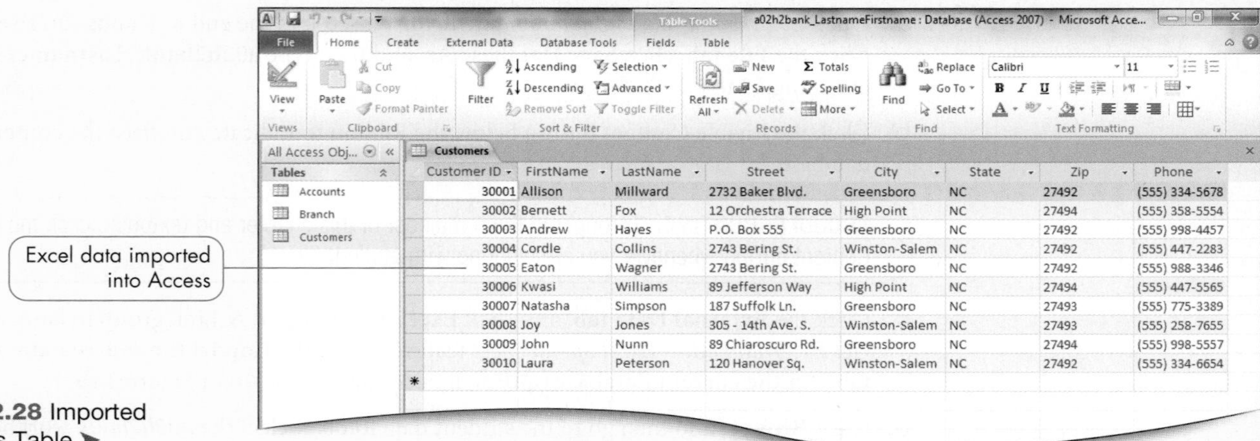

FIGURE 2.28 Imported Customers Table ➤

a. Click the **External Data tab**, and then click **Excel** in the Import & Link group to launch the *Get External Data - Excel Spreadsheet* feature. Select the **Import the source data into a new table in the current database option**, if necessary.

b. Click **Browse**, and then go to the student data folder. Select the *a02h2bank* workbook. Click **Open**, and then click **OK** to open the Import Spreadsheet Wizard.

   The Customers worksheet is active; you will import this worksheet.

c. Click **Next**.

d. Ensure that the *First Row Contains Column Headings* check box is checked to tell Access that column headings exist in the Excel file. Click **Next**.

   The CID will become the primary key in this table. It needs to be a unique identifier, so you change the properties to no duplicates.

e. Ensure that *CID* is displayed in the Field Name box in Field Options. Click the **Indexed arrow**, and then select **Yes (No Duplicates)**. Click **Next**.

f. Click the **Choose my own primary key option**. Make sure that the *CID* field is selected. Click **Next**.

   Access defaults to the table name Customers.

g. Click **Finish** to accept the Customers table name.

h. Click **Close** on the Save Import Steps dialog box.

   The Navigation Pane contains three tables: Accounts, Branch, and Customers.

i. Open the imported Customers table in Datasheet view, and then compare it to Figure 2.28. Close the table.

STEP 3 MODIFY AN IMPORTED TABLE'S DESIGN

The Excel worksheets became Access tables when you imported them into the Bank database. However, in order to answer all the auditor's questions (using queries), you need to modify the tables so that each field has the correct data type and field size. Refer to Figure 2.29 as you complete Step 3.

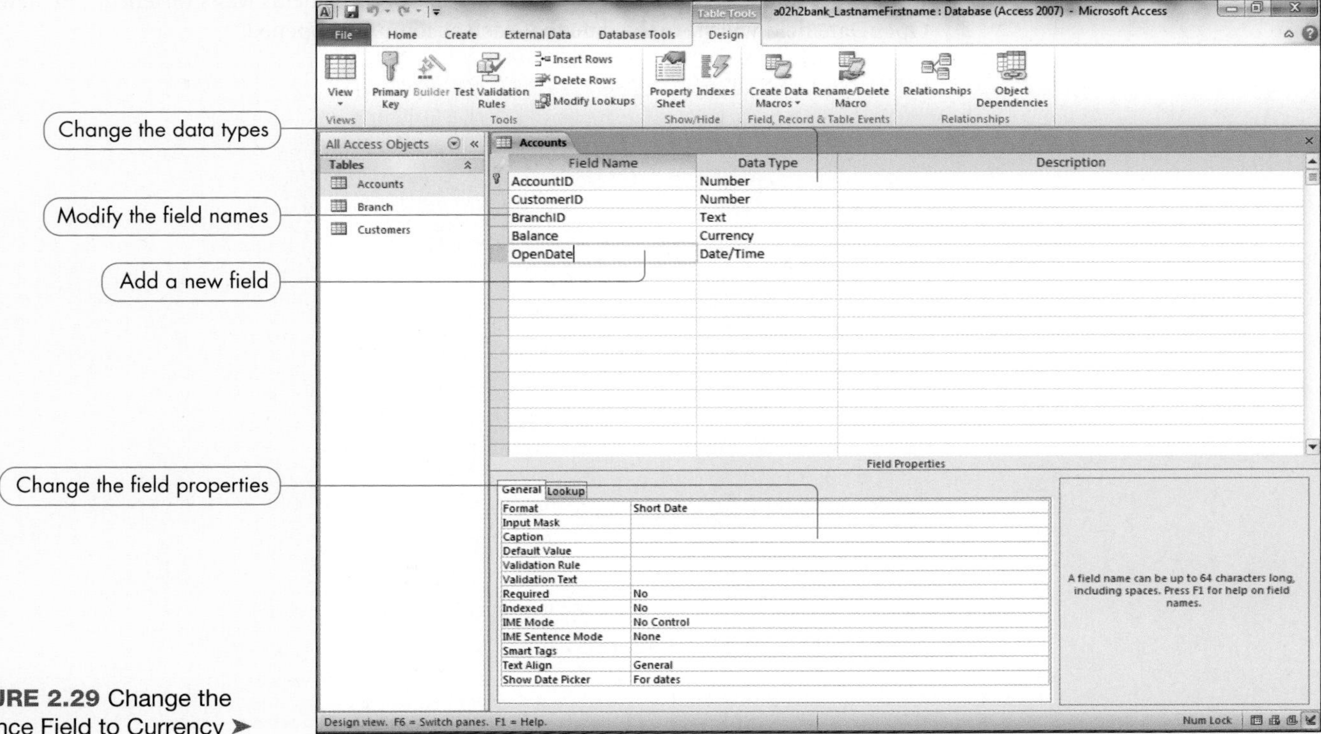

FIGURE 2.29 Change the Balance Field to Currency ➤

a. Double-click the **Accounts table** in the Navigation Pane to open it in Datasheet view.

b. Click **View** in the Views group on the Home tab to switch to Design view.

c. Change the AID field name to **AccountID**.

d. Change the Field Size property to **Long Integer** in the Field Properties at the bottom of the design window.

   Long Integer ensures that there will be enough numbers as the number of accounts grow over time. Importing data from Excel saves typing, but modifications will usually be required.

e. Type **Account ID** in the **Caption property box** for the AccountID field. The caption contains a space between *Account* and *ID*.

f. Change the CID field name to **CustomerID**.

g. Change the Field Size property to **Long Integer** in the Field Properties at the bottom of the design window.

   You can select the Field Size option using the arrow, or you can type the first letter of the option you want. For example, type *l* for Long Integer or *s* for Single. Make sure the current option is completely selected before you type the letter.

h. Type **Customer ID** in the **Caption property box** for the CustomerID field. The caption contains a space between *Customer* and *ID*.

i. Click the **BID field**. Change the BID field name to **BranchID**.

j. Type **5** in the **Field Size property box** in the Field Properties.

k. Type **Branch ID** in the **Caption property box** for the Branch ID field.

l. Change the Data Type of the Balance field from *Number* to **Currency**.

m. Type a new field name, **OpenDate**, under the Balance field name. Assign data type **Date/Time**, and then add the **Short Date format** in the Field Properties.

n. Click **View** in the Views group to switch to Datasheet View. Read the messages, and then click **Yes** twice.

   In this case, it is OK to click Yes because the size of three fields was shortened. The new OpenDate field will store the date that each account was opened.

o. Add the OpenDate values as shown below:

Account ID	OpenDate
1001	4/28/2007
1002	4/13/2005
1003	5/28/2004
1004	9/21/2003
1005	7/22/2005
1006	7/3/2003
1007	6/7/2006
1008	9/30/2007
1009	2/7/2006
1010	3/18/2010
1011	10/16/2012
1012	3/14/2007
1013	5/15/2009
1014	9/17/2007
1015	4/4/2003
1016	3/13/2003
1017	9/5/2004
1018	5/6/2003
1019	1/4/2012
1020	4/13/2005

p. Right-click the **Customers table** in the Navigation Pane, and then select **Design View** from the shortcut menu. Change the CID field name to **CustomerID**. Change the Field Size property of the CustomerID field to **Long Integer**, and then add a caption, **Customer ID**. Take note of the intentional space between *Customer* and *ID*.

   The Accounts table and the Customers table will be joined using the CustomerID field. Both fields must have the same data type.

q. Change the Field Size property to **20** for the FirstName, LastName, Street, and City fields. Change the Field Size for State to **2**.

r. Change the data type for Zip and Phone to **Text**. Change the Field size property to **15** for both fields. Remove the @ symbol from the Format property where it exists for all fields in the Customers table.

s. Click the **Phone field name**, and then click **Input Mask** in Field Properties. Click **Build** on the right side to launch the Input Mask Wizard. Click **Yes** to save the table, and then click **Yes** to the *some data may be lost* warning. Click **Finish** to apply the default phone number Input Mask.

   The phone number input mask will enable users to enter 6105551212 and Access to display (610) 555-1212.

t. Click **Save** to save the design changes to the Customers table. Read the Warning Box, and then click **Yes**.

STEP 4 ADD DATA TO AN IMPORTED TABLE

Now that you have created the Access tables, add data as directed by the auditor. You may also need to update and delete records if you and the auditor decide the information is no longer needed. Refer to Figure 2.30 as you complete Step 4.

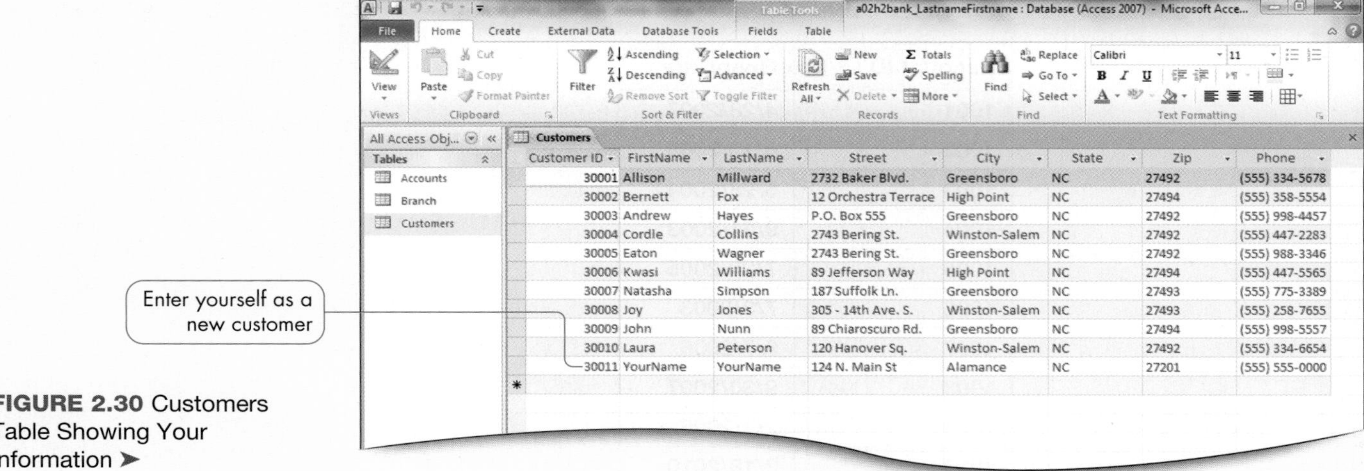

FIGURE 2.30 Customers Table Showing Your Information ➤

a. Click **View** in the Views group to display the Customers table in Datasheet view.

   The asterisk at the bottom of the table data in the row selector area is the indicator of a place to enter a new record.

b. Click the **Customer ID field** in the record after *30010*. Type **30011**. Fill in the rest of the data using your information as the customer. You may use a fictitious address and phone number.

c. Close the Customers table. Click the **Accounts table tab** if necessary.

d. Locate the new row indicator—the * in the row selector—and click in the **Account ID column**. Type **1021**. Type **30011** as the **Customer ID** and **B50** as the **Branch ID**. Type **21004** for the Balance field value. Type **7/2/2009** for the OpenDate.

e. Close the Accounts table; keep the database open.

STEP 5 ESTABLISH TABLE RELATIONSHIPS

The tables for the bank investigation have been designed. Now, you will need to establish connections between the tables. Look at the primary and foreign keys as a guide. Refer to Figure 2.31 as you complete Step 5.

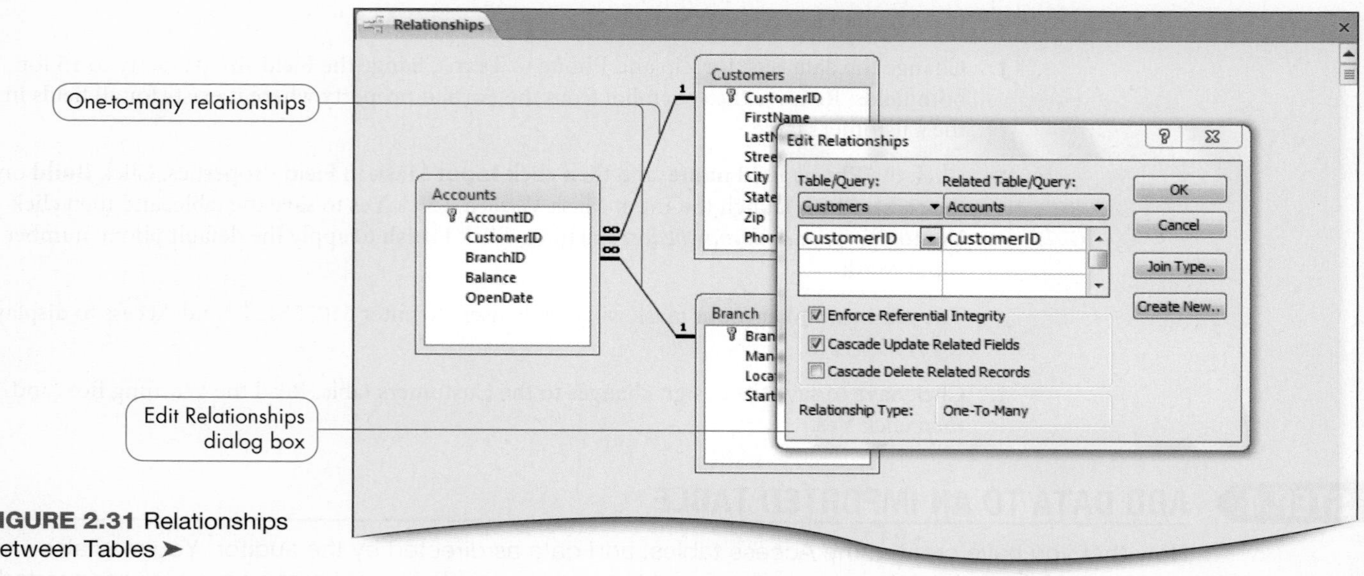

FIGURE 2.31 Relationships Between Tables ➤

a. Click the **Database Tools tab**, and then click **Relationships** in the Relationships group.

The Relationships window opens and the Show Table dialog box appears.

TROUBLESHOOTING: If the Show Table dialog box does not open, click Show Table in the Relationships group on the Relationships Tools Design tab.

b. Double-click each of the three tables displayed in the Show Table dialog box to add them to the Relationships window. (Alternatively, click a table, and then click Add.) Click **Close** in the Show Table dialog box.

TROUBLESHOOTING: If you have a duplicate table, click the title bar of the duplicated table, and then press Delete.

c. Resize the Customers table box so all the fields are visible. Arrange the tables as shown in Figure 2.31.

d. Drag the **BranchID field** in the Branch table onto the BranchID field in the Accounts table. The Edit Relationships dialog box opens. Click the **Enforce Referential Integrity** and **Cascade Update Related Fields check boxes**. Click **Create**.

A black line displays, joining the two tables. It has a 1 on the end near the Branch table and an infinity symbol on the end next to the Accounts table. You have established a one-to-many relationship between the Branch and Accounts tables.

e. Drag the **CustomerID field** in the Customers table onto the CustomerID field in the Accounts table. The Edit Relationships dialog box opens. Click the **Enforce Referential Integrity** and **Cascade Update Related Fields check boxes**. Click **Create**.

You have established a one-to-many relationship between the Customers and Accounts tables. A customer will have only a single CustomerID number. The same customer may have many different accounts: Savings, Checking, CDs, etc.

TROUBLESHOOTING: If you get an error message when you click Create, verify the data types of the joined fields are the same. To check the data types from the Relationships window, right-click the title bar of a table, and then select Table Design from the shortcut menu. Modify the data type and field size of the join fields if necessary.

f. Click **Save** on the Quick Access Toolbar to save the changes to the Relationships. Close the Relationships window.

STEP 6 TEST REFERENTIAL INTEGRITY

The design of the bank database must be 100% correct; otherwise, data entry may be compromised. Even though you are confident that the table relationships are correct, you decide to test them by entering some invalid data. If the relationships are working, the invalid data will be rejected by Access. Refer to Figure 2.32 as you complete Step 6.

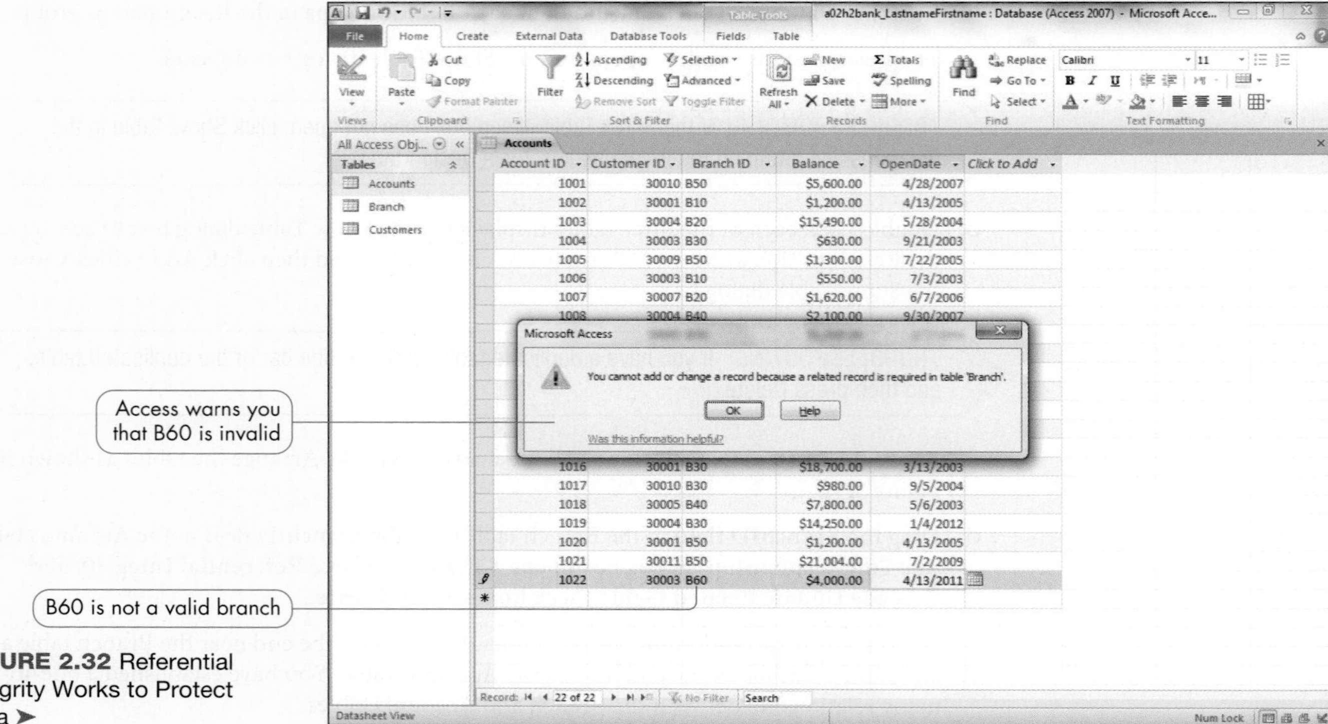

FIGURE 2.32 Referential Integrity Works to Protect Data ➤

a. Double-click the **Accounts table** to open it in Datasheet view.

b. Add a new record, pressing **Tab** after each field: Account ID: **1022**, Customer ID: **30003**, Branch ID: **B60**, Balance: **4000**, OpenDate: **4/13/2011**.

   A warning message is telling you that a related record in the Branch table is required since the Accounts table and the Branch table are connected by a relationship with enforce referential integrity checked.

c. Click **OK**. Double-click the **Branch table** in the Navigation Pane, and then examine the data in the BranchID field. Notice the Branch table has no B60 record. Close the Branch table.

d. Replace *B60* with **B50** in the new Accounts record, and then press **Tab** three times. As soon as the focus moves to the next record, the pencil symbol disappears and your data is saved.

   You successfully identified a BranchID that Access recognizes. Because referential integrity between the Accounts and Branch tables has been enforced, Access looks at each data entry item in a foreign key and matches it to a corresponding value in the table where it is the primary key. In Step 6b, you attempted to enter a nonexistent BranchID and were not allowed to make that error. In Step 6d, you entered a valid BranchID. Access examined the index for the BranchID in the Branch table and found a corresponding value for B50.

e. Close the Accounts table. Reopen the Accounts table; you will find that the record you just entered for 1022 has been saved. Close the table.

f. Close all open tables, if necessary.

g. Click the **File tab**, and then click **Compact & Repair Database**.

h. Click the **File tab**, click **Save & Publish**, and then double-click **Back Up Database**. Accept *a02h2bank_LastnameFirstname_date* as the file name, and then click **Save**.

   You just created a backup of the database. The *a02h2bank_LastnameFirstname* database remains open.

i. Keep the database onscreen if you plan to continue with Hands-On Exercise 3. If not, close the database and exit Access.

Single-Table Queries

A **query** enables you to ask questions about the data stored in a database.

If you wanted to see which customers currently have an account with a balance over $5,000, you could find the answer by creating an Access query. A ***query*** enables you to ask questions about the data stored in a database. Since data is stored in tables in a database, you always begin a query by asking, "Which table holds the data I want?" For the question about account balances over $5,000, you would reference the Accounts table. In some cases, the data may be held in two or more tables. Multi-table queries will be covered later; for now, you will limit your study of queries to only one table.

If you want to invite customers in a certain zip code to the Grand Opening of a new branch, you could create a query based on the Customers table.

Query Design view enables you to create queries; the Design view is divided into two parts—the top portion displays the tables, and the bottom portion (known as the query design grid) displays the fields and the criteria.

You use the ***Query Design view*** to create queries; the Design view is divided into two parts—the top portion displays the tables, and the bottom portion (known as the query design grid) displays the fields and the criteria.

Using the Query Design view, you select only the fields you want arranged in the order that you want them. The design grid also enables you to sort the records based on one or more fields. You can also create calculated fields to display data based on expressions that use the fields in the underlying table. For example, you could calculate the monthly interest earned on each bank account.

In this section, you will use the Query Wizard and Query Design to create queries that display only data that you select.

Creating a Single-Table Query

The **Simple Query Wizard** provides dialog boxes to guide you through the query design process.

You can create a single-table query in two ways—by using the Simple Query Wizard or by using the Query Design tool in the Queries group. Like all of the Microsoft wizards, the ***Simple Query Wizard*** provides dialog boxes to guide you through the query design process. The wizard is helpful for users who are not experienced with Access or with queries. More advanced users will usually use the Query Design tool to create queries. This method provides the most flexibility when creating queries (but without the prompting of the wizard). You can add criteria to a query while in the Query Design view, as compared to the wizard where you cannot add criteria while the wizard is running. After the query is created, you can switch to Design view and add criteria manually.

After you design a query (using either method), you can display the results of the query by switching to Datasheet view. A query's datasheet looks and acts like a table's datasheet, except that it is usually a subset of the records found in the entire table. The subset only shows the records that match the criteria that were added in the query design. The subset will usually contain different sorting of the records than the sorting in the underlying table. Datasheet view allows you to enter a new record, modify an existing record, or delete a record. Any changes made in Datasheet view are reflected in the underlying table.

TIP Caution: Changes Made to Query Results Overwrite Table Data

Be aware that query results display the actual records that are stored in the underlying table(s). On the one hand, being able to correct an error immediately while it is displayed in query results is an advantage. You save time by not having to close the query, open the table, find the error, fix it, and run the query again. However, you should use caution when editing records in query results since you might not expect to change the table data.

Create a Single-Table Select Query

As stated above, more experienced users create queries using the Query Design tool. To begin click the Create tab, and then click Query Design in the Queries group. The Show Table dialog box appears automatically. Select the table that you need in your query, and then click Add to add the table to the top section of the query design, as shown in Figure 2.33. After the table has been added, close the Show Table dialog box and begin dragging the fields from the table to the query design grid. The grid holds the fields as well as the criteria (for filtering records) and the sorting options. Figure 2.34 shows the Design view of a sample query with four fields, with criteria set for one field, and sorting set on another field. After the query design is finished, click Run in the Results group to show the results in Datasheet view, as shown in Figure 2.35.

A **select query** displays only the records that match the criteria entered in Design view.

By default, when you create a query, you create a select query, which is the most common type of query. A ***select query*** displays only the records that match the criteria entered in Design view. A select query does not change the data. Other types of queries, known as action queries, can update, append, or delete records when they are run. Examples include Update Query, Append Query, and Make Table Query.

TIP Examine the Records

An experienced Access user always examines the records returned in the query results. Verify that the records in the query results match the criteria that you specified in Design view. As you add additional criteria, the number of records returned will usually decrease.

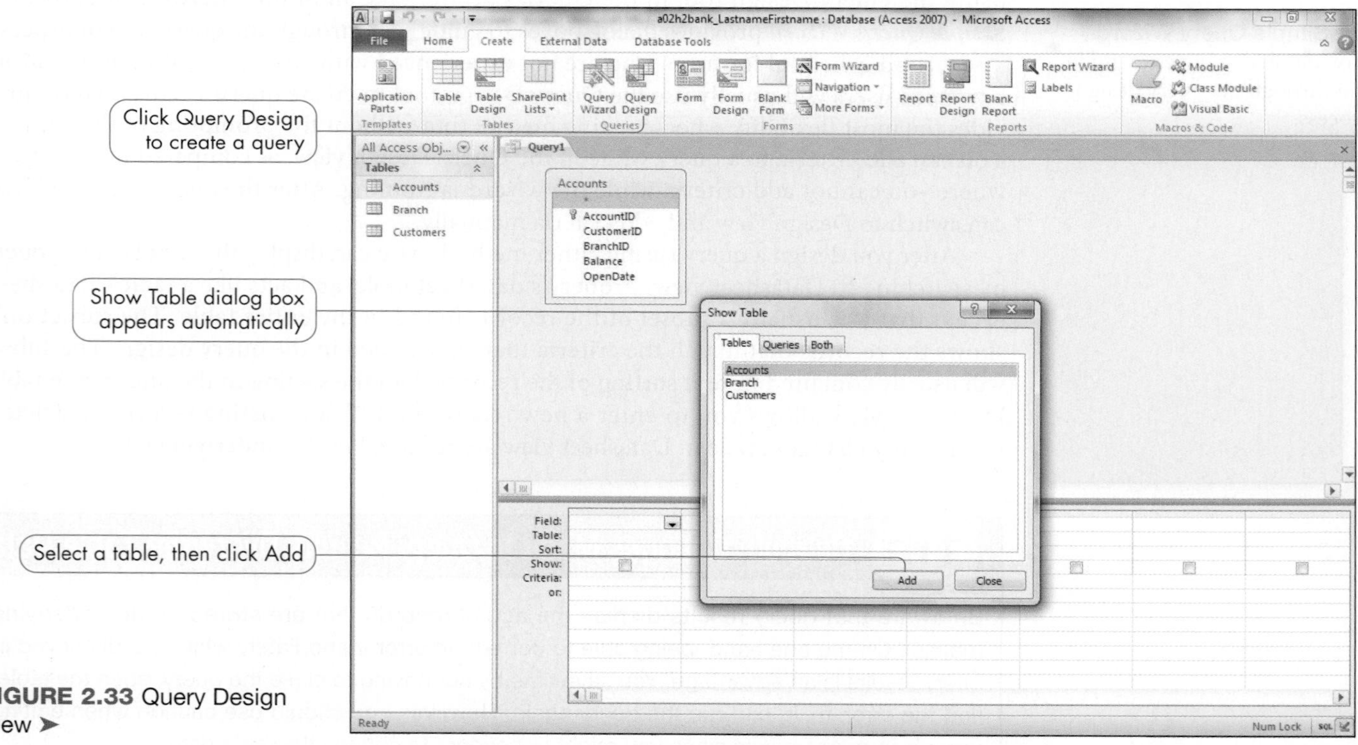

FIGURE 2.33 Query Design View ➤

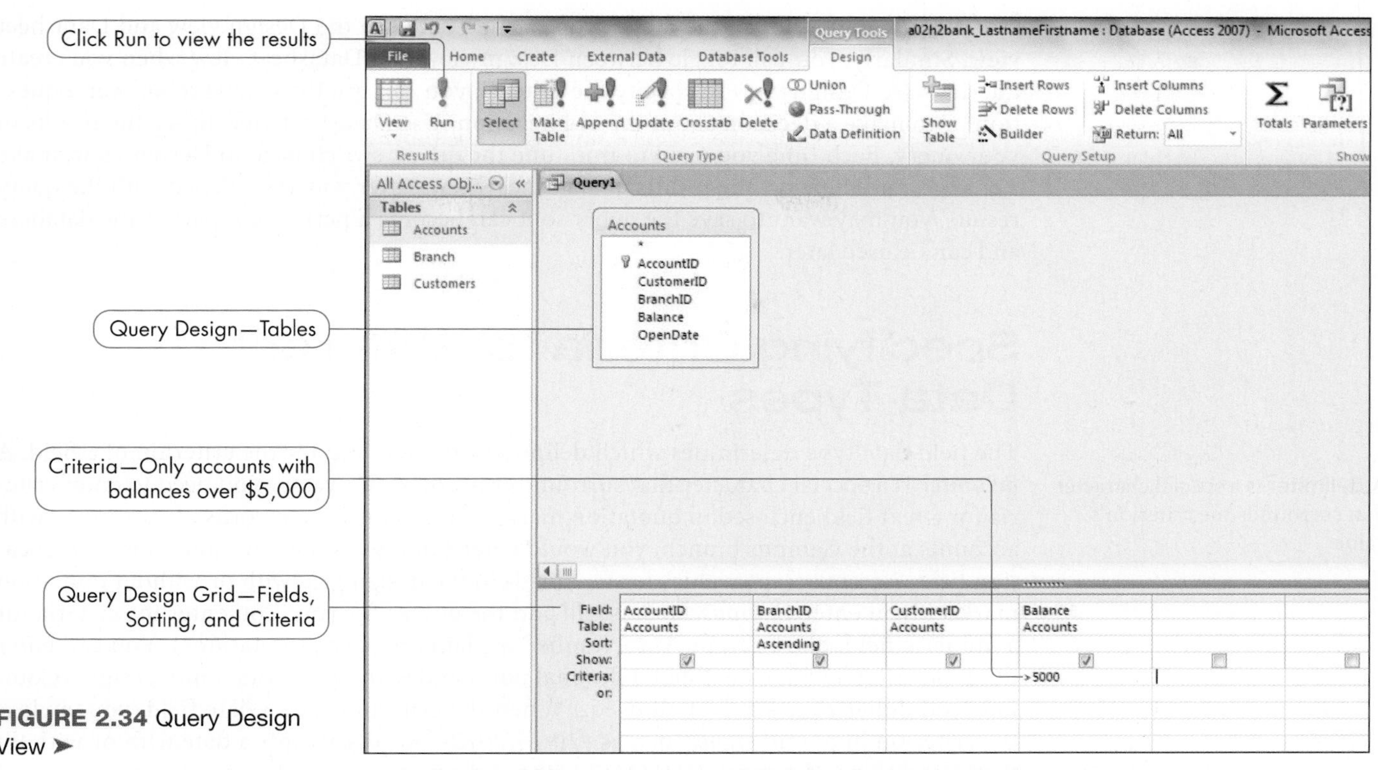

FIGURE 2.34 Query Design View ➤

Only accounts with a balance over $5,000

Query results in Datasheet view

Balance over 5000 Query

Account ID	Branch ID	Customer ID	Balance
1014	B10	30009	$16,700.00
1013	B20	30001	$10,000.00
1003	B20	30004	$15,490.00
1019	B30	30004	$14,250.00
1016	B30	30001	$18,700.00
1018	B40	30005	$7,800.00
1021	B50	30011	$21,004.00
1020	B50	30001	$12,000.00
1001	B50	30010	$5,600.00
*			

FIGURE 2.35 Query Results—Datasheet View ➤

The **Field row** in the Query Design view displays the field name.

The **Table row** in the Query Design view displays the data source.

The **Sort row** in the Query Design view enables you to sort in ascending or descending order.

The **Show row** in the Query Design view controls whether the field will be displayed in the query results.

The **Criteria row** in the Query Design view determines which records will be selected.

Use Query Design View

The Query Design view consists of two parts. The top portion contains tables with their respective field names. If a query contains more than one table, the join lines between tables will be displayed as they were created in the Relationships window.

The bottom portion (known as the query design grid) contains columns and rows. Each field in the query has its own column and contains multiple rows. The rows permit you to control the query results.

- The ***Field row*** in the Query Design view displays the field name.
- The ***Table row*** in the Query Design view displays the data source.
- The ***Sort row*** in the Query Design view enables you to sort in ascending or descending order.
- The ***Show row*** in the Query Design view controls whether the field will be displayed in the query results.
- The ***Criteria row*** in the Query Design view is used to set the rules that determine which records will be selected, such as customers with accounts greater than $5,000.

When you developed the tables, you toggled between the Design view and Datasheet view. Similarly, you will toggle between Design view and Datasheet view when you create queries. Use Design view to specify the criteria; you can use the results to answer a question or to make a decision about the organization. Use Datasheet view to see the results of your query. Each time you need to fine-tune the query, switch back to Design view, make a change, and then test the results in Datasheet view. After you are satisfied with the query results, you may want to save the query so it can become a permanent part of the database and can be used later.

Specifying Criteria for Different Data Types

A **delimiter** is a special character that surrounds the criterion's value.

The field data type determines which delimiters are required for the criterion of a field. A ***delimiter*** is a special character that surrounds the criterion's value. You need to enter criteria for a text field enclosed in quotation marks. To find only the records of customers with accounts at the Campus branch, you would enter *Campus* as the criterion under the Location field. Access accepts values for text fields in the design grid with or without quotation marks; if you enter *Campus*, Access will add the quotes for you. You enter the criteria for a numeric field, currency, or AutoNumber as plain digits (no quotations). You can enter numeric criteria with or without a decimal point and with or without a minus sign. (Commas and dollar signs are not allowed.) When the criterion is in a date field, you enclose the criterion in pound signs, such as *#10/14/2012#*. Access accepts a date with or without the pound signs; if you enter 1/1/2012 without the pound signs, Access will add the pound signs when you move to another column in the design grid. The date value should be in the mm/dd/yyyy format. You enter criteria for a Yes/No field as *Yes* or *No*.

Use Wildcards

A **wildcard** is a special character that can represent one or more characters in the criterion of a query.

Suppose you want to search for the last name of a customer but you are not sure how to spell the name; however, you know that his name starts with the letters Sm. You can specify the criteria in the LastName field as *Sm**, which would display all last names that begin with *Sm*. The asterisk is known as a wildcard. ***Wildcards*** are special characters that can represent one or more characters in a text value. You enter wildcard characters in the Criteria row of a query. A question mark is a wildcard that stands for a single character in the same position as the question mark; for example, *H?ll* will return *Hall*, *Hill*, and *Hull*. The asterisk wildcard stands for any number of characters in the same position as the asterisk; for example, *S*nd* will return *Sand*, *Stand*, and *StoryLand*. If you search the two-letter state code field using criterion Like *?C*, Access will return *DC*, *NC*, and *SC*. If you search the same field using criterion Like **C*, Access will return *DC*, *NC*, and *SC*. If you search the same field using criterion Like *C**, Access will return *CA*, *CO*, and *CT*.

Use Comparison Operators in Queries

A **comparison operator**, such as equal (=), not equal (<>), greater than (>), less than (<), greater than or equal to (>=), and less than or equal to (<=), can be used in the criteria of a query.

A ***comparison operator***, such as equal (=), not equal (<>), greater than (>), less than (<), greater than or equal to (>=), and less than or equal to (<=), can be used in the criteria of a query. Comparison operators enable you to limit the query results to only those records that meet the criteria. For example, if you only want to see accounts that have a balance greater than $5,000, you would type >5000 in the criteria row. Table 2.3 shows more comparison operator examples as well as other sample expressions.

TABLE 2.3 Sample Query Criteria

Expression	Example
>10	For a Price field, items with a price over $10.00.
<10	For a Price field, items with a price under $10.00.
>=10	For a Price field, items with a price of at least $10.00.
<=10	For a Price field, items with a price of $10.00 or less.
=10	For a Price field, items with a price of exactly $10.00.
<>10	For a Price field, items with a price not equal to $10.00.
#2/2/2012#	For a field with a Date/Time data type, such as a ShippedDate field, orders shipped on February 2, 2012.
"Harry"	For a Text field, find the name Harry.
Date( )	For an OrderDate field, orders for today's date.
Between #1/1/2012# and #3/31/2012#	For a specified interval between a start and end date, including the start and end dates.

Work with Null and Zero-Length Strings

Null is the term Access uses to describe a blank field.

Sometimes finding what is missing is an important part of making a decision. For example, if you need to know which orders have been completed but not shipped, you would ask for the orders with a missing ShipDate. Are there missing phone numbers or addresses for some of your customers? Ask for customers with a missing PhoneNumber. The term that Access uses for a blank field is ***null***. Table 2.4 gives two illustrations of when to use the null criterion in a query.

TABLE 2.4 Establishing Null Criteria Expressions

Expression	Example
Is Null	For an Employee field in the Customers table when the customer has not been assigned a sales representative.
Is Not Null	For the ShipDate field; a value inserted indicates the order was shipped to the customer.

Understand Query Sort Order

The **query sort order** determines the order of records in the query's Datasheet view.

The ***query sort order*** determines the order of records in a query's Datasheet view. You can change the order of records by specifying the sort order in the Design view. The sort order is determined from left to right. The order of columns should be considered when first creating the query. For example, a query sorted by Lastname and then by Firstname must have those two fields in the correct order in the design grid. Change the order of the query fields in the design grid to change the sort order of the query results. To change the order of fields, select the column you want to move by clicking the column selector. Release the mouse, then click again and drag the selected field to its new location. To insert additional columns in the design grid, first select a column, and then click Insert Columns in the Query Setup group. The inserted column will insert to the left of the selected column.

Establish AND, OR, and NOT Criteria

Recall the earlier question, "Which customers currently have an account with a balance over $5,000?" This question was answered by creating a query with a single criterion, as shown in Figure 2.34. At times, questions are more specific and require queries with multiple criteria. For example, you may need to know "Which customers from the Eastern branch currently have an account with a balance over $5,000?" To answer this question, you need to specify

The **AND logical operator** returns only records that meet all criteria.

The **OR logical operator** returns records meeting any of the specified criteria.

The **NOT logical operator** returns all records except the specified criteria.

criteria in multiple fields. When the criteria are in the same row of the query design grid, Access interprets the instructions using the ***AND logical operator***. This means that the query results will display only records that match *all* criteria. When the criteria are positioned in different rows of the design grid, Access interprets the instructions using the ***OR logical operator***. The query results will display records that match any of the specified criteria. The ***NOT logical operator*** returns all records except the specified criteria. For example, "Not Eastern" would return all accounts except those opened at the Eastern branch.

Figure 2.36a shows a query with an AND logical operator. It will return all of the B20 branch accounts with balances over $5,000. (Both conditions must be met for the record to be included.) Figure 2.36b shows a query with an OR logical operator. It will return all of the B20 branch accounts regardless of balance plus all accounts at any branch with a balance over $5,000. (One condition must be met for a record to be included.) Figure 2.36c shows a query that uses the NOT logical operator. It will return all of the accounts—excluding the B20 branch—with a balance over $5,000. Figure 2.36d shows a query that combines AND and OR logical operators. The top row will return B20 branch accounts with a balance over $5,000, and the second row will return B30 branch accounts with a balance over $15,000.

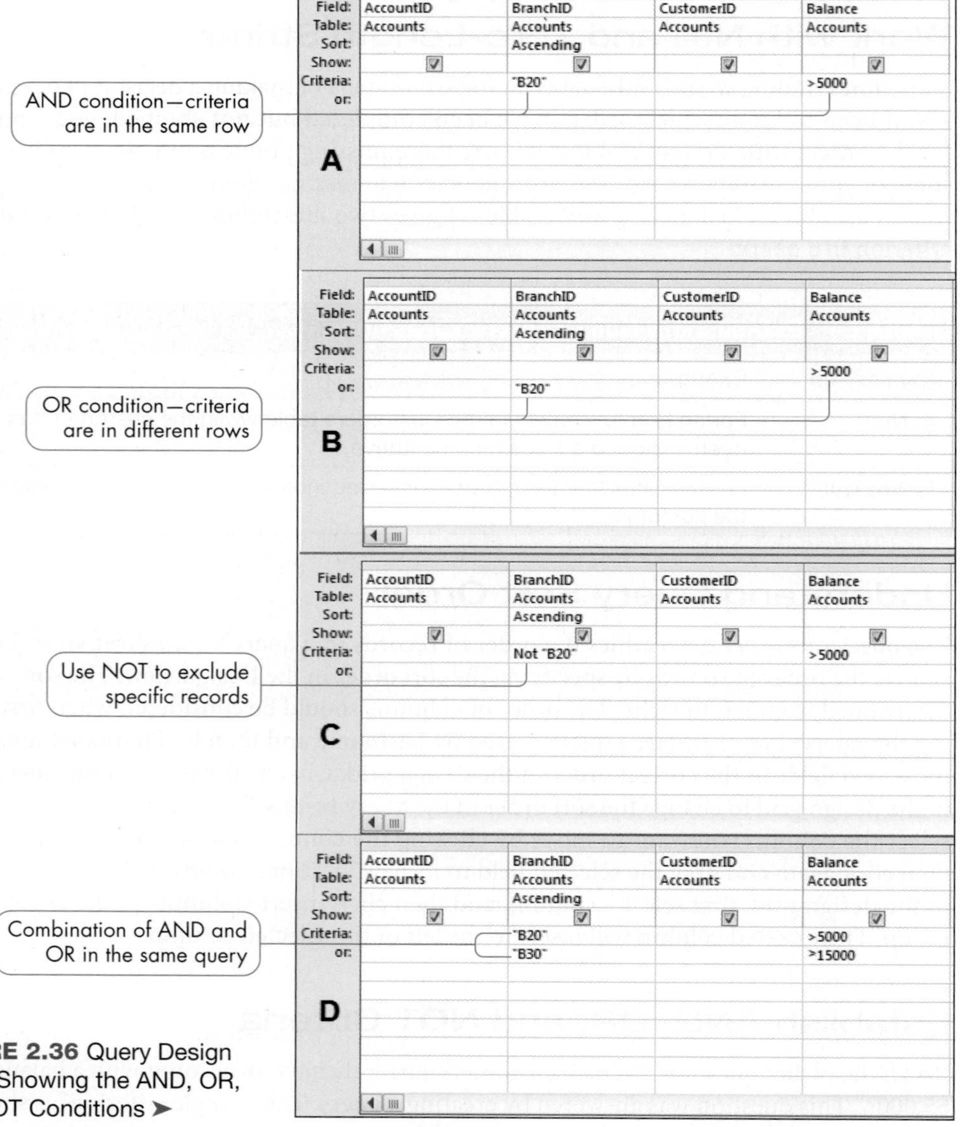

FIGURE 2.36 Query Design Views Showing the AND, OR, and NOT Conditions ➤

Copying and Running a Query

After you create a query, you may want to create a duplicate copy to use as the basis for creating a similar query. Duplicating a query saves time when you need the same tables and fields but with slightly different criteria.

Several ways exist to run a query. One method is to locate the query in the Navigation Pane, and then double-click it. A similar method is to select the query, and then press Enter. Another way is to click Run in the Results group, when you are in Design view.

Copy a Query

Sometimes you have a one-of-a-kind question about your data. You would create a query to answer this question and then delete the query. However, sometimes you need a series of queries where each query is similar to the first. For example, you need "Sales for This Month" in Houston, in Dallas, and in Chicago. In cases like this, you create a query for the first city and then save the query. Click Save As to save a copy of the query and name it for the second city. Change the criteria to match the second city. Repeat the process for the third city.

Run a Query

The **Run command** (the red exclamation point) is used to produce the query results.

After you create a query and save it, you can run it directly from the Design view. You run a query by clicking ***Run command*** (the red exclamation point) in the Results group. In the sample databases, the queries run quickly. For larger databases, query results may take several minutes to display. When you design queries in larger databases, include all necessary fields and tables, but do not include fields or tables that are not necessary to answer the question. You can also run a query from the Navigation Pane. Locate the query you want to run, and then double-click the query. The results will appear as a tab in the main window. (Note: This method is only recommended for select queries. This method is not recommended for action queries, which will be covered later.)

Using the Query Wizard

You may create a query directly in Design view or by using the Query Wizard. Even if you initiate the query with a wizard, you will need to learn how to modify it in Design view. Often, copying an existing query and making slight modifications to its design is much faster than starting at the beginning with the wizard. You also will need to know how to add additional tables and fields to an existing query when conditions change. To launch the Query Wizard, click the Create tab, and then click Query Wizard in the Queries group (see Figure 2.37).

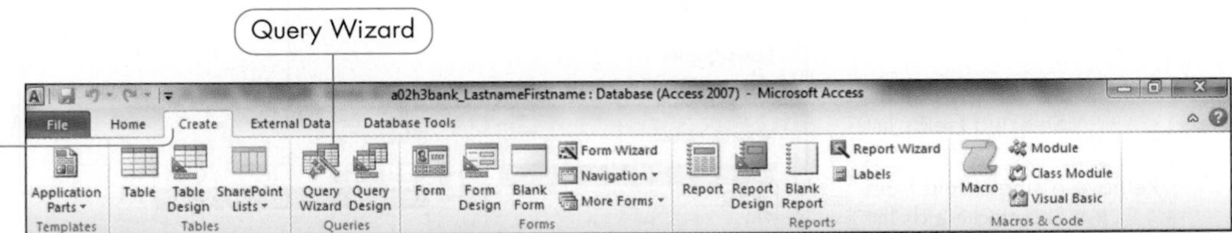

FIGURE 2.37 Launching the Query Wizard ➤

Select the Simple Query Wizard in the Query Wizard dialog box, as shown in Figure 2.38.

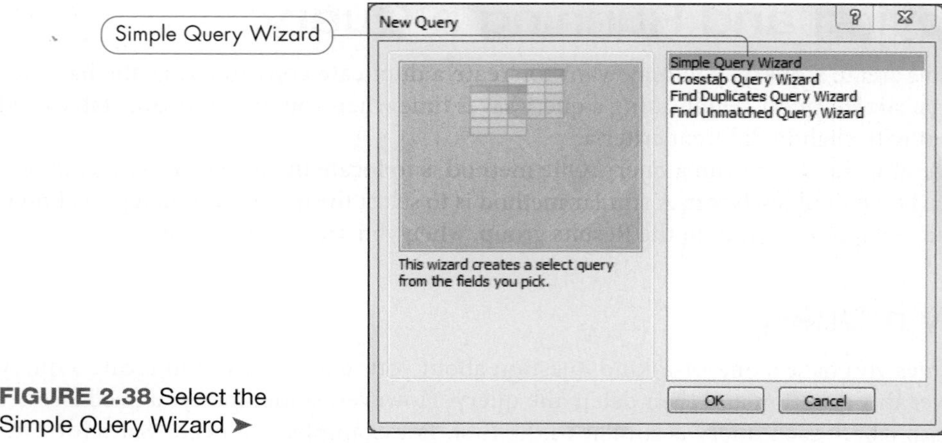

FIGURE 2.38 Select the Simple Query Wizard ➤

In the first step of the Simple Query Wizard dialog box, you specify the tables or queries and fields needed in your query. When you select a table from the Tables/Queries arrow, a list of the table's fields displays in the Available Fields list box. See Figures 2.39 and 2.40.

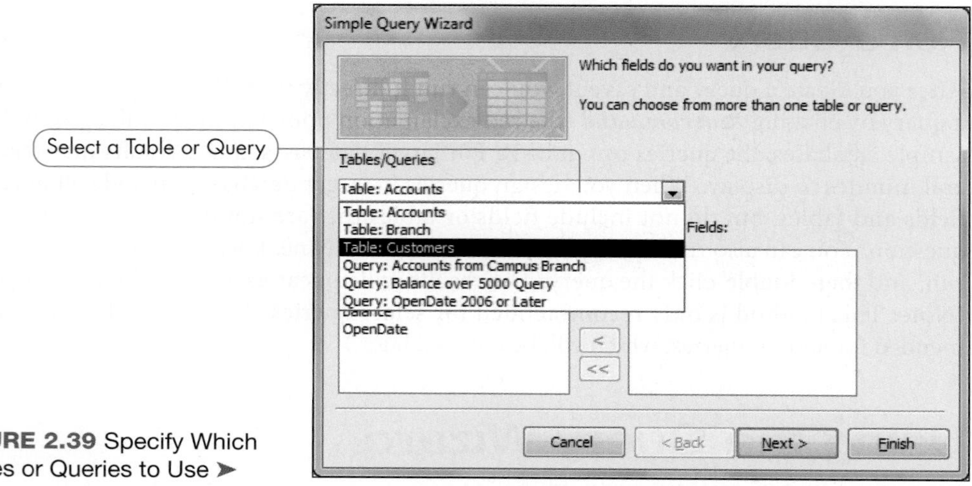

FIGURE 2.39 Specify Which Tables or Queries to Use ➤

Select the necessary fields, and then add them to the Selected Fields list box using the directional arrows shown in Figure 2.40.

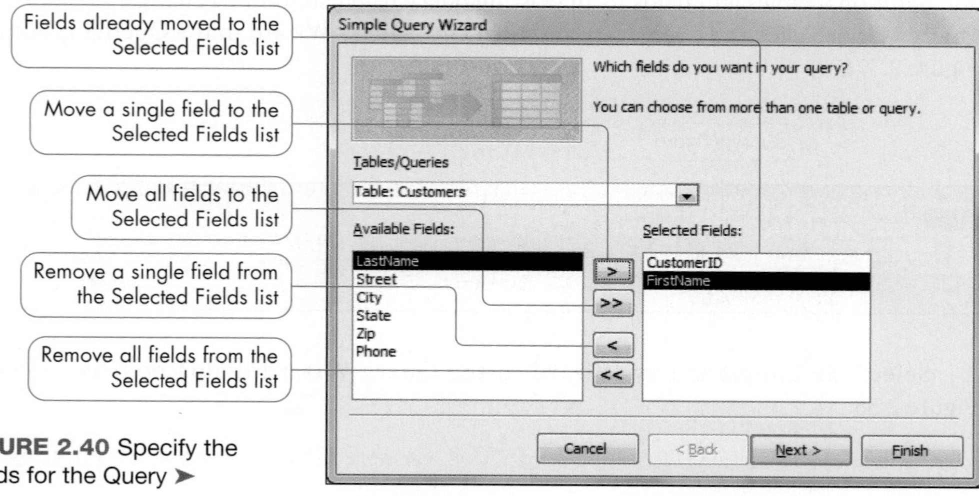

FIGURE 2.40 Specify the Fields for the Query ➤

In the next screen (shown in Figure 2.41), you choose between a detail and a summary query. The detail query shows every field of every record in the result. The summary query enables you to group data and view only summary records. For example, if you were interested in the total funds deposited at each of the bank branches, you would set the query to Summary, click Summary Options, and then click sum on the balance field. Access would then sum the balances of all accounts for each branch.

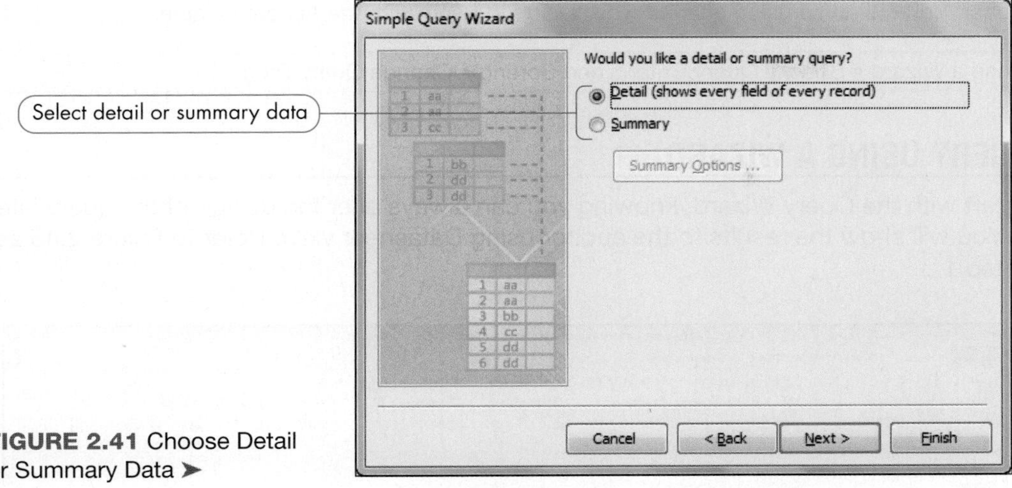

FIGURE 2.41 Choose Detail or Summary Data ➤

The final dialog box of the Simple Query Wizard asks for the name of the query. Assign a descriptive name to your queries so that you know what each does by looking at the query name. See Figure 2.42.

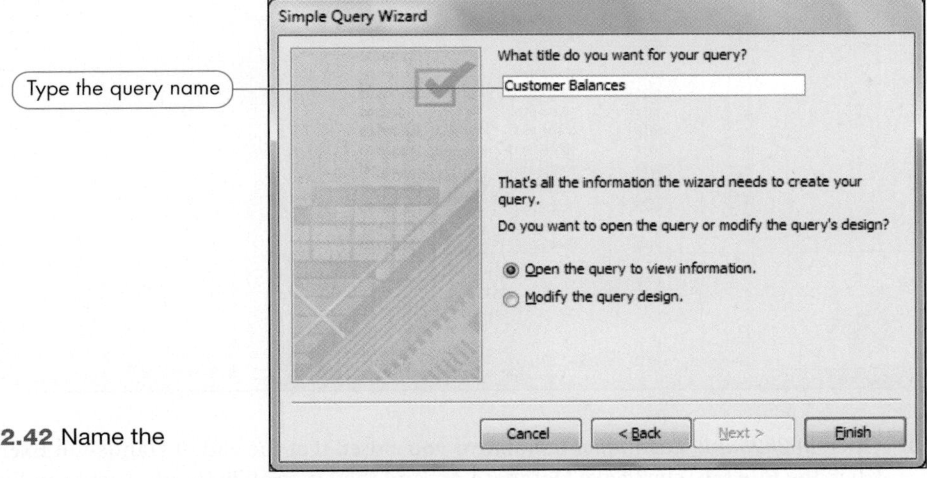

FIGURE 2.42 Name the Query ➤

The next Hands-On Exercise enables you to create and run queries in order to find answers to questions you have about your data. You will use the Query Wizard to create a basic query and then modify the query in Design view by adding an additional field and by adding query criteria.

Quick Concepts Check

1. Define a query. Give an example.
2. Give an example of how to use the criteria row to find certain records in a table.
3. When would you need to use the "is null" and "is not null" criteria?
4. When would you want to copy a query?

HANDS-ON EXERCISES

3 Single-Table Queries

The tables and table relationships have been created, and some data has been entered. Now, you need to begin the process of analyzing the bank data for the auditor. You will do so using queries. You decide to begin with the Accounts table.

Skills covered: Create a Query Using a Wizard • Specify Query Criteria and Sorting • Change Query Data

STEP 1 CREATE A QUERY USING A WIZARD

You decide to start with the Query Wizard, knowing you can always alter the design of the query later in Design view. You will show the results to the auditor using Datasheet view. Refer to Figure 2.43 as you complete Step 1.

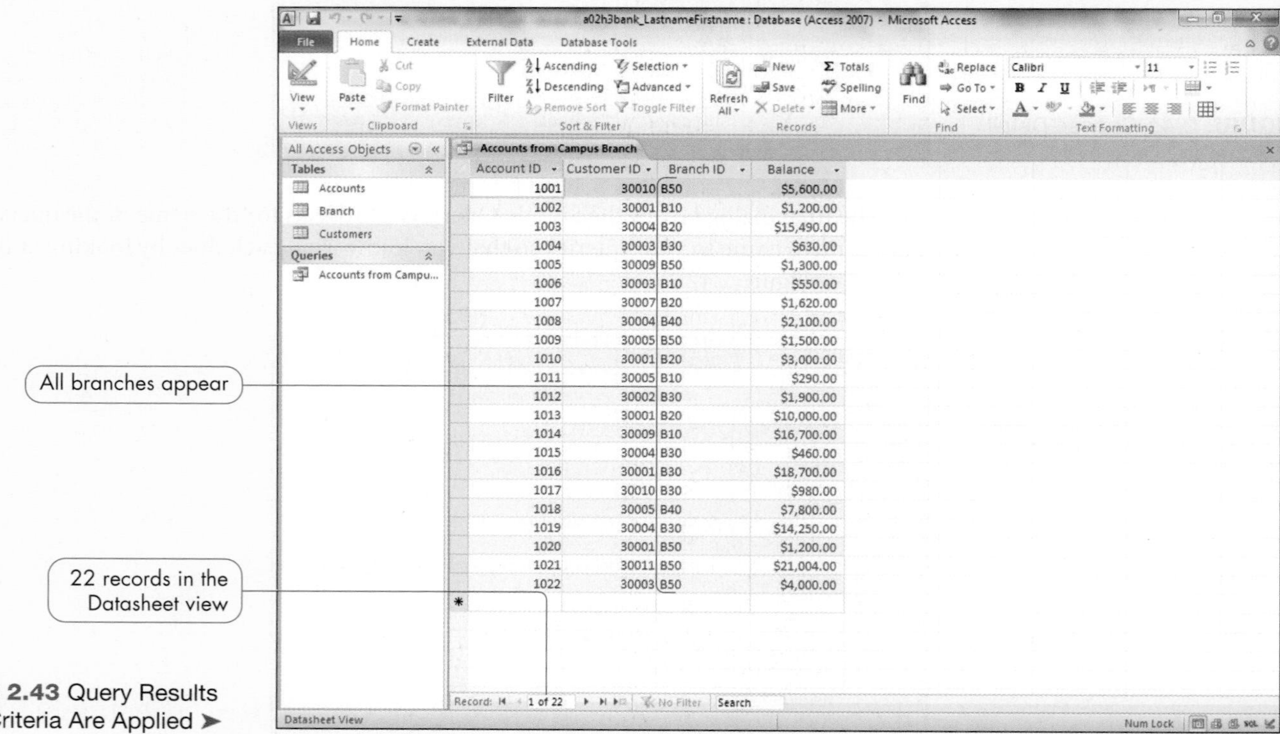

FIGURE 2.43 Query Results Before Criteria Are Applied ➤

a. Open *a02h2bank_LastnameFirstname* if you closed it at the end of Hands-On Exercise 2. Click the **File tab**, click **Save Database As**, and then type **a02h3bank_LastnameFirstname**, changing *h2* to *h3*. Click **Save**.

b. Click the **Create tab**, and then click **Query Wizard** in the Queries group to launch the New Query wizard.

   The New Query Wizard dialog box opens. Simple Query Wizard is selected by default.

c. Click **OK**.

d. Verify that **Table: Accounts** is selected.

e. Select **AccountID** from the **Available Fields list**, and then click >. Repeat the process with **CustomerID**, **BranchID**, and **Balance**. The four fields should now appear in the Selected Fields list box. Click **Next**.

f. Confirm **Detail** is selected, and then click **Next**.

g. Name the query **Accounts from Campus Branch**. Click **Finish**.

This query name describes the data in the query results. Your query should have four fields: AccountID, CustomerID, BranchID, and Balance.

STEP 2 SPECIFY QUERY CRITERIA AND SORTING

The auditor indicated that the problem seems to be confined to the Campus branch. You use this knowledge to revise the query accordingly. Refer to Figure 2.44 as you complete Step 2.

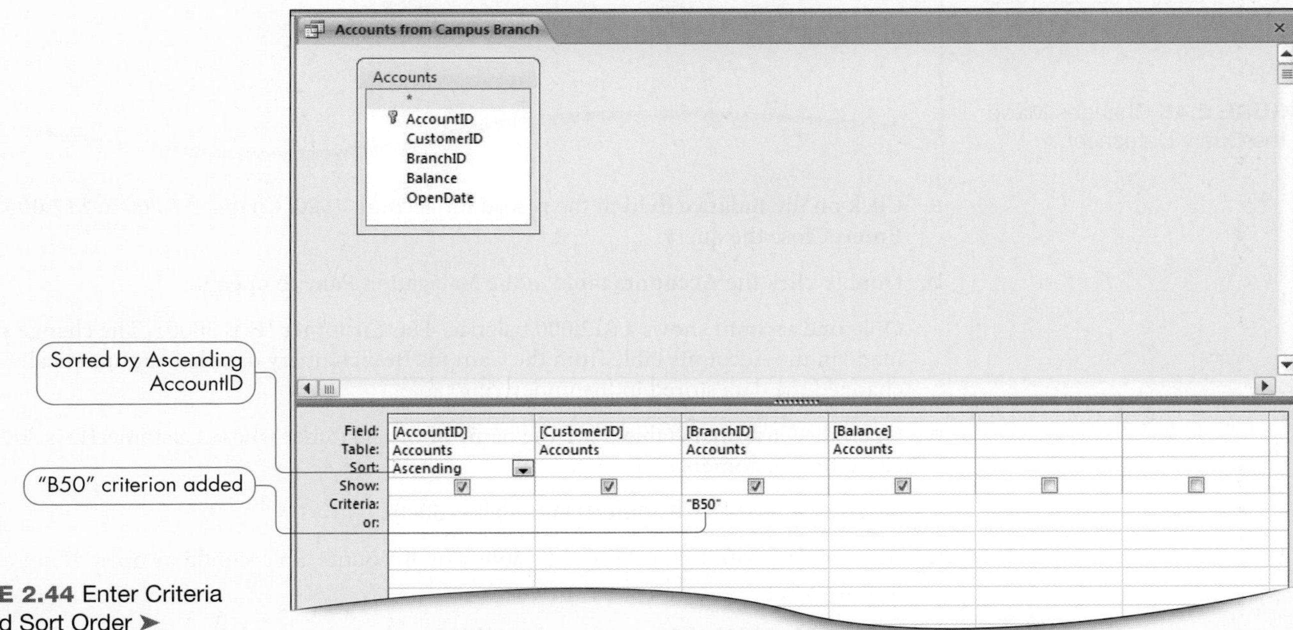

FIGURE 2.44 Enter Criteria and Add Sort Order ➤

a. Click the **Home tab**, and then click **View** in the Views group to views the Accounts from Campus Branch query in Design view.

You have created the Campus Branch Customers query to view only those accounts at the Campus branch. However, other branch's accounts also display. You need to limit the query results to only the records of interest.

b. Click in the **Criteria row** (fifth row) in the **BranchID column**, and then type **B50**.

B50 is the BranchID for the Campus branch. Access queries are not case sensitive; therefore, b50 and B50 will produce the same results. Access adds quotation marks around text criteria.

c. Click in the **Sort row** (third row) in the **AccountID column**, and then choose **Ascending** from the list.

d. Click **Run** in the Results group.

You should see six records, all from Branch B50, in the query results.

e. Save the query.

STEP 3 CHANGE QUERY DATA

When the query results are on the screen, the auditor notices that some of the data is incorrect, and one of the accounts is missing. From your experience with Access, you explain to the auditor that the data can be changed directly in a query rather than switching back to the table. Refer to Figure 2.45 as you complete Step 3.`

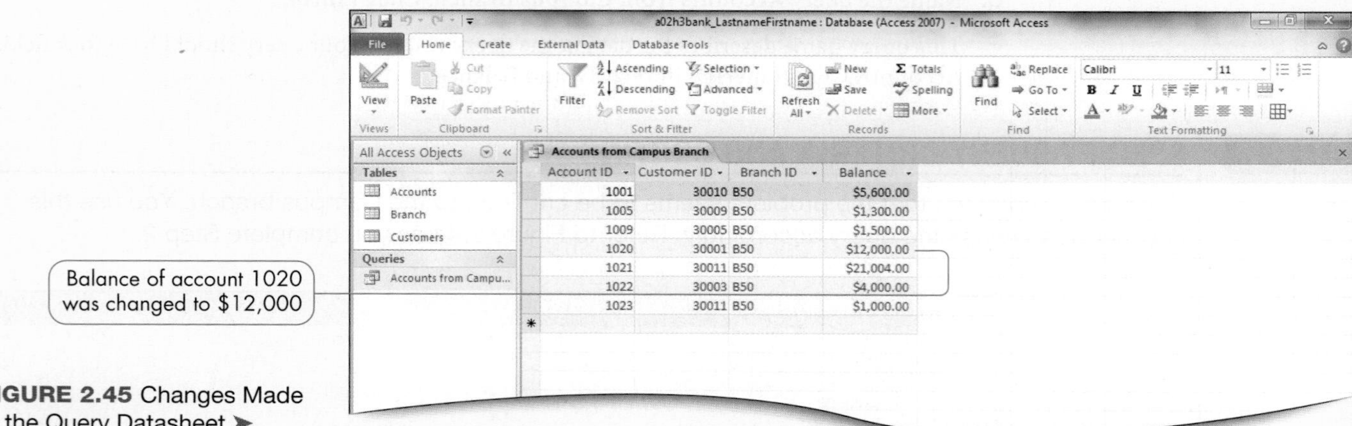

Account ID	Customer ID	Branch ID	Balance
1001	30010	B50	$5,600.00
1005	30009	B50	$1,300.00
1009	30005	B50	$1,500.00
1020	30001	B50	$12,000.00
1021	30011	B50	$21,004.00
1022	30003	B50	$4,000.00
1023	30011	B50	$1,000.00

FIGURE 2.45 Changes Made in the Query Datasheet ➤

a. Click on the **Balance field** in the record for account *1020*. Change *$1,200* to **$12,000**. Press **Enter**. Close the query.

b. Double-click the **Accounts table** in the Navigation Pane to open it.

Only one account shows a $12,000 balance. The Customer ID is 30001. The change you made in the Accounts table from the Campus Branch query datasheet automatically changed the data stored in the underlying table.

c. Open the Customers table. Find the name of the customer whose CustomerID is *30001*. Close the Customers table.

Allison Millward's CustomerID number is 30001.

d. Add a new record to the Accounts table. The Accounts table should be open. If not, open it now.

e. Type **1023**, **30011**, **B50**, **1000**, and **1/4/2012** in the new record. Press **Tab**.

f. Double-click the **Accounts from Campus Branch query** in the Navigation Pane.

Customer 30011 now shows two accounts: one with a balance of $21,004 and one with a balance of $1,000.

g. Close the Accounts from Campus Branch query. Close the Accounts table.

h. Click the **File tab**, and then click **Compact & Repair Database**.

i. Click the **File tab**, click **Save & Publish**, and then double-click **Back Up Database**. Accept *a02h3bank_date* as the file name, and then click **Save**.

You just created a backup of the database. The *a02h3bank_LastnameFirstname* database remains open.

j. Keep the database onscreen if you plan to continue with Hands-On Exercise 4. If not, close the database and exit Access.

Multi-Table Queries

A **multi-table query** contains two or more tables. It enables you to take advantage of the relationships that have been set in your database.

The sample bank database contains three tables: Customers, Accounts, and Branch. You learned how to connect the tables through relationships in order to store data efficiently and enforce consistent data entry. ***Multi-table queries*** contain two or more tables. They enable you to take advantage of the relationships that have been set in your database. When you need to extract information from a database with a query, most times you will need multiple tables to provide the answers you need.

One table may contain the core information that you need. Another table may contain the related data that makes the query relevant to the users. For example, the Accounts table will list the balances of each account at the bank—the key financial information. However, the Accounts table does not list the contact information of the owner of the account. Therefore, the Customers table is needed to provide the additional information.

Creating a Multi-Table Query

Related tables are tables that are joined in a relationship using a common field.

Creating a multi-table query is similar to creating a single-table query; however, choosing the right tables and managing the table relationships will require some additional skills. First, you should only include related tables in a multi-table query. ***Related tables*** are tables that are joined in a relationship using a common field. As a rule, related tables should already be established when you create a multi-table query. Using Figure 2.46 as a guide, creating a query with the Accounts and Branch tables would be acceptable, as would using Accounts and Customers tables, or Accounts, Branch, and Customers tables. All three scenarios include related tables. Creating a query with the Branch and Customers tables would not be acceptable, since these tables are *not* directly related.

TIP Print the Relationship Report to Help Create a Multi-Table Query

When creating a multi-table query, you should only include related tables. As a guide, you can print the Relationship Report in the Tools group on the Relationship Tools Design tab when the Relationships window is open. This report will help you determine which tables are related in your database.

In the previous example, you answered the question "Which customers from the Campus branch have an account with a balance over $5,000?" Figure 2.35 displays the datasheet results of the query. To make this report more useful, we can add the Branch Location (in place of the BranchID) and the Customer LastName (in place of the CustomerID). To make these changes we would need to add the Branch table and the Customers table to the query design.

Add Additional Tables to a Query

As discussed earlier, you can modify a saved query using Design view for the query. If you wanted to change the Balance Over $5000 query, first open the query in Design view. To add additional tables to a query, open the Navigation Pane, and then drag tables directly into the top portion of the query design grid. For example, the Branch and Customers tables were added to the query as shown in Figure 2.46. The join lines between tables indicate that relationships were previously set in the Relationships window.

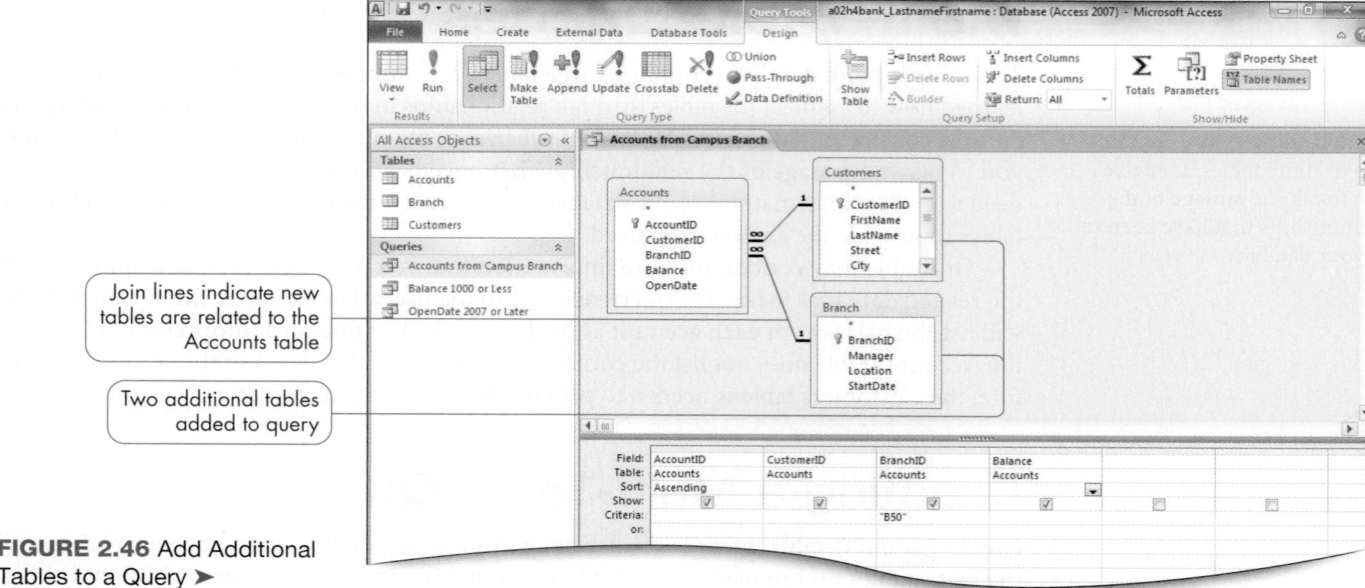

FIGURE 2.46 Add Additional Tables to a Query ➤

Get Answers Using a Multi-Table Query

You can get key information from your database using a multi-table query. For example, if you want to know how many orders each customer placed since the database was created, you would create a new query and add the Customers and Orders tables to the Query Design view. After you verify that the join lines are correct, add the CustomerID field from the Customers table and the OrderID field from the Order table to the query design grid. When you run the query, the results show duplicates in the CustomerID column because Customers place multiple orders.

To fix the duplicate CustomerID problem, return to the Query Design view, and then click Totals in the Show/Hide group. Both columns show the Group By option in the Total row. Change the total row of the OrderID field to Count, and then run the query again. This time the results show one row for each customer and the number of orders each customer placed since the database was created.

Modifying a Multi-Table Query

To modify multi-table queries, you use the same techniques you learned for single-table queries. Add tables using the Show Table dialog box; remove tables by clicking the unwanted table and then pressing Delete. Add fields by double-clicking the field you want; remove fields by clicking the column selector and then pressing Delete. Join lines between related tables should appear automatically in a query if the relationships were previously established, as shown in Figure 2.46.

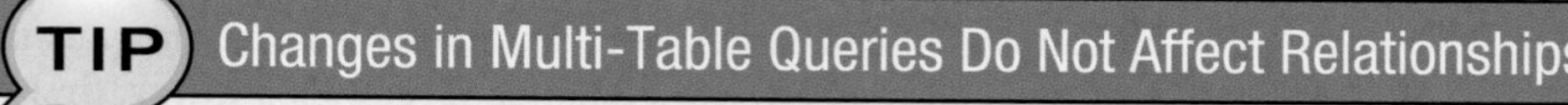

TIP Changes in Multi-Table Queries Do Not Affect Relationships

When you add two or more tables to a query, join lines appear automatically. You can delete the join lines in a query with no impact on the relationships themselves. Deleting a join line only affects the relationships in the individual query. The next time you create a query with the same tables, the join lines will be restored. And, if you open the Relationships window, you will find the join lines in tact.

Add and Delete Fields in a Multi-Table Query

In Figure 2.46, three tables, as well as the join lines between the tables, now appear in the top pane of the Query Design view. All the fields from each of the tables are available to be used in the query design grid. Figure 2.47 shows that Location (from the Branch table) and LastName (from the Customers table) have been added to the design, and BranchID and CustomerID have been deleted. The BranchID was deleted from the query; therefore, the 'B50' criterion was removed as well. 'Campus' was added to the Location field's criteria row in order to extract the same results. Because criteria values are not case sensitive, typing 'campus' is the same as typing 'Campus', and both will return the same results. Run the query to see that the datasheet is more useful now that the Location and LastName fields have been added. The results are shown in Figure 2.48.

Accounts from Campus Branch

Accounts: *, AccountID, CustomerID, BranchID, Balance, OpenDate

Customers: *, CustomerID, FirstName, LastName, Street, City

Branch: *, BranchID, Manager, Location, StartDate

Location replaced BranchID

LastName replaced CustomerID

Criteria was changed from 'B50' to 'Campus'

Field:	AccountID	LastName	Balance	Location	
Table:	Accounts	Customers	Accounts	Branch	
Sort:	Ascending				
Show:	☑	☑	☑	☑	☐
Criteria:				"Campus"	

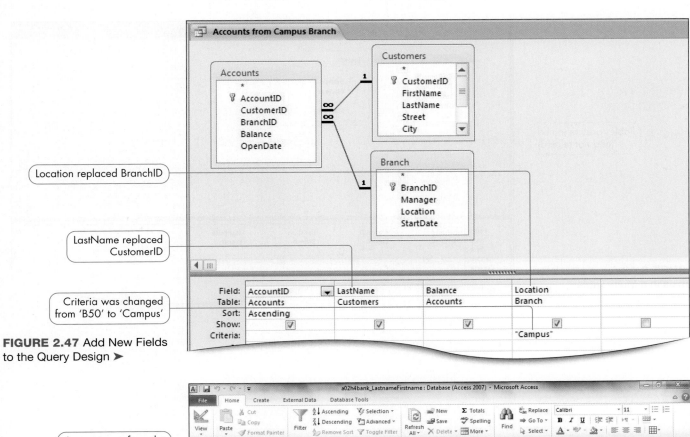

FIGURE 2.47 Add New Fields to the Query Design ➤

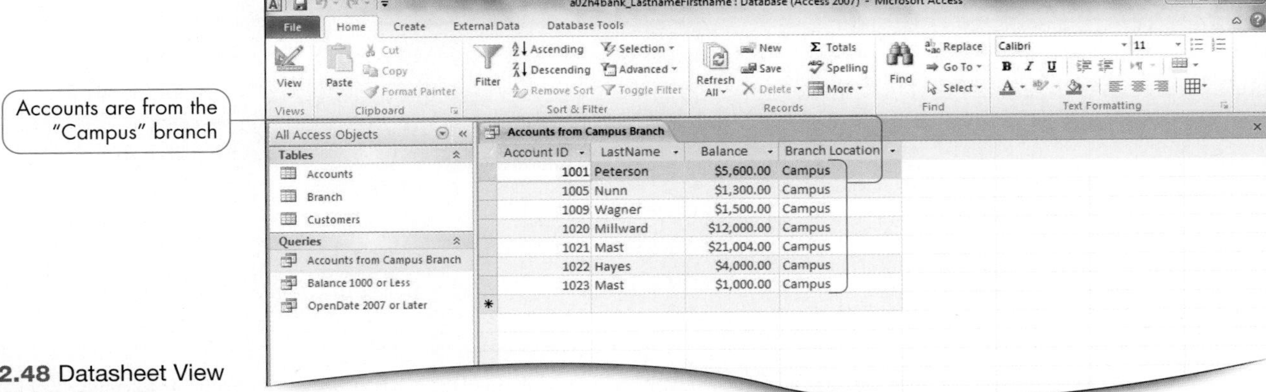

FIGURE 2.48 Datasheet View of a Multi-Table Query ➤

Fix a Common Problem in a Multi-Table Query

In Figure 2.49, two tables are added to the query design, but no join line connects them. The results of the query will be unpredictable and larger (i.e., more records) than expected. The Customers table contains 11 records, and the Branch table contains 5 records. Since Access does not know how to interpret the unrelated tables, the results will show 55 records—every possible combination of customer and branch (11 × 5). See Figure 2.50.

To fix this problem, you can create join lines using the existing tables if the tables facilitate this. Or you can add an additional table that will provide a join between all three tables. In the Branch query, you can add the Accounts table, which will facilitate a join between the two existing tables, Customers and Branch. As soon as the third table is added to the query design, the join lines appear automatically, as shown in Figure 2.47.

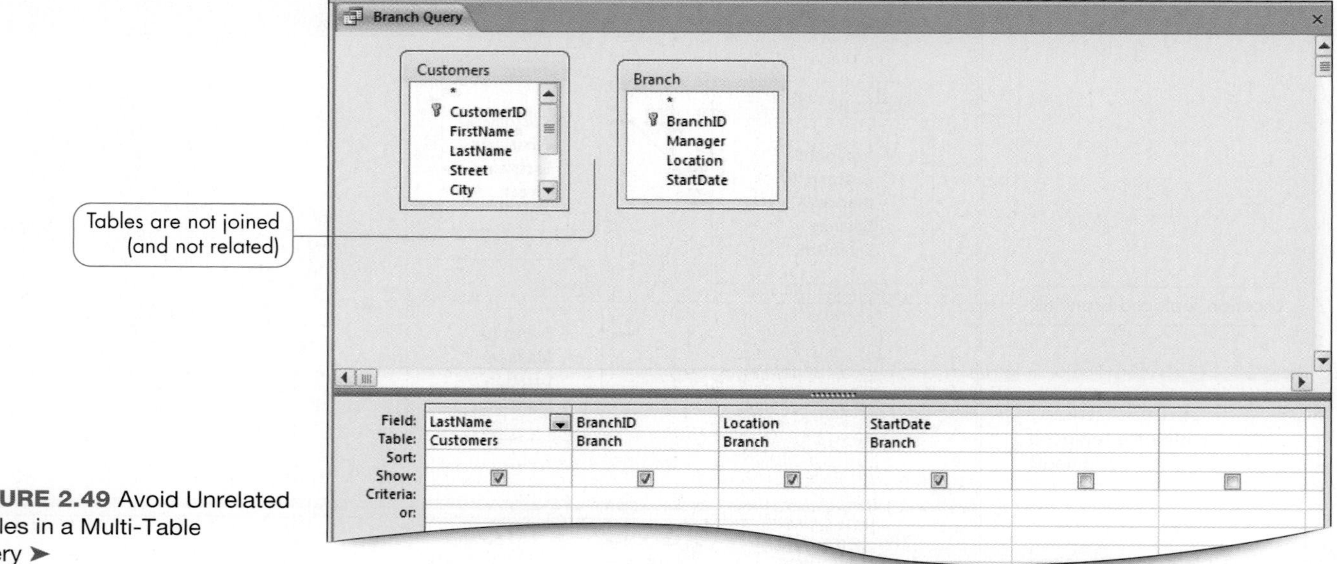

FIGURE 2.49 Avoid Unrelated Tables in a Multi-Table Query ➤

Access shows one record for every Branch for each Customer

Result shows 55 Records

Query1

LastName	Branch ID	Branch Location	Manager's Start Date
Millward	B10	Uptown	12/1/2007
Millward	B20	Eastern	6/17/2008
Millward	B30	Western	3/11/2006
Millward	B40	Southern	9/15/2009
Millward	B50	Campus	10/11/2011
Fox	B10	Uptown	12/1/2007
Fox	B20	Eastern	6/17/2008
Fox	B30	Western	3/11/2006
Fox	B40	Southern	9/15/2009
Fox	B50	Campus	10/11/2011
Hayes	B10	Uptown	12/1/2007
Hayes	B20	Eastern	6/17/2008
Hayes	B30	Western	3/11/2006
Hayes	B40	Southern	9/15/2009
Hayes	B50	Campus	10/11/2011
Collins	B10	Uptown	12/1/2007
Collins	B20	Eastern	6/17/2008
Collins	B30	Western	3/11/2006
Collins	B40	Southern	9/15/2009
Collins	B50	Campus	10/11/2011
Wagner	B10	Uptown	12/1/2007
Wagner	B20	Eastern	6/17/2008
Wagner	B30	Western	3/11/2006
Wagner	B40	Southern	9/15/2009
Wagner	B50	Campus	10/11/2011
Williams	B10	Uptown	12/1/2007
Williams	B20	Eastern	6/17/2008

Record: 1 of 55 No Filter Search

FIGURE 2.50 Query Result with Unrelated Tables ➤

Add a Join Line in a Multi-Table Query

Over time, your database will grow, and additional tables will be added. Occasionally, new tables are added to the database but not added to the Relationships window. When queries are created with the new tables, join lines will not be established. When this happens, you can create temporary join lines in the query design. These join lines will provide a temporary relationship between two tables and enable Access to interpret the query properly.

The process of creating a multi-table query works the same as creating a single-table query (covered previously in this chapter). In the Query Design view, you will add fields to the bottom portion (the query design grid), set the sorting, decide whether to show the fields, and add criteria as needed. You should take some precautions when working with multiple tables; these precautions will be discussed later.

Quick Concepts Check

1. Define a multi-table query.
2. What are the benefits of creating multi-table queries?
3. What is the result of creating a query with two unrelated tables?
4. Describe the purpose of a join line.

4 Multi-Table Queries

Based on the auditor's request, you will need to evaluate the data further. This requires creating queries that are based on multiple tables, rather than a single table. You decide to open an existing query, add additional tables, and then save the query with a new name.

Skills covered: Add Additional Tables to a Query • Create a Multi-Table Query • Modify a Multi-Table Query

STEP 1 ADD ADDITIONAL TABLES TO A QUERY

The previous query was based on the Accounts table, but now you need to add information to the query that is in the Branch table. You will need to add the Branch and Customers tables to the query. Refer to Figure 2.51 as you complete Step 1.

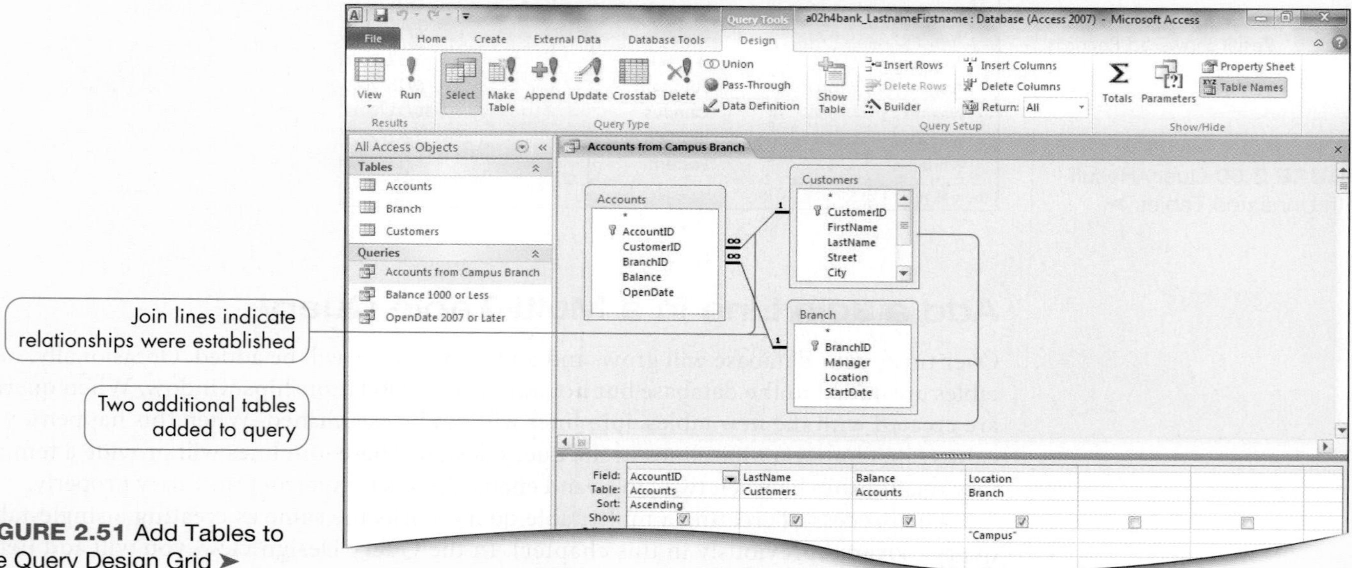

FIGURE 2.51 Add Tables to the Query Design Grid ➤

a. Open *a02h3bank_LastnameFirstname* if you closed it at the end of Hands-On Exercise 3. Click the **File tab**, click **Save Database As**, and then type **a02h4bank_LastnameFirstname**, changing *h3* to *h4*. Click **Save**.

b. Right-click the **Accounts from Campus Branch query** in the Navigation Pane, and then select **Design View** from the shortcut menu.

c. Drag the **Branch table** from the Navigation Pane to the top pane of the query design grid next to the Accounts table.

   A join line connects the Branch table to the Accounts table. The query inherits the join lines from the relationships created in the Relationships window.

d. Drag the **Location field** from the Branch table to the first empty column in the design grid.

   The Location field should be positioned to the right of the Balance column.

e. Click the **Show check box** under the BranchID field to clear the check box and hide this field in the results.

   The BranchID field is no longer needed since the Location field provides the same information. Because you unchecked the BranchID show check box, the BranchID field will not appear the next time the query is opened.

f. Delete the **B50 criterion** in the BranchID field.

g. Type **Campus** as a criterion in the **Location field**, and then press **Enter**.

   Access adds quotation marks around *Campus* for you; quotes are required for text criteria. You are substituting the Location criterion (*Campus*) in place of the BranchID criterion (B50).

h. Remove Ascending from the AccountID sort row. Click in the **Sort row** of the Balance field. Click the arrow, and then select **Descending** from the list.

   The query will be sorted by descending balance order. The largest balance will be listed first, and the smallest will be last.

i. Click **Run** in the Results group.

   Only Campus accounts should appear in the datasheet. Next, you will add the Customer LastName and criteria, and then delete CustomerID from the query.

j. Click **View** in the Views group to return to the Design view.

k. Drag the **Customers table** from the Navigation Pane to the top section of the query design grid.

   The one-to-many relationship lines automatically connect the Customers table to the Accounts table (similar to step c above).

l. Drag the **LastName field** in the Customers table to the second column in the design grid.

   The LastName field should be positioned to the right of the AccountID field.

m. Click the column selector in the CustomerID field to select it. Press **Delete**.

   The CustomerID field is no longer needed in the results because we added the LastName field.

n. Click **Run** in the Results group.

o. Save and close the query.

STEP 2 CREATE A MULTI-TABLE QUERY

After discussing the query results with the auditor, you realize that another query is needed to show those customers with account balances of $1,000 or less. You create the query and view the results in Datasheet view. Refer to Figure 2.52 as you complete Step 2.

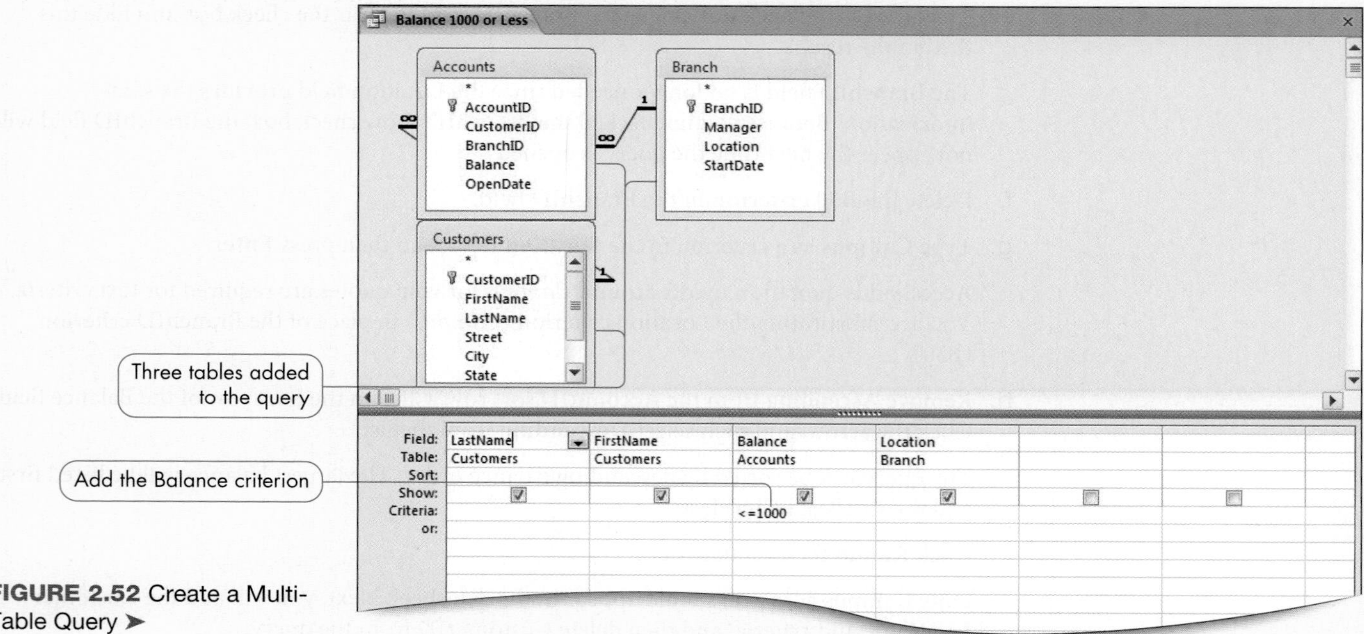

FIGURE 2.52 Create a Multi-Table Query ➤

a. Click the **Create tab**, and click **Query Design** in the Queries group.

b. Double-click each table name in the Show Table dialog box to add each one to the Query Design view. Click **Close** in the Show Table dialog box.

c. Double-click the following fields to add them to the design grid: **LastName**, **FirstName**, **Balance**, and **Location**.

d. Type <=**1000** in the **Criteria row** of the Balance column.

e. Click **Run** in the Results group to see the query results.

   Six records appear in the query results.

f. Click **Save** on the Quick Access Toolbar, and then type **Balance 1000 or Less** as the Query Name in the **Save As dialog box**. Click **OK**.

STEP 3 MODIFY A MULTI-TABLE QUERY

The auditor requests additional changes to the Balance 1000 or Less query you just created. You will modify the criteria to display the accounts that were opened after January 1, 2006, with balances of $2,000 or less. Refer to Figure 2.53 as you complete Step 3.

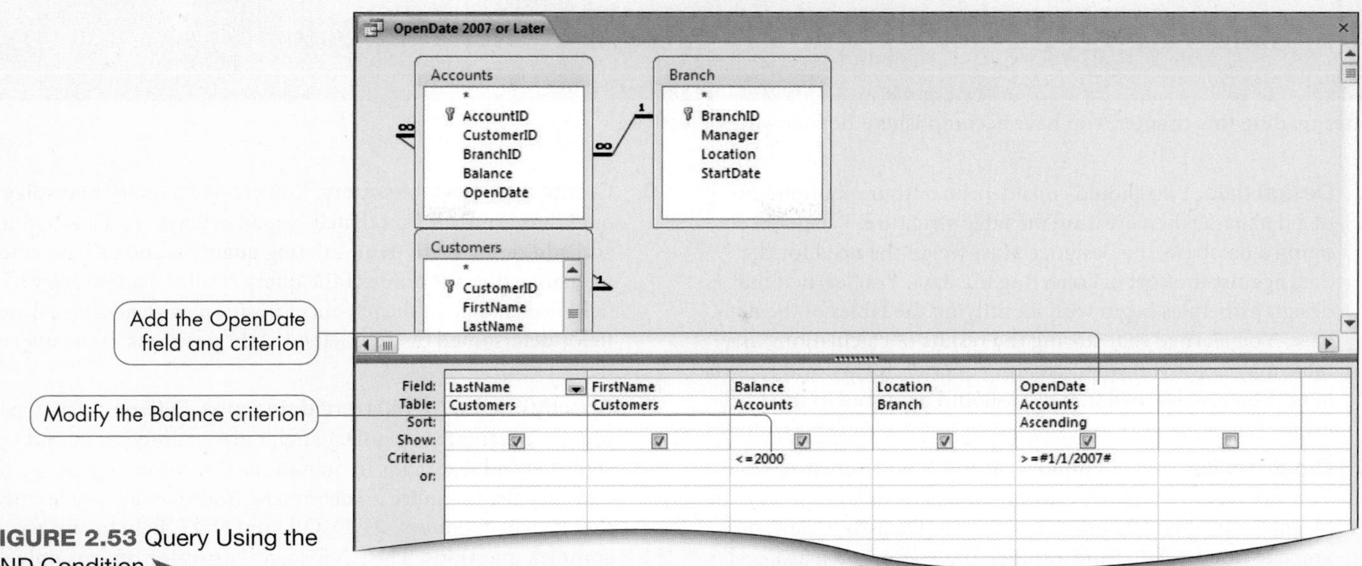

FIGURE 2.53 Query Using the AND Condition ➤

a. Click **View** in the Views group to switch the *Balance 1000 or Less* query to Design view.

b. Type **<=2000** in place of <=*1000* in the **Criteria row** of the Balance field.

c. Double-click the **OpenDate field** in the Accounts table in the top section of the Query Design view to add it to the first blank column in the design grid.

d. Type **>=1/1/2007** in the **Criteria row** of the OpenDate field to extract only accounts that have been opened since January 2007.

   After you type the expression and then move to a different column, Access will add the # symbols automatically.

e. Click **Run** in the Results group to display the results of the query.

   Three records appear in the query results.

f. Click the **File tab**, click **Save Object As**, and type **OpenDate 2007 or Later** as the query name. Click **OK**.

g. Click the **File tab** again to return to the database.

h. Click **View** in the Views group to return to the Design view of the query.

i. Click in the **Sort row** of the OpenDate field, and then select **Ascending**.

j. Click **Run** in the Results group to display the results of the query.

k. Save and Close the query.

l. Click the **File tab**, and then click **Compact & Repair Database**.

m. Click the **File tab**, click **Save & Publish**, and then double-click **Back Up Database**. Accept *a02h4bank_LastnameFirstname_date* as the file name, and then click **Save**.

   You just created a backup of the database. The *a02h4bank_LastnameFirstname* database remains open.

n. Click the **File tab**, and then click **Exit** (to exit Access).

o. Submit based on your instructor's directions.

CHAPTER OBJECTIVES REVIEW

After reading this chapter, you have accomplished the following objectives:

1. **Design data.** You should consider the output requirements of a database when creating the table structure. When developing a database, the designer must weigh the need for the data against the cost of collecting the data. You learned that design principles begin with identifying the tables of the database. You learned that storing the results of calculations in a table may assist you when creating queries, forms, and reports later. You also learned that data should be stored in its smallest parts.
2. **Create tables.** Access employs several ways to create a table. You can create a table by creating the fields in Design view or by entering table data into a new row in Datasheet view, or you can import data from another application such as Excel. You learned that each field needs a unique and descriptive name, and you were introduced to the CamelCase naming convention. Access accommodates many different types of data, including Text, Number, Date/Time, Yes/No, Memo, and others.
3. **Understand table relationships.** Relationships between tables are set in the Relationships window. In this window, join lines are created, and three options can be set: Enforce Referential Integrity, Cascade Update Related Fields, and Cascade Delete Related Records. When referential integrity is enforced, data cannot be entered into the related table unless it first exists in the primary table. Frequently, the primary key (unique identifier) from one table is entered as a foreign key in a related table. These two fields often become the basis of creating relationships between tables.
4. **Share data with Excel.** Microsoft Access can easily import and export data to (and from) Excel. You used the Import Wizard to import an Excel worksheet into an Access database table. The settings of the Import Wizard may be saved and reused when the import is cyclical.
5. **Establish table relationships.** You created relationship links between tables in the database and attempted to enter an invalid branch number in a related table. You discovered that the enforcement of referential integrity prevented you from creating an account in a nonexistent branch. The Cascade Update Related Fields option ensures that if the primary key is modified in one table, Access will automatically update all fields in related tables. Similarly, the Cascade Delete Related Records option ensures that if the primary key is deleted in one table, Access will automatically delete all records in related tables.
6. **Create a single-table query.** You created a query to display only those records that match certain criteria. You learned to add additional fields to an existing query, to add criteria, and to change the sort order of the query results. The primary sort field needs to be in the left-most position, with additional sort fields determined by their left-to-right positions in the query design grid.
7. **Specify criteria for different data types.** Different data types require different syntax. Date fields are enclosed in pound signs (#) and text fields in quotations ("). Numeric and currency fields require no delimiters. Additionally, you learned that logical operators, AND, OR, and NOT, help to answer complex questions. The AND logical operator returns only records that meet all criteria. The OR logical operator returns records meeting any of the specified criteria. The NOT logical operator returns all records except the specified criteria.
8. **Copy and run a query.** After specifying tables, fields, and conditions for one query, you can copy the query, rename it, and then modify the fields and criteria in the second query. Copying queries saves time since you do not have to select tables and fields again for queries that have a similar structure. To run a query during the design process, click Run in the Results group. To run a saved query, double-click the query name in the Navigation Pane.
9. **Use the Query Wizard.** An alternative way to create a select query is to use the Query Wizard. The wizard enables you to select tables and fields from lists. The last step of the wizard prompts you to save the query.
10. **Create a multi-table query.** Creating a multi-table query is similar to creating a single-table query; however, choosing the right tables and managing the table relationships requires some additional skills. You should only include related tables in a multi-table query. To add additional tables to a query, open the Navigation Pane, and then drag tables directly into the top section of the Query Design view.
11. **Modify a multi-table query.** To modify multi-table queries, you use the same techniques you used for single-table queries. Join lines between related tables should appear automatically in a query if the relationships were previously established. If join lines do not appear, the results will not be correct when you run the query. You can add temporary join lines from inside the query or set the Relationships permanently in the Relationships window.

KEY TERMS

AND logical operator ***p.658***
AutoNumber ***p.625***
Calculated field ***p.623***
CamelCase notation ***p.625***
Caption property ***p.629***
Cascade Delete Related Records ***p.638***
Cascade Update Related Fields ***p.638***
Comparison operator ***p.656***
Constant ***p.623***
Criteria row ***p.655***
Data redundancy ***p.623***
Data type ***p.625***
Date arithmetic ***p.623***
Delimiter ***p.656***
Field property ***p.628***
Field row ***p.655***
Indexed property ***p.638***
Multi-table query ***p.665***
NOT logical operator ***p.658***
Null ***p.657***
Number data type ***p.629***
One-to-many relationship ***p.642***
OR logical operator ***p.658***
Query ***p.653***
Query Design view ***p.653***
Query sort order ***p.657***
Referential integrity ***p.637***
Related tables ***p.665***
Run command ***p.659***
Select query ***p.654***
Show row ***p.655***
Simple Query Wizard ***p.653***
Sort row ***p.655***
Table ***p.620***
Table row ***p.655***
Text data type ***p.628***
Validation rule ***p.629***
Wildcard ***p.656***

MULTIPLE CHOICE

1. When entering, deleting, or editing table data:
   (a) The table must be in Design view.
   (b) The table must be in Datasheet view.
   (c) The table may be in either Datasheet or Design view.
   (d) Data may be entered only in a form.

2. Which of the following is true for the Query Wizard?
   (a) You can only select tables as the source.
   (b) No criteria can be added.
   (c) Fields from multiple tables are not allowed.
   (d) You do not need a summary.

3. Which of the following was not a suggested guideline for designing a table?
   (a) Include all necessary data.
   (b) Store data in its smallest parts.
   (c) Avoid calculated fields.
   (d) Link tables using common fields.

4. A query's specifications providing instructions about which records to include must be entered:
   (a) On the Show row of the query design grid.
   (b) On the Sort row of the query design grid.
   (c) On the Criteria row of the query design grid.
   (d) On the Table row of the query design grid.

5. An illustration of a one-to-many relationship would be:
   (a) A person changes his/her primary address.
   (b) A customer may have multiple orders.
   (c) A branch location has an internal BranchID code.
   (d) A balance field is totaled for all accounts for each person.

6. When adding criteria to the query design view:
   (a) The value you enter must be delimited by quotes (")(").
   (b) The value you enter must be delimited by pound signs (#).
   (c) The value you enter must be delimited by nothing ().
   (d) Access will add the correct delimiters for you ("),("), (#), or ().

7. Which of the following is true with respect to an individual's hire date and years of service?
   (a) Hire date should be a calculated field; years of service should be a stored field.
   (b) Hire date should be a stored field; years of service should be a calculated field.
   (c) Both should be stored fields.
   (d) Both should be calculated fields.

8. When importing data into Access, which of the following statements is true?
   (a) The Import Wizard only works for Excel files.
   (b) The wizard can be found on the Create tab.
   (c) You can assign a primary key while you are importing Excel data.
   (d) The wizard will import the data in one step after you select the file.

9. The main reason to enforce referential integrity in Access is to:
   (a) Limit the number of records in a table.
   (b) Keep invalid data from being entered into a table.
   (c) Make it possible to delete records.
   (d) Keep your database safe from unauthorized users.

10. It is more efficient to make a copy of an existing query, rather than create a new query, when which of the following is true?
    (a) The existing query contains only one table.
    (b) The existing query and the new query use the same tables and fields.
    (c) The existing query and the new query have the exact same criteria.
    (d) The original query is no longer being used.

PRACTICE EXERCISES

1 Tom & Erin's Bookstore

Tom and Erin Mullaney own and operate a bookstore in Philadelphia, Pennsylvania. Erin asked you to help her create an Access database because of your experience in this class. You believe that you can help her by creating a database and then importing the Excel spreadsheets they use to store the publishers and the books that they sell. You determine that a third table—for authors—is also required. Your task is to design and populate the three tables, set the table relationships, and enforce referential integrity. If you have problems, reread the detailed directions presented in the chapter. This exercise follows the same set of skills as used in Hands-On Exercises 1 and 2 in the chapter. Refer to Figure 2.54 as you complete this exercise.

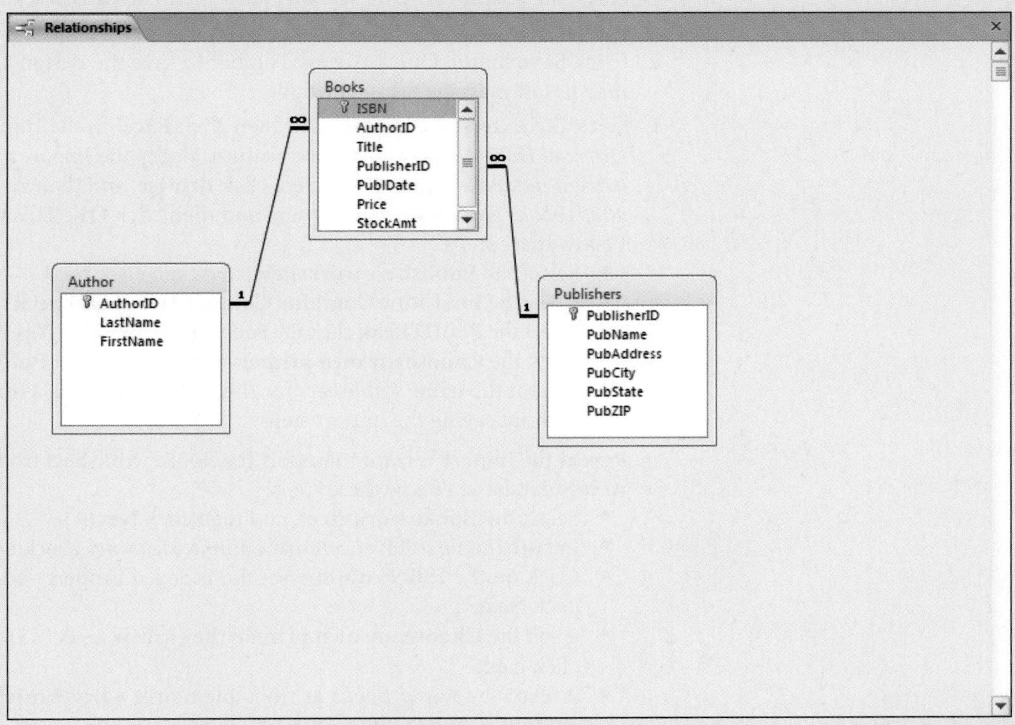

FIGURE 2.54 Access Relationships Window ➤

a. Open Access, and then type **a01p1books_LastnameFirstname** in the **File Name box**. Click **Browse** to locate your Student Data Files folder in the File New Database dialog box, click **OK** to close the dialog box, and then click **Create** to create the new database.

b. Type **11** in the **Click to Add column**, and then click **Click to Add**. The field name becomes *Field1*, and *Click to Add* now appears as the third column. Type **Wayne** and press **Tab**. The process repeats for the fourth column; type **John** and then press **Tab** twice.

c. The cursor returns to the first column where *(New)* is selected. Press **Tab**. Type the rest of the data using the following table. This data will become the records of the Author table.

ID	Field1	Field2	Field3
1	11	Wayne	John
(New)	12	Allen	Keith
	13	Scott	Michael
	14	Carl	Richard
	15	Keen	Clara
	16	Swartz	Millie
	17	Allen	John

d. Click **Save** on the Quick Access Toolbar. Type **Author** in the **Save As dialog box**, and then click **OK**.
e. Click **View** in the Views group to switch to the Design view of the Author table.
f. Select **Field1**—in the second row—in the top portion of the table design, and then type **AuthorID** to rename the field. In the *Field Properties* section in the lower portion of the table design, type **Author ID** in the **Caption property box**, and then verify that *Long Integer* appears for the Field Size property.
g. Select **Field2**, and then type **LastName** to rename the field. In the *Field Properties* section in the bottom portion of the table design, type **Author's Last Name** in the **Caption property box** and **20** as the field size.
h. Select **Field3**, and then type **FirstName** to rename the field. In the *Field Properties* section in the bottom portion of the table design, type **Author's First Name** as the caption, and then type **15** as the field size.
i. Click the **ID field row selector** (which shows the primary key) to select the row, and then click **Delete Rows** in the Tools group. Click **Yes** twice to confirm both messages.
j. Click the **AuthorID row selector**, and then click **Primary Key** in the Tools group to reset the primary key.
k. Click **Save** on the Quick Access Toolbar to save the design changes. Click **Yes** to the *Some data may be lost* message. Close the table.
l. Click the **External Data tab**, and then click **Excel** in the Import & Link group to launch the *Get External Data - Excel Spreadsheet* feature. Verify the *Import the source data into a new table in the current database* option is selected, click **Browse**, and then go to the student data folder. Select the *a02p1books* workbook, click **Open**, and then click **OK**. This workbook contains two worksheets. Follow these steps:
    - Select the **Publishers worksheet**, and then click **Next**.
    - Click the **First Row Contains Column Headings check box**, and then click **Next**.
    - Select the **PubID field**, click the **Indexed arrow**, select **Yes (No Duplicates)**, and then click **Next**.
    - Click the **Choose my own primary key arrow**, select **PubID**, if necessary, and then click **Next**.
    - Accept the name *Publishers* for the table name, click **Finish**, and then click the **Close button** without saving the import steps.

m. Repeat the Import Wizard to import the Books worksheet from the *a02p1books* workbook into the Access database. Follow these steps:
    - Select the **Books worksheet**, and then click **Next**.
    - Ensure the *First Row Contains Column Headings* check box is checked, and then click **Next**.
    - Click on the **ISBN column**, set the Indexed property box to **Yes (No Duplicates)**, and then click **Next**.
    - Click the **Choose my own primary key arrow**, select **ISBN** as the primary key field, and then click **Next**.
    - Accept the name *Books* as the table name. Click **Finish**, and then click the **Close button** without saving the import steps.

n. Right-click the **Books table** in the Navigation Pane, and then select **Design View**. Make the following changes:
    - Change the PubID field name to **PublisherID**.
    - Change the Caption property to **Publisher ID.**
    - Change the PublisherID Field Size property to **2**.
    - Click the **ISBN field** at the top, and then change the Field Size property to **13**.
    - Click the **Price field**, and then change the Price field Data Type to **Currency**.
    - Change the AuthorCode field name to **AuthorID**.
    - Change the AuthorID Field Size property to **Long Integer**.
    - Click the **ISBN field row selector** (which shows the primary key) to select the row, then release, press, and hold the mouse. Drag the row up to the first position.
    - Click **Save** on the Quick Access Toolbar to save the design changes to the Books table. Click **Yes** to the *Some data may be lost* warning.
    - Close the table.

o. Right-click the **Publishers table** in the Navigation Pane, and then select **Design View**. Make the following changes:
    - Change the PubID field name to **PublisherID**.
    - Change the PublisherID Field Size property to **2**.
    - Change the Caption property to **Publisher's ID**.
    - Change the Field Size property to **50** for the PubName and PubAddress fields.

- Change the Pub Address field name to **PubAddress** (remove the space).
- Change the PubCity Field Size property to **30**.
- Change the PubState Field Size property to **2**.
- Change the Pub ZIP field name to **PubZIP** (remove the space).
- Click **Save** on the Quick Access Toolbar to save the design changes to the Publishers table. Click **Yes** to the *Some data may be lost* warning. Close all open tables.

p. Click the **Database Tools tab**, and then click **Relationships** in the Relationships group. Click **Show Table** if necessary. Follow these steps:
  - Double-click each table name in the Show Table dialog box to add it to the Relationships window, and then close the Show Table dialog box.
  - Drag the **AuthorID field** from the Author table onto the AuthorID field in the Books table.
  - Click the **Enforce Referential Integrity** and **Cascade Update Related Fields check boxes** in the Edit Relationships dialog box. Click **Create** to create a one-to-many relationship between the Author and Books tables.
  - Drag the **PublisherID field** from the Publishers table onto the PublisherID field in the Books table.
  - Click the **Enforce Referential Integrity** and **Cascade Update Related Fields check boxes** in the Edit Relationships dialog box. Click **Create** to create a one-to-many relationship between the Publishers and Books tables.
  - Click **Save** on the Quick Access Toolbar to save the changes to the Relationships window.
  - Click **Relationship Report** in the Tools group on the Design tab.
  - Close the report; do not save it. Close the Relationships window.

q. Click the **File tab**, and then click **Compact & Repair Database**.

r. Click the **File tab**, click **Save & Publish**, and then double-click **Back Up Database**.

s. Click **Save** to accept the default backup file name with today's date.

t. Click the **File tab**, and then click **Exit** (to exit Access).

u. Submit based on your instructor's directions.

2 My Movie Collection

Over the years, you have collected over 300 movies and you decide to catalog them in an Access database. You will enter the title, genre, format, running time, director, actors, price, and year produced for each movie. You will create three tables—Movies, Genre, and Format—and then join each of them in a relationship. This exercise follows the same set of skills as used in Hands-On Exercises 1, 2, and 4 in the chapter. Refer to Figure 2.55 as you complete this exercise.

Movies

MovieID	Title	GenreID	Actors	FormatID	RunningTime	Director	Price	YearProduced
1	Black Swan	1	Natalie Portman	5	2:00	Darren Aronofsky	$9.95	2010
2	The Fighter	1	Mark Wahlberg	1	1:45	David O. Russell	$9.95	2010
3	Inception	1	Leonardo DiCaprio	1	1:45	Christopher Nolan	$5.99	2010
4	The Kids Are All Right	2	Annette Bening	1	1:45	Lisa Cholodenko	$9.95	2009
5	The King's Speech	3	Colin Firth	1	2:00	Tom Hooper	$9.95	2010
6	127 Hours	1	James Franco	4	1:55	Danny Boyle	$9.95	2011
7	The Social Network	1	Jesse Eisenberg	1	1:47	David Fincher	$9.95	2009
8	Toy Story 3	1	Tom Hanks	1	1:55	Lee Unkrich	$9.95	2010
9	True Grit	4	Jeff Bridges	3	2:00	Ethan Coen , Joel Coen	$12.95	2010
10	Winter's Bone	5	Jennifer Lawrence	1	2:00	Debra Granik	$9.95	2009
(New)								

FIGURE 2.55 Enter the Movie Data ➤

a. Open Access, and then type **a01p2movies_LastnameFirstname** in the **File Name box**. Click **Browse** to locate your Student Data Files folder in the File New Database dialog box, click **OK** to close the dialog box, and then click **Create** to create the new database.

b. Click **View** in the Views group to switch to Design view. Type **Movies** in the **Save As dialog box**, and then click **OK**.

c. Change the first Field Name to **MovieID**. Type **Title** in the second row of the Field Name column, and then press **Tab**. Accept **Text** as the Data Type, and then press **Tab** twice. Type **GenreID** in the third row of the Field Name column, and then press **Tab**. Select **Number** for the Data Type.

d. Add the remainder of the fields:

Actors	Text
FormatID	Number
RunningTime	Date/Time (Select Short Time as the Format in Field Properties.)
Director	Text
Price	Currency
YearProduced	Number

e. Click **View** in the Views group to switch to Datasheet view. Click **Yes** to save the table. Add the records as shown in Figure 2.55. Press **Tab** to move to the next field. Adjust column widths and column alignment to match Figure 2.55. Save and close the table.

f. Click the **Create tab**, and then click **Table Design** in the Tables group. Type **GenreID** for the first Field Name, and then select **AutoNumber** as the Data Type. Type **GenreDescription** for the second Field Name, and then accept **Text** as the Data Type.

g. Click the **GenreID field**, and then click **Primary Key** in the Tools group. Click **View** in the Views group, and then click **Yes** at the next prompt. Type **Genre** in the **Save As dialog box**, and then click **OK**.

h. Add the genre descriptions as shown below, and then save and close the table. GenreID will be generated automatically by Access.

GenreID	GenreDescription
1	**Drama**
2	**Action**
3	**Comedy**
4	**Animation**
5	**Western**

i. Click the **Create tab**, and then click **Table Design** in the Tables group. Type **FormatID** for the first Field Name, and then select **AutoNumber** as the Data Type. Type **FormatDescription** for the second Field Name, and then accept **Text** as the Data Type.

j. Click the **FormatID field**, and then click **Primary Key** in the Tools group. Click **View** in the Views group, and then click **Yes** at the next prompt. Type **Format** in the **Save As dialog box**, and then click **OK**.

k. Add the format descriptions as shown below, and then save and close the table. FormatID will be generated automatically by Access.

FormatID	FormatDescription
1	**DVD**
2	**VHS**
3	**Blu-Ray**
4	**MOV**
5	**MPEG**

l. Click the **Database Tools tab**, and then click **Relationships** in the Relationships group. Add all three tables to the Relationships window, and then close the Show Table dialog box.

m. Increase the height of the Movies table. Drag the **GenreID field** from the Genre table and drop it onto the GenreID field in the Movies table. Check the **Enforce Referential Integrity check box** in the Edit Relationships dialog box, and then click **Create**. Drag the **FormatID field** from the Format table and drop it onto the FormatID field in the Movies table. Check the **Enforce Referential Integrity check box** in the Edit Relationships dialog box. Click **Create**, and then close the Relationships window. Click **Save**.

n. Click the **File tab**, and then click **Compact & Repair Database**.

o. Click the **File tab**, and then click **Exit** (to exit Access).

p. Submit the database based on your instructor's directions.

MID-LEVEL EXERCISES

1 Quick Mart

You decide to open a Quick Mart food store in a vacant store near your home. The store is located near a community college and you hope to attract college students in the morning and at lunch time. You will provide coffee, breakfast sandwiches, lunch sandwiches, snacks, cold drinks, and a variety of other convenience products. You need to track your inventory and sales data with an Access database. Each product will be tagged with a product category. You need to track the total sales and the gross profit of each category. Refer to Figure 2.56 as you complete this exercise.

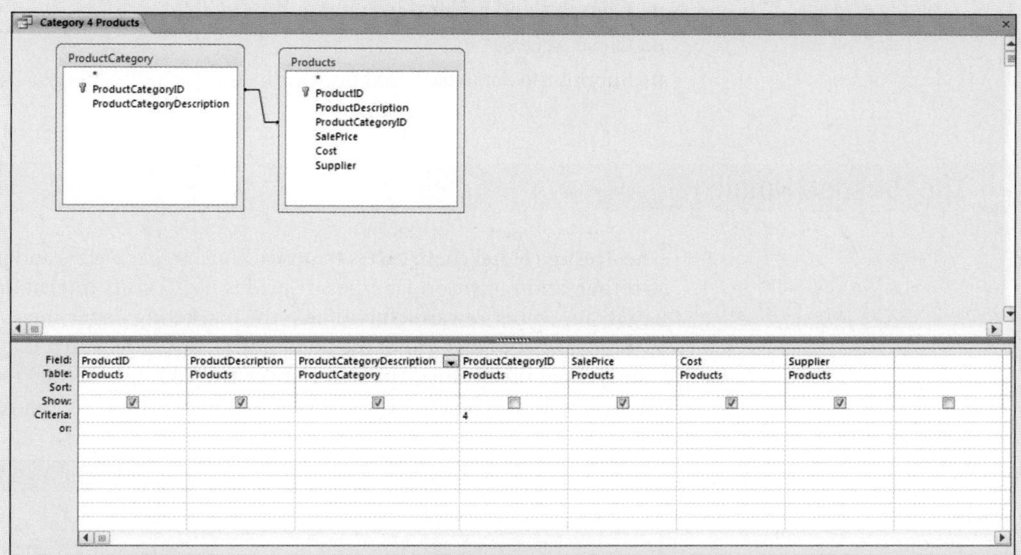

FIGURE 2.56 Category 4 Products Query ➤

a. Open Access, and then create a new database named **a02m1quickmart_LastnameFirstname**.
b. Click **View** in the Views group to switch to Design view. Type **ProductCategory** in the **Save As dialog box**, and then click **OK**.
c. Change the first Field Name to **ProductCategoryID**, and then accept the **AutoNumber data type**. Type **ProductCategoryDescription** in the second Field Name, and then press **Tab**. Accept **Text** as the Data Type.
d. Click **View** in the Views group to switch to Datasheet view. Click **Yes** to save the table. Add the following Product Categories—**Coffee**, **Breakfast sandwiches**, **Lunch sandwiches**, **Snacks**, **Cold drinks**, **News media**, and **Other**. Save and close the table.
e. Click the **Create tab**, and then click **Table Design** in the Tables group. Type **ProductID** for the first Field Name, and then select **AutoNumber** as the Data Type. Type **ProductDescription** for the second Field Name, and then accept **Text** as the Data Type.
f. Add the remainder of the fields:

ProductCategoryID	Number
SalePrice	Currency
Cost	Currency
Supplier	Text

g. Click the first field, and then click **Primary Key** in the Tools group. Click **View** in the Views group, and then click **Yes** at the next prompt. Type **Products** in the **Save As dialog box**, and then click **OK**.

h. Type the following products into the Products table—**Coffee**, **Iced Tea**, **Water**, **Egg and Cheese Sandwich**, **Turkey Club**, **Chips**, **Pretzels**, **Crackers**, **Snickers**, and **Daily News**. Enter one of the ProductCategoryIDs from the list you created in step d. Enter estimated values in the other fields. Save and close the table.

i. Create a relationship between the two tables using the ProductCategoryID field.

j. Click the **Create tab**, and then click **Query Design** in the Queries group. Add the Products and the ProductCategory tables to the query, and then click **OK**. (Access automatically adds a join line.) Drag all the fields from the Products table into the query design grid.

k. Type **4** in the criteria row of the ProductCategoryID column. Click **Run** in the Results group.

l. Switch to Design view. Drag the **ProductCategoryDescription field** to the third position in the query design grid. Uncheck the **Show check box** in the ProductCategoryID column. Compare your screen to Figure 2.56. Run the query.

m. Save the query as **Category 4 Products**, and then close the query.

n. Compact and repair the database.

o. Close Access.

p. Submit the database based on your instructor's directions.

2 The Prestige Hotel

The Prestige Hotel chain caters to upscale business travelers and provides state-of-the-art conference, meeting, and reception facilities. It prides itself on its international, four-star cuisine. Last year, it began a member reward club to help the marketing department track the purchasing patterns of its most loyal customers. All of the hotel transactions are stored in the database. Your task is to help the managers of the Prestige Hotel in Denver and Chicago identify their customers who stayed in a room last year and who had three persons in their party. Refer to Figure 2.57 as you complete this exercise.

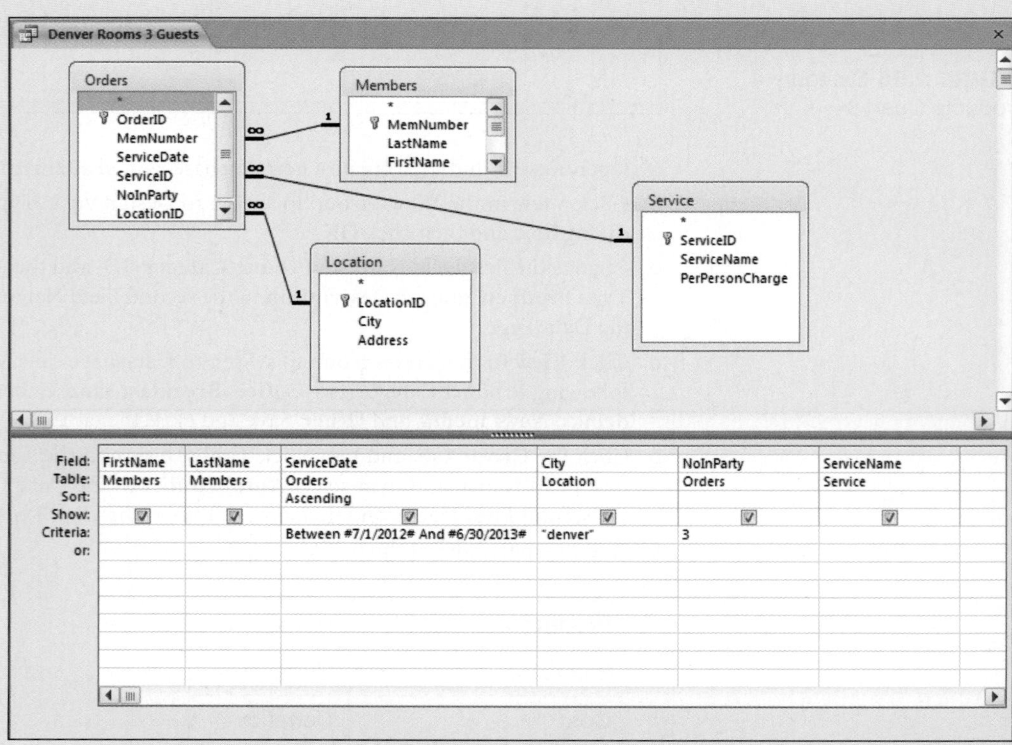

FIGURE 2.57 Denver Rooms 3 Guests Query ➤

a. Open *a02m2hotel*. Click the **File tab**. click **Save Database As**, and then type **a02m2hotel_LastnameFirstname**. Click **Save**. Review the data contained in the three tables. Specifically, look for the tables and fields containing the information you need: dates of stays in Denver suites, the members' names, and the numbers in the parties.

b. Import the Location data from the Excel file *a02m2location* into your database as a new table. Set the LocationID Indexed property to **Yes (No Duplicates)**, and then set the data type to **Long Integer**. Select the **LocationID field** as the primary key. Name the table **Location**.

c. Open the Relationships window, and then create a relationship between the Location table and the Orders table using the LocationID field. Enforce referential integrity, and then select **Cascade Update Related Fields**. Set the other two relationships as shown in Figure 2.57. Save and close the Relationships window.

d. Open the Members table, and then find Bryan Gray's name. Replace his name with your own first and last name. Now find Nicole Lee's name, and then replace it with your name.

e. Create a query with fields ServiceDate, City, NoInParty, ServiceName, FirstName, and LastName. Set the criteria to limit the output to **denver**. Use the Between command to only show services from **7/1/2012** to **6/30/2013**. Set the Number in Party criterion to **3**. Sort the results in ascending order by the Service Date.

f. Run the query, and then examine the number of records in the status bar at the bottom of the query. It should display *154*. If your number of records is different, examine the criteria.

g. Change the order of the query fields so that they display as FirstName, LastName, ServiceDate, City, NoInParty, and ServiceName. Compare your results to Figure 2.57.

h. Save the query as **Denver Rooms 3 Guests**. Close the query, and then copy it and rename the new query **Chicago Rooms 3 Guests**. One of your colleagues in Chicago asked for your help in analyzing the guest data.

i. Open the Chicago Rooms 3 Guests query in Design view, and then change the criterion for denver to **chicago**. Run and save the changes.

DISCOVER 

j. Combine the two previous queries into a third query named **Denver and Chicago Rooms 3 Guests**. Use the criteria from the two individual queries to create a combination AND – OR condition. The records in the combined query should equal the sum of the records in the two individual queries.

k. Compact, repair, and back up the database file. Close the database.

l. Submit based on your instructor's directions.

CAPSTONE EXERCISE

The Morris Arboretum in Chestnut Hill, Pennsylvania, tracks its donors in Excel. They also use Excel to store a list of plants in stock. As donors contribute funds to the Arboretum, they can elect to receive a plant gift from the Arboretum. These plants are both rare plants and hard-to-find old favorites, and they are part of the annual appeal and membership drive to benefit the Arboretum's programs. The organization has grown, and the files are too large and inefficient to handle in Excel. Your task will be to begin the conversion of the files from Excel to Access.

Create a New Database

You need to examine the data in the Excel worksheets to determine which fields will become the primary keys in each table and which fields will become the foreign keys. Primary and foreign keys are used to form the relationships between tables.

a. Locate the Excel workbook named *a02c1donors* and open it.

b. Locate the Excel workbook named *a02c1plants* and open it.

c. Examine the data in each worksheet and identify the column that will become the primary key in an Access table. Identify the foreign keys in each table.

d. Launch Access and create a new, blank database named **a02c1arbor_LastnameFirstname**.

Create a New Table

Use the new blank table created automatically by Access to hold the donations as they are received from the donors. Switch to Design view, and then save the table as **Donations**. Add the remaining field names in Design view. Note: The data for this table will be added later in this exercise.

a. Change *ID* to **DonationID** with an **AutoNumber Data Type**.

b. Add **DonorID** (a foreign key) as **Number (Long Integer) Data Type**.

c. Add **PlantID** (a foreign key) as **Number (Long Integer) Data Type**.

d. Enter two additional fields with an appropriate data type and field properties. Hint: You need the date of donation and the amount of donation.

e. Verify the primary key is *DonationID*.

f. Save the table. Close the table.

Import Data from Excel

You need to use the Import Spreadsheet Data Wizard twice to import a worksheet from each Excel workbook into Access. You need to select the worksheets, specify the primary keys, set the indexing option, and name the newly imported tables (see Figures 2.19 through 2.24).

a. Click the **Import Excel data command**.

b. Locate and select the *a02c1donors* workbook.

c. Set the DonorID field Indexed option to **Yes (No Duplicates)**.

d. Select **DonorID** as the primary key when prompted.

e. Accept the table name *Donors*.

f. Import the *a02c1plants* file, set the ID field as the primary key, and then change the indexing option to **Yes (No Duplicates)**.

g. Select the **ID** as the primary key when prompted.

h. Accept the table name *Plants*.

i. Open each table in Datasheet view to examine the data.

j. Change the ID field name in the Plants table to **PlantID**.

Create Relationships

You need to create the relationships between the tables using the Relationships window. Identify the primary key fields in each table and connect them with their foreign key counterparts in related tables. Enforce referential integrity, and check the Cascade Update Related Fields option.

a. Open the Donors table, and then change the Field Size property for DonorID to **Long Integer** so it matches the Field Size property of DonorID in the Donations table.

b. Open the Plants table, and then change the Field Size property for PlantID to **Long Integer** so it matches the Field Size property for PlantID in the Donations table.

c. Close the open tables, and then open the Relationships window.

d. Add the three tables to the Relationships window using the Show Table dialog box. Close the Show Tables dialog box.

e. Drag the **DonorID field** in the Donors table onto the DonorID field in the Donations table. Enforce referential integrity, and then check the **Cascade Update Related Fields option**. Drag the **PlantID field** from the Plants table onto the PlantID field of the Donations table. Enforce referential integrity, and then check the **Cascade Update Related Fields option**.

f. Close the Relationships window and save your changes.

Add Sample Data to the Donations Table

You need to add sample data to the Donations table. Add 20 records using the following guidelines:

a. Use any donor from the Donors table.

b. Enter the date of donation using dates from last month, this month, and next month.

c. Use any amount of donation.

d. Use any plant from the Plants table.

Use the Query Wizard

Use the Query Wizard to create a query of all donations greater than $100 in the Donations table. Use the following guidelines:

a. Include the DonorID and AmountOfDonation fields.

b. Name the query **Donations Over 100**.

c. Add criteria to include only donations of more than $100.

d. Sort by descending AmountOfDonation.

Create a Query in Design View

You need to create a query that identifies the people who have made a donation in the current month. The query should list the donor's full name, phone number, the amount of the donation, the date of the donation, and name of the plant they want. Sort the query by date of donation, then by donor last name and first name. This list will be given to the Arboretum staff so they can notify the donors that a plant is ready for pick up.

a. Click the **Create tab**, and then click **Query Design** in the Queries group.

b. Add the tables and fields necessary to produce the query as stated previously. Name the query **Plant Pickup List**.

c. Run and print the query from Datasheet view.

d. Compact, repair, and back up the file. Close the database.

e. Submit based on your instructor's directions.

Job Search

GENERAL CASE

FROM SCRATCH

You just graduated with an IT degree and now you are starting your job search. Create an Access database to keep track of the job openings that you find during your job search. Name the database **a02b1jobs_LastnameFirstname**. The database will require three related tables—Jobs, Source, and Sector. The Source and Sector tables should be created first; each will have an ID field and a description field. You will enter at least five records each for the Source and Sector tables. You will then create the Jobs table which will contain the following information: Source, Position, Description, Sector, Contact Person, Contact Phone, and Contact Email. Also include an ID field that will number the job openings sequentially. Add 10 sample job openings to the Jobs table. Create a query to demonstrate how to select jobs by sector. Save and close the database. Check with your instructor and submit the database based on your instructor's directions.

Database Administrator Position

RESEARCH CASE

FROM SCRATCH

You arrive at Secure Systems, Inc., for a database administrator position interview. After meeting the Human Resources coordinator, you are given a test to demonstrate your skills in Access. You are asked to create a database from scratch to keep track of all the candidates for the positions currently open at Secure Systems. Use these requirements:

a. Name the database **a02b2admin_LastnameFirstname**.
b. Create three tables: Candidates, JobOpenings, and Interviews.
c. Include a field to rank each candidate on a scale of 1 to 5 (5 is highest).
d. Set the table relationships.
e. Add 10 candidates—yourself and 9 other students in your class.
f. Add the Database Administrator job and four other sample jobs.
g. Add eight sample Interviews—four for the Database Administrator position and four others.
h. Create a query that lists all the Database Administrator interviews with a ranking of 4 or 5.
i. Add the last name and first name of the candidate to the query design. Sort by last name and first name. Run the query.
j. Close the database. Submit based on your instructor's directions.

Area of Expertise

DISASTER RECOVERY

Your company maintains a list of consultants that it can call on when the need arises. The consultants contact information as well as their area of expertise is stored in the *a02b3consultants* database file. Open the file, and then save the database as **a02b3consultants_LastnameFirstname**. The database contains one table—Consultants. Open the table and take note of the AreaOfExpertise field. To avoid data entry errors, such as misspellings and abbreviations, it is better to represent this information numerically. To do so, another table needs to be created. After the new table is created, add a new field to the existing table with a data type of number. You will then create a relationship between the two tables, and then enter the new area of expertise numeric data. After you finish your changes, save and close the database. Submit the database based on your instructor's directions.

ACCESS

3 CUSTOMIZE, ANALYZE, AND SUMMARIZE QUERY DATA

Creating and Using Queries to Make Decisions

CASE STUDY | Housing Slump Means Opportunity for College Students

Watch the
Set-up
Video
for this
Case Study!

Two students from Montgomery County Community College decided they would take advantage of the declining housing market. After taking several business courses at MCCC and a weekend seminar in real estate investing, Jeff Bryan and Bill Ryder were ready to test their skills in the marketplace. Jeff and Bill had a simple strategy—buy distressed properties at a significant discount, then resell the properties for a profit one year later when the market rebounds.

As they drove through the surrounding neighborhoods, if they noticed a For Sale sign in the yard, they would call the listing agent and ask for the key information such as the asking price, the number of bedrooms, square feet, and days on the market. Since they were just starting out, they decided to target houses that were priced at $100,000 or below and only houses that were on the market at least six months.

For the first two months, they gathered lots of information and began to get a feel for the houses and prices in the area. Some neighborhoods were definitely more distressed than others! But they still had not made any offers. The two MCCC investors realized they needed a more scientific approach to finding an investment property. Based on a tip from the real estate seminar, they decide to gather free lists of homes for sale and use that information to prequalify houses that meet their criteria. They have asked you to help them import the lists into Access. Once the data is in Access, Jeff, Bill, and you will be able to easily identify the qualifying properties.

This new database approach should help them become more successful and hopefully help them acquire their first investment property. And who knows, you might even become one of the partners.

OBJECTIVES AFTER YOU READ THIS CHAPTER, YOU WILL BE ABLE TO:

Calculations, Expressions, and Functions

Previously, you learned that Access now allows calculated fields to be added to tables. In previous versions of Access, you could not add calculated fields to tables; you could only add calculated fields to queries, forms, and reports. In Access 2010, many situations exist where you will still need to add arithmetic calculations—using expressions and functions—to queries, forms, and reports.

In Access 2010, many situations exist where you will still need to add arithmetic calculations ... to queries, forms, and reports.

For example, many Access developers prefer to create calculated fields in queries. Queries with calculated fields can then become the data source (or record source) for forms and reports. Calculated fields on a form cannot be edited the same way fields from a table can be edited. Calculated fields can only be displayed on a form. For example, if you store information about credit cards in a table, you would enter the bank (Chase), the credit card type (Visa), and the interest rate (9%). You would not enter the current amount due. That amount would be calculated and displayed on the form. You will recognize this restriction later when you create a form containing calculated fields.

In this section, you will learn about the order of operations and how to create a calculated field in a query.

Understanding the Order of Operations

The **order of operations** determines the sequence by which operations are calculated in an expression.

The ***order of operations*** determines the sequence by which operations are calculated in an expression. Evaluate expressions in parentheses first, then exponents, then multiplication and division, and, finally, addition and subtraction. Operations of equal value will be calculated from left to right. Table 3.1 shows some examples of the order of operations. You must have a solid understanding of these rules in order to create calculated fields in Access. Access, like Excel, uses the following symbols:

- Parentheses ( )
- Exponentiation ^
- Multiplication *
- Division /
- Addition +
- Subtraction –

TABLE 3.1 Examples of Order of Operations

Expression	Order to Perform Calculations	Output
=2+3*3	Multiply first, and then add.	11
=(2+3)*3	Add the values inside the parentheses first, and then multiply.	15
=2+2^3	Evaluate the exponent first, 2^3=2*2*2 or 8. Then add.	10
=(2+2)^3	Add the parenthetical values first (2+2=4), and then raise the result to the 3rd power. 4^3=4*4*4.	64
=10/2+3	Divide first, and then add.	8
=10/(2+3)	Add first to simplify the parenthetical expression, and then divide.	2
=10*2–3*2	Multiply first, and then subtract.	14

Creating a Calculated Field in a Query

When creating a query, in addition to using fields from tables, you may also need to create a calculation based on the fields from one or more tables. For example, a table might contain the times when employees clock in and out of work. You could create a calculated field to calculate how many hours each employee worked by subtracting the ClockIn field from the ClockOut field. You create calculated fields in the Design view of a query. A formula used to calculate new fields from the values in existing fields is known as an ***expression***. An expression can consist of a number of different elements to produce the desired output. The elements used in an expression may include the following:

An **expression** is a formula used to calculate new fields from the values in existing fields.

- Identifiers (the names of fields, controls, or properties)
- Arithmetic operators (e.g., * , / , + , or –)
- Functions (built-in functions like Date() or IIf())
- ***Constants*** (numbers such as 30 or .5)

A **constant** refers to a value that does not change.

You can use calculations to create a new value based on an existing field, verify data entered, set grouping levels in reports, or to help set query criteria.

Build Expressions with Correct Syntax

Expressions are entered in the first row of the query design grid. You must follow the correct ***syntax***—the set of rules that Access follows when evaluating expressions. You can create expressions to perform calculations using field names, constants, and functions. If you use a field name, such as Balance, in an expression, you must spell the field name correctly or Access will display an error. You should assign descriptive field names to the calculated fields. Access ignores spaces in calculations. An example of an expression with correct syntax is:

Syntax is the set of rules that Access follows when evaluating expressions.

```
MonthlyInterest: [Balance] * .035 / 12
```

In the above expression, if you omit the brackets [ ] around Balance, Access will add them for you. The arithmetic operators, the * symbol (multiply) and the / symbol (divide), first multiply the operands, [Balance] and .035, and then divide the result by 12. In calculated fields, the operands are usually a constant, a field name, or another calculated field. Figure 3.1 shows the NewBalance field which adds the [Balance] and the calculated field [MonthlyInterest]. This calculation will show the total amount owed.

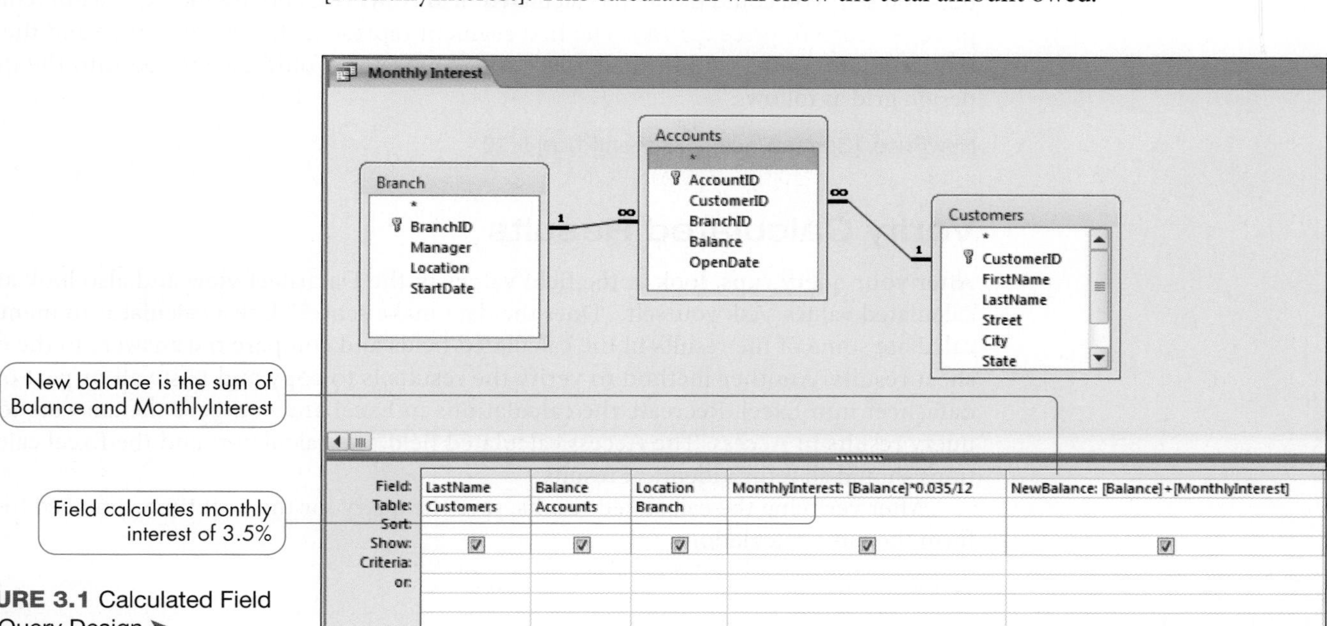

FIGURE 3.1 Calculated Field in a Query Design ➤

The query contains a second calculated field named NewBalance. Its value is derived from the sum of the original balance plus the monthly interest amount. The query results, as shown in Figure 3.2, display a decimal number in the Interest column. The NewBalance column appears to be rounded to two decimal places since the output is in currency format. However, when you click in the NewBalance field, Access displays the extra digits that are stored behind the scenes.

NewBalance appears to be rounded to two digits (currency format)

MonthlyInterest field shows a decimal number with many digits

Click in the NewBalance field to reveal a decimal number with four digits

Monthly Interest

LastName	Balance	Branch Locat	MonthlyInterest	NewBalance
Peterson	$5,600.00	Campus	16.3333333333333	$5,616.3333
Millward	$1,200.00	Uptown	3.5	$1,203.50
Collins	$15,490.00	Eastern	45.1791666666667	$15,535.18
Hayes	$630.00	Western	1.8375	$631.84
Nunn	$1,300.00	Campus	3.79166666666667	$1,303.79
Hayes	$550.00	Uptown	1.60416666666667	$551.60
Simpson	$1,620.00	Eastern	4.725	$1,624.73
Collins	$2,100.00	Southern	6.125	$2,106.13
Wagner	$1,500.00	Campus	4.375	$1,504.38
Millward	$3,000.00	Eastern	8.75	$3,008.75
Wagner	$290.00	Uptown	0.845833333333333	$290.85
Fox	$1,900.00	Western	5.54166666666667	$1,905.54
Millward	$10,000.00	Eastern	29.1666666666667	$10,029.17
Nunn	$16,700.00	Uptown	48.7083333333333	$16,748.71
Collins	$460.00	Western	1.34166666666667	$461.34
Millward	$18,700.00	Western	54.5416666666667	$18,754.54
Peterson	$980.00	Western	2.85833333333333	$982.86
Wagner	$7,800.00	Southern	22.75	$7,822.75
Collins	$14,250.00	Western	41.5625	$14,291.56
Millward	$12,000.00	Campus	35	$12,035.00
YourName	$21,004.00	Campus	61.2616666666667	$21,065.26
Hayes	$4,000.00	Campus	11.6666666666667	$4,011.67
YourName	$1,000.00	Campus	2.91666666666667	$1,002.92
*				

Record: 1 of 23 No Filter Search

FIGURE 3.2 Results of Calculated Fields in a Query ➤

Another example of when to use a calculated field is calculating a price increase for a product or service. Suppose you need to calculate a 10% price increase on certain products you sell. You could name the calculated field NewPrice and use the expression (current price) + (current price × 10%). The first segment represents the current price and the second segment adds an additional 10%. The expression would be entered into the query design grid as follows:

```
NewPrice: [CurrentPrice] + [CurrentPrice] * .10
```

Verify Calculated Results

After your query runs, look at the field values in the Datasheet view and also look at the calculated values. Ask yourself, "Does the data make sense?" Use a calculator to manually calculate some of the results in the calculated fields and compare the answers to the datasheet results. Another method to verify the results is to copy and paste all or part of the datasheet into Excel. Recreate the calculations in Excel and compare the answers to the query results in Access. The Access calculated field, the calculator, and the Excel calculations should all return identical results.

After verifying the calculated results, save the query for the next time you need to perform the same calculations.

TIP Resolve Rounding Problems

In Figure 3.2, the Balance field contains numbers in currency format; the MonthlyInterest field contains decimal numbers with many digits. When you add the two numbers, the sum—shown in the NewBalance field—appears to be in currency format. However, if you click the NewBalance field, the actual number is a decimal with four digits. Decimal numbers can cause rounding problems when you total the column. To resolve this problem, the MonthlyInterest field must be rounded to two decimal places prior to totaling the column.

Save a Query Containing Calculated Fields

As you already know, saving a query only saves the design of the query; saving does not save the data displayed in Datasheet view. While viewing the results of a query in Datasheet view, you can edit the data (and consequently update the data in the underlying table) providing the query is updatable. Calculated fields are the exception to this rule—calculated fields cannot be updated in Datasheet view. However, when the components of a calculated field are updated, the calculated field value will update automatically.

You can use a calculated field as input for other calculated fields. For example, calculate a 10% discount on an item (Calculation #1) and then calculate the sales tax on the discount price (Calculation #2).

In the first Hands-On Exercise, you will create calculated expressions, practice verification techniques, and recover from a common error.

TIP Avoid Spaces in Calculated Field Names

Although you can use spaces in calculated field names, it is a good habit to not use spaces. For example, use NewPrice: [Price]*1.1 rather than New Price: [Price]*1.1. If you avoid spaces in calculated field names, it will be easier to reference these fields in other queries, related forms, and related reports.

Quick Concepts Check

1. Briefly describe the order of operations. Give an example.
2. When might you need a calculated field in a query? Give an example.
3. Define syntax. How does Access respond to incorrect syntax?
4. Why is it important to verify calculated results?

HANDS-ON EXERCISES

1 Calculations, Expressions, and Functions

Using the data from the homes for sale lists that Jeff and Bill acquired, you are able to help them target properties that meet their criteria. As you examine the data, you discover other ways to analyze the properties. You create several queries and present your results to the two investors for their comments.

Skills covered: Create and Save a Query • Create a Calculated Field and Run the Query • Verify the Calculated Results • Recover from a Common Error

STEP 1 CREATE AND SAVE A QUERY

You begin your analysis by creating a query using the Properties and Agents tables. The Properties table contains all the properties the investors will evaluate; the Agents table contains a list of real estate agents who represent the properties' sellers. In this exercise, add the fields you need and only show properties that have not been sold. Refer to Figure 3.3 as you complete Step 1.

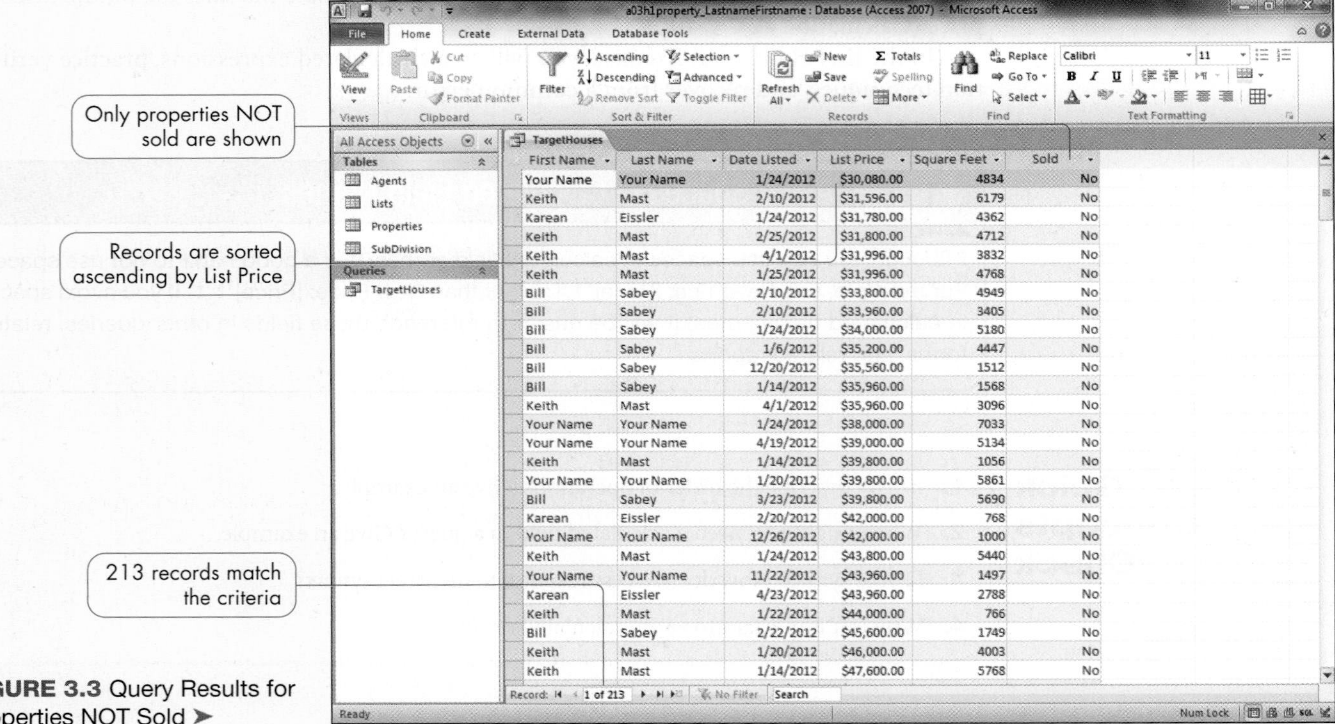

FIGURE 3.3 Query Results for Properties NOT Sold ➤

a. Open *a03h1property*. Click the **File tab**, click **Save Database As**, and then type **a03h1property_LastnameFirstname**. Click **Save**.

> **TROUBLESHOOTING:** Throughout the remainder of this chapter and textbook, click Enable Content whenever you are working with student files.

> **TROUBLESHOOTING:** If you make any major mistakes while completing this Hands-On Exercise, you can delete the *a03h1property_LastnameFirstname* file, repeat step a above, and then start over.

b. Open the Agents table, and then replace *Angela Scott* with your name. Close the table.

c. Click the **Create tab**, and then click **Query Design** in the Queries group to start a new query.

The Show Table dialog box opens so you can specify the table(s) and/or queries to include in the query design.

d. Select the **Agents table**, and then click **Add**. Select the **Properties table**, and then click **Add**. Close the Show Table dialog box.

e. Double-click the **FirstName** and **LastName fields** in the Agents table to add them to the design grid.

f. Double-click the **DateListed**, **ListPrice**, **SqFeet**, and **Sold fields** in the Properties table to add them to the query design grid.

g. Click **Run** in the Results group to display the results in Datasheet view.

You should see 303 properties in the results.

h. Click **View** in the Views group to switch to Design view. Type **No** in the **Criteria row** of the Sold field.

i. Select **Ascending** from the Sort row of the ListPrice field.

j. Click **Run** to see the results.

You only want to see properties that were not sold. There should now be only 213 properties in the datasheet. Compare your results to those shown in Figure 3.3.

k. Save the query as **TargetHouses**.

STEP 2 CREATE A CALCULATED FIELD AND RUN THE QUERY

You need to create a calculated field to evaluate the relative value of all unsold properties on the market. To do this, you create a calculated field to analyze the sale price compared to the square footage of each property. Refer to Figure 3.4 as you complete Step 2.

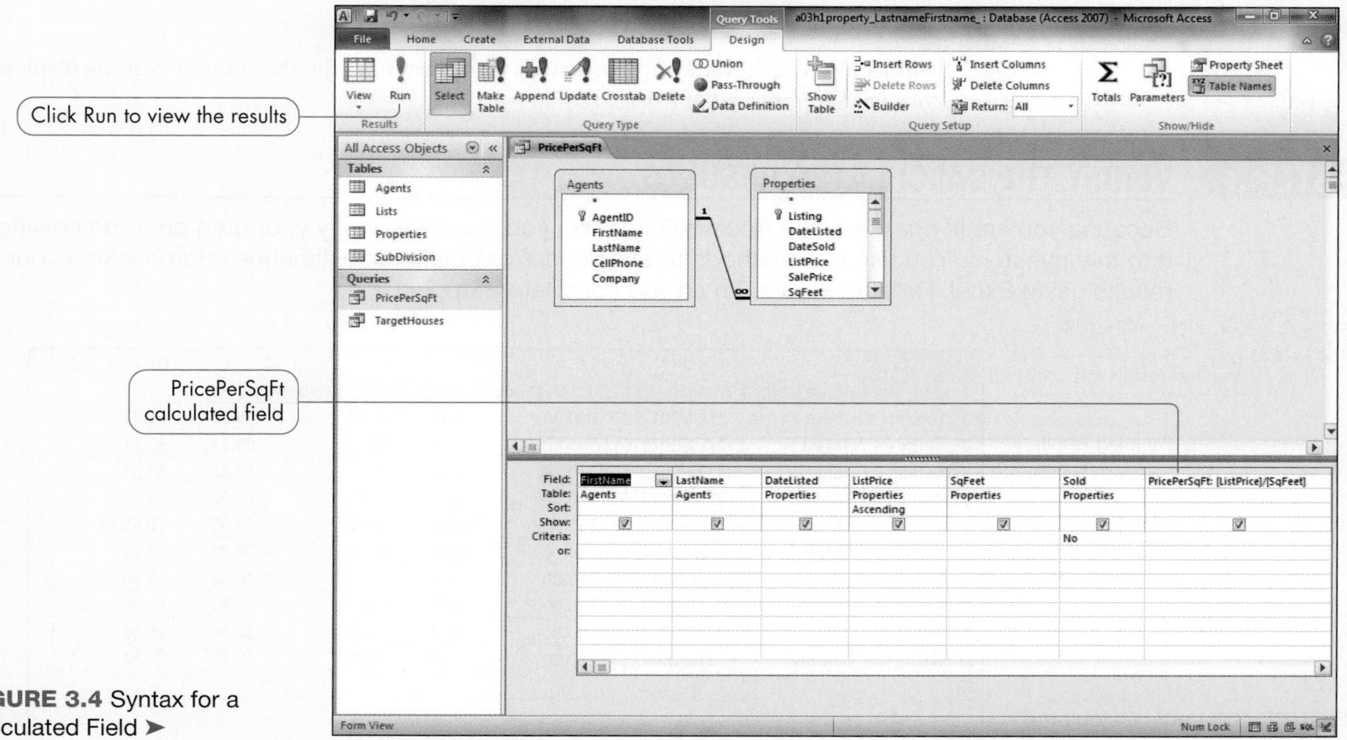

FIGURE 3.4 Syntax for a Calculated Field ➤

a. Click **View** in the Views group to switch to Design view.

TROUBLESHOOTING: If you accidentally click the View arrow, Access displays a list of options. Select the Design View option.

The TargetHouses query is based on two tables. The top portion of Query Design view displays the two tables, Agents and Properties, and the bottom portion (query design grid) displays the fields currently in the query.

b. Click the **File tab**, and then select **Save Object As**. Type **PricePerSqFt** in the **Save As dialog box**, and then click **OK**.

You made a copy of the TargetHouses query so you can add a calculated field to the new query but still preserve the original query.

c. Click the **File tab** to return to the query.

d. Scroll to the right until you see the first blank column in the query design grid.

e. Click in the top row of the first blank column, type **PricePerSqFt: ListPrice/SqFeet**, and then press **Enter**. Widen the PricePerSqFt column in order to see the entire expression.

Access inserts square brackets around the fields for you. The new field divides the values in the ListPrice field by the values in the SqFeet field. The : after *PricePerSqFt* is required.

f. Click **Run** in the Results group to view the results.

The new calculated field, PricePerSqFt, is displayed. Widen the PricePerSqFt column, if necessary, to see all the values.

g. Click **View** to switch back to Design view. Use Figure 3.4 to check your syntax. Click in the **PricePerSqFt calculated field cell**, and then click **Property Sheet** in the Show/Hide group.

The Property Sheet controls how the results of the calculated field will display in Datasheet view when you run the query.

h. Click the **Format property arrow**, and then select **Currency** from the list. Click in the **Caption box**, and then type **Price Per Sq Ft**. Close the Property Sheet.

i. Click **Run** to view your changes.

The calculated field values are formatted with Currency, and the column heading displays *Price Per Sq Ft* instead of *PricePerSqFt*.

STEP 3 VERIFY THE CALCULATED RESULTS

Because you are in charge of the Access Database, you decide to verify your data prior to showing it to the investors. You use two methods to check your calculations: estimation and checking your results using Excel. Refer to Figure 3.5 as you complete Step 3.

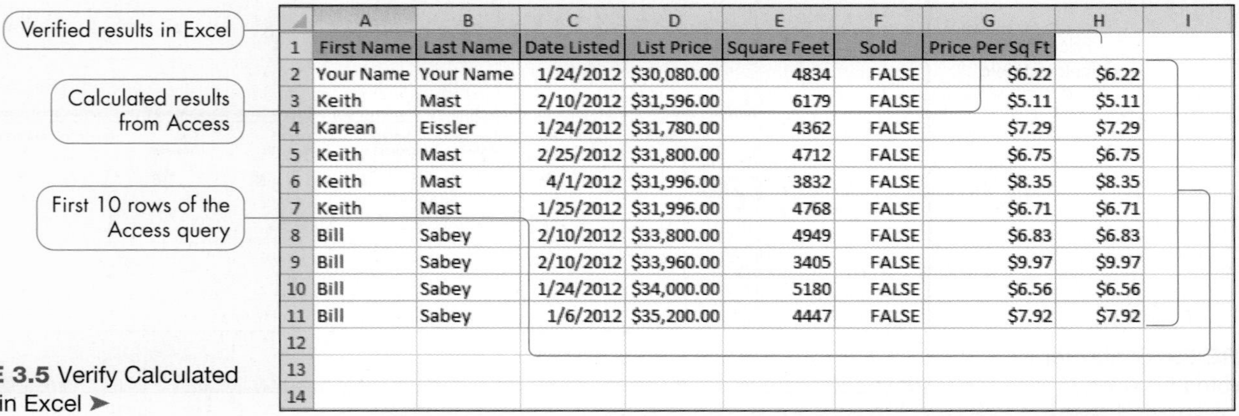

Verified results in Excel

Calculated results from Access

First 10 rows of the Access query

	A	B	C	D	E	F	G	H	I
1	First Name	Last Name	Date Listed	List Price	Square Feet	Sold	Price Per Sq Ft		
2	Your Name	Your Name	1/24/2012	$30,080.00	4834	FALSE	$6.22	$6.22	
3	Keith	Mast	2/10/2012	$31,596.00	6179	FALSE	$5.11	$5.11	
4	Karean	Eissler	1/24/2012	$31,780.00	4362	FALSE	$7.29	$7.29	
5	Keith	Mast	2/25/2012	$31,800.00	4712	FALSE	$6.75	$6.75	
6	Keith	Mast	4/1/2012	$31,996.00	3832	FALSE	$8.35	$8.35	
7	Keith	Mast	1/25/2012	$31,996.00	4768	FALSE	$6.71	$6.71	
8	Bill	Sabey	2/10/2012	$33,800.00	4949	FALSE	$6.83	$6.83	
9	Bill	Sabey	2/10/2012	$33,960.00	3405	FALSE	$9.97	$9.97	
10	Bill	Sabey	1/24/2012	$34,000.00	5180	FALSE	$6.56	$6.56	
11	Bill	Sabey	1/6/2012	$35,200.00	4447	FALSE	$7.92	$7.92	
12									
13									
14									

FIGURE 3.5 Verify Calculated Results in Excel ➤

a. Examine the Price Per Sq Ft column in the current query.

One of the ways to verify the accuracy of the calculated data is to ask yourself if the numbers make sense.

b. Locate the eighth record with *Bill Sabey* as the listing agent, an asking price of *$33,960*, and square footage of *3405*. Ask yourself if the calculated value of *$9.97* makes sense.

The sale price is $33,960 and the square footage is 3405. You can verify the calculated field easily by rounding the two numbers (to 34,000 and 3400) and then dividing the values in your head (34,000 div by 3400 = 10) to verify that the calculated value, $9.97 per sq ft, makes sense.

c. Launch Excel, and then switch to Access. Click the first row selector, and then drag through the first 10 records (the tenth record has a list price of *$35,200*). Click **Copy** in the Clipboard group on the **Home tab**.

You will also verify the calculation in the first 10 records by pasting the results in Excel.

d. Switch to Excel, and then click **cell A1** of the blank workbook. Click **Paste** in the Clipboard group on the Home tab.

The field captions appear in the first row, and the 10 records appear in the next 10 rows. The fields are located in columns A–G. The calculated field results are pasted in column G as values rather than as a formula.

TROUBLESHOOTING: If you see pound signs (#####) in an Excel column, use the vertical lines between columns to increase the width.

e. Type **=D2/E2** in **cell H2**, and then press **Enter**. Copy the formula from **cell H2** and paste it into **cells H3 to H11**.

The formula divides the list price by the square feet. Compare the results in columns G and H. The numbers should be the same. If the values differ, look at both the Excel and Access formulas. Determine which is correct, and then find and fix the error in the incorrect formula.

f. Close Excel without saving the workbook. Return to the Access database, and then click **Save** on the Quick Access Toolbar to save the design modifications made to the PricePerSqFt query.

TIP Use Zoom (Shift+F2) to View Long Expressions

To see the entire calculated field expression, click the field in Query Design view, and then press Shift+F2. A new window will appear to enable you to easily see and edit the entire contents of the cell. Access refers to this window as the Zoom dialog box, as shown in Figure 3.6.

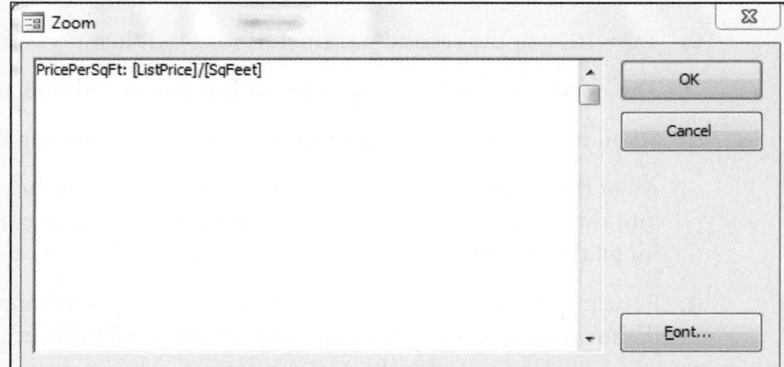

FIGURE 3.6 Use Zoom to See the Entire Calculated Field ➤

STEP 4 RECOVER FROM A COMMON ERROR

A few errors pop up as you test the new calculated fields. You check the spelling of the field names in the calculated field since that is a common mistake. Refer to Figure 3.7 as you complete Step 4.

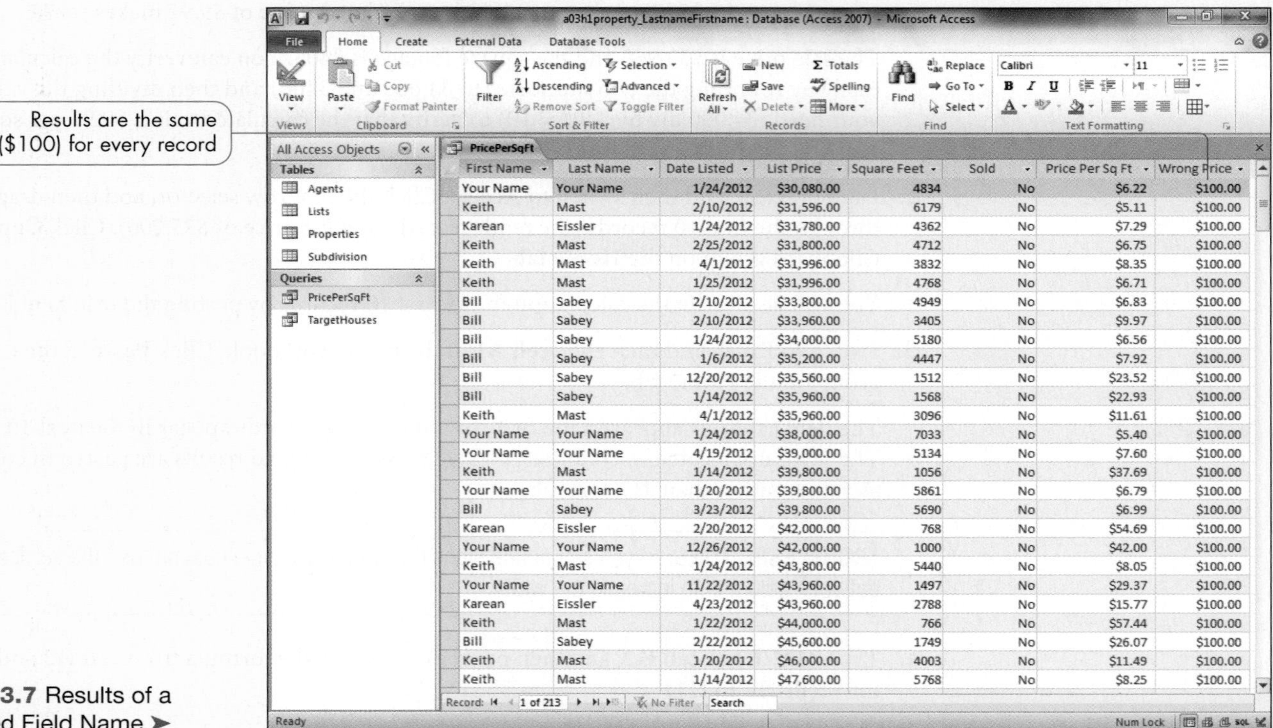
Results are the same ($100) for every record

FIGURE 3.7 Results of a Misspelled Field Name ➤

a. Click **View** in the Views group to switch to Design view. Scroll to the first blank column, and then click in the top row.

b. Type **WrongPricePerSqFt: xListPrice/xSqFeet**, and then press **Enter**. Widen the column to see the entire expression.

   Be sure that you added the extra *x's* to the field names. You are intentionally misspelling the field names to see how Access will respond. Access inserts square brackets around the fields for you.

c. Click **Run** in the Results group.

   You should see the Enter Parameter Value dialog box. The dialog box indicates that Access does not recognize xListPrice in the tables defined for this query in the first record. When Access does not recognize a field name, it will ask you to supply a value.

d. Type **100000** in the **first parameter box**. Press **Enter** or click **OK**.

   Another Enter Parameter Value dialog box displays, asking that you supply a value for xSqFeet. Again, this error occurs because the tables defined for this query do not contain an xSqFeet field.

e. Type **1000** in the **second parameter box**, and then press **Enter**.

   The query has the necessary information to run and returns the results in Datasheet view.

f. Scroll right and examine the results of the calculation for *WrongPricePerSqFt*.

   All of the records show 100 because you entered the values 100000 and 1000, respectively, into the parameter boxes. The two values are treated as constants and give the same results for all the records.

g. Return to Design view and correct the errors in the WrongPricePerSqFt field by changing the formula to **WrongPricePerSqFt: [ListPrice]/[SqFeet]**.

   Press Shift+F2 to view the calculated field and remove the *x* from the two field names.

h. Click in the **WrongPricePerSqFt calculated field**, click **Property Sheet**, and then change the Format property to **Currency**. Add the caption **Wrong Price Per Sq Ft**. Close the Property Sheet.

i. Run and save the query.

The calculated values in the last two columns should be the same.

j. Close the query.

k. Click the **File tab**, and then click **Compact & Repair Database**.

l. Click the **File tab**, click **Save & Publish**, and then double-click **Back Up Database**. Accept *a03h1property_LastnameFirstname_date* as the file name, and then click **Save**.

You just created a backup of the database you used to complete the first Hands-On Exercise. The *a03h1property_LastnameFirstname* database remains open.

m. Keep the database onscreen if you plan to continue with Hands-On Exercise 2. If not, close the database and exit Access.

TIP Learning from Your Mistakes

Following step-by-step instructions is a good way to begin learning about Access. If you want to become proficient, however, you must learn how to recover from errors. As you work through the rest of the Hands-On Exercises in this book, follow the instructions as presented and save your work along the way. Then go back a few steps and make an intentional error just to see how Access responds. Read the error messages (if any) and learn from your mistakes.

Expression Builder, Functions, and Date Arithmetic

In the last Hands-On Exercise, you calculated the price per square foot for real estate properties. That simple calculation helped you to evaluate all the properties on the investment list. You were able to type the expression manually.

The **Expression Builder** is a tool to help you create more complicated expressions.

When you encounter more complex expressions, you can use the ***Expression Builder*** tool to help you create more complicated expressions. When you create an expression in the field cell, you must increase the column width to see the entire expression. The Expression Builder's size enables you to easily see complex formulas and functions in their entirety.

In this section, you will learn how to create expressions using the Expression Builder. You also will learn how to use built-in functions. Finally, you will perform date arithmetic using the Expression Builder.

Creating Expressions with the Expression Builder

Launch the Expression Builder while in the query design grid to assist you with creating a calculated field (or other expression). The Expression Builder helps you create expressions by supplying you with the fields, operators, and functions you need to create them. When you use the expression builder to help you create expressions, you can eliminate spelling errors in field names. Another advantage is with functions; functions require specific arguments in a specific order. When you insert a function using the Expression Builder, the builder gives you placeholders that tell you where each argument belongs.

Launch the Expression Builder while in the query design grid to assist you with creating a calculated field.

After you create an expression in the Expression Builder, click OK to close the Expression Builder window. The expression is then entered into the current cell in the query design grid. From the query design, click Run in the Results group to view the results (in Datasheet view). If the results are incorrect, return to Design view and click the cell that contains the calculated field. Next, launch the Expression Builder again and make any corrections to the expression.

You can also use the Expression Builder when working with controls in forms and reports. For example, if you need a calculated field in a form, you can launch the Expression Builder by clicking Build on the right side of the control source box in the Property Sheet. You will learn more about this in later chapters. You can also use the Expression Builder to select a built-in function—for example, to calculate a payment on a loan. It will take some practice to master the Expression Builder; however, the effort will be well worth it as you learn to create more complication expressions.

Launch the Expression Builder

To launch the Expression Builder, open a query in Design view and verify the Design tab is selected on the Ribbon. Click Builder in the Query Setup group and the Expression Builder launches, as shown in Figure 3.8. (You can also launch the Expression Builder by right-clicking the cell where you want the expression and selecting Build from the shortcut menu.) The top section of the Expression Builder dialog box contains a rectangular area (known as the *expression box*) where you create an expression. You can type your expression in the box manually, or you can use the Expression Elements, Expression Categories, and Expression Values in the bottom portion of the Expression Builder. Double-click an item in the *Expression Categories* or *Expression Values* section and it will automatically be added to the expression box.

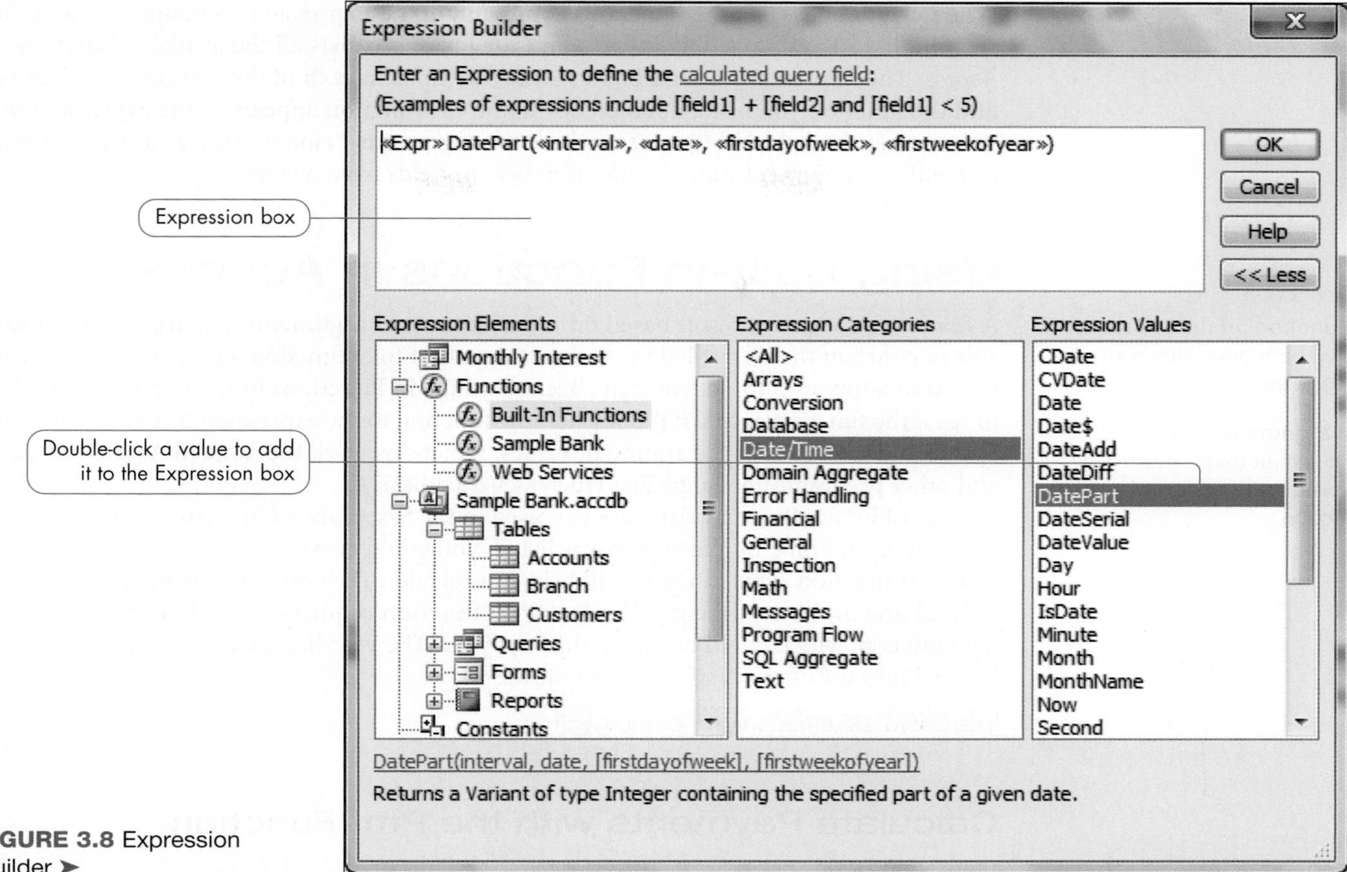

FIGURE 3.8 Expression Builder ➤

Create an Expression

The left column of the Expression Builder dialog box contains Expression Elements, which include the built-in functions, the tables and other objects from the current database, and common expressions. Select an item in this column; the middle column will show the list of options. For example, click a table in the left column and the fields from that table will appear in the middle column.

The middle column displays the Expression Categories based on the item selected in the Expression Elements box. For example, when the Built-in Functions item is selected in the Expression Elements box, the available built-in function categories are displayed in the Expression Categories box, such as the Date/Time category.

The right column displays the Expression Values, if any, for the categories that you selected in the Expression Categories box. For example, if you click Built-In Functions in the Expression Elements box, and then click Date/Time in the Expression Categories box, the Expression Values box lists all of the built-in functions in the Date/Time category, including DatePart.

You can create an expression by manually typing text in the expression box or by double-clicking the elements from the bottom section in the Expression Builder dialog box. For example, to create a calculated field using the fields in the tables, type the calculated field name, and then type a colon. Next, click the desired table listed in the *Expression Elements* section, and then double-click the field you want. Click the Operators item in the *Expression Elements* section, and then choose an operator (such as + or *) from the *Expression Categories* section (or just type the operator). The Expression Builder is flexible and will enable you to find what you need while still enabling you to modify the expression manually.

Calculated fields are relatively simple to create and most Access developers can create them without the Expression Builder. The main reason to use the builder for a calculated field is to eliminate spelling errors in field names. Using functions in Access almost always requires the Expression Builder since the syntax of functions can be difficult to remember.

When you double-click the Functions command in the Expression Elements box, and then click Built-In Functions, the Expression Categories box lists all the available functions in Access. The Expression Values box lists the functions in each of the categories. When you find the function you need, double-click it and the function appears in the expression box. You can see the «placeholder text» where the arguments belong; replace each placeholder text with the argument values, either numbers or fields from a table.

Using Built-In Functions in Access

A **function** produces a result based on inputs known as arguments.

An **argument** is a variable or constant that is needed to produce the output for a function.

A ***function*** produces a result based on inputs known as arguments. An ***argument*** is a variable or constant that is needed to produce the output for a function. Once you identify what you need a function to do, you can check the Built-in Functions in the Expression Builder to see if the function exists. If it does, add the function to the expression box and replace the «placeholder text» with the argument values. Functions work the same in Access and Excel and other programming languages (such as Visual Basic).

Consider the Property database you used in the first Hands-On Exercise. If you wanted to group each home by the year it was listed, you could create a year listed field using the DatePart function. This function will help you calculate the year listed using the DateListed field as one of the arguments. The DatePart function requires one other argument—the date interval, which could be day, month, or year. The year listed calculated field would be entered into the query design grid as follows:

```
YearListed: DatePart(“yyyy”, [DateListed])
```

Calculate Payments with the Pmt Function

The **Pmt function** calculates the monthly loan payment given the interest rate (monthly), term of the loan (in months), and the original value of the loan (the principal).

Figure 3.9 shows the ***Pmt function***, which calculates the monthly loan payment given the interest rate (monthly), term of the loan (in months), and the original value of the loan (the principal). To use this function, you need to supply the five arguments as field names from underlying tables or as constants.

The first argument is the interest rate per period. Interest rates are usually stated as annual rates, so you will need to convert them to monthly rates by dividing by 12. The second argument is the number of periods. Because loan terms are usually stated in years, you will need to convert the period to months by multiplying by 12. The next argument is the present value—or principal—of the loan. It tells you how much each customer has borrowed. The last two arguments, future value and type (both optional), are usually 0 or blank. The future value shows the amount the borrower will owe after the last payment has been made. The type argument tells Access whether the payment is made at the beginning or the end of the period.

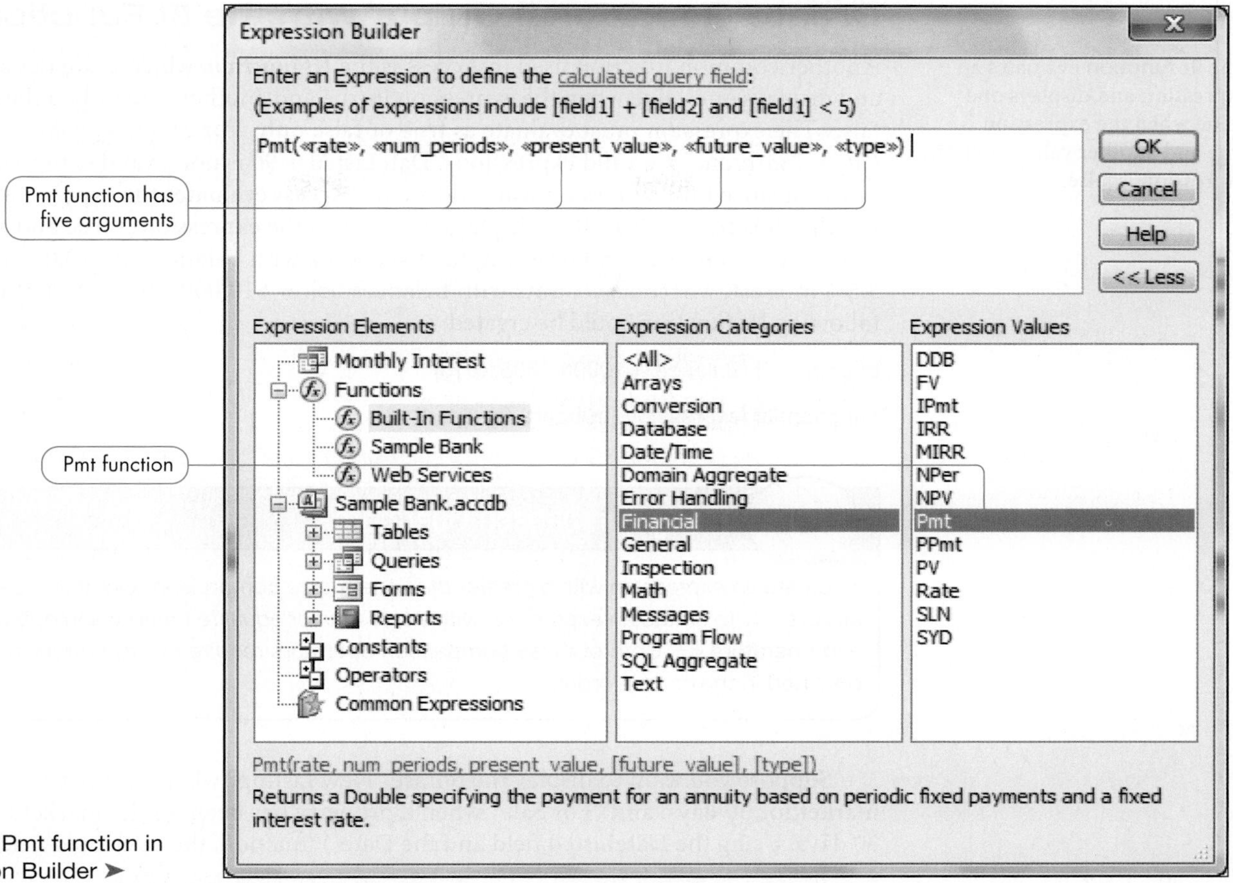

Pmt function has five arguments

Pmt function

FIGURE 3.9 Pmt function in the Expression Builder ➤

The following example shows how to use the Pmt function to calculate the monthly payment on a $12,500 loan, at a 6.0% interest rate, with a four-year payback term. Table 3.2 describes the arguments for the Pmt function in more detail.

Function: Pmt(*rate, num_periods, present value, future value, type*)

Example: Pmt(0.06/12, 4*12, 12500)

TABLE 3.2 Arguments of the Pmt Function

Part	Description
( )	Items inside the parentheses are arguments for the function. The arguments are separated by commas. Some arguments are optional; some arguments have a default value; in the Pmt function, the first three arguments are required and the last two are optional.
rate	Required. Expression or value specifying interest rate per period, usually monthly. A mortgage with an annual percentage rate of **6.0%** with monthly payments would have a rate entered as **0.06/12**. *The interest rate must match the period*.
num_periods	Required. Expression or integer value specifying total number of payment periods in the loan. For example, monthly payments on a four-year car loan give a total of 4 * 12 (or 48) payment periods.
present_value	Required. Expression or value specifying the present value of the money you borrow. If you borrow $12,500 for a car, the value would be 12500.
future_value	Optional. Expression or value specifying the future value after you've made the final payment. Most consumer loans have a future value of $0 after the final payment. However, if you want to save $50,000 over 18 years for your child's education, then 50000 is the future value. Zero is assumed if left blank.
type	Optional. Value (0 or 1) identifying when payments are due. Use 0 if payments are due at the end of the payment period (the default), or 1 if payments are due at the beginning of the period. Zero is assumed if left blank.

Create Conditional Output with the IIf Function

The **IIf function** evaluates an expression and displays one value when the expression is true and another value when the expression is false.

Another common function used in Access is the ***IIf function***, which evaluates an expression and displays one value when the expression is true and another value when the expression is false. The expression must evaluate as true or false only. For example, *balance >= 10000* or *City = "Sarasota"* are valid expressions. DateListed + *90* is not a valid expression for the IIf function since this expression will yield a date. Access evaluates the expression, determines whether it is true or false, then displays one value if the expression is true and another value if the expression is false. For example, if accounts with balances of $10,000 or more earn 3.5% interest, whereas accounts with balances below $10,000 earn only 1.5% interest, the following IIf function could be created:

Example: IIf (Balance>=10000, .035, .015)

Function: IIf (expression, truepart, falsepart)

Using Comparison Operators

To create an expression with a *greater than or equal to* comparison operator, type the two operators >=. To create an expression with a *less than or equal to* comparison operator, type the two operators <=. Both of these comparison operators require two operators and they must be typed in the correct order.

Suppose you want to display the phrase "New Listing" when a property has been on the market for 30 days, and "For Sale" when a property has been on the market for more than 30 days. Using the DateListed field and the Date() function, the calculated field would be:

PropertyStatus: IIf (Date() – [DateListed] <=30, "New Listing", "For Sale")

The expression Date() – [DateListed]<=30 evaluates each property and determines if the number of days on market is less than or equal to 30. When the expression is true, the function displays "New Listing." When the expression is false, the function displays "For Sale."

The IIf function can also evaluate text values. For example, to classify a list of customers based on whether they are in or out of the state of California, you could create the IIf function:

IIf([State]="CA", "CA", "Out of State")

Use a Nested IIf

Experienced Access users sometimes need to create nested IIf functions. This happens when two conditions are not sufficient to evaluate an expression. For example, in the earlier example where a property was classified based on days on market, the function PropertyStatus: IIf(Date() – [DateListed]<=30,"New Listing","For Sale") was used. If a third status were needed for properties that were on the market for six months, the nested PropertyStatus: IIf(Date() – [DateListed]<=30,"New Listing", IIf(Date() – [DateListed]>=180,"Stagnant","For Sale")) would be used.

When you finish the expression, click OK to close the Expression Builder dialog box. If you are working in a query, nothing will happen until you run the query. Your newly calculated field displays in the Datasheet view of the query. If you are working in a form, switch to Form view to see the results of your expression. And if you are working in a report, click Print Preview to see the results.

REFERENCE Use the Expression Builder to Create a Calculated Field

1. Open the query in Design view.
2. Click in the top row of the first blank column.
3. Verify the Design tab is displayed.
4. Click Builder in the Query Setup group to launch the Expression Builder (or right-click in the blank column and select Build from the list).
5. Type the name of the calculated field followed by a colon (:).
6. If the expression requires a field from a table, select a table from the Expression Elements box, and then double-click field names as needed to add them to the expression.
7. Type an arithmetic operator (such as + or *), or click Operators in the Expression Elements box, and then double-click a symbol in the Expression Values box.
8. If the expression requires a function, double-click the Functions folder, click Built-in Functions to see the function categories displayed in the Expression Categories box, and then select the function category. From the Expression Values box, double-click the specific function needed, and then fill in the correct arguments.
9. Click OK to exit the Builder box and place the expression in the field cell.
10. Run the query.
11. Examine and verify the output.
12. Return to the Design view.
13. Modify the new expression if necessary.
14. Run the query.
15. Save the query.

Performing Date Arithmetic

Working with dates in Access can be challenging, especially when performing date arithmetic. This can be even more problematic if your output will contain multiple formats for the United States, Europe, and Asia. Each has their own method of formatting dates. Fortunately, Access has some built-in functions to help work with dates and date arithmetic.

Date formatting affects the date's display without changing the actual underlying value in the table.

Date formatting affects the date's display without changing the actual underlying value in the table. All dates and times in Access are stored as the number of days that have elapsed since December 31, 1899. For example, January 1, 1900, is stored as 1, indicating one day after December 31, 1899. If the time were 9:00 PM on November 20, 2010, no matter how the date or time is formatted, Access stores it as 40502.875. The 40502 represents the number of days elapsed since December 31, 1899, and the .875 reflects the fraction of the 24-hour day that has passed at 9:00 PM. Because dates are stored by Access as sequential numbers, you can calculate the total numbers of hours worked in a week if you record the starting and ending times for each day. Using ***date arithmetic*** you can create expressions to calculate lapsed time, such as a person's age based on birth date or the number of days past due an invoice is based on the invoice date.

All dates and times in Access are stored as the number of days that have elapsed since December 31, 1899.

Using **date arithmetic** you can create expressions to calculate lapsed time.

Identify Partial Dates with the DatePart Function

Using a date function, you can isolate a portion of the date that is of interest to you. If your company increases the number of weeks of annual vacation from two weeks to three weeks after an employee has worked for five or more years, then the only part of the date of interest is the time lapsed in years. Access has a function, the ***DatePart function***, to facilitate this. Table 3.3 shows the DatePart function parameters.

The **DatePart function** enables you to isolate a specific part of a date, such as the year.

Example: DatePart("yyyy", [Employees]![HireDate])

Function: DatePart(interval, date), firstdayofweek, firstweekofyear

Useful date functions are:

- Date—Inserts the current date into an expression.
- DatePart—Evaluates a date and returns only the portion of the date that is designated.
- DateDiff—Measures the amount of time elapsed between two dates. This is most often today's date as determined by the date function and a date stored in a field. For example, you might calculate the number of days a payment is past due by comparing today's date with the payment DueDate.

TABLE 3.3 Using the DatePart Function

Function Portion	Explanation
DatePart	An Access function that examines a date and returns a portion of the date.
«**interval**»	The first argument, the interval, describes the portion of the date that you wish to return. Use "yyyy" for years, "m" for month, or "d" for day.
«**date**»	The second argument, the date, tells Access where to find the Date/Time information. In this case, it is stored in the Employee table in a field named HireDate.
«**firstdayofweek**»	Optional. A constant that specifies the first day of the week. If not specified, Sunday is assumed.
«**firstweekofyear**»	Optional. A constant that specifies the first week of the year. If not specified, the first week is assumed to be the week in which January 1 occurs.

After you practice using the DatePart function, the syntax for all date functions will become easier to understand. In the next Hands-On Exercise, you will copy and paste a query, use the Expression builder, and use functions.

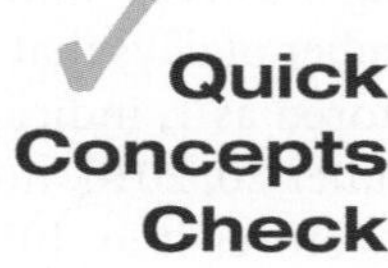

Quick Concepts Check

1. What are the benefits of creating expressions with the Expression Builder?
2. Give an example of a built-in function.
3. What is an argument in a function? Give an example.
4. What is the purpose of date arithmetic?

HANDS-ON EXERCISES

2 Expression Builder, Functions, and Date Arithmetic

As you learn more about Access, you find it easier to answer Jeff and Bill's questions about the properties using queries. When they ask you to calculate the price per bedroom and the price per room for each property, you use the Expression Builder to make the task easier. You also add two additional fields that calculate the days on market and the estimated commission for each property.

Skills covered: Copy and Paste a Query Using a New Name • Use the Expression Builder to Modify a Field • Use the Expression Builder to Add a Field • Use Functions • Work with Date Arithmetic and Add Criteria

STEP 1 COPY AND PASTE A QUERY USING A NEW NAME

You create a copy of the PricePerSqFt query from the previous Hands-On Exercise and paste it using a new name. You will add a few more calculated fields to the new query. Refer to Figure 3.10 as you complete Step 1.

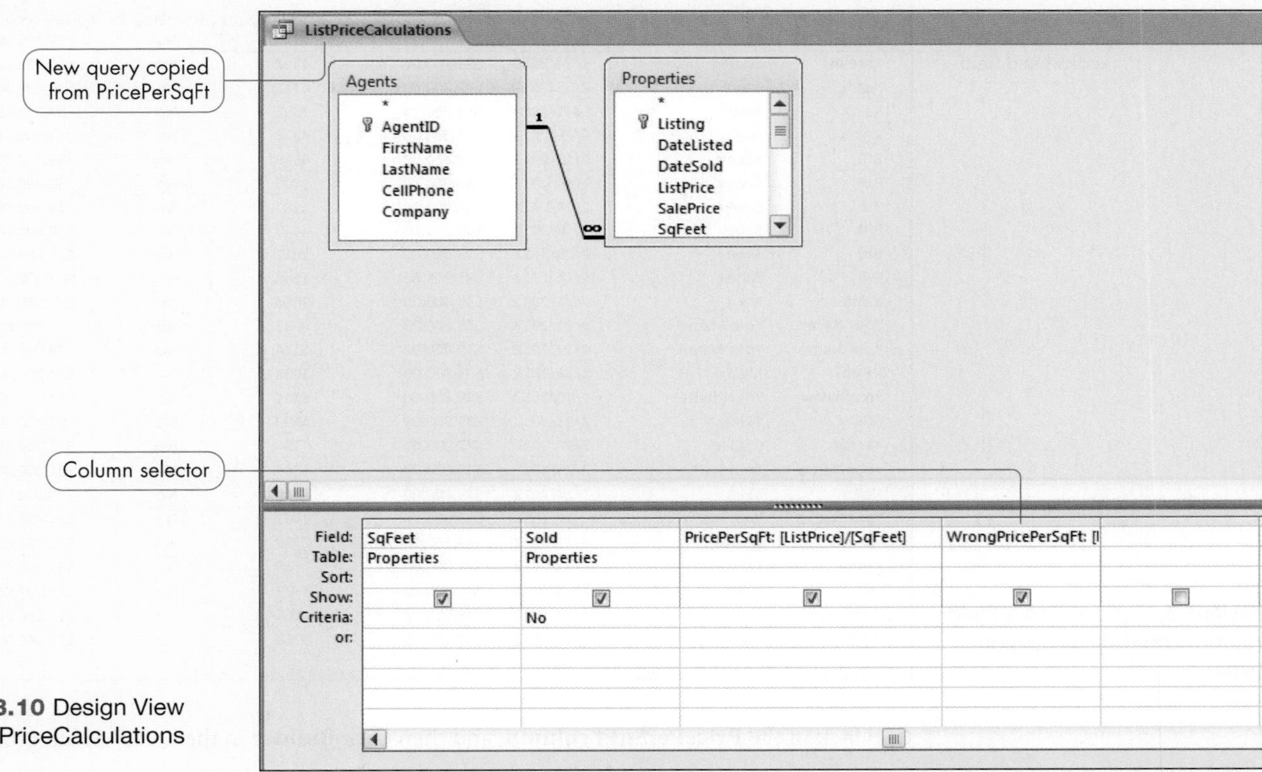

FIGURE 3.10 Design View of the ListPriceCalculations Query ➤

a. Open *a03h1property_LastnameFirstname* if you closed it at the end of Hands-On Exercise 1. Click the **File tab**, click **Save Database As**, and then type **a03h2property_LastnameFirstname**, changing *h1* to *h2*. Click **Save**.

b. Select the **PricePerSqFt query**, and then click **Copy** in the Clipboard group to copy the query.

c. Click **Paste**, and then type **ListPriceCalculations** as the query name. Click **OK**.

The new query is displayed in the Navigation Pane. The name of the query indicates that it contains calculations based on each property's list price.

d. Right-click **ListPriceCalculations**, and then choose **Design View** from the shortcut menu.

e. Delete the WrongPricePerSqFt field by clicking the column selector at the top of the column (as shown in Figure 3.10), and then pressing **Delete**.

The WrongPricePerSqFt field is not needed for this query.

f. Click **Run** to see the query results.

g. Click **View** to return to Design view. Save the query.

STEP 2 USE THE EXPRESSION BUILDER TO MODIFY A FIELD

You need another calculation to help Jeff and Bill determine which houses to purchase. You will use the Expression Builder to modify an existing field. Refer to Figure 3.11 as you complete Step 2.

Price Per Bedroom calculated field

ListPriceCalculations

First Name	Last Name	Date Listed	List Price	Square Feet	Sold	Price Per Bedroom
Your Name	Your Name	1/24/2012	$30,080.00	4834	No	$7,520.00
Keith	Mast	2/10/2012	$31,596.00	6179	No	$7,899.00
Karean	Eissler	1/24/2012	$31,780.00	4362	No	$10,593.33
Keith	Mast	2/25/2012	$31,800.00	4712	No	$10,600.00
Keith	Mast	4/1/2012	$31,996.00	3832	No	$7,999.00
Keith	Mast	1/25/2012	$31,996.00	4768	No	$7,999.00
Bill	Sabey	2/10/2012	$33,800.00	4949	No	$8,450.00
Bill	Sabey	2/10/2012	$33,960.00	3405	No	$8,490.00
Bill	Sabey	1/24/2012	$34,000.00	5180	No	$8,500.00
Bill	Sabey	1/6/2012	$35,200.00	4447	No	$8,800.00
Bill	Sabey	12/20/2012	$35,560.00	1512	No	$11,853.33
Bill	Sabey	1/14/2012	$35,960.00	1568	No	$11,986.67
Keith	Mast	4/1/2012	$35,960.00	3096	No	$17,980.00
Your Name	Your Name	1/24/2012	$38,000.00	7033	No	$7,600.00
Your Name	Your Name	4/19/2012	$39,000.00	5134	No	$9,750.00
Keith	Mast	1/14/2012	$39,800.00	1056	No	$19,900.00
Your Name	Your Name	1/20/2012	$39,800.00	5861	No	$7,960.00
Bill	Sabey	3/23/2012	$39,800.00	5690	No	$9,950.00
Karean	Eissler	2/20/2012	$42,000.00	768	No	$21,000.00
Your Name	Your Name	12/26/2012	$42,000.00	1000	No	$21,000.00
Keith	Mast	1/24/2012	$43,800.00	5440	No	$10,950.00
Your Name	Your Name	11/22/2012	$43,960.00	1497	No	$14,653.33
Karean	Eissler	4/23/2012	$43,960.00	2788	No	$21,980.00
Keith	Mast	1/22/2012	$44,000.00	766	No	$22,000.00
Bill	Sabey	2/22/2012	$45,600.00	1749	No	$15,200.00
Keith	Mast	1/20/2012	$46,000.00	4003	No	$11,500.00
Keith	Mast	1/14/2012	$47,600.00	5768	No	$11,900.00

Record: 1 of 213 No Filter Search

FIGURE 3.11 Calculated Field Created with the Expression Builder ➤

a. Click in the **PricePerSqFt column**, and then click **Builder** in the Query Setup group.

The Expression Builder dialog box opens.

b. Change the PricePerSqFt field name to **PricePerBR**.

c. Double-click the **[SqFeet] field** in the expression, and then press **Delete**.

d. Under Expression Elements, click the **plus sign** (+) next to the *a03h2property_LastnameFirstname* database in the Expression Elements box to expand the list. Click the (+) next to *Tables*, and then click the **Properties table**.

The fields from the Properties table are now listed in the middle column (Expression Categories).

e. Double-click the **Beds field** to add it to the expression box.

The expression now reads *PricePerBR: [ListPrice]/[Properties]![Beds].*

f. Select the **[Properties]! prefix** in front of *Beds*, and then press **Delete**.

   The expression now reads *PricePerBR: [ListPrice]/[Beds]*.

g. Click **OK**, and then click **Run** to view the query results.

h. Click **View** to switch to Design view, and then click the **PricePerBR field**. Click **Property Sheet** in the Show/Hide group, change the Format property to **Currency**, and then type **Price Per Bedroom** in the **Caption box**. Close the Property Sheet. Run the query and examine the changes.

i. Click **View** in the Views group to switch back to Design view. Save the query.

TIP **Switching Between Object Views**

You can switch between object views quickly by clicking View or you can click the View arrow and select the desired view from the list. Another way to switch between views is to right-click the object tab, and then select the view from the shortcut menu. See Figure 3.12.

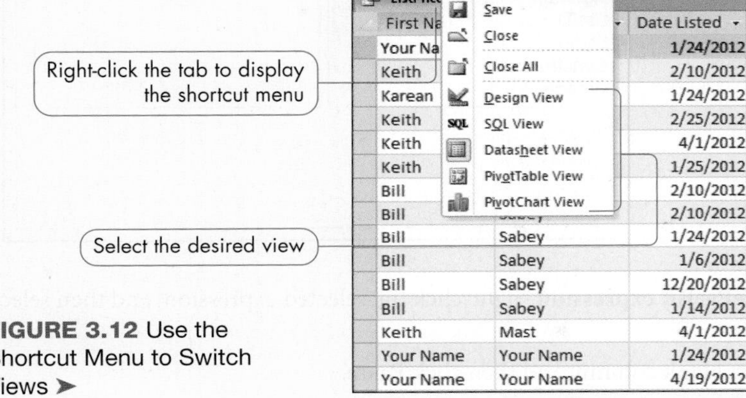

FIGURE 3.12 Use the Shortcut Menu to Switch Views ➤

TIP **Expression Builder and Property Sheet**

You can launch the Expression Builder by either clicking Builder in the Query Setup group on the Design tab or by right-clicking in the top row of the query design grid and selecting Build. Similarly, you can display the Property Sheet by clicking Property Sheet in the Show/Hide group on the Design tab or by right-clicking the top row of the query design grid and selecting Properties from the shortcut menu.

STEP 3 USE THE EXPRESSION BUILDER TO ADD A FIELD

The MCCC investors ask you for another calculation—the list price per room. For this calculation, you will assume that each property has a kitchen, a living room, a dining room, and the listed bedrooms and bathrooms. Refer to Figure 3.13 as you complete Step 3.

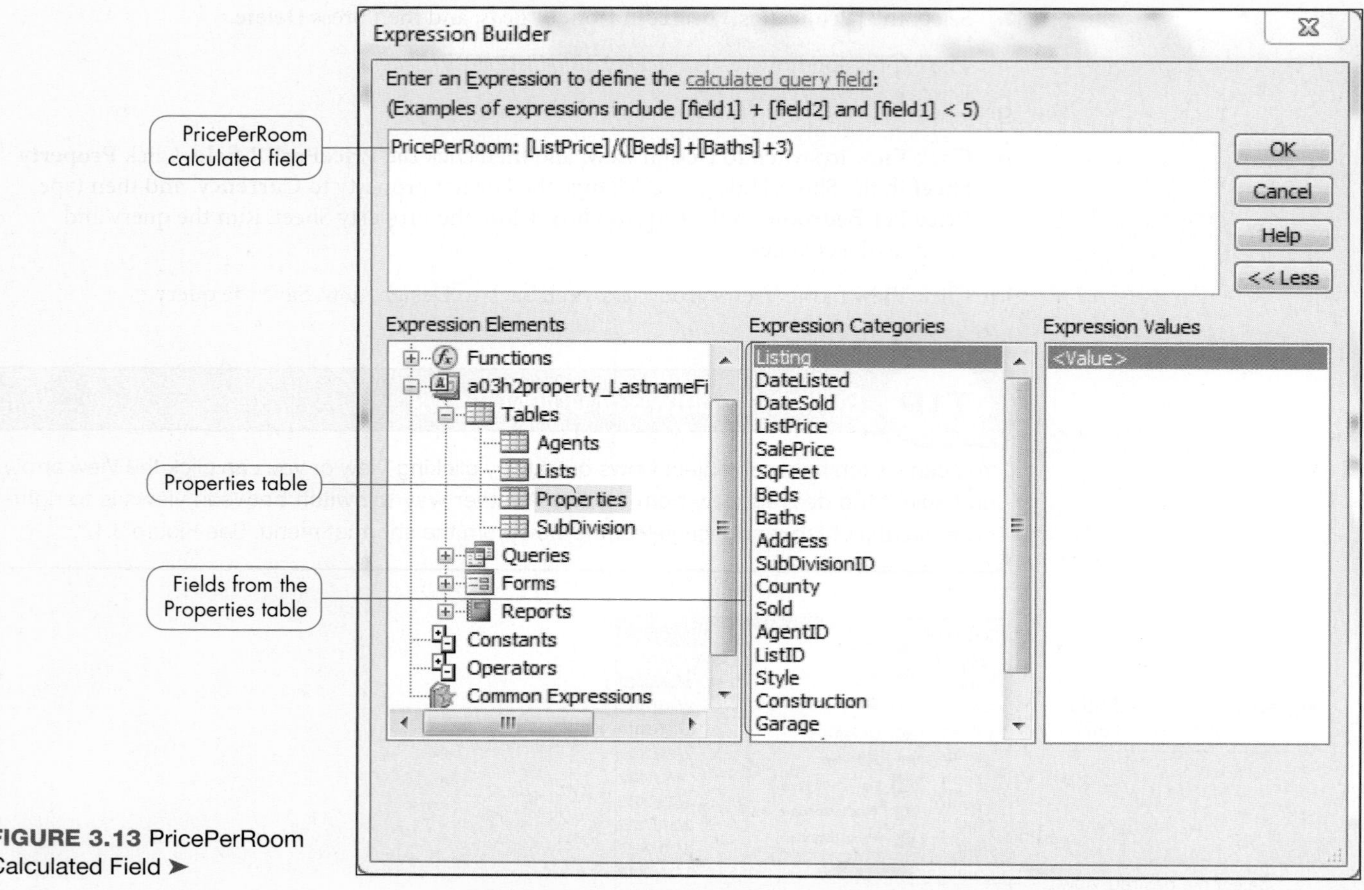

FIGURE 3.13 PricePerRoom Calculated Field ➤

a. Select the entire **PricePerBR expression**, right-click the selected expression, and then select **Copy**.

b. Right-click in the next blank column, and then click **Paste**.

   You will edit the copy so that it reflects the price per room.

c. Click the new field, and then click **Builder** in the Query Setup group.

d. Add **parentheses** around the [Beds] portion of the formula. Type a **plus sign** (+) after *[Beds]*, inside the parentheses.

   The expression box should read *PricePerBR: [ListPrice]/([Beds]+)*.

e. Click the **plus sign** (+) next to the *a03h2property_LastnameFirstname* database in the Expression Elements box to expand the list. Click the **plus sign** (+) next to *Tables*, and then click the **Properties table**.

   The fields from the Properties table are now listed in the Expression Categories box.

f. Double-click the **Baths field** to add it to the expression box.

   The expression now reads *PricePerBR: [ListPrice]/([Beds]+[Properties]![Baths])*.

g. Type another plus sign after *[Baths]*, and then type **3**.

   The expression now reads *PricePerBR: [ListPrice]/([Beds]+[Properties]![Baths]+3)*.

h. Delete the [Properties]! portion of the expression.

i. Change the PricePerBR field name to **PricePerRoom**.

   The expression now reads *PricePerRoom: [ListPrice]/([Beds]+[Baths]+3)*.

j. Click **OK** to close the Expression Builder. Run the query. Widen the PricePerRoom column in order to see all the values.

k. Switch to **Design view**, click the **PricePerRoom field**, and then click **Property Sheet**.

l. Change the Format property to **Currency**, and then type **Price Per Room** in the **Caption box**. Close the Property Sheet.

m. Run the query and examine the query results.

n. Save the query, and then close the query.

STEP 4 USE FUNCTIONS

Jeff and Bill feel like they are close to making an offer on a house. They would like to calculate the estimated mortgage payment for each house. You create this calculation using the Pmt function. Refer to Figures 3.14 and 3.15 as you complete Step 4.

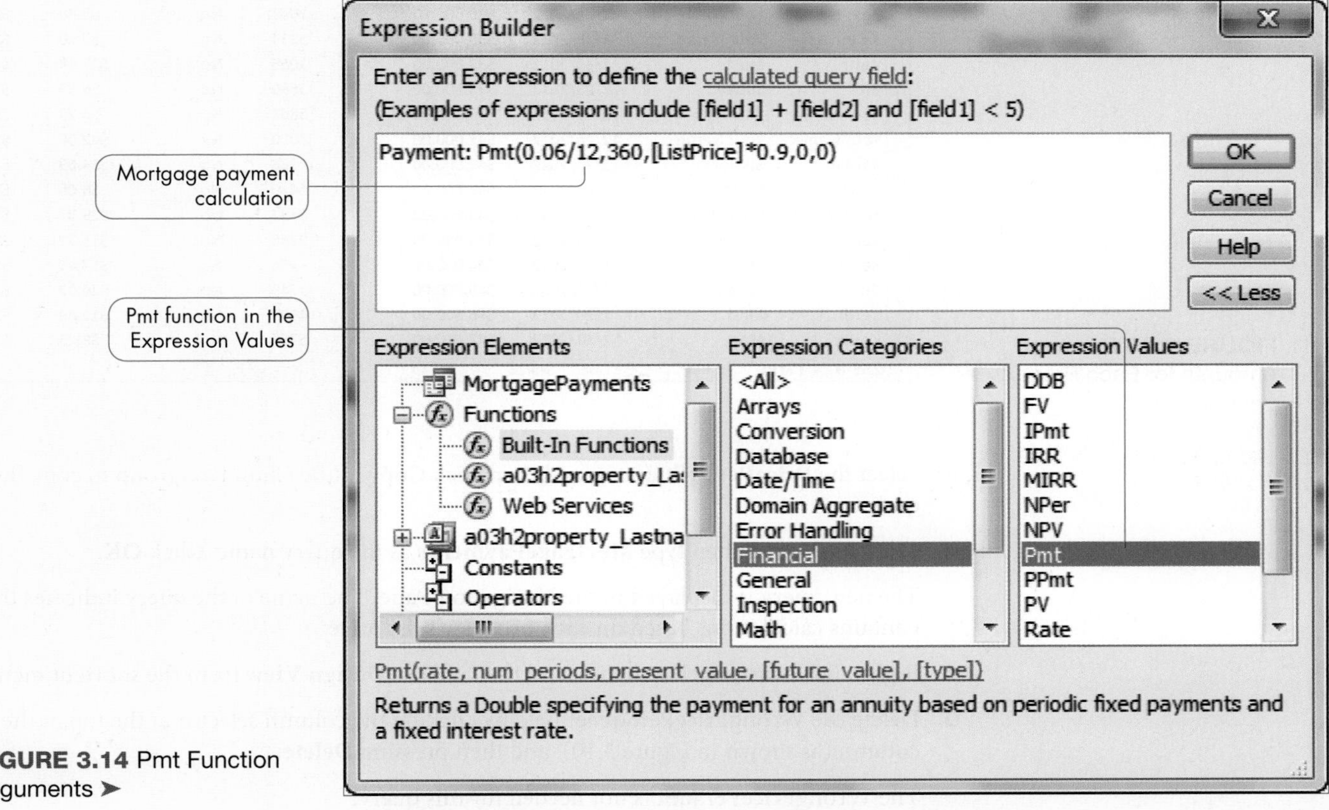

FIGURE 3.14 Pmt Function Arguments ➤

Mortgage payment calculation

MortgagePayments

First Name	Last Name	Date Listed	List Price	Square Feet	Sold	Price Per Sq Ft	Payment
Your Name	Your Name	1/24/2012	$30,080.00	4834	No	$6.22	$162.31
Keith	Mast	2/10/2012	$31,596.00	6179	No	$5.11	$170.49
Karean	Eissler	1/24/2012	$31,780.00	4362	No	$7.29	$171.48
Keith	Mast	2/25/2012	$31,800.00	4712	No	$6.75	$171.59
Keith	Mast	4/1/2012	$31,996.00	3832	No	$8.35	$172.65
Keith	Mast	1/25/2012	$31,996.00	4768	No	$6.71	$172.65
Bill	Sabey	2/10/2012	$33,800.00	4949	No	$6.83	$182.38
Bill	Sabey	2/10/2012	$33,960.00	3405	No	$9.97	$183.25
Bill	Sabey	1/24/2012	$34,000.00	5180	No	$6.56	$183.46
Bill	Sabey	1/6/2012	$35,200.00	4447	No	$7.92	$189.94
Bill	Sabey	12/20/2012	$35,560.00	1512	No	$23.52	$191.88
Keith	Mast	4/1/2012	$35,960.00	3096	No	$11.61	$194.04
Bill	Sabey	1/14/2012	$35,960.00	1568	No	$22.93	$194.04
Your Name	Your Name	1/24/2012	$38,000.00	7033	No	$5.40	$205.05
Your Name	Your Name	4/19/2012	$39,000.00	5134	No	$7.60	$210.44
Keith	Mast	1/14/2012	$39,800.00	1056	No	$37.69	$214.76
Bill	Sabey	3/23/2012	$39,800.00	5690	No	$6.99	$214.76
Your Name	Your Name	1/20/2012	$39,800.00	5861	No	$6.79	$214.76
Your Name	Your Name	12/26/2012	$42,000.00	1000	No	$42.00	$226.63
Karean	Eissler	2/20/2012	$42,000.00	768	No	$54.69	$226.63
Keith	Mast	1/24/2012	$43,800.00	5440	No	$8.05	$236.34
Your Name	Your Name	11/22/2012	$43,960.00	1497	No	$29.37	$237.21
Karean	Eissler	4/23/2012	$43,960.00	2788	No	$15.77	$237.21
Keith	Mast	1/22/2012	$44,000.00	766	No	$57.44	$237.42
Bill	Sabey	2/22/2012	$45,600.00	1749	No	$26.07	$246.06
Keith	Mast	1/20/2012	$46,000.00	4003	No	$11.49	$248.21
Keith	Mast	1/14/2012	$47,600.00	5768	No	$8.25	$256.85

Record: 1 of 84 No Filter Search

FIGURE 3.15 Payment Amounts for Each Property ➤

a. Select the **PricePerSqFt query**, and then click **Copy** in the Clipboard group to copy the query.

b. Click **Paste**, and then type **MortgagePayments** as the query name. Click **OK**.

   The new query is displayed in the Navigation Pane. The name of the query indicates that it contains calculations based on each property's list price.

c. Right-click **MortgagePayments**, and then choose **Design View** from the shortcut menu.

d. Delete the WrongPricePerSqFeet field by clicking the column selector at the top of the column (as shown in Figure 3.10), and then pressing **Delete**.

   The WrongPricePerSqFt is not needed for this query.

e. Click in the top row of the first blank column. Click **Builder** in the Query Setup group to open the Expression Builder dialog box.

   You will use the Pmt function to calculate an estimated house payment for each of the sold properties. You make the following assumptions: 90% of the sale price will be financed, a 30-year term, monthly payments, and a fixed 6.0% annual interest rate.

f. Double-click **Functions** in the Expression Elements box, and then click **Built-In Functions**.

g. Click the **Financial category** in the Expression Categories box.

h. Double-click the **Pmt function** in the Expression Values box. The expression box displays:

   Pmt(*«rate»*, *«num_periods»*, *«present value»*, *«future value»*, *«type»*)

i. Type **Payment:** to the left of the Pmt function. The expression box now displays:

   Payment: Pmt(«rate», «num_periods», «present value», «future_value», «type»)

TROUBLESHOOTING: If you forget to add the calculated field name to the left of the expression, Access will add *Expr1* to the front of your expression for you. You can edit the Expr1 name later, after the Expression Builder is closed.

j. Click each argument to select it, and then substitute the appropriate information. Make sure there is a comma between each argument.

Argument	Replacement Value
«rate»	0.06/12
«num_periods»	360
«present_value»	[ListPrice] * 0.9 *(this represents 90% of the list price)*
«future_value»	0
«due»	0

k. Examine Figure 3.14 to make sure that you have entered the correct arguments. Click **OK**. Run the query.

The Payment column shows ########. Widen the column and notice the payment amounts are negative numbers. You will edit the formula to change the negative payment values to positive.

l. Right-click the **MortgagePayments tab**, and then choose **Design View** from the shortcut menu. Right-click the **Payment field**, and then select **Build**. Add a **minus sign** (–) to the left of *[ListPrice]*.

The expression now reads *Payment: Pmt(0.06/12,360,–[ListPrice]*0.9,0,0)*.

m. Click **OK**. Open the **Property Sheet** for *Payment*, and then change the format to **Currency**. Close the Property Sheet.

The calculated field values should now appear as positive values formatted as currency, as shown in Figure 3.15.

n. Run and save the query.

STEP 5 WORK WITH DATE ARITHMETIC AND ADD CRITERIA

You need to limit the query results to only houses on the market at least six months. The investors also want you to add the commission fee to the query since they are getting ready to make a purchase and this information will help them figure out their commission cost. Refer to Figure 3.16 as you complete Step 5.

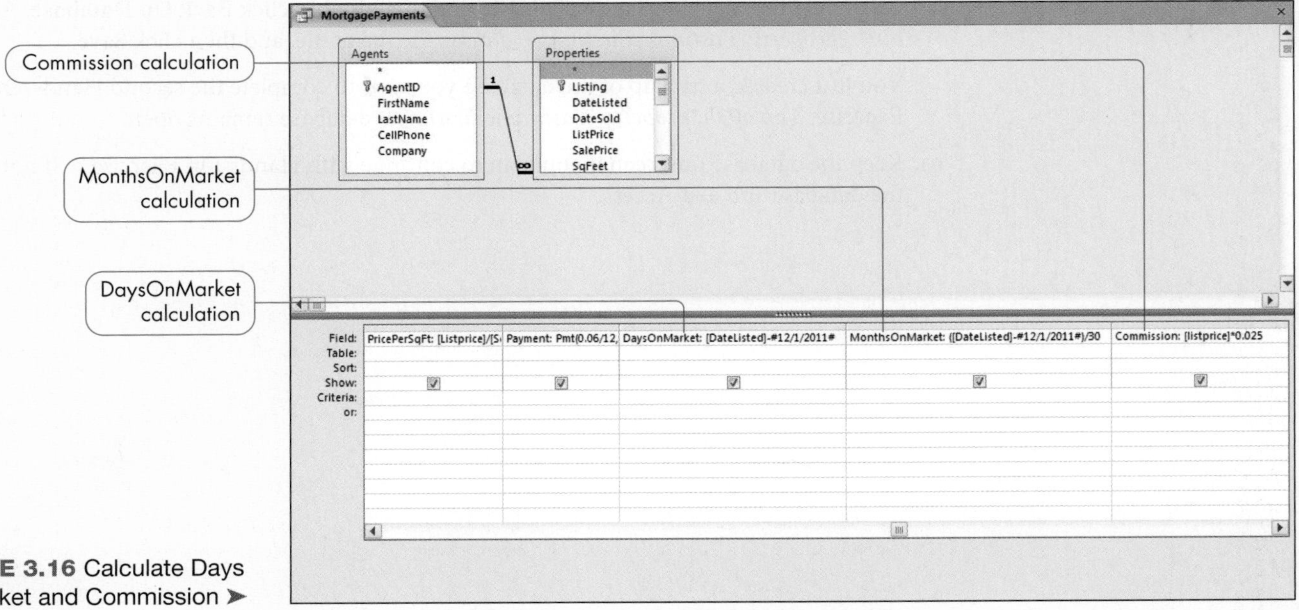

FIGURE 3.16 Calculate Days on Market and Commission ➤

a. Click **View** to return to the Design view of the MortgagePayments query. Click in the top row of the first blank column. Press **Shift+F2** to open the Zoom dialog box.

   You need to enter an expression to calculate the number of days that each property has been on the market.

b. Type **DaysOnMarket: [DateListed] – #12/1/2011#**.

   This will display the number of days a house has been on the market since 12/1/2011.

c. Click **OK** to close the Zoom dialog box. Open the **Property Sheet**, and then add the Caption to **Days on Market**. Close the Property sheet.

d. Type <=**100000** in the **Criteria row** of the **ListPrice column**. Run the query. Save the query.

   This expression will limit the query results to only houses with a list price of $100,000 or less. There should be 84 records.

e. Click **View** to switch to Design view. Click in the top row of the first blank column. Press **Shift+F2** to open the Zoom dialog box.

f. Type the formula **MonthsOnMarket: ([DateListed] – #12/1/2011#) / 30**.

   The formula for MonthsOnMarket requires placing parentheses around *[DateListed] – #12/1/2011#* and then dividing the result by 30. This is an example of how to control the order of operations.

g. Click **OK** to close the Zoom dialog box. Open the Property Sheet, and then change the Format to **Fixed**, and the Caption to **Months on Market**. Close the Property Sheet dialog box. Run the query. Save the query.

h. Switch to Design view. Click in the top row of the first blank column to create another calculated field. Open the Zoom dialog box, and then type the formula **Commission: ListPrice * .025**. Click **OK** to close the Zoom dialog box.

   The Commission field displays the projected commission for each house. The agent earns 2.5% of the sale price.

i. Right-click the **Commission field**, and then select **Properties**. Change the format to **Currency**, and then close the Property Sheet.

j. Run the query, examine the results, and then save the query. Close the query.

   The values in the Commission field now display in Currency format.

k. Click the **File tab**, and then click **Compact & Repair Database**.

l. Click the **File tab**, click **Save & Publish**, and then double-click **Back Up Database**. Accept *a03h2property_LastnameFirstname_date* as the file name, and then click **Save**.

   You just created a backup of the database you used to complete the second Hands-On Exercise. The *a03h2property_LastnameFirstname* database remains open.

m. Keep the database onscreen if you plan to continue with Hands-On Exercise 3. If not, close the database and exit Access.

Aggregate Functions

An **aggregate function** performs calculations on an entire column of data and returns a single value.

Aggregate functions perform calculations on an entire column of data and return a single value. Aggregate functions—such as Sum, Average, and Minimum—are used when you need to evaluate a group of record values rather than the individual records in a table or query.

Aggregate functions—such as Sum, Average, and Minimum—are used when you need to evaluate a group of record values rather than the individual records in a table or query.

Access refers to aggregate functions as Totals. In the Datasheet view of a query or table, click Totals in the Records group on the Home tab to add a Total row to the bottom of the datasheet. Each column can have its own aggregate function. Numeric fields are eligible for all of the functions, whereas text fields are only eligible for the count function.

When you create a query in Design view, click Totals in the Show/Hide group to change it to a totals query. The Total row now appears and you can select from the list of aggregate functions (e.g., Sum, Avg, Min).

The Datasheet view of a query or table displays individual records; users can edit these records, enter a new record, or delete a record in Datasheet view. However, when you work within a totals query in Datasheet view, no updates are allowed. A user cannot add, update, or delete records that have been totaled.

A car dealer's monthly inventory report is a good example of a report that might contain aggregate information. The cars would be grouped by model, and then by options package and color. At the end of the report, a summary page would list the count of cars in each model for quick reference by the sales reps. In the property database, aggregate information could be grouped by county or by subdivision. For example, the average home price per county could be presented in a query or a report. This would give prospective buyers a good idea of home prices in their target counties. Almost every company or organization that uses a database will require some type of aggregate data.

Almost every company or organization that uses a database will require some type of aggregate data.

A list of common aggregate functions is shown in Table 3.4.

TABLE 3.4 Aggregate Functions

Function	Description	Use with Data Type(s)
Average	Calculates the average value for a column. The function ignores null values.	Number, Currency, Date/Time
Count	Counts the number of items in a column. The function ignores null values.	All data types except a column of multivalued lists.
Maximum	Returns the item with the highest value. For text data, the highest value is 'Z.' The function ignores null values.	Number, Currency, Date/Time, Text
Minimum	Returns the item with the lowest value. For text data, the lowest value is 'a.' The function ignores null values.	Number, Currency, Date/Time, Text
Standard Deviation	Measures how widely values are dispersed from an average value.	Number, Currency
Sum	Adds the items in a column. Works only on numeric and currency data.	Number, Currency
Variance	Measures the statistical variance of all values in the column.	Number

In this section, you will learn how to create and work with aggregate functions. Specifically, you will learn how to use the Total row and create a totals query.

Adding Aggregate Functions to Datasheets and Queries

Aggregate functions are most commonly used in tables, queries, and reports. Occasionally, aggregate functions are also added to the form footer section of forms. Aggregate data helps users evaluate the values in a single record as compared to the average of all the records.

If you are considering buying a property in Bucks county for $150,000 and the average price of a property in Bucks county is $450,000, you know you are getting a good deal (or buying a bad property).

A **Total row** displays as the last row in the Datasheet view of a table or query and provides a number of aggregate functions.

Access provides two methods of adding aggregate functions to a query—a ***Total row*** displayed as the last row in the Datasheet view of a table or query and a totals query created in query Design view.

The first method enables you to add a Total row to the Datasheet view. This method is quick and easy and has the advantage of showing the total information while still showing the individual records. Adding a Total row to a query or table can be accomplished by most users (even those who are not familiar with designing a query).

The second method requires you to add a Total row in the Query Design view. This method has the advantage of enabling you to group your data by categories. For example, you can use the Count function to show the number of houses sold in each county in each subdivision. You could also use the Average function to show the average sale price for houses sold in each subdivision.

Once the totals data are assembled, you can use them to make decisions. Who is the leading salesperson? Which subdivisions are selling the most houses? This method requires the user to understand how to alter the design of a query.

Access also permits aggregates in reports. The Report Wizard gives users a choice to show all detail records or summary-only statistics. Select summary only to see aggregate data. You will learn to use both methods of creating aggregate data.

Add a Total Row in a Query or Table

Figure 3.17 shows the Total row added to the Datasheet view of a query. Using the balance column as illustrated, you can choose any of the aggregate functions that apply to numeric fields. To begin, click Totals in the Records group on the Home tab. The Total row is added at the bottom of the datasheet, below the new record row of the query or table. In the Total row, you can select one of the aggregate functions by clicking in the cell and then clicking the arrow. The list of aggregate functions includes Sum, Average, Count, and others.

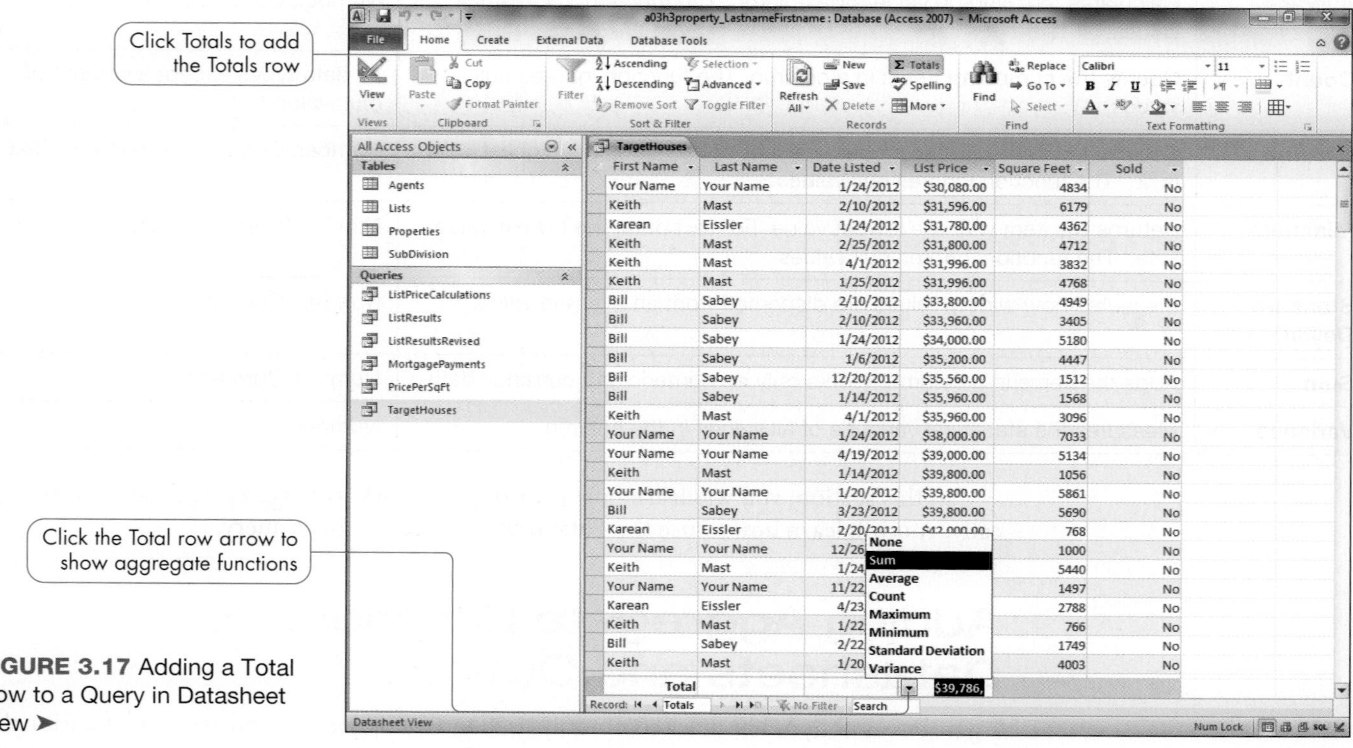

FIGURE 3.17 Adding a Total Row to a Query in Datasheet View ➤

Create a Totals Query

A **totals query** contains an additional row in the design grid and is used to display only aggregate data when the query is run.

A ***totals query*** contains an additional row in the query design grid and is used to display only aggregate data when the query is run. This is in contrast to using the Total row in a datasheet which shows both the detail records and the summary (as described in the previous section). The first column of a totals query will usually be a grouping field; the Total row will contain the Group function. The second and subsequent columns will usually contain the Count, Sum, or Avg function. Problems can arise when too many columns are included in a totals query; a typical totals query contains only two to five columns. Figure 3.18 shows the Design view of a totals query with three columns.

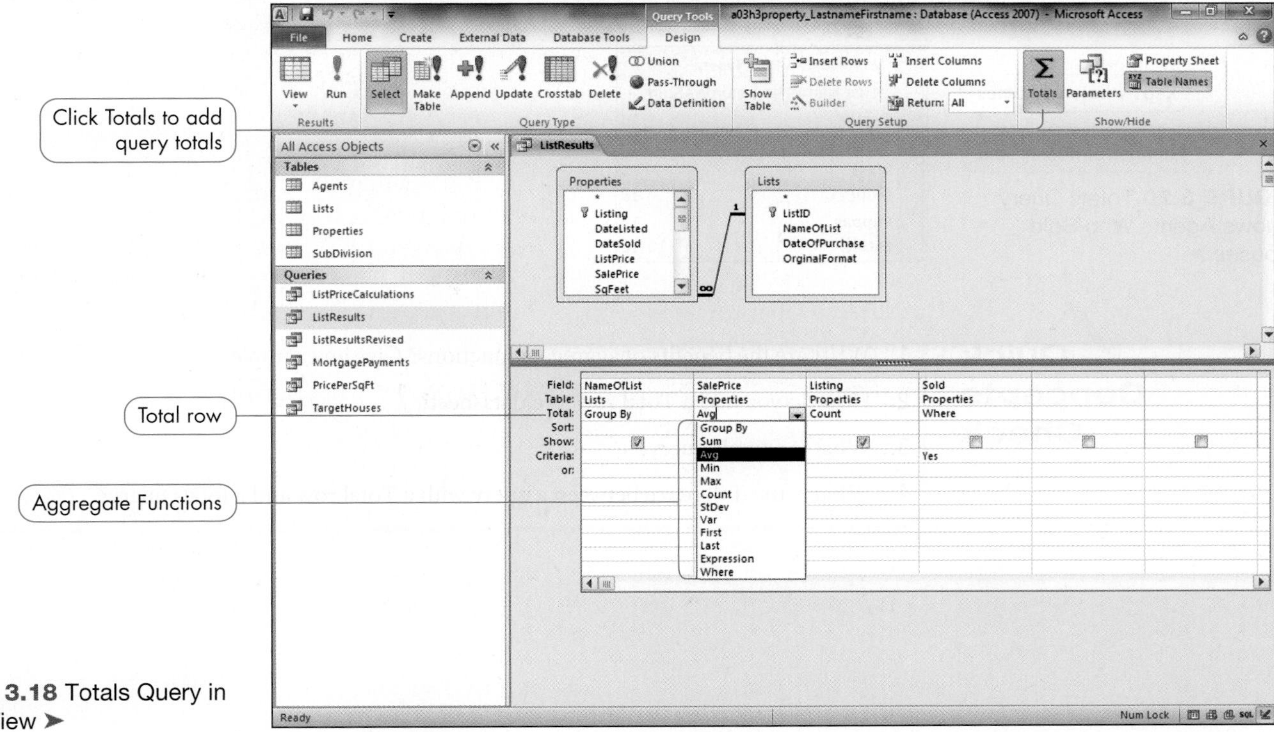

FIGURE 3.18 Totals Query in Design View ➤

Figure 3.18 groups the properties by county and then shows the count of houses and the average price in each county. You could add the Subdivision field to the second column of this query—to create a group within a group. The data will now be grouped by county and then by subdivision within each county. In order to show the subdivision field, you must add the Subdivision table to the query design. Figure 3.19 shows the results of the Housing Info by County by Subdivision totals query.

Grouped by county, then by subdivision

Count of homes

Average list price

Housing Info by County by Subdivision

County	Subdivision	Homes	Average Price
Berks	The Pines	40	$273,807.00
Bucks	Wood	49	$450,323.16
Chester	Fair Brook	1	$155,000.00
Chester	North Point	11	$62,264.55
Chester	Red Canyon	58	$93,569.07
Chester	The Courses	17	$127,537.65
Delaware	Fair Brook	17	$154,967.81
Lehigh	The Orchards	20	$169,077.70
Montgomery	Dale	26	$103,707.69
Philadelphia	Eagle Valley	10	$181,440.00
Philadelphia	Seeley Lake	26	$95,450.92
Philadelphia	The Estates	13	$68,040.00
Philadelphia	Water Valley	15	$145,229.33

FIGURE 3.19 Totals Query in Datasheet View ➤

A Totals Query Helps Evaluate a Database

If you were asked to evaluate a database that contains home sales information, you could quickly determine which agents sold houses by creating a totals query with two tables and three fields. From the Properties and Agents tables, you would add the LastName field, the Listing field, and the Sold field. Click Totals in the Show/Hide group. Accept Group By in column one; change column two to Count, and change column three to Where. Add Yes to the Criteria row of column three. The results of this query would show which agents sold homes, as shown in Figure 3.20.

Which Agents Sold Houses

Last Name	Homes Sold
Eissler	16
Keller	15
Mast	15
Mullock	16
Pappas	12
Sabey	16

Reps who sold homes

Number of homes sold

FIGURE 3.20 Totals Query Shows Agents Who Sold Houses ➤

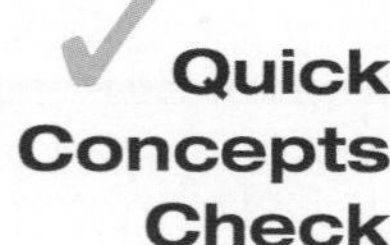

Quick Concepts Check

1. What are the benefits of aggregate functions? Give an example.
2. How do you add a Total row to a datasheet?
3. What is a totals query?
4. What is the difference between a query with a Total row and a totals query?

3 Aggregate Functions

The investors decide it would be helpful to analyze the property lists they purchased. Some of the lists do not have homes that match their target criteria. The investors will either need to purchase new lists or alter their criteria. You create several totals queries to evaluate the property lists.

Skills covered: Add a Total Row to Datasheet View • Create a Totals Query Based on a Select Query • Add a Calculated Field to a Totals Query

STEP 1 ADD A TOTAL ROW TO DATASHEET VIEW

You begin your property list analysis by creating a total row in the Datasheet view of the MortgagePayments query. This will give you a variety of aggregate information for each column. Refer to Figure 3.21 as you complete Step 1.

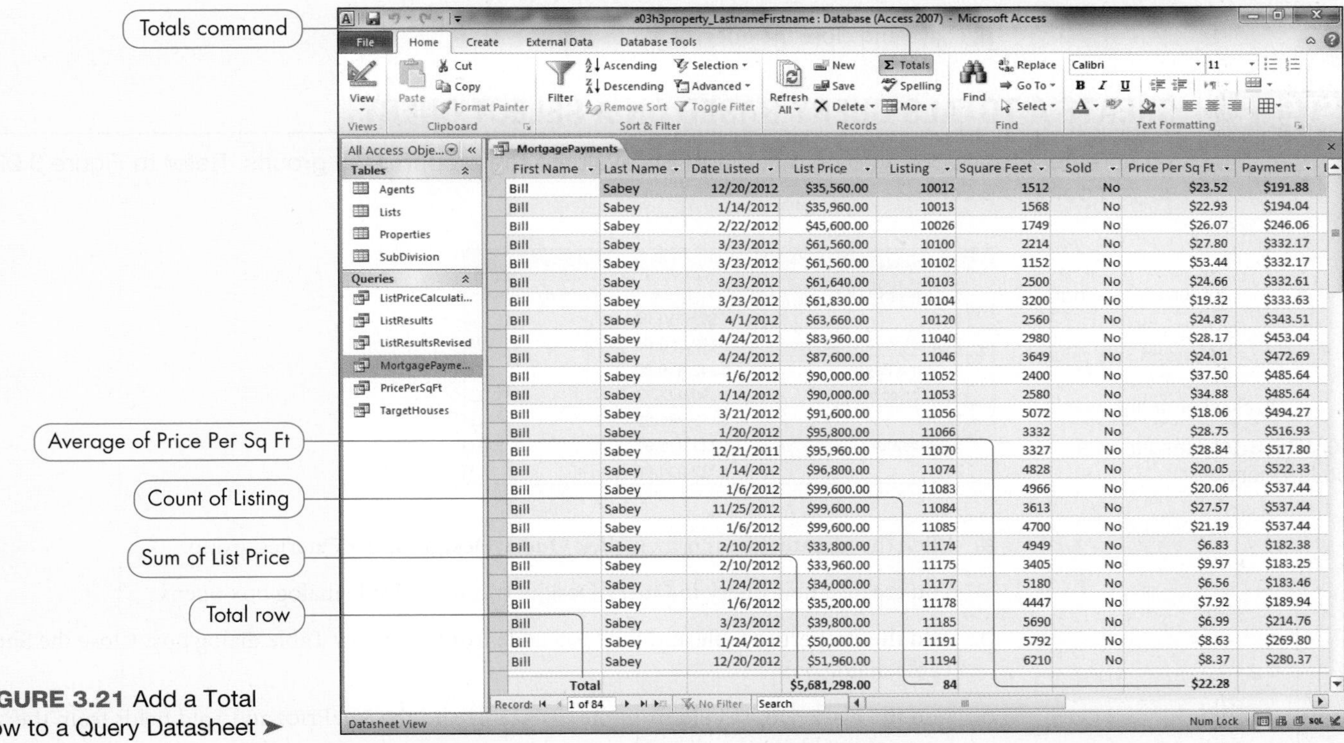

FIGURE 3.21 Add a Total Row to a Query Datasheet ➤

a. Open *a03h2property_LastnameFirstname* if you closed it at the end of Hands-On Exercise 2. Click the **File tab**, click **Save Database As**, and then type **a03h3property_LastnameFirstname**, changing *h2* to *h3*. Click **Save**.

b. Right-click the **MortgagePayments query** in the Navigation Pane, and then select **Design View** from the shortcut menu. Drag the **Listing field** from the Properties table to the fifth column.

The Listing field is now in the fifth column and the other columns shift to the right.

c. Click **View** to switch to Datasheet view. Click **Totals** in the Records group on the Home tab to show the Total row.

The Total row is now displayed as the last row of the query results. Click Totals again to hide the Total row, then one more time to show it.

d. Click in the cell that intersects the Total row and the List Price column.

e. Click the arrow, and then select **Sum** to display the total of all the properties that have not sold. Widen the List Price column if you can't see the entire total value.

The total list price of all properties is $5,681,298.00.

f. Click the arrow in the Total row in the Listing column, and then select **Count** from the list.

The count of properties in this datasheet is 84.

g. Click in the Total row in the Price Per Sq Ft column. Click the arrow, and then select **Average** to display the average price per square foot.

h. Save and close the query.

STEP 2 CREATE A TOTALS QUERY BASED ON A SELECT QUERY

You create a totals query to help Jeff and Bill evaluate the properties in groups. Refer to Figure 3.22 as you complete Step 2.

NameOfList	AvgOfSalePrice	Number Sold
MLS	$89,750.00	8
PhillyHousesForSale	$170,250.00	24
Reading Eagle	$242,450.00	8
Realtor.com	$130,422.73	11
Trulia	$145,781.82	18
Wholesaler	$223,316.67	16
ZIP	$322,000.00	5

FIGURE 3.22 Results of a Totals Query ➤

a. Click the **Create tab**, and then click **Query Design** in the Queries group.

You create a new query in Query Design; the Show Table dialog box opens.

b. Add the Properties table and the Lists table from the Show Table dialog box. Close the Show Table dialog box.

c. Add the NameOfList field from the Lists table and the SalePrice and Sold fields from the Properties table to the query design grid.

d. Click **Totals** in the Show/Hide Group to show the Total row.

e. Change the Total row to **Avg** in the SalePrice column.

f. Change the Total row to **Where** in the Sold column. Type **Yes** in the **Criteria row**.

This criterion will limit the results to sold houses only.

g. Click in the **SalePrice field**, and then click **Property Sheet** in the Show/Hide group. Change the SalePrice format to **Currency**. Close the Property Sheet. Run the query.

The query results indicate that the MLS list is the only source that is under the investor's target of $100,000 or less. They decide to continue using Realtor.com and Trulia even though the average price is over $100,000. The other sources will no longer be used.

h. Click **View** to switch to Design View. Add the Listing field from the Properties table to the fourth column in the design grid. Change the Total row for *Listing* to **Count**. Run the query.

   The query results now show the number of properties sold in each source, in addition to the average sale price. This will help determine which sources have been more effective.

i. Click **View** to return to the Design view of the query. Change the caption of the Listing column to **Number Sold**. Run the query, and then widen the columns as shown in Figure 3.22.

j. Save the query as **ListResults**. Keep the query open for the next step.

STEP 3 ADD A CALCULATED FIELD TO A TOTALS QUERY

The totals query helped group the houses into categories. However, the groups contain all the properties, even the ones that do not match the investor's criteria. You need to create a new query with the investor's criteria included. Refer to Figure 3.23 as you complete Step 3.

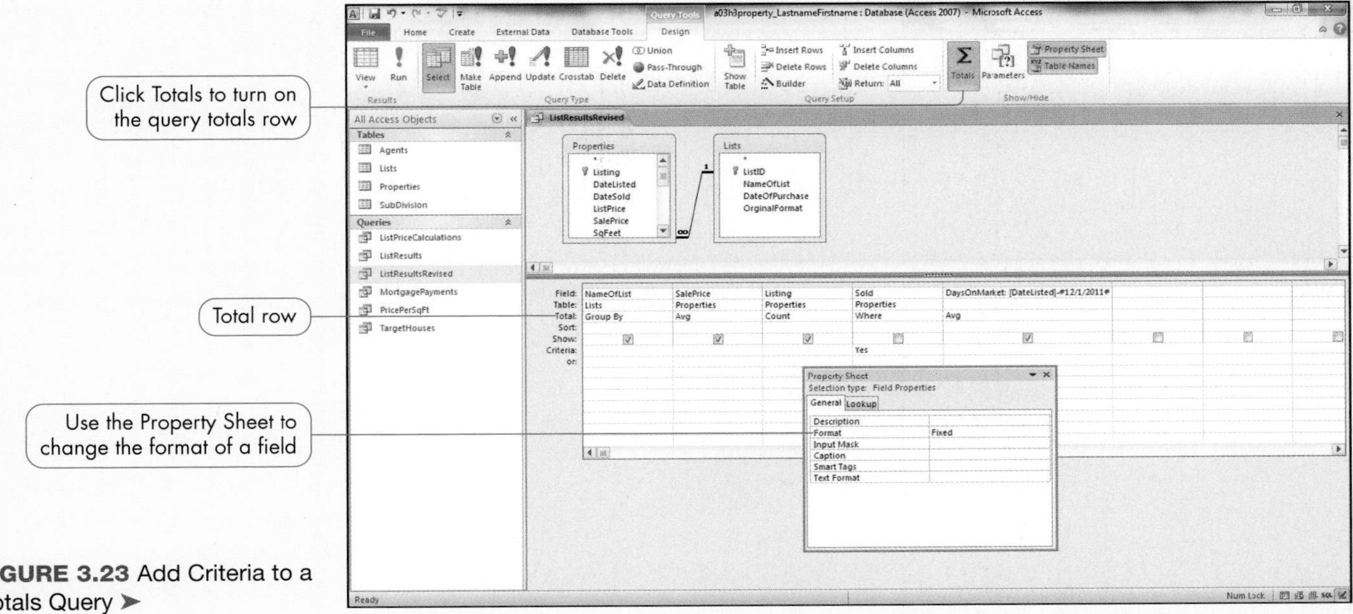

FIGURE 3.23 Add Criteria to a Totals Query ➤

a. Click the **File tab**, and then click **Save Object As**. Save the query as **ListResultsRevised**. Click the **File tab** to return to the query.

b. Click **Totals** in the Records group, and then add **Sum** to the Number Sold column.

   The total number of houses sold is 90.

c. Click **View** in the Views group to switch to Design view. In the first blank column, type **DaysOnMarket: [DateListed]** – **#12/1/2011#** to create a new calculated field. Change the Total row to **Avg**.

d. Right-click the **DaysOnMarket field**, and then select **Properties** from the shortcut menu. Change the Format property to **Fixed**, and then change the Decimal Places property to **0**. Close the Property Sheet.

e. Run the ListResultsRevised query, and then examine the DaysOnMarket.

f. Save and close the query.

g. Click the **File tab**, and then click **Compact & Repair Database**.

h. Click the **File tab**, click **Save & Publish**, and then double-click **Back Up Database**. Accept *a03h3property_LastnameFirstname_date* as the file name, and then click **Save**.

You just created a backup of the database you used to complete the third Hands-On Exercise. The *a03h3property_LastnameFirstname* database remains open.

i. Click the **File tab**, and then click **Exit** (to exit Access).

j. Submit based on your instructor's directions.

CHAPTER OBJECTIVES REVIEW

After reading this chapter, you have accomplished the following objectives:

1. **Understand the order of operations.** The order of operations determines the sequence by which operations are calculated in an expression. Evaluate expressions in parentheses first, then exponents, then multiplication and division, and, finally, addition and subtraction. Operations of equal value will be calculated from left to right. A solid understanding of these rules will enable you to easily create calculated fields in Access.
2. **Create a calculated field in a query.** When creating a query, you may need to create a calculation based on the fields from one or more tables. Add a calculated field in the Design view of a query to the first blank column or by inserting a blank column where needed. A formula used to calculate new fields from the values in existing fields is known as an *expression*. An expression can consist of a number of fields, operators (such as * , / , + , or –), functions (such as IIf), and constants (numbers). When creating a calculated field, you must follow proper syntax—the set of rules that Access follows when evaluating an expression.
3. **Create expressions with the Expression Builder.** Launch the Expression Builder while in the query design grid to assist you with creating a calculated field (or other expression). The Expression Builder helps you create expressions by supplying you with the fields, operators, and functions you need to create them. When you use the Expression Builder to help you create expressions, you can eliminate spelling errors in field names. Another advantage is with functions; functions require specific arguments in a specific order. When you insert a function using the Expression Builder, the builder gives you placeholders that tell you where each argument belongs.
4. **Use built-in functions in Access.** A function produces a result based on variable inputs known as *arguments*. Once you identify what you need a function to do, you can open the Built-In Functions folder in the Expression Builder to see if the function exists. If it does, add the function to the expression box and supply the required arguments. Functions work the same in Access and Excel.
5. **Perform date arithmetic.** All dates and times in Access are stored as the number of days that have elapsed since December 31, 1899. Working with dates in Access can be challenging, especially when performing date arithmetic. Fortunately, Access has some built-in functions to help work with dates and date arithmetic. Sample functions include DateDiff (), DateAdd(), Date(), and Now(). These functions help perform arithmetic on date fields.
6. **Add aggregate functions to datasheets and queries.** Aggregate functions perform calculations on an entire column of data and return a single value. Aggregate functions—such as Sum, Average, and Minimum—are used when you need to evaluate a group of records rather than the individual records in a table or query. Access refers to aggregate functions as Totals. In the Datasheet view of a query or table, click Totals to add a Total row to the bottom of the datasheet. When you create a query in Design view, click Totals to show the Total row.

KEY TERMS

Aggregate function ***p.713***
Argument ***p.700***
Constant ***p.689***
Date arithmetic ***p.703***
Date formatting ***p.703***
DatePart function ***p.703***
Expression ***p.689***
Expression Builder ***p.698***
Function ***p.700***
IIf function ***p.702***
Order of operations ***p.688***
Pmt function ***p.700***
Syntax ***p.689***
Total row ***p.714***
Totals query ***p.715***

MULTIPLE CHOICE

1. Which of the following correctly identifies the rules for the order of operations?
   (a) Exponentiation, parentheses, addition, subtraction, multiplication, division
   (b) Parentheses, exponentiation, addition, subtraction, multiplication, division
   (c) Parentheses, exponentiation, multiplication, division, addition, subtraction
   (d) Addition, subtraction, multiplication, division, exponentiation, parentheses

2. What is the result of the following expression?
   (3 * 5) + 7 – 2 – 6 * 2
   (a) 12
   (b) 7
   (c) 28
   (d) 8

3. The Builder command that opens the Expression Builder is found in the:
   (a) Manage group on the Databases Tools tab.
   (b) Query Setup group on the Design tab.
   (c) Database Management group on the Design tab.
   (d) Design group on the Query Setup tab.

4. Which function enables you to insert today's date into an expression?
   (a) Date()
   (b) DatePart()
   (c) Now()
   (d) DateDiff()

5. You correctly calculated a value for the OrderAmount using an expression. Now you need to use the newly calculated value in another expression calculating sales tax. The most efficient method is to:
   (a) Run and save the query to make OrderAmount available as input to subsequent expressions.
   (b) Create a new query based on the query containing the calculated Order amount, and then calculate the sales tax in the new query.
   (c) Close the Access file, saving the changes when asked; reopen the file and reopen the query; calculate the sales tax.
   (d) Create a backup of the database, open the backup and the query, then calculate the sales tax.

6. If state law requires that a restaurant's wait staff be at least 21 to serve alcohol and you have a database that stores each employee's birth date in the Employee table, which of the following is the proper syntax to identify the employees' year of birth?
   (a) Age:DatePart("yyyy",[Employee]![BirthDate])
   (b) Age=DatePart("yyyy",[Employee]![BirthDate])
   (c) Age:DatePart("yyyy",[BirthDate]![Employee])
   (d) Age=DatePart("yyyy",[BirthDate]![Employee])

7. Which statement about a totals query is true?
   (a) A totals query is created in Datasheet view.
   (b) A totals query may contain several grouping fields but only one aggregate field.
   (c) A totals query is limited to only two fields, one grouping field, and one aggregate field.
   (d) A totals query may contain several grouping fields and several aggregate fields.

8. After creating a calculated field, you run the query and a parameter dialog box appears on your screen. How do you respond to the Parameter dialog box?
   (a) Click OK to make the parameter box go away.
   (b) Read the field name specified in the parameter box, and then look for a possible typing error in the calculated expression.
   (c) Type numbers in the parameter box, and then click OK.
   (d) Close the query without saving changes. Re-open it and try running the query again.

9. An updatable query contains student names. You run the query and while in Datasheet view, you notice a spelling error on one of the student's names. You correct the error in Datasheet view. Which statement is true?
   (a) The name is correctly spelled in this query but will be misspelled in the table and all other queries based on the table.
   (b) The name is correctly spelled in the table and in all queries based on the table.
   (c) The name is correctly spelled in this query and any other queries, but will remain misspelled in the table.
   (d) You cannot edit data in a query.

10. Which of the following is not true about the Total row in the query design grid?
    (a) The Total row enables you to apply aggregate functions to the fields.
    (b) The Total row can apply to fields stored in different tables.
    (c) The Total row is located between the Table and Sort rows.
    (d) The Total row can only be applied to numeric fields.

1 Comfort Insurance

The Comfort Insurance Agency is a mid-sized company with offices located across the country. Each employee receives a performance review annually. The review determines employee eligibility for salary increases and the annual performance bonus. The employee data are stored in an Access database, which is used by the human resources department to monitor and maintain employee records. Your task is to calculate the salary increase for each employee; you will also calculate each employee's performance bonus for employees who have been employed at least one year. This exercise follows the same set of skills as used in Hands-On Exercises 1 and 2 in the chapter. Refer to Figure 3.24 as you complete this exercise.

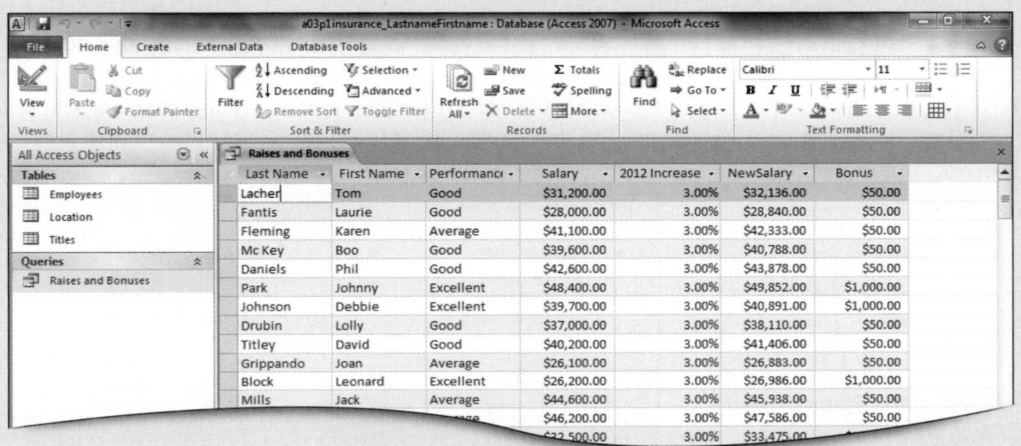

Last Name	First Name	Performance	Salary	2012 Increase	NewSalary	Bonus
Lacher	Tom	Good	$31,200.00	3.00%	$32,136.00	$50.00
Fantis	Laurie	Good	$28,000.00	3.00%	$28,840.00	$50.00
Fleming	Karen	Average	$41,100.00	3.00%	$42,333.00	$50.00
Mc Key	Boo	Good	$39,600.00	3.00%	$40,788.00	$50.00
Daniels	Phil	Good	$42,600.00	3.00%	$43,878.00	$50.00
Park	Johnny	Excellent	$48,400.00	3.00%	$49,852.00	$1,000.00
Johnson	Debbie	Excellent	$39,700.00	3.00%	$40,891.00	$1,000.00
Drubin	Lolly	Good	$37,000.00	3.00%	$38,110.00	$50.00
Titley	David	Good	$40,200.00	3.00%	$41,406.00	$50.00
Grippando	Joan	Average	$26,100.00	3.00%	$26,883.00	$50.00
Block	Leonard	Excellent	$26,200.00	3.00%	$26,986.00	$1,000.00
Mills	Jack	Average	$44,600.00	3.00%	$45,938.00	$50.00
			$46,200.00	3.00%	$47,586.00	$50.00

FIGURE 3.24 Raises and Bonuses ➤

a. Open *a03p1insurance*. Click the **File tab**, click **Save Database As**, and then type **a03p1insurance_LastnameFirstname**. Click **Save**.

b. Click the **Database Tools tab**, and then click **Relationships** in the Relationships group. Examine the table structure, relationships, and fields. Once you are familiar with the database, close the Relationships window.

c. Click the **Create tab**, and then click **Query Design** in the Queries group to start a new query. The Show Table dialog box opens. Add the Employees and Titles tables. Close the Show Table dialog box.

d. Add the **LastName**, **FirstName**, **Performance**, and **Salary fields** to the query. From the Titles table, add the **2012Increase field** to the query.

e. Click the top row of the first blank column in the query design grid, and then type **NewSalary: [Salary]*[2012Increase]+[Salary]** to create a calculated field.

f. Click **Run** in the Results group to run the query. (If you receive the Enter Parameter Value dialog box, check your expression carefully for spelling errors.) Look at the output in the Datasheet view. Verify that your answers are correct. Notice that the fourth column heading displays *2012 Increase*. This is the caption for the 2012Increase field in the Titles table that was carried over to the query. When a caption exists for a field in the table Design view, the caption also displays in the Query Datasheet view instead of the field name in the query.

g. Click **View** in the Views group to switch back to Design view. Open the Property Sheet, click in the **NewSalary calculated field**, and then change the format to **Currency**. Type **New Salary** in the **Caption box**. Close the Property Sheet.

h. Save the query as **Raises and Bonuses**.

i. Click the top row of the first blank column, and then click **Builder** in the Query Setup group. In the Expression Elements box, double-click the folder for **Functions**. Select the **Built-In Functions folder**. Scroll down the Expression Values box to locate the IIf function. Double-click **IIf** to insert the function.

j. Click «**expression**», and then replace it with **Performance = "Excellent"**. Click «**truepart**», and then replace it with **1000**. Click «**falsepart**», and then replace it with **50**.
k. Type **Bonus:** to the left of *IIf,* as the calculated field name. Click **OK**.
l. Change the format of the Bonus field to **Currency** in the Property Sheet.
m. Run the query. Save and close the query.
n. Click the **File tab**, and then click **Compact and Repair Database**.
o. Click the **File tab**, click **Save & Publish**, and then double-click **Back Up Database**. Click **Save** to accept the default backup file name.
p. Click the **File tab**, and then click **Exit** (to exit Access).
q. Submit based on your instructor's directions.

2 Analyze Orders

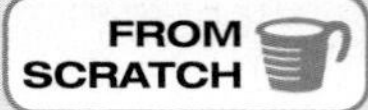

You are the marketing manager of your company and you must use the order information from an Access database to analyze sales trends. You need to determine the order revenue for all orders, grouped by Ship Country. You must also analyze shipping performance based on the number of days it takes to ship each order. This exercise follows the same set of skills as used in Hands-On Exercises 2 and 3 in the chapter. Refer to Figure 3.25 as you complete this exercise.

Shipping More Than 3 Weeks

OrderID	CustomerID	EmployeeID	OrderDate	ShippedDate	DaysToShip	ShipVia	Revenue	ShipCountry
10254	CHOPS	5	5/4/2011	6/23/2011	50	1	$54.68	Finland
10264	FOLKO	6	5/17/2011	6/15/2011	29	3	$2,606.81	USA
10430	ERNSH	4	11/23/2011	12/22/2011	29	1	$395.12	USA
10470	BONAP	4	1/2/2013	2/21/2013	50	1	$1,829.57	Austria
10514	ERNSH	3	3/14/2012	4/27/2012	44	3	$344.08	Austria
10579	LETSS	1	5/2/2012	5/28/2012	26	2	$117.88	Germany
11009	GODOS	2	2/6/2013	3/25/2013	47	2	$155.78	Belgium
11058	BLAUS	9	2/12/2013	5/3/2013	80	3	$115.46	Germany

FIGURE 3.25 Shipping More Than 3 Weeks Query ➤

a. Open Access, and then type **a03p2orders_LastnameFirstname** in the **File Name box**. Click **Browse** to locate your Student Data Files folder in the File New Database dialog box, click **OK** to close the dialog box, and then click **Create** to create the new database.
b. Click **View** in the Views group to switch to Design view. Type **Orders** in the **Save As dialog box**, and then click **OK**.
c. Change the first Field Name to **OrderID**, and then change the Data Type to **Number**. Type **CustomerID** in the second row, and then press **Tab**. Accept **Text** as the Data Type. Type **EmployeeID** in the third row, and then press **Tab**. Select **Number** for the Data Type.
d. Type the remainder of the fields:

OrderDate	Date/Time
ShippedDate	Date/Time
ShipVia	Number
Revenue	Currency
ShipCountry	Text

e. Verify the first field is set as the Primary Key.

f. Click **View** in the Views group to switch to Datasheet view. Click **Yes** to save the table. Add the three records as shown in table below. Press **Tab** to move to the next field.

Order ID	Customer ID	Employee ID	Order Date	Shipped Date	Ship Via	Revenue	Ship Country
10248	WILMK	5	4/27/2013	5/16/2013	1	$142.86	Belgium
10249	TRADH	6	4/28/2013	5/17/2013	2	$205.38	Germany
10250	HANAR	4	5/1/2013	5/20/2013	2	$58.60	Venezuela

g. Open the *a03p2orders_import* Excel file, and then click **Enable Editing** if necessary. Click and hold on row 2 and drag through row 828 so that all of the data rows are selected. Click **Copy** in the Clipboard group.

h. Return to Access, and then click on the **asterisk** (*) on the fourth row of the Orders table. Click **Paste** in the Clipboard group, and then click **Yes** to confirm that you want to paste all 827 rows into the Orders table. Save and close the table, and then close the spreadsheet and Excel. Do not save the data in the clipboard if prompted.

i. Click the **Create tab**, and then click **Query Design** in the Queries group to start a new query. The Show Table dialog box opens. Add the Orders table, and then close the Show Table dialog box.

j. Select all the fields in the Orders table, and then drag them to the query design grid. Click on the **ShipVia field**, and then click **Insert Columns** in the Query Setup group.

k. Click **Builder** in the Query Setup group. Double-click **Functions**, and then click **Built-In Functions** in the Expression Builder box. Click **Date/Time** in the Expression Categories box, and then double-click **DateDiff** in the Expression Values box.

l. Replace the placeholder fields with the following values:

«interval»	"d"
«date1»	[OrderDate]
«date2»	[ShippedDate]
«firstdayofweek»	*remove; also remove commas*
«firstweekofyear»	*remove; also remove commas*

m. Click **OK** to close the Expression Builder. Replace *Expr* with **DaysToShip** as the calculated field name. Run the query and verify that DaysToShip is displaying valid values.

n. Switch back to Design view. Add the criteria **>21** to the DaysToShip field. Run the query, and then compare your results to Figure 3.25. Save the query as **Shipping More Than 3 Weeks**. Close the query.

o. Click the **Create tab**, and then click **Query Design** in the Queries group to start a new query. The Show Table dialog box opens. Add the Orders table, and then close the Show Table dialog box. Click **Totals** in the Show/Hide group.

p. Add the following fields to the query design grid:

ShipCountry	Verify the Total row is set to *Group By*.
Revenue	Change the Total row to **Sum**.

q. Click **Run** to see the results, and then save the query as **Revenue by Ship Country**. Close the query.

r. Click the **File tab**, and then click **Compact & Repair Database**.

s. Click the **File tab**, and then click **Exit** (to exit Access).

t. Submit the database based on your instructor's directions.

MID-LEVEL EXERCISES

1 Small Business Loans

You are the manager of the small business loan department for the U.S. Government. You need to calculate the payments for the loans that are currently on the books. To do this, you will need to create a query and add the Pmt function to calculate the loan payments for each loan. You will also summarize each loan by loan type (M=Mortgage, C=Car, and O=Other). Refer to Figure 3.26 as you complete this exercise.

Loan Payments

	CompanyName	LoanID	Amount	InterestRate	Term	Type	Payment
	Jones and Co	10	$200,000	5.50%	15	M	$1,634.17
	Jones and Co	16	$150,000	6.50%	15	M	$1,306.66
	Jones and Co	17	$100,000	6.00%	30	M	$599.55
	Elements, Inc.	11	$25,000	5.00%	3	C	$749.27
	Elements, Inc.	19	$10,000	5.50%	5	C	$191.01
	Godshall Meats, LLC	15	$200,000	6.25%	15	M	$1,714.85
	Godshall Meats, LLC	18	$15,000	5.50%	3	O	$452.94
	Godshall Meats, LLC	20	$25,000	6.25%	4	C	$590.00
	Godshall Meats, LLC	23	$150,000	5.00%	15	M	$1,186.19
	Specialty Motor Cars	1	$475,000	5.90%	15	M	$3,982.70
	Specialty Motor Cars	2	$35,000	5.25%	5	C	$664.51
	Specialty Motor Cars	4	$12,000	3.99%	10	O	$121.44
	Specialty Motor Cars	24	$350,000	5.55%	30	M	$1,998.26
	Dairy Queen	3	$10,000	4.50%	3	C	$297.47
	Dairy Queen	12	$20,000	7.99%	5	O	$405.43
	Scooter's Bike Shop	5	$525,000	5.50%	30	M	$2,980.89
	Landis Plumbing, Inc.	6	$10,500	6.50%	5	O	$205.44
	Landis Plumbing, Inc.	25	$275,000	4.99%	15	M	$2,173.25
	Wait-a-While	7	$35,000	5.50%	5	O	$668.54
	Wait-a-While	8	$250,000	5.80%	30	M	$1,466.88
	Wait-a-While	9	$5,000	4.75%	3	O	$149.29
	Wait-a-While	21	$41,000	6.75%	4	C	$977.05
	Brother Atty PC	13	$56,000	6.50%	5	C	$1,095.70
	Expert Remodeling	14	$129,000	5.99%	15	M	$1,087.88
	Expert Remodeling	22	$350,000	6.50%	15	M	$3,048.88
*		(New)					
	Total		$3,453,500	5.74%			$29,748.25

FIGURE 3.26 Loan Payments Query Results ➤

a. Open Access, and then create a new database named **a03m1loans_LastnameFirstname**.

b. Switch to Design view. Type **Customers** in the **Save As dialog box**, and then click **OK**.

c. Change the first Field Name to **CustomerID**, and then accept AutoNumber as the Data Type. Type **CompanyName** in the second row, and then press **Tab**. Accept **Text** as the Data Type. Type **CustomerFirstName** in the third row, and then press **Tab**. Accept **Text** as the Data Type.

d. Type the remainder of the fields:

CustomerLastName	Text
City	Text
State	Text
ZipCode	Text

e. Verify the first field is set as the Primary Key.

f. Switch to Datasheet view. Click **Yes** to save the table. Add the records as shown in the table below. Press **Tab** to move to the next field.

CustomerID	CompanyName	Customer FirstName	Customer LastName	City	State	ZipCode
1	Jones and Co	Allison	Greene	Greensboro	NC	27401
2	Elements, Inc.	Laura	Peterson	Winston-Salem	NC	27101
3	Godshall Meats, LLC	Sam	Starber	Greensboro	NC	27402
4	Specialty Motor Cars	Bernett	Fox	High Point	NC	27261
5	Dairy Queen	Clay	Hayes	Greensboro	NC	27401
6	Scooter's Bike Shop	Cordle	Collins	Winston-Salem	NC	27102
7	Landis Plumbing, Inc.	Eaton	Wagner	Greensboro	NC	27403
8	Wait-a-While	Kwasi	Williams	High Point	NC	27260
9	Brother Atty PC	Natasha	Simpson	Greensboro	NC	27404
10	Expert Remodeling	Jay	Jones	Winston-Salem	NC	27101

g. Save and close the Customers table. Click the **External Data tab**, and then click **Access** in the Import & Link group. Click **Browse** to locate the a03m1import_loans database. Select the database, and then click **Open** at the bottom of the dialog box.

h. Click **OK** at the next dialog box. Select the **Loans table**, and then click **OK**. Click **Close** in the Save Import Steps dialog box.

i. Click the **Database Tools tab**, and then click **Relationships** in the Relationships group. Add both tables to the Relationships window, and then close the Show Table dialog box.

j. Drag the **CustomerID field** from the Customers table and drop it onto the CustomerID field in the Loans table. Check the **Enforce Referential Integrity check box** in the Edit Relationships dialog box, and then click **Create**. Save and close the Relationships window.

k. Create a query using the two tables that will calculate the payment amount for each loan. Add the following fields: **CompanyName**, **LoanID**, **Amount**, **InterestRate**, **Term**, and **Type**. Save the query as **Loan Payments**.

l. Add a calculated field named **Payment** in the first blank column to calculate the loan payment for each loan. Use the Pmt("rate", "num_periods", "present_value") function. Insert the field names in place of the placeholder arguments. Remember to divide the annual interest rate by 12 and multiply the loan's term by 12. Run the query.

 DISCOVER 

m. The format of the Payment values is not correct. Switch to Design view, and then change the display to a positive value with Currency format. Run the query again to verify your changes. Compare your results to Figure 3.26.

n. Switch to Datasheet view, and then add a **Total row**. Use it to calculate the sum of the amount column, the average interest rate, and the sum of payment. Save and close the query.

o. Click **Loan Payments**, and then click **Copy** in the Clipboard group on the Home tab. Click **Paste**, and then type **Loan Payments Summary** in the **Paste As dialog box**. Click **OK**.

p. Open the Loan Payments Summary query in Design view, and then rearrange the columns as follows: Type, LoanID, Amount, InterestRate, and Payment. Delete columns CompanyName and Term. Click **Totals** in the Show/Hide group. Change the Total row from left to right as follows: Group By, Count, Sum, Avg, and Sum. Run the query.

q. Switch to Design view, and then add a caption to each column; to add a caption, right-click on the column, and then click **Properties**. From left to right, add the following captions: *skip column one*, **Loans**, **Total Amount**, **Avg Interest Rate**, and **Total Payments**. Format the Avg Interest Rate field as **Percent**. Run the query. Save and close the query.

q. Compact the database. Exit Access.

r. Submit the database based on your instructor's directions.

2 Investment Properties

You are in charge of LGS Investment's database, which contains all of the information on the properties your firm has listed and sold. Your task is to determine the length of time each property was on the market before it sold. You also need to calculate the sales commission from each property sold. Two agents will receive commission on each transaction: the listing agent and the selling agent. You also need to summarize the sales data by employee and calculate the average number of days each employee's sales were on the market prior to selling and the total commission earned by the employees. Refer to Figure 3.27 as you complete this exercise.

Sales Summary

Subdivision	Avg Days On Mkt	Sale Price	Listing Comm	Sell Comm
The Orchards	22.8	$1,288,000.00	$45,080.00	$32,200.00
Fair Brook	24.8	$1,053,900.00	$36,886.50	$26,347.50
Eagle Valley	39.0	$4,012,000.00	$140,420.00	$100,300.00
Wood	47.9	$1,428,650.00	$50,002.75	$35,716.25
Red Canyon	52.0	$3,790,000.00	$132,650.00	$94,750.00
Total		$11,572,550.00	$405,039.25	$289,313.75

FIGURE 3.27 Sales Summary ➤

a. Open *a03m2homes*. Click the **File tab**, click **Save Database As**, and then type **a03m2homes_LastnameFirstname**. Click **Save**.

b. Open the Agents table, and then replace *David Royes* with your name. Close the table.

c. Create a new query, add the necessary tables, and then add the following fields: LastName, DateListed, DateSold, SalePrice, SellingAgent, ListingAgent, and Subdivision. Type **Is Not Null** into the criterion row of the DateSold field. Save the query as **Sales Report**. Format the SalePrice field as **Currency**.

d. Using the Expression Builder, create the DaysOnMarket calculated field by subtracting DateListed from DateSold. This will calculate the number of days each sold property was on the market when it sold. Add an appropriate caption.

e. Calculate the commissions for the selling and listing agents using two calculated fields. The listing commission rate is **3.5%** and the selling commission rate is **2.5%**. Name the newly created fields **ListComm** and **SellComm**. These fields contain similar expressions. They need to be named differently so that the proper agent—the listing agent or the selling agent—gets paid. Add captions and format the fields as **Currency**.

f. Save the query after you verify that your calculations are correct. In Datasheet view, add the Total row. Calculate the Average number of days on the market and the sum for the SalePrice and the two commission fields. Save and close the query.

g. Create a totals query based on the Sales Report query. Group by LastName, and then show the average of the DaysOnMarket. Show the sum of SalePrice, ListComm, and SellComm. Format the fields as **Currency**, and then add appropriate captions. Run the query. Adjust column widths.

h. Add a Total row to the Datasheet view that will sum the sale price and commission fields. Save the query as **Sales Summary**.

i. Format the average of the Days on Market fields as fixed, one decimal place. (Note: if you do not see the Decimal Places property in the Property Sheet, switch to Datasheet view, then switch back to Design view.) Format the remaining numeric fields as **Currency**. Run the query.

DISCOVER 

j. Modify the query so the grouping is based on Subdivision, not LastName. Sort the query results so the fewest Days on Market is first and the most Days on Market is last. Limit the results to the top five rows.

k. Compact the database. Back up the database. Exit Access.

l. Submit based on your instructor's directions.

CAPSTONE EXERCISE

Northwind Traders, an international gourmet food distributor, is concerned about shipping delays over the last six months. Review the orders over the past six months and identify any order that was not shipped within 30 days. Each customer that falls within that time frame will be called to inquire about any problems the delay may have caused. In addition, an order summary and an order summary by country will be created.

Database File Setup

Open the food database, use Save As to make a copy of the database, and then use the new database to complete this capstone exercise. You will replace an existing employee's name with your name.

a. Locate and open *a03c1food.*
b. Click the **File tab**, click **Save Database As**, and then type **a03c1food_LastnameFirstname**.
c. Click **Save**.
d. Open the Employees table.
e. Replace *Rachael Eliza* with your name. Close the table.

DaysToShip Query

You need to create a query to calculate the number of days between the date an order was placed and the date the order was shipped for each order. As you create the query, run the query at several intervals so you can verify that the data looks correct. The result of your work will be a list of orders that took more than three weeks to ship. The salespeople will be calling each customer to see if there was any problem with their order.

a. Create a query using Query Design. Include the fields CompanyName, ContactName, ContactTitle, Phone, OrderID, LastName, OrderDate, and ShippedDate. Use the Relationships window to determine which tables you need before you begin.
b. Run the query, and then examine the records. Save the query as **Shipping Efficiency**.
c. Add a calculated field named **DaysToShip** to calculate the number of days taken to fill each order. (*Hint*: The expression will include the OrderDate and the ShippedDate; the results will not contain negative numbers.)
d. Run the query, and then examine the results. Does the data in the DaysToShip field look accurate? Save the query.
e. Add criteria to limit the query results to include any order that took more than 30 days to ship.
f. Add the ProductID and Quantity fields to the Shipping Efficiency query. Sort the query by ascending OrderID. When the sales reps contact these customers, these two fields will provide useful information about the orders.
g. Switch to Datasheet view to view the final results. This list will be distributed to the sales reps so they can contact the customers. In Design view, add the **Sales Rep caption** to the LastName field.
h. Save and close the query.

Order Summary Query

You need to create an Order Summary that will show the total amount of each order in one column and the total discount amount in another column. This query will require four tables: Orders, Order Details, Products, and Customers. Query to determine if employees are following the employee discount policy. You will group the data by employee name, count the orders, show the total dollars, and show the total discount amount. You will then determine which employees are following the company guidelines.

a. Create a query using Query Design and add the four tables above plus the Products table. Add the fields OrderID and OrderDate. Click **Totals** in the Show/Hide Group; the Total row for both fields should be Group By.
b. In the third column, add a calculated field: **ExtendedAmount: Quantity*UnitPrice**. Format the calculated field as Currency. This calculation will calculate the total amount for each order. Change the Total row to **Sum**.
c. In the fourth column, add a calculated field: **DiscountAmount: Quantity*UnitPrice*Discount**. Format the calculated field as **Currency**. This will calculate the total discount for each order. Change the Total row to **Sum**.
d. Run the query. Save the query as **Order Summary**. Return to Design view.
e. Enter the expression **Between 1/1/2012 And 12/31/2012** in the criteria of OrderDate. Change the Total row to **Where**. This expression will display only orders that were created in 2012.
f. Run the query and view the results. Save the query.
g. Add the **Total Dollars caption** to the ExtendedAmount field and add the **Discount Amt caption** to the DiscountAmount field.
h. Run the query. Save and close the query.

Order Summary by Country Query

You need to create one additional query based on the Order Summary query you created in the previous step. This new query will enable you to analyze the orders by country.

a. Select the **Order Summary query**, and then use **Save Object As** to create a new query named **Order Summary by Country**.

b. In Design view of the new query, replace the OrderID field with the Country field.
c. Run the query, and then examine the summary records; there should be 21 countries listed.
d. In Design view, change the sort order so that the country with the highest Total Dollars is first, and the country with the lowest Total Dollars is last.
e. Run the query and verify the results.
f. Save and close the query, and then close the database and exit Access.
g. Submit based on your instructor's directions.

Vacation Time for Bank Employees

GENERAL CASE 

The *a03b1vacation* file contains data from a local bank. Open *a03b1vacation*. Click the File tab, click Save Database As, and then type **a03b1vacation_LastnameFirstname**. Click Save. Replace *Your Name* in the Customers table and the Branch table with your name. Use the skills from this chapter to perform several tasks. The bank's employee handbook states that a manager can take two weeks of vacation each year for the first three years of service, and three weeks of vacation after three years of employment. The Branch table stores the start date of each manager.

Create a query to determine how many years each manager has worked for the bank.

- Add a new field to calculate the number of weeks of vacation each manager is eligible to take.
- Use a nested IIf function to change the weeks of vacation to zero for any employee with a start date later than today.
- Change the format of each field to the appropriate type, and then add appropriate captions for the calculated fields.
- Save the query as **Vacation**.

Create another query to summarize each customer's account balances.

- List the customer's last name, first name, and a total of all account balances.
- Format the query results, and then add appropriate captions.
- Add the grand total of all accounts to the Datasheet view.
- Save the query as **Customer Balances**.

Close the query, and then close the database. Submit based on your instructor's directions.

Too Many Digits

RESEARCH CASE 

This chapter introduced you to calculated fields. Open the database *a03b2interest* and save the database as **a03b2interest_LastnameFirstname**. Open the Monthly Interest query in Datasheet view. Notice the multiple digits to the right of the decimal in the Monthly Interest column; there should only be two digits. Search the Internet to find a function that will resolve this rounding problem. You only want to display two digits to the right of the decimal (even when you click on a Monthly Interest value). Apply your changes to the Monthly Interest field, change the format to currency, and then run the query to test your changes. Save the query as **Monthly Interest Revised**. Close the query, and then close the database and exit Access. Submit your work based on your instructor's directions.

Payroll Summary Needed

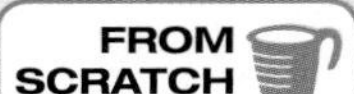

You were given an Excel spreadsheet that contains paycheck information for your company. Your task is to summarize this data by employee SSN and then report your results to your supervisor. Open the spreadsheet *a03b3paychecks_import* and examine the column headings and the data. You will use Access to summarize the data in this spreadsheet. Close the spreadsheet and close Excel. Create a new Access database named **a03b3payroll_LastnameFirstname**. Import the data from Sheet1 of the *a03b3paychecks_import* file into a table named **Payroll**. Let Access add a primary key field. Create a new totals query that summarizes the data by SSN; include the count of pay periods (using the ID field) and the sum of each currency field. Do not include the PayDate field in this query. Create a calculated field named **Total Compensation**, which displays the sum of Gross Pay, 401K Contributions, and Health Benefits. Add appropriate captions to shorten the default captions. Run the query, and then save the query as **Payroll Summary**. Close the query, and then close the database and exit Access. Submit the database based on your instructor's directions.

ACCESS

4 CREATING AND USING PROFESSIONAL FORMS AND REPORTS

Moving Beyond Tables and Queries

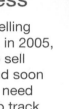

Watch the
Set-up Video
for this Case Study!

CASE STUDY | Coffee Shop Starts New Business

For over 10 years, the Santiago Coffee Shop was an ordinary coffee shop selling retail coffee, tea, and pastries to its loyal customers in Bucks County. Then, in 2005, owner Alex Santiago decided to use his knowledge of the coffee industry to sell coffee products to businesses in his area. This new venture grew quickly and soon became 25% of his annual revenue. Realizing that this new business would need more of his time each day, he decided to create an Access database to help track his customer, product, and order information.

With the help of a student from Bucks County Community College, he created tables for customers, products, sales reps, and orders. He is currently using these tables as his primary method of entering and retrieving information.

Alex wants to have one of his employees, Tonya, manage the database. But he does not want her to work in the tables; he wants her to work with forms. Alex heard that forms have an advantage over tables because they can be designed to show one record at a time—this will reduce data entry errors. Alex would also like to create several reports for his own benefit so he can stay on top of the business by reviewing the reports each week.

You have been hired to help Alex create the new forms and reports that he needs for his business. He will describe the forms and reports to you in detail and also provide written instructions. You will be expected to work independently to create the forms and reports. Remember to identify the data source for each new form and report.

OBJECTIVES AFTER YOU READ THIS CHAPTER, YOU WILL BE ABLE TO:

Form Basics

A **form** is a database object that is used to add data into or edit data in a table.

A ***form*** is a database object that is used to add data into or edit data in a table. Most Access database applications use forms rather than tables for data entry and for looking up information. Three main reasons exist for using forms rather than tables for adding, updating, and deleting data. They are:

You are less likely to edit the wrong record by mistake.
You can create a form that shows data from more than one table simultaneously.
You can create Access forms to match paper forms.

You are less likely to edit the wrong record by mistake … You can create a form that shows data from more than one table simultaneously … You can create Access forms to match paper forms.

If you are adding data using a table with many columns, you could jump to the wrong record in the middle of a record accidentally. For example, you could enter the data for one record correctly for the first 10 fields but then jump to the row above and overwrite existing data for the remaining field values unintentionally. In this case, two records have incorrect or incomplete data. A form will not allow this type of error since most forms restrict entry to one record at a time.

Many forms require two tables as their record source. For example, you may want to view a customer's details (name, address, e-mail, phone, etc.) as well as all of the orders he or she has placed. This would require using data from both the Customers and the Orders tables in one form. Similarly, you may want to view the header information for an order while also viewing the detail line items for the order. This would require data from both the Orders and Order Details tables. Both of these examples enable a user to view two record sources at the same time and make changes—additions, edits, or deletions—to one or both sources of data.

Finally, when paper forms are used to collect information, it is a good idea to design the electronic forms to match the paper forms. This will make data entry more efficient and reliable. Access forms can be designed to emulate the paper documents already in use in an organization. This facilitates the simultaneous use of both paper forms and electronic data. Databases do not necessarily eliminate paper forms; they supplement and coexist with them.

In this section, you will learn the basics of form design. You will discover multiple methods to create and modify Access forms. And you will learn how to create calculated controls.

Creating Forms Using the Form Tools

Access provides a variety of options for creating forms. One size does not fit all—some developers may prefer a stacked layout form, whereas others prefer the multiple items form. The multiple items form can be styled to match a company's standards, whereas the datasheet form is simple and requires very little maintenance. And let's not forget the users; they will have their opinions about the type of forms they want to use.

Access provides 16 different tools for creating forms. The Forms group, located on the Create tab, contains four of the most common form tools (Form, Form Design, Blank Form, and Form Wizard), a list of Navigation forms, and a list of More Forms, as shown in Figure 4.1. Navigation forms provides a list of six templates to create a user interface for a database; the More Forms command lists six additional form tools (Multiple Items, Datasheet, Split Form, and more). Select a table or query, click one of the tools, and Access will create an automatic form using the selected table or query. The most common of these tools, the ***Form tool***, is used to create data entry forms for customers, employees, products, and other primary tables. A primary table, introduced in a previous chapter, has a single field as its primary key and represents the "one" side of a one-to-many relationship. Once the form is created, as shown in Figure 4.2, you can customize the form using the Layout or Design views. After the form is created, it should be tested by both the database designer and the end users.

The **Form tool** is used to create data entry forms for customers, employees, products, and other primary tables.

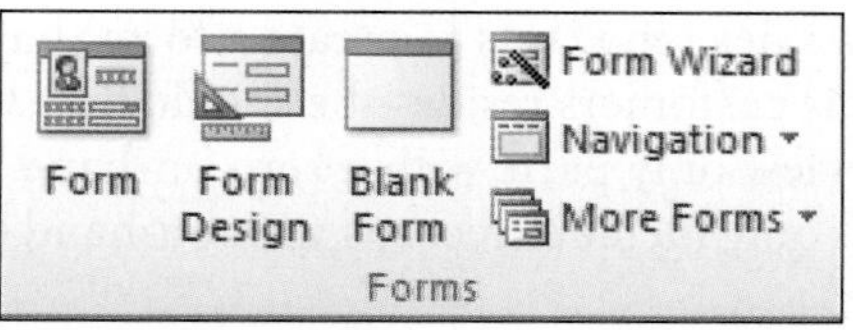

FIGURE 4.1 Forms Group ➤

A complete list of all the Form tools available in Access is found in the Form Tools Reference at the end of this section. Many of the tools will be covered in this chapter. Some will not be covered since they are not commonly used or because they are beyond the scope of this chapter (e.g., Form Design, Blank Form, Navigation forms, and Modal Dialog form). Use Microsoft Access Help to find more information about Form tools not covered in this chapter.

Employees

Employees Form

EmployeeID	1
LastName	Lacher
FirstName	Tom
Gender	M
Title	T01
Salary	$31,200.00
Location	L01
Performance	Good
HireDate	3/2/2009

Record: 1 of 311 No Filter Search

FIGURE 4.2 Employees Form Created with the Form Tool ➤

Ideally, a form should simplify data entry. Creating a form is a collaborative process between the form designer and the form users. This process continues throughout the life of the form, because the data needs of an organization may change. Forms designed long ago to collect information for a new customer account may not have an e-mail field; the form would have to be modified to include an e-mail field. The form designer needs to strike a balance between collecting the information users need to do their jobs and cluttering the form with extraneous fields. The users of the data know what they need and usually offer good feedback about which fields should be on a form. By listening to their suggestions, your forms will function more effectively, the users' work will be easier, and your data will contain fewer data entry errors.

Ideally, a form should simplify data entry.

Identify a Record Source

A **record source** is the table or query that supplies the records for a form or report.

Before you create a form, you must identify the record source. A ***record source*** is the table or query that supplies the records for a form or report. Use a table if you want to include all the records from a single table. Use a query if you need to filter the records in a table, or if you need to combine records from two or more related tables.

TIP Record Source vs. Data Source

The term *record source* can be interchanged with the term *data source*. Both terms refer to the source of data for a form or a report. In this chapter, the term *record source* will be used exclusively. As stated earlier, a record source can refer to either a table or a query.

For example, if a sales rep wants to create a form that only displays customers from a single state—where his customers reside—he should base the form on a query. Or, if a parts manager needs to review only parts with a zero on-hand quantity, he could create a form based on a query that only includes records with on-hand equal to zero.

Sketch the Form

It will help you to create the form in Access if you sketch the form first. A sketch may look similar to the form in Figure 4.2. After sketching the form, you will have a better idea of which form tool to use to create the form. After the form is created, use the sketch to determine which fields are required and what the order of fields should be.

Use the Form Tool

A **stacked layout form** displays fields in a vertical column, and displays one record at a time.

A **tabular layout form** displays records horizontally, with label controls across the top and the data values in rows under the labels.

Layout view is used to modify the design of a form.

As noted earlier, the Form tool is the most common tool for creating forms. Select a table or query from the Navigation Pane, and then click Form in the Forms Group on the Create tab, and Access creates a new form. You may need to modify the form slightly, but you can create a stacked layout form in a just one click. A ***stacked layout form*** displays fields in a vertical column, and displays one record at a time, as shown in Figure 4.3. Multiple Items and Datasheet forms, in contrast to stacked layout forms, are examples of tabular layout forms. A ***tabular layout form*** displays records horizontally, with label controls across the top and the data values in rows under the labels. When a new form is created using the Form tool, Access opens the form in Layout view ready for customizing. You can generate forms for your database using the Form tool, and then use ***Layout view*** to modify the design of a form. Figure 4.3 shows the Employees form in Layout view.

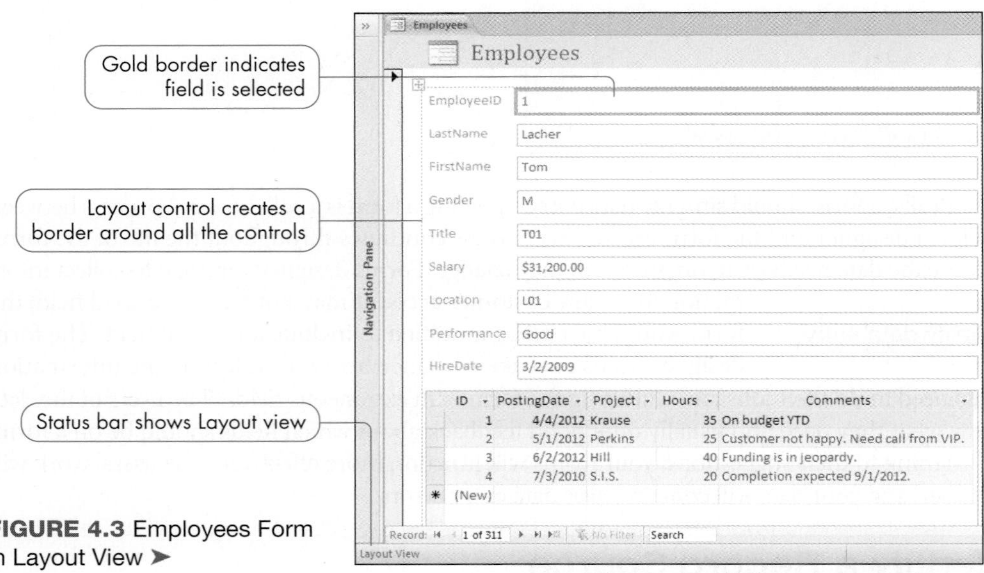

FIGURE 4.3 Employees Form in Layout View ➤

Work with a Subform

When you use the Form tool to create a form, Access will analyze the table relationships you created in the database and automatically add a subform to the main form. A subform displays records with foreign key values that match the primary key value in the main form. For example, assume you have a database that contains the tables Employees and Project Time, and a relationship exists between the two tables based on the EmployeeID field. If you create a new form based on Employees, using the Form tool, Access will add a Project Time subform to the bottom of the main form (see Figure 4.3).

At times, you may want the subform as part of your form; other times, you may want to remove it. To remove a subform control from a form, switch to Design view, click the subform control, and then press Delete. The subform is deleted!

Create a Split Form

A **split form** combines two views of the same record source—one section is displayed in a stacked layout and the other section is displayed in a tabular layout.

A ***split form*** combines two views of the same record source—one section is displayed in a stacked layout and the other section is displayed in a tabular layout. By default, the form view is positioned on the top and the datasheet view is displayed on the bottom; however, the orientation can be changed from horizontal to vertical in Layout view. If you select a record in the top half of the form, the same record will be selected in the bottom half of the form, and vice versa. For example, if you create a split form based on the Employees table, you can select an employee in the datasheet section and then see the employee's information in the *Form view* section (see Figure 4.4). If the selected employee is incorrect, click another employee in the datasheet section. The top and bottom halves are synchronized at all times.

The **splitter bar** divides the form into two halves.

To create a split form, first select a table or query in the Navigation Pane. Next, click the Create tab, click More Forms in the Forms group, and then select Split Form from the list of options. A new split form now appears. You can add, edit, or delete records in either section. The ***splitter bar*** divides the form into two halves. Users can adjust the splitter bar up or down unless the form designer disables this option.

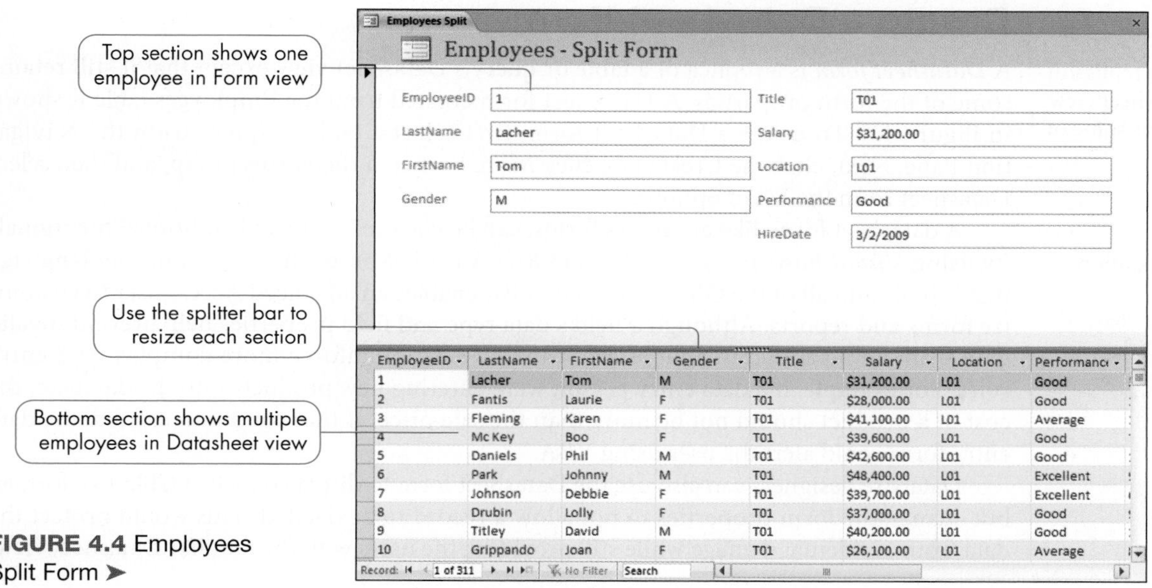

FIGURE 4.4 Employees Split Form ➤

Create a Multiple Items Form

A **Multiple Items form** displays multiple records in a tabular layout similar to a table's Datasheet view.

A ***Multiple Items form*** displays multiple records in a tabular layout similar to a table's Datasheet view. However, a Multiple Items form gives you more customization options than a datasheet, such as the ability to add graphical elements, buttons, and other controls. Figure 4.5 shows a Multiple Items form created from the Employees table. Compare this Multiple Items form to the Employees Datasheet form shown in Figure 4.6. The color scheme applied to the Multiple Items form could not be applied to the Datasheet form since the Datasheet form is much more limited in design and control options. To create a Multiple Items form, first select a table or query from the Navigation Pane. Next, click the Create tab, click More Forms in the Forms group, and then select Multiple Items from the list of options.

Layout resembles a table's Datasheet view

Employee records are displayed in tabular format

Employees Multiple

Employees - Multiple Items

EmployeeID	LastName	FirstName	Gender	Title	Salary	Location	Performance	HireDate
1	Lacher	Tom	M	T01	$31,200	L01	Good	3/2/2009
2	Fantis	Laurie	F	T01	$28,000	L01	Good	1/6/2009
3	Fleming	Karen	F	T01	$41,100	L01	Average	12/11/2007
4	Mc Key	Boo	F	T01	$39,600	L01	Good	7/25/1999
5	Daniels	Phil	M	T01	$42,600	L01	Good	1/31/2009
6	Park	Johnny	M	T01	$48,400	L01	Excellent	9/4/2009
7	Johnson	Debbie	F	T01	$39,700	L01	Excellent	6/19/2003
8	Drubin	Lolly	F	T01	$37,000	L01	Good	9/8/2007
					$40,200	L01	Good	

FIGURE 4.5 Multiple Items Form ➤

Create a Datasheet Form

A **Datasheet form** is a replica of a table or query's Datasheet view except that it still retains some of the form properties.

A ***Datasheet form*** is a replica of a table or query's Datasheet view except that it still retains some of the form properties. A Datasheet form created from the Employees table is shown in Figure 4.6. To create a Datasheet form, first select a table or query from the Navigation Pane. Next, click the Create tab, click More Forms in the Forms group, and then select Datasheet from the list of options.

Visual Basic for Applications (VBA) is Microsoft's programming language that is built into all of the Office products.

A datasheet form, like all Access forms, can be customized to add additional functionality using ***Visual Basic for Applications (VBA)***. VBA is Microsoft's programming language that is built into all of the Office products. VBA enables an advanced Access user to customize forms and reports. Although a field's data type and field properties help prevent invalid data from being added to a table, you can use VBA to enforce more complex data entry rules. For example, if a data entry person were entering new products into the database, the cost of a product should not be more than the sale price. If that condition existed, the data entry form could alert the user using VBA.

Database designers can also use the Datasheet form to display data in a table-like format, but change the form properties to not allow a record to be deleted. This would protect the data from accidental damage while still providing the users with the familiar Datasheet view.

Layout is a replica of a table's Datasheet view

Employees Datasheet

EmployeeID	LastName	FirstName	Gender	Title	Salary	Location	Performance
1	Lacher	Tom	M	T01	$31,200.00	L01	Good
2	Fantis	Laurie	F	T01	$28,000.00	L01	Good
3	Fleming	Karen	F	T01	$41,100.00	L01	Average
4	Mc Key	Boo	F	T01	$39,600.00	L01	Good
5	Daniels	Phil	M	T01	$42,600.00	L01	Good
6	Park	Johnny	M	T01	$48,400.00	L01	Excellent
7	Johnson	Debbie	F	T01	$39,700.00	L01	Excellent
8	Drubin	Lolly	F	T01	$37,000.00	L01	Good
9	Titley	David	M	T01	$40,200.00	L01	Good
10	Grippando	Joan	F	T01	$26,100.00	L01	Average
11	Block	Leonard	M	T01	$26,200.00	L01	Excellent
12	Mills	Jack	M	T01	$44,600.00	L01	Average
13	Nagel	Mimi	F	T01	$46,200.00	L01	Average
14	Rammos	Mitzi	F	T01	$32,500.00	L01	Excellent
15	Vieth	Paula	F	T01	$40,400.00	L01	Good
16	Novicheck	Deborah	F	T01	$46,800.00	L01	Good
17	Brumbaugh	Paige	F	T01	$49,300.00	L01	Average
18	Abrams	Wendy	F	T01	$47,500.00	L01	Good
19	Harrison	Jenifer	F	T01	$44,800.00	L01	Excellent
20	Gander	John	M	T01	$38,400.00	L01	Average
21	Sell	Mike	M	T01	$43,500.00	L01	Excellent
22	Smith	Denise	F	T01	$45,200.00	L01	Average
				T01	$42,700.00	L01	

FIGURE 4.6 Datasheet Form ➤

Create Forms Using the Other Form Tools

The Form Design tool and the Blank Form tools can be used to create a form manually. Click one of these tools and Access will open a completely blank form. Click Add Existing Fields, on the Design tab, in the Tools group and add the necessary fields.

The Navigation option in the Forms group enables you to create user interface forms that have the look and feel of a Web-based form, and enable users to open and close the objects of a database. These forms are also useful for setting up an Access database on the Internet. For more information about Navigation forms, visit www.microsoft.com.

PivotTables and PivotCharts, discussed in a later chapter, can also be converted to forms by selecting PivotChart or PivotTable in the More Forms option in the Forms group. After you create a PivotTable form or a PivotChart form, use the Layout view and Design view to customize the form.

The Modal Dialog Form tool can be used to create a dialog box. This feature is useful when you need to gather information from the user before working with another object. Dialog boxes are common in all Microsoft Office applications; creating a custom dialog box in Access can be useful when you need to collect information from the user.

REFERENCE Form Tools

Form Tool	Location	Use
Form	Create tab, Forms group	Creates a form with a stacked layout displaying all of the fields in the record source.
Form Design	Create tab, Forms group	Create a new blank form in Design view.
Blank Form	Create tab, Forms group	Create a new blank form in Layout view.
Form Wizard	Create tab, Forms group	Answer a series of questions and Access will create a custom form for you.
Navigation	Create tab, Forms group, Navigation button	Create user interface forms that can also be used on the Internet.
Split Form	Create tab, Forms group, More Forms button	Creates a two-part form with a stacked layout in one section and a tabular layout in the other.
Multiple Items	Create tab, Forms group, More Forms button	Creates a tabular layout form that includes all of the fields from the record source.
Datasheet	Create tab, Forms group, More Forms button	Creates a form that resembles the datasheet of a table or query.
PivotTable	Create tab, Forms group, More Forms button	The PivotTable form tool enables you to present data from a table or query using a multi-dimensional table format.
PivotChart	Create tab, Forms group, More Forms button	The PivotChart form tool enables you to present data from a table or query using a multi-dimensional chart format.
Modal Dialog	Create tab, Forms group, More Forms button	Creates a custom dialog box that forces the user to respond before working with another object.

Modifying a Form

After a form is generated by a Form tool, you will usually need to modify it. The most common form changes are add a field, remove a field, change the order of fields, change the width of a field, and modify label text. These changes, as well as adding a theme, can be made in a form's Layout view. Advanced changes, such as adding a calculated field or adding VBA code, can be made in a form's Design view.

Add a Field to a Form

To add a field to a form with a stacked layout, open the form in Layout view. Click Add Existing Fields in the Tools group on the Design tab to reveal the available fields from the form's record source. Drag the new field to the precise location on the form, using the orange line as a guide for the position of the new field. The other fields will automatically adjust to make room for the new field.

To add a field to a form with a tabular layout, follow the same steps for adding a field to a stacked layout form. The only difference is the orange line will appear vertically to help determine the insertion point of the new field.

Work with a Form Layout Control

Whenever you use one of the form tools to create a new form, Access will add a layout control to help align the fields. In general, form layout controls can help you create and modify forms. A ***layout control*** provides guides to help keep controls aligned horizontally and vertically, and give your form a uniform appearance. However, there are times when a layout control is too restrictive and will keep you from positioning controls where you want them. In this case, you can remove the layout control and position the controls manually on the grid.

A **layout control** provides guides to help keep controls aligned horizontally and vertically, and give your form a uniform appearance.

To remove a form layout control, switch to Design view, and then click anywhere inside the control you want to remove. On the Arrange tab, click Select Layout in the Rows & Columns group. (You can also click the Layout Selector, the small square with a cross inside, to select the layout.) Click Remove Layout in the Table group and the layout control is gone. All of the other controls are still on the form, but the rectangle binding them together is gone.

You can add a layout control to a form by first selecting all the controls you want to keep together. Then, click Stacked or Tabular in the Table group and the layout control appears.

Delete a Field from a Form

To delete a field in Layout view, click the text box control of the field to be deleted and note the orange border around the control. With the orange border showing, press Delete. The field's text box and label are both removed from the form and a space remains where the field used to be. Click the space, and then press Delete again, and the other fields will automatically adjust to close the gap around the deleted field.

Adjust Column Widths in a Form

When column widths are adjusted in a form with a stacked layout, all columns will increase and decrease together. Therefore, it is best to make sure that field columns are wide enough to accommodate the widest value in the table. For example, if a form contains first name, last name, address, city, state, ZIP, phone, and e-mail address, you will need to make sure the longest address and the longest e-mail address are completely visible (since those fields are likely to contain the longest data values).

To decrease column widths in a form with a stacked layout, open the form in Layout view. Click the text box control of the first field—usually on the right—to select it. Move the mouse over the right border of the field until the mouse pointer turns into a double arrow, then drag the right edge to the left until you arrive at the desired width. All the fields change as you change the width of the first field. Drag the same edge to the right to increase the width.

Add a Theme to a Form

You can apply an Office Theme to a form in order to give the form a more professional finish. An ***Office Theme*** is a defined set of colors, fonts, and graphics that can be applied to a form. Click the Themes picker in the Themes group on the Design tab, select a theme from the Themes Gallery, and Access will apply the theme to your form. You can apply a theme

An **Office Theme** is a defined set of colors, fonts, and graphics that can be applied to a form.

to a single form or to all the forms in your database that share a common theme. Applying the same theme to all forms will provide a consistent look to your database; most users prefer a consistent theme when using Access forms. The same Office Themes found in Access are also available in Excel, Word, and PowerPoint. Therefore, you can achieve a uniformed look across all Office applications.

Sorting Records in a Form

When a form is created using a Form tool, the sort order of the records in the form is dependent on the sort order of the record source—a table or a query. Tables are usually sorted by the primary key, whereas queries can be sorted in a variety of ways.

Change the Sorting in a Form

To modify the sort order of a form, open the form in Form view, and then select the field you want to use for sorting. Next, click Ascending in the Sort & Filter group on the Home tab and the records will immediately be reordered based on the selected field.

You can also modify the sort order of a form by modifying the underlying query's sort order. The method enables you to create a more advanced sort order, based on multiple fields. To begin, switch to Design view, and then open the Property Sheet. Select the form by clicking the arrow under Selection type at the top of the Property Sheet, and then clicking Form. Next, locate the Record Source property on the Data tab, click in the property box, and then click Build to the right of the property box. Answer Yes to the message that appears. Access opens the underlying query in Design view. Add the sorting you want, close the query, and save the query when prompted. You will also need to save the form.

Remove Sorting in a Form

To remove the sort order in a form, switch to Form view, and then click Remove Sort in the Sort & Filter group on the Home tab. If the form's sort order was modified, clicking this command will reset the form to the original order.

Quick Concepts Check

1. How does a form simplify data entry (when compared to entering data into a table)?
2. What is the record source of a form?
3. What is the difference between a form with a subform and a split form?
4. What is a layout control? What are the pros and cons of a layout control?

HANDS-ON EXERCISES

1 Form Basics

It is your first day on the job at Santiago Coffee Shop. After talking with Alex about his data entry needs, you decide to create several sample forms with different formats. You will show each form to Alex to get his feedback and see if he has a preference. Remember to select the correct record source prior to creating each new form.

Skills covered: Use the Form Tool and Adjust Column Widths in a Form • Create a Split Form • Create a Multiple Items Form • Create a Datasheet Form and Delete a Field from a Form • Add a Field to a Form • Change the Sorting in a Form and Remove Sorting in a Form

STEP 1 USE THE FORM TOOL AND ADJUST COLUMN WIDTHS IN A FORM

Use the Form tool to create an Access form to help Alex manage his customers. This form will enable Tonya to add, edit, and delete records more efficiently than working with tables. Refer to Figure 4.7 as you complete Step 1.

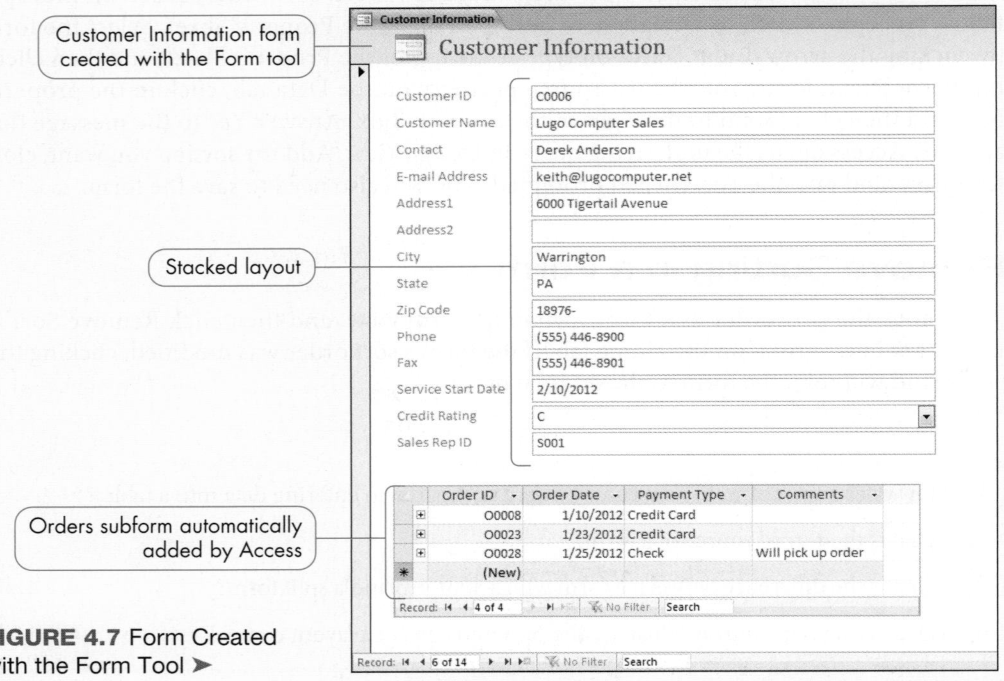

FIGURE 4.7 Form Created with the Form Tool ➤

a. Open *a04h1coffee*. Click the **File tab**, click **Save Database As**, and then type **a04h1coffee_LastnameFirstname**. Click Save.

> **TROUBLESHOOTING:** Throughout the remainder of this chapter and textbook, click Enable Content whenever you are working with student files.

> **TROUBLESHOOTING:** If you make any major mistakes in this exercise, you can close the file, repeat step a above, and then start over.

b. Click the **Customers table** in the Navigation Pane. Click the **Create tab**, and then click **Form** in the Forms group.

   Access creates a new form with two record sources—Customers (with stacked layout, on top) and Orders (with tabular layout, below). Access found a one-to-many relationship between the Customers and Orders tables. The form opens in Layout view.

c. Click the top text box containing *C0001*. The text box is outlined with an orange border. Move the mouse to the right edge of the orange border until the mouse pointer changes to a double-headed arrow. Drag the right edge to the left until the text box is approximately 50% of its original size.

   All the text boxes and the subform at the bottom adjust in size when you adjust the top text box. This is a characteristic of Layout view—enabling you to easily modify all controls at once.

   TROUBLESHOOTING: You may need to maximize the Access window, or close the Navigation Pane, if the right edge of the text box is not visible.

d. Click the Arrange tab, and then click **Select Layout** in the Rows & Columns group.

   All the controls are now selected.

   TROUBLESHOOTING: Click any control in the top part of the form before you click Select layout.

e. On the Arrange tab, click **Control Padding** in the Position group. Select **Narrow** from the list of choices.

   The space between the controls is reduced.

f. Click **Save** in the Quick Access Toolbar, and then type **Customer Information** as the form name in the **Save As dialog box**. Click **OK**.

g. Click the **Home tab**, and then click **View** in the Views group to switch to Form view, the view that most users will see. Advance to the sixth customer, *Lugo Computer Sales*, using the **Navigation bar** at the bottom of the form.

   TROUBLESHOOTING: Two Navigation bars exist, one for the main form and one for the subform. Make sure you use the bottom one that shows 14 records.

h. Double-click the **Customers table** in the Navigation Pane.

   Two tabs now appear in the main window. You will compare the table data and the form data while you make changes to both.

i. Verify the sixth record of the Customers table is *Lugo Computer Sales*, which corresponds to the sixth record in the Customer Information form. Click the tabs to switch between the table and the form.

j. Click the **Customer Information tab**, and then replace *Derek Anderson*, the contact for Lugo Computer Sales, with your name. Advance to the next record to save the changes. Click the **Customers tab** to see that the contact name changed in the table as well.

   The contact field and the other fields on the Customer Information form are bound controls. Changing the data in the form automatically changes the data in the underlying table.

   TROUBLESHOOTING: If the change to Derek Anderson does not appear in the Customers table, check the Customer Information form to see if the pencil appears in the left margin. If it does, save the record by advancing to the next customer, and then recheck to see if the name has changed.

k. Replace your name with **Derek Anderson**. Save the record by clicking on the record below *Lugo Computer Sales*. Click the **Customer Information tab**, and then find the sixth record. You should see the change you just made—Derek is back!

l. Switch to Layout view. Click the **Customers title** at the top of the form to select it, and then click again and change the title to **Customer Information**.

   The Customer Information title, a label control, is an example of an unbound control; an unbound control does not have a connection to an underlying table.

m. Click **Save** in the Quick Access Toolbar to save the changes to the form's title. Close the form and the table.

> **TROUBLESHOOTING:** If you make a mistake that you cannot easily recover from, consider deleting the form and starting over. The Form tool makes it easy to start over again.

STEP 2 CREATE A SPLIT FORM

Use the Split Form tool to create a different form to show to Tonya. She may prefer to use a split form to add, edit, and delete records rather than the Customer Information form that you created in the previous step. Refer to Figure 4.8 as you complete Step 2.

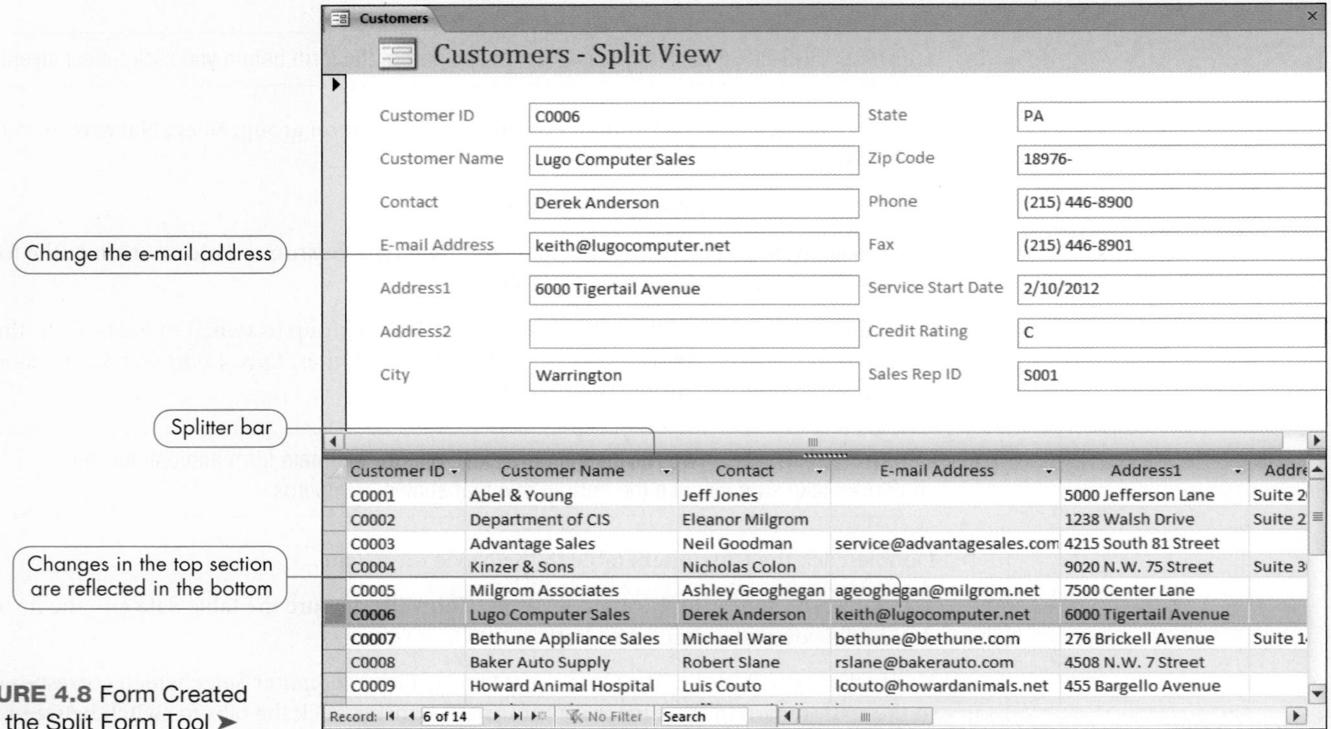

FIGURE 4.8 Form Created with the Split Form Tool ➤

a. Verify the Customers table is selected in the Navigation Pane. Click the **Create tab**, click **More Forms** in the Forms group, and then select **Split Form** from the list.

Access creates a new form with a split view, one view in stacked layout and one view in tabular layout.

b. Switch to Form view. In the bottom portion of the split form, click **Lugo Computer Sales**, the sixth record. Notice the top portion now displays the information for Lugo Computer Sales.

c. Change *service@lugocomputer.net* to ***yourname*@lugocomputer.net** in the top portion of the form.

The bottom portion reflects your change when you move to another field or advance to another record.

d. Click another record, and then click back on **Lugo Computer Sales**.

The pencil disappears from the record selector box and the changes are saved to the table.

e. Click anywhere on the Coulter Office Supplies customer in the bottom portion of the form (record 14).

The top portion shows all the information for this customer.

f. Modify the Contact, E-mail Address, and Address1 information in the top portion of the form, by typing **xyz** at the end of each cell. Save your changes by clicking anywhere in the bottom portion of the window.

   Notice the xyz characters appear in the bottom portion of the form.

g. Remove the xyz's from the Coulter Office Supplies record in the top section.

h. Switch to Layout view. Click the **Customers title** at the top of the form to select it, and then click **Customers** again and change the title to **Customers - Split View**.

i. Click **Save** on the Quick Access Toolbar, and then type **Customers - Split View** in the **Form Name box**. Click **OK**.

j. Move your mouse over the splitter bar, the border between the top and bottom portions of the window. When the pointer shape changes to a double-headed arrow, drag the splitter bar up until it almost touches the Sales Rep ID field.

k. Close the form and save the changes when prompted.

STEP 3 CREATE A MULTIPLE ITEMS FORM

You decide to use the Multiple Items tool to create a form for Alex to manage his products. Because of its tabular format, it will enable Alex and Tonya to view multiple records at one time. Refer to Figure 4.9 as you complete Step 3.

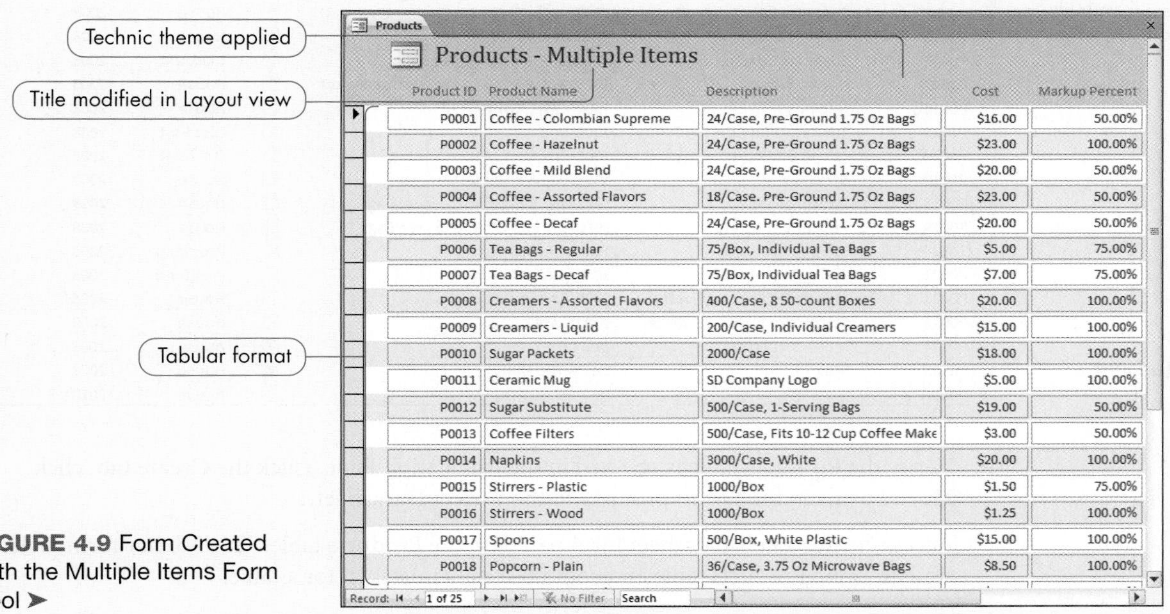

Product ID	Product Name	Description	Cost	Markup Percent
P0001	Coffee - Colombian Supreme	24/Case, Pre-Ground 1.75 Oz Bags	$16.00	50.00%
P0002	Coffee - Hazelnut	24/Case, Pre-Ground 1.75 Oz Bags	$23.00	100.00%
P0003	Coffee - Mild Blend	24/Case, Pre-Ground 1.75 Oz Bags	$20.00	50.00%
P0004	Coffee - Assorted Flavors	18/Case. Pre-Ground 1.75 Oz Bags	$23.00	50.00%
P0005	Coffee - Decaf	24/Case, Pre-Ground 1.75 Oz Bags	$20.00	50.00%
P0006	Tea Bags - Regular	75/Box, Individual Tea Bags	$5.00	75.00%
P0007	Tea Bags - Decaf	75/Box, Individual Tea Bags	$7.00	75.00%
P0008	Creamers - Assorted Flavors	400/Case, 8 50-count Boxes	$20.00	100.00%
P0009	Creamers - Liquid	200/Case, Individual Creamers	$15.00	100.00%
P0010	Sugar Packets	2000/Case	$18.00	100.00%
P0011	Ceramic Mug	SD Company Logo	$5.00	100.00%
P0012	Sugar Substitute	500/Case, 1-Serving Bags	$19.00	50.00%
P0013	Coffee Filters	500/Case, Fits 10-12 Cup Coffee Make	$3.00	50.00%
P0014	Napkins	3000/Case, White	$20.00	100.00%
P0015	Stirrers - Plastic	1000/Box	$1.50	75.00%
P0016	Stirrers - Wood	1000/Box	$1.25	100.00%
P0017	Spoons	500/Box, White Plastic	$15.00	100.00%
P0018	Popcorn - Plain	36/Case, 3.75 Oz Microwave Bags	$8.50	100.00%

FIGURE 4.9 Form Created with the Multiple Items Form Tool ➤

a. Click the **Products table** in the Navigation Pane. Click the **Create tab**, click **More Forms** in the Forms group, and then select **Multiple Items** from the list.

   Access creates a new multiple items form based on the Products table. The form resembles the datasheet of a table—both have a tabular layout.

b. Click **cell P0001**. Move the mouse over the bottom edge of cell P0001 until the pointer shape changes to a two-headed arrow. Drag the bottom edge up to reduce the height of the rows by 50%.

   Changing the height of one row affects the height of all the rows.

c. Click the **Products title** at the top of the form to select it, and then click again on **Products** and change the title to **Products - Multiple Items**.

d. Click the **Themes arrow** in the Themes group on the Design tab. Right-click the **Technic Theme** (near the bottom of the gallery), and then choose **Apply Theme to This Object Only**.

Hover over a theme and its name will display as a ScreenTip. The Technic theme is applied to the Products - Multiple Items form.

e. Close and save the form as **Products - Multiple Items**.

STEP 4 CREATE A DATASHEET FORM AND DELETE A FIELD FROM A FORM

You decide to use the Datasheet tool to create another form for Alex to manage his products. The Datasheet form is in tabular format and is similar to the Multiple Items form, but requires little or no maintenance, which Alex may like. Refer to Figure 4.10 as you complete Step 4.

Datasheet form based on the Products table

Field name modified

Datasheet form looks similar to Datasheet view

Products - Datasheet

Product ID	Product Name	Description	Refrig?	Brand	Year Introduce
P0001	Coffee - Colombian Supreme	24/Case, Pre-Ground 1.75 Oz Bags	☐	Discount	2008
P0002	Coffee - Hazelnut	24/Case, Pre-Ground 1.75 Oz Bags	☐	Premium	2008
P0003	Coffee - Mild Blend	24/Case, Pre-Ground 1.75 Oz Bags	☐	House	2008
P0004	Coffee - Assorted Flavors	18/Case. Pre-Ground 1.75 Oz Bags	☐	House	2008
P0005	Coffee - Decaf	24/Case, Pre-Ground 1.75 Oz Bags	☐	Discount	2008
P0006	Tea Bags - Regular	75/Box, Individual Tea Bags	☐	House	2008
P0007	Tea Bags - Decaf	75/Box, Individual Tea Bags	☐	House	2008
P0008	Creamers - Assorted Flavors	400/Case, 8 50-count Boxes	☐	Discount	2008
P0009	Creamers - Liquid	200/Case, Individual Creamers	☑	Premium	2008
P0010	Sugar Packets	2000/Case	☐	House	2008
P0011	Ceramic Mug	SD Company Logo	☐	House	2008
P0012	Sugar Substitute	500/Case, 1-Serving Bags	☐	Discount	2008
P0013	Coffee Filters	500/Case, Fits 10-12 Cup Coffee Maker	☐	House	2008
P0014	Napkins	3000/Case, White	☐	House	2008
P0015	Stirrers - Plastic	1000/Box	☐	Discount	2008
P0016	Stirrers - Wood	1000/Box	☐	Discount	2008
P0017	Spoons	500/Box, White Plastic	☐	House	2008
P0018	Popcorn - Plain	36/Case, 3.75 Oz Microwave Bags	☐	House	2008
P0019	Popcorn - Buttered	36/Case, 3.75 Oz Microwave Bags	☐	House	2008
P0020	Soup - Chicken	50 Envelopes	☐	Premium	2008
P0021	Soup - Variety Pak	50 Envelopes	☐	Premium	2008
P0022	Styrofoam Cups - 10 ounce	1000/Case	☐	House	2008
P0023	Styrofoam Cups - 12 ounce	1000/Case	☐	House	2008
P0024	Milk - 1 quart	Delivered Daily	☑	House	2008
P0025	Milk - 1 pint	Delivered Daily	☑	House	2008
* (New)			☐	House	2010

FIGURE 4.10 Datasheet Form ➤

a. Verify the Products table is selected in the Navigation Pane. Click the **Create tab**, click **More Forms** in the Forms group, and then select **Datasheet**.

Access creates a new datasheet form based on the Products table. The Tabular form looks similar to the Products table and could be easily mistaken for a table.

b. Click **Save** in the Quick Access Toolbar, and then type **Products - Datasheet** in the **Form Name box**. Click **OK**.

c. Widen the Navigation Pane so all object names are visible. Right-click the **Products - Datasheet form** in the Navigation Pane, and then choose **Layout View** from the list of options.

TROUBLESHOOTING: The View arrow does not contain the Layout view options.

d. Click anywhere in an empty area to deselect the controls.

e. Click the **Cost box**, the control on the right, to select it (you will see the orange border), and then press **Delete**. Click the blank space, and then press **Delete** to remove the blank space. Repeat the process to delete *MarkupPercent*.

You removed fields from the Products form and the other fields adjust to maintain an even distribution (after you remove the blank space).

f. Click the **Refrigeration Needed label** to select it. Change the label to the abbreviation **Refrig?**. Save the form, and then switch to Datasheet view.

g. Double-click the **Products table** in the Navigation Pane to open it.

The Products - Datasheet form and the Products table now appear different because the Cost and MarkupPercent fields were deleted from the form.

h. Close the Products Datasheet form and the Products table.

STEP 5 ADD A FIELD TO A FORM

The form tools made it easy to create forms for Alex's company. But Alex decided he needs a Website field, so you need to modify the form. Refer to Figure 4.11 as you complete Step 5.

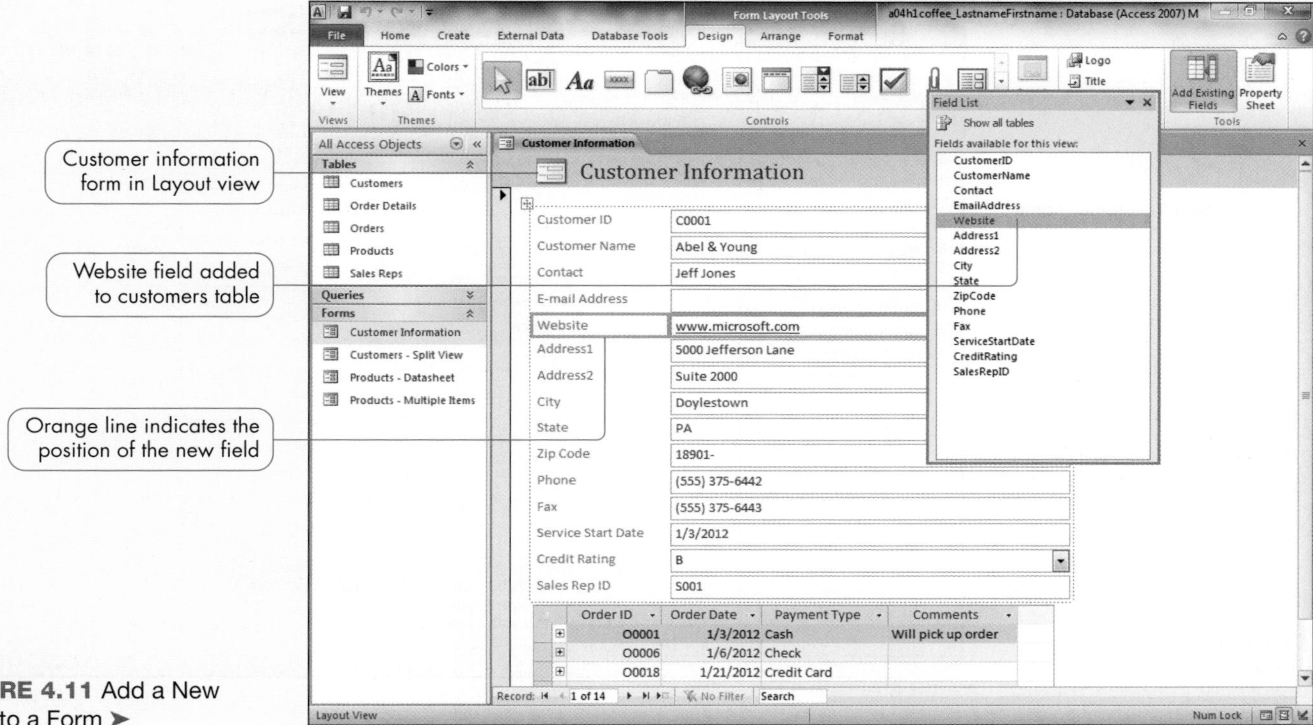
Customer information form in Layout view
Website field added to customers table
Orange line indicates the position of the new field

FIGURE 4.11 Add a New Field to a Form ➤

a. Right-click the **Customers table** in the Navigation Pane, and then click **Design View**.

You will add the Website field to the Customers table.

b. Click the **Address1 field**, and then click **Insert Rows** in the Tools group.

A new row is inserted above the Address1 field.

c. Type **Website** in the blank **Field Name box**, and then choose **Hyperlink** as the Data Type.

d. Close and save the Customers table.

e. Right-click the **Customer Information form** in the Navigation Pane, and then click **Layout View**.

You will add the Website field to the Customer Information form.

f. Click **Add Existing Fields** in the Tools group to display the Field List pane (if necessary).

g. Drag the **Website field** from the Field List pane to the form, below the E-mail Address field, until an orange line displays between E-mail Address and Address1 and release the mouse.

Access shows an orange line to help you place the field in the correct location.

h. Switch to Form view. Press **Tab** until you reach the **Website field**, and then type www.microsoft.com into the field.

i. Press **Tab** until the focus reaches the Orders subform to verify the tab order is correct.

j. Close and save the Customer Information form.

STEP 6 CHANGE THE SORTING IN A FORM AND REMOVE SORTING IN A FORM

Alex tested the Customer Information form and likes the way it is working. He asks you to change the sorting to make it easier to find customers with a similar Customer Name. Refer to Figure 4.12 as you complete Step 6.

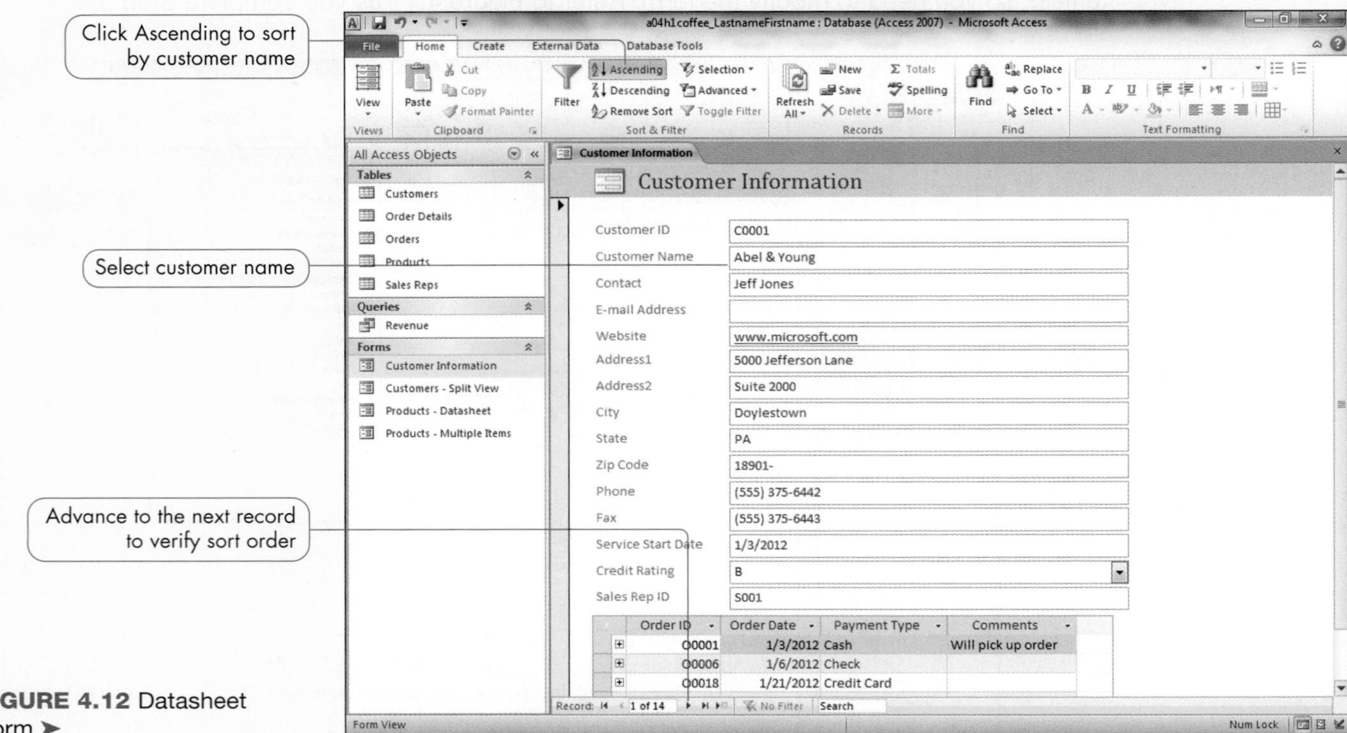

FIGURE 4.12 Datasheet Form ➤

a. Open the Customer Information form. Click **Next record** in the Navigation bar at the bottom several times to advance through the records.

Take note that the customers are in Customer ID order.

b. Click **First record** in the Navigation bar to return to customer Abel & Young.

c. Click the **Customer Name field**, and then click **Ascending** in the Sort & Filter group.

d. Click **Next record** in the Navigation bar at the bottom to advance through the records.

The records are now in Customer Name order.

e. Close the Customer Information form.

f. Click the **File tab**, and then click **Compact & Repair Database**.

g. Keep the database onscreen if you plan to continue with Hands-On Exercise 2. If not, close the database and exit Access.

Form Sections, Views, and Controls

As you work with the form tools to create and modify forms, you will often need to switch between the three form views in Access—Layout view, Form view, and Design view. Most of your design work will be done in Layout view; occasionally, you will switch to Design view to add a more advanced feature, such as a calculated field. Users of the form will only work in Form view. There should be no reason for a user to switch to Layout or Design view. Modifications to the form should be done by the designated form designer.

... you will often need to switch between the three form views in Access—Layout view, Form view, and Design view.

In this section, you will examine the different form sections. As you learn how to create forms, placing fields and labels in the right section will become second nature. You may have to use trial and error at first, switching between Form view and Layout view until the form is working correctly.

Controls are also covered in this section. You will learn the difference between bound and unbound controls. You will also learn how to add a calculated control. Because calculated fields were covered in the queries in a previous chapter, you should be familiar with the syntax found in calculated controls on forms.

Identifying Form Sections

Access forms, by default, are divided into three sections that can be viewed when you display a form in Design view. Each section can be collapsed or expanded as needed, but only in Design view.

Identify the Default Form Sections

Each form by default contains three main sections—*Form Header*, *Detail*, and *Form Footer*. These sections can vary depending on what type of form you create. Stacked layout forms will have different requirements than a tabular layout form. Form designers also have the option of removing certain sections from a form. Two additional sections—*Page Header* and *Page Footer*—are optional and can be added to a form as needed. These sections are visible in Design view and also during Print Preview and printing; however, page headers and footers are not visible in Form view or Layout view. Because these sections are less common in forms, they will not be explored further in this chapter. Use Microsoft Help for more information about the *Page Header* and *Page Footer* sections.

The **Form Header section** displays at the top of each form.

The ***Form Header section*** displays at the top of each form. This section will usually contain the form title, a logo or other graphic, and the current date and time. Column headings (labels) will also be located in this section for Multiple Item forms.

The **Detail section** displays the records in the form's record source.

The ***Detail section*** displays the records in the form's record source. Stacked forms will display one label and one text box for each field placed in the *Detail* section. Navigation controls enable the user to advance to the next, last, previous, and first record. Multiple Item forms will display multiple records (text boxes) in the *Detail* section, as many as can fit onto one screen.

The **Form Footer section** displays at the bottom of the form.

The ***Form Footer section*** displays at the bottom of the form. The Form Footer is commonly used to add totals for field values. For example, an invoice form would display the invoice subtotal, the shipping charges, the taxes, and the invoice total in the *Form Footer* section.

Modify the Default Form Sections

In Figure 4.13, three light grey section bars mark the top boundary of each form section. The top bar denotes the top boundary of the Form Header; the middle bar designates the top of the *Detail* section; and the bottom bar shows the top boundary of the Form Footer. The grid-like area under the bars shows the amount of space allotted to each section. If you decide that the allotted space for a particular section is not needed, you can collapse that section fully so that the section bars are touching. In Figure 4.13, the form has no space allocated to the Form Footer. The section remains in the form's design but will not take up space in Form view. If you want to remove the *Form Footer* section from the form, right-click the Form Footer bar, and then click Form Header/Footer from the list. When you remove the Form Footer, the *Form Header* section will also be removed. This may cause a problem since the title of the form usually resides in the Form Header.

To expand or collapse the space between sections, move your mouse over the bottom bar, and when the mouse pointer changes to a double-headed arrow, click and drag to expand or collapse the section. If you expand or collapse the space allotment for one section, the overall height of the form will be affected.

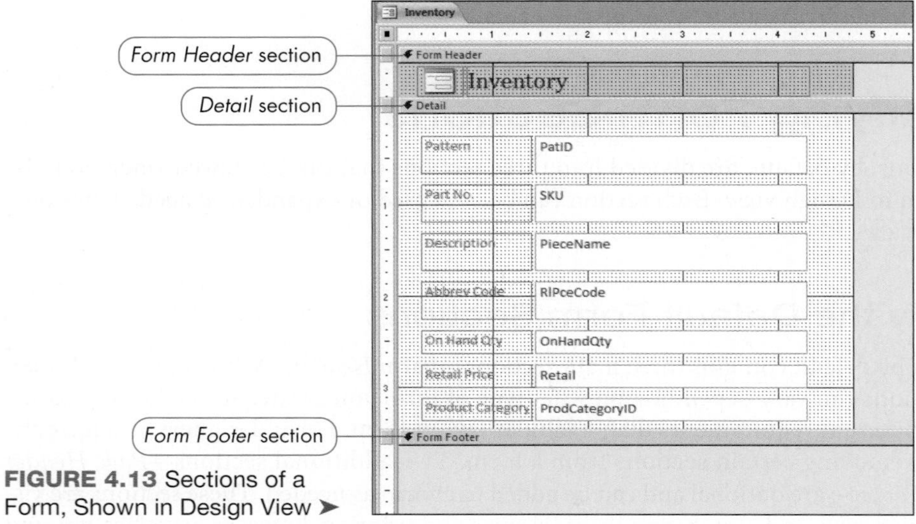

FIGURE 4.13 Sections of a Form, Shown in Design View ➤

Revising Forms Using Form Views

Access provides different views for a form, similar to the different views in tables and queries. Tables and queries have Design view and Datasheet view. Most forms have Layout view, Form view, and Design view. A Datasheet form has one additional view, the Datasheet view, but it does not have the Form view.

Switch Between Form Views

A variety of methods for switching between form views exist: click View in the Views group, click the View arrow, right-click a form in the Navigation Pane, right-click the form tab, or click one of the small view icons in the status bar at the bottom right of the form. Perhaps the quickest method for switching between views is clicking View. This will toggle the form between Layout view and Form view. Click the View arrow or right-click the form tab to switch to Design view. Each view is described in the sections below.

Edit Data in Form View

Use **Form view** to add, edit, and delete data in a form; the layout and design of the form cannot be changed in this view.

Use ***Form view*** to add, edit, and delete data in a form; the layout and design of the form cannot be changed in this view. Most users will only see Form view; if a form needs modification, the user will notify the database designer, who will make a change on the fly or during the next scheduled maintenance interval. Figure 4.14 shows a form in Form view. Users can print from this view by clicking the File tab and then selecting the Print option. However, printing from a form should be done with caution. A form with a stacked layout of 810 records could print as many as 810 pages (depending on how many records fit onto one page) unless you choose the Selected Record(s) option in the Print dialog box. The Selected Record(s) option will only print the current record or the number of records you selected.

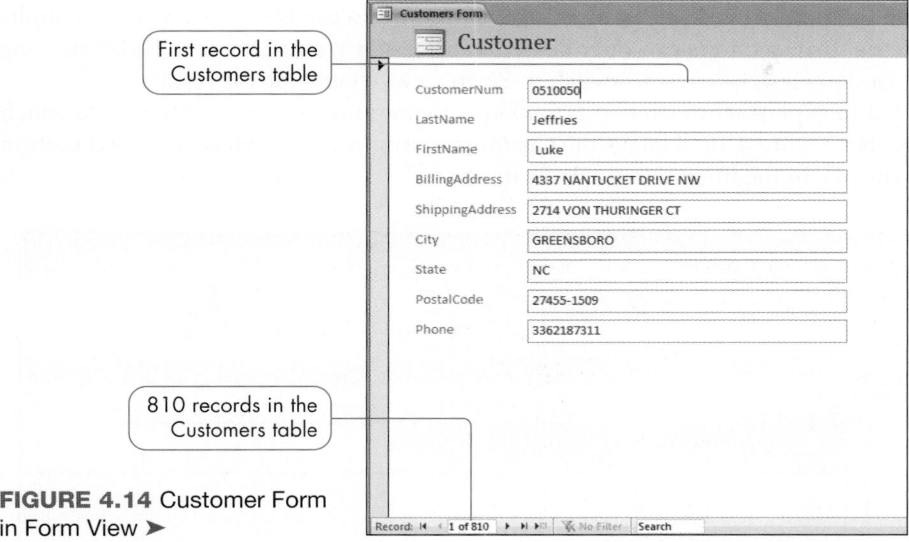

FIGURE 4.14 Customer Form in Form View ➤

Alter a Form in Layout View

Use Layout view to alter the form design while still viewing the data. You use Layout view to add or delete fields in a form, modify field properties, change the column widths, and enhance a form by adding a color scheme or styling. While you are working in Layout view, you can see the data as it would appear in Form view, but you cannot edit the data in Layout view. Seeing the data in Layout view makes it easier to size controls, for example, to ensure the data is visible (see Figure 4.15). It is good practice to test a form in Form view after making changes in Layout view.

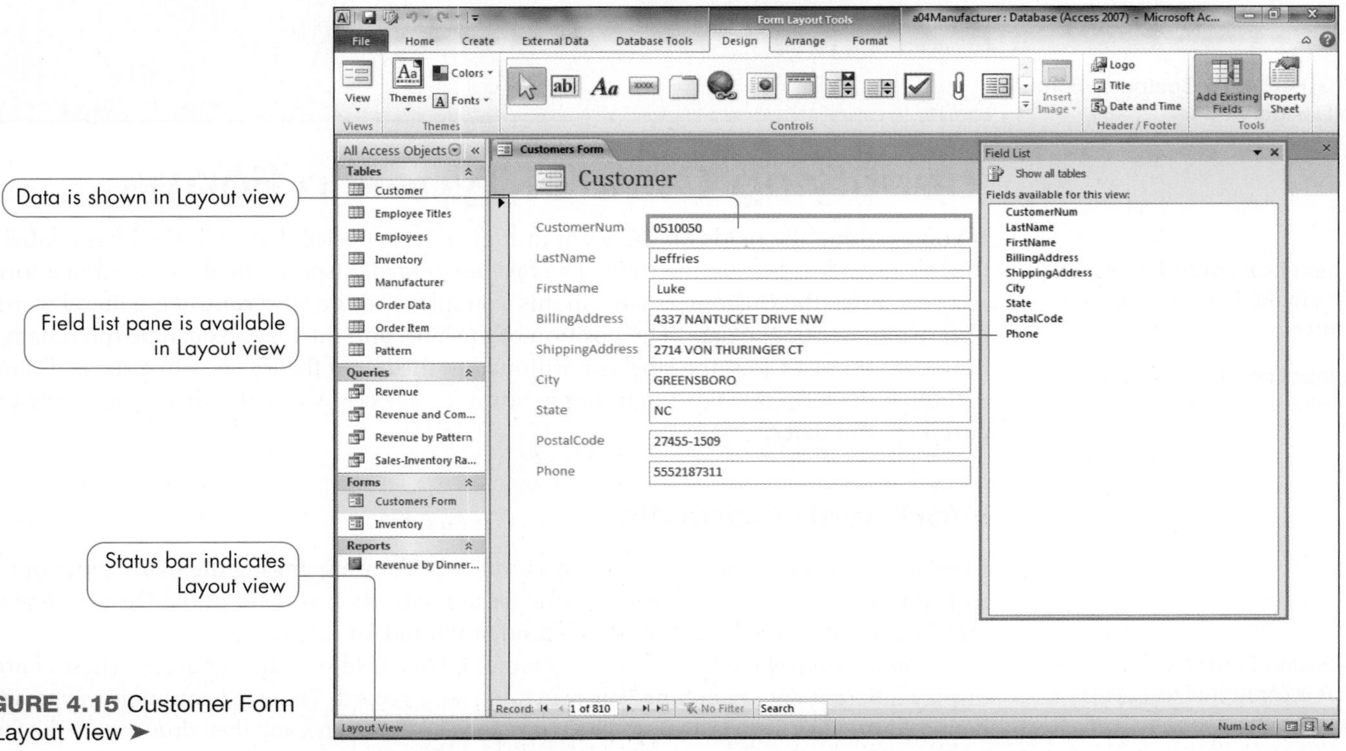

FIGURE 4.15 Customer Form in Layout View ➤

Perform Advanced Changes to a Form in Design View

Use **Design view** to perform advanced changes to a form's design.

Use ***Design view*** to perform advanced changes to a form's design. It provides you the most advanced method of editing an Access form. You can perform many of the same tasks in Design view as you can in Layout view—add and delete fields, change the field order, adjust field widths, modify labels, and customize form elements. But certain tasks cannot be done in Layout view, and Access displays a message telling you to use Design view. For example, changes to the form sections can only be made in Design view. After you finish making changes in Design view, it is best to switch to Form view to examine the results.

You need to experiment using both the Layout view and Design view to decide which view you prefer. Figure 4.16 displays the Customer form in Design view. The next section describes how to edit the finer details of a form.

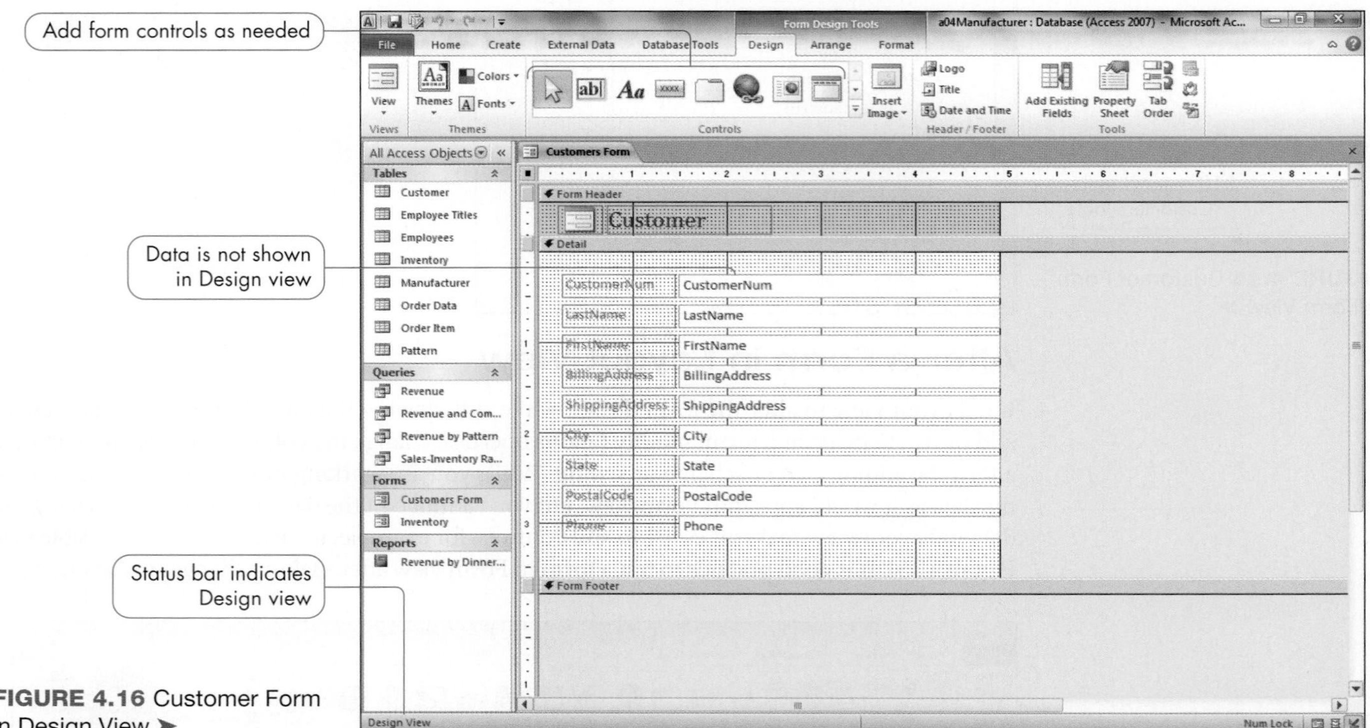

FIGURE 4.16 Customer Form in Design View ➤

Identifying Control Types in Forms

A **text box control** displays the data found in a form's record source.

A **label control** is a literal word or phrase to describe the data.

If you examine the fields on the form in Figure 4.16, notice that each field has a label on the left and a text box on the right. The ***text box control*** displays the data found in a form's record source (the Customers table in this example) and the ***label control*** is a literal word or phrase to describe the data. The position of the label and the text box can be interchanged; however, in most cases, the label is positioned to the left of the text box in a stacked layout. Although the term *text box* might imply *text only*, a text box can also display numeric data, currency, and dates.

Work with Controls

Label and Text Box objects are known as *controls*. They are among the many types of controls found in the Controls group on the Design tab when you are in the Design view of a form. Controls can be categorized as bound, unbound, or calculated.

A **bound control** is a text box that is connected to a field in a table or query.

A ***bound control*** is a text box that is connected to a field in a table or query. These controls display different data each time you switch to a new record. The most common way to add a bound control to a form is to drag a field from the Field List pane, and then drop it onto the form.

An **unbound control** is a label or other decorative design element, and is not connected to a source of data.

An ***unbound control*** is a label or other decorative design element, and is not connected to a source of data. These controls usually describe and decorate the data rather than display the data, and remain the same each time you switch to a new record. Unbound controls include labels, lines, borders, and images; they can be added to a form using the Controls group on the Design tab while in Design view. For example, a label that displays the title of the form is an unbound control.

A **calculated control** contains an expression that generates a calculated result when displayed in Form view.

A ***calculated control*** contains an expression that generates a calculated result when displayed in Form view. The expression can contain field names from the form's record source, constants, and functions. Use a text box, found in the Controls group, to create a calculated control.

Most forms include an unbound control (label) to describe each bound control (text box) on the form. In the form in Figure 4.17, each text box has a label describing it. As you add or delete fields from a form, be aware that many bound controls are connected to an unbound label. If you move the bound control, the label moves, too. Likewise, if you move the label, the bound control moves along with it. You can ungroup the controls and move them separately, but the default is that they are joined together.

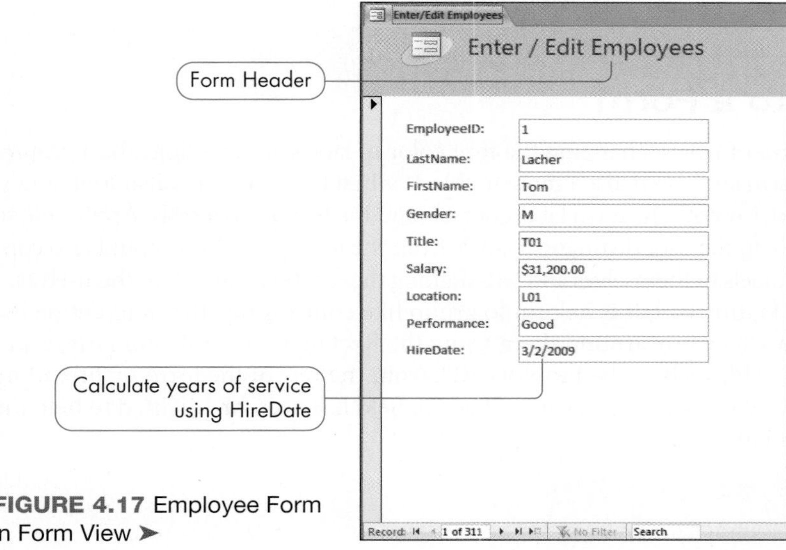

FIGURE 4.17 Employee Form in Form View ➤

Add a Calculated Control to a Form

Review the Enter/Edit Customers form in Figure 4.17 above. Users must manually calculate an employee's years of service using the HireDate field at the bottom of the form. Based on your knowledge of date arithmetic from a previous chapter, you could calculate each employee's years of service using the expression:

```
= (Date( ) – HireDate) / 365
```

To add this expression to the form, you add a calculated field using a text box. Open the form in Design view, and then click Text Box in the Controls group on the Design tab. Place a text box at the desired location, and then enter the expression *=(Date() – HireDate)/365* into the control source property of the new text box. Format the control as needed. Figure 4.18 shows the Years of Service text box formatted as fixed with one decimal.

FIGURE 4.18 Employee Form with Calculated Field ➤

Add Styling to a Form

Modifying the font size of labels, changing the font color of labels, and adding a background color can enhance a form and also make it more usable. It is best to choose a familiar font family, such as Arial or Calibri, for both the form label controls and the text box controls. Apply bold to the labels in order to help the user distinguish labels from the text boxes. You should also consider left-aligning the labels to themselves and left-aligning the text box controls to themselves.

As illustrated in Figure 4.19, it is helpful to group like controls together and define the group visually by drawing a box around them using the Rectangle control. Similarly, separate the primary key field, such as the EmployeeID, from the rest of the form by providing a sufficient visual boundary. Also, the Years of Service field has been highlighted to help the user locate this information quickly.

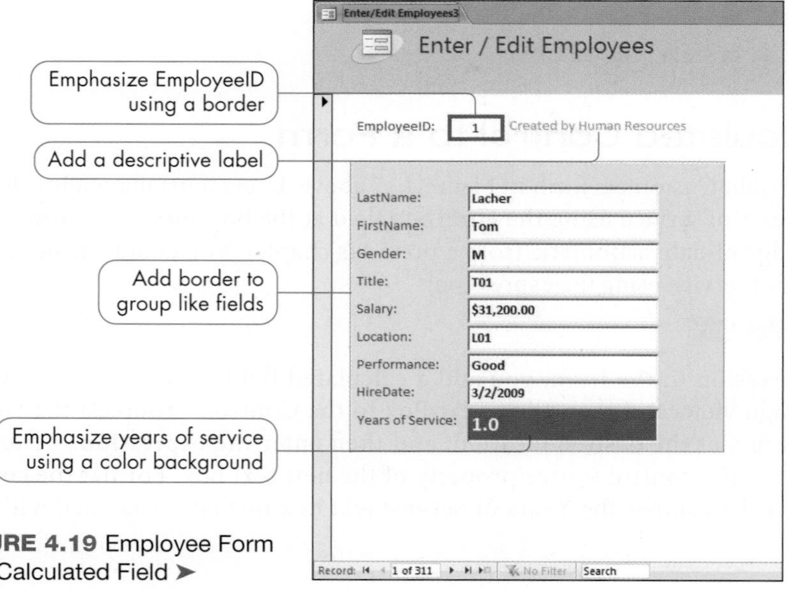

FIGURE 4.19 Employee Form with Calculated Field ➤

Quick Concepts Check

1. Name the three default form sections. Which section is required?
2. What is the difference between Layout view and Design view?
3. Define a bound control and an unbound control.
4. When would you need to use a calculated control? Give an example.

HANDS-ON EXERCISES

2 Form Sections, Views, and Controls

You already created several forms for the Santiago Coffee Shop; however, Alex would like some additional forms. After the new forms are created, you use the different views to make changes and test the forms.

Skills covered: Understand the Main Form Sections and Alter a Form in Design View • Edit Data in Form View • Work with Controls • Add a Calculated Control to a Form • Add Styling to a Form

STEP 1 UNDERSTAND THE MAIN FORM SECTIONS AND ALTER A FORM IN DESIGN VIEW

You have decided to use the Form tool to create a Revenue form. This form will enable Alex to track revenue for his company. You will use Design view to modify this form. Refer to Figure 4.20 as you complete Step 1.

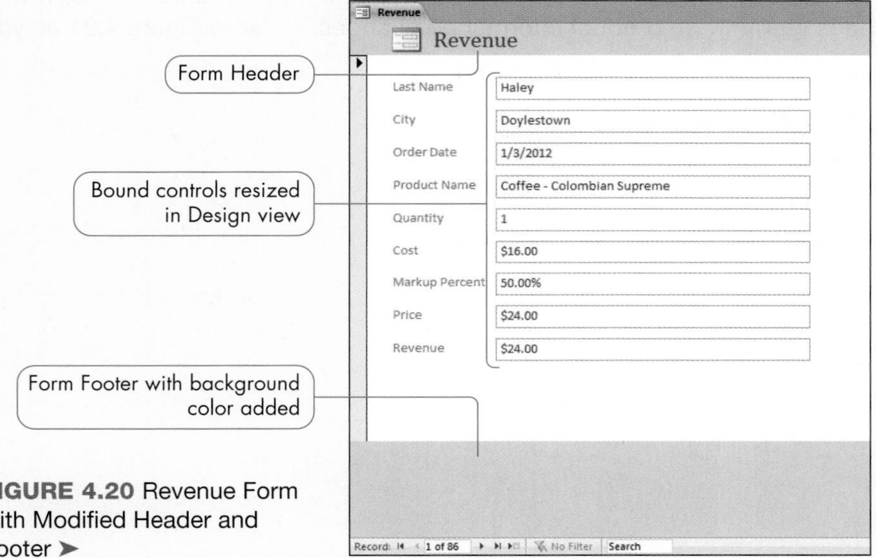

FIGURE 4.20 Revenue Form with Modified Header and Footer ➤

a. Open *a04h1coffee_LastnameFirstname* if you closed it at the end of Hands-On Exercise 1. Click the **File tab**, click **Save Database As**, and then type **a04h2coffee_LastnameFirstname**, changing *h1* to *h2*. Click **Save**.

b. Select **Revenue query** in the Navigation Pane. Click the **Create tab**, and then click **Form** in the Forms group.

   Access creates a new form based on the Revenue query. The form opens in Layout view, ready to edit.

c. Place the mouse on the right edge of the Last Name control so the mouse pointer changes to a double-headed arrow. Drag to the left to size the control section to 50% of its original size.

   Access simultaneously reduces the size of all the controls.

d. Switch to Design view.

   Notice the three sections of the form—*Form Header*, *Detail*, and *Form Footer*.

e. Place the mouse on the bottom edge of the Form Footer bar so the mouse pointer changes to a double-headed arrow. Drag the bar down until the size of the *Form Footer* section is **1"**, using the vertical ruler.

f. Switch to Form view.

With a white background, it is difficult to tell where the *Form Footer* section begins and ends.

g. Switch to Design view. Click **Property Sheet** in the Tools group. Click the **Selection type arrow**, and select **FormFooter**.

h. In the Property Sheet, click the **Format tab**, click the **Back Color arrow**, and then select **Background Light Header** from the list. Close the Property Sheet, and then switch to Form view.

With the new background color, the Form Footer is now evident. You will add content to the footer in a later step.

i. Switch to Design view.

j. Place the mouse on the top edge of the Detail bar so the mouse pointer changes to a double-headed arrow. Drag the bar down until the *Form Header* section is **3/4"**.

k. Click **Save** in the Quick Access Toolbar and save the form as **Revenue**. Close the form.

STEP 2 EDIT DATA IN FORM VIEW

You will use the Form tool to create an Access form to help Alex manage his products. This form will enable Tonya to make changes easily when product information changes. Refer to Figure 4.21 as you complete Step 2.

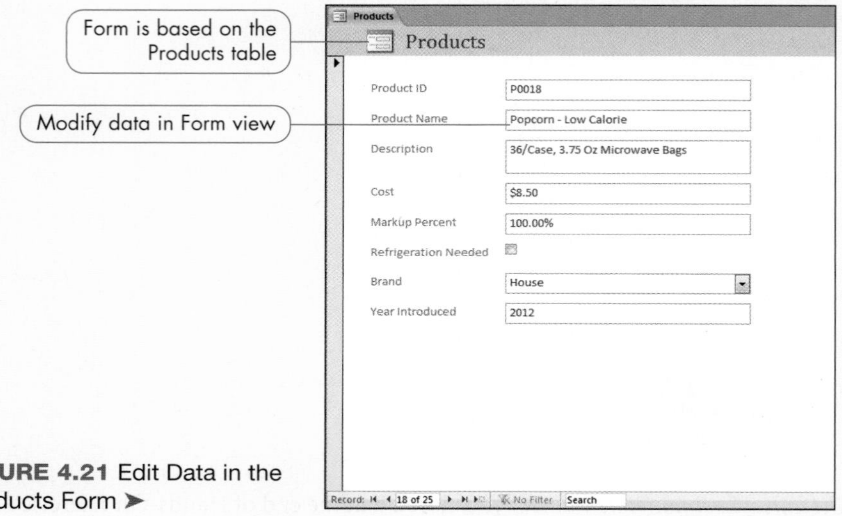

FIGURE 4.21 Edit Data in the Products Form ➤

a. Select the **Products table** in the Navigation Pane. Click the **Create tab**, and then click **Form** in the Forms group.

Access creates a new form based on the Products table.

b. Click anywhere in the subform at the bottom of the window, click the Layout Selector, and then press **Delete** to delete the subform. Click **View** in the Views group to switch to Form view.

c. Click **Next Record** in the Navigation bar to advance to the third record in the Products form.

Use Next Record to advance through the records.

d. Click in the **Product Name box**, and then change *Coffee - Mild Blend* to **Coffee - Light**.

e. Click **Last Record** in the Navigation bar to advance to the last record in the Products form. Click **Previous Record** to locate record 23.

Use Last Record to advance to the last record.

f. Click in the **Product Name box**, and change *Styrofoam Cups - 12 ounce* to **Heavy Paper Cups - 12 ounce**.

g. Click in the **Current Record box** in the Navigation bar, type **12**, and then press **Enter** to go to the 12th record in the Products form.

   Use the Current Record box to advance to a specific record.

h. Click in the **Product Name box**, and then change *Sugar Substitute* to **Splenda**.

i. Click in the **Search box** in the Navigation bar, and then type **pop** to locate any records with *pop* in any data value, in this case, record 18.

   Use the Search box to find a record with a value you type.

j. Click in the **Product Name box**, and then change *Popcorn - Plain* to **Popcorn - Low Calorie**.

k. Click **Save** in the Quick Access Toolbar and save the form as **Products**. Close the form.

STEP 3 WORK WITH CONTROLS

You make some enhancements to the Revenue form to increase its usability. Afterwards, Tonya and Alex test the form to determine if the changes are an improvement to the form. Refer to Figure 4.22 as you complete Step 3.

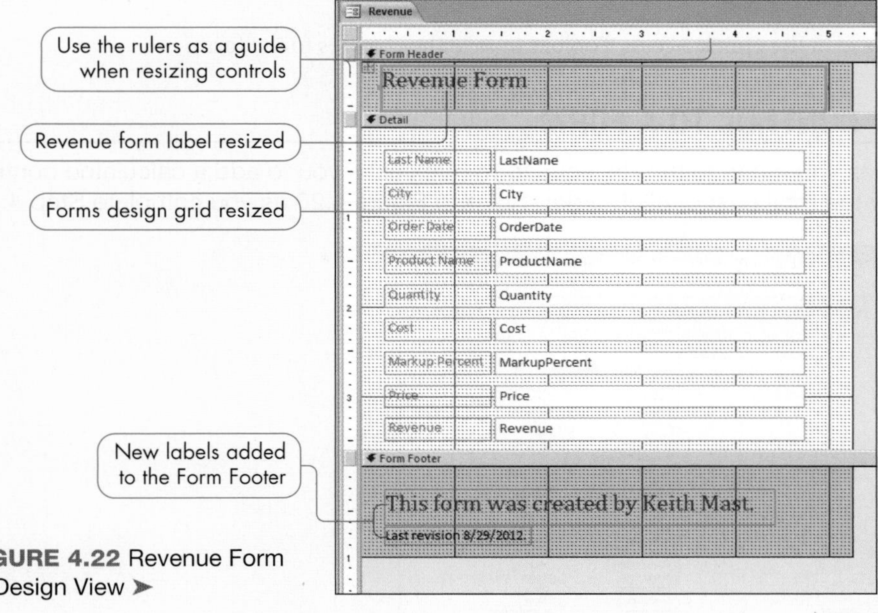

FIGURE 4.22 Revenue Form in Design View ➤

a. Right-click the **Revenue form** in the Navigation Pane, and then click **Design View**.

b. Click the **Revenue label** in the Form Header, and then click it again to edit it. Change the label to **Revenue Form**.

c. Click the **Form Logo** to the left of the Revenue Form label, and then press **Delete** to delete the image.

d. Click **Label** in the Controls group, and then click in the **Form Footer** at the 1/4" mark from both the horizontal and vertical rulers to insert a text box. Type **This form was created by *your name***.

e. Click the **Revenue Form label** in the Form Header, and then click **Format Painter** in the Clipboard group on the Home tab. Click the new label in the Form Footer to apply the same format. Click the label, and then drag the bottom-right sizing handle down and to the right so the entire text is visible.

f. Click **Label** in the Controls group on the Design tab, and then add a second label under the first label in the Form Footer at the 1/4" mark on the horizontal ruler. Type **Last revision *today's date***. Accept the default font.

g. Click the **Form Header bar**, and then open the Property Sheet if necessary. Change the Height property to **.65**.

You can change the height of the Form Header by dragging it with the mouse or by modifying the Height property.

h. Click the **Revenue Form label** in the Form Header. Modify the following properties:

- Change the Height property to **.5**.
- Change the Width property to **4.75**. Close the Property Sheet.

i. Place the mouse on the right edge of the form's design grid so the mouse pointer changes to a double-headed arrow. Drag the grid to the left to change the form's width to **5.25"**.

Use the horizontal ruler to locate the 5.25" mark.

TROUBLESHOOTING: If other Text box controls are too wide, reduce their width first, and then reduce the grid to 5.25".

j. Switch to Form view. Advance through the records using the Navigation bar at the bottom.

The controls in the Form Header and Form Footer do not change when you advance from one record to the next.

k. Click **Save** in the Quick Access Toolbar to save the changes to the form.

STEP 4 ADD A CALCULATED CONTROL TO A FORM

After reviewing the changes you made to the Revenue form, Alex asks you to add a calculated control. The new control will show the total cost of each order. Refer to Figure 4.23 as you complete Step 4.

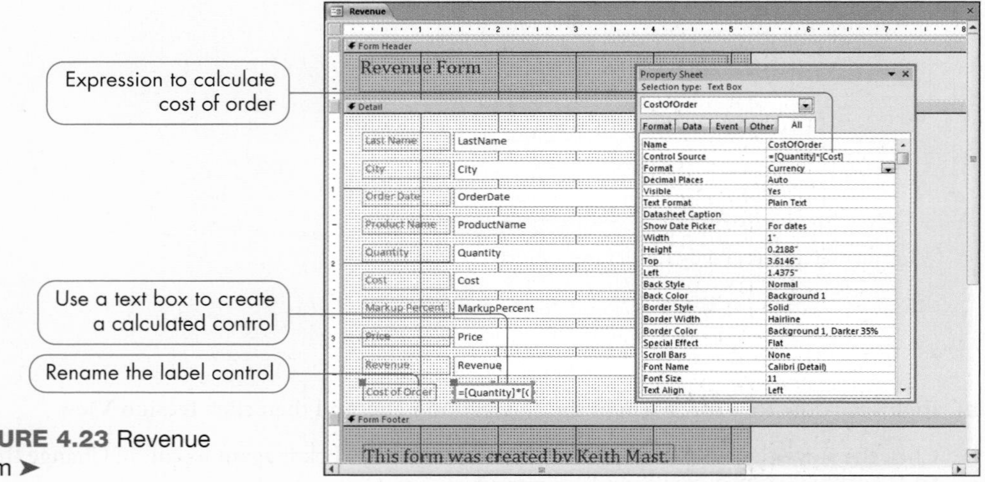

FIGURE 4.23 Revenue Form ➤

a. Switch to Design view.

b. Position the mouse on the top edge of the Form Footer bar until the mouse pointer changes to the double-arrow resizing shape. Drag the **Form Footer bar** down to increase the *Detail* section to **4"**.

c. Click **Text Box** in the Controls group, and then click just below the **Revenue text box** (the white rectangle) at the bottom of the *Detail* section.

d. Click in the **text box**, and then type =**[Quantity]*****[Cost]** in place of *Unbound*. Press **Enter**.

The expression you typed creates a calculated control that shows the total value of the current product.

e. Open the Property Sheet if necessary. Click the **All tab** in the Property Sheet, click in the **Name property box**, and then replace the existing text with **CostOfOrder**. Click the **Format property**, and then use the arrow to select **Currency** from the list of options.

f. Switch to Form view. Advance through the records using the Navigation bar at the bottom.

As you advance from one record to the next, the cost of each order is displayed in the calculated control.

> **TROUBLESHOOTING:** If you see #*Name* in the calculated control, you have typed the expression incorrectly. Be sure you begin the expression with =.

g. Switch to Design view.

h. Click the label control for the new calculated control, and then replace the existing label caption with **Cost of Order**. Resize label control to fit new text, if necessary.

i. Click the calculated control, and then click the **Other tab** on the Property Sheet. Locate the Tab Stop property and change it to **No**.

j. Click **View** in the Views Group to switch to Form view. Press **Tab** to advance through the fields to test the tab stop change.

A calculated control does not require data entry. It is now skipped when Tab is pressed.

k. Save the form.

STEP 5 ADD STYLING TO A FORM

The users of the Santiago Coffee Shop database have asked you to add some styling to the new form. You discuss their ideas with Alex, and then decide to apply the suggested styles. Refer to Figure 4.24 as you complete Step 5.

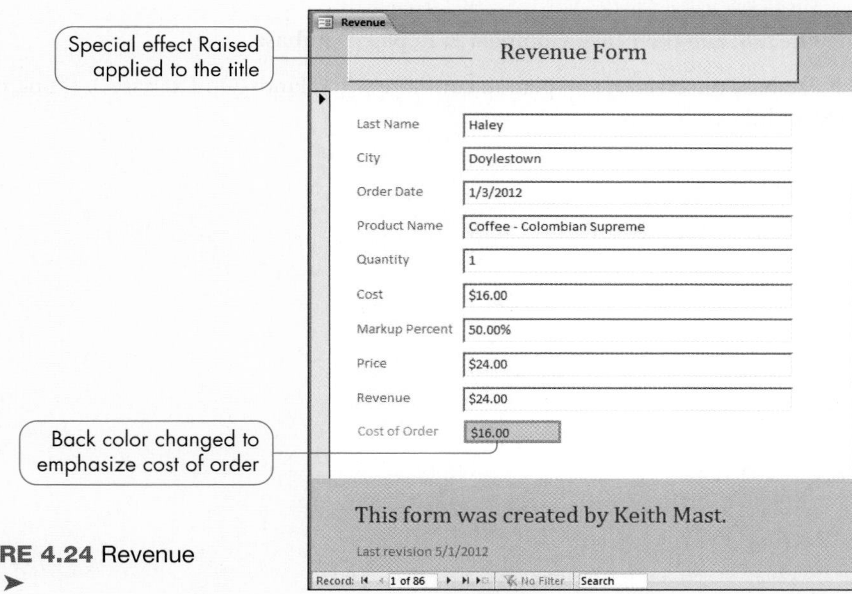

FIGURE 4.24 Revenue Form ➤

a. Switch to Design view.

b. Open the Property Sheet (if necessary), and then click the **Revenue Form label**.

c. Click the **Back Color arrow** on the Property Sheet Format tab, and then choose **Access Theme 2**.

The background color of the title changes to a light blue.

d. Click the **Special Effect arrow** on the Property Sheet Format tab, and then choose **Raised**.

The title now appears raised.

e. Click **Center** in the Font group on the Format tab on the Ribbon.

The form title is now centered within the control box.

f. Click just above the LastName box on the blank grid space, and then drag the mouse through all the fields, except Cost of Order.

All the text box fields are now selected as indicated with an orange border, except the Cost of Order field.

g. Click the **Special Effect arrow** on the Property Sheet Format tab, and then choose **Sunken**.

The fields now appear sunken.

h. Click the **Cost of Order box control**, click the **Border Width arrow** in the Property Sheet Format tab, and then click **2 pt**. Close the Property Sheet.

The border of the calculated control increases.

i. Click **Background Color arrow** in the Font group on the Format tab, and then select **Light Gray 2** (Standard Colors, first column, third row).

The background color of the calculated control is now gray to set it apart from the bound data entry fields.

j. Click the **Cost of Order label control**, click the **Font Color arrow** in the Font group, and then select **Light Gray 4** (Standard Colors, first column, fifth row).

The font color of the calculated control is now gray to set it apart from the bound data entry fields.

k. Switch to Form view. Compare your results to Figure 4.24, and then close and save the form.

l. Click the **File tab**, and then click **Compact & Repair Database**.

m. Keep the database onscreen if you plan to continue with Hands-On Exercise 3. If not, close the database and exit Access.

Report Basics

A **report** is a printed document that displays information from a database in a format that provides meaningful information to its readers.

By now, you know how to plan a database, create a table, establish relationships between tables, enter data into tables, and extract data using queries. You generated output by printing table and query datasheets. You also learned how to create several types of data entry forms. These forms can also be used for inquiries about the data in a database. In this section, you will learn how to create professional reports using the report-writing tools in Access. A ***report*** is a printed document that displays information from a database in a format that provides meaningful information to its readers.

Although you can print information from tables, queries, and forms, information printed from these database objects may not be in the best format. Most of the printed documents generated by Access will come from reports. Reports can be enhanced to help the reader understand and analyze the data. For example, if you print the Datasheet view from the Customers table, you will be able to locate the key information about each customer. However, using report tools, you can group the customers by sales rep, and then highlight the customers who have not placed an order in six months. This is an example of converting a list of customers into an effective business tool. To increase business, each sales rep could contact their customers who have not ordered in six months, and then review his or her findings with the sales manager. A sales report could be run each month to see if the strategy has helped produce any new business.

Most of the printed documents generated by Access will come from reports.

In this section, you will create reports in Access by first identifying a record source, then sketching the report, and finally choosing a Report tool. You will learn how to modify a report by adding and deleting fields, by resizing columns, and by adding a color scheme. You will also learn about the report sections, the report views, and controls on reports. After having worked through forms in the section above, you will discover that there are many similarities between forms and reports.

Creating Reports Using Report Tools

The **Report tool** is used to instantly create a tabular report based on the table or query currently selected.

Access provides five different report tools for creating reports. The report tools are found in the Reports group, as shown in Figure 4.25. Click one of these tools and Access will create an automatic report (or launch a wizard to guide you) using the table or query that is currently selected. The most common of the tools, the ***Report tool***, is used to instantly create a tabular report based on the table or query currently selected. The Blank Report tool is used to create a new blank report so that you can insert fields and controls manually and design the report. The Report Design tool is used to create a new blank report in Design view. In Design view, you can make advanced design changes to reports, such as adding custom control types and working with report sections. The Report Wizard tool will ask a series of questions and help you create a report based on your answers. The Labels tool is used to create a page of labels using one of the preformatted templates provided by Access. After you create a report using one of the report tools, you can perform modifications in Layout view or Design view.

FIGURE 4.25 Report Tools in the Reports Group ➤

Before you create a report in Access, you should ask these questions:

- What is the purpose of the report?
- Who will use the report?
- Which tables are needed for the report?
- What fields, labels, and calculations need to be included?
- How will the report be distributed? Will users pull the information directly from Access or will they receive it through e-mail, fax, or the Internet?
- Will the results be converted to Word, Excel, HTML, or another format?

Sample reports include a telephone directory sorted by last name, a customer list grouped by sales rep, an employee list sorted by most years of service, a financial statement, a bar chart showing sales over the past 12 months, a shipping label, and a letter to customers reminding them about a past due payment.

Identify the Record Source

The first step in planning your report is to identify the record source. You may use one or more tables, queries, or a combination of tables and queries as the report's record source. Sometimes, a single table contains all of the records you need for the report. Other times, you will need to incorporate several tables. When multiple tables are needed to create a report, you can add all the necessary tables into a single query, and then base the report on that query. (As stated earlier, multiple tables in a query must be related, as indicated with join lines. Tables with no join lines usually indicate an incorrect record source.)

Reports can also contain graphics as well as text and numeric data. For example, you can add a company logo, or a watermark to indicate the information is confidential or just a draft. After you identify the record source, you also need to specify which graphic images are needed (and the location of the images).

Sketch the Report

In the *Forms* section, you learned that it is helpful to sketch an Access form before you launch Access. The same holds true for creating an Access report. Design the report and indicate the record source (table names or query name), the title, the format of the report (stacked or tabular), the fields, and the order of fields. It would also be helpful to indicate the grouping and totals needed for the report. Sketch the report first and you will be happier with the results. A sample sketch is shown in Figure 4.26.

Physicians Report - Draft

First Name	Last Name	Address	City	State	Zip Code	Phone Number	Specialization
Bonnie	Clinton	10000 SW 59 Court	Coral Springs	FL	33071	(954) 777-8889	Obstetrics
Warren	Brasington	9470 SW 25 Street	Coral Springs	FL	33071	(954) 888-7654	Hematology
James	Shindell	Avenue	Coral Springs	FL	33070	(954) 773-4343	General Medicine
Edward	Wood	Avenue	Coral Springs	FL	33072	(954) 555-5555	Cardiology
Michelle	Quintana	3990 NW 3 Street	Coral Springs	FL	33071	(954) 888-1221	Internal Medicine
Kristine	Park	9290 NW 59 Steet	Coral Springs	FL	33072	(954) 777-1111	Exercise Physiology
William	Williamson	108 Los Pinos Place	Coral Springs	FL	33071	(954) 888-4554	General Medicine
Holly	Davis	8009 Riviera Drive	Coral Springs	FL	33072	(954) 388-7676	Cardiology
Steven	Fisher	444 SW 190 Street	Coral Springs	FL	33070	(954) 777-3333	Internal Medicine
David	Tannen	50 Main Street	Coral Springs	FL	33171	(954) 777-2211	Hematology
Jeffrey	Jacobsen	490 Bell Drive	Coral Springs	FL	33070	(954) 388-9999	Internal Medicine
Patsy	Clark	200 Harding Blvd	Coral Springs	FL	33070	(954) 777-1087	Cardiology
Keith	Mast	102 SCC	E. Norriton	PA	19401	(610) 555-1212	General Medicine

FIGURE 4.26 Sketch of the Physicians Report ➤

Use the Report Tool

After you sketch the report, you can decide which report tool is appropriate to produce the desired report. Access provides several tools that you can use to create a report, as shown in Figure 4.27. Which one you select depends on the layout of the report, the record source, and the complexity of the report design.

A **tabular layout report** displays data horizontally across the page in a landscape view.

The easiest way to create a report is with the Report tool. Select a table or query in the Navigation Pane, then click Report in the Reports group on the Create tab, and Access creates a tabular layout report instantly. A ***tabular layout report*** displays data horizontally across the page in a landscape view, as shown in Figure 4.27.

A **stacked layout report** displays fields in a vertical column.

You can also create a ***stacked layout report*** in Access, although this type of report is less common. A stacked layout report displays fields in a vertical column. The number of records on one page depends on the number of fields in the record source. You can also force a new page at the start of each record.

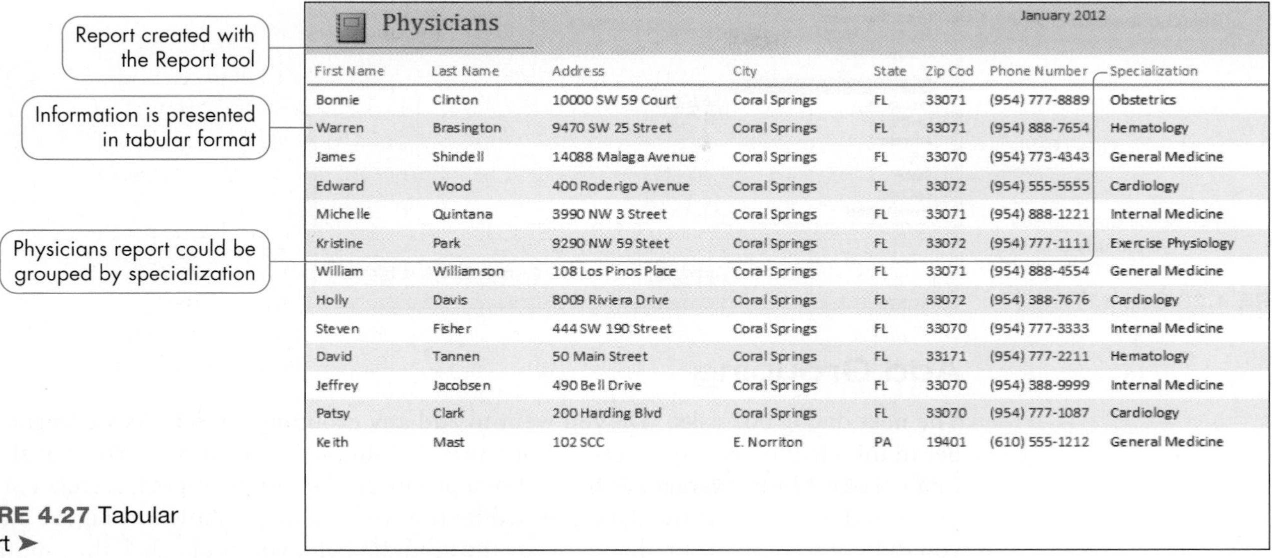

Report created with the Report tool
Information is presented in tabular format
Physicians report could be grouped by specialization

Physicians — January 2012

First Name	Last Name	Address	City	State	Zip Cod	Phone Number	Specialization
Bonnie	Clinton	10000 SW 59 Court	Coral Springs	FL	33071	(954) 777-8889	Obstetrics
Warren	Brasington	9470 SW 25 Street	Coral Springs	FL	33071	(954) 888-7654	Hematology
James	Shindell	14088 Malaga Avenue	Coral Springs	FL	33070	(954) 773-4343	General Medicine
Edward	Wood	400 Roderigo Avenue	Coral Springs	FL	33072	(954) 555-5555	Cardiology
Michelle	Quintana	3990 NW 3 Street	Coral Springs	FL	33071	(954) 888-1221	Internal Medicine
Kristine	Park	9290 NW 59 Steet	Coral Springs	FL	33072	(954) 777-1111	Exercise Physiology
William	Williamson	108 Los Pinos Place	Coral Springs	FL	33071	(954) 888-4554	General Medicine
Holly	Davis	8009 Riviera Drive	Coral Springs	FL	33072	(954) 388-7676	Cardiology
Steven	Fisher	444 SW 190 Street	Coral Springs	FL	33070	(954) 777-3333	Internal Medicine
David	Tannen	50 Main Street	Coral Springs	FL	33171	(954) 777-2211	Hematology
Jeffrey	Jacobsen	490 Bell Drive	Coral Springs	FL	33070	(954) 388-9999	Internal Medicine
Patsy	Clark	200 Harding Blvd	Coral Springs	FL	33070	(954) 777-1087	Cardiology
Keith	Mast	102 SCC	E. Norriton	PA	19401	(610) 555-1212	General Medicine

FIGURE 4.27 Tabular Report ➤

Use the Report Wizard

The Report Wizard.... uses six dialog boxes to collect information about your report.

The **Report Wizard** asks you questions and then uses your answers to generate a report.

You can also create a professional report with the Report Wizard. The ***Report Wizard*** asks you questions and then uses your answers to generate a report. The wizard uses six dialog boxes to collect information about your report.

Start the Report Wizard

After thinking through the structure, the layout, and the record source, you are ready to launch the Report Wizard. First, select the report's record source in the Navigation Pane, and then click Report Wizard in the Reports group on the Create tab. The wizard opens with the table or query (the record source) displayed in the first dialog box. Although you chose the record source before you started, the first dialog box enables you to select fields from additional tables or queries.

To demonstrate the Report Wizard, an Access database was created to track several health studies being conducted by a local physicians group. The studies are tracked using a StudyID code, S01, S02, S03, etc. The report that you need to create will list each volunteer alphabetically, grouped by study. See Figure 4.28 to review the fields in the Volunteers table—a key table in the Physicians database.

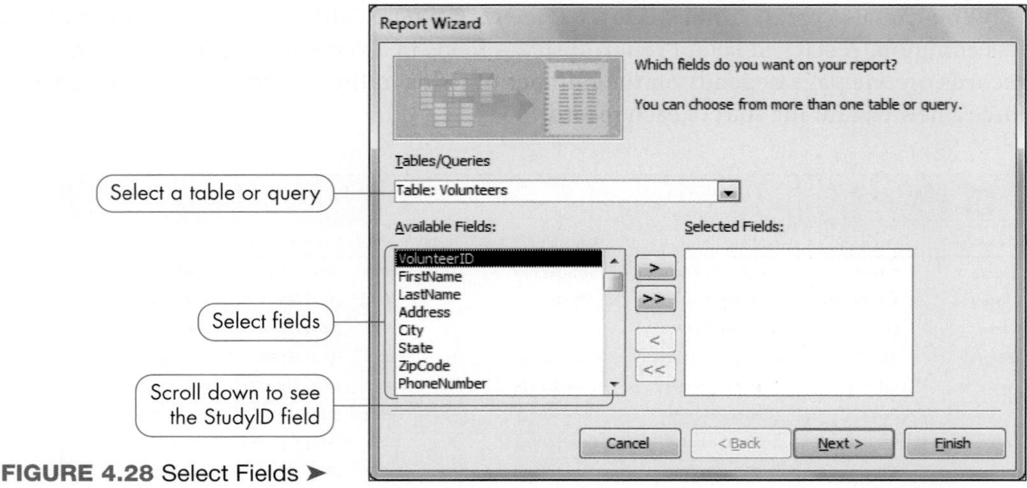

FIGURE 4.28 Select Fields ➤

Add Grouping

The next dialog box asks, "Do you want to add any grouping levels?" As we learned earlier in this chapter, grouping lets you organize and summarize your data. You can also add totals (sum, count, average) at the end of a group. In the sample report, Access correctly predicts that you want the data grouped by the study field (as shown in Figure 4.29). If you did not want to group the report by the StudyID field, you could click the < button to remove the group in step two of the Report Wizard. After you remove the unwanted grouping, select the field you want to group by, and then click the > button to add the new group. If you need a second or third grouping level, add those field names in order. The order in which you select the groups dictates the order of display in the report.

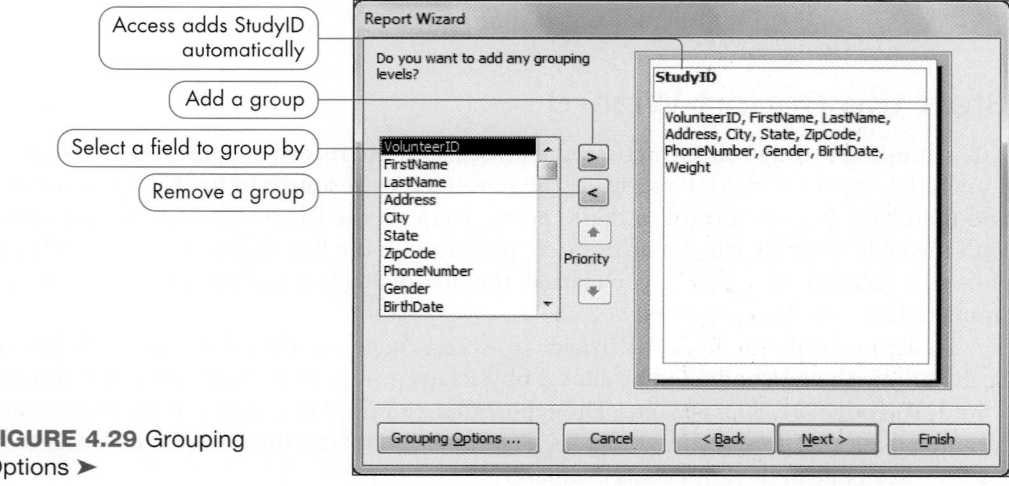

FIGURE 4.29 Grouping Options ➤

Add Sorting and Summary Options

The next dialog box asks, "What sort order and summary information do you want for detail records?" The summary information option will only appear if there is a numeric field in the selected fields (see Figure 4.30). Click Summary Options if you want to add aggregate functions (e.g., sum, average, minimum, and maximum) and to specify whether you want to see detail records on the report or only the aggregate results. Click OK or Cancel to return to the Report Wizard (see Figure 4.31). For the sort options, specify which field you want to sort by first, then second, third, and fourth. For each field, choose ascending order and/or descending order.

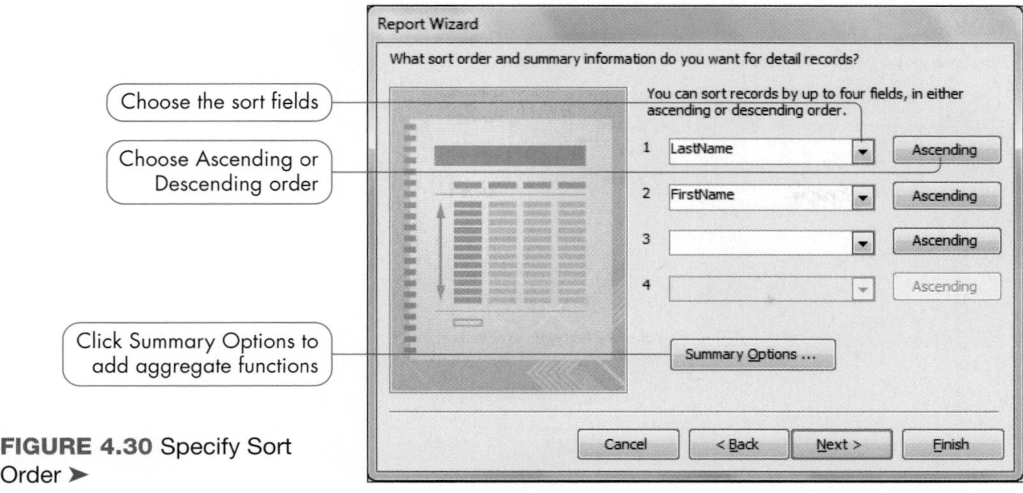

FIGURE 4.30 Specify Sort Order ➤

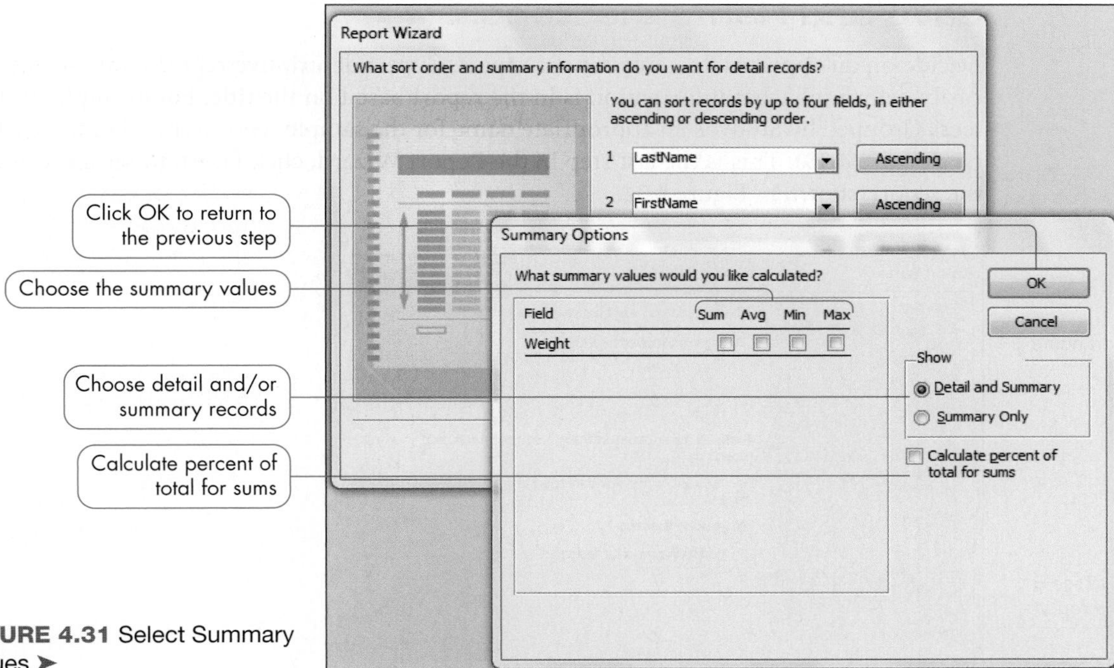

FIGURE 4.31 Select Summary Values ➤

Choose the Layout for the Report

The next dialog box will determine the report's appearance. First, you select the layout from three options—Stepped, Block, or Outline. Clicking an option will give you a general preview in the preview area. You can also select the orientation for the report, either Portrait or Landscape (see Figure 4.32). Select an appropriate format for the report.

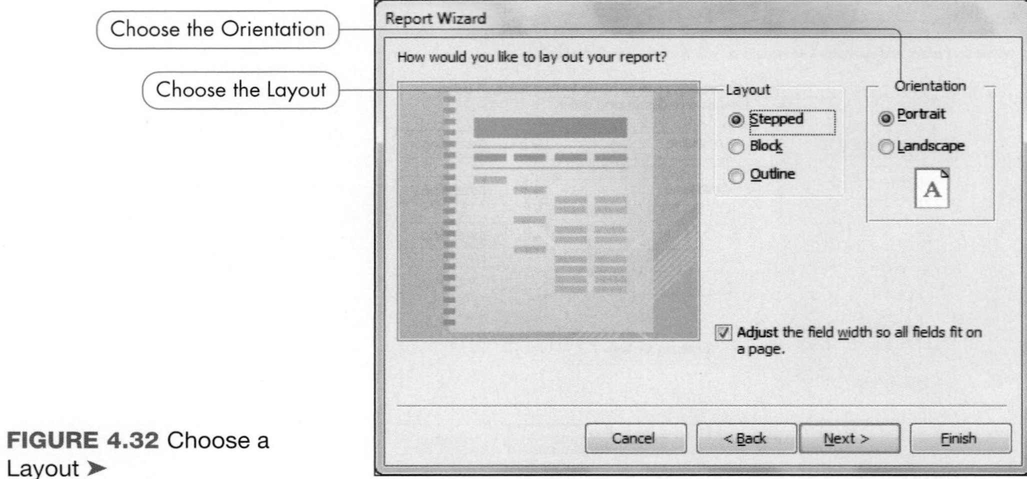

FIGURE 4.32 Choose a Layout ➤

Save and Name the Report

Decide on an appropriate name for the report. Type a descriptive report name so you can easily determine what information is in the report based on the title. For example, Volunteers Grouped by Study is an appropriate name for the sample report created in this section (see Figure 4.33). This is the last step in the Report Wizard; click Finish to see a preview of the report, shown in Figure 4.34.

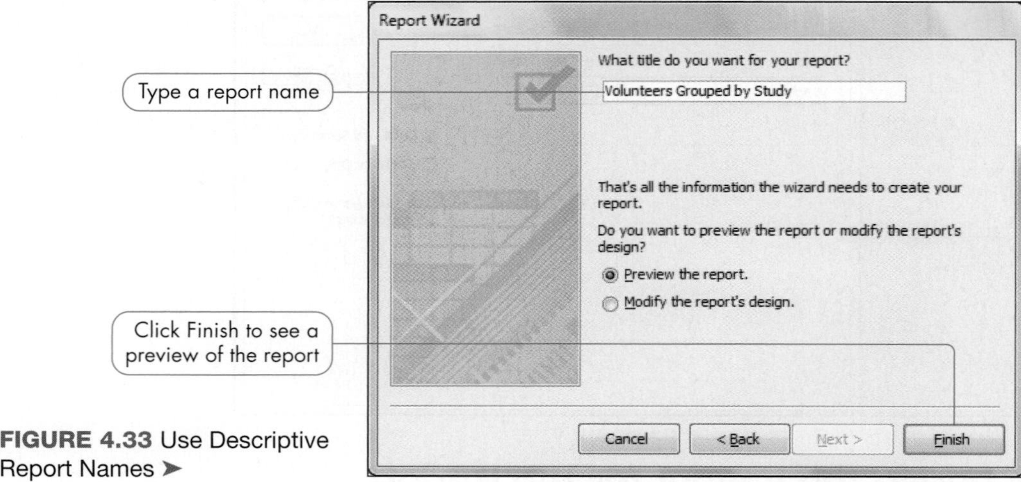

FIGURE 4.33 Use Descriptive Report Names ➤

Volunteers Grouped by Study

StudyID	Last Name	First Name	Weight	VolunteerID	Address	City	State
S01							
	Cooper	Deborah	150	V002	4000 SW 14 Stre	Coral Springs	FL
	Mullins	Bernard	175	V010	387 Hardie Road	Coral Springs	FL
	Newcomb	Jeff	210	V003	1900 Bird Road	Coral Springs	FL
	Roberts	Kevin	178	V014	7899 SW 56 Ave	Coral Springs	FL
Summary for 'StudyID' = 1 (4 detail records)							
		Avg	178.25				
S02							
	Campbell	Patsy	125	V001	900 Sunset Drive	Coral Springs	FL
	Miller	Joe	210	V007	310 West Drive	Coral Springs	FL
	Roberts	Betsy	145	V006	400 Granada Blv	Coral Springs	FL
Summary for 'StudyID' = 2 (3 detail records)							
		Avg	160				
S03							
	Glatstein	Victor	188	V017	2998 Leafy Way	Coral Springs	FL
	Mayhew	Mary	165	V018	200 SW 20 Stree	Coral Springs	FL
Summary for 'StudyID' = 3 (2 detail records)							
		Avg	176.5				
S04							
	North	Ned	312	V016	3 Main Street	Coral Springs	FL

FIGURE 4.34 Volunteers Grouped by Study Report ➤

Use the Label Wizard

The **Label Wizard** enables you to easily create mailing labels, name tags, and other specialized tags.

A **mailing label** is a specialized report that comes preformatted to coordinate with name-brand labels, such as Avery.

The ***Label Wizard*** enables you to easily create mailing labels, name tags, and other specialized tags. A ***mailing label*** is a specialized report that comes preformatted to coordinate with name-brand labels, such as Avery. You then use the Label Wizard to create a label that fits the 5660 template. To begin, click Labels in the Reports group on the Create tab, and then select the manufacturer, the product number, and the label type. Next, choose the font type and size, and then add the fields to the label template, as shown in Figure 4.35. The Physicians Labels report is shown in Figure 4.36.

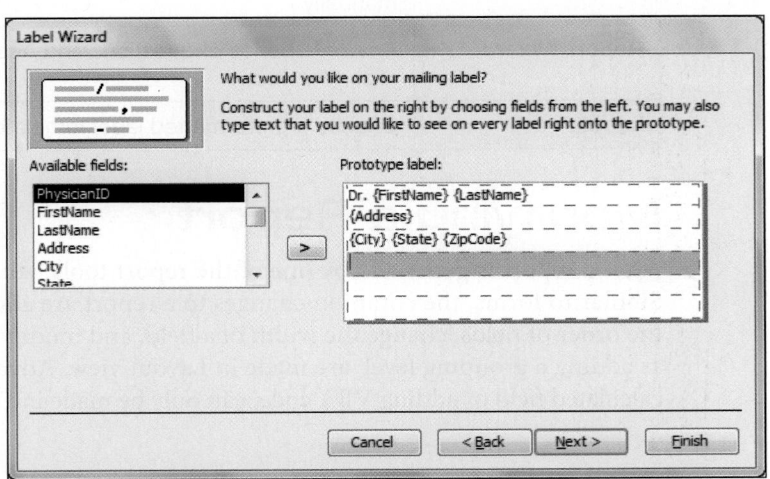

FIGURE 4.35 Create a Mailing Label ➤

Dr. Warren Brasington 9470 SW 25 Street Coral Springs fl 33071	Dr. Patsy Clark 200 Harding Blvd Coral Springs fl 33070	Dr. Bonnie Clinton 10000 SW 59 Court Coral Springs FL 33071
Dr. Holly Davis 8009 Riviera Drive Coral Springs FL 33072	Dr. Steven Fisher 444 SW 190 Street Coral Springs fl 33070	Dr. Jeffrey Jacobsen 490 Bell Drive Coral Springs fl 33070
Dr. Keith Mast 102 SCC E. Norriton PA 19401	Dr. Kristine Park 9290 NW 59 Steet Coral Springs fl 33072	Dr. Michelle Quintana 3990 NW 3 Street Coral Springs fl 33071

FIGURE 4.36 Physicians Label Report ➤

Table 4.1 provides a summary of the five report tools and their usage.

TABLE 4.1 Report Tools and Their Usage

Report Tool	Usage
Report	Create a tabular report showing all of the fields in the record source.
Report Design	Create a new blank report in Design view. Add fields and controls manually.
Blank Report	Create a new blank report in Layout view. Add fields and controls manually.
Report Wizard	Answer a series of questions and Access will design a custom report for you.
Labels	Choose a preformatted label template and create a sheet of labels.

Modifying a Report

After a report is generated by one of the report tools, you will usually need to modify it. Similar to forms, the common changes to a report are add a field, remove a field, change the order of fields, change the width of a field, and modify the title. These changes, as well as adding a grouping level, are made in Layout view. Advanced changes, such as adding a calculated field or adding VBA code, can only be made in Design view.

Add a Field to a Report

Adding a field to a report with a tabular layout is similar to adding a field to a form with a tabular layout. Right-click a report in the Navigation Pane, and then click Layout view. Next, click Add Existing Fields in the Tools group on the Design tab to reveal the available fields in the report's record source. Drag the new field to a precise location on the report, using the vertical orange line as a guide for the position of the new field, and release the mouse. The other fields will automatically adjust to make room for the new field.

The process of adding a field to a report with a stacked layout is the same as a tabular layout. The only difference is the orange line will appear horizontally.

Delete a Field from a Report

To delete a field from the *Detail* section of a tabular report, first switch to the Layout view or Design view of the report. Next, click the text box of the field to be deleted and note the orange border around the field. With the orange border visible, press Delete. Repeat the process to delete the associated label from the Page Header. After the controls are deleted, click in the blank space, and then press Delete again. After the text box and label are removed from the report, the other fields automatically adjust to close the gap around the deleted field.

Work with a Report Layout Control

Whenever you use one of the report tools to create a new report, Access will add a layout control to help align the fields. Layout controls in reports work the same as layout controls in forms. As discussed earlier in this chapter, the layout control provides guides to help keep controls aligned horizontally and vertically, and give your report a uniform appearance.

There are times when you may want to remove the layout control from a report in order to position the fields without aligning them to each other. If you want to remove the layout control from a report, switch to Design view, and then click anywhere inside the control you want to remove. On the Arrange tab, click Select Layout in the Rows & Columns group. Click Remove Layout in the Table group and the layout control is gone. All of the other controls are still on the report, but the rectangle binding them together is gone.

You can add a layout control to a report by first selecting all the controls you want to keep together. Then, click Stacked or Tabular in the Table group and the layout control appears.

Adjust Column Widths in a Report

You can adjust the width of each column in a tabular report individually so that each column is wide enough to accommodate the widest value. For example, if a report contains first name, last name, address and city, and e-mail address, you will need to make sure the longest value in each field is completely visible. Scroll through the records to make sure this is the case.

To modify column widths in a tabular report, first switch to the Layout view or Design view of the report. Click the text box of the field you want to adjust. The field will have an orange border around it, indicating it is selected. Move the mouse to the right border of the selected field; when the mouse pointer turns to a double arrow, drag the edge to the right (to increase) or the left (to decrease) until you arrive at the desired width.

Add a Theme to the Report

You can enhance the report's appearance by applying one of the themes provided by Access. To apply a theme, switch to Layout view, and then click Themes in the Themes group on the Design tab. Scroll through the themes until you find a theme you like; hover over one of the options to see a quick preview of the current report using the current theme. Right-click a theme, and then choose Apply Theme to This Object Only (as shown in Figure 4.37). You can also apply the theme to all matching objects.

1. What are the benefits of using the report wizard?
2. When would you need the label wizard?
3. What are the benefits of a report layout control when modifying a report?
4. Why is sorting the records in a report important?

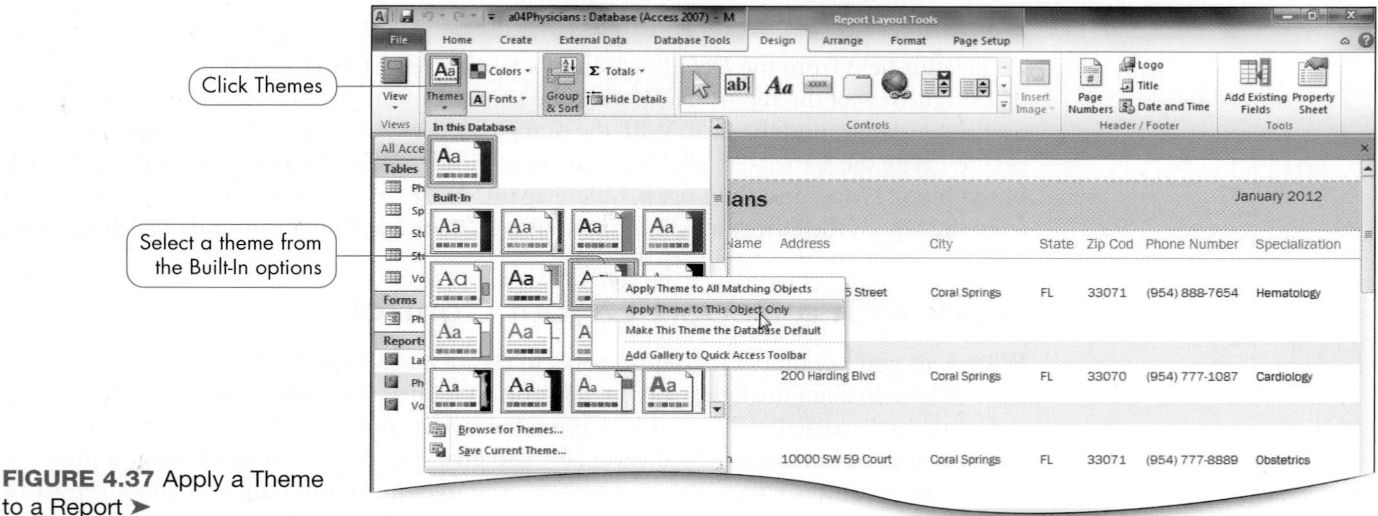

FIGURE 4.37 Apply a Theme to a Report ➤

Sorting Records in a Report

When a report is created using the Report tool, the sort order of the records in the report is initially dependent on the sort order of the record source—similar to the way records are sorted in a form. The primary key of the record source usually dictates the sort order. However, a report has an additional feature for sorting. While in Layout view or Design view, click Group & Sort in the Grouping & Totals group on the Design tab. The Group, Sort, and Total pane now appears at the bottom of the report. This section enables you to set the sort order for the report and override the sorting in the report's record source.

Change the Sorting in a Report

While working in the Layout view of a report, click Group & Sort to display the *Group, Sort, and Total* section, as shown in Figure 4.38. To sort the records in a report by last name, click Add a sort and select LastName from the list. The report records will instantly sort by LastName in ascending order. Next, you can set a second sort by clicking Add a Sort again. For example, you could add the FirstName sort after the LastName sort, as shown in Figure 4.38.

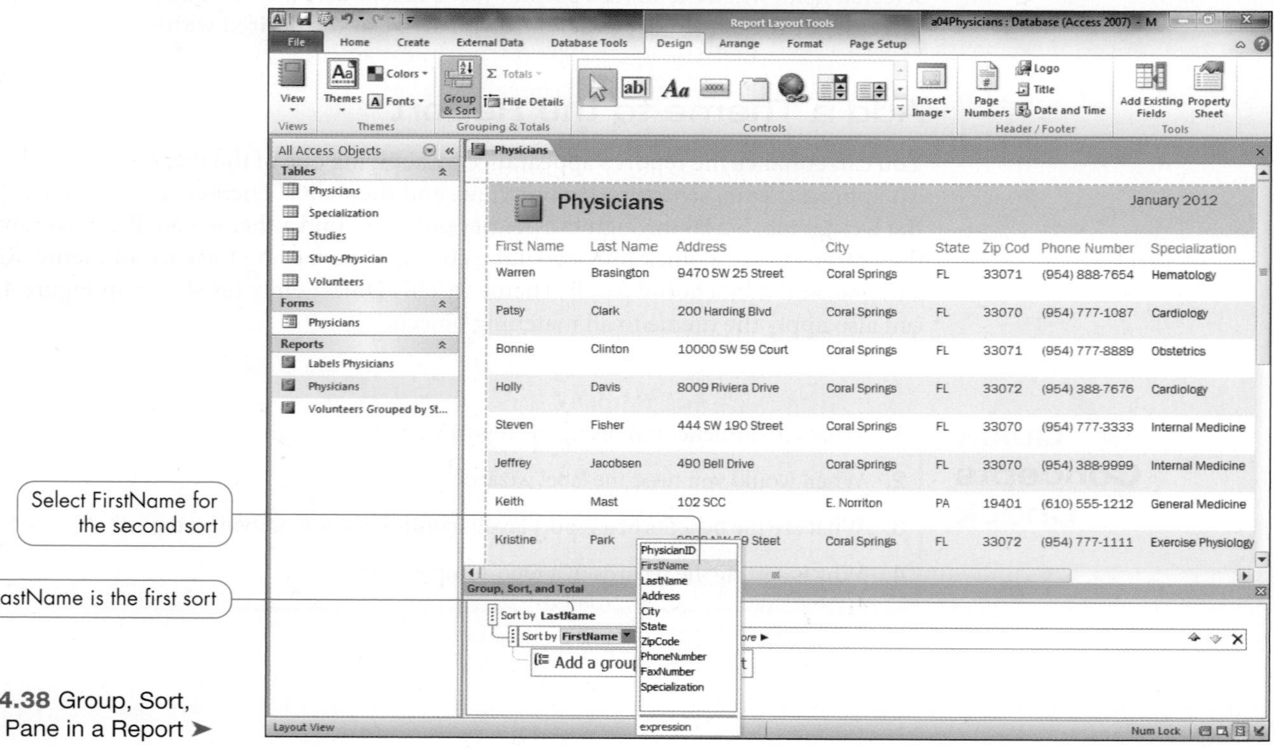

FIGURE 4.38 Group, Sort, and Total Pane in a Report ➤

HANDS-ON EXERCISES

3 Report Basics

You create a Products report using the Access Report tool to help Alex stay on top of the key data for his business. After Access creates the report, you modify the column widths so the entire report fits on one page (portrait or landscape, depending on the report). You also use the Report Wizard tool to create other reports for Alex.

Skills covered: Use the Report Tool • Add a Field to a Report • Delete a Field from a Report and Adjust Column Widths in a Report • Apply a Theme to the Report • Change the Sorting in a Report • Use the Report Wizard

STEP 1 USE THE REPORT TOOL

You use the Report tool to create an Access report to help Alex manage his product information. This report is especially useful for determining which products he needs to order to fill upcoming orders. Refer to Figure 4.39 as you complete Step 1.

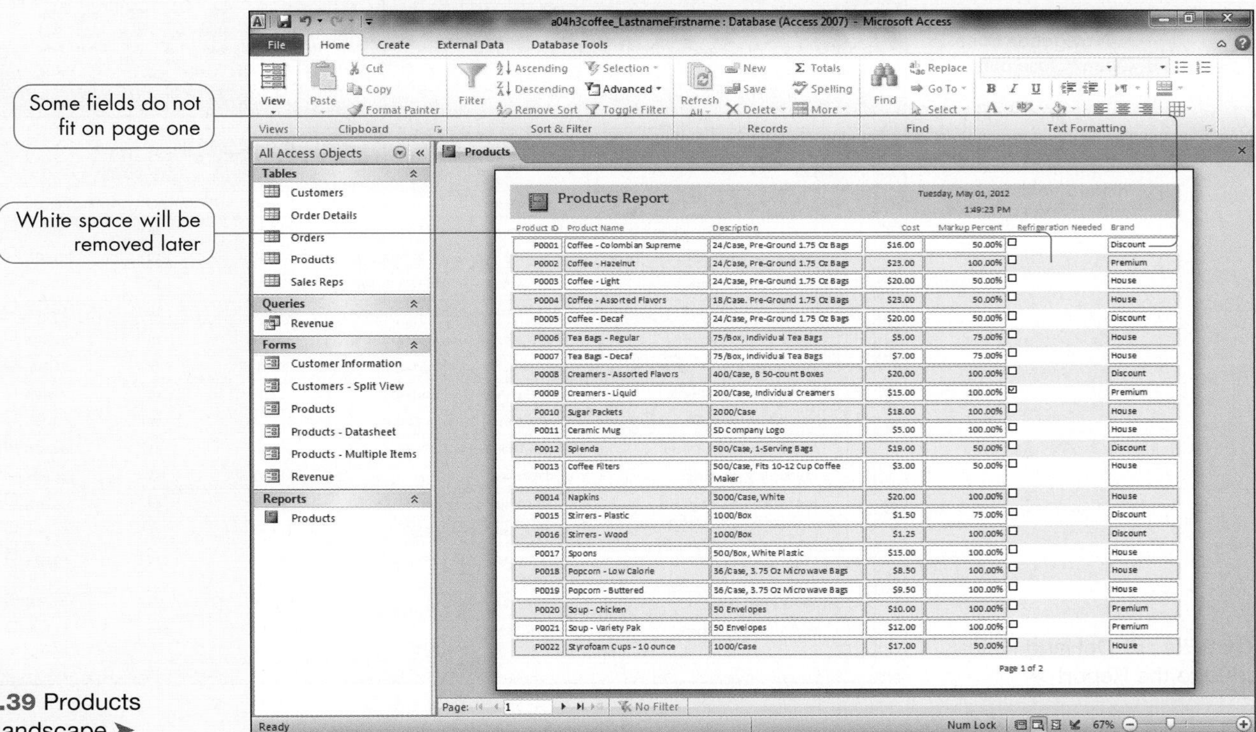

FIGURE 4.39 Products Report in Landscape ➤

a. Open *a04h2coffee_LastnameFirstname* if you closed it at the end of Hands-On Exercise 2. Click the **File tab**, click **Save Database As**, and then type **a04h3coffee_LastnameFirstname**, changing *h2* to *h3*. Click **Save**.

b. Select the **Products table** in the Navigation Pane. Click the **Create tab**, and then click **Report** in the Reports group.

   Access creates a new tabular layout report based on the Products table. The report opens in Layout view ready to edit.

c. Click the **Products title** at the top of the report to select it, and then click again on **Products** and change the title to **Products Report**.

d. Display the report in Print Preview.

The report is too wide for the page; you will change the orientation to Landscape.

e. Click **Close Print Preview**.

f. Click the **Page Setup tab**, and then click **Landscape** in the Page Layout group.

The report changes to Landscape orientation. Most of the columns now fit onto one page. You will make further revisions to the report later on so that it fits on one page.

g. Display the report in Print Preview.

h. Close and save the report as **Products**.

STEP 2 ADD A FIELD TO A REPORT

The Products report you created for Santiago Coffee looks very good (according to Alex). However, Alex asks you to add a new field to the Products table and incorporate that into the Products report. Refer to Figure 4.40 as you complete Step 2.

FIGURE 4.40 OnHand Field Added to the Report ➤

a. Open the Products table, and then click **View** in the Views group to switch to Design view.

You need to add the OnHand field to the Products table.

b. Click the **MarkupPercent field**, and then click **Insert Rows** in the Tools group.

A new blank row appears above the MarkupPercent field.

c. Type **OnHand** in the **Field Name box**, and then select **Number** as the Data Type. In the Field Properties at the bottom, change the Field Size to **Integer**.

d. Save the table. Click **View** to change to Datasheet view.

The new OnHand column appears empty in each row. Next you will add sample data to the new field.

e. Type the following OnHand values starting at the top and continuing through the last row: **10, 10, 10, 10, 10, 10, 10, 25, 25, 55, 40, 55, 125, 75, 200, 200, 200, 75, 75, 42, 42, 175, 175, 22, 37.**

f. Close the Products table.

g. Open the Products report in Layout view.

h. Click the **Open/Close button** on the Navigation Pane to collapse the Navigation Pane so more of the report is visible. Close the Property sheet, if necessary.

i. Click **Add Existing Fields** in the Tools group on the Design tab. Drag the **OnHand field** from the Field List pane onto the Products report between the Cost and MarkupPercent fields. Close the Field List pane.

   Because of the tabular layout control, Access adjusts all the columns to make room for the new OnHand field.

j. Insert a space in the OnHand label control in the Report Header so that it reads *On Hand.*

   A space was added to make the heading more readable.

k. Display the report in Print Preview.

   The report is still too wide for a single page. Next, you will modify the column widths.

l. Save the report.

STEP 3 DELETE A FIELD FROM A REPORT AND ADJUST COLUMN WIDTHS IN A REPORT

The Products report now contains the new OnHand value that Alex requested, but the report is too wide to print on one page. In this step, you delete unnecessary fields and read just the remaining column widths. Refer to Figure 4.41 as you complete Step 3.

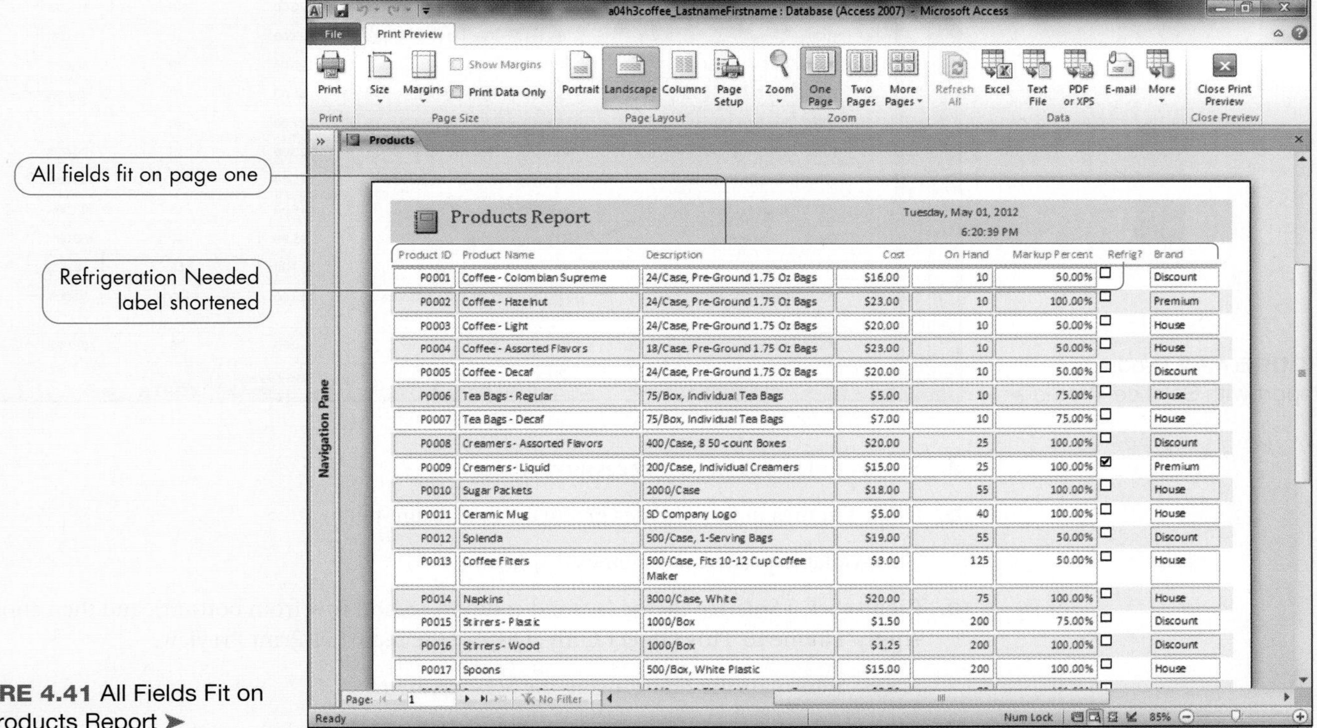

FIGURE 4.41 All Fields Fit on the Products Report ➤

a. Click **Close Print Preview**.

b. Scroll to the right, right-click anywhere on the **Year Introduced column**, and then click **Select Entire Column** from the shortcut menu. Press **Delete** to remove the column.

   The Year Introduced column is removed from the report.

c. Click the **ProductID column heading**, and then drag the right border to the left until the Product ID heading still fits, but any extra white space is removed.

d. Click the **Refrigeration Needed column heading**, and then rename the column **Refrig?**. Adjust the column width of the Refrig? column.

e. Adjust the width of the remaining columns until all fields fit on one page.

f. Display the report in Print Preview.

   This report now fits nicely onto one landscape page.

g. Click **Close Print Preview**, and then save the report.

STEP 4 APPLY A THEME TO THE REPORT

The Products report now contains the new OnHand value and the report fits nicely onto one landscape page. You create two color schemes for Alex and ask him to select one of them. Refer to Figure 4.42 as you complete Step 4.

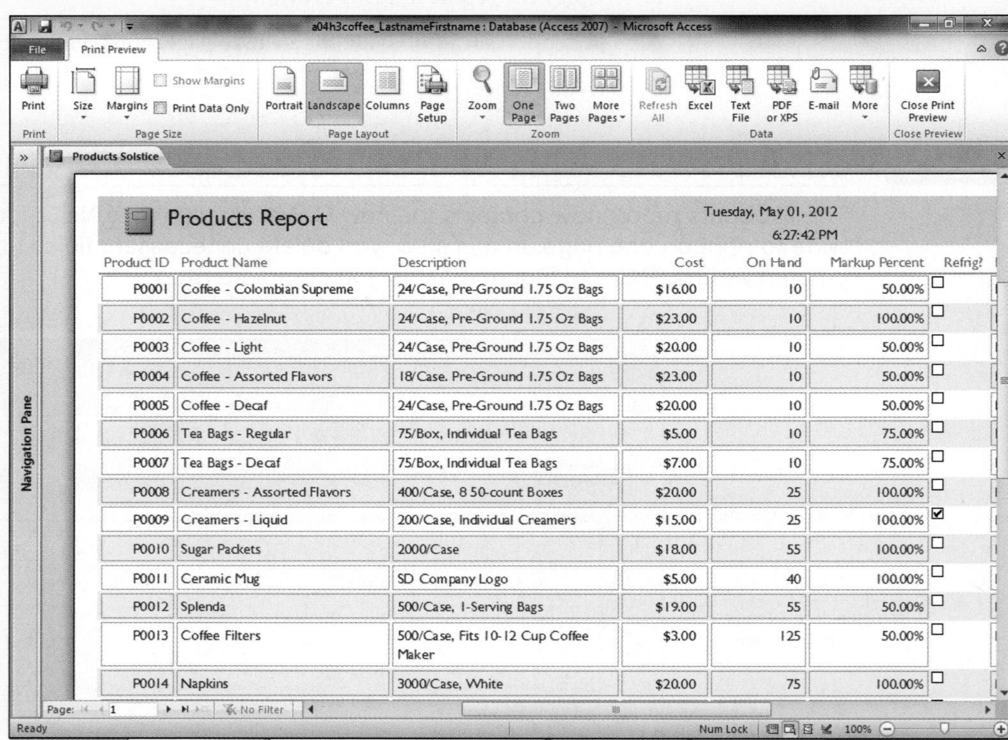

Product ID	Product Name	Description	Cost	On Hand	Markup Percent	Refrig?
P0001	Coffee - Colombian Supreme	24/Case, Pre-Ground 1.75 Oz Bags	$16.00	10	50.00%	☐
P0002	Coffee - Hazelnut	24/Case, Pre-Ground 1.75 Oz Bags	$23.00	10	100.00%	☐
P0003	Coffee - Light	24/Case, Pre-Ground 1.75 Oz Bags	$20.00	10	50.00%	☐
P0004	Coffee - Assorted Flavors	18/Case. Pre-Ground 1.75 Oz Bags	$23.00	10	50.00%	☐
P0005	Coffee - Decaf	24/Case, Pre-Ground 1.75 Oz Bags	$20.00	10	50.00%	☐
P0006	Tea Bags - Regular	75/Box, Individual Tea Bags	$5.00	10	75.00%	☐
P0007	Tea Bags - Decaf	75/Box, Individual Tea Bags	$7.00	10	75.00%	☐
P0008	Creamers - Assorted Flavors	400/Case, 8 50-count Boxes	$20.00	25	100.00%	☐
P0009	Creamers - Liquid	200/Case, Individual Creamers	$15.00	25	100.00%	☑
P0010	Sugar Packets	2000/Case	$18.00	55	100.00%	☐
P0011	Ceramic Mug	SD Company Logo	$5.00	40	100.00%	☐
P0012	Splenda	500/Case, 1-Serving Bags	$19.00	55	50.00%	☐
P0013	Coffee Filters	500/Case, Fits 10-12 Cup Coffee Maker	$3.00	125	50.00%	☐
P0014	Napkins	3000/Case, White	$20.00	75	100.00%	☐

FIGURE 4.42 Products Report with Solstice Theme ➤

a. Switch to Layout view, if necessary.

b. Click **Themes** in the Themes group on the Design tab.

   The available predefined themes display.

c. Right-click a **Solstice theme** (second column, second row from bottom), and then choose **Apply Theme to This Object Only**. Display the report in Print Preview.

   Access reformats the report using the Solstice theme.

d. Click **Close Print Preview**. Click the **File tab**, and then click **Save Object As**. Type **Products Solstice** as the report name, and then click **OK**. Click the **File tab** to return to the report.

   You saved the report with one theme. Now, you will apply a second theme to the report and save it with a different name.

e. Switch to Layout view, and then click **Themes** in the Themes group to apply a different theme.

f. Right-click a **Module theme** (first column, seventh row), and then choose **Apply Theme to This Object Only**. Display the report in Print Preview.

   Compare the Solstice theme to the Module theme.

g. Click **Close Print Preview**. Click the **File tab**, and then click **Save Object As**. Type **Products Module** as the report name, and then click **OK**. Click the **File tab** to return to the report.

STEP 5 CHANGE THE SORTING IN A REPORT

Alex would like the Products Module report to be sorted by Product Name order (rather than ProductID order). You change the sort order and preview again to see the results. Refer to Figure 4.43 as you complete Step 5.

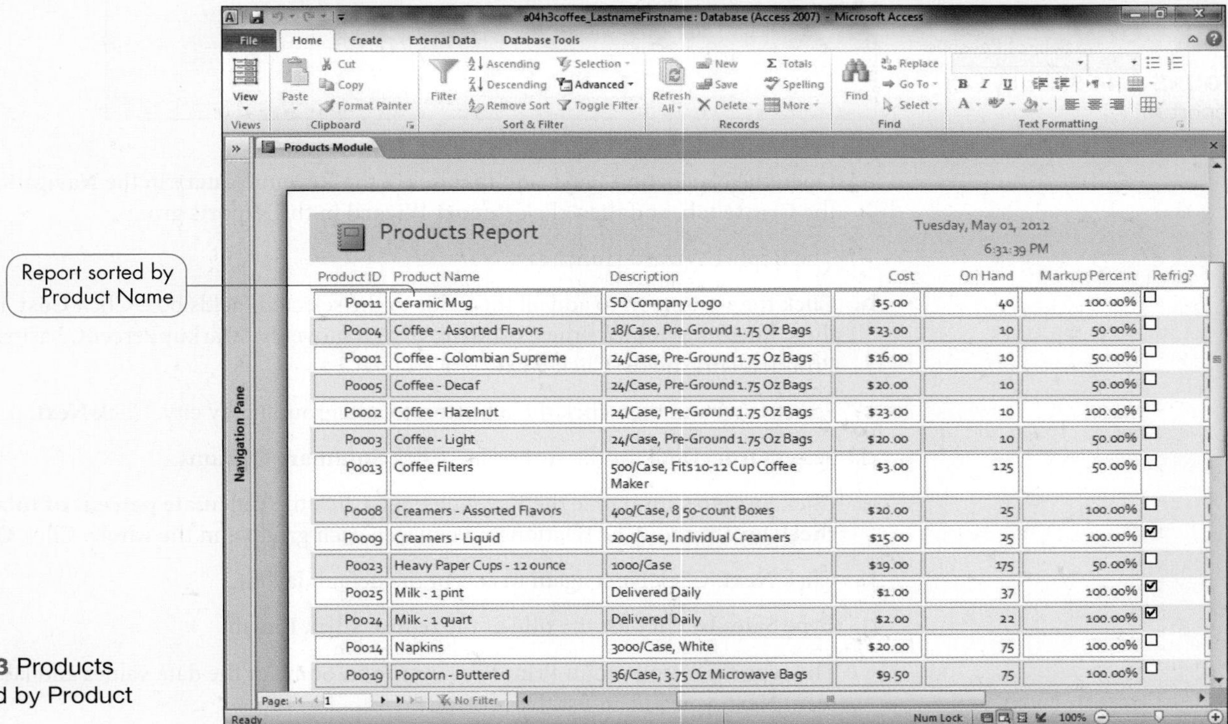

FIGURE 4.43 Products Report Sorted by Product Name ➤

a. Verify the Products Module report is in Layout view.

b. Click **Group & Sort** in the Grouping & Totals group.

   The Add a group and Add a sort options appear at the bottom of the report.

c. Click **Add a sort**.

   A new Sort bar appears at the bottom of the report.

d. Select **ProductName** from the list.

   The report is now sorted by ProductName.

e. Display the report in Print Preview.

f. Close Print Preview, and then save and close the report.

STEP 6 USE THE REPORT WIZARD

You decide to create the Sales by City report for Santiago Coffee. After discussing the report parameters with Alex, you decide to use the Report Wizard. Refer to Figure 4.44 as you complete Step 6.

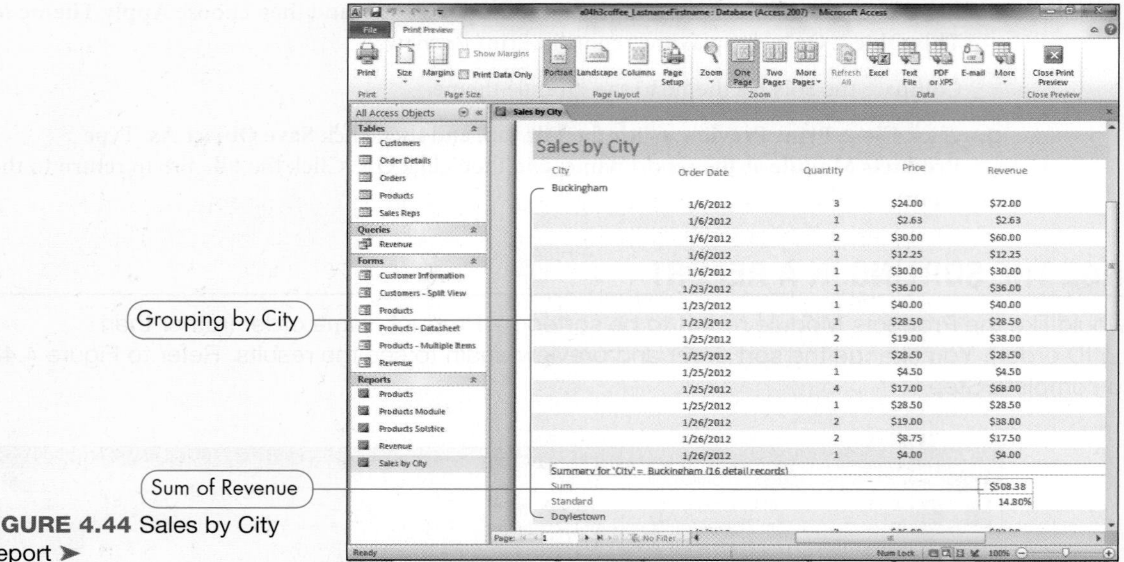

FIGURE 4.44 Sales by City Report ➤

a. Open the Navigation Pane, and then select the **Revenue query** in the Navigation Pane. Click the **Create tab**, and then click **Report Wizard** in the Reports group.

The Report Wizard launches.

b. Click the >> **button** to add all the fields to the selected Fields box. Click **Cost**, and then click the < **button** to remove the Cost field. Also remove the MarkupPercent, Lastname, and ProductName fields. Click **Next**.

c. Select **City**, and then click the > **button** to add grouping by city. Click **Next**.

d. Select **OrderDate** for the sort order. Click **Summary Options**.

e. Click **Sum** to summarize the Revenue field. Click the **Calculate percent of total for sums check box** to show the relationship between each group and the whole. Click **OK**.

f. Click **Next**. Click **Next** again to accept the default layout.

g. Type **Sales by City** for the title of the report. Click **Finish**.

The report is displayed in Print Preview mode. Some of the data values and labels cannot be seen. Next, you will adjust the controls.

h. Click **Close Print Preview**. In Layout view, adjust the controls so all the field values are visible, as shown in Figure 4.44. Widen the totals controls under the Revenue column. Click in the **Revenue total field**, open the Property Sheet, and then select the **Currency format**.

i. Display the report in Print Preview to verify your changes.

j. Close and save the report.

k. Click the **File tab**, and then click **Compact & Repair Database**.

l. Keep the database onscreen if you plan to continue with Hands-On Exercise 4. If not, close the database and exit Access.

Report Sections, Views, and Controls

You just created and modified reports in the previous section. In this section, you will learn about the various views you accessed while creating and modifying the reports. As you work with the report tools to create and modify reports, you will find the need to frequently switch between the four report views in Access—Layout view, Print Preview, Design view, and Report view. Most of your design work will be done in Layout view, but occasionally, you will need to switch to Design view to apply a more advanced feature, such as a calculated field. Users of the report will use Print Preview, Print, and occasionally Layout view. There should be no reason for a user to switch to Layout view or Design view. Modifications to the report should be done by the designated report designer.

To switch between the four views, click the View arrow in the Views group and select the desired view. Layout view and Print Preview are the most common views; Report view is useful for filtering a report based on a field value. You can also switch between views by right-clicking on the report tab or by right-clicking a report in the Navigation Pane. You can also click one of the small view icons in the bottom right of the Access window.

Even though reports have more default sections than forms, working with report sections will be similar to working with form sections.

In this section, you will learn how to identify report sections. You learned about the form sections earlier in this chapter; you can apply that knowledge as you learn about the report sections. Even though reports have more default sections than forms, working with report sections will be similar to working with form sections.

Controls are also covered in this section. Again, the overlap between forms and reports will become evident (and be helpful).

Identifying Report Sections

Access reports are divided into five main sections that can be viewed when you display a report in Design view. You need to become familiar with each section so you can manipulate reports to meet your needs.

Identify the Default Report Sections

In the forms section, you learned that Access divides forms into three main sections. For reports, Access creates five main sections—*Report Header*, *Page Header*, *Detail*, *Page Footer*, and *Report Footer* as shown in Figure 4.45. When in Design view, you can collapse or expand each section as needed, and delete any header or footer section.

The **Report Header section** prints once at the beginning of each report.

The ***Report Header section*** prints at the beginning of each report. This section will usually contain the report title, a logo or other graphic, and the date and time when the report was printed. You can remove this section by right-clicking on a section bar, and then clicking the Report Header/Footer option. Follow the same process to add the Report Header/Footer to a report. When you remove the Report Header, the Report Footer is also removed automatically.

The **Page Header section** appears once at the top of each page.

The ***Page Header section*** appears at the top of each page. Use this section to add or edit column headings on the top of each page. The Page Header will usually contain a horizontal line to separate the column headings from the data values. You can remove this section by right-clicking on a section bar, and then clicking the Page Header/Footer option. Follow the same process to add the Report Header/Footer to a report. If you remove the Page Header, the Page Footer is also removed automatically.

The *Detail* section prints one line for each record in the report's record source. Fields that are connected to the report's record source are known as *bound controls*. The *Detail* section can be hidden, if necessary, by clicking Hide Details in the Grouping & Totals group on the Design tab. For reports that only require summarized data, you will want to hide the details. Access makes it easy for you to show or hide detail levels. Click Hide Details again to redisplay hidden details.

Although the *Detail* section cannot be removed from a report, you can hide it from Print Preview, Layout view, and Design view to show only the headers and footers. This is relevant when the output only requires the totals of each category and not the details that make up the category.

The **Page Footer section** appears once at the bottom of each page.

The ***Page Footer section*** appears at the bottom of each page. Use this section to show page numbers at the bottom of each page. Totals should not be added to this section since the results will produce an error. You can remove this section by right-clicking on a section bar, and then clicking the Page Header/Footer option. Follow the same process to add the Report Header/Footer to a report. If you remove the Page Footer, the Page Header is also removed automatically.

The **Report Footer section** prints once at the bottom of the report.

The ***Report Footer section*** prints one time at the bottom of the report. The Report Footer is commonly used for displaying the grand total of certain columns. You can also display the count of all records in the *Report Footer* section. You can remove this section by right-clicking on a section bar, and then clicking the Report Header/Footer option. Follow the same process to add the Report Header/Footer to a report. If you remove the Report Footer, the Report Header is also removed automatically.

In Figure 4.45, each gray section bar marks the top boundary of a report section. The top bar denotes the top boundary of the Report Header. The bottom bar displays the top boundary of the Report Footer. The grid-like area under the bars shows the space allotted to that section. Notice that the report has no space allocated to the Report Footer. If you decide that the allotted space for a particular section is not needed, you can collapse that section fully so that the section bars are touching. The section remains in the report's design but will not be visible on the Print Preview or the printed page.

Similar to form sections, you can expand or collapse the space between report sections by moving your mouse over the section bar. When the mouse pointer shape changes to a double-headed arrow, drag to expand or collapse the section. A grid-like area appears as your mouse drags down. If you expand or collapse the space allotment for one section, the other sections may also be affected.

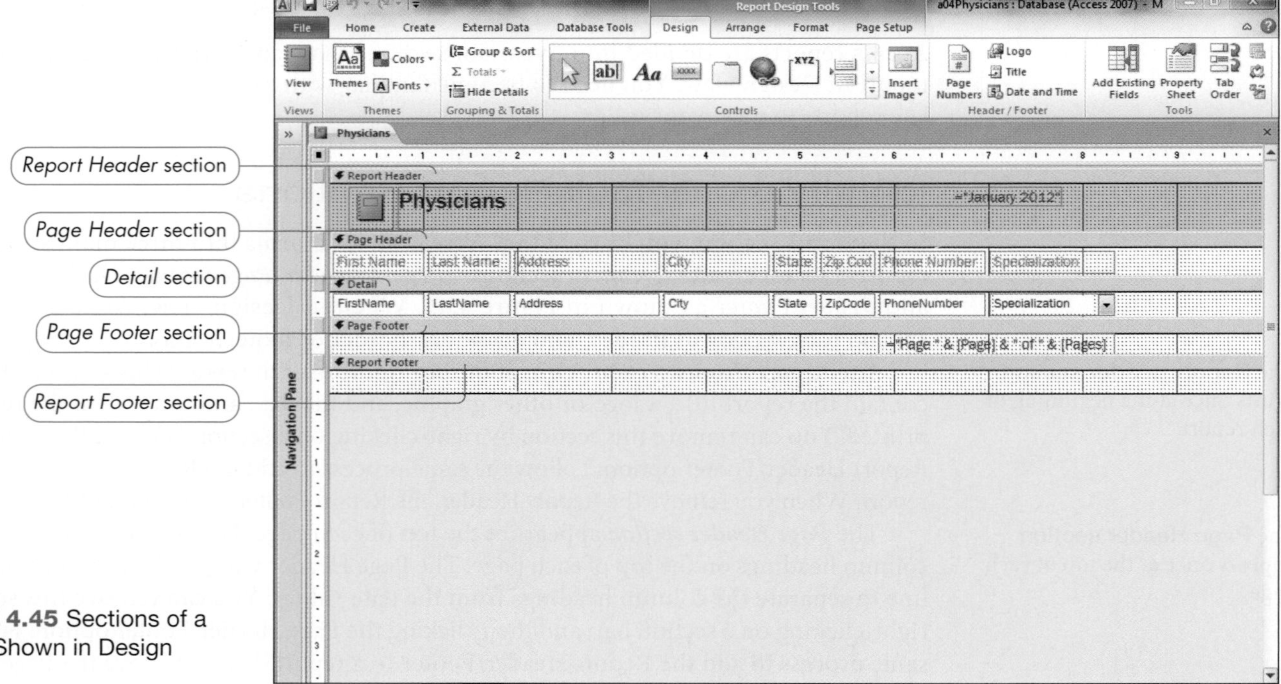

FIGURE 4.45 Sections of a Report, Shown in Design View ➤

Add a Group Header/Footer

In addition to the five main sections listed above, you can also add a custom *group header/footer* section to a report. For example, if you use the Report tool to create a report based on the Physicians table (as shown in Figure 4.46), you may want this report to be grouped by Specialization. It will be easier for users to locate a physician within a given specialization.

Otherwise, you would have to search through the entire list to locate a doctor within a certain specialization.

To add a custom group to a report, open the report in Layout view, and then click Group & Sort in the Grouping & Totals group on the Design tab. The Group, Sort, and Total pane appears below the report. This section enables you to add a custom group. Click Add a Group, and then select the field that you want to group by. For a field to be a candidate for grouping, field values must repeat in the *Detail* section. For example, since specialization repeats in the *Detail* section, it could be used for grouping.

A **Group Header section**, when activated, will appear just above the *Detail* section in Design view, with the name of the field you are grouping.

Once you establish the custom group, a ***Group Header section*** will appear just above the *Detail* section in Design view, along with the name of the field you are grouping. If you select the Specialization field as a custom group, the section will be named *Specialization Header*, as shown in Figure 4.46. Click Print Preview in the Views group to view the data in the report; each time the grouping field value changes, the group header will print with the new value. For example, in a physicians report with five specializations, grouped by Specialization, the group header will print five times, once for each specialization, with the physicians printed under each specialization.

The **Group Footer section**, when activated, will appear just below the *Detail* section in Design view, but only when you select this option in the Group, Sort, and Total pane.

A ***Group Footer section*** appears just below the *Detail* section in Design view, but only when you select this option in the Group, Sort, and Total pane. Locate the group header in question, and then click the More option on that group header bar; then click the *without a footer* arrow and select the *with a footer* option. The group footer is useful for totaling the data at the end of each group. If a group of physicians is part of a major practice, it would be good to know how many physicians are assigned to each specialization. The group footer could display the count of physicians for each specialization.

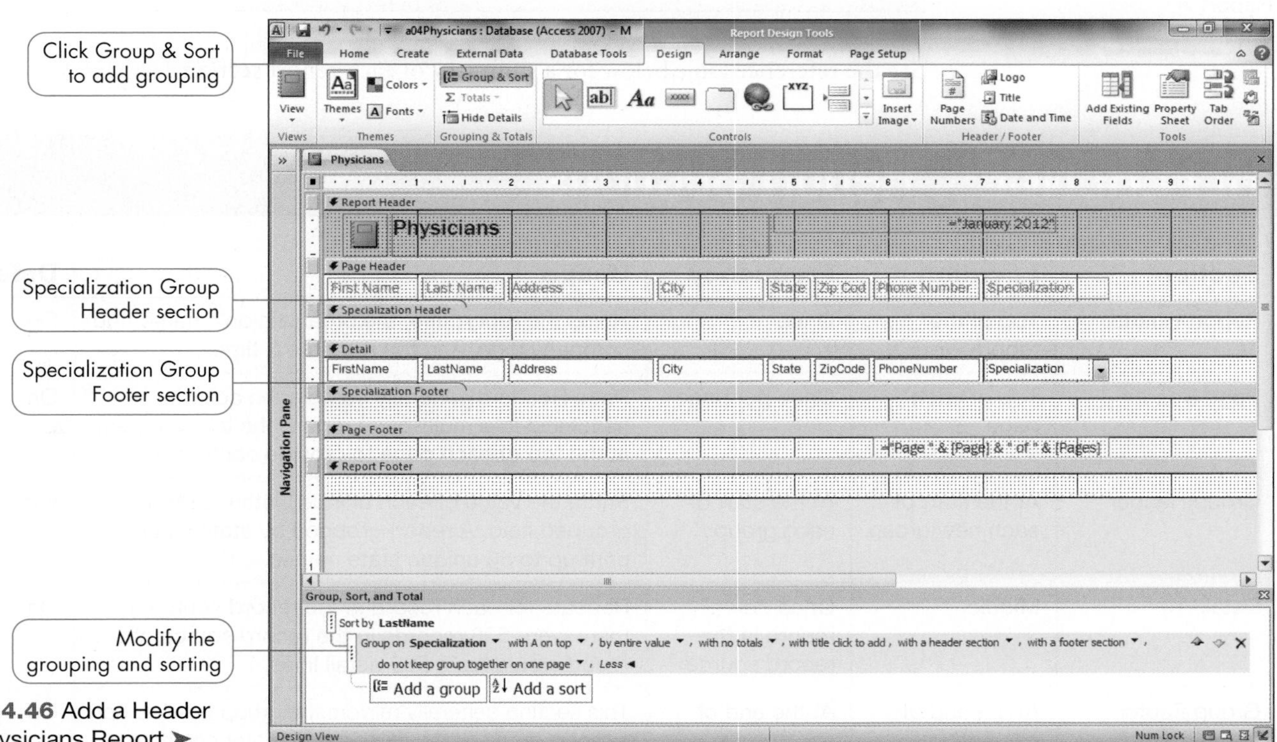

FIGURE 4.46 Add a Header to the Physicians Report ➤

Add Totals to a Group Footer/Report Footer

Often, reports require totals at the group level and/or at the grand total level. For example, the Physicians Report might contain a count of physicians in each Specialization group, and again at the end of the report. Figure 4.47 shows a report with a total number of customers for each sales rep and the total number of customers at the end of the report.

To add totals to a report, first create the group section required for the totals. For example, add the Sales Rep group to a Customers report. Next, in Layout view, click the field that contains the data you want to total, click Totals in the Grouping & Totals group on the

Design tab, and then select the appropriate option. Access will add a total after each group and again at the end of the report.

You remove a total from a report in the same way you add a total. First, select the field that contains the total, click Totals in the Grouping & Totals group, and then uncheck the option you want to remove.

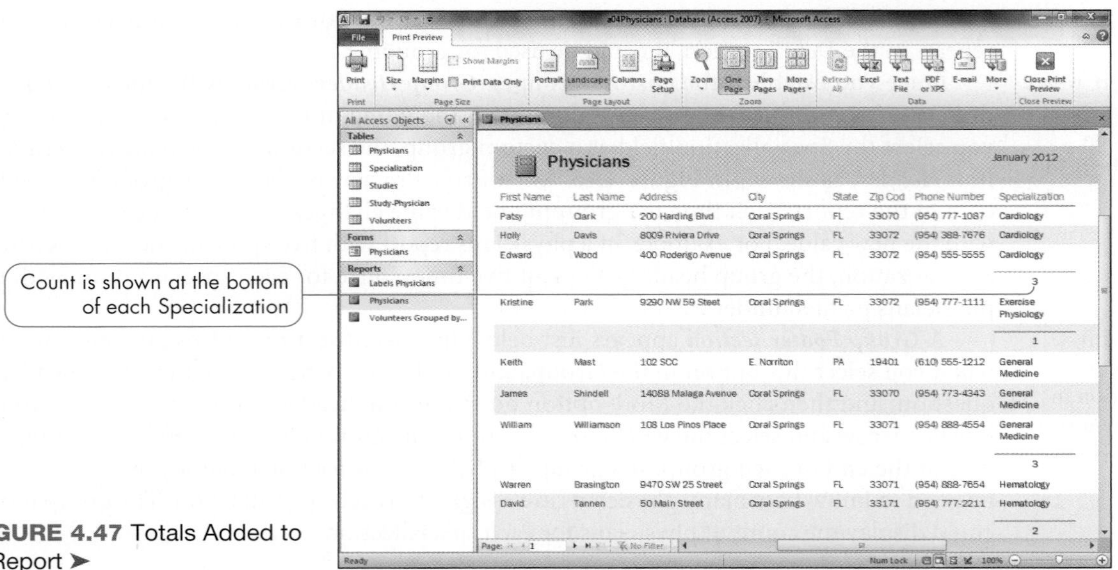

Count is shown at the bottom of each Specialization
Physicians
January 2012

FIGURE 4.47 Totals Added to a Report ➤

See the reference table below for a summary of each report section.

REFERENCE Report Sections

Section	Location	Frequency	Usage	Default
Report Header	Top of the report	Once	Holds the report title, the organization's name, the company logo, and the run date & time.	On
Page Header	Top of each page	Once per page	Page Headers generally contain the column headings. In a multi-page report, the labels repeat at the top of each page to provide continuity.	On
Group Header	At the start of each new group	At the start of each group	Prints the value of each unique instance for a grouped field. A report grouped by state would print up to 50 unique state names.	Off
Detail	Middle	Once per record in the record source	Repeats for each record in the record source. If there were 500 records in the record source, the report would have 500 detail lines.	On
Group Footer	At the end of each group	At the end of each group	This section generally mirrors the group header. For a report grouped by state, group footer could be used to show a count of the records in each state.	Off
Page Footer	Bottom of each page	Once per page	The Page Footer is generally used to print page numbers on the report.	On
Report Footer	End of the report	Once	Use the Report Footer to print grand totals or other aggregate information for the records.	On

TIP Report Footer Confusion

In Design view, the *Report Footer* section is located below the *Page Footer* section. However, in Print Preview, the Report Footer is positioned above the Page Footer. This may cause some confusion at first; however, the *Report Footer* section will be needed to produce grand totals at the end of a report.

Revising Reports Using Report Views

Access provides different views for a report similar to the different views in tables, queries, and forms. Tables and queries have Design view and Datasheet view. Forms have Layout view, Form view, and Design view. Reports have Layout view, Print Preview, Design view, and Report view. To switch between certain views, click View in the Views group, or click the View arrow, and then select a view from the list. Each view is described in the sections below.

Layout View

Use Layout view to alter the report design while still viewing the data. You should use Layout view to add or delete fields in the report, modify field properties, change the column widths, add grouping and sorting levels to a report, and to filter data by excluding certain records. Although Layout view appears similar to Print Preview, you will find sufficient variations between the two views, so that you will always need to verify the report in Print Preview to evaluate all the changes made in Layout view.

Print Preview

Print Preview enables you to see exactly what the report will look like when it is printed.

Print Preview enables you to see exactly what the report will look like when it is printed. Most users prefer to use Print Preview prior to printing the report. This enables you to intercept errors in reports before you send the report to the printer. You cannot modify the design in this view; switch to Layout view or Design view to modify the design. By default, Print Preview will display all the pages in the report. Figure 4.47 shows an Access report in Print Preview.

Design View

Design view displays the report's design without displaying the data. You can perform many of the same tasks in Design view as you can in Layout view—add and delete fields, add and remove sorting and grouping layers, rearrange columns, adjust column widths, and modify report elements. When a report is very long, Design view is useful because you can alter the design without needing to scroll through pages of data. However, after you make a change in Design view, it is best to switch to Layout view or Print Preview to examine the final output. You need to experiment using both the Layout view and Design view to decide which view you prefer. As with forms, some changes to reports can only be done in Design view. Figure 4.46 displays the Physicians report in Design view.

Report View

Report view enables you to see what the printed report will look like in a continuous page layout.

Report view enables you to see what a printed report will look like in a continuous page layout. Because Report view is similar to Layout view, but not used as frequently, this view will not be discussed further in this chapter.

TIP Always Preview Access Reports Before Printing

Because databases contain a great deal of information, Access reports may become very long, requiring many pages to print. Experienced Access users always use Print Preview prior to printing their reports. Some reports may require hundreds of pages to print—better to know that before sending it to the printer. Other reports may be formatted incorrectly and a blank page may print after each actual page. It would be better to correct this problem prior to sending it to the printer.

Identifying Control Types in Reports

If you examine the fields in a report, such as the one in Figure 4.47, you will notice that each field has a label (heading) at the top with a column of data values under the heading. As you learned in the forms section earlier in this chapter, a text box displays the data found in the record source and a label is a literal word or phrase to describe the data. The heading in Figure 4.47 is a label, and the data values are displayed using a text box.

The label and text box controls are among the many types of controls found on the Controls group on the Design tab when you are in the Design view of a report. As discussed earlier in the forms section, controls can be categorized as bound, unbound, or calculated.

> **TIP Report Column Headings**
>
> The column headings in reports are based on the captions used in the source table or query. If captions do not exist in the source table or query, you may need to edit the label controls that represent the column headings. For example, the Products table contains the MarkupPercent field, which includes the caption Markup Percent. Markup Percent becomes the column heading in the Products report. If the caption was not used in the Products table, then you would have to add a space between Markup and Percent in the column label.

Work with Controls

Bound controls are text boxes that are connected to a field in a table or a query. These controls display different data for each new record that is printed. To add a bound control to a report, switch to Layout view, and then drag a field from the Field List pane onto the report.

Unbound controls are labels and other decorative design elements. These controls usually describe and decorate the data rather than display the data. These controls remain the same each time a new record is printed. Unbound controls include labels, lines, borders, and images. Add an unbound control to a report using the Controls group on the Design tab in the Design view of a report.

Calculated controls contain an expression that generates a calculated result when displayed in Print Preview. The expression can contain field names from the report's record source, constants, or functions. Use a text box, found in the Controls group on the Design tab, while in Design view to create a calculated control.

Add a Calculated Control to a Report

To add a calculated control to the report, switch to Design view, and then click Text Box in the Controls group on the Design tab. Place a text box at the desired location, then enter the expression to create the calculation. Format the control as needed.

In Hands-On Exercise 4, you will create a report, add sorting and grouping to refine the content, work with data aggregates, and add a new field to the report.

Quick Concepts Check

1. Name the five default sections of a report.
2. What are the benefits of a Group Header and a Group Footer? Give an example.
3. What is the difference between Print Preview and Report view?
4. What is the difference between controls in forms and controls in reports?

4 Report Sections, Views, and Controls

The reports you created for Alex are working nicely. Alex would like you to modify the layout of the new reports to make them more attractive. You suggest he add grouping to one of the reports.

Skills covered: Identify the Default Report Sections and Add a Group Header/Footer in Layout View • Add Totals to a Group Footer/Report Footer in Layout View • Work with Controls in Design View • Add a Calculated Control to a Report in Design View

STEP 1 IDENTIFY THE DEFAULT REPORT SECTIONS AND ADD A GROUP HEADER/FOOTER IN LAYOUT VIEW

Alex asks you to make several changes to the Monthly Revenue by Salesperson report. First, you update the Sales Rep table with the latest information. Refer to Figure 4.48 as you complete Step 1.

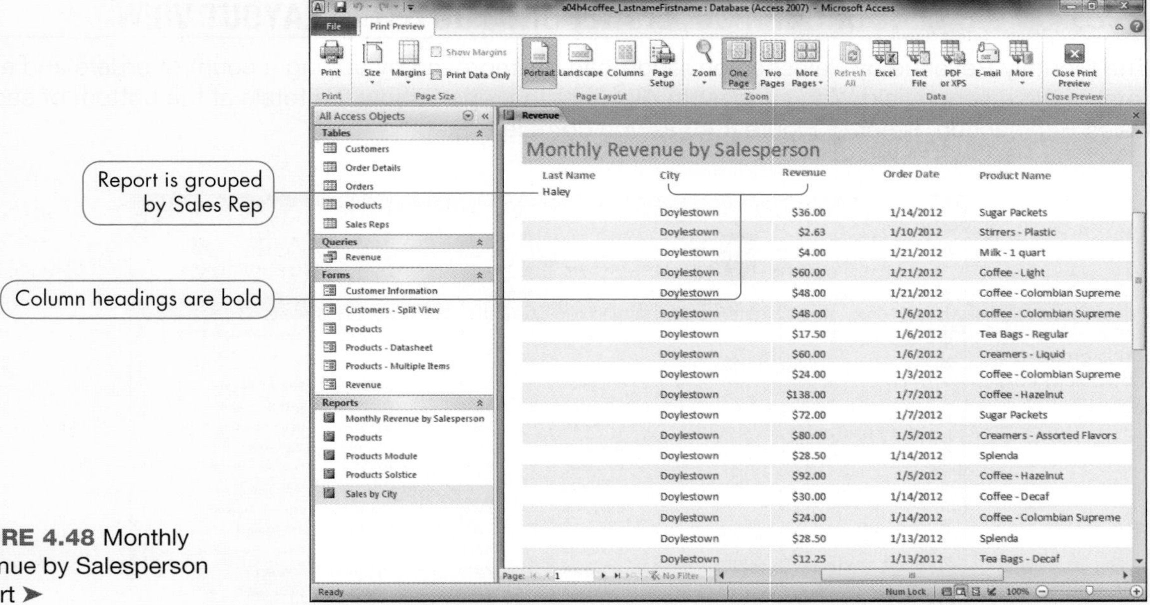

FIGURE 4.48 Monthly Revenue by Salesperson Report ➤

a. Open *a04h3coffee_LastnameFirstname* if you closed it at the end of Hands-On Exercise 3. Click the **File tab**, click **Save Database As**, and then type **a04h4coffee_LastnameFirstname**, changing *h3* to *h4*. Click **Save**.

b. Open the Sales Reps table. Add your first name and last name to sales rep S0002. Leave the other fields as they are. Close the table.

c. Open the Customers table. For all the customers in the city of Buckingham, change the Sales Rep ID to **003**. The leading *S* appears automatically due to the Format property. Close the table.

d. Select the **Revenue query** in the Navigation Pane, click the **Create tab**, and then click **Report Wizard** in the Reports group.

e. Add the **LastName**, **City**, **Revenue**, **OrderDate**, and **ProductName fields** to the Selected Fields list. Click **Next** four times to accept the default settings. The wizard now asks "What title do you want for your report?" Type **Monthly Revenue by Salesperson**.

The completed report is displayed in Print Preview.

f. Close Print Preview, and then switch to Layout view.

   Next, you will add the Last Name group.

g. Click **Group & Sort** in the Grouping and Sorting group. Click **Add a group**, and then select **LastName**. Close Group & Sort.

   The report now contains the LastName group.

h. Select the **Last Name column heading**, and then click **Bold** in the Font group on the Format tab. Apply bold to the rest of the column headings.

i. Select the **Last Name column heading**, and then type **Sales Rep**.

j. Modify the report column widths so the column spacing is uniform (as shown in Figure 4.48).

k. Switch to Print Preview.

   The report is now divided into Sales Rep groups.

l. Click **Close Print Preview**, and then save the report.

STEP 2 ADD TOTALS TO A GROUP FOOTER/REPORT FOOTER IN LAYOUT VIEW

The Monthly Revenue by Salesperson report can be improved by adding a count of orders and a total of the revenue field. You suggest to Alex that the report show the totals at the bottom of each *Sales Rep* section. Refer to Figure 4.49 as you complete Step 2.

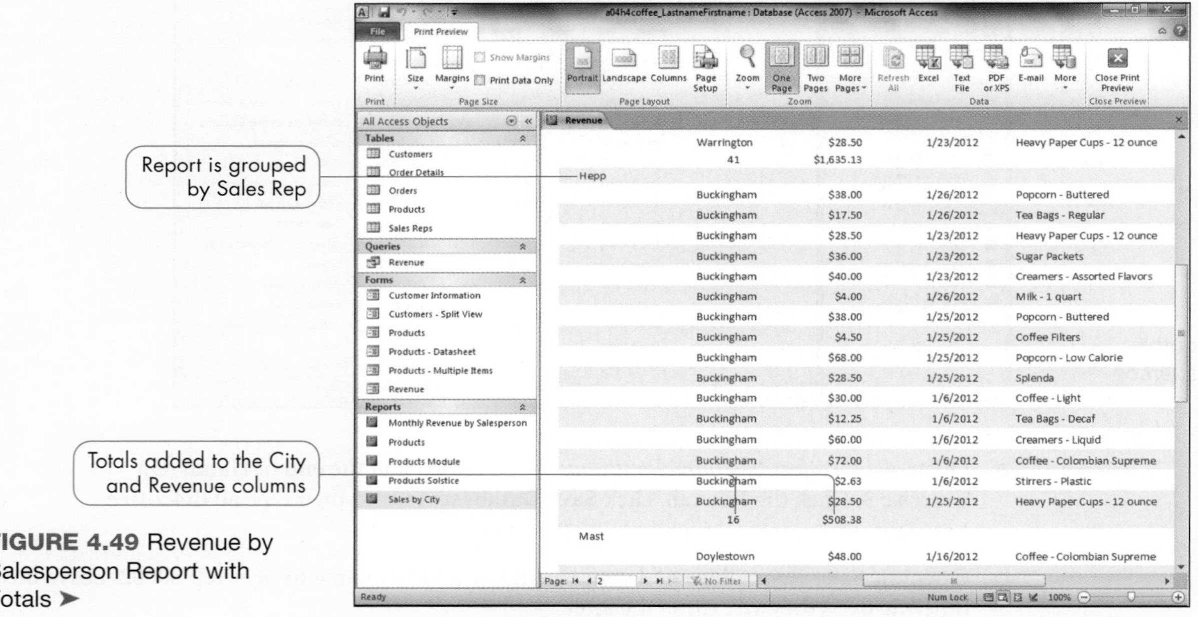

Report is grouped by Sales Rep
Totals added to the City and Revenue columns

FIGURE 4.49 Revenue by Salesperson Report with Totals ➤

a. Verify the Monthly Revenue by Salesperson report is open in Layout view. Click the **Revenue field**, click **Totals** in the Grouping & Totals group, and then select **Sum** from the list.

   A sum of revenue is now added to the group footer of each Sales Rep group.

b. Click the **View arrow** in the Views group, and then select **Print Preview**.

c. Advance to the next page to view the order count for each Sales Rep.

d. Click **Close Print Preview**, and then click the **City field**. Click **Totals** in the Grouping & Totals group, and then select **Count Records**.

e. Scroll down until the first totals control in the Revenue column is visible. Select the **totals calculated control box**, and then click **Property Sheet** in the Tools group. Click the **Format arrow** on the Format tab, and then choose **Currency** from the list.

   The totals are now formatted for currency.

f. Scroll down to the bottom of the report, and then click the **grand total calculated control box** under the Revenue column. Click the **Format arrow** on the Format tab, and then choose **Currency** from the list. Close the Property Sheet.

   The grand total is now formatted for currency.

g. Display the report in Print Preview. Advance through all the pages.

   The total revenue is now added to the group footer of each Sales Rep group.

h. Click **Close Print Preview**, and then scroll to the bottom of the report.

   The count of orders and the total revenue were automatically added to the Report Footer.

i. Switch to Design View.

   In Design view, you can see the seven sections of the Monthly Revenue by Salesperson report. The data is no longer visible.

j. Save the report.

STEP 3 WORK WITH CONTROLS IN DESIGN VIEW

Alex asks you to add Santiago Coffee Shop at the top of the Monthly Revenue by Salesperson report. You add a new label to the report section and make a few other formatting enhancements. Refer to Figure 4.50 as you complete Step 3.

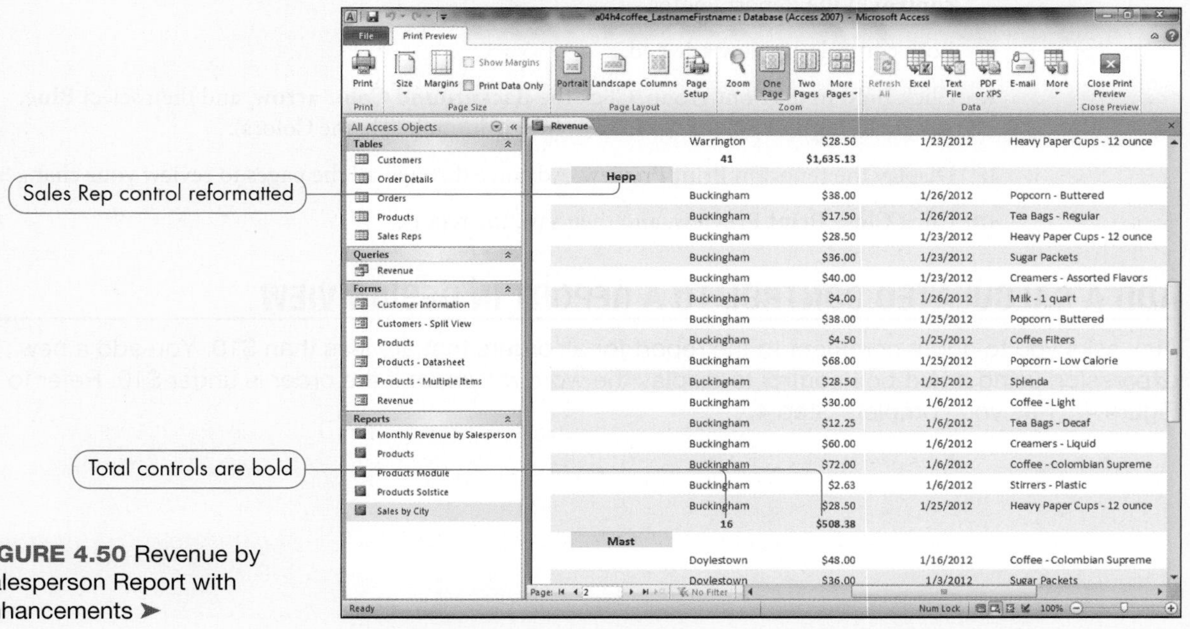

FIGURE 4.50 Revenue by Salesperson Report with Enhancements ➤

a. Click the **Monthly Revenue by Salesperson label** in the Report Header. Press ↓ to move the label down 1/4" to make room for another label.

When you move the title down using ↓, the *Report Header* section grows automatically.

b. Click **Label** in the Controls group on the Design tab, and then click just above the *M* in the Monthly Revenue title.

   The label control is ready for you to type a phrase.

c. Type **Santiago Coffee Shop** into the new label, and then press **Enter**.

   An orange border indicates the label control is still selected.

d. Click the **Format tab**, and then use the **Font group commands** to modify the new label:

   Font Size: **14**
   Font Color: **Dark Blue, Text 2, Darker 25%** (fifth row, fourth column)
   Style: **Italic**

e. Resize the new label using the bottom-right corner of the control box. Widen the box so the entire phrase is visible.

f. Click the **LastName text box** in the *LastName Header* section, and then modify the properties as follows:

   Font Size: **12**
   Font Color: **Dark Blue, Text 2** (first row, fourth column)
   Style: **Bold**
   Align: **Center**
   Background Color: **Yellow**

g. Resize the **LastName text box** using the bottom-right corner of the control box. Widen the field so the entire last name is visible when you switch to Layout view.

h. Click the **Count control** in the LastName Footer, and then click **Center** in the Font group. Hold down **Shift**, and then click the **Revenue Sum control** in the LastName Footer.

   Both controls are now selected.

i. Click **Bold** in the Font group.

j. Click the **Count control** in the Report Footer, hold down **Shift**, and then click the **Sum control** in the Report Footer.

   Both controls are now selected.

k. Click **Bold** in the Font group. Click the **Background Color arrow**, and then select **Blue, Accent 1, Lighter 80%** (second row, fifth column in Theme Colors).

l. Display the report in Print Preview. Advance through all the pages to review your changes.

m. Click **Close Print Preview**, and then save the report.

STEP 4 ADD A CALCULATED CONTROL TO A REPORT IN DESIGN VIEW

Alex asks you to add a comment to the report for all orders that are less than $10. You add a new expression using a text box control to display the word *minimum* if the order is under $10. Refer to Figure 4.51 as you complete Step 4.

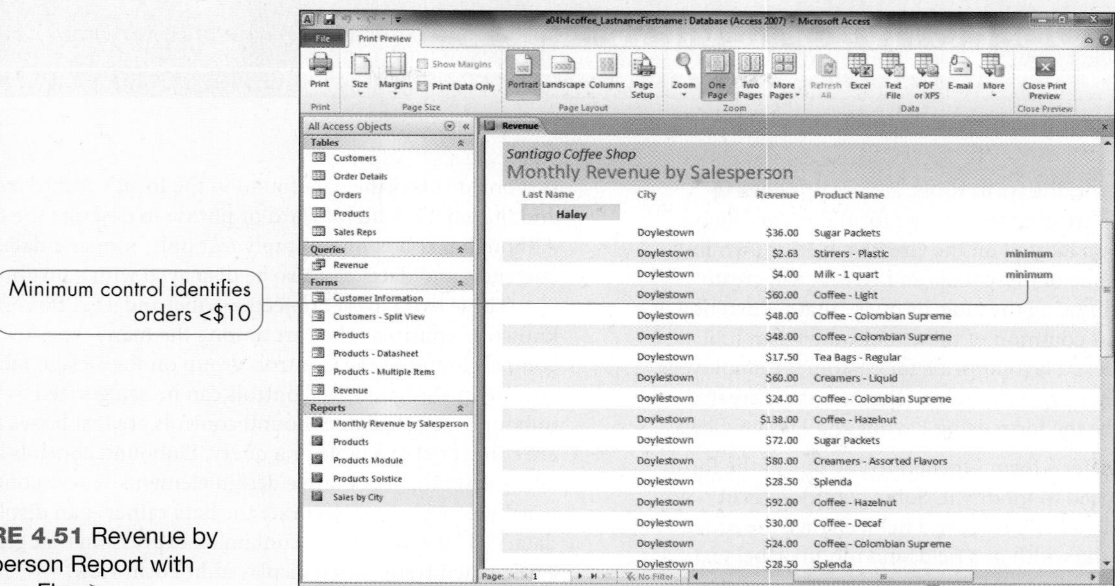

FIGURE 4.51 Revenue by Salesperson Report with Minimum Flag ➤

a. Switch to Design View if necessary. Click the **OrderDate box**, press **Delete**, and then delete the Order Date label. Drag the **Product Name box and label** to the **4 1/2"** mark on the horizontal ruler, moving the other labels and boxes, if necessary.

b. Click **Text Box** in the Controls group on the Design tab. Click in the **Detail section** to the right of the ProductName control.

   A new text box is created along with a label. The label overlaps the ProductName text box.

c. Click the new **Label control**, and then press **Delete**.

   The label control is deleted.

> **TROUBLESHOOTING:** If you delete the text box control, click Undo to restore the deleted control and delete only the Label control.

d. Click **Property Sheet** in the Tools group. Click the new text box, labeled *Unbound*, to select it.

e. Click the **All tab** in the Property Sheet pane. Type **MinimumOrder** in the **Name property box** and **="minimum"** in the **Control Source property box.** Change the Border Style property to **Transparent**.

f. Display the report in Print Preview.

   Minimum shows on all orders. You will now add an expression so that only orders less than $10 will show.

g. Click **Close Print Preview**. Verify the MinimumOrder control is selected.

h. Click the **Control Source**, and then press **Shift+F2** to expand the cell. Change the expression in the Control Source property to **=IIf(Revenue < 10, "minimum", "")**. Click **OK**.

   The second set of quote marks is an empty text string.

i. Display the report in Print Preview. Advance through all the pages to examine the minimum orders. Click **Close Print Preview**.

j. Click the **MinimumOrder control** in the *Detail* section, click **Bold** in the Font group on the Format tab, click the **Font Color arrow**, and then select **Red** under Standard Colors.

k. Display the report in Print Preview. Review the changes to the report, and then close and save the report.

l. Click the **File tab,** and then click **Compact & Repair Database**.

m. Exit Access.

n. Submit based on your instructor's directions.

CHAPTER OBJECTIVES REVIEW

After reading this chapter, you have accomplished the following objectives:

1. **Create forms using the form tools.** Access provides 16 different tools for creating forms. The form tools are found in the Forms group located on the Create tab, as shown in Figure 4.1. Click one of these tools and Access will create an automatic form using the table or query that is currently selected. The most common of these tools, the Form tool, is used to create stacked layout forms for customers, employees, products, and other primary tables. Once a form is created, you can customize the form using Layout and Design views.
2. **Modify a form.** After a form is generated by one of the form tools, you often need to modify it. Some common form changes are to add a field, remove a field, change the order of fields, change the width of a field, and modify label text. These changes, as well as adding a theme, can be made in a form's Layout view. Advanced changes, such as adding a calculated field or adding VBA code, can be made in a form's Design view.
3. **Sort records in a form.** When a form is created using a form tool, the sort order of the records in the form is dependent on the sort order of the record source. To modify the sort order of a form, open the form in Form view, and then select the field you want to use for sorting and click Ascending in the Sort & Filter group on the Home tab.
4. **Identify form sections.** Access forms, by default, are divided into three sections—Form Header, Detail, and Form Footer. These sections can vary depending on what type of form you create. Form designers also have the option of removing certain sections from a form. The *Form Header* section is displayed at the top of each form. This section will usually contain the form title, a logo or other graphic, and the date and time the report was printed. The *Detail* section displays the records in the form's record source. The *Form Footer* section is displayed at the bottom of the form. The Form Footer is commonly used to display totals for relevant field values.
5. **Revise forms using form views.** Access provides different views for a form, similar to the different views in tables and queries. Forms can be displayed in Layout view, Form view, and Design view. Use Layout view to alter the form design while still viewing the data. Use Design view to add or delete fields in a form, modify field properties, change the column widths, and enhance a form by adding a color scheme or styling.

   Most users will only see Form view; if a form needs modification, the user should notify the database designer. Use Design view to perform advanced changes to a form's design. It provides you the most advanced method of editing an Access form. You can perform many of the same tasks in Design view as you can in Layout view—add and delete fields, change the field order, adjust field widths, modify labels, and customize form elements.
6. **Identify control types in forms.** If you examine the elements on a form, you will notice that each field has a Label control box on the left and a Text Box control on the right. The text box displays the data found in the form's record source and the label is a literal word or phrase to describe the data. Although text box might imply text only, numeric data, currency, and dates can also be displayed with a text box.

   These two types of objects—Label and Text Box—are known as controls. They are among the many types of controls found in the Controls group on the Design tab when you are in Design view. Controls can be categorized as bound, unbound, or calculated. Bound controls are text boxes that are connected to a table or a query. Unbound controls are labels and other decorative design elements. These controls usually describe and decorate the data rather than display the data. Calculated controls contain an expression that generates a calculated result when displayed in Form view.
7. **Create reports using report tools.** Access provides five different report tools for creating reports. The report tools are found in the Reports group located on the Create tab, as shown in Figure 4.25. Click one of these tools and Access will create an automatic report using the table or query that is currently selected. The most common of the tools, the Report tool, is used to instantly create a tabular layout report based on the table or query currently selected. The Report Wizard will ask a series of questions and help you create the most appropriate report based on your answers. Use the Labels tool to create a page of labels using one of the preformatted templates provided by Access. After you create a report, you can perform modifications in Layout view and Design view.
8. **Modify a report.** After a report is generated by one of the report tools, you will usually need to modify it. The most common changes are to add a field, remove a field, change the order of fields, change the width of a field, and modify the title. These changes, as well as adding a grouping level, adding a sort order, and adding a theme, can be made in a report's Layout view or Design view. Advanced changes, such as adding a calculated field or adding VBA code, can be made in a report's Design view.
9. **Sort records in a report.** When a report is created using the Report tool, the sort order of the records in the report is initially dependent on the sort order of the record source. A report can be sorted while in Layout view or Design view by clicking Group & Sort in the Grouping & Totals group on the Design tab. The Group, Sort, and Total pane will appear at the bottom of the report. This section enables you to set the sort order for the report and override the sorting in the report's record source.
10. **Identify report sections.** Access reports are divided into five main sections, as shown in Figure 4.45. Each section can be collapsed or expanded as needed, but only in Design view. You can also remove any of the sections, except the *Detail* section, by right-clicking any section bar, and then clicking the *Header/Footer* section you wish to remove. The *Report Header* section prints once at the beginning of each report. The *Page Header* section appears once at the top of each

page. The *Detail* section prints one line for each record in the report's record source. The *Page Footer* section appears once at the bottom of each page. The *Report Footer* section prints once at the bottom of the report.

11. **Revise reports using report views.** Access provides different views for a report similar to the different views in tables, queries, and forms. Reports have Layout view, Print Preview, Design view, and Report view. To switch between views, click the View arrow in the Views group and select the Layout view or Design view. Use Layout view to alter the report design while still viewing the data. Print Preview enables you to see the closest approximation of what the report will look like when it is printed. Design view displays the report's layout without displaying the data. Report view enables you to see what the printed report will look like in a continuous page layout.

12. **Identify control types in reports.** If you examine the fields on a report, such as the one in Figure 4.47, you will notice that each field has a label (heading) at the top with a column of data values under the heading. A text box displays the data found in the record source and a label is a literal word or phrase to describe the data. The Label and Text Box controls are among the many types of controls found in the Controls group when you are in the Layout view or the Design view of a report. As discussed earlier, controls can be categorized as bound, unbound, or calculated. Bound controls are text boxes that are connected to a table or a query. Unbound controls are labels and other decorative design elements. Calculated controls contain an expression that generates a calculated result when displayed in Print Preview.

KEY TERMS

Bound control ***p.752***
Calculated control ***p.753***
Datasheet form ***p.738***
Design view ***p.752***
Detail section ***p.749***
Form ***p.734***
Form Footer section ***p.749***
Form Header section ***p.749***
Form tool ***p.734***
Form view ***p.750***
Group Footer section ***p.779***
Group Header section ***p.779***
Label control ***p.752***
Label Wizard ***p.767***
Layout control ***p.740***
Layout view ***p.736***
Mailing label ***p.767***
Multiple Items form ***p.737***
Office Theme ***p.740***
Page Footer section ***p.778***
Page Header section ***p.777***
Print Preview ***p.781***
Record source ***p.735***
Report ***p.761***
Report Footer section ***p.778***
Report Header section ***p.777***
Report tool ***p.761***
Report view ***p.781***
Report Wizard ***p.763***
Split form ***p.737***
Splitter bar ***p.737***
Stacked layout form ***p.736***
Stacked layout report ***p.763***
Tabular layout form ***p.736***
Tabular layout report ***p.762***
Text box control ***p.752***
Unbound control ***p.753***
Visual Basic for Applications (VBA) ***p.738***

MULTIPLE CHOICE

1. Which form tool does not place controls onto a form automatically?
   (a) Form Wizard
   (b) Form tool
   (c) Form Design tool
   (d) Datasheet tool

2. The Design view for a form enables you to do all of the following except:
   (a) Modify the form.
   (b) Add a new group.
   (c) View the data as it will be presented in the form.
   (d) Add a background color.

3. Which of the following guides you as you create a new report?
   (a) Report tool
   (b) Report Wizard
   (c) Blank Report tool
   (d) Report Design tool

4. Use the ____________ to see exactly what the printed report will look like before printing.
   (a) Report tool
   (b) Report Wizard
   (c) Report view
   (d) Print Preview

5. The easiest way to modify control widths in a form is in:
   (a) Layout view.
   (b) Form view.
   (c) Design view.
   (d) Report view.

6. What happens if you click a text box control in Layout view, and then press Delete?
   (a) The control is deleted from the report, but the other controls do not adjust to the empty space.
   (b) Nothing; you cannot change fields in Layout view.
   (c) The record is deleted from the report and from the database.
   (d) An error message appears stating that you should not attempt to delete records in a report.

7. The mouse pointer shape changes to a ____________ when you widen or narrow a column in Layout view.
   (a) single arrow
   (b) hand
   (c) two-headed arrow
   (d) four-headed arrow

8. Which of these is not a section in an Access form?
   (a) *Detail* section
   (b) *Group* section
   (c) *Form Header* section
   (d) *Form Footer* section

9. Which statement is true about controls?
   (a) Unbound controls are not used in reports.
   (b) Unbound controls are not used in the *Detail* section.
   (c) A calculated field is created with a text box control.
   (d) A form's title is usually created with the title control.

10. To organize your data in categories, you would use:
    (a) Sorting.
    (b) Grouping.
    (c) Queries.
    (d) Calculated fields.

1 Financial Management

You are working as a customer service representative for a financial management firm. Your task is to contact a list of prospective customers and introduce yourself and the services of your company. The list is currently in Excel but you decide it will be easier to create an Access database to store the data. You will create a Leads table and then copy and paste the Excel data into the new table. You decide that a form will help you add and update the data. After creating the form, you will customize it in Layout view. This exercise follows the same set of skills as used in Hands-On Exercises 1 and 2 in the chapter. Refer to Figure 4.52 as you complete this exercise.

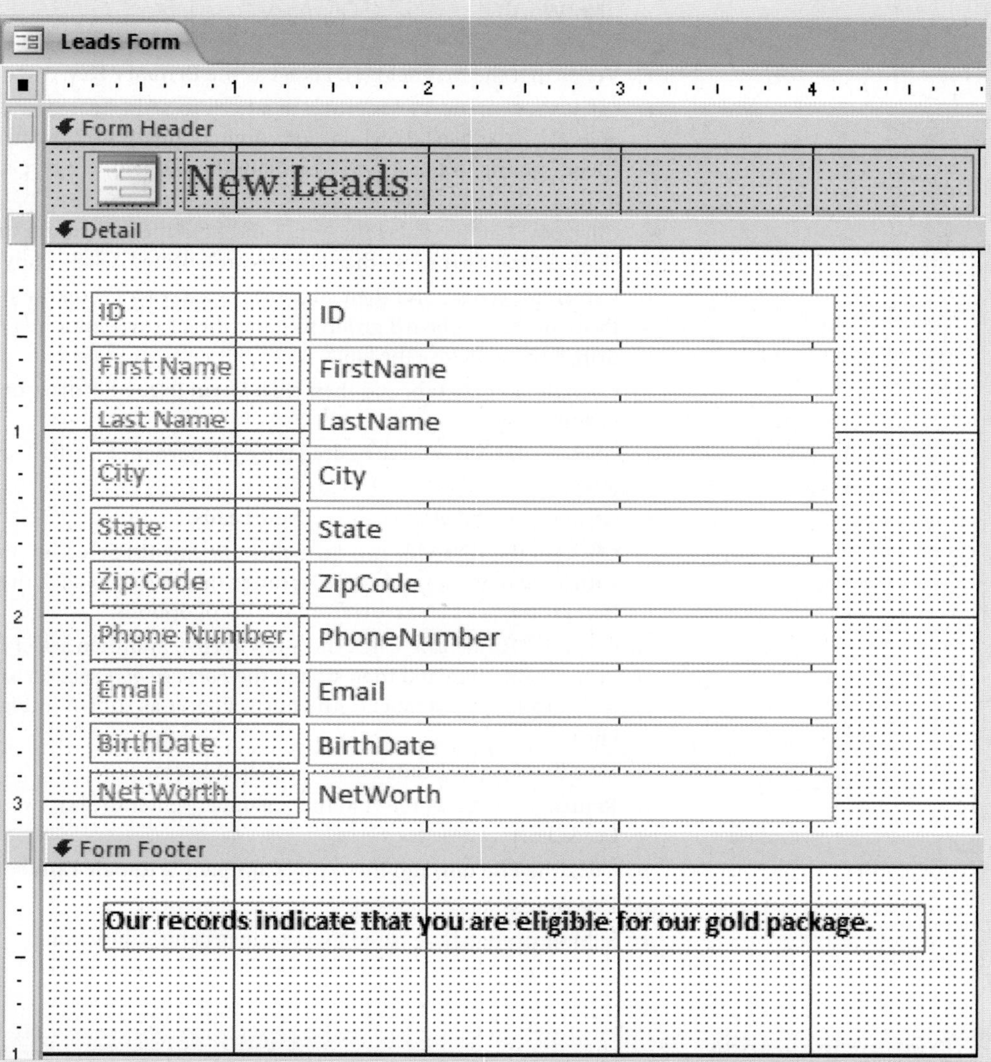

FIGURE 4.52 Leads Form in Form View ➤

a. Open Access, and then type **a04p1prospects_LastnameFirstname** in the **File Name box**. Click **Browse**. Locate your Student Data Files folder in the File New Database dialog box, click **OK** to close the dialog box, and then click **Create** to create the new database.
b. Click **View** in the Views group to switch to Design view. Type **Leads** in the **Save As dialog box**, and then click **OK**.
c. Type **FirstName** in the second row, and then press **Tab**. Accept **Text** as the Data Type. Type **25** in the **Field Size property** in Field Properties, and then type **First Name** in the **Caption property**.

d. Type the remainder of the fields and adjust the field properties as shown:

Field Name	Data Type	Field Size	Caption
LastName	Text	25	**Last Name**
City	Text	25	n/a
State	Text	2	n/a
ZipCode	Text	5	**Zip Code**
PhoneNumber	Text	14	**Phone Number**
Email	Text	30	n/a
BirthDate	Date/Time	n/a	n/a
NetWorth	Currency	n/a	**Net Worth**

e. Verify that the first field (ID) is set as the **Primary Key**.

f. Click **View** in the Views group to switch to Datasheet view. Click **Yes** to save the table. Open the *a04p1leads_import* Excel file, and then manually add the first three records into the Leads table. (Begin typing in the FirstName field; the ID field will be generated automatically.) Press **Tab** to move to the next field.

g. Click **row 5** in the Excel file, press and hold the **left mouse button**, and then drag through row 15 (Lynne Miller's row) so that 11 rows are selected. Click **Copy** in the Clipboard group.

h. Return to Access, and then click on the **asterisk** (*) on the first new row of the Leads table. Click **Paste** in the Clipboard group to paste the 11 rows into the Leads table, and then click **OK** to confirm. Save and close the table.

i. Click the **Create tab**, and then click **Form** in the Forms group to create a new form that opens in Layout view.

j. Click the **ID box**, and then drag the right border of the first field to the left to shrink the column by 50%.

k. Change the title of the form to **New Leads**.

l. Click on the **ID field**, and then click the **Layout Selector** (the small square in the top-left corner with a cross inside). Click the **Arrange tab**, and then click the **Control Padding arrow** in the Position group. Select **Narrow** from the list of options.

m. Click the **Home tab**. Click the **View arrow**, and then select **Design view**. Click the bottom of the Form Footer bar, and then stretch the *Form Footer* section to the 1" mark. Click **Label** in the Controls group. Add a label to the Form Footer as shown in Figure 4.52, and then apply bold to the label.

n. Save the form as **Leads Form**. Switch to Form view.

o. Return to the Excel file, and then manually enter the last two records into the Leads table using the Leads Form. Close the form.

p. Click the **File tab**, and then click **Compact & Repair Database**.

q. Exit Access.

r. Submit the database based on your instructor's directions.

2 Comfort Insurance

The Human Resources department of the Comfort Insurance Agency has initiated its annual employee performance reviews. The reviews affect employee salary increases and bonuses. The employee data, along with forms and reports, are stored in an Access database. You need to prepare a report showing employee raises and bonuses by city. This exercise follows the same set of skills as used in Hands-On Exercises 1, 3, and 4 in the chapter. Refer to Figure 4.53 as you complete this exercise.

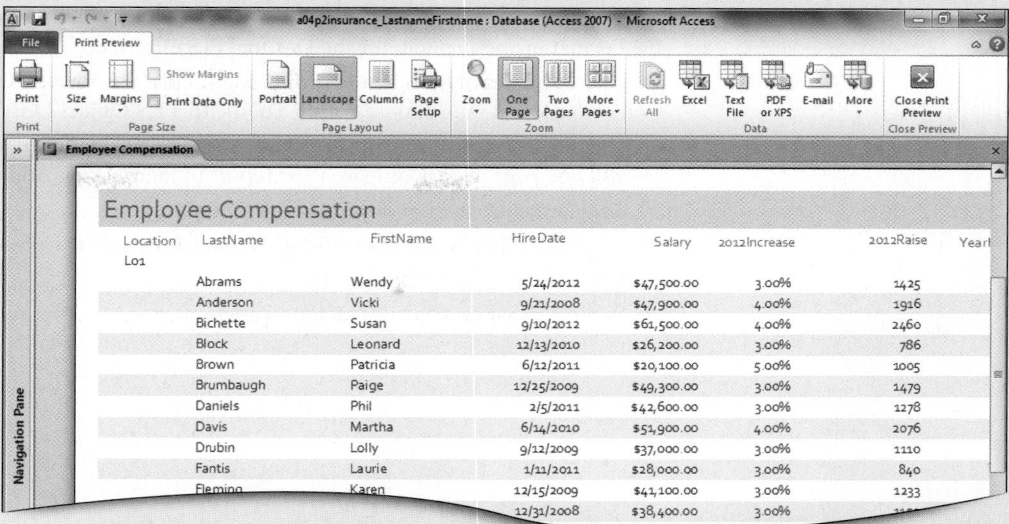

FIGURE 4.53 Employee Compensation Report with Totals ➤

a. Open *a04p2insurance*. Click the **File tab**, click **Save Database As**, and then type **a04p2insurance_LastnameFirstname**. Click **Save**.

b. Select the **Locations table**. Click the **Create tab**, and then click **Form** in the Forms group to create a new form that opens in Layout view.

c. Click the **LocationID text box** containing *L01*. Move the mouse to the right edge of the orange border until the mouse pointer changes to a double-headed arrow. Drag the right edge to the left to reduce the size of the text box to approximately 50% of its original size.

d. Click the subform at the bottom of the form, and then click the **Layout Selector** (the small square with a four-headed arrow inside). Press **Delete** to delete the subform.

e. Click **Themes** in the Themes group on the Design tab. Right-click a **Solstice theme** (second column, second row from bottom), and then choose **Apply Theme to This Object Only**.

f. Save the form as **Locations**. Close the form.

g. Select the **Locations table**. Click the **Create tab**, and then click **Report** in the Reports group to create a new tabular layout report in Layout view.

h. Click the **Locations label**, and then drag the right border of the label to the left to reduce the size of the control to **50%**.

i. Repeat the sizing process with the Zipcode label and the OfficePhone label. Adjust the other columns if necessary until there are no controls on the right side of the vertical dashed line.

j. Display the report in Print Preview. Verify that the report is only one page wide. Close and save the report using the name **Locations**.

k. Select the **Employee Query**. Click the **Create tab**, and then click **Report Wizard** in the Reports group to launch the Report Wizard. Respond to the questions as follows:
   - Click (>>) to add all the fields to the Selected Fields box. Click **Next**.
   - Accept grouping by Location. Click **Next**.
   - Select **LastName** for the first sort order and **FirstName** for the second. Click **Summary Options**.
   - Click **Sum** for Salary, **Avg** for 2012Increase, and **Avg** for YearsWorked. Click **OK**. Click **Next**.
   - Accept the Stepped layout. Change Orientation to **Landscape**. Click **Next**.
   - Type **Employee Compensation** for the title of the report. Click **Finish**.
   - The Report is displayed in Print Preview mode. Some of the columns are too narrow. Next, you will adjust the columns and summary controls.

l. Click **Close Print Preview**. Switch to Layout view.

m. Adjust the column widths so that all the data values are showing. Some of the columns will need to be reduced and some will need to be widened. Change the YearsWorked label to **Years**. Use Figure 4.53 as a guide.

n. Adjust the Summary controls at the bottom of the first Location (L01) so all the values are visible. Adjust the Summary controls in the Report Footer so all the values are visible. Align all the Summary controls with their associated detail columns.

o. Open the Property Sheet. Click the **Avg Of YearsWorked control**, and then select **Fixed** for the Format property and **0** for the Decimal Places property.
p. Click **Themes** in the Themes group. Right-click the **Module theme** (first column, fourth row from bottom), and then choose **Apply Theme to This Object Only**.
q. Display the report in Print Preview. Close the Navigation Pane, and then verify that the report is still one page wide. Compare your report to Figure 4.53. Adjust column widths if necessary.
r. Save and close the Employee Compensation report.
s. Click the **File tab**, and then click **Compact & Repair Database**.
t. Close the database. Exit Access.
u. Submit based on your instructor's directions.

MID-LEVEL EXERCISES

1 Hotel Chain

You are the general manager of a large hotel chain. You track revenue by categories: hotel rooms, conference rooms, and weddings. You need to create a report that shows which locations are earning the most revenue in each category. You also need to create a form that will enable you to enter and maintain member data for those guests who pay an annual fee in exchange for discounts and hotel privileges. Refer to Figure 4.54 as you complete this exercise.

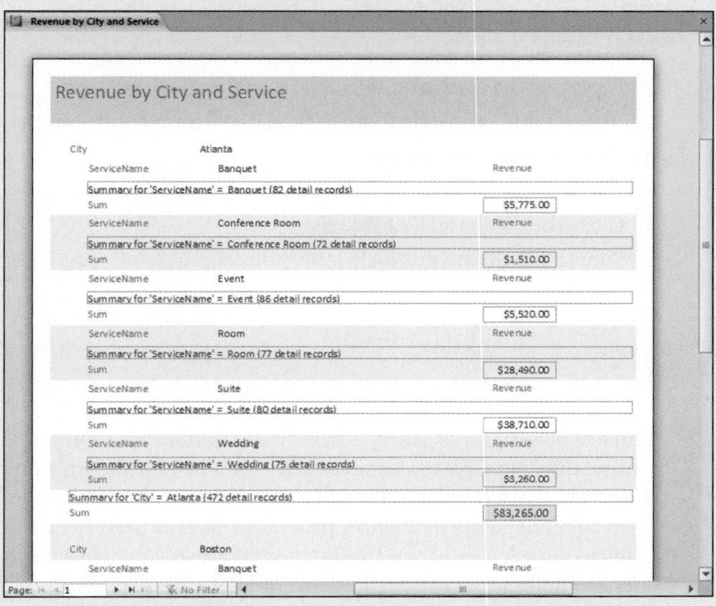

FIGURE 4.54 Revenue by City and Service, Summary Only ➤

a. Open *a04m1rewards*. Click the **File tab**, click **Save Database As**, and then type **a04m1rewards_LastnameFirstname**. Click **Save**.

b. Select the **Members table**, and then create a Multiple Items form. Save the form as **Maintain Members**.

c. Modify the form in Layout view as follows:
   - Reduce the row height by 50%.
   - Change the MemNumber label to **MemID**, and then reduce the MemNumber column width.
   - Adjust the column widths to eliminate extra white space.
   - Delete the form icon in the Form Header.

d. Switch to Design view, and then modify the form as follows:
   - Open the Property sheet, and then click the **Members title control** to change the Width property to **2.5"**.
   - Add the special effect **Raised** to the **Members title control**.
   - Increase the Form Footer to **1/2"**.
   - Add a new label control to the left side of the Form Footer.
   - Type **Form created by *your name***.
   - Reduce the width of the form to **12"** (reduce the e-mail column width, if necessary).
   - Add today's date to the right side of the Form Header using the **Date and Time command** in the Header/Footer group.

e. Switch to Form view. Verify that the controls in the *Header* and *Footer* sections remain constant as you advance through the records. Close and save the form.

f. Select the **Revenue query**, and then create a report using the Report Wizard. Answer the wizard prompts as follows:
   - Include all fields.
   - Add grouping by City and by ServiceName.
   - Add a Sum to the Revenue field.
   - Check the **Summary Only option**.

- Choose **Outline Layout**.
- Name the report **Revenue by City and Service**.

g. Scroll through all the pages to check the layout of the report while in Print Preview mode.

h. Switch to Design view, and then delete the NoInParty and PerPersonCharge controls in the *Detail* and *ServiceName Header* sections. Drag the remaining controls in the *ServiceName Header* section to the top of the section. Reduce the height of the *ServiceName Header* section as shown in Figure 4.54.

i. Open the Property Sheet, and then use the Width property to change the width of the Revenue control in the *Detail* section to **1.0"**, the width of the Sum of Revenue control in the ServiceName Footer to **1.0"**, the width of the Sum of Revenue1control in the City Footer to **1.0"**, and the width of the Revenue Grand Total Sum control in the Report Footer to **1.0"**.

j. Click each of the revenue controls while holding down **Shift**, and then set the Format property of all the selected controls to **Currency**.

k. Change the font size, font color, and background color of the Sum of Revenue1 control in the City Footer so the control stands out from the other controls.

l. Apply a different style to the Grand Total Sum control in the Report Footer.

m. Close and save the report.

n. Compact and repair the database.

o. Close the database. Exit Access.

p. Submit based on your instructor's directions.

2 Benefit Auction

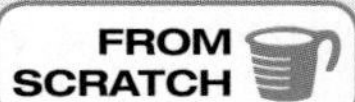

You are helping to organize a benefit auction to raise money for families who lost their homes in a natural disaster. Create a database that will store the description of items collected, their category, and the estimated sale price. You will also need to collect the name of the donor for each item. Create a form to manage the data entry process. You also need to create two reports: one that lists the items collected in each category and one for labels so you can send the donors a thank you letter after the auction. Refer to Figure 4.55 as you complete this exercise.

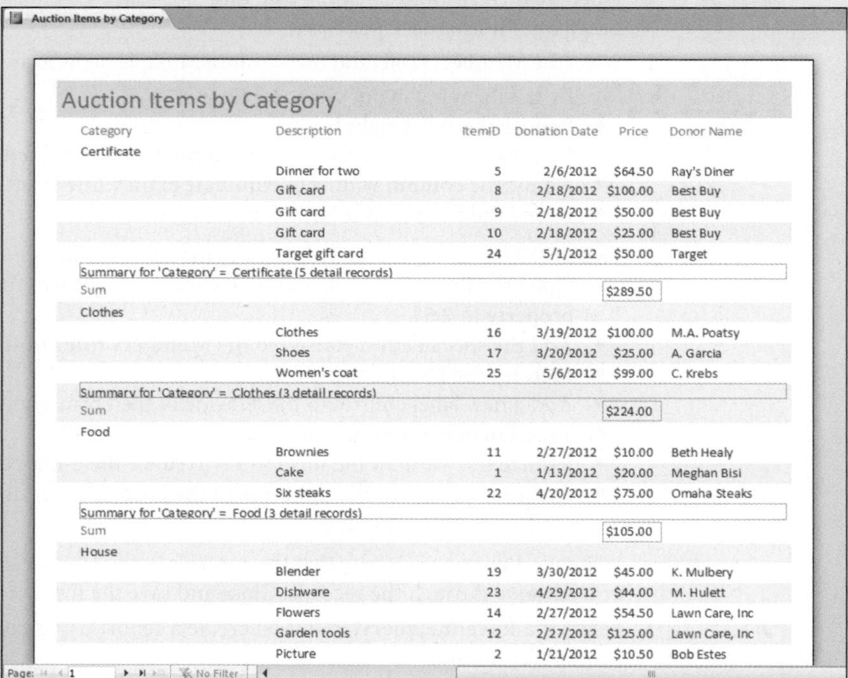

Auction Items by Category

Category	Description	ItemID	Donation Date	Price	Donor Name
Certificate					
	Dinner for two	5	2/6/2012	$64.50	Ray's Diner
	Gift card	8	2/18/2012	$100.00	Best Buy
	Gift card	9	2/18/2012	$50.00	Best Buy
	Gift card	10	2/18/2012	$25.00	Best Buy
	Target gift card	24	5/1/2012	$50.00	Target
Summary for 'Category' = Certificate (5 detail records)					
Sum				$289.50	
Clothes					
	Clothes	16	3/19/2012	$100.00	M.A. Poatsy
	Shoes	17	3/20/2012	$25.00	A. Garcia
	Women's coat	25	5/6/2012	$99.00	C. Krebs
Summary for 'Category' = Clothes (3 detail records)					
Sum				$224.00	
Food					
	Brownies	11	2/27/2012	$10.00	Beth Healy
	Cake	1	1/13/2012	$20.00	Meghan Bisi
	Six steaks	22	4/20/2012	$75.00	Omaha Steaks
Summary for 'Category' = Food (3 detail records)					
Sum				$105.00	
House					
	Blender	19	3/30/2012	$45.00	K. Mulbery
	Dishware	23	4/29/2012	$44.00	M. Hulett
	Flowers	14	2/27/2012	$54.50	Lawn Care, Inc
	Garden tools	12	2/27/2012	$125.00	Lawn Care, Inc
	Picture	2	1/21/2012	$10.50	Bob Estes

FIGURE 4.55 Auction Items by Category Report ➤

a. Open Access, and then create a new database named **a04m2auction_LastnameFirstname**.

b. Switch to Design view. Type **Items** in the Save As dialog box, and then click **OK**.

c. Change the ID Field Name to **ItemID**. Type **Description** in the second row, and then press **Tab**. Accept **Text** as the Data Type. Type **50** in the **Field Size property** in Field Properties.

d. Type the remainder of the fields and adjust the field properties as shown:

Field Name	Data Type	Field Size	Caption
DateOfDonation	Date/Time	n/a	**Donation Date**
Category	Text	20	n/a
Price	Currency	n/a	n/a
DonorName	Text	50	**Donor Name**
DonorAddress1	Text	50	**Donor Address 1**
DonorAddress2	Text	50	**Donor Address 2**

e. Verify the first field (ItemID) is set as the **Primary Key**. Save and close the table.

f. Verify that the Items table is selected. Create a new form using the Form tool.

g. Click the **ItemID box**, and then drag the right border of the field to the left to shrink the column by 50%.

h. Change the title of the form to **Items for Auction**.

i. Switch to Design View. Expand the *Form Footer* section, and then add a Label Control to the Form Footer that reads **The last day to receive items is May 31**. Increase the font size to **16 pt**, and then change the font color to **Red**.

j. Save the form as **Auction Items Form**. Switch to Form view.

k. Open the *a04m2items_import* Excel file and manually add the first three records into the form. (Begin typing in the Description field; the ItemID field will be generated automatically.) Close the form.

l. Open the Items table, and then copy and paste the remaining rows from the Excel file into the table. Close the table.

m. Select the **Items table** in the Navigation Pane, and then create a report using the Report Wizard. Include all fields except the donor address fields, group data by Category, sort by Description, add the Sum of Price, accept the default layout, and then title the report **Auction Items by Category**.

n. Switch to Layout view, and then adjust the controls so all data is visible (use Figure 4.55 as a guide). Add currency formatting to all the sum of price fields. Preview the report to verify the column widths are correct. Save and close the report.

o. Create mailing labels in the format shown below. You already purchased Avery 5260 labels. Sort the labels by Donor Name. Name the report **Donor Labels**. After you create the labels, display them in print preview mode and use the first six addresses to verify everything will fit onto the 5260 label template. Close the label report.

Label format:
Andrew Garcia
201 Denver St
Los Angeles, CA 90012

p. Compact and repair the database.

q. Back up the database using **a04m2auction_LastnameFirstname_*date*** as the file name.

r. Exit Access. Submit the database based on your instructor's directions.

CAPSTONE EXERCISE

Your boss asked you to prepare a schedule for each speaker for the national conference being hosted next year on your campus. She wants to mail the schedules to the speakers so that they can provide feedback on the schedule prior to its publication. You assure her that you can accomplish this task with Access.

Database File Setup

You need to copy an original database file, rename the copied file, and then open the copied database to complete this capstone exercise. After you open the copied database, you replace an existing employee's name with your name.

a. Open *a04c1natconf*.

b. Click the **File tab**, click **Save Database As**, and then type **a04c1natconf_LastnameFirstname**. Click **Save**.

c. Open the Speakers table.

d. Find and replace *Your_Name* with your name. Close the table.

Create a Form

You need to create a form to add and update Speakers. Use the Form tool to create the form, and then modify the form as explained.

a. Select the **Speakers table** as the record source for the form.

b. Use the **Form tool** to create a new stacked form.

c. Change the title to **Enter/Edit Speakers**.

d. Reduce the width of the text box controls to **50%**.

e. Delete the Sessions subform.

f. Add a new label control in the Form Footer that says **Contact Elaine Carey if you have questions about Speakers**.

g. View the form and data in Form view. Sort the records by LastName. Locate your record.

h. Save the form as **Edit Speakers**. Close the form.

Create a Report

You need to create a report based on the Speaker and Room Schedule query. You decide to use the Report Wizard to accomplish this task.

a. Select the **Speaker and Room Schedule query** as the record source for the report.

b. Activate the **Report Wizard** and use the following options as you go through the Wizard:
- Select all of the available fields for the report.
- View the data by Speakers.
- Verify that LastName and FirstName will provide grouping levels.
- Use **Date** as the primary sort field.
- Accept the **Stepped** and **Portrait options**.
- Name the report **Speaker Schedule**.
- Switch to Layout view, and apply the **Module theme** to only this report.

c. Preview the report, and then adjust the column widths if necessary.

d. Close and save the report.

Add an Additional Field

You realize the session times were not included in the query. You add the field to the query and then start over with the Report Wizard.

a. Open the Speaker and Room Schedule query in Design view.

b. Add the **StartingTime field** in the Sessions table to the design grid. Run the query.

c. Close and save the query.

d. Start the Report Wizard again and use the following options:
- Select the **Speaker and Room Schedule query**.
- Select all of the available fields for the report.
- View the data by Speakers.
- Use the **LastName, FirstName fields** as the primary grouping level.
- Use **Date** as the primary sort field.
- Use **StartingTime** as the secondary sort field.
- Select the **Stepped** and **Portrait options**.
- Name the report **Speaker Schedule Revised**.
- Switch to Layout view, and then apply the **Trek theme** to only this report.

e. Adjust the column widths in Layout View so that all the data is visible.

f. Increase the width of the StartingTime label control in the *Page Header* section in Design view, so that the entire phrase is visible. Add a space to the column heading labels as needed.

g. Close and save the report. Compact the database.

h. Close the database. Exit Access.

i. Submit based on your instructor's directions.

Inventory Value

GENERAL CASE 

The owner of a bookstore asked for your help with her database. Her insurance company asked her to provide an inventory report listing the values of the books she has in stock. Open *a04b1books*. Click the File tab, click Save Database As, and then type **a04b1books_LastnameFirstname**. Click Save. Use the skills you learned in this chapter to create three stacked layout forms for Authors, Publishers, and Books. Delete any attached subforms. Next, create the inventory report that shows the inventory values for the books on hand. The database contains a query that you can use to create the report. Group the records by publisher name; alphabetize authors by last name and first name within groups. Name the report **Bookstore Inventory Value**. In Layout view, create a total value control for each publisher and create a grand total. Resize and reposition the total controls so they are visible and aligned with the correct column. Add Currency formatting where applicable, and then modify column headings as needed. Preview the report and verify that all the columns are correct, and then save and close the report. Compact and repair the database, and then close the database and close Access. Submit based on your instructor's directions.

Create a Split Form

RESEARCH CASE 

This chapter introduced you to Access forms, including the Split Form. It is possible to turn an existing form into a split form if you modify a few form properties. Perform an Internet search to find the steps to convert a form to a split form. First, create a new database, and then name the file **a04b2split_LastnameFirstname**. Next, import the two objects (Books table and Books form) from the *a04b2books_import* database. To import the objects, click the **External Data tab**, and then click **Access** in the Import & Link group. After the new objects have been imported, use the information from the Internet to convert the Books form into a split form. Make sure the datasheet is on the bottom half; save the form as **Split Form Books**. Compact and repair the database, and then exit Access. Submit the database based on your instructor's directions.

Properties by City

DISASTER RECOVERY

A co-worker is having difficulty with an Access report and asked you for your assistance. Open the *a04b3sales* database and save the file as **a04b3sales_LastnameFirstname**. In the new database, open and examine the Properties report. The report was created incorrectly; change the report to **Landscape orientation**, and then adjust the column widths so they all fit onto one page. Add grouping by City. Save the new report as **Properties by City**. Compact and repair the database, and then exit Access. Submit the database based on your instructor's directions.

ACCESS APPLICATION CAPSTONE EXERCISE

You were recently hired by your local community college to help with registering all transfer students. Your skills in Access will be utilized because the college just created a new Access database for this purpose. Your tasks include importing an existing Excel worksheet as a table into your Access database, creating a relationship between two tables, creating a query with calculated fields and functions, and creating two reports. After you complete these tasks, compact and repair the database and then make a backup copy.

Database File Setup and Import an Excel Worksheet

You need to open an Access database, and then import an Excel worksheet into the database as a table.

a. Start Access. Open *a00c1college*.
b. Save the file as **a00c1college_LastnameFirstname**.
c. Import the Transfer_Schools Excel workbook from the location where you store your data files into the database using the name **Transfer_Schools**.
d. Set the StudentID field as the primary key of the Transfer Schools table. While importing the Excel data, choose **StudentID** as the primary key field.

Modify and Filter a Table

You need to revise the Transfer Schools table, and then create a filter for students from Pearson University.

a. Set the StudentID field size to **10**.
b. Remove the @ symbol from the StudentID format property.
c. Switch to Datasheet View, and then add a new field named **TuitionDue**. Set the Data Type to **Currency**.
d. Sort the Transfer Schools table on the Credits Transferred field in ascending order.
e. Use Filter By Selection to filter the table for Admitting School equal to Pearson University (three records will display). Save and close the table.

Create Relationships

Create a relationship between the two tables in the database.

a. Add the Transfer Schools and Transfer Students tables to the Relationships window.
b. Create a one-to-one relationship between the StudentID field in the Transfer Students (primary) table and the StudentID field in the Transfer Schools (related) table. Enforce referential integrity between the two tables.
c. Close the Relationships window. Save the changes.

Work with Data in a Form and a Table

You need to modify the data in the database. You will make modifications in a table and a form.

a. Open the Transfer Students Data Entry form.
b. Change the major for Cornelius Kavanaugh to **Elementary Education**. Close the form.
c. View the Transfer Students table in Datasheet view. Click **Advanced** in the Sort & Filter group, and then click **Filter by Form**. Create a filter to display the records where the Major is *Elementary Education*. Apply the filter to the table (four records will display).
d. Save and close the table.

Create a Query

You need to create a query to examine the transfer students' credits based on the admissions date criteria.

a. Create a new query using Design view. Add both tables to the design window. From the Transfer Students table, add the First Name, Last Name, and GPA fields. From the Transfer Schools table, add the Admission Date, TuitionDue, Credits Earned, and Credits Transferred fields.
b. Save the query as **Transfer Credits**.
c. Set the criteria in the Admission Date field to **8/1/2013**. Run the query (eight records will display). Save the query.
d. Enter the Tuition Due for Diana Sullivan as **5500** and for Adriana McGraw as **6000**. For all other students, enter **0**.

Create Calculated Fields

Add calculated fields that will show additional data about the transfer students.

a. Switch to Design view of the Transfer Credits query.
b. In the first empty field cell of the query, create a calculated field named **Credits Lost** that subtracts Credits Transferred from Credits Earned.
c. Create another calculated field named **Tuition Payments** that determines tuition paid in three installments. Using the Pmt(<<rate>>, <<num_periods>>, <<present_value>>, <<future_value>>, <<type>>) function, replace the rate argument with **0.025/12**, the num_periods argument with **3**, the present_value argument with the -[Tuition Due] field name, future_value argument with **0**, and type argument with **0**.
d. Format the Tuition Payments calculated field as **Currency**. Run the query.
e. Create another calculated field named **Deposit Date**. To calculate the deposit date, add **30** to today's date. Run the query and verify that the three calculated fields have valid data.
f. Add a total row to the query. Average the GPA column, and then sum the Credits Lost column. Save and close the query.

Create a Transfer Credits Report

You need to create a report based on the Transfer Credits query.

a. Create a report based on the Transfer Credits query using the Report Wizard. Add the Last Name, Credits Transferred, Credits Lost, and Tuition Payments fields to the report.
b. Do not add any grouping. Sort the report by Last Name, accept the default report name, and then view the report in Layout view.
c. Delete the Date and Time box from the report footer. Insert the Date and Time control into the right side of the report header using the default settings. View the report in Print Preview. Save and close the report.

Create a Transfer Students Report

Create another report based on the Transfer Students table using the Report tool.

a. Create a report based on the Transfer Students table using the Report tool. In Layout view, set the widths of the StudentID, Last Name, First Name, Year of Study, and GPA fields to **1"**. Set the width of the Major field to **2"**. Apply the **Trek Theme**. Save the report as **Transfer Students**.
b. Group the report on the Year of Study field. Sort the records within each group in ascending order by Last Name.
c. Add the average GPA for each year of study and overall in Layout view. Adjust the total boxes so the average values are completely visible.

d. Switch to Print Preview mode, and then verify the report fits on one page (portrait).
e. Click on the image in the report header in Layout view. Click **Insert Image** in the Controls group, and then browse to locate the file Student.wmf as a logo. Change the width of the image to **1.0"** and the height to **0.75"**. Set the size mode property to **Stretch**. Switch to Report view to verify that the image looks correct and that all the information fits onto one page. If necessary, return to Layout view, and then move the date and time controls to the left so the report fits on one page (portrait).
f. Save and close the report.

Close and Submit Database

a. Close all database objects.
b. Compact and repair the database, make a backup copy, and then exit Access.
c. Submit based on your instructor's directions.

ACCESS COLLABORATION EXERCISES

1 Used Cell Phones for Sale

You and a few of your classmates decide to start a new business selling used cell phones, MP3 players, and accessories. You will use an Access database to track your inventory. To begin, one person in your group will locate the Access database for this exercise, complete steps b through f, and then post the database to a SkyDrive folder. The next person in your group will retrieve the revised database and also complete the steps b through f (and so on until everyone has completed steps b through f). After everyone has completed steps b through f, you will retrieve the database again and complete step g. At the completion of this exercise, each person will submit his or her own Word document containing the answers to the questions below.

a. Open the *a01t1phones* database, and then save it as **a01t1phones_group*X***. (This step will be completed by only one person in your group. Replace X with the number assigned to your group by your instructor.)

b. Open the Inventory table, and then review the records in the table. Take note of the data in the TypeOfDevice column. Close the table, and then open the DeviceOptions table. Review the data, and then close the table.

c. Open the Relationships window. What is the benefit of the relationship between the Inventory table and the DeviceOptions table? Create a Word document with both the question and your answer. After you complete this exercise, you will submit this Word document to your instructor using the file name **a01t1phones_answers_LastnameFirstname**. Close the Relationships window.

d. Open the Inventory Form, and then add the information about your cell phone to the table (or search the Internet for any model if you do not have a cell phone) to the first new blank record. Enter your name in the SellerName field. With your information showing in the form, take a screen shot of the form using the Snipping Tool. Paste the image into the Word document you created in step c. Close the form.

e. Open the Inventory Report by Manufacturer in report view. Filter the records for only items that have not been sold. Take a screen shot using the Snipping Tool, and then paste the image into the Word document. Close the report, close the database, and then exit Access.

f. Create a folder on your Skydrive account named **Exploring Access**, and then share the folder with the other members in your group and the instructor. Upload the database to this new folder, and then notify another person in your group. The next person will complete steps b through f, and then the next person, until all group members have added their information.

g. After all the new phone records have been added, each person in the group should download the **a01t1phones_group*X*** database again, and then use filters to answer the following questions. Add the questions and your answers to the Word document you created in step c.

   1. How many phones are still for sale? ______________
   2. How many phones are made by Apple or Samsung? ______________
   3. How many phones were sold in the first half of 2012? ______________ List the ID numbers. ______________
   4. Sort the phones from smallest to highest asking price. Which phone is the least expensive? ______________ Most expensive? ______________
   5. How many items are not phones? ______________

h. Use e-mail or text messaging to communicate with the other members in your group if you have any questions.

i. Submit the Word document based on your instructor's directions.

2 Used Cell Phones for Sale

You and a few of your classmates started a new business selling used cell phones, MP3 players, and accessories. You have been using an Access database to track your inventory. You decide to improve the data entry process by adding three additional tables. After the new tables are added, and the relationships set, you will create several queries to analyze the data. In order to collaborate with the other members of your group, you will post an Access database and two Excel files to a SkyDrive folder. At the completion of this exercise, each person will submit his or her own Word document containing the answers to the questions below.

a. Open the *a02t1phones* database, and then save it as **a02t1phones_group*X***. Close the database. (This step will be completed by only one person in your group. Replace X with the number assigned to your group by your instructor.) Create a folder on your SkyDrive account named **Exploring Access**, and then share the folder with the other members in your group and the instructor. Upload the database to this new folder, and then notify the other members in your group.
b. Download the database from the Exploring Access Skydrive folder created in step a, and then save it locally as **a02t1phones_group*X*_LastnameFirstname**. (Everyone in the group will complete this step.) Open the database, and then open the Inventory table and review the records in the table. Take note of the data in the TypeOfDevice column; this field is joined to the DeviceOptions table, and the *enforce referential integrity* option has been set. Only the options in the DeviceOptions table are allowed to be entered. What other fields in this table could be joined to a table in the same way? Type your answer into a Word document named **a02t1phones_answers_LastnameFirstname**.
c. Import the data in the **a02t1carriers_import** Excel spreadsheet into a new table named **Carriers**. Let Access add a primary key field (ID). Open the table, and then verify that the data imported correctly. Change the ID field to **CarrierID**. Save and close the Carriers table.
d. Open the Inventory table if necessary, and then add a new field under the Carrier field named CarrierID with number data type. Save and close the table. Open the Relationships window, and then add the Carriers table. Create a relationship between the Carriers table and the Inventory table using the CarrierID field. Set enforce referential integrity to *yes*. Take a screen shot of the Relationships window using the Snipping Tool, and then paste the image into the Word document you created in step b. Close the Relationships window.
e. Open the Inventory table and the Carriers table. Using the CarrierID field in the Carriers table, enter the correct CarrierID into each record. Switch to Design view, and then remove the original Carrier field. Close the table.
f. Repeat steps c, d, and e for the fields Manufacturer and Color. To do this, one member of the group must create an Excel spreadsheet named **Manufacturers**, which contains all the manufacturers found in the Inventory table. Another member of the group must create an Excel spreadsheet named **Colors**, which contains all the colors found in the Inventory table. Both of these Excel spreadsheets must be saved to the Exploring Access folder created in step a so all members can access the data. Take a screen shot of the Relationships window using the Snipping Tool, and then paste the image into the Word document. Close the Relationships window.
g. After all the new tables have been added, each person in the group should create all of the following queries. Make sure the text fields from the supporting tables appear in the queries (not the ID fields from the Inventory table). Save each query as noted below. Take a screen shot of the datasheet of each query using the Snipping Tool, and then paste the image into the Word document.
    1. Display all the phones that are still for sale. Save as **qry1 Phones For Sale**.
    2. Display all the phones that are not made by Apple. Save as **qry2 Not Apple Phones**.
    3. List the Manufacturer and Model and asking price of sold phones; also include phones that are less than $50. Sort by asking price; only include tables that are required. Save as **qry3 Phones Sold and less than $50**.
    4. Display the phones that were purchased before 4/1/2012. Exclude the sold phones. Sort by purchase date. Save as **qry4 Obsolete Phones**.
h. Use e-mail or text messaging to communicate with the other members in your group if you have any questions.
i. Exit all open applications. Submit both the Word document and the database based on your instructor's directions.

3 Used Cell Phones for Sale

You and a few of your classmates started a new business selling used cell phones, MP3 players, and accessories. You have been using an Access database to track your inventory. You decide to increase your inventory by purchasing cell phones in bulk from an online provider. Once you purchase phones, you realize there is no easy way to enter the phones into the database (except manually). To find a solution to this problem, you and the other members of your group will search the Internet for "used cell phones" and test several methods for importing data from a Web page to an Access database. Once the sample data is imported, you will use aggregate functions to analyze your inventory. You will post your findings to a SkyDrive folder. At the completion of this exercise, each person will submit his or her own Word document containing the answers to the questions below.

a. Open the *a03t1phones* database, and then save it as **a03t1phones_group*X***. Close the database. (This step will be completed by only one person in your group. Replace *X* with the number assigned to your group by your instructor.) Create a folder on your SkyDrive account named **Exploring Access**, and then share the folder with the other members in your group and the instructor. Upload the database to this new folder, and then notify the other members in your group.
b. The first member of your group will download the database from the SkyDrive Exploring Access folder created in step a, and then save it locally as **a03t1phones_group*X*_*your initials***. Search the Internet for a site that sells used cell phones. When you locate a site, try to find a method for copying the phone data from the Web page to the Inventory table. Copy around 10 phones. It is OK to leave some fields blank. (Use the *a03t1web_phones_import* spreadsheet as a guide to show which fields must have data and which fields can be blank.). Use e-mail or text messaging to communicate with the other members in your group if you have any problems or ideas to share. If you cannot copy the data from the web page, type the new phones directly into the Inventory table.
c. After you add the phones to the Inventory table, take a screen shot of the Inventory table using the Snipping Tool, and then paste the image into a Word document named **a03t1phones_answers_LastnameFirstname**. Upload the revised database to the Exploring Access folder created in step a, and then notify the next member in your group.
d. The next member will then download the database from the SkyDrive Exploring Access folder created in step a, and then save it locally as **a01t3phones_group*X*_initials_*your initials***. The next member will search the Internet for a site that sells used cell phones. When you locate a site, try to find a method for copying the phone data from the Web page to the Inventory table. Copy around 10 phones. It is OK to leave some fields blank (open the Inventory table to see which fields must have data and which fields can be blank).
e. After the second member adds the phones to the Inventory table, take a screen shot of the Inventory table using the Snipping Tool, and then paste the image into a Word document named **a03t1phones_answers_LastnameFirstname**. Upload the revised database online to the Skydrive Exploring Access folder, and then notify the next member in your group.
f. Repeat steps d and e.
g. After all the new phones have been added, each person in the group should download the database and create all of the following queries. Make sure the text descriptions from the supporting tables appear in the queries (not the ID fields found in the Inventory table). Save each query as noted below. Take a screen shot of the datasheet of each query using the Snipping Tool, and then paste the image into the Word document.
    1. Display all the phones that are still for sale. Show the count of phones at the bottom of the database; also show the total value of the inventory (based on purchase price). Save as **qry1 Inventory Value**.
    2. Create a totals query that shows the value of phones grouped by Manufacturer (not ManufacturerID). Save as **qry2 Inventory by Manufacturer**.
    3. Show the Gross Profit, SellingPrice - PurchasePrice, of each sold phone. Also show the Gross Profit %, (SellingPrice - PurchasePrice) / SellingPrice. Save as **qry3 Gross Profit Sold Phones**.
    4. Revise Query #3 to include the count of phones, the total SellingPrice, PurchasePrice, Gross Profit, and the average gross profit %. Save as **qry4 Gross Profit Sold Phones II**.
    5. Is the average gross profit % in query #4 useful? Why or why not?
h. Use e-mail or text messaging to communicate with the other members in your group if you have any questions.
i. Submit both the Word document and the database based on your instructor's directions.

4 Used Cell Phones for Sale

You and a few of your classmates started a new business selling used cell phones, MP3 players, and accessories. You have been using an Access database to track your inventory. You need to create several forms and reports to improve database efficiency and analysis. You will post your findings to a SkyDrive folder. At the completion of this exercise, each person will submit his or her own Word document containing the answers to the questions below.

a. Open the *a04t1phones* database, and then save it as **a04t1phones_groupX**. Close the database. (This step will be completed by only one person in your group. Replace *X* with the number assigned to your group by your instructor.) Create a folder on your SkyDrive account named **Exploring Access**, and then share the folder with the other members in your group and the instructor. Upload the database to this new folder, and then notify the other members in your group.
b. The first member of your group will download the database from the Skydrive Exploring Access folder created in step a, and then save it locally as **a04t1phones_groupX_*your initials***. Create a form based on the Inventory table using the Form tool. Title and name the form Inventory Form *Your Name.* Add one new phone using the new form.
c. After you create the Inventory Form *Your Name*, take a screen shot of the form using the Snipping Tool, and then paste the image into a Word document named **a04t1phones_answers_LastnameFirstname**. Upload the revised database to the Exploring Access folder created in step a, and then notify the next member in your group.
d. The next member will then download the database from the online location created in step a, and then save it locally as **a04t1phones_groupX_initials_ *your initials***. The next member will create a form based on the Inventory table using the Multiple Items tool. Title and name the form Inventory Form *Your Name.* Add one new phone using the new form.
e. After you Create the Inventory Form *Your Name*, take a screen shot of the form using the Snipping Tool, and then paste the image into a Word document named **a04t1phones_answers_LastnameFirstname**. Upload the revised database online to your SkyDrive account or another similar file sharing service, and then notify the next member in your group.
f. The remaining members will repeat steps d and e using the Datasheet tool and the Split Form tool. Add one new phone using each of the new forms.
g. After all the new forms have been added, each person in the group should download the database and create an inventory report grouped by manufacturer and the total phones in each group and the total value in each group. Name the report **Inventory Report by Manufacturer**. Take a screen shot of the report in print preview using the Snipping Tool, and then paste the image into the Word document.
h. Use e-mail or text messaging to communicate with the other members in your group if you have any questions.
i. Submit both the Word document and the database based on your instructor's directions.

POWERPOINT

1 INTRODUCTION TO POWERPOINT

Presentations Made Easy

Watch the
Set-up
Video
for this
Case Study!

CASE STUDY | Be a Trainer

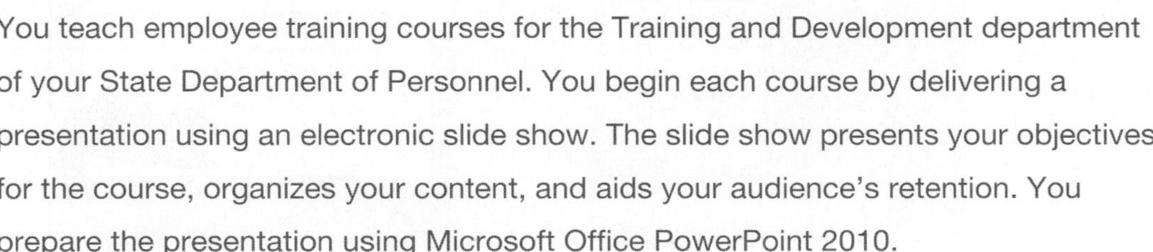

You teach employee training courses for the Training and Development department of your State Department of Personnel. You begin each course by delivering a presentation using an electronic slide show. The slide show presents your objectives for the course, organizes your content, and aids your audience's retention. You prepare the presentation using Microsoft Office PowerPoint 2010.

Because of the exceptional quality of your presentations, the director of the State Department of Personnel has asked you to prepare a new course on presentation skills. In the Hands-On Exercises for this chapter, you will work with two presentations for this course. One presentation will focus on the benefits of using PowerPoint, and the other will focus on the preparation for a slide show, including planning, organizing, and delivering.

OBJECTIVES AFTER YOU READ THIS CHAPTER, YOU WILL BE ABLE TO:

1. Use PowerPoint views ***p.809***
2. Save as a slide show ***p.813***
3. Plan a presentation ***p.817***
4. Assess presentation content ***p.820***
5. Use slide layouts ***p.820***
6. Apply themes ***p.821***
7. Review the presentation ***p.822***
8. Insert media objects ***p.828***
9. Add a table ***p.829***
10. Use animations and transitions ***p.829***
11. Insert a header or footer ***p.832***
12. Run and navigate a slide show ***p.839***
13. Print in PowerPoint ***p.841***

Introduction to PowerPoint

A **slide** is the most basic element of PowerPoint.

A **slide show** is a collection of slides that can be used in a presentation.

A **PowerPoint presentation** is an electronic slide show that can be edited or displayed.

You can use Microsoft PowerPoint 2010 to create an electronic slide show or other materials for use in a professional presentation. A ***slide*** is the most basic element of PowerPoint (similar to a page being the most basic element of Microsoft Word). Multiple slides may be arranged to create an electronic ***slide show*** that can be used to deliver your message in a variety of ways: you can project the electronic slideshow on a screen as part of a presentation, run it automatically at a kiosk or from a DVD, display it on the World Wide Web, or create printed handouts. A ***PowerPoint presentation*** is an electronic slide show saved with a .pptx extension after the file name.

Figure 1.1 shows a PowerPoint presentation with slides containing content, such as text, clip art images, and SmartArt. The presentation has a consistent design and color scheme. It is easy to create presentations with consistent and attractive designs using PowerPoint templates and slide layouts, which allow you to focus on the text, images, and other objects you will add to your slides.

It is easy to create presentations with consistent and attractive designs using PowerPoint templates and slide layouts.

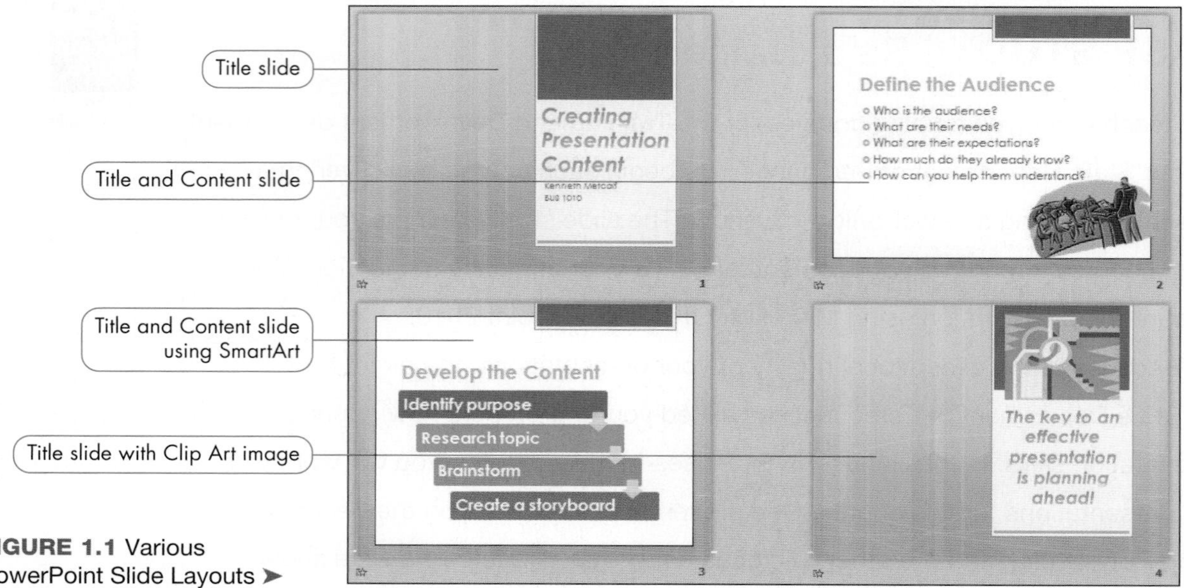

FIGURE 1.1 Various PowerPoint Slide Layouts ➤

In this section, you will start your exploration of PowerPoint by viewing a previously completed presentation so that you can appreciate the benefits of using PowerPoint. You will modify the presentation and add identifying information, examine PowerPoint views to discover the advantages of each view, and save the presentation. Finally, you will use Help to obtain assistance within PowerPoint.

TIP Polish Your Delivery

The speaker is the most important part of any presentation. Poor delivery will ruin even the best presentation. Speak slowly and clearly, maintain eye contact with your audience, and use the information on the slides to guide you. Do not just read the information on the screen, but expand on each bullet, paragraph, or image to give your audience the intended message.

Using PowerPoint Views

Normal view is the three-pane default PowerPoint view.

A **thumbnail** is a miniature of a slide that appears in the Slides tab.

Figure 1.2 shows the default PowerPoint view, ***Normal view***, with three panes that provide maximum flexibility in working with the presentation. The pane on the left side of the screen has two tabs: the Slides tab, which shows ***thumbnails*** (slide miniatures), and the Outline tab, which displays an outline of the presentation. The Slide pane on the right displays the current slide, and is where you make edits to slide content. The Notes pane, located at the bottom of the screen, is where you enter notes pertaining to the slide or the presentation. You can change the size of these panes by dragging the splitter bar that separates one pane from another.

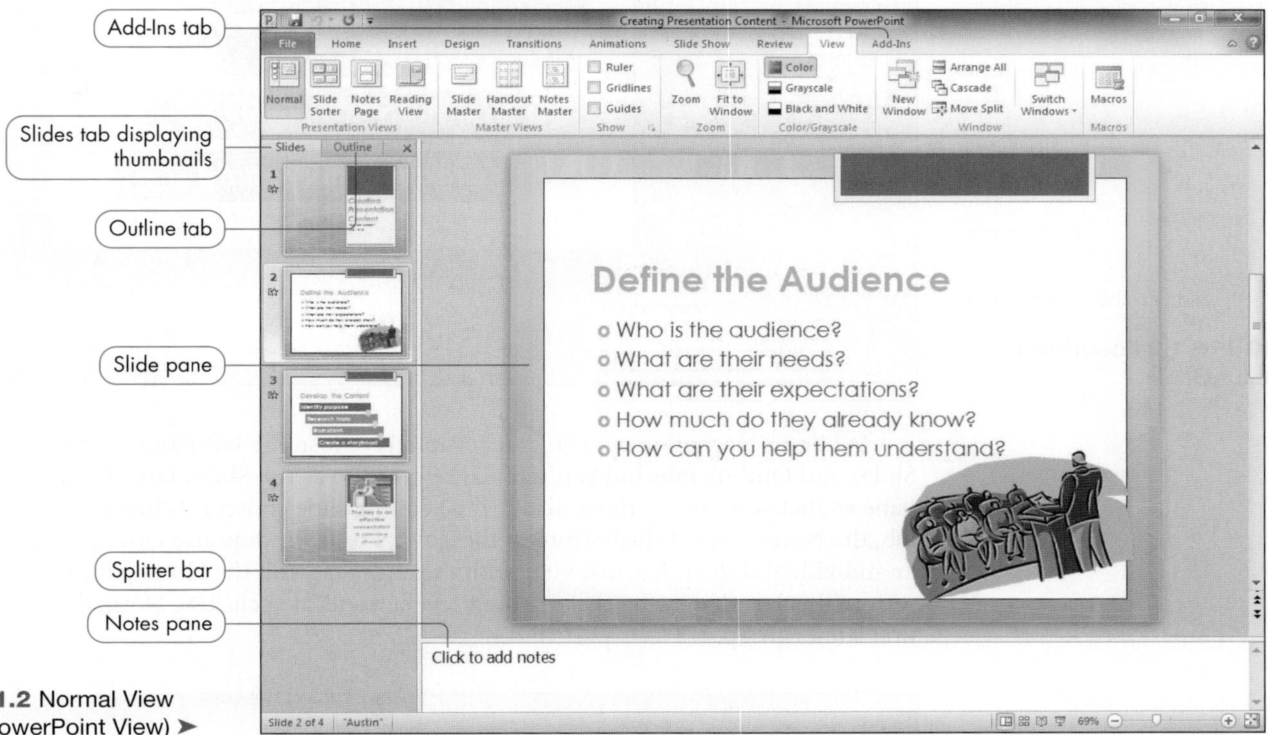

FIGURE 1.2 Normal View (Default PowerPoint View) ➤

The PowerPoint **status bar** contains the slide number, the design theme name, and View buttons.

Figure 1.3 shows PowerPoint's ***status bar***, which contains the slide number, the theme name, and options that control the view of your presentation: View buttons, the Zoom level button, a Zoom slider, and the Fit slide to current window button. The status bar is located at the bottom of your screen and can be customized. To customize the status bar, right-click it, and then click the options you want displayed from the Customize Status Bar list.

TIP Add-Ins Tab

You may see an Add-Ins tab on the Ribbon. This tab indicates that additional functionality, such as an updated Office feature or an Office-compatible program, has been added to your system. Add-Ins are designed to increase your productivity.

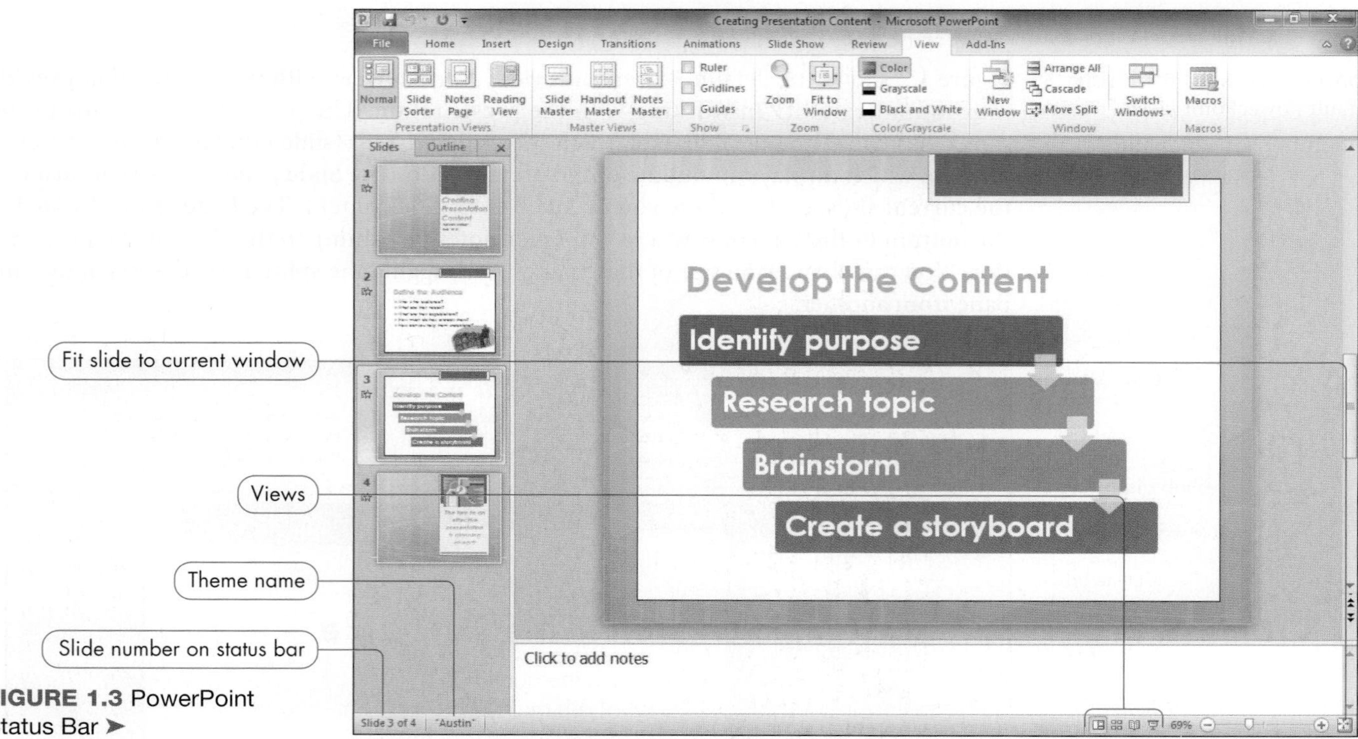

FIGURE 1.3 PowerPoint Status Bar ➤

While in Normal view, you can completely close the left pane—which includes the Slides and Outline tabs but is often just referred to as the Slides tab—to expand the Slide pane so that you can see more detail while editing slide content. When you close the Slides tab, the Notes pane at the bottom of the PowerPoint window also closes. Figure 1.4 shows an individual slide in Normal view with the Slides tab and the Notes pane closed. You can restore the default view by clicking the View tab, and then clicking Normal in the Presentation Views group.

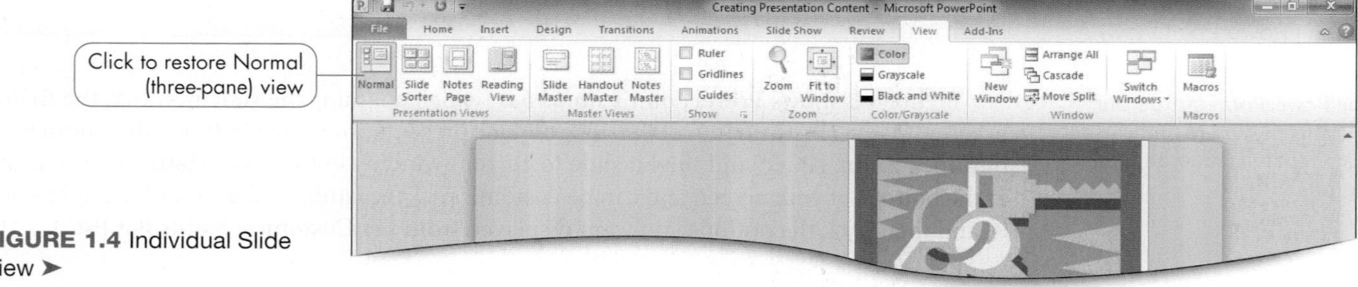

FIGURE 1.4 Individual Slide View ➤

PowerPoint offers views in addition to Normal view, including Slide Sorter, Notes Page, Reading View, and Slide Show views. Access Slide Sorter, Notes Page, and Reading View views from the Presentation Views group on the View tab. Access options for the Slide Show view from the Start Slide Show group on the Slide Show tab. For quick access, all of these views, except Notes Page, are available on the status bar.

Notes Page view is used for entering and editing large amounts of text to which the speaker can refer when presenting.

Notes Page view is used when you need to enter and edit large amounts of text to which the speaker can refer when presenting. If you have a large amount of technical detail in the speaker notes, you can use Notes Page view to print audience handouts that include the slide and associated notes. Notes do not appear when the presentation is shown, but are intended to help the speaker remember the key points or additional information about each slide. Figure 1.5 shows an example of the Notes Page view.

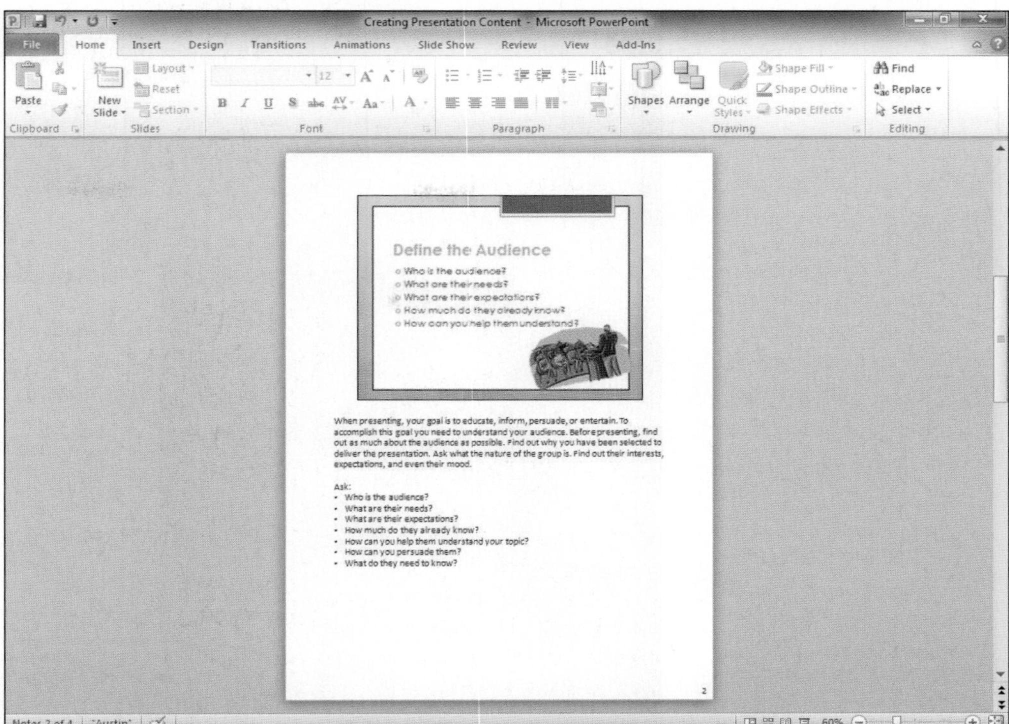

FIGURE 1.5 Notes Page View ➤

Slide Sorter view displays thumbnails of slides.

Slide Sorter view displays thumbnails of your presentation slides, which allow you to view multiple slides simultaneously (see Figure 1.6). This view is helpful when you wish to change the order of the slides or to delete one or more slides. You can set transition effects for multiple slides in Slide Sorter view. If you are in Slide Sorter view and double-click a slide thumbnail, PowerPoint returns the selected slide to Normal view.

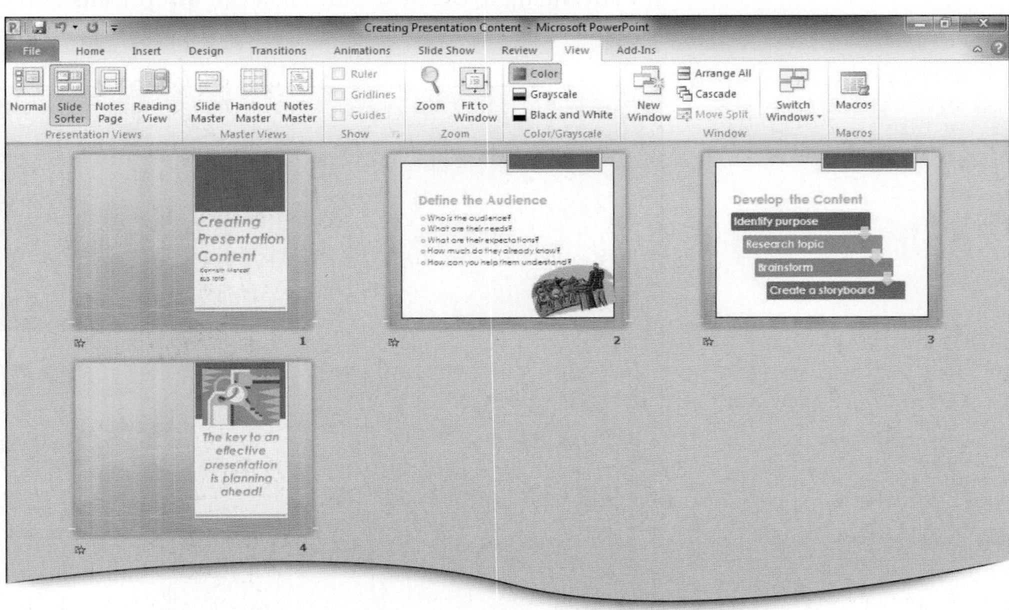

FIGURE 1.6 Slide Sorter View ➤

Reading View displays a full-screen view of a presentation that includes bars and buttons for additional functionality.

Reading View, a new view in PowerPoint 2010, is used to view the slide show full screen, one slide at a time. A Title bar including the Minimize, Maximize/Restore (which changes its name and appearance depending on whether the window is maximized or at a smaller size), and Close buttons is visible, as well as a modified status bar (see Figure 1.7). In addition to View buttons, the status bar includes navigation buttons for moving to the next or previous slide, as well as a menu for accomplishing common tasks such as printing.

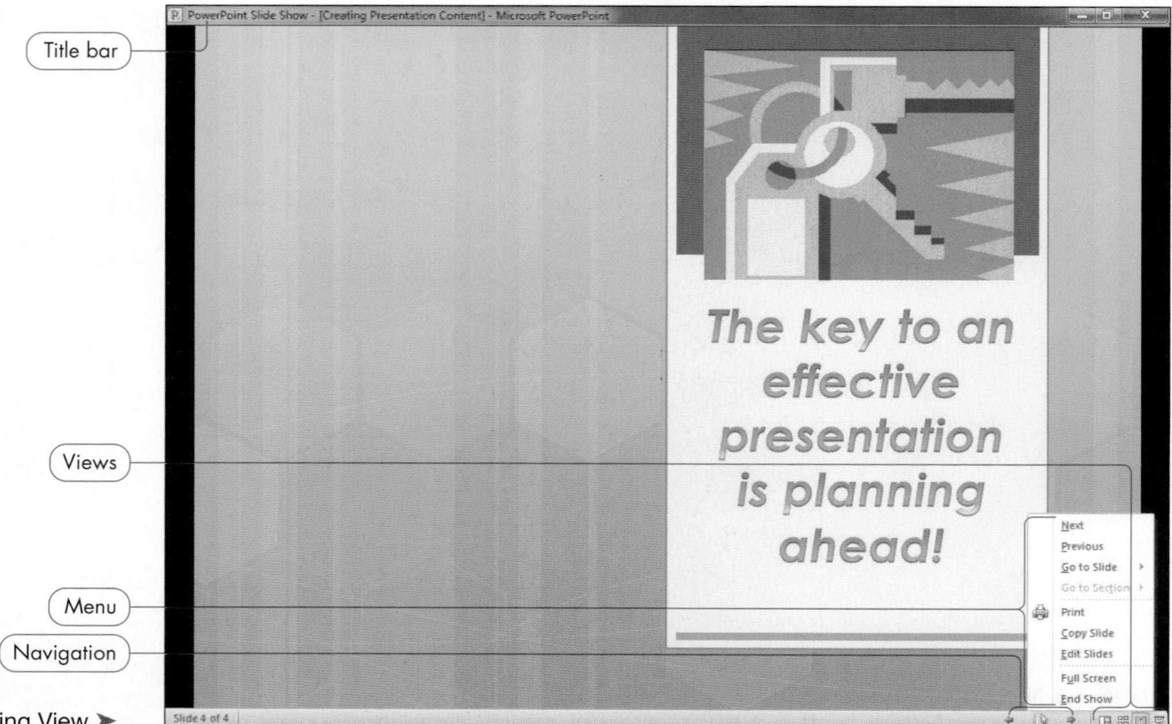

FIGURE 1.7 Reading View ➤

Slide Show view displays a full-screen view of a presentation to an audience.

Slide Show view is used to deliver the completed presentation full screen to an audience, one slide at a time, as an electronic presentation (see Figure 1.8). The slide show can be presented manually, where the speaker clicks the mouse to move from one slide to the next, or automatically, where each slide stays on the screen for a predetermined amount of time, after which the next slide appears. A slide show can contain a combination of both methods for advancing to the next slide. You can insert transition effects to impact the look of how one slide moves to the next. To end the slide show, you press Esc.

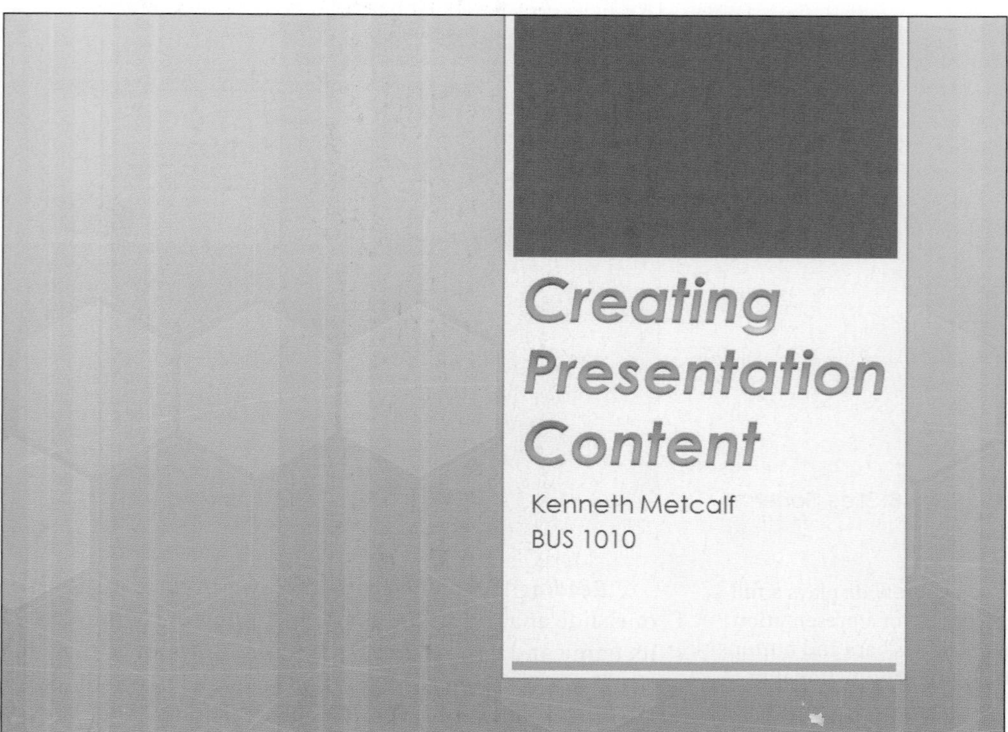

FIGURE 1.8 Slide Show View ➤

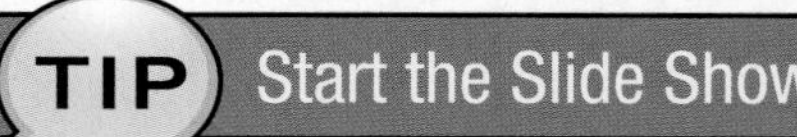

TIP Start the Slide Show

To start a slide show, click the Slide Show tab, and then click either From Beginning or From Current Slide in the Start Slide Show group.

Presenter view delivers a presentation on two monitors simultaneously.

Presenter view is a specialty view that delivers a presentation on two monitors simultaneously. Typically, one monitor is a projector that delivers the full screen presentation to the audience; the other monitor is a laptop or computer so that the presenter can see the slide, speaker notes, and slide thumbnails. This enables the presenter to jump between slides as needed, navigate using arrows that navigate to the previous or next slide, or write on the slide with a marker. A timer displays the time elapsed since the presentation began so that you can keep track of the presentation length. Figure 1.9 shows the audience view on the left side of the figure and the Presenter view on the right side. To use Presenter view, you must use a computer that has multiple monitor support activated.

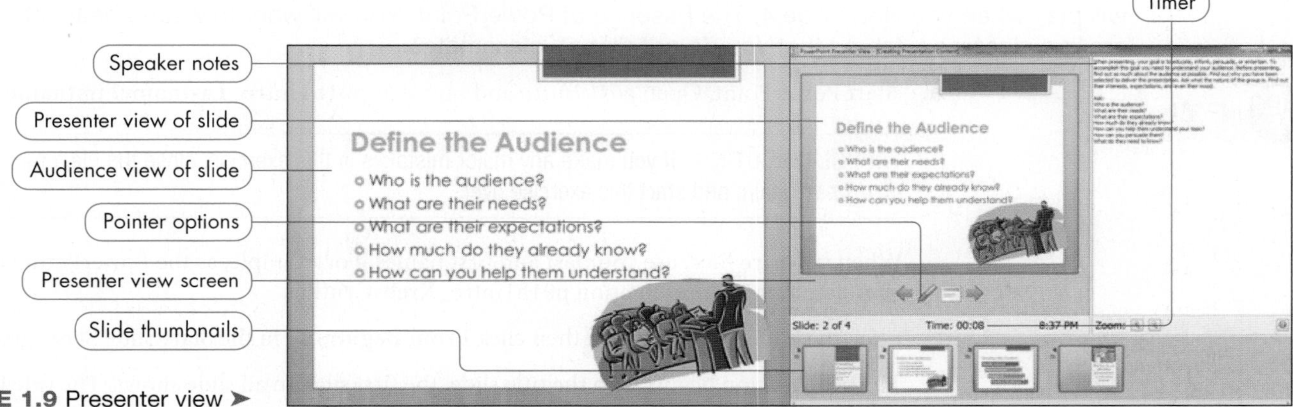

FIGURE 1.9 Presenter view ➤

Saving as a Slide Show

A **PowerPoint show** (.ppsx) is an electronic slide show format used for distribution.

PowerPoint presentations are saved with a .pptx file extension and opened in Normal view so that you can make changes to the presentation. You can save your presentation as a ***PowerPoint show*** with a .ppsx extension by using the Save As command. This file type will open the presentation in Slide Show view and is best for distributing an unchangeable version of a completed slide show to others for viewing. While the .ppsx file cannot be changed while viewing, you can open the file in PowerPoint and edit it. This file type is primarily used for distribution of a finished product.

Quick Concepts Check

1. Describe the main advantage for using each of the following views:
   a. Normal view
   b. Notes Page view
   c. Slide Sorter view
   d. Slide Show view
2. Explain the difference between a PowerPoint presentation (.pptx) and a PowerPoint show (.ppsx).

HANDS-ON EXERCISES

1 Introduction to PowerPoint

You have been asked to create a presentation on the benefits of PowerPoint for the Training and Development department. You decide to view an existing presentation to determine if it contains material you can adapt for your presentation. You view the presentation, add a speaker note, and then save the presentation as a PowerPoint show.

Skills covered: View the Presentation • Type a Speaker Note • Save as a PowerPoint Show

STEP 1 VIEW THE PRESENTATION

In this step, you view the slide show created by your colleague. As you read the contents, you use various methods of advancing to the next slide and then return to Normal view. As you experiment with the various methods of advancing to the next slide, find the one that is most comfortable to you and then use that method as you view slide shows in the future. An audio clip of audience applause will play when you view Slide 4, The Essence of PowerPoint. You will want to wear a headset if you are in a classroom lab so that you do not disturb classmates.

a. Start PowerPoint. Open *p01h1intro* and save it as **p01h1intro_LastnameFirstname**.

> **TROUBLESHOOTING:** If you make any major mistakes in this exercise, close the file, open *p01h1intro* again, and start this exercise over.

When you save files, use your last and first names. For example, as the PowerPoint author, I would name my presentation p01h1intro_KrebsCynthia.

b. Click the **Slide Show tab**, and then click **From Beginning** in the Start Slide Show group.

The presentation begins with the title slide, the first slide in all slide shows. The title has an animation assigned, so it comes in automatically.

c. Press **Spacebar** to advance to the second slide, and read the slide.

The title on the second slide automatically wipes down, and the arrow wipes to the right.

d. Position the pointer in the bottom-left corner side of the slide, and note the navigation bar that appears. Click the **right arrow** in the navigation bar to advance to the next slide. Read the slide content.

The text on the third slide, and all following slides, has the same animation applied to create consistency in the presentation.

e. Click the **left mouse button** to advance to the fourth slide, which has a sound icon displayed on the slide.

The sound icon on the slide indicates sound has been added. The sound has been set to come in automatically so you do not need to click anything for the sound to play. You can hide sound icons if desired.

> **TROUBLESHOOTING:** If you do not hear the sound, your computer may not have a sound card.

f. Continue to navigate through the slides until you come to the end of the presentation.

g. Press **Esc** to return to Normal view.

STEP 2 ➤ TYPE A SPEAKER NOTE

In this step, you add a speaker note to a slide to help you remember to mention some of the many objects that can be added to a slide. You also view the note in Notes view to see how it will print. Refer to Figure 1.10 as you complete Step 2.

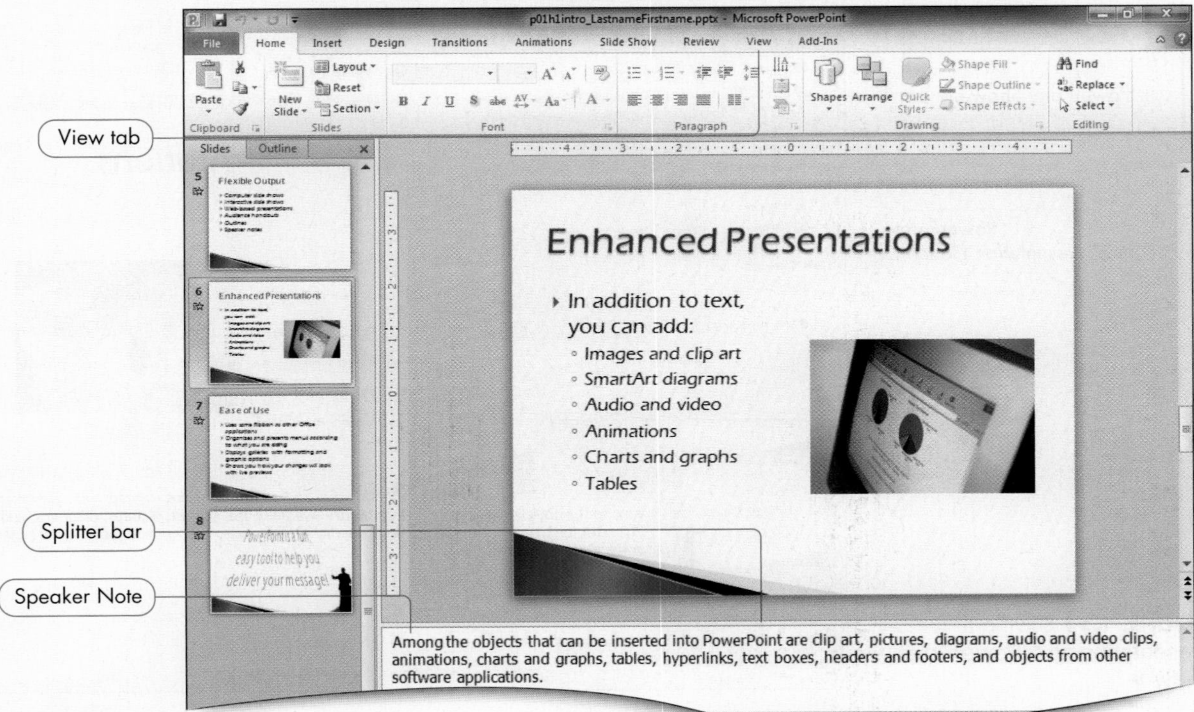

FIGURE 1.10 Speaker Note ➤

a. Scroll down in the **Slides tab**, if necessary, and then click the **Slide 6 thumbnail**.

   Slide 6 is selected, and the slide appears in the Slide pane.

b. Drag the splitter bar between the Slide pane and the Notes pane up to expand the Notes pane.

c. Type the following in the Notes pane: **Among the objects that can be inserted into PowerPoint are clip art, pictures, diagrams, audio and video clips, animations, charts and graphs, tables, hyperlinks, text boxes, headers and footers, and objects from other software applications.**

d. Click the **View tab**, and then click **Notes Page** in the Presentation Views group.

   The slide is shown at a reduced size, and the speaker note is shown below the slide. Drag the vertical scroll bar up to view the speaker note on the first slide.

e. Click **Normal** in the Presentation Views group on the View tab.

f. Save the presentation.

STEP 3 SAVE AS A POWERPOINT SHOW

You want to save the slide show as a PowerPoint show so that it opens in Slide Show view rather than Normal view. Refer to Figure 1.11 as you complete Step 3.

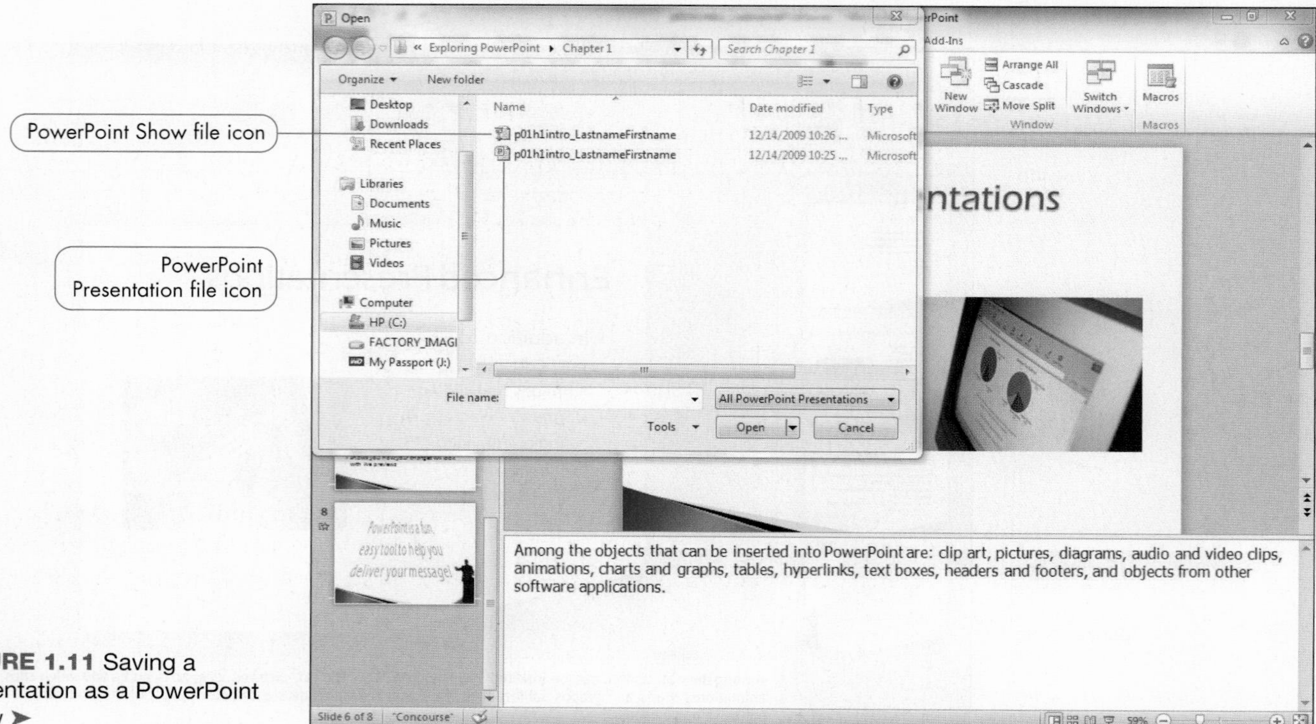

FIGURE 1.11 Saving a Presentation as a PowerPoint Show ➤

a. Click the **File tab**, click **Save As**, click the **Save as type arrow**, and then click **PowerPoint Show**.

b. Leave the file name *p01h1intro_LastnameFirstname* for the PowerPoint show.

   Although you are saving this file with the same file name as the presentation, it will not overwrite the file, as it is a different file type.

c. Click **Save**.

d. Click the **File tab**, and then click **Open**.

   The Open dialog box displays all of the presentations in the folder. Note two *p01h1intro_LastnameFirstname* files are listed. The gray icon is used to indicate the PowerPoint Show file that opens in Slide Show view. The orange icon listed is used to indicate the PowerPoint Presentation file. See Figure 1.11 to view these icons.

e. Click **Cancel**.

f. Save and close the *p01h1intro_LastnameFirstname* presentation, and submit based on your instructor's directions. Keep the presentation open if you plan to continue with Hands-On Exercise 2. If not, save and close the presentation, and exit PowerPoint.

Presentation Creation

You are ready to create your own presentation by adding content and applying formatting. You should create the presentation by adding the content first and then applying formatting so that you can concentrate on your message and its structure without getting distracted by the formatting and design of the presentation.

Planning a Presentation

Creating an effective presentation requires advance planning. First, determine the goal of your presentation. An informative presentation could notify the audience about a change in policy or procedure. An educational presentation could teach an audience about a subject or a skill. Sales presentations are often persuasive calls to action to encourage the purchase of a product, but they can also be used to sell an idea or process. A goodwill presentation could be used to recognize an employee or acknowledge an organization. You could even create a certificate of appreciation using PowerPoint.

Creating an effective presentation requires advance planning.

Next, research your audience—determine their level of knowledge about your topic. Find out what needs the audience has, what their expectations are, and what their level of interest is.

After determining your purpose and researching your audience, brainstorm how to deliver your message. Sketch out your thoughts on paper to help you organize them. After organizing your thoughts, add them as content to the slide show, and then format the presentation.

In this section, you will create a visual plan called a storyboard. You also learn to polish your presentation by using layouts, applying design themes, and reviewing your presentation for errors.

Prepare a Storyboard

A **storyboard** is a visual plan that displays the content of each slide in the slide show.

A ***storyboard*** is a visual plan for your presentation that helps you plan the direction of your presentation. It can be a very rough draft you sketch out while brainstorming, or it can be an elaborate plan that includes the text and objects drawn as they would appear on a slide.

A simple PowerPoint storyboard is divided into sections representing individual slides. The first block in the storyboard is used for the title slide. Subsequent blocks are used to introduce the topics, develop the topics, and then summarize the information. Figure 1.12 shows a working copy of a storyboard for planning presentation content. The storyboard is in rough-draft form and shows changes made during the review process. The PowerPoint presentation shown in Figure 1.13 incorporates the changes.

Storyboard

Purpose: [ ] Informative [X] Educational [ ] Persuasive [ ] Goodwill [ ] Other ______

Audience: IAAP membership
Location: Marriott Hotel
Date and Time: 9/20/12 7p.m.

	Content	Layout	Visual Element(s)
Title slide	Title Slide Planning ~~Before Creating~~ & Presentation Content	Title Slide	O Shapes O Chart O Table O WordArt O Picture O Movie O Clip Art O Sound O SmartArt O ______ Description:
Introduction	Introduction (Key Points, Quote, Image, Other) "If you don't know where you are going, you might end up someplace else." Casey Stengel	Section Header	O Shapes O Chart O Table O WordArt O Picture O Movie ⊗ Clip Art O Sound O SmartArt O ______ Description: ~~confusion image~~ Stengel pic
Key topics with main points	Key Point #1 Identify Purpose ~~Selling~~ (E-Commerce) Persuading Informing Advertising ~~Building~~ Good Will Entertaining Educating Motivation	Two Content	O Shapes O Chart O Table O WordArt O Picture O Movie O Clip Art O Sound O SmartArt O ______ Description:
	Key Point #2 Define Audience Who is ~~going to be~~ the audience? What are the audience's expectations? How much ~~does the audience~~ do they already know?	Title and Content	O Shapes O Chart O Table O WordArt ⊗ Picture O Movie O Clip Art O Sound O SmartArt O ______ Description: Audience Pic
	Key Point #3 Develop the Content Brainstorm ~~and write ideas down~~ Research ~~the topic and take notes~~ Storyboard ~~a rough draft and then refine~~	Title and Content	O Shapes O Chart O Table O WordArt O Picture O Movie O Clip Art O Sound O SmartArt O ______ Description: Smart Art
	Key Point #4 Edit the Content ~~Shorten the text from sentences, phrases~~ & make ~~it~~ text concise. Make bullets parallel + use active verbs	Title and Content	O Shapes O Chart O Table O WordArt O Picture O Movie O Clip Art O Sound O SmartArt O ______ Description:
Summary	Summary (Restatement of Key Points, Quote, Other) The key to an effective presentation is planning ahead.	Title	O Shapes O Chart O Table O WordArt O Picture O Movie ⊗ Clip Art O Sound O SmartArt O ______ Description: Key

FIGURE 1.12 Rough Draft Storyboard ➤

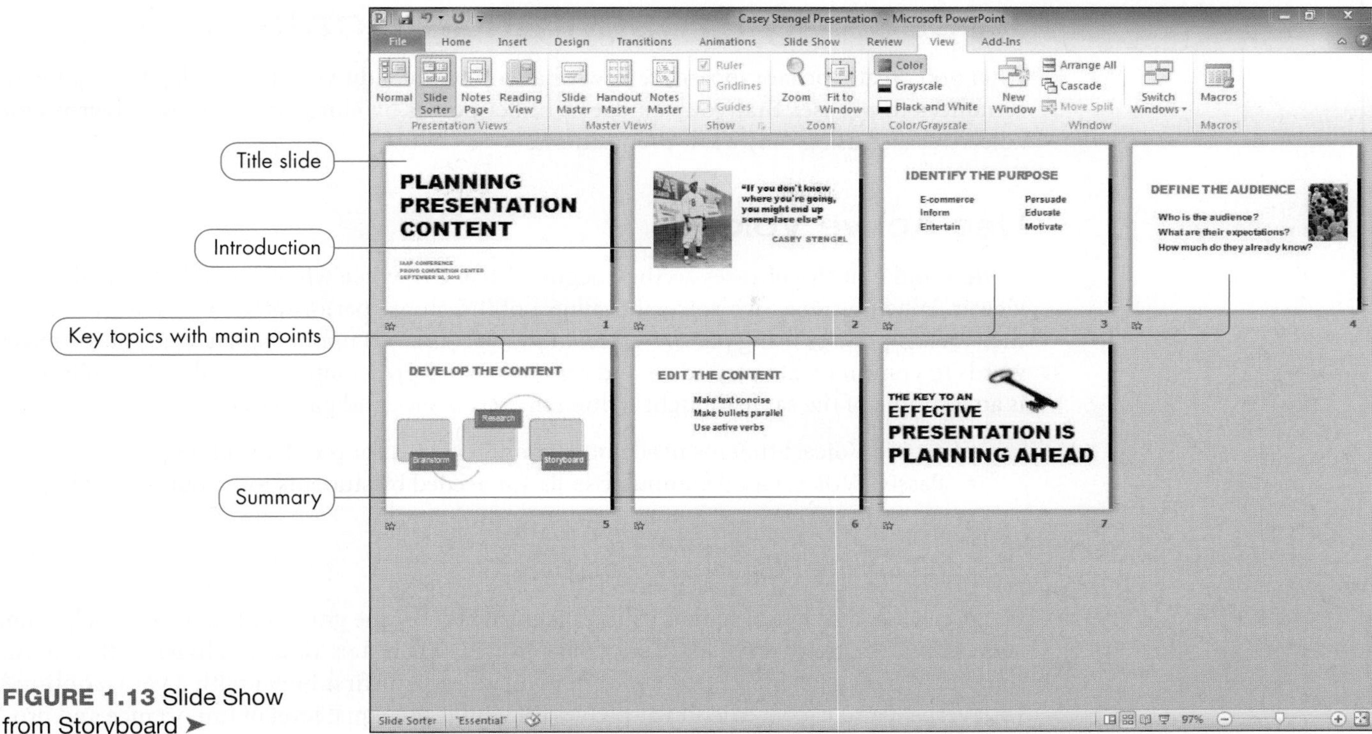

FIGURE 1.13 Slide Show from Storyboard ➤

> **TIP** Storyboard Template
>
> A sample storyboard template, *p01storyboard.docx*, is available in the Exploring PowerPoint Chapter 1 data files folder for you to use when planning your presentations.

Create a Title Slide and Introduction

The title slide should have a short title that indicates the purpose of the presentation. Try to capture the title in two to five words. The title slide should also contain information such as the speaker's name and title, the speaker's organization, the organization's logo, and the date of the presentation. This information is typically included as subtitles.

After the title slide, you may want to include an introduction slide that will get the audience's attention. The introduction could be a list of topics covered in the presentation, a thought-provoking quotation or question, or an image that relates to the topic. Introduction slides can also be used to distinguish between topics or sections of the presentation.

Create the Main Body of Slides

The content of your presentation follows the title slide and the introduction. Each key thought should be a separate slide with the details needed to support that thought. Present the details as bullets or a short paragraph that relates to the content. When determining the content, ask yourself what you want your audience to learn and remember. Support the content with facts, examples, charts or graphs, illustrations, images, or video clips.

Create the Conclusion

End your presentation with a summary or conclusion that reviews the main points, restates the purpose of the presentation, or invokes a call to action. You may also want to repeat your contact information at the end of the presentation so the audience knows how to follow up with any questions or needs.

Assessing Presentation Content

After you create the storyboard, review what you wrote. Edit your text to shorten complete sentences to phrases that you can use as bullet points by eliminating excess adverbs and adjectives and using only a few prepositions.

Use Active Voice

Review and edit the phrases so they begin with active voice when possible to involve the viewer. When using active voice, the subject of the phrase performs the action expressed in the verb. In phrases using passive voice, the subject is acted upon. Passive voice needs more words to communicate your ideas and can make your presentation seem flat. The following is an example of the same thought written in active voice and passive voice.

- Active Voice: Students need good computer skills for problem solving.
- Passive Voice: Good computer skills are needed by students for problem solving.

Use Parallel Construction

Use parallel construction so that your bullets are in the same grammatical form to help your audience see the connection between your phrases. If you start your first bullet with a noun, start each successive bullet with a noun; if you start your first bullet with a verb, continue with verbs. Parallel construction also gives each bullet an equal level of importance and promotes balance in your message. In the following example, the fourth bullet is not parallel to the first three bullets because it does not begin with a verb. The fifth bullet shows the bullet in parallel construction.

- Find a good place to study.
- Organize your study time.
- Study for tests with a partner.
- Terminology is important so learn how to use it properly. (Incorrect)
- Learn and use terminology properly. (Correct)

Follow the 7 × 7 Guideline

Keep the information on your slide concise. You will expand on the slide content when delivering your presentation with the use of notes. Follow the 7 × 7 guideline, which suggests that you use no more than seven words per line and seven lines per slide. Although you may be forced to exceed this guideline on occasion, follow it as often as possible.

After you complete the planning and review process, you are ready to prepare the PowerPoint slide show to use with your presentation.

Using Slide Layouts

A slide **layout** determines the position of objects containing content on the slide.

A **placeholder** is a container that holds content.

PowerPoint provides a set of predefined slide ***layouts*** that determine the position of the objects or content on a slide. Slide layouts contain any number and combination of placeholders. When you click the New Slide arrow on the Home tab, a gallery is displayed from which you can choose a layout. All of the layouts except the Blank layout include placeholders. ***Placeholders*** are objects that hold content, such as titles, subtitles, or images. Placeholders determine the position of the objects on the slide.

After you select a layout, click a placeholder to add your content. When you click a placeholder you can edit it. The border of the placeholder becomes a dashed line and you are able to enter content. If you click the dashed line placeholder border, the placeholder and its content are selected. The border changes to a solid line. Once selected, you can drag the placeholder to a new position or delete the placeholder. Any change you make impacts all content in the placeholder. Unused placeholders in a layout do not show when you display a slide show.

A new, blank presentation includes a title slide layout with a placeholder for the presentation title and subtitle. Add new slides using the layout from the layout gallery. By default, text on slides following the title slide appears as bullets. You can change the layout of an existing slide by dragging placeholders to a new location or by adding new placeholders and objects.

TIP New Slide Button

Click the New Slide arrow when you want to choose a layout from the gallery. Click New Slide, which appears above the New Slide arrow, to quickly insert a new slide. If you click New Slide when the Title slide is selected, the new slide uses the Title and Content layout. If the current slide uses any layout other than Title slide, the new slide uses the same layout.

Applying Themes

A **theme** is a collection of design choices that includes colors, fonts, and special theme effects.

PowerPoint enables you to concentrate on the content of a presentation without concern for its appearance. You focus on what you are going to say, and then use PowerPoint features to format the presentation attractively. The easiest method to format a slide show is to select a design by choosing a theme. A ***theme*** is a collection of formatting choices that includes colors, fonts, and special effects such as shadowing or glows. A theme is automatically applied to all slides, giving a consistent look to the presentation.

To choose a theme, click the Design tab, and then click the More button in the Themes group to display the Themes gallery. Position the pointer over each theme to display a Live Preview of the theme on the current slide, and then click a theme to apply it. The themes are listed alphabetically in the gallery. After applying a theme, be sure to review each slide to make sure the content still fits on the slide. As you gain experience with PowerPoint, you can use other formatting tools to create custom presentation designs. Figure 1.14 shows an image of four title slides, each with a different theme applied. Note the color, font, and text alignment in each theme.

FIGURE 1.14 Example of PowerPoint Themes ➤

Reviewing the Presentation

After you create the presentation, check for spelling errors and incorrect word usage. Nothing is more embarrassing and can make you appear unprofessional than a misspelled word enlarged on a big screen.

Use a four-step method for checking spelling in PowerPoint. First, read the slide content after you enter it. Second, use the Spelling feature located in the Review tab to check the entire presentation. Third, ask a friend or colleague to review the presentation. Finally, display the presentation in Slide Show view and read each word on each slide out loud. Although proofreading four times may seem excessive, it will help ensure your presentation is professional.

TIP Proofing Options

The Spelling feature, by default, does not catch contextual errors like *to*, *too*, and *two*, but you can set the Proofing options to help you find and fix this type of error. To modify the proofing options, click File, and then click Options. Click Proofing in the PowerPoint Options window, and then click Use contextual spelling. With this option selected, the spelling checker will flag contextual mistakes with a red wavy underline. To correct the error, right-click the flagged word, and then select the proper word choice.

Use the Thesaurus

As you create and edit your presentation, you may notice that you are using one word too often, especially at the beginning of bullets. Use the Thesaurus so your bullet lists do not constantly begin with the same word and so you make varied word choices.

Quick Concepts Check

1. Identify the three advanced planning steps you should follow before adding content to a slide show.
2. Define "storyboard" and describe how a storyboard aids you in creating a slide show.
3. Describe two guidelines you should follow when assessing your slide content.
4. Explain the difference between a slide layout and a presentation theme.

2 Presentation Creation

To help state employees learn the process for presentation creation, you decide to give them guidelines for determining content, structuring a slide show, and assessing content. You create a slide show to deliver these guidelines.

Skills covered: Create a New Presentation • Add New Slides • Modify Text and Layout • Reorder Slides • Apply a Theme

STEP 1 CREATE A NEW PRESENTATION

You begin creating the presentation for employees using the default slide layout. You start by entering the text of your presentation, knowing that you can format the presentation later.

a. Press **Ctrl+N** to create a new blank presentation.

   PowerPoint opens a new blank presentation using the default template with the Office theme. The slides have a white background, and the font for the placeholder text is Calibri.

TROUBLESHOOTING: Open PowerPoint if you closed it after completing Hands-On Exercise 1.

b. Save the presentation with the name **p01h2content_LastnameFirstname**.

c. Click inside the **title placeholder** containing the *Click to add title* prompt, and then type **Creating Presentation Content**.

d. Click inside the **subtitle placeholder**, and then type your name.

e. Click in the **Notes pane**, and then type today's date and the name of the course for which you are creating this slide show.

f. Save the presentation.

STEP 2 ADD NEW SLIDES

You continue creating your presentation by adding a second slide with the Title and Content layout. After adding a title to the slide, you create a bulleted list to develop your topic. After adding the presentation content, you proofread the presentation to ensure no errors exist. Refer to Figure 1.15 as you complete Step 2.

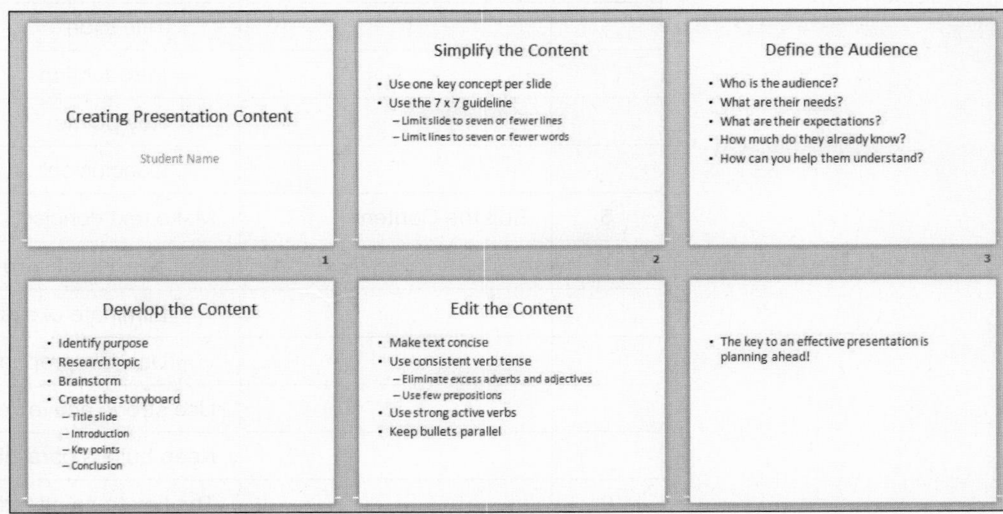

FIGURE 1.15 New Slides with Text Content ➤

a. Click **New Slide** in the Slides group on the Home tab.

The new Slide 2 contains two placeholders: one for the title and one for body content. You can insert an object, such as a table or image, by clicking a button in the center of the content placeholder. To enter text in a bulleted list, type the text in the content placeholder.

b. Type **Simplify the Content** in the **title placeholder**.

c. Click in the **content placeholder**, type **Use one main concept per slide**, and then press **Enter**.

By default, the list level is the same as the previous level.

d. Type **Use the 7 × 7 guideline** and press **Enter**.

e. Click **Increase List Level** in the Paragraph group.

The list level indents, and the bullet changes from a solid round bullet to a hyphen indicating this is a subset of the main level.

f. Type **Limit slide to seven or fewer lines** and press **Enter**.

g. Type **Limit lines to seven or fewer words**.

By default, the list level is the same as the previous level.

h. Click **New Slide** four times to create four more slides with the Title and Content layout.

i. Type the following text in the appropriate slide. Use Increase List Level and Decrease List Level to change levels.

Slide	Slide Title	Bullet Data
3	Define the Audience	Who is the audience?
		What are their needs?
		What are their expectations?
		How much do they already know?
		How can you help them understand?
4	Develop the Content	Identify purpose
		Research topic
		Brainstorm
		Create the storyboard
		Title slide
		Introduction
		Key points
		Conclusion
5	Edit the Content	Make text concise
		Use consistent verb tense
		Eliminate excess adverbs and adjectives
		Use few prepositions
		Use strong active verbs
		Keep bullets parallel
6		The key to an effective presentation is planning ahead!

FYI

j. Click **Spelling** in the Proofing group on the Review tab, and correct any errors. Carefully proofread each slide.

The result of the spelling check depends on how accurately you entered the text of the presentation.

FYI

k. Click the **Slide 2 thumbnail** in the Slides tab pane. Use the Thesaurus to change *main* in the first bullet point to **key**, and then click the **Close button** on the Thesaurus.

l. Save the presentation.

STEP 3 MODIFY TEXT AND LAYOUT

You want to end the slide show with a statement emphasizing the importance of planning and decide to modify the text and layout of the slide to give it more emphasis. You also leave space on the slide so that later you can add an animated clip. Refer to Figure 1.16 as you complete Step 3.

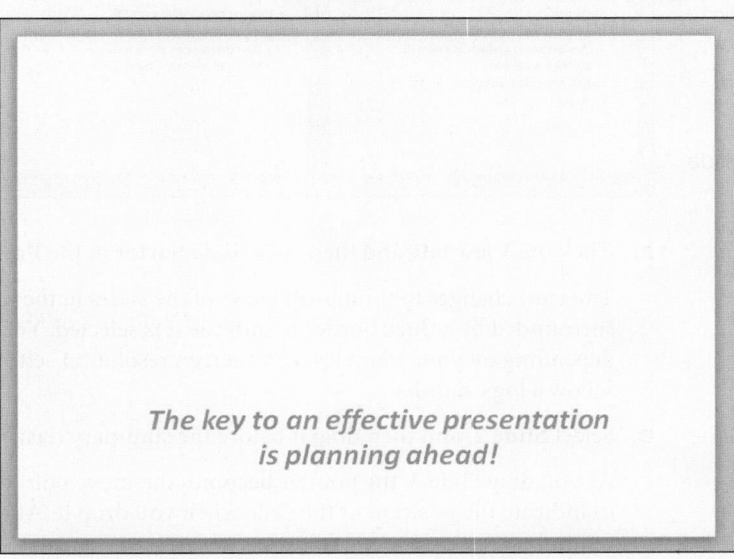
The key to an effective presentation
is planning ahead!

FIGURE 1.16 Slide with Modified Text and Layout ➤

a. Click the **Slide 6 thumbnail** in the Slides tab.

b. Click the **Home tab**, and then click **Layout** in the Slides group.

c. Click **Title Slide** from the Layout gallery.

The layout for Slide 6 changes to the Title Slide layout. The Title Slide layout can be used on any slide in a slide show if its format meets your needs.

d. Click the border of the title placeholder, and then press **Delete**.

The dotted line border becomes a solid line, which indicates the placeholder is selected. Pressing Delete removes the placeholder and the content of that placeholder.

e. Click in the subtitle text.

Clicking inside a placeholder shows the dashed line border, which indicates the placeholder is in edit mode.

f. Click the placeholder border to change it to a solid line, which selects the entire object, and then drag the border of the subtitle placeholder containing your text downward until it is near the bottom of your slide.

The layout of Slide 6 has now been modified.

g. Select the text in the subtitle placeholder if necessary, and then apply **Bold** and **Italic**.

h. Save the presentation.

STEP 4 REORDER SLIDES

You notice that the slides do not follow a logical order. You change the slide positions in Slide Sorter view. Refer to Figure 1.17 as you complete Step 4.

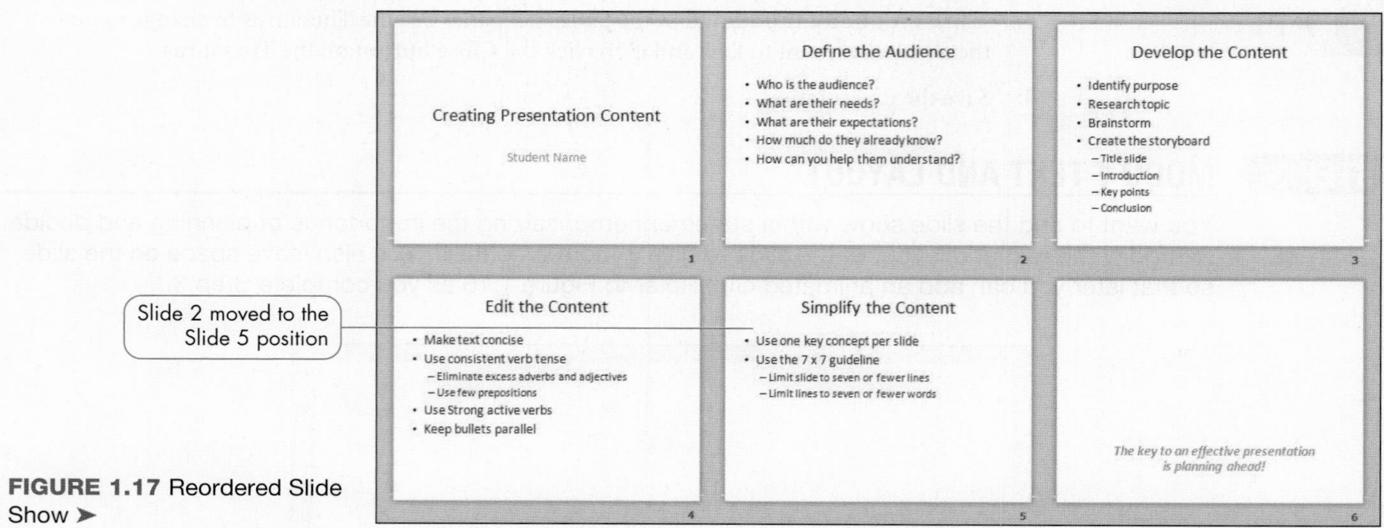

FIGURE 1.17 Reordered Slide Show ➤

a. Click the **View tab**, and then click **Slide Sorter** in the Presentation Views group.

   The view changes to thumbnail views of the slides in the slide show with the current slide surrounded by a thick border to indicate it is selected. Your view may differ from Figure 1.17 depending on your zoom level and screen resolution settings. Notice that the slides do not follow a logical order.

b. Select **Slide 2**, and then drag it before the summary (last) slide so that it becomes Slide 5.

   As you drag Slide 2, the pointer becomes the move pointer, and a vertical bar appears to indicate the position of the slide when you drop it. After you drop the slide, all slides renumber.

c. Double-click **Slide 6**.

   Your presentation returns to Normal view.

d. Save the presentation.

STEP 5 APPLY A THEME

To create a more consistent and business-like look for your presentation, you decide to apply a theme. After applying the theme, you reposition a placeholder to create a more attractive appearance. Refer to Figure 1.18 as you complete Step 5.

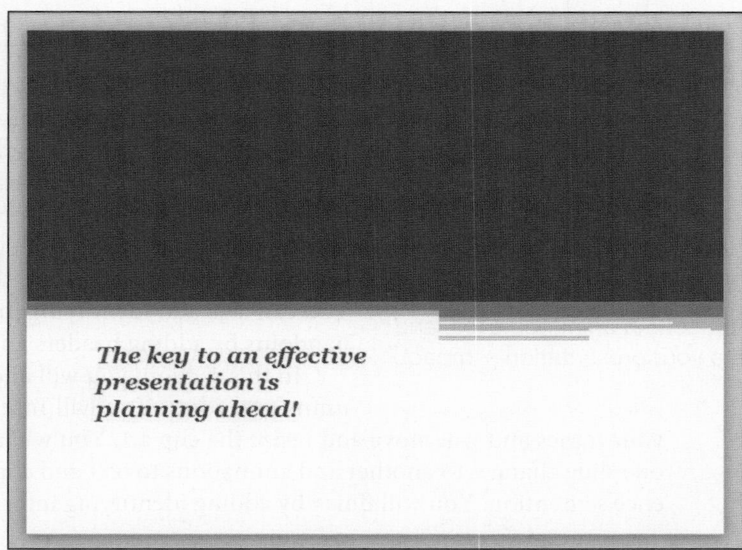
The key to an effective
presentation is
planning ahead!

FIGURE 1.18 Slide 6 with Urban Theme and Repositioned Placeholder ➤

a. Click the **Design tab**, and then click the **More button** in the Themes group.

Point to each of the themes that appear in the gallery to display the ScreenTip with the name of each theme and a Live Preview of the theme on the current slide.

b. Click **Urban** to apply the theme to the presentation.

The Urban theme has a clean, simple background with a business-like color scheme, making it a good choice for this presentation.

c. Click to select the placeholder at the bottom of the screen, and then drag a sizing handle to resize the placeholder so that it contains three lines.

d. Drag the placeholder to the left side of the slide and position it slightly under the double green lines.

e. Keep the presentation open if you plan to continue with Hands-On Exercise 3. If not, save and close the presentation, and exit PowerPoint.

Presentation Development

You can strengthen your slide show by adding objects that relate to the message and support the text. PowerPoint enables you to include a variety of visual objects to add impact to your presentation. You can add clip art, images, WordArt, sound, animated clips, and video clips to increase your presentation's impact. You can add tables, charts and graphs, and SmartArt diagrams created in PowerPoint, or you can insert objects that were created in other applications, such as a chart from Microsoft Excel or a table from Microsoft Word. You can add animations and transitions to catch audience attention. You can also add identifying information on slides or audience handouts by adding headers and footers.

Clip art, images, WordArt, sound, animated clips, and video clips increase your presentation's impact.

In this section, you will add a table to organize data in columns and rows. You will insert clip art objects that relate to your topics and will move and resize the clip art. You will apply transitions to control how one slide changes to another and animations to text and clip art to help maintain your audience's attention. You will finish by adding identifying information in a header and footer.

Inserting Media Objects

Adding media objects such as pictures, clip art, audio, and/or video is especially important in PowerPoint, as PowerPoint is a visual medium. In addition to using the Insert tab to insert media objects in any layout, the following layouts include specific buttons to quickly insert objects:

- Title and Content
- Two Content
- Comparison
- Content with Caption

Clicking Insert Picture from File or Insert Media Clip on the Insert tab opens an Insert dialog box you use to browse for files on your hard drive or a removable storage device. Clicking Clip Art opens the Clip Art pane. Figure 1.19 displays the layout buttons.

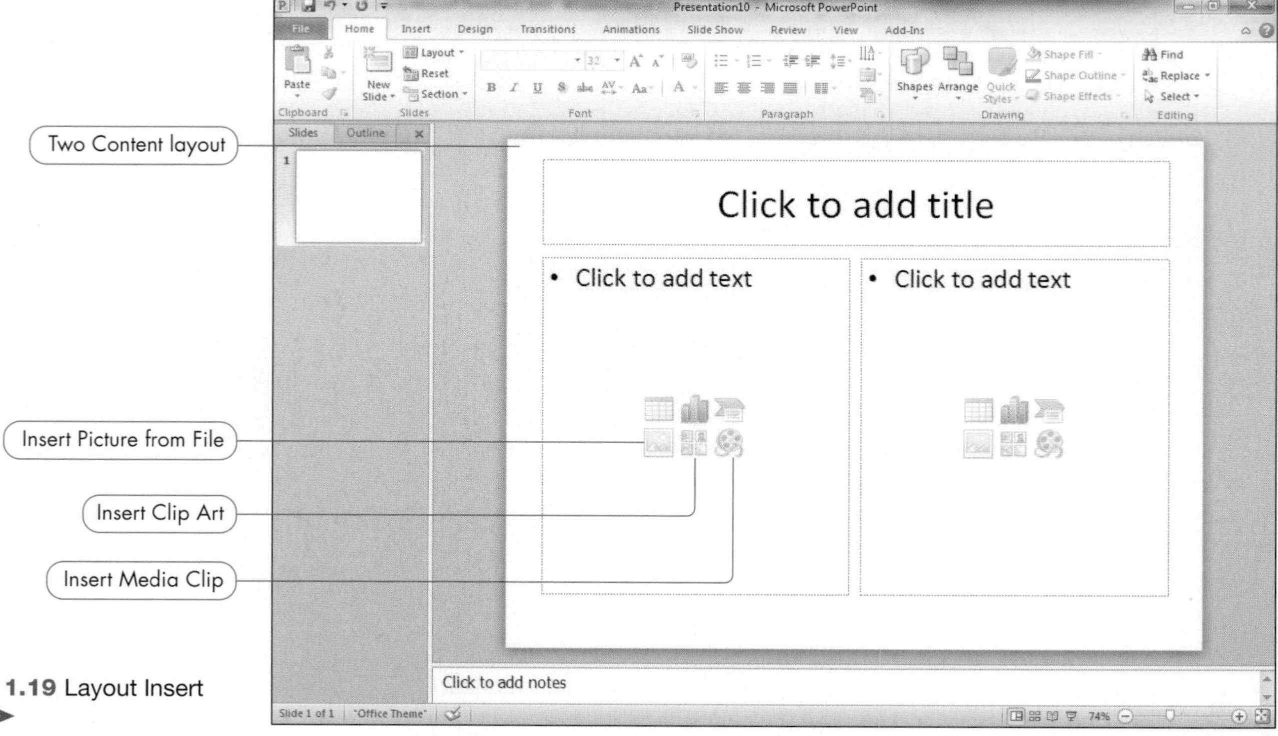

FIGURE 1.19 Layout Insert Buttons ➤

Adding a Table

A **table** organizes information in columns and rows.

A ***table*** organizes information in columns and rows. Tables can be simple and include just a few words or images, or they can be more complex and include structured numerical data.

To create a table on a new slide, you can select any layout, click the Insert tab, and then click Table in the Tables group. You can also click Insert Table on any slide layout that includes it. These two options create a table with a slightly different size, however. Figure 1.20 shows the same data entered into tables created in each of these ways. Once the table is created, you can resize a column or a row by positioning the pointer over the border you wish to resize and then dragging.

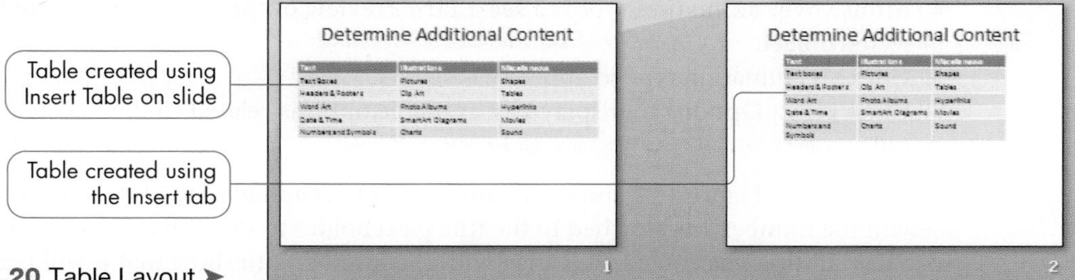

FIGURE 1.20 Table Layout ➤

> **TIP** Movement Within a Table
>
> The insertion point will show you where the text you type will appear in the table. Use the arrow keys or click anywhere in the table to move the insertion point to a new cell. You can also use the Tab key to move the insertion point. Press Tab to move to the next cell or press Shift+Tab to move to the previous cell. Pressing Ctrl+Tab inserts an indent within the cell. Pressing Tab in the last cell of a table creates a new blank row at the end of the table.

Using Animations and Transitions

An **animation** is movement applied to an object in a slide show.

A **transition** is an animation that is applied as a previous slide is replaced by a new slide.

An ***animation*** is a movement that controls the entrance, emphasis, exit, and/or path of objects in a slide show. A ***transition*** is a specific animation that is applied as a previous slide is replaced by a new slide while displayed in Slide Show view or Reading view. Animating objects can help focus the audience's attention on an important point, can control the flow of information on a slide, and can help you keep the audience's attention. Transitions provide visual interest as the slides change.

> **TIP** Animation Painter
>
> PowerPoint's new Animation Painter feature lets you copy an animation from one object to another. To use the Painter, select an object with an animation applied, click Animation Painter in the Advanced Animation group on the Animations tab, and then click the text or object to which you want to apply the animation.

Animate Objects

You can animate objects using a variety of animations, and each animation can be modified by changing its effect options. Keep animations consistent for a professional presentation. The options available for animations are determined by the animation type. For example, if you choose a Wipe animation, you can determine the direction of the wipe. If you choose an Object Color animation, you can determine the color to be added to the object.

To apply an animation to text or other objects, do the following:

1. Select the object you want to animate.
2. Click the Animations tab.
3. Click the More button in the Animation group to display the Animation gallery.
4. Mouse over animation types to see a Live Preview of the animation applied to the selected object.
5. Click an animation type to apply.
6. Click Effect Options to display any available options related to the selected animation type.

The slide in Figure 1.21 shows an animation effect added to the title and the subtitle. A tag with the number 1 is attached to the title placeholder to show that its animation will run first. The subtitle placeholder has a tag with the number 2 to show that it will play after the first animation. The picture is selected and ready for an animation to be attached from the Animation gallery.

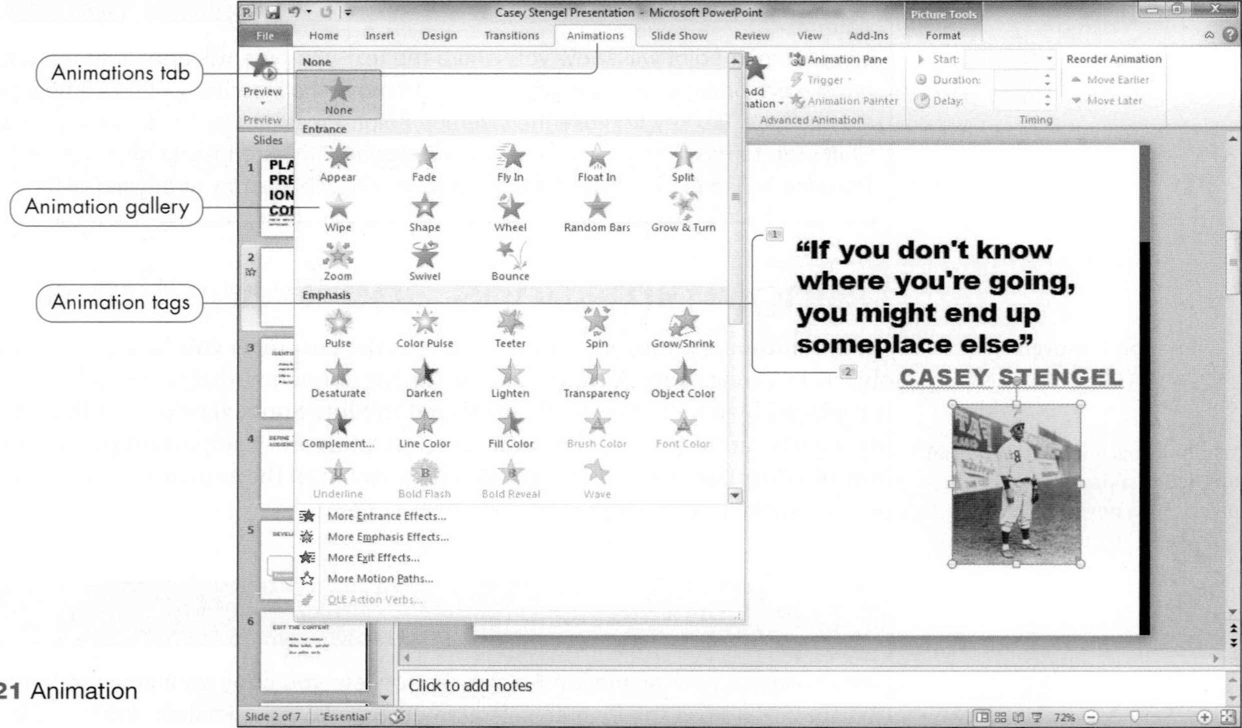

FIGURE 1.21 Animation Gallery ➤

The slide in Figure 1.22 shows a Fly In animation effect added to the picture. A tag with the number 3 is attached and is shaded orange to show that it is selected. The Fly In Effect Options gallery is open so that a direction for the image to fly in from can be selected. Click Preview in the Preview group to see all animations on the slide play. You can also see the animations in Reading View and in Slide Show view. Slides that include an animation display a star icon beneath the slide when viewing the slides in Slide Sorter view.

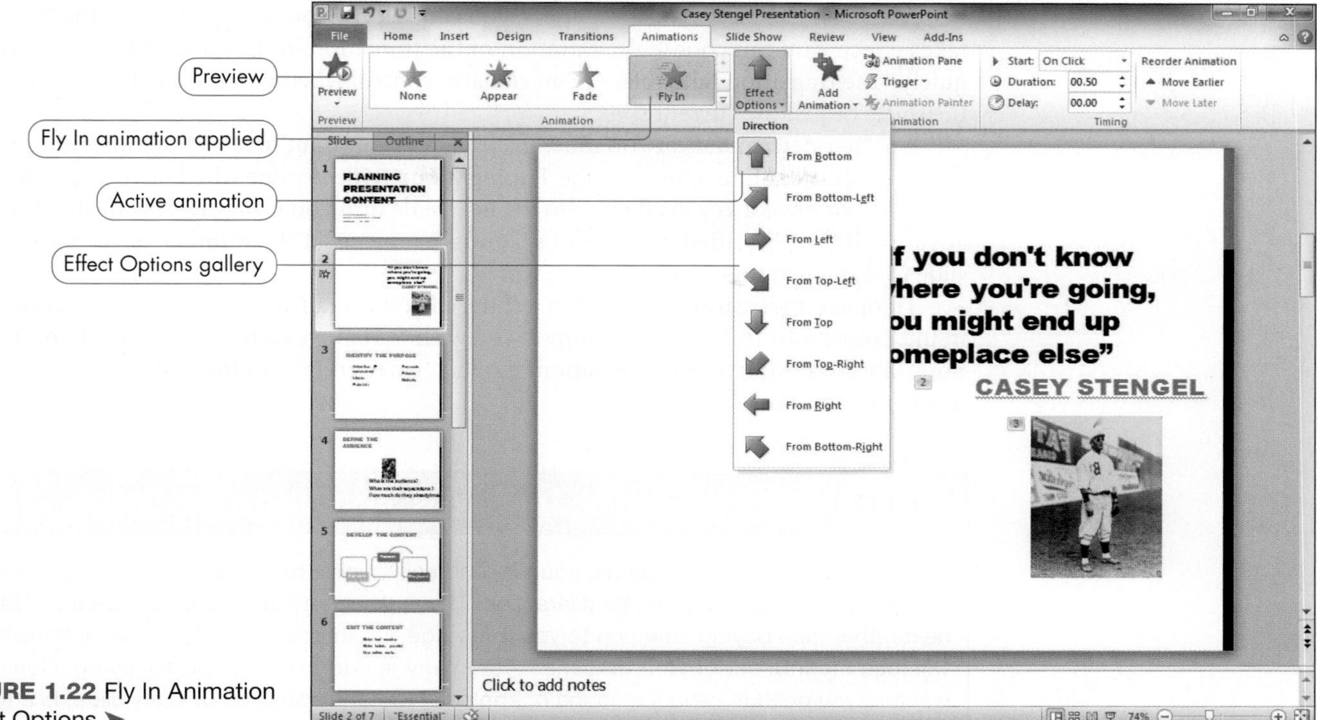

FIGURE 1.22 Fly In Animation Effect Options ➤

Apply Transitions

Transitions are selected from the Transitions to This Slide group on the Transitions tab. You can select from the basic transitions displayed or from the Transitions gallery. To display the Transition gallery, click the More button in the Transition to This Slide group on the Transitions tab. The gallery in Figure 1.23 displays the available transitions in the following groups: Subtle, Exciting, and Dynamic Content. Click Effect Options in the Transition to This Slide group to see any effects that can be applied to the transition. Figure 1.23 shows the Transition gallery.

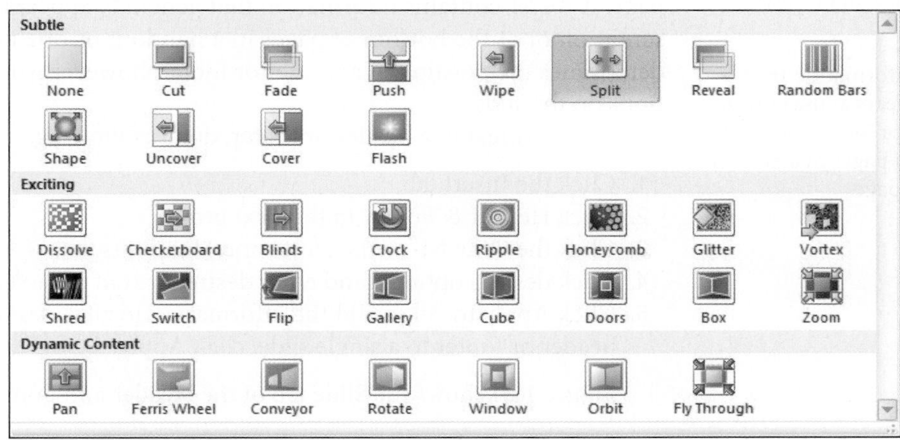

FIGURE 1.23 Transition Gallery ➤

TIP Slide Sorter View and Transitions

Transition effects also can be applied from the Slide Sorter view, where you can apply the same transition to multiple slides by selecting the slides prior to applying the effect. Once a transition is applied to a slide, a star icon appears beneath the slide when viewing the slides in Slide Sorter view.

After you choose a transition effect, you can select a sound to play when the transition takes effect. You can choose the duration of the transition in seconds, which controls how quickly the transition takes place. You can also control whether the transition applies to all the slides or just the current slide.

Another determination you must make is how you want to start the transition process. Use the Advance Slide options in the Timing group to determine whether you want to manually click or press a key to advance to the next slide or if you want the slide to automatically advance after a specified number of seconds. You can set the number of seconds for the slide to display in the same area.

To delete a transition attached to a slide, click the Transitions tab, and then click None in the Transitions to This Slide group. If you wish to remove all transitions, click the Transitions tab, click None in the Transitions to This Slide group, and then click Apply To All in the Timing group.

TIP Effectively Adding Transitions, Animations, and Sound

When you select your transitions, sounds, and animations, remember that too many transition and animation styles can be distracting. The audience will be wondering what is coming next rather than paying attention to your message. On the other hand, very slow transitions will lose the interest of your audience. Too many sound clips can be annoying. Consider whether you need to have the sound of applause with the transition of every slide. Is a typewriter sound necessary to keep your audience's attention, or will it grate on their nerves if it is used on every word? Ask someone to review your presentation and let you know of any annoying or jarring elements.

Inserting a Header or Footer

A **header** is information that generally appears at the top of pages in a handout or notes page.

A **footer** is information that generally appears at the bottom of slides in a presentation or at the bottom of pages in a handout or of a notes page.

The date of the presentation, the presentation audience, a logo, a company name, and other identifying information are very valuable, and you may want such information to appear on every slide, handout, or notes page. Use the Header and Footer feature to do this. A ***header*** contains information that generally appears at the top of pages in a handout or on a notes page. A ***footer*** contains information that generally appears at the bottom of slides in a presentation or at the bottom of pages in a handout or of a notes page. Because the template determines the position of a header or footer, however, you may find them in various locations on the slide.

To insert text in a header or footer, do the following:

1. Click the Insert tab.
2. Click Header & Footer in the Text group.
3. Click the Slide tab or the Notes and Handouts tab.
4. Click desired options, and enter desired text, if necessary.
5. Click Apply to All to add the information to all slides or pages, or if you are adding the header or footer to a single slide, click Apply.

Figure 1.24 shows the Slide tab of the Header and Footer dialog box.

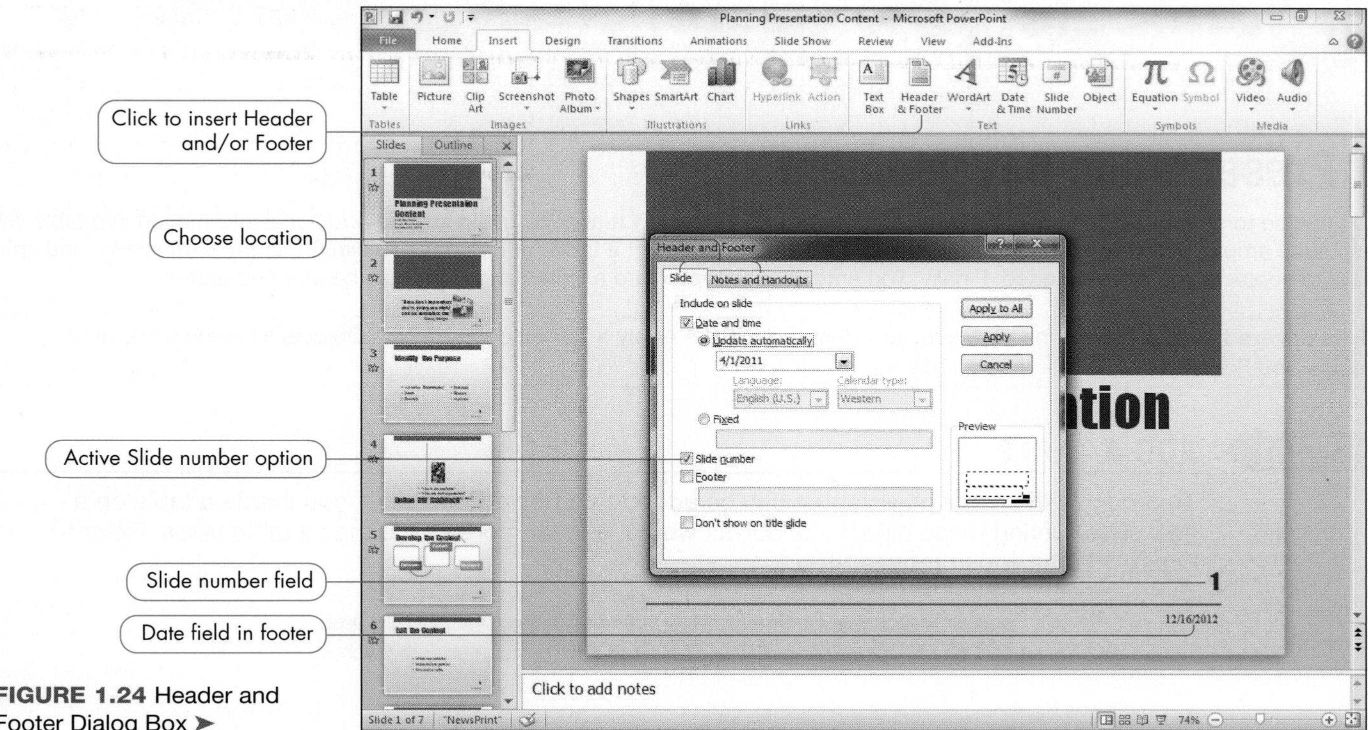

FIGURE 1.24 Header and Footer Dialog Box ➤

Click the Date and time check box to insert the current date and time signature. Click Update automatically if you wish the date to always be current. Once you select Update automatically, you can select the date format you prefer. Alternatively, you can choose the option to enter a fixed date to preserve the original date, which can help you keep track of versions.

Click in the Footer box to enter information. The Preview window allows you to see the position of these fields. Always note the position of the fields, as PowerPoint layouts vary considerably in Header and Footer field positions. If you do not want the footer to appear on the title slide, select *Don't show on title slide.* Click Apply All to apply the footer to every slide in the presentation, or click Apply to apply to the current slide only.

The Notes and Handouts tab gives you an extra field box for the Header field. Since this feature is used for printouts, the slides are not numbered, but the pages in the handout are. As you activate the fields, the preview window shows the location of the fields. The date and time are located on the top right of the printout. The Header field is located on the top left. The page number is located on the bottom right, and the footer field is on the bottom left.

Quick Concepts Check

1. Explain why adding media objects to a PowerPoint slide show is important.
2. How does a table organize information?
3. Describe three benefits that can occur when objects are animated in a slide show.
4. Give an example of when you would use the *Update automatically* option in the Header and Footer feature. When would you use the *Fixed date* option?

3 Presentation Development

You decide to strengthen the slide show by adding objects. You know that adding clip art and additional information in a table will help state employees stay interested and retain information. You insert a table, add and resize clip art, apply a transition, and animate the objects you have included. Finally, you enter a slide footer and a Notes and Handouts header and footer.

Skills covered: Add a Table • Insert, Move, and Resize Clip Art • Apply a Transition • Animate Objects • Create a Handout Header and Footer

STEP 1 ADD A TABLE

To organize the list of objects that can be added to a PowerPoint slide, you create a table on a new slide. Listing these objects as bullets would take far more space than a table takes. Refer to Figure 1.25 as you complete Step 1.

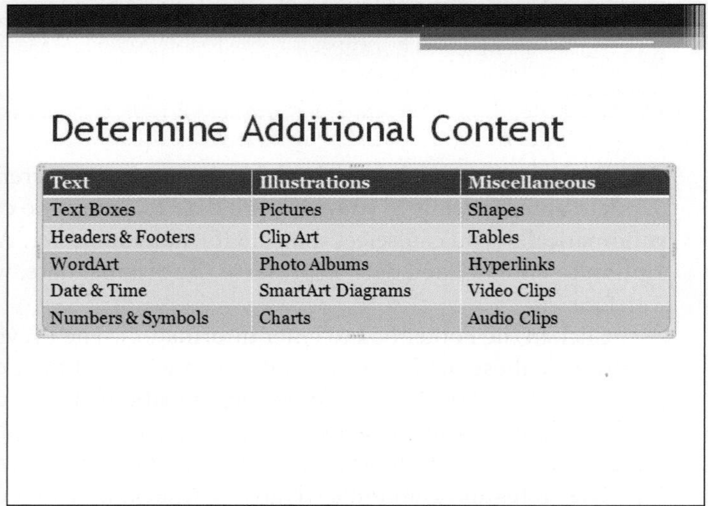

FIGURE 1.25 PowerPoint Table ➤

a. Open *p01h2content_LastnameFirstname* if you closed it at the end of Hands-On Exercise 2. Save the presentation as **p01h3content_LastnameFirstname**, changing *h2* to *h3*.

> **TROUBLESHOOTING:** If you make any major mistakes in this exercise, you can close the file, open *p01h2content_LastnameFirstname* again, and start this exercise over.

b. On Slide 5, click the **Home tab**, and then click **New Slide** in the Slides group.

   A new slide with the Title and Content layout is inserted after Slide 5.

c. Click in the **title placeholder**, and then type **Determine Additional Content**.

d. Click **Insert Table** in the center of the slide.

   The Insert Table dialog box opens.

e. Type **3** in the **Number of columns box**, press **Tab**, type **6** in the **Number of rows box**, and then click **OK**.

   PowerPoint creates the table and positions it on the slide. The first row of the table is formatted differently than the other rows so that it can be used for column headings.

f. Type **Text** in the **top-left cell** of the table. Press **Tab** to move to the next cell, and then type **Illustrations**. Press **Tab**, type **Miscellaneous**, and then press **Tab** to move to the next row.

g. Type the following text in the remaining table cells, pressing **Tab** after each entry.

Text Boxes	Pictures	Shapes
Headers & Footers	Clip Art	Tables
WordArt	Photo Albums	Hyperlinks
Date & Time	SmartArt Diagrams	Video Clips
Numbers & Symbols	Charts	Audio Clips

h. Save the presentation.

STEP 2 INSERT, MOVE, AND RESIZE CLIP ART

In this step, you insert clip art and resize it to better fit the slide. The clip art you insert relates to the topic and adds visual interest. You also add a Microsoft video clip to add movement to a slide. Refer to Figure 1.26 as you complete Step 2.

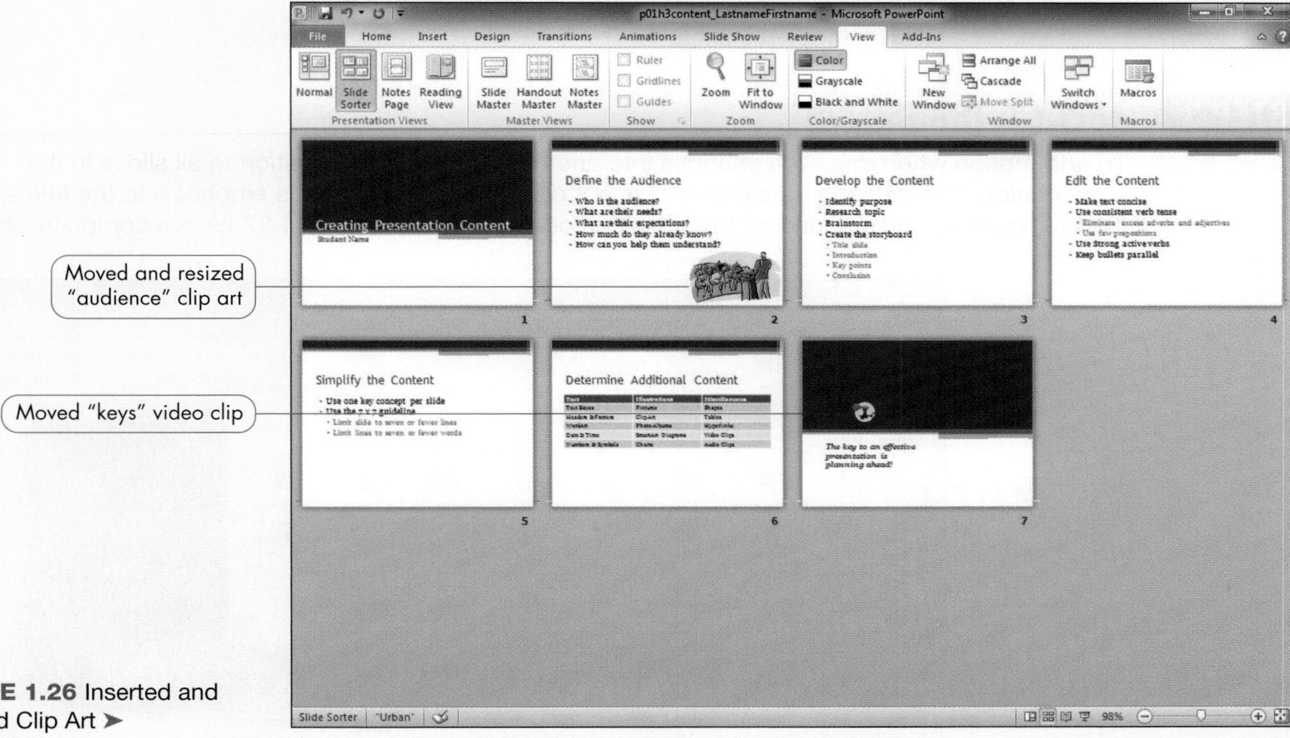

FIGURE 1.26 Inserted and Resized Clip Art ➤

a. On Slide 2, click the **Insert tab**, and then click **Clip Art** in the Images group.

The Clip Art pane displays on the right side of your screen.

b. Type **audience** in the **Search for box** in the Clip art pane.

c. Click the **Results should be arrow**, deselect all options except *Illustrations*, and then click **Go**.

d. Click the image shown in Figure 1.26 to insert it on Slide 2.

> **TROUBLESHOOTING:** If you cannot locate the image in Figure 1.26, select another clip art image that looks like an audience. Expand your search terms to include other result types if necessary.

e. Position the pointer in the center of the image, and then, with the mouse pointer showing as a four-headed arrow, drag the image to the bottom-right corner of the slide.

The clip art is too small. It is overwhelmed by the amount of text on the slide.

f. Position the pointer over the top-left sizing handle of the image, and then drag to increase the size of the clip art.

When you drag a corner sizing handle, the image retains its proportions.

g. Move the clip art image, if necessary, so that it is positioned attractively on the slide.

h. On Slide 7, change the *Search for* keyword in the Clip Art pane to **keys**, change the results to show **Videos**, and then click **Go**.

The videos in the Clip Art pane are animated clip art images that can be inserted in a slide.

i. Refer to Figure 1.26 to determine the keys movie clip to select, and then click the movie to insert it on Slide 7. Close the Clip Art pane.

TROUBLESHOOTING: If you cannot locate the video in Figure 1.26, select another video clip of keys.

j. Reposition the clip so that it is centered above the placeholder containing the text. Do not resize the clip art.

Since this clip is an animated movie clip, if it is enlarged, the image will become distorted.

k. Press **F5** to play the presentation to view the animation.

l. Save the presentation.

STEP 3 APPLY A TRANSITION

To add motion when one slide changes into another, you apply a transition to all slides in the presentation. You select a transition that is not distracting but that adds emphasis to the title slide (Slide 1) by including a sound as the transition occurs. Refer to Figure 1.27 as you complete Step 3.

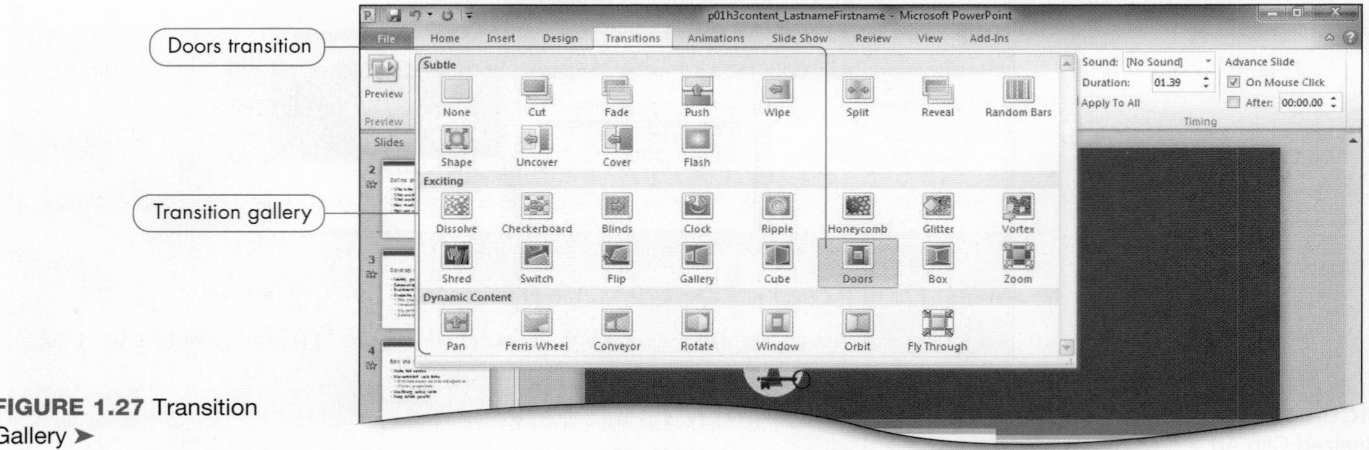

FIGURE 1.27 Transition Gallery ➤

a. Click the **Transitions tab**, and then click the **More button** in the Transition to This Slide group.

b. Click **Doors**.

c. Click **Apply To All** in the Timing group.

The transition effect will apply to all slides in the slide show.

d. On Slide 1, click the **Sound arrow** in the Timing group, and then select **Push**.

The Push sound will play as Slide 1 enters.

e. Click **Preview** in the Preview group.

Because Slide 1 is active, you hear the Push sound as the Doors transition occurs.

TROUBLESHOOTING: If you are completing this activity in a classroom lab, you may need to plug in headphones or turn on speakers to hear the sound.

f. Click the **View tab**, and then click **Slide Sorter** in the Presentation Views group.

The small star beneath each slide indicates a transition has been applied to the slide.

g. Click any of the stars to see a preview of the transition applied to that slide.

h. Save the presentation.

STEP 4 ANIMATE OBJECTS

You add animation to your slide show by controlling how individual objects such as lines of text or images enter or exit the slides. Refer to Figure 1.28 as you complete Step 4.

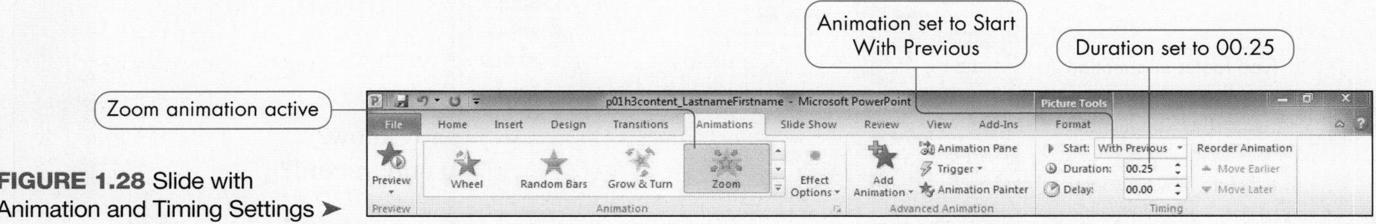

FIGURE 1.28 Slide with Animation and Timing Settings ➤

a. Double-click **Slide 1** to open it in Normal view, and then select the title placeholder.

b. Click the **Animations tab**, and then click the **More button** in the Animation group.

c. Click **Float In**.

The Float In animation is applied to the title placeholder.

d. On Slide 1, select the subtitle placeholder, and then select **Fly In** in the Animation group.

e. Click the **Start arrow** in the Timing group, and then select **After Previous**.

f. On Slide 2, select the clip art image.

You decide to apply and modify the Zoom animation and change the animation speed.

g. Click the **More button** in the Animation group, and then click **Zoom**.

h. Click **Effect Options** in the Animation group, and then select **Slide Center**.

The clip art now grows and zooms from the center of the slide to the bottom right of the slide.

i. Click the **Start arrow**, and then select **With Previous**.

The clip art animation will now start automatically when the bullets enter.

j. Click the **Duration down arrow** once.

The duration changes from *00.50* to *00.25*, so the animation is faster.

k. Save the presentation.

STEP 5 CREATE A HANDOUT HEADER AND FOOTER

Because you are creating this presentation to the Training and Development department, you include this identifying information in a slide footer. You also decide to include your personal information in a Notes and Handouts Header and Footer. Refer to Figure 1.29 as you complete Step 5.

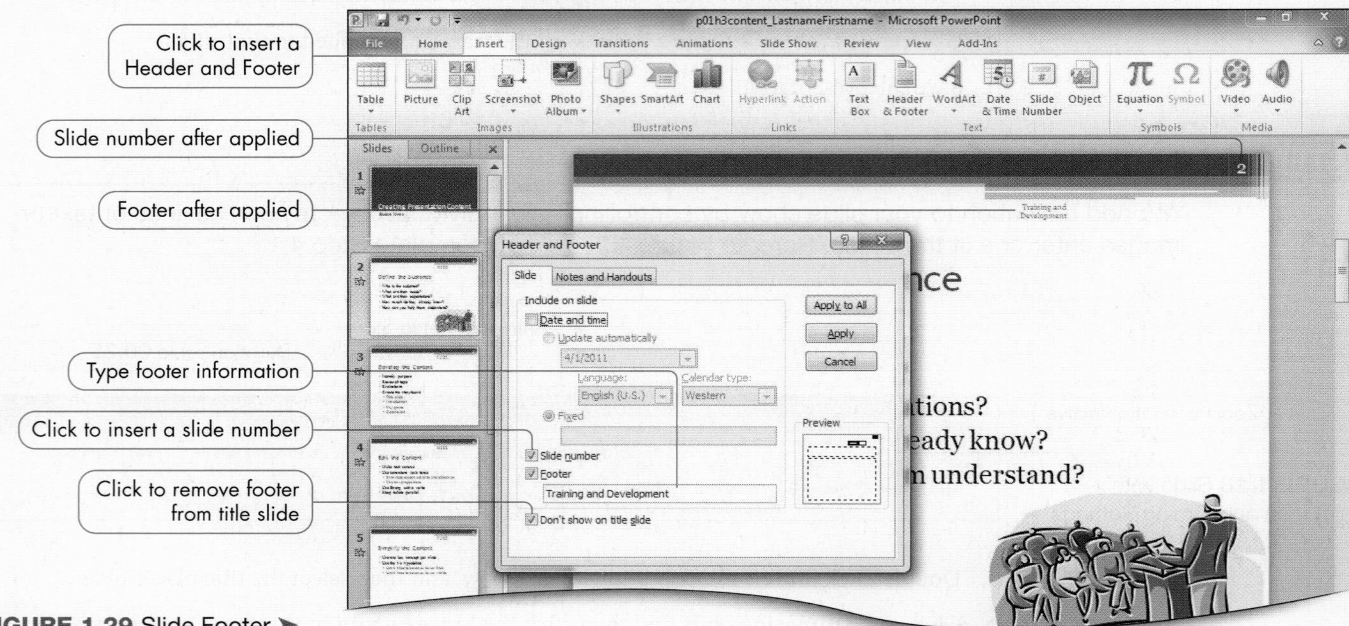

FIGURE 1.29 Slide Footer ➤

a. Click the **Insert tab**, and then click **Header & Footer** in the Text group.

   The Header and Footer dialog box opens, with the Slide tab active.

b. Click **Slide number**.

   The slide number will now appear on each slide. Note the position of the slide number in the Preview window: top right of the slide. The template determined the position of the slide number.

c. Click the **Footer check box**, and then type **Training and Development**.

   Training and Development will appear on each slide. Note the position of the footer in the Preview window: top right of the slide.

d. Click **Don't show on title slide**, and then click **Apply to All**.

   The slide footer appears at the top right on all slides except the title slide. The template positioned the footer at the top of the slide instead of the bottom.

e. Click **Header & Footer**, and then click the **Notes and Handouts tab**.

   The Notes and Handouts header and footer options become available.

f. Click the **Date and time check box**, click **Fixed**, and then type the current date in the **Fixed box**, if necessary.

   Using this option lets you use the date of the presentation on the handout rather than the date you edited the presentation.

g. Click the **Header check box**, and then enter your name in the **Header box**.

h. Click the **Footer check box**, and then type your instructor's name and your class in the **Footer box**.

i. Click **Apply to All**.

j. Switch to Notes Page view to see the header and footer. Return to Normal view, and then save the presentation.

k. Keep the presentation open if you plan to continue with Hands-On Exercise 4. If not, save and close the presentation, and exit PowerPoint.

Navigation and Printing

In the beginning of this chapter, you opened a slide show and advanced one by one through the slides by clicking the mouse button. Audiences may ask questions that can be answered by going to another slide in the presentation. As you respond to the questions, you may find yourself needing to jump back to a previous slide or needing to move to a future slide. PowerPoint's navigation options enable you to maneuver through a presentation easily.

Various options are available for audience handouts. Be aware of the options, and choose the one that best suits your audience's needs.

To help your audience follow your presentation, you can choose to provide them with a handout. Various options are available for audience handouts. Be aware of the options, and choose the one that best suits your audience's needs. You may distribute handouts at the beginning of your presentation for note taking, or provide your audience with the notes afterward.

In this section, you will run a slide show and navigate within the show. You will practice a variety of methods for advancing to new slides or returning to previously viewed slides. You will annotate slides during a presentation and will change from screen view to black-screen view. Finally, you will print handouts of the slide show.

Running and Navigating a Slide Show

PowerPoint provides multiple methods to advance through the slide show. You can also go backward to a previous slide, if desired. Use Table 1.1 to identify the navigation options, and then experiment with each method for advancing and going backward. Find the method that you are most comfortable using and stay with that method.

TABLE 1.1 Navigation Options

Navigation Option	Navigation Method
Advance Through the Slide Show	Press the Spacebar. Press Page Down. Press N for next. Press → or ↓. Press Enter.
Return to a Previous Slide or Animation	Right-click, and then choose Previous from the shortcut menu. Press Page Up. Press P for previous. Press ← or ↑. Press Backspace.
End the Slide Show	Press Esc. Press - (the hyphen).
Go to a Specific Slide	Type the slide number, and then press Enter. Right-click, point to Go to Slide, and then click the slide desired.

Slide Show Controls

You can press F1 at any time during your presentation to see a list of slide show controls. Familiarize yourself with these controls before you present to a group.

When an audience member asks a question that is answered in another slide on your slide show, you can go to that specific slide by using the Go to Slide command. The Go to Slide command is found on the shortcut menu, which displays when you right-click anywhere on the active slide during your presentation. Pointing to the Go to Slide command displays a list of your slide titles so you can easily identify and select the slide to which you want to go. This shortcut menu also lets you end the slide show as well as access other features.

After the last slide in your slide show displays, the audience sees a black slide. This slide has two purposes: It enables you to end your show without having your audience see the PowerPoint design screen, and it cues the audience to expect the room lights to brighten. If you need to blacken the screen at any time during your presentation, you can type B. If you blacken the screen in a darkened room, you must be prepared to quickly brighten some lights. When you are ready to start your slide show again, simply type B again.

If you prefer bringing up a white screen, type W. White is much harsher on your audience's eyes, however. Only use white if you are in an extremely bright room. Whether using black or white, you are enabling the audience to concentrate on you, the speaker, without the slide show interfering.

REFERENCE Delivery Tips

Practice the following delivery tips to gain confidence and polish your delivery.

Before the presentation:

- Practice or rehearse your presentation with your PowerPoint at home until you are comfortable with the material and its corresponding slides.
- Do not read from a prepared script or your PowerPoint Notes. Presenting is not karaoke. Know your material thoroughly. Glance at your notes infrequently. Never post a screen full of small text and then torture your audience by saying, "I know you can't read this, so I will …"
- Arrive early to set up so you do not keep the audience waiting while you manage equipment.
- Have a backup in case the equipment does not work: Overhead transparencies or handouts work well.
- Prepare handouts for your audience so they can relax and participate in your presentation rather than scramble taking notes.
- Make sure your handouts acknowledge and document quotes, data, and sources.

During the presentation:

- Speak to the person farthest away from you to be sure the people in the last row can hear you. Speak slowly and clearly.
- Vary your delivery. Show emotion or enthusiasm for your topic. If you do not care about your topic, why should the audience?
- Pause to emphasize key points when speaking.
- Look at the audience, not at the screen, as you speak and you will open communication and gain credibility.
- Use the three-second guide: Look into the eyes of a member of the audience for three seconds and then scan the entire audience. Continue doing this throughout your presentation. Use your eye contact to keep members of the audience involved.
- Blank the screen by typing B or W at any time during your presentation when you want to solicit questions, comments, or discussion.
- Do not overwhelm your audience with your PowerPoint animations, sounds, and special effects. These features should not overpower you and your message, but should enhance your message.

After the presentation:

- Thank the audience for their attention and participation. Leave on a positive note.

Annotate the Slide Show

An **annotation** is a written note or drawing on a slide for additional commentary or explanation.

You may find it helpful to add ***annotations*** (notes or drawings) to your slides during a presentation. To add written notes or drawings, do the following:

1. Right-click on a slide in Slide Show view.
2. Point to Pointer Options.
3. Click Pen or Highlighter.
4. Hold down the left mouse button and write or draw on the screen.

If you want to change the ink color for the Pen or Highlighter, right-click to bring up the shortcut menu, and then point to Pointer Options to select your pen type and ink color. To erase what you have drawn, press E. Your drawings or added text will be clumsy efforts at best, unless you use a tablet computer that includes a stylus and drawing screen. The annotations you create are not permanent unless you save the annotations when exiting the slide show and then save the changes upon exiting the file. You may want to save the annotated file with a different file name from the original presentation.

TIP Annotating Shortcuts

Press Ctrl+P to change the pointer to a drawing pointer while presenting, and then click and drag on the slide, much the same way your favorite football announcer diagrams a play. With each slide, you must press Ctrl+P again to activate the drawing pointer, in order to avoid accidentally drawing on your slides. Use Page Down and Page Up to move forward and backward in the presentation while the annotation is in effect. Press Ctrl+A to return the mouse pointer to an arrow.

Printing in PowerPoint

A printed copy of a PowerPoint slide show can be used to display speaker notes for reference during the presentation, for audience handouts or a study guide, or as a means to deliver the presentation if there were an equipment failure. A printout of a single slide with text on it can be used as a poster or banner. Figure 1.30 shows the print options in the Backstage view. Depending on your printer and printer settings, your button names may vary. To print a copy of the slide show using the default PowerPoint settings, do the following:

1. Click the File tab to display the Backstage view.
2. Click Print.
3. Click Printer to choose the print device you want to use.
4. Click Print All Slides to select print area and range.
5. Click Full Page Slides to select the layout of the printout.
6. Click Collated to change to uncollated.
7. Click Grayscale to select color, grayscale, or pure black and white.
8. Click Print.

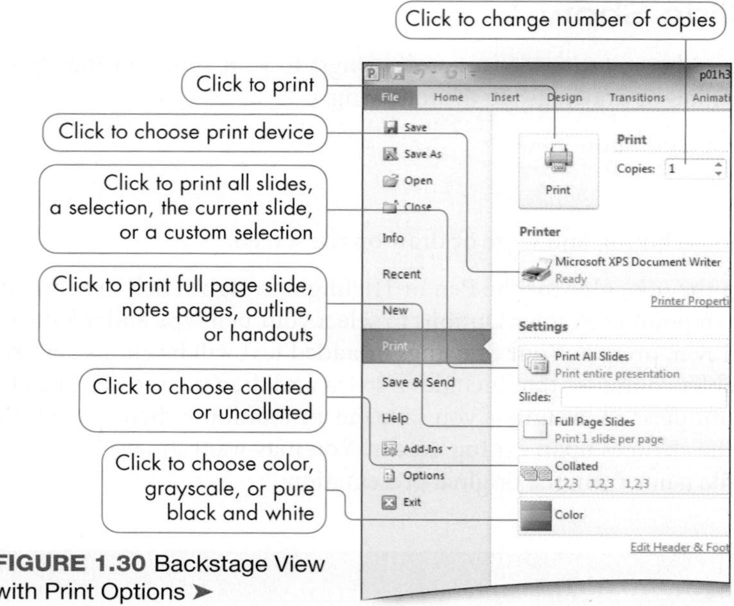

FIGURE 1.30 Backstage View with Print Options ➤

Print Full Page Slides

Use the Print Full Slides option to print the slides for use as a backup or when the slides contain a great deal of detail the audience needs to examine. You can also print the full slides on overhead transparencies to use with an overhead projector during a presentation. You will be extremely grateful for the backup if your projector bulb blows out or if your computer quits working during a presentation.

If you are printing the slides on transparencies or on paper smaller than the standard size, be sure to change the slide size and orientation before you print. By default, PowerPoint sets the slides for landscape orientation for printing so that the width is greater than the height (11" × 8.5"). If you are going to print a flyer or overhead transparency, however, you need to set PowerPoint to portrait orientation, to print so that the height is greater than the width (8.5" × 11").

To change your slide orientation, click the Design tab, click Slide Orientation in the Page Setup group, and then click Portrait or Landscape. If you are going to change the size of the slide as well as the orientation, click Page Setup, and then change the settings in the Page Setup dialog box. If you want to create a custom size of paper to print, enter the height and width.

After you click the File tab, then click Print, you can determine the color option with which to print. Selecting Color prints your presentation in color if you have a color printer or grayscale if you are printing on a black-and-white printer. Selecting Grayscale prints in shades of gray, but be aware that backgrounds do not print when using the Grayscale option. By not printing the background, you make the text in the printout easier to read and you save a lot of ink or toner. Printing with the Pure Black and White option prints with no gray fills.

When you click Full Page Slides in the Print Backstage view, additional options become available. The Frame Slides option puts a black border around the slides in the printout, giving the printout a more polished appearance. The Scale to Fit Paper option ensures that each slide prints on one page even if you have selected a custom size for your slide show, or if you have set up the slide show so that is it larger than the paper on which you are printing. If you have applied shadows to text or objects, click High Quality so that the shadows print. The final option, Print Comments and Ink Markup, is only active if you have used this feature.

Print Handouts

The principal purpose for printing handouts is to give your audience something they can use to follow and take notes on during the presentation. With your handout and their notes, the audience has an excellent resource for the future. Handouts can be printed with one, two, three, four, six, or nine slides per page. Printing three handouts per page is a popular option because it places thumbnails of the slides on the left side of the printout and lines on which the audience can write on the right side of the printout. Figure 1.31 shows the option set to Handouts and the Slides per page option set to 6.

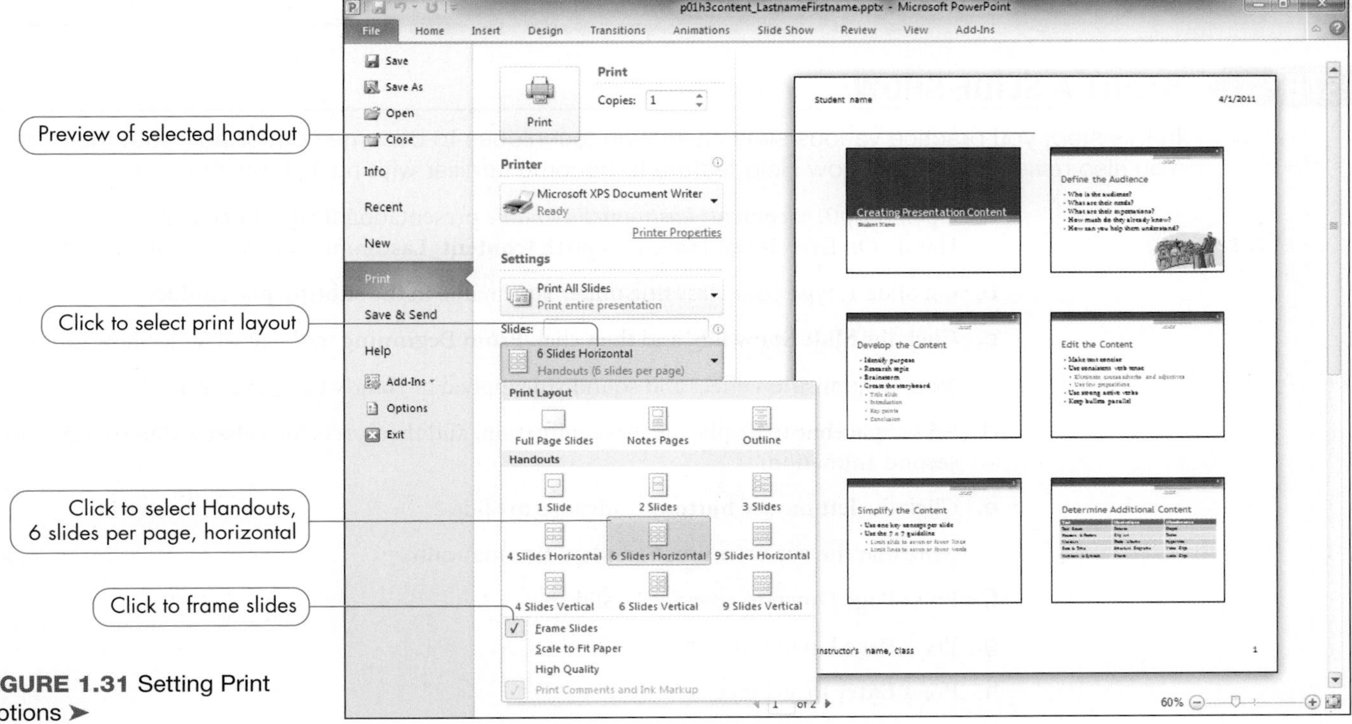

FIGURE 1.31 Setting Print Options ➤

Print Notes Pages

If you include charts, technical information, or references in a speaker note, you will want to print a Notes Page if you want the audience to have a copy. To print a specific Notes Page, change the print layout to Notes Pages, and then click the Print All Slides arrow. Click Custom Range, and then enter the specific slides to print.

Print Outlines

You may print your presentation as an outline made up of the slide titles and main text from each of your slides if you only want to deal with a few pages. The outline generally gives you enough detail to keep you on track with your presentation, but does not display speaker notes.

Quick Concepts Check

1. How do you access the *Go to Slide* command when displaying a slide show?
2. Describe at least three uses for a printed copy of a PowerPoint slide show.

HANDS-ON EXERCISES

4 Navigation and Printing

To prepare for your presentation to Training and Development department employees, you practice displaying the slide show and navigating to specific slides. You also annotate a slide and print audience handouts.

Skills covered: Start a Slide Show • Annotate a Slide • Print Audience Handouts

STEP 1 START A SLIDE SHOW

In this step, you practice various slide navigation techniques to become comfortable with their use. You also review the Slide Show Help feature to become familiar with navigation shortcuts.

a. Open the *p01h3content_LastnameFirstname* presentation if you closed it after the last Hands-On Exercise and save it as **p01h4content_LastnameFirstname**, changing *h3* to *h4*.

b. On Slide 1, type your class title under your name in the **subtitle placeholder**.

c. Click the **Slide Show tab**, and then click **From Beginning** in the Start Slide Show group.

   Note the transition effect and sound you applied in Hands-On Exercise 3.

d. Press **Spacebar** to display the first animation, and then press **Spacebar** again to display the second animation.

e. Click the **left mouse button** to advance to Slide 2.

   Note that the clip art animation plays automatically.

f. Press **Page Down** to advance to Slide 3.

g. Press **Page Up** to return to Slide 2.

h. Press **Enter** to advance to Slide 3.

i. Press **N** to advance to Slide 4.

j. Press **Backspace** to return to Slide 3.

k. Right-click, point to **Go to Slide**, and then select **5 Simplify the Content**.

   Slide 5 displays.

l. Press the number **3**, and then press **Enter**.

   Slide 3 displays.

m. Press **F1**, and then read the Slide Show Help window showing the shortcut tips that are available during the display of a slide show. Practice moving between slides using the shortcuts shown in Help.

n. Close the Help window.

STEP 2 ANNOTATE A SLIDE

You practice annotating a slide using a pen, and then you remove the annotations. You practice darkening the screen and returning to the presentation from the dark screen.

a. Press **Ctrl+P**.

   The mouse pointer becomes a pen.

b. Circle and underline several words on the slide.

c. Press **E**.

The annotations erase.

d. Press **B**.

The screen blackens.

e. Press **B** again.

The slide show displays again.

f. Press **Esc** to end annotations.

g. Press **Esc** to end the slide show.

STEP 3 PRINT AUDIENCE HANDOUTS

To enable your audience to follow along during your presentation, you print handouts of your presentation. You know that many of the audience members will also keep your handouts for future reference.

a. Click the **File tab** to display the Backstage view, and then click **Print**.

b. Click **Full Page Slides**, and then select **4 Slides Horizontal** in the *Handouts* section.

TROUBLESHOOTING: If you have previously selected a different print layout, Full Page Slides will be changed to that layout. Click the arrow next to the displayed layout option.

c. Click **Print** to print the presentation if your instructor asks you to print.

d. Save and close the file, and submit based on your instructor's directions.

CHAPTER OBJECTIVES REVIEW

After reading this chapter, you have accomplished the following objectives:

1. **Use PowerPoint views.** Slide shows are electronic presentations that enable you to advance through slides containing content that will help your audience understand your message. Normal view displays either thumbnail images or an outline in one pane, the slide in one pane, and a Notes pane. Slide Sorter view displays thumbnails of slides to enable you to organize slides. Notes Page view displays a thumbnail of the slide and speaker notes. Slide Show view displays the slide show in full-screen view for an audience. If a presenter has multiple monitors, Presenter view gives the presenter options such as a timer and notes, whereas the audience views the full-screen presentation.
2. **Save as a slide show.** You can save a presentation as a slide show, so that when the file opens it is in Slide Show mode. Slide shows cannot be edited and are saved with the file extension .ppsx.
3. **Plan a presentation.** Before creating your slide show, analyze your audience and research your message. Organize your ideas on a storyboard, and then create your presentation in PowerPoint. After completing the slide show, practice it so that you are comfortable with your slide content and the technology with which you will present it.
4. **Assess presentation content.** After creating presentation content, review what you wrote. Check bullet structure, word usage, and spelling.
5. **Use slide layouts.** When you add a slide, you can choose from a set of predefined slide layouts that determine the position of the objects or content on a slide. Placeholders hold content and determine the position of the objects on the slide.
6. **Apply themes.** PowerPoint design themes give the presentation a consistent look. The theme controls the font, background, layout, and colors.
7. **Review the presentation.** Use the Spelling and Thesaurus features, and review the presentation in Normal and Slide Show views to ensure no errors exist in the presentation.
8. **Insert media objects.** Media objects such as clip art, images, movies, and sound can be added to enhance the message of your slides and to add visual interest.
9. **Add a table.** Tables organize information in rows and columns.
10. **Use animations and transitions.** Animations control the movement of an object on the slide. Transitions control the movement of slides as one slide changes to another. Both features can aid in keeping the attention of the audience, but animations are especially valuable in directing attention to specific elements you wish to emphasize.
11. **Insert a header and footer.** Headers and footers are used for identifying information on the slide or on handouts and note pages. Header and footer locations vary depending on the theme applied.
12. **Run and navigate a slide show.** Various navigation methods advance the slide show, return to previously viewed slides, or go to specific slides. Slides can be annotated during a presentation to add emphases or comments to slides.
13. **Print in PowerPoint.** PowerPoint has four ways to print the slideshow. The Full Page Slide method prints each slide on a separate page. Handouts print miniatures of the slides using 1, 2, 3, 4, 6, or 9 slide thumbnails per page. Notes Page method prints a single thumbnail of a slide with its associated notes per page. Outline View prints the titles and main points of the presentation in outline format.

KEY TERMS

Animation ***p.829***
Annotation ***p.841***
Footer ***p.832***
Header ***p.832***
Layout ***p.820***
Normal view ***p.809***
Notes Page view ***p.810***
Placeholder ***p.820***
PowerPoint presentation ***p.808***
PowerPoint show ***p.813***
Presenter view ***p.813***
Reading view ***p.811***
Slide ***p.808***
Slide show ***p.808***
Slide Show view ***p.812***
Slide Sorter view ***p.811***
Status bar ***p.809***
Storyboard ***p.817***
Table ***p.829***
Theme ***p.821***
Thumbnail ***p.809***
Transition ***p.829***

MULTIPLE CHOICE

1. Which of the following print methods would you use for a large detailed table in your presentation?
   (a) Handout, 6 Slides Horizontal
   (b) Outline
   (c) Notes Pages
   (d) Full Page Slide

2. While displaying a slide show, which of the following will display a list of shortcuts for navigating?
   (a) F1
   (b) F11
   (c) Ctrl+Enter
   (d) Esc

3. PowerPoint's predefined slide arrangements are:
   (a) Placeholder views.
   (b) Slide layouts.
   (c) Slide guides.
   (d) Slide displays.

4. To add an object such as clip art to a slide, use the _______ tab.
   (a) Add-Ins
   (b) Design
   (c) Slide
   (d) Insert

5. Which of the following is a true statement regarding themes?
   (a) A theme must be applied before slides are created.
   (b) The theme can be changed after all of the slides have been created.
   (c) Themes control fonts and backgrounds but not placeholder location.
   (d) Placeholders positioned by a theme cannot be moved.

6. Which of the following views is best for reordering the slides in a presentation?
   (a) Presenter view
   (b) Reading view
   (c) Slide Sorter view
   (d) Slide Show view

7. Normal view contains which of the following components?
   (a) Slide Sorter pane, Slides and Outline tabs pane, and Reading pane
   (b) Slides and Outline tabs pane, Slide pane, and Reading pane
   (c) Slides and Outline tabs pane, Slide pane, and Notes pane
   (d) Slide pane, Notes pane, and Slide Sorter pane

8. Which of the following is the animation effect that controls how one slide changes to another slide?
   (a) Transition
   (b) Timing
   (c) Animation
   (d) Advance

9. Which of the following cannot be used to focus audience attention on a specific object on a slide during a slide show?
   (a) Put nothing on the slide but the object.
   (b) Apply an animation to the object.
   (c) Use the pen tool to circle the object.
   (d) Apply a transition to the object.

10. Which of the following bullet points concerning content development is not in active voice and is not parallel to the other bullets?
    (a) Identify the purpose of the presentation.
    (b) Storyboards are used to sketch out thoughts.
    (c) Brainstorm your thoughts.
    (d) Research your topic.

PRACTICE EXERCISES

1 Student Success

The slide show you create in this practice exercise covers concepts and skills that will help you be successful in college. You create a title slide, an introduction, four slides containing main points of the presentation, and a conclusion slide. Then, you review the presentation, and then edit a slide so that the text of the bulleted items is parallel. Finally, you print a title page to use as a cover and notes pages to staple together as a reference. This exercise follows the same set of skills as used in Hands-On Exercises 1–4 in the chapter. Refer to Figure 1.32 as you complete the exercise.

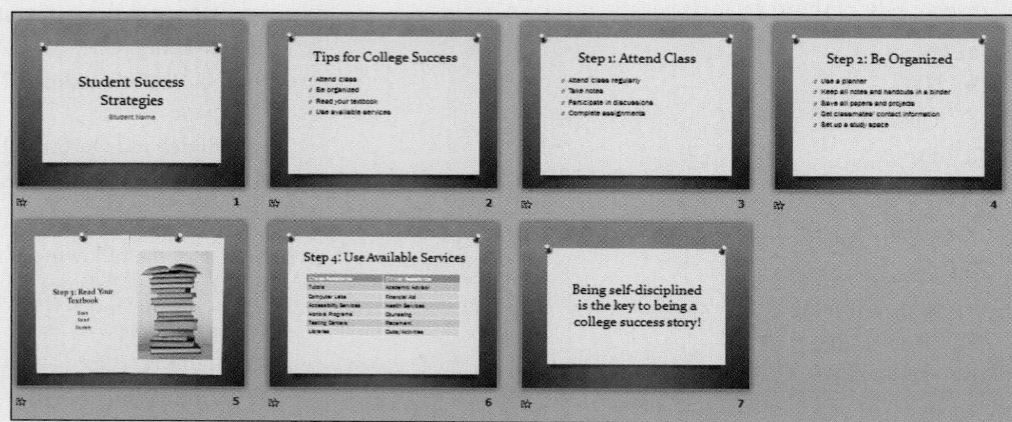

FIGURE 1.32 Student Success Strategies ➤

a. Open a new blank presentation and save it as *p01p1success_LastnameFirstname*.

b. Click the **Insert tab**, click **Header & Footer** in the Text group, and then click the **Notes and Handouts tab**. Make the following changes:
   - Click the **Date and time check box**, and then click **Update automatically** (if necessary).
   - Click the **Header check box**, and then type your name in the **Header box**.
   - Click the **Footer check box**, and then type your instructor's name and your class in the **Footer box**. Click **Apply to All**.

c. Click the **Design tab**, click the **More button** in the Themes group, and then click **Pushpin**.

d. On Slide 1, click in the **title placeholder**, and then type **Student Success Strategies**. Click in the **subtitle placeholder**, and then type your name.

e. Click **New Slide** in the Slides group on the Home tab to create a new slide (Slide 2) for the introduction of the slide show. Type **Tips for College Success** in the **title placeholder**, and then type the following bullet text in the **content placeholder**:
   - **Class Attendance**
   - **Be organized**
   - **Read your textbook**
   - **Use available services**

f. Click **New Slide** in the Slides group on the Home tab to create a new slide (Slide 3) for the first main point of the slide show. Type **Step 1: Attend Class** in the **title placeholder**, and then type the following bullet text in the **content placeholder**:
   - **Class attendance**
   - **Take notes**
   - **Participate in discussions**
   - **Complete assignments**

g. Type the following in the **Notes pane**: **Attend class even if you think your instructor won't notice or care. When you miss class, you lose the opportunity to listen to the lecture, take notes, participate in discussions, and you also miss assignments, quizzes, and tests. If you have to miss class, get notes and assignments from a classmate.**

h. Click **New Slide** in the Slides group on the Home tab to create a new slide (Slide 4) for the second main point of the slide show. Type **Step 2: Be Organized** in the **title placeholder**, and then enter the following bullet text in the **content placeholder**:

- **Use a planner**
- **Keep all notes and handouts in a binder**
- **Save all papers and projects**
- **Get classmates' contact information**
- **Set up a study space**

i. Type the following in the **Notes pane** for Slide 4: **Record every assignment, quiz, and exam date in a planner. Organize all of your class notes by date and put them in a 3-ring binder so you have everything you need in one location. Keep all returned papers, quizzes, and exams in the same binder so you not only have them to use as a resource for studying for a final exam, but you have a record of your grades for the course. Get phone numbers and/or e-mail addresses from at least two people in your class so if you have a question about an assignment or a test, or need notes, you can contact them. Designate a study area in your living space.**

j. Click the **New Slide arrow** in the Slides group on the Home tab. Click **Content with Caption** to create a new slide (Slide 5) for the third main point of the slide show. Type **Step 3: Read Your Textbook** in the **title placeholder**, and then enter the following text in the **content placeholder** on the left side of the slide following the title:

- **Scan**
- **Read**
- **Review**

k. Click the **Clip Art icon** in the content placeholder on the right side of the slide. Type **textbook** in the **Search for box**. Click the **Results should be arrow**, and deselect all categories except *Photographs*. Include results from Office.com, and then click **Go**. Click the image of stacked textbooks to insert it on the slide, as shown in Figure 1.32. Close the Clip Art task pane.

> **TROUBLESHOOTING:** If you cannot locate the image in Figure 1.32, select another clip art image of a textbook or textbooks. Expand your search terms to include other result types if necessary.

l. Type the following in the **Notes pane**: **Scan chapter titles, subtitles, everything in margins, and all bold or italic print. Look at all pictures, illustrations, and charts and graphs. Read the chapter summary and review questions. Next, read the entire chapter for detail and to increase your comprehension. Finally, review bold and italic information in the chapter again and ask why the author thought they were important enough to call attention to them. This is often the information an instructor focuses on when testing.**

m. Click the **New Slide arrow** in the Slides group on the Home tab. Click **Title and Content** to create a new slide (Slide 6) for the last main point of the slide show. Type **Step 4: Use Available Services** in the **title placeholder**.

n. Click the **Insert Table icon** in the content placeholder. Set *Number of columns* to **2** and *Number of rows* to **7**. Click **OK**. Type the following text in the columns:

Class Assistance	Other Assistance
Tutors	Academic Advisor
Computer Labs	Financial Aid
Accessibility Services	Health Services
Honors Programs	Counseling
Testing Centers	Placement
Libraries	Clubs/Activities

o. Type the following in the **Notes pane** for Slide 6: **You can use campus facilities like computer labs without charge because typically the cost is covered through fees you pay. You can also get questions answered and problems resolved by talking to personnel in campus offices.**

p. Click the **New Slide arrow** in the Slides group on the Home tab. Click **Title Slide** to create a new slide (Slide 7) for the conclusion slide of the slide show. Type **Being self-disciplined is the key to being a college success story!** in the **title placeholder**. Select the border of the subtitle placeholder, and then press **Delete**. Select the border of the title placeholder, and then drag the placeholder until the text is approximately centered in the white area.

q. Review Slide 2 and note that the slide bullets are not in parallel construction. The first bullet point needs to be changed to active voice. Select **Class Attendance**, and then type **Attend class**.

r. Click the **Tranisitions tab**, and then click the **More button** in the Transition to This Slide group. Click **Push** in the Transition to This Slide group.

s. Click **Apply to All** in the Timing Group.

t. On Slide 1, click the **File tab**, click **Print**, click **Full Page Slides**, and click **Frame Slides** to activate it. Click **Print All Slides**, and then click **Print Current Slide**. Click **Print Current Slide** if your instructor asks you to submit a printed slide.

u. Click the **File tab**, click **Print**, click **Print Current Slide**, and then click **Custom Range**. Type **2-7** as the slide range. Click **Full Page Slides**, and then select **Notes Pages**. Click **Notes Pages**, click **Frame Slides**, and then click **Print** if necessary.

v. Staple the title page you printed to use as a cover page to the front of the Notes Pages if your instructor asked you to print this exercise.

w. Press **Ctrl+S** to save the presentation. Click the **File tab**, click **Save As**, change the Save as type to **PowerPoint Show**, and then click **Save**. Close the presentation. Submit files based on your instructor's directions.

2 Tips for a Successful Presentation

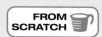

Your employer is a successful author who has been asked by the local International Association of Administrative Professionals (IAAP) to give tips for presenting successfully using PowerPoint. He created a storyboard of his presentation and has asked you to create the presentation from the storyboard. This exercise follows the same set of skills as used in Hands-On Exercises 2 and 3 in the chapter. Refer to Figure 1.33 as you complete this exercise.

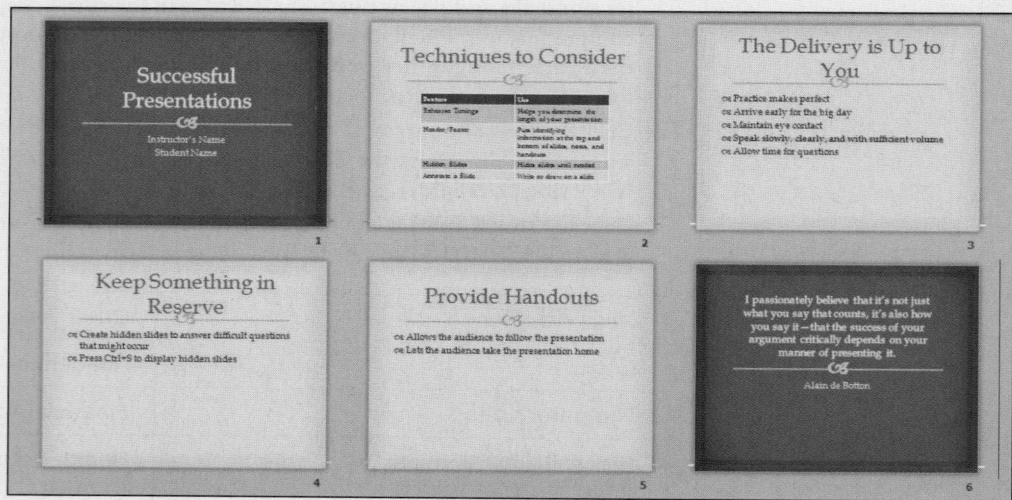

FIGURE 1.33 Successful Presentations ➤

a. Open a new blank presentation and save it as **p01p2tips_LastnameFirstname**.

b. Click the **Insert tab**, click **Header & Footer**, and then click the **Notes and Handouts tab**.

c. Click the **Date and time check box**, and then click **Update automatically**, if necessary.

d. Click the **Header check box**, and then type your name in the **Header box**.

e. Click the **Footer check box**, and then type your instructor's name and your class. Click **Apply to All**.

f. On Slide 1, click in the **title placeholder**, and then type **Successful Presentations**. Click in the **subtitle placeholder**, and then type your instructor's name. On the next line of the subtitle placeholder, type your name.
g. Click the **Home tab**, click the **New Slide arrow** in the Slides group, and then click **Title Only**.
h. Click in the **title placeholder**, and then type **Techniques to Consider**.
i. Click the **Insert tab**, click **Table** in the Tables group, and then use the grid to select two columns and five rows.
j. Type the following information in the table cells, pressing **Tab** to move from cell to cell. Position the table attractively on the slide.

Feature	Use
Rehearse Timings	Helps you determine the length of your presentation
Header/Footer	Puts identifying information on the top and bottom of slides, notes, and handouts
Hidden Slides	Hides slides until needed
Annotate a Slide	Write or draw on a slide

k. Click the **Home tab**, click the **New Slide arrow** in the Slides group, and then click **Title and Content**. Type **The Delivery is Up to You** in the **title placeholder**.
l. Click in the **content placeholder**, and then type the following bullet text:
   - **Practice makes perfect**
   - **Arrive early on the big day**
   - **Maintain eye contact**
   - **Speak slowly, clearly, and with sufficient volume**
   - **Allow time for questions**

m. Click **New Slide**, and then type **Keep Something in Reserve** in the **title placeholder**.
n. Click in the **content placeholder**, and then type the following bullet text:
   - **Create hidden slides to answer difficult questions that might occur**
   - **Press Ctrl+S while in Slide Show view to display hidden slides**

o. Click **New Slide**, and then type **Provide Handouts** in the **title placeholder**.
p. Click in the **content placeholder**, and then type the following bullet text:
   - **Allows the audience to follow the presentation**
   - **Lets the audience take the presentation home**

q. Click the **New Slide arrow**, and then click **Title Slide**.
r. Type **I passionately believe that it's not just what you say that counts, it's also how you say it—that the success of your argument critically depends on your manner of presenting it.** in the **title placeholder**, and then click the placeholder border. Change the font size to **28**.
s. Type **Alain de Botton** in the **subtitle placeholder**.
t. Check **Spelling**. Accept *Lets* in Slide 5, if necessary. Review the presentation in Slide Show view to fix any spelling or grammatical errors.
u. Click the **Design tab**, click the **More button** in the Themes group, and then click **Hardcover**.
v. Click the **Slide Show tab**, and then click **From Beginning** in the Start Slide Show group. Press **Page Down** to advance through the slides. When you reach the last slide of the slide show, press the number **3**, and then press **Enter** to return to Slide 3.
w. Right-click, point to **Pointer Options**, and then click **Highlighter**. Highlight **Speak slowly, clearly, and with sufficient volume**.
x. Press **Esc** when you reach the black slide at the end of the slide show, and then click **Keep** to keep your slide annotations.
y. Press **Ctrl+S** to save the presentation. Close the file and submit based on your instructor's directions.

3 Copyright and the Law

The ethics and values class you are taking this semester requires a final presentation to the class. You create a presentation to review basic copyright law and software licensing. You add clip art, a transition, and an animation. This exercise follows the same set of skills as used in Hands-On Exercises 2, 3, and 4 in the chapter. Refer to Figure 1.34 as you complete this exercise.

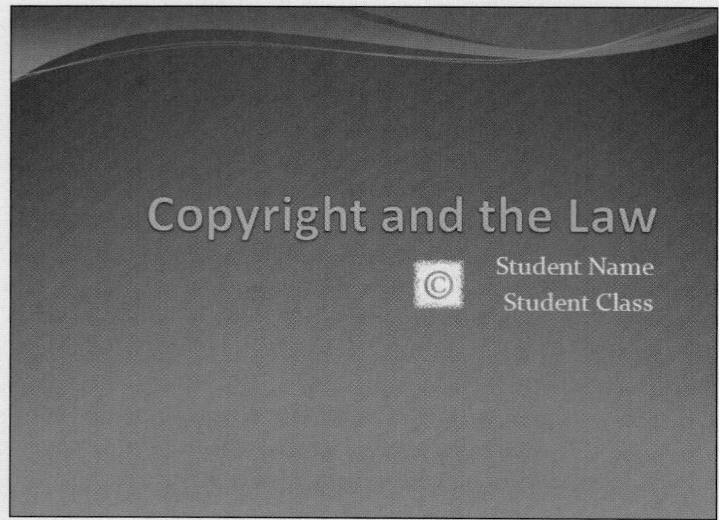

FIGURE 1.34 Copyright and the Law Presentation ➤

a. Open *p01p3copyright* and save it as **p01p3copyright_LastnameFirstname**.
b. Click the **Insert tab**, click **Header & Footer**, and then click the **Notes and Handouts tab**.
c. Click the **Date and time check box**, and then click **Update automatically**, if necessary.
d. Click the **Header check box**, and then type your name in the **Header box**.
e. Click the **Footer check box**, and then type your instructor's name and your class in the **Footer box**. Click **Apply to All**.
f. Click the **Slide Show tab**, and then click **From Beginning** in the Start Slide Show group. Read each of the slides' bullet items. Press **Esc** to return to Normal view.
g. Click the **Design tab**, click the **More button** in the Themes group, and then select the **Flow theme**.
h. On Slide 1, click in the **subtitle placeholder**, and then replace the words *Student Name* with your name. Replace *Student Class* with the name of the class you are taking.
i. Click the **Insert tab**, and then click **Clip Art** in the Images group. Type **copyright** in the **Search for box**. Click the **Results should be arrow**, and remove the check mark from all categories except *Videos*. Include results from Office.com. Select the **animated copyright symbol**, and then drag it to the title slide next to your name. Close the Clip Art pane.

> **TROUBLESHOOTING:** If the animated copyright clip does not appear when you search for the copyright keyword, change the keyword to law, and then select an image that relates to the presentation content and that uses the same colors.

j. Click the **Transitions tab**, and then click the **More button** in the Transition to This Slide group. Click **Rotate**, and then click **Apply To All**.
k. On Slide 6, select the **blue box** at the bottom of the slide.
l. Click the **Animations tab**, and then click **Fly In** in the Animation group.
m. Click **Effect Options**, and then click **From Bottom-Left**.
n. Click the **Start arrow** in the Timing group, and then click **After Previous**.
o. Click **Preview** in the Preview group to see the result of your custom animation.
p. On Slide 9, click the **Home tab**, and then click the **New Slide arrow** in the Slides group.
q. Click **Section Header** from the list of layouts.

r. Click in the **title placeholder**, and then type **Individuals who violate copyright law and/or software licensing agreements may be subject to criminal or civil action by the copyright or license owners**.

s. Click the placeholder border, change the font size to **40 pt**, and then click **Center** in the Paragraph group.

t. Click the border of the content placeholder, and then press **Delete**.

u. Resize the title placeholder until all of the text is visible and is centered vertically on the slide.

v. Save and close the file, and submit based on your instructor's directions.

1 Planning Presentation Content

Brainstorming a topic and creating a storyboard with the ideas is the first step in slide show development. After creating the slide show from a storyboard, however, the information should be accessed and edited so that the final slide show is polished and professional. In this exercise, you create a slide show from a storyboard and then edit the slide show following the tips contained in the content. Refer to Figure 1.35 as you complete this exercise.

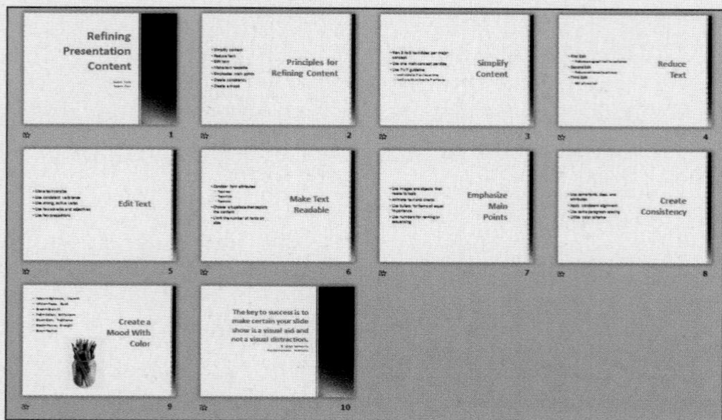

FIGURE 1.35 Refining Content Storyboard ➤

a. Create a new blank presentation, and then save it as **p01m1refine_LastnameFirstname**.

b. Create the following slides with the content contained in this table:

Slide Number	Slide Layout	Slide Title	Slide Content
1	Title	**Refining Presentation Content**	**Student Name** **Student Class**
2	Title and Content	**Principles for Refining Content**	• **Simplify content** • **Reduce text** • **Edit text** • **Make text readable** • **Emphasize main points** • **Create consistency** • **Create a mood**

3	Title and Content	**Simplify Content**	• **Plan 3 to 5 text slides per major concept**
			• **Use one main concept per slide**
			• **Use 7 × 7 guideline**
			    • **Limit slide to 7 or fewer lines**
			    • **Limit words in lines to 7 or fewer**

Slide Number	Slide Layout	Slide Title	Slide Content

4	Title and Content	**Reduce Text**	• **First Edit**
			  • **Reduce paragraph text to sentences**
			• **Second Edit**
			  • **Reduce sentences to phrases**
			• **Third Edit**
			  • **Edit phrase text**

5	Title and Content	**Edit Text**	• **Make text concise** • **Use consistent verb tense** • **Use strong, active verbs** • **Use few adverbs and adjectives** • **Use few prepositions**

6	Title and Content	**Make Text Readable**	• **Consider font attributes**
			  • **Typeface**
			  • **Type style**
			  • **Type size**
			• **Choose a typeface that depicts the content**
			• **Limit the number of fonts on slide**

7	Title and Content	**Emphasize Main Points**	• **Use images and objects that relate to topic** • **Animate text and charts** • **Use bullets for items of equal importance** • **Use numbers for ranking or sequencing**
8	Title and Content	**Create Consistency**	• **Use same fonts, sizes, and attributes** • **Apply consistent alignment** • **Use same paragraph spacing** • **Utilize color scheme**
9	Two Content	**Create a Mood with Color**	• **Yellow—Optimism, Warmth** • **White—Peace, Quiet** • **Green—Growth** • **Red—Action, Enthusiasm** • **Blue—Calm, Traditional** • **Black—Power, Strength** • **Grey—Neutral**
10	Title Slide	**The key to success is to make certain your slide show is a visual aid and not a visual distraction.**	**Dr. Joseph Sommerville** **Peak Communication Performance**

c. On Slide 9, insert a clip art image in the empty placeholder that illustrates the concept of color. Add other visual objects if you choose, but make sure the objects enhance the message.
d. Apply the design theme of your choice to the presentation.
e. Review the slide show and adjust font size, image size, and placeholder location until all elements fit attractively and professionally on the slides.
f. Assign the transition of your choice to all slides in the slide show, and then animate individual objects of your choice.
g. Save and close the presentation, and submit based on your instructor's directions.

2 University Housing Office Presentation

You are a work-study student employed by the housing office. Your boss has been asked to present to university officials about the purpose and goals of the housing office. You have been asked to take the administrator's notes and prepare a presentation.

a. Open the *p01m2university* presentation and save it as **p01m2university_LastnameFirstname**.
b. Add **University Housing Office** as a footer on all slides except the title slide. Also include an automatically updated date and time and a slide number.
c. Create a Notes and Handouts header with your name and a footer with your instructor's name and your class. Include the current date.
d. Apply the **Equity design theme**.
e. Add your name and the name of the class to the title slide.
f. Insert a new slide using the **Title and Content layout** as the second slide in the presentation. Type **Mission** as the title.
g. Type **The mission of the University Housing Office is to provide an environment that will enrich the educational experience of its residents. The office seeks to promote increased interaction between faculty and students through resident masters, special programs, and intramural activities.** in the **content placeholder.**
h. Move to the end of the presentation, and then insert a new slide with the **Blank layout**. Insert and position two photograph clips related to college life from the Clip Art pane. Resize the photos if necessary. Close the Clip Art pane.
i. On Slide 4, create a table using the following information:

Dorm Name	Room Revenue	Meal Revenue	Total Revenue
Ashe Hall	$2,206,010	$1,616,640	$3,822,650
Memorial	$1,282,365	$934,620	$2,216,985
Ungar Hall	$2,235,040	$1,643,584	$3,878,624
Merrick Hall	$1,941,822	$1,494,456	$3,436,278
Fort Towers	$1,360,183	$981,772	$2,341,955
Totals	$9,025,420	$6,671,072	$15,696,492

j. Select the cells containing numbers, and then right-align the numbers. Select the cells containing the column titles, and then center-align the text. Position the table attractively on the page.
k. Apply the **Cut transition** from the Subtle category to all slides in the slide show.
l. Add the **Bounce animation** from the Entrance category to each of the images on Slide 6. Set the animations so that they start automatically after the previous event.

m. Add an additional animation, **Float Out**, to the images on Slide 6. Set the animations so they float out at the same time.
n. Review the presentation and correct any errors you find.
o. Print the handouts, three per page, framed.
p. Save and close the file, and submit based on your instructor's directions.

CAPSTONE EXERCISE

The Entertainment Lair is a successful retail store. The Lair sells traditional board games, role-playing games, puzzles, and models, and is renowned for hosting game nights. The Lair is a place where gamers can find gaming resources, supplies, gaming news, and a good challenge. The store has been in operation for three years and has increased its revenue and profit each year. The partners are looking to expand their operation and need to prepare a presentation for an important meeting with financiers.

Entertainment Lair Mission Statement

You add your name to the title slide, apply a theme, and create a slide for the Entertainment Lair mission statement.

a. Open *p01c1capital* and save it as **p01c1capital_LastnameFirstname**.

b. Create a Notes and Handouts header with your name, and a footer with your instructor's name and your class. Include the current date. Apply to all.

c. On Slide 1, replace *Your Name* in the **subtitle placeholder** with your name.

d. Apply the **Thatch design theme**.

e. Insert a new slide using the **Title Only layout** after Slide 1. Type the following in the **title placeholder**: **The Entertainment Lair provides a friendly setting in which our friends and customers can purchase game equipment and resources as well as participate in a variety of challenging gaming activities.**

f. Change the font size to **40 pt**, apply **Italic**, and then resize the placeholder so all text fits on the slide.

Tables Displaying Sales Data

You create tables to show the increase in sales from last year to this year, the sales increase by category, and the sales increase by quarters.

a. On Slide 5, create a table of six columns and three rows. Type the following data in your table:

Year	Board Games	Role-Playing Games	Puzzles	Models	Events
Last Year	$75,915	$47,404	$31,590	$19,200	$25,755
This Year	$115,856	$77,038	$38,540	$28,200	$46,065

b. Format the table text font to **16 pt**. Center-align the column headings, and then right-align all numbers. Position the table on the slide so it is approximately centered.

c. On Slide 6, create a table of five columns and three rows. Type the following data in your table, and then apply the same formatting to this table that you applied in step b.

Year	Qtr 1	Qtr 2	Qtr 3	Qtr 4
Last Year	$37,761	$51,710	$52,292	$58,101
This Year	$61,594	$64,497	$67,057	$112,551

d. Check the spelling in the presentation, and review the presentation for any other errors. Fix anything you think is necessary.

e. View the presentation, and as you navigate through the slides, note that the presentation plan included the mission statement as the introduction slide, included supporting data in the body of the presentation, and included a plan for the future as the conclusion (summary) slide.

Clip Art and Animation

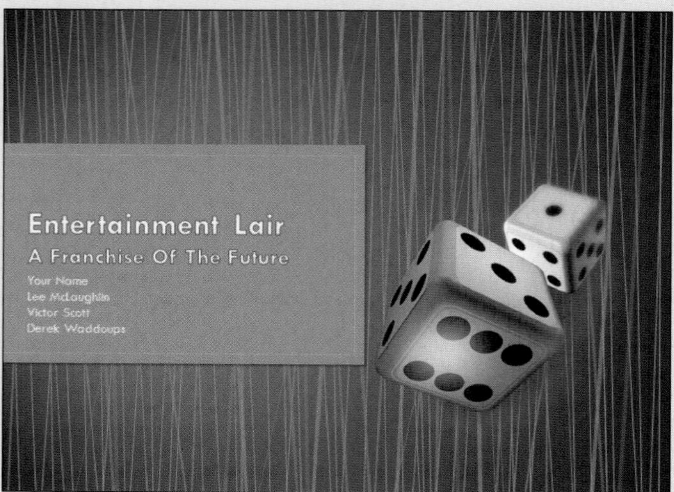

FIGURE 1.36 Dice Clip Art as Identifying Element

The Entertainment Lair uses dice in its logo. You use dice on the title slide to continue this identifying image.

a. On Slide 1, open the Clip Art pane. Use **dice** as your search keyword and locate the image of dice. Refer to Figure 1.36 to position and resize the image.

> **TROUBLESHOOTING:** If you cannot find the image of the dice, select an image that relates to games and that matches the color scheme.

b. Use the same clip art of dice on the last slide of your slide show. Position the clip in the bottom-right portion of your slide, and reduce its size.

c. On Slide 4, select the **Our first year was profitable box**, and then apply a **Fly In entrance animation**. Change the duration to **01.00**.

d. Select the **Our second year was significantly better box**, and then apply the **Fly In entrance animation**. Change the duration to **00.75**, and then change the Start option to **After Previous**.

Presentation View and Printout

You proofread the presentation in Slide Show view and check the transitions and animations. You print a handout with 4 slides per page.

a. Start the slide show and navigate through the presentation.

b. Annotate the conclusion slide, *The Next Steps*, by underlining *detailed financial proposal* and circling *two* and *ten* with a red pen.

c. Exit the presentation and keep the annotations.

d. Print handouts in Grayscale, four slides per page, horizontal, framed.

e. Save and close the file, and submit based on your instructor's directions.

BEYOND THE CLASSROOM

Be a Volunteer

GENERAL CASE 

FROM SCRATCH

You want to volunteer for the organization Big Brothers Big Sisters (www.bbbs.org), which helps children by providing mentors. You are invited to come in and meet representatives, introduce yourself, and complete an application. Because mentors and children are matched by interests, you decide to create a presentation to introduce yourself.

Create a storyboard for a presentation that includes four to six slides that introduce you, your background, and your interests. Be sure to include an introduction slide and a summary slide as well as your main point slides introducing you and your interests. Use the storyboard to create a slide show. Apply a design theme. Insert at least one clip art image or picture in an appropriate location. Add a transition and animations to enhance the show. Include a handout footer with your instructor's name and your class. Save your file as both a PowerPoint presentation and as a PowerPoint show using the file name **p01b1volunteer_LastnameFirstname**. Review each slide in Slide Show view to ensure that no errors exist. Display your slide show to at least one class member and get feedback. Edit the slide show as needed. Print handouts, four slides per page, framed, if requested by your instructor, and then submit your storyboard and presentation based on your instructor's directions.

Backup Strategy

RESEARCH CASE 

Do you have a computer backup strategy? Sooner or later, you will need to recover a file that you accidentally erased or are unable to read from a storage device like a flash drive. Backups can restore your files if you have a hardware failure in which you are unable to access the hard drive or if your computer is stolen.

Use the Internet to research ideas for backup strategies. Create a storyboard on paper or using Microsoft Word. Include a title slide and at least four slides related to a backup strategy or ways to protect files. Include a summary on what you plan to implement. Choose a theme, transitions, and animations. Insert at least one appropriate clip art image. Create a handout header with your name and the current date. Include a handout footer with your instructor's name and your class. Review the presentation to ensure there are no errors by viewing each slide in Slide Show view. Print as directed by your instructor. Save the presentation as **p01b2backup_LastnameFirstname**. Close the file and submit based on your instructor's directions.

Yard Care

DISASTER RECOVERY 

A neighbor has created a slide show to present to a local business explaining his company's services. He has asked you to refine the slide show so it has a more professional appearance. Open *p01b3green*, and then save the file as **p01b3green_LastnameFirstname**. View the slide show. Note that the text is difficult to read because of a lack of contrast with the background, there are capitalization errors and spelling errors, the bullet points are not parallel, and images are positioned and sized poorly.

Select and apply a design theme and a colors scheme. Modify text following the guidelines presented in Chapter 1. Reposition placeholders as needed. Size and position the images in the presentation, or replace them with your choice of images. Text may be included in speaker notes to emphasize visuals, if desired. Apply a transition to all slides. Add a minimum of two animations. Make other changes you choose. Create a handout header with your name and the current date. Include a handout footer with your instructor's name, and your class. Review the presentation to ensure there are no errors by viewing each slide in Slide Show view. Save your file, and then save it again as a PowerPoint show. Close the file and submit based on your instructor's directions.

POWERPOINT

2 PRESENTATION DEVELOPMENT

Planning and Preparing a Presentation

Watch the
Set-up Video
for this Case Study!

CASE STUDY | The Wellness Education Center

The Wellness Education Center at your school promotes overall good health to students and employees. The director of the Center has asked you to create two slide shows that she can use to deliver presentations to the campus community.

You create a presentation to inform campus groups about the center by downloading a template with a wellness theme from Microsoft Office Online. You modify several of the layouts the template provides to customize the template to your needs. To concentrate on the content of the slides, you use the Outline view to enter slide text and edit the presentation outline.

You create a second presentation for the center using an outline the director created in a word processor. You import the outline, supplement it with slides you reuse from another presentation, and divide the presentation into sections. Using standard slide show design guidelines, polish the presentation by editing the content and the theme.

OBJECTIVES

AFTER YOU READ THIS CHAPTER, YOU WILL BE ABLE TO:

1. Create a presentation using a template ***p.862***
2. Modify a template ***p.864***
3. Create a presentation in Outline view ***p.869***
4. Modify an outline structure ***p.870***
5. Print an outline ***p.871***
6. Import an outline ***p.877***
7. Add existing content to a presentation ***p.877***
8. Use sections ***p.882***
9. Examine slide show design principles ***p.883***
10. Modify a theme ***p.885***

Templates

One of the hardest things about creating a presentation is getting started. You may have a general idea of what you want to say but not how to organize your thoughts. Or you may know what you want to say but need help designing the look for the slides. PowerPoint's templates enable you to create professional-looking presentations and may even include content to help you decide what to say. In this section, you will learn how to create a presentation using a template that you modify to fit your needs.

Creating a Presentation Using a Template

A **template** is a file that incorporates a theme, a layout, and content that can be modified.

A ***template*** is a file that includes the formatting elements like a background, a theme with a color scheme and font selections for titles and text boxes, and slide layouts that position content placeholders. Some templates include suggestions for how to modify the template, whereas others include ideas about what you could say to inform your audience about your topic. These suggestions can help you learn to use many of the features in PowerPoint.

PowerPoint offers installed templates for you to use, or you can visit Microsoft Office Online to quickly and easily download additional professional templates in a variety of categories. These templates were created by Microsoft, a Microsoft partner, or a member of the Microsoft community. For example, you can select Presentations in the Browse Templates section of Office.com. Then you can select Business to download a template for a Renewable energy presentation created by a Microsoft partner, an Active Listening Presentation created by a Microsoft community member, or a Business financial report created by Microsoft. Figure 2.1 shows four PowerPoint templates.

Visit Microsoft Office Online to quickly and easily download professional templates in a variety of categories.

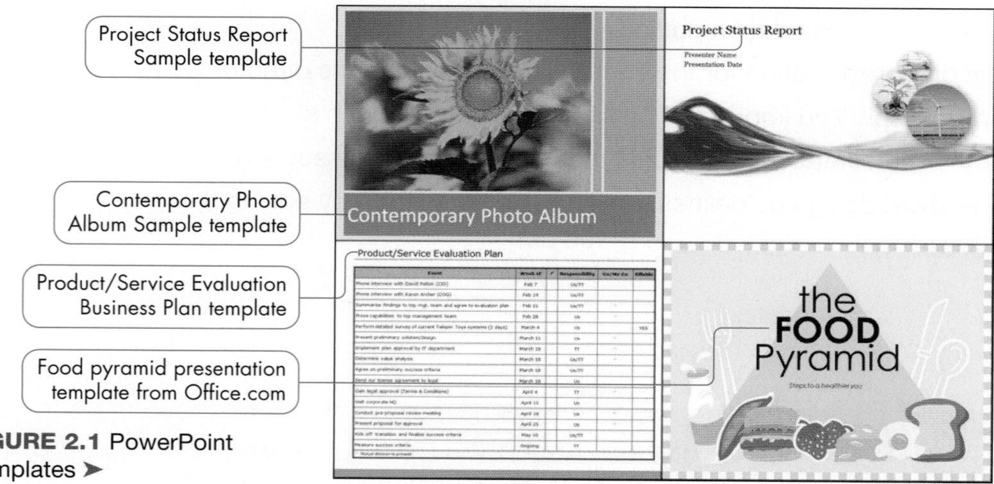

FIGURE 2.1 PowerPoint Templates ➤

> **TIP Submitting a Template to Microsoft Office Online**
>
> You can share a template you have created at Office.com/templates. Click the Submit a Template link in the Community group, and then follow Microsoft's instructions for uploading a template.

When you create a new blank presentation, PowerPoint uses the default template with the Office Theme. To begin a presentation using a different template or theme, do the following:

1. Click the File tab.
2. Click New.
3. Click a category in Home or Office.com Templates.
4. Click a template or theme to view it in the Preview pane.
5. Click Create or Download.

In the Home category, you can select from templates you have recently used, sample templates that were installed with the software, themes, templates you have created, or an existing template on the basis of which you created a new presentation. Click a folder in the Office.com Templates category to locate a specific type of presentation online, or enter the presentation type in the Office.com search box and click the Start search arrow.

TIP Downloading Templates in a Lab

Check with your instructor to find out if you are able to download and save Microsoft Office Online templates in your lab. If not, use an installed Sample template when completing assignments that ask you to download a template.

Figure 2.2 displays the Backstage view of Available Templates and Themes. Your view may show different template options, as Microsoft frequently updates the available templates.

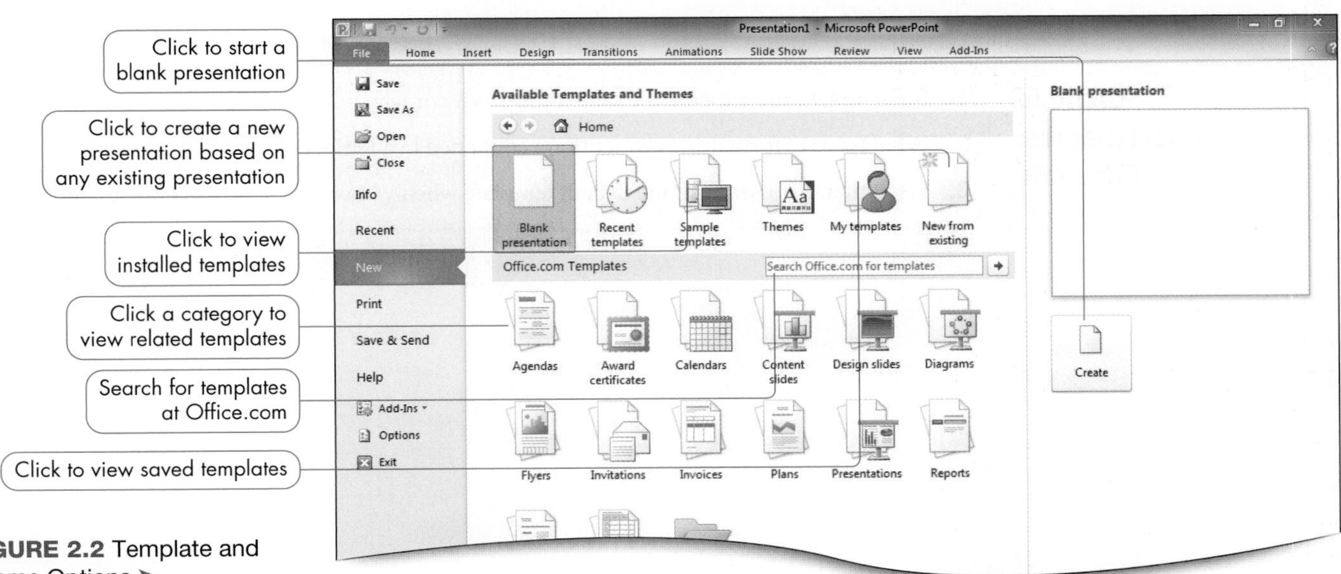

FIGURE 2.2 Template and Theme Options ➤

When you select the Sample templates option, templates installed with PowerPoint 2010 display. In Figure 2.3, the Classic Photo Album template is selected. The title slide for the template displays in the Preview pane.

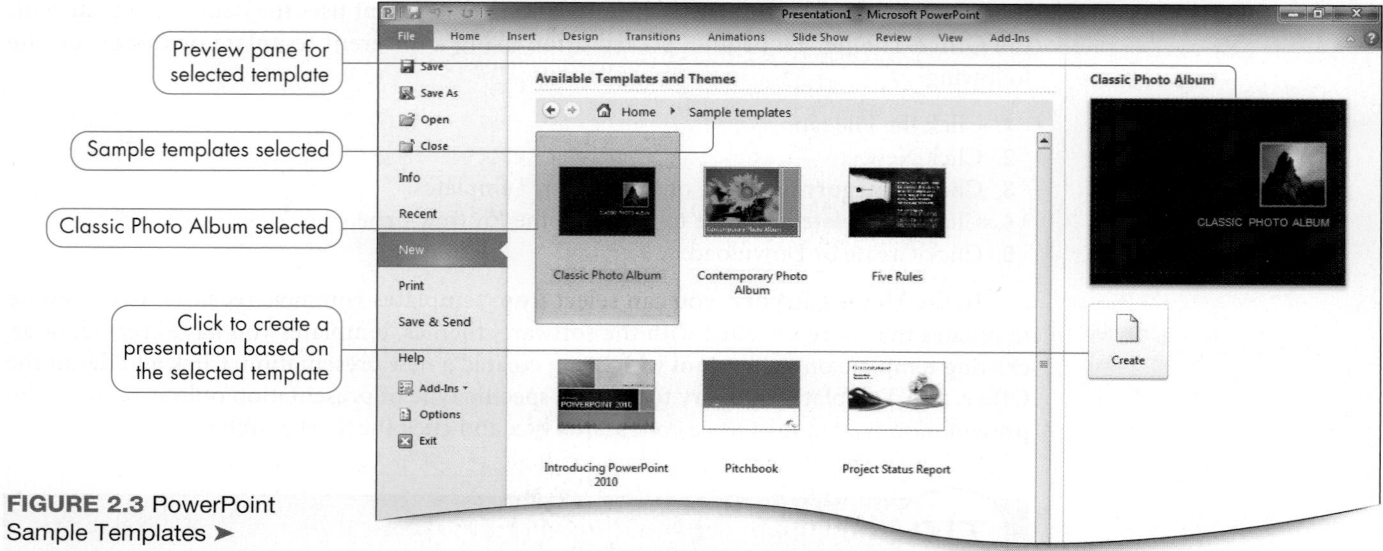

FIGURE 2.3 PowerPoint Sample Templates ➤

Modifying a Template

The templates you download may have custom layouts unique to that particular template. After you download a template you can modify it, perhaps by changing a font style or size, moving or deleting a placeholder, or moving an object on the slide. After you modify the template, you can save it and use it repeatedly. The ability to save changes to a template can save you a tremendous amount of time, since you will not have to redo your modifications the next time you use the template.

Quick Concepts Check

1. Is a template and a theme the same thing? Why or why not?
2. What types of formatting elements are contained in a template?
3. What theme is used with the default template when you open a new blank document?

HANDS-ON EXERCISES

1 Templates

To promote the Wellness Education Center at your school, you decide to create a presentation that can be shown to campus groups and other organizations to inform them about the center and its mission.

Skills covered: Create a New Presentation Based on an Installed Template • Modify a Template Placeholder • Modify a Template Layout • Add Pictures and Modify a Caption

STEP 1 CREATE A NEW PRESENTATION BASED ON AN INSTALLED TEMPLATE

You begin the Wellness Education Center presentation by looking for a template that is upbeat and that will represent the idea that being healthy makes you feel good. You locate the perfect template (a photo album with warm sunflowers on the cover) from the Sample templates category. You open a new presentation based on the template and save the presentation. Refer to Figure 2.4 as you complete Step 1.

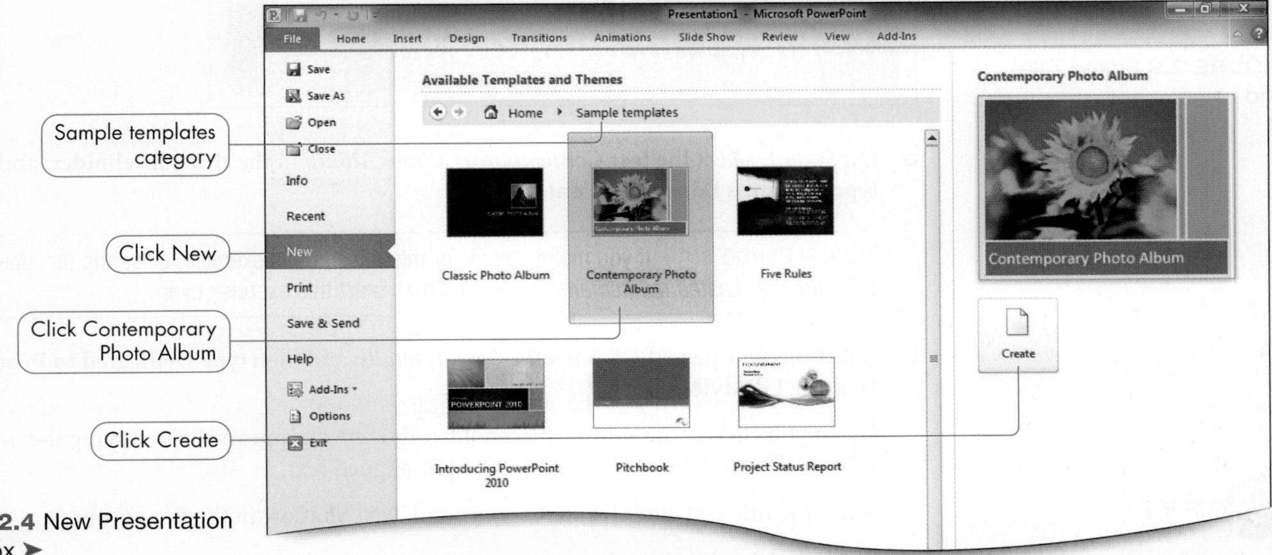

FIGURE 2.4 New Presentation Dialog Box ➤

a. Start PowerPoint, click the **File tab**, and then click **New**.

b. Click **Sample templates** in the Home category.

   Thumbnails of sample templates installed on your computer display.

c. Click **Contemporary Photo Album**, and then click **Create** in the Preview pane.

d. View the slide show, and then read each of the instructions included in the template.

   Templates may include instructions for their use or tips on the content that may be added to create a specific presentation. For example, Slide 2 includes instructions to follow for adding your own pages to the album.

e. Click the **Insert tab**, and then click **Header & Footer** in the Text group. Click the **Notes and Handouts tab** in the Header and Footer dialog box. Create a handout header with your name, and a handout footer with your instructor's name and your class. Include the current date.

f. Save the presentation as **p02h1center_LastnameFirstname**.

STEP 2 MODIFY A TEMPLATE PLACEHOLDER

The template you selected and downloaded consists of a Title Slide layout you like, but the text in the placeholders needs to be changed to the Wellness Clinic information. You edit the title slide to include the clinic name and slogan. You also modify the title placeholder to make the clinic name stand out. Refer to Figure 2.5 as you complete Step 2.

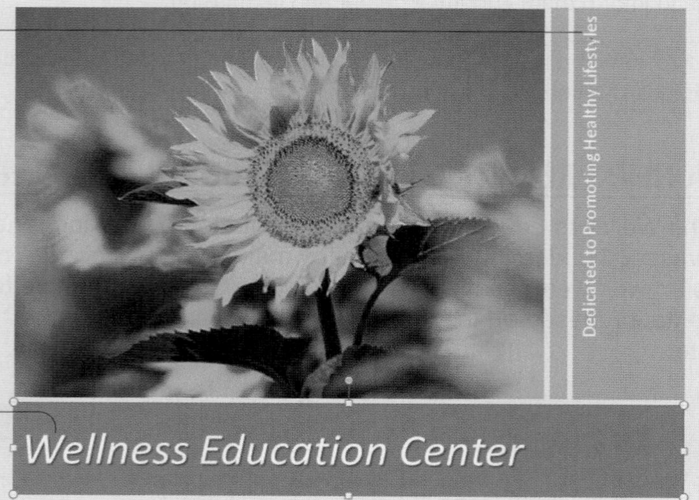

FIGURE 2.5 Edited Title Slide ➤

a. On Slide 1, select the text *Contemporary Photo Album* in the **title placeholder**, and then type **Wellness Education Center**.

> **TROUBLESHOOTING:** If you make any major mistakes in this exercise, close the file, open *p02h1center_LastnameFirstname* again, and then start this exercise over.

b. Select the subtitle text *Click to add date or details*, and then type **Dedicated to Promoting Healthy Lifestyles!**.

When you click in the subtitle placeholder, the text disappears. Begin typing the new subtitle text, and the text reappears as right-aligned text.

FYI

c. Select the title text, and then click **Italic** and **Text Shadow** in the Font group.

The template's title placeholder is modified to make the title text stand out.

d. Save the presentation.

STEP 3 MODIFY A TEMPLATE LAYOUT

The Contemporary Photo Album template includes many layouts designed to create an interesting photo album. Although the layout you selected conveys the warm feeling you desire, the layouts need to be modified to fit your needs. You modify a section layout and add a new slide with the layout of your choice. You also delete unnecessary slides. Refer to Figure 2.6 as you complete Step 3.

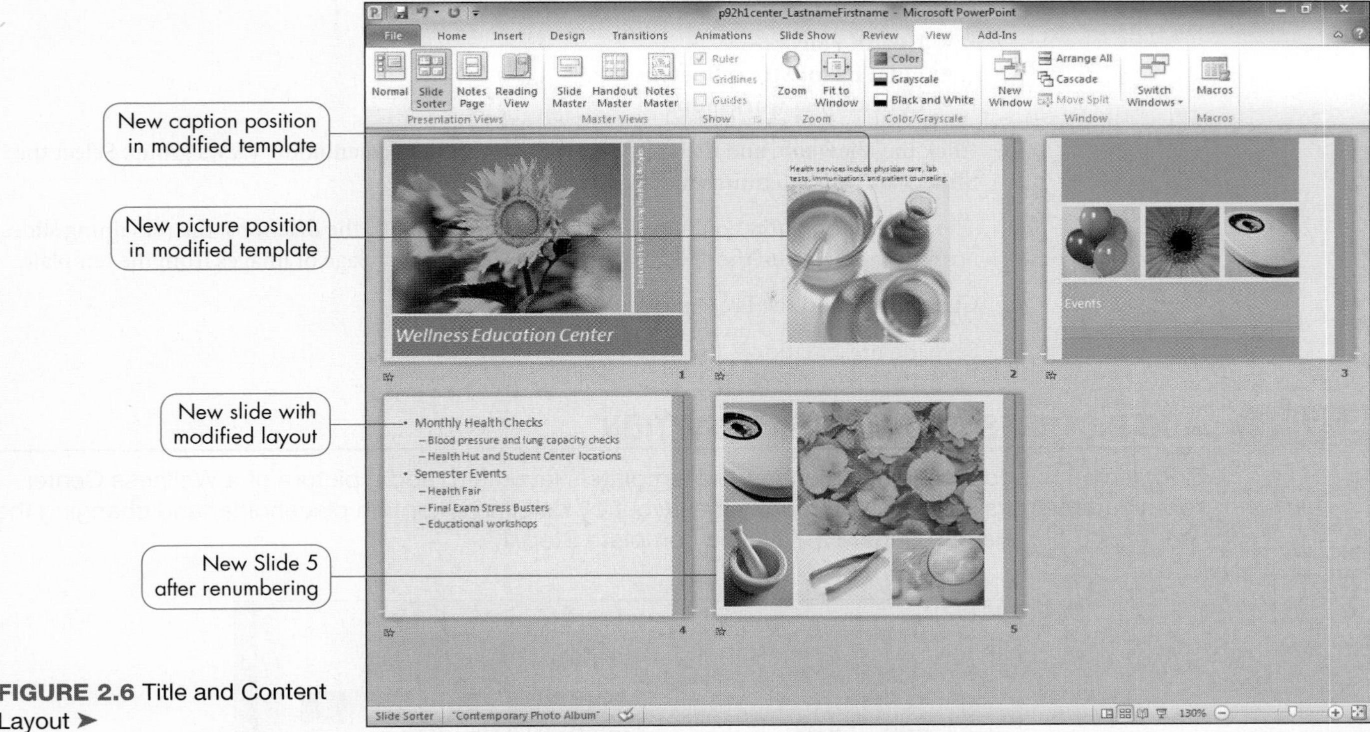

FIGURE 2.6 Title and Content Layout ➤

a. On Slide 2, replace the sample text with **Health services include physician care, lab tests, immunizations, and patient counseling.**

b. Click **Slide Layout** in the Slides group, and then click the **Square with Caption layout**.

Note that the Contemporary Photo Album template has many more layouts than the default Office Theme template. The number of layouts provided with a template varies, so always check to see your options.

c. Click the caption, hold **Shift**, and then drag the caption to the top of the picture (not above it).

Shift constrains the movement of the caption as you drag so that the new position of the caption is aligned left with its original position.

d. Select the picture, hold **Shift**, and then drag the picture below the caption.

The template layout is modified to show the caption above the picture.

e. On Slide 3, select the placeholder text that reads *Choose a layout…*, and then type **Events**. Delete the subtitle text.

When you delete existing text in a new template placeholder, it is replaced with instructional text such as *Click to add subtitle*. It is not necessary to delete this text, as it will not display when the slide show is viewed.

f. Click the **New Slide arrow**, and then click the **Title and Content layout**.

> **TROUBLESHOOTING:** Clicking the New Slide arrow opens the layout gallery for you to select a layout. Clicking New Slide directly above the New Slide arrow creates a new slide using the layout of the current slide.

g. Delete the title placeholder in the new slide, and then drag the content placeholder to the top of the slide. Enter the following information:

- **Monthly Health Checks**
  - **Blood pressure and lung capacity checks**
  - **Health Hut and Student Center locations**

- **Semester Events**
  - **Health Fair**
  - **Final Exam Stress Busters**
  - **Educational workshops**

h. Click the **View tab**, and then click **Slide Sorter** in the Presentation Views group. Select the **Slide 5** and **Slide 6 thumbnails**, and then press **Delete**.

   The presentation now contains five slides. After you make the deletions, the remaining slides are renumbered, and the slide that becomes Slide 5 is a collage of images from the template.

i. Click **Normal** in the Presentation Views group.

j. Save the presentation.

STEP 4 ADD PICTURES AND MODIFY A CAPTION

You decide to add a slide using one of the template's layouts to add a picture of a Wellness Center room and the nursing staff. You modify the layout by deleting a caption placeholder and changing the size of another. Refer to Figure 2.7 as you complete Step 4.

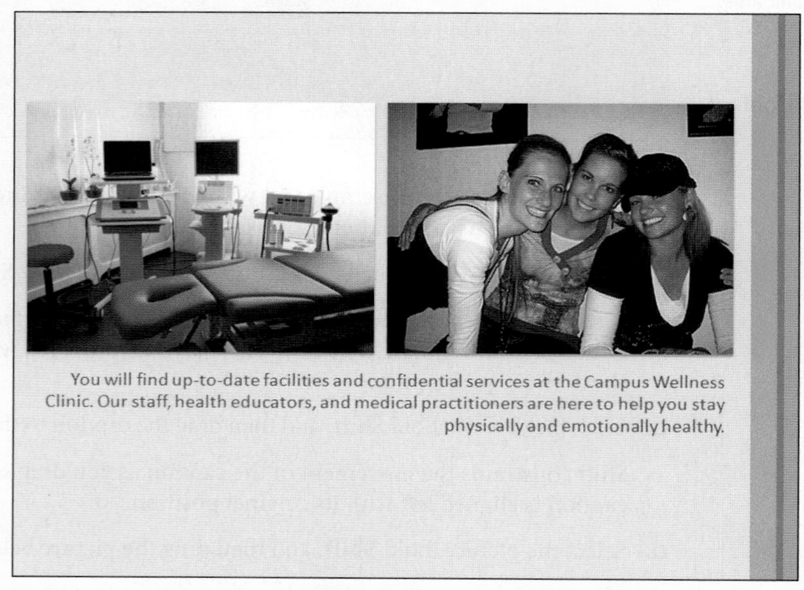
You will find up-to-date facilities and confidential services at the Campus Wellness Clinic. Our staff, health educators, and medical practitioners are here to help you stay physically and emotionally healthy.

FIGURE 2.7 Title and Content Layout ➤

a. On Slide 4, click the **New Slide arrow** on the Home tab, and then click **2-Up Landscape with Captions**.

   A new slide is created. The layout includes two picture placeholders and two caption placeholders.

b. Click the picture icon in the left picture placeholder, navigate to your student files, click *p02h1center*, and then click **Insert**.

   The image is sized to fit in the placeholder.

c. Click the picture icon in the right picture placeholder, navigate to your student files, click *p02h1nurses*, and then click **Insert**.

d. Delete one of the caption placeholders, and then drag a sizing handle on the remaining caption placeholder to stretch it to the width of the two pictures.

e. Type the following in the **caption placeholder**: **You will find up-to-date facilities and confidential services at the Campus Wellness Clinic. Our staff, health educators, and medical practitioners are here to help you stay physically and emotionally healthy.**

f. Keep the presentation open if you plan to continue with Hands-On Exercise 2. If not, save and close the presentation, and then exit PowerPoint.

Outlines

An **outline** is a method of organizing text in a hierarchy to depict relationships.

A **hierarchy** indicates levels of importance in a structure.

An ***outline*** organizes text using a ***hierarchy*** with main points and subpoints to indicate the levels of importance of the text. When you use a storyboard to determine your content, you create a basic outline. An outline is the fastest way to enter or edit text for a presentation. Think of an outline as the road map you use to create your presentation. Rather than having to enter the text in each placeholder on each slide separately, you can type the text directly into an outline.

In this section, you will add content to a presentation in Outline view. After creating the presentation, you will modify the outline structure. Finally, you will print the outline.

Creating a Presentation in Outline View

Outline view shows the presentation in an outline format displayed in levels according to the points and any subpoints on each slide.

To create an outline for your presentation you must be in Normal view; then you click the Outline tab to switch to ***Outline view***. In Outline view, the presentation is displayed as a list of all slides that illustrates the hierarchy of the titles and text in each individual slide. Beside each slide is a slide number, next to which is a slide icon, followed by the slide title if the slide contains a title placeholder. The slide title is bolded. Slide text is indented under the slide title.

One benefit of working in Outline view is that you get a good overview of your presentation without the distraction of design elements, and you can move easily from one slide to the next. You can copy text or bullets from one slide to another and rearrange the order of the slides or bullets. Outline view makes it easy to see relationships between points and to determine where information belongs. Figure 2.8 shows a portion of a presentation in Outline view.

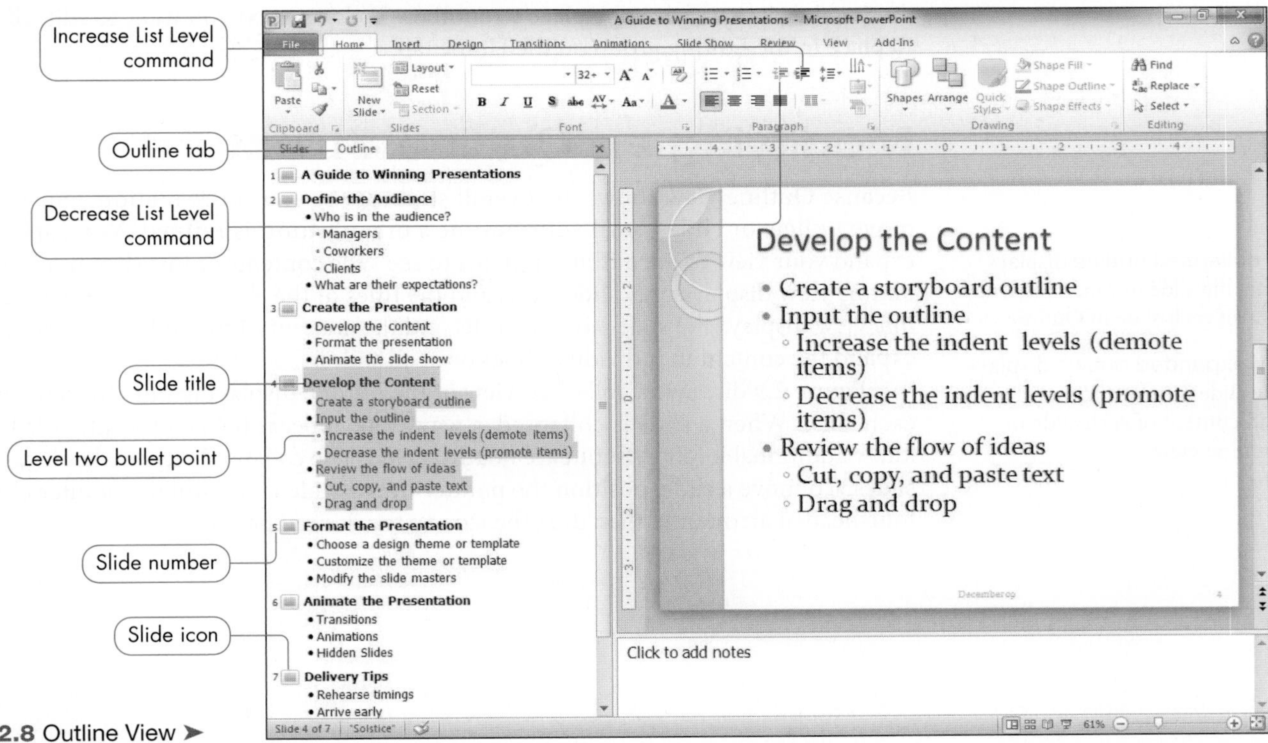

FIGURE 2.8 Outline View ➤

PowerPoint accommodates nine levels of indentation, although you will likely only use two or three per slide. Levels make it possible to show hierarchy or relationships between the information on your slides. The main points appear on Level 1; subsidiary items are indented below the main point to which they apply, and their font size is decreased.

You can promote any item to a higher level or demote it to a lower level, either before or after the text is entered, by clicking Increase List Level or Decrease List Level in the Paragraph group on the Home tab. When designing your slides, consider the number of subsidiary or lower-level items you add to a main point—too many levels within a single slide make the slide difficult to read or understand since the text size becomes smaller with each additional level. The level of an item in an outline indicates its importance: Level 1 items are main points, whereas level 9 items are less significant in comparison.

Level 1 items are main points, whereas level 9 items are less significant in comparison.

TIP Changing List Levels in an Outline

As a quick alternative to using Increase and Decrease List Level commands on the Home tab, press Tab to demote an item, or press Shift+Tab to promote an item.

On Slide 4 in Figure 2.8, the title of the slide, *Develop the Content*, appears immediately after the slide number and icon. The first-level bullet, *Create a storyboard outline*, is indented under the title. The next first-level bullet, *Input the outline*, has two subsidiary, or second-level, bullets. The following bullet, *Review the flow of ideas*, is moved back to Level 1, and it also has two subsidiary bullets.

Outline view can be an efficient way to create and edit a presentation. Press Enter to create a new slide or bullet at the same level. Demote or promote items as you type to create a hierarchy of information on each slide. Editing is accomplished through the same techniques used in other Office applications. Use the Cut, Copy, and Paste commands in the Clipboard group on the Home tab to move and copy selected text. Or you can simply drag and drop text from one place to another. To locate text you want to edit, click Find or Replace in the Editing group on the Home tab.

Modifying an Outline Structure

A **collapsed outline** displays only the slide number, icon, and title of each slide in Outline view.

An **expanded outline** displays the slide number, icon, title, and content of each slide in Outline view.

Because Outline view shows the overall structure of your presentation, you can use it to move bullets or slides until your outline's organization is refined. You can collapse or expand your view of the outline contents to see slide contents or just slide titles. A ***collapsed outline*** view displays only slide icons and the titles of the slides, whereas the ***expanded outline*** view displays the slide icon, the title, and the content of the slides. You can collapse or expand the content in individual slides or in all slides.

Figure 2.9 displays a collapsed view of the outline displaying only the icon and title of each slide. When a slide is collapsed, a wavy line appears below the slide title letting you know additional levels exist but are not displayed. The collapsed view makes it easy to move slides. To move a slide, position the pointer over a slide icon until the pointer changes to a four-headed arrow, and then drag the icon to the desired position.

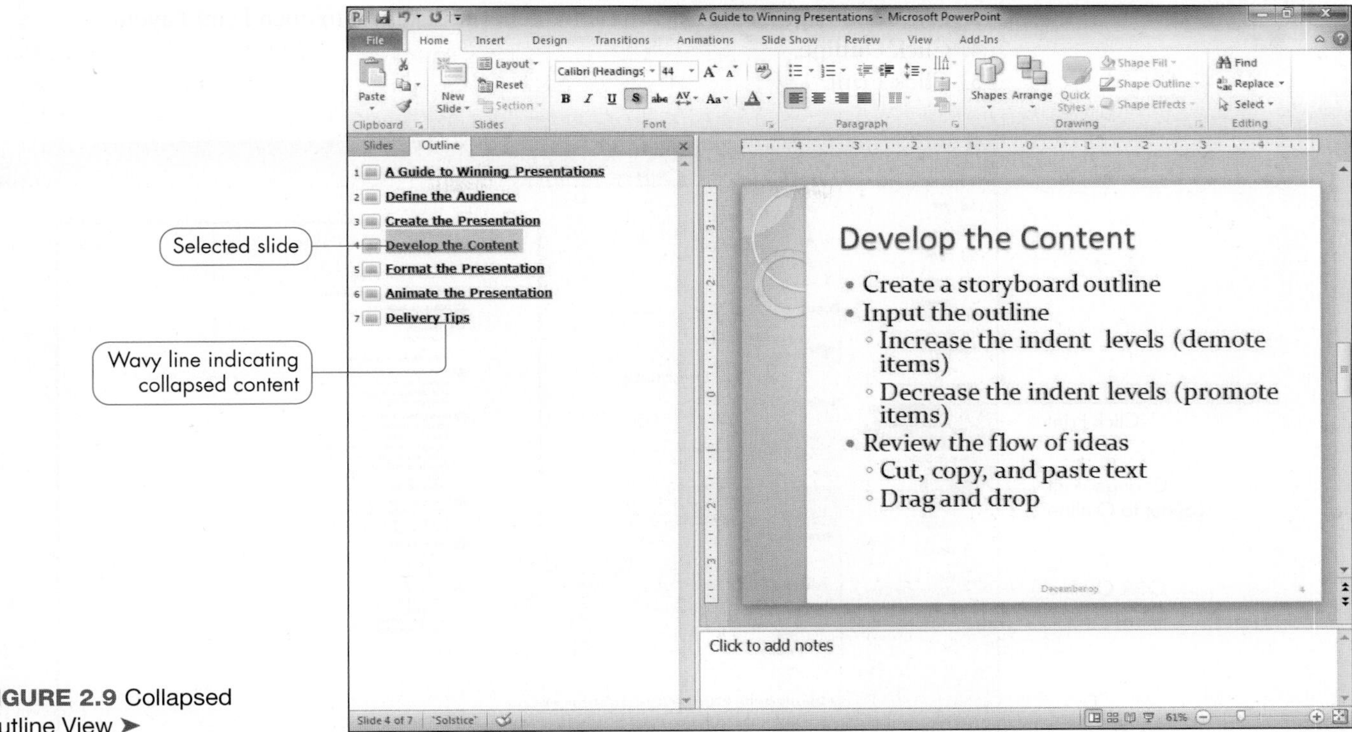

FIGURE 2.9 Collapsed Outline View ➤

To collapse or expand a slide, double-click the slide icon. Right-click the text following an icon to display a shortcut menu with options for collapsing or expanding the selected slides or all slides. Figure 2.10 shows the shortcut menu options.

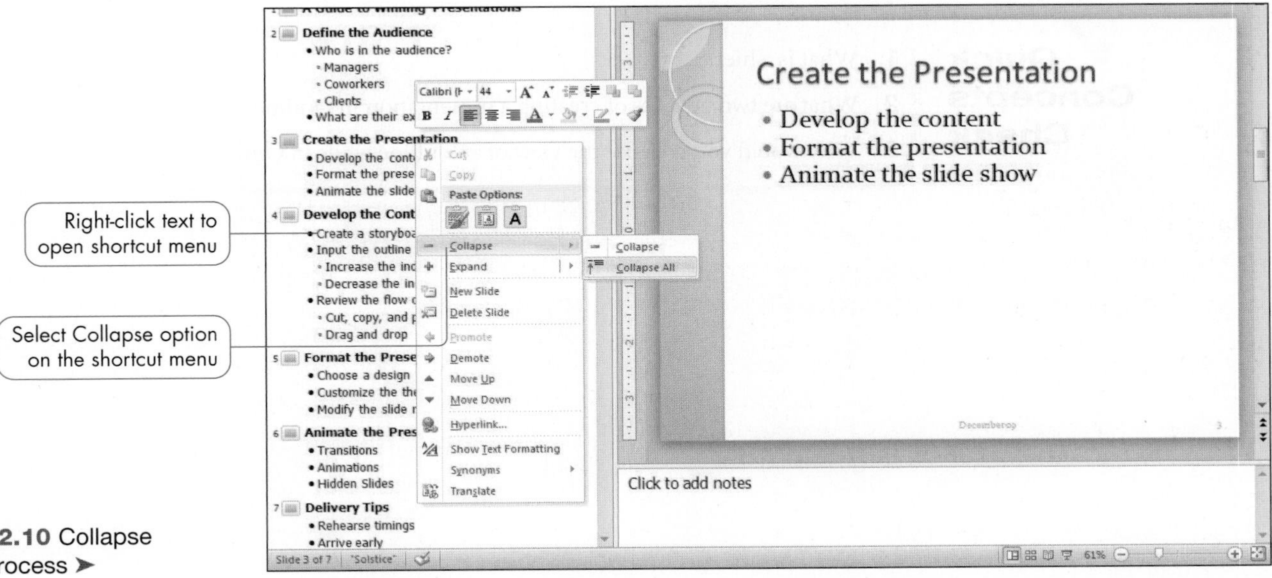

FIGURE 2.10 Collapse Outline Process ➤

Printing an Outline

You can print an outline in either expanded or collapsed view. Figure 2.11 displays a preview of an expanded view of the outline ready to print. The slide icon and slide number will print with the outline. To print the outline, do the following:

1. Click the File tab.
2. Click Print.

3. Click Full Page Slides or Outline (whichever displays) to open Print Layout.
4. Click Outline.
5. Click Print.

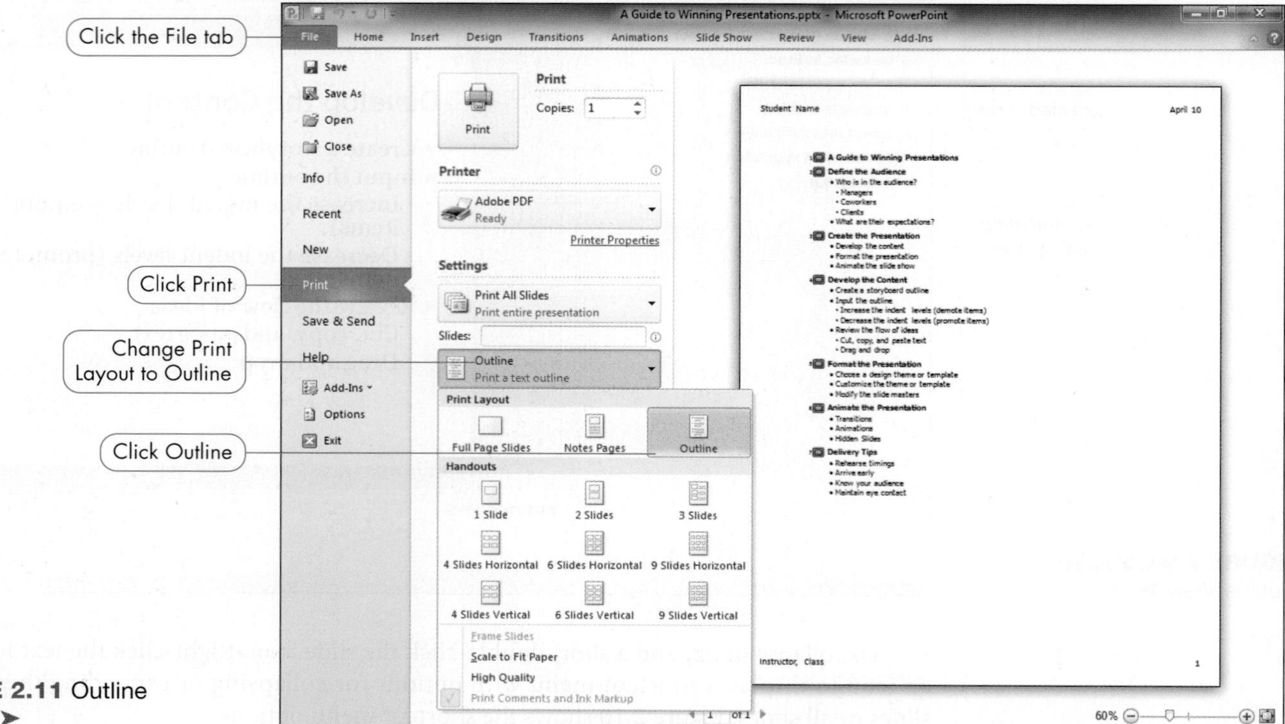

FIGURE 2.11 Outline Printing ➤

Quick Concepts Check

1. What is a hierarchy?
2. What are two benefits of creating a presentation in Outline view?
3. Why would you collapse the view of an outline while in Outline view?

HANDS-ON EXERCISES

2 Outlines

The Wellness Center sponsors a Walking Wellness group to help campus members increase their physical activity and cardio-vascular fitness. The director of the Wellness Center believes that joining a group increases a member's level of commitment and provides an incentive for the member to stay active. She asks you to edit the slide show you created in Hands-On Exercise 1 to include information about the walking group.

Skills covered: Use Outline View • Edit the Outline • Modify the Outline Structure and Print

STEP 1 USE OUTLINE VIEW

Because you want to concentrate on the information in the presentation rather than the design elements, you use Outline view. You add the information about the walking group as requested by the director. Refer to Figure 2.12 as you complete Step 1.

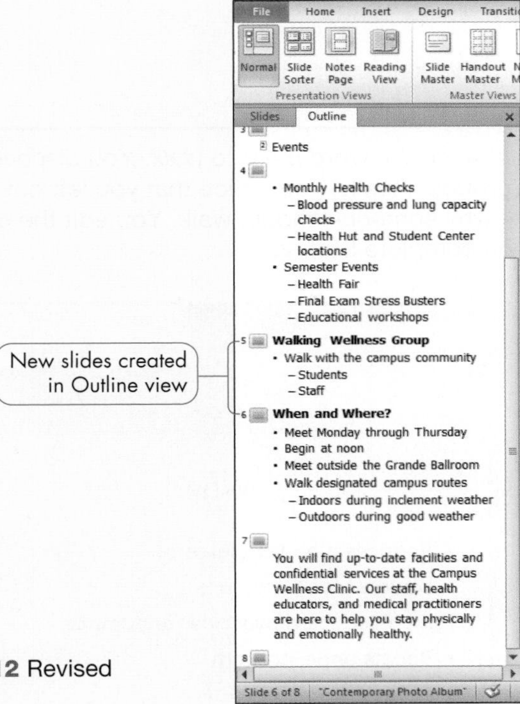

FIGURE 2.12 Revised Outline ➤

a. Open *p01h1center_LastnameFirstname*, if necessary, and save the presentation as **p02h2center_LastnameFirstname**, changing *h1* to *h2*.

b. Click the **Outline tab**.

   Note that each slide in the presentation is numbered and has a slide icon. Slides 1 through 5 include text on the slides. Slide 6 contains images only, so no text is displayed in the outline.

c. Click at the end of the last bullet on Slide 4, and then press **Enter**.

   The text in the outline is also displayed on the slide in the Preview pane. The insertion point is now positioned to enter text at the same level as the previous bullet point. To create a new slide at a higher level, you must decrease the indent level.

d. Click **Decrease List Level** in the Paragraph group on the Home tab twice.

   A new Slide 5 is created, the previous Slide 5 is renumbered as Slide 6, Slide 6 is renumbered as Slide 7, etc.

e. Type **Walking Wellness Group** and press **Enter**.

   Pressing Enter moves the insertion point to the next line and creates a new slide, Slide 6.

f. Press **Tab** to move to the next level.

   The insertion point is now positioned to enter bulleted text.

g. Type **Walk with the campus community** and press **Enter**.

h. Press **Tab** to move to the next level and type **Students**.

   Students becomes Level 2 text.

i. Press **Enter**, and then type **Staff**.

j. Press **Enter**, and then press **Shift+Tab** twice.

   Pressing Shift+Tab decreases the indent level and creates a new Slide 6.

k. Refer to Figure 2.12 to enter the information for Slide 6.

l. Save the presentation.

STEP 2 EDIT THE OUTLINE

While proofreading your outline, you decide to change the word *meet* to *walk*. You discover that you did not identify one of the campus community groups. Finally, you notice that you left out one of the most important slides in your presentation—why someone should walk. You edit the outline and make these changes. Refer to Figure 2.13 as you complete Step 2.

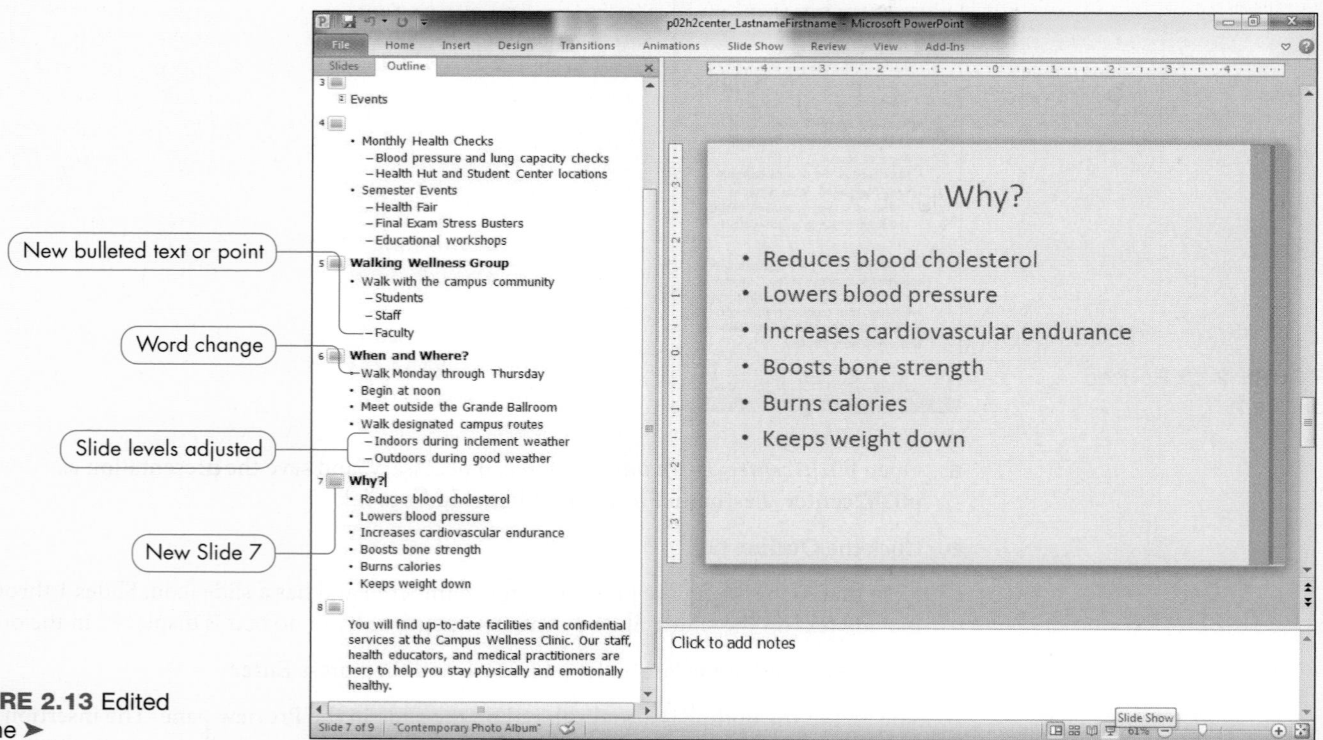

FIGURE 2.13 Edited Outline ➤

a. Select the word *Meet* in the first bullet on Slide 6. Type **Walk**.

b. Click at the end of the word *Staff* on Slide 5 of the outline.

c. Press **Enter**, and then type **Faculty**.

TROUBLESHOOTING: If your text does not appear in the correct position, check to see if the insertion point was in the wrong location. To enter a blank line for a new bullet, the insertion point must be at the end of an existing bullet point, not at the beginning.

d. Click at the beginning of the fifth bullet point, *Indoors during inclement weather*, on Slide 6, and then press **Tab**.

e. Click at the beginning of the sixth bullet point, *Outdoors during good weather*, and then press **Tab**.

Slide 6 now contains two levels of bullets.

f. Click at the end of the sixth bullet point, press **Enter**, and then press **Shift+Tab** twice.

A new slide is created.

g. Type **Why?** as the title on Slide 7, and then press **Enter**.

h. Press **Tab**, and then enter the following bullet points:

- **Keeps weight down**
- **Reduces blood cholesterol**
- **Lowers blood pressure**
- **Increases cardiovascular endurance**
- **Boosts bone strength**
- **Burns calories**

i. Save the presentation.

STEP 3 MODIFY THE OUTLINE STRUCTURE AND PRINT

The director of the Wellness Clinic has reviewed the slide show and made several suggestions about its structure. She feels that keeping weight down belongs at the bottom of the list of reasons for walking and asks you to reposition it. She requests that the "Why?" slide be moved before the "When and Where?" slide so people are motivated to find out when and where the group walks. To easily move the bullet point and the slide, you collapse the outline, position the slide, and then expand the outline. Refer to Figure 2.14 as you complete Step 3.

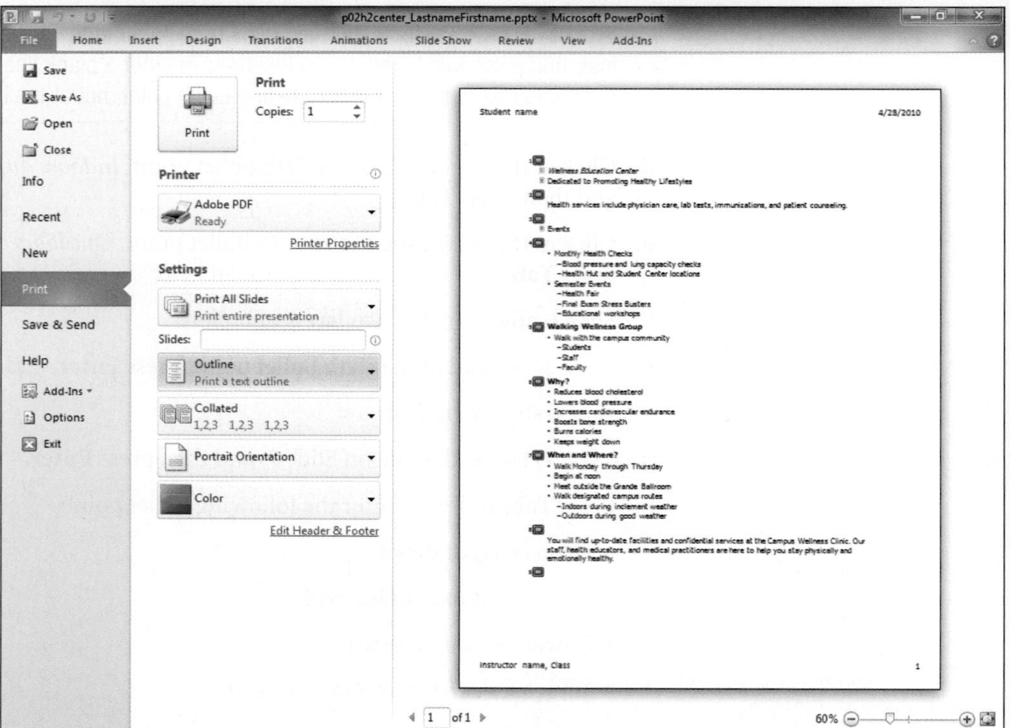

FIGURE 2.14 Expanded Outline in Print Preview ➤

a. Position the pointer over the first bullet, *Keeps weight down*, on Slide 7. When the mouse pointer looks like a four-headed arrow, drag the text until it becomes the last bullet on the slide.

b. Right-click the Slide 7 text, point to **Collapse**, and then click **Collapse All**.

c. Click the **Slide 6 icon** to select the collapsed slide, and then drag the **Slide 6 icon** below the Slide 7 icon.

> **TROUBLESHOOTING:** If you are unable to drag, check to make sure you are pointing at the icon, not the bullet text. Point directly at the icon until your mouse pointer looks like a four-headed arrow, and then drag.

d. Click the **File tab**, click **Print**, and then click the **Full Page Slides arrow**, if necessary. Click **Outline**.

   A preview of the collapsed outline shows in the Preview pane. Because so few slides contain titles, the collapsed outline is not helpful.

e. Click the **Home tab**.

   The Outline tab is once again visible.

f. Right-click any text visible in the Outline tab, point to **Expand**, and then select **Expand All**.

g. Click the **File tab**, and then click **Print**.

   The Outline Print Layout is retained from step d, and the expanded outline shows in the Preview pane.

h. Save and close the *p01h2center_LastnameFirstname* presentation, and submit based on your instructor's directions. Keep PowerPoint open if you plan to continue with Hands-On Exercise 3.

Data Imports

You can add slides to a presentation in several ways if the content exists in other formats, such as an outline in Word or slides from other presentations. PowerPoint can create slides based on Microsoft Word outlines (.docx or .doc formats) or outlines saved in another word processing format that PowerPoint recognizes. You can import data into a slide show to add existing slides from a previously created presentation. This is a very efficient way to add content to a slide show.

In this section, you will learn how to import an outline into a PowerPoint presentation and how to add slides from another presentation into the current presentation.

Importing an Outline

Rich Text Format (.rtf) is a file format that retains structure and most text formatting when transferring documents between applications or platforms.

Plain Text format (.txt) is a file format that retains only text, but no formatting, when you transfer documents between applications or platforms.

PowerPoint recognizes outlines created and saved in a ***Rich Text Format (.rtf)***, a file format you can use to transfer formatted text documents between applications such as word processing programs and PowerPoint. You can even transfer documents between different platforms such as Macintosh and Windows. The outline structure and most of the text formatting is retained when you import the outline into PowerPoint.

PowerPoint also recognizes outlines created and saved in a ***Plain Text format*** (which uses the file extension ***.txt***), a file format that retains text without any formatting. Because .txt outlines have no saved hierarchical structure, each line of the outline becomes a slide. Another alternative is to import a Web document (.htm), but in this case all the text from the file appears in one placeholder on one slide. Avoid saving outlines you create in these formats, but if you receive an outline in a .txt or .htm format, you can create a hierarchy in PowerPoint without having to retype the text.

To create a new presentation from an outline created in another format, do the following:

1. Click the File tab.
2. Click Open.
3. Click the All PowerPoint Presentations arrow.
4. Select All Outlines. (Any files in a format PowerPoint recognizes will be listed.)
5. Double-click the document you wish to use as the basis for your presentation.

TIP Problems Importing a Word Outline

If you import a Word document that appears to be an outline and after importing each line of the Word document becomes a title for a new slide, the Word document is actually a bulleted list rather than an outline. These two features are separate and distinct in Word and do not import into PowerPoint in the same manner. Open the bulleted list in Word, apply outline formatting, save, and then re-import it to PowerPoint. Or work on the bulleted list in Outline view and promote and demote text as necessary to create an outline format.

Adding Existing Content to a Presentation

You can also use an outline to add slides to a presentation that is currently open. The new slides that are created when you insert an outline appear after the current slide. To add slides to an existing presentation using an outline, do the following:

1. Click the New Slide arrow in the Slides group on the Home tab.
2. Click Slides from Outline.

3. Browse to navigate to the folder containing the outline.
4. Click Open.

You can reuse slides from a different file when creating PowerPoint presentations. To import existing slides without having to open the other file, do the following:

1. Click the New Slide arrow in the Slides group on the Home tab.
2. Click Reuse Slides.
3. Type the address of the presentation or Slide Library from which you want to use slides, or click Browse to navigate to the folder containing the presentation that has the slides you want to use.
4. Click Browse Slide Library or Browse File depending on whether the presentation is stored in a shared Slide Library or in your personal files.
5. Navigate to the presentation's saved location, and then click Open.
6. Point to a slide to view an enlarged thumbnail.
7. Click a slide to add it to the presentation, or right-click any slide and select Insert All Slides to add all of the slides to the presentation.

By default, when you insert a slide into the presentation it takes on the formatting of the open presentation. If the new slides do not take on the formatting of the open presentation, select the imported text in Outline view, and then click Clear all Formatting in the Font group of the Home tab. It will format the slides using the active theme. If you wish to retain the formatting of the original presentation, click the *Keep source formatting* check box at the bottom of the Reuse Slides pane, shown in Figure 2.15.

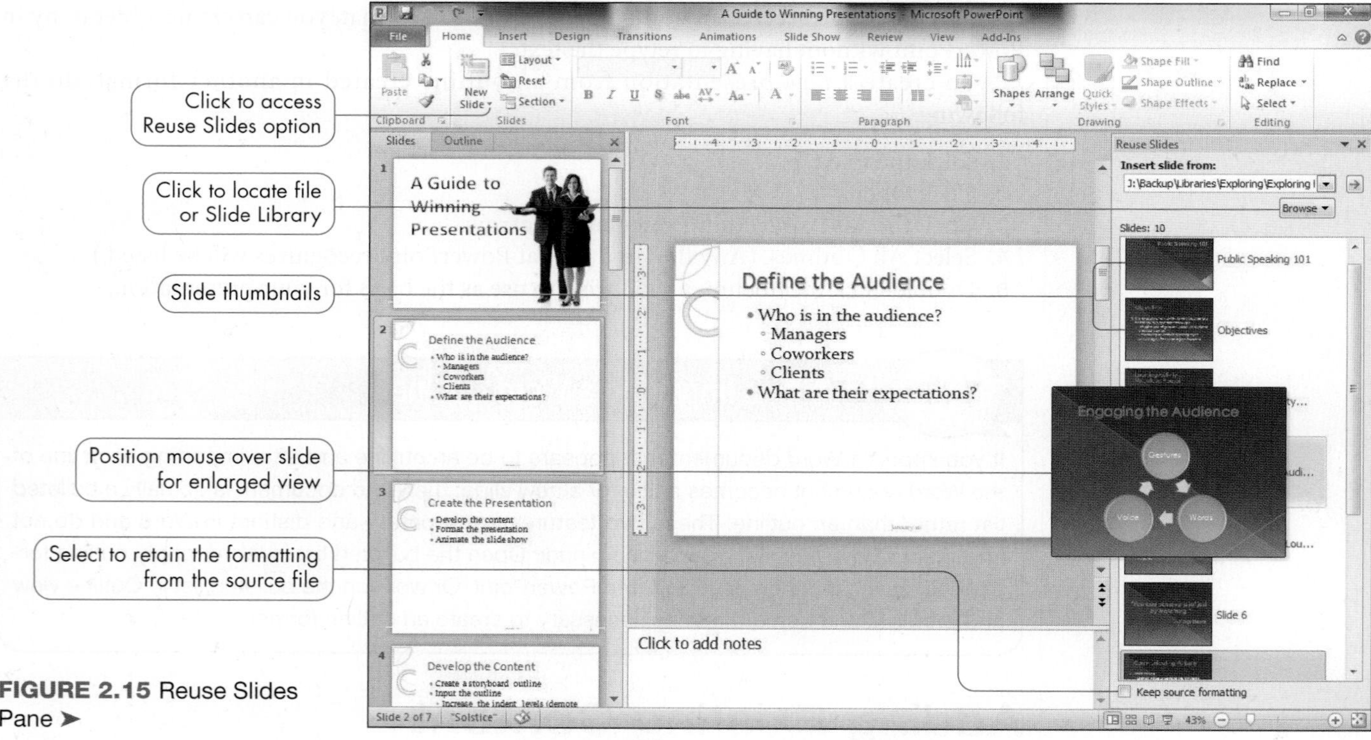

FIGURE 2.15 Reuse Slides Pane ➤

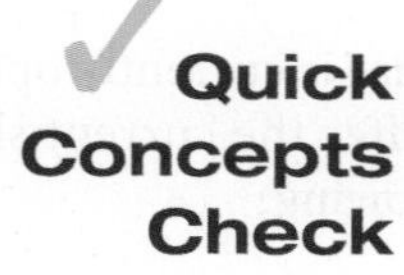

Quick Concepts Check

1. Explain the difference between an .rtf outline and a .txt outline.
2. Do you need to have another presentation open to reuse its content in your current presentation?

3 Data Imports

The director of the Wellness Clinic is impressed with the clinic overview presentation you created. She gives you an electronic copy of an outline she created in a word-processing software package and asks if you can convert it into a slide show. You create a slide show from the outline and then supplement it with content from another slide show.

Skills covered: Import a Rich Text Format Outline • Reuse Slides from Another Presentation

STEP 1 IMPORT A RICH TEXT FORMAT OUTLINE

The director of the Wellness Clinic saves an outline for a presentation in Rich Text Format. You import the outline into PowerPoint to use as the basis for a presentation about the clinic, its mission, and the services it provides to students, staff, and faculty. Refer to Figure 2.16 as you complete Step 1.

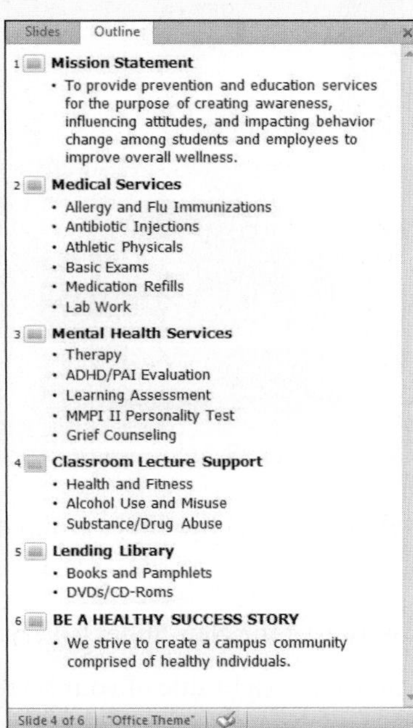

FIGURE 2.16 New Presentation Based on a Rich Text Format (.rtf) Outline ➤

a. Click the **File tab**, click **Open**, and then navigate to the location of your Chapter 2 student data files.

b. Click the **All PowerPoint Presentations arrow**, and then select **All Outlines**.

c. Open *p02h3medoutline*.

   The Rich Text Format outline is opened in PowerPoint, and a new presentation based on the imported document is created. Notice that the font is Cambria and the font color is blue, based on the outline imported into the presentation rather than the default template theme of a Calibri font with a black font color.

d. Click the **Outline tab**, and then review the outline.

   The Rich Text Format outline retains its hierarchy. Each slide has a title and bulleted text.

e. Create a handout header with your name, and a handout footer with your instructor's name, and your class. Include the current date.

f. Save the presentation as **p02h3mission_LastnameFirstname**.

STEP 2 REUSE SLIDES FROM ANOTHER PRESENTATION

While reviewing the Wellness Center presentation, you realize you do not have a title slide or a final slide inviting students to contact the center. You reuse slides from another slide show created for the center that has slides that would fit well with this presentation. Refer to Figure 2.17 as you complete Step 2.

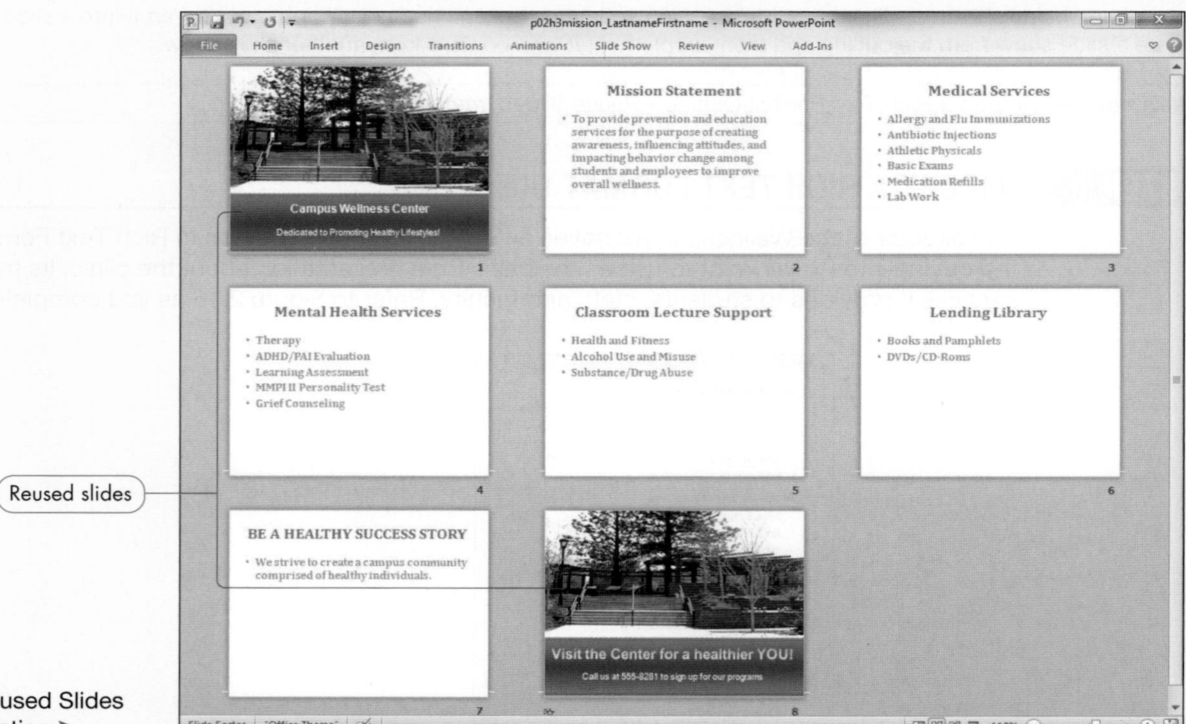

FIGURE 2.17 Reused Slides Added to Presentation ➤

a. On Slide 1, click the **New Slide arrow** in the Slides group on the Home tab.

   The New Slide gallery opens.

b. Click **Reuse Slides** at the bottom of the New Slides gallery.

   The Reuse Slides pane opens on the right side of your screen.

c. Click **Browse**, click **Browse File**, and then locate your student data files.

d. Select *p02h3health.pptx*, and then click **Open**.

> **TROUBLESHOOTING:** If you do not see the *p02h3health* file, click Files of type, and then select All PowerPoint Presentations.

e. Click the **Keep source formatting check box** at the bottom of the Reuse Slides pane.

   With Keep source formatting selected, the images and design of the slides you reuse will transfer with the slide.

f. Click the first slide (*Campus Wellness...*) in the Reuse Slides pane.

   The slide is added to your presentation after the current slide, Slide 1. The new slide needs to be in the Slide 1 position to serve as the title slide of your presentation.

g. Click the slide icon next to the *Mission Statement* slide on the Outline tab, and then drag it so it becomes the second slide.

h. Click the **Slide 7 icon** (*BE A HEALTHY SUCCESS STORY*).

i. Click **Slide 7** in the Reuse Slides pane, and then close the Reuse Slides pane.

The slide show now contains 8 slides. The last slide contains contact information for the Wellness Center.

j. Keep the presentation open if you plan to continue with Hands-On Exercise 4. If not, save and close the presentation, and then exit PowerPoint.

Design

When working with the content of a presentation, it can be helpful to work with the blank Office Theme template. Working in the blank template lets you concentrate on what you want to say. After you are satisfied with the content, then you can consider the visual aspects of the presentation. You should evaluate many aspects when considering the visual design of your presentation. Those aspects include dividing the content into sections, layout, background, typography, color, and animation.

You should evaluate many aspects when considering the visual design of your presentation.

Because the majority of people using PowerPoint are not graphic artists and do not have a strong design background, Microsoft designers created a variety of methods to help users deal with design issues. Using these features, you can create a slide show using a professional design and then modify it to reflect your own preferences. Before doing so, however, you need to consider some basic visual design principles for PowerPoint.

Using Sections

Content organization is an effective design element. Content divided into sections can help you group slides meaningfully. When you create a section, it is given the name *Untitled Section.* You can change the section name to give it a meaningful name, which enables you to jump to a section quickly. For example, you may be creating a slide show for a presentation on Geothermal Energy. You could create sections for Earth, Plate Boundaries, Plate Tectonics, and Thermal Features.

Slide sections can be collapsed or expanded. Use either Normal view or Slide Sorter view to create sections. Figure 2.18 shows a section added to a presentation in Normal view. To create a section, do the following:

1. Select the first slide of the new section.
2. Click Section in the Slides group on the Home tab.
3. Click Add Section.
4. Right-click Untitled Section, and then select Rename Section.
5. Type a new name for the section.

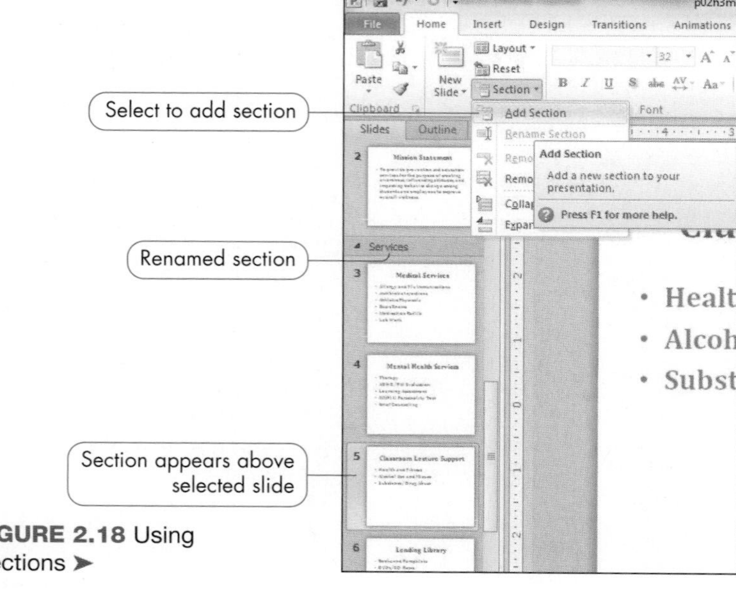

FIGURE 2.18 Using Sections ➤

Examining Slide Show Design Principles

When applied to a project, universally accepted design principles can increase its appeal and professionalism. Some design aspects may be applied in specific ways to the various types of modern communications: communicating through print media such as flyers or brochures, through audio media such as narrations or music, or through a visual medium such as a slide show. The following reference table focuses on principles that apply to slide shows and examines examples of slides that illustrate these principles.

REFERENCE Slide Show Design Principles

Example | **Design Tip**

FIGURE 2.19 Examples of Templates Appropriate for Different Audiences

- **Choose design elements appropriate for the audience.**
  Consider the audience's background. A presentation to elementary students might use bright, primary colors and cartoon-like clip art. Fonts should be large and easy to read. For an adult audience, choose muted earth tones and use photographs rather than clip art to give the slide show a more professional appearance. Figure 2.19 shows design examples suitable for grade school and business audiences, respectively.

FIGURE 2.20 Examples of a Cluttered Design (left) and a Clean Design (right)

- **Keep the design neat and clean.**
  This principle is often referred to as KISS: Keep it sweet and simple! Figure 2.20 shows an example of a cluttered and a clean design. Avoid using multiple fonts and font colors on a slide. Do not use more than three fonts on a slide. Avoid using multiple clip art images. Use white space (empty space) to open up your design.

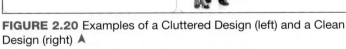

FIGURE 2.21 Examples of an Ineffective Focal Point (left) and an Effective Focal Point (right)

- **Create a focal point that leads the viewer's eyes to the critical information on the slide.**
  The focal point should be the main area of interest. Pictures should always lead the viewer's eyes to the focal point, not away from it. Images should not be so large that they detract from the focal point, unless your goal is to make the image the focal point. Figure 2.21 illustrates examples of ineffective and effective focal points.

(Continued)

REFERENCE Slide Show Design Principles (*Continued*)

Example

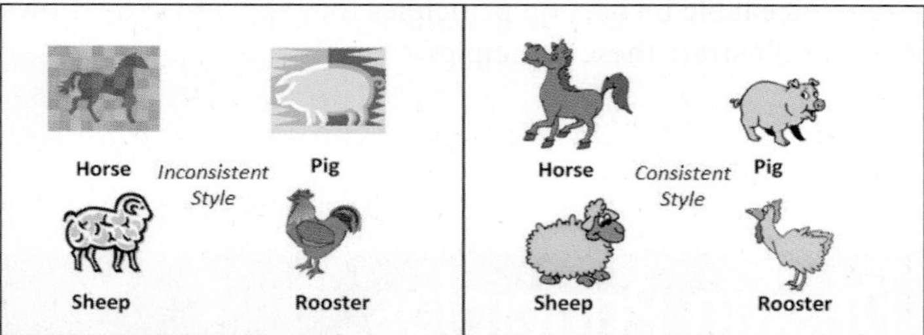

FIGURE 2.22 Examples of Disjointed (left) and Unified (right) Design Elements ▲

Design Tip

- **Use unified design elements for a professional look.**
  Visual unity creates a harmony between the elements of the slide and between the slides in the slide show. Unity gives the viewer a sense of order and peace. Create unity by repeating colors and shapes. Use clip art in only one style. Figure 2.22 shows a disjointed and a unified design.

Sans Serif **Serif**

FIGURE 2.23 Sans Serif (left) and Serif (right) Fonts ▲

- **Choose fonts appropriate for the output of your presentation.**
  If a presentation is to be delivered through a projection device, consider using sans serif fonts with short text blocks. If your presentation will be delivered as a printout, consider using serif fonts. Serif fonts help guide the reader's eyes across the page. You may use longer text blocks in printed presentations. Figure 2.23 displays an example of a sans serif font—a font that does not have serifs, or small lines, at the ends of letters. It also shows an example of a serif font with the serifs on the letter *S* circled. Decorative fonts are also available but should be used sparingly. When choosing a font, remember that readability is critical in a presentation.

Text Guidelines

- Do not underline text.
- DO NOT USE ALL CAPS.
- Use **bold** and *italics* sparingly.
- Avoid text that leaves one word on a line on its own.
- Avoid using multiple spaces after punctuation.

Space once after punctuation in a text block. Spacing more can create rivers of white. The white "river" can be very distracting. The white space draws the eye from the message. It can throb when projected.

FIGURE 2.24 Appropriate and Inappropriate Text Examples ▲

- **Do not underline text.**
  Underlined text is harder to read, and it is generally assumed that underlined text is a hyperlink.
- **Avoid using all capital letters.**
  In addition to being difficult to read, words or phrases in all caps are considered to be "yelling" at the audience.
- **Use italics and bold sparingly.**
  Too much emphasis through the use of italics and bold is confusing and makes it difficult to determine what is important.
- **Avoid creating lines of text that leave a single word hanging on a line of its own.**
  Modify the placeholder size so that more than one word is on a subsequent line.
- **Use just one space after punctuation in text blocks.**
  Using more than one space can create distracting white space in the text block. Figure 2.24 illustrates these principles.

(*Continued*)

REFERENCE Slide Show Design Principles (*Continued*)

Example

Title Text and Bullet Text

- Title text should be in title case and 36 pt or more
- Bulleted text should be in sentence case and 28 pt or more

FIGURE 2.25 Readable Text Guidelines ▲

Design Tip

- **Make text readable.**
  Title text should use title case and be 36 pt or higher.
  Bulleted text should be in sentence case and be 28 pt or higher.
  Figure 2.25 illustrates readable text.

Remember that these design principles are guidelines. You may choose to avoid applying one or more of the principles, but you should be aware of the principles and carefully consider why you are not following them. If you are in doubt about your design, ask a classmate or colleague to review the design and make suggestions. Fresh eyes can see things you might miss.

Modifying a Theme

Themes can be modified once they have been applied. You can change the colors, the fonts, and the effects used in the theme. You can even change the background styles. Each of these options is on the Design tab, and each has its own gallery. Figure 2.26 shows the locations for accessing the galleries.

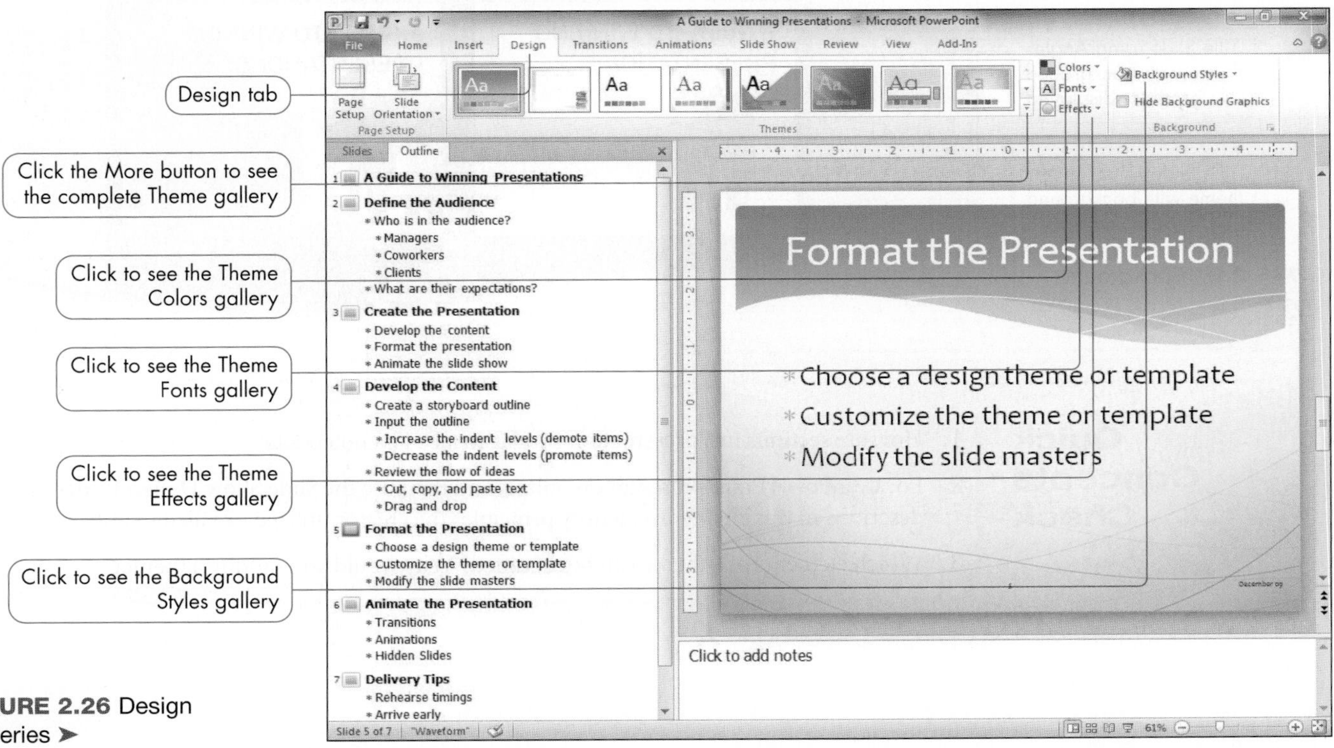

FIGURE 2.26 Design Galleries ➤

The **Colors gallery** provides a set of colors for every available theme.

Each PowerPoint theme includes a ***Colors gallery***, a gallery that provides a set of colors with each color assigned to a different element in the theme design. Once the theme is selected, you can click Colors to display the built-in gallery. Click one of the Theme Colors to apply it. You can even create your own color theme set by clicking Create New Theme Colors at the bottom of the gallery.

Selecting a font for the title and another for the bullets or body text of your presentation can be difficult. Without a background in typography, determining which fonts go together well is difficult. The ***Fonts gallery*** is a gallery that pairs a title font and a body font. Click any of the samples in the Fonts gallery, and the font pair is applied to your theme. You do not need to select the slides because the change applies to all slides.

The **Fonts gallery** contains font sets for title text and bulleted text.

The ***Effects gallery*** displays a full range of special effects that can be applied to all shapes in the presentation. Using effects aids you in maintaining a consistency to the appearance of your presentation. The gallery includes effects such as a soft glow, soft edges, shadows, or three-dimensional (3-D) look.

The **Effects gallery** includes a range of effects for shapes used in the presentation.

You can change the background style of the theme by accessing the ***Background Styles gallery***, a gallery containing backgrounds consistent with the selected Theme Colors. The backgrounds fall into one of three areas: subtle, moderate, or intense. Subtle backgrounds are a solid color, whereas intense backgrounds are designed with patterns such as checks, stripes, blocks, or dots. Simply changing your background style can liven up a presentation and give it your individual style.

The **Background Styles gallery** provides both solid color and background styles for application to a theme.

Some of the themes, like Angles, include background shapes to create the design. If the background designs interfere with other objects on the slide, such as tables, images, or charts, you can select Hide Background Graphics in the Backgrounds group, and the background shapes will not display for that slide. Figure 2.27 displays a Title slide with background graphics displayed and a slide with background graphics hidden.

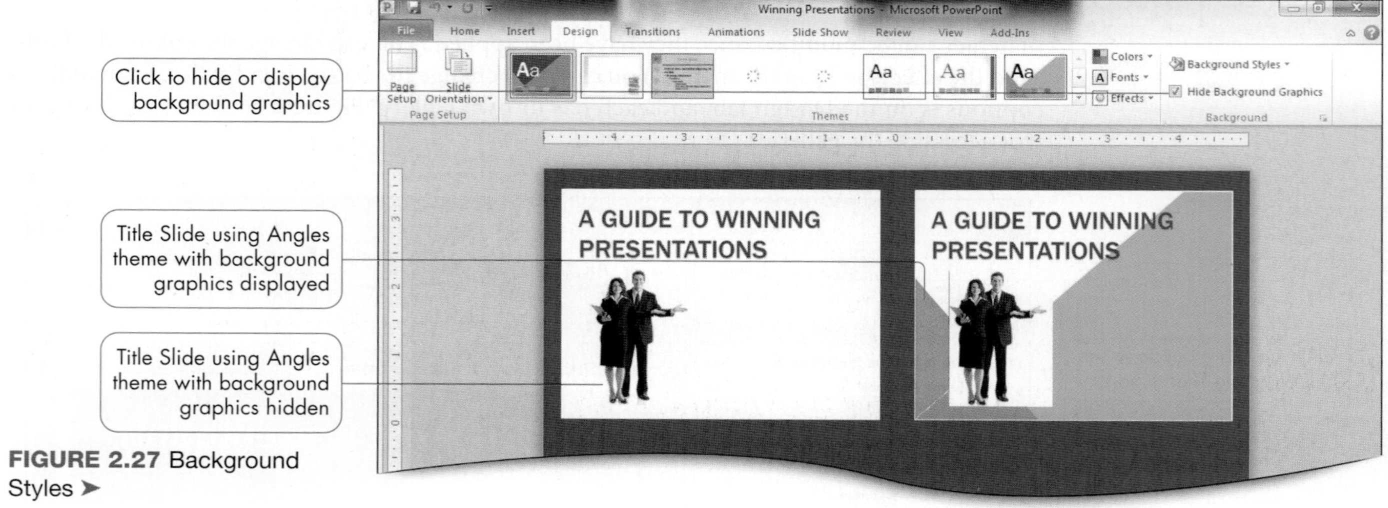

FIGURE 2.27 Background Styles ➤

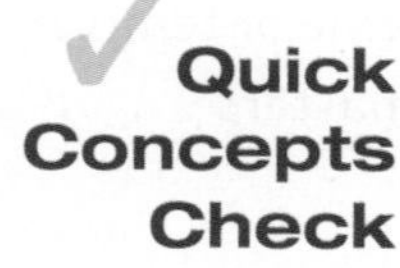

Quick Concepts Check

1. How are sections in a presentation similar to tabs in a notebook?
2. Locate a PowerPoint presentation online, and then use the Slide Show Design Principles described in this chapter to identify principles the creator utilized or failed to utilize.
3. Which elements of a theme can be modified? Why would you modify a theme?

4 Design

The director of the Wellness Clinic plans to add more content to the Campus Wellness Center mission presentation. To help her organize the content, you create sections in the slide show. You apply your knowledge of design principles to make the text more professional and readable. Finally, you change the theme and make modifications.

Skills covered: Create Sections • Apply Design Principles • Modify a Theme

STEP 1 CREATE SECTIONS

After reviewing the Campus Wellness Center mission slide show, you decide to create four sections organizing the content. Refer to Figure 2.28 as you complete Step 1.

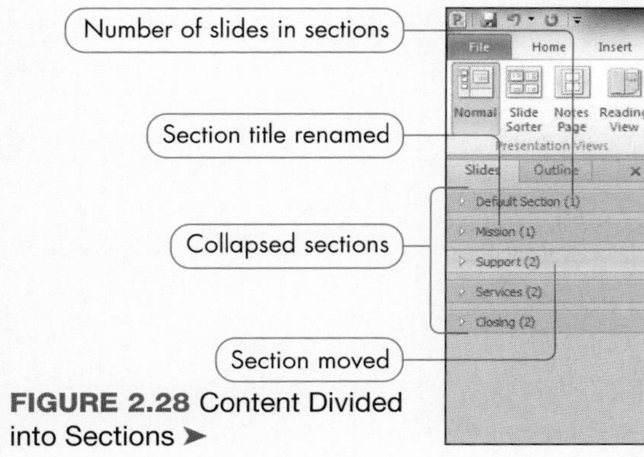

FIGURE 2.28 Content Divided into Sections ➤

a. Open *p02h3mission_LastnameFirstname*, if necessary, and save the presentation as **p02h4mission_LastnameFirstname**, changing *h3* to *h4*.

b. Click the **Slides tab**, and then click the **Slide 2 icon**.

c. Click **Section** in the Slides group on the Home tab, and then click **Add Section**.

   A section divider is positioned between Slide 1 and Slide 2 in the Slides tab. It is labeled *Untitled Section*.

d. Right-click the **Untitled Section divider**, and then click **Rename Section**.

   The Rename Section dialog box opens.

e. Type **Mission** in the **Section name box**, and then click **Rename**.

   The section divider name changes and displays in the Slides tab.

f. Create a new section between Slides 2 and 3.

g. Right-click **Untitled Section**, click **Rename**, and name the section **Services**.

h. Right-click between **Slide 4** and **Slide 5**, click **Add Section**, and then rename the section **Support**.

i. Right-click between **Slide 6** and **Slide 7**, and then create a section named **Closing**.

   The slide show content is divided into logical sections.

j. Right-click any section divider, and then click **Collapse All**.

The Slides tab shows the four sections you created: *Mission*, *Services*, *Support*, and *Closing*, as well as the *Default* Section. Each section divider displays the section name and the number of slides in the section.

k. Right-click the **Support section**, and then click **Move Section Up**.

The *Support* section and all its associated slides moved above the *Services* section.

l. Right-click any section divider, and then click **Expand All**.

m. Click the **View tab**, and then click **Slide Sorter**.

Slide Sorter view displays the slides in each section.

n. Save the presentation.

STEP 2 APPLY DESIGN PRINCIPLES

You note that several of the slides in the presentation do not use slide show text design principles. You edit these slides so they are more readable. Refer to Figure 2.29 as you complete Step 2.

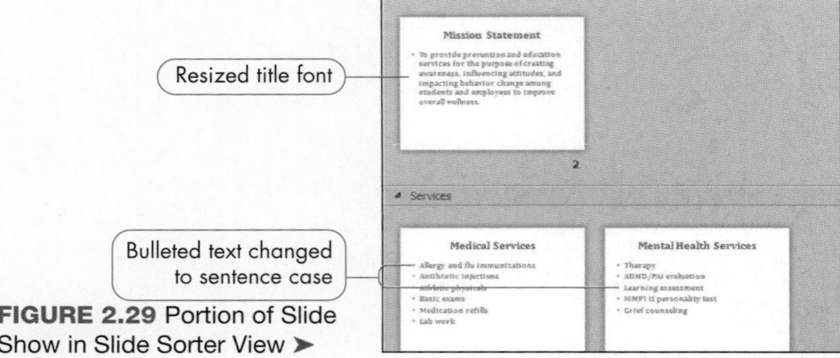

FIGURE 2.29 Portion of Slide Show in Slide Sorter View ➤

a. On Slide 1, select the title, and then change the font size to **44 pt**.

The title font now meets the guideline that title text should be 36 pt or greater.

b. On Slide 3, select the bulleted text, and then change the case to **sentence case**.

The bulleted text now meets the guideline and is more readable.

c. Change the bulleted text in Slides 4, 5, and 6 to **sentence case**.

d. On Slide 4, change the second bullet point to **DVDs/CD-ROMs**.

Always proofread to ensure that the case feature accurately reflects proper capitalization.

e. On Slide 7, select the title text, click **Change Case** in the Font group, and then click **Capitalize Each Word**.

Each word in the title begins with a capital letter.

f. Change the uppercase *A* in the title to a lowercase **a**.

Title case capitalization guidelines state that only significant parts of speech of four or more letters should be capitalized. Minor parts of speech including articles and words shorter than four letters should not be capitalized.

g. Click the **View tab**, and then click **Slide Sorter** in the Presentation Views group.

Note the sentence case in the *Services* section.

h. Save the presentation.

STEP 3 MODIFY A THEME

Although you are satisfied with the opening and closing slides, you think the main body of slides should be enhanced. You decide to change the theme and then modify the new theme to customize it. Refer to Figure 2.30 as you complete Step 3.

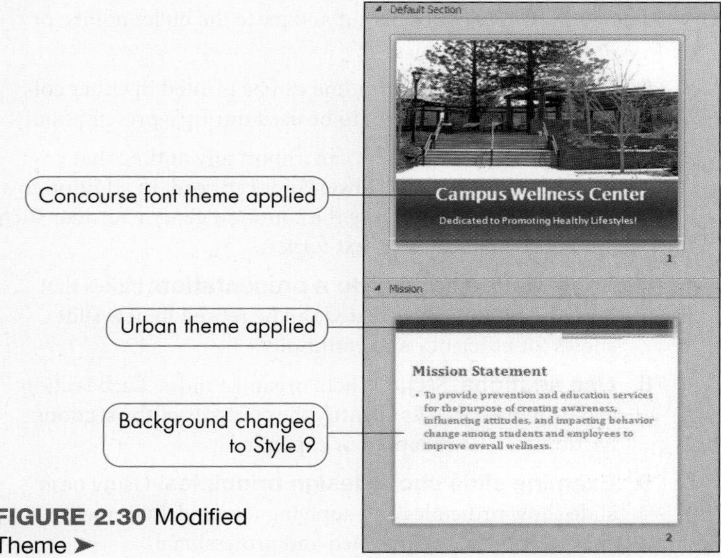

FIGURE 2.30 Modified Theme ➤

a. Click the **Design tab**, and then click the **More button** in the Themes group.

   The Themes gallery opens.

b. Click **Urban** in the Built-In category.

   The Urban theme, which provides a new background, is applied to the slide show.

c. Click **Background Styles** in the Background group, and then click **Style 9** (third row, first column).

d. On Slide 1, click **Fonts** in the Themes group, and then point to several Theme Fonts in the gallery to see how the different Theme Fonts impact the title and subtitle text.

e. Click the **Concourse Theme Font**.

   The title and subtitle text fonts are modified.

TROUBLESHOOTING: If you are on another slide, you will not see a font change. Slides created from outlines retain the original font. You can select individual placeholders and change the font, however.

f. Save and close the file, and submit based on your instructor's directions.

CHAPTER OBJECTIVES REVIEW

After reading this chapter, you have accomplished the following objectives:

1. **Create a presentation using a template.** Using a template saves time and enables you to create a more professional presentation. Templates incorporate a theme, a layout, and content that you can modify. You can use templates that are installed with Microsoft Office, or you can download templates from Microsoft Office Online.
2. **Modify a template.** You can modify the structure of a template. The structure is modified by changing the layout of a slide. To change the layout, drag placeholders to new locations or resize placeholders. You can even add placeholders so that elements such as logos can be included.
3. **Create a presentation in Outline view.** When you use a storyboard to determine your content, you create a basic outline. Entering your presentation in Outline view enables you to concentrate on the content of the presentation and saves time because you can enter information efficiently without moving from placeholder to placeholder.
4. **Modify an outline structure.** Because Outline view helps you see the structure of the presentation, you are able to see where content needs to be strengthened or where the flow of information needs to be revised. If you decide a slide contains content that would be presented better in another location in the slide show, use the Collapse and Expand features to easily move it. By collapsing the slide content, you can drag the slide to a new location and then expand it. To move individual bullet points, cut and paste the bullet points, or drag and drop them.
5. **Print an outline.** An outline can be printed in either collapsed or expanded form to be used during a presentation.
6. **Import an outline.** You can import any outline that has been saved in a format PowerPoint can read. In addition to a Word outline, you can use the common generic formats Rich Text Format and Plain Text format.
7. **Add existing content to a presentation.** Slides that have been previously created can be reused in new slide shows for efficiency and continuity.
8. **Use sections.** Sections help organize slides. Each section can be named to help identify the contents of the sections. Sections can be collapsed or expanded.
9. **Examine slide show design principles.** Using basic slide show principles and applying the guidelines make presentations more polished and professional.
10. **Modify a theme.** In addition to layouts, a template includes themes that define its font attributes, colors, and backgrounds. Themes can be changed to customize a slide show.

KEY TERMS

Background Styles gallery ***p.886***
Collapsed outline ***p.870***
Colors gallery ***p.886***
Effects gallery ***p.886***
Expanded outline ***p.870***
Fonts gallery ***p.886***
Hierarchy ***p.869***
Outline ***p.869***
Outline view ***p.869***
Plain Text format (.txt) ***p.877***
Rich Text Format (.rtf) ***p.877***
Template ***p.862***

MULTIPLE CHOICE

1. A format that incorporates a theme, a layout, and content that can be modified is a(n):
   (a) Theme.
   (b) Outline.
   (c) Background.
   (d) Template.

2. To create a presentation based on an installed template, click the:
   (a) File tab, and then click New.
   (b) File tab, and then click Open.
   (c) Insert tab, and then select Add Template.
   (d) Design tab, and then select New.

3. What is the advantage to collapsing the outline so only the slide titles are visible?
   (a) More slide titles are displayed at one time, making it easier to rearrange the slides in the presentation.
   (b) Transitions and animations can be added.
   (c) Graphical objects become visible.
   (d) All of the above

4. Which of the following is true?
   (a) Slides cannot be added to a presentation after a template has been chosen.
   (b) Themes applied to a template will not be saved with the slide show.
   (c) Placeholders downloaded with a template cannot be modified.
   (d) The slide layout can be changed after the template has been chosen.

5. Which of the following is the fastest and most efficient method for reusing a slide layout you have customized in another presentation?
   (a) Open the slide with the customized layout, delete the content, and enter the new information.
   (b) Open the slide with the customized layout, and cut and paste the placeholders to a new slide.
   (c) Save the custom slide layout, and reuse it in the new presentation.
   (d) Drag the placeholders from one slide to the next.

6. Which of the following is not an efficient method for adding existing content to a presentation?
   (a) Reuse Slides
   (b) Slides from Outline
   (c) Copy and paste slides from an existing slide show into a new slide show.
   (d) Retype the content from an existing slide show into a new slide show.

7. Which of the following demotes a bullet point from the first level to the second level in Outline view?
   (a) Shift+Tab
   (b) Tab
   (c) Decrease List Level
   (d) Ctrl+Tab

8. Which of the following is not true of sections?
   (a) A slide show can be divided into only six logical sections.
   (b) Sections can be created in Normal view or Slide Sorter view.
   (c) Sections can be collapsed.
   (d) Sections can be renamed.

9. Which of the following formats cannot be imported to use as an outline for a presentation?
   (a) .docx
   (b) .jpg
   (c) .txt
   (d) .rtf

10. You own a small business and decide to institute an Employee of the Month award program. Which of the following would be the fastest way to create the award certificate with a professional look?
    (a) Enter the text in the title placeholder of a slide, change the font for each line, and drag several clip art images of awards onto the slide.
    (b) Access Microsoft Office Online and download an Award certificate template.
    (c) Create a table, enter the award text in the table, and then add clip art.
    (d) Select a Theme, modify the placeholders, and then enter the award text information.

PRACTICE EXERCISES

1 Student Success

Figure 2.31 displays a Certificate of Training Completion, created from a template downloaded from Microsoft Office Online for Tesha Technology Training. You are the owner of the company, and you want to present a client, Aishah Batalo, with a certificate to certify she has completed the Digital Applications training offered by your company. This exercise follows the same set of skills as used in Hands-On Exercises 1 and 4 in the chapter. Refer to Figure 2.31 as you complete this exercise.

FIGURE 2.31 Certificate Created from Downloaded Template ➤

a. Click the **File tab**, and then click **New**.
b. Click **Certificates** in the Office.com Templates category, and then open the Business award certificates folder.
c. Click **Certificate of training completion**, and then click **Download**.
d. Save the file as **p02p1certificate_LastnameFirstname**.
e. Create a Notes and Handouts header with your name, and a footer with your instructor's name and your class. Include the current date set to update automatically.
f. Select the text *Company Name*, and then type **Tesha Technology Training**.
g. Select the text *Employee Name*, and then type **Aishah Batalo**.
h. Select the text *Class Name*, and then type **Digital Applications Training**.
i. Select the text *Presenter Name and Title*, and then type your name.
j. Click the **Design tab**, and then click **Background Styles** in the Background group.
k. Click **Style 9**.
l. Save and close the file, and submit based on your instructor's directions.

2 Classic Photo Album

You enjoy using your digital camera to record nature shots during trips you take on weekends. You decide to store these pictures in an electronic slide show that you can display for your family. You use the Classic Photo Album template. This exercise follows the same set of skills as used in Hands-On Exercises 1 and 4 in the chapter. Refer to Figure 2.32 as you complete this exercise.

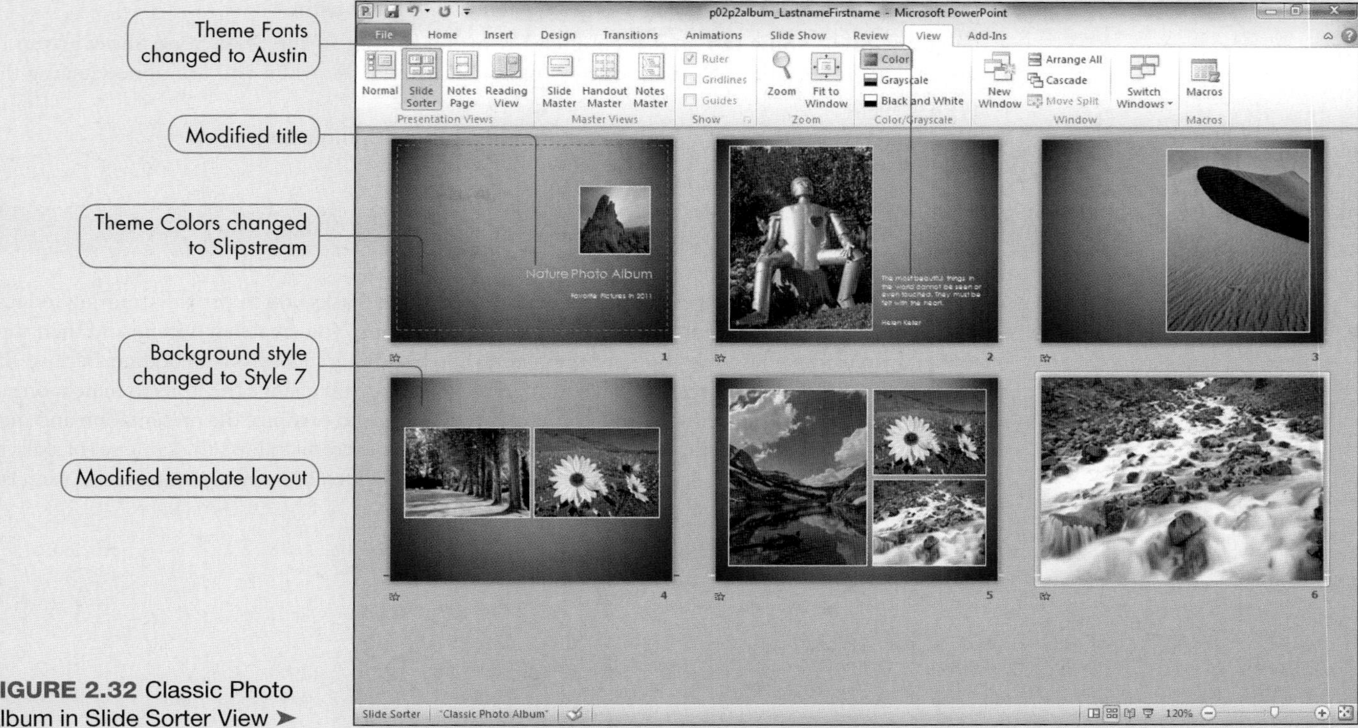

FIGURE 2.32 Classic Photo Album in Slide Sorter View ➤

a. Click the **File tab**, and then select **New**.
b. Click **Sample templates** in the Home category.
c. Select **Classic Photo Album**, if necessary, and then click **Create**.
d. Save the presentation file as **p02p2album_LastnameFirstname**.
e. Create a Notes and Handouts header with your name, and a footer with your instructor's name and your class. Include the current date set to update automatically.
f. Select the word *CLASSIC* in the **title placeholder** of the first slide, and then type **Nature**.
g. Change the case of the title to **Capitalize Each Word**.
h. Replace the text in the **subtitle placeholder**, *Click to add date and other details*, with **Favorite Pictures in 2011**.
i. Click the **New Slide arrow** to display the layout gallery.
j. Click the **Portrait with Caption layout** to add a new Slide 2.
k. Click the picture icon, locate the image *p02p2tinman* from your student data files, and then click **Insert**.
l. Click in the **caption placeholder**, and then type **The most beautiful things in the world cannot be seen or even touched. They must be felt with the heart.** Press **Enter** twice, and then type **Helen Keller**.
m. On Slide 3, read the text in the placeholder, and then click anywhere in the text.
n. Click the border of the caption placeholder, and then press **Delete** to remove the content. Select the placeholder again, and then press **Delete** to remove the placeholder. Modify the layout of the slide by dragging the picture placeholder to the right side of the slide.
o. Select the **Slide 4 thumbnail**, click **Layout** in the Slides group, and then click the **2-Up Landscape with Captions layout** to apply it to the slide.
p. Select the extra photograph (the smaller one), and then press **Delete**. Select a border surrounding one of the caption placeholders, and then press **Delete**. Repeat selecting and deleting until all caption placeholders have been deleted. Delete the CHOOSE A LAYOUT placeholder.
q. Select the **Slide 5** and **Slide 6 thumbnails** in the Slides tab, and then press **Delete**.
r. Click the **Design tab**, and then click **Colors** in the Themes group.
s. Click **Slipstream** to change the Theme Colors.
t. Click **Background Styles** in the Background group, and then click **Style 7** (second row, third column).

u. On Slide 1, click **Fonts** in the Themes group, and then select **Austin**.

v. Click the **Slide Show tab**, and then click **From Beginning** in the Start Slide Show group to view your presentation. Note the variety of layouts. Press **Esc** when you are done viewing the presentation.

w. Save and close the file, and submit based on your instructor's directions.

3 A Guide to Successful Presentations

Your community's Small Business Development Center (SBDC) asks you to provide training to local small business owners on preparing and delivering presentations. You create an outline and then supplement it by reusing slides from another presentation and by adding slides from an outline. Because the slides come from different sources, they have different fonts, and you change the fonts to match, one of the design principles discussed in the chapter. You create sections to organize the presentation and then polish the presentation by adding and modifying a theme. This exercise follows the same set of skills as used in Hands-On Exercises 2, 3, and 4 in the chapter. Refer to Figure 2.33 as you complete this exercise.

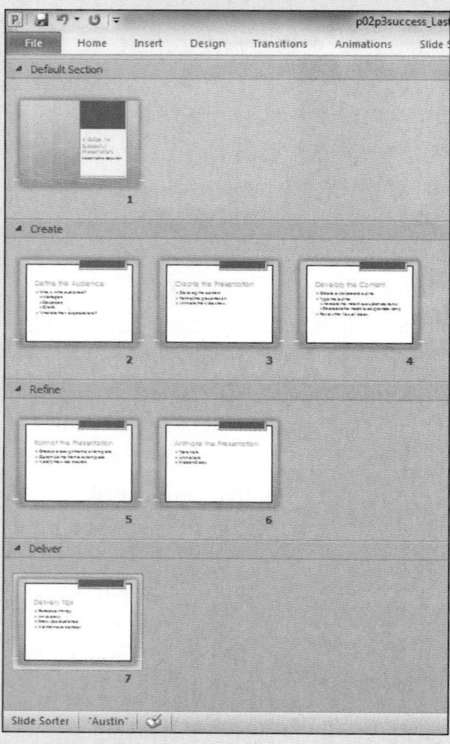

FIGURE 2.33 A Guide to Successful Presentations ➤

a. Click the **Outline tab** in a new blank presentation. Click next to the Slide 1 icon, and then type **A Guide to Winning Presentations**. Press **Enter**, and then press **Tab**. Type your name, and then add the title **Consultant**.

b. Save the new presentation as **p02p3success_LastnameFirstname**.

c. Create a Notes and Handouts header with your name, and a footer with your instructor's name and your class. Include the current date set to update automatically.

d. Click the **New Slide arrow** in the Slides group, click **Slides from Outline**, locate *p02p3tipsoutline* in your student data files, and then click **Insert**.

e. In Outline view, select the word *Winning* on Slide 1, and then type **Successful**.

f. Click at the end of the last bulleted text on Slide 3, press **Enter**, and then press **Shift+Tab** to create a new Slide 4. Type **Develop the Content**, and then press **Enter**.

g. Press **Tab**, type **Create a storyboard outline**, and then press **Enter**.

h. Type **Type the outline** and press **Enter**.

i. Press **Tab** to create a subpoint, and then type **Increase the indent levels (demote items)**. Press **Enter**.

j. Type **Decrease the indent levels (promote items)** and press **Enter**.

k. Press **Shift+Tab** to return to the previous level, and then type **Review the flow of ideas**.

l. Click at the end of the last bulleted text on Slide 5, and then click the **New Slide arrow** in the Slides group.

m. Click **Reuse Slides** at the bottom of the gallery to open the Reuse Slides pane. Click **Browse**, click **Browse File**, select *p02p3reuse*, and then click **Open**.

> **TROUBLESHOOTING:** If you do not see the *p02p3reuse* file, change the Files of type option to All PowerPoint Presentations.

n. Double-click each of the slides in the Reuse Slides pane to insert the slides into the slide show. Close the Reuse Slides pane.

o. Press **Ctrl+A** to select all text in the outline, change the font to **Calibri (Body)**, and then deselect the text.

p. Right-click any bullet point to collapse, point to **Collapse**, and then select **Collapse All**.

q. Drag the **Slide 5 icon** below the Slide 7 icon.

r. Right-click one of the slide titles, point to **Expand**, and then click **Expand All**.

s. Click the **Slides tab** to switch from Outline view to Slides view, and then click the **Design tab**.

t. Click the **More button** in the Themes group, and then click **Austin**.

u. On Slide 2, click the **Home tab**, click **Section**, and then select **Add Section**.

v. Right-click **Untitled Section**, select **Rename Section**, select **Untitled Section** (if necessary), and then type **Create**. Click **Rename**.

w. Repeat steps u and v to create a section named **Refine** before Slide 5 and a section named **Deliver** before Slide 7.

x. Click the **File tab**, click **Print**, click **Full Page Slides**, and select **Outline**. View the outline in the Preview pane, and then press **Cancel** to close the Print dialog box.

y. Save and close the file, and submit based on your instructor's directions.

MID-LEVEL EXERCISES

1 USDA Food Pyramid

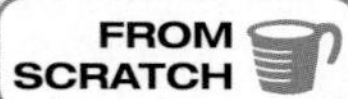

You have been asked to help in a local elementary school. The teacher would like you to teach the children about nutrition and healthy eating. You decide to create a presentation about the U.S. Department of Agriculture (USDA)'s recommended food pyramid. (Visit www.mypyramid.gov.) You locate a Microsoft Office Online template based on the food pyramid. After reading the content tips on the template slides, you think they would make excellent speaker notes for you to refer to during your presentation. You move the tips to the Notes pane. Figure 2.34 displays the downloaded template applied to the conclusion slide of your presentation. Refer to Figure 2.34 as you complete this exercise.

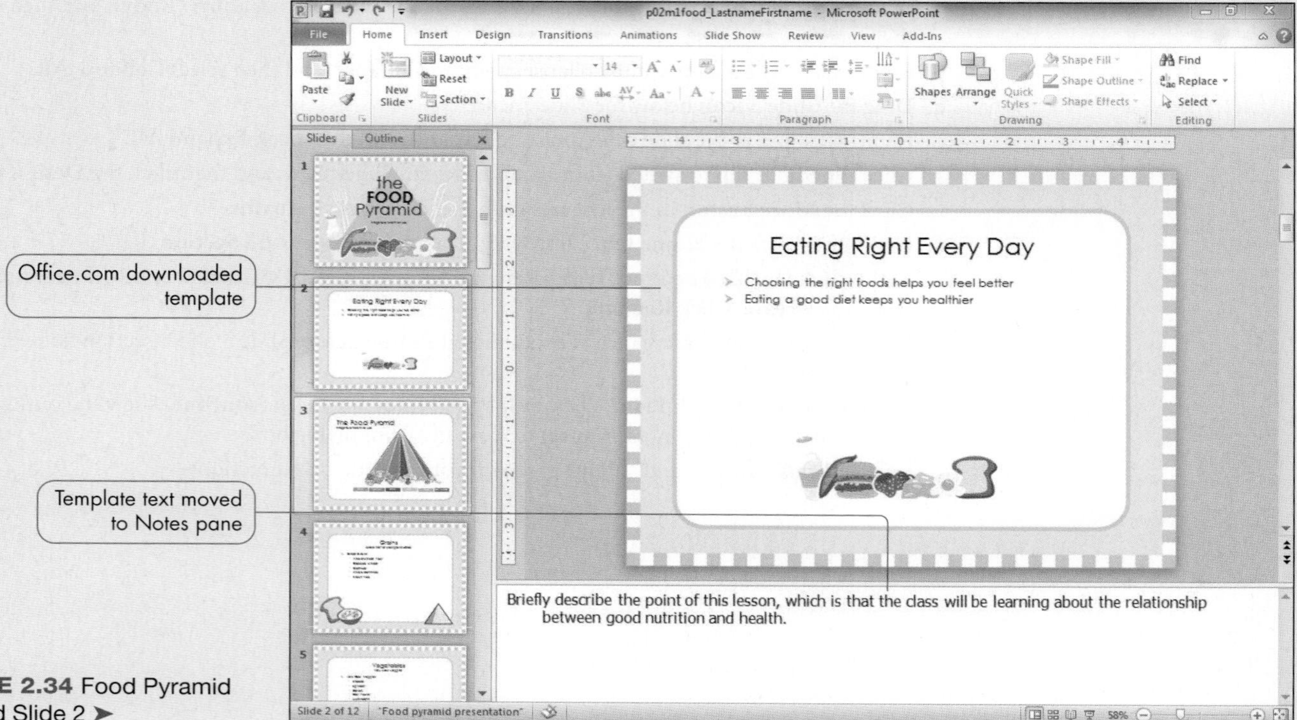

FIGURE 2.34 Food Pyramid Revised Slide 2 ➤

a. Download the Food pyramid presentation located in the Available Templates and Themes, Office.com Templates section, Presentations category, Healthcare folder. Save it as **p02m1food_LastnameFirstname**.

b. Create a Notes and Handouts header with your name, and a footer with your instructor's name and your class. Include the current date.

c. Click the **Slide 2 icon**, and then cut the text from the content placeholder on the slide. Click in the notes area, and then paste the cut text into the notes area. As you create each new slide in the rest of the exercise, cut the information on the slide and paste it to the notes as you did in this step.

d. Type the following bullet points on Slide 2:
   - **Choosing the right foods helps you feel better**
   - **Eating a good diet keeps you healthier**

e. Replace the text on the remaining slides with the information in the following table.

Slide	Bulleted Text

4	• Great Grains!
	  • Whole-wheat flour
	  • Cracked wheat
	  • Oatmeal
	  • Whole cornmeal
	  • Brown rice

5	• Very Cool Veggies!
	  • Broccoli
	  • Spinach
	  • Carrots
	  • Cauliflower
	  • Mushrooms
	  • Green beans

6	• Fresh Fruit!
	  • Apples
	  • Bananas
	  • Grapes
	  • Peaches
	  • Oranges

7	• Only a Little Oil!
	  • Olive oil
	  • Canola oil
	  • Sunflower oil
	  • Margarine
	  • Butter
	  • Mayonnaise (food containing oil)

8	• Magnificent Milk!
	  • Milk
	  • Cheese
	  • Yogurt
	  • Pudding

9	• Mighty Meats and Beans!
	  • Chicken
	  • Turkey
	  • Beef
	  • Pork
	  • Fish
	  • Beans and nuts

10	• Provide bonus calories to give you energy
	• Use for:
	  • Eating more of the foods on the list
	  • Eating higher calorie food
	• Eat more than advised, and you will gain weight

11	Delete slide
12	• Use the MyPyramid Worksheet provided by the USDA
13	• Follow the Food Pyramid Steps for a healthier you!

f. Change the layout for Slide 12, the conclusion, to a **Title Slide layout**.

g. Delete the graphic box with the white background that was left over when you changed the layout.

h. Check the spelling of your presentation and ignore any references to *MyPyramid*, the USDA worksheet name.

i. Save and close the file, and submit based on your instructor's directions.

The local senior citizens' center has asked you to speak on photography. The center has many residents interested in learning about digital photography. You decide to create a presentation with sections on learning the advantages of a digital camera, choosing a camera, taking pictures with a digital camera, and printing and sharing photos. In this exercise, you begin the presentation by creating the sections and completing the content for the first section. Figure 2.35 shows the four slides in the Advantages section in Slide Sorter view. Refer to Figure 2.35 as you complete this exercise.

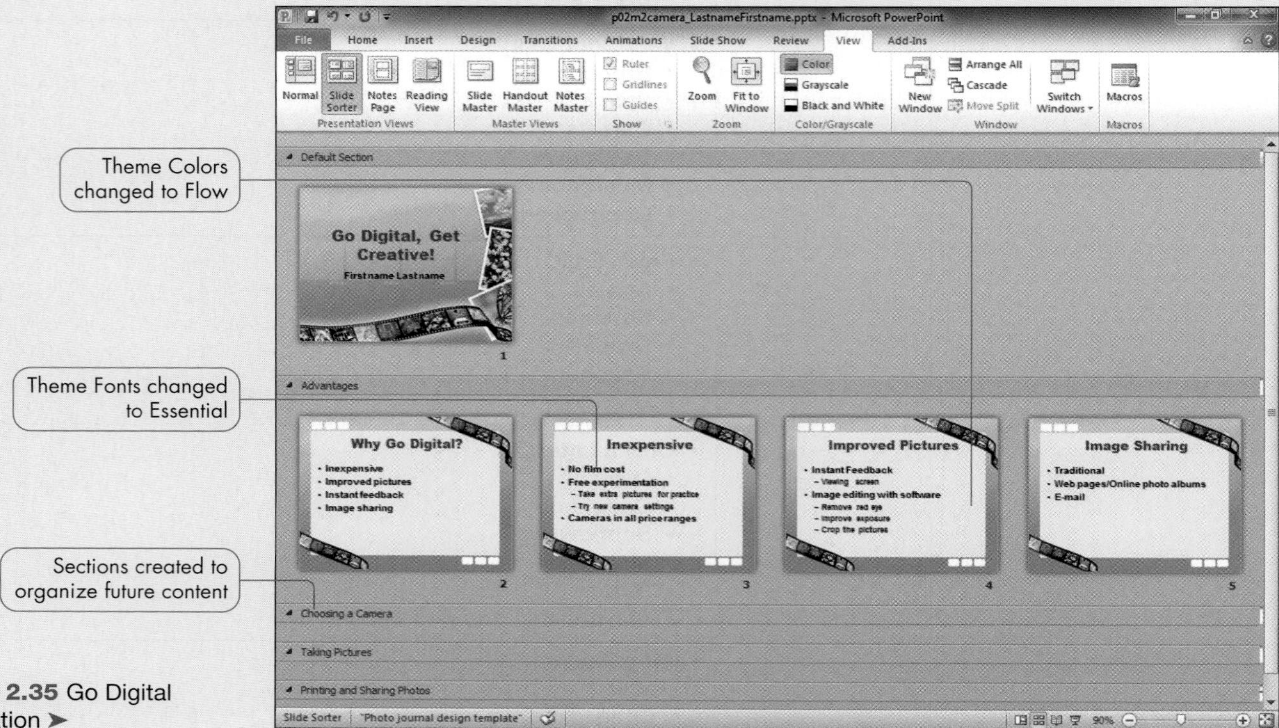

FIGURE 2.35 Go Digital Presentation ➤

a. Open Microsoft Word, click the **View tab**, and then click **Outline** in the Document Views group.

b. Create the following outline using **Tab** and **Shift+Tab** to promote and demote bullets the same way you do in PowerPoint.

Go Digital, Get Creative!
- **Your name in First name Last name format**

Why Go Digital?
- **Inexpensive**
- **Improved pictures**
- **Instant feedback**
- **Image sharing**

Inexpensive
- **No film cost**
- **Free experimentation**
- **Cameras in all price ranges**

Improved Pictures
- **Image editing with software**
  - **Remove red eye**
  - **Improve exposure**
  - **Crop the pictures**
- **Free experimentation**
  - **Take extra pictures for practice**
  - **Try new camera settings**

Instant Feedback

- **Viewing screen**

Image Sharing

- **Traditional**
- **Web pages/Online photo albums**
- **E-mail**

c. Save the outline as **p02m2word_LastnameFirstname**, and then close Microsoft Word.

d. Open PowerPoint, click **New Slide** in the Slides group, and then create slides from the *p02m2word_LastnameFirstname* outline. Save the slide show as **p02m2digital_LastnameFirstname**.

e. Delete the blank Slide 1, and then change the layout of the new Slide 1 to **Title Slide**.

f. Review the presentation in PowerPoint's Outline view and note that *Free experimentation* appears in two locations, that the *Instant Feedback* slide does not have enough information to be a slide on its own, and that the presentation does not contain a conclusion slide.

g. Cut the two bulleted items under *Free experimentation* on Slide 4, and then paste the two bulleted items as subpoints under *Free experimentation* on Slide 3.

h. Delete the Free experimentation bullet on Slide 5.

i. Cut the information on Slide 5, and then paste it as the first bullet point on Slide 4.

j. Use the spelling checker to check your presentation, and then save and close the presentation.

k. Create a new presentation by downloading a template from Office.com in the Design slides category. Open the Hobbies folder, and then download the **Photo journal design template**.

l. Open the Reuse Slides pane, and then browse to locate and open the *p02m2digital_LastnameFirstname* presentation you created in the previous steps. Right-click any slide, and then click **Insert All Slides**.

m. Delete the empty Slide 1.

n. Select all text in Outline view, and then click **Clear All Formatting** in the Font group on the Home tab.

o. Apply the **Flow Theme Colors** and the **Essential Theme Fonts**.

p. Create a section between Slide 1 and 2 named **Advantages**.

q. Create three sections after Slide 5 named **Choosing a Camera**, **Taking Pictures**, and **Printing and Sharing Photos**.

r. Create a Notes and Handouts header with your name, and a footer with your instructor's name and your class. Include the current date.

s. Save the file as **p02m2camera_LastnameFirstname**, close the file, and submit based on your instructor's directions.

3 Using Web Feeds

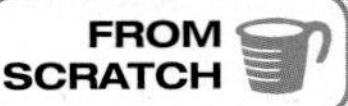

As the training manager of your company's Human Resources Department, you need to prepare a training presentation explaining how employees can stay up-to-date using Web syndication and Web feeds. In the presentation, you explain how they can register for a Web reader and then subscribe to the content for which they want updates. Figure 2.36 shows a sample of the completed presentation using the Median design theme and the Concourse color theme. Refer to Figure 2.36 as you complete this exercise.

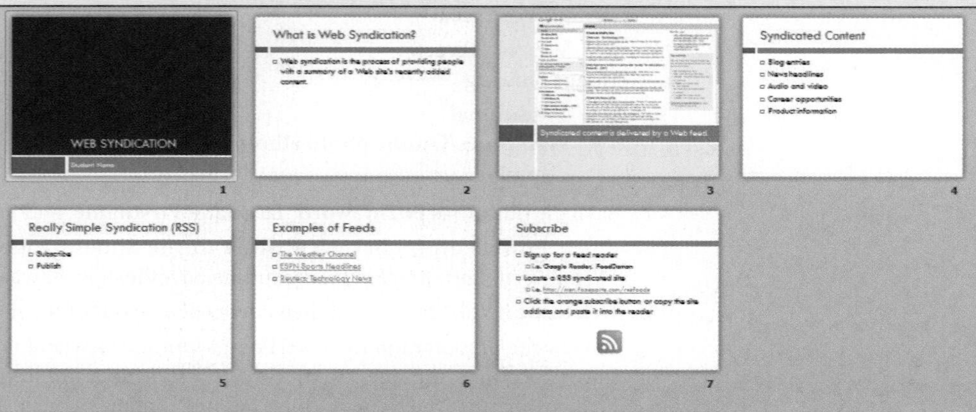

FIGURE 2.36 Refining Content Storyboard ➤

a. Create a new blank presentation and save it as **p02m3syndication_LastnameFirstname**.
b. Click the **Outline tab**, and then create the outline displayed in Figure 2.37.

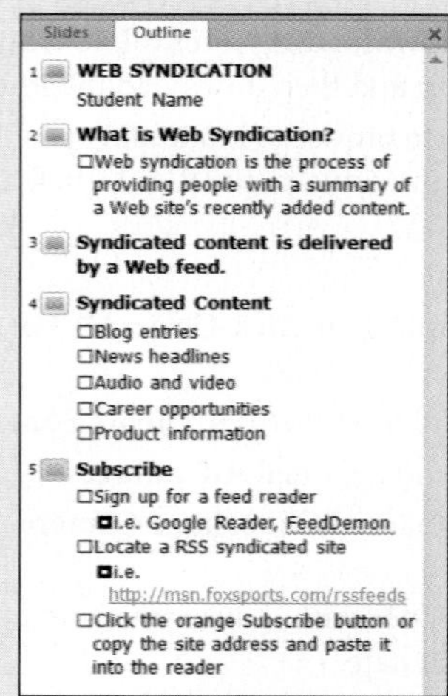

FIGURE 2.37 Web Syndication Outline ➤

c. Collapse all slides, and then drag **Slide 5** so that it becomes Slide 4.
d. Switch to Slides view, and then change the layout of Slide 3 to Picture with Caption. Insert *p02m3newsfeed.png*.
e. Move to Slide 6, and then insert *p02m3rssicon.png.png*. Resize and reposition the RSS icon so it is positioned beneath the last bullet.
f. Reuse the slide in the *p02m3feeds.pptx* presentation, and then position the new slide so it becomes Slide 6.
g. Apply the design theme of your choice to the presentation, and then apply the color theme of your choice.
h. Save and close the presentation, and submit based on your instructor's directions.

CAPSTONE EXERCISE

Your neighbors in your small southwestern subdivision are concerned about drought, fire danger, and water conservation. You volunteer to gather information about possible solutions and share the information with them in a PowerPoint presentation at the next neighborhood association meeting. In this capstone project, you concentrate on developing the content of the presentation.

Design Template

You download an Office.com template to create the basic design and structure for your presentation, save the presentation, and create the title slide.

a. Create a new presentation using one of the Available Templates and Themes in the Office.com Templates category. Open **Design slides**, open **Seasons**, and then download the **Sunny days design template**.

b. Save the presentation as **p02c1wise_LastnameFirstname**.

c. Type **Conserve** as the title on the title slide.

d. Type the subtitle **Waterwise Landscaping**.

e. Create a handout header with your name, and a handout footer with your instructor's name and your class. Include the current date.

Outline and Modifications

Based on the storyboard you created after researching water conservation on the Internet, you type the outline of your presentation. As you create the outline, you also modify the outline structure.

a. Click the **Outline tab**.

b. Type **Waterwise Options** as the title for Slide 2.

c. Enter each of the following as Level 1 bullets for Slide 2: **Zeroscaping**, **Xeriscaping**.

d. Type **Purpose of Landscaping** as the title for Slide 3.

e. Type each of the following as Level 1 bullets for Slide 3: **Beauty**, **Utility**, **Conservation**.

f. Add this speaker note to Slide 3: **With water becoming a limited resource, conservation has become a third purpose of landscaping.**

g. Modify the outline structure by reversing Slides 2 and 3.

Imported Outline

You have an outline on zeroscaping that was created in Microsoft Word and a slide show on xeriscaping. You reuse this content to build your slide show.

a. Position the insertion point at the end of the outline.

b. Use the **Slides from Outline option** to insert the *p02c1zero* outline.

c. Change the layout of Slide 4 from Title and Text to **Picture with Caption**.

d. Insert *p02c1zeropic* in the picture placeholder.

e. Position the point of insertion at the end of the outline.

f. Reuse all of the slides from *p02c1xeri* to add four slides to the end of the presentation.

g. Insert *p02cxeripic* in the picture placeholder on Slide 8.

Design

You know that the room in which you will be displaying the slide show is very light. You decide to change the color theme to darken the slides, which will increase the slide visibility. You also adjust the font size of two captions to increase their readability.

a. Change the Theme Colors to **Solstice**.

b. Change the background style to **Style 3** (first row, third column).

c. Increase the font size of the title and caption text two levels on Slides 4 and 8.

d. Use the spelling checker and proofread the presentation.

e. Apply the **Fade transition** to all slides.

Sections

To facilitate moving between the slides concerning zeroscaping and the slides concerning xeriscaping, you create sections.

a. Add a section before Slide 4, and rename it **Zeroscaping**.

b. Add a section before Slide 8, and rename it **Xeriscaping**.

c. Print the outline as directed by your instructor.

d. Save and close the file, and submit based on your instructor's directions.

Identity Theft

GENERAL CASE 

Import the *p02b1identity* outline and save the presentation as **p02b1identity_LastnameFirstname**. This partially completed presentation is intended to aid you in recognizing the global value of the Outline tab view and how it can be used to modify the structure of a presentation. A combination of slides containing only titles and slides containing content are randomly entered as if they were created from brainstorming. Organize the presentation so that each topic has content under it and so that the content matches the topic in the Title Slide. Create sections reflecting this organization. Create an appropriate conclusion. You may add additional slides, if desired. Good resources for your presentation include the Federal Trade Commission Web site (www.ftc.gov/idtheft) and the Identity Theft is a Crime: Resources from the Government Web site (www.idtheft.gov). Be sure to check the spelling and proofread the content of the presentation.

When you have completed the outline, save and close the presentation. Locate a template to use for the design, and reuse the *p02b1identity_LastnameFirstname* slides to create a new presentation. Apply a theme and modify the Theme Fonts, Theme Colors, and Background Style as desired. Keeping in mind good slide show design principles, you also may modify layouts and add appropriate clip art, transitions, and animations as desired. Create a handout header with your name, and a handout footer with your instructor's name and your class. Include the current date. Print the outline as directed by your instructor. Save the presentation and submit as directed by your instructor.

Explorers

RESEARCH CASE 

Create a presentation about a particular voyage, trip, expedition, or journey of interest in history. Create it as if you are the person undertaking the expedition and you are presenting to the financial sponsors of the trip requesting support. For example, create the presentation as if you are the explorer Marco Polo presenting a request for your expedition's funding to Pope Gregory X. Create the presentation in Outline view and include four to eight slides that explain why you want to go on the expedition, benefits that can be gained from sponsoring the expedition, the exploration plan, and provisions you need. Apply a design theme, and then modify the theme as desired. Insert at least one clip art image or picture of the explorer, the country visited, or some other relevant picture. in an appropriate location. Add a transition and animations to enhance the show. Include a Notes and Handouts footer with your instructor's name and your class. Save your file as **p02b2explorer_LastnameFirstname**. Submit based on your instructor's directions.

Alaska, My State

DISASTER RECOVERY 

Your brother spent a lot of time researching and creating a presentation on the state of Alaska for a youth organization merit badge. He located the information, but he has asked you for your help with the presentation's design. You help him download the template of his choice for the presentation. Save the new presentation as **p02b3meritbadge_LastnameFirstname**. Reuse his slides, which are saved as *p02b3alaska*. Cut and paste the images he gathered into the correct placeholders, or locate photographs for the presentation. Rearrange slides and content as needed to create an uncluttered appearance. You remind him that although federal government organizations allow use of their images in an educational setting, your brother should give proper credit if he is going to use their data. Credit is given to the State of Alaska's Web site for the information obtained from their student information site (www.commerce.state.ak.us/ded/dev/student_info/student.htm). Finalize the presentation by adding appropriate sections, modifying themes, proofreading, and applying transitions and animations as you desire. Create a handout header with your name, and a handout footer with your instructor's name and your class. Include the current date. Print the outline as directed by your instructor. Save the presentation and submit based on your instructor's directions.

POWERPOINT

3 PRESENTATION DESIGN

Illustrations and Infographics

CASE STUDY | Illustrations and Infographics Mini-Camp

Watch the
Set-up Video
for this Case Study!

Your city sponsors youth programs including art, sports, academics, and computers. As one of the youth program coordinators, you are responsible for scheduling the activities held in the high school's computer lab. You receive a request for a mini-camp to introduce students to drawing using computer-based drawing tools, creating infographics, and working with clip art. You decide to teach the mini-camp yourself because you want to introduce the young participants to PowerPoint's many tools for creating and modifying illustrations.

You begin the camp by teaching the participants how to create and modify lines and shapes, how to use shapes to create flow charts, how to use SmartArt diagrams, and how to modify clip art to meet their needs. You also teach participants WordArt manipulation because it is a creative way to enhance text used in illustrations and infographics.

OBJECTIVES AFTER YOU READ THIS CHAPTER, YOU WILL BE ABLE TO:

1. Create shapes *p.904*
2. Apply Quick Styles and customize shapes *p.909*
3. Create SmartArt *p.925*
4. Modify SmartArt *p.929*
5. Create WordArt *p.933*
6. Modify WordArt *p.933*
7. Modify objects *p.939*
8. Arrange objects *p.944*

Shapes

A **shape** is a geometric or non-geometric object, such as a rectangle or an arrow.

In addition to text, you can use a variety of visual elements to add impact to a presentation. One type of visual element is a ***shape***, a geometric or non-geometric object used to create an illustration or to highlight information. For example, on a slide containing a list of items, you could include a quote related to the items and create the quote inside a shape to call attention to it. You can combine shapes to create complex images. Figure 3.1 shows three PowerPoint themes utilizing shapes in each of these ways. The Apothecary theme uses a rectangular shape to draw attention to the information in the title placeholder. The Oriel theme utilizes circles and lines to create an interesting design. The ListDiagram theme from Office.com uses rectangles to emphasize each concept.

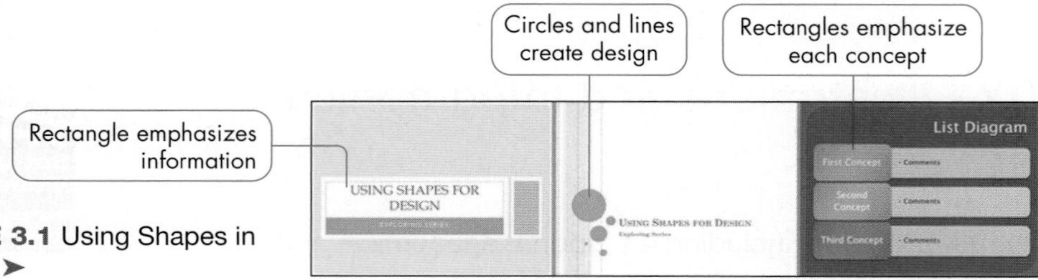

FIGURE 3.1 Using Shapes in Themes ➤

An **Infographic** is a visual representation of data or knowledge.

Infographics, a shortened term for information graphics, are visual representations of data or knowledge. Infographics typically use shapes to present complex data or knowledge in an easily understood visual representation. PowerPoint includes powerful drawing tools you can use to create lines and shapes, which are the basis for infographics. Because clip art is created with shapes, you learn to modify the shapes used for clip art to meet your needs. In addition to using the drawing tools, you can enhance shapes by warping or adding effects such as 3-D, shadow, glow, warp, bevel, and others. These effects are accessible through style galleries. Utilizing these visual effects makes it easy for you to create professional-looking infographics to enhance your presentation.

Utilizing … visual effects makes it easy for you to create professional looking infographics to enhance your presentation.

In this section, you will create and modify various shapes and lines. You will also customize shapes and apply special effects to objects. Finally, you will learn how to apply and change outline effects.

Creating Shapes

PowerPoint provides tools for creating shapes. You can insert a multitude of standard geometric shapes like circles or squares and hearts or stars. You can insert equation shapes, such as + and ÷, and a variety of banners. After you create a shape, you can modify it and apply fills and special effects.

To create a shape:

1. Click the Insert tab.
2. Click Shapes in the Illustrations group.
3. Click the shape you desire from the Shapes gallery.
4. Click the slide where you wish to place the shape, or drag the cross-hair pointer from the starting position of the shape until the shape is approximately the size you want.
5. Release the mouse button.

To resize the shape, drag any of the sizing handles that surround the shape after it is created. Figure 3.2 shows the Shapes gallery and the many shapes from which you can choose. Notice that the most recently used shapes are at the top of the list so you can conveniently reuse them.

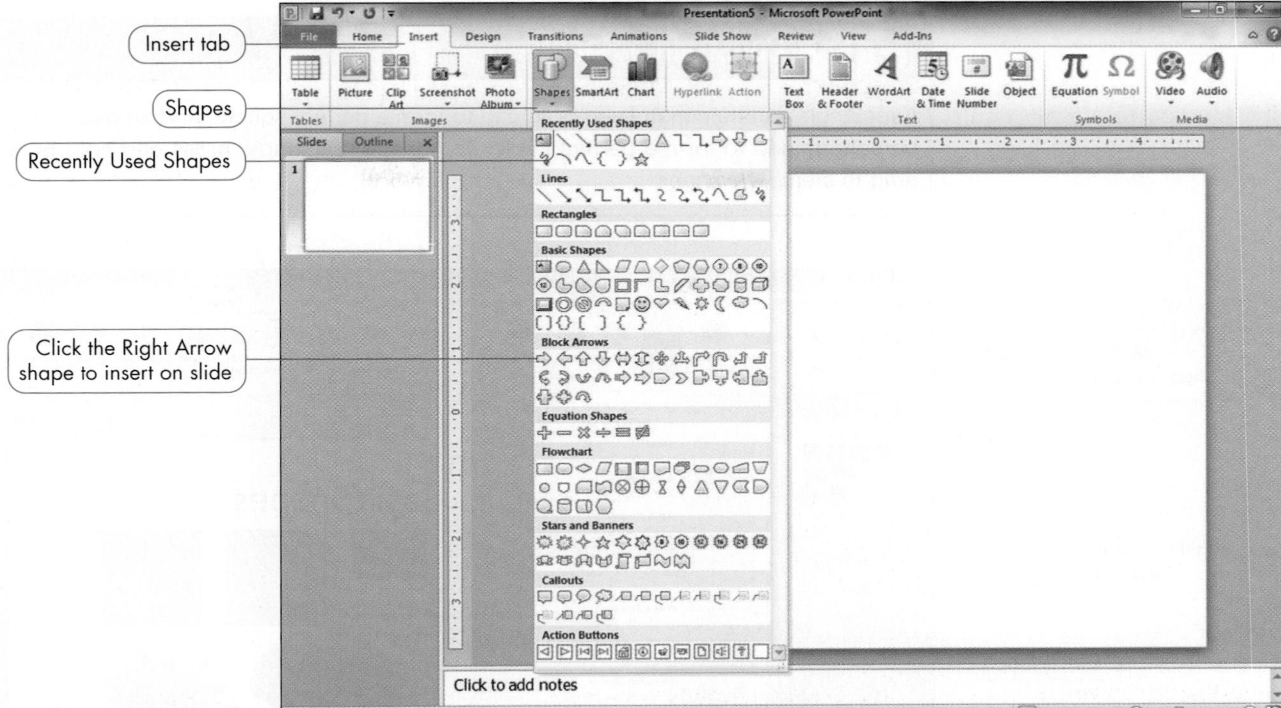

FIGURE 3.2 Shapes Gallery ➤

TIP Using the Drawing Group

You can also access the Shapes gallery from the Drawing group on the Home tab. This group allows you to choose a shape, arrange its order and position, apply a Quick Style, and change properties of the shape. If you have a widescreen monitor or if your monitor is set for a higher resolution, the Drawing group displays individual shapes instead of one Shapes command. If this is the case, click the More button to open Shapes gallery.

Lock Drawing Mode enables the creation of multiple shapes of the same type.

The Shapes command deactivates the selected shape after you draw it once, forcing you to reselect the shape each time you want to use it. By activating the ***Lock Drawing Mode*** feature, you can add several shapes of the same type on your slide without selecting the shape each time. To activate Lock Drawing Mode, right-click the shape you want to use in the Shapes gallery, and then select Lock Drawing Mode. Next, click anywhere on the slide, and then drag to create the first shape. Drag repeatedly to create additional shapes of the same type. To release the Lock Drawing Mode, press Esc.

A **callout** is a shape that includes a text box you can use to add notes.

An **adjustment handle** is a yellow diamond that enables you to modify a shape.

Figure 3.3 shows a series of squares created with the Lock Drawing Mode activated, a cloud created using the Cloud shape located in the Basic Shapes category, an explosion created using the Explosion 2 shape located in the Stars and Banners category, a Smiley Face located in the Basic Shapes category, and a ***callout*** created using the Oval Callout located in the Callouts category. A callout is a shape that includes a line with a text box that can be used to add notes, often used in cartooning. Notice that the Smiley Face shape is selected. The sizing handles display around the shape, and a yellow diamond appears at the curved line of the mouth. This yellow diamond is an ***adjustment handle*** that you can drag to change the shape. If you drag the adjustment handle downward, the smile becomes a frown. Some shapes have an adjustment handle, and some do not.

TIP Constrain a Shape

A rectangle can be constrained or forced to form a perfect square, and an oval or ellipse can be constrained to form a perfect circle. To constrain a shape, press and hold Shift as you drag to create the shape.

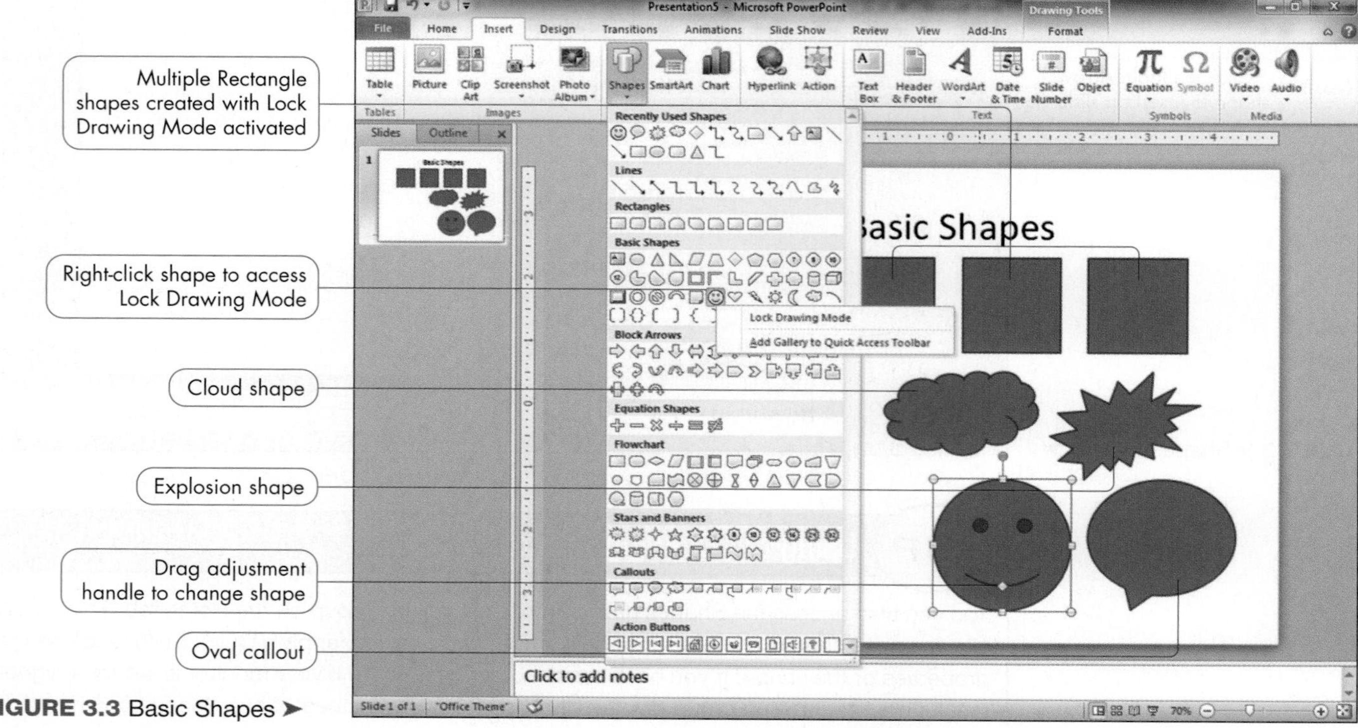

FIGURE 3.3 Basic Shapes ➤

Draw Lines and Connectors

Lines are shapes that can be used to point to information, to connect shapes on a slide, or to divide a slide into sections. Lines also are often used in slide design. Draw a straight line by selecting the line in the Lines category, positioning the pointer on the slide where you want the line to begin, and then dragging to create the line.

To create a curved line:

1. Click the Curve shape in the Lines category of the Shapes gallery.
2. Click the slide at the location where you want to start the curve.
3. Continue to click and move the mouse to shape the curve in the desired pattern.
4. Double-click to end the curve.

As you click while creating the curve, you set a point for the curve to bend around. To draw a shape that looks like it was drawn with a pen, select the Scribble shape.

TIP Create a Closed Shape

If you use the Curve, Freeform, or Scribble line tool to create a shape and end the shape at its starting point, the starting point and ending points join to create a closed shape. The advantage of joining the ends of the line and creating a closed shape is that you can include a fill, or interior.

A **connector** is a Lines shape that is attached to and moves with other shapes.

In addition to drawing simple lines to create dividing lines and waves, you may need ***connectors*** or lines that attach to the shapes you create. Connector lines move with shapes when the shapes are moved. The three types of connectors are straight, elbow (to create angled lines), and curved. To determine which line shapes are connectors, point to the line in the gallery and a ScreenTip will appear with the shape name.

The first step in working with connectors is to create the shapes you want to connect with lines. After you create the shapes, select a connector line from the Shape gallery. After you select the connector, red squares appear around the shapes when you move your pointer over them. These are the locations where you can attach the connector. Click one of the red squares and drag the line until it connects with the red circle that will appear on the next shape. The two shapes are now connected. You can also connect placeholders with a connector line.

If you move a shape that is joined to another shape with a connector line, the connecting line moves with it, extending or shortening as necessary to maintain the connection. Sometimes when you rearrange the shapes, the connectors may no longer extend to the shape that was not moved, or the connectors may cross shapes and be confusing. If that happens, you can use the yellow adjustment handle located on the connector line to reshape the connectors. Select the connector lines and drag the handles to obtain a clearer path.

A **flow chart** is an illustration showing the sequence of a project or plan.

A ***flow chart*** is an illustration that shows a sequence to be followed or a plan containing steps. For example, you could use a flow chart to illustrate the sequence to follow when taking a multiple-choice test. Connector lines join the shapes in a flow chart.

The typical flow chart sequence includes start and end points shown in oval shapes, steps shown in rectangular shapes, and decisions to be made shown in diamond shapes. Connectors with arrows demonstrate the order in which the sequence should be followed to accomplish the goal. Each shape has a label to which you can add text, indicating what the shape represents. When you select a shape and then type or paste text into it, the text becomes part of the shape.

A **text box** is an object that enables you to place text anywhere on a slide.

If you need to add text to a slide, create a text box. For example, use a text box to add a quote to a slide that you do not want in the slide content placeholder. A ***text box*** is an extremely useful object because it gives you the freedom to create and position text outside the slide content placeholders. Text inside a text box can be formatted just as text in placeholders is formatted. You can even add a border, fill, shadow, or 3-D effect to the text in a text box. Figure 3.4 shows a basic flow chart created with shapes, connectors, and text boxes.

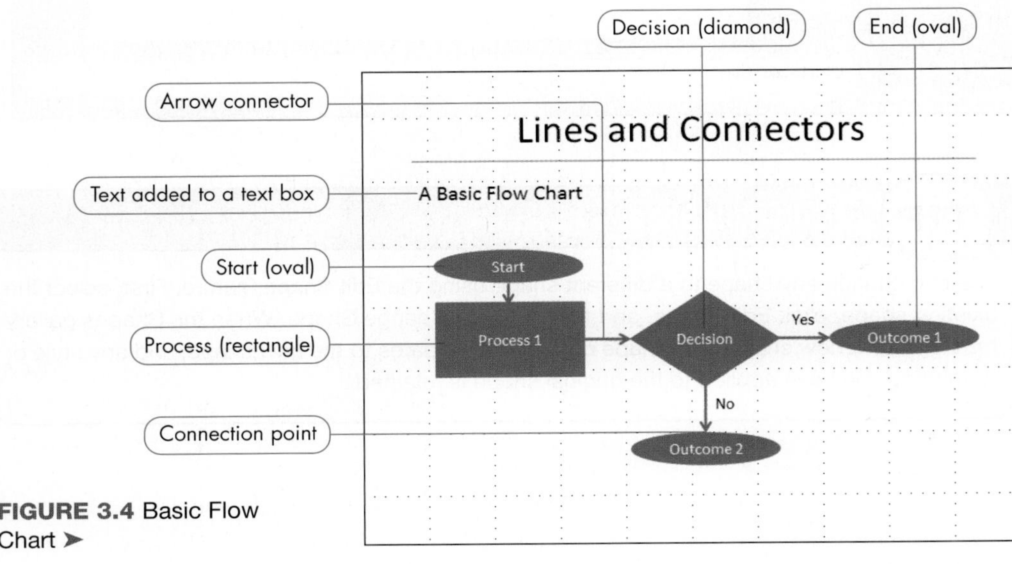

FIGURE 3.4 Basic Flow Chart ➤

Create and Modify Freeform Shapes

A **freeform shape** is a shape that combines both curved and straight lines to create a shape.

A ***freeform shape*** is a shape that can be used to create customized shapes using both curved and straight-line segments. Select the freeform shape in the Lines category of the Shapes gallery, and then click the slide. Drag to create curves; move the mouse and click to draw straight lines. Double-click to end the freeform shape. If you click the starting point of the shape, you create a closed shape just as you do with lines.

A **vertex** is the point where a curve ends or the point where two line segments meet in a freeform shape.

To modify a freeform shape, select the shape, and the Drawing Tools tab containing the Format tab displays. Click the Format tab, click Edit Shape in the Insert Shapes group, and then select Edit Points. ***Vertexes***, or black squares that indicate where a curve ends or the point where two line segments meet, will appear and can be moved if you click a point and drag it. A vertex can be deleted if you right-click the point, and then click Delete Point. Either moving a vertex or deleting it will redefine the object's shape. Figure 3.5 shows a freeform shape with its vertexes displayed. Figure 3.6 shows a selected vertex dragged to a new position. When you release the left mouse button, the freeform will take the new shape.

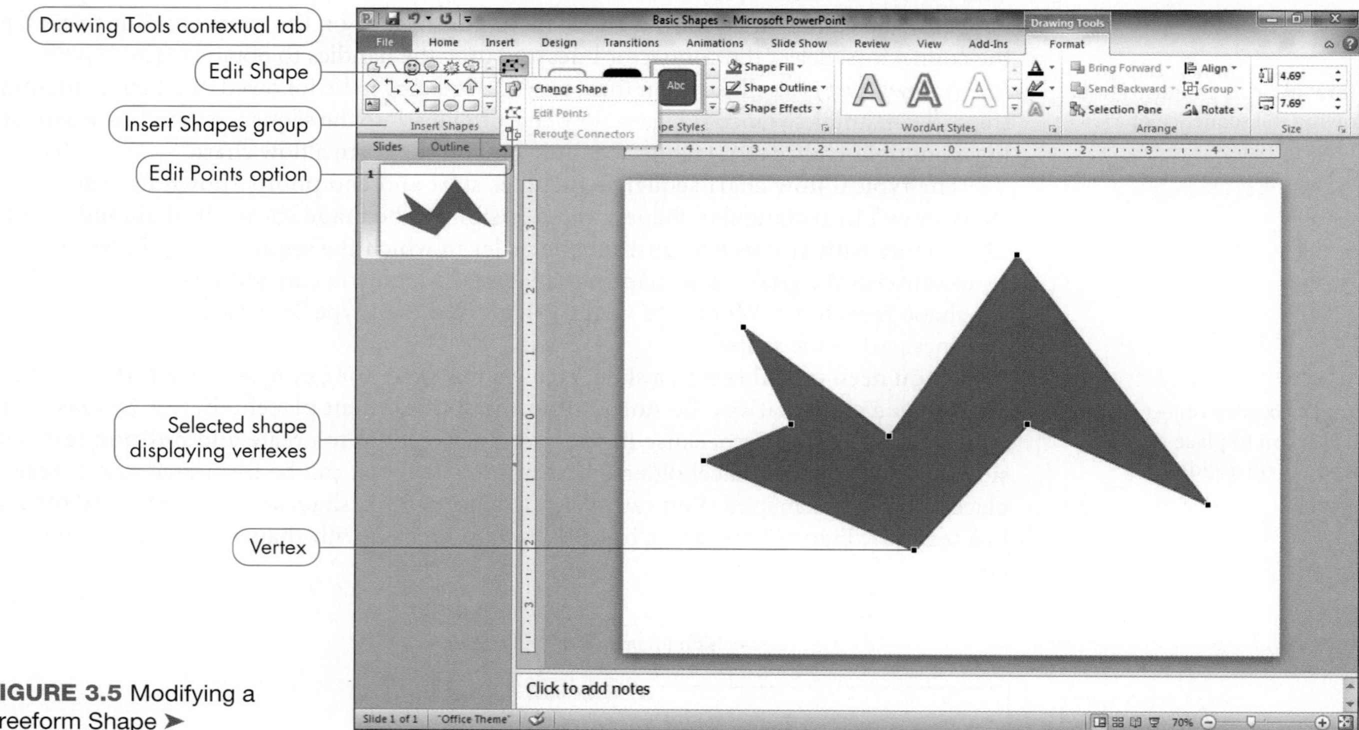

FIGURE 3.5 Modifying a Freeform Shape ➤

> **TIP** Changing a Shape
>
> You can change any shape to a different shape using the Edit Shape feature. First, select the existing shape, click Edit Shape, and then point to Change Shape. When the Shapes gallery opens, click a new shape. The shape on the slide updates to the new shape, and any style or formatting you have applied to the original shape is retained.

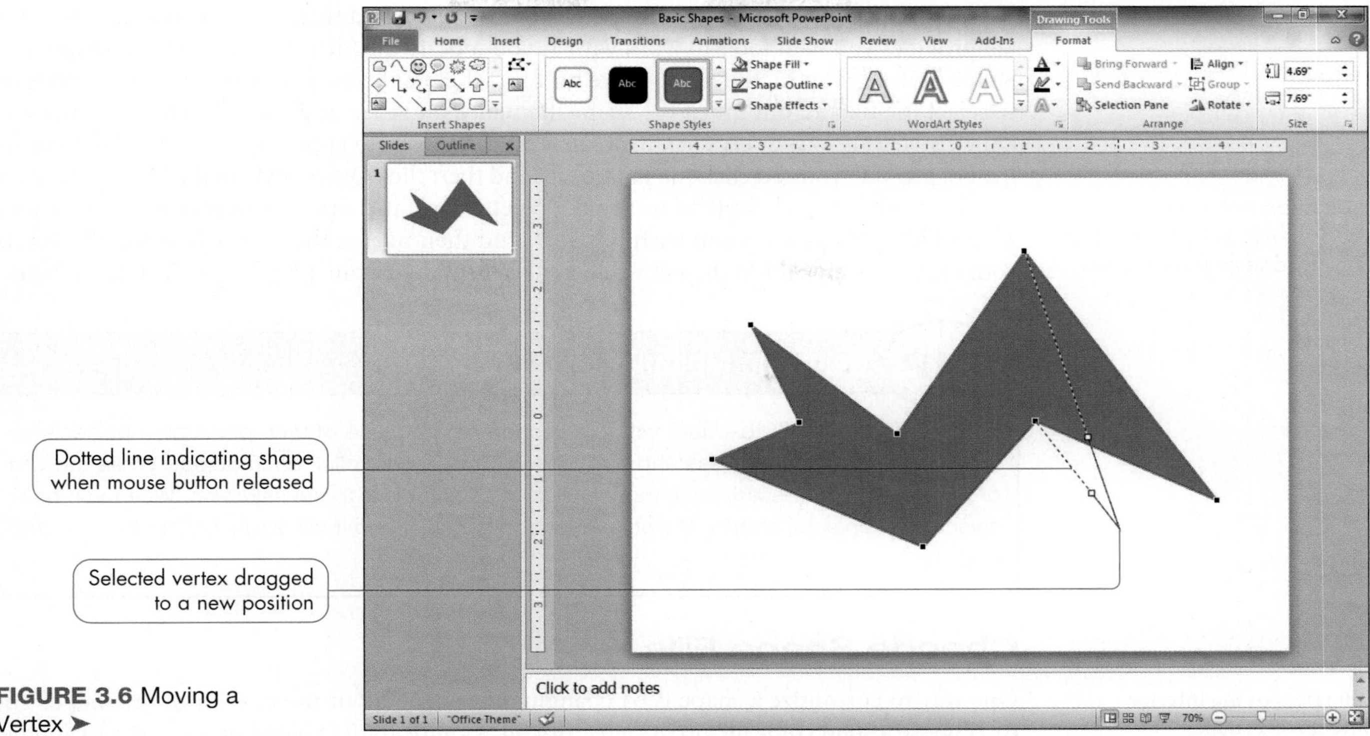

FIGURE 3.6 Moving a Vertex ➤

Applying Quick Styles and Customizing Shapes

A **Quick Style** is a combination of formatting options that can be applied to a shape or graphic.

A ***Quick Style*** is a combination of different formats that can be selected from the Quick Style gallery and applied to a shape or other objects. To see how a Quick Style would look when applied, position your pointer over the Quick Style thumbnail. When you identify the style you want, click to apply the style to a selected object. Options in the gallery include edges, shadows, line styles, gradients, and 3-D effects. Figure 3.7 shows the Quick Style gallery and several shapes with a variety of Quick Styles applied to them.

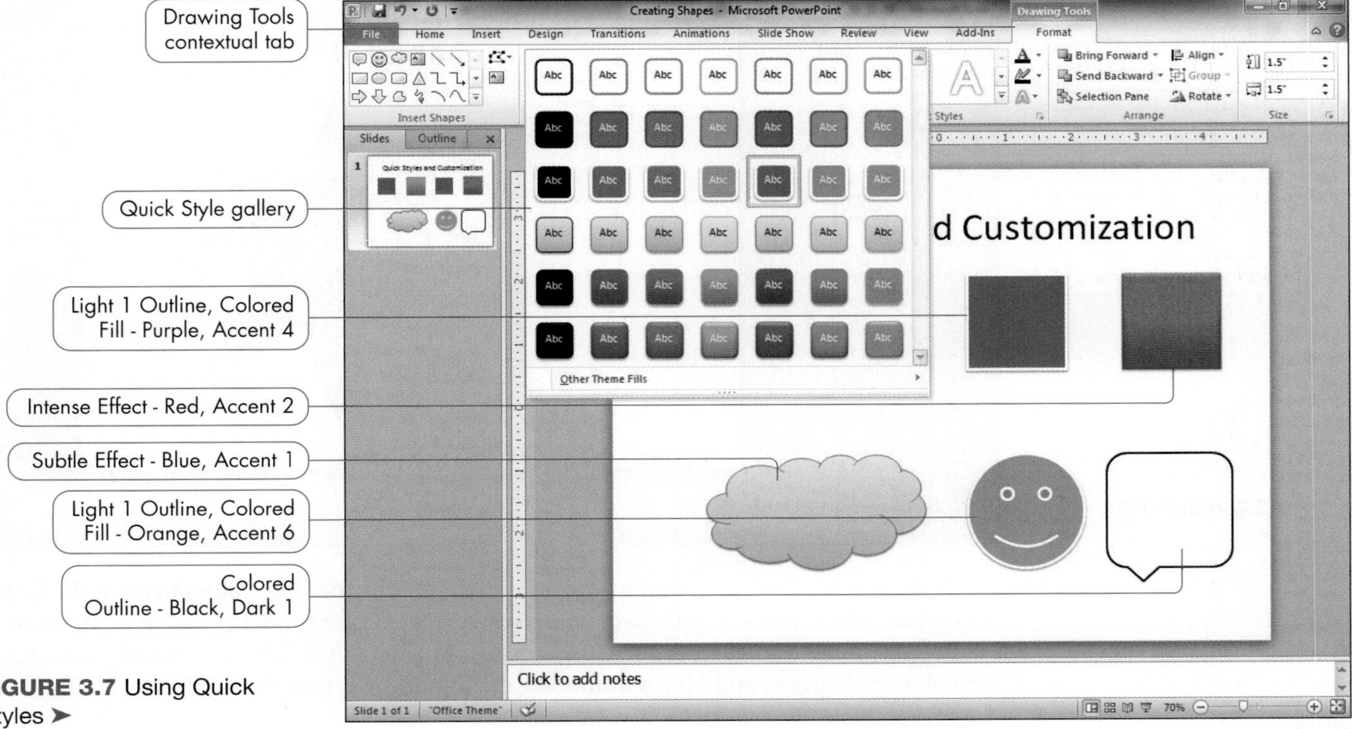

FIGURE 3.7 Using Quick Styles ➤

To apply a Quick Style to a shape, select the shape, and then click the Format tab. This tab provides you with tools to work with as you modify the format of the selected shape. The Shape Styles group includes the More button, which enables you to apply a Quick Style or to select the fill and outline of the shape manually, and then apply special effects. When the Quick Style gallery is open, click the Quick Style you wish to apply. As an alternative to using the Format tab, you can click the Home tab, and then click Quick Style in the Drawing group.

A **selection net** or marquee selects all objects in an area you define by dragging the mouse.

To apply a Quick Style to multiple objects, click and drag a ***selection net*** or marquee around all of the objects you wish to select, and then release the mouse button. All objects contained entirely within the net will be selected, and you can apply a Quick Style to them.

TIP Selecting Multiple Objects

If objects are difficult to select with a selection net because of their placement or because they are non-adjacent, press and hold Ctrl or Shift as you click each object. While the Ctrl or Shift keys are pressed, each mouse click adds an object to the selection. When you have selected all objects, choose the style or effect you want and it will apply only to the selected objects.

Change Shape Fills

A **fill** refers to the interior contents of a shape.

A **gradient fill** is a blend of two or more colors or shades.

One way to customize a shape is by changing the shape ***fill*** or the interior of the shape. You can choose a solid color fill, no fill, a picture fill, a ***gradient fill*** (a blend of one color to another color or one shade to another shade), or a texture fill. To change the fill of a selected object, click Shape Fill in the Shape Styles group on the Format tab. The Shape Fill gallery provides color choices that match the theme colors or color choices based on Standard Colors. Figure 3.8 shows the Shape Fill options and a shape filled with the Yellow Standard Color.

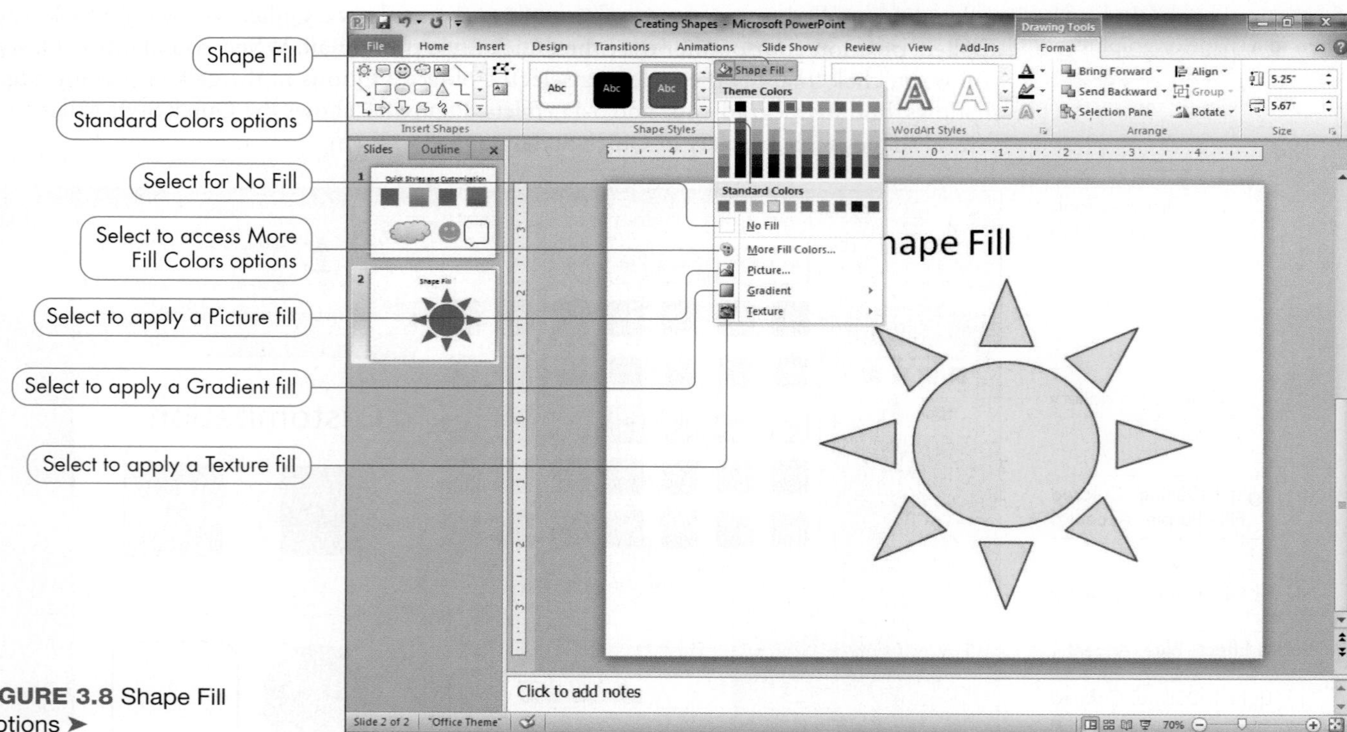

FIGURE 3.8 Shape Fill Options ➤

If these color choices do not meet your needs, select More Fill Colors to open the Colors dialog box where you can mix colors based on an RGB color model (Red Green Blue) or an HSL color model (Hue Saturation Luminosity). The default RGB color model gives each of the colors red, green, and blue a numeric value that ranges from 0 to 255. The combination of these values creates the fill color assigned to your shape. When all three RGB values are 0, you get black. When all three RGB values are 255, you get white. By using different combinations of numbers between 0 and 255, you can create over 16 million shades of color.

Transparency refers to how much you can see through a fill.

Opaque refers to a solid fill, one with no transparency.

The Color dialog box also enables you to determine the amount of ***transparency*** or visibility of the fill. At 0% transparency, the fill is ***opaque*** or solid, while at 100% transparency, the fill is clear. The Color dialog box enables you to drag a slider to specify the percentage of transparency. Figure 3.9 shows the Color dialog box with the RGB color mode selected, Red assigned a value of 236, Green assigned a value of 32, Blue assigned a value of 148, and a transparency set at 80%.

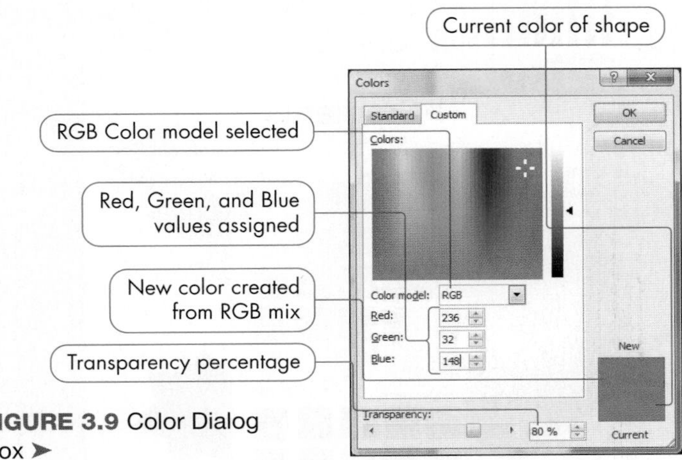

FIGURE 3.9 Color Dialog Box ➤

A **picture fill** inserts an image from a file into a shape.

You can fill shapes with images using the ***picture fill*** option. This option enables you to create unusual frames for your pictures and can be a fun way to vary the images in your presentation or create interesting frames for scrapbook images. To insert a picture as a fill, select Picture in the Shape Fill gallery, which is accessible from the Drawing Tools Format tab. Browse to locate the picture that you want to add, and then double-click the picture to insert it. Figure 3.10 shows the plaque shape filled with a casual snapshot taken with a digital camera.

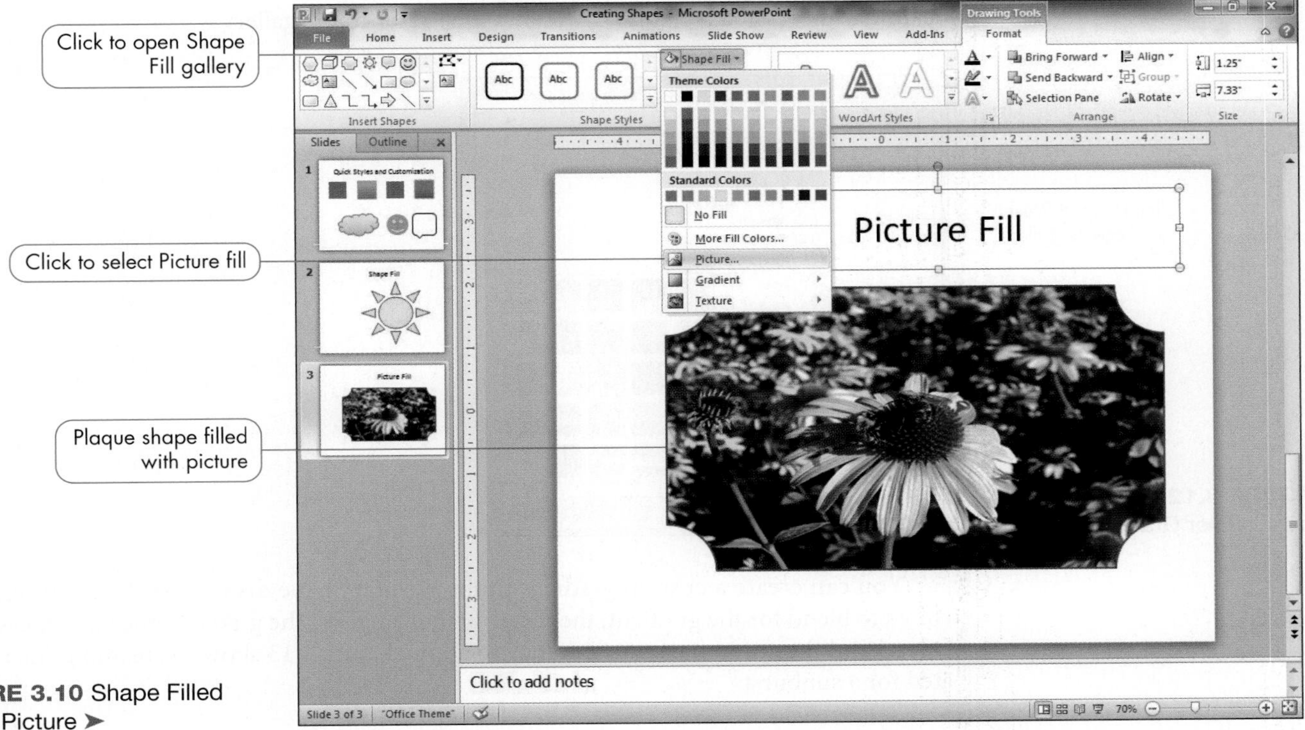

FIGURE 3.10 Shape Filled with a Picture ➤

As discussed earlier in the chapter, you can fill shapes with gradient fills, a blend of two or more colors. When you select Gradient from the Shape Fill gallery, another gallery of options opens, enabling you to select Light and Dark Variations that blend the current color with white or black in linear or radial gradients. Figure 3.11 shows the gradient options for a selected object.

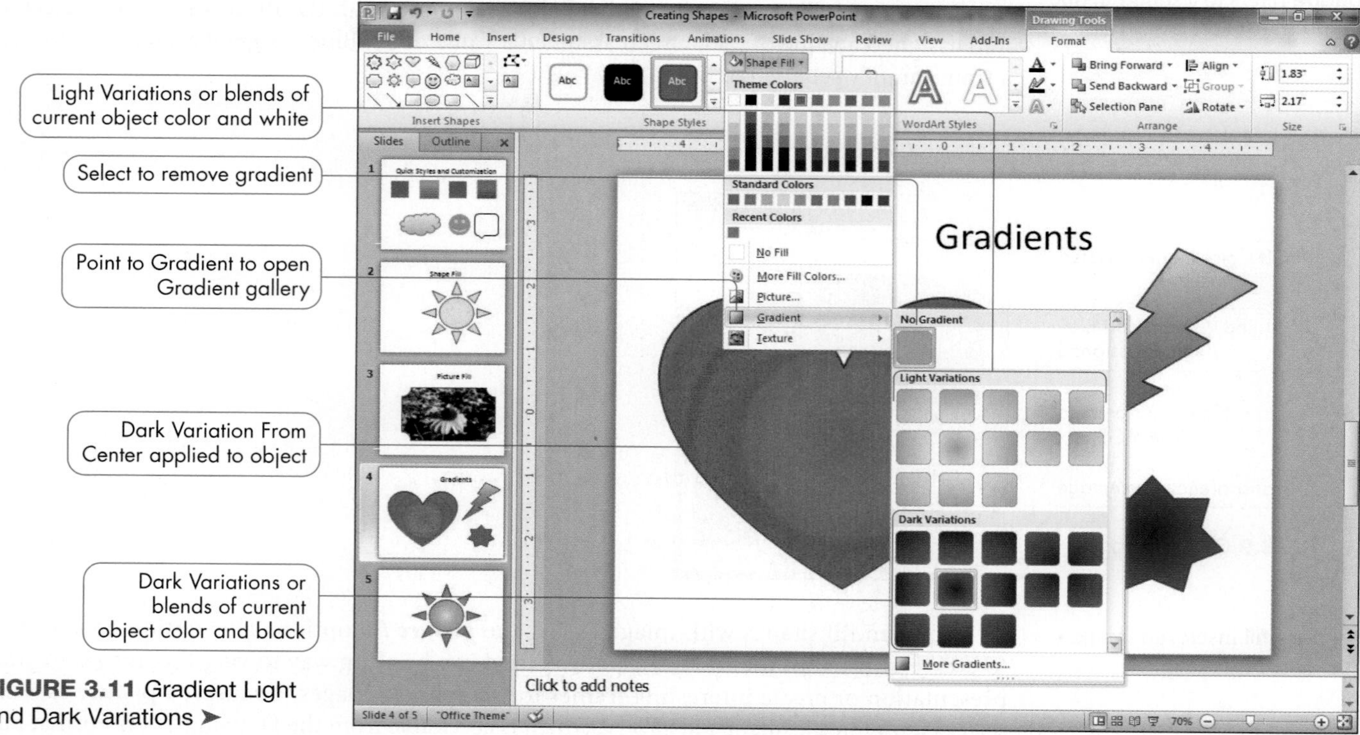

FIGURE 3.11 Gradient Light and Dark Variations ➤

When you select More Gradients at the bottom of the Gradients gallery, the Format Shape dialog box displays. The Gradient fill option provides access to the Preset colors gallery. This gallery gives you a variety of gradients using a multitude of colors to create truly beautiful impressions. Figure 3.12 shows the Preset colors gallery.

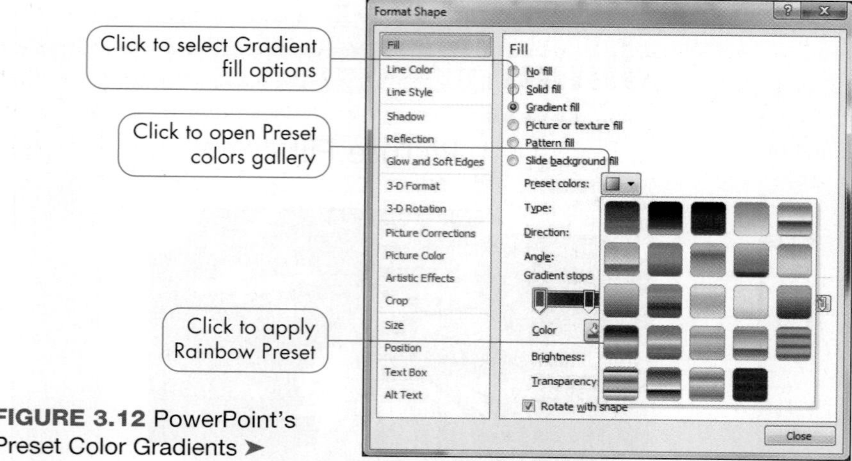

FIGURE 3.12 PowerPoint's Preset Color Gradients ➤

You can create a custom gradient in the Format Shape dialog box. You can select the colors to blend for the gradient, the direction and angle of the gradient, the brightness of the colors, and the amount of transparency to apply. Figure 3.13 shows a custom gradient created for a sunburst.

HANDS-ON EXERCISES

1 Shapes

You begin your mini-camp by having the participants create basic shapes using PowerPoint's drawing tools. You then ask the group to customize the shapes by adding styles and effects.

Skills covered: Create Basic Shapes • Draw and Format Connector Lines • Create and Modify Freeform Shapes • Apply a Quick Style and Customize Shapes • Change Shape Outlines • Change Outline Dash and Arrow Styles • Use Shape Effects

STEP 1 CREATE BASIC SHAPES

To teach participants how to create multiple shapes using the Lock Drawing Mode, you have them create several rectangles. You teach them to constrain the rectangles so they become squares. You have them create a cloud, an explosion, and a callout. Refer to Figure 3.18 as you complete Step 1.

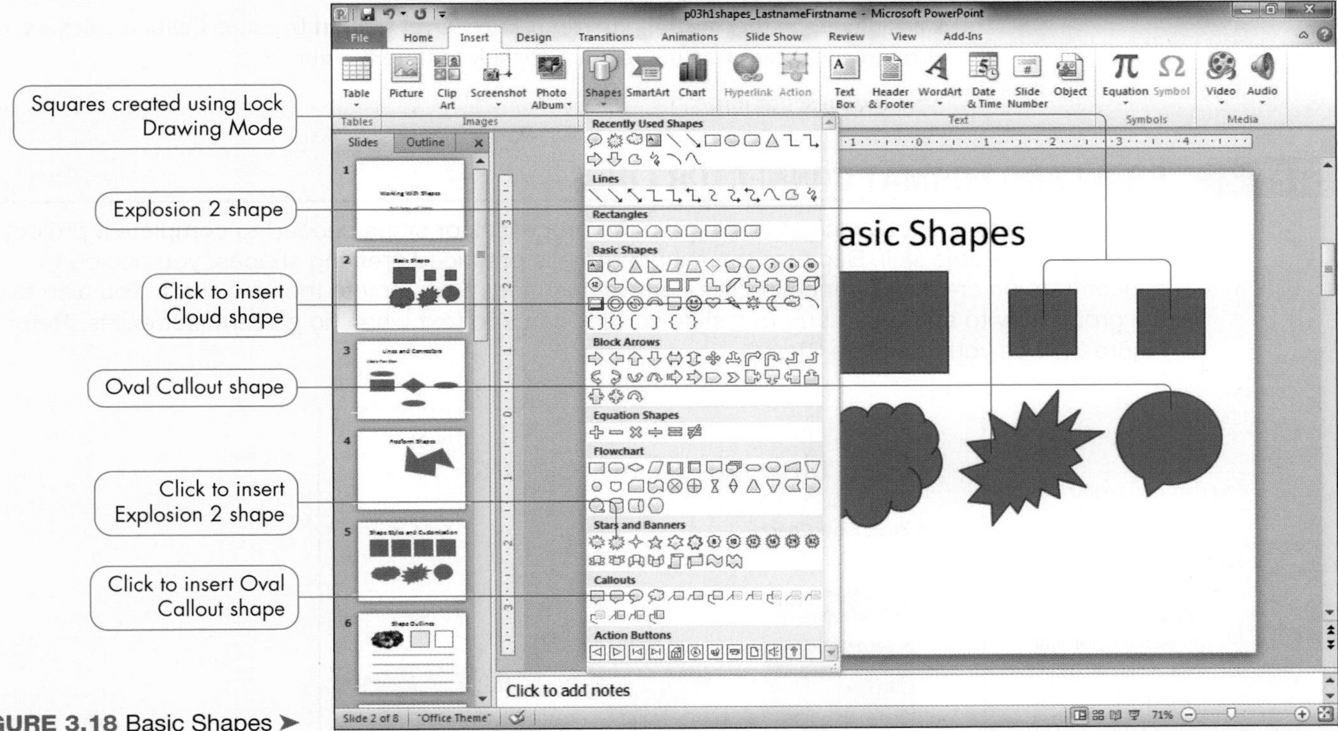

FIGURE 3.18 Basic Shapes ➤

a. Start PowerPoint, open *p03h1shapes*, and then save it as **p03h1shapes_LastnameFirstname**.

> **TROUBLESHOOTING:** If you make any major mistakes in this exercise, you can close the file, open *p03h1shapes*, and then start this exercise over.

b. On Slide 1, replace *First Name Last Name* with your name. Create a handout header with your name, and a handout footer with your instructor's name and your class. Include the current date.

c. On Slide 2, click **Rectangle** in the Drawing group on the Home tab. Position your pointer on the top-left side of the slide below the title, and then drag to create a rectangle.

> **TROUBLESHOOTING:** If you do not see the Rectangle shape, click Shapes.

Do not worry about the exact placement or size of the shapes you create at this time. You will learn how to precisely place and size shapes later in the chapter.

d. Click the **Insert tab**, and then click **Shapes** in the Illustrations group. Right-click **Rectangle** in the Rectangles category, and then select **Lock Drawing Mode**.

   You activate Lock Drawing Mode so that you can create multiple shapes of the same kind.

e. Press and hold **Shift**, position the pointer to the right of the previously created rectangle, and then drag to create a square. Repeat this process so that you have one rectangle and two squares on the slide.

   You create two squares by constraining the rectangle shapes.

f. Click **Shapes** in the Illustrations group, select **Cloud** from the Basic Shapes category, and then drag to create a cloud shape beneath the rectangle.

g. Click **Shapes** in the Illustrations group, select **Explosion 2** from the Stars and Banners category, and then drag to create an explosion shape on the right side of the cloud.

h. Click **Shapes** in the Illustrations group, select **Oval Callout** from the Callouts category, and then drag to create a callout on the right side of the explosion.

i. Save the presentation.

STEP 2 DRAW AND FORMAT CONNECTOR LINES

Knowing how to use a flow chart to diagram the processes or steps needed to complete a project or task is a valuable skill. Because the mini-camp has practiced creating shapes, you decide to concentrate on creating connecting lines between shapes to complete the flow chart. You also teach the group how to add a text box to a slide so they can add text when no placeholder exists. Refer to Figure 3.19 as you complete Step 2.

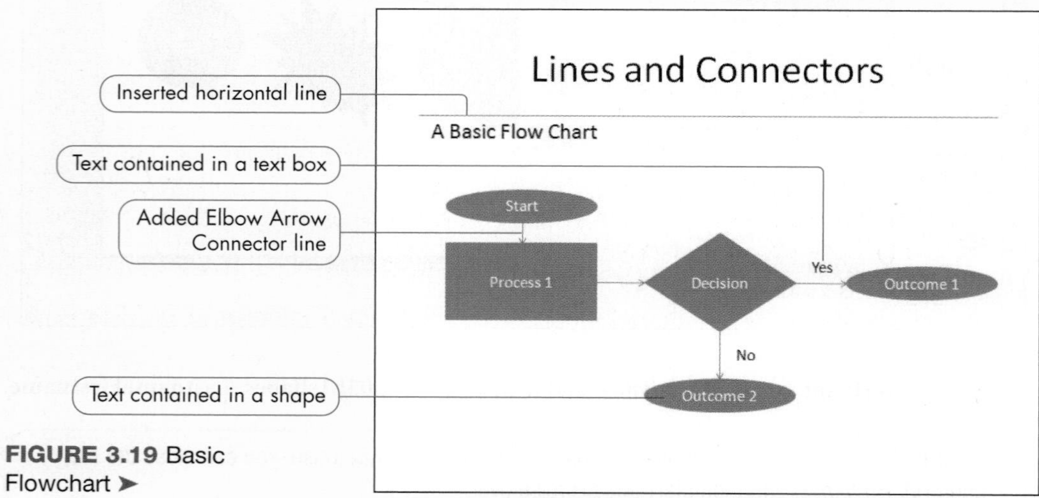

FIGURE 3.19 Basic Flowchart ➤

a. On Slide 3, click **Shapes** in the Illustrations group.

b. Click **Line** in the Line category, hold **Shift**, and then drag a horizontal line between the slide title, *Lines and Connectors*, and the words *A Basic Flow Chart*.

   You create a line to separate the title from the flow chart. Because this line is not used to connect shapes, you do not need to use a connector line.

c. Click **Shapes** in the Illustrations group, click **Arrow** in the Lines category, move the cross-hair pointer over the oval on the left side of the slide, and then position the pointer on the bottom-center red handle.

The shape's connector handles appear when a connector line is selected and the cross-hair pointer is moved onto the shape.

d. Drag a connecting line that attaches the bottom-center red connecting handle of the oval to the top red connecting handle of the rectangle below it.

The default line weight is very thin at 1/2 pt.

e. Create connecting arrows that attach the rectangle to the diamond and the diamond to each of the remaining ovals, as shown in Figure 3.19.

f. Select the oval on the top-left of the slide, and then type **Start**.

The text you typed becomes part of the oval shape.

g. Select each of the remaining shapes, and then type the text shown in Figure 3.19.

h. Click **Text Box** in the Text group on the Insert tab.

Clicking Text Box enables you to create text that is not contained in a shape or in a placeholder on the slide.

i. Position the pointer above the connector between the *Decision* diamond and the *Outcome 1* oval, click, and then type **Yes**.

> **TROUBLESHOOTING:** If the text box is not positioned above the connector line between the *Decision* diamond and the *Outcome 1* oval, click the border (not the sizing handle) of the text box, and then drag it into position.

j. Click **Text Box** in the Text group, position the pointer to the right side of the connector between the *Decision* diamond and the *Outcome 2* oval, click, and then type **No**. Reposition the text box if necessary.

k. Save the presentation.

STEP 3 CREATE AND MODIFY FREEFORM SHAPES

Knowing how to manipulate the vertexes of a freeform shape gives you the ability to change drawings and clip art—a powerful skill! You introduce this concept to your mini-camp participants by having them draw some freeform shapes and then manipulate the vertexes of a previously created shape. Refer to Figure 3.20 as you complete Step 3 (your shapes may vary from the figure).

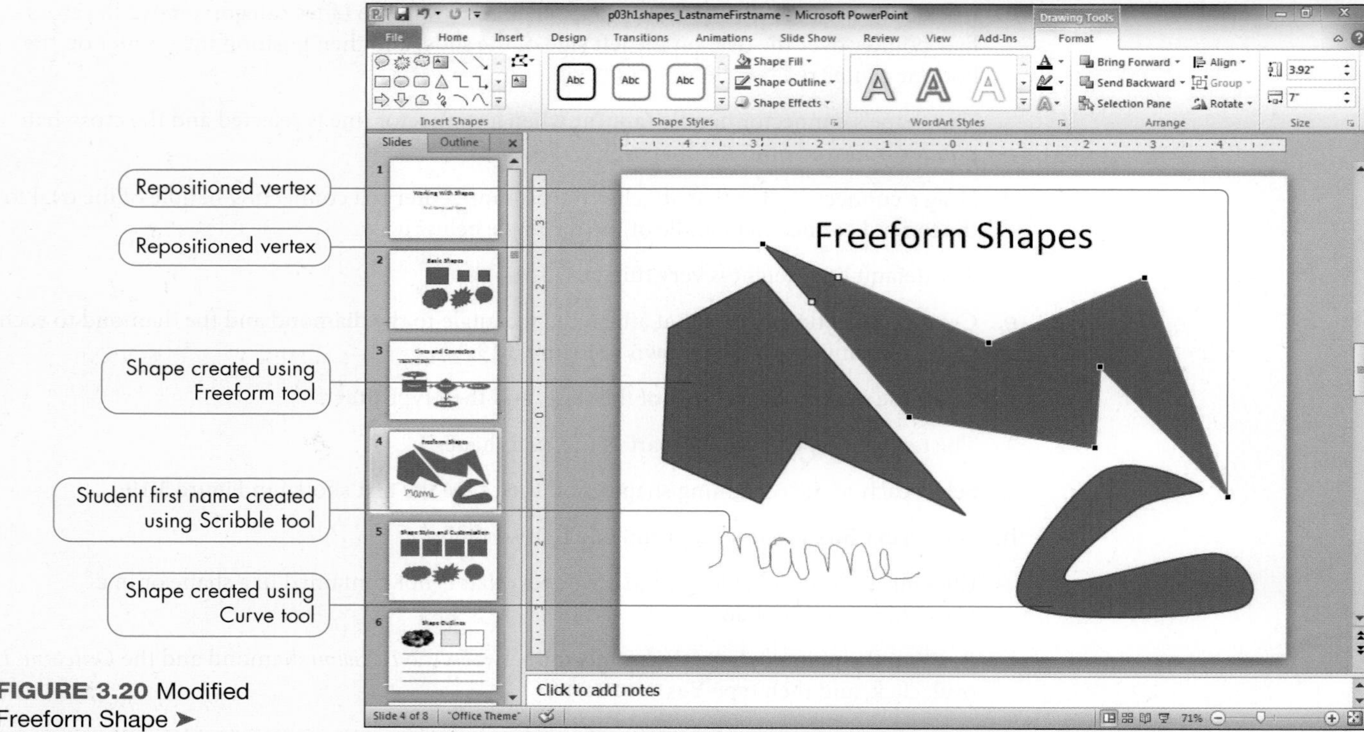

FIGURE 3.20 Modified Freeform Shape ➤

a. On Slide 4, click the **Insert tab**, if necessary, click **Shapes** in the Illustrations group, and then click **Freeform** in the Lines category.

b. To create the shape, click to the left of the existing freeform shape. Move your insertion point to a new location, and then click. Continue moving to new locations and clicking to set four new points, and then click the starting point to end your shape.

> **TROUBLESHOOTING:** Do not drag to create your lines, or they will not be straight.

The freeform shape you created consists of vertexes connected by straight lines.

c. Click **Shapes** in the Illustrations group, and then click **Curve** in the Lines category. Click anywhere on the bottom-right side of the slide to begin your shape. Position your insertion point in a new location, and then click. Continue moving to new positions and clicking to set new points, and then click the starting point to end your shape.

The curve shape you created consists of vertexes connected by lines curving around vertexes.

d. Click **Shapes** in the Illustrations group, and then click **Scribble** in the Lines category. Position your insertion point at the bottom of the slide, hold down the left mouse button, and then drag as you would a pencil. Continue dragging to create your name in cursive.

> **TROUBLESHOOTING:** If you release the mouse button, the line ends. If you end the line before completing your name, reselect the Scribble tool and continue.

e. Select the freeform shape in the top right of the slide. Click the **Format tab**, and then click **Edit Shape** in the Insert Shapes group.

f. Select **Edit Points**.

The freeform shape is selected—a red line surrounds its border, and the vertexes appear as black squares.

g. Select the vertex on the farthest right side of the slide, and then drag it down and to the left.

h. Select the vertex on the farthest top-left side of the shape, and then drag it toward the left of the slide title.

i. Modify the vertex locations on the forms you created as desired.

j. Save the presentation.

STEP 4 APPLY A QUICK STYLE AND CUSTOMIZE SHAPES

You encourage participants of the mini-camp to experiment with Quick Styles and to modify shape fills and outlines so that they are able to customize shapes. Then they set the shapes to styles of your choice to show they can meet specifications when asked. Refer to Figure 3.21 as you complete Step 4.

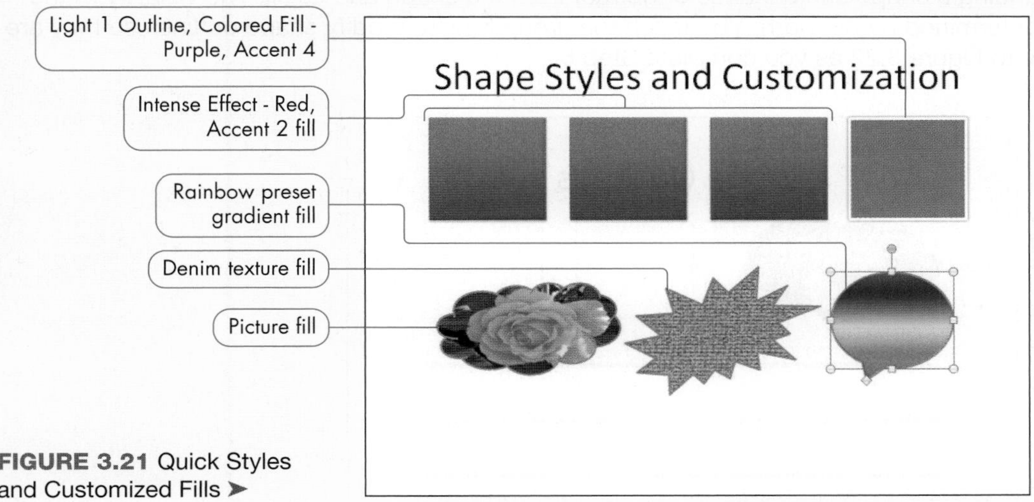

FIGURE 3.21 Quick Styles and Customized Fills ➤

a. On Slide 5, select the far-right square.

b. Click the **Format tab**, and then click the **More button** in the Shape Styles group.

The Quick Style gallery opens.

c. Move your pointer over the Quick Styles and note the changes in fill, outline, and effects to the shape as you do so. After you are through experimenting, click **Light 1 Outline, Colored Fill - Purple, Accent 4** (third row, fifth column). Deselect the square.

Live Preview shows the effects on your object as you move the pointer over the Quick Style options.

d. Press and hold **Ctrl**, click the remaining three squares to select them, and then click the **More button** in the Shape Styles group. Click **Intense Effect - Red, Accent 2** (sixth row, third column).

You apply a Quick Style to more than one shape at a time.

e. Click the cloud shape, click **Shape Fill** in the Shape Styles group, and then select **Picture**.

The Insert Picture dialog box opens.

f. Locate the file *p03h1rose.jpg* in your class files, and then double-click to insert the picture into the shape.

The rose picture fills the cloud shape.

g. Click the explosion shape, click **Shape Fill** in the Shape Styles group, point to **Texture**, and then select **Denim**.

h. Click the callout shape, click **Shape Fill** in the Shapes Styles group, point to **Gradient**, and then select **More Gradients** at the bottom of the gallery.

   The Format Shape dialog box opens with options for customizing the fill of the shape.

i. Click **Gradient fill**, click the **Preset colors arrow**, and then click the preset gradient of your choice. Make other selections to see different effects, and finally select **Rainbow**. Click **Close**.

   Live Preview does not work while in the Preset gallery, so you must apply selections to see the effect of the applied gradient.

j. Save the presentation.

STEP 5 CHANGE SHAPE OUTLINES

The line surrounding a shape can enhance or detract from the shape and its fill. The visibility of the line is mostly determined by its width. You teach the group how to modify shape outlines so they are effective. Refer to Figure 3.22 as you complete Step 5.

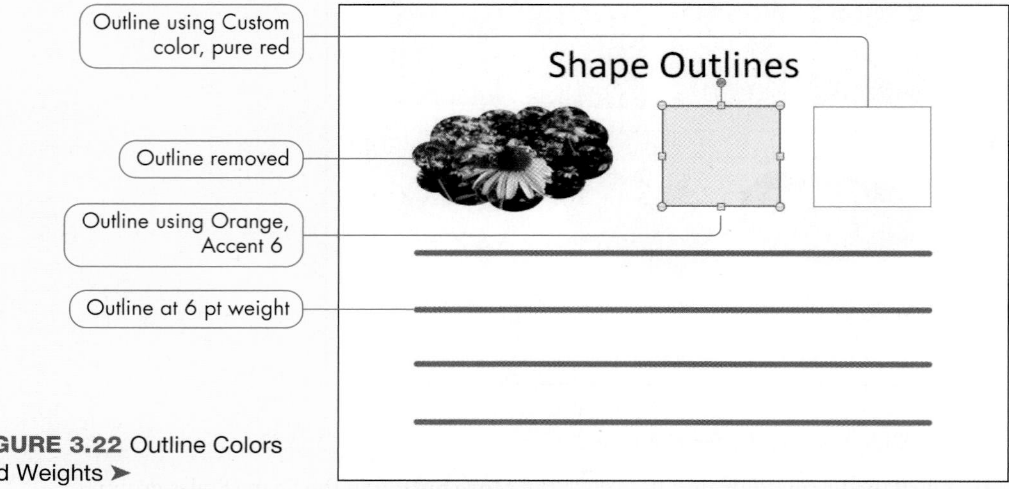

FIGURE 3.22 Outline Colors and Weights ➤

a. On Slide 6, click the cloud shape with the picture fill.

b. Click the **Drawing Tools Format tab** if necessary.

> **TROUBLESHOOTING:** If you see two Format tabs (one under Drawing Tools and one under Picture Tools), be sure to select the Drawing Tools Format tab. Picture Tools opens next to the Drawing Tools because of the picture fill.

c. Click **Shape Outline** in the Shape Styles group, and then select **No Outline**.

   The outline surrounding the shape is removed.

d. Select the square with the orange tint fill, click **Shape Outline**, and then select **Orange, Accent 6** (first row, last column) in the Theme Colors gallery.

e. Select the square on the far right that has no fill, click **Shape Outline**, and then select **More Outline Colors**. Click the **Custom tab**, if necessary.

f. Type **255** in the **Red box**, and then type **0** in each of the **Green** and **Blue boxes**. Click **OK**.

   This selection creates a pure red outline.

g. Beginning above and to the left of the top horizontal line, drag a selection net around the four horizontal lines.

   All four lines have open circle handles at each end indicating you have selected them.

h. Click the **Format tab**, if necessary, click **Shape Outline** in the Shape Styles group, select **Weight**, and then click **6 pt**. Click to deselect the lines.

i. On Slide 3, press and hold **Ctrl**, and then click each of the connecting lines in the flow chart.

   The endpoints of each connecting line turn red, indicating you have added the line to the selection.

j. Click the **Format tab**, click **Shape Outline** in the Drawing group, select **Weight**, and then select **2 1/4 pt**. Click to deselect the lines.

   All of the connecting line weights are increased.

k. Save the presentation.

STEP 6 CHANGE OUTLINE DASH AND ARROW STYLES

For additional experience in modifying outlines, you ask the mini-camp participants to modify the dash and arrow styles of lines. Dashed lines are effective in calling attention to a shape, and arrows are effective in directing attention. Refer to Figure 3.23 as you complete Step 6.

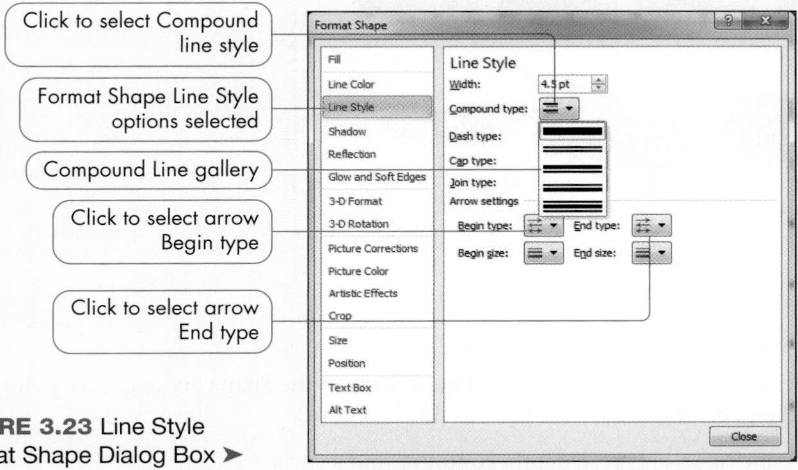

FIGURE 3.23 Line Style Format Shape Dialog Box ➤

a. On Slide 7, click the first horizontal line.

b. Click the **Format tab**, click **Shape Outline** in the Shape Styles group, point to **Dashes**, and then select **Long Dash Dot Dot**.

   The line style changes from the default solid line to a long dash dot dot style.

c. Click the second horizontal line, click **Shape Outline**, point to **Dashes**, and then select **Long Dash**.

d. Select the third horizontal line, click **Shape Outline**, point to **Dashes**, and then select **More Lines**.

   The Format Shape dialog box opens, providing you with options for creating custom lines, including compound line types.

e. Click the **Compound type arrow**, and then select **Triple** (last option).

   This selection creates a compound line composed of three lines of different weights: one thin line, one thick line, and then one thin line.

f. Click the **Width spin arrow**, and then change the width to **8 pt**. Click **Close**.

g. Select the fourth horizontal line, click **Shape Outline**, point to **Arrows**, and then select **Arrow Style 3**.

h. Select the fifth horizontal line, click **Shape Outline**, point to **Arrows**, and then select **Arrow Style 9**.

i. Select the last horizontal line, click **Shape Outline**, point to **Arrows**, and then select **More Arrows**.

j. Click the **Begin type arrow**, and then select **Stealth Arrow** (second row, first column).

k. Click the **End type arrow**, select **Oval Arrow** (second row, third column), and then click **Close**.

l. Save the presentation.

STEP 7 USE SHAPE EFFECTS

PowerPoint provides many shape effects that you can use for emphasis. You ask the participants to apply effects to shapes so they become familiar with the options available. Refer to Figure 3.24 as you complete Step 7.

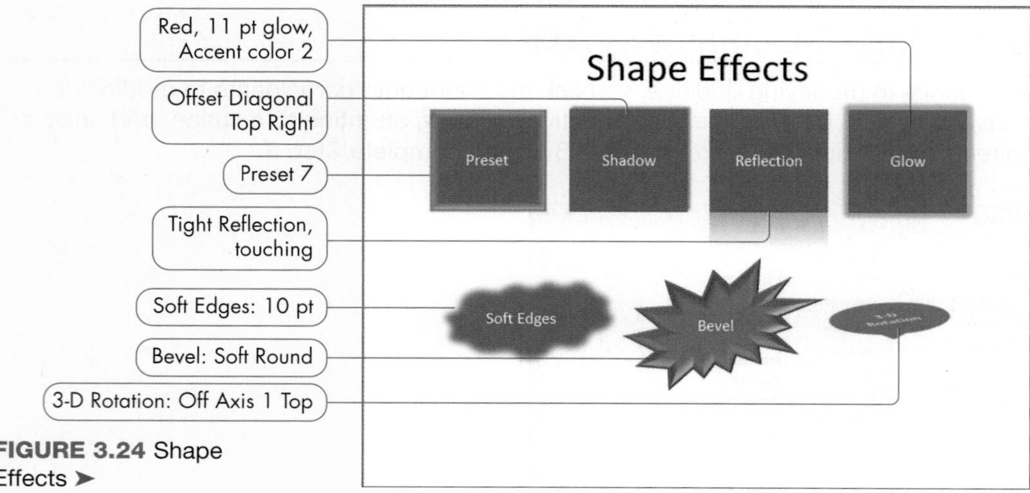

FIGURE 3.24 Shape Effects ➤

a. On Slide 8, click **Rectangle 1**.

b. Click the **Format tab**, if necessary, click **Shape Effects** in the Shape Styles group, point to **Preset**, and then click **Preset 7** (second row, third column).

   Preset 7 combines a bevel type, a depth, contours, and a surface effect.

c. Select the number **1**, and then type **Preset** to label the shape with the shape effect you applied.

d. Select **Rectangle 2**, click **Shape Effects** in the Shape Styles group, point to **Shadow**, and then click **Offset Diagonal Top Right** (third row, first column in the Outer category). Replace *2* with the word **Shadow**.

   The Offset Diagonal option applies a 4 pt soft shadow to the top right of the rectangle.

e. Select **Rectangle 3**, click **Shape Effects**, point to **Reflection**, and then click **Tight Reflection, touching** (first row, first column in the Reflection Variations group). Replace *3* with the word **Reflection**.

f. Select **Rectangle 4**, click **Shape Effects**, point to **Glow**, and then click **Red, 11 pt glow, Accent color 2** (third row, second column). Replace *4* with the word **Glow**.

g. Continue to use the Shape Effects options to apply effects to the remaining shapes, as indicated in the following table:

Shape	Effect and Name	Style
Cloud	Soft Edges	10 Point
Explosion	Bevel	Soft Round
Callout	3-D Rotation	Off Axis 1 Top (Parallel category)

h. Save the presentation, close the file, and exit PowerPoint if you do not want to continue with the next exercise at this time.

SmartArt and WordArt

Diagrams are infographics used to illustrate concepts and processes. PowerPoint includes a feature to create eye-catching diagrams: SmartArt. Attention is drawn to an infographic using text created by another eye-catching PowerPoint feature: WordArt. In this section, you will create and modify SmartArt diagrams and WordArt text.

Creating SmartArt

A **SmartArt** diagram presents in formation visually to effectively communicate a message.

The ***SmartArt*** feature enables you to create a diagram and to enter the text of your message in one of many existing layouts. The resulting illustration is professional looking and complements the theme you selected. You can also convert existing text to SmartArt, creating a visual representation of your information. Figure 3.25 compares a text-based slide in the common bullet format to a second slide showing the same information converted to a SmartArt diagram. The arrows and colors in the SmartArt diagram make it easy for the viewer to understand the message and remember the cycle. It is especially effective when you add animation to each step.

The arrows and colors in the SmartArt diagram make it easy for the viewer to understand the message....

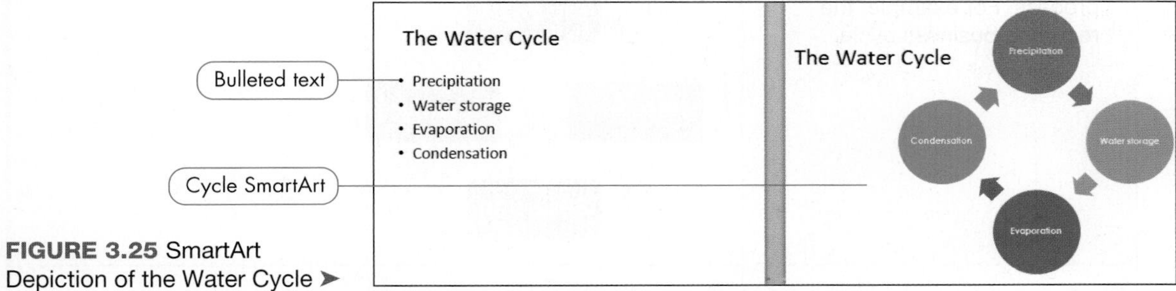

FIGURE 3.25 SmartArt Depiction of the Water Cycle ➤

A SmartArt diagram creates a layout for your information, provides a pane for quickly entering information, automatically sizes shapes and text, and gives you the ability to switch between layouts, making it easy to choose the most effective layout. Some layouts can be used for any type of information and are designed to be visually attractive, while other layouts are created specifically for a certain type of information. SmartArt types include options for presenting lists of information in ordered (steps to complete a task) or unordered (features of a product) formats.

To create a SmartArt diagram, choose a diagram type that fits your message. The SmartArt gallery has nine different categories of diagrams: List, Process, Cycle, Hierarchy, Relationship, Matrix, Pyramid, Picture, and Office.com. At the top of the list of categories is All, which you can click to display the choices from all categories. Each category includes a description of the type of information appropriate for the layouts in that category. The following Reference table shows the SmartArt categories and their purposes.

REFERENCE SMARTART DIAGRAM

Type	Purpose	Sample SmartArt
List	Use to show nonsequential information. For example: a list of items to be checked on a roof each year.	Flashing Shingles Soffits
Process	Use to show steps in a process or a timeline. For example: the steps to take to wash a car.	Hose Sponge Rinse
Cycle	Use to show a continual process. For example: the recurring business cycle.	Expansion Downturn Recession Recovery
Hierarchy	Use to show a decision tree, organization chart, or pedigree. For example: a pedigree chart showing the parents of an individual.	Reed J. Olsen Ivan Olsen Gladys Jones
Relationship	Use to illustrate connections. For example: the connections among outdoor activities.	Camping Hiking Fishing

(*Continued*)

REFERENCE SMARTART DIAGRAM (*Continued*)

Type	Purpose	Sample SmartArt
Matrix	Use to show how parts relate to a whole. For example: the Keirsey Temperament Theory of four groups describing human behavior.	Rationals / Idealists / Keirsey Temperaments / Artisans / Guardians
Pyramid	Use to show proportional relationships with the largest component on the top or bottom. For example: an ecology chart.	Indirect Consumers / Direct Consumers / Producers
Picture	Use to show nonsequential or grouped blocks of information. Maximizes both horizontal and vertical display space for shapes.	Xeriscaping / Zeroscaping
Office.com	Miscellaneous shapes for showing blocks of information.	Images / Audio / Video

Figure 3.26 shows the Choose a SmartArt Graphic dialog box. The pane on the left side shows the types of SmartArt diagrams available. Each type of diagram includes subtypes that are displayed in the center pane. Clicking one of the subtypes enlarges the selected graphic and displays it in the preview pane on the right side. The preview pane describes purposes for which the SmartArt subtype can be used effectively. Some of the descriptions include tips for the type of text to enter.

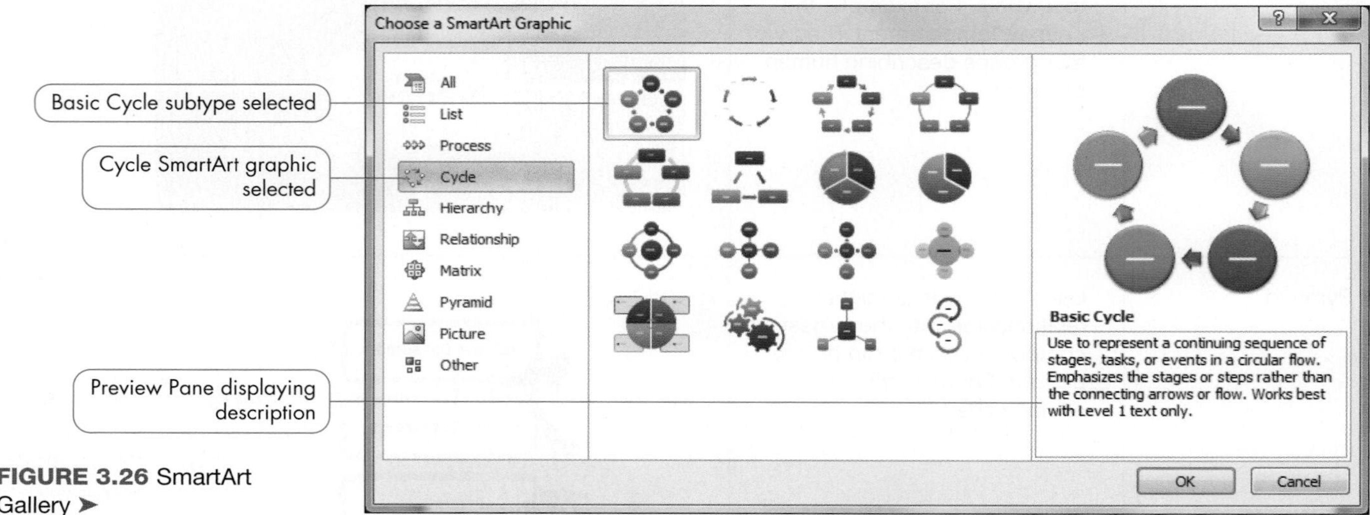

FIGURE 3.26 SmartArt Gallery ➤

To create a SmartArt diagram:

1. Click the Insert tab.
2. Click SmartArt in the Illustrations group.
3. Click the type of SmartArt diagram you want in the left pane.
4. Click the SmartArt subtype you want in the center pane.
5. Preview the selected SmartArt and subtype in the right pane.
6. Click OK.

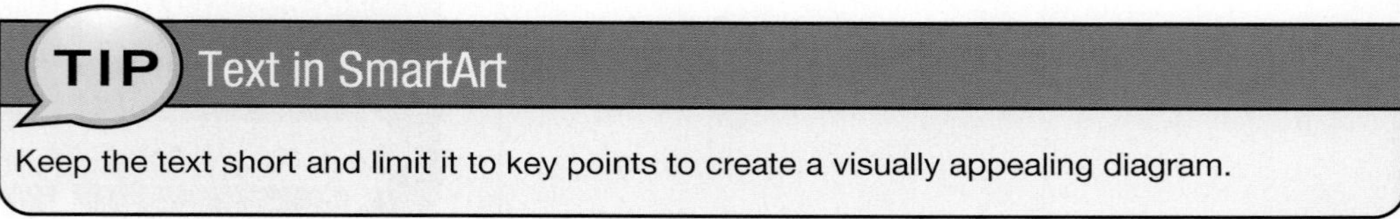

TIP Text in SmartArt

Keep the text short and limit it to key points to create a visually appealing diagram.

A **Text pane** is a pane for text entry that opens when you select a SmartArt diagram.

Once you select the SmartArt diagram type and the subtype, a ***Text pane*** opens in which you can enter text. If the Text pane does not open, click Text Pane in the Create Graphic group on the SmartArt Tools Design tab. The Text pane works like an outline—enter a line of text, press Enter, and then press Tab or Shift+Tab to increase or decrease the indent level. The font size will decrease to fit text inside the shape, or the shape may grow to fit the text, depending on the size and number of shapes in your SmartArt diagram. The layout accommodates additional shapes as you enter text unless the type of shape is designed for a specific number of shapes, such as the Relationship Counterbalance Arrows layout, which is designed to show two opposing ideas. If you choose a diagram with more shapes than you need, you may need to delete the extra shapes; then PowerPoint will automatically rearrange the shapes to eliminate any blank space. Figure 3.27 shows text entered into the Text pane for a Basic Cycle SmartArt diagram. Because five lines of text were entered, five shapes were created.

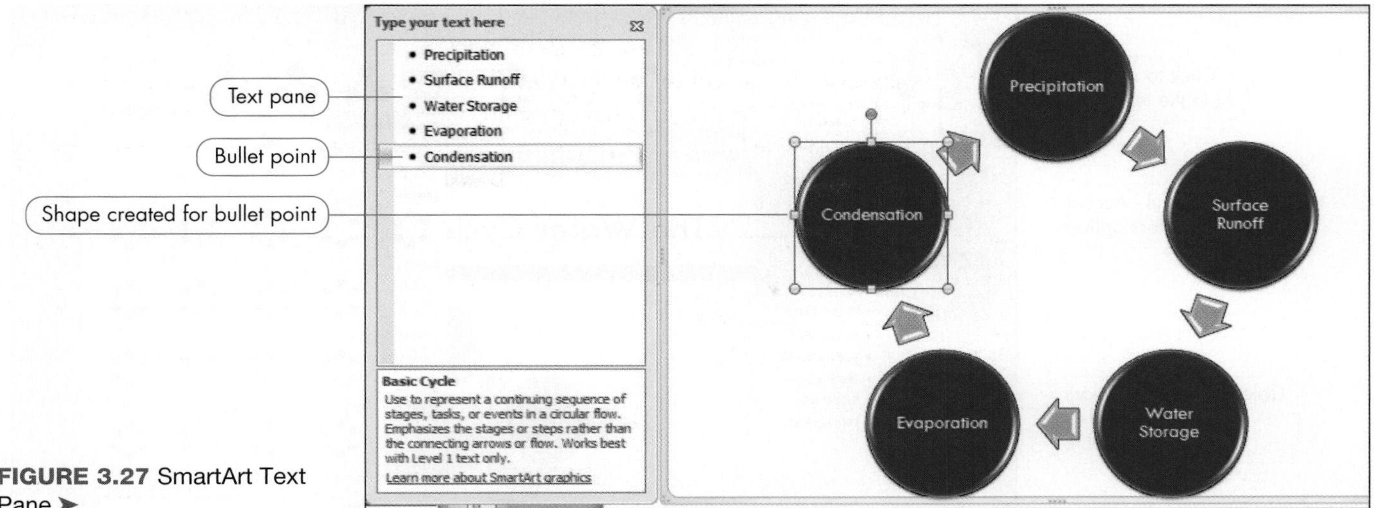

FIGURE 3.27 SmartArt Text Pane ➤

Modifying SmartArt

You can modify SmartArt diagrams with the same tools used for other shapes and text boxes. You can reposition or resize a SmartArt diagram by dragging its borders. You also can modify SmartArt text in the Text pane just as if it is in a placeholder, or you can modify the text in the shape itself. If you need an additional shape, click an existing shape in the diagram, position your insertion point in the Text pane at the beginning of the text where you want to add a shape, type the text, and then press Enter.

An alternative method for adding shapes is to use the Add Shape command. To use the Add Shape command, do the following:

1. Click an existing shape in the SmartArt diagram.
2. Click the SmartArt Tools Design tab.
3. Click the Add Shape arrow in the Create Graphic group.
4. Select Add Shape After, Add Shape Before, Add Shape Above, or Add Shape Below.

SmartArt diagrams have two galleries used to enhance the appearance of the diagram, both of which are located under the SmartArt Tools Design tab in the SmartArt Styles group. One gallery changes colors, and the other gallery applies a combination of special effects.

Change SmartArt Theme Colors

To change the color scheme of your SmartArt diagram, click Change Colors to display the Colors gallery (see Figure 3.28). The gallery contains Primary Theme Colors, Colorful, and Accent color schemes. Click a color variation to apply it to the SmartArt diagram.

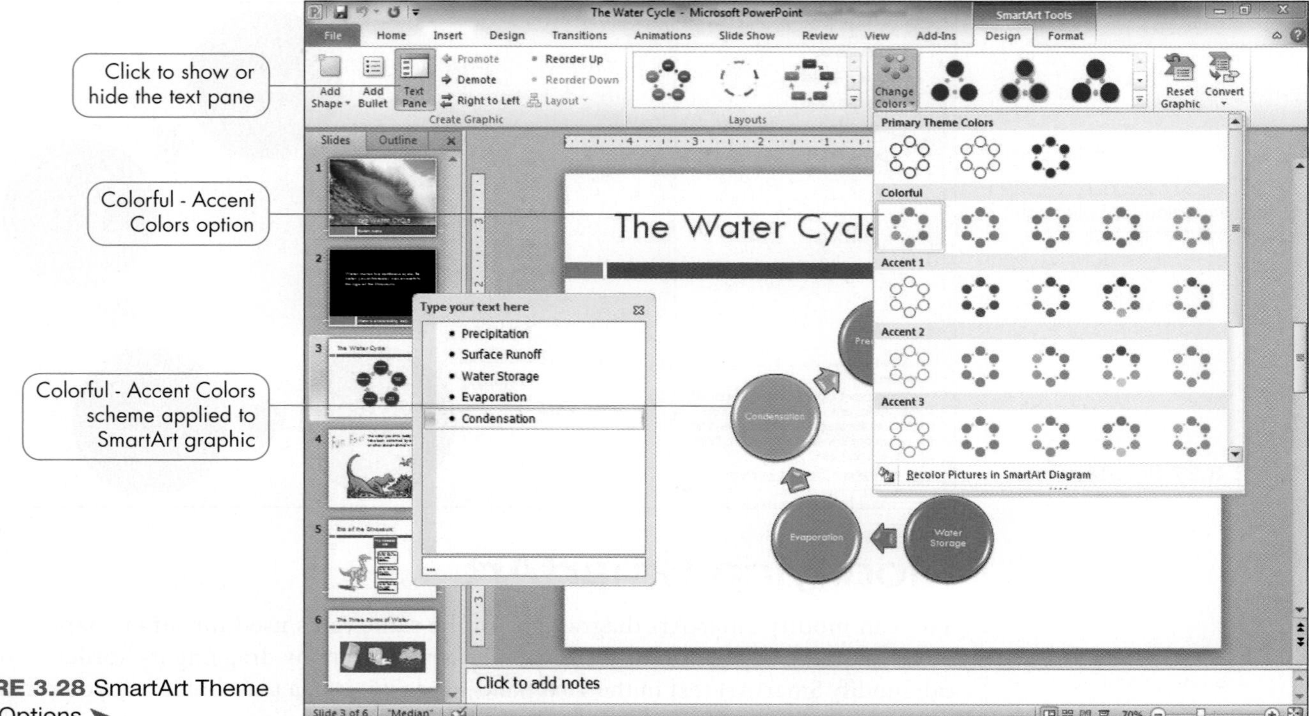

FIGURE 3.28 SmartArt Theme Color Options ➤

Use Quick Styles with SmartArt

After creating the diagram, you can use Quick Styles to adjust the style to match other styles you have used in your presentation or to make the diagram easier to understand. To apply a Quick Style to a SmartArt diagram, click the diagram, and then click the Quick Style from the SmartArt Styles gallery. To see the complete gallery, click the More button in the SmartArt Styles group on the SmartArt Tools Design tab. The gallery opens and displays simple combinations of special effects, such as shadows, gradients, and 3-D effects that combine perspectives and surface styles. Figure 3.29 displays the SmartArt Quick Styles gallery.

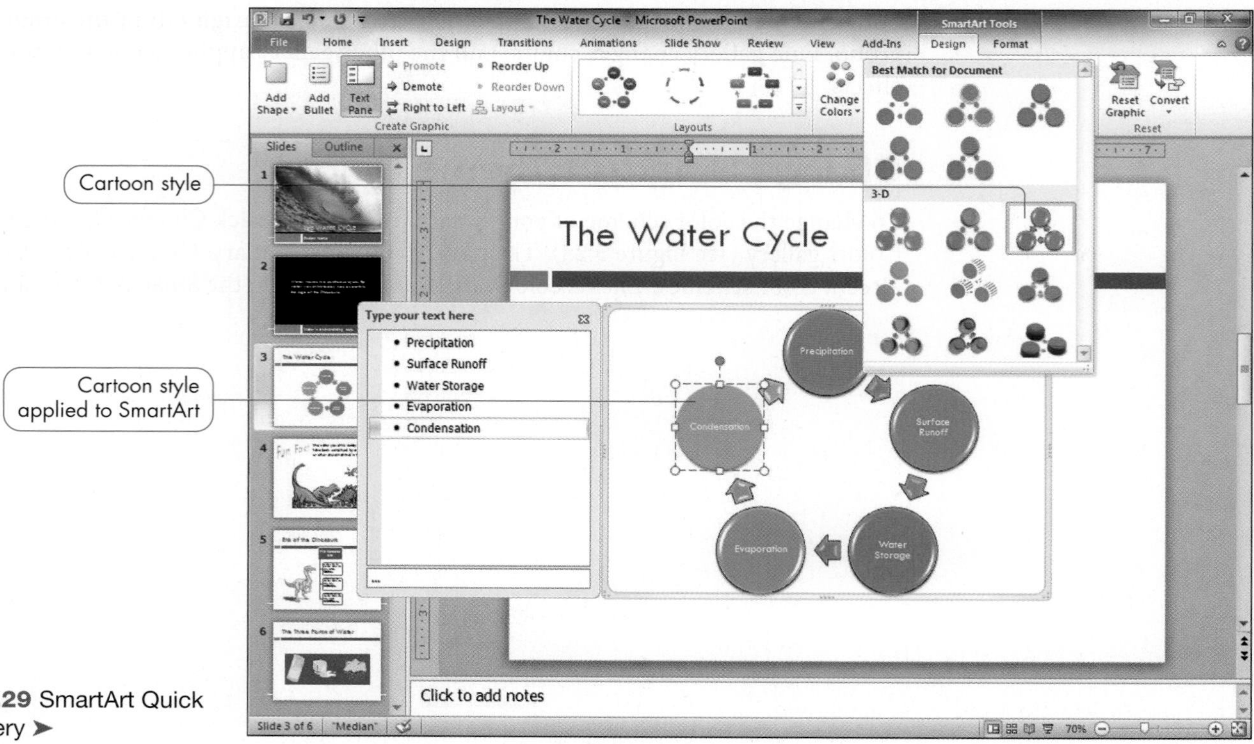

FIGURE 3.29 SmartArt Quick Styles Gallery ➤

Change the Layout

After creating a SmartArt diagram, you may find the layout needs adjusting. For example, as you enter text, PowerPoint reduces the size of the font. If you enter too much text, the font size becomes too small. Figure 3.30 shows a Hierarchy diagram displaying the relationship between the Mesozoic Era and its periods, along with the types of mammals and dinosaurs that lived during the period. To allow the text to fit in the shapes of the diagram, PowerPoint reduced the font size to 10 pt. Even projected on a screen, this text would be unreadable for most audience members.

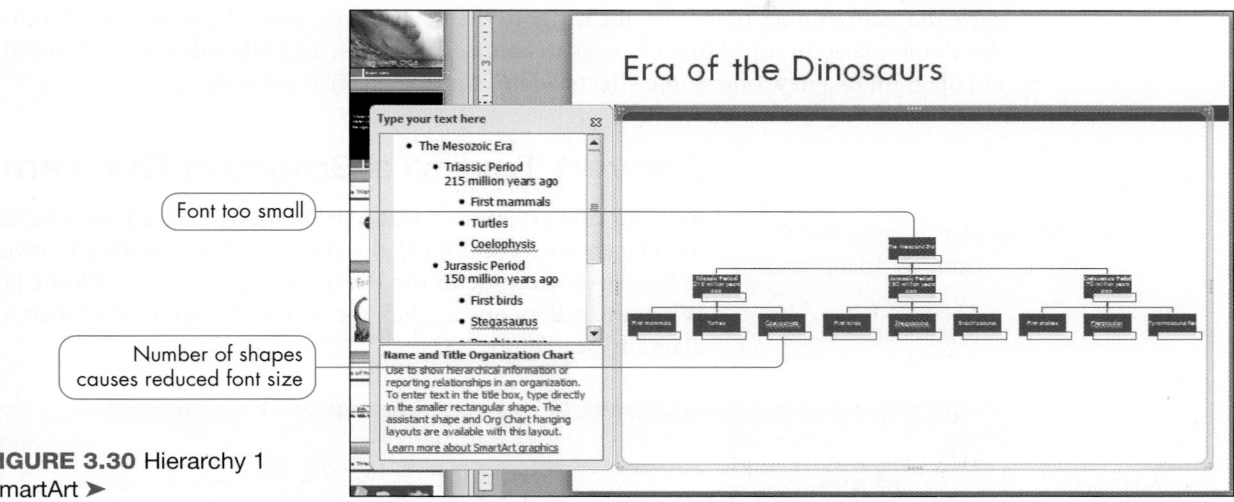

FIGURE 3.30 Hierarchy 1 SmartArt ➤

By adjusting the layout, you can make the Mesozoic Era diagram easier to read. First, select the SmartArt diagram, and then click the SmartArt Tools Design tab. Click the More button in the Layouts group to display the Layouts gallery. Layouts use combinations of effects such as shadowing, fills, box shapes and borders, and orientation, whether the layout is horizontally or vertically placed on the slide. Figure 3.31 shows the Mesozoic information in a Hierarchy List diagram that uses a vertical orientation.

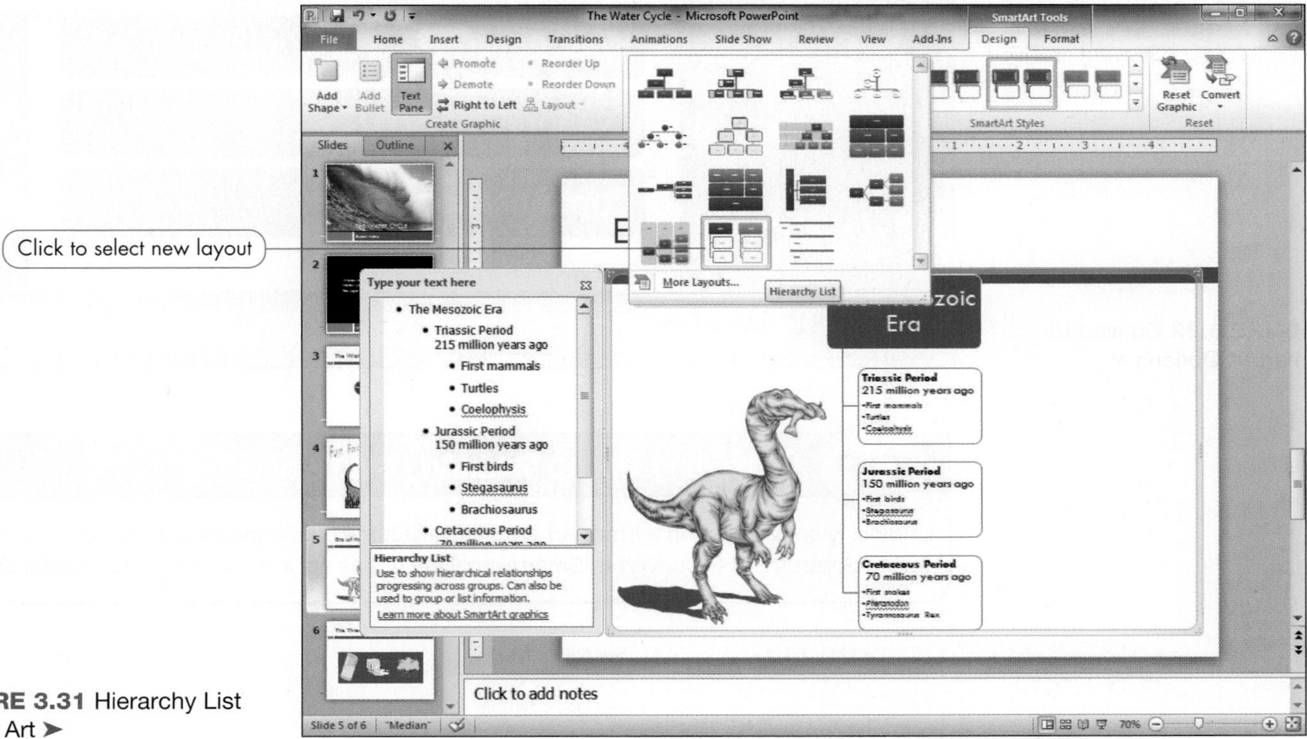

FIGURE 3.31 Hierarchy List Smart Art ➤

Change SmartArt Type

You can change the SmartArt diagram type if you decide a different layout would be better. The process is the same as changing the SmartArt layout. To change the SmartArt diagram type, click to select the SmartArt diagram. Click the More button in the Layouts group on the SmartArt Tools Design tab, and then click More Layouts. The Choose a SmartArt Graphic gallery opens, displaying all the layouts grouped by category. Click the type and layout you desire.

Changing diagram types alters the layout, which may affect the audience's perception of your diagram. For example, if you have created a list of unordered items, switching to a cycle diagram implies that a specific order to the items exists. Also, if you have customized the shapes, keep in mind that changes to colors, line styles, and fills will transfer from the old diagram to a new one. Some effects do not transfer, such as rotation.

Convert Text to a SmartArt Diagram

You can convert existing text to a SmartArt diagram....

You can convert existing text to a SmartArt diagram by selecting the placeholder containing the text, and then clicking Convert to SmartArt Graphic in the Paragraph group on the Home tab. When the gallery opens, click the desired layout for the SmartArt diagram (see Figure 3.32).

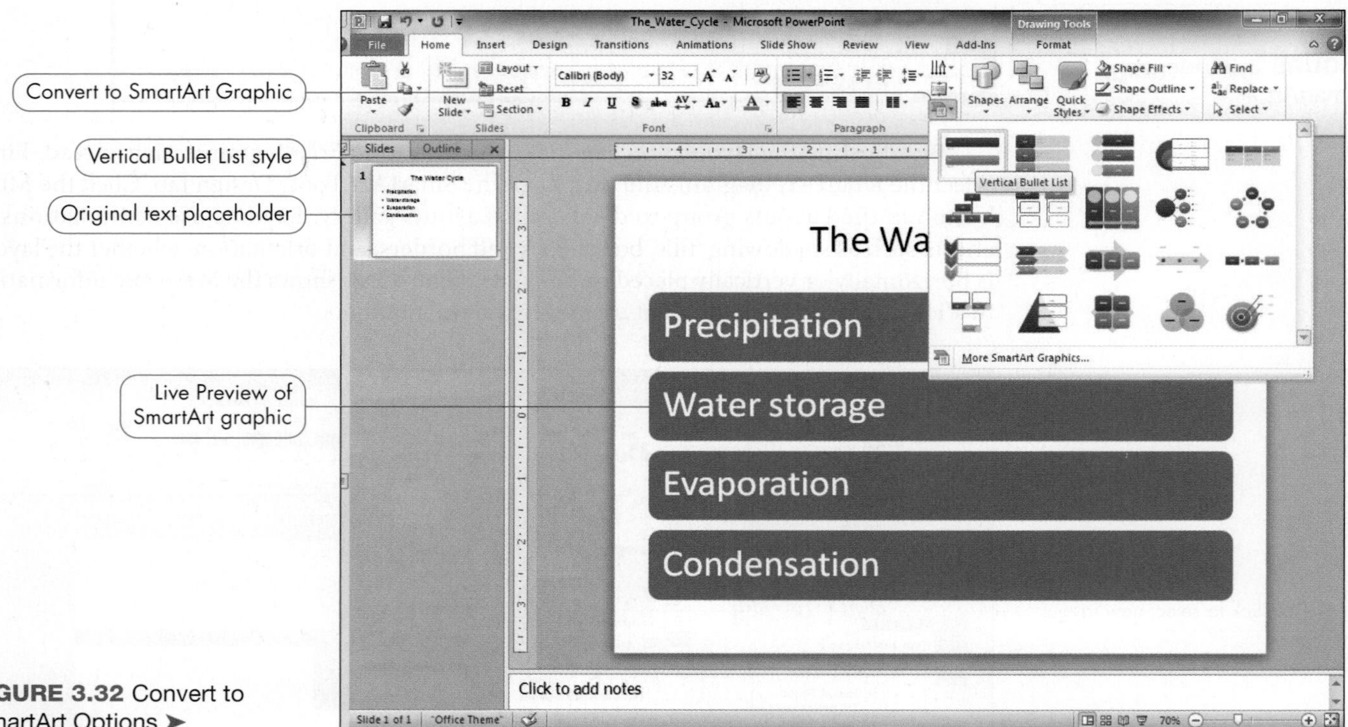

FIGURE 3.32 Convert to SmartArt Options ➤

TIP Converting Text to SmartArt Using a Shortcut

To quickly convert text to a SmartArt graphic, select the text, right-click, and then select Convert to SmartArt. The Convert to SmartArt gallery opens so you can select a SmartArt style.

Creating WordArt

WordArt is text that has a decorative effect applied.

WordArt is text that uses special effects based on styles in the WordArt gallery to call attention to the text. In WordArt, special effects apply to the text itself, not to the shape surrounding the text. For example, in a WordArt graphic the text would have a 3-D reflection rather than the box surrounding the text. By applying special effects, such as curves or waves, directly to the text, you can create text that emphasizes the information for your audience.

The WordArt gallery has a variety of text styles to choose from, as well as the option to change individual settings or elements to modify the style. You can convert existing text to WordArt text, or you can create a WordArt object and then enter text.

To create WordArt:

1. Click the Insert tab.
2. Click WordArt in the Text group.
3. Click the WordArt style of your choice.
4. Enter your text in the WordArt placeholder.

To convert existing text to a WordArt graphic:

1. Select the text to convert to WordArt text.
2. Click the More button in the WordArt Styles group on the Format tab.
3. Click the WordArt style of your choice.

Modifying WordArt

You can change the style of a WordArt object by clicking a Quick Style located in the WordArt Styles group on the Format tab. Alternatively, you can modify the individual elements of the WordArt by clicking Text Fill, Text Outline, or Text Effects in the WordArt Styles group. WordArt Text Effects includes a unique Transform option. Transform can rotate the WordArt text around a path or add a warp to stretch, angle, or bloat letters. Figure 3.33 shows the WordArt gallery options and Figure 3.34 shows the warp options available in the WordArt Transform category.

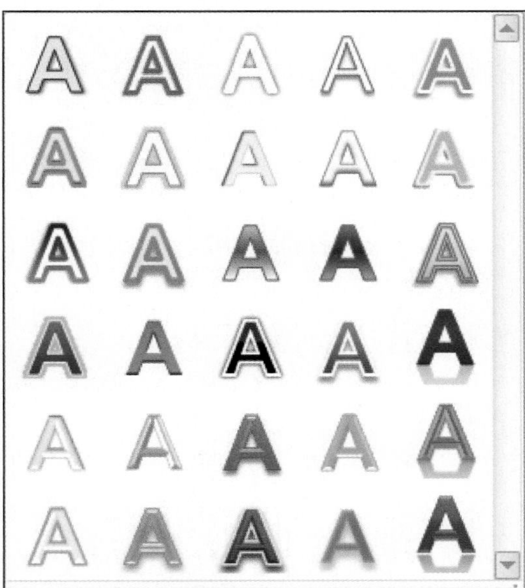

FIGURE 3.33 WordArt Quick Styles Gallery ➤

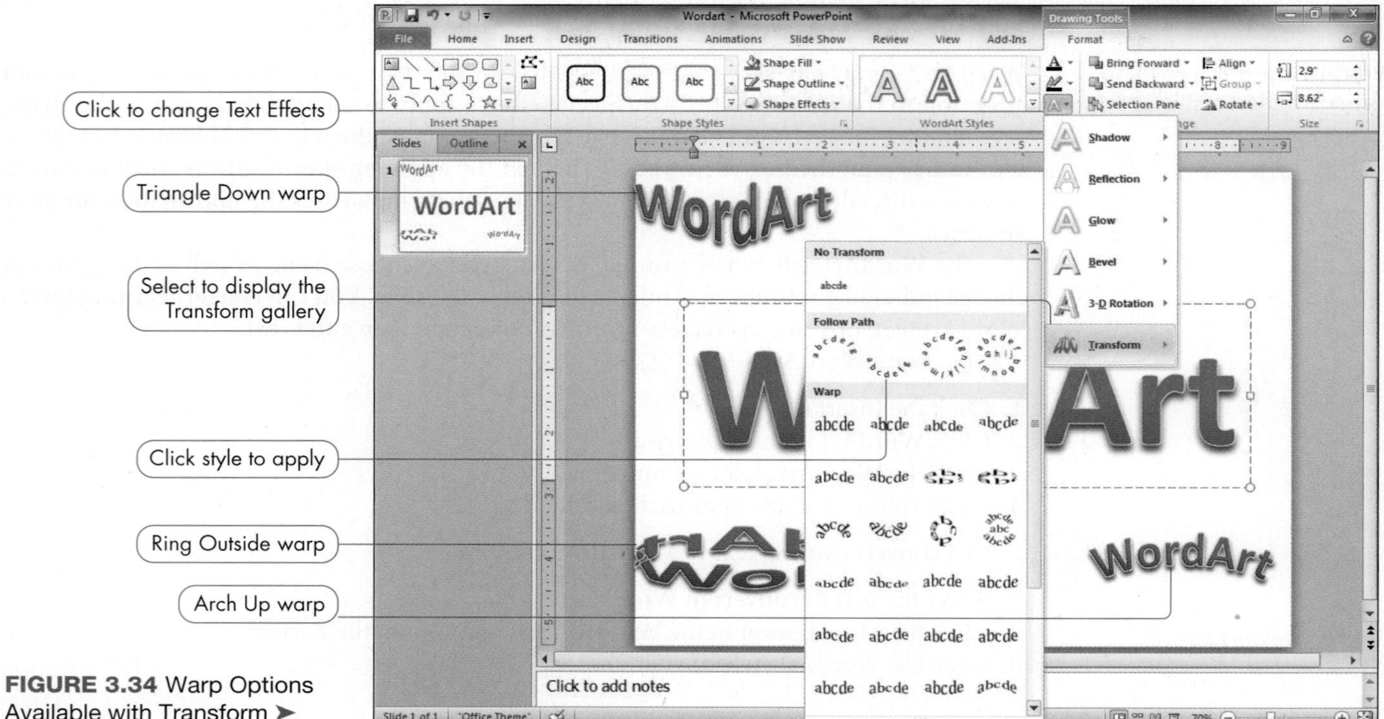

FIGURE 3.34 Warp Options Available with Transform ➤

Quick Concepts Check

1. Which SmartArt diagram type would be most effective to show a time line?
2. How does entering text in a SmartArt Text work like an outline?
3. How would you convert existing text to a SmartArt diagram?
4. List three text effects that can be modified when using WordArt.

2 SmartArt and WordArt

To teach your mini-camp participants how to work with SmartArt and WordArt, you choose to have the group work with a presentation about a process—the water cycle. To make the slide show interesting, you have included fun, interesting water facts.

Skills covered: Create SmartArt • Modify a SmartArt Diagram • Change SmartArt Layout • Create and Modify WordArt

STEP 1 CREATE SMARTART

A SmartArt diagram is perfect for introducing the concept of the water cycle and is an example of a simple infographic explaining a complex concept. You teach your students to diagram using PowerPoint's SmartArt feature. Refer to Figure 3.35 as you complete Step 1.

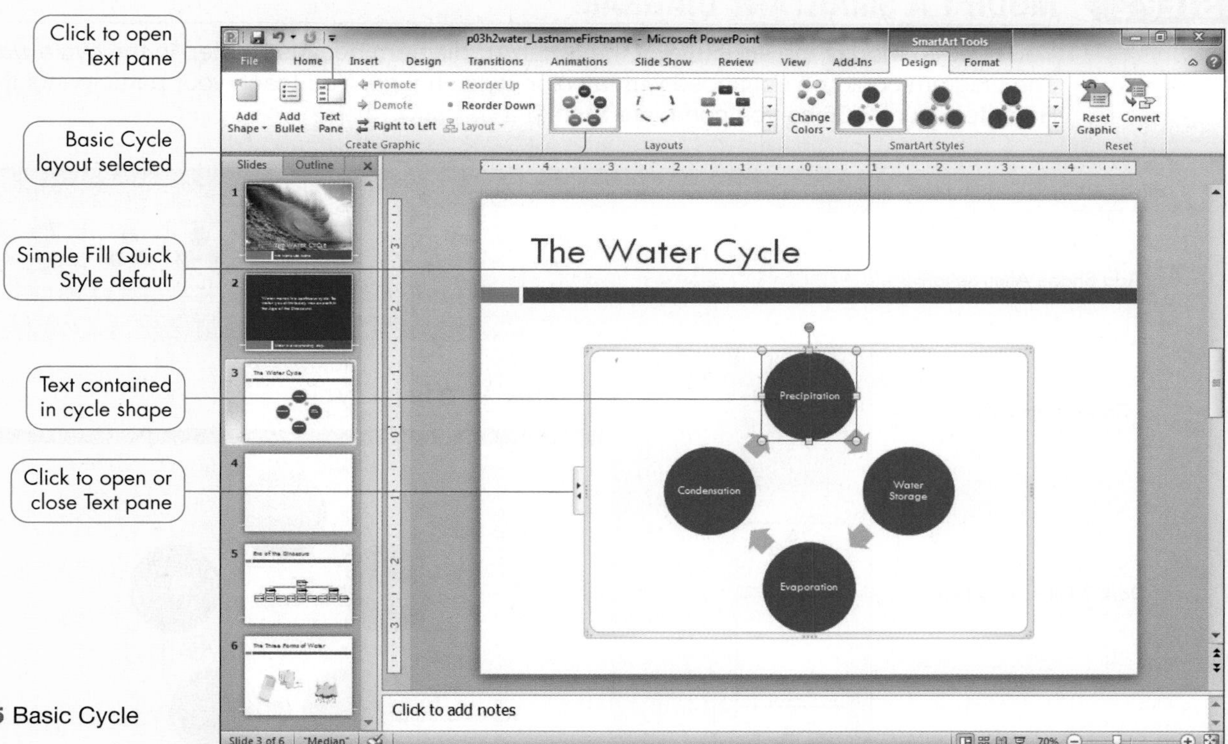

FIGURE 3.35 Basic Cycle SmartArt ➤

a. Open the *p03h2water* presentation and save it as **p03h2water_LastnameFirstname**.

b. On Slide 1, replace *First Name Last Name* with your name. Create a handout header with your name, and a handout footer with your instructor's name and your class. Include the current date.

c. On Slide 3, click the **Insert tab**, and then click **SmartArt** in the Illustrations group.

   The Choose a SmartArt Graphic dialog box opens.

d. Click **Cycle**, click the subtype **Basic Cycle**, and then click **OK**.

   The Text pane opens with the insertion point in the first bullet location so that you can enter the text for the first cycle shape.

TROUBLESHOOTING: If the Text pane is not displayed, click Text Pane in the Create Graphic group, or click the arrows on the left side of the SmartArt boundary.

e. Type **Precipitation**.

   As you type, the font size for the text gets smaller so the text fits in the shape.

f. Press ↓ to move to the second bullet, and then type **Water Storage**. Add two more bullet points: **Evaporation** and **Condensation**.

g. Press ↓ to move to the blank bullet point, and then press **Backspace**.

   The extra shape in the Basic Cycle SmartArt is removed.

h. Click the **Close button** on the top right of the Text pane to close it.

i. Drag the SmartArt object down so that it does not sit on the blue border.

j. Save the presentation.

STEP 2 MODIFY A SMARTART DIAGRAM

You need to modify the structure of the SmartArt diagram because a step in the cycle was omitted. The diagram could be enhanced with a color style change. You teach your participants these skills. Refer to Figure 3.36 as you complete Step 2.

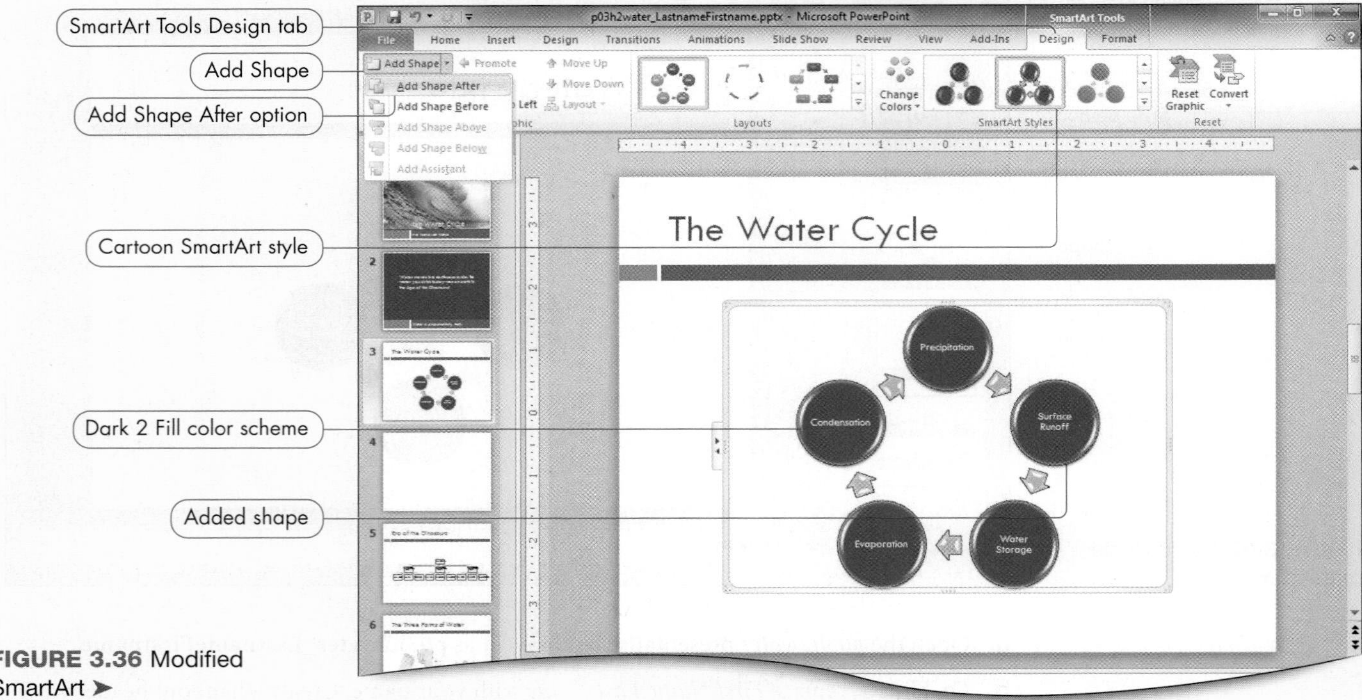

FIGURE 3.36 Modified SmartArt ➤

a. Click the **Precipitation shape**, and then click the **SmartArt Tools Design tab**, if necessary.

b. Click the **Add Shape arrow** in the Create Graphic group, and then select **Add Shape After**.

   You have added a new shape after *Precipitation* and before *Water Storage*.

TROUBLESHOOTING: If you had clicked Add Shape, you would have automatically added a shape after the selected shape. Using the Add Shape arrow gives you a choice of adding before or after.

c. Type **Surface Runoff** in the new shape.

d. Click the SmartArt border to select all the shapes in the SmartArt diagram, click **Change Colors** in the SmartArt Styles group, and then click **Dark 2 Fill** in the Primary Theme Colors category.

e. Click the **More button** in the SmartArt Styles group, and then move the pointer over the styles.

   Live Preview shows the impact each style has on the text in the SmartArt diagram.

f. Click **Cartoon** in the 3-D category (first row, third column).

   This choice makes the text readable and enhances the appearance of the SmartArt diagram.

g. Save the presentation.

STEP 3 CHANGE SMARTART LAYOUT

Many different layouts are available for SmartArt diagrams, and you teach the mini-camp group that for an infographic to be effective, it must be understood quickly. You ask the group to note the reduced font size on the hierarchy SmartArt showing the Era of the Dinosaurs, The Mesozoic Era. You teach them to change the layout of the SmartArt to make it more effective. Refer to Figure 3.37 as you complete Step 3.

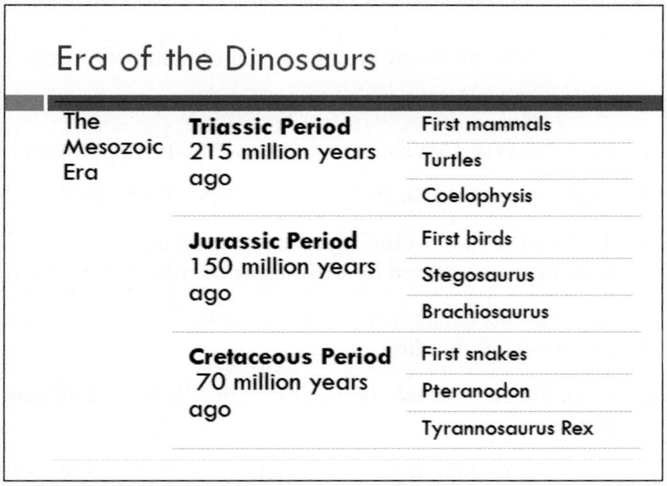

Era of the Dinosaurs

The Mesozoic Era	**Triassic Period** 215 million years ago	First mammals
		Turtles
		Coelophysis
	Jurassic Period 150 million years ago	First birds
		Stegosaurus
		Brachiosaurus
	Cretaceous Period 70 million years ago	First snakes
		Pteranodon
		Tyrannosaurus Rex

FIGURE 3.37 Line List Hierarchy SmartArt ➤

a. On Slide 5, select the **SmartArt Hierarchy shape** by clicking any shape.

b. Click the **SmartArt Tools Design tab**, click the **More button** in the Layouts group, select **More Layouts** at the bottom of the Layouts gallery, and then click **Lined List** under the *Hierarchy* section. Click **OK**.

c. Deselect the SmartArt diagram.

d. Save the presentation.

STEP 4 CREATE AND MODIFY WORDART

You teach the participants how to use WordArt to call attention to text and how to modify the Text effects applied to the WordArt. You also have them insert text in a text box so they can compare the options available with each method for adding text to a slide. Refer to Figure 3.38 as you complete Step 4.

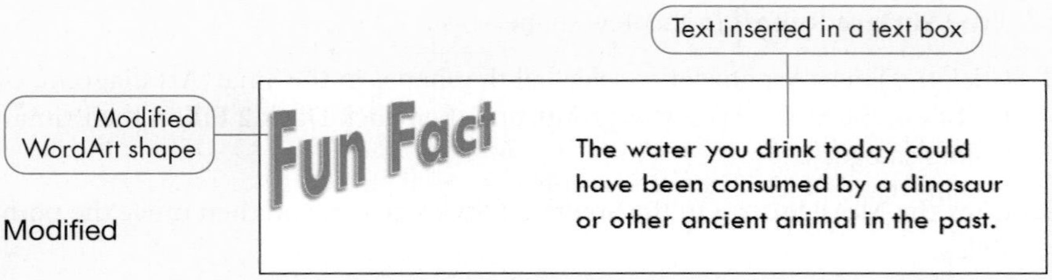

Text inserted in a text box

Modified WordArt shape

Fun Fact

The water you drink today could have been consumed by a dinosaur or other ancient animal in the past.

FIGURE 3.38 Modified WordArt ➤

a. On Slide 4, click the **Insert tab**, and then click **WordArt** in the Text group.

b. Click **Fill - Turquoise, Accent 3, Outline - Text 2** (first row, fifth column).

   A WordArt placeholder is centered on the slide.

c. Type **Fun Fact** in the **WordArt placeholder**.

d. Click the **Format tab**, if necessary, click **Text Effects** in the WordArt Styles group, and then point to **Transform**.

   The Transform gallery opens, showing No Transform, Follow Path, and Warp options.

e. Click **Cascade Up** (last row, third column).

TROUBLESHOOTING: If you do not see the Cascade Up option, scroll down until it becomes available.

f. Type **1.5** in the **Shape Height box**, and then press **Enter**.

   The height of the WordArt shape adjusts to 1.5".

g. Drag the WordArt shape to the top-left corner of the slide, and then deselect the shape.

h. Click the **Insert tab**, and then click **Text Box** in the Text group.

i. Click to the right of the WordArt shape, and then type **The water you drink today could have been consumed by a dinosaur or other ancient animal in the past.**

   The text box expands to fit the text with the result that the text is contained in one long line that flows off the slide.

j. Click the **Format tab**, type **5.75"** in the **Shape Width box** in the Size group, and then press **Enter**.

k. Click the **Size Dialog Box Launcher**, select **Text Box**, and then click the **Wrap text in shape checkbox**.

l. Change the font size of the text to **28 pt**, and then drag the text box until the top edge is aligned with the WordArt shape.

m. Save the presentation. Keep the presentation onscreen if you plan to continue with Hands-On Exercise 3. If not, close the presentation and exit PowerPoint.

Object Manipulation

As you add objects to your slides, you may need to manipulate them. Perhaps you have several shapes created, and you want them to align at their left edges, or you want to arrange them by their center points, and then determine the order of the shapes. You may have inserted a clip art image, and the colors used in the clip art do not match the color of the SmartArt on a slide. You may have added a clip art image that includes something you do not want.

In this section, you will learn to modify objects. You will isolate objects, flip and rotate objects, group and ungroup objects, and recolor clip art. You will also learn to determine the order of objects and align objects to one another and to the slide.

Modifying Objects

Clip art images are made from a series of combined shapes. You can modify existing clip art by breaking it into individual shapes and removing pieces you do not need, changing or recoloring shapes, rotating shapes, and combining shapes from several clip art objects to create a new clip art object. Figure 3.39 shows a picnic clip art image available from Microsoft Office Online. The clip art was broken apart; the fireworks, flag, fries, and tablecloth removed; the hamburger, hotdogs, and milkshake flipped and resized; and the chocolate milkshake recolored.

FIGURE 3.39 Modified Clip Art ➤

Resizing objects is the most common modification procedure. You have learned to resize an object by dragging a sizing handle; however, you may need a more precise resizing method. For example, you use PowerPoint to create an advertisement for an automobile trader magazine, and the magazine specifies that the ad must fit in a 2" by 2" space. You can specify the exact height and width measurement of an object or adjust to a specific proportion of its original size.

To enter an exact measurement, select the object, and then click the Format tab, which is located under any of the Tools contextual tabs (such as Drawing Tools, SmartArt Tools, Picture Tools, and Chart Tools). The Size group contains boxes to change the Shape Height and Shape Width of an object quickly. It also contains a Size Dialog Box Launcher that opens the Format Shape dialog box with more options.

The Size section in the Format Shape dialog box contains boxes for entering exact measurements for shape height and width. The Size section also allows you to use a precise rotation angle and to scale an object based on its original size (note that not all clip art entered from the Clip Art task pane is added at its full size).

Aspect ratio refers to the ratio of an object's width to its height.

To keep the original height and width proportions of a clip art object, make sure the *Lock aspect ratio* check box is selected. ***Aspect ratio*** is the ratio of an object's width to its height. The clip art image in Figure 3.40 was proportionally sized to 50% of its original size.

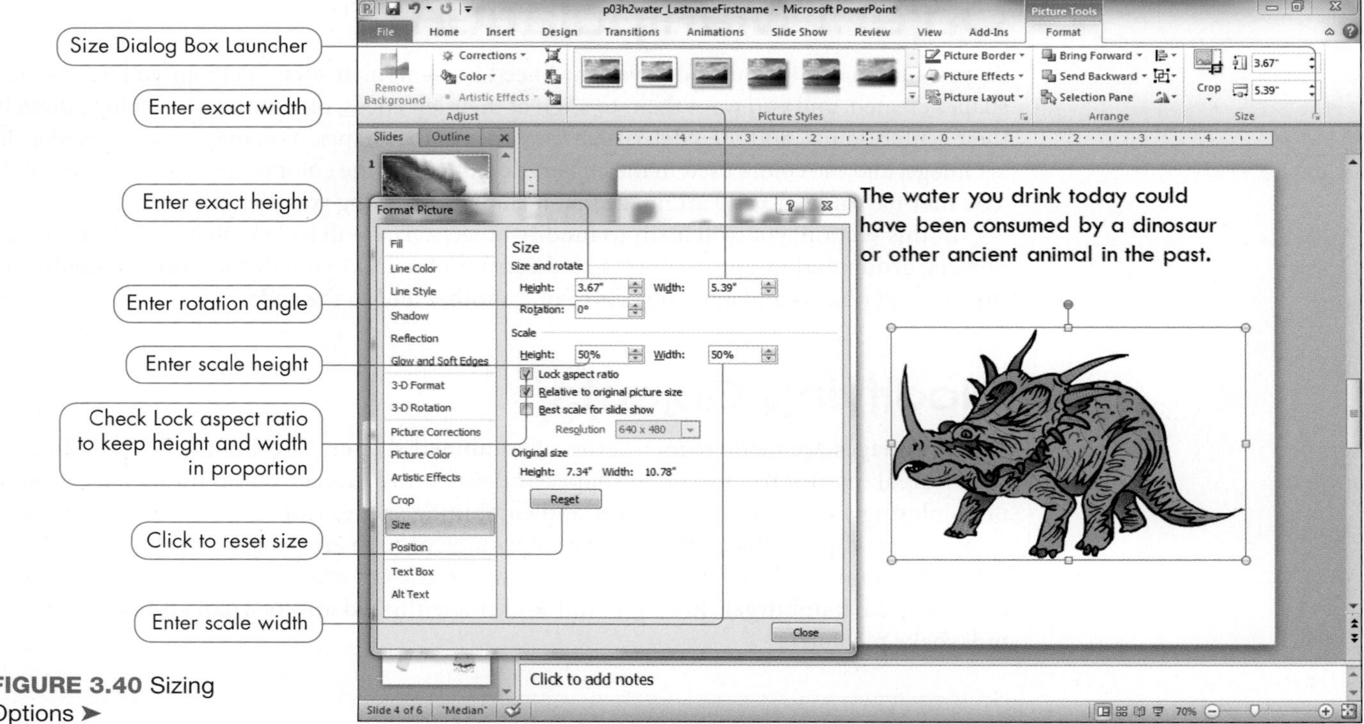

FIGURE 3.40 Sizing Options ➤

Flip and Rotate

To **flip** an object is to reverse the direction it faces.

To **rotate** an object is to move it around its axis.

Sometimes you will find that an object is facing the wrong way and you need to reverse the direction it faces or ***flip*** it. You can flip an object vertically or horizontally to get a mirror image of the object. You may find that you need to ***rotate*** or move the object around its axis. Perhaps you took a photograph with your digital camera sideways to get a full-length view, but when you download the image, it is sideways. You can quickly rotate an object left or right 90°, flip it horizontally or vertically, or freely rotate it any number of degrees.

You can rotate a selected object by dragging the green rotation handle located at the top of the object in the direction you want it to rotate. To constrain the rotation to 15° angles, press and hold Shift while dragging. To rotate exactly 90° to the left or the right, click Rotate in the Arrange group on the Format tab. If you need a mirror image, click Rotate, and then select Flip Vertical or Flip Horizontal. You can also drag one of the side sizing handles over the opposite side and flip it. If you do not drag far enough, you will distort the image. Figure 3.41 shows rotate options and a clip art image that has been flipped.

FIGURE 3.41 Rotating and Flipping Options ➤

Group and Ungroup Objects

Ungrouping is breaking a combined object into individual objects.

Grouping is combining two or more objects.

A **vector graphic** is an object-oriented graphic based on geometric formulas.

A clip art object is usually created in pieces, layered, and then grouped to create the final image. Clip art can be ***ungrouped*** or broken apart, so you can modify or delete the individual pieces. ***Grouping*** enables multiple objects to act or move as though they were a single object, while ungrouping separates an object into individual shapes.

In order for a clip art image to be ungrouped and grouped, you must create and save it as a vector graphic. ***Vector graphics*** are created using geometrical formulas to represent images and are created in drawing programs such as Adobe Illustrator and CorelDRAW. The advantage of vector files is that they are easily edited and layered, and they use a small amount of storage space. Many of the clip art images available from the Clip Art pane are vector graphics.

TIP Clip Art That Will Not Ungroup

If your selected clip art image will not ungroup for editing, it is not in a vector format. The Clip Art task pane also contains clips in bitmap, .jpg, .gif, and .png formats, which are not vector-based images and cannot be ungrouped.

Some non-vector graphics can be converted into drawing objects. Right-click the clip art image on the slide, and then select Edit Picture if the option is available. If the option is not available, the graphic cannot be converted into a drawing object. After you select Edit Picture, a message opens asking if you want to convert the picture into a drawing object. Click Yes. This action converts the object into a vector graphic.

After you convert the object into a drawing object, right-click the clip art image again, point to Group, and then select Ungroup. The clip art object ungroups and the individual pieces are selected. Complex clip art images may have more than one grouping. The artist may create an image from individual shapes, group it, layer it on other images, and then group it again. Figure 3.42 is an example of a complex Microsoft Windows Metafile that has multiple groups.

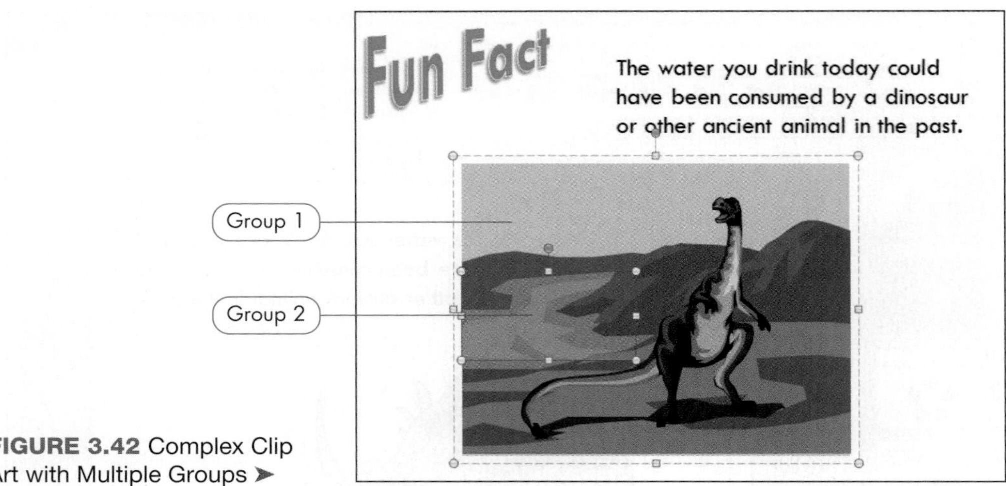

FIGURE 3.42 Complex Clip Art with Multiple Groups ➤

To continue ungrouping, select the clip, right-click, click Group, and then click Ungroup as many times as necessary to break the image down to all shapes. You can also select the clip, and then click the Drawing Tools Format tab. Click Group in the Arrange group, and if the clip art image can be broken down further, the Ungroup option will be active with Group and Regroup grayed out. Select Ungroup, and each individual shape is surrounded by adjustment handles. Click outside of the clip art borders to deselect the shapes, and then click the individual shape you wish to change. Figure 3.43 shows a clip art graphic that has been repeatedly ungrouped until only individual objects are left.

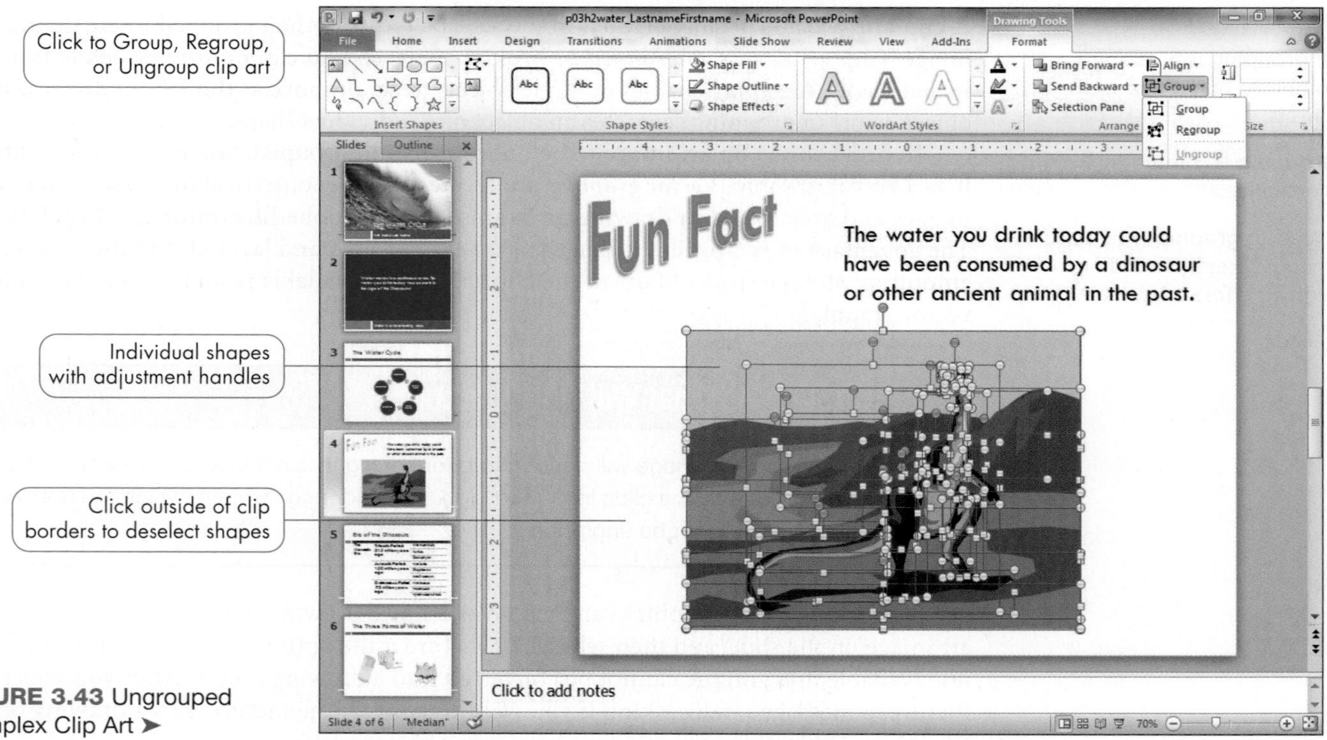

FIGURE 3.43 Ungrouped Complex Clip Art ➤

When working with the individual shapes of a clip art image, it is helpful to zoom in on the clip art. Zooming helps you make sure you have the correct shape before you make modifications. Figure 3.44 shows a selected shape that has had its fill changed to a theme color. Once you have made all of your needed changes, drag a selection net around all the shapes of the image and Group or Regroup the image. If you do not group the image, you risk moving the individual pieces inadvertently.

FIGURE 3.44 Modifying Ungrouped Shapes ➤

Recolor Pictures

You can quickly change the colors in a clip art image using the Recolor Picture option, which enables you to match your image to the color scheme of your presentation without ungrouping the image and changing the color of each shape. You can select either a dark or a light variation of your color scheme.

You also can change the color mode of your picture to Grayscale, Sepia, Washout, or Black and White. Grayscale changes your picture to up to 256 shades of gray. Sepia gives you that popular golden tone often used for an old-fashioned photo look. Washout is used to create watermarks, whereas Black and White is a way to reduce image color to black and white. Figure 3.45 shows a clip art image and three variations of color.

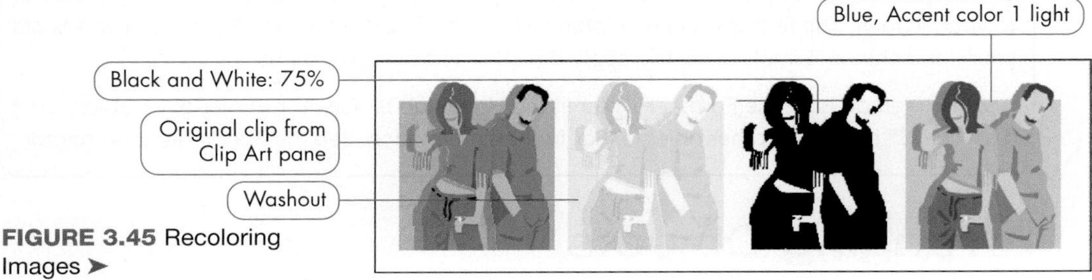

FIGURE 3.45 Recoloring Images ➤

To change the colors in your clip art image:

1. Select the clip art image you want to change.
2. Click the Format tab.
3. Click Color in the Adjust group.
4. Click the color variation of your choice, or select More Variations to open the Theme Colors options and select a theme color.

The Recolor gallery includes a Set Transparent Color option that is extremely valuable for creating a transparent area in many pictures. When you click Set Transparent Color, the pointer changes shape and includes an arrowhead for pointing. Move the pointer until the arrowhead is pointing directly at the color you wish to make transparent, and then click. The color becomes transparent so that anything underneath shows through. In Figure 3.46, the girl's shirt color is transparent so the white background shows.

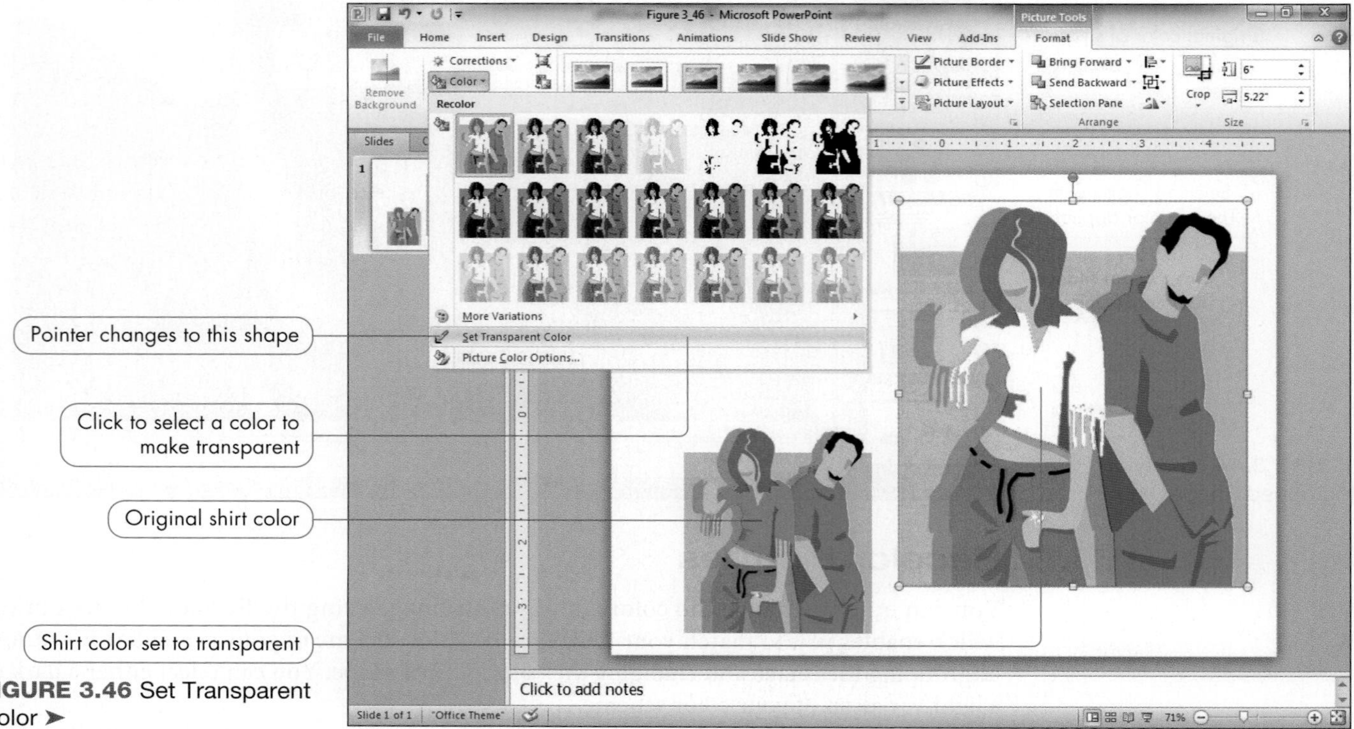

FIGURE 3.46 Set Transparent Color ➤

TIP Changing the Color of Multiple Shapes Easily

Press Ctrl as you click several shapes, and then apply a shape fill to all the selected shapes at the same time. You do not have to keep opening the Shape Fill gallery to apply the color to your shapes. The fill bucket immediately to the left of the Shape Fill command now reflects your color choice. Simply click it to apply the color to selected shapes.

Another method is to use Format Painter in the Home tab to select the color of an object, and then "paint" it over the other objects. For further information, see the Fundamentals chapter.

Arranging Objects

When you have multiple objects such as shapes, clip art, SmartArt, and WordArt on the page, it can become challenging and time consuming to arrange them. PowerPoint has several features to control the order and position of the objects, how the objects align to one another, and how they align to the slide. Before using any of these features, you must select the object(s). You can select the object(s) by using the ***Selection Pane***. The Selection Pane contains a list of all objects on the slide. Click any object on the list to select it, and then make changes to it. Click Selection Pane in the Arrange group on the Format tab to open the Selection Pane if an object is selected. If an object is not selected, click the Home tab, click Select in the Editing group, and then select Selection Pane. The object you selected is highlighted in the Selection Pane.

The **Selection Pane** is a pane designed to help select objects.

Order Objects

The **stacking order** is the order of objects placed on top of one another.

You can layer shapes by placing them under or on top of one another. The order of the layers is called the ***stacking order***. PowerPoint adds shapes or other objects in a stacking order as you add them to the slide. The last shape you place on the slide is on top and is the highest in the stacking order. Clip art images are comprised of shapes that have been stacked. Once you ungroup a clip art image and modify it, you may need to change the stacking order. You can open the Selection Pane to see the order in which objects are placed. The topmost object on the list is at the top of the stacking order.

To change the order of a stack of shapes, select a shape, and then click the Drawing Tools Format tab. The Arrange group on the Format tab includes the Arrange arrow to open a submenu that includes the Bring to Front option, which lets you move the shape all the way to the top of the stacking order, and Bring Forward, which lets you move the shape up one layer. The Send to Back option enables you to move the shape all the way to the bottom of the stacking order, and Send Backward lets you move the shape back one layer. Figure 3.47 shows the results of changing a square at the bottom of a stacking order to the top of a stacking order.

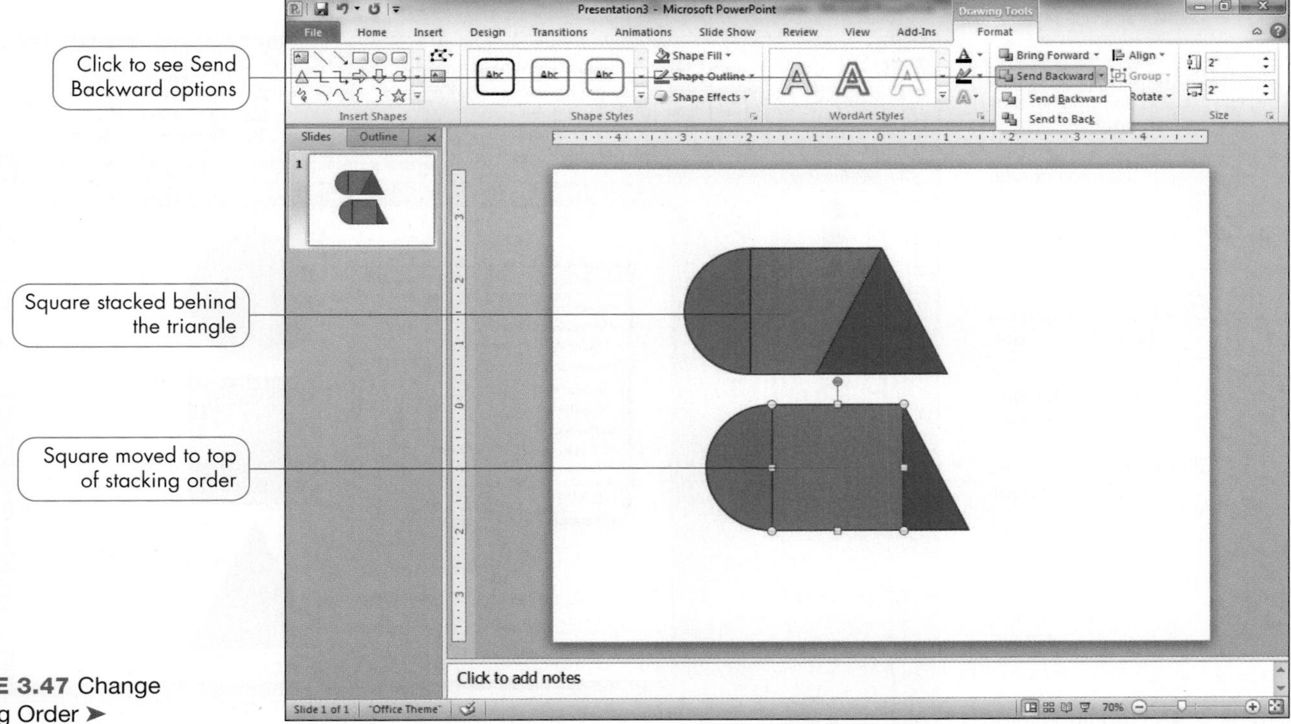

FIGURE 3.47 Change Stacking Order ➤

> **TIP** Ordering Shortcuts
>
> You can right-click a shape and select Bring to Front or Send to Back. Using this method, you can still choose whether to move one layer or all layers. You also can open the Selection Pane, select the object, and click the Re-order Bring Forward arrow or the Send Backward arrow to move the object up the list or down the list.

Align Objects

You can position objects precisely on the slide. For example, you can align a series of boxes at their tops or adjust the amount of space between the boxes so that they are evenly spaced. PowerPoint has rulers, a grid, and drawing guides that enable you to complete the aligning process quickly.

A **grid** is a set of intersecting lines used to align objects.

Each slide can display a ***grid*** containing intersecting lines, similar to traditional graph paper. Grids are hidden and are nonprinting, but you can display the grid to align your objects and to keep them evenly spaced. When you activate the grid, you will not see it in Slide Show view and it will not print. Rulers can also help keep your objects aligned by enabling you to see the exact size of an object, or the distance between shapes.

To view the grid and the ruler, click the View tab and click the check boxes for Gridlines and Ruler. To change the grid settings:

1. Click the Home tab.
2. Click Arrange in the Drawing group.
3. Point to Align, and then select Grid Settings.

By default, objects snap to the gridlines and measurement lines on the rulers. The *Snap to* feature forces an object to align with the grid by either the center point or the edge of the object, whichever is closer to the gridline. You can turn off the *Snap to* feature or change the setting so that objects snap to other objects and/or to the grid. To change the grid settings, select an object, click Align on the Drawing Tools Format tab, and then select Grid Settings.

Figure 3.48 displays the Grid and Guides dialog box options.

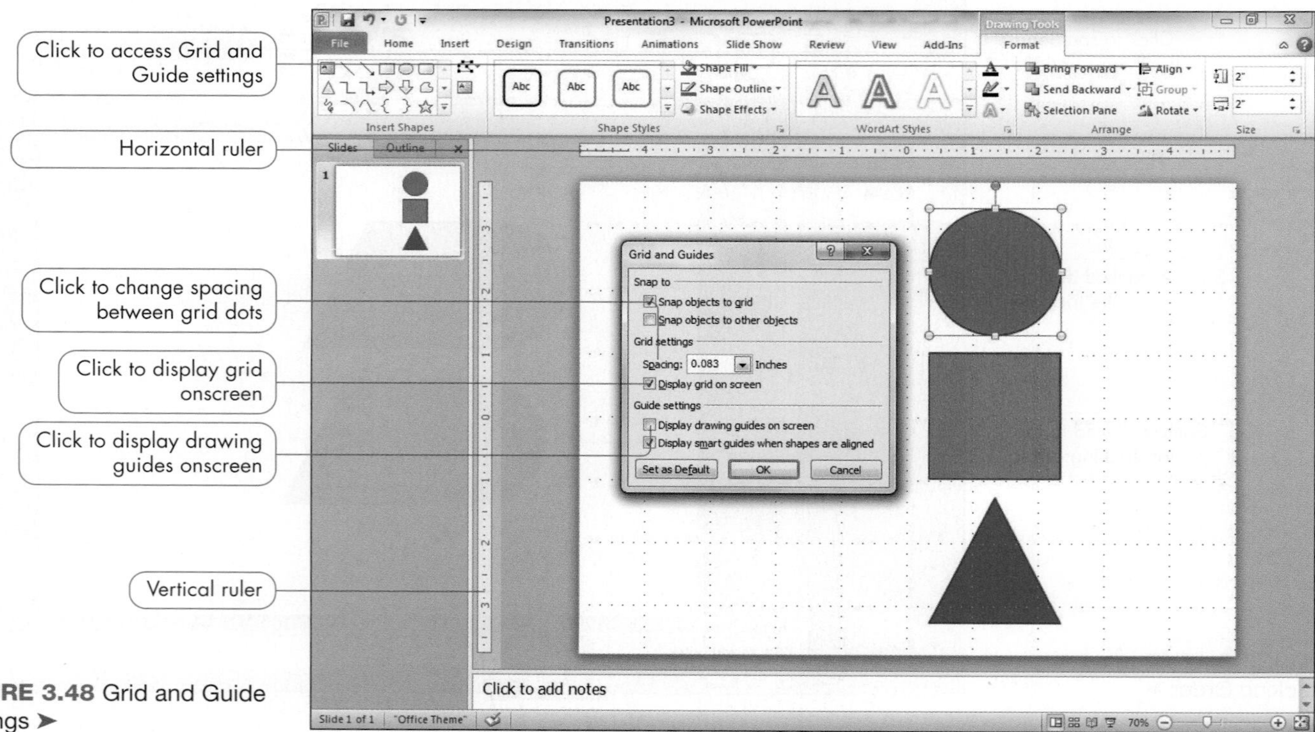

FIGURE 3.48 Grid and Guide Settings ➤

TIP Overriding Snap-to

To override the *Snap object to grid* feature temporarily so that you can freely move an object to any position, press Alt as you drag the object.

A **guide** is a straight horizontal or vertical line used to align objects.

Guides are nonprinting vertical or horizontal lines that you can place on a page to help you align objects or determine regions of the slide. For example, you can use guides to mark margins on a slide.

To activate guides:

1. Click the Home tab.
2. Click Arrange in the Drawing group.
3. Point to Align, and then select Grid Settings.
4. Click Display drawing guides onscreen.
5. Click OK.

When you first display the guides, you see two guides that intersect at the center of the slide (the zero setting on both the horizontal and vertical rulers). To move a guide, position your cursor over it and drag. A directional arrow will appear as well as a measurement telling you the distance from the center point you are moving the guide. To create additional guides, press Ctrl+Shift while dragging. To remove guides, drag them off the slide. Figure 3.49 displays the default guides and a new guide in the process of being created.

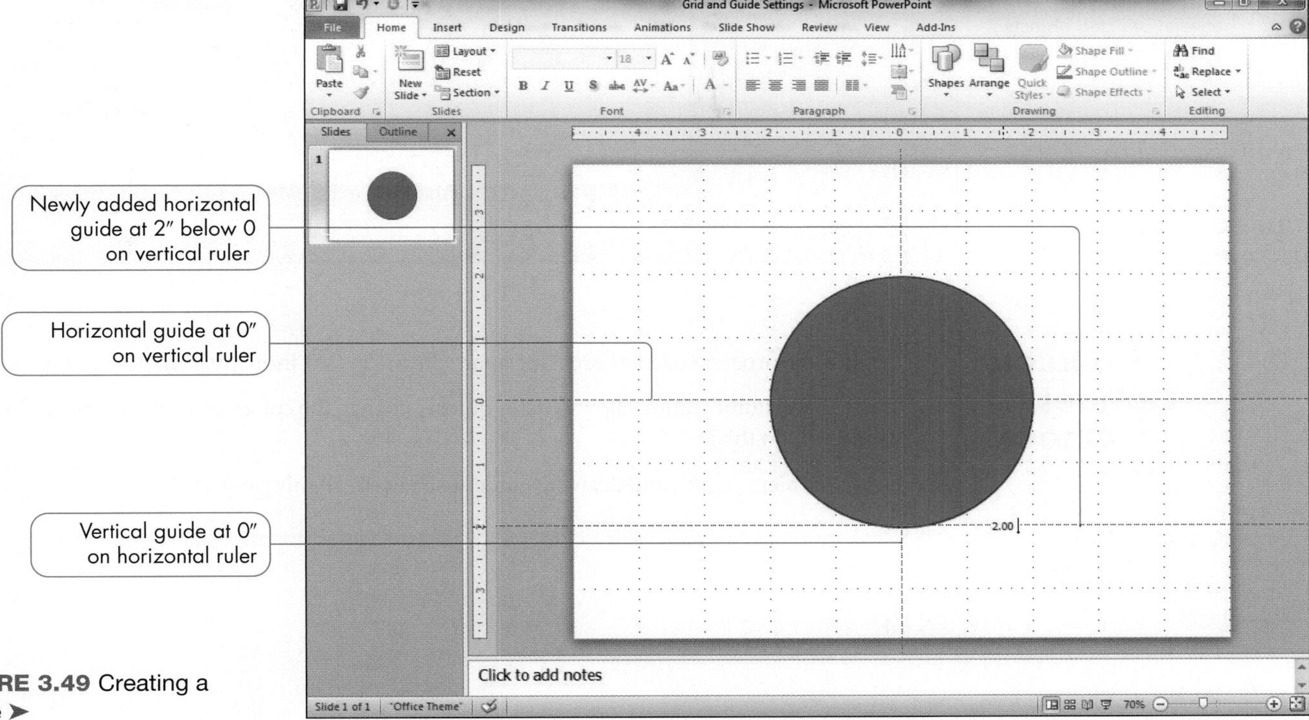

FIGURE 3.49 Creating a Guide ➤

To **align** is to arrange in a line to be parallel.

The ***Align*** feature makes it simple to line up shapes and objects in several ways. You can align with other objects by lining up the sides, middles, or top/bottom edges of objects. Or, if you have only one object or group selected, you can align in relation to the slide—for example, the top or left side of the slide. To align selected objects, click Align on the Format tab. When the alignment options display, select Align to Slide or Align Selected Objects. After you have determined whether you want to align to the slide or align objects to one another, determine which specific align option you want to use: Align Left, Align Center, Align Right, Align Top, Align Middle, or Align Bottom.

To **distribute** is to divide or evenly spread over a given area.

The Align feature also includes options to ***distribute*** selected shapes evenly over a given area. Perhaps you have shapes on the page but one is too close to another, and another is too far away. You want to have an equal amount of space between all the shapes. After selecting the shapes, click Align in the Arrange group on the Format tab. Then select Distribute Horizontally or Distribute Vertically. Figure 3.50 shows three shapes that are aligned at their middles, aligned to the middle of the slide, and distributed horizontally so that the space between them is equidistant.

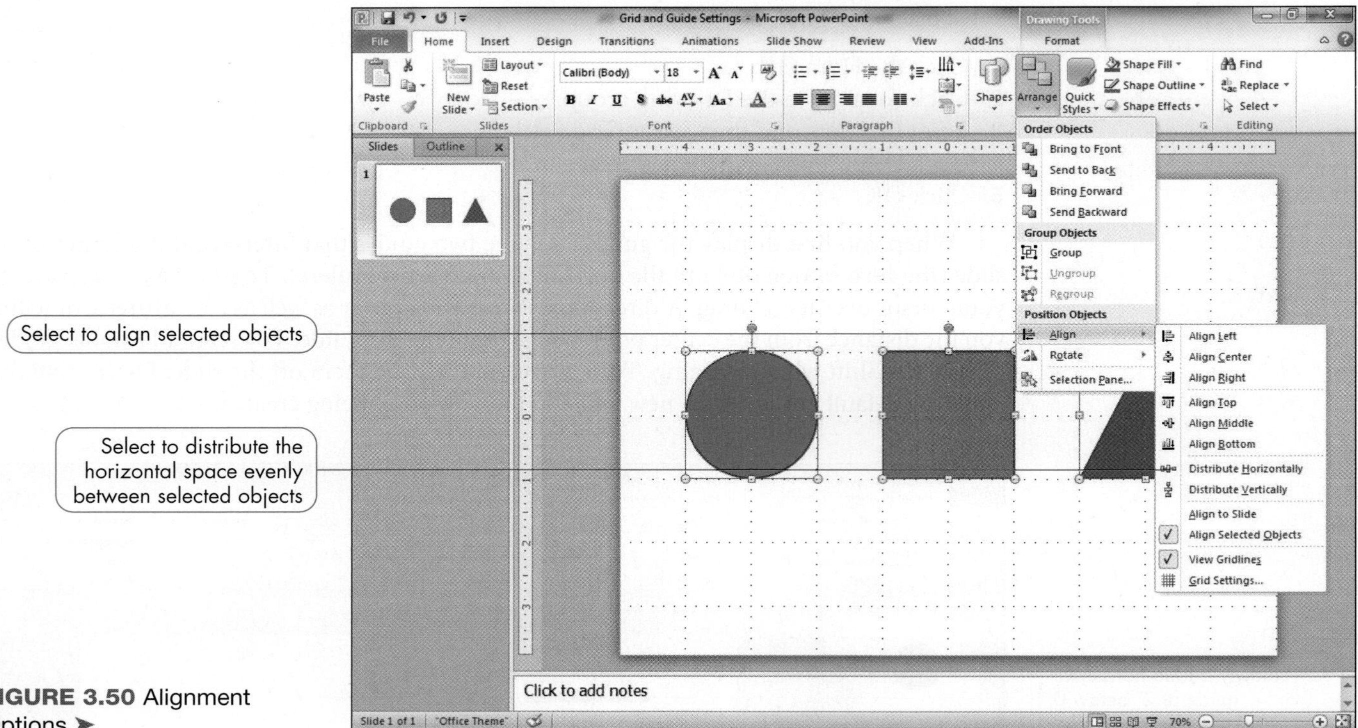

FIGURE 3.50 Alignment Options ➤

Quick Concepts Check

1. What is the process called of breaking apart clip art so that individual shapes can be modified?
2. What PowerPoint feature allows you to quickly change the colors in a clip art image? Why would you do this?
3. How are rulers, a grid, and drawing guides used when aligning objects?

HANDS-ON EXERCISES

3 Object Manipulation

While you could teach your mini-camp participants how to size, position, align, ungroup, and use other object manipulation techniques using shapes, you have them use clip art. The ability to manipulate clip art by grouping and ungrouping, recoloring, combining, and using other techniques turns the thousands of clip art images available from Microsoft Office Online into millions of possibilities. You want your group to have these skills.

Skills covered: Size and Position Clip Art • Flip Clip Art • Ungroup, Modify, and Regroup Clip Art • Recolor a Picture • Create and Reorder Shapes • Align and Distribute Clip Art

STEP 1 SIZE AND POSITION CLIP ART

You teach your mini-camp participants to use the Size Dialog Box Launcher. You want them to be able to precisely size and position objects on the slide. Refer to Figure 3.51 as you complete Step 1.

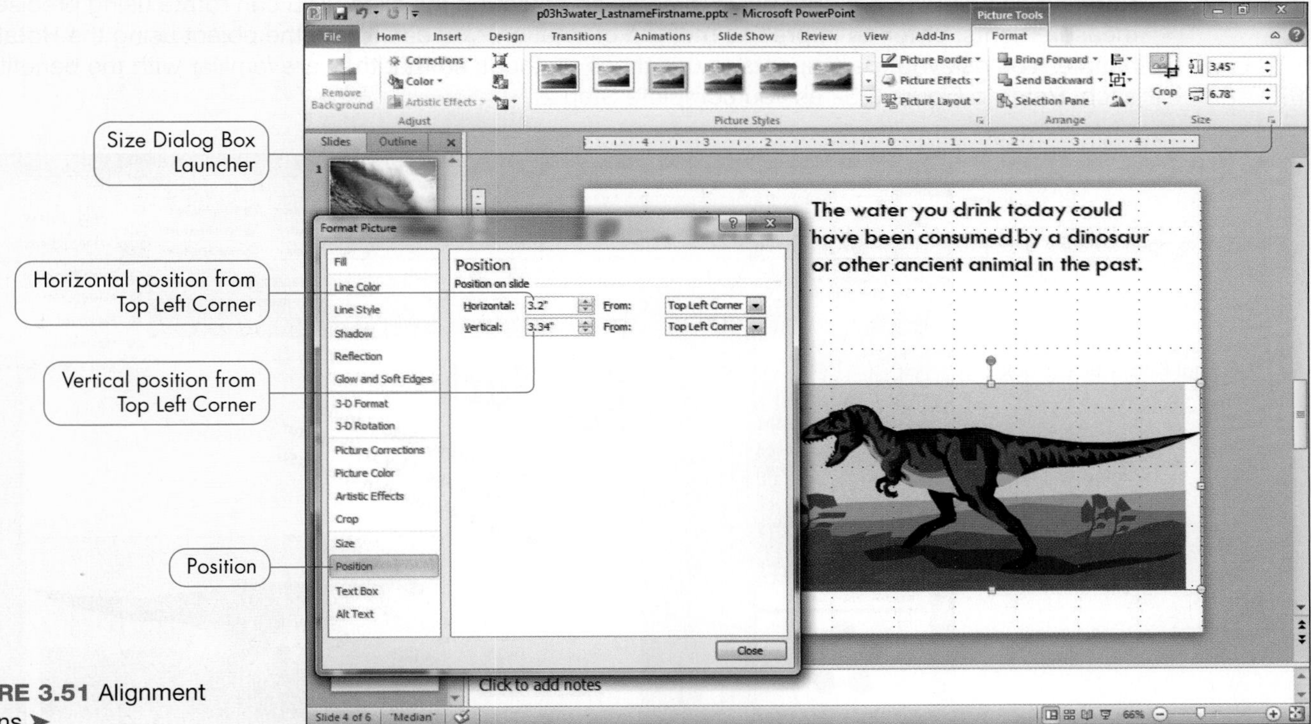

FIGURE 3.51 Alignment Options ➤

a. Open the *p03h2water_LastnameFirstname* presentation if you closed it after the previous exercise. Save the presentation as **p03h3water_LastnameFirstname**, changing *h2* to **h3**.

b. On Slide 4, click the **Insert tab**, and then click **Clip Art** in the Illustrations group.

   The Clip Art pane opens.

c. Select any text in the **Search for box**, type **dinosaurs**, check the **Include Office.com content checkbox**, and then click **Go**.

   Entering the keyword *dinosaurs* narrowed your search more than if you had entered the generic keyword *extinct.*

d. Insert the clip art image of the dinosaur as shown in Figure 3.51, and then close the Clip Art pane.

   You have inserted the clip art image in the center of Slide 4.

> **TROUBLESHOOTING:** If you cannot locate the image in Figure 3.51, select another clip art image of a dinosaur. Expand your search terms to include other result types if necessary.

e. Click the **Size Dialog Box Launcher** in the Size group on the Format tab.

f. Type **3.45** in the **Height box**, and then click in the **Width box**.

   Because Lock aspect ratio is selected, the width of the image changes to 6.78, keeping the image in proportion.

g. Click **Position** in the left pane, type **3.2** in the **Horizontal box**, type **3.34** in the **Vertical box**, and then click **Close**.

h. Save the presentation.

STEP 2 FLIP CLIP ART

Rotating and flipping are both ways to angle an object on the slide. You can rotate using precise measurements, or for an imprecise method of rotation, you can rotate the object using the Rotation handle. You ask your participants to use these methods so that they are familiar with the benefits of each. Refer to Figure 3.52 as you complete Step 2.

FIGURE 3.52 Flipping and Rotating ➤

a. Click the dinosaur clip art, and then click **Rotate** in the Arrange group on the Format tab.

   The rotate and flip options appear.

b. Select **Flip Horizontal**.

c. Click **Rotate** in the Arrange group, and then select **More Rotation Options**.

d. Type **180** in the **Rotation box**, and then click **Close**.

The picture is rotated upside down.

e. Click **Rotate**, and then select **Flip Vertical**.

The clip art picture appears to be in its original position, but the rotation angle is still set at 180°.

> **TROUBLESHOOTING:** If the rotation causes your clip art image to cover the text box, move the clip art toward the bottom of the slide. See Figure 3.52.

f. Select the text box in the top right of the slide, and then drag it down and to the left to the approximate center of the slide. Position the insertion point over the green rotation handle, and then drag the rotation handle to the left until the text box is rotated to approximately match the slant in the *Fun Fact* WordArt.

> **TROUBLESHOOTING:** As you change the angle of rotation for the text box, you will need to reposition it on the slide. An easy way to make small position adjustments is to press the arrow keys on the keyboard.

g. Save the presentation.

STEP 3 UNGROUP, MODIFY, AND REGROUP CLIP ART

Being able to change colors, remove shapes, add shapes, and group and regroup clip art images are important skills you want your participants to master. You ask the participants to change the color of plants, move the dinosaur shape, and regroup the dinosaur clip art image. Refer to Figure 3.53 as you complete Step 3.

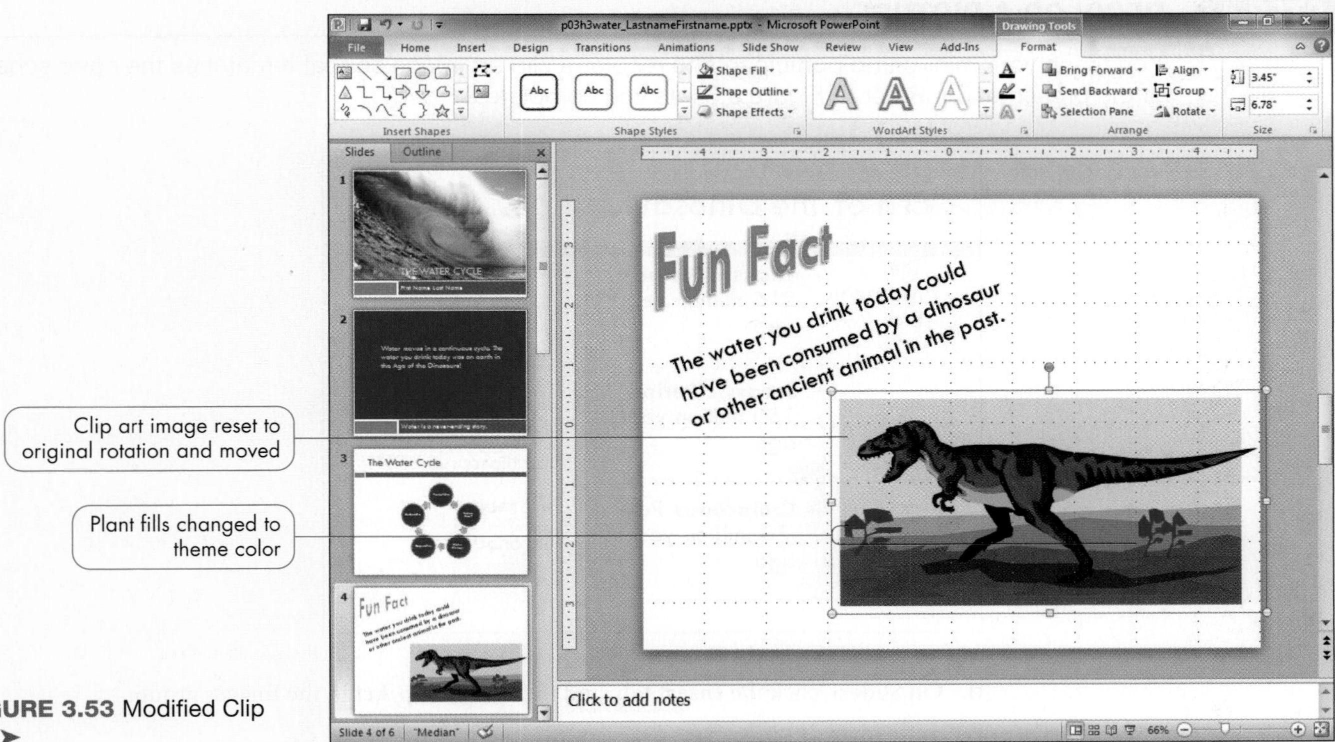

FIGURE 3.53 Modified Clip Art ➤

a. On Slide 4, right-click the dinosaur clip art, select **Edit Picture**, and then click **Yes** when the Microsoft Office PowerPoint message box opens.

The image has been converted to a drawing object and flips back to its original rotation angle.

b. Click the **Format tab**, click **Group** in the Arrange group, select **Ungroup**, and then click outside the clip art border.

   When you ungroup the clip art, each shape comprising the image is selected and surrounded with adjustment handles. Clicking outside the border deselects the shapes so that you can select just the one you wish to modify.

c. Drag the **Zoom slider** until the image is at a level with which you are comfortable, and then drag the scroll bars to locate the plant in the left side of the clip art.

   Zooming in makes selecting the individual shape you wish to modify easier.

d. Select the dull green shape of the plant, click the **Format tab** if necessary, click **Shape Fill** in the Shape Styles group, and then click **Turquoise, Accent 3, Darker 50%** (last row, seventh column).

   You change the dull green in the original clip art to a color that matches your theme color.

e. Change the fill color of the other dull green plants to **Turquoise, Accent 3, Darker 50%**.

f. Click the **View tab**, and then click **Fit to Window** in the Zoom group.

g. Drag a selection net around all the shapes used to make the dinosaur clip art image.

   All the shapes are selected. Pressing Ctrl and clicking the shapes would be time consuming because of the many shapes involved.

h. Click the **Format tab**, select **Group** in the Arrange group, and then select **Regroup**. Drag the new group to the bottom right of the slide.

   Because the WordArt and the text box were not part of the original group, they do not become part of the group.

i. Save the presentation.

STEP 4 RECOLOR A PICTURE

You teach your mini-camp participants to recolor a clip art image so that it matches the color scheme of the presentation. Refer to Figure 3.54 as you complete Step 4.

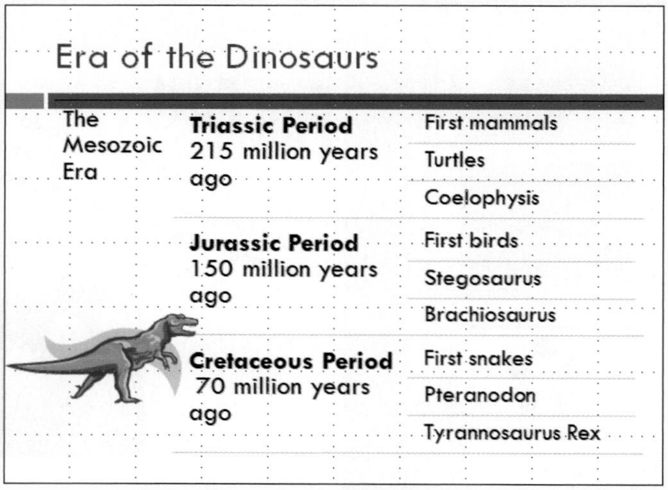

FIGURE 3.54 Recolored Picture ➤

a. On Slide 5, click the **Insert tab**, and then click **Clip Art** in the Images group.

b. Type **tyrannosaurus** in the **Search for box**, and then click **Go**.

c. Refer to Figure 3.54 to determine which tyrannosaurus to insert on the bottom left of your slide, drag the clip art object into position, and then close the Clip Art task pane.

d. Click the **Format tab**.

Because the clip art has not been converted to a drawing object, you can use the picture tools to modify it. Recoloring an image does not require clip art to be ungrouped.

e. Click **Color** in the Adjust group, and then click **Blue, Accent color 1 Light** (third row, second column).

The color of the clip art image now matches the colors in the theme.

f. Save the presentation.

STEP 5 CREATE AND REORDER SHAPES

Being able to create and reorder shapes allows you to be creative, enabling you to create backgrounds, borders, and corners. You ask your group to create a background for three clip art images, which unifies the images. Refer to Figure 3.55 as you complete Step 5.

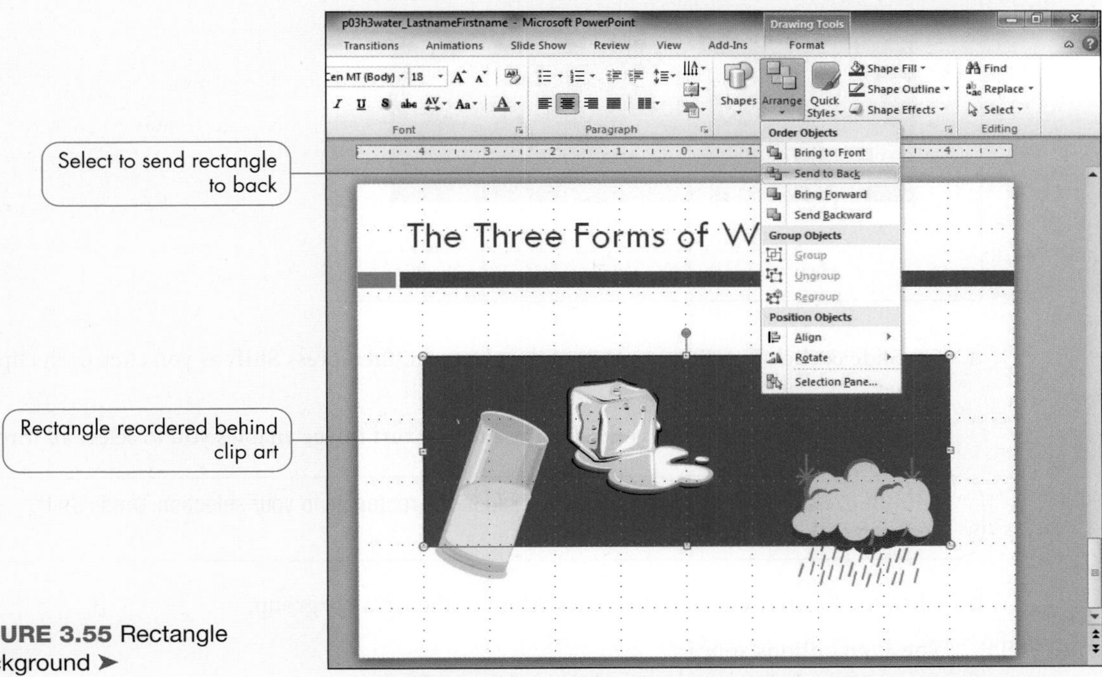

FIGURE 3.55 Rectangle Background ➤

a. On Slide 6, click the **View tab**, and then click the **Ruler check box** in the Show group (if necessary).

The horizontal and vertical rulers appear.

b. Click the **Home tab**, and then click **Rectangle** in the Drawing group.

TROUBLESHOOTING: Depending on your screen resolution, you may need to select Shapes first.

c. Position the cross-hair pointer on the slide so that the indicator on the ruler is at the 4" mark to the left of the zero point on the horizontal ruler and the 1" mark above the zero point on the vertical ruler.

This is the beginning point for the rectangle.

d. Drag to the 4" mark to the right of the zero point on the horizontal ruler and the 2" mark below the zero point on the vertical ruler, and then release.

A large rectangle shape in the theme color is created on top of the clip art on the slide. You will use the rectangle as a background for the clip art. Currently, it is hiding a portion of the clip art and must be reordered.

e. Click **Arrange** in the Drawing group, and then select **Send to Back**.

f. Save the presentation.

STEP 6 ALIGN AND DISTRIBUTE CLIP ART

Dragging objects into position on a slide can be a time consuming and frustrating process. You teach your group to align objects quickly and efficiently using the Drawing Tools Arrange feature. Refer to Figure 3.56 as you complete Step 6.

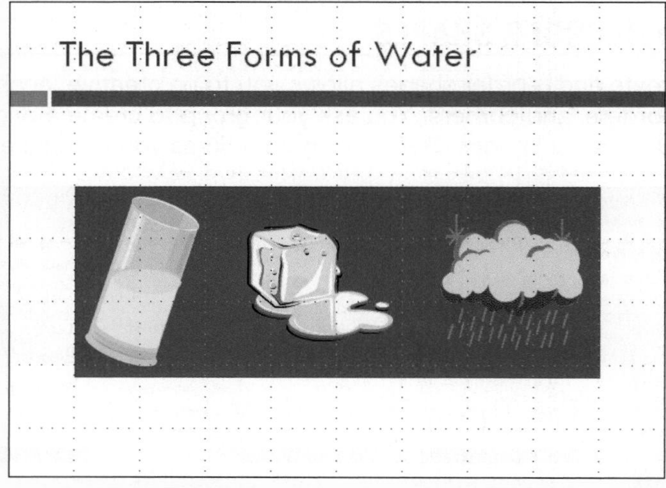

FIGURE 3.56 Arranged Objects ➤

a. On Slide 6, click the clip art image of the glass, and then press **Shift** as you click each clip art image.

   Pressing and holding Shift while clicking each clip art image enables you to select all three.

TROUBLESHOOTING: If you accidentally include the rectangle in your selection, press Shift, and then click the rectangle to deselect it.

b. Click the **Format tab**, and then click **Align** in the Arrange group.

   The align options appear.

c. Select **Align Middle**.

   You align the clip art images by their middles.

d. Click **Align**, and then select **Distribute Horizontally**.

   The objects are distributed evenly.

e. Click **Group** in the Arrange group, and then select **Group**.

   The three clip art images are grouped.

f. Press **Shift**, and then click the **blue rectangle**.

   The rectangle and the clip art group are now both selected.

g. Click **Align** in the Arrange group, and then select **Align Middle**.

   The rectangle and grouped clip art images are aligned by the horizontal middle. This ensures the blue rectangle is behind all of the images.

h. Deselect the objects.

i. Save and close the presentation.

CHAPTER OBJECTIVES REVIEW

After reading this chapter, you have accomplished the following objectives:

1. **Create shapes.** You can use shapes to highlight information, as a design element, as the basis for creating clip art illustrations, or to contain information in infographics. PowerPoint provides tools for creating, sizing, and positioning shapes.
2. **Apply Quick Styles and customize shapes.** A shape can be customized by changing its default fill to another color, to a picture, to a gradient, to a texture, or to no fill. The shape outline color, weight, or dash style can be modified. Special effects such as shadows, reflections, and glows may be added. Applying a Quick Style enables you to apply preset options. The vertexes of shapes can be edited.
3. **Create SmartArt.** SmartArt graphics are diagrams that present information visually to effectively communicate your message. SmartArt can be used to create effective infographics. You can convert text to a SmartArt diagram.
4. **Modify SmartArt.** SmartArt can be modified to include additional shapes, to delete shapes, to apply a SmartArt style, to revise the color scheme, or to add special effects. The direction of the SmartArt can be changed. SmartArt can be resized and repositioned.
5. **Create WordArt.** WordArt is text with decorative effects applied to draw attention to the text. Select a WordArt style, and then type the text you desire.
6. **Modify WordArt.** WordArt can be modified by transforming the shape of the text and by applying special effects and colors. The shape of the WordArt can be warped along a path. Text created as WordArt can be edited. Among the many special effects available are 3-D presets and rotations.
7. **Modify objects.** An object may be flipped horizontally or vertically, or rotated by dragging its green rotation handle. Vector clip art can be ungrouped so basic shapes can be customized, and then objects can be regrouped so they can be moved as one object. Pictures can be recolored by changing their color mode or by applying dark or light variations of a theme color or custom color.
8. **Arrange objects.** Objects are stacked in layers. The object at the top of the layer is the one that fully displays, while other objects in the stack may have some portions blocked. The stacking order of shapes can be reordered so that objects can be seen as desired. Features such as rulers, grids, guides, align, and distribute can be used to arrange objects on a slide and arrange objects in relation to one another.

KEY TERMS

Adjustment handle ***p.907***
Align ***p.949***
Aspect ratio ***p.941***
Callout ***p.907***
Connector ***p.908***
Distribute ***p.949***
Fill ***p.912***
Flip ***p.942***
Flow chart ***p.908***
Freeform shape ***p.910***
Gradient fill ***p.912***
Grid ***p.948***
Grouping ***p.943***
Guide ***p.948***
Infographic ***p.906***
Line weight ***p.916***
Lock Drawing Mode ***p.907***
Opaque ***p.913***
Picture fill ***p.913***
Point ***p.916***
Quick Style ***p.911***
Rotate ***p.942***
Selection net ***p.912***
Selection Pane ***p.946***
Shape ***p.906***
SmartArt ***p.927***
Stacking order ***p.947***
Text box ***p.908***
Text pane ***p.930***
Texture fill ***p.915***
Transparency ***p.913***
Ungrouping ***p.943***
Vector graphic ***p.943***
Vertex ***p.910***
WordArt ***p.935***

MULTIPLE CHOICE

1. Shapes are:
   (a) Images that you search for in the Shape Clip Organizer.
   (b) Graphics such as lines, arrows, and squares, which you add using the Shapes gallery.
   (c) A category of SmartArt.
   (d) Graphics that you create by clicking in the Shape group on the Design tab.

2. To rotate a shape on your slide:
   (a) Drag the green handle at the top of the image.
   (b) Drag one of the corner adjustment handles.
   (c) Double-click the lightning bolt, and then enter the number of degrees to rotate.
   (d) Do nothing because shapes cannot be rotated.

3. Which of the following is a reason for grouping shapes?
   (a) To be able to change each shape individually
   (b) To move or modify the objects as one
   (c) To connect the shapes with connectors
   (d) To create a relationship diagram

4. Which of the following is a reason for ungrouping a clip art object?
   (a) To resize the group as one piece
   (b) To move the objects as one
   (c) To add text on top of the group
   (d) To be able to individually change shapes used to create the composite image

5. You have inserted a clip art image of the ocean with a palm tree on the right side of the beach. If you flip the image vertically, what would the resulting image look like?
   (a) The image would show right side up, but the palm tree would be on the left side.
   (b) The image would be rotated 270°, and the palm tree would be at the top.
   (c) The image would be upside down with the palm tree pointing down.
   (d) The image would be rotated 90°, and the palm tree would be on the bottom.

6. Which of the following might be a reason for changing the stacking order of shapes?
   (a) To show a relationship by placing shapes in front of or behind each other
   (b) To hide something on a shape
   (c) To uncover something hidden by another shape
   (d) All of the above

7. Which of the following is not available from the SmartArt gallery?
   (a) Data table
   (b) Pyramid diagram
   (c) Process graphic
   (d) Matrix block

8. You have items needed for a camping trip in a bullet placeholder. Which of the following SmartArt diagrams would you use to display the data as an infographic?
   (a) Hierarchy
   (b) Cycle
   (c) List
   (d) Relationship

9. You are trying to align a shape directly on top of another, but it always jumps above or below where you need to place it. What feature should you deactivate?
   (a) Align to
   (b) Snap to
   (c) AutoAlign
   (d) Line Snap

10. Which of the following may be used to add emphasis to text on a slide?
    (a) Apply a WordArt Quick Style to the selected text.
    (b) Apply a Text Effect to the selected text.
    (c) Create the text using the WordArt feature.
    (d) All of the above

1 Greeting Card Template and Card

Because you give a lot of greeting cards, you decide to create your own PowerPoint template that you can use to quickly create personalized cards. You use guides and text boxes to create the card, and then you use PowerPoint's alignment and rotate features to help you position the text boxes on the slide. Finally, you create a "Sto lat" (good wishes, good health, and long life) card for your grandmother using the template. You customize the card to include modified clip art, a shape, and WordArt. This exercise follows the same set of skills as used in Hands-On Exercises 1–3 in the chapter. Refer to Figures 3.57 and 3.58 as you complete this exercise.

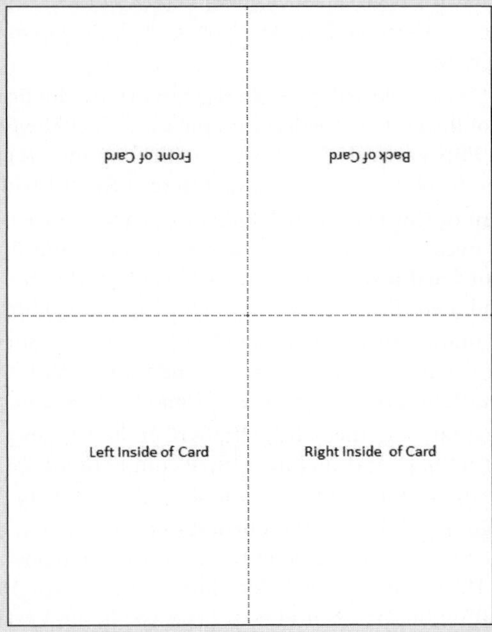

FIGURE 3.57 Greeting Card Template ➤

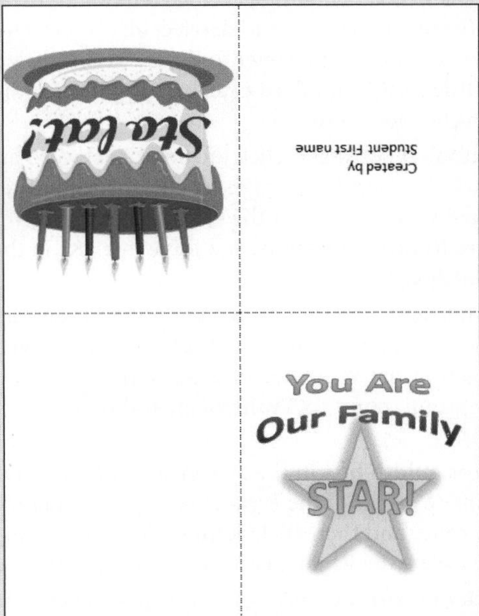

FIGURE 3.58 Birthday Card ➤

a. Open a blank presentation file and save it as **p03p1template_LastnameFirstname**. Create a Notes and Handouts header with your name, and a footer with your instructor's name and your class. Include the current date.
b. Click the **Design tab**, click **Slide Orientation** in the Page Setup group, and then click **Portrait.**
c. Click the **Home tab**, and then click **Layout** in the Slides group. Select the **Blank layout**.
d. Click **Arrange** in the Drawing group, point to **Align**, and then click **Grid Settings**. Click the **Display drawing guides on screen check box**, and then click **OK**.
e. Click the **Insert tab**, and then click **Text Box** in the Text group. Click on the approximate middle of the slide, and type **Front of Card** in the text box. With the text box still selected, click the **Format tab**, click **Rotate**, and then select **Flip Vertical**. Drag the selected text box to the top-left quadrant of the card. (This location will serve as a reminder that when the card is folded after printing, the top front of the page becomes the bottom.)
f. With the text box still selected, press **Ctrl+D** to duplicate the text box. Drag the duplicate text box to the top-right quadrant of the card, and edit the upside-down text to read **Back of Card**. When the card is folded, the text will be in the right position.
g. Drag a selection net around both text boxes, click the **Format tab** if necessary, click **Align**, and then click **Align Top**.
h. With both text boxes selected, press **Ctrl+D** to make a duplicate of the boxes. Drag the duplicates to the middle of the bottom quadrants of the card. Click the **Format tab** if necessary, click **Rotate**, and then click **Flip Vertical**. Edit the text on the bottom-left quadrant to read **Left Inside of Card** and the text on the bottom-right quadrant to read **Right Inside of Card**.
i. Select the **Front of Card** and **Left Inside of Card text boxes** on the left side of the card, click the **Format tab** if necessary, click **Align**, and then click **Align Center**. Select the **Back of Card** and **Right Inside of Card text boxes** on the right side of the card, click the **Format tab** if necessary, click **Align**, and then click **Align Center**. Deselect the text boxes.
j. Save the presentation using the PowerPoint Template (.potx) file type. This will enable you to open the file to create additional cards in the future. With the file still open, save the file again using the PowerPoint Presentation file type and the file name **p03p1card_LastnameFirstname**.
k. Click the **Insert tab**, and then click **Clip Art** in the Images group. Search for illustrations using the keyword **birthday** and include Office.com content. Click the **"Sto lat!" cake image** (see Figure 3.58) to insert onto your slide, and then close the Clip Art pane.
l. With the image selected, click the **Format tab** if necessary, and then click the **Size Dialog Box Launcher**. Click **Lock aspect ratio** in the Scale area to remove the check. Click in the **Height box**, and then type **190%**. Click in the **Width box**, and then type **185%**. Click **Position** in the left pane, and then type **0"** in the **Horizontal box**. Type **.69"** in the **Vertical box**. Click **Close**.
m. Right-click the selected image, and then click **Edit Picture**. Click **Yes** to convert the picture to a drawing object. Click the **Format tab**, click **Group** in the Arrange group, and then click **Ungroup**. Click in an empty area of the screen to deselect all objects, and then click the **pink frosting** on the top of the clip art cake to select it (refer to Figure 3.58). Click **Shape Fill** in the Shape Styles group, and then click **Blue** in the Standard category. Right-click anywhere in the cake image, point to **Group**, and then click **Regroup**.
n. Click the **Format tab** if necessary, click the **Send Backward arrow** in the Arrange group, and then click **Send to Back**. Deselect the borders by clicking somewhere else on the slide. Select and delete the **Front of Card text box**. Select the cake image again, and then click **Rotate** in the Arrange group, click **More Rotation Options**, and then type **180** in the **Rotation box** in the Format Shape dialog box. Click **Close**.
o. Click the **Insert tab**, and then click **WordArt** in the Text group. Click **Gradient Fill - Blue, Accent 1** (third row, fourth column). Type **You Are**, press **Enter**, type **Our Family**, press **Enter**, and then type **STAR!**. Position the WordArt over the star. On the Format tab, click **Text Effects** in the WordArt Styles group, point to **Transform**, and then click **Deflate Inflate** (seventh row, third column in Warp).
p. Click in the **Shape Width box** in the Size group, and then type **3.25"**. Drag the **WordArt object** into the approximate center of the *Right Inside of Card* quadrant. Click the **Send Backward arrow** in the Arrange group, and then click **Send to Back**. Deselect the borders by clicking somewhere else on the slide. Delete the **Right Inside of Card text box**.
q. Click in the **Back of Card text box**, select the existing text, and then type **Created by *Firstname*** (your first name). If the text is too long to fit in the quadrant, press **Enter** before your first name. Drag the text box into the approximate center of the back of the card.

r. Click the **Insert tab**, click **Shapes** in the Illustrations group, and then click **5-Point Star** in the *Stars and Banners* section. Press **Shift**, and then drag to create a star on the right inside of the card quadrant. With the image selected, click the **Format tab**, and then click the **Size Dialog Box Launcher**. Click in the **Height box** in the Size and rotate area, and then type **2.25"**. Click in the **Width box**, and then type **2.25"**. Click **Position** in the left pane, and then type **4.5"** in the **Horizontal box**. Type **6.85"** in the **Vertical box**. Click **Close**.

s. Click the **Format tab** if necessary, and then click **Shape Fill** in the Shape Styles group. Click **Yellow** in the *Standard Colors* section. Click **Shape Outline**, and then click **Orange** in the *Standard Colors* section. Click **Shape Effects** in the Shape Styles group, point to **Glow**, and then click **Orange, 18 pt glow, Accent color 6** (fourth row, last column in Glow).

t. Click the **Send Backward arrow** in the Arrange group, and then click **Send to Back**.

u. Delete the **Left Inside of Card text box**.

v. Click **Arrange** in the Drawing group, point to **Align**, and then click **Grid Settings**. Click the **Display drawing guides on screen check box** to turn off the display of drawing guides, and then click **OK**.

w. If directed to do so by your instructor, print the card, and then fold it to check the text rotations. Save and close the file. Submit *p03p1template_LastnameFirstname* and *p03p1card_LastnameFirstname* based on your instructor's directions.

2 Cloud Computing Infographic

To help you explain cloud computing to employees, you decide to create an infographic using a SmartArt Hierarchy diagram. You want the infographic to show the three categories of cloud computing: IaaS (Infrastructure-as-a-Service), PaaS (Platform-as-a-Service), and SaaS (Software-as-a-Service). You also want to show common providers in each category to help employees recognize the differences in the categories. This exercise follows the same set of skills as used in Hands-On Exercise 2 in the chapter. Refer to Figure 3.59 as you complete this exercise.

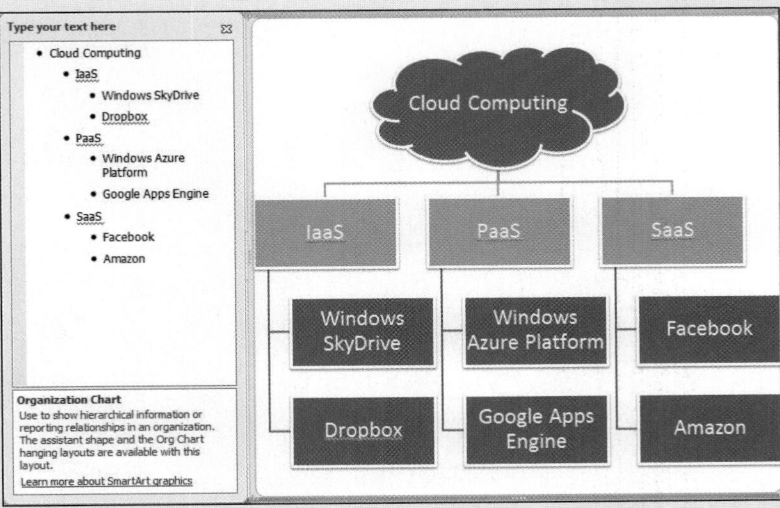

FIGURE 3.59 Cloud Computing Infographic ➤

a. Open a blank presentation file and save it as **p03p2cloud_LastnameFirstname**. Create a Notes and Handouts header with your name, and a footer with your instructor's name and your class. Include the current date.

b. Click the **Home tab**, and then click **Layout** in the Slides group. Select the **Blank layout**.

c. Click the **Insert tab**, and then click **SmartArt** in the Illustrations group. Click **Hierarchy** in the left pane. Click **Lined List** (fourth row, third column), and then click **OK**.

d. Click the **Format tab**, click **Size**, and then click the **Size Dialog Box Launcher** to open the Format Shape dialog box. Click in the **Height box**, and then type **7.5"**. Click in the **Width box**, and then type **8"**. Click **Position** in the left pane, and then type **1"** in the **Horizontal box** and **0"** in the **Vertical box**. Click **Close**.

e. Click the **Design tab** beneath the SmartArt Tools contextual tab, and then click **Text Pane** in the Create Graphic group to open the text pane (if necessary).
f. Type **Cloud Computing** in the first bulleted level in the text pane.
g. Select the second bullet point, and then type **IaaS**. Press **Enter**, press **Tab**, and then type **Windows SkyDrive**. Press **Enter**, and then type **Dropbox**. Press **Enter**
h. Press **Shift+Tab**, and then type **PaaS**. Press **Enter**, press **Tab**, and then type **Windows Azure Platform**. Press **Enter**, and then type **Google Apps Engine**. Press **Enter**
i. Press **Shift+Tab**, and then type **SaaS**. Press **Enter**, press **Tab**, and then type **Facebook**. Press **Enter**, and then type **Amazon**.
j. Delete remaining empty bullets.
k. Click the **More button** in the Layouts group, and then click **Organization Chart** (first row, first column).
l. Click **Change Colors** in the SmartArt Styles group, and then click **Colorful Range - Accent Colors 2 to 3**.
m. Click the **More button** in the SmartArt Styles group, and then click **White Outline** in the *Best Match for Document* section.
n. Select the **Cloud Computing shape**, and then click the **Format tab** beneath the SmartArt Tools contextual tab. Click **Change Shape** in the Shapes group, and then click **Cloud** in the *Basic Shapes* section. Click **Larger** in the Shapes group six times.
o. Save and close the file. Submit based on your instructor's directions.

3 Principles of Judo

You have created a slide show on Judo for your *sensei* (teacher) to show prospective students. You use infographics, shapes, and clip art to share his message. This exercise follows the same set of skills as used in Hands-On Exercises 1, 2, and 3 in the chapter. Refer to Figure 3.60 as you complete this exercise.

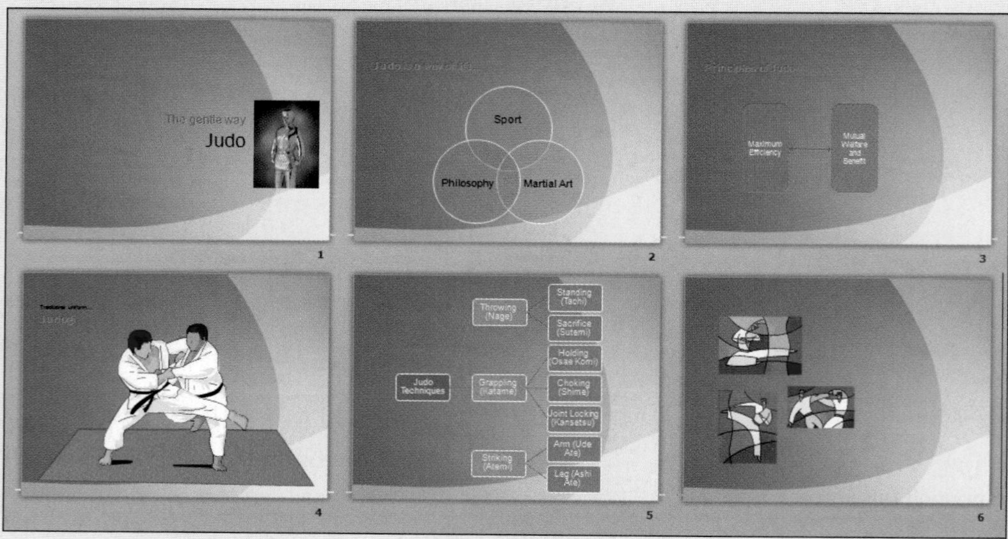

FIGURE 3.60 Judo, the Gentle Way ➤

a. Open *p03p3judo* and save it as **p03p3judo_LastnameFirstname**.
b. Create a handout header with your name, and a handout footer with your instructor's name and your class. Include the current date.
c. On Slide 2, click the placeholder containing the bullet points, and then click the **Home tab**.
d. Click **Convert to SmartArt Graphic** in the Paragraph group, and then select **Basic Venn**.
e. Click **Change Colors** in the SmartArt Styles group. Click **Colorful Range - Accent Colors 5 to 6** in the *Colorful* section.

f. On Slide 3, click the **Insert tab**, click **Shapes** in the Illustrations group, and then select **Double Arrow** in the *Lines* section. Drag an arrow from the right-center connecting point on the *Maximum Efficiency* shape to the left-center connecting point on the *Mutual Welfare and Benefit* shape.
g. On Slide 5, select the **Hierarchy SmartArt**, and then click the **SmartArt Tools Design tab**.
h. Select the **Striking (Atemi) shape**, and then click **Add Shape arrow** in the Create Graphic group. Select **Add Shape Below**, and then type **Leg (Ashi Ate)**.
i. Click **Simple Fill** in the SmartArt Styles group.
j. Click the **More button** in the Layouts group on the SmartArt Tools Design tab, and then select **More Layouts**. Click **Horizontal Hierarchy** in the *Hierarchy* section.
k. On Slide 1, select the image, click the **Format tab**, and then click **Color** in the Adjust group. Click **Grayscale** in the Recolor variations category (first row, second column).
l. On Slide 4, right-click the image, and then select **Edit Picture**. Click **Yes** to convert the picture into a drawing object. Select the image again.
m. Click the **Format tab**, and then click **Group** in the Arrange group. Select **Ungroup**.
n. Click the **View tab**, and then click **Zoom** in the Zoom group. Select **200%**, and then click **OK**. Deselect the shapes, and then scroll until you see the faces.
o. Press and hold **Ctrl**, and then click each of the lines and shapes that were used to create the eyebrows, eyes, and mouths on the two fighters. Press **Delete**.
p. Click **Fit to Window** in the Zoom group.
q. Drag a selection net around all the shapes composing the clip art image, click the **Format tab**, click **Group** in the Arrange group, and select **Regroup**.
r. Click the **Insert tab**, and then click **Shapes** in the Illustrations group. Click **Freeform** in the *Line* section.
s. Click approximately **1"** from the left knee of the fighter on the left to create the first point of a freeform shape you create to resemble a mat (see Figure 3.60).
t. Click approximately **1"** from the right foot of the fighter on the left to create the second point of the freeform shape.
u. Click approximately **1/2"** vertically and horizontally from the bottom right of the slide.
v. Click approximately **1/2"** vertically and horizontally from the bottom left of the slide.
w. Click the starting point of the freeform shape to complete the shape.
x. Click the **Format tab**, click the **Send Backward arrow**, and then select **Send to Back**.
y. View the slide show. Save and close the file, and submit based on your instructor's directions.

1 Project Management Life Cycle

CREATIVE CASE 

You have been asked to train the employees of a family-owned company about the life cycle of a project. You begin a slide show by creating an infographic, and then you apply Quick Styles and make customizations to create a professional look. Refer to Figure 3.61 as you complete this exercise.

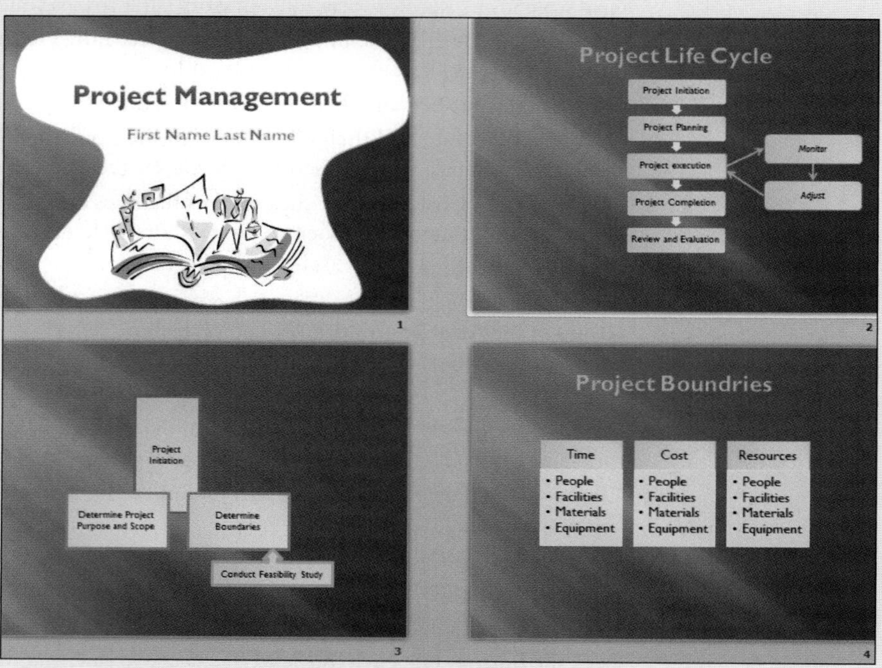

FIGURE 3.61 Project Management ➤

a. Open *p03m1projmgt* and save it as **p03m1projmgt_LastnameFirstname**. On Slide 1, replace *First Name Last Name* with your name.

b. Create a handout header with your name, and a handout footer with your instructor's name and your class. Include the current date.

c. On Slide 2, insert a **Process SmartArt diagram** using the **Vertical Process style**.

d. Type the following points in the **Text pane**, and then close the Text pane.
   - **Project Initiation**
   - **Project Planning**
   - **Project Execution**
   - **Project Completion**
   - **Review and Evaluation**

e. Apply the **Subtle Effect** from the SmartArt styles group.

f. Create two rounded rectangle shapes to the right of the SmartArt. Type **Monitor** in the top rounded rectangle shape, and then type **Adjust** in the bottom rounded rectangle shape.

g. Change the font style in the two new shapes to **Italic**.

h. Apply the Shape Style **Subtle Effect - Brown, Accent 2** (fourth row, third column) to the new shapes.

i. Apply the Shape Outline Theme Color **Brown, Accent 2, Darker 50%** to the new shapes.

j. Change the Shape Fill color of the Project Execution shape to **Subtle Effect -Brown, Accent 2**, and then change the Shape Outline Theme Color to **Brown, Accent 2, Darker 50%** (sixth row, sixth column).

k. Create arrows between the *Project execution*, *Monitor*, and *Adjust* rectangles to indicate the cycle. Change the Shape Outline weight to **3 pt**.

l. On Slide 3, create four shapes with the following specifications:

Shape	Fill	Position	Dimensions	Text
Rectangle 1	Subtle Effect - Brown, Accent 2	From Top Left Corner: Horizontal: 3.25" Vertical: 1.33"	Height: 3" Width: 2.17"	Project Initiation
Rectangle 2	Subtle Effect - Brown, Accent 5	From Top Left Corner: Horizontal: 1.61" Vertical: 3.75"	Height: 1.42" Width: 2.5"	Determine Project Purpose and Scope
Rectangle 3	Subtle Effect - Brown, Accent 5	From Top Left Corner: Horizontal: 4.58" Vertical: 3.83"	Height: 1.42" Width: 2.5"	Determine Boundaries
Up Arrow Callout (Block Arrows section)	Subtle Effect - Orange, Accent 1	From Top Left Corner: Horizontal: 5.17" Vertical: 5.25"	Height: .92" Width: 3"	Conduct Feasibility Study

m. Change the outline weight for all shapes to **4 1/2 pt**.

n. On Slide 4, create a SmartArt List diagram using the **Horizontal Bullet List style**.

o. Type the following as the first and second level bullets in the **Text pane**:

- **Time**
    - **People**
    - **Facilities**
    - **Materials**
    - **Equipment**

p. Copy the text you entered, and then paste it into the Text pane two times. Edit the second and third first level bullets so they read **Cost** and **Resources**, as shown in Figure 3.61.

q. Apply the **Subtle Effect** from SmartArt styles.

r. On Slide 1, insert your choice of *project* clip art. Ungroup the clip art image, and then change the fill color of several shapes to theme colors.

s. Use the Freeform tool or Curve tool to create a shape that covers the title, your name, and the clip art image. Move the shape you created to the back so all other objects on the slide are visible. Edit the shape fill and outline, and then move the objects on the slide until you are satisfied with your title slide.

t. Modify the WordArt Style used on the title in the title slide by changing the fill, outline, and shape effects. Apply a WordArt Style to your name in the subtitle placeholder.

u. View the slide show. Save and close the file, and submit based on your instructor's directions.

2 SmartArt and Clip Art Ideas

To help you become familiar with the SmartArt Graphic gallery and the types of information appropriate for each type of diagram, you create a slide show of "SmartArt ideas." You also manipulate clip art. In this activity, you work extensively with sizing, placement, and fills. Refer to Figure 3.62 as you complete this exercise.

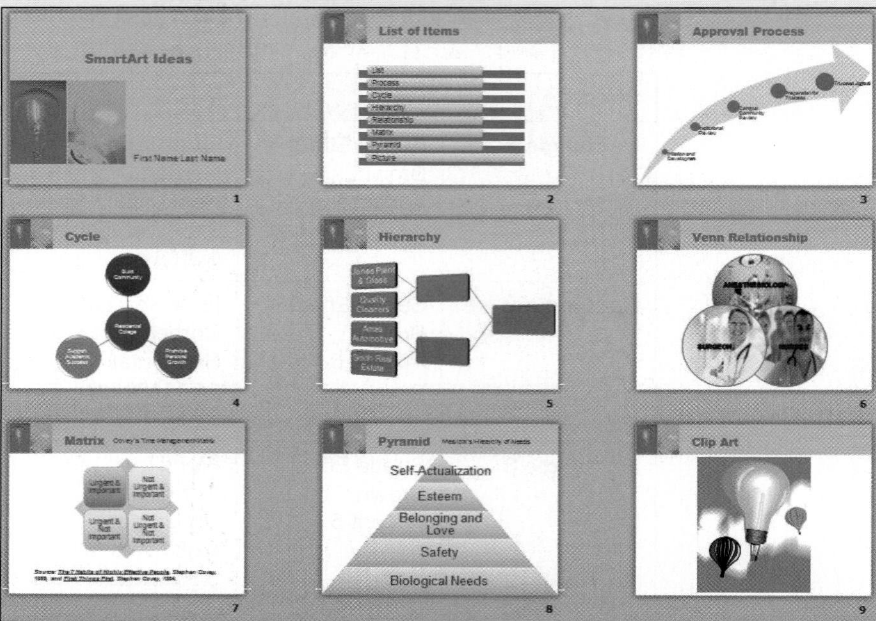

FIGURE 3.62 SmartArt and Clip Art ➤

a. Open *p03m2smart* and save it as **p03m2smart_LastnameFirstname**. On Slide 1, replace *First Name Last Name* with your name.

b. Create a handout header with your name, and a handout footer with your instructor's name and your class. Include the current date.

c. View the gridlines.

d. On Slide 2, insert a **Vertical Box List SmartArt diagram** (second row, second column in the List category), and then make the following modifications:
- Apply the **Subtle Effect** from SmartArt Styles.
- Change the text font size to **24 pt**.
- Type the following list items into the **Text Pane**:
  - **List**
  - **Process**
  - **Cycle**
  - **Hierarchy**
  - **Relationship**
  - **Matrix**
  - **Pyramid**
  - **Picture**
- Size the SmartArt diagram to 7" wide, and then drag it so that it is at the horizontal center of the page using the grid to help you determine placement.
- Align the bottom border of the SmartArt diagram with the last row of the gridline.

e. On Slide 3, insert an **Upward Arrow Process SmartArt diagram** (ninth row, third column in the Process category), and then make the following modifications:
- Apply the **Simple Fill SmartArt Style**.
- Type the following process steps in the **Text Pane**:
  - **Initiation and Development**
  - **Institutional Review**
  - **Campus Community Review**
  - **Preparation for Trustees**
  - **Trustees Approval**
- Change the height of the SmartArt diagram to **6.17"** and the width to **10"**.
- **Align Center** the diagram.
- Align the top border of the SmartArt with the green border of the title placeholder.

f. On Slide 4, insert a **Basic Radial SmartArt diagram** (third row, second column in the Cycle category), and then make the following modifications:
- Apply the **Polished SmartArt Style**.
- Change the SmartArt colors to **Transparent Gradient Range - Accent 2** (first row, fifth column, Accent 2 variation).

- Type **Residential College** as the center hub, and then type **Build Community**, **Promote Personal Growth**, and **Support Academic Success** as the spokes around the hub. Remove the extra shapes.
- Set the height of the SmartArt to **5.5"** and the width to **6.67"**.
- Change the text fill to **Light Green, Accent 3, Lighter 80%**.

g. On Slide 5, insert a **Horizontal Hierarchy SmartArt diagram** (third row, fourth column in the Hierarchy category), and then make the following modifications:
   - Apply the **Metallic Scene SmartArt Style** (third row, first column 1, 3-D variation).
   - Leave the first- and second-level bullets blank in the Text pane, and then type the following in the third-level bullets: **Jones Paint & Glass**, **Quality Cleaners**, **Ames Automotive**, and **Smith Real Estate**.
   - Use the Right to Left option in the Create Graphic group to change the orientation of the diagram.
   - Drag the borders of the SmartArt graphic until it fits the page and the text is large enough to read.
   - Change the text fill to **Light Green, Accent 3, Lighter 80%**.

h. On Slide 6, insert a **Basic Venn SmartArt diagram** (tenth row, fourth column in the Relationship category), and then make the following modifications:

   - Type the following as three bullets in the Text pane: **Anesthesiology**, **Nurses**, and **Surgeon**.
     - Insert a picture fill in the *Anesthesiology* shape using *p03m2anesth*.
     - Insert a picture fill in the *Nurses* shape using *p03m2nurses*.
     - Insert a picture fill in the *Surgeon* shape using *p03m2surgeon*.
   - Recolor all images using the **Grayscale variation**.
   - Format the SmartArt text with the **Gradient Fill - Dark Green, Accent 4, Reflection WordArt Style**.
   - Use the grid to center the Venn diagram in the available space.

i. On Slide 7, insert a **Basic Matrix SmartArt diagram** (first row, first column in the Matrix category), and then make the following modifications:
   - Apply the **Subtle Effect SmartArt Style**.
   - Change the colors to **Colorful - Accent Colors**.
   - Type the following text in the **Text pane**:
     - **Urgent & Important**
     - **Not Urgent & Important**
     - **Urgent & Not Important**
     - **Not Urgent & Not Important**

j. On Slide 8, insert a **Basic Pyramid SmartArt diagram** (first row, first column in the Pyramid category), and then make the following modifications:
   - Apply the **Subtle Effect SmartArt Style**.
   - Enter a blank space at the top pyramid level, and then add the following text to the remaining levels. You will add the text for the top pyramid level in a text box in a later step so that the font in the SmartArt is not reduced to a difficult-to-read font size.
     - **Esteem**
     - **Belonging and Love**
     - **Safety**
     - **Biological Needs**
   - Drag the border of the SmartArt diagram until it fills the available white space on the slide. Deselect the pyramid.
   - Create a text box on the top left of the slide, and then type **Self-Actualization** in the **text box**. Change the font size to **39 pt**. Drag the text box so it is centered over the top of the empty pyramid top.

k. On Slide 9, ungroup the complex clip art image until all grouping is undone. Make the following changes:
   - Use a selection net to select all the shapes that make up the bottom-right balloon, and then drag the balloon up into the white cloud area.
   - Click one of the bright red stripes in the balloon on the bottom left to select it. Shift-click, and then click the remaining two bright red stripes to add them to the selection. Change their fill color to **Yellow** in the Standard category.
   - Use a selection net to select all the shapes that make up the balloon on the left, and then apply a **Dark Blue outline** from the Standard category.
   - Click anywhere on the clip art image, click **Group** in the Arrange group, and then click **Regroup**.

l. View the slide show. Save and close the file, and submit based on your instructor's directions.

A presentation created by a local arts volunteer can be improved using shapes and SmartArt. Figure 3.63 shows a sample of the completed presentation using the Couture design theme, Inset SmartArt style, and Colored Fill - Accent 1 color scheme. Refer to Figure 3.63 as you complete this exercise.

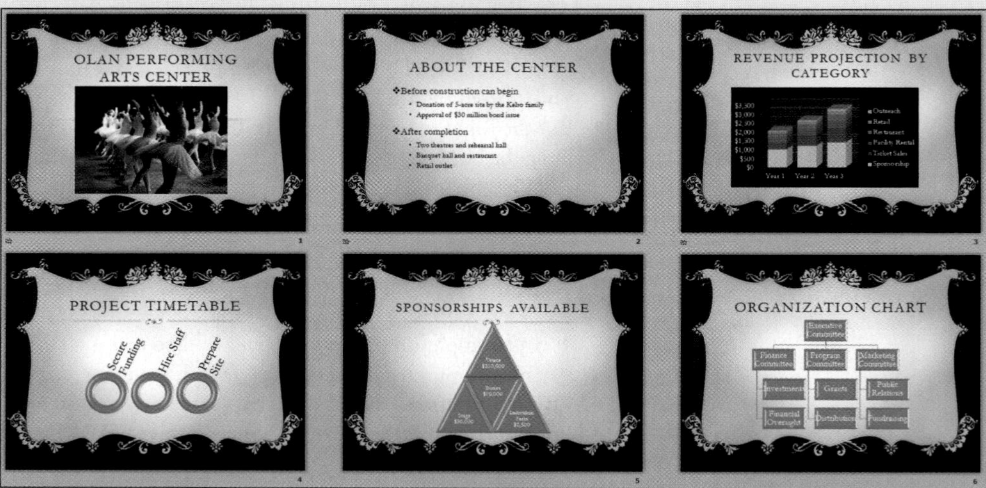

FIGURE 3.63 Partial Arts Presentation ➤

a. Open *p03m3arts* and save it as **p03m3arts_LastnameFirstname**. Create a Notes and Handouts header with your name, and a footer with your instructor's name and your class. Include the current date.
b. On Slide 4, select the bulleted text, and then convert it to a **Circle Accent Timeline** available in the Process SmartArt category. Apply the **Inset SmartArt Style** available in the 3-D category.
c. On Slide 5, select the existing SmartArt diagram, and then change the layout to a **Segmented Pyramid** in the Pyramid SmartArt category. Apply the **Inset SmartArt Style** available in the 3-D category. Resize the SmartArt to fit the available area, and then horizontally center the SmartArt.
d. On Slide 6, create an Organization Chart SmartArt diagram available in the Hierarchy category. The top level of management is the **Executive Committee**. The Executive Committee has the following subcommittees: **Finance Committee**, **Program Committee**, and **Marketing Committee**.
e. Add two shapes beneath each subcommittee (see Figure 3.63). Add the following committees to the Finance Committee: **Investments** and **Financial Oversight**. Add the following committees to the Program Committee: **Grants** and **Distribution**. Add the following committees to the Marketing Committee: **Public Relations** and **Fundraising**.
f. Delete the Assistant shape between the top level of management and the subcommittees.
g. Apply the **Inset SmartArt Style** available in the 3-D category.
h. Save and close the presentation, and submit based on your instructor's directions.

You began a presentation on Waterwise landscaping and concentrated on the content of the presentation. You decide to use the SmartArt feature to create infographics to demonstrate a process and to incorporate shapes to demonstrate concepts.

Create a "Fire Aware" Landscape

You decide to create shapes to explain the concept of creating zones to protect a home from fire and indicate the depth of the zones on the landscape. You stack three oval shapes to create the zones, and then you use a combination of text boxes and clip art to create the landscape. Refer to Figure 3.64 as you complete this exercise.

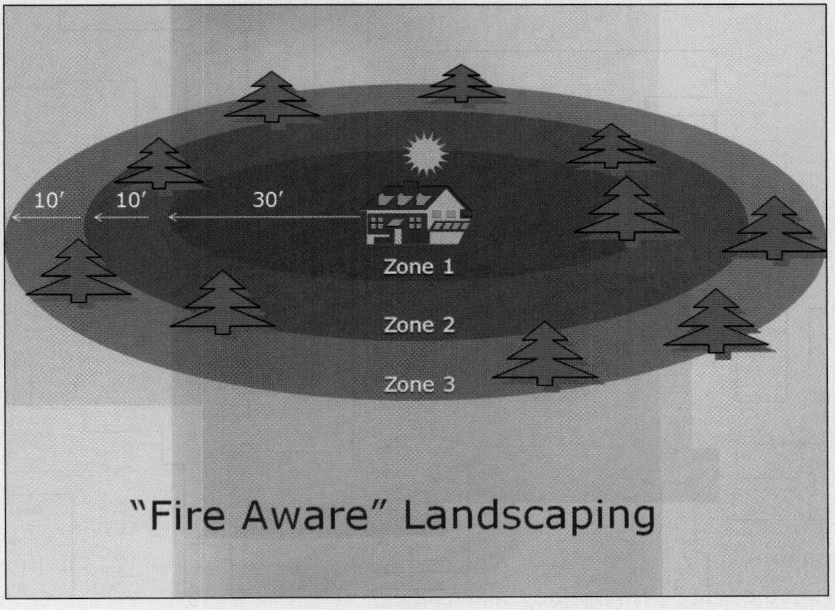

FIGURE 3.64 Fire Aware Landscaping ➤

a. Open *p03c1xeri* and save it as **p03c1xeri_LastnameFirstname**. Create a handout header with your name, and a handout footer with your instructor's name and your class. Include the current date.

b. On Slide 12, insert an oval shape in the approximate center of the blank area of the slide. This will be the center oval in a stack of ovals used to define the zones. Apply the following modifications to the shape:
   - Change the Shape Fill to a custom RGB color: **Red:51, Green:102, and Blue:0**, and a **Transparency** of **50%**.
   - Remove the outline from the shape.
   - Change the oval size to a height of **1.67"** and width of **6"**.

c. Make a copy of the oval you created in step b. Change the second oval size to a height of **2.92"** and width of **8.08"**.

d. Make a third copy of the oval, and then change the third oval size to a height of **4"** and width of **10"**.

e. Select all three ovals, and then **Align Center** and **Align Middle**. Group the three ovals so they will move as one, and then position the group at horizontal position: **0"** from the top-left corner and vertical position: **1"** from the top-left corner.

f. Insert a text box, type **Zone 1**, and then drag it to the bottom center of the small oval. Apply the **Fill - White, Outline - Accent 1 WordArt Quick Style** (use the **More button**) to the text. Make two copies of the text box, and then edit them to read *Zone 2* and *Zone 3*. Drag **Zone 2** to the bottom center of the medium-sized oval, and then drag **Zone 3** to the bottom center of the large oval.

g. **Align Center** the text boxes.

h. Locate and insert a clip art image of a house, and position it in the center of Zone 1. Size it appropriately.

i. Create an arrow that begins near the left edge of the house image and points left to the edge of the Zone 1 oval (see Figure 3.64). Create another arrow that begins near the end of the first arrow and ends at the edge of the Zone 2 oval, and a similar arrow for Zone 3. Set the weight for the arrows at **1 pt**. Set the arrow color to **White, Background 1**.

j. Create three text boxes and center one above each arrow. Label the Zone 1 text box **30'**, and then label the Zone 2 and 3 text boxes **10'**. Format the text color to **white**.

k. Locate and insert a clip art image of a tree. Duplicate it multiple times, and then position a few trees in Zone 2 and more trees in Zone 3. Size trees toward the top of the slide smaller than trees nearer the bottom of the zones. Refer to Figure 3.64, but your tree and tree placement can vary.

Convert Text to SmartArt

To add visual interest to slides, you go through the slide show and convert some of the bulleted lists to SmartArt graphics. Refer to Figure 3.65 as you complete this exercise.

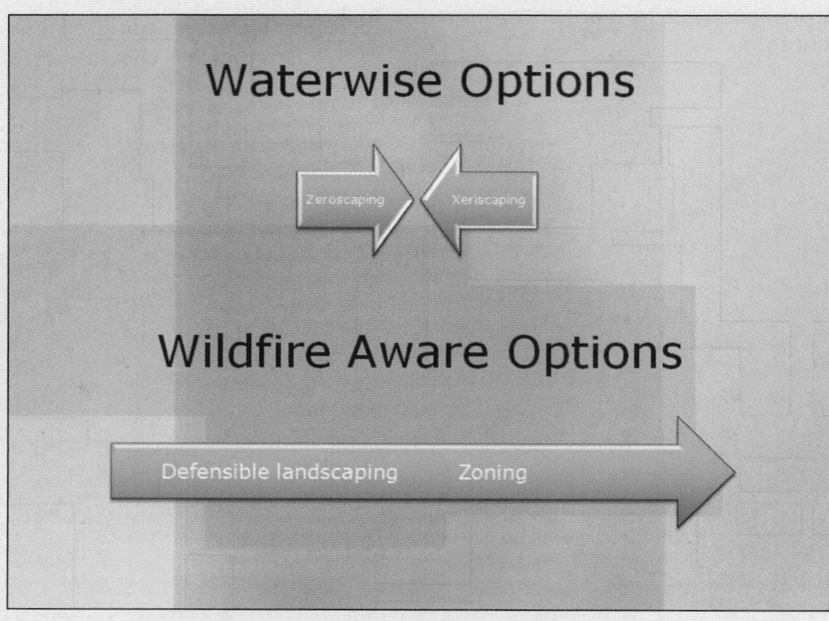

FIGURE 3.65 Text Converted to SmartArt ➤

a. On Slide 2, convert the bulleted text to a **Basic Venn SmartArt graphic**.

b. On Slide 3, select the **Waterwise Options bulleted text**, and then convert it to a **Converging Arrow SmartArt graphic**. Apply the following modifications to the graphic:
   - Resize the graphic so that the arrows almost touch in the middle to show the convergence of the methods around the theme of conserving water.
   - Align the SmartArt diagram in the middle of the horizontal space for *Waterwise Options*.
   - Apply the **Polished SmartArt Style**.

c. Select the **Wildfire Aware Options bulleted text**, and convert it to a **Continuous Arrow Process SmartArt graphic** to indicate that the creation of defensible landscaping leads to zones. Apply the **Polished SmartArt Style**, and then change the text color for each text block in the arrow to **White, Background 1**.

d. Check the spelling in the slide show, and then accept all spellings on the slide.

Create SmartArt

You have a list of waterwise landscaping principles that you decide would present well as a SmartArt list. Refer to Figure 3.66 as you complete this exercise.

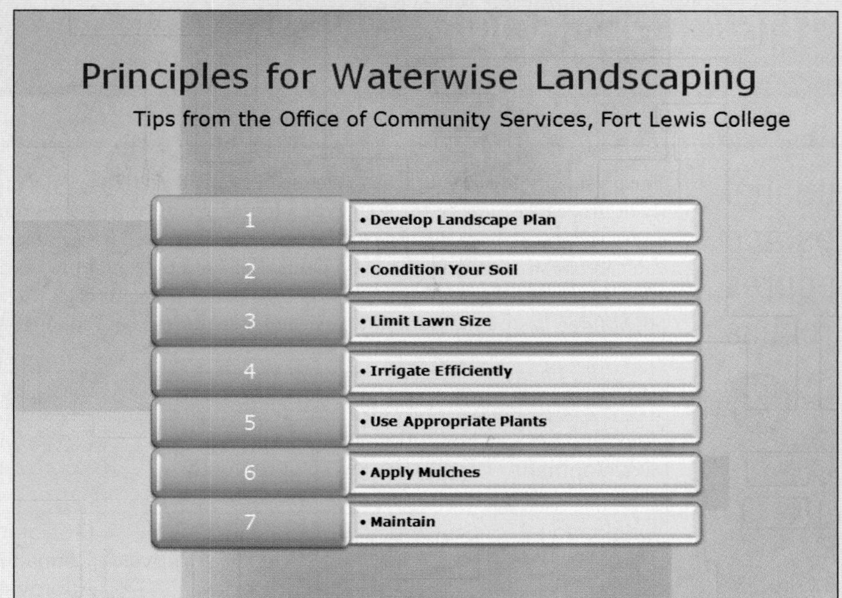

FIGURE 3.66 SmartArt Showing a Work-Flow Process ➤

a. Add a new slide after Slide 12 using a **Title Only layout**.

b. Type **Principles for Waterwise Landscaping** in the **title placeholder**. Change the title font size to **32 pt**, and then resize the placeholder so the title displays on one line.

c. Insert a text box, and then type **Tips from the Office of Community Services, Fort Lewis College** inside. Center the text under the title.

d. Insert a Vertical Block List SmartArt to show the steps, or work flow, in the Waterwise Landscaping process. Type the text in the following table in the **Text pane**. The number should be at Level 1, and the process text should be at Level 2.

Number	Process Text
1	Develop Landscape Plan
2	Condition Your Soil
3	Limit Lawn Size
4	Irrigate Efficiently
5	Use Appropriate Plants
6	Apply Mulches
7	Maintain

Convert Text to WordArt

The last graphic you want to insert is a WordArt object. After inserting the WordArt, you will apply an animation scheme.

a. On Slide 1, select the title.

b. Apply the **Gradient Fill - Indigo, Accent 6, Inner Shadow WordArt Style** (fourth row, second column) to the title.

c. Apply a **Transform Text Effect** to the title using the **Chevron Up Warp style** (second row, first column in the Warp category).

d. Apply the **Fill - White, Drop Shadow WordArt Style** (first row, third column) to the subtitle.

e. Apply the **Fly In animation** to the title, and then apply the **Fade animation** to the subtitle.

f. View the slide show. Save and close the file, and submit based on your instructor's directions.

Institutional Policies and Procedures Approval Process

GENERAL CASE 

The president of your college has asked you to create a one-page document that shows the process that a policy or procedure must go through to be adopted. Create the flow chart using grids and guides to place the necessary shapes. Refer to Figure 3.67 for the text to be placed in the shapes. Because your output will be printed, you can use smaller fonts than you would use for a presentation. Create a handout header with your name, and a handout footer with your instructor's name and your class. Include the current date. Save your file as **p03b1flow_LastnameFirstname**. Save and close the file, and submit based on your instructor's directions.

Stage 1	Stage 2	Stage 3	Stage 4	Stage 5
Initiation and Development	Institutional Entity Review	Campus Community Review	Procedures Approval	Policy Approval
Origination	Steward	President's Council Approval for Review	President's Council Final Approval	Board of Trustees Reviews Policy
President's Council Sponsorship	Dean's Council	Posted on Intranet for Review	Procedures Approved	Policies Approved
Policy Steward Assigned	Faculty Senate		Web Manager Notifies Campus Community	Web Manager Notifies Campus Community
Policy/ Procedure Development	PACE			Forward Policy to Board of Regents When Required
	Student Council			
	Others as Needed			

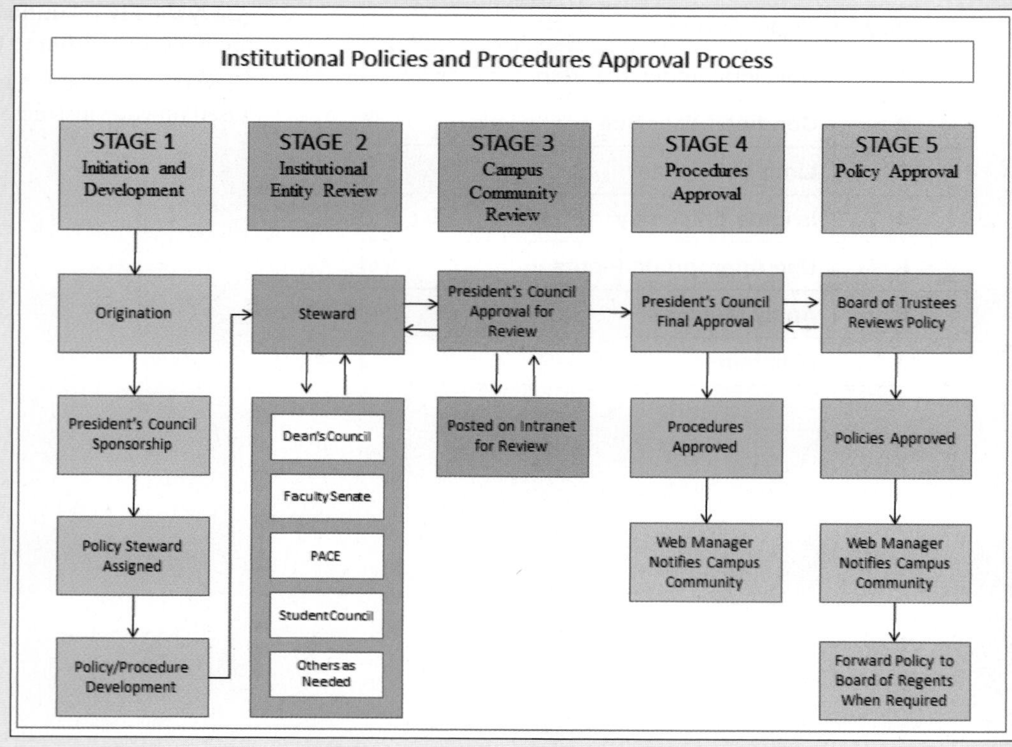

FIGURE 3.67 Policies and Procedures Approval Process Flow Chart ➤

Predators

RESEARCH CASE  

FROM SCRATCH

Create a presentation about a predator of your choice, such as a shark or lion. Include an introduction slide using a Pyramid SmartArt that shows the levels in a food chain. Use the following levels from top-level to bottom-level to create the pyramid: **Predators**, **Secondary Consumers**, **Primary Consumers**, and **Primary Producers**. The food chain is shown as a pyramid to show that meat-eating predators at the top of the food chain are more rare than plant-eating primary consumers, which are more rare than primary producers such as plants. Type a speaker note for the introduction slide that reads **Animals at the top-level of the food chain are predators. Predators are tertiary consumers or carnivores that eat other carnivores. The second level includes secondary consumers, or carnivores that eat herbivores. The third level includes primary consumers (herbivores) that live on plants alone, and finally the bottom level includes primary producers such as bacteria, plants, or algae.** After the introductory slide, research the predator of your choice, and then include a minimum of four slides sharing information about the predator. For example, create a presentation about sharks that could include where sharks are located, their classification, their prey, their hunting methods and tools, and their conservation status. Add speaker notes to clarify information. Add a title slide. Apply a design theme and modify it as desired. In addition to the Food Chain Pyramid, include several clip art images or pictures in appropriate locations. Add a transition and animations to enhance the show. Include a Notes and Handouts header with your name, and a handout footer with your instructor's name and your class. Save your file as **p03b2predator_LastnameFirstname**. Submit based on your instructor's directions.

My Nation

DISASTER RECOVERY 

Your student teaching supervisor has asked you to change the presentation she created about America's symbols to make it more visually and emotionally interesting for her students. If you desire, you may select another country, but be sure to include the inspirational symbols of the country you choose. Open *p03b3symbols* or create your own presentation, and then save the new presentation as **p03b3symbols_LastnameFirstname**. Apply the design theme of your choice and change other themes as desired. Add shapes, SmartArt, pictures, and clip art to add visual interest. Text can be moved to speaker notes, if desired, so that you can showcase symbols. Align and order objects attractively. Finalize the presentation by proofreading, and then applying transitions and animations. Create a Notes and Handouts header with your name, and a footer with your instructor's name and your class. Include the current date. Save the presentation and submit based on your instructor's directions.

POWERPOINT

4 POWERPOINT RICH MEDIA TOOLS

Enhancing with Multimedia

Watch the
Set-up Video
for this Case Study!

CASE STUDY | Wedding Albums

Your sister was recently married. As a gift to the couple, you decide to create two memory slide shows to celebrate. The first slide show will feature images of the couple in high school at their first formal dance, a few engagement photos, and two wedding photos. The second slide show will display photos taken during family vacations.

As you prepare the first slide show, you edit the images using PowerPoint's Picture Tools. Each slide in the first slide show is created individually, and each image is manipulated individually. You download an image from the Internet representing the couple's honeymoon and insert a video of fireworks recorded by the groom during the honeymoon. You insert a fireworks sound clip and also narrate a portion of the bride's vows. Finally, you create the second slide show of family vacations using PowerPoint's Photo Album feature. You utilize the Photo Album options for image manipulation.

OBJECTIVES AFTER YOU READ THIS CHAPTER, YOU WILL BE ABLE TO:

Pictures

Multimedia is multiple forms of media used to entertain or inform an audience.

Multimedia is multiple forms of media such as text, graphics, sound, animation, and video that are used to entertain or inform an audience. You can utilize any of these types of media in PowerPoint by placing the multimedia object on a slide. You already have placed text and graphics in presentations, and you have applied animations to objects and transitions to slides. In this chapter, you will expand your experience with multimedia by inserting pictures, sound, and video in slides.

Inserting a Picture

Multimedia graphics include clip art, objects created using drawing programs, diagrams and illustrations, pictures or photographs, scanned images, and more. You have worked extensively with clip art, diagrams, and illustrations using the Clip Organizer. In this section, you will concentrate on pictures.

Pictures are bitmap images that computers can read and interpret to create a photorealistic image. Unlike clip art vector images that are created by mathematical statements, ***bitmap images*** are created by bits or pixels placed on a grid or map. In a bitmap image, each pixel contains information about the color to be displayed. A bitmap image is required to have the realism necessary for a photograph. Think of vector images as connect-the-dots and bitmap images as paint-by-number, and you begin to see the difference in the methods of representation.

A **bitmap image** is an image created by bits or pixels placed on a grid to form a picture.

Each type of image has its own advantages and disadvantages. Vector graphics can be sized easily and still retain their clarity but are not photorealistic. Bitmap images represent a much more complex range of colors and shades but can become pixelated (individual pixels are visible and display square edges for a "jaggies" effect) when they are enlarged. A bitmap image can also be a large file, so ***compression***, a method applied to data to reduce the amount of space required for file storage, may be applied. The compression may be lossy (some data may be lost when decompressed) or lossless (no data is lost when decompressed).

Compression is a method applied to data to reduce the amount of space required for file storage.

Figure 4.1 displays a pumpkin created as a vector image and one created as a bitmap image. Note the differences in realism. The boxes show a portion of the images enlarged. Note the pixelation in the enlarged portion of the bitmap image.

FIGURE 4.1 Types of Graphics ➤

To display a photograph in a slide, you must save it in a computer bitmap format. You can accomplish this task by scanning and saving a photograph or piece of artwork, by downloading images from a digital camera, by downloading a previously created bitmap image from the Microsoft Clip Organizer or the Internet, or by creating an image in a graphics-editing software package like Photoshop. Table 4.1 displays the types of graphic file formats that you can add to a PowerPoint slide in alphabetical order by file extension.

TABLE 4.1 Types of Graphic File Formats Supported by PowerPoint

File Format	Extension	Description
Windows Bitmap (Device Independent Bitmap)	.bmp, dib	A representation consisting of rows and columns of dots. The value of each dot is stored in one or more bits of data. Uncompressed and creates large file size.
Windows Enhanced Metafile	.emf, .wmf	A Windows 32-bit file format.
Microsoft Windows Metafile	.wmf	A Windows 16-bit file format.
Graphics Interchange Format	.gif	Limited to 256 colors. Effective for scanned images such as illustrations rather than for color photographs. Good for line drawings and black-and-white images. Supports transparent backgrounds.
Joint Photographic Experts Group	.jpg, .jpeg	Supports 16 million colors and is optimized for photographs and complex graphics. Format of choice for most photographs on the Web. Uses compression, but it is lossy.
Macintosh PICT	.pict, pic, pct	Holds both vector and bitmap images. PICT supports 8 colors; PICT2 supports 16 million colors.
Portable Network Graphics	.png	Supports 16 million colors. Approved as a standard by the World Wide Web Consortium (W3C). Intended to replace .gif format. Uses compression, but it is lossy.
Tagged Image File Format	.tif, .tiff	Best file format for storing bitmapped images on personal computers. Can be any resolution. Lossless image storage creates large file sizes. Not widely supported by browsers.

TIP Scanning Images

You can scan and download images directly to Microsoft's Clip Organizer. Put your image on the scanner glass, and then open the Clip Organizer. To open the Clip Organizer in Windows 7, click the Start button, click All Programs, click Microsoft Office, click Microsoft Office 2010 Tools, and then click Microsoft Clip Organizer. In Microsoft Clip Organizer, click File, point to Add Clips to Organizer, and then click From Scanner or Camera. When the Insert Picture from Scanner or Camera dialog box opens, select your scanner from the Device box, and then click Insert. The clip you scanned appears in My Collections, not on your slide. You would then need to insert the scanned image as you do any other image from the Clip Organizer. If you are in a lab setting, do this only if you have permission to add to the Clip Organizer and have permission for the photo rights.

To add a picture using a placeholder, do the following:

1. Select a layout with a placeholder that includes an Insert Picture from File button.
2. Click Insert Picture from File to open the Insert Picture dialog box.
3. Navigate to the location of your picture files, and then click the picture you want to use.
4. Click Insert.

Figure 4.2 shows two examples of placeholders with Insert Picture buttons. When you insert a picture in this manner, the picture is centered within the placeholder frame and is sometimes cropped to fit within the placeholder. This effect can cause unwanted results, such as the tops of heads cropped off. If this situation occurs, undo the insertion, enlarge the placeholder, and then repeat the steps for inserting an image.

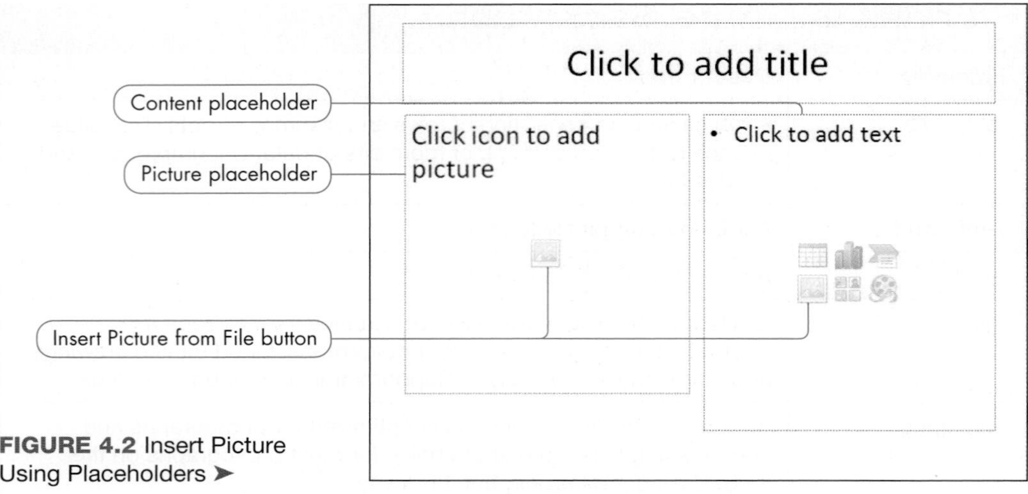

FIGURE 4.2 Insert Picture Using Placeholders ➤

Another way to insert an image is to click Picture on the Insert tab. The advantage of this method is that your image comes in at full size rather than centered and cropped in a placeholder, and you do not need a picture placeholder. You can then resize the image to fit the desired area. The disadvantage is you spend time resizing and positioning the image.

To add a picture using the Insert tab, do the following:

1. Click the Insert tab.
2. Click Picture in the Images group.
3. Navigate to the location of your picture files, and then click the picture you want to use.
4. Click Insert.
5. Adjust the size and position of the picture as necessary.

TIP Adding Images Using Windows Explorer

If you are adding multiple images to a slide show, you can speed up the process by inserting images directly from Windows Explorer. Open Windows Explorer and navigate to the folder where the images are located. Position the Windows Explorer window on top of the PowerPoint window, and then drag the images from the Explorer window onto the slides of your choice.

Transforming a Picture

Once you insert a picture onto a slide, PowerPoint provides powerful tools that you can use to adjust the image. Picture Tools are designed to adjust an image background, correct image problems, manipulate image color, or add artistic or stylized effects. You can also arrange, crop, or resize an image using Picture Tools. The Picture Tools are available when you select the picture in the slide and click the Picture Tools Format tab (see Figure 4.3).

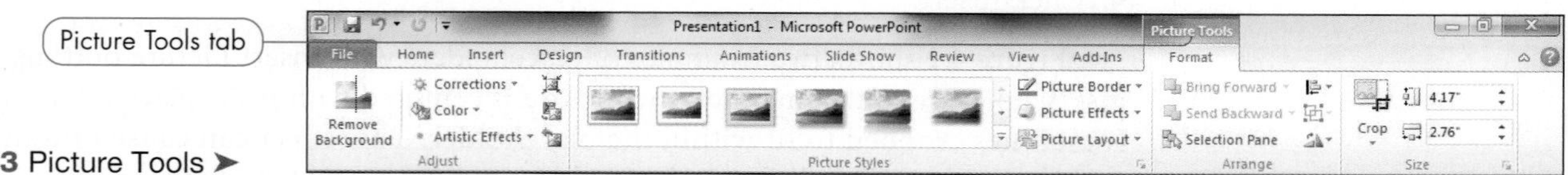

FIGURE 4.3 Picture Tools ➤

Remove a Picture Background

PowerPoint 2010's new feature, the Remove Background tool, enables you to remove portions of a picture you do not want to keep. Rather than have a rectangle-shaped picture on your slide, you can have an image that flows into the slide. When you select a picture and click the Remove Background tool in the Adjust group on the Format tab, PowerPoint creates an automatic marquee selection area in the picture that determines the ***background***, or area to be removed, and the ***foreground***, or area to be kept. PowerPoint identifies the background selection with magenta coloring. You can then adjust PowerPoint's automatic selection by marking areas you want to keep, marking areas you want to remove, and deleting any markings you do not want. You can discard any changes you have made or keep your changes. Figure 4.4 shows a picture in which the Remove Background tool has created a marquee identifying the foreground and background.

The **background** of a picture is the portion of a picture to be removed.

The **foreground** of a picture is the portion of the picture to be kept.

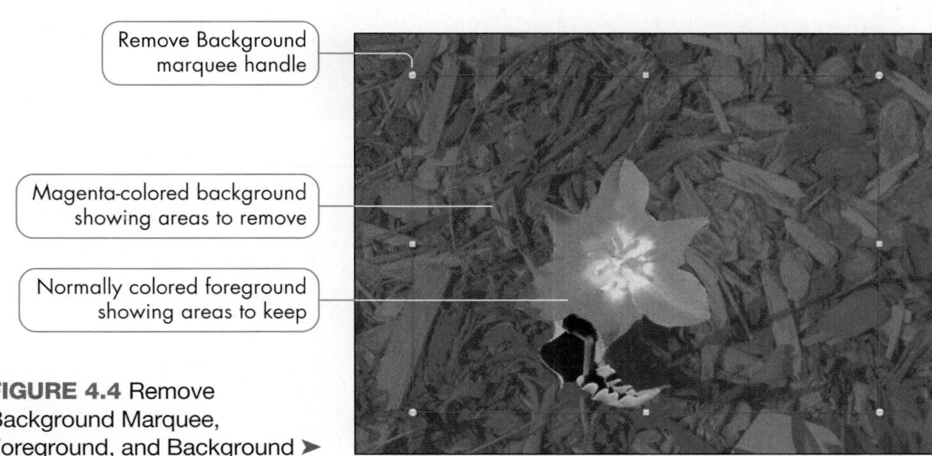

FIGURE 4.4 Remove Background Marquee, Foreground, and Background ➤

Once the background has been identified by the marquee, you can refine the marquee size and shape so that it contains everything you want to keep without extra areas. Resize the marquee by dragging a marquee handle, the same process you use to resize clip art. Refine the picture further by using the tools available in the Background Removal tab (see Figure 4.5).

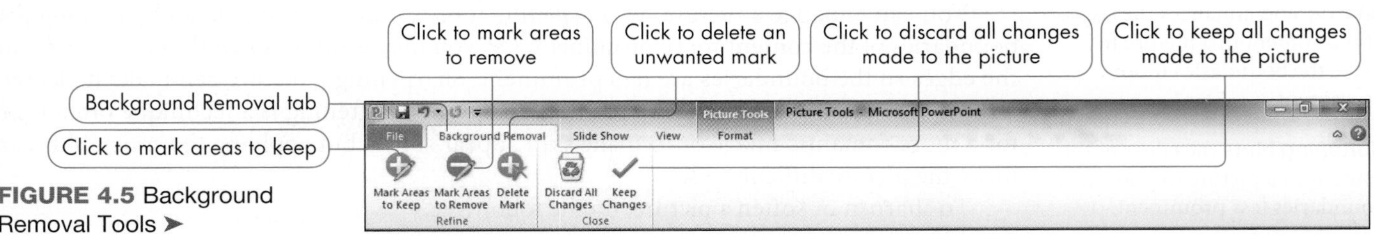

FIGURE 4.5 Background Removal Tools ➤

Use the Mark Areas to Keep tool to add to the foreground, which keeps the area. Use the Mark Areas to Remove tool to add to the background, which eliminates the area. To use both tools, click and drag a line to indicate what should be added or removed. At any time in the process, you can press Esc or click away from the selection to see what the picture looks like. Then you can return to Background Removal and continue working with your picture. Figure 4.6 shows a resized marquee with enlarged areas marked to show areas to keep and to remove. Figure 4.7 shows the flower picture with the background removed.

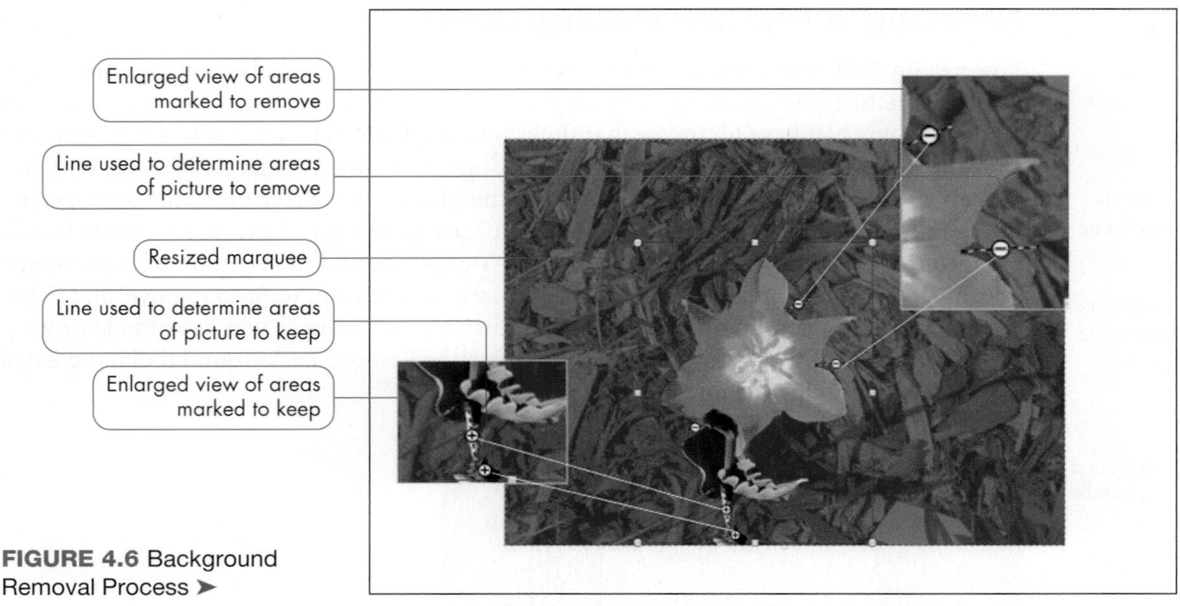

FIGURE 4.6 Background Removal Process ➤

FIGURE 4.7 Background Removed from Flower ➤

Correct a Picture

PowerPoint 2010 includes Corrections, a new set of tools in the Adjust group. As well as being able to adjust brightness and contrast as in previous versions, you can now soften or sharpen a picture. You can see what a correction will look like by previewing it in Live Preview.

Sharpening enhances the edges of the content in a picture to make the boundaries more prominent.

Softening blurs the edges of the content in a picture to make the boundaries less prominent.

You can enhance a picture by ***sharpening*** it or bringing out the detail by making the boundaries of the content more prominent. Or, you may want to ***soften*** the content or blur the edges so the boundaries are less prominent. Sharpening a picture can make it clearer, but oversharpening can make the picture look grainy. Softening is a technique often used for a more romantic image or to make skin appear softer, but applying too much blur can make the picture difficult to see.

To sharpen or soften a picture, do the following:

1. Select the picture.
2. Click the Picture Tools Format tab.
3. Click Corrections in the Adjust group.
4. Point to the thumbnails in the *Sharpen and Soften* section to view the corrections in Live Preview.
5. Click the thumbnail to apply the degree of correction you want.

You can make fine adjustments to the amount of brightness and contrast you apply to a picture. To make adjustments, follow Steps 1–3 above, and then click Picture Corrections Options at the bottom of the gallery. The Format Picture dialog box opens. Drag the Sharpen and Soften slider, or enter a percentage in the box next to the slider. Figure 4.8 shows the Corrections gallery, a picture that has been softened, and a picture that has been sharpened.

FIGURE 4.8 Corrections Gallery and Softened and Sharpened Pictures ➤

Brightness refers to the lightness or darkness of a picture.

The ***brightness*** (lightness or darkness) of a picture is often a matter of individual preference. You might need to change the brightness of your picture for reasons other than preference, however. For example, sometimes printing a picture requires a different brightness than is needed when projecting an image. This situation occurs because during printing, the ink may spread when placed on the page, making the picture darker. Or, you might want a picture as a background and need to reduce the brightness so that text will show on the background.

Contrast refers to the difference between the darkest and lightest areas of a picture.

Contrast refers to the difference between the darkest area (black level) and lightest area (white level). If the contrast is not set correctly, your picture can look washed out or muddy; too much contrast, and the light portion of your image will appear to explode off the screen or page. Your setting may vary depending on whether you are going to project the image or print it. Projecting impacts an image because of the light in the room. In a very light room the image may seem to need a greater contrast than in a darker room, and you may need to adjust the contrast accordingly. Try to set your control for the lighting that will appear when you display the presentation.

To adjust the brightness and contrast of a picture, do the following:

1. Select the picture.
2. Click the Picture Tools Format tab.
3. Click Corrections in the Adjust group.
4. Point to the thumbnails in the *Brightness and Contrast* section to view the corrections in Live Preview.
5. Click the thumbnail to apply the degree of correction you want.

You can make fine adjustments to the amount of sharpening or softening you apply. To make adjustments, follow Steps 1–3 above, and then click Picture Corrections Options at the bottom of the gallery. The Format Picture dialog box opens. Drag the Brightness and Contrast sliders until you get the result you want, or enter percentages in the boxes next to the sliders. Figure 4.9 shows the Format Picture gallery displaying an adjustment for Brightness, an adjustment for Contrast, the original picture, and the adjusted picture.

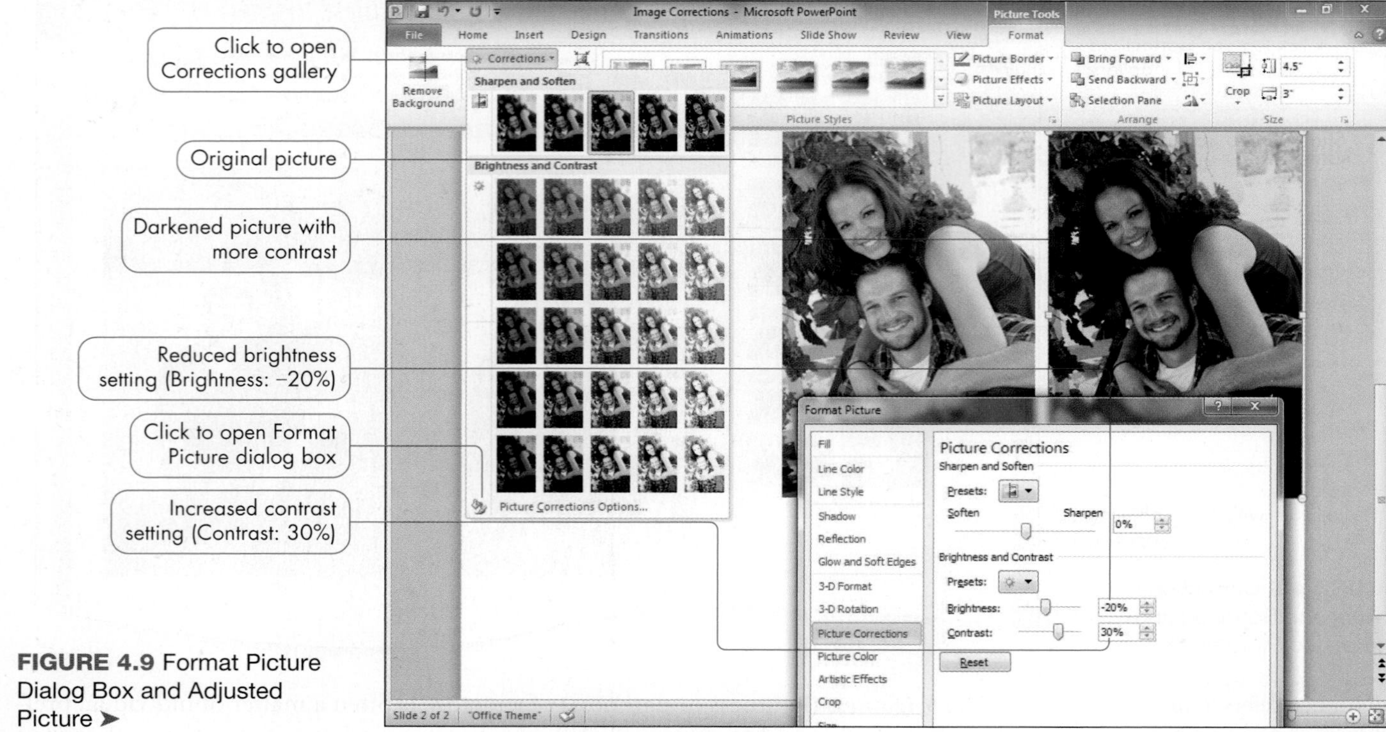

FIGURE 4.9 Format Picture Dialog Box and Adjusted Picture ➤

Change Picture Color

You can change the colors in your picture by using PowerPoint's color tools. To access the color tools, do the following:

1. Select the picture.
2. Click the Picture Tools Format tab.
3. Click Color in the Adjust group.
4. Point to the thumbnails in the gallery to view the corrections in Live Preview.
5. Click the thumbnail to apply the color effect you want.

Saturation refers to the intensity of a color.

You can change a picture's ***saturation***, or the intensity of the colors in an image. A high saturation level makes the colors more vivid, whereas 0% saturation converts the picture to grayscale. Figure 4.10 shows a picture at its original (100%) intensity and with various levels of intensity.

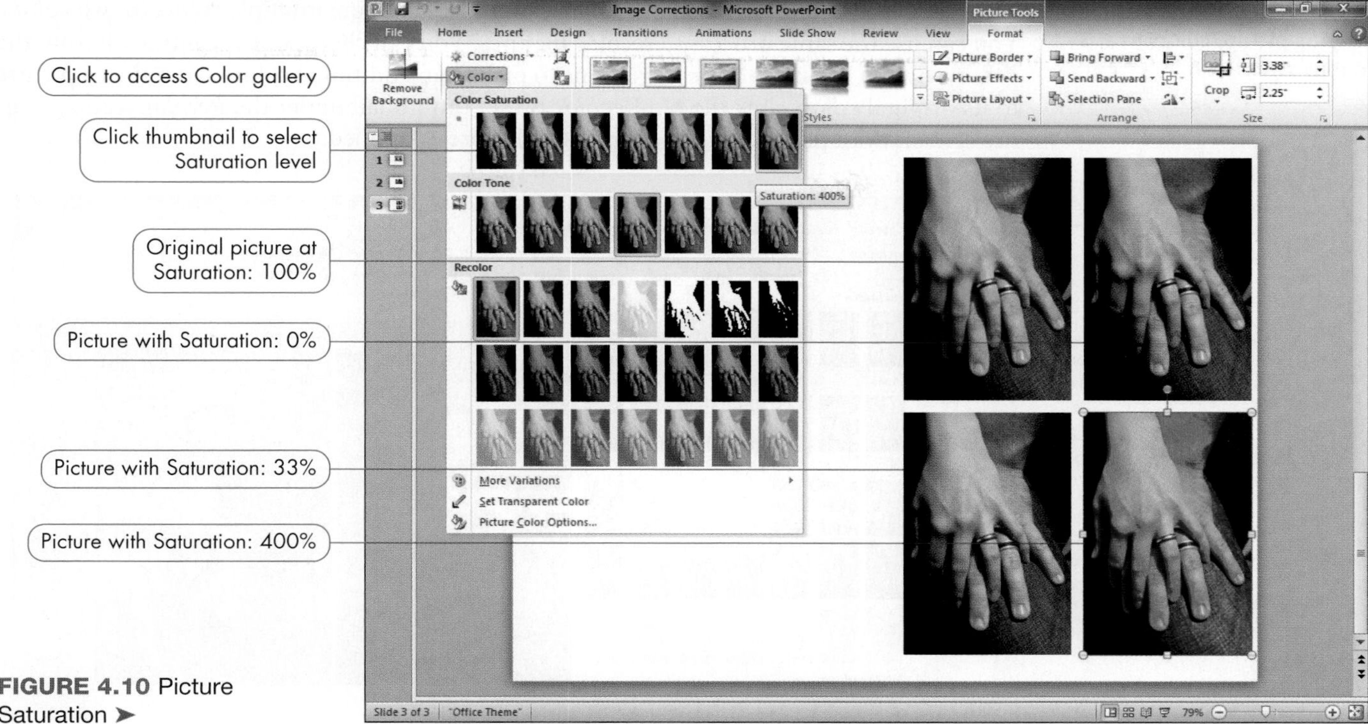

FIGURE 4.10 Picture Saturation ➤

Tone is the temperature of a color.

Kelvin is the unit of measurement for absolute temperature.

The ***tone*** or temperature of a color is a characteristic of lighting in pictures. It is measured in ***kelvin (K)*** units of absolute temperature. Higher color temperatures are cool colors and appear blueish white, whereas lower color temperatures are warm colors and appear yellowish to red. PowerPoint enables you to increase or decrease a picture's temperature to enhance its details. Point to a thumbnail to see the amount of temperature in Kelvin units that would be applied. Figure 4.11 shows a picture with its original cooler tone and a copy of the picture at a higher temperature with a warmer tone.

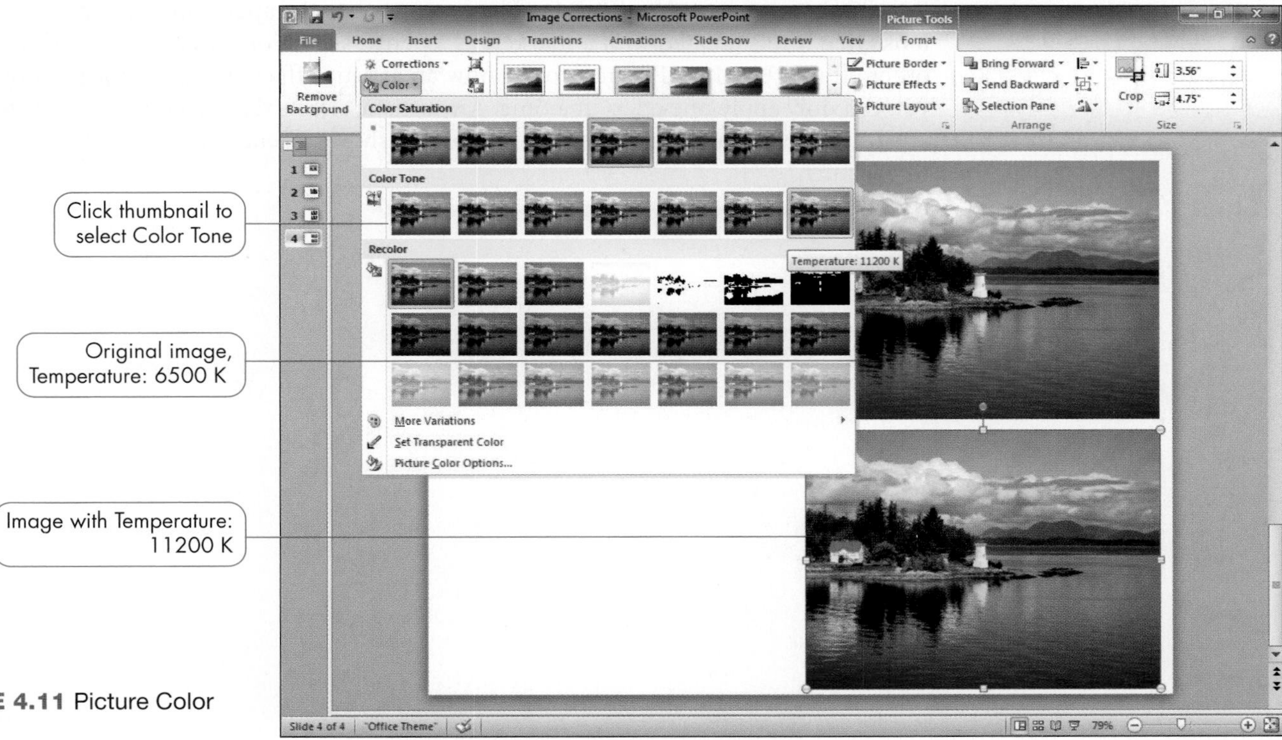

FIGURE 4.11 Picture Color Tone ➤

Recolor is the process of changing picture colors to a duotone style.

Previously you ***recolored*** clip art illustrations by changing multiple colors to two colors. You can use the same process to recolor pictures. You can click a preset thumbnail from the gallery, or you can click More Variations to pick from additional colors. To return a picture to its original color, click the No Recolor preset thumbnail under the *Recolor* section. Figure 4.12 shows a picture with the Sepia Recolor preset applied.

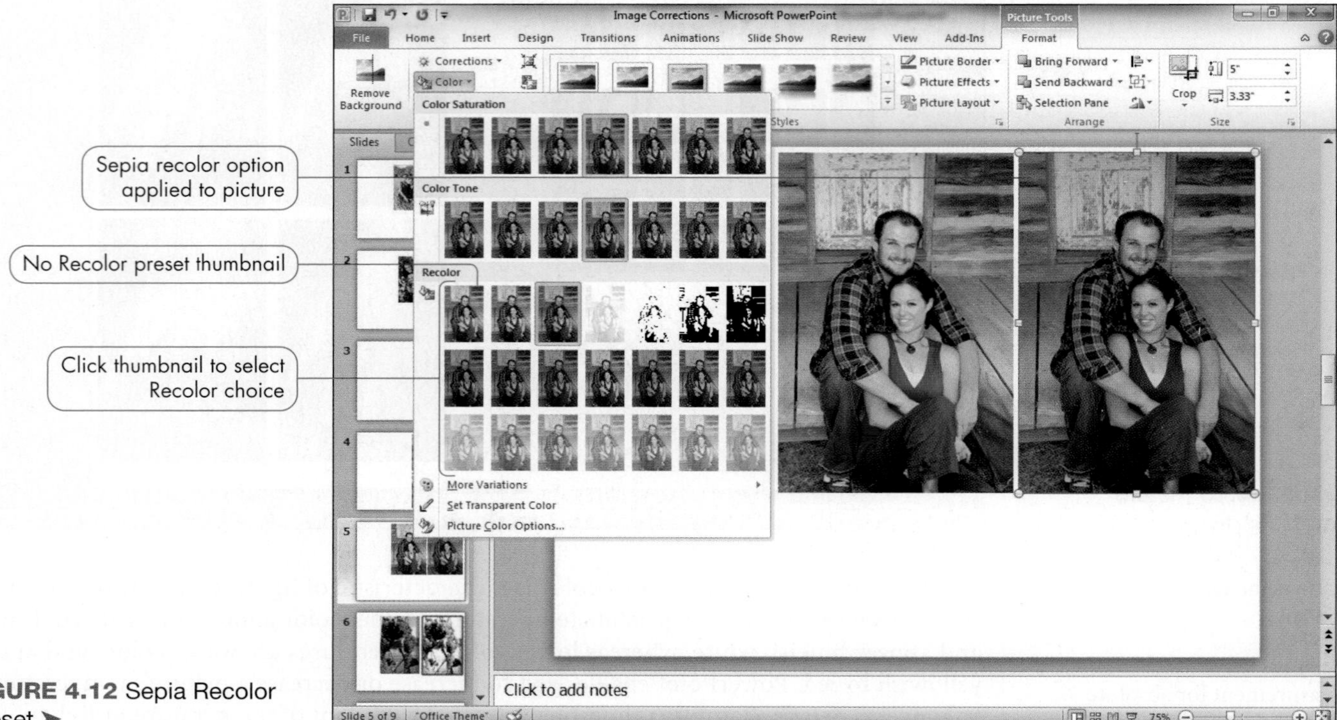

FIGURE 4.12 Sepia Recolor Preset ➤

Use Artistic Effects

PowerPoint's new artistic effects enable you to change the appearance of a picture so that it looks like it was created with a marker, as a pencil sketch or watercolor painting, or using other effects. Use Live Preview to see how an artistic effect changes your picture because you can only apply one effect at a time. Any artistic effects that you have previously applied are lost when you apply a new effect. Figure 4.13 shows a Pencil Sketch artistic effect applied to a picture.

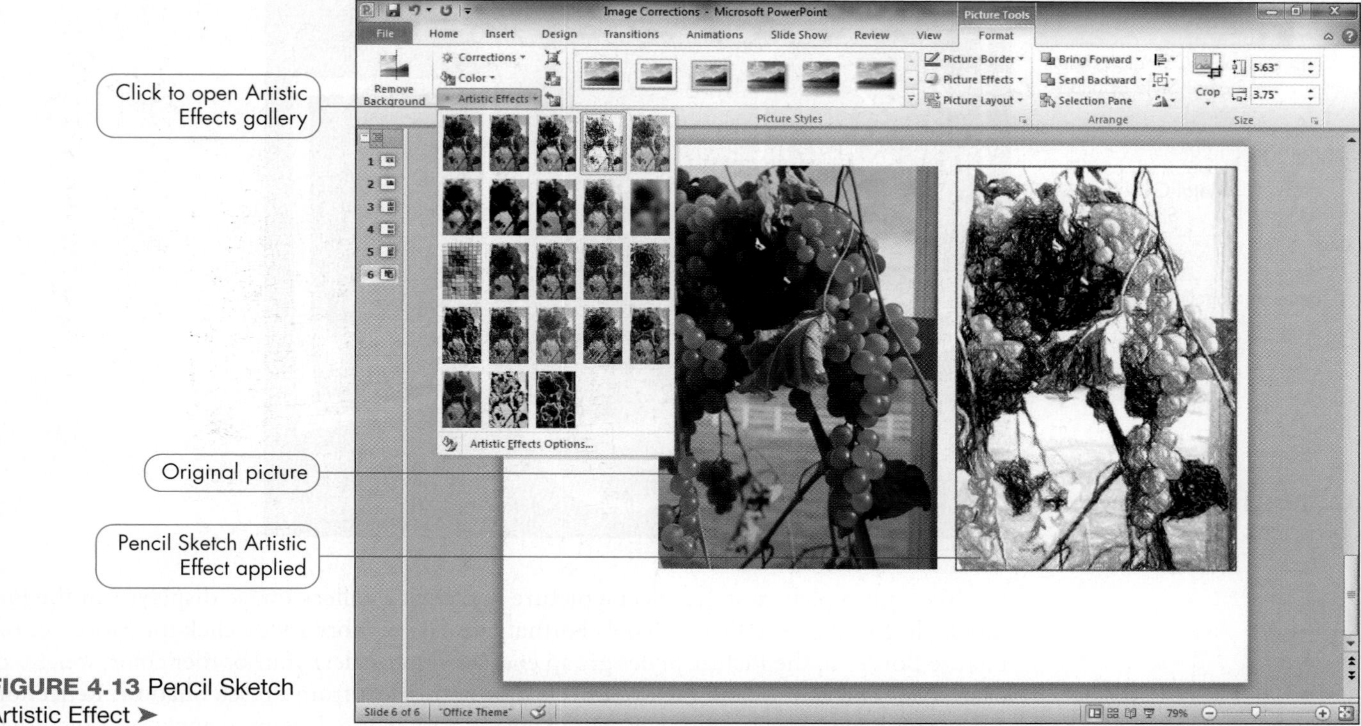

FIGURE 4.13 Pencil Sketch Artistic Effect ➤

To use an artistic effect, do the following:

1. Select the picture.
2. Click the Picture Tools Format tab.
3. Click Artistic Effects in the Adjust group.
4. Point to the thumbnails in the gallery to view the artistic effects in Live Preview.
5. Click the thumbnail of the artistic effect you want to use.

Apply Picture Styles

With Picture Styles, you can surround your picture with attractive frames, soften the edges of pictures, add shadows to the edges of pictures, apply 3-D effects to pictures, and add glossy reflections below your pictures. Many other effects are possible with Picture Styles, and when you consider that each of these effects can be modified, your creative opportunities are endless! Figure 4.14 shows a few of the possibilities.

Many … effects are possible with Picture Styles, and when you consider that each of these effects can be modified, your creative opportunities are endless!

FIGURE 4.14 Picture Style Applications ➤

To apply a picture style, select a picture and click a gallery image displayed in the Picture Style group on the Picture Tools Format tab. To see more styles, click the More button. Picture Border in the Picture Styles group enables you to select your border color, weight, or dash style. You can use the Picture Effects option to select from Preset, Shadow, Reflection, Glow, Soft Edges, Bevel, and 3-D Rotation effects. Use Picture Layout to apply your picture to a SmartArt diagram.

Crop a Picture

Cropping is the process of eliminating unwanted portions of an image from view.

Cropping a picture using the Crop tool lets you eliminate unwanted portions of an image from view, focusing the viewer's attention on what you want him or her to see. Remember that if you crop an image and try to enlarge the resulting picture, pixelation may occur that reduces the quality of the image. Figure 4.15 shows a picture with the areas to be cropped from view displayed in gray.

FIGURE 4.15 Use Crop to Focus Attention ➤

To crop a picture, do the following:

1. Select the picture.
2. Click the Picture Tools Format tab.
3. Click the Crop tool in the Size group.
4. Position the cropping tool over a cropping handle and drag inward to eliminate the portion of the image you do not want to view. Use a corner handle to crop in two directions at once.
5. Repeat Step 4 for the remaining sides of the picture.
6. Click the Crop tool.

When you crop a picture, the cropped part does not display on the slide, but it is not removed from the presentation file. This is helpful in case you decide later to reset the picture to its original state. When you crop an image, because the unwanted portions of the image are not deleted, the file size is not reduced. Use the Compress Pictures feature to reduce the file size of the image, or all images at once, to reduce the file size of the presentation.

Compress Pictures

When you add pictures to your PowerPoint presentation, especially high-resolution pictures downloaded from a digital camera, the presentation file size dramatically increases. It may increase to the point that the presentation becomes slow to load and sluggish to play. The increase in the file size depends on the resolution of the pictures you add. Use the Compress Pictures feature to eliminate a large part of this problem. The Compress Pictures feature is in the Adjust group in the Picture Tools Format tab.

The Compress Pictures option can help you manage large image files by changing the resolution of pictures and by permanently deleting any cropped areas of a selected picture. By default, you apply compression to only the selected image. If you remove the check, all pictures in the presentation are compressed. You select the amount of compression applied by determining your output. Select 220 pixels per inch (ppi) to ensure you will obtain a good quality printout. Select 150 ppi, however, if you will only be displaying the slide show onscreen or using it for a Web page. Select 96 ppi if you plan to e-mail the slide show. Figure 4.16 shows the Compress Pictures dialog box.

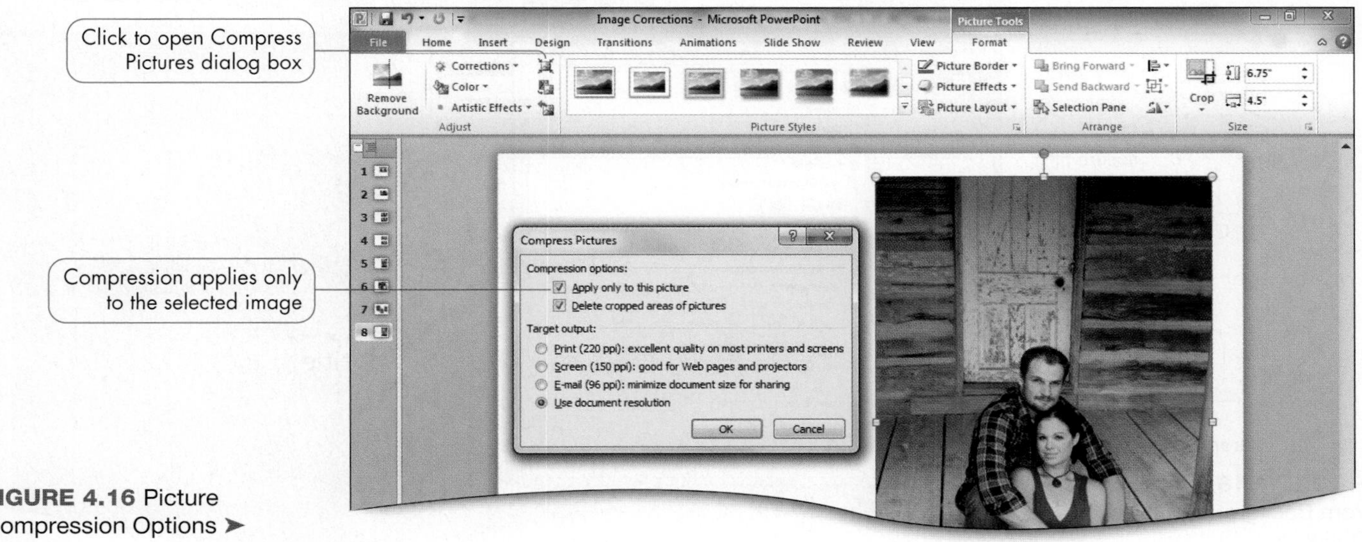

FIGURE 4.16 Picture Compression Options ➤

Create a Background from a Picture

Pictures can make appealing backgrounds if they are transparent enough that text on top of them can be easily read. Picture backgrounds personalize your presentation. To use a photograph as a background, use the Format Background command rather than the Insert Picture feature. Using Insert Picture involves more time because when the picture is inserted it must be resized and the order of the objects on the screen has to be changed to prevent the photograph from hiding placeholders. Figure 4.17 shows an image inserted using Insert Picture that must be resized if it is to be used as a background. It hides the placeholders, so it needs to be positioned at the back and its transparency must be adjusted. Figure 4.18 shows the same picture as Figure 4.17, but in this figure, it was inserted as a background. It is automatically placed behind placeholders and resized to fit the slide, and the transparency is adjusted.

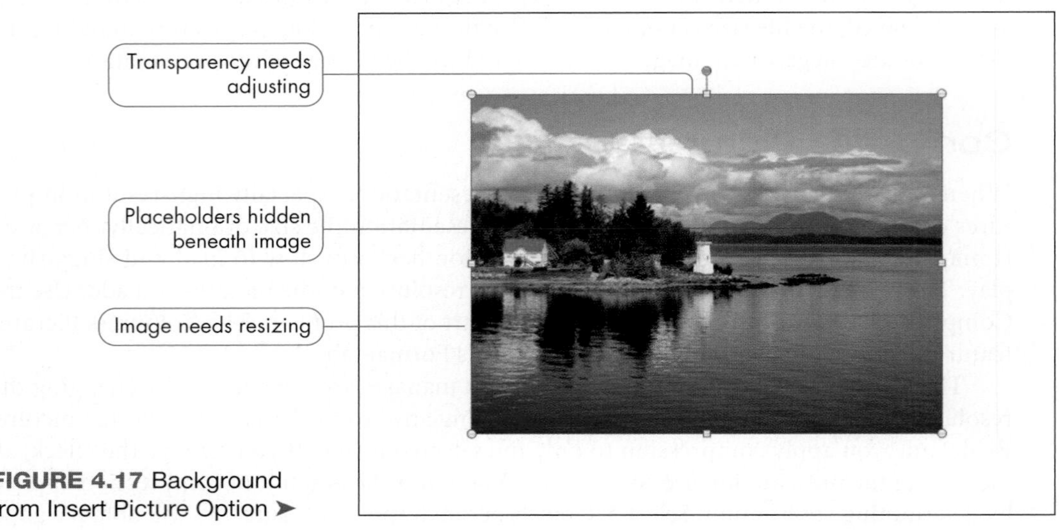

FIGURE 4.17 Background from Insert Picture Option ➤

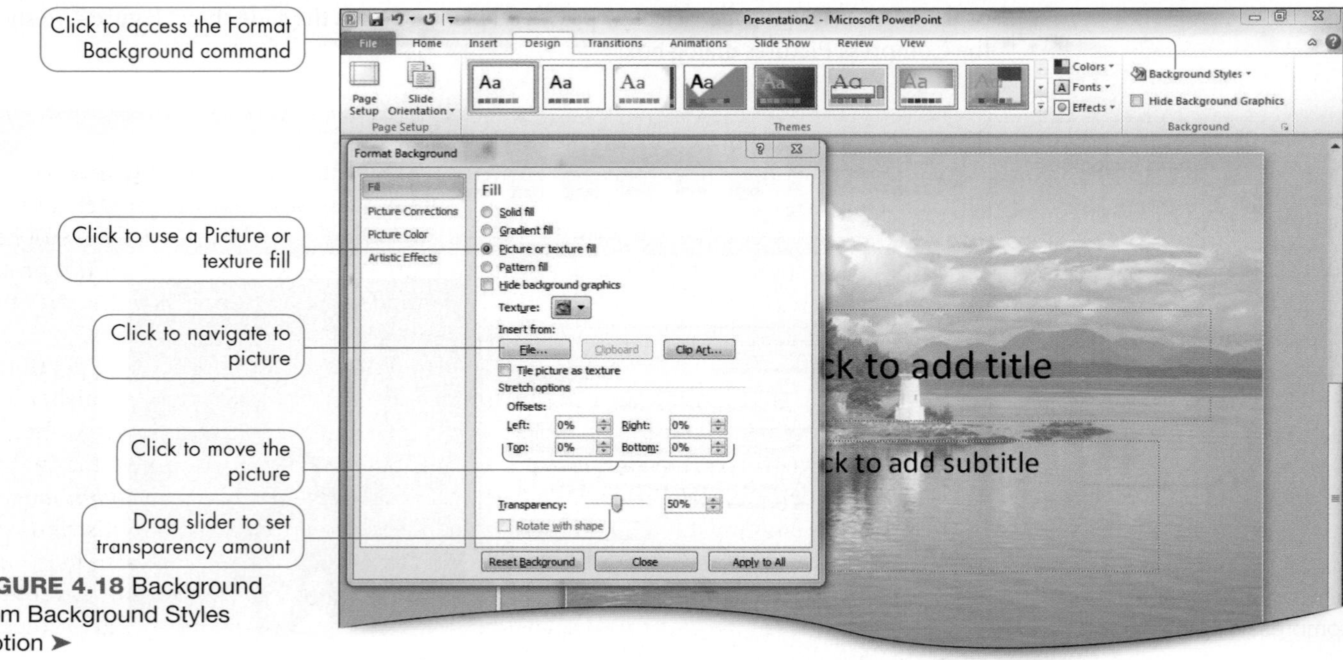

FIGURE 4.18 Background from Background Styles Option ➤

To create a background from a picture using the Background command, do the following:

1. Click the Design tab.
2. Click Background Styles in the Background group.
3. Select Format Background, and then click the Fill category.
4. Click *Picture or texture fill.*
5. Click File, and then navigate to the location where your picture is stored.
6. Click the picture file, and then click Insert.
7. Click Close to apply the picture background to the current slide, or click Apply to All to apply it to all slides in the presentation.

The dialog box also includes options for moving the picture by offsetting it to the left or right or the top or bottom, and for adjusting the transparency amount.

Using the Internet as a Resource

PowerPoint interacts with the Internet in three important ways. First, you can download resources from any Web page for inclusion in a PowerPoint presentation. Second, you can insert hyperlinks into a PowerPoint presentation, and then click those links to display the associated Web page in your browser. Finally, you can convert any PowerPoint presentation into a Web page. Be sure to check for copyright permissions and to give credit to sources. In this chapter, you will use the Internet as a resource for pictures, video, and audio.

Regardless of how you choose to use a photograph, your first task is to access the Web and locate the required image. After you choose an image, right-click it to display a shortcut menu, and then select Save Picture As to download the file to your hard drive. When you right-click the photograph, you can also select Copy to copy the picture onto the Clipboard.

To insert a downloaded picture in PowerPoint, click the Insert tab, and then click Picture in the Images group. If you copied the picture, simply paste it onto the slide. You also can click Insert Hyperlink in the Links group on the Insert tab to insert a hyperlink to the resource Web site. You can click the hyperlink during the slide show, and provided you have an Internet connection, your browser will display the associated page.

Understand Copyright Protection

Copyright is the legal protection afforded to a written or artistic work.

A ***copyright*** provides legal protection to a written or artistic work, including literary, dramatic, musical, and artistic works such as poetry, novels, movies, songs, computer software, and architecture. It gives the author of a work the exclusive right to the use and duplication of that work. A copyright does not protect facts, ideas, systems, or methods of operation, although it may protect the way these things are expressed.

Anything on the Internet should be considered copyrighted unless the site specifically says it is in the public domain....

Infringement of copyright occurs when a right of the copyright owner is violated.

Public domain refers to rights to a literary work or property owned by the public at large.

The owner of the copyright may sell or give up a portion of his or her rights; for example, an author may give distribution rights to a publisher and/or grant movie rights to a studio. ***Infringement of copyright*** occurs anytime a right held by the copyright owner is violated without permission of the owner. Anything on the Internet should be considered copyrighted unless th`e site specifically says it is in the ***public domain***, in which case the author is giving everyone the right to freely reproduce and distribute the material, thereby making the work owned by the public at large. A work also may enter the public domain when the copyright has expired. Facts themselves are not covered by copyright, so you can use statistical data without fear of infringement. Images are protected unless the owner gives his or her permission for downloading.

Using Microsoft Media Elements

Photos, clip art, fonts, sounds, and movies available from Microsoft are part of Microsoft's Media Elements and are copyright protected by Microsoft. To see what uses of Media Elements are prohibited, access Help, type the keyword *copyright*, and then press Enter. From the available links, click What is Clip Organizer? Scroll down and review the list of prohibited uses in the *WHAT USES OF PHOTOS, CLIP ART, AND FONT IMAGES ARE PROHIBITED* section.

The answer to what you can use from the Web depends on many things, including the amount of the information you reference, as well as the intended use of that information. It is considered fair use, and thus not an infringement of copyright, to use a portion of a work for educational or nonprofit purposes, or for critical review or commentary. In other words, you can use quotes, facts, or other information from the Web in an educational setting, but you should cite the original work in your footnotes, or list the resource on a bibliography page or slide. The Reference table below presents guidelines for students and teachers to help determine what multimedia can be used in an educational project based on the Proposal for Fair Use Guidelines for Educational Multimedia created in 1996. These guidelines were created by a group of publishers, authors, and educators who gathered to interpret the Copyright Act of 1976 as it applies to educational and scholarly uses of multimedia. You should note that although these guidelines are part of the Congressional Record, they are not law. They can, however, help you determine when you can use multimedia materials under Fair Use principles in a non-commercial, educational use.

REFERENCE Multimedia Copyright Guidelines for Students and Teachers

The following guidelines are based on Section 107 of the U.S. Copyright Act of 1976 and the Proposal for Fair Use Guidelines for Educational Multimedia (1996), which sets forth fair use factors for multimedia projects. These guidelines cover the use of multimedia based on Time, Portion, and Copying and Distribution Limitations. For the complete text of the guidelines, see www.uspto.gov/web/offices/dcom/olia/confu/confurep.pdf.

General Guidelines

- Student projects for specific courses may be displayed and kept in personal portfolios as examples of their academic work.
- Students in specific courses may use multimedia in projects with proper credit and citations. Full bibliographic information must be used when available.
- Students and teachers must display copyright notice if copyright ownership information is shown on the original source. Copyright may be shown in a sources or bibliographic section unless the presentation is being used for distance learning. In distance learning situations, copyright must appear on the screen when the image is viewed.
- Teachers may use media for face-to-face curriculum-based instruction, for directed self-study, in demonstrations on how to create multimedia productions, for presentations at conferences, and for distance learning. Teachers may also retain projects in their personal portfolios for personal use such as job interviews or tenure review.
- Teachers may use multimedia projects for educational purposes for up to two years, after which permission of the copyright holder is required.
- Students and teachers do not need to write for permission to use media if it falls under multimedia guidelines unless there is a possibility that the project could be broadly distributed at a later date.

(*Continued*)

REFERENCE Multimedia Copyright Guidelines for Students and Teachers (*Continued*)

Text Guidelines

- Up to 10 percent of a copyrighted work, or up to 1000 words, may be used, whichever is less.
- Up to 250 words of a poem, but no more than five poems (or excerpts) from different poets or an anthology. No more than three poems (or excerpts) from a single poet.

Illustrations

- A photograph or illustration may be used in its entirety.
- Up to 15 images, but no more than 15 images from a collection.
- No more than 5 images of an artist's or photographer's work.

Motion Media

- Up to 10 percent of a copyrighted work or 3 minutes, whichever is less.
- Clip cannot be altered in any way.

Music and Sound

- Up to 10 percent of a copyrighted musical composition, not to exceed 30 seconds.
- Up to 10 percent of a sound recording, not to exceed 30 seconds.
- Alterations cannot change the basic melody or fundamental character of the work.

Distribution Limitations

- Multimedia projects should not be posted to unsecured Web sites.
- No more than two copies of the original may be made, only one of which may be placed on reserve for instructional purposes.
- A copy of a project may be made for backup purposes, but may be used only when the original has been lost, damaged, or stolen.
- If more than one person created a project, each person may keep only one copy.

In the following Hands-On Exercise, you will insert pictures (bitmap images) into slides, both with and without using content placeholders. You will use Picture Tools to remove a background from an image, to soften and sharpen an image, and to adjust the brightness, contrast, saturation, and tone of a picture. You will apply a picture style and modify its effects. You will crop a picture and compress all the images in the slide show. You will also create a background for a slide from a picture. Finally, you will learn about using the Internet as a resource for images and review the Fair Use guidelines relating to student use of media downloaded from the Internet. You will download a picture from the Internet and insert the picture into a slide show.

Quick Concepts Check

1. What is the difference between bitmap images and vector graphics? Name one advantage and disadvantage of each type of graphic.
2. Why would you compress an image?
3. List five ways to transform an image by using PowerPoint's Picture Tools?
4. What is infringement of copyright? What is "fair use?"

HANDS-ON EXERCISES

1 Pictures

You decide to create a memories slide show for your sister and her husband, who were recently married. You include their high school Sweetheart Ball image, engagement and wedding pictures, and a picture to remind them of scuba diving on their honeymoon.

Skills covered: Insert Pictures and Remove a Background • Apply an Artistic Effect and a Picture Style • Correct a Picture and Change Picture Color • Crop and Compress Pictures • Create a Background from a Picture • Insert a Picture from the Internet

STEP 1 INSERT PICTURES AND REMOVE A BACKGROUND

You start the memory album with a picture from the couple's Sweetheart Ball. Because the Title Slide layout does not include a placeholder for content, you add a picture using the Insert Picture from File feature. You then insert images into content placeholders provided in the album layout. Refer to Figure 4.19 as you complete Step 1.

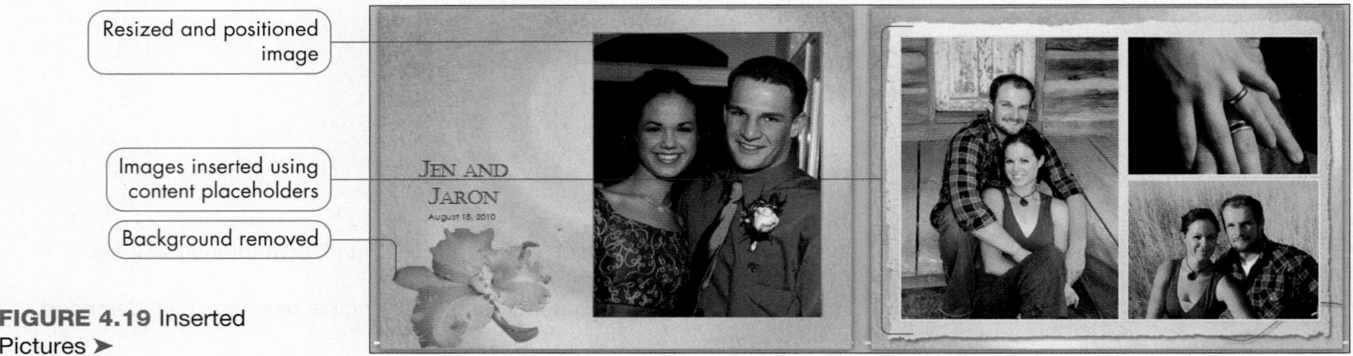

FIGURE 4.19 Inserted Pictures ➤

a. Open the *p04h1memory* presentation, and then save it as **p04h1memory_LastnameFirstname**. Use your last and first names. For example, as the PowerPoint author, I would name my workbook "p04h1memory_KrebsCynthia."

> **TROUBLESHOOTING:** If you make any major mistakes in this exercise, you can close the file, open *p04h1memory* again, and then start this exercise over.

b. Create a handout header with your name, and a handout footer with your instructor's name and your class. Include the current date.

c. On Slide 1, click the **Insert tab**, and then click **Picture** in the Images group.

   You add a picture using the Insert Picture from File command because the Title Slide layout does not include a placeholder for content. The Insert Picture dialog box opens.

d. Locate the *p04h1mem1.jpg* file in the *p04h1_3memory_media* folder, and then click **Insert**.

   The picture is inserted, sized to fit within the slide margins, and centered on the slide.

e. Click the **Size Dialog Box Launcher** in the Size group on the Picture Tools Format tab to open the Format Picture dialog box. Click in the **Height box** in the *Scale* section, select **100**, and then type **90**. Click in the **Width box** in the *Scale* section, and it will change to *90%* automatically.

   Typing 90 in the Height box automatically sets the scale for Width to 90% because the *Lock aspect ratio* check box is selected.

f. Click **Position** in the Format Picture dialog box, and then set the **Position on slide Horizontal option** to **4.5**" from the Top Left Corner. Set the **Position on slide Vertical option** to **.5**" from the Top Left Corner. Click **Close**.

g. Click the **Insert tab**, click **Picture** in the Images group, and then locate and insert *p04h1mem2.jpg.*

   The picture fills the slide. It is selected, and the Picture Tools Format tab is active.

h. Click **Remove Background** in the Adjust group.

   An automatic marquee appears around the image that includes most of the flower. Some petals are cut off and need to be added back in.

i. Drag the top-center sizing handle of the marquee to the top of the image.

   The top petal is now included in the marquee.

j. Drag the left-center and bottom-center sizing handles of the marquee until all petals are included in the picture (see Figure 4.20).

FIGURE 4.20 Adjusted Marquee ➤

k. Click **Keep Changes**.

   The background is removed from the flower.

l. Click the **Size Dialog Box Launcher** in the Size group to open the Format Picture dialog box, and then remove the check in the **Relative to original picture size checkbox** in the *Scale* section. Click in the **Height box**, and then type **40**. Click in the **Width box** in the *Scale* section, and it will change to *40%* automatically.

m. Click the **Position tab** in the Format Picture dialog box, and then set the **Position on slide Horizontal option** to **0.17**" from the Top Left Corner. Set the **Position on slide Vertical option** to **4.83**" from the Top Left Corner. Click **Close**.

n. On Slide 2, click **Insert Picture from File** in the large content placeholder on the left side of the slide. Click the *p04h1mem3.jpg* file to select it, and then click **Insert**.

o. Use the **Insert Picture from File buttons** in the two small content placeholders on the right side of the screen to insert *p04h1mem4.jpg* and *p04h1mem5.jpg* into your presentation.

   Note that in all three cases the images were centered inside the placeholders. The picture of the hands is cropped because it was in portrait orientation but placed in a landscape placeholder.

p. Save the presentation.

STEP 2 APPLY AN ARTISTIC EFFECT AND A PICTURE STYLE

The title slide includes a picture of the couple that you want to stand out. The Artistic Effects gallery includes many picture effects, and the Picture Styles gallery includes a variety of Picture Border effects. You decide to experiment with the options available in the galleries to see the impact they have on the title slide picture. You apply an artistic effect and a picture style. Refer to Figure 4.21 as you complete Step 2.

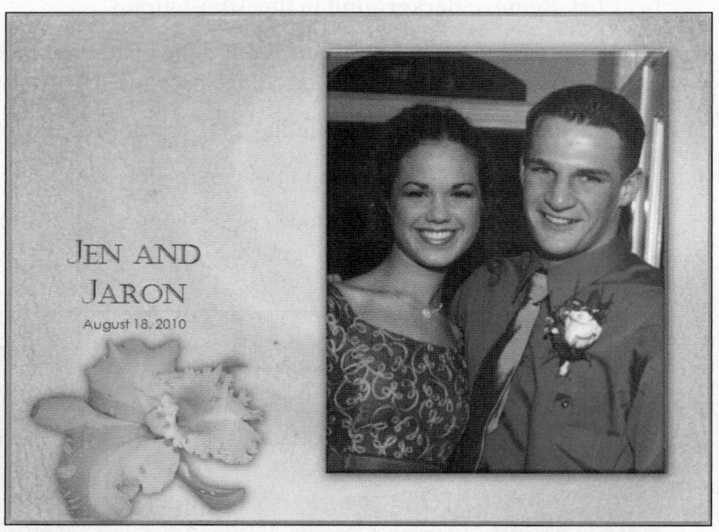

FIGURE 4.21 Applied Artistic Effect and Picture Styles ➤

a. On Slide 1, select the picture of the couple, and then click the **Picture Tools Format tab**.

b. Click **Artistic Effects** in the Adjust group.

   The Artistic Effects gallery opens. Point to the effects, and watch how each effect impacts the image.

   TROUBLESHOOTING: Some of the artistic effects involve extensive changes, so expect a slowdown as the preview is created.

c. Click **Texturizer** (fourth row, second column).

   A light texture is applied to the picture.

d. Click the **More button** in the Picture Styles group.

   The Picture Styles gallery opens. Point to the styles and watch how each style impacts the image.

e. Click **Center Shadow Rectangle** (third row, first column).

   A gray shadow appears evenly around the picture.

f. Click the **Home tab**, click **Format Painter**, and then click the flower picture.

   You copied the artistic effect and picture style and then applied it to the flower.

g. Select the picture of the couple again, and then click the **Picture Tools Format tab**.

h. Click **Picture Border** in the Picture Styles group, and then click **White, Accent 3, Darker 10%** (second row, seventh column) in the *Theme Colors* section.

i. Click **Picture Effects** in the Picture Styles group, point to **Bevel**, and then click **Cool Slant** (first row, fourth column of the *Bevel* section).

   The Bevel effect is applied to the outer edges of the picture.

j. Save the presentation.

STEP 3 CORRECT A PICTURE AND CHANGE PICTURE COLOR

You want to include two pictures of the couple in the memory album, but the pictures were taken in different lighting conditions. You decide to use PowerPoint's correction tools to enhance the pictures. You also change the color of a picture to match the cool-toned blue theme of the presentation. Refer to Figure 4.22 as you complete Step 3.

FIGURE 4.22 Applied Artistic Effect and Picture Styles ➤

a. On Slide 3, use **Insert Picture from File** in the content placeholders to insert *p04h1mem6.jpg* into the left placeholder and *p04h1mem7.jpg* into the right placeholder.

b. Select the image on the left, and then click **Corrections** in the Adjust group on the Picture Tools Format tab. Click **Brightness: −20% Contrast: +20%** (fourth row, second column of the *Brightness and Contrast* section).

   The image became slightly darker, and the increased contrast brings out the picture detail.

c. Select the image on the right, and then click **Corrections** in the Adjust group on the Picture Tools Format tab. Click **Brightness: +20% Contrast: −40%** (first row, fourth column of the *Brightness and Contrast* section).

   The image became brighter, and the contrast is reduced.

d. On Slide 4, select the picture of the bride.

e. Click **Color** in the Adjust group, and then click **Temperature: 4700 K** in the Color Tone gallery.

   The warm tones in the image are converted to cooler tones, which casts a blue hue over the picture.

f. Click the **More button** in the Picture Styles group, and then click **Soft Edge Oval** (fourth row, second column).

g. Save the presentation.

STEP 4 CROP AND COMPRESS PICTURES

You have included pictures of the groom dancing with the flower girl but decide to crop one image. You compress the image to delete the unwanted areas. You also compress all images in the slide show to reduce the file size of the slide show. Refer to Figure 4.23 as you complete Step 4.

FIGURE 4.23 Cropped and Compressed Pictures ➤

a. On Slide 6, examine the picture on the far right of the slide.

   Because the picture was framed with a window in the background, the light is a bright, white distraction. You decide to crop a portion of the window from view.

b. Click the **View tab**, and then click **Ruler** in the Show group, if necessary.

   Activating the ruler will make it easier for you to determine the area to crop.

TROUBLESHOOTING: The rulers are a toggle feature, so if yours are already displayed, skip step b or repeat it to redisplay the rulers if you closed them.

c. Select the large picture on the far right, click the **Picture Tools Format tab**, and then click **Crop** in the Size group.

d. Position the Crop tool over the right center cropping handle, and then drag inward until the guiding line on the vertical ruler reaches the +41/4" mark.

   The resulting size of the image is 7.5" high and 4.29" wide.

e. Click **Crop** in the Size group again to crop the area from view and to turn off the Crop feature.

f. Select the top-left picture, and then click the **Home tab**. Click **Format Painter**, and then click the picture you just cropped on the far right of the slide.

   The picture style is copied onto the cropped picture.

g. Select the cropped picture, and then click the **Picture Tools Format tab**.

h. Click **Compress Pictures** in the Adjust group.

   The Compress Pictures dialog box opens.

i. Click **Screen** in the *Target output* section.

j. Click the **Apply only to this picture check box** to deselect it.

   You need to compress all the pictures you have used in the presentation to reduce the presentation file size, not just the selected picture.

k. Click **OK**.

   The portions of the image that were cropped from view are deleted, and all pictures in the slide show are compressed.

l. Save the presentation.

STEP 5 CREATE A BACKGROUND FROM A PICTURE

The bride chose orchids for her table decorations, and you want to include a picture of one of the orchids as the background setting of a picture of the bride and groom. Refer to Figure 4.24 as you complete Step 5.

FIGURE 4.24 Background from a Picture ➤

a. Click the **Design tab**.

b. On Slide 5, click **Background Styles** in the Background group, and then select **Format Background**.

c. Click the **Hide background graphics check box** in the Format Background dialog box.

d. Click **Picture or texture fill**, and then click **File** to open the Insert Picture dialog box.

e. Select *p04h1mem2.jpg*, click **Insert**, and then click **Close**.

> **TROUBLESHOOTING:** If the orchid is not displayed, it may be blocked by the background graphics. Click the Hide Background Graphics check box in the Background group on the Design tab.

f. Save the presentation.

STEP 6 INSERT A PICTURE FROM THE INTERNET

CREATIVE CASE 

The couple went scuba diving in Cancun, Mexico, during their honeymoon so you want to insert a picture of an underwater scene to end the slide show. You insert an image from Image*After, a Web site that provides pictures free for personal or commercial use. Refer to Figure 4.25 as you complete Step 6.

FIGURE 4.25 Hyperlink to imageafter.com ➤

a. On Slide 7, note the text *Image*After* (imageafter.com) is a hyperlink.

The hyperlink will display if you view the presentation in Slide Show view.

b. Right-click the link, and then select **Open Hyperlink** to launch the Web site in your default browser.

> **TROUBLESHOOTING:** If you are not connected to the Internet, the hyperlink will not work. Connect to the Internet, and then repeat step b.

The Image*After Web site displays the nature-underwater group and shows thumbnails of images pertaining to underwater views.

c. Point, without clicking, to each thumbnail to see a bigger image.

d. Click the thumbnail of your choice to display a larger image. Right-click the image, select **Copy**, and then close the browser.

e. On Slide 7, paste the image using the **Picture paste option**.

f. Adjust the image size, depending on the size of the image you insert.

g. Drag the picture to position it on the slide, leaving the Image*After text box visible.

The Image*After text box should be visible to give credit to the image source.

h. Save the presentation, close the file, and then exit PowerPoint if you do not want to continue with the next Hands-On Exercise at this time.

Video

With video added to your project, you can greatly enhance and reinforce your story, and your audience can retain more of what they see. For example, a video of water tumbling over a waterfall would stir the emotions of a viewer far more than a table listing the number of gallons of water falling within a designated period of time. Anytime you can engage a viewer's emotions, he or she will better remember your message.

With video added to your project, you can greatly enhance and reinforce your story, and your audience can retain more of what they see.

In this section, you will learn the types of video file formats that PowerPoint supports, examine the options available when using video, and insert a video clip into the memories presentation.

Adding Video

Table 4.2 displays the common types of movie file formats you can add to a presentation listed in alphabetical order by file extension. Different file formats use different types of ***codec*** (coder/decoder) software, which use algorithms to compress or code movies, and then decompress or decode the movies for playback. Video playback places tremendous demand on your computer system in terms of processing speed and memory. Using a codec reduces that demand. In order for your video file to be viewed correctly, the video player must have the appropriate software installed. Even though your video file extension is the same as the one listed in Table 4.2 or in Help, the video may not play correctly if the correct version of the codec software is not installed.

A **codec** (coder/decoder) is a digital video compression scheme used to compress a video and decompress for playback.

TABLE 4.2 Types of Video File Formats Supported by PowerPoint

File Format	Extension	Description
Windows Media File	.asf	**Advanced Streaming Format** Stores synchronized multimedia data. Used to stream audio and video content, images, and script commands over a network.
Windows Video File	.avi	**Audio Video Interleave** Stores sound and moving pictures in Microsoft Resource Interchange File Format (RIFF).
Movie File	.mpg or .mpeg	**Moving Picture Experts Group** Evolving set of standards for video and audio compression developed by the Moving Picture Experts Group. Designed specifically for use with Video-CD and CD-i media.
Adobe Flash Media	.swf	**Flash Video** File format generally used to deliver video over the Internet. Uses Adobe Flash Player.
Windows Media Video File	.wmv	**Windows Media Video** Compresses audio and video by using Windows Media Video compressed format. Requires minimal amount of storage space on your computer's hard drive.

TIP Using Videos from the Clip Art Pane

Video clips available from the Clip Art pane are animated GIF files containing multiple images that stream to create motion. Although animated GIF files technically are not videos, Microsoft includes them in the Clip Art pane because the animations use motion to tell a story.

To **embed** is to store an object from an external source within a presentation.

To **link** is to establish a connection from a presentation to another location.

When you add video to your presentation, you can ***embed*** the video or store the video within the presentation, or you can ***link*** the video, which creates a connection from the presentation to another location such as a storage device or Web site. The advantage of embedding video is that a copy of the video file is placed in the slide so moving or deleting the original video will not impact your presentation. The advantage of linking a video file is that your presentation file size is smaller. A linked video is stored in its own file. Another advantage of linking over embedding is that the presentation video is updated automatically if the original video object is changed. One caution for using a linked video—the video is not part of the presentation, and if you save the presentation file to a different location, such as a flash drive, you must make sure you save the video to the new location, too. If you change the location of the video, you must make sure to change the link to the movie file in the presentation.

To insert or link a video in a presentation, do the following:

1. Click the Insert tab
2. Click the Video arrow in the Media group.
3. Click Video from File.
4. Browse, locate, and select the video you want to use in the presentation.
5. Click Insert to insert the video in your presentation, or click the Insert arrow and select Link to File to link the video to your presentation.

You can also embed video from an online video site such as YouTube. When you embed video from the online site, you have to copy and paste the Embed code from the online site into the Video from Web Site dialog box. Figure 4.26 shows the Embed code for the video in Figure 4.27 inserted into PowerPoint's Video from Web Site dialog box. Figure 4.27 shows a Commoncraft Video stored on YouTube (used with permission) and the location of the Embed code. If you have embedded video from an online site, you must be connected to the Internet when you display the presentation.

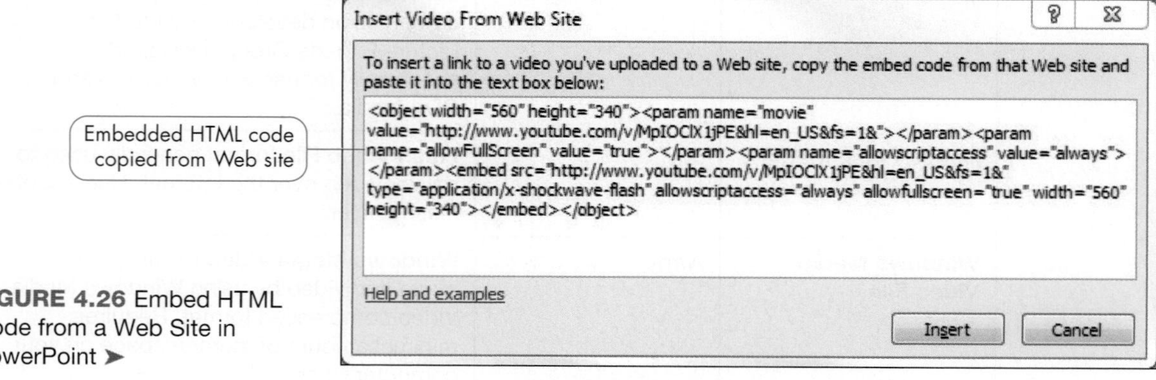

FIGURE 4.26 Embed HTML Code from a Web Site in PowerPoint ➤

FIGURE 4.27 Location of the Embed Code on YouTube ➤

To insert video from an online video site, do the following:

1. Locate video on an online video site.
2. Copy embedding code.
3. Click Insert tab in PowerPoint.
4. Click the Video arrow in the Media group.
5. Click Video from Web Site.
6. Paste the embedded HTML code into the box.
7. Click Insert.

Whether you have inserted your own video or video from a Web site, the video will include a Media Controls bar with a Play/Pause button, a Move Back 0.25 seconds button, a Move Forward 0.25 seconds button, a time notation, and a Mute/Unmute control slider. The Move Back and Move Forward 0.25 seconds buttons aid you when editing the video. The Media Controls bar is shown in Figure 4.28.

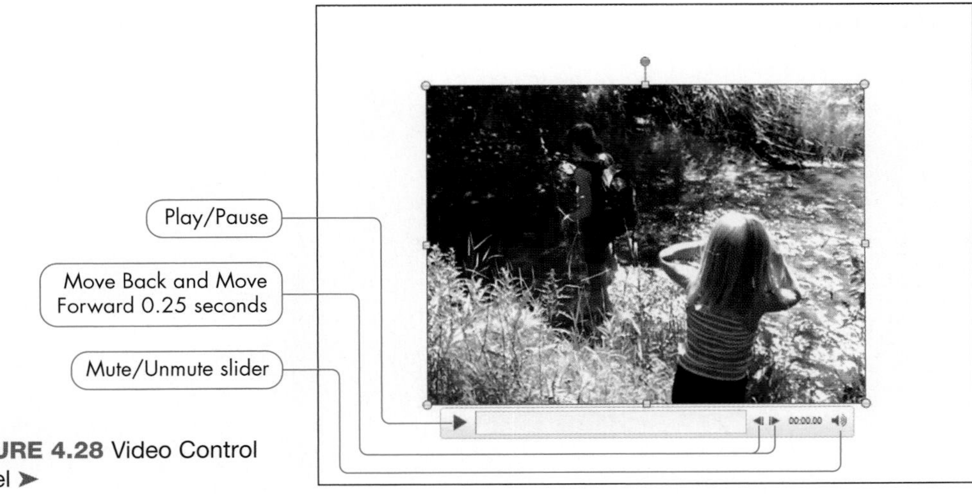

FIGURE 4.28 Video Control Panel ➤

Using Video Tools

PowerPoint 2010 includes wonderful new tools for working with video. You can format the video's brightness and contrast, color, and style. You can apply most artistic image effects, add or remove bookmarks, trim the video, and set fade in or fade out effects. When you select an inserted video, the Video Tools tab displays with two tabs: the Format tab and the Playback tab.

Format a Video

The Format tab includes options for playing the video for preview purposes, adjusting the video, applying a style to the video, arranging a video on the slide, and cropping and sizing the video. Figure 4.29 displays the Video Tools Format tab. Some of these tools will not work with embedded Web site videos.

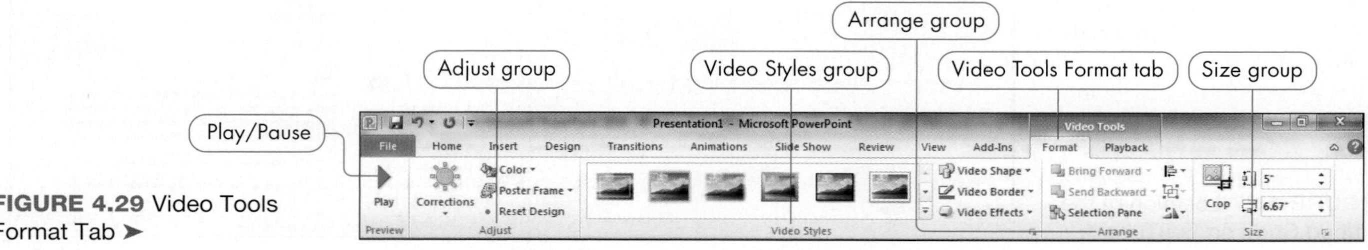

FIGURE 4.29 Video Tools Format Tab ➤

A **Poster Frame** is the frame that displays on a slide when a video is not playing.

Using the Adjust group, you can adjust video contrast and brightness, and you can recolor a video as you did when you worked with images. The Adjust group also includes the ***Poster Frame*** option, which enables you to choose a frame from within the embedded video or any image from your storage device to display on the PowerPoint slide when the video is not playing.

To create a poster frame from the video, do the following:

1. Click Play in the Preview group to display the video.
2. Pause the video when the frame you want to use as the poster frame appears.
3. Click Poster Frame in the Adjust group.
4. Click Current Frame.

To create a poster frame from an image stored in your storage device, do the following:

1. Click Poster Frame in the Adjust group.
2. Click Image from File.
3. Locate and select desired image.
4. Click Insert.

Figure 4.30 shows a video using the default first frame on the slide and a copy of the video with a poster frame set from the video.

FIGURE 4.30 Poster Frame Option ➤

The Style effects available for images are also available for videos. In addition to the styles in the Style gallery, you can edit the shape of a video, change the border of the video, and add style effects like Shadow, Reflection, Glow, Soft Edges, Bevel, and 3-D Rotation. Figure 4.31 shows a video formatted to fit a PowerPoint shape, with an olive green border and perspective shadow added.

FIGURE 4.31 Video Styles ➤

TIP Resetting a Video

To discard all formatting changes from a selected video, click the Reset Design arrow in the Adjust group on the Video Tools Format tab, and then select Reset Design or Reset Design & Size.

Set Video Playback Options

The Video Tools Playback tab includes options used when viewing a video. You can preview the video, add or remove bookmarks, trim the video, fade the video in and out, control the volume, determine how to start the video, set the video to play full screen, hide the video while not playing, loop the video until stopped, and set the video to rewind after playing. Figure 4.32 displays the Video Tools Playback tab.

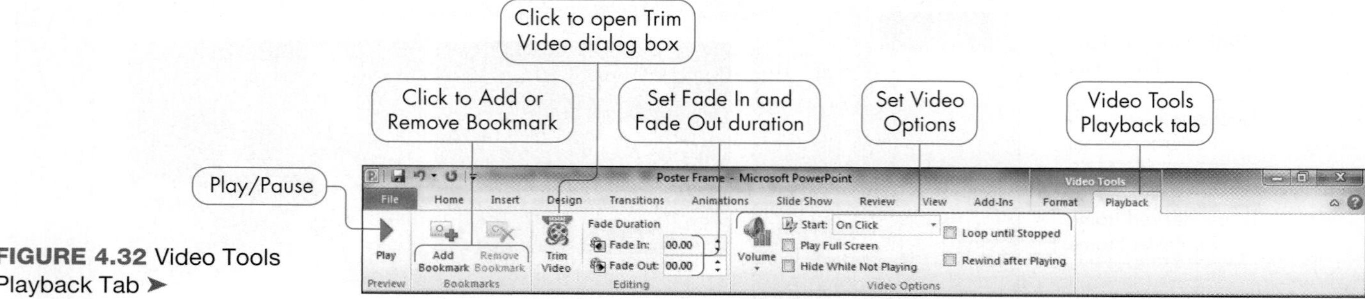

FIGURE 4.32 Video Tools Playback Tab ➤

You can use bookmarks to mark specific locations in a video, making it possible to quickly advance to the part of the video you want to display or to trigger an event in an animation.

To bookmark a video, do the following:

1. Select the video, and then click the Playback tab.
2. Click Play on the Media Control bar.
3. Click Add Bookmark in the Bookmarks group when the video reaches the location you want to quickly move to during your presentation.

A circle displays on the Media Control bar to indicate the bookmark location (see Figure 4.33). To remove the bookmark, click the circle on the Media Control bar, and then click Remove Bookmark in the Bookmarks group.

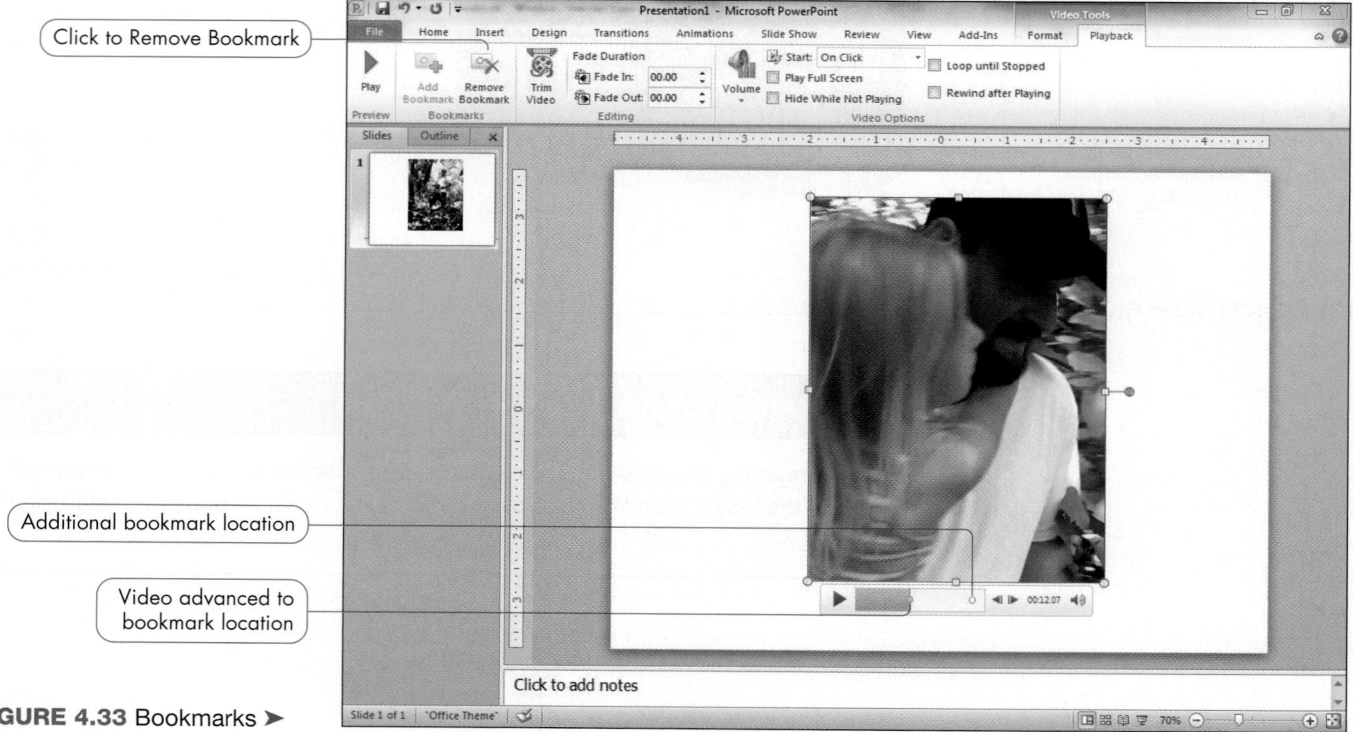

FIGURE 4.33 Bookmarks ➤

PowerPoint enables you to perform basic video editing by enabling you to determine the starting and ending of a video and setting a Fade In and Fade Out duration. In the Trim Video dialog box, which you access in the Editing group on the Playback tab, you can use the Trim option to specify the Start Time and End Time for a video, or you can drag the Start marker and the End marker on the Timing slide bar to select the time. The advantage to dragging the markers is that as you drag, you can view the video. Any bookmarks you set will also display in the Trim Video dialog box. Figure 4.34 shows the Trim Video dialog box.

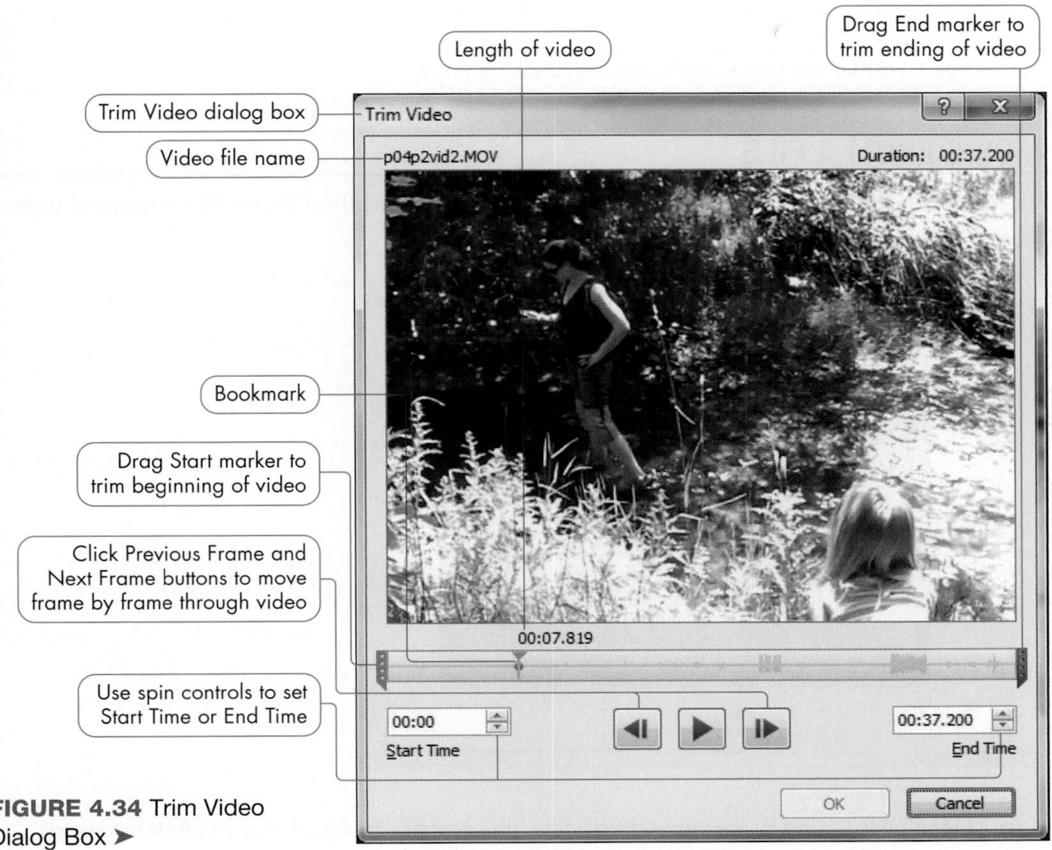

FIGURE 4.34 Trim Video Dialog Box ➤

To set a Fade In or Fade Out duration, click the spin buttons or enter an exact time in the appropriate boxes in the Editing group on the Playback tab. If you have selected a poster frame for your video, the poster frame will fade into the first frame of your video.

The Video Options group of the Playback tab enables you to control a variety of display options. You can control the volume of the video by clicking the Volume arrow and selecting Low, Medium, or High. You can also mute any sound attached to the video.

The Video Options group also enables you to determine whether the video starts on the click of the mouse (the default setting) or automatically when the slide displays. You can choose to play the video at full screen, hide the video when it is not playing, loop continuously until you stop the playback, and rewind after playing.

Quick Concepts Check

1. What is a video codec and why is it usually necessary?
2. Explain the difference between embedding a video and linking a video.
3. Why would you add a bookmark to a video?

2 Video

In Cancun, the couple recorded some fireworks displayed during a sports event. The groom gave you a copy of the fireworks because you think it would be an excellent finale to the slide show. You insert the video, add a photo frame, and set the video playback options.

Skills covered: Insert a Movie from a File • Format a Video • Set Video Playback Options

STEP 1 INSERT A MOVIE FROM A FILE

You create a blank slide at the end of the memories presentation, and then insert the fireworks video. Refer to Figure 4.35 as you complete Step 1.

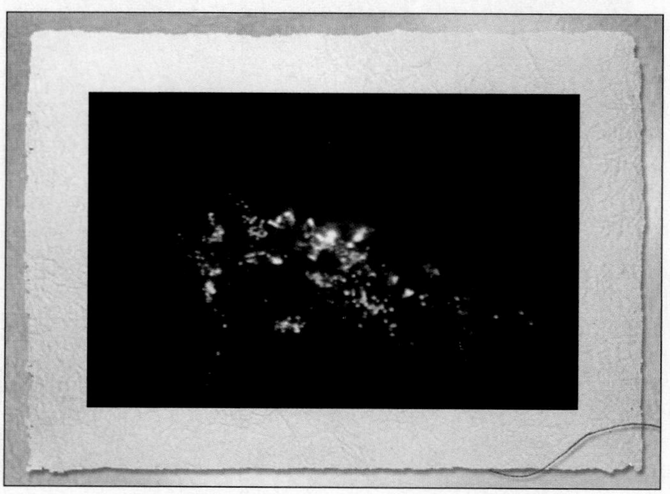

FIGURE 4.35 Inserted Windows Media Video File ➤

a. Open *p04h1memory_LastnameFirstname*, if necessary, and then save as **p04h2memory_LastnameFirstname**, changing *h1* to *h2*.

b. On Slide 7, click the **New Slide arrow** in the Slides group on the Home tab, and then click the **Blank layout**.

   A new slide (Slide 8) with the same presentation theme is created and should be positioned after Slide 7.

c. Click the **Insert tab**, and then click the **Video arrow** in the Media group.

d. Click **Video from File**, open the *p04h13memory_media* folder, select *p04h2fireworks.wmv*, and then click **Insert**.

e. Save the presentation.

STEP 2 FORMAT A VIDEO

The first image of the video shows the fireworks in the beginning stages. You decide to use a poster frame of the fireworks while they are fully bursting so the slide has an attractive image on display before the video begins. You also decide that a shape removing the edges of the video would be an improvement. Finally, you add a shadow video effect. Refer to Figure 4.36 as you complete Step 2.

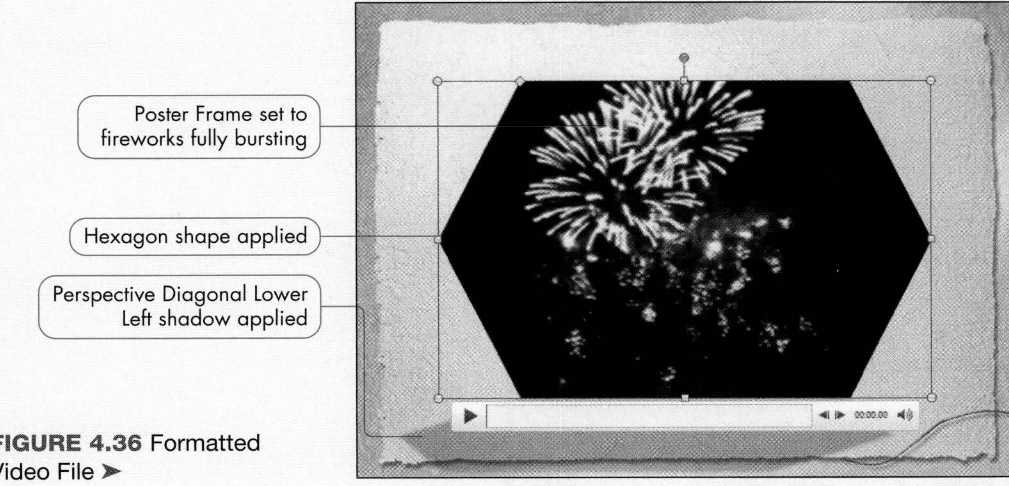

FIGURE 4.36 Formatted Video File ➤

a. Click **Move Forward 0.25 Seconds** on the Media Controls bar located beneath the video to advance the video to the frame at 2.00 seconds.

b. Click the **Video Tools Format tab**, if necessary, click **Poster Frame** in the Adjust group, and then click **Current Frame**.

   The frame you selected becomes the poster frame and displays on the slide.

c. Click **Video Shape** in the Video Styles group, and then click **Hexagon** in the Basic Shapes category.

   The video shape changes to a hexagon.

d. Click **Video Effects**, point to **Shadow**, and then click **Perspective Diagonal Lower Left** in the Perspective category.

   The shadow displays in a hexagon shape with a perspective view.

e. Click the **Slide Show tab**, and then click **From Current Slide** in the Start Slide Show group.

   Slide 7 opens with the video displayed on the slide. The poster frame shows the fireworks at full cascade with the video shadow.

f. Move the pointer to the bottom of the video to display the Media Controls bar, and then click **Play**.

g. Save the presentation.

STEP 3 SET VIDEO PLAYBACK OPTIONS

The last burst of fireworks does not finish its crescendo, so you decide to trim away this last portion of the video. Because you do not want the viewers of the presentation to have to click to begin the video, you change the start setting to start automatically. You decide to loop the video to play continuously until stopped because it is so short. Refer to Figure 4.37 as you complete Step 3.

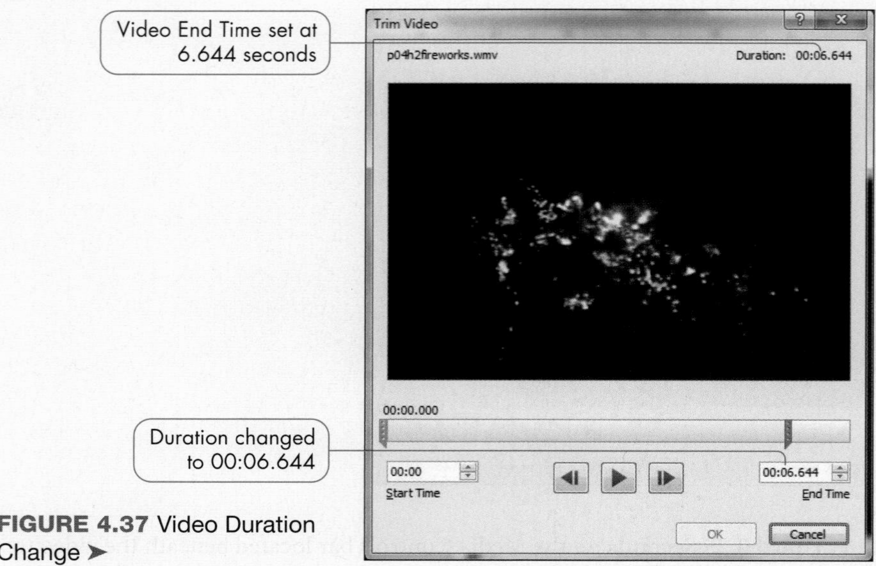

FIGURE 4.37 Video Duration Change ➤

a. Select the movie object, if necessary, click the **Video Tools Playback tab**, and then click **Trim Video** in the Editing group.

   The Trim Video dialog box opens.

b. Drag the red **End Time marker** on the slider until **00:06.644** appears in the End Time box or type **00:06.644** in the **End Time box**, and then click **OK**.

   The duration of the video changes from 7.755 seconds to 6.644 seconds.

c. Click the **Start arrow** in the Video Options group, and then click **Automatically**.

d. Check the **Loop until Stopped check box** in the Video Options group.

   The fireworks video will continue to play until you advance to end the slide show.

e. Click the **Slide Show tab**, and then click **From Beginning** in the Start Slide Show group.

   Advance through the slide show. Note the movie plays in the Hexagon shape.

f. Save the presentation, close the file, and then exit PowerPoint if you do not want to continue with the next Hands-On Exercise at this time.

Audio

Audio can draw on common elements of any language or culture—screams, laughs, sobs, etc.—to add excitement, provide a pleasurable background, set the mood, or serve as a wake-up call for the audience. Harnessing the emotional impact of sound in your presentation can transform your presentation from good to extraordinary. On the other hand, use sound incorrectly, and you can destroy your presentation, leaving your audience confused and with a headache. Keep in mind the guideline emphasized throughout this book—any added object must enhance, not detract from, your message.

Harnessing the emotional impact of sound in your presentation can transform your presentation from good to extraordinary.

In this section, you will review the methods for inserting sound and tips for each method. You insert sound from the Clip Organizer and learn how to determine the number of times a sound clip plays, the number of slides through which the sound plays, and the method for launching the sound. Finally, you record a short narration for a presentation.

Adding Audio

Your computer needs a sound card and speakers to play audio. In a classroom or computer laboratory, you will need a headset or headphones for playback so that you do not disturb other students. You can locate and play sounds and music from the Clip Art pane, or from a hard drive, flash drive, or any other storage device. You can also record your own sounds, music, or narration to play from PowerPoint.

Add Sounds from the Clip Art Pane

To insert sound from the Clip Art pane, click the Insert tab, and then click Clip Art in the Images group. When the task pane opens, enter a term in the *Search for* box, and then change the *Results should be* option to Audio. Point to a sound clip in the results pane to display a tip showing keywords, length of the sound track, file size, and the sound format of the clip. To hear a preview of the clip, click the bar that appears on the right side of the clip when your mouse points to it, and then select Preview/Properties. The Preview/Properties dialog box opens, playing the sound clip and providing you with information about the clip.

Insert Audio from a File

Table 4.3 lists the types of Audio file formats supported by PowerPoint in alphabetical order by extension.

TABLE 4.3 Types of Audio File Formats Supported by PowerPoint

File Format	Extension	Description
AIFF Audio File	.aiff	**Audio Interchange File Format** Waveform files stored in 8-bit monaural (mono or one-channel) format. Not compressed. Can result in large files. Originally used on Apple and Silicon Graphics (SGI) computers.
AU Audio File	.au	**UNIX Audio** Typically used to create sound files for UNIX computers or the Web.
MIDI File	.mid or .midi	**Musical Instrument Digital Interface** Standard format for interchange of musical information between musical instruments, synthesizers, and computers.
MP3 Audio File	.mp3	**MPEG Audio Layer 3** Sound file that has been compressed by using the MPEG Audio Layer 3 codec (developed by the Fraunhofer Institute).
Windows Audio File	.wav	**Wave Form** Stores sounds as waveforms. Depending on various factors, one minute of sound can occupy as little as 644 kilobytes or as much as 27 megabytes of storage.
Windows Media Audio File	.wma	**Windows Media Audio** Sound format used to distribute recorded music, usually over the Internet. Compressed using the Microsoft Windows Media Audio codec.

To insert audio from a file, do the following:

1. Click the Insert tab.
2. Click the Audio arrow in the Media group.
3. Click Audio from File.
4. Browse, locate, and select the desired file.
5. Click Insert.

A gray speaker icon representing the file appears in the center of the slide with a Media Controls bar beneath it. The same controls are available when you select audio as when you select video except the volume control is a slider for audio files.

Record and Insert Audio

Narration is spoken commentary that is added to a presentation.

Sometimes you may find it helpful to add recorded audio to a slide show. Although you could record music, ***narration*** or spoken commentary is more common. One example of a need for recorded narration is when you want to create a self-running presentation, such as a presentation displaying in a kiosk at the mall. Other examples include creating an association between words and an image on the screen for a presentation to a group learning a new language and vocabulary building for young children. Rather than adding a narration prior to a presentation, you could create the narration during the presentation. For example, recording the discussion and decisions made during a meeting would create an archive of the meeting.

Before creating the narration, keep in mind the following:

- Your computer will need a sound card, speakers, and a microphone.
- Comments on selected slides may be recorded rather than narrating the entire presentation.
- Voice narration takes precedence over any other sounds during playback, making it possible for a voice to play over inserted audio files.
- PowerPoint records the amount of time it takes you to narrate each slide, and if you save the slide timings, you can use them to create an automatic slide show.
- You can pause and resume recording during the process.

To record audio, do the following:

1. Click the Insert tab.
2. Click the Audio arrow in the Media group.
3. Click Record Audio.
4. Click Record (see Figure 4.38).
5. Record your message.
6. Click Stop.
7. Click Play to check the recording.
8. Type a name for the recording, and then press OK.

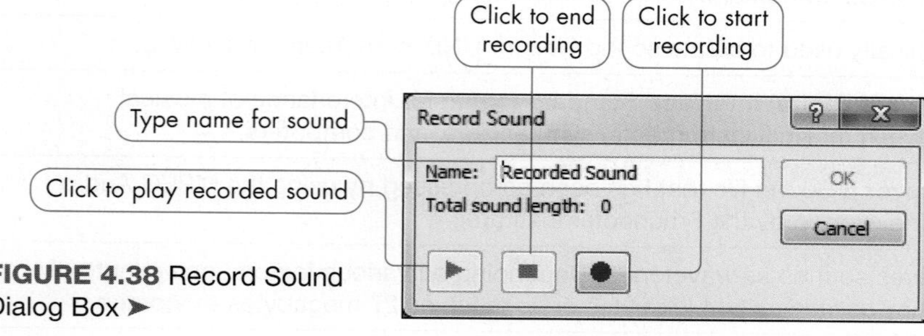

FIGURE 4.38 Record Sound Dialog Box ➤

TIP Create Notes of Your Narration

A transcript of your narration should be available for those in your audience who are hearing impaired. Providing the transcript lets this audience gain from your presentation, too. Put the transcript in the Notes pane, and then print the Notes to provide a transcript.

Changing Audio Settings

When an audio clip is selected, the Audio Tools tab appears with two tabs: Format and Playback. The Format tab is not relevant, as it provides options relating to images. The Playback tab provides options for playing and pausing the audio clip, adding a bookmark, trimming, fading in and out, adjusting volume, determining starting method, hiding the audio icon while playing, looping, and rewinding after playing. All of these features work similarly to the video features except that the Trim audio feature provides an audio time line rather than a video preview window.

Animate an Audio Sequence

Although the Audio Tools Playback tab gives you only two options for starting, On Click or Automatically, you have other options available through the Animation Timing group. You can choose whether the audio plays with a previous event or after a previous event; for example, you can have the audio play as a picture appears or after.

To set the audio to play with or after a previous event:

1. Select the sound icon.
2. Click the Animations tab.
3. Click the Start arrow in the Timing group.
4. Click With Previous or After Previous.

The Timing group on the Animations tab also includes a Delay spin box that you can use to delay the play of an audio clip (see Figure 4.39).

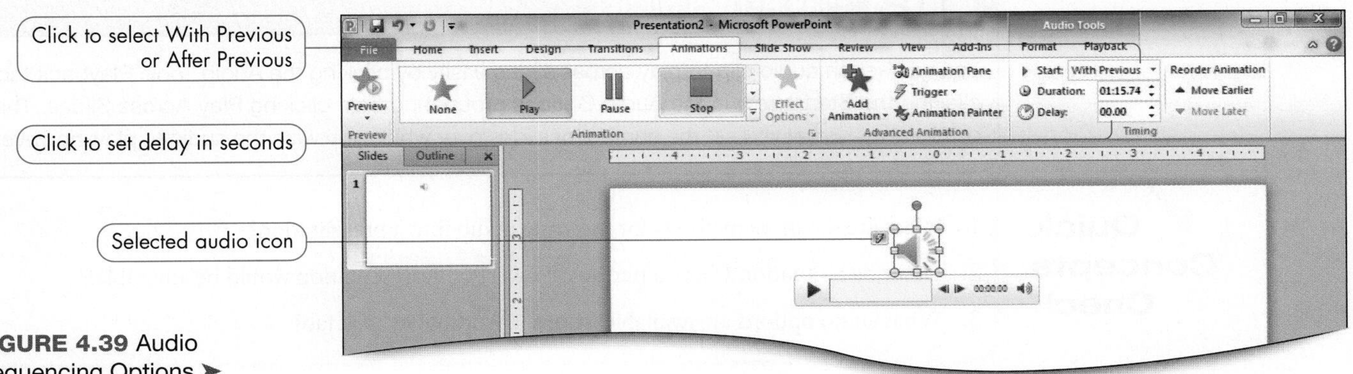

FIGURE 4.39 Audio Sequencing Options ➤

Play a Sound over Multiple Slides

By default, audio plays until it ends or until the next mouse click. If you are playing background music, this means the music ends when you click to advance to the next slide.

To continue audio over multiple slides, do the following:

1. Click the Animations tab.
2. Click Animation Pane in the Advanced Animation group.
3. Select the sound you want to continue over multiple slides.
4. Click the arrow to the right of the sound.

5. Click Effect Options.
6. Click the After option in the Stop playing section of the Effect tab.
7. Enter the number of slides during which you want the sound to play (see Figure 4.40).

If the background music stops before you get to the last slide, use the Loop Until Stopped feature to keep the sound repeating. Click the Audio Tools Playback tab, and then click the Loop Until Stopped check box in the Audio Options group.

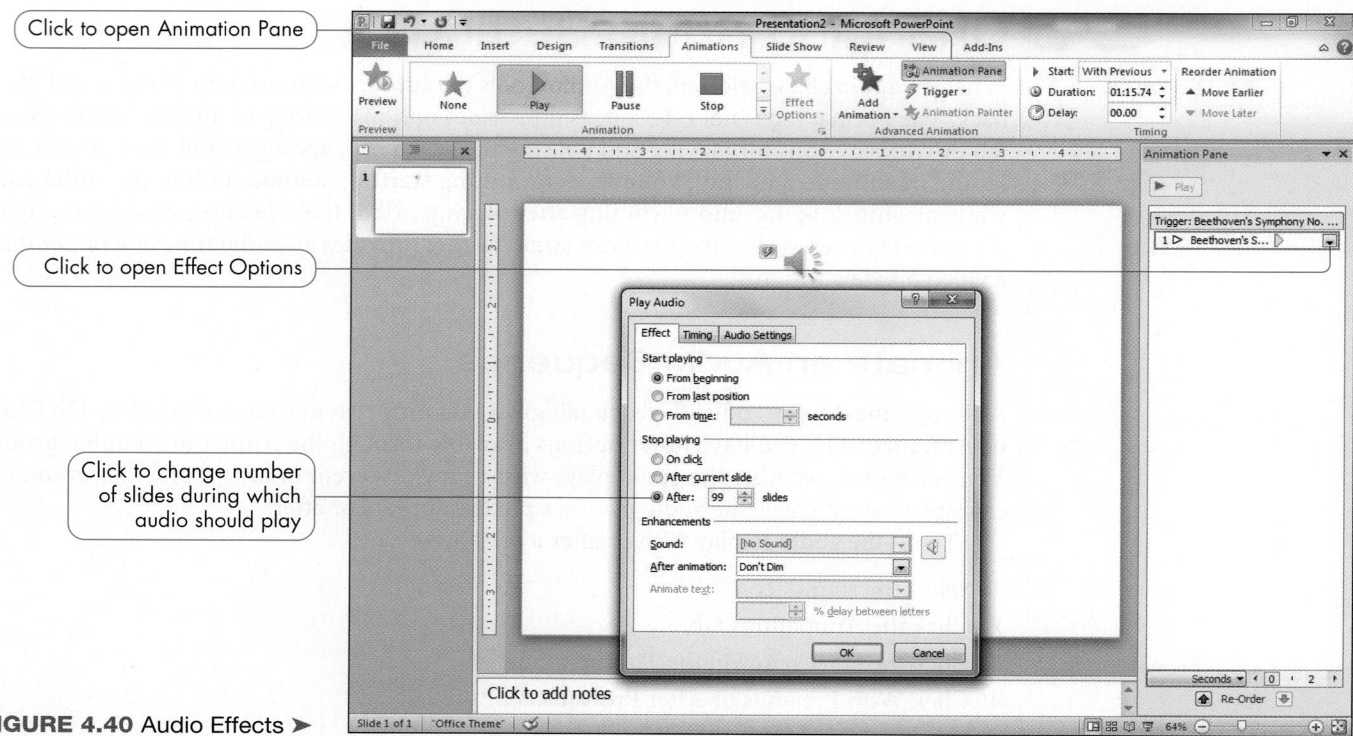

FIGURE 4.40 Audio Effects ➤

TIP Play Across Slides

You can set an audio clip to play across slides easily by clicking the Audio Tools Playback tab, clicking the Start arrow in the Audio Options group, and then clicking Play Across Slides. This option does not let you set the number of slides over which you wish the audio to play, however.

Quick Concepts Check

1. What are the three methods for inserting audio into a presentation?
2. Describe a situation where a narrated PowerPoint presentation would be advisable.
3. What audio options are available from the Audio Playback tab?

3 Audio

You decide to create a background mood for the memories presentation by inserting a favorite audio clip of the bride—Beethoven's Symphony No. 9. You also want to experience the full effect of the fireworks finale slide by adding the sounds of fireworks exploding.

Skills covered: Add Audio from a File • Change Audio Settings • Insert Sound from the Clip Art Pane • Add Narration

STEP 1 ADD AUDIO FROM A FILE

The bride is a classically trained pianist, so you decide to enhance the slide show with one of her favorite pieces. Refer to Figure 4.41 as you complete Step 1.

FIGURE 4.41 Slide 1 Audio Settings ➤

a. Open the *p04h2memory_LastnameFirstname* presentation if you closed it after the last exercise, and then save it as **p04h3memory_LastnameFirstname**, changing *h2* to *h3*.

> **TROUBLESHOOTING:** To complete this exercise, it is best that you have a sound card, a microphone, and speakers. Even if this equipment is not available, however, you can still perform these steps to gain the knowledge.

b. On Slide 1, click the **Insert tab**, click the **Audio arrow** in the Media group, and then select **Audio from File**.

   The Insert Audio dialog box opens.

c. Locate the *p04h1_3memory_media* folder, select **Beethoven's_Symphony_No_9**, and then click **Insert**.

   The sound icon and Media Controls bar are displayed in the center of the slide.

d. Click the **Audio Tools Playback tab**, click the **Start arrow** in the Audio Options group, and then select **Automatically**.

e. Drag the sound icon to the top-left corner of the slide.

f. Click the **Hide During Show check box** in the Audio Options group.

g. Click **Play** in the Preview group.

h. Save the presentation.

STEP 2 CHANGE AUDIO SETTINGS

Because PowerPoint's default setting ends a sound file when a slide advances, the Beethoven file is abruptly cut off when you advance to the next slide. You adjust the sound settings so the file plays continuously through all slides in the slide show. Refer to Figure 4.42 as you complete Step 2.

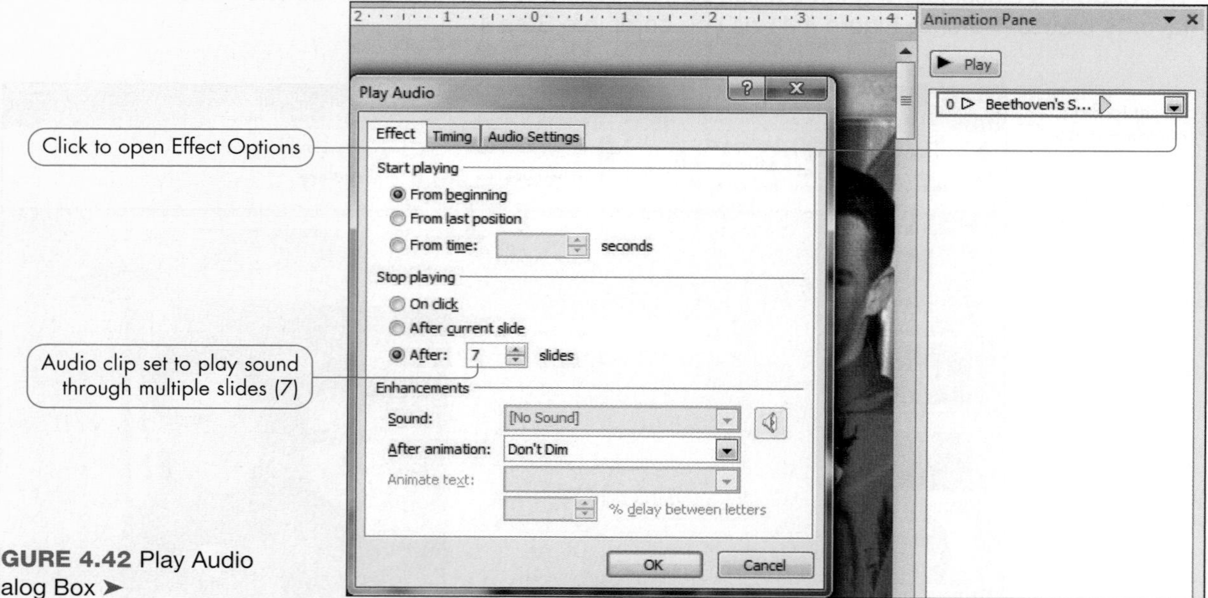

FIGURE 4.42 Play Audio Dialog Box ➤

a. Click the **Slide Show tab**, and then click **From Beginning** in the Start Slide Show group. Advance through the slides, and then end the slide show.

   Note that the sound clip on Slide 1 discontinues playing as soon as you click to advance to the next slide.

b. Select the sound icon on the top-left of Slide 1.

c. Click the **Animations tab**, and then click **Animation Pane** in the Advanced Animation group.

d. Click the **Beethoven's Symphony sound arrow** in the animation list, and then select **Effect Options**.

e. Click **After** in the *Stop playing* section, type 7 in the box, and then click **OK**. Close the Animation Pane.

f. Save the presentation.

g. Play the slide show and note the music plays through the seventh slide.

STEP 3 INSERT SOUND FROM THE CLIP ART PANE

The sound of fireworks exploding would make the finale slide more effective. You locate a fireworks audio clip in the Microsoft Clip Art pane, add it to the fireworks slide, set it to start automatically, and set it to loop until the presentation ends. After adding the audio clip, you modify its setting so it plays concurrently with the video. You move the audio icon so that it does not block the view of the fireworks. You also hide the audio icon during the presentation. Refer to Figure 4.43 as you complete Step 3.

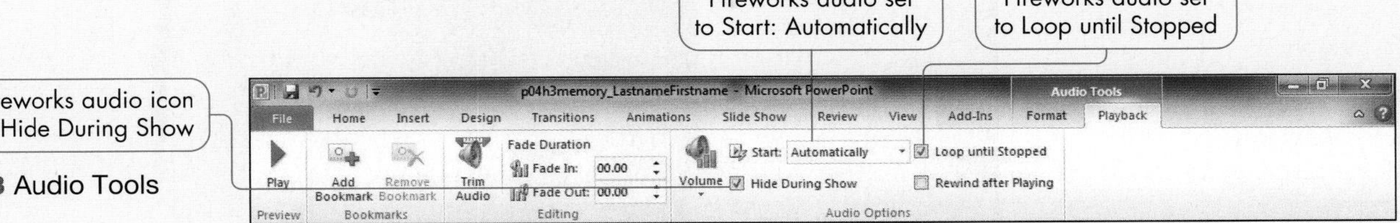

FIGURE 4.43 Audio Tools Tab ➤

a. On Slide 8, click the **Insert tab**, and then click **Clip Art** in the Images group.

b. Type the keyword **fireworks** in the **Search for box**, change Results to **Audio**, include Office.com content, and then click **Go**.

c. Point to the resulting sound clips to display the sound name, size, and file type. Locate and select the **Fireworks Loop, 5.00 sec, 29 KB, WAV clip**.

d. Click the arrow in the blue bar on the clip, and then click **Insert**. Close the Clip Art pane.

> **TROUBLESHOOTING:** If the sound clip speaker icon and Media Controls bar do not appear on the slide, you may be dragging the clip onto the slide instead of inserting the clip.

e. Select the sound icon if necessary, click the **Audio Tools Playback tab**, click the **Start arrow** in the Audio Options group, and then select **Automatically**.

f. Click the **Hide During Show check box** in the Audio Options group.

g. Click the **Loop until Stopped check box**.

h. Drag the sound icon down into the shadow of the video so that it will not block the fireworks on the slide.

i. Click the **Animations tab**, click the **Start arrow** in the Timing group, and then select **With Previous**.

j. Click the **Slide Show tab**, and then click **From Current Slide** in the Start Slide Show group.

k. Save the presentation.

STEP 4 ADD NARRATION

A small portion of the bride's vows is included on Slide 4. You narrate the vow and save it with the slide show so that it has a greater impact. Refer to Figure 4.44 as you complete Step 4.

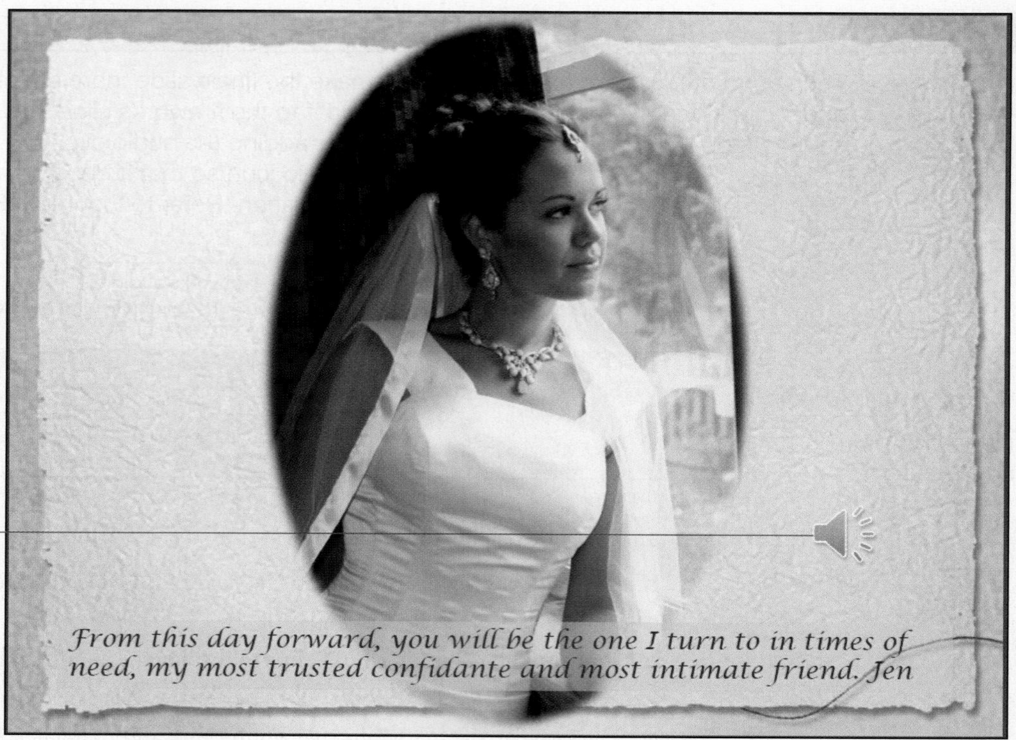

FIGURE 4.44 Audio Clip on Bride Slide ➤

a. On Slide 4, click the **Insert tab**.
b. Click the **Audio arrow**, and then click **Record Audio**.

> **TROUBLESHOOTING:** You will not be able to complete this step without a microphone, speakers, and a sound card.

c. Click the red **Record button** in the Record Sound dialog box, and then read.

   From this day forward, you will be the one I turn to in times of need, my most trusted confidante and most intimate friend.

d. Click the blue **Stop Recording button**, and then click **OK**.
e. Move the audio icon to the bottom-right of the slide.
f. Click the **Playback tab**, click the **Start arrow** in the Audio Options group, and then select **Automatically**.
g. Click the **Hide During Show check box** in the Audio Options group.
h. Click **From Beginning** in the Start Slide Show group so that you can hear the narration and sound clips you have added.
i. Save and close the slide show.

Photo Albums

PowerPoint has a Photo Album feature designed to speed up the album creation process. This feature takes the images you select and arranges them on album pages based on selections you make.

In this section, you will use the Photo Album feature to create an album and use the feature settings to customize your album.

Creating a Photo Album

A **Photo Album** is a presentation containing multiple pictures organized into album pages.

A PowerPoint ***Photo Album*** is a presentation that contains multiple pictures that are imported and formatted through the Photo Album feature. Because each picture does not have to be formatted individually, you save a considerable amount of time. The photo album in Figure 4.45 took less than two minutes to create and assign a theme. Because a four-per-page layout was selected, images were reduced to fit the size of the placeholder. This setting drastically reduced the size of some images, although it does create an interesting asymmetrical design on the page.

Because each picture does not have to be formatted individually, you save a considerable amount of time using the Photo Album feature.

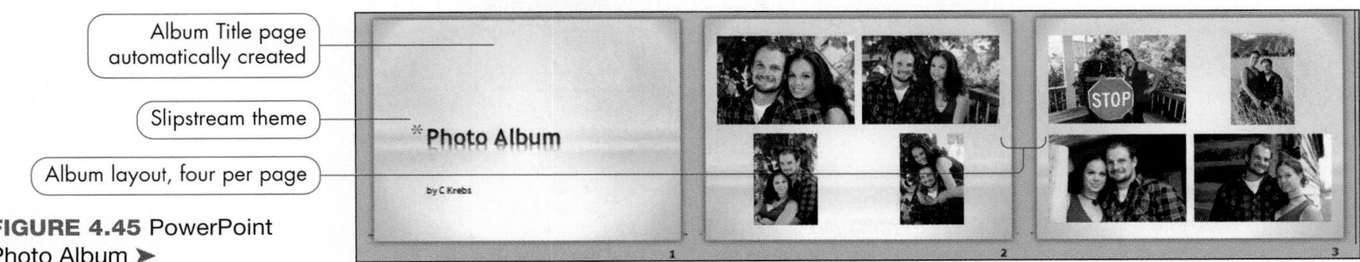

FIGURE 4.45 PowerPoint Photo Album ➤

To create a photo album, do the following:

1. Click the Insert tab.
2. Click Photo Album in the Images group.
3. Click File/Disk.
4. Navigate to your pictures, and then select the pictures to include in the album.
5. Click Insert.
6. Select the Photo Album options you want.
7. Click Create.

If you click the Photo Album arrow, you may choose between creating a new album and editing a previously created album. When you select the pictures you want to include in the album, do not worry about the order of the pictures. You can change the order later. Once an album has been created, you can edit the album settings by clicking the Photo Album arrow in the Images group on the Insert tab, and then selecting Edit Photo Album.

Creating Family Albums

After creating an album, add transitions and you have a beautiful presentation for a family gathering or special event. Loop the presentation, and let it run so people can watch as they desire. Burn the presentation to a CD and send it as a holiday greeting.

Setting Photo Album Options

After selecting pictures, they will appear in a list in the dialog box. Click the name of a picture to display a preview to help you determine the order of pictures in the album. Use the Move up arrow and the Move down arrow to reposition a selected photograph. Use Ctrl or Shift to select more than one image. Delete any unwanted photographs by selecting them and clicking Remove.

If you have downloaded photographs from a digital camera, you may need to rotate some images. Rotate buttons are included in the *Album Content* section. Contrast and brightness controls enable you to fine-tune your pictures. This section also includes the New Text Box button so that you can insert a text placeholder in the album. The text placeholder is the same size as the placeholders for pictures. The *Captions below ALL pictures* option will not become available until you choose a layout. When this option is active, the file name of the picture appears as a caption below the picture in the album. Figure 4.46 shows the location of these tools.

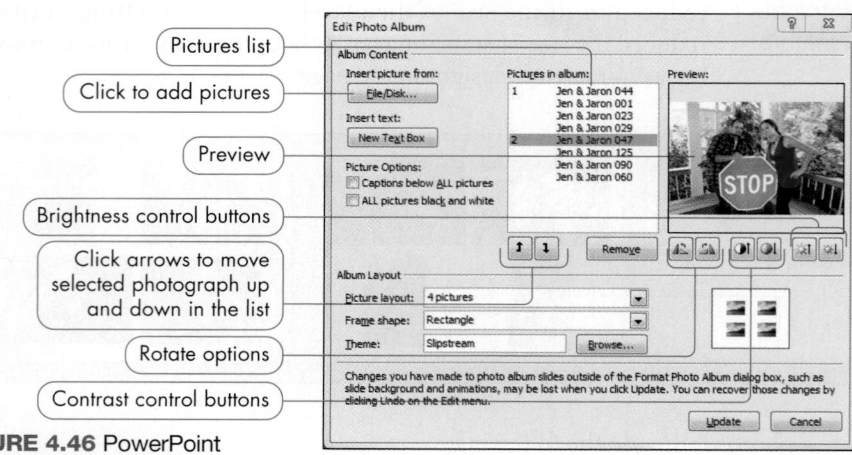

FIGURE 4.46 PowerPoint Photo Album Content Options ➤

The *Album Layout* section of the Photo Album dialog box gives many options for personalizing the album. First, you can select a layout: a single picture fitted to a full slide; one, two, or four pictures on a page; or one, two, or four pictures and a title placeholder per page. When you fit a single picture per page, the image is maximized on the page.

You can select from a variety of frame shapes in the *Album Layout* section. Options include rectangles, rounded rectangles, simple black or white frames, a compound black frame, a center shadow rectangle, or a soft edge rectangle.

You can apply a theme for the background of your album while in the Photo Album dialog box. If you are in a networked lab situation it may be difficult to navigate to the location where themes are stored. If this is the case, create the album, and then in the main PowerPoint window, click the Design tab, click the More button in the Themes group, and then select your theme from the gallery.

1. What advantages does the Photo Album feature offer?
2. List two image transformation tools available in the *Album Content* section of the Photo Album dialog box.
3. Describe one way to personalize an album.

HANDS-ON EXERCISES

4 Photo Albums

The bride's mother is a professional photographer and traveled with the couple, extensively capturing images from around the world. You prepare an album to help them preserve their memories.

Skills covered: Select and Order Pictures • Adjust Contrast and Brightness • Set Picture Layout • Select Frame Shape • Edit Album Settings and Apply a Theme

STEP 1 SELECT AND ORDER PICTURES

You have a folder in which you have saved the images you wish to use for the vacation album. In this step, you add the images to the album and order the images by the year during which the trip was taken. Refer to Figure 4.47 as you complete Step 1.

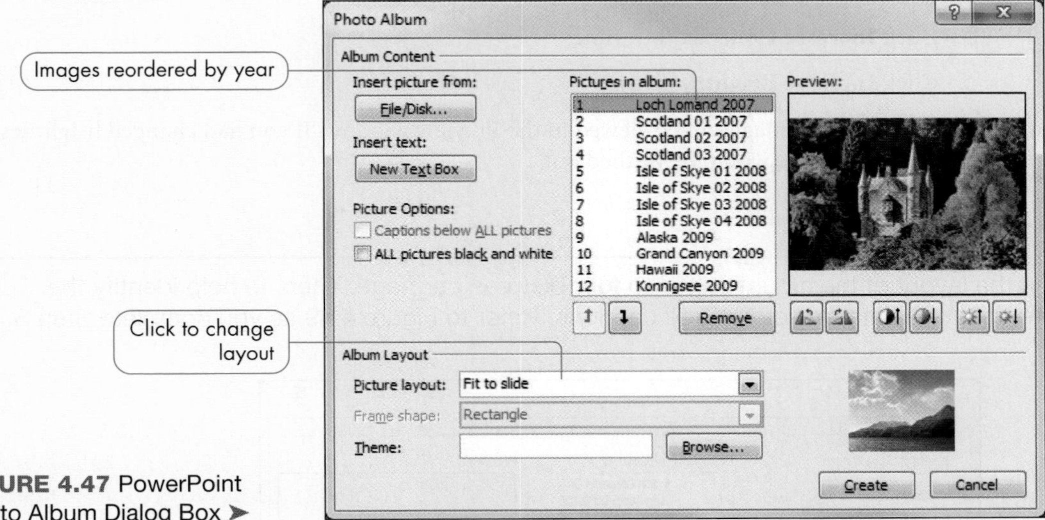

FIGURE 4.47 PowerPoint Photo Album Dialog Box ➤

a. In a new blank presentation, click the **Insert tab**, and then click **Photo Album** in the Images group.

   The Photo Album dialog box opens.

b. Click **File/Disk**. Open the *p04h4album_media* folder.

c. Press **Ctrl+A** to select all pictures in the folder, and then click **Insert**.

   The list of pictures displays in the *Pictures in album* box.

d. Use the **Move up arrow** to reposition *Loch Lomand 2007* so that it is the first picture in the list.

e. Continue using the **Move up arrow** and the **Move down arrow** to reposition each picture by the image number and by the year. Press and hold **Ctrl** to select multiple images to move them as a group. Refer to Figure 4.47 to ensure your images are in the correct order, and then click **Create**.

STEP 2 ADJUST CONTRAST AND BRIGHTNESS

The Photo Album feature includes buttons that enable you to adjust the contrast and brightness of images without having to access PowerPoint's Picture Tools. You use the Photo Album buttons to adjust the contrast in one of the Isle of Skye pictures. Refer to Figure 4.48 as you complete Step 2.

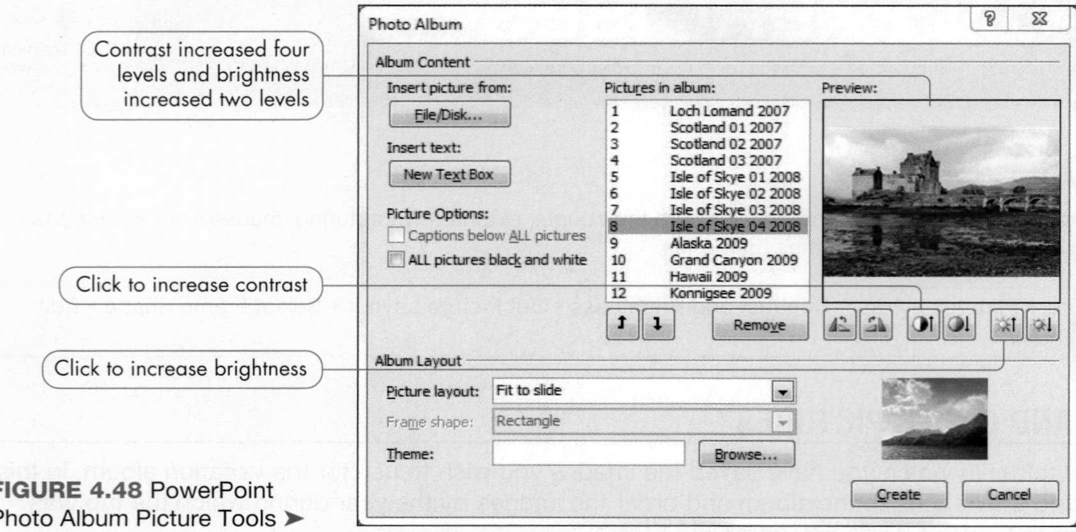

FIGURE 4.48 PowerPoint Photo Album Picture Tools ➤

a. Select **Isle of Skye 04 2008** in the **Pictures in album list**.

b. Click **Increase Contrast** four times.

c. Click **Increase Brightness** twice.

   The adjusted image can be viewed in the Preview window. If you had changed brightness only, the image would be washed out.

STEP 3 SET PICTURE LAYOUT

You change the layout of the album pages to four pictures per page. Then, to help identify the location and year of each trip, you include captions. Refer to Figure 4.49 as you complete Step 3.

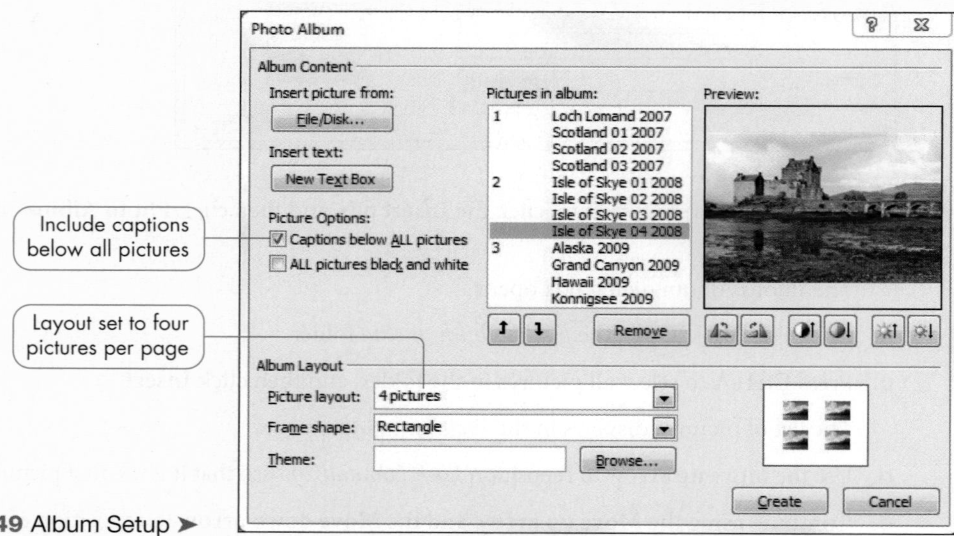

FIGURE 4.49 Album Setup ➤

a. Click the **Picture layout arrow** in the *Album Layout* section of the Photo Album dialog box.

b. Click each of the layouts and view the layout in the Album Layout Preview window on the right (below the larger Album Content Preview window), and then select **4 pictures**.

   Clicking 4 pictures will create an album of four pages—a title page and three pages with four pictures each.

c. Click the **Captions below ALL pictures check box** in the *Picture Options* section.

   Captions below ALL pictures only becomes available after the layout is selected.

STEP 4 SELECT FRAME SHAPE

You decide to use a simple white frame to enhance the pictures taken during the trips. Refer to Figure 4.50 as you complete Step 4.

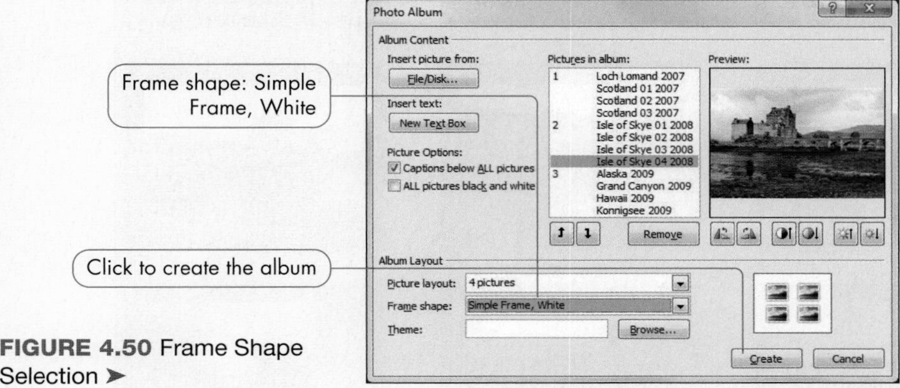

FIGURE 4.50 Frame Shape Selection ➤

a. Click the **Frame shape arrow** in the *Album Layout* section.

b. Select each of the frames, and then view the Preview window on the right.

c. Select **Simple Frame, White**, and then click **Create**.

The album is created, but because portrait and landscape pictures are included on the same page and portrait pictures are squeezed into small placeholders, the appearance of the album is not the best it can be. You will edit the appearance in the next step.

d. Create a handout header with your name, and a handout footer with your instructor's name and your class. Include the current date.

e. On Slide 1, enter your name in the subtitle placeholder.

f. Save the presentation as **p04h4album_LastnameFirstname**.

STEP 5 EDIT ALBUM SETTINGS AND APPLY A THEME

You decide to edit your album settings so that you include only one picture per page rather than four. This allows more space for the pictures so the bride and her mother can see more detail. You also change the frame shape. Finally, you apply a theme to the album. Refer to Figure 4.51 as you complete Step 5.

FIGURE 4.51 Slides 4–12 of the Revised Photo Album ➤

a. Click the **Insert tab**, click the **Photo Album arrow** in the Images group, and then select **Edit Photo Album.**

   The Edit Photo Album dialog box opens displaying the current settings, which you may now change.

b. Click the **Picture layout arrow**, and then select **1 picture**.

c. Click the **Frame shape arrow**, and then select **Center Shadow Rectangle**.

d. Click **Browse**, and then navigate to the location where your Microsoft Document Themes are located. Click **Paper**, and then click **Select** to apply the theme to the presentation.

> **TROUBLESHOOTING:** It may be difficult to locate Themes and Themed Documents in a networked laboratory. If this is the case, close your album and apply a theme from the Design tab.

e. Click **Update**.

   The pictures now appear one per page.

f. Save and close the file, and submit based on your instructor's directions.

CHAPTER OBJECTIVES REVIEW

After reading this chapter, you have accomplished the following objectives:

1. **Insert a picture.** Pictures are in a bitmap format and are photorealistic portrayals. They can be inserted using the Insert Picture option, which centers the image on the slide, or by using placeholders that might center and crop the image inside the placeholder.
2. **Transform a picture.** Pictures can be transformed in a variety of ways, including removing the background, applying corrections, changing colors, applying artistic effects and picture styles, and cropping. Pictures can be compressed to save file storage.
3. **Use the Internet as a resource.** The Internet can be extremely valuable when searching for information for a presentation. Although students and teachers have rights under the Fair Use Act, care should be taken to honor all copyrights. Before inserting any information or clips into your slide show, research the copyright ownership. To be safe, contact the Web site owner and request permission to use the material. Any information used should be credited and include hyperlinks when possible, although attribution does not relieve you of the requirement to honor copyrights.
4. **Add video.** You can insert video located on your hard drive or storage device or embed HTML coding from an online site.
5. **Use Video Tools.** PowerPoint includes video editing tools. You can adjust the brightness and contrast, recolor, set a poster frame, select a style, and arrange and size a video. You can also add a bookmark, trim, set a fade in and fade out effect, control the volume, determine how to start the video, set the video to play full screen, hide the video when not playing, loop until stopped, rewind after playing, and show media controls.
6. **Add audio.** Audio catches audience attention and adds excitement to a presentation. Take care when adding sound that it enhances your message rather than detracts from it.
7. **Change audio settings.** You can also add a bookmark, trim, set a fade in and fade out effect, control the volume, and determine how to start audio. You can hide the speaker icon when not playing, loop until stopped, rewind after playing, and show media controls. By default audio plays during one slide and stops when you advance to a new slide, but it can be set to play over multiple slides.
8. **Create a Photo Album.** When you have multiple images to be inserted, using the Photo Album feature enables you to quickly insert the images into a slide show. After identifying the images you wish to use, you can rearrange the order of the pictures in the album. You also can choose among layouts for the best appearance.
9. **Set Photo Album options.** Album options for contrast and brightness enable you to make image changes without having to leave the Photo Album dialog box. In addition to adjusting contrast and brightness, you can change the pictures to black and white. File names can be turned into captions for the pictures. A frame shape can be selected and a theme applied to complete the album appearance.

KEY TERMS

Background ***p.977***
Bitmap image ***p.974***
Brightness ***p.979***
Codec ***p.997***
Compression ***p.974***
Contrast ***p.979***
Copyright ***p.987***
Cropping ***p.984***
Embed ***p.998***
Foreground ***p.977***
Infringement of copyright ***p.987***
Kelvin ***p.981***
Link ***p.998***
Multimedia ***p.974***
Narration ***p.1008***
Photo Album ***p.1015***
Poster Frame ***p.1000***
Public domain ***p.987***
Recolor ***p.982***
Saturation ***p.980***
Sharpening ***p.978***
Softening ***p.978***
Tone ***p.981***

MULTIPLE CHOICE

1. Which of the following file formats supports 16 million colors, is optimized for photographs and complex graphics, and is the format of choice for most photographs on the Web?
   (a) .bmp
   (b) .jpg
   (c) .gif
   (d) .tiff

2. To transform a picture from cool colors (lower K) to warm colors (higher K), which of the following should you do?
   (a) Sharpen the picture.
   (b) Adjust the contrast of the picture.
   (c) Increase the saturation of the picture.
   (d) Change the tone of the picture.

3. Which of the following Picture Tools would help you adjust a scanned photograph that appears muddy and does not show much difference between the light and dark areas of the image?
   (a) Brightness
   (b) Contrast
   (c) Recolor
   (d) Compress Pictures

4. Which of the following is not permitted for a student project containing copyrighted material?
   (a) The educational project is produced for a specific class and then retained in a personal portfolio for display in a job interview.
   (b) Only a portion of copyrighted material was used, and the portion was determined by the type of media used.
   (c) The student received permission to use copyrighted material to be distributed to classmates in the project.
   (d) The student markets the project on a personal Web site.

5. Which of the following can be obtained from the Clip Art pane?
   (a) Windows Video files (.avi)
   (b) Moving Picture Experts Group movies (.mpg or .mpeg)
   (c) Animated GIF files (.gif)
   (d) Windows Media Video files (.wmv)

6. All of the following can be used to play a selected sound clip for preview except:
   (a) Click Play in the Preview group on the Audio Tools Format tab.
   (b) Click Play/Pause on the Media Controls bar.
   (c) Click Play in the Preview group on the Audio Tools Playback tab.
   (d) Click the blue bar on the right side of the clip in the Clip Art pane, and then select Preview/Properties.

7. Which of the following is a true statement regarding recording a narration?
   (a) Narration cannot play at the same time as other audio clips.
   (b) Narration is embedded on the slide on which it is recorded.
   (c) Narration time cannot be recorded for use in a self-running presentation.
   (d) Narrations cannot be paused during recording.

8. The Photo Album dialog box enables you to make all but this edit to pictures:
   (a) Rotate.
   (b) Crop.
   (c) Brightness.
   (d) Contrast.

9. Which of the following formatting options is available for video?
   (a) Brightness adjustment
   (b) Sharpen adjustment
   (c) Artistic effect application
   (d) Background removal

10. Audio Playback tools enables you to do all of the following except:
    (a) Add a bookmark.
    (b) Fade the audio out.
    (c) Loop the audio.
    (d) Apply an artistic effect.

PRACTICE EXERCISES

1 Geocaching Slide Show

The slide show in Figure 4.52 is designed to be used with a presentation introducing a group to the sport of geocaching. Geocaching became a new sport on May 2, 2000, when 24 satellites around the globe stopped the intentional degradation of GPS signals. On May 3, Dave Ulmer hid a bucket of trinkets in the woods outside Portland, Oregon, and the sport was born! It continues to grow at remarkable speed. Your Geocaching presentation is designed to teach the basics of taking something, leaving something, and signing the logbook. This exercise follows the same set of skills as used in Hands-On Exercises 1 and 3 in the chapter. Refer to Figure 4.52 as you complete this exercise.

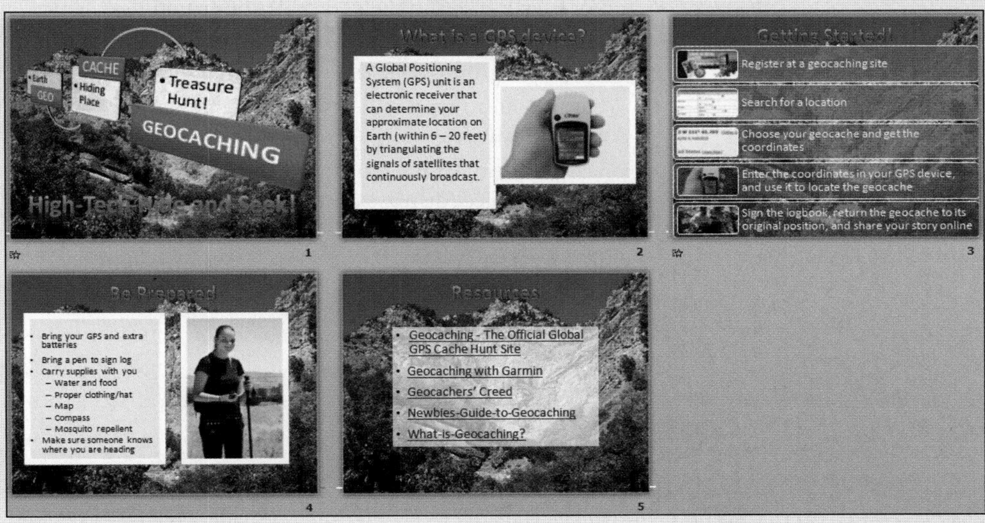

FIGURE 4.52 Geocaching Slide Show ➤

a. Open the *p04p1cache* slide show, and then save it as **p04p1cache_LastnameFirstname**.

b. Create a handout header with your name, and a handout footer with your instructor's name and your class. Include the current date.

c. Click the **Design tab** in any slide, click **Background Styles** in the Background group, and then select **Format Background**.

d. Click **Picture or texture fill**, select **File**, locate and open the *p04p1cache_media* folder, click **p04p1bkgd**, and then click **Insert**. Drag the **Transparency slider** to **10%**. Click **Apply to All**, and then click **Close**.

e. On Slide 2, click the **Insert Picture from File icon** on the toolbar in the right placeholder. In the *p04p1cache_media* folder, click and examine the **p04p1gps picture**. Click **Insert**, and then examine the image on Slide 2 and note the resizing of the placeholder to keep the image in proportion.

f. Click **Remove Background** in the Adjust group, and then drag the top, left, and bottom marquee handles to the edge of the picture. Click **Keep Changes**.

g. Click the border of the text box on the left side of the slide, click the **Home tab**, click **Format Painter** in the Clipboard group, and then click the gps picture.

h. Open your browser, and then type **garminuk.geocaching.com** in the **address bar** to open the Geocaching with Garmin Web site. Right-click **Geocaching with Garmin**, and then select **Save Background As**. Save the image as **p04p1garminlogo** (used with permission) to your student data folder for this chapter. Close your browser.

> **TROUBLESHOOTING:** The Save Background As option is available in Internet Explorer. If you are using Firefox, click View Background Image, and then right-click and save the image. If you are using another browser, right-click the image and select the appropriate option from the menu.

i. On Slide 3, click the first **Insert Picture from File icon** (next to *Register at a geocaching site)* in the top SmartArt diagram box, click the *p04p1garminlogo* image, and then click **Insert.**

j. Click the second **Insert Picture from File icon** in the SmartArt diagram, locate *p04p1seek*, and then click **Insert**.

k. Repeat Step j to enter *p04p1coordinates* in the third image location, *p04p1gps* in the fourth image location, and *p04p1locate* in the last image location.

l. On Slide 4, click the picture of the geocacher, and then click the **Format tab**. Click **Color** in the Adjust group, and then select **No Recolor** in the Recolor gallery.

m. Click **Corrections** in the Adjust group, and then click **Sharpen: 25%** in the Sharpen and Soften gallery.

n. On Slide 1, if you are able to record narration in your computer lab, click the **Insert tab**, click the **Audio arrow** in the Media group, and then select **Record Audio**. Click the red **Record Sound button**, and then read the Speaker Note at the bottom of Slide 1. When finished reading, click the blue **Stop button**, and then click **OK**.

o. If you are not able to record narration in your computer lab, click **Insert**, click the **Audio arrow** in the Media group, and then select **Audio from File**. Click *p04p1narration*, and then click **Insert**.

p. Click the **Audio Tools Playback tab**, and then click the **Hide During Show check box** in the Audio Options group. Drag the audio icon to the top right of the slide.

q. With the audio icon still selected, click the **Start arrow** in the Audio Options group. Select **Automatically**.

r. Click the **Animations tab**, and then click **Animation Pane** in the Advanced Animation group. The audio object displays on the Animation Pane. Click the **Re-Order up arrow** until the sound object moves to the top of the list.

s. Click the **Start arrow**, and then select **With Previous**. Close the Animation Pane.

t. View the slide show.

u. Save and close the file, and submit based on your instructor's directions.

2 Geocaching Album

Geocachers are asked to share their geocaching experience in the geocache logbook. The *Geocaching – The Official Global GPS Cache Hunt Site* includes some easy steps for logging a Geocache find and even enables you to upload a photo with your log entry. Often, geocachers also put their geocaching stories, photos, and videos online in the form of slide shows using a variety of software packages. In this exercise, you create a geocache slide show quickly and easily using the PowerPoint Album feature, and then add video and text to the slide show. This exercise follows the same set of skills as used in Hands-On Exercises 2 and 4 in the chapter. Refer to Figure 4.53 as you complete this exercise.

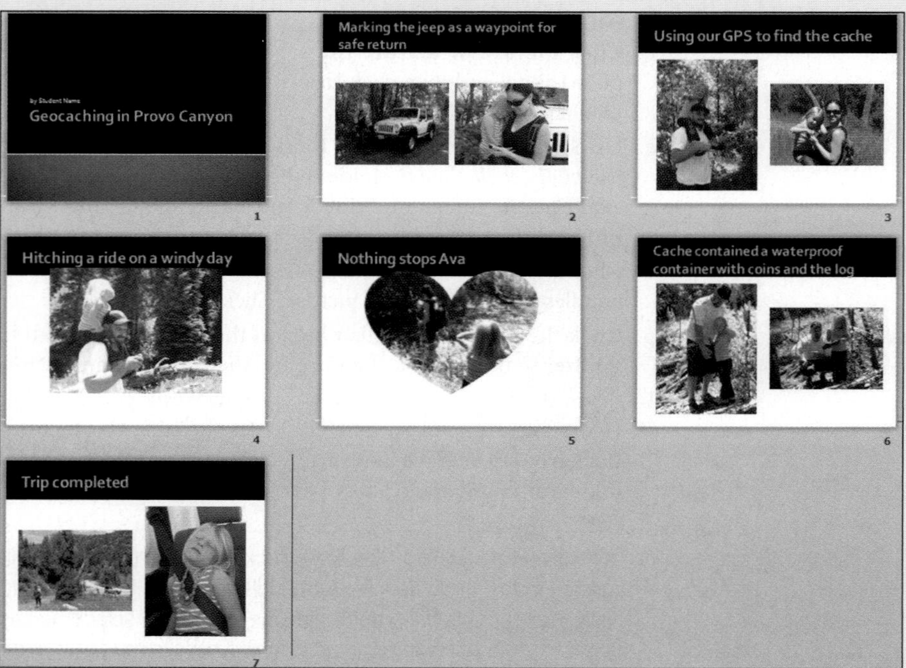

FIGURE 4.53 Geocaching Album ➤

a. In a new blank presentation, click the **Insert tab**, and then click **Photo Album** in the Images group.
b. Click **File/Disk**, open the *p04p2geo_media* folder, click one of the files, and then press **Ctrl+A** to select all pictures in the folder. Click **Insert**.
c. Click *p04p2img3* in the *Pictures in album* section, and then click **Rotate Right**. Repeat to rotate *p04p2img5* and *p04p2img8* to the right.
d. Click the **Picture layout arrow** in the *Album Layout* section, and then select **2 pictures with title**.
e. Click the **Frame shape arrow** in the *Album Layout* section, and then select **Center Shadow Rectangle**.
f. Click **Create**, and then save the album as **p04p2geo_LastnameFirstname**.
g. Create a handout header with your name, and a handout footer with your instructor's name and your class. Include the current date.
h. On Slide 1 of the resulting album, change the title to **Geocaching in Provo Canyon**. Change the subtitle to your name.

TROUBLESHOOTING: If you get an error message that says "PowerPoint cannot insert a video from the selected file" while inserting *p04p2vid1*, it is because, currently, the Windows operating system does not have a 64-bit video or audio codec for the three QuickTime media formats: MPEG-4 video (*.mp4), MPEG-4 audio (*.m4a), or QuickTime Movie (*.mov). Substitute any of the videos provided in your data files or a video of your choice. Do the same whenever asked to insert a QuickTime video in this exercise.

i. Click the **Design tab**, click the **More button** in the Themes group, and then click the **Module theme**.
j. Enter the following slide titles.

Slide 2	**Marking the jeep as a waypoint for safe return**
Slide 3	**Using our GPS to find the cache**
Slide 4	**Cache contained a waterproof container with coins and the log**
Slide 5	**Trip completed**

k. On Slide 3, click the **Home tab**, click the **New Slide arrow**, and then select **Title Only**. Change the title of the slide to **Hitching a ride on a windy day**.
l. Click the **Insert tab**, click the **Video arrow** in the Media group, and then select **Video from File**. Click *p04p2vid1* from the *p04p2geo_media* folder, and then click **Insert**.
m. Click the **Video Tools Playback tab**, and then click **Trim Video**. Type **00:17.491** in the **Start Time box**, and then click **Play**. Type **00:22.337** in the **End Time box**, and then click **OK**.
n. Type **00.01** in the **Fade Out box** in the Editing group.
o. Click the **Start arrow** in the Video Options group, and then select **Automatically**.
p. Click the **Video Tools Format tab**, and then move to the video frame at 4.75 seconds. Click **Poster Frame**, and then click **Current Frame**.
q. Insert a new Title Only slide, change the title to **Nothing stops Ava**, and then insert *p04p2vid2* from the *p04p2geo_media* folder.
r. Click the **Video Tools Playback tab**, and then click **Move Forward 0.25 Seconds** on the Media Controls bar to advance the video to the frame at 14 seconds. Click **Add Bookmark** in the Bookmark group.
s. Click the **Video Tools Format tab**, click **Video Shape** in the Video Styles group, and then click **Heart** in the Basic Shapes gallery.
t. Click the **Insert tab**, click **Clip Art** in the Images group, type the keyword **supplies**, change Results to **Audio**, and then click **Go**.
u. Point to the resulting audio clips to display the audio name, size, and file type. Locate the *Pencil Scratch, 1.00 Seconds [6 KB] WAV* clip, and then click the clip to insert it into the slide show. Close the Clip Art pane.
v. Drag the audio icon to the bottom of the screen.
w. Select one of the images in your album, click the **Picture Tools Format tab**, click **Compress Pictures** in the Adjust group, and then click the **Apply only to this picture check box** to deselect it. Click **OK**.

x. View the slide show. On Slide 5, point to the Media Controls bar, click the bookmark, and then click **Play** to begin the video at the bookmark site.
y. Save and close the file, and submit based on your instructor's directions.

3 Accident Record

You are involved in an accident on your bullet bike on the way to school one morning. You take pictures with your cell phone to keep a record of the damage to send to your insurance agent. You decide the quickest way to assemble the photographs is to create a Photo Album that is suitable for sending by e-mail. You then edit the Photo Album to include a text box so that you have a location in which to enter the accident details. This exercise follows the same set of skills as used in Hands-On Exercises 1 and 4 in the chapter. Refer to Figure 4.54 as you complete this exercise.

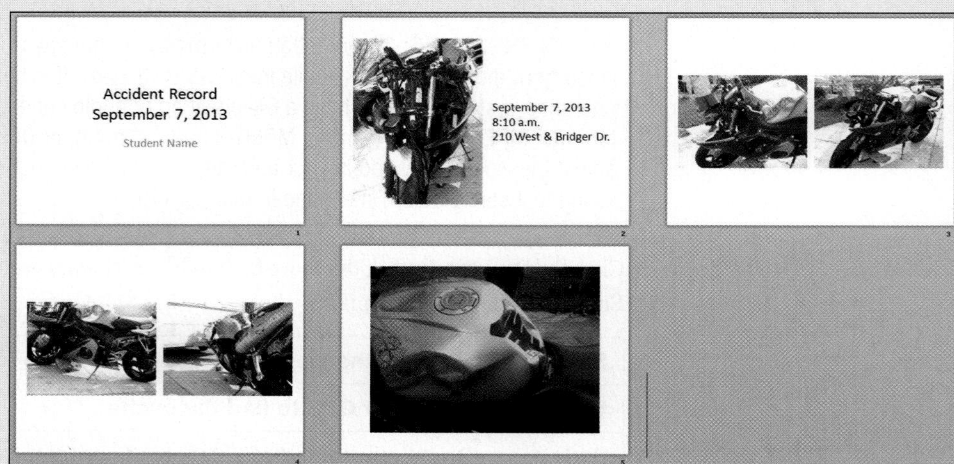

FIGURE 4.54 Accident Record Compressed for E-Mail ➤

a. Open a blank presentation document, click the **Insert tab**, and then click **Photo Album** in the Images group.
b. Click **File/Disk**, navigate to the p04p3accdnt_media folder, press **Ctrl+A**, and then click **Insert**.
c. Click **Create** to create the album, and then save the album as **p04p3accdnt_LastnameFirstname**.
d. Review the slides, and then note that each picture is placed on its own slide, that the photograph is dark in Slide 6, and that the photograph of the bullet bike is sideways in Slide 7.
e. Click the **Insert tab**, click the **Photo Album arrow**, and then click **Edit Photo Album**.
f. Use the **Move up arrow** to reposition *p04p3accdnt6* so that it is the first picture in the *Pictures in album* list.
g. Click the **Rotate left button** once to rotate *p04p3accdnt6* so that the bullet bike is upright.
h. With *p04p3accdnt6* still selected, click **New Text Box**.
i. Select *p04p3accdnt5*, click the **Increase Contrast button** five times, and then click the **Increase Brightness button** seven times.
j. Click the **Picture layout arrow** in the *Album Layout* section, and then click **2 pictures**.
k. Click the **Frame shape arrow** in the *Album Layout* section, and then select **Center Shadow Rectangle**.
l. Click **Update**.
m. Create a handout header with your name, and a handout footer with your instructor's name and your class. Include the current date.
n. Move to Slide 1, and then change the Photo Album title to **Accident Record** on one line and **September 7, 2013** on the following line. Change the subtitle to your name, if necessary.
o. Move to **Slide 2**, select the words *Text Box*, and then type the following information:
   - **September 7, 2013**
   - **8:10 a.m.**
   - **210 West & Bridger Dr.**

p. Select the image on Slide 5, and then click the **Format tab**. Change the height to **6"** in the Size group. The width automatically adjusts to 8".
q. Click **Align** in the Arrange group, and then click **Align Center**. Click **Align** in the Arrange group again, and then click **Align Middle**.
r. With the image still selected, click **Compress Pictures** in the Adjust group, and then deselect the **Apply only to this picture check box** so all pictures in the album will be compressed.
s. Click **E-mail** in the *Target output* section, and then click **OK**.
t. Save and close the file, and submit based on your instructor's directions.

MID-LEVEL EXERCISES

1 ATV for Sale

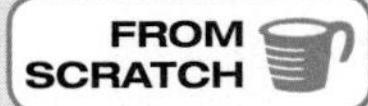

You have enjoyed riding your four wheeler ATV but now decide that you want to sell it to purchase a snowmobile. Using PowerPoint, you create a flyer advertising the four wheeler that you can reproduce to hang on bulletin boards at the college. Refer to Figure 4.55 as you complete this exercise.

FIGURE 4.55 ATV Sales Flyer ➤

a. Open a blank presentation and save it as **p04m1flyer_LastnameFirstname**.
b. Create a handout header with your name, and a handout footer with your instructor's name and your class. Include the current date.
c. Change the layout to a Blank layout.
d. Change the slide orientation to Portrait as you will be printing a single slide to use as a flyer.
e. Insert the **p04m1atv1 image** located in your student files in the p04m1flyer_media folder. Drag the image so that it aligns with the top edge of the page.
f. Create a WordArt object using **Fill – Olive Green, Accent 3, Powder Bevel** (row 5, column 4), and then type **FOUR WHEELER ATV**. Change the WordArt Text Outline to **Black, Text 1**. Change the WordArt font size to **60 pt**. Apply the Text Effect **Tight Reflection, touching** (row 1, column 1 in Reflection Variations).
g. Position the WordArt vertically at **5.5"** from the Top Left Corner. Verify that it is positioned horizontally at **0.12"** from the Top Left Corner.
h. Use the Clip Art pane to search for photographs only to locate the *For Sale* sign shown in Figure 4.55. Insert the image, and then use the Remove Background tool to remove the white background. (Tip: Zoom your view to 200%, and then drag to set areas in the sign to keep for greater accuracy.)
i. Change the scale of the *For Sale* image to 75% of its original size. Position the sign horizontally at **4.5"** from the Top Left Corner. Position it vertically at **6.36"** from the Top Left Corner.
j. Create a text box, and then type **Call 702-555-1212**. Apply a WordArt Style to the text using **WordArt Gradient Fill – Purple, Accent 4, Reflection** (row 4, column 5). Change the font size to **28 pt**.
k. Position the text box horizontally at **2.09"** from the Top Left Corner. Position it vertically at **7.1"** from the Top Left Corner.

l. Insert the **p04m1atv2 image** located in your student files in the p04m1flyer_media folder. Drag the image so that the image borders align with the bottom left corner of the flyer.

m. Adjust the sharpness of the image to +**50%**. Adjust the brightness and contrast to **Brightness: +40% Contrast: +40%**.

n. Create a text box, and then type the following information inside it:

Year: 2005

Usage: 195 hours, 754 miles

Color: Hunter Green

Price: $4,395

o. Change the font size of the text box to **24 pt**. Position the text box horizontally at **2.87"** from the Top Left Corner. Position it vertically at **8.03"** from the Top Left Corner.

p. Compress all the photographs on the flyer.

q. Save and close the file, and submit based on your instructor's directions.

2 Impressionist Paintings

In this exercise, you will use the Internet to obtain images of paintings by some of the masters of the Impressionist style. The paintings in Figure 4.56 may be viewed at the Web Museum (**www.ibiblio.org/wm/paint**) that is maintained by Nicolas Pioch for academic and educational use. On the Famous Artworks exhibition page, click the Impressionism Theme (or search for Impressionist paintings or painters).

a. Open the *p04m2painting* presentation and save it as **p04m2painting _LastnameFirstname.pptx**.

b. Create a handout header with your name, and a handout footer with your instructor's name and your class. Include the current date. On Slide 1, change the subtitle *First Name Last Name* to your name.

c. View the slide show, and then click the hyperlink to *The Web Museum* on Slide 1 to open the Famous Artworks exhibition. Locate the images you will copy and paste into the slide show.

d. When you locate a painting, click the thumbnail image to enlarge it, then right-click it and save the image to a new folder on your storage device named **Impressionist Paintings**. If necessary, change the name of the file to include the artist and the name of the painting. Repeat this process until you have saved each of the images of the paintings shown in the table below.

Slide #	Artist	Title
Slide 1	**Alfred Sisley**	***Autumn: Banks of the Seine near Bougival***
Slide 2	**Claude Monet**	***Impression: soleil levant***
Slide 4	**Edgar Degas**	***Ballet Rehearsal***
Slide 5	**Claude Monet**	***Waterlilies, Green Reflection, Left Part***
Slide 6	**Berthe Morisot**	***The Artist's Sister at a Window***
Slide 7	**Pierre-Auguste Renoir**	***On the Terrace***
Slide 8	**Camille Pissarro**	***Peasant Girl Drinking her Coffee***

e. Return to your slide show. Insert the picture for Slide 1 as a background, and then insert each of the remaining pictures on the appropriate artist's slide. Resize and postion the images as needed. Use picture styles. You do not need to compress the images, as they are already low resolution.

f. Insert an audio clip of your choice in Slide 1. As an alternative to providing your own audio clip, search for the keyword **classical** in the Clip Art pane. Find *Nocturne in ES-Dur* in the search results, and then insert it in Slide 1.

g. Position the audio icon on the slide, and then hide it during play. Loop the audio clip, and then set the song so it plays continuously across slides and does not stop with the next mouse click.

DISCOVER

h. Insert a blank slide after Slide 8. Search the Web for a video clip on Impressionist art, copy the Embed code for the video, and then insert the Embed code in PowerPoint. Apply a **Video Style**, and then choose other video settings as desired.
i. Save and close the file, and submit based on your instructor's directions.

3 Red Butte Garden

You visited Red Butte Garden, a part of the University of Utah, and enjoyed the natural gardens and the botanical garden. You want to create a Photo Album of the pictures you took that day.

a. Create a new Photo Album, and then insert all of the pictures in the *p04m3garden_media* folder.
b. Remove the *p04m3img1* (Red Butte Garden & Arboretum) picture.
c. Locate *p04m3img2*, increase the brightness six times, and then increase the contrast twice.
d. Locate *p04m3img14*, increase the brightness twice, and then increase the contrast six times.
e. Apply a **2 pictures layout** and the **Simple Frame, White frame shape style**.
f. Create the album, and then save it as **p04m3garden_LastnameFirstname**.
g. Create a handout header with your name, and a handout footer with your instructor's name and your class. Include the current date.
h. Edit the album so only one picture per page displays, and then click **Update**.
i. Insert *p04m3img1* as the background for Slide 1, and then remove the title and subtitle placeholders.
j. Move Slide 2 to the end of the slide show, and then apply the **Paint Brush Artistic Effect**.
k. On Slide 14, apply a **Sharpen: 50% correction**.
l. On any slide, apply the **Reveal transition**, and set the advance to automatically advance after **00:02:00**. Apply to all slides.
m. Save and close the file, and submit based on your instructor's directions.

CAPSTONE EXERCISE

A friend and his wife recently had a new baby. You volunteer to create a slide show announcing the birth of the baby that your friend can e-mail to family and friends. You use a modified version of Microsoft's Contemporary Photo Album template. The album has been modified to use a Surfer theme. In this activity, you will create the content, insert the photos, modify the photos, add sound, and insert a video clip of the baby. All media for this activity are located in the *p04c1birth_media* folder.

Insert Pictures

Using template layouts and picture placeholders, you insert photos of the expectant couple taken by Shanna Michelle Photography and photos taken by the family at the baby's birth. You modify template placeholders for better fit. Refer to Figures 4.56 through 4.60 as you complete this section.

a. Open the file named *p04c1birth*, and then save it as **p04c1birth_LastnameFirstname**.

b. Create a handout header with your name, and a handout footer with your instructor's name and your class. Include the current date.

c. On Slide 1, click **Insert Picture from File** in the large content placeholder. Locate the *p04c1birth_media* folder, and then insert *p04c1baby1*. Apply the **Paint Brush artistic effect** (refer to Figure 4.56).

d. Change the title to **IT'S A BOY!**, and change the title font size to **72 pt**.

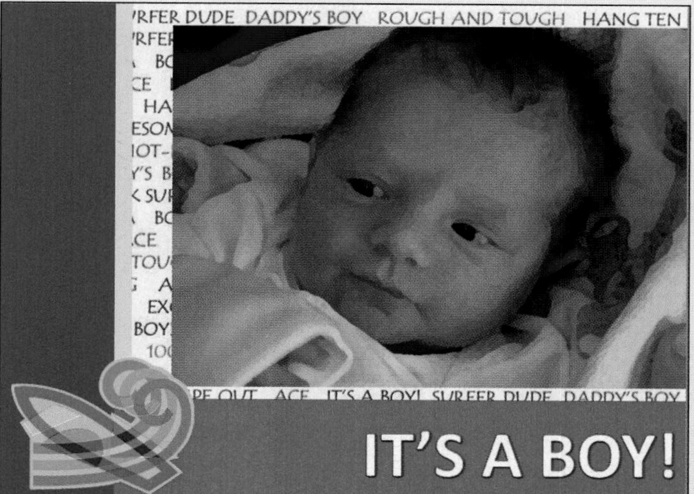

FIGURE 4.56 Slide 1 ▲

e. On Slide 2, insert *p04c1parents1*. Replace the text in the right placeholder with **A grand adventure is about to begin. *Winnie the Pooh***.

f. Select the text placeholder, right-click, and then select **Format Shape**. Modify the Text Box settings to resize the shape to fit the text (refer to Figure 4.57).

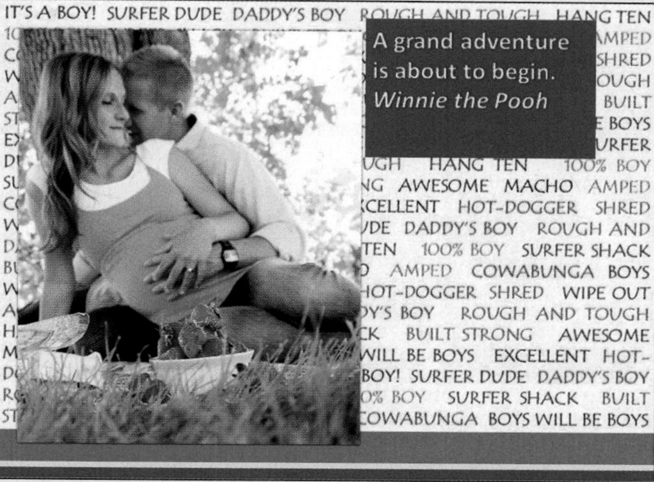

FIGURE 4.57 Slide 2 ▲

g. On Slide 3, change the slide layout to **Landscape with Caption**. Insert *p04c1family1*. Replace the caption text with **FIRST FAMILY PHOTO** (refer to Figure 4.58).

FIGURE 4.58 Slide 3 ▲

h. On Slide 4, replace the text in the blue placeholder with **Father**. Insert *p04c1dad1* in the left picture placeholder. Crop all but the father's head and shoulders. Resize the width of the picture to **2.83"**, let the height adjust automatically, and then drag the picture into a position above the caption (refer to Figure 4.59).

i. Replace the text in the green placeholder with **Mother**. Insert *p04c1mom1* in the right picture placeholder. Crop all but the mother's head and shoulders. Resize the width of the picture to **2.83"**. Drag the picture into a position above the caption (refer to Figure 4.59).

j. Replace the text in the red placeholder with **Baby Boy Jas**. Insert *p04c1baby2* in the center placeholder (refer to Figure 4.59).

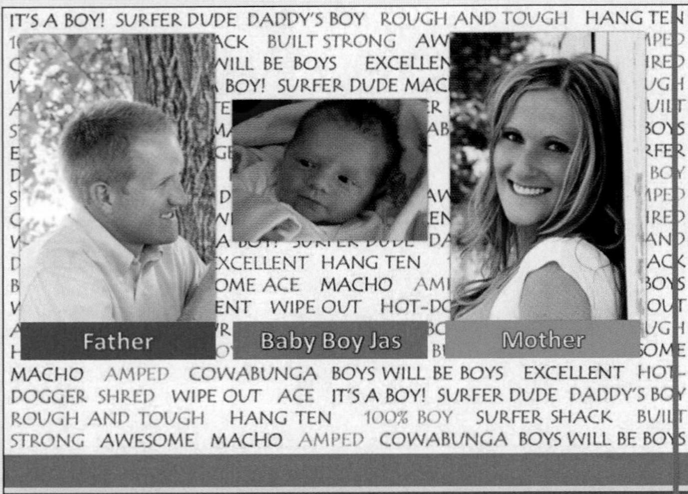

FIGURE 4.59 Slide 4 ▲

k. On Slide 5, insert *p04c1family2* in the large placeholder. Continue in a clockwise direction, and then insert *p04c1family3* through *p04c1family6* in the remaining placeholders (refer to Figure 4.60).

l. View and save the presentation.

Apply and Modify a Picture Style, Change Images

The pictures on Slide 4 would stand out better if they had a frame. You apply and modify a Picture Style. You replace the image of the parents (refer to Figure 4.61).

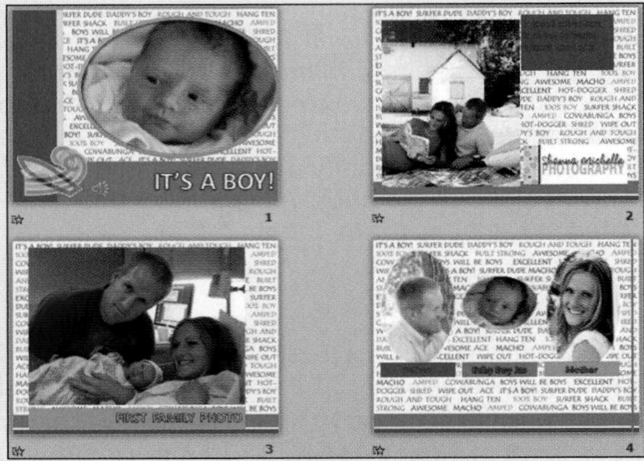

FIGURE 4.61 Picture Style Applied and Modified ▲

a. On Slide 4, select the picture of the father, and then apply the **Beveled Oval, Black picture style**.

b. Apply the **Preset 5 Picture Effect** (second row, first column).

c. Use the Format Painter to copy the effects applied to the center and right photographs.

d. Adjust the Text Box shapes to fit the text.

FIGURE 4.60 Slide 5 ➤

e. Correct the color tone of the baby picture so it is warmer by changing it to **Temperature 11200 K**.

f. On Slide 1, select the baby picture. Apply the **Metal Oval picture style**, and then change the color of the picture border to **Aqua, Accent 5** (first row, ninth column).

g. Select the image on Slide 2, and using the **Adjust tools group** on the Picture Tools Format tab, change the image to *p04c1parents2*.

h. Save the presentation.

Adjust and Compress Images

Some pictures on Slide 5 need the brightness, contrast, and color tones adjusted. You use Picture Tools to adjust the pictures, and then you apply an e-mail compression to all photographs (refer to Figure 4.62).

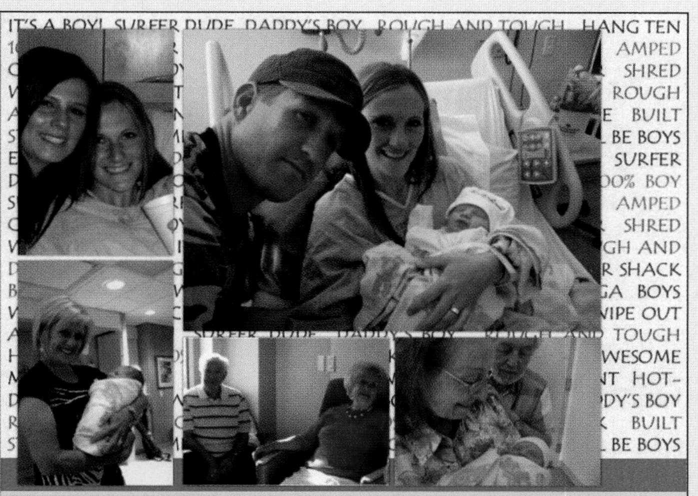

FIGURE 4.62 Image Adjustments ⮝

a. Select the bottom-center picture on Slide 5, and then increase the image brightness **+20%**.

b. Select the bottom-left picture, set the saturation to **66%**, and then set the color tone to **4700 K**.

c. Select the large picture of the parents, and then set the color tone to **8800 K**.

d. Compress all images for e-mail output.

e. Save the presentation.

Use the Internet as a Resource

Shanna Michelle Photography has given you permission to include photos in your presentation. You copy the company logo from their Web site and paste it into your presentation (refer to Figure 4.63).

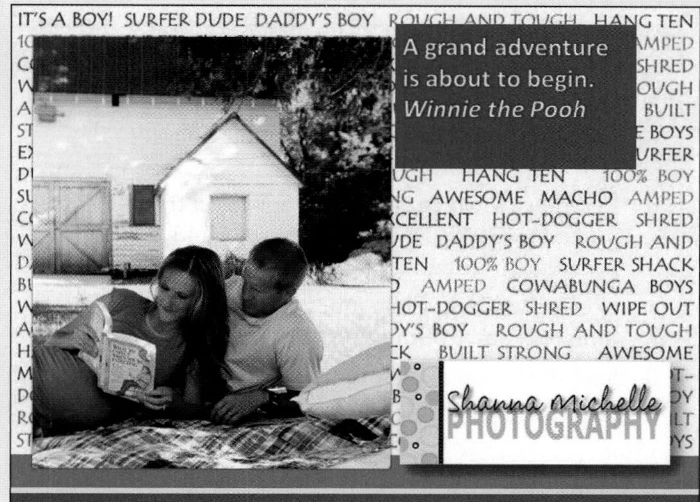

FIGURE 4.63 Image downloaded from Web site ⮝

a. Connect to the Internet, and then go to http://shannamichellephotography.blogspot.com/.

b. Right-click the **Shanna Michelle photography logo**, and then save it as **p04c1smlogo**.

c. Insert the logo on Slide 2.

d. Apply the **Drop Shadow Rectangle picture style**.

e. Positioning and size the logo (refer to Figure 4.64).

f. Save the presentation.

Insert a Movie and Add Sound

You insert a video clip of the baby, and then modify the settings. Finally, you add a soft lullaby music clip that plays continuously through all slides using the Clip Art pane.

a. On Slide 6, insert *p04c1babyvid.avi*.

b. Set a Poster Frame at **00:00:75**.

c. Set the movie to play automatically.

d. Change the Video Options to **Hide While Not Playing** and to **Rewind after Playing**.

e. On Slide 1, search the Clip Organizer for an audio clip using **lullaby** as the keyword for your search.

f. Insert *Kinderscenen* on Slide 1, and then have it **Play across Slides**.

g. Hide the audio icon during the show.

h. Activate the **Loop until Stopped sound option**.

i. Save and close the file, and submit based on your instructor's directions.

Create a Photo Album

Your friend asks you for a printed copy of all of the images. You prepare a photo album, and then print it.

a. Create a New Photo Album using the images in the *p04c1birth_media* folder.

b. Rearrange the pictures so they appear in the following order: berries, dad1, mom1, parents 1 and 2, baby 1 and 2, and then the family pictures in numerical order.

c. Create the album using four pictures per slide and a **Simple Frame, White**.

d. Save the album as **p04c1baby_LastnameFirstname**.

e. Create a handout header with your name, and a handout footer with your instructor's name and your class. Include the current date.

f. Edit the album to remove the *p04c1berries* picture on the first slide and the text box on the last slide (if necessary).

g. Apply *p04c1berries* at 10% transparency as the background image for all slides.

h. Modify the title on the Title Slide to **Baby Jas Photo Album**, and then type your name in the subtitle.

i. Move the title and subtitle above the strawberries.

j. Save and close the file, and submit based on your instructor's directions.

A Visit to the Zoo

GENERAL CASE

FROM SCRATCH

As a first-grade teacher, each year you take your students and parent helpers to the local zoo. The day your class visits, a zookeeper takes your students to specific animals and gives presentations on the animal, its habitat, its diet, and other fun facts. The keeper also teaches the children the difference between skin, fur, feathers, and scales. The keeper asks you to teach the students about animal facts before the visit. You prepare a presentation about the coverings of some of the animals you took pictures of during last year's visit to the zoo.

Create a new photo album with the file name **p04b1zoo_LastNameFirstName**. Include a handout header with your name, and a handout footer with your instructor's name and your class. Include the current date. The title of your slide show should be *OUR ZOO VISIT!*, and the subtitle should be *Animals and Their Coverings*. Use the pictures located in the *p04b1zoo_media* folder. Choose the layout and frame of your choice, but include a text box for each type of animal. Transform and crop images as desired. After creating the album, enter the type of covering for each animal in the text box (example: Crocodiles are covered with scales). Insert the movie *p04b1spray* on the Title slide. Create a Poster Frame and add a Bookmark. If it is possible to record narration in your classroom lab, read the text box on the first slide while recording. Add other narrations if desired. If you are unable to record the narration, insert sounds from the Clip Organizer in appropriate locations. Save and close the file, and submit based on your instructor's directions.

Zeroscaping vs. Xeriscaping

RESEARCH CASE

While on a trip through the Southwest, you took pictures of zeroscaping examples. You plan to use them in an existing slide show on Waterwise Landscaping. You want to know more about xeriscaping, however, so you research xeriscaping online. One site, XericUtah (xericutah.com), has beautiful images of xeriscaping, so you contact them and receive permission to use images from their Web site.

Open *p04b2landscape* and save it as **p04b2landscape_LastnameFirstname**. Add a handout header with your name, and a handout footer with your instructor's name and your class. Include the current date. Research zeroscaping and xeriscaping online, and include the Web sites on a Resources slide at the end of the slide show. Please remember that giving credit to your source does not mean you are released from copyright requirements. Create several speaker notes with information you find during your research. Use the zeroscaping images located in the *p04b2landscape_media* folder where appropriate, but visit xericutah.com to obtain images for the xeriscaping portion of the slide show. Use a xeriscaping picture for the background of the Title slide. You may change the template and add animations as desired. Add an audio clip, and set it to play across all slides. Save and close the file, and submit based on your instructor's directions.

Cascade Springs Ecosystem

DISASTER RECOVERY

You and another fifth-grade teacher are working together to create slide shows for your science students. The other teacher visited Cascade Springs, took pictures, and created a PowerPoint Photo Album of the pictures. Open *p04b3springs*, and then save the new presentation as **p04b3springs_LastnameFirstname**. Review the album and read the speaker notes created from National Forest Service signs available to hikers to help them understand the fragile ecosystem. Your role is to review the presentation created by the album and determine which slides and speaker notes to keep. When necessary, rotate images. You may also change the template or slides as desired. If it is possible to record narration in your classroom lab, read and record shortened versions of at least three speaker notes, and then add the audio files to the slides. If you are unable to record the narration, insert the audio files in the p04b3springs_media folder in appropriate locations. Set the audio files to play when the sound icon is clicked. This allows a teacher to determine if he/she wants to use recordings during the presentation or lecture himself or herself. Finalize the presentation by proofreading, applying transitions and animations, and testing sound icons to ensure they work properly. Compress all images to Screen Target Output. Finally, create a handout header with your name, and a handout footer with your instructor's name and your class. Include the current date. Save the album and submit as directed by your instructor.

POWERPOINT APPLICATION CAPSTONE EXERCISE

You are a student employee of your college's Student Success department. A previous employee created a presentation for students to view while they are waiting for their advisor. The goal of the presentation is to raise student awareness about available savings and discounts. You decide to modify the original slide show to add additional information and visual impact. You will insert and modify an image, a SmartArt graphic, and a presentation containing a table.

Presentation Setup and Slide Creation

You need to open the original slide show, rename the file, and save it. You insert a new slide for additional information.

a. Start PowerPoint. Open *p00ac1discounts*, and then save the file as **p00ac1discounts_LastnameFirstname**.

b. Create a Notes and Handouts Header and Footer with the date, your name in the header, and your instructor's name and your class in the footer.

c. Insert a new slide after Slide 4 with the Title and Content layout.

d. Move to the new Slide 5 if necessary, and then type **Travel Savings** in the **title placeholder**.

e. Type the following as Level 1 bullets for Slide 5: **Airfare discounts**, **Rail passes**, **Global phones**, pressing **Enter** after each.

f. Apply the **Module design theme**. Change the color theme to **Trek**.

Insert and Modify a Picture

You need to insert, resize, and position a picture. You also add a picture frame to the image.

a. On Slide 5, insert the picture file **p00ac1rooftops.jpg**.

b. Change the width of the picture to **3"** and the height to **2"**.

c. Move the picture to the bottom-right corner of the slide so that it aligns with the bottom and right edges of the slide.

d. Apply the Picture Style **Simple Frame, Black**.

Add a Shape

To draw attention to an instruction, you decide to add a shape to a slide and insert text. After adding the shape, you group it with another shape to form an attention-grabbing graphic.

a. On Slide 2, insert the **Horizontal Scroll shape** (row 2, column 6, Stars and Banners category).

b. Change the width of the shape to **2.5"** and the height to **1.75"**.

c. Position the shape horizontally at **7.5"** and vertically at **5"** from the Top Left Corner.

d. Type **Use a search engine to find "Software Discounts"** in the shape.

e. Select both the **Explosion1 shape** and the **Horizontal Scroll shape**, and then align them by their middles. Group the shapes.

f. With the shapes still selected, apply the shape style **Moderate Effect - Orange, Accent 1**.

Use WordArt, Format a Background, and Insert Audio

You decide to enhance the Title slide by changing text to WordArt, formatting the background to add an image, and by adding an audio clip.

a. On Slide 1, select the text in the title placeholder, and then apply the WordArt style **Gradient Fill - Orange, Accent 1**.

b. Switch to the Outline tab, and then on Slide 1, select the subtitle **Savings for cash-poor college kids**. Change the font style to **Italic** and the font size to **24 pt**.
c. Click the **Design tab**, and then access the Format Background options so that you can select a picture fill.
d. Select the picture file **p00ac1rooftops.jpg**, and then change the transparency to **20%**. Insert the picture.
e. Insert the audio file **p00ac1providence.wma**. Apply a **02.00 Fade Out duration**.
f. Change the audio clip playback from On Click to **Play across slides**. Insert a check in the **Loop until Stopped audio option**.
g. Align the sound icon to the bottom of the slide.

Add Content and Animation

You reuse a previously created slide to add content, and then you format the table on the reused slide. Next, you create a SmartArt graphic to include information about "free stuff" for students, and then you animate the graphic.

a. Switch to the Slides tab, and then use the Reuse Slides feature to add the slide in *p00ac1tips.pptx* at the end of the presentation.
b. On the new Slide 6, select the table, and then set the height of all the rows to **1"**.
c. Center align the text in the table. Apply the **Medium Style 1 table style** to the table.
d. Move the table so that its top-left corner is at the 1" mark above the 0 on the vertical ruler. Center align the table on the slide.
e. Insert a new slide after Slide 6 using the Title and Content layout. Type **Student Free Stuff** in the **title placeholder**.
f. On the new Slide 7, insert a **Vertical Box List SmartArt graphic**. Type **Ringtones** in the top shape, **Online video games** in the middle shape, and **Magazines and samples** in the bottom shape.
g. Change the SmartArt layout to a **Horizontal Bullet List**, and then change the SmartArt style to **Inset** (3-D category).
h. Align the SmartArt graphic to the bottom of the slide, and then resize as necessary so that it fits on the slide.
i. Apply the **Fly In animation** (Entrance category) to the SmartArt. Change the sequence of the animation to the **One by One effect**.

Finalize the Presentation

To ensure the professionalism of the presentation, you review the presentation and make changes.

a. Spell-check the presentation, and then correct any misspelled words. Ignore the error message that appears for *PacSun*.
b. On Slide 1, change the expression *cash-poor* to **cash-strapped**.
c. On Slide 2, use the Thesaurus to replace the word *generally* with an appropriate synonym.
d. Apply the **Cube transition** to all slides.
e. Change the transition timing so that all slides advance automatically after 8 seconds.
f. View the presentation.
g. Save the presentation. Close the presentation, and then exit PowerPoint. Submit the presentation as directed by your instructor.

1 Creating a Free Web Site and Blog for Your PowerPoint Experiences

Web 2.0 technologies make it easy for people to interact using the Internet. Web applications often combine functions to help us create our online identity, share information, collaborate on projects, and socialize. In this exercise, you will create an online identity for your use in your PowerPoint class, share information about your PowerPoint experience with others, and get to know a few of your classmates. You will create a Web site for use during your PowerPoint class, add information to the pages in your Web site, and then share the address of your site with others. You will also visit the Web sites of others in your class.

a. Open a Web browser, and then go to **www.weebly.com/**.
b. Enter your full name as the *Username* in the **Sign Up box**, enter your e-mail address, and then enter a password.
c. Type the security words in the **Please verify that you are human box** as requested, and then click **OK, let's go!**
d. Select the text in the **Welcome to Weebly box**, and then enter a title for your Web site as follows: use your first name followed by *PPT* to indicate this is your PowerPoint site, select the **Education category**, and then **Class Project** for your site type.
e. Select **Use a Subdomain of Weebly.com** in the Choose Your Website Domain box to set up the address where people will find your Web site online. Using a subdomain of Weebly.com is free. Click **Continue**. You have created your Web site, and you should note your Web site address as you will be sharing this address with your instructor and/or selected classmates.
f. Select the **Elements tab**, if necessary, and then drag elements from the top bar to the page to create your site. Add an element that can be used to introduce you to others (such as Paragraph with Title or Paragraph with Picture). Also, add a contact form so other students can get in touch with you if they have a comment or question.
g. Click the **Design tab**, and then select the Design theme of your choice for your site.
h. Click the **Pages tab**, and then click **Add Blog**. Click in the **Page Name box**, select **Blog**, type the name you want to use for your blog, and then click **Save Settings**. The left panel of the screen now shows that your Web site has two pages: your home page and your blog site.
i. Edit your blog by adding text that explains your previous experience with PowerPoint and why you have registered for this class. Search YouTube for a video about PowerPoint or Presentation skills. Create a second blog entry about what you learned and include the link for others to view, if interested.
j. Publish your Web site.
k. Exchange Web site addresses with at least three other students in your class. Visit your classmates' Web sites and use the contact form on their Home pages to leave your information and a comment. Then, revisit your Web site to see what comments your classmates entered.
l. E-mail your instructor the Web site address you created in step e so your instructor can visit your site.

2 Using Social Technologies for Ideas and Resources

Social networking enables us to use the Internet to connect with others through common interests. Social networking is also helpful to businesses who want to encourage their users to share ideas and who want to inform their users about the functionality of their products. Microsoft PowerPoint maintains a Facebook page that provides a wall where Microsoft posts information about their product and users post questions and ideas, a design gallery to inspire users, a support link where a user can post a question and have it answered, slidefest and video links that include both educational and fun media, and other options to help users. In this exercise, you will visit Microsoft's PowerPoint Facebook page, download a template from the Design Gallery, modify the template with your information, and then post the PowerPoint presentation you create to your Web site for others to view. *Note*: This exercise assumes you have done the Collaboration exercise for Chapter 1. If you have not completed that exercise, use Dropbox.com or another method for sharing your presentation with your instructor and classmates.

a. Access the Internet, and then go to your Facebook page. (Note: If you do not have a Facebook page and do not wish to create one, access the Internet and visit Office.com. Locate the available PowerPoint templates, select one, complete a presentation based on the template, and then post the presentation to the Web site you created in Collaborative Exercise 1, or save the presentation to a shared location your instructor recommends.)
b. Type **Microsoft PowerPoint** in the **Facebook Search box**, and then press **Enter**.
c. Scroll through Microsoft PowerPoint's wall to see the comment and question posts other people are making as well as the educational posts from Microsoft.
d. Click the **Design Gallery link** on the left panel of the page if necessary, and then click **Allow** on the permission screen if necessary.
e. Click the **View and Download the collections link**. The page you view displays a series of slides created by one of Microsoft's featured artists. Microsoft PowerPoint provides these slides as an exclusive benefit for their fans. Click **view all artist's collections** to see a thumbnail series of available presentation slides. Click a thumbnail to view the topic of the presentation, and then click **view all artist's collections** to return to the thumbnail view.
f. Select one of the presentations, and then download the slides to the location you use to store your files for this class. Open the saved slide show, and then modify the slides so they reflect your information and ideas. Make sure you create a final slide that credits the original artist for the slide design.
g. Load your edited presentation to an online location for others to review. If you are using the Weebly.com site from Exercise 1, open your Web site, and then click the **Multimedia link** on the Elements tab. Drag the **File element** to your Home page, and then upload the presentation you created from Microsoft's PowerPoint Facebook page Design Gallery. If you are not using the Weebly.com site from Collaborative Exercise 1, use Dropbox.com or another method for sharing your presentation with your instructor and classmates.
h. Create a blog entry about this experience if you are using the Weebly.com site created in Collaborative Exercise 1. Explain why you selected the artist's slides you used and what knowledge you gained from visiting Microsoft's PowerPoint Facebook page. Ask three classmates to go to the site, view the presentation you saved, and then add a comment about your presentation or blog entry. If you saved to Dropbox.com or another online storage location, share the location with three classmates, and then ask them to download the presentation. After viewing the presentation, ask them to e-mail you with their comments.
i. Visit three of your classmates' Weebly Web sites or download three classmates' presentations from their storage location. Use the contact form on their Weebly Home page to leave your information and a comment about their presentations, or e-mail your classmates sharing a comment about their presentations.
j. Review the comments of your classmates.
k. E-mail your instructor your Web site address or storage location so he or she can review your presentation.

3 Learning from an Expert

Video sharing sites such as YouTube.com make it possible to learn from PowerPoint industry experts as well as everyday PowerPoint users. You can learn through step-by-step instructions or by inspiration after seeing others use PowerPoint. The video source may also refer you to a professional Web site that will provide you with a wealth of tips and ideas for creating slide shows that move your work from ordinary to extraordinary. In this exercise, you will view a YouTube video featuring the work of Nancy Duarte, a well-known PowerPoint industry expert. After viewing the video and related Web site, you will use shapes and animation to re-create one of the effects in Duarte's presentation. Finally, you will post the slide you created to your Web site and blog about your experience. *Note*: This exercise assumes you have done the Collaboration exercise for Chapter 1. If you have not completed that exercise, use Dropbox.com or another method for sharing your presentation with your instructor and classmates.

a. Access the Internet, and then go to www.youtube.com. Search for the video *Powerpoint 2010: The Possibilities - Duarte HD.* View the video, click the supporting link beneath the video (**www.microsoft.eu**), and then note the additional resources available to viewers of the video. Close the Microsoft Europe Web site.

b. Advance to 2:29 seconds in the video clip on YouTube, and then rewatch Duarte's Rule 4—Practice Design Not Decoration.

c. Open *p00c3duarte.pptx*, which contains the slide *Duarte's Rule 4*. Apply animations to the shapes and text contained in the file to reproduce the effect of Duarte's slide. If you prefer, create your own slide reproducing any of Duarte's rules for effective presentations and animate it as desired. Save the file as **p00c3duarte_LastnameFirstname**.

d. Load your animated slide to your Weebly Web site if you completed Collaboration Exercise 1. Open the site, and then click the **Multimedia link** on the Elements tab. Drag the **File element** to your Home page, and then upload the *p00c3duarte_LastnameFirstname* file. If you are not using the Weebly.com site created during Collaborative Exercise 1, upload your animated slide to Dropbox.com or another online storage site.

e. Create a blog entry about this experience if you are using the Weebly.com site created in Collaborative Exercise 1. Discuss Duarte's rules and whether you have seen good examples and/or bad examples of these rules used in presentations. Ask three classmates to go to your Weebly Web site, view the presentation you saved, and then add a comment about your presentation or blog entry. If you saved to Dropbox.com or another online storage location, share the location with three classmates, and then ask them to download the presentation. Ask your classmates to view the presentation, and ask them to e-mail you with their comments.

f. Visit three of your classmates' Web sites after the due date for this exercise, and then use the contact form on their Home pages to leave your information and a comment about their presentations or blogs. Revisit your Web site to see what comments your classmates entered. Or, download and view three of your classmates' animated slides from the storage location they used.

g. E-mail your instructor your Web site address or storage location so your instructor can review your presentation.

4 Collaborating on a Group Project

In this exercise, you will collaborate with two to three students from your class to create a PowerPoint presentation advertising a product. Your group will determine the product you wish to sell. Be inventive! Find an existing product that you can use as a prop to represent your new product (see example in second paragraph). Create a storyboard for that product, and use a digital camera or cell phone to capture images for the product. You will upload your version of the pictures to a location all team members can access such as a SkyDrive account. You will then view your team's pictures, download the ones you wish to use, and create a presentation based on the storyboard—each group member prepares his or her own storyboard and presentation. Only the images are shared. You will insert the images you wish to use in the slides. You will edit the images as needed. You will create a final slide that lists all of the team members in your group. Finally, you will upload your version of the presentation to your Web site and blog about your experience.

For example, after talking using chat technology, a group decides to use green mouthwash as their product. But rather than have it represent mouthwash, they are going to use it as a "brain enhancer." They create a storyboard that lists Slide 1 as a Title and Content slide using the image of the mouthwash and the name of the product—Brain ++. For the second slide, they decide to illustrate the problem by having a picture of a person holding a test paper with the Grade F plainly visible. For the third slide, they decide to illustrate the solution by having the same person pretending to drink the Brain ++. The fourth slide demonstrates the result by showing the same person holding a test paper with the Grade A plainly visible. The last slide lists all members of the group. *Note*: This exercise assumes you have done the Collaboration exercise for Chapter 1. If you have not completed that exercise, use Dropbox.com or another method for sharing your presentation with your instructor and classmates.

a. Create a group with two to three class members and exchange contact information so you will be able to message each other. For example, have each member create a Windows Live account, a Yahoo! account, Facebook, Oovoo, or some other text or video chat technology.

b. Determine, as a group, the product you will be advertising and its use. Discuss the story line for your product with the group, and then each member should create a storyboard.

c. Each member should use a digital camera or cell phone to take pictures of the product.
d. Upload your images to a location on the cloud that will allow all group members to access the pictures. For example, your group could decide to load the images to Windows SkyDrive, Google, or Box.net.
e. View all of the images your group uploaded, determine which ones you want to use in your presentation, and then download those images.
f. Create a PowerPoint presentation, and then insert the product images into slides following the storyboard you created. Edit the slides and images as needed. Enhance slides as desired.
g. Save the completed presentation as **p00c4product_LastnameFirstname**.
h. Open your Web site, if you are using the Weebly.com site you created in Exercise 1, and then click the **Multimedia link** on the Elements tab. Drag the **File element** to your Home page, and then upload the *p00c3duarte_LastnameFirstname* file. If you are not using the Weebly.com site, upload your animated slide to Dropbox.com or another online storage site.
i. Create a blog posting about this experience, or write an essay using Microsoft Word. Was collaborating with others through a chat tool a good experience or was it difficult? What did you like about the experience? How could it have been improved? How easily did your group reach agreement on your product?
j. E-mail your instructor your Web site address if you uploaded the presentation and your comments to your Weebly Web site. If you stored your presentation on Dropbox.com, e-mail the location of your stored file to your instructor so he or she can download and view the presentation.

CAPSTONE EXERCISES

Using Office In the Legal, Medical, and Arts Professions

LEGAL EXERCISES

Application	Exercises	Skills Covered
1. WORD Data Files: w_pl_facts.docx Solution Files: w_pl_facts_LastnameFirstname.docx w_pl_saww_LastnameFirstname.docx	WORKERS' COMPENSATION REPORT (page 1047)	• Insert Page Breaks • Add Page Numbers • Insert a Cover Page • Insert Headers and Footers • Check Spelling and Grammar • Set Margins • Modify Document Properties • Apply Font Attributes • Control Word Wrapping • Use Tabs • Create, Use, and Modify Styles • Format a Graphic Element • Insert Clip Art and Images into a Document • Insert Comments into a Document • Acknowledge a Source • Create Footnotes • Add Legal References • Insert a Table • Format a Table
2. EXCEL Data Files: e_pl_trust.xlsx Solution Files: e_pl_trust_LastnameFirstname.xlsx e_pl_ledger_LastnameFirstname.xlsx	CLIENT LEDGER TRUST LEDGER (page 1051)	• Design a Worksheet • Enter and Edit Cell Data • Use Symbols and Order of Precedence in Formulas • Rename Worksheets • Copy Worksheets • Insert Columns and Rows • Hide and Unhide Columns and Rows • Select a Range • Use Paste Special • Insert and Delete Columns and Rows • Apply Alignment and Font Options • Apply Number Formats • Select Page Setup Options • Use Relative, Absolute, and Mixed Cell References • Use the SUM Function • Insert Statistical Functions • Insert the TODAY Function • Use the VLOOKUP Function • Use the IF Function • Create Nested Functions • Create a Bar Chart • Select the Data Source • Position and Size the Chart • Apply a Chart Layout and a Chart Style • Insert and Format the Chart Title • Customize the Legend • Freeze Rows and Columns • Set a Print Area • Create a Table • Apply a Table Style • Sort Data • Filter Data • Create a Total Row
3. ACCESS Data Files: a_pl_importcases.accdb Solution Files: a_pl_lawfirm_LastnameFirstname.accdb	LAW OFFICE DATABASE (page 1055)	• Navigate Among the Objects in an Access Database • Back Up, Compact, and Repair Access files • Create Filters • Sort Table Data on One or More Fields • Use the Relationships Window • Understand Relational Power • Design Data • Create Tables • Understand Table Relationships • Share Data with Excel • Establish Table Relationships • Create a Single-Table Query • Specify Criteria in a Query • Copy and Modify a Query • Create a Multi-Table Query • Modify a Multi-Table Query • Create a Calculated Field in a Query • Create Expressions with the Expression Builder • Use Built-In Functions in Access • Perform Date Arithmetic • Add Aggregate Functions to Datasheets and Queries • Create Forms using the Form Tools • Modify a Form • Revise Forms using Layout View • Identify Control Types in Forms • Create Reports using the Report Wizard • Modify a Report • Identify Report Sections • Revise Reports Using Layout and Design Views • Identify Control Types in Reports

4. POWERPOINT Data Files: p_pl_outline.rtf p_pl_lawbooks.jpg p_pl_relief.jpg Solution Files: p_pl_bankruptcy_LastnameFirstname	BANKRUPTCY PRESENTATION (page 1059)	• Plan a Presentation • Use Slide Layouts • Apply Themes • Insert Media Objects • Add a Table • Use Transitions and Animations • Run and Navigate a Slide Show • Print in PowerPoint • Create a Presentation Using a Template • Modify a Template • Import an Outline • Add Existing Content to a Presentation • Modify a Theme • Create Shapes • Create SmartArt • Create WordArt • Modify Objects • Arrange Objects • Insert a Picture • Transform a Picture • Use the Internet as a Resource • Add Video • Use Video Tools
5. INTEGRATED Data Files: i_pl_contacts.xlsx i_pl_letter.docx i_pl_responses.xlsx Solution Files: i_pl_contacts_LastnameFirstname.accdb i_pl_letter_LastnameFirstname.docx i_pl_responses_LastnameFirstname.xlsx i_pl_merge_LastnameFirstname	RECIPIENT NAMES DATABASE (page 1063) CAMPAIGN MERGED LETTERS (page 1063) APPROVAL RATING WORKSHEET (page 1064) PROMOTIONAL FLYER (page 1065)	• Create and Utilize a Database Containing Contact Information • Create a Merge Source File • Embed and Link Content from Multiple Sources • Choose Records or Fields to Merge

MEDICAL EXERCISES

Application	Exercises	Skills Covered
1. WORD Data files: w_md_vaccinations.docx Solution Files: w_md_vaccinations_LastnameFirstname.docx	VACCINATION GUIDE (page 1069)	• Insert Page Breaks • Add Page Numbers • Insert a Cover Page • Set Margins and Specify Page Orientation • Insert Headers and Footers • Create Sections • Check Spelling and Grammar • View a Document • Use Save Options • Select Printing Options • Modify Document Properties • Apply Font Attributes • Highlight Text • Control Word Wrapping with Nonbreaking Hyphens and Nonbreaking Spaces • Set Off Paragraphs with Tabs, Borders, Lists, and Columns • Apply Paragraph Formats • Copy Formats with the Format Painter • Create and Modify Styles • Insert Clip Art • Format a Graphic Element • Insert Symbols • Insert Comments • Track Changes • Create a Bibliography • Create and Modify Footnotes and Endnotes • Create a Table of Contents • Add Figure References • Insert a Table of Figures • Insert a Table • Format a Table • Convert Text to a Table
2. EXCEL Data Files: e_md_log.xlsx Solution Files: e_md_log_LastnameFirstname.xlsx	PATIENTS' PAYMENT LOG (page 1074)	• Enter and Edit Cell Data • Use Symbols and Order of Precedence in Formulas • Use AutoFill to Complete a Range and Copy Formulas • Display Cell Formulas • Rename and Copy Worksheets • Select a Range • Apply Alignment and Font Options • Apply Number Formats • Select Page Setup Options • Use Relative, Absolute, and Mixed Cell References • Use the SUM Function • Insert Statistical Functions • Insert Date Functions • Use the IF Function • Use the VLOOKUP Function • Assign Range Names and Use Range Names in Formulas • Create a Pie Chart • Select the Data Source • Apply a Chart Layout and a Chart Style • Move the Chart • Insert and Customize a Sparkline • Insert and Format the Chart Title • Customize the Data Labels • Freeze Rows and Columns • Create a Table • Apply a Table Style • Sort Data • Filter Data • Create a Total Row • Apply a Data Bar Conditional Format

3. ACCESS Data files: a_md_medical.accdb a_md_import_patients.accdb Solution files: a_md_medical_ LastnameFirstname.accdb	MEDICAL CLINIC (page 1078)	• Navigate Among the Objects in an Access Database • Back Up, Compact, and Repair Access Files • Create Filters • Sort Table Data on One or More Fields • Use the Relationships Window • Understand Relational Power • Design Data • Create Tables • Understand Table Relationships • Share Data with Excel • Establish Table Relationships • Create a Single-Table Query • Specify Criteria for Different Data Types • Copy and Run a Query • Create a Multi-Table Query • Modify a Multi-Table Query • Create a Calculated Field in a Query • Create Expressions with the Expression Builder • Use Built-In Functions in Access • Perform Date Arithmetic • Add Aggregate Functions to Datasheets and Queries • Create Forms Using the Form Tools • Modify a Form • Identify Form Sections • Revise Forms Using Form views • Identify Control Types in Forms • Create Reports Using Report Tools • Modify a Report • Sort Records in a Report • Identify Report Sections • Revise Reports Using Report Views • Identify Control Types in Reports
4. POWERPOINT Data Files: p_md_hypertension .pptx p_md_image1.jpg p_md _image2.jpg p_md_image3.jpg p_md_ image4.jpg p_md_image5.jpg Solution Files: p_md_ bloodpressure_ LastnameFirstname	BLOOD PRESSURE EDUCATION (page 1083)	• Use PowerPoint Views • Use Slide Layouts • Apply Themes • Insert Media Objects • Add a Table • Use Animations and Transitions • Insert a Header or Footer • Run and Navigate a Slide Show • Print in PowerPoint • Create a Presentation Using a Template • Modify a Template • Create a Presentation in Outline View • Import an Outline • Add Existing Content to a Presentation • Modify a Theme • Create Shapes • Apply Quick Styles and Customize Shapes • Create SmartArt • Modify SmartArt • Create WordArt • Modify WordArt • Modify Objects • Arrange Objects • Insert a Picture • Transform a Picture • Use the Internet as a Resource • Add Video • Use Video Tools • Add Audio • Change Audio Settings
5. INTEGRATED Data Files: i_md_receivables .accdb i_md_memo.docx Solution files: i_md_receivables_ LastnameFirstname.accdb i_md_clinics_LastnameFirstname .xlsx i_md_midwest_ LastnameFirstname.pptx i_md_memo_LastnameFirstname .docx	PATIENT BALANCES (page 1088)	• Maintain a Database Containing Patient and Physical Information • Merge Data Using Word and Excel (or Access) • Determine Which Application to Use When Creating Documents • Practice Good File Management (Including File Naming, Storing, and Backup Procedures)

ARTS EXERCISES

Application	Exercises	Skills Covered
1. WORD Data Files: w_a_presspacket .docx w_a_pricelist.docx Solution Files: w_a_presspacket_ LastnameFirstname.docx	PRESS PACKET (page 1091)	• Insert Page Breaks • Add Page Numbers • Insert a Cover Page • Insert Headers and Footers • Create Sections • Check Spelling and Grammar • Set Margins and Specify Page Orientation • Apply Font Attributes • Set Off Paragraphs with Tabs and Bulleted Lists • Apply Paragraph Formats • Copy Formats with the Format Painter • Use Styles • Insert Comments • Track Changes • Create Footnotes Insert a Table • Format a Table • Convert Text to a Table • Insert Formulas in a Table

2. EXCEL Data Files: e_a_theatre.xlsx Solution Files: e_a_theatre_ LastnameFirstname.xlsx	PRODUCTION BUDGETS (page 1095)	• Enter and Edit Cell Data • Use Symbols and the Order of Precedence • Display Cell Formulas • Manage Worksheets • Manage Columns and Rows • Apply Alignment and Font Options • Apply Number Formats • Specify Page Setup Options • Use Relative, Absolute, and Mixed Cell References in Formulas • Total Values with the SUM Function • Insert Basic Statistical Functions • Use Date Functions • Determine Results with the IF Function • Calculate Payments with the PMT Function • Create a Chart • Apply a Chart Layout and a Chart Style • Move a Chart • Insert and Customize a Sparkline • Select and Format Chart Elements • Customize Chart Labels • Freeze Rows and Columns • Create a Table • Sort Data • Filter Data • Apply Conditional Formatting
3. ACCESS Data Files: a_a_broadway.accdb a_a_import_casting.accdb Solution Files: a_a_broadway_ LastnameFirstname.accdb	ACTOR DATABASE (page 1099)	• Navigate Among the Objects in an Access Database • Back Up, Compact, and Repair an Access File • Sort Table Data on One or More Fields • Use the Relationships Window • Understand Relational Power • Create Tables • Understand Table Relationships • Share Data with Excel • Establish Table Relationships • Create a Single-Table Query • Copy and Modify a Query • Specify Criteria in a Query • Create a Multi-Table Query • Modify a Multi-Table Query • Create a Calculated Field in a Query • Use Built-In Functions in Access • Perform Date Arithmetic • Add Aggregate Functions to Datasheets and Queries • Create Forms Using the Form Tool • Modify a Form • Revise Forms Using Layout View • Identify Control Types in Forms • Create Reports Using the Report Wizard • Modify a Report • Identify Report Sections • Revise Reports Using Layout and Design Views • Identify Control Types in Reports
4. POWERPOINT Data Files: Christmas at the Andersons'.jpg p_a_brochure.pptx p_a_gmaudio.mp3 p_a_gmlogo.jpg p_a_outline.docx Paul's Kitchen 1.jpg Paul's Kitchen 2.jpg This Was Not In The Brochure.jpg Solution Files: p_a_kiosk_ LastnameFirstname.pptx p_a_season_LastnameFirstname .pptx	PRESENTATION OF PLAYS (page 1103) KIOSK PRESENTATION (page 1106)	• Use PowerPoint Views • Use Slide Layouts • Apply Themes • Insert Media Objects • Add a Table • Use Animations and Transitions • Insert a Header or Footer • Run and Navigate a Slide Show • Modify a Template • Modify an Outline Structure • Add Existing Content to a Presentation • Modify a Theme • Create Shapes • Apply Quick Styles and Customize Shapes • Create SmartArt • Modify SmartArt • Create WordArt • Modify WordArt • Modify Objects • Arrange Objects • Insert a Picture • Transform a Picture • Add Audio • Change Audio Settings
5. INTEGRATED Data Files: i_a_stats.docx i_a_seasontickets.accdb Solution Files: i_a_seasontickets_ LastnameFirstname.accdb i_a_seasontickets_ LastnameFirstname.xlsx i_a_stats_LastnameFirstname .docx i_a_stats_LastnameFirtname.pptx	TICKET HOLDER SALES REPORTS AND PRESENTATIONS (page 1107)	• Create a Summary Query • Export Query Results to an Excel Worksheet • Calculate Statistics Using MIN, MAX, and AVERAGE Functions • Create Charts from Data • Display the Statistics and Charts as Linked Objects in a PowerPoint Presentation • Embed Objects in a Word Document • Use Themes Across Applications to Create a Cohesive Appearance

Paralegals

Use Microsoft Word

Background

Word processors are the most used application program in a law office. Paralegals help create, modify, and disseminate a wide variety of legal documents. It is imperative that the paralegal knows the many features available in Microsoft Word and be comfortable using them without having to refer back regularly to a reference guide. Occasionally, however, the paralegal may need to refer to Microsoft Office Help to gain the knowledge needed to complete an unfamiliar task. The skills you use to complete the following tasks are taught in the four Word chapters and are all vital paralegal skills. In addition, you may want to use Microsoft Office Help to refresh your knowledge or to learn about more advanced skills.

Tasks

In a small office, the paralegal may be responsible for all kinds of document production. This could include the following:

- Correspondence and mailings (cover letters, face sheets, copies of pleadings)
- Presentations
- Forms, including billing
- Memoranda
- Reports and briefs

In a larger office, the office assistant may take care of general typing duties, but the paralegal might still be responsible for the following:

- Pleadings
- Research
- Case documentation

Skills

In addition to basic formatting skills, a paralegal should be able to do the following:

Chapter 1

- Insert page breaks (p. 127)
- Add page numbers (p. 128)
- Insert a cover page (p. 130)
- Insert headers and footers (p. 137)
- Check spelling and grammar (p. 141)
- Set margins (p. 145)
- Modify document properties (p. 155)

Chapter 2

- Apply font attributes (p. 172)
- Control word wrapping (p. 176)
- Use tabs (p. 180)
- Create, use, and modify styles (p. 195)
- Format a graphic element (p. 205)
- Insert clip art and images into a document (p. 211)

Chapter 3

- Insert comments into a document (p. 226)
- Acknowledge a source (p. 237)
- Create footnotes (p. 240)
- Add legal references (p. 242)

Chapter 4

- Insert a table (p. 272)
- Format a table (p. 274)

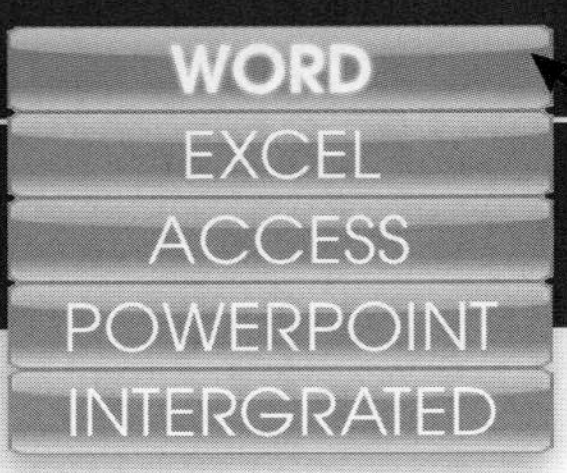

You work for a workers' compensation attorney who will be making a presentation at a State Bar function. Your boss wants to prepare a document to share with the attendees that will highlight the way workers' compensation intersects with other areas of law. You have been provided with a copy of his document to format, but it contains comments from one of his colleagues who reviewed the document. Prepare this document so that it has a professional appearance. It will be distributed in both paper and electronic form, so you will prepare it for appropriate viewing by either method.

Accept Document Revisions and Change File Properties

You review the document comments made by your attorney's colleague and notice that she has used a combination of methods to insert her suggestions. Your attorney has already authorized you to accept the revisions and apply her suggestions to his document.

a. Open *w_pl_facts*, and then save it as **w_pl_facts_LastnameFirstname**.

b. Accept all document revisions that were made in this document.

c. Delete all of the comments that were inserted throughout the document.

Use Find and Replace Commands

With the Show/Hide (¶) feature active to check spacing of headings, you note that in several locations there are two spaces between words and after periods instead of the correct single space. While scanning the document, you also noted that a contraction was used and you wish to change it to the more formal legal style, which does not use contractions.

a. Turn on the **Show/Hide (¶) feature**, if you have not already done so.

b. Use the Replace feature to locate two spaces and replace with one space. Replace all.

c. Search for the contraction "*don't*" and replace with "**do not**."

Apply Styles and Use Format Painter

Review the outline of the document to see how it is formatted. You decide to format the title, author's name, and each paragraph heading. The paragraph and section headings in the document are currently written in normal font, with individually applied attributes (such as bold). Use the existing Heading 1 style to reformat the headings.

a. Apply the **Book Title style** to the title of the document. Modify the style to use a font size of **16 pt**.

b. Select the **author identification line**. Apply the **Emphasis style**.

c. Select **Generally** (the first-level paragraph heading for the first paragraph), and then apply the **Heading 1 style**.

d. Use the Format Painter to apply this style to the remaining first-level paragraph headings.

Modify Styles

The attorney prefers a more traditional color scheme, so you modify the Heading 1 style. You also modify the Normal style to include a first line indent.

a. Right-click the **Heading 1 style** in the Styles group on the Home tab, and then click **Modify** to open the Modify Style dialog box. Modify the Heading 1 style so the font color applied is **Dark Blue, Text 2, Darker 50%.**

b. Click **Format** in the Modify Style dialog box, and then modify the Paragraph format to include 6 pt spacing after. Close the Modify Style dialog box.

c. Click within any paragraph using the Normal style. Modify the Normal style to include a First Line Indent.

Format the Document

You want the document to be formal, yet appealing. Apply additional formatting features to improve the appearance.

a. Set the left and right document margins to **1.5"**.

b. Insert a header using the Pinstripes style.

c. Type the header text **Workers' Compensation: A Few Facts Worth Knowing for the Non-Practitioner**.

d. Adjust the First Line Indent on the vertical ruler so it is set at the margin, so the header moves to the margin.

e. Insert a footer using the Pinstripes style. Type **Robert J. MacDonald**. The Pinstripes style automatically includes text on the left margin and the page number on the right margin.

f. Adjust the First Line Indent on the vertical ruler so it is set at the margin, so the footer moves to the margin.

Apply a Non-Breaking Space

You review the document to see how the formatting changes you made impacted line and paragraph endings. You notice on the top of page 3 in the paragraph headed *Family Law* that the MCL is on one line and the actual number of the law is on the next line. You fix that by applying a non-breaking space between the parts. (The MCL will move to the next line.)

a. Insert a non-breaking space between *MCL* and *552.625a(6)(d)*. Use the Find feature to locate this reference, if necessary.

b. Remove the existing space.

Add a Clip Art Image

Add a clip art image to the top of the document and position the image on the right side of the page. Add a picture style to the image.

a. Insert a clip art image at the beginning of the document. Type **crutches** in the **Search box**, and then set the results to display illustrations only. Choose the solid colored clip art image of a man with a crutch or any other similar image. Close the Clip Art task pane.

b. Change the height of the graphic to **1"**, allowing the width to change proportionately.

c. Change the position of the image to **Position in Top Right with Square Text Wrapping**.

d. Apply the **Snip Diagonal Corner, White picture style** to the image.

Add a Footnote

The author's credentials are currently located at the end of the document. You decide to position the qualifications in a footnote on the first page.

a. Locate the author's credentials at the end of the document, and then cut the italicized paragraph so it is copied to the clipboard.

b. Move your insertion point to the end of the author's identification line on the first page of the document. Add a footnote. Paste the paragraph containing the author's credentials so it appears as the footnote on the bottom of the first page.

Insert a Cover Page and Change the Theme Colors

As this document will be distributed at the State Bar meeting, it would be more professional to include a cover page. Because consistency gives a professional appearance, you use the Pinstripes format previously applied in your document to create the cover page. Your boss also likes the color blue, so you format the document with a blue color scheme.

a. Move to the top of your document.

b. Create a cover page using the Pinstripes style.

c. Complete the cover page information:

- The title should be in place. If not, copy the title from the header of your document.
- Delete the subtitle.
- Change the date to **9/23/2013**.
- Change the company name to **MacDonald, FitzGerald & MacDonald, PC**.
- Change the author's name to **Robert J. MacDonald**.

d. Make a copy of your graphic from page 2. Click before the page break on the cover page and paste.

e. Double-click the graphic to open the Format tab.

f. Change the height to **2"**. Change the position to the bottom center of the page. Click anywhere to deselect the graphic.

g. Open the theme colors; choose the **Metro color scheme** for the document. (Note: Change only the theme colors, not the document theme.)

Mark Citations and Add a Table of Authorities

A Table of Authorities references cases, rules, treaties, and other documents referred to in a legal document. You will create a Table of Authorities for this article. The Table of Authorities will be positioned at the end of the article, although the typical location of a Table of Authorities is at the beginning of a legal document. Your Table of Authorities is positioned at the end because it is not actually part of the article. You will locate and mark only the citations on the first page of the article.

a. Move to the first paragraph of the document. Locate the text *MCL 418.101-941*. Select the full text of the citation, beginning with *Michigan Workers'*, and ending with the case number. Be careful not to include any extra characters or punctuation in the selection.

b. Click the **References tab**, and then click **Mark Citation** in the Table of Authorities group. The selected text appears at the top of the dialog box. Mark this citation in the Statutes category. Click **Mark**, and then close the dialog box. The citation will appear within the paragraph. Turn off the **Show/Hide (¶)** feature to hide the citation.

c. Mark the following as citations to be included in the Table of Authorities:

Statutes:

IRC 104(a)(2)

Other Authorities:

IRS Publication 907

Cases:

Radecki v. Worker's Disability Compensation Director, 208 Mich App 19; 526 NW2d 611 (1994)

d. Move to the end of the document. Insert a page break.

e. Type the title **Table of Authorities**, and then format it with Heading 1 style. Insert two blank lines.

f. Insert a Table of Authorities. Accept all defaults in the dialog box.

Add a Document Comment

You need to get the attorney's approval for the citation format in the Table of Authorities. You add a comment to the article with this request before sending the article to him.

a. Insert the following as a comment on the Table of Authorities page: **Please check the formatting of the Table of Authorities' citations. If it appears as you want, I will mark the rest of the citations.**

Update Document Properties

It is important to develop the habit of using the document properties feature for your law office documents. Even though this document will be used for outside presentations, your office enforces the standard of always using the document properties.

a. Open the Document Panel, and then update the information. You may retype the information or copy/paste it from other locations in the document, as needed.

- Author: **Robert J. MacDonald**
- Title: **Workers' Compensation: A Few Facts Worth Knowing for the Non-Practitioner**

- Subject: **WC overview for Attys**
- Keywords: **WC, General, Attorney**
- Category: **Presentation**
- Status: **Completed**
- Comments: **Prepared for State Bar presentation, Sept 23, 2013. Formatted by <your name>**

Check Spelling and Grammar

Although a legal document contains many abbreviations and legal terms that may not be in the standard dictionary, a paralegal should still check a legal document for spelling and grammar errors. As standard abbreviations and terms are discovered, they should be added to the Custom Dictionary.

a. Save your document, and then run the spell checker.

b. Correct all misspelled words.

c. When prompted to change the abbreviation *Mich.*, click **Ignore All**.

d. Add any terms you feel would be common terms in a legal office to the Custom Dictionary.

Create a Table

In addition to the article, the attorney plans to distribute a table showing the Michigan State average weekly wages for the past five years.

a. Open a new document, and then create a table with six columns and six rows.

b. Save the document as **w_pl_saww_LastnameFirstname.docx**.

c. Enter the following information:

Year	SAWW	90% of SAWW (Maximum)	66% of SAWW	50% of SAWW (Minimum Benefit for Death Cases)	25% of SAWW (Minimum Benefit for Specific Loss and T&P)
2012	$820.04	$739.00	$546.69	$410.02	$205.01
2011	$803.17	$723.00	$535.45	$401.59	$200.79
2010	$784.31	$706.00	$522.87	$392.16	$196.08
2009	$765.12	$689.00	$510.08	$382.56	$181.28
2008	$744.49	$671.00	$496.33	$362.48	$186.12

d. Insert a footer using the Pinstripes style. Type **Source: Michigan State Workers' Compensation Agency**.

Format a Table

You format the table to make it easier to read and give it a more professional appearance.

a. Insert a new row above the row containing the column headings. Merge the cells in the new row, and then enter the table title: **State Average Weekly Wage Chart**. Bold the title and change the font size to **22 pt**.

b. Apply the **Medium Shading 2 – Accent 1 table style**.

c. Bold the column headings, and then change the font size to **12 pt**. Repeat the process with the years in the first column.

d. Change the alignment for the column headings to **Align Bottom Center**.

e. Set the alignment for rows 3 through 7 to **Align Top Center**.

f. Position the table so that it is centered horizontally on the page, if necessary.

Apply Text Effects to a Title

You will create an eye-catching title for the page with the table using Text Effects.

a. Type **Michigan Workers' Compensation** at the top of the page, and then apply the **Gradient Fill – Blue, Accent 1 text effect**.

b. Adjust the Shadow text effect, and then apply the **Offset Diagonal Bottom Right style**.

c. Increase the font size to **22 pt**.

d. Center the title horizontally on the page.

Save the Document

Now that you have made significant changes to the document, you want to be sure and save your work.

a. Save your document.

b. Close the document, and then submit based on your instructor's directions.

Paralegals

Use Microsoft Excel

Background

Microsoft Excel is such a versatile program that an experienced paralegal can find many valuable uses for Excel in the law office. Rather than knowing only a prescribed list of traditional uses, a paralegal should be alert to possible creative uses of Excel.

One of the tasks for which a paralegal may be responsible is recording transactions related to a trust account. A trust account is an account established by the lawyer and law firm for recording client fees and deposits. Each state has its own rules for trust account formatting and processing. For example, in Michigan, the distinction between retainer and advance fees has recently been clarified, and the distinction imposes some additional accounting requirements on the law office. Because a paralegal might be the person designated to set up and/or monitor the trust account, an accounting topic has been chosen for this exercise, even though many law offices use other programs for accounting purposes.

Tasks

In a small office, the paralegal may be responsible for all kinds of worksheet tasks, including the following:

- Completing accounting tasks
- Tracking client expenditures in a case
- Calculating probate expenses
- Determining real estate closure costs
- Preparing charts as trial exhibits

Skills

In addition to basic formatting skills, a paralegal should be able to do the following:

Chapter 1

- Design a worksheet (p. 328)
- Enter and edit cell data (p. 332)
- Use symbols and order of precedence in formulas (p. 337)
- Rename worksheets (p. 347)
- Copy worksheets (p. 348)
- Insert columns and rows (p. 349)
- Hide and unhide columns and rows (p. 352)
- Select a range (p. 353)
- Use Paste Special (p. 355)
- Insert and delete columns and rows (p. 358)
- Apply alignment and font options (p. 363)
- Apply number formats (p. 365)
- Select page setup options (p. 371)

Chapter 2

- Use relative, absolute, and mixed cell references (p. 394)
- Use the SUM function (p. 405)
- Insert statistical functions (p. 406)
- Insert the TODAY function (p. 409)
- Use the VLOOKUP function (p. 422)
- Use the IF function (p. 426)
- Create nested functions (p. 426)

Chapter 3

- Create a bar chart (p. 455)
- Select the data source (p. 460)
- Position and size the chart (p. 463)
- Apply a chart layout and a chart style (p. 471)
- Insert and format the chart title (p. 482)
- Customize the legend (p. 483)

Chapter 4

- Freeze rows and columns (p. 507)
- Set a print area (p. 509)
- Create a table (p. 517)
- Apply a table style (p. 519)
- Sort data (p. 525)
- Filter data (p. 527)
- Create a total row (p. 531)

Paralegals Capstone Exercises

An attorney in your office recently attended a continuing legal education seminar that emphasized the need for individual client tracking on a trust account. Although you had maintained a trust ledger, you had not been providing individual client ledgers. (Some professionals recommend having a ledger for every client, regardless of whether any of the client's funds are in the trust account!) While designing the worksheets, you realized that you could create the individual client ledgers and then construct the trust ledger as a set of links from the client ledgers. Just as Microsoft creates templates that can be used over and over again, you can create the individual client ledger as a template and use it for each client of the attorney.

Create a Client Ledger

As you plan the worksheet to be used as the template for the individual client ledgers, you determine the information you need to record and decide each type of information should be identified with a column label. When the attorney takes a case, the client pays a retainer for the attorney's services. This creates a deposit that is added to the account. If the attorney returns funds to a client, a check is issued, which is subtracted from the account. After planning the worksheet for use as the template, you create and name it. You will format the workbook so that all worksheets based on the template look alike.

a. Create a new workbook, and then save it as **e_pl_ledger_LastnameFirstname**.

b. Type the worksheet title **Client Ledger** in **cell A1**. Type the subtitle as an asterisk (*) in **cell A2** (this cell is used as a placeholder for the client name.) Apply **16 pt size** and bold to the **range A1:A2**.

c. Merge and center the **range A1:J1**, and then merge and center the **range A2:J2**.

d. Type **Case #** in **cell A3**, and then apply bold.

e. Type the following labels on row 5, pressing Alt+Enter as indicated:

- **DATE** in **cell A5**
- **CLIENT** in **cell B5**
- **SOURCE OF<Alt+Enter>DEPOSIT** in **cell C5**
- **PAYEE** in **cell D5**
- **CK #** in **cell E5**
- **PURPOSE** in **cell F5**
- **CHECKS<Alt+Enter>(SUBTRACT)** in **cell G5**
- **DEPOSITS<Alt+Enter>(ADD)** in **cell H5**
- **RUNNING<Alt+Enter>BALANCE** in **cell I5**
- **MEMO** in **cell J5**

f. Format the labels on row 5 with 12 pt. Apply **Top Align** and **Center** alignments. Adjust column widths as needed so that labels such as *SOURCES OF DEPOSIT* display on two lines within the respective cell.

g. Apply the **Short Date format** to the **range A6:A30**.

h. Apply the **Text format** to the **range B6:F30**.

i. Apply the **Accounting Number Format** to the **range G6:I30** (Checks, Deposits, and Running Balance columns).

j. Format the **range A5:J30** as a table. Select the option that indicates your table has headers.

k. Apply the **Table Style Light 2 format** to the table.

l. Add a Total Row.

m. Change the zoom to **75%** if columns A through J do not display onscreen.

n. Name the worksheet **Client Template**.

Change the Page Layout

Set the print options for this ledger template so that worksheets created from the template are ready to be printed and inserted into the client's file. Due to the amount of information, you will change the format so that the worksheet prints in landscape orientation.

a. Set the page orientation to **Landscape**.

b. Set the Print Area to the **range A1:J31**.

c. Use Print Preview to check that all columns display on one page.

d. Click the Home tab.

Create the Formulas for the Ledger

You have created this worksheet as a template for individual client ledgers. Just as you applied formats to the template, you create formulas in the template.

a. Type **Beginning Balance** in **cell F6**, and then enter **0** in **cell I6**. Note that the *0* changes to a hyphen and a *$* appears because it displays in Accounting Number Format.

b. Create a formula in **cell I7** that calculates the running balance after that row's transaction. The formula needs to subtract the check amount from and add the deposit amount to the running balance. Copy the formula down the table column.

c. Display the total row, and then display the totals for the CHECKS and DEPOSITS columns. Remove the total from the Memo column.

Create an Individual Client Ledger

Make a copy of the worksheet template containing the individual client ledger. Use it to set up a ledger for a new client, and then enter your own information.

a. Delete Sheet2 and Sheet3.

	A	B	C	D	E	F	G	H	I	J
1						**Client Ledger**				
2						**Student Name**				
3	Case #									
4										
5	DATE	CLIENT	SOURCE OF DEPOSI	PAYEE	CK #	PURPOSE	CHECKS (SUBTRACT)	DEPOSITS (ADD)	RUNNING BALANCE	MEMO
6	9/10/2012	Student Name				Beginning Balance			$ -	
7	11/14/2012	Student Name		US Mail	3164	Send Filing Packet	$ 10.50		$ (10.50)	
8	1/7/2013	Student Name	Ins. Co	Atty.		Settlement Proceeds		$ 10,000.00	$ 9,989.50	Check No. 1538603
9	1/15/2013	Student Name		Atty.	3201	Fee (25%)	$ 2,500.00		$ 7,489.50	
10	1/15/2013	Student Name		Client	3202	Balance Due Client	$ 7,489.50		$ -	

FIGURE 1.1 ▲

b. Create a copy of the Client Template worksheet. Change the worksheet tab name from *Client Template (2)* to your name.

c. Replace the asterisk (*) in the subtitle row with your name.

d. Use Figure 1.1 to enter information about your account in the ledger. The column I totals will automatically appear as you complete columns G and H. Adjust column widths to improve the appearance of the worksheet.

e. Create a footer with your name on the left side, the sheet name code in the center, and the file name code on the right side of each worksheet.

f. Set **0.2"** left and right margins and scale to fit to one page for the second worksheet.

g. Save and close the *e_pl_ledger_LastnameFirstname* workbook. Submit based on your instructor's directions.

Insert a Nested Function

Once the client ledgers have been set up and entries recorded, you make a trust ledger to consolidate all of the entries into one large document. This process would need to be automated if you had many clients and you would probably use a specialized program. In this small office, however, you can create the trust ledger using Excel. You need to be extremely careful using this process so that you do not introduce errors.

The template you created in the previous activity has been modified to include additional columns and revised column headings. Client ledgers have been created based on the template, and the template has been used to create a new worksheet titled Trust Ledger, Linda Ron, P.C. You enter the formulas for the trust ledger.

a. Open *e_pl_trust*, and then save it as **e_pl_trust_LastnameFirstname**.

b. Change the title of the Trust Ledger worksheet by replacing the attorney name in **cell A1**, *Linda Ron*, with your name.

c. Type **5000** in **cell K12** for the running balance (the amount from the end of the previous period).

d. Create a nested AND function within an IF function in **cell K13**: If the fees, charges, and payment received are all zero, display nothing by using "", two quotation marks without any text, values or formulas in between. This logical test detects the end of the transactions and will not repeat the same balance for rows that do not have transactions. Otherwise, add the previous row's running balance to the payment received and then subtract fees and charges to get the new running balance. Use Help to learn how to nest the AND function in an IF function. The goal is to have the balance display if a balance exists, but have empty cells in the running balance if it is the end of the entries. Copy this formula down the column. Enter and copy this same function in the other worksheets.

e. Insert today's date by function in **cell I3**.

Use the IF and VLOOKUP Functions

To help identify the type of fees charged to a client, a table was inserted at the top of each of the ledgers identifying the administrative fee code, an explanation of the fees, and the administrative fee charge. The ledgers include a column identifying the fee code and a column displaying the fee charged based on the code. Using the IF and VLOOKUP functions, you create the formula to have Excel search the table for the type of fee and then return the value for that fee. In addition, if there is no fee type specified in the ledger, the value returned should be a hyphen (-).

a. Display the Coolin, Tracy worksheet.

b. Create a nested VLOOKUP function within an IF function in **cell H13**. If the Admin Fees Type cell is empty for that row, display a zero. In the value_if_false argument, nest a VLOOKUP function that looks up the administrative fee code in cell G13, compares it to the lookup table in the range G6:I9, and then returns the administrative fee. (Note: Use absolute and relative cell references appropriately.)

c. Copy the administrative fees formula down the column.

d. Enter the same nested function from cell H13 in the Grab, Mark; Mattox, Brian; and Client Template worksheets, and then copy them down the table columns.

Enter the Data

You will create links from the original client ledgers to the trust ledger. By making links, subsequent changes to the client ledgers will show up in the trust ledger. Note: New entries will still have to be copied manually. Although you are familiar with copying cell contents to the clipboard, creating links with the content of the cell may be unfamiliar to you. Before completing this portion of the activity, review the Help topic Copy specific cell contents or attributes in a worksheet.

a. Select the **Coolin, Tracey worksheet**. Select the **range A13:J19** (the completed rows, but not the starter row). Copy the information.

b. Switch to the Trust Ledger worksheet. Select **cell A13**, the first empty row after the starter row.

c. Use the Paste Special option to link the pasted cells. Apply **General format** to the data in columns B and C and **Accounting Number Format** to data in columns H, I, and J.

d. Copy the **range L13:L19** from the Coolin, Tracey worksheet, and then use the Paste Special option to link the pasted cells, starting in cell L13 in the Trust Ledger worksheet.

e. Copy the contents of the next two client ledgers and paste the links below Tracey Coolin's data in the Trust Ledger worksheet. Correct any formatting issues that might occur after copying and pasting. Calculate the cumulative running balance.

Sort the Trust Ledger into Chronological Order and Apply Additional Formatting

You want to arrange the ledger entries in chronological order, freeze the panes so that the column headers and dates always remain on-screen, and filter the data to show deposits. Sort the entries in the Trust Ledger on the Date column, from oldest to newest.

a. Check the check numbers to be sure they appear in numerical order. If not, you have an accounting problem that will require account auditing.

b. Freeze the panes of the chart above and to the left of cell B12 so you can scroll down to the 100 rows you expect to have by the next accounting period.

c. Hide the Purpose column (F) because it is not relevant to the trust ledger.

d. Filter the Payment Received column to show only entries that have contents greater than zero. Four entries should remain.

Insert a Chart of Payments and Charges

For the convenience of your attorney, insert a chart showing the payments received and the payments made (Charges and Administrative Fees) for the trust account.

a. Select the column titles for columns H, I, and J in the Trust Ledger worksheet. Continue to select the **range H37:J37**.

b. Create a bar chart of type Clustered Horizontal Cylinder.

c. Move the chart below the table to span the **range D40:I60**.

d. Size the chart to a width of **7"** and height of **4.5"**.

e. Select the chart style of your choice.

f. Apply the **Layout 2 chart layout**.

g. Delete the legend.

h. Insert the following two-line title:
Trust Account, Your Name, P.C.
Payments and Charges July–December 2012

i. Change the title font color to **Blue, Accent 1**.

Print the Trust Ledger

Provide a printed copy of the trust ledger for your attorney and the accountant.

a. Change the scale until the entire Trust Ledger fits on one page width.

b. Hide the gridlines on the Trust Ledger worksheet.

c. Create a footer with this information: **Trust Ledger, Confidential, Page 1**.

d. Check the final version using Print Preview.

e. Save and close the workbook. Submit based on your instructor's directions.

Paralegals

Use Microsoft Access

Background

Much of the information used by attorneys in their offices can be tracked in a database. It is becoming more common to purchase an integrated case management software program to do this tracking, but many opportunities still exist for a paralegal to make good use of a Microsoft Access database. An Access database can be used to track every part of the law office operation, particularly in a small office that might not have purchased the larger programs due to cost. Even if an Access database is not used, the information in Chapters 1–4 will enhance one's ability to use third-party database programs more effectively.

Tasks

In a small office, a paralegal might be responsible for using Access to prepare the following:

- Client and case tracking
- Contact database, including courts and attorneys
- Trial preparation database (exhibits, documents, etc.)
- Statistical reports

Skills

In addition to basic data entry skills, a paralegal should be able to do the following:

Chapter 1

- Navigate among the objects in an Access database (p. 573)
- Back up, compact, and repair Access files (p. 581)
- Create filters (p. 589)
- Sort table data on one or more fields (p. 592)
- Use the Relationships window (p. 600)
- Understand relational power (p. 601)

Chapter 2

- Design data (p. 620)
- Create tables (p. 624)
- Understand table relationships (p. 636)
- Share data with Excel (p. 638)
- Establish table relationships (p. 642)
- Create a single-table query (p. 653)
- Specify criteria in a query (p. 656)
- Copy and modify a query (p. 659)
- Create a multi-table query (p. 665)
- Modify a multi-table query (p. 666)

Chapter 3

- Create a calculated field in a query (p. 689)
- Create expressions with the Expression Builder (p. 698)
- Use built-in functions in Access (p. 700)
- Perform date arithmetic (p. 703)
- Add aggregate functions to datasheets and queries (p. 713)

Chapter 4

- Create forms using the form tools (p. 734)
- Modify a form (p. 739)
- Revise forms using Layout view (p. 751)
- Identify control types in forms (p. 752)
- Create reports using the Report Wizard (p. 763)
- Modify a report (p. 768)
- Identify report sections (p. 777)
- Revise reports using Layout and Design views (p. 781)
- Identify control types in reports (p. 782)

Paralegals
Capstone Exercises

As a paralegal for a local law firm, you will be responsible for creating the firm's database, entering data, and also creating queries, forms and reports. The database will contain a main table named the Case table and several other supporting tables named CaseType table, County table, and Court table. You will also import the data from several Excel worksheets; the firm has been keeping case data on these worksheets.

Create the Database

Many excellent templates are available in Access, but you decide to create a new blank database for the law firm.

a. Create a blank database, and then save it as **a_pl_lawfirm_LastnameFirstname**.

Create the Case Type Table

The attorneys practice primarily family law and handle some criminal law cases. The firm would like to track statistics regarding case type. You need to create a table that stores the case type options.

a. Create a new table named **CaseType**.

b. Create a CaseTypeID field that will function as the primary key.

c. Add a second field named **CaseTypeDesc**. It will have a Data Type of Text and field size of 25.

d. Enter the following case types into the table: **Consultation**, **Separation**, **Domestic Violence**, **Divorce**, **Alimony**, **Custody**, **Child Support**, **Parenting Time**, **Paternity**, **Property Settlement**, **Misdemeanor**, **Felony**, and **Other**.

Create the County Table

The attorneys practice in several counties. Create another table listing the counties in which the attorneys practice.

a. Create a new table named **County**.

b. Create a field named **CountyID** that will function as the primary key.

c. Add a second field named **CountyDesc**. It will have a Data Type of Text and field size of 25.

d. Enter the following counties into the table: **Genesee**, **Lapeer**, **Shiawassee**, and **Oakland**.

Create the Court Table

The attorneys try cases in multiple jurisdictions: federal, state (civil and criminal courts), and municipal courts. Cases are tried in civil, criminal, appeals, and the Supreme Courts at each level. Create a table listing the courts in which your attorney tries cases.

a. Create a new table named **Court**.

b. Create a field named **CourtID** that will function as the primary key.

c. Add a second field named **CourtDesc**. It will have a Data Type of Text and field size of 25.

d. Enter the following courts into the table: **Civil**, **Criminal**, **Appeals**, and **Supreme**.

Create the Case Table

The main table is the Case table. As you create the fields for this table, you will create the field names that will link to the other three tables.

a. Create a new table named **Case**.

b. Type the field names and data types as indicated in Figure 1.2.

Case

Field Name	Data Type
CaseID	Number
OpenDate	Date/Time
CaseTypeID	Number
CountyID	Number
CourtID	Number
CaseNo	Text
ClientLastName	Text
ClientFirstName	Text
Trial	Yes/No
Settled	Yes/No
CloseDate	Date/Time
Summary	Memo

FIGURE 1.2 ▲

c. Set the following field sizes:

- CaseNo: **15**
- ClientLastName: **25**
- ClientFirstName: **20**

d. Add captions as needed (example: OpenDate should display as Open Date).

e. Save and close the table.

Create and Enforce Relationships

Before entering data into the Case table, create relationships between the tables and enforce referential integrity.

a. Close any open tables.

b. Open the Relationships window. Add the four tables to the Relationships window.

c. Create a relationship between the CaseType table and the Case table using the CaseTypeID field; enforce referential integrity.

d. Create a second relationship between the Court table and the Case table; enforce referential integrity.

e. Create a third relationship between the County table and the Case table; enforce referential integrity.

f. The Case table should be on the left side of the Relationships window; the other three tables should be on the right. This will help users to easily interpret the three relationships.

g. Save and close the Relationships window.

Import Excel Records into the Case Table

The law firm used to store cases in an Excel worksheet. Import these records into the Case table.

a. Import the records in *a_pl_importcases* into the Case table.

b. Open the Case table, and then replace Patricia Larkin's last name and first name with your last name and first name.

c. Filter the records for Case Type 12; remove the filter.

d. Sort the records by Client's Last Name; remove the sort.

e. Save and close the table.

Enter Case Data Using a Form

Create a simple form using the Form tool, and then enter the data as shown in the following section.

a. Create a form based on the Case table. Save the form as **Enter Case Data**.

b. Switch to Layout view, if necessary.

c. Change the title label to **Enter and Update Case Data**.

d. Reduce the text box widths to one-half of their original size.

e. Change the form's control padding to **Narrow**.

f. Switch to Form view. Enter the following two new case records:

CaseID	10123	10124
Open Date	April 1, 2012	March 18, 2012
Case Type	4	12
County1	1	3
Court	1	4
Case Number	08-499571	09-203381
Client Last Name	Jimenez	Deheer
Party First Name	Jaime	William
Trial	No	No
Settled	Yes	Yes
Close Date		
Summary	Divorce, 1 child	Possession

g. Close the form.

Create a Single-Table Query

You cannot remember a client's first name, so you create a query to find all clients with the last name Smith.

a. Create a query in Design view; include all fields in the Case table.

b. Add criteria to show all clients with the last name *Smith*.

c. Run the query.

d. Save the query as **Smith Cases**. Close the query.

Create a Multi-Table Query

Create a query that displays all cases for Genesee County. Include the Case, County, and CaseType tables.

a. Add the CaseID, OpenDate, CloseDate, CaseNo, ClientLastName, and ClientFirstName fields from the Case table, the CaseTypeDesc field from the CaseType table, and the County Desc and CountyID fields from the County table.

b. Add criteria to the CountyID field to show only cases for Genesee County, and then run the query. Do not show the CountyID field in the results. Run the query.

c. Save the query as **Genesee County Cases**. Close the query.

Copy and Modify a Query

Now that you have a query for Genesee County Cases, copy it and paste it using the name **Shiawassee County Cases**.

a. Copy the Genesee County Cases query; paste the query using the name **Shiawassee County Cases**.

b. Modify the CountyID field to locate the Shiawassee cases.

c. Run the query. Save and close the query.

Calculate Case Duration

The attorneys want to know approximately how long it takes to complete each case. Use the DateDiff() function to calculate the number of days.

a. Create a query using the Case table, the Court table, and the CaseType table.

b. Add the following fields: **CourtDesc**, **CaseTypeDesc**, **CaseNo**, **ClientLastName**, and **ClientFirstName**.

c. Use the Expression Builder to create a field called **Duration in Days**; this field should calculate the number of days from the date opened to the date closed using the DateDiff() function.

d. Sort in ascending order by Duration in Days. Run the query.

e. Modify the query to only include cases that have a close date. Run the query.

f. Save the query as **Case Duration**. Close the query.

Create a Totals Query

The attorneys want to know the average number of days it takes to complete each type of case.

a. Create a query using the Case table and the CaseType table.

b. Add the fields CaseTypeDesc and CaseID.

c. Copy the Duration in Days field from the Case Duration query; paste the field into the third column, and then change the field name to **Avg Duration in Days**.

d. Add the CloseDate field in the fourth column.

e. Display the Total row. Group by CaseTypeDesc, count the number of cases, and then calculate the average duration for each type of case. Only include cases with a close date.

f. Run the query, and then check it for accuracy. (Starting at the top, the Avg Duration by case type should read 136, 341.4, 928, 195, 167, 106, and 119.)

g. Save the query with the name **Avg Duration by Case Type**. Close the query.

Create a Report Using the Report Wizard

The attorneys want you to create a report that lists cases by case type. You decide to create a query first and then use the Report Wizard based on the query.

a. Create a query based on all four tables; add all the fields in the Case table except Trial, Settled, and Summary.

b. Replace the three ID fields with the corresponding Desc field in the related tables.

c. Run the query, and then examine the results. Save the query as **All Cases**. Close the query.

d. Create a report using the Report Wizard based on the All Cases query.

e. Include all the fields.

f. View by Case and Group by CaseTypeDesc.

g. Sort by OpenDate. Choose landscape, and then adjust the field width so all fields fit on a page.

h. Name the report **All Cases by Case Type**.

i. In Layout view, adjust the width of the columns so that all data is visible.

j. In Design view, add a CaseTypeDesc footer, and then add a text box control to the CaseID footer. Name the label **Total Cases**, and then type **=count(*)** in the **text box**. Display the report in Print Preview mode to test the new control. Align the new total control as needed.

Compact, Repair, and Back Up the Database

An Access database needs to be maintained regularly. It is a good idea to compact, repair, and back up the database each day.

a. Compact and repair the database.

b. Back up the database in the location where you save your student files. When naming the file, include today's date.

c. Submit the database according to your instructor's directions.

Paralegals

Use Microsoft PowerPoint

Background

Attorneys have historically focused on presenting their information by speaking or writing, and paralegals and legal assistants have aided the attorneys in the preparation for those tasks. Now, technology not only provides paralegals and legal assistants with highly effective tools for researching and document preparation, it has opened the doors to the use of multimedia as a tool for education and in the courtroom. Microsoft PowerPoint is a common tool used in trial openings and closings, and as a supplement to a formal presentation. This capstone exercise uses PowerPoint to educate potential clients within a law office. A paralegal or legal assistant would most likely be the person to prepare any kind of PowerPoint supplement that the attorney might want to use.

Tasks

In a small office, the paralegal may be responsible for using PowerPoint to prepare the following:

- Trial exhibits
- Formal presentation slides for a seminar
- Narrated presentations for clients
- Visual aids for the attorney to use when explaining concepts, in paper or electronic form
- Explanatory booklets for clients to take home for review

Skills

In addition to basic formatting skills, a paralegal should be able to do the following:

Chapter 1

- Plan a presentation (p. 817)
- Use slide layouts (p. 820)
- Apply themes (p. 821)
- Insert media objects (p. 828)
- Add a table (p. 829)
- Use transitions and animations (p. 829)
- Run and navigate a slide show (p. 839)
- Print in PowerPoint (p. 841)

Chapter 2

- Create a presentation using a template (p. 862)
- Modify a template (p. 864)
- Import an outline (p. 877)
- Add existing content to a presentation (p. 877)
- Modify a theme (p. 885)

Chapter 3

- Create shapes (p. 904)
- Create SmartArt (p. 925)
- Create WordArt (p. 933)
- Modify objects (p. 939)
- Arrange objects (p. 944)

Chapter 4

- Insert a picture (p. 974)
- Transform a picture (p. 976)
- Use the Internet as a resource (p. 987)
- Add video (p. 997)
- Use Video Tools (p. 1000)

Paralegals

Capstone Exercises

You have been hired by an attorney in the eastern district of Michigan, a consumer bankruptcy specialist, to prepare a PowerPoint presentation that he can use to explain the basics of bankruptcy to potential new clients. You will import the outline provided to you by the attorney, and then modify the presentation.

Import an Existing Outline

The basic outline has been sent to you by the attorney's office. You create new slides from the outline.

a. Create a new blank presentation, and then save it as **p_pl_bankruptcy_LastnameFirstname**.

b. Create a handout header with your name, and a handout footer with your instructor's name and your class. Include the current date.

c. Create new slides from the *p_pl_outline.rtf* outline.

d. Confirm that there is one slide for each major heading element, for a total of 16 slides, including the blank title slide at the beginning of the presentation.

e. View the slide show to familiarize yourself with the content.

Edit the Outline

The outline did not provide a title slide for you, so you must create your own. You edit the outline to create the title slide and edit text. You create both a title and subtitle in this section.

a. Switch to the Outline tab, and then enter **Bankruptcy Basics** as the title for Slide 1.

b. Add a two-line subtitle to Slide 1 that reads **Introductory Information for** on the first line, and on the second line, **Clients and Their Family**.

c. Reposition Slide 9 (*Chapter 7 Characteristics)* so that it becomes Slide 7.

d. On Slide 12, enter **Bekofske's** before *Seven Tests of a Plan* in the **title placeholder** to give credit to Carl Bekofske, the Flint Chapter 13 Trustee who delineated the tests.

e. Change the Bullets format of the text on Slide 12 in the content placeholder to the default Numbering format.

f. On Slide 13, increase the indent level of the bullet *All debtors must personally attend* so that it becomes a subtopic of the first bullet in the list.

g. On Slide 16, convert each of the referenced URLs to hyperlinks.

h. Use the Replace feature to search for the text *Web site:*, and then replace it with nothing so that the text does not appear before the hyperlinks you created in the previous step.

Modify the Template

With the text edited, you concentrate on the visual elements of the presentation. You set up the basic theme and color style so you can verify the format of the slides as you work.

a. Apply the **Apothecary design theme**.

b. Select the **Equity color theme**.

c. Apply the **Style 9 background style**, if necessary.

Modify Title Slide and Create Closing Slide

You modify the title and subtitle of the title slide. You also create a closing slide informing potential clients that there are alternatives to bankruptcy and that they should consult a legal professional. You then add an image and apply a picture style to give the slide dimension.

a. Switch to the Slides tab, and then on Slide 1 apply bold to the title text.

b. Apply an **Offset Diagonal Bottom Left outer shadow text effect** to the title text.

c. Change the settings of the shadow preset to:

- Transparency: **12%**
- Blur: **6 pt**.
- Angle: **160°**
- Distance: **5 pt**.

d. Change the font size of the subtitle to **16 pt** and the font to **Shadow**.

e. Create a new slide at the end of the slide show using the Picture with Caption layout. Enter **There are alternatives to Bankruptcy** in the **title placeholder**. (Note: The template style converts the text to all caps.)

f. Enter **Discuss Options with the Attorney** in the **subtitle placeholder**.

g. Insert *p_pl_lawbooks.jpg* into the picture placeholder. Apply a **Drop Shadow Rectangle picture style**.

Add SmartArt

You add SmartArt diagrams to the presentation to enhance its appearance and to provide the client a break from the bullet format used by the majority of slides. You apply a list SmartArt to the list of bankruptcy types on Slide 6, and then you apply a process SmartArt to the duties of Chapter 13 filers on Slide 13.

a. On Slide 6, convert the existing text to a Vertical Box List SmartArt.

b. Change the colors of the SmartArt to **Colorful Range–Accent Colors 2 to 3**.

c. Apply the **Moderate Effect style** to the SmartArt.

d. On Slide 13, convert the existing text to a Step Down Process SmartArt.

e. Apply the **Moderate Effect style** to the SmartArt.

Insert a Table

It would be useful to show statistics on the number of bankruptcy cases filed in the eastern district of Michigan where the attorney practices law.

a. Create a new slide after Slide 10 using the Title Only layout.

b. Enter a two-line title with **United States Bankruptcy Court** on the first line and **Eastern District of Michigan** on the second line.

c. Insert an eight-row by six-column table.

d. Merge and center the cells in the top row of the table, and then enter the table heading **201x Bankruptcy Statistics** where *x* is the year you chose (see step f).

e. Go to the Web site **www.mieb.uscourts.gov/**. Select **Court Statistics** from the menu bar.

f. View the newest year's statistics from the list at the bottom of the chart. (Note: If the current year does not include statistics for January through June, go to the previous year.)

g. Copy the column headings (*Chapter 7, Chapter 11, Chapter 12, Chapter 13, Totals*), and then paste the headings on the table you created in PowerPoint leaving the first cell blank. Copy all the data for the months January through June, and then paste the data in the table you created in PowerPoint.

h. Reposition the table attractively on the page so that it does not block the title placeholder.

Insert Images and Video

You decide to insert a bankruptcy-related image, and then modify it to further enhance the presentation. Also, the U.S. courts system has produced a nine-part video series to provide information about bankruptcy. You decide to embed the Part 1 video in the presentation.

a. On Slide 4, insert *p_pl_relief.jpg*, and then change the height of the image to **2.5"**.

b. Drag the image so that it is aligned at the bottom center.

c. Remove the white background from the image.

d. Open your Web browser, go to www.youtube.com, and then search YouTube for the video you want to insert, using the search phrase **Bankruptcy Basics–Part 1: Introduction**. Select the video.

e. Click **Share**, click **Embed**, click the **Use old embed code check box**, and then copy the embed code.

f. On Slide 2, insert a video from a Web site using the copied embed code. Set the Playback options to start automatically so that the Play button will automatically appear while viewing. Preview the video to ensure the video was embedded properly.

g. Position the video below the bullet list, and then center align the video.

Apply Animations and a Transition

a. Select the **title placeholder** on Slide 2, apply the **Zoom animation**, and then set the animation to start *After Previous*. Use the Animation Painter to copy the animation to all title placeholders in the presentation.

b. Select the **bullet placeholder** on Slide 2, and then apply the **Appear animation**. Set the animation effect options to *By Paragraph*, if necessary, and then set the animation to start *After Previous*. Use the Animation Painter to copy the animation to all bullet placeholders in the presentation except for the Resources list.

c. Apply the **Uncover transition** to all slides.

d. View the presentation.

e. Save and close *p_pl_bankruptcy_LastnameFirstname*, and then submit based on your instructor's directions.

Paralegals

Integrate Microsoft Office Programs

Background

In addition to working with individual Microsoft Office applications and legal management software, efficient paralegals and legal assistants often integrate content that has been created in different applications to complete projects.

Tasks

Microsoft Word is frequently the host program when integrating content created in other applications. Microsoft PowerPoint is often the host for training material, and is used for trial introductions and exhibits. Both Microsoft Excel and Microsoft Access are good programs for storing, organizing, retrieving, and indexing materials. In addition, Excel's ability to create charts from worksheet data could be particularly applicable in tax, probate, real estate, and trial work. Examples of integrated law office tasks that integrate data from multiple programs could include the following:

- Communicate clearly and effectively by creating merge documents in Word that utilize data from an Excel or Access file
- Embed or link Excel worksheets or charts into Word documents or PowerPoint slides
- Create PowerPoint presentations with various linked or embedded objects from Word and Excel

Skills

In addition to skills in each application program, a paralegal should be able to do the following:

- Create and utilize a database containing contact information
- Create a merge source file
- Embed and link content from multiple sources
- Choose records or fields to merge

Paralegals
Capstone Exercises

Donna DeWitt, an attorney in your state, has decided to run for the family court judicial vacancy. Because her legal staff performs specifically delegated tasks in her legal office, she is outsourcing her campaign materials to you, a paralegal. You will prepare many of her promotional materials. You will integrate data from Office programs to produce professional products for her.

Before starting, you make a call to the Genesee County Bar Association to speak with Ms. Ramona Sain, the executive director of the association, for advice on what to include in the publicity announcements. Ms. Sain suggests that you create a database of names of possible supporters, starting with local attorneys. She provides you with a list or supporters as well as the results of a candidate survey. You will send the attorneys a personalized letter announcing Donna's candidacy, outlining her qualifications, and including the results of a survey. She also suggests you prepare a flyer that can be printed and distributed in various sizes, as well as used in the DeWitt for Judge Web site. With those suggestions in mind, you prepare the promotional materials.

Create a Database of Recipient Names

Ms. Sain has provided you with an Excel worksheet that includes the names of attorneys in the area who should be recipients of the letter announcing Donna's candidacy. You import the Excel data into an Access database, and then create a new form so additional names can be added to the database. Because Donna will be visiting law offices in Flint next week, you query the database for Flint law office data, and then prepare a report for printing so that Donna has the addresses of the offices she can visit during her trip.

a. Open a new, blank Access database. Name it **i_pl_contacts_LastnameFirstname.accdb**.

b. Import external data from the Excel worksheet *i_pl_contacts.xlsx*. Complete the Get External Data–Excel Spreadsheet wizard, taking only information from Sheet1. Indicate that the first row contains column headings. All of the fields use the Text data type. Let Access add the Primary Key. Name the table **Contacts**. Do not save the import steps.

c. Use the Form tool to create a form that can be used to enter or modify records in the Contacts table.

d. Create a query from the Contacts table. Select the **City**, **Company**, **Address**, **Address2**, **LastName**, and **FirstName fields**.

e. Use *Flint* as the criterion for *City* to limit the output to only law offices located in Flint.

f. Sort the query fields first by Company, then by LastName and FirstName.

g. Save the query as **Flint Law Offices**.

h. Compact and repair the database.

i. Close the Access database.

Start the Mail Merge Process and Select the Recipient List

Ms. Sain indicated the first step in the campaign will be to send a letter to attorneys thanking them for their survey ratings and enlisting their support. You format a document that has already been created, and which will be the main document in the merge process. You modify the format so that the letter fits on one page, making it possible to mail it in a window envelope. Format the letter now, and in a later exercise, you will insert a chart and complete the merge.

a. Open the file *i_pl_letter.docx*. Save it as **i_pl_letter_LastnameFirstname.docx**.

b. Start the mail merge by using the Step by Step Mail Merge Wizard to select the Letters mail merge process.

c. Use the current document to start the letter.

d. Select recipients from the i_pl_contacts_LastnameFirstname.accdb database. Refine the recipient list by sorting it by LastName in ascending order.

e. Entering the following return address at the top of the Word document that was created as you began the Mail Merge Wizard.
Committee for the Election of Donna DeWitt
PO Box 12345
Flint, MI 48501-1234

f. Apply the **Metro theme** to the document.

g. Apply the **WordArt style 8** to the text *Committee for the Election of Donna DeWitt* in the return address. Set the WordArt text to bold, **16 pt**. Center the WordArt, and then press **Enter** twice to insert a blank line before the post office box.

h. Enter the following e-mail address at the right aligned with the right margin of the city, state, and zip line of the return address: **donnadewittforjudge@yahoo.com**.

i. Leave a blank line below the e-mail address, and then insert the date in the Month Day, Year format. Do not update automatically.

j. Insert a blank line, and then insert an address block using the default form of *Joshua Randall Jr.* as the recipient name. Be sure to include the three other default choices: *Insert company name*, *Insert postal address*, and *Format address according to the destination country/region*.

k. Insert a blank line, and then add a subject line, **RE: Peer Candidate Ratings**.

l. Insert a blank line, and then create a greeting line that will insert the greeting line fields in the format of *Dear Joshua Randall:*, and then add a blank line after the greeting.

m. Save and close the file for now, even though you are on Step 4 of the Mail Merge Wizard. You will complete the merge process later.

Format the Approval Rating Worksheet

Ms. Sain provided you with an Excel workbook displaying the approval rating statistics for Donna compiled from a survey of attorneys. Format the worksheet and prepare a chart depicting her ratings.

a. Open the Excel workbook *i_pl_responses.xlsx*, and then save it as **i_pl_responses_LastnameFirstname.xlsx**.

b. Apply the **Metro theme** to the worksheet.

c. Merge and center the *Opinion Responses: Donna DeWitt* title across columns A–I. Apply the **Accent5 style** to the resulting cell. Bold the selected title, and then increase the font size to **16 pt**.

d. Apply the **20% –Accent3 style** to **cell A3** (Summary Statistics). Bold the text.

e. Select the **range A3:C5**, and then apply the **Outside Borders border style**.

f. Format the **range A8:A142** as Text, and then center the text.

g. Format the **range A7:H142** as a table, and then apply the **Table Style Medium 20 style**.

h. Change the column width of columns A–I to **14 pt**.

i. Wrap the text in the column headings. Center the text in each of the column headings.

j. Proofread the column headings, and then edit the text so that the headings use consistent capitalization.

k. Remove the filter arrows from the column headings.

Insert Basic Statistical Functions into the Approval Rating Worksheet

With the formatting in place, add basic statistical functions to the worksheet. Calculate the number of responses to the survey, the average by question and average by person, and a final average score for the candidate. The final average score will be published in the promotional materials.

a. Add a new column heading **Average Rating by Person** in **cell I7**.

b. Insert a formula that computes the average rating by person in **cell I8** to compute the rating for each respondent in the survey. Display the results to one decimal place. (Note: If Excel prompts you that adjacent cells are not part of the formula, ignore the error. Column A is the Respondent # and should not be included in the calculations.)

c. Add a Total Row to the table, and then change *Total* to **Average**. Calculate the average for each column displaying the results to one decimal place.

d. Apply banding to the Last Column.

e. Enter the number of responses to the survey in **cell C4** using the appropriate function to count the responses.

f. Calculate the Final Average Score in **cell C5** using the information in column I, and then display to one decimal place.

Create a Chart of Approval Ratings

A visual depiction of the approval ratings will help most people quickly understand the ratings. Use the average ratings for each characteristic to format a chart for inclusion on promotional materials.

a. Select the column headings in rows B–H and the average for each characteristic.

b. Insert a clustered 2-D Clustered Bar chart.

c. Size the chart to **3"** high by **6"** wide, and then approximately center the chart below the worksheet.

d. Change the chart layout to **Layout 1**.

e. Apply **Chart Style 7**.

f. Change the chart title to **Donna DeWitt, Peer Approval Ratings**.

g. Change the chart title font to **12 pt**.

h. Switch the Row/Column data to display the characteristics on the vertical axis and the series in the legend.

i. Remove the legend.

j. Format the horizontal (Value) axis value by changing the settings to fixed values: *Minimum=0, Maximum=9, Major unit =3.*

k. Add a primary horizontal axis title that reads: **Average Points, Scale of 1-9**.

l. Add data labels to *Outside End*, remove the display of the primary horizontal axis, and then save the workbook.

Insert the Chart into the Letter

Copy the chart and paste it into the prepared letter.

a. Copy the chart you created in the *i_pl_responses_Lastname Firstname.xlsx* workbook. Save the workbook and close Excel.

b. Open the Word file *exp07_i_leg_cpt_letter_LastnameFirstname.docx*. When the Microsoft Word information dialog box appears telling you that data from your database will be placed in the document, click **Yes** to continue.

c. Use Paste Special and Paste link to embed the chart of approval ratings.

d. Move the pasted link between the first and second paragraphs. Set the text to wrap top and bottom. Make sure that you have a blank line before and after the chart.

e. Scale the chart proportionally to 70% of original size, and then center align the chart

f. Preview the results, and then make any adjustments necessary to fit the letters on a single page.

g. Your final letter should look like Figure 1.3. Save all documents.

Completing the Merge

After completing the main document and the data source file, you are ready to complete the merge process.

a. Finish and merge the main document and the data source file. Do **not** print the documents. (There will be 60 letters.) Save the merged letter file as **i_pl_merge_LastnameFirstname**, and then close the document.

b. Save *i_pl_letter_LastnameFirstname*, and then close the document.

c. Submit as directed by your instructor.

Committee for the Election of Donna DeWitt

PO Box 12345
Flint, MI 48501-1234

donnadewittforjudge@yahoo.com

September 21, 2011

«AddressBlock»

RE: Peer Candidate Ratings

«GreetingLine»

The results of the peer judicial candidate survey are back. Thank you for your support of me by rating me so highly at 7.2 out of 9. The results are summarized below:

For those of you who do not know me personally, here are a few of my qualifications:

- Family law attorney for 20 years;
- Domestic relations mediator;
- Women's shelter, member of the Board of Directors;
- GCBA Family Law committee member.

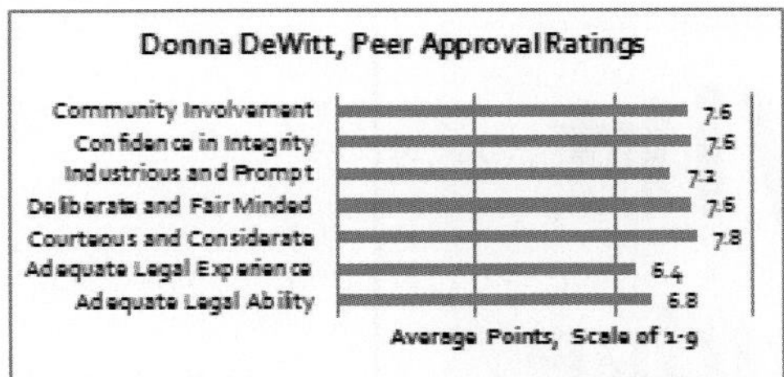

In addition, I am quite involved with other local charitable activities, including:

- Pro bono attorney for Easter Seals of Genesee County;
- Volunteer attorney for monthly family law pro bono legal session.

Your support in my bid for Family Court Judge will be greatly appreciated. Please contact me to volunteer or contribute.

Legally yours,

Donna DeWitt

FIGURE 1.3 ▲

Create a Flyer in PowerPoint

You need a simple, but attractive flyer that can be distributed around the city. It should outline the attorney's major qualifications.

a. Open a new PowerPoint presentation. Save it as **i_pl_flyer_LastnameFirstname.pptx**.

b. Change the layout of Slide 1 to **Title Only**, and then change the slide orientation to **Portrait**.

c. Select the **Concourse theme**, and then change the color scheme to **Median**.

d. Set the background to **Background Style 1**.

e. Create the following two-line main title:
Donna DeWitt for Family Court Judge

f. Center the title. Change the Text Fill to **Blue**. Change the font of the text in the title placeholder to **Calibri**.

g. Select the **title placeholder**, and then apply a Shape Style of **Subtle Effect–Ice Blue, Accent 1**. Resize the title placeholder to a height of **2"**.

h. Select the text *Donna DeWitt*, and then increase the font size until the text fills the width of the title placeholder.

i. Select the *for Family Court Judge* text, and then change the font size until the text is approximately as wide as the line *Donna DeWitt* above, but does not extend below the placeholder border.

j. With the text still selected, apply a Glow shape effect of **Ice Blue, 11 pt glow, Accent color 1**.

k. Insert the image *i_pl_dewitt.tif* below the title placeholder, and then resize the image to a height of **3.5"** and a width of **2.85"**. Increase the brightness of the image 20%. Flip the image horizontally. Position the image horizontally at 0.4" and vertically 2.7" from the top left corner.

l. Insert a Varying Width List SmartArt, and then add the text below:
   - **Family Law Attorney, 20 years**
   - **Domestic Relations Mediator**
   - **Women's Shelter, Board of Directors**

m. Resize the SmartArt and reposition it so that the right edge of the SmartArt aligns with the right edge of the title placeholder and the top of the SmartArt is aligned with the DeWitt image. (Do not allow SmartArt to cover any portion of the image.)

n. Apply the **Subtle Effect SmartArt style**.

o. Copy the *Donna DeWitt, Peer Approval Ratings* chart from *i_pl__responses_LastnameFirstname.xlsx*, and then paste it on the slide.

p. Position the chart so that it is horizontally 0.75" and vertically 6.35" from the top left corner.

q. Change the shape fill of the data bars to **Ice Blue, Accent 1, Darker 50%**.

r. Insert a text box at the bottom right of the flyer. Enter the following text:
Committee for the Election of Donna DeWitt
donnadewittforjudge@yahoo.com

s. Change the font size to **10 pt**.

t. The final flyer should look like Figure 1.4.

u. Save *i_pl_flyer_LastnameFirstname.pptx*. Submit according to the directions of your instructor.

Donna DeWitt
for Family Court Judge

Family Law Attorney, 20 years
Domestic Relations Mediator
Women's Shelter, Board of Directors

Donna DeWitt, Peer Approval Ratings

	Average Points, Scale of 1–9
Community Involvement	7.6
Confidence in Integrity	7.6
Industrious and Prompt	7.2
Deliberate and Fair Minded	7.6
Courteous and Considerate	7.8
Adequate Legal Experience	6.4
Adequate Legal Ability	6.8

Committee for the Election of Donna DeWitt
donnadewittforjudge@yahoo.com

FIGURE 1.4

Create a Running PowerPoint Slide Show

Donna DeWitt is planning to have an election table at the Genesee County Fair. She asked you to create a short PowerPoint slide presentation to run automatically at the fair. Because of the noisy, outdoor environment you do not use sound, but you insert animations on each slide to catch the attention of people passing the election table. Use the PowerPoint flyer and reconfigure it to run as a short kiosk presentation.

a. Save *i_pl_flyer_LastnameFirstname*, and then save it as **i_pl_fair_LastnameFirstname**.

b. Change the slide orientation to **Landscape**, and then make three duplicates of the existing slide.

c. In Slide 1, change the layout to the **Title slide layout**. Delete the SmartArt, the chart, the text box, and the subtitle placeholder.

d. Change the height and width scale of the image back to 100% so the image is not distorted. Apply the **Center Shadow Rectangle picture style** to the image. Arrange the title placeholder and the picture attractively on the slide.

e. Apply the **Shape animation** to Donna DeWitt's image, and then modify the effect options so that the direction is Out and the shape is Box. Set the animation to *After Previous*.

f. In Slide 2, change the layout to the **Blank layout**. Delete the chart, the photograph, and the text box.

g. Edit the title placeholder text to: **Qualifications**.

h. Change the SmartArt layout to **Vertical Box List**. Align the title placeholder and the SmartArt to the center of the slide.

i. Animate the SmartArt so each line fades in one by one after the previous animation. Set the delay to 01.50 seconds.

j. In Slide 3, change the layout to the **Blank layout**, and then remove all but the title placeholder and the chart.

k. Change the title placeholder text to **Peer Approval Ratings**, and then reduce the size of the text so that it to fits on one line. Center-align the title placeholder to the slide.

l. Change the chart height to **5"** and the chart width to **8"**.

m. Remove the chart title. Modify the vertical axis title font size to **18 pt**, and then modify the horizontal axis title to **12 pt**.

n. Position the chart attractively on the slide while ensuring that text is not hidden by the slide design elements.

o. Animate the chart so category information wipes from the left by the elements in the category. Set the animation to start *After Previous*.

p. In Slide 4, change the layout to **Title slide layout**. Delete the SmartArt, the chart, the picture, and the subtitle placeholder. Replace the title placeholder text with the following text:
Vote for
Donna DeWitt
Family Court Judge
November 6th

q. Format the title placeholder's box to resize the shape to fit the text. Position the placeholder so it is above the design elements at the bottom of the slide. Center-align the placeholder on the slide.

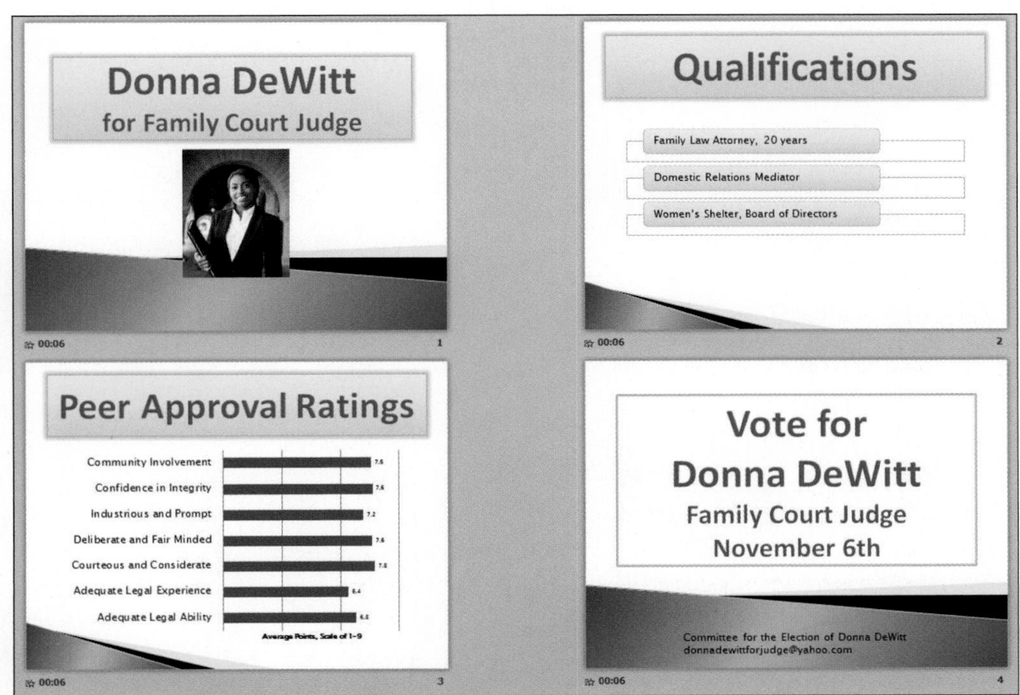

FIGURE 1.5 ▲

r. Change the placeholder's shape style to **Colored Outline – Ice Blue, Accent 1**.

s. Resize all of the text in the *Committee for the Election of Donna DeWitt* box to **18 pt**. Center-align the text box while maintaining its vertical position in the blue design element at the bottom of the slide.

t. Apply the **Zoom entrance animation** to the title placeholder, and then set it to animate *After Previous*.

u. Apply the **Flip transition** to all slides, and then advance slides automatically after 6 seconds.

v. Set up the slide show to be browsed at a kiosk using automatic timings.

w. View the presentation.

x. Save and close the *i_pl_fair_LastnameFirstname.pptx* presentation.

y. The final slides should look like Figure 1.5.

Medical Office Assistants

Use Microsoft Word

Background

Medical office assistants work in hospitals, clinics, and physician offices and are responsible for the administrative functions of the office. They use word processing software on a daily basis to create a wide variety of documents for physicians and patients. They transcribe dictation, prepare correspondence, and assist physicians with reports. Some documents they might develop include medical histories, patient invoices, order forms, and medical information pamphlets. It is imperative that medical office assistants understand the features of Microsoft Word and be comfortable using those features. The following word processing skills taught in the textbook are skills crucial to people employed in a medical office.

Tasks

Medical office assistants may be responsible for all kinds of document production. Such documents could include the following:

- Correspondence and mailings
    - Patient test results
    - Student health records
    - Medical histories
    - Memoranda and faxes
- Forms and reports
    - Patient information forms
    - Patient invoices
    - Patient schedules
    - Insurance forms
    - Lab reports
    - Purchase orders
- Brochures and pamphlets
    - Medical information brochures and pamphlets regarding health, diseases, and medicine

Skills

In addition to basic formatting skills, medical office assistants should be able to do the following:

Chapter 1

- Insert page breaks (p. 127)
- Add page numbers (p. 128)
- Insert a cover page (p. 130)
- Set margins and specify page orientation (p. 137)
- Insert headers and footers (p. 137)
- Create sections (p. 138)
- Check spelling and grammar (p. 141)
- View a document (p. 142)
- Use save options (p. 150)
- Select printing options (p. 153)
- Modify document properties (p. 155)

Chapter 2

- Apply font attributes (p. 172)
- Highlight text (p. 175)
- Control word wrapping with nonbreaking hyphens and nonbreaking spaces (p. 176)
- Set off paragraphs with tabs, borders, lists, and columns (p. 180)
- Apply paragraph formats (p. 186)
- Copy formats with the Format Painter (p. 195)
- Create and modify styles (p. 195)
- Insert clip art and images (p. 205)
- Format a graphic element (p. 205)
- Insert symbols (p. 209)

Chapter 3

- Insert comments (p. 226)
- Track changes (p. 229)
- Create a bibliography (p. 239)
- Create and modify footnotes and endnotes (p. 240)
- Create a table of contents (p. 245)
- Add figure references (p. 249)
- Insert a table of figures (p. 249)

Chapter 4

- Insert a table (p. 272)
- Format a table (p. 274)
- Convert text to a table (p. 285)

You work as a medical office assistant at a family practice. Your supervisor asked you to create a document about the vaccination program available to patients. You have been provided some of the text. Prepare the document so it has a friendly yet professional appearance. Include formatting, graphic elements, tables, and reference components.

Set Initial Document Formats

To ensure the vaccination guide is appealing and easy to read, you apply a larger, casual typeface and double-space the document.

a. Open *w_md_vaccinations* and save it as **w_md_vaccinations_LastnameFirstname**.

b. Set the left and right margins to **1"**.

c. Set the line spacing to double for the entire document.

d. Apply **Comic Sans MS**, **14 pt** to the entire document.

e. Set the paragraph Line Spacing Options to apply **6 pt** spacing before paragraphs for the entire document.

Insert a Cover Page

You decide to insert one of Word's preformatted cover pages, and then personalize the fields with your document title and physician's name.

a. Insert a cover page at the beginning of the document using the Austin cover page design.

b. Change the document theme to **Austin**.

c. Click **Show/Hide ¶** to view formatting marks.

d. Delete the page break that displays near the top of the cover page, and then insert a Section Break (Next Page) at the same location.

e. Change the document title to **A Guide to Vaccinations**. Change the font to **Comic Sans MS**, **bold**, and then shrink the font one size.

f. Type **For Infants, Children, and Adolescents** as the subtitle.

g. Type **Provided by Hilltop Family Practice** in the **abstract field**.

h. Change the author's name from *Exploring Series* to **Dr. Peter Mangas**.

Insert and Format Clip Art and a Symbol

Your physician, Dr. Mangas, asked that the document be very colorful and eye-catching, so you add a "colorful" image to the cover page to make it more interesting. You decide that using font effects will also add interest. You insert a smiley face to welcome readers to the Hilltop Family Practice immunization program.

a. Position the insertion point at the beginning of the page that contains the heading *Immunization Basics*. Insert the clip art image shown in Figure 1.1 using the following options:

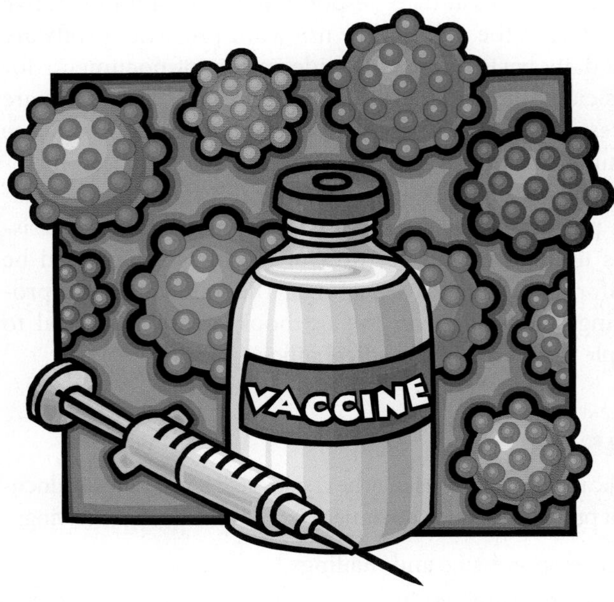

FIGURE 1.1 ▲

- Search for: **vaccines**
- Search in: **All media types**
- Include **Office.com content**

b. Scale the height to **63%**.

c. Position the clip art on the top left with square text wrapping.

d. Move the insertion point to the end of the sentence reading *Welcome to the Hilltop Family Practice immunization program.* Insert the **Wingdings:74 symbol** (the smiley face). Change the font size of the smiley face to **36 pt**.

Add a Footer

You want page numbers to appear on every page in the document because you plan on inserting a Table of Contents. You also want the medical practice name to appear on every page. Add a footer to the document to accomplish both of these tasks.

a. Position the insertion point on the second page, which is the first page in Section 2.

b. Double-click in the header or footer area to display the Header & Footer area as well as the Tools tab.

c. Remove the Different First Page option.

d. Insert a footer on that page, and then select the **Pinstripes style**. The Pinstripes style automatically includes text on the left margin and the page number on the right margin.

e. Type **Hilltop Family Practice** in the **Type text field**.

f. Format the footer using **Comic Sans MS, 11 pt**.

g. Format the page numbers so that the page numbers begin at *1*, and then close the footer.

Review a Document

You asked the physician's assistant, JM Behle, to review the document for accuracy. In addition, she also passed it along to supervisor Sherry Wright, who also reviewed the document. Both reviewers added comments to the document, some of which include specific instructions. You review the document using several of the reviewing features in Word to help you evaluate the changes to the document. After reviewing the document, you incorporate the changes in the document and remove all comments and highlighting.

a. Use the Show Markup feature to check the names of the reviewers. Make sure that your name, as well as *Sherry Wright* and *JM Behle*, displays.

b. Accept all changes in the document.

c. Delete the comment that displays in the beginning of the document on the heading *Welcome to the Hilltop Family Practice*.

d. Change the Show Markup options to hide the remaining comments in the document. You will display them again later to address the requests.

Create Sections and Apply Styles

The body of the document includes three distinct topics with information in each topic broken up as subtopics. You create sections, and format the titles and headings in each section using existing styles.

a. Apply the **Title style** to the section heading, *Immunization Basics*.

b. Use Find to locate the text *Recommended Vaccinations*, and then insert a Section Break (Next Page) at the beginning of the text. Apply the **Title style** to the section heading *Recommended Vaccinations*.

c. Use Find to locate the text *Suggested Schedules*, and then insert a Section Break (Next Page) at the beginning of the text. Apply the **Title style** to the section heading *Suggested Schedules*.

d. Apply the **Subtitle style** to the following paragraph headings in the document:

- *What is a vaccine?*
- *Are vaccines safe for my child?*
- *What side effects could my child experience?*
- *When should my child be vaccinated?*
- *HBV (Hepatitis B Vaccine)*
- *Rotavirus*
- *IPV (Inactivated Poliovirus)*
- *PCV (Pneumococcal Conjugate Vaccine)*
- *DTaP (Diptheria, Tetanus, Acellular Pertussis)*
- *Hib (Meningitis)*
- *Influenza*
- *MMR Vaccine*
- *Vericella (Chickenpox)*
- *MCV4 (Bacterial Meningitis)*
- *Hepatitis A*

e. Apply the **Heading 1 style** to the following text in the document (use only heading text in separate paragraphs—do not use text within paragraphs):

- *Diphtheria*
- *Pertussis*
- *Tetanus*
- *Measles*
- *Mumps*
- *Rubella*

Modify Styles

After reviewing the styles you applied, you decide to modify them so the headings reflect the casual friendly feel that you used on the cover page. Also, because the document includes short paragraphs with subtitles and headings, you format paragraphs to control widows and orphans. Modify the styles to include the following specifications:

a. Modify the Title style to use **Comic Sans MS**; **bold**; **Green, Accent 1, Darker 25%**. Apply **Align center**.

b. Modify the Subtitle style to use **Comic Sans MS**; **bold**; ***italic***; **16 pt**; **Orange, Accent 3**. Apply Align left. Adjust the paragraph spacing to **12 pt** before and **6 pt** after. Change paragraph settings to activate **Keep with next** and **Keep lines together**.

c. Modify the Heading 1 style to use **Comic Sans MS**. Adjust the paragraph spacing to **6 pt** before and **6 pt** after.

Use Find and Replace Commands

With the Show/Hide ¶ feature active to check spacing of headings, you note that in several locations there are two spaces between words and after periods instead of the correct single space. While scanning, you also decide that the title of one of the sections needs to be changed.

a. Move to the top of the document, and then turn on the Show/Hide ¶ feature, if you have not already done so.

b. Search for *Suggested Schedules*, and then replace it with **Immunization Schedules**.

c. Use the Replace feature to locate two spaces and replace with one space. Replace all, and then turn off **Show/Hide ¶**.

Format a Quote and Create a Footnote

You quoted a respected authority in the introduction to the document. You format the quote using an appropriate format, and then you insert the authoring information in a footnote on the first page.

a. Locate and select the quote regarding children in the United States (the second paragraph in the *Immunization Basics* section).

b. Single space the quote, and then apply a **.5"** left and right indent to the paragraph.

c. Italicize the quote using the Mini toolbar.

d. Move the insertion point to the end of the quote. Add a footnote using the following information: **Medline Plus, a service of the U.S. National Library of Medicine and the National Institutes of Health** (**www.nlm.nih.gov/medlineplus/childhoodimmunization.html**)

e. Apply **Century Gothic**, **bold**, **11 pt** font to the footnote.

Convert Text to a Table and Format Tables

The person who gathered the initial information for this document was unsure how to format the information for the immunization schedule, so she formatted one set of information as a table and one set as tabbed columns. You decide the table makes the information much easier to understand, so you convert the tabbed immunization information to a table.

a. Move to the end of the document. Locate and select all text after the existing table, and then convert the text to a table. Use three columns and separate text by tabs. (Text begins with *PPV* and ends with *Females only*.)

b. Insert two rows at the top of the newly created table.

c. Merge the cells in the first new row at the top of the table, and then set the alignment to **Center**. Change the row height to **0.7"**, if necessary. Type the table's title: **Recommended Immunization Schedule for Children 7–18 Years Old**.

d. Insert a footnote at the end of the title. Add the footnote text: **Centers for Disease Control and Prevention, 2008**.

e. Use the Format Painter to apply the same font to this footnote as you applied to the footnote on Page 1.

f. Type the column headings in the blank second row: **Vaccine**, **Age**, and **Comments**.

g. Apply the **Light List – Accent 5 table style** to both tables.

h. Change the table font size to **10 pt**, and then change the line spacing to **single** and apply this to the text in both tables. Do not change the font on the first two rows of either table.

i. Use the Show Markup feature to display comments. Insert information into the table as directed by the comments and then delete all comments from the document.

j. Insert a page break between the two tables at the end of the document. Remove extra line breaks so the second table displays at the top of the page.

Prepare the Document for Sharing and Change Document Properties

Before sending the final document to your supervisor for her approval, you make sure there are no misspellings, and no widows or orphans. You also check the tables to make sure that ages are not displaying improperly. You insert non-breaking spaces to correct the problem.

a. Check the spelling of the document, ignoring all occurrences of the correct spelling of the physician's name, *Mangas*. Assume all vaccination names and disease names are spelled correctly. Correct all other misspelled words.

b. Proofread the document. Not all errors can be identified by using the spell checker. Correct any errors you identify, such as the misspelling of Dr. Mangas' name.

c. Change the view to Full Screen Reading, and then scan the document to ensure there are no widows or orphans. Change back to Print Layout view.

d. Proofread the tables at the end of the document. Insert a non-breaking space between the age and the words *months* and *years* or *years old* to ensure they do not separate onto two lines in the cells (e.g., do not have *3* on one line and *years* on the next).

e. Set the document properties with the following information (the first two should be set already):

- The author is **Dr. Peter Mangas**.
- The title is **A Guide to Vaccinations**.
- Keywords are **Vaccinations, Immunizations, Shots**.
- Status is **Ready for Review**.

Insert Supplemental Components

You create captions for the two tables and then include a table of figures page. Then, you create a table of contents for the document. You feel that not only will this make the document more professional, it will make it easier for a reader to use. After creating the table of contents and reviewing it, you realize that the supplemental components should use roman numerals for page numbers and that the document should start on page 1. You change the format and starting number for page numbers as needed.

a. Create captions to display above each table at the end of the document. After the text that displays automatically in the Caption dialog box, type **: Schedule for Children 0–6 Years Old** as the caption for the first table. Type **: Schedule for Children 7–18 Years Old** as the caption for the second table.

b. Insert a blank page between the cover page and the first page of the document.

c. Type **Table of Figures**, and then insert two blank lines at the top of the new page. Apply the **Title style** to the heading.

d. Insert a table of figures using all defaults following the heading. Insert a Section Break (Next Page) between the cover page and the table of figures page.

e. Type **Table of Contents**, and then insert two blank lines at the top of the new page. Apply the **Title style** to the heading.

f. Click the **Table of Contents arrow** in the References tab, and then click **Insert Table of Contents**. Change the table of contents options to modify the *Build table of contents from* settings. In the *Available styles* section, set the TOC level for Heading 1 to **3**, Heading 2 to **4**, Heading 3 to **5**, and Title to **1**.

g. Change the footer page number for the table of contents section to use Roman numerals beginning with *i*. Change the footer page number for the table of figures to continue numbering from the previous section so that it displays the number *ii*.

h. Change the footer page number for the body of the document (beginning with the *Immunization Basics* section) to use the standard number format beginning with *1*.

i. Check all page numbering throughout the document, and then change the format to **Continue from Previous Section** where necessary so the pages are numbered sequentially.

j. Update the table of contents and the table of figures.

k. Change the font for the table of contents and the table of figures to **Comic Sans MS**, and then adjust spacing as necessary.

Change the Document Properties and Save Document

a. Change the status of your document to **Completed** in Document Properties.

b. Save and close the document.

c. Submit the file based on your instructor's directions.

Medical Office Assistants

Use Microsoft Excel

Background

Medical office assistants work in hospitals, clinics, and physician offices and are responsible for the administrative functions of the office. Medical office assistants use spreadsheet software on a daily basis to track data, calculate data, make decisions, and create charts. It is imperative that medical office assistants understand the features of Microsoft Excel and be comfortable using those features. The following spreadsheet skills taught in the textbook are skills crucial to people employed in a medical office.

Tasks

Medical office assistants may be responsible for creating and maintaining all types of spreadsheets. These types of spreadsheets could include the following:

- Patient logs
- Referral logs
- Test results logs
- Patient medical logs
- Triage forms
- Vaccine administration logs
- Patient schedules
- Receipt of payments

Skills

In addition to basic formatting skills, a medical office assistant should be able to do the following:

Chapter 1

- Enter and edit cell data (p. 332)
- Use symbols and order of precedence in formulas (p. 337)
- Use AutoFill to complete a range and copy formulas (p. 339)
- Display cell formulas (p. 340)
- Rename and copy worksheets (p. 347)
- Select a range (p. 353)
- Apply alignment and font options (p. 363)
- Apply number formats (p. 365)
- Select page setup options (p. 371)

Chapter 2

- Use relative, absolute, and mixed cell references (p. 394)
- Use the SUM function (p. 405)
- Insert statistical functions (p. 406)
- Insert date functions (p. 409)
- Use the IF function (p. 417)
- Use the VLOOKUP function (p. 420)
- Assign range names and use range names in formulas (p. 428)

Chapter 3

- Create a pie chart (p. 456)
- Select the data source (p. 460)
- Apply a chart layout and a chart style (p. 471)
- Move a chart (p. 472)
- Insert and customize a sparkline (p. 473)
- Insert and format the chart title (p. 482)
- Customize the data labels (p. 483)

Chapter 4

- Freeze rows and columns (p. 507)
- Create a table (p. 517)
- Apply a table style (p. 519)
- Sort data (p. 525)
- Filter data (p. 527)
- Create a total row (p. 531)
- Apply a data bar conditional format (p. 543)

Medical Office Assistant
Capstone Exercises

You work as a medical office assistant at the Diabetes Management Clinic at the Orland Medical Center. The Center provides specialty care for diabetes patients of all ages. Your supervisor asked you to create a workbook to log information about patients who come into the clinic for services each day. You keep track of the patient data as well as patients' insurance and payment information.

Enter and Format Identifying Information

Previously, you created a basic workbook serving as a log containing patient and insurance information. Your supervisor wants you to expand the workbook log to include payment information. The supervisor added column labels to the existing worksheet so that you would know the type of account information needed. Before creating the formulas and completing the log for a day's entries, you want to add a title, a subtitle, and the date at the top of the worksheet.

a. Open *e_md_log* and save it as **e_md_log_LastnameFirstname**.

b. Rename the sheet **Visit Log**, and then change the sheet tab color to **Aqua, Accent 5**.

c. Freeze the panes so that the column labels on row 6 will not scroll offscreen.

d. Change the font to **Calibri** for the entire worksheet.

e. Type **Diabetes Management Clinic at Orland Medical Center** in **cell A1**, and then do the following:
   - Merge and center the title in the **range A1:O1**.
   - Apply bold and **22 pt font size**.
   - Select the **Blue, Accent 1 font color**.
   - Apply the **White, Background 1, Darker 15% fill color**.

f. Type **Patient Log** in **cell A2**, and then do the following:
   - Merge and center the subtitle in the **range A2:O2**.
   - Use the Format Painter to copy the formatting from **cell A1**, and then reduce the font size to **16 pt**.

g. Apply the **Thick Box Border style** around the **range A1:O2**.

h. Use an appropriate date function in **cell A3** to display today's date in your worksheet. Use the **Short Date format**, apply **bold**, set the font size to **14 pt**, and then resize the column to display the date.

i. Use AutoFill to complete the patient numbers in column A, incrementing each number by 1.

Format Column Labels

The column labels in the worksheet need to show organization and have a professional look. Currently, some of the labels in the cells overlap or break inappropriately, making the text difficult to read. To assist with readability, you want to create a Patient Information categorical label to span over columns A:G and an Account Information categorical label to span over columns H:O on row 5. In addition, you will format the column labels.

a. Type **Patient Information** in **cell A5**, and then do the following:
   - Merge and center the label in the **range A5:G5**.
   - Apply bold and **14 pt font size**.
   - Apply the **Dark Blue, Text 2, Lighter 60% fill color** for the **range A5:G6** to color-code the two rows of column labels for Patient Information.

b. Type **Account Information** in **cell H5**, and then do the following:
   - Merge and center the label in the **range H5:O5**.
   - Apply bold and **14 pt font size**.
   - Apply the **Orange, Accent 6, Lighter 60% fill color** for the **range H5:O6** to color-code the two rows of column labels for Account Information.

c. Add these formatting features to the column headings in row 6.
   - Apply bold.
   - Apply the **Thick Bottom Border** to the **range A6:O6**.
   - AutoFit columns as needed.

Format Columnar Data

The Num column contains the order in which the patient arrives at the clinic. Instead of entering the numbers in the rest of the rows, use AutoFill to complete the series. The data in the other columns need to be formatted appropriately based on the data type. The date of birth data needs to be formatted with a date format, and the numerical data needs to be formatted to display dollar signs.

a. Use AutoFill to complete the series in the **range A7:A51**, increasing the number by one each for each row. Then do the following:
   - Select **Align Text Right**.
   - Increase the indent four times to shift the data more in the center while keeping the values aligned on the right side.

b. Format the **range C7:C51** using the **Short Date format**. Increase the column width as needed.

c. Format the **ranges I7:L51** and **N7:O51** with **Accounting Number Format with no decimal places**.

Enter Patient Information

You need to input the last two patients of the day in the Patient Log worksheet.

a. Enter the data for the second-to-the-last patient on row 50:
   - Num: **44**
   - Patient Name: **Olsen, Brad**

- Date of Birth: **February 23, 1949**
- Gender: **Male**
- Insurance Company: **Blue Cross**
- Insurance Type: **HMO**
- Insurance Policy Number: **XOF-6365167**
- Visit Code: **9211**
- Payment/Co-Pay: **30**
- Insurance Billing: **60**

b. Enter the data for the last patient on row 51:

- Num: **45**
- Patient Name: **Kizilsac, Yusuf**
- Date of Birth: **June 14, 1952**
- Gender: **Male**
- Insurance Company: **None**
- Visit Code: **8111**
- Payment/Co-Pay: **100**
- Insurance Billing: **0**

c. Apply **Calibri font** to the new records if Calibri is not automatically applied.

Use the VLOOKUP Function

The clinic has standard charges for the type of service a patient receives. The charges are stored in the Charges Lookup table. You need to assign a range name to the lookup table so that you can use the range name in a function. Then, you will create a VLOOKUP function using the stored information to determine the charge for the visit.

a. Assign the range name **charges** to the **range R8:S17**.

b. Insert a VLOOKUP function in **cell I7** that looks up the visit code in column H, compares it to the Charges Lookup table, and then returns the correct charge. Use the range name in the function, and then include the appropriate argument to ensure an exact match.

c. Copy the function down the Charge column.

Calculate the Insurance Adjustment

Your clinic participates in a managed fee-for-service plan with the insurance companies. The service plan sets an amount a patient pays (co-pay) and a maximum charge the insurance company pays. If a difference exists between the amount your clinic charges and the total of the patient co-pay and insurance payment, the difference must be adjusted off the books.

a. Create a formula in **cell L7** that adds the payment/co-pay to the insurance billing and then subtracts that amount from the charge.

b. Copy the formula down the Insurance Adjustment column.

Determine the Cash Discount and Adjusted Total Due

Your clinic has a policy that if a patient does not have insurance and pays cash the day of the visit, a 10% discount is applied to the amount due to reduce what the patient has to pay. First, insert an IF function to clearly display in a column that "Yes" an adjustment is applicable or "No" an adjustment is not applicable. Second, use another IF function to determine the amount of the discount. Finally, you use an IF function to determine the total due for the visit after the insurance adjustment or cash discount are applied. In most cases, the amount remaining after the co-pay and insurance payment is written off by the medical billing agency.

a. Create an IF function in **cell M7**. If the entry in the Insurance Company cell is *None*, the function returns *Yes*; any other value returns *No*.

b. Copy the function down the Discount Applicable column.

c. Create an IF function in **cell N7** that determines if a discount is applicable (based on *Yes* for the respective patient in column M). If the logical test is true, the function calculates a 10% discount based on the original charge in column I for the respective patient. If the logical test is false, the function returns 0. Use the cell reference to the cash discount below the lookup table.

d. Copy the function down the Cash Discount column.

e. Create an IF function in **cell O7**. If the Discount Applicable cell displays *Yes*, then subtract the Cash Discount from the Charge to determine the cash amount the patient owes; otherwise, subtract the insurance adjustment from the charge to determine the total amount owed between the patient and insurance company.

f. Copy the function down the Total Due After Adjustments column.

Create and Format a Table

You want to preserve the original worksheet, but you want to copy the worksheet so you can convert the data to a table and use Excel's table features to continue working with the data. After you convert a copied data set to a table, you will format it with a table style.

a. Copy the Visit Log worksheet. Place the copy to the right of the original worksheet. Rename the copied sheet **Visit Log Table**. Change the tab color of the new sheet to **Purple**.

b. Select the **range A6:O51**, and then convert the data to a table.

c. Apply **Table Style Light 14 table style**.

d. Apply **Black, Text 1, Lighter 5% font color** to the labels on row 6. (After you converted the data to a table, the style converted the font color to white, making it hard to read some of the column labels.)

e. Reduce the widths of columns L, N, and O.

f. Display the Total Row, and then display totals for these columns: Charge, Payment/Co-Pay, Insurance Billing, Insurance Adjustment, Cash Discount, and Total Due After Adjustment.

Create a Chart

You want to create a pie chart that depicts the percentage of co-pays, insurance billing, insurance adjustment, and cash discount of the original total charge. You will need to adjust the payment/co-pay after deducting the cash discount for those who pay cash. Use the Visit Log Table worksheet.

a. Set up data to chart:

- Type **=J6** in **cell J55**, **=K6** in **cell K55**, **=L6** in **cell L55**, and **=N6** in **cell M55**. Apply bold and wrap text to these labels, and then reduce the font size to **10 pt**.

- Click **cell J56**, and then enter a formula to subtract the Cash Discount total from the Payment/Co-Pay total. This is the net amount of cash payment and co-payments.
- Click **cell K56**, and then enter a formula to echo the Insurance Billing total.
- Click **cell L56**, and then enter a formula to echo the Insurance Adjustment total.
- Click **cell M56**, and then enter a formula to echo the Cash Discount total. (The total of all these formulas should sum to the original Charge total.)
- Format the formulas on row 56 with **Accounting Number Format with zero decimal places**.
- Type **Net** in **cell I56**.
- Apply the **Orange, Accent 6, Lighter 60% fill color** to the **range I56:M56**.

b. Create a column Sparkline in **cell N56** based on the **range J56:M56**. Do the following:

- Apply **Sparkline Style Accent 6, Darker 25% style** to the sparkline.
- Increase the height of row 56 to **48**.

c. Create a pie chart using the labels and formulas in rows 55 and 56.

d. Move the chart to a new chart sheet named **Pie Chart**.

e. Select chart **Layout 1** to display the percentages and category names by or within each slice and to remove the legend.

f. Apply chart **Style 26**.

g. Type the chart title: **Distribution of Total Charges**.

h. Apply **12 pt font size** to the data labels.

i. Explode the Payment/Co-Pay slice.

j. Move the Pie Chart sheet to the right of the Visit Log Table sheet. Change the tab color of the Pie Chart sheet to **Green**.

Sort the Table Data

A physician has requested the data in a different order. The physician wants to see the data sorted by insurance company and patient for one review. She then wants to see the visit code and total due after adjustments for a different perspective. You will create copies of the worksheets so that each sheet can display the data differently.

a. Copy the Visit Log Table sheet, and then place the duplicate to the right of the Pie Chart sheet. Rename the copied sheet **Sort by Insurance**. Change the tab color to **Yellow**.

b. Sort the table in the Sort by Insurance worksheet by Insurance Company in alphabetical order and then by Patient Name in alphabetical order.

c. Copy the Sort by Insurance sheet, place the duplicate to the right of the Sort by Insurance sheet, and then rename the copied sheet **Sort by Visit**. Change the tab color to **Red**.

d. Sort the data by Visit Code from smallest to largest and then by Total Due After Adjustments from largest to smallest.

e. Apply the **Gradient Fill Orange Data Bar conditional format** to the Total Due After Adjustments column in the **range O7:O51**.

Filter the Table Data

The physician has requested specific information regarding the number of patients with Blue Cross insurance. She also wants to know the number of patients without insurance. You need to filter the data to fulfill the physician's request.

a. Copy the Sort by Visit sheet, and then place the duplicate to the right of the Sort by Visit sheet. Rename the copied sheet **Filter Insurance**. Change the tab color to **Orange**. Remove the conditional formatting on the Filter Insurance sheet, if needed.

b. Create a filter that displays only patients who have Blue Cross Insurance.

c. Duplicate the Filter Insurance sheet, and then place the duplicate to the right of the Filter Insurance sheet. Rename the copied sheet **Filter No Insurance**. Change the tab color to **Dark Blue**.

d. Remove the filter in the copied sheet, and then set a filter to display records for only patients who do not have any insurance.

e. Create a footer with your name on the left side, the sheet tab code in the center, and the file name code on the right side of each worksheet.

f. Save and close the workbook. Submit based on your instructor's directions.

Medical Office Assistants

Use Microsoft Access

Background

Medical office assistants work in hospitals, clinics, and physician's offices and are responsible for the administrative functions of the office. They use database software to maintain records, including patient, physician, and insurance information, as well as create queries to locate and extract information from a database. In addition, medical office assistants design and create reports to display information in a professional manner. It is imperative that medical office assistants understand the features of Microsoft Access and be comfortable using those features. The following database skills taught in the textbook are skills crucial to people employed in a medical office.

Tasks

Medical office assistants may be responsible for creating and maintaining database information. This information could include the following:

- Creating tables and forms:
  - Physician data
  - Patient data
  - Medication data
  - Test results data
  - Scheduling data
  - Insurance data
- Sorting, filtering, and querying data
- Creating relationships between tables
- Creating reports:
  - Patient schedules
  - Payments received
  - Patient balance

Skills

A medical office assistant should be able to do the following:

Chapter 1

- Navigate among the objects in an Access database (p. 573)
- Back up, compact, and repair Access files (p. 581)
- Create filters (p. 589)
- Sort table data on one or more fields (p. 592)
- Use the Relationships window (p. 600)
- Understand relational power (p. 601)

Chapter 2

- Design data (p. 620)
- Create tables (p. 624)
- Understand table relationships (p. 636)
- Share data with Excel (p. 638)
- Establish table relationships (p. 642)
- Create a single-table query (p. 653)
- Specify criteria for different data types (p. 656)
- Copy and run a query (p. 659)
- Create a multi-table query (p. 665)
- Modify a multi-table query (p. 666)

Chapter 3

- Create a calculated field in a query (p. 689)
- Create expressions with the Expression Builder (p. 698)
- Use built-in functions in Access (p. 700)
- Perform date arithmetic (p. 703)
- Add aggregate functions to datasheets and queries (p. 713)

Chapter 4

- Create forms using the form tools (p. 734)
- Modify a form (p. 739)
- Identify form sections (p. 749)
- Revise forms using form views (p. 750)
- Identify control types in forms (p. 752)
- Create reports using report tools (p. 761)
- Modify a report (p. 768)
- Sort records in a report (p. 770)
- Identify report sections (p. 777)
- Revise reports using report views (p. 781)
- Identify control types in reports (p. 782)

Medical Office Assistant

Capstone Exercises

You work as a medical office assistant for Central Medical Clinics serving Chicago and the surrounding communities. The main office for the clinics has patient records stored in an Excel file. Information about the clinics and the physicians practicing in the clinics is stored in an Access database. Your supervisor asked you to update the Access database and to import the patient records from Excel. In addition to tracking patient, physician, and clinic information, the database needs to track insurance companies. The system will need to extract data from the tables and produce reports. The database needs to be set up according to the following instructions.

Create Tables

You have an existing database that contains the records of affiliated clinics and the physicians practicing in the clinics. You need to create a table in your database that will track the insurance information. You also need to modify the existing tables for better database design.

a. Open the *a_md_medical* file and save it as **a_md_medical_LastnameFirstname**.

b. Create a new table named **Insurance** using the following fields and properties:

Field Name	Data Type	Field Size	Comments
InsuranceID	AutoNumber		Set Primary Key
InsuranceName	Text	25	Caption: **Insurance Name**
Address	Text	25	
City	Text	25	
State	Text	2	
ZipCode	Text	10	Caption: **Zip Code**
Phone	Text	14	
Fax	Text	14	

c. Save the table.

d. Use the Input Mask Wizard to create an input mask for zip code in the Insurance table. Accept the hyphen as the placeholder and store the data without the symbols in the mask.

e. Use the Input Mask Wizard to create an input mask for the phone number and fax number using the default Input Mask format for Phone Number. Accept the underscore as the placeholder and store the data without the symbols in the mask.

f. Enter the following records into the Insurance table in Datasheet view.

	Record 1	Record 2	Record 3	Record 4
InsuranceID	AutoNumber	AutoNumber	AutoNumber	AutoNumber
InsuranceName	**United Healthcare**	**Aetna**	**Blue Cross**	**HMSP**
Address	**700 River Rd**	**1 Insurance Plaza**	**486 W Harrison**	**5873 W 68th**
City	**Chicago**	**Chicago**	**Chicago**	**Chicago**
State	**IL**	**IL**	**IL**	**IL**
ZipCode	**60614-3363**	**60290-1234**	**60637-4567**	**60645-7893**
Phone	**(773) 555-2367**	**(312) 555-8885**	**(773) 555-1115**	**(773) 555-5465**
Fax	**(773) 555-2377**	**(312) 555-9995**	**(773) 555-0550**	**(773) 555-0560**

g. Modify the Clinics table by applying the following changes:

Field Name	Data Type	Field Size	Comments
ClinicID	AutoNumber	Long Integer	Set as Primary Key
ClinicLocation	Text	20	Caption: **Clinic Location**
Address1	Text	30	
Address2	Text	30	
City	Text	25	
State	Text	2	
ZipCode	Text	10	Caption: **Zip Code**. Create input mask for a zip code using the default options.
Phone	Text	14	Create input mask using the default options for a telephone number.

h. Modify the Physicians table by applying the following changes:

Field Name	Data Type	Field Size	Comments
PhysicianID	AutoNumber	Long Integer	Confirm
FirstName	Text	20	Caption: **Physician First Name**
LastName	Text	25	Caption: **Physician Last Name**
Specialty	Text	25	
BoardCertification	Text	50	Caption: **Board Certification**
Cell	Text	14	Create input mask using the default options for a telephone number.
ClinicID	Number	Long Integer	

Share Data with Excel

Each day, the staff members compile the patient records in an Excel spreadsheet. Although this procedure enables the physicians and office manager to examine the patient data, your office manager wants to bring the data into the Access database; this will allow relationships to be created between the patient data, physician data, insurance data, and clinic data. After the relationships are created, queries can be created to analyze the data.

a. Import the data in the *a_md_import_patients* Excel file into a new table in the current database. Let Access add the primary key.

b. Name the table **Patients**.

c. View the data in the Patients table in Datasheet view and adjust column widths so all the data is visible.

d. Remove the @ symbol in the Format property if it exists in any field in the Patients table. Modify the fields as shown in the following table, and then save the table.

Field Name	Data Type	Field Size	Comments
PatientID	AutoNumber	Long Integer	
FirstName	Text	20	Caption: **Patient First Name**
LastName	Text	25	Caption: **Patient Last Name**
Phone	Text	14	Create input mask using the default options for a telephone number.
SSN	Text	11	Create input mask using the default options for a social security number.
Address	Text	30	
City	Text	25	

Field Name	Data Type	Field Size	Comments
State	Text	2	
ZipCode	Text	10	Caption: **Zip Code**. Create input mask using the default options for a zip code.
InsuranceID	Number	Long Integer	
Policy	Text	20	
PhysicianID	Number	Long Integer	
ClinicID	Number	Long Integer	
Charge	Currency		
CoPay	Currency		
InsurancePayment	Currency		Caption: **Insurance Payment**

Create Filters

You need to quickly find all patients who see Dr. Groves. You will open the Patients table and filter the records.

a. Open the Patients table in Datasheet view.

b. Filter the records for those patients who use Dr. Groves.

c. Close (but do not save) the table.

Create a Relationship

You need to create relationships between the tables to make the database more efficient.

a. Create the following relationships and enforce referential integrity:
   - Patients and Insurance tables
   - Patients and Physicians tables
   - Patients and Clinics tables

b. Save and close the Relationships window.

Create Single-Table Queries

The office manager would like to view a listing of the following data. Create a new query to accomplish each list.

a. Display a list of all patients that live in Chicago. Include last name, first name, address, city, state, zip code, and phone. Sort alphabetically by last name and then by first name. Save as **Chicago Patients**.

b. Display a complete list of all the patients of Dr. Mark Brody; include first name, last name, address-related fields, phone, and physician ID. Sort by patient's last name in ascending order. Save as **Brody Patients**.

c. Make a copy of the Brody Patients query and then modify the copy to create a query that displays all the patients that do not use Dr. Brody. Save as **Non-Brody Patients**.

Create Multi-Table Queries

The office manager would like to create two more queries. These queries require data from two tables.

a. Create a query of all patients sorted in alphabetical order by the insurance company name and then by the last name and first name of the patient. Include insurance ID, insurance name, last name and first name of patient, the patient policy number, and the amount of copay the patient is required to pay. Save as **Insurance by Patient**.

b. Create a query that lists clinic ID and location, then the last name of the physician, first name of the physician, the specialty of the physician, and the physician's cell phone number. Add criteria so that only CMC, Lake Shore physicians are included. Sort by physician last name. Save the query as **Lake Shore Physicians**.

Create a Patient Form

You create a new form to make it easier to enter new patients.

a. Create a new form based on the Patients table using the Form tool.

b. Change the title label control to **Enter Patient Data**.

c. Reduce the text box widths to one-half of their original size.

d. Change the form's control padding to narrow.

e. Save the form as **Enter Patient Data**, and then switch to Form view.

f. Enter a new patient record, **#46**, using your name. Enter a fictitious SSN and address. You have no insurance, and you see physician 13 at clinic 4. Your charge was $75 and you have no copay or insurance payment.

g. Close the form.

Use the Label Wizard

A new physician joined with the Oak Brook Clinic. A post-card has been prepared that will be sent to all patients to notify them of the new physician and the physician's specialty. Your office manager asks you to prepare labels for the postcards.

a. Use the Patients table to create address labels that can be printed on Avery 5660 labels, 1" × 2 13/16" (or similar label); use font type **Arial, 10 pt**.

b. Use all fields necessary to create a standard address block.

c. Sort the labels by Patient LastName and then by Patient First-Name.

d. Save the report as **Labels Patients**.

e. View the labels in Print Preview, and then save and close the labels.

Create a Report Using the Report Wizard

The office manager would like a report that lists each physician and his or her patients. Create the report using the Report Wizard.

a. Create a query and name it **Patients by Physicians**.
   - Add the LastName and FirstName fields from the Physicians table.
   - Add the LastName, FirstName, and Phone fields from the Patients table.
   - Add the InsuranceName field from the Insurance table.
   - Save and close the query.

b. Create a report based on the new query.
   - Group the data by physician Last name.
   - Sort the data by patient last name and then patient first name.
   - Select the **landscape orientation** for the report.
   - Type the report title and the report name as **Patients Grouped by Physician**.
   - Preview the report.

c. Change the column widths so all the data is visible. Widen the Report Header title control so the entire title is visible.

d. Preview the report. Close the report.

Revise a Report in Layout View

The office manager would like a revised report that lists each physician and his or her patients but that displays the insurance information more predominantly. You copy the Patients Grouped by Physician report and name the copied report Patients Grouped by Insurance.

a. Copy the Patients Grouped by Physician report and paste as **Patients Grouped by Insurance**. In Layout view, change the new report name to **Patients Grouped by Insurance**.

b. Add a new group for Insurance Name.

c. Remove the Physician's FirstName and LastName from the report in Design view.

d. Move the InsuranceName field into the first position in the InsuranceName header.

e. Remove the Physician's LastName group.

f. Reduce the width of the report, and then change the orientation to **Portrait**.

g. Preview the report and adjust the fields as necessary. Make any further adjustments so all information is visible. Save and close the report.

Create a Query and a Report with a Calculated Field

The office manager needs a report that displays all patients with an outstanding balance. You need to create a query to find all the patients that have a balance and then create a report based on the query results.

a. Create a query named **Balance Due**.
   - Add the Patient FirstName, Patient LastName, Phone, Charge, CoPay, and InsurancePayment fields in the query.
   - Use the Expression Builder to create a calculated field named Balance to determine the remaining balance. (The formula is Charge – Copay – InsurancePayment.)
   - Format the Charge, CoPay, InsurancePayment, and Balance fields as **Currency**.
   - Add a criterion that limits the results to only the patients that have a balance.
   - Sort the query so that the highest balances are displayed at the top of the query.
   - Add a total to the Balance column.
   - Save and close the query.

b. Use the Report tool to create a Balance Due report based on the Balance Due query.
   - Modify the column widths and column titles so that all fields fit onto one page.
   - Sort by Balance from largest to smallest.
   - Apply the **Civic theme** to the report.

Compact, Repair, and Back Up the Database

You compact the database to eliminate any unused space. You also back up the database and save it as another name.

a. Compact and repair the database.

b. Back up the database in the location where you save your student files. When naming the file, include today's date.

c. Submit the database based on your instructor's directions.

Medical Office Assistants

Use Microsoft PowerPoint

Background

Medical office assistants use presentation software on a regular basis. Medical presentations run the gamut from communicating research data to the scientific community to educating patients. Microsoft PowerPoint makes it possible for the user to create presentations with media elements, charts and graphs, and transitions and animations. It is imperative that medical office assistants understand the features of PowerPoint and be comfortable using those features. The following presentation skills taught in the textbook are skills crucial to people employed in a medical office.

Tasks

Medical office assistants may be responsible for creating all types of presentations and documents using PowerPoint. These could include the following:

- Presentations by a speaker at a conference or meeting
- Presentations for patient education
- Printed handouts for distribution to patients and audience members at a conference
- Informative presentations displayed in a kiosk

Skills

Medical office assistants should be able to do the following:

Chapter 1

- Use PowerPoint views (p. 809)
- Use slide layouts (p. 820)
- Apply themes (p. 821)
- Insert media objects (p. 828)
- Add a table (p. 829)
- Use animations and transitions (p. 829)
- Insert a header or footer (p. 832)
- Run and navigate a slide show (p. 839)
- Print in PowerPoint (p. 841)

Chapter 2

- Create a presentation using a template (p. 862)
- Modify a template (p. 864)
- Create a presentation in Outline view (p. 869)
- Import an outline (p. 877)
- Add existing content to a presentation (p. 877)
- Modify a theme (p. 885)

Chapter 3

- Create shapes (p. 904)
- Apply Quick Styles and customize shapes (p. 909)
- Create SmartArt (p. 925)
- Modify SmartArt (p. 929)
- Create WordArt (p. 933)
- Modify WordArt (p. 933)
- Modify objects (p. 939)
- Arrange objects (p. 944)

Chapter 4

- Insert a picture (p. 974)
- Transform a picture (p. 976)
- Use the Internet as a resource (p. 987)
- Add video (p. 997)
- Use Video Tools (p. 1000)
- Add audio (p. 1007)
- Change audio settings (p. 1009)

Medical Office Assistant
Capstone Exercises

The University of Michigan Hospital is a research hospital. You work as a medical office assistant for one of the physicians, Dr. Thomas Martin. He has been asked to present to a local service organization next week. He would like to educate the group about the dangers of high blood pressure and also teach the members ways to improve their blood pressure. He has asked you to prepare a PowerPoint slide show based on a presentation he gave at a local senior citizens center. Create the presentation according to the following instructions.

Set Up the Slide Show

The outline Dr. Martin used to prepare his previous presentation was created in Microsoft Word and saved as an .rtf (rich text format) file. You insert this outline into a blank presentation.

a. Create a new blank PowerPoint slide show and save it as **p_md_bloodpressure_LastnameFirstname**.

b. Enter the following text into the placeholders:
   - Title placeholder: **BLOOD PRESSURE**.
   - Subtitle placeholder: **Presented By: Tom Martin, M.D.**

c. Create a handout header with your name, and a handout footer with your instructor's name and your class. Include the current date.

d. Apply the **Concourse theme**.

e. Change the color theme to **Equity**.

Reuse Slides

Dr. Martin created a basic slide show about hypertension, which he presented to a local senior citizens group. His physician's assistant added speaker notes to this slide show for your use. For efficiency, you reuse this content in your slide show.

a. Reuse Slides 2 through 14 from *p_md_hypertension.pptx*.

b. Switch to Notes Page view, and then read the speaker notes for each slide.

c. Return to Normal view, and then apply the **Fade transition with the Through Black effect option** to all slides.

d. View the slide show.

Revise the Slide Show Structure

After reviewing the slide show you realize that, although it contains a strong body of information, it is missing an introduction slide. You also feel that the conclusion slide giving references is bland. You create an introduction to the presentation using an eye-opening statement. You also modify the conclusion by adding an attractive image that you hope will serve as a call to action to encourage the viewers to become more active.

a. Insert a new Slide 2 using the Section Header layout. Change the background style of the new slide to **Style 1**.

b. Enter the following text into the placeholders:
   - Title placeholder: **The "Silent Killer" Epidemic**.
   - Subtitle placeholder: **One in three U.S. adults has high blood pressure. Because there are no symptoms, nearly one third of these people do NOT know they have it!**

c. Insert a text box beneath the quote to credit the resource from which you are quoting. Type **American Heart Association**, and then change the font style to **Italic**, **16 pt**.

d. Enter the following speaker note: **High blood pressure usually has no symptoms, although sometimes headaches occur. Sometimes people only learn that they have high blood pressure AFTER it causes health problems. High blood pressure is a key risk factor for a stroke, heart attack, and kidney failure! (American Heart Association)**

e. Insert the image *p_md_image1.jpg*.
   - Change the height of the image to **3"**, and then position the image so that it is horizontally positioned at **0.8"** and vertically positioned at **1.25"** from the Top Left Corner.

f. Apply a **Reflected Perspective Right picture style** to the image, as shown in Figure 1.2.

g. Change the layout for the conclusion slide, Slide 15, to **Picture with Caption**.

h. Insert the picture *p_md_image2.jpg* into the picture placeholder.

i. Apply the **Double Frame, Black picture style** to the picture.

Modify the Outline and Change Slide Layouts

To be able to concentrate on the content of the slide show, you review the text in the Outline view. You check for slides with too much text and problems with parallel structure and make corrections. As a final step to reviewing the text in the document, use the spell checker and Find and Replace.

a. Switch from the Slides pane to the Outline pane, and then remove all unnecessary blank lines in the outline.

b. Reverse the *Diastolic Pressure* and *Systolic Pressure* families on **Slide 5** so that *Systolic Pressure* and its associated bullet point appear first.

c. Move to Slide 6, *Tips for Blood Pressure Readings*, and then modify the bullet points so each point begins with a verb and so that unnecessary text is removed.

d. Move to Slide 13, and then add the following bullet points:
   - **Rinse canned foods to reduce sodium**
   - **Choose convenience foods low in salt**

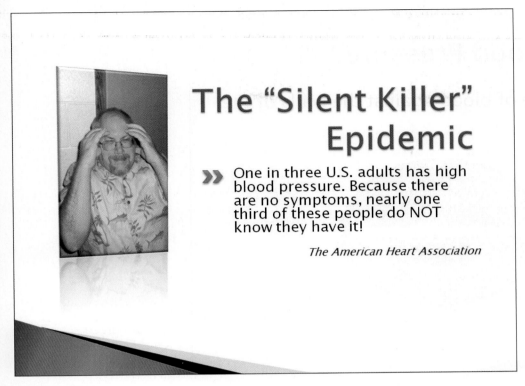

FIGURE 1.2 ▲

e. Check the spelling in the presentation, correcting all spelling errors.

f. Change the capitalization for the bulleted items on Slide 14 so that the first word of the medication type is capitalized and all other words are lowercase.

g. Switch back to the Slides pane, and then change the layout of Slide 14 to **Two Content**. Split the list of medications evenly between the two placeholders.

h. Move to Slide 4. Insert the picture *p_md_image3.jpg*, and change the height to **5"**. Apply **Align Center** and **Align Middle** to position the image.

i. Remove the white background from the image.

Add Media Objects

Recognizing that the majority of the slides are still text slides, you decide to add interest to the presentation by converting some text to SmartArt, adding shapes to illustrate points, and adding clip art.

a. Insert a picture fill for the background of Slide 1. Insert *p_md_image4.jpg*.

b. Format the title placeholder so that its Text Box shape resizes to fit the text. Position the title placeholder horizontally at **0"** and vertically at **6.5"** from the Top Left Corner.

c. Change the title text to WordArt Style **Fill – White, Drop Shadow**. Change the subtitle text to WordArt style **Fill – Dark Red, Accent 2, Warm Matte Bevel**.

d. On Slide 11, convert the text in the content placeholder to a **Continuous Block Process SmartArt**. Apply the SmartArt style of your choice.

e. On Slide 3, insert an oval, and then set the height to **3"** and the width to **4"**. Duplicate the oval and set the height to **2.85"** and the width to **3.8"**.

f. Change the shape style of the larger oval to **Colored Fill – Dark Red, Accent 2**.

g. Align Center and Align Middle the two ovals to create the appearance of an artery. Group the two ovals and position them attractively on the slide.

h. Insert a Left-Right Arrow shape that stretches from the left edge to the right edge of the smaller oval to illustrate pressure against the walls of an artery, as shown in Figure 1.3. Change the height and width of the arrow so it is easily visible inside of the oval group. Change the fill of the shape to **White, Background 1**. Align Center and Align Middle the arrow and the oval group. Group the ovals and the arrow.

i. On Slide 5, insert a text box below the bullets on the right side of the slide. Type **120** in the text box. Press **Enter**, and then type **80**. Change the font size to **80 pt**, and then apply **bold**. Center the text in the text box.

j. Insert a Line shape that stretches from the left alignment point of the text box to the right alignment point of the text box. Change the shape outline theme color to **Black, Text 1** and the shape outline weight to **3 pt**. Group the text box and the line shape.

k. Insert a heart shape, and then apply the shape style of your choice.

l. Size the heart shape to approximately the size of the text box and position it to the left of the text box.

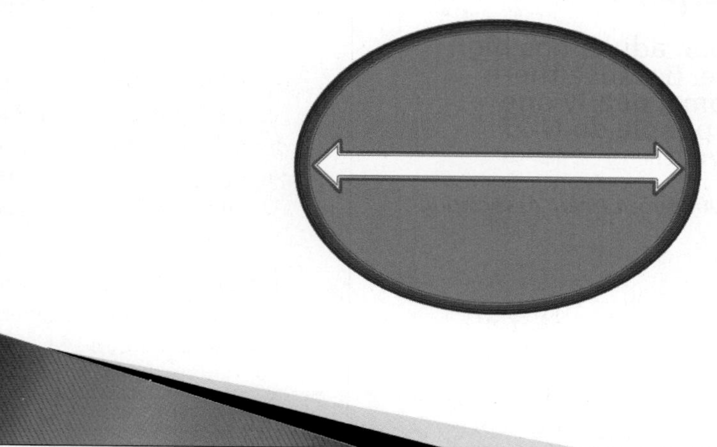

What is Blood Pressure?
The pressure of blood against the walls of the arteries.

FIGURE 1.3 ▲

m. Insert the **Heart Thuds sound Clip Art** using these options:
   - Search for: *heart*
   - Click the **Include Office.com content check box**.
   - Results should be: *Audio*

n. Start the sound automatically and hide the sound icon during the show. Loop the sound until stopped so it plays continuously until the next slide displays. Drag the sound icon to the bottom-right corner of the slide, as shown in Figure 1.4.

What Should Your Blood Pressure Numbers Be?
Systolic Pressure
The force in the arteries when the heart beats
Diastolic Pressure
The force in the arteries when the heart is at rest
120
80

FIGURE 1.4 ▲

o. On Slide 8, insert the following WordArt near the bottom of the slide, using **Gradient Fill – Orange, Accent 1**. Type **Check Your Blood Pressure Regularly!**, and then change the font size to **28 pt**.

p. Insert a video on blood pressure, diet, or exercise from a Web site on Slide 12 by locating a video on YouTube or another Web location, copying the Embed code, and then inserting the code in the Insert Video From Web Site dialog box.

Add a Table

- Add a table to display blood pressure levels.
- On Slide 7, insert a table with 3 columns and 5 rows.
- Enter the following information into the table cells:

Blood Pressure Category	Systolic	Diastolic
Normal	Less than 120	And less than 80
Prehypertension	120–139	Or 80–89
High Stage 1	140–159	Or 90–99
High Stage 2	160 or higher	Or 100 or higher

- Horizontally and vertically center the column titles.
- Resize the table to a width of **8"** and position it attractively in the white space.
- Apply the **Themed Style 1 – Accent 1 table style**.

Add Animation

Now that the presentation has been created, add animations to introduce elements at appropriate times and to create visual interest.

a. On Slide 1, apply the **Zoom entrance animation** to the title placeholder, having it start After Previous. Apply the same animation to the subtitle placeholder, having it start after the title placeholder has completed its animation.

b. On Slide 3, apply the **Grow/Shrink emphasis animation** to the oval and arrow group, and then set the timing to After Previous.

c. On Slide 4, insert *p_md_image5.jpg*. (*Note:* The image will cover the title placeholder, the content placeholder, and the previously inserted image of a sphygmomanometer.) Apply the **Random Bars entrance animation**, and then change the effect options to **Vertical**. Set the timing to **With Previous** with a delay of 02.00 seconds.

d. On Slide 6, apply the **Fly In animation** to the content placeholder. Have the text fly in by paragraph. Use the Animation Painter to apply the same scheme to Slides 8, 10, and 13.

e. On Slide 11, apply the **Wipe animation** to the SmartArt. Wipe the objects from the left and one by one.

Save and Close the Presentation

Save and close the presentation.

a. Save the *p_md_bloodpressure_LastnameFirstname* presentation, close the file, and then submit based on your instructor's directions.

Medical Office Assistants

Integrated Exercise

Capstone Integration Exercise

Each program in the Microsoft Office suite has its strength and specialty. Microsoft Word is the best program to use when creating documents, such as a letter to a patient. Microsoft Excel is the choice when the data requires extensive calculations, for example analyzing medical office financial data. Microsoft PowerPoint is a presentation program. It allows users to create unique, professional presentations and animate them. Microsoft Access is a database management program, capable of storing and analyzing patient and visit information over many years. Sometimes users will need to use all four programs together to create the desired result.

Tasks

Medical office assistants may be responsible for integrating data between Word, Excel, Access, and PowerPoint. This could include the following:

- Creating documents in one or all of the Office applications
- Copying and pasting data between applications
- Exporting data from Access to Excel
- Creating a chart in Excel and pasting into a PowerPoint slide

Skills

In addition to basic integration skills, a medical office assistant should be able to do the following:

- Maintain a database containing patient and physician information
- Merge data using Word and Excel (or Access)
- Determine which application to use when creating documents
- Practice good file management (including file naming, storing, and backup procedures)

Medical Office Assistant
Capstone Exercises

Retrieve the Past Due Account Information from Access

You use the Midwest Physician Center database to create a report that displays all patients with a balance due.

a. Open the *i_md_receivables* database and save it as **i_md_receivables_LastnameFirstname**.

b. Create a query called **Patient Balances** using the Patients and Physicians tables. This query should only display patients that have a remaining balance.

- Select the **FirstName**, **LastName**, **Charge**, **PatientPayment**, and **InsurancePayment fields** from the Patients table.
- Insert the Clinic field from the Physicians table between the LastName and Charge fields.
- Create a calculated field that shows the balance for each patient. Name the field **Balance**.
- Format the Charge, PatientPayment, InsurancePayment, and Balance fields as **Currency**.
- Add criteria that limit the results to only the patients that have a balance greater than zero.
- Sort the query on the Clinic field (ascending) and the Balance field (descending).
- Run the query and verify the accuracy of the Balance field.
- Save and close the query as **Patient Balances**.

c. Use the Report wizard to create a report named **Patient Balances** based on the Patient Balances query.

- Add the Clinic, LastName, FirstName, and Balance fields to the report.
- View by Patients; Group by Clinic.
- Sort the data by Balance in descending order.
- Add a sum to the Balance field.
- Accept the default settings for the rest of the wizard questions.
- Name the report **Patient Balances**.
- Switch to Layout view, and then adjust all the columns so that all the data is visible.
- Save and close the report.

Create a Totals Query

You need to create a totals query showing the account balances by clinic. Name the new query Patient Balances by Clinic. Then you export the data to Excel.

a. Copy the Patient Balances query, and then paste it using the name **Patient Balances by Clinic**.

b. In Design view, modify the new query as follows:

- Delete all the fields except Clinic and Balance.
- Add the Total row.
- Change the Total row for the Balance column to **Sum**.
- Remove the Descending sort from the Balance column.
- Run the query and verify that there are five records.
- Save and close the query.

Export Data to Excel

Export the Patient Balances by Clinic query to Excel. Use the data to chart the balances of the clinics.

a. Use the Export feature on the External Data tab to export the Patient Balances by Clinic query to Excel.

b. Save the worksheet in the same location as the Access database solution and name it **i_md_clinics_LastnameFirstname**.

c. Export the data with formatting and layout and open the destination file after the export operation is complete. Do not save the export steps. Close Access.

Create the Excel Chart

Use the exported data to create a pie chart of the balances by clinic.

a. Insert a 2D Pie Chart that shows the proportion of the total due by clinic.

b. Apply **Layout 1** for the Chart Layout, and then increase the height of the chart to **5"**.

c. Increase the font size of the labels to **12 pt**, and then increase the Chicago label font size to **20 pt**.

d. Change the title for the chart to **Midwest Physician Center**, and then add a second line **Patient Balances**.

e. Move the chart to a new separate chart sheet (following the worksheet), and then name the sheet **Clinic Balances Chart**.

f. Save the worksheet, but do not close the workbook.

Create the PowerPoint Slide Show

The chart you have prepared will be used as part of a presentation to the physicians by the finance department of the Midwest Physician Center. You begin this presentation by creating a logo for your department and then inserting the Patient Balances chart.

a. Open a blank PowerPoint presentation and save it as **i_md_midwest_LastnameFirstname**.

b. Create a Slide footer that displays the current date, the slide number, and your name on each slide.

c. Create a Notes and Handouts header that includes the current date, your name, and the page number; add the name of your instructor to the footer.

d. Add the title **Midwest Physician Center** and the subtitle **Finance Department** to Slide 1.

e. Apply the **Origin theme**.

f. Insert the clip art image of your choice using *caducei* as your keyword.

g. Change the height of the clip art image to **1.5"**.

h. Use WordArt to add both the center initials and department name next to the caducei. Group the WordArt and clip art to create a logo. Make other changes as desired, but do not exceed the 1.5" height requirement. Position the logo in the top-left quadrant of the slide. Figure 1.5 is an example of a possible logo.

FIGURE 1.5 ▲

i. Create Slide 2 using the Blank layout.

j. Copy the Excel chart and paste it into Slide 2.

k. Resize the chart to a height of **6"**, and then position it in the middle of the slide.

l. Apply a **Fly In animation** to the chart, animating By Category.

m. Run the slide show. Save the presentation.

Modify the Memo and Insert the Chart and Logo

Open the memo in Word, and then insert the information regarding the patient balances. The Excel chart will be inserted into the memo as well as the company logo from the PowerPoint slideshow.

a. Open the *i_md_memo* document and save as **i_md_memo_LastnameFirstname**.

b. Add your name after *From*, and then type the current date after the Date placeholder.

c. Calculate the total balance of all clinics in the Excel worksheet; copy and paste the total balance into the first paragraph, replacing *$xxx*.

d. Copy the Midwest Physician Center Patient Balances chart from the Excel worksheet, and then insert it below the first paragraph.

e. Resize the chart height to **5"** and width **6"** using the size controls on the Format tab. Center-align the chart.

f. Replace the word *MEMO* with the logo from Slide 1 of the *i_md_midwest_LastnameFirstname* slide show.

g. Save the document and submit the memo based on your instructor's directions. Close any open files; submit the Access database, the Excel workbook, and the PowerPoint presentation as directed.

Production Assistants

Use Microsoft Word

Background

A Word processing application is the most used program in a theater company business office. Production assistants create correspondence, contracts with actors, and theater rental space contracts, as well as memos, reports, press releases, and documents requiring desktop publishing. It is imperative that a production assistant becomes proficient in Microsoft Word and its many features.

Tasks

In a theater company's business office, a production assistant might be asked to create and develop many types of documents, including the following:

- Correspondence and mailings
- Contracts (actors and technicians of local and touring shows, crew, venue contact people)
- Mailing lists
- Tables
- Press releases
- Audition schedules
- Brochures

Skills

Production assistants should be able to do the following:

Chapter 1

- Insert page breaks (p. 127)
- Add page numbers (p. 128)
- Insert a cover page (p. 130)
- Insert headers and footers (p. 137)
- Create sections (p. 138)
- Check spelling and grammar (p. 141)
- Set margins and specify page orientation (p. 145)

Chapter 2

- Apply font attributes (p. 172)
- Set off paragraphs with tabs and bulleted lists (p. 180)
- Apply paragraph formats (p. 186)
- Copy formats with the Format Painter (p. 201)
- Use styles (p. 201)

Chapter 3

- Insert comments (p. 226)
- Track changes (p. 229)
- Create footnotes (p. 240)

Chapter 4

- Insert a table (p. 272)
- Format a table (p. 274)
- Convert text to a table (p. 285)
- Insert formulas in a table (p. 286)

Production Assistants
Capstone Exercises

You work as a production assistant in the offices of a new company, The Green Man Theatre. You have been asked to create a press packet for Paul's Kitchen, *a Green Man production. The packet will include a cover page, a cover letter, a press release, and a brochure advertising upcoming Green Man productions.*

Create a Cover Page

You create a cover page for the press packet that introduces the *Paul's Kitchen* production, and includes the date of the packet release and your name as the contact person for further information. You include the Green Man logo on the cover page and all other materials in the press packet for quick visual recognition.

a. Open *w_a_presspacket*, and then save it as **w_a_presspacket_LastnameFirstname**.

b. Turn on **Show/Hide ¶** to help you work with the multiple sections you will be creating for the press packet.

c. Set the document margins to **Normal**.

d. Insert a cover page in the Pinstripes style. Change the document theme to **Slipstream**. (*Note:* If the Slipstream theme is not available, download it from Microsoft Office Online or choose another theme.)

e. Type **Paul's Kitchen Press Release** as the document title. Type **Presented by Green Man Theatre** as the document subtitle.

f. Enter today's date using the Date Control. Remove the company name by removing the Content Control. Change the author to your name.

g. Place the insertion point on a blank line just below your name. Use the decrease indent feature, to align the text on the left margin. Type the following contact information on the line below your name and use your e-mail address for the requested e-mail address.

- **Production Assistant**
- **Green Man Theatre**
- **Phone: 1 (612) 555-1212**
- **Fax: 1 (612) 444-2323**
- **E-mail:**

h. Press **Enter** twice, insert the *w_a_gmlogo.jpg* file, and then apply the **Square text wrapping style**.

i. Create a WordArt object on the first page using **Green Man Theatre** as the text. Modify the WordArt format so that it uses the font of your choice, a fill that complements the colors in the logo, and any effects that you want to use. You might consider using the WordArt style **Gradient Fill – Blue, Accent 1, Outline – White, Glow – Accent 2**. Change the Font to **Broadway**, change the Text Fill color to **Green, Accent 4, Darker 50%**, change the Text Outline color to **Purple**, and then select the Shadow style named **Offset Diagonal Bottom Right**. Apply the **Square wrapping style**.

j. Position both the WordArt and the logo image together attractively in the center of the lower part of the cover page, resizing the objects as desired.

Create a Cover Letter

You write a cover letter to members of the press inviting them to the *Paul's Kitchen* production and offering them four complimentary tickets.

a. Place the insertion point before the Page Break paragraph symbol on the cover page if necessary, and then insert a Next Page section break. Position the insertion point on the first line of the second page, if necessary, and then insert a page break to add a blank page between the cover and the press release page. You will create a cover letter on this blank page.

b. Place the insertion point on the second page. Change the top and bottom margins of the cover letter section to **1"** if necessary.

c. Type a return address block using the following information.
Green Man Theatre
123 Main Street
Minneapolis, MN 55404

d. Insert three blank lines after the return address, and then add a date that will automatically update. Use the Month Day, Year format.

e. Press **Enter** four times, type **Greetings Members of the Press:** as a salutation line, and then press **Enter** two times.

f. Write the text of the cover letter making sure there is 6 pt spacing before and after each paragraph you create. Include the following information:

- An announcement that Green Man Theatre's 2013–2014 season is opening with a production of *Paul's Kitchen*, the story of seven friends, one van, and lots of laughs.
- The press will find the following information in the press packet:
  - Cover sheet
  - Cover letter
  - Press release
  - Ticket price list
  - Brochure
- The press member is personally invited to enjoy a performance of *Paul's Kitchen*. The press member needs to present the press packet at the box office to receive their four complimentary tickets.

g. Insert a complimentary closing line followed by a comma.

h. Leave three blank lines after the complimentary closing line, and then type **your name**.

i. Type **Production Assistant** as your title on the next line following your name.

j. Insert the **Pinstripes header** to the cover letter. Copy the WordArt and logo you created for the cover page, and then paste them into the header. Resize the objects so they fit attractively in the lower-right side of the header. Click **Link to Previous** in the Navigation group so that it is not selected.

k. Add a **Pinstripes footer**. In the area to type text, enter the theater's contact information displayed in two lines with no space above paragraphs:
123 Main Street, Minneapolis, MN 55404
(612) 555-1212

l. Replace the page number with **www.greenman-theatre.com**. Click **Link to Previous** in the Navigation group so that it is not highlighted. Scroll to the cover page, and then click in the footer area. Delete the address information that displays if necessary, and then scroll up to the Header and delete the graphic object that displays. Set the Footer from Bottom distance to .5" in each section. Close the header and footer.

m. Scroll to the second page, and then double-click anywhere. Change the page layout so that its vertical alignment is set to center.

Modify the Press Release

The basic information for the press release is on page 3 of the packet, but needs to be formatted professionally. You format the press release.

a. Apply the **Emphasis style** to the text *Press Release* on page 3 of the press packet.

b. Change the style of the text *Green Man Theatre Announces the Opening of Paul's Kitchen* to the **Title style**.

c. Apply the **Intense Emphasis style** to the paragraph that begins *Paul's Kitchen opens…*.

d. Change the style of the line that begins *Minneapolis…* to the **Emphasis style**.

e. Move the insertion point to the second blank line following the paragraph that introduces the playwright and actors, and describes the basic plot of the play. Type **Tickets are available at the box office or online at:**, and then press **Enter**.

f. Press **Tab**, and then type the following address information on the next three lines, adding a tab at the beginning of each line:

Green Man Theatre
123 Main Street, Minneapolis, MN 55404
(612) 555-1212

Convert the Showtimes Table

To make the showtimes of *Paul's Kitchen* easier to read, you apply a table format that matches the theme you used on the cover page.

a. Convert the text listing dates and showtimes to a 2-column table.

b. Format the table using the **Medium Shading 2–Accent 5 table style**.

c. Adjust the left edge of the table so it aligns with the paragraph text preceding it.

d. Adjust the width of the first column so that the month and the day are not split.

e. Change the row height to **0.3"**.

f. Center the text vertically in the table cells, and then align the text to the left edge of the cells.

g. AutoFit the table content.

h. Center the table horizontally on the page.

Create a New Ticket Price List

You add a table to the press packet that displays the ticket types available, and the costs per type of ticket. You format the table to match the theme colors.

a. Insert a Next Page section break after the table.

b. Change the top margin for the new page to **1.5"**.

c. Create a table with 4 columns and 4 rows.

d. Format the table using the **Medium Shading 1–Accent 5 table style**.

e. Merge the cells of the top row and create a title **Green Man Theatre Ticket Price List**, apply the **Title style** to the title, and then center the title in that cell.

f. In the second row and first column type the following headings:

Ticket Type	At the Door	Advance Purchase	Season Tickets
Adult			
Senior			

g. Insert a row above the *Adult* row, and then type **Student** as the *Ticket Type*.

h. Enter the *At the Door* ticket prices as shown:

Student	$15
Adult	$50
Senior	$25

i. Enter formulas in the table to calculate these discounts:
- A 20% discount for all advance purchase tickets.
- A 25% discount for season tickets. The season ticket price is the equivalent of purchasing tickets to all three productions.

j. Set the table preferred width to **6.65"**.

k. Add a footnote to the Advance Purchase column heading: **Advance Purchase Tickets earn a 20% discount off the door price and must be purchased at least two weeks before the show.**

l. Add a footnote to the Season Tickets column heading: **Season Tickets earn a 25% discount off the door price. All three tickets of the season must be purchased at once to qualify for season ticket pricing.**

Insert a Merchandise Price List

The Theater Shop manager asked you to include a price list of merchandise in the press packet. You create a link to the file containing these prices. The link should update the press packet information if there are any price changes in the Theater Shop.

a. Open the file *w_a_pricelist.docx*, copy the price list table, and then use Paste Special to include the table beneath the *Green Man Theater Ticket Price List*. Ensure that the link is in HTML format, and that it will update if there are any price changes in the Theatre shop price list document.

b. Format the table using the **Medium Shading 1–Accent 5 table style**.

c. Apply the **Title style** to the table title.

d. Format the new table to use the same column and row formats as the Ticket Price List table. Apply **Align Center Left** to the items, and then apply **Align Center** to the prices and discounts.

e. Adjust row heights to ensure that both tables fit on one page.

Complete a Document Review

You proofread the press packet and note that some of the references to Green Man Theatre use *Theater* in the name instead of *Theatre*. After proofreading, you review the document by checking the spelling and grammar of each page. Finally, before presenting the press packet to the Board of Directors for approval, you add a question to the Board.

a. Turn on **Track Changes**.

b. Find all occurrences of *Theater* within *Green Man Theater*, and then replace with **Theatre** so that the company name is *Green Man Theatre*.

c. Check the spelling and grammar of the packet. Accept all references to *showtimes* as the correct spelling, and then accept the sentence *Picture seven friends in a van driving from Minnesota to Cape Cod*.

d. Accept all changes in the packet.

e. Select the phrase *four complimentary tickets* in the cover letter, and then add a comment: **Did we decide on two tickets or four tickets?**.

f. Save and close *w_a_presspacket_LastnameFirstname*, and then submit based on your instructor's directions.

Production Assistants

Use Microsoft Excel

Background

Green Man Theatre is a local production company that puts on productions of plays and musicals. It has a small staff that takes care of production details, such as finances, scheduling, auditions, etc. Community actors audition for roles in plays and are paid a small stipend. A production assistant uses spreadsheets to prepare budgets for current and upcoming plays and musicals, as well as prepare rehearsal schedules for current shows and financial reports based on past shows. Therefore, it is imperative that theater production assistants are proficient in using Microsoft Excel.

Tasks

The theater production assistant may be responsible for creating and maintaining spreadsheets for many purposes, including the following:

- Mailing lists
- Budget for upcoming shows
- Budget reports for previous shows
- Charts to represent revenue or ticket sales
- Rehearsal schedules
- Mileage reimbursement

Skills

A production assistant should be able to do the following:

Chapter 1

- Enter and edit cell data (p. 332)
- Use symbols and the order of precedence (p. 337)
- Display cell formulas (p. 340)
- Manage worksheets (p. 346)
- Manage columns and rows (p. 349)
- Apply alignment and font options (p. 363)
- Apply number formats (p. 365)
- Specify page setup options (p. 371)

Chapter 2

- Use relative, absolute, and mixed cell references in formulas (p. 394)
- Total values with the SUM function (p. 405)
- Insert basic statistical functions (p. 406)
- Use date functions (p. 409)
- Determine results with the IF function (p. 417)
- Calculate payments with the PMT function (p. 422)

Chapter 3

- Create a chart (p. 460)
- Apply a chart layout and a chart style (p. 471)
- Move a chart (p. 472)
- Insert and customize a sparkline (p. 473)
- Select and format chart elements (p. 480)
- Customize chart labels (p. 482)

Chapter 4

- Freeze rows and columns (p. 507)
- Create a table (p. 517)
- Sort data (p. 525)
- Filter data (p. 527)
- Apply conditional formatting (p. 541)

You work as a production assistant for the Green Man Theatre. The director of operations asked that you prepare a packet to include an audition schedule and a budget for the upcoming show, Paul's Kitchen. *In addition, she asked you update the budget for the current show and create a chart. Finally, you need to create a forecast of ticket sales based on past shows. Rehearsals run for four weeks, starting Monday, August 4, 2013. The show opens Friday, August 30, 2013, just in time for the Labor Day weekend.*

Complete a Proposed Budget for *Paul's Kitchen*

You need to compile data to create a proposed budget for *Paul's Kitchen*, the first show of the Green Man Theatre's 2013 season. The workbook contains some of the weekly salary and expense data you have already received from the director, stage manager, prop master, costume designer, and tech crew. You need to enter and format some data and calculate total weekly expenses and categorical totals for the two-month period.

a. Open *e_a_theatre*, and then save it as **e_a_theatre_Lastname Firstname**.

b. Rename *Sheet1* **Budget Kitchen**. This sheet contains the proposed budget for the production of *Paul's Kitchen*.

c. Enter a function in **cell A2** that displays the current date each time you open the workbook.

d. Format the title *Budget for Paul's Kitchen* so that it is centered across columns A:J with **Calibri 16 pt font**, **White, Background 1 font color**, and **Blue, Accent 1 fill color**.

e. Format the **range A3:J18** using **Calibri 12 pt**. Center and bold the column labels. Widen columns as needed.

f. Enter data for salaries on the respective rows. The combined actors' salaries are $1,500 per week, and the stage manager earns $200 per week.

g. Format the **range B4:J18** with **Accounting Number Format** with no decimal places.

h. Insert a function in **cell J4** to calculate the total eight-week salary for the director. Copy the function for the rest of the employees.

i. Calculate the weekly total expenses in **cell B18**. Copy the formula for the rest of the totals on row 18.

j. Type **0** in each cell in the **range B17:H17**, and then apply a single underline for the **range B17:J17**.

Calculate Projected Revenue and Net Profit

The bottom portion of the Budget Kitchen worksheet contains ticket prices by group and projected number of advance and door tickets sold. Green Man Theatre gives a 20% discount for tickets purchased in advance. You need to insert cells to make room for the discounted ticket price per group and calculate the projected revenue.

a. Format the *Projected Ticket Sales* section. Merge and center the title across the **range A21:E21**. Use Format Painter to copy formatting from **cell A1** to **cell A21**.

b. Type **Advance Discount** in **cell I22**, and then bold the label. Type **.20** in **cell I23**. Apply **Percent Style** with no decimal places.

c. Add four new cells between the Door Ticket Prices (**range B22:B25**) and the Advance Seats (**range C22:C25**). Type **Advance Sales Price** in **cell C22**.

d. Format the labels on row 22 with wrap text, bold, and centering.

e. Create a formula in **cell C23** that calculates the advance purchase price for the Senior Citizens group. Copy this formula for the Adults and Students groups.

f. Enter a formula in **cell F23** that calculates total ticket revenue for projected senior citizen ticket sales. Copy the formula for the other two groups.

g. Calculate the total projected number of advance and door tickets sold in cells D26 and E26, respectively. Calculate the total projected ticket sale revenue in **cell F26**.

h. Apply a single underline to the **range D25:F25**.

i. Merge and center the **range A28:B28**. Use Format Painter to copy the formats from **cell A21** to **cell A28**.

j. Enter a formula in **cell B29** that displays the total projected ticket sales revenue that is stored in cell F26.

k. Enter a formula in **cell B30** that displays the total mounting costs that is stored in cell J18.

l. Enter a formula in **cell B31** that calculates the total profit after expenses.

m. Indent twice the total labels in **cells A18**, **A26**, and **A31**.

n. Apply **landscape orientation**. Create a footer that displays your name on the left side, the sheet tab code in the center, and the file name code on the right side.

Use the IF Function

Because actors work as independent contractors, they are reimbursed for mileage. The Green Man Theatre has an optional equal mileage payment plan that cast members can opt into to reduce the amount of paperwork. You have collected each of their round trip distances to the theater and have created an equalized mileage reimbursement based on whether they participate in the Mileage Payment Plan or not. The actors opting out of the equal mileage payment plan will turn in expense reports including their mileage logs and will receive mileage reimbursement in a lump sum at the end of the production based on their mileage logs.

a. Display the contents on the Mileage sheet.

b. Click **cell B7**, and then create a formula to calculate miles driven by Ellen Anderson for all rehearsals and performances. The total number of rehearsals and performances is stored in cell B12. Copy the formula for the rest of the cast. Use relative and absolute cell references appropriately.

c. Click **cell B8**, and then create a formula to calculate the total mileage reimbursement for Ellen Anderson. The reimbursement rate is stored in cell B11. Copy the formula for the rest of the cast. Use relative and absolute cell references appropriately.

d. Click **cell B9**, and then insert an IF function that equally divides the total mileage payments across the weekly pay periods for the production cycle of the show if the cast member opts into the Mileage Equal Payment Plan. If the cast member does not participate in the Mileage Equal Payment Plan, the function returns 0. Copy this function for the rest of the cast. The number of weeks of the production cycle is in cell B13.

e. Widen columns as needed.

Prepare Mileage Statistics

To help accurately prepare budgets for future productions, you prepare statistics on mileage expense reimbursement for each production. Because the number of actors varies from production to production, you need statistics on mileage reimbursement for a single actor.

a. Enter a function in **cell B16** to calculate the minimum total mileage reimbursement.

b. Enter a function in **cell B17** to calculate the maximum mileage reimbursement.

c. Enter a function in **cell B18** to calculate the average mileage reimbursement.

d. Enter a function in **cell B19** to calculate the total mileage reimbursement.

Calculate a Loan Payment

Part of your responsibility in managing the budget is to make recommendations on loan expenses. The Board of Directors has voted to replace the sound system and take out a loan to finance the cost. A theatre patron is the president of a local bank. She has guaranteed an interest rate of 4.25% on a five-year loan for the sound system. The board approved the purchase of an $18,995 sound system installed. How much will the monthly payment be on the loan?

a. Display the contents of the Sound System worksheet.

b. Enter the input values in column B, as mentioned in the above paragraph. Because Green Man Theatre will make monthly payments, type **12** for the number of payments in one year.

c. Insert a PMT function in **cell B6** to calculate the monthly payment. Be sure the result displays as a positive number.

Use a Lookup Function

The Green Man Theatre has created an Honor Circle to thank their generous patrons. The required donations for each level in the Honor Circle are listed in the table below. One of your responsibilities is to keep track of patrons' donations and give them appropriate acknowledgements in the play bill. You will use a lookup function to assign the appropriate Honor Level to your Patrons list.

Platinum	**$10,000**
Gold	**$1,000**
Silver	**$100**

a. Display the contents of the Patrons worksheet.

b. Create a lookup table starting in **cell A12**, using the above table. Apply **Accounting Number Format** to the values and **General format** for the text. Assign a range name **honor** to the lookup table.

c. Create a VLOOKUP function in **cell D3** that returns the honor level based on each patron's gift.

d. Copy this function for the rest of the patrons.

e. Select the **range A2:D8**, and then convert it to a table. Apply the **Table Style Light 9 style**.

f. Sort the table by Honor Level so Platinum patrons are at the top of the list, then by Gold, and finally Silver. (You will need to create a custom sort order to sort by Honor Level.) Sort the patrons alphabetically by last name inside the Honor Level groupings.

g. Save the workbook.

Create a Budget Summary

After a successful run of *Paul's Kitchen*, you create a budget summary and graphs summarizing ticket sales. Remarkably enough, the production stayed on budget and Green Man Theatre's ticket sales projections were pretty accurate.

a. Copy the Budget Kitchen worksheet, and then rename the copied sheet **Budget Summary**. Move the Budget Summary sheet after the Mileage worksheet.

b. Because *Paul's Kitchen* came in on budget, you do not need to make any changes to the budget section. Change the header for the *Projected Ticket Sales* section to **Ticket Sales**.

c. Enter these ticket sales numbers as your final sales figures, replacing the projected figures:

Ticket Type	Advance Purchase Seats	At Door Seats
Senior	202	84
Adult	604	163
Student	72	111

d. Use these final sales figures to construct two pie charts on this sheet to compare the percentage of ticket types. The first chart should have its top-right corner in or near **cell L4**, and should show percentage by ticket type of advanced tickets sold. The other should have its top-right corner in or near **cell L23**, and should show the percentage by ticket type of tickets sold at the door. Position and size the charts as necessary.

e. Include chart titles, legends, and data labels showing percentages.

f. Save and close the workbook. Submit based on your instructor's directions.

Production Assistants

Use Microsoft Access

Background

In order to store and analyze the data for a theater company, production assistants might use Microsoft Access. They create and maintain tables, create and edit queries, and create forms and reports. Theater data includes shows, theaters, actors, and casting. Producers and directors will use this data to determine which actors performed in which shows, which theaters were used more frequently, and which shows were profitable.

Tasks

In a theater company's business office, a production assistant might be asked to create and maintain many types of database objects, including the following:

- Tables
- Queries
- Forms
- Reports

Skills

A production assistant should be able to do the following:

Chapter 1

- Navigate among the objects in an Access database (p. 573)
- Back up, compact, and repair an Access file (p. 581)
- Sort table data on one or more fields (p. 592)
- Use the Relationships window (p. 600)
- Understand relational power (p. 601)

Chapter 2

- Create tables (p. 624)
- Understand table relationships (p. 636)
- Share data with Excel (p. 638)
- Establish table relationships (p. 642)
- Create a single-table query (p. 653)
- Copy and modify a query (p. 659)
- Specify criteria in a query (p. 663)
- Create a multi-table query (p. 665)
- Modify a multi-table query (p. 666)

Chapter 3

- Create a calculated field in a query (p. 689)
- Create expressions with Expression Builder (p. 698)
- Use built-in functions in Access (p. 700)
- Perform date arithmetic (p. 703)
- Add aggregate functions to datasheets and queries (p. 713)

Chapter 4

- Create forms using the Form tool (p. 734)
- Modify a form (p. 739)
- Revise forms using Layout view (p. 751)
- Identify control types in forms (p. 752)
- Create reports using the Report Wizard (p. 763)
- Modify a report (p. 768)
- Identify report sections (p. 777)
- Revise reports using Layout and Design views (p. 781)
- Identify control types in reports (p. 782)

Production Assistants

Capstone Exercises

You work as a production assistant in the offices of The Green Man Theatre. One of your duties is to maintain the company database. You will create and edit tables, queries, forms, and reports as well as maintain and back up the database. A database has already been created, so you decide to explore it.

Navigate Among the Objects in an Access Database

Open the Broadway database and examine the tables and other objects. You will also make one change in the Actors table.

a. Open the database *a_a_broadway*. Save it as **a_a_broadway_LastnameFirstname**.

b. Open each table and examine the data.

c. Close all the tables except the Actors table.

d. Sort the Actors table by Last Name in ascending order.

e. Find Stacie Henderson's record.

f. Replace the last name *Henderson* with **Tandbell**.

g. Remove the Sort.

h. Save and close the Actors table.

i. Open the Actors from NY query.

j. Switch to Design view. Modify the State criterion so the query displays all the actors who are not from NY.

k. Close (but do not save) the query.

Create a Casting Table

The database contains tables for Theaters, Shows, and Actors. However, there is no efficient way to keep track of which actors performed in which shows. You will create a Casting table that will contain the show, the actor, and the weekly pay.

a. Create a table using Table Design.

b. Add field names and data types as listed below.

Field Name	Data Type
CastingID	AutoNumber
ShowID	Number
ActorID	Number
WeeklyPay	Currency

c. Set ShowID and the ActorID together as the primary key.

d. Save the table as **Casting**, and then close the table.

Import Excel Data into the Casting Table

The Theater has been storing casting data in an Excel spreadsheet. You will import this spreadsheet data directly into the Casting table.

a. Append the data in Sheet 1 of the *a_a_import_casting* Excel file into the Casting table.

b. Open the Casting table and examine the data.

c. Verify the primary key is set correctly by changing the last record's ActorID from *12* to **9**. Click on the record directly above and Access will display the message *The changes you requested to the table were not successful...* Undo the change to ActorID.

d. Close the table.

Establish Table Relationships

Table relationships help users extract data more efficiently. Referential integrity will help eliminate common data entry mistakes. You will set two new relationships and enforce referential integrity.

a. Open the Relationships window, and then add the Actors and Casting tables.

b. Rearrange the tables so that Casting is in the left column, Shows and Actors are in the middle column, and Theaters is in the right column.

c. Set a relationship between the Shows and Casting tables; set Enforce Referential Integrity.

d. Set a relationship between the Actors and Casting tables; set Enforce Referential Integrity.

e. Make sure that no join lines are overlapping.

f. Save and close the Relationships window.

Create a Casting Query

You need to post the casting role for each new show. You will create a casting role for the latest show using a query.

a. Create a query based on the Casting table. Include only the ShowID and ActorID fields.

b. Add criteria to display all the actors who performed in *Jersey Boys*.

c. Run the query.

d. Save the query as **Jersey Boys Cast**.

e. Save and close the query.

Copy and Modify an Existing Query

The previous query does not show the name of the show or the name of the actor. You will copy the previous query and revise it to add the missing data.

a. Copy the Jersey Boys Cast query, and then paste it using the name **Jersey Boys Cast Enhanced**. Open the new query in Design view.

b. Add the Actors and Shows tables into the new query.

c. Add the ShowName field as the first column. Keep the ShowID field but change the Show row to **No**.

d. Replace the ActorID field with the LastName and FirstName fields.

e. Run the query. Verify the accuracy of the data.

f. Save and close the query.

Use a Calculated Field to Forecast Daily Revenue

The producers have asked you for the daily estimated revenue for each show, based on a sold-out house. You will create a query and use a calculated field to provide this information.

a. Create a new query based on the Shows and Theaters tables.

b. Include the ShowName, TheaterName, SeatingCapacity, and TicketPrice fields.

c. Save the query as **Estimated Daily Revenue**.

d. Use the Expression Builder to create the Daily Revenue calculated field in the fifth column. Double-click the field names to include them in the expression; manually type the operators.

e. Close the expression builder, run the query, and then manually verify the calculated field values are correct.

f. Save and close the query.

Use Functions in a Query

The producers ask you to modify and improve the Estimated Daily Revenue query. You will copy the existing query, rename it, and then add the required changes. The new query will require a Totals query so you can look up the total actors' salaries for each show.

a. Create a Totals query that can be used to lookup the total actor's salaries for each show. This query will be based on the Casting table. Add the ShowID and WeeklyPay fields. Use the Total row to Group by ShowID and Sum the WeeklyPay. Run the query, and then save the query as **Show Salaries**. Close the query.

b. Copy the Estimated Daily Revenue query, and then paste it using the name **Estimated Daily Revenue and Expenses**. Open the new query in Design view.

c. Add a Daily Rent calculated field to the sixth column using the expression below. Change the format property to **Currency**. Run the query, and then verify the calculated field is working.

Daily Rent: [WeeklyRentalFee]/7

d. Switch to Design view, and then add the Daily Salaries calculated field to the seventh column using the expression below. The DLookup() function directs Access to look up a value in the Show Salaries query you created in step a. Change the format property to **Currency**.

Daily Salaries: DLookUp("SumOfWeeklyPay","Show Salaries", "ShowID= " & [ShowID])/7

e. Run the query, and then manually verify the calculated field values are correct. Save and close the query.

f. Copy the Estimated Daily Revenue and Expenses query, and then paste it using the name **Estimated Net Income**. Open the new query in Design view. Add another calculated field for Daily Net. Daily Net is defined as Revenue minus Expenses. Add another calculated field for Total Net. Total Net is defined as Daily Net times the number of days the show runs. Total Net requires the DateDiff() function, as shown below. Run the query, and then verify the calculated fields are working.

Total Net: [Daily Net]*DateDiff("d",[StartDate],[EndDate])

g. Save and close the query.

Create a Form Using a Form Tool

You need to create a form to make it easier to add new actors. The same form will function as a maintenance screen for existing actors.

a. Create a form based on the Actors table using the Form tool.

b. Resize the width of the text box controls so they are about half the original size.

c. Select the subform at the bottom (using the layout control), and then delete it.

d. Change the title label to **Enter and Edit Actor Data**.

e. Save the form as **Maintain Actors**.

f. Add yourself as an actor using the new form. Include your real name, and make up the rest of the data.

g. Close the form.

Create a Report Using the Report Wizard

You need to create a report that lists all the actors grouped by show. The report should also show the weekly pay for each actor and a sum for each show, as well as display a sum for the weekly pay overall.

a. Create a query that will be used to create a report. Include the Casting, Shows, and Actors tables. Add the necessary fields based on the description above.

b. Name the query **Casting Summary**. Close the query.

c. Create a report based on the Casting Summary query using the Report Wizard. Answer the Report Wizard's questions using the description above. Name the report **Casting Pay by Show**.

d. Switch to Layout view, and then delete the Summary for 'ShowName' text box displayed in the ShowName footer. Preview the report.

e. Switch to Design view, and then move the Sum label and Sum text box up to the top of the ShowName footer. Reduce the height of the ShowName footer by one-half. Preview the report.
f. Save the report as **Casting Pay by Show**. Close the report.
g. Add yourself to the Jersey Boys show in the Casting table, and then preview the report again.
h. Close the report.

Compact, Repair, and Back Up the Database

An Access database needs to be maintained regularly. As a part of your daily routine, you will compact, repair, and back up the database.

a. Compact and repair the database.
b. Back up the database in the location where you save your student files. When naming the file, include today's date.
c. Save and close all open database objects, and submit the database based on your instructor's directions.

Production Assistants

Use Microsoft PowerPoint

Background

Microsoft PowerPoint can be a powerful tool for use in a theater company's business office. Production assistants use PowerPoint to create presentations, handouts, and scripts for presentations. It is important that a production assistant become familiar with planning a presentation, creating text, inserting media, and working with transitions and animation to utilize the benefits of this program. The following presentation skills are crucial to people employed as production assistants.

Tasks

In a theater company's business office, a production assistant might be asked to create and develop many types of presentations. Tasks involving PowerPoint could include:

- Planning and creating presentations centered upon a theme
- Preparing progress report presentations
- Creating advertisements and flyers
- Preparing process SmartArt diagrams
- Printing handouts for crews

Skills

Production assistants should be able to do the following:

Chapter 1

- Use PowerPoint views (p. 809)
- Use slide layouts (p. 820)
- Apply themes (p. 821)
- Insert media objects (p. 828)
- Add a table (p. 829)
- Use animations and transitions (p. 829)
- Insert a header or footer (p. 832)
- Run and navigate a slide show (p. 839)

Chapter 2

- Modify a template (p. 864)
- Modify an outline structure (p. 870)
- Import an outline (p. 877)
- Add existing content to a presentation (p. 877)
- Modify a theme (p. 885)

Chapter 3

- Create shapes (p. 904)
- Apply Quick Styles and customize shapes (p. 909)
- Create SmartArt (p. 925)
- Modify SmartArt (p. 929)
- Create WordArt (p. 933)
- Modify WordArt (p. 933)
- Modify objects (p. 939)
- Arrange objects (p. 944)

Chapter 4

- Insert a picture (p. 974)
- Transform a picture (p. 976)
- Add audio (p. 1007)
- Change audio settings (p. 1009)

Production Assistants
Capstone Exercises

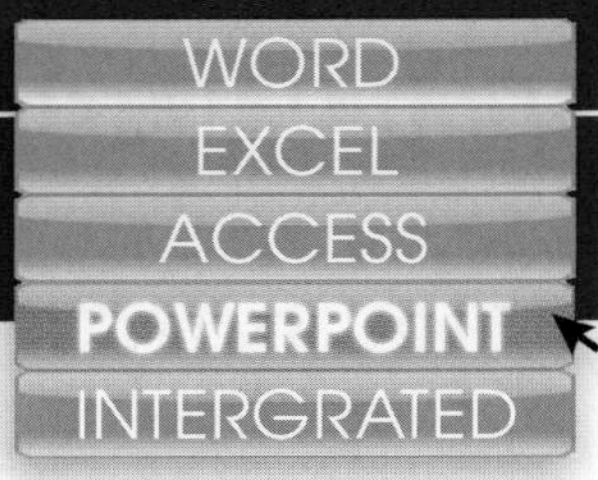

You work as a production assistant in the offices of a new company, The Green Man Theatre. You have been asked to create a presentation to display in a kiosk in the theater shop and box office to advertise season tickets.

Create a Title Slide

You create a title slide for the new presentation, and then you insert audio to catch the attention of viewers.

a. Create a new blank PowerPoint slide show and save it as **p_a_season_LastnameFirstname**.

b. Apply the **Angles theme**. Format the background style of this slide to apply the **Green marble texture**.

c. Add the title **GREEN MAN THEATRE** in the **title placeholder**. Select the **title placeholder**, and then apply WordArt **Fill–Orange, Accent 2, Warm Matte Bevel**. Resize the title font to **44 pt**.

d. Type **2013–2014 Season** in the **subtitle field** of the title slide. Change the font to **White, Background 1** and bold.

e. Insert the Green Man Theatre logo, **p_a_gmlogo.jpg**. Remove the white background from the logo, and then resize the logo to a height **3.5"** and a width **3.59"**.

f. Position the logo attractively in the blue section of the slide.

g. Insert the **p_a_gmaudio.mp3 audio file** on Slide 1. Set the playback options to play the audio across slides and hide the icon during the show. Position the audio icon on the bottom-left side of the slide.

h. Apply the following animations:

Object	Animation	Start	Duration	Delay
Title placeholder	Grow & Turn	With Previous	04.00	18.00
Subtitle placeholder	Swivel	With Previous	03.00	03.00
Logo image	Bounce	With Previous	06.00	10.00

Create a Mission Statement

You add a new slide for the mission statement, type content in the placeholders, format the text, adjust the indentation of the text, and then resize the placeholders.

a. Insert a new slide using the **Content with Caption layout**.

b. Type **Mission Statement** in the **title placeholder**, and then change the font size to **40 pt**.

c. Type **Green Man Theatre** in the **subtitle placeholder**, and then change the font color to **Orange, Accent 2**. Change the font size to **28 pt**.

d. Add this mission statement to the **content placeholder**:

We are committed to providing the environment and the resources for new artists, musicians, actors, and dancers to create and perform new works in the Twin Cities.

e. Inside the content placeholder, adjust the indent setting on the ruler so the second and remaining lines in the mission statement align with the first line. Adjust the size and position of the placeholder so that it is attractively placed in the white area of the slide.

Create a Title Slide

You insert a new slide, add and format a table, insert a logo, add a callout object, and apply an animation.

a. Insert a new slide using the Title Only layout. Title it **Green Man Theatre Presents**. Change the title text color to **Orange, Accent 2**.

b. Insert a two-column by four-row table on the slide. Enter the following information:

Show	Dates
Paul's Kitchen	September 4 - 27, 2013
Christmas at the Andersons'	November 27, 2013 - January 3, 2014
This Was Not in the Brochure	February 26 - March 28, 2014

c. Apply the **Light Style 2–Accent 4 table style** to the table, and then adjust the column widths and row heights so that no text in cells is split into two lines.

d. Copy the logo from the Title slide, and then paste it on Slide 3. Center-align the logo on the slide.

e. Create an **Oval Callout shape** to the right of the logo, and then type **2013–2014 Season** in the callout. Format the callout style to **Colored Outline – Orange, Accent 2**.

f. Position the callout so it is associated with the logo image, and then move the callout point so that it appears to come from the logo man's mouth. Group the logo and the callout, as shown in Figure 1.1.

g. Apply a **Float In entrance animation** to the title placeholder, having it start After Previous. Copy the animation to the logo group, and then to the table.

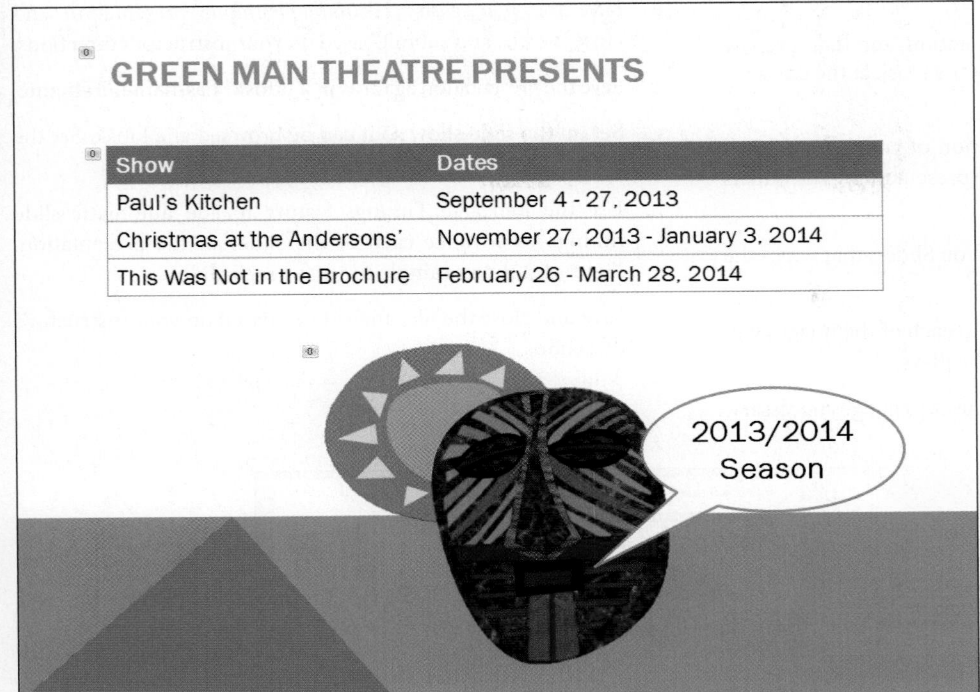

FIGURE 1.1 ▲

Add Existing Content to a Presentation

You have an outline describing two of the three plays of the season in a Word file. You also have the start of a slide show about the third play. You use this existing content to add the show descriptions to the presentation you are creating.

a. Use the Slides from Outline feature to add both slides contained in the *p_a_outline.docx* file to the end of *p_a_season_LastnameFirstname.pptx.*

b. Add a slide at the end of the presentation by reusing the slide in *p_a_brochure.pptx.*

c. Format the new Slides 4–6 so that all of the text content placeholders are in bulleted point format. Each slide should contain two first-level bullets with sub-level bullets for the descriptions of the play. Then modify the bulleted lists so they match one another using the format choices you want.

d. Modify the outline in Outline view by moving the bullets referring to the show running dates so they are the first bullet in each of the new Slides 4–6.

e. Photographs in your student data files are named *Paul's_Kitchen_1* and *Paul's_Kitchen_2*, *Christmas_at_the_Andersons'*, and *This_Was_Not_in_the_Brochure*. Insert these photos on the appropriate slides, or insert images of your choice that are relevant to the slides.

f. Position the images attractively on the slides.

g. Format each of the photos by removing backgrounds, applying color corrections, adjusting color, applying filters, and/or adding picture styles.

h. Insert a new slide after Slide 6 using the Content with Caption layout.

i. Add the title **Season Tickets**. Add these bullets:

- **Available in the Box Office and Theater Shop**
- **Discount on Season Tickets**
- **Patron Memberships available**

j. Insert the logo file **p_a_gmlogo.jpg**, remove the white background, and then position the logo above the slide title.

k. Type **Green Man Theatre** in the **subtitle placeholder**, and then change the font color to **Orange, Accent 2**. Change the font size to **28 pt**.

Create SmartArt

You create a SmartArt diagram to explain the three levels of giving and the amount required to achieve a particular level. Different benefits are available to patrons of different levels.

a. Insert a new slide after Slide 7 using the Title Only layout.

b. Type **Patronage Levels** in the **title placeholder**, and then format the text to match the other titles in the presentation.

c. Create a Pyramid List SmartArt to display three levels of giving.

- Platinum $10,000
- Gold $1,000
- Silver $100

d. Change the color of the SmartArt style to **Colorful Range–Accent Colors 4 to 5**.

e. Apply the SmartArt style **Moderate Effect**.

f. Apply a consistent transition effect for all slides.

Finalize the Presentation

You apply final animations to the presentation, and then prepare the presentation to play automatically at the kiosk at the entrance to the theatre.

a. Apply a consistent entrance animation of your choice to all bulleted content placeholders in the presentation. The bullets should enter one by one.

b. Apply an animation to the SmartArt on Slide 8 that wipes the objects from the left and one by one.

c. Apply an animation of your choice to each of the images you inserted on the slides introducing the plays.

d. View the presentation, and then make any changes necessary.

e. Save the *p_a_season_LastnameFirstname* presentation and close the file, and submit based on your instructor's directions.

f. Save the presentation again as **p_a_kiosk_LastnameFirstname.**

g. Set up the slide show so it can be browsed at a kiosk. Set the slide show to use slide timings.

h. Use the Rehearse Timings feature to add automatic slide timings to advance each of the slides in the presentation. Figure 1.2 shows sample times for each slide.

i. Save and close the file, and submit based on your instructor's directions.

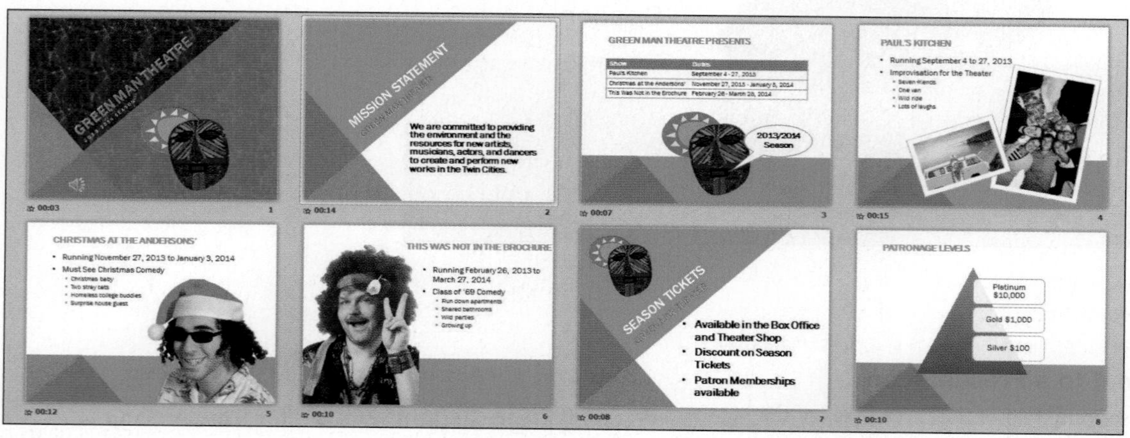

FIGURE 1.2 ▲

Production Assistants

Integrate Microsoft Office Software

Background

Each program in the Microsoft Office suite has its strength and specialty. The theater production office assistant needs to use each software program in the suite for the appropriate task. Microsoft Word is useful to create fliers and brochures for upcoming plays and musicals, letters to send to patrons and donors, etc. Microsoft Excel is appropriate to store budgets for the current and upcoming productions, develop schedules, and reimbursement forms that require mathematical calculations. Microsoft PowerPoint is beneficial for creating presentations for advertising the productions or when meeting with investors. Microsoft Access is a database management program that provides the capability to store and analyze large quantities of data. At times, the production office assistant needs to use all four programs together to create the desired result. For example, the production assistant may create a chart in Excel that can then be used in a PowerPoint presentation.

Tasks

In a theater company's business office, a production assistant might be asked to find data and present information using all the applications in Microsoft Office 2010. This could include the following:

- Create handouts in Word for a board meeting
- Calculate basic sales summary statistics in Excel
- Export data from Access database queries to Excel for quantitative manipulation
- Link data and charts from Excel into PowerPoint presentations

Skills

In addition to basic formatting skills, a production office assistant should be able to do the following:

- Create a summary query
- Export query results to an Excel worksheet
- Calculate statistics using MIN, MAX, and AVERAGE functions
- Create charts from data
- Display the statistics and charts as linked objects in a PowerPoint presentation
- Embed objects in a Word document
- Use themes across applications to create a cohesive appearance

Production Assistants

Capstone Exercises

You work as a production office assistant in the offices for The Green Man Theatre. You maintain the season tickets database. Your job entails creating and executing queries to help the production manager make critical decisions about the theater's operations. At times, you need to export Access data into an Excel worksheet for other data manipulations, create charts in Excel that you can import into a PowerPoint presentation, and import data into Word documents for distribution.

Export Queries to Excel

The sales manager asks you to create a query to determine how many seats each season ticket holder owns for the opening weekend and then import the results into an Excel workbook so he can analyze sales. You will export the tables and a few queries for just the opening weekend to a test database so you do not accidentally change any of the data in the actual database. If this becomes a regular function, you will move the queries into production. Season tickets are sold by the seat. Each show has its own set of seats in the run of the show. The tables of seats for each show are the following:

Table	Show
tblShow1	Opening Friday Night
tblShow2	Opening Saturday Night
tblShow3	Opening Sunday Matinee

a. Open the Access database *i_arts_seasontickets.accdb*, and then save it as **i_seasontickets_LastnameFirstname**.

b. Create a query for Friday night that includes Lastname, Firstname, Seat, and CustomerNum from the tblSeasonTicketHolders and tblShow1 tables. Group by Lastname, and then create a calculated field to count the number of seats each ticket holder owns for opening Friday night. Customize the column labels in Design view to display **First Of Seat** instead of *Seat* and **First Of Customer** instead of *CustomerNum*. Save the query as **qryShow1Count**.

c. Create a query for Saturday night that includes Lastname, Firstname, Seat, and CustomerNum from the tblSeasonticketHolders and tblShow2 tables. Group by Lastname, and then create a calculated field to count the number of seats each ticket holder owns for opening Saturday night. Customize the column labels in Design view to display **First Of Seat** instead of *Seat* and **First Of Customer** instead of *CustomerNum*. Save the query as **qryShow2Count**.

d. Create a query that includes Lastname, Firstname, Seat, and CustomerNum from the tblSeasonticketHolders and tblShow3 tables. Group by Lastname, and then create a calculated field to count the number of seats each ticket holder owns for opening Sunday matinee. Customize the column labels in Design view to display **First Of Seat** instead of *Seat* and **First Of Customer** instead of *CustomerNum*. Save the query as **qryShow3Count**.

e. Export the results of all three queries individually to Excel using Export to Excel in the Export group on the External Data tab. Select the export option that preserves formatting and layout for the exported data. Within the Export – Excel Spreadsheet dialog box, type **1_seasontickets_LastnameFirstname.xlsx**. The results of each query should create a separate worksheet in the same workbook. For example, the results of the Opening Friday Night query import into Sheet1 in the Excel workbook.

f. Save the Excel workbook.

g. Close the Access database, and submit based on your instructor's directions. Exit Access.

Perform Statistics Calculations on Imported Data in Excel

After you give the workbook to the sales manager, he comes by your office and admits he does not know what to do with it. He asks if you could do some analysis on the buying habits of the season ticket holders. He wants you to create a summary area in which you perform statistical calculations on each worksheet's data.

a. Open *i_a_seasontickets_LastnameFirstname.xlsx* in Excel. Make the first sheet the active sheet. Press and hold down **Shift** as you click the third sheet tab to group the three sheets together. Anything you do now will affect the grouped sheets.

b. Click **cell H1**, type **Sales Statistics for Opening Friday Night**, and then press **Enter**. Bold the label.

c. Start in **cell H2**, and then type the following labels down the column:

- **Total season ticket seats sold for this show**
- **Number of individual ticket holders for this show**
- **Maximum number of seats owned by an individual season ticket holder**
- **Minimum number of seats owned by an individual season ticket holder**
- **Average number of seats owned by an individual season ticket holder**

d. Adjust the width of column H.

e. Enter functions in column I for each respective label.

f. Select the function results, apply **Comma Style**, and then display one decimal place.

g. Click the second worksheet tab to ungroup the sheets.

h. Review each function on the other two worksheets, and then adjust the ranges within the function arguments as needed for each particular sheet of data. In **cell H1** for the other two worksheets, replace *Friday* with **Saturday** and **Sunday**.

i. Save the workbook and keep it open.

Create a Summary Chart

The sales manager wants you to create a column chart that depicts the total number of season tickets sold by opening night. You will consolidate the data on a new worksheet in order to be able to create a column chart.

a. Insert a new worksheet, and then name it **Summary**.

b. Type **Summary** in **cell A1**, and then press **Enter** twice.

c. Type **Friday Night**, **Saturday Night**, and **Sunday Matinee**, respectively, in the **range A3:A5**.

d. Click **cell B3**, type =, click the **qry1ShowCount sheet tab**, click the cell containing the total tickets sold function, and then press **Enter**.

e. Adapt step d to create formulas that point to the original respective functions for Saturday and Sunday.

f. Create a column chart on the same sheet. Add an appropriate chart title, delete the legend, add data labels, and then increase the font size of the data labels.

g. Move the chart below the data and increase its size.

h. Save the workbook and keep it open.

Link Data into a PowerPoint Presentation

The sales manager is pleased with the statistical analysis and chart you added to the Excel workbook. He decides to use the summary data and chart in a PowerPoint presentation that he can show at the next board meeting. You will create a presentation with a title slide, the three summary statistical tables on one slide, and the chart on a third slide.

a. Start PowerPoint, and then search for the theater template online. Download the Theater design template. Save the presentation as **i_a_stats_LastnameFirstname**.

b. Type **Green Man Theatre** in the **title placeholder**, and then type **Opening Night Ticket Sales** in the **subtitle placeholder** on the title slide.

c. Insert a second slide and do the following:
   - Link the Summary Statistics for Opening Friday Night range on the qryShow1Count sheet from the *i_e_seasontickets_LastnameFirstname* workbook on the second PowerPoint slide.
   - Link the Summary Statistics for Opening Saturday Night range on the qryShow2Count sheet from the *i_e_seasontickets_LastnameFirstname* workbook below the first linked range on the second PowerPoint slide.
   - Link the Summary Statistics for Opening Sunday Matinee range on the qryShow3Count sheet from the *i_e_seasontickets_LastnameFirstname* workbook on the second PowerPoint slide.
   - Increase the width of each summary area object on the slide show.
   - Apply a background fill color of your choice to each linked object to match the slide show theme.

d. Insert a third slide, and then link the column chart from the workbook on the PowerPoint slide.

e. Save and close the presentation. Exit PowerPoint. Submit based on your instructor's directions.

Copy Data into a Word Document

Finally, after you prepare the presentation, the sales manager asks you to create a Word document to e-mail to the board of directors before the meeting. This document should contain copies of the chart and the three sales statistics tables. However, because you are not sending the Excel workbook, you need to embed the data rather than link it to the Excel workbook.

a. Open *i_a_stats.docx* in Word, and then save it as **i_a_stats_LastnameFirstname**.

b. Copy each statistical summary table in the Excel workbook, and then paste it on the second page of the Word document. Use the Paste Special's Picture option.

c. Copy and paste the chart below the tables.

d. Type an introductory paragraph at the top of the second page that provides an overview to the tables and chart.

e. Adjust the size of the tables and chart to fit on the second page.

f. Save and close the document. Exit Word and Excel. Submit based on your instructor's directions.

GLOSSARY

100% stacked column chart A chart type that places (stacks) data in one column per category, with each column having the same height of 100%.

3-D chart A chart that contains a third dimension to each data series, creating a distorted perspective of the data.

Absolute cell reference A designation that provides a permanent reference to a specific cell. When you copy a formula containing an absolute cell reference, the cell reference in the copied formula does not change, regardless of where you copy the formula. An absolute cell reference appears with a dollar sign before both the column letter and row number, such as $B$5.

Access A database program that is included in Microsoft Office.

Access speed Measures the time it takes for the storage device to make the file content available for use.

Action Center A Windows 7 component that monitors maintenance and security settings, alerting a user when necessary. It provides alerts in pop-ups from an icon in the notification area.

Active cell The current cell in a worksheet. It is indicated by a dark border onscreen.

Adjustment handle A yellow diamond that enables you to modify a shape.

Aero Flip 3D A Windows feature that shows open windows in a rotating 3D stack from which you can click to bring a window to view on the desktop.

Aero Peek A preview of an open window, shown when you place the mouse pointer over the taskbar icon without clicking. Aero Peek also enables you to minimize all open windows, showing the desktop temporarily.

Aggregate function A function that performs calculations on an entire column of data and returns a single value.

Align To arrange objects by lining up the sides, middles, or top/bottom edges of the objects.

AND logical operator Returns only records that meet all criteria.

Animation A movement that controls the entrance, emphasis, exit, and/or path of objects in a slide show.

Annotation A written note or drawing on a slide for additional commentary or explanation.

Area chart A chart type that emphasizes magnitude of changes over time by filling in the space between lines with a color.

Argument A variable or constant input, such as a cell reference or value, needed to complete a function. The entire group of arguments for a function is enclosed within parentheses.

Ascending order A feature that arranges data in alphabetical order or sequential order from lowest to highest.

Aspect ratio The ratio of an object's width to its height.

Auto fill A feature that enables you to copy the contents of a cell or a range of cells or to continue a sequence by dragging the fill handle over an adjacent cell or range of cells.

AutoNumber A data type that stores a unique number for each record as it is added to a table and increments automatically each time a record is entered.

AutoRecover Enables Word to recover a previous version of a document.

AVERAGE function A predefined formula that calculates the arithmetic mean, or average, of values in a range.

Axis title A label that describes either the category axis or the value axis.

Background (Word) A color, design, image, or watermark that appears behind text in a document or on a graphical image. (PowerPoint) The portion of a picture to be removed during the Background Removal process.

Background Styles gallery Provides both solid color and background styles for application to a theme.

Backstage view Display that includes commands related to common file activities and that provides information on an open file.

Backup (Office Fundamentals) A copy of a file, usually on another storage medium. (Access) Creates a duplicate copy of the database.

Bar chart A chart type that compares values across categories using horizontal bars. In a bar chart, the horizontal axis displays values, and the vertical axis displays categories.

Bar tab Tab that inserts a vertical line at the location of a tab setting. Useful as a separator for text printed on the same line.

Bibliography A list of works cited or consulted by an author in his or her work and should be included with the published work.

Bitmap image An image created by bits or pixels containing color information and placed on a grid that forms a picture.

Border A line that surrounds a paragraph, a page, a table, or an image in a document, or that surrounds a cell or range of cells in a worksheet.

Bound control A text box that is connected to a field in a table or query.

Breakpoint The lowest value for a specific category or series in a lookup table.

Brightness The ratio between lightness and darkness of an image.

Bubble chart A chart type that shows relationships among three values by using bubbles to show a third dimension.

Bulleted list Itemizes and separates paragraph text to increase readability.

Calculated control A text box that contains an expression that generates a calculated result when displayed in Form view.

Calculated field Produces a value from an expression or function that references one or more existing fields.

Calculator A Windows 7 accessory program that acts as a handheld calculator with four different views—standard, scientific, programming, and statistical.

Callout A shape that includes a text box you can use to add notes.

CamelCase notation A style of writing which uses no spaces in multi-word field names, but uses uppercase letters to distinguish the first letter of each new word.

Caption A descriptive title for an image, an equation, a figure, or a table.

Caption property Used to create a more readable label instead of a field name; displays in the top row in Datasheet view and in forms and reports.

Cascade Delete Related Records An option that directs Access to automatically remove all records that are deleted from a primary table from those related tables that match the primary key.

Cascade Update Related Fields An option that directs Access to automatically update all foreign key values in a related table when the primary key value is modified in a primary table.

Category axis The chart element that displays descriptive group names or labels, such as college names or cities, to identify data.

Category label Text that describes a collection of data points in a chart.

Cell The intersection of a column or row in a worksheet or table.

Cell address The unique identifier of a cell, starting with the column letter and then the row number, such as A9.

Cell margin The amount of space between data and the cell border in a table.

Center tab Sets the middle point of the text you type; whatever you type will be centered on that tab setting.

Change Case Feature that enables you to change capitalization of text to all capital letters, all lowercase letters, sentence case, or toggle case.

Changed line A vertical bar in the margin to pinpoint the area where changes are made in a document when the Track Changes feature is active.

Character spacing The horizontal space between characters.

Character style Stores character formatting (font, size, and style) and affects only selected text.

Chart A visual representation of numerical data that compares data and helps reveal trends or patterns to help people make informed decisions.

Chart area A boundary that contains the entire chart and all of its elements, including the plot area, titles, legends, and labels.

Chart sheet A sheet within a workbook that contains a single chart and no spreadsheet data.

Chart title The label that describes the entire chart.

Circular reference A situation that occurs when a formula contains a direct or an indirect reference to the cell containing the formula.

Citation A note recognizing a source of information or a quoted passage.

Clip art An electronic illustration that can be inserted into an Office project.

Clipboard An Office feature that temporarily holds selections that have been cut or copied.

Clustered column chart A type of chart that groups or clusters similar data into columns to compare values across categories.

Codec (coder/decoder) A digital video compression scheme used to compress a video and decompress for playback.

Collapsed outline Displays only the slide number, icon, and title of each slide in Outline view.

Color scale A conditional format that displays a particular color based on the relative value of the cell contents to other selected cells.

Colors gallery Provides a set of colors with each color assigned to a different element for every available theme.

Column A format that sections a document into side-by-side vertical blocks in which the text flows down the first vertical block and then continues at the top of the next vertical block.

Column chart A type of chart that displays data vertically in columns to compare values across different categories.

Column index number The number of the column in the lookup table that contains the return values.

Column width The horizontal measurement of a column in a table or a worksheet. In Excel, it is measured by the number of characters or pixels.

Command A button or area within a group that you click to perform tasks.

Comment A private note, annotation, or additional information to the author or another reader about the content of a document.

Compact and Repair Reduces the size of the database, and repairs any corruptions to the database.

Comparison operator Used to evaluate the relationship between two quantities to determine if they are equal or not equal; and, if they are not equal, a comparison operator determines which one is greater than the other.

Compatibility Checker Looks for features that are not supported by previous versions of Word.

Compress The process of reducing the file size of an object.

Compression A method applied to data to reduce the amount of space required for file storage.

Conditional formatting A set of rules that apply special formatting to highlight or emphasize cells that meet specific conditions.

Connector A Lines shape that is attached to and moves with other shapes.

Constant An unchanging value, such as a birth date.

Contextual tab A Ribbon tab that displays when an object, such as a picture or clip art, is selected.

Contrast The difference between the lightest and darkest areas of an image.

Copy Duplicates a selection from the original location and places the copy in the Office Clipboard.

Copyright The legal protection afforded to a written or artistic work.

COUNT function A predefined formula that tallies the number of cells in a range that contain values you can use in calculations, such as numerical and date data, but excludes blank cells or text entries from the tally.

COUNTA function A predefined formula that tallies the number of cells in a range that are not blank; that is, cells that contain data whether a value, text, or a formula.

COUNTBLANK function A predefined formula that tallies the number of cells in a range that are blank.

Criteria row A row in the Query Design view that determines which records will be selected.

Criterion (criteria, pl**)** An expression used to filter the records in a table.

Cropping (or to **crop)** The process of reducing an image size by eliminating unwanted portions of an image or other graphical object.

Cross-reference A note that refers the reader to another location for more information about a topic.

Current List Includes all citation sources you use in the current document.

Cut Removes a selection from the original location and places it in the Office Clipboard.

Data bar A conditional format that displays horizontal gradient or solid fill indicating the cell's relative value compared to other selected cells.

Data label A descriptive label that shows the exact value of the data points on the value axis.

Data point A numeric value that describes a single value on a chart.

Data redundancy The unnecessary storing of duplicate data in two or more tables.

Data series A group of related data points that appear in row(s) or column(s) in the worksheet.

Data source A listing of information.

Data type Determines the type of data that can be entered and the operations that can be performed on that data.

Database Consists of one or more tables to store data, one or more forms to enter data into the tables, and one or more reports to output the table data as organized information.

Database table A collection of related records that contain fields to organize data.

Datasheet form A replica of a table's or query's Datasheet view except that it still retains some of the form properties.

Datasheet view A view of a database object, which displays data in row and column format, and in which you can add, edit, and delete the records of a table, form, or query.

Date arithmetic The process of manipulating dates, or adding or subtracting a constant from a date.

Date formatting Formatting that affects a date's display without changing the actual underlying value in the table.

Datepart function Enables you to isolate a specific part of a date, such as the year.

Decimal tab Marks where numbers align on a decimal point as you type.

Default A setting that is in place unless you specify otherwise.

Delimiter A special character that surrounds the criterion's value.

Descending order Arranges data in alphabetical or sequential order from highest to lowest.

Design view A view in which new database objects are created, and the design of existing objects is modified. Where you create tables, add and delete fields, and modify field properties.

Desktop The screen display that appears after you turn on a computer. It contains icons and a taskbar.

Detail section Displays the records in the form's record source and prints one line for each record in the report's record source.

Dialog box A window that opens when you are accomplishing a task that enables you to make selections or indicate settings beyond those provided on the Ribbon.

Dialog Box Launcher An icon in Ribbon groups that you can click to open a related dialog box.

Distribute To divide or evenly spread over a given area.

Document Inspector Checks for and removes different kinds of hidden and personal information from a document.

Document Panel Provides descriptive information about a document, such as a title, subject, author, keywords, and comments.

Doughnut chart A chart type that displays values as percentages of the whole but may contain more than one data series.

Draft view Shows a simplified work area, removing white space and other elements from view.

Effects gallery Includes a range of special effects that can be used on objects in the presentation.

Embed To store an object from an external source within a presentation.

Endnote A citation that appears at the end of a document.

Enforce referential integrity Ensures that data cannot be entered into a related table unless it first exists in the primary table.

Enhanced ScreenTip Provides a brief summary of a command when you place the mouse pointer on the command button.

Excel Software included in Microsoft Office that specializes in organizing data in worksheet form.

Expanded outline Displays the slide number, icon, title, and content of each slide in Outline view.

Exploded pie chart A chart type in which one or more pie slices are separated from the rest of the pie chart.

Expression A formula used to calculate new fields from the values in existing fields.

Expression Builder A tool in Access to help you create expressions.

Field The smallest data element contained in a table, such as first name, last name, address, and phone number.

Field property A characteristic of a field that determines how the field looks and behaves.

Field row A row in the Query Design view that displays the field name.

File A document or item of information that you create with software and to which you give a name.

File property A file identifier, such as author or date created.

Fill The interior contents of a shape.

Fill color The background color that appears behind data in a cell.

Fill handle A small black square at the bottom-right corner of a cell used to copy cell contents or text or number patterns to adjacent cells.

Filter Specifies criteria for including records that meet certain conditions, and displays a subset of records based on specified criteria.

Filter by Form A filtering technique that displays table records based on multiple criteria, and allows the user to apply AND conditions and OR conditions.

Filter by Selection A filtering technique that displays only the records that match the selected criteria.

Filtering The process of specifying conditions to display only those records that meet the conditions.

Final: Show Markup A view that displays inserted text in the body of the document and shows deleted text in a markup balloon.

Find Locates a word or phrase that you indicate in a document.

Firewall Software or hardware that protects a computer from unauthorized access.

First line indent Marks the location to indent only the first line in a paragraph.

Flip To reverse the direction and object faces.

Flow chart An illustration showing the sequence of a project or plan containing steps.

Folder A named storage location where you can save files.

Font A complete set of characters—upper- and lowercase letters, numbers, punctuation marks, and special symbols with the same design that includes size, spacing, and shape.

Fonts gallery Contains font sets for title text and bulleted text.

Footer Information that displays at the bottom of each document page, presentation slide, handout, or notes page.

Footnote A citation that appears at the bottom of a page.

Foreground (Word) Appears in front of text or images in a document or on a graphical image. (PowerPoint) The portion of the picture to be kept during the Background Removal process.

Foreign key A field in one table that is also the primary key of another table.

Form A database object that enables you to enter, modify, or delete table data.

Form Footer section A part of a form that displays at the bottom of the form in Display view.

Form Header section A part of a form that displays at the top of each form in Display view.

Form letter A letter with standard information that you personalize with recipient information, which you might print or e-mail to many people.

Form tool Used to create data entry forms for customers, employees, products, and other primary tables.

Form view Use to add, edit, and delete data in a form; the layout and design of the form cannot be changed in this view.

Format Painter A Clipboard group command that copies the formatting of text from one location to another.

Formula A combination of cell references, operators, values, and/or functions used to perform a calculation.

Formula AutoComplete A feature that displays a list of functions and defined names that match letters as you type a formula.

Formula Bar An element in Excel that appears below the Ribbon and to the right of the Insert command that shows the contents of the active cell so that you edit the text, value, date, formula, or function.

Freeform shape A shape that combines both curved and straight-line segments.

Freezing The process of keeping rows and/or columns visible onscreen at all times even when you scroll through a large dataset.

Full Screen Reading view A viewing format that eliminates tabs and makes it easier to read a document.

Function A predefined computation that simplifies creating a complex calculation and produces a result based on inputs known as arguments.

Function ScreenTip A small pop-up description that displays the arguments for a function as you enter it.

Gadget A desktop item that can represent things that change, such as the weather or a clock. Gadgets also include such things as puzzles and games.

Gallery A set of selections that appears when you click a More button, or in some cases when you click a command, in a Ribbon group.

Gradient fill A fill that contains a blend of two or more colors or shades.

Grid A set of intersecting lines used to align objects.

Gridline A horizontal or vertical line that extends from the horizontal or vertical axis through the plot area.

Group A subset of a tab that organizes similar tasks together.

Group Footer section When activated, will appear just below the *Detail* section in Design view, but only when you select this option in the Group, Sort, and Total pane. Provides aggregated information at the end of a group of records.

Group Header section When activated, will appear just above the *Detail* section in Design view; the name of the field you are grouping on provides information such as group name at the beginning of a group of records.

Grouping Combining two or more objects, which enables them to move or act as one object.

Guide A straight horizontal or vertical line used to align objects on a slide.

Hanging indent Aligns the first line of a paragraph at the left margin and indents the remaining lines.

Hard page break Forces the next part of a document to begin on a new page.

Hard return Created when you press Enter to move the insertion point to a new line.

Header Information that displays at the top of each document page, presentation slide, handout, or notes page.

Header row The first row in a data source that contains labels describing the data.

Help and Support A built-in library of help topics that is available from the Start menu. Using Help and Support, you can get assistance with specific questions or broad topics.

Hidden text Document text that does not appear onscreen.

Hierarchy Uses main points and subpoints to indicate levels of importance in a structure.

Highlighter Background color used to mark text that you want to stand out or locate easily.

HLOOKUP function A predefined formula that looks up a value in a horizontal lookup table where the first row contains the values to compare with the lookup value.

Horizontal alignment The placement of data or text between the left and right margins in a document, or cell margins in a spreadsheet.

Icon A small picture on the desktop that represents a program, file, or folder.

Icon set A conditional format that displays an icon representing a value in the top third, quarter, or fifth based on values in the selected range.

IF function (IIf in Access) A predefined logical formula that evaluates a condition and returns one value if the condition is true and a different value if the condition is false.

Index An alphabetical listing of topics covered in a document, along with the page numbers where the topic is discussed.

Indexed property A setting that allows quick sorting in primary key order and quick retrieval based on the primary key.

Infographic Information graphic that is a visual representation of data or knowledge.

Infringement of copyright Occurs when a right of the copyright owner is violated.

Input area A range of cells to enter values for variables or assumptions that will be used in formulas within a workbook.

Join lines Used to create a relationship between two tables using a common field.

Jump List A list of actions or resources associated with an *open window* button or a pinned icon on the taskbar.

Kelvin The unit of measurement for absolute temperature as a characteristic of lighting in pictures.

Kerning Automatically adjusts spacing between characters to achieve a more evenly spaced appearance.

Key Tip The letter or number that displays over features on the Ribbon and Quick Access Toolbar.

Label control A literal word or phrase to describe the data.

Label wizard A guide that steps you through the process of easily creating mailing labels, name tags, and other specialized tags.

Landscape Page or worksheet that is wider than it is tall.

Layout Determines the position of objects containing content on the slide.

Layout control Provides guides to help keep controls aligned horizontally and vertically, and to give your form a uniform appearance.

Layout view A view that is used to modify the design of a form or report while still viewing the data.

Leader character Typically dots or hyphens that connect two items, to draw the reader's eye across the page.

Left tab Sets the start position on the left so as you type, text moves to the right of the tab setting.

Legend A key that identifies the color, gradient, picture, texture, or pattern assigned to each data series in a chart.

Library An organization method that collects files from different locations and displays them as one unit.

Line chart A chart type that displays lines connecting data points to show trends over equal time periods, such as months, quarters, years, or decades.

Line spacing The vertical space between the lines in a paragraph and between paragraphs.

Line weight The width or thickness of a line.

Link To establish a connection from a presentation to another location.

Live Preview An Office feature that provides a preview of the results of a selection when you point to an option in a list.

Lock Drawing Mode Enables the creation of multiple shapes of the same type.

Logical test An expression that evaluates to true or false.

Lookup table A range that contains data for the basis of the lookup and data to be retrieved.

Lookup value The cell reference of the cell that contains the value to look up within a lookup table.

Mail merge A process that combines content from a main document and a data source.

Mailing label Specialized report that comes preformatted to coordinate with name-brand labels such as Avery.

Main document Contains the information that stays the same for all recipients in a mail merge.

Margin The blank space around the sides, top, and bottom of a document or worksheet.

Markup balloon A colored circle that contains comments, insertions, or deletions in the margin with a line drawn to where the insertion point was in the document prior to inserting the comment or editing the document.

Master List A database of all citation sources created in Word on a particular computer.

MAX function A predefined formula that finds the highest value in a range.

MEDIAN function A predefined formula that finds the midpoint value, which is the value that one-half of the population is above or below.

Merge field Serves as a placeholder for the variable data that will be inserted into the main document during the mail merge.

Microsoft Office A productivity software suite that includes word processing, spreadsheet, presentation, and database software components.

MIN function A predefined formula that finds the lowest value in a range.

Mini toolbar An Office feature that provides access to common formatting commands when text is selected.

Mixed cell reference A designation that combines an absolute cell reference with a relative cell reference. When you copy a formula containing a mixed cell reference, either the column letter or the row number that has the absolute reference remains fixed, whereas the other part of the cell reference that is relative changes in the copied formula. A mixed cell reference appears with the $ symbol before either the column letter or row number, such as $B5 or B$5.

Monospaced typeface Uses the same amount of horizontal space for every character.

Multilevel list Extends a numbered list to several levels, and is updated automatically when topics are added or deleted.

Multimedia Multiple forms of media used to entertain or inform an audience.

Multiple data series Two or more sets of data, such as the values for Chicago, New York, and Los Angeles sales for 2010, 2011, and 2012.

Multiple Items form Displays multiple records in a tabular layout similar to a table's Datasheet view.

Multi-table query A query that contains two or more tables. It allows you to take advantage of the relationships that have been set in your database.

Name Box An element in Excel that identifies the address or range name of the active cell in a worksheet.

Narration Spoken commentary that is added to a presentation.

Navigation Pane (Office Fundamentals) Located on the left side of the Windows Explorer window, providing access to Favorites, Libraries, Homegroup, Computer, and Network areas. (Access) Organizes and lists the database objects in an Access database.

Nested function A function that contains another function embedded inside one or more of its arguments.

Nonadjacent range A collection of multiple ranges that are not positioned in a contiguous cluster in an Excel worksheet.

Nonbreaking hyphen Keeps text of a hyphenated word on both sides of the hyphen together, thus preventing the hyphenated word from becoming separated at the end of a line.

Nonbreaking space A special character that keeps two or more words together.

Normal view The three-pane default PowerPoint view used when working with a presentation.

NOT logical operator A logical operator that returns all records except the specified criteria.

Notepad A text-editing program built into Windows 7.

Notes Page view Used for entering and editing large amounts of text to which the speaker can refer when presenting.

Notification area An area located on the right side of the taskbar. It displays icons for background programs and system resources. It also provides status information in pop-up windows.

NOW function A predefined formula that uses the computer's clock to display the current date and time in a cell.

Nper The number of payment periods over the life of the loan.

Null Missing or unknown data in a field.

Number data type A data type that can store only numerical data.

Numbered list Sequences and prioritizes the items in a list and is automatically updated to accommodate additions or deletions.

Object A main component in an Access database that is created and used to make the database.

Office Theme A defined set of colors, fonts, and graphics that can be applied to a form.

One-to-many relationship A relationship in which it is established when the primary key value in the primary table can match many of the foreign key values in the related table.

Opaque A solid fill, one with no transparency.

OpenType A form of font designed for use on all platforms.

Operand The part of an expression that is being manipulated.

Operating system Software that directs computer activities, performing such tasks as recognizing keyboard input, sending output to a display, and keeping track of files and folders.

Operator A mathematical symbol, such as +, –, *, and /.

OR logical operator A logical operator that returns records that meet any of the specified criteria.

Order of operations Determines the sequence by which operations are calculated in an expression.

Order of precedence A rule that controls the sequence in which arithmetic operations are performed.

Original: Show Markup A view that shows deleted text within the body of the document (with a line through the deleted text) and displays inserted text in a markup balloon.

Orphan The first line of a paragraph appearing by itself at the bottom of a page.

Outline A method of organizing text in a hierarchy with main points and subpoints to indicate levels of importance.

Outline view Displays varying amount of detail; a structural view of the document or presentation that can be collapsed or expanded as necessary.

Output area A range of cells that contains the results of manipulating values in an input area.

Page break An indication where data will start on another printed page. The software inserts automatic page breaks based on data, margins, and paper size. Users can insert additional page breaks.

Page Footer section Appears at the bottom of each page to display page summaries, dates, or page numbers at the bottom of every page in a form or report.

Page Header section Appears at the top of each page to display page summaries, dates, or page numbers at the top of every page in a form or report.

Paint A graphics program built into Windows 7 that enables you to create drawings and open picture files.

Paragraph spacing The amount of space before or after a paragraph.

Paragraph style Stores paragraph formatting such as alignment, line spacing, and indents, as well as the font, size, and style of the text in the paragraph.

Paste Places a cut or copied item in another location.

Photo Album A presentation containing multiple pictures organized into album pages.

Picture A graphic file that is retrieved from the Internet, a disk, or CD and placed in an Office project.

Picture fill Inserts an image from a file into a shape.

Picture Styles A gallery that contains preformatted options that can be applied to a graphical object.

Pie chart A chart type that shows each data point in proportion to the whole data series as a slice in a circular pie.

Pin The process of placing icons of frequently used programs on the taskbar or on the Start menu.

Placeholder A container that holds content.

Plagiarism The act of using and documenting the works of another as one's own.

Plain Text format (.txt) A file format that retains only text, but no formatting, when you transfer documents between applications or platforms.

Plot area The region containing the graphical representation of the values in the data series.

PMT function A predefined formula that calculates the periodic payment for a loan with a fixed interest rate and fixed term.

Point The smallest unit of measurement in typography.

Pointing The process of using the mouse pointer to select cells while building a formula. Also known as *semi-selection*.

Portrait Page or worksheet that is taller than it is wide.

Position Raises or lowers text from the baseline without creating superscript or subscript size.

Poster Frame The frame that displays on a slide when a video is not playing.

PowerPoint A Microsoft Office software component that enables you to prepare slideshow presentations for audiences.

PowerPoint presentation An electronic slide show that can be edited or displayed.

PowerPoint show (.ppsx) An unchangeable electronic slide show format used for distribution.

Presenter view Specialty view that delivers a presentation on two monitors simultaneously.

Primary key The field (or combination of fields) that uniquely identifies each record in a table.

Print area The range of cells within a worksheet that will print.

Print Layout view The default view that closely resembles the printed document.

Print order The sequence in which the pages are printed.

Print preview Allows you to see exactly what the report will look like when it is printed.

Proportional typeface Allocates horizontal space to the character.

Public domain Rights to a literary work or property owned by the public at large.

Pv The present value of the loan or an annuity.

Query A question that you ask about the data in the tables of your database.

Query Design view A view that allows you to create queries; the Design view is divided into two parts—the top portion displays the tables, and the bottom portion (known as the query design grid) displays the fields and the criteria.

Query sort order Determines the order of records in the query's Datasheet view.

Quick Access Toolbar Provides one-click access to commonly used commands.

Quick Style A combination of formatting options that can be applied to a shape or other objects.

Radar chart A chart type that compares aggregate values of three or more variables represented on axes starting from the same point.

Range A group of adjacent or contiguous cells in an Excel worksheet.

Range name A word or string of characters assigned to one or more cells. It can be up to 255 letters, characters, or numbers, starting with a letter.

Rate The periodic interest rate; the percentage of interest paid for each payment period.

Reading view Displays a full-screen view one slide at a time that includes bars and buttons for additional functionality.

Recolor The process of changing picture or illustration colors to a duotone style.

Record A group of related fields, representing one entity, such as data for one person, place, event, or concept.

Record source The table or query that supplies the records for a form or report.

Referential integrity Rules in a database that are used to preserve relationships between tables when records are changed.

Related tables Tables that are joined in a relationship using a common field.

Relational database management system (RDBMS) A database system in which you can manage groups of data (tables) and then set rules (relationships) between tables.

Relationship A connection between two tables using a common field.

Relative cell reference A designation that indicates a cell's relative location within the worksheet using the column letter and row number, such as B5. When a formula containing a relative cell reference is copied, the cell references in the copied formula change relative to the position of the copied formula.

Replace Finds text and replaces it with a word or phrase that you indicate.

Report An Access database object that displays professional-looking formatted information from underlying tables or queries.

Report Footer section A *report* section in Access that displays page numbers, dates, and/or aggregate totals once at the bottom of the report.

Report Header section A *report* section in Access that displays page numbers, dates, and/or aggregate totals and prints once at the beginning of each report.

Report tool A feature used to instantly create a tabular report based on the table or query currently selected.

Report view A view that allows you to see what the printed report will look like in a continuous page layout.

Report Wizard A guide that asks you questions and then uses your answers to generate a report.

Reviewing Pane A window that displays all comments and editorial changes made to the main document.

Revision mark Indicates where text is added, deleted, or formatted while the Track Changes feature is active.

Ribbon The long bar of tabs, groups, and commands located just beneath the Title bar.

Rich Text Format (.rtf) A file format that retains structure and most text formatting when transferring documents between applications or platforms.

Right tab Sets the start position on the right so as you type, text moves to the left of that tab setting and aligns on the right.

Rotate To move an object around its axis.

Row height The vertical measurement of a row in a table or a worksheet.

Run command Used to produce the query results (the red exclamation point).

Sans serif typeface A typeface that does not contain thin lines on characters.

Saturation The intensity of a color in an image.

Scaling (or to **scale)** Increases or decreases text or a graphic as a percentage of its original size.

Screen saver A series of images or a graphic display that continually moves over the screen when the computer has been idle for a specified period of time. Screen savers can be used for security purposes to keep others from viewing computer contents.

Section break A marker that divides a document into sections, thereby allowing different formatting in each section.

Select query A type of query that displays only the records that match criteria entered in Query Design view.

Selection net Selects all objects in an area you define by dragging the mouse.

Selection Pane A pane designed to help select objects from a listing of all objects on a slide.

Semi-selection The process of using the mouse pointer to select cells while building a formula. Also known as *pointing*.

Serif typeface A typeface that contains a thin line or extension at the top and bottom of the primary strokes on characters.

Shading A background color that appears behind text in a paragraph, a page, a table, or within a cell.

Shape A geometric or non-geometric object, such as a rectangle or an arrow, used to create an illustration or to highlight information.

Sharpen To enhance the edges of the content in a picture to make the boundaries more prominent.

Sheet tab A visual item in Excel that looks like a folder tab that displays the name of a worksheet, such as *Sheet1* or *June Sales*.

Shortcut A link, or pointer, to a program or computer resource.

Shortcut menu Provides choices related to the selection or area at which you right-click.

Show Markup Enables you to view document revisions by reviewer; it also allows you to choose which type of revisions you want to view such as comments, insertions and deletions, or formatting changes.

Show row A row in the Query Design view that controls whether the field will be displayed in the query results.

Show/Hide feature Reveals where formatting marks, such as spaces, tabs, and returns, are used in the document.

Simple Query Wizard A guide that walks you through the query design process to facilitate new query development.

Single data series A collection of data points for one set of data, such as the values for Chicago sales for 2010, 2011, and 2012.

Sizing handles (Word) The small circles and squares that appear around a selected object and enable you to adjust the height and width of an object. (Excel) A series of faint dots on the outside border of a selected chart; enables you to adjust the size of the chart.

Slide The most basic element of PowerPoint.

Slide show A collection of slides that can be used in a presentation.

Slide Show view Used to deliver the completed presentation full screen to an audience, one slide at a time, as an electronic presentation.

Slide Sorter view Displays thumbnails of your presentation slides, which allow you to view multiple slides simultaneously.

SmartArt A diagram that presents information visually to effectively communicate a message.

Snap A feature that arranges windows automatically on the left and right sides of the desktop.

Snip A screen display that has been captured and displayed by screen capture software.

Snipping Tool A Windows 7 accessory program that captures screen displays for saving or sharing.

Soft page break Inserted when text fills an entire page and continues onto the next page.

Soft return Created by the word processor as it wraps text to a new line.

Soften To blur the edges of the content in a picture to make the boundaries less prominent.

Sort Lists records in a specific sequence, such as ascending by last name or descending by employee id.

Sort Ascending Arranges a list of text data in alphabetical order or a numeric list in lowest to highest order.

Sort Descending Arranges a list of text data in reverse alphabetical order or a numeric list in highest to lowest order.

Sort row A row in the Query Design view that enables you to sort query results in ascending or descending order.

Sorting Listing records or text in a specific sequence, such as alphabetically by last name.

Sparkline A small line, column, or win/loss chart contained in a single cell.

Split form A type of form that combines two views of the same record source—one section is displayed in a stacked layout and the other section is displayed in a tabular layout.

Splitter bar A feature in Form design view that divides the form into two halves.

Spreadsheet An electronic file that contains a grid of columns and rows to organize related data and to display results of calculations.

Spreadsheet program A computer application, such as Microsoft Excel, that people use to create and modify spreadsheets.

Spyware Software that is installed from the Internet, usually without the user's permission. It can gather information for marketing purposes, and is sometimes capable of changing computer settings and recording keystrokes.

Stacked column chart A chart type that places stacks of data in segments on top of each other in one column, with each category in the data series represented by a different color.

Stacked layout form A type of form that displays fields in a vertical column and displays one record at a time.

Stacked layout report A type of report that displays fields in a vertical column.

Stacking order The order of objects placed on top of one another.

Start button A button located at the left side of the taskbar. Click the Start button to display the Start menu.

Start menu A menu that is displayed when you click the Start button. It is a list of programs, folders, utilities, and tasks.

Status bar (Office Fundamentals) The horizontal bar located at the bottom of an Office application containing information relative to the open file. (PowerPoint) Contains the slide number, the design theme name, and View buttons, in PowerPoint.

Stock chart A chart type that shows fluctuations in stock changes.

Storyboard A visual plan of a presentation that displays the content of each slide in the slide show.

Structured reference A tag or use of a table element, such as a column heading, as a reference in a formula.

Style A set of formatting options you apply to characters or paragraphs.

Subfolder A folder that is housed within another folder.

SUBTOTAL function A predefined formula that calculates an aggregate value, such as totals, for values in a range or database.

SUM function A predefined formula that calculates the total of values contained in two or more cells.

Surface chart A chart type that displays trends using two dimensions on a continuous curve.

Syntax The rules that dictate the structure and components required to perform the necessary calculations in an equation or evaluate expressions.

Tab (Office Fundamentals) Ribbon area that contains groups of related tasks. (Word) A marker that specifies the position for aligning text in a document.

Table (Access) An object in a database that stores related information. (Word, Excel, PowerPoint, Access) Organizes information in a series of records (rows), with each record made up of a number of fields (columns).

Table alignment The position of a table between the left and right document margins.

Table array The range that contains the body of the lookup table, excluding column headings. The first column must be in ascending order to find a value in a range, or it can be in any order to look up an exact value.

Table Move handle The graphical image that displays in the upper-left corner of a table and enables you to select a whole table at one time.

Table of authorities Used in legal documents to reference cases and other documents referred to in a legal brief.

Table of contents Lists headings in the order they appear in a document and the page numbers where the entries begin.

Table of figures A list of the captions in a document.

Table row A row in the Query Design view that displays the data source.

Table style The rules that control the fill color of the header row, columns, and records in a table.

Tabular layout form A type of form that displays records horizontally, with label controls across the top and the data values in rows under the labels.

Tabular layout report A type of report that displays data horizontally across the page in a landscape orientation.

Tag A file property, such as a rating, that a user can apply to a file for identification purposes.

Taskbar The horizontal bar located at the bottom of the desktop. It displays icons for open windows, a Start button, pinned icons, and a notification area.

Template A predesigned file that incorporates formatting elements, such as a theme and layouts, and may include content that can be modified.

Text One or more letters, numbers, symbols, and/or spaces often used as a label in a worksheet.

Text box An object that enables you to place text anywhere on a slide.

Text box control A control that displays the data found in a form's record source.

Text data type A data type that can store either text or numerical characters.

Text direction The degree of rotation in which text displays.

Text pane A pane for text entry that opens when a SmartArt diagram is selected.

Text wrapping style The way text wraps around an image.

Texture fill Inserts a texture such as marble, canvas, or cork into a shape.

Theme A collection of design choices that includes colors, fonts, and special theme effects used to give a consistent look to a presentation.

Thumbnail A miniature of a slide that appears in the Slides tab and Slide Sorter view.

Title bar A horizontal bar that appears at the top of each open window. The title bar contains the current file name, Office application, and control buttons.

TODAY function A predefined formula that displays the current date in a cell.

Toggle Commands such as bold and italic that enable you to switch from one setting to another.

Tone A characteristic of lighting in pictures (also called *temperature*).

Toolbar A collection of icons or items, usually displayed in a horizontal fashion, from which you can make selections.

Total row A table row that appears below the last row of records in an Excel table, or in Datasheet view of a table or query, and displays summary or aggregate statistics.

Totals query A query that contains an additional row in the design grid and is used to display only aggregate data when the query is run.

Track Changes Monitors all additions, deletions, and formatting changes you make in a document.

Transition A specific animation that is applied as a previous slide is replaced by a new slide while displayed in Slide Show view or Reading view.

Transparency The visibility of fill.

Trendline A line that depicts trends or helps forecast future data.

Type style The characteristic applied to a font, such as bold.

Typeface A complete set of characters—upper- and lowercase letters, numbers, punctuation marks, and special symbols.

Typography The arrangement and appearance of printed matter.

Unbound control A control that displays labels and other decorative design elements.

Ungrouping Breaking a combined object into individual objects, which enables them to move or act separately.

User Account Control (UAC) A Windows feature that asks a user's permission before allowing any changes to computer settings.

User interface A collection of onscreen components that facilitates communication between the software and the user.

Validation rule A property that prevents invalid data from being entered into a field.

Value A number that represents a quantity or an amount.

Value axis The chart element that displays incremental numbers to identify approximate values, such as dollars or units, of data points in the chart.

Vector graphic An object-oriented graphic based on geometric formulas.

Vertex The point where a curve ends or the point where two line segments meet in a shape.

Vertical alignment The position of data between the top and bottom cell margins.

View The way a file appears onscreen.

Visual Basic for Applications (VBA) Microsoft's programming language that is built into all of the Office products.

VLOOKUP function A predefined formula that looks up a value and returns a related result from the lookup table.

Watermark Text or graphic that displays behind text.

Web Layout view View to display how a document will look when posted on the Web.

Widow The last line of a paragraph appearing by itself at the top of a page.

Wildcard A special character used in a query to include all records that begin with a specific character or match one or more characters in the criterion of a query.

Window A rectangular bordered area of space on the desktop that represents a program, system resource, or data.

Windows Defender An antispyware program that is installed along with Windows 7.

Windows Explorer A Windows component that can be used to create and manage folders.

Windows Update A software patch, or fix, provided by Microsoft, that prevents or corrects problems. Many updates focus on security concerns.

Wizard A tool that makes a process easier by asking a series of questions, then creating a document structure based on your answers.

Word A word processing program that is included in Microsoft Office.

Word processing software A computer application, such as Microsoft Word, used primarily with text to create, edit, and format documents.

Word wrap The feature that automatically moves words to the next line if they do not fit on the current line.

WordArt Text that has a decorative effect applied.

WordPad A basic word processing program built into Windows 7.

Workbook A collection of one or more related worksheets contained within a single file.

Worksheet A single spreadsheet that typically contains labels, values, formulas, functions, and graphical representations of data.

Wrap text A formatting option that enables a label to appear on multiple lines within the current cell.

X Y (scatter) chart A chart type that shows a relationship between two variables using their X and Y coordinates. Excel plots one variable on the horizontal X-axis and the other variable on the vertical Y-axis. Scatter charts are often used to represent data in educational, scientific, and medical experiments.

X-axis A horizontal border that provides a frame of reference for measuring data horizontally on a chart.

Y-axis A vertical border that provides a frame of reference for measuring data vertically on a chart.

Zoom slider Enables you to increase or decrease the size of file contents onscreen.

INDEX

A

B

C

D

E

F

J

K

L

M

N

O

P

Q

R

S

T